Y0-BRT-558

ENCYCLOPAEDIA
JUDAICA

VOLUME 7
FR-HA

ENCYCLOPAEDIA JUDAICA

ENCYCLOPAEDIA JUDAICA JERUSALEM

Library of Congress Catalog Card Number: 72–90254

First printing

Produced and printed in Jerusalem, Israel

GLOSSARY

Asterisked terms have separate entries in the Encyclopaedia.

Actions Committee, early name of the Zionist General Council, the supreme institution of the World Zionist Organization in the interim between Congresses. The Zionist Executive's name was then the "Small Actions Committee."

***Adar,** twelfth month of the Jewish religious year, sixth of the civil, approximating to February-March.

***Aggadah,** name given to those sections of Talmud and Midrash containing homiletic expositions of the Bible, stories, legends, folklore, anecdotes, or maxims. In contradistinction to **halakhah*.

***Agunah,** woman unable to remarry according to Jewish law, because of desertion by her husband or inability to accept presumption of death.

***Aḥaronim,** later rabbinic authorities. In contradistinction to **rishonim* ("early ones").

Ahavah, liturgical poem inserted in the second benediction of the morning prayer *(*Ahavah Rabbah)* of the festivals and/or special Sabbaths.

Aktion (Ger.), expulsion from ghettos and other concentration points by the Nazis during the *Holocaust.

***Aliyah,** (1) being called to Reading of the Law in synagogue; (2) immigration to Ereẓ Israel; (3) one of the waves of immigration to Ereẓ Israel from the early 1880s.

***Amidah,** main prayer recited at all services; also known as *Shemoneh Esreh* and *Tefillah*.

***Amora** (pl. **amoraim**), title given to the Jewish scholars in Ereẓ Israel and Babylonia in the third to sixth centuries who were responsible for the **Gemara*.

Aravah, the willow; one of the "four species" used on *Sukkot ("festival of Tabernacles") together with the **etrog, hadas,* and **lulav*.

***Arvit,** evening prayer.

Asarah be-Tevet, fast on the 10th of Tevet commemorating the commencement of the siege of Jerusalem by Nebuchadnezzar.

Asefat ha-Nivḥarim, representative assembly elected by Jews in Palestine during the period of the British Mandate (1920–48).

***Ashkenaz,** name applied generally in medieval rabbinical literature to Germany.

***Ashkenazi** (pl. **Ashkenazim**), German or West-, Central-, or East-European Jew(s), as contrasted with *Sephardi(m).

***Av,** fifth month of the Jewish religious year, eleventh of the civil, approximating to July-August.

***Av bet din,** vice-president of the supreme court *(bet din ha-gadol)* in Jerusalem during the Second Temple period; later, title given to communal rabbis as heads of the religious courts (*see *bet din*).

***Badḥan,** jester, particularly at traditional Jewish weddings in Eastern Europe.

Bar, "son of . . ."; frequently appearing in personal names.

***Baraita** (pl. **beraitot**), statement of **tanna* not found in *Mishnah.

***Bar mitzvah,** ceremony marking the initiation of a boy at the age of 13 into the Jewish religious community.

Ben, "son of . . ."; frequently appearing in personal names.

Berakhah (pl. **berakhot**), *benediction, blessing; formula of praise and thanksgiving.

***Bet din** (pl. **battei din**), rabbinic court of law.

***Bet ha-midrash,** school for higher rabbinic learning; often attached to or serving as a synagogue.

***Bilu,** first modern movement for pioneering and agricultural settlement in Ereẓ Israel, founded in 1882 at Kharkov, Russia.

***Bund,** Jewish socialist party founded in Vilna in 1897, supporting Jewish national rights, Yiddishist, and anti-Zionist.

Cohen (pl. **Cohanim**), see Kohen.

***Conservative Judaism,** trend in Judaism developed in the United States in the 20th century which, while opposing extreme changes in traditional observances, permits certain modifications of *halakhah* in response to the changing needs of the Jewish people.

***Consistory** (Fr. consistoire) governing body of a Jewish communal district in France and certain other countries.

***Converso(s),** term applied in Spain and Portugal to converted Jew(s), and sometimes more loosely to their descendants.

***Crypto-Jew,** term applied to a person who although observing outwardly Christianity (or some other religion) was at heart a Jew and maintained Jewish observances as far as possible (see Converso; Marrano; Neofiti; New Christian; Jadīd al-Islām).

***Dayyan,** member of rabbinic court.

Decisor, equivalent to the Hebrew *posek* (pl. **posekim*), the rabbi who gives the decision (*halakhah*) in Jewish law or practice.

***Devekut,** "devotion"; attachment or adhesion to God; communion with God.

Diaspora, Jews living in the "dispersion" outside Ereẓ Israel; area of Jewish settlement outside Ereẓ Israel.

Din, a law (both secular and religious), legal decision, or lawsuit.

Divan, diwan, collection of poems, especially in Hebrew, Arabic, or Persian.

Dunam, unit of land area (1,000 sq. m., c. 1/4 acre), used in Israel.

Einsatzgruppen, in Nazi terminology, task force of mobile killing units (*Einsatzkommandos*) operating in the German-occupied territories during World War II.

***Ein-Sof,** "without end"; "the infinite"; hidden, impersonal aspect of God; also used as a Divine Name.

***Elul,** sixth month of the Jewish religious calendar, 12th of the civil, precedes the High Holiday season in the fall.

Endloesung (Ger. "Final Solution"), in Nazi terminology, the Nazi-planned mass murder and total annihilation of the Jews.

***Ereẓ Israel,** Land of Israel; Palestine.

***Eruv,** technical term for rabbinical provision permitting the alleviation of certain restrictions.

***Etrog,** citron; one of the "four species" used on *Sukkot together with the **lulav, hadas,* and *aravah*.

Even ha-Ezer, see Shulḥan Arukh.

***Exilarch,** lay head of Jewish community in Babylonia (see also *resh galuta*), and elsewhere.

***Final Solution,** see *Endloesung*.

***Gabbai,** official of a Jewish congregation; originally a charity collector.

***Galut,** "exile"; the condition of the Jewish people in dispersion.

***Gaon** (pl. **geonim**), head of academy in post-talmudic period, especially in Babylonia.

Gaonate, office of *gaon.

***Gemara**, traditions, discussions, and rulings of the *amoraim*, commenting on and supplementing the *Mishnah, and forming part of the Babylonian and Palestinian Talmuds (see Talmud).

***Gematria**, interpretation of Hebrew word according to the numerical value of its letters.

General Gouvernment (Ger.), territory in Poland administered by a German civilian governor with headquarters in Cracow after the German occupation in World War II.

***Genizah**, depository for sacred books. The best known was discovered in the synagogue of Fostat (old Cairo).

Get, bill of *divorce.

***Ge'ullah**, hymn inserted after the **Shema* into the benediction of the morning prayer of the festivals and special Sabbaths.

***Gilgul**, metempsychosis; transmigration of souls.

***Golem**, automaton, especially in human form, created by magical means and endowed with life.

***Ḥabad**, initials of *ḥokhmah, binah, da'at*: "wisdom, understanding, knowledge"; ḥasidic movement founded in White Russia by *Shneour Zalman of Lyady.

Hadas, myrtle; one of the "four species" used on Sukkot together with the **etrog*, **lulav*, and *aravah*.

***Haftarah** (pl. **haftarot**), designation of the portion from the prophetical books of the Bible recited after the synagogue reading from the Pentateuch on Sabbaths and holidays.

***Haganah**, clandestine Jewish organization for armed self-defense in Ereẓ Israel under the British Mandate, which eventually evolved into a people's militia and became the basis for the Israel army.

***Haggadah**, ritual recited in the home on *Passover eve at *seder* table.

Haham, title of chief rabbi of the Spanish and Portuguese congregations in London, England.

Ḥakham, title of rabbi of *Sephardi congregation.

***Ḥakham bashi**, title in the 15th century and modern times of the chief rabbi in the Ottoman Empire, residing in Constantinople (Istanbul), also applied to principal rabbis in provincial towns.

Hakhsharah ("preparation"), organized training in the Diaspora of pioneers for agricultural settlement in Ereẓ Israel.

***Halakhah** (pl. **halakhot**), an accepted decision in rabbinic law. Also refers to those parts of the *Talmud concerned with legal matters. In contradistinction to **aggadah*.

***Ḥaliẓah**, biblically prescribed ceremony (Deut. 25:9–10) performed when a man refuses to marry his brother's childless widow.

***Hallel**, term referring to Psalms 113–18 in liturgical use.

***Ḥalukkah**, system of financing the maintenance of Jewish communities in the holy cities of Ereẓ Israel by collections made abroad, mainly in the pre-Zionist era (see *kolel*).

Ḥalutz (pl. **ḥalutzim**), pioneer, especially in agriculture, in Ereẓ Israel.

Ḥalutziyyut, pioneering.

***Ḥanukkah**, eight-day celebration commemorating the victory of *Judah Maccabee over the Syrian king *Antiochus Epiphanes and the subsequent rededication of the Temple.

Ḥasid, adherent of *Ḥasidism.

***Ḥasidei Ashkenaz**, medieval pietist movement among the Jews of Germany.

***Ḥasidism**, (1) religious revivalist movement of popular mysticism among Jews of Western Germany in the Middle Ages; (2) religious movement founded by *Israel ben Eliezer Ba'al Shem Tov in the first half of the 18th century.

***Haskalah**, "Enlightenment"; movement for spreading modern European culture among Jews c. 1750–1880. An adherent was termed *maskil*.

***Havdalah**, ceremony marking the end of Sabbath.

***Ḥazzan**, precentor who intones the liturgy and leads the prayers in synagogue; in earlier times a synagogue official.

***Ḥeder** (lit. "room"), school for teaching children Jewish religious observance.

Heikhalot, "palaces"; tradition in Jewish mysticism centering on mystical journeys through the heavenly spheres and palaces to the Divine Chariot (see Merkabah).

***Ḥerem**, excommunication, imposed by rabbinical authorities for purposes of religious and/or communal discipline; originally, in biblical times, that which is separated from common use either because it was an abomination or because it was consecrated to God.

Ḥeshvan, see Marḥeshvan.

***Ḥevra kaddisha**, title applied to charitable confraternity (**ḥevrah)*, now generally limited to associations for burial of the dead.

***Ḥibbat Zion**, see Ḥovevei Zion.

***Histadrut** (abbr. for Heb. Ha-Histadrut ha-Kelalit shel ha-Ovedim ha-Ivriyyim be-Ereẓ Israel), Ereẓ Israel Jewish Labor Federation, founded in 1920; subsequently renamed Histadrut ha-Ovedim be-Ereẓ Israel.

***Holocaust**, the organized mass persecution and annihilation of European Jewry by the Nazis (1933–1945).

***Hoshana Rabba**, the seventh day of *Sukkot on which special observances are held.

Ḥoshen Mishpat, see Shulḥan Arukh.

Ḥovevei Zion, federation of *Ḥibbat Zion, early (pre-*Herzl) Zionist movement in Russia.

Illui, outstanding scholar or genius, especially a young prodigy in talmudic learning.

***Iyyar**, eighth month of the Jewish religious year, second of the civil, approximating to April-May.

I.Ẓ.L. (initials of Heb. ***Irgun Ẓevai Le'ummi**; "National Military Organization"), underground Jewish organization in Ereẓ Israel founded in 1931, which engaged from 1937 in retaliatory acts against Arab attacks and later against the British mandatory authorities.

***Jadīd al-Islām** (Ar.), persons practicing the Jewish religion in secret although outwardly observing Islam.

***Jewish Legion**, Jewish units in British army during World War I.

***Jihad** (Ar.), in Muslim religious law, holy war waged against infidels.

***Judenrat** (Ger. "Jewish council"), council set up in Jewish communities and ghettos under the Nazis to execute their instructions.

***Judenrein** (Ger. "clean of Jews"), in Nazi terminology the condition of a locality from which all Jews had been eliminated.

***Kabbalah**, the Jewish mystical tradition:

Kabbalah iyyunit, speculative Kabbalah;

Kabbalah ma'asit, practical Kabbalah;

Kabbalah nevu'it, prophetic Kabbalah.

Kabbalist, student of Kabbalah.

***Kaddish**, liturgical doxology.

Kahal, Jewish congregation; among Ashkenazim, *kehillah*.

***Kalām** (Ar.), science of Muslim theology; adherents of the Kalām are called *mutakallimūn*.

***Karaite**, member of a Jewish sect originating in the eighth century which rejected rabbinic (*Rabbanite) Judaism and accepted only Scripture as authoritative.

***Kasher**, ritually permissible food.

Kashrut, Jewish *dietary laws.

***Kavvanah**, "intention"; term denoting the spiritual concentration accompanying prayer and the performance of ritual or of a commandment.

***Kedushah**, addition to the third blessing in the reader's repetition of the **Amidah* in which the public responds to the precentor's introduction and connecting text with verses praising God.

Kefar, village; first part of name of many settlements in Israel.

Kehillah, congregation; see *kahal*.

Kelippah (pl. **kelippot**), "husk(s)"; mystical term denoting force(s) of evil.

***Keneset Yisrael**, comprehensive communal organization of the Jews in Palestine during the British Mandate.

Keri, variants in the masoretic (*masorah) text of the Bible between the spelling (*ketiv*) and its pronunciation (*keri*).

***Kerovah** (collective plural (corrupted) from **kerovẓ**), poem(s) incorporated into the **Amidah*.

Ketiv, see *keri*.

***Ketubbah**, marriage contract, stipulating husband's obligations to wife.

Kevuẓah, small commune of pioneers constituting an agricultural settlement in Ereẓ Israel (evolved later into *kibbutz).

***Kibbutz** (pl. **kibbutzim**), larger-size commune constituting a settlement in Ereẓ Israel based mainly on agriculture but engaging also in industry.

***Kiddush**, prayer of sanctification, recited over wine or bread on eve of Sabbaths and festivals.

***Kiddush ha-Shem**, term connoting martyrdom or act of strict integrity in support of Judaic principles.

***Kinah** (pl. **kinot**), lamentation dirge(s) for the Ninth of Av and other fast days.

***Kislev**, third month of the Jewish religious year, ninth of the civil, approximating to November-December.

Klaus, name given in Central and Eastern Europe to an institution, usually with synagogue attached, where *Talmud was studied perpetually by adults; applied by *Ḥasidim to their synagogue ("*kloyz*").

***Knesset**, parliament of the State of Israel.

K(c)ohen (pl. **K(c)ohanim**), Jew(s) of priestly (Aaronide) descent.

***Kolel**, (1) community in Ereẓ Israel of persons from a particular country or locality, often supported by their fellow countrymen in the Diaspora; (2) institution for higher Torah study.

Kosher, see *kasher*.

***Kristallnacht** (Ger. "crystal night," meaning "night of broken glass"), organized destruction of synagogues, Jewish houses, and shops, accompanied by arrests of individual Jews, which took place in Germany and Austria under the Nazis on the night of Nov. 9–10, 1938.

***Lag ba-Omer**, 33rd (Heb. **lag**) day of the **Omer* period falling on the 18th of *Iyyar; a semi-holiday.

Leḥi (abbr. for Heb. ***Loḥamei Ḥerut Israel**, "Fighters for the Freedom of Israel" also L.Ḥ.Y), radically anti-British armed underground organization in Palestine, founded in 1940 by dissidents from *I.Ẓ.L.

Levir, husband's brother.

***Levirate marriage** (Heb. *yibbum*), marriage of childless widow (*yevamah*) by brother (*yavam*) of the deceased husband (in accordance with Deut. 25:5); release from such an obligation is effected through **ḥaliẓah*.

LḤY, see Leḥi.

***Lulav**, palm branch; one of the "four species" used on *Sukkot together with the **etrog, hadas*, and *aravah*.

Ma'ariv, evening prayer; also called **arvit*.

Ma'aravit, hymns inserted into the evening prayer of the three festivals, Passover, Shavuot, and Sukkot.

***Ma'barah**, transition camp; temporary settlement for newcomers in Israel during the period of mass immigration following 1948.

***Maftir**, reader of the concluding portion of the Pentateuchal section on Sabbaths and holidays in synagogue; reader of the portion of the prophetical books of the Bible (**haftarah*).

***Maggid**, popular preacher.

***Maḥzor** (pl. **maḥzorim**), festival prayer book.

***Mamzer**, bastard, according to Jewish law, the offspring of an incestuous relationship.

***Mandate, Palestine**, responsibility for the administration of Palestine conferred on Britain by the League of Nations in 1922; mandatory government: the British administration of Palestine.

Maqâma (Ar.), poetic form (rhymed prose) which, in its classical arrangement, has rigid rules of form and content.

***Marḥeshvan**, popularly called Ḥeshvan; second month of the Jewish religious year, eighth of the civil, approximating to October-November.

***Marrano(s)**, descendant(s) of Jew(s) in Spain and Portugal whose ancestors had been forcibly converted to Christianity but who secretly observed Jewish rituals.

Maskil (pl. **maskilim**), adherent of *Haskalah ("Enlightenment") movement.

***Masorah**, body of traditions regarding the correct spelling, writing, and reading of the Hebrew Bible.

Masorete, scholar of the masoretic tradition.

Masoretic, in accordance with the masorah.

Meliẓah, in Middle Ages, elegant style; modern usage, florid style using biblical or talmudic phraseology.

Mellah, Jewish quarter in North African towns.

***Menorah**, candelabrum; seven-branched oil lamp used in the Tabernacle and Temple; also eight-branched candelabrum used on *Ḥanukkah.

Me'orah, hymn inserted into the first benediction of the morning prayer (*Yoẓer ha-Me'orot*).

***Merkabah**, *merkavah*, "chariot"; mystical discipline associated with Ezekiel's vision of the Divine Throne-Chariot (Ezek. 1).

Meshullaḥ, emissary sent to conduct propaganda or raise funds for rabbinical academies or charitable institutions.

***Mezuzah** (pl. **mezuzot**), parchment scroll placed in container and affixed to doorposts of rooms occupied by Jews.

***Midrash**, method of interpreting Scripture to elucidate legal points (*Midrash Halakhah*) or to bring out lessons by stories or homiletics (*Midrash Aggadah*). Also the name for a collection of such rabbinic interpretations.

***Mikveh**, ritual bath.

***Minhag** (pl. **minhagim**), ritual custom(s); synagogal rite(s); especially of a specific sector of Jewry.

***Minḥah**, afternoon prayer; originally meal offering in Temple.

***Minyan**, group of ten male adult Jews, the minimum required for communal prayer.

***Mishnah**, earliest codification of Jewish Oral Law.

Mishnayot, paragraph divisions of the *Mishnah.

Mitnagged (pl. ***Mitnaggedim**), originally, opponents of *Ḥasidism in Eastern Europe.

***Mitzvah**, biblical or rabbinic injunction; applied also to good or charitable deeds.

Mohel, official performing circumcisions.

***Moshav**, Smallholders' cooperative agricultural settlement in Israel, see moshav ovedim.

***Moshavah**, earliest type of Jewish village in modern Ereẓ Israel in which farming is conducted on individual farms mostly on privately owned land.

Moshav ovedim ("workers' settlement"), agricultural village in Israel whose inhabitants possess individual homes and holdings but cooperate in the purchase of equipment, sale of produce, mutual aid, etc.

Moshav shittufi ("collective moshav"), agricultural village in Israel whose members possess individual homesteads but where the agriculture and economy are conducted as a collective unit.

Mostegab, poem with biblical verse at beginning of each stanza.

***Muqaddim** (Ar., pl. **muqaddimūn**), "leader," "head of the community."

***Musaf**, additional service on Sabbath and festivals; originally the additional sacrifice offered in the Temple.

Musar, traditional ethical literature.

***Musar movement**, ethical movement developing in the latter part of the 19th century among Orthodox Jewish groups in Lithuania; founded by R. Israel *Lipkin (Salanter).

***Nagid** (pl. **negidim**), title applied in Muslim (and some Christian) countries in the Middle Ages to a leader recognized by the state as head of the Jewish community.

Nakdan (pl. **nakdanim**), "punctuator"; scholar of the 9th to 14th centuries who provided biblical manuscripts with masoretic apparatus, vowels, and accents.

***Nasi** (pl. **nesi'im**), talmudic term for president of the Sanhedrin, who was also the spiritual head and, later, political representative of the Jewish people; from second century a descendant of Hillel recognized by the Roman authorities as patriarch of the Jews. Now applied to the president of the State of Israel.

***Negev**, the southern, mostly arid, area of Israel.

***Ne'ilah**, concluding service on the *Day of Atonement.

Neofiti, term applied in southern Italy to converts to Christianity from Judaism and their descendants who were suspected of maintaining secret allegiance to Judaism.

***Neology; Neolog; Neologism**, trend of *Reform Judaism in Hungary forming separate congregations after 1868.

***Nevelah**, meat forbidden by the *dietary laws on account of the absence of, or defect in, the act of **sheḥitah* ("ritual slaughter").

***New Christians**, term applied especially in Spain and Portugal to converts from Judaism (as also from Islam) and their descendants; "Half New Christian" designated a person one of whose parents was of full Jewish blood.

***Niddah** ("menstruous woman"), woman during the period of menstruation.

***Nisan**, first month of the Jewish religious year, seventh of the civil, approximating to March-April.

Niẓoẓot, "sparks"; mystical term for sparks of the holy light imprisoned in all matter.

Nosaḥ (nusaḥ), "version"; (1) textual variant; (2) term applied to distinguish the various prayer rites, e.g., *nosaḥ Ashkenaz;* (3) the accepted tradition of synagogue melody.

***Notarikon**, method of abbreviating Hebrew words or phrases by writing single letters.

Novella(e) (Heb. **ḥiddush(im)*, commentary on talmudic and later rabbinic subjects that derives new facts or principles from the implications of the text.

***Nuremberg Laws**, Nazi laws excluding Jews from German citizenship.

Ofan, hymns inserted into a passage of the morning prayer.

***Omer**, first sheaf cut during the barley harvest, offered in the Temple on the second day of Passover.

***Omer, Counting of** (Heb. *Sefirat ha-Omer*), 49 days counted from the day on which the *omer* was first offered in the Temple (according to the rabbis the 16th of Nisan, i.e., the second day of Passover) until the festival of Shavuot; a period of semi-mourning.

Oraḥ Hayyim, see Shulḥan Arukh.

***Orthodoxy** (Orthodox Judaism), modern term for the strictly traditional sector of Jewry.

***Pale of Settlement,** 25 provinces of czarist Russia where Jews were permitted permanent residence.

***Palmaḥ** (abbr. for Heb. *peluggot maḥaẓ;* "shock companies"), striking arm of the *Haganah.

***Pardes,** medieval biblical exegesis giving the literal, allegorical, homiletical, and esoteric interpretations.

***Parnas,** chief synagogue functionary, originally vested with both religious and administrative functions; subsequently an elected lay leader.

Partition plan(s), proposals for dividing Ereẓ Israel into autonomous areas.

Paytan, composer of **piyyut* (liturgical poetry).

Peel Commission, British Royal Commission appointed by the British government in 1936 to inquire into the Palestine problem and make recommendations for its solution.

Pesaḥ, *Passover.

***Pilpul,** in talmudic and rabbinic literature, a sharp dialectic intellectual argumentation used particularly by talmudists in Poland from the 16th century.

***Pinkas,** community register or minute-book.

***Piyyut** (pl. **piyyutim**), Hebrew liturgical poetry.

Pizmon, poem with refrain.

Posek (pl. ***posekim**), decisor; codifier or rabbinic scholar who pronounces decisions in disputes and on questions of Jewish law.

Prosbul, legal method of overcoming the cancelation of loans with the advent of the *sabbatical year.

***Purim,** festival held on Adar 14 or 15 in commemoration of the delivery of the Jews of Persia in the time of *Esther.

Rabban, honorific title higher than that of rabbi, applied to heads of the *Sanhedrin in mishnaic times.

***Rabbanite,** adherent of rabbinic Judaism. In contradistinction to *Karaite.

Reb, rebbe, Yiddish form for rabbi, applied generally to a teacher or ḥasidic rabbi.

***Reconstructionism,** trend in Jewish thought originating in the United States.

***Reform Judaism,** trend in Judaism advocating modification of *Orthodoxy in conformity with the exigencies of contemporary life and thought.

Resh galuta, lay head of Babylonian Jewry (see exilarch).

Responsum (pl. ***responsa**), written opinion (*teshuvah*) given to question (*she'elah*) on aspects of Jewish law by qualified authorities; pl. collection of such queries and opinions in book form.

R.H.S.A. (initials of Ger. *Reichssicherheitshauptamt*: "Reich Security Main Office"), the central Security Department of the German Reich, formed in 1939, and combining the existing Security Police (Gestapo and Kripo) and the S.D.

Rishonim, older rabbinical authorities. Distinguished from later authorities (**aḥaronim*).

***Rishon le-Zion,** title given to Sephardi chief rabbi of Ereẓ Israel.

***Rosh Ha-Shanah,** two-day holiday (one day in biblical and early mishnaic times) at the beginning of the month of *Tishri (September-October), traditionally the New Year.

Rosh Ḥodesh, *New Moon; first of the Hebrew month.

Rosh yeshivah, see yeshivah.

***Sanhedrin,** the assembly of ordained scholars which functioned both as a supreme court and as a legislature before 70 C.E. In modern times the name was given to the body of representative Jews convoked by Napoleon in 1807.

***Savora** (pl. **savoraim**), name given to the Babylonian scholars of the period between the **amoraim* and the **geonim,* approximately 500–700 C.E.

S.D. (initials of Ger. *Sicherheitsdienst*: "security service"), security service of the *S.S. formed in 1932 as the sole intelligence organization of the Nazi party.

***Seder,** ceremony observed in the Jewish home on the first night of Passover (outside Ereẓ Israel first two nights), when the **Haggadah* is recited.

***Sefer Torah,** manuscript scroll of the Pentateuch for public reading in synagogue.

***Sefirot, the ten,** the ten "Numbers"; mystical term denoting the ten spheres or emanations through which the Divine manifests itself; elements of the world; dimensions; primordial numbers.

Seliḥah (pl. ***seliḥot**), penitential prayer.

***Semikhah,** ordination conferring the title "rabbi" and permission to give decisions in matters of ritual and law.

***Sephardi** (pl. **Sephardim**), Jew(s) of Spain and Portugal and their descendants, wherever resident, as contrasted with *Ashkenazi(m).

Shabbatean, adherent of the pseudo-messiah *Shabbetai Ẓevi (17th century).

Shaddai, name of God found frequently in the Bible and commonly translated "Almighty."

***Shaḥarit,** morning service.

Shali'aḥ (pl. **sheliḥim**), in Jewish law, messenger, agent; in modern times, an emissary from Ereẓ Israel to Jewish communities or organizations abroad for the purpose of fund-raising, organizing pioneer immigrants, education, etc.

Shalmonit, poetic meter introduced by the liturgical poet *Solomon ha-Bavli.

Shammash, synagogue beadle.

***Shavuot,** Pentecost; festival of Weeks; second of the three annual pilgrim festivals commemorating the receiving of the Torah at Mt. Sinai.

***Sheḥitah,** ritual slaughtering of animals.

***Shekhinah,** Divine Presence.

Shelishit, poem with three-line stanzas.

***Sheluḥei Ereẓ Israel** (or **shadarim**), emissaries from Ereẓ Israel.

***Shema** (*Yisrael*; "hear . . . (O Israel)," Deut. 6:4), Judaism's confession of faith, proclaiming the absolute unity of God.

Shemini Aẓeret, final festal day (in the Diaspora, final two days) at the conclusion of *Sukkot.

Shemittah, *Sabbatical year.

Sheniyyah, poem with two-line stanzas.

***Shephelah,** southern part of the coastal plain of Ereẓ Israel.

***Shevat,** eleventh month of the Jewish religious year, fifth of the civil, approximating to January-February.

***Shi'ur Komah,** Hebrew mystical work (c. eighth century) containing a physical description of God's dimensions; term denoting enormous spacial measurement used in speculations concerning the body of the **Shekhinah.*

Shivah, the "seven days" of *mourning following burial of a relative.

***Shofar,** horn of the ram (or any other ritually clean animal excepting the cow) sounded for the memorial blowing on *Rosh Ha-Shanah, and other occasions.

Shoḥet, person qualified to perform **sheḥitah.*

Shomer, Ha-Shomer, organization of Jewish workers in Ereẓ Israel founded in 1909 to defend Jewish settlements.

***Shtadlan,** Jewish representative or negotiator with access to dignitaries of state, active at royal courts, etc.

***Shtetl,** Jewish small-town community in Eastern Europe.

***Shulḥan Arukh,** Joseph *Caro's code of Jewish law (1564–65) in four parts:

Oraḥ Ḥayyim, laws relating to prayers, Sabbath, festivals, and fasts;
Yoreh De'ah, dietary laws, etc;
Even ha-Ezer, laws dealing with women, marriage, etc;
Ḥoshen Mishpat, civil, criminal law, court procedure, etc.

Siddur, among Ashkenazim, the volume containing the daily prayers (in distinction to the **maḥzor* containing those for the festivals).

***Simḥat Torah,** holiday marking the completion in the synagogue of the annual cycle of reading the Pentateuch; in Ereẓ Israel observed on Shemini Aẓeret (outside Ereẓ Israel a separate celebration on the following day).

***Sinai Campaign,** brief campaign in October-November 1956 when Israel army reacted to Egyptian terrorist attacks and blockade by occupying the Sinai peninsula.

Sitra aḥra, "the other side" (of God); left side; the demoniac and satanic powers.

***Sivan,** third month of the Jewish religious year, ninth of the civil, approximating to June-July.

***Six-Day War,** brief war in June 1967 when Israel reacted to Arab threats and blockade by defeating the Egyptian, Jordanian, and Syrian armies.

***S.S.** (initials of Ger. *Schutzstaffel*: "protection detachment"), Nazi formation established in 1925 which later became the "elite" organization of the Nazi Party and carried out central tasks in the "Final Solution."

Status quo ante community, community in Hungary retaining the status it had held before the convention of the General Jewish Congress there in 1868 and the resultant split in Hungarian Jewry.

***Sukkah,** booth or tabernacle erected for *Sukkot when, for seven days, religious Jews "dwell" or at least eat in the *sukkah* (Lev. 23:42).

***Sukkot,** festival of Tabernacles; last of the three pilgrim festivals, beginning on the 15th of Tishri.

Sūra (Ar.), chapter of the Koran.

Ta'anit Esther (Fast of *Esther), fast on the 13th of Adar, the day preceding Purim.

Takkanah (pl. ***takkanot**), regulation supplementing the law of the Torah; regulations governing the internal life of communities and congregations.

***Tallit (gadol),** four-cornered prayer shawl with fringes *(ẓiẓit)* at each corner.

***Tallit katan,** garment with fringes *(ẓiẓit)* appended worn during the day by observant male Jews under their outer garments.

***Talmud,** "teaching"; compendium of discussions on the Mishnah by generations of scholars and jurists in many academies over a period of several centuries. The Jerusalem (or Palestinian) Talmud mainly contained the discussions of the Palestinian sages. The Babylonian Talmud incorporates the parallel discussion in the Babylonian academies.

***Talmud torah,** term generally applied to Jewish religious (and ultimately to talmudic) study; also to traditional Jewish religious public schools.

***Tammuz,** fourth month of the Jewish religious year, tenth of the civil, approximating to June-July.

Tanna (pl. ***tannaim**), rabbinic teacher of mishnaic period.

***Targum,** Aramaic translation of the Bible.

***Tefillin,** phylacteries, small leather cases containing passages from Scripture and affixed on the forehead and arm by male Jews during the recital of morning prayers.

Tell (Ar. "mound," "hillock"), ancient mound in the Middle East composed of remains of successive settlements.

***Terefah,** food that is not **kasher*, owing to a defect in the animal.

***Territorialism,** 20th century trend in Jewish public life supporting the creation of an autonomous territory for Jewish mass-settlement outside Erez Israel.

***Tevet,** tenth month of the Jewish religious year, fourth of the civil, approximating to December-January.

Tikkun ("restitution," "reintegration"), (1) order of service for certain occasions, mostly recited at night; (2) mystical term denoting restoration of the right order and true unity after the spiritual "catastrophe" which occurred in the cosmos.

Tishah be-Av, Ninth of *Av, fast day commemorating the destruction of the First and Second Temples.

***Tishri,** seventh month of the Jewish religious year, first of the civil, approximating to September-October.

Tokhaḥah, reproof sections of the Pentateuch (Lev. 26 and Deut. 28); poems of reproof.

***Torah,** Pentateuch or the Pentateuchal scroll for reading in synagogue; entire body of traditional Jewish teaching and literature.

Tosafist, talmudic glossator, mainly French (12th–14th centuries), bringing additions to the commentary by *Rashi.

***Tosafot,** glosses supplied by tosafist.

***Tosefta,** a collection of teachings and traditions of the *tannaim*, closely related to the Mishnah.

Tradent, person who hands down a talmudic statement in the name of his teacher or other earlier authority.

***Tu bi-Shevat,** the 15th day of Shevat, the New Year for Trees; date marking a dividing line for fruit tithing; in modern Israel celebrated as an arbor day.

***Uganda Scheme,** plan suggested by the British government in 1903 to establish an autonomous Jewish settlement area in East Africa.

***Va'ad Le'ummi,** national council of the Jewish community in Ereẓ Israel during the period of the British *Mandate.

***Wannsee Conference,** Nazi conference held on Jan. 20, 1942, at which the planned annihilation of European Jewry was endorsed.

Waqf (Ar.), (1) a Muslim charitable pious foundation; (2) state lands and other property passed to the Muslim community for public welfare.

***War of Independence,** war of 1947–49 when the Jews of Israel fought off Arab invading armies and ensured the establishment of the new State.

***White Paper(s),** report(s) issued by British government, frequently statements of policy, as issued in connection with Palestine during the *Mandate period.

***Yad Vashem,** Israel official authority for commemorating the *Holocaust in the Nazi era and Jewish resistance and heroism at that time.

***Yeshivah,** Jewish traditional academy devoted primarily to study of the Talmud and rabbinic literature; *rosh yeshivah*, head of the yeshivah.

YHWH, the letters of the holy name of God, the Tetragrammaton.

Yibbum, see levirate marriage.

Yiḥud, "union"; mystical term for intention which causes the union of God with the **Shekhinah*.

Yishuv, settlement or popular group; more specifically, the Jewish community of Ereẓ Israel in the pre-State period. The pre-Zionist community is generally designated the "old yishuv" and the community evolving from 1880, the "new yishuv."

Yom Kippur, Yom ha-Kippurim, *Day of Atonement, solemn fast day observed on the 10th of Tishri.

Yoreh De'ah, see Shulḥan Arukh.

Yoẓer, hymn inserted in the first benediction *(Yoẓer Or)* of the morning **Shema*.

***Ẓaddik,** person outstanding for his faith and piety; especially a ḥasidic rabbi or leader.

***Ẓimẓum,** "contraction"; mystical term denoting the process whereby God withdraws or contracts within Himself so leaving a primordial vacuum in which creation can take place; primordial exile or self-limitation of God.

Zionist Commission (1918), commission appointed in 1918 by the British government to advise the British military authorities in Palestine on the implementation of the *Balfour Declaration.

Ẓiyyonei Zion, the organized opposition to Herzl in connection with the *Uganda Scheme.

***Ẓiẓit,** fringes attached to the **tallit* and **tallit katan*.

***Zohar,** mystical commentary on the Pentateuch; main textbook of *Kabbalah.

Zulat, hymn inserted after the **Shema* in the morning service.

Historiated initial letter "F" of the word *Fratibus* at the beginning of II Maccabees in a 12th-century manuscript from France. It illustrates the sending of the letter from the Jews of Jerusalem to their brethren in Egypt calling on them to observe the feast of Ḥanukkah. Bordeaux, Bibliothèque Municipale, Ms. 21, fol. 256v.

FRAENKEL (also **Frankel, Fraenckel, Frankl,** etc.), family widely scattered throughout Central and Eastern Europe. The name first appears in non-Jewish records as a designation for those who had immigrated to Vienna from "Frankenland," in the West. The family is traced back to two scholars in the Swabian town of Wallerstein in the 16th century, Moses ha-Levi Heller and Aaron Heller. Moses was the ancestor of Koppel Fraenkel ha-Levi "the rich" of Vienna (see below). Members of the family married into the patrician Teomim (called Munk in non-Jewish sources), Mirels, and Spiro families of Vienna and Prague. The name begins in Jewish use in the late 17th century, and after the expulsion of the Jews from Vienna (1670) is found throughout Central and Eastern Europe. KOPPEL FRAENKEL HA-LEVI (d. 1670), born in Baiersdorf, settled in Vienna around 1635 and became the richest man in the community. His sons DAVID ISAAC (Seckel), ISRAEL, and ENOCH (Hoenig) wound up the affairs of the Vienna community after the expulsion of 1670, giving 20,000 florins and the crown jewels of the principality of Moldavia (pawned to Koppel in 1665) as a security for the outstanding Jewish debts. They paid the city 4,000 florins for maintenance of the Jewish cemetery. With good conduct certificates, signed by Leopold I, they moved to Fuerth, where David Isaac became head of the community. Israel subsequently officiated as rabbi in Holesov, Uhersky Brod, Pinsk, and Wuerzburg. Enoch taught Hebrew to Johann Christoph *Wagenseil, and in 1683 sent him a letter stressing the importance of tolerance. Sons of Enoch were the ill-fated Ansbach Court Jews Elkan *Fraenkel and his brother Ẓevi Hirsch. GABRIEL and ZACHARIAS FRAENKEL, wealthy Court Jews to various south German principalities, resided in Fuerth but were not directly related to the Austrian levite branch. A son of David Isaac, ISSACHAR BERMAN (d. 1708), became chief rabbi of Schnaittach, Bavaria, **Landesrabbiner* of Ansbach, and rabbi of Brandenburg. Two of his sons, JUDAH LOEB and AARON LEVI, who published a collection of *seliḥot*, settled in Worms, where they and their descendants were prominent in communal life. The most noted of his numerous descendants was the founder of the Breslau seminary, Zacharias *Frankel. ISAAC SECKEL *FRAENKEL, the exponent of extreme Reform Judaism, was probably a descendant, as was L. A. *Frankl, the Austrian writer. Members of the family were among the Jews originally expelled from Vienna who settled in Berlin and Brandenburg, one of whom was appointed leader *(Obervorsteher)* of all the newly arrived Jews. BAERMANN FRAENKEL, another prominent communal leader, was fined 20 talers in 1705 for conducting a too-raucous Purim festival. The most famous of the Berlin Fraenkels was David ben Naphtali Hirsch *Fraenkel, teacher of Moses *Mendelssohn and rabbi of Berlin. His grandson JONAS FRAENCKEL (1773–1846), a wealthy Breslau merchant and philanthropist, donated the funds for the Breslau seminary. David Fraenkel's brothers, ABRAHAM and MOSES, were partners of V. H. *Ephraim in supplying precious metals to the mint. DAVID BEN MOSES FRAENKEL (d. 1865), director of the *Dessau Franzschule and editor of **Sulamith*, was a grandnephew of David Fraenkel; the wife of Leopold *Zunz was his grandniece. The Fraenkel family belonged to the upper stratum of Jewish society and through intermarriage was connected with numerous scholars and community leaders including Avigdor *Kara, Yom Tov Lippmann *Heller, Jacob *Emden, and Baruch *Fraenkel

Teomim. All Jews presently named Fraenkel may be descendants of the original Vienna family, though the exact relationship is no longer traceable.

Bibliography: L. Bato, in: *AJR Information* (July 1964), 12; M. M. Fraenkel-Teomim, *Der goldene Tiegel der Familie Fraenkel* (1928); Ger., Heb.); A. F. Pribram, *Urkunden und Akten zur Geschichte der Juden in Wien*, 1 (1918), index; D. Kaufmann, *Die letzte Vertreibung der Juden aus Wien* (1889), 144–8; Fraenkel, in: ZGGJT, 2 (1931/32), 67–80; E. K. Frenkel, *Family Tree of R. Moshe Witzenhausen* (1969); H. Schnee, *Die Hoffinanz und der moderne Staat*, 3 (1955), index; 4 (1963), index; S. Stern, *Der preussische Staat und die Juden* (1962), index. [Ed.]

FRAENKEL, DAVID BEN NAPHTALI HIRSCH (1707–1762), German rabbi and commentator on the Jerusalem Talmud. Fraenkel was born in Berlin. He was descended from the Mirels family that originated in Vienna and was also known as David Mirels. He studied under his father who was a *dayyan* in Berlin and under Jacob b. Benjamin ha-Kohen *Poppers, author of *Shev Ya'akov*. After living for a time in Hamburg, in 1737 he was appointed rabbi of Dessau, where Moses *Mendelssohn was one of his pupils. In 1739–42 his father Naphtali and his brother Solomon undertook the printing of Maimonides' *Mishneh Torah* on his initiative. In 1743 he was appointed chief rabbi of Berlin. Mendelssohn followed him to Berlin and continued to study under him (particularly Maimonides' *Guide of the Perplexed*) and also provided for his material needs. In Fraenkel's letter of appointment it was expressly stipulated that he was not to act as judge or give rulings in cases where members of his family, of whom there was a great number in Berlin, were involved. Fraenkel's jurisdiction extended to the districts of Brandenburg and Pomerania.

Fraenkel's main achievement is his commentary to the Jerusalem Talmud which constitutes his life work. It is divided into two parts: the first part, *Korban ha-Edah*, following Rashi's commentary to the Babylonian Talmud, is a running commentary aimed at elucidating the plain meaning of the text; the second part, *Shirei Korban*, in the manner of the *tosafot*, gives novellae and various notes to reconcile contradictions in the *Gemara* and correct the errors and inaccuracies that had accumulated in the text. At times his explanations in this commentary differ from those in *Korban ha-Edah*. The commentary appeared in parts: part one (Dessau, 1743) on *Mo'ed*, part two (Berlin, 1757) on *Nashim*, and part three (*ibid.*, 1760–62) on *Nezikin*. He commenced with *Mo'ed* because for *Zera'im* there already existed the commentary of Elijah b. Judah Leib of Fulda published in 1710. His commentary has become one of the two standard commentaries to the Jerusalem Talmud. He wrote Hebrew poems following various events in Prussia—the end of the Silesian wars (1745) and the victory of Prussia in the Seven Years' War (1757)—and published sermons that were translated, in part by Mendelssohn, into German.

Bibliography: E. L. Landshuth, *Toledot Anshei ha-Shem u-Fe'ullatam be-Adat Berlin* (1884), 35–60; M. Kayserling, *Moses Mendelssohn* (1862), 8ff.; M. Freudenthal, *Aus der Heimat Mendelssohns* (1900), 214ff., 229ff.; Z. Horowitz, in: *Ozar ha-Ḥayyim*, 6 (1930), 188; Waxman, Literature, 3 (1960[2]) 708ff.; E. Wolbe, *Geschichte der Juden in Berlin* (1937), 177, 188, 191; L. Ginzberg, *Perushim ve-Ḥiddushim ba-Yerushalmi*, 1 (1941), 55f. (Eng. introd.); J. Meisl, in: *Arim ve-Immahot be-Yisrael*, 1 (1946), 103; idem (ed.), *Pinkas Kehillat Berlin* (1962), index. [Y.Ho.]

FRAENKEL, EDUARD (1888–1970), classical scholar. Born in Berlin, Fraenkel studied under Ulrich von Wilamowitz-Moellendorff and was a member of the staff of *Thesaurus Linguae Latinae* in 1913. In 1917 he became a lecturer at Berlin University and in 1920 a professor. He was professor at Kiel in 1923, Goettingen in 1928, and in Freiburg in 1931. When Hitler came to power, he lost his chair and went to Britain where from 1935 to 1953 he was professor of Latin at Oxford. In 1941 he was elected a Fellow of the British Academy. Fraenkel had a remarkable range of scholarship. His Latin study led him to learn Greek; he used art to illuminate literature; studied archaeology; and always saw the life of the ancient people and how they lived behind the texts he worked on. His books include *Plautinisches im Plautus* (1922), an analysis of the Greek elements in Roman Comedy; *Aeschylus Agamemnon* (3 vols., edited in Eng., 1950); *Horace* (an examination of Horace's art in poetry, 1957); *Beobachtungen zu Aristophanes* (1962); *Kleine Beitraege zur klassischen Philologie* (2 vols., 1964); *Leseproben aus Reden Ciceros und Catos* (1968). [Ed.]

FRAENKEL, ELKAN (c. 1655–1720), *Court Jew in Ansbach. His father became rabbi in Fuerth and Bamberg after the expulsion of the Jews from Vienna in 1670. However Elkan antagonized the Fuerth community by advocating the interests of the margrave of Ansbach against the prelate of Bamberg, the traditional guardian of Fuerth Jewry. In 1703, Fraenkel became Court Jew of the margrave displacing the *Model family in this post, who thus became his bitter enemies. In 1704, he became an elder (*parnas*) of Fuerth and Ansbach Jewry. Although he could exercise magnanimity, reducing a fine of 30,000 florins imposed on the community for usurious practices to 20,000 florins, he was in general despotic and aroused much opposition. In 1712 he was denounced by Essaja (Jesse) Fraenkel, the spendthrift son of a Fuerth printer and a convert to Christianity, and falsely accused of 16 charges including witchcraft, lèse-majesté, debauchery, possession of blasphemous books, and hindering the confiscation of Hebrew books in Fuerth in 1702. He was sentenced to a public whipping and life imprisonment. His possessions were confiscated and his wife and daughter expelled. His brother Ẓevi Hirsch (d. 1723), appointed *Landesrabbiner* in 1709, was accused of witchcraft and use of kabbalistic devices to further Elkan's career. He received the same sentence and died in prison.

Bibliography: S. Stern, *The Court Jew* (1950), 193–4, 237–8, 244, 256–7; H. Schnee, *Die Hoffinanz und der Moderne Staat*, 4 (1963), 26–28; Ziemlich, in: MGWJ, 46 (1902), 88–93; idem, in: *Gedenkbuch D. Kaufmann* (1901), 457–86; Weinberg, in: MGWJ, 50 (1906), 94–99; S. Haenle, *Geschichte der Juden im ehemaligen Fuerstenthum Ansbach* (1867), 72–86; D. Y. Cohen, *Irgunei "Benei ha-Medinah" be-Ashkenaz* . . ., 1 (1968), 141ff.; 2 (1968), 135–7 (mimeographed dissertation; English summary). [Ed.]

FRAENKEL, FAIWEL (**Bar Tuviah**; 1875?–1933), Hebrew author and publicist. He was born in Vasilkov, in the district of Kiev. In 1893 he published his first article on Polish Jewish history in *Ha-Meliẓ*. He moved to Kiev, and in 1899 published a Hebrew translation of Pinsker's *Autoemancipation*, and a Hebrew translation and adaptation of Edward Bellamy's *Looking Backward* titled *Be-Od Me'ah Shanah* ("One Hundred Years Hence"). An active socialist, he was forced to leave Russia in 1901. He went to Switzerland, studied at the University of Berne, and received his doctorate in 1906 for his dissertation *Buckle und seine Geschichtsphilosophie* (Berner Studien, 1906). He lived in Geneva (1906–12), San Remo (1912–17), and Nice. Bar-Tuviah published many articles in Hebrew literary-scholarly periodicals, including *Ha-Dor*, *Ha-Me'orer*, *Ha-Olam*, *He-Atid*, *Ha-Tekufah*, *Miklat*, and *Hadoar*. They deal primarily with social science, Jewish studies, and with socialist theory. He was the first Hebrew writer to discuss social sciences in depth. In the field of Jewish studies he investigated the economic background of the formation of sects and parties in ancient Israel. His noteworthy contribution to this subject is his unfinished *Sefer ha-Nezirim,* a two-part history of asceticism among the Jews (1910). His more popular articles took up, in the main, questions of socialism and nationalism, and called for the negation of the Diaspora. His selected writings were published in 1964 by G. Elkoshi, accompanied by an evaluative biographical essay (9–40, and an annotated bibliography, 729–808).

Bibliography: Waxman, Literature, 4 (1960), 419ff. [G.El.]

FRAENKEL, ISAAC SECKEL (1765–1835), Hebrew translator and banker. Fraenkel, who was born in Parchim, Germany, was self-educated. He acquired extensive knowledge of religious and secular subjects and of ancient and modern languages. In 1798 he moved to Hamburg where he engaged in banking and became one of the community leaders, particularly in its Reform congregation. Fraenkel and M. I. Breslau edited a prayer book for the Hamburg Reform Temple (1818). His main literary project was the translation of the Apocrypha into Hebrew, entitled *Ketuvim Aḥaronim.* This work has frequently been reprinted since its first appearance in Leipzig (1830), its most recent edition appearing in Jerusalem in 1966. A bibliophile edition of the Books of the Maccabees, *Sefer ha-Ḥashmona'im,* appeared in Fraenkel's translation in 1964.

Bibliography: *Kitvei Menahem Mibashan ha-Ḥadashim* (1937), 145–58; S. Bernfeld, *Toledot ha-Reformaẓyon ha-Datit be-Yisrael* (1923), 72-73 and appendix B (excerpts from the prayer book). [G.K.]

FRAENKEL, JONAS (1879–1969), Swiss literary historian. Fraenkel was born in Cracow, Poland, studied at the Universities of Vienna and Berne, and became a lecturer at the latter in 1908 (professor extraordinary, 1921). He devoted himself to the investigation of German-Swiss literature and was the editor of the works of Gottfried Keller (17 vols., 1926–39). Other Swiss authors who engaged Fraenkel's attention were C. F. Meyer and his friend Carl Spitteler, whose unpublished works were bequeathed to Fraenkel for publication. In German literature Goethe and Heine were among his chief interests, and he published a new edition of Heine's poems (3 vols., 1911–13). Several of his essays were collected in *Dichtung und Wissenschaft* (1954). [L.W.K.]

FRAENKEL, LEVI BEN SAUL (Schaulsohn; 1761–1815), apostate member of the rabbinical *Fraenkel family. In 1806 he was nominated by the authorities assistant of the *Breslau *bet din* and *Oberlandesrabbiner* for Silesia (excluding Breslau), despite local objections. A year later he left the city, addressing an open letter to the community in which he acclaimed the French *Sanhedrin, advocated the unification of all religions, and expressed messianic hopes centered around *Napoleon. His letter caused consternation. In the same year in Paris he embraced Catholicism and thereafter wandered throughout Europe, until his death in extreme poverty and neglect in a Jewish hospital in Frankfort. He wrote a few mystical works.

Bibliography: M. Brann, in: *Jubelschrift . . . H. Graetz* (1887), 266–76; A. Freimann, in: ZHB, 4 (1900), 159. [Ed.]

FRAENKEL, LOUIS (1851–1911), Swedish financier. Born in Germany, Fraenkel moved to Stockholm in 1874 where in 1880 he established a successful banking firm. In 1893 he became executive manager of the Stockholm Handelsbank (now Svenska Handelsbanken), which he developed into one of the largest financial institutions in the country. Fraenkel's activity was characterized by the the personal manner in which he controlled his bank at a time when bureaucratic methods were becoming increasingly prevalent.

Bibliography: *Svenska män och kvinnor,* 2 (1944). [H.V./Ed.]

FRAENKEL-TEOMIM, BARUCH BEN JOSHUA EZEKIEL FEIWEL (1760–1828), rabbi in Poland and Moravia. Frankel-Teomim studied under Liber Korngold of Cracow, known as "Liber Ḥarif," and *David Tevele of Lissa. On the death in 1778 of Naphtali Herz Margolies, the *av bet din* of Wisznice, he was appointed his successor and served in this office until 1802. In that year he was appointed rabbi of Leipnik (Moravia), remaining there until his death. In Leipnik he founded a yeshivah which became renowned. Among his pupils were Ezekiel Panet, author of the *Mareh Yeḥezkel,* and Ḥayyim *Halberstamm, later his son-in-law (resp. *Ateret Ḥakhamim,* EH no. 9). During Fraenkel-Teomim's younger years *Ḥasidism began to spread in Poland and Galicia; at first he belonged to the circle of its opponents but later his opposition gradually diminished. Among the outstanding scholars with whom he was in contact may be mentioned Moses *Sofer (*ibid.,* ḤM nos. 12–15), with whom he was on intimate terms, David *Deutsch (*ibid.,* OḤ nos. 2,3), Ephraim Zalman *Margolies (*ibid.,* EH no. 21), and Mordecai *Banet of Nikolsburg.

Fraenkel-Teomim saw his main task in the strengthening of his yeshivah and the education of many pupils. He did not devote himself to the same extent to the writing of books, for fear of dissipating his time. Only individual pamphlets by him are extant. These were written by his pupils, who noted down his novellae and homilies. Among the first to collect his teachings and publish them were his son Joshua Hoeschel and Ḥayyim Halberstamm. They published his *Barukh Ta'am* (1841), a selection of his novellae to which Halberstamm added glosses. Fraenkel is often referred to by the name of this book. Among his other works may be mentioned: (1) *Ateret Ḥakhamim* (1866) in two parts: pt. 1, responsa on the four sections of the *Shulḥan Arukh;* pt. 2, novellae and **pilpulim* on talmudic themes; (2) *Margenita de-Rav* (1883; 2nd ed. with additions, 1957), a work on *aggadah* arranged in the order of the weekly scriptural readings, published by Menahem Eliezer Mahler from a manuscript in the possession of the author's grandchildren; (3) *Barukh she-Amar* (1905, 1966[2]), novellae on many tractates and talmudic themes.

Fraenkel-Teomim left glosses written in the margin of his books of the *rishonim* and *aḥaronim,* and there is a list of 53 such works. His glosses on the Shulḥan Arukh (OḤ, 1836; ḤM, 1860; YD, 1865; EH, 1904) under the title *Imrei Barukh* are highly regarded both in quality and quantity. His glosses to the Babylonian Talmud were published first in the Lemberg edition of the Talmud of 1862 and thereafter in all later editions; to the Jerusalem Talmud in Vilna in 1922; and to the Mishnah *Mishnot Rav* in Lemberg in 1862. His *Derushei Barukh Ta'am* (edited by B. S. Schneersohn and E. Heilprin, 1963) contains homilies for the festivals, and eulogies. Other works remain in manuscript.

His responsa and *pilpulim* on talmudic themes are based on the *rishonim,* and penetrating deeply into their meaning he arrives at the *halakhah.* Although he indulged in *pilpul,* a simple answer was more important to him than casuistic exercises. Even though he showed himself in his responsa to be a great authority he mentions in various places that he "fears to give directives" (*Ateret Ḥakhamim,* EH 18, 22). In certain cases he did not wish to rely on his own opinion and sought the consent of other outstanding scholars for his view, stressing: "I am afraid to give expression to new ideas" (*ibid.*, YD 2:24).

Bibliography: S. M. Chones, *Toledot ha-Posekim* (1910), 123; J. A. Kammelhar, *Dor De'ah* (1935), 143–9; J. Eibeschuetz, *Ohel Barukh* (1933); J. L. Maimon, in: *Sinai*, 44 (1959), 117–26, 204–12, 408–19; 45 (1959), 16–22, 97–106, 275–83; idem, *Middei Ḥodesh be-Ḥodsho*, 5 (1959), 49–57; Z. Horowitz, *Le-Korot ha-Kehillot be-Polanyah* (1969), 216f.; B. Fraenkel-Teomim, *Barukh she-Amar* (1966[2]), introd. 13–28 (biography).

[J.Ho.]

FRAGA, city in Aragon, N.E. Spain; information concerning Jews there dates to the 13th century. The privileges which the Jews enjoyed, later confirmed by Alfonso IV of Aragon (1327–36), include the usual definition of civil rights. The maximum annual tax payable by the community was specified. The Jews were given the right to elect their representatives, who were granted a limited jurisdiction and the right to impose levies for communal purposes. They were permitted to maintain a synagogue, cemetery, and slaughterhouse, and were given the right of defending themselves against attacks. In the 1380s there were 40 Jewish families living in Fraga. During the 1391 persecutions the synagogue was destroyed; many Jews left the town and others became converted to Christianity. In 1398 Queen Maria ordered 36 former members of the community to return to Fraga within a month, since they had undertaken not to leave without paying their share of the communal taxes. The most prominent member of the Fraga community, the physician Astruc Rimoch, embraced Christianity in 1414 as Franciscus de Sant Jordi. In September 1414 Ferdinand I ordered a number of converts to pay the tax they owed before their conversion. In 1436 John II permitted Jews to establish a new settlement in Fraga and the community apparently continued to exist until the expulsion in 1492.

Bibliography: Baer, Urkunden, index; Baer, Spain, index; Salarrullana, in: *Revista de archivos, bibliotecas, museos*, 40 (1919), 69, 183, 431; Romano, in: *Sefarad*, 13 (1953), 75, 78.

[Ed.]

FRAM, DAVID (1903–), South African Yiddish poet. Born in Ponevezh, Lithuania, he was a refugee with his parents in Russia during World War I, and on his return to Lithuania became a promising member of the Young Vilna school of poets. In 1927 he settled in South Africa, where he published his first book *Lider un Poemes* (1931), collected poems including nostalgic idylls of Jewish life in Lithuania, such as *"Baym Zeydn,"* as well as his first South African poems. Much of his later poetry dealt with South African themes and landscapes, but it remained rooted in the tradition and spirit of Lithuanian Jewry. Although not numerous, his writings are marked by a deep compassion for the underdog and a sensitive lyrical quality. Outstanding examples are two long poems, *"Efsher,"* largely biographical, and *"Dos Letste Kapitl"* (both 1947), an elegy on his destroyed Lithuanian homeland. Fram was also an editor (1934–42) of the Johannesburg Yiddish periodical, *Der Yidisher Ekspres*.

Bibliography: LNYL, 7 (1968), 439.

[G.Sa./L.Ho.]

FRANCE (Heb. פְּרַאנְצִיָּה and צָרְפַת), country in Western Europe. This entry is arranged according to the following outline:

From the First Settlements until the Revolution
- The Roman and Merovingian Periods
- From the Carolingians until the Eve of the First Crusade
- From the First Crusade until the General Expulsion from Provence (1096–1501)
- The Communities in Medieval France
- Scholarship in the Middle Ages
- From the Expulsion from Provence to the Eve of the Revolution

The Modern Period
- The Revolution
- Measures of Napoleon
- The Consistorial System
- Official Recognition
- Assimilation
- Abolition of the "Jewish Oath"
- Welfare and Education
- Protection of Jewish Rights
- Social and Economic Advances
- New Trends in Judaism
- Alliance Israélite Universelle
- Alsace-Lorraine and Algeria
- Anti-Semitism
- Separation of Church and State
- Demographic Changes
- World War I
- Inter-War Years
- Economic, Cultural, and Social Position

Holocaust Period
- Anti-Jewish Measures and Administration
- Deportations and Forced Labor
- Rescue and Resistance

Contemporary Period
- Native Population and Waves of Immigration
- Geographical Distribution
- Economic and Social Status
- Community Organization
- Cultural Life

Relations with Israel

This article deals with the history of the Jews living within the territory corresponding to present-day France; the territories beyond the present frontiers (more particularly those of the north and southwest) which were subjected to the authority of the kings of France for short periods are not considered here. The provinces neighboring on the kingdom of France or enclosed within it before their incorporation within the kingdom (in particular *Brittany, Normandy, *Anjou, *Champagne, *Lorraine, *Alsace, *Franche-Comté, *Burgundy, *Savoy, *Dauphiné, the county of *Nice, *Provence, *Comtat Venaissin, *Languedoc, *Auvergne, Guienne, *Poitou) are dealt with. Those areas which formed part of these provinces, but which are today beyond the borders of France, are not included.

From the First Settlements until the Revolution. THE ROMAN AND MEROVINGIAN PERIODS. The earliest evidence of a Jewish presence in France concerns an isolated individual, perhaps accompanied by a few servants; he was *Archelaus, the ethnarch of Judea, who was banished by Augustus in the year 6 C.E. to *Vienne (in the present department of Isère), where he died in 16 C.E. Similarly, his younger brother Herod *Antipas, tetrarch of Galilee and Perea, was exiled to *Lyons (if not to a place also called Lugdunum on the French side of the Pyrenees) by Caligula in 39. A story taken as legend (intended to explain the origin of the prayer *Ve-Hu Raḥum*) states that after the conquest of Jerusalem, the Romans filled three ships with Jewish captives, which arrived in *Bordeaux, *Arles, and Lyons. Recent archaeological findings tend to find a basis for this legend. Objects identified as Jewish because of the *menorah* portrayed on them have been discovered around Arles (first, fourth, and early fifth centuries), and in Bordeaux and the neighboring region (third and early fourth centuries). Written sources, previously treated with some reserve, affirm that during the Roman period Jews had been present in *Metz (mid-fourth century), *Poitiers (late fourth century), *Avignon (late fourth century), and Arles (mid-fifth century).

Evidence is abundant from 465 onward. There were then Jews in Vannes (Brittany), a few years later in *Clermont-Ferrand and *Narbonne, in *Agde in 506, in *Valence in 524, and in *Orléans in 533. After Clovis I (481–511), founder of the Merovingian dynasty, became converted to

Catholicism (496), the Christian population increasingly adopted Catholic doctrine. From 574 there were attempts to compel the Jews to accept the prevailing faith. In 576 Bishop *Avitus of Clermont-Ferrand offered the Jews of his town (who numbered over 500) the alternative of baptism or expulsion. His example was followed in 582 by Chilperic I, king of Neustria (the western part of the Frankish kingdom). In *Marseilles, where Jews from both these areas found refuge, there was also an attempt at forced conversion. Little information is available on a similar attempt made by Dagobert I between 631 and 639; had this been successful, the Jews would have been excluded from almost the whole of present-day France. However, this seems to have been far from the case; though documents make no mention of Jews for some time, there is a similar lack of information about other social and ethnic groups. Little is known of the Jews of Septimania (in southwest Gaul, then a Spanish province). The Jews there were spared the forced conversions and subsequent violent persecutions which befell their coreligionists in Visigothic *Spain.

During this period the number of Jews in France increased rapidly, initially through immigration, first from Italy and the eastern part of the Roman Empire and then from Spain, especially after Sisebut's persecutions, which began in 612. However, the increase in numbers was also due to Jewish proselytism, which found adherents mostly among the poorest classes and in particular among slaves.

At that time the Jews were mainly engaged in commerce, but there were already physicians and even sailors. In the absence of written Jewish sources, archaeological evidence once more provides information on the France of this early period. On a seal from Avignon (fourth century) the *menorah* is reproduced, although only with five branches. The same motif appears on the inscription of Narbonne (687/8), which also points to a scanty knowledge of Hebrew at the time; the whole text is in Latin with the exception of three words, *Shalom al Yisrael*, which are incorrectly spelled. Nothing at all is known of the internal organization of these Jewish groups, except for the presence of synagogues (*Paris 582; Orléans before 585), but it is known that there were contacts between them. The Marseilles community maintained relations with those of Clermont-Ferrand and Paris and even, beyond the borders, with that of Rome.

In spite of the attempts at forced conversion, relations between the Jewish and Christian populations seem to have been free, a state of affairs demonstrated by the repeated efforts of the church authorities to prohibit these relations. The main prohibition, frequently repeated, was on Jews and Christians taking meals together (Vannes, 465; Agde, 506; Epaon, 517; etc.); another, aimed at separating the population further, forbade the Jews to go out-of-doors during the Easter holidays (Orléans, 538; *Mâcon, 583; etc.); and finally—a measure designed to prevent Jewish proselytism—possession of not only Christian but also pagan slaves by the Jews was restricted or forbidden (Orléans, 541; Clichy, 626 or 627; etc.). Further, though at first sight negative, proof of good relations between Christians and Jews is provided by the frequent religious *disputations, discussions which were characterized by the great freedom in argument accorded to the Jews (particularly between King Chilperic I (561–84) and his Jewish purveyor *Priscus, 581). Another positive testimony—though this may be largely a pious invention—is to be found in the participation of the Jews in the obsequies of church dignitaries (Arles, 459 and 543; Clermont-Ferrand, 554).

From the Carolingians until the Eve of the First Crusade. The reign of the Carolingians was the most favorable period for the Jews in the kingdom of France. *Agobard's attempted forced conversion of Jewish children in Lyons and district around 820 brought the bishop into disfavor with Louis the Pious (814–840).

The important Jewish settlement in the Rhone Valley, which had been in existence during the Roman and Merovingian periods, increased and expanded through the Saône Valley. Continued immigration from Italy and Spain was a source of demographic growth, as was proselytism affecting also the higher social classes; the best-known example is *Bodo, deacon of Louis the Pious, who converted to Judaism in Muslim Spain. From the second half of the tenth century and, at the latest, from the second half of the 11th century, there was also a trend toward migration to England.

The most intensive economic activity of the Jews of France, especially in the commercial field, belongs to this period. Some were accredited purveyors to the imperial court and others administered the affairs of Catholic religious institutions. Privileges granted to the Jews by the Carolingian emperors became the model for those coveted by other merchants. Their great concentration in agriculture and especially viticulture enabled them practically to monopolize the market; even the wine for Mass was bought from Jews. The few cases of moneylending known from this period were in fact connected with this agricultural activity; they were related to deferred purchases of agricultural estates intended to round off existing Jewish estates. In view of the wealth of general information available on the Jews of this period, the paucity of evidence concerning physicians suggests that there was a great decrease of interest in this profession. In the public services, Jews were employed both in the subordinate position of tax collector and in the most respected office of imperial ambassador (*Isaac for *Charlemagne; Judah for Charles the Bald).

The personal privileges and ordinances granted by the Carolingians assured the Jews complete judicial equality. Moreover, any attempt to entice away their pagan slaves by converting them to Catholicism was penalized; their right to employ salaried Christian personnel was explicitly guaranteed; any offense against their persons or property was punishable by enormous fines. Even more, the Jews enjoyed a preferential status, because they were not subjected to the ordeals ("judgments of God") which normally formed part of the judicial process. An imperial official, the *magister Judaeorum*, who ranked among the *missi dominici*, supervised the meticulous enforcement of all these privileges.

The activities of the church councils had little effect during this period. The Councils of Meaux and Paris (845–6) sought to legislate on the subject of the Jews, and a series of hostile canons concerning them were drawn up; these were in fact a kind of canonical collection and the work of *Amulo, Agobard's successor to the see of Lyons, and the deacon *Florus of Lyons, faithful secretary of both bishops. However, Charles the Bald (840–77) refused to ratify these canons. Another center of intensive Jewish settlement and powerful anti-Jewish reaction was *Chartres, where at the beginning of the 11th century, Bishop *Fulbert delivered a series of sermons to refute the Jewish assertion that, since there might yet be Jewish kings in distant lands, the Messiah had not yet come. Toward the close of the same century, *Ivo of Chartres inserted a series of violently anti-Jewish texts in his canonical collection. All of these, however, precisely by their concern to combat Jewish influences on the Christian faithful, emphasize the cordiality of the relations prevailing between Jews and Christians.

The so-called "Carolingian Renaissance" in the intellec-

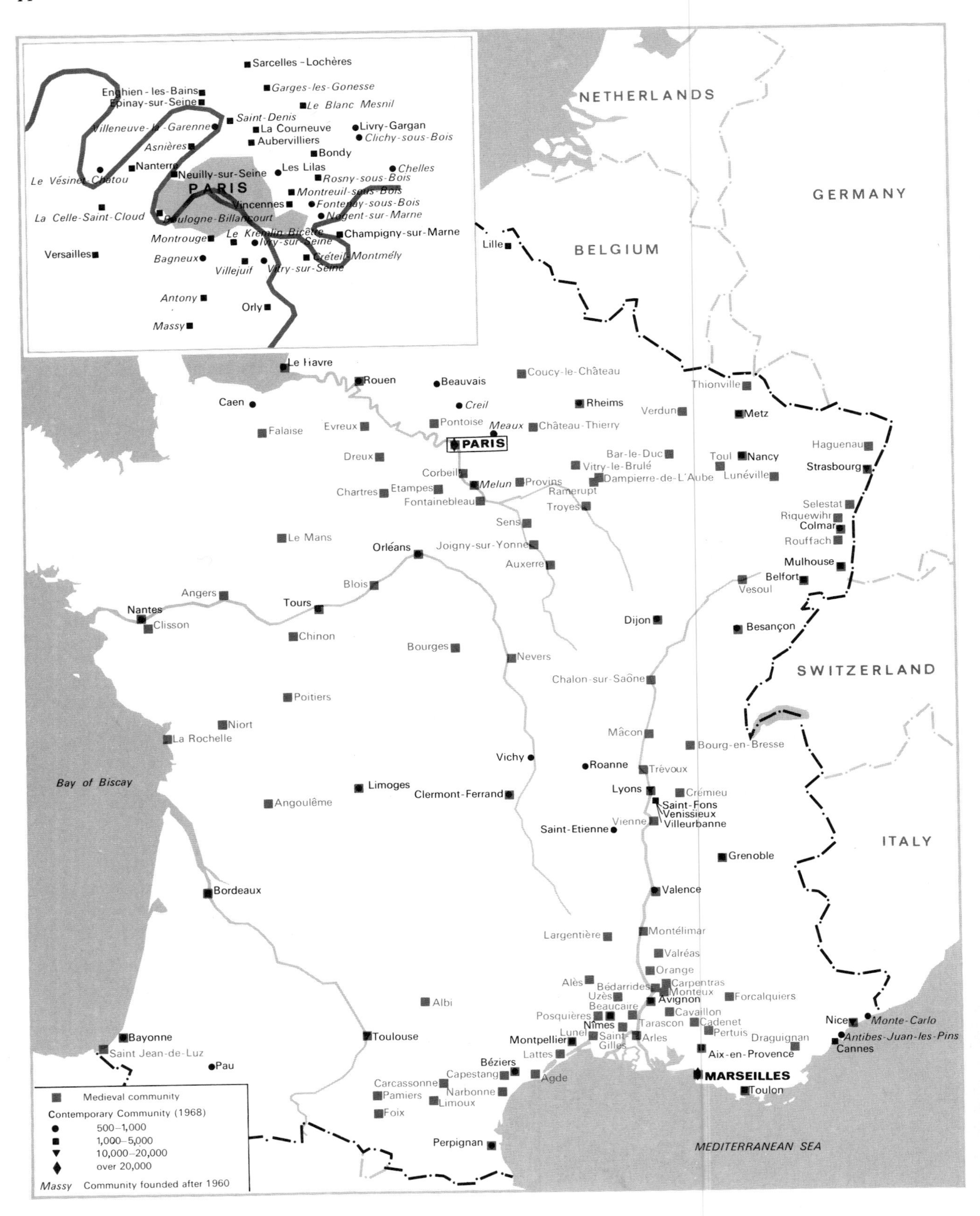

Main Jewish communities in France in the Middle Ages and in 1968.

tual sphere had no counterpart on the Jewish scene, but strangely enough, subsequent tradition also attributes the impetus of Jewish learning in the West to Charlemagne (768–814). Just as he actually brought scholarly Irish monks to France, he is said to have brought the Jewish scholar *Machir from Babylon. What is known of Hebrew works circulating in France derives from the testimony of Agobard, but, being a polemist, he mentions only those works he criticizes: a very ancient version of **Toledot Yeshu*, a parody of the Gospels, and **Shi'ur Komah*, a mystic work. The real upsurge of Jewish learning in France began during the 11th century. In the middle of the century, Joseph b. Samuel *Bonfils (Tov Elem) was active in Limoges, Moses ha-Darshan in Narbonne, and, a little later, *Rashi in Troyes. From the outset, the scholars' works comprised the principal fields of Jewish learning: liturgic poetry, biblical and talmudic commentaries, rabbinic decisions, grammar, and philology. The glory of Limoges and central France in general was shortlived, but Narbonne and Troyes heralded the great schools of Jewish scholars in both the extreme south and the extreme north of the country. The radical change in the situation resulted from the general upheaval which swept across the Christian West from the beginning of the 11th century and paved the way for the Crusades. Two local persecutions, in *Limoges at the end of the tenth and in the early 11th century, may be connected with the general persecution which raged through France from 1007 for at least five years. Launched by the clergy, it was rapidly supported by King Robert II the Pious (996–1031), then propagated by the general Christian population. The pretext for the riots was the accusation that the Jews of Orléans had joined in a plot against Christians with Sultan al-Ḥākim, who had indeed destroyed the Church of the Holy Sepulcher in Jerusalem. Thus the object of universal hatred, the Jews of France were then, if the sources are correct, either expelled from the towns, put to the sword, drowned in the rivers, or put to death in some other fashion, the only exceptions being those who accepted baptism. When one of the Jewish notables of France, Jacob b. Jekuthiel, intervened with Pope John XVIII (1004–09), the latter sent a legate to France to put a stop to the persecutions. Those Jews who had been forced to accept baptism immediately returned to Judaism. A similar situation arose in 1063: the "Spanish crusaders," who had set out to fight the Muslims, began by persecuting the Jews of southern France. On this occasion, however, they met with the opposition of the princes and the bishops, who were congratulated by Pope *Alexander II for their stand.

From the First Crusade until the General Expulsion from Provence (1096–1501). The First Crusade (1096–99) had little immediate effect on the situation of the Jews, but it was in France that the first murderous persecutions occurred, accompanied by forced conversions in *Rouen and Metz (but not in southern France, as some scholars have asserted recently). Although the brunt of the brutalities was borne by the Jews of Germany, it was in Rouen that the crusaders justified their persecutions of the Jews: "If it is our desire [so they said] to attack the enemies of God after having covered lengthy distances toward the Orient while before our eyes we have the Jews, a nation whose enmity to God is unequaled, we will then follow a path which leads us backward." The first written legal act of a king of France which is extant is *Louis VII's decree of 1144 in which he banished from his kingdom those Jews who had been converted to Christianity and later returned to Judaism, that is those who—from the Christian point of view—had "relapsed into heresy." The Second Crusade (1147–49) gave rise to a controversy between *Bernard of Clairvaux and *Peter of Cluny on the question of the Jews; although they were spared the confiscation of all their belongings, as the abbot of Cluny had recommended in order to finance this expedition, they were nevertheless compelled to make a considerable financial contribution.

France's first *blood libel occurred in *Blois in 1171, when 31 Jews—men, women, and children—were burned at the stake after a parody of a trial, and in spite of the fact that not even a body was produced as proof of the murder. A series of similar accusations followed in Loches, *Pontoise, Joinville, and Épernay. Although Louis VII declared to the leaders of the Jewish community of Paris when they appealed to him that he regarded the ritual murder accusation as pure invention and promised to prevent the renewed outbreaks of similar persecutions, popular rumors continued to indict the Jews. According to his biographer, King *Philip Augustus (1180–1223), when only six years old, learned from his playmates that the Jews were in the habit of killing Christian children. The hatred thus nurtured prevailed, and he acted upon it soon after his accession to the throne. In 1181 he had all the wealthy Jews of Paris thrown into prison and freed them only in return for a huge ransom. In the following year (1182) he decreed their expulsion from the kingdom and the confiscation of their real estate. If the number of Jews affected by this measure was comparatively small, this was the result of the small size of the actual kingdom of France and the lack of royal authority over the nobles of the neighboring provinces, where the exiles found immediate refuge. Such a haven, however, was not always safe from the tenacious hatred of the king of France. Thus, in 1190, he pursued the Jews in Champagne (in *Bray-sur-Seine or in Brie-Comte-Robert) and exterminated a whole community which had the temerity to condemn one of his subjects to death for assassinating a Jew.

Driven by financial considerations, Philip Augustus authorized the return of the Jews to his kingdom in 1198, extorting from them what profit he could. Possibly another concern was also involved: from 1182 Philip Augustus had considerably expanded his territory. In all the lands incorporated within the kingdom, he found Jews living among a population which raised no objection to their presence, and he might have seriously angered the populace by expelling the Jews. Since he tolerated the Jews in the newly acquired parts of his kingdom, their banishment from its heart was no longer justified. Two months after their readmission, the king reached an agreement with Thibaut II, count of Champagne, on the division of their respective rights over the Jews living in their territories.

The Third Crusade (1189–92), which had such grave consequences for the Jews of England, did not affect those of France, but the crusade against the *Albigenses in southern France also spelled ruin to the Jewish communities. That of *Béziers, in particular, mourned many victims when the town was taken in 1209; the survivors crossed the Pyrenees and reestablished their community in *Gerona.

During the reign of *Louis IX (1226–70), severe anti-Jewish persecutions took place in 1236 in the western provinces, in Brittany, Anjou, and Poitou, which were not subject to the direct authority of the monarch. In 1240 Duke Jean le Roux expelled the Jews from Brittany. During the same year the famous disputation on the Talmud took place in Paris. Properly speaking, it was a trial of the Talmud inspired by a bull issued by *Gregory IX in 1239. The verdict had already been given in advance: the Talmud was to be destroyed by fire, a sentence which was carried out in 1242. In Dauphiné, which was still independent of the kingdom, ten Jews were burned at the stake in *Valréas in 1247 following a blood libel. Anti-Jewish agitation which resulted in the imprisonment of Jews and the confiscation of their belongings spread to several places in Dauphiné. There is no reason to believe that Louis IX had intended to expel the Jews or that he had even issued an order to this effect. Yet his brother, *Alphonse of Poitiers, to whom the king had ceded the government of several provinces, ordered the expulsion of the Jews from Poitou in July 1249. However, the order was not rigorously applied or it took effect for a brief period only. Nevertheless, the territory governed by Alphonse was the scene of the first local expulsion: from Moissac in 1271. Louis IX and Alphonse of Poitiers rivaled one another in their brutal methods of extorting money from the Jews. The king, ostentatiously scrupulous of benefiting from money earned through the sin of usury, dedicated it to the financing of the Crusade. With the same pious motive Alphonse of Poitiers incarcerated all the Jews of his provinces so that he could lay his hands on

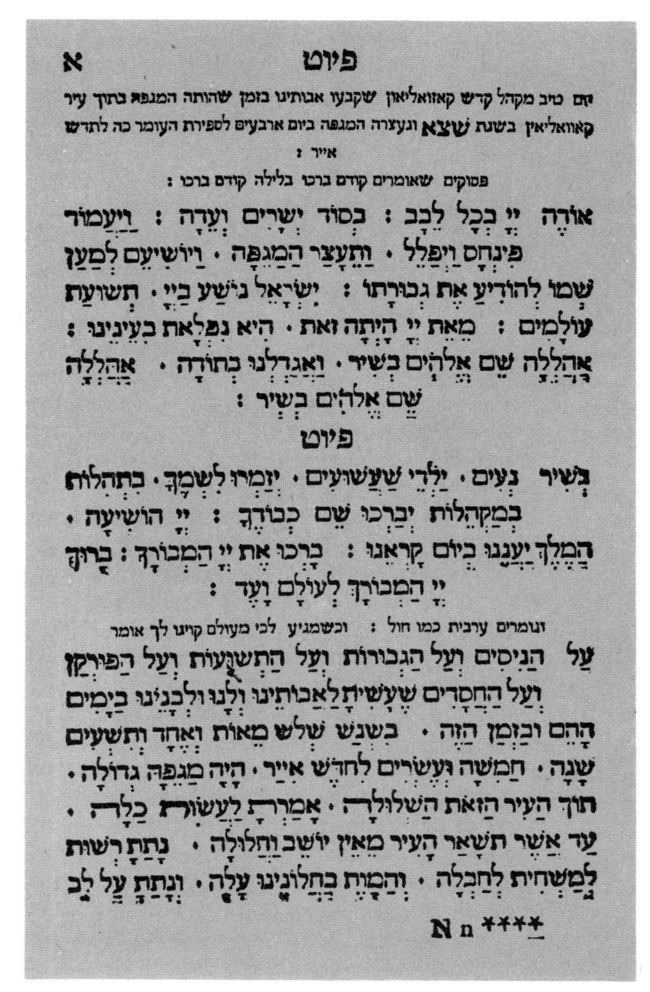

פיוט א

יום טוב מקהל קדש קאוואליאון שקבעו אבותינו בזמן שהותה המגפה בתוך עיר קאוואליאון בשנת שצא ונעצרה המגפה ביום ארבעים לספירת העומר כה לחדש אייר :

פסוקים שאומרים קודם ברכו בלילה קודם ברכו :

אודה יי בכל לבב : בסוד ישרים ועדה : ויעמוד
פינחס ויפלל · ותעצר המגפה · ויושיעם למען
שמו להודיע את גבורתו : ישראל נושע ביי · תשועת
עולמים : מאת יי היתה זאת · היא נפלאת בעינינו :
אהללה שם אלהים בשיר · ואגדלנו בתודה · אהללה
שם אלהים בשיר :

פיוט

בשיר נעים · ילדי שעשועים · יזמרו לשמך · בתהלות
במקהלות יברכו שם כבודך : יי הושיעה ·
המלך יעננו ביום קראנו : ברכו את יי המבורך : ברוך
יי המבורך לעולם ועד :

וגומרים ערבית כמו חול : וכשמגיע לכי מעולם קוינו לך אומר

על הניסים ועל הגבורות ועל התשועות ועל הפורקן
ועל החסדים שעשית לאבותינו ולנו ולבנינו בימים
ההם ובזמן הזה · בשנת שלש מאות ואחד ותשעים
שנה · חמשה ועשרים לחדש אייר · היה מגפה גדולה ·
תוך העיר הזאת השלולה · אמורה לעשורת כלה ·
עד אשר תשאר העיר מאין יושב וחלולה · נתת רשות
למשחית לחבלה · והמות בחלונינו עלה · ונתת על לב

N n ****

Figure 1. First page of a prayer book from Cavaillon, containing *piyyutim* recited at the special Purim celebrating the community's deliverance from a plague in 1631. Cecil Roth Collection.

their possessions with greater ease. *Philip III the Bold, who reigned from 1270, was responsible for a widespread migration of the Jews when he forbade them, in 1283, to live in the small rural localities. The accession of *Philip IV the Fair (1285) was ushered in by the massacre of *Troyes, once more following on a blood libel; several notables of the community were condemned and burned at the stake in 1288. In 1289, first *Gascony (which was an English possession) and then Anjou (governed by the brother of the king of France) expelled the Jews. In 1291, Philip the Fair hastily published an ordinance prohibiting the Jews expelled from Gascony and England from settling in France.

Although Philip the Fair denied the clergy in general (1288) and the inquisitors in particular (1302) any judicial rights over the Jews, this was not the better to protect them but merely because he objected to sharing his authority in any way. It was therefore probably royal judges who tried the first *host desecration cases brought against several Jews of Paris in 1290. In order to guarantee the greatest financial gain from the expulsion order of 1306, Philip the Fair issued oral instructions only. After the imprisonment of all the Jews (July 22, 1306) and the seizure of their belongings, numerous written ordinances were issued by the royal chancellery in order to secure for the king, if possible, the sum total of the spoils. Over this very question of the Jews, the resurgent royal authority was revealed; indeed, the expulsion order won the successive support of an ever-growing number of lords until its provisions even spread to the territories of those lords who had not been consulted. As well as in the provinces which still evaded royal authority—Lorraine, Alsace, Franche-Comté, Savoy, Dauphiné, Provence with the principality of *Orange and Comtat Venaissin, the counties of *Roussillon and Cerdagne (Cerdaña)—the Jews banished from France found asylum on the present territories of Belgium, Germany, Italy, and Spain. Philip the Fair granted safe-conducts to a number of Jews to enable them to stay in his kingdom or return to it; they were to assist him in collecting the debts which had been seized. In 1311 they too were "permanently" expelled. Although the expulsion itself encountered scarcely any objections on the part of the lords, this was far from the case when the king tried to seize all the booty for himself: bitter disagreements often followed, as in Montpellier.

The recovery of all the spoils was still far from complete when *Louis X the Quarreler (1314–16), son and successor of Philip the Fair, considered allowing the Jews to return (May 17, 1315), which actually came into effect before July 28, 1315. A decree of that date, repudiating the "evil advisers" who had incited his father to expel the Jews and justifying Louis' decision to recall them because of the "general clamor of the people," defined the conditions of Jewish residence for a 12-year period. Under Philip V the Tall (1316–22) anti-Jewish massacres were perpetrated by the *Pastoureaux in 1320, and the Jews of *Toulouse and areas to the west of the town suffered heavily. There the king, his officers, and the church authorities combined in efforts to suppress the movement, principally because it was a serious threat to the social order. Popular mania against lepers spread to the Jews in several places in 1321, particularly in *Tours, *Chinon, and Bourges (or elsewhere in Berry). Without even a legal pretext, Jews were put to death in all these places, 160 in Chinon alone. As well as the confiscation of the belongings of the Jews thus "brought to justice," an immense fine was imposed on the whole of French Jewry. The expulsion—no text of the decree ordaining it remains—took place between April 7 and Aug. 27, 1322.

In 1338 and 1347 over 25 Jewish communities of Alsace were the victims of persecutions which were limited to the eastern regions. On the other hand, the massacres connected with the *Black Death (1348 and 1349), struck Jewish communities throughout the eastern and southeastern regions, notably in Provence, Savoy, Dauphiné, Franche-Comté, and Alsace. It was only due to the intervention of the pope that the Jews of Avignon and Comtat Venaissin were spared a similar fate. In Franche-Comté, after they had been accused of spreading the plague, the Jews were imprisoned for long periods and their possessions confiscated; they were expelled in 1349, although they reappeared there at the latest in 1355. In that same year Dauphiné was practically incorporated within the kingdom of France, yet the Jews of this province continued to enjoy their former freedoms and immunities.

The crown never revealed the financial motive behind the readmission of the Jews so blatantly as in 1359. *Charles V (1364–80), regent for his father John II the Good who was held prisoner in England, then authorized their return for a period of 20 years simply in order to use the taxes to enable him to pay his father's ransom. Following the example of Louis the Quarreler, he allowed the Jews to reside in France for limited periods only, although in his case the residence periods which had been granted were more faithfully abided by. In 1360 John the Good (1350–64) ratified the authorization granted by his son.

When Charles V succeeded to the throne, he confirmed, in May 1364, the 20 years which were initially granted and prolonged the period by six years, then by a further ten years in October 1374. When *Charles VI (1380–1422) took over the government himself, in February 1388 and March 1389, he ratified the prolongations granted by Charles V; he did not ratify either the five or the six years accorded by Louis of Anjou, acting as regent for him (1380–88). Thus, after the decree of Sept. 17, 1394, stipulating that thenceforward the Jews would no longer be tolerated in the kingdom of France, the departure of the Jews became effective in 1395 (between January 15 and March 18), 36 years after the first concession for a new residence period granted by Charles V. Properly speaking, this was not actually an expulsion but rather a refusal to renew the right of residence. However, obviously it resulted in the departure of the Jews from the kingdom of France.

From 1380 the Jews were the victims of bloody persecutions, which followed in the wake of popular risings in several towns of the kingdom, especially in Paris and Nantes. There was a similar occurrence in 1382. Although the king exempted the Jews from returning the pawns which had been stolen from them on this occasion, he also granted a hasty pardon to the rioters. In 1389 the king allowed the town of Eyrieu the right of deciding for itself whether it would admit the Jews or not; although such a prerogative was subsequently granted to the towns of Alsace in general, this was at that time an exception within the kingdom. There was, however, no reason to regard this as a harbinger of the forthcoming generalized departure of the Jews. On the contrary, as late as July 15, 1394, the king issued a reasonably favorable decree to the Jews of Languedoc. When Charles VI terminated the residence of the Jews in his kingdom on September 17, he claimed that there had been "several grave complaints and outcries" concerning "the excesses and misdemeanors which the said Jews had committed and they continued to act in this manner every day against the Christians." He added that investigations had confirmed that the Jews had "committed and perpetrated several crimes, excesses, and offenses," particularly against the Christian faith, but such a justification for his action does not seem plausible. However, on this occasion there was no financial motive behind the expulsion, for it was not accompanied by confiscations. The move therefore remains inexplicable. This time the Jews of Franche-Comté shared the fate of their brothers in the kingdom, although the province did not then belong to the king of France.

From the second half of the 14th century, the voluntary movement of Jews from Dauphiné assumed ever greater proportions. The dauphin attempted to coax them back by offering fiscal advantages, but without success. By the early 16th century no more Jews lived in Dauphiné. In Savoy the situation of the Jews deteriorated throughout the 15th century: Jewish books were seized in 1417; there was a local expulsion from Châtillon-les-Dombes in 1429, a bloody persecution in 1466, and a general expulsion decree in 1492. In Provence, the greater part of the 15th century, especially during the reign of René I the Good (1431–80), was a favorable period for the Jews, aside from a few local incidents, for example in *Aix-en-Provence in 1430. Conditions changed from 1475 on when, for the first time since the Black Death, there were anti-Jewish outbreaks in several places. Between 1484 and 1486 attacks against the Jews occurred in numerous localities (notably in Aix, Marseilles, and Arles). After Provence was incorporated in France (1481), town after town demanded the expulsion of the Jews until the last remaining Jews were hit by a general expulsion order in 1498 which was completely enforced by 1501. There were therefore practically no Jews left within the present borders of France, with the exception of Alsace and Lorraine, Avignon, Comtat Venaissin, and the county of Nice.

THE COMMUNITIES IN MEDIEVAL FRANCE. *Benjamin of Tudela records valuable details on the southern communities of the third quarter of the 12th century. According to his figures—confirmed for Narbonne by other contemporary sources—in six communities there were 1,240 heads of families, that is more than 6,000 souls. Another document of the same period, the list of the martyrs of *Blois, notes there were about 30 families or about 150 souls in this community, which would have been totally unknown if it had not been for the tragedy which befell it. The greatest number and widest dispersion of Jews in France was attained during the third quarter of the 13th century. There were about 150 localities inhabited by Jews in Île-de-France and Champagne, about 50 in the duchy of Burgundy, about 30 in Barrois—in spite of its small area—and many others. From 1283, as a result of the prohibition on residing in small places, the communities in the towns grew larger. The total number of Jews continued to increase, and some have estimated that about 100,000 Jews were affected by the expulsion of 1306. Migration resulting from this banishment and the losses during the Black Death—both by the plague itself and in the persecutions which it sparked off—considerably reduced the Jewish population until the middle of the 14th century. There was a slight increase from then on, especially after the authorization to return in 1359. However, after the 1394/95 expulsion from the kingdom of France and the subsequent expulsions from the other provinces or voluntary departures due to hostile pressure combined with ever greater fiscal extortions, only about 25,000 Jews at the most remained during the 15th century. By 1501 they numbered a few thousand only. If Catholic missionary activity did achieve some tangible results—due mostly to coercion if not outright violence—this was the least factor in the demographic decline of the Jewish community.

From the 12th century onward, moneylending became increasingly prominent as a Jewish occupation. It was particularly pronounced—to the point of being sometimes their sole activity—in the places where the Jews settled at a later date or after the readmissions to the kingdom of France. In the main, these were private loans, with a multitude of creditors and a small turnover. In the east and southeast the Jews were principally traders in agricultural produce and livestock. Throughout the south, particularly in Provence, there were a relatively large number of physicians who, in addition to practicing among Jews, were sometimes also appointed by the towns to take care of the Christian population. The agriculture, and especially viticulture, subsisting mainly outside the kingdom, supplied the needs of the Jewish population and only exceptionally the general market. Petty public officials, watchmen, toll-gatherers, etc., were found especially in the south, but rarely after the 13th century (one of the few exceptions was the principality of Orange). Halfway between commerce and public office was the activity of broker, often found in Provence.

The regulations of the Fourth *Lateran Council (1215), interpreted as the compulsory wearing of the Jewish *badge, were at first imposed in Languedoc, Normandy, and Provence (by councils held in 1227, 1231, and 1234); a royal decree enforcing this in the kingdom of France was not promulgated until 1269. However, compulsory residence in a Jewish quarter dates from 1294 in the kingdom of France, although only from the end of the first half of the 14th century in Provence. Although the French crown often sought to protect the Jews from Church jurisdiction—especially that of the inquisitors—it imposed the legal disabilities or measures of social segregation which had been first advocated by the church itself. Following the example of the *magister Judaeorum* of the Carolingian period, "guardians" of the Jews were often appointed; in the kingdom of France there was one for the Languedoc and another for the Langue d'Oïl which included approximately the regions situated to the north of the River Loire. Their authority extended to all legal suits in which Jews were one of the parties. Jewish internal jurisdiction was increasingly limited; thus in Provence even simple administrative matters in the synagogue were brought before the public tribunal. A special form of oath (see *Oath, *more judaico*) was laid down for Jews who were witnesses or parties to a trial.

In the 13th century Christian polemical writings increased considerably: in practice Judeo-Christian disputations were relatively free and still quite frequent. After early warnings, followed by the explicit church prohibition on the participation of laymen in such discussions, they became increasingly rare. The Jews lost none of their sharpness in these confrontations: the most outstanding examples are the *Sefer ha-Mekanne* and the polemic treatise which goaded *Nicholas of Lyra into a reply.

The Jewish communities organized themselves with increasing efficiency. Although the earliest confirmation of internal statutes dates from 1413 (Avignon), these were certainly current practice long before then. As well as these statutes—which regulated internal administration through elected officials (actual power lay in the hands of the wealthiest), financial contributions toward communal expenses, and religious obligations—sumptuary regulations were often laid down, intended to limit the ostentatious display of riches. The first synods (gatherings of communal representatives) are known from the middle of the 12th century. At the synod of Troyes in 1150, the representatives of the French communities were joined by officials from German communities. The 1160 synod, also held in Troyes, convened only representatives from the kingdom of France, Normandy, and Poitou. Therefore it is evident that this was not a firmly established institution convened at regular intervals. If, as seems apparent, these synods normally involved the attendance only of communities directly concerned, it is astonishing that the synod of *Saint-Gilles (1215) convened the representatives of the communities between Narbonne and Marseilles only to discuss a problem of the greatest importance for the whole of Jewry living in Christian countries: how to prevent the promulgation of the projected anti-Jewish canons by the Fourth Lateran Council. With the proliferation and increase of Jewish taxes, the civil authorities rapidly realized that a Jewish inter-communal organization covering the area under their authority served their interests; it became the task of this organization to assess and to collect all the taxes levied on the Jews. Although some communities tried to make use of this arrangement to reach a direct, and more advantageous, agreement with the authorities, when misfortune struck an isolated community, others often spontaneously revealed their active solidarity. Thus, at the time of the tragedy of Blois, the communities of Orléans and Paris brought relief to the persecuted.

Scholarship in the Middle Ages. The leading centers of Jewish scholarship were found in Île-de-France (principally Paris, then *Dreux, *Melun, Pontoise, *Corbeil, *Coucy-le-Château, and Chartres) and in Champagne (led by Troyes, then *Dampierre-sur-Aube, *Vitry-le-Brulé, *Joigny-sur-Yonne, *Joinville, *Château-Thierry, and *Ramerupt); there was also a concentration of centers of learning in the Loire Valley (Orléans, Tours, and Chinon). As well as this, there were a number of schools in Languedoc (headed by Narbonne, then Argentière, *Beaucaire, *Béziers, Lattes, *Lunel, *Montpellier, *Nîmes,

Figure 2. The 18th-century Rue des Quatre Passeports in the Jewish quarter of Clermont-Ferrand. Courtesy Clermont-Ferrand Municipality.

*Posquières, *Capestang, and *Carcassonne) and in Provence (with Arles, *Trinquetaille, and Marseilles, then Salon and Aix-en-Provence). A few other provinces were also active, though on a much more modest scale; in the wake of Ile-de-France came Normandy (with *Evreux and *Falaise and possibly also Rouen) and Brittany (Clisson); in the wake of Champagne, Burgundy (with *Dijon); following Provence, Comtat Venaissin (with Monteux and *Carpentras), as well as Orange and Avignon; and after Languedoc, Roussillon (with *Perpignan). Lorraine (with *Verdun, *Toul, and Metz) and Alsace (with *Strasbourg and *Sélestat) assured a link between northern France and the Rhineland. By contrast, Dauphiné (with only Vienne), and especially Franche-Comté and Savoy, hardly played any part in this intellectual ferment.

The north was principally the home of talmudic and biblical commentaries, anti-Christian polemics, and liturgical poetry. In the south scholarly activities extended to grammatical, linguistic, philosophical, and scientific studies, and innumerable translations (mostly from Arabic, but also from Latin). Of particular importance were the mystic circles which gave an impetus to the kabbalist movement. Both north and south produced decorated and even richly illuminated manuscripts.

From the Expulsion from Provence to the Eve of the Revolution. As soon as the Jews had left the southeast or been converted to Christianity and thus become permanently absorbed within the general population, the southwest witnessed the arrival of secret Jews, the *Conversos. From 1550, these "Portuguese merchants" or "New Christians" were granted letters patent by Henry II, who authorized them to live in France "wherever they desired." They settled mainly in Bordeaux and in Saint-Esprit, near *Bayonne. They were subsequently to be found in small places nearby: *Peyrehorade, *Bidache, and Labastide-Clairence, and toward the north in La *Rochelle, Nantes, and Rouen. However, of all the Marranos who arrived in France from the beginning of the 16th century, only a tiny minority remained faithful to Judaism. Since they sought to evade detection by externally practicing Catholicism while maintaining their Iberian language and customs, they were suspected in Bordeaux in 1596 of attempting to deliver the town into the hands of the Spaniards, and in 1625 their possessions were confiscated as a reprisal for the confiscation of French belongings by the king of Spain. They were also subjected to particularly severe taxes, which rose to 100,000 livres in 1723 in exchange for new letters patent; for the first time these recognized them as Jews, although they did not grant them the right to practice their religion openly. The Jews of Comtat Venaissin had taken in some Spanish refugees on a temporary basis only, as was the case with the parents of *Joseph ha-Kohen, the author of *Emek ha-Bakha*, who was born in Avignon but lived there only during his early years. The communities of Comtat Venaissin were themselves threatened with expulsion on several occasions. These decrees were not finally enforced, but the Jews were nevertheless compelled to leave all towns in the Comtat with the exception of Avignon, Carpentras, *Cavaillon, and L'*Isle-sur-la-Sorgue. Even there, the quarters assigned to them were constantly reduced in area so as to limit the Jewish population.

Jews seem to have lived in Lorraine without interruption although in small numbers only. After the French crown had occupied the region, progressively greater facilities were offered to the Jews to induce them to settle there. From three families in Metz in 1565, their number increased to 96 families in 1657. In the meantime, as a result of the Treaty of Westphalia (1648), the three towns and bishoprics of Metz, Toul, and Verdun were formally ceded to France. Although theoretically the expulsion order against the Jews of the kingdom still remained in force—and it was even reiterated in 1615—the Jews in those parts of Lorraine which had become French were allowed to remain.

This was the first time since 1394 that Jews found themselves legally living in the kingdom of France. However, they were still confined to the town, or at best to the province, in which they lived. Considerable areas of Alsace were also incorporated within the kingdom of France by the Treaty of Westphalia. There also a firmly established Jewish population was not put in jeopardy by the new French administration; on the contrary, it was more effectively protected than in the past. In 1651, Jews from Holland settled in *Charleville, which belonged to the Gonzaga dukes (they had already admitted Dutch Jews for the first time from 1609 to 1633). Jews fleeing from the *Chmielnicki massacres in the Ukraine and Poland in 1648 arrived in Alsace and Lorraine. The general demographic decline which was a result of the Thirty Years' War (1618–48) explains the tolerance they encountered. Jews also arrived in the extreme southeast of France, where the duke of Savoy, to whom the county of Nice belonged, issued in 1648 an edict making Nice and *Villefranche de-Conflent free ports. Once more this was an indirect result of the Thirty Years' War, a search for an effective method of filling the economic vacuum it had created. Jews from Italy and North Africa immediately profited from the settlement facilities offered by this edict, strengthening the old Jewish community which had existed without interruption from the Middle Ages. However, Italian Jews who hoped to benefit from the apparently similar facilities offered in Marseilles by the edict of *Louis XIV in 1669 were disappointed; they were compelled to leave after a few years.

From the 17th century, the Jews of Avignon and Comtat Venaissin extended their commercial activity: besides frequenting the fairs and markets, mainly in Languedoc and Provence, they also attempted to remain in those towns and even to settle there. Following complaints from local merchants, the stewards of the king intervened on every occasion to remove them and restrict their presence at the fairs and markets as much as possible. With greater success, some Jews of Avignon and Comtat Venaissin—soon followed by Jews of Alsace—exploited the facilities granted to the "Portuguese" Jews, and from the beginning of the 18th century settled in Bordeaux. There they traded in the town or its environs, principally in textiles and to a lesser degree in livestock and old clothes.

From the beginning of the 18th century, some Jews began to settle in Paris, arriving not only from Alsace, Metz, and Lorraine, from Bordeaux, and from Avignon and Comtat Venaissin, but also from beyond the borders of France, mainly Germany and Holland. They were tolerated in Paris but no more. Even though they had benefited from most civil rights in their provinces of origin, they enjoyed no such privileges in the capital. In theory, if a Jew died in Paris his estate was confiscated in favor of the king and his burial had to be quasi-clandestine. In order to protect their rights and, initially, to obtain their own cemeteries, the Jews organized themselves into two distinct groups: southern Jews from Bordeaux, Avignon, and Comtat Venaissin, and Ashkenazim from Alsace, Lorraine, and a few other places. This was an early manifestation of the split which was later evident during the struggle for emancipation and afterward.

Just before the whole of Lorraine became part of France (1766), the request of some Jews of Lorraine to be admitted to the guilds gave rise to a lawsuit in which the advocate of Nancy, Pierre Louis de Lacretelle (1756–1824), called for their recognition as Frenchmen with rights equal to those of other citizens (1775). Although this suit was lost, nevertheless it left a powerful impression on the public who, from the beginning of the century, had become aware of the Jewish problem through the pronouncements of the great thinkers of the century, beginning with *Montesquieu. In 1781, Herz *Cerfberr, the representative of the Jews of Alsace, had the work of Christian Wilhelm von *Dohm (1751–1820), *Ueber die buergerliche Verbesserung der Juden* ("On the Civic Amelioration of the Jews"), translated into French. The first concrete result was Louis XVI's edict, drawn up in 1783 and published in January 1784, abolishing the humiliating "body tax" which for centuries had likened the Jews to cattle. In 1785 a competition by the Metz Société Royale des Arts et Sciences on the subject "Is there any way of rendering the Jews more useful and happier in France?" reflected this new trend of opinion, while strengthening it even further. The competition was initiated by P. L. *Roederer, a member of the *parlement* of Metz, and the best answers were submitted by the royal librarian Zalkind *Hourwitz (who defined himself as a "Polish Jew"), the advocate Thierry, and Abbé *Grégoire. Finally, in 1788, the minister *Malesherbes, who had successfully headed the commission charged with arranging civic rights for Protestants, was entrusted by Louis XVI with a similar mission with regard to the Jews. [B.Bl.]

The Modern Period. The Revolution. On the eve of the French Revolution some 40,000 Jews were living in France. Those of the "German nation" were mainly concentrated in Alsace-Lorraine or Paris, while the "Spanish, Portuguese, or Avignonese" Jews were chiefly concentrated in the south. The former who, excepting residents of Nancy, almost exclusively spoke or wrote in Yiddish, formed the vast majority (84%) of French Jewry while the latter were closer to French language and culture, less observant in religious practice, and more nearly integrated within local society. These various groups would no doubt have been fairly satisfied to obtain civic rights provided that they were consonant with the continuation of their internal communal autonomy. After much petitioning and long-drawn-out parliamentary and public discussion, the Jews of France finally became French citizens, the Portuguese Jews on Jan. 28, 1790, and the Ashkenazim on Sept. 27, 1791. The law of

1791, however, although conferring civic rights on Jews as individuals, was coupled with the abolition of their group privileges, i.e., their religious-legal autonomy.

Later the communities in France suffered from the Reign of Terror (1793–94) in company with the other religious denominations. Synagogues were closed down and the communal organization abolished as a consequence of the general tendency to suppress all religious institutions. When the synagogues reopened their doors, the character of the former communities had already greatly changed. The opening up of the ghettos and the abolition of restrictions on residence encouraged many Jews to leave their former areas of residence and to reject, either entirely or partly, the discipline imposed by their erstwhile community.

Measures of Napoleon. This anarchy, which led to complaints by former creditors of the dissolved Jewish communities, strengthened *Napoleon Bonaparte's determination to provide the Jews of France with a central organization supervised by the state and loyal to it, following the example of the arrangements he had already introduced for the other religions. Napoleon wished to create a Jewish "church organization" and at the same time to "reform" the Jewish way of life and Judaism, toward which he had an attitude of barely controlled hostility. Napoleon considered that the Jews were a "nation within a nation," and their emancipation had not produced the anticipated results. The Jews would therefore have to be corrected and regenerated; in particular a solution had to be found to solve the problem of usury, still a major Jewish occupation, especially in Alsace. With this in view, therefore, in 1806 he convened an assembly to serve as the "States General of French Judaism" (the *Assembly of Jewish Notables). Its first session was held on July 26. The Assembly had to reply to 12 questions put to it by the commissioners appointed by the government who were instructed to verify whether Jewish religious law held any principle contrary to the civil law. Having been informed of the deliberations of the Assembly and the answers it delivered, Napoleon determined on having them formulated into a type of religious code. He decided to convoke a Grand Sanhedrin (see French *Sanhedrin)—a gesture which was also within the framework of his European ambitions—whose religious authority could not be called in question. The Sanhedrin, composed of 45 rabbis and 26 laymen, met on Feb. 9, 1807, and dispersed two months later on March 9, having fulfilled its role by codifying "religious" decisions in the spirit of the answers to the 12 questions delivered by the Assembly of Notables. The Sanhedrin then gave way to the Notables, who continued their task with the intention of proposing the establishment of an organization of the Jewish religion and measures to control Jewish economic activities.

Figure 3. Interior of the Cavaillon synagogue, built in 1774. Courtesy Cavaillon Municipality.

The Consistorial System. The proposed regulation was amended by the Conseil d'Etat and promulgated by imperial edict in 1808, inaugurating what is usually called the consistorial system. This provided that a *consistory should be established for each department of France having a Jewish population of at least 2,000. Each consistory was constituted of a council composed of a *grand rabbin*, another rabbi, and three laymen elected by a small number of "notables." A central consistory composed of three *grand rabbins* and two laymen was to have its seat in Paris. Contrary to the provisions governing the organizations for the other recognized religions, expenses for religious purposes were still to be met by Jews. Thus, the new Jewish bodies were obliged, *ipso facto*, as inheritors, to repay the debts contracted by the former Jewish communities, whereas the other religions had been relieved of this burden. The consistorial system partially re-created the Jewish communities, and provided them with a means of action. It also constituted the recognition of Judaism as a religion, centralizing its organization, and placing it under strict government control. While the consistory was empowered to exercise absolute and exclusive authority in Jewish affairs, it mainly concerned itself with the strictly religious aspects. The consistory was supported by the rabbinate, which according to law was responsible for teaching the Jewish religion and the decisions of the Sanhedrin, promoting obedience to the civil laws, preaching in synagogue, and offering prayers for the imperial family. Although the authority of the rabbis was limited entirely to the religious sphere, it was nevertheless channeled into the service of the state.

These administrative measures were accompanied by complementary economic regulations. A decree abrogating a postponement previously granted on May 30, 1806, to persons owing money to Jews was issued, but it also laid down a mass of restrictive regulations. All debts contracted with Jews were to be annulled or liable to be annulled, reduced, or postponed by legal means (1808). As a result, a large section of the Jewish population of France, already in difficult circumstances, was brought to the verge of ruin. Any Jew who wished to engage in trade or commerce had to obtain a license to be renewed annually by the prefect of the department in which he resided. Further measures were issued in an attempt to compel the Jews of France to assimilate into French society by regulating their place of residence. Thus a Jew who had not previously been resident in Alsace was prohibited from settling there. A Jew might settle in other departments only if he exercised a profession regarded as useful. In order to preserve the educational value in performing military service in company with their non-Jewish compatriots, Jews drafted for the army were prohibited from procuring substitutes. Another decree which, however, confirmed an existing situation, made it obligatory for Jews to adopt surnames in the presence of an official of the registry. The central consistory was set up on July 17, 1808. Its three *grand rabbins* were the president and two vice-presidents of the Sanhedrin, David *Sinzheim, Joshua Benzion Segré, who died shortly afterward and was replaced by Emanuel *Deutz, rabbi of Coblenz, and Abraham Vita *Cologna, rabbi of Mantua. After the death of Sinzheim in 1812 and the resignation of Cologna in 1826, Deutz remained the only *grand rabbin* in the central consistory until his death in 1842. Subsequently only one *grand rabbin* served for the whole of French Jewry.

Official Recognition. The Restoration was not received with hostility by the Jews of France. The Napoleonic regulations, while having the merit of organizing communal affairs, had nevertheless represented a step backward in revolutionary ideals. Without major difficulties they were able to ensure that the Napoleonic decree determining their activities and means of livelihood, commonly referred to by Jews as the *décret infâme*, was not renewed after the expiry of its ten-year time limit (1818). Soon the need for new rabbis became a matter for concern. Until the Revolution rabbis for the Ashkenazi communities had been trained in the yeshivah in Metz, in the small local yeshivot of Alsace, or otherwise drawn from abroad. The Sephardi communities in the south generally recognized the authority of the Dutch or Italian Sephardi rabbinates. The closing of the Metz yeshivah under the Revolution had greatly curtailed the recruitment of rabbis. Thus, from 1820 numerous attempts were made to obtain permission for the opening of a rabbinical school in Metz to supply the needs of all sectors of French Jewry. In 1829 the Ministry of Religions authorized the opening of a central rabbinical seminary in Metz. It was transferred to Paris in 1859, where it continues to function. Judaism was placed on the same footing as the other recognized religions when the chamber of peers passed a law making the Treasury responsible for paying the salaries of ministers of the Jewish religion (from Jan. 1, 1831). Thus almost the last sign of anti-Jewish discriminatory legislation in France disappeared.

ASSIMILATION. These political successes did not conceal the profound crisis through which French Jewry was passing. Many Jews born after the grant of emancipation were unprepared for the new world they were now facing. A wave of conversions followed, in which members of the most firmly established families left Judaism. Deutz's own son, notorious for his role in the arrest of the duchess of Berry, and his son-in-law David *Drach, who had pursued rabbinical studies and directed the Jewish school in Paris, both embraced Christianity, the latter even taking orders. The eldest son of the president of the Bas-Rhin Consistory, Marie-Theodore *Ratisbonne, became converted in 1826. He subsequently took orders and in celebration of the conversion of his youngest brother founded the order of Notre Dame de Sion to be devoted to missionary work among the Jews. The brother, who was an active member of the order, later built a monastery in Jerusalem. Although the lower ranks of the Jewish population were hardly affected by these conversions, such cases were numerous among their leaders.

The disappearance of the generation which had known the Revolution and taken part in the work of the Sanhedrin, coupled with the new spirit of liberal democracy, and the pressure in the new communities by arrivals from the rural areas of Alsace and Lorraine now necessitated a reform of the consistorial system. By an order in council of May 25, 1844, French Jewry continued to be directed by the central consistory, which was henceforth composed of the *grand rabbin* and a lay member from each departmental consistory. The electoral college was enlarged in 1844 and 1848, when every Jewish male aged over 25 obtained the right to take part in the elections of the departmental consistories. The Paris consistory finally obtained an increase in the number of its representatives on the central consistory because it had a large population under its jurisdiction. This system continued, apart from some minor modifications, until 1905, with the separation of church and state (see below).

ABOLITION OF THE "JEWISH OATH." The final obstacle to complete equality for Jewish citizens was removed with the abolition of the humiliating oath *more judaico*. The various courts that had been called upon to decide whether it was necessary for Jews to take the oath in that form had rendered conflicting decisions. It was only on the advice given to the rabbis by Adolphe *Crémieux, who became a member of the central consistory in 1831, to refuse to take the oath in this form that some progress was made. The Supreme Court of Appeal decided on its abolition in 1846. In the same period the debts of the former Jewish communities were finally settled by partial repayments effected by the successor communities.

WELFARE AND EDUCATION. While French Jewry was concerned with defense of its rights and its religious organization, it also promoted charitable and educational activities. The local charitable committees were generally offshoots of the traditional Jewish mutual aid societies or of the *ḥevrot* (see *ḥevrah), which did not surrender their independence without hesitation or declared hostility. In the educational sphere, the first real development took place under the Restoration with the opening of Jewish primary schools. From 1818 schools were opened in Metz, Strasbourg, and Colmar. A boys' school had been functioning in Bordeaux from 1817 and a girls' school from 1831. In Paris the first Jewish boys' school was established in 1819 and the first girls' school in 1821. Parallel to these primary schools, the community also opened technical schools, at first in order to prepare their pupils for apprenticeship and later providing direct specialized training. The first Jewish trades school (Ecole de Travail) opened its doors in Strasbourg in 1825, and was followed by that of Mulhouse in 1842, and of Paris in 1865. This network grew in importance until the law making primary education compulsory was passed in 1882, and the church and state were separated in 1905, thus depriving it of state financial support.

PROTECTION OF JEWISH RIGHTS. The Jewish community in France was shocked into action to protect Jewish rights by the *Damascus Affair in 1840 and subsequently by the outbreak of anti-Jewish disorders in 1848. The hostile attitude shown by the French government and also by French public opinion when Jews in Damascus were accused of ritual murder, as well as the complicity of the French consul there, deeply stirred French Jewry. Crémieux therefore joined Sir Moses *Montefiore from England in a mission to Alexandria to intercede with *Muhammad Ali on behalf of the Damascus Jews. In February 1848, the peasants in Sundgau in Alsace took advantage of the general unrest to attack the Jews, some of whom managed to escape to Switzerland. The incidents spread northward, Jewish houses were pillaged, and the army was called out to restore order. Both this and the Damascus Affair strengthened the feeling among Jews in France that in certain situations they could rely only on self-defense. The formation of the provisional government, which included two Jews, Michel *Goudchaux and Crémieux, dispelled some of these anxieties, but Jewish concern was again heightened with the election of Prince Louis Napoleon to the presidency of the republic, and later his accession to the imperial title, since many feared that he would restore the discriminatory measures introduced by his uncle.

SOCIAL AND ECONOMIC ADVANCES. These fears proved unfounded. The Second Empire was a calm period for the Jews of France. Instances of anti-Jewish discrimination were the result of the influence of the Catholic circles surrounding the empress rather than of a determined will to start an anti-Semitic campaign. Jews, like other "nonbelievers," were often excluded from the universities. The social rise of the French Jews which had begun under the Restoration also continued under the Second Empire. In 1834 Achille *Fould became the first Jew to sit in the Chamber of Deputies, soon to be followed by Crémieux. The greatest and most rapid achievements were often

N° 576. Bulletin des Lois, n° 198.

DÉCRET IMPÉRIAL

Concernant les Juifs qui n'ont pas de nom de famille et de prénoms fixes.

A Bayonne, le 20 juillet 1808.

NAPOLÉON, EMPEREUR DES FRANÇAIS, ROI D'ITALIE, et PROTECTEUR DE LA CONFÉDÉRATION DU RHIN;

Sur le rapport de notre ministre de l'intérieur,

Notre Conseil d'État entendu,

Nous AVONS DÉCRÉTÉ et DÉCRÉTONS ce qui suit:

ARTICLE PREMIER.

Ceux des sujets de notre Empire qui suivent le culte hébraïque, et qui, jusqu'à présent, n'ont pas eu de nom de famille et de prénoms fixes, seront tenus d'en adopter dans les trois mois de la publication de notre présent décret, et d'en faire la déclaration par-devant l'officier de l'état civil de la commune où ils sont domiciliés.

2. Les Juifs étrangers qui viendraient habiter dans l'Empire, et qui seraient dans

Figure 4. First page of Napoleon's decree of July 20, 1808, ordering all Jews to adopt surnames. Cecil Roth Photo Collection.

through the civil service, candidates for which generally had to pass tests and competitive examinations. In 1836 Jacques *Halévy was elected a member of the Academy of Fine Arts. *Rachel, one of the greatest actresses of her time, never concealed her Jewish origin. In the commercial sphere, it was a period of success for the *Rothschild family and its head, Baron James, as well as for the *Pereire brothers to whom the Rothschilds were later violently opposed. Practically every career, including the army, was open to Jews.

NEW TRENDS IN JUDAISM. Events did not proceed without provoking the same unrest within the French community as had gripped German Jewry. The problem arose of maintaining Judaism in an open, modern society, and the influence of the *Reform movements from across the Rhine soon made itself felt. The French rabbinate was of a generally conservative frame of mind. Its members, who almost entirely hailed from the small towns of Alsace and Lorraine, were scarcely enthusiastic over the new ideas and the rabbinate found itself in retreat before the layman. A meeting of *grand rabbins* was held in Paris from May 13–21, 1856, to establish a common policy with which to confront the growing trend away from Judaism. The camps were clearly divided well before the meeting: the Alsatian communities, which were the most numerous, opposed the introduction of substantive reforms, for which they felt no necessity. However, since each consistory was represented by only one delegate, the majority of the representatives tended to opt for modifications. To prevent a breach, it was resolved that decisions would be taken according to a simple majority, but that the question of their application would be held in abeyance. The assembly decided to limit the number of *piyyutim*, to organize synagogue services for the blessing of newborn infants, to conduct the funeral service with more ceremonial, and to instruct rabbis and officiating ministers to wear a garb resembling that worn by the Catholic clergy. It was also resolved to make greater use of the sermon in synagogue, to reduce the length of services which were to be conducted in a more dignified manner, and to introduce the ceremony of religious initiation, particularly for girls, whose religious instruction was to be inspected and approved. The assembly also called for the transfer of the rabbinical seminary to Paris. Regarding the controversy which had arisen over the use of the organ in synagogue, it was decided that its use on Sabbath and festivals was lawful provided that it was played by a non-Jew. Its introduction would be subject to the authorization of the *grand rabbin* of the department concerned, at the request of the local rabbi. A breach in the community was therefore avoided at the price of compromises and half-measures. The different elements in French Jewry continued on good terms since the doctrinal independence of the local rabbi remained intact. Subsequently more ambitious attempts at reform were cut short by the Franco-German war of 1870–71. The French defeat cast an odium, a priori, on anything that smacked of German importation. As a result, French Jewry found itself in a state of arrested reform. Although moving away from Orthodoxy it remained firmly attached to the idea of an integrated community. To this day French consistorial Judaism has maintained great religious diversity, a situation which has always curbed the few attempts to establish dissident, Reform or Orthodox, communities. This flexibility later enabled the integration of immigrants from North Africa. The leading role still played in French communal affairs by the Rothschild family also helped to give the community a large measure of stability.

ALLIANCE ISRAÉLITE UNIVERSELLE. The *Mortara case in 1858 once again brought up the question of freedom of conscience and reminded French Jewry of the Damascus Affair and the troubles of 1848. It again demonstrated the importance of organizing Jewish self-defense, this time on an international scale. The French Jews, who had been convinced that they had succeeded in assimilation by reconciling fidelity to Judaism with the gains achieved by democracy, felt compelled to react. However, it was typical of the existing situation that action was taken outside the framework of the central consistory which had by then withdrawn into a religious and representational role. In 1860, a group of young Jewish liberals founded the *Alliance Israélite Universelle with a central committee permanently based in Paris. The activities of this body were mainly directed to helping communities outside France and it had the great merit of again demonstrating that Jewish solidarity extended beyond modern nationalism.

ALSACE-LORRAINE AND ALGERIA. The 1870 war not only revived Franco-German hostility and put an end to many of the hopes for greater unity, but cut off from French Jewry its vital sources in Alsace and Lorraine. There was also the problem of integrating the Alsatian Jews who had opted to stay in France. This immigration considerably increased the importance of the communities in Paris and that part of Lorraine which had remained French. It also led to the creation of new consistories in Vesoul, Lille, and Besancon. The effects of the war also speeded up the naturalization of the Jews of *Algeria, where at the time of the French conquest there were a number of old-established communities. The French authorities took their existing arrangements into account but limited the powers of the "head of the Jewish nation" by attaching to him a "Hebrew council." The powers of the rabbinical courts were also restricted. However the Jews of Algeria officially remained part of the indigenous population with a personal status which was variously interpreted. In 1870, on the eve of the war with Prussia, and following numerous petitions by the Jews in Algeria, the imperial government was on the point of declaring the collective naturalization of Algerian Jewry.

The Government of National Defense sitting at Tours, at the pressing insistence of Crémieux, then minister of justice, proclaimed this naturalization by a decree issued on Oct. 24, 1870. Having become French citizens, the Jews of Algeria gave up their personal status and were on the same footing as the Jews of France. The consistorial system, which had been introduced in Algeria in 1845, was modified to permit a more active participation of the members of the Algerian community in the consistorial elections. The appointment of rabbis and *grand rabbins* was made by the central consistory.

ANTI-SEMITISM. Withdrawn into itself but enriched by the Algerian accession, the Jewish community of France soon had to face a formidable test. The advent of the Third Republic was not received by Jews with unmixed enthusiasm. Concerned at the progress of secularism and of movements demanding reform, royalist and clerical circles in France attempted to create an anti-Jewish diversion. Anti-Semitic newspapers began to appear. In 1883 the Assumptionists established the daily *La *Croix* which, with other publications, set out to prove that the Revolution had been the work of the Jews allied with the Freemasons. This trend was strengthened by the socialist anti-Semitism of the followers of *Fourier and *Proudhon. The various shades of anti-Semitism converged in Edouard *Drumont's *La France Juive* (1886), which became a bestseller. After the collapse of the Union Générale, a leading Catholic bank, the Jews in France provided a convenient scapegoat. In 1889 Drumont's ideas culminated in the formation of the French National Anti-Semitic League (see *Anti-Semitic Political Parties and Organizations). In 1891, 32 deputies demanded that the Jews be expelled from France. In 1892 Drumont was able, with Jesuit support, to found his daily *La Libre Parole* which immediately launched a defamation campaign against Jewish officers who were accused of having plotted treason and of trafficking in secrets of the national defense. It also blamed Jews for the crash of the Panama Canal Company, creating a scandal which greatly increased its circulation. It was in this climate that Captain Alfred *Dreyfus was arrested on Oct. 15, 1894, on the charge of having spied in the interests of Germany. Many aspects of the affair are still unclear, although Dreyfus' innocence has been fully recognized. In any event, the affair went beyond the individual case of the unfortunate captain to rock the whole of France and Jews throughout the world.

In France the matter at stake was not the survival of the Jewish community: even its most virulent adversaries did not desire its physical disappearance, although cries of "death to the Jews" were uttered time and again by Paris crowds. On its part, the Catholic and right-wing press, and especially Drumont's *La Libre Parole*, frequently published "facts" about the machinations of a "World Jewish Syndicate" aimed at world domination. The *Dreyfus case hastened the crystallization of the ideas of Theodor *Herzl, then press correspondent in Paris and a bewildered witness of the unleashing of anti-Semitism in a country reputed to be the most enlightened in Europe. The affair, by opposing the general trends of public opinion in France, led to a crisis of conscience rarely equaled in intensity. Its repercussions caused an upheaval in French political life with similar consequences for Jewish life.

SEPARATION OF CHURCH AND STATE. The disproportion between the origin of the affair and its consequences does not fail to astonish. In 1905, as a result of the victory of Dreyfus' supporters, a law was passed separating church and state. With the other recognized religions, the Jewish religion lost its official status, and state financial support was withdrawn with the abolition of state participation in religious expenses. Like the Protestants, but in contradistinction to the Catholics, the Jews accepted this resolution with goodwill. It would also have been difficult for them to oppose those who had supported Dreyfus. At the same time *Grand Rabbin* Zadoc *Kahn died. His strong personality had dominated Jewish life since his election to the chief rabbinate of Paris in 1869 and a few years later to the chief rabbinate of France. His astonishing activity had revived French Judaism after the truncation of Alsatian Jewry, and he had interested Baron Edmond de *Rothschild in the colonization of Ereẓ Israel. The central consistory, disorientated after the passing of the 1905 act, thus had to transform itself while preserving its former framework as far as possible. Synagogues built with public subsidies were nationalized, but were immediately placed at the disposal of the successor religious associations. The central consistory became the Union des Associations Cultuelles de France et d'Algérie ("Union of the Religious Associations of France and Algeria"), and its office adopted the name Central Consistory. The regional consistories disappeared, but the large communities were changed into consistorial or religious associations. Practically all the departmental consistories remained in existence when the offices of the successor associations adopted the name consistory. The internal hierarchy, sanctioned by a century of tradition, continued. The perpetuation of the system, however, did not alter the fact that the organization of the Jewish community of France rested purely on a voluntary basis and on the recognition of a central authority freely accepted. In fact the French Jewish community became a federation of local communities which maintained a few joint central services, such as the chief rabbinate of France and the rabbinical seminary. Although this system increased the possibilities of fragmentation and disruption, the force of tradition maintained the moral authority of the various consistories, which became the principal, but not the exclusive, representation of a community undergoing a fundamental demographic transformation.

DEMOGRAPHIC CHANGES. During the 19th century, the relative importance of the Avignon communities had

Figure 5. Emanuel Deutz, *grand rabbin* of the Central Consistory of France from 1809 to 1842.

Figure 6. Deportation of French Jews from the Drancy transit camp to Auschwitz in 1943. Jerusalem, Yad Vashem Archives.

greatly decreased. The four Comtat communities had dispersed, their members moving to Marseilles and the large towns in southern France. The Bordeaux and Bayonne elements had never been very numerous. The extension of the French borders toward the north and east had opened up the country to a large Jewish immigration from Holland and the Rhineland. The Jewish population of Paris in 1789 numbered 500, out of the total French Jewish population of 40,000 to 50,000. There were 30,000 Jews living in Paris in 1869, out of a total of 80,000 for the whole of France. In 1880, following the loss of Alsace and Lorraine, 40,000 out of a total of 60,000 French Jews were living in Paris. This proportion has remained substantially unchanged. The pogroms in Russia of 1881 gave rise to a wave of Jewish emigration to the free countries and marked the beginning of the Russian, Polish, and Rumanian immigration into France. A second wave of immigration took place after the abortive 1905 Russian revolution. From 1881 to 1914 over 25,000 Jewish immigrants arrived in France. The Russian element was in the minority. From 1908 a large Jewish influx also began from the Ottoman countries, chiefly from Salonika, Constantinople, and Smyrna. However, for a large number of immigrants, France served as a country of transit and not of refuge.

World War I. The advent of World War I halted this immigration. In uniting all the forces of the nation, the war also put a stop to the anti-Semitic campaigns. The necessity for maintaining a common front *(union sacrée)* brought all the religions together. For some Jewish soldiers the war was to be a means of rejoining their families after the reconquest of Alsace and Lorraine. The victory restored to French Jewry these most vital communities. They had preserved their former consistorial organization since they had been in German territory in 1905 when the law separating church and state was passed. The French government, following a policy of pacification and taking into consideration the strong religious attachment of the population, did not apply the law to the regained territories. Thus religious life there continued to be organized on the old system.

Inter-War Years. After the war, Jewish immigration from the former Ottoman countries was resumed with greater intensity. The Jews from Turkey and Greece settled chiefly in Paris and in the large cities of the south. However, the largest immigration came from Eastern Europe in the wake of the Ukrainian and Polish pogroms. Rumania also provided a significant number of Jews. Once again the Russian and Lithuanian elements were not numerous. This trend increased after 1924 following the prohibition of free immigration into the United States. From 1933 many Jewish refugees from Nazi Germany passed through France en route for America or Palestine. The number remaining in France was relatively insignificant. It is estimated that there were 180,000 Jews resident in Paris in 1939, one-third of them belonging to the old French Jewish community. By then the use of Yiddish had become widespread and the "Ashkenazation" of the community had increased. The freedom of religious organization, which the law separating church and state had ratified by abolishing the official organization of religion, had enabled the different groups of immigrants to organize an appropriate framework for their religious and social life. Thus in 1923 the Fédération des Sociétés Juives de France (F.S.J.F.), a body which united the majority of Landsmanschaften, was created. However, these organizations did not impair the prestige of the old-established French Jewish communal bodies. The new bodies lost much of their meaningfulness as their members assimilated into French life, and with the progress of social security which deprived them of much of their usefulness. Many of their members subsequently joined the ranks of the established community.

Economic, Cultural, and Social Position. In the economic sphere, the position of French Jewry continued to improve. After 1850, the number of Jews engaged in crafts increased considerably, and many Jews entered the technical professions. Few were attracted to agriculture. In the period before World War I Jewish painters and sculptors had made the Paris school famous (see *Paris School of Art). Among a brilliant galaxy, the names of *Pissaro, *Soutine, *Pascin, *Kisling, *Chagall, and *Modigliani are well known. Sarah *Bernhardt, who was eventually baptized, brought luster to the French theater. Outstanding in literature and philosophy were Adolphe *Franck, Salomon *Munk, Henri *Bergson, Emile *Durkheim, Lucien *Lévy-Bruhl, Marcel *Proust, and André *Maurois.

Purely Jewish studies were not abandoned. From 1880 the *Société des Etudes Juives regularly published a learned periodical, *Revue des Etudes Juives,* and was responsible for the publication of the classic works of Heinrich *Gross (*Gallia Judaica,* 1897) and T. *Reinach (*Textes d'auteurs Grecs et Romains relatifs au Judaïsme,* 1895), and a modern translation of the works of Josephus. The French rabbinate published a magnificent translation of the Bible. On the other hand, talmudic studies in France ceased. The process of social assimilation continued, and in 1936 Léon *Blum became the first Jewish premier of France. [S.Sch.]

Holocaust Period. On May 10, 1940, the Germans invaded France. *Paris fell on June 14. The armistice, which was signed two weeks later, divided France into an unoccupied zone, an occupied zone (subdivided into the "general" and "forbidden" zones and several restricted areas), and into the departments of Nord and Pas-de-Calais attached to the *Militaerverwaltung* in Brussels, while Alsace-Lorraine was annexed to the Reich. No official figures exist on the number of Jews living in France in this period, since Jews were not singled out in the census and the documents on official and illegal entry or departure of refugees offer no satisfactory proof. It is estimated that about 300,000

Jews lived in France prior to the invasion. The Jews in France suffered from the combined impact of the Nazi "*Final Solution" and from traditional French anti-Semitism. By and large, French anti-Semitism did not tend to physical extermination, but its existence unquestionably helped the Nazis in carrying out their scheme. An estimated 85,000–90,000 Jews were deported (the former figure is more probable); barely 3,000 of these survived. In addition, a few thousand Jews were deported or executed for political and resistance activities without, however, having been singled out as Jews by the occupying powers.

Anti-Jewish Measures and Administration. The main legal and juridical anti-Jewish measures initiated after the subjugation were: the first *Verordnung (Ordonnance)* of Sept. 27, 1940, ordering a census of the Jews; the law of the Vichy government (Oct. 4, 1940), on the status of foreign nationals of Jewish "race"; the second *Verordnung* (Oct. 18, 1940), requiring the declaration of Jewish enterprises and appointment of so-called provisional administrators over them; the third *Verordnung* (April 26, 1941), extending the discriminatory category of "Jew" to groups of persons of Jewish origin who were not of the Jewish faith, and forbidding a number of economic activities; the fourth *Verordnung* (May 28, 1941), forbidding free negotiation of Jewish-owned capital; an unnumbered *Verordnung* (Aug. 13, 1941), for the confiscation of radios in Jewish possession; the fifth *Verordnung* (Sept. 28, 1941), blocking the proceeds from the forced sale of Jewish property; the proclamation of the *Militaerbefehlshaber Frankreich* (Dec. 14, 1941), announcing inter alia a fine of 1,000,000,000 francs, to be paid by the Jewish population; the execution of 53 Jewish members of the Resistance, and the deportation of 1,000 Jews (in fact, 1,100 Jews were actually deported on March 27, 1942, as a result of the proclamation); the sixth *Verordnung* (Feb. 7, 1942), establishing a curfew for Jews between 8 p.m. and 6 a.m., as well as forbidding change of residence; the seventh *Verordnung* (March 24, 1942), enlarging still further the scope of the definition of "the Jews"; the eighth *Verordnung* (May 29, 1942, enforced as from June 1, 1942), ordering all Jews to wear a yellow *badge; and the ninth *Verordnung* (July 8, 1942), forbidding Jews access to public places, squares, gardens, and sports grounds, and limiting them to one hour daily in which they might make their purchases in shops and food markets.

The German *Verordnungen* were valid only in the occupied zone; even after the occupation of the whole of France they were not extended to the newly occupied areas. Thus, for instance, the yellow badge never became compulsory in southern France. The statutes, laws, and ordinances of the Vichy government, on the other hand, were valid throughout France, as was the rubber stamp *Juif* ("Jew") on identity cards. Whereas German measures were directed without exception against all Jews, the Vichy measures mainly affected Jews who were either foreign nationals or stateless, and later Jewish immigrants who had recently become French nationals. French Jews of long standing were generally spared, sometimes by means of the exceptions made in favor of ex-servicemen and individuals of outstanding merit.

In occupied France, the Gestapo and specifically the Paris extension of *Eichmann's IV B (the latter already functioning in August 1940 and led by *SS-Hauptsturmfuehrer* Theodor *Dannecker), from Jan. 28, 1941, onward attempted to create a twin structure throughout France (including the unoccupied zone): a French government anti-Jewish agency and an all-French *Judenrat, to act as the French counterpart of the Gestapo's IV B branch and of the *Reichsvereinigung der Juden in Deutschland respectively. Their success in these undertakings was relative. After much German pressure, the Vichy government in April 1941 set up the *Commissariat Général aux Questions Juives, headed by Xavier *Vallat, an extreme-right member of parliament. Vallat was a French politician and an anti-Semite in the French tradition, according to which Jews were responsible for the very existence of democracy and the Third Republic which were "undermining" France. Being a disabled ex-serviceman and head of an important extreme-right organization of disabled soldiers, Vallat felt himself obliged to come to the help of Jews belonging to this category. Furthermore, as a Frenchman of the conservative camp, he was near to Pétain and no friend of Germany. He remained one year at the head of the Commissariat and had to leave when declared persona non grata by the German authorities. During his tenure of office, until May 1942, the Commissariat rarely acted outside the occupied zone, and even then limited its work, by and large, to the "aryanization" of Jewish businesses. Vallat was succeeded by *Darquier de Pellepoix, a rabid anti-Semite, reputed from prewar years to be a Nazi agent. Whereas Vallat was known to be personally honest, Darquier was considered both corrupt and mentally deranged. The Commissariat continued its activities, though without much help from the Vichy government. In a joint maneuver, the Commissariat and the German authorities pressured the Vichy government to bring about the mass cancellation of the naturalizations of foreign Jews (dating back to 1927), but they failed due to the obstinacy first of Pétain and then even of Pierre *Laval. The Vichy government created an official body called *Union Générale des Israélites de France (UGIF) in 1941 to represent French Jewry during the German occupation. It had two divisions—one in the occupied zone and one in the free one.

Deportations and Forced Labor. In practice, the Germans could not always insist on their policy against all Jews because the Vichy authorities, particularly the police, though prepared to enforce the regulations to persecute "foreign" Jews, were often reluctant to act against French Jews. For that reason, any *Aktion* against French Jews was executed by the Gestapo itself, whereas the roundups of non-French Jews ordered by the German authorities were carried out by the French police. In the main roundup, which took place on July 16–17, 1942, in Paris and its suburbs, about 12,884 people of all ages were arrested. Many more "*Aktions*" took place both before and after the main roundup. One of the most notorious was that of Aug. 15, 1942, carried out entirely by the Vichy police in the unoccupied zone, at which time over 7,000 foreign Jews were arrested and handed over to the Germans. Many of these Jews had not lived in France prior to the war. Some were from Belgium and the Netherlands, but the majority were refugees from Germany who had arrived in France after the invasion of May–June 1940; there were also about 7,000 German Jews from Baden, Wuerttemberg, the Saar, and the Palatinate expelled to France in the autumn of 1940 during the so-called *Buerckel-Aktion,* as well as a few hundred Jews from Luxembourg, shipped off to France under similar conditions. The great majority of these refugees went to the unoccupied southern part of France, where they joined several thousand French Jews who had also fled from the Germans. The cities of Toulouse, Marseilles, Lyons, and Nice thus had large Jewish concentrations, but also smaller towns, such as Limoges and Périgueux, sheltered thousands of Jews.

The refugees from abroad, except for a small number of particularly well-to-do, were liable to be interned either in detention camps, mainly at Saint-Cyprien, Gurs, Vernet, Argelès-sur-Mer, Barcarès, Agde, Nexon, Fort-Barraux, and Les Milles, or in smaller so-called *Détachements de prestataires de travail,* i.e., forced labor detachments. Thousands of foreign Jews who had volunteered in 1939–40 for the French army were not demobilized after the armistice, but kept for a time in similar forced labor battalions, both in continental France and in North Africa (Djerada, Djelfa, and on the Mediterranean-Niger railway project). Their living conditions were hardly better than those of criminals sentenced to terms of hard labor, nor was their work very different.

There were two main concentration camps for foreign Jews, *Pithiviers and Beaune-la-Rolande near Paris, and a few smaller ones. *Drancy, a northern suburb, was the main transit camp to *Auschwitz. A few Jews were deported from the Compiègne camp and a few deportation trains left from Pithiviers, Beaune-la-Rolande, and such towns as Angers, Lyons, and Toulouse, but the majority of convoys was dispatched from Drancy. Deportation came in several waves, beginning on March 27, 1942, and was largely handled by the military administration. The second deportation during the summer and fall of 1942 followed the main roundup throughout the country; a third wave during the spring of 1943 came after the clearance and destruction of the Vieux-Port quarter of Marseilles; a fourth wave in the fall of 1943 followed the occupation of the former Italian zone, where many Jews had found sanctuary from November 1942 until Sept. 8, 1943, when the Germans entered that zone (southeast France). They rounded up all the Jews they could find, and in Nice alone about 6,000 Jews (out of 25,000) were deported.

Rescue and Resistance. Jewish institutions, such as *HICEM, helped a few of the foreign Jews to emigrate overseas; the French rabbinate arranged for religious and social assistance, carried out in part by rabbis active in the resistance movement, such as René *Kappel and others in the Zionist-oriented groups which recruited considerable numbers of resistance members; other institutions cared for the social and physical well-being of the internees in France. The traditional Jewish organizations continued their activities mainly in southern France. This was true both for the official framework of religious communities called *Consistoire Israélite and the Fédération des Sociétés Juives de France consisting of immigrant Jews. The last carried out extensive activities for mutual aid and, as the persecution became more severe, these were transformed into resistance activities (falsification of identity and ration cards, of addresses, and help to fugitives from deportation).

The Jews of France played an outstanding role in the resistance movements, both in the general movements of all types and political opinion—from the right wing through the Communist and even Trotskyist groups—and within purely Jewish groups, set up through Jewish organizational affinities (e.g., Zionist) or through outside influences (Communist Jewish groups). The Zionist youth movements established a united Mouvement des Jeunesses Sionistes (M.J.S.), which became the nucleus of the Armée Juive (A.J.) and later on of the Organisation Juive de Combat (O.J.C.). Initially, the French-Jewish scout movement was, however, not insensitive to the Vichy ideology and particularly to the myth of Marshal Pétain; but when the deportations commenced in 1942, the myth was dispelled and the scouts played a major part, first in hiding hundreds of children, and then in the armed resistance movement, where together with the Armée Juive they established the O.J.C. Robert Gamzon (Castor), the national director of the Jewish Boy Scouts of France (Eclaireurs Israélites de France—E.I.F.), largely contributed to this evolution.

There was never any serious difficulty in hiding children with French families in the country and even in towns. Nor did adult Jews find it impossible to hide themselves in French villages or families. On the whole, the behavior of the French population toward the persecuted Jews was overwhelmingly positive. Many people, initially in sympathy with Pétain, were no longer so when they saw the yellow badge in the streets, and particularly when they realized that every single Jew—who often became known as such precisely because he wore the badge—including women and even children, was liable to arrest and deportation to an unknown destination. There were very few denunciations of Jews, and they were certainly less frequent than the denunciations of resistance fighters.

The Catholic Church as such disapproved of application of the anti-Jewish measures and particularly the deportations, although it did not denounce the anti-Jewish decrees as a whole. Alerted by Jewish circles, a number of higher ecclesiastics, such as the future cardinals Saliège and Théas, strongly condemned from the pulpit the deportations of the Jews. Many priests acted similarly, while convents and monasteries offered shelter to Jews, particularly to children. The Church as such did not attempt to proselytize Jewish children. The Protestant churches, numerically very small in France, were even more actively opposed to the persecution of Jews. The Protestant Cévennes area in Central France became a center for active rescue of Jews.

The rescue of children was by and large initiated by Jews, in which activity the Gentiles of necessity played a main role. A notable role was played by the scouts and *OSE (very often involving the same people), in a lesser measure by *WIZO in the Paris area, and, foremost of all, by communist Jewish groups, which succeeded in creating the Mouvement National contre le Racisme (M.N.C.R.), most of whose active members were non-communist Frenchmen. [L.St.]

Contemporary Period. Native Population and Waves of Immigration. France was the only country in Europe to which Jews immigrated in significant numbers after World War II, and in 25 years the Jewish population tripled. Although there has been no official census of the French Jewish population, it has been estimated that 550,000 Jews (about 1% of the total French population) were residing in France in 1968. (All statistics given in this article are estimates made by the Jewish community.) In the late 1960s the Jewish community of France, the largest in Western Europe and the fourth largest in the world, underwent a new geographical distribution, diversification in occupations and social status, a change in community structure, and a fundamental reorientation in religious, ideological, and cultural trends.

In 1945, there were 180,000 French Jews who had survived the Holocaust. The community was composed of established Jewish families and immigrants from Central and Eastern Europe and Mediterranean countries. Between 1945 and 1951 many Displaced Persons passed through France, and some of them settled there. In 1951, there were 250,000 Jews in the country, and between 1954 and 1961 approximately 100,000 Egyptian, Moroccan, Tunisian, and Algerian Jews moved to France. After the Bizerta incidents (1961) and the establishment of independent Algeria (1962), immigration increased; by 1963, almost the entire Jewish community of Algeria (110,000 persons) had moved to France. Moroccan and Tunisian Jews continued to arrive in the late 1960s, and their wave of immigration reached a new peak following the *Six-Day War (from the summer of 1967 to the summer of 1968, 16,000 Moroccan and Tunisian Jews sought sanctuary in France). Approximately 50% of the Jews who left North Africa settled in France, so that by 1968 the

Sephardim were in the majority in the French Jewish community.

Geographical Distribution. In 1939 the Jewish population was concentrated in Paris and the surrounding region, Alsace-Lorraine, and several large towns. In 1968 about 60% of the Jewish population lived in Paris and its surroundings, about 25% in the Midi, and the rest were scattered throughout France. Five provincial towns supported important communities: Marseilles (65,000), Lyons (20,000), Toulouse (18,000), Nice (16,000), and Strasbourg (12,000). Between 1957 and 1966 the number of localities in which Jews lived rose from 128 to 293. The dispersal of the immigrants from North Africa, which answered the need to absorb them into the economy, resulted in the establishment of Jewish communities throughout the country. In 1968, 76 rather isolated communities contained fewer than 100 Jews, and 174 communities numbered less than 1,000 (such communities were particularly numerous in the Paris district).

Economic and Social Status. French Jewry succeeded in normalizing its economic status during the first two or three years following the liberation. Each successive wave of immigration, however, included a large group of impoverished persons who were forced to make recourse to social services run by the community or the state. Among both Ashkenazim and Sephardim, rapid and important changes in social status took place. Artisans from Eastern Europe or North Africa abandoned their traditional occupations in the second, if not in the first, generation in order to find jobs in modern industry, where the need for technical skills was great and through which a rapid rise on the social scale was possible. This trend was encouraged by the education offered in the seven *ORT schools, whose pupils were mainly from immigrant families. About 80% of North African Jews continued in the same occupation they had pursued in their countries of origin, and their influx into France slightly modified the distribution of occupations and social status of French Jewry. An estimated 15% of Algerian Jews were clerks employed at all levels of public administration; these were absorbed into urban administrations. Despite the resettlement loans granted by the government to repatriated citizens, some small businessmen and artisans had to abandon their previous status as self-employed persons and become salaried employees. Social advancement was rapid among North African Jews who were French nationals, as racial barriers that had seriously handicapped their advancement under colonial rule did not exist in France. Their settlement there opened new prospects for them, and many made their way in the liberal professions, commerce, and industry. The economic absorption of Moroccan or Tunisian Jews was more difficult. Nevertheless, they also chose France as their new country of residence as a result of their varying degrees of assimilation into French culture in their native countries. The social status and occupational distribution of French Jewry resembled the principal traits of the Diaspora in the West, i.e., a preponderance of members of the liberal professions, white-collar workers, businessmen, and artisans.

Community Organization. The Consistoire Central Israélite de France et d'Algérie comprised 83 Jewish congregations in France and Algeria in 1965. Orthodox in orientation, the consistory was the official representative of French Judaism, responsible for the training, nomination, and appointment of rabbis, religious instruction for young people, the supervision of *kashrut*, and the application of religious law in matters of personal status. The central consistory maintained close contact with the three regional consistories in Alsace-Lorraine, where the law regarding the separation of Church and State did not apply, religious functionaries there being paid by the state. The synagogues of the consistory generally practiced Ashkenazi rites, but some followed the Portuguese or North African rites. The Chantiers du Consistoire building projects provided newly formed communities with synagogues and community centers. North African Jews often formed their own communal organizations, but were represented in all the consistorial organizations. After 1945, most of the pupils of the Ecole Rabbinique and the rabbinical seminary, the Séminaire Israélite de France, were of Egyptian and North African origin. After 1952, Orthodox Judaism was represented by the Conseil Représentatif du Judaisme Traditionnaliste de France (C.R.J.T.F.). In 1968, it comprised 49 bodies in Paris and the provinces. Its members were particularly active in aiding the social and religious absorption of North African Jews, whom they sought to organize into active communities. The Union Libérale Israélite, affiliated to the World Union for Progressive Judaism, was no less active. It had greater influence in more assimilated circles of established and North African families and trained its ministers at the Institut International d'Etudes Hébraïques. Lastly, there were the independent religious bodies, including Sephardi and North African communities practicing their various local rites, Poles, and Ḥasidim and kabbalists.

Despite the amount of effort expended, only a small minority of French Jewry practiced their religion. There were, however, hundreds of associations and institutions of a cultural, social, or philanthropic nature. From 1945 efforts made to coordinate and channel the rather anarchic development of such organizations met with a measure of success. The Conseil Représentatif des Juifs de France (C.R.I.F.) was founded in 1944. In 1968, it was composed of 27 important organizations of diverse trends, including religious, Zionist, Bundist, and even Communist bodies. According to its statutes, the Council's aim was "to protect the rights of the Jewish community in France." Under the terms of an agreement signed with the World Jewish Congress, the Council acquired the sole right to represent the interests of French Jewry before French authorities. Since 1945 C.R.I.F. played an active role in the fight against anti-Semitism. The Fonds Social Juif Unifié (F.S.J.U.), founded in 1949 to centralize the various efforts of the community, rapidly became the central organizational body of French Jewry. It coordinated, supervised, and planned the community's major social, cultural, and educational enterprises, which it financed through its unified fund-raising campaign and the contributions of the *American Jewish Joint Distribution Committee. Its community services played an important role in the integration of Jewish immigrants, and its numerous community centers aimed at involving peripheral elements without religious affiliations in community life. After the Six-Day War, the F.S.J.U. and the Appel Unifié pour Israël (United Israel Appeal) coordinated their activities and formed the Appel Unifié Juif de France, a joint fund-raising venture. Varied ideological and political orientations, from the assimilationists to the Zionists and from the left wing to the right, were freely expressed in the French Jewish community. Although the Landsmanschaften of Eastern European immigrants gradually died out, associations of immigrants from North African countries multiplied.

Cultural Life. The diverse cultural trends of French Jewry were expressed by its 40 or so weekly and monthly publications. In 1968, there were ten daily, weekly, or monthly publications in Yiddish. After 1945, due to the activities of the *Conference on Jewish Material Claims, many books on Jewish and Israel subjects were published

Figure 7. The Rothschild mansion on Avenue Foch, Paris. Photo M. Ninio, Jerusalem.

annually by large French publishing houses; there was also a weekly Jewish radio broadcast and a regular television program. Most French Jews preferred to provide their children with a secular state education. Less than 5% of Jewish schoolchildren studied in the Jewish day schools at all levels, but the numerous youth movements and organizations tried to attract as many young people as possible. Under an agreement between the French and Israel governments, Hebrew could be taught as a foreign language in the *lycées* (state high schools). Ten universities included Hebrew in their curriculum, the universities of Paris and Strasbourg taught Jewish history, literature, and sociology. All the major Zionist youth movements were represented in France. The French Zionist Federation included various Zionist parties; however, it was decimated by internal feuds and its influence was weak. Nevertheless, more and more French Jews expressed their solidarity with Israel.

Despite a certain latent but rarely virulent anti-Semitism (research conducted by the Institut Francais de l'Opinion Publique in December 1966 showed that about 20% of the French public held seriously anti-Semitic opinions), Jews felt well integrated into French society. The efforts of numerous Jewish organizations did not retard the rate of assimilation. After the Six-Day War (1967), the explicit anti-Israel stance of de Gaulle and his government (see below), came as a shock to French Jewry. The feeling of uneasiness increased when the anti-Israel utterances of de Gaulle, his officials and commentators assumed a half-disguised, sophisticated anti-Semitic quality, particularly through hints at the Jews' "double loyalty." It reached its peak when de Gaulle, at a press conference (Nov. 27, 1967), defined the Jews as *"un peuple d'élite, sûr de lui-même et dominateur"* ("an elite people, self-assured and domineering"), thus giving a great impetus to overt expressions of latent anti-Semitism. This dictum aroused a wide public controversy in France and abroad. The chief rabbi, Jacob Kaplan, voiced his protest, reaffirming Jewish attachment to Israel and stressing that it did not contradict in any way the fact that the Jews of France are loyal Frenchmen. De Gaulle later told the chief rabbi that his words were not meant to be disparaging. At the same time, from the other extreme of the political scene, came the violently aggressive anti-Israel propaganda of the *New Left and of the "students' revolution" of May 1968, who supported Arab-Palestinian terrorism against Israel, though many of the movement's leaders were themselves young Jews (Daniel Cohn-Bendit, Marc Kravetz, Alain Krivine, and others). This agitation was the cause of embarrassment to most French Jews, not only because of its enmity toward Israel but also because of its extremist ideology of violence (Troskyism, Maoism, anarchism, etc.), which could have easily aroused an anti-Semitic reaction in the mainly conservative French middle class, to whom most Jews belong. Physical clashes between Jews and Arabs in certain quarters of Paris, mostly provoked by pro-Palestinian North Africans, added to the malaise. As a result, migration from France to Israel, by both French and Algerian Jews, considerably increased in the late 1960's.

[D.Bs.]

Relations with Israel. France played a major role on the Middle Eastern scene especially from World War I (see *Zionism; *Sykes-Picot; *Lebanon; *Syria; *Israel, Historical Survey) until 1948. However, between the two world wars, France played a relatively minor role in Zionist policy, since the Zionist movement naturally directed its major political efforts toward London and Washington. Closer ties were established between the *yishuv* and "Free France" during World War II, against the background of the Nazi conquests and on the basis of the strong contact between the *yishuv* and the Free French in the Middle East. After the war, these ties were then reinforced by the joint opposition to British policy, which fostered the Arab League and tried to restrict both French and Jewish interests in the area. During the early postwar period, various French leaders provided moral and material support for the legal and "illegal" immigration of Jewish refugees to Palestine. When the State of Israel was established, however, France still largely considered her an unimportant factor. France had supported the U.N. partition resolution of Nov. 29, 1947, but the process of developing relations between the two countries was very slow at first and very restricted on France's side. When France did formally recognize Israel, her recognition was conditional upon Israel giving preferential rights to French educational and religious institutions in the country.

In the mid-1950s, various developments paved the way for a closer cooperation between Israel and France. Among these were: the inter-party relations that developed between the French Socialist Party, which played a prominent role in some governments of the Fourth Republic, and *Mapai; the accommodation of Israel's foreign policy to the new reality in postwar Europe with the trend toward some type of European unity, in which France held a special position; France's search for new markets, her aeronautics and arms industries finding an important outlet in Israel's defense needs; and France's confrontation with Arab nationalism in North Africa (particularly in Algeria), which resulted in an identity of interest between the Israelis and the French, in view of Egypt's direct intervention in the Algerian war and her infractions against French economic interests in the Middle East, which reached a climax with the nationalization of the Suez Canal in 1956.

Franco-Israel friendship, which reached its peak with the Sinai Campaign (1956) and during the years that followed, continued in part through the days of the Fifth Republic and almost until the Six-Day War (1967). Not only did France become Israel's major supplier of arms during that period, but there also developed a whole network of technical and scientific cooperation. A cultural agreement, which was signed in 1959, contributed greatly to the enhancement of cultural relations between the two countries. It included the establishment of chairs in French language and literature at Israel universities and in Hebrew language and literature at a score of French universities; the fostering of French and Hebrew instruction respectively in each other's secondary schools; and art exhibitions, exchanges of scientists and students, and joint scientific projects. On the other hand, even at the height of Franco-Israel military, economic, cultural, and scientific cooperation, the official representatives of France were always wary of expressing complete support for Israel's position, as, for example, on the issues of the Palestinian refugees and Jerusalem, or in Security Council discussions on border incidents. France also opposed Israel's application to join the European Economic Community and prevented her associate membership from coming into effect. In 1966, French exports to Israel amounted to $35,000,000, while her imports did not exceed $19,000,000. Tourism from France to Israel reached the figure of 40,000.

Not long after President de Gaulle assumed power in 1958, a reconsideration of French policy in the Middle East was begun. At first this review was undertaken slowly and was hardly felt at all; on the occasion of Ben-Gurion's visits to France in 1960 and 1961 and Eshkol's visit in 1964, de Gaulle hailed Israel as "our friend and ally." Over the years, however, changes in French policy toward Israel took more rapid effect, until they created an about-face position on the eve of the Six-Day War. Thereafter, Franco-Israel relations steadily and sharply deteriorated. The major stages in this development were the ending of Franco-Arab hostilities in Algeria, after which France began to renew her diplomatic relations with the Arab states; and her growing rejection of Israel's needs and claims on basic political and security matters culminating in the unilateral cancellation of French official political and economic commitments to Israel, exemplified by France's failure to implement her own declared policy of supporting free passage through the Straits of Tiran, her at first partial and later total embargo on arms to Israel, and French support of the Arab position after the Six-Day War. This policy resulted, to a large extent, from the personal stand of de Gaulle, who was said to have resented the fact that Israel did not heed his advice on the eve of the 1967 war, but

Figure 8. Charles de Gaulle at a memorial to Jewish soldiers who died for France in World War I. Courtesy *Ma'ariv*, Tel Aviv.

also from the constantly closing gap between Gaullist and Soviet policy on international matters. France's attitude toward Israel was further influenced by her increasing attempts to penetrate economically into the Arab states, and to receive special favors from the Arabs and exclusive rights to exploit their natural resources (especially oil). These factors continued to influence French policy after de Gaulle's resignation in 1969.

However, despite the grave deterioration in official relations, there was still considerable French public support for Israel. It found organized expression in the Alliance France-Israël, whose president was General Marie-Pierre Koenig (1898–1970). Koenig, a World War II hero of the Free French who twice served as minister of national defense, fought unremittingly for the cancellation of his country's embargo on the sale of arms to Israel. The official French line was also attacked by intellectuals such as Eugène *Ionesco and Nathalie *Sarraute, and by two former ambassadors to Israel, Pierre Gilbert and Jean Bourdeillette. Another vehement opponent of France's Middle East policy was Jacques Soustelle, a former Gaullist leader and onetime governor general of Algeria (1955–56), who sympathetically reviewed the Jewish national revival in *La longue marche d'Israël* (1968). The French government's pro-Arab stand—endorsed by ministers of Jewish origin such as Maurice Schumann, Michel Debré and Léo Hamon—nevertheless remained unaffected by this widespread public reaction. [Ed.]

See also *French Literature.

Bibliography: Until 1789: B. Blumenkranz, *Bibliographie des Juifs en France* (1961); idem, *Juifs et chrétiens* (1960); idem, in: *Fourth World Congress of Jewish Studies*, 2 (1968), 45–50; idem, in: *Annales de l'Est*, 19 (1967), 199–215; Aronius, Regesten; A. Neubauer and E. Renan, in: *Histoire littéraire de la France*, 27 (1877), 431–764; 31 (1893), 1–469; M. Schwab, *Inscriptions hébraïques en France . . .* (1899); L. Berman, *Histoire des Juifs en France* (1937); M. Catane, *Des croisades à nos jours* (1957); I. A. Agus, *Heroic Age of Franco-German Jewry* (1970); A. Hertzberg, *French Enlightenment and the Jews* (1968); L. Rabinowitz, *Social Life of the Jews of Northern France . . .* (1938); Z. Szajkowski, *Franco-Judaica* (1962); G. Nahon, in: REJ, 121 (1962), 59–80; R. Chazan, *ibid.*, 128 (1969), 41–65; G. I. Langmuir, in: *Traditio*, 16 (1960), 203–39; Gross, Gal Jud; E. E. Urbach, *Ba'alei ha-Tosafot* (1956); *Archives Juives* (1965–to date). Modern Period: L. Kahn, *Histoire des écoles communales et consistoriales israélites de Paris* (1884); idem, *Les professions manuelles et les institutions de patronage* (1885); idem, *Le Comité de Bienfaisance* (1886); idem, *Les Juifs à Paris depuis le VIe siècle* (1889); A. E. Halphen, *Recueil des lois, décrets . . . concernant les Israélites depuis la révolution de 1789* (1851); I. Uhry, *Recueil des lois, décrets . . . concernant les Israélites 1850–1903* (1903[3]); R. Anchel, *Napoléon et les Juifs* (1928); idem, *Les Juifs de France* (1946); E. Tcherikower, *Yidn in Frankraykh*, 2 vols. (1942); Elbogen, Century, passim; Z. Szajkowski, *Jews and the French Revolution of 1789, 1830 and 1848* (1970); idem, *Poverty and Social Welfare among French Jews (1800–1880)* (1954); M. Roblin, *Les Juifs de Paris* (1952), S. Schwarzfuchs, *Brève histoire des Juifs de France* (1957); P. Lévy, *Les noms des Israélites en France* (1960). Holocaust Period: L. Poliakov, *Harvest of Hate* (1954); G. Reitlinger, *Final Solution* (1968[2]), 327–51 and passim; R. Hilberg, *Destruction of European Jews* (1961), index; IMT, *Trial of the Major War Criminals*, 23 (1949), index; Z. Szajkowski, *Analytical Franco-Jewish Gazetteer 1939–1945* (1966); idem, in: *Yad Vashem Studies*, 2 (1958), 133–57; 3 (1959), 187–202; Ariel, *ibid.*, 6 (1967), 221–50; L. Steinberg, *Les autorités allemandes en France occupée* (1966); idem, *La révolte des justes—Les Juifs contre Hitler* (1970), 139–233. Contemporary Period: Bibliothèque du Centre de Documentation Juive Contemporaine, Catalogue no. 1, *La France de l'Affaire Dreyfus à nos jours* (1964); idem, Catalogue no. 2, *La France—le Troisième Reich—Israël* (1968); Rabi (pseud.), *Anatomie du judaïsme français* (1962); AJYB, 28 (1946/47–); *Annuaire du judaïsme* (1950–52); Fonds Social Juif Unifié, *Communautés juives de France* (1966); R. Berg et al., *Guide juif de France* (1968); G. Levitte, in:

JJSO, 2 (1960), 172–84; M. Catane, *Les Juifs dans le monde* (1962), 26–41; Donath, in: WLB, 21 no. 2 (1967), 24–26; Institut Français de l'Opinion Publique, *Sondages*, 2 (1967); E. Touati, in: *D'Auschwitz à Israël* (1968); *L'Arche* (1957–); *Information Juive* (1925–); *Community—Communauté* (French and English, 1958–); *Le Monde Juif* (1946–); *Les Nouveaux Cahiers* (1965–). ISRAEL-FRANCE RELATIONS: M. Bar-Zohar, *Suez, ultra-secret* (1964); Y. Tzur, *Yoman Paris 1953–1956* (1968); J. Bourdeillette, *Pour Israël* (1968); R. Aron, *De Gaulle, Israel and the Jews* (1969).

FRANCES, IMMANUEL BEN DAVID (1618–c. 1710), Hebrew poet. Born in Leghorn, he was educated by his father David, his brother Jacob *Frances, and especially by R. Joseph Fermo. Immanuel's life was filled with difficulties; not only was he forced to wander from one town to another to earn a living, but a succession of misfortunes befell him. His beloved father died in 1640, and his wife and two children in 1654. In 1657, he married Miriam, the daughter of R. Mordecai Visino, but both she and the son she bore him died in 1667. The same year saw the death of his brother, Jacob, to whom Immanuel was deeply attached, and together with whom he had fought against the supporters of Kabbalah. In his solitude, he devoted himself entirely to his literary work and to his activities as rabbi in Florence. In these he found his sole consolation for the remainder of his life.

His poetic work may be divided into three periods. The first extends from 1643 to 1660, when he was under the influence of two of Italy's most popular poets, Tasso and Guarini. At this time he wrote his love poems and his debates on women (*Vikku'aḥ Itti'el ve-Ukhal*), and rabbis (*Vikku'aḥ Rekhav u-Va'anah*), to which he appended satirical epigrams. The dramatic form he employed suited the literary style he had adopted to attack the corruption in contemporary Jewish society. During the second period, from 1664 to 1667, Immanuel, together with his brother Jacob, waged a literary war against Shabbetai Ẓevi, Nathan of Gaza, and their messianic movement, in which he saw a threat to the Jewish people. His book of satirical poems, *Ẓevi Muddaḥ* ("The Banished Gazelle *[Ẓevi]*"), belongs to this period and is the choicest of his literary work. The poems were published by M. Mortara (in *Kobez al jad*, 1 (1885), 99–131). In the final period, from 1670 until after 1685, the poet adapted his religious poetry for use in synagogue services, giving it a dramatic and recitative character. While the poet preferred to use the Spanish-Arabic meter, he also introduced into his Hebrew poetry the *terza rima* and the *ottava rima* of Italian prosody. His poetic works were edited by S. Bernstein in 1932 under the title *Divan le-R. Immanu'el b. David Frances;* his work *Metek Sefatayim*, written in 1667 during a period of residence in Algiers, deals with various aspects of poetry and rhetoric. It was published in 1892 by H. Brody.

Bibliography: M. Hartmann, *Die hebraeische Verskunst nach dem Metek Sefatajim des Immanuel Fransis und anderen Werken juedischer Metriker* (Berlin, 1894); Davidson, Oẓar, 4 (1933), 459; s.v. *Immanuel Frances (ben David);* Waxman, Literature, 2 (1960), 83–88. [Yo.D.]

FRANCES, ISAAC (18th century), preacher and the author of a collection of sermons, *Penei Yiẓḥak* (Salonika, 1753). No details are known of his life or where he lived. The sermons are based on the weekly portions of the Pentateuch, but there is usually more than one sermon for each portion, indicative of the author's long preaching career. Although Frances was influenced by the Kabbalah, often quoting and discussing kabbalistic sources in his sermons, he was not exclusively a kabbalist. He used both contemporary and ancient rabbinic sources extensively and even made some use of medieval philosophical writings, demonstrating the eclectic attitude common among 18th-century preachers. Frances's sermons are didactic, sometimes tending toward theological discourses, but more usually they are designed to foster the ethical improvement of his community, laying great emphasis on decent social behavior. [Y.D.]

FRANCES, JACOB BEN DAVID (1615-1667), poet; elder brother of Immanuel *Frances. Born in Mantua, Jacob, a highly educated man, mastered not only Hebrew and Aramaic, but Latin, Italian, and Portuguese as well. Aware of the fact that his brother was a better poet than he, Jacob would send his poems to him, which Immanuel corrected, completed, and to which he occasionally even attached additions of his own. Copyists inserted these additions into the poems without always noting that they were composed by Immanuel. At times they also attributed Immanuel's poems to Jacob, and vice-versa, because of the similarity in style, form, and content. There is still no definitive means of determining the true authorship of these poems; 54 sonnets, however, can almost certainly be ascribed to Jacob. These poems are rhymed, and their language beautiful and clear. After the manner of his contemporary poets, Jacob wrote on all subjects, including friendship, polemics, ethics, love, and marriage. As was customary in poetry at that time, some of his poems have a flavor of obscenity. Jacob quarreled fiercely with members of his community, chiefly attacking the sect of *Shabbetai Ẓevi that arose during his time, as well as the kabbalists who were closely associated with it. He and his brother regarded them as detrimental to Judaism and considered themselves duty-bound to stop them. Unike his brother, Jacob held no communal post but engaged in business. He died in Florence. Only isolated poems were published during his lifetime and afterward. A collection of all his poems from manuscripts and printed works was published by Peninah Naveh (see bibliography).

Bibliography: P. Naveh (ed.), *Kol Shirei Ya'akov Frances* (1969), incl. bibl.; A. M. Habermann, in: *Moznayim*, 29 (1969), 66–69; Davidson, Oẓar, 4 (1933), 415; Scholem, Shabbetai Ẓevi, 2 (1957), 425–8; E. Fleischer, in: KS, 45 (1969/70), 177–87. [A.M.H.]

FRANCHE-COMTÉ, region and former province in E. France, comprising the present departments of Haute-Saône, Doubs, and Jura. Since a document of 1220 mentions a Jewish quarter *(vicus Judaeorum)* in *Lons-le-Saunier, the Jews must first have come to Franche-Comté at a much earlier date, probably after the expulsion from the kingdom of France in 1182. From the middle of the 13th century, there is increased evidence of the presence of the Jews and the 40 or more places they had settled, including *Baume-les-Dames, *Besançon, Lons-le-Saunier, and *Vesoul. Because they were a valuable source of income, the Jews were eagerly welcomed by various local lords, who granted them advantageous privileges, but they were not admitted to the Church domains. From a detailed list of the fiscal contributions of the Jews drawn up in 1296, it is apparent that by then several localities no longer permitted Jewish residence; those remaining paid an annual tax of 975 livres. Though Franche-Comté was temporarily under the control of the French kingdom at the time, the Jews were not affected by the expulsion order of 1306; however, they were included in that of 1322, though possibly it was not rigorously enforced. From 1332/33 at the latest, new immigrants joined those who had been able to remain in their homes; in a census of 86 Jewish families, 32 are described as recent arrivals. As during the 13th century, their principal occupation was moneylending.

During the *Black Death persecutions in 1348, the count appointed two commissioners, who promptly arrested the

Jews and seized their belongings. They were imprisoned for many months (those of Vesoul for nearly ten months), some of them in Gray and the others in Vesoul. In spite of confessions extracted under torture, none was condemned to death but all were banished, and the regent, Jeanne de Boulogne, promised that Jews would no longer be tolerated in Franche-Comté. However, from 1355, there were Jews in the province once more, especially in Bracon and Salins-les-Bains, where a Christian loan bank was set up in 1363 so that there need be no recourse to Jewish moneylenders; the Jews were subsequently expelled from the town in 1374. In 1384, shortly after Franche-Comté was reunited with Burgundy, the duke authorized many Jewish families to settle there, but they did not escape the general expulsion from Burgundy ten years later. Many of them found refuge in Besançon, from where one Jew returned to settle in Champlitte. Driven out in 1409, he was the last Jew to live in Franche-Comté before the French Revolution.

Bibliography: J. Morey, in: REJ, 7 (1883), 1-36; L. Gauthier, in: *Mémoires de la Société pour l'Emulation du Jura* (1914), 90ff.; J. Fohlen, in: *Archives Juives,* 5 (1968–69), 12–13. [B.Bl.]

FRANCHETTI, RAIMONDO (1890–1935), Italian explorer. In 1910 Franchetti traveled alone through Indo-China and Malaysia. After World War I he explored the Sudan, East Africa, and Ethiopia. In *Nella Dancàlia Etiopica* (1935[3]) he described the Danakil region of northeastern Ethiopia. His sympathetic understanding encouraged many of the Ethiopian tribal chiefs to join an alliance with Italy before hostilities began in 1934. Franchetti was killed in a plane explosion near Cairo airport. [Ed.]

FRANCIA, FRANCIS (b. 1675), English conspirator. He was the grandson of Domingo Rodrigues Isaac Francia, an ex-Marrano of Vila Real (Portugal) who arrived in London from Bordeaux in 1655 and became a leading member of the London community. Francis himself was born in Bordeaux and dealt in wine. He subsequently went to London where in 1717 he was tried on a charge of treasonable correspondence with adherents of the exiled Old Pretender James. Despite the weighty evidence against him, he was acquitted. He then apparently turned government agent and betrayed his former associates.

Bibliography: Lipton, in: JHSET, 11 (1928), 190–205; L. Wolf, *Jews in the Canary Islands* (1926), 198–213; Roth, Mag Bibl, 248f. [C.R.]

THE

TRYAL

OF

Francis Francia,

FOR

High Treaſon,

AT THE

Sessions-House in the *Old-Baily*;

On Tuesday *Jan.* 22. 1716.

Peruſed by the Right Honourable
The Lord Chief-Baron Bury:
And alſo by
The Council *for* His MAJESTY, *and for the* Priſoner.

LONDON:

Printed for D. Midwinter, at the *Three Crowns* in St. *Paul's* Church-Yard. M DCC XVII.

Report of the trial of Francis Francia at the Old Bailey, London, in 1717. Cecil Roth Collection. Photo David Harris, Jerusalem.

°**FRANCIS I,** Austrian emperor 1792–1835, last Holy Roman Emperor (as Francis II) until 1806. In 1792 Francis ordered the *Judenamt* (office for Jewish affairs) to enforce the numerous restrictions on Jewish settlement in

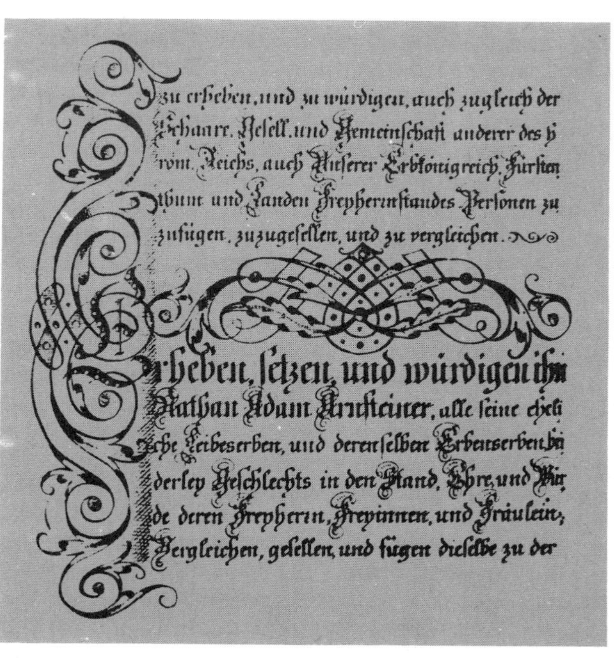
zu erheben, und zu würdigen, auch zugleich der Schaar, Geſell- und Gemeinſchaft anderer des h. röm. Reichs, auch Unſerer Erbkönigreich, Fürſtenthum und Landen Freyherrnſtandes Perſonen zu zufügen, zuzugeſellen, und zu vergleichen.

Erheben, ſetzen, und würdigen ihn Nathan Adam Arnſteiner, alle ſeine ehel. Leibeserben, und derenſelben Erbenserben bis derley Geſchlechts in den Stand, Ehre, und Würde deren Freyherren, Freyinnen, und Fräulein, vergleichen, geſellen, und fügen dieſelbe zu der

Decree of Francis I bestowing a barony on Nathan Adam Arnstein, 1798. From H. Spiel, *Fanny von Arnstein oder Die Emanzipation,* Frankfort, 1962.

*Vienna and raised the *Bolleten* (tax paid by a Jew each time he entered the city). The preamble to his 1797 patent granted to Bohemian Jewry (see *Bohemia), proclaiming equality as its ultimate aim, raised expectations which remained unfulfilled. Most of the petitions for improvement of the status of the Jews addressed to him by representatives of the Jews in the empire were unanswered, though in 1798 Francis authorized the existence of 52 communities in *Moravia. He agreed to the official use of "Mr." instead of "Jew" in reference to Jewish citizens. During the *Congress of Vienna a petition requesting partial equality presented by B. *Eskeles, A. *Arnstein, and L. *Herz met with no success (see also *Metternich). In Francis' Italian provinces, however, *emancipation measures were not revoked. In Galicia, Francis supported Naphtali Herz *Homberg; knowledge of his catechism *Benei Zion* was made compulsory in 1810 for all Jewish couples registering their marriages. While regularly making use of Jewish finance and financial advice, Francis unhesitatingly blamed Jewish financiers for all the economic ills of the empire.

Bibliography: A. F. Pribram, *Urkunden und Akten zur Geschichte der Juden in Wien,* 1–2 (1918), index; M. Grunwald, *Vienna* (1936), 168–71; Kisch, in: HJ, 8 (1946), 24; S. Baron, *Die Judenfrage an dem Wiener Kongress* (1920), 20–23, 118, 183; Dubnow, Weltgesch, 8 (1920–23), 280–93; R. Kestenberg-Gladstein, *Neuere Geschichte der Juden in den boehmischen Laendern,* 1 (1969), index. [Ed.]

FRANCISCANS, Roman Catholic Order of Friars Minor, established about 1209 by Francis of Assisi with the approbation of Pope Innocent III, known in Hebrew as *Ẓe'irim* ("Minorites") or *Yeḥefim* ("Barefooted"). In contrast to the *Dominicans, the Franciscans were not at the outset specifically interested in combating heresy or conducting propaganda among the unbelievers. On the other hand, they inevitably participated to some extent in the mainly Dominican activities of preaching conversionist *sermons, the *censorship of Hebrew literature, and the medieval disputations (e.g., at *Barcelona in 1263). The *blood libel at *Valréas in 1247 was stage-managed by Franciscan friars, while the inflammatory preaching of the Franciscan Peter Olligoyen was responsible for the bloody massacres in Navarre in 1328. In a later generation, the propaganda of the Franciscan *Alfonso de Espina stimulated the reaction against the *Conversos in Spain and led to the establishment of the Spanish *Inquisition. On the other hand, the mystical elements in Spanish Jewry in the 13th and 14th centuries seem to have been powerfully influenced by the outlook of the spiritual Franciscans.

A new phase in Franciscan history opened with the so-called Observantine Reform which began the close of the 14th century and professed to revert to the original intention of Francis of Assisi. Work among the poor, especially in Italy, made the friars conscious of the activities of the Jewish loan-bankers, then at the height of their prosperity, and the widespread indebtedness of the populace to them. From this point, the Franciscans adopted a fiercely anti-Jewish attitude, clamoring for the implementation of all the canonical anti-Jewish legislation, including physical segregation and the wearing of the Jewish *badge, and the restriction or prohibition of Jewish financial activities. The Lenten sermons which magnetic Franciscan preachers such as *Bernardino da Siena delivered in the early 15th century throughout Italy before enormous crowds, exhorting them to repentance, were partly devoted to anti-Jewish propaganda, as a result of which the Jews were expelled from a number of north Italian cities. John of *Capistrano extended these activities as far as Sicily in the south and Poland in the north. In due course, the Franciscans became the strongest supporters of instituting public loan-banks (see *Monte di Pietà) in order to replace the Jews and make it possible to drive them away with fewer complications. The greatest propagandist in favor of this in the second half of the 15th century was *Bernardino da Feltre, who was responsible for the expulsion of the Jews from several places in north Italy and for the tragic blood libel at *Trent in 1475. With the general anti-Jewish reaction at the time of the Counter-Reformation in the middle of the 16th century and the closing of the Jewish loan-banks in many areas, the specifically anti-Jewish activities of the Franciscan order were modified. Indeed, Lorenzo Ganganelli (Pope *Clement XIV), author of the 1759 report condemning the blood libel, was a Franciscan.

In Ereẓ Israel. Francis of Assisi arrived in Acre on a pilgrimage to the Holy Land in December 1219; the order established its first monastery in Jerusalem in 1335. When in 1426/27 the Franciscan chapel on Mount Zion was siezed by the Muslim authorities, the local Jews were blamed for instigating the action, this giving a further impetus to the anti-Jewish agitation in Italy. The position of custodian of the Christian Holy Places in Ereẓ Israel was vested in the head of the local Franciscans. In this capacity, in the 16th century Fra Bonifazio of Ragusa intrigued in Constantinople against Don Joseph *Nasi's plan for rebuilding Tiberias. The principal Franciscan monasteries in Israel in 1970 were in Jerusalem, Bethlehem, Nazareth, Tiberias, Capernaum, Acre, Jaffa, and Ramleh.

Bibliography: H. Holzapfel, *History of the Franciscan Order* (1948); *New Catholic Encyclopedia*, 6 (1967), s.v.; Colbi, *Christianity in the Holy Land* (1969).

[C.R.]

°**FRANCIS JOSEPH I OF HAPSBURG** (1830–1916), emperor of Austria 1848–1916. During his long reign he won popularity among all strata of Jewry in his empire and abroad. When he died the executive of the Austrian Zionists credited him with the betterment of the lot of the Jews in the empire, describing him as the "donor of civil rights and equality before the law, and their ever benevolent protector" (*Blochs Wochenschrift*, 33 (1916), 784). Anti-Semites nicknamed him "Judenkaiser." The Jewish masses referred to him as הקיר"ה (*ha-keisar, yarum hodo:* "the emperor, may his Majesty be exalted"), and many folklorist tales were told of him, among them that the prophet Elijah had promised him a long life. The synagogues were always full for the services held on his birthday, which were also attended by gentile dignitaries. Francis Joseph appreciated the role of the Jews as a sector of the population both devoted to and dependent on the monarchy at a time of growing internal national tensions. On the question of Jewish emancipation he assented to the liberal attitude of the 1848 Revolution (see also *Austria). In 1849 he granted the long-withheld recognition to the Vienna community simply by addressing its delegation as its representative (A. F. Pribram (ed.), *Urkunden und Akten . . .*, 2 (1918), 549). He intervened on behalf of the Jewish side in the *Mortara case. Francis Joseph signed the decree canceling restrictions on Jewish occupations and ownership of real estate (1860), and the Fundamental Law, which made Jews full citizens of the state (1867). In 1869 he met Jewish representatives in Jerusalem and gave a contribution to enable completion of the Nisan Bak Synagogue (Tiferet Yisrael). When visiting synagogues and other Jewish institutions he would assure Jews of his favor and praise their virtues, such as their devotion to family life and charity. He several times expressed his dislike of anti-Semitism, and in the Lower Austrian Diet called attacks on Jewish physicians a "scandal and disgrace in the eyes of the world" (1892). He twice refused to confirm the anti-Semite Karl *Lueger as mayor of Vienna, and on the day he finally did so conferred an order on Moritz *Guedemann, the chief rabbi of Vienna. He ennobled 20 Jews during his reign. After World War I many Jews of the former Hapsburg dominions looked back nostalgically to the reign of Francis Joseph as a golden age.

Bibliography: G. Deutsch, *Scrolls*, 2 (1917), 321–40; F. Coglievini, *Il viaggio in Oriente di S. M. Francesco Giuseppe I* (1869), 172–5; O. Gruen, *Franz Josef I in seinem Verhaeltniss zu den Juden* (1916); P. G. J. Pulzer, *The Rise of Political Antisemitism in Germany and in Austria* (1964), index; J. Fraenkel (ed.), *The Jews of Austria* (1967), index; F. Heer, *Gottes erste Liebe* (1967), 320–1; J. Roth, *Werke*, 3 (1956), 40f.; D. Bronsen, in: *Tribüne*, 9 (1970), 3556–64.

[Ed.]

FRANCK, ADOLPHE (Jacob; 1809–1893), French philosopher and writer. Franck, who was born at Liocourt, studied Talmud under Marchand Ennery, and later studied medicine and philosophy. He taught philosophy at several *lycées* (from 1840 in Paris) and lectured at the Sorbonne. In 1844 he was elected to the French Académie des Sciences Morales et Politiques, later being appointed to the Collège de France as extraordinary professor of ancient philosophy (1849–52) and professor of natural and international law (1854–86). In 1850 he represented the Jewish faith on the Conseil Supérieur de l'Instruction Publique. He was vice-president of the Consistoire Israélite and later president of the Alliance Israélite Universelle. Franck took part in the activities of the French society for the translation of the Bible and the Societé des Etudes Juives (whose chairman he became in 1888). In 1870 he interceded in Bucharest with Prince Carol in favor of the Rumanian Jews. Franck, who defended Judaism in several works, conceived it as an idealistic expression of monotheism and vigorously opposed pantheism, atheism, materialism, and communism. He established and managed the journal of the anti-atheistic league, *La Paix Sociale*, was coeditor of the *Journal des Savants*, and contributor to the *Journal des Débats* and the *Archives Israélites*. His works on general philosophy and the history of philosophy include: *Esquisse d'une histoire de la logique* (1838); *Le communisme jugé par l'histoire* (1848); *Philosophie de droit pénal* (1864), in which Franck and others put the case against capital punishment; *Philosophie du droit ecclésiastique* (1864); *La philosophie mystique en France à la fin du XVIIIe siècle* (1866); *Philosophie et religion* (1857); and *Philosophes modernes* (1879); he also edited the *Dictionnaire des sciences philosophiques* (6 vols., 1844–52; 1885[3]).

Franck's chief work is in the field of Jewish studies: *La Kabbale ou philosophie religieuse des hébreux* (Paris, 1843; 1892[3]; *The Kabbalah; Or The Religious Philosophy of the Hebrews*, 1926). This is the first attempt at a comprehensive, scientific description of the beginnings and contents of the Kabbalah in popular form. In the last (third) part Franck examines the religious and philosophic doctrines with which the Kabbalah has some traits in common (Platonism, the Alexandrinian school, the teachings of Philo, Christianity, the religions of the Chaldeans and the Persians). Two discussions on the Ḥasidim and the Frankists are appended. Franck's premises and hypotheses (early date for the beginnings of the Kabbalah; authenticity of *Sefer *Yeẓirah;* Persian influence) were strongly opposed (by Steinschneider, Jellinek, Jost, and Joel, among others). Other works of Jewish scholarly content are: *Sur les sectes juives avant le christianisme* (1853); *La religion et la science dans le judaisme* (1882); and *Le panthéisme oriental et le monothéisme hébreu* (1889). His articles on Jewish subjects (all of which appeared in *Archives Israélites*) include: *"De la Création"* (1845); *"Le rôle des juives dans la civilisation"* (1855); and *"Le péché original et la femme"* (1885).

Bibliography: H. Derenbourg, in: REJ, 4 (1882), 3–11; A. Kohut, *Beruehmte israelitische Maenner und Frauen* (1901); D. H. Joel, *Die Religionsphilosophie des Zohar* (1923); Jost, in: *Literaturblatt des Orients*, 6 (1845), 811; M. Steinschneider, *Jewish Literature from the Eighth to the Eighteenth Century* (1965), 299, 301; Pivacet, in: *Revue internationale de l'enseignement*, 40 (1920).

[Jo.H./Ed.]

FRANCK, HENRI (1888–1912), French poet. A great-grandson of Arnaud Aron (1807–1890), chief rabbi of Strasbourg, Franck was born into a well-to-do Parisian family. He studied under Henri Bergson and became one of the circle of young French intellectuals who, in the aftermath of the *Dreyfus affair, opposed the rising tide of nationalism and sought a new national and metaphysical ideal that would save France from fanatical individualism. Endowed with a consuming ardor for life and learning, Franck refused to spare himself and died of tuberculosis at the age of 24. His works include philosophical essays and literary criticism, but his major achievement was a magnificent 2,000-verse poem, *La Danse devant l'Arche* (1912), which secured his reputation as one of the most gifted French poets of his generation. Encouraged by his close friend André *Spire, Franck sought to harmonize biblical inspiration with the French Cartesian tradition and saw himself as a new David dancing before the Ark of the Covenant. His poem concludes on a note of disillusion because of the refusal of his fellow-Jews, so proud of their attenuated Judaism and atheistic French culture, to join him. Franck's spiritual conflict inspired his old friend and classmate, Jacques de *Lacretelle, to use him as a model for the tragic hero of his novel *Silbermann*.

Bibliography: J. Durel, *La sagesse d'Henri Franck, poète juif* (1931); C. Jean, in: *Revue littéraire juive*, 2 (1928), 675–99, 797–823; A. Spire, *Quelques juifs et demi-juifs*, 2 (1928), 107–69; H. Clouard, *Histoire de la littérature française du symbolisme à nos jours*, 1 (1947), 404–5.

[M.J.Go.]

FRANCK, JAMES (1882–1964), physicist and Nobel prize winner. Franck, who was born in Hamburg, studied chemistry at Heidelberg and Berlin. He then devoted himself mainly to physics. In 1920 he became a professor of experimental physics, directing the second Physical Institute at Goettingen. In 1925 he and Gustav *Hertz jointly received a Nobel prize for their discovery of the laws governing the impact of an electron on an atom, corroborating Bohr's "obstacle" theory of spectra, according to which atoms cannot absorb any energy below a certain level. In 1933, after the Nazi regime was established, Franck moved to the United States. He became a faculty member of Johns Hopkins and Chicago universities and made further investigations into the structure of matter, especially the kinetics of electrons. He also developed brilliant optical methods for determining the dissociation temperatures of chemical combinations from molecular spectra, and confirmed the assumptions on which modern atomic theory rests. In addition, he carried out important investigations in photochemistry.

James Franck, winner of the Nobel Prize for Physics. Jerusalem, Schwadron Collection, J.N.U.L.

Bibliography: McCallum and Taylor, *Nobel Prize Winners* (Zurich, 1938); *American Men of Science* (1965).

[J.E.H.]

FRANCO, English family. In the 18th century, Jacob de Moses Franco (d. 1777) settled in London and amassed a large fortune in the coral trade in conjunction with his brothers Raphael in Leghorn and Solomon (see below) in Fort St. George, Madras. He played a prominent part in the affairs of the London Sephardi community and was a member of the original Board of Deputies of British Jews in 1760. In that year, the College of Heralds accepted as evidence for his coat of arms the family badge which figured in the Leghorn synagogue. His brother Solomon (d. 1763) arrived in Bombay about 1743 under an agreement with the English East India Company as a "free merchant," moving to Madras in 1749. Described in his epitaph as "an eminent Hebrew merchant of Madras," he had huge interests in the coral and diamond trade. Ralph Franco, the great-grandson of Jacob, adopted the name of *Lopes, and was the ancestor of the barons Roborough.

Bibliography: A. Rubens, *Anglo-Jewish Portraits* (1935), 33; J. Picciotto, *Sketches of Anglo-Jewish History* (1956[2]), index; A. M. Hyamson, *Sephardim of England* (1951), index; Wolf, in: JHSET, 2 (1894–95), 159–68.

[C.R.]

FRANCO, GAD (1876–1954), Turkish jurist, son of the chief rabbi of Gallipoli, Ḥayyim Franco. In 1902 he went to Smyrna (Izmir), where, together with his cousin Hezekiah Franco, he published a number of periodicals, including the Ladino *El Nouvellists* (1902–06) and *El Commercial* (1906). At the same time he studied law and graduated as advocate at the University of Istanbul where he settled after World War I. Franco published a number of works in Turkish ("Guide to the Civil Code"; "The Theory of Education in Ancient Greece"; "The Theories of Education of Jean-Jacques Rousseau"). From 1929 to 1942 he published the "Review of Juridical Sciences" in Turkish. In 1943 he was one of the members of minority groups condemned to forced labor because he was unable to pay the *varlik vergisi* (property tax; see *Turkey). On liberation he returned to his professional activities. Both in Smyrna and later in Istanbul Franco was on the General Council of the Jewish community. [H.J.C.]

FRANCO-MENDES, DAVID (Ḥofshi-Mendes; 1713–1792), Hebrew poet of the early Haskalah period. Born into an esteemed and affluent Portuguese family in Amsterdam, he received an excellent education and had a command of six languages besides Hebrew. In honor of his marriage to Rachel da Fonseca in 1750, his friend Benjamin Raphael Dias Brandon composed *"Keter Torah,"* an epithalamium. Franco-Mendes was considered an outstanding talmudic scholar and often handed down halakhic decisions. He was a leading Hebrew poet of his time and was greatly influenced by M. Ḥ. *Luzzatto during his stay in Amsterdam (from 1735). A central figure among a group of Dutch Hebrew poets even prior to the appearance of *Ha-*Me'assef* in 1784, he became a member of Amadores das Musas, a Jewish literary society in 1769, and conducted an extensive correspondence with many Jewish literary personalities abroad. In the same year, he was also appointed honorary secretary of the Sephardi community of Amsterdam. A businessman, he was reduced to poverty in 1778, and compelled from then on to earn his living copying manuscripts. Franco-Mendes was one of the most zealous collaborators in the publication of *Ha-Me'assef; "Ahavat David"* (*Ha-Me'assef* (1785), 48), an article detailing a project for an encyclopedia in Hebrew, is one of his most noteworthy contributions to the periodical.

Franco-Mendes was a prolific writer. Among his dramas, most of them written in poetic form, his best-known work, *Gemul Atalyah* (Amsterdam, 1770), is reminiscent of Racine's tragedy *Athalie.* Many of his biographies of famous Sephardi Jews were published in *Ha-Me'assef* (1785ff.), and posthumously in *Ha-Maggid* (1860–66); some of his poems were also published in *Ha-Me'assef*, but the bulk is still in manuscript. *Nir-le-David*, responsa from the years 1735 to 1792, was partly published in *She'elot u-Teshuvot* of the yeshivah Ets Hayyim. *Sefer Tikkunim* is a critical work on some of the writings of Maimonides. His works on the Portuguese and Spanish Jews of Amsterdam (still in manuscript) are of historical value.

Bibliography: Klausner, Sifrut, 1 (1952), 200–3; J. Melkman, *David Franco-Mendes* (Eng., 1951), incl. bibl.; Schirmann, in: *Beḥinot*, 6 (1954), 44–52; Waxman, Literature, 3 (1960), 132–4; M. Gorali, in: *Taẓlil*, 6 (1966), 32–46. [Ed.]

FRANCOS (pl. of **Franco,** the Ladino equivalent of Arabic **Franji, Ifranjī**), term used in Muslim countries of the Eastern Mediterranean to designate all Europeans. *Benjamin of Tudela (12th century) used the term in the same sense (*Massa'ot*, ed. by M. N. Adler (1907), 19, 23). Since the time of the *capitulations treaties between France and the Ottoman Empire (1535), the term has been generally used for the protected (Christian) merchants who came from European countries. In later times Jewish merchants from Europe were also protected under the capitulations treaties. Consequently, one finds the name Franco in Sephardi rabbinic literature from the 16th century onward as a term for European Jews. In Eastern Europe it first came to mean a Jew who was a Turkish subject, and then a Sephardi, Ladino-speaking Jew. In modern Hebrew slang the term *Franji* is used with the same meaning.

Bibliography: Neubauer, Chronicles, 1 (1887), 157; E. W. Lane, *An Arabic-English Lexicon*, 6 (1877), 2389; R. Brunschvig (ed.), *Deux récits de voyage inédits en Afrique du Nord* (1936), 55, 121, 67, 135–6, 158, 192, and n. 3; Lutski, in: *Zion*, 6 (1940/41), 46–79; Baron, Community, 3 (1942), 101–2. [H.Z.H.]

FRANK, ALBERT RUDOLPH (1872–1965), German chemical engineer and industrial chemist. Born in Stassfurt, the son of Adolph Frank, he joined his father's company, the Cyanidgesellschaft, in 1899, and was its president from 1901 to 1908. In 1905 he also joined Stickstoffwerke A.G., succeeding his father as head of this company in 1916. With his father, Nikodem *Caro, and Linde, Frank worked on the production of sulfites and of hydrogen, and particularly on calcium carbide. Frank tried to make cyanides (then wanted for a process for extracting gold) from calcium carbide and

Albert Frank, chemical engineer. Courtesy American Cyanamide Co., New York.

atmospheric nitrogen, but instead he got calcium cyanamide, which he deduced could be used as a fertilizer. In 1914, when Germany was cut off from supplies of Chile saltpeter, calcium cyanamide became of vital importance to the country's agriculture, and it remains of some importance to this day. Frank also investigated the use of calcium cyanamide as a chemical intermediate, and later found a way of converting it into cyanides. Frank also worked on other uses for calcium carbide (such as making acetylene black for dry batteries). He held many patents and made numerous contributions to scientific literature. The advent of the Nazis compelled him to leave Germany in 1938. He went to the U.S.A., working for over 20 years with the American Cyanamid Company.

Bibliography: *Chemie-Ingenieur-Technik*, 24 (1952), 609; *New York Times* (March 19, 1965). [S.A.M.]

FRANK, ANNE (1929–1945), teen-age author of a diary composed while hiding from the Nazis in Amsterdam. She was the daughter of parents who fled from Germany to Amsterdam in 1933. Anne Frank was born in Frankfort, but received her entire education in Holland. In the summer of 1941, when public schools were closed to Jews under the German occupation, she transferred to the Jewish High School. In July, 1942 the deportations of Jews from Holland started, supposedly for *"Arbeitseinsatz"* ("forced labor") in the East. The Frank family decided to go into hiding in rooms at the back of the offices of Frank's

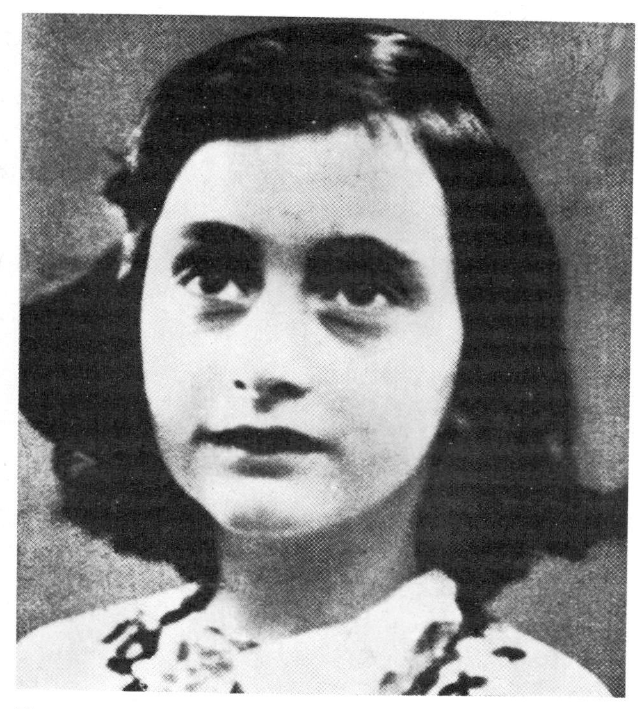

Figure 1. Anne Frank. Courtesy Yad Vashem Archives, Jerusalem.

business premises on the Prinsengracht. From July 9, 1942, until August 4, 1944, the Frank family remained in their hiding place, together with four other Jews, kept alive by friendly gentiles. An act of betrayal resulted in their discovery by the German police; they were transferred first to *Westerbork, and then (September 2, 1944) to *Auschwitz-Birkenau. In December 1944 Anne arrived in *Bergen-Belsen with her sister Margot; there she fell ill and died in March 1945. Anne had hoped to become an author, and during her period of hiding she wrote several short stories and the beginning of a novel. Her name became famous, however, as a result of the diary, found by the gentile friends immediately after the family's arrest. The life of the

Figure 2. The house (left) in Amsterdam, in which the Frank family was hidden, now a museum, the Anne Frank House.

eight people in hiding during the entire period is described with sharp observation, introspection, and clear formulation. It shows Anne's creative talent. Its great importance lies in the oppressing description of the all-pervading fear and the desolate life of the incarcerated Jews. Attempts to have the diary published after the war were initially frustrated by the unwillingness of numerous publishers. The first edition appeared in 1947, and was followed by many others. The book was widely translated and acclaimed, its author, Anne Frank, becoming the symbol of the persecuted Jewish child. After World War II an organization in the name of Anne Frank was set up and maintained in the house where the family had hidden during the war. The Anne Frank House serves as a museum and meeting place for youth to further the aims of peace.

Bibliography: *Works of Anne Frank* (1959), introduction by A. Birstein and A. Kazin, *Diary of Anne Frank*, dramatized by F. Goodrich and A. Hackett (1956); E. Schnabel, *Footsteps of Anne Frank* (1961); R. M. W. Kempner, *Edith Stein und Anne Frank* (1968).

[J.M.]

FRANK, BRUNO (1887–1945), German novelist and playwright. Born in Stuttgart, Frank studied philosophy and law at several German universities and then became a free-lance writer in Munich. After living for several years in Switzerland, he emigrated to the United States when the Nazis came to power. Frank began by writing lyric poetry, but his first published success was the novel *Die Fuerstin* (1915), a faithful portrait of contemporary society. He was at his best in recreating real or historical figures, as in *Tage des Koenigs* (1925), *Trenck* (1926), and *Politische Novelle* (1928), and in the plays *Die Schwestern und der Fremde* (1918) and *Zwoelftausend* (1927). In his last novel, *Die Tochter* (1943), one of the leading characters was a thinly veiled portrait of his mother-in-law, Fritzi Massary, the light-opera soubrette. It was in his novels rather than his plays that Frank's artistry and vivid imagination showed to their best advantage, but between the two world wars he was one of the most successful German dramatists.

Bibliography: F. Lennartz, *Deutsche Dichter und Schriftsteller unserer Zeit* (1959[8]), 208–10.

[R.K.]

FRANK, ELI (1874–1959), U.S. jurist. Frank was born in Baltimore. He taught law at the University of Maryland from 1900 on. In 1922, after serving on several state commissions, he was appointed judge on the Baltimore Supreme Bench. He held both positions until his retirement from public life in 1944. An authority on real estate law and the author of several books on the subject, Frank was highly active in Baltimore civic life and also in local Jewish activities. He served as president of the Hebrew Hospital and the Baltimore Federated Jewish Charities, was chairman of the American Jewish Relief Fund, and was a member of the executive committee of the American Jewish Committee. In 1929 he was appointed as one of the 44 non-Zionist American delegates to the Council of the Jewish Agency for Palestine.

[Ed.]

°**FRANK, HANS MICHAEL** (1900–1946), Nazi politician and lawyer responsible for the mass murder of Polish Jewry. A member of the Nazi Party from its inception, Frank participated in the Munich putsch of 1923. During the last years of the Weimar republic, Frank was the Nazis' leading lawyer, defending hundreds of party members accused of political crimes. With Hitler's accession to power, Frank was appointed head of the association of lawyers who were members of the Nazi party, and charged with the unification of the judiciary system of the Third Reich. After the Nazi conquest of Poland in the autumn of

1939, Frank was nominated governor general of the occupied Polish territories under the General Government. He was primarily responsible for the persecution of the population of Poland, the plundering of the country, and the extermination of its Jews. Frank exhorted the Nazi leadership first of all to exterminate the Jews living in Poland. He was thus responsible for greatly hastening the program of the death camps in the East. Frank succeeded in depriving the Jews of the benefits and protection of the laws, beginning with his promulgation of a law on Oct. 27, 1939 ordering forced labor by the Jewish population and culminating in a law on Oct. 15, 1941 by which Jews were forbidden to leave their special districts under penalty of death. He confiscated their goods, forced them to wear a special insignia (the yellow badge), and concentrated them into ghettos, where they starved. These acts were followed by deportations to the death camps.

During his rule over Poland, until January 1945, Frank kept a diary in which he noted every speech and official engagement. He never concealed his plans for the "Final Solution" for Polish Jewry. Condemned to death by the International Military Tribunal at Nuremberg, after admitting his own guilt and that of Nazi Germany as a whole, Frank was executed on Oct. 16, 1946.

Bibliography: E. Davidson, *Trial of the Germans* (1966), 427–45; IMT, *Trial of the Major War Criminals*, 24 (1949), index; G. M. Gilbert, *Nuremberg Diary* (1947), 276–90; S. Piotrowski (ed.), *Hans Frank's Diary* (1961). [Y.RE.]

FRANK, JACOB, AND THE FRANKISTS. Jacob Frank (1726–1791) was the founder of a Jewish sect named after him which comprised the last stage in the development of the Shabbatean movement. He was born Jacob b. Judah Leib in Korolowka (Korolevo), a small town in Podolia. His family was middle class, and his father was a contractor and merchant, apparently well respected. His grandfather lived for a time in Kalisz, and his mother came from Rzesow. Although Frank's claim before the Inquisition that his father used to serve as a rabbi appears to have no foundation there is reason to believe that he did conduct services in Czernowitz, where he moved in the early 1730s. His father is depicted as a scrupulously observant Jew. At the same time, it is very likely that he already had certain connections with the Shabbatean sect, which had taken root in many communities in Podolia, Bukovina, and Walachia.

Jacob Frank, pseudo-messiah and founder of the Frankist sect.

Frank was educated in Czernowitz and Sniatyn, and lived for several years in Bucharest. Although he went to *ḥeder*, he gained no knowledge of Talmud, and in later years boasted of this ignorance and of the qualities he possessed as a *prostak* ("simple man"). His self-characterization as an ignoramus *(am ha-areẓ)* must be seen in the context of the contemporary usage of the word to mean a man who knows Bible and the *aggadah*, but who is not skilled in *Gemara*. In his memoirs he makes much of the pranks and bold adventures of his childhood and adolescence. In Bucharest he began to earn his living as a dealer in cloth, precious stones, and whatever came to hand. Between 1745 and 1755 his trade took him through the Balkans and as far as Smyrna.

Early Associations with the Shabbateans. Frank's accounts of his earliest associations with the Sabbateans are full of contradictions, but there is no doubt that these contacts go back to his youth. Apparently his teacher in Czernowitz belonged to the sect and had promised that Frank would be initiated into their faith after marriage, as was often customary among Shabbateans. He began to study the Zohar, making a name in Shabbatean circles as a man possessed of special powers and inspiration. When in 1752 he married Hannah, the daughter of a respected Ashkenazi merchant in Nikopol (Bulgaria), two Shabbatean emissaries from Podolia were at the wedding. Shabbatean scholars like these, some of whom Frank mentions in his stories, accompanied him on his travels, and initiated him into the mysteries of "the faith." There is no doubt that these men were representatives of the extremist wing formed by the disciples of Barukhyah Russo (d. 1720), one of the leaders of the *Doenmeh in Salonika. It was in the company of these teachers, themselves Ashkenazim, that Frank visited Salonika for the first time in 1753, and became involved with the Barukhyah group of the Doenmeh, but he followed the practice of the Polish disciples and did not convert to Islam. After his marriage it seems that trading became secondary to his role as a Shabbatean "prophet," and as part of his mission he journeyed to the grave of *Nathan of Gaza, Adrianople, and Smyrna, and again spent a good deal of time in Salonika in 1755. Through their letters, his Shabbatean teachers and companions from Poland spread the news of the emergence of a new leader in Podolia, and finally persuaded him to return to his early home. Frank, who was a man of unbridled ambition, domineering to the point of despotism, had a low opinion of the contemporary Barukhyah sect in Salonika, calling it "an empty house"; whereas, as the leader of the Shabbateans in Poland, he envisaged a great future for himself. Although in the circle of his close friends he was given the Sephardi appellation *Ḥakham Ya'akov*, at the same time he was considered to be a new transmigration or a reincarnation of the divine soul which had previously resided in *Shabbetai Ẓevi and Barukhyah, to whom Frank used to refer as the "First" and the "Second." At the end of the 18th century, the story that Frank had gone to Poland on an explicit mission from the Barukhyah sect was still circulating in Doenmeh sects in Salonika. In the first years of his activity he did in fact follow the basic principles of this sect, both its teaching and its customs.

Frank in Podolia. On Dec. 3, 1755, Frank, accompanied by R. Mordecai and R. Naḥman, crossed the Dniester River and spent some time with his relatives in Korolewka. After this he passed in solemn state through the communities in Podolia which contained Shabbatean cells. He was enthusiastically received by "the believers," and in the general Jewish community the news spread of the appearance of a suspected *frenk*, which was the usual Yiddish term for a Sephardi. Frank, who had spent at least 25 years in Turkey and was thought to be a Turkish subject, actually conducted himself like a Sephardi and spoke Ladino when he appeared in public. Subsequently he assumed the appellation "Frank" as his family name. His appearance in Lanskroun (Landskron) at the end of January 1756 led to a great scandal, when he was discovered conducting a

Shabbatean ritual with his followers in a locked house. The opponents of the Shabbateans claimed that they surprised the sectarians in the midst of a heretical religious orgy, similar to rites which were actually practiced by members of the Barukhyah sect, especially in Podolia. Later Frank claimed that he had deliberately opened the windows of the house in order to compel the "believers" to show themselves publicly instead of concealing their actions as they had done for decades. Frank's followers were imprisoned but he himself went scot-free because the local authorities believed him to be a Turkish citizen. At the request of the rabbis an enquiry was instituted at the *bet din* in Satanow, the seat of the Podolia district rabbinate, which examined the practices and principles of the Shabbateans. Frank crossed the Turkish frontier; returning once more to his followers, he was arrested in March 1756 in Kopyczynce (Kopichintsy) but was again allowed to go free. After this he remained for at least three years in Turkey, first in Khotin on the Dniester, and afterward mainly in Giorgievo on the Danube. There, early in 1757, he became officially a convert to Islam, and was greatly honored for this by the Turkish authorities. In June and August 1757 he made secret visits to Rogatyn, in Podolia, in order to confer with his followers. During this period, he went to Salonika a number of times, and also paid one visit to Constantinople.

When Frank appeared in Poland he became the central figure for the vast majority of the Shabbateans, particularly those in Galicia, the Ukraine, and Hungary. It would appear that most of the Moravian Shabbateans also acknowledged his leadership. An inquiry of the *bet din* in Satanow had to a large extent uncovered the Shabbatean network of Barukhyah's followers, which had existed underground in Podolia. A considerable portion of the Satanow findings was published by Jacob *Emden. From this it is clear that the suspicions concerning the antinomian character of the sect were justified, and that "the believers," who conformed outwardly to Jewish legal precepts, did in fact transgress them, including the sexual prohibitions of the Torah, with the stated intention of upholding the higher form of the Torah, which they called *Torah de-aẓilut* ("the Torah of emanation"), meaning the spiritual Torah in contradistinction to the actual Torah of the *halakhah*, which was called the *Torah de-beri'ah* ("the Torah of creation"). The results of the inquiry were laid before a rabbinical assembly at Brody in June 1756, and confirmed at a session of the Council of the Four Lands held in Konstantynow in September. In Brody a *ḥerem* ("excommunication") was proclaimed against the members of the sect, which laid them open to persecution and also sought to restrict study of the Zohar and Kabbalah before a certain age (40 years in the case of Isaac *Luria's writings).

When printed and dispatched throughout the communities, the *ḥerem* provoked a wave of persecution against the members of the sect, particularly in Podolia. The Polish rabbis turned to Jacob Emden, well-known as a fierce antagonist of the Shabbateans, who advised them to seek help from the Catholic ecclesiastical authorities based on the argument that the Shabbatean faith, being a mixture of the principles of all the other religions, constituted a new religion, and as such was forbidden by canon law. However, the results of his advice were the opposite of what had been intended, as Frank's followers, who had been severely harassed, adopted the strategy of putting themselves under the protection of Bishop Dembowski of Kamieniec-Podolski, in whose diocese many of the Shabbatean communities were concentrated. If before they had acted in a two-faced manner with regard to Judaism, appearing to be outwardly Orthodox while being secretly heretical, they now decided, apparently on Frank's advice, to emphasize and even to exaggerate what beliefs they held in common with the basic principles of Christianity, in order to curry favor with the Catholic priesthood, although in fact their secret Shabbatean faith had not changed at all. Proclaiming themselves "contra-talmudists," they sought the protection of the Church from their persecutors, who, they claimed, had been angered precisely because of the sympathy shown by "the believers" toward some of the important tenets of Christianity. This extremely sucessful maneuver enabled them to find refuge with the ecclesiastical authorities, who saw in them potential candidates for mass conversion from Judaism to Christianity. In the meantime, however, members of the sect were constantly being impelled against their will by their protectors to assist in the preparation of anti-Jewish propaganda, and to formulate declarations which were intended to wreak destruction upon Polish Jewry. These developments strengthened mutual hostility and had dire consequences. Throughout these events Frank took great care not to draw attention to himself, except to appear as a spiritual guide showing his followers the way, as it were, to draw nearer to Christianity. It should be noted that the name "Frankists" was not used at this time, becoming current only in the 19th century. As far as the mass of Jews and rabbis were concerned there was no difference at all between the earlier Shabbateans and the Shabbateans in this new guise, and they continued to call them "the sect of Shabbetai Ẓevi." Even Frank's followers, when talking to one another, continued to refer to themselves by the usual term *ma'aminim* ("believers").

Disputations. In the events that followed, it is difficult to differentiate precisely between the steps taken by Frank's adherents and those that were initiated by the Church and resulted from ecclesiastical coercion, although there is no doubt that M. Balaban (see bibliography) is right in laying greater stress on the latter. Shortly after the *ḥerem* at Brody the Frankists asked Bishop Dembowski to hold a new enquiry into the Lanskroun affair, and they petitioned for a public disputation between themselves and the rabbis. On Aug. 2, 1756 they presented nine principles of their faith for debate. Formulated in a most ambiguous fashion, their declaration of faith asserted in brief: (1) belief in the Torah of Moses; (2) that the Torah and the Prophets were obscure books, which had to be interpreted with the aid of God's light from above, and not simply by the light of human intelligence; (3) that the interpretation of the Torah to be found in the Talmud contained nonsense and falsehood, hostile to the Torah of the Lord; (4) belief that God is one and that all the worlds were created by Him; (5) belief in the trinity of the three equal "faces" within the one God, without there being any division within Him; (6) that God manifested Himself in corporeal form, like other human beings, but without sin; (7) that Jerusalem would not be rebuilt until the end of time; (8) that Jews waited in vain for the Messiah to come and raise them above the whole world; and (9) that, instead, God would Himself be clothed in human form and atone for all the sins for which the world had been cursed, and that at His coming the world would be pardoned and cleansed of all iniquity. These principles reflect the belief of the antinomian followers of Barukhyah, but they were formulated in such a way that they seemed to refer to Jesus of Nazareth instead of to Shabbetai Ẓevi and Barukhyah. They constitute a blatant plan to deceive the Church which the priests did not understand, and which, quite naturally, they were not interested in understanding.

The rabbis managed to avoid accepting the invitation to the disputation for nearly a year. However, after great pressure from the bishop, the disputation finally took place at Kamieniec, from June 20 to 28, 1757. Nineteen opponents of the Talmud (then called Zoharites) took part, together with a handful of rabbis from communities in the area. The spokesmen for the Shabbateans were also learned men, some of them being officiating rabbis who had secret Shabbatean tendencies. The arguments in the accusations and the defense of the rabbis were presented in writing, and were later published in a Latin protocol in Lvov in 1758. On Oct. 17, 1757, Bishop Dembowski issued his decision in favor of the Frankists, imposing a number of penalties upon the rabbis, chief of which was a condemnation of the Talmud as worthless and corrupt, with an order that it be burned in the city square. All Jewish homes were to be searched for copies of the Talmud. According to some contemporary accounts many cartloads of editions of the Talmud were in fact burned in Kamieniec, Lvov, Brody, Zolkiew, and other places. The "burning of the Torah" had a crushing effect on the Jewish community and the rabbis declared a fast in memory of the event. Jews who had influence with the authorities tried to stop the burnings, which took place mainly in November 1757.

A sudden reversal of fortune, in favor of the "talmudists" and to the detriment of the sectarians, resulted from the sudden death of Bishop Dembowski on November 9, at the very time of the burnings. News of the event, in which Jews saw the finger of God, spread like wildfire. Persecutions of the sect were renewed with even greater vehemence, and many of them fled across the Dniester to Turkey. There several converted to Islam, and one group even joined the Doenmeh in Salonika, where they were known as "the Poles." Meanwhile the spokesmen for the "contra-talmudists" turned to the political and ecclesiastical authorities and sought the implementation of the privilege which had been promised them by Dembowski, who allowed them to follow their own faith. They also sought the return of their looted property and permission for the refugees to come back to their homes. After some internal disagreements among the Polish authorities, King Augustus III issued a privilege on June 16, 1758, which accorded the sectarians royal protection as men "who were near to the [Christian] acknowledgment of God." Most of the refugees returned to Podolia at the end of September, and gathered mainly in and around the small town of Iwanie (near Khotin). In December, or the beginning of January 1759, Frank himself also left Turkey and arrived in Iwanie. Many of "the believers" scattered throughout eastern Galicia were summoned there.

Iwanie. In fact, the Frankists constituted themselves as a special sect with a distinctive character only during those months when "the believers" lived in Iwanie, an episode which became engraved on their memory as a quasi-revelatory event. Here it was that Frank finally revealed himself as the living embodiment of God's power who had come to complete the mission of Shabbetai Ẓevi and Barukhyah, and as "the true Jacob," comparing himself to the patriarch Jacob who had completed the work of his predecessors Abraham and Isaac. It was here that he unfolded his teaching before his followers in short statements and parables, and introduced a specific order into the ritual of the sect. There is no doubt that it was here that he prepared them to face the necessity of adopting Christianity outwardly, in order to keep their true faith in secret, just as the Doenmeh had done with regard to Islam. He declared that all religions were only stages through which "the believers" had to pass—like a man putting on different suits of clothes—and then to discard as of no worth compared with the true hidden faith. Frank's originality at this time consisted in his brazen rejection of the Shabbatean theology which was well-known to "the believers" from the writings of Nathan of Gaza and from the writings which were based on the extreme Shabbatean Kabbalah in Barukhyah's version. He asked them to forget all this, proposing in its place a kind of mythology freed from all traces of kabbalistic terminology, although in fact it was no more than a popular and homiletical reworking of kabbalistic teaching. In place of the customary Shabbatean trinity of the "three knots of faith," i.e., *Attika Kaddisha, Malka Kaddisha,* and the *Shekhinah,* which are all united in the Divinity (see *Shabbetai Ẓevi), Frank went so far as to say that the true and good God was hidden and divested of any link with creation, and particularly with this insignificant world. It is He who conceals Himself behind "the King of Kings," whom Frank also calls "the Great Brother" or "He who stands before God." He is the God of true faith whom one must strive to approach and, in doing so, break the domination of the three "leaders of the world," who rule the earth at this moment, imposing upon it an unfitting system of law. The position of "the Great Brother" is connected in some way with the *Shekhinah,* which becomes in Frank's terminology the "maiden" *(almah)* or "virgin" *(betulah).* It is obvious that he tried consciously to make this concept conform as closely as possible to the Christian concept of the virgin. Just as the extreme Shabbateans from the sect of Barukhyah saw in Shabbetai Ẓevi and Barukhyah an incarnation of *Malka Kaddisha,* who is the "God of Israel," so Frank referred to himself as the messenger of "the Great Brother." According to him, all the great religious leaders, from the patriarchs to Shabbetai Ẓevi and Barukhyah, had endeavored to find the way to his God, but had not succeeded.

In order that God and the virgin be revealed, it would be necessary to embark upon a completely new road, untrodden as yet by the people of Israel: this road Frank called "the way to Esau." In this context, Esau or Edom symbolizes the unbridled flow of life which liberates man because its force and power are not subject to any law. The patriarch Jacob promised (Gen. 33:14) to visit his brother Esau in Seir, but Scripture does not mention that he fulfilled his promise, because the way was too difficult for him. Now the time had come to set out on this way, which leads to the "true life," a central idea which in Frank's system carries with it the specific connotation of freedom and licentiousness. This path was the road to consistent religious anarchy: "The place to which we are going is not subject to any law, because all that is on the side of death; but we are going to life." In order to achieve this goal it was necessary to abolish and destroy the laws, teachings, and practices which constrict the power of life, but this must be done in secret; in order to accomplish it, it was essential outwardly to assume the garb of the corporeal Edom, i.e., Christianity. The "believers," or at least their vanguard, had already passed through Judaism and Islam, and they now had to complete their journey by assuming the Christian faith, using it and its ideas in order to conceal the real core of their belief in Frank as the true Messiah and the living God for whom their Christian protestations were really intended.

The motto which Frank adopted here was *massa dumah* (from Isa. 21:11), taken to mean "the burden of silence"; that is, it was necessary to bear the heavy burden of the hidden faith in the abolition of all law in utter silence, and it was forbidden to reveal anything to those outside the fold. Jesus of Nazareth was no more than the husk preceding and concealing the fruit, who was Frank himself. Although it was necessary to ensure an outward demonstration of Christian allegiance, it was forbidden to mix with Christians or to intermarry with them, for in the final analysis Frank's vision was of a Jewish future, albeit in a rebellious and revolutionary form, presented here as a messianic dream.

The concepts employed by Frank were popular and anecdotal, and the rejection of the traditional kabbalistic symbolic terminology, which was beyond the comprehension of simple people, called into play the imaginative faculty. Frank therefore prepared his followers in Iwanie to accept baptism as the final step which would open before them, in a real physical sense, the way to Esau, to the world of the gentiles. Even in the organization of this sect Frank imitated the evangelical tradition: he appointed in Iwanie twelve emissaries (apostles) or "brothers," who were considered his chief disciples. But at the same time he appointed twelve "sisters," whose main distinction was to serve as Frank's concubines. Continuing the tradition of Barukhyah's sect, Frank also instituted licentious sexual practices among the "believers," at least among his more intimate "brothers" and "sisters." His followers who had been used to acting in this way did not see anything blameworthy in it, but they did not take kindly to this request that they eradicate from their midst all kabbalistic books, which had been superseded by Frank's teaching, and many of them continued to use ideas from Shabbatean Kabbalah, mixing them up in their writings with Frank's new symbols.

The group remained in Iwanie for several months until the spring of 1759. Frank established there a common fund, apparently in emulation of the New Testament account of the early Christian community. During this time, when they came into close contact with Frank, people were overcome and dominated by his powerful personality, which was compounded of limitless ambition and cunning, together with a facility of expression and marked imaginative faculty which even had a tinge of poetry. Perhaps it can be said of Frank that he was a mixture of despotic ruler, popular prophet, and cunning impostor.

The Disputation in Lvov. As events unfolded, an intermingling of two tendencies became manifest. On the one hand, it became clear to Frank and his disciples that they could not remain halfway between Judaism and Christianity. If they wished to restore their position after the severe persecutions they had suffered, baptism was the only course left open to them. They were even prepared to make a public demonstration of their conversion to Christianity, as the priests required as the price for their protection. On the other hand, there were quite different interests among important sections of the Church in Poland who from the very beginning did not associate themselves with the Frankist cause.

At this time there were several instances of the *blood libel in Poland, which were supported by some influential bishops and leading clergy. The Council of the Four Lands, Polish Jewry's supreme organized authority, was trying to act indirectly through different mediators with the ecclesiastical authorities in Rome, laying grave charges of deceit and insolence against those responsible for the promulgation of the blood libel. Their words did not go unheeded in Rome. It would appear that some priests in the bishoprics of Kamieniec and Lvov saw a good chance of strengthening their position with regard to the question of the blood libel, if Jews who represented a whole group could be found to come forward and verify this unfounded accusation. At the end of February 1759, when their position at Iwanie was at its peak, Frank's disciples requested Archbishop Lubieński in Lvov to receive them into the Church, claiming to speak in the name of "the Jews of Poland, Hungary, Turkey, Moldavia, Italy, etc." They asked to be given a second opportunity to dispute publicly with the rabbinic Jews, devotees of the Talmud, and promised to demonstrate the truth not only of the tenets of Christianity but also of the blood libel. Without doubt, the text of this request was composed after consultation with priestly circles and was formulated by the Polish nobleman Moliwda (Ignacy Kossakowski, who had once been head of the Philippovan sect), who was Frank's adviser in all these negotiations, right up to the actual baptism. Lubieński himself was not able to deal with the affair, since he was appointed archbishop of Gniezno and primate of the Polish Church. He handed over the conduct of the case to his administrator in Lvov, Mikulski, a priest who became extremely active in the preparation of the great disputation in Lvov, which was planned to end in mass baptism and verification of the blood libel.

In the months that followed, the Frankists continued to send various petitions to the king of Poland and to the ecclesiastical authorities in order to clarify their intentions, and to ask for specific favors even after their conversion. They claimed that 5,000 of their adherents were prepared to accept baptism, but at the same time requested that they be allowed to lead a separate existence as Christians of Jewish identity: they should not be compelled to shave their "sideburns" *(pe'ot);* they should be allowed to wear traditional Jewish garb even after conversion, and to call themselves by Jewish names in addition to their new Christian names; they should not be forced to eat pork; they should be allowed to rest on Saturday as well as on Sunday; and they should be permitted to retain the books of the Zohar and other kabbalistic writings. In addition to all this, they should be allowed to marry only among themselves and not with anyone else. In return for being allowed to constitute this quasi-Jewish unit, they expressed their willingness to submit to the other demands of the Church. In other petitions they added the request that they should be assigned a special area of settlement in Eastern Galicia, including the cities of Busk and Glinyany, most of whose Jewish inhabitants were members of the sect. In this territory they promised to maintain the life of their own community, and to establish their own communal life, setting up a "productivization" in contrast to the economic structure of the usual Jewish community. Some of these petitions, printed by the priests in Lvov in 1795, circulated very widely and were translated from Polish into French, Spanish, Latin, and Portuguese; they were also reprinted in Spain and Mexico and went through several editions there. The very presentation of these requests proves that Frank's followers had no thought of assimilating or of mixing with true Christians, but sought to gain for themselves a special recognized position, like that of the Doenmeh in Salonika, under the protection of both Church and State. It is obvious that they looked upon themselves as a new type of Jew and had no intention of renouncing their national Jewish identity. These petitions also show that the more extreme pronouncements of Frank within the closed circle of his followers had not wholly taken root in their hearts and they were not prepared to follow him in every detail. The prohibition against intermarriage with gentiles reiterates Frank's own words in Iwanie, yet on other matters there was apparently lively dispute between Frank and his followers. However, these isolated requests constituted only a transitional stage in the struggle which preceded the disputation in Lvov; and the spokesmen of the sect received a negative reply. The requirement of the Church was baptism without any precondition, although at this time the priests were convinced that the Frankists' intention was sincere, since they paid no heed to Jewish representatives who warned them continually about the secret Shabbatean beliefs of those who were offering themselves for baptism. The enormous publicity given to these events after the disputation at Kamieniec stimulated missionary activity on the part of some Protestant groups. Count Zinzendorf, head of "the Fellowship of the Brethren" (later the Moravian Church) in Germany, sent the convert David Kirchhof in 1758 on a special mission to "the believers" in Podolia in order to preach to them his version of "pure Christianity" (*Judaica,* 19 (1963), 240). Among the mass of Jews, the idea spread that Frank was in reality a great sorcerer with far-reaching demonic powers, prompting the growth of various legends, which had wide repercussions, concerning his magic deeds and his success.

The Frankists tried to postpone the disputation until January 1760, when many of the nobility and merchants would gather for religious ceremonies and for the great fair at Lvov. Apparently they hoped for considerable financial help because of their economic situation had suffered as a result of persecution. The authorities in Rome and Warsaw did not regard the proposed disputation favorably and, for reasons of their own, sided with the Jewish arguments against a disputation, especially one which was likely to provoke disturbances and unrest as a result of the section on the blood libel. The raising of this subject, with all the inherent risk of organized and unbridled incitement against rabbinic Judaism, was equally sure to plunge the Polish Jewish authorities into profound anxiety. In this conflict of interests between the higher authorities, who wanted the straightforward conversion of Frank's followers without any disputation, and those groups who were concerned mainly with the success of the blood libel, Mikulski acted according to his own views and sided with the latter. He therefore fixed an early date for the disputation, July 16, 1759, to be held in Lvov Cathedral, and he obliged the rabbis of his diocese to attend.

The disputation opened on July 17, attended by crowds of Poles, and was conducted intermittently at several sessions until September 10. The arguments of both sides, the theses of the "contra-talmudists" and the answers of the rabbis, were presented in writing, but in addition vehement oral disputes took place. About 30 men appeared for the rabbis, and 10–20 for the sectarians. However, the number of the actual participants was smaller. The chief spokesman, and the man who bore the main responsibility on the Jewish side, was R. Ḥayyim Kohen Rapoport, the leading rabbi of Lvov, a highly respected man of great spiritual stature. Supporting him were the rabbis of Bohorodczany and Stanislawow. The tradition which sprang up in popular accounts circulating years later that *Israel b. Eliezer Ba'al Shem Tov, the founder of Ḥasidism, was also a participant, has no historical foundation. Frank himself took part only in the last session of the disputation when the blood libel question was debated. The sect's spokesmen were three scholars who had previously been active in Podolia among the followers of Barukhyah: Leib b. Nathan Krisa from Nodwarna, R. Naḥman from Krzywicze, and Solomon b. Elisha Shor from Rohatyn. After each session, consultations took place between the rabbis and the *parnasim,* who drafted written replies. They were joined by a wine merchant from Lvov, Baer *Birkenthal of Bolechov, who, unlike the rabbis, spoke fluent Polish, and he prepared the Polish text of their replies. His memoirs of the disputation in *Sefer Divrei Binah* fill in the background of the official protocol which was drawn up in Polish by the priest Gaudenty Pikulsi, and printed in Lvov in 1760 with the title *Złość Żydowska* ("The Jewish Evil"). In Lvov the Frankists' arguments were presented in a form accommodated as far as possible to the tenets of Christianity, to an even greater extent than at the earlier disputation. However, even then, they avoided any explicit reference to Jesus of Nazareth, and there is no doubt that this silence served the express purpose of harmonizing their secret faith in Frank as God and Messiah in a corporeal form with their official support of Christianity. Indeed, according to Frank himself, Christianity was no more than a screen *(pargod)* behind which lay hidden the true faith, which he proclaimed to be "the sacred religion of Edom."

Seven main propositions were disputed: (1) all the biblical prophecies concerning the coming of the Messiah have already been fulfilled; (2) the Messiah is the true God who became incarnate in human form in order to suffer for the sake of our redemption; (3) since the advent of the true Messiah, the sacrifices and the ceremonial laws of the Torah have been abolished; (4) everyone must follow the religion of the Messiah and his teaching, for within it lies the salvation of the soul; (5) the cross is the sign of the divine trinity and the seal of the Messiah; (6) only through baptism can a man arrive at true faith in the Messiah; and (7) the Talmud teaches that the Jews need Christian blood, and whoever believes in the Talmud is bound to use it.

The rabbis refused to reply to some of these theses for fear of being offensive to the Christian faith in their answers. The disputation began at the behest of the Frankists with a statement by their protector Moliwda Kossadowski. The rabbis replied only to the first and second of the theological arguments. It was obvious from the outset that the main attention would be centered on the seventh proposition, whose effects were potentially highly dangerous for the whole of Jewry. This particular argument came up for discussion on August 27. In the preceding weeks Frank had left Iwanie and passed through the cities of Galicia, visiting his followers. He then waited a long time in Busk, near Lvov, where he was joined by his wife and children. The Frankist arguments in support of the blood libel are a mixture of quotations from books by earlier Polish apostates, and absurd arguments and nonsensical discussions based on statements in rabbinic literature containing only the slightest mention of "blood" or "red." According to Baer Birkenthal the rabbis too did not refrain from using literary stratagems in order to strengthen the impression that their replies would have on the Catholic priests, and in the oral debates they all rejected all Polish translations from talmudic and rabbinic literature without exception, which resulted in some violent verbal exchanges. Behind the scenes of the disputation, contacts continued between the rabbinic representatives and Mikulski, who began to waver, both because of the opposition of the higher church authorities to the blood libel and also as a result of rabbinic arguments concerning Frankist duplicity. The debate on this point was continued in the last session on September 10, when Rabbi Rapoport made a stringent attack on the blood libel. As the disputation came to an end, one of the Frankists approached the rabbi and said: "You have declared our blood permitted—this is your 'blood for blood.'" The confused ratiocinations of the Frankists did not achieve the desired effect, and, in the end, Mikulski resolved to ask the rabbis for a detailed written answer in Polish to the Frankists' charges. However, the time for their reply was postponed until after the end of the disputation. In the meantime nothing concrete emerged from all the upheaval about the blood libel.

On the other hand, the conversion of many of the Frankists did actually take place. Frank himself was received with extraordinary honor in Lvov, and he dispatched his flock to the baptismal font. He himself was the first to be baptized on Sept. 17, 1759. There is some disagreement about the number of sectarians who were converted. In Lvov alone more than 500 Frankists (including women and children) had been baptized by the end of 1760, nearly all of them from Podolia but some from Hungary and the European provinces of Turkey. The exact numbers of converts in other places are not known, but there are details of a considerable number of baptisms in Warsaw, where Frank and his wife were baptized a second time, under the patronage of the king of Poland, in a royal ceremony, on Nov. 18, 1759; from then on he is named Josef Frank in documents. According to oral tradition in Frankist families in Poland, the number of converts was far greater than that attested by known documents, and it speaks of several thousands. On the other hand, it is known that most of the sectarians in Podolia, and in other countries, did not follow Frank all the way, but remained in the Jewish fold, although they still recognized his leadership. It would appear that all his followers in Bohemia and Moravia, and most of those in Hungary and Rumania, remained Jews and continued to lead a double life, outwardly Jews and secretly "believers." Even in Galicia there remained many cells of "believers" in an appreciable number of communities, from Podhajce (Podgaytsy) in the east to Cracow in the west.

The Social Structure of the Sect. Contradictory evidence exists concerning the social and spiritual makeup of the sectarians, both of the apostates and of those who remained within the Jewish fold, but perhaps the two types of evidence are really complementary. Many sources, particularly from the Jewish side, show that a sizeable proportion of them were knowledgeable and literate, and even rabbis of small communities. Frank's closest associates among the apostates were doubtless in this category. As far as their social status was concerned, some were wealthy and owners of property, merchants and, craftsmen such as silver- and goldsmiths; some were the children of community leaders. On the other hand, a considerable number of them were distillers and innkeepers, simple people and members of the poorer classes. In Moravia and Bohemia they included a number of wealthy and aristocratic families, important merchants and state monopoly leaseholders, while in the responsa of contemporary rabbis (and also in the ḥasidic *Shivḥei ha-Besht*) incidents are related concerning scribes and *shoḥatim* who were also members of the sect. In Sziget, Hungary, a "judge of the Jews" *(Judenrichter)* is numbered among them, as well as several important members of the community.

The uncovering of the sect, which had hitherto practiced in secret, and the mass apostasy which had taken place in several of the Polish communities, received wide publicity and had various repercussions. The attitude of the Jewish spiritual leaders was not uniform, many rabbis taking the view that their separation from the Jewish community and their defection to Christianity were in fact desirable for the good of the Jewish people as a whole (A. Yaari in *Sinai*, 35 (1954), 170–82). They hoped that all the members of the sect would leave the Jewish fold, but their hopes were not realized. A different view was expressed by Israel Ba'al Shem Tov after the disputation at Lvov, namely, that "the *Shekhinah* bewails the sect of the apostates, for while the limb is joined to the body there is hope of a cure, but once the limb is amputated, there can be no possible remedy, for every Jew is a limb of the *Shekhinah.*" Naḥman of Bratslav, a great-grandson of the Ba'al Shem Tov, said that his great-grandfather died of the grief inflicted by the sect and their apostasy. In many Polish communities traditions were preserved concerning Frankist families who had not apostasized, while those who were particular about family honor took care not to marry into these families because of the suspicion of illegitimacy (see **mamzer*) which attached to them through their transgression of the sexual prohibitions.

Frank's Arrest. Frank's journey to Warsaw in great pomp in October 1759 provoked a number of scandalous incidents, particularly in Lublin. Even after their apostasy Frank's followers were continually watched by the priests who had doubts about their reliability and the sincerity of their conversion. Records vary of the evidence given to the ecclesiastical authorities of their real faith, and it is possible that these did in fact emanate from different sources. It was G. Pikulski in particular who in December 1759 obtained separate confessions from six of the "brethren" who had remained in Lvov, and it became apparent from these that the real object of their devotion was Frank, as the living incarnation of God. When this information reached Warsaw, Frank was arrested, on Feb. 6, 1760, and for three weeks he was subjected to a detailed investigation by the ecclesiastical court, which also confronted with many of the "believers" who had accompanied him to Warsaw. Frank's testimony before the inquiry was a mixture of lies and half-truths. The court's decision was to exile him for an unlimited period to the fortress of Czestochowa which was under the highest jurisdiction of the Church, "in order to prevent him having any possible influence on the views of his followers." These latter were set free and ordered to adopt Christianity in true faith, and to forsake their leader—a result which was not achieved. Nevertheless, the "treachery" of his followers in revealing their true beliefs rankled bitterly with Frank until the end of his days. The court also issued a printed proclamation on the results of the inquiry. At the end of February Frank was exiled and remained in "honorable"captivity for 13 years. At first he was utterly deserted, but he quickly found ways of reestablishing contact between himself and his "camp." At this time the apostates were scattered in several small towns and on estates owned by the nobility. They suffered a good deal until they finally settled down, mainly in Warsaw, with the remainder in other Polish towns like Cracow and Krasnystaw, and organized themselves into a secret sectarian society, whose members were careful to observe outwardly all the tenets of the Catholic faith. They also took advantage of the unstable political situation in Poland at the end of its independence, and several of the more important families demanded noble status for themselves, with some degree of success, on the basis of old statutes which accorded such privileges to Jewish converts.

Frank in Czestochowa. From the end of 1760 emissaries from the "believers" began to visit Frank and transmit his instructions. Following these, they became once more involved in a blood libel case in the town of Wojsłwiec in 1761, as the result of which many Jews were slaughtered. Their reappearance as accusers of the Jewish people aroused great bitterness among the Jews of Poland, who saw in it a new act of vengeance. The conditions of Frank's imprisonment were gradually relaxed and from 1762 his wife was allowed to join him, while a whole group of his chief followers, both men and women, were allowed to settle near the fortress, and even to practice secret religious rites of a typical sexual orgiastic nature inside the fortress. When talking to this circle Frank added a specifically Christian interpretation to his view of the virgin as the *Shekhinah*, under the influence of the worship of the virgin which, in Poland, was actually centered on Czestochowa.

In 1765, when it was apparent that the country was about to break up, Frank planned to forge links with the Russian Orthodox Church and with the Russian government through a Russian ambassador in Poland, Prince Repnin. A Frankist delegation went to Smolensk and Moscow at the end of the year and promised to instigate some pro-Russian activity among the Jews, but the details are not known. It is possible that clandestine links between the Frankist camp and the Russian authorities date from this time. These plans became known to the Jews of Warsaw, and in 1767 a counterdelegation was sent to St. Petersburg in order to inform the Russians of the Frankists' true character. From then on, Frankist propaganda spread once more through the communities of Galicia, Hungary, Moravia, and Bohemia, by means of letters and emissaries from among the learned members of the sect. Links were also formed with secret Shabbateans in Germany. One of these emissaries, Aaron Isaac Te'omim from Horodenka, appeared in Altona in 1764. In 1768–69 there were two Frankist agents in Prague and Possnitz, the Shabbatean center in Moravia, and there they were even allowed to preach in the synagogue. At the beginning of 1770 Frank's wife died, and thenceforth the worship of "the lady" *(gevirah),* which was accorded her during her lifetime, was transferred to Frank's daughter Eva (previously Rachel), who stayed with him even when practically all of his "believers" had left the fortress and gone to Warsaw. When Czestochowa was captured by the Russians in August 1772, after the first partition of Poland, Frank was freed by the commander in chief and left the town early in 1773, going with his daughter to Warsaw. From there, in March 1773, he journeyed with 18 of his associates disguised as the servants of a wealthy merchant to Bruenn (Brno) in Moravia, to the home of his cousin Schoendel *Dobruschka, the wife of a rich and influential Jew.

Frank in Bruenn and Offenbach. Frank remained in Bruenn until 1786, obtaining the protection of the authorities, both as a respected man of means with many connections and also as a man pledged to work for the propagation of Christianity among his numerous associates in the communities of Moravia. He established a semi-military regime in his retinue, where the men wore military uniform and went through a set training. Frank's court attracted many Shabbateans in Moravia, whose families preserved for generations the swords that they wore while serving at his court. Frank went with his daughter to Vienna in March 1775 and was received in audience by the empress and her son, later Joseph II. Some maintain that Frank promised the empress the assistance of his followers in a campaign to conquer parts of Turkey, and in fact over a period of time several Frankist emissaries were sent to Turkey, working hand in glove with the Doenmeh, and perhaps as political agents or spies in the service of the Austrian government. During this period Frank spoke a great deal about a general revolution which would overthrow kingdoms, and the Catholic Church in particular, and he also dreamed of the conquest of some territory in the wars at the end of time which would be the Frankist dominion. For this, military training would be a deliberate preparation. Where Frank obtained the money for the upkeep of his court was a constant source of wonder and speculation and the matter was never resolved; doubtless some system of taxation was organized among the members of the sect. Stories circulated about the arrival of barrels of gold sent, some say, by his followers, but according to others, by his foreign political "employers." At one particular period there were in Bruenn several hundred sectarians who followed no profession or trade, and whose sole and absolute master was Frank, who ruled with a rod of iron. In 1784 his financial resources failed temporarily and he found himself in great straits, but his situation subsequently improved. During his stay in Bruenn the greater part of his teachings, his recollections, and his tales were taken down by his chief associates. In 1786 or 1787 he left Bruenn, and, after bargaining with the prince of Ysenburg, established himself in Offenbach, near Frankfort.

In Bruenn and Offenbach, Frank and his three children played a part, which was unusually successful for a long time, in order to throw dust in the eyes of both the inhabitants and the authorities. While pretending to follow the practices of the Catholic Church, at the same time they put on a show of strange practices, deliberately "Eastern" in nature, in order to emphasize their exotic character. In his last years Frank began to spread even among his close associates the notion that his daughter Eva was in reality the illegitimate daughter of the empress Catherine of the house of Romanov, and that he was no more than her guardian. Outwardly, the Frankists shrank from social contact with Jews, so much so that many of those who had business or other dealings with the latter refused absolutely to believe Jewish charges concerning the true nature of the community as a secret Jewish sect. Even in the printed proclamations issued in Offenbach, Frank's children based their authority on their strong ties with the Russian royal house. There is some reliable evidence to show that even the prince of Ysenburg's administration believed that Eva should be regarded as a Romanov princess.

The last center of the sect was set up in Offenbach, where members sent their sons and daughters to serve at the court, following the pattern that had been established in Bruenn. Frank had several apoplectic fits, dying on Dec. 10, 1791. His funeral was organized as a glorious demonstration by hundreds of his "believers." Frank had preserved to the end his double way of life and sustained the legendary Oriental atmosphere with which his life was imbued in the sight of both Jews and Christians.

In the period between Frank's apostasy and his death the converts strengthened their economic position, particularly in Warsaw where many of them built factories and were also active in masonic organizations. A group of about 50 Frankist families, led by Anton Czerniewski, one of Frank's chief disciples, settled in Bukovina after his death and were known there as the sect of Abrahamites; their descendants were still living a separate life there about 125 years later. Several families in Moravia and Bohemia, who had remained within the Jewish fold, also improved their social status, had close connections with the *Haskalah movement, and began to combine revolutionary mystical kabbalistic ideas with the rationalistic view of the Enlightenment. Some of those who had converted in these countries under Frank's influence were accepted in the higher administration and the Austrian aristocracy, but they preserved a few Frankist traditions and customs, so that a stratum was created in which the boundaries between Judaism and Christianity became blurred, irrespective of whether the members had converted or retained their links with Judaism.

Only rarely did whole groups of Frankists convert to Christianity, as in Prossnitz in 1773, but a considerable proportion of the younger members who were sent to Offenbach were baptized there. Enlightening examples of family histories from the intermediate stratum mentioned above are those of the Hoenig (see *Hoenigsberg) and Dobruschka families in Austria. Some of the Hoenig family remained Frankist Jews even after their elevation to the nobility, and some of them were connected with the upper bourgeoisie and the higher Austrian administration (the families of Von Hoenigsberg, Von Hoenigstein, Von Bienefeld), while members of the Dobruschka family converted practically en bloc and several of them served as officers in the army. Moses, the son of Schoendel Dobruschka, Frank's cousin, who was known in many circles as his nephew, was the outstanding figure in the last generation of the Frankists, being known also as Franz Thomas von Schoenfeld (a German writer and organizer of a mystical order of a Jewish Christian kabbalistic character) and later as Junius Frey (a Jacobin revolutionary in France).

Apparently he was offered the leadership of the sect after Frank's death, and, when he refused, Eva, together with her two younger brothers, Josef and Rochus, assumed responsibility for the direction of the court. Many people continued to go up to Offenbach, to *"Gottes Haus"* as the "believers" called it. However, Frank's daughter and her brothers had neither the stature nor the strength of personality required, and their fortunes quickly declined. The only independent activity that emerged from Offenbach was the dispatch of the "Red Letters" to hundreds of Jewish communities in Europe in 1799 relating to the beginning of the 19th century. In these letters the Jews were requested for the last time to enter "The holy religion of Edom." By 1803 Offenbach was almost completely deserted by the camp of the "believers," hundreds of whom had returned to Poland, while Frank's children were reduced to poverty. Josef and Rochus died in 1807 and 1813 respectively, without heirs, and Eva Frank died in 1816, leaving enormous debts. In Eva's last years a few members of the most respected families in the sect, who were supported from Warsaw, remained with her. In the last 15 years of her life she acted as if she were a royal princess of the house of Romanov, and several circles tended to believe the stories circulating in support of this.

The sect's exclusive organization continued to survive in this period through agents who went from place to place, through secret gatherings and separate religious rites, and through the dissemination of a specifically Frankist literature. The "believers" endeavored to marry only among themselves, and a wide network of inter-family relationships was created among the Frankists, even among those who had remained within the Jewish fold. Later Frankism was to a large extent the religion of families who had given their children the approprate education. The Frankists of Germany, Bohemia, and Moravia usually held secret gatherings in Carlsbad in summer round about the Ninth of Av.

Frankist Literature. The literary activity of the sect began at the end of Frank's life, and was centered at first at Offenbach in the hands of three learned "elders," who were among his chief disciples: the two brothers Franciszek and Michael Wołowski (from the well-known rabbinic family, Shor) and Andreas Dembowski (Yeruḥam Lippmann from Czernowitz). At the end of the 18th century they compiled a collection of Frank's teachings and reminiscences, containing nearly 2,300 sayings and stories, gathered together in the book *Slowa Pańskie* ("The words of the Master"; Heb. *Divrei ha-Adon*), which was sent to circles of believers. The book was apparently written originally in Hebrew since it was quoted in this language by the Frankists of Prague. In order to meet the needs of the converts in Poland, whose children no longer learned Hebrew, it was translated, apparently in Offenbach, into very poor Polish which needed later revisions to give it a more polished style. This comprehensive book illuminates Frank's true spiritual world, as well as his relationship with Judaism, Christianity, and the members of his sect. A few complete manuscripts were preserved in a number of families in Poland, and some were acquired by public libraries and consulted by the historians Kraushar and Balaban. These manuscripts were destroyed or lost during the Holocaust, and now only two imperfect manuscripts in Cracow University Library are known, comprising about two-thirds of the complete text. Also in Offenbach, a detailed chronicle was compiled of events in the life of Frank, which gave far more reliable information than all other documents, in which Frank did not refrain from telling lies. It also contained a detailed and undisguised description of the sexual rites practiced by Frank. This manuscript was lent to Kraushar by a Frankist family, but since then it has vanished without trace. The work of an anonymous Frankist, written in Polish about 1800 and called "The Prophecy of Isaiah," which puts the metaphors of the biblical book to Frankist use, gives a reliable record of the revolutionary and utopian expectations of the members of the sect. This manuscript, parts of which were published in Kraushar's book, was in the library of the Warsaw Jewish community until the Holocaust. A book was recorded in Offenbach which listed the dreams and revelations of which Eva Frank and her brothers boasted, but when two younger members of the Porges family in Prague, who had been sent to the court and been disillusioned with what they saw, fled from Offenbach, they took the book with them and handed it over to the rabbinical court in Fuerth, who apparently destroyed it.

The Frankists in Prague. Another center of intensive literary activity emerged in Prague, where an important Frankist group had established itself. At its head were several members of the distinguished *Wehle and *Bondi families, whose forebears had belonged to the secret Shabbatean movement for some generations. They had strong connections with "the believers" in other communities in Bohemia and Moravia. Their spiritual leader, Jonas Wehle (1752–1823), was aided by his brothers, who were fervent Frankists, and his son-in-law Loew von Hoenigsberg (d. 1811), who committed to writing many of the teachings of the circle. This group acted with great prudence for a long time, particularly during the lifetime of R. Ezekiel *Landau, and its members denied in his presence that they belonged to the sect. However, after his death they became more conspicuous. In 1799 R. Eleazar *Fleckeles, Landau's successor, preached some fiercely polemical sermons against them, causing riotous disturbances in the Prague synagogue, and leading to the publication of libelous attacks on the group, as well as to both denunciations and defense of its members before the civil authorities. A great deal of evidence, extracted from "penitent" members of the sect in Kolin and other places, remains from this period. The important file on the Frankists in the Prague community archives was removed by the president of the community at the end of the 19th century, out of respect for the families implicated in it. The disturbances connected with the appearance of the "Red Letters" (written in red ink, as a symbol of the religion of Edom) helped to maintain a small, distinct Frankist group in Prague for years, and some of its members, or their children, were later among the founders of the first Reform temple in Prague (c. 1832). A similar distinct group existed for a long time in Prossnitz. Some of the literature of the Prague circle survived, namely, a commentary on the *aggadot* of *Ein Ya'akov* and a large collection of letters on details of the faith, as well as commentaries on various biblical passages written in German mixed with Yiddish and Hebrew by Loew Hoenigsberg in the early 19th century. Aaron Jellinek possessed various Frankist writings in German, but they disappeared after his death.

On Eva Frank's death the organization weakened, although in 1823 Elias Kaplinski, a member of Frank's wife's family, still tried to summon a conference of the sectarians, which took place in Carlsbad. After this the sect broke up, and messengers were sent to collect together the various writings from the scattered families. This deliberate concealment of Frankist literature is one of the main reasons for the ignorance concerning its internal history, allied to the decided reluctance of most of the sectarians' descendants to promote any investigation into their affairs. The only one of "the believers" who left any memoirs of his early days was Moses Porges (later Von Portheim). These he had recorded in his old age. A whole group of Frankist families from Bohemia and Moravia migrated to the United States in 1848–49. In his last will and testament, Gottlieb Wehle of New York, 1867, a nephew of Jonas Wehle, expresses a deep feeling of identity with his Frankist forebears, who appeared to him to be the first fighters for progress in the ghetto, a view held by many of the descendants of "the believers." The connection between the Frankists' heretical Kabbalah and the ideas of the new Enlightenment is evident both in surviving manuscripts from Prague, and in the traditions of some of these families in Bohemia and Moravia (where there were adherents of the sect, outside Prague, in Kolin, Horschitz (Horice), Holleschau (Holesov), and Kojetin).

There continued to be strong ties between the neophyte families in Poland, who had risen considerably in the social scale in the 19th century, and there may have been some kind of organization among them. In the first three generations after the apostasy of 1759/60 most of them married only among themselves, preserving their Jewish character in several ways, and only a very few intermarried with true Catholics. Copies of "the Words of the Master" were still being produced in the 1820s, and apparently it had its readers. The Frankists were active as fervent Polish patriots and took part in the rebellions of 1793, 1830, and 1863. Nevertheless the whole time they were under suspicion of Jewish sectarian separatism. In Warsaw in the 1830s most of the lawyers were descendants of the Frankists, many of whom were also businessmen, writers, and musicians. It was only in the middle of the 19th century that mixed marriages increased between them and the Poles, and most of them moved from the liberal wing of Polish society to the nationalist conservative wing. However, there still remained a number of families who continued to marry only among themselves. For a long time this circle maintained secret contacts with the Doenmeh in Salonika. An unresolved controversy still exists concerning the Frankist affiliation of Adam *Mickiewicz, the greatest Polish poet. There is clear evidence of this from the poet himself (on his mother's side), but in Poland this evidence is resolutely misinterpreted. Mickiewicz's Frankist origins were well-known to the Warsaw Jewish community as early as 1838 (according to evidence in the AZDJ of that year, p. 362). The parents of the poet's wife also came from Frankist families.

The crystallization of the Frankist sect is one of the most marked indications of the crisis which struck the Jewish society in the mid-18th century. Frank's personality reveals clear signs of the adventurer, motivated by a blend of religious impulses and a lust for power. By contrast, his "believers" were on the whole men of deep faith and moral integrity as far as this did not conflict with the vicious demands made on them by Frank. In all that remains of their original literature whether in German, Polish or Hebrew, there is absolutely no reference to those matters, like the blood libel, which so aroused the Jewish community against them. They were fascinated by the words of their leader and his vision of a unique fusion between Judaism and Christianity, but they easily combined this with more modest hopes which led them to become protagonists of liberal-bourgeois ideals. Their nihilist Shabbatean faith served as a transition to a new world beyond the ghetto. They quickly forgot their licentious practices and acquired a reputation of being men of the highest moral conduct. Many Frankist families kept a miniature of Eva Frank which used to be sent to the most prominent households, and to this day some families honor her as a saintly woman who was falsely reviled.

Bibliography: J. Emden, *Sefer Shimmush* (Altona, 1762); idem, *Megillat Sefer* (1896); E. Fleckeles, *Ahavat David* (Prague, 1800); M. Balaban, *Le-Toledot ha-Tenu'ah ha-Frankit* (1934); idem, in: *Livre d'hommage à . . . S. Poznański* (1927), 25–75; N. M. Gelber, in: *Yivo Historishe Shriftn*, 1 (1929); idem, in: *Zion*, 2 (1937), 326–32; G. Scholem, *ibid.*, 35 (1920/21); idem, in: *Keneset*, 2 (1937), 347–92; idem, in: *Sefer Yovel le-Yitzhak Baer* (1960), 409–30; idem, in: RHR, 144 (1953–54), 42–77; idem, *The Messianic Idea in Judaism, and Other Essays* (1920); idem, in: *Zeugnisse T. W. Adorno zum Geburtstag* (1963), 20–32; idem, in: *Max Brod Gedenkbuch* (1969), 77–92; idem, in: *Commentary*, 51 (Jan. 1971), 41–70; A. Yaari, in: *Sinai*, 35 (1954), 120–82; 42 (1958), 294–306; A. J. Brawer, *Galiẓyah vi-Yhudeha* (1966), 197–275; P. Beer, *Geschichte der religioesen Sekten der Juden*, 2 (1923); H. Graetz, *Frank und die Frankisten* (1868); idem, in: MGWJ, 22 (1873); S. Back, *ibid.*, 26 (1877); A. G. Schenk-Rink, *Die Polen in Offenbach* (1866–69); A. Kraushar, *Frank i frankiści polscy* (1895); T. Jeske-Choiński, *Neofici polscy* (1904), 46–107; M. Wishnitzer, in: *Mémoires de l'Académie . . . de St. Pétersbourg*, series 8, Hist.-Phil. Section, 12 no. 3 (1914); F. Mauthner, *Lebenserinnerungen* (1918), 295–307; C. Seligman, in: *Frankfurter Israelitisches Gemeindeblatt*, 10 (1932), 121–3, 150–2; V. Zacek, in: JGGJČ, 9 (1938), 343–410; O. Rabinowicz, in: *JQR 75th Anniversary Volume* (1967), 429–45; P. Arnsberg, *Von Podolien nach Offenbach* (1965); R. Kestenberg-Gladstein, *Neuere Geschichte der Juden in den boehmischen Laendern*, 1 (1969), 123–91; A. G. Duker, in: JSOS, 25 (1963), 287–333; idem, in: *Joshua Starr Memorial Volume* (1963), 191–201.

[G.Sch.]

FRANK, JEROME NEW (1889–1957), U.S. jurist and legal philosopher. Frank, who was born in New York City, practiced law in Chicago and New York City before being appointed general counsel to the Agricultural Adjustment Administration by President Franklin D. Roosevelt in 1933. Subsequently, he was appointed to important executive positions with the Federal Surplus Relief Corporation, the Reconstruction Finance Commission, and the Public Works Administration. As one of the more imaginative and articulate administrators of the New Deal program of President Roosevelt, he was often embroiled in argument and litigation in its defense, especially in the use of public power. Retiring to private practice in 1937, he was recalled by President Roosevelt in 1939 as commissioner and then chairman of the Securities and Exchange Commission. There, he played an important role in reorganizing the New York Stock Exchange. He also instituted new programs for public-utility holding companies under the 1935 Act. President Roosevelt named him to the U.S. Court of Appeals for the 2nd Circuit in 1941. He sat there, and lectured at Yale Law School as well, until his death.

Basically a "legal realist," Frank developed the juristic concept of fact-skepticism, or the continuous questioning of factual assumptions to expose the realities of the judicial process. Legal philosophers, he insisted, should not think only in terms of law to determine whether justice prevails in any given case, but rather to concentrate on the processes by which facts are found and judged. Fact-skepticism led him to infer that the jury was an inept institution and that it ought to be abolished. He also warned against relying on jury verdicts to inflict capital punishment. Frank sought through fact-skepticism to liberalize and reform the trial process. He developed his thoughts in challenging and provocative books entitled *Law and the Modern Mind* (1930) and *Courts on Trial* (1949), as well as in many law review articles. In 1945 he wrote *Fate and Freedom*, in which he attacked Freud's deterministic psychology, Marxism, and natural-law doctrines as endangering individual freedom and moral responsibility. In *If Men Were Angels* (1942), Frank replied to critics of the new administrative agencies of the New Deal. In *Not Guilty* (1957), written with his daughter, he commented on a number of cases in which innocent people were convicted of crimes.

[J.J.M.]

°**FRANK, KARL HERMANN** (1898–1946), Sudeten German Nazi politician, leader of the radical wing of the Sudeten German Party and close associate of *Himmler. In March 1939 he was appointed secretary of state to *Reichsprotektor* Constantin von Neurath in the Protectorate of Bohemia-Moravia. After the assassination of *Heydrich in 1942, Frank unleashed a wave of repression against the population of the Protectorate of Bohemia-Moravia, that culminated in the destruction of the town of Lidice. With the appointment of Wilhelm Frick as *Reichsprotektor,* Frank was nominated minister of state (1943) and became the virtual dictator of the Protectorate (see *Czechoslovakia). As S.S. and police officer with the rank of lieutenant-general, he was one of the persons mainly responsible for the annihilation of the Protectorate's Jewish population. Frank was hanged after the war (1946) by the verdict of a Czechoslovak court.

Bibliography: G. Wrighton, *Heydrich* ... (1962), index; IMT, *Trial of the Major War Criminals,* 24 (1949), index; E. Davidson, *Trial of the Germans* (1967), index. [Y.Re.]

FRANK, LEO MAX (1884–1915), engineer and the only Jew ever to have been murdered by a lynch mob in the United States. Frank, who was born in Cuero, Texas, of an immigrant German family, was raised in Brooklyn, and studied mechanical engineering. In 1907 he moved to Atlanta, Georgia, where his uncle, Moses Frank, owner of the National Pencil Company, offered him a job as plant superintendent. Here he became president of the local chapter of B'nai B'rith. On April 27, 1913, a 14-year-old employee of Frank's, Mary Phagan, was found murdered in the factory basement. Frank was arrested the next day and charged with the crime. The chief witness for the prosecution at his trial, which lasted for nearly two months, was a Negro employee of the factory, James Conley, who was suspected by many observers both at the time and subsequently of having been the true culprit. Despite the flimsy nature of the evidence, the dubious character of many of the prosecution's witnesses and Frank's own eloquent testimony on Aug. 23, 1913, the jury returned a verdict of guilty.

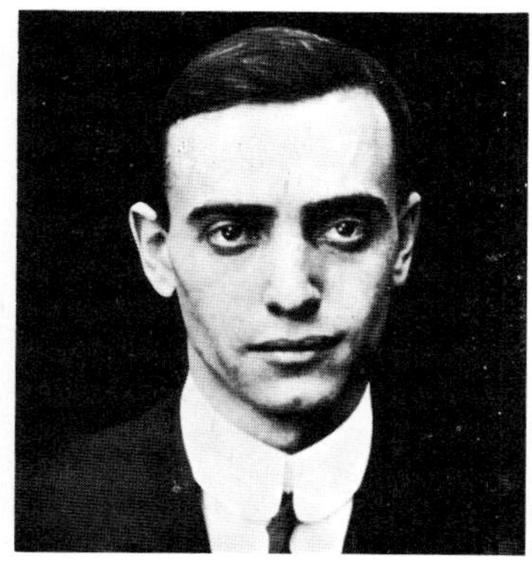

Leo M. Frank, lynched in Atlanta, Ga., in 1915. Courtesy American Jewish Archives, Cincinnati, Ohio.

The issue of Frank's Jewishness was first raised at his trial by his own lawyers, who claimed that he was a victim of prejudice, a charge that the prosecution vigorously denied. Whether or not this denial was sincere, it became clear as the trial progressed that the mobs in and out of the courtroom that continually called for Frank's blood were inspired by anti-Semitic passions, which undoubtedly influenced the decision of the jury. It was only when the case was already being appealed, however, that a vicious anti-Semitic campaign was launched around it by the ex-populist and racist politician Tom Watson, who in his weekly *Jeffersonian Magazine* repeatedly demanded the execution of "the filthy, perverted Jew of New York." Watson helped found the "Knights of Mary Phagan," an anti-Semitic society which sought to organize a boycott of Jewish stores and businesses throughout Georgia.

Frank's lawyers fought his case all the way to the United States Supreme Court on the grounds that he had not been given a fair trial, and it became a cause célèbre which enlisted the support of prominent Jews and gentiles. On May 18, 1915, however, the Court turned down Frank's final appeal. On June 21, shortly before his scheduled execution, his sentence was commuted to a life term by Governor John Slaton, who was personally convinced of his innocence. Slaton's decision, which was to cost him his political career, inflamed emotions in Georgia and did not save Frank's life for long: he was dragged from jail by a mob on Aug. 16, 1915, and lynched. There can be little doubt that Frank was innocent or that he would never have been brought to trial in the first place, much less convicted, had he not been a Jew.

Bibliography: H. Golden, *A Little Girl Is Dead* (1965, republished in England as *Lynching of Leo Frank* (1966)); L. Dinnerstein, *Leo Frank Case* (1968); idem, in: AJA, 20 (1968), 107–26. [H.Go.]

FRANK, MENAHEM MENDEL (late 15th–first half of 16th century), rabbi. He at first served as *av bet din* in Poznan, Poland, and from 1529 was rabbi of Brest-Litovsk, Lithuania. Frank was granted judicial authority by the king to assist Michael *Ezofovich in tax collection but met with opposition in Brest-Litovsk. In 1531, when Frank complained of the matter, the Jews under his jurisdiction were ordered by King *Sigismund I to obey him and submit to any *ḥerem* he imposed, being forbidden to appeal against his decisions to a non-Jewish tribunal. Encountering opposition by members of the nobility and state courts, possibly incited by Frank's Jewish opponents, in 1532 he sought the protection of Queen Bona. Upon her recommendation, the king prohibited royal officials and judges from intervening in the rabbi's affairs and declared that Frank could not be summoned to account before the throne. Decisions by Frank appertaining to divorce bills and contracts are mentioned by *Shalom Shakhna b. Joseph of Lublin. According to some records Frank ended his days in Jerusalem.

Bibliography: S. A. Bershadski (ed.), *Russko-yevreyskiy arkhiv,* 1 (1882), nos. 139, 147; A. L. Feinstein, *Ir Tehillah* (1886), 21–22, 64–65, 164–5. [A.Cy.]

FRANK, PHILIPP (1884–1966), philosopher and physicist. Born in Vienna, he was appointed professor of theoretical physics at the German University of Prague at 28, replacing Einstein. In 1938, he moved to the United States and taught mathematics and physics at Harvard. He established his reputation in physics by publishing with Richard von Mises, *Die Differential- und Integralgleichungen der Mechanik und Physik* (1925). Frank's most famous work was on philosophy of science. Following Duhem, Poincaré, Mach, and Einstein, Frank tried to clarify the philosophical foundations of the natural sciences. Frank's view is close to the positivism of the "Vienna Circle." He opposed the compartmentalization of individual sciences, stressing the unity of science. He also pointed out the neglected spheres between the individual sciences. Frank was a personal friend of Einstein and in 1947 wrote *Einstein: His Life and Times.* Frank opposed Mach's limited form of logical positivism and emphasized instead, relying on Einstein, that the principles of physics are the product of free human imagination and that they are symbols. These symbols are not arbitrary, but "true" ones, i.e., one should derive from them, by logical consequences, conclusions which are confirmed by experiment. This means that despite the emphasis on the empirical factor there still remains room for the researcher's productive activity. In his later years, he was especially interested in the sociological, historical, cultural, and psychological aspects of the natural sciences. Frank was a brilliant teacher and a lucid writer. A volume of *Boston Studies in the Philosophy of Science* (1965) was dedicated to him on his 80th birthday.

Frank's writings are an important source for the history of logical positivism and empiricism in the 20th century. They include: *Das Kausalgesetz und seine Grenzen* (1932); *Théorie de la connaissance et physique moderne* (1934); *Das Ende der mechanistischen Physik* (1935); *Interpretations and Misinterpretations of Modern Physics* (1938); *Between Physics and Philosophy* (1941); *Modern Science and Its Philosophy* (1949); *Relativity: A Richer Truth* (1950); and *Philosophy of Science: The Link Between Science and Philosophy* (1957). [Sh.H.B.]

FRANK, SEMYON LYUDVIGOVICH (1877–1950), Russian philosopher. Frank was born in Moscow. He became an enthusiastic Marxist in P. B. Struve's group, but later rejected Marx and in 1912 joined the Orthodox Church. He lectured at St. Petersburg from 1912 to 1917, was professor at Saratov (1917–21), and was then appointed to Moscow University, working with Berdyaev. The Soviets banished him in 1922 and he went to Germany. In 1937 he had to flee, spending eight years in France, before moving to England. A leading philosophical theologian, he contended that the world must be conceived as a "total-unity." He tried to give Christianity cosmic significance and to develop a religious humanism, seeing the glory of God in human creativity. His chief work, *Predmet Znaniya* ("The Object of Knowledge," 1915), appeared in French in 1937 as *La connaissance et l'être*. Two later works, *Nepostizhimoye* (1939; *God With Us*, 1946) and *Realnost i chelovek* (1956; *Reality and Man*, 1965), have appeared in English.

Bibliography: P. Edwards (ed.), *Encyclopedia of Philosophy*, 3 (1967), 219f.; N. O. Lossky, *History of Russian Philosophy* (1952), 266–92; V. V. Zenkousky, *History of Russian Philosophy* (1953), 852–72. [R.H.P.]

FRANK, WALDO DAVID (1889–1967), U.S. novelist, critic, and philosopher. Born in Long Branch, New Jersey, Frank was educated in Europe and at Yale. His early travels also took him to Latin America (where his books later enjoyed particular success). His father, an American-born son of German immigrants, was a wealthy and assimilated lawyer but Waldo Frank underwent a mystical reconversion to Judaism in 1920. His first published book was a novel, *The Unwelcome Man* (1917). He later made several outstanding experiments in poetic prose, such as *Rahab* (1922), *City Block* (1922), and *Holiday* (1923), the last a study of race relations in the South. A man of intellectual energy and literary skill, Frank wrote many books and essays evaluating American culture, notably *Our America* (1919), *The Re-Discovery of America* (1929), and *In the American Jungle* (1937). His books on other cultures include *Virgin Spain* (1926), *America Hispana* (1931), *Dawn in Russia* (1932), and *Cuba, Prophetic Island* (1962). As editor of the important, although short-lived, magazine *Seven Arts* (1916–17), which he founded with James Oppenheim, and of *The New Republic* (1925–40), Frank profoundly influenced American liberalism. His later writings were imbued with a prophetic and mystical philosophy that demanded the rejection of materialism and atheistic rationalism and the recognition of an immanent God. Frank also urged that private life should be guided by the ethical tenets of the Judeo-Christian tradition, enriched by the concepts of Marx and Freud. *The Bridegroom Cometh* (1939), a Marxist novel paradoxically inspired by Frank's religious beliefs, illustrates the author's conviction that the fundamental problem of the time was "how to transform the great traditional religious energies of Western civilization into modern social action." Two works by Frank on Jewish subjects are *The Jew in Our Day* (1944) and *Bridgehead: The Drama of Israel* (1957). The latter insisted on Messianism as the purpose of Jewish survival and on Jewry's mission of world redemption through the prophet Micah's principles of justice, mercy, and humility before God.

Bibliography: G. Munson, *Waldo Frank* (Eng., 1923); W. R. Bittner, *Novels of Waldo Frank* (1958); S. Liptzin, *Jew in American Literature* (1966), 223; R. L. Perry, *Shared Vision of Waldo Frank and Hart Crane* (1966); P. J. Carter, *Waldo Frank* (Eng., 1967). [B.W.]

FRANK, ẒEVI PESAḤ (1873–1960), chief rabbi of Jerusalem and halakhic authority. Frank was born in Kovno, Lithuania. His father, Judah Leib, was one of the leaders of the "Ḥaderah" society in Kovno which founded the village of *Ḥaderah in Ereẓ Israel. Frank studied under Eliezer *Gordon at Telz and under Isaac Rabinowitz at Slobodka. He attended the **musar* discourses of Israel *Lipkin of Salant. In 1893 he proceeded to Jerusalem where he continued his studies at the yeshivot of Eẓ Ḥayyim and Torat Ḥayyim. He acquired an outstanding reputation, combining a profound knowledge of the Talmud with sound common sense. Despite his youth, he was encouraged by Samuel *Salant, the rabbi of Jerusalem, who consulted with him in his halakhic decisions. In 1895 he married Gitah-Malkah, granddaughter of Ḥayyim Jacob Spira, head of the Jerusalem *bet din*. Subsequently he taught at a number of Jerusalem yeshivot. In 1902 he moved to Jaffa in order to be able to devote himself entirely to study. Rabbi A. I. *Kook had already taken up his appointment there, and later he and Frank associated in the efforts to establish the rabbinate of Israel.

In 1907 Frank was appointed by Salant and the scholars of Jerusalem as a member of the *Bet Din Gadol* in the Ḥurvah synagogue. Although he was its youngest member, the burden of the *bet din*, and the religious affairs of the city fell mainly upon his shoulders. He conducted single-handedly the spiritual administration of the city in the difficult days of World War I. The Turks tried to send him into exile in Egypt, but he hid in an attic from where he directed the rabbinical affairs of the city until the entry of the British (December 1917). The rabbinate was in a perilous state and Frank made strenuous efforts to raise its status, both materially and spiritually. He understood the importance of founding a central rabbinical organization, and immediately after the British occupation, took steps to found "The Council of Rabbis of Jerusalem." This organization, however, was shortlived. Later, however, he established the "Rabbinate Office," which became the nucleus of the chief rabbinate of Israel, and on his suggestion A. I. Kook was invited to become chief rabbi of Palestine in 1921. In the violent controversy which resulted, fomented by the extreme religious section which saw no halakhic precedent for such an appointment, Frank brought proof to bear. In 1936 he was elected chief rabbi of Jerusalem. In consequence of his preeminence as a halakhist, the appointment was accepted by all parties, including those who opposed him on political grounds.

Frank was a rare Torah personality. He was approached on all difficult halakhic problems in Israel or in the Jewish world, and unhesitatingly gave his ruling. He was especially concerned about *agunot* (see **Agunah*) and the laws

Ẓevi Pesaḥ Frank, chief rabbi of Jerusalem.

pertaining to the Land of Israel. Immediately after the *Balfour Declaration (1917) he expressed the opinion: "we have been worthy to see approaching signs of the redemption"; he began to clarify the laws of the Temple and sacrifices, and also headed the Midrash Benei Zion, an institute established for the clarification of the laws of the Land of Israel. He devised no novel procedure in halakhic ruling, but followed in the tradition of the renowned **posekim* Isaac Elhanan *Spektor and Samuel Salant. He fought against the military conscription of women and yeshivah students, exclusively secular education, and the desecration of the Sabbath. His statements sometimes raised a storm, but they were always received with respect. Together with Rabbi Isaac *Herzog he entered into an agreement with Hadassah Hospital on the circumstances under which autopsies could be performed according to the *halakhah.* He left many manuscripts, in particular responsa, constituting some 20 large volumes from which *Har Ẓevi* (1964), on *Yoreh De'ah; Mikdash Melekh* (1968); and *Har Ẓevi* (1969) on *Oraḥ Ḥayyim* were published.

Bibliography: *Keter Torah ve-Seder Hakhtarat ha-Rabbanut ... Ẓevi Pesaḥ Frank* (1936); *Ha-Ẓofeh* (Dec. 11, 1960). [S.De.]

FRANKAU, English literary family. Julia Frankau (1859–1916), novelist and critic, was a sister of the playwright James Davis (Owen Hall). She used the pseudonym "Frank Danby" for her fiction, and her first novel, *Dr Phillips, a Maida Vale Idyl* (1887), was a story of London Jewish life. Julia Frankau was an uneven craftsman, with an exuberant style. This is best shown in *Pigs in Clover* (1903),which deals with South Africans, *Uitlanders,* and Jews, all painted in lurid colors. Her son Gilbert (1884–1952) maintained no connection with Judaism. He introduced Jews into his novels, treating them mostly in theatrical style. *The Love Story of Aliette Brunton* (1922) is a plea for the liberalization of English divorce law. Gilbert Frankau wrote two topical novelettes in verse, *One of Them* (1918) and *One of Us* (1919). His daughter Pamela (1908–1967), who became a Catholic in 1942, was also a well-known novelist and magazine writer.

Bibliography: M.P. Modder, *The Jew in the Literature of England* (1939), 325–6. [Ed.]

FRANKEL, HIRAM D. (1882–1931), U.S. lawyer and community leader. Frankel, who was born in Mayfield, Ohio, served in appointive local and state government posts and was a member of the Minnesota Board of Regents. Frankel was also involved in journalistic and theatrical enterprises. He served as president of Mount Zion Hebrew Congregation in St. Paul, Minnesota, and of the Jewish Home for the Aged of the Northwest. He was a district president of B'nai B'rith, later director of the Canadian district, distinguishing himself in helping to break down barriers within the organization to Jews of East European origin. Frankel's large and meticulously preserved personal correspondence covering Jewish life in Minnesota and throughout the U.S. in the World War I period is housed in the Minnesota Historical Society, St. Paul.

Bibliography: W. Gunther Plaut, *Mount Zion, 1856–1956* (1956), 65, 89; idem, *The Jews in Minnesota* (1959), passim. [W.G.P.]

FRANKEL, LEE KAUFER (1867–1931), social worker and insurance executive. Born in Philadelphia, Pennsylvania, during the 1890s he taught chemistry at the University of Pennsylvania and also worked as a consulting chemist. Frankel's friendship with Rabbi Henry *Berkowitz helped arouse his interest in Jewish community affairs and social work. Frankel went to New York City in 1899 as manager of the United Hebrew Charities. A brilliant administrator, he helped introduce professional social work standards into Jewish philanthropy. He stressed the importance of adequate relief geared to rehabilitation, the development of a pension program for such dependents as widowed mothers, and a program of assisted migration to reduce the concentration of Jewish population in New York City. He became interested in the potential contribution of social insurance to the prevention and relief of poverty. The Russell Sage Foundation appointed him a special investigator in 1908; this led in 1910 to the publication of *Workmen's Insurance in Europe* which he wrote in cooperation with Miles M. Dawson and Louis I. Dublin. In 1909 Frankel became manager of the industrial department of the Metropolitan Life Insurance Company; he eventually advanced to the position of second vice-president. At Metropolitan, Frankel pioneered the development of social and health programs under private insurance auspices. These included the distribution of many pamphlets on communicable diseases and personal hygiene, the organization of public health nursing services, and community health demonstrations. Throughout his career Frankel retained an interest in Jewish affairs. He served on the board of the American Jewish Joint Distribution Committee, and in 1927 was chairman of the commission which surveyed Palestine for the Jewish Agency. Frankel published many articles on health and welfare issues and was the coauthor of several books, including *The Human Factor in Industry* (1920), *A Popular Encyclopedia of Health* (1926), and *Health of the Worker, How to Safeguard It* (1924).

Bibliography: Lowenstein, in: AJYB, 34 (1933), 121–40. [R.Lu.]

FRANKEL, LEO (1844–1896), Hungarian socialist. Born in Ó-Buda (now part of Budapest), Frankel was a goldsmith by trade. After living for a short time in Austria and Germany he settled in Paris in 1867, where he became an active socialist. He was imprisoned by the French Imperial government for his political activities but was released on the outbreak of revolution in 1870 and helped to organize the uprising in the Paris Commune. In March 1871 Frankel was made minister of labor of the Commune, and on its overthrow two months later fled to London, where he became a member of the council of the Socialist International. In 1875 Frankel left for Austria, where he participated in the workers' conference at Wiener-Neustadt. He was arrested by the Austrian authorities and extradited to Hungary. He was imprisoned from 1876 to 1878, when he went back to Paris as Engels' assistant in the Socialist International. In 1889 he represented the Hungarian Social Democrats at the inaugural conference of the Second Socialist International.

Frankel was in constant correspondence with Karl Marx, whom he much admired, but also became interested in Zionism as a result of meeting Theodor Herzl. After his death in Paris, French workers organized a campaign to raise funds for a memorial in his name. In 1951 his portrait

Leo Frankel, Hungarian member of the Socialist International.

was used on a Hungarian stamp and in 1968 his remains were transferred to Budapest for reburial in the Workers' Pantheon.

Bibliography: M. Aranyossi, *Leo Frankel* (Ger., 1957); T. Herzl, *Complete Diaries*, ed. by R. Patai, 1 (1960), 191–2. [Y.M.]

FRANKEL, NAOMI (1920–), Israel novelist. Born in Berlin into a wealthy, assimilated German-Jewish family, she joined Ha-Shomer ha-Ẓa'ir at an early age and went to Palestine in 1933. She served in the Palmaḥ in the War of Independence and later became a member of kibbutz Bet Alfa. Her panoramic trilogy, *Sha'ul ve-Yohannah* ("Saul and Joanna," 1956–67), describes the fate of German Jewry up to Nazi times, as reflected in the life of three generations of an assimilated Jewish family, whose granddaughter finds her way to a Zionist youth movement, and revolts against family tradition.

Bibliography: R. Gurfein, *Mi-Karov u-me-Raḥok* (1964), 122–5; J. Lichtenbaum, *Bi-Teḥumah shel Sifrut* (1962), 145–7. [G.K.]

FRANKEL, SALLY HERBERT (1903–), South African economist. He was born and educated in Johannesburg, where he was professor of economics at Witwatersrand University from 1931 to 1946. He did research in maize marketing and government railway policy in South Africa, compiled calculations of the national income for the South African treasury (1941–48), and was a member of the Treasury Advisory Council (1941–45). Frankel investigated the railway system (1942) and mining industry (1945) for the Rhodesian government. In 1946 he was appointed professor of the economics of underdeveloped countries at Oxford. From 1953 to 1955 he was a member of the East African Royal Commission, and from 1957 to 1958 adviser to South Rhodesia's Urban African Affairs Commission. Frankel's publications include: *Africa in the Re-Making* (1932), *Capital Investment in Africa* (1938), *Concept of Colonization* (1949), *Economic Impact on Underdeveloped Societies* (1953), *Some Conceptual Aspects of International Economic Development of Underdeveloped Territories* (1952), and *Investment and the Return to Equity Capital in the South African Gold Mining Industry, 1887–1965* (1967). [Ed.]

FRANKEL, SAMUEL BENJAMIN (1905–), U.S. naval officer. Born in Cincinnati, Ohio, Frankel graduated from the U.S. Naval Academy in 1929. He served on various U.S. warships between 1929 and 1936 before being sent to Riga, Latvia, to study Russian. During World War II he was assistant naval attaché at the United States embassy in Moscow and later assistant naval attaché for air in Murmansk-Archangel. Frankel was an intelligence officer in the United States Navy from 1946 to 1948 and was later naval attaché in Nanking, China. He remained in his post for a year after the Communist revolution before returning to the United States in 1950 to become director of the naval intelligence school. From 1953 to 1956 he was assistant head of naval intelligence in the Pacific fleet and was later a senior intelligence officer in the Navy Department in Washington, and promoted to rear admiral. In May 1960 Frankel became deputy director of naval intelligence and in the following year was appointed chief of staff of the Defense Intelligence Agency, a post he retained until his retirement in 1964. [Ed.]

FRANKEL, ZACHARIAS (1801–1875), rabbi and scholar. Frankel was born in Prague. After receiving a talmudic education under Bezalel *Ronsburg, he studied philosophy, natural sciences, and philology in Budapest (1825–30). In 1831 the Austrian government appointed him district rabbi *(Kreisrabbiner)* of Leitmeritz (Litomerice), and he settled in Teplitz (Teplice) where he was elected local rabbi. He was the first Bohemian rabbi with a secular academic education and one of the first to preach in German. In 1836 he was called by the Saxon government to *Dresden to act as chief rabbi. The publication of his study on the Jewish *oath (see below) led to its abolition in several German states. He declined a call to Berlin in 1843, mainly because the Prussian government would not meet his stipulations (complete legal recognition of the Jewish faith—until then merely "tolerated"; denial of support to missionary activities among the Jews, etc.). In 1854, after having actively advocated its establishment, Frankel became director of the newly founded *Juedisch-Theologisches Seminar at Breslau, where he remained until his death.

Religious Outlook. As a theologian, Frankel aimed at a synthesis between the historic conservative conception and contemporary needs, through gradual organic reform. Becoming the spiritual leader of the party advocating "moderate" reforms, he founded the so-called "positivist-historical" ("Breslau") school which later influenced the *Conservative movement in the United States. In the controversy over the Hamburg prayer book (1841) and in his subsequent reply to the circular of the Hamburg preacher, Gotthold *Salomon (*Literaturblatt des Orients*, 3 (1842), nos. 23–24), he declared that only changes that were not in conflict with the spirit of historical Judaism should be permitted in the traditional ritual. He believed that the messianic belief, which expressed the "pious wish for the independence of the Jewish people" was of importance for the survival and development of Judaism, and that it brought a new spirit and vigor into the life of German Jews, even though "they already had a fatherland which they would not leave." His monthly review, *Zeitschrift fuer die religioesen Interessen des Judenthums* (1844–46), was a platform for his opinions on Reform. At the second rabbinical conference at Frankfort in 1845 he pressed for the formulation of a firm principle as a guide to the adoption of slight additional reforms; the main opponents to his demand were A. *Geiger and S. *Holdheim. In protest against its rejection, and against the proposed gradual abolition of Hebrew as the language of prayer, Frankel withdrew from the conference. In the ensuing public controversy, though supported by Israel and David *Deutsch, Abraham Solomon Trier, and Solomon *Eger, he tried without success to call a conference of theologians to counter the aims of the earlier rabbinical conference. Frankel's views aroused opposition in both Reform and Orthodox quarters. As soon as the Juedisch-Theologisches Seminar at Breslau was opened, he was challenged by

Samson Raphael *Hirsch to state the religious principles that would guide instruction there. At the same time A. Geiger criticized the institution's casuistic method of talmudic instruction. On the publication of Frankel's *Darkhei ha-Mishnah* (1859), Hirsch attacked him in his periodical *Jeschurun*. An open letter addressed to Frankel by Gottlieb Fischer (*Jeschurun*, 1860) was followed by a series of critical essays in which Hirsch demanded that Frankel give a precise exposition of his views on rabbinical tradition and the revelation at Mount Sinai. Hirsch's stand was upheld by other Orthodox rabbis, notably B. H. *Auerbach (*Ha-Ẓofeh al Darkhei ha-Mishnah*, 1861), Solomon Ze'ev *Klein (*Mi-Penei Koshet*, 1861), Samuel *Freund, and the anonymous author of *Me'or Einayim*, while Frankel was supported by the conservative rabbis and scholars Solomon Judah *Rapaport (*Divrei Shalom va-Emet*, 1861), Wolf Landau, Saul Isaac *Kaempf (*Mamtik Sod*, 1861), and Raphael *Kirchheim. Confining himself to a brief statement in his journal *Monatsschrift fuer Geschichte und Wissenschaft des Judenthums* (vol. 10 (1861), 159–60), Frankel stressed that it was not his purpose to dispute the worth of rabbinical tradition or to deny its antiquity, adding that the question as to which of its halakhic elements were to be considered of Mosaic origin was not yet resolved.

Works. In his scholarly works Frankel dealt mainly with biblical-talmudic law (from a historical and systematic standpoint), the historical development of the halakhah, and talmudic exegesis. His first work, on the Jewish oath, *Die Eidesleistung bei den Juden* (1840), arose out of a practical political need and was at the same time a pioneering attempt at scientific analysis of halakhic problems using the method of comparative jurisprudence. He further examined the question in *Der gerichtliche Beweis nach talmudischem Rechte* (1846), a study of legal evidence according to talmudic law, and again in a series of articles in various periodicals: MGWJ, 2 (1853), 289–304, 329–47; 9 (1860), 321–31, 365–80, 406–16, 445–54; 16 (1867), 24–26, 70–72; and *Jahresbericht des Juedisch-Theologischen Seminars* (1860). Several of his works deal with the history of the oral tradition: in his first studies on the Septuagint, *Vorstudien zu der Septuaginta* (1841), he tried to show that traces of the Palestinian halakhah could be found in the Greek translation of the Bible; on this he based a further work on the influence of Palestinian exegesis on Alexandrian hermeneutics, *Ueber den Einfluss der palaestinischen Exegese auf die alexandrinische Hermeneutik* (1851). He published his research into the methodology of the Mishnah and the Talmud in *Darkhei ha-Mishnah* (1859; with supplement and index, 1867; new ed., 1923), which exercised a decisive inflence on further research on the Mishnah; and *Mevo ha-Yerushalmi* (1870), an introduction to the Jerusalem Talmud. He also wrote *Ahavat Ẓiyyon*, a commentary to several tractates of the Jerusalem Talmud (*Berakhot, Pe'ah*, 1874; *Demai*, 1875), and *Entwurf einer Geschichte der Literatur der nachtalmudischen Responsen* (1865), the outline for a history of post-talmudic responsa literature. In 1851 he founded the *Monatsschrift fuer Geschichte und Wissenschaft des Judenthums*, editing it for 17 years and publishing numerous articles on Jewish cultural history. In the Breslau seminary, Frankel set the standard for modern rabbinical training, and his curriculum of study and the qualifications he established for both students and lecturers were adopted by all similar institutions.

Bibliography: Kaufmann, Schriften, 1 (1908) 258–71; S. P. Rabinovitz, *Rabbi Zekharyah Frankel* (Heb., 1898); M. Braun, in: *Juedischer Volks- und Haus-Kalendar* (1899), 109–10; idem, in: ZHB, 20 (1917), 55; idem, in: *Geschichte des Juedisch-Theologischen Seminars* (1904), 28–40; J. Perles, in: ADB, 7 (1878), 266–8; Schwarz, in: JJGL, 5 (1902), 140–58; G. Deutsch, et al., in: *The Menorah*, 21 (1901), 329–66; D. Rudavsky, in: JJSO, 5 (1963), 224–44; idem, *Emancipation and Adjustment* (1967), 192–214; J. L. Blau, *Modern Varieties of Judaism* (1966), 91–95; A. Lewkowitz, *Das Judentum und die geistigen Stroemungen des 19. Jahrhunderts* (1935), 361–75; L. Ginzberg, *Students, Scholars, Saints* (1928), 195–216; I. Barzilay, *Sholomo Yehudah Rapoport (Shir) and His Contemporaries* (1969), index.

[Jo.H./Ed.]

FRANKENBURGER, WOLF (1827–1889), lawyer and politician in Germany. Born at Obbach in Bavaria and educated in Wuerzburg, he settled in Nuremberg in 1861 to practice law. Frankenburger was first elected to the Bavarian diet in 1869, and remained a member until the end of his life. From 1874 to 1878 he was also the representative for Nuremberg in the German Reichstag. The first motion he proposed in the assembly was for freedom of the press and freedom of sale of literature. Frankenburger managed to obtain the abolition of the Jewish taxes then still in force in Bavaria, and also obtained a salary increase for the poorly endowed rabbinical posts. Frankenburger was an eloquent advocate of the union of Bavaria with the German Empire.

Bibliography: A. Eckstein, *Beitraege zur Geschichte der Juden in Bayern—Die bayerischen Parliamentarier juedischen Glaubens* (1902), 23–33; E. Hamburger, *Juden im oeffentlichen Leben Deutschlands* (1968).

[B.M.A.]

FRANKENSTEIN, CARL (1905–), Israel psychologist and educator. Born in Berlin, he founded the Aid Society for Jewish Scientists, Artists, and Writers in Germany in 1928. Settling in Palestine in 1935, Frankenstein worked as probation officer of the Mandatory government until 1946. From 1948 to 1953 he was director of the Henrietta Szold Institute for Child Welfare, where he also founded and edited the education quarterly, *Megammot*. In 1951 Frankenstein began to teach at the Hebrew University first as a lecturer and later as professor of special education. He served on many government, municipal, and other public committees dealing with problems of welfare and education. In 1968 he was awarded the Israel Prize for education. He wrote books and essays in Hebrew, English, and German on depth psychology, juvenile delinquency, poverty, and impaired intelligence, including *Azuvat ha-No'ar* ("Neglected Youth," 1947), *Psychopathy* (1959), *Persoenlichkeitswandel durch Fuersorge, Erziehung und Therapie* (1964), *The Roots of the Ego* (1966), *Psychodynamics of Externalization* (1968), and *No'ar be-Shulei ha-Ḥevrah* (1970).

Bibliography: *Megammot*, 14 (1966), nos. 1–3 (articles on the occasion of Frankenstein's 60th birthday; in Hebrew, with English summaries).

[Z.L.]

FRANKFORT, HENRI (1897–1954), excavator, teacher, and author in the field of Near Eastern archaeology. Frankfort, who was born in Amsterdam, was concerned with the archaeology, culture, and religion of the entire Middle East. His wide-ranging scholarship enabled him to comprehend the ancient Near Eastern cultures in their totality, with a special awareness of their common features as well as the peculiarities of each. He participated in excavations at Tell el-Amarna, Abydos, and Armant in Egypt, and at Tell Asmar, Khafaje, and Khorsabad in Mesopotamia. From 1932 to 1938 he was also professor at the University of Amsterdam and from 1939 to 1949 he was professor at the Oriental Institute of the University of Chicago. In the last phase of his career, Frankfort produced "cultural syntheses," namely: *The Intellectual Adventure of Ancient Man, An Essay on Speculative Thought in the Ancient Near East* (with others, 1946; abridged by the elimination of the chapter on the Hebrews, republished as *Before Philosophy*, 1951); *Kingship and the Gods, A Study of Ancient Near Eastern Religion as the Integration of Society and Nature* (1948, 1955[2]); *The Birth of Civilisation in the Near East* (1951); and *The Art and Architecture of the Ancient Orient* (1954). During this phase he returned to Europe and became director of the Warburg Institute and professor of pre-classical antiquity at the University of London. Thus, Frankfort's development began with the treatment of excavated materials, progressed to classification and interpretation of Near Eastern archaeological remains (the *Cylinder Seals* . . ., 1939), and culminated in a cultural-historical-archaeological interpretation of these early civilizations.

Henri Frankfort, archaeologist. Courtesy Warburg Institute, University of London.

Bibliography: JNES, 14 (1955), includes bibliography. [P.P.K.]

FRANKFORT ON THE MAIN (Heb. פרנקפורט דמיין; abbr. פפד"מ), city in W. Germany with an ancient and important community.

Early History. Reports and legends about Jews residing in Frankfort go back to the earliest period in the city's history. Frankfort was an important trading center, and Jewish merchants probably visited its annual fall fairs. In 1074 Emperor Henry IV mentions Frankfort among the towns where the Jews of *Worms were permitted to trade without having to pay customs dues. During the 12th century Frankfort had an organized and flourishing community, though still numerically small. Financial transactions and tax payments by Frankfort Jews at that time are frequently mentioned: *Eliezer b. Nathan of Mainz makes repeated reference to the presence of Jewish merchants in Frankfort. In 1241 the Jewish houses were demolished by the populace and over three-quarters of the approximately 200 Jews of Frankfort were massacred. Among the victims were three rabbis, including the *ḥazzan;* many of the survivors accepted baptism. A special prayer for the martyrs has been retained in the liturgy for the Ninth of Av of the West German congregations. Subsequently Frederick II appointed a commission of inquiry, since the outbreak was an infringement of his imperial prerogative and interests. It apparently originated in a dispute over the forced conversion of a Jew. The city of Frankfort was ultimately granted a royal pardon. The safety of the Frankfort Jews was guaranteed and heavy penalties were ordered against Jew-baiters.

By around 1270 Frankfort had again become a busy center of Jewish life. Two Jewish tombstones dated 1284 were found under the altar of the cathedral in 1952. During the following decades all the customary Jewish institutions developed in Frankfort. The medieval community had a central synagogue ("Altschul"), a cemetery, a bathhouse, hospitals for local Jews and migrants, a "dance house" for weddings and other social events, and educational and welfare institutions. During the first half of the 14th century the financial burden on the Frankfort community, exploited by both the city and the crown, grew steadily greater, but the profit derived from the Jews protected them against the current waves of persecution. However, the surge of bloodthirsty hatred aroused by the *Black Death engulfed them along with almost all the other communities in Europe. In 1349, shortly after Emperor *Charles IV had transferred his "Jewish rights" to the city against a substantial consideration, the community was completely wiped out, many of its members setting fire to their own homes rather than meet death by the mob. In 1360 Frankfort reopened its gates to Jews. Their economic function was still vital to the flourishing city of merchants and craftsmen, proud of their political independence. However, the terms of resettlement imposed drastic changes. Jews had to apply individually for the privilege of residence, which usually had to be renewed annually in return for payment of heavy taxes and other dues. A set of statutes *(Staettigkeit)* regulated relations between the city and the community. Rabbis and communal leaders of note in the 14th century included Simeon Kayyara; Suesskind Wimpfen, who redeemed the body of *Meir b. Baruch of Rothenburg for ritual burial; and *Alexander Susslin ha-Kohen.

15th to 17th Centuries. In 1462 the Jews of Frankfort were transferred to a specially constructed street *(Judengasse)*, enclosed within walls and gates; this measure was

Der Juden zu Franckfurt Stättigkeit vñ Ordnung/
Wie dieselbe so wol von Vhralten Jahren hero/ als
hernacher biß auff das Jahr 1613. gefunden worden.

Dieser Ring
hat sich in dem Buch/
darinnen die Juden/ so Stättigkeit haben/ eingeschrieben seynd/
auff Pergament befunden/ vnd ist
vermuthlich/ daß es der Ring/ da-
von Nicolai Cardinalis Brieff/
in Cista Lit. A. N. 19. sub Anno 1452/ meldung
thut/ seye.

Getruckt zu Franckfurt am Mayn/ bey
Johann Saurn/ Anno 1614.

Titelblatt der Stättigkeit 1614.

Figure 1. Title page of the *Staettigkeit*, the statutes regulating relations between the city of Frankfort and the Jewish community, 1614. From E. Mayer, *Die Frankfurter Juden*, 1966.

Figure 2. Engraving of the plundering of the *Judengasse* of Frankfort, August 22, 1614, by G. Keller. From J. Gottfried, *Historische Chronica,* Frankfort, 1642.

put into effect only after repeated demands by the emperor and the church authorities, including the pope himself. Although existence in this ghetto entailed severe physical and social hardship to the community, its inner life developed even more intensively. There were 110 registered inhabitants of the ghetto in 1463, 250 in 1520, 900 in 1569, 1,200 in 1580, 2,200 in 1600, and about 3,000 in 1610. Since the ghetto was never permitted to expand beyond its original area, the existing houses were subdivided, and back premises and additional storeys were erected. The communal organization became stronger and more diversified. Religious and lay leaders *(Hochmeister* and *Baumeister)* were elected by the Jewish taxpayers, and a continual flow of *takkanot* laid the basis for powerful and jealously guarded local traditions in all spheres of religious, social, and economic life. Outstanding among the rabbis of the 15th century was Nathan *Epstein. Johannes *Pfefferkorn confiscated some 1,500 Hebrew books from Frankfort Jews. The Peasants' War and religious wars of the 16th century repeatedly endangered the community, and the guilds made serious inroads into their economic activities. Nevertheless, conditions were favorable to commercial enterprise, and by means of heavy financial contributions and skillful diplomacy the Frankfort Jews managed to safeguard their privileges. By the end of the 16th century the community reached a peak period of prosperity. It had become a center of Jewish learning, and students from far away flocked to the yeshivot of Eliezer *Treves and Akiva b. Jacob *Frankfurter. The Frankfort rabbinate and rabbinical court had become one of the foremost religious authorities in Germany. Decisions were made by the presiding rabbi in conjunction with the "members of the yeshivah" *(dayyanim).* General rabbinical *synods were held at Frankfort in 1562, 1582, and 1603.

However, economic and social antagonisms had long been simmering between the wealthy patrician families of the city and the guild craftsmen and petty traders, many of whom were in debt to Jews. The struggle flared into open rebellion when in 1614 the rabble, led by Vincent *Fettmilch, stormed the ghetto and gave vent to their anger by plundering the Jewish houses. The Jews were all expelled from the city, but the emperor outlawed the rebels, and their leaders were arrested and put to death (1616). Subsequently the Jews were ceremoniously returned to the ghetto, an event annually commemorated on Adar 20th by the Frankfort community as the "Purim Winz" ("Purim of Vincent"). Possibly a group of wealthy Frankfort Jews, among them Simeon Wolf, father of the celebrated Court Jew Samuel *Oppenheimer, used their influence at the imperial court to bring about this result. Among those who did not return to Frankfort after the Fettmilch rebellion was Isaiah *Horowitz, the celebrated author of *Shenei Luḥot ha-Berit,* who had occupied the rabbinate from 1606. Other leading rabbis of the period included his son Shabbetai *Horowitz, Ḥayyim Cohen, grandson of *Judah Loew (the Maharal) of Prague, and Meir b. Jacob ha-Kohen *Schiff, a native of Frankfort. Joseph Yuspa *Hahn recorded the ritual customs of the Frankfort community in his *Yosif Omeẓ.* These were a source of special pride to the Frankfort Jews, known for their local patriotism. Joseph Solomon *Delmedigo was for some years employed as communal physician. Aaron Samuel *Koidanover and his son Ẓevi Hirsh *Koidanover were also members of the Frankfort rabbinate. The community did not grow numerically during the 17th century owing to the unhealthy conditions of their overpopulated quarter and the excessive taxes imposed upon them during the Thirty Years' War. In addition, the terms of residence were designed to keep their number stationary, allowing a maximum of 500 families and 12 marriage licenses annually. At the end of the 17th century the community made successful efforts to prevent Johann *Eisenmenger from publishing his anti-Jewish book.

Figure 3. Frankfort Jewish costume, early 18th-century etching by C. Weigel. From A.A.S. Clara, *Neu Eroeffnete Welt-Gallerie,* Nuremberg 1703. Photo John R. Friedman, London.

18th Century. In 1711 almost the entire Jewish quarter was destroyed by a fire which broke out in the house of the chief rabbi, *Naphtali b. Isaac ha-Kohen. The inhabitants found refuge in gentile homes, but had to return to the ghetto after it had been rebuilt. J. J. *Schudt gave a detailed account of Jewish life at Frankfort in this period. The penetration of Enlightenment found the community in a state of unrest and social strife. Communal life had long been dominated by a few ancient patrician families, some of whom were known by signs hanging outside their houses, like the *Rothschild ("Red Shield"), Schwarzschild, *Kann, and *Schiff families. The impoverished majority challenged the traditional privileges of the wealthy oligarchy, and the city council repeatedly acted as arbitrator between the rival parties. Controversies on religious and personal matters such as the *Eybeschuetz-*Emden dispute further weakened unity in the community. Nevertheless, there was no decline in intellectual activity, and the yeshivot of Samuel Schotten and Jacob Joshua b. Ẓevi Hirsch *Falk attracted many students. The movement for the reformation of Jewish education fostered by the circle of Moses *Mendelssohn in Berlin found many sympathizers in Frankfort, especially among the well-to-do class who welcomed it as a step toward *emancipation. Forty-nine prominent members of the community subscribed for Mendelssohn's German translation of the Bible (1782), but the chief rabbi, Phinehas *Horowitz, attacked the book from the pulpit. When in 1797 a project was advocated for a school with an extensive program of secular studies, Horowitz pronounced a ban on it. He was supported by most of the communal leaders, though many had their children taught non-Jewish subjects privately. The ban had to be withdrawn by order of the magistrate. Some years previously, Horowitz had acted similarly against the kabbalist Nathan *Adler. Meanwhile the French revolutionary wars had made their first liberating impact on Frankfort Jewry. In 1796 a bombardment destroyed the greater part of the ghetto, and in 1798 the prohibition on leaving the ghetto on Sundays and holidays was abolished.

19th and 20th Centuries. The incorporation of Frankfort in Napoleon's Confederation of the Rhine (1806) and the constitution of the grand duchy of Frankfort (1810) gradually changed the status of the Frankfort Jews, bringing them nearer emancipation. In 1811 the ghetto was finally abolished, and a declaration of equal rights for all citizens expressly included the Jews, a capital payment of 440,000 florins having been made by the community. However, the reaction following Napoleon's downfall brought bitter disappointment. The senate of the newly constituted Free City tried to abolish Jewish emancipation and thwarted the efforts made by a community delegation to the Congress of *Vienna. After prolonged negotiations, marked by the *"Hep-Hep" anti-Jewish disorders in 1819, the senate finally promulgated an enactment granting equality to the Jews in all civil matters, although reinstating many of the old discriminatory laws (1824). The composition and activities of the community board remained subject to supervision and confirmation by the senate. Meanwhile the religious rift in the community had widened considerably. Phinehas Horowitz's son and successor, Ẓevi Hirsch *Horowitz, was powerless in face of the increasing pressure for social and educational reforms. He did in fact renew his father's approbation of Benjamin Wolf *Heidenheim's edition of the prayer book which included a German translation and a learned commentary. However, this first stirring of *Wissenschaft des Judentums could not satisfy those in the community desiring reform and assimilation. In 1804 they founded a school, the Philanthropin, with a markedly secular and assimilationist program. This institution became a major center for reform in Judaism. From 1807 it organized reformed Jewish services for the pupils and their parents. In the same year a Jewish lodge of *Freemasons was established, whose members actively furthered the causes of reform and secularization in the community. From 1817 to 1832 the board of the community was exclusively composed of members of the lodge. In 1819 the Orthodox *ḥeder* institutions were closed by the police, and the board prevented the establishment of a school for both religious and general studies. Attendance at the yeshivah, which in 1793 still had 60 students, dwindled. In 1842 the number of Orthodox families was estimated to account for less than 10% of the community. In that year, a Reform Association demanded the abolition of all "talmudic" laws, circumcision, and the messianic faith. The aged rabbi, Solomon Abraham Trier, who had been one of the two delegates from Frankfort to the Paris *Sanhedrin in 1807, published a collection of responsa from contemporary rabbis and scholars in German on the fundamental significance of circumcision in Judaism (1844). A year later a conference of rabbis sympathizing with reform was held in Frankfort. A leading member of this group was Abraham *Geiger, a native of Frankfort, and communal rabbi from 1863 to 1870. The revolutionary movement of 1848 hastened the emancipation of the Frankfort Jews, which was finally achieved in 1864. The autocratic regime of the community board weakened considerably. A small group of Orthodox members then seized the opportunity to form a religious association within the community, the "Israelitische Religionsgesellschaft," and elected Samson Raphael *Hirsch as their rabbi in 1851. The Rothschild family made a large donation toward the erection of a new Orthodox synagogue. When the community board persisted in turning a deaf ear to the demands of the Orthodox minority, the association seceded from the community and set up a separate congregation (1876). After some Orthodox members, supported by the Wuerzburg rabbi, Seligmann Baer *Bamberger, had refused to take this course, the community board made certain concessions, enabling them to remain within the community. A communal Orthodox rabbi, Marcus *Horovitz, was installed and a new Orthodox synagogue was erected with communal funds. From then on the Frankfort Orthodox community, its pattern of life and educational institutions, became the paradigm of German *Orthodoxy. The Jewish population of Frankfort

Figure 4. Bronze medal commemorating the 100th anniversary of the Philanthropin, the Jewish high school founded in 1804. New York, Dan Friedenberg Collection.

Figure 5. Drawing of the synagogue on the Boernestrasse, built in 1855–60 and burned down in 1938. Courtesy Frankfort Historical Museum.

numbered 3,298 in 1817 (7.9% of the total), 10, 009 in 1871 (11%), 21,974 in 1900 (7.5%), and 29,385 in 1925 (6.3%). During the 19th century many Jews from the rural districts were attracted to the city whose economic boom owed much to Jewish financial and commercial enterprise. The comparative wealth of the Frankfort Jews is shown by the fact that, in 1900, 5,946 Jewish citizens paid 2,540,812 marks in taxes, while 34,900 non-Jews paid 3,611,815 marks. Many civic institutions, including hospitals, libraries and museums, were established by Jewish donations, especially from the Rothschild family. The Jew Leopold *Sonnemann was the founder of the liberal daily *Frankfurter Zeitung,* and the establishment of the Frankfort university (1912) was also largely financed by Jews. Jewish communal institutions and organizations included two hospitals, three schools (the Philanthropin and the elementary and secondary schools founded by S. R. Hirsch), a yeshivah (founded by Hirsch's son-in-law and successor Solomon *Breuer), religious classes for pupils attending city schools, an orphanage, a home for the aged, many welfare institutions, and two cemeteries (the ancient cemetery was closed in 1828). Frankfort Jews were active in voluntary societies devoted to universal Jewish causes, such as emigrant relief and financial support for the Jews in the Holy Land (donations from Western Europe to the Holy Land had been channeled through Frankfort from the 16th century). The yearbook of the Juedisch-Literarische Gesellschaft was published in Frankfort, and the Orthodox weekly *Der Israelit* (founded in 1860) was published in Frankfort from 1906. The Jewish department of the municipal library, headed before World War II by the scholar A. *Freimann, had a rare collection of Hebraica and Judaica. During the first decade of the 20th century additional synagogues were erected, among them a splendid one situated at Friedberger Anlage. In 1920 Franz *Rosenzweig set up an institute for Jewish studies, where Martin *Buber, then professor at the Frankfort university, gave popular lectures. Two additional yeshivot were established, one by Jacob *Hoffmann, who in 1922 succeeded Nehemiah Anton *Nobel in the Orthodox rabbinate of the community. Others prominent in Frankfort Jewish life include the writer Ludwig *Boerne; the historian I. M. *Jost; the artists Moritz *Oppenheim and Benno *Elkan; the biochemist Paul *Ehrlich; the economist and sociologist Franz *Oppenheimer; rabbis Jacob *Horowitz and Joseph *Horowitz (Orthodox); Leopold Stein, Nehemiah Bruell, Caesar *Seligmann (Reform); and the Orthodox leaders Jacob *Rosenheim and Isaac *Breuer. [M.BRE.]

Holocaust Period. Nazi action against the Jews began on April 1, 1933, with a boycott of Jewish businesses and professionals, followed on April 7 by the dismissal of Jewish white-collar workers, university teachers, actors, and musicians. State and party pressure subsequently resulted in the closing or "aryanization" of almost all Jewish-owned firms, while local S.A. units and Nazi students terrorized Jewish citizens. Though originally prohibited, these arbitrary actions were in later years legalized by the Reich government which helped to organize and coordinate them. The Jewish community reacted by expanding existing services, establishing new agencies for economic aid, reemployment, occupational training, schooling, adult education, and emigration. All institutions were under strict surveillance by the Gestapo.

On Nov. 10–11, 1938, the big synagogues of the two Jewish communities, situated at Friedberger Anlage, Dominikanerplatz (formerly Boerneplatz), Am Grossem Wohlgraben (formerly Boernestrasse), and Freiherr-vom-Steinstrasse were burned down. Community buildings, Jewish homes, and stores were stormed and looted by the S.A., the S.S., and mobs they had incited. Hundreds of Jewish men were arrested and sent to *Buchenwald and *Dachau concentration camps. Members of the Orthodox Religionsgesellschaft were compelled to combine with the general community to form a single community organization which the Nazis named Juedische Gemeinde. In 1939 this autonomous community was forcibly merged into the state-supervised Reichsvereinigung. Jewish leaders were compelled to enter into Judenvertraege, transferring communal property to municipal ownership. Welfare foundations taken over by the municipal authorities in December 1938 were placed under direct Gestapo control in May 1940. Gestapo Officer Holland, who was also a city official, supervised Jewish welfare and emigration, later organizing labor recruitment and "orderly proceedings" before deportation.

Figure 6. The synagogue at the Boerneplatz, consecrated in 1882. Israel Museum Archives, Jerusalem.

The Frankfort community decreased by emigration from 26,158 in 1933, to 10,803 in June 1941, although there was an influx of Jewish families from the countryside. Deportations to Lodz began on October 19, 1941, and were followed by deportations to *Minsk, *Riga, *Theresienstadt, and other camps. In September 1943, after large-scale deportations stopped, the Jewish population in Frankfort totaled 602, including half-Jews. [E.S-O.]

After World War II. After the war, a new community was organized, consisting of those who had outlived the war in Frankfort, survivors from concentration camps, and displaced persons, totaling 1,104 in 1952. They were joined by a number of pensioners and Israelis, and the community increased to 2,566 by 1959 and 4,350 by 1970, to become the largest in West Germany (excepting that of Berlin); the average age of its members was 45.4, and two thirds were aged over 40. One of the large synagogues was rebuilt, and by 1970 five prayer rooms were also in use. The first postwar Jewish elementary school in Germany was opened there in 1965, and a communal periodical *Frankfurter juedisches Gemeindeblatt* commenced publication in March 1968. A 200-bed home for the aged was opened in 1968. The Frankfort municipal library contains the largest collection of Judaica in Germany (about 25,000 volumes and 325 Mss.). The ancient *Memorbuch of the community was presented to the Jewish National Library in Jerusalem in 1965. [H.W.]

Printing. The book fairs of Frankfort were visited by Jewish printers and booksellers as early as 1535. Some Hebrew printing was carried on in Frankfort as early as the 16th century; in 1512 the brothers Murner published "Grace after Meals." Hebrew printing seriously developed in Frankfort in the 17th century. The earliest work, *Megillat Vinẓenẓ* (Fettmilch), was published by Isaac Langenbuch after the Fettmilch riots (see above). From 1657 to 1707 Balthasar Christian Wust and later his son (?) Johann issued a great number of Hebrew books. For this part of their work they employed Jewish printers and other Jewish personnel, and found Jewish financial backing. (As Jews could not obtain printing licenses, they used Christian firms as a front.) They printed mainly liturgical items, but also a Pentateuch with a German glossary (1662), and bibles (1677, 1694); and Wallich's Yiddish *Kuhbuch* (1672). Several other Hebrew printers published books in the late 17th and early 18th centuries. An important publisher was Johann Koellner, who in 20 years of printing was responsible for about half of the books issued in Frankfort. Among his more important publications were the *Arba'ah Turim* (5 vols., 1712–16), and an excellent Talmud edition (1770–23). Soon after the completion of the latter, the whole edition was confiscated and was only released 30 years later. In the first half of the 19th century the names of seven non-Jewish printing houses are known. Subsequently Jewish printers emerged for the first time. Among them were J. H. Golda (1881–1920), E. Slobotzki (from 1855), and the bookseller J. Kauffmann, who took over the *Roedelheim press of M. Lehrberger in 1899. Hebrew printers were active in places like *Homburg, *Offenbach, *Sulzbach, Roedelheim, and others in the neighborhood of Frankfort, because Jewish printers were unable to establish themselves in Frankfort. [Ed.]

Figure 7. The remains of the Boerneplatz synagogue, after its destruction on *Kristallnacht,* November 1938. Israel Museum Archives, Jerusalem.

Music. The liturgical music and *ḥazzanut of the Frankfort community represent the archtype of the western Ashkenazi tradition. It can be traced to the 15th-century codifier Jacob *Moellin (Maharil), and is marked by an adherence to tradition which made any deviation from the customary melodies (some of which were credited with divine origin, "*mi-Sinai*") a religious offense. Thus the principal qualification required of cantors was a precise acquaintance with the details of musical custom *(minhag).* Liturgical poems *(piyyutim)* had a place of prime importance, especially as some of them were linked with the history of the community, and little scope was given to the cantor's capacity for musical invention or improvization. When at the beginning of the 16th century, the Sabbath hymn *Lekhah Dodi* came into vogue in many communities, it caused sharp controversy among Frankfort Jews, and though finally accepted, it had to be chanted for many years by an assistant cantor in order to stress its non-compulsory character. Every special event in the Jewish year was marked by a festive, solemn, or plaintive tune, as the occasion demanded. Every month and every festival had an appropriate melody of its own, which was intoned by the cantor at the Blessing of the New Moon. Thus the liturgical music served as a "musical calendar." When a festival or New Moon fell on a Sabbath, the cantor had to give each its musical share *("me-inyono").* This was achieved mainly by mingling variants of the Kaddish melodies, of which there existed more than 25. On Simḥat Torah the "Year's Kaddish" recapitulated the whole range of the "musical calendar." Great stress was laid on correct reading and cantillation of the Bible, and many verses of special importance were chanted to particularly solemn tunes. In spite of the strict traditionalism, many Frankfort melodies show the influence of German folksong; the one employed for the *Priestly blessing on the High Holidays is derived from the popular Frankfort "Fassbaenderlied" (Coopers' song). The melody sung in the synagogue on the annual celebration of Purim Winz (see above) was derived from the march tune of the military escort that led the Jews back to the Frankfort ghetto after the riots of 1616. In the 19th century the Reform movement installed an organ in the main Frankfort synagogue, whereupon the Orthodox congregation introduced a male choir in their own synagogue with I. M. *Japhet as musical director. [M.Bre.]

Bibliography: History: I. Kracauer, *Geschichte der Juden in Frankfurt a. M.,* 2 vols. (1925–27); A. Freimann and F. Kracauer, *Frankfort* (Eng., 1929); H. Schwab, *Memories of Frankfort* (1955); M. Horovitz, *Frankfurter Rabbinen,* 4 vols. (1882–85); J. Rosenheim, *Zikhronot* (1955), 9–111; T. Oelsner, in: *YIVO Bleter,* 20 (1942), 223–42; N. N. Glatzer, in: YLBI, 1 (1956), 105–22; A. Galliner, *ibid.,* 3 (1958), 169–86; Wiener Library, London, *German Jewry* (1958), index; E. Mayer, *Frankfurter Juden* (1966); Germ Jud, index; D. Andernacht and E. Sterling (eds.), *Dokumente zur Geschichte der Frankfurter Juden* (1963); D. Andernacht (ed.), *Das Philanthropin zur Frankfurt am Main* (1964); HJ, 10 (1948), 99–146; J. Katz, *Freemasons and Jews* (1970), index; M. Eliav, *Ha-Ḥinnukh ha-Yehudi be-Germanyah bi-Ymei ha-Haskalah ve-ha-Emanẓipaẓyah* (1960). Holocaust: PK Germanyah; P. Friedman (ed.), *Bibliografyah shel ha-Sefarim ha-Ivriyyim al ha-Sho'ah ve-al ha-Gevurah* (1960), index; N. Bentwich, in: *AJR Information,* 25 (Aug. 1970), 8. Printing: B. Friedberg, *Ha-Defus ha-Ivri be-Merkaz Eiropah* . . . (1935); 62ff. Music: I. M. Japhet, *Schirei Jeschurun* (1922[4]); S. Z. Geiger, *Divrei Kehillot* (1862); S. Scheuermann, *Die gottesdienstlichen Gesaenge der Israeliten fuer das ganze Jahr* (1912); F. Ogutsch, *Der Frankfurter Kantor* (1930).

FRANKFORT ON THE ODER, city in Brandenburg, E. Germany. Jews were living in Frankfort before 1294, when a dispute between Jews and the slaughterers' guild there was settled. The Jews were not permitted to own houses, and lived in rented dwellings, referred to as *Judenbuden.* They mainly engaged in small trading and moneylending. In 1399

Printer's mark from Frankfort on the Oder, showing a panorama of the city. Woodcut from a Pentateuch published in 1746. From A. Yaari, *Emblems of Hebrew Printers*, Jerusalem, 1943.

the community relinquished its cemetery for a larger one. From the second half of the 15th century the local merchants made continual complaints about economic competition by the Jews and the rate of interest they charged. In 1506 the synagogue was demolished and the new university was erected on the site. The Jews of Frankfort were expelled with the rest of *Brandenburg Jewry in 1510. They later returned, and in 1564 there were nine Jewish familes living in Frankfort, and 11 in 1567. They were again expelled in 1573. When a number of Jews were admitted to Brandenburg in 1671, a new community grew up in Frankfort. The university there was the first in Germany to admit Jews. The first two Jewish students registered at the faculty of medicine in 1678, and others followed from all over Europe and even Jerusalem. Between 1739 and 1810 about 130 Jews studied there, and between 1721 and 1794, 29 graduated in medicine. The community numbered 592 in 1801; 399 in 1817; around 800 in the 1840s; and 891 in 1880. Subsequently it declined to 747 around 1900; 669 in 1925; and 586 in 1933.

In the 18th century many Jews from Poland attended the fairs in Frankfort. In 1763 a conference of Polish rabbis headed by Gershon of Frankfort settled a dispute between the printing houses of Amsterdam and Sulzbach concerning the publication of the Talmud.

Following the spread of the *Reform movement in the first half of the 19th century, the Orthodox members in Frankfort seceded from the liberals and opened a prayer hall of their own. Samuel *Holdheim served as rabbi in Frankfort from 1836 to 1840. In 1861 the first society for the colonization of Ereẓ Israel was founded in Frankfort by Ḥayyim *Lorje. The scholar Judah *Bergmann officiated as rabbi there at the beginning of the 20th century, and the leader of liberal Judaism in Germany, Ignaz *Maybaum, was rabbi of the community between 1928 and 1936. In 1933 the community had a synagogue, a cemetery, three charitable societies, local chapters of the "Reichsbund Juedischer Frontsoldaten" and a *B'nai B'rith lodge. The Orthodox members rejoined the main community in 1934.

Under the Nazis the Frankfort Jews suffered the same fate as those in the rest of Germany. Rabbi Maybaum was arrested and confined to the notorious Colombia prison in Berlin; later the charges against him were suspended. There were 168 Jews living in Frankfort in 1939. Most were deported before the outbreak of World War II and eventually transported to Lublin Reservation. Twenty-four Jews from Frankfort were deported to *Theresienstadt on Aug. 27, 1942, and three on June 16, 1943. After the war a new community was organized. It had about 200 members in 1958, whose number subsequently declined.

Printing. The earliest Hebrew book printed in Frankfort on the Oder was a Pentateuch printed by J. and F. Hartman in 1595. Eighty years later J. C. Beckman, professor of theology at the local university, obtained a license to extend the privilege to print in Hebrew, and a Pentateuch with *haftarot* and the Five Scrolls, as well as other books, were published in 1677.

The most important work published there was a new edition of the Talmud (1697–99). The Court Jew Berend *Lehmann of Halberstadt invested in it and presented a large number of the 2,000 sets printed to various communities, *battei midrash*, and yeshivot. Further editions were printed in 1715–22 and 1736–39. Michael Gottschalk succeeded Beckman as manager and before 1740 Professor Grillo bought Gottschalk's press. It continued in his family until the end of the century, and in the hands of his successor, C. F. Elsner, until 1813. Grillos' turnover in trade of Hebrew books reached 80,000 Reichsthaler annually—a measure of the importance of the press for Germany and Eastern Europe. The main midrashim, *Yalkut Shimoni*, the Zohar, and other important rabbinic works were printed in Frankfort on the Oder. As the result of the Prussian legislation of 1812, it was possible in 1813 for Hirsch Baschwitz, a Jew, to acquire the Hebrew printing press from Elsner. In turn, he sold the business in 1826 to Trebitsch & Son of Berlin.

Bibliography: Germ Jud, 2 (1968), 251–2; FJW (1932), 65; A. Ackermann, *Geschichte der Juden in Brandenburg* (1906), 66, 70, 79, 80; S. L. Zitron, in: *Der Jude*, 2 (1917–18), 347–53, 670–7; L. Davidsohn, *Beitraege zur Sozial- und Wirtschaftsgeschichte der Berliner Juden vor der Emanzipation* (1920), 19, 39, 45, 46, 48; L. Lewin, in: JJLG, 14 (1921), 43–85, 217–38; 15 (1923), 59–96; 16 (1924), 43–85; idem, *Die Landessynode der grosspolnischen Judenschaft* (1926), 12, 14, 43, 49, 64; G. Kisch, in: *Juedische Familienforschung*, 10 (1934), 566–74, 598–602; B. Brilling, in: MGWJ, 80 (1936), 262–76; idem, in: SBB, 1 (1953–54), 84–94, 145–56, 183–96; 2 (1955–56), 79–96, 102–6; 8 (1966), 25–37; idem, in: *Archiv fuer Geschichte des Buchwesens*, 1 (1956), 325–30; idem, in: *Boersenblatt fuer den deutschen Buchhandel*, 13 (1957), 1537–48; S. Stern, *Der Preussische Staat und die Juden*, 2 (1962), Akten no. 1, 27, 43, 44, 142, 145, 149; PK Germanyah. [C.T.]

FRANKFURTER, DAVID (1909–), student of medicine who shot a Nazi official in protest against the persecution of Jews under the Nazi regime. The son of a rabbi, Frankfurter was born in Daruvar, Croatia (Yugoslavia). While studying in Germany, he witnessed the Nazi advent to power and the initiation of anti-Jewish measures. He left Germany and continued his studies in Switzerland. On Feb. 4, 1936, he shot and killed Wilhelm Gustloff, the leader of the Swiss branch of the Nazi party. A local court sentenced him to 18 years imprisonment, of which he served nearly nine. He was pardoned after the Nazi defeat but was banished forever from Switzerland. He settled in Israel and published a book about his experience, *Nakam* ("Vengeance," 1948). In 1969 the banishment order was rescinded and Frankfurter visited Switzerland. In Israel he worked for the Ministry of Defense.

Bibliography: E. Ludwig, *Davos Murder* (1937). [Y.Re.]

FRANKFURTER, FELIX (1882–1965), U.S. jurist. Frankfurter, who was born in Vienna, was taken to the United States at the age of 12. His parents settled on the Lower East Side of New York, where his father, scion of a long line of rabbis, was a modest tradesman.

Early Years. Frankfurter graduated with distinction from the College of the City of New York in 1902; his real education, however, as he liked to recount, was derived from the books and newspapers that he devoured at the Public Library, Cooper Union, and the coffee shops of the city. Throughout his life he had a compulsive passion for reading, and he regularly scanned the newspapers of several continents. These he absorbed in no merely passive spirit; he came to have a wide acquaintance among journalists and publishers, and frequently he would pepper them with notes of compliment or rebuke. At Harvard Law School, from which he received his degree in 1906, Frankfurter developed his deep, indeed reverent, attachment to the values of the Anglo-American system of government under law, and as the leading student in his class found new horizons of achievement opened to him. On the recommendation of

Dean Ames of Harvard Law School, he was invited by Henry L. Stimson, then United States Attorney in New York, to become an assistant in that office. Henceforth his professional life was divided between public service and teaching. The association with Stimson was one of the most significant experiences in Frankfurter's life, constituting living proof for him that the effective enforcement of the criminal law need not compromise the scrupulous standards of procedural decency that are encompassed in the guarantee of due process of law. When Stimson was appointed secretary of war in the administration of President Taft, Frankfurter became his personal assistant, with special responsibility for the legal affairs of overseas territories of the United States and the conservation of water resources. At this time his friendship began with Justice Oliver Wendell Holmes of the Supreme Court, which became a deep intellectual discipleship despite their disparity in background and temperament. Frankfurter admired not merely the style of Holmes—learning worn with grace—but his fastidiousness of mind and disinterestedness of judgment; and they shared an ardent love of country, instilled in the one by arduous service in the Civil War, in the other by the experience of seeing the vistas of opportunity opened to a gifted immigrant boy.

Professor and Public Servant. In 1914 Frankfurter accepted an appointment to a professorship at Harvard Law School, which he held until his appointment to the Supreme Court 25 years later. As a teacher and scholar he concentrated on the procedural aspects of law—the administration of criminal justice, the jurisdiction of the federal courts, the process of administrative tribunals, and the ill-starred use of the injunction in labor disputes. He earned a reputation as a radical reformer, but his concern was for the integrity of the law's processes, upon which a reasoned approach to the maintenance of a just society depended. Misunderstanding of his concern—its mistaken identification with the particular causes that motivated the victims of injustice—led some observers to conclude that Frankfurter was a radical who became a conservative on the bench. During World War I Frankfurter was called to Washington as legal officer of the President's Mediation Commission, charged with investigating and resolving serious labor disturbances. In that capacity he inquired into the vigilante action against strikers in the Arizona copper mines, finding that the companies' refusal to accept unionism was the root cause of the troubles, and he investigated the conviction of Tom Mooney on a bombing charge in California, finding that the trial had been vitiated by improper tactics of the prosecution. These were a forerunner of Frankfurter's involvement in the Sacco-Vanzetti murder case in Boston, the most bitter experience in his life, in which he fought unsuccessfully to have the verdict set aside on grounds of prejudicial conduct by the trial judge and prosecuting attorney, and thereby provoked against himself the burning hostility of the entrenched interests in the community. He was one of the founders of the American Civil Liberties Union, a legal adviser to the National Association for the Advancement of Colored People, and counsel to the National Consumers' League.

Zionist. Frankfurter became closely associated with Louis D. *Brandeis, who practiced law in Boston until his appointment to the Supreme Court in 1916. This association brought Frankfurter deeply into the Zionist movement, and in 1919 he went to Paris with the Zionist delegation to the peace conference. Through T. E. Lawrence he met Emir Feisal, head of the Arab delegation, and in consequence of their talks he received from Feisal the historic letter of February 3, 1919, stating that the Arab delegation regarded the Zionist proposal as "moderate and

Felix Frankfurter, U.S. Supreme Court Justice. Zionist Archives and Library, New York.

proper," that they "will wish the Jews a most hearty welcome home," and that the "two movements complete one another" and "neither can be a real success without the other." In 1921 Frankfurter withdrew from formal participation in the Zionist movement, when the Brandeis-Mack-Szold group seceded over issues of organization and fiscal autonomy for American Zionism. Thereafter, nevertheless, he maintained his active interest in the upbuilding of the Jewish national home in Palestine, and in 1931, disturbed by the tendency of Britain to shirk its responsibility as the mandatory power, he published a notable and much-cited critical article in *Foreign Affairs* (9 (1931), 409–34), entitled "The Palestine Situation Restated." Despite the break with the formal Zionist organization, his relations with Weizmann remained cordial.

In Politics. In politics Frankfurter was more concerned with men and policies than with party labels. He served under Stimson in a Republican administration, was an admirer of Theodore Roosevelt, and in 1924 supported Robert M. LaFollette, the Progressive third-party candidate, for the presidency. In 1928 he campaigned for Alfred E. Smith, to whom he had been an informal adviser on problems of public-utility regulation when Smith was governor of New York. In 1932, quite predictably, he warmly supported Franklin D. Roosevelt. Roosevelt, as assistant secretary of the Navy, served with Frankfurter on an interdepartmental board concerned with wartime labor relations. When Roosevelt became governor of New York, he called on Frankfurter for counsel, and upon his election as president, Roosevelt asked Frankfurter to become solicitor general, intimating that if he held this post it would be easier to appoint him in due course to the Supreme Court. Frankfurter declined, however, on the ground that he could be more useful to the President's program without an official place in the administration. He continued to teach at Harvard while advising Roosevelt on certain appointments and lending a hand in speech writing and in the drafting of legislation, notably in relation to the regulation of securities and the stock exchange. When, in 1938, Justice Benjamin N. *Cardozo died, there was widespread sentiment that by virtue of intellect and philosophy—not for reasons of religion—Frankfurter was the rightful successor to this chair, which had been occupied before Cardozo by Justice Holmes. Disregarding the advice of some timorous Jewish friends who pointed to the fact that Justice Brandeis was still on the Court, Roosevelt made the nomination, which was confirmed on January 17, 1939.

Supreme Court Justice. Upon assuming judicial office, Frankfurter's roving commission in law and public affairs was ended, but the gravity of the world situation made it impossible for him to become a judicial recluse. He had recognized the menace of Hitler before most of his compatriots, and when war came, his insight, experience, and judgment were drawn upon. Perhaps his most notable service in this regard was his recommendation of his old mentor, Henry L. Stimson, to be secretary of war. As a judge Frankfurter conceived his role to be more complex than that of a teacher or publicist, since a judge on the Supreme Court must subordinate his merely personal views when judging the validity of the acts of a coordinate branch of government. He rejected the claims of absolutism for even the most cherished liberties of speech, assembly, and religious belief, maintaining that they must be weighed against the legitimate concerns of society expressed through government. When those concerns were relatively tenuous or could be satisfied in a less intrusive way, the liberty of the individual must prevail. Thus when a state attorney general conducted an investigation into the teaching of a college lecturer, Frankfurter wrote a powerful opinion upholding the sanctity of the university classroom against the threat of domination by the state (*Sweezy v. New Hampshire,* 354 U.S. 234 (1957)). When a school board introduced released-time instruction in religion in the public schools, on a voluntary basis, Frankfurter joined in condemning the program as a breach of the "wall of separation" between church and state (*McCollum v. Board of Education,* 333 U.S. 203 (1948)). But when a compulsory flag-salute exercise in the public schools was resisted by Jehovah's Witnesses as a profanation of their religious tenets, Frankfurter concluded that the government had not gone beyond permissible bounds in seeking to inculcate loyalty and national pride in schoolchildren (*West Virginia State Board of Education* v. *Barnette,* 319 U.S. 624 (1943)). His dissenting opinion begins with his most explicit and deeply felt statement of his judicial philosophy in the troubled area of individual freedom:

> One who belongs to the most vilified and persecuted minority in history is not likely to be insensible to the freedom guaranteed by our Constitution. Were my purely personal attitude relevant I should wholeheartedly associate myself with the general libertarian views in the Court's opinion, representing as they do the thought and action of a lifetime.
>
> But as judges we are neither Jew nor gentile, neither Catholic nor agnostic. We owe equal attachment to the Constitution and are equally bound by our judicial obligations whether we derive our citizenship from the earliest or the latest immigrants to these shores. As a member of this Court I am not justified in writing my private notions of policy into the Constitution, no matter how deeply I may cherish them or how mischievous I may deem their disregard. . . . The only opinion of our own even looking in that direction that is material is our opinion whether legislators could in reason have enacted such a law.

He joined wholeheartedly in the decisions holding legally segregated public schools to be a denial of equal protection of the laws (*Cooper* v. *Aaron,* 358 U.S. 1 (1958)). But in another pathbreaking action of the Court, upsetting malapportionment in legislatures, he dissented vigorously, on the ground that the courts were entering a "political thicket" that would enmesh them in party politics (*Baker* v. *Carr,* 369 U.S. 186 (1962)).

Retrospect. In 1962 Frankfurter suffered a stroke, and resigned from the Court. Though invalided, he was able the following year to receive the Presidential Medal of Freedom, the highest civilian honor within the bestowal of the President. The citation read: "Jurist, scholar, counselor, conversationalist, he has brought to all his roles a zest and a wisdom which has made him teacher to his time." The citation suggested the many-sided liveliness of the man, but could not capture the full measure of what he liked to call the Blue Danube side of his nature: the bouncy step, the love of argumentation, the steely grip on his interlocutor's elbow, the roars of laughter, what Dean Acheson called affectionately the "general noisiness" of the man. Nor could the citation capture his astonishing range of friendships, which embraced statesmen, scholars, artists, former students, and writers around the world. His correspondence was prodigious. He was refreshed by uninhibited communication as others are refreshed by solitude. Although not an observing Jew ("a believing unbeliever," he called himself), he retained a familiarity with Jewish lore, and toward the end of his life he felt drawn closer to his heritage.

Writings. Frankfurter's own talk and writings of interest to the general reader include: *Felix Frankfurter Reminisces* (1960); *Law and Politics* (1939); *Of Law and Men* (1956); *Of Law and Life* (1965); *Roosevelt and Frankfurter; their Correspondence 1928–1945; Felix Frankfurter on the Supreme Court* (1970).

Bibliography: H. S. Thomas, *Felix Frankfurter: Scholar on the Bench* (1960); L. Baker, *Felix Frankfurter* (1969); W. Mendelson (ed.), *Felix Frankfurter: A Tribute* (1964); idem, *Felix Frankfurter: The Judge* (1964); Jaffe, in: *Harvard Law Review,* 62 (1949), 357–412; P. A. Freund, *On Law and Justice* (1968), 146–62; For further bibliography see R. Dahl and C. Bolden (eds.), *American Judge* (1968), nos. 4274–92 and 6366–437; P. B. Kurland, *Felix Frankfurter on the Supreme Court* (1970).

[P.A.F.]

FRANKFURTER, MOSES (1672–1762), author, *dayyan,* and printer in Amsterdam. Moses, the son of Simeon, established a printing press in 1721 from which he issued books both in Hebrew and Yiddish. He later moved to Frankfort where he died. Frankfurter wrote *Nefesh Yehudah* (1701), a commentary on Isaac Aboab's *Menorat ha-Ma'or* with a Yiddish translation of the text. This very popular tract was often reprinted, as was *Sheva Petilot* (1721), an abbreviated version of the same work. Frankfurter translated into Yiddish and published his father's *Sefer ha-Ḥayyim* (1712). From it he compiled *Sha'ar Shimon* (1714), prayers for the sick, in two parts, the second in Yiddish. He also wrote *Zeh Yenaḥamenu* (1712), a commentary on the *Mekhilta de-R. Ishmael.* When Frankfurter was in serious distress he sought comfort in dedicating himself to the laborious task of correcting the text and commenting upon it; *Tov Lekhet,* notes to the law of mourning of the Shulḥan Arukh, *Yoreh De'ah* (1746); *Ba'er Heitev,* glosses to the Shulḥan Arukh; *Ḥoshen Mishpat* (1749), patterned after Judah b. Simeon Ashkenazi's *Ba'er Heitev* (1736–42) on the other three parts of the Shulḥan Arukh. Frankfurter edited several works, the most important being a new edition of the rabbinic Bible *Mikra'ot Gedolot* (4 vols., Amsterdam, 1724–27), adding 16 previously unpublished commentaries on the various books of the Bible including his own commentary under the title *Kehillat Moshe;* another group of this compilation interpreting the whole Bible is *Komeẓ Minḥah, Minḥah Ketannah, Minḥah Gedolah,* and *Minḥat Erev.*

Bibliography: M. Horovitz, *Frankfurter Rabbinen,* 2 (1883), 74f.

[J.H.H.]

FRANKFURTER, SOLOMON FRIEDRICH (1856–1941), Austrian librarian, pedagogue, and classical philologist. Frankfurter was born in Pressburg and moved with his family to Vienna in 1859. In 1881 he began working as a volunteer at the University of Vienna library, where from 1919 to 1923 he was director. In 1909 he had been appointed consultant on Jewish community questions to the Austrian Ministry of Culture and Education, the first Jew to occupy such a position. Frankfurter was president of the Society for the Collection and Investigation of Jewish Historic Monuments, president of the B'nai B'rith, and member or consultant of many boards responsible for Jewish education and religion. He served briefly as director of the Vienna Jewish Museum. From 1934 to 1938 he was the only Jewish member of the Austrian Bundes-Kulturrat (Federal Board for Cultural Questions). When the Nazis invaded Austria (1938) he was arrested, but was released shortly after.

Frankfurter's publications deal with archaeology; education, particularly the important role of a classical gymnasium education; biographies; and Jewish subjects. His works include; *Unrichtige Buechertitel mit einem Exkurs ueber hebraeische Buechertitel* (1906); *Das altjuedische Erziehungs- und Unterrichtswesen im Lichte moderner Bestrebungen* (1910); *Josef Unger 1828–1857* (1917), dealing with Unger's youth; and *Zwei neugefundene mittelalterliche hebraeische Grabsteine in Wien* (1918).

U.S. Supreme Court Justice Felix *Frankfurter was his nephew. [Ed.]

FRANKINCENSE (Heb.לְבוֹנָה), the chief ingredient of the Temple *incense. It is mentioned a number of times among the treasures of the Temple (Neh. 13:5; I Chron. 9:29). It was burnt with the sacrifice of meal offering (Lev. 2:1) and placed upon the rows of showbread (Lev. 24:7). The frankincense on the meal offering along with a handful of the rest of its ingredients were scooped up by the priest as the "token portion" (Azkarah) of the offering which he deposited on the altar to go up in smoke as a "soothing odor" offered to the Lord (Lev. 6:8; cf. Isa. 66:3). Pure frankincense was one of the four ingredients of the incense of the Tabernacle (Ex. 30:34; and cf. Ecclus. 24:15). It was brought to Ereẓ Israel from Sheba (Jer. 6:20). The maiden in the Song of Songs (3:6) came from the wilderness perfumed with myrrh and frankincense; in the erotic imagery of the Song of Songs, the lover refers to the body of his mistress as "the mountain of myrrh" and "the hill of frankincense" (Song 4:6), while the beloved is compared to "an enclosed garden" in which grow exotic perfumes including "all trees of frankincense" (Song 4:14–15). Ben Sira emphasizes its aromatic scent (Ecclus. 39:14; 50:9). Frankincense is frequently mentioned in rabbinic literature in connection with the laws of meal offerings, where it was used in the form of globules or grains (Men. 1:2). A potion of wine and frankincense was prepared for those condemned to death, "that they should not suffer pain" (Sem. 2:9; cf. Sanh. 43a). The name *levonah* is common in Semitic languages. It has its origin in the white color of the fresh sap, "pure frankincense." From the Semitic the name passed also into the Greek λίβανος.

Frankincense was extracted from trees of the genus *Boswellia*, of which there are three species: in Somalia and southern Arabia, *B. carterii* and *B. frereana*, and in India, the species *B. serrata*. These trees are still the source for the frankincense used as incense in the Catholic Church. In ancient Egypt, as in other countries of the east, frankincense was very important and it seems that efforts were made to plant it locally. The bringing of pots of frankincense for planting in Egypt are depicted in ancient Egyptian drawings.

The high priest burning frankincense. Copper engraving from Jacques Basnage, *La République des Hébreux*, Amsterdam, 1713. Jerusalem, J.N.U.L.

Bibliography: Loew, Flora, 1 (1928), 312–4; J. Feliks, *Olam ha-Ẓome'aḥ ha-Mikra'i* (1968[2]), 260–2. [J.F.]

FRANKL, ADOLF (1859–1936), rabbi, banker, and communal leader in Hungary. Born in Debrecen, he studied in various yeshivot and received his rabbinical ordination at the yeshivah of Pressburg. From 1888 Frankl was *nasi* of the Hungarian *kolel* of Jerusalem. In 1905 he was elected president of the organization of Orthodox communities and honorary president of the Orthodox community of Budapest. After the death of Koppel *Reich, Frankl was elected chief rabbi of the Orthodox community in Budapest, and sat as the delegate of Orthodox Jewry in the Hungarian Upper House (1930). He won esteem in all circles of the Jewish population of Hungary.

Bibliography: *Magyar Zsidó Lexikon* (1929), 292. [B.Y.]

FRANKL, LUDWIG AUGUST (1810–1894), Austrian poet, secretary of the Vienna Jewish community, and founder of the *Laemel School in Jerusalem. Born in Chrast, Bohemia, Frankl was one of the first Jews to attend a Bohemian secondary school. He also received a sound Jewish education under his relative, Zacharias *Frankel. Although he studied medicine at Vienna and Padua, he devoted himself mainly to literature. The patriotic flavor of Frankl's first collection of ballads, *Das Habsburgerlied* (1832), brought him a reward from Emperor Francis I. It was followed by *Morgenlaendische Sagen* (1834), a volume of poems on Jewish themes, and by the epic *Christoforo*

Colombo (1836), for which he was made an honorary citizen of Genoa, the explorer's birthplace. In 1838 Frankl was appointed secretary and archivist of the Vienna Jewish community. The post enabled him to publish various works of Jewish interest, including a history of the Jews in Vienna (1853), but he really made his name as editor, from 1842, of the *Sonntagsblaetter*, which brought him into the circle of Austria's literary elite. In later years he was to publish studies of such of his new acquaintances as the dramatist Franz Grillparzer and the poet Nikolaus Lenau, but he also encouraged new writers, notably Moritz *Hartmann and Leopold *Kompert. His use of the elegant *Sonntagsblaetter* in support of the 1848 Revolution led to the paper's eventual suppression. During the Revolution Frankl served as an officer in the students' legion and achieved fame with his revolutionary lyric *Die Universitaet*, the first uncensored Austrian publication, which was circulated in half-a-million copies and was set to music no less than 28 different times: Frankl later edited the works of the revolutionary writer Anastasius Gruen (1877), and their correspondence was published by Frankl's son, Lothar. As the representative of Elisa *Herz, Frankl went to Jerusalem in 1856 and, in memory of her father, founded the Laemel School, which offered Jewish children a secular, as well as a religious, education. This aroused violent opposition on the part of the ultra-Orthodox Ashkenazi community, whose rabbinate placed Frankl under the ban of excommunication. He described his experiences in Ereẓ Israel in *Nach Jerusalem* (2 vols., 1858–60), which gives a valuable picture of the Jewish inhabitants of Jerusalem in the mid-19th century. The book was translated into Hebrew and other languages, and appeared in English as *The Jews in the East* (1859). A third volume, *Nach Aegypten*, appeared in 1860. Other works of Jewish interest are Frankl's *Elegien* (1842), *Rachel* (1842), *Libanon* (1855), and *Ahnenbilder* (1864). In 1876 he founded the Vienna Jewish Institute for the Blind, his philanthropic endeavors being rewarded with ennoblement as Ritter von Frankl-Hochwart. His memoirs appeared posthumously in 1910. His son LOTHAR (1862–1914), became professor of neurology at the University of Vienna in 1897.

Ludwig August Frankl, Austrian poet and communal leader. Engraving by C. Kotterba. New York, Leo Baeck Institute.

Bibliography: *Oẓar ha-Sifrut*, 5 (1896), 129–34, contains bibl.; E. Wolbe, *Ludwig August Frankl, der Dichter und Menschenfreund* (1910); S. Dollar, *Sonntagsblaetter von Ludwig August Frankl* (1932); Y. Yaari-Poleskin, *Ḥolemim u-Magshimim* (1967), 48–56; Schlossar, in: ADB, 48 (1904), 706–12. [ED.]

FRANKL, PINKUS (Pinḥas) FRITZ (1848–1887), German rabbi and scholar. Born in Uhersky Brod, Moravia, Frankl succeeded Geiger as rabbi of the Berlin community in 1877, and became lecturer in religious philosophy, medieval Hebrew literature, and homiletics at the Hochschule (Lehranstalt) fuer die Wissenschaft des Judentums in 1882. With Graetz he was coeditor of the journal **Monatsschrift fuer Geschichte und Wissenschaft des Judentums* (MGWJ). His studies were mainly about the Karaites: *Karaeische Studien* (1876); *Beitraege zur Literaturgeschichte der Karaeer* (1887); and articles in the Etsch-Gruber encyclopedia, MGWJ, and others. Frankl edited some *piyyutim* by Eleazar Kallir (in *Jubelschrift ... L. Zunz*, 1884). A collection of his sermons, *Fest- und Gelegenheits-Predigten 1877–87*, was published posthumously (1888). In 1884 Frankl was one of the initiators of a "General Assembly of German Rabbis."

Bibliography: S. Maybaum, *Trauerrede gehalten am 26. August, 1887 an der Bahre des Rabbiners Dr. P. F. Frankl* (1887). [ED.]

FRANKL, VICTOR E. (1905–), Austrian psychiatrist and founder of the school of existential psychotherapy known as logotherapy. During World War II, Frankl was sent to Auschwitz and other concentration camps for three years. During this period he gained new insights into human nature, which he later developed into his philosophy and theory of logotherapy. In contradistinction to the Freudian theories that analysed human behavior in terms of determinism, the sex drives, and the repressed experiences of the past, and contrary to the Adlerian school which based explanations on the human desire for power and self-assertion, Frankl's philosophy focused on the human need for purpose, self-fulfillment, and the need to attain a higher meaning in life. By observing the behavior of the Auschwitz inmates he came to the conclusion that, "The prisoner who had lost faith in the future—his future—was doomed. With his loss of belief in the future, he also lost his spiritual hold; he let himself decline and became subject to mental and physical decay." Frankl's books include *Ein Psychologe erlebt das Konzentrationslager* (1946; *From Death Camp to Existentialism*, 1959; republished as *Man's Search for Meaning*, 1964), and *Aerztliche Seelsorge* (1946; *The Doctor and the Soul*, 1955, 1965).

Bibliography: D. F. Tweedie Jr., *Logotherapy and the Christian Faith; an Evaluation of Frankl's Existential Approach to Psychotherapy* (1961); R. C. Campbell, *Jesus and Logotherapy* (1965); K. Dienelt, *Erziehung zur Verantwortlichkeit* (1955); Grollman, in: *Judaism*, 14 (1965), 22–38. [ED.]

FRANKL-GRUEN, ADOLF ABRAHAM (1847–1916), rabbi and historian in Moravia. Born in Uhersky Brod, Moravia, he officiated as rabbi of Kromeriz (Kremsier) from 1877 to 1911. Frankl-Gruen published many articles on biblical exegesis (see Gesamtindex of MGWJ (1966), 18) and homiletics, and a polemic against the anti-Semite H. S. *Chamberlain (1901). In 1903 he completed *Juedische Zeitgeschichte und Zeitgenossen*, on the contemporary Jewish scene. His three-volume *Geschichte der Juden in Kremsier* (1896–1901) and *Geschichte der Juden in Ungarisch-Brod* (1905), based mainly on documents previously unpublished, remain essential texts for the student of Jewish history in Moravia. In 1889 he became involved in a *blood libel in Kromeriz when a rumor was spread before

Passover that a box containing the body of a Christian girl had been sent to him by railway.

His son OSCAR BENJAMIN FRANKL (1881–1955) studied philology at Vienna University. In 1918 he founded in Prague the German Urania Institute for adult education which he headed until 1938. He was appointed chief of the German department of the Czechoslovakian government

Adolf Frankl-Gruen, Moravian rabbi and historian. Jerusalem, J.N.U.L., Schwadron Collection.

radio and became an international authority on broadcasting. In 1939 he managed to escape to the United States through France. There he served as a researcher for Columbia University (1942–55) and was appointed lecturer at the Rand School of Social Science. His *Der Jude in den deutschen Dichtungen des 15., 16., und 17. Jahrhundertes . . .*, on the image of the Jew in German literature of the 15th to 17th centuries, and *Friedrich Schiller in seinen Beziehungen zu den Juden und zum Judentum*, on Friedrich Schiller's relations to Jews and Judaism (both published in 1905), are noteworthy.

Bibliography: H. Gold (ed.), *Die Juden und Judengemeinden Maehrens . . .* (1929), 297.

[ED.]

FRANKLIN, English family active in communal, public, and economic life. BENJAMIN WOLF FRANKLIN (1740–1785), a teacher of Hebrew, went to England from Breslau about 1763. His youngest son, ABRAHAM (1784–1854), after spending his early life in Portsmouth, settled in Manchester and traded with the West Indies. Of Abraham's 12 children, three gained prominence: BENJAMIN (1811–1888) was a merchant in Jamaica where he was active in public and communal life. JACOB (1809–1877), first an optician and then a West Indies merchant, was a mathematician, accountant, and writer on accountancy. A staunch advocate of religious Orthodoxy, he founded and edited the *Voice of Jacob* as a mouthpiece against Reform (it was later merged with the *Jewish Chronicle*, to which he contributed as "She'erit Ya'akov"). Active in many communal organizations, he left the bulk of his fortune for educational projects, including the publication of Jewish textbooks. ELLIS ABRAHAM (1822–1909) moved from Manchester to London in 1842 and joined a banking house. Friendship with Samuel *Montagu, whose sister he married in 1856, led to his joining the firm established by Montagu and his brother in 1852. A patriarchal figure, he took an active interest in many communal organizations.

Ellis' daughter BEATRICE married Herbert *Samuel. His son, SIR LEONARD (1862–1944), senior partner in the family banking firm A. Keyser and Company, was a Liberal member of parliament, and was also active in synagogal administration. Another of his sons, ARTHUR ELLIS (1857–1938), besides his banking interests, was chairman of the Routledge publishing firm, president of the Jewish Religious Education Board, vice-president of the Board of Guardians, and vice-principal of the Working Men's College. He assembled a memorable collection of Jewish ritual art, now in the Jewish Museum, London. His son ELLIS (1894–1964) was similarly active in Anglo-Jewish communal life. Ellis' daughter, ROSALIND (1920–1957) was a distinguished chemist, particularly noted for her work on deoxyribonucleic acid (DNA).

Bibliography: A. E. Franklin, *Pedigrees of the Franklin Family* (1915); idem, *Records of the Franklin Family and Collaterals* (1935^2); J. Picciotto, *Sketches of Anglo-Jewish History* (1956^2), index; V. D. Lipman, *Century of Social Service 1859–1959* (1959), index.

[V.D.L.]

FRANKLIN, LEO MORRIS (1870–1948), U.S. Reform rabbi. Franklin was born in Cambridge City, Indiana. Upon ordination at Hebrew Union College (1892), he served in Omaha, Nebraska, for seven years, then became rabbi of Temple Beth El, Detroit, in 1899. Franklin was a proponent of classical Reform Judaism. He organized the United Jewish Charities (1899) and was a founder of the Jewish Welfare Federation (1926). He held many civic positions and was active in interfaith activities in Detroit. He belonged to the anti-Zionist American Council for Judaism until 1948, when he resigned and endorsed the State of Israel. Friendly with Henry Ford until the latter turned to anti-Semitic propagandizing, Franklin later opposed Ford. He wrote *Rabbi, the Man and his Message* (1938) and many articles.

Bibliography: Leo M. Franklin Section, Michigan Historical Collections, University of Michigan, Ann Arbor, Michigan.

[I.I.K.]

FRANKLIN, SELIM (1814–1883), Canadian politician. Born in Liverpool, England, Franklin was the son of a banker and acquired considerable wealth as a financier. He went to California during the gold rush of 1849 and in 1858 he and his brother, LUMLEY (1812–1873), were among the first Jews to settle in British Columbia, opening a real estate auctioneering business in Victoria. In 1860 Selim was elected to the Vancouver legislative assembly, despite allegations that he had brought in "black Yankees to stuff

Selim Franklin, 19th-century Canadian politician. Victoria, British Columbia, Provincial Archives.

the ballots." Trouble arose on his eligibility to take his seat because of the oath "on the true faith of a Christian." A committee of enquiry reported that the oath had been offered in good faith by the chief justice. Meanwhile Franklin's right to sit in the assembly had already been recognized. He was a member of the legislative assembly from 1860 to 1863 and from 1864 to 1866. In 1865 Lumley Franklin was elected mayor of Victoria. Together, the two brothers played a prominent part in the social and cultural life of both the general and the Jewish community of Victoria. A river running into the Alberni Canal on Vancouver Island and a street in Victoria were named after Selim Franklin.

Bibliography: D. Rome, *First Two Years* (1942), 52–105 and passim; B. G. Sack, *History of the Jews in Canada* (1945), 166.

[B.G.K.]

FRANKLIN (Frumkin), SIDNEY (b. 1903), U.S. matador who became the first non-Latin to win fame in the bull ring. Born in Brooklyn, he left the U.S. at the age of 18. He developed an interest in bullfighting in Mexico City. To disprove a widely held theory that only Latins were capable of fighting bulls he became a pupil of Rodolfo Gaona, Mexico's most famous matador. After successes in Mexican bull rings he made a sensational debut in Spain in 1929, being carried from the arena, surrounded by thousands of admirers. In 1929 he met Ernest Hemingway and the two became close friends. Hemingway wrote that Franklin was "one of the most skillful, graceful, and slow manipulators of the cape in his day." Franklin was a foreign correspondent during the Spanish Civil War, translated a Spanish book on bullfighting into English, and wrote his autobiography, *Bullfighter From Brooklyn* (1952). After dispatching over 5,000 bulls, he retired from the bull ring in 1959 to become a broadcaster of televised bullfights in Mexico City.

Sidney Franklin executing a classic kill. Wide World Photos, N.Y.

Bibliography: B. Postal et al. (eds.), *Encyclopaedia of Jews in Sports* (1965), 181; E. Hemingway, *Death in the Afternoon* (1932).

[J.H.S.]

FRANKS, English family, with an important branch in America. Benjamin Franks (c. 1650–c. 1716), son of an Ashkenazi merchant from Bavaria, was born in London but moved to the West Indies in the last decade of the 17th century. His checkered career took him to New York and Bombay where he made a deposition which was used in the piracy trial of Captain Kidd. He returned to London in 1698 and seems to have stayed there until his death. Abraham (Naphtali Hart) Franks (d. 1708/9) was a founder of the London Ashkenazi community admitted to the Royal Exchange in 1697. His son Aaron (d. 1777) attained great wealth as a jeweler, and was said to have distributed £5,000 yearly in charity without distinction of race or creed. At his country house in Isleworth near London he gave musical receptions and entertained members of the aristocracy. Like other members of the family, he was closely associated with the affairs of the Great Synagogue. He took the lead in 1745 in the attempt to secure the intervention of the English court on behalf of the Jews expelled from Prague. His brother Jacob *Franks was head of the American branch of the family, some members of which in due course returned to England and played a part in communal and public life.

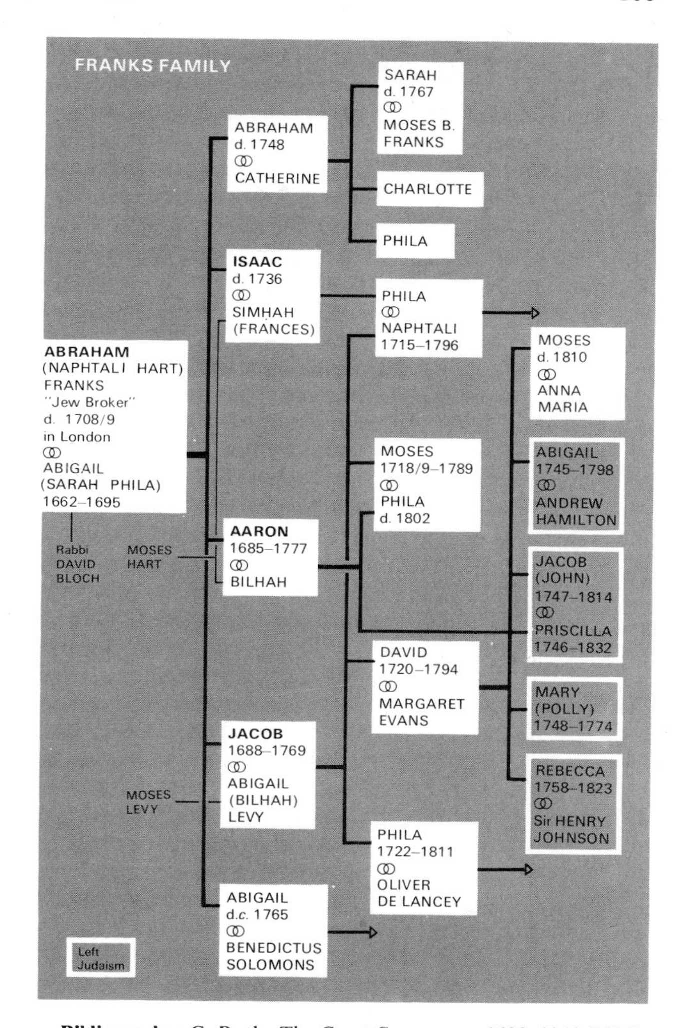

Bibliography: C. Roth, *The Great Synagogue, 1690–1940* (1950), passim; Oppenheim, in: AJHSP, 31 (1928), 229–34; L. Hershkowitz and I. S. Meyer (eds.), *Letters of the Franks Family, 1733–48* (1968).

[C.R.]

FRANKS, DAVID (1720–1794), Colonial American merchant and Loyalist. Franks, who was born in New York, began his extensive mercantile career with his arrival in

The home of David Franks in Woodford, Pa. Courtesy Philadelphia Museum of Art.

Philadelphia in 1738. In 1742 he entered a partnership with his uncle Nathan Levy. The following year he married a Christian and their children were baptized in Christ Church, Philadelphia. Franks, who had extensive holdings in Western lands, became an agent for the British Army in North America by 1754, along with his father. During the Revolution, Franks was deputy commissary of (British) prisoners for the Americas. However, because of dealings with his brother Moses and with England, he was relieved of his duties. In 1780, after several trials and a good deal of publicity, he was ordered out of Pennsylvania. Exiled to England, Franks vainly sought relief from the crown for his loyalty. [L.He.]

FRANKS, DAVID SALISBURY (c. 1743–1793), U.S. merchant, a Revolutionary War officer, and patriot. Franks was born in Philadelphia. Three years after his registration in 1760 at the Philadelphia Academy (University of Pennsylvania), he went to Montreal as a merchant. He returned in 1776 after aiding the invading army of generals Richard Montgomery and Benedict Arnold in their unsuccessful attack on Quebec. He became an aide to Arnold, serving in the Pennsylvania line as a major. Exonerated of complicity in the Arnold treason in 1780, Franks was promoted to the rank of lieutenant colonel. In 1781 he was sent to bring government dispatches and advice to John Jay in Madrid and to Benjamin Franklin in Paris. He served as courier, consular official, and confidant to Thomas Jefferson, Robert R. Livingston, and John Adams at various times in Europe until 1787. In 1790 he was appointed assistant cashier to the Bank of the United States. Franks

David Salisbury Franks, U.S. merchant and Revolutionary War officer. Courtesy American Jewish Historical Society, Waltham, Mass.

had served as *parnas* of the Congregation Shearith Israel in Montreal in 1775 and was a contributor to Mikveh Israel in Philadelphia.

Bibliography: Rosenbloom, Biog Dict, 39. [L.He.]

FRANKS, JACOB (1688–1769), New York City merchant and founder of a prominent mercantile family. Franks, born in London, arrived in New York in 1708 or 1709. He

Jacob Franks, American Colonial merchant. Oil painting by an unknown artist. From *Early American Jewish Portraiture*, New York, 1952.

became a freeman of New York in 1711. A year later he married Abigail Bilhah Levy, daughter of Moses *Levy, one of New York's wealthiest Jews. The couple had nine children, three of whom—Moses, David, and Naphtali—became successful merchants in England and the provinces. A daughter, Phila, married Oliver De Lancey in 1742, thus linking the family with New York aristocracy. Franks' vast trade activities, engaged in part with Moses Levy and Nathan Simpson, as well as his sons, included dry goods, liquor, and slaves. Other partners in trade were members of the Van Cortlandt, Philipse, and Livingston families. Franks was elected constable of the Dock Ward in New York City in 1720, but declined to serve. He did serve in the militia during the French and Indian Wars. Franks contributed to the building of the steeple on Trinity Church in 1711. Much involved in the congregational affairs of Shearith Israel in New York, he served in a variety of offices, including that of president (1729). He was a founder of the congregation's Mill Street synagogue, and also helped to purchase the congregation burial ground off present-day Chatham Square. Frank's interest in religious affairs was not continued by his descendants, and the family disappeared as Jews by the end of the 18th century.

Bibliography: L. Hershkowitz and I. S. Meyer (eds.), *Letters of the Franks Family (1733–1748)* (1968). [L.He.]

FRANKS, JACOB (c. 1766–c. 1823), merchant and civic leader in Wisconsin and Michigan. Franks, who was born in England, was a nephew of David Salisbury *Franks. He emigrated to Montreal and in 1792 was sent to Green Bay, Wisconsin, as agent for a Montreal firm. He soon purchased a large tract of land, opened his own trading post, and became one of the influential residents of the settlement, contributing much toward the development of the area. Franks moved to Mackinac, Michigan, in 1805 or earlier. During the War of 1812 Franks fought on the British side and aided in the capture of Mackinac. In 1815 he was listed as one of the "magistrates, merchants, traders and principal inhabitants of Michilimackinac and St. Josephs." When the British withdrew from Mackinac to Drummond Island, Michigan, in 1815, the Americans destroyed Franks' house at Mackinac. He returned to Montreal, where he became an army purveyor and was also a business associate of Henry Joseph, member of a leading Canadian Jewish family.

Bibliography: I. Katz, *The Beth El Story* (1955), index; B. Sack, *History of the Jews in Canada* (1945), index; *Wisconsin Historial Collections*, 19 (1903–11), 292.
[I.I.K.]

FRANZBLAU, ABRAHAM NORMAN (1901–), U.S. educator and psychiatrist. Franzblau was born in New York. He began a long association with Hebrew Union College in 1923 as principal of its school for teachers in New York, serving until 1931, when he became professor of education and pastoral psychiatry in the College at Cincinnati. Franzblau received a Ph.D. in education from Columbia (1935), and then took up the study of medicine, receiving his M.D. in 1937. During World War II he was attached to the Surgeon General's Office as colonel. Franzblau returned to New York in 1946 as professor of pastoral psychology and dean of the Jewish Institute of Religion school of education. In 1948 he became associated with the psychiatric department of Mount Sinai Hospital and in 1958 retired from Hebrew Union College to devote himself entirely to psychiatry. A pioneer in the application of psychiatric knowledge to the work of the ministry, Franzblau lectured in this field at many seminaries. Besides texts, monographs, and research studies, he wrote *Road to Sexual Maturity* (1954); *Primer of Statistics for Non-Statisticians* (1958); and (with his wife Rose Franzblau) *Sane and Happy Life* (1963).

His wife ROSE NADLER FRANZBLAU (1905–) was a psychologist and columnist. She was born in Vienna. Mrs. Franzblau wrote human relations columns for the *New York Post* from 1947 and discussed psychological problems submitted by listeners to her daily radio program. She wrote *Race Differences in Mental and Physical Traits* (1935); and coauthored *Final Report, National Youth Administration* (1944) and *Tensions Affecting International Understanding* (1950).
[S.D.T.]

FRANZOS, KARL EMIL (1848–1904), Austrian novelist and journalist. The son of a physician, Franzos was born in Czortkow, a focal point of ḥasidic life on the Russo-Galician border, which he later fictionalized as Barnow. While still a student of law at Vienna and Graz he was correspondent for the influential Viennese *Neue Freie Presse*. For a short time he edited the Budapest *Pester Journal* and also contributed to the *Pester Lloyd*. In 1873 Franzos began publishing in the *Neue Freie Presse* the tales and sketches which established his reputation. Entitled *Halb-Asien*... and collected in two volumes in 1876, they dealt in a realistic and compassionate manner with the life of East European Jewry. The stories in *Die Juden von Barnow* (1877), dedicated to his predecessor in this genre, Leopold *Kompert, combine a call for greater Jewish enlightenment and adaptation to Western culture with a deep understanding of the customs and superstitions of the Galician countryside. His best novel about the ghetto was *Der Pojaz*, which appeared posthumously in 1905. As editor of the Viennese *Neue Illustrierte Zeitung* (1884–86) and, even more, as editor of the biweekly *Deutsche Dichtung* (from 1886 until his death), Franzos exerted an important influence on German literary life and helped to spread the reputation of both new and established writers. His work as editor of Georg Buechner's collected works (1879) paved the way for Max *Reinhardt's production of Buechner's revolutionary drama *Dantons Tod* and for Alban Berg's musical adaptation of Buechner's *Wozzeck* as the first German proletarian opera. Franzos is credited with authorship of the saying: "Every country gets the Jews it deserves."

Bibliography: L. Geiger, *Deutsche Literatur und die Juden* (1910), 250–304.
[S.L.]

FRATERNAL SOCIETIES, organizations for mutual aid, fellowship, life insurance, relief of distress, and sick and death benefits, frequently modeled on the *Freemason pattern. Jewish fraternal societies originated in the 19th century. In England the Order Achei Brith and Shield of Abraham was organized in 1888, Ancient Maccabeans in 1891, Achei Ameth in 1897, Grand Order Sons of Jacob in 1900, followed by many others. In 1915 an Association of Jewish Friendly Societies was established there. In South and Central America these societies were organized as **Landsmannschaften*, e.g., the Galician Farband or Bessarabian Landsleit Farein. The main society in the United States is the Independent Order *Bnai B'rith. Other bodies are the True Sisters (1846), the *Free Sons of Israel (1849), *Brith Abraham (1859), the Independent Order Brith Abraham (1887), and the defunct Order Kesher Shel Barzel (1860). Many others originated as *Landsmannschaften*. Many small-scale *Landsmannschaften* later enrolled in general orders, some of which were formed along political lines: the *Workmen's Circle (1900) stressed socialism; the Jewish National Workers' Alliance (1910) combined Zionism with socialism; the International Workers' Order (1930), later renamed Jewish People's Fraternal Order, was controlled by Communists. They established elementary and high schools with instruction in Yiddish and Hebrew and promoted adult education. With the growing popularity of commercial insurance, the commercialization of the mortuary business, and leisure time activities, the membership of fraternal orders rapidly declined.

See also *Ḥevrah.

Bibliography: Baron, Community, index, s.v. *Landsmannschaften;* Weinryb, in: JSOS, 8 (1946), 219–44; AJYB, 39 (1938), 123–4; 50 (1949), 34–37; Levitats, in: *Essays on Jewish Life and Thought* (1959), 333–49.
[I.L.]

FRAUD, the prohibition against wronging another in selling or buying property (Lev. 25:14) is one of civil (see *Ona'ah) rather than criminal law—although, since it is a negative injunction, its violation by any overt act may result in the punishment of *flogging (Tos. and *Penei Yehoshu'a* to BM 61a; cf. Maim. Yad, Sanhedrin 18:1). Where reparation can be made by the payment of money, no such punishment may be inflicted in addition (cf. Yad, loc. cit., 2 and Mekhirah 12:1; Ket. 32a; Mak. 4b, 16a). The express repetition, "And ye shall not wrong one another, but thou shalt fear thy God" (Lev. 25:17), was interpreted to prohibit the "wronging" of another not only in commercial transactions but also in noncommercial intercourse: the prohibition extends to "wronging by words" as distinguished from wronging by fraudulent deeds and devices; and wronging by words includes pestering people in vain as well as offending or ridiculing them (BM 4:10). It is said that wronging by words is even more reprehensible than wronging by fraudulent deeds, because while the latter is an offense against property only and can be redressed by the payment of money, the former is an offense against the person and his reputation, for which money will not normally be an adequate compensation (BM 58b; Yad, Mekhirah 14:12–18; see *Slander). However, though not constituting a cause of action for damages, wronging by words is not punishable by flogging either, because the mere utterance of words is not considered such an overt act of violation as may be punished in this way (cf. Yad, Sanhedrin 18:2). The admonition "but thou shalt fear thy God" (Lev. 25:17) is said to indicate that even though the offender may escape human punishment, divine retribution is certain to follow (Yad, Mekhirah 14:18; Ibn Ezra to Lev. 26:17).

The fact that fraud, even in the civil law meaning of the term, was in biblical times regarded as eminently criminal in character is well illustrated in Ezekiel's discourse on individual criminal responsibility: the same responsibility attaches for wronging the poor and needy, converting property, and not restoring pledges, as for murder, robbery, and adultery (Ezek. 18:10–13), and for all those misdeeds the same capital punishment is threatened *(ibid.)*. Fraud and *oppression are usually found in the same context as *usury (Ex. 22:20, 24; Lev. 25:14, 17, 37; Deut. 23:17, 20; Ezek. 7–8; 12–13, 17). Fraud has also been held as tantamount to larceny (see *Theft and Robbery; Tur, ḤM 227). As fraud and oppression go hand in hand, their victims are often the weak and the underprivileged; hence there are particular prohibitions on fraud against strangers (Ex. 22:20), widows and orphans (Ex. 21), and slaves (Deut. 23:17). Wronging widows and orphans is so repulsive in the eyes of God that "if they cry at all unto Me . . . My wrath shall wax hot and I will kill you with the sword, and your wives shall be widows and your children fatherless" (Ex. 22:22–23). Wronging and vexing the poor and the stranger draws forth God's wrath (Ezek. 22:29–31 et al.) and is a cause of national disaster (Jer. 22:3–6).

In post-talmudic times, fraudulent business practices often resulted in the courts barring or suspending the offender from carrying on business. While isolated instances of fraud would be dealt with as civil matters, repeated and notorious fraudulent business practices might be punished by the sequestration of the offender's business, depriving him of his livelihood (S. Assaf, *Ha-Onshin Aḥarei Ḥatimat ha-Talmud* (1922), 43). On other aspects of fraud see also **Gerama*.

In the State of Israel, the criminal law on fraud and kindred offenses has been reformed and expanded by the Penal Law Amendment (Deceit, Blackmail and Extortion) Law, 5723–1963. Fraud is there defined as any representation of fact—past, present, or future—made in writing, by word of mouth, or by conduct, which the maker knew to be false or did not believe to be true. It is made a criminal offense not only to obtain anything by such fraud, but also to obtain anything by any trick not amounting to fraud or by the exploitation of another's mistake or ignorance. Particular instances of fraud mentioned in the Act are pretenses of sorcery or fortune-telling; forgeries and unauthorized alterations of documents and the use or uttering of the same; the fraudulent suppression or concealment of any document or chattel, and the fraudulent incitement of others to make, alter, or conceal documents; as well as the issue of a check where the drawer knew that the banker on whom it was drawn was not bound to honor it.

Bibliography: ET, 1 (1951[3]), 160f.; 2 (1949), 18f.; EM, 1 (1950), 149f. [H.H.C.]

FRAUENKIRCHEN (Hung. **Boldogasszony;** Heb. abbr. פ״ק), town in E. Austria; its Jewish community was one of the "Seven Communities" of *Burgenland, the last to be founded, in about 1678. The Jews who settled there had been expelled from an estate of the nearby monastery of Moenchhof. The charter of the community, granted in 1714, was renewed in 1800. The Jewish quarter was destroyed by fire in 1778 and 1781. The synagogue was built in 1837. The community adhered to Orthodoxy. Outstanding among its rabbis were Naphtali Herz Auerbach (d. 1737), a son of Menahem Mendel *Auerbach, and Shalom Ḥarif-Ullmann (d. 1825). The community numbered 195 persons in 1735; 782 in 1757 (33.1% of the total population); 629 in 1880; 399 in 1920; and 386 in 1934 (11.7%). After World War I the small Jewish settlements at Gattendorf and Kittsee in the vicinity were affiliated to the Frauenkirchen community. In 1938 the Jews were expelled and the synagogue and the Jewish street destroyed. There were no Jews living in Frauenkirchen in 1970. Nearly 6,000 items relating to the Frauenkirchen community are preserved in the central archives of Burgenland in Eisenstadt.

Bibliography: *Magyar Zsidó Lexikon* (1929), s.v. MHJ, 6 (1961), index locurum, s.v.; H. Gold (ed.), *Gedenkbuch der untergegangenen Judengemeinden des Burgenlandes* (1970), 77–79. [Y.M.]

FRAUENSTAEDT, JULIUS (Christian Martin; 1813–1879), philosopher. Frauenstaedt, who was born in Bojanowo, Posen, became a Christian at 20. He studied theology and philosophy at Berlin. Originally a Hegelian, he met Schopenhauer in 1846 and became a student and follower of his. Frauenstaedt published the first complete edition of Schopenhauer's works in 6 volumes (1873–74), and was his literary executor, publishing his posthumous writings. He differed with Schopenhauer on various aspects of his philosophy, especially regarding his voluntarism and pessimism. Frauenstaedt wrote extensively on religion and ethics. His best-known works are *Aesthetische Fragen* (1853); *Der Materialismus* (1856); and *Blicke in die intellektuelle, physische und moralische Welt* (1869). He also wrote a *Schopenhauer-Lexikon* (1871), *Briefe ueber die Schopenhauer'sche Philosophie* (1854), and *Neue Briefe* (1876).

Bibliography: H. Berger, *Julius Frauenstaedt, sein Leben, seine Schriften und seine Philosophie*, 1911). [R.H.P.]

Grand Duke Frederick I, a supporter of Theodor Herzl. Central Zionist Archives, Jerusalem.

°**FREDERICK I** (1826–1907), grand duke of Baden, son-in-law of Kaiser William I, and uncle by marriage of Kaiser William II. Frederick ruled Baden from 1852 until his death and was the first and almost the only influential political figure to help *Herzl wholeheartedly. When he learned of Herzl and *Der Judenstaat* from his sons' tutor, the Reverend William *Hechler, he followed Herzl's progress with deep sympathy. It was he who arranged the meeting between the German kaiser and Herzl when the former visited Ereẓ Israel in 1898, and he sent enthusiastic memoranda on political Zionism to the Russian czar. His efforts to arrange meetings between Herzl, the czar, and the king of England were unsuccessful, but the czar sent him a letter in support of political Zionism. Frederick received Herzl several times and they conducted an extremely friendly correspondence. The grand duke's picture, which he sent to Herzl, adorned the latter's study (and can be seen in the reconstruction of this room at the Herzl Museum, Jerusalem). After failures and disappointments in the diplomatic sphere, Herzl was greatly encouraged by his personal contacts with Frederick. The Zionist Organization sent a delegation (including David *Wolfsohn and Nahum *Sokolow) to Frederick's funeral in Karlsruhe.

The grand duke's correspondence with Herzl, the kaiser, the czar, and others in German, English, and French was found in 1959 by H. and B. Ellern, who published a facsimile edition in 1961. Later all the letters were published in the *Herzl Year Book*, 4 (1961–62), 207–70 by H. Zohn, together with an English translation of the letters in German and French. [G.K.]

°**FREDERICK II ("the Great")**, king of Prussia 1740–86. Like his predecessors, Frederick II followed the policy of allowing into the kingdom only fixed numbers of *Schutzjuden* ("protected Jews"), and took pains to ensure that these remained within defined limits. In keeping with this policy, the General Regulation he issued in 1750 distinguished between "ordinary" and "extraordinary" protected Jews; hereditary residential rights—to which only one child could succeed—were granted to the former alone while the rights of the "extraordinary" Jews lapsed with their death. Prussia's severe tax burden weighed more heavily on the Jews than other citizens. Apart from fixed "protection" money and the taxes levied in lieu of military service, they were also made responsible for the export of the state's manufactured products, and had to purchase a specified quantity of porcelain—the so-called *Judenporzellan*—from the royal factory. The trades and occupations they could follow were restricted, and the oath *more Judaico* was reimposed in 1747. Although freethinking and a lover of art and literature, the king was prepared only after much persuasion to extend to Moses *Mendelssohn the privilege of *Schutzjude*—and an "extraordinary" one, at that.

Prayer for the health of Frederick II from the *Memorbuch* of Arnswalde, Germany. Jerusalem, C.A.H.J.P., Ga. S 191/3.

Bibliography: Stern-Taeubler, in: JSOS, 11(1949), 129–52; S. Schwarz, in: YLBI, 11 (1966), 300–5. [R.M.]

°**FREDERICK II ("the Belligerent") OF BABENBERG**, duke of Austria 1230–1246. In 1244 he granted to Jews the privilege known as the "Fridericianum," following the basic lines of the charters granted by Emperor *Frederick II of Hohenstaufen in Germany in 1236, and to the city of Vienna in 1238. The "Fridericianum," regarded by the historian J. E. *Scherer as a "sparkling star in a dark night," served as the model for privileges granted to Jews in *Hungary in 1251, in *Bohemia in 1254, in *Poland in 1264, and in *Silesia in 1294. *Rudolf of Hapsburg confirmed it in 1278 in his capacity of Holy Roman Emperor. The charter remained valid in the territory of Austria proper, until the expulsion of the Jews in 1420 (see *Albert II; *Wiener Gesera). The "Fridericianum" granted the Jews autonomy and equality with Christians in civil law and equal rights for trading in wines, dyes, and medicaments. It prohibited forcible conversion and exempted Jews from having persons arbitrarily billeted in their houses. Jurisdiction over the Jews was transferred from the imperial to the ducal chamber. Security of their life and property was guaranteed including defense of their cemeteries and synagogues. Freedom of transit throughout Austria was permitted, including transportation of corpses for burial without paying tolls. In lawsuits between themselves Jews were entitled to judgment by their own *bet din*, while for settling disputes between Jews and gentiles the post of **Iudex Judaeorum* was created. If a gentile was suspected of murdering a Jew but the charge could not be substantiated, the duke was ready to supply a champion to fight him on behalf of the Jew. The transition of Jewish occupations from commerce to moneylending is reflected by the fact that 22 paragraphs out of 30 in the charter deal with matters connected with moneylending, fixing a weekly interest-rate of eight pfennigs on one mark, i.e., 173.33% yearly. The "Fridericianum" took over the concept of accepting the statement of a Jew on oath that he had taken a pledge bona fide if it was proved to have been stolen or lost though not through his fault, thus continuing to give the moneylender protection against malicious claims.

Bibliography: J. R. Marcus, *The Jew in the Medieval World* (1965), 28–33; J. E. Scherer, *Die Rechtsverhaeltnisse der Juden in den deutsch-oesterreichischen Laendern* (1901), 130–4; 173–315. [Ed.]

°**FREDERICK II OF HOHENSTAUFEN** (1194–1250), king of Sicily (with Apulia) from 1198; Holy Roman Emperor from 1215. He was in continuous and bitter conflict with the papacy, and was considered an arch-heretic by his opponents, who even termed him anti-Christ for his pamphlet *De tribus impostoribus* ("On the Three Impostors," i.e., Moses, Jesus, and Mohammed). However he had a lofty, if unusual, conception of the Christian religion, and of the royal duty to serve it. In his attitude toward the Jews and his reactions to them Frederick's complicated and powerful personality displayed an individual approach. Although in his Italian domains Frederick usually strictly enforced the Church canon relating to the Jews, including the compulsory wearing of the Jewish *badge (1221), he also invited Jewish translators and scholars to his court, among them Jacob *Anatoli, who took part in its lively and variegated intellectual life. In 1231 he made the dyeing and silk-weaving industries in south Italy crown monopolies administered by Jewish agents. In his German domains, Frederick finalized the legal definition governing the concept of Jewish servitude, which had evolved during the

12th century, describing the Jews in grants of privileges he issued in 1236 and 1237 as "**servi camerae nostrae.*"

The originality and force of Frederick's personality clearly emerged in the action he took in connection with the *blood libel. When the bodies of children alleged to have been murdered by the Jews in *Fulda (1238) were brought before him, he determined that he would finally settle the question. Frederick read about the problem himself and became convinced that the Jews were innocent of the charge. Being unable to obtain a clear-cut opinion or decision from the Church authorities or nobility, he had the original idea of convening a council of *apostates, who as former Jews and devout Christians should be able to give a definitive answer. Frederick subsequently published their unequivocal refutation of the blood libel and prohibited the libel's circulation throughout his domains.

Bibliography: Graetz, Hist, 3 (1949), 565–9; W. Cohn, in: MGWJ, 63 (1919), 315–32; A. Stern, in: ZGJD, 2 (1930), 68–77; J. P. Dolan, in: JSOS, 22 (1960), 165–74; G. Wolf, in: P. Wilpert (ed.), *Judentum im Mittelalter* (1966), 435–41; G. Kisch, *The Jews in Medieval Germany* (1949), index; L. I. Newman, *Jewish Influence on Christian Reform Movements* (1925), 291–9; *Der Adler: Mitteilungen der Heraldisch-Genealogischen Gesellschaft* (1931–34), 40–44; J. Cohn, *Die Judenpolitik der Hohenstaufen* (1934); S. W. Baron, in: *Sefer Yovel . . . Y. Baer* (1960), 102–24; R. Straus, *Die Juden im Koenigreich Sizilien unter Normannen und Staufen* (1910); Roth, Italy, index; S. Grayzel, *The Church and the Jews in the XIIIth Century* (1966²), index. [R.M.]

°**FREDERICK III OF HAPSBURG,** duke of Austria (as Frederick V), and king of Germany (as Francis IV, 1440–86); Holy Roman Emperor 1452–93. Frederick III favored the Jews, whose enemies described him as "more a Jewish than a Holy Roman Emperor." The general charter he granted to Carinthia in 1444 contained provisions for the protection of the Jews there. He resettled the Jews in *Austria (though not in Vienna) after their expulsion in 1421, for which he obtained a *bull from Pope Nicholas V in 1451 permitting their return since this would provide for the "Jews' livelihood and the Christians' benefit." He confirmed this permission when emperor. Frederick resisted the frequent protests by the Estates against admitting Jews (1458–63). As emperor he intervened on behalf of Israel *Bruna who was accused in a *blood libel in 1474, although earlier he had him imprisoned as a hostage to extort payment of a coronation tax. Frederick also intervened on behalf of the Jews in the blood libel cases of *Endingen (1470), *Trent (1476), and *Regensburg (1478). He persuaded Pope Paul II to issue a bull in 1469 ordering priests not to deny religious sacraments to officials who upheld the rights of the Jews. Jacob b. Jehiel *Loans was physician to Frederick III for many years, and according to tradition there was personal friendship between patient and physician. Frederick's attitude to the Jews was motivated both by the need to overcome his financial difficulties and to uphold the imperial authority including his jurisdictions over the Jews.

Bibliography: J. E. Scherer, *Die Rechtsverhaeltnisse der Juden in den deutsch-oesterreichischen Laendern* (1901), 422–20; S. Babad, in: HJ, 7 (1945), 196–98; R. Strauss, *ibid.*, 12 (1950), 20. [Ed.]

°**FREDERICK WILLIAM** (Ger. **Friedrich Wilhelm**), name of several kings of Prussia.

FREDERICK WILLIAM III was king of Prussia from 1797 to 1840. Although the liberal-inspired 1812 edict (see *Prussia) concerning the civil status of the Jews was issued by Frederick William III, it had been forced on him by the statesmen *Hardenberg and *Humboldt. The king himself made determined efforts to exclude the Jews from participation in army service: when, after the Napoleonic wars, Jewish war veterans and invalids applied for pensions and posts, he denied even the rights of those who had received decorations. The king explicitly ordered that conversion to Christianity should be made a condition for employment in state posts, including those in universities. Frederick William gave official support to a Prussian society for propagating Christianity among the Jews, and declared conversion to Judaism illegal. He opposed the *Reform movement and had the private prayer rooms of I. *Jacobson closed down. It was with reluctance that he awarded regular advancements and decorations to Meno *Burg, the first Jewish career officer in the Prussian army.

His son, FREDERICK WILLIAM IV, was king of Prussia from 1840 to 1861. Jewish hopes that he would follow a more liberal policy were soon disappointed. Imbued with a romantic-medieval concept of a Christian state, he proved even more reactionary than his father. He considered that Judaism was not a religion, but the remnant of a political constitution (see the ideas of Moses *Mendelssohn). Frederick William determined to reorganize the Jews as an independent corporation on medieval lines, alongside but not within the Prussian body. In December 1841, he ordered that the term "civil rights" should be replaced by "rights accorded by the 1812 edict," a preliminary for a new Jewish constitution under which the Jews were to have rights within their own community only. G. *Riesser, L. *Philippson, Johann *Jacoby, and Moritz *Veit led the struggle against the royal policy, supported by various Christian liberals as well as by the provincial estates, who were in favor of general and Jewish service in the army and full application of the 1812 edict. The king's most important supporters were F. J. *Stahl and *Bismarck. Despite vigorous opposition, he carried through his Jewish constitution in 1847 with only minor revisions. The king's "corporationist" plans were made obsolete by the 1848 revolution, but on the basis of the 1847 constitution the Prussian state recognized only individual Jewish communities.

Bibliography: H. Fischer, *Judentum, Staat und Heer in Preussen* (1968), index, s.v. *Friedrich Wilhelm.* [Ed.]

FREEDMAN, BARNETT (1901–1958), British artist and book illustrator. Freedman, who was born in the East End of London, was bedridden from the age of 9 to 12 years. He then became a draftsman for monumental masons and

Barnett Freedman, British painter and illustrator. Photo Colin Tait, London.

attended evening classes in art. In 1922 he obtained a small annual grant and admittance to the Royal College of Art. In 1940 he was appointed an official war artist to the British Army, and later to the admiralty. His most important artistic achievement was as a book illustrator. In 1927 he illustrated Laurence Binyon's poem *The Wonder Night*, followed two years later by an edition of *Memoirs of an Infantry Officer* by Siegfried *Sassoon. In 1935 he designed the commemorative stamp for the Jubilee of King George V. He illustrated a series of classics published by Limited Editions Club and the Heritage Club of America. His paintings of street scenes and itinerant musicians were influenced by memories of his childhood in the Jewish working-class area.

Bibliography: J. Mayne, *Barnett Freedman* (1948). [CH.S.S.]

FREEDMAN, SAMUEL (1908–), Canadian jurist. Born in Russia, Freedman was taken to Canada at the age of three. He lectured at the Manitoba law school from 1941 to

Samuel Freedman, Canadian jurist. Photo Jerry Cairns, Winnipeg.

1959, and from 1959 to 1968 was chancellor of the University of Manitoba. In 1952 he was made a queen's counsel and appointed a judge of the court of Queen's Bench in Manitoba. In 1960 he was promoted to the Manitoba Court of Appeal. A prominent figure in the Jewish community, Freedman was active in the *B'nai B'rith and was a governor of the Hebrew University of Jerusalem. [B.G.K.]

FREEDOM. The concept of freedom in the Bible is found in the injunction that on the advent of the *Jubilee, "liberty was proclaimed throughout the land unto all the inhabitants thereof... and ye shall return every man unto his family" (Lev. 25:10). Thus the freedom envisaged encompassed not only the emancipation of slaves, but the return to one's ancestral lands which had been alienated by sale. This concept is extended in Jeremiah 34, in which the prophet denounces the people for later disregarding the order given by Zedekiah "that every man should let his man-servant and every man his maid-servant, being a Hebrew man or a Hebrew woman, go free; that none should make bondsmen of them, even of a Jew his brother" (34:9). Although the Talmud also uses the word freedom in antithesis to slavery (BK 15a), in general it employs the word in a wider sense as denoting absence of subservience, and the concept that it was morally and legally wrong under any circumstances for a Jew to be dependent upon or subservient to another Jew became one of the fundamental principles of the rabbis, but to the evil of the denial of freedom to Jew by his fellow Jew was added that of the subservience of the Jew to foreign rule.

The concept of that freedom was unique in the insistence on the freedom of the individual in order that he might be free to devote himself utterly and without restraint to the service of God and the fulfillment of His will. The locus classicus of this conception is the rabbinical interpretation given to the verse "For unto Me are the children of Israel servants," which is emphasized by the repetition "they are My servants" (Lev. 25:55), upon which the rabbis comment: "they are My servants, but not the servants of My servants." It is the basis of the reason given by Johanan b. Zakkai for the law that a Hebrew slave who chose to remain in slavery when the time came for his emancipation had to have his ear bored (Ex. 21:6), an interpretation which is called "a species of *ḥomer*" (probably "an important ethical principle") "Why the ear of all the organs of the body? God said: Because it was the ear which heard Me say upon Mount Sinai 'Unto Me are the children of Israel servants, but not servants to My servants,' yet its owner went and acquired a [human] master for himself, therefore let that ear be bored" (Kid. 22b; in the *Mekhilta* to Ex. 21:6 Simeon b. Judah ha-Nasi derives the same ethical lesson from the fact that the ear had to be placed against the doorpost).

It was in accordance with this principle of freedom from man in order to be free for the service of God that R. Joshua b. Levi stated, "No man is free but he who labors in the Torah" (Avot 6:2), which may be a protest against those who thought of freedom in purely physical or rational terms. This principle was enshrined to such an extent that the Talmud actually asks how, in view of this interpretation, it is permitted for a Jew even to be the employee of another Jew and replies that the right of the laborer to withdraw his labor at any time preserves his essential liberty (see *Labor). This conception of the right of the Jew to individual freedom was extended to include national freedom from foreign rule. R. Judah interprets the freedom which comes from the study of the Torah as "freedom from exile" (Ex. R. 32:1), and the theme that failure to exercise this freedom brings in its train political servitude was a favorite theme of the rabbis in the period immediately following the destruction of the Temple, when foreign rule became a grim fact. Thus Johanan b. Zakkai homiletically interprets Song of Songs 1:8, "You were unwilling to subject yourselves to heaven; as a result you are subjected to the nations of the world"; and his contemporary Neḥunya b. ha-Kanah states, "He who accepts the yoke of Torah will have the yoke of foreign rule removed from him, and he who casts off the yoke of Torah, upon him will be laid the yoke of foreign rule" (Avot 3:5). The striking statement of Samuel in the Talmud (Sanh. 91b et al.) that the only difference between the present world and the Messianic age is subjection to foreign rule is actually accepted as the *halakhah* by Maimonides in the last chapter of the *Mishneh Torah*, but he also emphasizes that the "sages and prophets did not long for the days of the Messiah that Israel might exercise dominion over the world, or rule over the heathens, or be exalted by the nations, or that it might eat, drink, and be merry. Their aspiration was that Israel be free to devote itself to the Torah and its wisdom, with none to oppress or disturb it" (Yad, Melakhim 12:4).

Most extreme in their passion for liberty were the members of the "Fourth Philosophy," the *Zealots or *Sicarii as the case may be. Josephus states of them that "this school agrees in all other respects with the opinions of the Pharisees, except that they have a passion for liberty that is almost unconquerable, since they are convinced that God alone is their leader and master. They think little of submitting to death, if only they may avoid calling any man master" (Ant. 18:23), a principle which they carried into practice with their mass suicide at *Masada rather than submit to the Romans. It has been suggested that the differences between them and the Pharisees with regard to the love of freedom was that whereas the Pharisees, while

extolling the importance of liberty, did not include it among the cardinal principles for which one should suffer martyrdom rather than transgress, those members of the "Fourth Philosophy" did include it. The ideal of freedom was kept alive in the Jewish consciousness throughout the period of exile. The four cups of wine obligatory on the *seder night of Passover, the festival of freedom (Pes. 108b), are the symbol of freedom, and in the daily liturgy in the evening prayer, the Exodus from Egypt is referred to as the emergence of the children of Israel to "everlasting freedom."
[L.I.R.]

Freedom of Thought. Because there never was a single body of official doctrine, Jewish tradition not only permitted, but even encouraged freedom of thought. Speculation about the fundamentals of faith was held to be a desirable and meritorious activity. *Baḥya ibn Paquda, the 11th century moralist and philosopher, states explicitly that, "On the question whether we are under an obligation to investigate the doctrine of God's unity or not, I assert that anyone capable of investigating this and similar philosophical themes by rational methods is bound to do so according to his powers and capacities . . . Anyone who neglects to institute such an inquiry is blameworthy and is accounted as belonging to the class of those who fall short in wisdom and conduct" (*Ḥovot ha-Levavot, "Sha'ar ha-Yiḥud,"* ch. 3). Maimonides echoes this view, as do many other major Jewish thinkers. The last major Jewish philosopher of the Middle Ages, Joseph *Albo, summarized this tradition of freedom of thought: "It is clear now that every intelligent person is permitted to investigate the fundamental principles of religion and to interpret the biblical texts in accordance with the truth as it seems to him" (*Sefer ha-Ikkarim,* pt. 1, ch. 2). This freedom is evident in the lack of any one official Jewish creed. Proposed creeds vary in content, principles, and number of articles. From antiquity to the present Judaism has found room for almost every conception of God known to civilized man so long as it is consistent with the principle of God's unity.

The Israelites passing from slavery to freedom, from the *Barcelona Haggadah,* Spain, 14th century. London, British Museum, Add. Ms. 14761, fol. 66v.

Alongside this tradition of freedom of thought there was also a restrictive drive which sought to limit what Jews might think and even what they might read. A Mishnah teaches that certain categories of Jews forfeit their share in the world to come, either because they hold erroneous beliefs or because they read forbidden books (Sanh. 10:1). This repressive aspect of the tradition receives its most extreme form in the codified rule that certain kinds of heretics may, or even must be put to death (Av. Zar. 26b; Sh. Ar., YD 158; 2). There is, however, little evidence that such a rule was ever put into practice. David *Hoffmann argued that this rule was codified at a time of extreme Christian religious zealotry, and was intended to show that Jews were also devoted to their faith. He denied that this rule was ever intended to be enforced, adding that in modern times such a rule is a profanation of God's name. Restrictions were also enacted against the study of certain subjects. The Mishnah records the decree that "no man should teach his son Greek" which is interpreted to mean the study of Greek philosophy (Sot. 9:14; 49b). The study of mystic traditions as well was restricted. The Talmud relates that only one of the four sages who "entered the Garden" (i.e., engaged in esoteric speculation) departed unhurt (Ḥag. 14b). In codifying these laws Moses Isserles stated, "It is only permitted to 'enter the Garden' after one has satiated himself with meat and wine," i.e., the study of mysticism is only allowed for he who is thoroughly grounded in the study of *halakhah* and the details of the commandments (Sh. Ar., YD 246:4). In the Middle Ages bans were also imposed on the premature study of philosophy and sciences. Solomon b. Abraham *Adret proclaimed in his ban of 1305 that physics and metaphysics could be studied from the age of 25, but laid no restriction on the study of astronomy and medicine (other communities in southern France banned the study of philosophy until the age of 30; see *Maimonidean Controversy).

Freedom of thought was also threatened by those who banned or burned books which they found offensive. An almost continuous line leads from the talmudic prohibitions against certain works to the 20th-century zealot who burned a nonorthodox prayer book in New York in 1944. Over the centuries there were bans on and burnings of the works of some *Karaites, Maimonides' *Guide,* the *Me'or Einayim* of Azariah de *Rossi, and even of some books of M. Ḥ. *Luzzatto. The rise of *Ḥasidism and of the *Haskalah generated such intense efforts to suppress their literatures that one writer asserts that "there was no period in Jewish history in which so large a number of books . . . were banned or burned."

Such practical restrictions on freedom of thought came to an end in the 19th century. They can still be found only among some minor sects of the extreme orthodox right wing, but have no effect on the life and thought of the vast majority of Jews. In a peculiar way these restrictive elements in the Jewish tradition evoked a basic commitment to freedom of thought. Those who imposed bans on books could only enforce them locally, since there was no central authority. Such bans usually evoked counter-bans so that a book proscribed in one community found vigorous defenders in another. However great the stature of those who sought to prevent a book from being read, there were always men of equal stature who came to its defense and made it available. In this way, even when subjected to severe strains, freedom of thought was preserved and protected.
[Ma.Fo.]

Bibliography: In the Bible: L. I. Rabinowitz, in: *Sinai,* 55 (1964), 329–32; S. Goren, *Torat ha-Mo'adim* (1964), 334–45. In Jewish Philosophy: M. Carmilly-Weinberger, *Sefer ve-Sayif* (1966); R. Gordis, *The Root and the Branch* (1962), 31–53; D. J.

Silver, *Maimonidean Criticism and the Maimonidean Controversy* (1965); E. Shmueli, *Bein Emunah li-Khefirah* (1962), 161–78.

FREEHOF, SOLOMON BENNETT (1892–), U.S. Reform rabbi and scholar. Freehof, born in London, was taken to the United States in 1903 by his parents, who settled in Baltimore. He graduated from the University of

Solomon B. Freehof, U.S. Reform rabbi and scholar. Portrait by Joseph Margulies.

Cincinnati (1914) and a year later was ordained at Hebrew Union College, whose faculty he then joined. After serving as a chaplain with the American forces in Europe during World War I, Freehof became professor of liturgy at Hebrew Union College. In 1924 he became rabbi of Congregation Kehillath Anshe Maarav in Chicago, and in 1934 he was appointed rabbi of Congregation Rodef Shalom in Pittsburgh. Freehof's scholarly endeavors were largely in two fields. The first was Jewish liturgy. In 1930 he was appointed chairman of the Reform Committee on Liturgy of the Central Conference of American Rabbis, whose work led to the publication of the two-volume *Union Prayer Book* (1940–45) and the *Union Home Prayer Book* (1951), both of which stressed relevance to modern life and the inclusion of contemporary material in the service. His second main interest was the development of Jewish law as displayed in the literature of the responsa and its bearing on modern Jewish practice. He was appointed head of the Responsa Committee of the Central Conference of American Rabbis in 1955. He wrote: *Stormers of Heaven* (1931); *The Book of Psalms: A Commentary* (1938); *Modern Jewish Preaching* (1941); *The Small Sanctuary: Judaism in the Prayer Book* (1942); *In the House of the Lord* (1942); *Reform Jewish Practice and its Rabbinic Background* (1944); *Preface to Scripture* (1950); *The Responsa Literature* (1955); *The Book of Job: A Commentary* (1958); *Recent Reform Responsa* (1963); *A Treasury of Responsa* (1963); and *Current Reform Responsa* (1969).

Bibliography: Rodef Shalom Congregation, *Essays in Honor of Solomon B. Freehof* (1964).

[H.H.]

FREEMAN, JOSEPH (1897–1965), U.S. author, critic, and journalist. Freeman was taken to the U.S. from the Ukraine as a boy of seven. After his graduation in 1919, he joined the editorial staff of Harper's *Illustrated History of the World War*, but in the following year moved to Paris, where he worked for the *Chicago Tribune*, subsequently representing both the *Tribune* and the New York *Daily News* in London. In 1922 he returned to New York, where he used his journalistic talents in support of socialism, working first for *The Liberator* and later also for the *Partisan Review*. In 1926 he helped to found the monthly *New Masses*. He first represented the periodical in Moscow, and at various times during the 1930s was its editor. Freeman and Michael *Gold were the two outstanding American writers of the Left during the years preceding World War II. Freeman's works include *Dollar Diplomacy: A Study in American Imperialism* (1925), a radical assessment of U.S. foreign policy written in collaboration with S. Nearing; *Voices of October: Art and Literature in Soviet Russia* (1930), with J. Kunitz and L. Lozowick; and *The Soviet Worker* (1932). His autobiography, *An American Testament: A Narrative of Rebels and Romantics* (1936), is one of the most valuable source books on the radical literary politics of his time. Under the stress of the Nazi-Soviet pact of 1939 Freeman finally broke with the Communists. He later published two novels, *Never Call Retreat* (1943), which dealt with the frustrations of a political refugee, and *The Long Pursuit* (1947), set in postwar occupied Germany.

Bibliography: D. Aaron, *Writers on the Left* (1961), 68–90, 119–48, 365–75; S. J. Kunitz, *Twentieth Century Authors*, first supplement (1955), s.v.; *New York Times* (Aug. 11, 1965), 35.

[M.H.H.]

FREEMASONS, members of a secret society which developed out of craftmen's associations, originally consisting of masons proper. From the 17th century the society existed mainly as a social organization and cultivated a tradition of doctrines, passwords, and symbols, a ritual which is supposed to derive from the building of the First Temple in Jerusalem. The coat of arms of the English lodges is said to have been adapted from one painted by Jacob Judah Leon *Templo. Modern Freemasonry began in England around 1717; in 1723 the London Grand Lodge adopted a constitution formulated by the Reverend James Anderson, based on some older traditions. A printed constitution facilitated the foundation of new lodges on the basis of a recognized authority. During the next decades the lodges spread, in Britain, France, Holland, Germany, and many other countries. All the lodges regarded themselves as belonging to the same fraternity, and a Freemason appearing at any lodge with a certificate of membership was admitted to the work of the lodge and entitled to hospitality and help in case of need. The first paragraph of the constitution stated that anyone found to be true and honest, of whatever denomination or persuasion, was to be admitted. The constitution obliged the member only to hold "to that religion in which all men agree, leaving their particular opinions to themselves," a declaration of religious tolerance based on the current Deist trend, which postulated a Supreme Being who could be conceived of by any rational being. It is not known whether the possible aspiration of Jews to be accepted in the lodges influenced the wording of the constitution; yet it is formulated in a way that includes Jews as possible members. Thus, when a Jew asked for admission in 1732, one of the London lodges accepted him. The doors of the English lodges remained open to Jews in principle, although in practice there was some discrimination.

The Deistic declaration in the constitution did not remove some traces of Christian practice, including the New Testament, playing a part in the lodges. Nevertheless in the middle of the 18th century Jews joined the lodges, not only in England but also in Holland, France, and Germany. A Jewish lodge, the Lodge of Israel, was established in London in 1793.

Masonic tolerance weakened as a result of attacks made on it by the traditional sectors of all religions, who feared its all-embracing intentions. The Catholic Church banned—and still bans—Freemasonry in a bull promulgated by Pope Clement XII in 1738. The Deism of Freemasonry was clearly contrary to Church doctrines, and conservative Protestants and Jews also felt that its rituals were in conflict with their religious beliefs. To the objection of the Churches and other conservative elements in society, the Masons reacted by an apology which, in the main, tried to prove that Freemasonry was not an un-Christian institution, an argument supported by the fact that the Masonic fraternity consisted exclusively of Christians: Jews, Muslims, and pagans were not and should not be accepted. However, in England and Holland no objection in principle to Jewish applicants existed and in France the objections were swept away with the Revolution. Here Freemasonry became a kind of secular church in which Jews could participate freely. Adolphe *Crémieux was not only a Freemason from his early youth but in 1869 became the Grand Master of the Grand Lodge of the Scottish Rite in Paris.

In Germany objection to Jewish membership persisted, remaining a matter of controversy for generations. Until the 1780s only a few German Jews were admitted to Masonry. About this time Jewish applications for admission to the Masonic lodges became frequent. Though there were some attempts to open the lodges to Jews, no German Freemason of any standing at that time advocated Jewish admittance. Some German Jews became Freemasons when traveling abroad in England, Holland, and, particularly, in post-revolutionary France. In Germany itself French or French-initiated lodges were established during the Napoleonic occupation. A Jewish lodge, L'Aurore Naissante, was founded in Frankfort, authorized in 1808 by the Grand Orient in Paris. These ventures, however, hardened the resistance of the indigenous lodges in Frankfort and in other German towns, and some Masonic fraternities introduced amended constitutions specifically excluding Jews.

In the 1830s German intellectuals who were Freemasons protested against this exclusion, joined by Masons from Holland, England, France, and even by a lodge in New York, who resented the fact that their Jewish members were refused entrance to German lodges. By 1848 some lodges admitted Jews, if not as full members at least as visitors. The years of the 1848 Revolution swept away some of the paragraphs excluding Jews, and the Frankfort Jewish lodges were now acknowledged by their Christian counterparts. The exceptions were the Prussian lodges, controlled by law from 1798 by the mother lodges from Berlin. In 1840 there were 164 Prussian lodges with a membership of 13,000. No Jew could ever be admitted to these, not even as a visitor, but many members, and sometimes entire lodges, wanted to reintroduce the original English constitution which excluded the attachment of Freemasonry to any specific religion. By the early 1870s most branches admitted Jews as visitors, sometimes even as permanent visitors, and in one of the branches of the Prussian lodges the restrictive paragraph was removed in 1872. A new wave of anti-Semitism, however, soon swept over the Bismarckian Reich, and by 1876 the lodges were already adopting an anti-Semitic tone. Those Jews who had been accepted by Prussian lodges left during the anti-Semitic outbreaks, followed by some liberal-minded Christians who were shocked by the behavior of a society ostensibly committed to the ideal of brotherhood.

Some Freemasons genuinely believed that confessing the Jewish faith was a disqualification for Freemasonry, which they regarded as a Christian institution, a view contested by those who adhered to the original English constitution and called themselves humanistic Freemasons. The struggle between the two trends continued during the 19th century.

In Germany in the 1860s Jews and Freemasons began to be identified as twin agencies responsible for undermining traditional society. This combined criticism of the two groups was transplanted to France, where a succession of books stressed *"le peril judéo-maçonique."* The notion of a sinister alliance between the two played a conspicuous part in the *Dreyfus Affair and it became an anti-Semitic commonplace. *The Protocols of the *Elders of Zion* (first published in Russia in 1904) included the idea of a Jewish-Masonic plot to control the world. In Germany up to this time, Freemasonry was still thought of as a conservative and partly anti-Semitic association. When the *Protocols* were translated into German and English in the 1920s, Jews and Freemasons were identified as the sinister agents of the outbreak of World War I and of the German defeat. The slogan *Juden und Freimaurer* became a battle cry of the German right wing, and was utilized by Hitler in his rise to power. During World War II, Freemasons together with "Bolsheviks and Jews" were persecuted by the Nazis. [EH/ED.]

In the U.S. Jewish names appear among the founders of Freemasonry in colonial America, and in fact it is probable that Jews were the first to introduce the movement into the country. Tradition connects Mordecai Campanall, of Newport, Rhode Island, with the supposed establishment of a lodge there in 1658. In Georgia four Jews appear to have been among the founders of the first lodge, organized in Savannah in 1734. Moses Michael *Hays, identified with the introduction of the Scottish Rite into the United States, was appointed deputy inspector general of Masonry for North America in about 1768. In 1769 Hays organized the King David's Lodge in New York, moving it to Newport in 1780. He was Grand Master of the Grand Lodge of Massachusetts from 1788 to 1792. Moses *Seixas was prominent among those who established the Grand Lodge of Rhode Island, and was Grand Master from 1802 to 1809. A contemporary of Hays, Solomon *Bush, was deputy inspector general of Masonry for Pennsylvania, and in 1781 Jews were influential in the Sublime Lodge of Perfection in Philadelphia which played an important part in the early history of Freemasonry in America. Other early leaders of the movement included: Isaac da *Costa (d. 1783), whose name is found among the members of King Solomon's Lodge, Charleston, in 1753; Abraham Forst, of Philadelphia, deputy inspector general for Virginia in 1781; and Joseph Myers, who held the same office, first for Maryland, and later for South Carolina. In 1793 the cornerstone ceremony for the new synagogue in Charleston, South Carolina, was conducted according to the rites of Freemasonry.

The later history of Freemasonry in the United States shows a number of prominent Jewish names, but nothing corresponding to their influence in the earlier period. In 1843 the Grand Lodge in New York addressed a letter to the *Mutterloge* in Berlin complaining against the refusal of German lodges to accept registered Masons of the American Lodge because they were Jewish. Nonsectarianism in matters of religion has always characterized American Freemasonry, and regulations excluding Jews have not been part of their constitutions, though whether admissions policies have ever been restrictive would be difficult to establish. The apparatus of secrecy, ritual, and regalia which was a feature of *B'nai B'rith in its early years no doubt reflected the influence of Masonic practice as well as a desire to offer a substitute within the Jewish community. [S.D.T.]

In Israel. In the Masonic world Jerusalem has always been regarded as the birthplace of Freemasonry; according to its tradition, there were Masonic lodges in the Holy Land at the time of the erection of King Solomon's Temple. Lodges are known there from the middle of the 19th century. During the Ottoman regime, six lodges were established in the country. The first regular one was founded in Jerusalem in May 1873, under the jurisdiction of the Grand Lodge of Canada. In 1891 another was established in Jaffa under the National Grand Lodge of Egypt. During the years 1910–11 the Grand Lodge of Scotland founded three lodges. During the British mandatory regime, Freemasonry flourished under several jurisdictions, in the main those of the Grand Lodges of Palestine and of Scotland. In 1932, four lodges in Jerusalem, holding under the National Grand Lodge of Egypt, constituted themselves into the National Grand Lodge of Palestine. Later, three of other jurisdictions joined it.

With the establishment of the State of Israel, a number of changes occurred: the lodges holding under the Grand Lodge of England and one holding under the Grand Lodge of Scotland moved out of the area. The remaining lodges of foreign origin and the five holding under the German Symbolic Grand Lodge in Exile joined the National Grand Lodge of Palestine. The five remaining lodges holding under the Grand Lodge of Scotland started to negotiate with their Grand Lodge to consecrate a Sovereign Grand Lodge of the State of Israel, which would encompass all the Masonic lodges in the country. The United Grand Lodge of the State of Israel was constituted in 1953 and since its consecration is the only sovereign grand lodge in Israel. In 1970 it consisted of 64 lodges, with some 3,500 active members drawn from all communities; Jews, Muslims, Christians, and Druze. The activities of the Grand Lodge and its several lodges include: a mutual insurance fund; the Masonic old age home at Nahariyyah; Masonic temples all over the country; and a museum and library.

[AB.F.]

Bibliography: J. Katz, *Jews and Freemasons* (1970); idem, in: JJSO, 9 (1967), 137–47; J. G. Findel, *Die Juden als Freimaurer* (1901); D. Wright, *The Jews and Freemasonry* (1930); S. Oppenheim, in: AJHSP, 19 (1910), 1–94; A. M. Friedenberg, *ibid.*, 95–100; H. Loewe, in: *Masonic News*, 1 (1928), 14–15.

FREE SONS OF ISRAEL, U.S. Jewish fraternal order. The organization was founded by nine men in New York City on January 18, 1849. Its purpose was to seek the deletion of clauses in the New York City charter that restricted the appropriation of land for burial purposes, in order to obtain ground for a Jewish cemetery. The order long consisted primarily of German Jews. In 1970 the Free Sons of Israel consisted of 46 self-governing lodges throughout the U.S., with approximately 10,000 men and women members. Each lodge provided membership benefits, which usually included burial, medical, and other benefits. The order consisted of an Insurance Fund and Fraternal Division and was headquartered in New York City. The order maintained a toy distribution program for handicapped children; a scholarship fund for the benefit of members and their families; a Federal Credit Union, which by September 1969, had disbursed $2,000,000 in loans; an insurance fund; travel service; blood bank; athletic association; and a newspaper, *The Free Sons of Israel Reporter*.

[ED.]

FREE WILL, a philosophic and theological notion referring initially to the observation that man is able to choose between a number of possible courses of action, becoming, through his choice, the cause of the action which he selects. Among philosophers some accepted this observation as the true account of how men act, while others held that though man appears to be free to choose, his actions are, in fact, compelled, either by God or by laws of nature. While there were some Jewish philosophers who inclined toward a deterministic position, the majority affirmed that man, through choice, is the author of his own actions. Jewish philosophers generally considered a doctrine of free will as indispensable for accounting for man's moral responsibility for his own actions, and they considered it necessary for explaining God's justice in punishing evildoers. Closely related to the notion of free will are those of divine *providence and divine omniscience.

In Jewish Philosophy. PHILO. The question of the freedom of man's will is discussed in a number of places in the writings of *Philo, but his position on this matter is not sufficiently defined. On the one hand, he clearly posits the freedom of man's will, i.e., the ability to choose between good and evil out of a knowledge of the difference between the two. On the other hand, he expresses the notion that man's choosing between good and evil is predetermined by the struggle between his inclinations and by the influence of external forces. Thus it cannot be said that Philo rejected determinism, since he did assume that all the occurrences in the world are a result of a necessary chain of causes and effects. Again, Philo in a number of places points to the similarity between man's free choice, which was granted to him by God, and the free will of God himself. It is evident that this refers to voluntary action, which is independent of the previously mentioned causal chain. Moreover, Philo's notion of man's free will contains a certain innovation in contrast to traditional Greek philosophy, since Aristotelians, for example, tended to view man's free choice as a defect and deficiency, contingent on his material being. On this point too, however, Philo is not consistent, for he also expresses the opinion that all the activities of created beings, including man, are actually caused by God. Philo's attempts to bridge this contradiction are artificial.

In some places in his writings Philo expresses the opinion that it is impossible to attribute to God's will those sins which are committed intentionally, while sins against fellow-men which are committed unintentionally sometimes result from natural order, and sometimes are instruments of divine punishment for the sins of the victim. In performing his good deeds, man needs God's help and divine grace, and he cannot ascribe his virtues to himself.

SAADIAH GAON. It appears that according to Philo, there is almost no connection between the notion of man's free will and the problem of divine justice. In contrast, *Saadiah, who was heavily influenced by Mu'tazilite philosophy (see *Kalām), maintains that the idea of God's justice necessarily implies the freedom of man's will. According to Saadiah, it is impossible to think that God could compel a man to do something for which he would later punish him. Furthermore, if man has no freedom of choice, both the righteous and the wicked should be rewarded equally since they would be equally fulfilling God's will. Saadiah brings another proof for free will: man feels that he can speak or be silent, that he can take something or leave it. Similarly, he feels that there is no one to deter him from doing as he wishes (*Book of Beliefs and Opinions*, ch. 4). Therefore, Saadiah states, in accordance with Mu'tazilite teachings, that every activity is preceded in time by the ability to carry it out or to refrain from doing so. This ability can be viewed as having a real existence, and its being prior to every action is what underlies free choice. Refraining from performing a certain action is also to be counted as an action in this respect.

Since the notion of man's free will as held by Saadiah results, wholly or in part, from his need to justify God's actions, it necessarily rests on the assumption that man's primary conceptions of good and evil are fundamentally identical with those of God. God, too, acts and is bound to act in accordance with these conceptions and, contrary to the Aristotelians, Saadiah maintains that it is one of the major functions of the human intellect to apprehend these conceptions directly (without any intermediary aid).

Thus it follows that the human intellect is permitted to question God's actions, especially with regard to sins which serve as punishment, such as Absalom's rebellion against David. On the one hand, Absalom sinned in rebelling against his father, and this sin originated in his free will. On the other hand, Absalom's attempted seizure of his father's throne served as punishment for David's sins.

In contrast to the more extreme Mu'tazilites, Saadiah does not see any contradiction between man's freedom of activity and God's prior knowledge of what man will choose to do. This foreknowledge, according to Saadiah, does not limit man's freedom, since it does not cause his actions.

BAḤYA IBN PAQUDA. *Baḥya ibn Paquda (*Ḥovot ha-Levavot,* ch. 3) briefly presents the ideas of those who believe that all of man's actions are predetermined by God, as well as opposing views, which maintain that man's will is free. He reaches the conclusion that whoever delves into this question must necessarily fall into error. Therefore, man must both conduct himself like one who believes that his actions are in his own hands (i.e., that he has freedom of choice), and at the same time trust in God like one who is certain that all his actions are predetermined. This view, which rejects a theoretical solution to the problem, stems from a desire to reconcile Saadiah's theodicy with total devotion to God (including the renunciation of one's freedom of action), which is characteristic of the Muslim *Sufis by whom Baḥya was influenced.

JUDAH HALEVI. Like Saadiah, Judah *Halevi accepts the notion of the freedom of man's will, which he supports by means of various proofs, some of which are similar to Saadiah's. One such proof is that a man feels that he can speak or be silent, act or refrain from acting. A proof of the existence of free will is found by Judah Halevi in the fact that only those actions which proceed from free choice are considered to be praiseworthy or culpable. Unlike Saadiah, however, he develops, in his discussion of free will, a classification of causes, in which he is strongly influenced by the Aristotelian school of thought.

The first cause of everything, according to Judah Halevi, is God, who produces the intermediary causes, according to which all actions and occurrences are either natural (i.e., resulting from natural order), accidental, or voluntary (resulting from human choice). Even the first two classes are not entirely brought about by necessity, but only free choice belongs completely to the realm of the possible; before the actual deed there is no necessity that it should be done.

Like Saadiah, Judah Halevi also maintains that there is no contradiction between the notion of free choice and the view that God knows in advance what will happen. Like Saadiah, he also maintains that God's foreknowledge cannot be regarded as a cause which brings about the event. Nevertheless, Judah Halevi states that his definition of free will as an intermediary cause, which is produced by the first cause, makes it necessary to see the voluntary acts as being under the influence of divine decree.

Man must conduct himself to the best of his ability. Exaggerated dependence on God may bring him into danger, thus, the warning; "Do not try the Lord." Sometimes, however, God acts without recourse to the intermediary causes, thereby bringing about miracles, such as Moses' being saved from starvation during the 40 days he was on Mount Sinai, or the defeat of Sennacherib.

ABRAHAM IBN DAUD. Abraham *ibn Daud stated that he wrote his book *Ha-Emunah ha-Ramah* for the sole purpose of discussing the question of free will. Nonetheless, only a small section of the book (second treatise, 6:2, ed. by S. Weil, 93ff.) is devoted to this problem. Ibn Daud's position with regard to free will is similar to that of Judah Halevi. He classifies causes into divine, natural, accidental, and voluntary. There are some people, he says, in whom good or evil habits are so deeply ingrained that they are actually never required to exercise their free choice; but the majority of people are between these two extremes, and must therefore choose between good and evil. When they choose the good they become worthy of divine providence, while he who chooses evil is abandoned to his own resources. Ibn Daud is convinced that the existence of the possible in the world—and thus the non-existence of absolute determinism—is a defect. However, it should be pointed out, in this respect Ibn Daud departs from the teachings of his master, *Avicenna, whom he usually follows, since Avicenna believed that everything, including voluntary acts, is predetermined.

MAIMONIDES. In his *Guide of the Perplexed* *Maimonides deals with the question of free will in connection with providence (3:17). He distinguishes between five doctrines of providence, the last of which, that of the Torah, states that man can do everything according to his free choice. The question is whether Maimonides was convinced that man's choice and will are determined by prior causes, as was held by Muslim philosophers such as Avicenna, or whether he viewed the choice and voluntary activity of man as being uninfluenced by absolute determinism. There are various passages in the *Guide* which attest to his having followed the second opinion.

God's knowledge, which is only homonymous with human knowledge, controls each and every event, for God knows, "according to the view of our Torah," which of the possible outcomes will ultimately be actualized. This knowledge does not remove the things which are known, including human actions, from the realm of the possible. In his *Mishneh Torah,* which unlike the *Guide,* was intended for a popular audience, Maimonides takes a clearer position with regard to free will: every person may choose to be good or evil. God does not determine in advance whether a particular man will be righteous or wicked. A man can carry out any action, be it good or bad. If this were not so, the entire Torah would be purposeless; the wicked person could not be punished for his sins, nor the righteous be rewarded for his good deeds. In the same way that God instituted order in the universe, so it is His will that man be responsible for his own actions, by which he will be judged. Against the argument that God knows in advance whether a person will be righteous or wicked, Maimonides states that God's knowledge, being so unlike man's, cannot be apprehended by the human intellect. What is known beyond a shadow of a doubt is that man is responsible for his own deeds, and that God neither influences nor decrees that he should act in a certain manner. This is proven not only by religious tradition, but by clear arguments of reason (Yad, Teshuvah ch. 5).

Here, as in Saadiah, there is a clear connection between free will and the notion of God's justice. Unlike Saadiah and Judah Halevi, however, Maimonides does not avoid the difficulty involved in reconciling the idea of free will with the notion of God's omniscience. Contrary to some of his successors, he does not attempt to solve this difficulty, since he believes that its solution lies outside the scope of human understanding.

LEVI BEN GERSHOM. The post-Maimonidean Aristotelians placed great emphasis on the contradiction between God's all-inclusive foreknowledge and the idea of free will. *Levi b. Gershom accepts the notion of free will (*Milḥamot Adonai* 3:6), but offers his own solution to the difficulty by his interpretation of God's knowledge. According to him, God knows not only his own essence, but also (as does the active intellect) the general categories, i.e., the order of the universe, which is determined by the position of the stars. It is not necessary, however, that all events actually occuring in the world should correspond to his general order. By virtue of his free will man may act in contradiction to what has been predestined for him by the position of the stars. Thus, the knowledge of God and of the active intellect does not encompass those events which actually come into being, but they know only what should occur. Thus in his notion of free will Gersonides is following both the tradition of Jewish philosophy and Aristotelian Greek philosophy, which did not see absolute determinism as operating in the sublunar world.

Ḥasdai Crescas. A similar determinism underlies the idea of free will of Ḥasdai *Crescas (*Or Adonai* 2:5), which in some ways reverts to the Muslim philosophical tradition which held, following Avicenna, that man's choice is absolutely predetermined by a chain of prior causes: internal causes, based in man's character, and external causes, which are the factors influencing him. As Y. Baer has shown (in *Tarbiz,* 11 (1940), 188–206), Crescas was strongly influenced in this notion by *Abner of Burgos.

Crescas' notion, which is similar to that of Avicenna, is that voluntary actions are possible in themselves, but are necessary in terms of their causes. Crescas regards these actions as being necessary since they are known to God before their execution. He thinks, however, that this idea should not be made known to the masses who might use it as a justification for doing evil, since they will think that the punishment follows the sin in a causal chain of events. Despite this view, however, Crescas distinguishes between voluntary actions and acts carried out under compulsion. It is only proper, according to him, that only the former type should be subject to reward and punishment, and only in relation to this type of action can the commandments and prohibitions of the Torah act as a deterrent. Nevertheless, in this capacity, the commandments and prohibitions do not limit the activity of absolute determinism. On the other hand, man's beliefs and opinions do not depend on his own will and he should therefore not be rewarded or punished for them. [Sh.P.]

In Talmud and Midrash. The doctrine of free will, expressed in the idea that man is free to choose between good and evil, was at the core of the Pharisaic outlook. Josephus indeed characterizes the differences between the Pharisees and their Sadducean and Essene opponents as between those who accepted both the freedom of man and divine providence (the Pharisees), those who ascribed everything to chance, denying providential guidance (the Sadducees), and those who denied human freedom, maintaining a doctrine of predestination (the Essenes; Wars 2:162ff; Ant. 13:171; 18:12f.). Though some doubt has been cast on Josephus' account because of his tendency to explain matters in terms of Greek philosophical schools (see G. F. Moore, *Judaism* vol. 3 p. 139), there seems no grounds for rejecting the main outlines of his characterization (Urbach, *Ḥazal: Pirkei Emunot ve-De'ot* (1969), 227).

Though both the doctrine of man's freedom and that of divine providence were adhered to by the rabbis as central to their faith, they do not seem to have been integrated in any systematic way in the talmudic texts which deal with the subject. On the one hand, one finds constant reference to the notion that nothing happens in this world which is not in some way determined from on high: "No man can touch that which has been prepared in advance for his friend" (Yoma 38b); "No man injures his finger here below unless it has been decreed for him on high" (Ḥul. 7b); "Never does a snake bite . . . or a lion tear [its prey] . . . or a government interfere in men's lives unless incited to do so from on high" (Eccles. R. 10:11); "Everything is in the hands [i.e., control] of heaven except cold and heat" (Ket. 30a); "Forty days before a child is formed a heavenly voice decrees so-and-so's daughter shall marry so-and-so" (Sot. 2a). On the other hand the whole rabbinic theological structure of reward and punishment turns on the idea that man is free to do evil or good (see Deut. 30:15–19; and Sif. Deut. 53–54). As Josephus mentions, the rabbis wished to maintain both doctrines despite the tension between them, though they were aware of this tension. Before conception the angel appointed over conception takes a seminal drop and asks God:"What is to become of this drop? Is it to develop into a person strong or weak, wise or foolish, rich or poor?" (Nid. 16b). But no mention is made of its becoming wicked or righteous, because "Everything is in the hands of heaven except the fear of heaven" *(ibid.).*

The combination of these two doctrines within rabbinic theology may be understood, not so much from the philosophical point of view, but rather from the practical point of view which underlies all rabbinic thinking. On the one hand it is necessary to think of the world as under the complete surveillance and control of heaven, a thought which adds to the confidence and trust of the Jew in God, and on the other the individual needs to make his choices and decisions on the assumption that evil and good are both within his grasp. The conceptual integration of these two ideas did not enter rabbinic thought forms. The philosophical problems surrounding God's foreknowledge and man's free will are dealt with in an equally cursory way in the texts. The most striking is the saying of Akiva, "Everything is foreseen, but freedom of choice is given" (Avot 3:15). This has been taken by some commentators—Maimonides, for example—to be a statement of the position that though God has foreknowledge of all our acts, still this does not limit our freedom (Maimonides, commentary to the Mishnah, Avot 3:15). Though such a doctrine—that God's foreknowledge is such as not to be philosophically irreconcilable with human freedom—may have been held in some inchoate form by the rabbis, the saying of Akiva has been interpreted as an assertion that God sees all man's acts, even those performed in the privacy of his room (see Rashi on Avot 3:15; Urbach, op. cit., 229–30).

In Modern Jewish Thought. For Hermann *Cohen, freedom of the will—in the sense of being unaffected by mechanical causes—does not exist. However, while he relates causation to the individual man, Cohen holds that freedom of the will does exist in the ethical realm when applied to the goal of mankind. We must assume an independent ethical realm of being in which man can make his own decisions in accord with the rules of that realm. The freedom of the individual depends on how far the individual acts in accord with the goal of mankind. Real freedom will exist only in the future—in the ideal society which is mankind's goal; as of now, freedom is not given but a task to be worked at (*Juedische Schriften,* 1 (1924), 28).

For Martin *Buber free will is given even though in the realm I-It, causality rules. But in the realm of relation, I-Thou—real decision can, indeed must, take place: "if there were a devil it would not be one who decided against God, but one who, in eternity, came to no decision" (*I and Thou* (1958), 52, cf. 51f.). For Buber the main problem is not whether there is choice (in the realm of I-Thou), but the quality of the choices made—for good or evil. Since man is free to choose evil he is also free to overcome evil. Modern man because of prevalent ideologies based on scientific materialism or its counterparts (e. g., dialectical materialism) is even more of a believer in blind fate than pagan man. However, according to Buber, man is really free in his depths, and his destiny is not decreed by fate but is his true fulfillment when met in free will: ". . . the free man has no purpose here and means there, which he fetches for his purpose: he has only the one thing, his repeated decision to approach his destiny" (*I and Thou,* 60). Free man is not without influences from outside himself, but only he can really respond to outside events and perceive the unique in each event. External events are preconditioned for his action, not determining factors in his character. The free man responds where others react. Man's freedom lies not in the absence of external limitations but in the ability, despite them, to enter into dialogue, i.e., I-Thou relation.

A. J. *Heschel makes a distinction in external happenings, dividing them into what he calls "process," a regular pattern, and "event," an extraordinary, or unique thing. The essence of man's freedom is his ability to surpass himself. To a certain extent man is enslaved by his environment, society, and character, but man can think, will, and take decisions beyond these limitations. If men are treated as "processes" freedom is destroyed. Man is free at rare moments; freedom is an "event." Everyone has the potentiality for freedom, but only rarely achieves it. Free will, the ability to choose between two alternatives, is not the same as freedom, for though the latter includes choice, its achievement lies in the fact that one goes beyond oneself, and disregards the self as its own end. Thus man must choose, although he can choose even to ignore freedom—which would be to choose evil (see *God in Search of Man* (1955), 409–13; *Man is not Alone* (1951), 142, 146).

Mordecai *Kaplan believes that the idea of free will as it was formulated in the past is out of step with the spirit of the present which looks for causality in everything. He therefore interprets the doctrine of free will as the expression of the idea that there can be no responsibility without freedom. The problem of freedom therefore becomes a spiritual one having to do with the significance of individuality and selfhood on the one hand, and liberation of personality from self-worship and desire for power, on the other (see *Meaning of God in Modern Jewish Religion* (1937), 270–296). [Ed.]

Bibliography: H. A. Wolfson, *Philo*, 2 vols. (1947), index; idem, in: PAAJR, 11 (1941), 105–63; Husik, Philosophy, index, s.v. *Freedom of the Will;* Guttmann, Philosophies, index, s.v. *Will, freedom of the;* idem, in: *Jewish Studies in Memory of G. A. Kohut* (1935), 325–49; J. Guttmann, *Die Religionsphilosophie des Abraham Ibn Daud* (1879); idem, *Die Religionsphilosophie des Saadia* (1882); S. Schechter, *Some Aspects of Rabbinic Theology*, 285; J. B. Agus, *Modern Philosophers of Judaism* (1941), 73–74, 81–82; M. Friedman, *Martin Buber* (1960), 65–68, 198–9; F. Rothschild, *Between God and Man* (1959), 18–20, 26–30, 148–51.

FREIBERG, U.S. family, prominent from the mid-1800s to the 1930s. Julius Freiberg (1823–1905), who was born in Neu Leiningen, Germany, arrived in Cincinnati in 1847. In 1855 he established a distillery with Levi J. Workum. The business, which became quite successful, continued under family management until the passage of the Prohibition Amendment in 1918 forced it to close. Freiberg served as president of the Bene Israel (Orthodox) congregation for 25 years. Yet, when Isaac M. *Wise of Bene Jeshurun founded the Union of American Hebrew Congregations in 1873 and the Hebrew Union College two years later, Freiberg enthusiastically supported him. He served as vice-president of the UAHC from 1873 to 1889, and as president from 1889 to 1903. Freiberg was a member of the Board of Governors of the HUC from 1875 to 1904, and a vice-chairman for 26 years. He was a delegate to the Ohio Constitutional Convention of 1873 and held numerous other positions of public trust. In 1856 he had married Duffie Workum, the first Jewish female child born west of the Alleghenies. They helped found and support a number of Jewish charitable agencies.

His son Julius Walter Freiberg (1858–1921) also served as president of UAHC and served on the Cincinnati Charter Commission and several national Jewish organizations. His wife Stella (née Heinsheimer; 1862–1962) was one of the nine founders in 1894 of the Cincinnati Symphony Orchestra. One of the founders of the National Federation of Temple Sisterhoods, she served as its president from 1923 to 1929. J. Walter's brother Maurice J. Freiberg (1861–1936), who was president of the family business from 1905 to 1918, was also known as a philanthropist and public servant. He donated the maternity wing of Cincinnati's Jewish Hospital in memory of his wife, served as vice-president of the HUC Board of Governors, president of the Chamber of Commerce, and in many other Jewish and civic offices. Albert Henry Freiberg (1868–1940) and his son Joseph A. Freiberg (1898–) were noted orthopedic surgeons and served as faculty members of the University of Cincinnati College of Medicine. [K.D.R.]

FREIBURG IM BREISGAU, city in Baden, W. Germany. Jews were imprisoned there in 1230 by the town's overlord, and released by King Henry VII. *Rudolf of Hapsburg levied taxes from the Jews there in 1281. In 1300 the counts of Freiburg ratified the ancient rights of Freiburg Jewry. The rights to their taxes, which had been given for a short time to a Basle burgher, were restored in 1310 to the counts' authority, who granted the Jews a privilege in 1338. About this time the Jews owned 15 houses, near the synagogue and in other streets, shared by several families. The community, except pregnant women and children, was massacred by burning after one month's imprisonment, during the Black Death (January 1349). Emperor *Charles IV permitted the counts to resettle Jews in Freiburg in 1359. In 1373 a physician, master Gutleben, was admitted. In 1394 the Austrian overlord ordered that Jews should wear a special garb, with a coat and cap in dull shades; prohibited them from leaving their houses during Holy Week and from watching the religious procession; and set the weekly interest rate at 0.83%. In 1401 the Jews were expelled from the city although individual Jews were admitted from 1411–23; the expulsion became final in 1424 but Jews continued to live in the nearby villages and towns. In 1453 they were prohibited from doing business in the city.

Some Hebrew works were printed in Freiburg in the 16th century as the result of difficulties with Hebrew printing in Basle. Israel *Ẓifroni printed a number of Hebrew books for Ambrosius

The synagogue of Freiburg im Breisgau, destroyed by the Nazis in 1938. Courtesy Freiburg Municipality.

*Froben, among them Benjamin of Tudela's *Massa'ot* (1583), Jacob b. Samuel Koppelman's *Ohel Ya'akov*, and the first edition of Aaron of Pesaro's *Toledot Aharon* (1583–84). In 1503 and 1504, editions were issued of Gregorius Reisch's *Margarita Philosophica* including a page with the Hebrew alphabet in woodcut.

By the early 17th century Jews were able to enter Freiburg on business, accompanied by a constable. The first Jew received a medical degree from Freiburg University in 1791. There were 20 Jews living in Freiburg in 1846. Following the Baden emancipation law of 1862 a congregation was formed in Freiburg in 1863, and a synagogue was consecrated in 1885. It was burned down under the Nazis in 1938. The first rabbi, Adolf *Lewin, the historian of Baden Jewry, was succeeded by Max *Eschelbacher and Julius Zimmels. The legal historian Heinrich Rosen (1855–1927) was active in Jewish community life. Also of note at Freiburg University were the philosopher Edmund *Husserl, the economist Robert Liefmann, the jurist Otto Lenel, Fritz Pringsheim, the classical papyrologist, and the biochemist Siegfried Tannhauser. From 1933–35, along with six other professors, they were dismissed (Pringsheim returned from England in 1945). The Jewish population numbered 1,013 in 1903; 1,320 in 1910 (1.58% of the total), 1,399 in 1925 (1.44%), and 1,138 in June 1933 (1.5%). After the Nazi rise to power many left, and 474 remained in May 1939. In 1940, 350 Jews were expelled from Germany and interned by the French in *Gurs camp; 41 were deported to the east in 1941–42, as were almost all survivors from Gurs. After the war 15 survivors returned to Freiburg, and 78 displaced persons lived there in 1945. There were 58 Jews living in Freiburg in 1950, 111 in 1960, and 225 in 1968. A new prayer hall was consecrated in 1953. The university acquired the grounds where the synagogue once stood; it is commemorated by a memorial plaque. The *Freiburger Rundbrief*, a journal dedicated to Christian-Jewish understanding, is published in Freiburg.

Bibliography: T. Oelsner, *The Economic and Social Conditions of the Jews in Southwestern Germany* (1931); Germ Jud, 1 (1963), 108; 2 (1968), 253–7; S. W. Baron, *Social and Religious History of the Jews*, 11 (1965); A. Lewin, *Juden in Freiburg i. B.* (1890); A. Marx, *Studies in Jewish History and Booklore* (1944), 318; G. Kisch, *Zasius und Reuchlin* (1961), 1–2, 59–60; B. Schwinekoeper and F. Laubenberger, *Geschichte und Schicksal der Freiburger Juden* (1963); A. G. von Olenhausen, in: *Vierteljahreshefte fuer Zeitgeschichte*, 14 (1966), 175–206; F. Taddey and G. Hundsknurscher, *Die juedischen Gemeinden in Baden* (1967); P. Sauer, *Dokumente ueber die Verfolgung der juedischen Buerger Baden-Wuerttenbergs 1933–1945* (1965).

[T.O.]

FREIDLINA, RAKHIL KHATSKELEVNA (1906–), Russian organic chemist. She graduated from Moscow University in 1930 and worked until 1934 at the Scientific Research Institute of Insectofungicides. In 1935–39 and 1941–45, she was at the Institute of Organic Chemistry of the U.S.S.R. Academy of Sciences; in the intervening period she was at the Moscow Institute of Fine Chemical Technology. In 1945 she was appointed chief of the laboratory of the Institute of Organometallic Compounds of the U.S.S.R. Academy of Sciences, and in 1958 became a corresponding member of the Academy. She contributed many papers to Soviet scientific journals. Some have dealt with homolytic isomerization of organic compounds in solution, and her work on telomerization led to the development of the chemical precursors of some of the synthetic fibers now being made in Russia. Most of her work was with organometallic compounds. She is the author of *Sinteticheskiye metody v oblasti metalloorganicheskikh soyedineniy myshyaka* ("Synthetic methods . . . Organoarsenic Compounds," 1945) and coauthor of *Khimiya kvazikompleksnykh metalloorganicheskikh soyedineniy i yavleniya tautomerii* ("Chemistry of Quasicomplex Organometallic compounds . . .," 1947). [S.A.M.]

FREIDUS, ABRAHAM SOLOMON (1867–1923), U.S. librarian and bibliographer. Freidus was born in Riga, Latvia. He lived in Paris, in the Palestinian agricultural settlement of Zikhron Ya'akov, and in London before going to New York in 1889. Freidus completed a course in librarianship at Pratt Institute in 1894 and began working as a cataloger. In 1897 he was appointed first chief of the Jewish Division of the New York Public Library, where he developed the classification scheme used for Judaica; it was adopted for many other large American Judaica collections as well. Because of his remarkable bibliographical knowledge, Freidus was an indispensable guide to scholars in locating materials. The editors of the 12-volume *Jewish Encyclopedia* (1901–06) were especially indebted to him.

Bibliography: *Studies in Jewish Bibliography . . . in Memory of Abraham Solomon Freidus* (1929), contains a list of writings by and about Freidus, xi–xvii; N. Ausubel, in: *Morning Freiheit* (Oct. 28, 1944), section 2, pp. 4, 6 (Eng.).

[Sı.K.]

FREIER (née **Schweitzer**), **RECHA** (1892–), founder of *Youth Aliyah. She was born in Norden, Germany, and became a teacher and scholar of folklore. In 1932 she conceived the idea of Youth Aliyah and founded the first organization for the resettlement and agricultural training of young people in Palestine. After Hitler's rise to power, the idea was endorsed by the Zionist Congress of 1933, and the movement became a large-scale operation. After settling in Palestine in 1941, she founded the Agricultural Training Center for Israel Children for the education of underprivileged children in kibbutz boarding schools. She founded the Israel Composers' Fund in 1958 to foster original musical compositions, and, in 1966, established the Testimonium Scheme, a project aimed at recording major episodes in Jewish history in words and music based on authentic texts. She wrote the texts for two musical plays, *Massadah* and *Yerushalayim*. Her book *Let the Children Come: the Early History of Youth Aliyah* was published in 1961.

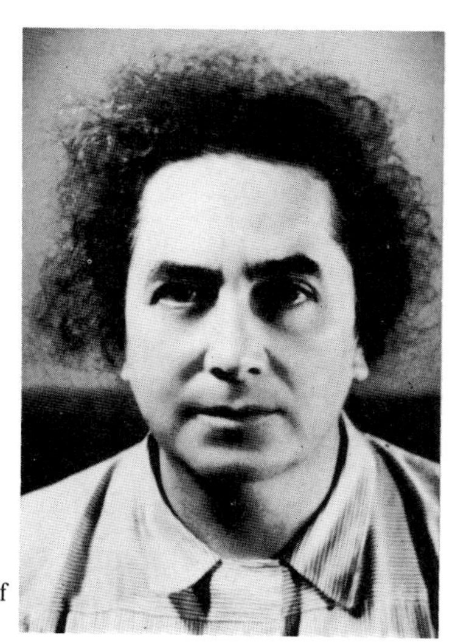

Recha Freier, founder of Youth Aliyah.

Bibliography: Tidhar, 6 (1955), 2668–69.

[A.L.]

FREILICH, MAX MELECH (1893–), Australian manufacturer and communal leader. Born in Lesko, Poland, Freilich went to Australia in 1927. From 1932 he was managing director of the Safre Paper industry in Sydney. An active zionist, he was president of the Australian Zionist Federation (1953–57) and of the Australian Keren Hayesod (1942–57). He was also vice-president of the

New South Wales Jewish Board of Deputies and chairman of the board of governors of the King David school. He published *Twenty-Five Years of Keren Hayesod* (1946). [ED.]

FREIMAN, Canadian family. MOSES BILSKY (1831–1923) was a Canadian pioneer figure and an ancestor of the Freiman family by way of his daughter Lillian. He was born in Kovno and at the age of 14 went to Montreal with his father, moving to Ottawa in 1857. In the years 1861–67 he traveled throughout North and Central America, going to the Caribou gold fields in British Columbia overland by way of the isthmus of Panama, and enlisting in the Union forces in the U.S. Civil War. He returned to Ottawa and entered the jewelry business. There he founded the Adath Jeshurun synagogue in 1895, helped found the city's first Zionist Society in 1899, and led in community activity.

LILLIAN (1885–1940) was born in Mattawa, Ontario. In 1903 she married Archibald J. Freiman (see below) of Ottawa. She was identified closely with Zionist work in Canada all her life and attended the third Canadian Zionist convention in Montreal at the age of 17. From 1919 to her death she was president of Canadian Hadassah. She took the initiative in 1920–21 in bringing 150 Jewish pogrom orphans to Canada and touring her native country to raise funds and recruit foster parents. In 1918, at the time of the great influenza epidemic, the mayor of Ottawa placed her in charge of efforts to combat the disease. She played a prominent and stimulating role in a wide range of activities of a nonsectarian and Jewish nature, involving relief and succor to others, locally and overseas, Jew and gentile.

ARCHIBALD JACOB FREIMAN (1880–1944) was a Canadian merchant and Zionist leader. He was born in Wirballen, Lithuania, and went to Hamilton, Ontario with his parents in 1893. In 1902 he settled in Ottawa, where he established a department store. He was president of the Adath Jeshurun synagogue from 1903 to 1929 and from 1920 to his death was national president of the Zionist Organization of Canada.

Their son LAWRENCE FREIMAN (1909–), a merchant, was born in Ottawa. He served twice as president of the Zionist Organization of Canada, and was honorary president of the Federated Zionist Organization of Canada, and was a member of the board of governors of the Weizmann Institute of Science at Reḥovot. Freiman played a leading role in cultural activities in Canada, and was a director of the Ottawa Philharmonic Orchestra, the Canadian Festival of Arts, and the National Arts Center in Ottawa.

Bibliography: H. M. Caiserman, *Two Canadian Personalities* (1948); A. D. Hart: *The Jew in Canada* (1926); Bernard Figler, *Lillian and Archie Freiman: Biographies* (1961). [B.G.K.]

FREIMANN, family of rabbis and scholars, ISAAC FREIMANN (d. 1886), who was born in Cracow, edited from a manuscript Abraham b. Ḥiyya's *Hegyon ha-Nefesh ha-Aẓuvah* (1860). His son ISRAEL MEIR FREIMANN (1830–1884) served as rabbi at Filehne (Wielen) and Ostrowo (Ostrow-Wielkopolski, both in Poznania), and declined an invitation to succeed Z. Frankel as head of the Breslau Jewish Theological Seminary. He prepared a critical edition of *Midrash Ve-Hizhir* (1875–80), and responsa of his were published in *Binyan Ẓiyyon* (1868), the responsa collection of his father-in-law Jacob Ettlinger, and elsewhere. His son was Aron *Freimann, his nephew and son-in-law was Jacob *Freimann, and Abraham (Alfred) *Freimann was his grandson. [ED.]

FREIMANN, ABRAHAM ḤAYYIM (Alfred; 1889–1948), jurist and rabbinical scholar. Freimann, born in Holleschau (Holesov), Moravia, the son of Jacob *Freimann, studied rabbinics with his father and law in Frankfort on the Main and Marburg. He served as a magistrate at Koenigsberg and county judge at nearby Braunsberg until the Nazis took power, when he emigrated to Palestine. There he at first worked for an insurance company, but in 1944 he began lecturing on Jewish law at the Hebrew University in Jerusalem. In 1947 Freimann was appointed head of an advisory committee for Jewish law concerning personal status in the proposed State of Israel. He was murdered by Arabs who attacked a convoy taking university staff to Mount Scopus.

Abraham Ḥayyim Freimann, jurist. Jerusalem, J.N.U.L., Schwadron Collection.

Freimann's scholarly work was concerned with medieval rabbinics; later he devoted his efforts to the adaptation of Jewish law to modern conditions in a Jewish state. He was about twenty when he published two important studies on *Asher b. Jehiel and his descendants (in: JJLG, 12 (1918), 237–317; 13 (1920), 142–254). He edited a series of important responsa collections by Maimonides and members of his family: *Teshuvot ha-Rambam* (1934); *Teshuvot R. Maimon ha-Dayyan Avi ha-Rambam* (1935); *Teshuvot Rabbenu Avraham ben ha-Rambam* (1938); *Teshuvot ha-R. Yehoshu'a ha-Naggid mi-Benei Banav shel ha-Rambam* (1940); and *Teshuvot ha-Rambam le-R. Yosef ha-Ma'aravi Talmido* (1940); and one by Rashi, *Teshuvot Rashi* (1941). Freimann also prepared a second edition of Filipowski's edition of *Sefer Yuḥasin* by Abraham *Zacut with an introduction and indexes (1925, repr. 1963). His major work *Seder Kiddushin ve-Nissu'in Aḥarei Ḥatimat ha-Talmud* (1945; repr. 1964), deals with changes in Jewish marriage laws after the talmudic period.

Bibliography: E. E. Urbach, in: KS, 25 (1948/49), 105–8 (with full bibl.); idem, in: *Yavneh*, 3 (1949), 125–7, 225–36; P. Dickstein, in: *Ha-Peraklit*, 5 (1948), 67–70; M. Elon, in: ILR, 3 (1968), 443ff., 448ff.

[ED.]

FREIMANN, ARON (1871–1948), German scholar, historian, and bibliographer. Freimann was born in Filehne (Wielen), Poznan, the son of the local rabbi, Israel Meir Freimann. In 1898 he began working at the municipal library in Frankfort, and under his direction the library in Frankfort assembled one of the richest collections of Judaica and Hebraica in the world. He retired in 1933 when the Nazis came to power, and emigrated to the United States in 1938. Between 1939 and 1945 he served as consultant in bibliography to the New York Public Library.

An industrious and erudite scholar, Freimann was the author or editor of scores of books and articles. In the field of bibliography one of his most important works is a systematic catalog of the Judaica collection of the Stadtbibliothek in Frankfort on the Main, *Stadtbibliothek Frankfurt a. M. Katalog der Judaica und Hebraica* (vol. 1: Judaica, 1932); unfortunately, he was unable to complete the second part of the catalog, which was to have included the Hebraica collection. In *Thesaurus Typographiae Hebraicae Seculi XV* (1924–31), Freimann provided a complete collection of samples of facsimiles of all known Hebrew incunabula; this work also remained incomplete, missing the introduction and the discussion of the facsimiles. A most useful bibliographical reference tool is his *A Gazetteer of Hebrew Printing* (1946), in which he listed all the cities where Hebrew books were known to have been printed. For many years Freimann was working on a union catalog of all Hebrew manuscripts, but this work also remained incomplete. Freimann's handwritten cards, representing the material culled from all major and minor collections of Hebrew manuscripts, were photographically reproduced after his death as *Union Catalog of Hebrew Manuscripts and Their Location* (1964). Between 1900 and 1922 Freimann was the editor of the journal *Zeitschrift fuer Hebraische Bibliographie,* in which many of his bibliographical articles appeared.

Among Freimann's important historical works are: *Geschichte der Israelitischen Gemeinde Ostrowo* (1896); a history of the Jews of Frankfort in collaboration with I. Kracauer, *Frankfort* (Eng., 1929); an edition of Ḥ. J. D. Azulai's diary, *Ma'gal Tov ha-Shalem* (1921–34); and a collection of texts relating to Shabbetai Ẓevi, *Inyanei Shabbetai Ẓevi* (1912; index 1931). He was coeditor of *Germania Judaica,* a collection of monographs on medieval German Jewish communities (2 vols., 1917–34, 1963–68). From 1929 to the Nazi take-over he was also one of the editors of *Zeitschrift fuer die Geschichte der Juden in Deutschland.* Of his works in other fields his edition of L. Zunz's *Die synagogale Poesie der Juden* (1920) is particularly valuable. Freimann supplied many references and indexes to this classic work, making it much more useful than it had been previously. He also edited several Festschriften in honor of scholars, such as *Berliner Festschrift* (1903), *Brann-Festschrift* (1919), and *Simonsen-Festschrift* (1923).

In addition to his scholarly activities Freimann was active in Jewish communal life and in Jewish educational institutions. He was affiliated with the *Mekizei Nirdamim society from 1909 to his death, serving as president and board member. He owned a private collection of rare Hebraica and Judaica, part of which he sold to the library of Hebrew Union College in Cincinatti. On the occasion of his sixtieth birthday a Festschrift was edited in his honor by A. Marx and H. Meyer (publ. 1935), which included a short poem by Ḥ. N. Bialik and contained a complete bibliography of his writings to that time.

Bibliography: A. Marx and B. Cohen, in: PAAJR, 17 (1947–48), xxiii–xxviii; S. D. Goitein, in: KS, 25 (1948/49), 109–12. [M.Sch.]

FREIMANN, JACOB (1866–1937), German rabbi, scholar, and editor. Freimann studied under Simon Sofer (see *Sofer) and Akiva *Kornitzer in his native Cracow, and under his uncle Israel Meir *Freimann at Ostrowo, as well as at Berlin and Tuebingen. He married Israel Meir Freimann's daughter. Jacob Freimann served as rabbi in Moravia at Kanitz (Dolni Kounice) and Holleschau from 1890 to 1913. In 1913 he succeeded Wolff *Feilchenfeld as chief rabbi of Posen. In 1928 he joined the rabbinate of the Berlin Jewish community. Freimann was a member of the board of *Mekizei Nirdamim, editor of the department of rabbinics for the Eshkol encyclopaedias of Judaica in German and Hebrew, and lecturer on rabbinics and Jewish history at the Berlin Rabbinical Seminary. Freimann's scholarly interest was medieval rabbinical literature. Particularly important in this field are his editions of Joseph b. Moses' *Leket Yosher* (1903–04), Nathan b. Judah's *Sefer Maḥkim* (1909), *Ma'aseh ha-Ge'onim* (1909), and *Siddur Rashi* (1911) which was prepared by S. *Buber but completed by Freimann. He also contributed an introduction and indexes to the second edition of Wistinetzki's edition of *Sefer Ḥasidim* (1924).

Bibliography: H. Levy (ed.), *Festschrift . . . Jacob Freimann* (1937), introd. 6–16 (includes bibliography); H. Gold. (ed.), *Juden und Judengemeinden Maehrens in Vergangenheit und Gegenwart* (1929), 233, 240, 270, 278; N. Lebovi, in: S. Federbush (ed.), *Ḥokhmat Yisrael be-Ma'arav Eiropah,* 2 (1959), 211–3.

[H.J.Z./J.Ro.]

FRENCH LITERATURE. This entry is arranged according to the following outline:

Biblical and Hebraic Influences. The influence of the Hebrew Bible and other Jewish writings on early French literature is limited. With the exception of the 12th-century *Jeu d'Adam,* an Anglo-Norman verse-play, and the 15th-century *Mistère du Viel Testament,* only New Testament themes appear in medieval French plays, poetry, and stories. However, there was one interesting case of "infiltration": the *Midrash and **aggadah* became important sources for the French *fabliaux.* Fables, parables, and didactic tales were not rare in talmudic literature, and they remained part of the Jewish literary heritage throughout the Middle Ages. Indian tales and Aesop's fables mingled with talmudic "Fox Fables" *(Mishlei Shu'alim),* as is testified by compilations of Jewish writers such as *Berechiah b. Natronai ha-Nakdan and *Isaac b. Joseph of Corbeil. These compilations, translated into Latin by baptized Jews such as *Petrus Alfonsi and *John of Capua, thus passed into the French heritage in the form of the *fabliaux.* Literary transpositions also occurred, the medievalist Gustave Cohen being the first to note that the midrashic tale of the blind man and the lame (Sanh. 91a; Lev. R. 4:5)—which has a parallel in Aesop—had become the French story of St. Martin. The "Three Rings" tale was the source of the anonymous 13th-century *Dit du Vrai Aniel,* a Christian author transforming the old fable into propaganda for the Crusades. This tradition elsewhere influenced *Boccaccio and, later still, *Lessing.

In the Middle Ages biblical knowledge was primarily the preserve of the clergy, and it was through churchmen that Hebrew words, biblical expressions, idioms, and proverbs found their way into the French language from the 12th century right up to the 17th. As elsewhere in Europe, various Hebrew terms were absorbed by way of Greek and Latin. Certain French borrowings from Hebrew extend or modify the original meaning: *tohu-bohu* (chaos, disorder); *capharnaüm* (lumber room); *jérémiade* (lament); *moïse* (wicker cradle); *sabbat* (tumult, uproar); and *cabale* (conspiracy, intrigue). Hebrew idioms from the Bible found their way into French, as into other European languages: *trouver grâce* (find favor), *amis de Job* (Job's comforters), *bouc émissaire* (scapegoat). The inclusion of Hebraisms was given a new impetus with two versions of the Bible: the *Bible Complète* of the University of Paris (c. 1235) and the *Bible Historiale* of Guyart des Moulins (c. 1295) which was not a literal translation. Until the Reformation, these were the only full versions of the Scriptures in French.

THE RENAISSANCE. Apart from some stray references in the works of François Villon (c. 1431–c. 1463), biblical subjects only make an appearance in French literature in the 16th century, under the combined impact of the Renaissance and the Reformation. At the same time there sprang up a widespread interest in the Hebrew language and the original biblical text. In 1530, Francis I established the Collège des Trois Langues (later renamed Collège de France) as a center of learning independent of the intolerant Sorbonne. Readers in mathematics and in Latin, Greek, and Hebrew were appointed in accordance with the humanistic principles of the Renaissance, and such was the liberalism of the era that the chair of Hebrew was first offered to a professing Jew, Elijah (Baḥur) *Levita, who declined the honor because of the exclusion of his fellow-Jews from the French realm. The post was not in fact given to a Jew until the late 19th century.

Humanism blazed a trail that was also followed by the new religious trends of the 16th century—early liberal Evangelism and Calvinism. The "return to the sources" inspired new Bible translations by Jacques Lefèvre d'Etaples (1523–30), Robert Olivétan (1535), a relative of John *Calvin and Sébastien Châteillon (1551). The Protestant poet Clément Marot composed beautiful metrical renderings of 50 of the Psalms (1545, and much reprinted), which John Calvin later accepted in his reformed hymnal, and which inspired many later imitations. François Rabelais placed considerable store on the study of the holy tongue and of the "thalmudistes et cabalistes," although he himself probably knew no Hebrew.

Later in the same century, Hebrew studies were pursued in a more systematic manner, by both Catholics and Protestants. Pontus de Tyard, a neoplatonist poet and later a bishop, published a French translation, *De l'Amour* (1551), of the *Dialoghi d'Amore* by Judah *Abrabanel (Leone Ebreo). Some leading French Christian Hebraists were Guillaume *Postel; Gilbert *Génébrard; Blaise de *Vignère; and Guy *Le Fèvre de la Boderie, a Bible scholar who wrote epic French verse full of kabbalistic references and Franco-Hebraic conceits. Two outstanding Protestant poets whose works owe much to biblical inspiration were Salluste *Du Bartas and Agrippa d'Aubigné, a militant Calvinist whose dramatic and satirical epic, *Les Tragiques* (1577–94), describes the sufferings of the French Protestants in a series of apocalyptic visions. Likening his coreligionists to the Children of Israel, d'Aubigné prophesies God's final vengeance on their persecutors.

Biblical drama also makes its appearance in the 16th century. *Saül le Furieux* (1572) by Jean de la Taille presents the theme of man's inability to understand the mysterious designs of Providence. Against God's command, Saul has spared the life of Agag, king of Amalek, and must be punished. This was a direct precursor of the classic French tragedy. In *Sédécie, ou les Juives* (1583), a drama in the Greek style by Robert Garnier, man's disobedience is again punished by God. Ignoring Jeremiah's injunction, Sédécie (Zedekiah) has sought an alliance with Egypt. The country and the Temple are destroyed, the king taken into captivity and blinded. Sédécie recognizes his sins and acknowledges God's justice. The chorus of Jewish women echoes the king's lament in strains reminiscent of Jeremiah. Minor biblical dramas of the period include: *Abraham Sacrifiant* (1576) by Théodore de Bèze; *Jephté* (1567) by Florent Chrestien, translated from the earlier Latin *Jephtes* (1554) by George Buchanan ("the Humanist"); and *Aman* and *David* (both 1601) by the talented Huguenot playwright and economist Antoine de Montchrestien.

THE CLASSICAL AGE. The 17th century manifests a dual character: classical and Christian. Naturally enough, biblical or post-biblical influences are felt primarily among writers of Christian inspiration; others return to the sources of classical antiquity. Among the great dramatists, Jean *Racine, deeply influenced by his Jansenist training and sympathies, was the only one for whom the Bible provided both subject matter and poetic inspiration. Racine's two biblical tragedies, *Esther* (1689) and *Athalie* (1691), rank among the great masterpieces of French drama. Two great French Christian writers of the century, Jacques-Bénigne Bossuet and Blaise *Pascal, were exceptionally aware of the importance of the biblical heritage. Bossuet, in his *Discours sur l'Histoire Universelle* (1681), presents a spiritual perspective of history in which the paths are traced by a mysterious but wise Providence. Here Israel is chosen for a particular mission to the world, and other nations of antiquity, however powerful and important they might appear in relation to the Jews, are but tools used by God to chastise or protect His chosen people. Israel is thus seen as the cornerstone of world history. Bossuet's biblical leanings are apparent in the lyrical and grandiose eloquence of his literary style; not only did biblical rhythm and imagery strongly influence all his works (including the sermons and the *Oraisons Funèbres*, 1663): he consciously transposed biblical passages and adapted them to contemporary circumstances. Pascal too, in his passionate search for God, saw in the Jews an exceptional and mysterious people, appointed by Providence to preside over human destiny. The Bible was to be read, studied, and interpreted symbolically, and Pascal drew heavily on the Midrash, which he considered a key to the understanding of the Scriptures. In his Platonic *Dialogues sur l'Éloquence* (1718), Fénelon regarded the Bible as a primary source of poetic inspiration and praised Judaism's religious purity.

In the 18th century, the "Age of Enlightenment," men like Denis *Diderot found it convenient to ridicule both the Bible and the Jewish people as an indirect method of attacking Christianity. Equally if not more virulent was *Voltaire, whose attitude was also more complex. Personally unfriendly toward the Jews, Voltaire, in his *Dictionnaire Philosophique* (1764), simultaneously attacked their alleged religious fanaticism and argued that Christians ought logically to practice Judaism, "because Jesus was born a Jew, lived a Jew, died a Jew, and said expressly that he was fulfilling the Jewish religion." Voltaire also condemned anti-Jewish persecution in his *Sermon du Rabin Akib* (1764). Another 18th-century writer, the atheistic Baron d'Holbach, strove in his *Esprit du Judaïsm* (1770) to prove that the Law of Moses was basically immoral, serving only to justify Jewish political ambitions. Although some other writers of the period, notably *Montesquieu and *Rousseau, made sympathetic references to Jews, they were not especially inspired by biblical or later Hebrew literature.

THE ROMANTIC AGE. The 19th-century Romantic movement brought with it a revival of interest in, and sympathy for, religion and Christian values. French poets displayed a noticeable reverence for the Bible and found inspiration in the Holy Land. Thus, François René de Chateaubriand praised the Bible's uniqueness and universality in his *Génie du Christianisme* (1802). In *Itinéraire de Paris à Jérusalem* (1811), he wrote a highly romanticized account of his journey to the Orient extolling the Jews' will to survive and their tenacious adherence to their heritage. Alphonse de Lamartine, a leading Romantic poet, acknowledged his debt to the Psalms and wrote a biblical drama, *Saül* (1818). After a grand tour which included Palestine, his *Souvenirs, Impressions . . . Pendant un Voyage en Orient* (1835) looked prophetically to the future: "Such a land, resettled by a new Jewish nation, tilled and watered by intelligent hands . . . would still be the Promised Land of our day, if only Providence were to give it back its people, and the tide of world events bring it peace and liberty."

Two other great French poets who were profoundly influenced by the Bible were Alfred de Vigny and Victor Hugo. Vigny, who knew the Bible by heart, based one-fifth of his poems on biblical themes and filled them with Hebrew images and expressions. They include "Moïse," "La fille de Jephté" (in *Poèmes Antiques et Modernes,* 1826) and "La colère de Samson" (in *Les Destinées,* 1864). Like all Vigny's heroes, the biblical figures are universal symbols—men of genius whose greatness condemns them to eternal solitude. Hugo was the preeminent biblical poet among the French Romantics. Despite his estrangement from Christian orthodoxy, Hugo constantly turns to biblical themes in such poems as "La Conscience," "Booz endormi," and "Salomon" (in *La Légende des Siècles,* 1859–83); "Le Glaive" (*Fin de Satan,* 1887); and "L'Aigle" (*Dieu,* 1891). He eulogized Isaiah and Ezekiel in *William Shakespeare* (1864); sought biblical support for his campaign against Napoleon III; and injected some basic knowledge of the Kabbalah (probably gained from his Jewish admirer, Alexandre *Weill) into *Les Contemplations* (1856).

Of the prominent 19th-century French novelists, Gustave Flaubert, another great traveler, recreated in his last work, *Hérodias* (the third of his *Trois Contes,* 1877), the Judea of the Roman era, the Dead Sea fortress of Machaerus, and the dramatic story of John the Baptist. Pierre Loti, a writer of Huguenot descent, wrote two travel books, *Jérusalem* (1895) and *La Galilée* (1896).

THE 20TH CENTURY. In more recent French literature, from the late 19th century onward, biblical and Christian inspiration again go hand in hand. Catholic writers such as Charles *Péguy, Léon *Bloy, and Paul *Claudel meditate on the Scriptures, and their poetic works (whether written in prose or verse) often take on a prophetic tone as they apply the biblical prophecies to contemporary events. Two biblically inspired dramas by Jean Giraudoux are his *Judith* (1932), a psychological tragedy; and *Sodome et Gomorrhe* (in *Théâtre complet,* vol. 10, 1947). In a class of his own stands the novelist and playwright André Gide, whose drama *Saül* (1898, publ. 1922) strips all heroism from its central character.

Some French Jewish poets of the early 20th century who rediscovered the Bible as a source of inspiration were Edmond *Fleg (*Ecoute Israël,* 1913, 1935[2]), André *Spire (*Poèmes juifs,* 1919), Henri *Franck (*La danse devant l'Arche,* 1912[2]), Albert *Cohen (*Paroles juives,* 1921), Gustave *Kahn (*Images bibliques,* 1929), and Benjamin *Fondane (*L'Exode*). Two important poets of the post-World War II era, both Catholic, both intoxicated with the Bible, were Pierre Emmanuel and Jean Grosjean. Emmanuel's mystical lyrics, reminiscent of Agrippa d'Aubigné and Victor Hugo, draw their images from the biblical text, and his vision (cf. *Babel,* 1951), like theirs, is prophetic, sometimes apocalyptic. Grosjean borrows almost all his themes from the Bible and the Kabbalah. The titles of his verse collections are eloquent: *Le livre du juste* (1952), *Fils de l'homme* (1953), and *Apocalypse* (1962). Other Jewish writers who sought inspiration in Jewish sources were Emmanuel *Eydoux, Arnold *Mandel, Armand *Lunel, Élie *Wiesel, and in Israel, three poets writing in French: Joseph *Milbauer, Jean *Loewenson, and Claude *Vigée.

The Image of the Jew. The appearance of Jewish characters in French literature is determined by the socio-historical role of the Jews in France, where they lived from Roman times until the expulsion of 1394. In medieval French literature, Jews generally appear in an unfavorable light. This attitude changes when they convert. Thus, in the 12th-century *Pèlerinage de Charlemagne a Jérusalem,* the Jew is presented like other "infidels" as a candidate for baptism. Confronted with the noble figure of the emperor, he readily accepts Jesus. In the 13th-century *Desputaison de la Synagogue et de la Saincte Eglise,* a play by Clopin which may reflect the Paris disputation of 1240, the representative of the Synagogue (i.e., the Jews) is a skillful woman debater who stubbornly refuses to acknowledge the superiority of the Church. A rare exception among medieval writers is Peter *Abelard (1079–1142), who composed a dialogue between a Jewish and a Christian philosopher which was quite favorable to Judaism.

The Jew's first appearance as a figure in French society in the 13th century is reflected in the literature of the period. The satirical poet Gautier de Coincy is particularly virulent against Jews, portraying them as not merely stubborn and blind, but also as rich oppressors of the poor. Two miracle plays, *Le Juif et le Chevalier* and *Le Miracle d'un Marchand et d'un Juif,* present a stereotyped Jew, crudely anticipating *Shakespeare's Shylock. In later mystery plays, the Pharisees represent the "hypocritical Jews," the "Christ-killers," filled with hatred and inspired by Satan. The performance of these plays in Paris was finally banned in 1548.

Throughout the 16th and 17th centuries the Jew is, by and large, absent from the French scene, and is virtually ignored by writers of that period. Even the liberal Michel de Montaigne (see below), a writer of partly Jewish descent who had personal contact with Jews in Italy, makes only a few random allusions to them in his *Essays.* Racine, however, defended the Jews in his drama *Esther,* where the heroine pleads their cause. The Jews, declares Racine, are peace loving, humble, and loyal to God and the king. Pascal also expresses his admiration for a Jewish people miraculously preserved through the ages and unique among nations for its unswerving loyalty to God, for its sincerity, and for its courageous devotion to the Law of Moses. Bossuet, too, marvels at Israel's miraculous survival. During his 17 years in Metz, whose Jewish community enjoyed royal protection, he met Jews and attempted to convert some of their youth. His unorthodox opponent in biblical controversies, the Hebraist Richard *Simon, was more enlightened. In 1690, he championed the Jews in the celebrated ritual murder trial of a Metz Jew, Raphaël Lévy, and in order to fight anti-Semitic prejudice, translated into French Leone *Modena's *Historia dei Riti Ebraici* (*Cérémonies et coustumes . . . parmi les Juifs,* Paris, 1674, 1681[2]).

THE 18TH-CENTURY PHILOSOPHERS. The few writers of the 18th century who were not blinded by anti-religious hatred expressed enlightened opinions about Jews and Judaism. Thus Montesquieu, who devotes no. 60 of his *Lettres Persanes* (1721) to the Jews, speaks of their passionate devotion to a religion which was the mother of Christianity and Islam. He then makes a plea for tolerance, repeated in the "Très humble remontrance aux Inquisiteurs d'Espagne et de Portugal" (*L'Esprit des Lois* (1748), 25:13), where the advocate of justice and humanity is a Portuguese Jew whose reasonableness makes a striking contrast to the violence of Christian fanatics. Among the many "oriental" works inspired by the *Lettres Persanes* were the *Lettres Juives* (1736) of the Marquis d'Argens, which present an exceptionally favorable image of Jewish values and morality.

Voltaire and the Encyclopedists, on the other hand, presented a generally unsympathetic image of the Jews, whom they held to be as guilty of religious fanaticism as the Christians. Diderot, in his *Encyclopédie* article "Juifs," also reflects the prejudices of his time, but in his novel *Le Neveu de Rameau* (written c. 1774) he introduces a gullible and cowardly Jew who is, for once, neither vicious nor evil. In the fourth book of his *Emile* (1762), Rousseau, though scarcely better informed than his contemporaries, makes a remarkable plea for a more objective and sympathetic understanding of the Jews. "We shall never know the inner motives of the Jews," he says prophetically, "until the day they have their own free state, schools, and universities, where they can speak and argue without fear. Then, and only then, shall we know what they really have to say."

THE JEW IN FICTION. Throughout the 19th century the Jew's growing importance in French society found its reflection in literature, but the image of the Jew in plays and novels generally lacks nuance. George Sand, in her drama *Les Mississipiens* (1866; originally *Le Château des Désertes*, 1851), introduces a Jewish capitalist, Samuel Bourset, who is merely a Shylock in modern dress. Jews like Gobseck and Elie Magus in the giant (17 volumes) cycle, *La Comédie Humaine*, of Honoré de Balzac, are largely stereotypes: bankers and art collectors, generally crafty, rapacious, and miserly, who only partially redeem themselves by their devotion to their womenfolk. Only Balzac's "beau Juif," Naphtaly, is a figure of chivalrous virtue. In *Manette Salomon* (1867), a novel by the Goncourt brothers Edmond and Jules, the Jewish heroine is unsympathetically treated. She is the corrupting influence who forces the artist Caridis to abandon his ideals. *Les rois en exile* (1879), by Alphonse Daudet, is a variation on the same theme.

In his dramas, Victor Hugo at first sacrificed truth to popular prejudice. The Great Protector's agent in *Cromwell* (1827) is a grotesque travesty of the historical *Manasseh Ben Israel, and another despicable Jewish usurer appears in *Marie Tudor* (prod. 1833; publ. 1834). Yet Hugo's last great play, *Torquemada* (1882), reveals the author's real sympathy for the Jewish victims of treachery and oppression—a sympathy he demonstrated publicly by presiding at a Paris rally on May 31, 1882, to protest against czarist persecution of Russian Jewry. Unpleasant Jewish types continued to make their appearance in the novels *Cosmopolis* (1893; Eng. tr. 1893) by Paul Bourget, *Mont-Oriol* (1887) by Guy de Maupassant, and *L'argent* (1891), part of the Rougon-Macquart novel cycle by Emile *Zola. Zola, however, by placing the Jewish Gundermann opposite a far more despicable Christian character, does succeed in restoring some sense of balance.

THE DREYFUS CASE. Some frankly anti-Semitic novels appeared at the turn of the century, reflecting the wave of ultranationalist feeling aroused by the *Dreyfus case. Such, for example, are *L'essence du soleil* (1890) by Paul Adam, Léon Cladel's *Juive-errante* (1897), and Léon *Daudet's *Le pays des parlementeurs* (1901) and *La lutte* (1907). In all these novels the Jew or Jewess is a rapacious intriguer, endangering the security of the nation and corrupting morals. A play in the same vein is *Le retour de Jérusalem* (1904) by Maurice Donnay. Bourget's *L'Etape* (1902) portraying an idealistic Jew, is a happy exception. Though often cast in the role of a prostitute, the Jewess in the short stories of Maupassant is treated sympathetically and proves herself more noble than her non-Jewish associates. Thus in *Mademoiselle Fifi* (1883), the Jewess Rachel alone resists the offensive Prussian officer, emerging as a symbol of French patriotism and courage. And in *La femme de Claude* (1873), a drama by Alexandre Dumas *fils*, it is the Jewess Rebecca who symbolizes feminine virtue and purity in a decadent and selfish society. The brothers J.-H. and S.-J. Rosny present a fierce and proud Jewess in *La Juive* (1907). The ambivalent Jewish characterization in the Erckmann-Chatrian novels of life in Alsace such as *L'ami Fritz* (1864; *Friend Fritz*, 1873), *Le blocus* (1867; *The Blockade*, 1869), and "Le Juif polonais" (in *Contes populaires*, 1866; *The Polish-Jew*, 1884) stems from their joint authorship: Emile Erckmann was a pro-Jewish Protestant, and Alexandre Chatrian a Catholic anti-Semite. Their best-known hero, Rabbi David Sichel (in *L'ami Fritz*), is a wholly admirable figure.

The Dreyfus case inspired not only a spate of nationalistic and anti-Semitic novels, but also some important works of an exactly opposite type by three great French writers. Zola's *Vérité* (1903) describes the "Affaire Simon," a romanticized Dreyfus case in which justice and secularism triumph over prejudice and clericalism. In *L'anneau d'améthyste* (1899), Anatole France presents a liberal who opposes bigotry, anti-Semitism, and racism, but it is in his charming *L'île des pingouins* (1908) that the *Affaire* is parodied with the most incisive wit. Society, eager to persecute the defenseless Jew Pyrot, is depicted in all its cowardice and greed. Anatole France also presents a likeable Jewish philologist, Schmoll, in *Le lys rouge* (1894). In *Jean Barois* (1913), Roger Martin Du Gard approaches the *Affaire* from a more philosophical standpoint. The central figure, a liberal journalist in search of truth and justice, speaks out on behalf of Dreyfus, under the influence of an admirable Jewish friend, Woldsmuth.

The *Affaire* also directed the attention of two great Catholic writers toward Jewry. Charles Péguy and Léon Bloy both devoted poems and meditations to the Jewish people, its destiny and mission. Paul Claudel did so too, in his drama *Le Père humilié* (1916), where the central figure is a blind Jewess, Pensée, who personifies the people of God. Two other writers of the period introduced Jewish figures. One was the poet Guillaume Apollinaire, who was fascinated by the figure of the *wandering Jew and used the Jew in his poems (particularly *Alcools*, 1913) and short stories as a symbol of exile and misfortune. The other was Marcel *Proust who, in the particular universe which he created, gave an important place to Jewish characters, including his own alter ego, the half-Jew Charles Swann.

WORLD WAR I AND AFTER. World War I marked a turning point in the treatment of Jewish characters in French literature, and they became increasingly numerous, varied, and interesting. Writers were preoccupied with the search for new social and moral values for a society shattered by war, and tended to give greater recognition to the Jew's specific identity. The Jew was no longer merely a persecuted human being to be defended for the sake of justice, but the bearer of a cultural and spiritual tradition worthy of a place in the broader French or European heritage. Such was the view of the former anti-Dreyfusard Maurice Barrès who, despite his ultranationalism and dislike of the Jew, assigned him in *Les diverses familles spirituelles de la France* (1917) a role akin to that of the Breton or Alsatian among the "families" constituting the French nation. With the brothers Jérôme and Jean *Tharaud, interest in the authentic Jew was transmuted into a search for the picturesque and the exotic in Jewish tradition. Even Zionism inspired a novel—*Le puits de Jacob* (1925) by Pierre Benoît, which deals with early pioneering in Ereẓ Israel. But it was Romain Rolland who, even before World War I, had given Jewish values a broad and universal meaning for modern civilization. Not only had the Jew his own traditions to contribute to the French heritage, he also had a special vocation in the western world, being the bearer of "Justice for all, of universal Right." The Jewish characters in Rolland's serial novel, *Jean Christophe*, are distinguished by their selfless devotion, their passion for improving the world, their boundless energy, and determination.

The first fully developed Jewish hero of 20th-century French literature was Silbermann, in the novel of that name by Jacques de *Lacretelle (1922). This deals with the friendship between two schoolboys, one a Christian and the other a Jew. The persecution of the brilliant and idealistic Silbermann by his anti-Semitic schoolmates forms the background to the story. The theme was taken up by André Gide in *Geneviève* (1936), which portrays a similar friendship between two girls. Henri de Montherlant, who otherwise dealt little with Jewish themes, wrote a "counterpart to Silbermann" in his autobiographical short story of World War I, "Un petit Juif à la guerre" (in *Mors et Vita*, 1932). The author, educated in a reactionary, anti-Semitic milieu, describes how he is attracted by a sensitive and intelligent young Jew whom he meets in the trenches. Georges Duhamel, in his serial novel *La chronique des Pasquier* (1933–41), presents a finely drawn Jew in Justin Weill, the loyal and idealistic friend of the storyteller-hero. Although the liberal Duhamel makes his Jewish hero an admirable figure, he is nevertheless presented as the perpetual stranger, alienated from both the French and the Jewish traditions. Throughout the *Chronicles* it is this fundamental alienation that accounts for the unsuccessful search for a Franco-Jewish synthesis. The same theme is given a slightly different interpretation by Paul Nizan in *La conspiration* (1938). Here the hero, Bernard Rosenthal, failing to involve the girl he loves in his own philosophical preoccupations, commits suicide. In all these works the Jewish hero has a central role, yet he is always analyzed in terms of the non-Jew's reactions.

To clarify the non-Jew's attitude toward the Jew, some French novelists have created minor, but striking, Jewish characters. Roger Martin Du Gard devotes *La belle saison* (1923), the third volume of his family cycle *Les Thibault*, to the story of Antoine Thibault, a young doctor, and Rachel, his Jewish mistress, who becomes intensely real although she is only seen through the eyes of her lover. Another interesting marginal character appears in *Thérèse Desqueyroux* (1927) by Francois Mauriac. It is a young Jew, Jean Azévédo, who brings a breath of fresh air into the stuffy atmosphere of a bigoted small town and precipitates Thérèse's revolt.

THE IMPACT OF NAZISM. The rise of racialism and Nazism between the two world wars led to the appearance of such anti-Semitic works as *Voyage au bout de la nuit* (1922; *Journey to the End of the Night*, 1959) by Louis-Ferdinand Céline and *Gilles* (1939) by Pierre Drieu La Rochelle. On the other hand, in 1941, Antoine de Saint Exupéry wrote to his Jewish friend, Léon Werth, the *Lettre à un ôtage* (New York, 1943) which was a unique message of comfort and encouragement from a French Gentile to a Jew. Saint Exupéry's meditative *Citadelle* (1948) contains mystical thinking of Jewish interest.

World War II and Nazi persecution inspired few Jewish characters among French writers. Some exceptions were *La marche à l'étoile* (1943) by *Vercors; some minor characters in works like *La mort dans l'âme* (1949) by Jean-Paul *Sartre; and *Le sang du ciel* (1961) by the Polish refugee Piotr Rawicz, a novel with a Jewish hero about the Nazi occupation of the Ukraine. The leading French writers of the postwar period did not introduce Jewish figures into their works, perhaps because of the irreparable mental shock caused by the war. Essays and theoretical writings on the Jewish question (by Sartre for example) were not rare, but Jewish characters and heroes became the exclusive concern of French Jewish writers.

The Jewish Contribution. Although Jews made no specific contribution to French literature before the 13th century, their links with French culture are more ancient. During the Middle Ages French Jews spoke Old French, which modified their pronunciation of Hebrew, and the somewhat Hebraized French dialect which they wrote in Hebrew characters is known as *Judeo-French. A parallel dialect in the south of France was *Judeo-Provençal. The **la'azim* (glosses) which *Rashi and other Jewish commentators used to explain difficult Hebrew terms are an immensely valuable source for philologists and Romance specialists. Even Hebrew-Old French dictionaries have survived. In the 13th century, liturgical poems and a festival prayer book (the fragmentary Heidelberg *maḥzor*) were composed in Old French, using Hebrew orthography. The most important document of the period is another fragment, the *Complainte de Troyes*, commemorating the martyrs of the *Troyes massacre of 1288 (text in: E. Fleg, *Anthologie juive* (1951[2]), 281). Its author was probably Jacob ben Judah de Lotra, who is known to have written a Hebrew *kinah* (elegy) on the same theme. Jews also began to write secular French verse: two 13th-century Provençal Jewish troubadours, Bonfils de Narbonne and Charlot le Juif, are mentioned and attacked in works by non-Jews; while some fragments have survived of poems by the convert Mathieu le Juif, a *trouvère* of Arras. With the expulsion of the Jews from France in 1394 this literary activity came to an end, although Alsace, and occasionally Provence, remained havens for Jewish refugees.

After a gap of nearly 200 years, writers of Jewish origin again made their appearance on the French literary scene. Outstanding among them were the celebrated astrologer and physician *Nostradamus (Michel de Nostre-Dame) and the great essayist Michel de Montaigne (1533–1592). The latter's mother, Antoinette de Louppes de Villeneuve, was a Christian descendant of Mayer Pacagon (Pazagón) of Calatayud who, after his forcible conversion at the beginning of the 15th century, took the baptismal name of Juan López de Villanueva. A skeptical humanist, more deistic than Christian, Montaigne in his *Essays* reveals a tolerant abhorrence of the Inquisition in Portugal, but only an outsider's interest in Jewish survival. In the revived Jewish community of Provence, *Purim plays had an honored place, a classic example being the dialect verse-drama *La Reine Esther*, written by Rabbi Mardochée Astruc and revised by *Jacob de Lunel, which was performed at Carpentras in 1774. But in French literature proper, Jews played no major literary role until the era of Louis Philippe (1830–48). Two early writers were the minor novelist Esther Foa and the prolific biographer, critic, and kabbalist Alexandre *Weill.

THE 19TH AND 20TH CENTURIES. Few of the many Jewish writers who rose to eminence in 19th-century France showed any real interest in Jewish themes. One rare exception was the poet and educator Eugène Manuel (1823–1901), author of *Pages intimes* (1866) and some very successful plays, who was a founder of the *Alliance Israélite Universelle. Other writers of this period were the poet and playwright Catulle *Mendès, the poet Ephraïm Mikhaël (1866–1890), the essayist and short-story writer Marcel *Schwob, and a host of playwrights and librettists—Adolphe Philippe d'Ennery (Dennery, 1811–1899); Hector Jonathan Crémieux (1828–1892) and his collaborator, Ludovic *Halévy; Georges de *Porto-Riche; Tristan *Bernard; and the stylish comedy writer Edmond Sée (1875–1959). By the beginning of the 20th century the number of Jewish playwrights had grown considerably.

Notable among them were Fernand Nozière (pseud. of F. Weyl; 1874–1931) and Alfred Savoir (1883–1934), who collaborated in the writing of successful comedies and farces; André Pascal (Henri de *Rothschild; 1872–1947), whose innovations at the Théâtre Pigalle included the revolving stage; the Belgians, Henry Hubert Kistemaeckers (1872–1938) and Francis de Croisset (1877–1937); Pierre Wolff (1865–1944) and Romain Coolus (1868–1952), two writers of popular comedies; and Jean Jacques *Bernard, son of the more distinguished Tristan Bernard, who became a Catholic. Overshadowing most of these were the social dramatist Henry *Bernstein and the converted literary critic Gustave Cohen. Prominent writers in other literary spheres were the essayists André *Suarès, Julien *Benda, and Benjamin *Crémieux. Maurice *Sachs, a depraved but talented writer, was a true war-time collaborator; and the eminent biographer André *Maurois at first supported Pétain. Outstanding poets of the early 20th century include the convert Max *Jacob, who died in a Nazi concentration camp; the half-Jew Oscar *Milosz, an esoteric writer detached from contemporary trends; and Yvan and Claire *Goll.

Almost all these authors, with the exception of Henry Bernstein, were Frenchmen who also happened to be Jews; but the Dreyfus case had a profound influence in reshaping the ideas of French Jewish writers. The publicists Victor *Basch and Bernard *Lazare were both roused to action by the affair. Even the half-Jew, Marcel *Proust, prevailed on Anatole France to intervene in Dreyfus' favor and, reassessing his own position in French society, gave a place of importance to Jewish characters in his great novel cycle *A la recherche du temps perdu.*

Two leading poets who rediscovered their Judaism were the symbolist Gustave *Kahn, who became an enthusiastic Zionist, and his even more militant contemporary, André *Spire, who inaugurated an entirely new Jewish and Zionist current in French literature. They were followed by Henri *Franck and Edmond *Fleg, the poet, playwright, and anthologist, whose rekindled devotion to Judaism led him to seek a symbiosis between the French and Jewish traditions.

In the 20th century the conflict of identity preoccupied several writers, including the novelists Jean-Richard *Bloch and Albert *Cohen. Their general approach was, however, very different. Bloch, a Communist, assigned to the Jew the role of "revolutionary ferment" in his adopted society; while Cohen, a Corfu-born poet and mystic, was strongly influenced by his Mediterranean background. The regional element is also important in the works of Armand *Lunel, who dealt primarily with Provençal culture, and Joseph *Kessel, who wrote some novels set in Israel. While Henri *Hertz, a leading French Zionist, devoted much of his attention to Jewish problems, other writers asserted their Jewishness mainly in their protests against anti-Semitism. Jean Finot (born Finkelstein, 1858–1922), a Warsaw-born lawyer, author of *Le préjugé des races* (1905; *Race Prejudice,* 1906), Emmanuel Berl (1892–), and Pierre Morhange (1901–) all belong to this category. So does Pierre Abraham (1892–), the brother of Jean-Richard Bloch, who directed the leftist monthly, *Europe,* and only recalled his Jewish identity in response to the Dreyfus case and, some 30 years later, to Hitler. A rare example of Jewish anti-Semitism was René Schwob (1895–1946), a convert to Catholicism, who wrote a series of unpleasant apologies, including *Moi, juif* (1928), *Ni grec ni juif* (1931), and *Itinéraire d'un juif vers l'église* (1940).

On the other hand, certain 20th-century writers were totally Jewish; they merely happen to have written in French. The problems they analyzed, the characters they depicted, the settings they chose were exclusively Jewish. Such were the half-Jewish Myriam *Harry; Lily Jean-Javal (1882–1958), a novelist and poet; Henry Marx (1882–), author of the poem *Sion;* Michel Matvéev (1893–), who evoked in novels such as *Ailleurs, autrefois* (1959) the tragic fate of the exiled and the persecuted; Pierre *Paraf; Josué Jéhouda; Pierre Neyrac; Joseph Schulsinger; Moïse Twersky, author of *L'Epopée de Menasché Foïgel* (3 vols., 1927–28, with André Billy), the story of a Russian immigrant in France; and Irène Némirowsky. Two other figures of note who dealt with the religious implications of Judaism were Raïssa *Maritain, a Russian Jewess who became a Catholic, and Aimé *Pallière, a Catholic who became a liberal pro-Jewish propagandist.

A phenomenon worth consideration is the large number of Rumanian-born Jews who either began or resumed their literary career in France. They include the novelist and playwrights Adolphe Orna (1882–1925); Tristan *Tzara; the political poet Claude Sernet (1902–); Ilarie *Voronca; the half-Jew Eugène *Ionesco; and Isidore Isou. Of these, only Orna and Ionesco showed any attachment to the Jewish people. Another French poet of Rumanian origin was the visionary Benjamin *Fondane.

THE HOLOCAUST. A number of French Jewish authors wrote about the Hitler era and the Holocaust of European Jewry. Anna *Langfus, in her semiautobiographical novels, described characters who, despite Nazi brutality, succeeded in retaining their human dignity and moral values. André *Schwarz-Bart, in the international best-seller, *Le dernier des justes* (1959; *The Last of the Just,* 1960), produced an epic on the age-old Jewish tragedy, while Élie Wiesel wrote a series of haunting novels on the Holocaust and its aftermath. A controversial best seller was *Treblinka* (1966) by Jean-François Steiner, son of Isaac Kadmi *Cohen. This semidocumentary, semi-fictional work attempted to provide a "psychological" explanation for Jewish passivity in the face of genocide.

After World War II some Jewish writers turned their attention to the problem of the contemporary Jew in a non-Jewish world. They include Léon *Aréga; Roger *Ikor—almost the only French Jewish author openly to advocate assimilation; André Gorz, a disciple of Sartre, whose novel, *Le traître* (1958), presents a hero fleeing his Jewish condition and in search of a new fatherland, which he professes to find in the world of literature; and the Tunisian-born Albert *Memmi. Other writers dealt more positively with questions of Jewish identity. Such were Elian-J. Finbert; Bernard *Lecache; Manès *Sperber; Rabi (pen name of Wladimir Rabinovitch; 1906–), a perceptive Jewish critic; Arnold Mandel; and Emmanuel Eydoux. The novelist Romain *Gary sided with the persecuted, as did the Belgian, David Scheinert.

Side by side with this postwar flowering of Jewish literature in France, the tradition of assimilation persisted, producing yet another generation of writers, some of great stature, who were Jewish in name only. Such were the poets Edmond Jabès, Jacques Givet, and Natalie *Sarraute; and the novelists Elsa *Triolet, Jean *Bloch-Michel, Jacques Lanzmann (1927–), and Bernard Frank (1929–). Three notable literary critics were Lucien Goldmann, Marie-Jeanne Durr (1901–), and Jean *Starobinski.

A group of French Jewish writers who settled in Israel deserves special mention: the poetess Yvette Szupak; the poet and storyteller Lionel Naaman; the Greek-born novelist Maurice Politi (1926–); Jean *Loewenson (Lavi); and the poets Joseph Milbauer, Pascal Thémanlys, and Claude Vigée. [D.R.G.]

Major Jewish French Authors. The individuals whose names are marked with an asterisk in the list below form the subjects of articles in their appropriate alphabetical position in the Encyclopaedia.

***ARÉGA, LÉON,** novelist.

BERL, EMMANUEL (1892–), author. A relative of *Bergson and Proust, Berl was a passionate political essayist and critic of the French bourgeoisie. His works include *Mort de la pensée bourgeoise* (1925), *La politique et les partis* (1932[2]), *Discours aux Français* (1934), *La culture en péril* (1948), and *Nasser tel qu'on le loue* (1968). Berl was chief editor of the weekly, *Marianne* (1933–37). He also wrote short stories, and novels including *Sylvia* (1952) and *Rachel et autres grâces* (1965), notable for their insight and an incisive style.

***BERNARD, TRISTAN** and **JEAN-JACQUES,** playwrights.

***BERNSTEIN, HENRY,** playwright.

***BLOCH, JEAN-RICHARD,** author and journalist.

***BLOCH-MICHEL, JEAN,** novelist and essayist.

***COHEN, ALBERT,** novelist.

***COHEN, GUSTAVE,** medievalist and literary critic.

***COHEN, ISAAC KADMI (Kadmi Cohen),** author and Zionist theoretician.

***CRÉMIEUX, BENJAMIN,** author and literary historian.

CROISSET, FRANCIS DE, pen name of **Frantz Wiener** (1877–1937), playwright. Born in Brussels, Croisset made his reputation in Paris, where he wrote many plays of the "boulevard" type, notably *Qui trop embrasse* (1899); *Chérubin* (1901), which was set to music by Jules Massenet; *Le paon* (1904); and *Le coeur dispose* (1912). He also wrote some plays in collaboration with R. de Flers; *Nos marionettes* (1928; *Our Puppet Show,* 1929), essays on the drama; a novel, *La Dame de Malacca* (1935; *Lady in Malacca,* 1936); and travel books such as *Le dragon blessé* (1936; *The Wounded Dragon,* 1937), on the Far East.

DUVERNOIS, HENRI, pen name of **Henri Simon Schwabacher** (1875–1937), author and journalist. His popular melancholy and ironical stories of everyday life in Paris, influenced by Maupassant, include the novels *Crapotte* (1908), *Faubourg Montmartre* (1914), *Edgar* (1919), and *Maxime* (1927). Duvernois also published a volume of one-act comedies (1928).

***EYDOUX, EMMANUEL,** poet and playwright.

FINBERT, ÉLIAN-J. (1899–), Jaffa-born author. Originally a camel driver and Nile boatman, Finbert published an anti-military novel, *Sous le règne de la Licorne et du Lion* (1925), for which Henri Barbusse wrote a preface. *Un homme vient de l'orient* (1930), the prizewinning *Le fou de Dieu* (1933), and *Le destin difficile* (1937) were novels on Jewish problems. Finbert edited a volume of essays, *Aspects du génie d'Israël* (1950); and wrote *Israël* (1955), a travel guide, and *Pionniers d'Israël* (1956).

***FLEG, EDMOND,** poet, playwright, and essayist.

FOA, ESTHER EUGÉNIE REBECCA (1799–1853), author. Born in Bordeaux, Esther Foa was the first Jewess to make her name as a French writer. Under various pen names, including Edmond de Fontanes, she wrote novels and stories on Jewish themes for juveniles. Among them are *Le Kiddouchim ou l'anneau nuptial des Hébreux* (4 vols., 1830); *La Juive, histoire du temps de la Régence* (1835); and *Le vieux Paris, contes historiques* (1840). She later abandoned Judaism.

***FONDANE, BENJAMIN,** French and Rumanian poet.

***FRANCK, HENRI,** poet.

***GARY, ROMAIN,** novelist.

GIVET (Vichniac), JACQUES (1917–), Swiss poet. Born in Moscow, Givet became prominent in Swiss intellectual circles. His verse collections, at first influenced by surrealism, include *Nous n'irons plus au bois* (1938), *Les cicatrices de la peur* (1954), and *L'eau et la mémoire* (1963). Givet also published a remarkable polemical tract on neo-anti-Semitism, *La gauche contre Israël* (1968).

GOLDMANN, LUCIEN (1913–1970), literary and philosophical writer. Born in Bucharest, Rumania, Goldmann settled in Paris, where he became director of studies at the Ecole Pratique des Hautes Etudes in 1958. His major work, *Le Dieu caché* (1955), deals with the tragic vision of life underlying the writings of *Pascal and *Racine. He also wrote *Sciences humaines et philosophie* (1952), *Jean Racine dramaturge* (1956), *Recherches dialectiques* (1959), and *Pour une sociologie du roman* (1964).

***GOLL, YVAN,** French and German poet.

***HALÉVY, DANIEL,** essayist.

***HALÉVY, LÉON,** essayist.

***HALÉVY, LUDOVIC,** playwright.

***HARRY, MYRIAM,** author.

***HERTZ, HENRI,** author and critic.

***IKOR, ROGER,** novelist and essayist.

***IONESCO, EUGÈNE,** playwright.

ISOU (Goldmann), ISIDORE (1925–), poet. Isou emigrated to France from Rumania. He wrote verse and created *Lettrisme,* an ephemeral literary theory which advocated the dislocation of the word and a return to the original letter; in this some critics have seen an unconscious echo of the Kabbalah. In his essay, *L'agrégation d'un Nom et d'un Messie* (1947), Isou pessimistically foretold a second Auschwitz that would engulf surviving Jewry.

JABÈS, EDMOND (1908–), poet. Born in Egypt, Jabès settled in Paris when the Egyptians expelled him after the 1956 Sinai Campaign. Revived awareness of his Jewish identity led to the verse trilogy *Le livre des questions* (1963–65), an esoteric work mingling surrealism and Kabbalah, aphorisms and poems in the romance of two concentration camp survivors. For Jabès, writing is the act of creation, and God an enigmatic "circle of luminous letters." Jabès also wrote *Je bâtis ma demeure* (1959) and *Yaël* (1967).

***JACOB, MAX,** poet.

JÉHOUDA, JOSUÉ (1892–1966), Swiss author and journalist. Born in Russia, Jéhouda settled in Switzerland, where he founded the *Revue juive de Genève.* He saw Israel's rebirth as an event of universal significance and viewed with alarm divisions between Orthodox and secular Jews, and between Israel and the Diaspora. His works include three novels, *Le royaume de Justice* (1933), *De père en fils* (1927), and *Miriam* (1928); and volumes of essays such as *La vocation d'Israël* (1947) and *Sionisme et messianisme* (1954).

***KAHN, GUSTAVE,** poet and critic.

***KESSEL, JOSEPH,** author and journalist.

***LANGFUS, ANNA,** novelist.

***LECACHE, BERNARD,** novelist and journalist.

***LOEWENSON (Lavi), JEAN,** translator and journalist.

***LUNEL, ARMAND,** novelist and librettist.

***MANDEL, ARNOLD,** novelist and journalist.

***MARITAIN, RAÏSSA,** author.

***MAUROIS, ANDRÉ,** author and biographer.

***MEMMI, ALBERT,** novelist and sociologist.

***MENDÈS, CATULLE,** poet, playwright, and critic.

MIKHAËL, EPHRAÏM, pen name of **Georges-Ephraïm Michel** (1866–1890), poet and playwright. Born in Toulouse, Mikhaël became a librarian at the Bibliothèque Nationale. An admired symbolist, he wrote sensitive poems that were later collected in *L'Automne* (1886) and *Oeuvres de Ephraïm Mikhaël: poésie, poèmes en prose* (1890). Some of his verse was translated into English by S.F. Merrill (in *Pastels in Prose,* 1890). His plays include *Le cor fleuri* (1888); *La fiancée de Corinthe* (1888), with Bernard *Lazare; and *Briséis* (1892), with Catulle Mendès.

***MILBAUER, JOSEPH,** poet.

***MILOSZ, OSCAR,** poet and playwright.

MORHANGE, PIERRE (1901–), poet. Born in Paris, Morhange gained his literary apprenticeship in the intellectual battles of the 1920s. He maintained that a special sensitivity identified the Jewish writer, and that French culture had been enriched by the Jewish contribution. In *Blessé* (1951) he described Jewish suffering with violence and anguish. A prophetic tone dominates collections such as *La vie est unique* (1933), *Autocritique* (1951), and *La robe* (1954).

NÉMIROWSKY, IRÈNE (1903–1944), novelist. Born in Kiev, Irène Némirowsky wrote several successful novels, including *Le vin de solitude* (1931), *L'Affaire Gourilof* (1933), and *Jézabel* (1936). Her best-known work was *David Golder* (1929; English trans., 1930), a powerful study of personal tragedy closer to the American than to the French tradition. She died in a Nazi concentration camp.

NEYRAC, PIERRE, pen name of **Naphtali Cohen** (1898–1960), novelist. A fourth-generation Palestinian, Neyrac immigrated to France in 1927 and practiced as a physician. He expressed nostalgia for his homeland in three novels, *L'indifférence perdue* (1933), *La mort de Frida* (1934), and *La jeunesse d'Elias* (1956).

***NOSTRADAMUS** or **MICHEL DE NOSTRE-DAME,** astrologer and physician.

***PORTO-RICHE, GEORGES DE,** playwright.

***PROUST, MARCEL,** novelist.

***SACHS, MAURICE,** novelist.

*SARRAUTE, NATHALIE, novelist.

SCHEINERT, DAVID (1916–), Belgian author. Born in Częstochowa, Poland, Scheinert was raised in Brussels, where he founded the *Revue juive de Belgique*. An aggressive style emphasized his sense of fellowship with the oppressed, whether Jews or non-Jews. Scheinert's works include the novels *L'apprentissage inutile* (1948), *Le coup d'état* (1950), and *Un silence provisoire* (1968); verse collections such as *Réquiem au genièvre* (1952), *Et la lumière chanta* (1954), and *Comme je respire* (1960); and literary essays, notably *Ecrivains belges devant la réalité* (1964).

SCHULSINGER, JOSEPH (d. 1943?), Belgian author. A religious Zionist active in Antwerp Jewish life, Schulsinger contributed to various Jewish periodicals. *La génuflexion d'Alénou* (1932), his historical drama about Jewish persecution in Ferrara, led to an interesting correspondence with the French poet and playwright Paul *Claudel (*Cahiers de Paul Claudel*, vol. 7, 1968). He was deported by the Nazis.

***SCHWARZ-BART, ANDRÉ,** novelist.

***SCHWOB, MARCEL,** essayist and biographer.

SÉE, EDMOND (1875–1959), playwright. Born in Bayonne, Sée foresook the law to write witty plays analyzing human emotions. Mainly comedies in the 18th-century French classical tradition, these include the highly successful *La brebis* (1896); *L'indiscret* (1903); *L'irrégulière* (1913); *La dépositaire* (1924); and *Charité* (1932). He also wrote two romantic novels, *Un cousin d'Alsace* (1918) and *Notre amour* (1920); and critical works such as *Le théâtre français contemporain* (1928).

***SPERBER, MANÈS,** novelist.

***SPIRE, ANDRÉ,** poet, critic, and Zionist leader.

***STAROBINSKI, JEAN,** literary critic.

***SUARÈS, ANDRÉ,** author and biographer.

THÉMANLYS, PASCAL (1907–), author. Descended from an old Bordeaux family, Thémanlys was born in Paris. A Zionist and a mystic, he believed in the reestablishment of Ereẓ Israel as Jewry's spiritual center. Settling in Israel in 1949, Thémanlys was cofounder with Joseph Milbauer of the Association des Amitiés Israël-France. His works include *Figures passionées* (1930), *Les merveilles du Becht* (1934), *Grands d'Israël, des Pharisiens à nos jours* (1938), *Influences* (1949), and *Un itinéraire de Paris à Jérusalem* (1963).

***TRIOLET, ELSA,** novelist.

***TZARA, TRISTAN,** French and Rumanian poet.

***VERCORS,** novelist and essayist.

***VIGÉE, CLAUDE,** poet and literary critic.

***VORONCA, ILARIE,** French and Rumanian poet.

***WEILL, ALEXANDRE ABRAHAM,** author, biographer and kabbalist.

***WIESEL, ÉLIE,** novelist and essayist.

Bibliography: J. Trénel, *L'Ancien Testament et la langue française du moyen âge* (1904); M. Debré, *Der Jude in der franzoesischen Literatur . . .* (1909; Eng.: *The Image of the Jew in French Literature from 1800–1908* (reprint, 1970)); A. Spire, *Souvenirs à bâtons rompus* (1962), 276–305; M. Lifschitz-Golden, *Les juifs dans la littérature française du moyen âge* (Thesis, Columbia University, 1935); E. S. Randall, *The Jewish Character in the French Novel, 1870–1914* (1941); R. Feigelson, *Ecrivains juifs de langue française* (1960), includes bibliography; F. Lehner, in: L. Finkelstein (ed.), *The Jews: Their History, Culture, and Religion*, 2 (1960[3]), 1472–86, includes bibliography; E.-J. Finbert (ed.), *Aspects du génie d'Israël* (1950); C. Lehrmann, *L'élément juif dans la littérature française*, 2 vols. (1960–61), includes bibliography; idem, *L'élément juif dans la pensée européene* (1947), 177–202; P. Aubery, *Milieux juifs de la France contemporaine* (1962[2]), includes bibliography; D. Goitein, *Jewish Themes in Selected French Works* (Thesis, Columbia University, 1967); L. Berman, *Histoire des juifs de France* (1937), 323–37, 460–9; N. J. E. Rothschild, *Le Mistère du Viel Testament*, 6 vols. (1878–91), includes bibliographies.

FRENCH REVOLUTION.

Position of the Jews Before the Revolution. The nature, status, and rights of the Jews became an issue of public consequence in *France in the last two decades before the outbreak of the Revolution in 1789. The Jewish population was then divided into some 3,500 Sephardim, concentrated mostly in southwestern France, and perhaps 30,000 Ashkenazim in eastern France. The Sephardim had arrived there after 1500 as *Marranos. By 1776, when the last *lettres patentes* in their favor had been issued by the crown, they had succeeded, step by step, in establishing their status as a merchant guild, avowedly Jewish, with at least the right to live anywhere within the authority of the *parlement* of *Bordeaux. The leading families of the Sephardim engaged in international trade. They were sufficiently assimilated to behave like bourgeois, and some were *Deists or nonbelievers before the Revolution. The Ashkenazim in eastern France were foreign and un-French in their total demeanor. This community spoke Yiddish and was almost totally obedient to the inherited ways of life. The power of the community over the individual was much larger among the Ashkenazim than among the Sephardim, for rabbinic courts were, in Metz and in Alsace, the court of first jurisdiction for all matters involving Jews. With the exception of a few rich army purveyors and bankers, Jews in eastern France made their living from petty trade, often in pursuits forbidden to them; by dealing in cattle; and from petty moneylending. More than any other, this last occupation embroiled the Jews in conflict with the poorest elements in the local population, the peasants.

Another economic quarrel involved the Jews in several places in France, and especially in Paris, with the traditional merchant guilds. In March 1767 a royal decree was issued creating new positions in the guilds and making these new posts freely accessible to purchase by foreigners. Jews managed to enter the guilds in a few places in eastern France, and to bid for entry in Bayonne. These efforts were fought in lawsuits everywhere. The new, Physiocratic insistence on productive labor had also helped sharpen the issue of "productivization" of the Jews in these years before the Revolution.

In the intellectual realm the Jews became a visible issue of some consequence in the 1770s and 1780s for a variety of reasons. The attack of the men of the Enlightenment on biblical religion inevitably involved these thinkers in negative discussion of the ancient Jews and, at least to some degree, of the modern ones. All of the newer spirits agreed that religious fanaticism, whether created by religion or directed against deviant faiths, needed to end. The Jews were thus an issue both as the inventors of "biblical fanaticism" and as the object of the hatred of the *Inquisition. Some of the great figures of the Enlightenment, with *Voltaire in the lead, argued that the Jews had an ineradicably different nature, which few, if any, could escape. The more prevalent, less ideological opinions were those of men such as the Marquis de *Mirabeau (the younger) and the Abbé *Grégoire, that the defects of the Jews had been created by their persecutors, who had excluded them from society and limited them to the most debasing of economic pursuits, leaving them entirely under the sway of their own leaders and their narrow tradition. With an increase in rights and better conditions, the Jews would improve.

Propaganda and pressure by Jewish leadership in eastern France, led by Herz *Cerfberr, the leading army purveyor in the region, had resulted in 1784 in the two last acts of the old order concerning Jews. In January 1784, Louis XVI, speaking in the accents of contemporary enlightened absolutism, forbade the humiliating body tax (see *Taxation) on Jews in all places subject to his jurisdiction, regardless of any local traditions to the contrary. In July of that year a much more general decree was published which attempted a comprehensive law for the Jews in Alsace. It was a retrograde act. A few increased opportunities were afforded the rich but no Jew could henceforth contract any marriage without royal permission and the traditional

Jewish pursuits in Alsace, the trade in grain, cattle, and moneylending, were surrounded with new restrictions. The rich were given new scope for banking, large-scale commerce, and the creation of factories in textiles, iron, glass, and pottery. The Jewish leaders in Alsace fought against this decree, and especially against that part of it which ordered a census in preparation of the expulsion of all those who could not prove their legal right to be in the province. This census was indeed taken and its results were published in 1785. Nonetheless, Jews continued to stave off the decree of expulsion until this issue was overtaken by the events of the Revolution. These quarrels and the granting of public rights to Protestants in 1787 kept the question of the Jews before the central government in Paris. Under the leadership of Chrétien Guillaume de Lamoignon de *Malesherbes, the question was again discussed by the royal government in 1788. Delegations of both the Sephardi and the Ashkenazi communities were lobbying in Paris during these deliberations. The prime concern of the Sephardim was to see to it that no overall legislation for Jews resulted in which their rights would be diminished by making them part of a larger body which included the Ashkenazim. The representatives of the Jews from eastern France followed their traditional policy of asking for increased economic rights and of defending the authority of the autonomous Jewish community.

The Era of Revolution. In the era of the Revolution the Jews did not receive their equality automatically. The Declaration of the Rights of Man which was voted into law by the National Assembly on Aug. 27, 1789, was interpreted as not including the Jews in the new equality. The issue of Jewish rights was first debated in three sessions, Dec. 21–24, 1789, and even the Comte de *Mirabeau, one of their chief proponents, had to move to table the question, because he saw that there were not enough votes with which to pass a decree of emancipation. A month later, in a very difficult session on Jan. 28, 1790, the "Portuguese," "Spanish," and "Avignonese" Jews were given their equality. The main argument, made by Talleyrand, was that these Jews were culturally and socially already not alien. The issue of the Ashkenazim remained unresolved. It was debated repeatedly in the next two years but a direct vote could never be mustered for their emancipation. It was only in the closing days of the National Assembly, on Sept. 27, 1791, that a decree of complete emancipation was finally passed, on the ground that the Jews had to be given equality in order to complete the Revolution, for it was impossible to have a society in which all men of whatever condition were given equal rights and status, except a relative handful of Jews. Even so, the parliament on the very next day passed a decree of exception under which the debts owed the Jews in eastern France were to be put under special and governmental supervision. This was a sop to anti-Jewish opinion, which had kept complaining of the rapacity of the Jews. The Jews refused to comply with this act, for they said that it was contrary to the logic of a decree of equality. Opinion thus had remained divided even in the last days, when Jews were being given their liberty.

This division of opinion about the status of the Jews was, to some degree, based on traditional premises. Such defenders of the old order as Abbé Jean Sieffrein Maury and Anne Louis Henry de la Fare, the bishop of Nancy, remained in opposition, arguing that the Jews were made by their religion into an alien nation which could not possibly have any attachment to the land of France. The more modern of the two, Maury, went further, to quote Voltaire to help prove that the Jews were bad because of their innate character and that changes of even the most radical kind in their external situation would not completely eradicate what was inherent in their nature. De la Fare was from eastern France, and he was joined in the opposition to the increase of Jewish rights by almost all of the deputies from that region regardless of their party. That this would occur had already been apparent in the *cahiers* from eastern France which, with the exception of one writer under the influence of Abbé Grégoire, were almost uniformly anti-Jewish. The most notable of the left-wing figures from Alsace in the revolutionary parliament, Jean François Rewbell, remained an uncompromising opponent. He held that it was necessary to defend "a numerous, industrious, and honest class of my unfortunate compatriots who are oppressed and ground down by these cruel hordes of Africans who have infested my region." To give the Jews equality was tantamount to handing the poor of eastern France over to counterrevolutionary forces, for the peasant backbone of the Revolution in that region would see the new era as one of increased dangers for them. The only organized body in eastern France which was publicly in favor of increased rights for the Jews was the moderate, revolutionary Société des Amis de la Constitution in Strasbourg, with which the family of Cerfberr had close connections. This group argued that the peasants were being artificially whipped up and that their hatred of the Jews would eventually vanish. A policy of economic opportunity would allow the Jews to enter productive occupations and become an economic boon to the whole region. It was along this general line that the Jews, if they were regenerated to be less clannish and more French and if they were dispersed in manufacture and on the land, would be good citizens, that their friends argued for Jewish emancipation. In the first debate on the "Jewish Question" on Sept. 28, 1789, when the Jews of Metz asked for protection against the threat of mob outbreaks (there had been outbursts in Alsace that summer and some Jews had fled to Basle), Stanislas de *Clermont-Tonnerre, a liberal noble from Paris, had agreed that the existing Jews did merit the hatred against them but ascribed what was wrong with the Jews to the effects of oppression. The Jews themselves could not maintain any separatism, for "there cannot be a nation within a nation." The emancipation of the Jews in France eventually took place on the basis sketched out by him: "The Jews should be denied everything as a nation but granted everything as individuals . . ." Such views were argued in the revolutionary years by the Jacobins of Paris, who were pro-Jewish (almost all the others and especially those in eastern France were anti-Jewish) and by the main body of moderate revolutionaries, who ultimately made their feeling prevail, that emancipation was a moral necessity, its purpose being to improve the Jews so that they could be part of a regenerated society.

The final decree of Sept. 27, 1791, did not end the tensions in eastern France. The structure of the Jewish community remained, and in some places in eastern France local civil powers continued, at least briefly, to enforce the taxation imposed by the *parnasim* for the support of the Jewish community. It soon became apparent that the revolutionary government itself needed to keep some kind of Jewish organization in being. The decree of nationalization of the property of the Church and of the émigrés (Nov. 2, 1789) had contained a provision for the assumption of the debts of the churches by the government, but it refused to assume responsibility for the debts contracted by the Jewish communities. The one in Metz was heavily in debt, largely to Christian creditors, and the issue of the payment of these debts remained a source of irritation and of repeated legal acts well into the middle of the 19th century. Those who had lived in Metz before 1789 and their descendants who had moved far away, even those who had converted from the faith, were held to be liable.

Throughout the era of the Revolution there was recurring concern about the patriotism of the Jews (their *civisme*) and about the channeling of their young into "productive occupations" and making them into good soldiers of the Republic; that is, whether the Jews were indeed "transforming" themselves as their emancipators had envisaged. During the first decade of the Revolution some economic changes were taking place. Jews did participate in the buying of nationalized property, and in particular lent money to the peasants in Alsace, who thus acquired their own farms. This splitting of the estates of the Church and of the émigré nobility into small farms gave the peasantry a stake in the Revolution, but the contribution of Jewish creditors and speculators to this trade (it was significant though not dominant) earned them no gratitude. It remained a fixed opinion, especially among Jacobins, that the Jews were usurers and that they were using the new opportunities of the Revolution to become even more obnoxious. In general, the occupational structure of the Jews changed very little in the 1790s. They continued mostly to be middlemen or peddlers; very few were beginning to work in factories or even to own land, despite much propaganda and occasional pressure on them to take up agriculture. There were some difficulties about their joining the armies of the Revolution. In many places the National Guard refused to accept Jews; sometimes it even attacked them and made minor pogroms, and it was regarded as a matter of unusual public importance that Max Cerfberr was accepted in Strasbourg in 1790. On the other hand, most Jews tried to avoid military service because of the problems of Sabbath and holiday observance which this created for them. A few of the sons of the richest families did become officers in the army as early as the 1790s, but the major military contribution of the Jews during the Republican period was in their traditional role as *contractors to the army. Jewish financiers were actually of minor importance, even here, but their visibility remained high and they were attacked with particular vehemence. Jews were involved in the military purchasing directory which was created in 1792, with Max Cerfberr as one of its directors. This body lasted just a few months, but it was at the center of much controversy during its existence, and thereafter. The Jews who were involved were subject to bitter criticism, but in this affair none was put to death for economic crimes or for treason.

The older Jewish leadership continued to dominate the Jewish community in the 1790s, but some newer forces were also arising. In southern France a group of Jewish Jacobins, whose club was named after Rousseau, became in 1793–94 the revolutionary government of Saint Esprit, the largely Jewish suburb of Bayonne. There were a few instances among both the Sephardim and the Ashkenazim of individual Jews who participated in the Religion of Reason. The overwhelming majority, however, both in the French Jewish communities and in those of the papal possessions, *Avignon and *Comtat Venaissin, which had been annexed to France in 1791, kept their religious traditions alive as best they could. No Jew was guillotined during the Terror (July 1793–July 1794) on the ground that his religious obduracy had made him an enemy of society, though such rhetoric was used by some of the Jacobins of eastern France in outraged reaction to the continuing practice of such traditions as Jewish burial. This was termed severely antisocial and a further expression of the supposed Jewish trait of hating the entire human race. During the Terror many synagogues and other Jewish properties were, indeed, nationalized and synagogue silver was either surrendered or hidden, as were books and Torah Scrolls. In some situations, such as in Carpentras in 1794, the Jews finally "willingly" gave their synagogue to the authorities. Nonetheless, religious services continued in hiding everywhere and after the Terror Jews were able not only to reopen many of their former synagogues but also to establish new conventicles in communities such as Strasbourg in which they had not had the right to live before the Revolution. As early as Aug. 4, 1794, within a few days after the fall of Robespierre, the Jews demanded the right to open a synagogue in Fontainebleau. There were a few cases of mixed marriage, though these remained very much the exception in the 1790s and did not become a trend of any significance until after the end of the century. The whole question of the status of Jewish acts in law remained confused, with many jurisdictions still continuing to restrict the personal freedom of Jews and the French courts still continuing to recognize Jewish law as determinant for Jews on matters of personal status, and especially marriage.

Anti-Jewish acts did not stop entirely with the end of the Terror. In November 1794, two Metz Jews were fined for carrying out Jewish burials and four years later five Jews were sentenced in Nice for building tabernacles for the Sukkot holiday. Thermidor was, however, regarded by Jews as a period in which religious persecution had ended. The problems of this period were mostly economic, for the civic tax rolls in various communities bore down heavily on Jews. From the very beginning of the Thermidor the central government ordered the protection of the Jews against agitation in eastern France. Occasional outbreaks continued and there were even some attacks on Jews for being in league, supposedly, with what remained of the Jacobins. Some angers that had been evoked by the emancipation of the Jews, and their involvement in the events of the first days of the Revolution, were evident during these days of reaction, but crucial was the fact that no change took place in the legal status of the Jews. Their emancipation was a fact and remained so; so was the economic conflict caused especially by their moneylending; so was the continued existence of their religious tradition and of their considerable communal apartness, even though the legal status of the community had been ended; so was the need of the central power to deal with the Jewish community in an organized way for many of its own purposes. All these questions, and an underlying concern about the "reform" of the Jewish religion and Jewish habits to accommodate the needs of the state, were deeded on to the next era, the period of *Napoleon.

Effects Outside France. The French Revolution brought legal equality to the Jews who dwelt in territories which were directly annexed by France. In addition to its operation in the papal possessions, Avignon and Comtat Venaissin, which were reunited with France in September 1791, just a few days before the final decree of emancipation for all of French Jewry, this legislation was applied to such border territories as Nice, which was conquered in 1792.

The German regions on the west bank of the Rhine were acquired by conquest in that same year, and the French conqueror, General A. P. de Custine, announced as his troops were entering the Rhineland that winter, that equality for Jews was one of his intentions. The formal enactments did not take place until 1797, when the supposedly independent Cisrhénane Republic was created. In the intervening years Jews who had begun by being suspicious of the new regime had become partisans of the Revolution.

In the *Netherlands there was a revolution in 1795, with help from the French army, and the Batavian Republic was proclaimed. A group of "enlightened" Jews had been among the prime organizers in Amsterdam of a body called *Felix Libertate. This association had as its purpose the furtherance of the ideas of "freedom and equality." There was substantial opposition in Holland even among some of the makers of the Revolution to the granting of full citizenship for Jews. The leaders of the official Jewish community were also opposed, for they fought bitterly against the disappearance of a Jewish separatist organization in a new regime of personal rights. There was a substantial debate, which culminated in eight days of discussion (Aug. 22–30, 1796), at the first session of the new revolutionary parliament. This debate was on a higher level than those held some years before in France; it resulted in the decision that Jews were to be given equal rights as individuals but that they had no rights as a people. The view of Clermont-Tonnerre in France in 1789 was thus upheld in Holland. In law this equality remained for the Jews in the Netherlands even after the fall of the Batavian Republic in 1806.

There were almost immediate echoes in *Italy of the French Revolution, but these stirrings were repressed in all of its various principalities. In the spring of 1790 the Jews were suspect of being partisans of the Revolution, and there were anti-Jewish outbreaks in both Leghorn and Florence; a comparable riot took place in Rome in 1793. There was almost no truth in all of these suspicions. A small handful of "enlightened" individuals were for the Revolution, but the organized Jewish communities looked forward only to some alleviations of their status by the existing regimes in Italy. Radical changes did take place toward the end of the decade, in 1796–98, when Napoleon Bonaparte conquered most of northern and central Italy, including the papal territories, in the course of two years of war. Everywhere the conquering French troops announced the end of the ghetto and equality for the Jews. In Italy the physical walls behind which Jews dwelt still existed in many places and the advent of the French armies gave the signal for the actual physical breaking down of these barriers by Jews and other partisans of the new order. Trees of liberty were planted in many places, especially in the Jewish quarters. Brief and even bloody revenge was taken on the Jews during Napoleon's absence in 1798–99 on his campaign in Egypt, as counterrevolutionary forces did battle against "Gauls, Jacobins, and Jews." In 1800 Napoleon, now as first consul, reconquered northern and central Italy and annexed it to France, ultimately to serve as the kernel of his future Kingdom of Italy. Jewish equality was secure in Italy until Napoleon's fall in 1815.

Elsewhere in Europe, the events of the French Revolution had enormous effects, but they did not lead to equality for the Jews. The French-inspired revolutionary Swiss regime of 1798 did not, even during its brief life, show any real desire to give the few Jews in Switzerland legal equality. In the Austrian Empire, the government was fearful of the Revolution and little was done in the 1790s that went beyond the several decrees of toleration that had been enacted in the spirit of enlightened absolutism by *Joseph II in 1781–82. The early years of the French Revolution coincided with the death agonies of independent Poland, leading to its partition and the end of Polish independence in 1795. Austria, Prussia, and Russia, among whom Poland was divided, were all either actively or passively arrayed against France throughout the 1790s. The influence of the French example, therefore, had no effect on their policy when these countries acquired among them the largest Jewish community, numbering some 800,000, in all of Europe. There was no change during the 1790s in the legal status of the Jews in any of the independent German principalities, not even those which sided with France in war. In the most important of the German states, *Prussia, despite notable and ongoing acculturation by members of the Jewish bourgeoisie in Berlin, the government refused to make any substantial changes in the regime of exclusion. A new decree that was issued at the beginning of 1790 spoke only of some future time, perhaps in three generations, when "regenerated Jews" might be admitted to civic equality. David *Friedlander answered on behalf of the leaders of Berlin Jewry that no changes at all were better than this "new imposition of chains"; what Jews wanted, he boldly added, was that such chains "be completely removed." To be sure, he and his circle were not insisting that equality be attained immediately by all Jews. Like the more successful Sephardim of France at that moment, the men whom David Friedlander led were interested almost entirely in their own rights. They proclaimed that the Jews in Berlin had already become culturally and intellectually the equal of the highest of German society, and they were, therefore, to be treated differently from their brethren in Bohemia or Poland, who were yet to wait until they had suitably prepared themselves by westernization for freedom.

The news from France was reported extensively and with exaltation in *Ha-Me'assef* for 1790, the Hebrew annual that was supported by this Berlin circle and by like-minded men on both sides of the Rhine and in Central Europe. These accents were soon suppressed in the name of patriotism, as Prussia went to war against France, but the example of equality in France, and of the United States Constitution of 1787, remained an ideal. For Jews everywhere in the next century after the French Revolution, the battle for emancipation became the central issue of their lives. Everywhere disabilities and exclusions were measured by the standards of France after 1791. In relation to the Jewish question Napoleon was the heir of the Revolution, and his victories after 1800 only extended the sphere of the emancipation. When he fell in 1815 the legal equality of Jews ended in much of his former empire, except in France and in Holland—and in Prussia, emancipation of 1812 had been a domestic decision, not forced upon Prussia by Napoleon. Nonetheless, the memory of the equality that Jews once held remained. Even in the many countries where nothing favorable to Jews had happened between 1789 and 1815, the example of the French Revolution was a dominant political force. Despite attempts at reaction in the 19th century the states of Europe had increasingly to contemplate full legal equality for all of their citizens, including Jews, as a central element of their entering modernity.

See also *Emancipation.

Bibliography: Z. Szajkowski, *Jews and the French Revolutions of 1789, 1830, and 1848* (1970); A. Hertzberg, *French Enlightenment and the Jews* (1968); Milano, Italia, 339–51; Roth, Italy, 421–45; S. Seeligman, *De Emancipatie der Joden in Nederland* (1913); Z. H. Ilfeld, *Divrei Negidim* (1799); I. Freund, *Emanzipation der Juden in Preussen* (1912); A. Kober, in: JSOS, 8 (1946), 291–322; M. Wiener, *Juedische Religion im Zeitalter der Emanzipation* (1933); R. Mahler, *Divrei Yemei Yisrael: Dorot Aḥaronim*, 1 (1952), 2 (1954), index.

[AR.H.]

FRENK, BEER (Issachar Dov; 1770–1845), Hungarian rabbinic author and painter. His father emigrated from Turkey—hence the name Frenk, which was the appellation used for Ashkenazi Jews in Turkey—and went to Pressburg. Frenk studied under Moses *Sofer, who gave his approbation to a number of Frenk's works. He served as *shoḥet* and beadle of the Pressburg community for 41 years. He possessed literary talent and was a skilled painter, especially of miniatures. Among the portraits he painted was one of Moses Sofer, which was done without his knowledge, and Sofer rebuked him for it. His books, all written in German with Hebrew characters, were popular presentations of religious duties, such as the salting of meat, *niddah*, Sabbath lights, recitation of the *Shema*, etc.

Bibliography: Ben-Menahem, in: *Sinai*, 64 (1968/69), 39–52; S. Schachnowitz, *Licht aus dem Westen* (1953[2]), ch. 21. [N.B.-M.]

FRENK, EZRIEL (or **Azriel**) **NATHAN** (1863–1924), Polish journalist and historian. Frenk was born in Wodzislaw to a ḥasidic family, but he was influenced by the Haskalah at an early age. In 1884 in Warsaw he began to write for the Jewish press, both in Hebrew and in Yiddish, and this remained his lifelong career. He published articles about current events, stories about ḥasidic life, and extensive studies on various subjects, mainly past and present problems of Poland's Jewry. Some of his historical writings, which had originally appeared in the daily press, were subsequently published in book form, notably, *Yehudei Polin bi-Ymei Milḥamot Napoleon* ("Jews of Poland in the Time of Napoleon," 1912); *Ha-Ironim ve-ha-Yehudim be-Polin* (The Burghers and Jews in Poland," 1921); and *Meshumodim in Poyln in Nayntsn Yorhundert* ("Apostates in Poland in the 19th century," 2 vols., 1923–24). However, the bulk of his writing, including important studies of Polish Jewish life in the first half of the 19th century, remains scattered in various Hebrew and Yiddish newspapers and periodicals. Frenk also undertook translations, e.g., H. Sienkiewicz's *Ogniem i mieczem* (*Ba-Esh u-va-Ḥerev*, 4 vols., 1919–21).

Bibliography: N. M. Gelber, in: S. K. Mirsky (ed.), *Ishim u-Demuyyot be-Ḥokhmat Yisrael be-Eiropah ha-Mizraḥit* (1959), 199–204; M. Balaban, *Yidn in Poyln* (1930), 314–9; idem, in: *Ha-Tekufah*, 21 (1924), 485–6; Kressel, Leksikon, 1 (1965), 682–3; Rejzen, Leksikon, 3 (1929), 228–37; LNYL, 7 (1938), 516–20. [I.Ha.]

FRENKEL, JACOB ILICH (1894–1952), Soviet physicist. Frenkel became an instructor at the University of the Crimea. From 1921 Frenkel lived in Leningrad. At first, he combined research work at the Physico-Technical Institute with lecturing at the Polytechnical Institute, where he headed the theoretical physics department for 30 years. He became a corresponding member of the Soviet Academy of Sciences in 1929. Frenkel's researches bore upon the physics of the atmosphere (particularly atmospheric electricity), terrestrial magnetism, biophysics, astrophysics, quantum theory, and the motion of electrons in metals. He laid foundations for the understanding of ferromagnetism and presented a theory of dielectric excitation, along with important ideas relating to defects in crystal lattices. He drew attention to certain similarities between liquid and solid structures, engaged in important researches on the liquid state, and presented his conclusions in his book on the kinetic theory of liquids (1945). Soon after the first artificial splitting of the uranium atom, Frenkel evolved a theory to account for the phenomenon of fission, which provided a basis for practical applications of nuclear energy. He was a pioneer in the writing of original Russian handbooks on modern theoretical physics.

Bibliography: *Bolshaya Sovetskaya Entsiklopediya*, 45 (1956[2]); T. Kuhn, et al., *Sources for History of Quantum Physics* (1967), index. [J.E.H.]

FRENSDORFF, SOLOMON (1803–1880), German masoretic scholar. Frensdorff was born in Hamburg, the son of a rabbi. He studied with Isaac *Bernays and later at the University of Bonn, where he took up Semitic languages. A. *Geiger and S. R. *Hirsch were his contemporaries and friends. Between 1834 and 1837 he was assistant rabbi in Frankfort; from 1837 he taught at the religious school in Hanover; and from 1848 he was head of the newly founded Teachers' Training College there. Frensdorff's major contribution to Jewish learning consists of a series of still valuable works on the masorah. He edited *Darkhei ha-Nikkud ve-ha-Neginot* (1847), ascribed to Moses ha-Nakdan, and the masoretic work *Okhlah ve-Okhlah* (1864, repr. 1969) from a Paris manuscript; the latter work had been published previously in a different version appended to rabbinic Bibles. Of a planned edition of *Die Massora Magna*, only the first part, an introduction, *Massoretisches Woerterbuch* (1876, repr. 1967), with a prolegomenon by G. E. Weil, appeared; the masorah notes are arranged alphabetically according to key words, giving the Bible passages where they occur. Part of Frensdorff's library is in the Jewish National and University Library in Jerusalem.

Bibliography: Kressel, Leksikon, 2 (1967), 681; *Zum Andenken an unsern Vater . . . Sal. Frensdorff* (1903), contains sermons by S. Groneman and L. Knoller. [Ed.]

FREUD, ANNA (1895–), psychoanalyst. Anna Freud was the youngest daughter of Sigmund *Freud, and was his companion on his vacation trips and his nurse during his prolonged illnesses. Her devotion to her father brought her into increasing contact with the developing thought and practice of psychoanalysis and she grew interested in child psychology. In 1927 she published a paper *Einfuehrung in die Technik der Kinderanalyse* (*Introduction to the Technique of Child Analysis*, 1928), in which she set out the analytical technique she had evolved. In 1936 she published *Das Ich und die Abwehrmechanismen* (*The Ego and the Mechanisms of Defence*, 1937) which described the ways by which painful ideas and emotions are warded off from consciousness and direct expression, e.g., by repression and replacement by the opposite idea. This book was a pioneer contribution to ego psychology and in understanding the adolescent.

She escaped from Austria with her father in 1938 and went with him to London, where she began to work as a children's analyst in the Hampstead nurseries. During World War II Anna Freud and her colleague, Dorothy Burlingham, wrote three books on their work at the Hampstead nurseries, describing the treatment of children separated from their families and under conditions of war stress. They also described the development of children from narcissism to socialization, and set out the problems in the emotional life of institutional children despite their receiving advantages in physical care. These books were: *Young Children in Wartime* (1942); *Infants without Families* (1943); and *War and Children* (1943).

The Hampstead nurseries closed in 1945. In 1947, with the help of Kate *Friedlander, Anna Freud founded the Child Therapy Course. In 1951 she became director of the clinic which was opened in conjunction with the course. Anna Freud's book *Normality and Pathology in Childhood* (1965) is a comprehensive summation of her thought. Anna Freud's contribution to child analytic therapy and child psychology was fundamental. She was able to demonstrate the validity of the reconstructions made by Freud of child development and pathology through his analysis of adults. Moreover she was able to add considerably to the information by her methods of direct observation of children. Of special interest was her employment of psychological understanding in the education of children and in preventive work with the child through its parents and educators. Her contribution to the knowledge of the reaction of young children separated from their parents and deprived of emotional relationships, particularly in institutions, has had a wide effect in social policy and direct child care. From 1968 her collected works appeared under the title *The Writings of Anna Freud*.

Bibliography: E. Pumpian-Mindlin, in: F. Alexander, et al. (eds.), *Psychoanalytic Pioneers* (1966), 519–33; Sandler, in: J. G. Howells (ed.), *Modern Perspectives in Child Psychiatry* (1965), includes bibliography, 250f. [Lo.M.]

FREUD, SIGMUND (1856–1939), Austrian psychiatrist, creator of psychoanalysis. Freud was born at Freiberg (Priber), Moravia. He went to school in Vienna and entered the university there as a medical student. He encountered anti-Semitism and a certain exclusion from the university community because of his Jewishness, but found a haven in Ernst Bruecke's physiological laboratory. He worked productively in research with Bruecke from 1876 to 1882.

In 1882, for financial reasons, he entered clinical practice as a resident in the Vienna General Hospital, working under the brain anatomist T. H. Meynert. He nevertheless continued to pursue his neurological interests and research in the wards. The work and reputation of the neurologist Jean Charcot in Paris attracted the young physician, and he began to study clinical manifestations of organic diseases of the nervous system. When Freud was awarded a traveling fellowship in 1885, he became a student of Charcot at the Salpetrière mental hospital. This period strengthened Freud's determination to investigate hysterical paralysis and anesthesias. Earlier, he had formed a friendship with the Viennese physician Josef *Breuer who told Freud of his treatment of hysteria and together they now began their epoch-making work on the treatment of hysteria. In 1895 they wrote *Studien ueber Hysteria* (*Studies in Hysteria,* 1936), which set out for the first time the theory that the damming-up of emotions in the unconscious could produce symptoms of hysterical illness. If a patient could discharge this emotion and the attendant fantasy, the symptom could disappear. Freud's growing conviction that disturbances in sexual life were important factors in the cause of neurosis was unacceptable to Breuer and in 1896 they parted company.

Working on his own, Freud gave up hypnosis and the method of cathartic discharge for a new therapeutic technique. He now asked the patient to abandon himself and say whatever came into his mind. This process, which he called free association, is the fundamental rule of psychoanalysis. By inducing the patient to recall to consciousness his forgotten memories, Freud was able to uncover the repressed experiences that gave rise to his neurosis. He realized that a conflict occurred between an unacceptable instinct and the resistance to it. The instinct was repudiated and repressed and, in the unconscious, sought substitute methods of gratification. Symptoms, mental or physical, resulted. The task of therapy was to uncover the repressions and allow normal judgment to accept or reject the repudiated impulse. This therapy Freud called psychoanalysis. Freud now established his conviction that repressed impulses were frequently sexual drives which the patient had resisted, and gratified in symptoms which were substitutes. His theories on the importance of sex from earliest infancy and on the Oedipus complex, elaborated over the next few years, were brought together in his *Drei Abhandlungen zur Sexualtheorie* (1905; *Three Essays on the Theory of Sex,* 1910).

In 1897 Freud began the heroic test of analyzing himself and of facing his own unconscious. His self-analysis was in the face of great personal struggle, mainly through his dreams. He discovered that the dream-thought is an impulse in the form of a wish, often of a very repellent kind, which is disavowed, but results in a dream after it has passed through a mental censorship. The dream thus serves as a disguised fulfillment of a repressed wish. He embodied this theory in *Die Traumdeutung* (1900; *The Interpretation of Dreams,* 1913). In 1904 Freud published *Zur Psychopatologie des Alltagslebens* (*The Psycho-Pathology of Everyday Life,* 1914), in which he demonstrated how psychoanalysis explains the numerous unconscious slips and mistakes that people make in everyday life—symptomatic actions, as they are called. These phenomena are not physiological or accidental; they have a meaning that can be interpreted.

Sigmund Freud. Photo Keystone Press Agency, London.

Freud's sexual theories were no more acceptable to the rest of the medical profession than they had been to Breuer, and for almost a decade he was virtually ostracized; but by 1905 a small circle of pupils had gathered around him and his isolation came to an end. In 1906 he heard that the group of psychiatrists in Zurich, which included C. G. Jung (1875–1961), were interested in psychoanalysis. He met Jung in the following year, and the Swiss psychiatrist became his foremost disciple. In 1909 Freud and Jung traveled to the United States and gave a week of lectures at Clark University in Worcester, Mass. It was then that Freud delivered his "Five Lectures on Psychoanalysis" (in *American Journal of Psychology,* 21 (1910), 181–218; *Ueber Psychoanalyse: fuenf Vorlesungen,* 1910). The association lasted until 1912, when Jung set forth his own theories, and founded his own school. It was at this time too that another prominent associate, the Austrian psychiatrist Alfred *Adler, withdrew from psychoanalysis. Like Jung he repudiated infantile sexuality and traced character and neurosis to the desire for power. In 1911 Freud began to set out general theoretical points of view in *Formulierungen ueber die zwei Prinzipien des psychischen Geschehens* (*Formulations Regarding the Two Principles in Mental Functioning,* 1925), in which he discussed the domination in infancy of the self-serving pleasure-pain principle and its displacement after maturation by the reality principle. From 1915 to 1917 he attempted to organize all mental processes according to the concepts of forces, conflicts, and systems of the mind, a "metapsychology." He then wrote such papers as "Instincts and their Vicissitudes," "The Unconscious," and "Mourning and Melancholia." His dissection of the mental apparatus led him to divide it into an ego, an id, and a superego. The ego represents reason and reality in contrast to the id, which contains the passions, while the superego developed out of the Oedipus complex and represents ethical standards.

After World War I Freud at last gave full vent to his inclination to theorize, especially about the instincts. In 1920 he published *Jenseits des Lustprinzips* (*Beyond the Pleasure Principle,* 1922); in 1921, *Massenpsychologie und Ich-Analyse* (*Group Psychology and the Analysis of the Ego,* 1922); and in 1923, *Das Ich und das Es* (*The Ego and the Id,* 1927). In the last-named he combined the instincts for the preservation of self and the species under the concept of Eros and contrasted it with an assumed death instinct. The latter was not accepted by many of his collaborators.

Freud applied his psychological theories to primitive cultures, mythology, and religion. In 1907 he established a relationship between obsessive acts and religious acts and rituals. *Totem und Tabu* (1913; *Totem and Taboo,* 1918) suggested that the dread of incest was even more marked among primitive than among civilized people. In *Die Zukunft einer Illusion* (1927; *The Future of an Illusion,* 1928), Freud denied the material truth of religion but accepted its historical truth. "In the long run," he said, "nothing can withstand reason and experience, and the contradiction which religion offers to both is only too palpable."

Freud was not a practicing Jew and noted that he did not understand Hebrew, was estranged from Judaism, and was unable to share Zionist ideals (preface to Hebrew edition of *Totem and Taboo*). He nevertheless rejected baptism and remained a steadfast member of the Jewish community. He was a loyal member of the Vienna B'nai B'rith lodge. In his book *Selbstdarstellung* (1925; *An Autobiographical Study,* 1935), he wrote, "My parents were Jews, and I remained a Jew myself." It is also noteworthy that almost all his colleagues (with Jung as the outstanding exception) were Jews. Freud made his final contribution to the subject of religion when he was over 80, in the last book he published, *Der Mann Moses und die monotheistische Religion* (1939; *Moses and Monotheism,* 1955). Here Freud tried to account for the origin and special characteristics of the Jewish people. He developed the idea that Moses had been an Egyptian, who taught an Egyptian monotheistic religion to the Children of Israel, that he had been killed when the Jews rebelled against him, and that this act of patricide had given rise to a self-perpetuating unconscious guilt feeling. There was a strong reaction against the book by Jews and non-Jews alike.

Freud—together with his daughter Anna Freud, the child psychoanalyst—was hurried out of Vienna by his colleagues after the Nazi occupation in 1938. He died in London after a long courageous battle with cancer.

The part played by Freud in the theoretical understanding of human psychology and mental disturbance is without parallel in history. Almost as great is the impact of his technique of psychoanalysis, or the more recent modified methods of analytic psychotherapy, in the treatment of neuroses and other lesser emotional disturbances. It should be noted, however, that his therapy has not yet been applied to individuals who have not acquired western methods of social organization. The application of both this theory of and treatment methods for insanity, especially by Eugen Bleuler (1857–1939) and Jung, has been at the core of the advances made in the knowledge of the functional psychoses, the schizophrenic and manic-depressive conditions. The application of psychoanalysis to medicine fostered the development of "psychosomatic medicine," permitting the rational explanation and care of emotionally colored conditions such as asthma and high blood pressure.

While Freud gave relatively little direct theoretical thought to education, it is in this field that his influence has been the greatest. The social, personal, and intellectual growth or stunting of the child in the light of the emotional relations in its family and at school are now understood through his work. This knowledge is at the core of modern preventive mental health practice. Freud's speculative work in sociology and anthropology stimulated psychologists, psychiatrists, and anthropologists to study the influences of the group and the socio-cultural environment on individual personality development, character, and deviation from the social norm. This added a new theoretical dimension to preventive mental health work which among other means tried where possible to modify the social environment.

A further educational impact of Freud's work has been its effect on moral thought and the application of legal and penal systems. Psychoanalysis helped to clarify the sources and motivation of ethical and delinquent behavior. The naughty child and the transgressor were seen not only from the point of view of their will to transgress but from the point of view of the failure of their will to control the universal impulse to transgress. Society's failure in moral education was at times a cause. These views shift some of the responsibility for the individual's delinquency and failure to others in his environment, if not to society as a whole. Freud's complete psychological works in English have been edited in 23 volumes by J. Strachey and others (1953–66), and his letters were published by E. L. Freud in 1961. [Lo.M.]

Freud's Place in the History of Psychology. Freud's place in the history of psychology is securely established, even though his theories present a paradox in that they were immensely influential, although his methods may be considered unscientific, even when measured against the standards of his day. Freud relied on nonsystematic clinical observations of his patients, of chance occurrences, and of himself. The early circle of disciples that collected around him left no room for dissent, and thus lacked even the stimulus to scientific adequacy that is normally supplied by the criticism of a peer group.

While Freud's theories may easily be faulted for the lack of control in data collection, the failure to check on the validity of their factual basis, and the impossibility of deriving testable hypotheses from them, they nevertheless gave rise to a flourishing and viable school of psychology. Beyond the field of psychology, psychoanalytic theory has widely influenced our culture in many ways, particularly in art and literature.

The answer to this apparent puzzle lies in the fact that Freud formulated his ideas at a propitious time. Psychology had passed from its philosophical period into the era of experimental science, but it had not been able to provide answers to some of the pressing problems of society. Freud was able to step into the gap and to turn psychology's interest into a new direction. In addition he wrote in a facile and attractive style and possessed a charming and dynamic personality, thus serving as his own best publicist and attracting a group of enthusiastic followers to spread his ideas.

Freud's systematic contribution actually involved three separate but related fields: human (especially childhood) development, the structure of personality, and techniques of dealing with behavior disorders. His developmental psychology is rooted in the concept of biological drives, especially the sex drive. Its natural science viewpoint and emphasis on opponent processes, such as attraction and repulsion, pleasure principle and reality principle, ego and object marks it as a typical example of 19th-century physicalism (see R. Lowry, in *Journal of the History of the Behavioral Sciences,* 3 (1967), 156–67). His stress on the sex drive and especially his hypothesis of infantile sexuality were the occasion for many vicious attacks, but ultimately worked in his favor in terms of the attention that they attracted and the changing attitudes toward sex that they brought about. Freud's role in opening up this topic for scientific discussion must be considered one of his major contributions.

His theory of personality hypothesized three major constructs, the id, the ego, and the superego. It also stressed dynamic processes such as repression, regression, and sublimation. Although his constructs were not open to verification and the processes he stressed were not new, his major contribution here lay in the realization of anxiety avoidance or reduction as a major source of behavior modification. His system also emphasized the unconscious nature of psychological processes. Finally, he was responsible for showing that much behavior has its roots in irrational causation, and thus laid the foundation for the downfall of the 18th-century notion of man as a rational being.

His third contribution, the process of psychoanalysis, was meant to provide a means of helping neurotic individuals. Its efficacy has been seriously doubted and its various components, such as cathexis, transference, and catharsis have not been confirmed in alternate methods of psychotherapy. Its value lies in the fact that it opened up the field of psychology to the practitioner. It freed the psychologist from the laboratory and projected him from academic isolation into the interpersonal relationships of the clinic. It also fulfilled a great need, felt even more today than in Freud's day, for a profession to help emotionally disturbed and troubled individuals. Freud's place in the history of psychology may best be gauged by the fact that, in the U.S. at least, clinical psychologists constitute by far the largest sector of professional psychology. [H.E.A.]

Bibliography: E. Jones, *Life and Work of Sigmund Freud*, 3 vols. (1953–57), includes bibliography; H. Sachs, *Freud, Master and Friend* (1945); T. Reik, *From Thirty Years with Freud* (1942); E. A. Grollman, *Judaism in Sigmund Freud's World* (1965), includes bibliography; D. Bakan, *Sigmund Freud and the Jewish Mystical Tradition* (1958); M. Freud, *Glory Reflected; Sigmund Freud, Man and Father* (1957); H. L. Philp, *Freud and Religious Belief* (1956), includes bibliographies; P. Rieff, *Freud: the Mind of a Moralist* (1950); M. H. Ruitenbeek, *Freud and America* (1966); A. Grinstein, *On Sigmund Freud's Dreams* (1969); M. Robert, *The Psychoanalytic Revolution: Sigmund Freud's Life and Achievement* (1966); B. B. Walman, *The Unconscious Mind* (1968).

FREUDEMANN, SIMḤAH (Ephraim ben Gershon ha-Kohen; c. 1622–1669), talmudist and author. Born in Belgrade, Freudemann studied under Judah Lerma II, the Sephardi rabbi of the Belgrade community, whom, despite his Ashkenazi descent, he succeeded as rabbi. In 1660 he was appointed rabbi of Ofen (Buda) in Hungary, but a dispute soon arose in the town on the grounds of his having relatives in the community, a disqualifying factor for the appointment of a rabbi under the terms of a ban included in the *takkanot* of the *dayyan* Aryeh Shraga Feivish of Vienna. In consequence, he left Ofen after a few months and returned to Belgrade where he remained until his death.

In 1647 he published Lerma's responsa, *Peletat Beit Yehudah* (Venice). Ten years later, there appeared in Venice his most important work, *Sefer Shemot* (referred to also as *Shemot ha-Gittin*), based on unpublished material of earlier Ashkenazi and Sephardi authorities, giving the correct Hebrew spelling of Jewish personal names of Hebrew, Latin, Spanish, and German origin, as well as the orthography of rivers and place-names for use in drawing up Jewish bills of divorce and other public documents in which accuracy was essential.

Bibliography: S. Bechler, *A zsidók története Budapesten* (1901), 140–7; Conforte, Kore, 51b; L. Greenwald, *Pe'erei Ḥakhmei Medinatenu* (1910), 19; idem, *Ha-Yehudim be-Ungarya* (1913), 19f.; *Arim ve-Immahot be-Yisrael*, 2 (1948), 126; P. Z. Schwartz, *Shem ha-Gedolim me-Ereẓ Hagar*, 2 (1913), 42a, no. 94; Zipser, in: *Ben-Chananja*, 2 (1859), 172f. [S.R.]

FREUDENTHAL, JACOB (1839–1907), German philosopher. His scholarly investigations were in the areas of Greek and Judeo-Hellenistic philosophy and the philosophy of Spinoza. Freudenthal was born in Hanover. In 1863 he taught at the Samson School in Wolfenbuettel and from 1864 lectured on classical languages and the history of religious philosophy at the Jewish Theological Seminary in Breslau. From 1875 he also taught at the Breslau University. He married a daughter of Michael *Sachs, the famous Berlin preacher and scholar.

Jacob Freudenthal, German philosopher. Jerusalem, J.N.U.L., Schwadron Collection.

Freudenthal was a foremost authority on Aristotle and published a series of works on his philosophy. In his studies of Xenophanes Freudenthal opposed the then prevalent opinion that Xenophanes was a consistent monotheist. His writings include: *Hellenistische Studien* (1875–79); *Flavius Josephus beigelegte Schrift: Ueber die Herrschaft der Vernunft* (1869); *Zur Geschichte der Anschauungen ueber die juedisch-hellenistische Religionsphilosophie* (1869); "Spinoza und die Scholastik" in: E. Zeller, *Philosophische Aufsaetze* (1887), 85–138; *Die Lebensgeschichte Spinoza's in Quellenschriften...* (1899); *Spinoza, sein Leben und seine Lehre*, vol. 1 (1904), vol. 2 (1927).

Bibliography: Baumgartner, in: *Chronik der Universitaet Breslau*, 22 (1907/8); Baumgartner and Wendland, in: *Jahresbericht ueber die Fortschritte der klassischen Altertumswissenschaft;* vol. 136, p. 152–63; M. Brann, *Geschichte des Juedisch-theologischen Seminars in Breslau* (1904), 129–30; B. Muenz, in: *Ost und West*, 7 (1907), 425–8; G. Kisch (ed.), *Das Breslauer Seminar* (1963), 322–3. [Jo.H./Ed.]

FREUDENTHAL, MAX (1868–1937), German liberal rabbi and writer. Freudenthal, who served as rabbi in Dessau, 1893–1900, Danzig, 1900–07, and Nuremberg, 1907–35, was one of the most resolute exponents of religious liberalism in Germany. His contributions to Jewish scholarship covered both philosophy and history. In philosophy he

Max Freudenthal, German liberal rabbi and scholar. Jerusalem, J.N.U.L., Schwadron Collection.

published *Die Erkenntnislehre Philos von Alexandrien* (1891); in history, *Aus der Heimat Moses Mendelssohns* (1900); *Die Familie Gomperz* (in collaboration with D. Kaufmann, 1907); *Die israelitische Kultusgemeinde Nuernberg, 1874–1924* (1925), which includes his autobiography; and *Leipziger Messgaeste* (1928). Freudenthal contributed a wealth of basic material to the study of modern Jewish history in Germany. He wrote for various learned publications, and was coeditor of the *Zeitschrift fuer die Geschichte der Juden in Deutschland.*

Bibliography: ZGJD, 7 (1937), 131–7. [Ed.]

FREUND, ERNST (1864–1932), U.S. jurist and legislative authority. Born in New York, Freund was educated in Germany and the United States. Freund practiced law in New York from 1886 to 1894, but was drawn to the teaching profession, concentrating on political and social sciences. As a professor at the University of Chicago from 1902, he made significant contributions in the field of public law, particularly in administrative law and legislation. Freund stressed the importance of social science in the legislative process. He served as a member of the National Conference of Commissioners on Uniform State Law from 1908 until his death, and took part in the drafting of uniform state laws relating to marriage and divorce, the guardianship of children, child labor, narcotics, and the improvement of the legal position of illegitimate children. Two important books among his writings are *The Police Power, Public Policy and Constitutional Rights* (1904) and *Standards of American Legislation* (1917).

Bibliography: *New York Times* (Oct. 21, 1932); *University Record* (January 1933); *Law Quarterly Review* (April 1933). [J.J.M.]

FREUND, ISMAR (1876–1956), writer, communal worker, and lawyer. From 1902 to 1938 Freund was the executive director of the Berlin Jewish community, and from 1905 a lecturer in religious community law at the *Hochschule (Lehranstalt) fuer die Wissenschaft des Judentums. He was the driving force behind the formation of the Preussischer Landesverband Juedischer Gemeinden (1922). Freund strove to achieve a nationwide Reichsverband Juedischer Gemeinden, but without success. He bitterly opposed the separate organization of Orthodox congregations (Halberstaedter Verband). Freund emigrated to Palestine in 1938, taking with him his valuable private archives, which he presented to the General Historical Archives in Jerusalem.

He wrote various works on German Jewish history, including the two-volume *Die Emanzipation der Juden in Preussen* (1912).

Bibliography: G. Kisch, *The Breslau Seminary* (1963), 414–6. [Ed.]

FREUND, MIRIAM KOTTLER (1906–), U.S. Hadassah leader. She was born in New York City and taught in the New York public high schools until 1944. From 1940 Miriam Freund was a member of the National Board of Hadassah,

Miriam Freund, U. S. Hadassah leader. Courtesy Hadassah, New York.

and held major positions in the organization. She was Youth Aliyah chairman (1953–56) and Hadassah national president from 1956 to 1960. Afterward, she filled a variety of Hadassah posts, and was instrumental in obtaining the services of Marc Chagall as creator of the stained-glass windows in the synagogue at the Hadassah Medical Center. She edited the *Hadassah Magazine* from 1966, and wrote *Jewish Merchants in Colonial America* (1939) and *Jewels for a Crown* (1963), as well as articles on Zionism and American history. [Gl.R.]

FREUND, PAUL ABRAHAM (1908–), U.S. constitutional lawyer, educator, and author. Freund, who was born in St. Louis, Missouri, was appointed law clerk to Justice *Brandeis for the 1932–33 term of the U.S. Supreme Court,

Paul A. Freund, U.S. constitutional lawyer.

and served on the legal staffs of the Treasury Department and the Reconstruction Finance Corporation (1933–35), and was special assistant to the solicitor general (1934–39) and to the attorney general of the U.S. (1942–46). Freund lectured at the Harvard Law School from 1939 (professor, 1940). He served as legal adviser to President Kennedy and to the State Department, and from 1957 as adviser to the American Law Institute on the drafting of the Restatement of the Conflict of Laws. A recognized authority on constitutional law, Freund believed that the U.S. Supreme Court in a federation has the responsibility of maintaining the supremacy of the Constitution and promoting the uniformity of law. His writings include: *On Understanding the Supreme Court* (1949); *The Supreme Court of the U.S.* (1961); and *On Law and Justice* (1968). [J.J.M.]

FREUND, SAMUEL BEN ISSACHAR BAER (1794–1881), rabbi and author of commentaries and glosses on the Mishnah and halakhic works. Born in Touskov, Bohemia, Freund was a pupil of Baruch Fraenkel-Teomim of Leipnik and Bezalel Ranschburg (Rosenbaum) of Prague. He served as rabbi in Lobositz, and afterward in Prague (1834–79), where he succeeded Samuel b. Ezekiel Landau as *dayyan*, or "Oberjurist." Freund initiated the founding of the "*Afike Jehuda" society for Jewish science in Prague (1869). He died in Prague.

Among his works are: *Zera Kodesh* (pt. 1, 1827); novellae and expositions of the tractates *Berakhot, Pe'ah* and *Demai; Musar Av* (Vienna, 1839), a commentary on Proverbs; *Teshuvat Keren Shemu'el* (Prague, 1841), a responsum on the subject of eating legumes, rice, and millet during Passover, his conclusion being that they cannot be permitted; *Et le-Ḥannenah* (1850), glosses on the order *Mo'ed; Ir ha-Ẓedek* (1863), an abridgment of the *Sefer Mitzvot Gadol (Semag)* of Moses of Coucy, with glosses, novellae, and expositions; *Amarot Tehorot* (1867), glosses to, and corrections of the works of commentators on the order *Tohorot*, together with his own *Ketem Paz* (1870), a commentary on *Avot*, and an appendix of glosses and novellae to *Berakhot*.

Bibliography: *Der Israelit*, 22 (1881), 609, 636–8, 725; G. Klemperer, in: HJ, 13 (1951), 80. [S.R.]

FREUND, WILHELM (1806–1894), classical philologist and educator. Freund, who was born in Kempen (now Kepno), Poznan province, was a Greek and Latin scholar, and until he was nearly 50 devoted himself mainly to the compilation of dictionaries and aids to the study of Greek and Latin classics. They included a Latin dictionary (1834–45), and a German-Latin-Greek dictionary for use in schools (1848–55). From 1855 to 1870 he was director of the Jewish high school in Gleiwitz (Gliwica). Freund wrote many educational pamphlets, as well as several on the legal position of the Jews in Germany. He was instrumental in bringing A. *Geiger as rabbi to Breslau. In 1843–44 he edited the periodical *Zur Judenfrage in Deutschland.* [ED.]

FREUNDLICH, OTTO (1878–1943), German painter, sculptor, graphic artist, and teacher. Freundlich, who was born in Pomerania, first studied art history and then art. From 1909 to 1914 he had a studio in Montmartre, and returned to Germany at the outbreak of World War I. Strongly sympathetic to the Left, Freundlich was a contributor to *Die Aktion,* a revolutionary anti-war publication in Berlin. Its September 1918 issue was dedicated to him, and was illustrated with his drawings and woodcuts. After the war, he joined the short-lived November Group, which vainly endeavored to narrow the gap between the masses and the artists. He returned to Paris in 1924. From 1932 to 1935 he took part in the exhibitions of the Abstraction-Création group. In Nazi Germany, his works were featured in the Degenerate Art show, and his near-abstract sculpture, "Homme Nouveau," was singled out as an example of "Bolshevik-Jewish" art. When France was invaded in 1940, he fled to the Pyrenees but was discovered by the Nazis and deported to Lublin extermination camp in Poland, where he died. His work was either close to

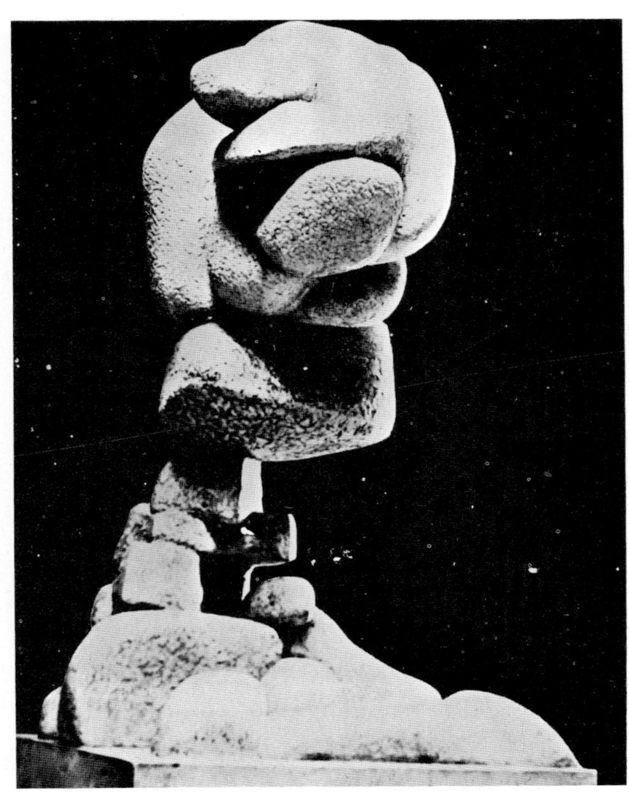

"Ascension," sculpture by Otto Freundlich, 1929. From *Deux sculptures monumentales,* Paris, 1962.

pure abstraction or completely nonfigurative. The sculptures, often related to architecture, consist of rolling, cloud-like masses, joined together with great subtlety. [A.W.]

°**FREY, JEAN BAPTISTE** (1878–1939), French priest and archaeological scholar. In 1925 Frey was appointed secretary of the papal Bible commission and in 1933 rector-consultor of the Congregation "De propaganda fide" ("For Propagating the Faith"). His most important publication, though incomplete, is the two-volume *Corpus Inscriptionum Judaicarum* (entitled in French *Recueil des inscriptions juives du troisième siècle avant au septième siècle après J. C.,* vol. 1, *Europe,* 1936; vol. 2, *Asie-Afrique,* 1952). The second volume, despite its title, deals with Egypt only. His other works include: *La théologie juive aux temps de Jésus-Christ . . .* (1910); *Une ancienne synagogue de Galilee récemment découverte* (1933); and *Il delfino col tridente nella catacomba giudaica di Via Nomentana* (1931). Frey also contributed numerous articles to learned periodicals, chiefly on Judaism in the time of Jesus and on Semitic epigraphy. [ED.]

FRIBOURG (Ger. **Freiburg**), capital of the Swiss canton of that name. Toward the middle of the 14th century, a number of Jews received permission to settle in Fribourg as citizens and to engage in moneylending. As elsewhere in Switzerland, they lived in their own part of the town, although not confined to a ghetto. On the outbreak of the *Black Death (1348–49), the Jews of Fribourg, like those in the rest of Europe, were accused of causing the epidemic by spreading poison. Jews were formally excluded from the city in 1428. From the end of the 17th century, Jewish cattle dealers were occasionally permitted to visit the city's open market, but the ban on Jewish commerce issued by nearby *Berne in 1787 also affected Fribourg. The restrictions remained in force until the middle of the 19th century. The present community was founded in 1895. In 1968 it numbered approximately 150 persons and had a synagogue.

The Ark of the Law in the synagogue of Fribourg, Switzerland, built in 1905. Courtesy Jean Nordmann, Fribourg. Photo B. Rast.

Bibliography: Kober, in: F. Boehm and W. Dirks (eds.), *Judentum, Schicksal, Wesen and Gegenwart,* 1 (1965), 162–3; A. Weldler-Steinberg, *Geschichte der Juden in der Schweiz* (1966), index s.v. *Freiburg.* [ED.]

FRIED, AARON (1812–1891), Hungarian rabbi. Born in Hajdúböszörmény, Fried studied under R. Moses Sofer in Pressburg from 1828 to 1831. In 1833 he married the daughter of Eleazar Loew (author of *Shemen Roke'aḥ*), the rabbi of Abaujszántó, and took up residence with him there until 1837. In the latter year, he was appointed rabbi of Mezőcsát where he remained until 1844. While there, all his possessions including his books and writings were lost in a fire. From 1844 to 1860 he was rabbi of Hajdusámson; he was then appointed to Hajdúböszörmény, where he remained for the rest of his life. Fried took a prominent part in the establishment of the organization of the Hungarian Orthodox Jewish community, and in conducting their affairs. He is the author of: *Omer le-Ẓiyyon* (1872), talmudic novellae; *Ẓel ha-Kesef* (1878), 24 aggadic excursuses (no. 21 contains interesting references to the Hungarian Jewish congress held in 1868/69); *Responsa Maharaf,* including a long aggadic introduction with some interesting autobiographical data entitled *Todat Aharon,* as well as a commentary on the Mishnayot of the order *Zera'im* and tractate *Mikva'ot,* entitled *Ḥallat Aharon* (1893); and *Zekan Aharon,* homilies (1904). The two latter books were published posthumously by Fried's son Eleazar (Lazar).

Bibliography: A. Fried, *She'elot u-Teshuvot Maharaf* (1893), 11a; P. Z. Schwartz, *Shem ha-Gedolim me-Ereẓ Hagar,* 1 (1913), no. 112; M. Stein, *Even ha-Me'ir,* pt. 1 (1907), 9b, no. 86; idem, *Magyar Rabbik,* 2 (1906), 72, no. 111. [A.SCHI.]

FRIED, ALFRED HERMANN (1864–1921), Austrian publicist and Nobel peace prize winner. Born in Vienna, Fried served as an Austrian diplomat for a short time but became discouraged and went to Berlin where he became a bookdealer and publisher. After 1891 he devoted himself to pacifist propaganda and founded and edited a number of journals for this purpose, among them *Die Waffen Nieder* which was owned by the famous Austrian pacifist-propagandist, Baroness von Suttner. Fried was the author of more than 70 books and pamphlets devoted to the advancement of peace and of nearly 2,000 newspaper articles. A member of the Berne Bureau and the International Institute for Peace, he was also European secretary of the Conciliation Internationale, secretary general of the Union Internationale de la Presse pour la Paix, and founder of the German and Austrian peace societies. Fried won the Nobel Prize for Peace in 1911. At the time of the Hague peace conferences (1899–1907) Fried was in constant touch with Ivan *Bliokh, the man who persuaded the czar to convene the conferences. His pacifist approach led to his being accused of treason; he left Austria on the outbreak of World War I and spent the war years in Switzerland. He was a prominent figure at the international workers meeting in Berne which fought to prepare a formula for a negotiated peace. After the war he advocated a European union of states similar to the Pan-American system. Fried's publications include *Handbuch der Friedensbewegung* (1905); *Die Grundlagen des revolutionaeren Pacifismus* (1908); *Der Kaiser und der Weltfrieden* (1910), a defense of Kaiser William II's policies; and *Der Weltprotest gegen den Versailler Frieden* (1920), an attack on the Versailles peace settlement.

Bibliography: R. Goldscheid, *Alfred Fried* (Ger., 1922); H. F. Peterson, *Power and International Order; an Analytical Study of Four Schools of Thought and their Approaches to the War, the Peace and a Post-War System, 1914–1919* (1964). [J.J.L.]

FRIED, MORTON HERBERT (1923–), U.S. anthropologist. Born and educated in New York City, Fried served in the U.S. Army, 1943–46, and then taught at New York City College, and later at Columbia, where he was chairman of the department from 1966 to 1969. He specialized in Asian studies and studied the Chinese in the Caribbean and Guianas (cf. his *Fabric of Chinese Society* (1953, 1968²), a study of the social life of a Chinese county seat). His other research interests included social kinship and social stratification in primitive society, especially China; evolution; and social and political organization, and evolution of the state. He was coeditor of *Readings in Anthropology* (2 vols., 1959, 1968²) and *Evolution of Political Society* (1967). [E.FI.]

FRIEDBERG, town in Hesse, W. Germany. A community existed there by 1260 when a Gothic-style *mikveh* was constructed. About this time the community had a

The "Jews' Street" in the Jewish quarter of Friedberg. Courtesy Municipality of Friedberg. Photo Schmidt.

well-developed organization and tax system (Responsa of Meir b. Baruch of Rothenburg (1891), no. 187, pp. 204–6). In 1275 *Rudolf of Hapsburg granted a charter to the Friedberg community. The Jews there suffered persecution in 1338 and following the Black Death in 1349, the property of those who had been killed or fled was sold to the city by the imperial bailiff in 1350–54. Jews had been readmitted to Friedberg by 1360. The charter of 1275 was confirmed by successive German emperors. The right of the Jews in Friedberg to engage in the retail trade was upheld by the burgrave in 1623. In 1603 the Friedberg *bet din* was declared one of the five central Jewish courts. Between 1588 and 1640 the community was administered by six to ten *parnasim* and from 1652 the community elected an electoral committee of nine from which the *parnasim* and a taxation committee were elected. The Jews of Friedberg lived in an enclosed quarter near a square below the castle. In the late 18th century the gates were closed on Sundays. Jewish residence in Friedberg was subject to permission from both the burgrave and the community, and by around 1600 was restricted to persons owning 1,500 guilders. Exemptions were made during the Thirty Years' War, and after the expulsion of the Jews from the towns of Upper Hesse in 1662. In 1540 the Jewries of 14 villages and towns formed the community of the *Land* (*Kehillat* Friedberg). Its rabbinate had jurisdiction over Upper Hesse and the adjoining principalities as far as Westphalia, and over Hesse-Kassel from 1625 to 1656. *Ḥayyim b. Bezalel, the brother of *Judah b. Bezalel Loeb of Prague, was rabbi there in 1566. Elijah b. Moses *Loanz (d. 1636) also officiated there. A *ḥevrat gemilut ḥasadim* (charitable institution) was founded in 1687. There were about 16 Jewish families in 1536, 32 in 1550, 107 in 1609, 99 in 1617–24, 72 in 1729, 42 families in 1805, 506 persons in 1892, 491 in 1910 (5.17% of the total population), 380 in 1925 (3.44%), and 305 in 1933. The community had a very active cultural and orthodox religious life. The synagogue was burned in November 1938 and by summer 1939 only 58 Jews were living in Friedberg; no record remains of their emigration or deportation. The medieval bathhouse was restored by the municipality in 1957–58, as an historical monument. In 1967 there were 21 Jews in Friedberg.

Bibliography: A. Kober, in: PAAJR, 17 (1947/48), 19–60; Baron, Social², 13 (1969), 200f.; Wagner, in *Jeschurun,* 2 (1902), 437–9; Germ Jud, 1 (1963), 110–1; 2 (1968), 260–3 (incl. bibl.); W. H. Braun, in: *Wetterauer Geschichtsblaetter,* 11 (1962), 81–84; 16 (1967), 51–78; F. H. Herrmann, *ibid.,* 2 (1953), 106–10; H. Wilhelm, *ibid.,* 11 (1961), 67–85; B. Brilling, *ibid.,* 14 (1965), 97–103; FJW; PK; S. Goldmann, in: *Zeitschrift fuer die Geschichte der Juden,* 7 (1970), 89–93; E. Keyser (ed.), *Hessisches Staedtebuch* (1957), 163f., 166.

[T.O.]

FRIEDBERG, ABRAHAM SHALOM (1838–1902), Hebrew author, editor, and translator. Born in Grodno, he received a traditional education and also studied watchmaking. After wandering from town to town in southern Russia, he returned to Grodno in 1858. His first book *Emek ha-Arazim* (adapted from *Vale of Cedars* by Grace Aguilar) was published in 1876 and enjoyed great popularity. After the pogroms of 1881 he joined the Ḥibbat Zion movement. In 1883 he went to St. Petersburg and became associate editor of **Ha-Meliẓ* and was influential in directing its editorial policy toward Zionism. He contributed numerous articles to the journal under the heading *Me-Inyanei de-Yoma* ("On Current Events"), which were signed H. Sh. for *Har Shalom*, the Hebrew translation of Friedberg. Failing to obtain a permit to remain in St. Petersburg, he left *Ha-Meliẓ* in 1886 and went to Warsaw, where he contributed to *Ha-Ẓefirah* and *Ha-Asif* and translated many books into Hebrew. He was an editor of the first Hebrew encyclopedia, *Ha-Eshkol* (1888), and was employed by the Aḥi'asaf publishing house. He wrote *Toledot ha-Yehudim bi-Sefarad* ("History of the Jews in Spain," 1893) based on Graetz, Kayserling, and others, translated into Hebrew M. Guedemann's *Geschichte des Erziehungswesens und der Kultur der abendlaendischen Juden*, 1880–88 (*Sefer ha-Torah ve-ha-Ḥayyim*, 1897–99), published *Sefer ha-Zikhronot* ("Book of Memoirs," 1899), a collection of literary articles and letters of well-known people, and edited the *Aḥi'asaf* yearbook (vols. 1–6). He also wrote for *Der Yid* and other Yiddish publications. His memoirs, which appeared in Sokolow's *Sefer ha-Shanah* (vols. 1 and 3) and in *Lu'aḥ Aḥi'asaf* (vol. 9), are important for the literary history of the period. His popular reputation was earned by his book *Zikhronot le-Veit David* ("Memoirs of the House of David," 1893–99), a series of stories embracing Jewish history from the destruction of the first Temple to the beginning of the Haskalah period in Germany. The first two volumes are an adaptation of *Geheimnisse der Juden* ("Secrets of the Jews") by H. Reckendorf, but the two remaining volumes were written by Friedberg himself. It was frequently republished and was translated into Arabic and Persian.

Bibliography: Y. Rawnitzki, *Dor ve-Soferav* (1927), 170–4; Maimon (Fishman), in: *Ha-Toren*, 9, no. 3 (1922), 88–90; 9, no. 4 (1922), 91–95; Waxman, Literature, 4 (1960), 160, 434.

[Y.S.]

FRIEDBERG, BERNARD (Bernhard, Ḥayyim Dov; 1876–1961), scholar and bibliographer. Friedberg was born in Cracow, and in 1900 moved to Frankfort, where he worked for the publisher and bookseller Isaac *Kauffmann. In 1904 he set up his own firm and by 1906 had published two catalogs; in the same year he and J. Saenger founded the publishing house of Saenger and Friedberg. In 1910 the partnership broke up, and Friedberg entered the diamond trade, moving to Antwerp. When the Nazis occupied Belgium, he lost his valuable library and all his papers. In 1946 he settled in Tel Aviv, continuing to deal in diamonds but with his heart in books and his bibliographical and genealogical researches.

Beginning in 1896 Friedberg published in Hebrew a number of biographies, e.g., Joseph Caro (1896), Shabbetai Kohen (1898), and Nathan Spira (1899); family histories, e.g., Schor (1901), Landau (1905), and Horowitz (1911, 1928[2]); and a study on the old Jewish cemetery of Cracow, *Luḥot Zikkaron* (1897, 1904[2], 1969). Friedberg's first bibliographical effort was a history of Hebrew printing in Cracow, *Ha-Defus ha-Ivri be-Cracow* (1900), followed by a similar study on Lublin, *Le-Toledot ha-Defus ha-Ivri be-Lublin* (1901). In 1932 he began publishing a series of works on the history of Hebrew printing, *Toledot ha-Defus ha-Ivri;* the series included volumes on Poland (1932, 1950[2]); on Italy, Spain, Portugal, Turkey, and the Orient (1934, 1956[2]); on Central Europe (1935); and on Western Europe (1937). His greatest achievement was his bibliographical lexicon *Beit Eked Sefarim* (1 vol., 1928–31; 4 vols., 1951–56[2], the second edition listing Hebrew books published by 1950). Though Friedberg's works are not always accurate, they are indispensable bibliographical reference books.

Bibliography: Tidhar, 5 (1952), 2268–69; Kressel, 2 (1967), 659.

[N.B.-M.]

FRIEDELL, EGON, pseudonym of **Egon Friedmann** (1878–1938), Austrian playwright and cultural historian. Born in Vienna, Friedell studied there and at Heidelberg. A witty and versatile bohemian, he not only wrote plays but often acted in them, particularly at Max Reinhardt's theaters in Berlin and Vienna. Among the plays he wrote was *Die Judastragoedie* (1920). Friedell's magnum opus was the three-volume *Kulturgeschichte der Neuzeit* (1927–31; *A Cultural History of the Modern Age*, 1931–32). Ranging from the Reformation to World War I, this highly original work is no solemn historical study but a brilliant, aphoristic, and sometimes ironic survey of world history and culture. He also wrote *Kulturgeschichte des Altertums* (2 vols., 1936–49) and *Das Jesusproblem* (1921). Friedell, who was only a "marginal" Jew, committed suicide to escape Nazi persecution.

Bibliography: W. Schneider, *Friedell-Brevier* (1947); H. Zohn, *Wiener Juden in der deutschen Literatur* (1964), 61–64.

[H.Zo.]

FRIEDEMANN, ADOLF (1871–1932), one of Herzl's first supporters. Born in Berlin, Friedemann was a founder of the Juedische Humanitaetsgesellschaft in Berlin (1893), which later developed into the Jewish Student Zionist Organization in Germany (1895). When Herzl became active in Jewish affairs, Friedemann was his faithful companion, carrying out various missions on his behalf and accompanying him on his trip to Egypt in connection with the El-Arish Project (1902). He was a member of the Zionist General Council from 1903 to 1920, and after the Keren Hayesod was established, worked in its behalf in several countries. Friedemann published numerous articles and books on Zionism and Ereẓ Israel. His book *Das Leben Theodor Herzls* (1914) was the first biography of the founder of political Zionism to be published in book form. Other books are *Reisebilder aus Palaestina* (1904, with illustrations by H. Struck) and a biography *David Wolffsohn* (1916). He was also the chief editor of the first lexicon of Zionism, *Zionistisches ABC Buch* (1908). He died in Amsterdam.

Bibliography: T. Herzl, *Complete Diaries*, 5 vols. (1960), index; R. Lichtheim, *Die Geschichte des deutschen Zionismus* (1954), index.

[G.K.]

FRIEDEMANN, ULRICH (1877–1949), German bacteriologist who made a significant contribution to the study of scarlet fever. Friedemann, who was born in Berlin, worked for two years as assistant to Paul Ehrlich, and then became professor of hygiene at Berlin University and head of the department of bacteriology at the Moabit city hospital in Berlin. He was also a member of the Robert Koch Institute. Friedemann left Germany soon after Hitler came to power in 1933 and, after three years as research worker at the National Institute for Medical Research in London, went to the United States. There he became chief of the division of bacteriology at the Jewish Hospital of Brooklyn, N.Y. In addition to his studies on scarlet fever, its causes and its effects, Friedemann did research on tetanus, virus diseases, latent infections and their significance to epidemiology, and the theory of anaphylactic shock.

Bibliography: S. R. Kagan, *Jewish Medicine* (1952), 259; *Journal of the American Medical Association*, 142 (Jan. 1950), 43.

[S.M.]

FRIEDENBERG, ALBERT MARX (1881–1942), U.S. lawyer and historian. Friedenberg was born in New York City. At the age of 19 he joined the *American Jewish Historical Society and became one of its leading members, and was largely responsible for the issuance of 17 volumes of the *Publications of the American Jewish Historical Society* (AJHSP, nos. 18–34). Friedenberg wrote numerous papers and articles on the early history of Jews in America, immigration, historical aspects of Zionism, Jews in Masonry, and the Jewish periodical press, and also on local German Jewish history, literature, and biography. He acted as the New York correspondent of the Baltimore *Jewish Comment* (1902–10) and the Chicago *Reform Advocate* (1905–31), and as contributing editor of the New York *Hebrew Standard* (1907–23).

Bibliography: Coleman, in: AJHSP, 35 (1939), 115–37; Friedman, *ibid.*, 37 (1947), 461–2.

[I.S.M.]

FRIEDENBERG, SAMUEL (1886–1957), U.S. collector of medals. Brought to New York from Poland at the age of seven, Friedenberg later built up a fortune in the textile business and then in real estate, and became active in philanthropic and cultural work. Beginning with the purchase of a small collection of medals in 1935 from a

Samuel Friedenberg, U.S. collector of medals.

German refugee, he built up what became the most complete collection of Jewish medals in existence. He commissioned from artists such as I. Sors, Benno *Elkan, Paul Vincze, F. Kormis, a supplementary series of portrait medals, mainly of contemporaries. He left the collection to the New York Jewish Museum, where his son, Daniel M. Friedenberg, who wrote widely on the subject, became honorary curator of Coins and Medals.

Bibliography: D. M. Friedenberg (ed.), *Great Jewish Portraits in Metal* (1963).

[C.R.]

FRIEDENWALD, U.S. family of ophthalmologists and Jewish communal leaders.

Jonas Friedenwald (1803–1893), a German immigrant who settled in Baltimore in 1831, was a businessman and one of the founders of the Hebrew Orphan Asylum and Chizuk Emunah Orthodox Congregation. His youngest son Aaron Friedenwald (1836–1902) was born in Baltimore and studied medicine at the University of Maryland. A distinguished ophthalmologist, he was the first president of the Medical and Chirurgical Faculty of Maryland and a prominent member of medical societies. In 1890 he organized the Association of American Medical Colleges. He was an active worker in local and national Jewish organizations, including the Baltimore

Bookplate of Harry Friedenwald, U.S. ophthalmologist, with reproduction of the etching, "The Healing of the Blind," by Rembrandt.

Hebrew Orphan Asylum, Jewish Theological Seminary of America, Federation of American Zionists, and American Jewish Historical Society. He also published articles of Jewish and general medical interest.

Harry Friedenwald (1864–1950), eldest of Aaron's five sons, was born in Baltimore. He excelled in studies at Johns Hopkins University, and after two years at the Baltimore College of Physicians and Surgeons, spent two years traveling and studying ophthalmology in Berlin. He returned to Baltimore in 1891 and began his practice, teaching ophthalmology at the Baltimore College of Physicians and Surgeons (1894–1929). Harry Friedenwald was a member of Hevras Zion in Baltimore, probably the first American Zionist society, and was president of the Federation of American Zionists, 1904–18. In 1911 and 1914 he went to Palestine, where he served as a consultant for eye diseases in several Jerusalem hospitals. He was a member of the Provisional Committee of Zionist Affairs during World War I, and in 1919 he was chairman of the Zionist Commission to Palestine, where he spent the year.

Friedenwald wrote on medical history with special emphasis on medieval Jewish doctors and the use of the Hebrew language in medical literature; he also lectured frequently on Jews in medicine. In 1944 his collected and expanded historico-medical writings, *The Jews and Medicine* (2 vols.), were published. He wrote *Jewish Luminaries in Medical History* (1946). His son Jonas Friedenwald (1897–1955) was also an ophthalmologist.

Bibliography: A. L. Levin, *Vision: the Story of Dr. Harry Friedenwald of Baltimore* (1964); G. Rosen, in: H. Friedenwald, *Jews and Medicine* (1967).

[Gl.R.]

FRIEDER, ARMIN (1911–1946), Slovakian rabbi in the *status quo community at Zvolen and the *Neolog community of Nove Mesto nad Vahom (from 1938), and an active Zionist. In 1942 he became a member of the underground "Working Group" (see *Slovakia, Holocaust) in Bratislava, set up to save the remaining Jews in

Slovakia, and served as the underground's contact with Slovak government circles. Under his influence, the Ohel David Home for the Aged at Nove Mesto became a refuge before deportations. Following the suppression of the Slovak Uprising in the autumn of 1944, Frieder found refuge in a Catholic monastery. After the war he was chief rabbi of the Jewish communities of Slovakia. [Li.Ro.]

FRIEDJUNG, HEINRICH (1851–1920), Austrian historian. Friedjung became professor of history in 1873 at Wiener Handelsakademie and participated in Georg von *Schoenerer's pan-German movement but parted with Schoenerer because of the latter's anti-Semitism. Dismissed from his post by the Education Ministry in 1881 for his radical political publicity, Friedjung entered upon a journalistic career. He founded and edited *Deutsche Wochenschrift* (1883–86) and became editor-in-chief of *Deutsche Zeitung*, the main publication of the Deutschnationale Partei. From 1891 to 1895, Friedjung was a member of the Vienna City Council. He then left politics and wrote scholarly works on the German Confederation, the Second German Empire, and the era of Francis Joseph. His *Der Kampf um die Vorherrschaft in Deutschland 1859–1869* (2 vols., 1907) went through 10 editions and spread his fame beyond the frontiers of Austria. His other works were *Benedeks Nachgelassene Papiere* (1904); *Oesterreich 1848–1860* (unfinished, 1907–12); *Krimkrieg und die oesterreichische Politik* (1911[2]). His scholarly *Das Zeitalter des Imperialismus* (3 vols., 1919–22) was completed after his death by A. F. Pribram. Friedjung's Jewish origin barred him from a post at Vienna University, and, while he had little interest in Jewish affairs, he considered it undignified to buy a career through conversion. [H.A.S.]

FRIEDLAENDER, DAVID (1750–1834), communal leader and author in Berlin, a pioneer of the practice and ideology of *assimilation and a forerunner of *Reform Judaism. Born in Koenigsberg, the son of a "protected Jew," Joachim Moses Friedlaender, a wholesale merchant, David settled in Berlin in 1770, and in 1776 established a silk factory there. As an expert in his field he was appointed counsellor of the state commission of inquiry into the textile industry. In 1791 he forwarded a memorandum in the name of the manufacturers, advocating changes in the economic system against excessive government supervision over industry and the granting of protective tariffs to individual manufacturers. However, his interests ranged far beyond his business activities. Entering Moses *Mendelssohn's circle at the age of 21, Friedlaender absorbed Mendelssohn's ideas and became prominent among his followers. Through his marriage in 1772 with Bluemchen Itzig, daughter of the banker Daniel *Itzig, he entered one of the wealthiest and most distinguished families of *Court Jews in Prussia.

In 1799 Friedlaender sent his famous *Sendschreiben* ("Open Letter") to Pastor Teller in which he expressed, "in the name of some Jewish householders," a deistic conception of religion. For this reason he rejected Christian dogma as well as the retention of Jewish ritual precepts. According to him the eternal truths around which enlightened Jews and Protestants should unite were synonymous with the pure teachings of Moses, i.e., with original Jewish monotheism. Throughout his life Friedlaender regarded Mosaic monotheism as an ideal to be followed; it was apparently the positive factor in his decision (in which he differed from many of his circle) against conversion to Christianity. "We are destined from time immemorial to guard and teach by example the pure doctrine of the unity and sanctity of God, previously unknown to any other people," Friedlaender wrote in 1815 in his *Reden der Erbauung* ("Edifying Speeches"). In his respect for biblical Judaism he was a faithful disciple of Mendelssohn, although Kant, who exercised a strong influence on Friedlaender, disparaged biblical Judaism. Friedlaender shared the educational ideals and belief in liturgical reform current among representatives of the Jewish enlightenment in Berlin after Mendelssohn, giving expression to these ideas in his writings.

David Friedlaender, communal leader. Jerusalem, J.N.U.L., Schwadron Collection.

After the issue of the 1812 edict in Prussia he published a paper on the reforms which he deemed necessary as a result of the new organization of the Jews in Prussia (reform of the divine service in the synagogues, of teaching institutions and subjects taught, and of their manner of education in general). Above all, he proposed substituting in the prayer in place of the expression of messianic hopes: "I stand here before God. I pray for blessing and prosperity for my compatriots, for myself and my family, not for the return to Jerusalem, not for the restoration of the Temple and the sacrifices. I do not harbor these wishes in my heart." He proposed that study of talmudic law should be replaced by study of the laws of the country. Friedlaender even wanted to enlist the help of the government in his endeavors for reform. In part as a result of his efforts, a "Jewish free school" was established in 1778; Friedlaender became the organizer and supervisor of the school, which he directed for almost 20 years, with his brother-in-law Isaac Daniel Itzig, along with the Hebrew press and bookshop associated with it. The institution aimed at putting into practice the ideals of enlightened education.

From 1783 to 1812 Friedlaender, as the representative of Prussian Jewry, fought assiduously for the implementation of its demands for equal rights. He headed the "general deputies" of the Jewish communities of Prussia who assembled in Berlin in order to submit their requests to the commission set up by *Frederick William II in 1787. Under Friedlaender's leadership, the deputies rejected the unsatisfactory "Plan for Reform" proposed by the commission. In 1793 he published the documents pertaining to these negotiations under the title *Aktenstuecke, die Reform der jued. Kolonien in den preussischen Staaten betreffend.* Continuing the struggle for emancipation, in 1810 he requested an audience with the Prussian chancellor, Carl August von *Hardenberg; as an argument in favor of granting emancipation he pointed to the "wave of baptisms" which indicated the degree of assimilation of Prussian Jewry. Friedlaender's efforts for the emancipation of Prussian Jews are especially important since in them are reflected the main dilemma of Jewish life in Prussia in the first generation after Mendelssohn: how to hold fast to a Jewish identity within a society based on universalist principles.

Bibliography: M. A. Meyer, *The Origins of the Modern Jew* (1967); H. Rachel and P. Wallich, *Berliner Grosskaufleute*, 2 (1938), ZGJD, 6 (1935), 65–71; V. Eichstaedt, *Bibliographie zur Judenfrage* (1938); M. Eliav, *Ha-Ḥinnukh ha-Yehudi be-Germanyah* (1961); *Gesamtregister zur MGWJ 1851–1939* (1966); H. Fischer, *Judentum, Staat und Heer in Preussen* (1968); L. Geiger, in: AZDJ, 77 (1913), 474ff.

[M.Gra.]

FRIEDLAENDER, ISRAEL (1876–1920), Semitist and U.S. communal leader. Friedlaender, born in Kovel, Poland, was raised in Warsaw, where he received an intensive education in both traditional and secular subjects with private tutors hired by his Orthodox but Haskalah-oriented father. In 1895 Friedlaender enrolled in the Hildesheimer Rabbinical Seminary in Berlin; at the same time he attended Berlin University, concentrating in Semitic languages. During his years in Berlin he also prepared German translations of works of Dubnow and Aḥad Ha-Am, two authors who influenced him greatly and whose works he was later to translate into English. By 1900 Friedlaender had discarded his plans for the rabbinate in favor of a career in Semitics. He left Berlin for the University of Strasbourg to study under the eminent orientalist Theodor Noeldeke, from whom he received his Ph.D. (1901) with a dissertation on the Arabic of Maimonides. The following year he was appointed lecturer in Semitics at the University of Strasbourg, a position he held until 1904, when he was invited to the Jewish Theological Seminary in New York City as professor of Bible.

Despite his new title, however, Friedlaender's major scholarly interest continued to be Semitics. Besides his post at the Seminary he also taught at Dropsie College in Philadelphia, which published his lectures in Judeo-Arabic studies in its *Jewish Quarterly Review* (1 (1910–11), 249–58; 2 (1911–12), 481–516; 3 (1912–13), 235–300). In 1909 Friedlaender published a study of Moslem heresies, *Heterodoxies of the Shiites in the Presentation of Ibn Hazm,* and in 1913 a study of Jewish influences on Arabic folklore, *Die Chadhirlegende und der*

Israel Friedlaender, Semitist and U.S. communal leader. Courtesy American Jewish Historical Society, Waltham, Mass.

Alexanderroman. His work on translating S. M. Dubnow's *History of the Jews in Russia and Poland* (Eng. tr., 3 vols., 1916–20) led to the appearance of his own *Jews of Russia and Poland: A Bird's-Eye View of their History and Culture* (1915). During these years Friedlaender also wrote a wide variety of essays on contemporary Jewish topics, which appeared not only in the Jewish press but in such national magazines as *The Atlantic Monthly, Harper's,* and *The Nation.* Many of these pieces were assembled in 1919 in a collection entitled *Past and Present* (new ed. 1961). A few of their titles—"The Hebrew Language," "The Problem of Polish Jewry," "The Function of Jewish Learning in America," "Ahad Ha'am," "Palestine and the World War"—give an idea of Friedlaender's broad range of interests, which were linked together by what he referred to as his "conception of Judaism as a living organism which is one and indivisible."

Friedlaender's literary productivity during this period was equaled by his no less energetic participation in Jewish communal life. The first chairman of New York City's Bureau of Jewish Education, he spoke and lectured frequently to various Jewish and Zionist organizations and was the first president of Young Judea and a trustee of the Educational Alliance. Between 1909 and 1912 he was active in the Achavah Club, an elite group of Jewish intellectuals that met under the leadership of Judah *Magnes. He was also a member of the National Executive Committee of the Federation of American Zionists for many years and strove in this capacity to reconcile the American Zionist movement and such anti-Zionist organizations as the American Jewish Committee. His public activity, as well as his writings, were characterized by his ability to see the different sides of the same question and to mediate between them.

In 1919 Friedlaender undertook a mission on behalf of the Joint Distribution Committee to the war-ravaged Jewish communities of Eastern Europe. He visited Poland and then proceeded to tour the Russian countryside, which was plunged at the time into Civil War. In July 1920 he, together with the U.S. rabbi and social worker Bernard Cantor (1892–1920), was waylaid and murdered by a party of bandits in the Ukraine. His wife Lilian (née Bentwich, the daughter of the British Zionist Herbert *Bentwich) later settled in Israel in Zikhron Ya'akov where she established and maintained Bet Daniel, a rest home for artists and authors.

Bibliography: B. Cohen, *Israel Friedlaender: A Bibliography of his Writing, with an Appreciation* (1936); Kohn, in: AJYB, 23 (1921–22), 65–79; A. Marx, *Essays in Jewish Bibliography* (1947), 280–9; 298 idem., *Studies in Jewish History and Booklore* (1944), 400–8; M. Bentwich, *Lilian Ruth Firedlaender; A Biography* (1957).

[Ed.]

FRIEDLAENDER, MICHAEL (1833–1910), orientalist, educator, and author. Born in Jutrosin (Posen province), Friedlaender served first as head of the *talmud torah* school in Berlin (from 1862), and from 1865 as principal of *Jews' College, London, Anglo-Jewry's rabbinical seminary, which under his leadership first became a fully developed rabbinical seminary. He remained in this position for 45 years, and exercised a great influence on generations of graduates. He published a German translation (with commentary) of the Song of Songs (*Das Hohelied,* 1867). His illustrated *Jewish Family Bible* (Hebrew and English, 1881, 1884, repr. 1953) became very popular, as did his standard work *Jewish Religion* (1891, 1913³) and its companion volume *Textbook of the Jewish Religion* (1891), which was also reprinted in many editions. Both represent a strictly traditionalist view.

He took an active part in the Society for the Diffusion of Jewish Literature under whose aegis he published his works on Ibn Ezra and Maimonides. The first was an edition of Abraham ibn Ezra's commentary on Isaiah with an English translation together with the English translation of Isaiah, revised in accordance with Ibn Ezra's commentary, as well as a volume of essays on the latter's writings (4 vols., 1873–77; vols. 1 and 3 repr. 1964). His translation into English (with annotations) of Maimonides' *Guide of the Perplexed* (3 vols., 1881–85; repr. 1953) was an edi-

Michael Friedlaender, principal of Jews' College, London, 1865–1907. Photo R. B. Fleming.

tion which owed much to S. Munk's Arabic text and translation (1856–66). A revised one-volume edition of the English translation (without the notes, 1904 and many reprints) was long the standard English version of the *Guide*. He took an active part in the communal and cultural life of Anglo-Jewry. His knowledge of mathematics and astronomy made him an expert on the Jewish calendar. Moses *Gaster was his son-in-law.

Bibliography: JC (May 8, 1903 and Dec. 16, 1910); I. Cohen, in: L. Jung, ed., *Men of the Spirit* (1964), 467–76; *Jews College Jubilee Volume* (1906), xxxi–lxvi.

[Ed.]

FRIEDLAENDER, MORITZ (1844–1919), writer, educator, and communal worker. Friedlaender, who was born in Hungary, studied for the rabbinate, but did not adopt it because of his liberal views. In 1875 he became secretary of the Israelitische Allianz, the Austro-Hungarian counterpart of the Alliance Israélite Universelle, and on behalf of both organizations visited Galicia to assist the emigration of Russian Jews to the United States. With the help of Baron Maurice de Hirsch and later of his widow, Friedlaender established and supervised more than 50 modern schools for boys, as well as vocational schools for girls in Galicia.

Friedlaender's scholarly interests lay in the direction of Hellenistic philosophy and the origins of Christianity. Among his published works are: *Ueber den Einfluss der griechischen Philosophie auf das Judentum und Christentum* (1872); *Patristische und talmudische Studien* (1878); *Philo's Philantropie des juedischen Gesetzes*, translation and commentary (1889); *Apion, ein Kulturbild* (1882); *Zur Entstehungsgeschichte des Christentums* (1894); *Der vorscristlich juedische Gnostizismus* (1898); *Geschichte der juedischen Apologetik* (1903); *Die religioese Bewegung innerhalb des Judentums im Zeitalter Jesu* (1906); *Der Kreuzestod Jesu* (1906). Friedlaender also wrote on his experiences in Galicia: *Fuenf Wochen in Brody* (1882); and *Reiseerinnerungen aus Galizien* (1900). He used the pseudonyms M. Freimann, Marek Firkowitsch, and Paul Frieda.

[Ed.]

FRIEDLAENDER, OSKAR EWALD (1881–), Austrian philosopher. Friedlaender, who was born in Slovakia, taught in Vienna. Writing under the name "Ewald," he dealt with Kantianism, history of philosophy, and philosophy of religion. He opposed ethical relativism and empiricism. Friedlaender dealt with the relationship of romanticism to contemporary philosophy, as well as offering an interpretation of Kant. In later writings, he sought to develop an undogmatic religion of humanity. His main works are: *Richard Avenarius als Begruender des Empiriokritizismus* (1905); *Die Probleme der Romantik als Grundfragen der Gegenwart* (1904); *Kants kritischer Idealismus als Grundlage von Erkenntnistheorie und Ethik* (1908); *Die Religion des Lebens* (1925); and *Freidenkertum und Religion* (1927).

[R.H.P.]

FRIEDLAENDER, SAUL (1932–), Israel historian. Born in Prague, Friedlaender lived in France from 1939 to 1948, when he emigrated to Israel. From 1964 to 1965 Friedlaender served as senior lecturer of the Institut des Hautes Etudes Internationales in Geneva and from 1965 to 1967 as professor. In 1967 he was visiting professor at the Hebrew University and in 1969 was appointed professor of history and international relations. Friedlaender specialized in Nazi history and wrote *Hitler et les Etats-Unis 1939–41* (1963; *Prelude to Downfall: Hitler and the United States*, 1967); *Pie XII et le IIIe Reich* (1964; *Pius XII and the Third Reich*, 1966) and *Kurt Gerstein, l'ambiguité du bien* (1967; *Kurt Gerstein; the Ambiguity of Good*, 1969). In 1969 he published *Reflexions sur l'avenir d'Israël*.

[Ed.]

FRIEDLAENDER (Friedland), SOLOMON JUDAH (c. 1860–c. 1923), author and literary forger. Friedlaender gave contradictory biographical accounts of his life, claiming at various times to have been born in Hungary, Turkey, and Rumania, but in all probability he was born in Beshenkovichi near Vitebsk, Belorussia. He supposedly studied at the yeshivah in Volozhin and afterward wandered throughout Europe. He was in Czernowitz (1880–1882), Mainz (1884), Frankfort on the Main (1885), Mulhouse (c. 1888–c. 1895), Waitzen (1900–1902), Naszod (1902–1906), and finally in Szatmar, from 1906 onward. It seems that he died in Vienna. Friedlaender published a number of works of doubtful authenticity or pure forgeries. Among these were: (1) *Ha-Tikkun*, published under the name of L. Friedland in Czernowitz in 1881. It pretends to be an authentic manual of ḥasidic customs, while in fact it is a crude and obscene parody of Ḥasidism in general and *Ḥabad Ḥasidism in particular; (2) *Tosefta, Seder Zera'im* and *Seder Nashim*, published in Pressburg in 1889 and 1890, with his commentary entitled *Ḥosak Shelomo*. He claimed to have edited a critical edition of the Tosefta text from an unpublished manuscript, but this was disputed by Adolf Schwarz and Rabbi Jacob Yanovsky of Kiev. Friedlaender responded to Schwarz's strictures in a pamphlet entitled *Kesher Bogedim* (Pressburg, 1891), replete with irrelevant matters and squalid abuse of his critics; (3) an edition of the tractate *Yevamot* of the Jerusalem Talmud, supposedly from a manuscript, along with a twofold commentary, *Ḥeshek Shelomo*, in Szinervaralja in 1905.

Friedlaender's most important forgery, however, was his pretended *Seder Kodashim* of the Jerusalem Talmud. Friedlaender proclaimed his fortunate discovery of an ancient Spanish manuscript, dated Barcelona 1212, which contained this long lost and most important talmudic text. He published *Zevaḥim* and *Arakhin* in 1907, and *Ḥullin* and *Bekhorot* in 1909, with his commentary *Ḥeshek Shelomo*. With these publications, he reached the summit of his audacity, claiming to be of pure Sephardi descent (*Sephardi tahor*) from the well-known Algazi family and a native of Smyrna. He asserted that he was assisted in the acquisition of the manuscript by his brother, Elijah Algazi, and a business associate of the latter, both citizens of Smyrna. Some of the leading scholars of this period, such as Solomon *Buber, Solomon *Shechter, and Shalom Mordecai *Schwadron of Brzezany accepted his story. However, the majority of scholars gave no credence to his tales, and B. Ritter of Rotterdam conclusively proved the fallaciousness of Friedlaender's claims. On the basis of internal evidence, Ritter showed that the text was an overt forgery. Ritter's conclusions were supported by many experts, including V. *Aptowitzer, W. *Bacher, D. B. Ratner and Meir Dan *Plotzki. The controversy continued for the next few years, and as late as 1913, Friedlaender still published booklets on this issue. He also edited a periodical entitled *Ha-Gan*, using the name of Judah Aryeh Friedland. It seems that only one issue appeared in Frankfort in 1885. After his death, his son, M. Friedlaender, published his *Mavo la-Tosefta*, in Tirnovo, 1930. Friedlaender claimed at various times to have published, among others, a critical and annotated edition of the entire Tosefta, the *She'iltot* of Rav Aḥai Gaon, and the Sifra. No bibliographical evidence can be found to support these claims.

Bibliography: B. Ritter, in: *Der Israelit*, 1907 and 1908; D. B. Ratner, in: *Haolam*, 1 (1907), 26ff.; *Tel-Talpioth*, 1907 and 1908. [A.Schl.]

FRIEDLAND, East European family originating in Bohemia, presumably from the Bohemian town Friedland (Frydlant). During the 17th century Nathan Friedland was known as the "head of the community and head of the province of Bohemia." During the 19th century, members of the family are found in Russia. Meshullam Feivel (1804–1854), a wealthy merchant of Slutsk, moved to Dvinsk in 1846 and was often among the delegates representing the communities of Lithuania before the authorities. His sons Meir (d. 1902) and Moses Aryeh Leib (1826–1899) moved to St. Petersburg, where they ranked among the wealthiest Jews and philanthropists in the community. Moses for more than 30 years was general army contractor for the Russian government. He founded a Jewish orphanage with a school of handicrafts in St. Petersburg, and erected an old-age home in Jerusalem. In 1892 he presented his collection of about 13,000 Hebrew books (including 32 incunabula) and 300 manuscripts which he had assembled over many years to the Asiatic Museum in St. Petersburg (now the Leningrad Institute for Oriental Studies). The thousands of Hebrew books already in the museum were combined with his collection, given the name of Bibliotheca Friedlandiana. The bibliographer S. *Wiener catalogued these books (up to the letter *lamed*) in *Kohelet Moshe* (8 pts., 1893–1936). The genealogy and some of the history of the family is given by I. T. Eisenstadt and S. Wiener in *Da'at Kedoshim* (1897).

Bibliography: S. Wiener, *Kohelet Moshe*, pt. 2 (1895), vii–xi. [Y.S.]

FRIEDLAND, ABRAHAM HYMAN (Ḥayyim Abraham; 1891–1939), poet, short-story writer, and educator. Friedland, who was born in Hordok, near Vilna, immigrated to America at the age of 15. In 1911 he founded the National Hebrew School in New York. In 1921 he assumed the post of superintendent of the Cleveland Hebrew Schools, and in 1924 was also appointed the first director of the Cleveland Bureau of Jewish Education. He was a leading member of the Jewish community in Cleveland and a champion of the community Jewish school which featured an intensive Hebraic curriculum and included a strong emphasis on the Zionist ideal. He wrote poems, short stories, and articles, edited educational texts, and published essays in Hebrew, English, and Yiddish on Hebrew literature. His poems and stories were collected in two volumes at the end of his life, *Sonettot* ("Sonnets," 1939), and *Sippurim* ("Stories," 1939), and in a posthumous volume of poems, *Shirim* ("Poems," 1940). His *Sippurim Yafim*, stories designed for children, were reissued in three volumes by the Cleveland Bureau of Jewish Education (1962). His narrative sonnets deal with the pathetic side of life, and his stories mainly portray American Jewish types.

Abraham H. Friedland, U.S. writer and educator. From *American Jewish Yearbook, 1940–41*, Jewish Publication Society, Philadelphia, Pa.

Bibliography: A. Epstein, *Soferim Ivrim be-Amerikah*, 2 (1952), 311–23; Waxman, Literature, 4 (1960), 1251–55; A. Ben-Or, *Toledot ha-Sifrut ha-Ivrit be-Dorenu*, 1 (1954), 139–41; *Sefer Zikhronot le-Ḥ. A. Friedland* (1940). [El.S.]

FRIEDLAND, NATAN (1808–1883), rabbi, precursor of the *Ḥibbat Zion movement. Born in Taurage, Lithuania, Friedland studied in various Lithuanian yeshivot. The *Damascus Affair (1840) made a deep impression on him. He believed that the redemption of the Jewish people could be realized gradually, as a natural process, and periods of liberalism and progress should be used to achieve this. The miraculous redemption would ultimately occur with the arrival of the Messiah. Friedland was unaware that some of his contemporaries held similar views (e.g., Judah *Alkalai), and he spread his ideas verbally in Belorussia, Lithuania, and Germany, where he met Ẓevi Kalisher. In 1859 he published two parts of his work *Kos Yeshu'ah u-Neḥamah* ("Cup of Salvation and Comfort"), in which he expounded his theories. Friedland met Adolphe *Crémieux and Albert *Cohen in Paris, and presented petitions from Kalischer and himself to Napoleon III, who granted him an audience. Sir Moses *Montefiore, whom he met in London, refused to cooperate with him. Friedland published a new edition of Kalischer's work *Derishat Ẓiyyon*, adding his own notes and essays. Friedland was an emissary of Ḥevrah le-Yishuv Ereẓ Israel ("Society for the Settlement of Ereẓ Israel"), established by Kalischer, and collected funds for it in Germany. During his visit to Holland, he handed the Dutch government a petition requesting their support for the restoration of Ereẓ Israel to the Jews. His greatest work, *Yosef Ḥen*, expounding his views, was published in a shortened version (1879). At the end of his life, he witnessed the beginnings of *aliyah* to Ereẓ Israel from Rumania and Russia. In 1882 he went to Ereẓ Israel from London and died in Jerusalem.

Bibliography: Klausner, in: *Ha-Ummah*, 18 (1967), 227–45. [I.K.]

FRIEDLANDER, ISAAC (1823–1878), U.S. businessman. Friedlander, born in Oldenburg, Germany, was taken to the U.S. as a child. After working in New York City and then in Savannah, Georgia, he went to San Francisco in 1849 to mine gold. Turning to business, Friedlander soon came to dominate the California flour market and in 1854 erected the Eureka Flour Mills, the largest in the state. He earned the title "Grain King" while speculating in the wheat market and by 1872 controlled nearly all California grain exported to foreign ports. A struggle by the California farmers' organization to circumvent him and export grain independently was unsuccessful. Friedlander also financed grain elevators and an irrigation project. He was one of the first regents of the University of California, and was president of the San Francisco Chamber of Commerce.

Bibliography: Paul, in: *Pacific Historical Review*, 27 (1958), 331–49; Anon, in: *California Mail Bag*, 9 (June 1876), 17–19; Reissner, in: YLBI, 10 (1965), 78. [Ed.]

FRIEDLANDER, KATE (1902–1949), criminologist and psychiatrist. After having completed her general medical studies in her native Innsbruck, she moved to Berlin where she specialized in mental and nervous diseases. She also trained as a psychoanalyst and worked as a specialist at the juvenile court in Berlin. In 1933 she migrated to London. Her main achievements were in the application of psychoanalysis to the theoretical and practical problems of dissocial character formation. Her book *The Psycho-Analytical Approach to Juvenile Delinquency* (1947, 1959²) is an important contribution to the understanding and treatment of juvenile delinquents. One of her principal interests, to which she devoted much of her life, was child guidance work for the elimination of unhappiness among children (in cooperation with Anna *Freud). She wrote many papers, most of which dealt with the emotional development of the child and were aimed at preventing juvenile delinquency and antisocial wayward behavior in general.

Bibliography: Hoffer, in: *International Journal of Psycho-Analysis*, 30 (1949), 138–9; Jacobs, in: *New Era*, 30 (1949), 101–3. [Z.H.]

FRIEDLANDER, WALTER (1891–), U.S. social welfare expert and educator, born in Berlin. Friedlander was trained in law, began his career as a welfare worker among children, and later served as a juvenile court judge in Berlin. From 1931 to 1933 he was president of the German Child Welfare League. Moving to Paris in 1933, he served three years as the director of the Legal and Social Services for Refugees. Emigrating to the United States, he lectured at the University of Chicago from 1934 to 1943 and then went to the University of California, Berkeley, as professor of social welfare. Friedlander wrote a number of textbooks on social welfare, including *Youth in Distress* (1922), *Introduction to Social Welfare* (1955), and *Individualism and Social Welfare* (1962). He also edited *Concepts and Methods of Social Work* (1958). [J.N.]

FRIEDMAN, BENJAMIN (Benny; 1905–), U.S. football player. Friedman, who was born in Cleveland, Ohio, played on the University of Michigan team, first as a halfback. As a quarterback, he led Michigan to the Western Conference championship in 1925, and a tie for the title in 1926, when he won a unanimous first team All-America selection. Friedman's entry into professional football in 1927 revolutionized the game. His liberal and accurate use of the forward pass led to a more open style of play which insured the success of the professional sport. He played with the Cleveland Bulldogs (1927), Detroit Wolverines (1928), and New York Giants (1929–31) and was player-coach of the Brooklyn Dodgers in 1932–33. Abandoning professional football in 1934, Friedman was head coach at the City College of New York for eight years. During World War II, he was a lieutenant commander in the U.S. Navy. In 1949 he became the first athletic director and head football coach at *Brandeis University. After leaving Brandeis in 1963, he devoted himself to his boys' summer camp in Maine.

Bibliography: B. Postal, et al., *Encyclopaedia of Jews in Sports* (1965). [J.H.S.]

FRIEDMAN, DÉNES (1903–1944), Hungarian rabbi and scholar. In 1927 he succeeded L. *Venetianer as rabbi of Ujpest, and in 1935 joined the staff of the Budapest rabbinical seminary. While still a student he edited, with D. S. *Loewinger, a manuscript of the Alphabet of Ben Sira (in *Ve-zot li-Yhudah*, 1926). He wrote *A zsidó irodalom főirányai* ("The Main Trends of Jewish Literature," 1928). He prepared *Bibliographie der Schriften Ludwig Blaus* (1926; enlargement of Hg. ed., 1926), and biobibliographies of graduates of the Budapest rabbinical seminary (in *Magyar Zsidó Szemle*, 44 (1927), 340–68). When the Nazis invaded Hungary in 1944, Friedman was deported to his death after witnessing the murder of his only son.

Bibliography: J. Wassermann (ed.), *Dr. Friedman Dénes irodalmi munkássága* (1943); List of his works; I. Hahn, *Az Országos Rabbiképzö Intézet Evkönyve*... (1946), 23–24. [B.Y.]

FRIEDMAN, HERBERT A. (1918–), U.S. rabbi and organization executive. Friedman was born in New Haven, Conn. He received a rabbinical degree from the Jewish Institute of Religion (1944) and from 1945 to 1947 was a chaplain with the army in Germany, where as assistant adviser on Jewish Affairs to the Commander of the U.S. Occupation Forces, he became acquainted with the problems of Jewish refugees. Returning to the U.S., Friedman was rabbi of Temple Emanuel in Denver (until 1952), and of Temple Emanu-El B'ne Jeshurun in Milwaukee (1952–55). In 1955 he became executive vice-chairman (from 1969, executive chairman) of the United Jewish Appeal, traveling widely to visit Jewish communities and Israel. He served on the national executive board of ORT from 1952, and on the board of governors of Israel Bonds from 1953. [H.H.]

FRIEDMAN, JACOB (1910–), Yiddish poet. Friedman, who was born in the small East Galician town of Mielnica, lived in Czernowitz, Bukovina, until the Rumanian authorities deported him to a camp in Transnistria during World War II. In 1947 he tried to make his way to Palestine, was intercepted by the British and spent a year in the Cyprus internment camp before reaching Israel in 1948. Immediately recognized as a significant Yiddish poet, his poems were translated into Hebrew and included in school textbooks. His lyrics are filled with religious fervor. From his first booklets *Adam* and *Shabos* (1939) to his *Pastekher in Yisroel* (1953) and *Libshaft* (1967), his poetry matured, reaching new heights in *Di Legende Noyakh Green* (1958) and in the dramatic poem *Nefilim* (1963).

Bibliography: J. Glatstein, *In Tokh Genumen*, 2 (1956), 366–72; M. Ravitch, *Mayn Leksikon*, 3 (1958), 345–7; S. Bickel, *Shrayber fun Mayn Dor* (1958), 175–81; M. Gross-Zimmermann, *Intimer Videranand* (1964), 202–7. [J.S.Z.]

FRIEDMAN, LEE MAX (1871–1957), U.S. lawyer, historian, and patron of learning. Friedman was born in Memphis, Tennessee, of German Jewish descent. He became a noted trial attorney in Boston and a teacher and scholar of law. He was vice-president and professor of law at Portia Law School, Boston, contributing learned articles to law journals. Friedman was deeply interested in American Jewish history, and in 1903 he began his association with the American Jewish Historical Society, eventually serving as president (1948–53) and honorary president (1953–57). In 1905 he was chairman of the celebration in Boston of the 250th anniversary of Jewish settlement in the United States, and half a century later he was the main speaker at Symphony Hall, Boston, on the occasion of the tercentenary. As a historian, Friedman contributed many articles and notes to the *Publications of the American Jewish Historical Society*, covering a wide range of subjects that included Judah Monis, Cotton Mather, and Aaron Lopez. The volumes he published in the field of Jewish history included some of European Jewish interest: *Robert Grosseteste and the Jews* (1934), and *Zola and the Dreyfus Case: His Defense of Liberty and Its Enduring Significance* (1937); and others on American Jewish themes: *Early American Jews* (1934), *Rabbi Haim Isaac Carigal: His Newport Sermon and His Yale Portrait* (1940), *Jewish Pioneers and Patriots* (1942), and *Pilgrims in a New Land* (1948). He presented books and manuscripts to the American Jewish Historical Society, and a bequest in his will enabled the Society to establish its own headquarters adjoining Brandeis University.

Lee M. Friedman, U.S. lawyer and Jewish historian. Courtesy American Jewish Historical Society, Waltham, Mass.

Friedman's approach to cultural, philanthropic, civic, and communal endeavors was conservative. He served in leading positions with the Boston Art Museum, Harvard College Library, General Theological Library, and Boston Public Library. He was active in Boston Jewish life and was prominent in such national bodies as the Union of American Hebrew Congregations and the World Union for Progressive Judaism.

Bibliography: Kozol, in: AJHSQ, 56 (1967), 261–7; Meyer, *ibid.*, 47 (1958), 211–5; Norden, *ibid.*, 51 (1961), 30–48 (bibl.). [I.S.M.]

FRIEDMAN, MILTON (1912–), U.S. economist. Friedman, who was born in Rahway, New Jersey, began working for the United States government in 1935 and taught at several American universities before becoming professor of economics at the University of Chicago. Here, he acquired an international reputation and served as consultant to national and international institutions. He also acted as adviser to President Nixon. Friedman became the leader of the "Chicago school" of economic thought opposed to those following the generally accepted theories of John Maynard Keynes. He argued that the United States government relied too much on changes in taxation and government spending instead of controlling the money supply, in order to regulate the economy. In addition he maintained that the U.S. Federal Reserve Board repeatedly erred in the rate at which it changed the money supply, and as a result intensified the fluctuations in economic growth.

Milton Friedman, U.S. economist. Courtesy University of Chicago.

Friedman favored a simplified taxation system, floating exchange rates, and the demonetization of gold. He also advocated the abolition of the social welfare system, which he considered paternalistic, ineffective, and inefficient. In its place he wanted a "negative income tax" which would provide ready cash for the poor to pay for their basic needs. A prolific writer, Friedman was the author of *A Monetary History of the United States* (1963; with Anna Schwarz), a major work on economic history in which he showed that declines in the supply of money led to nearly every recession in the U.S. economy in the last hundred years. Among his other writings were: *A Theory of Consumption Function* (1957); *A Program for Monetary Stability* (1960); and *Price Theory* (1962). [J.O.R.]

FRIEDMAN, NAPHTALI (1863–1921), Jewish deputy to the Russian *Duma (parliament). After graduating in law at the University of St. Petersburg, Friedman practiced in Ponevezh, Lithuania. In 1907 he was elected to the Third Duma for the district of Kovno. He joined the Kadets (Russian Constitutional Democratic Party), taking an active part in the committees of the Duma, and with the other Jewish delegate L. *Nisselovich several times defended the Jews from attacks by the anti-Semitic deputies. Friedman was also elected to the Fourth Duma (1912) where he continued to represent the interests of Russian Jewry with the two other Jewish delegates, M. Bomash and E. Gurewich. After the outbreak of World War I, Friedman joined with the representatives of the other national minorities in declaring that the Jews were ready to fight alongside the rest of the Russian peoples for victory. Friedman combated the allegations of Jewish treason trumped up by military circles in an attempt to cover up their defeats at the front. He returned to Lithuania on the outbreak of the Communist revolution.

Bibliography: M. Sudarski et al. (eds.), *Lite* (Yid., 1951), 1411–18. [Y.S.]

FRIEDMAN, PHILIP (1901–1960), Polish-Jewish historian. Friedman studied at the universities of Lvov and Vienna, and obtained his doctorate for a thesis on *Die*

Philip Friedman, Jewish historian. Courtesy YIVO, New York.

Galizischen Juden im Kampfe um ihre Gleichberechtigung (1848–1868), 1929. In further research on the history of Polish Jewry, mainly in the 19th century, Friedman described changes in the economic structure and the growth of the great Jewish center at Lodz. He took part in editing periodicals in Hebrew, Yiddish, and Polish, and contributed to *Miesiecznik Żydowski* ("The Jewish Monthly"). Friedman published Hebrew textbooks for Jewish high schools, and taught Jewish history at the Jewish High School in Lodz and at the Institute of Jewish Studies in Warsaw. During World War II he went into hiding in Lvov. After the liberation, Friedman moved to Lublin, where he organized the Central Jewish Historical Commission, later the Jewish Historical Institute, in Warsaw, which undertook extensive documentation on the fate of Polish Jewry. In 1946 Friedman was appointed to organize an educational project for the Holocaust survivors in the American zone of occupation in Germany. In 1948, after the displaced persons camps were closed, Friedman immigrated to the United States, where he directed the Jewish Teachers' Institute in New York. He also lectured on Jewish history at Columbia University. Friedman was a member of the YIVO staff and director of the bibliographical series of the Joint Documentary Projects of YIVO and Yad Vashem. Almost all Friedman's postwar publications dealt with the Holocaust period, on which he became a leading expert. His writings up to 1955 are listed in *Writings of Philip Friedman. A Bibliography* (1955). His later works include *Martyrs and Fighters* (1954), a collection of sources on the Warsaw Ghetto uprising; and *Their Brothers' Keepers* (1957), about non-Jews who saved Jewish lives in occupied countries. The bibliographies of the Holocaust which he edited are: *Guide to Jewish History under Nazi Impact* (coeditor J. Robinson, 1960), *Bibliography of Books in Hebrew on the Jewish Catastrophe and Heroism in Europe* (1960), and *Bibliography of Yiddish Books on the Catastrophe and Heroism* (coeditor J. Gar, 1962).

Bibliography: S. W. Baron, in: PAAJR, 29 (1960/61), 1–7; JBA, 18 (1960/61), 76–80 (Yid.); *Yad Vashem Bulletin* 6/7 (1960), 3–7; YIVO, *Newsletter*, no. 74 (1960), 1,7; B. Orenstein, *Das Leben un Shafen fun Ph. Friedman* (1962). [Sh.E.]

FRIEDMAN, THEODORE (1908–), U.S. Conservative rabbi and scholar. Friedman was born in Stamford, Conn. Ordained at the Jewish Theological Seminary (1931), he was rabbi of the Jewish Center of Jackson Heights, N.Y., during 1939–54, and of Beth El of South Orange, N.J., from 1954 until his retirement in 1970 when he moved to Jerusalem. A leader of the centrist group within Conservative Judaism which advocates controlled change within Jewish law, Friedman served as chairman of the Law Committee, and as president of the Rabbinical Assembly of America (1962–64). He was managing editor of *Judaism*, a journal of Jewish thought, during 1953–61. He was coeditor of *Jewish Life in America* (1955), and wrote *Letters to Jewish College Students* (1965), relating Jewish teachings to the concerns of contemporary college students, and of *Judgment and Destiny* (1956), sermons. [J.R.]

FRIEDMANN, ABRAHAM (d. 1879), chief rabbi of Transylvania. Among the first rabbis there to introduce the preaching of sermons in the synagogue in Hungarian, he encountered strong opposition from Orthodox rabbis. When officiating in Simánd (province of Arad) in 1845 he preached in Hungarian on the occasion of the birthday of King Ferdinand I. The address, entitled *Egyházi beszéd*, was published the same year. Previously Friedmann published a pamphlet, also in Hungarian, in defense of Jewish rights entitled *Az izraelita nemzetnek védelmére* (1844). In 1845 the council of electors of the Jews of Transylvania, convened by the Catholic bishop of *Alba-Iulia, elected him chief rabbi of the grand principality. He subsequently settled in the capital, Alba-Iulia. During his period of office he also played a political role as representative of Transylvanian Jewry, and became involved in bitter disputes and polemics. In 1872 his opponents obtained his removal from office. He was the last chief rabbi to hold office for the whole of Transylvania. One of his main opponents was Hillel *Lichtenstein.

Bibliography: *Magyar Zsidó Lexikon* (1929), 295. [Y.M.]

FRIEDMANN, DAVID ARYEH (1889–1957), Hebrew critic and editor. After studying medicine at Moscow University, he migrated in 1925 to Palestine, where he was a practicing ophthalmologist and active member of the Medical Association. Friedmann wrote many articles in the Hebrew press on medicine, literature, and the arts, most of which were published posthumously in two volumes: *Iyyunei Shirah* (1964), and *Iyyunei Prozah* (1966). He was an editor of Ayanot Publishing Co., as well as of *En Hakore* (1923); he also edited the Medical Association's journal, *Ha-Refu'ah* from 1929.

Bibliography: B. Shmueli, *Maḥberet ha-Ayinin* (bibliography of works by Dr. D. A. Friedmann, 1912–42, 280 items); idem, in: *Ha-Refu'ah*, 39 no. 1 (1950), 13 (summary as well as comprehensive appreciation by Y. L. Roke'aḥ); *Hadoar* (Sept. 20, 1957). [G.K.]

FRIEDMANN, DAVID BEN SAMUEL (also called **"Dovidel" Karliner;** 1828–1917), Lithuanian rabbi and *posek*. Friedmann was born in Biala and lived for a time in Brest-Litovsk after 1836. On the advice of Leib Katzenellenbogen he moved to Kamenets-Litovsk where he studied under the supervision of his older brother Joseph until 1841. In that year he made the acquaintance of the philanthropist Shemariah Luria of Mohilev, who entrusted to him the education of his brother-in-law Zalman Rivlin of Shklov. Friedmann later married Luria's daughter. From 1846 to 1866 he devoted himself to concentrated study in the house of his father-in-law, where he compiled his *Piskei Halakhot*. After the death of his father-in-law in 1866 he accepted the rabbinate of Karlin near Pinsk (in 1868) where he remained until his death.

Friedmann's renown rests upon his *Piskei Halakhot* (pt. 1, 1898; pt. 2, 1901), an exposition and summary of matrimonial law, with a commentary entitled *Yad David*, an appendix entitled *She'ilat David* containing responsa on the laws of **mikva'ot* ("ritual baths"). The text of the *Piskei Halakhot* follows that of Maimonides. In his comprehensive exposition, Friedmann endeavors to establish clear-cut decisions. His work is distinguished by the fact that he relies to an overwhelming extent on the Babylonian and Jerusalem Talmuds and on the **rishonim*, disregarding the **aḥaronim*. He eschewed casuistry and tried to penetrate to the essence of the *halakhah* by a logical approach. Among the rabbis who turned to him with their problems were Menahem Mendel *Schneersohn, the head of the Lubavich (Ḥabad) dynasty, and David *Luria. When religious extremists in Jerusalem excommunicated the *bet midrash* of his brother-in-law, Jehiel Michael *Pines, because he supported the establishment in Jerusalem of an orphanage "where they would also learn a foreign language," Friedmann attacked them in his *Emek Berakhah* (1881). It consists of four essays in which he discusses the question of a ban and the regulations and conditions under which it should be imposed, emphasizing that a handful of rabbis of Jerusalem had no right to impose such a ban. Pines wrote a long introduction to the book. Even though he tended to view with favor secular knowledge and the study of languages, Friedmann was opposed to compromise with regard to Torah education and the character of the traditional **ḥeder* and in 1913 vehemently opposed the plan of the society Mefiẓei Haskalah be-Rusyah ("Disseminators of Secular Education in Russia") to change the accepted curriculum of the *ḥeder*.

During a certain period of his life, Friedmann participated actively in the Ḥibbat Zion movement. From 1863 he published articles in the *Levanon* which reflect his favorable attitude towards this movement, and he thus influenced many observant Jews to join it. He debated with Ẓ. H. *Kalischer on the problems of the movement and, together with L. *Pinsker and Samuel *Mohilever, participated in the *Kattowitz conference of 1885 as a delegate of the Pinsk branch of the Ḥovevei Zion. In a letter to A. J. Slucki he stressed that the noble idea of the nationalist movement deserves to become dear to "our brethren who are anxious for the word of God," and he testifies of himself that "the fire of love for our holy land burns in my heart" (ed. by A. J. Slucki, *Shivat Ẓiyyon*, 1 (1891), 18–19. In the course of time, however, he changed his attitude and following the decision of Zionist parties to include national secular education among their activities became an opponent of the Zionist idea. His grandson SHMUEL ELIASHIV (Friedmann, 1899–1955), jurist and author, served as first ambassador of the State of Israel to the U.S.S.R.

Bibliography: S. N. Gottlieb, *Oholei Shem* (1912), 172–4; Masliansky, in: *Hadoar*, 17 (1938), 455f.; *Toyzent yor Pinsk* (1941), 87, 93, 171, 269–71; Zinovitz, in: *Ba-Mishor*, 6 (1945), no. 255 p. 4f.; *Yahadut Lita*, 1 (1960), 250f., 344, 494, 513; 3 (1967), 79; S. Eliashiv, in: *Sefer Biala-Podlaska* (1961), 334–6.

[Y.H.]

FRIEDMANN, DESIDER (1880–1944), lawyer and Zionist leader. Born in Boskovice, Moravia, he was an active Zionist from 1898. When Vienna became the first great Jewish community in the West with a Zionist majority, Friedmann was elected vice-president of its Israelitische Kultusgemeinde (Jewish community; 1920–24) and from January 1933 its president. In May 1934 Friedmann was appointed a member of the Austrian Council of State (*Staatsrat*). He was a courageous fighter for Jewish rights and enlarged the cultural, educational, and social activities of the Kultusgemeinde. The Austrian chancellor Schuschnigg dispatched him abroad in 1938, a few weeks before the annexation of Austria to Nazi Germany (the *Anschluss*), to negotiate support for Austrian currency. Immediately after the *Anschluss*, the Nazis arrested him, allegedly for his financial aid to the Schuschnigg government. He was sent to various concentration camps, and in the autumn of 1944 he, his wife, and other Zionist leaders of Vienna were transferred from Theresienstadt to the gas chambers at Auschwitz.

Bibliography: J. Fraenkel (ed.), *Jews of Austria* (1967), index; H. Gold (ed.), *Die Juden und Judengemeinden Maehrens...* (1929), 92.

[JO.FR.]

FRIEDMANN, GEORGES (1902–), French sociologist, born in Paris, educated at the Ecole Normale Supérieure and the University of Paris. During World War II he organized the resistance movement in the Toulouse region. Friedmann, an expert in vocational education and the sociology of work and industry, was appointed inspector general of technical education in France in 1945 and participated in the work of the commission for educational reform. He became professor for the history of labor at the Conservatoire des Arts et des Métiers in 1946, director of studies at the Ecole Pratique des Hautes Etudes at the Sorbonne in 1948, and was administrator of the Centre d'Etudes Sociologiques, 1949–51. In 1956 he was president of the International Sociological Association. His position in industrial sociology is that the psycho-physiological problems of labor in industry must be considered not only within the individual enterprise, but also in the context of the larger social structure and cannot be solved without thoroughgoing changes in the social order. Among his major works are: *Problémes du machinisme en U.R.S.S. et dans les pays capitalistes* (1934); *La crise du progrès: Esquisse d'histoire des idées (1895–1935)* (1936; *De la Sainte Russie à l'U.R.S.S.* (1938); *Liebniz et Spinoza* (1946); *Les problèmes humains du machinisme industriel* (1946); *Humanisme du travail et humanités* (1950); *Où va le travail humain?* (1951), and *Le travail en miettes; spécialisation et loisirs* (1956). Friedmann was editor and coeditor of *L'Homme et la machine* and of *Annales des Economies, Sociétés, Civilisations*, and author of numerous articles on human and technological problems in industrial development. Several of his works were translated into English and German. In 1965, after an extended stay in Israel, Friedmann published *La Fin du peuple Juif?* (1965; *The End of the Jewish People?*, 1967). In this book he dealt with the present problems and future prospects of the State of Israel and the Jewish people. He held that the decline of religious orthodoxy, the growth of cultural assimilation in Israel and elsewhere, and the rise of a secular Israel nationalism will endanger the continued existence of the Jewish people in the Diaspora, as well as the Jewishness of Israelis.

[W.J.C.]

FRIEDMANN, MEIR (pen name **Ish-Shalom**; 1831–1908), rabbinic scholar. Friedmann was born in Horost, Slovakia. From 1843 to 1848 he studied in Ungvar at the yeshivah of his relative Meir Asch. Between 1848 and 1858 he underwent several crises and changes. Successively, he lived as an ascetic Ḥasid preparing for immigration to Ereẓ Israel, temporarily came under the influence of the Haskalah, returned to the study of the Talmud and was ordained, married, and became a farmer; his wife died, he was impoverished, and he became a *maggid*. In 1858 he settled in Vienna and attended the university as a non-matriculated student. From 1864 on he served as librarian, Bible teacher to adults, and Talmud teacher to the young at the *bet midrash* in Vienna. After 1894 he also taught at the rabbinical seminary there. Among his students were V. *Aptowitzer, Z. P. *Chajes, and S. *Schechter.

In his lifetime Friedmann was known for his studies of and lectures on *aggadah*, and even earned the title *mara de-aggadeta* ("master of *aggadah*"). His most important contributions are concerned with the halakhic Midrashim. He discovered lost sources, determined correct versions, and illuminated difficult passages; his writing is exceptionally erudite, profound, logical, and elegant of expression. His influence on Jewish scholarship was considerable. Many of the commentaries and interpretations of later talmudic scholars and researchers originated in his work. Friedmann maintained that "the Talmud is the foundation of Judaism and whoever abandons it is abandoning life"; this conviction affected all his creative work and activities. At the height of the Haskalah Friedmann was calling for traditional education, even drawing up plans for traditional Jewish secondary schools and universities. He was also active in the Zionist movement and founded the Association for the Dissemination of the Hebrew Language.

Friedmann edited midrashic texts with introductions and commentaries, the commentaries entitled *Me'ir Ayin*. The halakhic Midrashim include *Mekhilta* (1870), *Baraita de-Melekhet ha-Mishkan* (1908), and *Sifrei* (1864); a part of the *Sifra*, which he had begun editing, was published posthumously (1915). He published *Pesikta Rabbati* (1880) and *Tanna de-vei Eliyahu* (1902), aggadic texts; *Talmud Bavli: Massekhet Makkot* (1888) with a short interpretation as an example of a scientific edition of the Talmud; and a pamphlet about translating the Talmud, *Davar al Odot ha-Talmud* (1885). He published many works on the literature of *halakhah* and *aggadah*, its characteristics and principles, as well as books and articles on other Jewish

Meir Friedmann, rabbinic scholar. Jerusalem, Schwadron Collection, J.N.U.L.

subjects, including Bible, particularly commentaries on the Pentateuch, Judges, Samuel, Isaiah, Hosea, and Psalms; and the Targums of Onkelos and Aquila; the Holy Land; and Jewish prayer and poetry. He produced a number of sample textbooks on the Talmud and Mishnah for schools, and several of his lectures and sermons were published, although most of them can only be found incorporated into the works of his contemporaries. With I. H. Weiss Friedmann edited the periodical *Beit ha-Talmud* (1881–89). Most of his articles appeared in that and other publications under his pen name "Ish Shalom."

Bibliography: B. Z. Benedikt, in: KS, 24 (1947/48), 263–75; idem, in: *Aresheth*, 2 (1960), 269–84; T. Preschel, *ibid.*, 3 (1961), 468; J. Friedmann (ed.), *Lector M. Friedmann zur 100 Wiederkehr seines Geburtstages...* (1931), a bibliography; Kressel, Leksikon, 1 (1965), 98; J. Bergman, in: *Sefer ha-Zikkaron le-Veit ha-Midrash le-Rabbanim be-Vina* (1946), 37–45; S. Schechter, *Seminary Addresses and Other Papers* (1915, repr. 1959), 135–43.

[B.Z.B.]

FRIEDMANN, MORITZ (1823–1891), Hungarian *ḥazzan*. Born in Hraboc, Friedmann was a noted boy soprano. When he went to Budapest as a youth the *ḥazzan* David Broder accepted him in his choir. Later he went to Oedenburg (Sopron) and obtained a post as assistant cantor and Hebrew teacher in a nearby congregation. In 1857 he was appointed chief *ḥazzan* in Budapest, where he conducted services in the *Sulzer style, with a large choir and set psalms and prayers to music for solo and choir. His collection of Jewish synagogue songs, *Izráelita vallásos énekek...* (1875), was used in the synagogues of most Hungarian communities. He also edited the paper *Ungarische Israelitische Kultusbeamtenzeitung* (1883–97), in which he published articles on cantorial music.

Bibliography: *Friedmann Album*, 2 vols. (1877–85); Sendrey, Music, indexes; M. Rothmueller, *The Music of the Jews* (1967).

[J.L.N.]

FRIEDMANN, PAUL (1840–?), philanthropist and author, initiator of a settlement scheme for Jews in Midian. A Protestant of Jewish descent, Friedmann was born in Koenigsberg, Prussia, but the place and year of his death are unknown. After accumulating a vast fortune, he traveled over Europe to gather material for his works, *Les Dépêches de G. Michiel, Ambassadeur de Venise en Angleterre pendant les années 1554 à 1557* (1896) and *Anne Boleyn—A Chapter of English History 1527–1535*, 2 vols. (1885[2]). In 1891 he privately published *Das Land Madian* (Arabic for Midian), in which he described the possibilities of colonizing this land without mentioning Jews as the prospective settlers. Influenced by the Russian pogroms of the 1880s, he envisioned the unpopulated land of Midian as a haven for the victims of such persecution, and ultimately even as a Jewish state. With the assent of Sir Evelyn Baring (later Lord Cromer), Britain's representative in Egypt, Friedmann opened negotiations with the British authorities. He simultaneously set out to enlist the first settlers and was finally able to persuade a group of 17 men, 6 women, and 4 children from Austrian Galicia to join his expedition. He acquired a yacht, which he called *"Israel,"* that reached Suez on December 1, 1893, with a total of 46 persons. The Prussian officer in command exercised strictest discipline, which proved unbearable, and 18 persons left the group. After one of them was found dead in the Sinai desert, Friedmann was blamed for the "murder." Leaving the women and children in Cairo, the group finally reached the Sinai Peninsula and prepared to cross the Red Sea to Midian. News reached them, however, that the Turks had occupied the Midianite city of Dhaba and that in accordance with Turkish law no non-Muslim was permitted to settle in this area, which is part of the Hejaz.

A number of Friedmann's group deserted the camp and arrived in Cairo, spreading gruesome stories about the enterprise. As Friedmann's scheme had been favored by Baring, it was branded in the local press as a British attempt to occupy Midian, and bitter controversies arose between the British and Turkish authorities. Finally Friedmann was compelled to abandon his efforts. He was then a broken man, financially as well as spiritually, and although he brought successful court actions against a number of newspapers that attacked him, the litigation took many years and was, ultimately, of no avail.

Bibliography: O. K. Rabinowicz, in: *In Time of Harvest: Essays in Honor of Abba Hillel Silver* (1963), 284–319; J. Fraenkel, in: *Herzl Year Book*, 4 (1961), 67–117; N. M. Gelber, in: B. Dinur et al. (eds.), *Shivat Ẓiyyon* (1953), 251–74.

[O.K.R.]

FRIEDRICHSFELD, DAVID (c. 1755–1810), German author. In 1781 Friedrichsfeld settled in Amsterdam, where he became one of the leaders in the fight for Jewish emancipation. After Amsterdam was occupied by the French revolutionary forces, he became one of the leaders of the *Felix Libertate society. A follower of Moses Mendelssohn, he expounded his views in works such as *Beleuchtung... in Betreff des Buergerrecht der Juden* (Amsterdam, 1795); *De Messias der Jooden...* (The Hague, 1796); *Appell an die Staende Hollands* (Amsterdam, 1797); and *Kol Mevasser* (Amsterdam, 1802). He also wrote a work on Hebrew phonetics, *Ma'aneh Rakh* (Amsterdam, 1808); and contributed short articles and poems to *Ha-Me'assef*.

Bibliography: Graetz, Hist, 5 (1895), 400–1, 454; Klausner, Sifrut, 1 (1952[2]), index.

[ED.]

FRIEDSAM, MICHAEL (1858–1931), U.S. businessman, public servant, philanthropist, and art collector. Friedsam, who was born in New York, began working for the B. Altman & Company department store at the age of 17. He became a company partner in 1900 and a vice-president in 1909. Upon the death of company president Benjamin Altman in 1913, Friedsam became president of the company and of the Altman Foundation, established to disburse the bulk of Altman's fortune for charitable and educational purposes. During World War I Friedsam, as a New York State representative of the Federal Food Administration, participated in government efforts to regulate consumption and check profiteering. He also held the rank of colonel in the New York State National Guard. In 1925 Friedsam chaired the committee appointed by Governor Al Smith which recommended increased New York State financial aid to public schools. Friedsam willed portions of his extensive fine arts collection to the New York Metropolitan Museum of Art and the Brooklyn Institute of Arts and Sciences. In 1932, under the terms of his will, the Friedsam Foundation was established, for assisting the young and aged and for educational purposes.

[R.SK.]

FRIEND, HUGO MORRIS (1882–1966), U.S. lawyer and judge. Friend, who was born in Prague, was brought to the United States when he was two. In his youth he distinguished himself as an athlete and was a member of the U.S. team at the 1906 Olympic Games. In 1908 he was admitted to the Illinois bar and started practice in Chicago. Friend was made a master in chancery for Cook County, and in 1920 was appointed to fill a vacancy in the circuit court. He was reelected to office until 1930, when he was appointed to the appellate court for the first district. Friend took some part in the charitable work of the Jewish community. In 1917–18 he was president of the Young Men's Jewish

Charities; he was a vice-president of the Jewish Home Finding Society, board member of Mount Sinai Hospital, president of the Jewish Children's Bureau (1945–48), and a director of the Jewish Charities of Chicago. [S.D.T.]

FRIENDLY, FRED W. (**Fred Wachenheimer;** 1915–), U.S. television writer and director. Friendly began his career as a radio announcer in 1937. During World War II he was a correspondent for army publications, and in 1948 joined the National Broadcasting Company. He collaborated with Edward R. Murrow in the *Hear It Now* radio series. These were followed by several years of *C.B.S. Reports* for Columbia Broadcasting System, where he headed the news department from 1964. Two years later he resigned when his decision to carry the U.S. Senate Vietnam hearings at times normally used for commercially sponsored programs was overruled. Friendly then became a television adviser to the Ford Foundation, where he developed the Public Broadcast Laboratory, and a professor of journalism at Columbia University. [B.Hea.]

FRIENDSHIP, a relationship between people arising from mutual respect and affection. The ideal of friendship in the western world is largely derived from classical Greece. Not only do the myths and legends point to friendship as one of the great human achievements, but the philosophers make it one of the primary virtues of existence. The Romans continued this exaltation of friendship, as is evident in Cicero's essay on the topic, *De amicitia.* Biblical tradition seems to take friendship, as it does so many other general values, for granted and accords it respect; yet it never raises the close relationship between one person and a chosen companion to the status of a major ideal. There can be no question that the significance of true friendship is recognized in the Bible. A friend *(re'a)* is defined, almost accidentally, in Deuteronomy 13:7 as "one who is like your very self"; in Proverbs 18:24 a friend *(ohev)* is one "who sticks closer than a brother." There are few depictions of friendship in the Bible; the most notable examples are those of David and Jonathan (I Sam. 20), David and Barzillai (II Sam.17:27–29, 19:32–40), and Ruth and Naomi (Ruth 1:7–3:17). When Jephthah's daughter goes off to bewail her fate she asks permission to do so with her companions (Judg. 11:37). The Bible seems to emphasize proper concern for one's neighbor as a means for the creation of a sacred society, rather than intense person-to-person relationships. This may be a safeguard against homosexuality, which was so much a part of the Greek conception of friendship.

Typical of the Bible's ethical concern in human relations is the frequent reference to false friendship in the book of Proverbs. As the worthy friend is he who stands by you, so the bad friend is he who deserts you when you are in need. Thus the warning is issued that the rich, not the poor, have many friends (14:20); that friends flock to the gift giver (19:6); and that he who has many friends has reason to worry (18:24). The rabbinic tradition, like the biblical, shows appreciation of friendship. The friendship of David and Jonathan is held up as the supreme example of altruistic love (Avot 5:19). It does not consider it a major concern, however, though the good *ḥaver* (associate or colleague, *ibid.,* 1:6; 2:13) and the good neighbor (2:13) are mentioned as ideals to be sought. The *amora* Rav is reported to have praised the friends of Job for going to see him when they learned of his suffering, even though they lived at a great distance from him. In response to Rav, Rabbah quoted the popular saying "Either a friend like the friends of Job or death" (BB 16b). The Talmud reports that Rabbi Zera showed friendship even to some lawless men

The friendship of David and Jonathan (bottom left) in the illuminated manuscript *Somme le Roi,* France, late 13th century. On the right, Saul threatens David with a spear. The dove and hawk in the upper register symbolize, respectively, love and hate. London, British Museum, Add. Ms. 23162, fol. 6v.

who lived near him. It chides some of the other sages who did not do so for their hardness of heart but praises them for their repentance (Sanh. 37a). Modern Jewish thought, responding to the ethical implications of the concept of friendship, has shown a renewed interest in this subject, exemplified in the writings of Martin *Buber (*I and Thou,* 1952^{2}, passim) and Hermann *Cohen (*Religion der Vernuft* (1929^{2}), 510). [E.B.B.]

°**FRIES, JAKOB FRIEDRICH** (1773–1843), German anti-Semitic philosopher. He lectured in both Jena and Heidelberg and published authoritative works on philosophy and psychology. Immediately after the Napoleonic wars, Fries took part in the nationalistic student agitation and was the only member of the professional staff present at the 1817 Wartburg demonstration organized by the ultranationalist German students. His popularity with the students contributed to the success of his anti-Jewish writings. Under his influence, the Burschenschaft (students' associations) decided not to accept Jews as members. In his pamphlet *Ueber die Gefaehrdung des Wohlstandes und Charakters der Deutschen durch die Juden* (Heidelberg, 1816) he protested violently against the emancipation of the Jews and recommended that they be treated as they had been by the Pharaohs: that is, "destroyed root and branch." According to Goethe, Fries was "the most savage enemy of the Jews" in his day.

Bibliography: L. Poliakov, *Histoire de l'antisémitisme,* 3 (1968), index; E. Sterling, *Er ist wie du* (1954), 163, 226; O. F. Scheuer, *Burschenschaft und Judenfrage . . .* (1927); Graetz, Gesch, 11 (1900), 313ff.; H. Fischer, *Judentum, Staat und Heer in Preussen* (1968), 84–86.

[L.Po.]

FRIGEIS, LAZARO DE (16th century), physician. Scholars disagree on whether he was a native of Hungary or Holland. When Andrea Vesalius (1514–1564), the great anatomist, came to Padua, Frigeis became a member of his close circle of friends. He furnished Vesalius with the Hebrew names for some of the anatomic structures described in Vesalius' epoch-making work *De Humani Corporis Fabrica* and possibly also those appearing in *Tabulae Anatomicae.* The Hebrew anatomical terms used are for the most part taken from the Hebrew translation of the *Canon* of Avicenna and in some cases directly from the Talmud.

Bibliography: S. E. Franco, in: RMI, 15 (1949), 495–515, incl. bibl.; C. Singer and C. Rabin, *Prelude to Modern Science* (1946), xxvi, 24, 30. [S.M.]

FRISCH, DANIEL (1897–1950), U.S. Zionist leader. Frisch, who was born in Ereẓ Israel, was taken by his family to Rumania when he was one year old. He went to the U.S. in 1921, settled in Indianapolis, Indiana, and eventually became an investment broker and the head of a large salvage firm. In 1934 Frisch, a militant General Zionist from his youth, became a member of the Zionist Organization of America's (ZOA) Administrative Council. In the course of the next 25 years he held numerous other Zionist posts before being elected ZOA president in 1949. In that same year, largely through Frisch's efforts, the ZOA, the Jewish Agency, and the World Confederation of Zionists reached agreement for financing various projects in Israel. Frisch's approach to Zionism was reflected in his belief that Israel's growth and welfare was dependent upon the strength of the General Zionist movement and in the need for the development of a strong private sector in the Israel economy. A collection of his essays, sketches, and letters was published as *On the Road to Zion* (1950). [Ed.]

FRISCH, EFRAIM (1873–1942), Austrian author and journalist. Born at Stry in the Ukraine, Frisch was a member of an Orthodox family. Following the success of his novel *Das Verloebnis* (1902), he worked at Max *Reinhardt's Deutsches Theater in Berlin as director of drama from 1904 to 1908. His views on the stage are contained in *Von der Kunst des Theaters* (1910). After some years with a Munich publishing house, Frisch edited *Der Neue Merkur* (1914–1925), a literary and political monthly whose contributors included Gottfried Benn, Bertholt Brecht, Martin Buber, André Gide, Yvan Goll, Bernard Shaw, and Arnold Zweig. He also published translations from the French (Giraudoux, Cocteau), English (Priestley), Polish, and Yiddish (Mendele Mokher Seforim).

Zenobi (1927), a brilliantly written novel generally considered Frisch's masterpiece, shows how a gentle, impractical and naïve fool becomes the touchstone for a depersonalized and corrupt world of materialism, militarism, and technology. Frisch's positive attitude toward Judaism is clear from the frequent and sympathetic presentation of the East-European Jewish milieu in his fiction. He once published a special Jewish issue of *Der Neue Merkur* and in 1935 delivered four public lectures on Judaism at Ascona, Switzerland, where he later died.

Bibliography: Stern, in: YLBI, 6 (1961), 125–49. [H.Zo.]

FRISCH, EPHRAIM (1880–1957), U.S. Reform rabbi. Frisch, who was born in Lithuania, was taken to the United States in 1888. He received rabbinic ordination at Hebrew Union College (1904), and held pulpits in Pine Bluff, Ark. (1904–12), Far Rockaway, N.Y. (1912–15), New York City (1915–23), and San Antonio, Tex. (1923–42). After becoming rabbi emeritus of the San Antonio congregation in 1942, Frisch settled in New York. An active member of the Central Conference of American Rabbis, he served on several of its committees. He was an outspoken liberal on social questions and an active supporter of the American Civil Liberties Union and Americans for Democratic Action. Frisch wrote *A Historical Survey of Jewish Philanthropy from the Earliest Times to the Nineteenth Century* (1924), and a number of pamphlets.

Bibliography: *New York Times* (Dec. 26, 1957). [S.D.T.]

FRISCH, OTTO ROBERT (1904–), British physicist. Born in Vienna, the nephew of the physicist Lise *Meitner. Frisch did research on atomic energy in Berlin. With the coming of the Nazis he fled to Copenhagen and then went to England, where he worked at Liverpool and Oxford and later at Los Alamos, U.S.A., where the atomic bomb was produced. After World War II he was appointed head of the nuclear physics division at the United Kingdom Atomic Energy Establishment at Harwell. In 1947 he became professor of natural philosophy at Cambridge University.

Frisch invented the term "nuclear fission," based on the term "fission" used by biologists to describe the way bacteria divide themselves. He was elected a fellow of the Royal Society in 1948. Among his books are: *Meet the Atoms* (1947), *Atomic Physics Today* (1961), *Working with Atoms* (1965), and *The Nature of Matter* (1968). [M.Gol.]

FRISCHMANN, DAVID (1859–1922), one of the first major writers in modern Hebrew literature. Versatile and prolific in his literary creativity, Frischmann was an innovator in style and in the treatment of his subject, especially in the Hebrew short story, the ballad, the essay, criticism, and the lyric-satiric feuilleton. He also distinguished himself as a translator of world literature, and as an editor. In introducing western aestheticism into Hebrew literature, Frischmann was a major influence in the development of Hebrew literature according to the aesthetic concepts of the world.

Early Career. He was born in Zgierz, near Lodz, into a well-to-do mercantile family which, although traditional, approved of the Haskalah. His education included Hebrew religious studies as well as humanities. At a young age, Frischmann already showed signs of literary talent and was considered a prodigy. At 15, his first writings were published—the sonnet *"Yesh Tikvah,"* a translation of Heine's "Don Ramiro," and *"Tarnegol ve-Tarnegolet,"* an original short story (*Ha-Boker Or,* 1874). He published satirical writings in **Ha-Shaḥar,* whose editor, *Smolenskin, hailed him as a "brilliant star that has risen in our literary spheres—Boerne and Heine in German and Frischmann in Hebrew."

Short Stories. Frischmann's early satirical narratives, with their inherent social criticism, influenced by the writings of J. L. *Gordon and K. E. *Franzos, gave way to the short story whose purpose was mainly aesthetic. Jewish life was now portrayed more objectively. Frequently, the main characters were Jews who had come into direct conflict with the mores of the traditional society in which they lived and who, because of these conflicts, had either become estranged from it, or were rejected by it. In *"Yom ha-Kippurim"* (1881), a Jewish girl attracted to the world of music becomes a famous singer but abandons her people and traditions. At a recital in the church of her native town, on the Day of Atonement, she meets her death at the hand of her widowed mother who, out of shame and pain, has become demented. In *"Ha-Ish u-Miktarto,"* a famous rabbi is so addicted to smoking that he is forced to violate the Sabbath, first furtively, and later publicly; as a result, he is excommunicated. Frischmann empathizes with these protagonists who succumb to human weaknesses and describes them with compassion and understanding.

Ba-Midbar (1923), a series of fictional biblical tales, alluding to biblical motifs and written in a biblical style and language, are original both in their choice of subject and in form. Set in the desert, immediately after the exodus of the Israelites from Egypt, the characters are torn between the half-pagan primitive habits and lusts that still cling to them, and the new moral life preached by Moses as the word of God. Their leaders and priests, responsible for the observance and teaching of the new precepts, are themselves not always faithful to them. These stories, while evoking nostalgia for the ancient era, also reflect universal themes relevant to Frischmann and his time: the conflict between religion as an act of faith and as law, and instinct.

Literary Critic. Frischmann frequently was a scathing literary critic. Thus in an article, *"Mi-Misterei Sifrutenu"* (*Ha-Boker Or,* 1880), he violently admonished P. Smolenskin, the leading authority in Hebrew literature at that time, whom he accused of plagiarizing from M. *Hess's *Rome and Jerusalem.* In *Tohu va-Vohu* (1883), he mocks and scorns the Hebrew literary journalism of his day because of its inefficiency and provincialism. In due course, Frischmann became an authoritative arbiter of good taste and a champion of literary writing for art's sake. He defended J. L. Gordon against the attacks of M. L. *Lilienblum—who had accused Gordon of not being sufficiently nationalistic in his writings (in a critical article published in **Ha-Asif,* 1894). His admiration for Gordon did not, however, prevent him from criticizing Gordon on another matter. He claimed that Gordon, after joining the editorial board of **Ha-Meliẓ,* had abandoned those liberal views which he had propounded for 30 years previously.

An Iconoclast Poet. Frischmann's literary nonconformism, expressed in two of his earliest poems *"Lo Elekh Immam"* and *"Elilim"* were to become the motto of his life and his literary credo. In *"Lo Elekh Immam,"* he voices his refusal to follow the old path and expresses his fearless criticism:

I shall not go with them, I shall not go; their ways are not mine,
I cannot bear their prattle, their expressions, their talk or their conversation.
I cannot tolerate their ways, their manners, or their thoughts,
Their prophets are not my prophets, their angels are not my angels.
Thoughts repel me, thoughts without minds,
I detest feelings, feelings without hearts.

"Elilim" points to Frischmann the iconoclast; the poem harks back to the patriarch Abraham whom he sees as the first iconoclast. The poet claims that Abraham in smashing the idols had not completed the act, since the largest of the idols still survived. He calls upon the patriarch to endow him with his ancient venerated spirit, so that he might smite surviving idols.

A non-observant Jew, Frischmann rejected as futile and impractical the attempts at religious reforms in the 19th century, whose purpose was the adaptation of Judaism to the spirit of the times. In *"Ani va-Avi Zekeni,"* Frischmann argues that the grandfathers who cling to Judaism would not assent to any reform of the *mitzvot* which, in their view, were all "given to Moses at Sinai"; whereas the younger generation, with which the author identifies, does not need the sanction of tradition to act according to its conscience.

Frischmann and European Culture. Like many of his contemporaries, Frischmann's introduction to European culture was by way of German, a language he had studied in his youth. Two German-Jewish authors, *Heine and *Boerne, exercised a profound influence upon his writing. Frischmann visited Germany several times, and during his 1882 stay, became personally acquainted with a number of authors and scientists, among them B. Auerbach, a German-Jewish writer, and A. *Bernstein, whose large popular scientific work, *Knowledge of Nature,* Frischmann was to translate in part. Between 1890 and 1895, he studied philology, philosophy, and the history of art at the University of Breslau. He returned to Warsaw in 1895, and until 1910, translation became his regular occupation. The works he rendered from German, Russian, and English into Hebrew during that period include: J. Lippert's *The History of the Perfection of Man* (1894–1908); George Eliot's *Daniel Deronda* (1893); legends and tales of Hans Christian Andersen (1896); selected poems of Alexander Pushkin (1899); Byron's *Cain* (1900); and Nietzsche's *Also sprach Zarathustra* (1900). Frischmann devoted his entire life to literature and avoided all public office or public involvements. His many opponents accused him of anti-Zionism. In actuality, it was his rejection of the use of art for ideological or propagandistic purposes that caused him to refrain from advocating social or political views.

Frischmann as a Hebrew Journalist. In the 19th century, the dividing line between belles lettres and journalism had not been clearly defined, and most authors engaged in both disciplines without differentiating between them. Frischmann published a series of short stories, *Otiyyot Poreḥot* (1893), a series of book reviews, and a series of feuilletons on practical subjects, called *"Ba-Kol-mi-Kol-Kol"* in *Ha-Asif.* His adversaries often dismissed him as "merely a feuilletonist." Frischmann, who did not accept the old forms, and left on all the genres he employed his mark as innovator—in style, structure, choice of content and its treatment—saw the feuilleton as a new form of poetry whose range extended far beyond that of any other type of poetry. In his eulogy of Theodor *Herzl, Frischmann wrote:

"I knew him as an artist in his field long before he became famous as the father of Zionism. My enthusiasm for Herzl, the feuilletonist, was so great, that for a time I almost hated Zionism because it had robbed me of his poetic powers and transformed a great poet into a man of public affairs concerned with petty politics. However immense his contribution to Zionism may have been, the loss to literature is immeasurable."

Frischmann had a special affinity for political leaders who had literary talents. He wrote with enthusiasm about the diary of Ferdinand *Lassalle, and about the private letters of Rosa *Luxemburg.

Editor and Publisher of Journals. Frischmann published several short stories in the German literary monthly *Salon* (Leipzig, in 1885), in *Ha-Meliẓ* (whose editor, J. L. Gordon, invited him to join its editorial board in 1896); and in *Ha-Yom,* the first Hebrew daily. Frischmann preferred *Ha-Yom* because it was an independent journal and its editor and principal contributors, among them J. L. *Kantor, and J. L. *Katznelson, shared the same liberal outlook as he. Frischmann served as assistant editor and published his feuilletons almost daily; the series "Letters Concerning Literature" became one of the foundation stones of modern Hebrew criticism.

In 1901 Frischmann became editor of *Ha-Dor,* a literary weekly whose high literary standard attracted the most talented writers of the day. After one year it was forced to close down, due to its small circulation. Frischmann tried to revive it three years later, but failed after publishing 38 additional issues. Zalman *Shneour, describing the *Ha-Dor* period in his memoirs, says: "Frischmann was generally considered a quarrelsome man; his antagonists considered him a cynic. In truth, he was a mild, pleasant man who loved talented and promising young people."

In 1903, Frischmann became editor of the literary

supplement of the Vilna daily newspaper *Ha-Zeman*, in 1909, in Warsaw, of the short-lived *Ha-Boker;* between 1908 and 1910 of the literary collections *Sifrut* (1909–10); and of *Reshafim* (1909–10; pocket-sized literary anthologies) in which he published, in serial form, his translation of *Also sprach Zarathustra*.

Frischmann in Yiddish. Hebrew was Frischmann's literary vehicle of expression, and he was faithful to biblical Hebrew, which he had mastered probably better than any contemporary author, rejecting the "synthetic" Hebrew developed by *Mendele Mokher Seforim and his school. Occasionally, however, he also wrote in Yiddish and in German. The few poems that he composed in Yiddish are lyrical in tone. He also wrote short stories and feuilletons in that language. His first Yiddish articles were published in *Shalom Aleichem's *Yudishe Folksbibliothek* (1888–89), but he also contributed Yiddish poems and articles to the literary annual *Hoys-Fraynd*, the weekly *Der Yud*, and the daily *Fraynd*. From 1908, he was a regular contributor of weekly feuilletons to the Warsaw Yiddish daily *Haynt*. His collected Yiddish stories were published in two volumes by the Lodz Pedagogue editions, and his Yiddish articles on drama and literature were published by the Warasw Progress editions. These collected works are only a small part of Frischmann's Yiddish writings, most of which are still uncollected.

Frischmann's Visits to Palestine. Frischmann visited Palestine twice, in 1911 and 1912, each time with groups organized by *Haynt*, in which he published his travel impressions. These he also published in Hebrew in a small book entitled *Ba-Areẓ* (1913). Overwhelmed by his experiences he wrote emotionally about the holy places he had visited, the landscape, his meetings with the pioneers, and the beginnings of the revival of Hebrew. His initial skepticism gave way to enthusiasm, and he candidly and openly retracted his reservations about the rebirth of Hebrew as a vernacular.

Frischmann in Russia During World War I and the Revolution. At the outbreak of World War I, Frischmann was on a visit in Berlin, where he was interned as an enemy alien. Eventually, he was set free and allowed to return to Poland. When the conquering German army neared Warsaw, he left for Odessa where he remained until the Russian Revolution. While in Odessa, he wrote some of his most beautiful lyrical poems, translated *The Conversations of the Grimm Brothers* for the Moriah editions of Bialik-Rawnitzki and the poetry of the Indian poet Rabindranath Tagore. Frischmann's translation of Tagore's poetry is a masterpiece. The translation, together with several original poems, and a series of literary obituaries, were published in *Keneset* (1917), edited by *Bialik. During his stay in Odessa, he also contributed weekly feuilletons to the Odessa Yiddish newspaper *Undzer Lebn*, until the Russian authorities closed down the paper.

After the revolution of February 1917, a Hebrew literary center was formed in Moscow, and Frischmann was invited to be the chairman of the editorial board of the A. J. Stybel publications. He was named editor of **Ha-Tekufah*, the quarterly published by Stybel. There he published his translations of Goethe, Heine, Byron, Oscar Wilde, Anatole France, and Tagore. He also continued his biblical stories of the *Ba-Midbar* series. Stybel's generous support enabled him, as well as many other authors, to devote themselves entirely to writing. The publication program of the house was outlined by Frischmann in his address on "Belles Lettres" at the second Hebrew Language and Culture congress in Vienna (1913).

In 1919, the Stybel publishing house was closed down in Moscow, and reestablished in Warsaw, where Frischmann

David Frischmann, Hebrew and Yiddish writer. Portrait drawing by Hermann Struck. Central Zionist Archives, Jerusalem.

continued in his capacity of editor. There he also published a series of "New Letters Concerning Literature" in the monthly *Miklat* (another Stybel project, edited by Y. D. *Berkowitz in New York), and translated the "Legends" (*Aggadot*) of Max Nordau (1923[2]) and Shakespeare's *Coriolanus* (published in 1924). His grave illness compelled him to be in Berlin to seek medical treatment; there he died and was buried.

Frischmann's Conversations and Letters. Besides his great literary prolificacy, perseverance in pursuing an idea or belief, and his immense contributions to the different branches of literature, Frischmann's talent also revealed itself in his letters to friends (few unfortunately survive), and in conversation. Some of his conversations were written down later, from memory, by his admirers: J. *Fichmann, E. *Steinman, and Z. *Shneour. His letters to his contemporaries, rarely personal, are a valuable source of information on Frischmann and on the history of the Hebrew literature of his period. Eleven of his letters, *Iggerot David Frischmann* ed. by E. R. Malachi, were collected and published in New York (1927), others were published in different periodicals.

Collected writings of Frischmann have been published in various editions: (1) *Ketavim Nivḥarim* (4 vols., Piotrokow-Warsaw, 1899–1905), a selection of his writings with an introduction by Y. L. Kantor; (2) *Ketavim Ḥadashim* (5 vols., Warsaw, 1909–12); (3) *Kol Kitvei David Frischmann u-Mivḥar Tirgumav* (16 vols., Warsaw, 1922[2]), his complete writings and a selection of his translations, as well as an additional volume (vol. 17) of his articles; (4) *Kol Kitvei Frischmann* (8 vols., Warsaw-New York, 1939), his complete writings; (5) *Kol Kitvei Frischmann* (8 vols. published until 1968), his complete works; (6) *Tirgumim* (1954), a collection of all his literary translations. Four books of Frischmann's collected Yiddish writings were published by the Pedagogue editions (1909) in Lodz, and the Progress editions (1911) in Warsaw. Many of Frischmann's writings in Hebrew, as well as in Yiddish and German, have not yet been collected in book form and are still scattered in different periodicals. For English translations see Goell, Bibliography, 674–81, 2046–91, 2794–95.

Bibliography: D. Frischmann, in: *Ha-Tekufah*, 16 (1923; autobiographical letter, written in 1893 to S. L. Zitron); E. R. Malachi (ed.), *Iggerot Frischmann* (1927); N. Sokolow, in: *Ha-Tekufah*, 16 (1923); J. Fichmann, *Ruḥot Menaggenot* (1952), 117–74; E. Steinman, *Mi-Dor el Dor: Seder Frischmann* (1951); Z. Shneour, *David Frischmann ve-Aḥerim* (1959); Y. D. Berkowitz, *Ha-Rishonim ki-Venei Adam, bein Shalom Aleikhem u-Frischmann* (1943); Y. H. Rawnitzki, *Dor ve-Soferav* (1927; in memory of D. Frischmann); Lachower, Sifrut, 3 pt. 1 (1963), 123–78; R. Brainin, *Ketavim Nivḥarim, Avot: David Frischmann* (1950); A. A. Ben-Yishai, in: *Sefer ha-Shanah shel ha-Ittona'im be-Yisrael* (1961); Rejzen, Leksikon, 204–28; Z. Fishman, in: *En Hakore* (1923); Waxman, Literature, index; N. Slouschz, *David Frischmann* (Fr., 1913).

[A.Z.B.-Y.]

°**FRITSCH, THEODOR** (1852–1933), German anti-Semitic publicist and politician. One of the leading early racists, in 1886 he joined the Deutsche Antisemitische Vereinigung (see *Anti-Semitic Political Parties and Organizations) which strove to repeal the emancipation law. In 1887 he founded the Hammer publishing house whose first production *Antisemiten-Katechismus* . . . (1887) was a catalog of "Jewish misdeeds." Later renamed *Handbuch der Judenfrage*, it went through more than 40 editions, inspiring the Nazis, who honored Fritsch as their *Altmeister*. Following Adolf *Stoecker, Fritsch expounded, in his *Antisemitische Flugblaetter*, the need for a new Aryanized Christianity, purged of all Judaic elements. He became a member of the Nazi Reichstag, and on his death was eulogized by Julius *Streicher.

Bibliography: P. G. J. Pulzer, *Rise of Political Anti-Semitism in Germany and Austria* (1964), passim; P. W. Massing, *Rehearsal for Destruction* . . . (1949), passim; G. L. Mosse, *Crisis of German Ideology* . . . (1964), passim; W. Buchow, *50 Jahre antisemitische Bewegung* . . . (1937), 55ff.; R. G. Phelps, in: *Deutsche Rundschau*, 87 (1961), 442–9.

[Ed.]

FRITTA (**Friedrich Taussig**; 1909–1944), Czech painter and graphic artist. In 1942 he was deported to the concentration camp at *Theresienstadt. Here, together with fellow artists Leo *Haas, Otto Ungar, Friedrich Bloch (an Austrian painter), and later Karel Fleischmann, he formed a group of painters who assigned themselves the task of creating a pictorial record of the last days of men facing death. Fritta's contribution to this unique documentary was probably the largest. Their works were smuggled out of Theresienstadt over a two-year period. In July 1944 the Nazis discovered some of Fritta's works depicting shocking scenes of ghetto life. Fritta was imprisoned and deported to Auschwitz, where he died after undergoing torture. About 150 of his Theresienstadt drawings, buried in a tin case, were unearthed after the war, together with the works of other Theresienstadt artists. They are now in the Jewish Museum in Prague.

Bibliography: Frýd, in: *Terezin*, published by the Council of Jewish Communities in Czech Lands (1965), 206–18; Haas, *ibid.*, 156–62.

[Av.D.]

FRIULI, N.E. part of the Veneto province, N.E. Italy. Between 1028 and 1420 the patriarch of Aquileia ruled over Friuli. Under his protection, Jewish merchants and money-lenders settled in *Cividale, Udine, and from the 13th century in Gemona and *San Daniele. Within a brief period, prosperous Jewish communities formed around them. When Friuli was annexed by the Republic of Venice in 1420 there was no essential change in the status of the Jews. However, at the end of the 15th and during the 16th centuries the preaching of friars and the Counter-Reformation movement led to the expulsion of the Jews from most of the towns in Friuli, though a small Jewish community continued to exist in San Daniele and even smaller centers in Genars and Spilimbergo. In 1714 lending money on interest was prohibited and in 1779 the Jews were expelled.

Bibliography: C. Roth, *Venice* (1930), 269, 349; F. Luzzatto, *Cronache storiche della Università degli ebrei di San Daniele del Friuli* . . . (1964); idem, in: RMI, 16 (1950), 140–6; Modona, in: *Vessillo Israelitico*, 47 (1899), 327–34, 366–8; Roth, Dark Ages, index.

[D.C.]

FRIZZI, BENEDETTO (1756–1844), Italian physician and author from Ostia. He graduated from Pavia and practiced in Trieste. In 1790 he founded the first Italian medical journal and published six *Dissertazioni* (Pavia, 1787–90) on precepts of the Law, presenting them in a modern scientific manner. He also wrote apologetic and polemical works: *Difesa contro gli attacchi fatti alla Nazione Ebrea* (1784) and *Dissertazione in cui si esaminano gli usi ed abusi degli Ebrei* (1789), which intended to disprove the accusations by a contemporary Italian that Jews hated Christians and that their economic activities tended to impoverish the countries they lived in. He described Jewish theology, philosophy, and ethics and then analyzed in great detail and with many examples the economic role of Jews in Europe, particularly in Italy. He outlined the valuable functions they fulfilled historically and attributed their success as merchants to attention to details and to quality, setting of realistically low prices, avoidance of borrowing at interest, decision to

DIFESA

CONTRO

GLI ATTACCHI FATTI

ALLA

NAZIONE EBREA

nel libro intitolato

DELLA INFLUENZA DEL GHETTO

NELLO STATO.

PAVIA. MDCCLXXXIV.

Nella Stamperia del R. I. Monistero di S. Salvatore

Con licenza de' Superiori.

Title page of Benedetto Frizzi's "Defense Against the Attacks Made on the Jewish People," Pavia, 1784. Cecil Roth Collection.

trade in perennially useful products rather than luxury goods for which demand varies. Frizzi enumerated markets and services opened and developed by Jews and described their business methods at length. He wrote his Hebrew work, *Petaḥ Enayyim* (Leghorn, 1815–25), to demonstrate that the rabbis' teachings were based on scientific knowledge. He hoped both to increase his contemporaries' respect for Torah and to attack traditionalists who saw Jewish law as untouchable and untouched by the modern spirit. A man of great learning and wide renown, Frizzi was considered one of the most outstanding Jewish scholars of the Enlightenment in Western Europe.

Bibliography: Nissim, in: RMI, 34 (1968), 279–91; Dinaburg, in: *Tarbiz*, 20 (1948/49), 241–64. [D.N.]

FROEHLICH, ALFRED (1871–1953), pharmacologist. He was born in Vienna and became professor of pharmacology and toxicology at the University of Vienna in 1912. In 1939 he settled in the U.S. and became associated with the Jewish Hospital in Cincinnati. He was the first to describe in 1901 adiposo-genital dystrophy, a form of obesity which is associated with a tumor in the pituitary gland and deficient development of the sex organs. He collaborated with Otto *Loewi on the pharmacology of the autonomous nervous system and as a result of their discoveries, the use of a combination of adrenalin and cocaine was established in medical practice. Together with the neurologist L. F. Hochward, Froehlich recommended the use of hypoglysin during delivery, a practice that became universally accepted. He and H. H. Mayer investigated the contracture of striated muscle fibers under influence of tetanus toxin. He carried out experimental research in increasing the effect of certain drugs and made extensive investigations into the effect of theophylline.

Bibliography: S. A. Kagan, *Jewish Medicine* (1952), 209–12. [S.M.]

Frogs swarming through an Egyptian oven as an illustration of the second plague in the *Sarajevo Haggadah* (fol. 22), Spain, 14th century. Above, the first plague, blood. National Museum, Sarajevo.

FROG (Heb. צְפַרְדֵּעַ, *ẓefarde'a*). One of the ten plagues visited upon Egypt was that of frogs (Ex. 7:29; Ps. 78:45; 105:30). They apparently made life intolerable for the Egyptians by their shrill croaking and by contaminating food with their moist bodies. The frog, *Rana esculenta*, is found in Israel near bodies of water. The word *ẓefarde'a* may also refer to the toad *(Bufo)*. While the frog is, according to the laws of the Torah, prohibited as food, it is not included among the swarming things which, by contact, make man, vessels, and food unclean (cf. Lev. 11:29–30; Toh. 5:4).

Bibliography: Tristram, Nat Hist, 280f.; J. Feliks, *Animal World of the Bible* (1962), 112. [J.F.]

FROHMAN, U.S. family of theatrical figures, born in Sandusky, Ohio. DANIEL (1851–1940), theater manager and producer, began his career as a journalist, but later turned to theater management. In 1880 he became business manager of the Madison Square Theater. Later he bought the Lyceum Theater (1885) and appointed David *Belasco as stage manager. He staged plays by Belasco, A. W. Pinero, V. Sardou, and H. A. Jones, and such stars as William Faversham, Henry Miller, and E. H. Sothern acted under his management. He also managed Daly's Theater (1899–1903) and, after the Lyceum closed, opened the New Lyceum (1903). Later he went into film production and became a director of the Paramount Company. In 1933 he returned to Broadway to produce an English version of the Yiddish drama *Yoshe Kalb* at the National Theater, but the play closed after four performances. Daniel was president of the Actors' Fund of America from 1903 till his death and remained a revered figure of the American stage. He recalled his career in *Memories of a Manager* (1911), *Daniel Frohman Presents* (1935), and *Encore* (1937).

His brother, GUSTAVE (1855–1930), a theater manager, interested Charles (see below) in the theater and persuaded Daniel to leave journalism.

A third brother, CHARLES (1860–1915), theater manager and producer was for some years a booking agent with connections throughout the United States. Later he helped organize a theatrical syndicate which controlled U.S. theaters for several years. Frohman acquired the Empire Theater in New York and had controlling shares in others. He also had interests in five theaters in England. As a producer he scored his first real success with *Shenandoah* (1889). He was the first U.S. producer to become famous outside the country and produced some 125 plays in London. Charles managed and developed many stars of the stage of his day, some of the best known being Maude Adams, Ethel Barrymore, John Drew, William Gillette, and Otis Skinner. He also introduced Oscar Wilde and Somerset Maugham to the American public. Frohman dominated the U.S. stage in his time and with his death, on the torpedoed *Lusitania*, an era ended. [Jo.R.]

FROMM, ERICH (1900–), U.S. psychoanalyst, social philosopher, and author. Fromm, who was born in Frankfort of rabbinic descent, studied at German universities and received his professional training at the Psychoanalytic Institute of Berlin. He worked at the Institute for Social Research in Frankfort from 1929 to 1932, but emigrated to the U.S. when Hitler came to power in Germany. His first appointment in America was at the International Institute for Social Research in New York City (1934–39). He was on the faculty of Bennington College, Vermont, from 1941 to 1950. In 1951 he was appointed professor at the National University of Mexico. He was also professor at Michigan State University (1957–61) and New York University (1962). A theoretician of the neo-Freudian school, he pursued an independent road in the application of psychoanalysis to the problems of culture and society. His psychological studies on the meaning of freedom for modern man have had a wide influence on western thought.

Erich Fromm, U.S. psychoanalyst and social philosopher. Photo Bender, New York.

A student of the Bible and the Talmud, "brought up in a religious family where the Old Testament touched me and exhilarated me more than anything else I was exposed to," Fromm was a disciple of Ludwig Krause and Nehemia Nobel, and was greatly influenced by Hermann Cohen. Fromm believes that everyone has a religious need and that religion is "the formalized and elaborate answer to man's existence." He postulates two major kinds of religion: the authoritarian and the humanistic. He rejects the former, for here man is utterly powerless, and adopts the humanistic religion in which man experiences oneness with the All, achieving his greatest strength and self-realization, as in the Jewish prophets, where their doctrines have an underlying humanity and where freedom is the aim of life. He differs from Freud, and considers "the religious cult as vastly superior to neurosis, because man shares his feelings, his oneness, security, and stability with his fellow men, which the neurotic person lacks in his isolation."

Fromm claims that Judaism is an "untheological religion, where the stress is on the underlying substratum of human experience." Making extensive use of Judaic texts and practices, he demonstrates their contemporary relevance to the human condition, showing, in a nontheological way, how the idea of God is a permanent challenge to all kinds of idolatry. In Fromm's view, alienation, which is identical with idolatry in the Bible, is the sum and substance of human misery in our society. To save Western man from "depersonalization," society must recognize the sovereignty of the individual. In contrast to Freudian orthodoxy, Fromm emphasizes the need for a social and cultural orientation in psychoanalysis.

Fromm's belief in the need for a society which recognizes man as a responsible individual is expounded in *The Sane Society* (1955). This society he regards as the best antidote to the totalitarianism which he denounced in *Escape from Freedom* (1941). His other studies deal with the interrelation of psychology and ethics, psychoanalysis and social history, myth and religion, and dream symbolism. These books include: *Man for Himself* (1947); *Psychoanalysis and Religion* (1950); *The Forgotten Language* (1952); *The Art of Loving* (1956); and *You Shall Be As Gods* (1967), a psychiatric commentary on the biblical view of God.

Bibliography: J. S. Glen, *Erich Fromm: a Protestant Critique* (1966); Friedenberg, in: *Commentary*, 34 (1962), 305–13. [M.M.Br.]

FROMM-REICHMANN, FRIEDA (1889–1957), U.S. pioneer of psychoanalytic psychiatry and psychotherapeutic teaching and research. Born in Karlsruhe, Germany, Frieda Fromm-Reichmann studied medicine, practiced in several German cities and founded the South West German Psychoanalytic Institute. She worked at the "Weisse Hirsch" Sanatorium in Dresden, which was a crossroads of psychoanalysis, social reform, Jewish orthodoxy, and existentialist philosophy. With the advent of Hitler she left Germany in 1933 and went to the U.S., where she joined the Washington Psychoanalytic Society in 1935, worked at the William Alanson White Institute in New York, and at Chestnut Lodge in Rockville, Maryland. She believed in the voluntary acceptance of life's commitments and in acquiring the strength to accept criticism. She was also fearlessly critical, for instance, of Freud's concept of narcissistic neurosis, a psychotic withdrawal which he held to be inaccessible to treatment. She stimulated the application of linguistic and communications research to psychoanalysis, when participating in 1955 and 1957 at the Center for Advanced Studies in the Behavioral Sciences, Stanford, California. She influenced a wide circle of pupils. Her major books include *Principles of Intensive Psychotherapy* (1950) and *Psychoanalysis and Psychotherapy* (1959, with full bibliography).

Bibliography: A. Grinstein, *Index of Psychoanalytic Writings*, 2 (1957), 701–3; 6 (1964), 3256–58; *Journal of the American Medical Association*, 164 (Aug. 3, 1957), 1601. [J.A.Sch.]

FRUG, SHIMON SHMUEL (1860–1916), Yiddish poet. Frug was born in a Jewish agricultural colony in Kherson province, Russia; he was self-educated. He began his poetic career writing in Russian, published three volumes of verse, and was the first poet to treat Jewish themes in Russian verse. His poem "The Goblet," written under the impact of the pogroms of 1881, was translated into Yiddish as *Der Kos* by I. L. Peretz and sung by Jews the world over. Soon Frug himself began to write in Yiddish, but his first collection of Yiddish songs and ballads did not appear until 1896. A complete edition in three volumes followed in 1904 and again, with additions, in 1910. His Yiddish national songs were keyed to the needs of his generation. In his popular song *Zamd un Shtern* ("Sand and Stars") he argues with God, asking why He had only fulfilled half His promise to Abraham, making Jews as numerous as sand: but "where are the stars?" The song *Hot Rakhmones* ("Have Pity"), composed after the Kishinev Pogrom of 1903, bore the refrain "Have pity, give shrouds for the dead and for the living—bread." It was recited and sung at mass meetings protesting against Czarist oppression of Jews. In his socialist and Zionist lyrics, he pleaded for a return of the Jews to productive labor on their ancestral soil. His songs

Shimon Shmuel Frug, Yiddish poet.

inspired the early Zionist pioneers. He also composed ballads based on Jewish folklore, of which the best known is *"Dem Shames Tokhter,* "The Sexton's Daughter," a Jewish parallel to the Greek tale of Admetus and Alcestis. Frug, who suffered from poverty, misfortune, illness, and family troubles in his last years in Odessa, characterized himself as a poet who wept all his life.

Bibliography: Rejzen, Leksikon, 3 (1929), 138–62; Feinberg, in: JBA, 17 (1959/60), 65–72; Singer, *ibid.*, 24 (1966/67), 87–90; S. Liptzin, *Flowering of Yiddish Literature* (1963), 65–72; E. H. Jeshurin, *S. Frug, Bibliografye* (1960); L. Wiener, *History of Yiddish Literature* (1899).

[M.RAV.]

FRUMKIN, ALEKSANDR NAUMOVICH (1895–), Russian physical chemist. He graduated from the University of Odessa in 1915, where he taught 1920–22. In 1928–29 he was lecturer on colloid chemistry at the University of Wisconsin, and from 1930 professor of electrochemistry at the University of Moscow. Frumkin was director of the Institute of Physical Chemistry of the U.S.S.R. Academy of Sciences 1939–49, and from 1958 of the Academy's Institute of Electrochemistry. He became an academician in 1932, and was awarded the Lenin Prize in 1931 and the Stalin Prize in 1941. He wrote on surface phenomena, the theory of electrochemical processes, the electric double layer, diffusion processes in solution under the influence of electric fields, and other topics. His work has been applied in the U.S.S.R. to the generation of electricity by chemical means, the wetting of metals by electrolytes, flotation, and heterogenous catalysis. He was the author of *Elektrokapillyarnye yavleniya i elektrodnye potentsialy* ("Electrocapillary Effects and Electrode Potentials," 1919) and a co-author of *Kinetika elektrodnykh protsessov* ("Kinetics of Electrode Processes," 1952). [S.A.M.]

FRUMKIN, ARYEH LEIB (1845–1916), rabbinical scholar and writer; pioneer of Jewish settlement in Ereẓ Israel. Frumkin studied rabbinics in his native Kelme, Lithuania, and at the Slobodka Yeshivah. He visited Ereẓ Israel in 1867, and after two years in Odessa, returned to Jerusalem in 1871. There he began research for a history of the rabbis and scholars of Jerusalem, *Toledot Ḥakhmei Yerushalayim* (Vilna, 1874; ed. by E. Rivlin, Jerusalem, 1928–30, repr. 1969, with biography and index). Frumkin's account of his first visit to Jerusalem, *Massa Even Shemu'el* (1871), gives important source material on conditions in Ereẓ Israel at the time. Returning to Lithuania, Frumkin was ordained a rabbi and took a rabbinical post at Ilukste, Latvia. After

Aryeh Leib Frumkin, pioneer settler of Ereẓ Israel. Courtesy Sarah Epstein, Tel Aviv.

the 1881 pogroms, Frumkin participated, representing Ḥovevei Zion, in the consultations held in Germany to consider the plight of Russian Jewry. There he advocated settlement in Ereẓ Israel as a solution, opposing emigration to the United States. With the financial support of Emil Lachman, a wealthy Berlin Jew, he bought land in *Petaḥ Tikvah, built the first house there, and began a heroic ten-year period as a farmer-scholar, braving malaria and other dangers, establishing a *talmud torah* and a small yeshivah, and persuading more settlers to move there from *Yehud. Lachman eventually refused to continue endowing the enterprise and Frumkin was compelled to leave the settlement. In 1894 he went to London and was active in Jewish life in the East End. He established a wine business, using the income to return to Ereẓ Israel in 1911, where he lived first in Jerusalem and then returned to Petaḥ Tikvah.

Apart from *Toledot Ḥakhmei Yerushalayim*, Frumkin's main contribution to Jewish scholarship is his edition of *Seder Rav Amram* (of *Amram ben Sheshna) which he published as a large *siddur* (from an Oxford Ms.), with a commentary and notes (Jerusalem, 1910–12). He also published a biographical sketch of his uncle, Elias b. Jacob, called *Toledot Eliyahu* (1900), a Passover *Haggadah* (with *Gei Ḥizzayon* commentary, 1913), and an edition of the Book of Esther with two commentaries (1893).

Bibliography: M. Harizman and J. Poleskin, *Sefer ha-Yovel le-Fetaḥ Tikvah* (1929), 321–51; E. Rivlin, in: A. L. Frumkin, *Toledot Ḥakhmei Yerushalayim*, 1 (1928), 11–56, first pagin.; A. I. Trywaks and E. Steinman, *Sefer Me'ah Shanah* (1938), 399–410.

[ED.]

FRUMKIN, BORIS MARKOVICH (1872–after 1939), pioneer of the *Bund and among its most prominent publicists; first historian of the Jewish labor movement in Russia. From the middle 1890's, Frumkin ranked among the leading ideologists of the Jewish Social Democrat circles in Minsk. He was the editor of the *Arbayter Bletel* of Minsk (1897), the first periodical published by the Jewish Social Democrats in Russia. He helped to organize the Bund in Lodz, where he was imprisoned in 1898 for revolutionary activity. In 1906 he left Russia and became a member of the "Committee Abroad" of the Bund and secretary of the Organization of Workers' Societies and Relief Groups for the Bund Abroad. After his return to Russia, he was again active in Lodz and edited (1913–14) the principal legalized organ of the Bund in St. Petersburg, *Di Tsayt, Undzer Tsayt*. After the February 1917 Revolution, Frumkin wrote for the Bundist press. Later, he disappeared from the literary and public scene. He appears to have been still alive on the eve of World War II, but there is no information available on his end.

Frumkin's historiographical writings include: *Iz istorii revolyutsionnogo dvizheniya sredi yevreyev v 1870-kh godakh* ("From the History of the Revolutionary Movement among the Jews in the 1870s"), in: *Yevreyskaya Starina*, 4 (1911), 221–48, 513–40; *Ocherki iz istorii yevreyskogo rabochego dvizheniya v Rossii 1885–1897* ("From the History of the Jewish Labor Movement in Russia 1885–1897"), *ibid.*, 6 (1913), 108–22, 245–63; and *Zubatovshchina i yevreyskoye rabocheye dvizheniye* ("The Zubatov Movement and the Jewish Labor Movement"), in: *Perezhitoye*, 3 (1911), 199–223. Over the signature of "B. Gorenberg" he wrote the Bund's report on the problem of emigration, *Zur Emigrationsfrage* (also Yid., *Emigratsye un Imigratsye*) for the Stuttgart congress of the Second International (1907). He was coauthor of *Der "Bund" in der Revolutsye fun 1905–06* ("The 'Bund' in the Revolution of 1905–06" 1930), which also appeared in *Archiv fuer Sozialwissenschaft und Sozialpolitik*.

Bibliography: F. Kursky, *Gesamlte Shriftn* (1952), index; *Di Geshikhte fun Bund*, 2 vols. (1960–62), indexes.

[M.M.]

FRUMKIN, ISRAEL DOV (1850–1914), pioneer journalist in Ereẓ Israel. Frumkin was born in Dubrovno, Belorussia and was taken to Jerusalem when he was nine. In 1870 he started contributing to the weekly *Ḥavaẓẓelet* founded by his father-in-law, Israel *Bak. Frumkin soon became its publisher and editor, and turned it into a militant paper that attacked financial corruption in the Jerusalem community. His enemies caused the sporadic banning of his paper and even his imprisonment. In *Ḥavaẓẓelet* he advocated the consolidation of the separate communities in Jerusalem, higher standards in education, and the inclusion of secular studies and vocational training in the schools. His early support of agricultural settlement in Ereẓ Israel turned to adamant opposition as its secular character became apparent. Frumkin was especially hostile to Aḥad Ha-Am, the Ḥovevei Zion, and the Herzl brand of Zionsim in Ereẓ Israel. He also fiercely opposed missionary activities. *Ḥavaẓẓelet* declined after the turn of the century and ceased publication in 1910.

Bibliography: I. Kressel, in: *Mivhar Kitvei I. D. Frumkin* (1954), 13–114, 205–29; G. Frumkin, *Derekh Shofet bi-Yrushalayim* (1955), opening chapters; *Tidhar*, 1 (1947), 489–91. [Y.S.]

FRÝD, NORBERT (or **Nora**; 1913–), Czech novelist. Frýd wrote several significant books about the Holocaust. He spent World War II in the concentration camps of Theresienstadt, Birkenau, and Dachau. A Communist from his youth, Frýd entered the Czechoslovak Foreign Service after the war and spent several years as cultural attaché in Mexico. His tour of duty there inspired a novel based on the social struggle of the Mexican Indians, *Studna supů* ("Well of Vultures," 1953), and three fiercely anti-American works—*Mexiko je v Americe* ("Mexico Is in America," 1952), *Případ majora Hogana* ("The Case of Major Hogan," 1952) and *Usměvavá Guatemala* ("Smiling Guatemala," 1955). He recorded his experiences as an inmate of the Nazi death camps in his best novel, *Krabice živých* ("A Box of Living People," 1956). In 1963 Frýd received a government decoration for his literary achievements, and in 1966 was awarded one of the highest Czech literary prizes for a trilogy of novels dealing with the fate of several Jewish families from the Sudetenland. These were: *Vzorek bez ceny* ("Sample without Value," 1966), *Hedvábné starosti* ("Silken Worries," 1968), and *Omíč národů* ("Ball of Nations").

Bibliography: J. Kunc, *Slovník českých spisovatelů beletristů* (1957). [Av.D.]

FUBINI, GUIDO (1879–1943), Italian mathematician. Fubini was professor of mathematics at Catania in 1901, at Genoa in 1906, and at Turin from 1908 until the Fascist anti-Jewish laws resulted in his dismissal in 1938. He emigrated in the following year to the United States and worked successively at the Institute of Advanced Studies, Princeton, and New York University. Fubini, who was a member of the Accademia Nazionale dei Lincei, made important contributions to projective differential geometry, theory of Lie groups and analysis. His collected works in three volumes entitled *Opere Scelte* (1957–62) were publishing two monographs, *Alfred de Vigny* (1922), and record of his publications together with a biographical introduction. [B.S.]

FUBINI, MARIO (1900–), Italian literary historian and critic. Born in Turin, Fubini was first a schoolteacher and later a professor of Italian literature at the universities of Palermo (1937–39), Trieste (1945–49), and Milan (from 1949). He took an early interest in French literature, publishing two monographs, *Alfred de Vigny* (1922) and *Jean Racine e la critica delle sue tragedie* (1925), but subsequently concentrated on Italian literature, particularly that of the Renaissance and Romantic periods. He wrote a number of studies of fundamental importance including *Ugo Foscolo* (1928); *Studi sulla critica letteraria del Settecento* (1934); *Vittorio Alfieri: il pensiero—la tragedia* (1937, 1960[3]); *Dal Muratori al Baretti* (1946); *Foscolo Minore* (1949); *Ritratto dell'Alfieri e altri studi alfieriani* (1951, 1963[2]); *Romanticismo italiano* (1953); and *La cultura illuministica in Italia* (1957). Stressing the indissolubility of the connection between culture and literature, Fubini formulated various modifications of Croce's aesthetics, to which he basically adhered. The results of Fubini's research on linguistic problems are contained in *Stile e umanità di Giambattista Vico* (1946); *Studi sulla letteratura del Rinascimento* (1947); and *Metrica e poesia* (1962). An authority on Dante, Fubini also published a collection of essays, *Il peccato di Ulisse e altri studi danteschi* (1966). He was editor of the *Giornale Storico della Letteratura Italiana*.

Bibliography: Attisano, in: *Momenti e Problemi di Storia dell' Estetica*, 4 (1961), 1533–35. [L.C.]

FUCHS, ABRAHAM MOSHE (1890–), Yiddish short-story writer. Born in Ozerna, East Galicia, Fuchs lived variously in Lemberg, New York, and Vienna, where he served until 1938 as correspondent of the New York *Jewish Daily Forward*. Many of his manuscripts were lost in 1938 when he fled from the Nazis and went to London. In 1950 he settled in Israel. Fuchs began to publish short stories in periodicals in 1911. His books are: *Eynzame* (1912), *Oyfen Bergl* (1924), *Unter der Brik* (1924), *Di Nakht un der Tog* (1961), which includes *Der Alter Volf*, a masterpiece of narrative art, which was translated into Hebrew. Fuchs' protagonists are poor Galician Jewish villagers, and he describes their natural surroundings. His later tales are set in Israel.

Bibliography: Rejzen, Leksikon, 3 (1929), 26–32; M. Ravitch, *Mayn Leksikon*, 3 (1958), 334–8; S. Bickel, *Shrayber fun Mayn Dor*, 2 (1965), 361–6. [J.S.]

FUCHS, ALFRED (1892–1941), Czech journalist and author. In his youth he was a Zionist, but later he became an assimilationist and edited publications of the organized assimilationist movement of Czech Jews (see *Čechů Židů, Svaz). Ultimately he was baptized and became one of the leading Catholic publicists in Czechoslovakia. He learned Hebrew in order to read kabbalistic literature (together with his friend, the ḥasidic poet Jiří Mordechai *Langer), but found greater affinity in the Catholic mystic philosophers. After a career with the Catholic press, he became chief of the press department of the prime minister's office. He was a leading expert on canon law and published a number of penetrating studies on Vatican policy. Fuchs described his road to Catholicism in an autobiographical novel *Oltář a rotačka* ("Altar and Printing Press"). He never concealed his Jewish origin, and at the peak of the anti-Semitic wave under Hitler, he wrote that if he were forced to wear the yellow star of David, he would wear that and his Vatican decorations with equal pride. In 1941 he was taken by the Gestapo from a monastery where he had found refuge and died in the Dachau concentration camp.

Bibliography: O. Donath, *Židé a židovství v české literatuře 19. a 20. století* (1930); F. Langer, *Byli a bylo* (1963); E. Hostovský, in: *Jews of Czechoslovakia*, 1 (1968), index. [Av.D.]

FUCHS, MOSES ẒEVI (1843–1911), Hungarian rabbi. He was born in Lovasbereny, where his father, Benjamin Ze'ev Wolf, was rabbi, and Moses succeeded him in 1873. In 1882 he moved to Grosswardein (now Oradea), Rumania, where he served until his death. His *Yad Ramah* (1940) includes important halakhic responsa, many of which reflect the problems facing European Jewry in his time.

Fuchs saw in Ḥasidism an antidote to Haskalah and assimilation, stating in one of his responsa: "The love of God and His Torah is the essence and source of Ḥasidism. When economic circumstances permit, one should occupy oneself in the study of Torah with deep deliberation and spiritual joy. It is also important to visit the *zaddik* from time to time, in order to learn from his ways. The wise man should learn from the *zaddikim* and their true disciples but pay no attention to the masses who go running after them."

Bibliography: S. N. Gottlieb, *Oholei Shem* (1912), 226; Z. Schwartz, *Shem ha-Gedolim me-Erez Hagar*, 2 (1914), 14b–15a; E. Goldmann, *Shalshelet Zahav* (1942), 9–46.

[N.B.-M.]

FUENN, SAMUEL JOSEPH (1818–1890), Hebrew writer of the more traditional wing of the Russian Haskalah and an early member of Ḥovevei Zion. Fuenn, who was born in Vilna, received a traditional Jewish education, and afterward joined the circle of Haskalah supporters there. He was a founder of the first Jewish school in the city (1841) where he taught Bible and Hebrew. Together with L. Hurwitz he published the literary magazine *Pirḥei Zafon* (1841–44), the first such Hebrew work to appear in Russia. When the government rabbinical school opened in Vilna in 1847 he joined it as a teacher of Bible and Hebrew language. In 1856 he was appointed inspector of the government Jewish schools in the Vilna District. In 1863 he opened a Hebrew printing press in Vilna. He edited and published *Ha-Karmel* (1860–81) which appeared first as a weekly and then as a monthly. Fuenn wrote extensively in Hebrew and Russian for this periodical, and his articles included studies of the history of Russian Jewry and literary criticism, as well as the first chapters of his autobiography, *Dor ve-Doreshav*. Because of his moderate views on the Haskalah, his traditional way of life, and his financial independence, Fuenn achieved a prominent role in the leadership of the Vilna Jewish community. He was also highly respected by the civilian authorities and was the recipient of government medals. When the Ḥibbat Zion movement began, he helped establish a society in Vilna and headed it, together with L. Levanda. He was later elected to the central committee in Russia. In his later years Fuenn devoted himself to two important works. The first was a biographical lexicon of notable Jews, *Keneset Yisrael* (1886–90). The second was an extensive Hebrew dictionary, *Ha-Ozar*, which was the first in the history of Hebrew lexicography to cover the Bible, Mishnah, Talmud, the Hebrew poets, and medieval philosophers; the dictionary also included a translation of terms into Russian and German. Only the first volume, comprising the first seven letters *alef* to *zayin*, appeared in the author's lifetime; the remaining three volumes were completed from Fuenn's notes by S. P. *Rabbinowitz (1900–03). For the meaning of Hebrew words Fuenn relies upon the works of the medieval grammarians, especially Ibn Janaḥ and David Kimḥi, as well as modern lexicographers. His Hebrew dictionary is a summary of the knowledge available in his generation, which still lacks systematic etymological insight. Its strong point is the collection of references to the sources, the Mishnah, the Jerusalem Talmud, liturgical, and Aramaic texts. He died in Vilna. Fuenn's other works include a history of the Second Temple, *Divrei ha-Yamim li-Venei Yisrael* (Vilna, 1871–77), *Kiryah Ne'emanah* (Vilna, 1860), a monograph on the Vilna community, and a number of textbooks and translations of juvenile historical novels and short stories.

Bibliography: Klausner, Sifrut, 4 (1953[2]), 115–20; Z. Vilnai, in: *Gilyonot*, 15 (1943), 236–43; G. Elkoshi, in: *Yahadut Vilna*, 1 (1959), 438–41.

[Y.S.]

FUERST, JULIUS (pseudonym **Alsari**, 1805–1873), Polish Hebraist, bibliographer, and historian. Fuerst was born in Zerkow, Poland, the son of a *darshan* ("expounder" of the Bible). He studied at the University of Berlin, where Hegel was one of his teachers, and at the universities of Breslau and Halle, where he was the pupil of *Gesenius. He settled in Leipzig and taught Hebrew, Syriac, Aramaic grammar and literature, Bible exegesis, and other subjects at the university there (professor, 1864).

Fuerst owes his reputation to his monumental bibliographical work *Bibliographica Judaica* (2 vols., 1849–51, 2 vols. in 3, 1863[2], reprint 1960). The work is based solely on his findings without taking into account the important research done in the field by his contemporary M. *Steinschneider. His history of the Karaites, *Geschichte des Karaeerthums* (3 vols., 1862–69), was superseded by later works, even by the time of its publication. Fuerst also wrote *Lehrgebaeude der aramaeischen Idiome* (1835), *Ḥaruzei Peninim* (1836), *Ozar Leshon ha-Kodesh* (1837–40), a revision of *Buxtorf's Bible concordance in collaboration with Franz *Delitzsch, and *Hebraeisches und Chaldaeisches Handwoerterbuch ueber das Alte Testament* (2 vols., 1851–61), with the supplement *Zur Geschichte der Hebraeischen Lexicographie* (1867[3]; translated into English by S. Davidson, *A Hebrew and Chaldee Lexicon to the Old Testament*). He translated Saadiah Gaon's *Emunot ve-De'ot* into German (1845), and wrote a comprehensive history of Hebrew literature, *Geschichte der juedischen Literatur und des juedisch-hellenistischen Schrifttums* (2 vols., 1867–70); *Der Kanon des Alten Testaments nach den ueberlieferungen in Talmud und Midrasch* (1868); and several Hebrew-Aramaic dictionaries and grammars. He collaborated with L. *Zunz and also worked on the publication of an edition of the Bible, *Illustrierte Prachtbibel* (1874), comprising 24 books with German translation and explanatory notes. He was a close friend of Franz Delitzsch, whom he assisted in writing his work on the history of Jewish poetry.

Fuerst founded and edited the weekly magazine *Orient* (1840–52), in whose scientific supplement *Literaturblatt des Orients* many of his scientific articles were published. Although most of Fuerst's works are by now obsolete, he is thought to be one of the forerunners of scientific research in all branches of Judaic studies. His library was bequeathed to the *Hochschule fuer die Wissenschaft des Judentums in Berlin.

Bibliography: M. Steinschneider, in: HB, 13 (1873), 140; Fuenn, Keneset, 438–40; W. Schochow, *Deutsch-juedische Geschichtswissenschaft* (1969), 286–7.

[Ed.]

FUERSTENBERG, CARL (1850–1933), German banker. Born in Danzig, Fuerstenberg worked for the Berlin banking house of S. *Bleichroeder from 1871 to 1883, when he left to join the Berliner Handels-Gesellschaft, another prominent issuing and investment bank. Under Fuerstenberg's guidance the Berliner Handels-Gesellschaft developed close connections with the German mining, heavy, and electrical industries, and introduced Russian and United States securities on the Berlin Stock Exchange. Fuerstenberg also established firm relations with the New York firm of *Hallgarten and Company which were useful after World War I, when Germany needed foreign credit. Fuerstenberg, who was known for his caustic wit, refused all offers of titles and decorations. His memoirs were published by his son Hans (*Erinnerungen*, 1965).

Bibliography: H. Fuerstenberg, *Carl Fuerstenberg* (Ger., 1962); *Berliner Handels-Gesellschaft in einem Jahrhundert deutscher Wirtschaft* (1956).

[J.O.R.]

FUERTH (Heb. פיורדא, פירד), city in Bavaria, W. Germany. Jewish moneylenders are mentioned there in 1440. They were later expelled, but in 1528 Jews were allowed to resettle in the town. There were 200 Jewish residents in 1582. A rabbi is mentioned in 1607. The Jews were

Figure 1. The Jewish cemetery in Fuerth; early 18th-century etching by J. A. Boener. Courtesy Fuerth Municipality. Photo Knut Meyer.

represented on the municipal council by two of their *parnasim*. The community dispersed during the Thirty Years' War (1618–48). In 1670 refugees from Vienna augmented the Jewish community, which was concentrated around the Geleitsgasse. The "old synagogue" (near Koenigstrasse) was built in 1617, a new one in 1697, and that of the *Fraenkel family in 1707. The first cemetery dates from 1607 and the hospital *(hekdesh)* from 1653.

In 1719 the status of the community (consisting of 400 households) was regulated by the bishop. In return for annual payments, the Jews were promised protection for their lives and property; they were allowed to build synagogues and to employ a cantor, beadle *(Schulklopfer)*, and gravedigger; cases between Jews were to be tried by a Jewish court, while litigation between Jews and gentiles came under the jurisdiction of the cathedral court. The Fuerth community regulated its internal affairs by a series of *takkanot* in 1728. The first Jewish orphanage in Germany was established in Fuerth in 1763 and from the 17th century until 1824 there was an important yeshivah in the town. An Orthodox elementary school was established in 1862 and officially recognized as a secondary school in 1899. In 1811 Elkan *Henle of Fuerth published a pamphlet calling for emancipation of the Jews in Bavaria; Gruensfeld of Fuerth became the first Jewish lawyer in Bavaria (1843), David Morgenstern, the first Jewish deputy to the Landtag (1849), and Solomon Berolzheimer, the first Jewish judge (1863). Fuerth Jews contributed much to the economic, cultural, and political development of the city.

Figure 2. Portal of the main synagogue of Fuerth, destroyed by the Nazis in 1938. Courtesy Fuerth Municipality. Photo Knut Meyer.

Hebrew printing was begun in Fuerth in 1691 by S. S. Schneur and his sons Joseph and Abraham and son-in-law Isaac Bing. From 1691 to 1698 they issued 35 works, including **Sifra* with commentaries. Hirsch Frankfurter opened a press which issued nine books, between 1691 and 1701. Confiscations of Hebrew books from 1702 onward account for a pause in printing until it was resumed by the Schneur family from 1722 to 1730. Between 1737 and 1774, Ḥayyim b. Hirsch of Wilhermsdorf published 80 works and his press continued in the family till 1868; their non-Jewish successor issued a Pentateuch with *haftarot* as late as 1876. Between 1760 and 1792 Isaac b. Loeb Buchbinder (not Bamberg) printed 73 Hebrew books. Joseph Petschau and his son Mendel Beer printed 17 books between 1762 and 1769. S. B. Gusdorfer was active as a printer from 1852 to 1867.

The Jewish population numbered 1,500 in 1720; 2,434 in 1816 (19% of the total); 3,336 in 1880; and 2,000 (2.6% of the total) in 1933. On Nov. 10, 1938, the main synagogue was burned down; the other six synagogues and innumerable Jewish shops and homes were demolished. By May 17, 1939, only 785 Jews remained; the last 38 were deported to *Auschwitz on June 18, 1943. In 1967 the synagogue was restored and consecrated. There were 200 Jews living in Fuerth in 1970.

Bibliography: F. Neubuerger, in: MGWJ, 45 (1901), 404–22, 510–39; M. Brann, in: *Gedenkbuch D. Kaufmann* (1900), 385–450; L. Loewenstein, *Zur Geschichte der Juden in Fuerth* (1913, 1967[2]) (=JJLG, 6 (1909), 153–233); S. Schwarz, *Juden in Bayern* (1963); PK; *Nachrichten fuer den juedischen Buerger Fuerths* (1961–to date); H. Barbeck, *Geschichte der Juden in Nuernberg und Fuerth* (1878).

[Z.F.]

FUERTH, HENRIETTE (1861–1938), German social worker. Fuerth was born in Katzenstein, Germany. Herself the mother of 11 children, she was one of the founders of the Mother's Welfare Movement, an organization which concerned itself with family and health problems affecting mothers and their families. She established and directed the Organization for the Prevention of Venereal Diseases. Interested in politics as a means of achieving her welfare goals, she served for nine years as a socialist member of the Frankfort City Council.

She wrote a great number of books and articles on social welfare, especially in relation to working women, sexual problems in society, and population policy. Among her works: *Staat und Sittlichkeit* (1912), *Die soziale Bedeutung der Kaeufersitten* (1917), *Kulturideale und Frauentum* (1906).

[J.N.]

FUKS, ALEXANDER (1917–), Israel historian. Fuks was born in Wloclawiek, Poland, and joined the history faculty of the Hebrew University in 1949, being appointed professor of ancient history and classics. Fuks is the author of numerous scholarly articles, including studies of political life in classical Athens, and social revolution in Sparta in the Hellenistic period. In the field of Jewish history, he wrote "Aspects of the Jewish Revolt in A.D. 115–117" (*Journal of Roman Studies*, 51 (1961), 98–104) and "The Jewish Revolt in Egypt (A.D. 115–117) in the Light of the Papyri" (*Aegyptus*, 33 (1953), 131–58). He collaborated with Victor *Tcherikover on the *Corpus Papyrorum Judaicorum* (3 vols., 1957–69), a collection of papyri written in Greek relating to Jews and Jewish affairs.

[Ir.M.]

FUKS, LAJB (1908–), librarian and Yiddish scholar. Born in Poland, Fuks went to Holland in 1939. In 1946 he became assistant librarian of the Bibliotheca Rosenthaliana, the Hebraica and Judaica Department of the Amsterdam University Library (see Jewish *Libraries), and was its librarian from 1949. He lectured in modern Hebrew and Yiddish at the University of Amsterdam from 1964. His main scholarly interest was the history of Old-Yiddish language and literature. He wrote *The Oldest Known Literary Document of Yiddish Literature (c. 1382)*, 2 vols. (1957); and *Die hebraeischen und aramaeischen Quellen des altjiddischen Epos Melokîm-Bûk* (1964). His other works deal with the history of Dutch Jewry, especially the history of Hebrew printing and bibliography in Holland (1957). He was the editor of and frequent contributor to the *Studia Rosenthaliana* from its founding in 1967. [H.Bo.]

°**FULBERT OF CHARTRES** (d. 1028 or 1030), bishop of Chartres (France). In 1009, Fulbert delivered a series of three sermons based on Genesis 49:10: "The scepter shall not depart from Judah." They dealt with Jewish objections to the Christian argument that since royalty no longer existed among the Jews, the Messiah had already come and that he was Jesus. The Jews claimed that their present distress was only temporary, as had been their captivity in Babylon; moreover, there might be Jewish kings in other parts of the world and there were still wise and powerful Jews who enjoyed an almost royal power.

Bibliography: J.-P. Migne (ed.), *Patrologia Latina*, 141 (1880), 305–18; B. Blumenkranz, *Juifs et Chrétiens* . . . (1960), index; idem, *Les auteurs chrétiens latins* . . . (1963), 237–43. [B.Bl.]

FULD, AARON BEN MOSES (1790–1847), defender of Orthodoxy and communal worker in his native Frankfort. Fuld in his early youth met R. Phinehas ha-Levy Horowitz, author of the *Hafla'ah*, and was close to the circle of his son, Ẓevi Hirsch Horowitz. He was also a pupil of Solomon Zalman Trier who headed the Frankfort *bet din*, and to whom he used to refer as: "my esteemed teacher, the high priest." Fuld engaged in business and never held any rabbinical post. Although opposed to the Reform movement, he strove for the inclusion of secular subjects in the curriculum of Jewish schools. In a letter to Akiva *Eger, Fuld asked for the approval of a curriculum in which secular subjects were included, stressing that the rabbis of "every city and province should strive with all their might that there be no slackening of the study of these subjects, essential nowadays so as not to provide an opening for the criticism of those who have risen against us" (*Beit Aharon*, Introd., V–VI). In another letter, of 1843, written on behalf of the Frankfort rabbinate, he protested strongly against the desecration of the Sabbath and the abolition of circumcision, attendant upon the strengthening of the Reform movement. On one occasion, when Fuld was rebuked by Moses *Sofer (Schreiber) for having, according to his informant Akiva b. Abraham Moses *Lehren, permitted shaving during the intermediate days of a festival, he wrote a letter of vindication, stating, "Those who said I permitted shaving during the intermediate days have spoken falsely about me, for such a thing never entered my mind" (*Beit Aharon*, introd., II). At the same time, Sofer mentions Fuld with respect in his responsa as "the sharp-witted, learned rabbi" (responsa *Ḥatam Sofer*, YD (1841), nos. 88, 224, 319, 323).

Fuld's work, *Beit Aharon* comprises five sections: (1) *Meshivei Milḥamah Sha'rah*, 17 responsa written between 1823 and 1830; (2) glosses to the Talmud; (3) glosses to the Arukh (also published as an appendix to the 1959 edition of Arukh); (4) *Haggahot ha-Tishbi* to the *Sefer ha-Tishbi* (Isry, 1541) of Elijah b. Asher ha-Levi Baḥur; (5) *Haggahot ha-Meturgeman* to the *Sefer ha-Meturgeman* (*ibid.*, 1541) of Elijah b. Asher ha-Levi Baḥur. Fuld's notes to the *Shem ha-Gedolim* of Ḥ. J. D. Azulai were published at the end of volume two of the Frankfort edition (1847).

Bibliography: Ḥ. M. Horowitz, in: A. Fuld, *Beit Aharon* (1890), i–xiv (introd.); S. A. Trier, *Rabbinische Gutachten ueber die Beschneidung* (1844), xix. [Y.Ho.]

FULD, STANLEY HOWELLS (1903–), U.S. attorney. After occupying a number of state legal offices in New York, Fuld was appointed to the New York Court of Appeals in 1946. In 1966 he was elected chief judge of the Court of Appeals in the State of New York. Fuld defended personal rights against what he believed was infringement by the state, often dissenting in cases such as eavesdropping, public school prayers, and the Fifth Amendment. He was a member of the New York County Republican Committee and was active in communal and Jewish affairs. He was chairman of the law division of the Joint Defense Appeal (1945–46), the National Hillel Commission (1947–56), and the board of the Jewish Theological Seminary (1966–). [Ed.]

FULDA, city in Hesse, W. Germany. Jews are first mentioned there in 1235, when 34 martyrs were burned to death following a *blood libel. Emperor *Frederick II, after inquiries, refuted the charge in his judgment of the case. The martyrs were commemorated by Pesaḥ ha-Kohen, a relative and friend of some of the victims, in three *seliḥot*. In 1301 King Albert I pledged the taxes of the Jews of the diocese to the abbot of Fulda. In 1310 Henry VII transferred full authority over them to the abbot. In 1349 they fell victim to the *Black Death persecutions. Jews had been readmitted to Fulda by 1399. By the 16th century Fulda became the seat of a rabbinate which extended its jurisdiction over the entire region, for some time as far as *Kassel. At the Frankfort *synod of 1603 Fulda was made the seat of one of the five Jewish district courts in Germany. *Aaron Samuel b. Moses Shalom of Kremenets taught at the yeshivah from 1615 to 1620, and Meir b. Jacob ha-Kohen *Schiff (Maharam Schiff) from 1622 to 1640. Judah b. Samuel Mehler, who studied in Fulda and left the city in 1629 at the age of 20, wrote an informative autobiography. Jews of Fulda dealt in wine-retailing but were opposed by the burghers. Regulations restricting Jewish trade were issued in 1699, 1739, 1788, and 1792. There were 75 Jewish families living in Fulda in 1633 (compared with 292 Christian households). The whole community, apart from five families, was expelled in 1677. By 1708 their number had increased to 19 taxpayers. The community had a well, and owned houses, homesteads, and stables in the Jews' street (first mentioned in 1367); by 1740 some lived outside this area. The synagogue and bathhouse were located on the "Jews' Hill" near the community's hospital, and the cemetery in a suburb. A Jewish school was established in 1784. The community numbered 321 in 1860; 675 in 1905; 957 in 1913 (4.26% of the total population);

The old synagogue of Fulda, destroyed by the Nazis in 1938. Courtesy Magistrat der Stadt Fulda.

1,137 in 1925 (4.44%); and 1,058 in June 1933 (3.8%). Under its rabbi, Michael Cahn (1849–1919), Fulda was a center of Orthodoxy. Its yeshivah remained open until 1939. The synagogue was set on fire in November 1938, and in 1940 the cemetery was destroyed. Four hundred and fifteen Jews remained in Fulda on May 17, 1939; 131 of those unable to leave were deported to Riga on Dec. 12, 1941, and an additional 122 in 1942 to *Theresienstadt and unknown destinations in the East. The few Jews who survived the Holocaust and returned to Fulda after the war turned their cemetery into a paved courtyard to protest against the frequent desecrations there. There were 17 Jews living in Fulda in 1967.

Bibliography: Germ Jud, 1 (1963), 113–4, 2 (1968), 267–8; G. Kisch, *Jews in Medieval Germany*... (1949), index; Bloch, in: *Festschrift... Martin Philippson* (1916), 114–34; Baron, Community, 1, 341–43; Baron, Social², 9 (1967), 143f., 311f.; 10 (1967), 146f., 359; 13 (1969), 201f.; Salfeld, Martyrol; M. Stern, in: ZGJD, 2 (1888), 194–9; L. Loewenstein, in: ZHB, 19 (1917), 26–37; A. Schmidt, *Führer durch Fulda* (1955³), 35; A. Jestadt, in: *Veroeffentlichungen des Fuldaer Geschichtsvereins*, 38 (1937), 55, 62–70; 40 (1950), 59; S. M. Auerbach, *The Auerbach Family: The Descendants of Abraham Auerbach* (1957), 78–80; FJW, 86, 200, 318; P. N. Emeking, *Das Hochstift Fulda unter seinem letzten Fuerstbischof* (1935), 119f.; E. Keyser (ed.), *Hessisches Staedtebuch* (1957), 174–76; PK.

[T.O.]

FULDA, LUDWIG (1862–1939), German playwright. Born in Frankfort, Fulda's early interest was the German baroque poets; his first play was *Christian Guenther* (1882), and this was followed by the study, *Die Gegner der zweiten schlesischen Schule* (1883). Fulda then came under the influence of Sudermann's Naturalism in Berlin, became an Ibsen enthusiast, and in 1889 helped to found the *Freie Buehne*. During this period he wrote plays of a sociological nature, such as *Das verlorene Paradies* (1892) and *Die Sklavin* (1892), remarkable for their clever stage effects and insight into social problems, but lacking in great depth or

Ludwig Fulda, German dramatist. Courtesy D.P.A., Frankfort.

style. Fulda's greatest success came with his change to a neo-romantic mood in *Der Talisman* (1892). This comedy on the theme of the fairy tale, "The Emperor's New Clothes," was awarded the Schiller Prize, but its performance was banned by the kaiser. *Die Zwillingsschwester* (1901) displayed his talent for writing graceful verse. Fulda published translations of Beaumarchais' *Figaro* (1897), Molière's plays (1892), Rostand's *Cyrano de Bergerac* (1898), Shakespeare's *Sonnets* (1914), Ibsen's poems and *Peer Gynt* (1916), and the Spanish dramatists' *Meisterlustspiele der Spanier*, 2 vols. (1925). In 1928 he was elected president of the Prussian Academy. He was dismissed after Hitler's rise to power and lived in retirement until the Nazis stripped him of his most prized possessions. He then committed suicide.

Bibliography: A. Klaar, *Ludwig Fulda* (Ger., 1922).

[S.L.S.]

FULVIA (1st century C.E.), Roman proselyte. A lady of high rank, she was attracted to Judaism and entered the Jewish faith. She was then persuaded by a certain Jew, who had come from Ereẓ Israel, to send presents of purple and gold to the Temple in Jerusalem. The gifts, deposited with this Jew and his three confederates, were never delivered. Fulvia urged her husband to report the matter to Emperor Tiberius. The latter thereupon expelled all the Jews from Rome (19 C.E.). Four thousand young Jews were drafted into military service and sent to fight the brigands in the island of Sardinia. The expulsion is mentioned by the Roman historians, Suetonius, Tacitus, and Dio Cassius, all of whom connect the incident in some manner with proselytism.

Bibliography: Jos., Ant., 18:81–84; Schuerer, Gesch, 3 (1909⁴), 168; Heidel, in: *American Journal of Philology*, 41 (1920), 38–47; Rogers, *ibid.*, 53 (1932), 252–6; Roth, Italy, 9f.; Vogelstein-Rieger, 1 (1896), 14f.

[I.G.]

FUNES, town in Navarre, northern Spain. A charter granted to Funes and the neighboring town of Viguera at the beginning of the 12th century also regulated relations between Jews and Christians, including the mode of establishing evidence in litigation. Ordeal by battle between Jews and Christians was prohibited and a high blood price was fixed for the murder of a Jew. Jewish landowners were required to pay tithes to the church. In 1171 King Sancho VI extended the same privileges to the Jews of Funes as those he had granted to the Jews of *Tudela in 1170, based on the *fuero* ("municipal charter") of Nájera. The Jews were freed from other dues in return for undertaking maintenance of the citadel of Funes, and they were not to be held responsible for the death of a Christian killed by them during an attack on the citadel, where they were living. The Jewish community had its own executive official, the *bedinus*. Much may be learned of life in the community in the 13th century from the list of fines imposed on members who had transgressed the law. Little of importance is known of the Jews in Funes from the 14th century onward.

Bibliography: M. Kayserling, *Die Juden in Navarra* (1861), index; Baer, Urkunden, 1 (1929), index.

[Ed.]

FUNK, CASIMIR (1884–1967), U.S. biochemist, originator of the word "vitamin." He was born in Warsaw, and obtained his doctorate at the University of Berne in 1904. In 1910 he went to the Lister Institute in London where he studied beriberi, a deficiency disease in rice eaters. He found a substance in rice shavings (and also in yeast and milk) which prevented the disease, and called it "vitamine." This was vitamin B, later known to be a complex of several vitamins. He worked as head of the department of chemistry at the Cancer Hospital Research Institute until he went to America in 1915. With the support of the Rockefeller Foundation, he went back to Warsaw as head of biochemistry at the School of Hygiene (1923–27). During 1928–39 he operated his own Casa Biochemica at Rueil-Malmaison, France, also serving as consultant from 1936 to the U.S. Vitamin Corporation. During World War II he returned to America, and from 1948 was president of the Funk Foundation for Medical Research. Funk contributed numerous papers to scientific periodicals on various matters of synthetic organic chemistry, and on other biochemical topics such as internal secretions, diabetes, and cancer. He wrote the books *Die Vitamine* (1914; *The Vitamins*, 1922). Funk's hypotheses on the importance of vitamins A, Bs, C and D to normal growth and development stimulated other investigators in the field of nutrition and laid the foundation of rational child nutrition and modern dietetics in general.

Bibliography: B. Harrow, *Casimir Funk, Pioneer in Vitamins and Hormones* (1955); S. R. Kagan, *Jewish Medicine* (1952), 192–3.

[S.A.M.]

FUNK, SOLOMON (1867–1928), rabbi and scholar. Funk was born in Hungary and served as rabbi at Sarajevo, Bosnia, Boskovice, Czechoslovakia, and in Vienna. Among his published works are: *Die haggadischen Elemente in den Homelien des persischen Weisen Aphraates* (1891); *Die Juden in Babylonien 200–500* (2 vols., 1902–08); *Grundprinzip des biblischen Strafrechts*... (1904), a comparative discussion of the Bible and the Hammurapi Code; *Entstehung des Talmuds* (1919²); and *Talmudproben* (1921²). The last two small but well-presented volumes, which appeared as volumes 479 and 583 in the popular Goeschen series, did much to convey a balanced view of the world of the Talmud to non-Jewish readers. Other publications of Funk were *Die Hygiene des Talmuds* (1912); "Bibel und Babel" (in *Monumenta Talmudica*, 1913); and a pro-Zionist tract, *Der Kampf um Zion*... (1921).

Bibliography: S. Krauss, in: *Die Wahrheit* (Dec. 11, 1925), 7; *Wiener Morgen-Zeitung* (Dec. 12, 1925); JJLG, 20 (1929), 7; *Arim ve-Immahot be-Yisrael*, 1 (1946), 279.

[N.B.-M.]

FURAYDIS, AL- (Ar. فُرَيْديس), Arab village in Israel at the foot of Mt. Carmel, near *Zikhron Ya'akov. The village of al-Furaydis and the nearby Jewish settlers developed close economic and social ties, which date back to the founding of Zikhron Ya'akov. During the *War of Independence (1948), the Arab village did not participate in the attacks on Jewish traffic in the vicinity. It was the only Arab village of the region which remained fully populated and unchanged after Israel's independence (1948). Al-Furaydis, with 2,810 inhabitants in 1969, engaged in intensive farming. Like the Hebrew word "Pardes," the village's name is assumed to be derived from the Greek "paradeisos" (the origin also of "paradise"). [E.O.]

FURST, MORITZ (1782–1840), early U.S. medalist. Furst was born near Pressburg (Bratislava), and after emigrating to the United States in 1807, he worked as an engraver for the United States Mint in Philadelphia from 1812 to 1839. He received quick recognition and 33 of his patriotic commemoratives and portraits are still issued by this mint; his best-known work was struck commemorating the War of 1812. He also did the first recorded American Jewish medal, the homage on the death in 1816 of the patriot and religious leader Gershom Mendes Seixas. Official portraits were struck by him for presidents James Monroe, John Quincy Adams, Andrew Jackson, and Martin Van Buren.

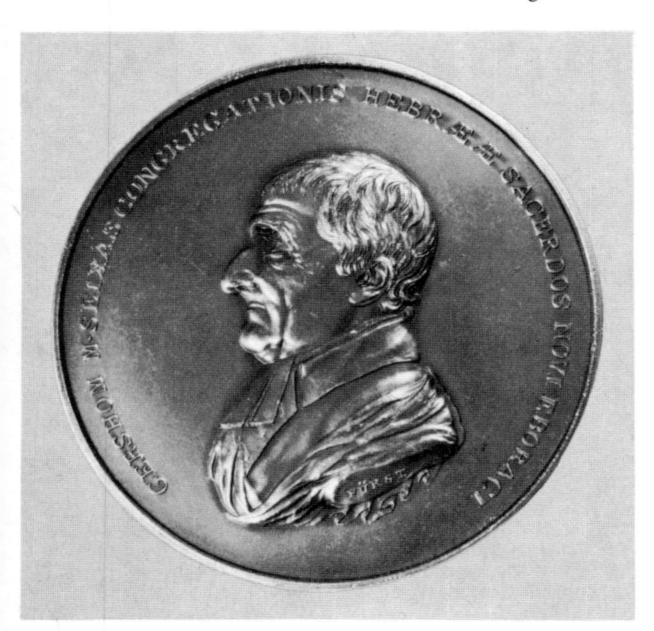

Medal engraved by Moritz Furst in memory of Gershom Mendes Seixas. New York, Daniel Friedenberg Collection.

Bibliography: *Magyar Zsidó Lexikon* (1929) 300; *Price List of Bronze Medals for Sale by the U.S. Mint;* D. M. Friedenberg, in: *The Numismatist* (July 1969), 904–5.

[D.M.F.]

FURTADO, ABRAHAM (1756–1817), politician and communal leader in France. His parents originally lived in Portugal as Marranos, but after his father's death in the

Abraham Furtado, French politician and communal leader. Lithograph portrait after a painting by Antoine Maurin, 1834. Courtesy J. Michman-Melkman, Jerusalem.

Lisbon earthquake (1755), his mother moved to London, where Abraham was born, and returned to Judaism. In 1756 she settled in Bayonne. They later moved to Bordeaux, where Furtado was educated. His dealings in property eventually enabled him to devote himself to literature, philosophy, and history, and to enter politics. In 1788 he and David *Gradis were invited to sit on the *Malesherbes commission for considering proposals for the amelioration of the Jewish position, as representatives for southern France. Furtado became a municipal councillor in Bordeaux shortly before the French Revolution. A sympathizer with the federalist-minded Girondins, Furtado was proscribed with them in 1793. After the downfall of Robespierre, however, he was reinstated in civic office in Bordeaux. He was elected president of the *Assembly of Jewish Notables (1806–07) convened by Napoleon and acted as secretary of the Paris *Sanhedrin (1807). Furtado, who knew Napoleon personally, traveled to Tilsit in June 1807 to present a memorandum to the emperor in the hope of preventing restrictive measures against the Jewish community. His efforts were only partially successful. In 1808 he published in Paris his *Mémoire d'Abraham Furtado sur l'Etat des Juifs en France jusqu' à la Révolution.* After Napoleon's return from Elba, Furtado refused the appointment of vice-mayor of Bordeaux, but accepted it from Louis XVIII when the monarchy was restored for a second time.

Bibliography: M. Berr, *Eloge de M. Abraham Furtado* (1817); AI, 2 (1841), 361–8 (biography); R. Anchel, *Napoléon et les Juifs* (1928), index.

[Ed.]

FUR TRADE AND INDUSTRY. Jews arrived at the fur trade and industry through their commerce between the Mediterranean littoral and Continental Europe, in particular Eastern Europe. Their active participation in the central European fairs enabled them to play an important role in the development of the fur trade. During the ninth century the Jewish merchants known as *Radanites were among the principal agents in the international fur trade. They may have purchased the furs at the northern end of their European itinerary, but more likely bought them in the land of the *Khazars, since pelts could be obtained there cheaply, and secured for the Khazar kingdom a central position in the international trade (taxes there were occasionally collected in furs). The report of *Ibrahim b. Yakub in the tenth century shows that Jewish and Muslim merchants in Prague dealt in furs and hides of various kinds, among other goods. The fur trade must have remained an important part of the business of Jewish merchants visiting Russia *(holkhei Russia)* in the 11th and 12th centuries. Furs were among the wares of the 11th-century Mediterranean merchant Naharay b. Nissim. The extent to which the fur trade and payment in furs figured in Jewish life and imagination is shown in a 13th-century tale about "a Jew who went afar and saw in his dreams a Jew whom exalted ones were weighing in a balance, and his sins were found to weigh heavier; they said: as his sins are heavier he will have no part in the world to come. [Then] others came and said: you did not weigh fairly, and they put pelts and other furs on the man, and he was heavier; they said: he shall enter the world to come . . . And they said: those furs they put on him were furs he paid in tax" (*Sefer Ḥasidim*, ed. R. Margalioth (1924), no. 654, p. 421).

In the 13th century Jewish merchants imported furs from Hungary into Little Poland. The Jews of Volhynia and Red Russia, especially at the close of the 14th and beginning of the 15th centuries, held a prominent place among the merchants who imported oriental goods and traded at the fairs of Lvov and Kiev—these imported, among other articles, furs and horses. During the second half of the 15th century, and especially after 1454, following the extension of Polish rule to *Gdansk (Danzig), participation of Jews in the northern trade intensified; among the cargoes rafted down the rivers there were hides and furs. Furs held an important place among the goods supplied by Jews to the courts of the Polish kings. Sebastian *Miczyński (1618) tells that "there are two Israelite brothers who, upon arriving in Lvov where various goods arrive from Turkey . . . took into their possession almost all the furs . . . and this is not all . . . they [the Jews], despite existing laws and privileges, import from Bohemia, Moravia, and Germany finished goods and prepared furs, fox furs made from the hide of the belly." Throughout the 17th century, the Jewish merchants of Poland played a main role in the overland export of hides and furs. The regulations of the furriers' guild of Cracow of 1613 show that its members were, in fact, fur merchants. In Bohemia during the 15th to 16th centuries the Jews were prominent in the fur retail trade. In 1515, when the municipal councillors of Prague sought to reduce Jewish competition in trade, they prohibited them, among other things, from preparing or selling cloths and new furs. On the other hand, they were authorized to sell used clothes and furs at the fairs. During the 17th and 18th centuries the Jews of Amsterdam also engaged in the trade of furs, which they imported from Frankfort. The city of *Leipzig was an important center of the fur trade. Here, the Jewish merchants of Austria, Germany, and Russia played a pioneering role through their participation in the fairs of the city from the beginning of the 16th century. In recognition of their contribution toward the import of raw materials for the hide and fur industries, the Jews of Poland and Russia were authorized in 1747 to settle in Leipzig without paying taxes. Jewish merchants from Brody, Lissa (Leszno), and Shklov were among the most active fur traders at the fairs of Leipzig. During this period, the other principal centers of the fur trade in Germany were Breslau and Gross-Glogau (for furs imported from Russia, from the region of Crimea), as well as Luebeck and Hamburg (for furs from Siberia and the Scandinavian countries).

Mink breeding at a farm in Talpiot, Jerusalem, 1970. Government Press Office, Tel Aviv.

In North America the Jews played an important role in the fur trade during the colonial period. George Croghan, a prominent fur trader in the second half of the 18th century, was assisted by many Jewish suppliers. In 1765 the brothers Barnard and Michael *Gratz established an extensive commercial partnership with non-Jewish merchants and their activities included trade in furs. Other important fur traders in the colonial period were Hayman *Levy, Joseph *Simon, Salomon Simson, and David *Franks. In Canada, the town of Trois Rivières became the center of the fur trade, in which Aaron *Hart and Samuel *Judah, who exported furs to England, played a considerable role. The sales of the American-Russian Fur Company were handled by the J. M. Oppenheim firm, London's largest fur house. Before the purchase of Alaska by the United States in 1867 the Russian firm began selling furs to independent fur traders of San Francisco, many of whom were Jews, eager to penetrate the lucrative seal islands of Alaska. Indeed the negotiations of Hutchinson, Kohn, and Co. for purchasing the Alaskan fur monopoly influenced the decision to purchase the territory. The Russian company's rights and assets were subsequently bought by this firm. Californian Jews were prominent in the "fur rush" to Alaska. The Alaska Commercial Company, headed by Lewis *Gerstle and Louis Sloss, continued to dominate the fur trade after Alaska was purchased by the United States. On the east coast a number of German-Jewish firms sprung up for the processing of fur products, the largest being A. Hollander and Sons of Newark, New Jersey.

The year 1815 was the start of a prosperous period for the fur trade of Leipzig as a result of which a local fur industry was established. The first Jewish company, founded by Marcus Harmelin in 1830, existed until 1939. With the unification of Germany in 1871, the Jewish fur industry of Leipzig received new momentum when Jewish fur merchants of Berlin, Breslau, Brody, Frankfort, Fuerth, and Hamburg settled there or opened branches of their businesses. Even the new Jewish companies then beginning trade in New York, such as Ullmann and Boskovitz, opened branches there. The fur trade between Russia and Germany remained at a peak level until World War I, and the important Jewish furriers of Leipzig took part annually in the large fairs of Russia. According to the census of 1897 Jews formed 90% of the fur merchants in Congress Poland, and according to the census of 1900 in Galicia they formed 80% of the hide and fur merchants. Even though World War I brought a crisis to the fur trade, the principal companies in Germany recuperated immediately afterward, when trade relations with the United States intensified. In 1921 the trade was also renewed with the Soviet Union. It has been estimated that in 1929 there were about 1,228 fur industry enterprises in Leipzig of which at least 513 were owned by Jews. Of the 794 fur merchants then living there, 460 were Jews. Before Hitler's rise to power, the Leipzig fur industry saw a period of prosperity during which many Jewish companies began to open branches in other places. Subsequently the Jewish fur industry throughout Germany was brought to an end. The centers of the Jewish fur industry were then transferred to other places, with refugees who had succeeded in escaping Nazi Germany occasionally occupying leading positions.

Though the fur-working industry in the United States in the 19th century was largely in the hands of Germans, the large Jewish immigration from Eastern Europe from the 1880s on had brought a flood of Jewish workers into the profession, many of whom were forced to labor under sweatshop conditions. In 1912 an estimated 7,000 out of 10,000 fur workers in the United States were Jewish, the great majority concentrated in New York, Philadelphia, and Chicago. A Jewish Furriers Union was organized in 1906 but soon dissolved. In 1913 the International Fur Workers Union came into being, the leadership and rank and file of which were both heavily Jewish. Under the leadership of Benjamin *Gold, the Furriers International was for years among the most politically radical unions in America.

A study undertaken in 1937 indicated that approximately 80% of the employees in the fur industry in the United States, and over 90% of the employers, were Jewish. The largest of these Jewish fur firms was Eitington-Schild of New York City, whose president, Motty Eitington, was a leading figure for many years in the Associated Fur Manufacturers, as was another large Jewish fur dealer, Samuel N. Samuels. In Canada, Jews became prominent in this branch, notably in Montreal, Toronto, Winnipeg, and Vancouver. A census held in 1931 shows that 48.65% of the employers and directors and 31.82% of the workers in this industry were Jews. Most had acquired their professional knowledge in their countries of origin in Eastern Europe, and they contributed largely to promoting the industry in Canada.

In London Jewish companies were estimated in the 1960s to constitute about two-thirds of the city's fur enterprises. They contributed considerably toward the development and improvement of methods employed in the fur industry, such as the preparation and dyeing of furs. In Argentina in the same period about 80% of the fur enterprises were owned by Jews who organized a trade association, the Sociedad Mercantil de Peleteros. In Israel the fur trade and industry employed in 1969 about 500 workers in 70 firms specializing mainly in broadtail and karakul. Production, primarily aimed at export, earned approximately $1,000,000 in 1963 and over $3,500,000 in 1969. A small number of minks and chinchillas are reared on farms.

Bibliography: I. Schipper, *Di Virtshaftsgeshikhte fun di Yidn in Poiln be-Eysen Mitelalter* (1926), passim; F. Dublin, in: PAJHS, 35 (1939), 14–16; L. Rosenberg, *Canada's Jews* (1939), 178–9, 186; N. Barou, *Jews in Work and Trade* (1948[3]), index; L. Rabinowitz, *Jewish Merchant Adventurers* (1948), 82ff., 164ff.; P. S. Foner, *Fur and Leather Workers Union* (1950), 20–21, 24–26; R. Glanz, *Jews in American Alaska* (1953), 46; M. U. Schappes, *Jews in the United States* (1958), index; W. Harmelin, in: YLBI, 9 (1964), 239–66; J. R. Marcus, *Early American Jewry*, 2 vols. (1951–53), index; idem, *American Jewry Documents* (1959), index; H. A. Immis, *Fur Trade in Canada* (1956); M. Wischnitzer, *History of Jewish Crafts and Guilds* (1965), index. [Ed.]

FURTUNĂ, ENRIC (pseudonym of **Henry Peckelmann**; (1881–1965), Rumanian poet. Born in Botoşani, Furtună practiced as a physician in Jassy. He spent much of his time writing poetry which he published both in Jewish periodicals, such as *Ha-Tikvah* and *Adam*, and in general Rumanian journals. Two important verse collections were *De pe Stâncă* ("From the Rock," 1922) and *Poemele resemnării* ("Poems of Resignation," 1940). Many of Furtună's poems had Jewish themes and he showed particular concern for the tragic homelessness of the Jewish people, for which the only remedy he saw was a return to Zion. Some of his poems are on biblical themes, the last being *Abişag*, a dramatic work published in Tel Aviv in 1963 when Furtună was over 80. There are other poems which show a biblical influence. Furtună also wrote plays and translated Hebrew poetry, especially that of Ḥ. N. Bialik and David Shimoni, and Yiddish writers, notably Itzik Manger and Halper Leivick. Furtună emigrated to Ereẓ Israel in 1944 but he left after two years and returned to Rumania. In 1958 he settled in Brazil where he died in São Paulo.

Bibliography: E. Lovinescu, *Evolutia poeziei lirice* (1927), 161–3; S. Lazar, in: *Viăţa noastră* (July 20, 1965). [A.Fe.]

Initial letter "G" of the word "Ge" ("I" in old French) at the opening of a paraphrase of and commentary on I Sam. 19:11 in Old French and Latin. The historiated initial in this 13th-century manuscript depicts Saul sending messengers after David. Munich, Bayerische Staatsbibliothek, Cod. gall. 16, fol. 36r.

GAAL (Heb. גַּעַל), the son of Ebed, head of a band that fought *Abimelech son of Gideon (Judg. 9:26–41), who, with the help of mercenaries, had imposed his rule over Mt. Ephraim. During Abimelech's absence from Shechem, Gaal incited the inhabitants to revolt and took advantage of the social, and possibly also of the racial, tension prevailing among the various sections of the town's population. It appears that Gaal conspired with the ancient nobility in the locality, which claimed descent from Hamor the father of Shechem (9:28) and which apparently belonged to the Canaanite population hostile to Abimelech. The immediate cause of the friction was the highway robbery conducted by the Shechemites (9:25). Apparently, the ruling families seized control of the roads and interfered with Israelite commerce. Informed by Zebul, the city prefect, Abimelech quickly returned and, by a clever stratagem, crushed the revolt. Gaal was driven from the city (9:30–41) and was not heard of again.

Bibliography: A. Malamat, in: B. Mazar (ed.), *Ha-Historyah shel Am Yisrael* (1967), 226–8; idem, in: H.H. Ben-Sasson (ed.), *Toledot Am Yisrael bi-Ymei Kedem* (1969), 77. [Ed.]

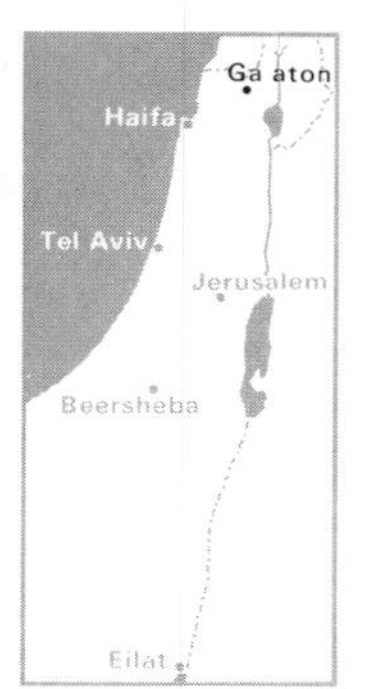

GA'ATON (Heb גַּעְתּוֹן), kibbutz in the hills of northern Israel, east of *Nahariyyah, affiliated with Kibbutz Arẓi Ha-Shomer ha-Ẓa'ir. It was founded in October 1948 while under fire from nearby Arab positions. The founding group of settlers hailed from Hungary; later, Israel-born members and immigrants from Egypt and other countries formed the majority. The local hill farming consists mainly of deciduous fruit trees, but the kibbutz works land in the Acre Plain further west and also has a metal factory. The name is historical, mentioned (Tosef., Shev. 4:11) as an enclave on the northern border of the area occupied by the returning exiles from Babylonia, having been preserved in the Arabic names of the nearby ruin Khirbat Ja'tūn and the Ga'aton brook, which runs down from there to its outlet in Nahariyyah. [E.O.]

GABBAI (Heb. גַּבַּאי, גַּבַּי), lay communal official. Derived from the Hebrew *gavah* (גָּבָה—to exact payment), the word is actually part of the complete title *gabbai ẓedakah* (charity warden) and all the relevant regulations, such as that individuals could not act as a *gabbai*, but collectors had to work in pairs, refer to this charity collector. In the Middle Ages, however, the meaning of the word was extended to include other communal officials. The original meaning of collector of taxes or treasurer merged in the usage of the medieval community with the parallel ancient meanings of collector for charities or administrator of them, and also came to connote supervisor and executive leader. The executive officer of a **ḥevrah* or *guild was named *gabbai*. He was an unpaid lay-elected officer who administered the affairs of the particular association, whether burial, sick care, or the host of other purposes served by these groups. Very large societies had as many as 12 *gabba'im*, each serving one month in the year, when he was *gabbai ḥodesh*. Smaller organizations elected only one or more executives. Where the work was plentiful, the *gabbai* had the services of a beadle and other paid employees. In the small association the *gabbai* usually did all the work himself. In the communal administration the *gabbai* was an officer in charge of a particular committee or activity. In the Cracow community there were officers termed exalted, *gabba'im gevohim*. Some served as *gabba'im* in the synagogue, managing its affairs and distributing honors, especially at the Reading of the Torah. There were also *gabba'ei Ereẓ Yisrael*. In 1749, for example, at the Jaroslaw session of the Polish *Council of Four Lands, such officers were appointed in local or regional communities to make collections for the maintenance of the poor in Ereẓ Israel. In modern times there were also *gabba'im* of the *kolelim* (see also **ḥalukkah*). The manager and supervisor of the affairs of a ḥasidic rabbi was also named *gabbai*. Female heads of associational activities were called *gabbaites*. The elected heads of the synagogues, mainly among Ashkenazi Jewry, were titled *gabbai*. British Jews employed the term **parnas* in a congregational context instead of *gabbai*, using the latter for the warden of the synagogue; the president is called *parnas* in Hebrew.

Bibliography: Baron, Community, index s.v. *Gabba'im, Elders;* J. Marcus, *Communal Sick-Care* (1947); I. Levitats, *Jewish Community in Russia* (1943); Halpern, Pinkas, 329, 338; C. Roth, *Records of the Western Synagogue* (1932), 58. [I.L.]

GABBAI, family with many branches in Baghdad and India. Noteworthy members include: ISAAC BEN DAVID BEN YESHU'AH (d. 1773), known as Sheikh Isḥāq Pasha because he ruled with the firmness of a pasha from 1745 to 1773 as *nasi* of the Jewish community and as *ṣarrāf bāshī* ("chief banker") for the governor of Baghdad. On the other hand, his contemporaries praised his good deeds, especially his efforts to encourage R. Ẓedakah *Ḥusin who was very active in propagating the study of the Torah among Iraqi Jewry. He died together with his three sons in the plague of 1773. EZEKIEL BEN JOSEPH NISSIM MENAHEM GABBAI (d. 1826), also known as Baghdadali, was a prominent banker in Baghdad. With his assistance, Ṭalʿat Effendi succeeded, in 1811, in suppressing the rebellion of Suleiman Pasha, the governor of Baghdad. Gabbai was called to Constantinople, where he became a favorite of Khālid Effendi, the secretary to the Sultan. He was introduced to the court of the sultan and appointed *ṣarrāf bāshī.* In this position he revealed exceptional talents and wielded tremendous unofficial influence; many honors were bestowed upon him, and he succeeded in displacing the Armenian faction from the court. He exploited his position for the benefit of his coreligionists and family in the leadership of the Baghdad community. The *nasi* Sasson ibn Ṣāliḥ was replaced by his brother EZRA who held the position from 1817 until 1824. When the Armenian faction regained its influence Ezekiel was exiled, and both brothers were later executed as a result of libels brought against them. EZEKIEL GABBAI (1825–1898), a grandson of Ezekiel b. Joseph, was the first Jew to hold office in the Ottoman Ministry of Education and later became president of the Supreme Criminal Court. He was also an active member of the Constantinople community. In 1860 he founded a Ladino newspaper, *El Zhurnal Izraelit,* in which he fought for reforms within the Jewish community. He also summarized the laws of the Ottoman State in regard to the Jews. His son ISAAC published until 1930 the newspaper *El Telegrafo,* which followed a similar policy to that of his father. EZEKIEL BEN JOSHUA GABBAI (1824–1896), the disciple and nephew of R. Abdallah *Somekh of Baghdad, traveled in 1842 to India, where he became wealthy. He was accustomed to set aside *ma'aser* ("a tenth") of his income for charities in India, Iraq, and Ereẓ Israel. He extended his business to China in 1843, becoming one of the first Baghdadis to trade there. In 1853, he married ʿAzīza (d. 1897), the daughter of Sir Albert (Abdallah) *Sassoon. The traveler Jacob *Saphir wrote of him in 1860 that he was a distinguished scholar, sharpwitted and shrewd, cultured and industrious. His five sons and five daughters included Flora (Farḥa), the wife of Sir Solomon *Sassoon, David, president of the Jewish community in Shanghai, and one son who became a judge in Bombay. EZEKIEL BEN ṢĀLĪḤ GABBAI (1812–1887) traveled in 1842 from Baghdad to India, where he was "*gabbai* ("treasurer") of the Four Lands" (Jerusalem, Hebron, Tiberias, and Safed) for 40 years. Under his direction, large sums were collected for Ereẓ Israel. In 1870, the traveler Solomon *Reinmann (*Masot Shelomo,* 182) stated that Ezekiel possessed a fortune amounting to several million francs. He later lost most of his wealth and became the manager for David Sassoon and Company in Calcutta.

AARON (d. 1888) and ELIJAH (d. 1892), sons of Shalom Gabbai, were born in Baghdad. In 1840, they journeyed to Calcutta and amassed a fortune in the opium trade between India and China. Outstanding philanthropists, they contributed generously to charitable causes in India, Iraq, and Ereẓ Israel. Elijah lived in China for a time and later returned to Calcutta, where he became a member of the municipal council and an agent for David Sassoon and Company. RAPHAEL BEN AARON GABBAI (d. 1923) was also born in Baghdad and later settled in Calcutta. Another noted philanthropist, he left a bequest of £100,000 to be distributed among charitable institutions in Ereẓ Israel, Baghdad, Calcutta, and London. SASSON BEN EZEKIEL MORDECAI GABBAI, "*gabbai* of the Four Lands" in Bombay during the 19th century, raised considerable funds for charities in Ereẓ Israel. JOSHUA BEN SIMEON GABBAI (1828–1898) settled in Calcutta in 1851, where he was a communal worker and *gabbai* of the Maghen David Synagogue. [A.B.-Y.]

SOLOMON ṢALAḤ GABBAI (1897–1961), poet and educator in Iraq. After having taught for many years in Baghdad, he became rabbi of Amara (1943–1944) and later rabbi of the Iraqi community in Teheran. He wrote many poems in Hebrew and collected them in two booklets entitled *Shirei ha-Kerem* (Baghdad, 1925–26); some of these are poems on Zion. He also wrote an elegy on the massacre of the Jews in Baghdad during June 1941. He settled in Israel in 1951.

Bibliography: A. Ben-Jacob, *Yehudei Bavel* (1965), index; D. S. Sassoon, *Ohel Dawid,* 1 (1932), 36, 430–1; idem, *History of the Jews in Baghdad* (1949), index. [H.J.C.]

GABBAI, family of Hebrew printers. ISAAC BEN SOLOMON (b. second half of 16th century) lived in Leghorn and was the author of the Mishnah commentary *Kaf Naḥat* (appended to Mishnah, ed. Venice, 1614). Early in the 17th century he worked as a typesetter for *Bragadini in Venice. His son JEDIDIAH acquired the Bragadini type and

טור פטדה והוא
חלק שני ממקור חיים
הנה זה עומד אחר כתלנו לבאר היטב בדרך נגלה ונסתר הלכות שבת
ועירובין כפי מסקנת מהר"י קארו ז"ל
ב שלחן ערוך שלו
חיברו חכינו וגם חקרו הרב בקי בחדרי החכמה הנפלאה כמהר"ר
חיים הכהן נ"ע
ליוורנו
תחת ממשלת אדוננו הדוכוס הגדול
פירדינאנדו די מידיצי
שנת ואני בקול תודה אזבחה לך
Con Licenza De Supriori.

Title page of *Tur Piteda,* the second part of *Mekor Ḥayyim,* by Ḥayyim ha-Kohen, printed by Jedidiah b. Isaac Gabbai in Leghorn, Italy, 1655. Jerusalem, J.N.U.L.

decorations and set up the first Hebrew press in *Leghorn, which was active there from 1650 to 1660, issuing a number of important works. With part of the equipment and staff of this press, Jedidiah's son ABRAHAM in 1657 established a printing house in Smyrna, which existed until 1675. Abraham himself moved to Constantinople in 1660, where he was a printer for a number of years. His corrector (proofreader) was SOLOMON BEN DAVID GABBAI—probably not of the same family—author of the kabbalistic work *Me'irat Einayim* (between 1660 and 1665) and a theological work *Ta'alumot Ḥokhmah* (Bodleian Library, Ms. Opp. 602). [ED.]

GABBAI, MEIR BEN EZEKIEL IBN (1480–after 1540), kabbalist of the generation of Spanish exiles. The details of his life are not known. Apparently he lived in Turkey and possibly died in Ereẓ Israel. He wrote three books dealing with the principal problems of Kabbalah. They are: *Tola'at Ya'akov* (written in 1507 and first printed in Constantinople, 1560), on the prayers; *Derekh Emunah* (written in 1539 and first printed Constantinople, 1560), an explanation of the doctrine of the *sefirot* in the form of questions and answers, based on *Sha'ar ha-Sho'el* by *Azriel of Gerona and incorporating views of the *Zohar; and *Avodat ha-Kodesh,* on the entire doctrine of the Kabbalah, in four parts—on the unity of God, the worship of God, the purpose of man in the universe, and an explanation of esoteric aspects of the Torah—an important work which he wrote from 1523 to 1531. The last is the most comprehensive and organized summary of the doctrine of the Kabbalah prior to the Safed period and was one of the most popular books on Kabbalah even with recent generations. It was first printed 1566–68 under the name *Marot Elohim.* Gabbai was one of the leading proponents of the view that the *Sefirot* are the essence of divinity.

Bibliography: Yaari, in: KS, 9 (1933), 388–93; Zunz, Lit Poesie, 381; Blau, in: ZHB, 10 (1906), 52–58.

[G.SCH.]

GABBAI, MOSES BEN SHEM-TOV (d. c. 1443), scholar of Spain and North Africa. He lived for a time in Calatayud and then moved to Teruel where he served as rabbi. He settled in Majorca (before 1387) but during the riots of 1391 escaped to North Africa and was appointed rabbi of Honein. Gabbai was closely connected with the royal Spanish court and King John I of Aragon granted him freedom of passage between Spain and Majorca to attend to his affairs in Majorca (from a document dated 1394). His sister was the wife of Simeon b. Ẓemaḥ *Duran; Gabbai corresponded with the latter and with *Isaac b. Sheshet Perfet, both of whom he greatly respected. The poet Solomon b. Meshullam *Da Piera praised him in several of his poems. The latest mention of his name is in a responsum of Duran (*Tashbeẓ,* 2:99) addressed to him at Honein. From its contents it is clear that it was written in 1443, and not in 1427, as has been erroneously stated by his biographers. His extant writings are: a supercommentary (written in 1421) on the commentary of Rashi on the Pentateuch (in manuscript); and a *bakkashah* (petitional prayer) which is also in manuscript.

Bibliography: I. Epstein, *The Responsa of Rabbi Simon ben Ẓemaḥ Duran* (1903), index; A. Hershman, *Rabbi Isaac bar Sheshet Perfet and his Times* (1943); Baer, Urkunden, 1 (1929), 720f.

[I.T.-S.]

GABBAI IZIDRO (Ysidro), ABRAHAM (d. 1755), Sephardi rabbi. A Spanish Marrano, his wife was tried by the Inquisition while he escaped to London and reentered Judaism. He studied later with David Israel *Attias in Amsterdam and published in 1724 a sermon containing some interesting autobiographical details. Thereafter he was rabbi in *Surinam and then *Barbados. In old age, he returned to London where he died. He left in manuscript a kabbalistic verse commentary, *Yad Avraham* on the **Azharot,* which was published (Amsterdam, 1758) by his widow, who had settled in Bayonne.

Bibliography: Kayserling, Bibl, 48; JHSAP, 29 (1925), 13.

[C.R.]

GABÈS (Ar. **Qābis;** the ancient **Tacapae**), maritime town in Tunisia, situated in a luxuriant palm forest. Gabès was an important commercial and industrial center. Under Arabic rule the Jews were farmers and manufacturers,

Jewish women of Gabès. Jerusalem, Israel Museum Photo Collection, Department of Ethnography. Photo Shulman, 1953.

who wove silk and exported—mainly precious cloth; they gained considerable wealth as a result of their trade with Sicily, the Orient, and the interior of Africa. Some of them were merchants of worldwide importance. In Gabès many Jews devoted themselves to poetry and music, and their intellectual leaders, such as the Ibn Jamaʿ family, succeeded in converting their academy into a religious center whose importance was comparable to that of Kairouan. These rabbinical scholars maintained contact with Sura and Pumbedita, where the *gaon* Abraham al-Qābisi (i.e., of Gabès) had already settled at the beginning of the ninth century. During the 12th century they frequently communicated with the Jews of Spain; Abraham ibn Ezra stayed in Gabès. After incursions by the Normans of Sicily (1117, 1147) the community was destroyed by the Almohads in 1159. Once reconstituted, the community did not return to its former importance. During the following centuries, the Jews of Gabès generally lived in peace. Many of them were engaged in commerce. The weaving of cloth and the wood and jewelry trades were principally Jewish crafts. The community, which numbered about 3,200 before World War II, suffered extensively under the German occupation of 1942–43. From 1948 its members emigrated to France and Israel. Only about 200 families of wealthy Jewish landowners still lived in Gabès in 1970.

Bibliography: R. Brunschwig, *La Berbérie orientale sous les Hafṣides,* 2 vols. (1940–47), index; Hirschberg, Afrikah, index; S. D. Goitein, *A Mediterranean Society,* 1 (1967), index.

[D.Co.]

GABIN (Pol. **Gąbin;** Rus. **Gombin**), small town in Warszawa province, central Poland. Of the 352 houses there in 1564, seven were owned by Jews. The wooden synagogue was erected in 1710. The community numbered 365 in 1765, 2,539 in 1897, and 2,564 in 1921 (out of a total population of 5,777). Abraham Abele b. Ḥayyim ha-Levi *Gombiner, author of *Magen Avraham,* was born there. Yehuda Leib *Avida (Zlotnik) was rabbi of Gabin from 1911 to 1919. [Ed.]

Holocaust Period. At the outbreak of the war, there were 2,312 Jews living in Gabin. When the Germans entered the town, the Jews were immediately subjected to compulsory hard labor. At the end of September 1939, German soldiers set fire to the synagogue and to nearby Jewish houses. The Germans imposed a "contribution" (fine) on the Jewish community, placing the blame for the blaze on the Jews themselves. In October 1939 a Judenrat was formed, consisting of six members and presided over by Moshe Want. Early in 1940 a ghetto was created for 2,100 Jews, 250 of whom were deportees from surrounding localities. Most of the ghetto inhabitants continued to perform hard physical labor for the Germans in the town and neighborhood. During the ghetto period, the Jews were compelled to pay some "contributions," and when the collection took too long the Germans seized hostages and plundered the Jewish houses. In the first half of 1941, the Germans began sending transports of Jews to labor camps—the majority of them to Konin. In the beginning, the Judenrat called up young men by lists for the transports, and they appeared, but when the tragic conditions of the camps became known the men began to hide. Then, German police, with the help of Jewish policemen, raided the streets and houses. In 1942, 2,150 Jews lived in Gabin, and despite transports to labor camps the Jewish population grew, because of an influx of Jews from the region. But on May 12, 1942, all Jews in Gabin were dispatched to the death camp in *Chelmno. Only 212 Jews from Gabin survived—32 on the "Aryan side" and in concentration camps, and about 180 in the U.S.S.R. Nearly all of them subsequently left Poland. [De.D.]

Bibliography: S. Pazyra, *Geneza i rozwój miast mazowieckich* (1959), index; *Miasta polskie w tysiącleciu* (1967), index; S. Huberband, *Kiddush ha-Shem* (1969), 278; D. Dabrowska, in: BŻIH, no. 13–14 (1955), 122–84 and passim.

°**GABINIUS AULUS,** Roman governor of Syria from 57 to 55 B.C.E. He was granted extensive authority, and his system of rule was characteristic of Roman imperialistic methods toward the end of the period of the republic. He put into effect Pompey's decision to diminish the area of the territory of Judea, deprived Hyrcanus of the title ethnarch, divided the country into five districts, and rehabilitated the Greek cities which the Hasmoneans had destroyed. He defeated the efforts of Aristobulus II and his son Alexander to seize power in Judea.

Bibliography: A. Schalit, *Ha-Mishtar ha-Roma'i be-Ereẓ Yisrael* (1937), 4–5, 32ff.; idem, *Hordos ha-Melekh* (1964), index; A. H. M. Jones, *The Herods of Judaea* (1938), 20, 24–26. [Ed.]

GABIROL, SOLOMON BEN JUDAH, IBN (c. 1020–c. 1057; Ar. **Abū Ayyūb Sulaymān ibn Yaḥyā ibn Gabīrūl;** Lat. **Avicebron**), Spanish poet and philosopher.

His Life. The main source of information on Gabirol's life is his poems, although frequently they offer no more than hints. A number of details can be found in the works of *Ibn Saʿīd and in *"Shirat Yisrael"* by Moses *ibn Ezra (published by B. Halper, 1924), and some information can be deduced from Gabirol's introduction to his ethical work, *Tikkun Middot ha-Nefesh* (Constantinople, 1550). He was apparently born in Malaga—or at any rate he lived there and regarded it as his native city, signing a number of his poems "Malki," i.e., from Malaga—but as a child he was taken to Saragossa, where he acquired an extensive education. Orphaned at an early age, he wrote a number of elegies on the death of his father; on his mother's death in 1045, he mourned both his parents in *"Niḥar be-Kore'i"* (14). Gabirol complained of his weak physique, small stature, and ugliness, and it is apparent that he was frequently ill in his childhood, suffering particularly from a serious skin disease that he seems to describe in his strange and terrifying poem *"Ha-Lo Ezdak."* Beginning to write poetry at an early age, at the latest 16 when he wrote *Azharot* (Venice, 1572), Gabirol likened himself to a 16-year-old with the heart of an 80-year-old (*"Ani ha-Sar,"* 8). His self-esteem, at times verging on arrogance, brought him into frequent conflict with influential men of his day, whom he attacked virulently. Since he wanted to devote his life to philosophy and poetry, he was dependent on the support of wealthy patrons, a subservience against which he rebelled from time to time. One of his more important supporters was Jekuthiel b. Isaac ibn Ḥasan, whom he praised in a number of poems for his knowledge of the Talmud and the sciences, his interest in poetry, and his generosity *("Ve-At Yonah").* In 1038 Gabirol wrote a number of elegies on the death of *Hai b. Sherira Gaon. At the age of 19, he completed his great didactic poem, *"Anak."* In the next year, when Jekuthiel was killed as a result of court intrigues, Gabirol wrote two elegies, one of which *("Bi-Ymei Yekuti'el Asher Nigmaru")* is regarded as one of the greatest of Jewish medieval secular poems. With the loss of his patron, Gabirol's financial status and social standing were drastically lowered and his incessant squabbling with the town nobles caused him considerable suffering. It is thought that he wrote *Tikkun Middot ha-Nefesh* ("The Improvement of the Moral Qualities") in 1045, and soon afterward he seems to have left Saragossa; from then on few details are available on his life and work. Some scholars believe that he lived for some time in Granada, where his patron was *Samuel ha-Nagid, with whom he later quarreled as a result of his criticisms of Samuel's poems. Gabirol appears to have spent the year 1048–49 under the patronage of *Nissim b. Jacob ibn Shahin, but it is doubtful if he ever was actually Nissim's student. He was on friendly terms with Isaac ibn Khalfun and Isaac Kapron. According to Ibn Ezra, Gabirol died in Valencia at the age of 30, while Abraham b. David states that he died in 1070, when he was approximately 50. However, the most exact date seems to be that given by Ibn Saʿid: 450 A. H. or 1057–58, when he was between 35 and 38. The many legends surrounding his life attest to the awe in which the man and his works were held after his death. One legend (found in the commentary to *Sefer Yeẓirah* (publ. Mantua, 1562), attributed to Saadiah Gaon) relates how Gabirol made a female *golem* out of wood; another (in *Shalshelet ha-Kabbalah* by Gedaliah ibn Yaḥyā, Venice, 1587) tells how he was murdered by an Arab.

Works. In one of his poems, Gabirol boasts of having written 20 books, but only two are extant that can certainly be attributed to him: *Mekor Ḥayyim* and *Tikkun Middot ha-Nefesh. Sefer Al ha-Nefesh (Liber de Anima),* which has been preserved in Latin, and *Mivḥar Peninim* (Venice, 1546) are frequently attributed to Gabirol, but in both cases there is insufficient proof of his authorship. In their commentaries on the Bible, Abraham ibn Ezra and David Kimḥi quote some of his interpretations, mostly allegorical, but it is not known if he composed a complete commentary of his own. The difficult task of recovering and identifying Gabirol's poems, which were scattered in prayer books, anthologies, and single pages dispersed in many libraries, was first undertaken in the 19th century by J. L. Dukes, S. D. Luzzatto, S. Sachs, and H. Brody, who brought out the first collection of his verse. The discovery in the *Genizah* in the early part of the 20th century of an ancient index of poems by Gabirol, Ibn Ezra, and Judah Halevi proved that there had been a very early collection of Gabirol's poems, and later a complete *divan* was found in manuscript (Schocken 37). Bialik and Ravnitzky did not regard their seven-volume edition of Gabirol's collected works (1924–32) as complete, but it has not yet been superseded by any better collection.

Poetry. In his poetic works Gabirol displays his great knowledge of biblical Hebrew and his linguistic virtuosity, while avoiding the complexity of many of his predecessors, including Samuel ha-Nagid. Employing images and idioms from Arabic poetry, he fuses them into an original style. In spiritual tone his poetry is shaped by Bible and talmudic literature as well as by early mystical Midrashim. In its mystical tendencies, his work is closely akin to Sufi poetry. Both his scientific knowledge, especially of astronomy, and his neoplatonic leanings are evident in his poems.

SECULAR POETRY. In accordance with contemporary tradition, most of Gabirol's secular poetry was composed in honor of patrons whom he describes in extravagant panegyric. As he employs the full range of the Hebreo-Arabic rhetoric of the time in poems of praise and poems of friendship, it is often difficult to differentiate between the two. His pride is evident in his references to himself as a "violin unto all singers and musicians" *("Ani ha-Sar")* before whom are opened the "doors of wisdom" that are closed to the rest of his nation *("Ha-Tilag le-Enosh")*. Following convention, especially that of the great Arab pessimistic poets, he emphasizes the contrast between himself and the society in which he lives, frequently voicing complaints against time, i.e., fate, and his inability to find his place among his fellows, involved as they are in mundane matters and temporal successes. Nonetheless, he was alive to the impulses of youth and while he composed few love poems those few are powerful lyrics. An erotic note is sounded in his description of his relation to poetry, which he portrays as a desirable young girl. Primarily, however, he mourns his inability to enjoy the pleasures of the world and of love, finding refuge from these afflictions in wisdom and in God.

In his "wisdom poetry" he depicts himself as devoting his life to knowledge in order to prepare his soul to rejoin the "Source of Life" on its release from its bodily prison. Knowledge has two aspects consisting both of the effort of the intellect to scale the heights of the heavenly spheres and of the soul's introspection. At first pleading with God to let him live, the poet soon begins to deride the world and time, regarding them as valueless and insignificant obstacles on the way to eternity. From the height of his identification with the infinity of the Godhead and of eternity, he regards with disgust the trials of the world below, the illusions of the senses, and the weakness of the flesh.

In accordance with the rules of rhetoric, some of Gabirol's extensive nature poetry seems to have served as an introduction to his laudatory verse, for the patron's generosity was often likened to the ordained plenitude of nature. It is clear from his nature poetry that he was influenced by the predominantly Islamic culture prevalent in Spain at the time, but within this traditional framework, the fine descriptions are accurately observed. Some of his winter poems ("autumn" according to the poet) include a few of his finest creations, e.g., *"Avei Sheḥakim,"* and *"Yeshallem ha-Setav Nidro."*

In another large section of Gabirol's work, his ethical poems, he addresses the reader directly, propounding an

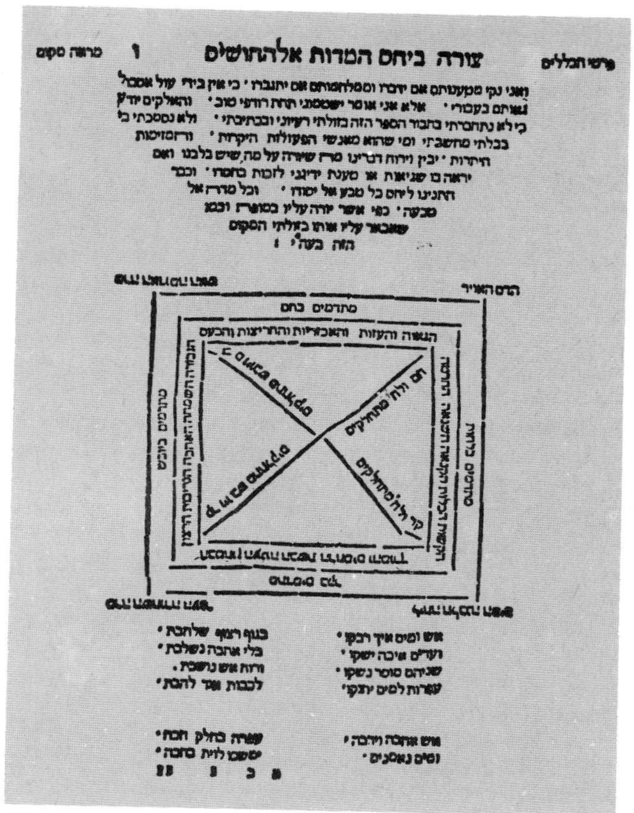
פירושי המלים צורה ביחס המדות אלהחושים ו מראה מקום

ואני נקי מטענותם אם יחברו וממלחמותם אם יתגברו · כי אין בידי עול אסכל
נשאתם בעבורי · אלא אני אומר ישמעתני תחת רודפי טוב · והאלקים יודע
כי לא נתחכמתי בחבור הספר הזה בזולתי רעיוני ובבחינתי · ולא נסמכתי כי
בבלתי מחשבתי ומי שהוא מאנשי הפעולות היקרות · והרומזיות
היתרות · יבין וירוה דברינו פרי שירה על מה שיש בלבנו ואם
יראה בו שגיאות או טענת ידיעני לזכות בחסדו · וכבר
התנינו ליחס כל טבע אל יסודו · וכל מדה אל
טבעה · כפי אשר יורה עליו בצורת וכמו
שנבאר עליו אותו בזולתי המקום
הזה בעה"י :

בגוף רגזף שלהבת ·
בלי אהבה נשלבת ·
ורוח אש נשבת .
לכבות אשר להבת ·

אש ומים איך רכשו ·
ועדים ואיבה ישקו ·
שניהם סומר נשקו ·
עפרות למים יתקו ·

עפרה בחלק וחבה ·
ישענו לוית סובה ·

אש ואהבה ויהבה ·
ומים נאמנים ·

Figure 1. Page from Solomon ibn Gabirol's *Tikkun Middot ha-Nefesh*. The diagram illustrates the grouping of the basic characteristics of human nature. Riva di Trento, Italy, 1562. Jerusalem, J.N.U.L.

ethic based upon individual introspection. These poems deal with the transience of life and the worthlessness of bodily existence in all its aspects as opposed to the eternal values of spiritual life and the immortality of the soul. Gabirol's didactic tendency also finds expression in the many riddles he composed, which were possibly appended to letters, and it is also apparent in the dialogue form in which many of the longer poems were written. This style, developed in medieval Arabic poetry, was also used to introduce variety into the long poems which otherwise tended to be monotonous as a result of the identical rhyming of all the stanzas. The only secular verse he wrote in a strophic form is *"Ki-Khelot Yeini"*—a humorous poem that became a popular Purim song.

RELIGIOUS POETRY. Through his combination of pure Hebrew with the varied meters of Arabic poetry, Gabirol enhanced his poetic stature in the estimation of his contemporaries. Today, however, these qualities are dimmed by the great wealth of complex strophic forms he employed in his religious poetry. Stylistically, liturgical poets were always the elite of medieval Jewish poetry and Gabirol's works in this genre are the apogee of the tradition. Gabirol composed a substantial number of religious poems in the difficult style of the early school of liturgical poets, possibly because they were commissioned by various communities or synagogues. Despite this, the freshness and vivacity of his imagery is striking. Many of these liturgical poems have been preserved, not only in Sephardi and Ashkenazi prayer books but also in those of the Karaites. It is on the basis of these poems that Gabirol is regarded as the major religious poet of Spanish Jewry, and many of them, such as *"Reshut"* and *"Shaḥar Avakkeshkha,"* are outstanding lyrical-religious creations even outside this particular context. Although his God is a personal deity, to whom he may turn in confession or supplication, Gabirol, unlike Judah Halevi, does not describe his great love for God as the relationship between the lover and the beloved. The poet, who in his secular verse is strong-willed and contemptuous of the base world about him, becomes humble in his religious poetry as he begins to understand himself and man in general. When addressing God, he realizes his insignificance and his inability either to combat desire or to understand the essential evil of the senses for which there is no succor except in the compassion of God (*"Adonai, Mah Adam," "Shokhenei Battei Ḥomer"*). At times, these expressions of longing and of profound love for God are akin to the emotions expressed in the love poems (*"Shaḥar Aleh Elai Dodi"*).

As it was customary to compose liturgical poems according to a system of acrostics, most of the religious poems begin with the letter *shin* (S). In his shorter poems, Gabirol set out his own name "Shelomo" in the first letters of each verse, whereas in the longer ones he duplicated this name a number of times, combining it with that of his father Judah ibn (or ben) Gabirol. Other poems were composed according to an alphabetical sequence, but even in these he wove his own name, at times beginning an alphabetically arranged poem with a verse containing his name. Although surpassed by Judah Halevi's poems in the same vein, Gabirol's national poetry overshadows the modest efforts of Samuel ha-Nagid and should be regarded as a link between the two. This poetry emerged from a combination of the traditional longing for deliverance and the particular fate of Spanish Jewry. Political events, the fate of Jekuthiel, and the murder of an anonymous Jewish statesman by Christians in the forests along the border (*"Asher Teshev Shekhulah"; "Lekhu Bo'u ve-Hikkaveẓu"*) must have reinforced Gabirol's awareness of the dangers of exile. In *"Ge'ullot"* and *"Ahavot"* the people of Israel speak to their God as a woman to her lover, telling of her sorrows, while her lover comforts her with promises of her deliverance. In these poems fear of the final destruction and of the end of the prophetic vision mingle with a fervent belief in the advent of the Messiah. *Rashuyyot*, a collection of limpid short poems, is marked by extreme yearning for the savior. According to Abraham ibn Ezra, Gabirol was among those who tried to predict the Day of Judgment and this tendency is apparent in his poetry. The concepts and visions in Gabirol's mystical poems are very difficult to reconcile with the philosophical concepts expressed in his other works. In these poems, knowledge of the Divinity can be apprehended only by the elect who have plumbed the mysteries of creation through which God manifests Himself. The very names of God are endowed with mystical significance, becoming potent symbols of the power of the Creator and the wonders of His creation. The account of the creation is similar to that which appears in *Sefer Yeẓirah*. Many midrashic elements, as well as God's reply out of the whirlwind in Job, join to form a dynamic, mystery-shrouded account of creation breaking forth from the turmoil of primordial chaos into reality and form. There are detailed descriptions of the upper spheres, the curtain of the heavens, and the abodes of the angels, written in the spirit of *heikhalot literature and the *Pirkei de-Rabbi Eliezer*. The close relationship between imagery and content in some of these poems, e.g., *"Ha-Ra'ash ha-Gadol," and "Shinanim Sha'ananim,"* suggests that they may have been written in moments of ecstasy. *Ha-Anak* is a didactic poem apparently intended to teach the basic rules of Hebrew. According to Abraham ibn Ezra (introduction to *Moznayim*, 1809), the poem contained 400 stanzas, of which only 88 are extant, and was based upon a series of acrostics. An introduction on the superiority of the Hebrew language is followed by an explanation of how the words in the language are related to 22 letters of the alphabet in the same way that form is related to matter. *"Ha-Anak,"* which Gabirol called *Iggeret* and *Maḥberet*, is written in plain, flowing language, and was apparently designed for study, perhaps for teachers. The book was greatly admired by Abraham ibn Ezra, who regarded it as an important contribution to the understanding of the Hebrew language. The peak of Gabirol's poetic achievement is *Keter Malkhut* (see below). The many editions, manuscripts, translations, and imitations (most important by David ibn Zimra) of the work bear witness to the widespread and continuing admiration it has aroused.

Judah *Al-Ḥarizi has the highest praise for Gabirol's poetry: "All the poets of his age were worthless and false in comparison . . . He alone trod the highest reaches of poetry, and rhetoric gave birth to him in the lap of wisdom . . . all the poets before him were as nothing and after him none rose to equal him. All those who followed learned and received the use of poetry from him" (*Tahkemoni*, "Third Gate"). [E.H.]

Philosophy. METAPHYSICS. Gabirol presents his philosophic views in his major work, *Mekor Ḥayyim* ("The Source of Life"). Written in Arabic, but no longer extant in that language, the full work has been preserved in a medieval Latin translation under the title *Fons Vitae*. A Hebrew translation of several extracts by Shem Tov ibn Falaquera (13th century), who claimed that it contained all of Gabirol's thought, is also extant under the title *Likkutim mi-Sefer Mekor Ḥayyim*. In studying *Mekor Ḥayyim*, however, the loss of the Arabic original makes it difficult to explain certain terms.

Mekor Ḥayyim is written in the form of a dialogue between master and pupil, a style also current in Arabic philosophic literature of that period. However, it is not a typical Platonic dialogue, in which the student discovers true opinions for himself through discussion with the master; instead, the student's questions serve to enable the master to expound his views. *Mekor Ḥayyim*, divided into five treatises, is devoted primarily to a discussion of the principles of matter and form. The first treatise is a preliminary clarification of the notions of universal matter and form, a discussion of matter and form as they exist in objects of sense perception, and a discussion of the corporeal matter underlying qualities. The second treatise contains a description of the spiritual matter that underlies corporeal form. The third is devoted to demonstrating the existence of simple substances. The fourth deals with the form and matter of simple substances, and the fifth, with universal form and matter as they exist in themselves. The doctrine of matter and form is, in Gabirol's view (*Mekor Ḥayyim*, 1:7), the first of the three branches of science, the other two being, in ascending order, the science of (God's) will and the science of the First Essence, God. Gabirol states (5:40) that he has written a special book devoted to God's will, but no further evidence of such a book is available.

Gabirol's cosmological system generally has a neoplatonic structure but with modifications of his own. The first principle is the First Essence, which can be identified with God. Next in order of being are the divine will, universal matter and form, then the simple substances—intellect, soul, and nature, and finally the corporeal world and its parts. Gabirol holds that all substances in the world, both spiritual and corporeal, are composed of two elements, form and matter. This duality produces the differences between various substances, but, according to some passages, it is specifically the forms that distinguish one substance from the other, while according to others, it is matter. Matter is the substratum underlying the forms;

forms inhere in it. All distinctions between matter and form in the various substances stem from the distinction between universal matter and universal form, the most general kinds of matter and form, which, according to Gabirol's account of being, are the first created beings. However, Gabirol presents conflicting accounts of their creation. According to one account (5:42), universal matter comes from the essence of God, and form, from the divine will, but according to another (5:36–38), both of these principles were created by the divine will. In some passages Gabirol holds that universal matter exists by itself (2:8, 5:32), which deviates from the Aristotelian account of matter, but in other passages he states, in accord with Aristotle's view, that matter is akin to privation, and form to being, and that matter exists only in potentiality (5:36).

All forms, in addition to appearing in various levels of being, are also contained in universal form. Matter and form do not exist by themselves; their first compound is intellect, the first of the spiritual substances, from which the soul emanates, it, too, being composed of matter and form. Hence, as opposed to the Aristotelian views, spiritual matter exists, and it is found in all incorporeal substances. All spiritual, or simple, substances emanate forces that bestow existence upon substances below them in the order of being. Thus, soul is emanated from intellect. There are three kinds of soul, rational, animate, and vegetative, which, besides being cosmic principles, also exist in man. In contrast to the opinion of the Aristotelians, nature as a cosmic principle emanates from the vegetative soul. Nature is the last of the simple substances, and from it emanates corporeal substance, which is below nature in the order of being. Corporeal substance is the substratum underlying nine of the ten Aristotelian *categories. The tenth category, substance, is universal matter as it appears in the corporeal world, and the nine other categories are universal form as it appears in the corporeal world.

For soul to be joined to body a mediating principle is required. The mediating principle joining the universal soul to the corporeal world is the heavens; the mediating principle joining the rational soul of man to the body is the animal spirit. The relation of man's body to his soul is also said to be like the relation between form and matter (a parallel which is difficult to reconcile with Gabirol's account of these two principles). The soul comprehends the forms but not matter, since the latter principle is unintelligible. In order to comprehend sensible forms the soul must use the senses, because these forms do not exist in the soul as they are in the corporeal world. The forms which always exist in the soul are the intelligible forms. However, since the soul was deprived of its knowledge as a result of its union with the body, these forms exist in the soul only potentially, not actually. Therefore, God created the world and provided senses for the soul, by means of which it may conceive tangible forms and patterns. It is through this comprehension of the sensible forms and patterns that the soul also comprehends ideas, which in the soul emerge from potentiality to actuality (5:41).

All forms exist in intellect, also, but in a more subtle and simple manner than in soul. Furthermore, in intellect they do not have separate existence, but are conjoined with it in a spiritual union. "The form of the intellect includes all the forms, and they are contained in it" (4:14). Intellect, which is composed of universal form and matter, is below these two principles, and therefore can conceive them only with great difficulty.

Above the knowledge of form and matter there is a far more sublime knowledge: that of the divine will, which is identical with divine wisdom and divine logos. This will in itself, if considered apart from its activity, may be thought of as identical with the Divine Essence, but when considered with respect to its activity, it is separate from divine essence. Will according to its essence is infinite, but with respect to its action is finite. It is the intermediary between divine essence and matter and form, but it also penetrates all things. In its function as the efficient cause of everything, it unites forms with matter. The will, which causes all movement, be it spiritual or corporeal, is in itself at rest. The will acts differently on different substances, this difference depending upon the particular matter, not upon the will (5:37). The First Essence, i.e., God, cannot be known because it is infinite and because it lacks any similarity to the soul. Nevertheless, its existence can be demonstrated.

The goal to which all men should aspire is defined in *Mekor Ḥayyim* (1:1, 2:1) as knowledge of the purpose for which they were created, i.e., knowledge of the divine world (5:43). There are two ways to achieve this goal: through knowledge of the will as it extends into all matter and form and through knowledge of the will as it exists in itself apart from matter and form. This knowledge brings release from death and attachment to "the source of life."

Sources. On a number of points, Gabirol's philosophy is close to the neoplatonic system current in medieval thought, for example, the concept of emanation that explains the derivation of simple substances and the concept of the parallel correspondence between different grades of being. Nevertheless, it differs on two very important points from the Muslim neoplatonism: the concept of form and matter (especially the latter) and the concept of will.

Gabirol's concept of matter is not internally coherent. On the one hand, it reflects distinct Aristotelian influence, but on the other, the occasional identification of matter with essence *(substantia)* suggests a Stoic influence, possibly the result of Gabirol's reading of the Greek physician Galen (second century). A concept that particularly characterizes Gabirol's system is spiritual matter. One possible source of this concept is the neoplatonist Plotinus (205?–270) in his *Enneads* (2:4), but there is no known Arabic translation of the latter's text (see *Neoplatonism). Theorem 72 of Proclus' *Elements of Theology*, which was translated into Arabic, sets forth a view of matter akin to Gabirol's. Like Gabirol, Plotinus and the Greek neoplatonist Proclus (c. 410?–485) regard matter as the basis of all unity in the spiritual world as well as in the physical. However, they do not maintain that universal form and matter are the first simple substances after God and His will. Pseudo-Empedoclean writings set forth the view that matter (Heb. *yesod*) and form are the first created beings and are prior to intellect. Ibn Falaquera states explicitly that Gabirol followed the views expressed by "Empedocles," that is, in the Pseudo-Empedoclean writings. It is even more likely that Gabirol's views on form and matter were influenced by certain texts of the tenth-century philosopher Isaac *Israeli or by a pseudo-Aristotelian text (see J. Schlanger, *La philosophie de Salomon Ibn Gabirol* (1968), 57–70) that appears to have influenced the latter as well as other authors.

In the identification of divine will and the logos and in the concept of the omnipresence of will, Gabirol's concept of will finds a parallel in *Saadiah Gaon's commentary to *Sefer Yeẓirah*. There is also a partial similarity of Gabirol's teachings to those of the Muslim Ismaili sect. In the text of *Mekor Ḥayyim* Plato is the only philosopher mentioned.

Influence of Mekor Ḥayyim. *Mekor Ḥayyim* is unique in the body of Jewish philosophical-religious literature of the Middle Ages, because it expounds a complete philosophical-religious system wholly lacking in specifically

Jewish content and terminology. The author does not mention biblical persons or events and does not quote the Bible, Talmud, or Midrash. To some extent this feature of the work determined its unusual destiny. Among Jewish philosophers *Mekor Ḥayyim* is quoted by Moses ibn Ezra in his *Arugat ha-Bosem*. Abraham ibn Ezra was apparently influenced by it, although he makes no direct reference to the work, and Joseph ibn Ẓaddik, the author of *Ha-Olam ha-Katan* ("The Microcosm"), also drew on it. There is also a clear similarity between the views of the Spanish philosopher and kabbalist Isaac ibn *Latif and those of *Mekor Ḥayyim*. Traces of Gabirol's ideas and terminology appear in the Kabbalah as well.

On the other hand, *Mekor Ḥayyim* was severely attacked by Abraham *ibn Daud, an Aristotelian, in his book *Emunah Ramah*. Despite these influences, however, *Mekor Ḥayyim* was slowly forgotten among Jews. In its own time it was not translated into Hebrew, and the original Arabic text was lost.

In the 12th century *Mekor Ḥayyim* was translated into Latin by Johannes Hispalensus (Hispanus) and Dominicus Gundissalinus. Hispalenus, also known as Aven Dauth, may possibly have been the same Ibn Daud who criticized Gabirol. Gabirol's name was corrupted to Avicebron, and he was generally regarded a Muslim, although some Christians thought he was a Christian. Some Christian thinkers were greatly influenced by *Mekor Ḥayyim*. Aristotelians, such as Thomas *Aquinas, sharply criticized Gabirol's views, but the Franciscan philosophers, who favored Augustine, accepted some of them. The Jewish philosophers Isaac *Abrabanel and his son Judah *Abrabanel, better known as Leone Ebreo, seem to have been familiar with some of Gabirol's works. Leone Ebreo, who quotes him by the name Albenzubron, regards him as a Jew, and states his own belief in Gabirol's views. It was only in the 19th century, 350 years after the Abrabanels, that Solomon *Munk, the French scholar, rediscovered the Falaquera extracts and through them identified Avicebron as Solomon ibn Gabirol, a Jew. Among modern philosophers, Schopenhauer noted a certain similarity between his own system and that of Gabirol.

Ethical Work. *Tikkun Middot ha-Nefesh* ("The Improvement of the Moral Qualities"), Gabirol's book on ethics, was written around 1045 and has been preserved in the original Arabic as *Kitāb Iṣlāḥ al-Akhlāq* and in Hebrew by Judah ibn Tibbon's Hebrew translation (1167). In this work Gabirol discusses the parallel between the universe, the macrocosmos, and man, the microcosmos. There is no mention in the book of the four cardinal virtues of the soul, a Platonic doctrine which was popular in Arabic ethical writings. Gabirol developed an original theory, in which each of 20 personal traits is assigned to one of the five senses: pride, meekness, modesty, and impudence are related to the sense of sight; love, mercy, hate, and cruelty, to the sense of hearing; anger, goodwill, envy, and diligence, to the sense of smell; joy, anxiety, contentedness, and regret, to the sense of taste; and generosity, stinginess, courage, and cowardice, to the sense of touch. Gabirol also describes the relation between the virtues and the four qualities: heat, cold, moistness, and dryness, which are incorporated in pairs in each of the four elements of which the earth is composed: earth, air, water, and fire.

Philosophical Poetry. Gabirol gives poetic expression to the philosophical thought of *Mekor Ḥayyim* in the first part of his poem *Keter Malkhut* (*The Kingly Crown*, tr. by B. Lewis, 1961). Although the conceptual framework of *Keter Malkhut* is not identical in every detail to that of *Mekor Ḥayyim*, the differences are in many cases only of phrasing or emphasis. The conceptual variations reflect the contradictions apparent in *Mekor Ḥayyim* itself. *Keter Malkhut* opens with praise for the Creator and an account of His attributes: His unity, existence, eternity, and life and His greatness, power, and divinity. God is also described as "Light," according to the neoplatonic image of the deity, "Thou art the supreme light and the eyes of the pure soul shall see thee" (tr. Lewis, 31). Nevertheless, Gabirol stresses that God and his attributes are not distinguishable: we refer to attributes only because of the limited means of human expression.

The next section speaks of divine "Wisdom" and the "predestined Will" (*ha-Ḥefeẓ ha-Mezumman*), which together parallel the single concept of will (*Raẓon*) in *Mekor Ḥayyim*. "Thou art wise, and from Thy wisdom Thou didst send forth a predestined will, and made it as an artisan and a craftsman, to draw the stream of being from the void ..." (*ibid.*, 33). His description of the creative activity of the predestined will corresponds with the concept of will in *Mekor Ḥayyim*, but despite the close ties between them, wisdom and will are not as closely identified with each other in *Keter Malkhut* as in *Mekor Ḥayyim*. In *Mekor Ḥayyim* Wisdom is seated upon the Throne, which is the first matter; in *Keter Malkhut* the link between these two substances is not clearly stated: "Who can come to Thy dwelling place, when Thou didst raise up above the sphere of intelligence the throne of glory, in which is the abode of mystery and majesty, in which is the secret and the foundation to which the intelligence reaches ..." (*ibid.*, 47). Apparently, in *Keter Malkhut* the foundation or element (*ha-Yesod*) is the first matter.

The will is the instrument and the means of creation;

Figure 2. Statue of Solomon ibn Gabirol by the U.S. sculptor Reed Armstrong, erected in Malaga, Spain, by the municipal council. Courtesy *Jewish Chronicle*, London.

after the description of the will the poet goes on to describe the structure of the world according to Ptolemaic cosmology. The earth, "half water, half land," is surrounded by a "sphere of air," above which there is a "sphere of fire." The world of the four elements is circumscribed by the spheres of the moon, Mercury, Venus, the sun, Mars, Jupiter, Saturn, the zodiac, and the diurnal sphere, "which surrounds all other spheres." The distance of these spheres from the world, the length of their orbit, the magnitude of the heavenly bodies found within them, and, particularly, their forces and their influence upon nature, worldly events, and the fate of man are all described according to Ptolemaic and Muslim astronomy. However, beyond the nine spheres there is yet another, which is the result of philosophical abstraction: "... the sphere of the Intelligence, 'the temple before it,'" from whose luster emanates the "radiance of souls and lofty spirits ... messengers of Thy Will" (*ibid.*, 45). Above this sphere is "the throne of glory, in the abode of mystery and majesty," and beneath it is "the abode of the pure souls" (*ibid.*, 47). In this exalted sphere, also, the punishment of sinful souls will be meted out. This part of the poem ends with a description of the soul that descends from the upper spheres to reside temporarily in matter, the source of sin, from which the soul can escape only by "the power of knowledge which inheres" in it (*ibid.*, 50). The concluding section of the poem contains a confession of sins *(viddui)*, and for that reason *Keter Malkhut* was included in the Day of Atonement prayer book of some Jewish rites.

Among the translations and editions of Gabirol's philosophical works are: the Hebrew text of Ibn Falaquera's *Likkutim mi-Sefer Mekor Ḥayyim*, with a French translation by S. Munk, in the latter's *Mélanges de philosophie juive et arabe* (1859, 1927[2]); a German edition by C. Baemker of the Latin translation by Johannes Hispanus (Hispalensus) and Dominicus Gundissalinus (1895); *Fountain of Life*, a partial translation by H. E. Wedeck with an introduction by E. James (1962); *La Source de Vie, Livre III*, translated with introduction, notes, and bibliography by F. Brunner (1950); *Sefer Mekor Ḥayyim*, a modern Hebrew translation by J. Bluwstein (1926); *Improvement of the Moral Qualities*, including the Hebrew text, translated with an introduction by S. Wise (1901); *Keter ha-Malkhut*, edited by I. A. Zeidman (1950). [Sh.P.]

Bibliography: Poetry: Moses ibn Ezra, *Shirat Yisrael*, ed. by B. Halper (1924), 69–72; M. Sachs, *Die religioese Poesie der Juden in Spanien* (1845), 213–48; Zunz, Lit Poesie, 187–94; S. Sachs, *Shelomo b. Gabirol u-Keẓat Benei Doro* (1866); A. Geiger, *Salomo Gabirol und seine Dichtungen* (1867); D. Kahana, in: *Ha-Shilo'aḥ*, 1 (1897), 38–48, 224–35; J. N. Simhoni, in: *Ha-Tekufah*, 10 (1921), 143–223; 12 (1922), 149–88; 13 (1923), 248–94; Solomon b. Gabirol, *Selected Religious Poems* tr. by I. Zangwill, ed. by I. Davidson (1923), introd.; J. Klausner, introd. to *Mekor Ḥayyim* tr. by J. Bluwstein (1926); A. Marx, in: HUCA, 4 (1927), 433–48; D. Yellin, *Ketavim Nivḥarim*, 2 (1939), 274–318; A. M. Habermann, in: *Sinai*, 25 (1943), 53–63 (bibliography on *Mivḥar ha-Peninim*); A. Orinowski, *Toledot ha-Shirah ha-Ivrit bi-Ymei ha-Beinayim*, 1 (1945), 85–133; J. Millás-Vallicrosa, *Selomo ibn Gabirol como poeta y filósofo* (1945); H. Schirmann, in: *Keneset*, 10 (1947), 244–57; J. Schirmann, *Shirim Ḥadashim min ha-Genizah* (1966), 166–84 (166f. a bibliographical list of poems published since 1935); D. Jarden and N. Allony (eds.), *Kovez Shirei Ḥol le-R. Shelomo ibn Gabirol* (1969); D. Jarden (ed.), *Kovez Shirei Kodesh le-R. Shelomo ibn Gabirol* (1969). Philosophy: J. Schlanger, *La Philosophie de Salomon ibn Gabirol* (1968); Guttmann, Philosophies, index s.v. *Ibn Gabirol;* idem, *Die Philosophie des Salomon ibn Gabirol* (1889); F. Brunner, *Platonisme et aristotélisme: La Critique d'Ibn Gabirol par St. Thomas d'Aquin* (1965), incl. bibl.; idem, in: REJ, 128 (1970), 317–37; Heschel, in: *Festschrift J. Freimann* (1937), 68–77; idem, in: MGWJ, 82 (1938), 89–111; idem, in: HUCA, 14 (1939), 359–85; R. Palgen, *Dante und Avencebrol*, 1958; Pines, in: *Tarbiz*, 27 (1957/58), 218–33; 34 (1964/65), 372–8; Husik, Philosophy, index; G. Scholem, in: *Me'assef Soferei Ereẓ Yisrael* (1960), 160–78.

GABOR, DENNIS (1900–), British physicist and electrical engineer of Hungarian birth. Gabor wrote on electrical transients, gas discharges, electron dynamics, communication theory, and physical optics. He was also greatly concerned with the impact of science and technology upon society. Gabor taught at the University of Berlin-Charlottenburg as an assistant for two years. From 1926 to 1933 he worked first for the German research association for high voltage equipment and then as a research engineer in an engineering company. Gabor settled in England in 1933. Gabor theorized about a process of photographic recording which he named holography (1947). In the 1960s with the invention of laser beams the theory was realized, permitting cameraless three-dimensional full color photographic images. He was elected a Fellow of the Royal Society of London in 1956 and became professor of applied electron physics at the Imperial College of Science and Technology, University of London, two years later. [J.E.H.]

GÁBOR (originally **Lederer**), **IGNÁC** (1868–1944), Hungarian philologist. Born in Abaujkomlos, Gábor studied at the Budapest rabbinical seminary and at the universities of Budapest and Paris, where he specialized in Semitic and Indo-European philology. His research was confined mainly to the theory of rhythm, and he translated medieval Hebrew poetry and various Sanskrit, Norse, French, Italian, Dutch, and other works into Hungarian. He initiated the "Popular Jewish Library," and edited a French-language newspaper, *Le Progrès* (1896–99). His works include a translation into Hungarian of the 13th-century Icelandic *Poetic Edda* (1905); *Manoello élete és költészete* ("Poems and Life of Imanuel of Rome," 1922); *A magyar ritmus problémája* ("The Problem of Rhythm in Hungarian," 1925); and *Der hebraeische Urrhytmus* (1929). Gábor and most of his family died in the Holocaust at the end of 1944.

Bibliography: *Magyar Zsidó Lexikon* (1929), 302; *Magyar Irodalmi Lexikon*, 1 (1963), 375. [B.Y.]

GAD (Heb. גָּד), one of the 12 tribes of Israel, tracing its descent to Gad, a son of Jacob, borne to him by Zilpah, the maidservant of Leah (Gen. 30:10–11). The tribe was comprised of seven large families, the Zephonites, Haggites, Shunites, Oznites, Erites, Arodites, and Arelites, named after the seven sons of Gad (Num. 26:15–17; with slight differences in Gen. 46:16). During the period of the Conquest of Canaan, Gad's fighting men numbered 40,500 (Num. 26:18). According to Jacob's blessing, "Gad shall be raided by raiders; but he shall overcome at last" (Gen. 49:19). Moses declared: "Poised is he like a lion to tear off arm and scalp" (Deut. 33:20), showing that Gad was a tribe of fighting warriors. Indeed, in the era of the monarchy, the Gadites are described as "expert in war," as having faces "like the faces of lions," and as being "as swift as gazelles upon the mountains" (I Chron. 5:18; 12:9).

Its Territory. When Transjordan was conquered by Israel in the time of Moses, the Gadites (together with the Reubenites and half of Manasseh) requested permission to settle in the pasture lands east of the Jordan because of their abundant cattle. Moses acceded to their request, but stipulated that they first cross the Jordan and participate fully with all the tribes in the wars of conquest (Num. 32; Deut. 3:12–20; Josh. 1:12–18; 22:1 ff.). Accordingly, the Gadites settled in Gilead, which was in the center of Transjordan, between the territory of Reuben in the south

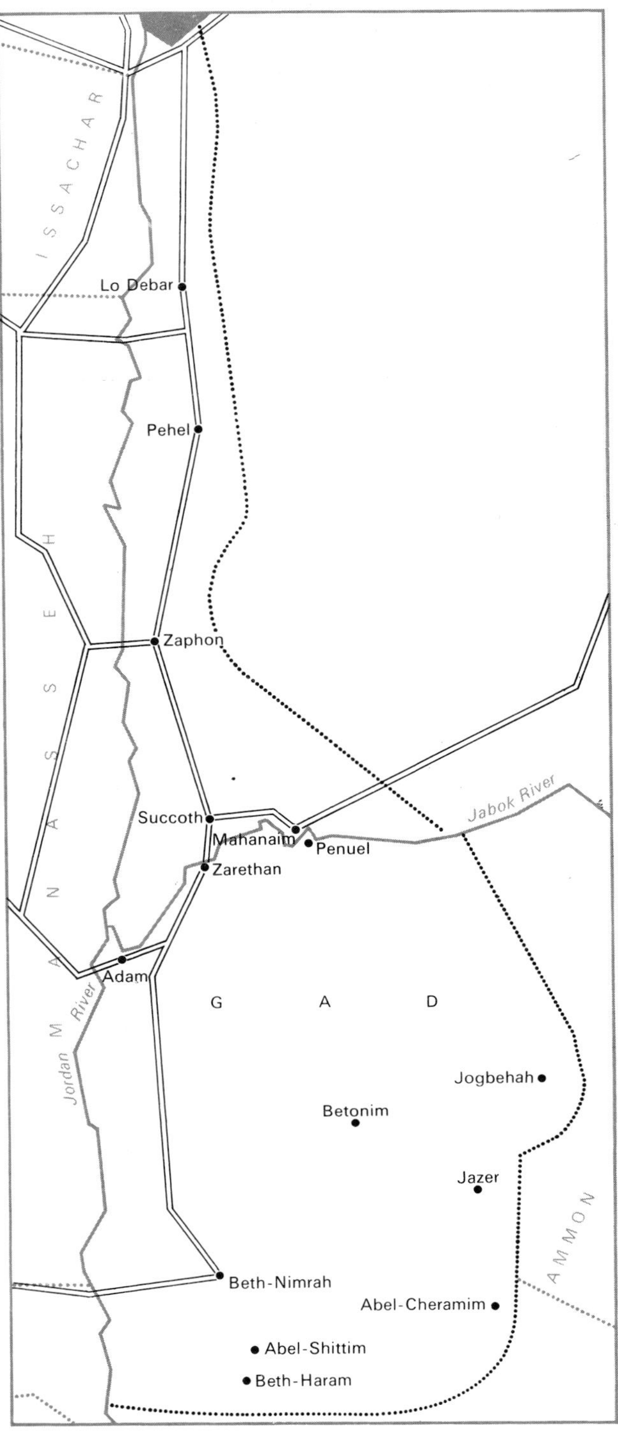

Territory of the tribe of Gad. After Y. Aharoni in *Lexicon Biblicum*, Dvir, Tel Aviv, 1965.

and that of the half tribe of Manasseh in the north. In the east their territory bordered that of the Ammonites and that of various nomadic desert tribes. On the west was the Jordan, from the sea of Chinnereth to the Dead Sea; in the south, the vicinity of Heshbon and the northern tip of the Dead Sea; in the north the border passed by way of Mahanaim (Khirbet Mahna south of Nahal-Jabesh) and Lidbir (probably Lo-Debar (II Sam. 9:4), south of Naḥal-Arav) to the edge of the sea of Chinnereth. The eastern border apparently receded westward to the region of Rabbath-Ammon, then extended northeastward to the region of the upper Yarmuk whence it turned to Mahanaim. This description of the territory of Gad in accordance with the Book of Joshua (13:24–28; 20:8; 21:36–37) certainly reflects the reality of a definite period; however, some hold it to be very early and, like most of the borders of the Book of Joshua, merely theoretical and ideal. Political developments subsequently caused changes in the region of the tribe's settlement, sometimes for the worse (e.g., I Kings 22:3; II Kings 10:33) and sometimes for the better (e.g., I Chron. 5:11).

Its History. The history of the tribe consists of a succession of wars with Ammon and Moab in the south, with the Kedemites, the Hagrites, and nomadic tribes in the east, and with Arameans in the north. During the era of the Judges, the submission of the people of Succoth and Penuel to the Midianites and the Kedemites led them into a fratricidal war with *Gideon (Judg. 8; cf. verse 5; Josh. 13:27). The Gileadites as a whole were saved from the Ammonites by Jephthah (Judg. 11). At this time the Gileadites (=Gad) and the Benjamites entered into marital ties and a fraternal alliance (Judg. 21). In addition, the reign of the Benjamite Saul was a period of relief and respite for the tribes of Transjordan (I Sam. 11; I Chron. 5). Hence, the notable act of loyalty of the Gileadites to the slain Saul (I Sam. 31:11–13) and to his family. The capital of Saul's son Ish-Bosheth was Mahanaim (II Sam. 2:8–9). Saul's grandson Mephibosheth took refuge in Lo-Debar (II Sam. 9:4–5), but this, in northern Gilead, was probably not Gadite but Manassite.

David's wars with Aram, Ammon, and Moab greatly strengthened the position of Israelite Transjordan. In consequence the Gileadites supported David, and Mahanaim became his base, in his war against Absalom (II Sam. 17:24–27; 19:33). Mahanaim later became the station of one of Solomon's twelve commissioners (I Kings 4:14). In the era of the divided kingdom, Gad belonged to the kingdom of Samaria. Elijah the prophet was a native of Gilead (I Kings 17:1). When King Mesha of Moab rebelled against Israel, he dealt harshly with the Gadites of Ataroth (*Mesha Stele*, 10–13, in: Pritchard, Texts, 320). The Gileadites suffered greatly from the Arameans and the Ammonites during Israel's weakness in the first half of the rule of the House of Jehu (see *Jehu, *Jehoahaz; cf. Amos 1:3, 13); but Gilead was reconquered by Jeroboam II (cf. Amos 6:13; Lo-Dabar and Karnaim=Lo-Debar and Ashteroth- Karnaim). The reign of Jeroboam son of Joash seems to have been a period of respite in their history (II Kings 14:28; cf. I Chron. 5:17). There are allusions to some sort of ties between Gilead and the kingdom of Judah during the reign of Jotham king of Judah, on the eve of the destruction of Gilead (I Chron. 5:17; II Chron. 27:5). In 732 B.C.E. the territory of Gad was laid waste by Tiglath Pileser III, and most of its inhabitants were exiled from their land (II Kings 15:29), which was then invaded by the Ammonites (Jer. 49:1). However, there are indications that a remnant of the Gadites remained in southern Gilead, and it is possible that the Tobiads known at the beginning of the Second Temple period derived from them. The Gadite remnant and the Judean refugees in Ammon (Jer. 41) formed the foundation of the Jewish community that developed in Transjordan in the days of the Second Temple. [YE.BL.]

In the Aggadah. Gad was born on the tenth of Ḥeshvan and lived to the age of 125 (Yal. Ex. 162). He was born circumcised (Rashi to Gen. 30:11). His name "Gad" was a portent of the manna (which was "like coriander seed," Heb. *gad*, Ex. 16:31; Ex.R. 1:5). He was among the brothers whom Joseph did not present to Pharaoh, lest Pharaoh, when he saw their strength, would enlist them in his bodyguard (Gen. R. 95:4). Gad was ultimately buried in Ramia, in the portion of his tribe, on the east bank of the Jordan (*Sefer ha-Yashar*, end). According to some, Elijah was a descendant of Gad (Gen. R. 71:8). [ED.

Bibliography: A. Bergman, *The Israelite Occupation of Eastern Palestine in the Light of Territorial History* (1934); A. Alt, in: PJB, 35 (1939), 19ff.; Abel, Geog, 2 (1938), 67, 77, 82, 103, 123, 138; N. Glueck, in: AASOR, 18–19 (1939), 150ff.; idem, in: D. Winton Thomas (ed.), *Archaeology and Old Testament Study* (1967), 429ff.; Albright, Arch Rel, 218; idem, in: *Miscellanea Biblica B. Ubach* (1954), 131–6; M. Noth, in: MNDPV, 58 (1953), 230ff.; idem, in: ZDPV, 75 (1959); S. Yeivin, in: EM, 2 (1954), 423–9; Y. Kaufmann, *The Biblical Account of the Conquest* (1954), 26–28, 46–52; Y. Aharoni, *Ereẓ Yisrael bi-Tekufat ha-Mikra* (1962), 178–9, 228, 304–5; B. Mazar (ed.), in: *Historyah shel Am-Yisrael, ha-Avot ve-ha-Shofetim* (1967), 191–2, 197; Y. Aharoni, *ibid.*, 214–5; Z. Kallai, *Naḥalot Shivtei Yisrael* (1967), 221–8.

GAD (Heb. גָּד, "fortune"; cf. Gen. 30:11), a deity of fortune, equivalent in meaning to the Greek Tyché. In Isaiah 65:11 Gad is mentioned together with Meni. Although the name appears here (according to the masoretic pointing) preceded by the definite article, it refers to the deity. The rite described here is the lectisternium in which food was spread before an image of the deity. This is the only unequivocal mention of the deity in the Bible. There are other references, however, which might be connected with the deity. Thus a place named Baal-Gad, "Lord of fortune," is mentioned as the extreme northern limit of Joshua's conquest (e.g., Josh. 11:17); Migdal-Gad, "Tower of Gad," appears as a place in the southwest lowlands of Judah (Josh. 15:37). The word *gad* also occurs in proper names, but probably as the appellative meaning "(good) fortune" rather than as the name of a god, e.g., Gaddi (Num. 13:11), Gaddiel (Num. 13:10), and Azgad (Ezra 2:12). This is almost certainly the case in the name Gaddiyo ("YHWH is my fortune"), which occurs on one of the Samaria ostraca. The character of the element *gad* in the names Gad Melekh and Gad-Marom, on seals from the fifth to fourth centuries B.C.E. and an earlier period respectively, found in Jerusalem, is uncertain.

Gad also appears in other Semitic religions as an element in names. Though the meaning cannot always be determined, in most cases it is possible to interpret the element *gad* as an appellative meaning "fortune." Thus in a number of Palmyrene inscriptions the word occurs in combinations where the second element is the name of Nabū, Bēl, and other Babylonian deities. One Palmyrene inscription found at a sacred spring (Efka), reading "Gadda," clearly points to a deity to whom the spring was sacred. In Phoenicia the word is found as an element in personal names (e.g., גַּדְעַזִּיז, גָּדִי). It appears also as an element in Nabatean (e.g., גדטב), Aramaic (e.g., גַּדְיָא), and South Arabian (e.g., עַמְגַּד) names.

Bibliography: R. Dussaud, *Notes de mythologie syrienne* (1905), 73ff.; idem, *La pénétration des Arabes en Syrie avant l'Islam* (1955), 91, 110ff., 144; J. Hastings (ed.), *Encyclopaedia of Religion and Ethics*, 1 (1908), 662; E. Littmann, *Thamūd und Ṣafā* (1940), 108; O. Eissfeld, in: *Der alte Orient*, 40 (1941), 94, 123; S. Bottéro, in: S. Moscati (ed.), *Le Antiche Divinità Semitiche* (1958), 56; H. B. Huffmon, *Amorite Personal Names in the Mari Texts* (1965), 179; M. Hoefner in: H. W. Haussig (ed.), *Woerterbuch der Mythologie*, 1 (1965), 438–9.

[Ed.]

GAD (Heb. גָּד), the seer; one of the three prophets during the days of King *David. Gad joined David when the latter fled from Saul to Adullam and he persuaded him to return to Judah (I Sam. 22:5). He also instructed David to purchase the threshing floor of *Araunah the Jebusite and to build an altar there (II Sam. 24:18ff.); this later became the site of Solomon's Temple (I Chron. 22:1). It is known that he remained in the court of David when the latter reigned in Jerusalem (II Sam. 24:11–14; I Chron. 21:9–30). He was also one of the organizers of the levitical service in

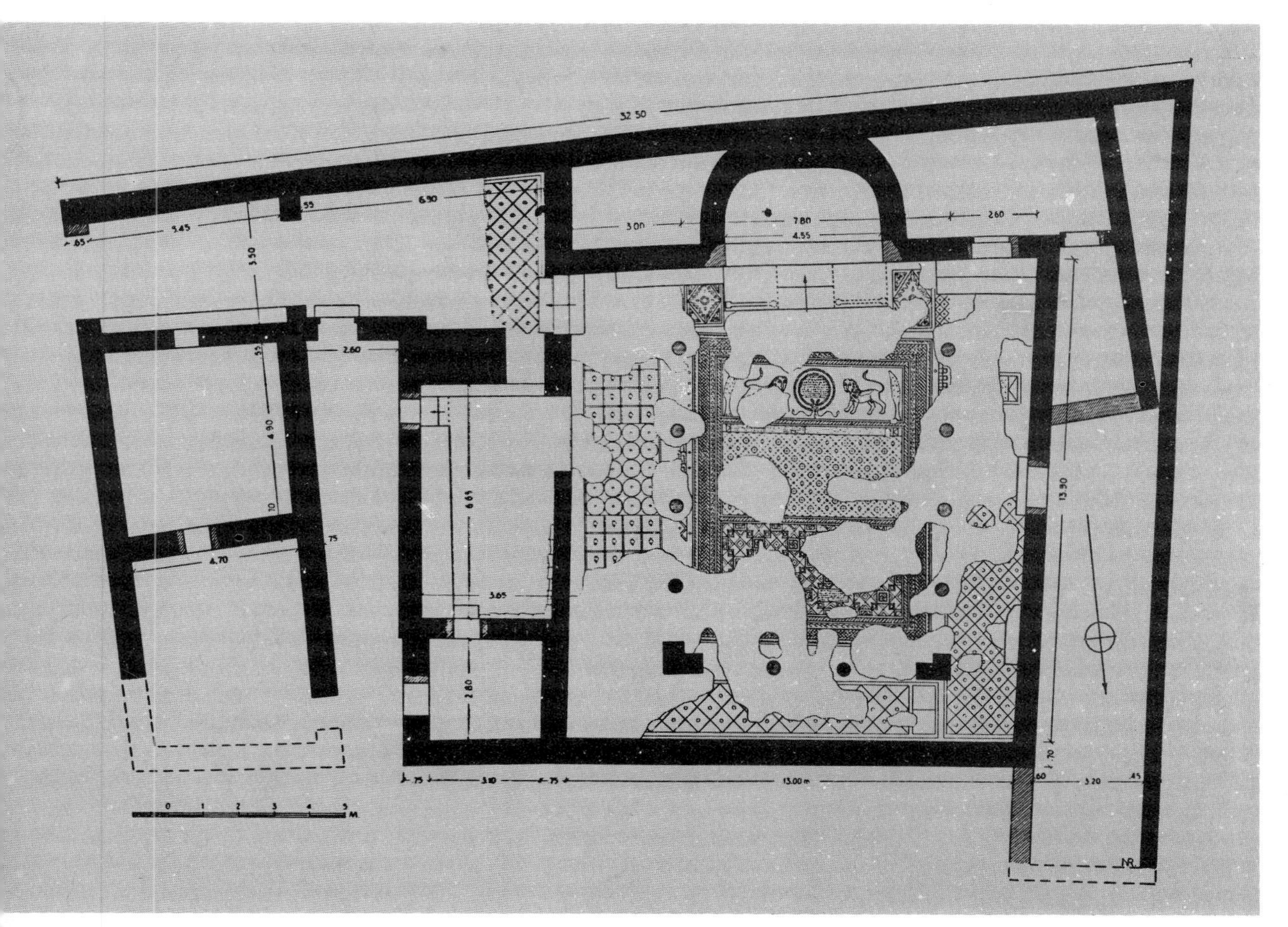

Figure 1. Ground plan of the synagogue of Ḥammat Geder (Gadara), fifth century C.E., showing the excavated floor mosaics. From *Journal of the Palestine Oriental Society*, Vol. XV, 1935.

the Temple (II Chron. 29:25) and one of the chroniclers of the history of David (I Chron. 29:29).

Bibliography: M.Z. Segal, *Sifrei Shemu'el* (1961), 178; Yeivin, in: VT, 3 (1953), 149–65; O. Eissfeldt, *The Old Testament. An Introduction* (1965), 55, 533. [Jo.S.]

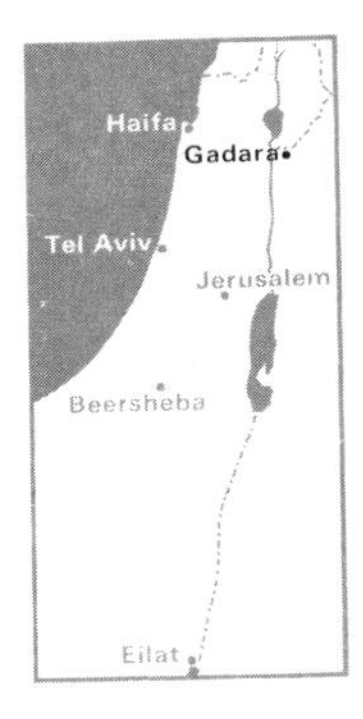

GADARA, ancient city of Gilead. It is first mentioned as a Hellenistic settlement in the description of the conquest of Ereẓ Israel by *Antiochus III (Polybius, 5:71, 3). Although the name is of Semitic origin, the new settlers called it Gadara after a Macedonian city. It was among the cities captured by Alexander *Yannai, but *Pompey took it from the Jews and included it in the *Decapolis. It was part of *Herod's domain in the Roman period and later became autonomous with the right of minting coins. An important center of Hellenistic culture, it was the birthplace of the poets *Meleager and Menippus and the philosopher *Philodemus. Jews lived there both during and after the Jewish War (60–70/73). In the days of R. Gamaliel and R. Akiva there is a reference to "Shizpar, the head of Geder" (RH 22a); the philosopher Oenomaus of Gadara (called "ha-Gardi" in the Talmud) was a friend of R. Meir (Lam. R., Proem 2; cf. Ḥag. 15b). In the Byzantine period, bishops of Geder are mentioned up to the sixth century. Under Arab rule the city declined and is the present-day village of Muqays (Umm Qays) situated at a height of 1,194 ft. (364 m.) with a splendid view of the Sea of Galilee, the Jordan Valley, Galilee, and Mt. Hermon. It contains many traces of ancient habitation: a colonnaded street paved with basalt stones; two theaters; ruins of houses, including a synagogue from the mishnaic period; tombs with sarcophagi, inscriptions and statues, etc. At the foot of the city are hot springs known as *Ḥammat Geder. The city's area may have extended to the Sea of Galilee as indicated in the New Testament story of the "Gadarene swine" but variants of the text mention different cities, e.g., Gerasa (Matt. 8:28; Mark 5:1, Luke 8:26).

Figure 2. Detail from the Ḥammat Geder floor mosaic showing one of the lions which flanks a Hebrew inscription. Courtesy Israel Department of Antiquities, Jerusalem.

Bibliography: S. Klein (ed.), *Sefer ha-Yishuv*, 1 (1939), s.v.; G. Schumacher, *Northern Aylun* (1890), 46ff.; Schuerer, Gesch, 2 (1907[3]), 157–61. [M.A.-Y.]

GADNA (Heb. גַּדְנַ"ע; abbr. for גְּדוּדֵי נֹעַר, *Gedudei No'ar;* "Youth Corps"), Israel government youth movement for training 13- to 18-year-olds in defense and national service. Gadna, whose membership is voluntary, functions in high schools and youth clubs. It trains its members in firsthand knowledge of Israel's geography and topography, physical fitness, marksmanship, scouting, field exercises, comradeship, teamwork, and mutual aid. It is administered by the Gadna Command which functions in the framework of the Israel Defense Forces and the Ministry of Defense and cooperates with the Ministry of Education and Culture. The corps may be activated in an emergency by special permission of the chief of staff.

In addition to regular training, Gadna organizes route marches for 16-year-olds, sharpshooting clubs with nationwide contests on Lag ba-Omer, and an international Bible contest for youth. In its air section (Gadna-Avir) youngsters construct model planes, study aviation, and practice gliding, under the direction of Air Force officers. In the naval section (Gadna-Yam) naval officers teach swimming, rowing, sailing, navigation, diving, and underwater fishing. There is a Gadna orchestra, which has played abroad. During vacations third-year high school students go to Gadna work and training camps in border settlements and immigrant villages, or participate in national service projects in landscape improvement, archaeological excavation, and assistance in hospitals. The corps also helps to reeducate and reintegrate delinquent youth.

Gadna, established in 1948, was the successor to Ḥagam (*Ḥinnukh Gufani Murḥav;* "Extended Physical Training"), which was founded in 1939, and Alummim, a general organization for the 14- to 18-year-old group. Its purpose, defined by Prime Minister Ben-Gurion in 1949, was "training for peace and not for war." In 1951 a Gadna training farm was set up at *Be'er Orah in the Negev,

Figure 1. Members of Israel's Gadna youth corps in training at Nurit, 1963. Courtesy Government Press Office, Tel Aviv.

Figure 2. A contingent of flag bearers passing the Jerusalem Citadel during the Gadna parade on Independence Day, 1970. Courtesy Government Press Office, Tel Aviv.

followed by others at Nurit in the Gilboa Hills, and at *Sedeh Boker and Keẓiot in the Negev. In the early 1950s Gadna youngsters went out to help newcomers in immigrant villages and introduce them to Israel life through Hebrew lessons, Israel songs, and games. Gadna's work has been of interest to visitors from African and Asian countries, and a Gadna delegation traveled to Ghana, Nigeria, and Liberia in 1959. The first Gadna course for youth from Africa and Asia was organized in 1961, and Gadna instructors were later sent to various countries. In 1968 a Gadna unit was organized for *Druze youth. The corps publishes a monthly newspaper *Be-Maḥaneh Gadna* ("In the Gadna Camp").

During the Sinai Campaign of 1956 and the Six-Day War of 1967, Gadna youngsters effectively replaced personnel in the postal system, civil defense, schools, hospitals, industry, and agriculture.

Bibliography: E. Shomroni, *Maggal va-Ḥerev* (1955²), 7–22, 159; *Israel Year Book* (1949–). [DA.CO.]

GADYACH, city in Poltava oblast, Ukrainian S.S.R. From the beginning of the 19th century, the city had a small Jewish community and was renowned as the burial place of the founder of Ḥabad Ḥasidism, R. *Shneur Zalman of Lyady. He died in 1813 while fleeing from the armies of Napoleon and was brought to Gadyach, where a monument was built over his tomb. The Jewish community numbered 883 in 1847, and by 1897 had increased to 1,853 (24% of the total population). With the outbreak of pogroms in October 1905, Jewish property was looted. Under the Soviet regime the Jewish population declined as many left for the larger towns. In 1926 Gadyach had 1,764 Jews (17. 3% of the total). Toward the end of 1941, on the eve of the German occupation, there were about 500 Jews in the city, all of whom were exterminated. The life of the Jews under German occupation is described in A. Ẓefoni's *Esh ha-Tamid* (1966). In 1970 the number of Jews in Gadyach was estimated at about 75 (15 families). [Y.S.]

GAETA, town N.W. of Naples. According to the Chronicle of *Ahimaaz (1054), *Aaron of Baghdad lived for a time in Gaeta in the ninth century, teaching his mystical and esoteric doctrines. The main occupation of the Jews of Gaeta in the 12th century was dyeing, on which they had to pay a special tax. From the 15th century Jewish loan-bankers were also active there. In 1492–93 a number of refugees from Sicily and Spain settled there. The expulsion of the Jews from the kingdom of Naples in 1510–11 brought the Gaeta community to an end.

Bibliography: Roth, Italy, index; Milano, Italia, index; N. Ferorelli, *Ebrei nell' Italia meridionale* . . . (1915). [A.To.]

°**GAFFAREL, JACQUES** (1601–1681), French Catholic theologian and Hebrew scholar. Gaffarel, who was particularly interested in kabbalistic literature, published a description of the manuscripts used by *Pico della Mirandola (Paris, 1651). Gaffarel's writings include: (1) *Les tristes pensées de la fille de Sion sur les rives de l'Euphrate* (*ibid.*, 1624); (2) *Abdita divinae cabalae mysteria contra sophistarum logomachiam defensa* (*ibid.*, 1625; translated into French by Samuel b. Ḥesed as *Les profonds mystères de la Cabale divine*, Paris, 1912); and (3) *Jom JHWH, Dies Domini* (*ibid.*, 1629; according to *Steinschneider the fictitious author's name Elḥa b. David was invented by Gaffarel). He also published, with an introduction—without the author's consent—the *Historia de gli riti Hebraici* by Leone *Modena, whom he had met in Venice in 1633. His *Curiosités inouyés sur la sculpture talismanique des Persans; Horoscope des Patriarches et lecture des estoilles* (first published in 1632 or 1637) was published in a Latin translation with an extensive commentary by M. G. Michaelis (Hamburg, 1676).

Bibliography: Wolf, Bibliotheca, 1 (1715), 223; 2 (1721), 1244; 3 (1727), no. 223; Steinschneider, Cat Bod, 919 no. 4526; G. Scholem, *Bibliographia Kabbalistica* (1933), 51 no. 396–400; S. Stern, *Der Kampf der Rabbiner gegen den Talmud im 17. Jahrhundert* (1902), 184; *Biographie Universelle*, 15 (1856), 347. [JO.H./ED.]

GAGIN, ḤAYYIM (b. c. 1450), Moroccan rabbi and poet, first known member of a family which produced many talmudic scholars. Gagin was born in Fez, but when still young, probably at the time of the massacre of the Jews of Fez in 1465, he left for Spain. There he studied under R. Isaac Aboab, the last *gaon* of Castile, and the talmudist R. Joseph Uzziel. Having acquired a vast and profound knowledge, he returned to Fez where he was appointed *av bet din* of the native-born community to which his family belonged. Disputes often broke out between this community and the newly constituted one of the Spanish and Portuguese refugees, both over economic questions and differences in customs. Gagin was a staunch defender of the customs of the native Jews and of their manner of interpreting the laws. His intransigence on the subject of the insufflation of the lungs of slaughtered animals was the origin of the lengthiest and most severe controversy in which his community came into conflict with that of the Spanish Jews who had settled in Fez. It was only in 1535, after 10 years of disputes in which the Muslim authorities were also involved, that this struggle, first of a purely religious character but which had degenerated into a social conflict, ended with the victory of the viewpoint of the Spanish Jews. The vicissitudes which resulted from this dispute were described by Gagin in *Eẓ Ḥayyim*, lengthy extracts of which were published by J. M. Toledano in his *Ner ha-Ma'arav* (1911). He also wrote numerous *kinot*, particularly on the Spanish expulsion. Nothing is known of his descendants until the 18th century, when they emigrated to Jerusalem, where the Gagin family produced a number of talmudic scholars, among whom was R. ḤAYYIM ABRAHAM *GAGIN, the first *Ḥakham Bashi* of Ereẓ Israel.

Bibliography: J. M. Toledano, *Ner ha-Ma'arav* (1911), index; J. Benaim, *Malkhei Rabbanan* (1931), 36a; M. D. Gaon, *Yehudei ha-Mizraḥ be-Ereẓ Yisrael*, 2 (1938), 178–9.

[D.Co.]

GAGIN, ḤAYYIM ABRAHAM BEN MOSES (1787–1848), chief rabbi of Jerusalem. Gagin was born in Constantinople. He became *rishon le-Zion* (Sephardi chief rabbi) in 1842 and was the first to bear the official title of *ḥakham bashi*. Gagin was responsible for the taxes of the Jews to the government, and was granted authority to impose taxation within the community on meat ("gabela"), *maẓẓot*, wine, etc. He lived in the Old City of Jerusalem in the courtyard of his grandfather, Shalom *Sharabi, the kabbalist, and the government placed a guard of ten soldiers near his dwelling to protect the Jewish quarter. In his time a violent dispute broke out among the rabbis of Jerusalem with reference to the **Kolelim* and the distribution of the funds for them which arrived from abroad. The following of his works were published: *Minḥah Tehorah* (Salonika, n. d. c. 1825–36), *Ḥukkei Ḥayyim* (1843); *Ḥayyim mi-Yrushalayim* (1882); and *Yeri'ot ha-Ohel* (2 pts., 1886–1904).

Bibliography: Frumkin-Rivlin, 3 (1929), 276–8; M. D. Gaon, *Yehudei ha-Mizraḥ be-Ereẓ Yisrael*, 2 (1938), 179–82.

[A.B.-Y.]

GAGIN, SHALOM MOSES BEN ḤAYYIM ABRAHAM (d. 1883), talmudist and emissary of Ereẓ Israel. He was the son of Ḥayyim Abraham *Gagin, from whom he inherited a large library, of which *Frumkin made use in his *Toledot Ḥakhmei Yerushalayim*. Shalom was a member of the kabbalist circle of scholars at the yeshivah "Bet El" in Jerusalem. From 1862–65, as an emissary of Jerusalem, he visited Tripoli and Algeria, as well as Tunis, where he influenced Caid Nissim Shamama to bequeath a large sum of money to Ereẓ Israel. In 1870, on a second mission, Shalom spent some time in Rome. He died in Jerusalem.

His works, most of whose titles include the word *Samaḥ* (from the initials of his name), include: (1) *Yismaḥ Lev*, responsa, pt. 1 (1878), pt. 2 (1888); (2) *Yismaḥ Moshe* (1878), rulings relevant to the testament of Nissim Shamama; (3) *Samaḥ Libbi* (1884), homilies; (4) *Saviv ha-Ohel* pt. 1 (1886), pt. 2 (1904), on the tent of meeting, consisting of additions to *Yeri'ot ha-Ohel*, the commentary of Ḥayyim Abraham Gagin (Agan) on the *Ohel Mo'ed* of Samuel b. Meshullam *Gerondi; (5) *Samaḥ Nefesh* (1903), on the laws of blessings. Shalom also arranged the publication of *Sha'ar ha-Pesukim* (1863) of Ḥayyim Vital, and *Ḥayyim mi-Yrushalayim* (1888), a collection of his father's sermons. Some of his poems were published in *Devar Adonai mi-Yrushalayim* (1873) of Aaron b. Isaac Pereira.

Bibliography: M. D. Gaon, *Yehudei ha-Mizraḥ be-Ereẓ Yisrael*, 2 (1938), 188; Yaari, Sheluḥei, 738f.; Frumkin-Rivlin, 1 (1929), 60, 66 (introduction); 3 (1929), 121, 277, 312. [S.Mar.]

GAḤAL (abbreviation for Heb. **Gush Tenu'at ha-Ḥerut—ha-Miflagah ha-Liberalit;** Ḥerut Movement—Israel Liberal Party Bloc), Israel party established in 1965 by two opposition parties, *Ḥerut and the *Liberal Party. The two parties agreed that while maintaining a separate political and organizational existence, they would establish a joint leadership for the implementation and coordination of mutually planned activities. The two parliamentary factions in the Fifth Knesset amalgamated and, at the elections in 1965, Gaḥal submitted joint lists of candidates. It obtained 256,957 votes (23.6%) and 26 seats in the Knesset; 223,695 votes (23.9%) in the municipal elections; and 99,559 votes (15.2%) in the elections to the Histadrut conference. Early in 1967, three Ḥerut Knesset members split from Gaḥal and established a separate party, Ha-Merkaz ha-Ḥofshi (The Free Center), but Gaḥal still constituted the second largest party in the Knesset (after the Alignment of Mapai-Aḥdut ha-Avodah) and provided the main opposition until the Six-Day War. In May 1967, under the threat of Arab attack, Gaḥal supported the establishment of the Government of National Unity, and its representatives, Menahem *Begin and Yosef *Sapir, joined the cabinet. In 1969 Gaḥal obtained in the elections for the Knesset 296,294 votes (21.66%) and 26 seats; in the municipal elections 287,114 votes (25.3%) and in the elections to the Histadrut 104,614 votes (16.85%). In the coalition cabinet which was formed after the elections it was represented by six ministers. Gaḥal resigned from the coalition in August 1970, after the government accepted a U.S. initiative implying the principle of withdrawal from occupied territories in exchange for peace, and returned to the position of the major opposition party. [Y.Ba.]

GAISIN (Gaysin), city in Vinnitsa oblast, Ukrainian S.S.R., formerly within Poland. There were 65 Jews living in the town in 1765. After it passed to Russia Gaisin became a district capital. The Jewish population numbered 2,018 Jews in 1847, 4,321 (46% of the population) in 1897, and 5,190 (34%) in 1926. In World War II, during spring 1942, under the German occupation Gaisin was made a center for labor camps whose prisoners were employed in road construction in the surrounding area. In addition to the remaining local Jews, others who had been expelled from Rumania were concentrated in the camps. Most of them were "liquidated" in "selections" and *"Aktionen."*

Bibliography: YE, 6 (c. 1910), 31; PK Romanyah, 1 (1970), 518–22. [Y.S.]

°GALACTION, GALA (pen name of **Grigore Pişculescu;** 1879–1961), Rumanian novelist and writer. Galaction was one of Rumania's outstanding literary figures, and his humanitarian outlook made him an unrivaled friend of the Jews. Jewish types abound in his novels and stories, and their high moral character is contrasted with their bitter struggle for survival. He attributed this survival to a divine miracle. In two novels, *Roxana* (1930) and *Papucii lui Mahmud* ("Muhammad's Slippers," 1932), he makes a plea for understanding between Christians, Muslims, and Jews. As a result of his friendship with Jewish intellectuals Galaction used to deliver lectures to Jewish organizations, and he also wrote articles on Jewish festivals and religious lore for Rumanian-Jewish periodicals.

An admirer of Theodor *Herzl, whom he considered a successor to the biblical prophets, Galaction wrote many pro-Zionist essays which were collected in *Sionismul la prieteni* ("Zionism among Friends," in *Herzl*, 1929). A visit to Palestine (1926) inspired a series of articles in *Adam* (1929) and the novel *Scrisori către Simforoza: In pămîntul făgăduinței* ("Letters to Simforoza: In the Promised Land," 1930). Galaction exerted an incalculable influence on the Rumanian people in general through his translation of the Bible (1938; in collaboration with Vasile Radu). He produced a version of the Old Testament that has great artistic merit. His translations of the Song of Songs and the Book of Psalms are particularly remarkable. It is significant that, even at the height of World War II, Galaction courageously maintained his close ties with the Jewish community of Rumania, and when the Jews were forced to clear the streets of snow, he insisted on joining them.

Bibliography: G. Călinescu, *Istoria literaturii române . . .* (1941) 601–3; T. Vianu, *Arta prozatorilor români* (1941), 257–63; M. Sevastos, *Aminitiri de la "Viața Românească"* (1957), 117–20; F. Aderca, *Mărturia unei generații* (1967), 85–94; T. Virgolici, *Gala Galaction* (Rum., 1967). [D.L.]

GALAI, BINYAMIN (1921–), Hebrew writer and poet. Born in Vladivostok, Siberia, his family went to Palestine in 1926. He lived in Tel Aviv for many years, then moved to Haifa where he served as press adviser to the municipality. His volumes of poetry include *Im ha-Ru'aḥ* (1946); *Armonim* (1949), *Shivah Shelishit* (1953), and his collected poems *Al Ḥof ha-Raḥamim* (1958), and *Massa Ẓafonah* (1968). He also published a volume of plays, *Sedom Siti* ("Sodom City," 1952); a selection of sketches, *Al Kafeh Hafukh* ("Over White Coffee," 1960); radio plays, *Mayim Genuvim* (1964); and two volumes of children's stories. A list of his works translated into English appears in Goell, Bibliography, 23f.

Bibliography: Y. Zmora, *Sifrut al Parashat Derakhim*, 2 (1949) 288–93; M. Shamir, *Be-Kulmos Mahir* (1960), 117–26; Kressel Leksikon, 1 (1967), 480. [G.K.

GALANT, ELIAHU (Ilya) VLADIMIROVICH (1868–after 1929), historian of Ukrainian Jewry. Galant, who was born in Nezhin, Ukraine, taught Jewish religion in high schools in Kiev. His studies of the persecution of Ukrainian Jewry from the 17th to the 19th centuries, particularly the blood-libels charged against them, appeared in *Yevreyskaya Starina* and other Russian-Jewish papers. In 1919 Galant was associated with the establishment of a Jewish Historical-Archeographical Commission, known as the "Galant commission," founded under the auspices of the Ukrainian Academy of Sciences. The commission's task was to conduct research on the history of Ukrainian Jewry based on government archival material, which was not accessible under the czarist regime. The commission's work was interrupted by the ensuing civil war and it was not revived until 1924 with Galant as secretary. He edited the first two volumes of its proceedings, *Zbirnyk prats Zhydivskoy istorychno-arkheografichnoy komisiyi* (1928–29). Shortly afterward, Galant became suspect to the *Yevsektsia, which criticized his work, and was forced to discontinue his scholarly activities in 1929.

Bibliography: A. Greenbaum, *Jewish Scholarship in Soviet Russia 1918–41* (1959), passim; B. A. Dinur, *Bi-Ymei Milḥamah u-Mahpekhah* (1960), 393–7. [Y.S.]

GALANTA, town in N.W. Slovakia, Czechoslovakia. Gravestones indicate that the community was founded before 1700. From the end of the 19th century there were two Orthodox communities and a well-known yeshivah, which attracted pupils from all over Europe. One of the teachers there was R. Ḥayyim *Duschinsky. The yeshivah was listed among the institutions of higher theological studies recognized by the Czechoslovakian government. In 1930, there were 1,274 Jews in the town. In 1944, 1,400 Jews were deported to Nazi extermination camps. Some 200 returned in 1945 and restored the community and its institutions.

Bibliography: R. Iltis (ed.), *Die aussaeen in Traenen . . .* (1959), 142–5. [S.R.-G.]

GALANTE, family of Spanish origin which produced a large number of scholars. An ancestor of the family was MORDECAI GALANTE, who was among the Spanish exiles of 1492 and lived in Rome during the first half of the 16th century, dying there after 1541. His original family name was Angello. Because of his handsome appearance and his dignified behavior he was nicknamed by the Roman nobility *galant' uomo,* from which was derived the surname Galante adopted by his descendants. Both of his sons, Moses *Galante and Abraham *Galante, migrated to Safed. The former had three sons: JONATHAN (d. 1678), who became a rabbi in Jerusalem, Jedidiah *Galante, the author of *Ḥiddushei Galante* (Willhermsdorf, 1716), and ABRAHAM, who served as *dayyan* in the *bet din* of Damascus. Moses *Galante II, the son of Jonathan, succeeded his father in Jerusalem. Around the year 1700 a certain JOSEPH GALANTE functioned as rabbi in Tyre. During the latter half of the 18th century another MORDECAI GALANTE (d. 1781), who was a scion of the same family, was rabbi and head of a yeshivah in Damascus. He corresponded about matters of Jewish law with the foremost Sephardi rabbinical authorities of his time. A number of his halakhic dissertations are contained in the responsa *Berekhot Mayim* by Mordecai *Meyouhas (Salonika, 1789), Solomon *Laniado (Constantinople, 1775) and *Bigdei Yesha* of Isaiah *Attia (1853). A collection of his sermons was published in Leghorn under the heading of *Divrei Mordekhai.* To these were appended responsa by him entitled *Gedullat Mordekhai* as well as homilies by his son Moses under the title of *Kolo shel Moshe.* Mordecai Galante of Damascus was succeeded by his son MOSES (d. 1806). The latter also wrote responsa, which were published in Leghorn in 1809 under the name of *Berakh Moshe.* Attached to the volume was an appendix entitled *Zikkaron la-Rishonim.* It included also glosses on Joseph Caro's Shulḥan Arukh *Ḥoshen Mishpat* by Moses b. Mordecai (I) Galante, as well as notes by Ḥayyim *Modai on Shulḥan Arukh *Oraḥ Ḥayyim* and *Yoreh De'ah,* and on *Hezekiah da Silva's *Peri Ḥadash,* and Ḥayyim *Benveniste's *Keneset ha-Gedolah.* Moses Galante died in Damascus. Abraham *Galanté, the historian, also belonged to this family.

Bibliography: Azulai, 1 (1852), 10 no. 36, 132 no. 111; Michael, Or, no. 176; S. Hazan, *Ha-Ma'alot li-Shelomo* (1894), 43a no. 20, 55b no. 1, 57a no. 14, 57b no. 15, 58b no. 23; Ghirondi-Neppi, 251 no. 41; Frumkin-Rivlin, 1 (1929), 56, 150; Rosanes, Togarmah, 3 (1938²), 281–2; Fuenn, Keneset, 16; Vogelstein-Rieger, 2 (1896), 35, 86; J. Rivlin, in: *Reshumot,* 4 (1926), 114; A. Elmaleh, in: *Talpioth,* 9 (1964), 364–86. [S.R.]

GALANTÉ, ABRAHAM (1873–1961), Turkish politician, scholar, and historian born in Bodrum, Turkey. Galanté was a teacher and inspector in the Jewish and Turkish schools of Rhodes and Smyrna. He fought the misrule of Sultan Abd al-Hamid II and partly in consequence of this he left for Egypt, where from 1905 to 1908 he edited the Ladino newspaper *La Vara* and also contributed to Arabic, French, and Turkish newspapers and periodicals. He encouraged the acculturation of Turkish Jewry to its homeland, and conducted an active campaign for the adoption of the Turkish language by the Jews. At the same time he fought vigorously for Jewish rights. After the revolution of the Young Turks, Galanté returned to Istanbul, at whose university he was appointed professor of Semitic languages in 1914 and later professor of the history of the Ancient Orient. Galanté was a delegate to the first Turkish National Assembly after World War I and also a member of the Parliament which met in 1943. His principal field of scientific activity was the study of Jewish history in Turkey. His works (mainly in French) include: *Don Joseph Nassi, Duc de Naxos* (1913); *Esther Kyra* (1926); *Documents officiels turcs concernant les Juifs de Turquie* (collections, 1931–54); *Nouveaux documents sur Sabbetai Sevi* (1935); *Histoire des Juifs d'Anatolie* (1937–39; appendix 1948); and *Histoire des Juifs d'Istanbul* (1941–42).

Bibliography: A. Elmaleh, *Le Professeur Abraham Galanté* (1947); idem, *Ha-Profesor Abraham Galanté* (1954), incl. bibl.; Shunami, Bibl, index. [M.PL.]

GALANTE, ABRAHAM BEN MORDECAI (second half 16th century), kabbalist in Safed. He was the brother and a pupil of Moses b. Mordecai *Galante and a disciple of Moses *Cordovero. Galante, who was known as a distinguished and modest Ḥasid, received the title, *"Ha-Kadosh"* ("the saint"). He was the first to cite Joseph Caro's *Maggid Meisharim.* His works include: (1) *Yare'aḥ Yakar,* a commentary on the *Zohar (extant in manuscripts, to Exodus-*Terumah* 140:2). The work was abridged by Abraham Azulai, entitled *Zohorei Ḥammah,* and published in Venice (1655, and later in Piotrkow, 1881); (2) *Kinat Setarim,* a kabbalistic commentary on Lamentations (publ. by R. I. Gershon in the work *Kol Bokhim,* Venice, 1589); (3) *Zekhut Avot,* a kabbalistic commentary on the tractate *Avot* (in the work *Beit Avot,* Bilgoraj, 1911); and (4) *Minhagei Ḥasidut,* published by S. Schechter (1908). Ḥ. J. D. *Azulai relates that Galante built the court of Meron where the graves of *Simeon b. Yoḥai and his son Eleazar are located.

Bibliography: S. Schechter, *Studies in Judaism,* 2 (1908), 208–9, 273–5, 294–7; G. Scholem, *Kitvei Yad be-Kabbalah* (1930), 102–4; idem, *Bibliographia Kabbalistica* (Ger., 1933), 187–8; M. Benayahu, *Toledot ha-Ari* (1967), 111–5, index; D. Tamar, *Meḥkarim be-Toledot Yehudim be-Ereẓ Yisrael u-ve-Italyah* (1970), 101–6. [D.TA.]

GALANTE, JEDIDIAH BEN MOSES (17th century), scholar and emissary. From 1607 to 1613 Galante visited the Italian communities as an emissary of Safed, possibly on behalf of its Italian community to which his family belonged. During his travels he wrote several halakhic responsa in reply to problems addressed to him and relayed the remarkable deeds attributed to Isaac *Luria (the *Ari*). In 1608 he published in Venice the responsa of his father, Moses *Galante. When some Italian Jews, who objected to one of Jedidiah's rulings on a subject that divided the rabbis of Italy, accused him of embezzling the donations for Ereẓ Israel, he took dramatic action. On a Sabbath in Elul 1609, after his sermon to a large Venetian congregation before which he had been invited to preach, he took a Scroll of the Law from the Ark and in the presence of the whole congregation swore to his complete innocence. The incident, which made a profound impression, was publicized by the lay leaders and rabbis of Venice in a specially printed notice circulated among the Italian communities.

Bibliography: Sonne, in: *Koveẓ-al-Yad*, 5 (1950), 205–12; Yaari, Sheluḥei, 152, 247, 842–3. [A.Ya.]

GALANTE, MOSES BEN JONATHAN (II) (1620–1689), Jerusalem rabbi. Galante was called *"Ha-Rav ha-Magen"* after his major work *Elef ha-Magen* which includes one thousand responsa and cases (unpublished). He was the grandson of Moses b. Mordecai *Galante (I). He studied in Safed and later moved to Jerusalem where he became a leading rabbi and headed the yeshivat Bet Ya'akov. His students included *Hezekiah b. David Da Silva, author of *Peri Ḥadash*, Israel Jacob Ḥagiz, his son-in-law (the father of Moses *Ḥagiz), and Abraham Yiẓḥaki, the rabbi of Jerusalem. He and other scholars instituted an ordinance *(takkanah)* that the scholars of Jerusalem would not use the title "rabbi" (in order that one scholar would not have authority over another). From 1667–68 he served as an emissary of Jerusalem to the cities of Turkey and Hungary. In 1673 he was again in Jerusalem. Galante was influenced by the Shabbatean movement for a time. In 1665 he and other rabbis from Jerusalem went to Gaza in order to seek purification of the soul from *Nathan of Gaza. At the end of 1665 or early in 1666 Galante was in Aleppo where he was among the leading Shabbatean "prophets." According to the testimony in a letter from Aleppo (in Ms. Epstein, Vienna, Jewish Community Library 141[8]), Galante was the "*ḥakham* Moses Galante" who accompanied Shabbetai Ẓevi to Smyrna at the end of 1665 and was appointed by him "King Yehoshaphat." He also accompanied Shabbetai Ẓevi to Constantinople. R. Abraham Yiẓḥaki testified that Galante said "Although I would not believe in Shabbetai Ẓevi, I would not deprecate him. But after I saw that in writing to one of his followers here, he signed himself 'I the Lord your God' [i.e., he wrote the Tetragrammaton in his own handwriting], I excommunicate him daily." His published works include: *Zevaḥ ha-Shelamim*, commentaries on the Torah with the glosses of Galante's grandson Moses Ḥagiz (Amsterdam, 1708); *Korban Ḥagigah*, sermons for the Three Festivals and novellae on the tractate *Ḥagigah* and on Maimonides' *Yad ha-Ḥazakah* (Venice, 1704, 1709).

Bibliography: Frumkin-Rivlin, 2 (1928), 56–60, 150; Habermann, in: *Koveẓ-al-Yad*, 13 (1940), 210; Yaari, Sheluḥei, 290–1; I. Tishby, *Ẓiẓat Novel Ẓevi le-Rabbi Ya'akov Sasportas* (1954), 74f.; Scholem, Shabbetai Ẓevi, name index. [D.Ta.]

GALANTE, MOSES BEN MORDECAI (I) (fl. 16th century), talmudist and kabbalist, one of the scholars ordained in Safed in the second half of the 16th century. Galante, who was born in Rome, was the brother of Abraham b. Mordecai *Galante. He was well acquainted with Ḥayyim *Vital's disciples. Galante was a disciple of Joseph *Caro who ordained him at the age of 22 (Responsa of Moses Galante, par. 124). His teacher in the field of Kabbalah was Moses *Cordovero. From 1580 he served as *av bet din* in Safed as the successor of Moses di Trani. He lived

Title page of Moses ben Jonathan Galante's *Korban Ḥagigah*. Venice, 1704. Jerusalem, J.N.U.L.

קהלת יעקב
יסודותו בהררי קדש
צפת
תוב"ב שבגליל העליון קרית מלך רב היא היום תחת
ממשלת ארונינו המלך סולטן מארד יר"ה :

Title page of Moses ben Mordecai Galante's *Kohelet Ya'akov*, Safed, 1578. Jerusalem, J.N.U.L.

to be over 90 and apparently died after 1612. His works include: (1) responsa, only partly published (124 paragraphs) by his son Jedidiah, with the addition of his novellae (Venice, 1608); (2) *Mafte'aḥ ha-Zohar,* an index of the biblical passages interpreted in the Zohar (incomplete; Venice, 1566); and (3) *Kohelet Ya'akov,* a partly homiletic and partly kabbalistic commentary on Ecclesiastes (Safed, 1578). Some of his sermons were published in the commentary on Ruth of Obadiah of Bertinoro (Venice, 1585).

Bibliography: G. Scholem, *Bibliographia Kabbalistica* (Ger. 1927), 195; Benayahu, in: *Sinai,* 35 (1954), 60; Tamar, in: *Tarbiz,* 27 (1958), 111–6.

[D.TA.]

GALATI (Rum. **Galaţi;** Ger. **Galatz**), port on the River Danube, in Moldavia, eastern Rumania. Jews first settled there at the end of the 16th century. There are Jewish tombstones dating from between 1590 and 1595. A second cemetery was established in 1629 and a third in 1774. Until the beginning of the 18th century the *ḥevra kaddisha* was responsible for the communal administration. Following a *blood libel in 1796, outrages were perpetrated against the Jews. In 1812 Greek revolutionaries, who entered the town, set fire to several synagogues, and in 1842 there were renewed attacks on the community by local Greeks. In 1846 anti-Jewish outbreaks again occurred in which synagogues were looted and Jewish houses and shops were destroyed. In 1859, in a similar attack, many Jews were killed. In 1867 a number of Jews among those expelled from the country drowned in the Danube near Galati: the catastrophe provoked a storm of protest throughout Europe. The Jewish bakers were expelled from Galati for refusing to break the strike of their fellow workers and party members in 1893. The Jewish population numbered 14,500 in 1894, 12,000 in 1910 (22% of the total), 19,912 in 1930 (20%), and 13,000 in 1942. Jewish artisans and merchants contributed considerably to the city's economic and commercial development. Before World War II the community had 22 synagogues, a secondary school, two elementary schools for boys and one for girls, a kindergarten, a trade school, a hospital, an orphanage, an old-age home, and two ritual bathhouses. There was also a cultural-religious society, a Zionist society, a youth organization Ẓe'irei Zion, and a "culture" club. The Jews in Galati were subjected to constant persecution by the pro-Nazi authorities during World War II. The community was not destroyed during the Holocaust, but subsequently diminished through emigration. It numbered 13,000 in 1947, 9,000 in 1950, and 450 families in 1969, with two synagogues.

Bibliography: *Monografia Comunităţii Israelite din Galaţi* (1906); *Almanahul Ziarului Tribuna Evreească,* 1 (1937/38), 260–3; L. Preminger-Hecht, in: *Ostjuedische Zeitung,* 10 (1928), no. 1107; PK Romanyah, 90–99.

[H.K.B./ED.]

¶ Epigramma Hebraicum, in laudem Libri & Autoris.

¶ Mosis Aharon Hebræi, in laudem Autoris & Libri, Epigramma.

¶ Ishac Hispani Hebræi medici physici, in laudem Autoris & Operis, carmina.

A page from *De arcanis catholicae veritatis* by Pietro Columna Galatinus, Italian theologian and Christian kabbalist. Basle, 1550 edition. London, British Museum, Catalog no. 6, fol. 3.

GALATIA, district in Asia Minor, which became a Roman province in 25 B.C.E. Evidence of the existence of Jews in Galatia is scanty, but it is likely that Jewish settlement began with the establishment of Jewish military colonies by Antiochus III in adjoining Phrygia and Lydia (Jos., Ant. 12:147ff.) toward the end of the third century B.C.E. Jews lived in the neighboring countries of *Pergamus, *Cappadocia (I Macc. 15:22), and *Bithynia (Philo, *Embassy to Gaius,* 281) in the second century B.C.E., and the first century C.E. Josephus tells of an edict of Augustus published in Ancyra, capital of Galatia, granting the Jews, among other privileges, the right to practice their ancestral traditions, and to transfer funds to Jerusalem (Ant. 16:162–5). However, "Ancyra" is a correction proposed by Scaliger from a faulty text which cannot be absolutely relied upon. Clearer evidence is available from accounts of the missionary activities of the apostle Paul among the various communities in the first century (I Cor. 16:1; Acts 16:6; 18:23), in particular his *Epistle to the Galatians.* Jewish names in inscriptions found in the precincts of Galatia include "Esther" and "Jacob," appearing on a tomb at Germa, southwest of Ancyra (Frey, Corpus, 2 (1952), 48, no. 796) and "Levi," inscribed elsewhere (Henderson, in *Journal of Hellenistic Studies,* 19 (1899), 285, no. 178). The word "Galia," recurring a number of times in talmudic literature, is in some instances considered to refer to Galatia, e.g., the journey of R. Akiva to "Galia" (RH 26a). It is similarly thought that Nahum or Menahem of "Galia" came from Galatia although others identify "Galia" with France or with a settlement in Judea. (Ket. 60a; Tosef., Er. 11:10; TJ, Ber. 4:4, 8b). In II Maccabees 8:20, it is specifically mentioned that Jews fought against the Galatians at the side of Seleucid kings in Babylonia, defeating them and taking much loot, but there is no available information as to which war is referred to, or its details.

Bibliography: Schuerer, Gesch, 3 (1909[4]), 22–23; Juster, Juifs, 1 (1914), 193; W. M. Ramsay, *Cities and Bishoprics of Phrygia,* 2 (1897).

[L.RO.]

°**GALATINUS, PIETRO COLUMNA** (1460–1540), Italian theologian and Christian kabbalist. A Franciscan friar who believed himself to be the "Angel Pope" first prophesied by followers of Joachim of Fiore in the 13th century, Galatinus wrote a monumental work of Christian mysticism, *De arcanis catholicae veritatis* (Ortona, 1518), first printed by Gershom *Soncino. Though anti-Jewish in tone, it was published in defense of the great German humanist Johann *Reuchlin and did much to promote Christian Hebraism. The book, which assembled a vast number of polemical texts, inspired many later Christian kabbalists, including the French visionary Guillaume *Postel. It was prefaced by laudatory Hebrew verses and laid great stress on numerology. The most popular work of its kind in the 16th century, the *Arcana* was praised by *Amatus Lusitanus. Galatinus anticipated Daniel *Bomberg by advocating the publication of the Talmud. He "explained" early Christianity's lack of explicit reference to the Kabbalah by citing a passage in the Babylonian Talmud (Ḥag. 11b ff.), which forbids the indiscriminate transmission of the creation and chariot mysteries (see *Merkabah Mysticism), especially in writing.

Bibliography: D. W. Amram, *Makers of Hebrew Books in Italy* (1909), 124–6; C. Roth, *Jews in the Renaissance* (1959), 182; F. Secret, *Les kabbalistes chrétiens de la Renaissance* (1964), 102–6; idem, in: *Studi francesi*, 3 (1957), 379ff. [G.E.S.]

GALBANUM (Heb. חֶלְבְּנָה, *ḥelbenah*), a gum resin mentioned among the ingredients of the incense in the Tabernacle (Ex. 30:34) and by Ben Sira as a spice (Gr. χαλβάνη). It was included in a *baraita* (Ker. 6a), dating from Second Temple times, among the constituents of the incense used in the Temple. The *Gemara* (Ker. 6b) states that it was an ingredient of incense despite its offensive smell, thus demonstrating that a malodorous substance, when mixed with fragrant spices, also contributes to the general pleasant odor, thereby symbolizing that sinners of Israel are an integral part of its society. Greek and Roman natural and medical writers, referring to the medicinal qualities of galbanum, praise the spices imported from Syria (Pliny, *Historia Naturalis*, 12:25; Dioscorides, *De Materia Medica*, 3:87). In Israel six species of galbanum grow wild, but their resin is not used for any known purpose. A substance called umbelliferone, employed as a remedy for convulsions, is extracted from two species of galbanum, from *Ferula galbaniflua* which grows in Syria and *Ferula schair* which grows in Turkestan. These plants are of the Umbelliferae family whose stems contain a milk-like resin congealing on contact with air. It is also used in the lacquer industry.

Bibliography: Loew, Flora, 3 (1924), 455–7; J. Feliks, *Olam ha-Ẓome'aḥ ha-Mikra'i* (1968²), 276–7. [J.F.]

°**GALEN (Galenus), CLAUDIUS** (131–c. 201 C.E.), prominent physician in antiquity and author of important philosophical works. Galen was born in Pergamum (Asia Minor) and died in Rome. Medieval Hebrew authors and translators regarded Galen as "the greatest physician" *(gedol ha-rofe'im, rosh ha-rofe'im)*. A popular legend among the Jews in the Middle Ages identified Galen with the patriarch Gamaliel II, who was said to have written a handbook of medicine for Titus after the destruction of Jerusalem. This did not, however, prevent *Maimonides and other Jewish authors from sharply criticizing Galen for his attacks on the law of Moses (see R. Waltzer, *Galen on Jews and Christians*, 1949) and denying his authority in any field other than medicine (*Pirkei Moshe* (1888), 25). *Jedaiah ha-Penini launched a sharp attack on Galen (*Iggeret Hitnaẓẓelut*, in *Iggerot ha-Rashba* (1881), 61), and *Immanuel of Rome relegated him to hell (*Maḥbarot*, vol. 2 (1967), no. 28, p. 515). A derogatory opinion on Galen as a philosopher is also found in a work by Shem-Tov ibn *Falaquera (*Ha-Mevakkesh*, 33). On the other hand, on the question of the eternity of the world, Maimonides sided with Galen against al-*Fārābī (*Guide of the Perplexed*, 2:15). As a physician and author of medical works, Galen's reputation among Jews was beyond dispute. Maimonides wrote Arabic compendia of the 16 "canonical" books and of several other works by Galen, and his Arabic commentary on Hippocrates' *Aphorisms* is based primarily on Galen. Maimonides' own aphorisms *(Pirkei Moshe)* are also primarily a selection from Galen's works and the latter's commentary on Hippocrates (as stated by Maimonides in the introduction).

The following works by Galen appeared in Hebrew translation (generally based on the Arabic text of Ḥunayn ibn Isḥāq, but in some instances also on Latin versions) or as Hebrew adaptations: (1) *Ars Parva (Melakhah Ketannah)*, translated by Samuel ibn *Tibbon in 1199 (manuscripts in Leiden and Paris) together with the Arabic commentary by the Egyptian physician Ali ibn Riḍwān. This commentary was translated again under the title of *Sefer ha-Tegni* (manuscript in Rome and extracts in Paris) by *Hillel b. Samuel, but this time from the Latin translation by Gerard of Cremona. (2) Four books dealing with various diseases, their causes, and symptoms, were translated by Zeraḥiah b. Isaac *Gracian under the title of *Sefer ha-Ḥola'im ve-ha-Mikrim* (manuscript in Munich). (3) Three treatises on compound drugs were also translated by Gracian under the title of *Katagenē* (manuscript in Hamburg). (4) The "Book of Crises" was translated by Solomon Bonirac of Barcelona under the title *Sefer Baḥran*, based on the Arabic text by Ḥunayn. (5) The treatise on bloodletting exists in two Hebrew translations: one, based on the Arabic text was made by Kalonymus b. Kalonymus in Arles (manuscript in Leiden); the other is an anonymous work based on the Latin translation and bears in the title *Sefer ha-Hakkazah shel Gidim* (manuscript in Guenzburg collection). (6) *De clysteriis et colica*, translated by Kalonymus from the Arabic of Ḥunayn (manuscript in Leiden). (7) Treatise on the regimen to be followed by epileptic boys, anonymous translation under the title *Sefer be-Hanhagat ha-Na'ar ha-Nikhpeh*, based on Ḥunayn's Arabic text (manuscript in Munich). (8) *De malitia complexionis diversae* translated by David b. Abraham Caslari in Narbonne under the title *Sefer Ro'a Mezeg Mitḥallef*, probably on the basis of the Latin text by Gerard of Cremona (Bodleian manuscript). (9) The Alexandrians' compendia of Galen's 16 "canonical" writings were translated from the Arabic version by Samson b. Solomon under the title *Sefer ha-Kibbuẓim la-Aleksandriyyim*. Several manuscripts are extant, all fairly complete.

Apart from the compendia translated by Samson b. Solomon, there existed several compendia of individual works by Galen. Two of these exist in anonymous Hebrew translations: *Kelalei Sefer Galenus ba-Marah ha-Sheḥorah* (on melancholy), based on the translation by Stephanus, as revised by Ḥunayn; and *Asifat Marot ha-Sheten*, on the colors of urine (three manuscripts). A second translation of the latter work bears the title *Kibbuẓei Sifrei Galenus be-Minei ha-Sheten* (manuscript in Leiden).

Galen's commentary on the Aphorisms by Hippocrates was translated from the Arabic by Nathan b. Eliezer ha-Me'ati in Rome, together with Hippocrates' own work (many manuscripts have been preserved). A second translation from the Arabic of both works was made by Jacob b. Joseph ibn Zabara (manuscript in New York), and a third, based on the Latin version of Constantinus Africanus, is probably the work of Hillel b. Samuel.

A large number of works attributed to Galen were also translated into Hebrew, including *Sefer ha-Em*, *Sefer Issur ha-Kevurah*, *Panim le-Fanim*, *Sefer ha-Nefesh*, and *Likkutei Segulot u-Refu'ot mi-Galeno*.

Other works by Galen also influenced medieval Jewish literature, even though they were not translated into Hebrew. Thus, for example a work by Galen was quoted in *Saadiah Gaon's commentary on *Sefer Yeẓirah* (4:5), in *Baḥya ibn Paquda's *Ḥovot ha-Levavot* (2:5), in Judah *Halevi's *Kuzari* (5:8), and in a letter by Zerahiah b. Isaac Gracian addressed to Hillel b. Samuel (in *Oẓar Neḥmad*, 2 (1857), 141).

Bibliography: D. Kaufmann, *Die Sinne* (1884), 6, 192, and passim; M. Steinschneider, *Alfarabi* (1869), 31, 34, 134, 142; Steinschneider, Uebersetzungen, index; Steinschneider, Arab Lit, 214ff., 217, 232; Steinschneider, Cat Bod, 2 (1931), 997; A. Marx, in: *Devir*, 2 (1924), 208–12.

[M.N.Z./ED.]

GALICIA (Pol. **Galicja;** Ger. **Galizien;** Rus. **Galitsiya**), geographical-political region of E. Europe, in S.E. Poland and N.W. Ukrainian S.S.R., extending northward from the Carpathians into the Vistula Valley to the San River. After numerous changes in the Middle Ages, Galicia was incorporated within the kingdom of Poland. The major part passed to the Hapsburg monarchy during the first partition of Poland in 1772; with the third partition of Poland the area under Hapsburg rule was extended to the north and northwest of the region. From 1803 Galicia formed a separate administrative unit (province). With the dissolution of the monarchy after World War I Galicia again passed to Poland (1918–19). In 1939, after the outbreak of World War II, western Galicia was occupied by the Germans and eastern Galicia by the Soviet Union, which incorporated it in the Ukrainian S.S.R. Eastern Galicia was also occupied by the Germans in 1941. After the war western Galicia returned to Poland, while eastern Galicia remained within the Ukrainian S.S.R.

During the period of Polish rule until 1772 Galicia was known as Little Poland (see *Lesser Poland), which within the Jewish organizational framework of the *Council of the Lands formed one of the four "lands" (provinces). For the history of the Jews in this period, see *Poland-Lithuania.

For the period of Hapsburg rule and within independent Poland, see article *Galicia in the Supplementary Entries. For the position of the Jews in eastern Galicia after World War II, see *Ukrainian S.S.R. [S.K.]

GALILEE (Heb. הַגָּלִיל, *Ha-Galil*), the northernmost region of Ereẓ Israel.

Name. The name Galilee is derived from the Hebrew *galil* which comes from the root גלל ("to roll"), and thus means a circle. It appears in the Bible in the combination *Gelil ha-Goyim* "Galilee of the nations" (Isa. 8:23), a formula repeated in I Maccabees 5:15. The town of Kedesh (see *Kadesh) is mentioned several times with the addition "in Galilee" (Josh. 20:7; 21:32; I Chron. 6:61); in I Kings 9:11 the 20 cities Solomon gave to *Hiram of Tyre (in the region of Cabul) are defined as being "in the land of Galilee." In the *Zeno papyri (259 B.C.E.) the name appears as Galila. The form Galilee as the name of the northernmost region of Ereẓ Israel west of the Jordan is firmly established in the writings of *Josephus, the New Testament, and talmudic literature.

History. In prehistoric times the eastern part of Galilee was settled by Neanderthal man in the Lower Paleolithic period (see *Israel: History, to the beginning of the monarchy): remains of human skeletons have been found in the *Arbel and 'Amūd valleys. With the establishment of urban civilization in the Early Canaanite period, cities were founded in the plains surrounding the Galilean mountain massif and in its northern plateau while the wooded core of the country was left unoccupied. Egyptian documents mention only the cities (apart from those in the Jordan Valley and the coastal plain) lying on the branch of the Via Maris (the road leading from Damascus to the sea) which crosses the southeastern corner of Lower Galilee: Shemesh-Adom, Adummim, Anaharath, Hannathon, and apparently cities in northern Galilee: Beth-Anath, Kanah, Meron, and probably Kedesh. The armies of the Pharaohs and of the invading *Hyksos avoided the difficult mountain region as far as possible. Archaeological evidence indicates that the Israelite tribes exploited this situation by infiltrating into the forested hill country before attacking the Canaanite strongholds in the plains (see *Archaeology). The victories of Joshua at the waters of Merom and of *Deborah at Mt. *Tabor ensured Israelite supremacy over the whole of Galilee. In biblical times Galilee was divided

Figure 1. The Sea of Galilee, with Mount Hermon in the background, 1920s. Jerusalem, State Archives, Sir Herbert Samuel Album.

between four tribes: *Asher in the northwest, *Zebulun in the southwest, *Naphtali in most of the eastern half, and *Issachar in part of the southeast (see Twelve *Tribes: Tribal territories). By conquering the remaining Canaanite cities in the *Jezreel Valley, David annexed the whole of Galilee to his kingdom. Under *Solomon, Galilee was divided into three districts, each roughly corresponding to a tribal area: the ninth district included Zebulun and probably Asher, the eighth, Naphtali, and the tenth, Issachar. With the division of the monarchy Galilee became part of the northern kingdom of *Israel and was in the forefront of the struggle with Aram-Damascus (see *Aram-Damascus). In 732 B.C.E. *Tiglath-Pileser III, king of Assyria, conquered Galilee and turned it into the Assyrian province of Magiddu (*Megiddo). Some of the Israelite inhabitants were deported but the remaining remnant renewed its relations with Jerusalem in the time of Josiah who may have reunited Galilee with his kingdom (see Lost Ten *Tribes). Nothing is known of Galilee under the Babylonians and Persians; it was possibly administered from *Acre or Hazor since Megiddo had lost its importance by this time (see *Israel; History, Second Temple). In the Ptolemaic period some estates in Galilee were held by Greeks; it appears in the Zeno papyri as a supplier of wheat to Tyre. It was part of the eparchy of Samaria in Seleucid times (see *Seleucia); its administrative center was the royal fortress on Mt. Tabor (Itabyrion). According to I Maccabees 5:15 there were Jewish settlements in western Galilee in the confines of Acre-Ptolemais. These were evacuated by Simeon but others remained in eastern Galilee; *Bacchides, the Seleucid general, is reported to have attacked the Jews of Arbel on the Sea of Galilee. Galilee was incorporated into the Hasmonean kingdom by *Judah Aristobulus I (104 B.C.E.). It rapidly became completely Jewish, for only two years later at the beginning of the reign of Alexander *Yannai, its cities could be attacked on a Sabbath for an easy victory. After *Pompey's conquest (63 B.C.E.) Galilee was left to Judea; *Gabinius' attempt to cut it off from Jerusalem by establishing a separate council *(synedrion)* at *Sepphoris did not succeed. Galilee was then a province *(meris)*, a division established by Alexander Yannai, containing the sub-districts of Sepphoris, Araba, Tarichaea, and Gischala in Upper Galilee. Under Hyrcanus II, *Herod was governor of Galilee for a time; when he became king, Galilee was one of the centers of opposition to his rule and it remained a *Zealot stronghold until the fall of Jerusalem. After Herod's death Galilee was inherited by Herod Antipas, who founded its second largest city—*Tiberias. From Herod *Antipas it passed to *Agrippa I and then to

Roman *procurators. In the last years of Nero, Tiberias and its vicinity were granted to *Agrippa II. In 66 C.E. Galilee joined in the Jewish revolt against Rome; it was the home of *John of Giscala, one of the foremost Zealot leaders. The defense of the Galilee was in the hands of the historian Josephus who lost it to Vespasian in 67. The Romans took no measures against the Jews of Galilee, some of whom, especially those of Sepphoris and Tiberias, favored the Roman cause. Under Trajan Tiberias became an autonomous city; Hadrian turned Sepphoris into a Roman city called Diocaesarea but its population remained largely Jewish. Galilee did not take part in the *Bar Kokhba War (132–135; although historians dispute this point); what is certain is that after the expulsion of the Jews from Judea, Galilee was throughout the mishnaic and talmudic periods the stronghold of Judaism in Ereẓ Israel. The activities of *Jesus and the early Christian apostles had no effect on the Jewishness of Galilee. The national authority of the patriarchate was reconstituted there in the second century, and the *Sanhedrin continued to sit in various cities, settling later in Sepphoris and finally in Tiberias. The priestly families which had been dispersed from Judea settled in Galilee. The remains of a score of synagogues and of a central necropolis at *Bet She'arim are material evidence of the prosperity and vitality of Galilean Jewry from the second to the sixth centuries, and the completion of the Mishnah and the Palestinian Talmud, of its spiritual productivity. The establishment of Christianity as the official religion did not at first influence the Jewishness of Galilee even though the Church set up an ecclesiastical hierarchy there and built numerous churches in the sixth century. Galilee was the center of the Jewish revolts against *Gallus Caesar (351) and the Byzantines (614). It fell to the Muslim Arabs in 635/6 and became part of the province of al-Urdunn (Jordan) with its capital in Tiberias. The Jewish villages continued diminishing but some existed until the time of the *Crusades. Under Crusader rule Galilee was formed into a principality held by the Norman *Tancred. It was lost in 1187 after their disastrous defeat at the Horns of Hittin, but part of it was regained in 1198 and all of it in 1240 only to be lost again during the 1260s. Ruins of crusader castles (at *Miʿilyā, *Montfort, etc.) attest to their rule. Under the *Mamluks Galilee was part of the *mamlaka* ("province") of *Safed; under the Turks it was ruled by the semi-independent pashas of Acre. In the 16th century Safed became the center of Jewish kabbalism and Tiberias was resettled by Don Joseph *Nasi as the center of a proposed Jewish province. [M.A.-Y.]

In the second half of the 19th century, Galilee's population increased and, on the whole, progressed, thanks to an extended period of peace. The Jewish community, concentrated mainly in Safed, somewhat improved its standard of living, although it continued to be dependent on **ḥalukkah* (donations from the Diaspora). In 1856, Ludwig August *Frankl found 2,100 Jews in Safed, and 50 in *Peki'in, the only other Jewish community in Upper Galilee at that time. Until 1895, the number of Jews in Safed increased to 6,620, and in Peki'in to 96. Even before the arrival of settlers of the Ḥovevei Zion and Bilu movements, there were stirrings within the Safed community for a more productive way of life, and in 1878 a group formed to settle at Gei Oni, the forerunner of *Rosh Pinnah; later a second group which formed to settle in the Golan eventually established Benei Yehudah. Rosh Pinnah became the cornerstone of a Jewish settlement network in eastern Upper Galilee and on the rim of the *Ḥuleh Valley. In 1891, Russian Jews founded Ein Zeitim north of Safed. A second phase began in 1900 when the *Jewish Colonization Association (ICA) bought rather flat land with basalt soil in eastern Lower Galilee with the object of establishing "true" farming villages, i.e., based on grain crops, and *Ilaniyyah, *Kefar Tavor, *Jabneel, and other settlements were founded. More moshavot were added through private initiative, and a training farm was set up on *Jewish National Fund (JNF) land at *Kefar Ḥittim. The Galilean moshavot set the stage for the beginnings of the cooperative movement of Jewish laborers and of *Ha-Shomer ("Guardsmen's" Association). In the following decade, however, the Galilean moshavot and the Tiberias community stagnated, and those of Safed and Peki'in even decreased. As a result of World War I Safed's Jewish community was decimated, whereas Galilee's Arab rural society, based on a solid foundation of agriculture, emerged from the war unscathed and was even consolidated.

The Third, Fourth, and Fifth *aliyot,* which gave a powerful impulse to Jewish settlement in other regions, hardly touched Galilee, although all around it new Jewish areas were created, in the Jezreel Valley to the south in the 1920s, and in the Zebulun Valley to the southwest in the 1930s. The expansion of the *Tower and Stockade network during the 1936–39 Arab riots completed this outer ring, in the Acre Coastal Plain to the northwest, in the Bet Shean Valley to the southeast, and in the Ḥuleh Valley to the northeast. In Galilee proper, only the kibbutz Kefar ha-Ḥoresh was established in 1935 near Nazareth.

It was at the end of the decade that settlement spread into the hills near the Lebanese border in the northwest (*Ḥanitah, *Eilon, *Maẓẓuvah), while *PICA and the JNF, reacting to the British *White Paper of 1939, strengthened the "settlement bridge" in southeastern Lower Galilee connecting the *Jezreel and the *Kinnarot valleys (e.g., the settlements *Sharonah, *Ha-Zore'im, etc.). In the 1940s, several more outpost settlements were set up, some of them at particularly difficult and isolated sites (e.g., *Manara, *Yeḥi'am, *Misgav Am).

The largest part of Galilee, however, continued to be exclusively non-Jewish, causing the UN partition plan of 1947 to allocate to the proposed Arab state the bulk of the area, from the Lebanese border south to, and including, Nazareth and from the shore of the Acre Plain east to the vicinity of Safed; only a strip of eastern and southeastern Galilee was left to the Jewish state. In the War of Independence, the Jewish villages, many of them isolated, held their ground without exception. In battles before the State of Israel was proclaimed (May 14, 1948), new positions were gained and continuous fronts consolidated: the southeastern corner of Lower Galilee was cleared of enemy strongholds; Tiberias and Safed became unexpectedly all-Jewish towns when the Arabs left them;

Figure 2. The hills of upper Galilee. Courtesy Keren Hayesod, United Israel Appeal, Jerusalem.

Figure 3. The coast of western Galilee near Rosh ha-Nikrah. Photo Zev Radovan, Jerusalem.

and when on May 12–13, 1948, the Acre Plain was occupied by Jewish forces, direct contact was renewed in western Upper Galilee with the Ḥanitah bloc and Yeḥi'am. In the ten days of fighting between the first and second truces ("Operation Dekel," July 9–18, 1948), western, southern, and more of southeastern Galilee were taken, Arab forces were dislodged from their positions, and *Sepphoris and Nazareth came into Israel hands. The rest of Galilee, corresponding to the previous British Mandate borders, was brought under Israel control in "Operation Ḥiram" (Oct. 29–31, 1948); this fact was endorsed in the 1949 Armistice Agreement with Lebanon, in which a strip of territory west of the Naphtali Ridge which Israel had occupied returned to Lebanon.

In contrast with the events in other parts of the country, the movement of Israel forces in Galilee was followed by only a minor exodus of the Arab population; although a considerable part of the Muslims left, most of the Christians and almost all of the Druzes remained. This caused a relative increase of the latter two communities in Galilee's total population, with the following pattern of ethnic distribution thus emerging: Druze inhabit villages in western Upper Galilee, between Acre and Mount Meron, and one village, al-Maghār, further southeast. Around Nazareth in southwestern and central Lower Galilee, there are mostly Greek Orthodox and Roman Catholic villages, but also a number of Muslim villages which remained intact. Two villages of the Greek Catholics, Miʿilyā and Fassūta, lie in western Upper Galilee, and one of the Maronite faith (Gush Ḥalav = Jish), near the Lebanese border further east. During and immediately after the War of Independence, new kibbutzim were created, not only in the Acre Plain (*Sa'ar, *Gesher ha-Ziv, *Kabri, etc.) but also in the hills near the Lebanese border (*Ga'aton, *Yiftaḥ, *Sasa, Baram, etc.) and in Lower Galilee (*Lavi, *Ein-Dor, etc.). In the beginning of the 1950s, about 30 moshavim were added, many of them initially in the form of "work villages," the settlers earning their livelihood as hired workers in soil reclamation, afforestation and other projects until a minimum of land became available for their own farms. This was intended to create more or less continuous chains of Jewish settlements across Galilee from west to east. In the same period many newcomers were absorbed in Tiberias and Safed, but the growth of both towns later slowed down. Two new urban centers were established in southern Galilee—*Migdal ha-Emek in 1952, and Upper Nazareth in 1957. In the northwest, *Ma'alot and *Shelomi were founded as nuclei of development towns, but their progress was far from satisfactory. The new moshavim in the hills also encountered difficulties, as their infrastructure of cultivable land and available water proved too narrow and the choice of farming branches was limited by local conditions. The non-Jewish villages of Galilee, on the other hand, entered a phase of prosperity. Provided through government aid with access as well as internal roads, water installation, electricity, educational facilities, and municipal and social services, they modernized their farming methods and added new branches (e.g., deciduous fruit orchards) to the traditional ones (such as olives, tobacco, sheep, goats); many inhabitants worked in the cities as skilled or semi-skilled laborers, but kept their dwellings and holdings in the villages. Housing improved, and the built-up areas of the villages expanded, as most of them doubled or even tripled their population between 1948 and 1968. When surveys showed that Galilee's opportunities were still far from being fully used and that more settlers could be absorbed there, both urban and rural settlement was furthered. Upper Nazareth grew quickly in the 1960s, and the initial stagnation at Migdal ha-Emek was overcome by industrialization. In 1963 a Central Galilee development project was started by the Israel government, the JNF, and the Jewish Agency settlement department. Within its framework, a new village bloc was established near the Lebanese border (Biranit, Shetulah, Netu'ah, Zarit) and development work was carried out in the Yodefat-Mount Ḥazon area. In 1964, the town of *Karmi'el was founded, which expanded mostly after 1967.

Northern Israel, comprising in addition to the Galilean hill regions areas in the Upper and Central Jordan Valley, in the Jezreel Valley, and in the Acre Plain, increased its population from 53,400 in the 1948 census to 194,300 in 1961, and to 240,900 in 1968; accordingly, the population density increased from about 1,145 per sq. mi. (44.2 per sq. km.) in 1948 to about 362.6 (101.4) in 1961, and to almost 339.4 (131.0) in 1968. In 1968 Galilee proper (i.e., the natural regions of eastern Upper and Lower Galilee, the Hazor Region, the Nazareth-Tir'an hills, and western Upper and Lower Galilee) had 145 inhabited places, of which 88 were Jewish and 57 non-Jewish, and its population totaled 237,400, of which 66,800 were Jews and 170,600 non-Jews. [E.O.]

Bibliography: Maisler, in: BJPES, 11 (1944), 39ff.; Alt, in: PJB, 33 (1937), 52ff.; idem, in: ZDPV, 52 (1929), 220ff.; S. Klein, *Ereẓ ha-Galil* (1946); Y. Aharoni, *Hitnaḥalut Shivtei Yisrael ba-Galil ha-Elyon* (1957); Avi-Yonah, Land, index; Abel, Geog, 2 (1938), passim; Aharoni, Land, passim; EM, 2 (1965), 506–7; R. Dafni, *Galilee* (1961).

GALILI, ISRAEL (1910–), labor and *Haganah leader in Ereẓ Israel. Born in Brailov, in the Ukraine, Galili was taken to Ereẓ Israel by his family at the age of four. In 1924 he was among the founders of Ha-No'ar ha-Oved, the youth wing of the *Histadrut, and was among the organizers of the first agricultural collective of this organization, kibbutz Na'an (1930). With the establishment of the Youth Center in the Histadrut, Galili was called upon to work in the new framework, and at the same time he worked at the center of the Haganah. In 1941 he joined its central command as one of three Histadrut representatives. He was in the minority (Si'ah B) in the controversy that led to the split in Mapai in 1944 and became a leader of *Aḥdut ha-Avodah (B) upon its establishment. From 1945 to 1947, during the anti-British struggle of the *yishuv*, Galili was one of the principal organizers of underground armed activities, and on "Black Saturday" (June 29, 1946) he was among the heads of the Haganah who evaded imprisonment by the British. In the spring of 1947, David *Ben-Gurion appointed him head of Haganah's territorial command, and in this capacity he did much to prepare it for the *War of Independence (1948) against Arab guerrillas and the invading Arab armies. During the war itself, he was in charge of all army matters, especially the purchase of arms. He was deputy minister of defense in the provisional government (1948–49) and opposed the dissolution of the *Palmaḥ command ordered by Ben-Gurion. Galili was a member of the Knesset from its foundation.

Israel Galili, Haganah leader and Israel labor politician. Israel Government Press Office.

In January 1948 Galili supported the union of left Zionist parties in *Mapam; but when Mapam faced a crisis over the question of its attitude to the Soviet Union, he contributed decisively to the resurrection of Aḥdut ha-Avodah as an independent party (1954). During deliberations over the alignment of Aḥdut ha-Avodah with Mapai (1961), which eventually led to the union of the two parties in the *Israel Labor Party (1967), he strongly supported unification. From 1966 he was a minister without portfolio in the Israel government, being responsible for the information services in Israel, including broadcasting (until 1970). From 1969 he was one of Prime Minister Golda *Meir's main advisers. [Y.S.]

GALIPAPA, ELIJAH MEVORAKH (d. 1740), Turkish rabbi. Galipapa was born in Sofia and went to Jerusalem in 1702. He fled from there after being imprisoned for his inability to pay the heavy taxation imposed on him, and reached Rhodes where, in 1704, he became deputy to the chief rabbi, Elijah ha-Kohen ibn Ardut. Galipapa is the author of *Yedei Eliyahu* (Constantinople, 1728) in two parts: (1) the *takkanot* (ordinances) instituted by the prophets; (2) novellae. Many more of his novellae remain unpublished. His tombstone still stands in Rhodes.

Bibliography: Azulai, 1 (1852), 21 no. 155; 2 (1852), 59 no. 7; Fuenn, Keneset, 104; Frumkin-Rivlin, 2 (1928), 158f.; Rosanes, Togarmah, 4 (1935), 240, 348–9. [S.Mar.]

GALIPAPA, ḤAYYIM BEN ABRAHAM (1310–1380), Spanish talmudist. Galipapa was born in Monzon, Aragon. He served as rabbi of Huesca and subsequently of Pamplona. The following works by him are known: *Emek Refa'im,* a commentary to the tractate *Semaḥot* which includes a description of the *Black Death and the persecutions of the Jews which came in its train in Catalonia and Provence during the years 1347–50—extracts from it are given by *Joseph ha-Kohen in his *Emek ha-Bakha* and *Divrei ha-Yamim le-Malkhei Ẓarefat; Iggeret ha-Ge'ullah,* mentioned by Joseph Albo in his *Ikkarim* (4:42); a commentary on the *Seder Avodah* (for the Day of Atonement) of Joseph b. Isaac ibn *Avitur, extracts from which are given in the *Kovez Ma'asei Yedei Ge'onim Kadmonim* (1856; pt. 2, 120–2). There is also extant a letter by *Isaac b. Sheshet (Resp. Ribash 394) to Galipapa from which the latter's views on *halakhah* can be seen. Galipapa's place in the Spanish Judaism of his time was determined by the great daring he displayed both in thought and in *halakhah.* According to Joseph Albo (loc. cit.), Galipapa maintained that all Isaiah's prophecies of deliverance had reference to the Second Temple and Daniel's vision in chapter 7 to the Hasmoneans. It is evident that in his work Galipapa intended to abolish belief in the coming of the Messiah or at least to deny that there was a basis for such belief in the Bible. Galipapa also showed an exceptional tendency toward leniency in *halakhah.* He maintained that there was no need to conceal permissive laws out of fear that the permission would cause the ignorant to fall into error with regard to things forbidden "for they are all wise and with understanding, knowing the Torah, expert in the minutiae of the precepts, and as full of precepts as is the pomegranate of seeds" (Isaac b. Sheshet, loc. cit.). In opposition to the opinions of all authorities before him he ruled that combing the hair on the Sabbath is not forbidden. To find a basis for this permissiveness Galipapa was compelled arbitrarily to amend the text of the Talmud, thus aggravating still more the opposition to him.

Bibliography: Michael, Or, no. 866; Graetz-Rabbinowitz, 5 (1897), 309–11; Weiss, Dor, 5 (1904[4]), 147f.; I. F. Baer, *Toledot ha-Yehudim bi-Sefarad ha-Noẓerit* (1959[2]), 271. [J.Lev.]

GALIPAPA, MAIMON (14th–15th century?), Spanish satirical poet. Galipapa, called "En" (=Don) Maimon Galipapa, was possibly identical with the Galipapa mentioned in a document of 1353 from Valencia. He is the author of *Ma'amarei ha-Rofe'im,* a parody on the *Aphorisms* of Hippocrates, a medical work highly popular in the Middle Ages, and *Neder Almanah,* a satire about a widow who quickly forgets her late husband. Presumably he also wrote the anonymous humorous pamphlet *Midyenei Ishah* ("Contentions of a Wife") which appeared together with *Ma'amarei ha-Rofe'im* in Ferrara in 1551.

Bibliography: I. Davidson, *Shalosh Halaẓot . . . Meyuḥasot le-R. Yosef Zabara* (1904); J. Zabara, *Sefer Sha'ashu'im,* ed. by I. Davidson (1914[2]) xcix–ci, 73; Davidson, Oẓar, 4 (1933), 433; H. Friedenwald, *Jews and Medicine,* 1 (1944), 69–83; Schirmann, Sefarad, 2 (1956), 547–54. [J.H.Sch.]

GALLEGO, JOSEPH SHALOM (d. 1624), Hebrew poet. Originating in Salonika, Gallego was for 14 years *ḥazzan* in Amsterdam. He later migrated to Ereẓ Israel. His *"Imrei No'am"* (Amsterdam, 1628) is a collection of devotional poems for the festivals, fast days, weddings, and circumcisions. The Spanish songs according to whose tune they were to be sung are generally indicated. Some of the poems are by Gallego; other poems of his are included in the collection *Kol Tefillah ve-Kol Zimrah* by David *Franco-Mendes (Ms.). He also translated into Spanish the ethical writings of Jonah *Gerondi (*Sendroe* [Sendero] *de Vidas,* Amsterdam, n.d. and 1640[2]).

Bibliography: Dukes, in: *Litteraturblatt des Orients,* 5 (1844), 440–1; 6 (1845), 146; Steinschneider, Cat Bod, 485 no. 3216; I. S. da Silva Rosa, *Geschiedenis der portugeesche Joden te Amsterdam* (1925), 8, 26; Davidson, Oẓar, 4 (1933), 408, s.v. *Yosef Shalom Galliano.* [J.H.Sch.]

GALLICO (or **Gallichi**), Italian family of French origin. The family first lived in Rome where it was known from the 14th century. In 1323, a "Gallichi" (which may however imply "French") synagogue is mentioned there. Later the Gallico family spread to other Italian towns. MALACHI (Angelo) GALLICO was physician and rabbi in Cori, a village of Rome, in 1565 when the community decided to accept the invitation of Joseph *Nasi and move en masse to Tiberias. SAMUEL GALLICO, rabbi and kabbalist, published a summary of Moses *Cordovero's *Pardes Rimmonim,* under the title of *Asis Rimmonim* (Venice, 1601). In the

Crest of the Gallico family, an illumination added to the 14th-century *Golden Haggadah* on the occasion of the marriage of Rosa, daughter of R. Joab Gallico, to R. Menahem Rava in Carpi, 1603. London, British Museum, Add. Ms. 27210, fol. 16r.

16th, 17th, and 18th centuries several other rabbis and scholars belonging to this family are mentioned in Mantua, Modena, and Siena. Another member of the family was the Hebrew scholar and poet Abraham b. Hananiah de Gallichi *Jagel.

Bibliography: A. Milano, *Ghetto di Roma* ... (1964), index; Mortara, Indice; C. Roth, *The House of Nasi: Duke of Naxos* (1948), 125–30; D. Kaufmann, in: JQR, 2 (1889/90), 291–7, 305–10. [A.Mil.]

GALLICO, ELISHA BEN GABRIEL (c. 1583), talmudic scholar and kabbalist in Safed. Gallico was a pupil of Joseph *Caro and a member of the latter's *bet din.* After the death of Caro he was a member of Moses *di Trani's *bet din.* Gallico was the teacher of Samuel *Uceda. Gallico's signature appears—once together with the other scholars of Safed—on several responsa (in Caro's *Avkat Rokhel,* etc.). After Caro's death, according to his instructions, Gallico banned Azariah *dei Rossi's *Me'or Einayim.* The collection of Gallico's responsa has been lost; however several of them are quoted both in the work *Keneset ha-Gedolah* and in the responsa, *Ba'ei Ḥayyei* by Ḥayyim *Benvenisti. Gallico wrote homiletic and kabbalistic commentaries on all the five scrolls. The commentaries on Ecclesiastes (Venice 1578), Esther (Venice 1583), and the Song of Songs (Venice 1587) have been published. Toward the end of his life he headed a yeshivah in Safed.

Bibliography: L. Zunz, in: *Kerem Ḥemed,* 5 (1841), 141; Michael, Or, no. 474; D. Tamar, in: *Sefunot,* 7 (1963), 173; idem, in: KS, 33 (1958), 378. [D.Ta.]

°**GALLING, KURT** (1900–), German Lutheran biblical scholar. He was professor at Halle from 1928 to 1945, at Mainz from 1946 to 1954, from 1955 at Goettingen, and from 1962 at Tuebingen. A versatile and prolific scholar, Galling published works and articles on archaeology and biblical history, theology, and exegesis, including: *Der Altar in den Kulturen des Alten Orients* (1925); *Die Erwaehlungstraditionen Israels* (1928); *Biblisches Reallexikon* (1937); *Der Prediger Salomo* (1940, 1964²); *Das Bild vom Menschen in biblischer Sicht* (1947); *Die Buecher der Chronik, Esra, Nehemia* (1954); and *Studien zur Geschichte Israels im persischen Zeitalter* (1964). From 1957 to 1962 Galling edited the third edition of *Die Religion in Geschichte und Gegenwart,* to which he contributed scores of articles in various fields.

Bibliography: RGG³, Registerband (1965), 69–70; *Theologische Literaturzeitung,* 85 (1960), 153–8, incl. extensive bibl. [Ed.]

GALLIPOLI, port in European Turkey, on the S. coast of the Gallipoli peninsula. Benjamin of Tudela, the 12th-century traveler, found 200 Jews in Gallipoli; they are also mentioned during the reign of Michael VIII Palaeologus in 1261. In 1354 Gallipoli came under Turkish rule. The number of Jews increased at the end of the 15th century, when the Romaniot Jews were joined by refugees from Spain and Portugal. In 1576, during a period of prosperity, a conflict broke out between the Romaniots and the Sephardim over the division of taxes. In 1666 the pseudo-messiah *Shabbetai Ẓevi was confined to the fortress of Abydos (called by the Jews *Migdal Oz,* "Tower of Strength") in the vicinity of Gallipoli; his prison became a center of Shabbatean activity.

During the 19th century the Jewish community prospered. Among the Jews were merchants, artisans, and civil servants. In 1912 there were 2,500 Jews in Gallipoli. The earthquake in the same year destroyed the Jewish quarter, but no Jews were killed. During the Balkan Wars (1912–13) refugees, including Jews, streamed into Gallipoli. The

באור

ספר קהלת

לחכם השלם הגאון כמהר״ר
אלישע גאליקו נר״ו ריש
מתיבתא בצפת
תעב״ו

נדפס בבית זואן

פה ויניציאה

Title page of *Be'ur Sefer Kohelet,* a commentary on Ecclesiastes by Elisha b. Gabriel Gallico, 16th-century Safed kabbalist. Venice, 1578. Jerusalem, J.N.U.L.

Va'ad ha-Hazzalah ("Rescue Committee"), founded then, aided the refugees, as well as the Jewish soldiers from Syria and Iraq. In 1915 the Zion Mule Corps, as part of the British Army, fought the Turks on the Gallipoli peninsula (see *Jewish Legion). From 1933 all religious and administrative affairs of the Gallipoli community were subordinated to the district rabbinate of *Canakkale. As a result of emigration to Istanbul and the United States between the two world wars and subsequently to Israel, the number of Jews in Gallipoli decreased. In 1948 there were about 400 Jews in Gallipoli, and in 1951 about 200. By 1970 the few remaining families in Gallipoli were mainly engaged in commerce.

Bibliography: Angel, in: *Almanakh Izraelit* (1923), 109–11 (Ladino); Rosanes, Togarmah, 1 (1930²), 4; 3 (1938²), 127–8; Scholem, Shabbetai Ẓevi, index. [S.MAR.]

GALON (Heb. גַּלְאוֹן), kibbutz in southern Israel, northeast of *Kiryat Gat, affiliated with Kibbutz Arẓi ha-Shomer ha-Ẓa'ir. It was founded on the night of Oct. 6, 1946, as one of 11 settlements established simultaneously in the Negev. The founding members hailed from Poland, where a number of them lived in ghettos or were partisans fighting the Nazis. In the *War of Independence (1948), Galon served as a vantage point for Israel columns in dislodging Arab forces from the Bet Guvrin and southern foothills area. Its economy was based on intensive crops, livestock, and a factory for electric appliances. Its name, meaning "Monument to Strength," commemorates fallen ghetto fighters. In 1968 it had a population of 350 inhabitants. [E.O.]

GALUT (**Golah**; Heb. (גּוֹלָה) גָּלוּת), exile.

The Concept. The Hebrew term *galut* expresses the Jewish conception of the condition and feelings of a nation uprooted from its homeland and subject to alien rule. The term is essentially applied to the history and the historical consciousness of the Jewish people from the destruction of the Second Temple to the creation of the State of Israel. The residence of a great number of members of a nation, even the majority, outside their homeland is not definable as *galut* so long as the homeland remains in that nation's possession.

Only the loss of a political-ethnic center and the feeling of uprootedness turns Diaspora (Dispersion) into *galut* (Exile). The feeling of exile does not always necessarily accompany the condition of exile. It is unique to the history of the Jewish people that this feeling has powerfully colored the emotions of the individual as well as the national consciousness. The sense of exile was expressed by the feeling of alienation in the countries of Diaspora, the yearning for the national and political past, and persistent questioning of the causes, meaning, and purpose of the exile. Jewish mystics perceived a defectiveness in the Divine Order which they connected with alienation in this world—"the exile of the Divine Presence."

The Diaspora Pattern. The process of Jewish dispersion in various countries during different periods was due to the combination of national catastrophes, military defeats, destructions, persecutions, and expulsions, as well as to normal social and economic processes—migration to new places of settlement and transition to new means of livelihood. The expression "Egyptian Exile" for the period before the Exodus is merely a homiletic conception of later date; but there is no doubt that Jewish dispersion had already begun in a normal way a long time before the concept of exile developed. The conquests of the Arabs between 632 and 719 changed the pattern of the Diaspora by uniting large parts of the Jewry of the Roman Empire with that of the Persian Kingdom. The Muslim armies extirpated the Jews from the Arabian peninsula, with the exception of those in Yemen and Wadi al-Qara, but created favorable conditions of development for the exiles in the remainder of the lands of Islam. In the Christian world, this period is marked by the progress of the Jewish dispersion in Gaul and later in Germany and Britain. From the 11th century, the Jewry of the West (see *Germany) managed to maintain itself under increasingly difficult conditions and even spread to central Germany. The changes in the territorial supremacies of Christianity and Islam as a result of the Crusades and the Reconquest in Spain, as well as the *expulsions in the Christian countries, brought changes in the configuration of the Jewish Diaspora from one period to another.

By processes of both expulsion and attraction, the Jews penetrated the expanses of Poland-Lithuania during the 15th century. The migration eastward was halted by the total prohibition imposed on the admission of Jews by the grand duchy of Moscow (see *Russia). After 1497 there were no professing Jews (except for the underground of forced converts—*anusim) left in all of the lands bordering the Atlantic including England. During the 17th century, however, the Jews returned and penetrated to the Netherlands and England. The Jewish population in the Ottoman Empire had increased in numbers after the Spanish Expulsion. The largest Jewish concentrations during the 16th to 18th centuries were to be found in the Ottoman Empire and the kingdom of Poland-Lithuania. The persecutions of 1648–49 (see Bogdan *Chmielnicki) started off the migration of Jews in Eastern Europe toward the West, a process which continued and intensified throughout the modern era.

At the close of the 18th century, the partitions of Poland as well as the French Revolution led to a Jewish expansion toward the western provinces of Russia, the northeastern provinces of Austria, the Kingdom of Prussia and the French territories. Economic, social, cultural, and political developments made Ashkenazi European Jewry the most important in the Diaspora, both numerically and in dynamism, throughout the 19th century and the first 30 years of the 20th. As formerly, liberalist or restrictive trends in this period also determined the pattern of Jewish dispersion in the world. It was only in 1917 that the revolution in Russia abolished the *Pale of Settlement and removed the last barriers to the settlement of Jews throughout the territory of the great Eurasian power.

In America individual Sephardi Jews had already begun to arrive during the 16th century. However, the emigration of considerable groups of Jews there was only to begin during the mid-19th century when many left Germany; the transfer of masses of Jews from Eastern Europe to the new world, especially the United States, only began during the last quarter of the 19th century. The flow of mass emigration to the United States and later also to Canada and the South American countries, coupled with the impetus of Zionism and trends of modern nationalism, have contributed to the shift to new centers of gravity. The catastrophe of the persecutions in Germany from 1933, the conquests of the Nazis until 1939, and the decimation of European Jewry in the Holocaust from 1939 until 1945, have created the present situation (the 1970s) when the numerical majority in the Jewish Diaspora is to be found on the American continent, while Ereẓ Israel has the third largest Jewish concentration in the world (Soviet Russia is the second). In Ereẓ Israel, the independent Jewish politico-national center has been revived. As in the Second

Temple era, through the State of Israel, the Jewish nation has regained the basic pattern of a Diaspora with a state as its center (see *Diaspora).

Second Temple and Mishnah Period. It can be assumed that the severe persecutions in the days of Antiochus Epiphanes and the success of the ensuing rebellion contributed to the Jews' feeling of being out of place in the Diaspora and their yearning for Judea. Despite this, the growth of the Diaspora was more pronounced in the hellenistic kingdoms and in the Roman Empire. Prophecies and poems of pietists gave expression to the tragedy of the *galut* combined with the feeling of the inevitability and continuity of the Diaspora. In the second half of the second century B.C.E. the sibyls explain to their nation, "it is thy fate to leave thine holy soil" (Or. Sibyll. 3:267), a fate described as encompassing the whole world and causing hatred toward those who are dispersed because of their way of life (*ibid.*, 3:271–2). In the second half of the first century it was stated that, "among every nation are the dispersed of Israel according to the word of God" (Ps. of Sol. 9:2); the conquests of Pompey were also seen as a cause of the *galut* (*ibid.*, 17:13–14, 18). Even prior to the destruction of the Temple were sensed the dangers which stemmed from the general dispersion, as foretold in the biblical warnings (Test. Patr., Ash. 7:2–7). On the other hand there were groups who expressed the feelings of the people in their own cultural terms and wrote favorably of the Diaspora and their neighbors, tending to regard the dispersion as a normal and even desirable situation (Philo, *De Legatione ad Gaium*, 281; Jos., Ant. 4:115–6).

After the destruction of the Temple the question of the *galut* as existence under foreign rule without a Temple and without a spiritual center was discussed. In the spirit and the style of the Bible, it was said that "behold we are yet this day in captivity, where Thou hast scattered us, for a reproach and a curse and a punishment" (I Bar. 3:8); but thought was directed mainly to the possibility of existing in a land of gentiles and under their rule (*ibid.*, 1:12, 4:6). The question of the meaning and the justification of the exile begins to be asked in all earnestness: the evil nations dwell in prosperity and the chosen people suffer; the author of IV Ezra (3:32–34, 6:59) argues with his Creator, asking: "Have the deeds of Babylon been better than those of Zion? Has any other nation known Thee besides Zion? . . . If the world has indeed been created for our sakes, why do we not enter into possession of our world?—How long shall this endure?" He is bitter about the fact of "the reproach of the nations" and the profaning of God's name which occurs in the *galut* (*ibid.* 4:23–25), but he lays no stress on the physical suffering entailed. Accepting neither the cosmic explanation of the exile, nor the mysteriousness of the ways of the Lord, nor the world to come, which nullify the valuation of the events in this world (*ibid.* 4:9–10), he seeks to explain the exile as a road of suffering which must be traveled in order to reach the good (*ibid.* 7:3–16). He is comforted in the exile by the vision of the lion—the Messiah—who will destroy the eagle—Rome (*ibid.* ch. 12).

The author of II Baruch (10:9–16) almost despairs of all life, from the survival of the people to cultivating the land, a mood which is also found in the "ascetics who multiplied" (BB 60b) after the destruction of the Temple. The essence of the tragedy of the exile seems to him, too, to be a diminution of the honor of God in the eyes of the gentiles and the degradation of the Jewish people (II Bar. 67:2–8). The deep spiritual shock which followed in the wake of the dispersion is expressed in this book: There were Jews who despaired of the possibility of spiritual leadership of the people after the destruction of the Temple and the cessation of the sacrifices and the priesthood (*ibid.* 77:13–14). In the spirit of Jabneh and from the power of the Torah, which exists even in the *galut*, the author answers their despondency: "Shepherds and lamps and fountains come from the law . . .if therefore ye have respect to ponder on the law and are intent upon wisdom the spiritual leadership will not be lacking" (*ibid.* 77:15–16).

Thus the problems of the *galut*, its meaning, and its essence were considered in great depth and with considerable apprehension during the first two generations after the destruction of the Temple. It is true that the ideas voiced in the Apocrypha were not heard by the people in general and their influence was not noticeable, but they reflect a feeling and emotional state which are similar to those expressed in the Mishnah, the Talmud, and the Midrashim.

The thinking of the *tannaim* and *amoraim* on the *galut* and its meaning is extensive and varied, developing in the light of the changes which took place from the days of the Second Temple until about the fifth century C.E. In general the patterns of thought and the imagery of the Bible prevail, together with those of many apocryphal works. However, they express their feelings with greater and more penetrating detail, arising from the depths of their degradation and the suffering occasioned by the rise of Christianity, when they passed from subjugation to alien pagans to subjugation to the rule of a Jewish heresy.

Apprehension of the pain of the destruction was so severe that "the ascetics in Israel who refused to eat meat and to drink wine increased"; this recourse to complete abstinence, whose intention was self-annihilation of the nation ("it is fitting that we should decree upon ourselves not to marry nor beget children") was not accepted, and the moderate path of limited mourning and remembering the destruction of the Temple was followed instead (BB 60b). Yet from the beginning the *galut* was a phenomenon which demanded an explanation: even the gentiles asked: "And His people, what did they do to Him that He exiled them from their land?" (ARN[2] 1, 4). The sages could not be satisfied with a general answer about the sins of the people, and they gave their opinion about the specific causes of the destruction of the Second Temple. Unlike the first exile, which resulted from idol worship, incest, and the shedding of innocent blood, the second destruction was caused by baseless hatred and the love of money (Yoma 9b). Alongside these realistic types of explanation, there is a widespread tendency to connect the *galut* with the past and to find in it links for the future. Abraham had to decide whether to choose for his children either "Gehinnom or foreign kings," and some say that Abraham chose Gehinnom for himself and God chose the foreign kings for him (Gen. R. 44:21). Even the ram struggling among the thorns was a symbol for Abraham that "thy children will be trapped by iniquities and be entangled by troubles . . . and by foreign kings" (TJ, Ta'an. 2:4, 65d; Gen. R. 56:9; Mid. Ḥag. to Gen. 22, 13). When the tribes in the desert "wept without cause," "from that hour it was determined that the Temple would be destroyed in order that Israel would be exiled among the nations" and there would then be a reason for their weeping (Num. R. 16:20; Ta'an. 29a). R. Abbahu, at the end of the third century, compares the expulsions of the people and their banishment as punishment for violating the covenant with the expulsion and banishment of Adam from the Garden of Eden after he had transgressed the commandment of the Lord (PdRK 119b). The exile from "country to country" was considered one of the ten decrees proclaimed against Adam (ARN[2] 42, 116). The sages give varied interpretations to the dispersion and its temporary nature, regarding as a specially severe decree the fact that the Jews were not concentrated in one place, but scattered among the nations "as a man scatters grain with a winnowing shovel and not one grain sticks to another" (Sifra. 6:6). Everywhere the Jews are only "temporary" (i.e., wanderers) and the "dwellers" (the permanent population) are the children of Esau (Deut. R. 1, 22). The suffering of the exile is equal to all other suffering combined (Sif. Deut. 43); it is "like death and the abyss" (Mid. Ps. to 71:4). In the *galut* Israel is a mendicant (*ibid.* to 9:15), deprived of its pride, which has been given to the gentiles (Ḥag. 5b). There is no way for the exiled nation to defend itself since "Israel is among the 70 mighty nations; what can [Israel] do?" (PR 9:32a).

The very soul of the Jew is affected in the *galut*, which renders him "unclean with iniquities" (Song R. 8:14). Nor is the individual soul alone affected: the *galut* detracts from the completeness of the Kingdom of Heaven (Mid. Ps. to 97:1). The *Shekhinah* "moans like a dove" and the "Holy One blessed be He roars like a lion" over the destruction of the Temple and over the children of Israel . . . "Whom I have exiled among the nations" (Ber. 3a; cf. Ḥag. 5b). From the time of R. Akiva it became accepted belief that "in every place where Israel was exiled the *Shekhinah* was exiled with them" (Mekh., Pisḥa 14; Meg. 29a; TJ, Ta'an. 1:1, 64a; etc.). This idea connected the exile of Israel with the fate of the world as a whole and became a source of encouragement and faith.

Despite the feeling of suffering and the oppression of the exile, the rabbis at all times firmly believed that the *galut* would not mean total destruction. God had made the nations of the world swear that "they would not subjugate Israel overmuch"; the great sufferings in the *galut* consisted a violation of this oath, and this would hasten the advent of the Messiah (Ket. 111a; Song R. 2:7).

The rabbis saw a cause for satisfaction even in the negative aspects of the *galut*. The suffering emphasizes the faithfulness of Israel and gives it an opportunity to say to God "How many religious persecutions and harsh edicts have they decreed against us in order to nullify Thy sovereignty over us, but we have not done so" (Mid. Ps. to 5:6). The sages saw the dispersion as a prerequisite for the redemption: in the settlement of Jews throughout the whole Roman Empire ("if one of you is exiled to Barbary and another to Sarmatia") they saw (in the second half of the second century) a fulfillment of this condition (Song R. 2:8; PdRK 47a–48a; PR 15:71b). Nevertheless, according to the opinion of Rav: "When Israel merits it, the majority of them will be in the land of Israel and a minority in Babylonia, but when they are unworthy of it, the majority will be in Babylonia and the minority in Ereẓ Israel" (Gen. R. 98:9).

The increase in the number of converts in the Roman Empire gave added meaning to the dispersion. At the beginning of the third century the *amoraim* R. Johanan and R. Eleazar gave the interpretation that "the Lord did not exile Israel among the nations except in order that there should be added to them converts" (Pes. 87b). In the eyes of the homilists who expressed similar sentiments, the people of Israel was like a "flask of perfume," which emits its scent only when it is shaken, and to Abraham, who made converts, it was said, as a sign for his descendants, "Wander about in the world, and your name will become great in my world" (Song R. 1:4). This evaluation of the Diaspora is similar to that of Philo and Josephus, and it is possible that the *amoraim* are only repeating views which were widespread for a long time before them, when the conversion movement was at its height. With the adoption of Christianity by the Roman Empire and with the decrease in conversion, the dispersion took on an additional aspect of national security. When a Christian sectarian boasted, "We are better than you," for "when you were given permission to destroy Rome, you left none in it except a pregnant woman" and "you have been with us many years and we do not do anything to you," R. Oshaiah answered that it is not the mercy of the rulers which assured survival in exile, but the political situation. Their wide dispersion saves the Jewish people from total destruction and thus "the Lord did a righteous thing to Israel in scattering them among the nations" (Pes. 87b; cf. SER 11:54). As a favor to His exiled people the Lord sees to it that no one kingdom dominates the world: "He divided His world into two nations, into two kingdoms . . . in order to preserve Israel" (*ibid.*, 20:11, 4). In the ancient promise to the patriarchs that their children would be "as the dust of the earth," the rabbis found a symbol of the *galut;* "As the dust of the earth is scattered from one end of the world to the other, thus your children will be scattered from one end of the world to the other, as the dust of the earth causes even metal vessels to wear out but exists forever, so Israel is eternal but the nations of the world will become nought . . . as the dust of the earth is threshed, so thy children will be threshed by the nations . . ." (Gen. R. 41:9).

Like Ezekiel, and in the same language and spirit, the sages deal with the problem of religious observance in the Diaspora. The absence of sacrifices and of the Temple was liable to undermine the foundations of the religion. Some maintained that from a religious point of view the Jewish people in exile could be compared to a slave who had been sold and the laws obtaining in his former master's house did not apply to him: "When we were in His city and in His house and in His Temple we served him; now that we have been exiled among the nations—let us act as they do" (SER 29:159; Sifra, Be-Ḥukkotai 8:4). An echo of the fear expressed by the author of I Baruch is heard in the saying of the sages that in the exile "knowledge has been taken from them . . . they will be lacking in the study of the Torah" (Mekh., Ba-Ḥodesh, 1). These were, however, the effects of the first shock. The people overcame them, finding solace in the teaching of the sages. The commandments assumed new value in the *galut* and the Torah was studied. When the national organism sought means of defense and survival for its separate life as a community in an alien environment, it was realized that in exile the nation had lost all signs of social-national unity; "for what has remained to them . . . all the boons which had been given to them have been taken from them; and were it not for the Torah which remained to them, they would be no different from the nations of the world" (Sifra, Be-Ḥukkotai 8:10). In the *galut* the Torah was both the anchor and the protective wall for survival, preserving unity: this had already been symbolized in the promise of the "dust of the earth": "As the dust of the earth is not blessed except with water, so Thy children are not blessed except by the virtue of the Torah" (Gen. R. 41:9). Even God wondered at the way they maintained their religious-national status in the long exile: "My child I am full of wonder, how did you wait for Me all these years?—and Israel answered . . . were it not for the *Sefer Torah* which Thou hast written for us the nations of the world would already have made us lost to Thee" (PdRK). The Torah is the marriage contract which was given to the faithful wife.

To the sages, the social and psychological battle of the people as a whole and of each individual to resist the blandishments of *assimilation in the exile gave meaning to the trouble and sufferings which resulted from it. From their knowledge of the conditions of life in the exile they understood that "had they found a refuge, they would not have returned" (Gen. R. 33:6). In interpreting the ideas expressed by Ezekiel, they saw the social disabilities and the physical suffering of the exile as a means of annulling the desire to abandon the Torah: "Without your consent, against your will, I imposed My sovereignty upon you . . . for they immediately humble their heart in repentance" (Sifra, Be-Ḥukkotai 8:4–5). It is stated even more emphatically, perhaps as a result of the increase in their troubles and persecutions: "When your bones are crushed and your eyes are put out and the blood of your mouths spill to the ground, you cause His kingdom to reign over you" (SER 29:159). The sufferings on their part add a special reward and meaning to the observance of the Torah and its study: "The later generations are better than the former; although there is subjugation to foreign kings, there is study of Torah" (Yoma 9b).

The spiritual struggle to explain and justify the exile became intensified from the time that Judaism was obliged, from the fourth century onward, to contend with Christianity, which saw in the exile of Israel a witness and a sign that the divine favor had been taken from Israel and given to the church and its adherents. This polemic tone is particularly noticeable in the words of the *paytanim* and in late Midrashim (see *Apologetics).

As the duration of the exile extended, fears grew: when they saw that oppression increased "with taxes . . . and with poll taxes . . . Jacob became afraid . . . would it last forever?" The people found their consolation in Messianic promises which were bound up with the liquidation of the *galut* and the ingathering of the exiles—"from Babylonia . . . from Gaul and from Spain" (PdRK 151a–b). When despair grew until they even went as far as to complain, "Is there any remedy for a servant whose master creates evils and troubles for him?" The remedy for this weakness of spirit was found in the doctrine that the troubles themselves were a sign of the true election of Israel (Ḥag. 5a).

The concept of exile and the description of the feelings it inspired which occur in the Mishnah, Talmud, and Midrashim reveal a community battling against adverse conditions and finding a rationale for accepting its sufferings and looking forward to the end of the *galut*. Through this concept the essence of the phenomenon, the reason for the dispersion among the nations, the religious, social, and national qualities of the nation for whom there remained only the Torah were considered; and in it expression was also given to the struggle against the religion which sought to find in the condition of the exile itself support for its claim that Judaism had come to an end, and that it could claim to be its heir.

Ideology in the Medieval World. During the Middle Ages both the reality of *galut* and its image acquired new intensity. Changes were wrought by the power and violence of events, the strength and fervor of continuous religious *disputations with the surrounding nations, and the soul searchings among Jews on the implications of *galut*, which appeared as a central element of both faith and world destiny. Every change in the fate of the exiles of "Edom" (as Christendom was termed) or "Ishmael" (Islam), in their legal position, and in their spiritual confrontation with Christianity and Islam, required fresh adaptation of the concept of *galut* to the new challenges.

In fact the position of the Jews and their status differed with time, place, and the attitude adopted in principle and practice toward them by Christian and Muslim rulers and peoples (see *History of the Jews; *Image of the Jew; *Blood Libel; Jewish *Badge; Covenant of *Omar; *Dhimmi).

Despite these distinctions, however, a fundamental conception of *galut* remained. Basically, throughout the Middle Ages exile was for the Jews everywhere a political and social condition characterized by alienation, humiliation, and servitude, and regarded as such by both non-Jews and Jews. Danger to life and limb and the actuality of expulsion were its permanent accompaniments. It was this situation which gave rise to ideas and imagery concerning the exile and its meaning in the minds of the dispersed and downtrodden nation.

The challenge of exile induced in response a system of thought which viewed *galut* as a course of suffering which uplifted the spirit, a penance for sins in this world, and a preparation for redemption. As an outcome both of medieval thinking in general and of the Jewish spiritual legacy in particular, Jewish thinkers emerged who, while they viewed exile against all its horrors, showed the majesty of God's purpose, and the greatness of the Jewish heritage, and who reinforced the faith of fellow Jews and countered the arguments of gentiles. The attitude of the Jews to exile during the Middle Ages can be measured by the extent of the response made by different generations to the appearance of pseudo-messiahs and *messianic movements, which were a direct and spontaneous expression of the desire to abolish the exile. The condition of alienation in the Diaspora also found perpetual expression in tradition, customs of mourning for Jerusalem, and the symbols perpetuating the memory of the destruction of the Temple. The immediate preparedness of individuals or groups of Jews to return and settle in Ereẓ Israel, the support given by the Diaspora for the immigrants, and the calls for aid and immigration from those in the Holy Land and their emissaries continued in all periods. The stories current in Jewish tradition concerning the Lost Ten *Tribes criticize under the veil of utopian legend Israel's lack of kingship and sovereignty and express the desire for their restoration. In conjunction with these popular expressions of the condition of *galut*, in which ideas concerning the exile and redemption are interwoven, Jewish thinkers advanced their views on the meaning of the sufferings and purpose of *galut*, and developed the ideology a stage further.

During the seventh century, with the rise of Islam and its victories over Christianity, it appeared to the Jews that contemporary events constituted a retribution on Israel's enemies and that it was the intent of Providence to ease the yoke of the exile (see *Nistarot de-Rabbi Shimon bar Yoḥai*). During the eighth century, *Anan b. David confirmed the custom of preserving strict mourning for Zion, and prohibited the eating of meat and drinking of wine. During the tenth century, after a number of messianic movements had failed, rationalist and skeptical outlooks increased within the community and a Judaism was conceived which did not anticipate redemption (Saadiah Gaon, *Beliefs and Opinions*, treatise 8). The ideas of the Karaite Al-*Kirkisānī testify that a similar attitude was emerging among certain Karaites (L. Nemoy, in HUCA, 7 (1930), 395; J. Mann, in JQR, 12 (1921/22), 283). However, the majority of the people did not agree with such extremes.

With time, the constant humiliation to which Jews in the Islamic Empire were subjected was felt more intensely, and in the period of unrest, when the Abbasid caliphate was in process of disintegration, the misfortunes of exile multiplied. Exile under Islam appeared a terrible fate to those living in it. Saadiah Gaon expressed the sentiments of those who remained among the faithful despite all adversities: "the servitude has been drawn out and the yoke of the [alien] kingdoms has been prolonged, behold every day we are increasingly impoverished and our numbers are reduced as time advances" (prayer for period of misfortune, in *Siddur Rav Sa'adyah Ga'on* (1963), 77–78, see also 350–1).

Out of this conception of the harshness of the exile, systematic arguments were advanced to prove that the *galut* was only temporary, and explanations were given on the meaning of the sufferings it entailed and the methods to be followed to bring about its termination. The Karaite "Mourners of Zion" (*Avelei Zion) gathered in Jerusalem, where they mortified themselves and prayed for the end of the exile, proclaiming their emotions in words saturated with the feeling of the misery of exile and expressing in their poetry the pain for the condition "of our poor mother," "whom we lifted up our eyes to see and could not recognize as a result of her ill appearance" (*Kovez le-Divrei Sifrut* ... (1941), 141–2). They considered that "Karaism is the path toward redemption, while the Rabbanite prolongs the exile" (J. Mann, in JQR, 12 (1921/22), 283).

Saadiah Gaon developed a theory of his own to explain the meaning of the exile: he considered that its imposition as a temporary punishment had substantial internal sense. Exile had befallen the nation "partly as punishment and partly as a test" (*Beliefs and Opinions,* treatise 8, 291), while this trial also had a purifying value: "to refine our dross ... and to terminate our impurities ... He has exiled us and scattered us among the nations, so that we have swum in the roaring waves of the kingdoms, and, as the smelting of silver in the furnace, in their fires ... we have been purified (*Siddur Rav Sa'adyah Ga'on* (1963), 78). Because of these principles "we patiently await" (*Beliefs and Opinions,* treatise 8, 292).

According to this conception, the endurance of the nation is a result of its historical experience and religious faith, and cannot be conceived by one "who has not experienced what we have experienced nor believed as we have believed" (*ibid.* 293). Saadiah Gaon points to the certainty of the justice of God as perceived by the believer, and the strength which he has revealed in his struggle against the severity of the exile as manifested in the present time, to prove that there must be meaning and end to *galut:* It is inconceivable "that He is not aware of our situation or that He does not deal fairly with us or that He is not compassionate ... nor ... that he has forsaken us and cast us off" (*ibid.* 294). In the exile "some of us are being subject to punishment and others to trials." This is the correct religious manner of explaining "every universal catastrophe ... such as famine, war, and pestilence" (*ibid.* 295). In this respect, *galut* is not to be distinguished from other natural and historical calamities which do not differentiate between the righteous and the wicked.

An explanation advanced by an anonymous profound thinker in some fragments extant from the tenth century gives the meaning of the exile as a mark of Israel's election, as a divine gift and the "blessing of Abraham" (HUCA, 12–13 (1937–38), 435ff). In his opinion, as far as can be discerned from the fragments, the purpose of the dispersion among the nations is that Israel should assume the function of the priest of the world, who atones for the sins of the nations and guides them by means of the yoke of the sufferings which he bears on his back and by the arguments which he constantly voices in their ears. The anonymous author is firmly convinced that "just as the dispersion has come about and materialized, so will the ingathering come about and be realized without delay" (*ibid.*).

From the beginning of the 11th century the academies of Babylonia were in a state of continuous decline, while Islam not only failed to disintegrate but also received additional strength by the accession of the Turks. The political situation with which Jews were faced was that of a hostile Islamic and Christian world composed of fragmented states. This situation called forth *Hai b. Sherira Gaon's description of the nation as "a threshold over which every passerby tramples" (Ḥ. Brody, *Mivḥar ha-Shirah ha-Ivrit,* ed. by A. M. Habermann (1946), 59). Protests emerged against God that the nation is "like Job ... forgotten ... in judgment and not remembered in mercy ... the King has rejected me ... He has seen me slaughtered and devoured and has not rebuked those who consumed me" (*ibid.* 59–60).

From the beginning of the tenth century, plentiful evidence is available concerning the feelings of exile among the Jews of Christian Europe. In Germany, *Simeon b. Isaac (Simeon the Great) described the state and feeling of exile during the period. Next to the fact of material suffering, he places especial stress on the spiritual danger which faced Jews in the Christian arguments that the exile is a proof of the Jews' responsibility for the sin of the crucifixion and their punishment for it, so that the exile can only be ended by their conversion to Christianity (*Piyyutei R. Shimon ha-Gadol,* ed. by A. M. Habermann (1938), 40–41). *Gershom b. Judah also felt the pressure of missionary arguments based on *galut* during the 10th to 11th centuries: "the enemy urges ... your yoke to remove ... to accept a despised idol as a god" (Ḥ. Brody, op. cit., 69–71).

Conditions deteriorated after the massacres of the First Crusade (1096) and the numerous cases of martyrdom (see **Kiddush ha-Shem*) that accompanied it (see *Crusades). A thousand years had elapsed since the destruction of the Temple and the beginning of the exile, and pertinence was thus added to the claim of the Christians that an exile of over one thousand years was a proof that God had abandoned the nation. The Reconquest in Spain transferred many Jews under Islamic rule to Christian dominance. Rashi was a witness of this change for the worse. He explains the hatred of the Christians for Jews because Israel does not "pursue after their lie in order to accept their erroneous belief" (on Ps. 69:5). He felt strongly the degradation of Israel and the mocking that their mourning evoked (on Isa. 52:14; Ps. 69:11; 88:9). The root of the evil was that the nation "is exiled ... from Erez Israel" (on Isa. 53:8). With a vivid plasticity of expression his commentaries (particularly to Isa. 53) convey the feeling of calamity experienced by the generation which underwent the persecutions of 1096. The sufferings related of the "servant of God" by the prophet are understood by Rashi in terms of the tragedy which befell his nation in Germany. There is a special religious justification for the acceptance of these sufferings in the concept of sanctification of the Holy Name: "His soul [of the martyr] is given over and sacrificed for My holiness, to return it to me as a trespass offering for all that he has transgressed ... this is an indemnity [Old French: *amende*] which a man gives to the one whom he has sinned against." Even so, Rashi is unable to reconcile himself to the flourishing state of the cruel nations, which weakens the hands of the God-fearing from His service as well as undermining their trust in Him (on Ps. 69:7; 88:11). On the subject of the sufferings of the righteous in the exile, Rashi follows the doctrine of Saadiah Gaon. In the climate of perpetual controversy with Christianity, Rashi conceives that the cause for the cruel persecution of the Jews originates in the jealousy of the nations of the Divine election of Israel, a fact which—despite everything—still applies (e.g., on Ps. 102:11). This explanation came to be generally accepted by Jews.

During the 12th century, *Eliezer of Beaugency, in France, advanced in his commentaries the idea that the perseverance of Jews in their faith in the Christian environment is the outcome of divine decree: "I will not put it in your heart to worship wood and stone, so that you become one nation with them and they do you no further evil; but I will harden your hearts against their faith ... and they will hate you so that among them you will fall by the sword, by fire, by captivity, and by plunder" (on Ezek.

20:32–33). Jews long to die "in battle," but their endurance of the life of exile is also an exposure to mortal danger. Ezekiel's vision of the "valley of the dry bones" is interpreted by Eliezer as referring to the House of Israel which had died in exile, to be "a great comfort to all those who have died for the unity of His Name, and even if they have not been done to death, since all their lives they have endured disgrace and shame and have been smitten and struck because they do not believe in their idol—and with this they have also died" (on Ezek. 37:9–15; cf. *Sefer Ḥasidim,* no. 263).

Of the tosafists (see **Tosafot*) *Eliezer b. Samuel of Metz, the disciple of Jacob b. *Meir Tam, emphasizes the bane of the exile from its spiritual aspect and attributes it to lack of political independence: "... our intelligence is confused, because we are in captivity without a king or country, and people who are not settled have neither heart nor knowledge" (*Sefer Yere'im ha-Shalem,* ed. by A. A. Schiff (1892), 72, nos. 31–32). *Moses b. Jacob of Coucy ascribes to the exile an ecumenical significance and purpose for drawing proselytes by serving as an example of moral conduct: "now that the exile has been prolonged more than necessary, Israel must abstain from the vanities of the world and take up the seal of God, which is truth, so as not to lie either to Israel or to the nations and not to lead them into error in any matter, and [Israel] must sanctify themselves even in that which is permitted ... and when God shall come to deliver them, the nations will say: He has done justly, because they are honest men and their Law is sincerely observed by them. But if they behave toward the Gentiles with deceit, they will say: see what the Lord has done, that He has chosen as His portion thieves and swindlers ... God sows Israel in the lands so that proselytes may be added to them, and so long as they deal deceitfully, who will join them? ..." (*Semag,* Assayin 74).

The conception of exile of the *Ḥasidei Ashkenaz is dominated by the phenomenon of *Kiddush ha-Shem,* which permeates all their thoughts on life. A description of the rigor of exile in 12th-century France was put into the mouth of the Jew in the disputation composed by Peter *Abelard (cf. Baer, in *Zion,* 6 (1934), 152–3). Spanish Jewry from the 11th century envisioned exile as an element in specific ideological-mystical configurations. In his *Megillat ha-Megalleh,* *Abraham b. Ḥiyya ha-Nasi considers that history was immanent in the Creation; thus even "this harsh exile in which we find ourselves today was decreed by the King in the six days of Creation"; the sins of the nation, which were its direct cause, were also foreseen in this primordial decree. Thus predestinational-astrological conception moves exile away from the notion of punishment, facilitating the discussion of the subject with Christians and especially with the mystics among them.

Powerful expression of the inner dilemma arising from the search for the reason for the exile is given by *Judah Halevi in his poetry and thought. His *Kuzari* was written "to defend the humiliated religion," and its dominant motif is the knowledge that the Christian and Muslim worlds "despise us for our degradation and poverty" (Judah Halevi, *The Kuzari,* tr. by H. Hirschfeld (1964), pt. 1 no. 113). To meet the arguments of the oppressors who claim that the degradation of the Jews in the exile shows that "their degree in the next world [will be] according to their station in this world" (*ibid.* no. 112), he advances his theory on the ethnic election of the Jewish people. Israel suffers for the sins of the nations which are by nature inferior to itself; "Israel among the nations is like the heart amid the organs of the body," and the diseases with which it is afflicted—its degradation—are a sign of its central position in human history and the nobility of its character (pt. 2 nos. 29–44). The Jewish nation is entitled to be proud of its affliction in the exile, as all monotheistic religions glory in martyrdom. However, only a minority of Jews willingly and lovingly accept the yoke of the exile, while for the remainder the affliction is enforced, a fact which explains the length of the exile. Every Jew who suffers in the exile nevertheless has great merit, whether he bears the yoke of exile by compulsion or out of free choice "for whoever wishes to do so can become the friend and equal of his oppressor by uttering one word, and without any difficulty" (pt. 1 nos. 112–5). Judah Halevi did not relinquish his optimistic faith in final victory. He enlarges upon the ancient simile that the nation in exile is to be compared to "the seed which falls into the ground": to the person who observes the external condition of the seed, its sowing signifies its destruction; but to the one who has real knowledge, the sowing "transforms earth and water into its own substance, carries it from one stage to another until it refines the elements and transfers them into something like itself" (pt. 4 no. 23). Judah Halevi admits that for some Jews the acceptance of the yoke of exile is no more than merely passive agreement (pt. 2 nos. 23–24). The survival of the sick and dispersed nation which resembles "a body without a head ... scattered limbs ..." in this lengthy exile is in itself a proof that "He Who keeps us ... in dispersion and exile" is "the living God" (*ibid.* nos. 29–32). The sorrows of exile continue: "we are burdened by them, whilst the whole world enjoys rest and prosperity. The trials which meet us are meant to prove our faith, to cleanse us completely, and to remove all taint from us" (no.44). With realistic insight into the sensation of exile, Judah Halevi promises the one who accepts these consolations with sincerity the peace of mind required to lead a human existence in the exile, because "he who bears the exile unwillingly loses his first and his last rewards" (pt. 3 no. 12).

During the second half of the 12th century, despair also seized the exiles of the Islamic world. In about 1160, *Maimon b. Joseph addressed to his brothers in Arabic the *Iggeret ha-Neḥamah* ("Letter of Consolation"), when he himself had left his place of residence from fear of the Muslim *Almohads. He particularly stresses the constant terror and anguish of a life where security is absent. To fortify the souls which find themselves in this distress, Maimon formulated his meditation on exile in metaphor. The Torah is a lifeline which is thrown to one who is drowning in the sea of exile, "and whoever seizes it has some hope." The exile is only lengthy viewed in human dimensions. From the terrifying description of the storms of the sea and the weakness of the man caught up in them, he evokes a picture of consolation, "it so happens ... that while the current overthrows walls and hurls up rocks, the frail thing remains standing. Thus with the exile ... the Holy One, blessed be He, will save the frail nation ..."

His son, *Maimonides, considered the exile of his time to be part of the continuous attempts through history to turn the Jewish people from its religion. Some have attempted this by force and others by persuasion; Christianity has merely introduced the innovation "that for its purpose it combined the two, that is coercion and arguments ... because it realized that this was more effective for achieving the effacement of the nation and the Torah" *(Iggeret Teiman).* Islam learned this combined method from Christianity. However, the attitude of Islam is the hardest and most degrading: "there has never risen against Israel a worse nation" than Ishmael *(ibid.).* When Maimonides imputes responsibility for "the loss of our kingdom and the destruction of our Temple" to "our ancestors ... who did not study the art of war and the conquest of lands" because they believed in the foolishness of astrology (from his responsa to the rabbis of Marseilles), this realist-political explanation is only considered by him a description of the natural punishment which had resulted from having sunk into one of many sins. Born into a generation which had been tried by forced *conversions, and having witnessed religious coercion and escaped from it, he conceived the exile as a furnace whose purpose is to purify and test "until religion is retained only . . . by the pious of the offspring of Jacob . . . who are pure and clean, who fear God" *(Iggeret Teiman)*. The exile and the sufferings of the people "and all that will befall them is as a holocaust upon the altar" *(ibid.)*; these words are accompanied by an enumeration of the sacrifices actually demanded of his contemporaries.

The feeling of exile as experienced in Spain during the Reconquest period, with the changes in political situations and conjunctions where the plight of the Jew remained unaffected, was expressed by David *Kimḥi in his simile of the animals which were ensnared within a circle in the forest and which, in turn, the lion encircled with his tail; "thus, we in the exile are as within the circle, we cannot leave it without falling into the hands of the carnivores: for if we can extract ourselves from the rule of the Ishmaelites, we fall under the dominion of the uncircumcized . . . we therefore withdraw our hands and feet for fear of them" (commentary to Ps. 22:17); Jewish adherence to faith in persecution and suffering is stressed (on Isa. 26:13; Ps. 44:21).

During the middle of the 13th century, a period bringing an upsurge of mystical thought and an intensification of rationalistic tendencies among Jews, Moses b. Naḥman (*Naḥmanides) attributed a most profound and penetrating religious significance to exile, and his thought was to exercise tremendous influence within Judaism in coming generations. Naḥmanides visualized exile as a crisis in Divinity itself. He explains the sayings of the rabbis on the special bond with which the inhabitants of Ereẓ Israel are linked to God as an allusion to the distinction between "the venerable God, blessed be He, the God of gods when abroad" and the "God of Ereẓ Israel, which is the possession of God" (on Lev. 18–25); there is "additional" power in God as lord of His own estate compared with the power which He has in the remainder of His world; exile is the disruption of the link with this special "emanation" of the Divinity. This divine crisis is followed by a religious crisis, "because the precepts are essentially intended for those living in the land of God" *(ibid.)*. Ereẓ Israel, the earthly Temple, and the condition of exile in the lower world become symbols of the situation and the events in the celestial world (*ibid.;* also on Deut. 4:28; 11:18). It is not only the property of prophecy which is impaired as the result of the exile, but the nature of faith, world, and God. Another aspect of Naḥmanides' approach is his theory—based on the passage of Sifra, Be-Hukkotai 10:5, and Rashi (on Lev. 26:32) and his own historical experience—that the desolation of Ereẓ Israel is a sign that though the alliance between God and the Jews has been broken in some of its elements, the alliance of the "Owner of the estate" has not been established with any other nation. The estate will not be cultivated and the Owner will not be worshiped in this aspect of His Divinity until His children return to His land (on Lev. 26:16). Naḥmanides' profound recognition of the religious aspect of the tragedy of exile did not overshadow his realistic appraisal of the actual situation in the 13th century. He recognizes the potentials of the physical and spiritual existence of the remainder of the nation and the possibility of preservation to a certain degree of the link with God (on Deut. 4:27; and in other words in *Sefer ha-Ge'ullah*, 4). Naḥmanides minimizes the extent of the economic decadence in the exile, no doubt influenced by the flourishing condition of the Jews in Spain in his time (on Deut. 28:42). Like *Baḥya b. Joseph ibn Paquda (*Ḥovot ha-Levavot, "Sha'ar ha-Beḥinnah,"* 5), who had preceded him during the prosperous days under Islamic rule, Naḥmanides concludes that "as a result of our exile in the lands of our enemies, our affairs have not fared for the worse . . . for in these lands we are as the other nations living there, or even better than them" (on Deut. 28:42). Menahem b. Solomon *Meiri, in the generation which followed Naḥmanides, criticized Christian persecution of the Jews since they pray for the peace of the monarchy, "and our prayer is pure and sincere, unlike their thoughts; if only our prayers for them would be fulfilled in our own persons" (on Ps. 35). This lends a new note to the feeling of exile—the bitterness over suffering even while the Jews demonstrate sincere loyalty to Christian rule.

The conception of Naḥmanides that the world and the Divinity had become impaired as a result of the exile assumed a more practical and concrete meaning for the generations which followed the expulsion from Spain, Portugal, and Sicily (1492, 1497). Exile presented itself from the viewpoint of Kabbalah as the misery arising from a cosmos fractured internally, as the terror of a world in which a struggle was taking place between light and darkness, purity and impurity; a world situation in which Israel, the nation of light, is delivered into the hands of the children of darkness, that is the children of Edom, who in this array of symbols are subjected to a double measure of hatred. A dynamic mystic-universal meaning was attributed to efforts to amend the world by deeds, knowledge, and example (a meaning taken up by the kabbalists of *Safed, and the *Shabbateans).

An explanation of the negative phenomena of the exile and the manifestations of continuing survival in it were given 15th-century realities and concepts by Isaac *Arama. Its torments and persecutions are attributed to being in close relation to gentiles by residence "in their towns and settlements." Yet in its state of semi-serfdom and semi-protection, and to a large measure thanks to this enslavement and protection by the crown, the nation has been able to survive exile. Isaac Arama also places the forced converts within his tableau of the exile: "even though they have become assimilated within the nations . . . their feet have not found complete rest; because they [the nations] constantly insult and despise them and contrive against them . . . libels . . . and they always consider them as reverting to Judaism" (*Akedat Yiẓḥak*, Deut., *sha'ar* 98). The underground life of the *anusim* is depicted as exile accompanied by even heightened terrors. To the question of the length of the exile, of the shining of the Divine countenance on the Christian world and its success, which had already been asked in former generations and disturbed the generation of the Expulsion with even greater urgency *(ibid.*, Lev., *she'arim* 70 and 60), Isaac Arama attempted to offer several answers. Jewish history until this exile "was merely to be considered as a betrothal . . ."; the marriage had not yet taken place. There is therefore no reason to speak of a divorce (*ibid.*, Ex., *sha'ar* 50). Moreover, even according to Christian thinking, the Law was only revealed thousands of years after the Creation, while Jesus came to redeem souls from the original sin long after this revelation. By comparison Israel's wait for redemption is not long, even if anguished (*ibid.*, Deut., *sha'ar* 88). Purification from sins and removal of the evil inclination from the heart are also advanced as reasons for the intensification of the sufferings and their prolongation (*ibid.*, Gen., *sha'ar* 14).

Isaac *Abrabanel vividly contrasts the kind fate accorded to the gentile nations and the evil which had befallen Israel in the exile (introduction to *Ma'yenei ha-Yeshu'ah*).

He distinguishes between the cause of the hatred by the Christians—the crucifixion of Jesus—and that of the hatred by the Ishmaelites—the rejection of the Koran (on *Hinneh Yaskil Avdi*). Exile is also characterized for him by the fact that "the exiles . . . will not become tillers of the land . . . but will engage to a limited extent in the commerce of goods . . ." (*Yeshu'ot Meshiḥo, iyyun* no. 2 ch. 1), but he considers this laudable, because the acquisition of land abroad would reduce the yearning for redemption (*ibid., iyyun* no. 1 ch. 1). The steadfastness of Israel as manifested in endurance of suffering, in holding fast to the faith in disputations and in maintaining purity of religion and worship, Abrabanel regards as a threefold gain from the *galut* (on *Hinneh Yaskil Avdi*). The steadfastness of the faithful stands out in contrast to the conduct of the *anusim*, who silenced their voices and hid their faith; he stresses the merit of those who gave up their homes and belongings and went into exile with pride in order to practice Judaism openly. Even during those evil days Abrabanel believed that by its spiritual strength the nation would yet succeed in its desire to "bring the Gentiles under the wings of the Divine Presence, . . . by its knowledge and wisdom . . . it would remove them from their false beliefs"; Israel will act kindly toward its tormentors and will instruct its torturers *(ibid.)*.

The words of these scholars preserve the strength and originality of men who observed the condition of a physically stricken but spiritually intact and healthy nation, of thinkers who drew from the sources of tradition and who perceived the past in the light of the present and the present in the light of the past. However, the words of Solomon *ibn Verga, written about 30 years after the Expulsion, reveal the mood of a man who has lost contact with the social framework against which he should direct the sharpness of his rebuke. His thought is abstract and presented in the form of analogies detached from concrete situations. The subsidiary reason for the exile advanced by Maimonides—that the Jews were defeated because they did not study the art of war and relied upon astrology—becomes a recurrent argument of Ibn Verga, that "at first, when the Jews found favor in the eyes of God, He fought their wars . . . they did therefore not study . . . war . . . and when they sinned . . . they were not familiar with the instruments of war, and God was not with them . . . and they fell as a flock without a shepherd" *(Shevet Yehudah)*. The condition of exile caused the Jews to forfeit their wisdom: "our mind is in exile, being enslaved to the exile, to the search for means of livelihood, to the taxes and decrees of the state; how can it preoccupy itself with wisdom?" *(ibid.)*. Analysis of the situation, accompanied by wishful inclination, leads Ibn Verga to conclude that it is the Christian masses who hate the Jews, while "the kings in general . . . the princes, the wise, and all the notables of the land loved them"; even the pope "loves the Jews" because he authorizes them to live in his country and trade there. Ibn Verga, however, realizes that the fury of mass passions is an overwhelming power "and if the king safeguard us and the populace rise against us, how can we be secure?" *(ibid.)*.

Ibn Verga is preoccupied with searching for "the reason for the great hatred felt by the Christians against the Jews." This he finds in a combination of religious and natural factors: on the one hand, religious fanaticism which paves the way to belief in fantastic libels against the Jews, on the other, the desire for loot and the fact that every community "seeks to absorb its neighbor and to integrate it within itself"; the Gentiles therefore hate the Jews who refuse to assimilate into them. He also echoes the steadfast pride of the exile who declares to the "Master of the world: You go to great lengths that I should abandon my religion . . .despite the dwellers of heaven, I am a Jew . . . and will remain as such" *(ibid.)*. This divine persecution is explained through the ancient and powerful answer of the prophet: "You only have I known of all the families of the earth; therefore, I will visit upon you all your iniquities" (Amos 3:2). But concomitantly, exile continues naturally because of religious hatred, "the jealousy of women, the envy of money," and the accusations brought against the totality of Jewry because of the sins of individuals "who have sought to dominate the nations."

The thought of *Judah Loew b. Bezalel (the Maharal of Prague) on the exile at the beginning of the 17th century bears the imprint of the situation which followed the Spanish Expulsion on the one hand and the relative prosperity in his country, Bohemia-Moravia, in his time; it is based upon both the fundamentals of Kabbalah and the rabbinical systems of *halakhah* and homiletics current during the 16th to 17th centuries. The mainstream of his thought is expressed in *Neẓaḥ Yisrael*, and marginally in *Gur Aryeh*, *Or Ḥadash*, and *Be'er ha-Golah*. The Maharal divides the "night of exile" into three "watches": the first is one of painful slavery, the second of massacres and forced conversions, while the third—that in which he is living and which appears to him the last before dawn—consists essentially of consecutive expulsions. Like Ibn Verga, he too preferred the order of the king's peace and protection according to God's will against the popular frenzy and violence which did not spare the weak. The Maharal analyzed the religious-spiritual-social nature of the exile in terms which anticipate the theories of organic nationalism of the 19th century: "Exile is a change and a departure from order: for God has situated every nation in the place which is appropriate to it . . . According to the natural order the suitable place for them [the Jews] is Ereẓ Israel where they are to live in independence . . . As with every natural existing object, they are not to be divided into two . . . since the Jewish people is one nation, more indivisible and inseparable than all the other nations . . . dispersion is unnatural to them . . .; moreover, according to the natural order, it is improper that one nation be enslaved by another . . . because God has created every nation for itself . . . It is therefore unbecoming that in the order of nature Israel should be under the dominion of others." In several aspects, exile is thus an anomaly in the eternal natural order, every deviation from which cannot be but casual and temporary.

This combination of natural factors is the guarantee for the redemption from the unnaturalness of exile. For "all things which are removed from their natural place are unable to survive in a place which is not natural to them . . . because if they subsisted . . . the unnatural would become natural and this is impossible . . . therefore, from the exile, we can perceive the redemption." In the meantime, however, the exile continues by the express will of God (because "that which . . . departs from the limits of reality requires excessive supervision and reinforcement in order to survive"), and it is by Him also that assimilation in the exile is prevented. So long as this anomaly is maintained, it has its own legitimacy and roots to feed on by the laws of nature: the rule of Edom over the world becomes the defective condition of this world. There is an essential spiritual contrast, even if the depths of its profundity cannot be perceived, between Edom and Jacob: as between "water and fire, although not endowed with intelligence or will, are opposed to each other by nature." The struggle between the two is for the totality of the creation, because "each desires the possession of all that exists, which is this world . . . and the world to come, and thus repels his opponent." In the present stage of this struggle "Esau has gained for himself out of the quarrel a world of shame and disgrace . . . to which he is related; Jacob is removed from it, because impurity is foreign to him and he was born the last"; it is impossible that Jacob and Esau should possess both worlds together, because, if so, there would be two extremes in one subject. With pride he sees the exile as an expansion into far-flung regions where the dispersed Jews await the era of perfection of the world, which they will rule.

In opposition to the physical dispersion of the material reality, there are spiritual factors which unite the nation. This is unity created and symbolically expressed both by consciousness of national solidarity and by Torah study and prayer. Engaged in the latter the nation is in a state resembling redemption. To the question: "If . . . the Divine Presence is indeed with Israel in exile . . . why does Israel spend most of its days in this world undergoing oppression and expulsions?" the Maharal replies that "this world is not the portion of Israel"; hence, it is to the advantage of the Jews to be removed from its benefits. The Maharal developed a theory against censorship of thought and literature and religious coercion which regarded these as the exercise of tyranny, and the struggle against them as the true and full expression of the free divine spirit in man.

The *galut* feeling in Poland-Lithuania, an exile which appeared relatively easy during the 16th to 17th centuries, is reflected in the commentaries of Samuel Eliezer b. Judah ha-Levi *Edels (the Maharsha) on the *aggadot* of the Talmud. He was grateful to the Turks for the refuge which the exiles had found in their country, and he considered the "Kings of Ishmael" "merciful kings" (*Ḥiddushei Aggadot,* on BB 74b), while "Esau and his offspring . . . have tormented us in every generation more than all the other nations . . ." (*ibid.* on Meg. 11a). With their persecutions, the Christians are intent on placing obstacles in the path of the Jewish people toward perfection (*ibid.* on Bek. 8a).

Edels accepted the viewpoint of the author of *Shevet Yehudah* concerning the difference of attitude toward the Jews on the part of the various classes: "It is obvious that by the king and the princes they will be not humiliated and despised also when in exile, but only by the populace and the masses of the nations" (on Ta'an. 20a). On the other hand, the hatred of the populace saves the Jews from being appointed officials in "most contemptible crafts" *(ibid.)*. Of special interest is the discussion of Edels with the Christians on the subject of the destruction of the Temple, the cessation of its existence, the revelation of the Divine Presence within its walls, and the length of the exile as evidence of the departure of the Holy Spirit from Israel. The Jew insists that the Divine Presence is not really bound up fully with one location only; partially at least the Jews can carry on the divine task even in dispersion and exile (*ibid.* on Bek. 8a and Ar. 10b).

*Ephraim Solomon b. Aaron of Luntschitz (Leczyca) regarded the exile as a social problem, part of the problem of justice in the world. He arranges a kind of double confrontation, between the wealthy of Israel and the condition of their nation and between the nations of the world and the distribution of material bounty among them; as result of this comparison "the superiority of victory is always upon my lips to reply to the nations who adduce a proof for their religion from their success . . . to refute their opinion and to overthrow their towers: because in every generation . . . our eyes witness that God has handed over all the benefit of temporary success to those who are unworthy of it, and this forms part of His profound and wonderful counsel—in order that the axe should not become proud against him that hews therewith, and that the nations should not say our hand is powerful; because they [i.e., the Gentiles] also agree that there are among them wicked people that are unworthy of success and even so they see their houses filled with wealth, while according to their evil ways [i.e., the Christian faith] they do not deserve that God should bestow of his abundance on them." However, the goods of this world, which are putrid flesh and stale bread, are thrown to the dogs of this world (*Olelot Efrayim,* 1 (1883), 3 nos. 5–6). He warns the "blind in the camp of the Hebrews" not to rely on their prosperity and to remember the communities which have been destroyed.

Once Italian Jewry had established itself in a renewed structure in the towns and states of the post-Renaissance period, it became imperative to explain the exile to the urban dwellers whose minds were inclined toward rationalistic reasoning and commercial considerations. In 1638 Simone (Simḥah) *Luzzatto completed his *Discorso circa il stato de gl'hebrei . . .* ("Discourse on the State of the Hebrews . . ."), in which he attempted to shed light on the exile in a manner most acceptable to the rulers in Venice—by the exploitation of humanist trends of thought and mercantile considerations. This apologetic tractate, which was intended to convince despots governed by cold political considerations and commercial-utilitarian motivations of the usefulness of the Jews, also reflects the self-criticism resulting from feelings of inferiority induced by the contrast with gentile existence. Many ideas which had formerly been expressed within the Jewish framework of the concept of exile were now brought out to the non-Jewish world and illumined with the cold and harsh light of realistic calculation.

In the 17th century *Manasseh Ben Israel also addressed himself to Gentiles in order to overcome objections to the return of Jews to England by the members of the Protestant sects who were prejudiced by religious fervor in addition to their economic considerations. Manasseh Ben Israel expressed not only the desire for survival of the *galut* but also its tendency toward extension with the expansion of the known world and the discoveries of new territorial and social horizons. Much of his reasoning is drawn from the arguments of Luzzatto, but, voiced by Manasseh, they assume a more religious content and a less submissive tone. He is not deterred from declaring to the nations in their own language, in the manner of the early medieval debators, that the sufferings of the "Servant of God" had befallen the Nation of God, and that the nations in their various countries "have slaine them, not for wickednesses, which they did not commit, but for their riches which they had" (*The Hope of Israel,* sec. 29). Even the expulsions serve the process of the expansion of the exile, because when one ruler expels them, the second accepts them with affability and grants them a "thousand priviledges" (*ibid.* sec. 33). Commerce enables the Jews to live in wealth and with the acquisition of properties, as a result of which they "not only become gracious to their Princes and Lords" but also causes "that they should be invited by others to come and dwell in their Lands," because "wheresoever they go to dwell, there presently the Traficq begins to florish" (*A Declaration to the Common-wealth of England,* fol. 1–2). The central theory of Manasseh on the continuation of the exile and its extension is that so long as the prophecy of Daniel remains unfulfilled and the exiles have not yet been scattered to the extremities of the world, the redemption will not come.

Ideology in Modern Times. The feeling that there was room for expansion and progress for the Jews in general society, the apologetic trend of appeal to the non-Jewish world, and the awareness of new attitudes intensified with the changes in society and opinions of 18th-century Europe. In the modern era the nature of the debate on the exile assumed a different character as a result of social experiments made by Jews and non-Jews to abolish the exile. From the

18th century, ideas on and explanations of the exile were channeled to new methods of expression, both through organized movements which attempted to remold the character of Judaism and through individual thinkers (see *Emancipation; *Reform; *Haskalah; *Assimilation; *Ḥasidism; *Ḥibbat Zion; *Zionism; *Agudat Israel; M. *Mendelssohn; S. R. *Hirsch; J. L. *Pinsker; *Aḥad Ha-Am; S. *Dubnow; M. J. *Berdyczewski (bin Gorion); J. Ḥ. *Brenner; J. *Klatzkin; A. D. *Gordon; A. I. *Kook; F. *Rosenzweig; S. *Rawidowicz). The conception of the exile of these movements and personalities cannot be separated from their essential standpoints and lines of thought and should be considered within their specific contexts. Even those whose thinking followed ancient paths ascribed their views to innovations brought about by these movements in the modern era. Until the second half of the 19th century, it appeared that supremacy was being achieved both in reality and in ideology by the trends which sought to abolish the exile through integration within the surrounding nations or through continuing a respected existence within their midst by finding a meaning in this situation either as a divine punishment or as part of a sublime religious purpose. However, from the second half of the 19th century, this reality deteriorated in the emergent world of nationalism. Jews increasingly viewed the exile in terms of anger and despair, which even though presented in modern idioms, resembled in content the ancient conception of the exile expressed by former generations. Numerous efforts were made toward finding a means of preserving the distinctiveness and historic continuity of the nation within new and changing circumstances.

By the second half of the 20th century, the two fundamental conceptions in Jewish ideology of the modern era on the subject of the exile have resumed their struggle with renewed intensity. One line of thinking points to the Holocaust in Europe, the brutality of its perpetrators and the apathy manifested by the majority of the nations of the world during the years 1939–45. It was argued that hatred of the Jews has not disappeared even after the atrocities of Hitler, while the Jews are subject to powerful forces of assimilation in places where they have free social interchange. There is the reality of the establishment of the State of Israel in contrast to the difficulties of maintaining the unity of world Jewry and the ties between the nation in its country and the minorities abroad. All these phenomena are interpreted as signaling the degeneration of the Jewish position and the danger attached to the continuation of the exile, and are put forward as decisive proofs for the necessity of its liquidation.

Adherents of the other line of thinking point to the political freedom and equality of rights legally granted to individual Jews in all the countries of the world and the authorization accorded in most states to Jewish organizations to pursue their cultural and social activities. They stress the organizational, spiritual, literary, and philanthropic achievements of the Diaspora communities; the political and material strength which is added to the State of Israel by the support of Diaspora Jewry; and the role of the Diaspora as exemplified in the Second Temple era. The success that the Germans achieved in modern times in uniting their dispersed nation around their country is noted. These believe—in common with the Jews in the days of *Philo and *Josephus, the geonic period, and the 19th century—that the Diaspora has a reason, and a right of existence; that there is national utility in the maintenance of the Diaspora according to its potentialities in its diffusion throughout the world. In fact, many who approve the existence of the exile are inclined to consider the state as a more favorable form of Jewish survival and sympathize with the principle of the "ingathering of the exiles." On the other hand, the majority of those who condemn the exile recognize that there is no possibility in sight of terminating the Diaspora. The Six-Day War (1967) and its aftermath strengthened both the consciousness of identity and feelings of interdependence between Israel and the Diaspora for the majority of Jews. However, a radical and vocal minority expresses strong disapproval of this tie. The link with Israel has become a touchstone and testing furnace for the existence of Jews in present-day Communist-ruled countries.

Down through its history the feeling of *galut* has been one of the most permanent and prolific incentives in Jewish thought. It has expressed the desire for redemption and preservation as a nation even in the most difficult days. The discussion between Jews and adherents of other monotheistic religions on this subject, the spiritual pride and religious feeling it engendered, resulted in the formulation of new patterns of explanation of the exile from generation to generation which enabled the Jew to bear his suffering without losing his humanity or his faith in God and justice. The spirit of Jacob has been saved out of the tragedy of the exile because the feeling of exile has been one of the principal factors creating the particular sensitivity to questions of divine and social justice among most Jews. As the result of a specific situation, according to Judah Loew b. Bezalel, the Jewish nation has become different from the other nations of the world through its experience of suffering and humiliation and detachment from the rest of society for generation after generation, and through alert and proud reaction to this trial.

Bibliography: S. Dubnow, *Mikhtavim al ha-Yahadut* (1937), 96–103; Aḥad Ha-Am, *Parting of the Ways . . .* (1905); EM, 2 (1965), 496–506; J. M. Guttmann, *Mafte'aḥ ha-Talmud,* 3 pt. 2 (1930), s.v. *Ereẓ Yisrael, Malkhuyyot;* G. Rosen, *Juden und Phoenizier* (1926[2]); A. Posnanski, *Schiloh* (Ger., 1904); Y. Kaufman, *Golah ve-Nekhar,* 2 vols. (1954–61); *Galut: Le-Verur Mashma'ut ha-Galut ba-Mikra u-ve-Sifrut ha-Dorot* (1959); J. Klatzkin, *Galut ve-Ereẓ* (1920); *Soẓyologyah shel Toledot ha-Golah ha-Yehudit le-Or ha-Marxism* (1951); S. Rawidowicz, *Bavel vi-Yrushalayim* (1957); M. Kamrat (ed.), *Mashma'utah shel Galut ba-Amerikah . . .* (1964); H. H. Ben-Sasson, *Ha-Yehudim mul ha-Reformaẓyah* (1969); N. Rotenstreich, *Jewish Philosophy in Modern Times* (1968); Y. Baer, *Galut* (Eng., 1947); idem, in: *Zion,* 5 (1933), 61–77; 6 (1934), 149–71; B. Dinur, *Israel and the Diaspora* (1969); L. Baeck, *This People Israel* (1965); J. B. Agus et al., in: *Midstream,* 9 (1963), 3–45; D. Polish, *Eternal Dissent* (1961), 147–61; Baron, Social[2], index; Scholem, Mysticism, index s.v. *Exile, Tikkun;* idem, *Ra'yon ha-Ge'ullah ba-Kabbalah* (1946).

[H.H.B.-S.]

GALVESTON PLAN, a project to divert European Jews immigrating to the United States from the large eastern ports of the United States to the southwestern states. In 1907 Jacob H. *Schiff initiated and financed the plan, hoping to alleviate the concentration of immigrants in the big cities of the northeast and middle west. The Jewish Territorial Organization undertook to continue the task. A Jewish Immigrants' Information Bureau, directed by Morris D. *Waldman, was established in 1907 in Galveston, Texas, to settle and sustain the immigrants, who began to arrive in July of that year. Rabbi Henry *Cohen of Galveston was instrumental in the entire effort. However, several major Jewish immigration organizations refused to assist, and in 1910 the U.S. Department of Commerce and Labor deported a large number of immigrants who had arrived at the port of Galveston, alleging that the immigrants had violated the contract labor laws or were liable to become public charges. Nevertheless, the Galveston plan managed to settle 10,000 immigrants before it ceased operations at the outbreak of World War I.

For Galveston, see *Texas.

Bibliography: M. D. Waldman, in: *Jewish Social Service Quarterly*, 4 (1926); Z. Szajkowski, in: JSOS, 29 (1967), 22–26, 81; L. Shpall, in: *Jewish Forum*, 28 (June–Aug. 1945), 119–20, 139–40, 156–8. [Ed.]

GAMA, GASPAR DA (c. 1440–1510), Jewish traveler; his original name is unknown. Born, according to one account, in Posen (Poland), he made his way to Jerusalem and then Alexandria, was taken prisoner and sold as a slave in India, where he obtained his freedom and entered the service of the ruler of Goa. When the Portuguese explorer Vasco da Gama arrived off Angediva in 1498, he was greeted in a friendly fashion by this long-bearded European on behalf of his master, but Vasco da Gama treacherously seized the Jew and compelled him to embrace Christianity under the baptismal name of Gaspar da Gama. He now had to pilot the fleet in Indian waters and was subsequently brought back to Portugal. In Lisbon, Gaspar was granted a pension by the king, who employed his linguistic ability in subsequent Portuguese naval expeditions. In 1500 he accompanied Cabral on his voyage in western waters and was with Nicolau Coelho when he first stepped ashore in Brazil. On the return voyage he met Amerigo Vespucci, the Tuscan explorer after whom America is named, at Cabo Verde and was consulted by him. Later he went to India once more with Vasco da Gama (1502–03) and again in 1505 with Francisco d'Almeida. He took part in the latter's expedition against Calicut in 1510, when he may have died.

Bibliography: A. Wiznitzer, *Jews in Colonial Brazil* (1960), 3–5; Huemmerich, in: *Revista da Universidade de Coimbra* (1927); W. J. Fischel, *Ha-Yehudim be-Hodu* (1960), 15–30; M. Kayserling, *Christopher Columbus* . . . (Eng., 1928²), 113–9. [W.J.F.]

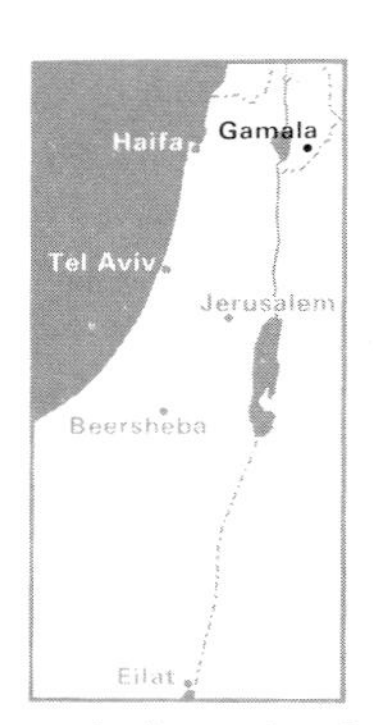

GAMALA, ancient city in lower Golan, opposite Tarichaea. It was called Gamala because it was situated on a hill shaped like a camel's hump (Heb. *gamal*, "camel"). According to the Mishnah it was fortified in the time of Joshua (Ar. 9:16). Alexander Yannai captured the city and it continued to be inhabited by Jews (Jos., Ant. 13:394); it belonged to the Herodian territory of Gaulanitis (Wars 1:105). During the Jewish War against Rome it was fortified by Josephus and since the Jewish rebels could maintain contact with Babylonia by way of Gamala, the city underwent a prolonged siege in 67 C.E. Because of its nearly impregnable position and strong fortifications, it was captured only after very severe fighting; Vespasian killed many of its inhabitants while others committed suicide (Wars 4:11–54, 62–83). The name is preserved in the Arab village of Jamla, on the Nahr al-Ruqqād 11 mi. (18 km.) east of the Sea of Galilee. The fortress was located at nearby Tell al-Ahdab.

Bibliography: G. Schumacher, *Across the Jordan* (1886), 74–76, 84–85; Dalman, in: PJB, 7 (1911), 25–26; 8 (1912), 52ff. [M.A.-Y.]

GAMALIEL, RABBAN, the name and title of six sages, descendants of *Hillel, who filled the office of *nasi* in Ereẓ Israel.

(1) Rabban Gamaliel ha-Zaken ("the elder"), a grandson of Hillel, lived in the first half of the first century. As president of the Sanhedrin he maintained close contact not only with the Jews of Ereẓ Israel, but also with those in the Diaspora. The Talmud has preserved three letters with the original text, containing reminders about the times of separating tithes and information about the leap year, which Rabban Gamaliel dictated to the scribe Johanan, while seated in the company of sages upon the steps of the Temple Mount. In these letters he addresses "our brethren in Upper Galilee and in Lower Galilee," "our brethren of the Upper South and of the Lower South," and "our brethren of the exile of Babylon, the exile of Media, and the other exiles of Israel" (Sanh. 11b; Tosef., Sanh. 2:6; TJ, Sanh. 1:2, 18 d). Like his grandfather, Hillel, Gamaliel was responsible for many **takkanot*, many of them bearing the formula, "for the benefit of humanity" (Git. 4:2–3), particularly on behalf of women *(ibid.)*. Of particular importance is his decision permitting a woman to remarry on the evidence of a single witness to the death of her husband (Yev. 16:7). Stories have been preserved testifying to his ties with the royal family, apparently that of *Agrippa I (Pes. 88b). Among his pupils were Simeon of Mizpeh, Joezer of Ha-Birah, and Nehemiah of Bet Dali (Pe'ah 2:6; Or. 2:12; Yev. 16:7). According to Acts Gamaliel was tolerant toward the first Christians, and Paul was one of his pupils (22:3). Of his children there are known Simeon, who succeeded him, and a daughter who married Simeon b. Nethanel ha-Kohen (Tosef., Av. Zar. 3:10). The sages' regard for Gamaliel was expressed in their saying: "When Rabban Gamaliel the elder died the glory of the Torah ceased, and purity and saintliness [lit. "separation"] perished" (Sot. 9:15).

(2) Rabban Gamaliel II, also called Rabban Gamaliel of Jabneh, grandson of (1), succeeded *Johanan b. Zakkai as *nasi* c. 80 C.E. He saw his life's work as the strengthening of the new center at Jabneh and the concentration and consolidation of the people around the Torah, constituting an authority that would be capable of filling the place of the Temple and of the Sanhedrin which had met in the Chamber of Hewn Stones. To this end he worked energetically for the elevation of the dignity of the *nasi's* office, and for the unification of *halakhah.* The heavenly voice "that was heard in Jabneh" establishing the *halakhah* in accordance with Bet Hillel (Er. 13b; TJ, Ber. 1:7, 3b) is probably an allusion to the activity of Gamaliel. He stressed that his vigorous exertions were not directed to increasing his own honor or that of his household but to preserving the unity of the nation and the Torah (BM 59b). In his private life and in his personal relationships he was modest and easygoing, showed love and respect toward his pupils and friends, and even to his slave, and was tolerant of gentiles (Tosef, BK 9:30; Ber. 2:7; Sanh. 104b; et al.; Sif. Deut. 38). In respect to laws and prohibitions he was at times lenient to others and strict with himself (Ber. 2:6; TJ, Ber. 1:2, 3a). In spite of this, his firmness as *nasi* and his endeavors to increase the power of the new center aroused the strong opposition of the elder scholars of his generation and led to a severe struggle in which Gamaliel did not hesitate to excommunicate his own brother-in-law, *Eliezer b. Hyrcanus (BM 59b). Of greatest consequence was Gamaliel's dispute with *Joshua b. Hananiah on the fixing of the new moon (see *Calendar). Gamaliel regarded the affair as a test of the authority of his *bet din* and ordered R. Joshua to demonstrate publicly that he accepted the discipline of the *nasi*: "I charge you to appear before me with your staff and your money on the day which according to your reckoning should be the Day of Atonement." On the advice of his colleagues, Akiva and Dosa b. Harkinas, R. Joshua bowed to the command. When he came before Rabban Gamaliel, the *nasi* rose, kissed him on his head and said to him: "come in peace my teacher and pupil—my teacher in wisdom and my pupil because you have accepted my decision" (RH 2:8–9). The clashes between Gamaliel and Joshua, however, did not cease with this affair. The firmness of Gamaliel was regarded by most of the scholars as an insult to the dignity of R. Joshua and led to a revolt against his authority which ended with his removal from the office

Rabban Gamaliel teaching two pupils. Full page miniature from the *Pollak-Pratto Haggadah* (fol. 26v), Italy, c. 1300. New York, Jewish Theological Seminary.

of *nasi* and the appointment of *Eleazar b. Azariah in his place (Ber. 27b–28a). The nobility of Rabban Gamaliel's character was vindicated, however, by his not absenting himself from *bet ha-midrash* and by his participation in the establishment of the *halakhah* under the direction of the new *nasi*. In the end Gamaliel appeased Joshua, and the scholars, meeting him halfway "out of respect for his father's house," reinstated him as *nasi*. According to the Jerusalem Talmud (Ber. 4:1) he alone was *nasi*, Eleazar b. Azariah only serving as his deputy, *av bet din*, but according to the Babylonian Talmud *(ibid.)* Eleazar b. Azariah continued to share the post of *nasi* with him.

Rabban Gamaliel was recognized as one of the greatest scholars of his generation by his colleagues, by his many pupils, and even by his opponents. His halakhic pronouncements, among them traditions from his father and grandfather, are abundantly cited in the Mishnah and *beraitot*. His activity, together with that of his colleagues and pupils in Jabneh, laid the foundation of the Mishnah. Exceptionally important *takkanot* with respect to religion and worship are associated with the name of Rabban Gamaliel, their aim being to face up to the new reality created by the destruction of the Temple by the implementation of laws and customs designed to serve as a "reminder of the Temple." Rabban Gamaliel played a large part in formulating Passover eve ceremonial after the destruction of the Temple (Pes. 10:5), in determining the final version of the 18 benedictions *(*Amidah)*, in making it a duty for each individual to pray, and in deciding in favor of the custom of praying three times a day. It is clear that Rabban Gamaliel was close to the general culture and learning of his time, permitting among other things the study of Greek (Tosef., Sot. 15:8). His son Simeon's testimony that many youngsters studied Greek wisdom in his father's house (Sot. 49b) seemed incomprehensible to the scholars, who later explained the phenomenon in terms of the political activity of the *nasi* and in the light of the need to maintain good relations with the ruling powers. He did not refrain from bathing in the bathhouse of Aphrodite in Acre, regarding the image there as serving a decorative purpose only (Av. Zar. 3:4). Gamaliel's son, Ḥanina, testified that it was customary in his father's house to use seals which had figures in relief (TJ, Av. Zar. 3:1, 42c). He was apparently also acquainted with the principles of Greek science. He used astronomical diagrams to examine the witnesses of the new moon (RH 2:8) and he fashioned an instrument to measure distances (Er. 43b). Gamaliel was not only the chief religious authority but also the recognized national-political leader. It is probable that the Roman government also recognized him as the spokesman of the Jews. In any event he made journeys—either alone or in the company of other scholars—to the governor in Syria to receive "authority" (Eduy. 7:7; Sanh. 11a) and also to Rome in order to intercede for his people (TJ, Sanh. 7:19, 25d). In his contacts with non-Jews, he also appeared as the spokesman of Judaism in its battle against idolatry and heresy (Av. Zar. 3:4, 4:7, et al.). Associated with his name is the introduction of the **Birkat ha-Minim* in the *Amidah*, aimed at excluding the Christians from the Jewish fold (Ber. 28b; Meg. 17b).

The year of his death is not known, but in all probability he did not live to witness the revolt in the time of Trajan (c. 116 C.E.). The life and death of the great *nasi* are embellished in the *aggadah*. Tradition assigns to him the great *takkanah*—on behalf of the poor—of abrogating ornate and expensive funerals and introducing the practice of burying the dead in simple flaxen raiment.

(3) GAMALIEL III or Rabban Gamaliel be-Rabbi, the son of *Judah ha-Nasi, lived in the first half of the third century. He was appointed *nasi* in accordance with the testament of his father who instructed him to conduct his office with firmness (Ket. 103b); his brother Simeon was appointed *ḥakham* in the same testament. In the Mishnah Gamaliel rejects the extremist desideratum of isolation from the affairs of the world, takes a positive view of occupation and labor, and exhorts those occupied with communal affairs to work for the sake of heaven and not for their own benefit and honor. He counsels (apparently on the basis of his own experience) caution and suspicion in one's dealings with the government (i.e., Roman authority), even when it appears friendly (Avot 2:2–3). It is reported of Rabban Gamaliel and his *bet din* that they voted to invalidate ritual slaughter performed by Samaritans (Ḥul. 5b and Rashi, *ibid.*). Not many of his halakhic saying have been preserved, but the greatest *amoraim* of the first generation—Samuel, Hosea, Ḥanina, and Johanan—were his disciples and highly valued his teachings. Among the discoveries in the *Bet She'arim excavations of 1954 were two adjoining decorated sepulchers, bearing the inscriptions in Hebrew and Greek, "Rabbi Gamaliel" and "Rabbi Simeon" respectively, which are thought to be the graves of the *nasi* and his brother.

(4) RABBAN GAMALIEL IV, the son of *Judah Nesiah, lived in the second half of the third century.

(5) RABBAN GAMALIEL V, the son of Hillel II, lived in the second half of the fourth century; very little is known of either father or son.

(6) RABBAN GAMALIEL VI, the last *nasi*. An order of the emperors Honorius and Theodosius II, dated 415, has been preserved, which deprived Gamaliel of the post of *nasi* and of the titles of honor given by the government to that office as a penalty for having built a synagogue without authorization and for having defended the Jews against the Christians. Gamaliel's death in 426 brought to an end the institution of the *nasi*. From an allusion in the works of the medical author Marcellus (fifth century) it would seem that this Gamaliel was also a physician.

See also *Nasi.

Bibliography: Graetz, Hist, index; Weiss, Dor, 1 (1924[4]), 234 (index), s.v.; 2 (1924[4]), 236 (index), s.v.; 3 (1924[4]), 38ff.; Halevy, Dorot, vol. 1, pt. 5 (1923), 41ff.; Hyman, Toledot, 304–21; Urbach, in: *Beḥinot*, 4 (1952/53), 66; Alon, Toledot, 1 (1958[3]), 114ff.; L. Finkelstein, 775–7 and index; idem, ed., *The Jews*, 1 (1949), 149–52; 2 (1949), 1790–91 and index; Baron, Social[2], index; G. F. Moore, *Judaism*, 2 (1946), index.

[Ed.]

GAMALIEL BEN PEDAHZUR (fl. first half of 18th century), pseudonym of the author of *The Book of the Religion, Ceremonies, and Prayers of the Jews* (London, 1738). This comprises the earliest translation of the Jewish prayer book, published in English with a scurrilous introduction. It appears from a letter in *The Gentleman's Magazine* (28 (Oct. 1758), 468) that the author was an apostate named Abraham Mears. The work throws interesting light on the life and customs of London Jewry in the 18th century.

Bibliography: Roth, in: JHSEM 2 (1935), 1–8; Singer, in: JHSET, 3 (1896–98), 51–53.

[C.R.]

GAMBLING. Gambling was known to the ancient world. Games of chance were an appreciated pastime, often turning into addiction, among the Greeks—Herodotus relates that the Lydians supposedly invented some games (*History* 1:94); among the Romans, who are known to have bet heavily on chariot races; and among the Teutons, of whose gambling habits Tacitus states that in their less sober moments they even gambled themselves into slavery (*Germany*, 24). While the Hebrews were also acquainted with gambling (Judg. 14), it was only from mishnaic days onward that the rabbis took a definitive attitude toward gambling.

Professional and Compulsive Gambling. Professional gambling in any shape or form, whether among Jews or non-Jews, was severely frowned upon. The professional gambler was considered a parasite who was engaged in a useless endeavor and contributed nothing to better the world. Some rabbis went so far as to declare the professional gambler a robber whom the Mishnah (Sanh. 3:3) disqualified from giving testimony; he was looked upon as a spineless wastrel who, instead of engaging in the study of Torah or in the pursuit of an honest livelihood (Maim., Comm. to Mishnah, Sanh. 3:3), frittered his time and efforts away on a demeaning occupation and unseemly conduct (*Rabban* (ed. 1920), 224d; *Mordekhai*, Sanh. nos. 690, 695).

The rabbis recognized the inability of the compulsive gambler to control his passion for the game (*Shiltei ha-Gibborim*, Sheb. 756), considered him a moral weakling, and consequently dealt with him severely. One medieval rabbi advised: "Do not show pity to the gambler who pleads 'pity me in order that I may not be shamed and disgraced by him who has won a gulden.' Better he be disgraced . . ." (Judah he-Ḥasid, *Sefer Ḥasidim*, ed. by R. Margaliot (1957) no. 1026 cf. no. 400). So vehement was his opposition to the gambler that if the latter were to lose his money and require assistance from charity, it was to be denied to him.

Public calamities that befell the Jewish community were often considered the consequence of, and the punishment for, excessive gambling. In 1576, in Cremona, three scholars proposed a ban on gambling after a pestilence had abated. They maintained that the popular passion to gamble was the main source of all calamities that had befallen the community. A similar view had been expressed earlier by Judah Katzenellenbogen (Isaac Lampronti, *Paḥad Yiẓhak*, 3 (Venice, 1798), 54a).

Effects of Gambling. Community leaders, keenly aware of the painful and destructive effects of gambling upon an individual's character, meted out severe punishment. Gambling debts could not be collected through the Jewish courts (Resp. Rashba, vol. 7, no. 445). The gambler was often placed under ban, dismissed from the burial society (*ibid.*, nos. 244, 270; Resp. Rosh 13:12), at times prohibited from holding his wedding in the synagogue courtyard (Loewenstein, in JJLG, 8 (1910), 184f.), not called to the Torah (Finkelstein, Middle Ages, 282–95), etc. Family life was also disrupted by gambling habits, and there is much evidence readily available to show how difficult relationships were between gamblers and their wives (Resp. Rashba, vol. 2, nos. 35, 286; vol. 7, no. 501; Rosh, resp. 82:2, inter alia). Women refused to live with such husbands; wife-beating and drinking were common (*Zikhron Yehudah* no. 71; responsa Maharyu no. 135) and the education of children was jeopardized (Rosh, resp. 82:2). Repelled by the conditions under which they were forced to live, gamblers' wives often sought divorce. The gambler's desertion of his family was not an uncommon occurrence. One moralist even suggested that women should join their husbands in their acts of gambling in order to save their marriages (Moses of Jerusalem (Moses Henochs), *Brant-Shpigel*, ch. 10).

Gambling was denounced not only by Jewish law and by Jewish moralists, but its evils and terrible consequences were warned against by popular folk singers, in colloquial expressions, and in proverbs. "Gambling poems," describing the sorrow of a home where the man gambles, speak pitifully of the mental anguish of the gambler's "widow," the hidden tears, and the neglect of the children.

Curbs on Gambling. Jewish writings mention many gamblers who made conscious efforts to curb their passion and activities. A common practice among them was to take an oath not to indulge in games of chance, although this usually resulted in a double violation: gambling and breaking a vow. The vows varied: some gamblers set a time limit to their vows; others excluded specific days or special occasions; while still others only refrained from placing monetary stakes, but played, for example, for stakes of fruit (Resp. Rashba, vol. 3, no. 305; Maharshal resp. no. 185). Rabbis discouraged hasty vows, realizing that these did not lessen the lure of games of chance.

Exemptions. Communal restrictions to suppress gambling were often enacted; the frequency of these enactments, however, shows how futile the prohibitions were and how popular the games. Taking into consideration the attraction of games and gambling, the enactments were flexible: on many festive occasions (e.g., Ḥanukkah, Purim, the intermediary days of Passover and Sukkot, and the New Moon) the restrictions were lifted (Israel Bruna resp. no. 136). Special family occasions also received communal dispensation for gambling (Finkelstein, Middle Ages, 228–42, 284–91). In general, however, the prohibitions were enforced and accompanied by severe penalties: excommunication and flagellation were commonly meted out to transgressors (Resp. Rashba, vol. 7, nos. 244, 270); fines were imposed and honorary functions within the synagogue withheld.

Types of Games of Chance. The medieval gambler was enticed by all sorts of games. Dice were known from ancient times, and games such as "odds or evens" played with pebbles, knucklebones, and bowling were also quite old. Games with nuts, although often played by children, were also a pastime for the gambler (*Haggahot Mordekhai*, Sanh. nos. 722–3; Resp. Maharam of Rothenburg, ed. Prague, no. 94). Not until the 15th century did cards capture the fancy of the Jewish masses (I. Abrahams, *Jewish Life in the Middle Ages* (1932[2]), 415ff.). Tennis, popular among the

Jews of Italy during the 16th century, was, just as chess, not merely played as a pastime but enormous stakes were wagered upon the outcome of such matches (Henderson, in JQR 26 (1935/36), 5; for cards and chess see *Games). By the 18th century, lotteries were very popular. The different types of gambling were not universal; each country had its own fads and favorite games.

Many authorities felt that it was permissible to indulge in games of chance on occasions (*Mordekhai,* Sanh. 690f.). Gambling, however, carried with it a stigma; but while public opinion looked down upon it, all the private and communal efforts to stem the tide of gambling did not stop Jews from indulging frequently. One scholar even urged the abolition of all decrees against gambling since men could not withstand such temptation (*Mordekhai,* Shev. 787).

Synagogue Gambling. Gaming in the synagogue was not uncommon; a sharp contrast was drawn, however, between the usual forms of gambling and cases where the primary motive was not personal gain. A multitude of responsa cite instances where the winnings at games of chance were not considered fruits of sin (e.g., Resp. Maharam of Rothenburg, ed. Prague, no. 493). One of the clearest statements was made by Benjamin *Slonik who differentiated between gambling for private gain and that in which the winnings, even if only in part, went to charity. He saw no violation in the latter case and demanded full payment of gambling debts to charity. There were many instances where the rabbis and communities joined in games of chance. One rabbi ruled that he who wins at a lottery should pronounce the blessing *She-Heḥeyanu;* should one win together with a partner, one must also add the blessing *ha-tov ve-ha-metiv* (B. Levin, *Shemen Sason* (1904), 53 no. 27; see *Benedictions). It seems hardly likely that any blessing should be required if the winnings were considered the rewards of sinful acts. It would thus appear that Jewish law proscribes the professional and compulsive act of gambling; frowns severely and condemns the occasional act of gambling when indulged in for personal gain; while occasional gambling, where all or part of the winnings go to charity, has never aroused condemnation and frequently even has had the approval of the Jewish communities.

These findings might have bearing on the modern controversy over congregationally sponsored bingo and card games organized to raise funds to meet the tremendous budgets of the synagogues. Jewish history and rabbinic literature shows that such methods are not new. Synagogues and communities have indulged in similar games in the past, and the revenues have been used to meet their financial obligations. Rabbis not only did not frown upon such acts but frequently encouraged them. The *United Synagogue of America at successive conventions has, however, ruled that bingo is a form of fund-raising not to be permitted by their congregations, the opinion being that it is not in keeping with the spirit of Judaism. [L.LA.]

In Jewish Law. It is said that people who play games of dice are the sinners "in whose hands is craftiness" (Ps. 26, 10), calculating with their left hand and covering with their right, and defrauding and robbing each other (Mid. Ps. to 26:7). Dice are variously named in the Talmud as *kubbiyyah* (RH 1:8; Sanh. 3:3; et al.), *pesipas* (Sanh. 25b), or *tipas* (Tosef., Sanh. 5:2), apparently all words of Greek origin denoting small, wooden, mostly painted cubes. The player is sometimes called *kubiustos,* and it is said of him that he is afraid of daylight (Ḥul. 91b). Slaves are said to be notorious gamblers—which is the reason given for the rule that the sale of a slave could not be rescinded where it turned out that he was a *kubiustos* (BB 92b–93a and Rashbam *ibid.*).

However sinful and reprehensible gambling may be, it was not regarded as a criminal offense in talmudic law. A gambler who had no other trade but lived by gambling was disqualified as a judge and as a witness (RH 1:8; Sanh. 3:3), and in order to have his disqualification removed, had first to pay back (or to distribute to charities) all the money he had earned from his gambling (Sanh. 25b; *Piskei ha-Rosh,* Sanh. 3:10). For the purpose of such disqualification, moreover, the concept of gambling was expressly extended to include betting on animal races and the flights of pigeons and other birds (Sanh. 25a–b). Opinions differ as to the reason for such disqualification: some hold that taking money from another by way of game or sport, without giving valuable consideration in return, is like larceny; others hold that wasting time and money in gambling, instead of engaging in studies or in a trade or profession, amounts to ignoring the "general welfare of the world" *(yishuvo shel olam)*; both schools conclude that gamblers cannot, therefore, be reliable (*ibid.;* and Yad, Gezelah Va-Avedah 6:10–11 and Edut 10:4). The rule did not apply to occasional gamblers who earned their livelihood by an honest trade (Sanh. 3:3; *Rema,* ḤM 370:3; *Mordekhai,* Sanh. 690; *Kesef Mishneh,* Edut 10:4; et al.). A vow not to earn money was understood to mean not to win money by gambling (TJ, Ned. 5, 4, 39b). As gambling easily grows into an irresistible obsession, vows and oaths to abstain from it in the future were frequently taken, and the question arose whether such vows were irrevocable: those who held that they were regarded gambling as offensive and prohibited anyway (cf. e.g. TJ, Ned. *ibid.* and *Korban Edah* and *Penei Moshe ibid.*; Resp. Rashba, vol. 1, no. 756; Resp. Radbaz 214; Resp. Maharashdam, YD 84; et al.); others also considered the psychological aspect and held such vows to be impossible to maintain (Resp. Ribash 281, 432; et al.). But so long as the vow had not been lawfully revoked, any gambling in contravention of it would be punished with *flogging and heavy *fines (Resp. Rosh 11:9).

In the Middle Ages, the playing of games of chance came to be recognized in many communities as a criminal offense: with the impoverishment of ghetto populations, the public danger of gambling and the necessity to suppress it called for drastic measures. The following is an example of a communal law *(*takkanah)* on gambling: "Nobody may play at cards or dice or any other games whatsoever that the mouth could speak or the heart think, even on Rosh-Ḥodesh, Ḥanukkah, Purim, *ḥol ha-mo'ed,* and other days on which no *Taḥanun* is said, and even at the bed of a woman confined in childbirth or at a sickbed—and everybody whoever it may be, including boys and girls, manservants and maidservants, shall be punished if they should (God forbid) contravene and play; if the offender is well-to-do, he shall pay for every occasion two silver coins, one for the *talmud torah* and one for the poor of Jerusalem; and if he is poor so that he cannot be punished by fine, he shall be punished by *imprisonment and tortured by iron chains as befits such offenders—always according to his blameworthiness and the exigencies of the day; and in any case shall his shame be made public, by announcing that this man has contravened this law" (*Takkanot Medinat Mehrin,* ed. I. Halpern, 92f.).

The modern distinction between games of skill (which are lawful) and games of chance (which are prohibited) was already made in Jewish medieval sources: some scholars held that games of skill were allowed and games of chance prohibited on a Sabbath (*Shiltei ha-Gibborim,* Er. 35b); some doubted the validity of the distinction and held that all games, even chess, were prohibited on Sabbath (several responsa on the subject are printed in full in *Paḥad Yiẓḥak* (by Isaac Lampronti) s.v. *Shevu'ah she-Lo Lishok*). Games of skill, such as chess, were never made a criminal offense, though disapproved of as a waste of time which should properly be devoted to study; and domestic gambling, even for money, became customary during the night of Christmas.

The Israel Penal Law Amendment (Prohibited Games; Lottery and Betting) Law, 5724–1964, provides for the punishment, with imprisonment up to one year and a fine of up to 5,000 pounds, of professional gamblers (and much lighter punishment for occasional gamblers); the prohibition attaches to games in which money or other material benefits can be won, and the results of which depend more on chance than on understanding or skill, or—as in the case of bets—depend purely on guesswork.

See also *Cards and Card-Playing; *Games. [H.H.C.]

Bibliography: L. Loew, *Die Lebensalter in der juedischen Literatur* (1875), 323–37; V. Kurrein, in: MGWJ, 66 (1922), 203–11; I. Rivkind, in: *Tarbiz*, 4 (1932/33), 366–76; idem, in: *Horeb*, 1 (1934), 82–91; idem, *Der Kamf kegen Azartshpilen bay Yidn* (1946); I. Jakobovits, *Jewish Law Faces Modern Problems* (1965), 109–12; L. Landman, in: JQR, 57 (1966/67), 298–318; 58 (1967/68), 34–62; idem, in: *Tradition*, 10 no. 1 (1968/69), 75–86; I. Abrahams, *Jewish Life in the Middle Ages* (1932²), 397–422; ET, 2 (1949), 113; 5 (1953), 520–2; J. Bazak, in: *Ha-Peraklit*, 16 (1960), 47–60; idem, in: *Sinai*, 48 (1961), 111–27.

GAMES. Jews, like all other peoples, have played games from earliest times. There are ample references to games in the Bible. Guessing games were played in biblical days (Judg.14:12ff.; I Kings 10:1–3). Jews were also acquainted with sports and military games such as horseback riding, racing, and archery (I Sam. 20:20–21; Jer. 12:5; Ps. 19:6). Twelve young men from Benjamin waged a fencing contest with twelve of David's followers (II Sam. 2:14ff.). Children played at home and in the streets (Zech. 8:5). During the Second Temple period, games of Babylonian, Persian, Greek, and Roman origin were introduced into Israel. Jews rarely originated games, usually adopting them from their neighbors (see *Sports). There are many reports on the mass games held on the nights of Sukkot during the *Feast of Water Drawing. The leaders of the people, such as Hillel the Elder and Simeon b. Gamaliel, took an active part in the proceedings. The levites played and danced on the steps, and platforms were erected from which the people could view the scene. Here men and women mixed together, although in later times they were separated at social functions. The national leaders set the tone by engaging in acrobatic exercises, in dancing and juggling with eight burning torches, knives, or eggs (Suk. 5:1–4; Tosef. Suk. 4:1–5). The custom of holding youth festivals in the vineyards was observed as late as the Second Temple period (Ta'an. 4:8). Traces of it are still found in the traditions observed by some communities, such as Caucasia and Yemen, on the conclusion of the Day of Atonement.

The paraphernalia of games in ancient times included nuts, fruits, eggs, balls, bones, and stones. The Jerusalem Talmud (Ta'an. 4:8, 69a) states "Tur-Shimon [?] was destroyed because its inhabitants played ball" (on the Sabbath, see *Korban ha-Edah*, ad loc.). Certain games with nuts and apples were played by women on the Sabbath (Er. 104a). Other games mentioned in the Talmud are akin to modern dominoes, checkers, and chess. There was betting (on pigeon races, called "*Mafrihei Yonim*") and *gambling with dice. Persons who engaged in these pursuits were not regarded as trustworthy witnesses (San. 3:3). Weddings were another occasion for joyous play. To fulfill the commandment of helping the bridal pair to rejoice, the sages would leave their studies and perform juggling tricks, pour oil and wine, and dance with the bride on their shoulders (Ket. 17a). Holding live fowl in their hands, they would dance before the bride or clap their hands and stamp their feet (Git. 57a). The tradition of merrymaking in honor of the bride and groom developed further in the Middle Ages with the *Marshalek*, a professional comedian who would amuse the wedding party by telling jokes, extemporaneously composing songs, and putting on various acts. Weddings were a time for the abandonment of restraint, when public entertainment was permitted. A "guard" of men wearing extravagant uniforms, some of them mounted on horses, accompanied the bridal parade, dancing women beat the cymbals, and children raced along with burning torches. Bearded old men danced and clapped their hands, or sang songs and prayers.

Figure 1. Game board, Middle Bronze Age IIb (1750–1550 B.C.E.), from Tell Beit Mirsim in the northern Negev, Israel. Jerusalem, Israel Department of Antiquities and Museums.

Under the new medieval environment in which the Jews found themselves, the form of entertainment likewise changed. The carnival made its way into the Jewish quarter, and on Purim especially there would be masquerades, death dances, stage shows, and street parades. *Purim was the only season of the year during which Jewish communities, in all times and places, observed unlimited rejoicing. The period of merrymaking began on the first of Adar, when wandering musicians appeared in the Jewish quarter. People donned Purim costumes and danced in the streets, and stage shows were performed with the story of Esther and Ahasuerus as their theme. Young men on horseback amused the public by trying to push one another off their mounts. Children made stuffed dolls and burnt Haman in effigy. Shots were fired, and the sound of the "*grager*" (noisemaker) filled the air. Jews in Italy held sports tournaments in which boys fought on foot throwing nuts, while their fathers rode on horses, and, amidst a background of horns and bugles blowing, attacked a model of Haman with wooden staves, later burning it on a mock funeral pyre. In some communities, such as Hebron, Yemen, and Baghdad, Hanukkah was observed in a similar manner, though on a smaller scale, as was Simhat Torah and the second day of Shavuot. In the yeshivot, the great occasion for play was Purim. Preparations would start right after Hanukkah, and the usual theme for the play was "The

Sale of Joseph" or "David and Goliath." Young artisans would also put on Purim plays, their favorite theme being the Esther story. In Sephardi communities, the play would be a parody based on the life of Esther, Haman's wedding to Zeresh, Haman's funeral, etc. In Iraq and other communities, a Haman figure would be put up on Purim to serve as a target for young and old alike. The games played at home were *cards, *chess, dominoes, and checkers. Card playing was sharply condemned, and the rabbis often excluded card players from religious functions and social life. Yet the habit persisted. The 14th century *Kalonymus b. Kalonymus in his *Even Boḥan* sharply criticized those card players who reduced their opponents to utter despair. Maimonides compared such persons who gamble to robbers (Yad, Gezelah ve-Avedah 6:7). A synod in Forli, Italy, enacted a ruling in 1416 that the Jewish community must refrain from playing dice, cards, and other games of chance, except on fast days and in time of illness, in order to relieve the distress. Similar measures were taken in Bologna and Hamburg. The numerical value of the letters making up *karten* (Yid. for cards) was found to be the same as that of "Satan," and hence a pious Jew should keep away from them. The 17th century *Ḥavvot Ya'ir* of Jair Ḥayyim *Bacharach permitted card playing without money on Ḥanukkah, Purim, and **ḥol ha-mo'ed* (p. 126). On Christmas eve, playing for money was tolerated. Leone Modena was plagued by his obsessive love for card playing. The rabbis of Venice issued a ruling in 1628 excommunicating any member of a congregation who played cards, and there were many instances of oaths taken by individuals who wanted to avoid all games of chance. In the course of time, Yiddish terms were introduced into the card games: a six became a *"vover"* (the letter *"vav"* having the numerical value of six), a seven a *"zayner,"* a nine a *"teser"*; hearts became *"lev"* and trumps were *"yom tov"* (holiday). The card deck was called the small *"Shas"* (the Talmud) or the *"Tillim'l"* (the Book of Psalms), etc. Chess, on the other hand, was a respected pastime, although some rabbis disapproved of the game. There was a legend ascribing its invention to King Solomon. Rashi observed that chess drives boredom away and causes the player to contemplate (Ket. 61b). Poets and philosophers set down the rules of the game, and R. Abraham *ibn Ezra composed a poem on it as did Bonsenior *ibn Yahia in the 15th century (both translated into Latin by Thomas Hyde in *De Ludis Orientalium*, Oxford, 1694). There were rabbis who excelled in the game of chess. One legend has it that R. Simeon, the chief rabbi of Mainz (11th century), played chess with the pope and recognized in him his long lost son. The *Magen Avraham* of Abraham Abele b. Ḥayyim ha-Levi *Gombiner (17th century) tells of people who had special silver chess sets for use on the Sabbath. Here, too, Yiddish and Hebrew terms were introduced into the game. Checkers was also a popular game. Yeshivah students would draw a checkerboard on the blank inside cover of the Talmud volume and make their own black and white pieces of wood. Rabbi Nahum of Shtipensht found in the game an allegory of life: you take one step in order to gain two. You must not take two steps at once. You may only go up; once you have reached the top, you may go wherever you like (A. Y. Sperling, *Ta'amei ha-Minhagim* (1957), 367).

The world of children in both Ashkenazi and Sephardi communities was a world of games. For every holiday the Jewish child prepared special toys, made up out of whatever material was available, with the assistance of the rabbi in the *ḥeder* or of older children. The Jewish child was said to be a jack-of-all-trades: On Passover he makes holes in the *maẓẓot*, on Shavuot he becomes a gardener, on Lag ba-Omer he is a soldier, on Sukkot a builder, on Ḥanukkah he pours lead, on Purim he is a gunsmith, and for Rosh Ha-Shanah he trains as a trumpeter (to blow the *shofar*). For Ḥanukkah the boys would prepare a *"dreydel"* (a four-sided top), either carving it out of wood or pouring lead into a form. This game is still popular and has also been adopted by Yemeni and Sephardi children. It came upon the Jewish scene in the early Middle Ages, and the four sides of the *dreydel* were marked with the Hebrew letters *Nun, Gimmel, He, Shin* (standing for Yiddish words *Nimm, Gib, Halb, Shtell* meaning take, give, half, and put). Soon, however, the letters were interpreted as standing for the Hebrew *Nes Gadol Hayah Sham* ("a great miracle happened there"). In modern Israel the last word was changed to *Po*, so as to read "a great miracle happened here." *Dreydel* spinning was one form of Ḥanukkah gambling. Older children made their own Yiddish cards known as *"Lamed-Alef-niks"* or *"Kvitlakh."* For Purim, noise-making toys, *"gragers"* or boxes, to drown the sound of Haman's name in the synagogue reading of the Book of Esther, masks, costumes, and Haman dolls were made by young folk. Passover games were played with walnuts. For Lag ba-Omer the equipment was bows and arrows, and the children spent the day in the woods, engaging in various warlike operations under the command of the "Lag ba-Omer general." On Shavuot girls decorated the windows with paper roses, and the boys brought field flowers and ivy from the forest and adorned the doors, windows, and lamps. There was also a custom of piercing eggs, emptying them of their contents, drawing a string through the empty shells, gluing feathers to them, and hanging them up in the open to swing in the wind like birds. On the eve of the Ninth of Av children armed themselves with wooden swords and played as soldiers fighting the Turks for possession of Ereẓ Israel. The "Rabbi" game in which boys mimicked their teachers was popular between the 17th of Tammuz and the Ninth of Av, when children were free from punishment. Even adults enjoyed this game on Purim. Throughout the year in their spare time children played war games (often based on biblical themes), cops and robbers, hide-and-go-seek, "Simple Simon," etc. More sedate games were played with buttons, pocketknives, heads or tails, paper cutouts, and drawing on walls.

Concerning adults, there are records of Jews dueling. In Spain, some enjoyed wearing arms, considering themselves knights and using stately names. In Provence, Jews used trained falcons in hawking while riding horses. Occasional-

Figure 2. Engraving of a Ḥanukkah celebration with children playing games and adults gambling. From Kirchner, *Juedisches Ceremoniel*, Nuremberg, 1734. Jerusalem, J.N.U.L.

Figure 3. First round of the 16th Chess Olympics, held in Tel Aviv in 1964. Courtesy Government Press Office, Tel Aviv.

ly, they joined Christian friends in hunting, although they could not eat the game killed that way because of the *dietary laws (see Cruelty to *Animals and *Hunting). All ages enjoyed a variety of word games, often based on biblical verses. A *"samekh-pe"* game, relating to finding open or closed lines in the Pentateuch was popular. The "Moses" game was played by children who would turn to pages of the Bible and compete with each other to be the first to locate the Hebrew letters of Moses' name among the last letters on the page. Letter games with *Gematria, i.e., in which corresponding words and phrases were searched for with each having the same numerical value, were enjoyed, for example, the identical numerical value of the Hebrew phrases for "blessed is Mordecai" and "cursed be Haman." Riddles were a form of amusement, and early examples were found in the series of moral riddles in the 13th chapter of Proverbs. **Eḥad mi Yode'a,* a song from the Passover *seder,* is an illustration. Hebrew *acrostics were popular, combined with arithmetical puzzles. Abraham ibn Ezra wrote several of these, some expressly for Ḥanukkah. Judah Halevi also composed poetic riddles. In the 13th century riddles about general folk legends like "Solomon and Marcom" were also known to Jews. Yet at this time the most common games involving words were table riddles, such as found abundantly in the Hebrew romances of Al-Ḥarizi and Joseph Zabara. The Talmud reported an example of such a riddle from Adda the fisherman: "Broil the fish with his brother (salt), plunge it into its father (water), eat it with its son (sauce), and drink after it its father (water)" (MK 11a). Jewish gatherings in later times were often enlivened by witty puzzles. *Kabbalah also had a part in such wordplay, as when children would direct some invocation to the angel *Sandalfon at the start of their games. There were formal occasions for performances by teenagers at the end of the school term or the conclusion of a tractate of the Talmud (see **Siyyum*) on the 15th of Shevat, etc. In Ashkenazi communities, *Shabbat Naḥamu* (the Sabbath following the Ninth of Av) would be marked by a festive meal and children's show. Sephardi children in the old city of Jerusalem, Hebron, Baghdad, etc. would mark the last day of Ḥanukkah with a play, *"Miranda di Ḥanukkah."* In Tripoli, Tunis, and Salonika, on the sixth or seventh day of Ḥanukkah, a celebration would be held for girls who had reached the age of twelve. Also on Ḥanukkah, Sephardi children would play "Caricas di Sol" ("Face of Salt"), or act as soldiers fighting the Greeks. This was also the custom among the children of Yemen, who wore blue clothes for the occasion. Jewish children in Persia marked Ḥanukkah by playing various games of chance known as *"Kab," "Kemar,"* and *"Tachte-ner"* (a kind of checkers, known as *"Shesh-Besh"* in Arabic). Yemeni children played with fruit stones (now played in Israel with apricot stones). Their Ḥanukkah top (*"Duame"*) was made of nutshells; the Purim *"grager"* was called *"Khirye."* Other games were *"Umey"* (blindman's buff), *"Kez Almakez"* ("horses," or jumping over one another's bent backs), etc. In Tripoli the young men had the custom of holding donkey races on the Ninth of Av, for on that day the Messiah was expected to come riding on a donkey. On Shavuot they would pour water on the passers-by (also customary in other eastern communities). The last day of Passover was the occasion for a "*Maimuna" carnival, when young and old would pelt one another with flowers and vegetable leaves. In all communities, girls had their own games, such as playing ball, dolls, "cat-and-mouse," "golden bridges," etc. They also played an elaborate form of "bride-and-groom," accompanied by songs. Rarely did boys and girls join in games together, although girls would also engage in games usually reserved for boys. After World War I, various forms of modern sports and gymnastics were introduced into the Jewish communities, taking the place of the traditional forms of entertainment. Some of the old games, however, still survive and are handed over by children from one generation to the next.

Bibliography: J. J. Schudt, *Juedische Merckwuerdigkeiten,* 2 (1714), 312; 3 (1714), 202; A. Berliner, *Aus dem inneren Leben der deutschen Juden im Mittelalter* (1871); M. Steinschneider, *Schach bei den Juden* (1873); M. Guedemann, *Geschichte des Erziehungswesens und der Cultur der abendlaendischen Juden,* 3 vols. (1880–88); I. Abrahams, *Jewish Life in the Middle Ages,* ed. by C. Roth (1932), 397–422; I. Rivkind, *Der Kamf kegen Azartshpiln bay Yidn* (1946); Y. Stern, *Kheyder un Bes-Medresh* (1950); C. Roth, *Jews in the Renaissance* (1959), 28–30; M. Molho, *Literatura sefardita de Oriente* (1960), 177–82; *Yahadut Luv* (1960), 367–99; Y. Kafih, *Halikhot Teiman* (1961), passim; J. Yehoshua, *Yaldut bi-Yrushalayim ha-Yeshanah* (1965). [Y.-T.L.]

GAMORAN, EMANUEL (1895–1962), U.S. educator. Born in Belz, Russia, he was taken to the U.S. in 1907. From 1917 to 1921 Gamoran was associated with the New York Bureau of Jewish Education, becoming in 1923 the educational director of the Commission of Jewish Education of the Union of American Hebrew Congregations, a post he held until his death. He was also president of the National Council for Jewish Education in 1927–28. Under Gamoran's direction, the Reform Commission on Jewish Education produced numerous textbooks and curricula for its affiliated schools, and pioneered the use of audiovisual aids in Jewish education. Gamoran wrote *Changing Conceptions in Jewish Education* (1924), as well as graded textbooks for Jewish schools and many articles on Jewish education.

Bibliography: *Jewish Education,* 34 (1964), 67–86 (several articles in honor of Gamoran). [L.Sp.]

GAMZU, ḤAYYIM (1910–), Israel drama and art critic. Born in Chernigov, Russia, he went to Palestine with his parents in 1923, and later left to study art and philosophy at the Sorbonne and the University of Vienna. The director of the Tel Aviv Museum, from 1962 he taught at the Ramat Gan School of Drama, and wrote regularly on painting, sculpture, and the theater, mainly for the daily *Haaretz.* His criticism was erudite and often harsh. Insisting that Hebrew drama must maintain European standards, he often expressed dissatisfaction with its achievements. His books, consisting of reproductions of works of art and accompanying text, include *Ḥannah Orloff* (1949), *Ẓiyyur u-Fissul be-Yisrael ve-ha-Yeẓirah ha-Ommanutit be-Ereẓ Yisrael ba-Ḥamishim Shanah ha-Aḥaronot* ("Painting and Sculpture in Israel and Artistic Creation in the Land of Israel in the

Past 50 Years," 1957); *Ze'ev Ben-Zvi* (1955); *Ommanut ha-Pissul be-Yisrael* ("The Art of Sculpture in Israel," 1957). [G.K.]

GANDZ, SOLOMON (1887–1954), Semitics scholar and historian of mathematics. Gandz was born in Austria. He studied mathematics, Semitics, and rabbinics in Vienna and taught at a Viennese high school from 1915 to 1923. He emigrated to the United States in 1924 and was librarian and instructor in medieval Hebrew and Arabic at the Rabbi Isaac Elchanan Theological Seminary until 1935. From 1942 until his death he taught the history of Semitic civilization at Dropsie College.

Gandz's particular field of study was ancient oriental mathematics, astronomy, and science and Jewish study of these specialties in the Middle Ages. Among his works in this field is a translation of *Mishnat ha-Middot* (in *Quellen und Studien zur Geschichte der Mathematik, Astronomie und Physik,* Abteilung A, 2, 1932), a second-century Hebrew geometry and its ninth-century Arabic version. A selection of his many essays was collected in *Studies in Hebrew Astronomy and Mathematics* (1970). In Semitics, he contributed an annotated German translation of Imruʾ al-Qays' sixth-century poems, "Die Muʿallaqa des Imrulqais" (in *Sitzungsbericht der Kaiserlichen Akademie der Wissenschaften in Wien,* 170, Abhandlung 4, 1913). He was associate editor of the international periodical *Osiris,* devoted to the history of science, to which he contributed "The Dawn of Literature" (7 (1939), 261–522). He also contributed the section on public law to the second volume of *Monumenta Talmudica* (Ger., 1913). For the Yale Judaica Series English edition of Maimonides' Mishneh Torah, Gandz did the translation of Book 3, *Book of Seasons* (1961; with Hyman Klein) and of Book 3, Treatise 8, published separately as *Treatise on the Sanctification of the New Moon* (1956).

Bibliography: J. Dienstag, in: *Hadoar,* 34 (May 14, 1954), 528–9; Levey, in: *Isis,* 46 (1955), 107–10, includes bibliography. [Ed.]

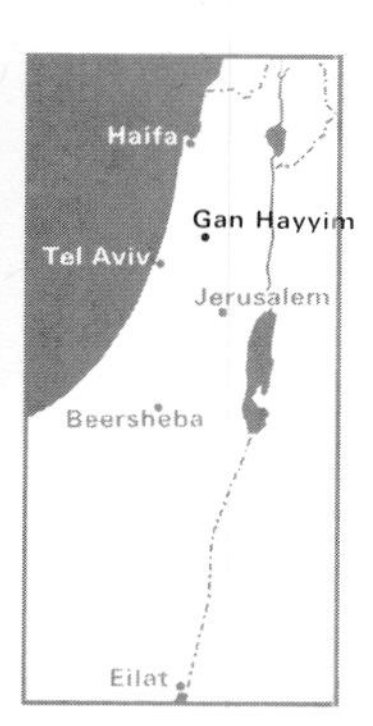

GAN ḤAYYIM (Heb. גַּן חַיִּים), moshav in central Israel in the southern Sharon near *Kefar Sava, affiliated with Tenu'at ha-Moshavim. It was founded in 1935 by veteran farm workers from Russia and other East European countries. The moshav expanded in 1949 when settlers from Rumania joined it. Citriculture constituted a prominent farm branch. The moshav, which had a population of 220 in 1968, is named after Chaim *Weizmann. [E.O.]

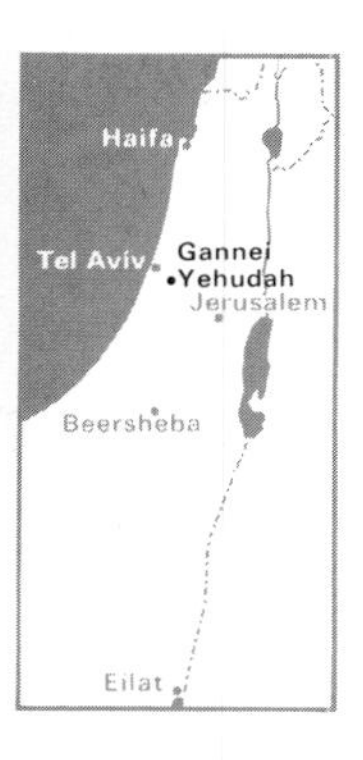

GANNEI YEHUDAH (Heb. גַּנֵּי יְהוּדָה; "Gardens of Judea"), moshav with municipal council status in the Judean coastal plain of Israel near Petaḥ Tikvah, affiliated with Ha-Iḥud ha-Ḥakla'i, founded in 1950. The founding settlers were mainly immigrants from South Africa. In 1968, Gannei Yehudah, with 580 inhabitants, engaged principally in citriculture. [E.O.]

GANS, BIRD STEIN (1868–1944), U.S. educator. She was born in Allegheny City, Pennsylvania. In 1896 she became director of the Society for the Study of Child Nature in New York, the first organization in the U.S. engaged in the field of parent education. With the growth of similar societies in other cities the organization changed its name to the Federation for Child Study in 1898 and Bird Gans was elected its first president. In 1924 the organization became the Child Study Association of America. Bird Gans organized similar groups in Japan (1924) and England (1929). By 1941 the association was conducting extensive experiments and research in child psychology, and providing its results to approximately 100 groups throughout the country. Bird Gans was president of the organization until 1933 and honorary president for the next six years. She served on the National Board of Review, the film censorship organization, and was associated with several organizations devoted to the investigation and solution of youth welfare problems. [Ed.]

GANS, DAVID BEN SOLOMON (1541–1613), chronicler, astronomer, and mathematician. Born in Lippstadt, Westphalia, Gans studied rabbinics with Reuben Fulda in Bonn; Eliezer Treves in Frankfort; Moses Isserles in Cracow; and Judah Loew (the *Maharal*) in Prague. Encouraged, so it is said, by Isserles, he devoted himself to the study of mathematics and astronomy. In the house of his first father-in-law Gans apparently found a Hebrew translation of Euclid by Moses ibn Tibbon; his second father-in-law was the physician Samuel Rofe who had become famous for his mercury cures of syphilis. Gans was one of the few German Jews of his time, when rabbinics ruled supreme, to undertake serious secular studies for which he found and quoted older Jewish authorities. In Prague he corresponded with the astronomer Johann Mueller (Regiomontanus) and was in friendly contact with Johann Kepler and Tycho Brahe, for whom he translated the Alfonsine Tables from Hebrew into German.

Gans's main astronomical (and also geographical) work was *Neḥmad ve-Na'im* ("Delightful and Pleasant," Jesnitz, 1743; shortened version *Magen David,* Prague, 1612) in which he rejects the new Copernican system in favor of Ptolemy's, the former going back (according to Gans) to the Pythagorean system. Astronomy (and mathematics)—he held—was first studied by Jews from whom the Egyptians had learned the science, passing it on to the Greeks. Ptolemy had studied with Alexandrian Jewish scholars. The study of astronomy was important not only for the Jewish calendar but as proof for the cultural achievements of the Jewish people. Other works by Gans on mathematics, the calendar, and the geography of Ereẓ Israel remained unpublished.

Gans wrote his chronicle *Ẓemaḥ David* ("Offspring of David," Prague, 1592) in two parts, one dealing with Jewish history to the date of publication, the other with general history. He had written it for "householders like myself and of my worth," while justifying the inclusion of general history by the fact that it contained ethical teachings of emperors, which ordinary people would accept coming from such illustrious mouths. The first part of the work summarizes that of his predecessors, such as *Ibn Daud and *Zacuto, but he dissociates himself from the untraditional approach of Azariah dei *Rossi. For the second part his sources are contemporary German chroniclers like Cyriak Spangenberg and Laurentius Faustus, though in his introduction he expresses doubts as to their reliability. Gans shows an interest in economics; his description of historical events and situations reflects the spirit and taste of the 16th-century Jewish "householder" in Bohemia and Poland. The *Ẓemaḥ David* remained a standard work up to the Haskalah period. The second edition by David b. Moses of Reindorf (Frankfort, 1692) brings the chronicle up to the date of publication, also giving a long poetical description

Tombstone of the historian David b. Solomon Gans in the Prague cemetery. Courtesy State Jewish Museum, Prague.

of the *Fettmilch riots of 1614. It was translated into Latin by W. H. Vorst (Leyden, 1692); into Yiddish by Solomon Zalman Hanau (Frankfort, 1698); and parts of it into German by G. Klemperer (ed. Moritz Gruenwald, 1890). The Warsaw edition of 1849, also brought up to date, was reproduced in 1966 with introductions in Hebrew and English and an index.

Bibliography: K. Lieben, *Gal-Ed* (1856), Hebrew section 4; German section 10–12; M. Steinschneider, *Geschichtsliteratur der Juden* (1905), para. 132; idem, *Copernikus nach dem Urteil des David Gans* (1871); M. Grunwald, in: D. Gans, *Ẓemaḥ David*, Ger. tr. by G. Klemperer (1890), introd.; S. Steinherz, in: JGGJČ, 9 (1938), 171–97; G. Alter, *Two Renaissance Astronomers* (1958).

[Ed.]

GANS, EDUARD (1798–1839), jurist and historian in Berlin. From 1816 to 1819 he studied law and philosophy in the universities of Berlin and Heidelberg; at Heidelberg he was influenced by *Hegel and his system. In 1820 Gans was appointed lecturer in the university of Berlin where he became celebrated for his inspiring lectures. He considered that Judaism had to relinquish its separate existence and distinctiveness and assimilate to become one of the currents in the evolving European culture. He founded in 1819, in conjunction with Leopold *Zunz and Moses *Moser, the *Verein fuer Cultur und Wissenschaft der Juden, whose object was to bring general education to Jewish youth by expanding their cultural horizons and reform of traditional Jewish thinking. The society was dissolved in 1824. His inclination to *assimilation, and the government's objection to the appointment of a Jew to a permanent academic position, led Gans to become an apostate to Christianity at the end of 1825. In 1826 he was appointed associate professor in Berlin University, and in 1829 a full professor. In his lectures on jurisprudence, which attracted an enormous audience, Gans developed the Hegelian philosophical system rejecting the historical system of Savigny. On history, he elaborated the concept of the Prussian state and its sovereignty, and the central role of the ruler as the incarnation of the concept of the state. He saw the French Revolution as a new and crucial factor in European history, and explained the historical concept of "Europe" as a synthesis of different peoples incorporating the best in the cultures of Israel, Greece, Rome, Christianity, and the West in its development; Gans was opposed to nationalism and the romantic glorification of the Middle Ages and its Christian culture.

His works include (on law): *Scholien zum Gaius* (1821); *System des roemischen Civilrechts im Grundrisse* (1827); *Ueber die Grundlage des Besitzes* (1839); *Beitraege zur Revision der preussischen Gesetzgebung* (1830–32); *Das Erbrecht in weltgeschichtlicher Entwicklung* (4 vols., 1824–35; repr.), a fundamental work on comparative law; and a historical work, *Vorlesungen ueber die Geschichte der letzten fuenfzig Jahre* (1833–34). He also edited Hegel's lectures on the philosophy of history (vols. 8 and 9 of G. W. F. Hegel's *Werke*, 1833–37). In 1827 he founded the *Jahrbuecher fuer wissenschaftliche Kritik*. An essay on the principles of the law of inheritance in the Pentateuch and Talmud, a chapter from his work *Das Erbrecht in weltgeschichtlicher* appeared in the *Zeitschrift fuer die Wissenschaft des Judenthums* (vol. 1 (1822–23), 419–71), which also published his study of the Roman legislation concerning the Jews ("Gesetzgebung ueber Juden in Rom"). The reports of the society, including several of his addresses, are preserved in manuscript in the Zunz archives in Jerusalem.

Eduard Gans, German jurist. Jerusalem, J.N.U.L., Schwadron Collection.

Bibliography: H. G. Reissner, *Eduard Gans: ein Leben in Vormaerz* (1965); idem, in: YLBI, 2 (1957), 179–86; 4 (1959), 92–110; M. Wiener, in: YIVOA, 5 (1950), 190–3; B. Kurzweil, in: *Haaretz* (April 24, 1967).

[N.N.G.]

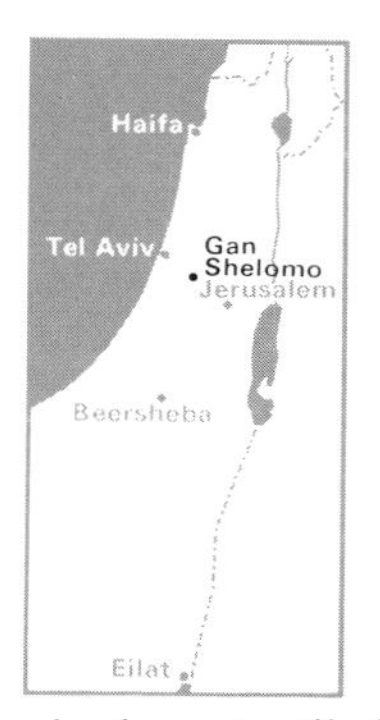

GAN SHELOMO (Heb. גַּן שְׁלֹמֹה; previously known as **Kevuẓat Schiller**), kibbutz near Reḥovot, affiliated with Iḥud ha-Kevuẓot ve-ha-Kibbutzim. It was founded in 1927 by a pioneer group of former students from Galicia. Affiliated with *Ḥever ha-Kevuẓot (of *Mapai orientation), the settlers nevertheless preserved their political ties with Ha-Oved ha-Ẓiyyoni (Independent Liberals). Citriculture and dairy cattle constitute principal farm branches, and the kibbutz also has a textile factory. Gan Shelomo is named in memory of Solomon *Schiller. In 1968 its population was 265.

[E.O.]

GAN SHEMU'EL (Heb. גַּן שְׁמוּאֵל), kibbutz in central Israel near *Ḥaderah, affiliated with Kibbutz Arẓi Ha-Shomer ha-Ẓa'ir. Members of Odessa's Ḥovevei Zion first settled there in 1884, laying out plantations of *etrogim* ("citrons"). They named the place "Samuel's Garden" after Samuel *Mohilever. In 1912 a laborers' group settled there temporarily, and in 1921, settlers from Eastern Europe, took over. In 1968 Gan Shemu'el had 700 inhabitants and its economy was based on intensive irrigated farming and a food preserves factory. [E.O.]

Shavuot celebration at kibbutz Gan Shemu'el. Government Press Office, Tel Aviv.

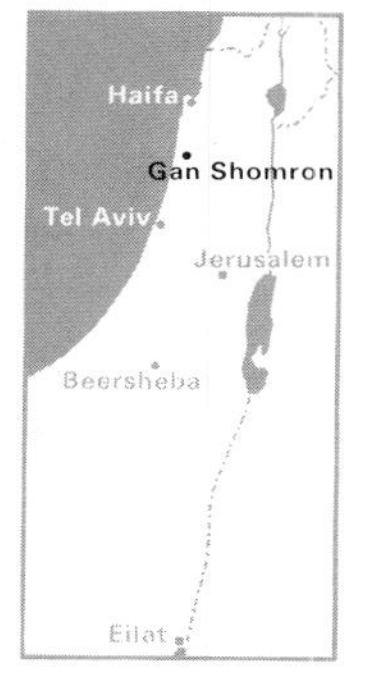

GAN SHOMRON (Heb. גַּן שׁוֹמְרוֹן), moshav in central Israel, northeast of *Ḥaderah, founded in 1934 by middle-class settlers from Germany and unaffiliated with any moshav association. It expanded after 1945, when World War II veterans and new immigrants settled there. Its economy is based on intensive farming (especially citriculture). The name Gan Shomron refers to the locality of the Samaria Hills. In 1969 its population was 322. [E.O.]

GANSO, JOSEPH (17th century), rabbi, author, and *paytan.* He lived in Bursa, Turkey, and, in his old age, emigrated to Jerusalem, where he died. Famed as a leading hymnologist he composed a book of *piyyutim* of which only one incomplete copy is extant (in the library of the Jewish Theological Seminary in New York). The hymns, written in a lucid style, reveal the influence of R. Israel *Najara, but they are also original in a manner typical of his contemporaries and of his time. Several of the hymns are in Aramaic. The most important of Ganso's pupils was R. Solomon *Algazi.

Bibliography: Conforte, Kore, 50a, 51a; Ghirondi-Neppi, 197; Rosanes, Togarmah, 3 (1914), 160; Davidson, Oẓar, 4 (1933), 493–4. [A.M.H.]

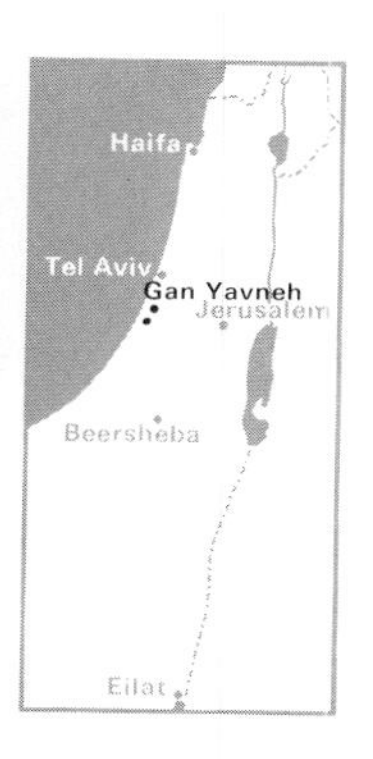

GAN YAVNEH (Heb. גַּן יַבְנֶה), moshavah in the coastal plain of Israel, southwest of *Yavneh, founded in 1931 by a Zionist group, the Aḥuzah society in New York, most of whose members failed to arrive. The moshavah was considerably enlarged by new immigrants in 1949 and in October 1968 had 2,840 inhabitants. Gan Yavneh's economy is based on farming (especially citriculture) and small industries. Its name refers to the historical site of Jabneh, which is 5½ mi. (9 km.) away. [E.O.]

GANZFRIED, SOLOMON BEN JOSEPH (1804–1886), rabbi and author. Ganzfried was born in Ungvar, Hungary, where he also died. Orphaned in his childhood, he was brought up in the house of the local rabbi Ẓevi Hirsch Heller, one of the outstanding scholars of his time. From 1830 to 1849 Ganzfried served as rabbi of Brezewicz and subsequently as head of the *bet din* of Ungvar. He was one of the chief speakers for orthodox Jewry at the Jewish congress which took place in Budapest in 1869. He also published a polemic against the Reform movement. His first published work, *Keset-ha-Sofer* (1835; 1871[2] with additions by the author), was on the laws of writing a *Sefer Torah,* and was highly recommended by Moses *Sofer as a necessary textbook for scribes of Torah scrolls, *tefillin,* and *mezuzot.* Ganzfried's fame, however, rests mainly upon his *Kiẓẓur Shulḥan Arukh* ("Abridged Shulhan Arukh," 1864); it achieved great popularity and widespread circulation and was accepted as the main handbook for Ashkenazi Jewry. It encompassed all the laws relating to the mode of life of the ordinary Jew living outside Ereẓ Israel (including such subjects as etiquette, hygiene, etc.), but omitting such details as were common knowledge and practice at that time (see his introduction to ch. 80) or that were not essential knowledge for the ordinary man (see especially the laws of matrimony, ch. 145). The *Kiẓẓur Shulḥan Arukh* is based upon the Shulḥan Arukh of Joseph *Caro with the glosses of Moses *Isserles. It is written in simple, popular language, with a lively style, and interest is sustained by the ethical maxims with which it is interlaced. Unlike his predecessor Abraham *Danzig, author of the *Ḥayyei Adam,* Ganzfried does not detail and explain the different views but usually gives his decision without the reasoning. The book had already achieved 14 editions during its author's lifetime, and since then it has gone through scores of editions, displacing all previous abridgments of the Shulḥan Arukh. It also became a basic work to which many scholars added marginal notes and novellae.

The important editions of the work are: Lublin, 1888, with the commentaries, *"Pe'at ha-Shulḥan"* by the author himself, *Ammudei ha-Shulḥan* by Benjamin Isaiah b. Jeroham Fishel ha-Kohen, and *Misgeret Zahav,* by Moses Israel; Leipzig, 1924, with source references *(Meẓudat Ẓiyyon),* supplements *(Meẓudat David)* and with illustrations, edited by D. Feldman; Jerusalem, 1940, a vocalized edition with the addition of the laws and customs applying in Ereẓ Israel at the present day, edited by J. M. Tucazinsky, and one with the additions *Misgeret ha-Shulḥan* and *Leḥem ha-Panim* of Ḥayyim Isaiah ha-Kohen Halbersberg and a summary of those precepts connected with the land of Israel in accordance with the rulings of Abraham Isaiah *Karelitz, edited by K. Kahana (Jerusalem, 1954).

The book was also translated into many languages (English by H. E. Goldin (1928)). Ganzfried's other published works are: a commentary on the prayer book with notes and supplements to the prayer-book commentary *Derekh ha-Ḥayyim* of Jacob Lorbeerbaum (first published in the prayer book printed in Vienna in 1839); *Penei Shelomo* (1845), novellae to Bava Batra; *Torat Zevaḥ* (1849), on the laws of *sheḥitah; Leḥem ve-Simlah* (1861), on the laws of menstruation and ritual immersion; *Appiryon* (1864; with the author's additions in 1876), homilies on the Pentateuch and on some *aggadot; Oholei Shem* (1878), on the laws of names in bills of divorce and on the writing of deeds; and *Shem Shelomo* (1908), on talmudic themes. There have remained in manuscript *Leshon ha-Zahav,* on Hebrew grammar; *Penei Adam,* notes to the *Ḥayyei Adam; Kelalim be-Ḥokhmat ha-Emet,* a commentary on the Zohar; and his responsa.

Bibliography: Brody, in: *Oẓar ha-Sifrut*, 3 (1889/90), 55–61 (4th pagination); J. Banet, in: S. Ganzfried, *Shem Shelomo* (1908), introd.; J. L. Maimon, in: S. Ganzfried, *Kiẓẓur Shulḥan Arukh* (1950), introd. [J.Lev.]

GAON (pl. **Geonim**), formal title of the heads of the academies of Sura and Pumbedita in Babylonia. The *geonim* were recognized by the Jews as the highest authority of instruction from the end of the sixth century or somewhat later to the middle of the 11th. In the 10th and 11th centuries this title was also used by the heads of academies in Ereẓ Israel. In the 12th and 13th centuries—after the geonic period in the exact sense of the term—the title *gaon* was also used by the heads of academies in Baghdad, Damascus, and Egypt. It eventually became an honorific title for any rabbi or anyone who had a great knowledge of Torah. Apparently, the term *gaon* was shortened from *rosh yeshivat ge'on Ya'akov* (cf. "the pride of Jacob," Ps. 47:4). Other explanations of the origin of the term offered by modern scholars are not acceptable.

The Geonim of Sura and Pumbedita. The exact time when the title of *gaon* came into use cannot be established. *Sherira and later rabbis automatically designated as *gaon* the heads of the two academies from the year 900 according to the Seleucid calendar (589 C.E.), when the academies renewed their normal activity. But *Sherira also mentions a tradition that Ravai, of Pumbedita (c. 540–560), was already *gaon*. However, some hold that this title and the special privileges of the academies were not granted until after the Arab conquest of Babylonia (657 C.E.), Sura receiving them first and later Pumbedita. Together with the title *gaon* they also used the titles *resh metivta* or *rosh yeshivah* ("head of the academy") as was customary in the talmudic period, and the title *rosh yeshivah shel golah* ("head of the academy of the exile") which is not found in the Talmud. According to a tradition which originated in the Sura academy (Neubauer, Chronicles, 2 (1895), 78), only the heads at Sura were called *gaon* and not their counterparts in Pumbedita. This was accepted by some historians, but is contradicted by R. Sherira's account and other sources. The existence of separate traditions, one in Sura which enumerates "the qualities in which Sura is superior to Pumbedita" *(ibid.)*, and that of Pumbedita which emphasizes that "the rabbis of Pumbedita are the leaders of the Diaspora from the time of the Second Temple" (*Iggeret Rav Sherira Ga'on*, ed. B. M. Lewin (1921), 82) emphasizes the competition between the two. Hints of tension and even open quarrels are found in other sources.

In the talmudic period the heads of the academies were chosen by the scholars of the academies (BB 12b) while in the geonic period they were appointed by the exilarchs. *Geonim* usually (although not always) rose through the hierarchy of positions in the academies until they attained this highest office. Persons of average ability therefore also attained the gaonate, and in the entire period of 400 years only a few *geonim* were outstanding men who made a lasting impact on Judaism. These included *Yehudai, *Amram, *Saadiah, Sherira, *Samuel b. Hophni, and *Hai. At times the exilarchs misused their authority and appointed *geonim* whom they expected to be subservient to them and who were not outstanding scholars. For example, it is related that an exilarch rejected *Aḥa of Shabḥa, author of the *She'iltot*, and appointed his disciple Natronai Kahana to the gaonate in Pumbedita (Ibn Daud, Tradition, 47–49). Thus, the academy in Sura was generally disturbed by the interference of the exilarchs. Sherira, *Iggeret Sherira Ga'on*, 105) argues that because of the interference of the exilarchs he could not exactly record the names of the *geonim* of Sura until the year 1000 of the Seleucid calendar (689 C.E.). After the authority of the exilarchs had weakened under *David b. Judah (*ibid.* 93) in the times of the caliph al-Ma'mun, from 825, the influence of the group of scholars on the appointment of the *gaon* increased, especially in Pumbedita.

There were cases when the exilarch and the group of scholars could not agree on the appointment of the *gaon* and each side appointed its own candidate. If the two sides did not reach a compromise as a result of the pressure of public opinion, the quarrel might last until the death of one of the candidates. Generally, assistants to the heads of academies were appointed *gaon* and were called *dayyanei de-bava* or *av* (abbreviation of *av bet din*). Distinguished *geonim* such as Sherira, Samuel b. Hophni, and Hai had first served as *av bet din;* a deviation from this practice was considered derogatory. Because only those who already possessed such honorific titles as **aluf* and **resh kallah* and who had formerly served as scribes or assistants to heads of *yeshivot*, were appointed to the gaonate, the choice often fell on old men who could fill the position for only a few years.

In this period the academies in Babylonia served as the cultural center for world Jewry, and not only Babylonian-Persian Jewry as was the case in talmudic times. Hence, the influence of the *geonim* was now all-important. They interpreted the Talmud in the form which they received from the **savoraim*, with the aim of making it the accepted code of law in all social and religious matters. The *geonim* made the academies a supreme court and source of instruction for all Jewry. Thousands of persons, occupied with their personal affairs for most of the year, would assemble in the academies in the **kallah* months of Elul and Adar in order to hear lectures on *halakhah*. During those months the *geonim* would answer all the questions sent to them from the Diaspora.

The gaonate had jurisdiction over the organization of the courts in all the districts of Babylonia. However, the judges were appointed by the exilarch with the assent of the *geonim*. Only under Hai Gaon did the supreme court *(bet din ha-gadol)* of Pumbedita appoint the judges (Neubauer, Chronicles, 2 (1887), 85; *Teshuvot ha-Ge'onim*, ed. Harkavy, no. 180). The *geonim* were not satisfied with halakhic conclusions derived from the Talmud; they also made new regulations regarding contemporary needs. Their *takkanot* ("ordinances") had legal validity because the *geonim* considered themselves presidents of the Sanhedrin of their generation. All these tasks required a large establishment; therefore, the academies employed scribes, directors of the *kallah* assemblies, and other officials. Their expenditure was covered by taxes levied on districts, which were directly subject to their authority. In addition, the communities which addressed their questions to the *geonim* sent them contributions. In isolated instances the *geonim* would turn to the communities in the Diaspora with a request for financial support and usually their request was answered. Real estate also served as a source of income for the academies. The requests for support of the academies increased, especially, toward the end of the geonic period. Thus, the candidates for the office of head of the academies had to be not only learned, but they also had to possess administrative talents. Descent was also a factor; six or seven families provided most of the *geonim* of Sura and Pumbedita. Three of these were priestly, while Sherira traced his ancestry to King David (*Iggeret Sherira Ga'on*, 92). His family produced several *geonim*, many assistant heads of academies, and other important officials in Pumbedita. In Sura positions were held for 200 years by three families. The *geonim* Jacob, Ivomai, Moses, and *Kohen Ẓedek (b. Ivomai) belonged to one priestly family; another such family produced the *geonim* *Hilai (788),

*Natronai b. Hilai (853), Jacob, and Joseph (942), while a third priestly family produced the *geonim* Kohen Ẓedek of Pumbedita, his son *Nehemiah, Samuel b. Ḥophni grandson of Kohen Ẓedek, his son *Israel, and his grandson Azariah of Sura. The *geonim* *Zadok, Kimoi, *Nahshon, *Ẓemah b. Ḥayyim, and Hai b. Nahshon were members of one family. However, the position of *gaon* was not hereditary. Although Hai attained the gaonate immediately after his father Sherira, Nahshon did not become *gaon* until 53 years after the death of his father Zadok, seven members of other families serving as *geonim* in the interim. The difference in time between the death of Hilai and the appointment of his son Natronai was similar. *Dosa did not attain the gaonate until 71 years after the death of his father Saadiah and when he was more than 80 years old.

On the appointment of a new *gaon* a festive ceremony was held, in which the scholars of the two academies and the dignitaries of all the communities in Babylonia, headed by the exilarch, participated. According to *Nathan ben Isaac ha-Bavli (Neubauer, Chronicles 2 (1895), 86), the ceremony resembled the installation of the exilarch and the people honored the *geonim* royally. Following the method of talmudic references to heads of academies, Sherira throughout used the word *"malakh"* ("reigned") to designate the term of service of the *gaon*.

The *geonim* were considered the intellectual leaders of the entire Diaspora and their decisions and responsa had absolute legal validity in most Jewish communities. It cannot be assumed that they attained their influence without a struggle and conflict with other centers, especially Ereẓ Israel. Ben Baboi (see *Pirkoi Ben Baboi) the pupil of Yehudai Gaon, attested to the intervention of the *geonim* in the affairs of Ereẓ Israel, "and he wrote to Ereẓ Israel regarding . . . all the *mitzvot* which are not observed properly according to the *halakhah* but according to practice in times of persecution and they did not accept his intervention and they replied to him: 'a custom suspends a *halakhah*' " (Ginzberg, *Ginzei Schechter*, 2 (1929), 559). Baboi attacked practices of Ereẓ Israel (*Tarbiz*, 2 (1931), 396–7). Seventy years later Amram polemized against those who followed the customs of the westerners who deviated from the right path. The aim of the Babylonian *geonim* was to impose the Babylonian Talmud and the doctrines of their academies also in Ereẓ Israel and in this way to lessen the attachment of the Diaspora to Ereẓ Israel.

The gaonate had a specific political, communal function at the side of the exilarch. The recognition of the gaonate as a political representation of the Jewish community is attested by the fact that on the death of the exilarch his income was given to the *gaon* of Sura until the appointment of a new exilarch. The *geonim* also attempted to influence the policy of the government toward the Jews via Baghdad Jewry, who had representatives in the court of the caliphs. However, the particular achievement of the *geonim* was their success in giving legal validity to the laws of the Talmud and spreading the knowledge of the Talmud among the thousands of people who came to Babylonia from all parts of the world. Their writings in the fields of commentary and *halakhah* made an impact on the entire period which is named after them. Their great importance to Jewry is attested by the paragraph in the **Kaddish* where the *geonim* are mentioned together with the exilarch (*Gedenkbuch . . . D. Kaufmann* (1900), Hebrew section, 52ff.; *Ginzei Kedem*, 2 (1923), 46; 3 (1925), 54). They and other high officials in the academies are also mentioned with the exilarch in the prayer *Yekum Purkan*. R. *Ẓemaḥ b. Ḥayyim, the *gaon* of Sura, expressed this feeling of authority in his responsa to the community in Kairouan: "And when Eldad said that they pray for the scholars of Babylonia and then for those in the Diaspora, they are right. For the major scholars and prophets were exiled to Babylonia, and they established the Torah and founded the academy on the Euphrates under Jehoiachin, king of Judah until this day, and they were the dynasty of wisdom and prophecy and the source of Torah for the entire people . . ." (*Eldad ha-Dani*, ed. by Abraham Epstein (1891), 8).

Even though the leading *geonim* were those of the later generations, the gaonate already had declined as the cultural, religious center of Judaism far before it had ceased to exist. This was as a result of a combination of internal and external causes. A sign of its public decline was that from the late ninth century most *geonim* no longer lived in the cities of the two academies. They lived in Baghdad, the center of the authorities and the residence of the exilarch. On the one hand, the decline of the academies in the eyes of the Diaspora was caused by the competition between Sura and Pumbedita and the quarrels in the academies regarding the appointment of the *gaon*. On the other hand, the essence of the fulfillment of the mission of the *geonim*—the spread of the Talmud—lessened its importance. With the emergence of new centers for talmudic studies and the appearance of great scholars throughout the Diaspora, its dependence on the two academies and on the *geonim* ceased and its attachment to them weakened. Independent-minded scholars stopped sending questions to the academies and their *geonim*, and even important *geonim* such as Sherira and Hai expressed their anger at the weakening of the links with North Africa and with Spain (Mann, Texts, 1 (1931), 109, 120–1). *Ḥanokh b. Moses of Cordoba did not even answer the letters of *Sherira. The scholars of Spain found encouragement from the authorities in their tendency to break their dependence on the *geonim* of Babylonia. The Umayyad caliphs in Cordoba did not approve the Jewish attachment to the academies in Babylonia which were under the Abbasids (cf. Abraham ibn Daud's statement, "The king was delighted by the fact that the Jews in his domain no longer had need of the people of Babylon," Ibn Daud, Tradition, 66).

The decline of the Baghdad caliphate, the impoverishment of Babylonian Jewry which caused the academies to depend completely on contributions from abroad, the greatness and the independent intellectual development of the Diaspora, and the persecutions by the Abbasid and Seljuk rulers put an end to the institution of the gaonate in about 1040.

List of the Geonim of Sura and Pumbedita. Because of the dearth of sources the exact chronology of the *geonim* cannot be established. The letter of R. Sherira serves as the basis for the list but it contains contradictions and many variant versions. The list of Abraham *Ibn Daud in the *Sefer ha-Kabbalah* does not clarify these contradictions. Nonetheless, the letter of Sherira remains the major source for the chronology of the Babylonian *geonim*. But there is much material on the history of their period, both in Babylonia and in other countries, in the collections of the responsa of the *geonim* (see bibliography). [Si.A./J.Br.]

The collecting of scattered material in the anthologies of geonic responsa, both printed and in manuscript, and in their editing, according to the order of the tractates of the Babylonian Talmud, was begun by B. M. Lewin in *Oẓar ha-Ge'onim*, which he published in 12 volumes to *Bava Kamma* (1928–43). The 13th volume was published posthumously to part of *Bava Meẓia* and one volume of *Oẓar ha-Ge'onim* to *Sanhedrin* was published by H. Z. Taubes (Jerusalem, 1966).

The following are the editions of geonic responsa: *Halakhot Pesukot min ha-Ge'onim* (Constantinople, 1516, and again published by J. Mueller, 1893):

She'elot u-Teshuvot me-ha-Ge'onim (Constantinople, 1575); *Sha'arei Ẓedek* (Salonika, 1792; Jerusalem, 1966); *Sha'arei Teshuvah* (in *Naharot Dammesek* of Solomon Kamondo, Salonika, 1802,

Chronological List of the Geonim in Sura and Pumbedita (Dates according to year of appointment)

Sura		Pumbedita
	589	Hanan of Iskiya
Mar bar Huna	591	(?) Mari b. Dimi (formerly of Firuz-Shapur and Nehardea)
Ḥanina	614	Ḥanina of Bei-Gihara (Firuz-Shapur)
	. . .	Ḥana (or Huna)
Huna	650	
Sheshna (called also Mesharsheya b. Taḥlifa)	. . .	
	651	Rabbah
	. . .	Bosai
Ḥanina of Nehar-Pekod	689	Huna Mari b. Joseph
	. . .	Ḥiyya of Meshan
	. . .	Ravya (or Mar Yanka)
Hilai ha-Levi of Naresh	694	
Jacob ha-Kohen of Nehar-Pekod	712	
	719	Natronai b. Nehemiah
	. . .	Judah
Samuel	730	
	739	Joseph
Mari Kohen of Nehar-Pekod	748	Samuel b. Mar
	752	(?) Natroi Kahana b. Mar Amunah
	. . .	Abraham Kahana
Aḥa	756	
Yehudai b. Naḥman	757	
Aḥunai Kahana b. Papa	761	Dodai b. Naḥman (brother of Yehudai the *gaon* of Sura)
	764	Hananiah b. Mesharsheya
Ḥaninai Kahana b. Huna	769	
	771	Malkha b. Aḥa
	773	Rabbah (Abba) b. Dodai
Mari ha-Levi b. Mesharsheya	774	
Bebai, (Bivoi, Bivi) ha-Levi b. Abba of Nehar-Pekod	777	
	781	Shinoi
	782	Ḥaninai Kahana b. Abraham
	785	Huna ha-Levi b. Isaac
Hilai b. Mari	788	Manasseh b. Mar Joseph
	796	Isaiah ha-Levi b. Mar Abba
Jacob ha-Kohen b. Mordecai	797	
	798	Joseph b. Shila
	804	Kahana b. Ḥaninai
	810	Ivomai (in both academies)
Ivomai, uncle of his predecessor	811	
	814	Joseph b. Abba
Zadok b. Jesse (or Ashi)	816	Abraham b. Sherira
Hilai b. Ḥanina	818	
Kimoi b. Ashi	822	
Moses (Mesharsheya)	825	
Kahana b. Jacob		
	828	Joseph b. Ḥiyya
	833	Isaac b. Hananiah
	836[a]	
Kohen Ẓedek b. Ivomai	838	
	839	Joseph b. Ravi
	842	Paltoi b. Abbaye
Sar Shalom b. Boaz	848	
Natronai b. Hilai	853	
	857	Aḥa Kahana b. Rav
Amram b. Sheshna[b]	858	Menahem b. Joseph b. Ḥiyya
	860	Mattathias b. Mar Ravi
	869	Abba (Rabbah) b. Ammi
Nahshon b. Zadok	871	
	872	Ẓemaḥ b. Paltoi
Ẓemaḥ b. Ḥayyim	879	
Malkha	885	
Hai b. Nahshon	885	
	890[c]	Hai b. David
Hilai b. Natronai	896	
	898	Kimoi b. Aḥai
Shalom b. Mishael	904	
	906	Judah b. Samuel (grandfather of Sherira)
Jacob b. Natronai	911	
	917–926	Mevasser Kahana b. Kimoi
Yom Tov Kahana b. Jacob	924	
	926–936	Kohen Ẓedek b. Joseph (appointed during the life time of his predecessor)
Saadiah b. Joseph	928	
	936	Ẓemaḥ b. Kafnai
	938	Hananiah b. Judah
Joseph b. Jacob	942–944[d]	
	943	Aaron b. Joseph ha-Kohen Sargado
	960	Nehemiah b. Kohen Ẓedek
	968	Sherira b. Hananiah
Ẓemaḥ b. Isaac (descendant of Paltoi)	988	
(?) Samuel b. Hophni ha-Kohen	997	
	998	Hai b. Sherira
Dosa b. Saadiah	1013	
Israel b. Samuel b. Hophni	1017	
Azariah ha-Kohen (son of Israel?)	1034	
(?) Isaac	1037	
	1038–(1058)	Hezekiah b. David (exilarch and head of the academy)

a. Until 838 position not filled in Sura. b. Ruled with above 853–858. c. The first of the *geonim* who lived in Baghdad (R. Isaac ibn Ghayyat, *Sha'arei Simḥah*, pt. 1 no. 64). d. The academy was closed for about 45 years, however, apparently several teachers and pupils remained.

and separately; Leipzig, 1858; Leghorn, 1869; New York, 1946); *Teshuvot Ge'onim Kadmonim* (Berlin, 1848); *Ḥemdah Genuzah* (Jerusalem, 1863); *Toratam shel Rishonim* (published by Ch. M. Horowitz, Frankfort, 1881); *Teshuvot Ge'onei Mizraḥ u-Ma'arav* (published by J. Mueller, Berlin, 1888); *Kohelet Shelomo* (published by S. A. Wertheimer, Jerusalem, 1899); *Ge'on ha-Ge'onim* (published by S. A. Wertheimer, Jerusalem, 1925); *Mi-Sifrut ha-Ge'onim* (published by S. Assaf, Jerusalem, 1933); *Teshuvot ha-Ge'onim* (standard title for different texts): published by J. Musafia (Lyck, 1864); by N. N. Coronel (Vienna, 1871); by A. Harkavy (Berlin, 1887); by S. Assaf (Jerusalm, 1927, 1928, 1942); by A. Marmorstein (Déva, 1928). Geonic responsa appeared also in several anthologies and periodicals such as *Ta'am Zekenim* (ed. by E. Askenazi, 1855); *Ozar ha-Ḥayyim* (ed. by Ch. Ehrenreich, 1925–38); *Ginzei Kedem* (1922–44); in REJ, JQR, *Tarbiz, KS, Sinai* (see their index volumes), and in various Festschriften.

The Geonim of Baghdad after the Geonic Period. The heads of the Baghdad academy saw themselves as the successors of the *geonim* of Sura and Pumbedita because the last of them had lived in Baghdad after the tenth century. It may be assumed that many students and teachers from the older academies came to the academy that opened in the second half of the 11th century. The heads of the academies in Baghdad attempted to preserve, if at all possible, the continuity of their connection with the geonic period and called themselves, in the manner of their predecessors in Sura and Pumbedita, *rosh yeshivat ge'on Ya'akov* and *rosh yeshivah shel golah.* The first known Baghdad *gaon* was Isaac b. Moses b. Sakri who came to the East from Spain in about 1070 after he failed to receive recognition in his native country. There is no information on the academy of Babylon, except for the period of 1140–50 when its head was Eli ha-Levi, the rabbi of David *Alroy. The names of the *geonim* who followed him are known from letters and responsa. The most famous was *Samuel b. Ali ha-Levi who opposed *Maimonides; he is praised by the travelers *Benjamin of Tudela and *Pethahiah of Regensburg. Judah *Al-Ḥarizi found that the liturgical poet *Isaac b. Israel ibn Shuwaykh was the head of the Baghdad academy. He was also known because of his connections with *Abraham Maimuni. In 1258 Baghdad Jewry was threatened by the attack of the Mongols and with the decline of Babylonian Jewry the position of gaonate declined as well. In 1288 the head of the Baghdad academy was *Samuel b. Abi al-Rabi'ah ha-Kohen. This is known from his letter concerning the Maimonidean controversy (published by Halberstam in J. Kobak's *Jeschurun,* vol. 7, pp. 76–80). Henceforth, nothing is known about the fate of the Baghdad academy in the Middle Ages.

Chronological List of the Baghdad Geonim

1070	Isaac b. Moses
1140	Ali ha-Levi
1150	Solomon
1164	Samuel b. Ali ha-Levi
1194	Zechariah b. Barachel
1195	Eleazar b. Hillel
1209	Daniel b. Eleazar b. Ḥibbat Allah
1218	Isaac b. Israel ibn Shuwaykh
1240	Daniel b. Abi al-Rabīʿa ha-Kohen
1250	Eli II
1288	Samuel b. Daniel b. Abi al-Rabīʿa ha-Kohen.

The Gaonate in Ereẓ Israel. Little information on the beginnings of the gaonate in Ereẓ Israel is available. Sources increase only in the beginning of the 10th century as a result of the dispute between Saadiah Gaon and Aaron *ben Meir and the bitter polemic between Rabbanites and Karaites. However, even here there is no reliable information on the gaonate in Ereẓ Israel, as was the case with the letter of R. Sherira regarding Babylonia, and was similarly true concerning the chronology of the *geonim* in Ereẓ Israel as given by Ben Meir. In any case it is clear that the title of *gaon* was not used in Ereẓ Israel until the academy of Tiberias moved to Jerusalem, which was several generations after its use in Babylonia. One may assume that the Babylonian *geonim* did not recognize the right of the heads of academies in Ereẓ Israel to use this title which they called *rosh ḥavurah* or *rosh yeshivah.* Since the Jerusalem academy was considered the successor to that of Tiberias, its leaders were sometimes called *"ge'on Teveryah."* The leadership of the academy of Ereẓ Israel was held by a group of seven scholars, often called *"Sanhedrin Gedolah,"* and at its head was *ha-shelishi ba-ḥavurah* ("the third of the group of scholars"), the *gaon* and the *av bet din* or his substitute. The rest of the five members were called *ha-revi'i ba-ḥavurah* ("the fourth of the group of scholars"), etc., or briefly, *ha-shelishi,* etc. The appointment to positions was done according to a fixed hierarchy. After the death of the *gaon,* his position reverted generally to the *av bet din* and the rest of the leadership was promoted according to the hierarchy of positions. It is possible, however, that this order began only after the death of Ben Meir. Contrary to the Babylonian practice, the position of the *gaon* in Ereẓ Israel was hereditary. Sometimes the father would serve as *gaon,* one of his sons as *av bet din,* and the second son would be *shelishi* or *revi'i* in the *ḥavurah;* there is no doubt that this practice negatively influenced the matters of study in the academy of Ereẓ Israel.

The *geonim* of Ereẓ Israel in the 10th and 11th centuries were mainly from the family of Ben Meir, which claimed relation to *Judah ha-Nasi and thus to King David, and two families of kohanim, one of which was the family of *Abiathar and was related to *Eleazar b. Azariah. However, S. Abramson concludes that the family of kohanim that claimed relation to the House of David stemmed from the academy in Ereẓ Israel in one family. Abramson discovered in the *Genizah* fragments of an unknown document, which contained a list of the heads of academies for several generations. From this document it is apparent that one family of kohanim was merely a branch of the Ben Meir family. Thus, the gaonate of Ereẓ Israel was held by one family and its different branches for perhaps 200 years. *Solomon b. Judah, a native of Fez, next to Ben Meir the most famous of the *geonim* in Ereẓ Israel and whose family is not known, and his successor *Daniel b. Azariah, a descendant of one of the families of the exilarchate in Babylonia, were heads of academies and were not descendants of the *geonim* of Ereẓ Israel. Daniel was known as a strong leader, was esteemed by his contemporaries, and was a friend of Samuel ha-Nagid (Ibn Nagrela).

Besides managing the academy, the work of the *gaon* included all Jewish affairs in Ereẓ Israel. The designation of powers among the heads of academies and exilarchs, as was practiced in Babylonia, was not known in Ereẓ Israel. The *geonim* ordained the *ḥaverim,* appointed the *dayyanim* in Ereẓ Israel and Syria, and managed the economic affairs of the Jewish community in Ereẓ Israel. They were recognized by the foreign ruler as the representatives of the Jewish community in Ereẓ Israel. After Ereẓ Israel was politically allied with Baghdad and later with Egypt, the *geonim* corresponded with highly influential Jewish dignitaries in the two capitals. In these cases of emergency they were accustomed to travel there in order personally to negotiate in the court of the rulers. The halakhic and literary activity of the *geonim* is attested by some responsa. Hundreds of letters asking the *geonim* to aid the Jewish community and the academies were discovered in the Cairo *Genizah.* The *geonim* of Ereẓ Israel were not as learned as the *geonim* in

Babylonia. Their major achievement was the maintenance of the continuity of the tradition of the academies in Ereẓ Israel under difficult political conditions.

Chronological List of the Geonim of Ereẓ Israel

...	Moses (head of the academy?)
...	Meir I (head of the academy?)
884–915	Ẓemaḥ
915–932	Aaron b. Moses Ben Meir
932–934	Isaac (son of Aaron)
934–948	... Ben Meir (brother of Aaron)
948–955	Abraham b. Aaron
c.955	Aaron
...	Joseph ha-Kohen b. Ezron (ruled two years)
...	... (ruled thirty years)
988–?	Samuel b. Joseph ha-Kohen
...	Yose b. Samuel
...	Shemaiah
1015	Josiah b. Aaron ("member of the Great Synagogue") b. Abraham (lived in Ramleh)
1020–1027	Solomon b. Joseph ha-Kohen
1027–1051	Solomon b. Judah
1051–1062	Daniel b. Azariah (*nasi* and *gaon*)
1062–1083	Elijah b. Solomon b. Joseph ha-Kohen
1084–1109	Abiathar b. Elijah.

Abrahamson assumes that Ẓemaḥ, who served as head of the academy from about 884–915, was a fourth-generation descendant of *Anan b. David, the founder of the Karaites, and he was a *nasi* and a *gaon.* Aaron ben Meir succeeded in deposing Anan's family only after a bitter struggle in which he was assisted by the scholars and heads of the Baghdad community.

The Geonim of Ereẓ Israel in Damascus, and the Geonim of Egypt. The occupation of Jerusalem by the Seljuks in 1071 completely destroyed the city's Jewish community. The *gaon* *Elijah b. Solomon moved the academy to Tyre, which was subject to Fatimid rule. Elijah's son Abiathar headed the Tyre academy until the conquest of the city by the crusaders. Afterward he moved to Tripoli, Syria, where he died before 1110. His brother Solomon, who served as an *av bet din,* fled in 1093 to Hadrak (near Damascus) because of the decrees of David b. Daniel b. Azariah, head of Egyptian Jewry. In Hadrak he assembled the survivors of the Ereẓ Israel academy which apparently included his brother's son Elijah b. Abiathar. Later his position was given to his son Maẓli'aḥ, who went to Egypt in 1127 where he received the title of *gaon.* The academy of Ereẓ Israel was moved from Hadrak to Damascus and still existed during the 12th century when *Benjamin of Tudela reported that it was subject to the rule of the Babylonian gaonate (Baghdad). The names of two *geonim* who were descendants of the Abiathar family, Abraham b. Mazhir and his son Ezra, are known. The latter was ordained by Samuel b. Ali of Baghdad. In his time or shortly afterward the continuity of the *geonim* of Ereẓ Israel was broken. It is possible that he was followed by Zadok, who was dismissed from his position (*Taḥkemoni,* ed. by A. Kaminka (1899), 354).

In Fostat, Egypt, the academy existed in the time of Elhanan, the father of Shemariah, who is known from the story of the "*Four Captives." His title "chief rabbi" and his position were inherited by his son and then his grandson Elhanan who called himself *rosh ha-seder* or "*rosh ha-seder* of all Israel." *Shemariah and Elhanan, both of whom had previously studied in the Pumbedita academy, corresponded with Sherira and Hai. Only after the decline of the Babylonian and Palestinian academies did the large communities in Egypt request the establishment of their own gaonate. David b. Daniel (1083–89) was the first who attempted to do this. Like his strict father, he hoped to become *nasi* and *gaon* and to exert his power even over the head of the Tyre academy and on the communities in the coastal cities of Ereẓ Israel. However, the *nagid* Mevorakh, who supported him at first, later rejected him. In 1127 Maẓliaḥ b. Solomon, the aged head of the Ereẓ Israel academy, moved from Hadrak to Fostat and called himself *rosh yeshivat ge'on Ya'akov.* Several of his documents and letters are extant. After his death in 1138, his position was apparently given to Moses ha-Levi b. Nethanel; however, it is possible that Samuel b. Hananiah, who met Judah Halevi when he traveled from Egypt to Ereẓ Israel, was given the position. After Moses, his son Nethanel was *gaon* (1160–70) and was followed on his death by his brother Sar Shalom who was appointed *gaon* at Fostat. Sar Shalom, who was perhaps of Palestinian geonic descent, sometimes called himself *rosh yeshivat Ereẓ ha-Ẓevi,* as if his activities were a continuation of the academies of Ereẓ Israel not only in Damascus but also in Fostat. With his death the gaonate in Egypt ceased to exist. Maimonides, who lived at that time in Egypt, did not possess the title of *gaon.*

The Title of Gaon in Other Countries. The title of *gaon* was also used by great scholars in other countries. Maimonides writes in his introduction to the *Mishneh Torah,* "the *geonim* of Spain and France." The *geonim* of Africa, Lotharingia (Lorraine), Mainz, and Narbonne are mentioned in the literature of the early *posekim.* Thus, the title was given to well-known individuals from the early rabbinic period, such as R. *Hananel, R. *Nissim, R. *Moses b. Ḥanokh and his son *Ḥanokh, R. *Joseph b. Abitur, R. Kalonymus of Lucca and his son R. Meshullam, and others.

[Sl.A./Ed.]

Bibliography: General: Assaf, Ge'onim; Abramson, Merkazim; Mann, Egypt; Mann, Texts. Babylonia: L. Ginzberg, *Geonica,* 2 vols. (1909, repr. 1968); idem, *Ginzei Schechter,* 2 (1929); J. Mueller, *Mafte'aḥ li-Teshuvot ha-Ge'onim* (1891); B. M. Lewin, *Meḥkarim Shonim bi-Tekufat ha-Ge'onim* (1926); V. Aptowitzer, *Meḥkarim be-Sifrut ha-Ge'onim* (1941); M. Ḥavaẓẓelet, *Ha-Rambam ve-ha-Ge'onim* (1967); H. Tykocinski, *Die Gaonaeische Verodnungen* (1929); S. D. Goitein, *Sidrei Ḥinnukh* (1962); *Iggeret Rav Sherira Ga'on,* ed. by B. M. Lewin (1921); S. Abramson, in: *Sinai,* 54 (1963/64), 20–32; 56 (1964/65), 303–17; Epstein, in: *Festschrift . . . A. Harkavy* (1908), 164–74 (Heb. sect.); Y. L. Fishman (Maimon), in: *Sefer ha-Yovel . . . B. M. Lewin* (1940), 132–59; Krauss, in: HḤY, 7 (1923), 229–77; J. Mann, in: JQR, 7 (1916/17), 457–90; 8 (1917/18), 339–66; 9 (1918/19), 139–79; 10 (1919/20), 121–51, 309–65; 11 (1920/21), 409–71; idem, in: *Hebrew Union College Jubilee Volume* (1925), 223–62; idem, in: *Tarbiz,* 5 (1933/34), 148–79, 273–304; 6 (1934/35), 66–88; I. Schepanski, *Ereẓ Yisrael be-Sifrut ha-Teshuvot,* 1 (1966), 1–107; Ḥ. Tchernowitz, *Toledot ha-Posekim,* 1 (1946), 18–130; Baron, Social[2], index; Graetz, Hist, 3 (1949), 86–230; Graetz-Rabbinowitz, 3 (1894); Z. Jawetz, *Toledot Yisrael,* 9 (1922); Weiss, Dor, 4 (1904). Babylonia, Post-Gaonic Times: S. Poznański, *Babylonische Geonim im nachgaonaeischen Zeitalter* (1914); A. Marmorstein, in: REJ, 70 (1920), 97–111; S. Assaf, in: *Tarbiz,* 1 (1930); A. Ben-Jacob, *Yehudei Bavel* (1965), 1–34. Ereẓ Israel: S. Assaf and J. A. Mayer (eds.), *Sefer ha-Yishuv,* 2 (1944); S. Schechter, *Saadyana* (1903), 86–104; S. Poznański, in: *Festschrift A. Schwarz* (1917), 471–87; idem, in: ZDMG, 68 (1914), 118–28; A. Marmorstein, *ibid.,* 67 (1913), 635–44; idem, in: REJ, 68 (1914), 37–48; idem, in: JQR, 8 (1917/18), 1–29; A. Marx, *ibid.,* 1 (1910/11), 62–78; W. Bacher, *ibid.,* 15 (1902/03), 79–96.

GAON, MOSES DAVID (1889–1958), Israel educator, journalist, and writer. Gaon was born in Travnik, then under Austro-Hungarian administration (now in Yugoslavia), and studied in the University of Vienna. He emigrated to Ereẓ Israel in 1909. He taught Hebrew and was principal of elementary schools in Jerusalem, Smyrna, and Buenos Aires. In his last years he was an official of the Jerusalem municipality and was active in the Committee of the Sephardi Community. He co-founded the Mizrachi Pioneers' Federation. For several decades Gaon contributed articles to the Hebrew press on oriental Jewry and its relation to the Holy Land, which was also the subject of his book *Yehudei ha-Mizraḥ be-Ereẓ Yisrael* (2 vols., 1928–37). He also wrote a study of a popular Ladino moralistic work, *Maskiyyot Levav* on **Me-Am Lo'ez* (1933), *Ba-Mishol* (1936) on the history of the Hebrew press in Palestine up to 1914, etc. He edited the jubilee volume in honor of Jacob *Meir *Zikhron Me'ir* (1936) with M. Laniado; *Sefer ha-Zikhronot* (1938) by Ben-Zion Koinka; and a volume on the Jerusalem family Azriel (1950). He compiled a bibliography of the Ladino press in *Ha-Ittonut be-Ladino—Bibliografyah* (1965). His son Yehoram, a popular Israel entertainer, was one of the leading singers of the *Ladino Romances. He also appeared in several films and on the musical stage notably in the Israel musical *Kazablan*.

Bibliography: Tidhar, 1 (1947), 500; 10 (1959), 3648. [G.K.]

GAON, SOLOMON (1912–), English Sephardi rabbi. Born in Travnik (Yugoslavia), Gaon studied for the

Solomon Gaon, haham of the Sephardi congregations of the British Commonwealth.

rabbinate at Jews' College, London. After acting as senior *ḥazzan*, he was in 1949 appointed haham of the Spanish and Portuguese Jews' Congregations in the British Commonwealth. He also acted for some time as visiting minister to the She'erit Israel Sephardi Congregation of New York. He published *Influence of Alfonso Tostado on the Pentateuch Commentary of Abravanel* (1943). [Ed.]

GARBER, MICHAEL (1892–), Canadian lawyer, communal leader, and Zionist. Garber was born in Lithuania and immigrated to Montreal in 1906. He was a delegate to the founding assembly of the Canadian Jewish Congress in 1919 and remained active in it, serving as national president (1962–68). He also was president of the Zionist Organization of Canada (1956–58). Garber wrote a column for the *Canadian Jewish Chronicle* 1925–29 ("The Calumnist") and contributed to the Yiddish *Keneder Odler*. He served as alderman in the city of Westmount, Quebec (1955–59). [B.G.K.]

GARDEN OF EDEN (Heb. גַּן עֵדֶן), a garden planted by the Lord which was the first dwelling place of *Adam and Eve (Gen. 2–3). It is also referred to as the "garden in Eden" (Gen. 2:8, 10; 4:16), the "garden of YHWH" (Gen. 13:10; Isa. 51:3), and the "garden of God" (Ezek. 28:13; 31:8–9). It is referred to by Ben Sira 40:17 as "Eden of blessing." There existed in early times an Israelite tradition of a "garden of God" (i.e., a mythological garden in which God dwelt) that underlies the story of the Garden of Eden in Genesis 2–3. Ezekiel (28:11–19; 31:8–9, 16–18) in his description introduces new and variant details not present in the Genesis narrative of the Garden of Eden. Thus, in Genesis there is no trace of the "holy mountain" of Ezekiel 28:14 and no mention of the "stones of fire" of Ezekiel 28:14, 16. While Genesis speaks only in general terms about the trees in the garden (2:9), Ezekiel describes them in detail (31:8–9, 18). The term "garden of YHWH" occurs in a metaphorical sense in a number of other passages in the Bible (Gen. 13:10; Isa. 51:3; Joel 2:3). The name Eden is commonly explained by the Akkadian *edinu*, borrowed from the Sumerian *eden*, meaning "plain." Thus, Eden would be a geographical designation, a fact which is indicated by the references to the rivers in that region. The exact location, however, is unknown despite the many attempts that have been made to identify it.

For a fuller treatment see *Paradise, and for Islam, *Eschatology.

"Paradise" by Jan Brueghel the Elder (1568–1625). Adam and Eve are shown under a tree in the background. Budapest, Magyar Nemzeti Museum.

In the Aggadah. The Garden of Eden appears in the *aggadah* in contradistinction to Gehinnom—"hell." However, talmudic and midrashic sources know of two Gardens of Eden: the terrestrial, of abundant fertility and vegetation, and the celestial, which serves as the habitation of souls of the righteous. The location of the earthly Eden is traced by the boundaries delineated in Genesis 2:11–14. Resh Lakish declared, "If paradise is in the land of Israel, its gate is Beth-Shean; if it is in Arabia, its gate is Bet Gerem, and if it is between the rivers, its gate is Dumaskanin" (Er. 19a). In *Tamid* (32b) its location is given as the center of Africa. It is related that Alexander of Macedon finally located the door to the Garden, but he was not permitted to enter. The *Midrash ha-Gadol* (to Gen. 2:8) simply states that "Eden is a unique place on earth, but no creature is permitted to know its exact location. In the future, during the messianic period God will reveal to Israel the path to Eden." According to the Talmud, "Egypt is 400 parasangs by 400, and it is one-sixtieth of the size of Ethiopia; Ethiopia is one-sixtieth of the world, and the world is one-sixtieth of the Garden, and the Garden is one-sixtieth of Eden..." (Ta'an. 10a). The rabbis thus make a clear distinction between Eden and the Garden. Commenting upon the verse "Eye hath not seen, O God, beside Thee," R. Samuel b. Naḥamani states, "This is Eden, which has never been seen by the eye of any creature." Adam dwelt only in the Garden (Ber. 34b., cf., Isa. 64:3). The word *le-ovedah* ("to dress it"; Gen. 2:15) is taken to refer to spiritual, not physical, toil, and is interpreted to mean that Adam had to devote himself to the study of the Torah and the fulfillment of the commandments (Sif. Deut. 41). Although the eating of meat was forbidden him (Gen. 1:29), it is stated nevertheless that the angels brought him meat and wine and waited on him (Sanh. 59b; ARN 1, 5).

The boundary line between the earthly and heavenly Garden of Eden is barely discernible in rabbinic literature. In fact, "The Garden of Eden and heaven were created by one word [of God], and the chambers of the Garden of Eden are constructed as those of heaven. Just as heaven is lined with rows of stars so the Garden of Eden is lined with rows of the righteous who shine like the stars" (Ag. Song 13:55).

Bibliography: In the Bible: M. D. Cassuto, in: *Studies in Memory of M. Schorr* (1944), 248–53; idem, in: EM, 2 (1954), 231–6; J. L. McKenzie, in: *Theological Studies*, 15 (1954), 14–20; idem, *Oriental and Biblical Studies*, ed. by J. J. Finkelstein and M. Greenberg (1967), 23–34; N. M. Sarna, *Understanding Genesis* (1966), 23–28. In the Aggadah: Ginzberg, Legends, index.

[Ed.]

GARDOSH, KARIEL (**Charles, "DOSH"**; 1921–), Israel cartoonist. He created the figure of "Little Israel," a young boy who became the popular symbol of the State and its people. "Dosh," as he signed himself, was born in Budapest and educated there and in Paris. He emigrated to Israel in 1948 and five years later joined the staff of the afternoon paper *Ma'ariv* as editorial cartoonist. His drawings were marked by comic irony which won him a wide following. They were regularly reprinted in the *Jerusalem Post*, in the Tel Aviv Hungarian daily *Uj Kelet*, and in many newspapers abroad. Gardosh illustrated books, wrote short stories and one-act plays, and held exhibitions in Israel and other countries. He published several collections of cartoons, including *Seliḥah she-Nizzaḥnu!* (1967; *So Sorry We Won!*, 1967) and *Oi la-Menazzeḥim* (1969; *Woe to the Victors*, 1969) with text by Ephraim *Kishon, dealing with the Six-Day War and after.

Bibliography: Tidhar, 8 (1957), 3048. [Ed.]

Cartoon by Kariel Gardosh (Dosh) depicting Israel's position before the Six-Day War of 1967. Courtesy *Ma'ariv*, Tel Aviv.

GARLIC (Heb. שׁוּם, *shum*), plant mentioned once in the Bible among the vegetables which the Israelites ate in Egypt and for which they longed when wandering in the wilderness (Num 11:5). Garlic (*Allium sativum*) is a condiment which was extremely popular among the peoples of the East from very early times. Herodotus states that an inscription on the pyramid of the pharaoh Cheops refers to the large sum spent on garlic as food for the men who worked on the pyramids. The ancients attributed to garlic aphrodisiac qualities (Pliny, *Historia Naturalis*, 20:23), and

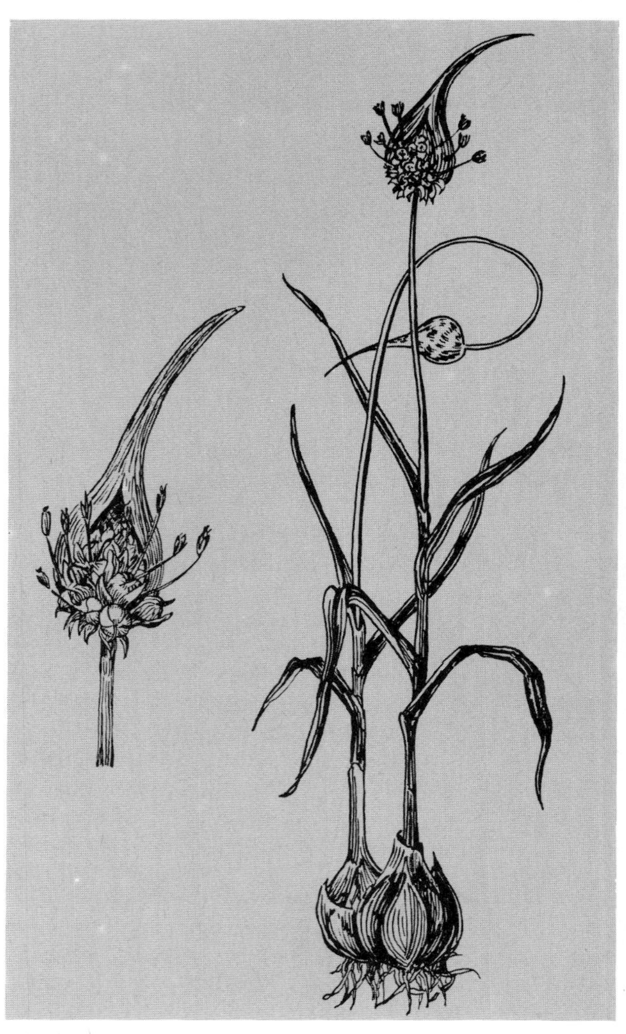

The flowering garlic plant (*Allium sativum*). Courtesy J. Feliks, Jerusalem.

an enactment ascribed to Ezra decrees that it is to be eaten on Friday evenings since "it promotes love and arouses desire" (TJ, Meg. 4:1, 75a). Because it was their custom to eat garlic, the Jews referred to themselves as "garlic eaters" (Ned. 3:10). The fastidious loathed the smell, and it is related of Judah ha-Nasi that he asked those who had eaten garlic to leave the *bet midrash* (Sanh. 11a). In this he may have been influenced by the Roman aristocracy's objections to garlic eating, the emperor Marcus Aurelius having criticized Jews for exuding its smell (Ammianus Marcellinus, *Res gestae*, 22:5). Garlic was regarded as a remedy for intestinal worms (BK 82a), a view also held by Dioscorides (*De Materia Medica*, 2:181). It belongs to the genus *Allium*, to which belong also the *onion and the *leek (*ḥaẓir*, to be distinguished from its usual sense of grass: *fodder), which are mentioned together with garlic in the Bible (Num. 11:5). Many species of the genus *Allium* grow wild in Israel, and are picked and eaten by the local population.

Bibliography: Loew, Flora, 2 (1924), 139–49; J. Feliks, *Olam ha-Ẓome'aḥ ha-Mikra'i* (1968²), 172f. [J.F.]

GARLOCK, JOHN HENRY (1896–1965), U.S. surgeon. Born and educated in New York City, Garlock was assistant attending surgeon at the New York Hospital and instructor in surgery at the Cornell Medical College from 1924 to 1937. He was then appointed chief of surgery at New York's Mount Sinai Hospital and clinical professor of surgery at Columbia University. He was consultant in surgery to many hospitals and held membership in numerous professional societies. Among his many contributions to medical literature are several chapters in standard textbooks of surgery. His book, *Garlock's Surgery of the Alimentary Tract* (1967), was published posthumously by his colleagues. Garlock was chairman of the American Jewish Physicians Committee, which raised money to start the Hebrew University Faculty of Medicine. [F.R.]

GARMISON, SAMUEL (17th century), scholar and prolific author. Born in Salonika, Samuel emigrated to Jerusalem. In about 1647 he traveled as an emissary of Jerusalem apparently to Italy but was taken captive during the journey by Maltese pirates, from whom he was ransomed by a society for the redemption of captives centered in Venice. He was rabbi in Malta until c. 1660. Subsequently he seems to have officiated in Jerusalem. In 1666 he attacked Shabbetai Ẓevi in a sermon which is included in his *Imrei No'am*. Only one of his works has been published: *Mishpetei Ẓedek* (1945), responsa on the Shulḥan Arukh, *Arba'ah Turim* and *Beit Yosef*. Among others still in manuscript are: *Kevod Ḥakhamim*, sermons on the Bible; *Imrei No'am*, sermons on the Pentateuch; *Imrei Tevunah ve-Imrei Kodesh*, on the Talmud and codes; a commentary on the Mishnah; novellae to the tractates *Ḥullin, Bekhorot, Zera'im, Tohorot*, and *Berakhot;* works on the tractates *Beẓah, Kiddushin*, and *Ḥullin*.

Bibliography: Benayahu, in: *Scritti . . . S. Mayer* (1956), 25–31 (Heb. part); M. D. Gaon, *Yehudei ha-Mizraḥ be-Ereẓ Yisrael*, 2 (1938), 208; Scholem, Shabbetai Ẓevi, 1 (1957), 152, 156, 201, 290; Frumkin-Rivlin, 2 (1928), 53f. [S.MAR.]

°**GARSTANG, JOHN** (1876–1956), British archaeologist; professor of archaeology at the University of Liverpool from 1907 to 1941. From 1900 to 1908 he conducted excavations in Egypt, Nubia, Asia Minor, and northern Syria, and from 1909 to 1914 he worked at ancient Meroë in Sudan uncovering important remains of the Roman-Nubian culture. After the British conquest of Palestine, Garstang was director of the British School of Archaeology in Jerusalem (1919–26). At the same time he served in the British Mandatory government as the first director of its Department of Antiquities, organizing the department and excavating at Ashkelon. In 1930–36 he resumed work in Palestine at Jericho, his findings there attracting wide attention at the time, although some of his conclusions were not borne out by subsequent investigations. After resigning from the University of Liverpool, Garstang continued working in Asia Minor (at Mersin, etc.) on behalf of the British Institute of Archaeology at Ankara. His publications, all characterized by a conservative trend, include studies in Hittite history, historical topography of Palestine and the Bible, and numerous excavation reports. During the controversy aroused by the 1939 White Paper, Garstang adopted an anti-Zionist position and was active in British public affairs on behalf of the Arabs. He was the author of *Hittite Empire* (1929), *Joshua, Judges* (1931), and *Heritage of Solomon* (1934). [M.A.-Y.]

GARY, "The Steel City," founded in 1906 by the United States Steel Corporation; situated on the southern tip of Lake Michigan; the second largest city in Indiana. Gary has a population of approximately 180,000, about 3,300 of them Jewish. Jewish families made their way into Gary's sand dunes and swamps along with the earliest pioneers, and in September 1908 the first Orthodox Jewish house of worship was dedicated. Subsequent years brought a series of ever larger structures, and in 1955 the modern Temple Beth El was completed. The Reformed Congregation was incorporated in 1910. Services are now conducted in the large, new Temple Israel.

Gary's Jewish community is active in government, business, civic, and philanthropic circles. During most of the time from 1964 to 1968 the mayor, city attorney, superintendent of schools, health commissioner, and municipal judge were Jewish. There is little overt anti-Semitism, but Jews are excluded from the all-white Gary Country Club and the University Club. The Gary Jewish Welfare Federation was formed in 1941. Enlarged in 1958–59 to include East Chicago and Hammond, the name was changed to the Northwest Indiana Jewish Welfare Federation. This Federation possesses archives which include historical material on the Jewish communities in the area. [I.K.S.]

GARY (originally **Kacew**), **ROMAIN** (1914–), French novelist. Gary, who was of mixed parentage, "part Cossack and Tartar, part Jew" to use his own phrase, was born in Vilna. When he was seven, his family moved to Poland and finally, in 1926, to Nice. He was a fighter pilot in the French Air Force at the outbreak of World War II, then joined De Gaulle's Free French in England in 1940. After the liberation, he entered the French diplomatic service. His final appointment was that of consul-general in Los Angeles (1956–60).

Gary's first novel *Education européenne* (1945; *Forest of Anger*, 1944, reissued as *A European Education*, 1960) includes many elements of Jewish interest, notably the description of a clandestine Friday evening service held by Jewish underground fighters. His other novels include *Tulipe* (1946); *Le grand vestiaire* (1948; *The Company of Men*, 1950); *Les Racines du ciel* (1956; *The Roots of Heaven*, 1958), an adventure story about a group of idealists bent on saving a herd of elephants from hunters, which won the Prix Goncourt; *La Promesse de l'aube* (1960; *Promise at Dawn*, 1961), memories of the author's Jewish mother, and *Le Mangeur d'étoiles* (1966; *The Talent Scout*, 1961). Two works which first appeared in English are *Lady L* (1958), a social satire, and *The Ski Bum* (1965). Jewish characters constantly make an appearance in Gary's novels, but they were mostly viewed from the outside until the writer's traumatic experience in a Warsaw war museum savagely wakened him to reality. *La Danse de Gengis Cohn* (1967; *The Dance of Genghis Cohn,* 1969), the title of which sardonically reflects Gary's own ancestry and predicament,

Romain Gary, French novelist and diplomat. From *Livres de France,* Paris, March 1967.

tells with cruel humor the story of a Jewish comedian shot by the Nazis, who relentlessly haunts his executioner. He also wrote *La Tête Coupable* (1968; *The Guilty Head,* 1969).

Bibliography: C. Lehrmann, *L'Elément juif dans la littérature française,* 2 (1961), 198–205; *Livres de France,* 18 no. 3 (1967), special issue devoted to Gary. [M.C.]

GASCONY, a duchy under English rule from 1152 to 1453, and later (with Guyenne) a province of the kingdom of France. There have been Jews in Gascony from at least the fourth century, especially in *Bordeaux. From 1242 or earlier the English ruler appointed special judges over the Jews, who were particularly numerous in *Agen and its vicinity. A first expulsion order was issued in 1289, even before the expulsion from England itself. Debts owing to the Jews were confiscated and collected at half their value for the king's treasury. Royal agents were appointed to seize the Jews and their belongings. However, the expulsion order was not vigorously enforced or rapidly became obsolete, for in 1292 there were again Jews in Gascony; the king ordered their expulsion once more. In 1305 they returned and must this time have obtained official authorization since in 1308 a judge was again in charge of Jewish affairs. A further expulsion order followed in 1310, which was repeated in 1313 and 1316. However, there were Jews in Gascony in 1320, when they were massacred by the *Pastoureaux. Some Jews were still found in Bordeaux until at least 1362. Jews bearing the surname of Gascon may have originated from there. Marrano refugees from Spain took refuge in this region from the close of the 15th century. Through them the Bordeaux community later became important again.

Bibliography: Gross, Gal Jud, 144–5; E. Gaullieur, in: REJ, 11 (1885), 78–100; I. Rosenthal, in: PAAJR, 26 (1957), 127–34; Ch. Bemond and Y. Renouard (eds.), *Rôles Gascons,* 2 (1900), nos. 1067, 1128, 1181, 1192; 3 (1906), nos. 2054, 4786; 4 (1962), nos. 246, 488, 489, 490, 1127, 1138, 1233, 1670; Ch. Samaran, *La Gascogne dans . . . Trésor des Chartes* (1966), nos. 43, 44, 428; H. G. Richardson, *English Jewry under Angevin Kings* (1960), 225–7, 232–3. [B.Bl.]

GASKELL, SONJA (1904–), artistic director of Het Nationaal Ballet of Amsterdam. Sonja Gaskell was born in Kiev, and became a teacher and ballet teacher in Paris during the 1930s. She went to Holland in 1939, and after World War II founded her own group, Ballet Recital. She established the first Netherlands academy of ballet in The Hague, and was director of Het Nederlands Ballet there before assuming leadership of the Amsterdam company in 1961. [M.B.S.]

GASSER, HERBERT SPENCER (1888–1963), U.S. neurophysiologist and Nobel Prize winner. Gasser was born in Platteville, Wisconsin. He collaborated with Joseph *Erlanger in investigating the electrical properties of nerve fibers. Utilizing a cathode-ray oscilloscope and a sensitive amplification system they recorded the electrical impulses passing over isolated nerve fibers. The measurements of the potential cycles of different nerve fibers revealed three distinct patterns indicating that there were three major types of fibers. It was also shown that the rate of conduction varied directly with the thickness of the fiber. These studies were the foundation of the modern knowledge of action currents in nerves and were of great importance toward an understanding of the complexities of nerve impulse transmission. As a result of this work Gasser and Erlanger shared the 1944 Nobel Prize for Medicine and Physiology. Working with Erlanger and others, Gasser also contributed much to the understanding of the differences between sensory and motor nerves. He also dealt with problems involving the perception of pain and the contraction of muscle as well as the coagulation of blood.

Bibliography: L. G. Stevenson, *Nobel Prize Winners in Medicine and Physiology, 1901–1950* (1935), 223–8; *Biographical Memoirs of Fellows of the Royal Society,* 10 (1964), 75–82. [N.Lev.]

GASSNER, JOHN (1903–1967), U.S. author, critic, and anthologist. He was playreader in the 1930s for Theater Guild, and in 1940 established the playwriting seminar of Erwin Piscator's Dramatic Workshop. Gassner also functioned as dramatic critic for various publications. He was professor of playwriting and dramatic literature at Yale from 1956. He was one of two members of the drama jury of the Pulitzer Prize who resigned in 1963 when the trustees rejected the verdict for Edward Albee's *Who's Afraid of Virginia Woolf?* and made no award. His writings include (with B. Mantle) *Treasury of the Theater* (3 vols., 1935), *Masters of the Drama* (1940), *The Theater in Our Times* (1954), *Heritage of World Literature* (1946, vol. 7 of *Literature,* ed. by E. A. Cross), and *Best American Plays 1918–1958* (1961). [Ed.]

GASTER, MOSES (1856–1939), rabbi, scholar, and Zionist leader. Gaster was born in Bucharest and studied at the University of Breslau and the Jewish Theological Seminary of Breslau, where he was ordained in 1881. He taught Rumanian language and literature in the University of Bucharest, 1881–85, published a popular history of Rumanian literature, *Literatura Populară Română* (1883), and began his great chrestomathy of Rumanian literature *Chrestomatie Română* (2 vols., 1891). In 1885, because of his protests against the treatment of the Jews, he was expelled from Rumania. He settled in England where he was appointed to teach Slavonic literature at Oxford University in 1886. In 1887 he was appointed haham of the English Sephardi community.

Gaster's abilities as a scholar and an orator gave him an outstanding position both in the Anglo-Jewish community and in those areas of intellectual life in which he became a recognized authority, e.g., folklore and Samaritan literature. However, Gaster had a stubborn and combative personality, and this led to an unwillingness to retreat from a position once taken, which did not enhance his reputation. When he was principal of Judith Montefiore College, Ramsgate (1891–96), he endeavored to make it an institution for training rabbis, but the attempt failed. In 1918, after disagreements with his congregation, Gaster retired from the office of haham.

Gaster was active in Ḥibbat Zion and later in the Zionist movement. He accompanied L. *Oliphant on his visits to

Painting of Moses Gaster, haham of English Sephardi community. London, Spanish and Portuguese Jews' Congregation. Photo John R. Freeman.

Rumania, Constantinople, and Ereẓ Israel, and also played a considerable part in the establishment of Zikhron Ya'akov and Rosh Pinnah in Palestine, the first colonies settled by Rumanian Jews. He became one of Herzl's early supporters but opposed him on the *Uganda Plan, and this also brought him into conflict with the leaders of the English Zionist Federation, of which he was president in 1907. Throughout these years Gaster was a prominent figure at Zionist Congresses, being elected a vice-president at the first four. It was to Gaster that Herbert *Samuel, then in the British Cabinet, turned when he wished to establish contact with the Zionists. The conference held at Gaster's home in February 1917 between the Zionist leaders and Sir Mark Sykes of the British Foreign Office was an important stage in the events leading to the *Balfour Declaration. After World War I he returned to his dissociation from official Zionist policy; this was partly the result of his failure to satisfy his ambition of becoming the official leader of the organization.

Gaster's writings covered many branches of learning, including Rumanian literature, comparative and Jewish folklore, Samaritan history and literature, rabbinic scholarship, liturgy, Anglo-Jewish history, and biblical studies. A selection of Gaster's scattered essays appeared under the title *Studies and Texts in Folklore, Magic, Medieval Romance, Hebrew Apocrypha* . . . (3 vols., 1925–28). Other publications are listed in the bibliographies below. Gaster assembled a magnificent library, including many manuscripts, most of which he sold to the British Museum in 1925, but he continued his literary work, despite almost total blindness.

His son, THEODOR HERZL GASTER (1906–), educator and scholar, was born in London, and taught comparative religion at Dropsie College, Philadelphia, and at several universities in the United States and elsewhere. His writings include *Passover; its History and Traditions* (1949), *Purim and Hanukkah in Custom and Tradition* (1950); *Thespis; Ritual, Myth and Drama in the Ancient Near East* (1950, 1961²), *Festivals of the Jewish Year* (1953), *Holy and the Profane* (1955), and *New Year; Its History, Customs and Superstitions* (1955). He edited J. G. Frazer, *The New Golden Bough* (1959), edited and translated *Oldest Stories in the World* (1952), and translated the *Dead Sea Scriptures* into English.

Bibliography: B. Schindler (ed.), *Occident and Orient . . . Gaster Anniversary Volume* (1936), includes bibliography; idem, *Gaster Centenary Publication* (1958), contains revised bibliography; C. Roth, in: JHSET, 14 (1940), 247–52; DNB, supplements, 5 (1949), 309–10. [C.R.]

GAT (Heb. גַּת), kibbutz in southern Israel, N.E. of *Kiryat Gat, affiliated with Kibbutz Arẓi ha-Shomer ha-Ẓa'ir, founded by East European settlers in 1942, as one of the first outposts established in the framework of the program to extend the settlement network to the South and northern Negev. The kibbutz economy is based on highly intensive farming and a factory for wood products. The kibbutz name was chosen due to its proximity to the tell, then identified with biblical *Gath. In 1968 there were 435 inhabitants. [E.O.]

GATESHEAD ON TYNE, industrial town in N.E. England. The first known Jew to settle in Gateshead was Zachariah Bernstone in the 1890s, a Russian immigrant who rebelled and broke away from the lesser observant congregation of adjoining *Newcastle on Tyne. With his protégé E. Adler and their families from Eastern Europe he attempted to establish a community at the beginning of this century. On the initiative of a group of scholars, including *shoḥet* David Dryan, David Baddiel, and Moshe David Freed (son-in-law of Z. Bernstone), a yeshivah, now world famous with some 250 pupils, was opened in 1929 under the direction of Rabbi N. Landynski and his assistant, L. Kahan. It represented the realization of a dream of those scholars who had seen their own yeshivot in Europe destroyed in pogroms. The first students from the U.K. were joined in the 1930s by refugees fleeing Nazi Germany and later by students from all over the world. Rabbi N. Shakowitzky, formerly of Lithuania, became community leader in the 1930s, up to which time the community and its houses of learning were of a strictly Russian-Polish character.

When refugees from Nazi Germany came to England only the strictly observant were attracted to Gateshead. A college for advanced talmudical students *(kollel),* the first of its kind in Britain, was founded by E. G. *Dessler. German Jews who came to Gateshead after the war established further institutions of learning—a teachers' training college for girls, founded by A. Kohn, and a boarding school founded by M. L. Bamberger, 1944. Other institutions include a Jewish primary school, a kindergarten, and a *ḥeder*. The first scientific **shaatnez* bureau in Britain was

The Gateshead Yeshivah. From C. H. Stark, *This is Gateshead*, 1967.

established in Gateshead. In 1966 the Gateshead Foundation for Torah was established to further the publication of Jewish literature. The community numbered 350 in 1970.

Bibliography: M. Donbrow, in: *Jewish Chronicle* (London, 1959). [ED.]

GATH (Heb. גַּת), name of several Canaanite cities often appearing with a toponymic addition to differentiate them (e.g., Gath-Hepher, Gath-Rimmon, Gath-Gittaim, etc.). Four cities called Gath are listed among the conquests of Thutmose III and several Gath (or Gintis) are mentioned in the *Tell el-Amarna letters: Ginti, Ginti-Kirmel, and Giti-Padalla. The last, which also appears in the city list of Pharaoh Shishak, is identified with the Arab village of Jatt in the Sharon. Pliny mentions a Gitta north of Mt. Carmel (*Natural History* 5:75); it was the home town of the famous sorcerer Simon Magus (Justinus Martyr, *Apologia* 1:26, 5–6). Eusebius locates a Gath between Antipatris and Jamnia (Jabneh; Onom. 72:2) and it is similarly situated on the Madaba Map. This is probably Gath-Gittaim, which Jewish tradition identifies with Ramleh and for which B. Mazar proposes the site of Ras Abu Ḥumayd (or Ḥamīd), east of Ramleh.

The best known Gath is "Gath of the Philistines." It was originally inhabited by Anakim ("giants"; Josh. 11:22; I Chron. 20:6, 8; II Sam. 21:20, 22) and later by one of the five Philistine lords (Josh. 13:3; etc.). It was one of the cities to which the Ark was brought after its capture (I Sam.5:8). The Philistines fled from Gath after the defeat of Goliath (*ibid.* 17:52). Persecuted by Saul, David escaped to take refuge with Achish king of Gath (*ibid.* 21:11) from whom he received Ziklag in the Negev, a fact which indicates the extent of the territory ruled by Gath in the south. When Israel again became strong and united under David, Gath is mentioned in connection with his victory over the Philistines (I Chron. 8:13); the parallel account in II Samuel 8:1, however, contains the enigmatic "Metheg-Ammah" instead of Gath. The people of Gath were subdued and Ittai the Gittite became one of the captains of David's guard and remained faithful to him when Absalom rebelled (II Sam. 15:19–22; 18:2). A descendant of Achish, however, continued to rule Gath at the beginning of Solomon's reign (I Kings 2:39ff.); thus the Gath fortified by Rehoboam cannot be Gath of the Philistines and is possibly Moresheth-Gath, as proposed by Y. Aharoni. In his campaign of c. 815–814 B.C.E., Hazael of Aram-Damascus advanced as far as Gath (II Kings 12:18); his destruction of the city may be that alluded to by Amos (6:2). Gath was conquered by Uzziah, king of Judah (II Chron. 26:6) and Sargon mentions the capture of Gath (Ginti) during his campaign against Ashdod in 711 B.C.E. It is doubtful, however, whether these two references are to Gath of the Philistines or to the more northern Gat-Gittaim. In later times Eusebius mentions a village called Gath, five Roman miles from Eleutheropolis on the road to Diospolis-Lydda (Onom. 68:4ff.); it is also mentioned by Jerome (*Epistulae* 108:14).

The identification of Gath is a much debated problem. Albright proposed to locate it at Tell al-ʿUrayna, west of Bet Guvrin (Eleutheropolis) but six seasons of excavations by S. Yeivin have shown that most of the site contained no Iron Age (Philistine) remains. Only on the upper mound were remains from that period found, but its small size (3–4 acres) precludes an identification with Gath. A subsequent proposal to identify Gath with Tell al-Najīla has also been disproved so far by excavations; in two seasons of excavations a large Middle Bronze Age city was found but almost no Iron Age remains. The current proposal returns to its old identification with Tell al-Ṣāfī (as suggested by Elliger, Galling, and later, Aharoni). This large mound, excavated in 1899/1900, has produced large quantities of Philistine pottery.

Bibliography: EM, s.v.; F.J. Bliss and R.A.S. Macalister, *Excavations in Palestine* (1902), pl. 44; Albright, in: AASOR, 2–3 (1923), 7–17; Elliger, in: ZDPV, 57 (1934), 148–52; Bulow and Michell, in: IEJ, 11 (1961), 101–10; S. Yeivin, *First Preliminary Report on the Excavations at Tel Gat* (1961); Mazar, in: IEJ, 4 (1954), 227–35; Aharoni, Land, index. [M.A.-Y.]

GATH-HEPHER (גַּת חֵפֶר), a town on the border of the territory of *Zebulun, between *Japhia and Eth-Kazin (Josh. 19:13). It is referred to as the birthplace of the prophet *Jonah (II Kings 14:25). The biblical site has been identified with Khirbat al-Zurraʿ (now called Tel Gath Hepher), near the Arab village of Mashhad, 2½ mi. (4 km.) southeast of *Sepphoris. An examination of the tell has revealed Iron Age pottery on its surface. A tomb in the village traditionally that of Jonah (al-Nabī Yūnis) attests the existence of a local tradition which was already noted by Jerome in the preface to his Latin commentary on the Book of Jonah.

Bibliography: Albright, in: BASOR, 35 (1929), 8; EM, s.v. [M.A.-Y.]

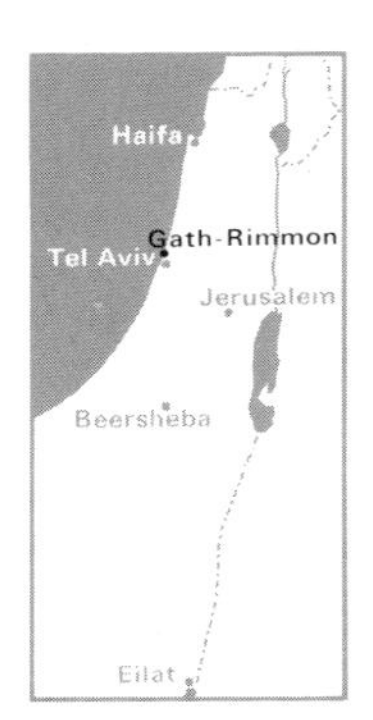

GATH-RIMMON (Heb. גַּת רִמּוֹן). (1) Levitical city in the territory of Dan (Josh. 21:24; I Chron. 6:54). It is located in the vicinity of Jehud, Bene-Berak, and Me-Jarkon ("the waters of Yarkon") in Joshua 19:45 and it is possibly mentioned in the list of conquests of Thutmose III in c. 1469 B.C.E. (line 63) in the same general area, between Jaffa and Lydda. In the opinion of some scholars, the Giti-rimunima in the *Tell el-Amarna letters (ed. by Knudtzon, 250) refers to this locality. Gath-Rimmon is commonly identified with Tell Jarīsha, which was excavated from 1934. The finds included remains of a Hyksos wall and glacis of the Middle Bronze II Age, a Late Bronze Age tomb, and evidence of a settlement up to the ninth century B.C.E. (2) Levitical city of the tribe of Manasseh west of the Jordan (Josh. 21:25). Some scholars consider it identical with the Giti-rimunima of the el-Amarna letters mentioned above, and as evidence that a second Gath-Rimmon existed in the region, they cite the worship of Hadadrimmon in the Jezreel Valley (Zech. 12:11). In the parallel text of levitical cities in I Chronicles 6, however, Bileam (Ibleam) appears instead of Gath-Rimmon, and the mention of the latter twice in Joshua 21 may have been due to an error.

Bibliography: EM, s.v. (includes bibliography); QDAP, 4 (1935), 208–9; 6 (1938), 225; 10 (1944), 55ff., 198–9, excavation reports of Gath Rimmon (1); Aharoni, Land, index. [M.A.-Y.]

GATIGNO, family of rabbis and scholars that first appeared in Spain and Portugal in the 14th century and settled in Turkey after the expulsion. Some consider the name to derive from the French province of Gatines. EN SOLOMON ASTRUC of Barcelona, called the *"kadosh,"* is regarded as one of the first members of this family, but others cast doubt upon his connection with them. He was the author of the commentary on the Pentateuch called *Midreshei ha-Torah,* apparently composed after 1376. Some identify him with EZRA B. SOLOMON, while others maintain that Ezra was his son, who lived in the second half of the 14th century in Saragossa and Acrimonte. Ezra wrote a supercommentary (still in manuscript) on Abraham ibn Ezra's commentary to the Pentateuch, explaining his exegesis and his homiletical interpretations. ḤAYYIM BEN SAMUEL GATIGNO was among the exiles from Spain in 1492 who reached Italy. He worked in Rome as a copyist between the years 1542 and 1553 and then as a proofreader in Cremona.

From the beginning of the 18th century members of the family are found especially in Smyrna and Salonika. ELIAKIM BEN ISAAC GATIGNO served as rabbi of Smyrna, where he died in 1795. He was the author of: *To'afot Re'em* (Smyrna, 1762), an exposition of Elijah *Mizraḥi's super-commentary to Rashi; responsa, *Agurah be-Ohalekha* (Salonika, 1781), which include responsa taken from manuscripts by David b. Zimra (Radbaz), Isaac Escapa, and Abraham ha-Kohen of Safed, and appended to the volume are passages which he omitted from the *To'afot Re'em;* and *Yiẓḥak Yerannen* (*ibid.,* 1786), glosses to Maimonides' *Mishneh Torah.* Eliakim's son, ISAAC, was the author of: *Beit Yiẓḥak* (*ibid.,* 1792), also glosses to the *Mishneh Torah; Beit Mo'ed* (*ibid.,* 1839), novellae to the tractates *Mo'ed Katan* and *Makkot* with additions by his pupil Ḥayyim *Palache, who also wrote an introduction to the work; and *Mi-Yagon le-Simḥah* (*ibid.,* 1795), a commentary on the laws of mourning (nos. 1–32) of *Meir of Rothenburg. Among the rabbis of this family who served in Salonika during the 18th and 19th centuries are: ḤAYYIM ABRAHAM BEN BENVENISTE, kabbalist, a pupil of Solomon *Amarillo, and the author of *Tirat Kesef* (*ibid.,* 1736), sermons on the weekly scripture portions; and *Ẓeror ha-Kesef* (*ibid.,* 1756), responsa, glosses, and novellae on the Shulḥan Arukh, talmudic themes, and on the *Mishneh Torah.* These were published by BENVENISTE (Mercado), son of Ḥayyim Abraham, with an introduction and additions. Benveniste was the author of a halakhic work, *Terumat ha-Kesef,* which, together with a work by his son Abraham, *Elef Kesef,* was published with the comprehensive title *Maẓref le-Kesef* (1867). ABRAHAM BEN BENVENISTE GATIGNO was elected *ḥakham bashi* ("chief rabbi") of Salonika in 1875. He died in 1895. He was the author of the responsa *Ẓel ha-Kesef* (1872) to which are appended ten homilies. Abraham was the founder of the first modern Jewish school in the town. BENVENISTE BEN MOSES was the author of homilies on the Torah which were published together with additions by his son JUDAH under the title, *Meḥushakim Kesef* (1839). Judah's son SAMUEL (d. 1885) was a *dayyan* in Salonika.

Bibliography: S. Eppenstein (ed.), *Midreshei ha-Torah* (1899), introd.; A. Freimann (ed.), *Inyanei Shabbetai Ẓevi* (1912), 147 nos. 142, 146; M. Steinschneider, *Gesammelte Schriften,* 1 (1925), 1–8; Baer, Urkunden, 1 (1929), 579f.; B. Wachstein, *Mafte'aḥ ha-Hespedim,* 1 (1922), 18, 24, 31, 54, 62; 2 (1927), 3, 25, 31, 41; 3 (1930), 4, 18, 50, 63, 84; 4 (1932), 33; I. S. Emmanuel, *Maẓẓevot Saloniki* (1963), no. 531; Molḥo and Amarijlio, in: *Sefunot,* 2 (1958), 55f.; *Saloniki Ir va-Em be-Yisrael* (1967), 15, 19, 77.

[Y.Ho.]

GAUNSE, JOACHIM (d. 1619), mining engineer; member of the Gans family of Prague. In 1581 he was in England, where he reorganized the copper mining at Keswick in Cumberland, and later at Neath, Wales. He was arrested in Bristol (1596) for incautious remarks during a theological dispute and declared himself a Jew. He was sent to London for trial before the Privy Council and presumably was expelled from England. He is probably identical with the Zalman b. Zeligman Gans whose tombstone in Prague (S. Hock, *Die Familien Prags,* 1892, no. 997) describes him as having endangered his life to wreak vengeance among the gentiles.

Bibliography: M. B. Donald, *Elizabethan Copper . . .* (1956), passim; Abrahams, in: JHSET, 4 (1903), 83–101.

[C.R.]

GAVISON (or **Gavishon**), Spanish family. In the 14th century the Gavison family were among the most respected Jews of Seville, but they were forced to flee to Granada during the persecutions of 1391. There, in the 15th century, almost all the Gavisons were murdered; only JACOB and ABRAHAM, the sons of JOSEPH GAVISON, escaped in 1492 to Tlemcen, Algeria, JACOB BEN JOSEPH was a physician and the author of *Derekh ha-Sekhel,* a work directed against the opponents of Maimonides, no longer extant. Poems in praise of this work were written by Solomon al-Malaki, Jacob Berab, and Abraham (2?) Gavison. One of Joseph Gavison's descendants was ABRAHAM (2) BEN JACOB (d. 1578) of Tlemcen, a physician, who lived for some time in Algiers, author of *Omer ha-Shikhḥah* (unfinished). His son JACOB edited the poetical portion of this work and added poems written by himself and his own son ABRAHAM (3) (1586–1605), a gifted young man who died of the plague (see *Omer ha-Shikhḥah,* 127b–128a, and Abraham's poems, 120b). MOSES (d. 1696), a merchant of Algiers, belongs to the same branch of the family; he also died of the plague. The same fate overtook in 1745 the two sons of ABRAHAM (4), who in 1748 published his ancestor's *Omer ha-Shikhḥah* in Leghorn. MEIR and SOLOMON were contemporaries of R. Jacob de *Castro in Egypt in the second half of the 16th century. Meir Gavison, originally from Damascus, went to Egypt as a merchant and later joined the academy of the *dayyan* Ḥayyim Kaposi; his responsa were seen in manuscript by Ḥ.Y.D. *Azulai. Solomon Gavison, also a halakhic authority (see responsa of Solomon ha-Kohen (Maharshak) III, Salonika 1594), was sharply attacked by Castro (responsa *Oholei Ya'akov,* no. 33), because he delivered a halakhic opinion favorable to the Karaites. In the second half of the 19th century VIDAL served as a rabbi in Gibraltar.

Bibliography: A. Gavison, *Omer ha-Shikhḥah* (1746), preface and supplement; A. Cahen, *Juifs dans l'Afrique septentrionale* (1867), 104ff.; M. Mendez-Bejarano, *Histoire de la Juiverie de Séville* (1922), 125; Rosanes, Togarmah, 3 (1938), 246, 247, 250ff.; Hirschberg, Afrikah, 2 (1965), 46–47.

[J.H.SCH.]

GAVSIE, CHARLES (1906–1967), Canadian lawyer and public official. Born in New York, Gavsie went into practice with a law firm in Montreal. In 1941 he joined the Canadian civil service and from 1945 to 1948 served as general counsel to the Canadian Department of Munitions and Supply. He was assistant deputy minister of National Revenue for Taxation (1948–51) and from 1951 to 1954 was deputy minister of National Revenue for Taxation. Gavsie was appointed vice-president of the St. Lawrence Seaway Authority in 1954 and three years later became president. He served for a year and then resumed law practice.

[B.G.K.]

°**GAWLER, GEORGE** (1796–1869), English Christian who propagated the idea of Jewish settlement of Ereẓ Israel. Gawler took part in the Battle of Waterloo as a senior commander and was the first governor of the newly established colony of South Australia (1838–41). On his return to England he took up the cause of the agricultural settlement of Ereẓ Israel by Jews and persisted in the propagation of this idea until the end of his life. He sought to provide a solution both to the permanent unrest in the Middle East and to the Jewish problem in Europe and proposed that his plan should be executed by the British. He first introduced his ideas in a pamphlet entitled *Tranquilization of Syria and the East: Observations and Practical Suggestions in Furtherance of the Establishment of Jewish Colonies in Palestine . . . the Most Sober and Sensible Remedy for the Miseries of Asiatic Turkey* (London, 1845), and followed this up with a series of pamphlets in which he discussed plans, including *Emanicipation of the Jews Indispensable for the Maintenance of the Protestant Profession of the Empire; and Most Entitled to the Support of the British Nation* (1847). His experience in Australia led him to believe that it was possible to settle an uninhabited land within a few years. He accompanied Sir Moses *Montefiore on the latter's third trip to Ereẓ Israel (1849) and seems to have been the one who persuaded Montefiore to initiate agricultural settlement in the country, in spite of the opposition of large sections of the Jewish population to the idea. In the course of the years, Gawler contributed numerous articles to the Jewish press in Britain *(Voice of Jacob, Jewish Chronicle);* in one of these articles he stated: "I should be truly rejoiced to see in Palestine a strong guard of Jews established in flourishing agricultural settlements and ready to hold their own upon the mountains of Israel against all aggressors, I can wish for nothing more glorious in this life than to have my share in helping them do so" (JC, Aug. 10, 1860). The only result of his plans was Montefiore's acquisition of an orange grove near Jaffa on his fourth trip to the Holy Land (1855), where Jewish workers were employed (now known as the Montefiore Quarter in Tel Aviv).

His son, JOHN COX GAWLER, took up his father's cause and in 1874 published a detailed plan for the settlement of Ereẓ Israel by Jews on businesslike and technological principles. He also sought to gain Montefiore's interest in the plan. The plan aroused great interest in Jerusalem, and a Hebrew translation of it by I. D. *Frumkin was published in *Ḥavaẓẓelet.* By publishing the plan, Frumkin encouraged certain groups of the old *yishuv* to put the plan into practice, and, as a result, four years later *Petaḥ Tikvah was founded.

Bibliography: M. Montefiore, *Diaries of Sir Moses and Lady Montefiore,* 2 (1890), 15; N. Sokolow, *History of Zionism,* 2 vols. (1919), index; G. Kressel (ed.), *Mivḥar Kitvei I. D. Frumkin* (1954), index; G. Yardeni, *Ha-Ittonut ha-Ivrit be-Ereẓ-Yisrael* (1969), index. [G.K.]

GAY (Froehlich), PETER JACK (Joachim; 1923–), U.S. historian. Gay, who was born in Berlin, Germany, went to the United States in 1941 and began teaching at Columbia University in 1948. In 1969 he became professor of comparative European intellectual history at Yale. Gay's chief interest was the Enlightenment of which he presented a sympathetic view. His major publications in this field are: *Voltaire's Politics* (1959); *Party of Humanity: Essays in the French Enlightenment* (1964); and *The Enlightenment, an Interpretation: The Rise of Modern Paganism* (1966). He also wrote *The Dilemma of Democratic Socialism: Eduard Bernstein's Challenge to Marx* (1952); *A Loss of Mastery: Puritan Historians in Colonial New England* (1966) and *Weimar Culture* (1968). [J.I.S.]

GAZA (Heb. עַזָּה, **Azzah**), city on the southern coastal plain of Ereẓ Israel. From earliest times it served as the base of Egyptian operations in Canaan. Gaza was held by Thutmose III (c. 1469 B.C.E.) and in his inscriptions it has the title of "that-which-the-ruler-seized" signifying its role as the chief Egyptian base in Canaan. In the reliefs of Seti I (c. 1300 B.C.E.) it is called "the [town of] Canaan." It is also mentioned in the Tell el-Amarna and Taanach tablets as an Egyptian administrative center. According to biblical tradition its original inhabitants were the Avvites (Deut. 2:23; Josh. 13:3). At the time of the Israelite conquest it was alloted to the tribe of Judah (Josh. 15:47; Judg. 1:18) but it remained in the possession of the Canaanites until the beginning of the 12th century B.C.E. when it was occupied by the Philistines—possibly at first as an Egyptian garrison. It became the southernmost city of the Philistine Pentapolis (Josh. 13:3; I Sam. 6:17; Jer. 25:20). At Gaza Samson performed some of his famous deeds and there too he perished in the temple of Dagon in the great slaughter of his enemies (Judg. 16). With the weakening of Egyptian support, the Philistines finally submitted to David (II Sam. 5:25). In 734 B.C.E. Tiglath-Pileser III of Assyria took Gaza but it remained a Philistine city and the short conquest of Hezekiah (II Kings 18:8) did not alter its status. Pharaoh Necho II occupied Gaza briefly in 609 B.C.E. Under the Persians (after a siege in 529 B.C.E. by Cambyses) Gaza became an important royal fortress called Kadytis by Herodotus (2:159). In 332 B.C.E. it was the only city in Ereẓ Israel to oppose Alexander who besieged it and sold its people into slavery. In the Hellenistic period Gaza was the outpost of the Ptolemies until its capture by Antiochus III in 198 B.C.E. Its commercial importance increased in Persian and Hellenistic times when it served as the Mediterranean outlet of the Nabatean caravan trade and as the gateway for Greek penetration into southern Ereẓ Israel. The city was attacked by Jonathan the Hasmonean in 145 B.C.E. (I Macc. 11:61–62) but was taken only by Alexander Yannai in 96 B.C.E. after a long siege. It was restored by Pompey and rebuilt by Gabinius in 57 B.C.E. It was held by Herod for a short time. Gaza prospered under Roman rule and contained a famous school of rhetoric. It was fanatically devoted to its Cretan god Marnas, even under Christian rule; only in the fifth century was its temple destroyed and Christianity made the ruling religion. Although Jews were settled there in the talmudic period the city was regarded as being outside the halakhic boundaries of the Holy Land. Gaza is shown as a large city on the Madaba Map—"splendid, delicious" are the words of the traveler Antoninus—with colonnaded streets crossing its center and a large basilica in the middle, probably the church erected on the temple of Marnas. In antiquity Gaza controlled an

Figure 1. Greek inscription in the mosaic floor of the ancient synagogue in Gaza, indicating the donors as two brothers who were wood traders and giving the Greek date, Loos 589 (508/9 C.E.). Courtesy Asher Ovadia, Israel Department of Antiquities, Jerusalem.

Figure 2. Detail from the floor of the ancient Gaza synagogue showing King David as Orpheus. He is identified by his name in Hebrew characters. Courtesy Asher Ovadia, Israel Department of Antiquities, Jerusalem.

extensive territory, including the areas of Anthedon and its harbor Maiumus. The sources mention an "Old Gaza." This was probably at Beth-Eglaim—Tell al-Ajūl (the tell at the city proper however contains evidence of settlement from the Bronze Age onward). "Gaza the desert" in the New Testament (Acts 8:26), which is the city proper, was so called because of its devastation by Alexander Yannai. The "New City" (Neapolis) was the harbor; a synagogue was found there paved with mosaics and dated 508/9. In 1965 a mosaic floor was uncovered on the seashore of Gaza's harbor. Its figures include one of King David as Orpheus, dressed in Byzantine royal garments and playing the harp. The name "David" in Hebrew letters appears above it. A Greek inscription at the center of the floor, which mentions the names of the two donors (Menahem and Jesse) of the mosaic to the "holy place," and the name "David," testify to the fact that a synagogue stood there. The synagogue was cleared by A. Ovadiah in 1967/68. Evidence of a considerable Jewish population during the talmudic period in Gaza is provided also by a relief of a *menorah,* a *shofar,* a *lulav,* and an *etrog,* which appear on a pillar of the Great Mosque of Gaza; and various Hebrew and Greek inscriptions. According to the Karaite Sahl b. Maẓli'aḥ, Gaza, Tiberias, and Zoar were the three centers of pilgrimages in Ereẓ Israel during the Byzantine period. Gaza was situated 3 mi. (5 km.) from the sea in a fertile plain rich in wheat, vineyards, and fruits. Its fair *(panegyris)* was one of the three main fairs in Roman Palestine.

In a great battle fought near Gaza in 635, the Arabs vanquished the Byzantines; the city itself fell soon afterward. It remained the seat of the governor of the Negev, as is known from the Nessana Papyri. The Jewish and Samaritan communities flourished under Arab rule; in the eighth century, R. Moses, one of the masoretes, lived there. In the 11th century R. Ephraim of Gaza was head of the community of Fostat (old Cairo). King Baldwin I of Jerusalem occupied the city which was known in Crusader times as Gadres; from the time of Baldwin III (1152) it was a Templar stronghold. In 1170 it fell to Saladin. Under Mamluk rule Gaza was the capital of a district *(mamlaka)* embracing the whole coastal plain up to Athlit. After the destruction of Gaza by the Crusaders the Jewish community ceased to exist. Nothing more was heard of it until the 14th century. Meshullam of Volterra in 1481 found 60 Jewish householders there and four Samaritans. All the wine of Gaza was produced by the Jews (A. M. Luncz, in *Yerushalayim,* 1918). Obadiah of Bertinoro records that when he was there in 1488, Gaza's rabbi was a certain Moses of Prague who had come from Jerusalem (*Zwei Briefe,* ed. by A. Neubauer (1863), 19). Gaza flourished under Ottoman rule; the Jewish community was very numerous in the 16th and 17th centuries. The Karaite Samuel b. David found a Rabbanite synagogue there in 1641 (*Ginzei Yisrael be-St. Petersburg,* ed. by J. Gurland (1865), 11). In the 16th century there were a *bet din* and a yeshivah in Gaza, and some of its rabbis wrote scholarly works. Farm-owners were obliged to observe the laws of *terumah* ("priestly tithe"), *ma'aserot* ("tithes"), and the sabbatical year. At the end of the 16th century the Najara family supplied some of its rabbis; Israel *Najara, son of the Damascus rabbi Moses Najara, author of the *"Zemirot Yisrael"* was chief rabbi of Gaza and president of the Bet Din in the mid-17th century. In 1665, on the occasion of Shabbetai Ẓevi's visit to Gaza, the city became a center of his messianic movement, and one of his principal disciples was *Nathan of Gaza. The city was occupied by Napoleon for a short time in 1799. In the 19th century, the city declined. The Jews concentrated there were mainly barley merchants; they bartered with the Bedouins for barley which they exported to the beer breweries in Europe. It was a Turkish stronghold in World War I; two British attacks made on Gaza in 1916–17 failed and it was finally taken by a flanking movement of *Allenby. Under Mandatory rule Gaza developed slowly; the last Jews left the town as a result of the anti-Jewish Arab disturbances in 1929.

[M.A.-Y.]

In 1946 Gaza's population was estimated at 19,500, all Muslim except for 720 Christians. In the Israel *War of Independence, the invading Egyptian army occupied Gaza (May 1948). The town, together with the newly formed *Gaza Strip, was put under Egyptian administration by the armistice agreement of 1949. The influx of Arab refugees from the areas which became part of Israel swelled the city's population at least fourfold. The 1967 census showed that 87,793 inhabitants lived in the city proper, while 30,479 lived in the refugee camp within municipal boundaries. Of these 1,649 were Christian, and the rest Muslim. In the *Sinai Campaign (1956), Gaza was occupied by the Israel army (Nov. 2, 1956) and evacuated in March 1957. The Egyptian army reinstalled itself in the Strip, but in the Six-Day War (1967), Israel forces captured the town on June 6, and an Israel military government was set up in the town. From 1969, there were frequent acts of terrorism and sabotage in the town.

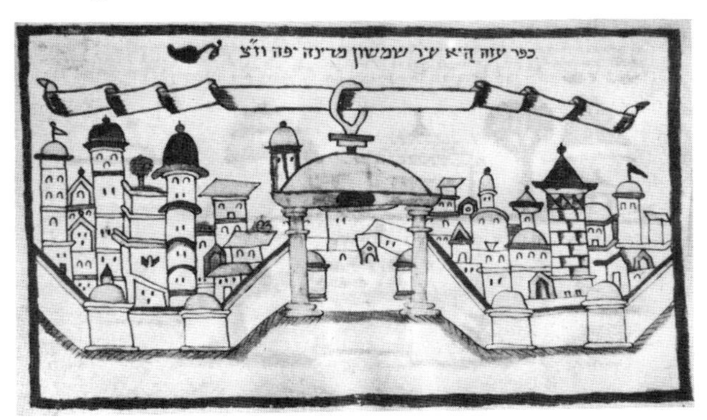

Figure 3. Miniature of Gaza, "City of Samson," from the manuscript of the Casale Pilgrim, Casale Monferrato, Italy, 1568, fol. 9v. Cecil Roth Collection. Photo Werner Braun.

It appears that in the historic past Gaza's built-up area alternately expanded and decreased in size, particularly in the area between the city core and the seashore about 2 mi. (3 km.) distant. This expanse of dunes lay waste in the 20th century, until the British Mandate authorities allocated land for a nominal fee to anyone promising to build his house there within five years of signing a contract. Gaza's principal east-west artery now runs through this area, up to the shore. From the 1940s the city also expanded eastward. In the northwest Gaza gradually links up with Jabalya and Nazala. Within the municipal area, there are orchards, fields, and kitchen gardens. Farming and sea fishing retain a place with small commerce and industries in the city economy, while pottery constitutes a prominent branch. After 1967, larger manufacturing plants (food, textiles, and other branches) were established there. [ED.]

Bibliography: M. A. Mayer, *History of the City of Gaza* (1907); G. Downey, *Gaza in the Early Sixth Century* (1963); Kena'ani, in: BJPES, 5 (1937), 33–41; Benayahu, *ibid.*, 20 (1955), 21–30; Avi-Yonah, *ibid.*, 30 (1966), 221–3; M. Ish-Shalom, *Masei Noẓerim le-Ereẓ Yisrael* (1965), index; Ben Zvi, Ereẓ Yisrael, index; J. Braslavski (Braslavi), *Le-Ḥeker Arẓenu—Avar u-Seridim* (1954), index; idem, *Mi-Reẓu'at Azzah ad Yam Suf* (1957); S. Klein, *Toledot ha-Yishuv ha-Yehudi be-Ereẓ Yisrael* (1935), index; S. Assaf and L. A. Mayer (eds.), *Sefer ha-Yishuv*, 2 vols. (1939–44).

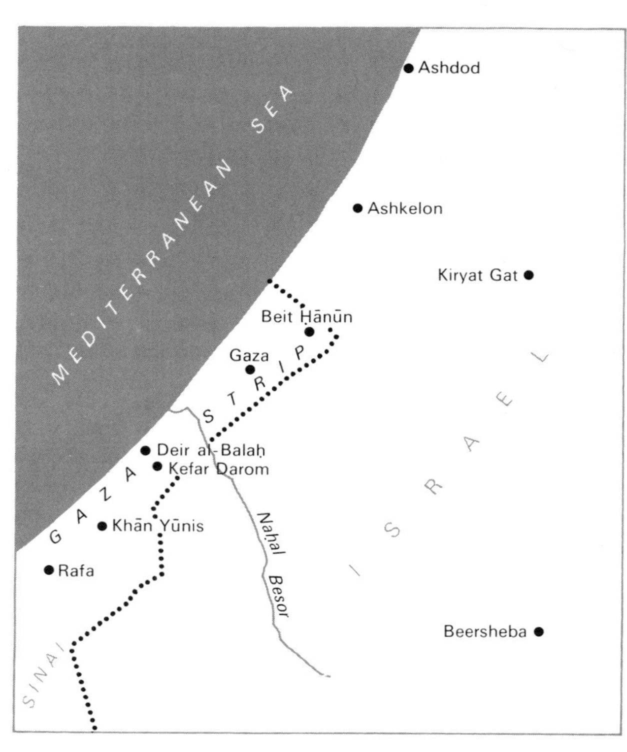

The Gaza Strip.

GAZA STRIP (Heb. רְצוּעַת עַזָּה), area in the southern Coastal Plain of Ereẓ Israel, covering 140 sq. mi. (362 sq. km.), between 3 and 4.5 mi. (5–7 km.) wide from west to east and 28 mi. (45 km.) long from the vicinity of Yad Mordekhai in the northeast to Rafiaḥ (Rafa) in the southwest. The Gaza Strip is not a separate geographical unit, as the part south of Naḥal Besor belongs to the Negev Coastal Plain and the rest forms part of the southern (Philistine) Coastal Plain (see Land of *Israel, Physiography). The Gaza Strip came into being as a separate administrative unit in the final stages of the War of Independence (1948), when it was the only part of the territory under the former British Mandate over Palestine still held by Egyptian forces. In the Armistice Agreement between Israel and Egypt (February 1949), it was placed under Egyptian administration, but it was never incorporated into Egypt. The border of the Gaza Strip drawn in 1949 generally mirrors military positions occupied by both sides when the War of Independence battles came to a halt in that region in December 1948, but Israel consented to evacuate two small areas it then held—Beit Ḥānūn at the Strip's northern end and ʿAbasān and vicinity at its southern extremity—and to permit them to be added to the Strip's territory.

Contrary to the wording and spirit of the Armistice Agreement, in the first half of the 1950s, Egypt placed considerable armed forces in the Gaza Strip, which it made the principal base of the Fedayeen terrorists. From 1954 onward, the terrorists infiltrated into Israel, perpetrating murderous attacks on civilians in villages and towns, which drew retaliatory attacks by Israel on military objects inside the Strip. In the spring of 1956, increased terrorist attacks from the Strip became one of the causes provoking the *Sinai Campaign. The Gaza Strip was in Israel's hands between its occupation on Nov. 2, 1956, and the withdrawal of Israel forces on March 8, 1957. The withdrawal was effected on the assumption that neither the Strip nor Sinai would be remilitarized by Egypt. Thereafter U.N. troops were posted to watch the border and a comparatively quiet era ensued. However in 1967 aggression against Israel was again launched from there in the weeks preceding the Six-Day War, when U.N. forces were asked by Nasser to leave their border observation posts. The occupation of the Gaza Strip by the Israel army was completed on June 6, 1967, and the area was put under Israel military administration.

Last parade of the United Nations emergency force in the Gaza Strip before the Six-Day War, 1967. Courtesy Government Press Office, Tel Aviv.

The Gaza Strip's demographic structure underwent radical changes during and after the War of Independence. Arab refugees, practically all of them Muslims, swelled the Strip's population from an estimated 50,000–60,000 in 1947 to about 180,000–200,000 in 1949. Kefar Darom, the only Jewish settlement within the Strip's area, was evacuated in June 1948 (but resettled in 1970). According to the census on Sept. 10–14, 1967—the first reliable count in contrast to British Mandate statistics and the grossly exaggerated figures of the Egyptian administration—the Strip's total population numbered 356,261 persons (22% less than the 1966 Egyptian estimate of 454,960).

Even these figures, however, show the Gaza Strip as having one of the highest population densities in the world (2,560 inhabitants per sq. mi. or 973 per sq. km. in 1967). In contrast with other Arab countries, the urban population is in the majority in the Gaza Strip with 79.4% in 1967; without counting the refugee camps, there were 149,489 urban inhabitants against 31,368 villagers, 1,105 nomads, and 1,778 people living outside settlements. These figures, however, do not reflect the occupational structure, as many inhabitants of towns and camps—in fact, the great majority of wage earners—derive most of their livelihood from farming, either on their own holdings or as hired laborers.

In 1967, the number of persons described as refugees was 207,250 or 58.9% of the total population. Of these, 149,396 lived in camps, which also accommodated 23,000 persons who were not refugees. Muslims accounted for 99% of the 1967 population. Approximately 20% of the population in 1967 were under four years old, and 50.6% below the age of 14, indicating a very high birthrate.

The high population density makes great demands on the available land and water resources. In 1967, 103.1 sq. mi. (267 sq. km.)—73% of the area—were under cultivation. This included even sand dunes (as long as a more fertile layer of earth was shallowly concealed beneath), roadsides, and plots in built-up areas. Excessive exploitation of groundwater is a serious problem: in 1967 there were about 1,200 wells, from which some 17,000,000,000 gal. (about 65,000,000 cu. m.) of water were extracted annually. The proximity of the sea caused the intrusion of seawater into the water table, and there was an imminent danger of salination of the well water. Steps were taken after 1967 to reduce pumping and local irrigation considerably and allocate some water from Israel sources. Of the cultivated area, 52.9 sq. mi. (137 sq. km.) were irrigated in 1967, of which 35.5 sq. mi. (92 sq. km.) were citrus groves producing an average of between two and four million cases of export fruit annually; 3.9 sq. mi. (10 sq. km.) were planted with olives, vines, and deciduous fruit trees; and about 13.5 sq. mi. (35 sq. km.) with vegetables and field crops. The main unirrigated crops were wheat, date palms (mainly near Deir al-Balaḥ), and ricinus bushes (in the south). After the Six-Day War, growing terrorist attempts were made to disrupt normal conditions. At the same time guidance by the Israel authorities, provision of seed, fertilizers, pesticides, and machinery, and aid in marketing and export brought about noticeable progress in farming. In manufacturing, the region made its first steps toward modernization. Pottery, domestic weaving and clothmaking, and food processing (milling, baking) are traditional trades. Beginning in 1968, a number of industrial enterprises, primarily based on local farm produce, were set up in cooperation with the Israel authorities and private individuals, alleviating local unemployment. From 1967, thousands of laborers from the Gaza Strip found work in building, farming, industry, and development projects in various parts of Israel. In 1969 work started on an industrial zone, with the cooperation of Israel and local Arab investors, on the northern border of the Strip.

See also *Gaza; *Israel, State of, Frontiers, Arab Refugees, Arab Population. [E.O.]

GAZELLE (Heb. צְבִי, *ẓevi*). The gazelle is included among the seven wild animals permitted as food (Deut. 14:5; 12:15), and is the only one among them that has survived in Israel. Though it was almost extinct in the early 1940s, there has been a considerable increase in the number since the passing of the Wild Life Protection Law by the State of Israel, which made hunting the gazelle an offense, and today hundreds of them are to be found in the Judean hills and in the Negev. There are two species of gazelle in Israel; the more common is the *Gazella gazella,* which is grayish-brown in color, 55 inches (140 cm.) in length, and up to 27½ inches (70 cm.) in height. The other species, *Gazella dorcas,* which is found in the Negev, is light-brown in color, has large ears and diverging horns, and stands only 23½ inches (60 cm.) high. The gazelle's delicate appearance, its slender legs, narrow body, and beautiful eyes, made it a symbol of grace and beauty (Song 2:9; 4:5; 7:4). It was hunted extensively for its delicious meat (Isa. 13:14; Prov. 6:5). Its light-footedness became a symbol of speed (II Sam. 2:18). In Song of Songs (2:7; 3:5) there twice occurs the

Gazelles in the Biblical Zoo, Jerusalem. Photo David Harris, Jerusalem.

adjuration "by the gazelles and by the hinds of the field," the reference being to the habit of the males and females of living apart during most of the year and meeting again at the mating season. Perhaps the maiden here intimates that her beloved will surely return to her. Because the gazelle is not found in Europe, the translators of the Bible there identified the *ẓevi* with the *deer (Heb. אַיָּל), which abounds there. Whereas, however, the horns of the deer are branched and solid ("antlers"), the Talmud clearly states that those of the *ẓevi* are unbranched (Ḥul. 59b) and hollow (TJ, Er. 1:17, 19b). "Gazelle" and not "deer" is also the meaning of the Aramaic and Arabic cognates of *ẓevi.* The *halakhah* refers to the prohibition of crossbreeding the gazelle with the goat, which it resembles (Kil. 1:6), the progeny of such cross-breeding being, according to some, the animal known as the *koi* (Ḥul. 132a). It was used as the symbol of the Israel Postal Service.

Bibliography: I. Aharoni, *Torat ha-Ḥai,* 1 (1923), 87; F. S. Bodenheimer, *Ha-Ḥai be-Ereẓ Yisrael* (1953), 246; Tristram, Nat Hist, 127–30; J. Feliks, *Animal World of the Bible* (1962), 11. [J.F.]

GAZIT (Heb. גָּזִית; "hewn building stones," Isa. 9:9), kibbutz in eastern Lower Galilee, Israel, S.E. of Kefar Tavor, affiliated with Kibbutz Arẓi Ha-Shomer ha-Ẓa'ir, first founded in 1943 by a group known as "Irgun Borochov," and taken over by a Ha-Shomer ha-Ẓa'ir group in the summer of 1947. A year later, the present kibbutz was established, while the battles of the *War of Independence were in progress nearby. Its members are pioneers from Argentina, Rumania, and other countries. The kibbutz economy is based on field crops, orchards, beef cattle, and a factory for mosaic stones; the kibbutz is also a partner in a paints factory in the Haifa Bay area. Its population in 1968 was 415. [E.O.]

GDANSK (Pol. **Gdańsk;** Ger. **Danzig**), major commercial port in Poland, situated at the estuary of the Vistula on the Baltic. In 1308 the city passed to the Teutonic Order, which prohibited Jewish settlement there. During the first half of the 15th century Jews from Poland and Lithuania frequently visited the town but this tolerance was limited in 1438. Around 1440 a "Judengasse" ("Jewish Lane") existed on the bank of the Motława. Toward the end of the 15th century, after the town had been incorporated in Poland, it became the wealthiest city of Poland, and the entrepôt for the large commerce in grain and goods between Western and Eastern Europe. This created many commercial possibilities for Jews. However, their activities were restricted by the autonomous status of Gdansk, which enabled the city to discriminate against them. In 1476 the Polish king recommended the city council to permit two Jews to enjoy equal rights with the other merchants.

A Jewish settlement grew up in Gdansk after 1454, but owing to the opposition of the merchants in 1520 the Jews had to move to the Schottland suburb which was not under municipal jurisdiction. Subsequently Jews also settled in other places outside the jurisdiction of the city. On the intervention of King *Sigismund I in 1531, the council withdrew the regulation prohibiting Jews from trading at the fair, but a resolution of the *Sejmik* (small parliament) of Prussia prohibited the extension of further rights to the Jews. In retaliation, the Jews of Lithuania boycotted the Gdansk banking house in Kaunas (Kovno) which had to be liquidated, and ousted the merchants of Gdansk from the Lithuanian salt trade. In 1577 an agreement was concluded between King Stephen Báthory and Gdansk approving the existing restrictions. The citizens also demanded that Jewish residence and trade in the city should be entirely prohibited. Jews were not allowed to hold religious services there, and in 1595 the city council permitted them to stay in Gdansk during fair days only. In 1616 the Gdansk authorities had to pay large indemnities for their arbitrary exclusion of Jewish merchants coming from Polish cities; subsequently Jews were allowed to stay six days in Gdansk against payment of a high poll tax.

Around 1616 about 400 to 500 Jews were living in Gdansk in addition to those settled in lands owned by the gentry or clergy. In 1620 the king permitted Jewish residence in Gdansk. They were permitted to trade in grain and timber in the commercial sector and Langengarten which belonged to the port area, and after these quarters were incorporated into Gdansk in 1626 these rights were extended to the whole of the city. However, the Polish-Swedish wars of the 17th century interrupted the trading activities of the Gdansk Jews. In the middle of the 17th century about 50 Jews became apostates to Christianity. One of them, Johann Salama, a teacher in the seminary of Gdansk, carried on missionary activity among Jews. Cramer, the pastor of Gdansk, in a sermon published in 1664, *Der verstockte Jude,* describes the martyrdom of a Jew who refuses to accept Christianity. During the 18th century, the main opposition to the Jews in Gdansk came from the representatives of small trades and crafts. The third Northern War, strengthening the position of Catholicism in Gdansk, aggravated the hostility to the Jews, and they were moved away from some of their quarters. However, a *ḥevra kaddisha* and *bikkur ḥolim* were founded in the old Jewish quarter in Schottland (Stary Schottland) in 1724. The Jews who had been expelled returned in 1748, although according to a regulation endorsed by the king in 1750 they could only stay temporarily in Gdansk. There were about 1,098 Jews living in Gdansk in the areas outside the city jurisdiction in 1765, of whom 504 were living in Schottland and Hoppenbruch, 230 in Langfuhr, and 364 in Weinberg. In 1773, 50 families received the rights of citizenship in Gdansk and 160 Jews were permitted to reside there.

After Gdansk was incorporated into Prussia on the second partition of Poland in 1793 the restrictions on the Jews remained in force. In 1813 Langfuhr and Schottland were destroyed, and the Jews there moved within the city. Between 1807 and 1814 Gdansk was a Free City, and after its renewed occupation by Prussia the Jews there obtained rights of citizenship by the Prussian liberation decree. There were anti-Jewish incidents during the *Hep! Hep! riots in September 1819 and again in August 1821. Thirty-three Jews were received into the merchants' guild, but by then the city's commercial importance had declined. Jews were permitted to engage in crafts, and in 1823 the Society for the Promotion of Crafts Among the Jewish Population was founded.

Some Hebrew printing was done there in the 16th century in connection with Phillip Wolff's *Spiegel der Juden.* In 1843 the printing house of Rathke and Schroth issued the Mishnah with the *Tiferet Yisrael* commentary by Israel *Lipschuetz, who was rabbi at Danzig. They also published some works of Ẓevi Hirsch *Edelmann from 1844 to 1845, including an edition of his Passover *Haggadah, Leil Shimmurim.* Abraham Stein, an adherent of Reform and later preacher in Prague, was rabbi of Schottland from 1850 to 1864. In 1888 the communities of Schottland, Langfuhr, Weinberg, Mattenbunden, and Breitegasse were amalgamated. The Jewish population numbered 3,798 in 1816, 2,736 in 1880 (2. 4% of the total), 2,390 in 1910 (1. 4%), and 4,678 in 1924.

In 1920 Gdansk was again declared a Free City, having a population of approximately 356,000. There were 7,292 Jews living in the territory of the Free City in 1923, and 9,230 in 1924, of whom 53.4% lived in Gdansk itself. A large number of Jewish emigrants passed through the port on their way to the United States and received assistance from the *American Jewish Joint Distribution Committee and *Hias. The community had four synagogues and various Jewish organizations. The "Jung-Juedischer Bund–Danzig" was founded in 1920. A communal organ, *Juedisches Wochenblatt,* was published from 1929 to 1938. The Jews in Gdansk engaged in commerce and the liberal professions; over 150 Jews were employed in crafts. Adjoining Sopot was a popular summer and sea resort for many Polish Jews between the two world wars. It also attracted a number of Jewish émigrés from Soviet Russia. Despite large Nazi gains in the elections of 1933 and 1935, civil and economic order was upheld by Hermann Rauschning, president of the senate, until 1937, when the *minority rights provided for under the League of Nations lapsed. Albert Forster, the Nazi gauleiter, dismissed almost all Jews from practice in the liberal professions. In 1937 a full-scale pogrom was initiated. Half of the Jews left Gdansk within a year, the Polish government offering them no protection. Between Nov. 12 and 14, 1938, two synagogues were burned down and two others were desecrated. Shops and homes were looted. The Jewish community decided to organize emigration and many left. By September 1939 only 1,200 remained, mostly elderly persons. Three hundred and ninety-five Jews were deported during February and March 1941 to Warsaw and the rest in small groups to concentration camps. Twenty-two Jewish partners of mixed marriages who remained in Gdansk survived the war. After the city reverted to Poland in 1945, a number of Jews settled there. Few remained by the end of the 1960s.

Bibliography: P. Simson, *Geschichte der Stadt Danzig,* 4 vols. (1913–18); E. Keyser, *Danzig's Geschichte* (1923); A. Stein, *Die Geschichte der Juden zu Danzig* (1933[2]); *Gdańsk, przeszłość i teraźniejszość* (1928); M. Aschkewitz, *Zur Geschichte der Juden in Westpreussen* (1967); J. Kirschbaum, *Geshikhte fun di Yuden in Dantsig* (1926); C. J. Burckhardt, *Meine Danziger Mission 1936–1939* (1960); MGWJ, 6 (1857), 205–14, 241–50, 321–31, 401–11; E. Lichtenstein, in: ZGJD, 4 (1967), 199–218; K. Sander, in: *Unser Danzig,* 12 (1960), 21–24; *Zeitschrift fuer Demographie und Statistik der Juden,* 4 (1927), 126–7; E. Cieślak and C. Biernat, *Dzieje Gdańska* (1969); S. Echt, in: BLBI, 6 (1963), 352–94; E. Soidekat, *ibid.,* 8 (1965), 107–49; T. Loevy, *ibid.,* 9 (1966), 190–2; AJYB, 32 (1930/31), 249–51; D. Weinryb, in: PAAJR, 19 (1950), 1–110 (Heb. sect.); Halpern, Pinkas, index.

[J.Go.]

GEBA (Heb. גֶּבַע; "hill"), common name of inhabited places in Ereẓ Israel from biblical times onward; its Arabic form (Jabaʿ جبع) has survived in the names of several Arab villages. Important places bearing this name include:

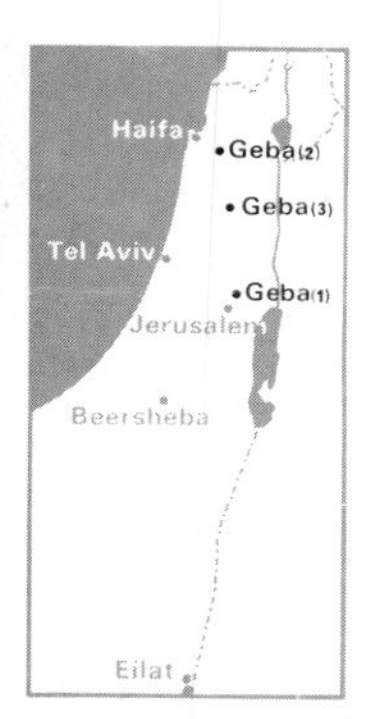

(1) A city of *Benjamin, near the northern border of the tribe, the present-day Jabaᶜ, a Muslim village some 5½ mi. (9 km.) north of *Jerusalem and 2 mi. (3 km.) east of al-Rāma, situated on an ancient tell containing Iron Age remains. Because of the similarity between the names Geba, Gibeah, and other places in the area, it is sometimes difficult to determine exactly which place the Bible refers to, expecially since there are also interchanges and probable errors in the text (e.g., in Judg. 20:10 *Gibeah is meant and in II Sam. 25 Gibeon, according to the parallel verse in I Chron. 14:16). It is therefore not certain whether Geba of the Benjaminite cities (Josh. 18:24) is the one under discussion or a more northerly city known to Eusebius, 5 Roman miles north of *Gophnah (Onom. 74:2). Geba is one of the levitical cities (Josh. 21:17; I Chron. 6:45) and was apparently the seat of the family of Ehud, the son of Gera (Judg. 3:13; I Chron. 8:6, following the Septuagint reading Ehud (ʼΑωδ) instead of Eḥud). Strategically located south of Wadi Ṣuwaynīṭ, opposite *Michmas, it played a central role in Saul's wars with the Philistines. His son Jonathan seized control of the city after his victory over its Philistine garrison (I Sam. 13:3). From the continuation of the war between Geba and Michmas (*ibid.*, 13:16; 14:5), it is clear that this Geba is meant. Moreover, the assumption that a Philistine garrison was stationed at Gibeah before Saul established his capital there has been refuted by excavations at this site. It thus also appears that the "hill of God" (Gibeath ha-Elohim), which was the site of the Philistine garrison (I Sam. 10:5), is identical with the Geba being discussed, and this indicates that a "high place" existed there during the time of Saul.

Asa fortified Geba with stones taken from nearby Ramah (I Kings 15:22; II Chron. 16:6); excavations at Geba have also established that this reference is not to Gibeah, as some scholars have claimed. Geba's strategic position on the eastern branch of the northern highroad is described by Isaiah (10:29) and it is logical that this is the same city which is mentioned on the border of the kingdom of Judah in the latter days of the First Temple (II Kings 23:8; Zech. 14:10; Neh. 11:31). From the statement that *Josiah brought the priests to Jerusalem "from Geba to Beer-Sheba" (II Kings 23:8) it seems likely that up to his time a sanctuary was located in the city (especially after the discovery of an Israelite temple of this period at *Arad on the southeastern border of the kingdom). Geba's destruction came about with the fall of the First Temple and it was rebuilt in the post-Exilic period; the exiles who returned to it are listed together with those from neighboring Ramah (Ezra 2:26; Neh. 7:30; and see Neh. 12:29). [Yo.A.]

(2) Geba-Parashim (Gr. *Geba Hippeon,* "Geba of the Horsemen"), city in Lower Galilee near the Jezreel Valley founded by Herod who settled demobilized cavalrymen there (Jos., Ant. 15:294; Wars 3:36). It served as a Herodian and Roman administrative center in the valley and enjoyed several urban privileges, including the right to mint city-coinage. During the Jewish War (66–70/73) fighting between the Romans and the Galilean rebels under the command of Josephus took place near Geba (Jos., Life 115). The city was in existence until the fourth century C.E. and was the seat of a Christian bishop. Most scholars identify it with Khirbat Ḥarithiyya near a key road at the entrance of the Jezreel Plain. Another suggestion is that Hellenistic Geba corresponds to the Geba mentioned in the list of Thutmose III's conquests (No. 41, Geba-Shemen) which has been identified with Tell al-ᶜAmr in the same neighborhood.

(3) Geba, a place mentioned in the Mishnah (Kelim 17:5) and Tosefta (Kelim, BM 6:10) as being inhabited by Kutim (Cutheans). This city has been identified with the Arab village of Jabaᶜ, 3¾ mi. (6 km.) north of Samaria. It is also mentioned in the Samaria ostraca from the eighth century B.C.E. [M.A.-Y.]

Bibliography: Abel, Geog, 2 (1938), 328–9; Aharoni, Land, index; EM, s.v.; IDB, s.v. *Gibeah;* Maisler (Mazar), in: BJPES, 11 (1945), 37ff.; Avi-Yonah, Geog, 145.

GEBIHA OF BE-KATIL (first half of the fifth century), Babylonian *amora.* Gebiha headed the academy of Pumbedita during the years 419–33 (*Iggeret Sherira Ga'on* (1921), 96), and lectured on *halakhah* at the *bet ha-midrash* adjoining the house of the *exilarch. His younger contemporaries *Amemar and *Ashi discussed the meaning of his pronouncements (Beẓah 23a). Gebiha, who spanned a number of generations of *amoraim,* mentions the rulings of Abbaye (Ḥul. 64b; Me'il. 10a), transmits cases that came before Rava (Av. Zar. 22a), and is also frequently found debating halakhic topics with Ashi (Ḥul. 26b; et al.).

Bibliography: Hyman, Toledot, 300. [J.E.E.]

GEBINI (first century), Temple crier of the Second Temple. His role was to rouse those on duty to the performance of the Temple rites; the *baraita* gives his cry as, "Priests, bestir yourselves to your service, levites to your platform (for song), Israelites to your posts" (**Ma'amad;* Yoma 20b; TJ, Shek. 5:2, 48d). His stentorian voice became legendary. The *baraita* adds that King Agrippa heard his voice at a distance of three (another version, eight) parasangs, and sent him a gift in admiration. An early Mishnah states that his voice could even be heard as far as Jericho (Tam. 3:8). It is believed that the name became an eponym for all subsequent Temple criers.

Bibliography: Hyman, Toledot, 300. [J.E.E.]

GEBIRTIG, MORDECAI (1877–1942), Yiddish poet. Gebirtig was born in Cracow and worked as a carpenter all his life. He attained fame as a Yiddish bard, composing both words and melodies for his songs. His songs were sung throughout the Diaspora long before literary critics recognized their value and originality. They were first collected in 1936, in a volume edited by the folksinger M. Kipnis, and were reprinted with additions in 1942 and 1948. Gebirtig's most famous song, *Undzer Shtetl Brent* ("Our Town is Burning"), was written in 1938 under the impact of the Polish pogrom in Przytyk. The tragic topicality of the theme and the prophetic vision of the doomed *shtetl*-culture made this song into a hymn which is often sung at Jewish memorial assemblies. The poet was murdered by the Nazis in June 1942, together with his wife and two daughters. However, his last songs, written in the Cracow Ghetto, were miraculously saved. A selection of Hebrew translations of his poems appeared in 1967 under the title *Ha-Ayarah Bo'eret* ("The Town is Burning").

Bibliography: Rejzen, Leksikon, 1 (1926), 595ff.; LNYL, 2 (1958), 286–90; B. Mark, *Umgekumene Shrayber fun die Ghettos* (1954), 187–94; M. Neugroeschel, in: *Fun Noentn Over* (1955), 349–51; J. Leftwich (ed.), *The Golden Peacock* (1939). [M.Rav.]

GECKO, reptile of the order Lacertilia. Six genera belonging to the Gekkonidae family are to be found in Israel. The most common is the house gecko, *Hemidactylus turcicus,* a nocturnal lizard up to about 4¾ inches (12 cm.) in length, with a soft speckled hide and prehensile feet which enable it to climb walls. Two animals referred to in the Bible are likely to be identical with the gecko. The *anakah* is included among the unclean swarming things (Lev. 11:30) and has, according to the Mishnah (Ḥul. 9:2), a soft hide. The word *anakah* means "groan," and the gecko does in

House gecko *(Hemidactylus turcicus),* the most common of the Gekkonidae family found in Israel. Courtesy J. Feliks, Jerusalem.

fact emit a sound reminiscent of the groan of a sick person. The Book of Proverbs, in its enumeration of the "things which are little upon the earth, but . . . are exceeding wise" (30:24), mentions the *semamit,* which "taketh hold with her hands, and is in kings' palaces" (*ibid.,* 28). This description fits the ubiquitous gecko which climbs on walls with feet that resemble hands. Although many other identifications have been suggested for the *anakah* and the *semamit,* the gecko fits them best.

Bibliography: I. Aharoni, *Torat ha-Ḥai,* 1, pt. 3 (1930), 62–66; Tristram, Nat Hist, 265f.; J. Feliks, *Animal World of the Bible* (1962), 97.

[J.F.]

GEDALIAH (Heb. גְּדַלְיָה, גְּדַלְיָהוּ), son of Ahikam. Gedaliah was appointed by the Babylonians as governor of Judah after the capture of Jerusalem in 586; members of his family had held important posts during the last decades of the kingdom of Judah. His grandfather *Shaphan and his father *Ahikam supported Josiah during the latter's reforms (II Kings 22:3ff., 12ff.). Ahikam held an important post during the reign of Jehoiakim and was able to save Jeremiah from the anger of the people after his speech at the Temple gate (Jer. 26:24). Evidently this family followed a line of moderation and submission to Babylon, which explains the choice of one of its members to govern the remnant in Judah (see also *Elasah, *Jaazaniah). Gedaliah may even have been a man of influence and status before

Seal inscribed "To Gedaliah who is in charge of the house." It comes from a papyrus letter sent from Jerusalem to Lachish shortly before the destruction of the fortress in 587/6 B.C.E. Jerusalem, Israel Department of Antiquities.

this time (II Kings 25:22; Jer. 40:5). He has been identified with the official of the same name, who was "in charge of the house"; the identification was made by means of the impression of a seal which was found at the town gate of *Lachish, a town burned and destroyed in the last days of the kingdom of Judah.

Gedaliah resided at *Mizpah in the territory of Benjamin. The remaining people of Judah who gathered around him included army officers who had escaped capture and deportation by the Babylonians. May and other critics claim that Gedaliah served as the representative of the exiled *Jehoiachin who was still considered king of Judah, but there is no real basis for this assumption. The center at Mizpah was not long lived and Gedaliah, together with the Judahites and Babylonians stationed at Mizpah, was murdered by *Ishmael b. Nethaniah, who was in contact with *Baalis, king of the Ammonites. The assassination was instigated apparently with the hope of overthrowing Babylonian rule. Those who were spared, including several army officers, fled to Egypt, taking Jeremiah with them, out of fear that the Babylonians might consider them responsible for the murder of Gedaliah (II Kings 25:25–26; Jer. 41:1ff.).

Several scholars have suggested that the Babylonian Exile from Judah in the 23rd year of Nebuchadnezzar's reign (Jer. 52:30) is connected with the murder of Gedaliah (cf. Jos., Ant. 10:181), but this assumption requires the dating of the murder in 582/1 B.C.E., whereas according to the biblical record, Gedaliah governed only for a short time, either until the seventh month of the year of destruction (587/6) or the seventh month of the following year (586/5). The day of Gedaliah's death was observed as a fast day, and is called "the fast of the seventh month" in the Bible (Zech. 7:5; 8:19) and, at a later date, the Fast of Gedaliah (see *Fasts and Fasting). According to tradition it occurs on the third of Tishri (RH 18b).

Bibliography: Bright, Hist, index; Yeivin, in: *Tarbiz,* 12 (1940/41), 253, 255–8, 266–8; May, in: AJSLL, 56 (1939), 146–8; C. C. McCown et al., *Excavations at Tell en-Nasbeh,* 1 (1947), 30–34, 46–48; EM, 2 (1965), 440–2.

[J.Li.]

GEDALIAH, (Don) JUDAH (d. c. 1526), Hebrew printer. Gedaliah, who was born in Lisbon, worked there at *Eliezer Toledano's Hebrew press (1489–95) until the expulsion from Portugal (1497). He settled in Salonika, establishing the first Hebrew printing press there using fine typefonts he had brought from Lisbon. Between 1515 and 1535 he, his daughter, and his sons (who continued the firm after his death) carefully edited and printed about 30 Hebrew books including the first edition of *Ein Ya'akov* of R. Jacob ibn Ḥabib (1516–22). The latter, in his introduction, highly praised Gedaliah for his efforts in spreading the knowledge of Torah among the other Iberian refugees in Salonika.

Bibliography: A. Freimann, in: ZHB, 11 (1907), 52–53; J. Bloch, *Early Hebrew Printing in Spain and Portugal* (1938), 34–54; H. D. Friedberg, *Toledot ha-Defus ha-Ivri bi-Medinot Italyah . . .* (1956), 130ff.

[J.H.H.]

GEDALIAH, JUDAH BEN MOSES (16th century), scholar in Salonika. Nothing is known of his life, but his important works remain. They are: *Masoret Talmud Yerushalmi,* indexes of parallels to the Jerusalem Talmud (Constantinople, 1573); notes on the *Midrash Rabbah* and the Five Scrolls (Salonika, 1593/94). In this latter work Gedaliah reveals a sound critical aptitude and extensive philological knowledge. He explains most of the difficulties found in the Midrash, and is extensively quoted by later commentators. His notes on the *Zohar Ḥadash* (Salonika,

1596/97) also reveal his critical insight. In the Bodleian Library there are preserved a few volumes of the Bomberg edition of the Babylonian Talmud with his notes in manuscript.

Bibliography: Michael, Or, no. 980; Fuenn, Keneset, 393; Steinschneider, Cat Bod, no. 1326. [Y.AL.]

GEDALIAH HA-LEVI (d. after 1610), kabbalist and rabbi in Safed, Ereẓ Israel. Gedaliah, the brother-in-law of Ḥayyim *Vital, was one of the "initiates" of Isaac *Luria, i.e., one of his important and early disciples. His signature appears on the writ of association of Luria's disciples (1575). He edited and arranged according to Luria's instructions the *Derushei ha-Melakhim she-Metu,* which appeared in *Kol ba-Ramah* (Korets, 1785) and exists in several unsigned manuscripts. Solomon Shlomel Dresnitz, author of *Shivḥei ha-Ari,* heard tales about Luria directly from Gedaliah.

Bibliography: A. Z. Aescoly (ed.), *Sefer ha-Ḥezyonot* (1954), 56, 221; G. Scholem, *Kitvei Yad be-Kabbalah* (1930), 138; idem in: *Zion,* 5 (1940), 146–7, 149; D. Tamar, *Meḥkarim be-Toledot ha-Yehudim be-Ereẓ Yisrael u-ve-Italyah* (1970), 171. [D.TA.]

GEDALIAH OF SIEMIATYCZE (early 18th century), Jerusalem emissary. Gedaliah, followed by his brother R. Moses of Siemiatycze, arrived in Jerusalem on Oct. 14, 1700, in the group headed by R. *Judah Ḥasid. For most of the immigrants, including Gedaliah, the objective of this *aliyah* was to hasten the redemption by ethical conduct, repentance, prayer, fasting, and self-mortification. Gedaliah was sent later on, as the emissary of the Ashkenazi community of Jerusalem, to Western Europe where he published his work on the virtues of Ereẓ Israel, *Sha'alu Shelom Yerushalayim* ("Pray for the Peace of Jerusalem," Berlin, 1716). In it Gedaliah describes the *aliyah* of R. Judah Ḥasid and his group; the arrival of the group in Jerusalem and the death of their leader soon after; the arrangements of the "courtyard" which they acquired; the oppression of the authorities who extorted a great sum of money from them in the form of taxes and bribery; and the methods of collecting the poll tax. He also depicts Jerusalem life in general: the food, the fruits and vegetables, the methods of baking and cooking, the water supply, clothing, the means of travel, the houses, the bathhouses, and the markets, the holy places, and especially the prayers at the Western Wall. An account is also given of the decrees issued by the government and the unrest during the first years after the arrival of the group.

His brother, R. Moses of Siematycze, was accepted in 1702 as one of the teachers in the yeshivah founded by Abraham *Rovigo in Jerusalem; about 1711, he visited Metz as the emissary of the Ashkenazi community of Jerusalem. He died after 1716. [A.YA.]

°**GEDDES, ALEXANDER** (1737–1802), Catholic Bible scholar. He studied in Paris and was a priest in various places in Scotland in the years 1764–80, and afterward in London. A versatile scholar and prolific writer, Geddes published after many preparatory works *The Holy Bible . . . translated from the corrected Text of the Original; with various readings, explanatory notes, and critical remarks* (2 vols., 1792–97; embracing only the historical books). Already in conflict with the Church, Geddes was suspended from exercising his priestly functions on account of the critical attitude contained in his *Critical Remarks on the Hebrew Scriptures, Corresponding with a New Translation of the Bible; Containing Remarks on the Pentateuch* (1800). He disputed Moses' divine inspiration, explained the miracles in a natural way, and saw in the Pentateuch an assemblage of numerous and mostly post-Mosaic fragments. He thus established the "fragments" hypothesis, which was accepted and further developed by J. S. Vater, and one of whose outstanding exponents was W. M. L. de *Wette.

Bibliography: DNB, 7 (1889/90), incl. bibl. [R.SM.]

GEDERAH, GEDEROTH (Heb. גְּדֵרָה, גְּדֵרוֹת), name of several localities in Ereẓ Israel formed from the root גדר ("to wall in"). (1) A place in the northern Shephelah of Judah mentioned in Joshua 15:36. It may be identical with the home of Jozabad, a "mighty man" of David (I Chron. 12:5), and of Baal-Hanan, the overseer of David's olive and sycamore trees (the latter being especially plentiful in the Shephelah; I Chron. 27:28). The city has been tentatively identified with Khirbat Jadīra (Judayra), ½ mi. (1 km.) south of Beit Nattif. (2) A Gederoth mentioned in Joshua 15:41 together with Beth-Dagon and Naamah is perhaps identical with the Gedrus of Eusebius (Onom. 68:22). The Kedron in I Maccabees 15:39, the tell of Qaṭra, has been suggested as its site. (3) A locality appearing among the cities conquered by the Philistines during the reign of Ahaz. Since it is mentioned together with Soco, Timnah, Gimzo, Beth-Shemesh, and Aijalon (II Chron. 28:18), *Albright has identified it with Khirbat el-Jadīra (Judayra), 1 mi. (2 km.) west of Latrun, in the Aijalon Valley. (4) A place mentioned in I Chronicles 4:23 (JPS translation, "hedges"), probably identical with (1) or (2) above.

Bibliography: EM, s.v. (includes bibliography). [M.A.-Y.]

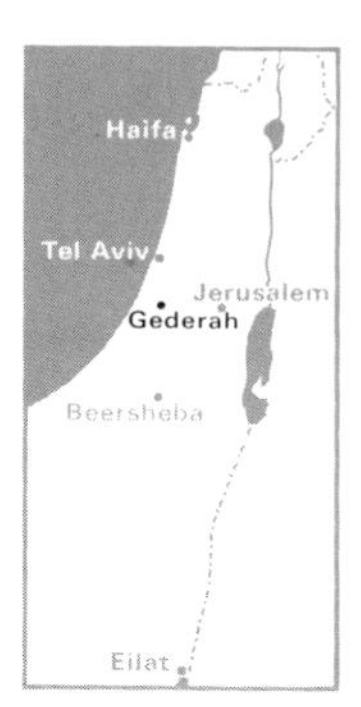

GEDERAH (Heb. גְּדֵרָה), moshavah with municipal council status, in the Coastal Plain of Israel, 8 mi. (13 km.) S.W. of Reḥovot. It was founded in 1884 by young members of the *Bilu movement from Russia. Gederah was for a long time the southernmost Jewish settlement in the country and also the only veteran moshavah independent of Baron Edmond de *Rothschild's aid and administration. Initially, grapes and grain constituted Gederah's principal farm branches, later citrus orchards, cotton, and other intensive field crops were added. In the 1930s a number of rest houses, among them sanatoriums for respiratory ailments, were established there. The moshavah has a few small industrial enterprises in food and other branches. Its municipal boundaries include Uri'el, a village for the blind who are employed in certain branches of agriculture and handicrafts, and Kannot, a *Youth Aliyah children's village. Gederah's name is derived from the neighboring Arab village Qaṭra—abandoned since 1948. Most scholars assume Qaṭra to be identical with the town of *Gederah belonging to the tribe of Judah (Josh. 15:36), and, with greater certainty, with the town Kedron mentioned in I Maccabees (15:39; 16:9) as the scene of one of Judah's victories over Syrian forces. The Greek form of the name has been preserved by moshav Kidron founded north of Gederah in 1949. [E.O.]

GEDILIAH, ABRAHAM BEN SAMUEL (d. 1672), rabbi and author. Born in Jerusalem, Abraham journeyed to Italy in 1648 and resided in Leghorn and Verona. On his return journey in 1660, he stayed for a time in Egypt. In Italy he was friendly with Samuel *Aboab and Moses b. Mordecai *Zacuto. While in Leghorn, he worked as a proofreader in the printing works of Jedidiah Gabbai. In 1657–60 he published the **Yalkut Shimoni* with his own commentary, *Berit Avraham.* In 1665 he sent a letter from Gaza to the rabbis of Italy, expressing his belief in the messianic claims of *Shabbetai Ẓevi and in the prophecy of *Nathan of Gaza. This letter, the first of its kind to be sent by a scholar of Ereẓ Israel, made a deep impression. Abraham died in Jerusalem. Some of his homilies are included in the *Mizbaḥ Eliyahu* of *Elijah ha-Kohen of Smyrna (Smyrna, 1867). Many members of the Gediliah family were rabbis in Hebron, and some in Tiberias and Safed. His grandson, Abraham Gediliah of Hebron, was an emissary of Ereẓ Israel.

Bibliography: Frumkin-Rivlin, 2 (1928), 33f.; Yaari, Sheluḥei, 158, 272, 845; idem in: KS, 25 (1948/49), 113f.; Tishbi, *ibid.*, 230f.; Scholem, Shabbetai Ẓevi, 198, 289f., 478. [A.YA./ED.]

GEDOR (Heb. גְּדוֹר). (1) A city of Judah mentioned in the Bible together with *Halhul and *Beth-Zur (Josh. 15:58). It has been identified with Khirbat Jadūr, 2½ mi. (4 km.) north of Beth-Zur, where surface pottery from the Early Iron (Israelite) Age has been found. (2) The city Gedor appears in I Chronicles 4:18. It is probably identical with *Gederah (1). Another Gedor—the home of two of David's "mighty men," Joelah and Zebadiah, sons of Jeroham (I Chron. 12:8), may be identical with either (1) or (2). (3) One of the cities of Simeon (I Chron. 4:39). It is called Geder in Joshua 12:13, Gerar in the Septuagint, and is not listed among Simeon's cities in Joshua 19:1–9. (4) The capital of Perea in post-Exilic times (now al-Tell near ʿAyn Jadūr in the vicinity of al-Ṣalṭ in Transjordan (Jos., Wars 4:413)). In the Mishnah it is included among the cities fortified in the time of Joshua (Ar. 9:6).

Bibliography: L. Haefeli, *Samaria und Peraea* ... (1913), 107ff.; Dalman, in: PJB, 6 (1910), 22–23; Aharoni, Land, index. [M.A.-Y.]

GEHUD HA-AVODAH (Heb. "The [Yosef Trumpeldor] Labor Legion"), first countrywide commune of Jewish workers in Palestine. The Gedud was founded in the autumn of 1920 by 80 pioneers of the Third Aliyah, disciples of Yosef *Trumpeldor. In the winter of 1920 the Gedud contracted to build part of the Tiberias-Tabgha road in Galilee. The members decided to establish a permanent form of communal life at their camp near Migdal, with a common treasury. In the spring of 1921 some of the members were sent to Rosh ha-Ayin to lay the branch railroad to Petaḥ Tikvah and at the same time to serve as the nucleus of a second Gedud, which soon grew to 300 members. In early summer representatives of the groups met at Migdal and defined the Gedud's aim as "the building of the land by the creation of a general commune of the workers of the Land of Israel." The members were to be organized in disciplined groups, which would be at the disposition of the *Histadrut for labor and defense. In the course of time it was intended that the Gedud would encompass all workers and merge with the Histadrut. Among its leaders were M. Elkind and Y. Kopeliovitz (*Almog); Yiẓḥak *Sadeh was an active member. As road work diminished, "companies" of the Gedud went to the Jezreel Valley, where they founded *Ein Ḥarod (1921) and *Tel Yosef (1923), forming a single farming unit. A large group went to Jerusalem to work in building and quarrying and to strengthen the armed defenses of the *yishuv* there. Others worked in agriculture and building and provided services at British army camps. At its zenith the Gedud had some 700 members. In July 1923 the Tel Yosef-Ein Ḥarod group split over a minority demand for economic autonomy, about one-third of the members settling in Ein Ḥarod and the majority in Tel Yosef. A minority attempt to turn the Gedud into a political party, with syndicalist and pro-Communist tendencies, resulted in another split, in 1926, into right-wing and left-wing factions. The left wing soon disintegrated, as some of its members, including Elkind, went to the Soviet Union. They set up a communal farm in the Crimea, Via Nova, which was disbanded in 1931–32. The Gedud was seriously weakened, and in December 1929 the three surviving groups—Tel Yosef, Kefar Giladi, and Ramat Raḥel—joined *Ha-Kibbutz ha-Me'uḥad.

At its peak the Gedud played an important pioneering role in settlement, defense, and labor. Over 2,000 pioneers passed through its ranks, and its influence was out of proportion to its membership. It published a periodical, *Me-Ḥayyenu* and maintained a dramatic studio, *Massad* ("Foundation").

Bibliography: Al Inyenei Ein Ḥarod (1923); *Koveẓ Ḥavrei Gedud ha-Avodah ba-Kibbutz ha-Me'uḥad* (1932); *Koveẓ ha-Kibbutz ha-Me'uḥad* (1932); I. Bar-Ḥayyim, *Mi-Naftulei Gedud ha-Avodah ba-Kur* (1941); Sh. Lavi, *Megillati be-Ein Ḥarod* (1947); D. Horowitz, *Ha-Etmol Shelli* (1970), 160–98. [ED.]

GEFFEN, TOBIAS (1870–1970), U.S. Orthodox rabbi. Geffen, who was born in Kovno, Lithuania, studied first under Isaac Elhanan Spektor and later at the Slobodka Yeshivah. After holding a rabbinic position in Kovno he went to the U.S. in 1903 and served congregations in New York and Canton, Ohio. In 1910 he was appointed to Congregation Shearith Israel, Atlanta, Georgia, where he remained active until the end of his life. Geffen published an autobiography in Yiddish and several volumes containing sermons, responsa on Jewish law and talmudic dissertations. He was a zealous teacher and an energetic worker for public causes, and these qualities, together with his talmudic scholarship, gave him an authoritative position among Orthodox Jews in the southern U.S. [ED.]

GEHAZI (Heb. גֵּיחֲזִי ,גֵּחֲזִי), servant of *Elisha. In the story of the wealthy Shunammite woman (II Kings 4:8–37), Gehazi is portrayed as Elisha's faithful messenger and loyal protector (4:27). In the story of Naaman (II Kings 5), he is portrayed as a greedy character who, contrary to the instructions of Elisha, cunningly solicited a reward from the Syrian general and then tried to practice deception on his master, the prophet Elisha. In punishment, Elisha cursed Gehazi and his descendants forever with the leprosy of Naaman. The third time that Gehazi appears is in connection with the woman from Shunem and the king of Israel (II Kings 8:1–6). In this story Gehazi reported to the king on the great deeds which Elisha had performed. These three stories, so it would appear, did not occur in the chronological order in which they are now arranged in the Kings, since it is unlikely that Gehazi would have stood before the king recounting Elisha's great deeds after he had been cursed with leprosy. It is reasonable to assume that they reflect two separate traditions. The first and third stories, which are related in content, constitute one tradition, while that of Naaman stems from a different circle. [Is.A.]

In the Aggadah. Gehazi is one who set his eyes upon that which was not proper with the result that he was not granted that which he sought, and lost whatever he possessed (Sot. 9b). Although learned, he was jealous of Elisha's learning, sensual (in his actions toward the Shunamite), and did not believe in the resurrection of the dead. Instead of obeying Elisha's order not to greet anyone on his way to the Shunamite's son (II Kings 4:29), he made sport of his mission and deliberately asked everyone he met whether they really believed that Elisha's staff, which he was carrying, could restore the dead to life (PdRE 37).

Gehazi was punished with leprosy because Elisha had been studying the law of the eight unclean creeping things when Naaman first consulted him. When Elisha accused Gehazi of taking eight things from Naaman (II Kings 5:26), he implied that he would be punished as would one who caught any of the eight creeping things—with leprosy (AdRN 9). According to another tradition, Gehazi was thus punished because he showed disrespect by calling his master by name (cf. II Kings 8:5; Sanh. 100a). Gehazi never repented. Instead, he sinned further either by hanging a magnet over Jeroboam's idol and suspending it between heaven and earth in order to deceive people, or by engraving the name of God on it, so that it spoke the first two commandments (Sanh. 107b). When Elisha met him in Damascus and exhorted him to repent, he replied: "Thus have I learnt from thee. He who sins and causes the multitude to sin, is not afforded the means of repentance" *(ibid.)*. Elisha, however, is criticized for "thrusting Gehazi away with both hands," instead of using only one for that purpose, and the other for drawing him toward himself (Sot. 47a). Gehazi is one of the four commoners who have no share in the world to come (Sanh. 10:2). He was even undeserving of speaking the praises of God and His servant Elisha.

Bibliography: Ginzberg, Legends, index; I. Ḥasida, *Ishei ha-Tanakh* (1964), 97–98.

[ED.]

GEHINNOM (Heb. גֵּי בֶן־הִנֹּם, גֵּי בְנֵי הִנֹּם, גֵּיא בֶן־הִנֹּם, גֵּיא הִנֹּם; Gr. Γέεννα; "Valley of Ben-Hinnom, Valley of [the Son(s) of] Hinnom," Gehenna), a valley south of Jerusalem on one of the borders between the territories of Judah and Benjamin, between the Valley of *Rephaim and *En-Rogel (Josh. 15:8; 18:16). It is identified with Wadi er-Rababi.

During the time of the Monarchy, Gehinnom, at a place called *Topheth, was the site of a cult which involved the burning of children (II Kings 23:10; Jer. 7:31; 32:35 et al.; see *Moloch). Jeremiah repeatedly condemned this cult and predicted that on its account Topheth and the Valley of the Son of Hinnom would be called the Valley of the "Slaughter" (Jer. 19:5–6).

In Judaism the name Gehinnom is generally used metaphorically as an appellation for the place of torment reserved for the wicked after death. The New Testament uses the Greek from Gehenna in the same sense. For fuller details see *Nether World; *Paradise. [ED.]

GEIGER, ABRAHAM (1810–1874), rabbi, son of an old-established family in Frankfort, one of the leaders of the *Reform movement in Judaism, and an outstanding scholar of *Wissenschaft des Judentums. Geiger received a traditional education. His principal teacher was his elder brother, Solomon Geiger. He was also influenced by the teachings of B. W. *Heidenheim. Subsequently, he began to study oriental languages and Greek, from 1829 in Heidelberg and then in Bonn. In Bonn Geiger became acquainted with his future Orthodox adversary S. R. *Hirsch, whom he greatly admired at the time, setting up in conjunction with him and several other young men a circle for developing the art of preaching. In 1832, Geiger became rabbi in *Wiesbaden, where he took his first steps to introduce reform of the synagogue services, and began publication of the *Wissenschaftliche Zeitschrift fuer juedische Theologie* (6 vols. in 5, 1835–47), to which the most important Jewish scholars of his day contributed. In 1837 he convened the first meeting of Reform rabbis in Wiesbaden. In 1838, Geiger was chosen as *dayyan* and assistant rabbi by the Breslau community, but, owing to the strong opposition of its rabbi, S. A. *Tiktin, Geiger was not able to take up his position until 1840. After Tiktin's death in 1843, Geiger was accorded the rabbinate by the majority of the community, thus causing the Orthodox minority to secede. In Breslau Geiger established a school for religious studies and a group for study of Hebrew philology. Geiger was one of the most active participants in the *Synods held by the Reform rabbis in Frankfort (1845) and Breslau (1846). He was among the initiators of the *Juedisch-Theologisches Seminar in Breslau in 1854, but contrary to his wishes was not appointed its principal because of opposition from the conservatives. From 1863 Geiger served as rabbi of the Reform congregation in his hometown Frankfort, and from the beginning of 1870 was rabbi of the Berlin congregation; in 1872, the *Hochschule fuer die Wissenschaft des Judentums was established in Berlin with his assistance and Geiger directed it until his death.

Abraham Geiger, early German Reform rabbi. Jerusalem, J.N.U.L., Schwadron Collection.

During his lifetime Geiger combined the work of a militant reforming theologian and a philologist-historian. He was active in all affairs of German Jewry of his time, while his scientific research ranged over almost every sphere of Judaism. His theoretical and practical activities were stamped by intellectual daring and profound knowledge of both Jewish and general subjects, and served his aspiration to make Judaism an integral part of the general European culture in its German context. Geiger valued prophecy in Judaism, and wished to maintain the feeling of Jewish continuity, but he was radically opposed to Orthodoxy which he regarded as ossified by nomism and lacking aesthetic forms to satisfy the cultured man. He aspired to lead Jewry to a form of *assimilation which would both further fulfillment of the Jewish "mission" to spread rational faith in the One God and His moral law, and lead to a modification of the Jewish way of life and thinking. He was, therefore, interested, although he did not express this publicly, in abolishing every institution of Judaism in its existing form and constructing a new edifice upon its ruins (according to his letter to J. Derenbourg of Nov. 8, 1836). The new edifice, however, was to be constructed from materials to be found in the historical and halakhic tradition of the past, and by utilizing the immanent forces of the tradition itself for change and renewal. In order to attain this objective, Geiger concentrated his wide research on the history of the religion. The historiographical picture resulting from his work served the requirements of religious reform and civic emancipation.

In his desire to see Judaism solely as a religious community Geiger set out to eliminate from Judaism every mark of national uniqueness and of dissociation from the gentile nations. Hence, his attitude was negative toward all manifestations of Jewish solidarity, as at the time of the *Damascus affair (1840), and in 1845 he opposed prayer in Hebrew, which he further justified by the ignorance of the language among most worshipers. In the course of time his approach to religious reform became more moderate; while he omitted all reference to the Return to Zion from the prayer book which he brought out in 1854 for his community in Breslau, he retained Hebrew corresponding in its essentials with the original version alongside several prayers in German; but Geiger changed the German translation accompanying the prayers, in accordance with Reform spirit (for example, *meḥayyeh ha-metim*—"reviver of the dead"—is translated in his version as *Quell ewigen Lebens*—"the source of eternal life"). In his last years his moderation became even greater; and in Berlin he reinstated celebration of the second day of the festivals (as customary in the Diaspora), which he had abolished in Breslau. This change of outlook was actuated by two reasons: his wish to avoid a sudden split in Judaism, and his antagonism to Christianity. On these grounds, he did not agree to changing the Sabbath to Sunday, even though he permitted instrumental music on the Sabbath in synagogue and permitted several prohibited kinds of work on the Sabbath. These arguments also underlay Geiger's opposition to the abolition of circumcision, although he regarded it (according to his letter to L. Zunz of March 18, 1845) as "a barbaric act of bloodletting." Geiger's prayer book was the product of social and religious aims in conjunction with aesthetic considerations. He considerably shortened the order of prayer to enable worshipers to pray with devotion. He established prayers for rain in summer also, to suit conditions in Germany, and omitted portions from various prayers that he regarded as empty verbiage.

Writings. In his doctoral dissertation *Was hat Mohammed aus dem Judenthume aufgenommen* (1833), Geiger demonstrated the influence of Jewish tradition upon the Koran. Geiger's principal work was *Urschrift und Uebersetzungen der Bibel . . .* (1857; 1928[2]), in which he correlates the history of the biblical translations with the history of the sects in Israel (particularly the Pharisees and Sadducees). He also supplemented the work with comments, written in a fine rabbinic Hebrew (*Oẓar Neḥmad,* 3 (1860), 1–15, 116–21). Geiger enlarged upon his discussion of the division between the Pharisees and the Sadducees in a separate work, *Sadducaeer und Pharisaeer* (1863, 1928[2]). His *Urschrift . . .* won high praise at the time but was also sharply criticized (S. J. *Rapaport, *Ner Mitzvah ve-Or Torah,* in *Sefer Naḥalat Yehudah,* 1867). Geiger summarized his historical view of Judaism in general in a series of popular lectures that he delivered in Frankfort, *Das Judenthum und seine Geschichte* (3 vols., 1865–71; *Judaism and its History,* 1865, 1911). Also important are Geiger's *Lehr- und Lesebuch zur Sprache der Mischnah* (1845); and *Parschandatha; die nordfranzoesische Exegetenschule* (1855). Other writings included a study of Maimonides (1850); an edition of the *Divan* of Judah Halevi (1851); a study of Ibn Gabirol (1867); translations of a number of their poems in German verse; a treatise on the Karaite Isaac b. Abraham Troki (1853); and a study on Leone Modena (1856). He published several valuable manuscripts (collected in *Melo Chofnajim,* 1840). Geiger contributed regularly to the *Zeitschrift der Deutschen Morgenlaendischen Gesellschaft,* and from 1862 to 1875 published *Juedische Zeitschrift fuer Wissenschaft und Leben,* where he wrote a severe criticism of *Rome and Jerusalem* by Moses Hess (1862), and many scholarly and publicist articles. Collections of Geiger's articles in Hebrew were published by R. Kirchheim (*Nachgelassene Schriften,* 5 (1877), Heb. pt.), and by S. A. Posnański (1910–12), and were also appended to the second issue of the *Urschrift . . .* (1928), and to the Hebrew edition *Ha-Mikra ve-Targumav* (1949). Other writings by Geiger were published posthumously by his son, Ludwig *Geiger (1875–78) and a collection of Geiger's letters to Joseph Derenbourg appeared in 1896.

Bibliography: M. Wiener, *Juedische Religion im Zeitalter der Emanzipation* (1933); idem (comp.), *Abraham Geiger and Liberal Judaism* (1962); idem, in: *Judaism,* 2 (1953), 41–48; idem, in: YIVOA, 11 (1956/57), 142–62; H. Liebeschvetz, in: *Essays Presented to Leo Baeck* (1954), 75–93; idem, *Das Judentum im deutschen Geschichtsbild* (1967); Klausner, Sifrut, 257–61; idem, in: A. Geiger, *Ha-Mikra ve-Targumav* (1949), introduction; G. Scholem, in: *Lu'aḥ ha-Areẓ* (1944), 101–2; N. Rotenstreich, *Ha-Maḥashavah ha-Yehudit ba-Et ha-Ḥadashah,* 1 (1945), 90–146; L. Geiger, *Abraham Geigers Leben in Briefen* (1878); idem, *Abraham Geiger, Leben und Lebenswerk* (1910); S. Schechter, *Studies in Judaism,* 3 (1924), 47–83; F. A. Levy, in: JBA, 18 (1960/61), 86–94; D. Philipson, *History of the Reform Movement* (1931), index; W. G. Plaut, *The Rise of Reform Judaism* (1963), index; M. Waxman, in: S. Federbusch (ed.) *Ḥokhmat Yisrael be-Eiropah* (1965), 55–78; M. Vogelstein, in: *Tradition und Erneuerung,* 8 (1960), 117–25; J. J. Petuchowski, *Prayerbook Reform in Europe* (1968); M. M. Kaplan, *Greater Judaism in the Making* (1960), 31–46; I. Barzilay, *Shlomo Yehudah Rapoport (Shir) and His Contemporaries* (1969), 16–17, 145–60. [J.Lev.]

GEIGER, BERNHARD (1881–1964), Austrian philologist. Geiger, born in Bielitz (Bielsko), Upper Silesia, attended the universities of Vienna, Bonn, and Heidelberg. Originally his field of study was Hebrew, but one of his teachers in Vienna aroused his interest in Iranian and Sanskrit, and it was in those languages that he made his principal contributions to scholarship. From 1909 to 1938 he taught at the University of Vienna, being forced to leave that position by the Nazis. In 1938 he immigrated to the United States and from 1938 to 1951 was professor of Indo-Iranian philology at the Tibetan-Iranian Institute (later the Asia Institute), New York. In 1951–56 he taught Indo-Iranian at Columbia University. In 1949 the shah of Iran conferred upon him the Order of Humayoun.

Geiger's publications include *Die Aməša Spəntas* (1916); *Die Religion der Iranier* (1929); and *Middle Iranian Texts* (1956; repr. from *The Excavations at Dura-Europos, Final Report,* 7 pt. 1 (1936), 283–317). Geiger was one of the contributors to the volume of *Additamenta* to A. Kohut's *Aruch Completum* (1937), being mainly responsible for the detailed philological study of talmudic words of Iranian origin. [Ed.]

GEIGER, LAZARUS (Eliezer Solomon; 1829–1870), German philosopher and philologist. Geiger, who was born in Frankfort, was a nephew of Abraham *Geiger. He studied classical philology at the Universities of Marburg, Heidelberg, and Bonn. Unlike his uncle, he belonged to the Orthodox religious group of German Jewry. From 1861 until his death he was a teacher at the Jewish educational institute *Philanthropin in Frankfort. He saw in language the source of human reason. Language, according to Geiger, was formed from meaningless expressions—the reactions of early man to his visual impressions. These expressions became fixed and stabilized into permanent concepts. Geiger's research won a certain amount of contemporary approval, but his conclusions were rejected by subsequent scholarship. His main works are: *Ursprung und Entwicklung der menschlichen Sprache und Vernunft* (2 vols., 1868–72); *Der Ursprung der Sprache* (1864).

Bibliography: G. Peschier, *Lazarus Geiger, sein Leben und Denken* (1871); L. A. Rosenthal, *Lazarus Geiger* (Ger., 1883).

[Ed.]

GEIGER, LUDWIG (1848–1919), German literary historian; a fervent adherent of assimilation. Son of Abraham *Geiger, he studied at his father's Hochschule in Berlin and concluded his academic studies with a dissertation, presented to Leopold von Ranke, on the attitude of Greek and Roman authors to Judaism and Jews. In 1880 he was appointed professor of German literature and cultural history at Berlin University. Geiger was a versatile scholar, editor, and translator. His major contributions were to Renaissance, Humanism, and Reformation studies, German-Jewish history, and research on Goethe. Even when treating the first and last subjects he remained particularly conscious of the Jewish aspect. Appreciation of Geiger's work on the Rennaissance led the Swiss historian, Jacob Burckhardt—a notorious anti-Semite—to appoint him editor of all future editions of his *Die Cultur der Renaissance in Italien* ("Civilization of the Renaissance in Italy"). Geiger's major work in this subject was *Renaissance und Humanismus in Italien und Deutschland* (1882). He published the letters of Johann *Reuchlin (1875, 1962) and the latter's biography: *Johann Reuchlin, sein Leben und seine Werke* (1871). Founder and editor of *Zeitschrift fuer die Geschichte der Juden in Deutschland* (1887–92), he also wrote *Geschichte der Juden in Berlin* (2 vols., 1871), *Die deutsche Literatur und die Juden* (1910), and numerous articles on German Jewish history. The *Goethe Jahrbuch* was founded by him in 1880; he continued to edit it until 1913, when he had to leave in the aftermath of an acrimonious dispute. His major works on Goethe were *Goethe und die Seinen* (1908) and *Goethe, sein Leben und Schaffen* (1910); he also wrote on Goethe's relationship to Jews and Judaism. Geiger edited his father's *Nachgelassene Schriften* (5 vols., 1875–78) and other works; he also wrote a biography of his father, *Abraham Geiger, Leben und Lebenswerk* (with others, 1910).

Geiger was a vigorous exponent of liberalism and Reform Judaism and an opponent of political Zionism. In 1911, in his birthday letter to the kaiser, he courageously protested against the social discrimination to which German Jews were subjected. From 1909 he edited the leading Jewish newspaper, *Allgemeine Zeitung des Judentums.* His unpublished works include a projected edition of the correspondence of Leopold *Zunz.

Bibliography: M. Guedemann, *Ludwig Geiger als Kritiker der neuesten Geschichtsschreibung* (1889); Stern, in: AZDJ, 82 (1917), supplement. [R.K.]

GEIGER, MORITZ (1860–1937), philosopher. Moritz Geiger, a nephew of Abraham *Geiger, was born in Frankfort and became professor in Munich and Goettingen. After the rise of the Nazis in 1933 he moved to the U.S. and was professor at Vassar College. Geiger was first a disciple of Th. Lipps, then a fellow student of *Husserl, and the first to apply the objective "eidetical" method developed in Husserl's *Logische Untersuchungen* in aesthetics. Geiger did not accept the "transcendental-subjective" method that was already Husserl's main concern. Geiger saw the aesthetic values of the object as based, not on its real characteristics, but on its phenomenal ones. From this he concluded that a student of aesthetics is obliged to investigate its objects from the point of view of their phenomenal characteristics. In this way Geiger brought about a change toward the objectivity of aesthetics, which was adopted by many in the teaching of art and beauty, and became the basis for interpreting "aesthetic pleasure" in the school of phenomenalism. Other studies led Geiger to an analysis of the unconscious. He showed that the laws of psychological reality are not to be understood as laws of consciousness. Additional studies were devoted to philosophical problems of mathematics and physics, the theory of relativity and axiomatic geometry. His work on essential relations and essential meaning in aesthetics induced him to turn to metaphysics; the philosophy of ontology and the question of the division of the sciences caused him to reconsider the problem of "the ultimate existence, the unattached existing within itself," and "independent metaphysics." He wrote: *Bemerkungen zur Psychologie der Gefuelselemente und Gefuelsverbindungen* (1904); *Die philosophische Bedenkung der Relativitaetstheorie* (1921); *Systematische Axiomatik der euklidischen Geometrie* (1924); *Aesthetik* (1921); and *Die Wirklichkeit der Wissenschaften und die Metaphysik* (1930).

Bibliography: Zelker, in: *Zeitschrift fuer philosophische Forschung,* 14 (1960), 452–66. [ED.]

GEIGER, SOLOMON ZALMAN (ben Abraham, d. 1775), community notable of Frankfort on the Main. In 1738 he published a philosophic-kabbalistic homiletical commentary *Kerem Shelomo* which was at first well received. However, in 1742 the rabbis of Frankfort withdrew his right to be chosen as *gabbai,* interdicted him from serving as precentor in the Great Synagogue for nine years, and apparently made a public declaration against his book, the official reason being that Geiger had not comported himself correctly in the community meetinghouse. Geiger compiled an anthology of writings of medieval Jewish philosophers (unpublished).

Bibliography: M. Horovitz, *Frankfurter Rabbinen,* 2 (1883), 90; 3 (1884), 15, 19–21, 60; 4 (1885), 35. [J.LEV.]

°**GELASIUS I,** pope, 492–6. A council convened in Rome by Gelasius in 494 established the Catholic canon of biblical texts. On a personal level, Gelasius was not hostile to the Jews; among his favorites was a Jew, Telesinus, who won the pope's trust to the extent that in 495 Gelasius recommended Telesinus' nephew, the Jew Antius or Antonius, to the bishop Quinigesius. In 496, when the pope was apprised that the slave of a Jew had claimed that, although he had been a Christian from childhood, his Jewish master had forced him to be circumcised, Gelasius ordered the investigators to act with scrupulous justice so that religious interests should not be wronged nor the slave unfairly removed from his master's authority.

Bibliography: Vogelstein-Rieger, 127f.; B. Blumenkranz, *Auteurs chrétiens latins* (1963), 48f. [B.BL.]

GELB, IGNACE JAY (1907–), U. S. Assyriologist. Born in Tarnow, Poland, Gelb studied in Rome with the Sumerologist, Anton Deimel. He went in 1929 to the Oriental Institute at the University of Chicago, with which he remained associated. After serving in the armed forces in World War II, he returned to the Institute as professor of Assyriology in 1947 and began the reorganization and replanning of the monumental *Assyrian Dictionary of the Oriental Institute of the University of Chicago* (1956ff.; 10 vols. by 1970) a project which had been begun in 1921. He served as editor of the dictionary from 1947 to 1955. He was also the editor and chief contributor of the auxiliary project, *Materials for the Assyrian Dictionary* (from 1951). His contributions to the field of Assyriology are centered around the ethno-linguistic foundations of the Ancient Near East. Among his works on this subject are *Hurrians and Subarians* (1944); *Nuzi Personal Names* (with M. Puryes and A. A. MacRae, 1943); *La lingua degli Amoriti* (1958); "The Early History of the West Semitic Peoples" (in: *Journal of Cuneiform Studies,* 15 (1961), 27ff.). Of fundamental importance are his penetrating studies of the Old Akkadian dialect: *Sargonic Texts from the Diyala Region* (1952), *Old Akkadian Writing and Grammar* (1952, 1961^2), *Glossary of Old Akkadian* (1957), and *A Sequential Reconstruction of the Proto-Akkadian* (1969). He published a popular scientific work, *A Study of Writing* (1952, 1965^2).

Bibliography: Chicago University, Oriental Institute, *Assyrian Dictionary,* 1 (1956), introd.

[E.D.M./P.A.]

GELBER, Canadian family. Moses Gelber (1876–1940), born in Brzezany, Galicia, settled in Toronto in 1892, where he established a wool importing business. He was a founder of Jewish education in Toronto, serving as first president of the Toronto Hebrew Free School (later the Associated Hebrew Schools). A vice-president of the Zionist Organization of Canada, Gelber was among the first supporters of the project to reclaim the Sharon Valley in Palestine. His son Edward Elisha (1903–) was born in Toronto. He studied at Columbia and the Jewish Theological Seminary, and was admitted to the Ontario bar (1934) and the Palestine bar (1937). Gelber played a leading role in Jewish education in Toronto; in the Canadian Jewish Congress; and in the Zionist Organization of Canada, of which he was national president in 1950–52. In 1954 he moved to Jerusalem where he served as chairman of the executive of the Hebrew University, and vice-chairman of Yad Vashem.

Louis Gelber (1878–1968), brother of Moses, was born in Brzezany, Galicia, and in 1896 went to Canada where he was associated in business with his brother Moses. He was a founder of the Toronto Hebrew Free Loan Association. His son Lionel Morris (1907–), born in Toronto, was a writer on international affairs. Lionel Gelber was a Rhodes scholar and studied at Oxford. He wrote *Rise of Anglo-American Friendship* (1938); *Peace by Power* (1942); *Reprieve from War* (1950); *American Anarchy* (1953); and *Alliance of Necessity* (1966). He served as special assistant to Canada's prime minister John Diefenbaker during 1960–61. Louis' daughter Sylva (1910–) was born in Toronto. During 1934–37 she was a social worker in Jerusalem and became probation officer in the Magistrate's Court, appointed to the department of labor of the Palestine government in 1942. She joined the Department of National Health and Welfare in Ottawa in 1950, and in 1969 was appointed head of the women's bureau of the Canadian Department of Labor. Her brother Marvin (1912–), also born in Toronto, was a student of economics and politics. He wrote for various journals and was a Liberal member of parliament for York South (1963–65). He was national president of the United Nations Association of Canada; head of the Canadian delegation to the UN Economic and Social Council (1967); and delegate to the UN General Assembly (1968). He was closely associated with Zionist and Jewish community activity. Another brother Arthur E. (1915–), born in Toronto, was a Jewish community leader. He was president of the United Jewish Welfare Fund of Toronto and active in the United Jewish Appeal, Canadian Jewish Congress, and United Jewish Refugee Agencies. He took a leading role in settling Jewish refugees in Canada in the post-World War II period. Prominent in cultural activities in Canada, he was president of the Canadian Conference of the Arts and the National Ballet. A fourth brother Sholome Michael (1918–), born in Toronto, served in the RCAF during World War II. He then worked for the Joint Distribution Committee in postwar Europe. He served as dean of the Academy for Higher Jewish Religion in New York, then in 1966 began teaching at New York University in the department of religion. He wrote *Failure of the American Rabbi* (1961).

Bibliography: A. D. Hart (ed.), *Jew in Canada* (1926), 133, 319; *Who's Who in Canadian Jewry* (1965), 310, 387. [B.G.K.]

GELBER, NATHAN MICHAEL (1891–1966), Austrian historian and Zionist leader. Gelber was born in Lvov, Galicia. He served in World War I as an officer in the Austro-Hungarian army; thereafter he assumed the post of general secretary of the Eastern Galician delegation of the Va'ad Le'ummi in Vienna (1918–21) and, subsequently, became first secretary of the Austrian Zionist Organization (1921–30). In 1934 he immigrated to Palestine where, until his retirement in 1954, he worked in the Keren Hayesod head office in Jerusalem. His last years were devoted to Jewish scholarship, which he had pursued extensively, though not professionally, all his life.

Gelber was a prolific author who published close to 1,000 books and articles, in Hebrew, German, Yiddish, and Polish, on Jewish history and contemporary Jewish life, in addition to scores of articles on contemporary issues in daily newspapers. He was a major contributor to the *Juedisches Lexikon*, the *Encyclopaedia Judaica*, the *Encyclopaedia Hebraica*, and other encyclopedias. His most significant works deal with the history of Zionism and Galician Jewry. Among them are: *Zur Vorgeschichte des Zionismus* (1927); *Hazharat Balfour ve-Toledoteha* (1939); *Toledot ha-Tenu'ah ha-Ziyyonit be-Galizyah, 1875–1918* (2 vols., 1958); *Aktenstuecke zur Judenfrage am Wiener Kongress 1814–1815* (1920); *Die Juden und der polnische Aufstand* (1923); a volume on Brody (vol. 6 of *Arim ve-Immahot be-Yisrael*, 1955); and "Toledot Yehudei Lvov" (in EG, 4 (1956), 22–390).

Bibliography: H. Gold, in: *Sefer ha-Yovel le-Nathan Michael Gelber* (1963), 235–64. [M.A.M.]

GELBHAUS, SIGMUND (Joshua Samuel; c. 1850–1928), East European rabbi and writer. Gelbhaus was born in Tysmienica (Galicia) and served as rabbi in Karlovac (Karlstadt, Croatia), Nordhausen (Germany), Prague, and Vienna. In Vienna he also lectured at the Israelitisch-Theologische Lehranstalt and at the Hebrew Paedagogium. A prolific writer, he published numerous articles, books, and translations into Hebrew. Among them are *Rabbi Jehuda Hanassi und die Redaktion der Mischna* (1876); *Die Mittelhochdeutsche Dichtung in ihrer Beziehung zur biblisch-rabbinischen Literatur* (3 vols., 1889–93); *Esra und seine reformatorischen Bestrebungen* (1903); *Religioese Stroemungen in Judaea waehrend und nach der Zeit des babylonischen Exils* (1912); and *Die Metaphysik der Ethik Spinozas im Quellenlichte der Kabbala* (1917).

Bibliography: Wininger, Biog, 2 (1928), 399; 6 (1931), 614. [Ed.]

GELDERN, SIMON VON (1720–1788), German adventurer and traveler. Von Geldern, who was born in Duesseldorf into a family of Court Jews (see Van *Geldern), studied at yeshivot, and also acquired a secular education. He went wandering through many countries and eventually reached Palestine where he spent six months studying the Kabbalah in Safed. Armed with letters of recommendation from Safed scholars headed with the words *Kitvei Kodesh u-Melizot Hakhamei Yisrael* (printed in Amsterdam, c. 1759) and with contributions from public and private charity chests, he set off on another journey, calling himself "an emissary from the Holy Land." Von Geldern engaged in the book trade, mainly selling copies of the *Zohar. Assuming the title of "Chevalier von Geldern" and posing as an oriental sage, he led a life of adventure, gambling, and the pursuit of amorous affairs in Christian society and among royalty. His grandnephew, Heinrich *Heine, speaks admiringly of his exploits in North Africa. Von Geldern was the first person to mention the Cairo *Genizah.* He made an English adaptation, entitled *The Israelites on Mount Horeb* (1773), of a French oratorio by the Abbé de Voisinon, which in its turn was based on the Italian original by a fellow adventurer, Giacomo Casanova. Von Geldern also published a Hebrew version of the Book of Judith. He spent the last ten years of his life in the service of the grand duke of Hesse-Darmstadt. He provided Abbé *Gregoire with the material for his *Essai sur la regénération physique, morale et politique des Juifs*

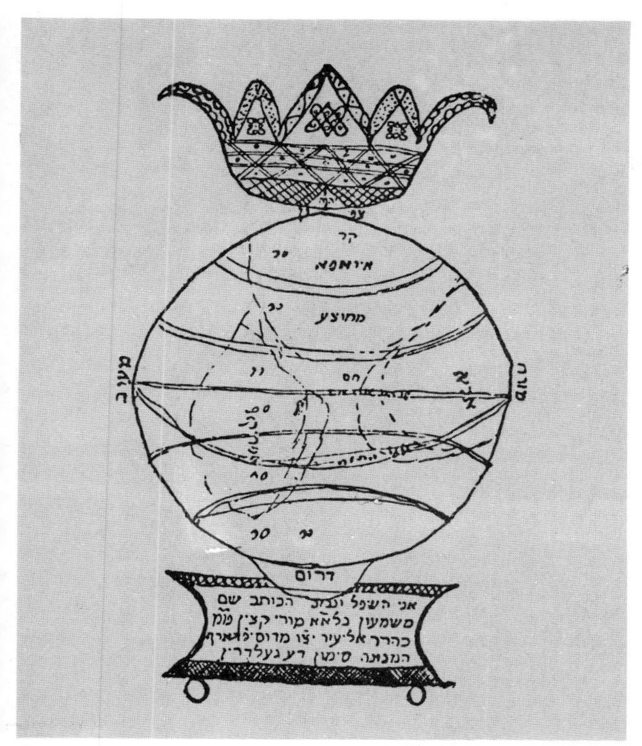

Drawing of the globe from Simon von Geldern's travel diary. Formerly in the possession of the Berlin Jewish Community.

(1789). Von Geldern's travel diaries (facsimile of Ms. (original probably lost) in Schocken Library, Jerusalem) and his personal papers, including a family tree, have survived.

Bibliography: F. Heymann, *Der Chevalier von Geldern* (1963[2]); Brilling, in: BLBI, 8 (1965), 315ff; D. Kaufmann, *Aus Heinrich Heines Ahnensaal* (1896); *Archiv fuer juedische Familienforschung*, 1 nos. 2–3 (1913), 18ff., nos. 4–6, 32ff; Loewenstein, in: MGWJ, 51 (1907), 205ff.; idem, in: JJLG, 10 (1912), 121; Yaari, Sheluḥei, 180, 446ff.

[Ed.]

GELDERN, VAN, Duesseldorf family of *Court Jews. The prefix in the surname indicates the family's origin from the Dutch province or from the village near Duesseldorf where Joseph Jacob (Juspa) van Geldern (1653–1727) established himself as supplier and banker to the elector of Hanover, who had made Duesseldorf his capital. Juspa maintained business connections with Leffmann *Behrends and his daughter married the son of Jost *Liebmann. He built a synagogue for the community, of which he was *Obervorgaenger* ("chief representative") for more than 30 years; he paid one tenth of the community's dues. His son, Lazarus (d. 1769), inherited the office in the community and became Court Jew of *Juelich and *Berg, but lost most of the immense family fortune in lawsuits. Lazarus' son, Gottschalk, was a prosperous physician whose daughter Betty married Samson Heine, descendant of the Schaumburg-*Lippe family of Court Jews. Their son Heinrich Heine, the poet, immortalized his great-uncle, the adventurer Simon van *Geldern, Lazarus' other son.

Bibliography: D. Kaufmann, *Aus Heinrich Heine's Ahnensaal* (1896); G. Wilhelm (ed.), *Heine Bibliographie* (1960[2]), 44f.; S. Stern, *The Court Jew* (1950), index; H. Bieber and M. Hadas, *Heinrich Heine, A Biographical Anthology* (1956), 38–40.

[Ed.]

GELERTER, LUDWIG LITMAN (1873–1945), physician; one of the pioneers of the general and Jewish socialist movements in Rumania. In 1895 he was among the founders in Jassy of *Lumina, the first Jewish socialist society in Rumania, and signed the memorandum of the society to the London Congress of the Second International (1896). A notable speaker, organizer, and writer, Gelerter continued to uphold his views during the disintegration of the movement and assisted in the reorganization of the Jewish socialist society in Jassy in 1915 and in publication of a weekly, *Der Veker*. After World War I he moved to Bucharest. Although Gelerter held similar views to those of the Bund, he did not join that movement. He established the Socialist Workers' Party of Rumania (1929) which was affiliated to the Fourth International but rejoined the Social Democratic Party of Rumania on the eve of World War II. Gelerter headed the Jewish hospital of Bucharest and helped to promote popular Jewish cooperative credit banks. While not a Zionist, he was sympathetic toward pioneering enterprises in Palestine, especially cooperatives and kibbutzim. Rumanian immigrants named a New York branch of the Workmen's Circle after him.

Bibliography: LNYL, 2 (1958), 310.

[M.M.]

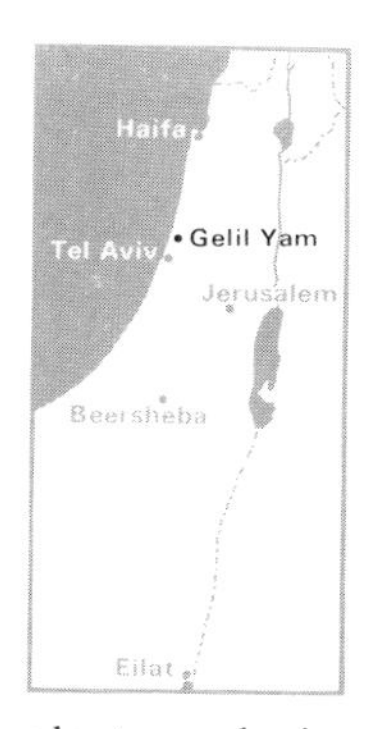

GELIL YAM (Heb. גְּלִיל יָם), kibbutz in central Israel near Herzliyyah, affiliated with Ha-Kibbutz ha-Me'uḥad. It was founded in 1943 by a group which had maintained a transitory camp near Tel Aviv for over a decade, while working as hired laborers in the Tel Aviv port and on the railways. The founding settlers from Russia and Poland were later joined by immigrants from different countries. Its economy was based on intensive farm branches, a weaving and sewing plant, a plant producing water meters, and a metal factory. Gelil Yam's name is based on the Arabic denomination of the site, Jalīl. In 1968 its population was 310.

[E.O.]

GELLÉRI, ANDOR ENDRE (1907–1945), Hungarian novelist. Gelléri, who was born in Budapest, worked as a dyer and as a locksmith. His literary talents were first discovered in a short-story competition run by the evening newspaper *Az Est*. His prize enabled him to complete his education in Germany. Gelléri's first novel, *Nagymosoda* ("The Laundry," 1931), combined reality with dreams and visions. His characters were wretched slum dwellers, some of them Jews. His other works include *Szomjas inasok* ("Thirsty Apprentices," 1933); a book of short stories, *Hold utca* ("Hold Street," 1934); *Kikötö* ("The Harbor," 1935); and *Villám és esti tüz* ("Lightning and Evening Fire," 1940). Following the Nazi occupation of Hungary he was sent to the Mauthausen concentration camp at the end of 1944 and died at the Wells camp in Germany, a victim of typhus, two days after the liberation in May 1945. Gelléri's autobiography, *Egy önérzet története* ("The Story of One Man's Self-Respect"), appeared posthumously in 1957.

Bibliography: M. Szabolcsi (ed.), *A magyar irodalom története*, 6 (1964), 757–66; *Magyar Irodalmi Lexikon*, 1 (1963), 390–1.

[B.Y.]

GELLMAN, LEON (1887–), U. S. Zionist journalist and leader. Gellman, who was born in Yampol, Russia, went to the U. S. at the age of 23. He settled in St. Louis where he worked as a principal of various Hebrew schools (1911–17), and later as editor (1918–35) and publisher (1923–35) of the Yiddish *St. Louis Jewish Record*, in which he advocated the creation of a great religious Zionist movement. An organizer of the U. S. Mizrachi movement, he subsequently served as its executive secretary (1914–17), national vice-president (1930–35), and president (1935–39). Moving to New York, he was editor of Mizrachi publications from 1935 to 1949, including *Der Mizrachi Weg* (1936–49) and (with Pinkhos Churgin) the *Mizrachi Jubilee Publication* (1936).

Gellman moved to Israel in 1949 and became chairman of the World Mizrachi Organization in that year, later becoming honorary chairman. From 1948 to 1953 he was a deputy member of the Executive of the Jewish Agency. He was a frequent contributor to *Ha-Ẓofeh*, the Israel national religious daily, and to New York Yiddish newspapers. A prevalent theme in Gellman's writing is that the survival of Israel is contingent upon adherence to traditional Jewish faith and values. Among his numerous books, primarily collections of essays, are: *Eynem Kampf far der Yidishe Medine* (1948), *Ha-Yahadut be-Ma'avakah* (1956), *Neẓaḥ ha-Ummah* (1958), *Bi-Shevilei ha-Yahadut* (1967), and *Be-Darkhei No'am* (1969). [ED.]

GELL-MANN, MURRAY (1929–), U.S. physicist and Nobel laureate, especially noted for his work in the theory of elementary particles of matter. Gell-Mann, who was born in New York City, joined the Institute for Advanced Study at Princeton in 1951 and Chicago University's Institute of Nuclear Studies in 1952, becoming an associate professor in 1954. In 1955 he moved to the California Institute of Technology, and was appointed professor of physics the following year.

A baffling phenomenon of modern physics is the multiplicity of subatomic particles described as "elementary." Physicists have searched for relationships to classify the particles, in a theoretical structure comparable with Mendeleyev's periodic table. A great advance was made in 1961 when Gell-Mann announced his "Eightfold Way" system of classification. The theory was advanced independently in the same year by Yuval *Ne'eman of Tel Aviv. When the known particles were arranged according to this scheme, one particle required by the theory—Omega Minus—was missing. It was discovered in January 1964 at the Brookhaven National Laboratory, confirmation of the theory that could mark a turning point in particle physics. It was in 1964 that Gell-Mann and Ne'eman published their book, *The Eightfold Way*. Gell-Man received the Nobel Prize for Physics in 1969 for his research into the behavior of the subatomic particles. He called these mysterious new particles "quarks"—a name taken from James *Joyce's *Finnegans Wake*.

Bibliography: McGraw-Hill, *Modern Men of Science* (1966), 188–90. [M.GOL.]

GELLNER, FRANTIŠEK (1881–1914), Czech poet and cartoonist, and the outstanding Czechoslovak satirist of his time. Born in Mlada Boleslav into a poor family, Gellner studied painting first in Munich and then in Paris, where he published his early cartoons in *Rire, Cri de Paris,* and other French periodicals. He soon found, however, that he could express his anarchist creed better through the medium of verse, and his three books of poetry, modeled on the style of François Villon, contain some of the best satirical verse ever written in Czech. They are: *Po nás at přijde potopa* ("After us the Deluge," 1901), *Radosti života* ("Pleasures of Life," 1903), and *Nové verše* ("New Poems," 1919). In 1911 he joined the leading Czech newspaper *Lidové Noviny,* as a cartoonist and feature editor, and then began writing prose. *Cesta do hor a jiné povídky* ("Trip to the Mountains and Other Stories") appeared in 1914 and *Povídky a satiry* ("Stories and Satires," 1920) after his death. Because in many of his articles and short stories Gellner did not hesitate to subject Jewish weaknesses to the merciless lash of his satire, he has been criticized as an anti-Jewish writer. He disappeared while serving on the Russian front early in World War I. New editions of his works appeared in 1952 and 1964.

Bibliography: F. Gellner, *Spisy,* 3 (1928), postscript by M. Hýsek; P. Váša and A. Gregor, *Katechismus dějin české literatury* (1925); O. Donath, *Židé a Židovství v české literatuře 19. a 20. století,* 2 (1930), index. [AV.D.]

GELMAN, MANUEL (1910–), Australian educator. Born in London, Gelman was taken to Australia as an infant. From 1946 to 1964 he was a lecturer in methods of modern languages at Melbourne University's Faculty of Education. From 1950 he headed the department of languages at the Secondary Teachers' College. From 1961 to 1964 Gelman was president of the Modern Languages Teachers' Associations of Victoria and founded the Australian Federation of Modern Language Teachers' Associations. His activities within the Jewish community included membership of the Board of Governors of Mount Scopus College, Melbourne (1959–61) and chairmanship of its Education Committee. [H.FR.]

GELNHAUSEN, town in W. Germany. The Gelnhausen Jews paid their annual tax to the imperial treasury jointly with the Frankfort community in 1241. In 1347 Emperor Louis IV offered the revenues from Gelnhausen Jewry as security on a loan. The community was annihilated during the *Black Death persecutions (1349) and the burghers were released from their debts to the Jews. By 1360 Jews had again settled in the town. In the late 17th century they were active as moneylenders, despite restrictions and threats of expulsion. A burial society was founded in 1711 and in 1734 the synagogue was rebuilt. The community then numbered 33 families. It remained approximately the same size in the 19th century (some 200 persons) and until the Nazi advent to power. The last Jew left Gelnhausen on Oct. 1, 1938. After World War II several Jews returned to the region but no organized community was formed. They numbered 27 in 1960.

Bibliography: Roth, in: ZGJO, 5 (1892), 188; *Aus Alter und Neuer Zeit* (June 25, 1925); Germ Jud, 2 (1968), 273–5; FJW, 187; Yad Vashem Archives; PKG. [ED.]

GELSENKIRCHEN, city in North Rhine-Westphalia, W. Germany. A community was established there in 1874 and a synagogue built in 1885. There were 120 Jews living in Gelsenkirchen in 1880; 1,171 in 1905; and 1,400 in 1933. The community maintained an elementary school which in 1906 had 121 pupils. Max *Eschelbacher officiated as rabbi before World War II. In Gelsenkirchen, as in most Westphalian congregations, Reform Judaism was dominant but an Orthodox congregation was established with its own synagogue and institutions. For some time from 1922 the rabbi of the Association for the Safeguarding of Traditional Judaism in Westphalia (founded 1896) had his seat in Gelsenkirchen. Under the Nazi regime most of the Jews left. The synagogue was destroyed in the *Kristallnacht,* Nov. 9, 1938. By June 17, 1939, only 720 Jews remained. On Sept. 9, 1939, the men were deported to the *Sachsenhausen concentration camp. Their families followed in 1942. There were again 69 Jews in Gelsenkirchen in 1946. In 1958, a synagogue and communal center was built for the newly established *Kultusgemeinde.* The community numbered 110 in 1967—mostly new residents—and had its own cantor and teacher.

Bibliography: *Festschrift der Synagogen-Gemeinde Gelsenkirchen* . . . (1924); H. C. Meyer (ed.), *Aus Geschichte und Leben der Juden in Westfalen* (1962), 63–66, 162–3, 188, incl. bibl.; PKG. [ED.]

GEMARA (Aram. גְּמָרָא; lit. "completion" or "tradition"), a word popularly applied to the Talmud as a whole, or more particularly to the discussions and elaborations by the *amoraim* on the Mishnah. The word appears (abbreviated) in the printed editions of the Babylonian Talmud to indicate the beginning of that discussion and it has been adopted in the Vilna (Romm) edition of the Jerusalem Talmud. There is a *Gemara* to both the Babylonian and the Jerusalem Talmuds, though not to all or to the same tractates.

For a fuller discussion of the precise meaning of the word see *Talmud. [ED.]

GEMARIAH (Heb. גְּמַרְיָה, גְּמַרְיָהוּ; "Yahu has accomplished"), two biblical figures. (1) Gemariah son of Hilkiah was one of Zedekiah's emissaries to Nebuchadnezzar, who brought the letter written by Jeremiah to the elders in exile (Jer. 29:3). (2) Gemariah son of Shaphan was a high official in the time of Jehoiakim (Jer. 36:10). He was a member of one of the influential pro-Babylonian families in the last days of Judah (see *Shaphan), and was also one of the royal officers on friendly terms with Jeremiah. Baruch read Jeremiah's scroll in Gemariah's chamber (Jer. 36:10–12). The latter's son Micaiah reported this to Jehoiakim, who ordered the scroll destroyed after it was read to him. Gemariah was among the officials who tried to dissuade him. The mention of Gemariah's chamber in the Temple is interesting, yet the reason for his having one is not entirely clear. Such chambers were commonly intended for priests and levites (Neh. 10:38–39; 13:4–9; I Chron. 9:26, 33) and also for high officials of the king (II Kings 23:11; Jer. 35:4), but the purpose of these chambers is unknown (cf. I Sam. 9:22; Neh. 13:4–9).

The name Gemariahu son of Hizziliahu occurs on the *Lachish Ostraca.

Bibliography: Yeivin, in: *Tarbiz*, 12 (1940–41), 255, 257–8. [ED.]

GEMATRIA (From Gr. γεωμετρία), one of the aggadic hermeneutical rules for interpreting the Torah (*Baraita of 32 Rules, no. 29). It consists of explaining a word or group of words according to the numerical value of the letters, or of substituting other letters of the alphabet for them in accordance with a set system. Whereas the word is normally employed in this sense of manipulating according to the numerical value, it is sometimes found with the meaning of "calculations" (Avot 3:18). Similarly where the reading in present editions of the Talmud is that Johanan b. Zakkai knew "the heavenly revolutions and *gematriot*," in a parallel source the reading is "the heavenly revolutions and calculations" (Suk. 28a; BB 134a; Ch. Albeck, *Shishah Sidrei Mishnah*, 4 (1959), 497).

The use of letters to signify numbers was known to the Babylonians and the Greeks. The first use of *gematria* occurs in an inscription of Sargon II (727–707 B.C.E.) which states that the king built the wall of Khorsabad 16,283 cubits long to correspond with the numerical value of his name. The use of *gematria* (τὸ ἰσόψηφον) was widespread in the literature of the Magi and among interpreters of dreams in the Hellenistic world. The *Gnostics equated the two holy names Abraxas (Ἀβράξας) and Mithras (Μίθρας) on the basis of the equivalent numerical value of their letters (365, corresponding to the days of the solar year). Its use was apparently introduced in Israel during the time of the Second Temple, even in the Temple itself, Greek letters being used to indicate numbers (Shek. 3:2).

In rabbinic literature numerical *gematria* first appears in statements by *tannaim* of the second century. It is used as supporting evidence and as a mnemonic by R. Nathan. He states that the phrase *Elleh ha-devarim* ("These are the words") occuring in Exodus 35:1 hints at the 39 categories of work forbidden on the Sabbath, since the plural *devarim* indicates two, the additional article a third, while the numerical equivalent of *elleh* is 36, making a total of 39 (Shab. 70a). R. Judah inferred from the verse, "From the fowl of the heavens until the beast are fled and gone" (Jer. 9:9), that for 52 years no traveler passed through Judea, since the numerical value of *behemah* ("beast") is 52. The Baraita of 32 Rules cites as an example of *gematria* the interpretation that the 318 men referred to in Genesis 14:14 were in fact only Eliezer the servant of Abraham, the numerical value of his name being 318. This interpretation, which occurs elsewhere (Ned. 32a; Gen. R. 43:2) in the name of *Bar Kappara, may also be a reply to the Christian interpretation in the Epistle of Barnabas that wishes to find in the Greek letters τιη, whose numerical value is 318, a reference to the cross and to the first two letters of Jesus' name, through which Abraham achieved his victory; the Jewish homilist used the same method to refute the Christian interpretation.

The form of *gematria* which consists of changing the letters of the alphabet according to *atbash*, i.e., the last letter ת is substituted for the first א, the penultimate ש for the second ב, etc., already occurs in Scripture: Sheshach (Jer. 25:26; 51:41) corresponding to Bavel ("Babylon"). The Baraita of 32 Rules draws attention to a second example: *lev kamai* (Jer. 51:1) being identical, according to this system, with *Kasdim ("Chaldeans"). Another alphabet *gematria* is formed by the *atbaḥ* system, i.e., ט is substituted for א, ח for ב, etc., and is called "the alphabet of Ḥiyya" (Suk. 52b).

Title page of *Megalleh Amukot*, a work utilizing *gematria*, by Nathan Nata b. Solomon Spiro, Lemberg, 1795. Jerusalem, J.N.U.L.

Rav, the pupil of Ḥiyya, explained that Belshazzar and his men could not read the cryptic writing because it was written in *gematria*, i.e., according to *atbaḥ* (Sanh. 22a; cf. Shab. 104a).

Gematria has little significance in *halakhah*. Where it does occur, it is only as a hint or a mnemonic. The rule that when a man takes a nazirite vow for an unspecified period, it is regarded as being for 30 days, is derived from the word *yihyeh* ("he shall be") in Numbers 6:5, whose numerical value is 30 (Naz. 5a). Even in the *aggadah*, at least among the early *amoraim*, *gematria* is not used as a source of ideas and homilies but merely to express them in the most concise manner. The statements that Noah was delivered not for his own sake but for the sake of Moses (Gen. R. 26:6), that Rebekah was worthy to have given birth to 12 tribes (*ibid.* 63:6), and that Jacob's ladder symbolizes the revelation at Sinai (*ibid.* 68:12), do not depend on the *gematriot* given there. These homilies are derived from other considerations and it is certain that they preceded the *gematriot*.

Gematriot, however, do occupy an important place in those Midrashim whose chief purpose is the interpretation of letters, such as the *Midrash Ḥaserot vi-Yterot*, and also in the late aggadic Midrashim (particularly in those whose authors made use of the work of *Moses b. Isaac ha-Darshan) such as *Numbers Rabbah* (in *Midrash Aggadah*, published by S. Buber, 1894), and *Bereshit Rabbati* (published by Ḥ. Albeck, 1940; see introduction, 11–20). Rashi also cites *gematriot* that "were established by Moses ha-Darshan" (Num. 7:18) and some of the *gematriot* given by him came from this source even if he does not explicitly mention it (Gen. 32:5, e.g., "I have sojourned with Laban"—the *gematria* value of "I have sojourned" is 613, i.e., "I sojourned with the wicked Laban but observed the 613 precepts," is the interpretation of Moses ha-Darshan, *Bereshit Rabbati*, 145). Joseph *Bekhor Shor, one of the great French exegetes of the Torah, made extensive use of *gematriot*, and nearly all the tosafists followed him in this respect in their Torah commentaries (S. Poznański, *Mavo al Ḥakhmei Ẓarefat Mefareshei ha-Mikra*, 73). A wealth of *gematriot* occur in *Pa'ne'aḥ Raza*, the commentary of *Isaac b. Judah ha-Levi (end of 13th century), and in the *Ba'al ha-Turim*, the biblical commentary of *Jacob b. Asher. The Kabbalah of the *Ḥasidei Ashkenaz also caused *gematriot* to enter the *halakhah*. In his *Ha-Roke'aḥ*, *Eleazar of Worms uses *gematriot* to find many hints and supports for existing laws and customs; with him the *gematria* at times embraces whole sentences. Thus he establishes by *gematria* from Exodus 23:15 that work which can be deferred until after the festival may not be performed during the intermediate days (*Ha-Roke'aḥ*, no 307). *Gematriot* of the Ḥasidei Ashkenaz occupy a prominent place in their commentaries on the liturgy and on *piyyutim*. Abraham b. Azriel incorporated the teachings of Judah he-Ḥasid and Eleazar Roke'aḥ in his *Arugat ha-Bosem*, and followed their lead. These *gematriot*, which were part of the Kabbalah of the Ḥasidei Ashkenaz, established the definitive text of the prayers, which came to be regarded as sacrosanct. Some authorities forbade it to be changed even when the text did not conform with the rules of grammar. *Naḥmanides, on the other hand, tried to limit the arbitrary use of *gematriot* and laid down a rule that "no one may calculate a *gematria* in order to deduce from it something that occurs to him. Our rabbis, the holy sages of the Talmud, had a tradition that definite *gematriot* were transmitted to Moses to serve as a mnemonic for something that had been handed down orally with the rest of the Oral Law . . . just as was the case with the *gezerah shavah* [see *Hermeneutics] of which they said that no man may establish a *gezerah shavah* of his own accord" (*Sefer ha-Ge'ullah* ed. by J. M. Aronson (1959), *Sha'ar* 4; see his commentary to Deut. 4:25). [EH]

In Kabbalah. The use of *gematria* was developed especially by the Ḥasidei Ashkenaz and circles close to them in the 12th and 13th centuries. It is possible that traditions of *gematriot* of Holy Names and angels are from an earlier date, but they were collected and considerably elaborated only in the aforesaid period. Even among the mystics *gematria* is not generally a system for the discovery of new thoughts: almost always the idea precedes the inventing of the *gematria*, which serves as "an allusion **asmakhta*." An exception is the *gematria* on the Holy Names, which are in themselves incomprehensible, or that on the names of angels whose meaning and special aspect the German Ḥasidim sought to determine via *gematria*. Often *gematria* served as a mnemonic device. The classic works of *gematria* in this circle are the writings of *Eleazar of Worms, whose *gematriot* are based—at any rate partially—on the tradition of his teachers. Eleazar discovered through *gematria* the mystical meditations on prayers which can be evoked during the actual repetition of the words. His commentaries on books of the Bible are based for the most part on this system, including some which connect the midrashic legends with words of the biblical verses via *gematria*, and some which reveal the mysteries of the world of the *Merkabah ("fiery chariot") and the angels, in this way. In this interpretation the *gematria* of entire biblical verses or parts of verses occupies a more outstanding place than the *gematria* based on a count of single words. For example, the numerical value of the sum of the letters of the entire verse "I have gone down into the nut garden" (Songs 6:11), in *gematria* is equivalent to the verse: "This is the depth of the chariot" *(merkavah)*. Several extensive works of interpretation by means of *gematria* by the disciples of Eleazar of Worms are preserved in manuscript.

In the beginnings of Sephardi Kabbalah *gematria* occupied a very limited place. The disciples of *Abraham b. Isaac of Narbonne and the kabbalists of Gerona hardly used it and its impact was not considerable on the greater part of the Zohar and on the Hebrew writings of *Moses b. Shem Tov de Leon. Only those currents influenced by the tradition of the Ḥasidei Ashkenaz brought the *gematria* into the kabbalistic literature of the second half of the 13th century, mainly in the work of *Jacob b. Jacob ha-Kohen and Abraham *Abulafia and their disciples. The works of Abulafia are based on the extensive and extreme use of *gematria*. His books require deciphering before all the associations of the *gematriot* in them can be understood. He recommended the system of developing power of association in *gematria* in order to discover new truths, and these methods were developed by those who succeeded him. A summary of his system is found in *Sullam ha-Aliyyah* by Judah *Albotini, who lived a generation after the Spanish expulsion (*Kirjath Sefer*, 22 (1945–46), 161–71). A disciple of Abulafia, Joseph *Gikatilla, used *gematria* extensively as one of the foundations of the Kabbalah in *Ginnat Egoz* (Hanau, 1615; the letters *gimmel, nun, tav* of *Ginnat* are the initials of *gematria notarikon*, and *temurah*—the interchange of letters according to certain systematic rules). This work influenced considerably the later Zohar literature, *Ra'aya Meheimna* and *Tikkunei Zohar*.

Two schools emerged as the Kabbalah developed: one of those who favored *gematria*, and another of those who used it less frequently. In general, it may be stated that new ideas always developed outside the realm of *gematria;* however, there were always scholars who found proofs and wide-ranging connections through *gematria*, and undoubtedly attributed to their findings a positive value higher than that of a mere allusion. Moses *Cordovero presented his entire system without recourse to *gematria,* and explained matters of *gematria* only toward the end of his basic work on Kabbalah *(Pardes Rimmonim).* A revival of the use of *gematria* is found in the Lurianic Kabbalah, but it is more widespread in the kabbalistic works of Israel *Sarug and his disciples (mainly Menahem Azariah of *Fano and Naphtali *Bacharach, author of *Emek ha-Melekh*) than in the works of Isaac *Luria and Ḥayyim *Vital. The classic work using *gematria* as a means of thought and a development of commentative ideas in the Kabbalah in the 17th century is *Megalleh Amukot* by Nathan Nata b. Solomon Spira, which served as the model for an entire literature, especially in Poland. At first only the part on Deut. 3:23ff. was published (Cracow, 1637) which explains these passages in 252 different ways. His commentary on the whole Torah (also called *Megalleh Amukot*) was published in Lemberg in 1795. Apparently Nathan possessed a highly developed sense for numbers which found its expression in complex structures of *gematria.* In later kabbalistic literature (in the 18th and 19th centuries) the importance of the methods of commentary via *gematria* is well-known and many works were written whose major content is *gematria,* e.g., *Tiferet Yisrael* by Israel Ḥarif of Satanov (Lemberg, 1865), *Berit Kehunnat Olam* by Isaac Eisik ha-Kohen (Lemberg, 1796; complete edition with commentary of *gematria,* 1950), and all the works of Abraham b. Jehiel Michal ha-Kohen of Lask (late 18th century).

In the Shabbatean movement, *gematriot* occupied a place of considerable prominence as proofs of the messianism of *Shabbetai Ẓevi. Abraham *Yakhini wrote a great work of Shabbatean *gematriot* on one single verse of the Torah (*Vavei ha-Ammudim,* Ms. Oxford), and the major work of the Shabbatean prophet Heshel *Zoref of Vilna and Cracow, *Sefer ha-Ẓoref,* is based entirely on an elaboration of *gematriot* surrounding the verse *Shema Yisrael* ("Hear O Israel"; Deut. 6:4). In ḥasidic literature *gematria* appeared at first only as a by-product, but later there were several ḥasidic rabbis, the bulk of whose works are *gematria,* e.g., *Igra de-Khallah* by Ẓevi Elimelekh Shapira of *Dynow (1868), *Magen Avraham* by Abraham the Maggid of Turisk (1886), and *Sefer Imrei No'am* by Meir Horowitz of Dzikow (1877).

The systems of *gematria* became complicated in the course of time. In addition to the numerical value of a word, different methods of *gematria* were used. In Ms. Oxford 1,822, one article lists 75 different forms of *gematriot.* Moses Cordovero (*Pardes Rimmonim,* part 30, ch. 8) lists nine different types of *gematriot.* The important ones are:

(1) The numerical value of one word (equaling the sum of the numerical value of all its letters) is equal to that of another word (e.g., גבורה *(gevurah)*=216= אריה *(aryeh)*).

(2) A small or round number which does not take into account tens or hundreds (4 = ת ; 2 = כ).

(3) The squared number in which the letters of the word are calculated according to their numerical value squared. The Tetragrammaton, יהו״ה $= 10^2+5^2+6^2+5^2 = 186 =$ מקום ("Place"), another name for God.

(4) The adding up of the value of all of the preceding letters in an arithmetical series (ד*(dalet)*$=1+2+3+4=10$). This type of calculation is important in complicated *gematria* that reaches into the thousands.

(5) The "filling" (Heb. *millui*); the numerical value of each letter itself is not calculated but the numerical values of all the letters that make up the names of the letter are calculated (בי״ת =412; דל״ת =434; יו״ד =20). The letters ה and ו have different "fillings"—הו, הה, הא and וו, ואו, ויו; *millui de-alefin* (*alef* "filling"), *millui de-he'in* ("*he* filling"), or *millui de-yudin* (*yod* "filling"), respectively. These are important in Kabbalah with regard to the numerical value of the Name of God (יהו״ה), the Tetragrammaton, which varies according to the four different "fillings" יוד, הא, ואו, הא (= 45, in *gematria* אָדָם (Adam), symbolizing the 45-letter Name of God); יוד, הה, וו, הה (= 52, in *gematria* ב״ן, representing the Holy Name of 52 letters); יוד, הי, ואו, הי (= 63, in *gematria* ס״ג, the 63-letter Name); יוד, הי, ויו, ה׳ (= 72, in *gematria* ע״ב, representing the Holy Name of 72 letters).

Other calculations in *gematria* involve a "filling" of the "filling," or a second "filling." The *gematria* of the word itself is called *ikkar* or *shoresh,* while the rest of the word (the "fillings") is called the *ne'elam* ("hidden part"). The *ne'elam* of the letter י is וד = 10; the *ne'elam* of שד״י is ין, לת and וד = 500.

(6) There is also a "great number" which counts the final letters of the alphabet as a continuation of the alphabet (500 = ם ; 600 = ן; 700 = ץ ; 800 = ף ; 900 = ך ; etc.). However, there is a calculation according to the usual order of the alphabet whereby the numerical values of the final letters are as follows: ך = 500, ם = 600, ן = 700, etc.

(7) The addition of the number of letters in the word to the numerical value of the word itself, or the addition of the number "one" to the total numerical value of the word.

Criticism of the use of *gematria* as a justified means of commentary was first voiced by Abraham *ibn Ezra (in his commentary on Gen. 14:14) and later by the opponents of the Kabbalah (in *Ari Nohem,* ch. 10). But even several kabbalists (e.g., *Naḥmanides) warned against exaggerated use of *gematria.* Joseph Solomon *Delmedigo speaks of false *gematriot* in order to abolish the value of that system. When the believers in Shabbetai Ẓevi began to widely apply *gematriot* to his name (*shaddai* (God) and its "filling" = 814), those who denied him used mock *gematriot* (*ru'aḥ sheker* = ("false spirit") = 814). In spite of this, the use of *gematria* was widespread in many circles and among preachers not only in Poland but also among the Sephardim. To this day the homiletical and allegorical literature according to the method of **Pardes* (the four levels of meaning of a text), expecially of the North African rabbis, is full of *gematria.* [G.Sch.]

Bibliography: W. Bacher, *Exegetische Terminologie . . .,* 1 (1899), 125–8; 2 (1905), 124; F. Dornseiff, *Das Alphabet in Mystik und Magie* (1925²), 91–118; A. Berliner, *Ketavim Nivḥarim,* 1 (1945), 34–37; S. Lieberman, *Hellenism in Jewish Palestine* (1950), 69–74; H. Waton, *Key to the Bible* (1952); T. Wechsler, *Ẓefunot be-Masoret Yisrael* (1968); Scholem, Mysticism, index; S. A. Horodetzky, in: EJ, 7 (1931), 170–9.

GEMEN, town in Westphalia, W. Germany. Jews are known to have lived there from the mid-16th century. After 1771 they came under the jurisdiction of the rabbi of *Muenster. The community numbered 28 persons in 1809; 49 in 1911; and 52 in 1933. The synagogue (erected in 1912) was destroyed in November 1938, and shortly afterward the congregation ceased to exist.

Bibliography: E. Loewenstein, *Aus Vergangenheit und Gegenwart der israelitischen Gemeinde Gemen* (1912); PKG. [Ed.]

GEMILUT ḤASADIM (Heb. גְּמִילוּת חֲסָדִים; lit., "the bestowal of lovingkindness"), the most comprehensive and fundamental of all Jewish social virtues, which encompasses the whole range of the duties of sympathetic consideration toward one's fellow man. The earliest individual rabbinic statement in the Talmud, the maxim of *Simeon the Just, mentions it as one of the three pillars of Judaism ("Torah, the Temple service, and *gemilut ḥasadim*) upon which the [continued] existence of the world depends" (Avot 1:2).

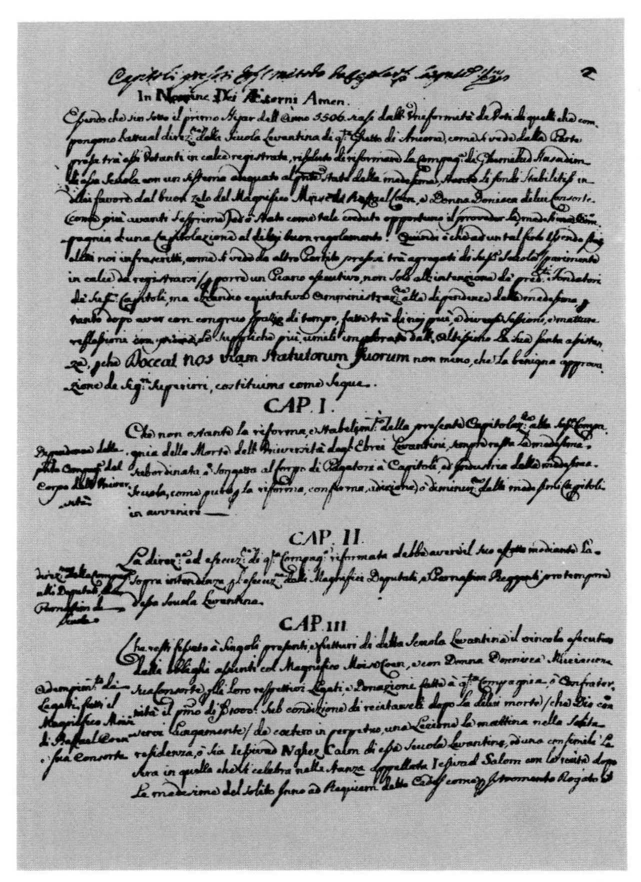
In Nomine Dei Aeterni Amen.

CAP. I.

CAP. II.

CAP. III

Figure 1. New regulations of the *Gemilut Ḥasadim* society of the Scuola Levantina of Ancona, Italy, 1746, drawn up upon the bequest of 1,000 scudi by Moses Raphael Coen on condition that special prayers be recited for him daily. Jerusalem, C.A.H.J.P.

The first Mishnah of *Pe'ah* enumerates it both among the things "which have no fixed measure" and among those that "man enjoys the fruits thereof in this world, while the stock remains for him in the world to come," i.e., its practice affords satisfaction in this world while it is accounted a virtue for him on the Day of Judgment. This, incidentally, is an exception to the general rule that pleasure in this world is at the expense of one's spiritual assets. With regard to the former, the Jerusalem Talmud (Pe'ah 1:1, 15b) differentiates between *gemilut ḥasadim* expressed in personal service ("with his body") and with one's material goods. It maintains that only the former is unlimited in its scope, whereas the latter is limited by the general rule that one should not "squander" more than a fifth of one's possessions on good works. With regard to the latter, the text of the Mishnah mentions only "honoring one's parents, *gemilut ḥasadim,* and bringing about peace between man and his fellow." The prayer book version adds, inter alia, "hospitality to wayfarers, visiting the sick, dowering the bride, attending the dead to the grave." These additions, culled from various *beraitot* and other passages, are actually redundant since they are merely aspects of the comprehensive virtue of *gemilut ḥasadim* which embraces them and many other expressions of human sympathy and kindness (cf. Maim. Yad, Evel 14:1).

Gemilut ḥasadim encompasses a wider range of human kindness than does *charity: "Charity can be given only with one's money; *gemilut ḥasadim,* both by personal service and with money. Charity can be given only to the poor; *gemilut ḥasadim,* both to rich and poor. Charity can be given only to the living; *gemilut ḥasadim,* both to the living and the dead" (Suk. 49b). Thus, helping a lame man over a stile is an act of *gemilut ḥasadim,* though not of charity; a gift given with a scowl to a poor man may be charity; the same amount given with a smile and a word of good cheer raises it to the level of *gemilut ḥasadim.* Almost humorously the rabbis point out that the only provable example of genuine altruistic *gemilut ḥasadim* is paying respect to the dead, for in it there is not the unspoken thought that the recipient may one day reciprocate (Tanḥ., Va-Yeḥi, 3; cf. Rashi to Gen. 47:29).

Gemilut ḥasadim is regarded as one of the three outstanding, distinguishing characteristics of the Jew, to the extent that "whosoever denies the duty of *gemilut ḥasadim* denies the fundamental of Judaism" (Eccles. R. 7:1); he is even suspected of being of non-Jewish descent. Only he who practices it is fit to be a member of the Jewish people (Yev. 79a), for the Jews are not only practicers of *gemilut ḥasadim* but "the scions of those who practice it" (Ket. 8b). That *gemilut ḥasadim* is essentially a rabbinic ethical conception, is explicitly stated by Maimonides (loc. cit.).

During the Middle Ages the grand conception of *gemilut ḥasadim* as embracing every aspect of benevolence and consideration to one's fellow both in attitude and in deed became severely limited to the single aspect of giving loans without interest to those in need. It is not unlikely that this limitation was due to the fact that the main source of economic existence for the Jew was moneylending (to non-Jews), with the result that in lending money without interest he was depriving himself of his essential stock in trade. It is to this connotation of *gemilut ḥasadim* that the free-loan *gemilut ḥasadim* societies refer.

See also *Charity. [L.I.R.]

Modern Period. Burial societies in the communities of Central and Eastern Europe in the 18th century were known as **ḥevra kaddisha* or *kabranim* with the added appellation *gemilut ḥasadim.* They were also called *gomelei ḥesed shel emet* (Gen. 47:29). This application came to signify the acts of lovingkindness connected with burial and consolation of the bereaved. The Prague community in 1792 had an association with triple functions: the provision of *gemilut ḥasadim,* of burial duties, and of *sandakim* at circumcisions. In Koenigsberg and many other communities the local *bikkur ḥolim* was also called *gemilut ḥasadim.* The Hambro Synagogue in London in 1795 had a ladies'

Figure 2. Seal of the Hebrew Benevolent Society of Charleston, South Carolina, founded in 1784.

auxiliary, *ḥevra kaddisha u-gemilut ḥasadim mi-nashim.* In the United States *ḥesed shel emet* societies have specialized in burial of the poor. Such an association, founded in 1888 in St. Louis, Missouri, amassed considerable wealth from its large cemetery holdings and was able to support local, national, and overseas charities from its considerable income. [I.L.]

Bibliography: ET, 6 (1954), 149–53; C. G. Montefiore and H. Loewe (eds.), *A Rabbinic Anthology* (1938), ch. 16; Rabinowitz, in: *Fourth World Congress of Jewish Studies, Papers,* 1 (1967), 145–8 (Heb. pt.); J. Marcus, *Communal Sick-Care in the German Ghetto* (1947); I. Levitats, *Jewish Community in Russia* (1943); idem, in: *Essays . . . in Honor of S. W. Baron* (1959), 337ff.

GENEALOGY.

In the Bible. Genealogical lists in the Bible are of two main types: (1) those which are simply lists of historical, ethnographic, and even legendary traditions, and which constitute most of the lists in Genesis that are called "generations" or "books of generations" (Gen. 5:1; 6:9; 10:1; et al.); (2) those which are tribal genealogies or lists reflecting clan traditions, the census lists in Numbers, and the genealogical accounts in Chronicles and those in which several detailed lists give the genealogical background of individual families, usually where that family played an important historical role, such as in the case of the house of David (I Chron. 2:10–15; 3:1–24), the house of Zadok (I Chron. 5:28–41; et al.), and the house of Saul (I Chron. 8:33 ff.; et al.). Sometimes, less important families (I Chron. 2:31–41; 5:14; et al.), and also individuals (II Kings 22:3; Jer. 36:14), are represented in the same way as in the third type of list. The Bible does not distinguish these different types from each other, and the historico-ethnographic and tribal genealogies are all based on the view (common also among the Arabs) that nations, tribes, and clans all develop in the same way: every human grouping is descended from a single father. Nor is it always easy to classify a genealogy as belonging to one or another type.

It is not known when the tradition of recording genealogies became established in Israel, but it is undoubtedly an ancient one, as only by proving connection with some family or clan could an individual claim the privileges of citizen status. The important role of the genealogy is indicative of a society based on a tribal, patriarchal tradition. Consequently, certain family groups or individuals from among the local population or from closely related tribes, who joined the Israelites during the period of the Conquest or in the early monarchy, were included in the genealogical framework of the tribe as one way of truly incorporating them into the community. In like manner artisans, wise men, and poets, whose profession was customarily hereditary, were generally linked with some ancient ancestor (cf. I Chron. 2:55; 4:21, 23), and whoever joined such a group was as a matter of course attached to it genealogically even though he did not actually stem from its line.

Such written lists were definitely family and clan genealogies and not those of individuals; in part they were composed for official purposes, such as for a national census, military service, or the levying of taxes. Genealogical lists in Israel are known from the time of the First Temple, from what is related in Ezra 2:62 of priestly families who on returning to Zion sought proof of their pedigree but could not find it. Nehemiah (7:5) also mentions the "book of the genealogy of those who came up at first." It seems that the institution of genealogical lists is the background of certain figurative expressions in the Bible (cf. Ex. 32:32; Ezek. 13:9; Ps. 139:16; et al.). Apparently genealogies of individual families were based on oral traditions passed down among the families concerned, or even on national traditions. Some think that the list of Aaron's priestly descendants (I Chron. 5–6) goes back to a text in which many generations were missing, and that the editors filled some of the gaps by repeating some of the names.

In the period of the return to Zion the question of genealogy acquired a special significance. Of primary importance was the lineage of the priests and the levites, for without proving their priestly descent they could not qualify for service in the Temple; but the other returning families were no less keen to prove their descent in order to claim family property. Consequently, a special interest developed in the ancient genealogical lists, some of which are reproduced in the opening chapters of Chronicles and presumably were written toward the end of the Persian period. Similarly, in the short historical stories of Esther, Judith, and Tobit, also written at the end of the Persian period, the lineage of the main hero of the story is given in detail, e.g., those of Mordecai (Esth. 2:5; cf. I Sam. 9:1), Tobit (1:1; cf. Gen. 46:24), and Judith (8:1; cf. Num. 1:6). It is hard to suppose that these are authentic genealogies, yet each of these books claims to relate an event that happened long before the time of composition.

In the genealogical lists, particularly those of I Chronicles, there are three main elements which are usually combined. One represents the relationship of clans through lines of descent from father to son; another sees it in the names of settlements (usually so-and-so, the "father" of the settlement); and a third, in the names of families (e.g., the Tirathites (I Chron. 2:55)). The line of Caleb's descendants (I Chron. 2:42–49) illustrates the mixture (see table).

Various scholars have sought to find in the genealogical schemes of the Bible a conventional way of handing down ethnographic records and information concerning regional history and the pattern of settlement of local clans and families. These scholars have even attempted to establish rules to interpret the various genealogical schemes. Thus, the fusing of two ethnic groups or tribes can be expressed by an account of a marriage; and the integration of a newly settled tribe in the indigenous population can be indicated by the head of the tribe marrying one of the native women, or taking one as a concubine. Daughters generally represent settlements subject to a larger urban center, and sons naturally represent the strongest and oldest of these. Individuals from outside the "family" circle who appear in a genealogy usually symbolize weak families who joined a stronger tribe and so on.

Though such rules cannot provide the sole interpretation of the genealogical lists, they are an aid to the unraveling of the complicated process of Israelite settlement. One, of course, must bear in mind that several of the stories and traditions concerned derive from a combination of schematic descriptions, as regards the historic reality, together with legends and folktales.

It frequently happens that a given name—of a nation, tribe, or family—occurs in different genealogical contexts, or even in a compound list, once as father, once as son, uncle, or brother. For example, Aram is listed in Genesis 10:23 as the father of Uz, whereas in Genesis 22:20–21 Uz is a son of Nahor and an uncle of Aram. In Genesis 36:5, 14 Korah is a son of Esau, but in Genesis 36:16 the clan of Korah is descended from Esau's son Eliphaz. In I Chronicles 2:9 Ram is a son of Hezron and brother of Jerahmeel, yet in the same chapter, verse 27, Ram is the eldest son of Jerahmeel. Sometimes one name can be included in several genealogical lists in association with different ethnic or tribal units. For instance, Zerah, Korah, and Kenaz, who are included in the Edomite list in Genesis

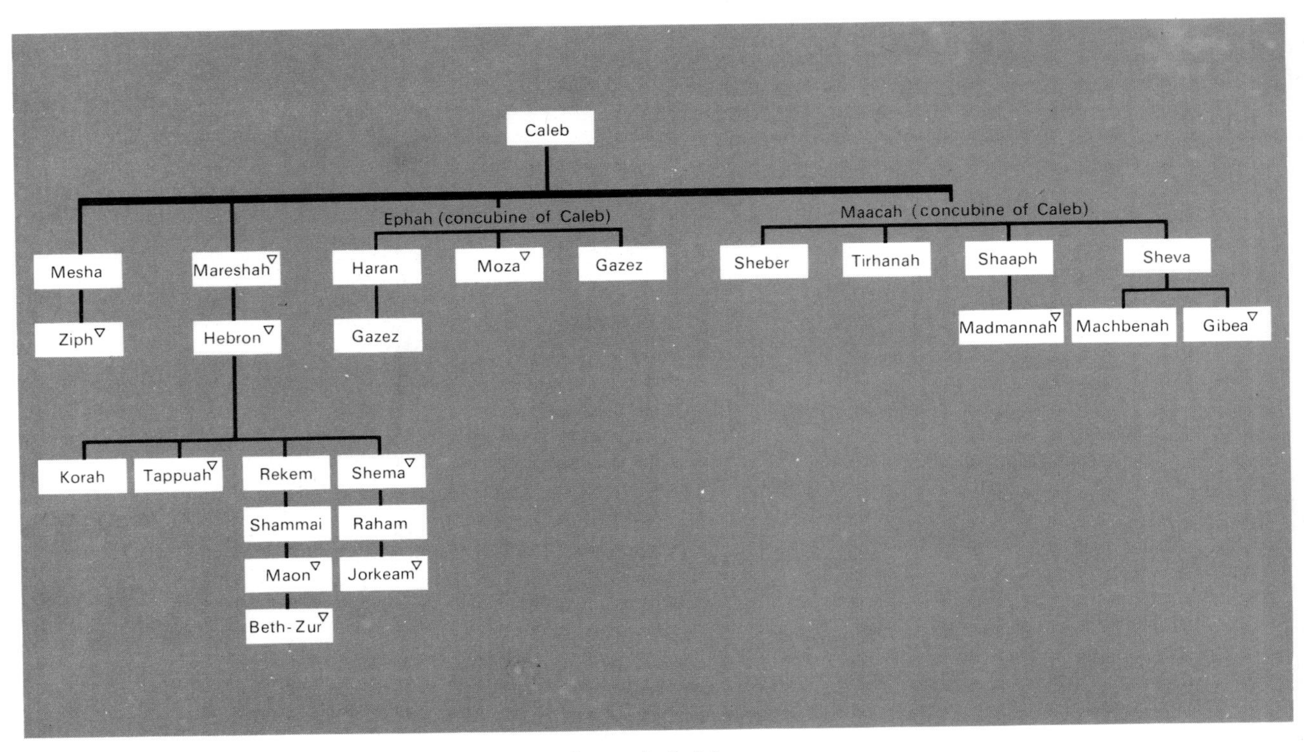

The line of Caleb (I Chron. 2:42–49). ∇ indicates names of towns in Judah.

36, are also found on the list of families in the tribe of Judah in I Chronicles 2 and 4; Beriah appears as one of the sons of Ephraim (I Chron. 7:23), and also as one of the sons of Asher (Gen. 46:17); and Hezron is listed as the son of Reuben (Gen. 46:9), and also as one of the sons of Perez son of Judah (Gen. 46:12). At times it may seem plausible that two entirely separate ethnic groups bore the same name, but generally such duplication is caused by uncertainty concerning genealogical attribution or the existence of parallel traditions. These may have had various causes; sometimes they reflect changes in historical circumstances—the power relations between tribes, families and clans; the migration of several tribes or clans from one region to another; or a mingling of various ethnic elements.

The editors of the genealogical lists in the Bible, particularly those of I Chronicles, were confronted with conflicting lists and traditions, often mutually contradictory. The combination of the various lists, without altering their different, individual character, was possible because the editors of the comprehensive lists regarded them as genealogies of individuals, the progenitors of families and tribes. Thus, the repeated recurrence of the same name provided no difficulty. They did not regard such recurrences as conflicting data concerning families and clans, but merely as showing that the same name kept recurring among individuals related to one another. [J.Li.]

In the Second Temple Period. Purity of descent played an important role in the Second Temple period. It concerned mainly the kohanim ("priests") and those Israelite families who laid claim to the eligibility of their daughters to marry kohanim. Other families, who had no record of their descent but on the other hand were not suspected of impure lineage, were referred to as *issah* ("dough"). The kohanim, in order to preserve their pure status, were restricted to marital ties with families whose purity of descent was not in doubt, and were therefore required to know in detail their own genealogy and that of the families whose daughters they married. Families laying claim to purity of blood kept ancestral lists, which served as evidence of their seniority and legitimacy, for the very possession of such lists enhanced their standing. For the kohanim, a general genealogical list was maintained in the Temple, which recorded genealogical information on all priestly families; even the kohanim who lived in the Diaspora provided this genealogical center in Jerusalem with full details of their marriages (cf. Jos., Apion, 1:7).

A priestly tribunal, which convened in a special room in the Temple, was responsible for the upkeep of the genealogical lists and the verification of genealogical data. They functioned in accordance with established rules, and also based their findings on the evidence of witnesses and genealogical documents. One such rule followed in the Second Temple period was that families who traditionally performed certain functions were beyond suspicion and their purity of descent required no further examination: priestly families who served in the Temple "from the altar and upward" and "from the *dukhan* [the place from which the kohanim blessed the people] and upward," and members of the *Sanhedrin and other families who performed certain official functions (Kid. 4:4–5; Sanh. 4:2; Ar. 2:4). Other duties, such as participation in the priestly blessing or partaking in the *terumah* (the contribution made to kohanim), did not in themselves put the priestly family in question beyond the need for further proof. It should be pointed out that the various offices in the Temple service passed from father to son.

It is important to note that the sages did not owe their positions of leadership to their descent from prominent families. Some of the sages, it is true, were of noble lineage (such as *Judah ha-Nasi), but others came from families with no genealogical record and there were even a few who were the descendants of proselytes. In their society, the rabbi took the place of the father, and the tradition of the academies (the yeshivot) took precedence over the tradition of the family. Talmudic legends went so far as to "invent" a gentile origin for some sages, including some of the greatest (*Akiva, *Meir, and others); some sages were even said to have been descended from infamous and evil gentiles (Sisera, Sennacherib, Haman, Nero) who had repented of their ways and had become Jews. The evident purpose of such legends was to demonstrate that the acquisition of

Torah learning and piety was not dependent upon noble descent.

Purity of blood did, however, play a role in the struggle for secular power among the prominent families, and even the royal houses had to resort to genealogical proofs in order to strengthen their position. Thus the *Hasmoneans, who had to defend themselves against the contention that only Davidic descendants could lay claim to kingship, in turn questioned the purity of David's blood, in view of his descent from Ruth the Moabite. *Herod, who also had to face a challenge to the legitimacy of his rule, forged for himself a pedigree going back to David, after first destroying the genealogical records maintained in the Temple (according to the third-century Christian historian Africanus). Later sources reflect the great danger inherent in any attempt to probe the purity of leading families, for the latter would not hesitate to use force against anyone casting doubt upon their pure descent (Kid. 71a). *Johanan b. Zakkai therefore decreed (apparently on the eve of the destruction of the Temple) that no rabbinical court would deal with matters concerning genealogy (Eduy. 8:3). A similar consideration led to an early rejection of *Sefer Yuḥasin,* which seems to have been a Midrash on Chronicles (Pes. 62b).

After the destruction of the Temple, when the kohanim lost their function, they prized even more their purity of descent, for it was the only symbol left to them of their exalted status. This emphasis on descent continued up to the end of the era of the *amoraim* (sixth century), in both Ereẓ Israel and Babylon. One result was that a man who wished to ensure the continued purity of his family would marry only his sister's daughter (Yev. 62b, et al.); many of the great sages followed this practice. The Damascus Sect (see Book of the Covenant of *Damascus) disapproved of it. It is doubtful whether the rabbis of the tannaitic and talmudic era had real knowledge of their own—and contemporary—genealogy. Numerous families are mentioned in the Mishnah and the *Gemara,* and some of these are described as being of traceable descent (Tosef., Pe'ah 4:11; Yev. 16b; Ta'an. 4:5, etc.). The list in the Mishnah Ta'anit 4:5 originates from the Persian period. Some of the genealogies ascribed to these families are undoubtedly of a legendary character, while the rest are disputed by scholars. A special problem is posed by the later genealogy of the house of David, a subject which also concerned the early Christians (Matt. 1:1–17, Luke 3:23–38).

The Mishnah (Kid. 4:1) lists ten social groups who returned from the Babylonian exile, in the order of their genealogical precedence. The first three—kohanim, levites, and Israelites—are of equal status, except that the kohanim are restricted in their choice of wives; the *ḥalalim* are the sons of the marriages of disqualified kohanim and are themselves disqualified from service in the Temple and marital ties with kohanim; next are *gerim* (converts to Judaism) who are equal to Israelites in most respects, except that they may enter certain marriages which are prohibited to an Israelite by descent; the sixth group are the *ḥarurim,* manumitted slaves; the seventh are the **mamzerim,* i.e., bastards, the children of one of the unions prohibited on pain of death or **karet;* next are the *nethinim,* the descendants of the Gibeonites who were circumcised at the time of Joshua and were not regarded as full Jews because their ancestors' conversion was incomplete; the ninth group are the *shetukim* ("the silent ones") who do not know the identity of their father; and the tenth, and lowest, group are the *asufim* ("foundlings") who know neither mother nor father. A chapter in the Talmud (Kid. 4) is devoted to the relationships between these groups, i.e., the rules applying to intermarriage between one group and another. Not included in the scale are gentiles and slaves; these have no genealogical status at all, and when they convert or are set free achieve their own "descent" and are legally free to marry even their closest relatives. This genealogical scale applied to marriage and honorific matters; it was not deemed relevant in respect of Torah learning and piety, and the Mishnah states clearly that "a learned bastard takes precedence over an uneducated high priest" (Hor. 3:8).

Babylonian Jewry considered that the purity of its descent was of a higher order than that of Ereẓ Israel, basing its claim on the tradition that all those whose purity was in doubt had returned to Ereẓ Israel with Ezra. In the course of time, however, Babylonian *amoraim* declared the population of entire areas as Jews who were not fit "to enter the assembly of God" (i.e., for marriage with other Jews; Kid. 70b). The rabbis of Ereẓ Israel made several attempts to change the existing rule which regarded Babylonian lineage as superior but failed in their attempt; this was a result of the general reluctance to take up genealogical questions prevailing in Ereẓ Israel, as well as the rising importance of Babylonian Jewry at this time (beginning of third century). Babylonian Jews continued to claim greater purity, and the Talmud (Kid. 71b) tells of an impostor who feigned a Babylonian accent to claim Babylonian descent.

This development testifies to the degeneration of the concept of genealogy which, with the destruction of the Temple ceased to have practical significance and merely became a symbol of social status. The Talmud makes frequent references to honorable families and individuals who quarreled with one another about their lineage, even stating: "When men quarrel among themselves, they quarrel over birth" (Kid. 76a). The *amoraim* tackled the problem from two angles: on the one hand they decided that "anyone with a family stigma stigmatizes others and never praises anyone" (according to the correct reading in DER 1), and Samuel added that "he stigmatizes with his own stigma" (Kid. 70b). It is also related in this same spirit of the people of Ereẓ Israel: "When two people quarrel they see which becomes silent first and say to him 'This one is of superior birth'" (*ibid.* 71b); on the other hand they included within their homilies abundant praise of birth, such as "When the Holy One causes His divine Presence to rest, it is only upon Israelite families of pure birth" (Kid. 70b); "The Holy One is reluctant to uproot a name from its place in a genealogical tree" (Gen. R. 82:11; cf. TJ, Suk. 5:8). The sages also protested against "anyone who takes a wife not fit (i.e., with a stigma) for him" (Kid. 70a) because he disregards the importance of birth. The sages included among their homilies sayings in the style of prophecies of comfort that God will purify Israel's genealogy in time to come. They stressed, however, that for the time being one can only act carefully and be guided by the rule that "a family once mixed up remains so" (Kid. 70b)—an important rule which they regarded as "a charity shown by God to Israel" since it is likely to abolish the obstacles of genealogical stigmas: one should not reveal the truth concerning families that have become mixed up and whose stigma has been forgotten (see also *Family).

The Talmud records the Davidic descent of the patriarchs of the Ereẓ Israel community in the talmudic era, and of the Babylonian *exilarchs. Similarly, in the post-talmudic era the exilarchs were regarded as descending from the house of David. The same claim was made about some of the *geonim* (such as *Hai Gaon). In the Middle Ages, Davidic lineage was claimed for some great scholars, e.g., *Rashi, and in consequence his grandsons Jacob b. Meir *Tam and *Samuel b. Meir were said to have descended from *Johanan ha-Sandlar, who in turn was regarded as being of Davidic descent.

In the Modern Period. From the 12th century onward, the term **yiḥus* (birth) assumed additionally a new and positive meaning among the Jews of Central and Eastern Europe. Dynastic connection not only ensured the family concerned against any suspicion of impure birth, but also provided it with family privileges *(zekhut avot)* applicable in many matters. These dynastic genealogies stemmed from superiority of their pious and scholarly forefathers, the founders of the family, and its main importance was in connection with arranging marriages. Many families possessed genealogical trees—whether of substance or otherwise—which they took great pains to preserve. Some of these lists were published in order to add further luster to the family name. Many rabbis strongly criticized this custom and stressed the value of a man creating his own good name. In *Ḥasidism, descent from the **ẓaddik* was endowed with special significance, rooted in the belief that the *ẓaddik* transmitted some of his sanctity to his descendants. With the development of dynasties of *ẓaddikim* the term *yiḥus* acquired also great formal institutional value. In 19th-century Germany the study of genealogy held an important place in Jewish public affairs, because of the aspiration to prove that the Jewish community was deeply rooted in the locality. Scientific journals dealing with this topic were founded and much scientific and archival material published. [I.T.-S.]

Bibliography: BIBLICAL: Klein, in: *Zion (Me'assef),* 2 (1927), 1–16; 3 (1929), 1–16; 4 (1930), 14–30; Maisler (Mazar), in: *Zion,* 11 (1946), 1–16; U. Cassuto, *A Commentary on the Book of Genesis,* 1 (1961), 249–89; 2 (1964), 141–224, 250–77; J. Liver, *Toledot Beit David* (1949); idem, in: *Sefer D. Ben-Gurion* (1964), 486–99; S. Yeivin, *Meḥkarim be-Toledot Yisrael ve-Arẓo* (1960), 131ff.; Luther, in: ZAW, 22 (1901), 33–76; E. Meyer, *Die Israeliten und ihre Nachbarstaemme* (1906); W. Robertson Smith, *Kinship and Marriage in Early Arabia* (1903[3]), 3–39; Freund, in: *Festschrift A. Schwarz* (1917), 265–311; M. Noth, *Das System der zwoelf Staemme Israels* (1930); W. Duffy, *The Tribal Historical Theory on the Origin of the Hebrew People* (1944); De Vaux, Anc Isr, 4–7; Malamat, in: JAOS, 88 (1968), 163–73. POST-BIBLICAL AND MODERN: A. Buechler, in: *Festschrift Adolf Schwarz* (1917), 133–62; L. Freund, *ibid.,* 163–209; A. S. Hershberg, in: *Devir,* 2 (1923), 92–100; idem, in: *Ha-Tekufah,* 28 (1935), 348–62; V. Aptowitzer, *Parteipolitik der Hasmonaeerzeit im rabbinischen und pseudoepigraphischen Schrifttum* (1927); idem, in: *Sefer Zikkaron . . . A. A. Poznański* (1927), 145–69; S. Klein, in: *Zion,* 4 (1939), 30–50, 177–8; idem, in: *Sefer ha-Yovel . . . B. M. Lewin* (1939), 86–92; J. Katz, in: *Zion,* 10 (1945), 21–54; H. L. Poppers, in: JSOS, 20 (1958), 153–79; Shunami, Bibl, 466–9; E. E. Urbach, in: *Divrei ha-Akademyah ha-Le'ummit ha-Yisre'elit le-Madda'im,* 2 (1969), 31–54.

°**GÉNÉBRARD, GILBERT** (1537–1597), French theologian and Hebraist. Born in Riom, Auvergne, Génébrard, a pupil of the Provençal convert Abraham de Lunel, who is said to have reverted to Judaism in his latter years, was a polymath, specializing in biblical exegesis, theology, patristics, liturgy, chronology, and rabbinics. Unlike many of his contemporaries, he was in general opposed to the Kabbalah. From 1569 Génébrard was professor of Hebrew and Bible at the Collège de France and from 1593 he was archbishop of Aix-en-Provence. His outspoken support for the Catholic League—which opposed Henry of Navarre, a Protestant—incurred official wrath after the latter's accession (as Henry IV). Génébrard died in disgrace. As a Hebraist, he was considered an expert on the correct pronunciation of the "holy tongue." He was a prolific writer, translator, and editor: Steinschneider lists about two dozen of his publications.

His works include: *Commemoratio divorum et ritus nuptiarum, e libro Mahzor* (published with *Symbolum fide*); *Eldad Danius . . . De Judaeis clausis* (Paris, 1563), a Latin version of the Travels of *Eldad ha-Dani; *De metris Hebraeorum ex libro R. David Jechiae . . .* (Paris, 1562–63), an edition of the *Sha'ar bi-Melekhet ha-Shir* of R. David b. Solomon *ibn Yaḥya; ΕΙΣΑΓΩΓΗ *rabbinica ad legenda et intelligenda Hebraeorum Rabbinorum Commentaria sine punctis scripta . . .* (Paris, 1563); *Alphabetum Hebraicum* (Paris, 1564); and *Symbolum fidei Judaeorum . . . Precationes . . . DCXIII legis Praecepta e capitulis ultimis More Nebuchim* (Paris, 1569), based on *Maimonides. Génébrard also published *Chronologia Hebraeorum Major* (Paris, 1578), a Latin version of the *Seder Olam* of *Jose b. Ḥalafta, a shortened version of which, *Hebraeorum breve Chronicon usque ad 1112,* had appeared earlier (Paris, 1573); there are various later editions of this book. Two other works by Génébrard are *Jakob Salomonis cap. Chelek* (published with the *Chronicon*), a Latin edition of the commentary by Jacob b. Solomon *Ḥabib on a chapter of the tractate *Sanhedrin* (of the Babylonian Talmud) much studied by Renaissance Christian Hebraists and kabbalists; and an edition of the Song of Songs with three rabbinical commentaries (Paris, 1570). Gilbert Génébrard's pupils included the French diplomat and kabbalist, Blaise de *Vigenère.

Bibliography: F. Secret, *Les Kabbalistes Chrétiens de la Renaissance* (1964), 201–3; idem, *Le Zôhar chez les Kabbalistes Chrétiens de la Renaissance* (1964[2]), 88–91; Steinschneider, Cat Bod, nos. 1006–08; *Dictionnaire de théologie catholique,* 6 (1920), 1183–85. [G.E.S.]

GENERAL ZIONISTS, Zionist party. When the first parties (*Po'alei Zion and *Mizrachi) were established in the Zionist movement, those Zionists who did not join any faction or draw up a program of their own in addition to the *Basle Program came to be known as "General Zionists." Having no separate organizational framework, their delegates at Zionist Congresses formed a loose group and their numbers dwindled from one Congress to another.

In 1929, Yiẓḥak *Schwarzbart of Cracow, who was trying to consolidate and unify General Zionism, succeeded in establishing the World Union of General Zionists. At its founding conference, held in Basle in 1931, the following principles were adopted (1) the priority of the interests of the Land of Israel and the Jewish people over class and sectional interests; (2) united effort by labor and property to serve the people; (3) the encouragement of private enterprise and the settlement of persons with limited means, in addition to support for the national funds and aid to the *ḥalutzim;* (4) abolition of party control over educational, health, and similar institutions. The principles remained the basis of the General Zionist program throughout the years.

Among the founders of the World Union were Leo *Motzkin, Stephen S. *Wise, Louis *Lipsky, Kurt *Blumenfeld, Menahem *Ussishkin, Benzion *Mossinson, Moshe *Gluecksohn, Yehoshua *Suprasky, Peretz *Bernstein, A. Schmorak, and Y. Schwarzbart.

The World Union did not survive for long; there were frequent splits and reunifications among the General Zionists. The factions that came into being bore a variety of names: General Zionists A and General Zionists B; the Union of General Zionists and the Confederation of General Zionists; the Organization of General Zionists and the Progressive Party. The causes of the splits varied. On one occasion the differences were of a political nature, and as a result, Chaim *Weizmann headed one list of General Zionist delegates to the Congress, while Ussishkin headed another. For the most part, it was a question of economic priorities: town versus village, national capital against private capital, agricultural settlement of *ḥalutzim* or middle-class settlement, etc. Every split among General Zionists in Ereẓ Israel resulted in a corresponding split abroad; this, however, was not true of mergers, and in several instances General Zionists reunited in Israel without the factions abroad following suit.

A split among General Zionists the world over took

place in 1963, over the question of identification with one of the parties in Israel. In consequence, there developed the World Confederation of General Zionists, headed by Rose *Halprin and Israel *Goldstein, which stands for non-identification with any Israel political party, and the World Union of General Zionists, headed by Emanuel *Neuman, which maintains ties with the *Liberal Party and the *Independent Liberal Party in Israel. In 1965, at the 26th Zionist Congress, the Confederation had 81 delegates, and the Union 95.

General Zionists in Israel. General Zionists in Ereẓ Israel began to organize in 1922, the first meetings being attended by *Aḥad Ha-Am, M.*Dizengoff, B. Mossinson, Z. *Gluskin, Y. Suprasky, Y. Grasovsky-*Goor, and others. Here, too, there were splits, the main reason being that one faction opposed the policy of the Zionist Organization and the *Va'ad Le'ummi, and later the Government, preferring to conduct its struggle from the outside, while the other sought to achieve its program by working within the national institutions, and the government. In 1948, the two groups, as the General Zionist Party and the Progressive Party, participated in the provisional government, but the former did not join the first regular government in 1949 and was represented in the government coalition only in 1952–55.

Both parties opposed over-politicization and the "party key," and were especially critical of the separate "trends" in education and party control of labor exchanges and medical insurance. They were, in part, successful in their struggle, when a unified state educational system and a state employment service were introduced. They continued to campaign for a national health insurance system.

In 1961 the General Zionist Party and the Progressives established the Liberal Party. Four years later, in 1965, the general council of the party voted in favor of the establishment of a joint bloc with the *Ḥerut movement for elections to the Knesset and the local authorities (*Gaḥal); one section, mainly the former Progressives, would not accept this decision and broke away, to form the Independent Liberal Party. In the ensuing Knesset elections, the Gaḥal bloc gained 26 seats, of which 12 were held by Liberals, while the Independent Liberals gained five. In the 1969 elections the Gaḥal bloc held 26 seats and the Independent Liberals four.

In the Zionist Organization, both parties belonged to the World Union and participated in its work, but by the late 1960s the Independent Liberals became an independent group on the Zionist scene as well.

The Youth. General Zionist youth organizations were first established in the 1920s, especially in Eastern Europe, under such names as Ha-No'ar ha-Ivri, Ha-Shomer ha-Tahor, Ha-No'ar ha-Ẓiyyoni, and Akiva. These movements gradually grew to encompass tens of thousands of members; some of them chose to become *ḥalutzim* and established the General Zionist He-Ḥalutz.

The splits in the parent organization brought about corresponding splits among the youth. Eventually there were two world movements of General Zionist youth: Ha-No'ar ha-Ẓiyyoni and Israel ha-Ẓe'irah. Both belong to the World Union, but Israel ha-Ẓe'irah is linked to the Liberal Party in Israel while Ha-No'ar ha-Ẓiyyoni is linked to the Independent Liberals.

General Zionist Labor. The first group of General Zionist youth, made up of members of Ha-No'ar ha-Ivri in Galicia, settled in Ereẓ Israel in 1930 and established the first General Zionist kibbutz, near Petaḥ Tikvah. They were followed by others, from various countries, and thus a General Zionist labor movement came into existence, in both rural and urban areas, and its members founded kibbutzim and moshavim.

In the initial stage, they all joined the *Histadrut, the General Federation of Labor, but they did not accept its policies and methods, opposing class consciousness, the celebration of the First of May, the maintenance of a labor trend in education and a labor sports organization, and so forth. Their belief was that the Histadrut should confine itself to trade union affairs and refrain from such activities as contracting and the establishment of industries in competition with the private sector. They also felt that the Histadrut was dominated by socialist parties and discriminated against them.

As a result, an independent General Zionist Workers Organization was established in 1934 by some of the General Zionist members of the Histadrut. The rest, who adhered to the principle of a single labor federation, formed their own faction, Ha-Oved ha-Ẓiyyoni, to struggle for the principles of General Zionism within the Histadrut. It was this split that eventually led to the split among General Zionists in Israel and abroad.

In 1946, when General Zionists the world over were reunited, it was agreed that General Zionist workers should belong to the Histadrut, and the General Zionist Workers' Organization became a separate faction in it, side by side with *Ha-Oved ha-Ẓiyyoni. In 1961, the two factions joined to form the Liberal Workers' Movement, but split again in 1965, when the Liberal Party again divided, into the Liberal Workers' Movement, linked to the Independent Liberal Party, and the Organization of Liberal Workers, linked to the Liberal Party. The latter, together with Ḥerut Workers, forms the Gaḥal bloc, which secured 15.3% of the votes at the Histadrut elections in 1965, the Liberal Workers' Movement getting 4.4%, and in the 1969 elections the Gaḥal list received 16.85% and the Liberal Workers' Movement 5.69%.

Bibliography: K. Sultanik (ed.), *General Zionist Movement* (1956); Y. Nedava (ed.), *Sefer Pereẓ Bernstein* (1961), 149–76 and passim; M. Kol, *Misholim* (1964); J. Klausner, *Mahutah u-She'ifoteha shel ha-Ẓiyyonut ha-Kelalit* (1943); M. Gluecksohn, *Im Ḥillufei Mishmarot,* 1 (1939), 98–105 and passim; M. Kleinman, *Ha-Ẓiyyonim ha-Kelaliyyim* (1945); I. Schwarzbart, *Tsvishen Bayde Velt-Milkhomes* (1958), 279–357; F. Weltsch, *Allgemeiner Zionismus* (1937); H. N. Shapira, *Der Algemeyner Tsionism* (Yid., 1936); L. J. Fein, *Politics in Israel* (1967), index.

[CH.L.]

GENESIS, BOOK OF, the first book of the Pentateuch. The English title refers to the opening theme of the book and is derived, via the Latin transliteration, from the tradition of the Alexandrian Jews as reflected in the Septuagint (Γένεσις, "origin"). The popular Hebrew name בְּרֵאשִׁית is based on the initial word (cf. TJ, Meg. 3:1, 74a; TJ, Sot. 1:10, 17c; Gen. R. 3:5; 64:8). Some medieval Hebrew manuscripts also use the titles "First Book" *(Sefer Ri'shon)* and the "Book of the Creation of the World" *(Sefer Beri'at ha-Olam).* Another title occasionally in use was the "Book of the Upright" *(Sefer ha-Yashar),* referring to the patriarchal narratives (cf. Av. Zar. 25a; TJ, Sot. 1:10, 17c).

The book is traditionally divided into 12 *parashiyyot,* "annual pericopes," and 43 (in some Mss. 45) *sedarim,* "triennial pericopes." There are 43 *petuḥot,* "open sections," and 48 *setumot,* "closed sections." Printed Hebrew Bibles, based upon the Vulgate system, divide the book into 50 chapters containing 1,534 verses in all.

The Contents. Genesis is a narrative account of the span of history from the creation of the world to the death of Joseph. It divides naturally into two main parts, the first dealing with the universal history of early mankind (chapters 1–11), the rest being devoted to the story of the patriarchs and their families (chapters 12–50). The time span purportedly covered by the book is 2,307 (or 2,309 cf. 11:10) years according to the accepted received Hebrew text. This may be calculated by combining the sum of the ages of the fathers of mankind at the birth of their respective successors (1,946 or 1,948 years; Table 1) with the years that elapsed between the birth of Abraham and the death of Joseph (36; Table 2). Great imbalance in the presentation of the material is evident, for the first 11 chapters deal with a time span of over 2,000 years while the other 39 are devoted to only one eighth of the period treated. Moreover, the only themes elaborated in detail in the universal history are Creation, the Flood, and the ethnic division of mankind. This disproportion may be taken as indicative of the aims and purposes of Scripture. It is less interested in recording history for its own sake than in the utilization of events as vehicles for the demonstration, objectification, and transmission of the verities of biblical faith.

Composition—The Critical View. Genesis itself contains no information about its authorship, nor can any biblical passage be cited in support of a tradition concerning it. Post-biblical Judaism accepted the unitary origin of the entire *Pentateuch as the divinely inspired work of *Moses, so that Genesis in its present form is regarded as being a homogeneous composition, the product of Mosaic authorship. (For the traditional view see *Pentateuch; Traditional View.) This belief has come under increasing challenge during the past few centuries. The presence of anachronisms, the use of different Hebrew names for God, diversity of style and vocabulary, and the existence of duplicate and sometimes varying and even contradictory accounts of the same event all serve as the criteria for literary analysis that leads proponents of the critical school to postulate that Genesis is really a composite work put together from different documents deriving from varying periods.

ANACHRONISMS. Abraham's native city is called "Ur of the Chaldeans" (11:28, 31; 15:7) although the people known by that

BOOK OF GENESIS — CONTENTS

1:1–11:32	**PART 1: Universal History.**
1:1–6:4	**Creation. From Adam to Noah.**
1:1–2:4a	The story of Creation; the Sabbath.
2:4b–3:24	Adam and Eve in the Garden of Eden.
4:1–16	Cain and Abel.
4:17–26	The genealogy of Cain; the rise of civilization.
5:1–32	The line of Adam to Noah.
6:1–4	The "sons of God" and the daughters of men.
6:5–11:32	**From Noah to Abraham.**
6:5–8:32	The Flood.
9:1–17	The blessing and the covenant with man.
9:18–29	Noah's drunkenness;
10:1–32	The table of nations.
11:1–9	The Tower of Babel.
11:10–32	The line of Shem to Abraham.
12:1–50:26	**PART 2: Patriarchal History.**
12:1–25:18	**Abraham.**
12:1–9	The call of Abraham; the migration to Canaan.
12:10–20	Abraham and Sarah in Egypt.
13:1–18	Abraham and Lot.
14:1–24	The battle of the kings; Abraham blessed by Melchizedek.
15:1–21	The covenant with Abraham.
16:1–16	Abraham, Sarah and Hagar; Divine promises regarding Ishmael.
17:1–27	The covenant concerning circumcision.
18:1–33	Abraham and the three messengers; the intercession for Sodom.
19:1–29	The destruction of Sodom and Gomorrah.
19:30–38	Lot and his daughters; the birth of Moab and Ammon.
20:1–18	Abraham and Sarah at Gerar.
21:1–8	The birth of Isaac.
21:9–21	The expulsion of Hagar and Ishmael.
21:22–34	Abraham and Abimelech at Beer-Sheba.
22:1–19	The binding of Isaac *(Akedah).*
22:20–24	The line of Nahor.
23:1–20	The purchase of Machpelah and the burial of Sarah.
24:1–67	The marriage of Isaac to Rebekah.
25:1–6	The line of Keturah.
25:7–18	The death and burial of Abraham; the line of Ishmael.
25:19–36:43	**Isaac and Jacob.**
25:19–34	The birth of Jacob and Esau; the sale of the birthright.
26:1–33	Isaac,Rebekah and Abimelech at Gerar.
26:34–35	Esau's Hittite wives.
27:1–28:5	Jacob's deception of Isaac.
28:6–9	Esau's Ishmaelite wife.
28:10–22	Jacob at Bethel.
29:1–30:43	Jacob with Laban.
31:1–54	Jacob's flight from Laban.
32:1–32	Jacob at Mahanaim and Penuel; Jacob wrestles with the angel.
33:1–20	Jacob meets Esau; his purchase of land at Shechem.
34:1–31	The rape of Dinah.
35:1–15	Jacob revisits Bethel.
35:16–29	Family affairs in Canaan.
36:1–43	The lines of Esau and Seir the Horite; early kings of Edom.
37:1–50:26	**Joseph and his brothers.**
37:1–36	Joseph and his brothers.
38:1–30	Judah and Tamar.
39:1–23	Joseph in Potiphar's house.
40:1–23	Joseph in prison.
41:1–57	Pharoah's dreams; Joseph's rise to power; the years of abundance and the start of the famine.
42:1–44:34	Joseph encounters his brothers.
45:1–28	Joseph discloses his identity.
46:1–47:10	The migration of the Israelites to Egypt.
47:11–27	Joseph's agrarian policy.
48:1–50:21	Jacob's farewell blessings; his death and burial.
50:22–26	The death of Joseph.

name did not penetrate southern Mesopotamia before the end of the second millennium B.C.E., long after the patriarchal period. Genesis 13:7 states that "the Canaanites and Perizzites were then dwelling in the land," implying that neither people existed at the time of the writer, whereas both survived as late as Solomon's time (I Kings 9:16, 20; cf. Josh. 16:10; Judg. 1:27–33; II Sam. 24:7). The reference to Dan (Gen. 14:14) is irreconcilable with later history (Josh. 19:47; Judg. 18:29). The mention of Philistines (Gen. 21:32, 34; 26:1, 8, 14, 15, 18; cf. 10:14) presents a similar problem since that particular ethnic group did not settle on the Canaanite coast before the end of the 12th century B.C.E. A phrase like "committing an outrage in Israel" (34:7) is difficult as a direct quotation from Jacob's time, but seems rather to be of a proverbial nature (cf. Judg. 20:6, 10; Jer. 29:23) deriving from a period when "Israel" was already designated as an established ethnic or cultic community. The list of eight Edomite kings (Gen. 36:31–39) would cover about 150 years of history. Since the Edomites were not settled in Transjordan before the 13th century B.C.E., the list cannot be earlier than about the middle of the 11th century. This conclusion is buttressed by the phrase "before any king reigned over the Israelites" (36:31) which would set the passage in the time of the Israelite monarchy.

DUPLICATIONS. It is asserted that there are two irreconcilable accounts of Creation. In the one (1:26–28), man and woman are created simultaneously as the climax of creation after the birds and animals; in the other (2:7, 18, 19, 22), the order is man, animals, birds, then woman. The Flood story seems to present similar contradictions. One passage demands a single pair of each species of beast, bird, and creeping things to be taken into the ark (6:19–20), while another has orders to Noah to take aboard seven pairs of clean animals and birds and one pair of unclean (7:2–3), and still a third passage reports that Noah took two of each species irrespective of their clean or unclean status (7:8–9). One account appears to refer to 40 days of rain and a further 14 days until the waters had finally subsided (7:4, 12, 17; 8:6–11); another speaks of a duration of 150 days (7:11; 7:24–28:1; 8:3–4) and an entire year and ten days before Noah was able to emerge from the ark (7:11; 8:13–14). Sarah was twice taken from her husband, once by Pharaoh (12:11–20) and once by Abimelech (20:1–18). A similar story is related about Rebekah and Abimelech (26:6–11). In all three accounts the wife is passed off by the spouse as his sister for his own protection. Hagar twice leaves her mistress in flight to the wilderness (16:6–14; 21:9–19). Both narratives have in common the presence of a well, an angelic visitation, and divine assurances of greatness for Ishmael. Two accounts of the origin of the name Beer-Sheba in the days of Abimelech are given, one concerning Abraham (21:22–32) and the other concerning Isaac (26:26–33). The story of Isaac's expectation of imminent death (27:1–2) does not seem to be compatible with his still being alive at least 20 years later (35:28). The names of Esau's wives given in 26:34 and 28:9 do not correspond with those recorded in 36:2–3. There are duplicate etiologies for the names Bethel (28:17–19; 35:14–15) and Israel (32:29; 35:10). Rachel's death (35:19) seems not to be in consonance with Jacob's reaction to Joseph's dream 17 years later (37:10), and the birth of Benjamin near Bethlehem (35:16–17) makes difficult his inclusion in the list of Jacob's sons born in Paddan-Aram (35:23–26). Finally there seem to be two separate traditions about the identity of those who bought and sold Joseph; they are variously called Midianites (37:28a, 36) and Ishmaelites (37:27, 28b; 39:1).

THE DIVINE NAMES. The foregoing material has to be supplemented by the variant use of divine names. Genesis employs YHWH about 150 times whether in direct quotation (cf. 4:1; 14:22; 15:2, 7, 8 and so about 30 times), or in the narrative (over 100 times). The patriarchs built altars to YHWH (12:7, 8; 13:18, cf. 8:20) and invoked His name (12:8; 13:4; 21:33; 26:25; cf. 4:3; 25:21, 22). According to 4:26 this practice began as early as the days of Enosh. It is clear, however, from Exodus 3:14 and 6:2–3, as interpreted by the critical school, that another tradition existed which ascribed the initial revelation of the name YHWH to the time of Moses. Indeed, large sections of Genesis do not use that divine appellative at all, employing Elohim or some other name instead.

On the basis of all the phenomena just described, critical scholars have attempted to reconstruct the literary history of Genesis. It is postulated that there once existed a Judahite history which began with the creation of the world and which preserved the tradition of the early use of the name YHWH (J source). Later on, a parallel Ephraimite history appeared which commenced with Abraham and which, preserving the tradition of a later origin of YHWH, used ʾElohim (E source) exclusively in the patriarchal narratives. A redactor (R) fused the two accounts into a single narrative (JE). Still another source, this time of priestly origin (P), which had the same tradition about YHWH as did E, was interwoven with JE, so that the present Genesis is a composite of JEP with admixtures of R. Each source, it is claimed, betrays its own peculiarities of literary style and phraseology and displays its own distinctive religious and theological outlook.

The basic distribution of Genesis according to the classical three-source hypothesis of the Graf-Wellhausen school appears on the next page.

It should be noted that chapter 14 cannot be fitted into any of the sources. In some instances such as chapters 31 and 45:1–28, the J and E sources have been so interwoven that disentanglement of the strands is precarious.

In the course of time the inadequacies of the original Graf-Wellhausen hypothesis have led to an expansion of the three sources through the continuous subdividing of each document and by the isolation of still other sources. O. Eissfeldt has recognized an L (lay) document which he claims is the oldest narrative strand.

The Distinctiveness of Genesis within the Pentateuch. There is much evidence to show that Genesis constitutes a distinct unit within the pentateuchal complex, for the book has a character all its own, distinguished by numerous features not shared by the other four. It is almost entirely narrative, and in the number and variety of its stories it is unparalleled. Unlike the rest of the Torah it contains the biographies of individuals, not an account of the fortunes of the nation.

The patriarchal sagas have preserved certain social institutions that are unknown elsewhere in the Bible, although they are now documented in cuneiform sources from the second millennium B.C.E. These institutions are the thrice-repeated wife-sister motif (12:11–20; 20:1–18; 26:6–11), concubinage as a remedy for childlessness (16:2; 30:2–3), service-adoption which seems to be behind the relationship of Eliezer and Abraham (15:2–4) and of Jacob and Laban (chapters 29–31), fratriarchy, which explains Laban's status in the marriage negotiations of Rebekah (24:29, 50, 53ff.; 25:20), and the transference of the birthright (see below).

The book is peculiar, too, in its onomasticon. Of the 38 personal names connected with the patriarchal family, 27 never recur in the Bible. Nowhere else is there mention of the place-name Paddan-Aram used here so frequently (25:20; 28:2, 5, 6, 7), or is Hebron referred to as Mamre (13:18; 14:13, 18:1; 23:17, 19; 25:9; 35:27; 49:30; 50:13).

Genesis is further differentiated by some stylistic characteristics. It employs the phrase "These are the generations of" ((ו)אֵלֶּה תּ(וֹ)לְד(וֹ)ת) ten times (2:4; 6:9; 10:1; 11:10, 27; 25:12, 19; 36:1, 9; 37:2; cf. 5:1; 10:32; 25:13), which occurs only once in the rest of the Torah (Num. 3:1; cf. Ruth 4:18). It has God speaking in the first person plural (Gen. 1:26; 3:22; 11:7; otherwise only Isa. 6:8) which is unusual, combines the divine names YHWH-ʾElohim, "Lord God," nearly 22 times in two chapters (2–3), such a conjunction appearing otherwise only once in the Pentateuch (Ex. 9:30).

The patriarchal narratives contain such material actually at variance with the Torah legislation. Deuteronomy 21:15–17 explicitly interdicts the transference of the birthright in contrast to what takes place in the case of Jacob and Esau (Gen. 25:23, 30–34; 27:1–33), Reuben (49:3–4; cf. I Chron. 5:1–2) and Ephraim and Manasseh (Gen. 48:13–20). Abraham entered into marriage with his paternal half-sister (20:12), something repeatedly forbidden in the Torah code (Lev. 18:9, 11; 20:17; Deut. 27:22). Jacob was simultaneously married to two sisters (Gen. 29:23, 28, 30), a state of affairs to which Leviticus 18:18 is opposed. Judah had a relationship with his daughter-in-law (and the offspring was not thereby illegitimized; Gen. 38:16; cf. Ruth 4:18). This contrasts strongly with pentateuchal law (Lev. 18:15).

Turning to the area of the cult, the same anomalous situation is apparent. Abraham planted a sacred tree in connection with worship (Gen. 21:33; cf. 12:6–7; 13:18), a practice abhorred in the legislation (Deut. 16:21; cf. Ex. 34:13; Deut. 12:3). Jacob set up sacred stone pillars at Bethel (Gen. 28:18, 22; 31:13; 35:14) and Gilead (31:44–53), cultic paraphernalia otherwise outlawed by the Torah (Deut. 16:22; cf. Ex. 23:24; 34:13; Lev. 26:1; Deut. 7:5; 12:3).

ANALYSIS OF THE BOOK OF GENESIS

Chapter	J	E	P
1			1
2	4b–25		1–4a
3	3		
4	4		
5	29		1–28, 30–32
6	1–8		9–22
7	1–5, 7–10, 12, 16b, 17b, 22–23		6, 11, 13–16a, 17a, 18–21, 24
8	2b–3a, 6–12, 13b, 20–22		1–2a, 3b–5, 13a, 14–19
9	18–27		1–17, 28–29
10	8–19, 21, 24–30		1–7, 20, 22–23, 31–32
11	1–9, 28–30		10–27, 31–32
12	1–4a, 6–20		4b–5
13	1–5, 7–11a, 12b–18		6, 11b–12a
(14?)			
15	1–2a, 3b–4, 6–12, 17–21	2b–3a(?), 5(?), 13–16(?)	
16	1b–2, 4–14		1a, 3, 15–16
17			17
18	18		
19	1–28, 30–38		29
20		20	
21	1a, 2a, 33	6–32, 34	1b, 2b–5
22	20–24	1–19	
23			23
24	24		
25	1–6, 11b, 18, 21–26a, 27–34		7–11a, 12–17, 19–20, 26b
26	1–33		34–35
27	1–45		46
28	10, 13–16, 19, 21b	11–12, 17–18, 20–21a, 22	1–9
29	1–14, 31–35	15–23, 25–28a, 30	24, 28b–29
30	3–5, 7–16, 20b, 24–43	1–2, 6, 17–20a, 21–23	
31	} 1–18a, } 19–54	} 1–18a, } 19–54	18b
32	4–33	1–3	
33	1–17	18b–20	18a
34	34		
35	14, 21–22a	1–8, 16–20	9–13, 15, 22b–29
36			36
37	2b–20, 25–27, 28b	21–24, 28a, 28c–36	1–2a
38	38		
39	39		
40		40	
41		1–45, 46b–57	46a
42	27–28	1–26, 29–38	
43	43		
44	44		
45	} 45	} 45	
46	1, 28–34	2–5	6–27
47	1–5a, 6b, 13–27a, 29–31		5b–6a, 7–12, 27b–28
48	} 8–22	1–2, } 8–22	3–7
49	1b–28a		1a, 28b–33
50	1–11, 14	15–26	12–13

The religious situation is further distinguished by other extraordinary features. The war on idolatry is unknown and there is no religious tension between the patriarchs and their neighbors. The appellation "the God of my (your/his) father" (Gen. 26:24; 28:13; et al.) is peculiarly characteristic of the book as is also the employment of numerous Divine Names, several of them unique: *ᵓEl ᶜElyon* (14:18, 22), *ᵓEl Roᵓi* (16:13), *ᵓEl ᶜOlam* (21:33), *ᵓEl Bet-ᵓEl* (31:13; 35:7), *ᵓEl ᵓElohe Yisrael* (33:20), *ᵓEl Shaddai* (17:1; 28:3; et al.), *Paḥad Yiẓḥaq* (31:42), *ᵓAbbir Yaᶜaqov* (49:24). Another peculiarity is the frequent appearance of angels, which are encountered by Hagar (16:7ff.; 21:17), Abraham (18:1ff.; cf. 22:11,15; 24:7, 40), Lot (19:1, 15), and Jacob (28:12; 31:11; 32:2; cf. 48:16). Finally, the idea that the future nation promised to the Patriarchs is to be the collective recipient of a divine revelation, thereby achieving a unique spiritual status, is not to be found in Genesis.

The Antiquity of the Material. The data presented above has an important bearing upon the problem of the age of the material, irrespective of the date of the final redaction of the book in its present form. When combined with other evidence, there can be no doubt of the great antiquity of many of the traditions.

One such piece of evidence is the continuous and consistent association of the patriarchs with Mesopotamia. The family originated in Ur (11:28; 15:7; cf. Josh. 24:2–3) and moved to Haran (Gen. 11:31). To this city came Abraham's servant to find a wife for Isaac (24:4ff.), and Jacob fled to Haran from the wrath of Esau (28:2, 10) and spent a good part of his adult life there. All the tribes, with the exception of Benjamin, originated in this area. However, the association with Mesopotamia comes to an abrupt end with the return of Jacob to Canaan. Since there is no conceivable reason either for its invention or for its sudden discontinuance, it must be presumed to represent an authentic tradition of great antiquity. This conclusion receives independent support from the fact that the personal names of the patriarchal ancestry are often identical with place-names in the vicinity of Haran. This is true of Terah, Abraham's father (11:24–32), of Nahor, the name of his grandfather (11:22–25) and of his brother (11:26–27, 29), of Serug, Terah's grandfather (11:20–23) and of Peleg, the grandfather of Serug (10:25; 11:16–19). Another piece of evidence is provided by the undoubted literary affinities between the Creation, Flood, and Tower of Babel narratives and Mesopotamian traditions.

Further testimony to the antiquity of many a Genesis report are the peculiarities of the onomasticon, the unique social and religious institutions, and the contradictions with Torah legislation, all described above. These traditions must have crystallized very early for they have generally remained intact, no attempt having been made to harmonize them with the moral standards, social conventions, legal norms, or cultic practices of a later age. The very presence of anachronisms, in fact, makes this point all the more salient. In addition, unless the religious situation reflects an earlier phase of Canaanite religious development, it would be difficult to understand the absence of any reference to Baal who figures so prominently in later times as the chief god of the Canaanites.

Other striking contrasts between the known historic realities of the post-settlement period and the traditions about Jacob's sons make it certain that these cannot be later retrojections. Thus, Reuben is depicted as Jacob's firstborn son (29:32; 49:3), and his name always takes pride of place in the tribal lists (35:23; 46:8) even though he lost the birthright (49:3–4; cf. I Chron. 5:1–2). Nevertheless, Reuben enjoyed no tribal supremacy in the recorded post-patriarchal history of Israel (cf. Deut. 33:6; Judg. 5:15–16). The identical situation exists in respect of Manasseh, firstborn of Joseph (Gen. 41:51; 48:14, 18–19) who likewise lost the birthright (48:1–20). The tribe was wholly eclipsed by Ephraim in later times. The image of Levi in Genesis is of a warlike and ruthless adversary (34:1–31; 49:5–7). This is at variance with the priestly and cultic functions of the tribe which played no role in the wars of conquest. Simeon is depicted as the partner of Levi in its act of violence (34:1–31), but in Joshua's campaigns Simeon was allied with Judah (Josh. 19:9; Judg. 1:3). The organization of the tribes according to matriarchs does not correspond to the post-conquest reality. Maternally related tribes did not enjoy any special political associations and their tribal territories were not always contiguous. All this can have no other explanation than that the Genesis narratives have preserved authentic reminiscences of early tribal history.

The same conclusion holds true in respect to the generally harmonious relationships that prevail between the Patriarchs and their neighbors in sharp contrast to the implacable hostility of the conquest and post-conquest periods. Abraham and Isaac enter into pacts with various peoples (14:13; 21:22–32; 26:28–31); Jacob's sons Judah and Simeon intermarry with Canaanites (38:2; 46:10); the Arameans and the Patriarchs are portrayed as being consanguineous (22:21; 24:24, 38; 25:20), notwithstanding the continuous series of wars between them and Israel from David's time on, just as there is no ambiguity about the blood relationship between Jacob and Edom (36:1) despite the inveterate and traditional enmity between the Israelites and Edomites. In both instances a late invention of close ethnic kinship would be unthinkable and the traditions, therefore, must represent early history. Even the apparently anachronistic usage of "Philistine" is instructive in this connection, for the narratives concerning them paint quite a different picture from that of Judges and Samuel. There is no mention of the pentapolis governed by *seranim* (cf. Josh. 13:3; Judg. 3:3; 16:1ff.; et al.). Instead, they are concentrated in the more southerly Gerar region and are ruled by a king and they are not listed among the nations inhabiting the land (15:19–21).

The Major Themes and Teachings. The distinctive nature of Genesis within the pentateuchal complex does not mean that it can be understood apart from the other books. On the contrary, it is the indispensable prologue to the drama that unfolds in Exodus. It provides the ideological and historical background for the relationship between God and Israel as it found expression in the events connected with the national servitude and the liberation. Its unique concept of God, of man, of the nature of the world, and of their interrelationships is essential to the understanding of those events.

THE GOD OF CREATION. The external points of contact between the Genesis creation account and the ancient Near Eastern cosmologies are sufficiently numerous and detailed as to leave no doubt about the influence of the latter on the former. Nevertheless, the differences and contrasts are so great that the biblical narrative constitutes a wholly original production. Unlike its pagan counterparts, the theme of Creation occupies a secondary place in the national religion, and the *cosmology serves neither to validate the social and political institutions nor to fill the needs of the cult. It does, however, embody the basic Israelite concept of *God.

The pagan pantheon inevitably involved a plurality of wills inherent in which was a clash between them. In other words, polytheism did not permit the existence of an omnipotent God whose will was sovereign and who was not capricious. The Genesis creation narrative, on the other hand, presupposes a single God who is totally outside the realm of nature which is His creation and which cannot be other than fully subservient to His will. Creation by divine fiat (1:3, 6, 9, 11, 14, 20, 24) emphasizes just this very concept of the omnipotent, transcendent God Whose will is unchallengeable. In this connection, the external literary form in which the account of cosmogony has been cast is highly instructive (Table 3). The creative process is divided into two groups of three days each, the first of which represents the stage of preparation or creation of the elements, the second the stage of completion or creation of those who are to make use of them. Each three-day group embraces the same number of creative acts, and in each case the first day witnesses a single deed, the second a bipartite act, and the third two distinct creations. The products of the middle days in the two groups are chiastically arranged. The seventh day is climactic and pertains to God alone. (The human institution of the Sabbath is not mentioned.)

This symmetrically arranged literary pattern serves to underscore the fundamental idea that the world came into being as the free, deliberate, and meaningful expression of divine will.

MAN. Another basic reaching is the exalted concept of *man that emerges from the narrative and that is expressed through several unique literary features. The creation of man is the culmination of the cosmogonic process. Only here is the divine act preceded by an annunciation of intention (1:26). Only man is created "in the image of God" (1:26, 27), and to him alone is the custody and exploitation of nature's resources entrusted (1:26, 28, 29). In the second account of the creation of man, his unique position is emphasized by the fact that his appearance constitutes the sole exception to creation by divine fiat and requires, as it were, a special and personal effort by God, from Whom he directly receives the breath of life (2:7). At the same time, the exceptional mention of the material out of which he was formed (2:7) is suggestive of the limitation of his God-like qualities.

EVIL. Another revolutionary departure from polytheism is to be found in the understanding of evil. The sevenfold affirmation of the goodness of God's creative acts (1:4, 10, 12, 18, 21, 25, 31) opposes the pagan concept of an inherent primordial evil in the world. This, too, is the import of the Garden of Eden narrative which implies that evil is moral, not metaphysical, it being the product of the free, but rebellious, exercise of man's will.

THE MORAL LAW. The divine punishment of Cain for fratricide (4:3–16) and the visitations upon the generation of the Flood for its corruption (6:9–8:22) and upon Sodom and Gomorrah for their wickedness (chapters 18–19) all presuppose the existence of a divinely ordained order of universal application, for the infraction of which men are ultimately and inevitably brought to account.

THE UNITY OF MANKIND. The idea of the derivation of all mankind from one common stock is manifested through the divine creation of a single pair of humans as ancestors to all humanity. It is reinforced by the genealogical lists that illustrate the process of development from generation to generation. This concept of the family of man and the unity of mankind receives its consummate expression in the "Table of Nations" (chapter 10), in which the totality of ethnic entities is schematized in the form of a family genealogical tree deriving from the three sons of Noah and their wives, the only human survivors of the Flood. The attribution of all nations to a primary father serves not only to teach the unity of mankind but also to emphasize God's universal sovereignty. It prefigures the consistent biblical preoccupation with the active role of God in human history.

DIVINE ELECTION. The universal focus in Genesis is gradually narrowed through a process of divine selectivity. Noah is singled out for salvation from the rest of mankind (6:8). Of his sons, Shem is especially blessed (9:26), and his line receives outstanding attention (10:21–31; 11:10–32). His genealogy is continued to the birth of Abraham (11:26) who becomes the elect of God and founder of a new nation (cf. 18:19). Again, of Abraham's two sons, Ishmael is rejected and Isaac chosen (17:7–8, 19, 21; 21:14; 25:6; 26:3–4), and the selective process is repeated in respect of his offspring (35:9–12). The divine blessing of Jacob is the final stage, since at this point the patriarchal period ends and the national era begins. Nevertheless, the universal interest is not neglected entirely for the divine promises involve Israel in the international community (12:1–3; 18:18; 22:18; 26:14; 28:14).

THE COVENANT AND THE PROMISES. One of the most extraordinary features of Genesis is its conception of the relationship between God and man in terms of a covenant by which, as an act of grace, God commits Himself unconditionally to the welfare of man. This is first explicated in the case of Noah (6:18; 9:8–17; cf. 1:28–29). With the advent of Abraham, the covenant becomes the dominant theme of the entire book, to which all else is preparatory and which itself becomes prologue to the rest of the Bible. The oft-repeated promises to the Patriarchs consist basically of two parts—a future national existence and the possession of national territory. Abraham is to father a great people destined to inherit the land of Canaan (12:2–3; 13:14–17; 15:4–5, 18–21; 17:2, 4–8; 22:17–18). The same is reaffirmed to Isaac (26:3–4) and Jacob (28:13–14; 35:10–12; cf. 46:2–4; 48:3–4). In fact, most subsequent scriptural references to the three Patriarchs are in connection with these promises, and the measure of their paramount importance may be gauged both by the frequency of their repetition and by the fact that the book closes on this very theme (50:24).

The first page of Genesis from the *De Castro Pentateuch*, S. Germany, 1344. Above the title word, the pictures of Adam and Eve and the tree of knowledge are flanked by the hand of God upraised in blessing (right) and the gates of paradise. Letchworth, England, Sassoon Collection, Ms. 506, fol. 2.

The promissory covenant in Genesis lacks mutuality. It is a unilateral obligation freely assumed by God. The solemnity and immutable nature of the act of divine will is conveyed through a dramatic covenant ceremonial (chapter 15). Abraham's worthiness is indeed stressed (18:19; 22:12, 16; 26:5), and his offspring to come, throughout the ages, are to observe the rite of circumcision as the symbol of the covenant (17:9–14). It should be noted, though, that the idea of a national covenant on Sinai with all its implications for the religion of Israel is beyond the horizon of Genesis, which sees in the promises to the Patriarchs the guarantee of God's eternal grace to Israel and the assurance of eventual deliverance from Egypt (cf. 15:14; 50:24; Ex. 6:4–5).

GOD AND HISTORY. The concepts of God and the covenant in Genesis inevitably mean that the presence of

The full-page frontispiece of the *Schocken Bible*. It contains the initial-word *Bereshit* (Genesis), and a carpet of forty-six historiated circles, arranged from right to left, depicting Pentateuch episodes from Adam and Eve to Balaam's she-ass. Written by Ḥayyim the Scribe, in South Germany, about 1300. Jerusalem, Schocken Library, ms. 14 940, fol. 1v ($8\frac{3}{8} \times 6$ ins/22×15 cm.).

God is to be felt on the human scene. History is thus endowed with meaning. A literary characteristic of the Genesis narratives is the employment of schematized chronology, the featuring of neatly balanced periods of time and the use of symbolic numbers to give prominence to this idea.

The ten generations from Adam to Noah are paralleled by a like number separating Noah from Abraham. The birth of each personality represents, from the biblical point of view, the arrival of an epochal stage in history. It is not accidental that the arts of civilization appear precisely in the seventh generation after Adam (Gen. 4:20–22), through the sons of Lamech who himself lived 777 years (5:31).

Turning to the period of the Patriarchs, it is significant that Abraham lived 75 years in the home of his father and the same number of years in the lifetime of his son Isaac, that he was 100 years of age when Isaac was born, and sojourned 100 years in Canaan (12:4; 21:5; 25:7). Jacob lived 17 years with Joseph in Canaan and 17 years with him in Egypt (37:2; 47:9, 28).

The Patriarchs resided a total of 250 years in Canaan (21:5; 25:26; 47:9), which is exactly half the duration of their descendants' stay in Egypt (Ex. 12:40; according to the Greek and Samaritan versions the correspondence is exact). The important events in their lives are recorded in terms of a combination of the decimal and sexagenary systems with the occasional addition of seven (Table 4). The idea is clearly projected that what is happening is the stage by stage unfolding of the divine plan of history.

Table 1. The time span from Adam to Abraham's birth

Genesis	Personality	Age at birth of first-born
5:3	Adam	130
5:6	Seth	105
5:9	Enosh	90
5:12	Kenan	70
5:15	Mahalalel	65
5:18	Jared	162
5:21	Enoch	65
5:25	Methuselah	187
5:28	Lamech	182
5:32	Noah	500
11:10	Shem	100
11:12	Arpachschad	35
11:14	Shelah	30
11:16	Eber	34
11:18	Peleg	30
11:20	Reu	32
11:22	Serug	30
11:24	Nahor	29
11:26	Terah	70
		1946*

* or 1948 according to Gen. 11:10

Table 2. The time span from Abraham's birth to the death of Joseph

Genesis	Personality	Age
21:5	Abraham at the birth of Isaac	100
25:26	Isaac at the birth of Jacob	60
47:28	Life span of Jacob	147
41:46 45:6 47:28 50:26	From the death of Jacob to the death of Joseph	54
		361

Table 3. The process of Creation (Gen. 1:1—2:3)

Group I		Group II	
Day	Element	User	Day
1	Light (1:3–5)	Luminaries (1:14–19)	4
2	Sky Terrestial Waters (1:6–8)	Marine life (fish) Sky life (fowl) (1:20–23)	5
3	Dry land Vegetation (1:9–13) (Lowest form of organic life)	Land animals Man (1:24–31) (Highest form of organic life)	6
7	*Divine cessation from creativity (2:1–3)*		

Table 4. Important events in the lives of the Patriarchs

Personality	Event	Age	Source
			Genesis
Abraham	Migrated from Haran	75	12:4
	Married Hagar	85	16:3
	At birth of Isaac	100	21:5
	At death	175	25:7
Sarah	At birth of Isaac	90	17:17
	At death	127=2× 60+ 7	23:1
Isaac	Married Rebekah	40	25:20
	At birth of twins	60	25:26
	At Esau's Marriage	100	26:34
	At death	180=3× 60	35:28
Jacob	At migration to Egypt	130	47:9
	At death	147=2× 70+ 7	47:28
Joseph	At sale to Egypt	17=10+ 7	37:2
	At rise to power	30	41:46
	At death	110	50:26

Bibliography: COMMENTARIES: H. E. Ryle (Eng., 1921); B. Jacob (Ger., 1934); J. Skinner (Eng., 1930[2]); S. R. Driver (Eng., 1948[15]); C. A. Simpson and W. R. Bowie (Eng., 1952); U. Cassuto (Eng., 2 vols. 1961–64); G. Von Rad (Eng., 1961). GENERAL STUDIES: A. T. Chapman, *An Introduction to the Pentateuch* (1911); Kaufmann Y., Toledot, 1 (1960), 207–11; idem, in: *Molad,* 17 (1959), 331–8; M. H. Segal, in: JQR, 46 (1955/56), 89–115; 52 (1961/62), 41–68; 53 (1962/63), 226–56; B. Gemser, in: OTS, 12 (1958), 1–21; J. Finegan, *In the Beginning* (1962); U. Cassuto, *The Documentary Hypothesis* (1965[4]); O. Eissfeldt, *The Old Testament . . .* (1965), 194–9; N. M. Sarna, *Understanding Genesis* (1966); B. Mazar, in: JNES, 28 (1969), 73–83. ON CHAPTERS 1–11: W. F. Albright and S. Mowinckel, in: JBL, 58 (1939), 87–103; U. Cassuto, in: *Knesseth,* 8 (1943), 121–42; S. N. Kramer, in: JAOS, 63 (1943), 191–4; 64 (1944), 7–23, 83; idem, in: *Studia Biblica et Orientalia,* 3 (1959), 185–204; R. A. F. Mackenzie, in: CBQ, 15 (1953), 131–40; K. Cramer, *Genesis 1–11* (1959); B. S. Childs, *Myth and Reality in the Old Testament* (1960); A. Heidel, *The Babylonian Genesis* (1963); idem, *The Gilgamesh Epic* (1963); G. C. Westerman, *The Genesis Accounts of Creation* (1964). On patriarchal period see bibliographies to *Abraham, *Isaac, *Jacob, *Joseph, *Patriarchs.

[N.M.S.]

GENESIS RABBAH (Heb. בְּרֵאשִׁית רַבָּה), aggadic Midrash on the Book of Genesis, the product of Palestinian *amoraim*.

Title. The earlier title of the Midrash was apparently *Bereshit de-Rabbi *Oshaya Rabbah (Genesis of R. Oshaya Rabbah)* so named after its opening sentence, "R. Oshaya Rabbah took up the text..." (Gen. R. 1:1), this being later abbreviated to *Genesis Rabbah*. It has however been suggested that it was so called in order to distinguish it from the biblical Book of Genesis of which it is an expansion (*rabbah* means "great").

Structure. *Genesis Rabbah* is an exegetical Midrash which gives a consecutive exposition of the Book of Genesis, chapter by chapter, verse by verse, and often even word for word. It is a compilation of varying expositions, assembled by the editor of the Midrash. The work is divided into 101 sections (according to the superior manuscript, which is in the Vatican library; other manuscripts and the printed versions have minor variations in the number of sections). Often the division into sections was fixed according to the open and closed paragraphs of the Torah (see *Masorah), and at times according to the triennial cycle of the weekly readings in the Torah in Ereẓ Israel which had been customary in earlier times. All of the sections, with seven exceptions, are introduced by one or several proems, one section having as many as nine. The total for the entire work is 246. The proems are of the classical type common to amoraic Midrashim, opening with an extraneous verse which is then connected with the verse expounded at the beginning of the section. Most (199) of the proems in *Genesis Rabbah* are based on verses from the Hagiographa (principally Psalms and Proverbs), only a small number being from the Prophets (37) and the Pentateuch (10). The proems are largely anonymous and in most instances commence without any of the conventional introductory formulae or *termini technici*. Those that are ascribed to the authors are mostly amoraic, only two being tannaitic. Generally, the sections have no formal ending, but some conclude with the verse with which the following section begins, thus providing a transition. On rare occasions the ending carries a message of consolation. Characteristic of *Genesis Rabbah*, as of the other early amoraic Midrashim, tannaitic literature, and the two Talmuds, are its repetitions. An exposition or story is often transferred in the Midrash where an expression appears in more than one context.

Language. The language of *Genesis Rabbah* closely resembles that of the Jerusalem Talmud. It is mostly written in mishnaic Hebrew with some Galilean Aramaic. The latter is used especially for the stories and parables, in which many Greek terms and expressions are also interspersed.

The Redaction of the Midrash. In the early Middle Ages, some scholars ascribed the work to the author of the opening proem of the Midrash, *Oshaya, of the first generation of Palestinian *amoraim*. The fact, however, that *Genesis Rabbah* mentions the last group of Palestinian *amoraim* who flourished in the second half of the fourth century C.E. (about 150 years after Oshaya) shows this ascription to be erroneous.

The editor used early Aramaic and Greek translations of the Bible (the translation of *Aquila is quoted three times in the Midrash), but was unacquainted with Targum *Onkelos on the Pentateuch, which was edited apparently in the fifth century C.E. He used the *Mishnah and the **beraitot*, but not the *Tosefta, the extant *halakhic Midrashim, or **Avot de-Rabbi Nathan*, these having been unknown to him, as was *Seder Olam Rabbah*. Although there are many parallel passages in *Genesis Rabbah* and the Jerusalem *Talmud, a careful examination reveals that the latter was not the source of the former. The *aggadot* which occur in both *Genesis Rabbah* and the Jerusalem Talmud were sometimes derived from earlier common sources (probably from oral traditions). The *halakhot* in *Genesis Rabbah* were either incorporated in the *aggadot* in the earlier sources or originated close to the period of the Mishnah, in which case they were derived from an edition of the Jerusalem Talmud different from the extant one, but which was also redacted and arranged not later than 425 C.E. *Genesis Rabbah*, too, was apparently edited at about the same time. On the basis of its language, of the names of sages mentioned in it (most of whom were Palestinian *amoraim*), and of various historical allusions, it is clear that the work was edited in Ereẓ Israel. *Genesis Rabbah* is thus the earliest amoraic aggadic Midrash extant; it is also the largest and the most important. The other amoraic aggadic Midrashim, including Leviticus Rabbah and Lamentations Rabbah, already made use of it. The first explicit reference to the work, however, occurs in *Halakhot Gedolot*.

The editor drew upon both written and oral sources. *Ben (or Bar) Sira is mentioned four times in *Genesis Rabbah*, on one occasion being introduced by the phrase, "As it is written in the book of Ben Sira" (Gen. R. 91:4). *Genesis Rabbah* contains many *aggadot* which also occur in the other Apocrypha, the Pseudepigrapha, and in the works of *Philo and *Josephus. No conclusions, however, are to be drawn from this regarding any relation between *Genesis Rabbah* and these works, it being highly probable that they drew upon a common source or early oral traditions. In addition, *aggadot* and ideas from Jewish-Hellenistic literature often reached the sages through indirect channels. In addition to amoraic statements, *Genesis Rabbah* naturally contains much tannaitic aggadic material. Having assembled all of this material, the editor arranged it according to the order of the verses in the Book of Genesis, abbreviating, or modifying as he saw fit.

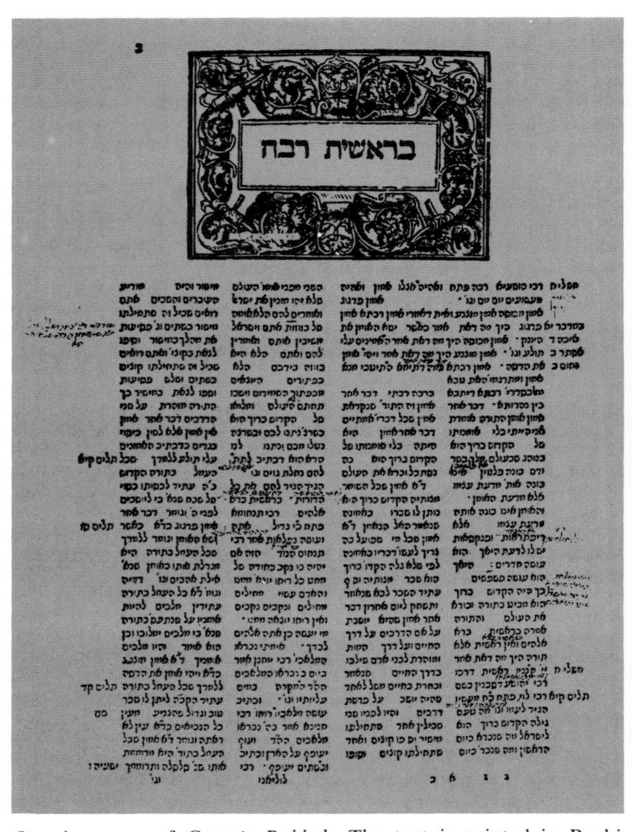
בראשית רבה

Opening page of *Genesis Rabbah*. The text is printed in Rashi script, Salonika, 1593. Jerusalem, J.N.U.L.

Later Additions. In *Genesis Rabbah* there are several parts (in 75, 84, 88, 91, 93, 95ff.) whose language, style, and exegetical character do not form an integral part of the original Midrash but are later additions. In most manuscripts the original expositions on the end of the pentateuchal portion of *Va-Yiggash* and the beginning of that of *Va-Yeḥi* are omitted and replaced by others of later origin and which belong to a type of **Tanḥuma* Midrash, *Midrash *Yelammedenu.*

Editions. *Genesis Rabbah* was first published in Constantinople in 1512 together with four other Midrashim on the other books of the Pentateuch, though these latter have nothing in common, as regards style and date of editing, with *Genesis Rabbah.* This edition and Midrashim on the five scrolls (which were previously published separately) were reprinted in Venice in 1545 and reissued several times.

Genesis Rabbah has appeared in a scholarly, critical edition based on manuscripts and containing variant textual readings and comprehensive commentary. This edition is one of the finest such works of modern rabbinic scholarship. It was begun by I. *Theodor in 1903 and completed in 1936 by Ḥ. *Albeck, who also wrote the introduction. From the numerous manuscripts at his disposal, Theodor chose the London manuscript, written about the middle of the 12th century. Careful examination of the manuscripts by Albeck, however, established the manuscript Vatican 30, copied in the 11th century, as superior. The London manuscript is probably a later formulation of the same tradition recorded in the Vatican manuscript. This conclusion has been subsequently confirmed by Y. *Kutscher's linguistic studies of the Vatican manuscript which have shown it to represent an accurate archetype of Galilean Aramaic. *Genesis Rabbah* was translated into English in the Soncino series by M. Friedman (1939).

Bibliography: Frankel, Mevo, 51b–53a; M. Lerner, *Anlage und Quellen des Bereschit Rabba* (1882[2]); Weiss, Dor, 3 (1883), 252–61; Ḥ. Albeck, *Mavo le-Midrash Bereshit Rabbah* (1936); idem, *Midrash Bereshit Rabbati* (1940), 1–54 (introd.); J. Mann, *The Bible as Read and Preached in the Old Synagogue,* 1 (1940); Zunz-Albeck, *Derashot,* 76–78, 123–124. [M.D.H.]

GENESIS RABBATI (Heb. בְּרֵאשִׁית רַבָּתִי), a Midrash on the Book of Genesis usually ascribed to *Moses ha-Darshan of Narbonne (first half of 11th century). The Midrash was published from the only extant manuscript by Ḥ. Albeck (Jerusalem, 1940). However *Raymond Martini in his *Pugio Fidei* included many excerpts from "*Genesis Rabbah* of Moses ha-Darshan," which he termed "The large *Genesis Rabbah,*" calling the well-known **Genesis Rabbah* "The Minor [or short] *Genesis Rabbah.*" The relationship between these extracts and *Genesis Rabbati* has been a subject of dispute among scholars. Zunz, whose sole knowledge of it was derived from S. J. Rapoport, assumed that the quotations found in Martini's work had been extended and given the name *Genesis Rabbati.* In this way he explained the differences between *Genesis Rabbati* and the fragments in the *Pugio Fidei.* S. Buber argued that *Genesis Rabbati* should not be ascribed to Moses ha-Darshan on the specious ground that he could not find in it certain quotations from Moses ha-Darshan cited by Rashi, the *tosafot,* and Abrabanel in his *Yeshu'ot Meshiḥo.* Epstein held that *Genesis Rabbati* is an abridged form of "the large *Genesis Rabbah*" mentioned in the *Pugio Fidei,* finding support for his view in the very fact that many of the quotations cited by Martini in the name of Moses ha-Darshan do not occur in *Genesis Rabbati.* He came to the conclusion that in fact "the large *Genesis Rabbah*" was not the work of Moses ha-Darshan, but of an anthologist who used some of Moses' work. Ḥ. Albeck accepted the view of Epstein concerning the relationship between *Genesis Rabbati* and "the large *Genesis Rabbah.*" He reinforced his view by a comparison between the *Midrash Aggadah* published by Buber (which is based upon the Midrash of Moses ha-Darshan) and with *Numbers Rabbah* to the portions *Ba-Midbar* and *Naso* (chapters 1–15), which is also based, as he succeeded in proving, upon the Midrash of Moses ha-Darshan (an opinion already expressed by S. D. Luzzatto in his notes to *Numbers Rabbah*).

Genesis Rabbati is based upon the classical sources of the *halakhah,* viz., the two Talmuds, the *targumim, Sefer Yeẓirah,* and all the known Midrashim, but reveals an especially wide knowledge of variant readings in the Midrashim. In the main, however, it is based upon *Genesis Rabbah* (of which it also gives variant readings). The unique quality of *Genesis Rabbati* lies in its quotations from the Apocrypha and Pseudepigrapha, and particularly from the Testaments of the Twelve Patriarchs, quoting it either directly or from the *Midrash Tadshe* which is to a considerable extent dependent upon these works. Epstein even maintains that *Midrash Tadshe* is the work of Moses ha-Darshan. Quotations from the latter are mostly cited in the name of *Phinehas b. Jair to whom the *Midrash Tadshe* is attributed because of its opening words. Similarly, in quoting from other Midrashim which were attributed to definite authors, Epstein attributes such statements to their presumed author. *Genesis Rabbati* does not quote its sources verbatim but adapts them (as is the case with the other Midrashim based upon the Midrash of Moses ha-Darshan). Moses was accustomed to combine sources, to change one source in order to equate it with another, to explain one by means of the other, etc. He also added his own explanations and made great use of **gematria.* His treatment of the sources and his additions, while having a precedent in the early Midrashim, clearly indicate his desire to create a new Midrash which would however reflect the biblical exegesis of the rabbis of the Midrash, and this aim is equally evident in the additions. The importance of this Midrash lies not only in its quoting of the sources but also in its biblical exegesis and in its exposition of the Ashkenazi **piyyut* which came into being at about this time. There are no clear proofs of the direct use of *Genesis Rabbati* by authors of this period, though certain references by authors to *Genesis Rabbah,* which do not occur there, may refer in fact to *Genesis Rabbati.*

Bibliography: A. Epstein, *R. Moshe ha-Darshan mi-Narbona* (1891); Ḥ. Albeck, *Midrash Bereshit Rabbati* (1940), introduction. [Y.El.]

GENEVA, capital of Geneva canton, Switzerland. Jews apparently first settled there after their expulsion from France by *Philip Augustus in 1182, receiving protection from the local bishop. The first mention of a Jew in an official document dates from the end of the 13th century. At first Jews were not authorized to settle in Geneva itself but only in the vicinity. They engaged in moneylending and moneychanging as well as in commerce on a partnership basis with Christian merchants. There were also some physicians among them. Jews having to pass through Geneva on business paid a poll tax of four denarii (pregnant women paid a double tax). In 1348, at the time of the *Black Death, the Jews were accused of having poisoned the wells and many were put to death. From the early 15th century, the merchants and the municipal council restricted the Jewish activities, and from 1428 Jewish residence was confined to a separate quarter (near the present Rue des Granges). The relations between the Jews and the Christian merchants were strained and the Jewish quarter was frequently attacked by the populace. The most serious attack occurred at Easter 1461. The duke's representatives admonished the city authorities but the situation of the Jews continued to deteriorate. In 1488, Jewish physicians were forbidden to practice there and in 1490 the Jews were expelled from the city.

Subsequently no Jews lived in Geneva for 300 years. A proposal to allow a group from Germany to settle if they undertook to pay a high tax and perform military service obligations was rejected by the municipal council in 1582. In 1783 Jewish residence was permitted in the nearby town of Carouge, which was then under the jurisdiction of the dukes of Savoy. After the French Revolution, Geneva was annexed by France and remained under French rule until 1814. During this period, the Jews enjoyed equal rights of citizenship. However, in 1815 Geneva became a canton within the Swiss confederation, and subsequently their position deteriorated. The acquisition of real estate by Jews throughout the territory of the canton was now prohibited. The Jews in Geneva were not granted civic rights until 1841, and freedom of religious worship until 1843. The Jewish community was officially recognized in 1853 and a synagogue was inaugurated in 1859. The first rabbi of Geneva was Joseph Wertheimer, who also lectured at the University of Geneva. At the turn of the century, Geneva University attracted many Jewish students from Russia. Chaim *Weizmann lectured there in organic chemistry in 1900–04. [Z.Av./Ed.]

Modern Period. As the seat of the *League of Nations, Geneva was also the seat of the Comité pour la Protection des Droits des Minorités Juives, headed by Leon *Motzkin, and of the Agence Permanente de l'Organisation Sioniste auprès de la Société des Nations, represented by Victor *Jacobson and, after his death, by Nahum *Goldmann. The *World Jewish Congress was founded in Geneva in 1936, and the last Zionist Congress before World War II took place there in August 1939. During World War II, the city served as an important center for information about the fate of Jews in Nazi-occupied Europe. After the war, although the headquarters of the United Nations were established in New York, Geneva preserved its international importance as seat of the European office of the United Nations and of many U.N. and other international agencies. Consequently, many Jewish organizations, including the *Jewish Agency, the World Jewish Congress, the *American Jewish Joint Distribution Committee, and *ORT, established their European headquarters there. The government of Israel maintains a permanent delegation to the European office of the United Nations, headed by an ambassador. The Jewish community of Geneva numbered 2,245 in 1945, and 2,700 in 1968. After World War II a number of East European Jews settled in Geneva, and later Jews from North Africa and the Middle East also settled there. The community, which consists of separate Ashkenazi and Sephardi congregations, has two synagogues, a *mikveh,* and a community center (Bâtiment de la Communauté) with a library. From 1948 Alexandre *Safran, former chief rabbi of Rumania, served as chief rabbi of the Geneva Jewish community. [Ch.Y.]

Synagogue at Geneva, built 1859. Courtesy Alexandre Safran, Geneva.

Hebrew Printing. From the 16th to the 19th centuries, non-Jewish printers issued a considerable number of Hebrew books in Geneva, mostly Bibles or individual books of the Bible with the Greek or Latin versions, or Hebrew grammars, primers, and dictionaries using Hebrew type. Thus Robert Estienne printed a Hebrew Bible with Latin translation in 1556, and a year later a Hebrew-Chaldee-Greek lexicon. Calvin's commentaries on Daniel (1561) and Psalms (1564) were printed in Geneva with the Hebrew text. J. H. Otho's *Lexicon rabbinico-philogicum* ... of 1675 included the Mishnah tractate *Shekalim* in the original with a Latin translation. The 18-volume duodecimo edition of the Hebrew Bible (1617–20) is usually ascribed to Geneva, and so is the volume of Proverbs, with interlinear Latin translation of 1616 by the same printer (כאפא אילן). The possibility that the Hebrew transcription גנווא should be read as Genoa cannot be excluded. [Ed.]

Bibliography: E. Ginsburger, in: REJ, 75 (1922), 119–39; 76 (1923), 7–36, 146–70; A. Nordmann, *Histoire des Juifs à Genève de 1281 à 1780* (1925); J. Jéhouda, *L'histoire de la colonie juive de Genève, 1843–1943* (1944); A. Weldler-Steinberg, *Geschichte der Juden in der Schweiz* (1966), index, s.v. *Genf;* K. J. Lucetti, *Hebraeisch in der Schweiz* (1926), 35ff.

GENIZAH (Heb. גְּנִיזָה; literally "storing"), a place for storing books or ritual objects which have become unusable. The *genizah* was usually a room attached to the synagogue where books and ritual objects containing the name of God—which cannot be destroyed according to Jewish law—were buried when they wore out and could no longer be used in the normal ritual. As a result ancient synagogues can preserve books or sections thereof of great antiquity. The word is derived from the root גנז from the Persian *ginzakh* ("treasury"), the root meanings of which are to "conceal," "hide," or "preserve." Eventually it became a noun designating a place of concealment. In Scripture there occur *ginzei ha-melekh* ("the king's treasuries"; Esth. 3:9; 4:7) and *beit ginzayya* (Ezra 5:17; 6:1; 7:20) with the sense of a "treasury" or "archive." In talmudic and midrashic literature, however, it is used as a *nomen actionis* (Shab. 16:1; Lev. R. 21:12; Meg. 26b), as a place for the putting away of all kinds of sacred articles, such as sacred books no longer usable, as well as the books of Sadducees and heretics, and other writings of which the sages disapproved but which were not required to be burned (Mid. 1:6; Shab. 116a); whence the expression *sefarim genuzim* ("books to be hidden away"). The expression *beit genizah* ("storeroom," Pes. 118a) means a treasury "powerfully and strongly guarded" (Rashbam, ad loc.). There was an ancient custom of honoring a dead man by putting holy books next to his coffin (BK 17a; see also Meg. 26b; MGWJ, 74 (1930), 163). In times of war and forced conversion, Jews used to hide their books in caves or tombs in order to preserve them. The letter of *Ḥisdai ibn Shaprut to the king of the Khazars relates, in the name of

Figure 1. Solomon Schechter examining fragments from the Cairo *Genizah* at Cambridge University. Courtesy Jewish Theological Seminary, New York.

the elders *(yeshishei ha-dor),* that during a period of forced conversion "the scrolls of the law and holy books" were hidden in a cave. In 1947 certain scriptural scrolls, books, and fragments were discovered in a cave at ʿAyn al-Fashkha in the Judean wilderness and later in other caves in that vicinity. It is probable that the sectarians who lived there hid the books when compelled to leave (see *Dead Sea Scrolls). There were also *genizah* sites between the stone courses of sacred buildings (Shab. 115a), under the foundation stones of synagogues (as in Mainz), and attics and special cupboards kept in synagogues. When the cupboards and attics could take no more, the tattered pages, which, because they contained the Divine Name, were known as *shemot* ("names," i.e., of God), were buried in the cemetery. The day on which the *shemot* were conveyed from the *genizah* for burial in "one of the caves on the slope of Mount Zion" was celebrated in a festive way in Jerusalem, even during the modern period. The participants in the ceremony would play musical instruments, sing, dance, and play games "facing one another with drawn swords in order to magnify the joyousness of the affair" (*Yerushalayim* (ed. Luncz), 1 (1882), 15–16). There is evidence that a similar custom prevailed in other areas.

Such *genizot* existed in a great number of both Eastern and Western communities. Although they usually contained only the worn-out remnants of books in daily use such as the Pentateuch and the prayer book, rare or historically important books and documents were sometimes hidden among them. In the majority of cases the material of the *genizot* was so damaged by dampness and mildew that the collections were of no value for the purposes of historical research.

Cairo Genizah. There are some notable exceptions to this, the best-known of which is the *Genizah* from Fostat (Old Cairo), rediscovered mainly by Solomon *Schechter. In fact the Cairo *Genizah* had already been seen by Simon von *Geldern in 1753, and by Jacob *Saphir in 1864. They had not been allowed to examine its contents because of the local superstition which claimed that disaster would befall anyone who touched the sacred pages. Nevertheless various leaves were occasionally extracted without permission and sold to visitors. These included the Karaite Abraham *Firkovich, the Russian archimandrite Antonin of Jerusalem, and A. E. *Harkavy, who transferred the fragments to Russia. Many *Genizah* fragments came into the possession of S. A. *Wertheimer who published them at the close of the 19th century. Further fragments were bought by Elkan *Adler and others. In 1896 two Christian visitors bought some Hebrew fragments in Cairo, and on returning to England showed them to Schechter who recognized them as being from the Hebrew original of the Book of *Ben Sira, which had been lost and was known only in its Greek translation. Toward the end of 1896 Schechter traveled to Cairo and after several months of strenous effort, was able to extract from the *Genizah* about 100,000 pages which he took to Cambridge. Researchers and bibliophiles were responsible for the discovery of about another 100,000 pages, which were later deposited in large libraries throughout the world.

The Cairo *Genizah* was found in the attic of the Ezra Synagogue, whose worshipers had preserved ancient Palestinian customs, and in which Maimonides, his son Abraham, and other great scholars had taught. This synagogue was built in 882 on the ruins of a Coptic church sold to the Jews. In 1890 it was rebuilt, but the attic was not touched. The attic was situated at the end of the women's gallery; it was without doors or windows and could only be reached by means of a ladder through a large hole at the side.

The Cairo *Genizah* brought to light literary treasures and historical documents, including: (1) most of the Hebrew Ben Sira; (2) fragments of *Aquila's Greek translation of the Bible; (3) The Covenant of *Damascus; (4) ancient Palestinian, Babylonian, and Spanish *piyyutim;* (5) a large number of documents relating to the history of the Jews of Israel and Egypt from the time of the Islamic conquests until the First Crusade, a period about which nothing had previously been known; (6) abundant material on the history of Karaism; (7) authentic documents and the signatures of important personages; (8) an exceptional variety of historical and cultural material, including Ashkenazi *piyyutim* and writings (letters and poems) from the 13th and 15th centuries in Judeao-German (Yiddish). The most ancient dated document, *Zikhron-Edut* is from Fostat itself and is dated 1062, of the "era of contracts" (i.e., Seleucid), corresponding to 750 C.E. In other places, too, such as Kafa (Crimea), Lublin (Poland), Tripoli, and Jerusalem, *genizot* have been opened but nothing of value has been found. The *genizot* of Egypt and the Judean

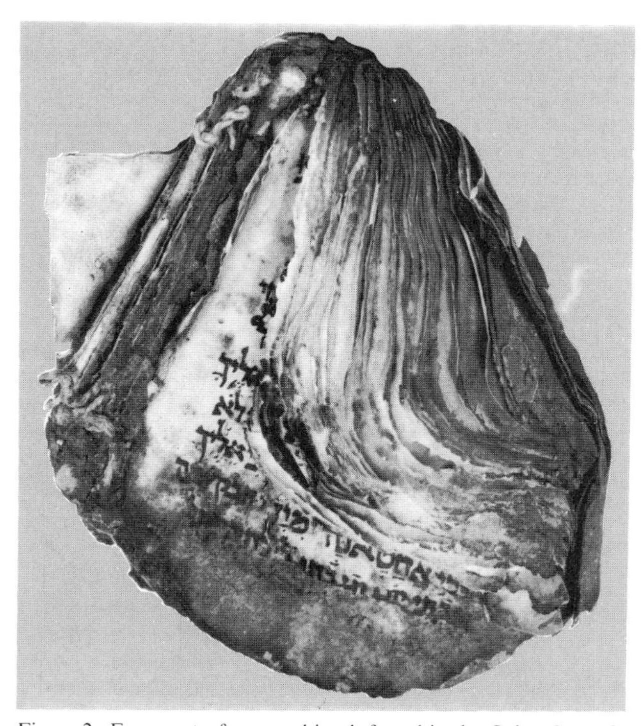

Figure 2. Fragment of a sacred book found in the Cairo *Genizah*, 1896. Cambridge University Library.

wilderness were preserved by the clear, dry climate, whereas the *genizot* of less arid climes soon rotted away.

Until recently research on the Cairo *Genizah* was pursued in an uncoordinated manner by scholars who, interested only in their own fields of study, never attempted to record and classify the entire collection. Even the thousands of fragments that were published by different scholars appeared in a large variety of periodicals which themselves were not arranged in an orderly and coordinated bibliographical manner. Over the years several books and periodicals were devoted particularly to the publication of *genizah* fragments from various fields, like *Ginzei Schechter* (3 vols., 1928), and *Ginzei Kedem* (4 vols., 1922–30). Recent years have witnessed the appearance of certain books that begin to summarize the vast body of material found in the *genizah*. Among these are: *Rav Nissim Gaon* (1965) and *Ba-Merkazim u-va-Tefuẓot* (1965) by S. Abramson; and the anthology *Shirim Ḥadashim min ha-Genizah* (1966) by H. Schirmann (see S. Shaked, *A Tentative Bibliography of Genizah Documents* (1964)).

Bibliography: Masseri, in: *Mizraḥ u-Ma'arav*, 1 (1920), 27–31 (English version in *Jewish Review*, 4 (1913), 208–16); Halper, in: *Ha-Tekufah*, 19 (1923), 261–76; 20 (1924), 261–84; A. M. Habermann, *Ha-Genizah* (1944); idem, *Edah ve-Edut* (1952), introd.; E. L. Sukenik, *Megillot Genuzot*, 1 (1948), introd.; 2 (1950), introd.; idem (ed.), *The Dead Sea Scrolls of the Hebrew University* (1955), introd.; Zulay, in: *Lu'aḥ Haaretz li-Shenat 5710* (1950), 110–26; Teicher, in: JJS, 1 (1948/49), 156–8; Golb, in: *Judaism*, 6 (1957), 3–16; P. E. Kahle, *The Cairo Genizah* (1960[2]); S. D. Goitein, *A Mediterranean Society*, 1 (1967), 1–28; idem, in: PAAJR, 23 (1954), 29–40; Allony, in: *Aresheth*, 3 (1961), 395–425.

[A.M.H.]

GENNAZANO, ELIJAH ḤAYYIM BEN BENJAMIN OF (second half of 15th century), writer and disciple of R. Benjamin of Montalcino. Gennazano wrote: (1) *Iggeret Ḥamudot*, on the Kabbalah, dedicated to David b. Benjamin of Montalcino, whom he wished to instruct in Kabbalah (ed. A. W. Greenup, 1912); (2) a poem about women, in which Gennazano arbitrates between Abraham of Sarteano who published a poem against women, and Avigdor of Fano who composed a poem in their defense (all three ed. by Neubauer in *Israelitische Letterbode*, 10 (1884/85), 97–105); (3) two anti-Christian parodies of the "*Yigdal*" hymn (A. Marx, in JQR, 9 (1918/19), 306–7 and *Freidus Memorial Volume*, 1 (1929), 276ff.); and (4) a polemic against Christianity, a compilation of the arguments he used in a disputation with the monk Francesco de Aquapendete in Orvieto (Ms.).

Bibliography: HB, 10 (1870), 104; 21 (1881), 21; D. Kaufmann, in: REJ, 34 (1897), 309–11; I. Davidson, *Parody in Jewish Literature* (1907), 32.

[U.C./Ed.]

GENOA, seaport in N. Italy. There were Jews living in Genoa before 511, since in that year Theodoric the Ostrogoth confirmed through his minister Cassiodorus the Jewish privilege of restoring, but not enlarging, the synagogue, which had been destroyed by Christian fanatics. From 1134 Jews who came to Genoa had to pay toward the illumination of the cathedral—this obviously discouraging their settlement. *Benjamin of Tudela (c. 1165) found only two Jews (brothers) in Genoa, dyers from North Africa. Notarial documents of 1250–74 show a number of Jews established there or in transit. In 1492 refugees from Spain arriving in Genoa in overcrowded ships were allowed to land for three days, but on Jan. 31, 1493, this concession was withdrawn through fear that the Jews had introduced the plague. In following years some well-to-do Jews were allowed to stay in Genoa under the supervision of an "Office of the Jews."

The policy of the Genoese doges and senate toward the Jews subsequently varied, alternately influenced by fear of competition and the need to exploit Jewish experience in overseas trade. The Jews were expelled from the city in 1515, readmitted a year later, and again expelled in 1550. In 1567 the expulsion was extended to the whole territory of the republic. However, between 1570 and 1586, permission to engage in moneylending and to open shops in Genoa was granted four times to the Jews. In 1598 a further decree of expulsion was issued, but many Jews succeeded in evading it. In 1660 the 200 Jews living in Genoa were confined to a ghetto, although two years later many were still living outside it. What is possibly the first polyglot Bible (or part of it) was published here in 1516: the Psalter in the Hebrew original, with the Greek Septuagint, the Latin Vulgate, the Aramaic Targum and its Latin translation, and an Arabic version together with some notes by Bishop Agostino Giustiniani, to whose scholarly initiative this magnificent edition was due. The last decree of expulsion was issued in 1737 but was not rigorously enforced. Finally, in 1752 a more liberal statute was issued, but owing to the uncertain conditions the Jewish population remained small, numbering only 70 in 1763. The number increased during the 19th century, after Genoa's development as Italy's major port, especially after full equality was granted to the Jews in 1848. The community numbered about 1,000 in the middle of the 19th century.

[A.Mil.]

The Holocaust Period. In 1931 the Jews in Genoa numbered 2,500. On Nov. 3, 1943, about 300 Jews were deported (among them the rabbi and historian of the community, Riccardo Pacifici, and 100 foreign nationals). The delegation of Assistance to Emigrants worked in Genoa, in cooperation with Italian authorities, to save

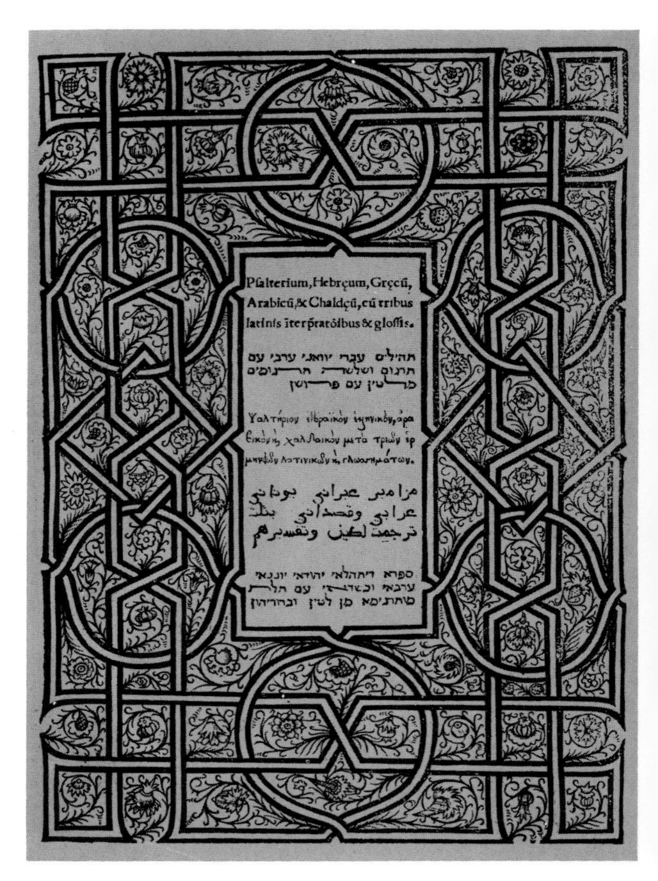
Psalterium, Hebręum, Gręcū, Arabicū, & Chaldęū, cū tribus latinis īterp̄ratōibus & glossis.

תהלים עברי יוני ערבי עם
תרגום ושלשה תרגומים
לטין עם פירושן

Ψαλτήριον ἑβραϊκὸν ἑλληνικὸν, ἀρα
βικὸν καὶ χαλδαϊκὸν μετὰ τριῶν ἑρ
μηνειῶν λατινικῶν καὶ γλωσσημάτων.

مزامير عبراني يوناني
عربي وكلداني بثلث
ترجمة لطين وتفسيرهم

ספרא דתהלאי יהודאי יונאי
ערבאי וכשדאי עם תלת
תרגמא מן לטין ובחריהון

Title page of the first polyglot Psalter, with notes by Agostino Giustiniani, the bishop of Genoa. Text in Latin, Hebrew, Greek, Arabic, and Aramaic, Genoa, 1516. New York, Rabbinical Seminary of America.

Jewish lives and property. None of the Jews from Genoa deported to the death camps returned.

Contemporary Period. At the end of World War II, 1,108 Jews were left in Genoa. Subsequently, the Jewish population maintained its size, notwithstanding a constant outnumbering of deaths over births, and in 1965 it numbered 1,036 persons out of a total of 840,000 inhabitants. The port of Genoa was the transit center for various groups of Jewish emigrants who came mainly from Eastern Europe and were heading for Israel. In 1969 the community of Genoa had a synagogue of Sephardi rite, a kindergarten, and an elementary Hebrew school. The review *La Fiamma* ("The Flame") was published monthly. [S.D.P.]

Bibliography: Milano, Bibliotheca, index, s.v. *Genova*; Roth, Italy, index; idem, in: *Speculum*, 25 (1950), 190–7; idem, *Jews in the Renaissance* (1959), 155; R. Pacifici, *Nuovo Tempio di Genova con illustrazioni e notizie storiche nella comunità nei secoli XVII e XVIII* (1939); Perreau, in: *Vessillo Israelitico*, 29 (1881), 12–14, 37–40, 70–73; D. W. Amram, *Makers of Hebrew Books in Italy* (1909), 266ff.; A. Marx, *Studies in Jewish History and Booklore* (1944), 312; S. Jona, *Persecuzione degli ebrei a Genova* (1965).

GENOCIDE CONVENTION. The Genocide Convention for the prevention of genocide and the punishment of the organizers of genocide arose out of a general reaction to the Nazi crimes against the Jewish people. Though several mass liquidations had already previously occurred in the history of mankind, none of these had reached the proportions and planning of the slaughter of European Jewry by the Third Reich. After World War II, a movement developed demanding that such acts be condemned as an international crime, and their perpetrators be punished. This condemnation was to be upheld by the coordinated activity of all civilized nations. The term "genocide" was coined by the Polish-Jewish lawyer Raphael *Lemkin in his book *Axis Rule in Europe* (1944), 79–95. It was also due to a large extent to his personal efforts over the years that the Convention was later ratified.

The Genocide Convention was directly connected with the trials of the major Nazi war criminals at the International Military Tribunal at Nuremberg, where the Nazi plan to exterminate Jews wherever possible was publicly revealed in all its brutality (see *Nuremberg Trials). The *United Nations, which in the preamble to its Charter had renewed the affirmation of basic human rights and the recognition of the value of human life, could not ignore what had happened in this sphere. Consequently, at its first session on Dec. 11, 1946, after it had confirmed Resolution No. 95 (I) on the principles of international law which had been introduced by the legislation of the Nuremberg tribunal, the General Assembly adopted Resolution No. 96 (I), condemning genocide as a crime in international law, and determining that all nations have an interest in punishing such cases. After two years of preparation the text of the Convention was unanimously adopted by the General Assembly of the U.N. (Dec. 8, 1948). By January 1969, 67 countries had ratified it, some with important reservations.

The Convention outlaws not only mass murder but also several other actions of a less extreme nature, taken against groups of individuals. It does not give a legal definition of the term "genocide." The characteristic trend of all the actions which can be defined as genocide is their inherent intention to destroy, wholly or partially, a national, ethnic, racial, or religious group *per se*. The following actions are classified as genocide: the killing of persons belonging to the group; the causing of grievous bodily or spiritual harm to members of the group; deliberately enforcing on the group living conditions which could lead to its complete or partial extermination; the enforcement of measures designed to prevent birth among the group; the forcible removal of children from one group to another.

Since the Convention aims at the prevention as well as the punishment of genocidal action, it determines that not only those who carry out such actions are liable to punishment, but also those who take certain measures liable to bring about genocide, such as a plot to carry out genocide; direct and public incitement to genocide; an attempt at genocide; participation in such action. This list clearly shows that the activities included within the framework of genocide are related only to the biological and physical existence of the group in question.

One of the main achievements of the Convention is its application to every criminal, regardless of his status, i.e., it applies equally to rulers who bear the legislative responsibility for the act, on public functionaries, and on private individuals. This directive overrrules the argument of an "act of state," which contends that leaders of the state are free of responsibility, performing their action not in their own name but in the name of the state. Although the convention does not deal explicitly with the plea of "superior order," it is clear that this plea is invalid unless it refers to instances in which the intent to murder a group cannot be attributed to the accused. The Convention provided for national implementation (by local courts), for international implementation (by an international penal court, not yet in existence), and for prevention and suppression of genocide by the General Assembly which may be called upon to do so.

The effectiveness of the Convention had in the first 20 years of its existence not been put to the test. Claims of genocide being committed were made, *inter alia*, in regard to Negroes in Southern Sudan, to Kurds in Iraq, to Nagas in India, and to communists, Chinese in Indonesia, and the Ibos in the Biafran War in Nigeria, but no attempt was made to "seize" the General Assembly with these claims.

Bibliography: N. Robinson, *Genocide Convention* (1960); P. N. Drost, *Crime of State*, 2 vols. (1959), incl. bibl.; Perlman, in: *Nebraska Law Review*, 30 (1950); Stanciu, in: *Yad Vashem Studies*, 7 (1968), 185–7; Lemkin, in: *Revue internationale de droit pénal*, 17 (1946); G. Percy, *La Convention pour la prévention et la répression du crime de génocide* (1950); Landsberg, in: *Aussenpolitik* (May 1953), 310–21; Société Internationale de Prophylaxie Criminelle, *La prophylaxie du génocide*, 1 no. 11–13 (1967); 2 no. 14–15 (1968); Fawcett, in: *Patterns of Prejudice* (Nov.-Dec. 1968), 23–25.

[N.Ro.]

GENTILE, non-Jew. It was only during the later Second Temple period that a sharp distinction and a barrier of separation was erected between the Jew and the gentile. The prohibition of marriage, which in the Bible was limited to the seven Canaanite nations (Deut. 7:1–4), was extended, following the reforms of Ezra to include all non-Jews; the acceptance of monotheism was made the distinguishing mark of the Jew (Meg. 13a, Esth. R. 6:2); the Jews were regarded as having completely discarded *idolatry which was, however, uniformly characteristic of the non-Jew. In addition to that the low moral, social, and ethical standards of the surrounding gentiles were continuously emphasized, and social contact with them was regarded as being a pernicious social and moral influence. As a result, during this period the world was regarded as divided, insofar as peoples were concerned, into the Jewish people and the "nations of the world," and insofar as individuals were concerned, into "the Jew" and the idolater (*"oved kokhavim u-mazzalot,"* usually abbreviated to *"akkum,"* literally "a worshiper of stars and planets" but applied to all idolaters). Only considerations of humanity, such as relief of their poor, visiting their sick, affording them last rites (Git. 61a) and discretion ("one greets a gentile on their festivals for the sake of peace"—Tosef. Av. Zar. 1:3) were reasons for breaking the otherwise impenetrable barrier. As a result, the conception of and the attitude toward the non-Jew from the Talmudic period onward are strikingly different from that during the biblical period.

For the biblical period see *Stranger. [Ed.]

In the Talmud. Since talmudic literature spans over half a millennium, covering a wide geographic area, attitudes toward gentiles expressed in it vary considerably. In fact, it reveals a whole spectrum of opinions from the extreme antipathy of the tormented Jew of Hadrian's time—e.g., Simeon b. Yoḥai's statement: The best of gentiles should be killed (TJ, Kid. 4:11, 66c)—to the moderate views expressed in the more friendly atmosphere of early Sassanid Babylon—witness Samuel's making no distinction between Israel and the nations on the Day of Judgment (TJ, RH 1:3, 57a). Thus all such statements must be seen in their specific geographical-historical context. Nevertheless, in general it may be said that the Jew's attitude toward the gentile was largely conditioned by the gentile's attitude toward him (see Esth. R. 2:3), so that a gentile's friendship to a Jew would be warmly and uninhibitedly reciprocated (see BK 38a, and witness the relationships between Meir and Avnimos ha-Gardi, Judah ha-Nasi and Antoninus, Samuel and Sapor, etc.).

Jewish antipathy to the gentile in talmudic times stemmed from a number of causes and functioned on several levels. Thus, gentiles were condemned for their cruelty to Jews (see BK 117a; Av. Zar. 25b, etc.), their morals were considered reprehensible (Yev. 98a; Av. Zar. 22b; Song R. 6:8, etc.), and throughout the period one finds reiterated the (theological) accusation that though they were offered the Torah, they rejected it (Av. Zar. 2b; Tahh. B., Deut. 54, etc.). Thus, the Jewish antipathy to the gentile was not due to the fact that he was of non-Jewish stock, i.e., it was not a racial prejudice, but rather motivated by their idolatry, moral laxity, and other such faults (see Av. Zar. 17a–b). Those that were righteous (by Jewish standards), however, were fully entitled to the rewards of the world-to-come (Tosef., Sanh. 13:2; BB 10b), and a further distinction was made by Johanan who declared that gentiles outside Palestine were not really idolaters, but only blind followers of their ancestral customs (Ḥul. 13b).

Terms. In rabbinic literature the distinction between gentile *(goi, akkum)* and Christian *(Noẓeri)* has frequently been obscured by textual alterations necessitated by the vigilance of censors. Thus "Egyptian," "Amalekite," "Zadokite" (= Sadducee) and *kuti* (Samaritan) often stand in place of the original *noẓeri*, as well as *goi, akkum*, etc. (see *Paḥad Yiẓḥak*, s. v. *Goi*). Probably when Resh Lakish stated that a gentile (*akkum* etc., in existing texts) who observed the Sabbath is punishable by death (Sanh. 58b), he had in mind Christians (see A. Weiss, in *Bar Ilan*, 1 (1963), 143–8, xxxi–ii). The same may be so in the case of R. Ammi who ruled that one may not teach a gentile Torah (Ḥag. 13a; cf. Sanh. 59a). Numerous anti-Christian polemic passages only make real sense after *noẓeri* has been restored in place of the spurious *kuti* or *ẓedoki*, etc.

In Law. The gentile figures very widely in talmudic law, in various legal categories, such as laws of personal status, marriage and inheritance, proselytization, laws of accession, contract, agency, evidence and damages, purity and impurity, laws concerning the types of property, and offerings he may present to the Temple, to name but a few. The basic assumption is that all non-Jews are subject to certain universal laws, religious, moral, and social (called the seven *Noachian laws): (1) institution of courts of justice; (2) idolatry; (3) blasphemy; (4) incest; (5) homicide; (6) robbery; (7) eating the limb of a living animal, and according to other opinions, castration, mixing of breeds, witchcraft, etc. (Sanh. 56a–b, et al.). Thus the gentile is a legal personality in Jewish law, and though sometimes discriminated against, is generally treated equitably. Thus, the Talmud relates that once the Roman government sent two officials to learn the Jewish law. After careful study, they said: "We have scrutinized all your laws and found them just *(emet)*, except for the following instance. You say that if a Jew's ox gores that of a gentile, the owner is free from damages, while if a gentile's ox gores that of a Jew, he is obliged to pay damages. But if, as you say, 'neighbor' (in Ex. 21:35) excludes the gentile, then he should be free even when his ox gores that of a Jew. And if, on the other hand 'neighbor' includes the gentile, then the Jew should have to pay damages when his ox gores that of a gentile . . ." (BK 38a).

Where there is legal discrimination against a gentile, it is usually based on objective reasoning, such as the fact that he does not subscribe to the Jewish "social contract" (nonreciprocity). Thus, the Talmud rules that the commandment to restore lost property to its owner (Deut. 22:1–3) does not apply when the gentile is the owner (BK 113b). This is because gentiles do not act reciprocally in such cases. Similarly, a gentile cannot act as witness (BK 15a) because (according to one opinion) he is dishonest and unreliable (cf. Bek. 13b). Here it should be noted that Jews suspected of the same faults were liable to identical discrimination. Other apparently discriminating rulings were intended to discourage intimacy with the non-Jew, or, in other words, primarily to guard the Jews from the dangers of assimilation, such as the interdict against non-Jewish wines and cooked foods etc. In practice discrimination against gentiles was frowned upon and even forbidden as it might jeopardize friendly relations (*mi-penei darkhei shalom*, Git. 5:8–9, *mi-penei eivah* Av. Zar. 26a) and bring about a profanation of the Divine Name (*ḥillul ha-Shem*, BK 113b)—so much so, that the Talmud enjoins that gentile poor be supported with charity like Jewish poor (Git. 61a) and does not even tolerate the charging of interest to gentiles (BM 70b). [D.S.]

In the Middle Ages. The talmudic laws, referred to above, whose purpose was to minimize contacts between Jews and idolaters ran counter to the social and economic realities of Jewish life in the Middle Ages. Unlike the talmudic period, Jews no longer lived in compact, economically self-sufficient communities. (This historical explanation for lifting many of the talmudic restrictions on Jewish-gentile relationships was already put forth by the Tosafists; see Tos. to Av. Zar. 15a, beg. *Eimor.*) Economic—and, as a result, a measure of social—contact with non-Jews was an inevitable necessity. Hence, in daily life, many of the talmudic restrictions in this area simply became dead letters. Taking this fact into cognizance, R. Menahem Meiri could write: "In our times, no one observes these practices, neither gaon, rabbi, sage, pietist, nor pseudo-pietist" (*Bet ha-Beḥirah*, Av. Zar. introd.). Under the circumstances, the halakhists of the period were confronted with the problem of reconciling talmudic law with common practice that patently ignored it. Among the tosafists, this was accomplished by a process of dialectically reinterpreting the talmudic sources. Each specific law was reinterpreted so as to make it conform to the current practice. For example, the talmudic law prohibiting business dealings with gentiles on their festivals was construed as in consonance with doing business with Christians on Sundays (Tos. to Av. Zar. 2a, beg. *Asur*). Rashi (quoted in *Or Zaru'a*, Sanh. 2a) declares that such dealings are forbidden only on Christmas and Easter. A similar attitude is taken by the Tosafist R. Elhanan in the matter of renting to a Christian a house owned by a Jew (Tos. to Av. Zar. 21a beg. *Af;* see also Tos. to Av. Zar 13a beg. *Kal va-ḥomer*). Occasionally the discrepancy between law and practice was overcome by drawing a distinction between idolaters referred to in the Talmud and Christians who reside outside the land of Israel (Maharam of Rothenburg, Resp., ed. Berlin, no. 386). While the tosafists declare that "we are certain that the Christians do not worship idols" (Tos. to Av. Zar. 2a beg. *Asur*), an attitude already adumbrated by R. Gershom, they fail to apply the principle categorically. The hesitation of the medieval halakhists to fully accept the implications of an absolute distinction between a Christian and an idolater is apparent in their legal discussions. The prominent tosafist R. Isaac of Dampierre held that since Christians could not be regarded as strict monotheists, according to the halakhah they come under the category of Noachides who are not enjoined against trinitarian belief (Tos. to San. 63b beg. *Asur;* Tos. to Bek. 2b beg. *Shema*). Confronted by the exigencies of daily life, the medieval halakhists tended toward leniency in such talmudic prohibitions as the use of gentile bread, butter, and wine. R. Menahem Meiri constitutes the single significant exception to the attitude of the halakhists. Strongly influenced by the rationalistic philosophy of his time, he drew a basic distinction between idolaters and between Christians and Muslims. The latter, he writes, are "peoples disciplined by religion" and, on principle, are to be regarded as Jews in so far as economic and social relations with them are concerned. In these matters, no invidious distinctions are to be made between Jews and Christians (*Bet ha-Beḥirah,* BK 113b; *ibid.,* Av. Zar. 20a). He hesitates however in his practical decisions to waive all the ancient restrictions lest their total abolition lead to a loss of Jewish identity. Maimonides in his role as halakhist offers a position that is at odds both with that of the medieval decisors and with that of R. Menahem Meiri. He flatly states (Yad, Akum 9:4)—deleted by censors in the ordinary editions—that the talmudic limitations on Jewish-pagan relations are applicable in his own time. Moralistic literature of the period, notably, *Sefer Ḥasidim,* displays a marked ambivalence. In a number of instances, it goes far beyond talmudic law in warning against any contact with Christianity and its ritual objects. Thus, while the tosafists broadly qualify and virtually abolish the prohibition against dealing in the ritual objects of an alien faith, *Sefer Ḥasidim* makes the prohibition absolute. Yet, in its moral teachings, the book exhorts to an ethical scrupulosity in dealings with a gentile who observes the seven Noachide commandments. Such a person, it is averred, should be more honored than a Jew who does not engage in the study of Torah. However, such moral promptings were frequently motivated by considerations of expediency. Nevertheless, in a significant passage (no. 58), the book holds up a noble act performed by a Christian as one most worthy of emulation by Jews. A motive frequently invoked in warning against unethical acts committed by Jews toward Christians is that of *ḥillul ha-Shem* (desecration of God's name; no. 1080). Despite a social atmosphere saturated with Christian contempt, repression, and persecution of Jews, R. Moses of Coucy could write: "We have already explained concerning the remnant of Israel that they are not to deceive any one whether Christian or Muslim. Thus, the Holy One, Blessed be He, scatters Israel among the nations so that proselytes shall be gathered unto them; so long as they behave deceitfully toward them (non-Jews), who will cleave to them? Jews should not lie either to a Jew or to a gentile, nor mislead them in any matter" (*Semag Asayim* no. 82). [TH.F.]

Bibliography: IN THE TALMUD: G. F. Moore, *Judaism,* 1 (1946), 274–5, 339, 453; 2 (1946), 75; B. M. H. Uzid, in: *Ha-Torah ve-ha-Medinah,* 4 (1952), 9–21; ET, 5 (1953), 286–366; E. E. Urbach, in: IEJ, 9 (1959), 149–65, 229–45; M. D. Herr, in: *Sefer Zikkaron le-Binyamin De Vries* (1968), 149–59; E. E. Urbach, *Ḥazal* (1969), 482–3, 488–9. IN THE MIDDLE AGES: J. Katz, *Exclusiveness and Tolerance* (1961); Y. F. Baer, in: Zion, 3 (1937/38), 37–41; E. E. Urbach, *Ba'alei ha-Tosafot* (1955²), index, s.v. *Avodah Zarah;* G. Tchernovitz, *Ha-Yaḥas Bein Yisrael la-Goyim le-fi ha-Rambam* (1950).

GENTILI (Ḥefeẓ), family in northern Italy, particularly in Gorizia, Trieste, Verona, and Venice. The name Gentili was rendered in Hebrew as Ḥefeẓ, and it is the latter name which appears in the Hebrew writings of the members of this family.

MOSES BEN GERSHOM (1663–1711), rabbinical scholar. Born in Trieste, Moses was active in Venice. He was a pupil of Solomon b. Isaac Nizza, who was active in Venice around 1700, and supported himself by being a private tutor. He dealt with philosophy, mathematics, and the natural sciences. He composed poems, one of which, written when he was 13, can be found in the Venice edition of the Bible (1675–78). His main work was a homiletical-philosophical commentary on the Pentateuch (*Melekhet Maḥashevet,* Venice, 1710, with tables and a portrait of the author; second edition, Koenigsberg, 1810, with super-commentary, *Maḥashevet Ḥoshev,* by Judah Leib *Jaffe). Moses also wrote *Ḥanukkat ha-Bayit,* dealing with the construction of the Second Temple (Venice, 1696, with plan). On the occasion of his wedding, the poet Yomtov Valvasson composed a poem (Venice, 1682), and a dirge on his death was published (Ghirondi-Neppi, 241). The

בן מאה שנה אנכי היום
צורת הרב הגאון מו"ה משה חפץ זצ"ל

Frontispiece of *Melekhet Maḥashevet* by Moses Gentili, showing the author at the age of 46, Venice, 1710. This was the first portrait ever published in a Hebrew book. Jerusalem, J.N.U.L.

beginning of an address by Moses is found in an Oxford manuscript (Neubauer, Cat. 1123). [U.C./ED.]

GERSHOM BEN MOSES (1683–1700), son of Moses b. Gershom. Gershom wrote: *Yad Ḥaruzim*, a Hebrew rhyme-lexicon containing an introduction, 12 rules for Hebrew usage in poetry and rhyme scheme, and an appendix devoted to a poetical version of the 613 commandments *(azharot)*, according to Maimonides' enumeration. After Gershom's untimely death at the age of 17, the work was published by his father who added an introduction containing his son's biography. A eulogy by Solomon b. Isaac Nizza, Gershom's teacher, appears as an appendix to the work (Venice, 1700; second edition, without the *azharot* and the eulogy, but with additional notes by Simḥah *Calimani, Venice, 1738–45). Moses Gentili quotes some of his son's interpretations in his *Melekhet Maḥashevet*. [SH.A.H./ED.]

Bibliography: Ghirondi Neppi, 70, 239; Steinschneider, in: *Vessillo Israelitico*, 27 (1879), 204 n.2; Soave, *ibid.*, 28 (1880), 46; Fuenn, Keneset, 219; Cowley, Cat, 212, 469.

GEOGRAPHY.

In the Bible. The geographic horizon in the early biblical period was the *lu'aḥ ha-ammim*, a table of 70 nations listed in Genesis 10. The identification of the names and the location of the countries are the subject of differences of opinion among scholars. It is clear however that included are all of Arabia, Syria, Asia Minor as far as the Caucasus, all the lands of the Tigris and Euphrates, the western part of the highlands of Iran, the regions of the middle and lower Nile including the desert extending to their west, and Greece and its islands (see *Table of Nations).

In the Talmud. Scattered throughout the Talmuds, the Targums, and the Midrashim are various geographic references connected with the *halakhah* and with expositions and homilies on the Bible and Midrash. Most of these references are associated with Ereẓ Israel: with laws about "commandments applying to Ereẓ Israel," which are to be observed only in Ereẓ Israel, with praise of the country, and with the identification of biblical place-names.

The *mitzvot* dependent on Ereẓ Israel have full application only within "the territories occupied by those who came back from Babylonia" (Ereẓ Israel); have partial application within the borders of those who came up from Egypt; and refer only marginally to that territory which lies within the wider borders promised to the patriarchs but outside the area of those who came up from Egypt—territory conquered by David on his own responsibility and known in the Talmud as Syria. Within the obligatory territories were exempted enclaves, such as Caesarea in the Sharon, Susita (Hippos) in the Golan, Ashkelon in the Judean coastal lowland, and within the exempted territories obligatory enclaves such as Kefar Ẓemaḥ on the southeastern shore of Lake Kinneret. The boundaries of these areas and also of the enclaves are laid down in the *halakhah* (Shev. 6:1; Tosef., Shev. 6:6–11; Tosef., Oho. 18:14; Sif. Deut. 51; TJ, Shev. 6:1, 36b). In connection with the laws of usucapion, Ereẓ Israel was divided into three districts: Judea, Transjordan, and Galilee (BB 3:2). Concerning the laws for the removal of fruit from the house in the sabbatical year when they had stopped growing in the field, each of the three districts was subdivided into three regions: mountain, valley, and lowland. The phytogeographical features of these were: for mountains the *Cillin* pine, for valleys the palm, and for lowlands the sycamore *(Ficus sycamora)* (Tosef., Shev. 7:11, cf. Shev. 9:2). The area between Judea and Galilee was called "the country of the Cutheans" or contemptuously "the Cuthean Strip" (*Matlit shel Kutim;* Lam. R. 3:7). The question also arose as to whether the law applicable to levitically unclean heathen countries applied also to the country of the Cutheans. The sages decided that the law was applicable in those cities which had been surrounded by a wall since the time of Joshua and in which *Megillat Esther* is read on Adar 15th (Ar. 9:6; Ar. 32a; Meg. 4a; TJ, Meg. 1:1, 70a).

Many identifications of geographic and ethnographic names in the Bible are in the nature of expositions. Onkelos contented himself with a few which he considered to be beyond doubt. Targum Pseudo-Jonathan and the Palestinian Targum frequently identified places solely on the basis of the similarity of names without regard to any geographic considerations. Among the identifications of the table of nations, given in the Midrashim and Targums, none includes all the nations and countries known to the sages. These identifications are frequently inconsistent and contradictory. The equation of Rome with biblical Edom which was apparently intended at first to allow for open criticism of the Roman authorities was later accepted as fact and hence the former and latter halves of the verse: "Behold, of the fat places of the earth shall be thy dwelling, and of the dew of heaven from above" (Gen. 27:39) were interpreted in the Midrash (Gen. R. 67:6) as referring respectively to Italy (Rashi, ad loc., adds "of Greece," i.e., Magna Graecia, southern Italy) and to Bet Guvrin. On the identification of Kenites, Kenizzites, and Kadmonites, who are mentioned in the covenant with Abraham (Gen. 15:19), and who were not conquered by those who came up from Egypt, there are divergent opinions: in a plausible interpretation R. Judah held that they were Arab tribes on the border of the land of the seven nations which the Israelites

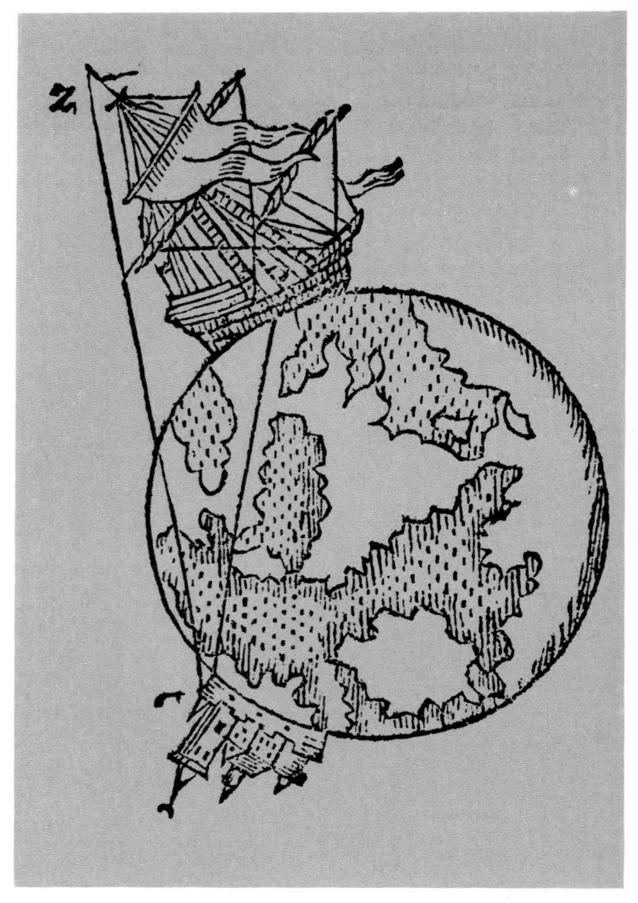

Figure 1. Eighteenth-century schematic map of the world with lines representing navigational directions, from *Ma'aseh Tuviyyah*, by Tobias Cohn, a physician and Hebrew scholar. Jessnitz, Germany, 1721. Jerusalem, J.N.U.L.

inherited, whereas R. Eliezer contended that they refer to Asia Minor, Thrace, and Carthage (Gen. R. 44:23, end; BB 56a). The identification of places in Ereẓ Israel, particularly in Galilee, is mostly realistic and is of aid in a scientific study of the historical topography of the country (TJ, Meg. 1:1, 70a, b; TB, Meg 5b).

The sages thought that geographic and hydrologic factors exerted a great influence on man's physical and spiritual being. On Moses' instructions to the spies: "And see the land, what it is; and the people that dwelleth therein, whether they are strong or weak" (Num. 13:18), the *Tanḥuma* (Shelaḥ Lekha, 6) comments: "There is a country that raises strong men, and there is a country that raises weak men." A similar view is expressed in the midrashic statement: "Some springs raise strong, others weak men, some handsome, others ugly men, some modest, other dissolute men." The spring of Shittim (Num. 25:1), which was a place of licentiousness, watered Sodom (Num. R. 20:22).

From the statements of the sages one can reconstruct the geographic concept of the world current in talmudic times. The earth with its seas was seen as a circle ringed around by the ocean *(Okyanos)* with the center of the circle being the **even shetiyyah* ("foundation stone") in the Holy of Holies, which was thought to be in the middle of the earth *(tabbur ha-areẓ),* not only in a geometrical sense. This was thought to be the beginning of creation. Around the center are concentric circles in order of importance: the Holy of Holies, the Temple, Jerusalem, Ereẓ Israel, and the world (Tanḥ. Kedoshim, 6); this particular idea was devised by a man who had never seen Jerusalem. The idea of the centricity of the Holy Land occurs first in the Apocrypha, influenced by the Greek concept of *omphalos,* that the center of the earth is at Delphi. The sages based the idea that the start of creation is with the *even shetiyyah* on biblical passages (Tosef. Yom ha-Kippurim 3:6; Yoma 54b), but not the centricity of Jerusalem, which was not of such great significance to Jews as to Christians who transferred the center to the cross of Jesus, a concept which the Church Fathers based on biblical verses (Ezek. 5:5; 38:12; Ps. 74:12). Thus the center of circular medieval maps is Jerusalem with the cross. The view that Ereẓ Israel is higher than all countries, Jerusalem than the whole of Ereẓ Israel, and the Temple Mount than all Jerusalem (Sif. Deut. 152 and 37; Sanh. 87a) is a literal homiletical interpretation of the verse: "Then shalt thou arise, and get thee up unto the place which the Lord thy God shall choose" (Deut. 17:8). The sages were however not unaware of the fact that the spring of Etam, from which water flowed to the Temple, was higher than the Temple Mount.

An estimate of the size of the "world" ranged between the extremes of 6,000 and 1,440,000 parasangs. But a still more exaggerated view held that the earth was only 1/12,960,000 part of Gehinnom (TJ, Ber. 1:1, 2c; Pes. 94a). On the area of the inhabited world (οἰκουμένη) there were divergent opinions: (1) a third is inhabited, the remaining two-thirds being sea and desert; (2) the whole inhabited world is situated under one star; (3) the inhabited world is located between the Wain and Scorpio, that is, about 80° from north to south (54° north of the equator and 26° south of it); (4) it extends from east to west, a distance of one hour of the sun's course, that is 15° (Pes. 94a). Even those sages who were aware that the earth is round did not deal with the problem of the date line. Alexander the Great during his campaigns is said to have risen upward until he saw the earth like a globe partially submerged in an enormous bowl of water, that is, the ocean (TJ, Av. Zar. 3:1, 42c; Num. R. 13:14). The Zohar (Lev., *s.v. ve-im zevaḥ shelamim* (3:1), Soncino ed., 346) states that according to the Book of R. Hamnuna the Elder the earth is a revolving globe, that when it is day on one side, it is night on the other, that there is a place where there is no day and opposite it a place where there is no night. The comprehension of this is said to be the secret of the mystics and not of geographers. How this individual view came to be included in the Zohar is not clear.

The problem of the density of the earth occupied the aggadists. There was a widespread view that the circle of the earth is like a dish that floats on the face of the *deep namely, the water, and that below the deep are mountains, so that the whole rests on a solid base. Another view holds that the earth rests on pillars which apparently reach down to those mountains. Views on the thickness of the earth range from a thousand cubits (about 500 m. = 547 yds.) to a 50-year journey. There was a generally accepted view that the "water of the deep" is close to the surface of the ground which accounts for the origin of springs and the moistening of the ground: to a handbreadth of rain the deep responds with two handbreadths (Ta'an. 25b). Some thought that these springs originated in the Euphrates. The four rivers that went out of the Garden of Eden were higher than all the rivers in the world, the highest of them being the Euphrates, and hence R. Judah in the name of Rav prohibited all the water in the world to anyone who took a vow not to drink from the Euphrates (Bek. 55a). Hot springs have their origin in the deep, and pass over the entrance to Gehinnom (Shab. 39a). "All the rivers run into the sea, yet the sea is not full . . . they return (to their source)" (Eccles. 1:7). How do they return? There are three views: (1) through the channels of the deep; (2) through vapors that rise from the sea and form clouds, the desalination of the seawater taking place in the deep or in the clouds; (3) that river water disappears in the ocean because the latter has water which "absorbs water" even if brought up in a barrel on to dry land (a view which is apparently not an exposition of the passage in Ecclesiastes). The phenomenon of how such absorption takes place is not explained (Ta'an. 9b; Gen. R. 13:9; et al.). The Jordan flows from the Dead Sea to the ocean below the earth (Bek. 55a). The idea that the ocean is higher than the land is apparently based on the homiletic interpretation of biblical verses (Jer. 5:22; Amos 9:6); the sand on the seashore prevents the flooding of the land, which happened twice, once in the generation of Enosh, when the flood reached Calabria, and once in the generation that witnessed the confusion of the tongues when the flood stretched as far as the ends of Barbaria (TJ, Shek. 6:2, 50a; Gen. R. 23:7, end). In the sea there are river-like currents and waves whose height reaches 300 parasangs which is also the distance between one wave and another. Among the big waves there are small ones (BB 73a).

The sages distinguished between floral zones in Ereẓ Israel on the basis of differences in altitude and hence in temperature. But there are other universal reasons for such diversity, *viz.* the distinctive features of water and of soil. Koheleth-Solomon planted in his gardens and parks "trees . . . of all kinds of fruit" (Eccles. 2:5), which means, according to the *aggadah,* literally all the kinds in the world. That they might flourish he sent demons, over whom he had dominion, to irrigate each tree by bringing water from its country of origin. Another view held that arteries spread out from the center of the earth through the entire world, and Solomon, knowing how to distinguish them, planted on each artery the appropriate trees, even those from Africa and India (Eccles. R. 2:5, no. 1).

From the praise of Ereẓ Israel contained in the *aggadah* it is possible to put together an aggadic geography of the country before its destruction. The love of the Holy Land,

די״ם מלה יונית ופירושו נכח רגליו לפי שהאנשים
בצד אחר של הכדור הלז רגליהם הם נוכח רגלינו :
ומכאן שהארץ היא כדורית יותר מן הי׳

Figure 2. Illustration showing the globe with men standing at both poles, from Tobias Cohn's *Ma'aseh Tuviyyah.*

the anguish at its impoverishment and at the depletion of its children, and the expectation of its future glory engendered exaggerations that are logically incomprehensible. Ereẓ Israel's situation in the center of the world and its altitude did not change even after the destruction of the Second Temple, nor did the weight of its stones, which was greater than those of the neighboring countries (PdRE 13). The *aggadah* is responsible for the extension of the western boundary up to the Atlantic Ocean, this being, for the aggadist, the interpretation of "the Great Sea" in the verse: "And for the western border, ye shall have the Great Sea for a border" (Num. 34:6). Extravagant conclusions were reached by Targum Pseudo-Jonathan. All the countries on the continent as well as the islands opposite Ereẓ Israel within the limits assigned to the patriarchs (from the Brook of Egypt to Taurus Amanus) up to the "primeval waters" at the furthermost extremity of the world and even the ships sailing the sea are all included in the Promised Land *(ibid).* It was said that after the destruction of the Second Temple Ereẓ Israel "drew together," i.e., diminished inside. Alexander Yannai had 60 myriad "cities" in the King's Mountain and in each of them were 60 myriad people, except for three in which there were twice as many. To feed this population the country produced enormous crops of excellent quality. By the fourth century, the country had deteriorated to such an extent that it did not produce even a large number of reeds (TJ., Meg. 1:1, 170a; TJ., Ta'an. 4:8, 69a; Git. 57a). In the days of Simeon b. Shetaḥ rain fell at the right time, the grains of wheat were as large as kidneys, the grains of barley like olives, the lentils like golden denarii (Ta'an. 23a). Several species of trees, such as cinnamon, brought from distant lands in the time of Solomon, still grew in the Second Temple period, and Indian pepper continued to grow until the destruction of Bethar (Eccles. R. 2:8). In fulfillment of the biblical passage: "Thou shalt not lack any thing in it" (Deut. 8:9), there were exiled with Israel to Babylonia through the channels of the deep 700 species of fish permissible as food and through the air 800 species of locusts permissible as food. The fish and the locusts returned with those who came back from Babylonia (Lam. R., Proem 34).

The fate of the Lost Ten Tribes has stirred the imagination of Jews from the days of the Second Temple to our times. A miraculous existence was invented for them in distant and unknown lands, the legend of the tribes being connected with those of the river *Sambatyon and the Mountains of Darkness. Thus the Ten Tribes were exiled across the *Sambatyon, Σαββατεῖον, the Sabbath river, which rages and hurls stones on six days of the week but rests on the Sabbath, thus proving through nature the holiness of the Sabbath (Sanh. 65b; Gen R. 11:5, 73:6); Josephus describes it as a river in Syria which flows on one day and rests on six days of the week (Jos., Wars 7:96–99); the origin of the legend being apparently to be found in rhythmically intermittent springs, such as Ein Farah in the Judean desert.

Medieval Jewish Geography. Knowledge of the spherical form of the earth, derived from observing the height of the stars in different latitudes, reached Jewish scholars in Islamic countries through Arab astronomy. The first Jew to consider the earth as a sphere was the Cordovan rabbi, Ḥasan b. Mar Ḥasan ha-Dayyan, in his book on intercalation (end of the 10th cent.). At approximately the same time in Baghdad *Sherira b. Ḥanina Gaon, followed by his son *Hai Gaon, rejected the opinion that the heavens are like a cap over a flat earth. Only fragments remain of the stories of Abraham b. Jacob who traveled in Germany and the Slavic countries in the 950s. The two letters from Joseph b. Aaron, king of the Khazars, to R. *Ḥisdai ibn Shaprut, which comprise not only historical, but also geographical material, were transmitted by Jewish merchants from Germany (about 950). The books of medieval travelers frequently contained material of geographic interest (see *Travelers).

By the 11th century the spherical form of the earth was accepted among Jewish scholars in Islamic countries, and from there the idea passed to Provence and Italy. Solomon ibn *Gabirol states in *Keter Malkhut:* "The terrestrial globe is divided into two, half is dry land and half water." The first work in Hebrew about the round shape of the earth and its division into climatic regions, together with a list of the countries in each region, was *Sefer Ẓurat ha-Areẓ* ("The Book of the Shape of the Earth" (late 11th or beginning of the 12th century)), by *Abraham b. Ḥiyya. His system, like that of his Muslim teachers, is that of Ptolemy, the Alexandrian (c. 150 C.E.). According to Abraham b. Ḥiyya, the earth, with the seas upon it, is a globe. The western or lower half of the globe is entirely water. The eastern half is mostly dry land (except for seas such as the Mediterranean and the Red Sea), but there is no human settlement except in seven regions. North of latitude 66° there is no settlement because of the cold. In the far south (there are those who say from the equator to the south and those who say from a few degrees south of the equator) there is no populated area because of the heat, which increases as one progresses in a southerly direction. *Ẓurat ha-Areẓ* was published with a Latin translation by D. Schreckenfuchs and notes by Sebastian Muenster (Basle, 1546).

The discoveries at the end of the 15th and the beginning of the 16th century refuted the limitation of the earth's population to seven regions. Information regarding this refutation was conveyed to readers of Hebrew by Abraham b. Mordecai *Farissol in chapter 13 of his book *Iggeret Orḥot Olam* ("Epistle on the Ways of the World," 1525), but geographical ideas derived from legends or books are still to be found in homiletic and ḥasidic works, and they persisted in "scholarly" books until the 19th century. Still in 1550, Mattathias b. Solomon *Delacrut, in his short treatise *Ẓel ha-Olam* ("Shadow of the World"), based on a 13th-century French work, speaks of a quarter of the area of dry land which was not populated and where no human foot trod. As late as the end of the 18th century, Phinehas Elijah *Hurwitz of Vilna in *Sefer ha-Berit [ha-Shalem]* ("The [Complete] Book of the Covenant," 1797–) maintains that most of the globe is water, either surface or underground, that the waters of the oceans are higher than the land, and that sand prevents their flooding the earth. It served as a basic text to those who wished to learn about nature, but were apprehensive of the work of the new *maskilim* who belittled traditional literature. Geographic literature in Hebrew and the part played by Jews in systematic geographic research are slight compared with the Jewish contribution to other branches of science, such as astronomy, mathematics, and medicine.

Geography Textbooks. Abraham Farissol's *Iggeret Orḥot Olam* served as a Hebrew geography textbook until the 19th century. Like other 16th-century Jewish and Christian thinkers, Farissol believed in the existence of the Ten Tribes and the river Sambatyon, and devoted much space to them. Approximately 300 years later, Samson ha-Levi *Bloch, a *maskil* of the Galician school, published *Shevilei Olam* ("The Paths of the World": vol. 1, "Asia," 1822; vol. 2, "Africa," 1827), basing himself on German literature. The treatise is in the rhetorical and witty style of the times. Abraham Menaḥem Mendel *Mohr, still using only German sources, continued the work (1856) after Bloch's death. The information on Jewish communities and Jewish scholars, known to the two authors without having to do any special research, is their original contribution. In the 1780s with the establishment of schools that included secular instruction in the curriculum, special short textbooks began to appear. *Reshit Limmudim* ("The Beginning of Instruction," first ed. 1796; last ed. 1869), by Baruch Linda, the first such textbook in Hebrew, also has chapters on geography. A geography book, *Ha-Kaddur* ("The Globe," Prague, 1831), by Moses S. Neumann, was written partly in Hebrew and partly in German, though in Hebrew characters. Asher Radin's *Ge'ografyah ha-Ketannah* ("The Short Geography," Koenigsberg, 1860), is an abridgment of a German textbook. Two works on the principles of geography: *Meẓukei Ereẓ* ("The Foundation of the Earth," 1878), by Nahum *Sokolow, and *Gelilot ha-Areẓ* ("The Regions of the Earth," 1880), based on German literature, by Hillel Kahana, an experienced pedagogue who is one of the last of the Galician school, appeared about the same time. As was customary among writers who did not know any Western European language other than German, Kahana transcribed French and English names according to the German pronunciation. An innovation was a colored Hebrew map, and sketches and pictures with Hebrew captions. In this way he educated the Hebrew reader to map study and observation.

Writers of textbooks solved problems in Hebrew geographical terminology and paved the way for the teaching of geography in schools in Ereẓ Israel from the end of the 19th century. [A.J.Br.]

Modern Geography. In modern geography there has been development in the concentration on limited areas and specialization in particular fields of study. One of these limited areas is the city. *Die Stadt Bonn, ihre Lage und raeumliche Entwicklung* (1947), by Alfred *Philippson, a German geographer, is one of the most important works on urban geography. Another significant contribution was made by Norton Sidney *Ginsberg, a U.S. geographer, who at the invitation of the Japanese government studied Tokyo's urban problems and incorporated his findings in "Tokyo Memorandum" (*Reports on Tokyo Metropolitan Planning,* 1962). Another specialized field is economic geography. Julius *Bien, a U.S. cartographer, not only prepared atlases for a number of major cities but carried out a full-scale survey of intercontinental railways for the U.S. War Department. Saul Bernard *Cohen, who specialized in a number of geographic fields, wrote *Store Location Research for the Food Industry* (1961), considered a standard guide. In addition, in the sphere of political geography he wrote *Geography and Politics in a World Divided* (1963).

On physical geography Victor A. *Conrad wrote *Fundamentals of Physical Climatology* (1942) and *Methods in Climatology* (1944); the Israel meteorologist Dov *Ashbel published *A Bio-Climatic Atlas of Israel* (1950), and *Climate of the Great Rift; Arava, Dead Sea, Jordan Valley* (1966). Joseph Ḥefeẓ Gentilli (1912–), an Australian geographer, wrote *Australian Climates and Resources* (1947) and *Geography of Climate* (1958). In connection with the study of the geography of soils David *Amiran, an Israeli, edited for UNESCO "Land Use in Semi-Arid Mediterranean Climates" (in *Arid Zones Research,* vol. 26, 1964). Morton Joseph *Rubin, a U.S. meteorologist, did research in oceanography, meteorology, and in glaciology, particularly in connection with his studies on the Antarctic. Another specialized branch of modern geography is biogeography; a monumental work in this field is *Studies in Medical Geography* (7 vols., 1958–67), by Jacques Meyer May (1896–), a French-born American scientist. Nautical geography is another division which has drawn the interest of Jewish geographers, among them the Italian Carlo *Errera, who wrote the pamphlet *L'italianità dell' Adriatico* (1914). The modern period has also produced an increasing number of historians of geography. Gustavo Uzielli (1889–1911), an Italian, did extensive research on

ספר
צורת הארץ
הנכתב ע״י הנשיא ר׳ אברהם בר׳ חייא
הספרדי· כבר היה נדפס עם איזה פי׳
מחכמי האומות בלשון לטין·
וגם ספר אשפירא הגדול
נקרא מראות אופנים
והקצר נקרא ספר הגלגל
אשר לא היו בדפוס מעולם· וכעת
כולם עולים ע״י חד מזעירא חכימיי׳·
התוכן ה״ה האלוף התורני מוהר״ר
יהונתן בעל מחבר ספר ישועה
בישראל· לא כראשונים שנחסרו
שערים ופתחים· וברוב בקיאתו איזן
ותיקן הרבה· כאשר עיניכם תחזנה
מישרים· לתלפיות מסודרים:
בשנת אלה תולדות שמים וארץ
פה קק אופי באך
בדפוס הארון באנא
פענטורא דע לא נאיי

Figure 3. Title page of Abraham b. Ḥiyya's *Sefer Ẓurat ha-Areẓ,* Offenbach, 1720. Jerusalem, J.N.U.L.

the explorations of Christopher Columbus, Toscanelli, and Amerigo Vespucci. His best known work is *La vita e i tempi di P. Dal Pozzo Toscanelli* (1894).

A number of geographers have turned their attention to the history of cartography. Roberto *Almagià, one of Italy's most distinguished geographers, edited *Monumenta Italiae Geographica* (1929) and *Monumenta Cartographica Vaticana* (4 vols., 1944–55). Erwin J. *Raisz, an American, wrote *General Cartography* (1938) and *Principles of Cartography* (1962).

See also *Mapmakers. [Ed.]

Bibliography: Neubauer, Géogr; J. Z. Hirschensohn, *Sheva Ḥokhmot* (1912²); A. J. Brawer, in: *Yerushalayim*, 10 (1914), 117–32; idem, *Palaestina nach der Agada* (1920); S. Klein, *Zur Geographie Palaestinas in der Zeit der Mischna* (1917); J. Obermeyer, *Die Landschaft Babylonien im Zeitalter des Talmuds...* (1929); J. M. Guttmann, *Ereẓ Yisrael be-Midrash ve-Talmud* (1929); M. Avi-Yonah, *Atlas Karta li-Tekufat Bayit Sheni, ha-Mishnah ve-ha-Talmud* (1966); F. Taeschner, in: ZDMG, 77 (1923), 31–80; Zunz, Schr, 1 (1875), 146–216.

GEORGE (Cohn), MANFRED (1893–1965), journalist and editor. Born in Berlin, he took a degree in law and became a prominent newspaper editor and writer. George excelled as a political writer and as a film and drama critic. Among his books is *Theodor Herzl, sein Leben und sein Vermaechtnis* (1932). When the Nazis came to power, George went to Prague, worked there for several years, and in 1938 emigrated to the U.S. In New York, he took over *Aufbau* (subtitled "Reconstruction"), founded in 1924, originally the newsletter of the German-Jewish "New World Club." Under his editorship, *Aufbau* became a German-language weekly representing the German-Jewish immigrant community and acquired a circulation of more than 30,000. George was one of the outstanding figures of America's German-Jewish community.

GEORGIA (Rus. **Gruziya**), Soviet Socialist Republic in W. Transcaucasia. There is a tradition among the Jews of Georgia (the "Gurjim") that they are descended from the Ten Tribes exiled by Shalmaneser, which they support by their claim that there are no *kohanim* (priestly families) among them. According to another tradition, their ancestors were the exiles from Judah under Nebuchadnezzar. Some scholars believe the "אפריקי" mentioned in the Talmud (Tam. 32a; Sanh. 94a) lies in the vicinity of Georgia and that Rabbi Akiva traveled as far as Georgia (RH 26a). In any case Jewish settlement in Georgia has ancient origins. According to the "History of Armenia" of Moses of Chorene (5th century) the Bagrat family which gave kings to Georgia and Armenia was descended from one of the noblemen of Judah taken captive by Nebuchadnezzar. This source also relates that other families of the Georgian aristocracy were of Jewish origin.

The Georgian and Armenian traditions emphasize the role played by the Jews in the spread of Christianity in this region. In the vicinity of Mtskheta an Aramaic inscription in Hebrew characters was found on the tomb of a certain Judah Gurk. Possibly the Jews of Georgia took part in the anti-talmudic *messianic movements from the ninth century on. At least one tradition which associates Abu ʿImrān Mūsā al-Zaʿfarānī with Georgia refers to him as *Abu ʿImrān al-Ṭiflisī. *Kirkisānī testifies that in his day there were still members of the sect known as the Tiflisites. The Georgian Jews were neighbors of the *Khazars and there were presumably cultural relations between the Khazars, the Alans, and the Georgian Jews.

Abraham *ibn Daud testifies to the faithfulness of the Jewish communities of Georgia ("the Land of the Girgasite and it is called Girgan") to Rabbanite Judaism. *Benjamin

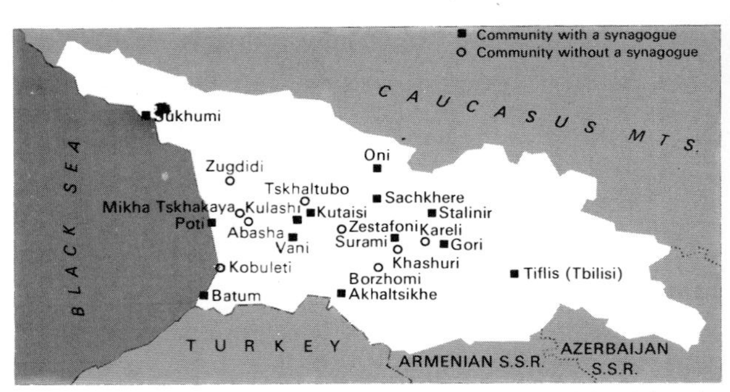

Jewish communities in Georgian S.S.R. From M. Neistadt, *Yehudei Gruzyah: Ma'avak al ha-Shivah le-Ẓiyyon*, Tel Aviv, 1970.

of Tudela (after 1160) includes the Jews of Georgia ("the Land of Goron, known as Garganin, they live along the bank of the Giḥon River, they [the Georgians] are the Girgasites and practice the Christian religion") among those whom "the exilarch authorizes in all these communities to appoint over every community a rabbi and *ḥazzan*, because they come to him to receive *semikhah* and permission and they bring him gifts and presents"; this indicates that by the second half of the 12th century the Jews of Georgia recognized the authority of the Babylonian academies. About ten years after the visit of Benjamin of Tudela, *Pethahiah of Regensburg mentions the small number of Jews in the towns of Georgia. Marco Polo, who passed through Georgia in 1272, reports that there were Jews living in Tiflis, though they were not numerous. The institution of **servi camerae regis* also appears to have reached Georgia. In 1428 King Alexander I conferred 27 Jewish families on the former Catholicos and the patriarch Diometius. Persecutions of the Georgian Jews are connected with the name of this king.

With the feudal disintegration of the kingdom and the general insecurity of the 15th century, the sufferings of the Jews increased. Their dependence on the landowners grew and they had to perform onerous duties. Some Jews were actually degraded to the status of slaves and Jewish girls were sold to the harems of the Muslim rulers. This situation continued until the beginning of the 19th century, when Georgia passed to Russia. Memories of the oppressions and injuries they underwent in this period were still alive within the Georgian communities during the second half of the 19th century. In 1780 a German traveler reported that the village Jews of Georgia did not observe the precepts and were therefore referred to by their coreligionists in the towns as "Canaanites." The belated contacts with the Jewish culture of Babylonia, prolonged oppression, and constant migration were apparently responsible for the absence of creative cultural achievement among Georgian Jewry. Their spoken language is that of the local inhabitants.

Figure 1. The synagogue in Kuolashi, Georgian S.S.R.

The Russian authorities did not differentiate the Jews of Georgia from the rest of the population. During the first period of Russian rule at least, the restrictive legislation imposed on the Jews throughout Russia was not applied to them. The statute of 1804 authorized the settlement of "European" Jews in the Caucasus; however, only a limited number of craftsmen arrived in Georgia. The senatorial decree of 1825 prohibited Jews from settling in the Caucasus, and the regulation concerning the Jews of 1835 excluded Georgia from the territories in which Jewish residence was permitted. The expulsion of the Jews was even mooted, but the local authorities violently opposed it claiming that a considerable number were engaged in agriculture and commerce while others were serfs. In 1835 there were 1,363 Jews with 113 Karaites living in the town of *Kutais (Kutaisi) and its surroundings, 1,040 in Gori, 623 in Akhaltsikhe, and 61 in *Tiflis (Tbilisi). The total Jewish population of Georgia and the region beyond the Caucasus was 12,234.

In 1878 a *blood libel case occurred in Georgia, the Jewish inhabitants of a village in the vicinity of Kutaisi being accused of the murder of a six-year-old girl. The trial took place in 1879, and the accused, who were defended by noted Russian advocates, were declared innocent.

According to the census of 1897, there were 18,574 Jews living in Georgia (9,710 in the province of Tiflis, 8,864 in the province of Kutais) of whom 6,665 were local Georgian Jews; however, the latter figure may not be accurate. The largest communities were in Kutaisi (4,843), Tiflis (3,668), Akhaltsikhe (1,533), and *Batum (1,179). Communities of European Jews had already been established in Georgia by the end of the 19th century, and the relations between these and the local Jews were strained. A number of Georgian rabbis who studied at the *yeshivot* of Poland and Lithuania helped to promote better relations between the two groups. Jewish soldiers from European Russia who served in the Caucasus also made contacts with the Georgian Jews and spread Zionism there. Extensive Zionist activity was initiated by communal leaders from among the many refugees who reached Georgia during World War I from the western regions of Russia, and a number of pioneers stayed in Georgia on their way to Ereẓ Israel. Georgian Jews began to settle in Ereẓ Israel in 1863. In 1914 there were about 500 members of the "Gurji" community in Ereẓ Israel, most of them in Jerusalem. By 1920–21, their numbers had increased to approximately 1,700.

After the establishment of the short-lived independent Republic of Georgia in 1918, the Jews were granted full equality of rights and a number held important positions. According to the 1926 census, there were 21,105 Jewish inhabitants (0.8% of the population) in the Soviet Georgian Republic though in fact the number was greater; it has been estimated at 30,000. They succeeded in maintaining their communal organization and way of life, the Soviet authorities showing relative tolerance to their customs and religious institutions in line with general Soviet policy toward this region. Apparently attempts to organize kolkhozes of Georgian Jews were unsuccessful, and some migrated to the towns. A historico-ethnographic museum devoted to the study of the history of the Georgian Jews was founded in Tbilisi in 1933. The museum published three volumes of studies in Russian and Georgian between 1940 and 1945. After its director was imprisoned and sent to Siberia, the museum was closed down in 1949 and its large collection was transferred to the Georgian Museum in Tbilisi.

During World War II Jews from the Nazi-occupied territories temporarily settled in Georgia. The encounter with the stream of Jewish refugees from Eastern Europe who arrived in Georgia did much to stimulate national awareness among Georgian Jewry. The support given by the Soviet Union in establishing the State of Israel also encouraged national feelings. According to the 1959 census the Jewish population of Georgia numbered 51,582 (1.3% of the population) of whom 36,745 spoke Georgian and the remainder were Russian and Yiddish-speaking ("Ashkenazim"). One-third of the Jews of Georgia lived in Tbilisi. An estimate based on unofficial local sources puts the number of Jews in Georgia in the 1960s much higher, in one estimate even at 80,000.

[S. Ett.]

Figure 2. Sukkah of the synagogue in Sukhomi, Georgian S.S.R.

Despite anti-religious indoctrination by the Soviet authorities and the complete lack of Jewish educational facilities, many Georgian Jews succeeded in maintaining Jewish traditions among their families, celebrating Jewish festivals and keeping Jewish customs with their children both in the synagogues and in their homes. Contacts between Ḥabad Ḥasidim who reached Georgia and Orthodox Georgian Jews were somehow established, and in the 1960s the urge to settle in Israel became even more explicit among Georgian Jews. In November 1969 Israel's Prime Minister Golda Meir announced the contents of a letter which she had received from 18 heads of Georgian Jewish families. It expressed a deep-felt religious and historical attachment to the land of Israel and a protest, directed to the United Nations Human Rights Committee, against the Soviet authorities who withheld their exit permits for emigration to Israel. The letter inaugurated a spate of similar written statements and protests of Jews from various parts of the Soviet Union. See also *Mountain Jews.

[Ed.]

Figure 3. Three members of the congregation in the Sukhomi synagogue.

Georgian Jewish Writers and Intellectuals.

***BAAZOV, HERZL** (1904–1945).

BABALIKASHVILLI, NISSAN, orientalist; son of a Tbilisi rabbi; he specialized in Jewish subjects and investigated the history of Jewish settlement in Georgia. He discovered manuscripts relating to Jewish history there in the 9th and 10th centuries.

DANIELOSHVILI, MOSHE, stage producer; he translated S. *An-Ski's play "The Dybbuk" into Georgian and produced it at the state theater at Tbilisi.

DAVIDASHVILI, ROSA, ethnologist and author of children's literature of the generation preceding the Revolution.

DAVIDASHVILI, YIZḤAK, philologist; he graduated in Semitic languages at Tbilisi in the late 1960s, and acquired knowledge of Hebrew, Yiddish, and Arabic, as well as of the Bible and modern Hebrew literature. He specialized in medieval Spanish poetry, and translated works by Judah Halevi, Moses ibn Ezra, Abraham ibn Ezra, and other Jewish authors into Georgian from versions in Yiddish, German, or Spanish as the original works in Hebrew were not available. Some of these were published in the Georgian literary quarterly *Homli* in 1969.

GAPONOV, BORIS, translator of the national Georgian epic by Shota Rust'haveli, *Vep'khis-taosani* ("The Man in the Panther's Skin," 12th century), into a perfect and rich Hebrew. It was published only in Israel (1969) and its author was awarded the Tchernichowsky Prize for translations into Hebrew.

KOKASHVILI, GYORGI, poet, playwright, and literary critic; his play "The Children of the Sea" was performed at the state theater at Tbilisi.

KOTSISHVILI, JOSEPH, author of an historical novel on the beginning of Jewish settlement in Georgia; he translated Shalom Aleichem into Georgian, as well as works by Lion *Feuchtwanger.

MAMISTABOLOB, ABRAHAM, poet, born in the village of Staliniri, formerly Tskhinvali; a collection of his poems published in 1957 includes two poems based on Jewish themes, "Wedding in the Jewish Quarter" and "The Family."

MIKHAELASHVILI, SHALOM, historian; he investigated the history of his native community at Kulashi.

[Mo.N.]

Bibliography: E. Salgaller, in: JSOS, 26 (1964), 195–202; A. Harkavy, *Ha-Yehudim u-Sefat ha-Slavim* (1867), 106–20; J. J. Chorny, *Sefer ha-Massa'ot be-Ereẓ Kavkaz u-va-Medinot asher me-Ever la-Kavkaz* (1884); A. L. Eliav (Ben-Ammi), *Between Hammer and Sickle* (1969), passim; M. Neistadt, *Yehudei Gruzyah* (1970); *Histoire de Géorgie depuis l'antiquité jusqu'au XIXè siècle* (attrib. uncertain, trans. M. F. Brosset (Rus. name M. I. Brosse), 7 vols., 1849–58); J. Baye, *Les Juifs des montagnes et les Juifs géorgiens* (1902); A. Katz, *Die Juden im Kaukasus* (1894); D. M. Maggid, in: *Istoriya yevreyskogo naroda,* 12 (1921; = *Istoriya yevreyev v Rossii,* 2 bk. 1) 85–95; M. S. Plisetski, *Religiya i byt gruzinskikh yevreyev* (1931); *Yevreyskaya Biblioteka,* 7 no. 12 (1880), 1–188 (on the Kutaisi blood libel); *Al Yehudei Berit ha-Mo'aẓot,* published by the Israel Ministry of Education and Culture (1970).

GEORGIA, state in S.E. United States. The Jewish population of Georgia was approximately 27,000 in 1968. Georgia was first settled at *Savannah by Gen. James Oglethorpe in February 1733. Two shiploads of Jews, about 90 persons, arrived during the same year and were permitted to stay

Премьер-министру Израиля
госпоже Голде Меир

Уважаемая госпожа Меир,
мы, 18-ть верующих еврейских семей Грузии, всё ещё ждём и молимся.
Мы обратились с одинаковыми просьбами /разница только в заключительных строчках/ к главам трёх великих держав и пересылаем Вам копии всех трёх писем.
Мы делаем всё, что можем сделать; сделайте и Вы всё, что сможете, для нашего освобождения.
Мы вновь предоставляем Вам право, если потребуется, опубликовать полные тексты писем, приведя полностью фамилии, имена, отчества и домашние адреса.
Мы вновь просим Вас принять любые меры, которые Вы сочтёте необходимыми.
Не думайте о нашей безопасности: жребий брошен и пути назад уже нет.
Мы верим: Бог поможет вам и нам.

ПОДПИСИ /на следующей странице/:

ПОДПИСИ:

1. ЭЛАШВИЛИ Шабата Михайлович — Кутаиси, Джапаридзе, 53.
2. ЭЛАШВИЛИ Михаил Шабатович — Кутаиси, Джапаридзе, 33.
3. ЭЛАШВИЛИ Израиль Михайлович — Кутаиси, Кирова, 31.
4. ЭЛУАШВИЛИ Яков Аронович — Кутаиси, Маяковского, 5.
5. ХИХИНАШВИЛИ Мордех Исакович — Кутаиси, Махарадзе, 19.
6. ЧИКВАШВИЛИ Михаил Самуилович — Кутаиси, Хаханашвили, 38.
7. ЧИКВАШВИЛИ Моше Самуилович — Кутаиси, Церетели, 82.
8. БЕБЕРАШВИЛИ Михаил Рубенович — Кутаиси, Клара Цеткин, 9.
9. ЭЛАШВИЛИ Яков Израйлович — Кутаиси, Церетели, 54.
10. МИХЕЛАШВИЛИ Хаим Аронович — Поти, Цхакая, 57.
11. МИХАИЛАШВИЛИ Альберт Хаимович — Поти, Цхакая, 57.
12. МИХЕЛАШВИЛИ Арон Хаимович — Поти, Джерахидзе, 18.
13. ТЕТРУАШВИЛИ Хаим Давидович — Кутаиси, Джапаридзе, 42.
14. ЦИЦУАШВИЛИ Исро Захарович — Кутаиси, Шаумяна, 1-й пер., 5.
15. ЦИЦУАШВИЛИ Ефрем Исрович — Кутаиси, Шаумяна, 1-й пер., 6.
16. ЯКОБИШВИЛИ Бенсион Шаломович — Тбилиси, 4, до востребования /проживал по ул. Барнова, 91/
17. БАТОНИАШВИЛИ Михаил Рафаелович — Кутаиси, Джапаридзе, 53.
18. ТЕТРУАШВИЛИ Михаил Шаломович — Кулаши, Сталина, 114.

Figure 4. Letter received by the Israel Prime Minister from 18 Georgian families in 1969, enclosing their appeal to the heads of the three Western Great Powers for help in emigrating from the Soviet Union to Israel. The text reads:

"Dear Mrs. Meir, We, 18 religious families of Georgia, are still waiting and praying. We have applied with identical requests (there is a difference only in the concluding lines) to the Heads of the three Great Powers and we are sending you copies of all the three letters. We are doing everything we can; please, do also everything you can for our liberation. We again give you the right, if necessary, to publish the full texts of the letters, giving in full our family names, given names, patronyms and addresses. We again ask you to undertake any measures that you consider necessary. Do not think of our safety: the lot has been cast and there is no way back any more. We believe: God will help you and us."

(signed)

1. Elashvili Shabata Mikhailovich—Kutaisi, Dzhaparidze 53
2. Elashvili Mikhail Shabatovich—Kutaisi, Dzhaparidze 33
3. Elashvili Izrail Mikhailovich—Kutaisi, Kirova 31
4. Eluashvili Yakov Aronovich—Kutaisi, Mayakovskogo 5
5. Khikhinashvili Mordekh Isakovich—Kutaisi, Makharadze 19
6. Chikvashvili Mikhail Samuilovich—Kutaisi, Khakhanashvili 38
7. Chikvashvili Moshe Samuilovich—Kutaisi, Tsereteli 82
8. Beberashvili Mikhail Rubenovich—Kutaisi, Klara Tsetkin 9
9. Elashvili Yakov Izrailovich—Kutaisi, Tsereteli 54
10. Mikhelashvili Khaim Aronovich—Poti, Tskhakaya 57
11. Mikhailashvili Albert Khaimovich—Poti, Tskhakaya 57
12. Mikhelashvili Aron Khaimovich—Poti, Dzherakidze 18
13. Tetruashvili Khaim Davidovich—Kutaisi, Dzhaparidze 42
14. Tsitsuashvili Isro Zakharovich—Kutaisi, Shaumyana, 1st alley, 5
15. Tsitsuashvili Efrem Isrovich—Kutaisi, Shaumyana, 1st alley, 6
16. Yakobishvili Bension Shalomovich—Tbilisi 4, poste restante (formerly at Baranova 91)
17. Batoniashvili Mikhail Rafaelovich—Kutaisi, Dzhaparidze 53
18. Tetruashvili Mikhail Shalomovich—Kulashi, Stalina 114

Temple Albany Hebrew Congregation, Albany, Georgia. Courtesy Union of American Hebrew Congregations, N.Y. Photo Holland.

due to Oglethorpe's personal influence. Many were of German origin, poor and financed by the Jewish community of London. Notable among them were Benjamin Sheftall, Abraham de Lyon, Abraham Minis, and Dr. Nunez who, as the colony's only physician, made himself and his coreligionists more welcome by stemming an epidemic. The first settlement failed. By 1741 all but three or four Jewish families had moved north. Most returned during the 1750s, prospered, and established the congregation Mikveh Israel in 1790. Its first president was Philip Minis. His father Abraham Minis probably was the first white male born in Georgia. A Masonic lodge and a welfare society founded by Oglethorpe during the 1750s listed Jews among the charter members.

There were 400 Jews in the state by 1829; a few families lived in Augusta and isolated areas, while the majority were in Savannah. More rapid growth began during the 1840s with increased immigration from Germany. Jews then settled throughout the state in almost every community, establishing congregations in Augusta in 1850; Columbus, 1854; and Macon, 1859. Although many moved north just before and during the Civil War, they returned in greatly increased numbers immediately after the war. By 1877 there were Jewish communities of 100 or more persons in seven cities, with congregations in *Atlanta; Rome, established in 1871; Athens, 1872; and Albany, 1876. Groups from Eastern Europe began to arrive in the 1880s, settling primarily in Atlanta, Savannah, and Brunswick, which had a

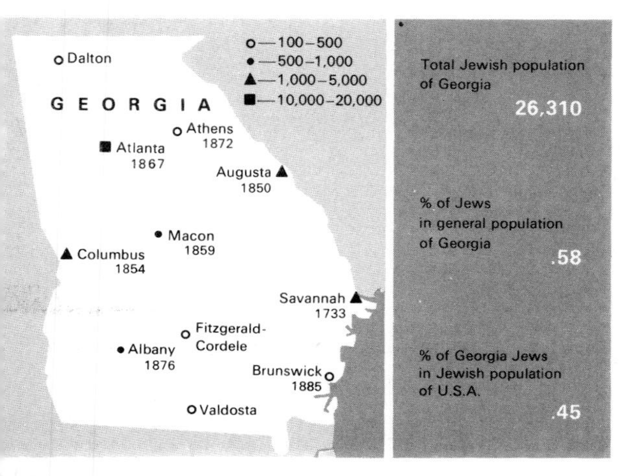

Jewish communities in Georgia and dates of establishment. Population figures for 1968.

congregation by 1885. In 1900 there were 6,400 Jews in Georgia.

Georgian Jews have always enjoyed full civil and religious freedom, including the holding of public office and service in the militia, although the requirement to take a Christian oath restricted them from elective office until 1789. They served as commissioned officers as well as enlisted men in every war, providing all-Jewish companies from Macon and West Point to defend Savannah in 1862. A county is named for David Emmanuel, president of the Georgia Senate in 1797 and governor in 1801, who is believed to have been the first Jewish governor of any U.S. state. Capt. Abraham Simons went to the State Legislature in 1804. Col. Raphael Moses, of Columbus, went to the legislature in 1868 and became chairman of the House Judiciary Committee in 1877. The University of Georgia Law School Building is named for Harold Hirsch (1881–1939), who was a distinguished Atlanta attorney. Several communities have elected Jewish mayors and other city officials. A Jewish woman from Columbus was the first director of the Georgia Department of Public Welfare.

Although relatively free from anti-Semitism, Georgia Jews have suffered hostility on several occasions. During the Civil War they were temporarily banned from Thomasville, and Jewish-owned stores were broken into in Talbottom. A discriminatory newspaper and the Ku Klux Klan exercised widespread influence in the early 20th century, becoming exceptionally bitter during the Frank case (see *Atlanta; Leo *Frank).

Organized Jewish communities exist at present in 12 Georgia cities, the major ones in Atlanta; Savannah, 3,500; Augusta, 1,200; Columbus, 1,000; Macon, 785; and Albany, 525. There is a home for the aged in Atlanta, serving the entire state, and Jewish community centers exist in Atlanta, Savannah, and Columbus. Two summer camps, one operated by the Southeastern Region of the Union of American Hebrew Congregations and the other by the Atlanta Jewish Community Center, are located at Cleveland. There is a Hillel Foundation at the University of Georgia in Athens, and an Anglo-Jewish newspaper published in Atlanta serving the area.

Bibliography: W. G. Plant, in: HUCA, 14 (1939), 575–82; M. H. Stern, in: AJHSP, 53 (1963/64), 169–99; L. Huehner, *ibid.*, 10 (1902), 65–95; C. C. Jones, *ibid.*, 1 (1893), 5–12; J. R. Marcus, *Early American Jewry*, 2 (1953), 277–373; J. O. Rothschild, *As But a Day* (1967); B. W. Korn, *American Jewry and the Civil War* (1951), passim.

[Ja.O.R.]

GERAMA AND GARME (Aram. גְּרָמָא, גַּרְמֵי), terms variously used in the Talmud to describe tortious damage caused indirectly by the tortfeasor's person. The following acts are examples cited of *garme* damage: a judge delivering an erroneous decision resulting in damage to another; burning another's bond—thus preventing him from recovering his debt; a banker giving an erroneous valuation of coins—causing them to be acquired at a loss; damaging mortgaged property held by a creditor—thus reducing the value of his security; informing on another's property to bandits—thus causing them to take it away. Opinion is divided in the Talmud over the question of liability for this kind of tort (BK 98b; 100a; 117b); some of the sages maintain that liability does exist, while others exclude it. In other cases—similar to those cited above—the damage is termed *gerama* (BK 48b; 60a; BB 22b), but here liability is excluded. Examples of *gerama* damage are: placing a ladder by a pigeon loft, enabling a weasel to climb up and eat the pigeons; setting a fire by means of the wind resulting in a conflagration; allowing an animal to trespass onto another's land, where it falls into a well so that its corpse pollutes the water. Other cases which were later interpreted as *gerama* are: bending the stalks of grain in another's field toward an approaching fire so that they catch fire; placing poison in the path of another's animal, causing it to eat this and die; sending a burning object through a minor or an idiot, who is irresponsible and thus causes damage; inciting another's dog to bite a third person; frightening another to the extent that he suffers injury or damage from such fright; leaving a broken vessel on public ground so that the pieces cause injury (BK 24b; 55b–56a). Even the earliest of the post-talmudic commentators found difficulty in explaining the difference between *gerama* damage, for which Talmud does not impose any liability, and *garme* damage, for which talmudic opinion differs as to whether there is liability or not. According to Rashi (to BB 22b, s.v. *gerama;* see Sh. Ar., ḤM 386:4), there is no difference between the two concepts—and that those sages who exclude liability for *garme* damage also exclude it in cases of *gerama* damage, and vice versa. Some of the tosafists maintain (BB 22b s.v. *zot omeret*) that, indeed, in strict law there is no distinction and that there is no liability in either case—save that the more common injuries are called *garme* and that those sages who impose liability for *garme* damage do so in the sense of fining the tortfeasor for the sake of public order. However, according to the majority of the tosafists, all indirect damage that is an immediate result of the tortfeasor is termed *garme,* whereas all other acts of indirect damage are called *gerama*—in respect of which the sages are unanimous in excluding liability. There are also further distinctions between *gerama* and *garme* damage, which all present difficulties and which are all less acceptable. It appears that the two categories can be distinguished by using *gerama* to refer to indirect damage that is too remote to have been foreseeable, and *garme* to refer to indirect damage that should have been foreseeable—but which was caused solely by the independent act of a second person who acted negligently following the first person's act, while he could have refrained from doing that which resulted in the damage. In the latter situation, some sages maintain that the first person is exempt from liability, even though he could have foreseen that his act would result in the negligent act of the second person—who is held to be solely responsible. On the other hand, others hold the first person liable, just because he should have foreseen that his own act would result in the negligent act of the second person. According to this distinction, therefore, the loss sustained by someone acting on the advice of an expert is *garme* damage—because he should have realized that other experts should be consulted before he acted on one expert's advice and he was himself negligent in failing to take such second opinions. If, however, the matter is such that only one suitable expert is available and there is no choice but to rely exclusively on his advice, it is not a case of *garme* damage, and it is the unanimous opinion that the expert is liable for the consequences of his negligent advice. The *halakhah* is that a person is liable for *garme* damage, although it is disputed in the codes whether such liability stems from the strict law or is in the nature of a fine for the sake of public order, as mentioned above. The law applicable in the State of Israel is the Civil Wrongs Ordinance, 1947, which makes a person liable for the natural consequences of his conduct—but not if the decisive cause of the damage is the fault of another. An expert is held liable for giving negligent declarations and opinions.

Bibliography: Gulak, Yesodei, 1 (1922), 157; 2 (1922), 24, 182, 206–9; 4 (1922), 162f.; Herzog, Institutions, 2 (1939), 311 (index), s.v.; ET, 6 (1954), 461–97; 7 (1956), 382–96; S. Albeck, *Pesher Dinei ha-Nezikin ba-Talmud* (1965), 43–61; B. Cohen, *Jewish and Roman Law,* 2 (1966), 578–609, addenda 788–92.

[Sh.A.]

GERAR (Heb. גְּרָר), a city and region in the Negev in which Abraham and Isaac dwelt (Gen. chs. 20, 26). Gerar was located on the way to Egypt and is mentioned in connection with Kadesh (identified in ancient sources with Petra and now mainly with ʿAyn Qudayrāt) and Shur (the fortifications on the Egyptian frontier). In the north it bordered on the territories of Beersheba and Gaza (Gen. 10:19; 26:1–2; II Chron. 14:12–13). Its area included Rehoboth (which some scholars identify with the later Ruheibah, 12½ mi. (20 km.) south of Elusa, Sitnah, Esek, the valley of Gerar, and the royal city of Gerar. Through Abraham's oath to Abimelech, the land of Gerar was excluded from the territory destined to be conquered by the Israelites (Gen. 21:22–32; cf. Ḥul. 60b) and it was outside the area of Israelite settlement (Josh. 15). According to the patriarchal tradition, the land of Gerar was inhabited by Philistines originating from Casluhim who lived in Gerar as shepherds ruled by a king; a treaty existed between them and the Hebrew Patriarchs (Gen. 10:14; 21:32–34; 26:1, 15ff.). These references to the Philistines, however, are considered an anachronism. Gerar is again mentioned in the time of Asa king of Judah (c. 908–867 B.C.E.) who pursued Zerah the Ethiopian from Mareshah to Gerar and destroyed all the cities in its vicinity (II Chron. 14:8–14). If the Septuagint version of I Chronicles 4:39–41 is correct (reading Gerar instead of Gedor), the land of Gerar was inhabited in the period of the monarchy by remnants of Ham and by Meunim. The name Gerar survived as a geographical term even after the destruction of the city and designated the district occupied by the former land of Gerar. The reference to it in II Chronicles 14:12 may already have this meaning and it certainly has it in II Maccabees 13:24 (cf. I Macc. 11:59). The district was later known by its Greek name Geradike (TJ, Shev. 6:1, 36c; Gen. R. 52:6; 64:3) or Geraritike (Eusebius, Onom. 60:6ff.) which was identified with the biblical Gerar. Eusebius (loc. cit.) locates it 25 Roman miles "from Eleutheropolis (Bet Guvrin) toward the south"; it is similarly represented on the Madaba Map southwest of Beersheba. Various scholars have accordingly proposed to identify it with Tell al-Sharīʿa, 12 mi. (19 km.) northwest of Beersheba or with Tell Yamma further to the west. Y. Aharoni, however, has suggested a site midway between these two mounds—Tell Abu Hurayra (Tell Haror), the largest tell in the area and containing pottery dating from the Middle Bronze Age and later periods.

Bibliography: Horowitz, Ereẓ Yis, s.v.; I. Ben Zvi, *Sefer ha-Shomeronim* (1935), 116ff.; Grintz, in: *Koveẓ . . . M. Schorr* (1944), 96ff.; idem, in: *Tarbiz,* 17 (1945/46), 32ff.; 19 (1947/48), 64; Aharoni, in: IEJ, 6 (1956), 26ff.; Aharoni, Land, index.

[Y.M.G.]

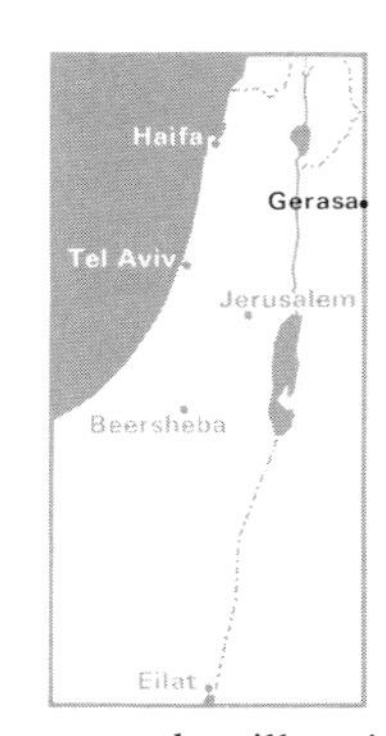

GERASA (**Jarash,** Heb. גְּרַשׁ, Ar. جَرَش), ancient city in Transjordan, north of the Jabbok River. Its ruins are situated 1,870 feet (570 m.) above sea level near the small Circassian village Jarash between Amman and Irbid in a fertile region with extensive fields, remains of forests, and scenic surroundings. Wadi Jarash (called Chrysorrhoas in antiquity) passed through the ancient city. According to pottery finds, the site was inhabited as early as the Neolithic period in the seventh millennium B.C.E. and settlement continued into the Early Bronze Age (Canaanite period). Although the name Gerasa, of Semitic origin, also testifies to its early occupation, the first mention of the city appears in the Hellenistic period when it was called "Antioch on the River

Figure 1. The Roman forum at Gerasa (Jarash), Transjordan, with a cardo (columned street) heading to the north. Courtesy Israel Department of Antiquities, Jerusalem.

Chrysorrhoas"—a name indicating that the Hellenistic settlement was established under the Seleucid dynasty. It was apparently founded by Antiochus IV, although a Greek legend attributes its establishment to Alexander the Great. The city's jurisdiction extended in the south beyond the Jabbok, in the north beyond Wadi Yābis, in the west as far as Regev (Ragaba, Rājib), and in the east to the desert. During the decline of the Seleucid kingdom, control of Geresa was seized by Zeno and Theodorus, the rulers of Philadelphia (Ammān), from whom it was captured by Alexander Yannai. It remained a Hasmonean possession until the time of Pompey after which a Jewish community continued to live in the city and maintained friendly relations with the other inhabitants. Under Roman rule the importance of the autonomous city of Gerasa increased, especially after the conquest of the Nabatean kingdom by Trajan (105 C.E.) and the establishment of the Province of Arabia. The great highway connecting Boẓrah (*Basrah) with Elath and the Red Sea passed through Gerasa making it one of the centers of the caravan trade. During the disturbances leading to the Jewish War the inhabitants of Gerasa sent the Jewish population away unharmed. Under the emperor Hadrian—who visited the city in 129/30—and his successors, Gerasa reached the peak of its development and possessed several splendid buildings. In the time of Caracalla in the third century, the title of Roman colony was conferred on Gerasa. In the middle of the century a period of decline set in and continued until the mid-fifth century. Subsequently, however, Gerasa experienced renewed prosperity as a Christian city: its temple of Dionysus was converted into a center of Christian worship and during the years 464 to 611, 11 churches were built, one of them on the ruins of a synagogue. Gerasa's final decline was precipitated by the Muslim conquest (635). In the eighth century the city was destroyed by a series of earthquakes and during the Middle Ages it lay deserted and in ruins until Circassians settled there some time after 1878. The excavation of Gerasa by an Anglo-American expedition began in 1928. It uncovered a triumphal arch, the city wall, a hippodrome, the temple of Zeus, two theaters, the forum (circular marketplace), a columned street 2,624 feet (800 m.) long running through the city, a public fountain *(nymphaeum)*, the temple of Artemis with a magnificent entrance connected to the bridge, baths, as well as the ruins of numerous churches containing mosaic pavements, decorated with representations of cities and animal and plant motifs. More than 500 Greek and Latin inscriptions were discovered in the city. The mosaic pavement of a synagogue with a Greco-Jewish inscription and representations of the animals entering Noah's Ark, a candelabrum, and various sacred objects, was found under the foundations of a church built in 430. R. Joshua, "the Garsi," a pupil of R. Akiva (Er. 21b; Lam. R. 3:43, no. 9) may have been named after Gerasa.

Figure 2. Columns of the portico to the inner court of the temple of Artemis at Gerasa. Courtesy Israel Department of Antiquities, Jerusalem.

Figure 3. Drawing of part of the floor mosaic from the synagogue at Gerasa, depicting the animals entering the ark. Fourth–fifth century C.E. From E. L. Sukenik, *The Ancient Synagogue at Beit Alpha*, Jerusalem, 1934.

Bibliography: Guthe, in: *Das Land Der Bibel*, 3 pt. 1–2 (1919); C. H. Kraeling (ed.), *Gerasa, City of the Decapolis* (1938); G. Lankester Harding, *The Antiquities of Jordan* (1959), 78ff.
[M.A.-Y.]

GERCHUNOFF, ALBERTO (1884–1950), Argentine author and journalist. Born in Proskurov, Russia, Gerchunoff was taken to Argentina as a child when his father became a pioneer settler of Moisés Ville, in the province of Santa Fé, one of the ICA agricultural colonies financed by Baron Maurice de *Hirsch. Later the family moved to Alcaraz in the province of Entre Ríos. When he finished school, Gerchunoff settled in Buenos Aires, where he became a journalist. In 1908 he joined the staff of *La Nación*, a leading daily, with which he was associated for over 40 years, part of the time as chief editor. Gerchunoff's first, and most famous, book was *Los Gauchos Judíos* (1910; *The Jewish Gauchos of the Pampas*, 1955). This collection of articles from *La Nación* described the life of Jewish colonists in Entre Ríos during the first decade of the 20th century. It was the first Latin-American account of emigration to the New World as well as the first work of literary value to be written in Spanish by a Jew in modern times. Gerchunoff wrote several other distinguished books, some of which—notably *Entre Ríos, Mi País* (1950)—have an autobiographical content. A number appeared posthumously.

Gerchunoff was the founder and first president of the Argentine Writers' Association and was an active radical politician. He was detached from Jewish life for many years and much of his writing was strongly tinged with Christian mysticism. Following the rise of Hitler, however, he became a bitter opponent of the Nazis and Fascists and an enthusiastic Zionist. From 1945 onward he canvassed the support of Latin-American statesmen and politicians for the establishment of a Jewish state and was instrumental in securing their aid at the United Nations in 1947–48.

Alberto Gerchunoff, Argentine author and journalist, drawing by Alejandro Siro.

Bibliography: S. Jaroslasky de Lowy, *Alberto Gerchunoff: Vida y Obra, Bibliografía-Antología* (1957), offprint from *Revista Hispánica Moderna,* 23, no. 3–4 (1957); M. Kantor, *Sobre la obra y el anecdotario de Alberto Gerchunoff* (1960), lists all his published and unpublished work (3,000 articles and essays), offprint from *El hombre importante* (1934); *Davar,* no. 31–33 (Buenos Aires, 1951), special issue.

[Ed.]

GEREZ, JOSEF HABIB (1928–), Turkish poet and communal worker. Born in Istanbul, where he studied law, Gerez later became chief secretary to the Istanbul chief rabbinate. The most prominent Jewish poet in mid-20th-century Turkey, Gerez published several collections of verse which were highly praised by literary critics. They include *Gönülden Damlalar* ("Drops from the Heart," 1952), *Renklerin Akini* ("The Flow of Color," 1954), *Savrulan Zaman* ("The Scattered Time," 1955), *Acili Bitimler* ("Sad Ends," 1960), *Dar Açılar* ("Narrow Angles," 1965), and *Arayiş Içınde* ("In Search," 1967), *Büyük Güzel* ("The Great Beauty," 1969), and *Başini Alip Giden Dünya* ("The World that Goes Alone," 1970). Some of Gerez's poems were translated into French and published in the *Journal d'Orient.* He also wrote Ladino poetry on Jewish themes. Gerez was also a painter who exhibited in Istanbul. [S.Ko.]

GERHARDT, CHARLES FREDERIC (1816–1856), French chemist. Gerhardt, who was born in Strasbourg, was one of the earliest scientists to bring order into the chaos besetting organic chemistry in the first half of the 19th century. He worked in Paris at the beginning of the 1840s as an assistant to Jean Baptiste Dumas (1800–1884) and with Auguste Laurent (1807–1853), and the three of them were mainly responsible for reviving the radical theory of structure. Gerhardt helped Laurent to develop a classification of organic compounds, and it was he who gave the name "phenol" to the acid produced by Laurent from coal tar in 1841. He also produced a detailed exposition of the concept of atoms and molecules. Gerhardt continued to spend much of his time working in Paris after receiving a professorship at the University of Montpellier in 1844, and his appointment was terminated in 1851. He taught chemistry privately in Paris until 1855, when he was appointed professor of chemistry and pharmacy at Strasbourg University. His main works were *Précis de chimie organique* (2 vols., 1844–45) and *Traité de chimie organique* (4 vols., 1853–56). He was also editor of the *Journal chimique.* [S.A.M.]

GERIZIM, MOUNT (Heb. הַר גְּרִזִּים), mountain in Ereẓ Israel, S. of Shechem. After crossing the Jordan River, the children of Israel were commanded to build a stone altar on Mt. Ebal, to engrave upon it "all the words of this law" (Deut. 27:4–8), and to "set the blessing upon Mt. Gerizim, and the curse upon Mt. Ebal" (*ibid.* 11:29; 27:12–13). According to Joshua 8:30, this was Joshua's first act after the conquest of Ai. Har-Gerizzim (as written in the masoretic text; Har Gerizim, according to *Ben-Asher; usually Hargerizim in the traditional Samaritan text of the Pentateuch) is the present-day Jebel al-Ṭūr (shortened from the Samaritan name Tura Brikha). Mt. Gerizim and Mt. Ebal rise above the city of Shechem (Nablus), in the south and north respectively; Gerizim is approximately 2,600 ft. (881 m.) high and Ebal approximately 2,800 ft. (940 m.). Between them lies the valley of Shechem. Both hills are composed of monolithic limestone, ten springs descending from their slopes to the fertile and well-watered valley. Mt. Ebal has comparatively little vegetation and no water issuing along its southern side, because the slope of the tilted rock is northward; one exception is at the southeast end of Ebal, where a spring makes it possible for the village of Askar to exist. The slopes of Mt. Gerizim, on the other hand, are covered with trees to the very top of the ridge, and the slope of the rock causes the main springs to issue on the side of the valley facing the city of Shechem. The contrast in the amount of water on the two sides of the valley is very marked. A pilgrim's legend from the Middle Ages, which is recited even today, relates that Mt. Gerizim, the blessed mountain (Deut. 11:29), is pleasant and fertile, while Mt. Ebal, cursed by divine decree *(ibid.),* is desolate and barren.

The identification of the two mountains is made clear in the Bible (Deut. 11:29–30; cf. Gen. 12:6; Judg. 9:7), and this identification is maintained throughout the sources (Sot. 7:5; Jos., Ant. 4:305; 11:340) down to modern times. As a result of an obscure topographical identification in Deuteronomy 11:30—"Are they not beyond the Jordan, behind the way of the going down of the sun, in the land of the Canaanites that dwell in the Arabah, over against Gilgal, beside the terebinths of Moreh?"—and apparently in the wake of a dispute with the Samaritans, another tradition, ascribed to R. Eliezer, appears in the Talmud, which identifies the two mountains with two mounds which the children of Israel erected for themselves near Gilgal, and not with the two mountains near Shechem (TJ, Sot. 1:3, 21c; TB, Sot. 33b). This view was later adopted by the fathers of the Christian Church (Eusebius, Onom. 64:19–20). On the Madaba Map, both traditions appear: next to Shechem is written Tur Garizin, and next to Jericho Ebal-Gerizin. Apparently, the Bible does not mean to imply that these two mountains are situated in the Arabah near Gilgal, but simply refers to the general direction in order to distinguish between this Arabah and the Arabah associated with the hill-country of the Amorites (Deut. 1:1; 4:49). Perhaps "behind the way of the going down of the sun" indicates the region west of the road which passes through the northern Arabah (from Jericho to Beth-Shean).

Later Mt. Gerizim is mentioned when the Samaritans erected their temple there about the time of Nehemiah (in the time of Alexander the Great, according to Jos., Ant. 11:310–11, but this is apparently a mistake; cf. Neh. 13:28, according to which a man of priestly stock was cast out by Nehemiah for intermarriage with the Samaritans). From then on, the Samaritans considered this temple to be their most holy spot, and their tradition ascribes nearly all of the biblical account of the patriarchs' deeds and the places associated with them (the land of Moriah, Beth-El, etc.) to Mt. Gerizim. There are 13 names for Mt. Gerizim, the "Kibla" of the Samaritans, the place toward which they turn in prayer. The fourth of the five articles in the declaration of their creed proclaims its holiness. *Markah dedicated a whole chapter in his *Memar* to the praise of this mountain (II, 10) in connection with Ex. 15. He enumerates it as one of the choicest things created by God and set apart as divine. The Samaritan text for Deuteronomy 27:4–5 reads: "And it shall be when ye are passed over the Jordan, that ye shall set up these stones, which I command you this day, in Mt. Gerizim" (in place of Mt. Ebal in the masoretic text; cf. Sot. 33b). It is of interest that they even add Mt. Gerizim at the end of the Ten Commandments in both Exodus 20:17 and Deuteronomy 5:21, considering it to be the chosen mountain (Har ha-Mivḥar), even from the time of the creation of the world. (The Samaritans read *baḥar*, "has chosen," for the masoretic text *yibḥar*, "will choose," in Deut. 12:14.) The Samaritans gave it the title "mountain of blessing" or "blessed mount" (Tūrbarīk; Samaritan Book of Joshua, ch. 21; Gen. R. 32:10; Song. R. 4:4, no. 5: Tura Brikha; Deut. R. 3:6; Tura Kaddisha) and they claimed that the mountain was not submerged at the time of the Flood *(ibid.)*.

Mt. Gerizim became the main point of divergence between the Samaritans and the Jews. (Cf. the end of Kut.: "At what point can the Samaritans be accepted into Judaism? When they reject their belief in Mt. Gerizim.") In the time of Ptolemy I Soter (323–284 B.C.E.), there was an argument over this point between the Samaritans and the Jews of Alexandria (Jos., Ant. 12:1ff.). When Antiochus IV Epiphanes passed decrees against the Jews, he converted the Samaritan temple on Mt. Gerizim into a pagan shrine in honor of Zeus Xenios or Hellenios (II Macc. 5:23; 6:1; Jos., Ant. 12:257ff.). This temple was destroyed in 129 B.C.E. by John Hyrcanus (Jos., Ant. 13:255ff.; cf. Meg. Ta'an. 333). However, it remained a holy site for the Samaritans, and all religious acts were performed "in the name of Mt. Gerizim" (TJ, Yev. 8:1, 9a). Due to the Samaritan belief in the ancient sanctity of the mountain, the Roman procurator Pontius Pilate massacred a large gathering of Samaritans who had assembled to look at vessels which Moses allegedly made for the Tabernacle and which one of the Samaritans claimed he would show them (these vessels had supposedly been concealed on Mt. Gerizim; Jos., Ant. 18:85).

In the war against Rome (66–70), the Samaritans joined the rebellion and assembled on Mt. Gerizim to halt the Romans, in spite of the news they had received that the Jews of Galilee had been defeated. Vespasian sent Cerialis, commander of the fifth legion, against them and he besieged them with 3,000 infantry and 600 cavalry. The Roman troops massacred more than 11,000 of the Samaritans on the 27th of Sivan, 67 C.E. (Jos., Wars, 3:307ff.). After the war of Bar Kokhba (132–135) the emperor Hadrian erected a pagan shrine to Zeus Hypsistos (or to Serapis) on the top of Mt. Gerizim and placed the bronze gates from the Temple in Jerusalem there. From the time of Antoninus Pius onward, this sanctuary appears on the coins of Neapolis, the city which Titus had built on the site of the village of Ma'abarta, near ancient Shechem. In the time of the emperor *Julian, this sanctuary was destroyed and the Samaritans used the bronze gates as the door of the synagogue *(ha-knishah)* called Ḥelkat ha-Sadeh, which their priest Akbon built in the city of Neapolis. Another synagogue was erected by Akbon's predecessor, Baba Rabbah, "near Mt. Gerizim, Beth-El," "below the mountain" (apparently the site of the present-day Rijl al-ʿAmūd), in the time of Theodosius I (379–395 C.E.).

Samaritan encampment on Mount Gerizim during the sacrifice of the paschal lamb, 1942. Courtesy Keren Hayesod, United Israel Appeal, Jerusalem.

With the predominance of Christianity in the country, the religious status of the Samaritans suffered. Judging from John 4, Gerizim was also a sacred spot for the Christians. After a Samaritan uprising in the time of Zeno (474–491 C.E.), the Samaritans were expelled from the mountain and their synagogue was taken from them by command of the emperor (484 C.E.). The Christians erected a Church of the Virgin Mary there and placed a stone from Calvary in it. Following a Samaritan rebellion in the time of Justinian, the area around the church on Mt. Gerizim was encompassed by a fortified wall. In the time of the caliph al-Manṣūr (754–755), the Christian church was destroyed, and under al-Ma'mūn (813–833) Justinian's wall was razed.

Remains of buildings sacred to the Samaritans still stand on the mountain (Khirbat al-Lūza; al-Ṣakhra ("the rock"); the place of the 12 stones). There are also remains of the Church of the Virgin Mary and Justinian's wall. The remains of the church were excavated by a German expedition in 1927–28 and by the Department of Antiquities of the British Mandatory government in 1946. It is on Mt. Gerizim that the Samaritans still observe all their festivals and all public holy ceremonies, as the sacrifice of the paschal lamb, and prayers on all their feasts and holidays. The entire congregation dwells on its slopes from the 10th of Nisan until the day after the end of the Maẓẓot Festival. Today houses have been built to accomodate them instead of the tents of former years. The offering takes place not on the top of the mountain, the holiest spot where their temple once stood, but at a lower place to the west of it, possibly because the holy spot has been defiled by a Muslim cemetery.

Bibliography: N. Adler (ed.) *The Travels of R. Benjamin of Tudela* (1908), 22–23; I. Ben Zvi, *Sefer ha-Shomeronim* (1935); Conder-Kitchener, 2 (1882), 186ff.; J. Montgomery, *The Samaritans* (1907; repr. 1968); Abel, Geog, 1 (1933), 360ff.; A. Reifenberg, in: *Eretz Israel*, 1 (1951), 74ff.; A. M. Schneider, in: ZDPV, 68 (1951), 211ff.; G. E. Wright, *Shechem: The Biography of a Biblical City* (1965).

[Y.M.G.]

GERMAN, YURI PAVLOVICH (1910–), Soviet Russian novelist. Born in Riga, German began his literary career in 1929. His first major work was *Nashi znakomye* ("Our Acquaintances"; 1936), which was translated into English as *Antonina* (1937; U.S. ed. *Tonia*, 1938). This is a story of a starry-eyed Soviet girl who progresses from a fleeting adolescent love affair with a glamorous actor, through a placid and comfortable but loveless marriage to an older man, to a "mature" union with a stern, though kindly, secret policeman. German was popular with rank-and-file Soviet readers, as one of the very few authors who avoided heroics, portraying ordinary Soviet men and women in familiar surroundings, and allowing his audience some cathartic melodrama. Later works included *Zhmakin* (1938; *Alexei the Gangster,* 1940); *Rossiya molodaya* ("Russia the Young," 1952), a historical novel set in the era of Peter the Great; and *Delo, kotoromu ty sluzhish* ("The Cause You Serve," 1958). During the post-World War II, "anti-cosmopolitan" purges, German was violently attacked as a result of the publication of the first instalment of the novel *Podpolkovnik meditsinskoy sluzhby* ("Lieutenant Colonel of the Medical Corps") in the literary monthly *Zvezda* (no. 1, 1949). The ire of the Party critics was provoked by the fact that the novel's Jewish central character, the elderly and ailing Dr. Levin, overwhelmed by purely "personal" problems, displayed little of the enthusiasm and optimism required of positive heroes in Soviet literature. The novel's publication was interrupted by *Zvezda,* which also expressed its regret at its "error" in publishing the first part. As to the trauma of Dr. Levin in the Holocaust, the "criticism" had clear anti-Semitic overtones. The work only reappeared, in a completely revised version, in 1956, at the height of the "liberal," post-Stalin "thaw." [M.F.]

GERMAN LITERATURE.

Biblical and Hebraic Influences. Before the *Aufklaerung* (Age of Enlightenment), Jewish influences in German literature were essentially biblical and Hebraic. The medieval miracle or mystery plays, in Germany as in England and France, dramatized Old Testament themes and treated the Hebrew patriarchs with reverence, but the "passion plays" based on the New Testament made the post-biblical Jew a demonic ally of the Devil. For special historical reasons, this latter portrayal came to have serious popular repercussions. The impact of the Bible itself has been traced to the earliest contact of the Germanic tribes with missionary Christianity. In the fourth century the Gothic bishop Ulfilas (or Wulfila) wrote a Teutonic version of the Bible, from which only a few verses are extant, and, early in the 11th century, Job and the Psalms were translated into Old High German by Notker Labeo of St. Gallen (c. 950–1022), whose Psalter alone is extant. A late 11th-century prose version of the Song of Songs (c. 1065) by Williram familiarized the Germans with its traditional author, King Solomon, whose legendary wisdom, fortified by tales brought back to Europe by the crusaders, soon became a stock literary theme.

Bible Translations. The first printed version of the Bible in High German (1466) has been traced to an anonymous 14th-century translator. Based on the Latin (Vulgate) text and printed in Strasbourg, this was the model for 13 subsequent pre-Lutheran editions. The first printed version of the Bible in Low German appeared in 1477. Both German versions, of course, conformed with Roman Catholic doctrine. By contrast, the German reformer Martin *Luther produced a complete translation of the Bible (6 vols., 1534, revised eleven times up to 1545) which was based on the original tongues, notably the Hebrew of the Old Testament. Luther's text injected the thought patterns of the Hebrew Bible into the German language, where the Hebrew simile and metaphor were speedily absorbed. His magnificent version was written in the Saxon dialect, which thus became the principal vehicle of High German language and literature. This was a somewhat curious achievement, since High German was the language of predominantly Catholic south Germany, whereas Low German was spoken in the Protestant north; but the fact that German Catholics found Luther's Bible readily accessible ensured its widespread success. The German Protestant Bible had a greater influence on the language of its readers than any other comparable work except the English Authorized Version. It became the most widely read book in the German tongue, constituted Germany's greatest literary achievement in the 16th century, and was of immeasurable significance in stabilizing the language. Although other German translations were attempted by Luther's contemporaries and successors, it was not until the 20th century that, under Jewish auspices, a comparable version of the Hebrew Bible appeared, published by Martin *Buber and Franz *Rosenzweig.

See also *Bible, Translations.

A post-biblical Hebraic influence on German literature much in evidence during the 16th century was the Kabbalah, the Christian interpretation of which found a pioneer exponent in Johann *Reuchlin. His *De verbo mirifico* (1494) and *De arte cabalistica* (1517), though written in Latin, created a vogue for Hebrew studies in German scholarly circles, and Reuchlin's followers included Wolfgang Fabricius *Capito, Conrad *Pellicanus, Sebastian *Muenster, and *Fagius Paulus. The movement gained its widest support among the Lutherans. Another Protestant, Jacob Boehme (1575–1624), developed a mystical system largely inspired by the Christian Kabbalah.

Biblical Drama. Martin Luther and his fellow-reformers fostered the writing of biblical plays in both Latin and German. Sixtus Birck dramatized not only episodes from the Bible—*Zorobabel* (1538), *Ezechias* (1538), and *Joseph* (1539)—but also the apocryphal tales of *Susanna* and *Judith* (both 1532). The Judith story was also dramatized in 1551 by the Nuremberg poet and *Meistersinger,* Hans Sachs. Sachs' biblical plays included among others *Der Wueterich Herodes* (1552) and *Tragedia Koenig Sauls* (1557), and others on themes such as Esther (1530), Job (1547), Adam and Eve (1548), Cain and Abel (1553), and David (1556). A century later, Christian Weise took all the themes of his religious plays from the Old Testament, believing that the figure of Jesus ought not to appear on the stage. His dramas included *Der verfolgte David* (1683), *Nebukadnezar* (1683), *Athalia* (1687), and *Kain und Abel* (1704). Weise was followed by the Swiss poet and playwright Johann Jacob Bodmer, who published a German translation of *Milton's *Paradise Lost* in 1732 and later wrote dramatic poems about Joseph (*Jakob und Joseph,* 1751; *Joseph und Zulika,* 1753), the Flood (*Die Synd-Flut,* 1751), Noah (1752^2), Adam (1763), Solomon (1764), and Abraham (1778). Bodmer's fellow-Swiss, Solomon Gessner, roused interest in the Cain theme with his sentimental prose epic, *Der Tod Abels* (1758). Its English translation (1761) enjoyed enormous success and is said to have inspired works on the same subject by Coleridge and *Byron. Germany's first major modern poet, Friedrich Gottlieb Klopstock, who was influenced by Milton and Bodmer, is best remembered for his epic *Der Messias* (1749–73). He also wrote the plays *Der Tod Adams* (1757), *Salomo* (1764), and *David* (1772). Another 18th-century Swiss author, Johann Kaspar Lavater, wrote *Abraham und Isaak* (1776). The biblical element in German literature received a valuable stimulus in the late 18th century with the publication by Johann Gottfried *Herder of his two-volume work *Vom Geist der Ebraeischen Poesie* (1782–83). In his *Adrastea* (1802) Herder published a German version of the **Lekhah Dodi* hymn by Solomon *Alkabeẓ. Friedrich *Schiller wrote essays on biblical themes and echoed the Bible in tragedies such as *Die Jungfrau von Orleans* (1802). Johann Wolfgang von *Goethe drew inspiration from the Bible for his great tragedy, *Faust* (1808), whose "Prologue in Heaven" is modeled on the early chapters of Job. Other 19th-century playwrights who wrote on biblical themes were Karl Ferdinand Gutzkow (*Koenig Saul*, 1839), Friedrich Rueckert (*Saul und David*, 1843; *Herodes der Grosse*, 1844), and Austria's leading playwright, Franz Grillparzer (*Esther*, 1877), while a theme from the Apocrypha was dramatized by Otto Ludwig (*Die Makkabaeer*, 1854). Gutzkow's very popular *Uriel Acosta* (1847) entered the Yiddish as well as the German repertoire. Friedrich Hebbel wrote *Judith* (1841), about the heroine of the Apocrypha, but his outstanding "Hebraic" drama was *Herodes und Mariamne* (1850), based on Josephus.

Only a few Jewish writers in 19th-century Germany and Austria dealt with biblical or later historical themes of Jewish interest. Ludwig *Robert wrote the drama *Die Tochter Jephthas* (1820) and Karl *Beck the tragedy *Saul* (1841). Poems on biblical and post-biblical Jewish subjects were written by Heinrich *Heine and Seligmann *Heller, whose works include *Die letzten Hasmonaeer* (1865) and *Ahasver* (1868).

THE BIBLE IN 20TH-CENTURY GERMAN LITERATURE. From 1900 onward there was a considerable increase in German works of biblical inspiration. *Das Buch Joram* (1907) by Rudolf Borchardt, who was of partly Jewish descent, was a pastiche of the Book of Job set in the time of Jesus. *Die juedische Witwe* (1911) by Georg Kaiser, based on the heroic apocryphal tale of Judith and Holofernes, was, unlike so many of these works, a comedy. Jewish writers played an increasingly important role, with Siegfried *Lipiner dramatizing the story of *Adam* (1911), a theme that similarly inspired Arno *Nadel (1917). The same subject was dealt with in some post-World War I poems by the Viennese lyricist Josef Weinheber and in the epic *Erschaffung der Eva* (1941) by the Austrian Franz Karl Ginzkey. The story of Cain prompted a tragedy by another Viennese writer, Anton Wildgans (1920), and that of Noah, Ernst Barlach's drama, *Die Suendflut* (1924). Richard *Beer-Hofmann wrote a mystical drama, *Jaakobs Traum* (1918).

Thomas *Mann's trilogy, *Joseph und Seine Brueder* (1933–42; *Joseph and His Brothers*, 1934–45), was the climax of a vast array of German works based on the story of Joseph, headed by some 26 dramas in the 16th century and by the 17th-century novels of Hans Jakob Christoffel von Grimmelshausen (1667) and Philipp von Zesen (*Assenat*, 1670). Hugo von *Hofmannsthal's only biblical work was *Die Josephlegende* (1914), written for a ballet. The Samson theme was dramatized by Herbert Eulenberg (1910), Frank Wedekind (1914), Hermann Burte (1917), and Karl Roettger (1921). The tragic figure of King Saul attracted Karl *Wolfskehl (1905), Paul *Heyse (1909), and Beer-Hofmann (*Der junge David*, 1933). The romance of David and Bathsheba was dramatized by Lion *Feuchtwanger in *Das Weib des Urias* (1905), and another episode in the life of the Psalmist inspired Arnold *Zweig's *Abigail und Nabal* (1913). Feuchtwanger also wrote a novel on the sacrifice of Jepthah's daughter (1957), a theme previously dramatized by Ernst *Lissauer (1928). The best-known work of Sammy *Gronemann is his comedy *Der Weise und der Narr: Koenig Salomo und der Schuster* (1942).

Other 20th-century writers were drawn to stories from the Prophets and Hagiographa. Jeremiah inspired an anti-war drama by Stefan *Zweig (1917) for which Arno Nadel wrote the music, and Job was the subject of a popular novel by Joseph *Roth (1930). Esther provided the theme of a drama by Felix *Braun (1926), another by Max *Brod (1918), and a Purim play by Sammy Gronemann (*Hamans Flucht*, 1926). Later Jewish historical figures who inspired 20th-century German fiction were Josephus, the hero of a trilogy by Feuchtwanger (1932–42); Rabbi Akiva, in a play by Moritz *Heimann (1922); the hero of Max *Brod's novel, *Rëubeni, Fuerst der Juden* (1925); and the *Jewess of Toledo, who figures in a late novel by Feuchtwanger (*Spanische Ballade*, 1955). The legend of the **golem* formed the theme of a novel by Gustav Meyrink (1915) and *Jew Suess was the hero of Feuchtwanger's most famous novel (1925).

Hebrew and Yiddish Influences on the German Language. As with English and French, so in the case of German, certain biblical terms entered the language at a fairly early stage, mainly through the writings of churchmen. Luther's Bible brought a vastly increased number of words and phrases into general usage. Some have become German idioms, including *Kainszeichen* (the mark of Cain, Gen. 4:15); *Suendenbock* (scapegoat, Lev. 16); *Salomonisches Urteil* (the judgment of Solomon, I Kings, 3:16 ff.); *Gott mit uns* (*Immanuel*, Isa. 7:14); *Menschensohn* (son of man, Ezek. 2:1ff.). Hebrew loanwords also entered German at various periods. These include *Abt* (abbot<Aramaic *abba*), *Ebenholz* (ebony<*even*), *Fratze* (face, mug<*parẓuf*), and *Natro* (soda<*neter*). More than any other European language, not excluding English, German is peculiarly rich in other terms and expressions, mainly slang or colloquialisms, which entered everyday speech through *Yiddish and the *Juden-Deutsch* (West Yiddish) dialect spoken by German Jews. Most of these were, of course, restricted to Jewish circles, including *Schabbes, Jonteff, Mischpoche* or *Muschpoke, Goi, Schickse, Schadchen, meschugge, benschen, daffke*, and *nebbich* (< *nicht bei Euch*). In the 15th and 16th centuries, however, others entered general use, probably by way of thieves' slang; *acheln*, to eat (<*akhal*), *ganfen*, to steal (< *ganav*), *Schaute*, fool (< *shoteh*). The 18th century added words like *Mackes*, blows (<*makkot*), *schmusen*, to chat, *Schmuser*, chatterbox (<*shemu'ot*) and *Stuss*, nonsense (<*shetut*). In the 19th century a host of other such expressions became familiar, notably *Golem, Kaffer*, boor (<*kefar*), *koscher, Rischess*, anti-Semitism (<*rishut*), *schaechten*, to defraud, overreach (<*shaḥat*), *Schlemihl*, schelemiel (<*Shelumiel?*), and *Zores*, trouble (<*ẓarot*). Despite periodic "purifications" of the German language, a vast number of these Hebraisms and Yiddishisms still occur in German dictionaries and other works of reference. Heine, in his poem "Prinzessin Sabbat" (*Romanzero*, 1851), humorously alluding to Schiller's "Ode to Joy," described *tcholent* as "koscheres Ambrosia"; while Adelbert von Chamisso entitled his world-famous story about the man who lost his shadow *Peter Schlemihls wundersame Geschichte* (1814). Conversely, Heine's pathetic "Jewish" refrain in the poem "Gedaechtnisfeier" (in the collection *Romanzero*), "Nicht gedacht soll seiner werden," is taken directly from Luther's translation of Ezek. 21:37.

The Image of the Jew in German Literature. German attitudes toward the Jews, shaped by religious, economic, and social factors, were clearly mirrored in German literature. The earliest recorded Old High German literature, largely written by Christian clerics, depicted Jews as simultaneously God's chosen people and as the "people accursed." On the one hand, Jews were kinsmen of the Christian savior and descendants of revered patriarchs and prophets; on the other, they were supposedly guilty of deicide, had fallen from grace, and had been condemned to eternal scorn and wandering (see also the *Wandering Jew).

THE MEDIEVAL STEREOTYPE. Medieval German drama, from the primitive mystery plays dealing with the life and death of Jesus to the spectacular passion plays staged at Easter, presented a cruel and abhorrent image of the Jew. In these plays Jews were shown to be far more the people of

Judas than of Jesus. The most famous of the passion plays—that of Oberammergau, Bavaria—has been performed roughly once every ten years since 1634. It was banned for a time in the 18th century and, strangely enough, during the Hitler era, the Nazis evidently allowing anti-religious policy to outweigh their hatred of the Jews. In 1969 a few textual modifications were made on the recommendation of the Catholic Church in order to remove offensive anti-Jewish passages. Folktales and folksongs also spread the legend that Jews habitually engaged in the crucifixion of Christian boys to provide blood for the Passover ritual. The stories of "Good Werner" (1286) and Simon of *Trent (1475) popularized the *blood libel in Germany and provided a counterpart to the English martyrologies of *Hugh of Lincoln and William of Norwich.

Upon the earliest literary image, which had its source in religion, was superimposed another, which had its source in economics: the Jew as usurer. Usury was defined by the Church as the lending of money at interest. Since Christians were forbidden to engage in such moneylending, Jews had a virtual monopoly until the Lombards arrived on the German scene. In the sermons of Berthold von Regensburg (c. 1210–1272), the most popular Franciscan preacher of the mid-13th century, Jew and usurer were synonymous. Easter plays included a comic interlude: the three Marys buying oil to anoint the body of the crucified Jesus from a merchant depicted as a wily, haggling Jew. As an object of ridicule, the Jew also made his entry into the *Fastnachtsspiele* (Shrovetide plays). Hans Folz (c. 1450–c. 1515), a *Meistersinger* of Worms and Nuremberg, was a notable exponent of this genre. In one of his plays rabbinic Judaism is unfavorably contrasted with Christianity and the **Adon Olam* hymn is sung in a German rhymed adaptation. In another farce, a student seduces a Jewess and then mocks her parents and her religion. The Middle High German stereotype of the grasping Jew passed into early New High German literature. In the first published version of the Faust legend—the anonymous *Faustbuch* of 1587—Faust borrows money from a Jew, who accepts one of his legs as security. Faust saws off the leg, but when he comes to redeem his pledge the Jew cannot return it and has to pay compensation. *Der Jude von Venetien,* a German adaptation by Christoph Bluemel of *Shakespeare's *Merchant of Venice* performed in the 1660s, stressed the greed and hardheartedness of the Jew who insists on his pound of flesh and finally loses his entire investment.

The dominant literary image of the Jew throughout the 16th and 17th centuries was characterized by hostility and ridicule. Though a spirited defense of Hebrew literature was undertaken by Johann Reuchlin and other German humanists in their struggle against the slanders of the apostate Johannes *Pfefferkorn, Martin Luther's embittered diatribe, *Wider die Juden und ihre Luegen* (1544), subsequently reinforced the hostile image of the Jew.

18TH-CENTURY ASSESSMENTS. Not until the 18th century was a major breach made in this portrayal. Gotthold Ephraim *Lessing gave the first favorable presentation of Jews in his comedy, *Die Juden* (1749), and later in his internationally famous *Nathan der Weise* (1779). The hero of this philosophical drama, a wise and benevolent Jew, was the mouthpiece for the writer's doctrines of religious tolerance and universal brotherhood. Lessing's model for Nathan was Moses *Mendelssohn, whose mind and character deeply impressed contemporary German intellectuals. "Nathan the Wise" thus became the symbol of the enlightened Jew.

From the late 18th century German Jews and Christians mingled in Berlin salons and influenced each other's religious, philosophical, and literary expression. Jewish salon hostesses inspired German poets and were mirrored in German novels, creating the image of the educated, dignified, and freethinking Jewess. The Romantic movement, which succeeded the Enlightenment, was also ambivalent in its portrayal of Jews. Some Romantic writers, such as Adelbert von Chamisso, Bettina von Arnim, and Karl August *Varnhagen von Ense, treated Jewish themes, characters, and legends in a sympathetic manner. On the other hand, some writers—especially those in the Berlin circle of Bettina's husband, Achim von Arnim—regarded Jews with enmity and disdain. Arnim himself perpetuated the idea of the Jew's dual nature as eternal witness and repulsive merchant in his drama, *Halle und Jerusalem* (1811).

THE 19TH-CENTURY PORTRAIT. The intensification of German nationalism during the struggle against Napoleon led writers to depict Jews as outsiders and eternal wanderers. It encouraged virulent anti-Semitism at a time when Jewish intellectuals were straining toward complete integration in German society, baptism being accepted by many as a corollary of assimilation and as (in Heine's sardonic phrase) "a ticket of admission to German culture." Ludwig *Boerne and Heine both had a profound impact upon the post-Napoleonic generation. As the leaders of *Jungdeutschland* ("Young Germany"), a liberal literary movement, they paved the way for the Revolution of 1848 and both were outspoken champions of Jewish emancipation. Heine's onetime ally, Wolfgang Menzel, derided "Young Germany" as in reality "Young Palestine." While Berthold *Auerbach, in his polemic pamphlet, *Das Judenthum und die neueste Literatur* (1836), defended the Jews against the charge of revolutionary radicalism hurled at them by the apostles of Teutonism, the prominence of Jews among the pioneers of Socialism—men such as Moses *Hess, Karl *Marx, and Ferdinand *Lassalle—reinforced the image of the Jew as a subversive element undermining the established political and social systems. The gifted orator and pamphleteer Gabriel *Riesser denied the existence of a distinct Jewish nationality, but Moses Hess, parting company with the Socialist doctrinaires, strongly affirmed Jewish nationalism in his *Rom und Jerusalem* (1862; *Rome and Jerusalem,* 1918), which called for the reestablishment of a Jewish state in Zion.

During the 19th century Jewish themes increasingly infiltrated German drama and fiction. In her novella *Die Judenbuche* (1842), Annette von Droste-Huelshoff told a grim tale of the avenging of the murder of a Jew, even inserting a cryptic Hebrew phrase into her story. Franz Grillparzer, Friedrich Hebbel, and Otto Ludwig extolled the Jewish past and presented biblical and Jewish historical characters quite different from the old stereotypes. Grillparzer's *Die Juedin von Toledo* (1873), based on the tragic romance of Alfonso VII of Castile and the Jewess of Toledo, was the forerunner of many other treatments of this theme. On the other hand, novelists who dealt with the Jewish present continued to portray the Jew as a villain. Gustav Freytag wrote a best-selling novel, *Soll und Haben* (1854), which reinforced the image of the Jewish usurer, contrasting the noble, loyal, and hardworking Christian apprentice Anton with his rascally Jewish fellow-worker, Veitel Itzig, who comes to a sorry end. In *Der Hungerpastor* (1864), the best-known novel of Wilhelm Raabe, another Jew follows the wicked example of Veitel Itzig; while Felix Dahn's novel, *Ein Kampf um Rom* (1876), extols German racial purity and presents the Jew, Jochem, as cowardly and treacherous.

A somewhat glamorized picture of Jewish life was presented by Leopold *Kompert (*Boehmische Juden,* 1851; *Neue Geschichten aus dem Ghetto,* 1860) and Karl Emil *Franzos (*Die Juden von Barnow,* 1877). The setting of

Kompert's tales was Bohemia and that of Franzos', Galicia. Austrian Galicia was also the setting of many novels and stories by the non-Jewish writer, Leopold Ritter von Sacher-Masoch. Sacher-Masoch, whose later erotic works gave rise to the term "masochism," was the son of an Austrian police chief in Lemberg (Lvov), and his early impressions of Jewish life there inspired his *Judengeschichten* (1878), *Polnische Ghetto-geschichten* (1886), and *Juedisches Leben in Wort und Bild* (1890). His obvious sympathy for the East European Jew's tenacious adherence to his religion and culture subjected him to considerable abuse. The works of Kompert, Franzos, and Sacher-Masoch enjoyed quite a vogue as exotic literature, but it was not until Georg *Hermann wrote the novels *Jettchen Gebert* (1906) and its sequel, *Henriette Jacoby* (1909), that cultured German Jewry received adequate treatment in German fiction.

LATER REACTIONS. When Friedrich Nietzsche wrote in 1886 in *Jenseits von Gut und Boese* that he had never yet met a German who was favorably inclined to Jews, he was undoubtedly exaggerating, but he correctly recognized that in Germany the age-old image of the Jew was an unflattering one. Although his close association with Richard *Wagner had brought him into contact with an outspoken anti-Semite, Nietzsche himself abhorred anti-Semitism as the revolt of the rabble against culture, and condemned it in the most violent terms. While Nietzsche foresaw a glorious future for Jews on the world scene, another influential German philosopher, Oswald Spengler, held that Judaism had already completed its historic function and was on the verge of disappearing. In *Der Untergang des Abendlandes* (1922) he was at pains to stress the intense mutual hatred between Germans and Jews, and the "inevitable conflict" between a vigorous young culture rooted in the soil and a senile, overripe civilization of landless cosmopolitans. Spengler's vaunted objectivity was soon to supply Nazi ideologists and literary racists with ammunition for their perverted theories.

The late 19th century saw a reaction to German literary anti-Semitism on the part of a few isolated Jewish writers, notably Max *Nordau and Theodor *Herzl, both of them fathers of the Zionist movement. Nordau's tragedy, *Doktor Kohn* (1898), concluded that assimilation was impossible and that a solution to Jewish misery had to be found elsewhere; while Herzl, in his utopian novel *Altneuland* (1902), projected his answer into an idealized Jewish state. Arthur *Schnitzler, neither a Zionist nor an assimilationist, presented an admirable Jewish physician in his drama *Professor Bernhardi* (1912), which attacked anti-Semitism. With few exceptions, the major non-Jewish writers sided with the Jews in their battle for self-preservation. Although Artur Dinter anticipated the Nazis with his hate-filled *Die Suende wider das Blut* (1917), modern authors of the stature of Gerhart Hauptmann and Thomas Mann remained aloof from the rising tide of nationalism. In his tragicomedy, *Der rote Hahn* (1901), and in his drama, *Die Finsternisse* (1947), which had to be smuggled out of Nazi Germany, Hauptmann paid tribute to the fruitful liberalism of German Jewry. There were sympathetic Jewish characters in Mann's works, too, especially in *Koenigliche Hoheit* (1909) and *Der Zauberberg* (1924). A certain objectivity characterizes the Jewish portrayals of Ernst Glaeser (*Jahrgang 1902,* 1928) and Gertrud von Le Fort (*Der Papst aus dem Ghetto,* 1930).

PRELUDE TO CATASTROPHE. During the first third of the 20th century, the Jewish influence on German literature reached its climax. The image which Jewish writers incorporated in their works ranged from the self-hatred of Maximilian *Harden, Karl *Kraus, Kurt *Tucholsky, and Otto *Weininger to the strong affirmation of national resurgence by Martin Buber, Richard Beer-Hofmann, Max Brod, and Arnold Zweig. Joseph Roth dramatized the conflict between the authentic and the assimilated Jew; Walter *Mehring identified the Jews with the capitalists responsible for the inflation; and Hans José *Rehfisch and Wilhelm Herzog dramatized European anti-Semitism in *Die Affaire Dreyfus* (1929). Stefan Zweig saw the Jew as the precursor of the good European and Ernst *Toller fought German racial conceit by espousing cosmopolitanism and utopian Socialism.

Aryan mythmakers from Houston Stewart *Chamberlain to Alfred *Rosenberg propagated the fiction of blood as the determining psychic factor. Nazi writers fed the Germans an image of the Jew as an hereditary criminal, and branded as a fairy tale the possibility that baptism could emancipate the Jew from his criminal tendencies. With the triumph of Nazi ideology in 1933, all favorable images of the Jew were suppressed by literary, stage, and radio censors. Only in exile could Thomas and Heinrich Mann and other writers of non-Jewish origin present a more balanced image of the Jew. Most German émigré writers on Jewish themes were, however, either Jews or of Jewish descent. They included Arthur *Koestler, Lion Feuchtwanger, Karl *Wolfskehl, Arnold Zweig, Hermann *Kesten, Alfred *Doeblin, and Else *Lasker-Schueler. The few courageous voices that were heard from the "Aryan" side included those of the baptized half-Jew Carl *Zuckmayer, who had shown Jewish faults and virtues to be common to all men in such works as his drama *Der Hauptmann von Koepenick* (1930); Wolfgang Langhoff, whose *Die Moorsoldaten* (1935) was the first literary account of Nazi brutality in the concentration camps; and Bertolt Brecht, who developed a similar theme in *Furcht und Elend des Dritten Reiches* (1941). Like their Jewish fellow-writers, however, Zuckmayer, Langhoff, and Brecht were finally compelled to take refuge abroad, and it was not until after World War II that a more dispassionate assessment of the Jewish image in German literature could be attempted. [S.L./ED.]

The Jewish Contribution to German Literature. Jews first settled along the Rhine in Roman times and they have thus been an integral element in German culture from its earliest beginnings. In the Middle Ages, the Middle High German which they spoke became interspersed with Hebrew words and, following waves of persecution, was carried eastward to become the Yiddish language (i.e., *Juedisch-Deutsch*). Those Jews who remained in Germany developed a kindred dialect, *Judendeutsch,* and it was in this more distinctly Germanic tongue that *Glueckel of Hameln wrote her famous memoirs at the end of the 17th century. German Jewry can, however, lay claim to one authentic Jewish contributor to medieval German literature—the *Minnesaengèr* (minstrel) *Suesskind von Trimberg, who flourished in the first half of the 13th century. The handful of lyrics still extant, notable for their Jewish feeling and inspiration, are of perennial interest to German literary historians. A century later, in 1336, Samson Pine was one of three German writers who collaborated in the translation of a French version of the *Parsifal* romance. The prefatory acknowledgements of his Strasbourg colleagues clearly indicate that Pine was a Jew and that he was responsible for most of the work. In 1519 Johannes *Pauli, a Jew turned Franciscan preacher, published his *Schimpf un Ernst,* an important and influential collection of humorous and didactic anecdotes.

THE AGE OF ENLIGHTENMENT. It was not until 250 years later, during the late 18th century, that Jewish writers first appeared in significant numbers on the German cultural scene, utilizing the German language as their literary medium. The doctrines of tolerance and human equality propounded by the philosophers of the Enlightenment made a profound impression on Jewish intellectuals. The Jewish elite wished to contribute to the stream of German culture, and at first the German elite welcomed them. The finest expression of this rapprochement between the two ethnic groups was the friendship of Moses Mendelssohn, the Jew from Dessau, and Gotthold Lessing, Germany's most influential literary critic, who both stressed the common ethical heritage of Judaism and Christianity. A towering figure of both the German Enlightenment and the Jewish Emancipation, Moses Mendelssohn was also the first modern Jewish writer to master the German idiom in all its subtleties. His philosophical and aesthetic works—notably the *Briefe ueber die Empfindungen* (1755), *Phaedon, oder Ueber die Unsterblichkeit der Seele* (1767), and *Morgenstunden* (1785)—had an enormous impact in Germany itself and abroad. The reputation he came to enjoy in the outside world enhanced his standing within German Jewry, which thereafter involved itself increasingly in German cultural and literary affairs. Mendelssohn also founded German Jewry's first newspaper, *Kohelet Musar* (Berlin, 1750), and in 1778 began publishing an original German translation of the Bible with a Hebrew commentary. German enlightenment found its finest philosophical formulation in the critical reasoning of Immanuel *Kant, and it is no accident that the first enthusiastic adherents of Kantian philosophy were Jews. From Marcus Herz, the friend and physician of Lessing and Mendelssohn, Lazarus *Bendavid, Solomon *Maimon, and David *Friedlaender to the outstanding neo-Kantians of the 20th century—Hermann *Cohen and Ernst *Cassirer—Jews played a leading role in the exposition of Kant's philosophy.

Hartwig *Wessely, who died in 1805, was the last of the Hebrew lyrical poets in Germany, and German steadily replaced Hebrew among the Jewish writers of Central Europe. Moses Ephraim *Kuh attacked anti-Semitism in witty German epigrams, and the Polish physician Issachar Falkensohn *Behr wrote *Gedichte von einem pohlnischen Juden* (1772), which were reviewed by Goethe. Michael *Sachs, through his translations, introduced the religious poetry of medieval Spanish Jewry to the Jews of Germany.

THE AGE OF ROMANTICISM. During the ensuing Romantic era the German theologian Friedrich *Schleiermacher, who wished to see a revival of religion along with the pursuit of poetry and the fine arts, strenuously opposed all attempts to convert Jews to Christianity, since he doubted the sincerity of the converts. Romanticism delayed the process of Jewish emancipation by developing a nationalist philosophy that led to a new form of anti-Semitism, based not on religious differences, but rather on differences in national origin. This "Teutonism" condoned hatred of the Jews.

From the 1780s, German Jews and non-Jews had mingled in Berlin salons, where Jewish hostesses of charm, learning, and wit furthered the cultural exchange between statesmen, philosophers, and Romantic artists. The most distinguished salon in Berlin was that of the brilliant Henriette *Herz, wife of the philosopher Marcus Herz and an admirer of Goethe and the Romantics, who fostered the doctrines of the new generation. Other Berlin hostesses were Rahel Varnhagen von Ense (whom Goethe claimed as the first person to understand and recognize him); Moses Mendelssohn's daughter, Dorothea von *Schlegel, who introduced Victor Hugo and Mme. de Staël to the German reader; and Fanny *Lewald, a writer and feminist. Their Viennese counterparts were Fanny, Baroness von *Arnstein; and the von Wertheimsteins, Josephine, her sister Sophie, Baroness Todesco, and her daughter Franziska.

THE AGE OF LIBERALISM. Romanticism promoted the revival of historical studies and taught that history does not merely interpret the past but affords an understanding of the present and guidance to the future. Preeminent among Jewish historians during the first half of the 19th century was Leopold *Zunz, the originator of the *Wissenschaft des Judentums ("Science of Judaism"). Together with Abraham *Geiger, Moses Moser (1796–1838), and Eduard *Gans, he founded in 1819 the *Verein fuer Cultur und Wissenschaft des Judentums. Heine, who joined this organization, gave a detailed record of its achievements in a eulogy of his friend Ludwig Marcus (1798–1843). The impact of Zunz and of the *Verein* was felt throughout the 19th century. Geiger wrote his three-volume study, *Das Judentum und seine Geschichte* (1864–71), from the standpoint of Reform Judaism, but the concept of Jewish history was broadened when the positive historical (Conservative) school emerged with the *Monatsschrift fuer Geschichte und Wissenschaft des Judentums,* under the editorship of Zacharias *Frankel. The first universal history of the Jewish people in German, *Geschichte der Israeliten* (1820–47) written by Isaac Markus *Jost paved the way for Heinrich *Graetz, whose *Geschichte der Juden von den aeltesten Zeiten bis auf die Gegenwart* (11 vols., 1853–75) is generally considered one of the outstanding works of historical scholarship in the German language.

Prussian and Austrian reactionaries were the most rabid anti-Semites, and Jews saw in political liberalism a powerful ally in their battle for emancipation. The aim of German liberalism was to develop the capacities of the individual irrespective of race, sex, class, or economic status; it therefore enabled Jews to develop their talents to the fullest extent. Berthold Auerbach, who was for many years the literary spokesman of German-Jewish liberalism; became the outstanding Jewish master of the sentimental novel and short story. However, although Jews finally succeeded in obtaining full legal rights as citizens of the German states, their inner conflict did not abate. Ferdinand Lassalle, the leading German socialist, summoned his "martyr people" to join the revolutionary working classes in the fight against the common oppressor. Jews in general joined the opposition parties, and some became influential contributors to the liberal and socialist press.

DISILLUSIONMENT. Heinrich Heine, the greatest Jewish poet in the German language, tried to disguise the conflicts arising from his opportunist conversion to Christianity by satirical irony, but at heart he always remained a Jew. Some of his most Jewish poems (e.g., the "Hebraeische Melodien" of his *Romanzero*) were written years after his baptism. Heine and Ludwig Boerne were the originators of the German *feuilleton,* a literary genre of great artistic charm in which Jews—from Moritz Gottlieb *Saphir and Daniel Spitzer (1835–1893) to Herzl, Nordau, Peter *Altenberg, Felix *Salten, and Alfred *Polgar—particularly excelled. Some German revolutionary poets such as Karl *Beck and Moritz *Hartmann were Jewish merely by the accident of birth and both converted. It was only when revolutionary ardor gave way to disappointment verging on despair that these writers turned to authentic Jewish subjects. Karl Emil Franzos discovered *Halbasien* ("Semi-Asia," i.e., Galician Jewry) and described the tension between Eastern and Western Jews.

With few exceptions, 19th-century German dramatists suppressed any Jewish feelings they may have had. Ludwig *Robert, the converted brother of Rahel Varnhagen, was always sensitive to the ambiguities of his position; while Michael *Beer, brother of the composer Giacomo *Meyerbeer, wrote a play, *Der Paria* (1826), which betrays the depressing effect of his Jewish origin. A third playwright,

Solomon Hermann von *Mosenthal, in his *Deborah* (1850), dramatized the story of a Jewess living among Christian peasants.

During the first half century of Jewish emancipation, the dichotomy was resolved for many German Jews by assimilation or conversion. Of the direct descendants of Michael *Creizenach, a scholarly advocate of religious reform, his son Theodor (1818–1877), a poet and authority on Goethe, abandoned Judaism, as did Theodor's son Wilhelm (1851–1919), an eminent literary scholar. Friedrich Wolters (1876–1930), who belonged to the circle of Stefan George, was the non-Jewish grandson of the Odessa-born poet and translator Wilhelm Wolfsohn (1820–1865). Heinrich Stieglitz (1801–1849), a melancholic lyricist, was the son of a baptized banker; and Betty Paoli (Barbara Elisabeth Glueck, 1815–1894) was a Viennese society poet born of a Hungarian nobleman and a Belgian Jewess.

The Struggle Between the Two Souls. The novelist Jacob *Wassermann, reviewing his own life in *Mein Weg als Deutscher und Jude* (1921), wrote: "I am a German and a Jew, each as completely as the other; neither can be separated from the other." This held true for most German-Jewish writers of the late 19th and early 20th centuries, although the proportion between the German and the Jewish ingredients of this amalgam varied. Some wished for total assimilation; others were willing to identify themselves within the German-Jewish group but denied all kinship with East-European Jews, whom they considered foreign and inferior. Jewish history was for this class of writer far more remote than the history of the Germans whom they idealized.

Three writers who appear to have been untouched by the problem were the half-Jewish poet Paul Heyse, who was awarded the Nobel Prize for literature in 1910; and two humorists, Julius Stettenheim (1831–1916) and C. Karlweis (Karl Weiss, 1850–1901), an Austrian railroad inspector who wrote popular comedies and short stories. On the other hand, Arthur Schnitzler, the sensitive, delicate analyst of a dying Viennese society, was a vigorous opponent of anti-Semitism. Stefan Zweig despaired of the survival of European culture, and the European tragedy finally drove him to suicide. He nevertheless felt that Jewry would endure, but he himself was not primarily of it, despite his awareness of Jewish nobility and martyrdom. Some writers were impelled to stress the positive aspects of the Jewish heritage and identity. They include Jacob Loewenberg (1856–1929), whose verse was collected in *Lieder eines Semiten* (1892) and *Aus juedischer Seele* (1901); and the proselyte Nahida Ruth *Lazarus, noted for her expository works conceived in the spirit of Liberal Judaism. Ludwig *Jacobowski, in his novels *Werther der Jude* (1892) and *Loki* (1899), portrayed the struggle between the Jew and his anti-Semitic surroundings. The pioneer Zionist Samuel *Lublinski emphasized the Jewish thirst for knowledge and truth; another Jewish nationalist, Fritz Mordechai *Kaufmann, became an expert on Yiddish folklore; while Georg Hermann wrote about Berlin's Jewish society with benevolent satire. Two other writers who took a positive Jewish stand were Moritz *Heimann and Alfred *Kerr.

By contrast, several leading literary figures of the era revealed themselves to be either unsympathetic to the fate of their own people or even outspokenly hostile. Carl *Sternheim anticipated the Fascists with his attacks on the Jewish middle classes, but Rudolf Borchardt, who tried to disguise his origin by the adoption of reactionary nationalism, only narrowly escaped deportation to Auschwitz concentration camp. The philosophical father of "Jewish self-hatred" was Otto Weininger; his leading disciple was Arthur *Trebitsch, whose pathological detestation of the Jews and Judaism led him to offer his services an an anti-Semitic propagandist to the Austrian Nazis. Two other writers influenced by Weininger were Karl *Kraus and Kurt *Tucholsky. Somewhat less violent was the ostentatious Catholic convert Ernst *Lothar. Ernst Lissauer, composer of World War I's notorious "Hymn of Hate" against England, also supported the postwar reactionary nationalists. A double irony attaches to Ferdinand Bronner (1867–1948), a naturalistic dramatist who wrote under the pen name Franz Adamus: he was born in the Polish town of Oświęcim (Auschwitz), and in his comedy, *Schmelz, der Nibelunge* (1905), a son denies his Jewish parentage. His own son, Arnolt Bronnen (1895–1959), swung from support of the extreme left to the far right, and held important radio and television posts under the Nazis. After World War II the erstwhile Nazi became a respectable public figure in Austria and at the end of his life was a drama critic in East Berlin.

The Jewish Renaissance. Under the impact of their military disaster in World War I the Germans experienced a temporary spiritual revulsion against war, brutality, lust for power, and materialism. The literary movement of Expressionism thereafter engaged in a fervent struggle for peace, world brotherhood, and the dignity of man. It included a high proportion of Jewish writers, notably Ernst Toller, Alfred Doeblin, Franz *Werfel, Alfred *Mombert, Albert *Ehrenstein, Alfred *Wolfenstein, Jacob von Hoddis (1887–1942), Ludwig *Rubiner, and the Franco-German poet Yvan *Goll.

Together with this rebellious movement in the arts, there arose a second movement aiming at the intellectual, moral, and political rebirth of the Jewish people. Martin Buber and Franz Rosenzweig were the outstanding philosophical leaders of this Jewish renaissance. Richard Beer-Hofmann was the major poet of this German-Jewish revival and gave expression to Jewish suffering and glory in a biblical cycle about King David. His *Schlaflied fuer Miriam* (1897) is regarded as the finest philosophical lullaby in the German language. Karl Wolfskehl, who began his career as a member of the Stefan George circle, also found his way to Jewish poetry. Max Brod, whose Zionism led him to settle in Ereẓ Israel in 1939, considered Judaism a rampart against the black void toward which events were pointing, and felt that his "best service to humanity was to work in all humility for the perfection of my own people." Franz *Kafka and Hermann *Broch broke new ground in German fiction with works on the ultimate goal of human existence. Although their novels never directly touch on Jewish themes, they reflect the Jewish character of their authors. Kafka himself studied Hebrew and even planned to settle in Ereẓ Israel.

Vivid pictures of Jewish life in Germany were painted by the novelists Lion Feuchtwanger (*Jud Suess,* 1925) and Arnold Zweig. Feuchtwanger also wrote a celebrated trilogy based on the story of Josephus. Zweig, long an ardent Zionist, lived in Haifa for many years before settling in East Germany after 1948. In *Der Gezeichnete* (1936), Jacob *Picard portrayed with affection the Orthodox folklore and traditions of Jews long settled in southwest Germany. Else Lasker-Schueler, regarded by many as the greatest German poetess after Annette von Droste-Huelsoff, dreamed of an imagined oriental world, celebrated the "Land of the Hebrews," and ended her days in Jerusalem. Gertrud *Kolmar, whose poems, some of them in Hebrew, expressed tragic loneliness, remained in Germany and perished in a death camp. A third important woman poet, Nelly *Sachs, who was awarded the Nobel Prize for literature in 1966, expressed both the anxiety and the restlessness of her age and her loyalty to the Jewish people and its destiny.

Jewish writers of the 1930s echoed the torment and despair of their era. On the one hand there was a messianic belief in the future of mankind and, on the other, a nihilistic mistrust of any system of values. The Jews who fled Germany from 1933 and Austria from 1938 included some of the most prominent Jewish writers, although there were many who either chose to remain or could not escape. With the onslaught of the Hitler regime on German-speaking Jewry, the cherished dream of a German-Jewish symbiosis abruptly collapsed and the history of German-Jewish literature was, so far as Europe was concerned, at an end.

LITERARY SCHOLARS. The Jews of Germany and Austria also made an important contribution to literary history and research, many of them writing scholarly works that continue to be regarded as classics. Some outstanding literary historians were the convert Emil Kuh (1828–1876), who "discovered" the dramatist Friedrich Hebbel, editing his works (1866–68) and writing his biography (1877); Julius Leopold *Klein, the Hungarian-born author of a 13-volume *Geschichte des Dramas* (1865–76); Richard Moritz *Meyer, who wrote his *Deutsche Literatur des neunzehnten Jahrhunderts* (1900); Friedrich *Gundolf, an authority on Shakespeare, Goethe, and Kleist; Alfred Kerr, author of *Die Welt im Drama* (1917) and *Die Welt im Licht* (1920); Egon *Friedell, the Austrian playwright, who was also a cultural historian and author of a *Kulturgeschichte der Neuzeit* (3 vols., 1927–31); Hugo *Bieber, who wrote *Der Kampf um die Tradition* (1928) and was an authority on Heine; and Arthur *Eloesser, author of *Die deutsche Literatur vom Barock bis zur Gegenwart* (1930–31).

Other scholars in this field include Julius *Bab, Albert Bielschowsky (1847–1902), Ernst *Heilborn, Rudolf *Kayser, Alfred Klaar (1848–1927), Victor Klemperer (1881–1960), Samuel *Lublinski, Kurt Pinthus (1886–), Otto Pniower (1859–1932), and Julius Wahle (1861–1940). Two outstanding authorities on Goethe were Michael Bernays (1834–1897), the baptized son of Ḥakham Isaac *Bernays of Hamburg, who was a professor at Munich; and Ludwig *Geiger, a son of the German reformer Abraham Geiger, who was a professor in Berlin and wrote *Die deutsche Literatur und die Juden* (1910). Three other academic scholars were Robert F. Arnold (Robert Frank Levisohn, 1872–1938), who was professor of German literature at Vienna; Jonas *Fraenkel, an expert on Swiss-German literature, who held a chair at Berne; and Fritz *Strich, who was professor successively at Munich and Berne universities. Georg Witkowski (1863–1941), the baptized brother of Maximilian *Harden, wrote *Das deutsche Drama des neunzehnten Jahrhunderts* (1923–25) and ended his career as a professor in Leipzig. Eduard Engel (1851–1938) published a *Geschichte der deutschen Literatur* that reached its 38th edition in 1929; and the Czech anthologist Camill *Hoffmann wrote *Die deutsche Lyrik aus Oesterreich seit Grillparzer* (1912). The literary and dramatic critic Monty Jacobs (1875–1945), who was a coeditor of the *Goldene Klassikerbibliothek,* had an English father and took refuge in London after the Nazis came to power; while Werner Kraft (1896–), a German poet, editor, and critic, eventually settled in Israel. An outstanding scholar, Daniel *Sanders, published several authoritative German dictionaries, including a *Handwoerterbuch der deutschen Sprache* (3 vols., 1859–65).

From the age of Heine onward, German Jews also distinguished themselves as cultural mediators, especially with the English and French. Heine's contemporary, the royal physician David Ferdinand *Koreff, was also a writer and did much to promote the interchange of ideas between leading authors through his circle in Paris. Later contributions were made by German-Jewish translators from various languages, notably Julius Elias (Ibsen), Alexander Eliasberg (Dostoyevski, Tolstoy), F. Gundolf (Shakespeare), Siegfried *Trebitsch (Shaw), and Stefan Zweig (Verhaeren).

WORKS ON PALESTINE AND ISRAEL. Discounting biblical poems, and plays and novels set in ancient Palestine, most of the literature on the Holy Land written in German was produced by a few German-Jewish authors. One of the very few 19th-century works was *Nach Jerusalem* (1858–60; *The Jews in the East,* 1859), travel sketches by the poet and Viennese communal leader, Ludwig August *Frankl. The *Gesaenge aus der Verbannung* (1829) by Solomon Ludwig *Steinheim anticipated the return to Zion, as did Theodor Herzl's novel, *Altneuland* (1902), three-quarters of a century later. Moshe Ya'akov *Ben-Gavriel (Eugen Hoeflich), who had been an Austrian liaison officer with the Turkish army during World War I, wrote a series of Zionist works based on personal experience, beginning with books such as *Der Weg ins Land* (1918) and *Feuer im Osten* (1920). Rudolf *Lothar included an account of a visit to Palestine in *Zwischen drei Welten* (1926), and other German and Austrian Jews—not always Zionists—brought back glowing reports of Jewish pioneering achievements in Ereẓ Israel. They include Alfred Kerr, who has a chapter entitled "Jeruschalajim" in his *Die Welt im Licht* (1920); Arthur Holitscher, who wrote *Reise durch das juedische Palaestina* (1922); Richard Arnold *Bermann, who collaborated with another non-Zionist, Arthur Rundt, in the publication of *Palaestina* (1923); and Felix Salten (*Neue Menschen auf alter Erde,* 1925). Else Lasker-Schueler's poetic impressions of the land in which she spent her last years, illustrated with her own quaint drawings, were conveyed in *Das Hebraeerland* (1937). Another refugee, the historical biographer Josef *Kastein, wrote many works in Palestine after 1933, including *Jerusalem; Die Geschichte eines Landes* (1937) and *Eine palaestinensische Novelle* (1942).

After World War II, Hans José Rehfisch wrote *Quelle der Verheissung* (1946), a play about German Jews who settled in Ereẓ Israel. Max Brod's novel, *Unambo* (1949), dealt with Israel's War of Independence, while Aryeh Ludwig *Strauss, a refugee poet and literary historian who settled in Palestine and later wrote in Hebrew as well as German, reflected both the Israel scene and his own intimate experience in the lyrical *Heimliche Gegenwart* (1952). M. Y. Ben-Gavriel found a new and valuable outlet for his talents in the many books of anecdotes and travel which became best sellers in post-Hitler Germany, such as *Kumsitz* (1956). His descriptions of life in the State of Israel did much to win sympathy and support for the infant Jewish state in Federal Germany. [R.K./ED.]

The Holocaust and Its Aftermath. The liquidation of German writers of Jewish origin was set in motion almost as soon as the Nazis came to power in 1933. Two early victims were the philosopher Theodor *Lessing (murdered at Marienbad in 1933) and the poet and dramatist Erich *Muehsam (tortured to death at the Oranienburg concentration camp in 1934). The massacre increased after the outbreak of World War II. Ernst Heilborn died at the hands of the Gestapo in Berlin in 1941, Paul *Kornfeld in the Lodz Ghetto in 1942, and Gertrud Kolmar somewhere in Eastern Europe in the following year. Writers who perished at *Auschwitz include Georg Hermann (1943), Arno Nadel (1943), and Camill Hoffmann (1944). By a grim irony, Herwarth *Walden, who fled to the U.S.S.R. in 1933, is thought to have been executed during a Soviet purge in 1942. A number of Jewish writers, unable to accept the shattering of their illusions, committed suicide. They include the cultural philosopher and historian Walter

*Benjamin (Paris, 1940), Egon Friedell (Vienna, 1938), Ludwig *Fulda (Berlin, 1939), Ernst Toller (New York, 1939), Kurt Tucholsky (Sweden, 1935), Ernst *Weiss (Paris, 1940), Alfred Wolfenstein (Paris, 1945), and Stefan Zweig (Brazil, 1942). In fear of the Nazi invaders, the half-Jewish expressionist poet Walter *Hasenclever took his own life at a detention camp in southern France in 1940.

Many other German and Austrian writers of Jewish birth, more fortunate, found refuge abroad. Among those who settled in England were Felix Braun, Kurt *Hiller, Alfred Kerr, Arthur Koestler, Theodor *Kramer, Robert *Neumann, Hans José Rehfisch, and Carl *Roessler. Karl Wolfskehl died an exile in New Zealand, Nelly Sachs and Peter *Weiss settled in Sweden, while Paul *Adler survived the Holocaust in hiding in Czechoslovakia. Switzerland provided a haven for Efraim *Frisch, Margarete *Susman, Siegfried Trebitsch, and the converted half-Jew, Carl Zuckmayer, who spent the war years in the U.S. By far the largest number fled to the United States or Palestine. Those who emigrated to Ereẓ Israel include Max Brod, Martin Buber, M. Y. Ben-Gavriel, Sammy Gronemann, Josef Kastein, Leo *Perutz, Else Lasker-Schueler, Aryeh Ludwig Strauss, and Arnold Zweig. The U.S. welcomed scores of refugee writers, among them literary figures such as Julius Bab, Richard Beer-Hofmann, Hugo Bieber, Ferdinand *Bruckner, Alfred Doeblin, Lion Feuchtwanger, Manfred *George, Hermann *Kesten, Ernst Lothar, Ludwig *Marcuse, Walter *Mehring, Alfred *Neumann, Alfred *Polgar, Roda Roda (Sandor Rosenfeld, 1872–1945), Felix Salten, Friedrich *Torberg, Berthold *Viertel, Ernst *Waldinger, and Franz Werfel. Refugee writers who returned to Europe after World War II include Braun, Bruckner, Doeblin, Lothar, Marcuse, Rehfisch, Salten, Torberg, and Viertel. Several leftist writers abandoned the West for Iron Curtain countries: from Mexico, Egon Erwin *Kisch, the "rushing reporter," returned to Prague and Anna *Seghers to East Germany; Friedrich *Wolf moved from the U.S.S.R. to East Berlin and was for a time East Germany's envoy in Warsaw; while Arnold Zweig, who left Israel in 1948, also settled in East Berlin. Hans *Habe, who had fought first with the French and later with the U.S. army, finally made his home in Austria. A postwar playwright, Wolfgang Hildesheimer (1916–), was in Ereẓ Israel during the 1930s and World War II, but eventually settled in Munich.

THE LITERATURE OF REMORSE. After the collapse of Nazi Germany, non-Jewish writers of a new, repentant generation experienced a feeling of revulsion against the mass murder of the Jews. They tended to idealize the figure of the Jew, endowing him with biblical grandeur, immense wisdom, and great moral stature. As the prime victim of the European Holocaust, the Jew continued to trouble and preoccupy the conscience of postwar Germany. The poet and novelist Johannes Bobrowski, who had served on the Russian front during World War II, wrote affectionately of the heterogeneous population and folk world of pre-Nazi East Prussia, and spoke of Germany's treatment of the Jews as "a long story of misfortune and guilt, for which my people has been to blame ever since the days of the Teutonic Knights. " Similar feelings pervaded the works of postwar novelists such as Heinrich Boell (*Wo warst du, Adam?*, 1951), Albrecht Goes (*Das Brandopfer*, 1954), Guenter Grass (*Die Blechtrommel*, 1959; *Hundejahre*, 1963), Walter Jens (*Der Blinde*, 1951), Wolfgang Koeppen, and Felix Lutzendorf. The anti-Nazi refugee novelist Erich Maria Remarque dealt with the fate of German Jews immediately before and during the Holocaust: *Arc de triomphe* (1946; *Arch of Triumph*, 1946); *Der Funke Leben* (1952; *Spark of Life*, 1952); and *Die Nacht von Lissabon* (1962); and other novels on the theme of anti-Jewish persecution were written by Stefan Andres (*Die Sintflut*, 1949–59), Friedrich Duerrenmatt (*Der Verdacht*, 1953), Hermann Kasack (*Die Stadt hinter dem Strom*, 1947), and Rudolf Lorenzen (*Alles andere als ein Held*, 1959).

The fate of the Jews was also presented on the stage in plays by Stefan Andres (*Sperrzonen*, 1959), Max Frisch (*Andorra*, 1962), Fritz Hochwaelder (*Der Fluechtling*, 1948; *Der oeffentliche Anklaeger*, 1954), Erwin Sylvanus (*Korczak und die Kinder*, 1959), and Martin Walser (*Eiche und Angora*, 1962). The most influential—and controversial—postwar German drama about the Jews in the Nazi era was Rolf *Hochhuth's *Der Stellvertreter* (1963), which condemned Pope Pius XII as an accessory to Hitler's "Final Solution of the Jewish Problem." *Der Stellvertreter* was translated into many languages and was staged in the U.S. as *The Deputy* and in England as *The Representative*. In postwar German literature the Jew thus became a symbol of man's inhumanity to man and an instrument of national self-flagellation. This process was encouraged by the appearance of works in German by Jewish victims of the Hitler era—the moving diary of Anne *Frank; *Das unausloeschliche Siegel* (1946), a novel by the baptized half-Jewess, Elisabeth Langgaesser (1899–1950); *Eine Seele aus Holz* (1962; *A Soul of Wood*, 1964), a grim volume of tales about Hitler's "death doctors" and their victims by Jakov Lind (1927–); the visionary poems of Paul Celan (1920–1970), a Rumanian-born writer and translator, whose works include *Der Sand aus den Urnen* (1948) and *Mohn und Gedaechtnis* (1952); and the poems of Nelly Sachs. Two half-Jews who saw the problem from both sides of the fence were Carl Zuckmayer, in his plays *Des Teufels General* (1947) and *Das kalte Licht* (1955), and Peter Weiss with *Die Ermittlung*, an oratorio based on the Auschwitz trial held in Frankfort in 1965 (Eng., *The Investigation*, 1966). [S.L./ED.]

Alphabetical List of Entries of German-language Authors. The authors in the list below form the subjects of articles in their appropriate alphabetical position in the Encyclopaedia.

***ADLER, PAUL** (1878–1946), author.
***ALTENBERG, PETER** (1859–1919), author.
***AUERBACH, BERTHOLD** (1812–1882), novelist and protagonist of Jewish emancipation.
***AUERNHEIMER, RAOUL** (1876–1948), author and journalist.
***BAB, JULIUS** (1880–1955), literary critic and historian.
***BAUM, OSKAR** (1883–1941), Czech author.
***BAUM, VICKI** (1888–1960), novelist.
***BECK, KARL ISIDOR** (1817–1879), Hungarian poet.
***BEER, MICHAEL** (1800–1833), playwright.
***BEER-HOFMANN, RICHARD** (1866–1945), poet and playwright.
***BEHR, ISACHAR FALKENSOHN** (1746–1817), Polish poet.
***BEN-GAVRIEL, MOSHE YA'AKOV (EUGEN HOEFLICH,** 1891–1965), Austrian and Israel author.
***BENJAMIN, WALTER** (1892–1940), cultural philosopher and literary historian.
***BERG, LEO** (1862–1908), literary critic and essayist.
***BERMANN, RICHARD ARNOLD** (1883–1938), author and journalist
***BERNSTEIN, ARON** (1812–1884), author, journalist, and protagonist of religious reform.
***BIEBER, HUGO** (1883–1955), literary historian.
***BIRNBAUM, URIEL** (1894–1956), poet and painter.
***BLUMENTHAL, OSKAR** (1852–1917), playwright.
***BOERNE, LUDWIG** (1786–1837), essayist and protagonist of Jewish emancipation.
***BRAUN, FELIX** (1885–), poet, playwright, and novelist.
***BROCH, HERMANN** (1886–1951), novelist.
***BROD, MAX** (1884–1968), Czech and Israel novelist, playwright, essayist, and composer.
***BRUCKNER, FERDINAND** (1891–1958), playwright.
***BUBER, MARTIN** (1878–1965), philosopher, author, and Zionist.

*CALÉ, WALTER (1881–1904), poet.
*CANETTI, ELIAS (1905–), Anglo-Austrian playwright and novelist.
*DOEBLIN, ALFRED (1878–1957), novelist.
*DONATH, ADOLF (1876–1937), poet and art critic.
*EHRENSTEIN, ALBERT (1886–1950), poet and author.
*ELOESSER, ARTHUR (1870–1938), literary historian and critic.
*FEUCHTWANGER, LION (1884–1958), novelist.
*FRAENKEL, JONAS (1879–1965), Swiss literary historian.
*FRANK, BRUNO (1887–1945), novelist and playwright.
*FRANKL, LUDWIG AUGUST (1810–1894), poet, editor, and Jewish communal leader.
*FRANZOS, KARL EMIL (1848–1904), novelist and editor.
*FRIEDELL, EGON (1878–1938), playwright and cultural historian.
*FRISCH, EFRAIM (1873–1942), author, literary critic, and translator.
*FULDA, LUDWIG (1862–1939), playwright and translator.
*GEIGER, LUDWIG (1848–1909), literary scholar and cultural historian.
*GEORGE, MANFRED (1893–1965), author and editor.
*GOLL, YVAN (1891–1950), French and German poet.
*GRONEMANN, SAMMY (1875–1952), German Israel novelist, playwright, and Zionist leader.
*GUMPERT, MARTIN (1897–1955), author and scientific writer.
*GUNDOLF, FRIEDRICH (1880–1931), literary historian.
*HAAS, WILLY (1891–), literary critic and essayist.
*HABE, HANS (1911–), novelist
*HARTMANN, MORITZ (1821–1872), poet and novelist.
*HASENCLEVER, WALTER (1890–1940), poet.
*HEILBORN, ERNST (1867–1941), author and cultural historian.
*HEIMANN, MORITZ (1868–1925), author and essayist.
*HEINE, HEINRICH (1797–1856), poet and essayist.
*HELLER, SELIGMANN (1831–1890), poet and literary critic.
*HERMANN, GEORG (1871–1943), novelist and essayist.
*HERZL, THEODOR (1860–1904), author, journalist, and founder of political Zionism.
*HESS, MOSES (1812–1875), novelist and essayist.
*HEYMANN, WALTER (1882–1915), poet.
*HEYSE, PAUL (1830–1914), novelist, poet, and playwright.
*HILLER, KURT (1885–), essayist and editor.
*HIRSCHFELD, GEORG (1873–1942), playwright.
*HITZIG, JULIUS EDUARD (1780–1849), author and biographer.
*HOFFMANN, CAMILL (1878–1944), Czech poet, editor, and translator.
*HOFMANNSTHAL, HUGO VON (1874–1929), poet and playwright.
*HOLITSCHER, ARTHUR (1869–1941), novelist and playwright.
*HOLLAENDER, FELIX (1867–1931), novelist and stage critic.
*JACOB, HEINRICH EDUARD (1889–1967), playwright and biographer.
*JACOBOWSKI, LUDWIG (1868–1900), novelist, poet, and Jewish apologist.
*JACOBSOHN, SIEGFRIED (1881–1926), drama critic and editor.
*KAFKA, FRANZ (1883–1924), Czech novelist.
*KAHANE, ARTHUR (1872–1932), novelist, critic, and editor.
*KALISCH, DAVID (1820–1872), playwright.
*KAUFMANN, FRITZ MORDECHAI (1888–1921), essayist and Yiddish folklorist.
*KAYSER, RUDOLF (1889–1964), author and biographer.
*KERR, ALFRED (1867–1948), essayist and literary critic.
*KESTEN, HERMANN (1900–), novelist
*KISCH, EGON ERWIN (1885–1948), author and journalist.
*KLEIN, JULIUS LEOPOLD (1810–1876), playwright and literary historian.
*KOLMAR, GERTRUD (1894–1943), poet.
*KOMPERT, LEOPOLD (1822–1886), novelist.
*KOREFF, DAVID FERDINAND (1783–1851), author and physician.
*KORNFELD, PAUL (1889–1942), playwright.
*KRAMER, THEODOR (1897–1958), poet.
*KRAUS, KARL (1874–1936), author, satirist, and editor.
*KUH, EPHRAIM MOSES (1731–1790), poet.
*LANDSBERGER, ARTUR (1876–1933), novelist and editor.
*LASKER-SCHUELER, ELSE (1869–1945), poet.
*LAZARUS, NAHIDA RUTH (1849–1928), author and proselyte.
*LEONHARD, RUDOLF (1889–1953), author and essayist.
*LEWALD, FANNY (1811–1889), novelist, salon hostess, and feminist.
*LIPINER, SIEGFRIED (1856–1911), poet and playwright.
*LISSAUER, ERNST (1882–1937), poet and playwright.
*LORM, HIERONYMUS (1821–1902), novelist and poet.
*LOTHAR, ERNST (1890–), novelist and stage director.
*LOTHAR, RUDOLF (1865–1936?), playwright and author.
*LUBLINSKI, SAMUEL (1868–1910), playwright and literary historian.
*LUDWIG, EMIL (1881–1948), author and biographer.
*MARCUSE, LUDWIG (1894–), essayist, literary scholar, and biographer.
*MEHRING, WALTER (1896–), poet and satirist.
*MENDELSSOHN, MOSES (1729–1786), philosopher and Bible translator.
*MEYER, RICHARD MORITZ (1860–1914), literary historian.
*MOMBERT, ALFRED (1872–1942), poet.
*MOSENTHAL, SALOMON HERMANN (1821–1877), playwright and author.
*MUEHSAM, ERICH (1878–1934), poet, playwright, and anarchist leader.
*NADEL, ARNO (1878–1943), poet and liturgical composer.
*NEUMANN, ALFRED (1895–1952), novelist.
*NEUMANN, ROBERT (1897–), Anglo-Austrian novelist and writer on the Holocaust.
*NORDAU, MAX (1849–1923), novelist, playwright, and Zionist leader.
*PAULI, JOHANNES (c. 1455–1530), humorist.
*PERUTZ, LEO (1884–1957), novelist.
*PICARD, JACOB (1883–), author
*POLGAR, ALFRED (1873–1955), author and literary critic.
*REHFISCH, HANS JOSÉ (1891–1960), playwright and novelist.
*ROBERT, LUDWIG (1778–1832), playwright.
*RODA RODA (SÁNDOR ROSENFELD; 1872–1945), author and satirist.
*RODENBERG, JULIUS (1831–1914), author and editor.
*ROESSLER, CARL (1864–1948), playwright.
*ROSENZWEIG, FRANZ (1886–1929), religious philosopher and translator.
*ROTH, JOSEPH (1894–1939), novelist and journalist.
*RUBINER, LUDWIG (1881–1920), poet and essayist.
*SACHS, NELLY (1891–1970), poet.
*SALTEN, FELIX (1869–1947), novelist, playwright, and essayist.
*SALUS, HUGO (1866–1929), Czech poet.
*SANDERS, DANIEL (1819–1897), literary historian and lexicographer.
*SAPHIR, MORITZ GOTTLIEB (1795–1858), satirist and literary critic.
*SCHLEGEL, DOROTHEA VON (1763–1839), author and salon hostess.
*SCHNITZLER, ARTHUR (1862–1931), playwright and physician.
*SEGHERS, ANNA (1900–), novelist.
*STEINHEIM, SALOMON LUDWIG (1789–1866), poet, philosopher, and protagonist of Jewish emancipation.
*STERNHEIM, CARL (1878–1942), playwright, author, and essayist.
*STRAUSS, ARYEH LUDWIG (1892–1953), German and Israel (Hebrew) poet.
*STRICH, FRITZ (1882–1963), literary historian.
*SUESSKIND VON TRIMBERG (c. 1200–1250), poet and *Minnesaenger*.
*SUSMAN, MARGARETE (1872–1966), poet and essayist.
*TAU, MAX (1897–), author and publisher.
*TOLLER, ERNST (1893–1939), playwright, poet, and revolutionary.
*TORBERG, FRIEDRICH (1908–), novelist and editor.
*TREBITSCH, ARTHUR (1880–1927), author and anti-Semite.
*TREBITSCH, SIEGFRIED (1869–1956), novelist, playwright, and translator.
*TUCHOLSKY, KURT (1890–1935), author, editor, and satirist.
*VIERTEL, BERTHOLD (1885–1953), poet, playwright, and stage director.

*WALDEN, HERWARTH (1878–1942?), author and editor.
*WALDINGER, ERNST (1896–1969), poet.
*WASSERMANN, JAKOB (1873–1933), novelist and essayist.
*WEILL, ALEXANDRE ABRAHAM (1811–1899), French and German author and biographer.
*WEISS, ERNST (1884–1940), novelist.
*WEISS, PETER (1916–), playwright, and author.
*WERFEL, FRANZ (1890–1945), novelist, playwright, and poet.
*WIHL, LUDWIG (1807–1882), poet and journalist.
*WOLF, FRIEDRICH (1888–1953), playwright, author, and essayist.
*WOLFENSTEIN, ALFRED (1888–1945), poet and playwright.
*WOLFSKEHL, KARL (1869–1948), poet.
*ZUCKERMANN, HUGO (1881–1914), poet and translator.
*ZUCKMAYER, CARL (1896–), playwright and author.
*ZWEIG, ARNOLD (1887–1968), playwright, novelist, and essayist.
*ZWEIG, STEFAN (1881–1942), playwright, essayist, and biographer.

Bibliography: GENERAL: L. Geiger, *Die deutsche Literatur und die Juden* (1910), 1–24. BIBLICAL AND HEBRAIC INFLUENCES: G. Karpeles, *Geschichte der juedischen Literatur,* 2 (1921³), 346–54; E. Tannenbaum, *Philo Zitaten-Lexikon: Worte von Juden, Worte fuer Juden* (1936), 17–61 (includes bibliography); F. Lehner, in: L. Finkelstein (ed.), *The Jews*... 2 (1960³), 1472–86 (includes bibliography). IMAGE OF THE JEW: O. B. Frankl, *Der Jude in den deutschen Dichtungen der 15., 16. und 17. Jahrhunderten* (1905); L. Geiger, *Die deutsche Literatur und die Juden* (1910), 25–45. THE JEWISH CONTRIBUTION: A. Soergel and C. Hohoff, *Dichtung und Dichter der Zeit,* 2 vols. (1961–63), index, s.v. names of authors; G. Karpeles, *Geschichte der juedischen Literatur,* 2 (1921³), 320–43 and index (includes bibliography); G. Krojanker (ed.), *Juden in der deutschen Literatur* (1926); A. Zweig, *Juden auf der deutschen Buehne* (1928); A. Myerson and I. Goldberg, *The German Jew* (1933), 119–42; A. Lewkowitz, *Das Judentum und die geistigen Stroemungen des neunzehnten Jahrhunderts* (1935); E. Tannenbaum, *Philo Zitaten-Lexikon: Worte von Juden, Worte fuer Juden* (1936), 124–44, 149–53 (includes bibliography); F. R. Bienenfeld, *The Germans and the Jews* (1939), 126ff.; R. Kayser, in: D. D. Runes (ed.), *The Hebrew Impact on Western Civilization* (1951), 556–64; C. Roth, *The Jewish Contribution to Civilization* (1956³), 79–80, 93, 94–98, and index (includes bibliography); S. Liptzin, *Germany's Stepchildren* (1944, repr. 1961); A. Zweig, *Bilanz der deutschen Judenheit* (1961), 239–49; S. Kaznelson (ed.), *Juden im deutschen Kulturbereich* (1962³), 1–67; H. Zohn, *Wiener Juden in der deutschen Literatur* (1964); H. Friedmann and O. Mann, *Deutsche Literatur im 20. Jahrhundert,* 2 vols. (1967⁵), index, s.v. authors' names; H. Zohn, in: *The Jews of Czechoslovakia,* 1 (1968), 468–522 (includes bibliography); W. Jakob, in: *Studies in Bibliography and Booklore,* 6 (1962–63), 75–92 (an extensive bibliography on the subject). THE HOLOCAUST AND ITS AFTERMATH: L. Kahn, in: JBA, 24 (1966), 14–22; I. Elbogen, *A Century of Jewish Life* (1944), 636–74 (includes bibliography); *Exil Literatur 1933–45. Eine Austellung aus Bestaenden der deutschen Bibliothek, Frankfurt am Main* (1967³), index, s.v. names of authors.

GERMANY, country in north central Europe. The Talmud and the Midrash use "Germania" (or "Germamia") as a designation for northern European countries, and also refer to the military prowess of these peoples and to the threat they posed to the Roman Empire (Meg. 6b; Gen. R. 75:9; etc.). Medieval Jewish sources first refer to Germany as "Allemania"; later the biblical term *"Ashkenaz" came into use, and was retained in Hebrew literature and Jewish vernacular until recent times.

The entry is arranged according to the following outline:

Middle Ages. There is no substance to the legends extant in the Middle Ages relating that Jews were present in Germany "before the Crucifixion." The first Jews to reach Germany were merchants who went there in the wake of the Roman legions and settled in the Roman-founded Rhine towns. The earliest detailed record of a Jewish community in Germany, referring to *Cologne, is found in imperial decrees issued in 321 and 331 C.E. (Cod. Theod., 16:8, 3–4; Aronius, Regesten, no. 2). There is, however, no evidence of continuous Jewish settlement in Germany, although the Jews' Street in Cologne remained inside the Roman town in the early days of the German Empire. Jews entered Central

Figure 1. The synagogue of Worms, one of the first centers of Jewish settlement in Germany. Built in 1034, the synagogue was destroyed by the Nazis in 1938 and reconstructed after World War II by the Federal German government. Photo Westenfelder, Worms.

Europe in this period from the west and the southwest; Jewish merchants from southern Italy and France were welcomed in Germany, and settled in the towns along the great rivers and trade routes. The *Kalonymos family from Lucca established itself in *Mainz in the tenth century. Like the Jews of France, German Jewry in its early stages drew its inspiration in matters of religion and religious practice straight from the centers of Jewish creative activity in Ereẓ Israel: a 12th-century Jewish scholar speaks of a letter he saw in *Worms, which Rhine Jews had sent to Ereẓ Israel in 960, asking for verification of the rumor that the Messiah had come (REJ 44 (1902), 238). Until the end of the 11th century the Jews of Germany engaged in international trade, especially with the East, and were a respected element of the urban population. They were concentrated along the west bank of the Rhine, in Lorraine, and in ancient episcopal seats and trade centers, such as Cologne, Mainz, *Speyer, Worms, and *Trier, as well as religious and political centers situated more eastward, such as *Regensburg and *Prague. The extant reports of Jewish settlement in Germany are of a haphazard nature, and the dating of such records does not necessarily establish the sequence of settlement. The first mention of Jewish settlement in Mainz dates from c. 900, of Worms from 960, and of Regensburg from 981. Jewish communities in south central Germany (*Bamberg, *Wuerzburg) and *Thuringia (*Erfurt) are mentioned in documents from the 11th century. The persecutions to which the Jews were exposed in the 12th to 14th centuries forced them to move from the south to the east and north of Germany, and they were drawn in the same direction by opportunities for trade and *moneylending. Thus, although this coincided with the general migratory trend within Germany, the Jews joined the move for independent reasons. In *Breslau and *Munich Jews are mentioned at the beginning of the 13th century, in *Vienna in the middle of that century, and in *Berlin (and other places) at its end. German Jews maintained close ties with France. At the end of the tenth century (or the beginning of the 11th), *Gershom b. Judah *("Me'or ha-Golah")* moved from *Metz to Mainz and that city became noted for Torah learning; the yeshivot of Mainz and Worms became spiritual centers for all the Jews in Central Europe and even attracted students from France, among them the famous *Rashi. For the Jews, the Carolingian Empire, although no longer a political entity, still remained a single social and cultural unit. In Christian Germany, which had retained many of the concepts of a tribal society, the Jews figured as aliens as well as infidels. Their social and legal status was distinct from that of the general population, and, as people who had no country and were not Christians, they required special protection to safeguard their existence. The first reports of persecution of Jews in Germany date from the 11th century (the expulsion of the Jews of Mainz in 1012), and the first written guarantees of rights, granted to them by emperors and bishops, also date from that century. In 1084 the archbishop of Speyer invited them to settle in his enlarged city "in order to enhance a thousandfold the respect accorded to our town" (Aronius, Regesten, 70 no. 168), and granted the Jews far-reaching trading rights and permission to put up a protective wall around their quarters. This evidence of the high value attached to Jews for settlement of a new town and the expansion of its trade precedes by only 12 years the *"gezerot tatnav"* (1096; see below). In 1090 Emperor *Henry IV issued charters of rights to the Jews of Speyer and Worms (*ibid.,* 71–77 nos. 170–1), and succeeding emperors followed his example. All these writs acknowledged the right of the Jews to be judged "by their peers and no others . . . according to their law" (from a charter of 1090). In another such document, granted to the Jews of Worms in 1157, the emperor reserves for himself the exclusive right of judging the Jews "for they belong to our treasury." The guarantees of rights were given to the community leaders, who were also the spiritual leaders of the community, and were well-to-do men belonging to respected families. Communities that were accorded guarantees already possessed a synagogue (the Worms synagogue was founded in 1034) and public institutions. No reliable figures on the size of these Jewish communities are available; to judge by figures mentioned in the narratives of their martyrdom, there were communities of 2,000 persons (Mainz), but in general they consisted of several hundred, or several dozen. The community regula-

Figure 2. Pillar believed to be from the Kalonymos house, Mainz, dating from the 10th century, the period when this family settled in Germany. The royal symbol of the eagle on the capital is a mark of privilege. Mainz, Mittelrheinisches Landesmuseum.

tions enacted by the Jewish communities in Germany, and the commentaries and *piyyutim* written by their scholars (such as Gershom b. Judah and *Simeon b. Isaac) reveal a strong and simple faith, and readiness to die for it (and see *takkanot* of the period).

First Crusade. Their faith was put to the supreme test during the first *Crusade, from April to June 1096. The brutal massacres that then took place are remembered in Jewish annuals as the *gezerot tatnav* (i.e., the massacres of 4856=1096). The first waves of crusaders turned upon the Jews of the Rhine valley. Although the emperor, the bishops, and Christian neighbors were reluctant to take part in this onslaught and tried to protect the Jews, this defense had small success. It was then that the Jews of Germany revealed their indomitable courage and religious devotion and chose a martyr's death (**kiddush ha-Shem*). In Mainz, it is related in a contemporary description of these acts of heroism that "in a single day one thousand and one hundred martyrs were slaughtered and died" (A. M. Habermann (ed.), *Gezerot Ashkenaz ve-Ẓarefat* (1945), 32). The martyrdom of Mainz Jewry was preceded by negotiations with the emperor by Kalonymos ben Meshullam; in response, Henry IV published an order in defense of the Jews, but this was of little help. The Jews offered armed resistance and it was only in the final stage that they committed suicide. Similar events took place in many communities on the Rhine and along the crusaders' route; many Jews chose martyrdom; others managed to save their lives by going into hiding (Speyer, Cologne, Worms, *Xanten, Metz). Some accepted temporary conversion, as in Regensburg, where "all were coerced" (*ibid.* 56). Later the emperor permitted their return to Judaism. The beginning of the Crusades inaugurated far-reaching changes in the social and economic structure of the Christian peoples in Western Europe and in their general outlook, and as a result also mark a turning point in the history of German Jewry. Henceforth the mob came to regard physical attacks on Jews as permissible, especially in periods of social or religious ferment. The city guilds forced the Jews out of the trades and the regular channels of commerce; this coincided with the stricter appliance of the church ban on usury in the 12th to 13th centuries. The combination of circumstances made moneylending and pawnbroking the main occupation of Jews in Germany. They also continued in ordinary trade; as late as the 13th century they dealt in wool, attended the Cologne fairs, and traded with Russia and Hungary; during most of the Middle Ages there were even Jewish *craftsmen and Jews had some contact with *agriculture.

However moneylending, conceived by the Church as usury, became the hallmark of Jewish life in Germany. About 100 to 150 years after usury became the main occupation of Jews in England and France, it became central to the livelihood of Jews in Germany also. Jew hatred and the evil *image of the Jew as conceived in the popular imagination were nourished by this economic pattern. Owing to the scarcity of money and lack of firm securities the rate of interest was extremely high. In 1244 the Jews of *Austria were given a bill of rights by Duke *Frederick II based on the assumption that interest was the Jews' main source of income; the bill contained detailed regulations on moneylending, and the rate of interest was fixed at $173\frac{1}{3}$%. This kind of charter for Jews became typical of those granted in central and eastern Germany (and Poland) in the 13th and 14th centuries. Borrowing money from Jews against pawns became usual among the nobility and the townspeople, and enabled rabble-rousers to accuse the Jews of "sucking Christian blood" and of associating with gentile thieves who pawned their loot with the Jewish

Figure 3. A Jewish moneylender with his family in the background negotiating with a peasant and a townsman. A woodcut from Foltz, *Die Rechnung Kolpergers von dem Gesuch der Juden*, Nuremberg, 1491.

moneylenders. The Jews insisted on their right to refuse to return pawns unless reimbursed, a right confirmed as early as 1090. After the end of the 11th century the social status of the Jews steadily deteriorated. The *Landesfrieden* ("peace of the land") issued in 1103 includes the Jews among persons who bear no arms and are therefore to be spared violence and defended. The concepts which had determined the status of the Jews from the beginning of their settlement in Germany were now applied with increasing cruelty and vigor. The German political view was molded by a combination of tribal and state concepts which could not regard those who were alien in blood and faith as citizens of the state, while the Church had always claimed that the sins of the Jews condemned them to perpetual serfdom and degradation. The need of the Jews for refuge and protection was now utilized by the urge to oppress and exploit them. A long-drawn-out process of legal and social development was finally summed up in 1236 by Emperor Frederick II, when he declared all the Jews of Germany **Servi camerae nostri* ("servants of our treasury"; Aronius, Regesten, 216 no. 496). This meant that from the legal point of view the Jews and their property were possessions of the emperor and hence entirely at his mercy. However they never fully experienced the severity of this concept as it was never fully applied to them; in a way, their status as servants of the imperial treasury was even welcomed for it assured them of imperial protection, protection which no other German authority was able or willing to afford them. Long after the concept of the servitude of the Jews had been applied in Germany, *Meir b. Baruch of Rothenburg conceived that "the Jews are not *glehae* [*adscripti*=bound] to any

Map 1. Major medieval Jewish communities in Germany in the 13th century.

particular place as gentiles are; for they are regarded as impoverished freemen who have not been sold into slavery; the government attitude is according to this" (Responsa, ed. Prague, no. 1001; cf. Tos. to BK 58a). The concepts that Jewish lives were not inviolable and that the Jews were in servitude to the country's rulers led to renewed outbursts of anti-Jewish violence whenever a critical situation arose. The second Crusade (1146), which was again accompanied by widespread anti-Jewish agitation, was also a living nightmare for the Jews. However the experience of 1096 had taught a lesson both to the Jews and to the authorities: the Jews took refuge in the castles of the nobility, whenever possible having the entire citadel to themselves until the danger passed (see A. M. Habermann, op. cit. 117). The preaching of *Bernard of Clairvaux against doing the Jews physical harm also helped to restrain the masses. Thus a repetition of the earlier terrorization and slaughter did not take place. Between the second Crusade and the beginning of the 13th century the Jews were subjected to numerous attacks and libels but relatively few lost their lives as a result.

Spiritual Life. The events of 1096 had shaken German Jewry to the core; its response came in the form of tremendous spiritual and social creativity. Succeeding generations glorified the deeds of the martyrs and created a whole doctrine around the sanctification of God by martyrdom *(kiddush ha-Shem)*. The ideas of self-sacrifice, **akedah*, of choosing to meet "the Great Light" rather than apostasy, and of standing up to the attacker, were now formulated and transmitted as permanent principles. A special blessing was inserted into the prayer book to be recited by those who were about to be slain. The martyrs of Xanten had their own prayer: "May the Almighty avenge the blood of His servants which has been shed, and will be shed after us, in the days of those who survive us and before their very eyes: may the Almighty save us from men of evil, from destruction and idolatry and from the impurity of the gentiles" (A. M. Habermann, op. cit., 49). This prayer expresses the general mood of the German Jews in this period and of the "leaders in martyrdom" in particular. In the 12th and 13th centuries a group known as Ḥasidim (pious men) came into being, distinguished by their piety in thought and deed (see *Ḥasidei Ashkenaz). The way of life to which this group adhered was established, in the main, by the members of a single family: *Samuel b. Kalonymos he Ḥasid of Speyer, his son *Judah b. Samuel he-Ḥasid of Regensburg, and their relative *Eleazar b. Judah (ha-Roke'aḥ) of Worms. These formulated the principles of perfect piety: observance of "Heavenly Law" *(din shamayim)* which is above and beyond the "Law of the Torah," for the latter was given to man taking into account his *yeẓer ha-ra* ("evil urge"). They taught that one should regard property as being held on trust (from God) only, and that one should abstain from lust without retiring from family and public life. *Sefer Ḥasidim* and *Sefer ha-Roke'aḥ*, two works written by these men, express the feelings and ideas of the Ḥasidim of Germany on the greatness of God, on man's conduct in life, on ghosts and spirits, on sexual temptation and how to withstand it, on the true observance of commandments, and on love of learning as a foremost religious value.

Social Life. During this period further consolidation of the Jewish communal leadership in Germany took place. Jews increasingly restricted themselves to the Jewish quarter in the town, which gave them a greater feeling of security and made possible the development of an intense social life. The *meliores* (leading families) accepted the authority of the most eminent scholars. Torah learning was not interrupted in times of trouble and danger. It even received additional impetus from the need to provide leadership for the Jewish public and guidance to the individual, while the number of outstanding scholars also increased. Even the source of livelihood that was forced upon the Jews—lending money against interest—came to be appreciated as an advantage since it left time to spare for Torah study. Moneylending also determined the artificial structure of Jewish life; the Jews derived their income mainly from non-Jews, and there was hardly any economic exploitation of one Jew by another. As a result, there was a large measure of social cohesion in the German communities. The average community maintained a synagogue, a cemetery (or, if it was too small, obtained burial rights in a neighboring town), a bathhouse, and a place for weddings and other public festivities. A scholar attracted groups of students who lived in his home and were cared for by the scholar's wife (A. M. Habermann, op. cit., 165–6). Meir b. Baruch of Rothenburg attests that his house was spacious and included "a *bet midrash* . . . a winter house [i.e., the main living quarters] . . . a courtyard for public use . . . a cool upper room where I eat in summer and . . . a room . . . for each student" (Responsa, ed. Cremona, no.. 108). Community institutions developed. The community leaders and scholars—in gatherings on fair-days— issued *takkanot* regulating many spheres of life which were binding upon individual communities or groups of several communities. In the 13th century, *Eliezer b. Joel ha-Levi of Bonn established the principle that a majority decision also obligated the opposing minority, and unanimity was not required (contradicting the 12th-century French scholar Jacob b. Meir *Tam). Communal offices which had come into existence in the 12th and 13th centuries are listed in a document issued by the Cologne community in 1301: *Nos Episcopus, magistratus Judeorum ac universi Judei civitatis Coloniensis* ("We the bishop [i.e., the leader], and officers of the Jews and the entire Jewish community of Cologne"; see *Judenschreinsbuch*, 92–93). From 1220 onward, the *"Takkanot Shum,"* regulations issued by three of the great communities on the Rhine—Speyer, Worms, and Mainz (שו"ם, the initials of the three names)—have been preserved; joint meetings of the leaders of these three communities had a decisive influence on all the Jewish communities in Germany. German Jewry developed an independent leadership with a series of honors and degrees of rank. The intimacy of the small community enabled a person who felt wronged to turn to the public by means of interruption of prayer (see ***bittul ha-tamid*) in synagogue until he received redress. Families experienced the usual sorrows and joys, and also had their share of frivolities: "wild young men . . . who liked gambling" (*Sefer Ḥasidim*, ed. by J. Wistinetzki (1924[2]), no. 109) and practical jokes at festivities (see also Tos. to Suk. 45a, s.v. *Mi-Yad Tinnokot*). The main purpose of the *takkanot* was to strengthen religious life and especially to provide for increased study of the Torah, the observance of sexual purity laws, of the Sabbath, etc. They also introduced innovations designed to strengthen community life: the obligation on the part of each individual to pay his tax assessment and to refrain from false declarations, and the right of the community officers to transfer funds from one purpose to another, when the common good required it. Considerable emphasis was put on strengthening the authority of the community leadership: members of the community were not permitted to accept appointments by the authorities or to ask the authorities for exemption from community taxes; every dispute between Jews had to be brought before Jewish judges, and Jews were not allowed to apply to non-Jewish courts. Excommunication of an individual required the consent of the community, as did the divorce of a wife. Gambling was outlawed and regulations were issued for the preservation of order in the synagogues and law courts and at public celebrations. Lending money to Jews against the payment of interest, and insulting anyone in public were also prohibited. In the 12th century the Jews still took part in the defense of the towns in which they lived. Eleazar b. Judah tells of "the siege of Worms by a great host on the Sabbath, when we permitted all the Jews to take up arms . . . for if they had not helped the townspeople they would have been killed . . . therefore we permitted it" (*Sefer ha-Roke'aḥ* (Cremona, 1557), 23a, *Hilkhot Eruvin*, no. 197). In this period, Jews also moved with the eastward trend of the population, and new Jewish communities were established in the east and southeast. Those who joined in the movement of the urban population eastward encountered the terrors and problems of new colonists: "When you build houses in the forest you find the inhabitants stricken with plague since the place is haunted by spirits . . . They asked the sage what they should do; he answered: Take the Ten Commandments and a Torah Scroll and stretch out a cord the length of the ground, and bring the Torah Scroll to the cord . . . and then at the end say: 'Before God, before the Torah, and before Israel its guardians, may no demon nor she-demon come to this

Figure 4. Illustration showing Jews receiving a charter of privileges from Emperor Henry VII in 1312. From *Codex Baldvini*, Koblenz, Municipal Archives.

Figure 5. Fifteenth-century woodcut showing the burning of Jewish martyrs. From Schedel's *Weltchronik*, 1493.

Figure 6. Fifteenth-century woodcut published and widely disseminated in Germany showing the martyrdom of the Jews of Trent following the blood libel of 1475.

place from today and for ever' " (*Sefer Ḥasidim* (ed. Wistinetzki), no. 371).

13TH CENTURY. The 13th century brought new troubles upon the Jews. The Fourth *Lateran Council (1215) decreed that the clergy were to restrict business relations between Christians and Jews, that Jews had to wear signs distinguishing them from the Christians (see *badge), and that they were not to hold any public office. In 1235 the first case of *blood libel occurred in Germany (in *Fulda) and in the second half of the 13th century the libel of *Host desecration began to spread in the country. These accusations were to cost many Jewish lives, to cause Jews much anxiety and anguish, and to bring about further deterioration of their image in the eyes of their Christian neighbors, who now came to regard them as corrupt beings, capable of the most abominable crimes. The acceptance of such views of the Jews by the masses occurred at a time when imperial rule was weakening, and the right to the Jews' "servitude to the treasury" was passed on or transferred in different ways and for differing reasons to various local competencies. Religious fanaticism was rising and caused a social ferment in the cities, where the mob vented their anger on the Jews. In 1241, when the Jews of *Frankfort on the Main tried to prevent one of their people from converting to Christianity, a *Judenschlacht* (Jews' slaughter) took place, in which the entire community was butchered by the Christian mob. In 1259 a synod of the Mainz archdiocese ordered that Jews within its borders should wear the yellow badge. In 1285 the entire Jewish community of *Munich—some 180 persons—was burned to death, victims of a libel that had been spread against them. The Jews also had a heavy tax burden. A partial list of imperial revenue, dating from 1241, reveals that in 25 Jewish communities the Jews paid 857 marks, amounting to 12% of the entire imperial tax revenue for the year (7,127.5 marks) and 20% of the total raised in the German cities. In addition to the regular taxes the Jews also had to make payments in the form of "presents" and bribes, or money was simply extorted from them. In this period—the second half of the 13th century—German Jewry produced great spiritual leaders. Foremost was Meir b. Baruch of Rothenburg, whose responsa and instructions guided several generations of Jews. He attacked manifestations of injustice or high-handedness in communal affairs, and in his threnodies and other writings gave expression to the sufferings of his people. In the end, his own fate symbolized the distress of the Jews: trying to escape overseas, like other persecuted Jews in Germany, he was arrested, handed over to the emperor, and died in jail in 1293.

PERSECUTIONS OF THE 14TH CENTURY. At the end of the 13th century and the first half of the 14th, anti-Jewish excesses by the mob increased in vehemence and frequency, and the authorities were also increasingly oppressive. In 1342 Louis IV of Bavaria decreed that "every male Jew and every Jewish widow, of 12 years and above, is obliged to pay a yearly tax of one gulden." This poll tax was designed to increase the income that the emperor derived from the Jews, which had declined as the result of their "transfer" to lower authorities, and came in addition to the other taxes exacted from the Jews. In 1356 Emperor *Charles IV transferred his claim over the Jews to the Imperial Electors. Within a period of 50 years the Jews of Germany suffered three devastating blows. In 1298–99, when civil war had broken out in southwest Germany, the Jews were accused of Host desecration, and the Jew-baiter, *Rindfleisch, gathered a mob around him which fell upon the Jews of Franconia, Bavaria, and the surrounding area, destroying no less than 140 communities (including *Rothenburg, Wuerzburg, *Nuremberg, and Bamberg). Many Jews chose a martyr's death and in many places also offered armed resistance. The period 1336–37 was marked by the catastrophe of the *Armleder massacres, in the course of which 110 communities, from Bavaria to Alsace, were destroyed by rioting peasants. Finally, in the massacres during the *Black Death, in 1348–50, 300 Jewish communities were

Figure 7. Woodcut of the blowing of the shofar in the synagogue, with women and children behind the screen in the foreground. From J. J. Pfefferkorn, *Judenbeichte*, Cologne, 1508.

destroyed in all parts of the country, and the Jews either killed, or driven out as "poisoners of wells." The greatest Jewish scholar of the time, *Alexander Suslin ha-Kohen, was among those slain in Erfurt, in 1349. As a result of these three onslaughts, the structure of Jewish life in Germany suffered a severe blow. Nevertheless, only a short while later, Jews were again permitted to take up residence in German cities, where there was no one else to fulfill their function in society of moneylenders. Only a few weeks after the slaughter of the Jews of *Augsburg the bishop permitted some to return to the city; between 1352 and 1355 Jews reappeared in Erfurt, Nuremberg, *Ulm, Speyer, Worms, and Trier. Their residence was now based on contracts which contained severe restrictions and imposed numerous payments on them. There was also increased exploitation of the Jews by the emperor; a moratorium on debts, declared by *Wenceslas in 1385 and again in 1390, dealt a severe blow to the economic situation of the Jews. Jewish vitality, however, was able to assert itself even in the adverse conditions that prevailed after the Black Death massacres. The scholars assured the continuity of Jewish creativity. In 1365, *Meir b. Baruch ha-Levi established a new school in Vienna, based upon the customs and traditions of the Rhine communities, and his disciples—the "Sages of Austria"—became the spiritual leaders of German Jewry. In east and south Germany, with fewer towns and a relatively backward economy, Jews found it easier to earn their livelihood. This was also the route to *Poland, which gradually turned into a refuge for the Jews. Until the Reformation there was no change in the precarious situation of the Jews of Germany. On the one hand, the disintegration of the Empire prevented large-scale countrywide expulsions: when the Jews were driven out of one locality they were able to bide their time in a neighboring place, and after a short while return to their previous homes; on the other hand, the lack of a central authority put the Jews at the mercy of local rulers. In general, the emperor, the princes, and the leading classes in the towns gave their protection to the Jews; yet a single fanatic anti-Jewish preacher, John of *Capistrano, found it possible to inflame the masses against the Jews and to initiate a new wave of persecutions (1450–59) which culminated in the expulsion of the Jews from Breslau.

15th Century. The 15th century was generally marked by libels against Jews and their expulsion from certain areas: in 1400 the Jews were expelled from Prague; in 1420, 1438, 1462, and 1473 there were successive expulsions from Mainz; in 1420–21 from Austria; in 1424 from Cologne; in 1440 from Augsburg; in 1475 the blood libel was raised in *Trent, resulting in anti-Jewish agitation and riots all over Germany, and the expulsion of the Jews from *Tyrol; in 1492 it was the turn of the Host desecration libel in *Mecklenburg, and the expulsion of the Jews from there; in 1493 they were driven out of *Magdeburg, and in the period 1450–1500, out of many towns in Bavaria, Franconia, and Swabia; in 1499 from Nuremberg; in 1510 there was another Host desecration libel and expulsion from *Brandenburg; in the same year expulsion from Alsace; and in 1519 from Regensburg. Nevertheless, in the course of the 15th century, amid these tribulations, Jews were also able to branch out into occupations other than moneylending. In the south German communities, there were Jewish wine merchants and petty traders. Jews also began to play a role in the expanding commercial life, acting as intermediaries between the large agricultural producer (such as the monasteries) and the rising city merchant; expelled from the cities and forced to live in the small towns and villages, the Jews bought wool, flax, etc., from the large storehouses and sold these commodities to the wholesale merchant. This

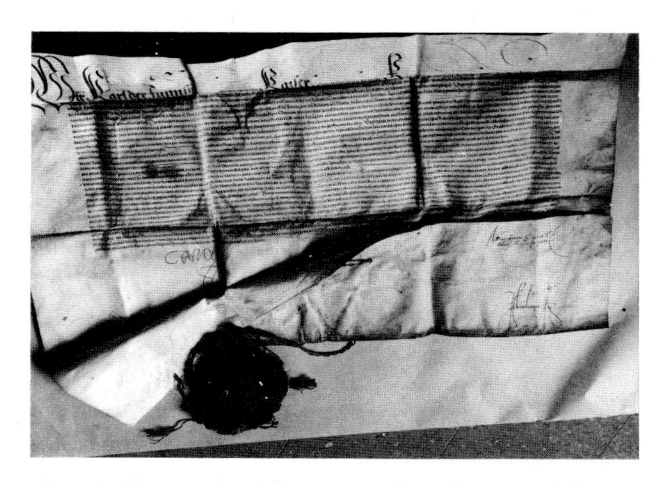

Figure 8. Charter of privileges granted to the Jews of Worms by Charles V in 1552. Jerusalem, C.A.H.J.P. Rh/w, A1.

was the beginning of a process which culminated in Poland in the 16th and 17th centuries with the Jews entering the service of the nobility as managers of their estates. Jewish life in the small communities of Germany was frequently marked by great material and spiritual hardship. Yet the Jews did all in their power to fulfill the commandments of their faith. Israel *Isserlein's *Pesakim u-Khetavim* (Venice, 1545), para. 52, records a "curious event" in south Germany, when several communities had only a single *etrog* to share among them on the Sukkot festival; they cut the fruit up and sent a piece to each community, and although shriveled by the time it reached its destination, the Jews made the prescribed blessing over their slice of *etrog* on the first day of the festival. Despite their poverty and sufferings, Jews held on to the normal joys of life. Jacob Moses *Moellin permitted "placing tree branches in water on the Sabbath . . . in order to provide a source of joy for the house" (Jacob b. Moses Moellin, *Maharil* (Cremona, 1558), 38b); when asked about celebrating a wedding in a community where a local ordinance forbade the participation of musicians, the same rabbi advised that the wedding be moved to another community, where music could be made, rather than have the bride and bridegroom forego the pleasure (*ibid.*, 41b). Even at a time when persecutions were actually taking place, the Jews persisted in their way of life and in study of the Torah. Thus Moses *Mintz, while writing a halakhic decision, records that "the time limit given us by the bishop [of Bamberg] for leaving the town has been reached, for he would not allow us a single additional day or even hour" (Resp. Maharam Mintz, para. 48). The rabbis' position became widely acknowledged in this period, and they were regarded as "the leaders." It may be assumed that it was Meir b. Baruch ha-Levi's school that established the custom of *semikhah* (rabbinical ordination) and of awarding the title of **Morenu* ("our teacher") to a graduate rabbi, a custom which Ashkenazi Jews have still retained. At the same time the rabbis often engaged in bitter quarrels over the question of jurisdiction, and the position of the rabbi. These quarrels largely resulted from the difficulties facing the Jewish spiritual leaders, who tried, in a permanent state of insecurity, to rebuild communities that had been destroyed. The rabbinical leaders of this period—Meir b. Baruch ha-Levi and his disciples, Jacob b. Moses Moellin, Israel Isserlein (author of *Terumat ha-Deshen*), Moses Mintz, Israel b. Ḥayyim *Bruna, and others—were dedicated men who did all in their power to establish new yeshivot and spread the study of Torah, but they did not achieve the degree of leadership displayed by their predecessors. An extreme example of a scholar devoted to his yeshivah was that of Jacob b. Moses Moellin "who would live in a house alone with his students, next to the house of his wife the 'rabbanit,' while her sons were with her in her house; nor did he enjoy a mite of his wife's property during her lifetime or eat with her. Only the communal leaders supplied him with sufficient means to support the students of his yeshivah, while he himself earned a livelihood as a marriage broker" (*Maharil* 76a). His yeshivah was attended not only by poor scholars, but by "those rich and pampered youths who had tables made for them—when they sat down in their seats they could turn the table in any direction they pleased, and kept many books on them" (*Leket Yosher,* ed. by J. Freimann (1903), YD 39). The debate with Christianity did not die down in this period, and Yom Tov Lipmann *Muelhausen raised it to new heights of sharp polemical argument in his *Sefer ha-Niẓẓaḥon* (see *Disputations).

Emperors resorted to the most extreme measures in order to extort money from the Jews. The most extortionate was Sigismund who demanded one-third of their property. Their desire to increase the income extracted from the Jews induced the emperors to utilize the high prestige enjoyed by the rabbis by attempting to appoint one of them "chief rabbi" (*Hochmeister*). In 1407, Rupert of Wittelsbach appointed Israel b. Isaac of Nuremberg to this office, and sought to give him sole powers of sequestering Jewish property. The communities, however, refused to acknowledge the authority of a Jew appointed by gentiles and eventually the king abandoned his attempt. Sigismund named several "chief rabbis" for the purpose of improving the collection of the oppressive taxes that he imposed upon the Jews, including well-known rabbinical leaders. It is not clear, however, to what extent these appointments were recognized by the communities, and the responsa literature of the period contains no specific references to such appointments. At any rate, a proposal made by Seligmann Oppenheim Bing (see *Bingen) to convene a conference which would create a chief rabbinate was rejected by most of his rabbinical colleagues.

In sum, the last few centuries of the Middle Ages were a period of severe and difficult changes for the Jews of Germany. The center of gravity, both in population and intellectual activity, shifted steadily eastward. From their position as desirable traders the Jews were driven by the religious and social forces which gained ascendancy in the 12th and 13th centuries into the despised occupation of usury. The 50 years from 1298 to 1348 took a tragic toll in both life and property. Throughout the trials and tribulations of the Middle Ages the Jews of Germany succeeded in preserving their human dignity and ancestral heritage. They displayed their own creative powers in halakhic literature and religious poetry, and in the establishment of communal institutions. Although they did not disdain the innocent joys of life, they were exacting in the application of the Law and were imbued with the spirit of ascetic piety. *Kiddush ha-Shem*—martyrdom for the sanctification of God—and their particular pietism (*Ḥasidut Ashkenaz*), in both theory and practice, were authentic contributions of German Jewry to the realm of supreme Jewish values. When the age of the Reformation set in, German Jewry, although of lesser stature than their ancestors on the Rhine in organization, learning, and religious spirit, was strong enough to stand up to the challenge of a changing world. [H.H.B.-S.]

From The Reformation To World War I. The age of the Reformation was characterized by upheavals in all spheres of life—political, economic, social, religious, and cultural. It also produced new attitudes to Jews and Judaism often of a conflicting nature. When the Middle Ages came to an end, the Jews had suffered expulsion from most German cities, as well as from many other dioceses and localities:

Figure 9. The plundering of the Frankfort ghetto in 1614. Engraving by H. Merian, from Gottfried, *Chronica,* Frankfort, 1642.

*Heilbronn 1475, *Tuebingen 1477, Bamberg 1478, *Esslingen 1490, Mecklenburg 1492, Magdeburg 1493, *Reutlingen 1495, Wuerttemberg and Wuerzburg 1498, Nuremberg and Ulm 1499, *Noerdlingen 1507, the state of Brandenburg 1510, Regensburg 1519, Rottenburg 1520, and *Saxony 1537. Jews were prohibited from practicing most occupations. From engaging in commerce at the beginning of the Middle Ages and in finance at the end, they now had to earn a livelihood from hawking haberdashery, peddling, moneylending, and pawnbroking in the small towns and villages. Interest rates were subject to severe regulations, and wearing of the humiliating badge was enforced. In various states Jews were prohibited from building new synagogues and from holding discussions on religious questions without Church authorization. However, Emperor *Charles V (at assemblies of the Reichstag in Augsburg 1530, Regensburg 1541, Speyer 1544, and Augsburg 1548) authorized in full the charters granted to the Jews by previous emperors.

At the very time that humanism was coming to the fore, the libels against the Jews, accusing them of using human blood for ritual purposes and of desecrating the Host, were continually resuscitated, and resulted in further killings and expulsions: *Endingen 1470, Regensburg 1476, *Passau 1477, *Trent 1475, Sternberg (Mecklenburg) 1492, Engen (Swabia) 1495, Berlin 1500, Langendenzlingen 1503, Frankfort 1504, Brandenburg 1520. Some humanists acknowledged the religious and moral values inherent in Judaism and took up its defense, but in folk literature and the mystery plays the Jew was depicted as a usurer and bloodsucker, as the Christ-killer and reviler of the Virgin Mary, an associate of Satan and ally of the Turk. Yet there was also Johann *Reuchlin who led a courageous struggle against the defamation of the Talmud and called for equal rights for the Jews, as "cocitizens of the Roman Empire." Martin *Luther, after failing to win them, showed vehement hatred for the Jews, and in his writings called upon the secular rulers to deprive them of their prayer books and Talmud, to destroy their homes, to put them on forced labor or expel them from the land. There were, however, other reforming movements, especially the Anabaptists, who appreciated the Jewish Bible and Judaism and displayed sympathy and love for the Jews. The Jews were also caught in the struggle between the emperor, on the one hand, and the princes and cities, on the other. The emperors, whose power was on the decline, made efforts to retain their control of the Jews, to protect them against local potentates and to remain the sole beneficiaries of the taxes paid by the Jews. The opposing forces, bent upon establishing their independence of the emperor, also tried to extend their supremacy over the Jews and tax them. When attacking the Jews the princes and city governments were not only motivated by the traditional hatred, but also by their desire to reduce the emperor's authority and force the Jews to seek protection from them rather than the emperor. As a result, the Jews were often forced to pay taxes to two or even three different authorities. This situation, however, also prevented a general expulsion of the Jews from Germany at a time when this had become the lot of the Jews in most countries of Western Europe. The Jews also became the subject of controversy between the local rulers and the Estates *(Staende)*—the nobility, the ruling clergy, and the privileged townsmen. The latter had the power of levying taxes and tried to extend their power in various ways, including control of the Jews. To some degree the persecutions of Jews in the 15th and 16th centuries, which coincided with a rise in the power of the Estates, were the result of this struggle; thus, the Host desecration libel against Jews in Brandenburg, in 1510, was also an expression of the opposition of the Estates to Elector Joachim I, who had given several Jews permission to settle in the country, despite the Estates' objections. Other internal differences also affected the situation of the Jews, such as the antagonism between the princes and the landed gentry, and the cities. The former would permit Jews who had been expelled from the cities to settle on their lands, thereby gaining additional taxpayers who were also skilled merchants able to compete with the hated townsmen and provide the princes and estate-owners with better and cheaper supplies. For example, the Jews who had been expelled from Augsburg were offered refuge in the nearby villages; those who had been driven out of Nuremberg were permitted to settle in *Fuerth; the Count of *Oettingen accepted the Jews of Noerdlingen; and the Count of *Hanau lent his protection to the Portuguese Jews to whom the neighboring municipality of Frankfort had refused permission to settle. The sweeping economic changes that took place in the 16th and 17th centuries also had their effect upon the situation of the Jews. The early manifestations of nascent capitalism caused much suffering among the masses of the people. Failing to grasp the meaning of the social and economic upheaval, they found in the Jew a scapegoat on whom they could blame their troubles, whom they had always been taught to regard as their enemy and exploiter. The demands for equality and justice which emerged from the social unrest in the cities included a call for the expulsion of the Jews "for the devastating harm that their presence brings to the plain people." The patrician class, which had supported the Jews in the cities, made way to the guilds, who adhered to a narrow social and economic outlook and would not tolerate any competition. They were also opposed to foreigners, especially if these were infidels. The numerous instances of expulsion that occurred in this period were to a large degree the outcome of these new developments in the structure of the economy. An outstanding Jewish personality of this period was *Joseph (Joselman) b. Gershon of Rosheim who in the course of his life made tremendous efforts to ease the lot of German Jewry and enable them to withstand the onslaught of the diverse forces arraigned against them.

THE ABSOLUTIST PRINCIPALITIES. Absolutism, followed by enlightened absolutism, and the mercantile system of economy introduced into kingdoms and principalities, brought far-reaching changes in the situation of the Jews. In its enlightened and mercantilist version, the system that now evolved regarded interests of state as supreme and attached the greatest value to money, commerce, and increase of population; it also came to judge the Jews from the point of view of these interests. The taxes paid by the Jews were highly lucrative, for they were among the few paid directly into the coffers of the ruler, and did not depend upon the consent of the Estates. Rulers welcomed wealthy Jews with capital and economic experience who could make important contributions to internal and international trade and to the development of industry. In *Hamburg, Portuguese Jews who had been expelled from their native country founded the Hamburg Bank which promoted commerce with Spain and Portugal and traded in tobacco, wine, textiles, cotton, etc. Saxony invited Jews to the *Leipzig Fair in order to forge new trade links with Switzerland, Holland, Italy, and England. Karl Ludwig, the enlightened elector of the Palatinate—a land which had been devastated by the Thirty Years' War—invited Jews to settle there in order to help restore trade and found industries. In Brandenburg, Frederick William, "the Great Elector," permitted 50 Jewish families who had been driven out of Austria to settle in Berlin and elsewhere, granting them extensive privileges and unrestricted trade throughout the country (1670/71). Jews were allowed to settle in *Frankfort on the Oder, in order to infuse new life into the fair held in that city; in *Cleves, in order to facilitate transit trade with Holland; in *Pomerania and East Prussia, in order to attract commerce to the eastern portion of the country, and in Berlin itself, in order to make it the commercial center of Brandenburg and northeast Germany. The regime of the absolutist states instituted a system of supervision of the Jews which both regulated every detail of their lives and exploited them (see *Frederick II of Prussia). An unending series of laws and regulations, ordinances, decrees, patents, and privileges, circumscribed the entry and settlement of Jews, the length of their stay, the number of marriages and number of children, matters of inheritance and guardianship, the conduct of business and their moral behavior, their taxes, and even the goods they had to buy, for instance, china—*Judenporzellan*—in Prussia. Violation of these provisions resulted in severe penalties (and see *Austria, *Berlin, *Prussia.)

SOCIAL AND SPIRITUAL LIFE. In their internal organization, the Jewish communities, up to the 18th century, continued to base themselves in the main upon the pattern

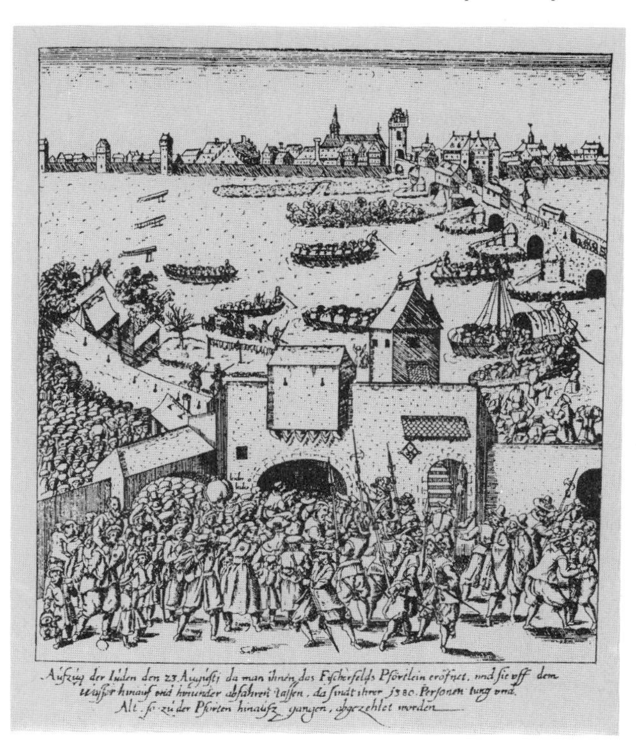

Figure 10. The expulsion of Frankfort Jews after the *Fettmilch* riots of 1614. Engraving by Georg Keller. Munich, Kupferstichkabinet.

Figure 11. Jonathan Eybeschuetz, kabbalist suspected of Shabbatean leanings. Jerusalem, Sir Isaac and Lady Wolfson Museum in Hechal Shlomo. Photo David Harris, Jerusalem.

established in the Middle Ages. In the smaller communities the *shtadlan* was usually also the local leader. In many of the communities that had reestablished themselves after an earlier expulsion, leadership became largely a function of wealth. It was not until after the *Chmielnicki massacres of 1648 that scholars, preachers, and teachers from Poland who took refuge in Germany began to play an important role in Jewish education. At the end of the 17th century the absolutist rulers adopted a policy of interfering in the internal affairs of the communities; as a result, the authority of the autonomous community organs was gradually reduced—a development which corresponded with the abolition of the powers that had previously been vested in the guilds and city councils.

Following upon the Thirty Years' War, proper *conferences of rabbis and community leaders were convened, to which "all the Jewish residents" of the country were invited, in order to decide upon a fair distribution of the tax burden. The powers of these conferences were severely restricted; they could not be held without official permission, and the authorities fought to confine their activities to tax collection. Nevertheless, the conferences in fact became an overall community forum and dealt with all matters that had traditionally been the concern of Jewish autonomous bodies (and see *Landjudenschaft). The authority of the rabbis was reduced in the 18th century by both the secular leaders of the communities and by the authorities, and when *emancipation was introduced, they were divested of their juridical powers. The ferment and crisis caused by the *Shabbateans had a profound effect upon Jewish social and spiritual life in Germany at the end of the 17th century. The two great scholars and spiritual leaders of this period were Jair Ḥayyim *Bacharach and Ẓevi Hirsch *Ashkenazi. The memoirs of *Glueckel of Hameln reflect the life of well-to-do Jews in the 17th to 18th centuries—their business methods, piety, family life, and ties maintained with neighbors. She gives a vivid description of messianic fervor in Germany with the appearance of Shabbetai Ẓevi. *Messianism and *Kabbalah remained at the center of Jewish spiritual life in Germany until the middle of the 18th century as a result of the passions aroused by the fierce controversy between Jonathan *Eybeschuetz and Jacob *Emden.

Court Jews. A characteristic innovation of the era of absolutism and the mercantile system was the appearance of the *Court Jews. Some of the Court Jews abandoned Jewish tradition and their ties with the Jewish people; others remained faithful and used their wealth and position to help their brethren. In some instances their intervention succeeded in averting anti-Jewish measures; they built synagogues at their expense, published religious books, and founded institutions of learning. Court Jews were instrumental in reestablishing communities that had been destroyed during the Reformation (e.g., in *Dresden, Leipzig, *Kassel, *Brunswick, and *Halle). The precariousness of their position could affect both themselves and the Jewish community; as they were dependent upon the whim of the absolutist ruler, any change in his attitude could mean their downfall, and this was often followed by anti-Jewish measures of a general nature. In fact the Court Jews led a double life, often marked by tragedy—as instanced by such figures as Samuel *Oppenheimer, Samson *Wertheimer, and Joseph Suess *Oppenheimer.

Haskalah. Toward the end of the 18th century there were significant changes in the situation of German Jewry. Large parts of Poland were incorporated into Prussia and their substantial Jewish population became a reservoir of manpower and spiritual values for German Jewry as a whole. At the same time certain groups of wealthy Jews began to turn toward *assimilation in German society, especially in the large cities—such as Berlin—where the Jewish communities were comparatively new and unencumbered by age-old local tradition and custom. The background to this development was the Haskalah (enlightenment) movement, which was met in its aspirations by the claims of enlightened gentiles for the "moral and social betterment" of the Jews and the abolishment of all social and legal discrimination (see also C. W. von *Dohm; W. von *Humboldt; *Joseph II; G. E. *Lessing). These developments gave rise to considerable ferment in German Jewry. Moses *Mendelssohn, although widely esteemed as the representative figure of German Jewry in the enlightenment period, did not really succeed in becoming the guide of his generation. Many of the "enlightened" Jews—especially among the wealthy—placed general social and cultural values above the traditions of their people, and in their desire for radical assimilation contemplated and often took the road of apostasy which at the beginning of the 19th century assumed the dimensions of a mass movement. Rabbis of the period, such as David Tevele *Schiff of Lissa and Akiva *Eger, took up the struggle against the "enlightened" and the assimilationists, but the bans and excommunications they issued failed to halt the desertion of Judaism by many wealthy Jews.

Effects of French Revolution. The emancipation granted to the Jews of France by the *French Revolution was soon carried over into Germany by the revolutionary armies. In the states on the left bank of the Rhine, which were incorporated into the French Republic, the Jews became French citizens. When more German states were conquered by *Napoleon, and the Confederation of the Rhine was created, these states, upon French insistence, also declared equal rights for the Jews and granted them freedom to engage in commerce on the same basis as all other citizens (e.g., in Wuerttemberg and the grand duchy of *Berg). In Frankfort and in the Hanseatic cities emancipation was announced in 1811. In 1808 the Jews of

*Baden were declared "free citizens of the state for all time" and in 1809 a "Supreme Israelite Council" was formed in that state, which had the task of reforming Jewish education so that the Jews should reach the same cultural and spiritual standards as their environment and eventually achieve full equality. In Prussia, where the Jews were more advanced economically than in other German states, and more in tune with the prevailing culture, their emancipation was part of the reforms introduced by H. F. K. von *Stein and K. A. *Hardenberg after the defeat suffered by the kingdom in 1806/07. This was followed by the edict of 1812 granting equal rights and privileges to the Jews, and the abolition of the special taxes imposed on them.

Post-Napoleonic Reaction. The fall of Napoleon and the victory of the Holy Alliance resulted, almost everywhere, in the restoration of the previous state of affairs and the withdrawal of the equality that the Jews had achieved. Although the Congress of *Vienna had decided that the rights granted to the Jews in the various German states should be retained, the newly restored governments interpreted this decision as not applicable to the rights given to the Jews by the French or by the governments appointed by Napoleon. The "Jewish statutes," enacted by the Prussian provincial governments, repealed the 1812 emancipation edict in fact, although the edict as such was not canceled. Anti-Jewish feelings revived in the post-Napoleonic period, not only because the political and economic emancipation of the Jews was regarded as one of the Napoleonic reforms that had to be removed, but also as part of a spiritual and cultural reaction, an expression of a Christian-Teutonic, romantic and nationalist *Weltanschauung*. The new conservatism sought to replace the ideals of equality of the French Revolution with the harsh tradition of the past, and regarded the patriarchal state and feudal institutions as the natural political way of life for the German people. This view of state and society was accompanied by an emotional religious revival, and the concept of a "Christian-Teutonic" or "German-Christian" state came into being. A sharp literary debate was waged over the Jewish problem and the place of the Jews in the "Christian-German" state. The Jews, it was said, had to renounce their ethnic and religious ties, and accept Christianity, for a proper moral life among Christian peoples could only be a Christian life. The least that the Jews had to do was to renounce their ethnic distinctiveness. It was this clash between the rationalist and romantic concept of society which marked the relations between Germans and Jews in the period from 1815 to 1848. There were tragic overtones to these relations; thus, in 1819 there were the *Hep-Hep riots in which the masses gave vent to their anger over the social and economic rise of the Jews.

Assimilation and Reform. The reactions of Jews to the concept of the Christian state were mixed. Some became apostates because they had lost their faith in Judaism and Jewish values and acknowledged the superiority of Christian-German spirit and culture; others did so because they cynically looked for their own advancement in whatever way they could achieve it; or because of personal relations with Christians. In most cases it was a combination of all these factors. Among the apostates were the sons and daughters of Mendelssohn, as well as Rachel *Varnhagen, Henriette *Hertz, Eduard *Gans, Friedrich Julius *Stahl, August *Neander, Ludwig *Boerne, Heinrich *Heine, and many others; in the first decades of the 19th century most of the entire class of educated and wealthy German Jews was lost to Judaism by conversion. There were others who, while denying the validity of Jewish ethnic identity and the distinct nature of Jewish life, sought to preserve what they regarded as the essence of Judaism. They initiated *Reform in Jewish religion, to ease the burden of the precepts which prevented Jews from establishing close relations with the people among whom they lived, and to stress and develop in Judaism spiritual and ethical concepts of faith and life. This was the attitude of the "Society for the Culture and Science of Judaism," among whose founders were I. L. *Auerbach, E. Gans, H. Heine, I. M. *Jost, M. *Moser, and L. *Zunz—most of whom eventually took the road of apostasy. This attitude was also adopted by the actual reformers—A. *Geiger, S. *Holdheim, and their associates; these wished to be termed "Germans of the Mosaic Faith," a beautiful and pure faith which would be compatible with the spirit and culture of the time and facilitate the achievement of equal rights and creation of close relations with Christians. These reformers were violently opposed by the leaders of traditional Judaism of the time, and bitter strife ensued. Other trends emerged which attempted to find a compromise between the two extremes—the "historical-positive" school of Zacharias *Frankel, and "*Neo-Orthodoxy," founded by Samson Raphael *Hirsch and Azriel (Israel) *Hildesheimer. The unwillingness of the Neo-Orthodox to retain organizational ties with their Reform brethren led to the formation of two Jewish communities in many places in Germany where previously there had been only one: a "general" community, which included the Reform Jews and the Conservatives, with the former usually in control, and an Orthodox community. In 1876 Prussia adopted the *Austrittsgesetz* ("Law on withdrawal from the Jewish Community") under which Jews were permitted to dissociate from the Jewish community for religious reasons, and yet be recognized as Jews. By this act the compulsory membership of the community, provided for in a law adopted in 1847, was abolished; the "separatist" Orthodox communities *(Austrittsgemeinde)* were legalized and at the same time

Figure 12. Painting of Ẓevi Hirsch Ashkenazi, a major opponent of the Shabbateans. Formerly Berlin, Museum of the Jewish Community.

individual Jews were enabled to leave the organized Jewish community without having to go through formal conversion. These various trends in German Jewry gave rise to the *Wissenschaft des Judentums which, at the end of the 19th and beginning of the 20th centuries, made Germany the center of scientific study of Jewish history and culture. In the initial stage, the men associated with the Wissenschaft des Judentums were nearly all leaders of the Reform movement, but later on scholars of all the trends in German Jewry took part.

Economic and Social Life. From the political and sociological aspect, the history of German Jewry in the first half of the 19th century is marked by their economic and social rise, and by the struggle for emancipation. The political reaction of the "Holy Alliance" period, while succeeding in depriving the Jews of most of their political achievements, had little effect upon their rights in economic and commercial matters. Jews entered all branches of economy in the cities, contributing to the development of industry and capitalism and benefiting from it. At the end of the 18th century most of the German Jews still lived in small towns, their communities rarely exceeding a few dozen families; even in the "large" communities such as Hamburg or Frankfort they numbered no more than several hundred families (1,000 to 2,000 persons). In the course of the 19th century many Jews left the small towns for the large centers of commerce. Augmented also by the influx of Jews from the east, the communities expanded rapidly, and by the end of the century most of the Jews of Germany lived in the large cities—Breslau, Leipzig, Cologne, in addition to Hamburg and Frankfort, and particularly in Berlin, which eventually comprised one-third of German Jewry. Most of the Jews were well off and some became wealthy. The standard of living of many Jewish merchants, industrialists, and bankers equaled that of the German middle and upper classes. A large class of Jews in the liberal professions came into being and Jews took an increasingly active part in cultural life, in literature, and science. This development served to step up the Jewish demand for emancipation. Both Reform and Neo-Orthodox felt that the grant of equal rights should not depend upon any demand for diminution of their Jewish identity according to the conceptions of each trend. In this they encountered opposition even on the part of Christian liberals, such as H. E. G. Paulus and H. von *Treitschke, who held that so long as the Jews clung to their religious practice and maintained their specific communal cohesion they were not entitled to participation in the political life of the country. While these liberals did not demand apostasy, they felt that full rights should not be granted to the Jews unless they abandoned their distinctive practices, such as *kashrut,* observance of the Sabbath, and even circumcision. The Jews, on the other hand, encouraged by their economic progress and the rise of their educational level, took strong exception to this view, voicing their opinion that equality was a natural right that could not be withheld from them, whatever the pretext. Convinced that their struggle was intimately connected with the full social and political liberation of the German people and the creation of a free, democratic, and liberal German state, they pleaded their cause before the German public in word and print and took an active part in the German movement for national and political liberation. They refused to make their religion a bargaining counter in the struggle for equal rights and rejected the government's demand for the abolition of *kashrut* and observance of the day of rest on Sunday. The chief spokesman of the Jewish struggle for emancipation was Gabriel *Riesser; others were J. *Jacoby and Ludwig Boerne (himself an apostate).

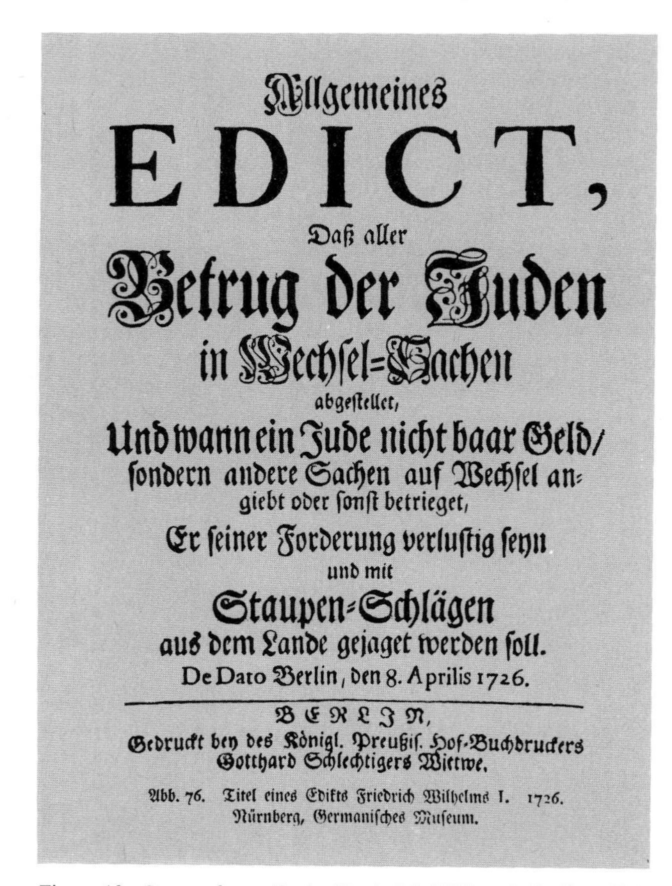
Allgemeines
EDICT,
Daß aller
Betrug der Juden
in Wechſel=Sachen
abgeſtellet,
Und wann ein Jude nicht baar Geld/
ſondern andere Sachen auf Wechſel an=
giebt oder ſonſt betrieget,
Er ſeiner Forderung verluſtig ſeyn
und mit
Staupen=Schlägen
aus dem Lande gejaget werden ſoll.
De Dato Berlin, den 8. Aprilis 1726.

BERLIN,
Gedruckt bey des Königl. Preußiſ. Hof-Buchdruckers
Gotthard Schlechtigers Wittwe.

Abb. 76. Titel eines Edikts Friedrich Wilhelms I. 1726.
Nürnberg, Germaniſches Muſeum.

Figure 13. Cover of an edict by Frederick William I, Berlin, 1726, forbidding Jewish deceit in monetary matters, with confiscation and expulsion as the punishment. Nuremberg, Germanisches Museum.

Emancipation. Jews took part in the 1848–49 revolution and there were several Jews among the members of the Frankfort Parliament (including Gabriel Riesser). The "Basic Laws of the German People" promulgated by this parliament extended equal rights to the Jews by accepting the principle that religious affiliation should in no way influence the full enjoyment of civil and political rights. This achievement was curtailed by the reaction that set in during the 1850s, following the collapse of the revolutionary movement; however, the rise of the middle classes, including the Jews, did not come to a halt, and liberal tendencies continued to make headway. Nor did the Jews themselves give up the struggle. In 1869 the North German Confederation abolished the civil and political restrictions that still applied to the members of certain religions; after the 1870 war, the same law was adopted by the south German states and included in the constitution of the newly established German Reich. Many German Jews now felt that the attainment of political and civil equality had also erased their separate Jewish identity, not only in their own estimation but in that of the Germans as well. In the period from 1871 to 1914, German Jews indeed became a part of the German people from the constitutional point of view, and, in a large measure, also from the practical point of view. According to the law, every sphere of German life became open to them, whether economic, cultural, or social, with one exception: they were not permitted to participate in the government of the country. But usually, in spite of the constitutional guarantees, Jews were not appointed to official positions, nor could they become officers in the army. In general, Jews were also barred from appointments as full professors at the universities, although there were large numbers of Jews of lower academic rank. Jews were active in the economy of the country and some

Table 1. Jewish Socio-Economic Structure (percent)

	1895	1907
Agriculture	1.4	1.3
Industry and trades	19.3	22.0
Commerce and transportation	56.0	50.6
Hired workers	0.4	0.6
Public services and liberal professions	6.1	6.5
Self-employed with no profession	16.7	19.0

became leading bankers, industrialists, and businessmen; there was also a large number of Jews in the liberal professions. Jews were among the founders and leaders of the political parties; the Liberal and Social-Democrat parties usually had a number of Jewish members in the Reichstag. In the sciences and technology, in literature, the press, the theater and the arts the share of Jews was disproportionately high. Almost all were radically assimilated, and for Jewish history they are significant only as the target of German *anti-Semitism, and, in some instances, for actions they undertook on behalf of the Jewish people.

The Jewish population in Germany numbered 512,158, in 1871 (1.25% of the total), 562,612 in 1880 (1.24%), 567,884 in 1890 (1.15%), 586,833 in 1900 (1.04%), and 615,021 in 1910 (0.95%). Demographically, German Jewry was among the first communities to feel the effects of the practice of birth control. At the beginning of the 20th century natural increase among German Jewry came to a complete end; this, in addition to the many cases of apostasy and *mixed marriages, threatened the very existence of the community. It was only the steady influx from the east which enabled German Jewry to maintain its numerical strength.

ANTI-SEMITISM. In the period following the foundation of the German Reich a shadow fell across the tranquility and prosperity enjoyed by German Jewry which darkened increasingly: the manifestation of anti-Semitism among the German public. Although its virulence varied, it existed throughout this period, and took on the form of political movements. It did not, however, affect the formal legal status of the Jews who therefore regarded anti-Semitism as mainly a social, cultural, and spiritual problem; its potential political strength and danger were not recognized by either Jews or non-Jews.

INTERNAL LIFE. Despite widespread assimilation, independent Jewish creativity did not come to an end. For a significant minority of German Jews, Jewish consciousness retained its strength. The constant influx of Jews from the east ("Ostjuden") was also an important factor in preventing total assimilation. The presence of these newcomers created a certain amount of tension, both among Germans who resented their successful integration into economic life, and among the "old" Jewish families, who disapproved of the Ostjuden manners and of the way they had of making themselves conspicuous in the community. Zionism had an early start among German Jewry. Although small in numbers, the Zionists were well organized and worked effectively for their cause. German Jews were among the leaders of the World Zionist Movement; two of the presidents of the World Zionist Organization—D. *Wolfsohn and O. *Warburg—were German Jews, as was the founder and organizer of agricultural settlement in Ereẓ Israel, A. *Ruppin. After the death of Theodor Herzl, the headquarters of the Zionist Organization was moved to Germany and remained there even during World War I. By their high standard of general education and strict separation from Reform Jews, the German Neo-Orthodox exercised a profound influence upon observant Jews in other parts of the world. They had created a new type of Jew, who could be a qualified professional man, highly educated and versed in the manners of the world, and yet at the same time strictly observant of religious practice. It was men of this type who became the leaders of the world movement of *Agudat Israel after the founding of that organization in 1912. Orthodox chaplains serving in the German forces during World War I did a great deal to spread the principles of Agudat Israel among East European Jews. The confrontation with East European Jewish life also had a profound influence on German Jews serving in the forces; they were attracted by the wholesomeness of the life led by the Jewish masses, and many became convinced Zionists. German Jewish life was well organized. Organizations were established for the consolidation of the communities and for combating anti-Semitism (see *Centralverein), for social welfare (the *"Hilfsverein"), for research and studies (the rabbinical seminars—the Breslau *Juedisch-theologisches Seminar, established in 1854; the Berlin *Hochschule fuer die Wissenschaft des Judentums, founded in 1872; the *Rabbinerseminar fuer das orthodoxe Judentum in Berlin, also founded in 1872; the Historical Commission established in 1885, etc.). All were active and highly efficient. Throughout the second half of the 19th century and the early years of the 20th, German Jewry occupied a highly respected place among world Jewry, exercising a profound influence on Jewish centers in Eastern and Western Europe, in America, and in Ereẓ Israel. [S.M.S.]

Figure 14. Charter of privileges granted by Maximilian of Bavaria to Samuel Wertheimer in 1765. Courtesy Central Zionist Archives, Jerusalem.

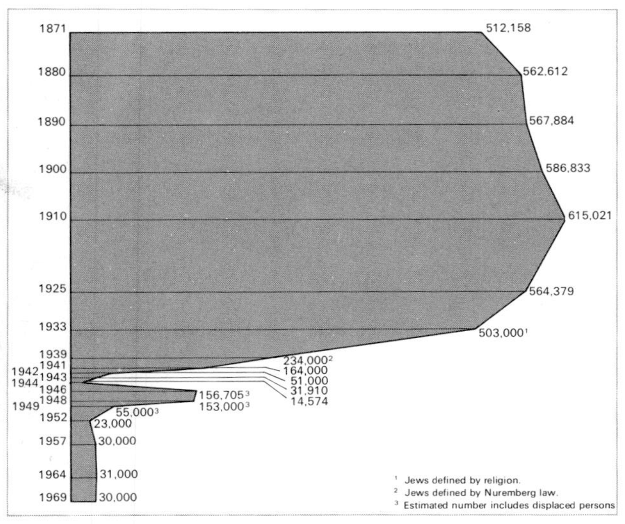

Jewish population in Germany, 1871–1969.

1914–1933. The history of German Jewry in the interwar period is sharply divided into two chapters: the period up to 1933, which was a time of great prosperity; and the period which began in 1933, a year which was to mark the beginning of the tragic end of German Jewry.

Figure 15. Engraving showing 18th-century synagogue attire with a heart-shaped Jewish badge. From *Tyroff'schen Trachtenbuch*, Nuremberg, 1766.

Over 100,000 Jews had served in the German army during World War I, and 12,000 Jews fell in battle. At the end of the war, when the monarchy had fallen and a democratic republic was established, it seemed that the Jews had achieved full emancipation. Any restrictions that were still in force were abolished by the Weimar Republic, and Jews could now participate in every sphere of public life. Their share and influence in the political life of the country reached unprecedented proportions. Many of the leaders of the democratic and socialist parties were Jews, as were two of the six "people's commissars" which made up the first post-revolutionary German government (O. *Landsberg and H. *Haase). In Bavaria, Jews played an even more significant role; the head of the revolutionary government was a Jew, Kurt *Eisner, and the majority of the Soviet-type government set up after Eisner's murder consisted of Jewish intellectuals (Eugen *Leviné, Gustav *Landauer, Ernst *Toller, etc.). The inquiry commission which was to determine the responsibility of the military leadership for Germany's defeat had among its members Oscar *Cohn, a Social Democrat and Zionist. The Weimar Constitution was drafted by a Jew, Hugo *Preuss; another Jew, Walter *Rathenau, first became minister of reconstruction and later foreign minister: his murder by young extremists was motivated largely by anti-Semitism. Several Jews were appointed to high positions in the civil service, especially in Prussia. The rise of Jews to positions of political power, added to their economic and social advance, increased hostility among the population, and facilitated the growth of the Nazi movement. Anti-Semitic propaganda exploited a series of financial scandals and bankruptcies in which Jews were involved. The background to these events was the great social and economic crisis which gripped Germany as a result of the terrible inflation after the war. Right-wing circles in Germany, anxious to divert public attention from the real beneficiaries of inflation—the "pure Aryan" industrial and financial barons and their giant enterprises—were more than ready to use the anti-Jewish propaganda for their purposes. The middle class, heavily hit by the economic upheaval, the nobility and the officer class who felt their honor besmirched by the defeat and whose privileges were abolished in the revolution, were all easily swayed by the idea that it was the Jews who were to blame for all of Germany's misfortunes—that "the Jews had stabbed the undefeated German army in the back," and thus forced it to surrender; that Capitalism and "Marxism" (i.e., Bolshevism and Socialism) were the result of the machinations of "World Jewry." In the 1920s, however, the full implications of this anti-Semitic mood had not yet become apparent, and the situation of the Jews seemed satisfactory. It was not until 1933, when the Nazis came to power and based their program upon the "doctrine of race"—i.e., hatred of Jews—that the role of the Jewish problem for the internal historical development of Germany stood fully revealed.

Even in the best years of the Weimar Republic the Jewish problem had not really been solved. Socially and spiritually the German people had not absorbed the Jews. Even the assimilationists among the Jews had to acknowledge this fact, and some reacted by over-emphasizing their German nationalism, thereby hoping to set themselves apart from the rest of the Jews. As a result of the large increase of Jewish immigration from Eastern Europe, the old difference between "Eastern" and "Western" Jews became much more pronounced and had many practical implications. Jewish organizations did their best to facilitate the absorption of the newcomers and created special institutions

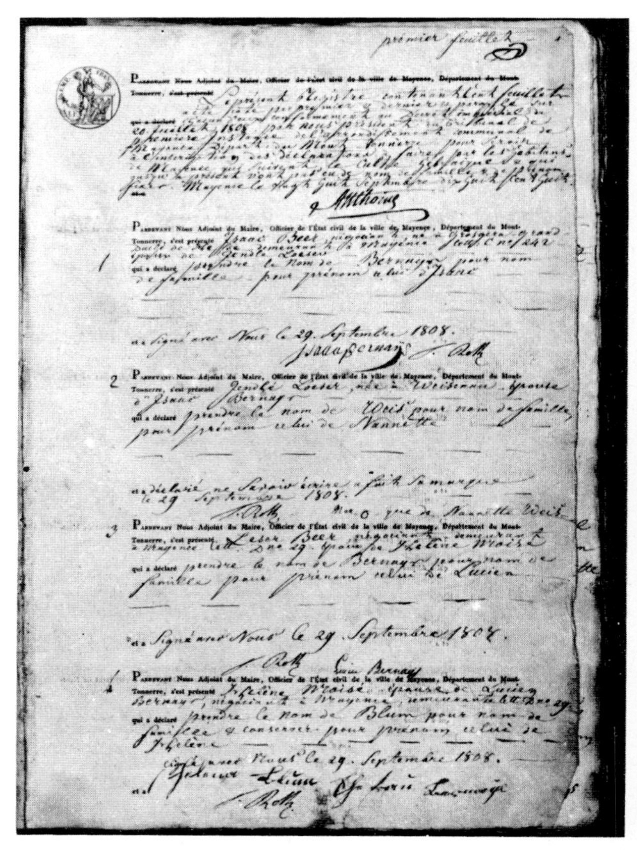

Figure 16. First page of a register of changes of name under the Napoleonic occupation, Mainz, 1808. The third entry records Leser Beer as becoming Lucien Bernays. Courtesy C.A.H.J.P., Jerusalem.

for this purpose, such as the Welfare Bureau for Jewish Workers. According to the 1925 census, there were 564,379 Jews in Germany, representing 0.9% of the total population. One-third lived in Berlin, another third in the other large cities, while the remaining third lived in 1,800 different places with organized Jewish communities and another 1,200 places where there were no organized communities. Most of the Jews made their living in commerce and transportation and in the liberal professions; in the large cities, one-third or even more of the lawyers and doctors were Jews; they also played a prominent role in the press, in literature, in the theater, and in other forms of entertainment. In general, the Jews belonged to the middle class and were well off. Although many had lost their savings in the inflation, they recovered from the effects of this crisis, and when the Nazis came to power, there was again a great deal of capital in the hands of individual Jews and the Jewish communities. The absorption of Jews into all spheres of German life was accompanied by record numbers of mixed marriages and conversions; in the period 1921–27, 44.8% of all Jewish marriages were mixed, conversions took place at the rate of 500 annually, and a similar number of Jews formally "dissociated" themselves from the community.

COMMUNAL ORGANIZATION. Between the two World Wars, the Jewish communities presented a model of organization. The Weimar Constitution retained official recognition of the Jewish communities as entities recognized by public law and their right to collect dues. In general, a Jewish community had a representative body, elected by the community members, and an executive committee, elected in turn by the representative body and consisting of three to seven members. A point under dispute was the voting rights of Jews of foreign nationality (the Ostjuden), who in some communities amounted to a substantial proportion of the total membership. Although the "foreigners" had equal rights to the religious and social services provided by the community, in many places they had no right to vote, or were given that right only after long years of local residence. In the various states of which the Reich was made up, there existed "state unions" of Jewish communities. For a long time the need was felt for a national union of Jewish communities, but there were differences of opinion as to the form this should take; some thought that it should be a union of individual communities, others preferred a national union of the state unions, while a third proposal called for a kind of Jewish parliament, elected by direct democratic vote (the last plan was supported by the Zionists). By the time a national union was finally established, shortly before Hitler came to power, the organizational form of the communities, and the tasks they faced, were about to undergo a radical change. Apart from the religious and cultural tasks they performed, the community organizations were most active in social welfare; this was true of the period preceding 1933, and became even more important after that turning point. In 1917 a central welfare bureau for German Jewry was set up, the *Zentralwohlfahrtstelle, whose membership consisted of the communities as well as of many private institutions, trusts, and societies. The bureau cooperated with the main non-Jewish welfare agencies in the country, as well as with the *American Jewish Joint Distribution Committee, and published its own monthly. It supervised hospitals, clinics, counseling centers, bureaus, and a variety of other public institutions, and had some 2,000 welfare agencies affiliated with it. In the large communities expenditure on welfare amounted to as much as 30% of the total budget. Agencies concerned with youth, and with immigrants passing through Germany on their way overseas, also played an

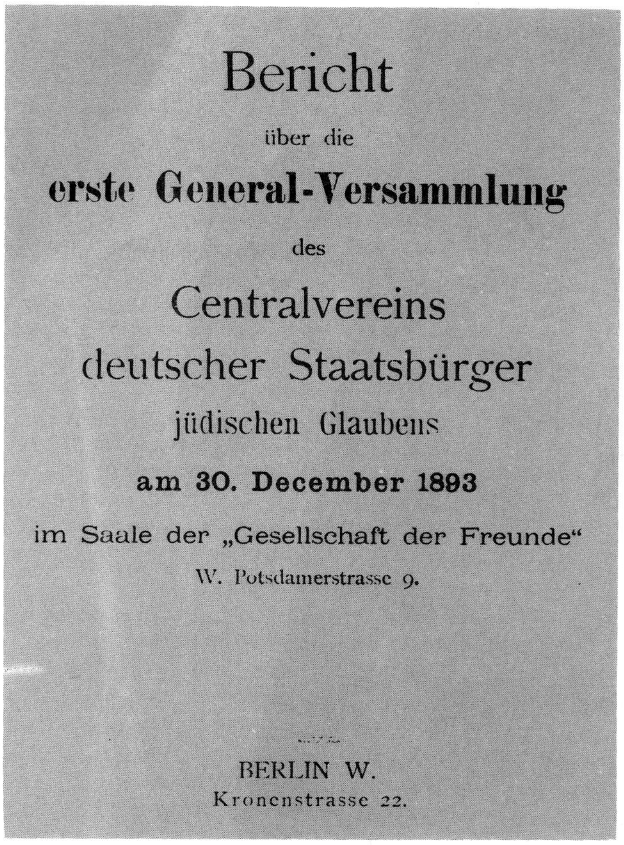

Bericht
über die
erste General-Versammlung
des
Centralvereins
deutscher Staatsbürger
jüdischen Glaubens
am 30. December 1893
im Saale der „Gesellschaft der Freunde"
W. Potsdamerstrasse 9.

BERLIN W.
Kronenstrasse 22.

Figure 17. Title page of the first report of the *Centralverein*, the general organization of German Jews. Berlin, December 30, 1893. Jerusalem, C.A.H.J.P., T.D. 809.

important role. In addition to the organizations based on the communities, there were also a large number of other societies, as well as cultural and scientific institutions. Jewish life in general was marked by the struggle between Jewish nationalism and various degrees of assimilation. Zionism succeeded in revolutionizing the life of the communities, and the councils, in addition to "notables," now also contained democratically elected members who represented national-Jewish interests.

The following were the main organizations of German Jewry in the period: Centralverein (C.-V.) deutscher Staatsbuerger juedischen Glaubens ("Central Organization of German Citizens of the Jewish Faith"); Zionistische Vereinigung fuer Deutschland (Z.V.f.D.; "Zionist Organization of Germany"); Hilfsverein der deutschen Juden ("Aid Society of German Jews"); the religious organizations—Agudat Israel, Aḥdut, *Vereinigung fuer das liberale Judentum; *B'nai B'rith; *Verband nationaldeutscher Juden ("Union of Jews of German Nationality"); *Reichsbund juedischer Frontsoldaten ("Reich Association of Jewish War Veterans"); the various rabbinical associations, and associations of teachers and cantors; etc. An important role in the cultural life of German Jewry was played by the academic organizations: *Kartell-Convent (K.-C.) deutscher Studenten juedischen Glaubens ("National Fraternity of German Students of the Jewish Faith"), affiliated to the Centralverein; Bund juedischer Akademiker (B.J.A., an association of Orthodox academies); Kartell juedischer Verbindungen, the Zionist student organization. A substantial number of Jewish youth in Germany were members of Jewish youth movements. Some of the youth organizations were sponsored by the Centralverein, and others by the Orthodox; a third type were the Zionist youth organizations. The latter encouraged pioneer settlement in Ereẓ Israel, maintained training centers, and supplied a

Map 2. Major Jewish communities in Germany in 1933 and 1970.

small but steady flow of immigrants. The Centralverein was the largest and most important organization, which published its own newspaper. It advocated a synthesis of Judaism and "Germanism," emphasized defense of Jewish civil rights, and regarded German Jewry as an integral part of the German people. Other periodicals were *Der *Israelit* (published by Agudat Israel); *Juedisch-liberale Zeitung; Der Schild* (published by the veterans' organization); *Der *Jude,* a Zionist monthly, edited by Martin *Buber; and *Der Morgen,* a monthly published by the Centralverein. The official organ of the Zionist movement, **Juedische Rundschau,* a weekly (which in its last years appeared twice a week), eventually became the leading Jewish paper published in Germany.

Despite differences of outlook, there was close cooperation between the various organizations. An outstanding example was the establishment of the *Keren Hayesod in Germany in 1922 which was based on cooperation between Zionists and non-Zionists, and served as a preliminary stage to the enlarged *Jewish Agency (1929). The Zionist Organization included Zionist party organizations (Mizrachi, *Poalei-Zion, *Hapo'el ha-Ẓair-Hitaḥdut, etc.).

CULTURAL LIFE. After World War I, when many Hebrew writers and publishers fled from Russia and took refuge in Germany, the country became a center of Hebrew publishing and Hebrew literature. Some of the greatest Hebrew poets and writers became residents of Germany, and Hebrew publishing houses were established. This was in addition to the many books published in German, on Judaism, Zionism, and Jewish studies. In Berlin and Breslau, the Zionist Organization founded schools for the study of modern Hebrew by adults and the youth. In 1920 Franz *Rosenzweig established the Freies Juedisches Lehrhaus ("Free Institute of Jewish Learning") in Frankfort, and it gained great prestige. Other cultural institutions were the Juedische Volkshochschule ("Jewish College of Adult Education"); the Toynbee-Halls, which also served as centers of social work; and the Juedisches Volksheim (Jewish Social Center) established in Berlin in 1916. There were Jewish elementary schools in several communities and Jewish teachers' seminaries in Wuerzburg and Cologne. There were also Jewish secondary schools, originally maintained by Orthodox Jews only, but in later years also supported by the Zionists.

1933–1939. As a result of the Nazi seizure of power on Jan. 30, 1933, the entire existing structure of Jewish life in Germany collapsed. At the same time (1933–38), German Jewry underwent a spiritual awakening and achieved a peak of vitality in Jewish communal life. In the national-socialist racist state, the Jews, branded as an "alien race," were automatically excluded by law from general life. Anti-Jewish measures gradually reduced the Jews to self-confinement and seclusion; the majority of the Jews were, however, unable unreservedly to sever the ties that had integrated them into German life. The racist decree that "no Jew could be a German" gravely affected the premise for the flourishing life of German Jewry, since the vast majority had considered themselves Germans and were completely assimilated in German culture.

On April 1, 1933, the first large-scale anti-Jewish

demonstration took place, in the form of a boycott of all Jewish-owned shops and offices of Jewish professionals. The yellow *badge was posted on Jewish business concerns and many residences; windows and doors were smeared with anti-Semitic and indecent cartoons; and S.A. (storm troop) guards ensured the observance of the boycott. The boycott was abandoned two days later due to sharp reaction from abroad and for fear of potential damage to the economy of the country. This demonstration, far from being "a spontaneous eruption of the people's wrath," was organized by the Nazi Party on government orders. In the beginning there were even some signs of resistance among the German public to actions of this sort, until eventually the Nazi Party succeeded in suppressing all opposing political trends and concentrated absolute power in its own hands (see also *S.S.). This was achieved soon after the Nazi takeover, initiated by a wave of arrests of political opponents, for whose internment concentration *camps were set up. The first victims were political opponents of the regime, or people with whom it had personal accounts to settle, or whom it sought to deprive of their property. On April 7, 1933, the term *Nichtarier* ("non-Aryan") was adopted as legal designation. This facilitated the removal, step by step, of the Jews from various professions. The first to suffer were lawyers, judges, public officials, artists, newspapermen, and doctors. (At the beginning, veterans of World War I were not included in the ban.) The Jews were methodically pushed out of their remaining employment.

The adoption of the *Nuremberg Laws on Sept. 15, 1935, marked a new phase. It provided a precise definition of the "Jew" by origin, religion, and family ties; deprived the Jews of their status as citizens of the Reich; and reduced them to "subjects of the state." Intermarriage was prohibited while special provisions were made to deal with already-existing mixed marriages. Sexual intercourse between Jews and non-Jews was branded as *Rassenschande* ("defiling of the race") liable to severe punishment. In order to stigmatize the Jews further and brand them as a licentious people, the employment of "Aryan" maids in their households was also forbidden. From time to time, addenda were made to the Nuremberg Laws, further reducing the Jews' status, until July 1, 1943, when the 13th such order was promulgated, declaring Germany *judenrein* ("clean of Jews"). Several Nazi leaders declared that with the adoption of the Nuremberg Laws the "regulation of the Jewish problem" was completed, and that the government had no intention of ousting the Jews from the economic positions they still held. In the period 1935–37, despite all the destructive measures, a large amount of capital still remained in Jewish hands and some Jews continued to run profit-making enterprises. To an extent, the Jews also benefited from the economic prosperity brought about by rearmament. Confiscation of Jewish capital, or enforced sale of Jewish enterprises *(Arianisierung)* did, however, become more and more frequent, along with arrests and other anti-Jewish measures.

The decisive turning point in Nazi policy against the Jews came in March 1938, when Austria was annexed to the Reich. The anti-Jewish excesses that took place in Austria, especially in *Vienna, were far worse than any that had occurred thus far in Germany, and the general population's part in them was much greater. The Jews in the Sudetenland were to undergo like persecution when the Nazis annexed it on the basis of the October 1938 Munich Conference. The gravest incident in this stage in the entire area of "Greater Germany" occurred on Nov. 9, 1938 (see **Kristallnacht*). The pretext for this action was the assassination of a member of the German Embassy in Paris by a Jew, Herschel *Grynszpan. A collective fine of one billion marks was also imposed upon the Jews. These measures put the Jews of Germany in jeopardy and all subsequent measures only further aggravated their situation, culminating in 1940 with the commencement of systematic deportations to extermination camps.

The April 1, 1933, anti-Jewish demonstration filled many with consternation, but only a few Jews were brought to the brink of despair (resulting in some cases in suicide). In the initial stage, both Jews and some non-Jews protested. The Jews sought to remind the Germans of the contributions they had made to Germany's cultural and economic life, of their loyalty to the country, and of the medals they had earned on the field of battle. They soon realized that their efforts were futile. Gradually, the majority of the Jews understood that their fate was bound up with the Jewish people. Their only defenders were the Jews throughout the world who protested against the ill-treatment to which their brethren in Germany were being exposed. Emigration from Germany was their only hope but this too they could not achieve without the aid of international Jewish bodies. Judaism was also their only source of moral comfort. The persecution aroused in them a sense of pride in being a Jew, which gave them the moral strength to endure.

German Jewry now began to cooperate as a single body because external events erased the differences that had previously divided the assimilationists and those Jews who identified themselves with the Jewish culture and people. The anti-Jewish policies were directed against the assimilationist Jews as well, forcing them to recognize that they too

Figure 18. Synagogue in Dusseldorf daubed with anti-Semitic slogan and swastika, 1933. Courtesy Yad Vashem, Jerusalem.

Figure 19. Nazi mass rally at the Grunewald Stadium, Berlin, 1933. Courtesy Yad Vashem, Jerusalem.

were members of the Jewish people. The Nazi doctrine propounded that "blood" determined everything, so even converts and persons of mixed parentage were labeled Jews. Among the latter were persons who for two or three generations had had no spiritual tie with Judaism. Of these "non-Aryan" Christians, or persons not adhering to any religion, only a few found their way back to active Jewish life. The rest, however, who still regarded themselves as Jews, now closed ranks, irrespective of the divergent views they had held in the past. Many who had played important roles in German life, but had been remote from Jewish activities, were now eager and ready to accept Jewish public activity. At first, the existing Jewish organizations united under the Zentralausschuss fuer Hilfe und Aufbau ("Central Committee for Aid and Construction"), providing welfare and emigration services. This was followed by the creation of the *Reichsvertretung der Juden in Deutschland ("Reich Representation of the Jews in Germany") headed by Rabbi Leo *Baeck. (The use of the term "Jews in Germany" was imposed when the Nazis prohibited the term "German Jews.")

From the outset, one of the principal tasks confronting the Reichsvertretung was to organize emigration, which had taken various forms. There was first of all the spontaneous flight to neighboring countries. In 1933, this was comparatively easy, for the Jews bore German passports which permitted entry to most European countries without visas. Regulations on removal of currency from Germany were not that strict, and a uniform regulation had not as yet been reached. In the course of time, however, the countries of reception placed obstacles in the way of the refugees from Germany, especially by refusing them work permits. Thus, the Swiss government refused such permits to all foreign nationals. Only in a few instances were the emigrants able to maintain themselves on the funds they had brought with them. Emigration was also directed to overseas countries, mainly to the United States, but also to South America, Canada, and Australia. The consulates of these countries were thronged, but the existing regulations were not slackened to help the persecuted Jews. Except for Britain in 1938–39, no entry visas were issued outside the scope of existing immigration laws. The third and principal form of emigration was to Palestine. This was more than a simple rescue operation, for it had ideological overtones, reinforced by the feeling of attachment to the "Jewish National Home," while emigration to other

Table 2. Emigration of Jews from Germany in the Period April 1933 to May 1939[1], including Areas occupied by Germany by May 1939[1]

Country of Reception	No. of German immigrants
U.S.A.	63,000
Palestine	55,000
Great Britain	40,000
France	30,000
Argentina	25,000
Brazil	13,000
South Africa	5,500
Italy	5,000
Other European countries	25,000
Other South American countries	20,000
Far Eastern countries	15,000
Other	8,000
Total	304,500

[1] Estimated figures.

Figure 20. The 19th-century neo-oriental synagogue of Darmstadt, destroyed by the Nazis in 1938. Courtesy Darmstadt Municipality. Photo Immo Beyer, Darmstadt.

countries was dictated by utilitarian reasons only. Most of the Zionists who left Germany made their way to Palestine. A systematic campaign on behalf of *aliyah* was conducted, and as the dangers grew, an immigration certificate to Palestine became a valuable document, coveted also by non-Zionists.

According to estimates of the League of Nations *High Commissioner for Refugees, 329,000 Jews fled from the Nazis in the period 1933–39, of whom 315,000 left Germany itself. In June 1933 there were 503,000 Jews by religion in Germany (including the Saar Region, incorporated in Germany in 1935), while in the first six years of the Nazi regime, the number of Jews was reduced by 289,000, leaving 214,000 Jews in May 1939. According to the census, there were 234,000 Jews (as defined by the Nuremberg Laws) in Germany in 1939, a reduction of 330,000 since 1925.

Efforts were also made to bring about a change in the occupational structure of the Jews, in order to prepare them for emigration. A large part of the Jewish students had been expelled from their German schools and universities and were now taught new trades on farms or in vocational and agricultural schools. Schools to teach Hebrew, English, Spanish, and other languages were also established to prepare Jews for future emigration. *Aliyah* to Palestine, and *hakhsharah*, preparation for *aliyah*, were organized by the Zionist *Palestine Office *(Palaestina-Amt)*, which greatly expanded in this period. The Palestine Office acted in an advisory capacity and was in charge of the transfer of capital through the *Ha'avara Company, which, with the approval of the authorities, succeeded in removing Jewish capital from Germany in the form of exports to Palestine, valued at about $16,200,000. Emigrants to the United States were rendered aid primarily by the Hilfsverein der Deutschen Juden and the American Jewish *Joint Distribution Committee. For the Jews in Germany the last few years preceding the war were marked by a desperate race to discover possible emigration outlets. The number of outlets, however, was continually reduced and, when the last exit to safety was finally closed, there was still a sizable Jewish community left in Germany.

In the period 1933–38, the Jews of Germany stepped up

in considerable measure their own public and cultural life. They were now called upon to provide not only for their strictly "Jewish" needs, but also to engage in activities of a general nature, especially in education and culture. The Jewish community had to set up its own elementary and high schools for Jewish children, who had been expelled from the public schools. The teaching staff for these new schools consisted of the Jewish teachers who had been dismissed from the German school system. The "Center for Jewish Adult Education," an institution created by Martin Buber under the auspices of the Reichsvertretung, included among its tasks the training of these teachers for their duties in Jewish schools. In general, the educational and cultural activities of the Reichsvertretung may be regarded as the beginning of a Jewish moral resistance movement.

Among the Zionist youth movements, the largest was Ha-Bonim, No'ar Ḥaluẓi, which was founded in 1933 and based on a merger of Kadimah and Berit Olim. Makkabbi Hazair was a General Zionist youth movement, while the Werkleute were absorbed by Ha-Shomer ha-Ẓa'ir. After 1928, religious youth was organized in the Berit Ḥaluẓim Datiyyim. He-Ḥalutz, the largest organization preparing its members for settlement in Ereẓ Israel, established *hakhsharot*—agricultural training centers—with the support of the Reichsvertretung. Non-Zionist youth was organized in the Deutsch-juedische Jugend and Vortrupp societies. The Zionist Organization of Germany, which grew tremendously in strength, gained half of the seats in the community council and the national organizations in 1935.

The Jewish press played a great role in strengthening the spirit of German Jews. The *C.-V. Zeitung* gained a circulation of 40,000 and a similar number subscribed to the *Juedische Rundschau.* (A front-page article of the *Rundschau,* published under the title, *Tragt ihn mit Stolz, den gelben Fleck* ("Wear it proudly, the yellow badge"), electrified the Jews with its call for courage in the face of adversity.) The pro-Zionist *Israelitisches Familienblatt* also jumped to a circulation of 35,000.

In art and literature a similar development took place. Jewish artists and writers who had not succeeded in immediately leaving Germany were forced to restrict their work to the realm of Judaism; in many instances this was a "return to Judaism" in name only, but in others it was accompanied by a profound spiritual change. The *Juedischer Kulturbund was created to organize Jewish cultural life. Jewish newspapers enlarged their scope, Jewish publishing houses increased their activities, and books on Jewish subjects, poetry, history, and essays, gained a wide distribution. Like their cultural activities, the publishing activities of Jews were under the official supervision of the Juden-Referat, a separate body established within the framework of Goebbels' Ministry of Propaganda. From time to time certain publications were prohibited and newspaper editions were confiscated. The Zionist organ, *Juedische Rundschau,* was closed down and reopened on numerous occasions. In the course of time, the officials of the Juden-Referat came to show personal interest in the continued functioning of Jewish cultural life. The events of Nov. 9–10, 1938, however, put an end to this situation, and the ensuing months, up to the outbreak of the war, were marked by general alarm among the Jews, cessation of all social activities, mass emigration, and Gestapo persecution of the remaining Jews. [R.W.]

World War II. In the course of the war, when German rule was extended over large areas, Jews were sent to or transferred from Germany and other European countries. Many German Jews were put to death in Germany itself, along with foreign Jews interned there. In the period 1933–39, the communal and occupational life of German Jewry had undergone a radical change. After expulsion from commercial life and the professions, many Jews switched over to manual labor and agriculture. Although in 1933, 48.12% of German Jews had steady employment, by 1939 this figure had been reduced to 15.6% (Jews "by faith"). Of breadwinners in 1939 who no longer had any regular employment, over 40% were able to live off their capital and property, while others had some income from other sources and insurance. By 1939, thousands of Jews were already imprisoned in concentration camps. The Nazis planned, or pretended to be planning, the transfer of German Jews to special, remote, areas—in *Madagascar or in the occupied territories of Poland or Russia. At the beginning of 1942, when the physical destruction of Jews was already in full swing, these plans were finally abandoned. A law passed on July 4, 1939, transformed the Reichsvertretung into the Reichsvereinigung der Juden in Deutschland ("Reich union of Jews in Germany"), and charged the new organization with promoting Jewish emigration, running the Jewish schools, and social welfare. Leo Baeck remained head of the new organization. The work of the Reichsvereinigung was defined by law, and subject to orders from the minister of the interior. The Nazis regarded it as an instrument which could be maneuvered to rid the country of all its Jews in the shortest possible time. In May 1939, there were still 214,000 Jews left, of whom 90% lived in 200 cities and the rest in 1,800 different places without an organized Jewish community. There were an additional 20,000 persons who had been classified as Jews under the Nuremberg Laws.

The outbreak of the war (Sept. 1, 1939) did not bring about any change in the legal status of the Jews. Until November 1941, i.e., at a time when the mass killing of Jews in Eastern Europe had been in process for several months, some still succeeded in leaving Germany. German Jews were admitted to some neutral countries, others were able to escape across the Atlantic. In fact they reached every corner of the globe, including *Shanghai. Until June 20, 1940, Jews who had some means at their disposal were able to reach Palestine by way of the Italian ports, and until Nov. 11, 1942, they could go to *Lisbon and *Casablanca by way of unoccupied France. On May 1, 1941, there were 169,000 Jews in Germany, and by Oct. 1, 1941, 164,000. In the period that had elapsed since May 1939 their number had therefore been reduced by some 50,000 to 70,000. A substantial number of these had succeeded in leaving Germany, although some of them only moved to countries which soon came under German occupation. About 8,000 Jews were deported by the Nazis, to make room for Germans who were repatriated after the outbreak of war.

Figure 21. Waiting at the Palestine Office, Berlin, for permits to enter Ereẓ Israel, 1939. Courtesy Yad Vashem, Jerusalem.

Figure 22. Deportation of Wuerzburg Jews to Eastern Europe, 1941/42. Courtesy Yad Vashem, Jerusalem.

These Jews were sent in the first shipment to the *Lublin district, and later to unoccupied France. Many Jews were put into the existing concentration camps, or into newly established ones. The mortality rate among the Jews also rose to unprecedented heights.

Some time in March 1941, Hitler issued his verbal order for the "Final Solution of the Jewish Question" by a physical extermination program. On Sept. 1, 1941, the Jews were ordered to wear the yellow badge (*Judenstern*= "Jewish star"). In mid-October 1941, their mass "transfer" (*"Evakuierungen"* or *"Abwanderungen"*) to ghettos in Eastern Europe (*Lodz, *Minsk, *Riga, *Kovno) and to concentration and forced labor camps was begun, under Adolf *Eichmann's supervision. By the end of the year, 30,000 Jews had been thus "transferred." In the period from October 1942 to March 1943, Jews from Germany were "transferred" to *Auschwitz and other extermination centers, at first by way of concentration camps and, later, directly. Many synagogues were turned into collection points for those about to be deported. It was in this period that the rate of suicide among the Jews took a sudden rise. The property of the "transferred" Jews, or of those who had committed suicide, was taken over by the state, as property of "enemies of the people and the country."

German Jewry's public activities were carried on within the framework of the Reichsvereinigung, which in accordance with the law had absorbed all the 1,500 organizations and institutions and the 1,600 religious communal bodies which had existed in Germany in 1939. The last to be absorbed, in January 1943, was the Berlin Community. When emigration ceased, the work of the Reichsvereinigung was restricted to education and social welfare. It supported elementary schools, several high schools and colleges, vocational and agricultural training courses, and language courses, as well as the famous Hochschule fuer die Wissenschaft des Judentums. In July 1942 all Jewish educational institutions were closed down. The Reichsvereinigung also supported Jewish hospitals, children's homes, and homes for the aged. It was forced to assist the Nazis in gathering the Jews who had been earmarked for "transfer." The Reichsvereinigung derived its income from contributions, membership dues, and special taxes imposed on emigrants. In July 1943 the activities of the Reichsvereinigung came to an end. By then, most of its officials, as well as most of those whom it had cared for, had been "transferred" to their deaths, or put into prison. The assets of the Reichsvereinigung (about 170 million marks) were confiscated by the Nazis. A new national body was created, headed by Walter Lustig, at the Jewish hospital in Berlin.

In the "privileged camp" which was known as the *Theresienstadt Ghetto, of the 139,606 Jews interned, 42,103 were from Germany. In January 1943, Leo Baeck was interned there. This ghetto allowed the continuation of Jewish life in some measure. But by the end of the war, only 5,639 German survivors were left in the ghetto.

By the end of 1942 the number of Jews in Germany had been reduced to 51,000, and by the beginning of April the following year to 32,000. On May 19, 1943, Germany was declared *judenrein*. On Sept. 1, 1944, there were still 14,574 Jews in Germany who were not imprisoned. These were, for the most part (97.8%), the spouses of non-Jews, or "half-Jews," who had been defined as Jews by the Nuremberg Laws. On the other hand, in January 1945, there were in concentration and forced labor camps in Germany hundreds of thousands of Jews from various European countries.

The number of Jews who remained free in Germany—openly or underground—has been estimated at 19,000, and those who returned from the concentration camps after the war (including Theresienstadt) at 8,000. Late (January 1942) and doubtful figures provided by the Nazis state that from the beginning of Nazi rule 360,000 Jews had emigrated from Germany. About 160,000 to 180,000 German Jews are estimated to have been murdered by the Nazis in Germany, or to have died as a result of persecution.

See also *Holocaust. [J.LEV.]

Contemporary Period. When the Nazi regime in Germany ended, the general assumption was—in the words of Leo Baeck—that the Holocaust had terminated the thousand-year history of German Jewry and that Jews would not resettle in the country where the massacre of European Jewry had been conceived. This forecast has not proven completely accurate. Jews are again living in Germany and they have rebuilt their communal and social organizations; but numerically they do not exceed 5% of the Jewish population of the country at the time of Hitler's rise to power. Although the Jews form a very diversified group, their relative influence in all spheres of life is but a faint shadow of what it was. After a period of consolidation the Jews of Germany consisted of three main groups: the remnants of German Jewry who had survived the war in Germany; *Displaced Persons (D.P.s) who took temporary refuge in Germany after the war, especially in the American zone; and Jews who returned to Germany or settled there after the war. Those who survived the persecutions and the war in Germany itself had, on the whole, only a tenuous attachment to Judaism. Many had been baptized, and the majority had entered mixed marriages (surviving the Holocaust only with the help of their "Aryan" relatives) and had raised their children as Christians. Among them were also several hundred women who had married Jews, and converted to Judaism. The average age of this group was over 50. The number of Jews in Germany grew in the immediate postwar period, when several thousand German Jews who had survived the concentration camps (especially Theresienstadt) and did not go into D.P. camps returned to Germany. Soon after, a few thousand were able to emigrate to the United States and several hundred went to other countries. Of those who remained, only a part (estimated by H. Maor between 6,000 and 8,000) joined the reestablished Jewish communities.

The D.P.s who arrived in Germany after the war were a "community in transit" and did not regard themselves as a part of German Jewry. At the end of 1946, there was a record number of 160,000 Jewish D.P.s in Germany; the total number of Jewish D.P.s who spent some time in the country is estimated at 200,000. Most of them were in the American Zone, where they neither joined the communities nor had much contact with German Jews. The D.P.s formed their own organization, She'erit ha-Peletah (The Saved Remnant), which had local regional and central committees. In the British Zone (northwest Germany), however, it was the reestablished communities that joined the She'erit ha-Peletah, which had its headquarters at *Bergen-Belsen. In time the refugees, especially those who lived outside the D.P. camps in the urban D.P. assembly centers, established contacts with members of the Jewish communities. When the great stream of *aliyah* and emigration of the She'erit ha-Peletah came to an end in the early 1950s, 12,000 former D.P.s were left in Germany. There were in 1960, according to Maor, about 6,000 former D.P.s in Germany who had become members of the Jewish communities. They represented a sizable portion of the total membership of some of the communities, e.g., 80% in Munich and 40% in Frankfort. No precise data are available on the remaining 6,000. Some may have emigrated, others may be listed as returnees, and still others may have severed all links with the organized Jewish community.

From the end of the war to the beginning of the 1960s, about 6,000 German Jews returned to Germany and some 2,000 Jews from other countries settled there. Since the early 1960s, Germany has received a few hundred more Jewish immigrants, in addition to several thousand returnees. For the most part, these were people who had not adjusted in the countries to which they had emigrated (including Israel). Others hoped that their presence in Germany would speed up the restitution of their property, or the indemnification payments due to them (see *Restitution and Compensation). Still others were simply attracted to Germany by the prevailing economic prosperity. Some prominent people, mostly artists and men-of-letters, returned to Germany, but as a rule they did not join the Jewish communities. In general, the former D.P.s and the returnees were the more active groups, having much closer ties with Judaism than the group of survivors who never left the country.

REESTABLISHMENT OF JEWISH COMMUNITIES. The reestablishment of Jewish communities began shortly after the war, but in the early stages the means at their disposal were quite limited. Various organizations were operating in Germany to care for the victims of Nazism, and included the Jews in their activities. Among these were the organizations of Nazi victims and the Bavarian Red Cross. In Bavaria, the ministry of the interior established a State Commissariat for the care of people who had been persecuted on the basis of race, religion, or political convictions. (The first commissioner, appointed in the fall of 1945, was a non-Jewish Social Democrat; in 1946 a leading Jew, Philip Auerbach, was appointed to this post.) A bureau of the same kind was also established in Hessen. The American Jewish Joint Distribution Committee helped the communities establish themselves, and gradually they were able to assume the main burden of the religious and social services required by their members. The Berlin Jewish community at this time included the four zones of the city. In June 1947 a coordinating committee of Jewish communities in Germany, covering all the zones of occupation, was formed. When the *aliyah* and emigration of the D.P.s came to an end, the communities grew in importance. It was at this time that the German Federal Republic (West) and the German Democratic Republic (East) were established. The interest of the newly founded government of West Germany in strengthening the Jewish communities was shared by the occupation authorities, especially in the American Zone (headed by High Commissioner John J. McCloy). On July 17, 1950, a Zentralrat der Juden in Deutschland ("Central Council of Jews in Germany") was set up with headquarters at Duesseldorf. The formation of the council was encouraged by the authorities, and it became the supreme organ of the Jewish communities in West Germany, achieving that status first in fact and later in law.

While in the immediate postwar years the Jews in Germany had insisted that their stay in the "accursed land" was temporary and that they would soon leave it, by the early 1950s voices began to call for the building of bridges between the Jewish and German peoples. One community leader declared that the Jewish-sponsored idea of dissolving the Jewish communities in Germany should be abandoned, and a rabbi who had returned to Germany even stated that the Jews remaining in the country were charged with reminding the German people of their guilt and their obligation to atone. Such ideas were supported by the government of West Germany and especially by Chancellor Konrad *Adenauer, who felt that in addition to the reparations agreement with Israel, the existence of a Jewish community in Germany and good relations between that community and the German people would be important contributions to the moral and political rehabilitation of Germany in the eyes of the world. To help bring about a reconciliation with the Jewish people, various German organizations and movements, such as the Aktion Suehnezeichen ("Operation Atonement") led by the Protestant theologian Helmut Gollwitzer, the Society for Christian-Jewish Understanding, the Peace With Israel movement headed by Erich Lueth, and others, were formed. It is doubtful, however, whether any of these movements would have made headway had it not been for West Germany's rapid economic recovery, which facilitated the economic absorption of the Jews (most of whom had hitherto maintained themselves by grants or black market activities).

World Jewish organizations, especially the Zionist movement, disapproved of Jewish integration into German life. They regarded it as morally wrong for Jews to be permanently resident in Germany and tried to persuade them to leave the country. When, however, the reparations agreement was signed between the State of Israel, the *Conference on Jewish Material Claims, and the Federal

Figure 23. World War II refugees waiting for Passover supplies from the American Jewish Joint Distribution Committee in Berlin, April 1946. Courtesy A.J.D.C., New York.

Figure 24. Signing of the German-Israel reparations agreement at the Luxembourg Municipality, 1952. Seated from left: Felix Shinnar, Giora Josephthal, Moshe Sharett, Nahum Goldmann. From R. Vogel, *The German Path to Israel*, 1969.

Republic in September 1952, the psychological and political basis for ostracizing the Jews of Germany no longer existed. The Zentralrat became a member of the Claims Conference, and in 1954 the Zionist Executive approved the reestablishment of the Zionist Organization of Germany. (This is not to be confused with the Zionist Organization of the She'erit ha-Peletah, which was disbanded in 1951 as were all other institutions of the She'erit Ha-Peletah.) The Zentralrat also became affiliated with the *World Jewish Congress. Following the reparations agreement and the legislation for indemnification and the restitution of property, the federal government of West Germany and governments of the *Laender* adopted a liberal policy toward the restitution of property to the communities and provided them with regular subsidies for their needs. As a result, the Jewish communities of Germany became among the wealthiest in the world. This process of consolidation was not without its upheavals, struggles, and public scandals, which came before the German courts. Among those sentenced to imprisonment were Aaron Ohrenstein, the rabbi of Munich, and Philip Auerbach, who committed suicide in prison. There were also court proceedings contesting the legality of several community councils.

Anti-Semitism continued to exist in the country, perhaps exacerbated by the problem of bringing Nazi criminals to justice and the demand for the exclusion of Nazis from public office and government service. In fact, Neo-Nazi movements sprang up, Jewish cemeteries were desecrated, swastikas were daubed on walls, and anti-Semitic propaganda was disseminated. On the other hand, there were signs of a genuine change of heart: German youth was educated toward democracy, Jewish literature and literature on Jews appeared on the bookstands, there were exhibitions on Jewish themes, etc. The authorities assisted the communities in the construction of new synagogues and undertook the reconstruction of synagogues of historical value in places where there was no Jewish community (such as the Rashi Synagogue in Worms).

In October 1967, the number of Jews registered with the Jewish communities in West Germany, including West Berlin, was 26,226 (this includes 1,300 Jews living in Frankfort who were not members of the community but registered as Jews in the census). It is estimated that there are 5,000 to 10,000 additional Jews in the country who are not listed with the communities. According to the figures for Oct. 1, 1966, the largest communities were in West Berlin (5,991 members), Frankfort (4,168), Munich (3,345), Duesseldorf (1,579), Hamburg (1,500), and Cologne (1,304). Because of the high average age, the demographic composition of German Jewry is highly abnormal. The death rate greatly exceeds the birth rate, e.g., in 1963–64 there were 482 deaths and only 69 births. In spite of the wide gulf between Jews and Germans, the rate of intermarriage is among the highest in the world. In the period 1951–58, there were 679 marriages in which both partners were Jewish, as against 2,009 mixed marriages; 72.5% of the Jewish men and 23.6% of the Jewish women who married chose non-Jewish partners. (For the period 1901–30 the respective figures were 19.6% for men and 12.2% for women.)

Several aged rabbis returned to Germany, and a few came there from other countries, e.g., the United States, Israel, and Britain, to serve for a limited period.There was a serious scarcity of teachers, religious articles, and community workers. The work of the communities was generally in the hands of a salaried staff. Jewish schools were established in Frankfort and Munich, while elsewhere the community provided religious instruction during after-school hours. There were social welfare departments in the communities and a central welfare office (Zentralwohlfahrtsstelle) in Frankfort. Many communities maintained homes for the aged and summer camps for children. German-language Jewish weeklies were published in Duesseldorf and Munich. The Juedischer Verlag (Jewish Publishing Co.) in Berlin was reestablished, and another publishing house, Ner Tamid, was opened. The Zionist organization had branches in most of the communities, as did Jewish women's organizations and youth movements. In most places there were local committees of the *Keren Hayesod and the *Jewish National Fund, and in Berlin, Frankfort, and Munich there were B'nai B'rith Lodges. An outstanding contribution to the postwar rehabilitation of Jews in Germany was made by Karl Marx (1897–1966), who returned to Germany in 1945, joined the Zionist movement, and founded the *Allgemeine Wochenzeitung des Judentums* ("General Jewish Weekly") in Duesseldorf. He regarded as his task the "building of a bridge" between the Jewish people and Israel, on the one hand, and Germany, on the other. He had close connections with the first president of the Federal Republic, Theodor Heuss, with Chancellor Adenauer, and with Social Democratic leaders and tried to serve as a link between them and the leaders of Israel and world Jewry. A number of Jews assumed important public offices. Among them were Paul Hertz, a Social Democratic senator in Berlin; Herbert A. *Weichmann, President of the Bundesrat and mayor of Hamburg; Joseph Neuberger, the minister of justice in North Rhine-Westphalia (who returned to Germany from Israel); and Ludwig Rosenberg, chairman of the Federation of Trade Unions. Several scholars and prominent artists, including the actors Ernst *Deutsch and Fritz *Kortner, also returned to Germany.

Despite their manifold activities, the Jewish communities in Germany rest on weak foundations because of their abnormal demographic structure, the inadequacy of Jewish education, and the abyss that continues to exist between the Jews and German society. The replacement of the expression *Deutsche Juden* ("German Jews") by the term *Juden in Deutschland* ("Jews in Germany") may be taken as an indication of the strangeness that Jews feel in Germany and their anxiety about the future.

There is only a tiny remnant of Jews in the German Democratic Republic. Their number is estimated at 1,500, of whom 900 live in East Berlin. Although there is no ban on religious practice, the communist regime makes an effort to obscure the identity of Jews. Only a few of the public figures who are of Jewish origin have retained any connection with organized Judaism. One of these was the author Arnold *Zweig who was president of the Academy of Arts. [CH.Y.]

Relations With Israel. Prior to the establishment of diplomatic relations between the State of Israel and the German Federal Republic (West Germany) in March 1965, relations between the two states were confined to the agreement of Sept. 10, 1952, for global recompense of the material damage inflicted on the Jewish people by the National-Socialist regime (see *Restitution and Indemnification). An Israel Mission was in charge of the implementation of this agreement as the only official representative of Israel in the Federal Republic. No German counterpart existed in Israel, in view of vehement opposition there to extending relations beyond the commercial limits of the agreement. The Israel mission was, however, authorized to grant entry visas to Israel, where the British consulate, acting for the Federal Republic, granted entry visas to West Germany. The value of Israel's purchases under the agreement amounted to 60–80 million annually. As a result of the contact with the large number of suppliers, relations developed and reached far beyond the field of commerce. Consequently, and in view of the Federal Republic's impressive economic and political recovery from 1953 onward, a need was felt for more clearly defined relations, as well as for the presence of an official representative in Israel. In a letter to the Israel mission, written in March 1956, the then foreign secretary, H. von Brentano, officially proposed the establishment of a mission in Israel whose status would be parallel to that of the Israel mission. Although this proposal was accepted by Israel, it was not implemented by Germany, since the German Foreign Office feared the Arab States would react to the establishment of diplomatic relations between Israel and the Federal Republic by recognizing the German Democratic Republic (East Germany) as a second sovereign German state. Such a development would be contrary to the Hallstein Doctrine (adopted in May 1958), whose basic aim was Germany's reunification.

Figure 25. The new synagogue of Hanover, built with the assistance of the Federal German government. Courtesy Hanover Municipality. Photo Hermann Friedrich, Hanover.

Figure 26. Rolf Pauls, first German ambassador to Israel, presenting his credentials to President Zalman Shazar, Jerusalem, 1965. From R. Vogel, *The German Path to Israel*, 1969.

On March 7, 1965 (two years after Ludwig Erhard had become chancellor of the Federal Republic) an offer to establish diplomatic relations with Israel was made; the timing of the offer was due to an official visit to Cairo by Walter Ulbricht, head of the Democratic Republic. Ulbricht's visit was considered by the Federal Republic's government as provocation by President Nasser of the United Arab Republic and an overture to the establishment of diplomatic relations with the Democratic Republic. In consequence of this visit and the publicity campaign initiated by Nasser against the supply of defensive arms to Israel by the Federal Republic (although Egypt received incomparably more weapons from the Soviet Union), diplomatic relations were broken off between Germany and Egypt and most of the Arab States. The Israel government and the Knesset accepted the West German offer, and on May 12, 1965, diplomatic relations were finally established; exchange of ambassadors followed in July 1965. From July 1965, relations developed satisfactorily between the Federal Republic and Israel. The visit to Israel of the former Chancellor, Konrad Adenauer, in May 1966 was a significant event. It demonstrated his friendship for Israel and for the former prime minister, David *Ben-Gurion. In November 1967 the former chancellor, Professor Erhard, paid a visit to Israel, which also symbolized the gradual normalization of relations. At the inauguration of the new Knesset building in 1966, the Federal Republic was represented by the president of its parliament, Eugen Gerstenmaier. An Israel-German chamber of commerce was established with Walter Hesselbach, a leading figure in the West German economy and an ardent friend of Israel, and the former minister of finance, Franz Etzel, at its head. Long-term loans for development were granted by the Federal Republic to Israel in 1966 and subsequent years under an agreement of May 12, 1965. Similar loans had been granted for the development of the Negev in the years 1961–65, agreed upon at the historic meeting between Ben-Gurion and Adenauer at the Waldorf Astoria Hotel in New York on March 14, 1960. Visitors from all walks of life subsequently went from the Federal Republic to Israel, and these visits furthered better understanding between the two countries. Even in the five years preceding the establishment of diplomatic relations, about 40,000 young people aged between 18 and 25 years from the Federal Republic had visited Israel. The first German ambassador to Israel, Rolf Pauls, made unceasing efforts for the improvement of relations. Asher Ben-Nathan was Israel's first ambassador to the Federal Republic. [F.E.S.]

Bibliography: The major bibliography is *German Jewry* (1958), supplemented by *From Weimar to Hitler: Germany 1918–1933* (1964[2]); *Persecution and Resistance under the Nazis* (1960[2]); and

After Hitler (1963), all published by the Wiener Library, London. These are brought up to date in the *Yearbooks of the Leo Baeck Institute* (YLBI, 1956ff.). The *Bibliography of Jewish Communities in Europe* (BJCE), compiled by B. Ophir in the Yad Vashem Institute, Jerusalem, is the most complete for an economic, social and regional history. The following periodicals are indispensable: BLBI; HJ; *Juedische Familien-Forschung;* JJGL; JJLG; JJV; MGADJ; MGWJ; *Zeitschrift fuer Demographie und Statistik der Juden;* ZGJD. GENERAL: *Festschrift zum siebzigsten Geburtstage Martin Philippsons* (1916); J. R. Marcus, *Rise and Destiny of the German Jew* (1934); F. Kobler, *Juden und Judentum in deutschen Briefen* (1935); M. Lowenthal, *Jews of Germany* (1939); Baron, Social[2]; H. G. Adler, *Die Juden in Deutschland* (1960); K. Schilling (ed.), *Monumenta Judaica,* 3 vols. (1963); W. Kampmann, *Deutsche und Juden* (1963); F. Boehm and W. Dirks, *Judentum: Schicksal, Wesen und Gegenwart,* 2 vols. (1965); I. Elbogen and E. Sterling, *Geschichte der Juden in Deutschland* (1967); H. H. Ben-Sasson (ed.), *Toledot Am Yisrael,* 3 vols. (1969); idem, *Ha-Yehudim mul ha-Reformazyah* (1969); H. M. Graupe, *Die Entstehung des modernen Judentums* (1969); M. Kreutzberger (ed.), *Bibliothek und Archiv* (1970). MEDIEVAL: Aronius, Regesten; G. Caro, *Sozial- und Wirtschaftsgeschichte der Juden im Mittelalter,* 2 vols. (1924); Finkelstein, Middle Ages; Germ Jud; B. Altmann, in: PAAJR, 10 (1940), 5–98; G. Kisch, *Jewry-Law in Medieval Germany* (1949); idem, Jews in Medieval Germany (1949); S. Landau, *Christian-Jewish Relations* (1959); J. R. Marcus, *Jews in the Medieval World* (1960); J. Trachtenberg, *The Devil and the Jews* (1961); C. Roth (ed.), *Dark Ages* (1966), 122–42, 162–74; I. A. Agus, *Heroic Age of Franco-German Jewry* (1969). MERCANTILISM AND ABSOLUTISM: J. R. Marcus, *Communal Sick-Care in the German Ghetto* (1947); H. Schnee, *Die Hoffinanz und der moderne Staat,* 6 vols. (1953–67); H. Kellenbenz, *Sephardim an der unteren Elbe* (1958); S. Stern, *Der Preussische Staat und die Juden,* 2 vols. (1962); idem, *Court Jew* (1950); B.-Z. Abrahams (ed. and tr.), *The Life of Glueckel of Hameln* (1962). ENLIGHTENMENT AND EMANCIPATION: I. Freund, *Die Emanzipation der Juden in Preussen,* 2 vols. (1912); M. J. Kohler, *Jewish Rights at the Congresses of Vienna (1814–15) and Aix-la-Chapelle (1818)* (1918); M. Eliav, *Ha-Ḥinnukh ha-Yehudi be-Germanyah bi-Ymei ha-Haskalah ve-ha-Emanzipazyah* (1960); A. Shohet, *Im Ḥillufei Tekufot* (1960); J. Katz, *Tradition and Crisis* (1961); N. N. Glatzer, *Dynamics of Emancipation* (1965); M. A. Meyer, *Origin of the Modern Jew* (1967); H. Fischer, *Judentum, Staat und Heer in Preussen* (1968). 19TH AND 20TH CENTURY: F. Theilhaber, *Der Untergang der deutschen Juden* (1921); G. Krojanker (ed.), *Juden in der deutschen Literatur* (1922); H. Silbergleit, *Die Bevoelkerungs- und Berufsverhaeltnisse der Juden im deutschen Reich* (1930); J. Lestschinsky, *Das Wirtschafliche Schicksal des deutschen Judentums* (1932); F. R. Bienenfeld, *The Germans and the Jews* (1939); H. Schwab, *History of Orthodox Jewry in Germany* (1950); idem, *Jewish Rural Communities in Germany* (1956); R. Lichtheim, *Die Geschichte des deutschen Zionismus* (1954); S. Adler-Rudel, *Ostjuden in Deutschland 1880–1940* (1959); S. Kaznelson, *Juden im deutschen Kulturbereich* (1959); E. Simon, *Aufbau im Untergang* (1959); S. Liptzin, *Germany's Stepchildren* (1961); R. Weltsch (ed.), *Deutsches Judentum* (1963); W. G. Plaut (ed.), *Rise of Reform Judaism* (1963); A. Altmann, *Studies in Nineteenth Century Jewish Intellectual History* (1964); W. Schochow, *Deutsch-juedische Geschichtswissenschaft* (1966); J. Toury, *Die Politschen Orientierungen der Juden in Deutschland* (1966); E. G. Loewenthal (ed.), *Bewaehrung im Untergang* (1966); H. Liebschuetz, *Das Judentum im deutschen Geschichtsbild von Hegel bis Max Weber* (1967); D. Philipson, *Reform Movement in Judaism* (1967); E. Hamberger, *Juden im oeffentlichen Leben Deutschlands* (1968); U. Tal, *Yahadut ve-Nazrut ba-Reikh ha-Sheni* (1969). ANTI-SEMITISM: P. Massing, *Rehearsal for Destruction* (1949); A. Leschnitzer, *Magic Background of Modern Antisemitism* (1956); P. G. J. Pulzer, *Rise of Political Antisemitism in Germany and Austria* (1964); J. Toury, *Mehumah u-Mevukhah be-Mahpekhat 1848* (1968); E. Sterling, *Judenhass* (1969); G. L. Mosse, *Germans and Jews* (1970). HOLOCAUST: N. Bentwich, *Refugees from Germany* (1936); G. O. Warburg, *Six Years of Hitler* (1939); E. H. Boehm, *We Survived* (1949); E. Kogon, *Theory and Practice of Hell* (1950); E. Reichmann, *Hostages of Civilization* (1951); B. Blau, *Das Ausnahmerecht fuer die Juden Deutschlands* (1954[2]); L. Poliakov, *Harvest of Hate* (1954); L. Kochan, *Pogrom, 10 Nov. 1938* (1957); H. Tramer (ed.), *In zwei Welten, Siegfried Moses zum 75. Geburtstag* (1962); S. Colodner, *Jewish Education in Nazi Germany* (1964); H. H. Freeden, *Juedisches Theater in Nazideutschland* (1964); W. Mosse and A. Paucker (eds.), *Entscheidungsjahr, 1932* (1965); H. Buchheim et al., *Anatomy of the SS State* (1965); H. Eschwege, *Kennzeichen* (1966); H. Genschel, *Die Verdraengung der Juden aus der Wirtschaft im Dritten Reich* (1966); R. Hilberg, *Destruction of the European Jews* (1967); G. Reitlinger, *Final Solution* (1968); L. Poliakov and J. Wulf, *Das Dritte Reich und die Juden* (1955); International Military Tribunal, *Trial of the Major War Criminals,* 23 vols. (1949), index; W. Scheffler, *Judenverfolgung im Dritten Reich* (1964); idem, *Die Nationalsozialistsche Judenpolitik* (1960); K. J. Ball-Kaduri, *Das Leben der Juden in Deutschland im Jahre 1933* (1963); idem, *Vor der Katastrophe—Juden in Deutschland 1934–1939* (1967); idem, in: *Yad Vashem Studies,* 7 (1968), 205–18; S. Esh, *ibid.,* 2 (1958), 79–93; S. Colodner, *ibid.,* 3 (1959), 161–85; Simon, in: YLBI, 1 (1956), 68–104; Freeden, *ibid.,* 142–62; Gaertner, *ibid.,* 123–41; Edelheim-Muesham, *ibid.,* 5 (1960), 308–329; S. Esch, in: YWSS 7 (1968), 19–38; D. Schoenbaum, *Hitler's Social Revolution: Class and Status in Nazi Germany, 1933–39;* G. Mosse, *Germans and Jews* (1970). POST-WAR: L. W. Schwarz, *The Redeemers* (1953); H. Maor, *Ueber den Wiederaufbau der juedischen Gemeinden in Deutschland seit 1945* (1961); N. Muhlen, *The Survivors* (1962); A. Elon, *Journey through a Haunted Land* (1967); K. Gershon, *Postscript* (1969); L. Katcher, *Post Mortem: The Jews of Germany Today* (1968); AJYB (1945–); F. E. Shinnar, *Be-Ol Koraḥ u-Regashot* (1967); *Die Juden in Deutschland 1951/52–1958/59: ein Almanach* (1959); *Vom Schicksal gepraegt . . .* (1957); H. G. van Dam, *Die Juden in Deutschland seit 1945* (1965); B. Engelmann, *Deutschland ohne Juden* (1970). RELATIONS WITH ISRAEL; R. Vogel, *The German Path to Israel* (1969); I. Deutschkron, *Israel und die Deutschen* (1970).

GERNSHEIM, FRIEDRICH (1839–1916), German composer, conductor, and teacher. Born in Worms, of an old Rhineland family, Gernsheim was a child prodigy, both as performer and composer. He taught and conducted at Cologne and Rotterdam, and from 1890 in Berlin. Finally he became director of a master class in composition at the Prussian Academy of Fine Arts. During his early years as conductor he promoted the works of Brahms. His own compositions, which number over a hundred, include piano and chamber works, four symphonies, cantatas, choral compositions, and songs. Their idiom is generally conservative, although innovations appear in his late period. A

Friedrich Gernsheim, German composer. Etching by Hermann Struck, 1904. Jerusalem, J.N.U.L., Schwadron Collection.

renewal of interest in Gernsheim's compositions was noticeable in the 1960s, especially in Germany. His attitude to Judaism seems to have been passive although he gave the subtitle *Mirjam* to his third symphony, op. 54, in which he depicted Miriam's song of triumph at the Red Sea; and he also wrote an *Elohenu* for cello and orchestra or piano (1882). The greater part of his papers and manuscripts were deposited in 1966 at the Jewish National and University Library in Jerusalem.

Bibliography: K. Holl, *Friederich Gernsheim: Leben, Erscheinung und Werk* (1928); Grove, Dict; MGG, s.v. (includes bibliography).

[B.B.]

GERONA (Lat. **Gerunda**; Heb. גירונא), city in Catalonia, northeastern Spain. It had one of the most important Jewish communities in the region, probably dating back to the end of the ninth century. Houses in the Jewish quarter are mentioned in documents from the mid-tenth century. Jews who owned land in Gerona and its surroundings had to pay a tithe to the Church. In 1160 they were permitted to lease shops built outside the city walls. The community was concentrated in a locality still called Montjuich (Jews' Mount). Remains of the public baths and tombstones have been preserved. Jews began to take part in the administration in the 13th century. Noteworthy were the *baile* (bailiff) Bondia Gracián, *Benveniste de Porta, and Astruc *Ravaya and his son Joseph, both members of the court of Pedro III of Aragon. They served as administrative officers and their signatures in Hebrew appear on numerous documents. Solomon b. Abraham *Adret cooperated with them in the Jewish communal leadership. About 1271 the communities of Gerona and *Besalú, which formed a joint *collecta*, or tax administrative unit, paid a total of 20,000 sólidos, approximately half the sum paid by the community of *Barcelona. In the 13th century the priests of the local cathedral chapter instituted the custom of casting stones on the Jewish quarter from the cathedral tower at Easter, sometimes causing much damage. In 1278 Pedro III threatened to hold the bishop responsible for such actions. At Easter 1331 rioters broke into the Jewish quarter. In 1285 the Jews in Gerona took part in its defense against the French; they suffered when the latter occupied the city, and again when it was recaptured by Pedro III. From the end of the 13th century Jews were forced out of their positions in the local administration, as well as from various economic activities: no further mention is made of Jewish landowners cultivating their own land, and some Jews of Gerona settled in other cities under royal protection. Nevertheless, the Gerona community absorbed Jews expelled from France in 1306.

In 1258 James I of Aragon empowered the Jews in Gerona and nearby Besalú to appoint five persons to punish tax offenders. In 1279 Pedro III granted Benedict Jonah of Gerona and Solomon b. Abraham Adret sole jurisdiction over the community. In 1341 certain notables from Barcelona drafted regulations for the Gerona community concerning the election of trustees, auditors, "criers" *(makhrizim)*, and a dual council with 26 members in one section and 16 members in the other. The community was dominated by an oligarchy, which in 1386 was torn by a violent quarrel resulting in the intervention of the authorities. In April 1391 the community of Gerona was given a new constitution, specifying the names of 23 persons entitled to serve on the council, some for life and others for a three-year term. The council was to appoint magistrates *(borerim)*, trustees, and a salaried treasurer and tax collector. The latter had to be chosen from among the lesser taxpayers, and relatives of trustees were not eligible for the post. In 1459 John II provided for the election by lot of a treasurer, trustees, two magistrates, and two tax assessors.

Part of the old Jewish quarter in Gerona, Spain. Photo S. Marti, Gerona.

During the 1391 persecutions the majority of the Jews of Gerona chose martyrdom. A few were converted to Christianity, mainly merchants and artisans. Some Jews found refuge in the citadel and others managed to escape to *Perpignan. The community had already been reconstituted by 1392. The Jews of Gerona were compelled to send two representatives to the disputation of *Tortosa, which resulted in an intensified tendency to conversion as well as increased attacks on Jews. However, the city authorities and King Ferdinand took action to protect the Jews in Gerona (1413–14). In 1415 the king ordered that the synagogue in Calle San Lorenzo, and the adjoining public bath, should be restored to the Jews. The synagogue was partly destroyed during the civil war in 1462–72.

The decline of the Gerona community continued throughout the 15th century. In 1431 the last treasurer *(gabbai)* of the charitable trust *(hekdesh)* became converted; Alfonso V ordered him to remain in office and to distribute the money at his disposal to both Christian and Jewish poor, but mainly to the Christians as the majority of the Jews had become converted. In 1442 the area of the Jewish quarter was reduced. A reflection of the state of affairs in the community in 1470 is the will of the widow of one Solomon Shalom, expressing the desire that her Jewish son and Christian daughter should live in peace and unity. In 1486 the Jews were prohibited from owning shops with windows and doors facing the main street. When the edict of expulsion of the Jews from Spain was issued in 1492, there was a small community in Gerona. Most of its members went into exile. The remains of the synagogue were sold for ten florins to a canon of the cathedral and the remaining property owned by Jews to the municipal notary and other citizens.

At the height of its prosperity the Gerona community was a center of learning and produced celebrated scholars, many of whom are known by the cognomen "Gerondi," i.e., originating from Gerona: their Italian descendants called themselves *Ghirondi. In the 1230s Gerona was one of the centers of the movement opposing the teachings of *Maimonides. Distinguished scholars active there at the period were *Jonah Gerondi and his great disciple *Naḥmanides, who wrote an account of the disputation of *Barcelona for the bishop of Gerona. The primary importance of Gerona in Jewish history is that it became the first center of kabbalism in Spain; a group was formed there in the mid-13th century, in which *Ezra b. Solomon, *Azriel b. Menahem, and their associates were leading figures. Naḥmanides also had connexions with their *Ḥavurah Kedoshah* ("Sacred Association"), which had a decisive influence on the development of Kabbalah. Other noteworthy personalities included *Zeraḥiah ha-Levi Gerondi, who left Gerona while a youth; Jonah Gerondi the Younger (active 1270s); *Nissim b. Reuben Gerondi (mid-14th century); David Bonjorn, a native of Perpignan (lived in Gerona at the end of the 14th century); *Abraham b. Isaac ha-Levi, a distinguished communal leader (14th century); and in the 15th century, Bonastruc *Desmaestre and Bonjudah Yeḥasel Hakashlari who both took part in the Tortosa disputation.

Bibliography: Baer, Spain, index; Baer, Urkunden, index; J. Girbal, *Los Judíos de Gerona* (1870); G. Scholem, *Reshit ha-Kabbalah* (1948), 127–61; A. Masiá de Ros, *Gerona en la guerra civil en tiempo de Juan II* (1943); Prats and Millás-Vallicrosa, in: *Sefarad*, 5 (1945), 131ff.; 12 (1952), 297–335; Angeles, *ibid.*, 13 (1953), 287–309; Gallarty, *ibid.*, 19 (1959), 301–20; Prats, *ibid.*, 21 (1961), 48–57; Casanovas, *ibid.*, 23 (1963), 22–25; 25 (1965), 49–58.

[H.B.]

GERONDI (Gerundi), ISAAC BEN JUDAH (13th century), Spanish Hebrew poet. It has been suggested that Gerondi may perhaps be identified with Isaac ha-Nasi of Barcelona (a nephew of Sheshet ha-Nasi) whose poetry is lauded by *Al-Ḥarizi (*Taḥkemoni*, ed. by A. Kaminka (1899), 350–1). Gerondi's surname, Ibn Fasad (בן פשאד), has so far not been satisfactorily explained. The Latin transcription of this name, *Avenpesat*, is that of many Jews of Aragon, Navarre, and Marseilles (Baer, Urkunden, 1 (1929), 1095 s.v. *Avenpesat*). The designation *ha-Nadiv*, found in some of his acrostics, may refer to his father only. About 20 of Gerondi's poems are extant; among these are the individual parts of his *kerovah*, *"Va-Areẓ Etnappal Lifnei Dar Gevohai"* for *Rosh Ha-Shanah. The composition, in which poems by other authors are interpolated, is to be found in the rites of Algiers, Tunis, Constantine, and Tlemcen; and while the text in all four is the same, the incidental poems vary.

Bibliography: Derenbourg, in: WZJT, 5 (1844), 404, 407, 478; Landshuth, Ammudei, 120–1; Zunz, Lit Poesie, 481–2; Halberstam, in: *Jeschurun*, 7 (1871), 38 (Heb. pt.); Luzzatto, in: *Oẓar Tov*, 3 (1880), 42; Davidson, Oẓar, 4 (1933), 421.

[J.M.Sch.]

GERONDI, JACOB BEN SHESHET (mid-13th century), kabbalist in Gerona, Catalonia. His works include: *Meshiv Devarim Nekhoḥim* (ed. G. Vajda, 1969), directed against Samuel ibn Tibbon's *Ma'amar Yikkavu ha-Mayim; Sha'ar ha-Shamayim* (published in *Oẓar Neḥmad* (1860), 153–65, and previously in *Likkutim me-Rav Hai Ga'on* (Warsaw, 1798), 15–25)—a treatise also known as *Moshe Kibbel* from its opening words; and *Ha-Emunah ve-ha-Bittaḥon* (first published in *Arzei Levanon* (Venice, 1601)) and in *Kitvei ha-Ramban* (ed. Chavel, 1964). In early manuscripts *Ha-Emunah ve-ha-Bittaḥon* was attributed to *Naḥmanides. Jacob Reifmann suggested that it was written by *Baḥya b. Asher, and other scholars accepted his conjecture. After this had been disproved by A. Tauber, G. Scholem was the first to assign the composition to Jacob b. Sheshet on the basis of comparing *Ha-Emunah ve-ha-Bittaḥon* with *Meshiv Devarim Nekhoḥim*. Recently it has become apparent that in several places in *Meshiv Devarim Nekhoḥim*, Jacob b. Sheshet makes reference to some items, stating "as I have written"; in these cases the subject under discussion is not found in *Meshiv Devarim Nekhoḥim* but in *Ha-Emunah ve-ha-Bittaḥon*. The work has been published in several editions; that by C. B. Chavel retains the errors of previous printings.

Although Jacob b. Sheshet and his works are not widely mentioned in the kabbalistic literature of the late 13th and early 14th century, they had a marked influence on this literature. Large sections of *Ha-Emunah ve-ha-Bittaḥon* were included in the works of Baḥya b. Asher, and Menahem b. Benjamin *Recanati also used the work in several places. *Meshiv Devarim Nekhoḥim*, too, had great influence. Entire homilies were copied by important kabbalists such as Baḥya b. Asher, Recanati, the anonymous author of **Ma'arekhet ha-Elohut*, and Todros *Abulafia. Traces of *Sha'ar ha-Shamayim* have been discovered in the works of Baḥya b. Asher, and *Isaac b. Samuel of Acre copied an important section of it. Jacob b. Sheshet was an outstanding opponent of what he believed to be the heretical tendencies of philosophy, which, he believed, deny: (1) the true essence of the Torah, considering it merely as a sociopolitical theory designed only to regulate the physical needs of the man and society; (2) the creation of the world; (3) divine providence; (4) retribution. Such heresy results in the denial of the value of prayer and of the possibility of man's asking his needs of God.

In *Meshiv Devarim Nekhoḥim* he formulates the kabbalistic meaning of these basic conceptions. A great part of the work is devoted to the question of the creation of the world. Like other kabbalists he is far from holding the traditional conception of creation out of nothing; however, his commentary to Genesis differs from that of his contemporary kabbalists whose works he knew well. Jacob b. Sheshet posits a continuous emanation from the divine realm, i.e., the world of the *Sefirot*, to the physical world. To construct this continuity two main elements, heavenly matter and earthly matter, are found in the world of the *Sefirot;* they evolved until the heavenly and the earthly hylic substances were formed. Thus, according to Jacob b. Sheshet, Genesis is not an expression of a paradigm, i.e., a description of the creation of the physical world which repeats the formation of the world of the *Sefirot*. It is rather a continuous description, beginning with the creation within the world of the *Sefirot* and ending with the physical stage of the primal divine element.

Bibliography: G. Scholem, *Reshit ha-Kabbalah* (1948), 132; idem, *Ursprung und Anfaenge der Kabbala* (1962), 334–9; G. Vajda, *Recherches sur la philosophie et la Kabbale* (1962), 8–113; idem (ed.), in: J. B. S. Gerondi, *Meshiv Devarim Nekhoḥim* (1969), 11–17, 67–215; E. Gottlieb, *ibid.*, 18–63; idem, *Ha-Kabbalah be-Khitvei R. Baḥya b. Asher* (1970), 10–13, 96–143; idem, in: *Tarbiz*, 37 (1968), 294–317.

[E.G.]

GERONDI, MOSES BEN SOLOMON D'ESCOLA (second half of 13th century), *paytan* of Gerona, Catalonia. Gerondi was related to *Naḥmanides, who in 1267 sent a letter from Jerusalem requesting that his greetings be conveyed to Gerondi—his "son and pupil"—whose poem he had read with great emotion on the Mount of Olives. He may have had in mind the *seliḥah, "Yerushalayim Ir ha-Kodesh," printed at the conclusion of Naḥmanides' commentary to the Pentateuch. Gerondi is known to be the author of some other liturgical poems.

Bibliography: Gross, Gal Jud, 147; Landshuth, Ammudei, 235, 259; Zunz, Gesch, 482; Davidson, Oẓar, 4 (1933), 448. [Jo.H./Ed.]

GERONDI, SAMUEL BEN MESHULLAM (c. 1300), scholar of Gerona, Catalonia. Hardly any biographical details are known of him. Gerondi's fame rests primarily on his *Ohel Mo'ed* (1 (Jerusalem, 1886); 2 (Jerusalem, 1904)), a comprehensive code consisting only of such laws as are of practical application. The book is divided into 4 parts: (1) *Ma'arekhet Tamid,* on the reading of the *Shema,* prayer, blessings, *tefillin, mezuzah, ẓiẓit;* appended is a separate section ("gate") devoted to morals and ethics; (2) *Avodat ha-Mishkan,* the laws of ritual slaughter, *terefot,* ritual law, including laws of marriage; (3) *Mishmeret ha-Kodesh,* on the Sabbath and the **eruv;* (4) *Yare'aḥ le-Mo'adim,* on the festivals. Each part is subdivided into chapters, sections, and subsections called "gates," "roads," and "paths," respectively. In this work, written after 1320, the author quotes extensively from the early Spanish, Provençal, and German scholars. Like the *Toledot Adam ve-Ḥavvah* of his contemporary, *Jeroham b. Meshullam, Gerondi's work was to a large extent superseded by the *Arba'ah Turim* of *Jacob b. Asher, which fulfilled essentially the same task in a far more comprehensive manner and which was superior both in form and style. Joseph *Caro is almost the sole authority to quote Gerondi. His work, as it has come down, is an abridged version by the author himself of a larger work which is no longer extant.

Bibliography: Gruenhut, in: JQR, 11 (1898/99), 345–9. [I.T.-S.]

GERONDI, SOLOMON BEN ISAAC (13th century), Spanish liturgical poet. Gerondi was a student of *Naḥmanides (see *Tashbeẓ,* no. 456). According to L. Zunz he composed five poems which include his variation of a favorite theme among medieval poets, the "Thirteen Attributes of God"; *"Shav min ha-Pesilim,"* a hymn on the patriarch Abraham; and an elegy for the Ninth of *Av (*Shekhurat ve-Lo mi-Yayin*). The latter became very popular among Sephardi and Ashkenazi Jews.

Bibliography: Zunz, Lit Poesie, 482f.; Zunz, Poesie, 144, 309; Schirmann, Sefarad, 2 (1956), 326–8; Davidson, Oẓar, 4 (1933), 474. [Ed.]

GERONDI, ZERAHIAH BEN ISAAC HA-LEVI (12th century), rabbinical scholar and poet. His father, Isaac ha-Yiẓhari ben Zerahiah ha-Levi Gerondi, was a Hebrew poet and talmudic scholar in Spain. His poetry was included in the rites of the communities of Avignon, Carpentras, Montpellier, Oran, and Tlemcen. Zerahiah, born in Gerona, Spain, left his native city in his youth, possibly to escape from his many enemies there, and settled in Provence. In Narbonne he studied under *Moses b. Joseph, as well as under *Abraham b. Isaac and *Joseph ibn Plat. He lived for many years in Lunel, which he was compelled to leave on several occasions because of disputes. In Lunel he was the teacher of Samuel, the son of Judah ibn *Tibbon. Judah characterized Zerahiah as unique in his generation, called him his superior in knowledge, and extolled the stylistic excellence of his letters and poems (I. Abrahems (ed.), *Hebrew Ethical Wills,* 1 (1926), 72). Zerahiah was proficient in Arabic as well as in philosophy and astronomy, having acquired a knowledge of the latter in Provence. At the age of 19 he composed a *piyyut* in Aramaic and began to write his chief halakhic work, *Ha-Ma'or* ("The Luminary"), which he completed in the 1180s. It is divided into two parts—*Ha-Ma'or ha-Katan* ("The Lesser Luminary"—a play on Lunel, "the moon") on *Berakhot,* many tractates of the order *Mo'ed,* and *Ḥullin*; and *Ha-Ma'or ha-Gadol* ("The Great Luminary"—a play on his name Zerahiah), on *Nashim* and *Nezikin.* (These have several times been published separately, often together with Isaac Alfasi's commentary, and from 1552 appeared in the Venice edition of the Talmud.) This work, which is deeply critical of *Alfasi, constitutes part of the literature of criticism and is representative of the approach adopted by *Abraham b. David of Posquières in his criticism of Maimonides. In many instances Zerahiah preferred the version of the talmudic text as emended by Rashi, and he relied to a considerable extent on the methodology adopted by the northern French commentators, thus combining in his work the principles of the halakhic and exegetical schools of Spain and France which merged in Provence. The *Ma'or* on *Rosh Ha-Shanah* 20b contains a comprehensive exposition on the calendar and the principles of intercalation, Zerahiah having found it necessary to reaffirm the views of the Talmud against those who deviated from it. Many generations of halakhists were influenced by the *Ma'or,* which, however, was strongly criticized by several scholars (especially Naḥmanides) who composed works in defense of Alfasi.

Zerahiah also wrote *Sefer ha-Ẓava,* a sequel to his earlier work, in which he endeavored to show that Alfasi had disregarded the accepted principles of talmudic interpretation (see Rabad, *Temim De'im,* 28a–29b, no. 225). In the acrimonious dispute between Abraham b. David and himself, Zerahiah came off second best in a halakhic exchange of letters (D. Crachman, *Divrei ha-Rivot,* 1908). Zerahiah wrote a criticism of Abraham's *Ba'alei ha-Nefesh* (published together with that work, Venice, 1741; Berlin, 1762) and attacked him in *Sela ha-Maḥaloket,* to which Abraham retaliated by severely criticizing *Ha-Ma'or* (*Katuv Sham,* ed. by I. D. Bergman (1957), introd., 26, 39, 42). Zerahiah was also the author of *Hilkhot Sheḥitah u-Vedikah, Sefer Pitḥei Niddah,* a commentary on the tractate *Kinnim,* and of responsa. The Sephardi *maḥzor* contains 18 of his *piyyutim,* one of which contains a reference to the Crusader rule in Jerusalem. [H.H.B.-S.]

His brother Berechiah ben Isaac ha-Levi, also called "Yiẓhari" (12th century), was a Spanish liturgical poet and Talmud scholar. According to Gross, the epithet "Yiẓhari" refers to the name of a Spanish town (perhaps Oliva or Olivares) where his ancestors had lived. He also was born in Gerona (Spain) but lived in Lunel, Provence. In one section of his *Sefer ha-Ma'or,* Zerahiah ha-Levi answers a halakhic question posed by his brother, and he also refers to Berechiah in a poem at the end of his *Hassagot al Sefer Ba'al ha-Nefesh le-ha-Rabad.* Berechiah was the author of a number of *piyyutim,* some extant only in manuscript.

[Jo.H./Ed.]

Bibliography: Zerahiah: J. Reifmann, *Toledot R. Zeraḥyah ha-Levi* (1853); Marx, in: REJ, 59 (1910), 200–24; S. M. Chones, *Toledot ha-Posekim* (1910), 107–13; Ch. Tchernowitz, *Toledot ha-Posekim,* 1 (1946), 149–63; Urbach, index; Rabad, *Katuv Sham,* ed. I. D. Bergman (1957), introd., 26, 39, 42; I. Twersky, *Rabad of Posquières* (1962), 120ff. and passim; C. B. Chavel, *Ramban, his Life and Teachings* (1960), 20ff. Berechiah: Zunz, Lit Poesie, 463, 495; Landshuth, Ammudei, 56; Michael, Or, no. 648; Fuenn, Keneset, 202; Gross, Gal Jud, 255–6; Davidson, Oẓar, 4 (1933), 373.

GEROVICH, ELIEZER MORDECAI BEN ISAAC (1844–1913), Russian *ḥazzan* and composer. Gerovich, who was born in the Ukraine, was gifted with a rich tenor voice. At the age of 18 he went to study music at Berdichev where he became assistant *hazzan* at the so-called Choral Synagogue (i.e., a synagogue with a choir). After studying cantoral music under Nissan *Blumenthal in Odessa, he attended the St. Petersburg Conservatory. In 1887 he was appointed chief *ḥazzan* at the Choral Synagogue at Rostov-on-Don, a post he held for 25 years. Gerovich became famous for his own compositions of synagogue music, based on traditional Jewish melodies but written in an original style. Most of them were collected in his two-volume *Schire Tefilla* and *Schire Simra* (1897).

Bibliography: Idelsohn, Music, 310f.; A. Friedmann, *Lebensbilder beruehmter Kantoren,* 3 (1927), 32; E. Zaludkowski, *Kultur-Treger fun der Yidisher Liturgye* (1930), 163–8; H. H. Harris, *Toledot ha-Ḥazzanut be-Yisrael* (1950), 11, 425–7; Sendrey Music, 368 and 394 (indexes), s.v.; A. Holde, *Jews in Music* (1959), 356 (index), s.v. [J.L.N.]

GERSHENZON, MIKHAIL OSIPOVICH (1869–1925), Russian literary historian, philosopher, and essayist. Born in Kishinev, Gershenzon studied in Berlin and Moscow. An anti-Marxist liberal, he nevertheless became the best-known exponent of the thesis that the Bolshevik Revolution would ultimately benefit Russian culture by freeing it from the shackles of tradition. This idea was expressed in his *Perepiska iz dvukh uglov* ("Correspondence From Two Corners," 1921), an exchange of letters with the Symbolist poet Vyacheslav Ivanov. Gershenzon's other works include monographs dealing with several 19th century Russian revolutionaries and men of letters, as well as such major studies as *Mechta i Mysl I. S. Turgeneva,* ("The Dream and Thoughts of Turgenev," 1919), and *Mudrost Pushkina,* ("The Wisdom of Pushkin," 1919). One of the foremost Russian intellectuals of his age, Gershenzon was one of the earliest enthusiasts of the revival of Hebrew literature and fought for its recognition as a potentially major contribution to modern writing. According to Gershenzon, "A free Jew does not cease being a Jew. On the contrary, only a free Jew is fully capable of absorbing Jewish spirit and merging it with his totally liberated humanity". He published an article on *Bialik (1914) and essays on Judaism, but attacked the Zionist movement.

Bibliography: Y. Z. Berman, *M. O. Gershenzon* (Rus., 1928), includes bibliography. [M.F.]

GERSHOM (Heb. גֵּרְשֹׁם, גֵּרְשׁוֹם), elder son of Moses and Zipporah (Ex. 2:22; 18:3). Gershom was born in Midian. The meaning of the name is unknown, but is explained as "a stranger there," symbolizing Moses' flight from Egypt. According to I Chronicles 23:16 and 26:24, Gershom's son was Shebuel. Since, however, he is described as "the chief officer in charge of the treasuries" in the time of David, Shebuel was very likely a more distant descendant of Gershom. Another descendant was Jonathan who acted as a priest at the idol of Micah (Judg. 18:30; MT has "Moses" deferentially written with a suspended *nun*). The Gershomites had no functions in connection with the Tent of Meeting and no Levitical cities were apportioned to them. They apparently were priests to the tribe of Dan *(ibid.)*. [N.M.S.]

GERSHOM BEN JUDAH ME'OR HA-GOLAH (c. 960–1028), one of the first great German talmudic scholars and a spiritual molder of German Jewry. Few biographical details are known of Gershom, most of the stories about him being of a legendary nature. He was apparently born in Metz, but his home was in Mainz (Isaac of Vienna, *Or Zaru'a* (1862), 2, 275), where he conducted a yeshivah, and where he wrote the *ketubbah* for his second wife Bona in 1013. A tombstone in Mainz of which the extant words are ". . . in memoriam: R. Gershom ben R. . . ." is thought to be his. Gershom mentions only one of his teachers, *Judah b. Meir ha-Kohen Leontin "from whom I received most of my knowledge" (Responsa Meir of Rothenburg (Prague, 1895), 264). His own best-known pupils are *Eliezer the Great, *Jacob b. Jakar, and *Isaac b. Judah, the last two of whom were the teachers of *Rashi. His brother Machir compiled a lexicon known as *Alfa Beta Rabbi Makhir,* now lost. An unconfirmed tradition maintains that Gershom had a son Eliezer, who headed a yeshivah. The **rishonim,* however, mention a son who was forcibly converted to Christianity and died before he could repent, yet his father fulfilled the laws of mourning for him (*Or Zaru'a, ibid.,* 428). The probable time for this is 1012, when Heinrich II issued an edict of expulsion against the Jews of Mainz.

The reverence in which Rabbenu Gershom was held in subsequent generations was already expressed by Rashi: "Rabbenu Gershom, may the memory of the righteous and holy be for a blessing, who enlightened the eyes of the exile, and upon whom we all depend and of whom all Ashkenazi Jewry are the disciples of his disciple" (J. Mueller (ed.), *Teshuvot Ḥakhmei Ẓarefat ve-Lutir* (1881), no. 21). This is apparently also the source of the title *"Me'or ha-Golah"* ("Light of the Exile").

Gershom's name is connected with many *takkanot,* most famous of which is his *ḥerem* ("ban") against bigamy. Well known, too, is the *ḥerem* forbidding the unauthorized reading of private letters. This latter *takkanah* in particular, and several others ascribed to him, may not really be his. Rashi cites only one *takkanah* in his name, the prohibition against reminding forcibly converted Jews, who have repented and returned to the fold, of their transgressions. Jacob *Tam mentions his *takkanah* against emending talmudic texts. The two important *takkanot* enforcing monogamy and prohibiting the divorce of a wife against her will are attributed to him by *Meir of Rothenburg (loc. cit., nos. 866 and 1121), but *Eliezer Nathan, who lived in Mainz a century after Gershom, refers to them as communal *takkanot* (*Sefer Raban* (Prague, 1610), 121b). Fifteenth-century scholars attribute to him the ancient *takkanah* known as the **ḥerem ha-yishuv* (Israel of Krems' gloss to Asher b. Jehiel, BB 2:12). It is possible that they were attributed to the great luminary in order to give these *takkanot* the weight of his great authority. On the other hand, there is no valid reason that *takkanot* ascribed to Gershom should not really be his.

Rabbenu Gershom's responsa and halakhic decisions are scattered throughout the works of the French and German scholars, and have been collected by S. Eidelberg (1955). Most items deal with civil law. In them he bases himself upon the Bible and Talmud alone, and only seldom refers to the early *geonim.* In one place he writes that he prefers the opinion of his teacher Leontin, who likewise based himself on Scripture and Talmud (Meir of Rothenburg, loc. cit., no. 264), to that of the famous *geonim* Yehudai and Sherira, but the sources of Leontin's teaching are obscure. From his works it appears that Gershom was acquainted with the general German law of his time and was even influenced by it. His legal decisions were regarded as authoritative, particularly by French and German scholars throughout the centuries, and influenced the major direction of the *halakhah* in these countries.

The commentaries attributed to R. Gershom which were published in the Vilna Romm edition of the Talmud to tractates *Bava Batra, Ta'anit,* and the whole of *Seder Kedoshim* (except *Zevaḥim*), are now considered not to be his. He probably laid the foundations for them, but the present work is that of his pupils and their pupils. *Nathan b. Jehiel, in the *Arukh,* refers to it sometimes as "the commentary of the sages of Mainz," and sometimes as that of Rabbenu Gershom, but mostly quotes it anonymously (over 550 times). It was superseded by Rashi's commentary and remained almost unknown until the time of Bezalel

*Ashkenazi, who was also the first to ascribe them to Rabbenu Gershom.

Gershom transcribed the Mishnah and the *Masorah Gedolah* of the Bible and corrected them. These copies were highly regarded by the *rishonim*, on account of their accuracy. He was the first Franco-German scholar to compose *seliḥot* and other *piyyutim* (collected by A. M. Habermann, 1944). His *seliḥot* were accepted in all German communities; most popular is the *piyyut Zekhor Berit*, included in the *seliḥot* of Rosh Ha-Shanah. They reflect the troubles and tribulations of his generation and are noteworthy for their simplicity and naturalness of expression and the emotion with which they are imbued.

Bibliography: Epstein, in: *Festschrift ... M. Steinschneider* (1896), 115–43; Naphtali b. Shemu'el (J. N. Simḥoni), in: *Ha-Shilo'aḥ*, 28 (1913), 14–22, 119–28, 201–12; Tykocinski, in: *Festschrift ... M. Philippson* (1916), 1–5; Finkelstein, Middle Ages, index; idem, in: MGWJ, 74 (1930), 23–31; Baer, *ibid.*, 71 (1927), 392–7; 74 (1930), 31–34; idem, in: *Zion*, 15 (1950), 1–41; A. Aptowitzer, *Mavo le-Sefer Ravyah* (1938), 330–5; Eidelberg, in: *Zion*, 18 (1953), 83–87; Z. W. Falk, *Jewish Matrimonial Law in the Middle Ages* (1966), index s.v. *Gershom*.

[S.E.]

GERSHOM BEN SOLOMON (13th century), Provençal scholar of Béziers. No biographical details are known about him. He compiled a halakhic work, *Shalman*, giving the halakhic rulings of the Talmud according to the order of the *halakhot* of Isaac Alfasi, and approximating the order of Maimonides in his *Mishneh Torah*. In some sources Gershom's work is erroneously called *Shulḥan* and is not to be confused with the *Sefer Shulḥan* in the Paris National Library, Zotenberg, no. 415; (see Benjacob, 583 no. 687, and Lubetzky, bibl.). Gershom's book was completed by his son SAMUEL BEN GERSHOM who also participated in the composition of the earlier portion. Lubetzky corrected the name Meshullam b. Gershom to Samuel b. Gershom in *Bet ha-Beḥirah* (Introduction to *Avot*). The book and its author are referred to in *Mikhtam* by David b. Levi of Narbonne (ed. by A. Sofer (1959), 223), the commentary of Manoah b. Jacob of Narbonne on Maimonides' Yad (Constantinople, 1718, 11b, et al.), *Kol Bo* and *Orḥot Ḥayyim* (see index), *Avudarham* (ed. by C. L. Ehrenreich (1927), 29), and in *Sefer Ba'alei Asufot* (still in manuscript; see Lubetzky). Samuel was the teacher of *Judah b. Jacob, the author of the last-named work.

Bibliography: Isaac de Lattes, *Sha'arei Ẓiyyon*, ed. by S. Buber (1885), 44; Michael, Or, no. 687; Gross, Gal Jud, 99f.; Meshullam b. Moses of Beziers, *Sefer ha-Hashlamah*, ed. by J. Lubetzky, 1 (1885), introd. xv; Benedikt, in: *Sinai*, 29 (1951), 191–3; idem, in: KS, 27 (1951), 143 and n. 60; Sussman, in: *Koveẓ al Yad*, n.s. 6, pt. 2 (1966), 283, 285.

[S.Z.H.]

GERSHON, GERSHONITES (Heb. גֵּרְשׁוֹן; in Chron. usually **Gershom,** גֵּרְשׁוֹם, גֵּרְשֹׁם), the eldest son of Levi, from whom a division of the Levites traced their descent (Gen. 46:11; Ex. 6:16–17; Num. 3:17ff.; Josh. 21:6, 27; I Chron. 5:27; 6:1). The clan descended from Gershon is designated "Gershonites" (Heb. הַגֵּרְשֻׁנִּי; e.g., Ex. 6:17). Two sons of Gershon, Libni and Shimei, are also mentioned (Ex. 6:17; Num. 3:18; I Chron. 6:2); in I Chronicles 23:7 and 26:21 Ladan is used in place of Libni. After the exile, very little mention is made of the Gershonites as such. However, the distinguished guild of Asaphites is said to be descended from Gershon (I Chron. 6:24–28 [39–43]), and 128 (Ezra 2:41), or 148 (Neh. 7:44), of the Asaphites are reported to have taken up residence in Jerusalem. They led the music at the laying of the foundation of the Temple (Ezra 3:10) and blew the trumpets at the dedication of the city walls (Neh. 12:35).

The history of the Gershonites, as reflected in the biblical sources, can be divided into four stages:

(1) During the desert wanderings, the clans encamped behind the Tabernacle, to the west (Num. 3:23). In the census of the Levites from the age of one month up, the recorded entries of all the Gershonite males came to 7,500 (3:22), and the entries of males from the age of 30 through 50 came to 2,630 (4:39–40). Their duty was to carry the hangings which comprised the Tabernacle proper, the outer coverings and the hangings of the court, with their cords, and the altar and accessories (3:25–26; 4:24–26; cf. 10:17), for which they were assigned two carts and four oxen, as required for their service (7:7). They were under the direction of Ithamar, the youngest son of Aaron the priest.

(2) After the settlement in the land, the Gershonites were assigned 13 cities in the tribal territories of the half-clan of Manasseh on the eastern side of the Jordan and of the clans of Issachar, Asher, and Naphtali, on the western side (Josh. 21:6, 27–33; I Chron. 6:47, 56–61).

(3) According to the Chronicler, at the direction of David the Temple music was conducted partly by Asaph, a Gershonite, and his family (e.g., I Chron. 25:1–2). David also appointed the clan to undertake service in the Temple when he organized the Levites into divisions "according to the sons of Levi" (23:6–11; 26:20ff.).

(4) The last time the Gershonites are mentioned as such is in the list of Levites who took part in the cleansing of the Temple under Hezekiah (II Chron. 29:12–13). [SH.BA.]

GERSHON, ISAAC (d. after 1620), scholar and proofreader. His full name was Isaac b. Mordecai Gershon Treves but he is usually referred to simply as Isaac Gershon. Gershon was born in Safed and studied under Moses *Alshekh. He went to Venice not later than 1576, and on his journey there published his *Shelom Esther* (Constantinople, c. 1575–76), an anthology of the commentaries of the French and Spanish scholars to the Book of Esther. For more than 30

Title page of *Sefer Einei Moshe* by Moses Alshekh, text proofread by Isaac Gershon, Venice, 1601. Jerusalem, J.N.U.L.

years he worked as proofreader of books published in Venice, mainly by the Safed scholars. Among the works he saw through the press were: *Beit Elohim* (1576) by Moses di *Trani; *Reshit Ḥokhmah* (1579) by Elijah di Vidas; *Manot ha-Levi* (1585) by Solomon *Alkabeẓ; *Zemirot Yisrael* (1599–1600) by Israel *Najara; the Pentateuch commentary by Moses Alshekh (1601–1607); the *Sefer Ḥaredim* (1601) by Eleazar *Azikvi; and responsa by Moses Galante (1608). Isaac Gershon was a member of the Venice *bet din* and his signature appears on its resolutions and edicts together with those of the Venice rabbis Ben Zion Sarfaty and Judah Leib *Saraval. He published *Mashbit Milḥamot* (Venice, 1606), containing the rulings of those rabbis who were lenient in connection with the *Rovigo *mikveh*. He wrote commentaries to other books of the Bible; his commentary on Malachi was published in *Likkutei Shoshannim* (*ibid.*, 1602). Together with the other rabbis of Venice, he defended the emissary, Jedidiah b. Moses b. Mordecai Galante, who was accused of embezzling money he had collected for Ereẓ Israel. Some of Isaac's responsa are extant, published in the works of his contemporaries or in manuscript. Toward the end of his life, apparently in the 1620s, he returned to Safed, and died there.

Bibliography: Montefiore, in: REJ, 10 (1885), 185, 195, 199; Sonne, in: KS, 7 (1930/31), 281f.; 34 (1959), 135f.; idem, *Kobez al Jad*, 5 (15) (1950), 206, 211; Yaari, Sheluḥei, 251, 844; idem, *Meḥkerei Sefer* (1958), 135, 159, 171f., 174, 421; Judah Aryeh of Modena, *Ziknei Yehudah*, ed. by S. Simonsohn (1956), 37 (introd.); Tamar, in: KS, 33 (1957/58), 377f.

[D.TA.]

GERSHON BEN SOLOMON OF ARLES (late 13th century), Provençal scholar. There is almost no exact information about his life. The period in which he lived is estimated from the sources he used for his book *Sha'ar ha-Shamayim* (*The Gate of Heaven*, tr. by F. S. Bodenheimer, 1953), the only work by him which is extant, and probably the only one he wrote. It has been estimated that this work was written between 1242 and 1300.

It is now agreed that Gershon lived in Arles in southern France (Provence). The traditional notion that he lived in Catalonia is shown to be incorrect by his own words: "For in the area of Catalonia the sheep and goats are smaller than those in our area" (*Sha'ar ha-Shamayim* (Roedelheim, 1801), 30b, 26-27). Spain is also not his place of residence: "One in our provinces and one in the provinces of Spain" (*ibid.*, 20a, 4). It also appears that Gershon regarded France as outside his homeland (*ibid.*, 16a, 11).

Sha'ar ha-Shamayim is a brief popular summary of the natural sciences, astronomy, and theology of Gershon's day. It is divided into three parts: natural sciences, theology, and astronomy. The first part contains ten treatises, on the following subjects: the four elements (including a discussion of meteorology); inanimate objects; plants; animals; fowls; bees, ants, and spiders; fish; man; parts of the body; sleeping and waking (including a discussion on dreams). The chapters on man include also psychological data, the law of heredity, and even clinical prognoses.

The first part is the longest and most detailed. In the extant editions of the work it takes up five-sixths of the entire book, but in some manuscripts there are obvious additions, which are not found in the printed version.

Gershon lists a great number of Greek, Latin, Arabic, and Jewish authors, and cites from their works. Among the authors cited by him are Homer, Plato, Pythagoras, Aristotle, Galen, Hippocrates, Al-Farabi, Avicenna, and Averroes. It appears that he received this knowledge from Hebrew translations of earlier scientific and philosophic literature rather than from original sources. He states in his

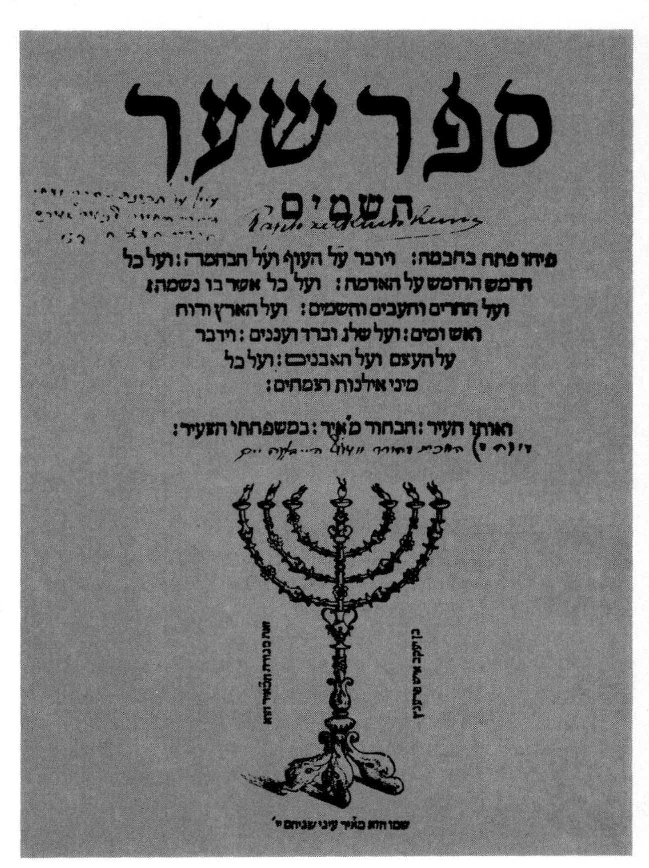
ספר שער
השמים
פיהו פתח בחכמה: וידבר על העוף ועל הבהמה: ועל כל
הרמש הרומש על האדמה: ועל כל אשר בו נשמה:
ועל ההרים והעבים והשמים: ועל הארץ ורוח
אש ומים: ועל שלג וברד ועננים: וידבר
על העצם ועל האבנים: ועל כל
מיני אילנות וצמחים:
האותו העיר: הבחור מאיר: במשפחתו הצעיר:

Title page of *Sha'ar ha-Shamayim*, by the 13th-century scholar Gershon b. Solomon of Arles, Venice, 1547. Jerusalem, J.N.U.L.

introduction that he had "some of the books of the philosophers which had been translated from their languages to his own." He further states, with regard to the second and third parts of the book, that he based himself primarily on those writings of *Maimonides and the Arabic scholar Al-Farghani (ninth century), which suited his purposes. It is not known which direct sources were used for the first part of the book.

In addition to citing from written sources, Gershon also set down what he had heard through reports from Jews or Christians. He was not an independent thinker; even where he makes statements in the first person, these are often taken literally from other sources.

Because there were not enough adequate words in Hebrew, and perhaps also in order to make for easier understanding, Gershon expressed many scientific concepts and objects by their foreign names, which he probably found in his sources. These names, usually Latin or Arabic, are an integral part of the text, unlike the foreign usages in other medieval writings, such as the commentaries of *Rashi, whose purpose in using foreign words is merely to clarify the meaning of difficult Hebrew terms.

Sha'ar ha-Shamayim served for hundreds of years as a popular book of sciences for readers of Hebrew. It was widely circulated and is extant in many manuscripts. The extant editions are all imperfect and incomplete in comparison with a few of the manuscripts. The first edition (Venice, 1547) apparently served as a basis for all subsequent editions (Roedelheim, 1801; Zolkiew, 1805; Warsaw, 1876; Jerusalem, 1944), in which corrections were made only on the basis of conjecture.

Bibliography: L. Kopf, in: *Tarbiz*, 24 (1955), 150–66, 274–89, 410–25; A. Neubauer, in: MGWJ, 21 (1872), 182–4; H. Gross, *ibid.*, 28 (1879), 20ff., Gross, Gal Jud, 82–83, 94; Steinschneider, Uebersetzungen, 9–16; idem, in: REJ, 5 (1882), 278; Renan, Rabbins, 589–91.

[L.KO.]

GERSHOVITZ, SAMUEL (1907–1960), U.S. social worker and Jewish Welfare Board (JWB) executive. Gershovitz was born in New Rochelle, New York, but raised in the midwest. Gershovitz's association with JWB began in 1939 with his position as field secretary for the midwest. In 1942 Gershovitz received his first position with National JWB. He became executive director in 1947 and executive vice-president in 1952. He traveled widely, organizing USOs, community centers, and similar projects in Europe, Central America, and the Pacific. In Anchorage, Alaska, he set up the first Jewish community council. [Ed.]

GERSHUNI, GRIGORI ANDREYEVICH (1870–1908), Russian revolutionary; founder and leader of the terrorist arm of the Socialist-Revolutionary (S.-R.) Party. Gershuni was born in Tavrova, an estate in the Kovno province where his father was a tenant. After a short period in *ḥeder* he was educated in a Russian high school in Shavli (Šiauliai), but at the age of 15, before graduating, he was sent by his parents to another town to be a pharmacist's apprentice. He eventually settled in Minsk (1898) where he opened a bacteriological laboratory. There he took part in semi-legal educational activities among working-class people and was gradually drawn into clandestine circles, partly under the influence of Yekaterina Breshkovskaya, the "grandmother of the Russian Revolution." The turning point in his revolutionary career was a fortnight of arrest and interrogation in 1900, when the czarist police officer Zubatov tried to enlist him into the loyalist workers' movement organized by himself as a counterforce to terrorism and revolutionary ideology. The effect on Gershuni was exactly the opposite. He became an ardent supporter of anti-czarist terrorism, and when several revolutionary groups merged into the S.-R. Party, it was Gershuni who organized and headed its terrorist arm, the famous Fighting Organization (Boyevaya Organizatsiya), which, under his personal guidance, assassinated some of the highest and most hated officials and dignitaries. Yevno *Azeff, who was later unmasked as an agent provocateur of the police, became his closest collaborator in leading the Fighting Organization and took it over in 1903, when Gershuni was denounced by another police agent and arrested. A military tribunal sentenced Gershuni to death, but the sentence was later commuted to life imprisonment. He was imprisoned in the old Schluesselburg fortress in 1906, but after having been transported to a Siberian prison, he was smuggled out in a cabbage barrel and in a daring flight, by way of China (where he met Sun Yat-sen) and Japan, he reached the United States. There he addressed in many cities socialist mass meetings of Jewish and other workers and collected funds for the Russian S.-R. Party. Several weeks later he appeared in Finland where he publicly attended the second S.-R. Party congress. After his death in a Zurich hospital, his friends arranged for his burial in the Montparnasse cemetery in Paris alongside other famous Russian revolutionaries. His funeral grew into an impressive demonstration of international sympathy for the Russian revolutionary movement.

Gershuni became a legendary figure in his lifetime. Although completely assimilated in Russian language and culture, he was always conscious of being a Jew. In his revolutionary speech before the military tribunal in 1903 he stressed the plight of the Jewish masses in Russia. In his behavior in prison and in his dealings with the czarist authorities he was always proud and courageous, so as not to play into the hands of anti-Semitic propaganda which tried to present the Jewish revolutionaries as cowardly manipulators behind the scenes. To his friend Chaim *Zhitlowsky he said that after the revolution, when liberty would be achieved in Russia, he would join those who devote themselves completely to Jewish interests. Gershuni's reminiscences *Iz nedavyago proshlago* ("From the Recent Past") were published in Paris by the S.-R. central committee (1908).

Bibliography: A. I. Spiridovich, *Zapiski zhandarma* (1928[2]); V. Chernov (ed.), *Grigory Gershuni: Zayn Leben un Tetikeyt* (1934); M. Rosenbaum, *Erinerungen fun a Sotsyalist-Revolutsyoner*, 2 vols. (1924).

[B.E.]

GERSHWIN, GEORGE (1898–1937), U.S. composer. Born in New York, he wrote his first songs while working as a pianist with a music publishing firm. His first revue, *Half Past Eight* (1918), was followed by the successful *La La Lucille* (1919) and in the same year his song "Swanee," sung by Al *Jolson in the revue *Sinbad*, caused a sensation. He was commissioned by Paul Whiteman to compose a jazz symphony. The resultant work, *Rhapsody in Blue* for piano and orchestra, was first performed in New York in 1924, with the composer at the piano. It made jazz "respectable" for the American concert stage and made Gershwin famous. He composed the *Concerto for Piano in F Major* (1925), *Three Preludes for Piano* (1926), *An American in Paris* (1928), *Second Rhapsody* (1931), and *Cuban Overture* (1932). Gershwin had little formal training, and after the success of the *Rhapsody in Blue*, in which he had received the help of an orchestrator, he studied with Rubin *Goldmark and Joseph *Schillinger.

George Gershwin, U.S. composer. Courtesy Jewish Theatrical Guild, New York.

He continued composing music for films and Broadway shows, his most successful revues being *Lady Be Good* (1924), *Oh Kay* (1926), *Strike Up The Band* (1927), *Girl Crazy* (1930), and *Of Thee I Sing* (1931), a political satire. Most of the lyrics for his revues and songs were written by his brother Ira (1896–). His last and greatest work was the folk opera *Porgy and Bess* (1935), based on DuBose Heyward's play, *Catfish Row*, about the life of southern Negroes. Gershwin's musical style was rooted in the jazz idiom of his time, and stimulated by the traditions of the southern Negroes. Influences of cantorial style may be discerned in certain wide-ranging phrases, notably the clarinet solo which opens the *Rhapsody in Blue*.

Bibliography: R. Rushmore, *Life of George Gershwin* (1966); I. Goldberg, *George Gershwin: A Study in American Music* (1931); M. Armitage (ed.), *George Gershwin* (1938); D. Ewen, *A Journey to Greatness, The Life and Music of George Gershwin* (1956); G. Chase (ed.), *American Composer Speaks* (1966), 139–45.

[J.T./B.B.]

GERSONI, HENRY (Heb., **Gershoni, Ẓevi Hirsch;** 1844–1897), journalist and author. Born in Vilna, he studied in the Vilna Rabbinical Seminary. Moving to St. Petersburg he married a Christian girl and converted to Christianity. In 1868 he publicly confessed his conversion in *Ha-Maggid*, a leading Hebrew periodical, but announced his repentance and reaffirmed his loyalty to Judaism. After

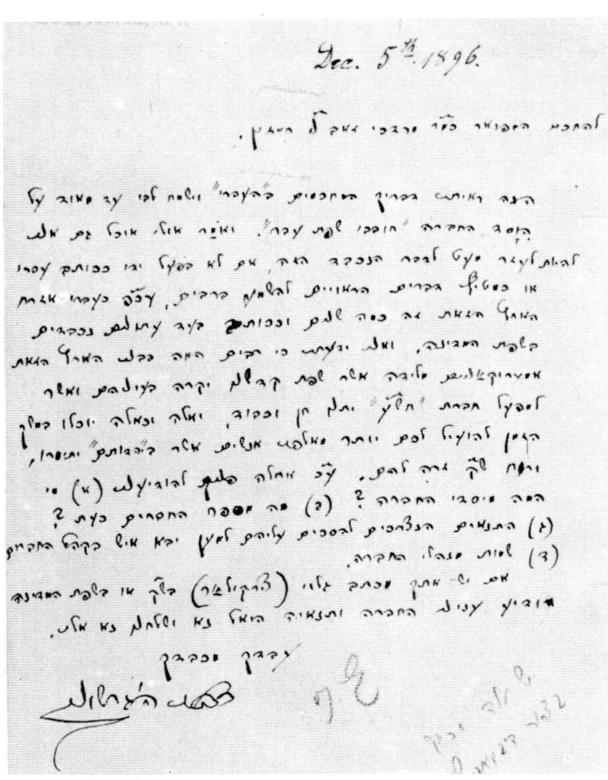
Dec. 5th 1896.

Letter from Henry Gersoni, New York, 1896, offering assistance to an association for promoting the Hebrew language. Jerusalem, Schwadron Collection, J.N.U.L.

many wanderings, he settled in New York in 1869. In 1874 he became a rabbi in Macon, Georgia. He also served as rabbi in Atlanta and in Chicago, where he published his short-lived weekly *The Jewish Advance* and, later, *The Maccabean*. He returned to New York in 1893 where he lived by his pen until his death.

Devoted to the new Hebrew literature, Gersoni published articles in the leading Hebrew periodicals. He was also a pioneer of the Yiddish press in America, editor of the *Post* in New York (1870) and a contributor to Jewish periodicals in the English language. He translated Turgenev into English and Longfellow's *Excelsior* into Hebrew.

Gersoni wrote on the burning problems of the day: Orthodoxy and Reform, immigration to America and to Palestine, ethical culture, organizational life of Jewry. His subjective and acute observations of the American scene are still of historic importance, e.g., in his *Sketches of Jewish Life and History* (1873).

Bibliography: J. Kabakoff, *Ḥalutzei ha-Sifrut ha-Ivrit ba-Amerikah* (1966), 79–130. [EI.S.]

GERSON-KIWI, EDITH (Esther; 1908–), Israel musicologist. Born in Berlin, she studied with the harpsichordist Wanda *Landowska. Settling in Ereẓ Israel in 1935, she devoted herself to teaching and to ethnomusicological research. Her work at the Institute of Jewish Music at the Hebrew University was sponsored at different periods from 1950 by the Ministry of Education and Culture. It included the collection of musical recordings which, by 1970, comprised 7,000 items. From 1967 she also lectured at Tel Aviv University. Her writings deal with the musical traditions of Jewish communities and the mutual influences to be found in Jewish, Christian, and Muslim music. Her publications include *The Persian Doctrine of Dastga Composition* (1963) and "Vocal Folk Polyphonies of the Western Orient in Jewish Tradition" (in *Yuval*, 1 (1968), 169–93).

Bibliography: B. Bayer, in: *Bat Kol*, 3 (1961), 33–35. [ED.]

°**GERSTEIN, KURT** (1905–1945), German anti-Nazi. The son of a bourgeois family, a German nationalist, and a Christian, Gerstein joined the Nazi Party in 1933, while remaining in the Protestant youth movement. He was expelled from the Nazi Party for activities on behalf of the dissident Bekenntniskirche ("Professing Church") and was twice incarcerated in concentration camps (1936 and 1938). Anxious to know more about the Nazis' horrifying activities, he volunteered for the Waffen-S.S. in March 1941 and became an employee at its Hygiene Service. There are, however, other versions of the reason for his entry into the S.S. A professional engineer, Gerstein reached officer's rank and due to his technical abilities was named chief of the disinfection department. In 1942, as an expert in the use of Zyklon B—a poison gas used in fumigations—Gerstein was sent by the *RSHA to *Belzec and *Treblinka, where his task was to substitute Zyklon B for diesel exhaust fumes as a means of mass murder. At Belzec he witnessed the killing of several thousand Jews from Lvov. Upon his return to Berlin, Gerstein tried to stop the murders, informing Swedish and Swiss legations, the Holy See, and underground Church groups of his experiences, but encountered disbelief and indifference. Charged with the task of continuing to supply the murderous gas to the camps, Gerstein succeeded in destroying two consignments. At the end of the war, he submitted to an Anglo-American intelligence team a detailed report in French on Nazi atrocities which was used at the Nuremberg trials. Another, in German, was published after his death in *Vierteljahreshefte fuer Zeitgeschichte* (vol. 1, 1953), entitled "Augenzeugenbericht zu den Massenvergasungen." Arrested by the French as a suspected war criminal, Gerstein was found hanged in his cell on July 25, 1945.

Bibliography: S. Friedlaender, *Kurt Gerstein, the Ambiguity of Good* (1969); idem, in: *Midstream*, 13 no. 5 (1967), 24–29; F. Helmut, *K. Gerstein* (Ger., 1964); R. Hochhuth, *The Representative* (1963), (U.S. title—*The Deputy*). [Y.RE.]

GERSTLE, LEWIS (1824–1902), U.S. merchant. Gerstle, born in Ichenhausen, Bavaria, emigrated to America about 1845, settling in Louisville, Ky., and then in California. After prospecting for gold briefly, he joined Louis Sloss and Company of Sacramento, general merchandise dealers. During this time, Gerstle and Sloss married the sisters Hannah and Sarah Greenebaum. Moving to San Francisco in about 1860, Gerstle and Sloss entered the stock brokerage business, bought and sold hides, operated a tannery, and acquired shipping interests. In 1868, after the American purchase of Alaska, they and others organized the highly successful Alaska Commercial Company for trade in the new territory. They received a fur seal concession, established trading posts, and supplied miners during the Klondike gold strike of 1897. Gerstle was a director of Congregation Emanu-El and the Pacific Hebrew Orphan Asylum and Home Society, a member of the Vigilance Committee, and treasurer of the University of California. He promoted manufacturing establishments and directed two banks.

Bibliography: G. Mack, *Lewis and Hannah Gerstle* (1953); M. A. Meyer, *Western Jewry* (1916); R. Glanz, *Jews in American Alaska (1867–1880)* (1953); L. D. Kitchener, *Flag Over the North* (1954); M. Zarchin, *Glimpses of Jewish Life in San Francisco* (1964). [R.E.L.]

GERTLER, MARK (1891–1939), English artist. Born in London, Gertler was one of the most talented and romantic first generation painters to emerge from the wave of Jewish immigration into England at the turn of the century. Until he went to school at the age of eight, his only language was Yiddish. Later he began attending evening classes in art and worked for a firm of glass painters. In 1908, on the advice of Sir William *Rothenstein, the Jewish Educational Aid Society sent him to the Slade School of Art. Here he found himself among the brilliant group of Jewish students which included David *Bomberg, Jacob *Kramer, Bernard *Meninsky, and Isaac *Rosenberg. In 1911, before he was 20, he painted one of his finest pictures, "The Artist's Mother," one of the collection of his works in the Tate Gallery, London. When he left the Slade, in 1912 he began to receive important portrait commissions. Handsome, volatile, and a brilliant raconteur, he was taken up by the Bloomsbury Group of intellectuals, and seemed destined for greatness. Gertler's early works were influenced by his life in the Whitechapel ghetto. In addition to the studies of his parents and neighbors, often in fancy dress, these include "Rabbi and Grandchild" (1913) and "Rabbi and Rebbitzen" (1914). Gertler was later influenced by post-impressionism. From 1919 onward he regularly visited the south of France. His health began to deteriorate and eventually, depressed by his condition, by Hitler's anti-Jewish campaign, and by financial problems resulting from decreasing success, he committed suicide in 1939.

"The Artist's Mother," by Mark Gertler, oil, 1911, 22×26 in. (66×55.8 cm.). London, Tate Gallery.

Bibliography: Bell, in: M. Gertler, *Selected Letters*, ed. by N. Carrington (1965), introduction; J. Rothenstein, *British Art Since 1900* (1962), 172, plates 85, 86. [Ch.S.S.]

GERTSA (Rum. **Herta**), town in N. Bukovina, Chernovtsy oblast, Ukrainian S.S.R., which passed from Rumania to the Soviet Union in 1940. The locality was founded by Jews in the first quarter of the 18th century, when the local landowner invited a number of Polish Jews to found a settlement. Its first institution was a *talmud torah* of which a minute-book dating from 1764 has been preserved. The oldest tombstone in the cemetery dates from 1766. The community had four synagogues, of which the oldest was built at the end of the 18th century; a *mikveh* was founded in 1820, and a mixed school was established in the early 20th century. The community numbered 1,200 in 1803, 1,554 (56.4% of the total population) in c. 1859, 1,939 in 1899 (66.1%), 1,876 in 1910, and 1,801 in 1930 (25%). During the peasants' revolt in 1907 the Jews in Gertsa prevented attacks and pillaging by organizing *self-defense. After the conferment of Rumanian nationality in 1919, Jews were elected to the municipal council, and at one time a Jew served as vice-mayor. In 1927 the Rumanian governing party appointed a communal board from its own adherents, but the Jews boycotted it and two years later ensured its resignation. During World War II the Jews in Gertsa were deported to *Transnistria.

Bibliography: E. Schwarzfeld, *Impopularea, reimpopularea şi întemeires tîrgurilor şi tîrguşoarelor în Moldova* (1914), 63, 79; V. Tufescu, *Tîrguşoarele din Moldava şi importanţa lor economiaš* (1942), 115, 118, 140. [Th.L.]

GERTZ, ELMER (1906–), U.S. lawyer. Gertz, who was born in Chicago, practiced law there from 1930. He became known for his vigorous opposition to capital punishment, his defense of freedom of expression, and his fight for civil rights and liberties. In 1958 he obtained parole for Nathan Leopold, and in 1962 secured commutation of the death sentence of William Crump for murder, on the ground that Crump had been rehabilitated in prison while surviving nine stays of execution. Gertz helped to save the life of William Witherspoon, another convicted murderer, when the U.S. Supreme Court (1968) upheld his contention that prospective jurors should not have been challenged for their conscientious scruples against imposing the death penalty. He was also instrumental in the setting aside of the death penalty imposed on Jack *Ruby (1966). Gertz's court pleas brought about the removal of the ban on the sale of Frank Harris' *My Life and Loves*, Henry Miller's *Tropic of Cancer* (1964), and the works of the Marquis de Sade. He also secured the abolition by the U.S. Supreme Court of the Chicago motion picture censorship ordinance (1968). In the 1940s, as special counsel for the National Association for the Advancement of Colored People, Gertz was successful in a test case to make housing restrictions in Illinois illegal. He helped secure passage of the Illinois Fair Employment Practices Law and defended its validity before the Illinois Supreme Court in the late 1950s.

Active in many Jewish communal affairs, Gertz was president of the Greater Chicago Council of the American Jewish Congress (1959–63). He wrote *Frank Harris: A Study in Black and White* (1931, with A. I. Tobin); *The People vs. The Chicago Tribune* (1942); *A Handful of Clients* (1965), dealing with many of his cases; and *Moment of Madness: The People vs. Jack Ruby* (1968).

Bibliography: M. Myerson and E. C. Banfield, *Politics, Planning, and Public Interest* (1955). [M.M.B.]

GERUSIA (Gr. γερουσία), council of elders, common throughout the Hellenistic world (e.g., Sparta, Cyrene). Since the "elders" or "city elders" *(Ziknei ha-Ir)* are mentioned repeatedly in the Bible (cf. Deut. 19:12, 21:2ff.; Josh. 20:4; Judg. 8:14; I Sam. 9:3; I Kings 21:8, 11; Ruth 4:2ff.), Josephus concludes that the earliest Jewish *Gerusia* dates back to biblical times, functioning as a high court together with the high priest and prophets (Ant. 4:218). During the Hellenistic period the *Gerusia* appears not merely as a legislative and judicial body, but as representative of the Jewish population of Judea. Thus in the famous edict of Antiochus III the Great, following his conquest of Palestine, the Seleucid monarch describes the splendid reception given him by the Jews—in the person of the *Gerusia* (and not, as might have been expected, the high priest). As a result, the members of the *Gerusia* were exempted from a number of taxes, together with officials of the Temple (Ant. 12:138ff.). Similarly, Antiochus IV Epiphanes, in an epistle to the Jews, addresses his remarks to the *Gerusia* and not the high priest (II Macc. 11:27). That the Jews of this period considered the *Gerusia* their official representative body is further apparent from the correspondence of "those in Jerusalem and Judea, the *Gerusia*, and Judah" to their brethren in Egypt during the early years of the Hasmonean rebellion (II Macc. 1:10). When Jonathan became leader of the Jewish nation, the office of high priest was apparently formally recognized as representative of the people, and thus in a correspondence with the Spartans "Jonathan the high priest and the *Gerusia*" are listed together (I Macc. 12:6; Jos., Ant. 13, 166).

It would be a mistake, however, to identify the *Gerusia*, which appears to be a permanent representative body of elders dating back to the Persian period (cf. Judith 4:8,

11:14, 15:8), with the "Great Assembly" *(keneset ha-gedolah),* a body representing the total Jewish population of Palestine, and convened only when important constitutional decisions were taken. The "elders" are thus mentioned as a part of the Great Assembly that appointed Simeon high priest and leader of the Jewish nation (I Macc. 14:28). It is feasible, however, that the *Gerusia* eventually evolved into what became known as the "Sanhedrin" of Jerusalem, although the precise date of the introduction of this term is unknown (cf. H. Mantel, *Studies in the History of the Sanhedrin* (1961), 49–50, 61–62, for a summation of the numerous views on this problem). According to Philo (Flaccus, 10:74) there also existed a Jewish *Gerusia* in Alexandria, which during the rule of Augustus replaced the previous form of local Jewish leadership, the ethnarchate.

Bibliography: S. B. Hoenig, *Great Sanhedrin* (1953); Y. M. Grintz, *Sefer Yehudit* (1957), 105. [I.G.]

GESANG, NATHAN-NACHMAN (1886–1944), one of the founders and president of the Zionist Organization of Argentina. Born in Cracow, Gesang went to Berlin to study and became active in the Zionist movement. When he moved to Britain (in 1909) he became secretary of the British Zionist Organization. In 1910 he settled in Argentina and after a short while was one of the leaders of Argentine Jewry and a founder of the Zionist movement, serving as its president in 1922–23 and 1930–31. Gesang was active in the propagation of the Hebrew language and culture and published articles in Hebrew, Yiddish, and Spanish on Zionist affairs and Jewish studies. Among his published books are *Der Khoyveve Tsiyonism un der Politisher Tsiyonizm* ("Ḥovevei Zion Movement and Political Zionism," Yid. and Sp., 1937) and a new edition of the *Kuzari* by Judah Halevi, with a detailed introduction (1943).

Bibliography: *Haolam,* 24 (1936), 650. [G.K.]

GESELLSCHAFT DER JUNGEN HEBRAEER (Ger. "Society of Young Hebrews"), society founded in Prague at the beginning of the 19th century by two young enlightened Jews, Judah and Ignaz *Jeiteles. Unlike the Gesellschaft der Freunde in Berlin, on which it was modeled, the society's aim was not only to provide mutual aid for its members, but also to propagate the ideas of the Haskalah among the working youth and uneducated members of Jewish society in Prague. Thus their *Yidish Daytshe Monatshrift,* of which six numbers appeared in 1802, was published neither in Hebrew nor in German but in *Vayber-Daytsh* ("Women's German," i.e., the Yiddish language of *Ẓe'enah u-Re'enah* printed in the Hebrew alphabet). Both the society and its periodical were forerunners of the particular Bohemian brand of Haskalah that was influenced by rising Czech nationalism, Jewish consciousness, and loyalty to the house of Hapsburg.

Bibliography: R. Kestenberg-Gladstein, in: *Molad,* 23 (1965), 221–33; idem, *Neuere Geschichte der Juden in den boehmischen Laendern,* 1 (1969), 191–253. [M.La.]

GESELLSCHAFT ZUR FOERDERUNG DER WISSENSCHAFT DES JUDENTUMS (Ger. "Society for the Advancement of Jewish Scholarship"), Jewish scholarly society in Berlin, Germany, 1902–1938. In pursuit of its goal the Gesellschaft zur Foerderung der Wissenschaft des Judentums published and subsidized scholarly volumes, took over as its organ the established periodical **Monatsschrift fuer die Geschichte und Wissenschaft des Judentums,* held annual meetings featuring scholarly lectures, and provided grants to individual scholars. In order to create a comprehensive synthesis of the field of Judaica, the society planned a 36-volume "Grundriss der gesamten Wissenschaft des Judentums," which was not, however, completed. Membership in the society, whose first chairman was the historian Martin Philippson, was open to both individuals and organizations; it reached a high point of 1,742 members in 1920.

The first volume to be published by the organization was Leo Baeck's classic *Das Wesen des Judentums* (1905). Among the other important publications were M. Guedemann, *Juedische Apologetik* (1906); M. Philippson, *Neueste Geschichte des juedischen Volkes* (1907–11); G. Caro, *Die Sozial- und Wirtschaftsgeschichte der Juden* (1908–20); K. Kohler, *Grundriss einer systematischen Theologie des Judentums* (1910); I. Elbogen, *Der juedische Gottesdienst* (1913); H. Cohen, *Die Religion der Vernunft aus den Quellen des Judentums* (1919); and the not completed *Corpus Tannaiticum* and *Germania Judaica.* The society, which for more than a generation provided great impetus and organization for all branches of Jewish scholarship, was forced to cease its activities following the **Kristallnacht* riots.

Bibliography: L. Lucas, in: MGWJ, 71 (1927), 321–31; I. Elbogen, *ibid.,* 72 (1928), 1–5. [M.A.M.]

°GESENIUS, HEINRICH FRIEDRICH WILHELM (1786–1842), German orientalist, lexicographer, and Bible scholar. Born at Nordhausen, he taught in several German towns (Helmstedt, Goettingen, Heiligenstadt), and was appointed professor of theology at the University of Halle in 1881. He wrote a number of studies in Semitic language including *Versuch ueber die maltesische Sprache . . .,* Leipzig (1810); *De Pentateuchi Samaritani origine, indole et auctoriate . . .,* Halle (1815); *De Samaritanorum theologia ex fontibus ineditis commentatio,* Halle (1822); *Palaeographische Studien ueber phoenizische und punische Schrift* (1835); *Scripturae linguaeque phoeniciae monumenta quotquot supersunt edita et inedita* (1837). Gesenius' main field of interest was the scientific investigation of biblical Hebrew based on comparison with other Semitic languages and his studies remained basic for subsequent research. His work was the first in a field of research that freed the study of Hebrew from theological considerations. His most important contributions to the knowledge of Hebrew language and grammar are: (1) *Hebraeisch-deutsches Handwoerterbuch . . .,* in two volumes (Leipzig, 1810–12); an improved edition *"Hebraeisches und chaldaeisches Handwoerterbuch ueber das Alte Testament"* (Leipzig, 1815; after the tenth edition *aramaeisches* was substituted for *chaldaeisches*). The book has appeared in German in 16 editions. The 16th edition (1915) was reprinted several times and was translated into English (*A Hebrew and English Lexicon of the Old Testament,* ed. F. Brown, S. R. Driver, and Ch. A. Briggs, 1907[2]; corrected impression 1952). (2) *Thesaurus philologicus criticus linguae Hebraeae et Chaldaeae veteris testamenti* (started to appear in 1829 but was completed only posthumously by his pupil E. Roediger, in 1858). In this dictionary, Gesenius drew on talmudic sources and quotes Jewish Bible commentators such as *Rashi, Abraham *ibn Ezra, and David *Kimḥi. (3) *Hebraeische Grammatik* (Halle, 1813), a Hebrew grammar which appeared in German in 29 editions (editor G. Bergstraesser, 1929[29]; 29th edition not completed) and was also translated into English (*Gesenius' Hebrew Grammar,* ed. A. E. Cowley, 1910[2]). (4) *Hebraeisches Lesebuch* ("A Hebrew Reader," Halle, 1814); (5) *Geschichte der hebraeischen Sprache und Schrift* ("A History of the Hebrew language and script," Leipzig, 1815). (6) *Ausfuehrliches grammatisch-kritisches Lehrgebaeude der hebraeischen Sprache mit Vergleichung der verwandten Dialekte* (Leipzig, 1817). In it, he explained his scientific linguistic system based on comparative Semitic philology. Gesenius wrote one exegetical work, a commentary (together with a translation) on Isaiah, in three volumes (Leipzig 1820–21, 1829[2]).

Bibliography: E. F. Miller, *The Influence of Gesenius on Hebrew Lexicography* (1927); R. Haym, *Gesenius, eine Erinnerung fuer seine Freunde* (1842). [IR.G./ED.]

GESHER (Heb. גֶּשֶׁר), kibbutz in the Jordan Valley, Israel, near the confluence of the Jordan and Jarmuk rivers, affiliated with Ha-Kibbutz ha-Me'uḥad. Its land, belonging to the Palestine Jewish Colonization Association, was previously settled by another group which later established itself permanently at *Ashdot Ya'akov. Gesher was taken over in 1939 by Youth Aliyah graduates from Germany joined by Israel-born youth and settlers from various countries. In the War of Independence (1948) Gesher held out against a heavy bombardment when the Arabs attempted to cross the Jordan in order to reach Haifa. Gesher developed intensive farming and runs a gypsum plant. After the Six-Day War, it became a target for frequent artillery attacks from the other side of the Jordan. Its name, "Bridge," refers to a Roman bridge nearby and to modern railway and road bridges spanning the Jordan and Jarmuk. [E.O.]

GESHER BENOT YA'AKOV (Heb. גֶּשֶׁר בְּנוֹת יַעֲקֹב; "Bridge of the Daughters of Jacob"), a bridge on the Jordan situated at the southern end of the Huleh Valley where the riverbed enters the valley about 6 mi. (9 km.) E. of Rosh Pinnah, near kibbutz Gadot. In excavations conducted near the bridge by M. Stekelis (1935–36), remains of the Early Stone Age were uncovered including remains of elephants. Built of basalt arches, the original bridge was erected at the end of the 13th century on the site of a natural ford of the Jordan (cf. Isa. 8:23) which served as one of the most important links between Ereẓ Israel and Damascus via Galilee and the Golan. A branch of the ancient route, the Roman *Via Maris,* passed through the ford. The name of the bridge is derived from an Arab tradition according to which the patriarch Jacob crossed the Jordan here and his daughters were buried nearby. The crusaders called the ford Vadum Jacob. Because of its strategic importance, it was the scene of several famous battles. In 1157 Baldwin III, crusader king of Jerusalem, was defeated there by the Muslim ruler of Damascus, Nur al-Din. A fortress ("chastellet"), remains

Gesher Benot Ya'akov, bridge over the Jordan, 1969. Photo Zev Radovan, Jerusalem.

of which still stand, erected by Baldwin IV in 1178 and assigned to the Knights Templar, was captured by Saladin within a year of its construction. In 1799 soldiers of Napoleon were stationed at the bridge to prevent reinforcements from Damascus from reaching Acre which his army was besieging. A battle between British and Turkish forces took place at the bridge in 1918. It was one of the bridges blown up by members of the *Haganah* on the night of June 17, 1946. In May 1948 the Syrians entered Israel near the bridge and captured *Mishmar ha-Yarden, but later withdrew under the cease-fire agreements. After the Six-Day War (June 1967) the bridge served traffic to the Golan Heights.

Bibliography: Stekelis, in: BRCI, 9 (1960), 61–88. [Y.B.-AR.]

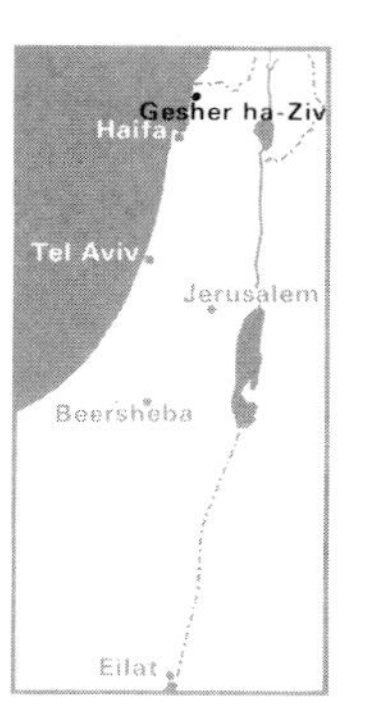

GESHER HA-ZIV (Heb. גֶּשֶׁר הַזִּיו), kibbutz in the northern Coastal Plain (Acre Valley) of Israel, N. of *Nahariyyah, affiliated with Iḥud ha-Kibbutzim. It was founded in 1949 by members of the former kibbutz Bet ha-Aravah evacuated during the War of Independence (1948). The founding members, some from Central Europe and some Israel-born, were later joined by pioneers from North America, South Africa, and other countries. The kibbutz engages in highly intensive farming and has a wood factory. It also runs a guest house. Gesher ha-Ziv, meaning "Bridge of Splendor,"

Memorial at kibbutz Gesher ha-Ziv to 14 Haganah men killed in the area in 1946. Courtesy Government Press Office, Tel Aviv.

commemorates a unit of 14 Haganah men who fell in the area on June 17, 1946, when they blew up a bridge over the Keziv River, during the struggle against the British; the name also refers to the nearby ancient city *Achzib. In 1968 its population was 328. [E.O.]

°**GESSIUS FLORUS,** the last procurator of Judea before the Jewish War; governed from 64–66 C.E. He was appointed on the recommendation of Nero's consort Poppaea Sabina (Tacitus, Historiae, 5:10). Florus showed himself to be an oppressive and rapacious ruler. On the occasion of a visit to Jerusalem of the Roman governor of Syria, *Cestius Gallus Gaius, the Jews complained bitterly to him of the procurator's conduct. On his departure the situation deteriorated. With the renewal of the quarrel at Caesarea between the Jews and the Syrians over the local synagogue, Florus promised the Jews his support but later adopted an anti-Jewish attitude (TJ, Bik. 2:3, 65d). The arrest of Jewish leaders who had come to Sebaste to enlist his aid, and his plundering of 17 talents from the Temple treasury, aroused the anger of the people against him, and the Jews sarcastically collected money in the streets of Jerusalem for the "indigent procurator." Florus demanded that those responsible should be handed over to him for punishment and finally ordered his soldiers to sack Jerusalem, paying no attention to the intercession of *Berenice, the sister of *Agrippa II. For a while the leading citizens were able to calm the people, but when Florus led his troops on the city the Jews rose in arms and succeeded in halting the Roman advance. Fearing a second attempt, the Jews now broke down the porticoes connecting the Temple Mount with the fortress of Antonia, whereupon Florus returned to Caesarea. Agrippa tried to calm the people, but they refused to submit any more to the orders of the procurator. Both Florus and the Jews gave the governor of Syria their own version of what had taken place. The latter sent an emissary to Jerusalem to learn the truth of the matter and subsequently informed Nero that the blame for the outbreak of war rested on Florus. There is no doubt that Florus's conduct was one of the chief causes of the ensuing war which resulted in the destruction of the Second Temple.

Bibliography: Jos., Ant., 20:252–68; Jos., Wars, 2:277ff., 558; Schuerer, Gesch, 1 (1901[4]), 585, 601ff.; Pauly-Wissowa, 13 (1910), 1325–28, no. 5.

[L.Ro.]

GESTAPO (abb. **GEheime STAatsPOlizei,** "Secret State Police"), the secret police of Nazi Germany that persecuted Jews at the outset of the Nazi regime and later played a central role in carrying out the "*Final Solution." The right-wing revolution in Prussia in late 1932 brought about a sweeping purge of "left-wing and Jewish elements" in its political police and paved the way for the changes of the Nazi era. The new Prussian minister of the interior after Hitler's rise to power, Hermann *Goering, completed the purge and gave the secret police executive powers, transforming it from a shadowing and information agency into a wide executive arm to persecute enemies of the Nazi regime. The head office of the secret state police—the Geheimes Staatspolizeiamt, or Gestapa—was given powers to shadow, arrest, interrogate, and intern; however, it had to struggle against the Nazi party organizations, the S.A. (Storm Troops) and *S.S., which also "fought" the regime's opponents, but without the supervision of traditional state bodies.

Simultaneously, with relatively few changes in the Prussian political police, the *Reichsfuehrer* of the S.S., Heinrich *Himmler, achieved control over the Bavarian political police and established direct ties between the S.S., the political police, and concentration camps. Thus Himmler snatched the secret police administration out of the hands of the state conservatives and in collaboration with the Bavarian minister of justice, Hans *Frank, and with Hitler's direct support, created an independent organization for shadowing, interrogation, arrest, imprisonment, and execution along the lines of the Nazi ideology (see *S.S. and S.D., and *Hitler). The Bavarian political police under Reinhard *Heydrich's direction was able to evade the laws that still applied in Germany in order to influence individuals, disband political parties, and liquidate trade unions. It led campaigns through the newspapers and radio against political opponents, interrogated individual "enemies," and sent them to the central concentration camp *Dachau. The officials of the political police all remained civil servants but were simultaneously drafted into the S.S. and subordinated to Himmler, both through the civil service and Nazi Party. Many of the officials had never been members of the Nazi Party, as was the case of Heinrich *Mueller, an old Weimar secret police man who became Heydrich's assistant and eventually headed the Gestapo.

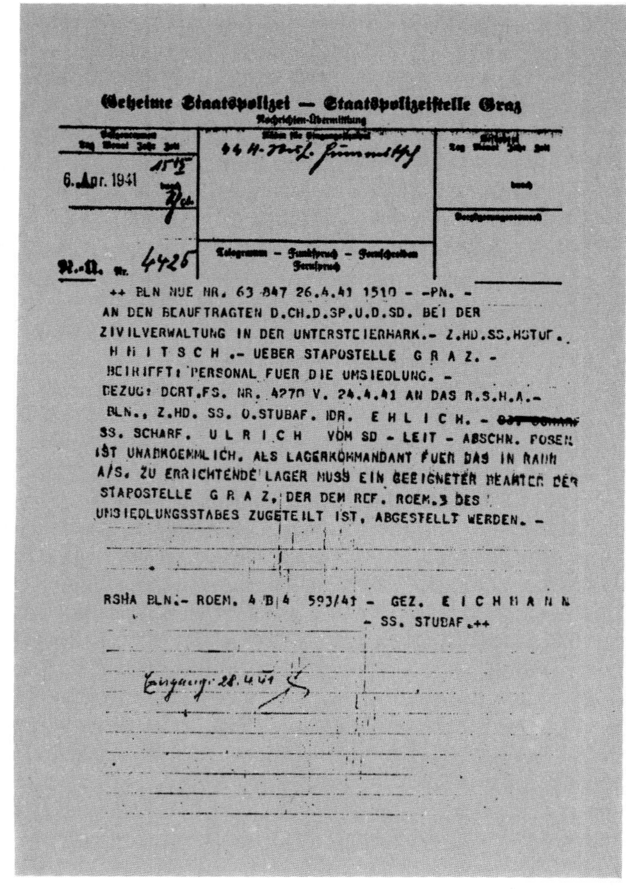
Geheime Staatspolizei — Staatspolizeistelle Graz
Nachrichten-Übermittlung

6. Apr. 1941 1515

N.-Ü. Nr. 4425

Telegramm — Funkspruch — Fernschreiben
Fernspruch

++ BLN NUE NR. 63 847 26.4.41 1510 - -PN. -
AN DEN BEAUFTRAGTEN D.CH.D.SP.U.D.SD. BEI DER
ZIVILVERWALTUNG IN DER UNTERSTEIERMARK.- Z.HD.SS.HSTUF.
H H I T S C H .- UEBER STAPOSTELLE G R A Z. -
BETRIFFT: PERSONAL FUER DIE UMSIEDLUNG. -
BEZUG: DORT.FS. NR. 4270 V. 24.4.41 AN DAS R.S.H.A.-
BLN., Z.HD. SS. O.STUBAF. DR. E H L I C H. -
SS. SCHARF. U L R I C H VOM SD - LEIT - ABSCHN. POSEN
IST UNABKOEMMLICH. ALS LAGERKOMMANDANT FUER DAS IN RANN
A/S. ZU ERRICHTENDE LAGER MUSS EIN GEEIGNETER BEAMTER DER
STAPOSTELLE G R A Z, DER DEM REF. ROEM.3 DES
UMSIEDLUNGSSTABES ZUGETEILT IST, ABGESTELLT WERDEN. -

RSHA BLN.- ROEM. 4 B 4 593/41 - GEZ. E I C H M A N N
- SS. STUBAF.++

Eingang: 28.4.41

Figure 1. Telegram from Adolf Eichmann to the Gestapo in Graz, Austria, April 1941, on the appointment of a commander for a new concentration camp in the region. Jerusalem, Israel Police, Section 06.

From the outset Heydrich's prisoners included many Jews, most of whom were intellectuals or active in left-wing parties. During 1933 the political police began shadowing and investigating Jewish organizations and Jewish community life and thus set up its own network for imprisonment and uniform repression of all the Jews of Bavaria, in the wake of the policy of isolating Jews that was part of the first stage and was followed by exerting pressure, openly and insidiously, on the Jews to emigrate.

Unification of the Political Police. From August 1933, Himmler managed to rise from his starting point in Bavaria to take over the political police of the various *Laender,* including Prussia. From the head office of the Prussian Gestapo in Berlin, which also became the headquarters of the S.S., Himmler and Heydrich directed all the political police services in Germany. The Gestapo then became the authority that investigated, along with the S.D., every aspect of life in Germany, and especially watched over the regime's "enemies of alien race." The Jews headed the list. Until the end of 1939, the Gestapo's Jewish Department was directed by Karl Haselbacher, a lawyer who was among those who drafted the first anti-Jewish laws. Until the outbreak of World War II, most of the murders in the camps were carried out on Gestapo orders under various cover-ups, such as "killed while attempting escape," but eventually these pretenses were dispensed with, especially where Jews were concerned.

From 1938. As an institution in charge of shadowing, interrogating, arresting, and imprisoning "enemies of the Reich," the Gestapo became a massive authority employing thousands of government officials and S.S. men who together persecuted the regime's "enemies" or other opponents. Various groups in the population were turned over and left to the

Gestapo's sole discretion; they were subjected to "neutralization" in camps without prior trial or forced to emigrate or face physical liquidation. From 1938 onward, the Gestapo began increasingly to deal with Jews who had previously been subject to other Nazi authorities. It had a hand in the **Kristallnacht* and enforced Jewish emigration. In competitive cooperation with the S.D., the Gestapo set up the *Zentralstelle fuer juedische Auswanderung in annexed Austria, directed by Adolf *Eichmann and headed by Mueller. Other centers for forced emigration were set up in 1939 in the Protectorate of Bohemia-Moravia and in Germany proper to accelerate the emigration of Jews by eviction and persecution, impoverishment, and degradation. When the Gestapo and part of the S.D. were joined under the *R.S.H.A. of the S.S. in November 1939, Office IV (Gestapo) of the new main office acquired sole authority over all Jews who were not yet imprisoned in camps.

During World War II the Gestapo, along with the S.D. and Security Police, constituted part of the *Einsatzgruppen* (mobile killing units) in Poland and other occupied countries. These units dealt with the murder and internment of numerous Jews and especially with the expulsion of the inhabitants of the small towns in Poland to mass concentration centers. Afterward Gestapo officials were appointed supervisors over the mass concentration of Jews. In Berlin headquarters the Gestapo in the first year of the war laid plans for various temporary "solutions for the Jewish problem," such as the establishment of a "reservation" in Poland or the mass transfer of Jews to Madagascar. At the end of 1940, when the Jews in Eastern Europe were interned in ghettos, the Gestapo, along with the German occupational civil administration, was charged with guarding and supervising the ghettos, imposing forced labor, and causing starvation and disease in an effort to decimate the ghetto inhabitants. In the Western occupied countries the Gestapo saw to registering the Jews and isolating them from the rest of the population for purposes of their eventual removal from economic life and confiscation of property. Under Eichmann, Section IVB4 of the Gestapo was *"federfuehrend"* (leading) in the "Final Solution."

The Einsatzgruppen. After the invasion of Russia in 1941, the *Einsatzgruppen,* headed by Gestapo men and directly responsible to Heydrich and Mueller, renewed the massacres on an enormous scale. The *Einsatzgruppen* carried out executions of Jews in the Baltic states and in Belorussia and wiped out part of the Ukrainian Jews. Later in 1941, the decision was made to kill all the Jews of Europe in gas chambers and the Gestapo was to supervise the dispatch of the Jews to the camps specially adapted or constructed for the program of mass murder (see *Holocaust, General Survey). The Gestapo section headed by Eichmann was in charge of the dispatch of Jews to the camps, and it also directly supervised at least one camp, *Theresienstadt, in Czechoslovakia. The section also supplied some of the gas used in the chambers, negotiated with countries under Nazi domination to accelerate the liquidation, and dealt with Jewish leaders, especially in Hungary (see *Kasztner) in an effort to smooth the process of the impending liquidation of various Jewish communities (see *Judenrat). The local Gestapo offices in Germany supervised the dispatch of Jews to death trains and the confiscation of their property. The Gestapo was largely responsible for the actual implementation of the dispatch orders and could choose its victims. It especially held the fate of people of mixed parentage *(Mischlinge)* in its hands. It excelled in its unabated and premeditated cruelty, in its ability to delude its intended victims as to the fate that awaited them, and in the use of barbaric threats and torture to lead the victims to their death, all as part of the "Final Solution."

At the same time the Gestapo acted as the principal executive arm of the Nazi regime in all the campaigns of terror, liquidation, looting, starvation, confiscation of property, and theft of cultural treasures (see Desecration and Destruction of *Synagogues; *Poland) throughout Europe. The Gestapo also repressed the anti-Nazi partisan movement and stamped out resistance in the Western European countries. Thus the term Gestapo became an accepted synonym for horror. After the war, very few of the important members of the Gestapo were caught and brought to trial. The courts in the Federal German Republic from 1969 discussed the question of several principal contingents of the Gestapo.

See also *Holocaust, General Survey.

Bibliography: G. Reitlinger, *SS, Alibi of a Nation* (1956); H. Hoehne, *The Order of the Death's Head: The Story of Hitler's SS* (1969); K. D. Bracher, W. Saver, and W. Schulz, *Die Nationalsozialistische Machtergreifung* (1968); S. Aronson, *Reinhard Heydrich und die Fruehgeschichte von Gestapo und SD* (1970); H. Krausnick et al., *Anatomy of the SS State* (1968); F. Zipfel, *Gestapo und SD in Berlin* (1961); R. Hilberg, *Destruction of the European Jews* (1961).

[SH.AR.]

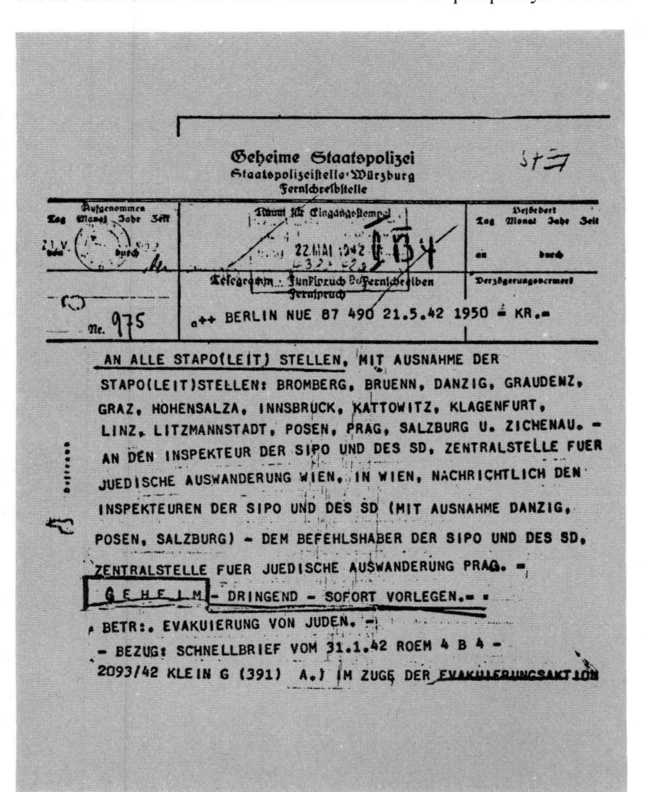

Geheime Staatspolizei
Staatspolizeistelle Würzburg
Fernschreibstelle

++ BERLIN NUE 87 490 21.5.42 1950 = KR.=

Nr. 975

AN ALLE STAPO(LEIT) STELLEN, MIT AUSNAHME DER STAPO(LEIT)STELLEN: BROMBERG, BRUENN, DANZIG, GRAUDENZ, GRAZ, HOHENSALZA, INNSBRUCK, KATTOWITZ, KLAGENFURT, LINZ, LITZMANNSTADT, POSEN, PRAG, SALZBURG U. ZICHENAU. – AN DEN INSPEKTEUR DER SIPO UND DES SD, ZENTRALSTELLE FUER JUEDISCHE AUSWANDERUNG WIEN, IN WIEN, NACHRICHTLICH DEN INSPEKTEUREN DER SIPO UND DES SD (MIT AUSNAHME DANZIG, POSEN, SALZBURG) – DEM BEFEHLSHABER DER SIPO UND DES SD, ZENTRALSTELLE FUER JUEDISCHE AUSWANDERUNG PRAG. =

GEHEIM – DRINGEND – SOFORT VORLEGEN.=

BETR:. EVAKUIERUNG VON JUDEN. –

– BEZUG: SCHNELLBRIEF VOM 31.1.42 ROEM 4 B 4 – 2093/42 KLEIN G (391) A.) IM ZUGE DER EVAKUIERUNGSAKTION

Figure 2. Secret telegram from Berlin to the Wurzburg Gestapo, May 1942, concerning the deportation of Jews. Jerusalem, Israel Police, Section 06.

GESTETNER, DAVID (1854–1939), British industrialist. Born in Csorna, Hungary, he was the inventor of the cyclostyle duplicating process and was credited with being the founder of modern stencil duplicating. At 17, chafing at the monotony of clerking on the Vienna Stock Exchange, he went to New York, where, after experimenting with papers for duplicating, he moved on to London to sell his invention and set up business. The firm he founded now has worldwide branches and factories, employing thousands of people. Entering communal life, he was a founder of the Green Lanes Synagogue, London (1897). SIGMUND (1897–1956), David's son, was chairman and managing director of the Gestetner business when he was 23, and made a name as a progressive industrialist. Influenced by Chaim Weizmann, he was a devoted Zionist, and as chairman of the *Keren Hayesod in England at the time of the Nazi regime in Germany he helped Jewish craftsmen to escape, and through the *Central British Fund for German Jewry and the Children's Movement, he helped to resettle refugees. He served in the army in World War I, and in World War II he turned his factory over to war work and organized the Balfour Club

Sigmund Gestetner, British industrialist and Zionist. Courtesy J.N.F., London.

for the Jewish Forces in London. He was treasurer of the Jewish National Fund in Britain in 1949, and became its president in 1950. He was treasurer of the Joint Palestine Appeal and honorary treasurer of the Weizmann Institute Foundation. He was also a successful farmer, and lent his farm to the Zionist movement for training agricultural pioneers for Ereẓ Israel.

Bibliography: *The Times*, London (March 16, 1939; April 21, 1956). [J.M.S.]

GESUNDHEIT, JACOB BEN ISAAC (1815–1878), Polish rabbi and author. Gesundheit was born in Praga, a suburb of Warsaw. He studied there under Leib Zinz of Plotsk. On the death of Dov Berush b. Isaac Meisels, rabbi of Warsaw, Gesundheit was chosen to succeed him (1870). Possessed of considerable means, he had not previously held a rabbinic post despite the fact that he was a great talmudist, headed a yeshivah, and had already written a number of books. Gesundheit fought strongly against *Ḥasidism, which was on the increase in Warsaw. The Ḥasidim fought back and together with the assimilationists under Ludwig Nathanson compelled him to resign from the rabbinate after four years. He died four years later. All his published books are entitled *Tiferet Ya'akov*. He wrote novellae on the Shulḥan Arukh (1842–1926), and on tractates *Gittin* (1858) and *Ḥullin* (2 pts., 1867–1910). His responsa and other talmudic novellae have remained in manuscript.

Bibliography: Fuenn, Keneset, 542f.; "Toledot Rabbenu Ya'akov Gesundheit," in: *Reshimat ha-Sefarim mi-Sifriyyat Gesundheit* (1939), 5–8. [Y.Al.]

GE'ULEI TEIMAN (Heb. גְּאוּלֵי תֵימָן; "The Redeemed from Yemen"), moshav and housing quarter in the Ḥefer Plain, Israel, founded in 1947 by settlers from Yemen as an extension of the neighboring village of *Elyashiv. The farming community is affiliated with Ha-Po'el ha-Mizrachi Moshavim Association (since 1967). In 1968 its population was 181. [E.O.]

GE'ULIM (Heb. גְּאוּלִים; "Redeemed Ones"), moshav in central Israel, S.E. of *Netanyah, affiliated with Tenu'at ha-Moshavim, founded in 1938 by settlers from Yemen. Ge'ulim engages in intensive farming, mainly in citrus orchards. Its population in 1968 was 480. [E.O.]

GE'ULLAH (Heb. גְּאֻלָּה; "Redemption"), title of several prayers. That section in the morning and evening prayer which is recited between the *Shema* and the **Amidah* is known as *Ge'ullah*. This ancient prayer is mentioned in the Mishnah (Ber. 1:4; 2:2; Tam. 5:1) and referred to as *Ge'ullah* in the Talmud (Pes. 117b). The original text was probably much shorter; according to Zunz it contained only 45 Hebrew words. The present wording varies considerably in different rites. The prayer starts with the words *"emet ve-emunah"* ("true and trustworthy") in the evening prayer and with *"emet ve-yaẓiv"* ("true and firm") in the morning prayer (Ber. 12a). It opens with a profession of faith, enumerates the miracles of the redemption of Israel from Egypt, and closes with a plea to the Redeemer of Israel to deliver them again. In some Sephardi rituals, however, there is a longer variant ending. The Talmud (Ber. 4b, 9b) insists that there be no interruption between *Ge'ullah* and the *Amidah* and so even the response *"Amen"* is omitted after the *Ge'ullah* benediction in the morning prayer. In the evening prayer **Hashkivenu* is inserted between them, the interruption being permitted because the recitation of the evening prayer was not considered obligatory in the Talmud.

The name *Ge'ullah* applies also to the *piyyutim* which are inserted before the closing formula of this prayer on special Sabbaths and on the three pilgrimage festivals.

The Mishnah uses the term *Ge'ullah* for the benediction recited at the end of *Hallel* during the Passover *seder* (Pes. 10:6).

The term *Ge'ullah* is also used to designate the seventh benediction of the *Amidah* which ends with the words "the Redeemer of Israel."

Bibliography: ET, 5 (1953), 43–46; Elbogen, Gottesdienst, 22ff., 101, 211f., 514; Eisenstein, Dinim, 67f.; Idelsohn, Liturgy, 41, 92, 99. [Ed.]

GEVA (Heb. גֶּבַע; "Hill"), kibbutz in the Valley of Jezreel, Israel, affiliated with Iḥud ha-Kevuẓot ve-ha-Kibbutzim, and founded in 1921 by Third Aliyah pioneers from Russia who were later joined by new settlers from different countries. In 1968 the kibbutz had 510 inhabitants, engaged in highly intensive mixed farming, and ran a factory for electronic instruments. [E.O.]

GEVARAM (Heb. גְּבַרְעָם; "the People Overcomes"), kibbutz in the southern coastal plain of Israel, S. of Ashkelon, affiliated with Ha-Kibbutz ha-Me'uḥad, founded in 1942. The settlers, mainly pioneers from Slovakia, Austria, Holland, and Germany, previously maintained a transitory camp at *Kefar Sava as hired agricultural workers. They initially suffered from the lack of water, but sufficient groundwater table was discovered to cover local needs and to supply other settlements. The siege of the Egyptian army during the War of Independence was lifted in Operation Ten Plagues (October 1948). Gevaram's economy is based on intensive and largely irrigated farming, dairy cattle, and a metal factory. In 1968 its population was 240. [E.O.]

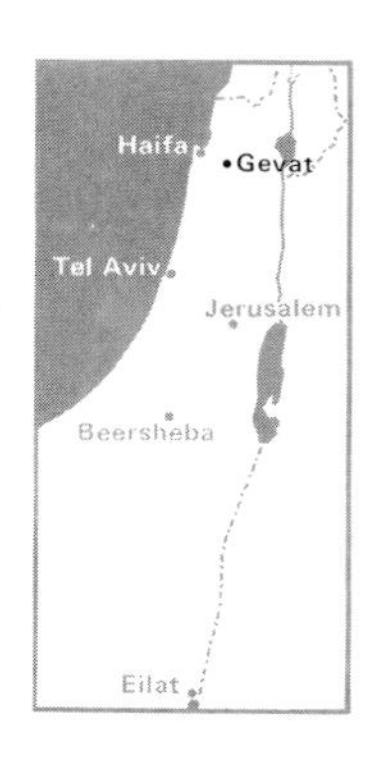

GEVAT (Heb. גְּבַת), kibbutz in northern Israel, in the *Jezreel Valley, at the foot of the *Nazareth Hills, affiliated with Ha-Kibbutz ha-Me'uḥad. It was founded in 1926 by pioneers from Pinsk, Poland. The kibbutz participated in the draining of the Jezreel Valley swamps. With the split in Ha-Kibbutz ha-Me'uḥad in 1951–52, some of its members established a separate kibbutz, *Yifat, further east. In 1968, Gevat had 625 inhabitants and its economy was based on intensive mixed farming. The kibbutz produces plastic products and runs metal workshops. Gevat is a historical name, mentioned by Eusebius (Onom. 70:9ff.) in its Aramaic form Gabata. [E.O.]

GÉVAUDAN, region in France, corresponding to the present department of Lozère. Jews were first recorded in Gévaudan in 1229, in the town of *Mende, and they were also found in Marvejols and Meyrueis. The supposition that the names of localities like Salmon, Gimel, etc. indicate an earlier presence of Jews can be dismissed as fantasy. However, it is probable that the place name Montjézieu derives from an earlier name *mons judaeus.* Gulielmus Durandus, bishop of Mende (1285–96), enforced in his diocese the canonical laws prohibiting Christians from entering the service of Jews and forbidding the Jews to appear in public during Easter or to work on Sundays and Christian holidays; they were also compelled to wear the *badge. When they were expelled in 1306, Gévaudan's Jews had an estimated capital of 15,000 livres. A few Jews were living in Marvejols in 1322.

Bibliography: N. Pinzuti, in: *Archives Juives*, 2, no. 3 (1965/66, 2ff.
[B.BL.]

GEVIM (Heb. גְּבִים), kibbutz in the coastal plain of Israel, 8 mi. (13 km.) E. of Gaza, affiliated with Iḥud ha-Kevuẓot ve-ha-Kibbutzim, founded in August 1947. Gevim was one of the first links in the settlement chain extending to the south and Negev that had to defend itself against the Egyptian forces in the *Israel War of Independence (a few months after its establishment). The founding members were Israel-born and *Youth Aliyah graduates from Central Europe. Irrigated and unirrigated field crops and dairy cattle are its prominent farm branches. Gevim means "Water Holes," an allusion to the first Negev water pipeline, which passes through the kibbutz. [E.O.]

GEVULOT (Heb. גְּבוּלוֹת), kibbutz in southern Israel, 20 mi. (32 km.) W. of Beersheba, affiliated with Kibbutz Arẓi ha-Shomer ha-Ẓa'ir, founded in 1943 as the first of the three "observation outposts" established to explore settlement conditions in the Negev (the other two were *Bet Eshel and *Revivim). The sandy loess soil of the region proved cultivable despite the severe lack of water. In 1946, on the basis of Gevulot's successful experiments, 11 additional settlements were erected in the south and the Negev. In the *War of Independence (1948) the isolated kibbutz held out against the long Egyptian siege until Operation Ten Plagues (October 1948). With water made available through the Yarkon-Negev pipeline in the 1950s, the kibbutz developed intensive farm branches in addition to its unirrigated grain fields. Its factory makes spraying equipment and other farm implements. Gevulot's name, "Borders," was chosen as the kibbutz was, at the time of its founding, the Jewish settlement nearest to the Egyptian border. [E.O.]

GEWITSCH, AARON WOLF (c. 1700–c. 1770), Austrian scribe, illuminator, one of the most gifted and prolific of the school of Jewish manuscript artists who flourished in Central Europe in the 18th century. His work was somewhat uneven in quality, probably because later he

Title page of *Haggadah* designed and illustrated by Aaron Wolf Gewitsch in Pressburg, 1730. Budapest, Library of the Hungarian Academy of Sciences, Kaufmann Collection.

employed an assistant. Born in Posen, he settled first in Gewitsch and then in Vienna, and from about 1724 acquired a reputation by a series of Hebrew illuminated manuscripts. A dozen of his Haggadah manuscripts are extant in various collections, but he was responsible also for other manuscript books of Psalms (one executed for an Austrian archduke), occasional prayers, and other miscellaneous volumes. Although like other Hebrew manuscript artists of the period, he followed traditional lines in his compositions, he introduced new groupings and an exceptional freshness of approach. In 1735 he was in the employment of the Imperial Library in Vienna. He also engaged in calligraphic work in other languages.

Bibliography: Naményi, in: REJ, 116 (1957), 61–63; Roth, Art, 488–9.
[C.R.]

GEZER (Heb. גֶּזֶר). (1) Major city in ancient times located in the northern Shephelah at Tell Jazar (also called Tell Abu-Shūsha). Gezer was first settled in the Chalcolithic period (fourth millennium B.C.E.); in the Early Bronze Age I it was occupied by a non-Semitic people who followed the custom of burning their dead. Semitic settlers established there in the Early Bronze Age II–IV (3rd millennium B.C.E.) enclosed the city with a wall. The Canaanite occupation reached its peak of prosperity in the Middle Bronze and Late Bronze I

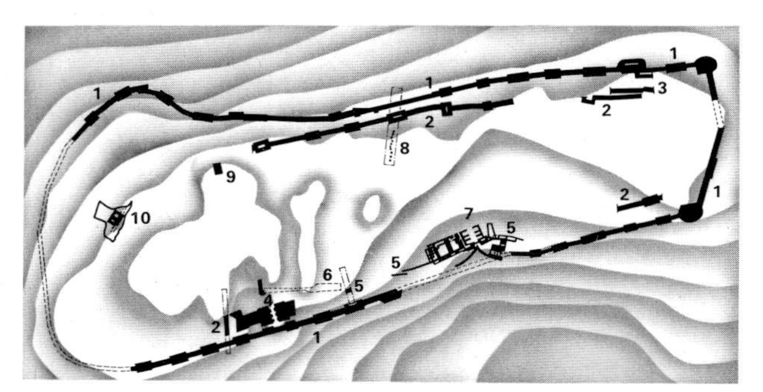

1. Outer wall of the Late Bronze Age.
2. Inner wall of the Middle Bronze Age.
3. Part of the inner wall.
4. Gate of the inner wall, three entry way.
5. Part of the casemate wall.
6. Water tunnel of the Late Bronze Age.
7. Four entry way gate of the Solomonic period.
8. High place of the Middle Bronze Age.
9. Wêli (a hole to obtain water).
10. Part of the inner wall (excavation of 1934).

Plan of the Gezer excavations. Courtesy William G. Dever, Hebrew Union College, Biblical and Archaeological School, Jerusalem.

Ages (20th–14th centuries B.C.E.), when a stone wall 10ft. (3 m.) wide with square towers was built around the city. This period at Gezer also yielded objects testifying to links with Egypt as well as a potsherd in ancient Canaanite script. The city is first mentioned in Egyptian documents in the list of cities captured by Thutmose III (c. 1469 B.C.E.). The importance of Gezer in the 14th century is evident from the *Tell el-Amarna letters. Milkilu, king of Gezer, and his successor Yapahu controlled an extensive area which also included Aijalon and Zorah; their chief rival was the king of Jerusalem. The capture of Gezer is mentioned in the "Israel stele" of Pharaoh Merneptah (c. 1220 B.C.E.) together with Ashkelon and Yeno'am. During the Israelite conquest, Horam, king of Gezer, was defeated in battle by the Israelites (Josh. 10:33). His city was assigned to the Levites in the territory of Ephraim but its population remained predominantly Canaanite (Josh. 16:3, 21:21). Pharaoh Siamun (?) conquered Gezer and ceded it to Israel "for a portion unto his daughter, Solomon's wife." Commanding the approaches to Jerusalem, the city became one of the major strongholds of Solomon who built a gate there identical in plan with gates he erected at Hazor and Megiddo (I Kings 9:15–17). Part of the Solomonic city gate, built of dressed stones, and an adjacent casemate wall have been discovered there. A stepped tunnel 216 ft. (66 m.) long cut to provide access to the water table may date to this period. Also found there is a small contemporary stone tablet of seven lines ("the *Gezer Calendar"). Gezer was conquered by Shishak according to that Pharaoh's inscriptions (c. 924 B.C.E.) and archaeological finds indicate that the city declined at that time. Tiglath-Pileser III's capture of the city (probably in 74 B.C.E.) is depicted on a relief found at Calah. In the Assyrian period Gezer's population was augmented by foreign settlers; contracts of two of these, written in cuneiform from the years 651 and 649 B.C.E., have survived. The city recovered in the Persian period and under the Hellenistic kings it again became an important royal fortress. During the Hasmonean wars Gezer was a major Greek base and remained in Greek hands until its capture in 142 B.C.E. by Simeon who expelled the aliens. He refortified the city and made it the military center of his state, under the command of his son John Hyrcanus, second only to Jerusalem (I Macc. 4:15; 9:52: 13:43; 16:19). A Hasmonean palace discovered there was apparently built by Greek prisoners of war; a curse was found scratched on one of its stones: "May fire descend from heaven and devour the house of Simeon." Gezer's importance declined after the Hasmonean period and the center of the district was transferred to Emmaus. Eusebius mentions it as a village four miles north (this should read "south") of Emmaus (Onom. 66:19ff.). It does not appear in other ancient sources but a Roman bathhouse and several Christian lamps found there testify to its continued occupation. On the Madaba Map, the legend "Gedor also Gidirtha" apparently refers to Gezer. It was known as Montgisart in the crusader period; there King Baldwin II defeated the forces of Saladin in 1177 but by 1191 it was in the hands of the Muslims and served as their headquarters in the war against Richard the Lionhearted.

Figure 1. A "high place" at Gezer, with ten pillars and a stone basin or altar. Middle Bronze Age II, c. 1600 B.C.E. Courtesy William G. Dever, Hebrew Union College, Biblical and Archaeological School, Jerusalem.

Figure 2. Solomonic city gate at Gezer, with finely dressed ashlar masonry at the threshold. (1) On the sides of the street, divided by a large drain (2), are four sets of piers guarding the entry. Courtesy William G. Dever, Hebrew Union College, Biblical and Archaeological School, Jerusalem.

After crusader times the site was completely forgotten. It was reidentified by C. Clermont-Ganneau in 1873 and investigated in excavations conducted at Tell Jazar by R.A.S. Macalister from 1902 to 1912, A. Rowe in 1934–35, and from 1964, by the Hebrew Union College under G. E. Wright, William G. Dever, and others. [M.A.-Y.]

(2) Gezer is a kibbutz in central Israel, E. of *Ramleh, and is affiliated with Iḥud ha-Kevuẓot ve-Kibbutzim. Its land was originally acquired by the Ancient Order of Maccabaeans in England because of its proximity to *Modi'in. The settlement was founded in 1945 by settlers from Central Europe together with Israel-born youth. In the Israel *War of Independence (1948), Gezer, located in the thin chain of settlements connecting Jerusalem with the

Figure 3. Boundary stone at Gezer, Herodian period, first century B.C.E. The stone is inscribed "boundary of Gezer" in Hebrew and "[belonging to] Alkios" in Greek. Courtesy William G. Dever, Hebrew Union College, Biblical and Archaeological School, Jerusalem.

Coastal Plain, was involved in a hard battle with the Arab Legion and served as a vantage point in Operation Dani (July 1948), which resulted in the inclusion of the towns of Ramleh and Lydda in the State of Israel. Gezer runs various farms branches and has a workshop for wood products. A pumping station of the Yarkon-Negev water pipeline is located nearby. [E.O.]

Bibliography: Clermont-Ganneau, Arch, 2 (1899), 224ff.; R. A. S. Macalister, *Excavation of Gezer,* 3 vols. (1912); Abel, in: RB, 35 (1926), 513ff.; Rowe, in: PEFQS, 67 (1935), 19ff.; EM, 2 (1965), 465–71; A. Malamat (ed.), in: *Bi-Ymei Bayit Rishon* (1961), 35ff.; Yadin, *ibid.*, 66ff.; idem, in: IEJ, 8 (1958), 80ff.; W. G. Dever, in: *Jerusalem Through the Ages* (1968), 26–32); idem, in: *Qadmoniot,* 3 (1970), 57–62; idem, in: *The Biblical Archaeologist,* 30 (1967), 47–62; H. Lance, in: *ibid.*, 34–47; J. Ross, in: *ibid,* 62–71.

The "Gezer Calendar," an ancient Hebrew record of the annual cycle of agricultural occupations, late tenth century B.C.E. Replica in the Israel Museum, Jerusalem.

GEZER CALENDAR, a Hebrew inscription of seven lines, engraved on a limestone tablet written in ancient Hebrew script; discovered in Gezer by R. A. S. *Macalister in 1908. The Gezer Calendar is dated by its script to the tenth century B.C.E. and cites an annual cycle of agricultural activities that seem to begin with the month of Tishri. The word *yeraḥ* ("his month") or *yerḥu* (*yrḥw;* "his two months") precedes the name of each month. According to an accepted view, the inscription first lists two months of fruit picking, particularly olives (Tishri-Ḥeshvan). Then follow two months of grain sowing (Kislev-Tevet), two months concerned with the late sowing (Shevat-Adar), one month of flax harvest (by uprooting with a mattock; Nisan), one month of barley harvest (Iyyar), a month of wheat harvest (Sivan), two months of vine pruning or of vintage (Tammuz-Av), and, at the end, the month of *kayiẓ,* i.e., the picking or drying of figs (Elul). In the left lower edge of the inscription "Aby[...]" is written vertically. It is possible that the name indicates the owner of the inscription. The nature and purpose of the calendar are not clear, and many different explanations have been proposed. According to some scholars, the calendar was written as a schoolboy exercise in writing. This view derives from the fact that the script is rather crude. Another view holds that the Gezer Calendar was designated for the collection of taxes from farmers. It is also possible that the content of the inscription is a popular folk song, listing the months of the year according to the agricultural seasons.

Bibliography: R. A. S. Macalister, *Excavation of Gezer,* 2 (1912), 24–28; Albright, in: BASOR, 92 (1943), 16–26; L. Finkelstein, *ibid.*, 94 (1944), 28–29; Wright, in: BA, 18 (1955), 50–56; Segal, in: JSS, 7 (1962), 212–21; Talmon, in: JAOS, 83 (1963), 177–87; Wirgin, in: *Eretz Israel,* 6 (1960), 9–12 (Eng. section); Rathjen, in: PWQ, 93 (1961), 70–72; Honeyman, in: JRAS (1953), 53–58; Pritchard, Texts, 320; Pritchard, Pictures, 272; EM, 2 (1965), 471–4 (incl. bibl.).

[B.O.]

°**GHAZĀLĪ, ABU ḤAMID MUHAMMAD IBN MUHAMMAD AL-ṬŪSĪ AL-** (1058–1111), Persian Muslim theologian, jurist, mystic, and religious reformer, who wrote mainly in Arabic.

Al-Ghazālī's best-known work is his *Iḥyāʾ ʿUlūm al-Dīn* ("Revival of the Religious Sciences") in which he successfully reconciled orthodox Islam and *Sufism. The four large volumes of this work constitute one of the major works of Sunni Islam and were able decisively to blunt the threat that Sufism posed to orthodoxy. As a result, some of the warmth and emotional religious feeling inherent in Islamic mysticism was infused into the legalistic approach of Sunni Islam. In his early career, al-Ghazālī wrote his famous *Tahāfut al-Falāsifaʾ* ("Incoherence of the Philosophers") in which he directly confronted the claims of the philosophic systems of al-*Fārābī and *Avicenna. The book is divided into 20 topics, the most important of which is the discussion of the createdness of the world. At the end of his work, he offers the legal opinion that the philosophers are guilty of heresy and are liable to the death penalty on three counts: they believe in the eternity of the world, they disbelieve in the omniscience of God, and they do not accept the dogma of bodily resurrection. *Averroes wrote his *Tahāfut al-Tahāfut* ("Incoherence of the Incoherence") in reply, but philosophy as a major discipline of study disappeared from the Islamic world, except for Persia.

Al-Ghazālī had summed up the philosophic system of al-Fārābī and Avicenna in his *Maqāṣid al-Falāsifaʾ* ("Intentions of Philosophers"), which was supposed to serve as an introductory volume to his *Incoherence* but was used as a handy, independent compendium of philosophy. In his

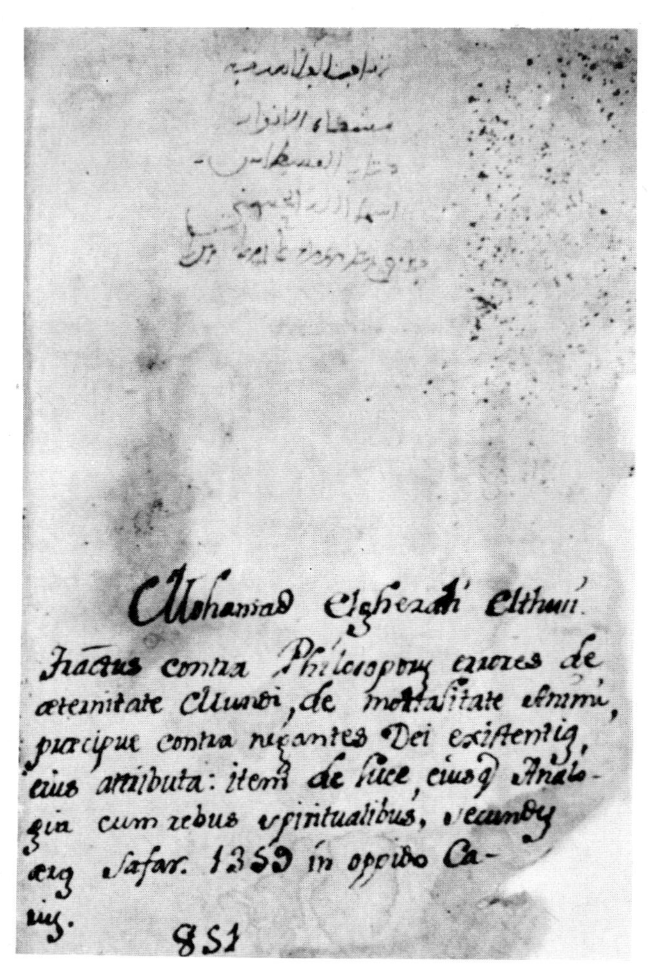

Flyleaf of the Escorial manuscript containing works of al-Ghazālī, Madrid, Escorial Library, Arabic Ms. 631, leaf 1b.

Deliverance from Error he discussed his initial skepticism concerning the possibility of knowledge, and then his search for enlightenment in *Kalām (scholastic theology), philosophy, the doctrine of certain Islamic sects that there exists an authoritative Imām, or religious guide to absolute knowledge (Ismaʿilism), and finally Sufism, in which he found the solution to his quest for certainty.

Influence on Jewish Philosophy. Al-Ghazālī's influence on Jewish thought falls into two periods: (1) through the 13th century when he influenced Jewish thinkers who thought and wrote in Arabic, and (2) from the 13th century onward when a number of his works were translated into Hebrew, some more than once, commented on, and read by the Jewish thinkers of Provence and Spain, who did not know Arabic. In the first period al-Ghazālī influenced *Judah Halevi, who followed al-Ghazālī's *Incoherence* in attacking the Aristotelian philosophy then current in Spain. One of Judah Halevi's main arguments refers to the difference of opinion among philosophers, except in matters of mathematics and logic, to which al-Ghazālī had already referred. However, in a more general and profound sense, al-Ghazālī made apparent the great danger of philosophy for revealed religion, and it is in this sense that Judah Halevi was a true disciple of his great Islamic predecessor. Judah Halevi also quotes textually from an early work of al-Ghazālī that sums up the dogmatic bases of the belief of a religious person. This early work of al-Ghazālī was later incorporated into his *Revival*.

Although it cannot be demonstrated conclusively, most probably *Maimonides had read al-Ghazālī's *Incoherence* and was influenced by it in formulating the contrasting conceptions of a god of religion, who exercises free will, and a god of philosophy, who is restricted by the immutability of the order of nature (Maimonides, *Guide of the Perplexed*, ed. by S. Pines (1963), cxxvii). The parallel between al-Ghazālī, who attempted to reconcile Islam and Sufism in his *Revival*, and Maimonides, who attempted to reconcile the law of Judaism with philosophy in his *Guide*, is instructive, and Maimonides' idea of an all-inclusive legal work including non-legal aspects may have been influenced by al-Ghazālī's *Revival* as well.

The number of works of al-Ghazālī translated into Hebrew during the 13th century also indicates his popularity during the preceding period, in which they had become well known and were considered worth translation. His *Intentions of the Philosophers* was translated into Hebrew three times. Isaac *Albalag, who was one of the translators, used it as point of departure for his own views, which he expressed in excursuses appended to his translation. *Moses of Narbonne composed a full commentary to the work; his commentary was the object of further comments and commentaries to the beginning of the 16th century. Even a poetical version in Hebrew was composed in the second half of the 14th century by *Abraham Avigdor b. Meshullam. Al-Ghazālī's *Incoherence* was translated into Hebrew once independently and more than once in the form in which Averroes quotes it in his *Incoherence of the Incoherence;* the latter was translated into Hebrew a number of times. Altogether, at least six works ascribed to al-Ghazālī were translated into Hebrew during the Middle Ages. Transliterations into Hebrew letters of al-Ghazālī's *Intentions, Incoherence,* and *Deliverance* are extant, which is another indication of al-Ghazālī's popularity among the Jewish intellectuals who knew Arabic.

It is interesting to note that on the flyleaf of a manuscript containing some of his works in Arabic letters, the contents are described in Hebrew letters as being by "Abu Ḥāmid al-Ghazālī, the memory of the righteous be blessed," the usual designation for a pious Jew (see illustration). This illustrates how congenial his general outlook was felt to be by Jewish medieval thinkers and is a striking example of Jewish-Islamic medieval symbiosis. In general, one may say that the influence of al-Ghazālī on Jewish thinkers who wrote in Arabic and Hebrew was considerable throughout the 15th century and, through Judah Halevi, on religious Jews to the present day. His case presents an example of Jewish assimilation of Islamic thought during the Middle Ages.

For a detailed list of his writings see W. M. Watt, in: EJ², s.v. *al-Ghazālī*. For a list of his writings translated into Hebrew see H. Baneth, in: EJ, 2 (1928), 287–91, s.v. *Algazali*.

Bibliography: Steinschneider, Uebersetzungen, 296–348; Guttmann, Philosophies, index.

[L.V.B.]

GHELERTER, LITMAN (1873–1946), Rumanian physician and socialist leader. Ghelerter studied medicine in his native Jassy, where he joined the socialist movement. In 1895 he founded *Lumina* ("The Light"), a socialist group and a journal of the same name. He was also active in the struggle for granting political rights to Jews deprived of Rumanian citizenship, and thereby came into conflict with the official leadership of the party. In 1896 he edited a Yiddish periodical *Der Veker* ("The Awaker"). After World War I, Ghelerter went to Bucharest and started a new party, *Partidul Socialist Unitar* (The United Socialist Party). He founded a hospital which existed until the advent of the Fascist regime in Rumania.

Bibliography: J. Kisman, *Shtudien tsu der Geshikhte fun Rumenishe Yidn in 19-tn un Onheyb 20-tn Yorhundert* (1944).

[I.Be.]

GHENT (Flemish: **Gent;** Fr. **Gand**), city in N.W. Belgium. That there was a Jewish settlement in Ghent in the eighth century, as indicated in some early Christian chronicles, is difficult to believe. The Jews were expelled from the city as from the rest of Flanders in 1125, but they were apparently permitted to return in the 13th century. The Jews were again expelled during the *Black Death, 1348–49. Jews began to settle again only in the 18th century. In 1724, the municipal council decided on a special formula of oath for the Jews. However, by 1756, only one Jewish resident, a jeweler, was still in Ghent. When the area passed to France, at the end of the 18th century, the Jewish population increased. It numbered 20 families (107 persons) in 1817, and maintained a synagogue. The majority were peddlers, some of whom were lottery-ticket dealers. Apparently the Jewish street *(Jodenstraatje)* received its name at this time. In 1847, the municipal council granted a plot of land to the community for establishing a Jewish cemetery. In May 1940, before the Nazi occupation, the Jewish population numbered 300. In 1941 the Nazis prohibited the Jews of Belgium to live outside Brussels, Antwerp, Liège, and Charleroi, so that any Jews who remained in Ghent did so illegally. After the liberation in September 1944, there were 150 Jews in Ghent. There were an estimated 80 Jews living in Ghent in 1969.

Bibliography: E. Ouverteaux, *Notes et documents sur les Juifs de Belgique sous l'ancien régime* (1885), 21, 27; E. Ginsburger, *Les Juifs de Belgique au XVIIIe siècle* (1932), 86–97; S. Ullmann, *Histoire des Juifs en Belgique jusqu'au 19è siècle* (1934), 37–49, 50, 58; E. Sperling-Levin in *Regards* (Dec. 1970), 20–27.

[Ed.]

GHEREA-DOBROGEANU, CONSTANTIN (originally **Solomon Katz;** 1855–1920), Rumanian literary critic and Socialist theoretician. Born in Slavianka, Ukraine, Katz became involved in revolutionary politics as a student at Kharkov University. His subsequent political career was colorful and adventurous. Pursued by the czarist police, he crossed into Rumania in 1875, but three years later the Russian authorities found him masquerading as an American citizen, and he was kidnapped and taken back to Russia. After a year's imprisonment, Katz, who had by now formally converted to Christianity, succeeded in making his way back to Rumania, where he changed his name to Constantin Gherea-Dobrogeanu. He obtained the restaurant concession at the Ploesti railway station, and the place became an asylum for writers and Rumanian and Russian refugee socialists. Gherea-Dobrogeanu's career as a writer followed separate literary and political roads. As a literary theorist and critic, his great achievement was the introduction into Rumania of the scientific concept of art as opposed to "art for art's sake." He insisted that art was a product of society and reflected the outlook of different social groups and classes. The articles he began publishing in various periodicals in 1885 were collected in his *Studii critice* (3 vols., 1890–97; 2 vols., 1925–27[2]), to which a fourth volume was subsequently added. The work became the main guide to the materialist viewpoint in Rumanian literature. As a political writer, Gherea-Dobrogeanu was the great popularizer of Marxist socialism in Rumania. Outstanding among his political works was his *Concepţia materialistă a istoriei* ("The Materialist Concept of History," 1892), which remained a classic text for generations, as did *Ce vor socialiştii* ("What do the Socialists Want," 1886; 1946[4]), *Anarhism şi socialism* (1894), and *Socialismul in România.* In his social study *Neoiobăgia* ("The New Finality," 1910), Gherea-Dobrogeanu declared that even a bourgeois revolution had still to take place in Rumania. In 1941, at the height of Antonescu's dictatorship, the Bucharest authorities exhumed Gherea-Dobrogeanu's remains and induced the Jewish community to rebury them in the Jewish cemetery. After World War II the new communist government severely criticized his ideas, seeing in him a typical representative of the social democratic camp, and declared him guilty of "grave ideological errors."

Caricature of Constantin Gherea-Dobrogeanu, Rumanian socialist theoretician. Courtesy D. Litani, Tel Aviv.

Bibliography: G. Călinescu, *Istoria literaturii Romîne . . .* (1941), 484–8; F. Aderca, *Viaţa şi Opera lui Dobrogeanu-Gherea* (1948); A. Dima, *Studii de Istorie a teoriei literare româneşti* (1962), 61–86, 270–8; J. Peltz, *Cumi-am cunoscut* (1964), 145–56; Yad Vashem, *Dr. Filderman Archives,* 17 (1941), 104; M. Bucur, in: *Lupta de clasă,* 11 (1969), 96–102.

[D.L.]

GHERON, YAKKIR MORDECAI BEN ELIAKIM (d. 1817), Turkish rabbi (the Italian branch of the family write the name Ghiron, and the Turkish, Gheron). Gheron succeeded his father as rabbi and *dayyan* of Adrianople and district in 1800. He devoted himself particularly to the building of synagogues and supervised the studies in a *talmud torah* which he had established during his period of office in Adrianople. A certain scholar who had converted to Islam was found burnt to death, and the pasha of the town accused the Jews of having been responsible. Gheron was imprisoned and sentenced to death. The pasha's secretary, to whom the rabbi had previously shown kindness, succeeded in having the death sentence repealed, and in its stead a fine was imposed on the Jewish community. In 1812 he went to Jerusalem and was appointed a member of the *bet din* of Jacob Moses *Ayash. His name appears as a signatory to a **takkanah* of 1814 with reference to milk milked by gentiles. His responsa appear in the *Dera Dakhya* (Salonika, 1819) of Mordecai b. Menahem *Bekemoharar. He wrote an approbation for the *Nimmukei Yosef* (Leghorn, 1795) of Joseph *ibn Ḥabib.

Bibliography: S. Markus, in: *Sinai,* 41 (1957), 49–52.

[S.Mar.]

GHETTO, urban section serving as compulsory residential quarter for Jews. Generally surrounded by a wall shutting it off from the rest of the city, except for one or more gates, the ghetto remained bolted at night. The origin of this term has been the subject of much speculation. It was probably first used to describe a quarter of Venice situated near a foundry (*getto,* or *ghetto*) and which in 1516 was enclosed by walls and gates and declared to be the only part of the city to be open to Jewish settlement. Subsequently the term was extended to all Jewish quarters of the same type. Other theories are that the word derives from the Hebrew *get* indicating divorce or separation; from the Greek γέιτων (neighbor); from the German *geheckter [Ort],* or fenced place; or from the Italian *borghetto* (a small section of the town). All can be excluded, except for *get* which was sometimes used in Rome to mean a separate section of the city. In any case the institution antedates the word, which is commonly used in several ways. It has come to indicate not only the legally established, coercive ghetto, but also the voluntary gathering of Jews in a secluded quarter, a process known in the Diaspora time before compulsion was exercised. By analogy the word is currently used to describe similar homogeneous quarters of non-Jewish groups, such as immigrant quarters, Negro quarters in American cities, native quarters in South African cities, etc.

For historical survey see *Jewish Quarter.

In Muslim Countries. In Muslim countries the Jewish quarter in its beginnings never had the character of a ghetto. It was always built on a voluntary basis, and it remained so in later times in the vast Ottoman Empire. Istanbul (Constantinople) was the classic example of a capital in which the Jewish quarters were scattered all over the city. In Shīʿite countries (Persia, Yemen) and in orthodox North Africa (Malikite rite) all non-Muslims were forced to live in separate quarters—for religious reasons (ritual uncleanness). Embassies from Christian countries had to look for their (even temporary) dwellings among the Jews. Christian travelers and pilgrims to the Holy Land always remark that in case there was no Christian hospice in a town, they had to look for hospitality among the Jews. After the regulations compelling the Jews to dwell in separate quarters had been repealed (in the 19th and 20th centuries), and they could freely move out, the majority voluntarily remained in their old quarters. Only after the establishment of the new independent states in North Africa did most of the Jews abandon their old dwellings.

See *Jewish Quarter, in Muslim Countries. [Ed.]

Holocaust Period. The Crystallization of German Policy. During the Holocaust period, the ghetto was substantially different from its character during the Middle Ages. In 1939 Hitler expressed the idea of concentrating the Jews in ghettos: "Out with them from all the professions and into the ghetto with them; fence them in somewhere where they can perish as they deserve ..." He did not, however, give orders to realize this idea, probably because allocating the Jews a defined status by placing them in ghettos was not in accordance with plans for their physical extermination. The suggestion to establish ghettos was raised from time to time (for example, by Goering in 1938), but it was not accepted. In his letter of Sept. 21, 1939, to the commanders of the *Einsatzgruppen,* Heydrich ordered the dissolution *(Aufloesung)* of communities that numbered less than 500 persons and the concentration of the Jews in the large cities, where they would be restricted to specified neighborhoods. By that time, however, it is almost certain that the Nazi leaders did not intend to turn the ghettos into permanent living quarters, and there is no doubt that with the acceptance of the decision on the "*Final Solution" (March 1941), the fate of the various ghettos was sealed, even though a few continued to exist for some time. The ghetto, therefore, was conceived as a way station to the labor and extermination camps, and its purpose was to aid in the control and supervision of Jews by concentrating them in specific areas. It may be assumed that the Germans also hoped that as a result of hard labor, malnutrition, overcrowding, and substandard sanitary conditions, a large number of Jews would perish. Likewise, the life-span of some ghettos was extended because they provided a large reservoir of cheap labor; but even this consideration did not prevent the extermination process. Thus the commander of Galicia, for example, sent out an order in the fall of 1942 to decrease the number of ghettos from 1,000 to 55, and in July 1943 Himmler decided to transfer the surviving inhabitants of ghettos throughout *Ostland* to concentration

Street in the Warsaw ghetto during the Nazi occupation. Courtesy Yad Vashem, Jerusalem.

camps. The last ghetto on Polish soil (*Lodz), which had been in existence since April 1940, was liquidated in August 1944.

Special ghettos were established for Jews deported from Rumania to Transnistria and resettled in cities or towns and in neighborhoods or on streets that had been occupied by Jews who had been exterminated shortly before by the German army. One exception was the ghetto at *Theresienstadt, which was established at the end of 1941 to house Jews from Bohemia and Moravia and later Jews from Germany and other Western countries were deported there as well. The Germans intended Theresienstadt to be a showcase to the world of their mass treatment of the Jews and thus mask the crime of the "Final Solution."

The Jewish Reaction to the Establishment of the Ghettos. The Jews, who were unaware of the Nazis' intentions, resigned themselves to the establishment of ghettos and hoped that living together in mutual cooperation under self-rule would make it easier for them to overcome the period of repression until their country would be liberated from the Nazi yoke. It seemed to them that by imprisoning Jews in ghettos, the Nazis had arrived at the final manifestation of their anti-Jewish policy. If the Jews would carry out their orders and prove that they were beneficial to the Nazis by their work, they would be allowed to organize their community life as they wished. However, the cruel treatment by the Nazi authorities and especially the *Aktions,* in which large portions of the Jewish communities were arrested and transported to places from which no one returned, quickly destroyed this illusion. In addition, the Jews had practically no opportunity to express armed opposition that would prevent the Germans from carrying out their plans. The constant changes in the composition of the population (effected by transfers and roundups) and in living quarters made it more difficult to realize the expressions of opposition; the hermetic imprisonment from the outside world prevented the acquisition of arms; and conditions in the ghetto (malnutrition, concern for one's family, etc.) weakened the power of the opposition. On the other hand, the Germans had the manpower and technical equipment to repress any uprising with ease, and the non-Jewish population collaborated with them, or at best remained apathetic. Any uprising in the ghettos was thus predestined to failure.

Typology of the Ghettos. In most cases, the ghetto was located in one of the poor neighborhoods of a city that had previously housed a crowded Jewish population. Jews were transferred from the other neighborhoods in the city, and in many cases from nearby villages, to housing there, while the non-Jewish inhabitants of the neighborhood were forced to move to another area. These transfers caused great overcrowding from the outset. In Lodz, for example, the average was six people to a room; in Vilna there were even eight to a room during one period. Whenever the overcrowding lessened because of the deporting of Jews to extermination camps, the area of the ghetto was decreased drastically. At first there were two types of ghettos: open ones, which were marked only by signs as areas of Jewish habitation; and closed ones, which were surrounded by fences, or in some cases even by walls (as in *Warsaw). This difference, however, lost all significance during the period of deportations for before an open ghetto was liquidated, all access roads were blocked by the German police, whereas in closed ghettos shifts of German police or their aides constantly guarded the fences and walls. A more significant distinction was the fact that the Germans regarded the closed ghettos as large concentration camps, and therefore most of them were liquidated later than the open ghettos. In contrast to these ghettos, which were all in Polish and Russian territory, the ghettos in Transnistria were not predestined for liquidation. Neither was the ghetto in Theresienstadt. Transnistria even succeeded in maintaining contact with the outside world and received assistance from committees in Rumania. Theresienstadt was, in fact, cut off from the world (except for the transports that came in and went out), but the standard of living was higher there than in Eastern European ghettos.

Jewish Administration. For every ghetto, the German authorities appointed a *Judenrat, which was usually composed of Jewish leaders acceptable to the community. The Judenrat was not a democratic body, and its power was centered in one person, not always the chairman, who was responsible for its cooperation in matters relating to the ghetto. The leader of the Judenrat was subordinate to the German authorities, who delegated to him much authority with regard to the Jews but treated him disrespectfully and often cruelly. Many Jews appointed to the Judenrat believed that they were placed in their position in order to serve the Jewish people in its time of great need.

From the beginning, the Jewish leadership was faced with the impossible task of organizing ghetto life under emergency conditions and under the ceaseless pressure of threats of cruel punishment. Jewish institutions, to the extent that they existed, continued to function, either openly, such as the institutions that fulfilled religious needs, or in secret, such as the various parties. The major function of the leadership, however, was the provision of sustenance and health and welfare services (including hospitals), and this had to be accomplished without adequate means. Despite supreme effort, in the course of time these institutions collapsed in most ghettos. It was even more difficult to establish those services which had not existed within the Jewish community before the Holocaust, such as police, prisons, and courts. The authority vested in these institutions was broad within the narrow autonomous framework that existed in the ghettos, and in many instances they were, of course, not properly utilized under conditions of the life-and-death struggle imposed on the inhabitants of the ghetto.

Liquidation of the Ghettos. The liquidation of the ghettos was conducted as part of the policy of the "Final Solution," for which purpose the Germans prepared special extermination camps. When it was decided to liquidate a ghetto, they would call on the Jews to present themselves voluntarily to be transferred to labor camps (sometimes with false promises of improved living conditions), but when this method proved unsuccessful, they would round up the residents and bring them by force to areas of concentration, from where they would be transported, usually by train, to their destination. The great majority of the ghetto inhabitants were killed immediately upon their arrival in the camps; a minority were employed in forced labor and were killed after a short time by one of the regular means of extermination. Only a very small number remained alive, sometimes after having been shunted from camp to camp.

See also *Holocaust, and for more information on specific ghettos see *Kovno, Lodz, *Lublin, *Theresienstadt, and *Warsaw. [J.M.]

Bibliography: G. Reitlinger, *Final Solution* (1968[2]), index; R. Hilberg, *Destruction of the European Jews* (1961), index; P. Friedman, in: JSOS, 16 (1954), 61–88 (incl. bibl.).

GHETTO FIGHTERS' HOUSE (Heb. בֵּית לוֹחֲמֵי הַגֶּטָאוֹת; *Beit Loḥamei ha-Getta'ot*), a ghetto uprising and Holocaust remembrance authority, established in kibbutz *Loḥamei ha-Getta'ot, on April 19, 1950, by a group of former ghetto fighters and partisans. The house serves as a memorial and research and documentation center on the Holocaust period, and on Jewish resistance under Nazi rule in Europe. It contains an important historical archives on the Holocaust, and particularly on organized resistance; papers left

Part of the permanent exhibit of the Ghetto Fighters' House at kibbutz Loḥamei ha-Getta'ot.

by the poet Itzhak *Katzenelson, after whom it is named; documents from the *He-Ḥalutz archives in the Warsaw and Bialystok ghettos; a collection of the publications of the Jewish underground in occupied Poland; on the Jewish underground in Holland and France; a register of names of Jewish partisans who fought in Italy and Yugoslavia; and photographs, films, and pictures. The museum maintains a permanent display as well as special exhibits dealing with different aspects of the Holocaust and Jewish resistance; models of the Warsaw Ghetto and the *Treblinka death camp are on show. On the national Holocaust Remembrance Day in Israel (27th of Nisan), a mass memorial assembly is held at the amphitheater outside the museum. The Ghetto Fighters' House has published a series of books and periodicals, *Dappim le-Ḥeker ha-Sho'ah ve-ha-Mered* (1951–52, 1969); and *Yedi'ot Beit Loḥamei ha-Getta'ot al shem Yiẓhak Katzenelson* (1951–60). [Ed.]

GHEZ, Tunisian family, whose most eminent members were David (second half of 18th century), author of a number of works of which only one, *Ner David,* part 1 (Leghorn, 1868), has been published; the others include a commentary to the tractates *Shabbat, Pesaḥim,* and *Sukkah,* as well as novellae to various other tractates. Moses (end of 18th century) wrote commentaries to the tractate *Shevu'ot* and Elijah *Mizrachi's supercommentary on Rashi to the Pentateuch under the titles *Yeshu'at Ya'akov* and

Yedei Moshe. He also wrote *Yismah Moshe* (Leghorn, 1863), a commentary to the Passover *Haggadah,* notes on the Pentateuch, and three poems. JOSEPH (b. 1800), son of David, was a kabbalist. He left numerous works in manuscript, including a commentary to Maimonides' *Mishneh Torah,* sermons, glosses on the Talmud, on the Zohar, etc. In *Pi ha-Medabber* (Leghorn, 1854), his kabbalistic commentary to the Passover *Haggadah,* he cites explanations by his cousin Ḥayyim Ghez.

Another member of the family was MATHILDA GHEZ (1918–), a communal leader in Tunisia. In 1957 she moved to Israel and was elected to the Knesset (in 1965 representing Rafi, and in 1969, the Israel Labor Party).

Bibliography: D. Cazès, *Notes Bibliographiques sur la Littérature Juive-Tunisienne* (1893), 194–205 (= *Mizrah u-Ma'arav,* 2 (1928), 353–6). [ED.]

°**GHILLANY, FRIEDRICH WILHELM** (1807–1876), German theologian. As a municipal librarian in Nuremberg, Ghillany wrote on various historical subjects but he was chiefly concerned with religious questions, and adopted the teachings of G. F. Daumer (1800–1875), a deist in search of "true religion." Following the Damascus blood libel, Ghillany wrote *Die Menschenopfer der alten Hebraeer* (Nuremberg, 1842), in which he accused the Jews of "cannibalism" and "molochism" in both ancient and modern times and of the ritual murder of Jesus. He gave further expression to his anti-Semitism in *Die Judenfrage; eine Beigabe zu Bruno Bauer's Abhandlung ueber diesen Gegenstand* (*ibid.,* 1843), and *Das Judenthum und die Kritik* (*ibid.,* 1844). Both Daumer and Ghillany were praised by Nazi propagandists.

Bibliography: L. Poliakov, *Histoire de l'antisémitsme,* 3 (1968), 425–6; R. W. Stock, *Die Judenfrage durch fuenf Jahrhunderte* (1939), 391–427; V. Eichstaedt, *Bibliographie zur Geschichte der Judenfrage 1750–1848* (1938), index; M. Loewengard, *Jehowa, nicht Moloch, war der Gott der alten Hebraeer . . .* (1843). [ED.]

GHIRON, family of scholars whose name derives from Gerona in N. Spain. Among its most important members are: JOHANAN GHIRON (1646–1716), born in Casale Monferrato, Italy. Johanan was rabbi of Florence for 34 years, and was given the title *Alluf Torah* ("Master of the Torah") in appreciation of his great erudition. Though by upbringing and inclination he sided with the Shabbatean movement, he willingly signed the excommunication on Nehemiah *Ḥayon. After his death, all the *takkanot* he had instituted were repealed. Johanan was the author of: (1) *Mishtah ha-Ramim,* an apology for his attitude in connection with the dispute over Ḥayon, with an appendix consisting of his letters (still in manuscript); (2) prayers, on the occasion of the earthquakes in Lugo in 1688 and in Ancona in 1690. The prayer on Ancona was also recited in Florence on the occasion of the earthquake in Leghorn in 1742. It was published in the *Shever ba-Mezarim* of Raphael Meldola (Leghorn, 1742); (3) responsa mentioned in the *Paḥad Yiẓḥak* of Isaac *Lampronti, in the *Shemesh Ẓedakah* of Samson Morpurgo, and elsewhere (Montefiore collection); (4) glosses on the *Arba'ah Turim* and halakhic novellae (unpublished).

JUDAH ḤAYYIM GHIRON, his son, was born in Casale Monferrato and was rabbi of Florence from 1719 to 1738. His *Mekor Dimah,* on his father's activities in connection with Nehemiah Ḥayon and on his *takkanot,* together with a selection of letters on Nehemiah Ḥayon and an appendix to his father's *Mishtah ha-Ramim,* are still in manuscript.

JUDAH ḤAYYIM LEONTI GHIRON (1739–1761) was rabbi of Casale. His halakhic correspondence with contemporary scholars is preserved in the Asiatic Museum in Leningrad.

SAMUEL ḤAYYIM GHIRON (1829–1895) was born in Ivrea. In 1854 he qualified as a teacher of literature and in 1877 was appointed rabbi of Turin. He published a prayer book according to the Italian rite, with an Italian translation (Leghorn, 1879). In the National Library, Jerusalem, there is an elegy on the death of Hillel Cantoni in Italian and Hebrew, the latter by Samuel Ghiron (Turin, 1857). In 1880, with the assistance of B. Peyron, he published a catalog of the Hebrew manuscripts in Turin. He also wrote essays, sermons, and poems. ISAIAH GHIRON (1837–1888), director of the Braidense Library in Milan, wrote books in Italian on Hebrew numismatics and inscriptions. In 1874 he was editor of *Rivista di Lettere, Scienze ed Arti.*

Bibliography: Ghirondi-Neppi, 161; Levi, in: RI, 8 (1911), 169–85; Mortara, Indice, 27; Nacht, in: *Zion Me'assef,* 6 (1934), 121; Sonne, in: *Zion,* 4 (1938/39), 86–88; Wilensky, in: KS, 24 (1946/47), 195 no. 68. [S.MAR.]

GHIRONDI, MORDECAI SAMUEL BEN BENZION ARYEH (1799–1852), Italian scholar and biographer. Ghirondi was a descendant of a rabbinic family. His grandmother Mazal-Tov Benvenida Ghirondi (c. 1760), wife of Mordecai, rabbi of Cittadella, was famous for her Jewish learning and educated many disciples to a relatively high grade of knowledge. Ghirondi was born in Padua. He taught theology at the rabbinical college of Padua, where he had studied, beginning in 1824. He was assistant rabbi of Padua 1829–31, and from 1831 to his death was chief rabbi.

Apart from a juvenile moral treatise, *Tokho Raẓuf Ahavah* (1818), Ghirondi's minor works include some scattered essays and a number of unpublished works, mainly in the Montefiore collection and in the Jewish Theological Seminary of America. His major work is *Toledot Godolei Yisrael* (1853), a biographical dictionary of Jewish scholars and rabbis composed as an extension of *Zekher Ẓaddikim li-Verakhah,* a similar biographic work by Hananel Graziadio *Neppi. The *Toledot* was published by Ghirondi's son Ephraim Raphael (1834–57) at Trieste. Although naive and badly proportioned, the work retains its importance for information, based in some entries on personal acquaintance or oral tradition, on Italian rabbis of the 18th and early 19th centuries; these are the vast majority of the entries. Ghirondi also annotated *Azulai's *Shem ha-Gedolim* (publ. in E. Gartenhaus, *Eshel ha-Gedolim,* 1958).

Ghirondi was a notable book collector; many of his manuscripts are in the Montefiore Library in Jews' College, London, and his printed books and some manuscripts are in the Jewish Theological Seminary in New York.

Bibliography: Ghirondi-Neppi, 56, 374–6. [C.R.]

GHIRSHMAN, ROMAN (1895–), French archaeologist, specialist in Iranian studies. Ghirshman was born and educated in Paris. He had his first experience in excavation at Tello in Iraq in 1930. In 1931 he was sent to Iran as leader of an expedition and this was the beginning of a long series of successful excavations of important early settlements in Iran and Afghanistan. These included Tepe Giyan, Tepe Sialk, and Tchoga Zanbil in Elam. Ghirshman, who held a professorship at the University of Aix-en-Provence, was head of the French archaeological mission to Afghanistan from 1941 to 1943 and director of the Suse mission in Iran from 1946 to 1967. His numerous publications on Iranian art, history, and culture include: *Fouilles de Tépé Giyan 1931 et 1932* (with G. Contenau, 1935); *Fouilles de Sialk* (2 vols., 1938–39); *Iran: From the Earliest Times to the Islamic Conquest* (1954); and *Iran: From the Origins to Alexander the Great* (1964). [P.P.K.]

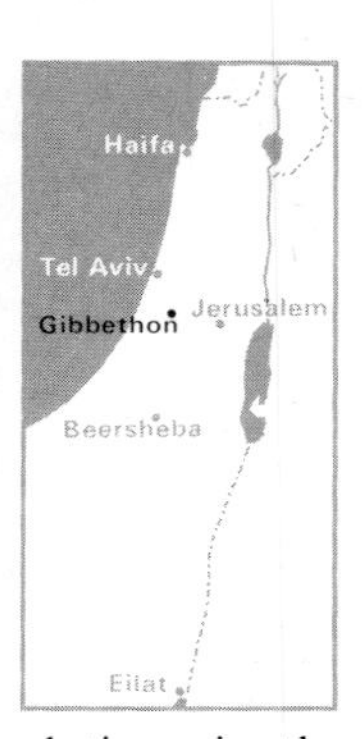

GIBBETHON (Heb. גִּבְּתוֹן). (1) Town in the territory of Dan, mentioned with Eltekeh and Baalath (Josh. 19:44). It is also listed as a levitical city of the Kohathite family (*ibid.* 21:23) and was thus apparently a Davidic administrative center (its name is absent in the parallel text of levitical cities in I Chron. 6). Gibbethon appears twice in the Book of Kings as a Philistine city that was beseiged by Nadab and "all Israel" and again by Elah; both seiges, however, were interrupted by revolutions in the besieging armies and were unsuccessful (I Kings 15:27; 16:15). It may also be included in the list of cities captured by Thutmose III in c. 1469 B.C.E. (no. 103). Gibbethon is generally identified with Tel al-Malāt (now called Tell Gibbethon), southwest of Gezer, a prominent mound containing pottery from the Chalcolithic to the Arabic periods. [M.A.-Y.]

(2) Moshav Gibbethon in central Israel, near *Reḥovot, affiliated with Tenu'at ha-Moshavim, was founded in 1933 by settlers from Eastern Europe as one of the villages of the "Thousand Families Settlement Scheme." Citriculture constitutes a prominent farm branch. No identification with the ancient site has been suggested.

Bibliography: Von Rad, in: PJB, 29 (1933), 30ff., 35; EM, 1 (1963), 354. [E.O.]

GIBBOR, JUDAH BEN ELIJAH (b. c. 1460), Karaite author and poet living in Constantinople. His writings include a poetical commentary on the Pentateuch *Minḥat Yehudah* (published in the Karaite ritual, Venice, 1529). In this poem, often commented upon by Karaite scholars, Gibbor refers with deep respect to Maimonides; it deals with the three pillars of Karaism—Scripture, analogy, and (Karaite) tradition. He also wrote three works which are no longer extant: *Hilkhot Sheḥitah,* on the laws of ritual slaughter, *Sefer Mo'adim,* regulations for the festivals, and *Mo'ed Katan,* on the secondary festivals, which also contained the essential teachings of the Kabbalah. Gibbor's eldest son, Elijah Shubshi (1483–1501), who died at the age of 18, wrote a commentary on *Shesh Kenafayim,* an astronomical work by Immanuel b. Jacob *Bonfils of Tarascon.

Bibliography: Danon, in: JQR, 15 (1924/25), 313–5; 17 (1926/27), 179–81; Mann, Texts, 2 (1935), 296, n.7, 732, n.176, 1177, 1421. [I.M./Ed.]

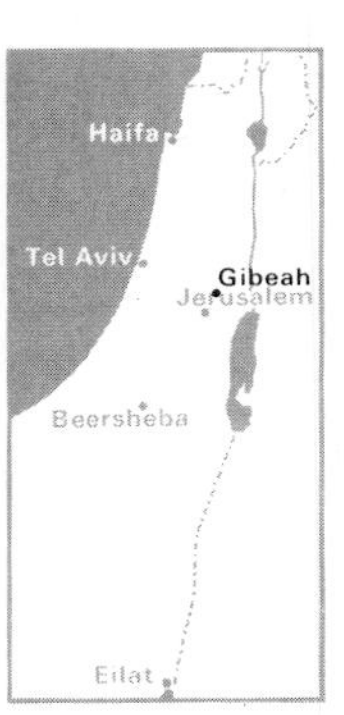

GIBEAH (**Gibeath-Benjamin, Gibeath-Shaul;** Heb. גִּבְעַת שָׁאוּל, גִּבְעַת בִּנְיָמִן, גִּבְעָה), the center of the territory of the tribe of Benjamin (Josh. 18:24; Judg. 19–20) and Saul's royal city. It was identified by E. *Robinson (1837) with Tell al-Fūl, 3 mi. (5 km.) north of Jerusalem, at a height of about 2,755 ft. (840 m.) on the road from Jerusalem to Shechem, which was the highroad leading from the territories of Judah to Ephraim during the period of the Judges (Judg. 19:11–13). It was excavated by W. F. *Albright in 1922–23 and 1933 and by P. W. Lapp in 1964. According to biblical and archaeological evidence, the site passed through four main phases: (1) The earliest settlement belongs to the Early Iron Age and was in existence until about the middle of the 12th century B.C.E. Its destruction can be connected with the biblical tradition of the war waged by the tribes against Benjamin because of its crime against the levite's concubine (Judg. 19–20). (2) The city was rebuilt in the latter part of the 11th century B.C.E. Excavations have uncovered a rectangular citadel; its wall, made of undressed blocks, and a square tower in the excavated corner. The latest investigations have refuted the view that this fortress was built by the Philistine garrison at Geba (I Sam. 10:5; 13:3), which was routed by Jonathan (I Sam. 13–14; cf. *Geba (1)). It was thus apparently built by Saul, served as his royal residence and was henceforth named after him (*ibid.* 11:4; 15:34; 22:6; 23:19). Gibeah's importance ended with the fall of Saul's monarchy, and the fortress was perhaps destroyed by the Philistines after the battle of Gilboa, but its repair and reconstruction probably date from the days of David. One of David's warriors came from Gibeah (II Sam. 23:29). (3) Gibeah was rebuilt a third time in the latter part of the monarchy, when it was surrounded by a feeble casemate fortification. This is the city mentioned by Isaiah on the northern approach of Jerusalem (Isa. 10:29), probably along the route taken by part of Sennacherib's army. It was destroyed by the Chaldeans. (4) A new fortress, built in the late fourth century B.C.E., survived until the second century B.C.E. Josephus (Wars 5:51) mentions Gibeah as a settlement situated 30 ris ($3\frac{1}{2}$ mi.) north of Jerusalem. Titus camped there on his march to Jerusalem, and his troops demolished it. Excavations indicate that an impoverished settlement existed there down to the period of the Bar Kokhba war (132–135 C.E.). By Eusebius' time (early fourth century), the site was already forgotten.

Bibliography: Albright, in: BJPES, 1 (1925), 53; idem, in: AASOR, 4 (1924), 1–160; idem, in: BASOR, 52 (1933), 6; Sinclair, in: AASOR, 34–35 (1960), 1–52; idem, in: *Enziklopedyah la-Ḥafirot Arkhe'ologiyyot be-Ereẓ Yisrael,* 1 (1970), 109–11; Lapp, in: BA, 28 (1965), 2–10; Aharoni, Land, index. [M.A.-Y.]

GIBEON (Heb. גִּבְעוֹן), levitical city in the territory of the tribe of Benjamin (Josh. 18:25; 21:17). Gibeon was the capital of a league of cities northwest of Jerusalem ("Gibeon, and Chephirah, and Beeroth, and Kiriath-jearim") in the period of the Israelite conquest (*ibid.* 9:17). Joshua's great battle with the Canaanite kings, headed by Adoni-Zedek, king of Jerusalem, was fought nearby; during this event the miracle commanded by Joshua took place: "Sun, stand thou still upon Gibeon; and thou, Moon, in the valley of Aijalon" (*ibid.* ch. 10). Gibeon also figures in accounts of events during the time of David. It was the scene of the clash between the armies of David and Ish-Bosheth, commanded by Joab and Abner, and of David's victory over the Philistines (II Sam. 2:12ff.; I Chron. 14:16). In the description of the former battle, the Bible mentions several topographical features of

Figure 1. The Arab village al-Jīb, identified with the biblical town of Gibeon. Photo Richard Cleave, Jerusalem.

Figure 2. Spiral staircase leading to the ancient pool of Gibeon. Photo Richard Cleave, Jerusalem.

the surroundings including a pool beside which David's men prevailed over Ish Bosheth's followers. At the beginning of the monarchy the "great high place" was located at Gibeon; there Solomon offered sacrifices and had his famous vision (I Kings 3:4–15). According to other biblical references this "great high place" was connected with the "tabernacle of the Lord" which was also located at Gibeon at that time (I Chron. 16:39; 21:29; II Chron. 1:3, 13, etc.). In the same period the Bible calls the "wilderness of Gibeon" the eastern slopes of the hills of Benjamin from Gibeon to the plains of Jordan (II Sam. 1:24). Gibeonites were among the returning Babylonian exiles; they resettled the city and took part in building the walls of Jerusalem (Neh. 7:25, 3:7). Josephus locates Gibeon about 40 or 50 stadia ($4\frac{1}{2}$–$5\frac{1}{2}$ mi.) from Jerusalem (Ant., 7:283; Wars, 2:516). The city is identified with al-Jīb, a small Muslim Arab village situated on an oval-shaped hill about $3\frac{1}{2}$ mi. (6 km.) northwest of Jerusalem's northernmost suburbs (with a 1967 population of 1,173). It is already called al-Jīb by the 13th-century Arab geographer Yakut. In excavations conducted at the site by J. P. Pritchard (1956–62), parts of the city wall were uncovered in the western and northeastern section of the city. Near the wall the above-mentioned round pool was discovered, measuring 37 ft. (11.3 m.) in diameter and 35 ft. (10.8 m.) deep, with a spiral staircase going down to a tunnel 148 ft. (45 m.) long with 93 steps leading outside the city wall to a cistern which was connected by another tunnel 112 ft. (34 m.) long with the main spring of the city. Debris filling the round pool contained numerous jar handles inscribed with the name Gibeon, Gdn (or Gdd) Gibeon, and names of persons such as Damlah, Shebuel, Azariah, Hananiah, Amariah, etc. Wine cellers, containing sherds of storage jars, silos, seals, and weights, were discovered near the pool. The excavations also uncovered remains dating from the Early, Middle, and Late Canaanite periods, but the earliest wall found was built sometime in the 12th century B.C.E. The city flourished in the Israelite period and was destroyed during the Babylonian invasion. There was also evidence of a small settlement in the Persian and Hellenistic periods and of a thriving city, not defended by a wall, from Hasmonean to Roman times.

Bibliography: B. Maisler, *Toledot Ereẓ Yisrael* (1938), 224–5; R. Amiran, in: *Eretz Israel*, 1 (1951), 136 n. 12 (Heb.); Dalman, in: PJB, 8 (1912), 12; Albright, in: AASOR, 4 (1924), 10ff.; idem, in: BASOR, 35 (1929), 4; idem, in: JQR, 22 (1931–32), 415ff.; idem, in: JBL, 58 (1939), 179; Jirku, in: JPOS, 8 (1928), 178ff.; C.C. McCown, *Tell-en-Nasbeh* (Eng. 1947), 40ff.; S. Yeivin, in: RHJE, 1 (1947), 143ff.; J. B. Pritchard, *Gibeon* (1962); idem, in: *Enẓiklopedyah la-Ḥafirot Arkhe'ologiyyot be-Ereẓ Yisrael* (1970), 107–9; Reed, in: D. Thomas (ed.), *Archaeology and Old Testament Study* (1967), 231ff.

[Y.EL.]

GIBEONITES AND NETHINIM (Heb. גִּבְעֹנִים, נְתִינִים). The Gibeonites, residents of four important cities in the vicinity of Jerusalem, feared that they might share the fate of Jericho and Ai, which were destroyed by the Israelites, and tricked *Joshua into a treaty that would spare them (Josh. 9). Had Joshua known that these people were actually Canaanites whom he was pledged to dispossess, he would not have concluded a treaty with them, but the Gibeonites had disguised themselves as coming from a distant land, and had made overtures of devotion to the God of Israel. As they were returning to their nearby cities, the ruse was discovered, but by that time the Israelites were bound by the treaty, and could not drive them out or destroy their cities, which were strategically located to control access to Jerusalem and the roads through the Judean mountains. As a result of this treaty, five Canaanite rulers immediately formed a coalition under the king of Jerusalem and attacked Gibeon. Under the terms of the treaty, the Gibeonites called upon Joshua to come to their aid, and he routed the Canaanite coalition (Josh. 10:cf. 11:19). Thus deceived by the Gibeonites, the Israelites adopted an alternative measure, that of forced labor: "On that day Joshua gave them over to be hewers of wood and drawers of water for the assembly and for the altar of the Lord until this day, at the place which He will choose" (Josh. 9:27). The Gibeonites appear again in connection with a famine during the reign of *David (II Sam. 21). David learned that the famine was a punishment for an offense committed by *Saul, who had put a number of Gibeonites to death out of zeal for Israel and Judah, but in violation of Israel's ancient oath. In expiation, David was obliged to hang seven of Saul's descendants on a hill at Gibeath-Shaul, where Saul had resided, and where at least some of his descendants undoubtedly still lived.

The designation Nethinim is derived from the Hebrew verb *natan* ("to give over"), which can mean devoting someone to cultic service. The verb is used in this sense with respect to Joshua's action toward the Gibeonites in Joshua 9:27, where cultic servitude is involved ("for the altar of the Lord"). The Book of Ezra (8:20) states that David and his commanders "devoted" (Heb. *natan*) the Nethinim "to the service of the *levites" which may reflect the ancient practice of committing captives and conquered peoples to temple slavery, which was a widespread phenomenon in the ancient Near East. The Bible itself offers other indications of its operation in ancient Israel. Many modern scholars consider that such was the status of the Nethinim, and cite certain data in support of this view. The Nethinim are listed together with "the sons of the servants of Solomon" in the census of Israelites returning from Babylonia in about 538 B.C.E. (Ezra 2 = Nehemiah 7), and the latter are generally considered to have been royal slaves. Furthermore, a large number of foreign names in the list of Nethinim suggests that they were captives of war.

There are, however, counterindications. It is possible that "servants of Solomon" were not slaves but royal merchants (see: Servants of *Solomon). The verb *natan*, discussed above, need not necessarily imply servitude, but was used to designate other types of cultic devotion as well. It was applied to the levites, who were hardly temple slaves, and was used to characterize a relationship to the cultic establishment which was primarily administrative and religious; one not based on the economic institution of temple property, under which temple slaves are to be classified.

A later tradition identifies the Gibeonites of Joshua's time with the Nethinim mentioned in the post-Exilic literature. This tradition probably arose in Palestine during the late Hellenistic or early Roman period, at a time when the Jews had become familiar with temple slavery among the pagans, especially in the form of sacred prostitution. It was probably known to the historian Josephus of the first Christian century who translates the term Nethinim in Ezra, chapter 2, by the Greek term *hierodoulos* (from δοῦλοι ἱεποί, "sacred slaves"). On the other hand, it probably arose after the completion of the Septuagint translation to the Bible which never renders Nethinim as *heirodoulos,* but either translates the term literally into Greek as *dedomenoi* (so in I Chron. 9:2), or uses Greek transcriptions of the original Hebrew term. Modern scholarship, though recognizing that identification of the Gibeonites with the Nethinim represents a later tradition, nevertheless tends to accept the identification of the Nethinim as "uncircumcised" temple personnel, such as those referred to by Ezekiel (44:7). Conclusive clarification of the exact social status and precise cultic functions of the Nethinim must await further evidence, but the possibility that they represented a guild of free cultic practitioners should not be disregarded.

I Chronicles 9:1–2 states that in the days of David the Nethinim were among the first settlers in the land, but they are never actually mentioned in the pre-Exilic books of Samuel and Kings, nor in any other biblical book presumed to be pre-Exilic. Some scholars claim that this term occurs in Numbers 3:9 and 8:19, which speaks of the dedication of the levites; however, this is unlikely, and it is better to take the repeated *netunim netunim* ("devoted, yea, devoted") as mere passive participles. Although Ezra 8:20 associates the Nethinim with the levites, they are left as two separate groups elsewhere in the Bible (cf. Ezra 2; 7:7; Neh. 10:29; 11:3; I Chron. 9:2). However, there is evidence to support the tradition of I Chronicles 9 concerning the pre-Exilic existence of the Nethinim. A hoard of Hebrew ostraca dating from the last days of the kingdom of Judah has been uncovered at the site of ancient *Arad in the Negev, where an Israelite sanctuary was in use throughout most of the pre-Exilic period. An official named "the Kerosite" appears in one of the ostraca. The personal name Keros otherwise occurs only once, and that in the list of Nethinim in Ezra 2:44 (=Neh. 7:47): "the sons of Keros." Therefore it is probable that the Kerosite at Arad was a member of a group of Nethinim, who would logically be located at a sanctuary. If true, this would be the first contemporary attestation of the existence of Nethinim in the pre-Exilic period. Evidence of a comparative nature also suggests that the Nethinim were a very ancient group. The administrative archives at Ugarit have yielded a list of *ytnm,* the Ugaritic form of Hebrew *nethinim* (C. H. Gordon, *Ugaritic Text-Book,* 301:1, 1). They are also mentioned in a poetic ritual text (*ibid.,* 52:3) and it is reasonable to consider them some sort of cultic personnel, as in Palestine. One of the families or groups of *ytnm* at Ugarit had the same name as a group of Nethinim listed in Ezra (cf. Ugaritic *bn ḥgby, ibid.,* 301:2, 5 with *benei Hagab, Hagabah* in Ezra 2:45–46). It is therefore possible that the Nethinim were an international group of persons skilled in certain cultic arts, who had attached themselves to the Israelites at an early period. The manner in which they are listed suggests that they were organized according to family groups, as was customary.

Akkadian sources also throw light on the semantic and institutional background of the Nethinim. Neo-Babylonian documents refer to members of a religious order dedicated to the service of different Babylonian deities, called *širku,* "devotees, oblates" (from Akk. *šarāku,* "to give, present"). This word is the semantic equivalent of the Hebrew Nethinim, and the members of both orders were temple servitors (Speiser). The Bible provides several more references to the Nethinim which are instructive. About the middle of the fifth century B.C.E. Ezra recruited Nethinim along with other personnel preparatory to his return to Judah (Ezra 7:7, 24; 8:1–20). Nehemiah 3 describes the resettlement of Jerusalem, whose recruited population of skilled persons included Nethinim. In about 438 B.C.E. the leaders of the people convoked a great assembly in Jerusalem to ratify a new covenant (Neh. 10:1–40), and the Nethinim were among the principal signatories (10–29; cf. 11:3). Only *bona fide* Israelites would have been admitted to the covenant, especially at a time when there was great concern in rooting out foreign strains from the community. [B.A.L.]

Post-Biblical Period. Nothing more is heard of the Nethinim until they appear in the legislation of the Mishnah which classes them with proselytes, freedmen, *mamzerim,* waifs, and foundings with whom alone they are permitted to intermarry (Kid. 4:1). The Mishnah (Hor. 3:8), however, classifies the Nethinim as being one level lower than *mamzerim* but preceding proselytes and freedmen. They were regarded as the descendants of the Gibeonites (Yev. 78b–79a) and the prohibition in their marrying Jews of pure pedigree as having been established by King David (*ibid.* 78b) and reconfirmed by Ezra (Num. R. 8:4). It is impossible to explain this loss of status since the days of Nehemiah. It is possible that, in employing the classification Nethinim, the talmudic sages did not have the actual biblical group in mind at all, but merely reapplied an ancient term to contemporary groups of declassed persons who were the subject of their own legislation, thus stigmatizing them with traditional associations. An attempt by the rabbis to abolish the inferior status of the Nethinim was rejected by Judah ha-Nasi on the grounds that when the Temple was rebuilt it would be deprived of hewers of wood and drawers of water, and the matter was relegated to "the time to come" (Yev. 79b). Maimonides, too, regards the Nethinim as the descendants of the Gibeonites (Yad, Issurei Bi'ah, 12:23–24).

Gibeonites in the Aggadah. Although the Gibeonites deserved no better fate than all the rest of the Canaanite nations, in that the covenant made with them was obtained through subterfuge, Joshua nevertheless kept his promise to them, in order to show the world the sanctity of an oath to Israel (Git. 46a). He hesitated to defend them when they were attacked, but God reminded him, "if you estrange those who are distant you will ultimately estrange also those who are near" (Num. R. 8:4). In the course of time it became obvious that the Gibeonites were not worthy of being received into the Jewish fold and Joshua, therefore, left their fate to be decided by the one who was to build the Temple (TJ, Sanh. 6:9, 23c–d).

During David's reign Israel suffered from a drought which was ascertained to be God's punishment for the murder of seven Gibeonites by the descendants of Saul. When David sought to make restitution through ransom, the Gibeonites firmly refused, insisting upon lives from the household of Saul. This cold-bloodedness clearly demonstrated to David the absence in the Gibeonite character of Israel's three basic attributes—mercy, humility, and benevolence—and he consequently excluded them from the assembly of Israel (TJ, Kid. 4:1, 65c). Ezra renewed the edict, which is to be in force even in the Messianic era *(ibid.).* [ED.]

Bibliography: B. A. Levine, in: JBL, 82 (1963), 207–12 (incl. bibl.); idem, in: IEJ, 19 (1969), 49–51; M. Haran, in: VT, 11 (1961), 159–69; E. A. Speiser, in: IEJ, 13 (1963), 69–73, Ginzberg, Legends, index.

GIBRALTAR, British crown colony, south of *Spain. Jews lived in Gibraltar in the 14th century, and in 1356 the community issued an appeal for assistance in the ransoming of Jews captured by pirates. In 1473 a number of Marranos fleeing from Andalusia applied for permission to settle in Gibraltar. The Treaty of Utrecht (1713), which ceded the fortress to England, excluded the Jews from Gibraltar in perpetuity. However, by an agreement in 1729 between England and the sultan of Morocco, his Jewish subjects were empowered to come there temporarily for purpose of trade, and the establishment of a permanent community was not long delayed. The majority of the Jewish settlers were from adjacent parts of North Africa. By 1749, when the legal right of Jewish settlement was recognized, the community numbered about 600, being about one-third of the total number of civilian residents, and there were two synagogues. During the siege of 1779–83 many took refuge in London, reinforcing the Sephardi community there. Subsequently, the community in Gibraltar resumed its development. During the period of the Napoleonic wars, Aaron Nuñez *Cardozo was one of the foremost citizens of Gibraltar; his house on the Almeida subsequently became the city hall. In the middle of the 19th century, when the Rock was at the height of its importance as a British naval and military base, the Jewish community numbered about 2,000 and most of the retail trade was in their hands, but thereafter the number declined. During World War II, almost all the civilian population, including the Jews, was evacuated to British territories, and not all returned. In 1968 the community numbered 670 (out of a total population of 25,000); it still maintained four synagogues and many communal organizations. Sir Joshua A. *Hassan was the first mayor and chief minister of Gibraltar from 1964 to 1969.

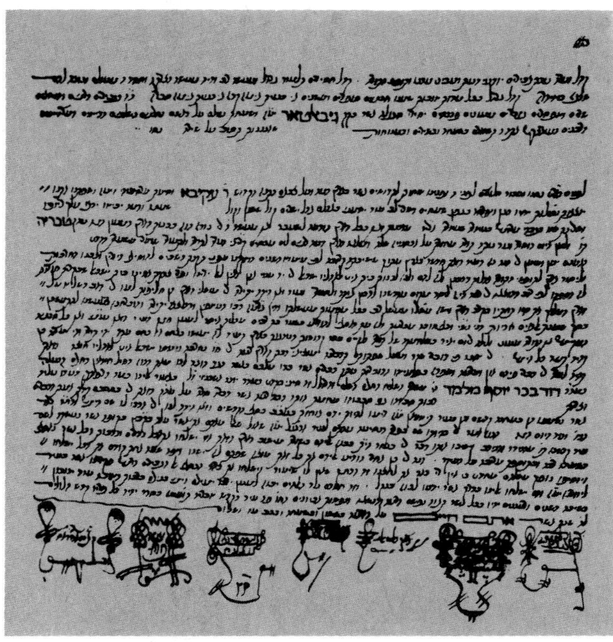

Figure 1. Letter introducing *sheliḥim* from Tiberias to the Gibraltar community, 1748. Cecil Roth Collection.

Figure 2. *Ketubbah* from Gibraltar, 1872. Cecil Roth Collection.

Bibliography: A. B. M. Serfaty, *Jews of Gibraltar under British Rule* (1958²); H. W. Howes, *The Gibraltarian: Origin and Development of the Population of Gibraltar from 1704* (1950); Beinart, in: *Sefunot*, 5 (1961), 87–88; Cano de Gardoqui and Bethencourt, in: *Hispania*, 103 (1966), 325–81; Hirschberg, in: *Essays Presented . . . I. Brodie* (1968), 153–81; JYB (1968), 140.

[C.R.]

GIDDAL (end of third century C.E.), Babylonian *amora*. He was one of the best-known younger pupils of *Rav, for whom he had an overwhelming respect and awe. This is reflected in the fact that most of Giddal's sayings in the Talmud are in the name of this teacher, often via *Ḥiyya b. Joseph, but only a few in the name of Ḥiyya b. Joseph himself. Once Giddal defended himself by swearing on the Holy Scripture and Prophets that his saying was that of Rav (Er. 17a). After Rav's death he studied in the academy of *Huna in Sura, and there came into contact with *Zeira (Ber. 49a). He appears to have had heated debates with Huna ("Giddal became impotent through the discourses of Huna": Yev. 64b). However, he was also ruled by the decisions of Judah b. Ezekiel of Pumbedita (Av. Zar. 11b). Later in life he went to Palestine (Kid. 59a). He interpreted Song of Songs 5:13 in an allegorical way, to teach that one should not study lightheartedly. "Any scholar who sits before his teacher and his lips do not drip bitterness shall be burnt" (Shab. 30b). He interpreted Psalms 39:7 to the effect that anyone who quotes a saying should imagine himself as standing in the presence of the one who originally said it (TJ, Shab. 1:2, 3a et al.). A man who writes a Torah Scroll was regarded by Giddal as if he had received it at Mount Sinai (Men. 30a). His keen sense of justice is revealed in the story about a field which he intended to buy but was anticipated by another buyer. When Isaac Nappaḥa (the Palestinian) ruled that the owner of the field should sell it to Giddal, he declined even to accept it as a gift (Kid. 59a). This explains his sharp critique of people who dealt unjustly (although he gives it in the name of Rav): "If an inhabitant of Naresh has kissed you, then count your teeth. If a man of Nehar Pekod accompanies you, it is because of the fine garments he sees on you. If a Pumbeditan accompanies you, then change your quarters" (Ḥul. 127a). Giddal was accustomed to sit at the gates of the ritual bath and to instruct the women about the rules of immersion. When asked whether he was not afraid lest his passion get the better of him, he replied that to him the women looked like so many white geese (Ber. 20a).

Bibliography: Bacher, Pal Amor; Hyman, Toledot, s.v.

[ED.]

GIDEON (Heb. גִּדְעוֹן, derived from גדע; "to cast down"), also called *Jerubaal (Heb. יְרֻבַּעַל; "let Baal contend," Judg. 6:32), son of Joash, the Abiezrite from *Ophrah, in the area of the tribe of Manasseh. Gideon is regarded as one of the *Judges although his biography (Judg. 6:11–8:32) does not contain the usual formula that "he judged Israel." He was appointed to leadership in an angelic revelation reinforced by signs and wonders of folkloristic nature, which were intended to confirm his divinely ordained mission and to emphasize his charismatic personality (6:34).

Gideon was destined to deliver Israel from the Midianites and their allies, Amalek and "the children of the east" (6:3; cf. *Midian, *Amalek, *Kedemites *(Benei Kedem)*), described as camel-mounted bedouin who came marauding from the fringes of the desert into the cultivated areas west of the Jordan. In the course of their invasions they menaced those Israelite tribes, especially Manasseh, whose settlements bordered on the Valley of Jezreel. These areas made good targets for plunder, and provided convenient passage to the interior and to the coast. Gideon's brothers appear to have been among those killed in such an attack (8:18–19). At first, only the Abiezrites responded to his call, but he was later joined by the tribes of Asher, Zebulun, and Naphtali (6:34–35; cf. 7:23). From more than 30,000 followers, a carefully selected force of 300 men was assembled at his camp at *En-Harod (7:2–7). Upon gathering intelligence as to the state of the enemy's morale, Gideon struck with a surprise night attack which wrought havoc in the Midianite camp. The Midianites and their allies withdrew eastward to the Jordan, and Gideon summoned support from Naphtali,

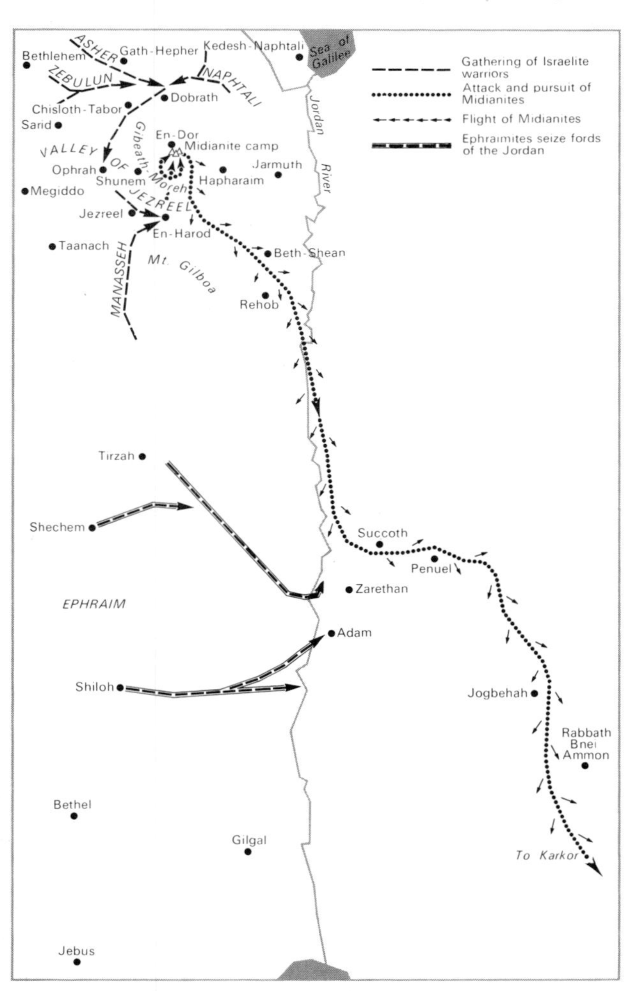

The war of Gideon against the Midianites. After Y. Aharoni and M. Avi-Yonah, *Macmillan Bible Atlas,* Carta, Jerusalem, 1968.

Asher, Manasseh, and Ephraim to block the escape routes, thereby ambushing the retreating enemy. In the pursuit, two Midianite princes, Oreb and Zeeb, were captured and beheaded (7:25; cf. Ps. 83:12–13). At this point, the Ephraimites complained about their exclusion from the original operations, but Gideon diplomatically settled the affair (Judg. 8:1–3). Gideon then resumed the pursuit of the enemy beyond the Jordan, requesting material support, meanwhile, from the non-Israelite cities of Succoth and Penuel. The rulers of these cities refused, fearing Midianite reprisals should Gideon fail. After decisively defeating the enemy, who retreated deeper into the desert, Gideon returned to Succoth and Penuel to settle accounts there (8:4–21). The military victory over the Midianites was remembered and cited for many generations (Isa. 9:3; 10:26; Ps. 83:10; cf. I Sam. 12:11).

There can be no doubt about the outstanding position Gideon occupied in the period between the conquest and the founding of the monarchy. Not only are his exploits recorded with unwonted detail, but also, and most exceptionally, the narrative is concerned with his post-military activities. Clearly, he enjoyed some special leadership status, though its precise nature is unclear. For the first time in Israelite history there is encountered a desire for change from tribal, charismatic rule to a more comprehensive, hereditary type when the "men of Israel" offer to make Gideon the founder of a dynasty (Judg. 8:22). However, it should be noted that the verb employed is "rule" *(mshl)* rather than "reign" *(mlkh),* the word usually employed for kingship. Apparently, the incident represents an intermediary stage in the movement toward the establishment of a permanent monarchy.

Despite his refusal of the offer, Gideon continued to play a leading role. He had a large harem and fathered 70 sons (8:30). Through his concubine in Shechem (8:31) he was related to some of the leading families in that town (9:1–4), and a son born of the union, *Abimelech, was later crowned king of that city-state (9:6). Gideon also exercised authority in the sphere of the cult. At the outset of his career he had built an altar to the Lord at Ophrah and had dared to destroy a local Baal altar, an act which earned him the name *Jerubaal (6:24–32; cf. I Sam. 12:11; II Sam. 11:21). Subsequent to his military victories he fashioned an *ephod from the spoils of war (Judg. 8:24–27), which, while it did not meet with the approval of the editor of Judges, illustrates the deeply religious character of Gideon. [N.M.S.]

In the Aggadah. Gideon, Jephthah, and Samson were the three least worthy of the Judges (RH 25a and b). Because on the eve of one Passover Gideon said of the Lord, "Where are all the miracles which God did for our fathers on this night" (Judg. 6:13), he was chosen to save Israel (Yal. Judg. 62) and that victory was also gained on Passover (cf. Yannai, *"Az Rov Nissim,"* Passover *Haggadah*). Another reason was his filial piety (Mid. Hag., Gen. 48:16). When Gideon sacrificed his father's bullock after the angel appeared to him, he would have transgressed no less than seven commandments, were it not that he was obeying an explicit divine command (TJ, Meg. 1:14, 72c). The cake of barley bread seen by the Midianite soldier in his dream (Judg. 7:13) indicated that the children of Israel would be vouchsafed victory as a reward for bringing the offering of an omer of barley (Lev. R. 28:6). On the breastplate of the high priest the tribe of Joseph was represented by Ephraim alone. To remove this slight upon his own tribe Manasseh, he had a new ephod made after his victory, substituting the name of Manasseh. Although he consecrated it to God, after his death it became an object of adoration (Yalkut, Judg. 64). He is identified with Jerubaal of I Samuel 12:11

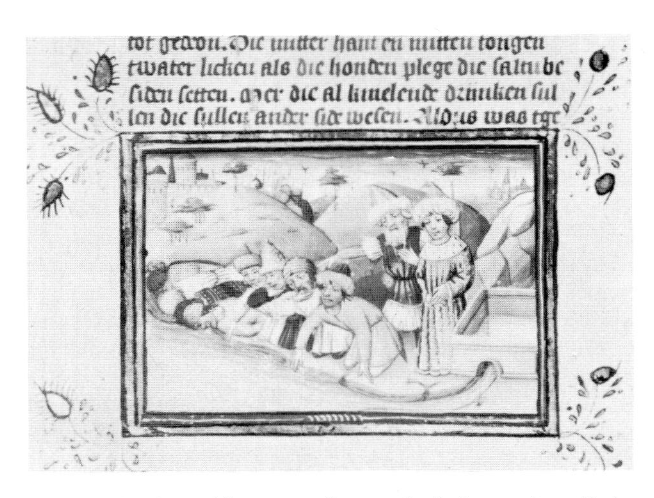

Gideon selecting soldiers according to God's instructions (Judg. 7:4–7). Illumination from a 13th-century Dutch manuscript. London, British Museum, Add. Ms. 10043, fol. 126v.

and from the juxtaposition of this name in that verse with that of Samuel, the rabbis deduce that even the most worthless of individuals, once he is appointed as leader of the community, is to be accounted as the greatest (RH 25a and b).

In the Arts. Literary works on this theme have tended to stress Gideon's heroism and patriotic motivation. Probably the first treatment occurs in the early 17th-century Old Testament dramatic cycle known as the *Stonyhurst Pageants,* in which an English writer devoted some 300 lines to the Hebrew judge. Several works in verse and prose dealt with the subject from the 18th century onward, including *Gideon; or the Patriot* (London, 1749), a fragmentary epic poem by the English dramatist Aaron Hill, a rival of Alexander Pope. In the 20th century, Grete Moeller wrote the verse play *Gideon* (Ger., 1927), two other dramas being August Schmidlin's *Gedeon, biblisches Heldendrama . . . aus der Zeit der Richter* (1932) and *Gideon* (1953), a "tragedy in 22 scrolls" by the Yiddish writer David *Ignatoff. An unusual modern interpretation of the story was the U.S. writer Paddy *Chayefsky's play *Gideon* (1962), which dramatizes man's alternate dependence on and rebellion against God.

In art the typology of Gideon is particularly subtle. The miracle of the fleece was interpreted as a symbol of the Jews, first chosen and favored (or wet), and then rejected (or dry). The fleece also became the emblem of the Burgundian Order of the Golden Fleece, one of the supreme honors of knighthood. Gideon is usually represented as a knight in armor, helmeted, and with a broken pitcher in his hand, as in the 17th-century statue in Antwerp Cathedral. Narrative cycles are rare (though Chartres offers a 13th-century sequence of four episodes), most representations concentrating on the appearance of the angel, the miracle of the fleece and the dew, the selection of the 300 warriors, or the victory over the Midianites. The angel's appearance and Gideon's incredulity, seen as a prefiguration of the Annunciation, are depicted at Chartres and in the tapestry of La Chaise-Dieu (1510). The miracle of the fleece occurs frequently at Chartres; in the Amiens and Avignon cathedrals (15th century); in the *Petites Heures d'Anne de Bretagne* (15th century); in a 16th-century fresco in Chilandari, Mount Athos; and in a fresco by Salvator Rosa (1615–1673) in the Quirinal. The selection of the warriors is illustrated in the French *Psalter of Saint Louis* and the English *Queen Mary's Psalter* (both dating from the 13th century) and by Federico Zuccaro (1540/43–1609) in a drawing at the Louvre. The victory is again portrayed at Chartres.

An early musical interpretation of the Gideon theme occurs in *Daz Gedeones wollenvlius* ("Gideon's Woollen Fleece"), an allegorical song by the *minnesaenger* Rumelant (c. 1270), which typically combines the search for biblical prototypes of the knightly ideal with the mystical concept of divine love. The martial atmosphere also prevails in at least some of the later compositions on this subject, beginning with "Gideon—Der Heyland Israels," the fifth of J. Kuhnau's *Biblische Sonaten* for keyboard instruments (1700). Johann Mattheson's oratorio *Der siegende Gideon,* written for the Hamburg celebration of Prince Eugene of Savoy's victory at Belgrade (1717), was begun, completed, and performed in the record time of 11 days. One of J. Chr. Smith's oratorios for which the music was taken wholly or largely from Handel was his *Gideon* (1769). Other compositions inspired by the subject include oratorios by Friedrich Schneider (1829) and Charles Edward Horsley (1959) and a choral work for eight male voices, *Les soldats de Gédéon* (1868), by Camille Saint-Saëns. [Ed.]

Bibliography: Bright, Hist, index; S. Tolkowski, in: JPOS, 5 (1925), 69–74; Malamat, in: PEQ, 85 (1953), 61–65; Yeivin, in: *Zion Me'assef,* 4 (1930), 1ff.; idem, in: *Ma'arakhot,* 26–27 (1945), 67ff.; idem, in: BIES, 14 (1949), 85ff.; Kutscher, *ibid.,* 2 (1934), 40–42; Kaufmann Y., Toledot, 2 (1942), 118; M. Buber, *Koenigtum Gottes* (1936[2]), 3–12, 27–30; Ginzberg, Legends, 4 (1913), 39f.; 6 (1928), 199f. In Art: G. Reese, *Music in the Middle Ages* (1940), 235–6; L. Réau, *Iconographie de l'art chrétien,* 2 pt. 1 (1956), 230–4.

GIDEON, SAMSON (originally **Gideon Abudiente;** 1699–1762), English financier. His father Reuel Gideon Abudiente was descended from the Hamburg scholar of the same name. Gideon early made a considerable fortune by speculation. In the mid-18th century, he was the principal agent for raising English government loans. His advice helped to preserve the financial stability of the country during the Jacobite rebellion in 1745. During the Seven Years' War (1755–63), he advised the English government in financial matters, and in 1758 was thanked by the king for his services in raising a loan for Hanover. Gideon left more than £500,000. In his younger days he supported the synagogue, and in 1720 contributed a sonnet in English to the Spanish translation of the Psalms by D. Lopez *Laguna. Subsequently, however, he bought a country estate, married out of the faith, had his children baptized, and, on the pretext of disapproving of the Jewish Naturalization Bill (1753), resigned his synagogue membership. He continued nevertheless to contribute to the synagogue secretly and left it a large legacy on condition that he would be buried in its cemetery. In 1759 he obtained the title of baronet for his son, also Samson Gideon (1745–1824), who became Lord Eardley in 1789. The latter had no contacts with Judaism.

Bibliography: Sutherland, in: JHSET, 17 (1953), 79–90; A. M. Hyamson, *Sephardim of England* (1951), 128–33; C. Roth, *Anglo-Jewish Letters* (1938), 130–2, 176; DNB, s.v. [C.R.]

GIESSEN, city in Hesse, W. Germany. A persecution of the Jews took place there in 1350. Jews are again mentioned in 1375. In the 17th century the few dozen Jews of Giessen were compelled to listen to missionary sermons by Christian preachers. In 1662 they were expelled from the town. Jews were permitted to return and to settle in Giessen in 1708. Some Hebrew printing took place in Giessen during the 17th and 18th centuries, most of it by non-Jewish printers. The community numbered 200 in 1828, 458 in 1871, and 1,035 (3.3% of the total population) in 1925. In 1933, under the Nazi regime, Richard *Laquer, rector of the university, was dismissed from his office because he was Jewish, as were F. M. *Heichelheim, K. *Koffka, Erich *Stern, and Margarete *Bieber. The synagogues erected in 1867 and 1899 were destroyed during **Kristallnacht* in November 1938. A year later only 259 Jews remained. About 110 were deported in 1942. There were 27 Jews living in Giessen in 1967.

Bibliography: Germ Jud, 2 (1968), 278–9; PK; A. Freimann, *A Gazetteer of Hebrew Printing* (1946). [A.P.]

GIFT, the transfer of legal rights without any consideration or payment. It is essentially no more than a sale without payment and all the principles of the law of sale apply (see *Sale).

The Da'at of the Parties. The decision *(gemirat ha-da'at)* of the parties to conclude a gift transaction—the intention of one to give and the other to receive—is established by means of an act of *kinyan*, i.e., by the performance of one of the recognized acts whereby property is acquired (see *Acquisition, Modes of). Upon performance of the *kinyan*, ownership of the property passes from the donor to the donee and neither may any longer withdraw from the transaction. The test as to whether or not the *gemirat ha-da'at* exists is an objective one, namely: if the parties performed an act customarily performed by people in order to conclude such a transaction and if in the particular circumstances of the case there existed no reason why most people would not conclude the transaction, the gift will be effective (Kid. 49b). A gift may be conferred on a person without his knowledge, because it is assumed that he agrees to get a benefit, the rule being that "a benefit may be conferred on a person in his absence, but an obligation may only be imposed on him in his presence" (Git. 11b). Similarly, the *gemirat ha-da'at* of the parties does not require a *consensus ad idem* between the parties. If it is manifest that the donor made up his mind to effect the gift, whereas the donee has not made up his mind to receive it, the latter may retract but the former may not, since the *gemirat ha-da'at* of a party to a transaction precludes him from retracting from it. Consequently, when a person confers a gift on another through a third party, the donee may refuse to accept it until it has reached his hands, even if he has heard of the intended gift—but the donor may not withdraw, since the person acquiring the gift on behalf of the donee performed a *kinyan* whereby the donor's decision to conclude the transaction was made (Yad, Zekhiyyah 4:2). If the donee should discover a defect in the gift, and it is of such nature that people would generally not want such a gift, the donee may retract even after the gift has come to his hands (*Kesef Mishneh*, Zekhiyyah 4:1, concl.).

When it is manifest to all that there was an absence of *gemirat ha-da'at* on the part of both parties, the transaction will be void. A person cannot transfer to another, by way of gift, something which is not yet in existence, or which is not his own; nor can a gift be conferred on someone who is not yet born; nor can a gift be conferred of something which one owns but which is not at the present time in his possession, such as where the owner has been robbed (see *Theft and Robbery). According to some scholars, however, even these kinds of gifts may validly be conferred in certain circumstances (see *Sale). Similarly, if a person promises a valuable gift to another verbally, but without a *kinyan*, so that the latter does not rely on the promise, there would not even be any moral sanction against him if he should withdraw (BM 49a).

If it is clear, notwithstanding an act of *kinyan*, that the donor did not really intend to effect the gift (for example, he was compelled to make the gift under duress), it will be void. Even if there was no duress, but prior to the gift the donor had declared before witnesses that he was not making it of his own free will, the transaction will also be void, even if the witnesses were not themselves aware of any duress exercised against him, because by his declaration he manifests an intention of not making the gift (Yad, Zekhiyyah, 5:4; see **Ones*). Moreover, as a gift must be made openly and publicly, an undisclosed gift is invalid, since "the donor is not presumed to have made up his mind to a gift, but is scheming for the loss of other people's property" (*ibid.* 5:1). Similarly, if a person makes a written disposition of all his property to one of his sons, the latter does not acquire it all since the assumption is that the father intended to do no more than appoint this son administrator so that his brothers should accept his authority. This is also the case if he made a disposition in favor of his wife. However, where he disposes of only part of his assets to his wife or son, or where he expressly states that an absolute gift is intended, the gift will be effective (*ibid.* 6:2–4). A gift by a woman before her marriage by way of a written disposition in favor of a person other than her prospective husband becomes ineffective if the latter should die or be divorced from her, since the disposition of her assets to another was made in order to keep these from her husband in the event of his inheriting her (*ibid.* 6:12). On the other hand, one who gives money for *kiddushin* (*marriage) which is known to be invalid, e.g., to one's own sister, intends to do so for the sake of gift (Kid. 46b). According to another opinion he gives the money as bailment.

A deaf-mute, an idiot, and a minor lack the legal capacity to make a gift, since they have no *da'at*, but the scholars prescribed that minors or deaf-mutes, depending on the degree of their understanding of the nature of the transaction, may effectively make certain gifts, by virtue of the rule of "for the sake of his sustenance" (Yad, Mekhirah 29; see *Sale). According to many opinions, they may also receive gifts, even in terms of biblical law (Tos. Kid. 19a). The sages also prescribed that someone may acquire and receive a gift on behalf of a minor, even if the latter is no more than one day old (Rashbam to BB 156b).

Conditions of the Gift. The donor may make the gift conditional upon certain terms, failing which the gift will be void (see *Conditions). As in the case of a sale, the stipulating party must impose his conditions in such a manner as to make it clear and known to all that he intends in all seriousness that the gift be considered void if the conditions should not be fulfilled and that he is not merely making a statement at large (Yad, Zekhiyyah 3:6–7). When it is apparent from the circumstances that he intends to make his gift subject to the happening of certain events, the condition will be operative even if not expressly stated and, at times, even if not stated at all (Tos. to Kid. 49b). Thus a gift would be void if made by a person who transfers all his assets to another on hearing of his son's death, but subsequently finds out that his son is still alive—since the circumstances show that he would not have given away all his assets if he had known that his son was really alive (BB 164b). Similarly, a gift made to the family of one's bride is returnable, if the marriage should fail to take place and the gift was not of a perishable kind *(ibid.)*. So too, where it is customary for wedding gifts to be sent to a friend in order that the latter shall give his own similar gifts to the donor upon his own marriage; the latter may claim such from the former if they are not given, gifts of this kind being regarded as similar to loans (Yad, Zekhiyyah 7).

The donor may stipulate that the gift is to be returned, in which event the gift is valid but the recipient is obliged to return it after the expiry of the stipulated period. During this stipulated period, however, this gift is the property of the recipient, like all his other property; but after the stipulated period, the recipient must return the property to its former owner, and failure to do so will amount to the nonfulfillment of a condition, voiding the transaction of a gift *ab initio* (Sh. Ar., ḤM 241:6). Similarly, the donor may stipulate that he is making a gift, first for the benefit of one person and then for another (see *Wills). Where the true intention of the donor is in doubt, his ultimate purpose may be deduced with the aid of the rule that "he who gives a gift gives in a liberal spirit." Thus if one says, "give to so-and-so a house capable of holding 100 barrels," and it is found to hold 120 barrels, the donee will have acquired the whole house (BB 71a). Generally, no responsibility is imposed in connection with the gift, and if it should be foreclosed, the donee will have no recourse against the donor, unless expressly provided for between the parties (Yad, Shekherim 13:1).

In the State of Israel the rules of gift are ordered in terms of the Gift Law, 1968, consisting of six material paragraphs. On the question of the degree of its reliance on Jewish law, see Elon in bibliography.

See also *Wills.

Bibliography: M. Bloch, *Das mosaisch-talmudische Erbrecht* (1890), 40ff.; idem, *Der Vertrag nach mosaisch-talmudischen Rechte* (1893), 87–90; Gulak, Yesodei, 1 (1922), 39, 76 n. 3, 118, 129ff.; 2 (1922), 159–63; Gulak, Oẓar, xxii, 38, 182–91, 346f.; Herzog, Instit, index; ET, 1 (1951[3]), 165f., 216f., 219, 291; 3 (1941), 203; 5 (1953), 400–3; 6 (1954), 89–92, 550f., 606f., 613f., 619, 625–31; 7 (1956), 30, 43f., 57, 170–3; 8 (1957), 435f.; 9 (1959), 161f.; 10 (1961), 64–66; 12 (1967), 140–6; B. Cohen, in: *Wolfson Jubilee Volume*, 1 (1965), 227f.; M. Elon, in: ILR, 4 (1969), 96–98.

[Sh.A.]

GIFTER, MORDECAI (1916–), U.S. rabbi and talmudic scholar. Gifter was born in Portsmouth, Virginia. He graduated from Yeshiva College in 1933, and also studied at Telz Yeshivah in Lithuania. After serving congregations in Baltimore and Waterbury, Conn., from 1945 Gifter taught Talmud, religion, and ethics at the Telz Yeshiva in Cleveland. He was appointed president and dean in 1965.

[C.Sc.]

GIKATILLA (Chiquatilla; Heb. גִּיקַטִילְיָא), ISAAC IBN (fl. end of 10th century), Spanish Hebrew poet and grammarian. A student of *Menahem b. Jacob ibn Saruq, he took part in the controversy on grammar between him and *Dunash b. Labrat. Moses *ibn Ezra in his *Shirat Yisrael* (ed. by B. Halper (1924), 64) states that Isaac ibn Gikatilla and his contemporary the poet R. Isaac Mar Saul surpassed their immediate predecessors—Dunash b. Labrat, Menahem ibn Saruk, and other contemporary poets—in "nobility and eloquence," and that "both came from Lucena and competed with each other (for literary supremacy), but Ibn Gikatilla was the more diligent and superior because of his greater knowledge of Arabic literature." Moses ibn *Tibbon in his commentary (still in manuscript) to the *azharot* of Solomon ibn *Gabirol mentions that Isaac ibn Gikatilla had also written some *azharot*. Only in 1950, however, were four manuscripts containing the majority of these *azharot* published by M. Zulay. The influence of *Saadiah Gaon is strongly marked in these poems. This type of *azharah* is the first of its kind to be written in Spain, and at the end of each the name "Isaac" appears. Besides this work, Moses ibn Ezra ascribed another verse to Gikatilla. This ascription has been authenticated by a number of scholars.

Isaac ibn Gikatilla, together with Judah Ḥayyuj and Isaac ibn Kapron, who were also students of Menahem ibn Saruk, actively defended their teacher against the attacks of Dunash b. Labrat. In their reply (ed. by S. G. Stern together with Yehudi ben Sheshet's reply, see bibl.), they praise the grammatical works of Menahem, enumerate Dunash's errors one by one, and invalidate his system of comparisons between Hebrew and other Semitic languages, Arabic and Aramaic. They accuse Dunash of having corrupted the Hebrew language by adapting it to the Arabic meter. *Yehudi b. Sheshet, the pupil of Dunash, replied and from his words "Behold, the greatest among you, ben Gikatilla" (Stern, pt. 2, p. 17) it can be deduced that Gikatilla was presumably the most outstanding scholar among his colleagues. Yehudi b. Sheshet's enumeration of the errors of Gikatilla makes it possible to estimate the extent of the latter's contribution to the jointly written reply of Menahem's disciples. Gikatilla was a teacher of the grammarian Jonah *ibn Janaḥ whom he encouraged in the study of the Arabic language. Ibn Janaḥ, in many of his own works, cites Gikatilla without, however, mentioning the source. Other grammarians of the Middle Ages, such as Judah *ibn Bal'am, also quote him.

Bibliography: S. Pinsker (ed.), *Likkutei Kadmoniyyot* (1860), in: Supplements 159, 161, 165; S. G. Stern (ed.), *Sefer Teshuvot Talmidei Menaḥem ve-Talmidei Dunash* . . . (1870), lxxv (introd.); Jonah ibn Janaḥ, *Sefer ha-Shorashim*, ed. by W. Bacher (1896), x (introd.); D. Yellin, *Toledot Hitpatteḥut ha-Dikduk ha-Ivri* (1945), 94–106; Zulay, in: *Tarbiz*, 20 (1949/50), 161–76; Schirmann, Sefarad, 2 (1956), 702, s.v. *Azharot*.

[N.N.]

GIKATILLA (Chiquatilla), JOSEPH BEN ABRAHAM (1248–c. 1325), Spanish kabbalist whose works exerted a profound and permanent influence on kabbalism. Gikatilla, who was born in Medinaceli, Castile, lived for many years in Segovia. Between 1272 and 1274 he studied under Abraham *Abulafia, who praises him as his most successful pupil. Gikatilla, who was at first greatly influenced by Abulafia's ecstatic, prophetic system of kabbalism, soon showed a greater affinity for philosophy.

His first extant work, *Ginnat Egoz* (1615), written in 1274, is an introduction to the mystic symbolism of the alphabet, vowel points, and the Divine Names. The title derives from the initial letters of the kabbalistic elements *gematria* ("numerology"), *notarikon* ("acrostics"), *temurah* ("permutation"). In common with his mentor, Gikatilla also links this mystic lore with the system practiced by *Maimonides. This work makes no suggestion of the theosophical doctrine of *Sefirot* or "spheres" (see *Kabbalah), later adopted by Gikatilla. The *Sefirot* here are identified with the philosophical term "intelligences." On the other hand, the author shows himself familiar with the revelatory mysticism of *Jacob b. Jacob ha-Kohen, although the latter is not mentioned by name. Several of Gikatilla's other writings also deal with the theory of letter combinations and alphabetical mysticism. However, in the 1280s, Gikatilla evidently made contact with *Moses b. Shem Tov de Leon, and thereafter the two exerted a mutual influence on each other's kabbalistic development.

Before writing *Ginnat Egoz*, Gikatilla had written a commentary on the Song of Songs (but not the one in the Paris manuscript 790 which bears indications that Gikatilla wrote it in 1300 in Segovia). The later work endorses the doctrine of *Shemitot*, a theory of cosmic development based on the sabbatical year, as expounded in the **Sefer ha-Temunah*. Gikatilla also compiled *Kelalei ha-Mitzvot*, explaining *mitzvot* by a literal interpretation of *halakhah* (Ms. Paris 713); a number of *piyyutim* (Habermann, in *Mizraḥ u-Ma'arav*, 5 (1932), 351; Gruenwald, in *Tarbiz*, 36 (1966/67), 73–89), some devoted to kabbalistic themes; and *Sefer ha-Meshalim*, a book of proverbs to which he added his own commentary, whose ethical precepts were close to kabbalistic principles. (The proverbs alone published by I. Davidson, in *Sefer ha-Yovel shel "Hadoar"* (1927), 116–22; the book with commentary, in Ms. Oxford 1267). While Gikatilla wrote numerous works on Kabbalah, many others have been attributed to him erroneously. A. Altmann, for instance, has shown that Gikatilla was not the author of the lengthy *Sefer Ta'amei ha-Mitzvot*. Written by an unknown kabbalist about 1300 (Cambridge Ms.) and also attributed to Isaac ibn Farḥi, it had a wide circulation. A number of treatises await clarification as to authorship.

Gikatilla's most influential kabbalistic work, written before 1293, is his *Sha'arei Orah* (1559), a detailed explanation of kabbalistic symbolism and the designations of the ten *Sefirot*. He adopted a system intermediate between that of the Geronese school of kabbalists and the *Zohar. This is one of the first writings to disclose knowledge of portions of the Zohar, although it departs from its approach in several fundamental respects.

Sefer Sha'arei Ẓedek (1559) provides another explanation of the theory of *Sefirot*, reversing their normal succession. Other published works by Gikatilla are: *Sha'ar ha-Nikkud* (1601), a mystical treatise on vocalization; *Perush Haggadah shel Pesaḥ*, a kabbalistic commentary on the Passover *Haggadah* (1602); a number of essays on various subjects (publ. in *Sefer Erez ba-Levanon*, ed. by Isaac Perlov, Vilna, 1899); kabbalistic works remaining in manuscript are: mystical treatises on certain *mitzvot;* a commentary on the Vision of the Chariot of Ezekiel (numerous manuscripts); and considerable portions of a biblical commentary continuing the system followed in *Ginnat Egoz* (manuscript in JTS, New York, Deinard 451). A work on disciplines *("pe'ulot")* in practical Kabbalah was extant in the 17th century (Joseph Delmedigo, *Sefer Novellot Ḥokhmah* (1631), 195a). A collection of kabbalistic responsa on points of *halakhah* from the second half of the 14th century has been erroneously ascribed to Gikatilla. Joseph *Caro made use of them in his *Beit Yosef*. Problems of Kabbalah put to Joshua b. Meir ha-Levi by Gikatilla are in manuscript, Oxford, 1565. Also extant are a number of prayers, such as *Tefillat ha-Yiḥud, Me'ah Pesukim* ("100 Verses," on the *Sefirot*), and *Pesukim al-Shem ben Arba'im u-Shetayim Otiyyot* ("Verses on the 42-Lettered Divine Name"). Commentaries were written on *Sha'arei Orah* by an anonymous 15th-century kabbalist (publ. by G. Scholem, in his *Kitvei Yad be-Kabbalah* (1930), 80–83) and by Mattathias *Delacrut (mainly included with the work). A summary was translated into Latin by the apostate Paul Riccius (1516).

Gikatilla made an original attempt to provide a detailed yet lucid and systematic exposition of kabbalism. He was also the originator of the doctrine equating the infinite, **Ein Sof*, with the first of the ten *Sefirot*. The conception was rejected by the majority of kabbalists from the 16th century onward, but his works continued to be highly esteemed and were published in many editions.

See also *Kabbalah.

Bibliography: S. Sachs, *Ha-Yonah* (1850), 80–81; G. Scholem, *Kitvei Yad ba-Kabbalah* (1930), 218–25; idem, in: *Sefer ha-Yovel le-Ya'akov Freimann* (1937), 163–70 (Heb. section); Altmann, in: KS, 40 (1965), 256–76, 405–12; idem, in: *Sefer ha-Yovel le-Israel Brodie* (1967), 57–65; Weiler, in: HUCA, 37 (1966), 13–44 (Heb. section); Steinschneider, Cat Bod, 1461–70; A. Jellinek, *Beitraege zur Geschichte der Kabbala*, 2 (1852), 57–64; Scholem, Mysticism, 194–5, 405–6; Werblowsky, in: *Zeitschrift fuer Religion und Geistgeschichte*, 8 (1956), 164–9.

[G.SCH.]

GIKATILLA (Chiquatilla), MOSES BEN SAMUEL HA-KOHEN (11th century), Spanish Jewish liturgical poet and grammarian. Born in Córdoba of good family, he lived principally in Saragossa and, it seems, traveled extensively. One of a group of youths favored and supported by *Samuel ha-Nagid, Gikatilla wrote poems of praise dedicated to his benefactor and to the latter's son Joseph. His works in the fields of grammar, Bible exegesis, and other subjects have been lost except for quotations in the works of others, and are now known only through laudatory or critical references to them. Abraham *ibn Ezra refers to him as the "greatest of the grammarians." From the quotations ascribed to him, it can be deduced that he wrote commentaries in Arabic to most of the books of the Bible. He mentions *Saadiah Gaon, Samuel ha-Nagid, Yeshu'ah, and others. He wrote a *Sefer Dikduk* ("Book of Grammar"), and translated some of the works of Ibn Ḥayyuj and possibly also of Samuel ha-Nagid from Arabic into Hebrew. The extant fragments of his exegetical writings suggest that he was a bold and original commentator. He usually adopted the literal meaning of the text and was among the few who explained the aspirations of the prophets as applying to their own times and not to those of the Messiah. He was the first commentator to attribute the chapters from Isaiah 40 onward to a prophet other than Isaiah. On Isaiah 41, the following is reported in his name: "These first consolations, from the middle of the book onward, refer to the Second Temple" (i.e., not to the messianic age). Concerning Psalm 106:47 he said, "This psalmist was in Babylon." Similar comments on other chapters are also cited in his name.

The scanning excerpts of Gikatilla's commentaries were collected by S. Poznański. Of his Hebrew hymns and poems, only ten have been published. Moses *ibn Ezra said of him: "He was among the greatest of the exalted rhetoricians and poets in both languages" (*Shirat Yisrael* (1924), 69). His poems, which are rhymed and stylistically characteristic of his time, include religious compositions, friendship and love poems, and drinking songs.

Bibliography: Brody, in: YMḤSI, 3 (1937), 64–90; Schirmann, Sefarad (1956), 294–7; S. Poznański, *Moses b. Samuel ha-Kohen Chiquitilla nebst den Fragmenten seiner Schriften* (1895).

[A.M.H.]

GILADI (Butelbroit), ISRAEL (1886–1918), Ereẓ Israel pioneer and leader of *Ha-Shomer. Born in Calarasi, Bessarabia, Giladi was a member of Po'alei Zion and an advocate of Jewish self-defense. In 1905 he went to Ereẓ Israel and joined the Jewish laborers in the settlements. In 1907 he was one of the founding members of the Bar Giora secret defense society and a year later joined the collective labor group in *Sejera. When Ha-Shomer was founded in 1909, Giladi was elected to its committee and put in charge of the defense of settlements in Galilee, Samaria, and Judea. He became acting head of the organization in 1913 when Israel *Shochat, its leader, left for Constantinople. During World War I he proposed the establishment of an agricultural settlement to serve as a base for Ha-Shomer and, in the summer of 1917, he and a group of friends established Kefar Bag (named after the Bar Giora society) south of Metullah. He died in an influenza epidemic. Giladi was the author of *Divrei Yemei ha-Aguddah* ("History of the Association"), a source for the history of Ha-Shomer (published in *Koveẓ ha-Shomer*, 1937). After his death, the village he had helped found, Kefar Giladi, was named after him.

Bibliography: Dinur, Haganah, index; J. Yaari-Poleskin, *Ḥolemim ve-Loḥamim* (1946), 363–9; S. Sheva, *Shevet ha-No'azim* (1969).

[Y.S.]

GILBERT, FELIX (1905–), U.S. historian. Born in Baden, Germany, Gilbert emigrated to the U.S. in 1936. During World War II he served as research analyst in the Office of Strategic Services and the U.S. Department of State (1943–46). In 1946 he joined the faculty of Bryn Mawr College, rising to the rank of professor of history in 1948. From 1962 he was professor at the School of Historical Studies at the Institute for Advanced Study in Princeton.

Gilbert's principal scholarly interests were the Italian Renaissance and diplomatic history of the 18th and 20th centuries. Among his major works were: *Hitler Directs His War* (1951); *To the Farewell Address: Ideas of Early American Foreign Policy* (1961); *Niccolò Machiavelli e la vita culturale del suo tempo* (1964); *Machiavelli and Guicciardini: Politics and History in Sixteenth-century Florence* (1965). With G. A. Craig he edited *The Diplomats, 1919–1939* (2 vols., 1953–63).

[O.I.J.]

GILBERT, MILTON (1909–), U.S. economist. Gilbert, who was born in Philadelphia, joined the U.S. Department of Commerce in 1938 as editor of the department's *Survey of Current Business,* later becoming director of national and statistical accounts. From 1960 he served as economic adviser to the Bank of International Settlements in Basle. His major interests were social accounting, business fluctuations, foreign exchange, and international finance. Gilbert's publications include *International Comparison of National Products and the Purchasing Power of Currencies* (1954); *Problems of the International Monetary System* (1966), and *The Gold-Dollar System* (1968). [J.O.R.]

GILBERT, SHLOMO (1885–1942), Yiddish writer. Born in Radzymin, Poland, he spent his adult years in Warsaw. He was poor and consumptive, and spent most of his time poring over religious tracts in synagogues. He perished in the extermination camp at Treblinka. His realistic tales and short dramas, with kabbalistic-mystic overtones, appeared from 1907 in Polish Yiddish journals. His dramatic poem *Moshiakhs Trit* ("The Steps of Messiah," 1924), was translated into Hebrew. A definitive edition of his works appeared posthumously in 1954, with an introduction and evaluation by the critic S. *Niger.

Bibliography: LNYL, 2 (1958), 209ff.; M. Ravitch, *Mayn Leksikon,* 1 (1945), 52–54. [M.Rav.]

GILBOA (Heb. גִּלְבֹּעַ), mountain ridge branching off to the N.E. from the Samarian Hills and lying on a S.E.-N.W. axis. The ridge is an upfaulted block that drops precipitously to the Beth-Shean Valley in the east and the Harod Valley in the northeast and more gradually to the southern Jezreel Valley in the west. Along the fault lines at the mountain's foot in the east and the northeast are some of the most

Figure 1. Philistines discover King Saul and his sons dead on Mount Gilboa (I Sam. 31:8), an illumination from the *Pierpont Morgan Picture Bible*, France, 13th century. The lower register shows Saul's armor being placed in the house of Ashtaroth and his head being paraded through the land. New York, Pierpont Morgan Library, Ms. 368, fol. 35r.

Figure 2. Kibbutz Bet Alfa, at the foot of Mount Gilboa in the Jezreel Valley. Courtesy Keren Hayesod United Israel Appeal, Jerusalem.

plentiful natural springs in Israel. The entire length of the ridge is $10\frac{1}{2}$ mi. (about 17 km.). The summit is 479 m. high, lying $1\frac{1}{4}$ mi. (about 2 km.) south of Kafr Faqūʿa. It is from this village that the Arabic name for the mountain, Jebel Faqūʿa, was derived.

Mt. Gilboa was the scene of the battle in which Saul and his sons were killed (I Sam. 31:1–6). David cursed the mountain in his lament over Saul and his sons (II Sam. 1:21): "Ye mountains of Gilboa, let there be no dew nor rain upon you, neither fields of choice fruits." The ancient name is preserved in the present-day Arab village of Jalbūn, situated southeast of Kafr Faqūʿa. Jalbūn is mentioned by Eusebius as Gelbous (Onom., 72:10). In September 1921 kibbutz *En-Harod was established at the foot of the mountain, next to the En-Harod spring (the kibbutz was transferred in 1929 to the northern side of the Harod Valley; on the side of the mountain itself is moshav *Gidonah—established in 1949—which initially bore the name Gilboa). In the time of the British Mandate, especially between 1936 and 1939, Gilboa served as a base for Arab raids on the Jewish settlements in the Harod and Beth-Shean valleys. Similarly, the Arab Legion and irregulars fortified positions on Mt. Gilboa during the *War of Independence in the spring of 1948, with the aim of cutting off the Harod and Beth-Shean Valley settlements from the west. This danger was overcome with the occupation of the villages of Zarʿīn (see *Yizre'el) and Mazār by a *Palmaḥ detachment. The 1949 armistice border, following the military front, gave Israel a foothold on the northern and eastern rims of the mountain and left to Jordan most of its inhabited parts in the west and south. After the *Six-Day War, this border marked the northeastern corner of the occupied region of Samaria.

Apart from the new villages founded in the 1950s and 1960s at the foot of Mt. Gilboa in the west, north, and east, two settlements came into being on the mountain proper—Nurit, established in 1950 as a moshav and later transformed into a *Gadna training camp and nature study center, and Ma'aleh Gilboa, founded in 1962 as a Naḥal outpost, which became a civilian kibbutz affiliated with *Ha-Kibbutz ha-Dati in 1967. The Jewish National Fund planted a forest on Mt. Gilboa with over 3,000,000 trees—one of the country's largest—and built many access roads and paths opening the mountain for tourism. A large area has been declared a nature reserve where plant species exclusive to Mt. Gilboa are afforded protection.

Bibliography: Weitz, in: *Bikat Beit-She'an* (1962), 124–8; Levinsohn, *ibid.*, 96–101; EM, 2 (1965), 486. [A.J.Br./Ed.]

GILBOA, AMIR (1917–), Israel poet. Born in Radzywilow, Volhynia, Gilboa went to Palestine in 1937, working initially as a laborer. He began to publish poetry while serving in the Jewish Brigade during World War II. The accent on linguistic sensitivity in the 1940s prompted Gilboa to abandon flowery rhetoric, but he nevertheless preserved the multilevel allusions inherent in this style. His poetry with its developed lyrical sense and complex structure speaks with compassion, and his blending of personal and national motifs is reminiscent of Bialik. Gilboa sensitively and at times enigmatically describes the feelings of the individual within the crowd in a surrealistic dream atmosphere. These feelings range from the fear and expectation of the apocalypse to an expression of wild and childlike joy. A similar atmosphere envelops his poems about biblical characters, but the aura of nightmare is present as the landscapes and figures of his childhood and youth are darkened by the Holocaust and the death of his relatives. Gilboa's use of various levels of language without the perspective of distance or irony draws him into a confrontation with the primordial element in Hebrew poetry, particularly the Psalms. His confidence in his own personal vision enables him to create poems wherein ancient words and experiences are suffused with wonder and freshness. The same compassion that typifies his attitude toward human beings is also seen in Gilboa's relationship with trees and plants, their tactile values and biological vitality replacing human attributes.

Gilboa's four volumes of poetry are: *Le'ut* ("Fatigue," 1942); *Sheva Rashuyyot* (1949); *Shirim ba-Boker ba-Boker* (1953); *keḥulim va-Adumim* (1963); and *"Raẓiti Likhtov Siftei Yesheinim"* (1968). For English translations of his works see Goell, Bibliography, 24.

Bibliography: D. Tsalka (ed.), *Amir Gilboa: Mivḥar Shirim u-Devarim al Yeẓirato* (1962); Sachs, in: S. Burnshaw et al. (eds.), *The Modern Hebrew Poem Itself* (1965), 136–47.

[D.Ts.]

GILEAD (Heb. גִּלְעָד), the central region east of the Jordan, approximately between the river Yarmuk in the north and the northern end of the Dead Sea in the south. The name Gilead is explained in the Bible as deriving from Gal-ed, in Aramaic Yegar-Sahadutha (Gen. 31:47), and there are some scholars who relate its meaning to the Arabic *Jalʿad,* meaning "harsh," "rude," because of the mountainous and rocky nature of the region.

According to the Bible, Israelite Transjordan was divided in three main regions: the plain, Gilead, and the Bashan (Deut. 3:10; Josh. 20:8; II Kings 10:33). The plain is the flat height north of the Arnon which was the scene of constant battle between Israel and Moab. The Bashan is the northern part of Transjordan north of the Yarmuk, for which Israel competed with the Arameans. Gilead is the clearly Israelite section of Transjordan and, therefore, in its broad meaning, encompassed central Transjordan, on both sides of the Jabbok, from the Sea of Galilee to the Dead Sea (Gen. 37:25; Josh. 22:9, 15; II Sam. 2:9; II Kings 10:33; Ezek. 47:18; Amos 1:3; etc.). Different parts of the Bible mention the two halves of Gilead, north and south of the Jabbok (Deut. 3:12; Josh. 12:2, 5; 13:31).

The allotted settlements of tribes on the other side of the Jordan are described according to this geographic division: "From Aroer, which is by the valley of Arnon, and half the hill-country of Gilead, and the cities thereof, gave I unto the Reubenites and to the Gadites; and the rest of Gilead, and all Bashan, the kingdom of Og . . . gave I unto the half-tribe of Manasseh" (Deut. 3:12–13).

On the other hand, there are some places in the Bible from which it appears that the name Gilead designates a smaller area. Numbers 32:1 separates the land of Jazer from the territory Gilead. In Deuteronomy 3:15–16 the name Gilead includes only the northern part, between the Jabbok and the Yarmuk (though "from the Gilead to the valley of Arnon" is not separated—it is a part of the territory of the tribes of Reuben and Gad). On the other hand, "the land of Gilead" which is enumerated among the 12 regions of Solomon (I Kings 4:19) is in southern Transjordan, including the plain. In place of "the land of Gilead," however, the Septuagint reads "the land of Gad."

In light of these different descriptions several scholars have concluded that the name Gilead originally comprised a more limited area and broadened only with the continuation of Israelite settlement.

According to R. Smend, the name Gilead originally referred to ʿAjlūn, the region between the Jabbok and the Yarmuk. He bases this opinion on the names of the cities Jabesh-Gilead and Ramoth-Gilead, both of which belong to this region, and also on the genealogical lists of Manasseh which mention Gilead, the son of Machir (Num. 26:29; Josh. 17:1; see *Manasseh). R. de Vaux, on the other hand (and also M. Noth), prefers a more southerly location, between al-Ṣalt and the Jabbok, because of the present-day Jebel Jalʿad, Khirbat Jalʿad, and Khirbat Jalʿūd, which preserved the name, as well as various biblical statements (especially Num. 32).

Gilead was described in the Bible as pasturage land (Num. 32:1; Jer. 50:19; Micah 7:14). It was known for its spices, among other things (Jer. 8:22; 46:11). There are iron deposits in the vicinity of the Jabbok that were exploited in early times. Archaeological research has shown that the first great settlement of Gilead flourished around the 24th–21st centuries B.C.E. During the 20th century B.C.E. there was a definite decline in the settlement of Gilead and the southern parts of Transjordan, and it seems that these areas were occupied mainly by a nomadic population. This decline was not present in the Bashan and in northern Gilead, up to the area of Bet Arbel (Irbid), around 20 mi. (30 km.) south of the Yarmuk. Heavy population of the whole Gilead and the southern regions of Transjordan was resumed around the beginning of the 13th century, with the establishment of the kingdoms of Amman, Moab, and Edom. According to biblical tradition most of the areas of Gilead were then occupied by two Amorite kings, Og king of Bashan and Sihon king of Heshbon, from whom these areas were conquered by the settling Israelite tribes (Num. 21:32; Deut. 1:4; 3:10–13; Josh. 1:12–15; 9:10; 12:1–6; Judg. 11; etc.). The southern part of Gilead was settled by the tribes of Reuben and Gad, and north of the Jabbok—the half-tribe Manasseh. The latter comprised several family units, such as Machir and the villages of Jair (I Kings

The mountains of Gilead, with the Jordan river in the foreground. Courtesy Keren Hayesod, United Israel Appeal, Jerusalem.

4:13), and the Gadites, too, spread southward up to the Sea of Galilee (Josh. 13:27). According to biblical tradition, the name Israel was given to Jacob at Peniel which is on the Jabbok in central Gilead (Gen. 32:29–31).

The Bible records the war, during the time of the judges, between the Gileadites and Amman, under the leadership of Jephthah the Gileadite (Judg. 11), which resulted in bloody conflict between the Gileadites and the Ephraimites (*ibid.* 12:1–6). This period saw the weakening of the bonds between the tribes of the Gilead and western Ereẓ Israel, as can also be seen from their nonparticipation in the war of Deborah (*ibid.* 5:17) and from the building of the altar by the tribes from the other side of the Jordan "over against the land of Canaan in the borders of Jordan" (Josh. 22:11).

Nevertheless, the Ammonites' attempt to conquer Jabesh-Gilead and its being saved by Saul were the direct motivations for the establishment of the Israelite monarchy (I Sam. 11). The mountainous nature of the Gilead and its broad pasture-lands helped preserve desert customs and early Israelite traditions to which prophetic vision became attached. It is not, therefore, a coincidence that this was the place of origin of Elijah the Gileadite whose spirit greatly affected the development of prophecy.

The Gileadites remained loyal to the ruling house of Israel that protected them from their neighbors in the east and plunderers from the desert. In time of trouble the Israelite kings sought refuge in Mahanaim and Penuel on the Jabbok (II Sam. 2:8; I Kings 12:25). The Gilead is mentioned as one of three places over which Abner son of Ner appointed Ish-Baal (Ish-Bosheth) son of Saul as king (II Sam. 2:8–9). In the time of Solomon Transjordan was divided into three areas (I Kings 4:13–14, 19): (1) the vicinity of Ramoth-Gilead, the village of Jair in the Gilead and the region of Argob in the Bashan, i.e., northern Gilead and the Bashan; (2) the vicinity of Mahanaim, i.e., central Gilead on both sides of the Jabbok; (3) "the land of Gad" according to the Septuagint (masoretic text, "the (southern) land of Gilead"), i.e., southern Gilead and the plain up to the Arnon River.

With the division of the kingdom Gilead remained in the area of northern Israel. However, the Bashan and the northern part of Gilead were quickly conquered by the Arameans (I Kings 22; II Kings 9:14; II Chron. 18), and Ramoth-Gilead thereafter became an area of perpetual conflict between them and Israel. The Arameans also took the opportunity to broaden their boundaries in Gilead (Amos 1:13). In around 814 B.C.E. Hazael of Aram Damascus conquered the whole land of Gilead from Israel (II Kings 10:32–33). At the beginning of the eighth century Damascus was weakened under Assyrian pressure (*ibid.* 13:5), and the Gilead was restored to the area of Israel (*ibid.* 13:25; 14:25, 28). In 733 the Gilead was conquered by Tiglath-Pileser III, king of Assyria, and many of its inhabitants were exiled to Assyria (*ibid.* 15:29; I Chron. 5:26). The Assyrian satrapy Gal'aza (=Gilead) was established in the place, except for the regions of southern Gilead which were occupied by the Ammonites (Jer. 49:1).

Gilead in the Persian period was included in the fifth satrapy called Abirnahara ("beyond the river," i.e., Trans-euphrates) whose capital was at Damascus. During the rule of the Ptolemies the name Galaaditis (Gilead) designated a small district in Transjordan and in the Seleucid period it was the name of one of the four large eparchies into which Coele-Syria was organized (I Macc. 5:17–45).

Bibliography: R. de Vaux, in: RB, 47 (1938), 398ff.; idem, in: *Vivre et Penser,* 1 (1941), 16ff.; N. Glueck, in: AASOR, 18–19 (1939), passim; 25–28 (1951), passim; M. Noth, in: PJB, 37 (1941), 50ff.; idem, in: ZDPV, 75 (1959), 14ff.; Abel, Geog, 1–11, passim; Aharoni, Land, passim.

[Yo.A.]

GILEAD, ZERUBAVEL (1912–), Hebrew poet, writer, and editor. Born in Bendery, Bessarabia, his family emigrated to Palestine in 1922 and settled in the newly founded kibbutz *En-Harod, where he grew up. He was active in the Ha-No'ar ha-Oved and He-Ḥalutz youth movements, served as an emissary of the latter in Poland and was information officer of the *Palmaḥ and a member of its general staff during Israel's War of Independence. His poems, stories, and articles appeared in numerous journals and newspapers from 1929. His works include: *Ne'urim* (poems, 1936); *Marot Gilbo'a* (sketches, 1943); *Aggadot Yaldut* (poems, 1947); *Siḥah al ha-Ḥof* (stories, 1954); *Nahar Yarok* (poems, 1956); *Siḥah she-Lo Tammah* (essays, 1965); and *Yam shel Ma'alah* (poems, 1967). From 1956, he was one of the editors of *Mi-Bifenim* (a periodical of Ha-Kibbutz ha-Me'uḥad), and was on the board of the movement's publishing house. (For English translations see Goell, Bibliography, index.)

Bibliography: G. Yardeni, *Siḥot im Soferim* (1961), 133–42; D. Sadan, *Avenei Boḥan* (1951), 140–5; Sadan, in: *Bein Din le-Ḥeshbon* (1963), 115–23; Y. Keshet, *Maskiyyot* (1953), 273–81.

[G.K.]

GILELS, EMIL GRIGORYEVICH (1916–), Russian pianist. Born in Odessa, he became a teacher at the Moscow Conservatory in 1939 and in that same year won the first prize at the international piano competition in Brussels. He was awarded the Stalin Prize in 1946 and the Lenin Prize in 1962. Gilels became popular on concert platforms all over the world. The virtuosity of his early days was enhanced by a depth of interpretation and range of expression which made him one of the foremost pianists of the time.

Bibliography: V. Delson, *Emil Gilels* (Rus., 1959); S. M. Khentova, *Emil Gilels* (Rus., 1967[2]).

[M.Go.]

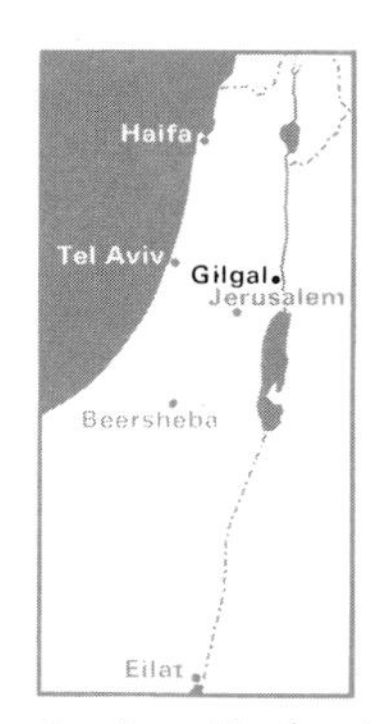

GILGAL (Heb. גִּלְגָּל), name indicating an ancient sacred site on which a circle of large stones was erected. *Gilgalim* ("circles") were constructed in Canaan from very early times; the Bible mentions several places called Gilgal which were named after *gilgalim* in their vicinity.

(1) The best-known Gilgal is the place "on the east border of Jericho" where the Israelites encamped after crossing the Jordan. There Joshua set up the 12 stones which the Israelites had taken from the Jordan (Josh. 4:19–20). At Gilgal *Pesaḥ* (Passover) was celebrated and those born in the desert were circumcised. "This day have I rolled away (*galloti* from root *galol*) the reproach of Egypt from off you" is the biblical explanation given for the place-name (5:7–10). The camp at Gilgal

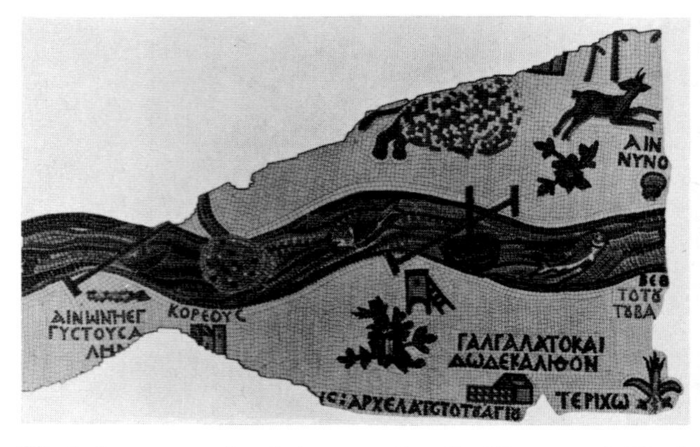

Gilgal shown as a church incorporating the 12 stones of Gilgal (lower center), in a detail from the sixth-century Madaba mosaic map of Ereẓ Israel.

served as a base during Joshua's wars (9:6; 10:6–9; 14:6). After the conquest of Canaan, the site continued to be sacred; in times of national crisis sacrifices were offered there; Samuel judged Israel there; and Saul was crowned king at Gilgal (I Sam. 10:8; 7:16; 11:14–15). Later its cult aroused the wrath of the prophets (Hos. 4:15; Amos 4:4; 5:5). In the period of the Second Temple it was called Beth-Gilgal and was inhabited by levites who were sons of the Temple singers (Neh. 12:29). The 12 stones in Gilgal are mentioned in the Talmud (Sot. 35b). Eusebius locates it east of Jericho (Onom. 64:24ff.). The Madaba Map shows a church, in which the stones have been embodied, east of the tell of Jericho. Khirbat al-Mafjar or Khirbet al-Athala have been suggested for its identification.

(2) Another Gilgal is perhaps referred to in the verse: "in the Arabah, over against Gilgal, beside the terebinths of Moreh" (Deut. 11:30); its location is not clear.

(3) The Gilgal from which "they went down to Beth-El" which is associated with the activities of Elisha (II Kings 2:1–2; 4:38–44) is identified by some scholars with Jaljūliya, north of Ramallah; others suggest that it is identical with Gilgal (1).

(4) The Gilgal mentioned in the description of the frontier of Judah near "the ascent of Adummim" (Josh. 15:7; but called Geliloth in Josh. 18:17) is unidentified.

(5) The Gilgal whose king Joshua defeated (Josh. 12:23; LXX—"Galilee") is also unidentified.

Bibliography: Maisler (Mazar), in: BJPES, 11 (1945), 35–41; S. Klein, *Ereẓ ha-Galil* (1946), 13; E. Sellin, *Gilgal* (1917); Albright, in: BASOR, 11 (1923), 7ff.; M. Noth, *Das Buch Josua* (1953²), 32–33; Abel, Geog, 2 (1938), 336–8; Kelso, in: BASOR, 121 (1951), 6ff.; Kelso and Baramki, in: AASOR, 29–30 (1955).

[M.A.-Y.]

GILGUL (Heb. גִּלְגּוּל, "transmigration of souls," "reincarnation," or "metempsychosis"). There is no definite proof of the existence of the doctrine of *gilgul* in Judaism during the Second Temple period. In the Talmud there is no reference to it (although, by means of allegoric interpretations, later authorities found allusions to and hints of transmigration in the statements of talmudic rabbis). A few scholars interpret the statements of Josephus in *Antiquities* 18:1, 3, and in *Jewish Wars* 2:8, 14 on the holy bodies which the righteous merit, according to the belief of the Pharisees, as indicating the doctrine of metempychosis and not the resurrection of the dead, as most scholars believe. In the post-talmudic period *Anan b. David, the founder of Karaism, upheld this doctrine, and in some of his statements there is an echo and a continuation of the ancient sectarian traditions. The doctrine of transmigration was prevalent from the second century onward among some Gnostic sects and especially among Manicheans and was maintained in several circles in the Christian Church (perhaps even by Origen). It is not impossible that this doctrine became current in some Jewish circles, who could have received it from Indian philosophies through Manicheism, or from Platonic and neoplatonic as well as from Orphic teachings.

Anan's arguments on behalf of *gilgul*, which were not accepted by the Karaites, were refuted by *Kirkisani (tenth century) in a special chapter in his *Sefer ha-Orot;* one of his major points was the death of innocent infants. Some Jews, following the Islamic sect of the Muʿtazila and attracted by its philosophic principles, accepted the doctrine of transmigration. The major medieval Jewish philosophers rejected this doctrine (*Saadiah Gaon, *The Book of Beliefs and Opinions*, treatise 6, ch. 7; Abraham ibn Daud, *Emunah Ramah*, treatise 1, ch. 7; Joseph *Albo, *Ikkarim*, treatise 4, ch. 29). *Abraham b. Ḥiyya quotes the doctrine from neoplatonic sources but rejects it (*Meditations of the Sad Soul*, 46–47; *Megillat ha-Megalleh*, 50–51). *Judah Halevi and *Maimonides do not mention *gilgul*, and *Abraham b. Moses b. Maimon, who does refer to it, rejects it completely.

In Early Kabbalah. In contrast with the conspicuous opposition of Jewish philosophy, metempsychosis is taken for granted in the Kabbalah from its first literary expression in the *Sefer ha-*Bahir* (published in late 12th century). The absence of any special apology for this doctrine, which is expounded by the *Bahir* in several parables, proves that the idea grew or developed in the circles of the early kabbalists without any affinity to the philosophic discussion of transmigration. Biblical verses (e.g., "One generation passeth away, and another generation cometh" (Eccles. 1:4), taken as meaning that the generation that passes away is the generation that comes) and talmudic *aggadot* and parables were explained in terms of transmigration. It is not clear whether there was any connection between the appearance of the metempsychosic doctrine in kabbalistic circles in southern France and its appearance among the contemporary Cathars (see *Albigenses), who also lived there. Indeed the latter, like most believers in transmigration, taught that the soul also passes into the bodies of animals, whereas in the *Bahir* it is mentioned only in relation to the bodies of men.

After the *Bahir* the doctrine of *gilgul* developed in several directions and became one of the major doctrines of the Kabbalah, although the kabbalists differed widely in regard to details. In the 13th century, transmigration was viewed as an esoteric doctrine and was only alluded to, but in the 14th century many detailed and explicit writings on it appeared. In philosophic literature the term *ha'atakah* ("transference") was generally used for *gilgul;* in kabbalistic literature the term *gilgul* appears only from the **Sefer ha-Temunah* onward; both are translations of the Arabic term *tanāsukh*. The early kabbalists, such as the disciples of *Isaac the Blind and the kabbalists of Gerona, spoke of "the secret of *ibbur*" ("impregnation"). It was only in the late 13th or 14th centuries that *gilgul* and *ibbur* began to be differentiated. The terms *hitḥallefut* ("exchange") and *din benei ḥalof* (from Prov. 31:8) also occur. From the period of the *Zohar on, the term *gilgul* became prevalent in Hebrew literature and began to appear in philosophic works as well.

Biblical verses and commandments were interpreted in terms of *gilgul*. The early sects to whom Anan was indebted saw the laws of ritual slaughter (*sheḥitah*) as biblical proof of transmigration in accordance with their belief in transmigration among animals. For the Kabbalists the point of departure and the proof for *gilgul* was the commandment of levirate marriage (see **Ḥaliẓah*): the brother of the childless deceased replaces the deceased husband so that he may merit children in his second *gilgul*. Later, other *mitzvot* were interpreted on the basis of transmigration. The belief in metempsychosis also served as a rational excuse for the apparent absence of justice in the world and as an answer to the problem of the suffering of righteous and the prospering of the wicked: the righteous man, for example, is punished for his sins in a previous *gilgul*. The entire Book of Job and the resolution of the mystery of his suffering, especially as stated in the words of Elihu, were interpreted in terms of transmigration (e.g., in the commentary on Job by *Naḥmanides, and in all subsequent kabbalistic literature). Most of the early kabbalists (up to and including the author of the Zohar) did not regard transmigration as a universal law governing all creatures (as is the case in the Indian belief) and not even as governing all human beings, but saw it rather as connected essentially with offenses against procreation and sexual transgressions. Transmigration is seen as a very harsh punishment for the soul which must undergo it. At the same time, however, it is an expression of the mercy of the Creator, "from whom no one is cast off forever"; even for those who should be punished with "extinction of the soul" *(keritut), gilgul* provides an opportunity for restitution. While some emphasized more strongly the aspect of justice in transmigration, and some that of mercy, its singular purpose was always the purification of the soul and the opportunity, in a new trial, to improve its deeds. The death of infants is one of the ways by which former transgressions are punished.

In the *Bahir* it is stated that transmigration may continue for 1,000 generations, but the common opinion in the Spanish Kabbalah is that in order to atone for its sins, the soul transmigrates three more times after entering its original body (according to Job 33:29, "Behold, God does all these things, twice, three times, with a man"). However, the righteous transmigrate endlessly for the benefit of the universe, not for their own benefit. As on all points of this doctrine, opposing views also exist in kabbalistic literature: the righteous transmigrate as many as three times, the wicked, as many as 1,000! Burial is a condition for a new *gilgul* of the soul, hence the reason for burial on the day of death. Sometimes a male soul enters a female body, resulting in sterility. Transmigration into the bodies of women and of gentiles was held possible by several kabbalists, in opposition to the view of most of the Safed kabbalists. The *Sefer Peli'ah* viewed proselytes as Jewish souls which had passed into the bodies of gentiles, and returned to their former state.

GILGUL AND PUNISHMENT. The relationship between transmigration and hell is also a matter of dispute. *Baḥya b. Asher proposed that transmigration occurred only after the acceptance of punishment in hell, but the opposite view is found in the *Ra'aya Meheimna,* in the Zohar, and among most of the kabbalists. Because the concepts of metempsychosis and punishment in hell are mutually exclusive, there could be no compromise between them. Joseph of Hamadan, Persia, who lived in Spain in the 14th century, interpreted the entire matter of hell as transmigration among animals. The transmigrations of souls began after the slaying of Abel (some claim in the generation of the Flood), and will cease only with the resurrection of the dead. At that time the bodies of all those who underwent transmigrations will be revived and sparks *(niẓoẓot)* from the original soul will spread within them. But the other answers to this question were proposed by many kabbalists, especially in the 13th century. The expansion of the notion of transmigration from a punishment limited to specific sins into a general principle contributed to the rise of the belief in transmigration into animals and even into plants and inorganic matter. This opinion, however, opposed by many kabbalists, did not become common until after 1400. Transmigration into the bodies of animals is first mentioned in the *Sefer ha-Temunah,* which originated in a circle probably associated with the kabbalists of Gerona. In the Zohar itself this idea is not found, but some sayings in *Tikkunei Zohar* attempt to explain this concept exegetically, indicating that this doctrine was already known to the author of that work. *Ta'amei ha-Mitzvot* (c. 1290–1300), an anonymous work on the reasons for the commandments, records many details (partly quoted by Menahem *Recanati) on the transmigration of human souls into the bodies of animals, the great majority of which were punishments for acts of sexual intercourse forbidden by the Torah.

In the Later and the Safed Kabbalah. A more general elaboration of the entire concept appears in the works of *Joseph b. Shalom Ashkenazi and his colleagues (early 14th century). They maintain that transmigration occurs in all forms of existence, from the *Sefirot* ("emanations") and the angels to inorganic matter, and is called *din benei ḥalof* or *sod ha-shelaḥ.* According to this, everything in the world is constantly changing form, descending to the lowest form and ascending again to the highest. The precise concept of the transmigration of the soul in its particular form into an existence other than its original one is thus obscured, and is replaced by the law of the change of form. Perhaps this version of the doctrine of *gilgul* should be seen as an answer to philosophical criticism based on the Aristotelian definition of the soul as the "form" of the body which consequently cannot become the form of another body. The mystery of true *gilgul* in this new version was sometimes introduced instead of the traditional kabbalistic teaching as found in *Masoret ha-Berit* (1916) by *David b. Abraham ha-Lavan (c. 1300). The kabbalists of Safed accepted the doctrine of transmigration into all forms of nature and, through them, this teaching became a widespread popular belief.

In Safed, especially in the Lurianic Kabbalah, the idea of *niẓoẓot ha-neshamot* ("sparks of the souls") was highly developed. Each "main" soul is built in the spiritual structure of "mystical limbs" (parallel to the limbs of the body), from which many sparks spread, each of which can serve as a soul or as life in a human body. The *gilgulim* of all the sparks together are aimed at the restitution of the hidden spiritual structure of the "root" of the principal soul; it is possible for one man to possess several different sparks belonging to one "root." All the roots of the souls were in fact contained in Adam's soul, but they fell and were scattered with the first sin; the souls must be reassembled in the course of their *gilgulim* which they and their sparks undergo and through which they are afforded the opportunity to restitute their true and original structure. The later Kabbalah developed much further the idea of the affinity of those souls which belong to a common root. In the kabbalistic commentaries on the Bible many events were explained by such hidden history of the transmigration of various souls which return in a later *gilgul* to situations similar to those of an earlier state, in order to repair damage which they had previously caused. The early Kabbalah provides the basis of this idea: there Moses and Jethro, for example, are considered the reincarnations of Abel and Cain; David, Bathsheba, and Uriah, of Adam, Eve, and the serpent; and Job, of Terah, the father of Abraham. The anonymous *Gallei Razayya* (written 1552; published partly Mohilev, 1812), and *Sefer ha-Gilgulim* (Frankfort, 1684) and *Sha'ar ha-Gilgulim* (1875, 1912) by Ḥayyim *Vital present lengthy explanations of the histories of biblical characters in the light of their former *gilgulim.* *Luria and Vital expanded the framework to include talmudic figures. The transmigrations of many figures are explained in *Gilgulei Neshamot* by Menahem Azariah da *Fano (edition with commentary, 1907). Many kabbalists dealt in detail with the function that was fulfilled by the several *gilgulim* of Adam's soul; they also explained his name as an abbreviation of Adam, David, Messiah (first mentioned by *Moses b. Shem-Tov de Leon).

Ibbur. In addition to the doctrine of *gilgul,* that of *ibbur* ("impregnation") developed from the second half of the 13th century. *Ibbur,* as distinct from *gilgul,* means the entry of another soul into a man, not during pregnancy nor at birth but during his life. In general, such an additional soul dwells in a man only for a limited period of time, for the purpose of performing certain acts or commandments. In the Zohar it is stated that the souls of Nadab and Abihu were temporarily added to that of Phinehas in his zeal over the act of Zimri, and that Judah's soul was present in Boaz when he begat Obed. This doctrine was a respected one in the teachings of the kabbalists of Safed, especially in the

Lurianic school: a righteous man who fulfilled almost all of the 613 *mitzvot* but did not have the opportunity to fulfill one special *mitzvah* is temporarily reincarnated in one who has the opportunity to fulfill it. Thus the souls of the righteous men are reincarnated for the benefit of the universe and their generation. The *ibbur* of a wicked man into the soul of another man is called a *Dibbuk in later popular usage. The prevalence of the belief in *gilgul* in the 16th and 17th centuries also caused new disputes between its supporters and detractors. A detailed debate on the doctrine of transmigration took place in about 1460 between two scholars in Candia (Ms. Vatican 254). Abraham ha-Levi ibn Migash disputed against the doctrine of *gilgul* in all its manifestations (*Sefer Kevod Elohim*, 2, 10–14, Constantine, 1585) and Leone *Modena wrote his treatise *Ben David* against transmigration (published in the collection *Ta'am Zekenim*, 1885, pp. 61–64). In defense of transmigration, *Manasseh Ben Israel wrote *Sefer Nishmat Ḥayyim* (Amsterdam, 1652). Works of later kabbalists on the subjects are *Midrash Talpiyyot, Anaf Gilgul* (Smyrna, 1736) by Elijah ha-Kohen ha-Itamari and *Golel Or* (Smyrna, 1737) by Meir *Bikayam.

Bibliography: S. Rubin, *Gilgulei Neshamot* (1899); S. Pushinski, in: *Yavneh*, 1 (1939), 137–53; G. Scholem, in: *Tarbiz*, 16 (1945), 135–50; S. A. Horodezki, *Torat ha-Kabbalah shel ha-Ari ve-Ḥayyim Vital* (1947), 245–52; S. Poznański, in: *Semitic Studies in Memory of A. Kohut* (1897), 435–56; N. E. David, *Karma and Reincarnation in Israelitism* (1908); G. Scholem, *Von der mystischen Gestalt der Gottheit* (1962), 193–247; 297–306; E. Gottlieb, in: *Sefunot*, 11 (1969), 43–66. [G.Sch.]

GILYONOT (Heb. גִּלְיוֹנוֹת), an independent literary monthly published in Tel Aviv from 1934 to 1954, founded and edited by Yiẓhak *Lamdan. Lamdan's strong Zionist and socialist ideas were expressed both in his literary and editorial policy. He viewed modern Hebrew literature as a "continuation of the Hebrew literature" of the past. In addition to recognized Hebrew writers, Lamdan encouraged younger writers to publish in *Gilyonot* and several contemporary writers of stature published their first works in its pages (S. *Yizhar, for example). He also invited the participation of Hebrew writers living in Europe and the U.S. He manifested great interest in U.S. Jewry, devoting an issue of *Gilyonot* to that community (vol. 31, no. 8–10). Of interest also is the 18th anniversary issue (vol. 26, no. 5–6) which dealt with the history of Hebrew periodical literature. The final issue of *Gilyonot* appeared after Lamdan's death and was dedicated to his memory. [G.K.]

GIMBEL, U.S. merchant family. ADAM GIMBEL (1817–1896), who emigrated from Bavaria, settled in New Orleans in 1835. Six brothers and two sisters followed him to the United States. Adam was a peddler along the Mississippi River before opening a dry goods store in Vincennes, Indiana, in 1842. By the time he sold his firm 40 years later, he owned four stores in Vincennes. He was a member of the city council from 1842 to 1866. The two eldest of Adam's seven sons, JACOB (1851–1922) and ISAAC GIMBEL (1857–1931), established a department store in Danville, Illinois, in the 1880s. When they found the undertaking unprofitable, they moved to Milwaukee, Wisconsin, where they founded Gimbel Brothers. In 1894 they opened a second department store in Philadelphia, which was run by their brothers CHARLES (1861–1932) and ELLIS GIMBEL (1865–1950). The Gimbels' first New York venture came in 1910 with the establishment of a department store at Herald Square, which grew rapidly when two older firms were merged with it. In 1923 Gimbel Brothers bought Saks and Co. and shortly thereafter built a Saks subsidiary on Fifth Avenue. The Gimbel chain was further extended in 1926, when they took over Kaufman and Baer of Pittsburgh. In the next decades, Saks branches were opened in Chicago, Detroit, Beverly Hills, and San Francisco. BERNARD F. GIMBEL (1885–1966), Isaac's son, became president of Gimbel Brothers in 1927. He was a distinguished civic figure who played a large part in the organization and direction of New York City's World Fairs in 1939 and 1964–65. He was a generous contributor to a number of scholarly institutions and was active in the work of the National Conference of Jews and Christians. Bernard's son, BRUCE A. GIMBEL (1913–), succeeded his father as president of Gimbel Brothers, Inc. in 1953. Sales during the fiscal year ending Jan. 31, 1961, in altogether 53 urban and suburban stores in the chain reached a record $61.6 million, and ten additional stores were opened over the next three years. [H.G.R.]

GIMMEL (Heb. גִּמֶל), third letter of the Hebrew alphabet; its numerical value is therefore "three." The basic shape of this letter consists of two strokes forming an angle; thus in the Proto-Sinaitic ∟, Proto-Canaanite ⋀, and Proto-Arabian ˥ scripts. In the tenth-century B.C.E. Phoenician script two types occur: ˥ and ⋀. The first type was adopted by the ancient Hebrew and Greek scripts (cf. the gamma Γ), while the second one prevailed in the later Phoenician and Aramaic scripts. From the Aramaic ⋀ developed the Jewish ⋏, Syriac ܓ and Arabic ج. The modern Hebrew cursive *gimmel* evolved as follows: ⋏→⋏→ ג. [Jo.Na.]

GINGOLD, PINCHAS M. (1893–1953), U.S. Labor Zionist and Yiddish educator. Gingold was born near Grodno, Lithuania, and emigrated to the United States at the age of 16. A founder of the Jewish Legion at the start of World War I, Gingold enlisted and saw action with the British Army in Palestine. Upon his return to New York (1920), he joined the Labor Zionist movement and was active in the American and the World Jewish Congress. During the 1920s and 1930s Gingold was the director of the Yiddish Teachers Seminary. In 1932 he edited the *Yidishe Dertsiung*, an educational journal sponsored by the Jewish National Workers' Alliance (Farband). After 1930 he headed the national committee of the Jewish Folk Schools. The committee published the *Pinchas Gingold Book* (1955), a commemorative Yiddish volume containing Gingold's essays on Jewish education and culture and his reminiscences of the Jewish Legion. [Ed.]

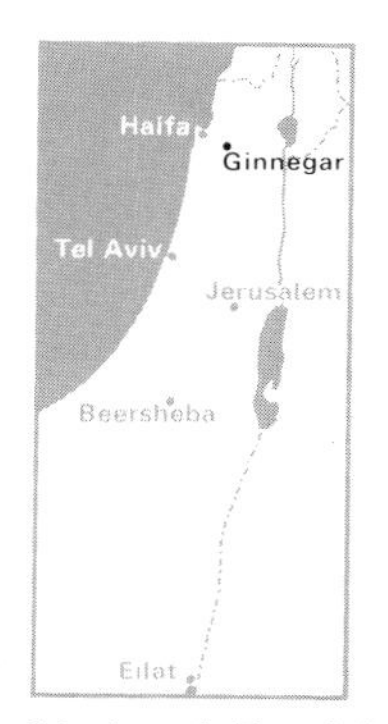

GINNEGAR (Heb. גִּנֵּיגַר), kibbutz on the northern rim of the Jezreel Valley, Israel, S.W. of Nazareth, affiliated to Iḥud ha-Kevuẓot ve-ha-Kibbutzim. It was founded in 1922 by pioneers of the Third Aliyah. Its settlers had previously set up kibbutz Deganyah Gimmel in the Jordan Valley. Ginnegar was one of the earliest Jezreel Valley settlements, and in the initial years of struggle, the settlers were employed in the planting of the Balfour Forest, at the time the largest *Jewish National Fund forest in the country, located on the slopes above the kibbutz. The kibbutz' economy is based on highly intensive farming. Ginnegar is a historical name mentioned, in forms like Neginegar (נְגִינַגַר) in the Talmud (TJ, Er. 1:9, 19c; Kil. 4:4, 29b; et al.), and is preserved in the Arabic name of the site Jinjār. [E.O.]

GINNOSAR (גִּנּוֹסַר), kibbutz on the shore of Lake Kinneret, Israel, founded by Israel-born youth and Youth Aliyah graduates of *Ben Shemen. The kibbutz was set up at the time of the Arab riots early in 1937, serving initially as a guard outpost on *Palestine Jewish Colonization Association (PICA) lands. In spite of PICA's opposition, the settlement became permanent. Before 1948, in the pre-State period, Ginnosar served as a training and organizational center of the *Palmaḥ. It developed subtropical intensive farming and engaged in fishing in Lake Kinneret and its own fish ponds. Later Ginnosar opened a large guest house. [E.O.]

GINNOSAR, PLAIN OF (Heb. בִּקְעַת גִּנּוֹסָר), narrow plain on the N.W. shore of Lake *Kinneret. The plain extends c. 3½ mi. (5½ km.) along the coast and its width in the center from the sea to the edge of the alluvial soil and the foot of the hills is c. 1¼ mi. (2 km.). In antiquity the name Ginnosar apparently also applied to the rim of the hills since Josephus states that it is 2½ mi. (3.7 km.) wide (Wars, 3:516ff.). Its area covers over 1,600 acres (6,450 dunams). The plain of Ginnosar was created by alluvial soil deposited by three brooks which pass through the plain: Naḥal Ammud and Naḥal Zalmon, perennial brooks, and Naḥal Arbel, a brook flowing intermittently. The extreme fertile basaltic red soil washed down from the hills to which the sea added moisture and dew produced the famous fruits praised by Josephus *(ibid.)* and the Talmud. The fruits are described as being large, easily digested, and causing the skin to become smooth. Several interesting anecdotes are told about rabbis who partook of them, including a story about *Simeon b. Lakish whose mind began to wander (Ber. 44a). The plain of Ginnosar was included in the territory of Naphtali and the Talmud attributes the blessings of Jacob and Moses to Naphtali to this plain: "It is the plain of Ginnosar which hastens its fruits like a hind [which runs swiftly]" (Gen. R. 99:12); "Naphtali, satisfied with favor, And full with the blessing of the Lord: that is the plain of Ginnosar" (Sif. Deut. 355). The name appears in ancient sources in various forms of which the most correct appears to be the Greek form Gennesar as in I Maccabees 11:67 and in talmudic sources, but the form Ginnosar is most frequently used and has become generally accepted. The lands of the plain of Ginnosar are now cultivated by the settlements of *Migdal and *Ginnosar. [A.J.Br.]

GINSBERG, ALLEN (1926–), U.S. poet and leader of the mid-20th century "Beat Generation." Born in New Jersey, Ginsberg graduated from Columbia University. He worked as a dishwasher, spot-welder, night porter, actor, and market research worker while writing his early poems. He specialized in readings of his own works in coffee shops and on college campuses, and was a co-founder of various magazines, such as the *Evergreen Review.* Following the appearance of his first book of verse, *Howl and Other Poems* (1955), Ginsberg became identified with the "Beat" movement centered in San Francisco, and was soon its acknowledged leader. *Howl,* which involved its publisher in a highly publicized obscenity trial, dramatizes modern man's destruction by a dehumanized technological society. Ginsberg's later works include *Empty Mirror* (1960); *Kaddish and other Poems 1958–60* (1960); and *Reality Sandwiches 1953–60* (1963). Stylistically, all of Ginsberg's works are notable for their jazz rhythms and hallucinatory imagery. They contain descriptions of madness, homosexuality, drug-induced hallucinations, and physical anguish, all illuminated by an exalted Blakean vision of man's perfectibility in innocence. Some of the poems reveal the author's bizarre, even apocalyptic, sense of humor. His later works *Wichita Vortex Sutra* (1966) and *Planet News* (1968), reflect Buddhism's mystical notion of man's oneness with a benevolent universe. His balding head, black beard, bespectacled face, and patriarchal demeanor became familiar to millions all over the world. His poetry has been translated into many languages and has given rise to a new freedom of subject matter and style. His father, LOUIS GINSBERG (1896–), was born in New Jersey and after graduating from Rutgers and Columbia universities became a teacher. He published two books of poetry, *The Attic of the Past and Other Lyrics* (1920) and *The Everlasting Minute and other Lyrics* (1937), which at its best gives literary freshness and color to everyday things.

Bibliography: *Midstream,* 7 no. 4 (1961); J. Kramer, *Allen Ginsberg in America* (1969). [D.I.]

GINSBERG, EDWARD (1917–), U.S. attorney and business executive. Ginsberg was born in New York City and became a partner in the Cleveland law firm of Gottfried, Ginsberg, Gruen & Merritt; a director of Rusco Industries; and a board member of Orlite, an Israel company. Active in Jewish communal life, Ginsberg has been a leader in the *American Jewish Joint Distribution Committee, the Cleveland Jewish Community Federation, and the *United Jewish Appeal. [ED.]

GINSBERG, HAROLD LOUIS (1903–) U.S. Bible scholar and Semitist. Born in Montreal (Canada), Ginsberg studied at the University of London, then went to the United States in 1936, where, from 1941, he was professor of Bible at the Jewish Theological Seminary of America, New York. While the bulk of his publications in the biblical field are philological—word studies, text restorations, and exegesis—he also elucidated problems of biblical history religion. Ginsberg made contributions to Aramaic linguistics, being a pioneer in the interpretation of Ugaritic texts and their application to the Bible. His Semitistic and exegetical skills are combined luminously throughout his work.

Ginsberg was an editor of the new Bible translation of the American Jewish Publication Society (editor in chief of the translation of the Prophets from 1962). He edited the Bible division of the *Encyclopaedia Judaica.*

Ginsberg was a fellow of the American Academy for Jewish Research (vice-president, 1969–70) and was the honorary president of the American Society of Biblical Literature (1969). He was a member of the Israel Academy for the Hebrew Language.

His works include: *Kitvei Ugarit* (1938); *The Legend of King Keret* (1946); *Studies in Daniel* (1948); *Studies in Koheleth* (1950); a new Hebrew commentary on Ecclesiastes (1961); and translations from Aramaic and Ugaritic in J. B. Pritchard (ed.), *Ancient Near Eastern Texts Relating to the Old Testament* (1950; 1955²; 1969³). He also edited *The Five Megilloth and the Book of Jonah* (JPS, 1969). [Mo.G.]

GINSBERG, MITCHELL I. (1915–), U.S. social worker and educator. Ginsberg, a native of Boston, served as director of a number of Jewish community centers before moving to the personnel and training bureau of the National Jewish Welfare Board in New York. He joined the faculty of the Columbia University School of Social Work and in 1953 he became full professor, serving as associate dean (1960–66). He was a consultant in various training programs of the U.S. Peace Corps project and to the City of New York. In 1966 Ginsberg was appointed commissioner of public welfare, New York City, and in 1968 administrator of the city's Human Resources Commission, serving also as consultant on the community action program of the U.S. Office of Economic Opportunity. [J.N.]

GINSBERG, MORRIS (1889–1970), English sociologist. He studied at University College, London, where he was lecturer in philosophy from 1914 to 1923. From 1929 to 1954, he was professor of sociology at the London School of Economics. Ginsberg's position in sociology was derived from the evolutionary theory of his teachers Hobhouse and Westermarck. His works deal with the systematic evaluation of sociology, the study of social structures, institutions and groups, and the comparative study of custom and religion in a variety of cultures. Ginsberg was actively interested in Jewish problems. His book *The Jewish People Today*, a survey of the structure and the institutions of contemporary Jewish life, appeared in 1956. He was associated with the World Jewish Congress and was an editor of *The Jewish Journal of Sociology*. His works include *The Material Culture and Social Institutions of the Simpler Peoples* (with L. T. Hobhouse and G. C. Wheeler, 1915); *The Psychology of Society* (1921); *L. T. Hobhouse: His Life and Work* (with J. A. Hobson, 1931); *Studies in Sociology* (1932); *Sociology* (1934); *Moral Progress* (1944); *Reason and Unreason in Society* (1947); *The Idea of Progress: a Reevaluation* (1953); *Essays in Sociology and Social Philosophy* (3 vols., 1956–61); *Reason and Experience in Ethics* (1956); *Law and Opinion in England in the 20th Century* (1959); *Evolution and Progress* (1961); and *Nationalism: A Reappraisal* (1961). [W.J.C.]

GINSBERG, NORTON SIDNEY (1921–), U.S. geographer. Ginsberg was born in Chicago. In World War II he served in the navy and participated in actions with the Sixth Marine Division in north China. After the war he remained in the Far East as chief of the Research and Intelligence Center at Shanghai. In 1947 he taught geography at the University of Chicago (full professor, 1960). His major interests lay in urban geography, political geography, and economic development, with particular stress on East and Southeast Asia. In 1961 he was appointed director of the Association for Asian Studies. Apart from many papers, he published (with C. F. Roberts) *Malaya* (1958), was the coauthor and editor of *Pattern of Asia* (1958), and edited *Essays on Geography and Economic Development* (1960). In 1961 he compiled the *Atlas of Economic Development*. The Japanese government invited him in 1962 to study Tokyo's urban problems, on which he reported in the *Tokyo Memorandum: Reports on Tokyo Metropolitan Planning* (1962). He edited A. Harmann's *Historical Atlas of China* (1968, new edition). [ED.]

GINSBURG, CHRISTIAN DAVID (1831–1914), Bible scholar. Born in Warsaw, he converted to Christianity in 1846 and soon afterward moved to England. There he devoted himself to research on the masoretic text of the Bible; *The Massorah* (his magnum opus), published between 1880–1905 in four volumes, is the fruit of his labor. In the first two volumes, the original text of the masorah (in Hebrew) is arranged alphabetically with many additional notes drawn from manuscripts. The third volume contains supplements, and some masoretic tractates; the fourth renders into English all Hebrew entries of the first volume up to the letter *"yod,"* with explanatory notes. In his work, Ginsburg amassed rich and rare material; some of it, however, is not accurate. He also published two standard editions of the Hebrew Bible (1894, 1911) based on the same research. In *Introduction to the Massoretico-Critical Edition of the Hebrew Bible* (1897, repr. 1966) and in *A Series of 15 Facsimiles of MSS of the Hebrew Bible* (1897; second edition: *A Series of 18 Facsimiles* ..., 1898), he explains his system. In 1904, on the occasion of its centennial, the British Bible Society entrusted Ginsburg with the publication of a new critical Hebrew Bible text; it was completed only in 1926. Before his death, however, he edited and published the Pentateuch (1908), Isaiah (1909), the Prophets (1911), and Psalms (1913). In his research he based himself on 75 manuscripts and 25 earlier Bible editions.

Ginsburg also wrote commentaries on the Song of Songs (1857), Ecclesiastes (1861), Leviticus (1882); and published: *The Karaites, their History and Literature* (1862); *The Essenes* (1864); *The Kabbalah, its Doctrines, Development and Literature* (1863, 1920²); *Massoret ha-Massoret*, by Elijah *Levita, with an English translation and critical explanatory notes (1867); Jacob b. Chajim ibn Adonijah's Introduction to the *Mikra'ot Gedolot* Bible edition (Hebrew and English) with explanatory notes (1867, repr. 1968); *The Moabite Stone* (1870). He also published the New Testament in Hebrew, translated by the convert J. E. Salkinson (1885). Ginsburg spent the last years of his life in Middlesex. His collection of Bible manuscripts is in the possession of the British Bible Society.

Bibliography: C. D. Ginsburg, *Introduction to the Massoretico-Critical Edition of the Hebrew Bible* (1966), introduction by H. M. Orlinsky; C. D. Ginsburg, *Commentary to Jacob ben Chajim ibn Adonijah's Rabbinic Bible and E. Levita's Massoret ha-Massoret* (1968), introduction by N. Snaith. [ED.]

GINSBURG, JEKUTHIEL (1889–1957), mathematician and Hebrew writer, brother of Simon and Pesaḥ *Ginzburg. Born in Russia, he emigrated to the United States in 1912, studied at Columbia University and, later, taught mathematics at Teachers College of Columbia University. In 1930 he was appointed professor and head of the department of mathematics at Yeshiva College. In 1932 he founded the quarterly *Scripta Mathematica*, edited the *Scripta Mathematica Library*, and coauthored (with D. E. Smith) the *History of Mathematics in America before 1900* (1936). His Hebrew feuilletons appeared in *Hadoar* under the pseudonym of J. L. Gog. His articles on the role of Jews in mathematics were collected in his *Ketavim Nivḥarim* ("Selected Writings," 1960), which includes his biography and data on his literary and scientific works.

Bibliography: Kressel, Leksikon, 1 (1965), 472f. [EI.S.]

GINSBURG, SAUL (1866–1940), author and historian of Russian Jewry. Born in Minsk he received a traditional Jewish as well as secular education. He was active in the Ḥovevei Zion movement. Ginsburg became a contributor to *Voskhod* in 1892, and in 1896 published a historical study in that journal, *"Zabytaya epokha"* ("A Forgotten Era") concerning the first Russian-Jewish periodical *Razsvet*. The following year he began contributing a regular review of the Hebrew press (under the pseudonym of "Ha-Kore") to *Voskhod*, as well as a literary column, and in 1899 was appointed to the editorial board. Together with P. *Marek he published *Yevreyskiye narodnye pesny* ("Jewish Folk Songs," 1901), which became a landmark in the study of Jewish folklore. In 1903 Ginsburg established *Der Fraynd*, the first Yiddish daily in Russia, which played an important role in the development of Yiddish journalism and was noted for its high literary standards. In 1908 Ginsburg left *Der Fraynd* in order to devote himself completely to the study of the cultural history of the Jews in Russia. He took part in the historical periodical *Perezhitoye* (4 vols., 1908–13). In 1913 he published *Yevrei i otechestvennaya voyna 1812 goda* ("Jews and the War of 1812"), a study of the history of Russian Jews during the Napoleonic Wars, and was a cofounder of the Jewish Literary and Scientific Society (which was closed down by the authorities in 1910). When the Bolshevist Revolution broke out, Ginsburg was one of a small group who strove to carry on independent Jewish scientific work under the Soviet regime. From 1922 to 1928 he edited *Yevreyskaya mysl* ("Jewish Thought") and *Yevreyski vestnik* ("Jewish Herald"). In this period several of his studies of the history of Russian Jews also appeared in *Zukunft*, the New York Yiddish monthly. In 1930 Ginsburg left the Soviet Union and was able to take his voluminous archive with him. He first settled in Paris, but moved to New York in 1933. Here the Yiddish daily *Forward* regularly published his popular historical essays. A collection of his studies, *Historishe Verk*, appeared in three volumes in 1937–38 with a bibliography by I. Rivkind. Two posthumous volumes were *Amolike Peterburg* ("Petersburg

Saul Ginsburg, historian of Russian Jewry. Jerusalem, Schwadron Collection, J.N.U.L.

as it Was," 1944), and *Meshumodim in Tsarishn Rusland* ("Jewish Apostates in Czarist Russia," 1946). Among his articles and studies some are devoted to personal memoirs.

Bibliography: Rejzen, Leksikon, 1 (1926) 567–72; LNYL, 2 (1958), 227–9.
[Y.S.]

GINSBURGER, ERNEST (1876–1943), French rabbi and Jewish historian; born in Héricourt (Haute-Saône), France. During World War I he volunteered as rabbi of the French 18th Army Corps, and was awarded the Médaille Militaire. He was subsequently chief rabbi of Geneva, Belgium, and Bayonne. Arrested in March 1942, he was interned at Compiègne and deported to a death camp in February 1943. Ginsburger left valuable essays on Jewish history, including *Les Juifs de Belgique au XVIIIe siècle* (1932), *"Les Juifs de Frauenberg"* (in REJ, 47 (1903), 87–122), and *Le Comité de Surveillance de Jean-Jacques Rousseau—Saint-Esprit-les-Bayonne* (1934), based on the minutes of the only committee in revolutionary France with a majority of Jewish members. [Ed.]

GINZBERG, ELI (1911–), U.S. economist and social planner. Ginzberg was born in New York City, the son of the rabbinic scholar Louis *Ginzberg. He studied economics at Columbia University and in 1935 was appointed to the Columbia School of Business, where he subsequently taught. In addition, after 1950 he was director of Columbia's Conservation of Human Resources Department. He also served with the United States War Department (1942–44 and 1946–48), the Surgeon General's Office, the White House Conference on Children and Youth (1959–63), and the National Manpower Council (1951–), of which he became chairman in 1962. His activities as a consultant, which were widely sought, embraced the United States Departments of State, Defense, Labor, and Health, Education and Welfare, the Hoover Commission, and the National Advisory Mental Health Council. From 1953 to 1959 he was a governor of the Hebrew University of Jerusalem.

A specialist in labor economics, Ginzberg was particularly interested in problems of manpower utilization and economic growth, especially as they affected underdeveloped countries and minority groups. He was a leading expert on the economic aspects of the Negro problem in the United States, and he frequently traveled abroad in an advisory capacity to the governments of developing nations, especially Israel.

Eli Ginzberg, U.S. economist.

Among his many publication were *The House of Adam Smith* (1934), *Grass on the Slag Heaps: The Story of the Welsh Miners* (1942), *Agenda for American Jews* (1950), *The Negro Potential* (1956), and *Manpower Utilization in Israel* (1962). He edited a wide series of studies for the Columbia Conservation of Human Resources Department, including *The Uneducated* (1953), *Life Styles of Educated Women* (1966), and *Manpower Strategy for the Metropolis* (1968), and was coauthor of *The Troublesome Presence: American Democracy and the Negro* (1964). His biography of his father, *Keeper of the Law*, appeared in 1966.

Bibliography: *Current Biography Yearbook, 1966* (1967), 126–9.
[M.P.]

GINZBERG, LOUIS (1873–1953), scholar of Talmud, Midrash, and *aggadah*, whose comprehensive works in Jewish law and lore made him the doyen of Jewish scholars in the U. S. Ginzberg was born in Kovno, Lithuania, and studied at the yeshivot of Kovno and Telz. Ginzberg was the great-grandnephew of the Vilna Gaon (*Elijah ben Solomon Zalman), whose life and work greatly influenced him. After leaving Lithuania he studied history, philosophy, and oriental languages at the universities of Berlin, Strasbourg, where his teacher was T. *Noeledeke, and Heidelberg, completing his studies in 1898.

In 1899 Ginzberg immigrated to the United States to accept a position at Hebrew Union College, but when he arrived the invitation was withdrawn. He joined the staff of the *Jewish Encyclopedia* as editor of the rabbinic department in 1900. Many of his contributions to that publication have remained classical statements of his subject. In 1903 he resigned to accept a position teaching Talmud at the Jewish Theological Seminary, where he remained until his death. In teaching future rabbis and by his halakhic decisions and scholarly output, he became a principal architect of the Conservative movement. He was a founder (1919–20) and president for several years of the American Academy of Jewish Research. In 1928–29 Ginzberg was the first professor of *halakhah* at the Hebrew University of Jerusalem, and in 1934 he was a member of the Hartog Commission, whose recommendations led to important changes in the administration of the Hebrew University.

Ginzberg's work dealt mainly with the origins of *aggadah, halakhah*, and the literature of the *geonim*. While exploring the origins of *aggadah*, Ginzberg uncovered many lost legends of Jewish origins preserved only in early Christian texts. In his major work *The Legends of the Jews* (7 vols., 1909–38) he combined hundreds of legends, maxims, and parables from the entire midrashic literature into a continous narrative taken from the lives of the fathers of the people of Israel, its heroes, and its prophets. He analyzed the evolution of the legend from rabbinical texts, the external books and Hellenist literature, the early Christian texts, translations, exegeses, and the Kabbalah, correlating the material with the legends of other cultures and attempting to differentiate popular from scholarly creations.

Ginzberg researched the *Genizah,* culling from it fragments of the Jerusalem Talmud, the midrashim and legends, much geonic literature, and fragments of ancient Karaite texts. His introductions to the various texts are important studies in obscure and difficult problems of talmudic and rabbinical literature. His commentaries and suggestions are actually analyses of the evolution of *halakhah* and *aggadah* in Ereẓ Israel and Babylon and include extensive interpretations of the Jerusalem Talmud, the Babylonian Talmud, Mishnah, and Tosefta; comprehensive explorations of historical questions, e.g., the Shammai and Hillel schools, the presidency of R. Eleazar ben Azariah, and the rivalry between Judea and Galilee; and the emergence and development of various customs and institutions, e.g., the Great Knesset, the Sanhedrin, the direction of prayer, kneeling and bowing in prayer, and the interchange of customs between Ereẓ Israel and Babylonia. Among his publications are *Fragments of the Yerushalmi* (1909); *Geonica* (2 vols., 1909); *Excerpts of Midrash and Agadah* (1925); *Pirkoi ben Baboi* (1929); *The Significance of the Halakhah for Jewish History,* (1929); *Commentaries and Innovations in the Yerushalmi* (3 vols., 1941); *Die Haggada bei den Kirchenvaetern* (1899–1900); *Genizah Studies* (2 vols., 1928–29); and *Studies in the Origins of the Mishnah* (1920). In his study of the Damascus Sect *Eine unbekannte juedische Sekte* (1922) he stated that it consisted of extreme Pharisees who had first organized during the reign of Alexander Yannai, were not content with the changes made during the reign of Salome Alexandra, and left for Damascus, splitting away from the main body of moderate Pharisees. In *Students, Scholars and Saints* (1928) Ginzberg presented portraits of great leaders of Jewry, including the Gaon of Vilna, Israel Lipkin Salanter, Zechariah Frankel, and Solomon Schechter. One note which Ginzberg sounded in all his writings was that it was not possible to understand Jewish history and culture without a thorough knowledge of *halakhah.*

Louis Ginzberg, talmudic scholar. Courtesy Jewish Theological Seminary, New York.

Bibliography: D. Druck, *Reb Levi Ginzberg* (1934), in Yiddish, including a bibliography of his works, in Hebrew (1960); *Louis Ginzberg Jubilee Volume* (1945), with bibliography; Finkelstein, in: AAJR, 23 (1954), xliv–liii; idem, in: AJYB 56 (1955), 573; E. Ginzberg, *Keeper of the Law: Louis Ginzberg* (1966).

[AR.H.]

GINZBURG, ISER (1872–1947), Yiddish author, journalist, and physician. Ginzburg was born in Russia and received a yeshivah education. He settled in the United States in 1893, and graduated from the Cornell University Medical School. Ginzburg, who had been early influenced by Jewish socialism, contributed articles to Yiddish journals and was on the staff of the *Jewish Daily Forward.* He wrote on contemporary problems and reviewed books dealing with Jewish religion, literature, and history. Despite his erudition, he lacked the discipline of a scholar and his style was unpolished. His major works are: *Der Talmud, Zayn Entshtehung un Entviklung* ("The Talmud, Its Origins and Development," 1910); *Di Entshtehung fun Kristentum* ("The Origin of Christianity," 1917); *Idishe Denker un Poeten in Mitelalter* ("Jewish Thinkers and Poets in the Middle Ages," 2 vols., 1918–9); *Maimonides* (1935).

Bibliography: LNYL, 2 (1958), 223f.

[E.SCH.]

GINZBURG, NATALIA (1917–), Italian novelist and playwright. Natalia Ginzburg, who was born in Palermo, was the daughter of the biologist, Giuseppe Levi, and a non-Jewish mother. She studied in Turin, where her associates were the Jewish anti-fascist intellectuals who were active in the Italian resistance. Her first husband, Leone Ginzburg, a victim of the Nazis, died in a Roman prison in 1944. Her first story, *La strada che va in città* (1942; *Road to the City,* 1949), appeared under the pen name "Alessandra Tornimparte." Later works are *È' stato così* (1947), the novel *Tutti i nostri ieri* (1952; Eng. ed. *Dead Yesterdays,* 1956; U.S. ed. *A Light for Fools,* 1957), the short story volume *Valentino* (1957), *Le voci della sera* 1961; *Voices in the Evening,* 1963), and *Le piccole virtù* (1962). Natalia Ginzburg's characters, who are lonely, persecuted, and engaged in a hopeless quest for sympathy and understanding, include many Jews. Her deep pessimism was overcome, for once, in her outstanding work, *Lessico famigliare* (1963; *Family Sayings,* 1967). This is a psychological novel based on the author's recollections of her own family and the events of her youth. The characters range from the bourgeois, assimilated Jews of the late 19th century, personified by her father, to the anti-fascist circles of Turin and her first friends. But the book's main achievement lies in the distinctive language of the narrative. Natalia Ginzburg uses her family's private phraseology, including many expressions from Spanish- and German-Jewish dialects, in such a way that it plays a leading role in recreating the flavor of an age. Natalia Ginzburg's three plays are: *Ti ho sposato per allegria, La segretaria,* and *L'inserzione.* The last was produced as *The Advertisement* by the National Theater in London.

Natalia Ginzburg, Italian novelist and dramatist. Courtesy Guilio Einaudi, Turin, Italy.

Bibliography: O. Lombardi, *La giovane narrativa* (1963); G. Romano, in: *Scritti in memoria di L. Carpi* (1967), 202–4; S. Pacifici, *A Guide to Contemporary Italian Literature* (1962), index.

[G.R.]

GINZBURG, SIMON (1890–1944), poet and critic. Ginzburg was born in the village of Lipniki, Volhynia, where he received a traditional education. He published his first poem in *Ha-Shilloʾaḥ* in 1910. In 1912 he settled in the

U.S., studied at Columbia University, and obtained a doctorate from Dropsie College in 1923. He immigrated to Palestine in 1933, but returned to America shortly before World War II as the emissary of the Hebrew Writers' Association. He was one of the editors of *Ha-Toren* (1913–15) and *Lu'aḥ Aḥi'ever* in 1918, and a contributor to numerous Hebrew publications. Both in content and language, Ginzburg was greatly influenced by Bialik to whom he dedicated his book of poems *Shirim u-Fo'emot* ("Songs and Poems," 1931). Essentially a romantic poet, the American rural landscape attracted him, but he was repelled by the noise of New York. In *Ahavat Hoshe'a* ("Love of Hosea," 1935), he reveals dramatic ability; the twilight of the Northern Kingdom and the regeneration of the Jews on the eve of disaster are used to point a significant lesson for contemporary Jewry. In addition to a biography in English of Moses Ḥayyim Luzzatto (1931), Ginzburg published three of his plays, with critical notes, including *Ma'aseh Shimshon* from a manuscript in the New York Public Library, his poetry, *Sefer ha-Shirim* ("Book of Poems," 1944–45), and an edition of his letters, under the title *R. Moshe Ḥayyim Luzzatto u-Venei Doro* ("R. Moshe Ḥayyim Luzzatto and his Contemporaries," 1936). These works, and his critical essays on the poet, are a major contribution to Luzzatto scholarship. His other critical essays were collected in *Be-Massekhet ha-Sifrut* ("In the Web of Literature," 1945). He translated Coleridge's *The Rime of the Ancient Mariner* into Hebrew, as well as D. H. Lawrence's *Sons and Lovers,* and poems by Tennyson, Hood, Byron, and Poe.

His younger brother PESAḤ (1894–1947), also born in the village of Lipniki, studied in Odessa, and lived for a time in the United States (1913 to 1918), England, Canada, and the Scandinavian countries before settling in Palestine in 1922. He published several newspapers, which were, however, short-lived; edited various magazines, and was a night editor of *Haaretz* for about 20 years. Pesaḥ's poems, short stories, and articles appeared in the Hebrew press, a number of them also as separate booklets, including *Regina Ashkenazi* (1919) and *Sippur Ereẓ Yisraeli* (1945). He translated extensively, mainly Scandinavian and English literary works.

Bibliography: A. Epstein, *Soferim Ivriyyim ba-Amerikah,* 1 (1952), 92–103; Waxman, Literature, 4 (1960[2]), 1067–69. [EI.S.]

GINZBURG, VITALII LAZAREVICH (1916–), Soviet physicist. Ginzburg joined I. E. *Tamm's group at FIAN (Physics Institute of the Academy of Sciences) and from 1951 was deputy director of a division. From 1945 he was also in charge of the department of radiation and radio wave propagation at Gorkii state university. He was editor in chief of the journal *Radiofizika* and on the editorial staff of other journals. In his work Ginzburg was greatly influenced by the scientific atmosphere created by L.I. *Mandelshtam and Tamm, as well as by L.D. *Landau with whom he collaborated, developing a close friendship. He published a great number of scientific papers, monographs, and books on subjects ranging from astrophysics to superconductivity. Ginzburg was the recipient of several prizes, including the Lenin Prize for his work on the Cerenkov effect. Ginzburg was not only a physicist, but was also interested in general scientific and cultural problems and his lectures attracted large audiences.

Bibliography: *Prominent Personalities in the USSR* (1968). [G.E.T.]

°**GIORGIO (Zorzi), FRANCESCO (Franciscus Georgius Venetus;** 1460–1540), kabbalist of the Franciscan Order of Minor Friars. Giorgio was the author of *De Harmonia Mundi* (1525) and *In Scripturam Sacram et Philosophos Tria Millia Problemata* (1522), which was placed on the *donec corrigatur* ("till it is corrected") list of prohibited books. After the censorships of G. Contarini, *Sixtus of Siena, R. Bellarmino, etc., the most famous is that of Marin Mersenne, *Quaestiones . . . in Genesim, cum . . . textus explicatione. In volumine Atheir . . . expugnatur, et F. Georgii . . . cabalistica dogmata . . . repelluntur* (1623). Giorgio was a cousin of Marin Sanudo, who mentions him in his *Diarii,* a friend of Gershom *Soncino, and the sponsor of several converts; his Hebrew library awakened the interest of H. C. Agrippa. He was one of the active intermediaries in the controversial divorce case of Henry VIII of England. His pupil Archangelus of Burgunuovo, the defender of Giovanni *Pico della Mirandola, plagiarized his works. A disciple of G. *Postel, Guy *Le Fèvre de la Boderie, translated the *De Harmonia* into French in 1579 and dedicated it to a member of the heterodox Family of Charity. A manuscript of his detailed commentaries on the kabbalistic theses of Pico della Mirandola is in the National Library in Jerusalem (Yahuda Collection).

Bibliography: C. Vasoli, *Testi scelti* (1955); *Biographie Universelle,* s.v. *Georges;* A. Mercati and A. P. M. J. Pelzer, *Dizionario Ecclesiatico,* 3 (1958), s.v. *Zorzi;* D. W. Amram, *The Makers of Hebrew Books in Italy* (1909); L. Thorndike, *A History of Magic and Experimental Science,* 6 (1941); R. Wittkower, *Architectural Principles in the Age of Humanism* (1962[2]); F. Secret, *Le Zôhar chez les Kabbalistes chrétiens* (1958); idem, *Les kabbalistes chrétiens de la Renaissance* (1964); idem, in: *Bibliothèque d'Humanisme et Renaissance,* 30 (1968). [FR.S.]

GIOVANNI MARIA (c. 1470–c. 1530), Italian lute player, born in Germany. His original Jewish name is unknown and when, after settling in Florence, he was baptized, he took his new name in honor of Cardinal Giovanni de' Medici. He was still often referred to, however, as "Giovanni Maria, the Jew." In 1492 he was condemned to death for murder, but fled to Rome, where he entered the service of the Cardinal de' Medici. When the cardinal became Pope Leo X, Giovanni Maria was given the revenues of the township of Verrocchio, with the title of count. He was subsequently in the service of Pope Clement VII, the doge of Venice, and the dukes of Mantua and Urbino. A few of Giovanni Maria's own compositions were published and he is referred to with admiration in various literary works of the period. His son Camillo was also a musician in the papal service.

Bibliography: Pirro, in: *Mélanges . . . H. Hauvette* (1934); C. Roth, *The Jews in the Renaissance* (1959), 281–3; U. Cassuto, *Gli Ebrei a Firenze nell'età del Rinascimento* (1918), 192f. [C.R.]

GIRGASHITES (Heb. גִּרְגָּשִׁי), one of the nations inhabiting the land of Canaan (Gen. 15:21; Deut. 7:1; Josh. 3:10; Neh. 9:8). The name also appears as that of the fifth ethnic group descended from Canaan (Gen. 10:16; I Chron. 1:14). Although the Girgashites are not referred to in the narrative of the wars of conquests, and their locality is not stated, they are named by Joshua among the peoples the Israelites dispossessed (24:11).

They have been uncertainly identified with the Qaraqisha, allies of the Hittites in their wars with Ramses II. A personal name *grgš* appears in Ugaritic, but its connection with this people is unknown. The sibilant termination of the biblical name suggests a Hurrian origin.

Bibliography: B. Maisler (Mazar), in: ZAW, 50 (1932), 86–87; E. A. Speiser (ed.), *Genesis* (Eng., 1964), 69. [ED.]

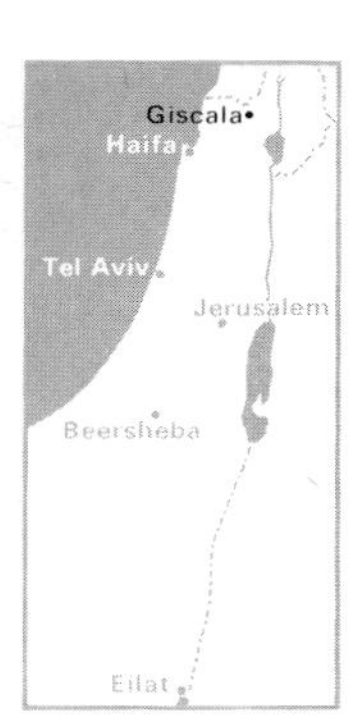

GISCALA (**Gush Ḥalav**; Heb. גּוּשׁ חָלָב), ancient Jewish city in Upper Galilee, today the Christian-Arab village of al-Jish, 5 mi. (c. 8 km.) N.W. of Safed. According to the Mishnah, "the acropolis of Gush Ḥalav" was surrounded by a wall built in the time of Joshua (Ar. 9:6). Canaanite and Israelite remains from the Early Bronze and Iron Ages have been uncovered there but the city is first mentioned (as Giscala) in connection with the history of the Jewish War (66–70/73). It was the birthplace of the Zealot leader *John (Johanan) b. Levi of Giscala, a dealer in oil, who fortified the city at his own expense and escaped to Jerusalem with his followers when the Romans surrounded it; Giscala thereupon surrendered—the last city in Galilee to fall to the Romans (Jos., Wars, 2:275, 590; 4:92–120, 208; Life, 70, 75, 189). After the destruction of the Second Temple, during the days of the *amoraim* and *tannaim*, Jews also lived there. The city was situated in the center of an olive growing district and derived its main livelihood from oil; the inhabitants also engaged in the production of silk (Tosef., Shev. 7:15; Eccl. R. 2:8, no. 2). A Jewish community continued into the Middle Ages, at least until the 13th century.

On the summit of the hill on which Giscala stands is a Christian church with remains of an ancient synagogue and, at its foot, near a spring, are the ruins of a second synagogue in which an inscription was found mentioning a Joseph b. Nahum who erected one of the columns. A hoard of Roman coins was also found in the village. Numerous rock tombs are scattered through the village and its vicinity; according to an unsubstantiated local tradition, these include the graves of *Shemaiah and *Avtalyon. The village was severely damaged by an earthquake in 1873. [M.A.-Y.]

Modern Period. In October 1948 when it was taken by the Israel Army, the Muslims left and the Christian inhabitants of the neighboring *Kafr Birʿim came to settle in the village soon afterwards. Since then, the village population has been made up almost exclusively of members of the Maronite sect, forming Israel's major Maronite community. In 1968, it had 1,650 inhabitants. Its economy is based on olives, figs, deciduous fruits, vineyards, tobacco fields, and beef cattle. The historical name Gush Ḥalav ("Milk Clod") assumedly points to the production of milk and cheese for which the village has been famous at least since the early Middle Ages; some scholars, however, assume that the name refers to the light color of the local limestone, in contrast with the dark-reddish basalt rock of the neighboring village Ra's al-Aḥmar ("Red Mountain Top"), today moshav Kerem Ben Zimrah. [Ed.]

Bibliography: Y. Aharoni, *Hitnaḥalut Shivtei Yisrael ba-Galil ha-Elyon* (1957), 14; S. Klein (ed.), *Sefer ha-Yishuv*, 2 vols. (1939–44), s.v.; H. Kohl and C. Watzinger, *Antike Synagogen in Galilaea* (1916), 107ff.; Hamburger, in: IEJ, 4 (1954), 201ff.

GISER, MOSHE DAVID (1899–1952), Yiddish poet. Born in Radom, Poland, Giser was deported from Poland during World War I for labor in Germany. Returning to Warsaw in 1921, he joined the Yiddish expressionistic group *Khaliastre. He emigrated to Argentina in 1924 and to Chile in 1933, where he earned a living by operating a printing press. While his early lyrics centered about Polish Jews in cities and villages, his later lyrics dealt with Latin-American scenes and people. A posthumous edition of his selected works appeared as *Dos Gezang fun a Lebn* ("The Song of a Life," 1953).

Bibliography: LNYL, 2 (1958), 241–3; M. Ravitch, *Mayn Leksikon*, 1 (1945), 55ff. [M.Rav.]

GISSIN, AVSHALOM (1896–1921), pioneer in the military defense of the *yishuv*. Born in Petaḥ Tikvah, Gissin studied at the officers' school of the Turkish Army in Istanbul and Damascus. At the end of World War I he returned to Palestine and founded *Maccabi and the scout movement in Petaḥ Tikvah, where he schooled local youth in the use of arms. When Arab riots broke out in 1921, Gissin left his work as a surveyor in the south and returned to his home to organize the defense of the settlement. He was killed with three others in battle while defending Petaḥ Tikvah against armed Bedouins. Maccabi Avshalom, the Petaḥ Tikvah soccer team, is named after him. His grandfather, Ephraim Gissin (1835–1898), born in Mohilev, Belorussia, was an early member of Ḥovevei Zion and went to Ereẓ Israel in 1895 joining his three sons and daughter who had settled in Petaḥ Tikvah.

Bibliography: Tidhar, 2 (1947), 741–2, 770. [Ed.]

GISZKALAY (**Gush Ḥalav**), **JÁNOS** (pseudonym of **Dávid Widder**; 1888–1951), Hungarian poet and journalist, and leader of the Hungarian and Transylvanian Zionist movements. Born in Nyitra (now Czechoslovakia), Giszkalay worked in Budapest, where he contributed to the Jewish press and, from 1918, edited the Zionist newspaper, *Zsidó Szemle*. During the "White Terror" which followed the defeat of Béla *Kun in 1918, he wrote justifying a Jewish girl's protest in a school essay against the Hungarian persecution of the Jews. Giszkalay maintained that anti-Semites had no moral right to demand patriotism of the oppressed Hungarian Jews. This led to an order for his arrest and he fled to Rumania, where he joined the staff of *Uj Kelet*, the Hungarian-language Jewish daily in Kolozsvár (Cluj), Transylvania. Giszkalay's verse betrays the influence of E. Ady, the leading modern Hungarian poet, who was himself greatly influenced by the Bible. Outstanding for their enthusiasm and richness of language, Giszkalay's poems deeply impressed Zionist youth. His best-known poems were *Kezét fel az égre, ki férfi ki bátor!* ("Whoever is a man, whoever is courageous, let him raise his hand!"); *A messiás heroldja* ("The Herald of the Messiah"); and *Péntek a háboruban* ("A Wartime Friday Night"). Anthologies of his poems include *Új prófeciák* ("New Prophecies," 1923). He also wrote a children's story, *Vitéz Benája három utja* ("Three Journeys of Knight Benayahu," 1928). Giszkalay's Zionist activities encouraged many Hungarian Jews to settle in Ereẓ Israel. In 1941 he immigrated to Palestine, where he worked as a shepherd on kibbutz Ma'agan. Later he moved to Haifa, where he translated his own works into Hebrew.

Bibliography: H. Danzig, in: *Davar* (April 13, 1951); *Magyar Zsidó Lexikon* (1929); *Száz év zsidó magyar költői* (1943), 241, 243. [B.Y.]

GITLIN, JACOB (1880–1953), South African communal leader. For half a century Gitlin was the moving spirit in Zionist activities in *Cape Town, where he arrived from Vilna, Lithuania, in 1902. His furniture business became the unofficial headquarters of the Zionist movement there. As chairman of the Western Province (Cape) Zionist Council, he helped to make the organization one of the most influential Zionist centers in South Africa. Active in many spheres, he helped to found the Cape Board of Jewish Education.

Bibliography: M. Gitlin, *The Vision Amazing* (1950), index. [L.Ho.]

GITLOW, BENJAMIN (1891–1965), U.S. Socialist and onetime Communist. Gitlow was born in New Jersey. He early became active in the Socialist Party and in the Retail Clerks Union of New York. Nominated in 1917 by the Socialist Party for the New York assembly, Gitlow was elected, but became convinced that more revolutionary action was necessary and helped form the American Communist Labor Party. Elected to its Labor Committee at its 1919 founding convention, Gitlow was arrested that same year for publishing revolutionary material, and served a three-year term. Gitlow then became a member of the Communist International executive committee and presidium, and also held a high position in the American Communist Party. While serving as general secretary in 1929, he and some associates were expelled by Moscow for not following the international communist line. In 1933, along with Lazar Becker, a colleague, he formed the Workers Communist League, later the Socialist Party. Disillusioned with Marxism, he became involved in investigations to expose the Communist movement and eventually wrote a bitter attack on the movement in his autobiography, *I Confess: The Truth About American Communism* (1940).

[AL.A.B.]

GITTAIM (Heb. גִּתַּיִם), biblical city in the northern Shephelah. Its name is derived from Gath, and some of the biblical verses mentioning Gath may, in fact, refer to Gittaim (e.g., I Sam. 7:14; I Kings 2:39; II Kings 12:18; I Chron. 7:21; 8:13; II Chron. 26:6). Since, according to the Bible, the Beerothites of the tribe of Benjamin fled to Gittaim (II Sam. 4:3), the city must have been situated in the vicinity of this tribe. It is mentioned together with Hadid, Neballat, Lydda, and Ono in Nehemiah 11:33. Some scholars identify Gi-im-tu, the city captured by Sargon II in 712 B.C.E., with Gittaim, and not Gath. Eusebius locates it between Antipatris and Jabneh (Onom. 72:2–3); it appears as Gitta on the Madaba Map. The most recent studies have shown that it was probably located at Tel Raʾs Abu Ḥumayd near Ramleh, a large site of some 100 dunams containing surface pottery dating from the Early Iron Age to the Arab period.

Bibliography: Mazar, in: IEJ, 4 (1954), 227–35.

[M.A.-Y.]

GITTELSOHN, ROLAND BERTRAM (1910–), U.S. rabbi. Gittelsohn, who was born in Cleveland, Ohio, was ordained at the Hebrew Union College in 1936. After serving as rabbi from 1936 to 1953 at the Central Synagogue of Nassau County in Long Island, he was appointed rabbi of Temple Israel, Boston, Mass. Gittelsohn served as a U.S. Navy chaplain from 1943 to 1946 and preached the address of dedication of the Jewish section of the Iwo Jima cemetery. In 1968 he was elected president of the Central Conference of American Rabbis. He repeatedly called on the American Jewish community to adopt a more activist position on social and political issues, particularly in opposition to the war in Vietnam. Gittelsohn wrote: *Modern Jewish Problems* (1935); *Little Lower Than the Angels* (1955); *Man's Best Hope* (1961); *My Beloved Is Mine* (1969), on the Jewish view of marriage; and *Fire in My Bones* (1969).

[AB.V.G.]

GITTIN (Heb. גִּטִּין; "divorces"), sixth tractate of the order *Nashim* in the Mishnah, Tosefta, and Babylonian and Jerusalem Talmuds. *Gittin* is placed before *Kiddushin* because of the custom of arranging the tractates in the order

Figure 1. Copperplate engraving illustrating the tractate *Gittin* from a Hebrew-Latin edition of the Mishnah, Amsterdam, 1700–1704, depicts the husband handing the wife the bill of divorce. Jerusalem, J.N.U.L.

of their length, *Gittin* containing nine chapters and *Kiddushin* only four. From a statement of Rashi (Git. 71b, s.v. *ta'ama*) and others, it seems that there was a different order of chapters, the present seventh chapter, according to Rashi, preceding the sixth. But from the *geonim, tosafot* (to Git. 62b, s.v. *ha-omer*), and Naḥmanides (in his novellae at the end of chapter 6) it appears that the present order is correct. The entire tractate deals with bills of divorce, with few digressions on other topics. The first chapter deals with the bringing of a bill of divorce *(get)* from outside Ereẓ Israel, the bearer of which has to testify that "it was written and signed in my presence." The question of the borders of Ereẓ Israel are dealt with in this connection. The first Mishnah of the second chapter, in fact, is a continuation of the first chapter and deals with the same topic. A similar phenomenon also occurs at the beginning of the seventh chapter; its first two *mishnayot* are a direct continuation of the theme of *agency in the writing and delivery of a *get* dealt with in the sixth chapter. The second chapter discusses the materials used for writing a *get* and the persons who may write and deliver it. The third chapter contains a group of *halakhot* based upon the principle that a previous condition may be presumed to exist: e.g., "If a man brings a *get* and has left the husband aged or sick, he may deliver it on the presumption that he is still alive" (3:3); the possibility of his death and the consequent invalidity of the *get*, necessitating a levirate marriage if he is childless, is ignored.

The fourth and fifth chapters cite a series of *halakhot* enacted for "general welfare" or in the interests of peace; e.g., "Scrolls of the Law, **tefillin*, and **mezuzot* should not be bought from gentiles at more than their value, for the general good" (4:6), i.e., so that gentiles should not be encouraged to steal such religious requisites from Jews; similarly, "one does not prevent the gentile poor from gathering gleanings, the forgotten sheaf, and the corner of the fields in the interest of peace" (5:8). The sixth chapter discusses agency and clarifies the difference between an agent for the delivery of a *get*, in which case the woman is not divorced until the *get* reaches her, and an agent for the reception of the *get*, where the agent represents the wife with the result that she is divorced as soon as the agent receives the *get*. The seventh chapter deals with the laws of conditional divorces. The eighth chapter, which derives from the Mishnah of R. Meir ("the whole of this chapter is R. Meir"—TJ, 8:5, 49c), contains a list of invalid divorces; should the woman remarry on the strength of them, she would need to receive a divorce from both husbands (a formula repeated in *mishnayot* 5–9). The ninth chapter contains parts of formulae of bills of divorce (9:3), from which it may be inferred that in early days there was no fixed formula (cf. also Tosef., Git. 9:6; Kid. 5b) and that divorces were written in Aramaic or Hebrew. The tractate concludes with a dispute between Bet Shammai and Bet Hillel about the grounds on which a man is permitted to divorce his wife. "Bet Shammai says, 'a man may not divorce his wife unless he has found unchastity in her,' while Bet Hillel says, 'even if she spoilt his food.' " According to Akiva, he may even divorce his wife if he finds another more attractive. This additional opinion is not a third one but an explanation of the words of Bet Hillel (see also Halevy, Dorot, 1, pt. 3 (1923), 569), and the radical wording is apparently intended to reject the views of Christians, who forbade divorce entirely (Mark 10:2–12, et al.).

The Tosefta, which in the printed edition contains seven chapters (the Mss. have nine like the Mishnah), supplements the Mishnah and gives the continuation of the development of the *halakhah*. Thus Mishnah 7:8 teaches: "(If the husband said) 'This is your *get* if I do not return within 12 months,' and he died within 12 months, it is not valid"—for the *get* only becomes effective at the end of 12 months and a divorce cannot be effected after death. To this the Tosefta (7:11) adds: "but our rabbis permitted her to marry." The Babylonian and Jerusalem Talmuds remark: "who are meant by 'our rabbis'? *Judah Nesiah . . . ," *Judah (II) the son of Gamaliel and the grandson of Judah ha-Nasi redactor of the Mishnah (76b; TJ, 7:3, 48d). This is one of three instances in which Judah Nesiah is called "our rabbi," although in general "our rabbis" refers to the generation of quasi-*tannaim* following Judah ha-Nasi (see Epstein, Tannaim, 231). Tosefta 5:4–5 affords information about cooperation between Jews and gentiles in the field of social welfare. In a city containing Jews and gentiles the communal leaders collect from both in the interest of peace. The gentile poor are supported together with the Jewish poor, in the interest of peace. Eulogies are delivered over them; when in mourning they are comforted; and their burial is undertaken in the interest of peace.

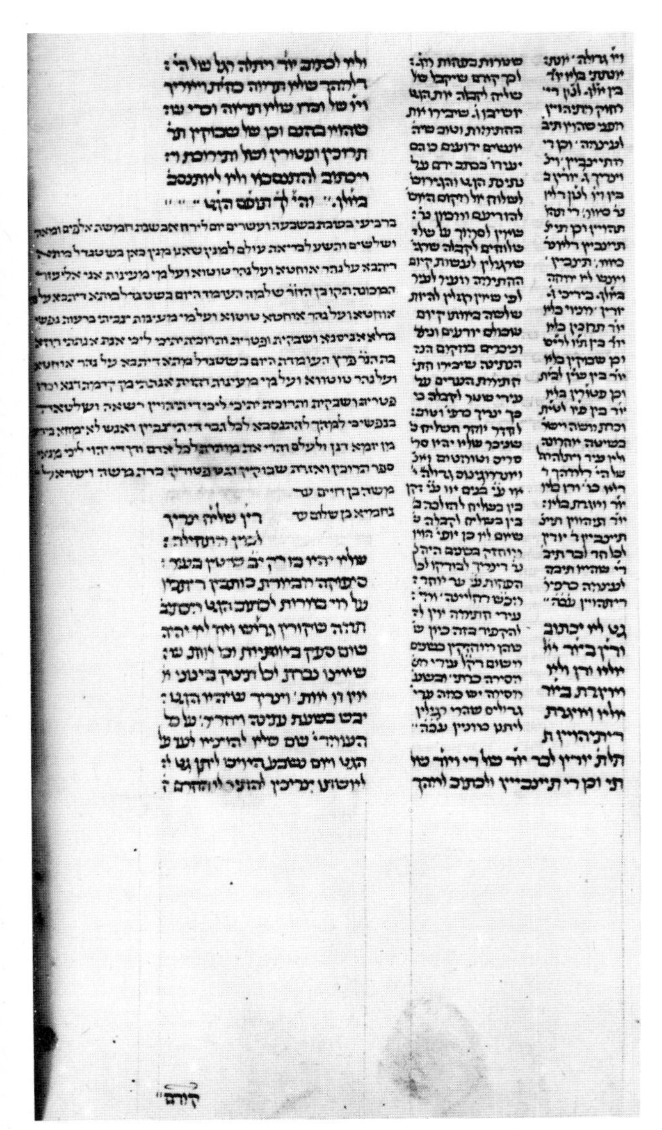

Figure 2. An example of a bill of divorce from *Sefer Mitzvot Katan* by Isaac of Corbeil, 1379. London, British Museum, Ms. Harl. 5584, fol. 74b.

From the tractate it is possible to prove that there existed a kind of official recognition by the government of Jewish civil jurisdiction and that government sanctions were invoked to execute the decisions of the Jewish courts. Thus the Mishnah (9:8) teaches: "A bill of divorce given under compulsion is valid if ordered by a Jewish court, but if by a gentile court it is invalid; but if the gentiles beat him and say, 'Do what the Jews bid thee,' it is valid." Thus even a bill of divorce arranged by gentiles can also be valid, i.e., if the Jewish court requests the gentile court forcefully to compel the husband to give a divorce. So too in the Jerusalem Talmud (9:10, 50d) "and if gentiles compel on the initiative of (the *bet din* of) Jews, it is valid." The Jerusalem and Babylonian Talmuds explain and clarify the subjects raised in the Mishnah; e.g., Mishnah 4:2 cites a **takkanah* of Rabban Gamaliel the Elder that for the general good the husband is forbidden to annul a bill of divorce that has been handed over to a messenger but has not yet reached the wife. According to Simeon b. Gamaliel in a *baraita* (33a), should the husband disobey the *takkanah* and annul the divorce, the annulment is of no effect, and the divorce is valid. On this, the Talmud asks: "And is it possible that where a divorce has been annulled according to Torah law, we should, to uphold the authority of the court, allow a married woman to remarry?" To this the Babylonian Talmud replies: "Yes. When a man betroths he does so on the conditions laid down by the rabbis, and in this case the rabbis annul his betrothal." The Jerusalem Talmud (4:2), however, holds that the rabbis do have the power to annul Torah law, even without the premise that all who betroth do so on the conditions laid down by the rabbis.

Aggadic sayings are sometimes interwoven with the *halakhah*. Mishnah 5:6 quotes various *takkanot* in connection with the law of buying land from the sicaricon (i.e., those usurping the owner's land by decree of the Roman government), the purpose of these *takkanot* being to normalize economic conditions and the purchase of property. In connection with this, the Talmud (55bff.) cites a collection of interesting *aggadot* relating to events connected with the destruction of the Temple and its causes (67bff.). The beginning of the seventh chapter enumerates a long list of popular remedies, and the passage includes the story of *Asmodeus (Ashmedai) and his demons.

Mishnah 5:8 lays down, "in the interest of peace," the order in which men are called to the public reading of the Pentateuch: "A priest reads first, after him a levite, and after him an Israelite." The Babylonian Talmud (60a) completes the order in which Israelites are called to the reading of the law. From this list the degree of importance of the functionaries in Jewish society can be inferred: "First scholars appointed *parnasim* over the community, then scholars fit to be appointed *parnasim* over the community, then the sons of scholars whose fathers have been appointed *parnasim* over the community, after them heads of synagogues and the general public." The Babylonian Talmud (67a) quotes a *baraita* specifying the distinctive merits of scholars: "Meir was wise and a scribe; Judah was wise when he desired to be; Tarfon was like a heap of nuts; Ishmael was like a well-stocked shop; Akiva was like a storehouse with compartments; Johanan b. Nuri was like a basket of fancy goods; Eleazar b. Azariah was like a basket of spices; the Mishnah of Eliezer b. Jacob is scant but clear. Yose always had his reasons; Simeon used to grind much and produce little . . . and what he discarded was only the bran" (cf. ARN[1] 18, 68). The following dicta and apothegms are worthy of note: **dina de-malkhuta dina,* "the law of the government is binding" (a halakhic rule of great importance in the Diaspora; 10b); "a man should not terrorize the members of his household" (6b); "The words of the Torah abide only with one who sacrifices himself for their sake" (57b); "If a man divorces his first wife, even the altar sheds tears" (90b). In the Soncino translation of the Talmud tractate Gittin was translated by M. Simon (1936). For the commentators, editors, and translations of the tractate, see *Talmud.

Bibliography: Ḥ. Albeck (ed.), *Shishah Sidrei Mishnah*, 3 (*Seder Nashim*, 1954), 265–72. [Y.D.G.]

°**GIUSTINIANI (Pantaleone), AGOSTINO** (1470?–1536), Italian orientalist and Hebraist. Born in Genoa, Giustiniani, a friend of Erasmus, *Pico della Mirandola, and Sir Thomas More, taught in Bologna, and in 1513 wrote a kabbalistic work inspired by J. *Reuchlin's *De verbo mirifico* and *De arte cabalistica.* He then made a bold, but unsuccessful, attempt to publish the first modern polyglot Bible, of which only the first part, *Psalterium octaplum* (Genoa, 1516), appeared. This contained the Hebrew text of Psalms, the Targum, an Arabic translation, two Greek and two Latin translations, and a commentary based largely on rabbinic sources. On Psalm 19:5 there is a curious marginal allusion to Christopher *Columbus (Giustiniani's Genoese compatriot) and his voyages of discovery, which is the first such allusion in Hebrew literature. Although this Psalter, dedicated to Pope Leo X, was well received, it did not enjoy great commercial success, and the project then came to an end.

In 1514 Giustiniani was made bishop of Nebbio in Corsica, but political considerations led to his acceptance of the chair of Hebrew in Paris. From 1517 until 1522 he taught at the new College of the Three Languages, founded by Francis I, and published various works, including an edition of R. David *Kimḥi's Hebrew grammar (*Liber Viarum Linguae Sanctae,* Paris, 1520?), and *Rabi Mossei Dux seu Director dubitantium aut perplexorum* (Paris, 1520), a Latin version of the *Guide of the Perplexed* of *Maimonides. The latter, which Giustiniani produced with the aid of Jacob *Mantino, was marred by its reliance on faulty texts. Many of his kabbalistic writings appeared in the *De arcanis catholicae veritatis* (Ortona, 1518) of P. Columna *Galatinus. Giustiniani bequeathed his library of rare books and manuscripts to Genoa. Little is known about the last years of his life. In 1536, on a trip to Corsica, he was lost at sea.

Bibliography: Steinschneider, Cat Bod, 5 no. 1564–66; C. Roth, *The Jews in the Renaissance* (1959), 124f., 155; F. Secret, *Le Zôhar chez les Kabbalistes Chrétiens de la Renaissance* (1964²), 30ff.; idem, *Les Kabbalistes Chrétiens de la Renaissance* (1964), 99–102. [G.E.S.]

°**GIUSTINIANI, MARCO ANTONIO** (fl. 16th century), printer of Hebrew books in Venice, Venetian patrician. His master printer Cornelius *Adelkind printed a fine edition of the Babylonian Talmud (1546–51). Soon, this very active press faced a formidable competitor in the house of *Bragadini which issued Maimonides' *Mishneh Torah,* with the notes of Meir Katzenellenbogen. Giustiniani then printed the full text of that code without R. Meir's notes. The mutual recriminations that the rivals engaged in at the Papal Court ultimately resulted in the confiscation and burning of all Hebrew books (1553).

Bibliography: D W. Amram, *Makers of Hebrew Books in Italy* (1909), index. [Ed.]

GIVAT ADA (Heb. גִּבְעַת עָדָה), moshavah in central Israel on the slopes of the Manasseh Hills. Founded in 1903 by the Jewish Colonization Association (ICA) on land purchased by Baron Edmond de Rothschild, after whose wife Ada (Adelaïde) it was named, it provided homesteads for the children of farmers from *Zikhron Ya'akov. The village's progress was very slow and it suffered from attacks during the Arab riots of 1920 and 1936–39. After World War II additional families received land at Givat Ada, and after 1948, when the village received the status of a municipal council, new immigrants were absorbed. In 1968 Givat Ada had 1,330 inhabitants and its economy was based on vineyards, fruit orchards, field and garden crops, and cattle. [E.O.]

GIVATAYIM (Heb. גִּבְעָתַיִם; "Two Hills"), township in central Israel, between Tel Aviv and Ramat Gan, founded in 1922 as a workers' suburb named Shekhunat Borochov (after Ber (Dov) *Borochov). In 1942, this quarter was united with four others in the vicinity to form the municipal unit of Givatayim. The town's population increased from 7,000 in 1947 to 42,100 in 1968. Compared with other urban communities, Givatayim's population was characterized in 1969 by an exceptionally high percentage of Israel-born and veteran Israelis (over 70%), while among those born abroad, 79.6% originated from Europe and America. Standards of living and education were above the average. Industry employed 30.1% of the city's manpower in 1968. In 1968 202 local industrial enterprises, mostly small, engaged in a large variety of branches (metals and machines, textiles, leather, and food). The city is situated within the Tel Aviv conurbation and its built-up area links up with that of the neighboring municipalities. [E.O.]

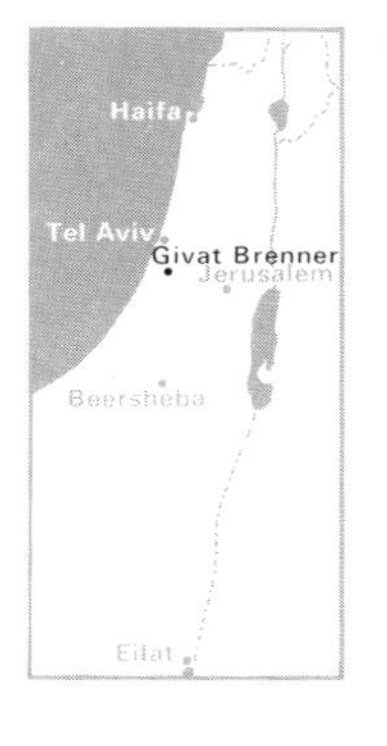

GIVAT BRENNER (Heb. גִּבְעַת בְּרֶנֶר), kibbutz in central Israel, south of *Reḥovot, affiliated with Ha-Kibbutz ha-Me'uḥad. It was founded in 1928 by pioneers from Lithuania and Italy who were later joined by immigrants from Germany and several other countries. The members initially derived a livelihood mainly as hired laborers on farms and in industries nearby, but they quickly developed their own intensive farming branches and industrial enterprises (including plants for metal sprinkler parts, textiles, fruit and vegetable preserves, ceramics, furniture, baby food), and became

Kibbutz Givat Brenner, with its industrial area in the foreground. Courtesy Government Press Office, Tel Aviv.

the largest collective settlement in the country. Following the split in Ha-*Kibbutz ha-Me'uḥad in 1951–52, a number of its members joined a new kibbutz, *Neẓer Sereni. In 1968, Givat Brenner had 1,520 inhabitants. Its "Bet Yesha" rest home and resort was the first of its kind in a labor settlement. The kibbutz has a cultural center named after Enzo *Sereni, who was one of its members. The settlement is named after Joseph Ḥ. *Brenner. [E.O.]

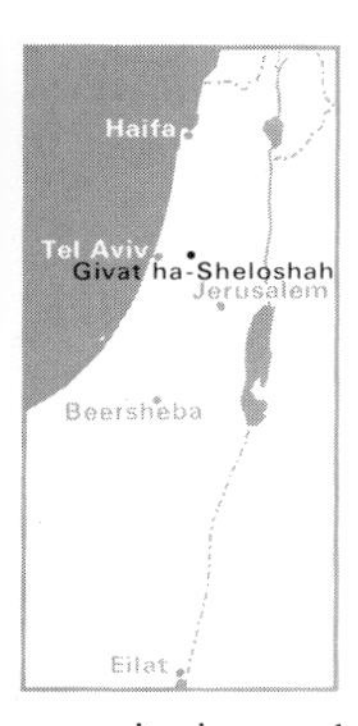

GIVAT HA-SHELOSHAH (Heb. גִּבְעַת הַשְּׁלוֹשָׁה), kibbutz in central Israel, east of Petaḥ Tikvah, affiliated with Ha-Kibbutz ha-Me'uḥad, first founded in 1925 on a site west of Petaḥ Tikvah by pioneers from Eastern Europe. The kibbutz initially subsisted mainly on its members' wages as hired laborers in local farms and industry. Gradually it developed its own farm branches and industrial enterprises. With the urbanization of the vicinity, the kibbutz was allocated a new site in rural surroundings of Rosh ha-Ayin further east. The transfer also made possible the establishment of two separate kibbutzim for the two sectors created as a result of the 1951–52 split in Ha-Kibbutz ha-Me'uḥad (the kibbutz that joined Iḥud ha-Kevuẓot ve-ha-Kibbutzim assumed the name *Einat). In 1968, Givat ha-Sheloshah had 510 inhabitants. Its farming is highly intensive, with citrus and other orchards, irrigated crops, and dairy cattle. The kibbutz has a shoe factory and a plant for building materials. The name, "Hill of the Three," commemorates three Jewish laborers from the Petaḥ Tikvah area who were executed by the Turks during World War I. [E.O.]

GIVAT ḤAYYIM (Heb. גִּבְעַת חַיִּים), two kibbutzim in central Israel 4 mi. (6 km.) south of Ḥaderah. The founding settlers from Austria and Czechoslovakia were among the first pioneers on the Ḥefer Plain lands. They worked on drainage of the local swamps and planted eucalyptus groves. In 1932, the group established a kibbutz and was joined by immigrants from other countries. They developed intensive farming and set up a cask factory and a food preserves plant. Givat Ḥayyim was affiliated with Ha-Kibbutz ha-Me'uḥad, and after a split in that movement in 1951–52, was partitioned into two neighboring kibbutzim—Givat Ḥayyim and Givat Ḥayyim Bet. In 1968, Givat Ḥayyim (Ha-Kibbutz ha-Me'uḥad) numbered 705 persons and Givat Ḥayyim Bet (Iḥud ha-Kevuẓot ve-ha-Kibbutzim) had 690 inhabitants. The name commemorates Chaim *Arlosoroff. [E.O.]

GIVAT ḤEN (Heb. גִּבְעַת חֵ"ן), moshav in central Israel near *Ra'ananah, affiliated with Tenu'at ha-Moshavim, founded in November 1933 in the framework of the "Thousand Families Settlement Scheme" by settlers from Eastern Europe who had become agricultural workers in Ra'ananah. They began by developing auxiliary farms which later became full-fledged farmsteads mainly based on citriculture, vegetable gardens, and dairy cattle. The moshav's name is composed of the initials of Ḥayyim Naḥman *Bialik's first names. [E.O.]

GIVENS, PHILIP S. (1922–), Canadian politician. Born in Toronto, Givens was admitted to the bar in 1949 and was a Toronto alderman from 1950 to 1961. From 1963 to 1966 he was mayor of Toronto. Givens was elected to the Canadian parliament as a Liberal in 1968. In parliament he concentrated on the problems of the large urban areas. Givens was an active figure in Jewish affairs and Jewish community causes, and he was elected national vice-president of the Federated Zionist Organization of Canada.

Philip Givens, Canadian politician. Courtesy Toronto Municipality. Photo Cavouk, Toronto.

Givens was chairman of the Toronto emergency campaign for Israel at the time of the Six-Day War and later chairman of the *United Jewish Appeal. [B.G.K.]

GLADIATOR, professional fighter in Roman public games. Little information is available about the gladiatorial contests held in the Middle East under Roman imperial rule. The performances were arranged by the authorities of cities with a predominantly Hellenistic culture; in Judea, for instance, they were sponsored by *Herod in *Caesarea. The Jewish sources make mention of Jews in this connection, and it was common knowledge that gladiators were bought for "large sums" (TJ, Git. 4:9, 46a–b). Rabbinical opinion was in general opposed to providing a ransom for a man who had sold himself as a gladiator, although an opinion is expressed that he should be ransomed since his life was in danger (Git. 46b–47a). "It is the accepted custom that a gladiator does not make a will," since he might be killed at any moment (Gen. R. 49:1, ed. by Theodor and Albeck, 1200). Some Jewish gladiators deliberately infringed the dietary laws to annoy their coreligionists and lived in Roman style (Git., loc. cit.). Others, however, were obliged to sell themselves out of financial stress "in order to exist" (TJ, loc. cit.). The expression "meal for gladiators" denoted an early repast consisting of an enriched diet (Pes. 12b; Shab. 10a). It is related of the *amora* Resh Lakish (see *Simeon R. Lakish) that he sold himself as a gladiator but that by combining courage with guile he managed to outwit the promoters of the contest and kill them all (Git. 47a). The rabbinical attitude toward the gladiatorial contests is clear from their association in the Midrash with brothels, gaming, and sorcery (Tanh. B., Gen. 24).

Bibliography: Schuerer, Gesch, 2 (1907[4]), 60f.; Krauss, Tal Arch, 3 (1912), 114f.; S. Lieberman, *Greek in Jewish Palestine* (1942), 148f. [H.H.B.-S.]

GLANVILLE, BRIAN LESTER (1931–), English novelist and journalist. Glanville's first novel was *The Reluctant Dictator* (1952). He emerged as the leading young Anglo-Jewish novelist of the decade with *The Bankrupts* (1958) which exposed the sham culture of Anglo-Jewry's nouveaux riches, but proved controversial. Glanville was attacked in various quarters for his unsympathetic attitude toward and relative ignorance of Judaism. *A Bad Streak* (1961) and *Diamond* (1962) also incorporate critical portrayals of Jewish types. Three later novels on general themes were *The Director's Wife* (1963), *A Roman Marriage* (1966) and *The Olympia* (1969). Glanville became a sports writer for the *Sunday Times* in 1960 and published books on association football. [ED.]

GLANZ, JACOB (1902–), Mexican Yiddish poet. Born in the Ukraine, Glanz emigrated to Mexico in 1925. In 1928 he collaborated with two other pioneering Yiddish poets of Mexico, Isaac Berliner and Moses Glikovski, in a joint volume, *Dray Vegn* ("Three Ways"). The poems of his period in Mexico were collected in *Trit in di Berg* (1939). Glanz's most prolific period was the decade from 1936 to 1946, during which he edited the literary supplement of *Der Veg* in Mexico and published three volumes of eclectic verse. In *A Kezayes Erd* ("A Bit of Earth," 1950), he glorified his native Ukrainian village, now surviving only as a memory.

Bibliography: LNYL, 2 (1958), 263ff.; S. Kahan, *Meksikaner Viderklangen* (1951), 193–6; 201–8; idem, *Literarishe un Zhurnalistishe Fartsekhnungen* (1961), 315–9. [S.L.]

GLANZ, LEIB, (1898–1964), cantor and composer. He was born in Kiev, where his father was cantor at the synagogue of the Talna Ḥasidim. He led congregational prayers at the age of eight. After holding cantorial posts at Kishinev and in Rumania, he emigrated to the United States in 1926 to

Leib Glanz, cantor. Photo Western Photographic Service, Los Angeles.

become cantor of the Ohev Shalom Synagogue in Brooklyn, N.Y. Glanz had a lyric tenor voice which had great appeal both in its technical range and warmth of expression. He rebelled against the "sobbing" style favored in his time by many cantors and disapproved of the excessive use of the minor scale. The music he arranged for the synagogue had grace as well as devotional fervor. While holding his post at Brooklyn, he toured extensively and then accepted a post as cantor of Heikhal Sinai Synagogue and the Sha'arei Tefillah Synagogue in Los Angeles. In 1954 he settled in Israel and was chief cantor of the Tiferet Ẓevi Synagogue in Tel Aviv until his death. Glanz regarded the pentatonic scale as the ancient basis of Jewish music. He did research on liturgical melodies, and arranged choral music in ḥasidic style. He aimed at creating a new tradition of *ḥazzanut*, and for this purpose founded the Tel Aviv Institute of Religious Jewish Music, to which the Cantorial Academy he headed became affiliated. He left more than 100 compositions in manuscript and many recordings of his own performances.

Bibliography: E. Steinmann (ed.), *Zoharim* (1965); E. Zaludkowski, *Kulturtreger fun der Yidisher Liturgie* (1930), 263; Sendrey, Music, index. [J.L.N.]

GLANZ-LEYELES, AARON, (1889–1966), U.S. Yiddish poet and essayist. Born in Vloclawek, Poland, he was educated in his father's *talmud torah* in Lodz, studied literature at the University of London (1905–08) and, after emigrating to New York in 1909, at Columbia University (1910–13). He taught at Yiddish schools, lectured on Yiddish literature, edited Yiddish journals, and for more than half-a-century wrote articles on literary, social, and political events for the New York Yiddish daily *The Day*. His prose appeared under his own name, A. Glanz, and his verse under the pseudonym A. Leyeles. In 1919, together with Jacob *Glatstein and N. B. *Minkoff, he founded the *In-Zikh movement of Yiddish poetry and the literary organ *In Zikh* for the propagation of the Inzikhist credo.

While his first book of poetry, *Labirint* (1918), rejected impressionistic effects and intricate traditional forms, his second book, *Yungharbst* ("Young Autumn," 1922), followed the Inzikhist doctrines. *Fabius Lind* (1937), an autobiography in verse, told the story of his spiritual odyssey and was prefaced by a vigorous restatement of his literary beliefs. *A Yid Oyfn Yam* ("A Jew at Sea," 1947) consisted of lyrics composed under the impact of the European Jewish catastrophe during the Nazi domination. It was followed by the volume of poems *Baym Fus Fun Barg* ("At the Foot of the Mountain," 1957), in which Leyeles again emphasized his opposition both to abstract poetry stripped of emotional content and to poetry as the expression of untamed feeling devoid of intellectual content. He held that poetry must always be concrete, the direct or indirect expression of a real experience, in which thought and feeling were to be inextricably intertwined. In the lyrics of *Amerike un Ikh* ("America and I," 1963) Leyeles voiced his faith in America's historical ideals.

Of Leyeles' experiments in poetic drama, only *Shlomo Molkho* (1926) aroused real interest. This drama dealt with the conflict between the two messianic aspirants David *Reuveni and Solomon *Molcho. While Reuveni sought to redeem the Jewish people by force of arms and to restore them to a normal existence on their ancestral soil, Molcho, influenced by kabbalistic lore, wished the Jews to remain in the Diaspora and to become the self-sacrificing redeemers of all mankind. Through the mouth of the 16th-century Marrano martyr, Leyeles voiced his own Territorialist philosophy. In a second drama, *Asher Lemlen* (1928), Leyeles dealt with the conflict between Jewish messianic longing and the reality of political and social life. A Hebrew translation of the two plays was made by Shimshon Melzer and a Hebrew rendering of selected poems by B. Ḥrushovski (1960), with a literary analysis by Dov Sadan. In the volume *Velt un Vort* ("World and Word," 1958), Aaron Glanz-Leyeles collected the best of his essays on poets, novelists, and memoirists. In his analysis of poetry, he revealed great critical penetration and perception. In his

Aaron Glanz-Leyeles, Yiddish poet and essayist.

75th year, Leyeles visited Israel for the first time and was stimulated to a new burst of lyric creativity. He was never harsh or bitter and never emphasized the literary failings of the writers concerned, holding that a critic should call attention to the way in which a work enriched literature rather than to its failings.

Bibliography: Rejzen, Leksikon, 2 (1927), 255–8; LNYL, 5 (1963), 330–8; N.B. Minkoff, *Literarishe Vegn* (1955), 219–49; J. Glatstein, *In Tokh Genumen*, 1 (1947), 97–105, 295–302; 2 (1956), 291–6; S. Lestchinsky, *Literarishe Eseyen* (1955), 116–26; S. Bickel, *Shrayber fun Mayn Dor* (1958), 84–98; Waxman, Literature, 5 (1960), 93–95; *Jewish Book Annual*, 25 (1968), 116–122. [S.L.]

GLAPHYRA (first century B.C.E.), daughter of Archelaus, king of Cappadocia. Glaphyra's first husband was *Alexander, son of Herod the Great. After Alexander's execution (7 B.C.E.) Herod returned her to her father. However, her two sons by the marriage, Tigranes and Alexander, remained with the king. Glaphyra then married Juba, king of Libya. This marriage seems to have ended abruptly, and the princess returned home again. There she met Archelaus, son of Herod, who immediately divorced his wife Mariamne and married her. This marriage constituted a transgression of Jewish law, since Glaphyra had already borne children to the brother of Archelaus. Glaphyra died shortly after her arrival in Judea.

Bibliography: Jos., Ant., 16:11, 193, 206, 303, 328–32; 17:12, 341, 349–53; Jos., Wars, 1:476–8, 552f.; 2:114–6; Schuerer, Hist, 152, 154, 176; A.H.M. Jones, *Herods of Judaea* (1938), index; Klausner, Bayit Sheni, 4 (1950[2]), 154ff., 179. [I.G.]

GLASER, DONALD ARTHUR (1926–), U.S. physicist and Nobel Prize winner. Glaser was born in Cleveland,

Donald A. Glaser, U.S. physicist and Nobel laureate. Courtesy University of California at Berkeley.

Ohio. At school he was so inattentive that only the intervention of a psychologist prevented his being transferred to a school for backward children. He went on to take his physics degrees at the California Institute of Technology. He taught physics at the University of Michigan. There in his work in nuclear physics Glaser felt limited by the cloud chamber apparatus used for recording the high-speed trajectories of nuclear particles. In 1952, by reversing the process used in the cloud chamber, Glaser designed a small "bubble chamber." This became the basis of what is now an indispensable research tool in nuclear physics. This invention and the use of it won for him the Nobel Prize for physics in 1960. Subsequently he became professor of molecular biology at the University of California.

Bibliography: *New Scientist*, 9 (1961), 474f.; *Les Prix Nobel en 1960* (1961), 21–24, 58f. [J.E.H.]

GLASER, EDUARD (1855–1908), explorer and Arabist. Born in Deutsch-Rust, Bohemia, he made four journeys to Arabia between 1883 and 1894. He identified many localities in Yemen. He discovered numerous inscriptions in the interior of Arabia, as well as archaeological remains and Arabic manuscripts. On his third trip in 1887–88, he penetrated to Marib and ancient Saba (Sheba), making important geographical discoveries and collecting over 1,000 inscriptions in Sabean and Himyaritic. In 1892 he made his fourth journey to Arabia, reaching the interior, mapping the region, and collecting innumerable manuscripts, inscriptions, and specimens of diverse dialects. Glaser's writings include: *Skizze der Geschichte und Geographie Arabiens ...*, 2 vols. (1889–90); *Abessinier in Arabien und Afrika* (1895); *Punt und die suedarabischen Reiche* (1899);

Eduard Glaser, explorer and Arabist. Jerusalem, J.N.U.L., Schwadron Collection.

and *Zwei Inschriften ueber den Dammbruch von Marib* (1897).

Bibliography: Akademie der Wissenschaften, Wien, *Sammlung Eduard Glaser*, 2 vols. (1944–61). [E.Fi.]

GLASER, JULIUS ANTON (**Joshua**; 1831–1885), Austrian jurist. Born in Postelberg, Bohemia, he converted to Christianity in his youth. He obtained doctorates in law from the universities of Zurich and Vienna. In 1856 he was appointed assistant professor of criminal law at Vienna University and four years later became full professor. From 1871 to 1879 he was minister of justice and later attorney general. Glaser's principal contribution to Austrian jurisprudence was the introduction of a new penal code in 1873. The code was largely concerned with protecting the rights of the accused and remained in force in Austria until 1938. Among his numerous legal publications are: *Das englisch-schottische Strafverfahren* (1850); *Anklage, Wahrspruch und Rechtsmittel im englischen Schwurgerichtsverfahren* (1866). [G.T.]

GLASGOW, city in S.W. Scotland. The first Jew to settle in the city was Isaac Cohen in 1812; however there was no sizable community or synagogue until 1833, when services were held in the house of the *shoḥet*, Moses Lisenheim. By 1831, 47 Jews lived in the city, most of them originating from Eastern Europe, though six had already been born in Glasgow. Four years later the community acquired its first burial ground, which was used until 1851. There was a split in the congregation in 1842 when a hall attached to Anderson College was leased for religious services; a minority of community members objected that since human bodies were dissected at the college it was an unfit place for a synagogue. Subsequent bitterness between the two groups led to court proceedings over the right to use the cemetery; the majority won the case. However, at the election of Nathan Marcus *Adler as chief rabbi of Great Britain in 1844 both parties exercised a vote. By 1850 there were 200 Jews in the city and eight years later they consecrated a new synagogue, known as the Glasgow Hebrew Congregation. In 1879 the community had a synagogue built at Garnethill, with E. P. Phillips as minister,.which was soon followed by two others in the South Side. As elsewhere in Britain, an influx of immigrants followed the Russian persecutions of 1881; in 1897 there were 4,000 Jews in the city and in 1902, 6,500. Many of the newcomers, who settled in the Gorbals district, were tailors or furriers.

The community was always active in Zionism, supporting *Ḥovevei Zion in the 19th century and Zionist Associations in modern times. Mainly because of the stimulus of the *Habonim movement, a large number of young Glasgow Jews settled on kibbutzim in Israel. A charity board originally known as The Glasgow Hebrew Philanthropic Society (1858) and later called The Glasgow Jewish Board of Guardians also helped in the organization of the Jewish Old Age Home for Scotland, situated in the south of the city. The Glasgow *talmud torah* and Board of Jewish Religious Education organized classes for children (as do the individual synagogues), directed the Hebrew College (for post-bar mitzvah Jewish education), and assisted in running the yeshivah. In 1970 there was a Jewish day school at primary level and Hebrew was taught in two municipal secondary schools; Glasgow University taught both biblical and modern Hebrew.

The Jewish Echo (weekly, established in 1928) was Scotland's only Jewish newspaper until 1965, when *The Jewish Times* (later renamed *Israel Today*) was established. The community had many organizations of Jewish interest, e.g., Benei Akiva, ORT, and the Jewish Lad's Brigade (which claimed the world's only Jewish bagpipe band). Ten Orthodox and one Reform synagogue served the community. Religious leaders of note included Samuel I. *Hillman, Kopul *Rosen, I. K. Cosgrove (b. 1903), and Wolf Gottlieb (b. 1910). Among the community's outstanding members were Sir Maurice *Bloch, Sir Isaac *Wolfson, Sir Ian M. *Heilbron, Sir Myer Galpern (b. 1903, lord provost and lord lieutenant of Scotland (1958–60) and Labor M. P. (1959)), Samuel Krantz (b. 1901) and L. H. *Daiches. Notable in the university as well as in the community were Noah Morris (professor of medicine), Michael Samuel (professor of English language), and David Daiches Raphael (professor of political and social theory).

In 1969 the Jewish population numbered about 13,400 (out of a total of 1,045,000).

Bibliography: A. Levy, *Origins of Glasgow Jewry, 1812–1895* (1949); idem, *Origins of Scottish Jewry* (1959), 27–29; idem, in: JHSET, 19 (1960), 146–56; C. Roth, *Rise of Provincial Jewry* (1950), index; J. Gould and S. Esh (eds.), *Jewish Life in Modern Britain* (1964), index; C. Bermant, *Troubled Eden* (1969), index; idem, in: *Explorations*, 1 (1967), 99–106.

[Ed.]

GLASMAN, BARUCH (1893–1945), Yiddish novelist. Stemming from a family of artisans in the Belorussian village of Mozyr, Glasman was educated in Kiev, and emigrated to the United States in 1911. He graduated from Ohio State University in 1918 and served in the U.S. Army from 1918 to 1919. For some years he wandered in Poland, Russia, and the United States and alternated between English and Yiddish as his literary medium, and between different philosophies of life, eternally dissatisfied with himself and the world, and especially with his Jewish environment. In choice of themes for his short stories and novels, Glasman was the most American of Yiddish writers, combining a brooding, psychoanalytic approach with exciting action. He sympathized with the underprivileged members of society. His novel *In Goldenem Zump* ("In the Golden Swamp," 1940) is a violent attack upon New York's Yiddish literary and journalistic milieu. His selected works appeared in eight volumes (1927–37).

Bibliography: LYNL, 2 (1958), 249–52; A. Beckerman, *Baruch Glasman* (Yid., 1944); B. Rivkin, *Undzere Prozayker* (1951), 274–84; S. D. Singer, *Dikhter un Prozayker* (1959), 145–52; A. Tabachnik, *Dikhter un Dikhtung* (1965), 441–51.

[M.Rav.]

GLASNER, MOSES SAMUEL (1856–1924), rabbi and early leader of the *Mizrachi movement in Hungary and Transylvania. Glasner, a great-grandson of R. Moshe *Sofer, was born in Pressburg. From 1878 until 1923, when he settled in Ereẓ Israel, he was the rabbi of Klausenburg. He was one of the two Orthodox rabbis in Hungary (the other being Moses Aryeh Roth) who joined the Zionist movement and Mizrachi, and at the founding convention of Mizrachi (Pressburg, 1904) he spoke out against the Orthodox Hungarian rabbis for their attacks upon Zionism and the Mizrachi. He propagated the Zionist idea in speeches and writings among Orthodox circles. He also published several halakhic works (*Or Bahir*, 1908; *Halakhah le-Moshe*, 1912; *Dor Revi'i*, 1921) and a work on the *aggadah*, *Shevivei Esh* (1903). In Jerusalem, he took part in the educational and cultural activities of Mizrachi and was especially close to Rabbi A. I. *Kook.

Bibliography: L. Jung (ed.), *Men of the Spirit* (1964), 459–66; EẒD, 1 (1958), 523–7.

[G.K.]

GLASS.

Earliest Times. The earliest manufacture of glass does not antedate the late third millennium B.C.E., when the first glass beads were made in Mesopotamia and Egypt. The invention of glass vessel-making dates to the mid-second millennium B.C.E., when the first core-formed glass vessels appear almost simultaneously in Egypt and Mesopotamia. Egypt's glass industry was particularly flourishing in the el-Amarna period (the first half of the 14th century B.C.E.). Some Mesopotamian glass vessels have been found in northern Syria, though none in Palestine, but several Palestinian sites have yielded Egyptian glass vessels of the 14th–13th centuries B.C.E. A rich collection of such vessels was found in the small Canaanite Fosse Temple at Lachish; others were found at Beth Shean and Tell Dayr ʿAllā (the ancient Sukkoth). Egyptian glass vessels were also found in tombs at Tell al-ʿAjūl, Beth Shemesh, and Ẓahrat al-Ḥumrāya south of Jaffa. Gezer and Megiddo yielded similar glass vessels. There is no positive evidence that there was any manufacture of glass vessels in Canaan in the Late Bronze Age. A complete decline in glassmaking set in toward the end of the second millennium B.C.E. and it is only in the second half of the eighth and the seventh centuries B.C.E. that glass vessels appear again. None of the molded and cut luxury glass bowls and other colored vessels of that period has come to light in Palestine, but a core-formed vessel of the seventh century was found in a tomb at Achzib. Glass-inlay pieces of the late ninth and eighth centuries were found together with the ivories in the palace of the kings of Israel at Samaria, but whether they were made of Syrian or imported glass is not known. An

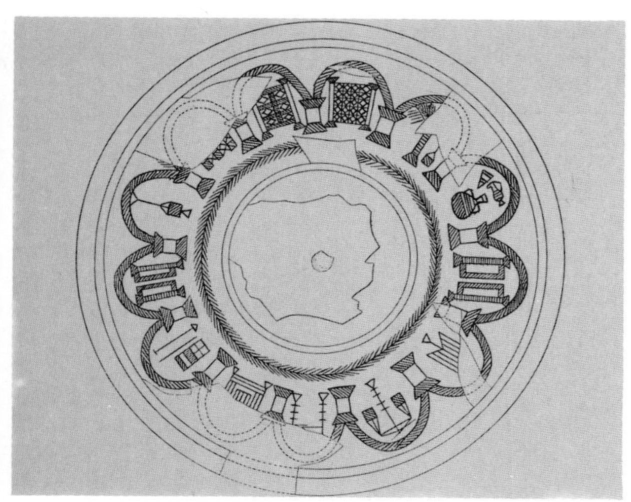

Figure 1. Drawing of engraved glass plate from a catacomb at Beth She'arim, third–early fourth century, diam. 20 in. (52 cm.). Courtesy N. Avigad and Israel Exploration Society, Jerusalem.

active production center of core-formed glass vessels, probably on the island of Rhodes, began making small amphoriskoi, aryballoi (short-necked flasks), alabastra, and juglets late in the seventh century B.C.E., and specimens have been found in an early sixth-century tomb at Gibeah, north of Jerusalem, and in Ammonite tombs in Jordan. Other vessels of this type have been found in Israel at Athlit, Achzib, Hazor, Beth Shean, and En Gedi. Molded and cut luxury glass vessels continued to be made in the Achaemenid period (sixth to fourth centuries) and the remains of an alabastrow of this type were found in a tomb at Athlit. Core-formed glass vessels of the Hellenistic period have occasionally been found in Palestine. The fragments of molded bowls found in second- and first-century B.C.E. levels at Ashdod, Jerusalem, Samaria, and other sites, may be products of local glass factories, possibly situated somewhere along the coast. There is, however, no indication whatsoever that Jews had any connection with glassmaking during the Hellenistic period, either in Palestine or in the Diaspora.

Glass in Hellenistic and Roman Periods. Glass is mentioned only once in the Bible, in Job 28:17, where it is equated with gold. This reflects the early situation when glass was of great value. The obscure statement in Deuteronomy 32:18–19 about Zebulun's hidden treasures in the sand was explained by Targum Jonathan as referring to glass, but this seems anachronistic. The Septuagint followed a very different line when it chose to render this passage as close as possible to Genesis 49:13. This probably indicates that when the Greek version of the Bible was prepared, this area had not had the obvious connection with glass that it had later on. A very early tradition seems to be preserved in the Palestinian Talmud (TJ, Pes. 1:6, 27b) and in the Babylonian Talmud (Shab. 14b, 15a), according to which Jose b. Joezer and Jose b. Johanan, who lived in the first half of the second century B.C.E., declared that glass vessels are liable to become impure. The U.S. talmudist Louis Ginzberg suggested that this declaration had an economic basis—it was meant to protect local pottery and metal ware from competition with foreign glass imports. Glass was, however, rare and valuable all through the Hellenistic period, and could not have presented competition to any local products. An explanation must therefore be sought in the cultural-religious sphere. The edict is contemporary with the first large-scale production of glass drinking bowls, and the two Jewish authorities may have objected to them because they identified them with Hellenistic influence, manners, and customs.

A revolutionary event was the invention of glassblowing toward the end of the first century B.C.E., which made it possible to produce glass vessels cheaply and in great variety. The invention seems to have taken place during the reign of Augustus (31 B.C.E.–14 C.E.) somewhere along the Phoenician coast, perhaps at Sidon, an area where a glass production center was apparently already in existence. The fame of Sidonian glass must have been considerable, since glassmakers working in Rome in the first century C.E. boasted of their Sidonian origin when they stamped the handles of their canthari in Greek or Latin, as, for example, Artas Sidon.

Several Jewish tombs of the first and second centuries C.E. have yielded glass vessels. Glass vessels are relatively rare in ossuary tombs around Jerusalem, which are no later than 70 C.E. A tomb excavated at Ramat Raḥel in 1931 (Tomb I) contained a small bottle with a spheric body and a short cylindrical neck. Several tombs in a cemetery on the Mount of Olives yielded simple, small glass bottles with pear-shaped bodies and elongated necks. All these glass vessels are typical of the first-century vessels common throughout the Roman Empire. A Jewish tomb of the middle of the first century at Carthage yielded a shallow glass bowl of a shape very common in the early imperial period. So-called "candlestick" bottles which have small convex bodies and long tubular necks were found in a few ossuary tombs in and around Jerusalem which can be dated to the second century. To the relatively limited testimony from Jewish tombs were added in 1960–61 the finds from the Judean desert caves in which fugitives of the *Bar Kokhba revolt took refuge. The finds included typical glass vessels of the early part of the second century C.E. It appears, then, that the only Jewish glass vessels of this period were the normal ware of the day. It stands to reason that some of the vessels, perhaps even many of them, were made by Jews but this is no more than a logical assumption. The Mishnah includes passages which refer specifically to glassmaking. Kelim 8:9 mentions עוֹשֵׂי זְכוּכִית—those who make glass (the "metal")—and זַגָּגִין—those who make glass vessels and their furnaces. Makers of glass vessels are also mentioned in Kelim 24:8. The Mishnah would not have included regulations about these trades if they had not been part and parcel of the daily life in Palestine, at any rate in the second century C.E. and possibly earlier. This, then, proves the existence of Jewish glassmakers in this period.

GOLD GLASS. The first group of glass vessels which is distinctly Jewish by reason of its decoration is the famous gold glass with Jewish symbols. The term is used to describe

Figure 2. Glass pendant from Tyre. On the left of the *menorah* is a *shofar*, on the right a *lulav* and *etrog*. London, British Museum E.C. 703.

decorations of thin gold foil encased between two layers of glass medallion; and must not be confused with gilding, where the gold is left uncovered. The commonest type of gold glasses are those which were used, in the third and the

Figure 3. Hexagonal glass bottle, sixth century C.E., probably made in Jerusalem. A *menorah* can be seen on the left face. Height 5 in. (13 cm.). Berlin, Staatliches Museum, Antiken-Abteilung, 30219.168. Photo Isolde Luckert.

fourth centuries C.E., as a decorated base of very shallow plates, bowls, or beakers. The thinly hammered gold foil was pasted on a round piece of clear or dark blue glass, within the boundaries of a low raised glass base. The outlines and the designs of the desired pictures, patterns, and inscriptions were prepared by removing the superfluous gold from the background, and leaving the designs in gold. Enamel paints were used at times to enrich the decoration. In the final stage the decorated base was reheated and joined to the outer surface of a large, hot, clear glass "bubble" which was later given the shape of the required bowl. A similar method was used to decorate the body of a vessel by smaller medallions of gold foil on blue glass. This technique was not exclusively Jewish. In the third and fourth centuries C.E. this particular craft flourished on an unprecedented scale. The center of the industry was Rome, and most of the pieces were found in pagan, Christian, or Jewish catacombs in and around the city. The vessels were broken deliberately, often skillfully chiseled around the edges, and stuck into the plaster near or on the graves of the deceased. The reasons for this custom have not yet been convincingly explained. Of the 500 bases and decorative medallions that have survived, only about a dozen bear definitely Jewish symbols. The earliest was found in 1882 in the catacomb of the saints Peter and Marcellinus (now in the Vatican Museum; color plate 9) and another around 1894 in the catacomb of Saint Ermete. A gold glass now in Berlin (color plate 11) is said to have been found in the Jewish catacomb of Vigna Randanini in Rome and another which is now in the Cologne City Museum (color plate 3) is said to have come from the Villa Torlonia catacomb. Other Jewish gold glass pieces are now in the Vatican (color plates 4, 9, 10, 12) and in the British (color plate 6), the Ashmolean (color plate 8), the Metropolitan (color plate 7), the Wuerzburg University (color plate 5), and the Israel (color plates 1, 2) Museums. Most of the Jewish gold glass bases have their decorations presented in two registers. These include representations of the Ark of the Covenant flanked by a pair of lions or doves, temple vessels like *menorot*, amphorae, and *shofarot*, and objects relating to Sukkot, the Feast of the Temple, such as *lulavim*, *etrogim*, and motifs found in other Jewish objects and catacombs of the period. Of a different type is the Vatican fragment found in 1882 (color plate 9). This bears a miniature painting of a tetrastyle temple inside a peristyle court surrounded by palm trees. The temple is approached by four steps and on the tympanum of the gable is a *menorah*. In front of the temple are a *lulav*, an *etrog*, two amphorae, and other objects. The temple is flanked by two free-standing columns. Most scholars seem to agree that this is a representation of Solomon's Temple, and it can be assumed that it was copied from an early illuminated Bible manuscript. This fragment bears a Greek inscription. Other Jewish gold glasses have inscriptions in Latin, similar to those found on the non-Jewish glasses such as *ANIMA DULCIS* ("sweet soul"; color plate 3). Only one Jewish small gold glass medallion is known (color plate 12). This shows a *shofar* between two *etrogim*. It is now in the Vatican Library. These Jewish gold glasses are generally thought to have been drinking vessels, perhaps for ritual purposes. The fragment with Solomon's Temple may tentatively be attributed to the third or early fourth century C.E.; the rest are more likely to be of the fourth century. Their decoration has numerous parallels in Jewish art. It is possible to assume that they were made by Jews.

In addition to the gold glasses and cut bowls from Rome there are further specimens worth noting: Moshe *Schwabe and Adolf *Reifenberg uncovered and published in 1935 a Jewish gilded glass sepulchral inscription in Greek ending with *Shalom* in Hebrew, with a *menorah* below the inscription and a *shofar* on its right. They also published a stamped glass medallion from Rome bearing a *menorah* and the name of the glassmaker: *EX OF[FICINA] LAVRENTI.*

Figure 4. Opaque glass oil or wine decanter with inscription in Hebrew, and another in Arabic on the neck. Damascus(?), Syria, 18th century. Jerusalem, Israel Museum. Photo Manning Bros.

Figure 5. Colored *ḥevra kaddisha* glass with enameled decoration. It is inscribed as a presentation to the burial society of Polin by Moses son of Jacob Polin on Ḥanukkah, 1692. Bohemia or Hungary, height 9¾ in. (24 cm.). New York, Jewish Museum, Harry G. Friedman Collection. Photo Sandak, Inc.

The Eastern Mediterranean: Third Century to Arab Conquest. The excavations at the Jewish cemeteries at Beth She'arim have yielded some finds of glass. Several vessels and many fragments were found in catacombs 12–20 and date to the third and first half of the fourth century C.E. These are, with very few exceptions, fragments of various common types of receptacles of the period, mainly bottles, and do not have any characteristics which could identify them as Jewish. An exceptional decorated glass plate was discovered in catacomb 15. With a diameter of 52 cms. (c. 20 ins.), it is unusually large, and engraved on its exterior are 13 arches under which are vessels, tools, doors, and hanging lamps and several unidentified objects. Although this may represent a temple facade, nothing in the designs on the plate is specifically Jewish. The remains of a glass factory were found at Beth She'arim during the excavations in 1940 and were attributed to the first half of the fourth century C.E. and to the Byzantine period. A large slab of glass—3.40×1.94×0.45 m. (11×6½×1½ ft.)—apparently the bottom of a glassmaker's tank was also discovered in a cistern. This too possibly dates to the Byzantine period. It is therefore reasonable to assume that some of the vessels found in the cemeteries around the site were local products. Several glass vessels, also of contemporary Palestinian types, were found in a Jewish tomb of the late fourth to fifth centuries at Gezer (Tomb 201). Glass lamps having three handles for suspension and cups of the type used for bronze polycandela were in use in Palestinian synagogues of the Byzantine period. Lamps suspended from seven-branched candlesticks are depicted on the mosaic pavement of the synagogue of Naaran (sixth century C.E.). Several other synagogue mosaic pavements have representations of seven-branched candlesticks with glass lamps. A complete glass lamp and many fragments of lamps of various types were found in the Beth She'an synagogue. They belong to its last phase in the first half of the seventh century and are now in the collection of the Israel Department of Antiquities. Similar fragments of lamps from the late sixth or early seventh centuries were also found in the synagogue of Maon near Nir Am, southeast of Gaza. Exactly the same types of lamp were used in contemporary churches in Palestine and Syria, so the glass finds in such Jewish contexts as the catacombs of Beth She'arim, Gezer (Tomb 201), or the ruins of synagogues do not differ from the normal glassware of their times. Between the late fourth and early seventh centuries there are a few groups of ornamental glass objects such as pendants and bracelets, bearing symbols which identify them as specifically Jewish. In a tomb excavated at Tarshīḥā in western Galilee a small circular pendant of greenish glass with a loop for suspension was found stamped with a *menorah*. The tomb was in use in the fourth and fifth centuries. The pendant is now in the Rockefeller Museum, Jerusalem (31.286B). The British Museum has a pendant made of light brownish glass, said to be from Tyre, with a *menorah*, a *shofar* on the left and a *lulav* and *etrog* on the right. There are similar pendants in the Israel Museum and in the Reifenberg collection. Of unknown provenance is a small greenish glass medallion in the Jewish Museum, New York, representing a *menorah* in a wreath. It was originally applied to a vessel and dates to the fourth century C.E. An identical piece from Egypt is in the Israel Museum. A fragment of a blue glass bracelet with the *menorah* stamped on it several times was found in the western part of the Jezreel Valley. It is now in a private collection. A complete bracelet of blue glass with 14 impressions of a *menorah* and *shofar* on its right side was acquired in New York in 1965. It is said to be of east Mediterranean provenance. Both the fragment and the complete example are probably of the fourth or fifth century. Another bracelet of very dark green glass with similar impressions but of unknown provenance is in the Museum Haaretz, Tel Aviv.

HEXAGONAL BOTTLES FROM PALESTINE. By far the most interesting Jewish glass from Palestine are the mold-blown hexagonal and octagonal small jugs or jars. These were blown into hexagonal or octagonal metal molds which were open top and bottom. The designs which were hammered into the molds appeared on the lower part of the jug, as an impression and not as a relief. Some hexagonal jugs have a long neck and a handle while others have a short neck and outsplayed rim. Nearly all these vessels were made of a bubbly brown glass, but there are few known examples made of greenish glass. Of many such mostly Christian jugs, only about 30 survived bearing Jewish symbols, such as *menorot* (Fig. 3), often with a *shofar* on the left and a *lulav* and *etrog* on the right, sometimes with an incense shovel on the right. The other sides are decorated with trees, arches, and other objects or patterns. Similar jugs and jars bearing Christian symbols have identical features, indicating that they were made in the same workshops. They are believed to have been used as containers for oil taken from the lamps of the Church of the Holy Sepulcher to be blessed at Golgotha, and there can be no doubt that they were made in Jerusalem. These are attributed to the late sixth or early seventh century, and by analogy the Jewish vessels can be attributed to the same period. It can be assumed that Jewish pilgrims used the vessels for carrying away oil from lamps at their center of veneration—

Figure 6. Wine goblet, England, late 18th century. Inscribed around the rim is the phrase "The righteous shall flourish like the palm tree" (Ps. 92:13), New York, Jewish Museum.

probably the Western Wall. During the excavations at Ephesus in Asia Minor a bottle was found on which are painted in black a *menorah,* a *shofar,* a *lulav,* and an *etrog.* Though this seems to be the only known Jewish glass vessel from the eastern Mediterranean area, apart from Palestine and Syria, the existence of Jewish glassmakers in the region in the sixth century C.E. can be deduced from two popular Byzantine fables of that time, one from Emesa (Homs), the other from Constantinople, in both of which the central figure is a Jewish glassmaker.

In the East from Medieval to Modern Times. The fact that Jews were active in glassmaking in medieval times is borne out by references in sources of the period. Arab historians have preserved the interesting information that the Khalif ʿAbd al-Malik (685–705) employed a group of Jews to make the glass lamps and vessels for the Mosque in Jerusalem but that Omar ibn Abd al-Aziz deprived them of this office. Very important data have been preserved in the Cairo *Genizah.* A document signed in the spring of 1011 deals with a dispute over the payment for a consignment of 50 "bales of glass" sent by three Jews from Tyre to Cairo. This ties up with a statement made by *Benjamin of Tudela, who visited Palestine in 1170, that at Tyre were "Jews, makers of good glass which is called Tyrian glass and is famous in all countries." Benjamin of Tudela also mentions that at Antioch "are about ten Jews and they are glassmakers." In an article on the Cairo *Genizah* published in 1961, S. D. Goitein mentions four contracts of partnership in glass workshops, one of which refers to a Jewish glassmaker who arrived in Cairo "from the west." He appears to have traveled overland from Tunis. Goitein believes that Jews were connected with the issue of the well-known Islamic glass weights. However, no actual survivals of Jewish glass manufactured in this period are known.

It has been suggested that Jews were connected with the age-old glass works at Hebron. The first to mention these works seems to have been the Augustine monk, Jacob of Verona, who visited Hebron in 1335; but he made no reference to any Jews there, although production was already on a large scale (Fig. 8). [D.P.B.]

L. A. Mayer assumed that a group of clumsily inscribed Syro-Egyptian glass mosque lamps were executed by "Jewish craftsmen, who were literate, but in a different script." During the Ottoman period, in the 17th century, there was in Damascus a Jewish center for the manufacturing of similar glass lamps. One such lamp in the Jewish Museum in London bears a Hebrew inscription and dates from 1694. Of Middle Eastern 18th-century origin are bottles of opaque glass, which have Hebrew dedicatory inscriptions cut in them. One which belonged to the Charles Feinberg Collection is now in the Israel Museum (Fig. 4). Another specimen in the Victoria and Albert Museum in London has a metal top and decorative chains. These were probably used as oil or wine containers.

In the West From Medieval to Modern Times. The art of glassmaking was reintroduced into Europe during the period of the Crusades. Numbers of Eastern glassmakers settled in northern Italy, Spain, and southern France. Jewish craftsmen may have been among them; though it cannot be proven.

Figure 7. Set of decanters made by the Jacobs family of Bristol, England, 18th–19th century. Bristol Art Gallery.

EASTERN EUROPE. There were, however, Jewish glassmakers in Central and Eastern Europe after the 15th century. There are also records of Jewish glaziers and glassmakers in Bohemia and Moravia from the 15th century onward, and the craft was frequently practiced by Bohemian Jews in the latter half of the 16th century.

From glass vessels and from contracts between Jewish glassmakers and the aristocracy it is clear, for instance, that the Jews took an active part in the flowering of glassmaking in Hungary in the 17th and 18th centuries.

Ḥevra Kaddisha Beakers. In the 17th and 18th centuries Hungarian and Bohemian Jews apparently participated in the general practice of manufacturing decorated jugs or beakers for special occasions. Among them were prominent beakers used by members of a guild or a fraternity at their annual banquets and given each year by the men chosen head of the guild. Interesting are some painted and cut-glass beakers which were executed for the Jewish Burial Society, the **ḥevra kaddisha*, in some German and Bohemian communities. Several such beakers survived, mostly in the Jewish Museum in Prague. Their most common decoration is the burial procession. One such beaker dated 1692 is now in the New York Jewish Museum (Fig. 5).

In modern times too Jews were prominent in the marketing and industrial production of Czechoslovakian glass, centered in Bohemia. In the period between the world wars there were many Jewish firms which produced sheet glass, plate glass and mirrors, as well as glass pastes for artificial jewelry. When Hitler occupied Czechoslovakia some of the leading Jewish producers of artificial gems and costume jewelery moved their firms to the United States.

ENGLAND. In the late 18th and 19th centuries Lazarus Jacobs (d. 1796) of Bristol and his son Isaac (d. 1833) were important glass manufacturers and merchants, the latter holding a royal appointment as glass manufacturers to George III (Fig. 7). They were especially celebrated for their opaque white, and the elegant royal blue glassware for which Bristol was famous. Another eminent Jewish glassmaker was Meyer Oppenheim, who came from Pressburg in Hungary. He invented a ruby flint glass which he produced in Birmingham from 1756 to 1775. A number of Jews were associated with the glass industry in Birmingham, where the lead glass used for artificial gems was known as "Jew's glass" in the middle of the 19th century.

THE UNITED STATES. The earliest known American glass cutter was a Jew named Lazarus Isaacs who arrived from England in 1773. He was employed by Stiegel at his factory at Manheim, Pennsylvania, where the first fine glassware in America was produced. Jews do not reappear in American glassmaking until the late 19th century, when Lazarus Straus and Sons of New York was a leading producer of high quality cut glass in the United States and Europe (see *Straus family).

ISRAEL. On their return to Ereẓ Israel, the Jews revived the glass industry on the Phoenician coast, where it existed in ancient times. In the late 19th century, the Baron de *Rothschild set up a glass factory at Tantura near the site of the Phoenician harbor of Dor to provide bottles for the nascent wine industry, and in 1934 Phoenicia, the Israel Glass Works, was founded in the Haifa Bay Area. Under the patronage of Baroness Bathsheva de Rothschild, a new style of art glass was evolved in the early 1960s, based on forms of the talmudic period.

From the end of the 19th century a school of primitive glass paintings developed in Safed, Jerusalem, and other centers. One of its later offsprings is the painter Shalom of Safed. Their subjects were *holy places, **Mizraḥ* panels, amulets, and biblical topics. [ED.]

Figure 8. Arab glassblowers at work in Hebron. Courtesy Government Press Office, Tel Aviv.

Bibliography: Mayer, Art, index s.v. *glass, glass blowing, glass bottle, glass cutters, glass makers, gold glasses;* Goodenough, 1 (1953), 168–77; 2 (1953), 108–119, 218; Krauss, Tal Arch, 2 (1911), 285–8; A. B. Engle, in: *Miscelanea de Estúdios Arabes y Hebráicos* (1969), 15–16; E. H. Bryrne, in: JAOS, 38 (1918), 176–87; C. J. Lamm, *Mittelalterliche Glaeser und Steinschnitt-Arbeiten aus dem Nahen Osten,* 1 (1930), 522–44 (a general bibliography); J. C. Pick, in: *The Jews of Czechoslovakia,* 1 (1968), 379–400; Roth, Art, 242–3, 355.

GLASS, MONTAGUE MARSDEN (1877–1934), U.S. humorist. Glass, who was born in Manchester, England, was taken to the U.S. at the age of 13. He studied and practiced law in New York but in 1909 abandoned his profession to become a full-time writer. The Jewish clients whom Glass met in his law office inspired a series of short stories which he began publishing in various magazines in 1908. The first collection, *Potash and Perlmutter,* appeared in 1910 and this was followed a year later by *Abe and Mawruss.* Though treated humorously, the two clothing manufacturers, Abe Potash and Morris Perlmutter, were sympathetically presented and their entertaining foibles and typically Jewish family virtues endeared them to Jewish readers. Both story collections became the basis of stage successes. The first *Potash and Perlmutter* play, produced in 1913, had long runs in New York and London. Glass also wrote *Elkan Lubliner—American* (1912), *Worrying Won't Win* (1918), and *You Can't Learn Them Nothing* (1930).

Bibliography: Waxman, Literature, 4 (1960[2]), 974–5; S. Liptzin, *Jew in American Literature* (1966), 116–7. [Jo.R.]

GLATSTEIN (Gladstone), JACOB (1896–), Yiddish poet, novelist, and critic. Glatstein was born in Lublin, Poland, and emigrated to the United States in 1914.

Glatstein started to write at an early age, but it was in the United States that his first poems appeared (in *Poezye,* 1919). Then he published his first book of verse, *Yankev Glatshteyn* ("Jacob Glatstein," 1921). In 1920, together with Aaron *Glanz-Leyeles and N. B. *Minkoff, Glatstein inaugurated the "Inzikhist," or introspectivist, tendency in American Yiddish poetry. Taking their name from the journal *In Zikh,* which was to appear irregularly from 1920 to 1939, and from the group anthology, *In Zikh, A Zamlung Introspektive Lider* (1920), the Inzikhistn announced their mission of revitalizing Yiddish poetry and making it truly contemporary.

In the historically important essay, "Introspectivism,"

which introduces the *In Zikh* anthology, the aims of the group are set forth. In contrast to the established poets, known as Di Yunge ("The Young Ones"), the introspectivists rejected decorum and formal elegance in favor of free verse whose rhythms were to be correlates of unique, individual experience. In their own day Di Yunge, too, had

Jacob Glatstein, U.S. Yiddish poet and writer.

been rebels: they had turned against didacticism, rhetoricism, and ideology in Yiddish literature; they had absorbed the currents of European symbolism, widened the range of subject matter, and cultivated formal perfection. The introspectivists appreciated many of their predecessors, yet cautioned against emulating any of them. Like their Anglo-American contemporaries, whose work they knew, they emphasized the concrete image and favored suggestion and association over direct statement and logical development. They distrusted metrical regularity and fixed patterns and sought to capture the rhythms of the human voice and of modern urban life. In their search for new forms and for a poetry of relevance and universality, they saw themselves as continuing the work begun by Di Yunge. The mood paintings of the latter, however, were to give way to a poetry fusing thought and feeling. Glatstein was from the outset the most talented of the introspectivists and one of the least bound by the group's dogmas. He abandoned his early strictures against rhyme and meter and experimented freely in a variety of forms. Yet his early rhythmic principle, striking imagery, use of suggestion and association, and partiality to prose and irony remained constant features of his poetic practice.

From his earliest poems onward Glatstein is the poet in love with his medium, the Yiddish language, which he not only uses but remakes and endlessly celebrates. No poet in Yiddish has been so richly inventive in coining new words and word combinations. No poet in Yiddish has had a better ear for folk idiom and, indeed, for the sound structure of Yiddish generally. Many of Glatstein's poems seem to grow out of the latent powers hidden in the shape, sound, and history of individual words.

The introspectivists early declared that a Yiddish poem was Jewish by virtue of its medium; no subject was barred. They often wrote on themes far removed from Jewish life. Yet there is relatively little strained cosmopolitanism in the early Glatstein, who even before the ominous pre-Hitler years wrote poems dense with traditional allusion and echo. The war years and the Holocaust transformed Glatstein into one of the great elegists of Eastern European Jewish life. From about 1938 onward, Glatstein's major poetic purpose was to meditate on, to mourn, and to celebrate a shattered way of life. In *"A Gute Nakht, Velt"* ("Good Night, World"), he bitterly rejects European culture and defiantly and joyously declares his return to the narrow confines of traditional Jewish life. No Yiddish poem has aroused as much comment as this seemingly xenophobic and anti-universalist poem of execration and affirmation. Yet no careful reader will fail to read it in dramatic terms. Neither in this nor in any other of his poems is Glatstein an obscurantist. It is often in his most Jewish poems such as the Reb *Naḥman of Bratzlav cycle that his universalism is most pronounced.

Glatstein's distinction rests primarily on his poetry: *Yankev Glatshteyn* (1921); *Fraye Ferzn* (1926), *Kredos* (1929), *Yidishtaytshn* (1937), *Gedenklider* (1943), *Shtralendike Yidn* (poems, 1946), *Dem Tatns Shotn* (1953), *Fun Mayn Gantser Mi* (poems, 1965), *Di Freyd fun Yidishn Vort* (1961), and *A Yid fun Lublin* (1966). However, he was also a distinguished writer of both imaginative and critical prose. There are no novelistic travel narratives in Yiddish literature comparable to *Ven Yash Iz Geforen* ("The Peregrinations of Yash," 1938) and *Ven Yash iz Gekumen* ("When Yash Arrived," 1940; Eng., *Homecoming at Twilight*, 1962). These loosely autobiographical works, part of a projected trilogy, deal with the author's visit to his birthplace prior to the outbreak of World War II and are notable for their style and their brooding sense of impending catastrophe. *Emil un Karl* (1940), a novel of a Jewish and a Christian boy in Hitler-occupied Austria, is particularly suited to the young reader.

As columnist for the New York Yiddish daily *The Day-Morning Journal* and as regular contributor of the column *In Tokh Genumen* to the weekly *Idisher Kemfer* (for the years 1945–57) and other periodicals, Glatstein commented on virtually every significant event in Jewish literary and cultural life and on world literature generally. As critic of Yiddish literature he exerted great influence and helped to raise the level of critical awareness both among writers and readers. Occasionally, as in his essays on Frost and Yeats, his critical acumen failed him. His essays and reviews appeared in a series of volumes entitled *In Tokh Genumen* (1947; 1956; 1960), continued in *Mit Mayne Fartogbikher* (1963) and *Oyf Greyte Temes* (1967).

Jacob Glatstein, seated between Itzik Manger and Raizel Zhichlinski, welcomed by Yiddish writers in Paris, 1950. Among those standing are (seen left to right) Shmerle Kaczerginsky (second), Joseph Wolf (fifth), Abrah Zak (eighth), Israel Ashendorf (eleventh), and Leib Rochman (last). Courtesy L. Rochman, Jerusalem.

Translations into English: I. Howe and E. Greenberg, *A Treasury of Yiddish Poetry* (New York, 1969), 245–256, 326–337.

Bibliography: M. Starkman (ed.), *Hemshekh Antologye fun Amerikaner-Yidisher Dikhtung* (1945), 17–24; D. Sadan, in: J. Glatstein, *Mi-Kol Amali: Shirim u-Fo'emot* (1964), 28–32; bibliographical notes; LNYL, 2 (1958), 256–61; includes bibliography; E. Greenberg, *Yankev Glatshteyns Freyd fun Yidishn Vort* (1964); Ch. Faerstein, in: *Judaism*, 14 (1965), 414–31; S. Gutman, in: *Traditsye un Banayung* (1967), 262–9; S. D. Singer, in: *Dikhter un Prozayker* (1959), 67–83. [L.P.]

GLATZER, NAHUM NORBERT (1903–), scholar, teacher, and editor. Glatzer was born in Lemberg (Lvov), and pursued his higher education in Germany, and at the

Breuer Yeshivah in Frankfort on the Main (1920–22). He became a disciple and associate of Franz *Rosenzweig, whose life and work so influenced him that he decided to devote himself to scholarship rather than pursue a career in the rabbinate. In 1932 he succeeded another mentor, Martin *Buber, in the University of Frankfort's chair of Jewish philosophy and ethics. In 1933 Glatzer left Germany

Nahum Glatzer, Judaic scholar. Courtesy Brandeis University, Waltham, Mass.

for Israel, where he taught at Bet Sefer Reali in Haifa. From 1938 he was in the United States, teaching at several colleges before joining the faculty of Brandeis University in 1950; he was professor and chairman of the Department of Near Eastern and Judaic Studies there from 1956. He served as editorial adviser to *Schocken Books, where he was chief editor (1945–51), and was a director of the Leo Baeck Institute from 1956.

In his doctoral dissertation, *Untersuchungen zur Geschichtslehre der Tannaiten* (1933), Glatzer maintained that the rabbis of the first and second centuries C.E. retained their faith in the God of history in the face of apocalyptic tendencies and the consequent denigration of this world. Glatzer's *Geschichte der Talmudischen Zeit* (1937) elaborates and continues his earlier work. He wrote a number of studies on particular problems of talmudic history. Glatzer also wrote extensively on the history of 19th-century Jewry, especially on the history of the Wissenschaft des Judentums. His book *Franz Rosenzweig: His Life and Thought* (1953, 1961[2]) is considered the definitive volume on Rosenzweig. Glatzer edited more than a dozen anthologies, which are widely used in teaching Jewish history and ideas. Among his many works are *Hillel the Elder* (1956, 1962); *Anfaenge des Judentums* (1966); *The Rest is Commentary* (1961, 1969[2]); *Faith and Knowledge* (1963, 1969[2]); *Dynamics of Emancipation* (1965, 1969[2]), *The Dimensions of Job* (1969); he edited *A Jewish Reader* (1961, 1966[2]), *Hammer on the Rock* (1962), *Parables and Paradoxes* by Franz Kafka (1961), and *The Essential Philo* (1970).

Bibliography: A. Altmann, in: *Judaism,* 12 (1963), 195–202, contains a list of Glatzer's writings. [A.L.S.]

GLAZER, NATHAN (1923–). U.S. sociologist. Born in New York, Glazer was a member of the editorial staff of *Commentary* (1945–53), urban sociologist with the Housing and Home Finance Administration in Washington, D.C., and lecturer and instructor at the Universities of Chicago and California and at Bennington College. From 1963 he was professor of sociology at the University of California at Berkeley. Glazer coauthored with David Riesman and Reuel Denney *The Lonely Crowd* (1950), with David Riesman *Faces in the Crowd* (1952), and with Daniel Patrick Moynihan *The Social Basis of American Communism* (1961). He also wrote *Beyond the Melting Pot* (1963), an analysis of the persistence of ethnic groups—Negroes, Puerto Ricans, Jews, Italians, and Irish—in the New York metropolitan area, and *Remembering the Answers* (1970). Glazer published numerous papers and articles on housing problems and on problems of American ethnic groups, including papers on the specific problems of American Jews; the latter appeared chiefly in *Commentary.* He wrote *American Judaism* (1957) and also contributed the article "Social Characteristics of American Jews" to *Jews: Their History, Culture and Religion 1694–1735* (vol. 2 (1960[3]), ed. by L. Finkelstein).

Bibliography: *Contemporary Authors,* 5–6 (1963), 179–80.
[W.J.C.]

GLAZER, SIMON (1878–1938), U.S. Orthodox rabbi and author. Glazer, who was born in Kovno, Lithuania, was ordained in 1896. He went to the U.S. in 1897 and subsequently served as rabbi in several cities in the Midwest before becoming chief rabbi of the United Synagogues of Montreal and Quebec (1907–18). He moved to New York in 1923 and was rabbi of Beth Hamidrash Hagadol (1923–27); Temple Beth-El, Brooklyn (1927–30); and the Maimonides Synagogue (1930–38). Glazer was a founder (1907) and the first editor of the Yiddish daily, the *Canadian Jewish Eagle (Keneder Adler)* and was active in rabbinic and Zionist organizations. His published works include: *Jews of Iowa* (1904); *Guide of Judaism* (1917); *The Palestine Resolution* (1922); *History of Israel* (6 vols., 1930), a reworking of Graetz's *History of the Jews;* and *Visions of Isaiah* (1937), a collection of sermons.

His son, B. BENEDICT GLAZER (1902–1952), was a prominent Reform rabbi in the U.S. He was rabbi of Temple Beth El in Detroit, Michigan, from 1942 until his death.
[ED.]

GLICENSTEIN, ENRICO (Henoch; 1870–1942), sculptor, painter, and print maker. The son of a tombstone carver, Glicenstein was born in Turek, Poland, and began studying for the rabbinate. After working as a sign painter and wood-carver in Lodz he went to study art in Munich, where he won the Prix de Rome in 1894 and 1897. He went to live in Italy in 1897 with his wife, Helen, daughter of the painter Samuel *Hirschenberg, but had to leave the country in 1928 because of his refusal to join the Fascist Party and settled in New York. He died in an automobile accident. Glicenstein, who had been elected an honorary mem-

"The Player" by Enrico Glicenstein, mahogany, 1935–40. Height 1¾ ft. (58.5 cm.). New York, Brooklyn Museum.

ber of the Société des Beaux-Arts in 1906 on Rodin's recommendation, had one-man shows in nearly all the art centers of the world including the 15th Venice Biennale (1928). Glicenstein was predominantly a carver. The majority of his works were done in wood, mostly oak or walnut. Spurning mechanical aids, he preferred the arduous, time-consuming method of cutting directly into his material. He created stern monolithic pieces, in solid, sturdy forms, devoid of any unnecessary detail. Like the expressionists, he felt free to exaggerate, to abbreviate, to elongate, and to distort, although he showed that a sculpture can be expressive while maintaining a firm equilibrium between form and content. Form is maintained, too, in Glicenstein's drawings, etchings, and his few paintings. As a draftsman, he was never indecisive. Likewise, the mastery of a knowledgable hand is seen in the prints, cut with a needle into copper by vigorous strokes that aim straight to the core of a face, action, or scene. Among his dry points, more than 60 plates for the *Book of Samuel* must be singled out for mention. Among the outstanding men of his time who sat for Glicenstein's portrait busts were Ludwig *Mond, Hermann *Cohen, Gabriele D'Annunzio, Sir Israel *Gollancz, Ignace Paderewski, and Franklin D. Roosevelt. His works were acquired by many museums and a Glicenstein Museum containing his library was established in Safed, Israel. His son, EMANUEL ROMANO (1897–), was a painter. Born in Rome, he changed his name and in 1928 emigrated to New York with his family. Romano was best known for his portraits but also did murals for many buildings. He was an outstanding colorist.

Bibliography: J. Cassou, *Glicenstein* (Eng., 1958), album with introd. by J. Cassou; F. Orestano, *Enrico Glicenstein e la sua arte* (1926). [A.W.]

GLICK, HIRSH (1922–1944), Yiddish poet. Born in Vilna, he began to write in Hebrew but, under the influence of the Yiddish poets of the "Young Vilna" group, turned to Yiddish. In 1939 he edited and published four issues of *Yungvald,* an organ of young Vilna poets. His own poems *Lider un Poemes* were published posthumously in 1953.

Glick spent the war years in the Vilna ghetto and in various forced labor camps; he escaped while being transferred to the camp at Goldfield (Estonia) but all trace of him was then lost. He is known primarily for his stirring poem *"Mir Zaynen Do,"* which became the battle song of the Vilna partisan fighters and after the war was the hymn sung at gatherings commemorating the Jewish struggle against the Nazis. The poem was translated into Hebrew (by A. Shlonsky), English, and other languages. Glick is one of the heroes of Perez *Markish's monumental poem *"Milkhome."*

Bibliography: LNYL, 2 (1958), 271–3; N. and M. Ausubel (eds.), *A Treasury of Jewish Poetry* (1957), 270, 445; N. Meisel, *Hirsch Glick un Zayn Lid "Zog Nisht Keyn Mol"* (1949); M. Dvorjetski, *Hirshke Glick . . .* (Yid., 1966). [E.SCH.]

GLID, NANDOR (1924–), Yugoslav sculptor. Glid was born in the town of Subotica. During the Nazi occupation he was in a forced labor camp and later fought with the Yugoslav partisans. After the war he studied at the Academy of Fine Arts in Belgrade. He began as a portrait sculptor but later worked on monuments to commemorate concentration camp victims. He was commissioned to carry out his projects for monuments in the former Nazi camps of Mauthausen and Dachau. The monument in Subotica to a group of anti-Nazis (mainly Jews) who were hanged there is also his work. He has exhibited monotype graphics on war and camp subjects.

Memorial by Nandor Glid at the site of Dachau concentration camp, erected 1968. Bronze, 21×52 ft. (6.3×16 m.).

Bibliography: A. Rieth, *To the Victims of Tyranny—Den Opfern der Gewalt* (1968), 45–47, pls. 53, 75. [ZD.L.]

GLIÈRE, REINHOLD MORITZEVICH (1874–1956), Soviet Russian composer and conductor. He was born in Kiev where his father, following a family tradition, was a maker of musical instruments. Glière began composing at 14, entered the Kiev Music School in 1891 and the Moscow Conservatory in 1894. He taught for some time in St. Petersburg, spent two years (1905–07) in Berlin, and became director of the Kiev Conservatory in 1914. In 1920 he went to the Moscow Conservatory as professor and held this post until his death. Glière was a prolific composer. He studied the folk music of various national groups and used folklore elements in his compositions. His symphonic works reflect Russian traditional harmony. Prokofieff, Miaskovsky, and Mossolov were among his pupils. A tireless conductor, Glière appeared in remote regions of the country. From 1938 to 1948 he was chairman of the Union of Soviet Composers. His major works are: three symphonies (1900, 1907, and 1911), several operas, among them *Shah-Senem* (1923–34) on an Azerbaijan subject, and *Rachel* (1943) after Maupassant's novel. His ballets include: *Cleopatra* (1925), *Red Poppy* (1927), *The Bronze Horseman* (1949), and *Taras Bulba* (1952). His concerto for harp and orchestra (1938), and especially the concerto for voice and orchestra (1942) won great popularity. He composed chamber music, songs, and piano works. Glière received many awards including orders of Lenin and the Stalin Prize.

Bibliography: I. F. Belza, *R. M. Glière* (Russ., 1962); N. E. Petrova, *Reyngold Moritsevich Glière* (1962); S. V. Katanova, *Balety R. M. Gliera* (1960); R. M. Glière, *Statyi, vospominaniya, materialy* (1965); M.G.G., s.v.; Rieman-Gurlitt, s.v.; Grove, Dict, s.v. [M.GO.]

GLIKIN, MOSHE (1874–), Zionist and *yishuv* leader. Born in Moscow, in 1892 Glikin went to Ereẓ Israel, where he worked as a laborer at Ein Zeitim. He returned to Russia in 1894 and later studied in Leipzig, where he was secretary of a student Zionist association. He attended the Fifth and Sixth *Zionist Congresses and voted against the *Uganda

Jewish Gold Glass from Rome (third to fourth century C.E.)

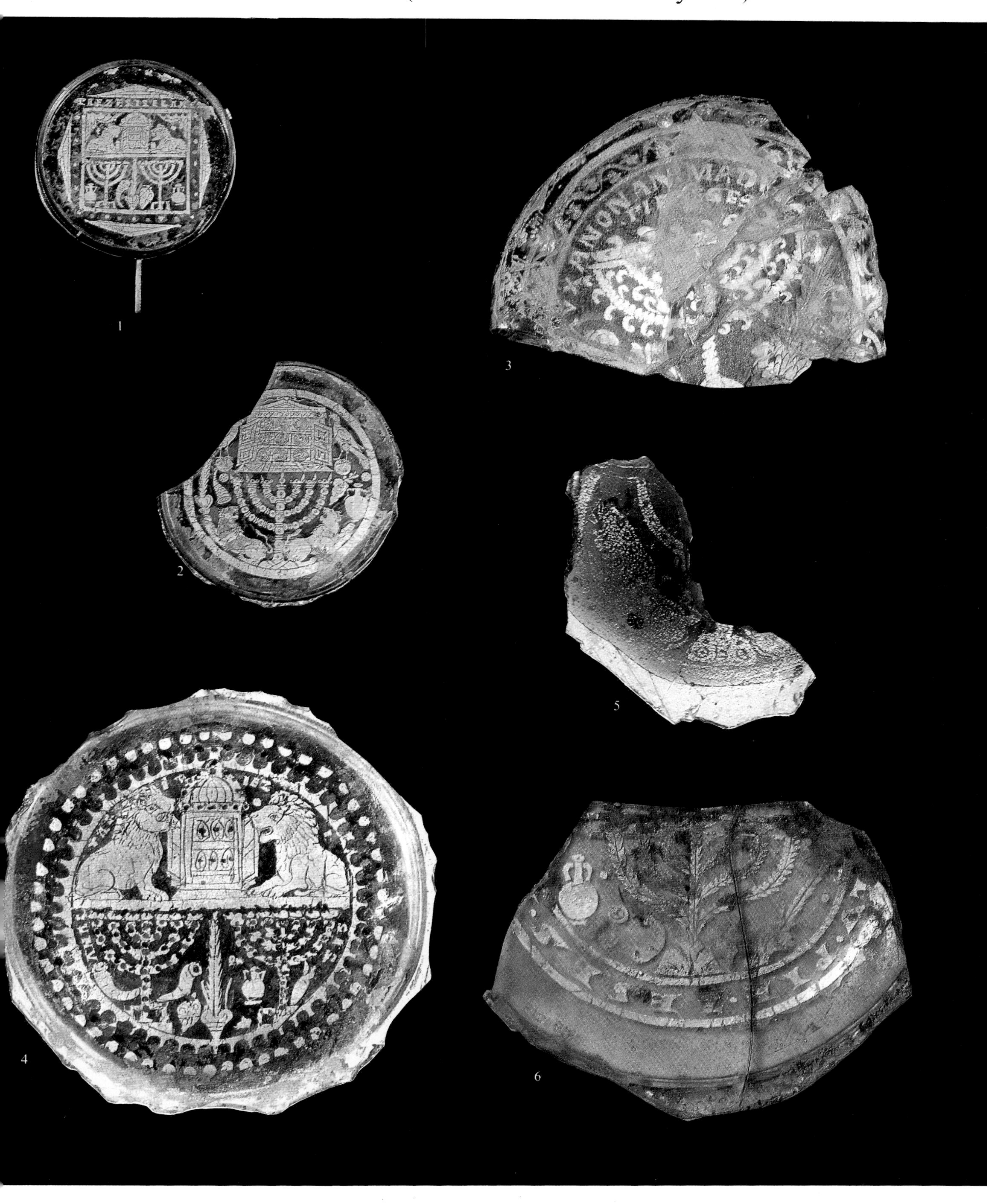

PLATE 1. Jerusalem, Israel Museum. Diameter 9 cm. (3½ in.). Photo David Harris, Jerusalem. PLATE 2. Jerusalem, Israel Museum. Diameter 11.4 cm. (4½ in.). Photo David Harris, Jerusalem. PLATE 3. Cologne, Roemisches Germanisches Museum, Inv. N.6254, Morey 426. Diameter 5.5 cm. (2 in.). PLATE 4. Rome, Vatican Library, Morey 114. Diameter 11 cm. (4⅓ in.). Photo Leonard von Matt, Switzerland. PLATE 5. Wuerzburg University, Martin von Wagner- Museum. Maximum diameter 4.3 cm. (1¾ in.). PLATE 6. London, British Museum, E.C. 615, Morey 346. Maximum diameter 7.8 cm. (3 in.).

PLATE 7. New York, Metropolitan Museum of Art, Morey 458. Maximum diameter 9 mm. ($\frac{3}{4}$ in.). PLATE 8. Oxford, Ashmolean Museum, Pusey House Coll., Morey 359. Diameter 8.7 cm. ($3\frac{1}{3}$ in.). Photo Ashmolean Museum. PLATE 9. Rome, Vatican Library, Morey 116. Diameter 6.4 cm. ($2\frac{1}{2}$ in.). PLATE 10. Rome, Vatican Library, Morey 115. Diameter 10 cm. (4 in.). PLATE 11. Berlin, Staatliche Museen, Fruehchristlich-Byzantinische Sammlung, Inv. J. 6700. Maximum diameter 10.5 cm. (4 in.). PLATE 12. Rome, Vatican Library, Morey 173. Diameter 2.5 cm. (1 in.). Photo Leonard von Matt, Switzerland.

scheme. He directed the office of the Zionist *Democratic Fraction in Berlin in 1902 and later worked at the offices of various Zionist periodicals in Russia. In 1908 Glikin returned to Ereẓ Israel, where he worked first in the Atid edible oil factory in Haifa and then at the Bezalel School of Arts and Crafts in Jerusalem. From 1910 he was director of *Migdal Farm. During World War I, he was exiled by the Ottoman authorities to Nazareth. In 1920 he was a delegate to the first Asefat ha-Nivḥarim ("the Elected Assembly" of the *yishuv*) and was a founder of the Hadar ha-Karmel, the new Jewish quarter of Haifa, where he then lived.

Bibliography: I. Klausner, *Oppoziẓyah le-Herzl* (1960), index; Tidhar, 1 (1947), 479–80. [I.K.]

GLINYANY (Pol. **Gliniany;** Yid. **Gline**), small town in Lvov oblast, Ukranian S. S. R. Some Jews lived there in the 12th century. An organized community existed from 1474. The Jews of Glinyany suffered during the Tatar raids and Cossack massacres in 1624, 1638, and 1657, and particularly in 1648–49 (see *Chmielnicki). The first synagogue, built of wood, was erected there in 1704. Glinyany was a stronghold of the Shabbateans and later of the Frankists (see Jacob *Frank); in 1758 King Augustus III assigned Glinyany to the latter as one of their places of residence before baptism. In the 18th century Glinyany became a center of Ḥasidism. A Jewish-German school in Glinyany, established under Joseph II after Austrian annexation of Galicia, remained open until 1806. A public school in the name of Baron Hirsch existed there from 1816 to 1914. The center of Zionist activity was a club, "National Home," founded in 1906. The community numbered 688 in 1765, 1,708 in 1880 (out of a total population of 3,695), 2,177 in 1900 (out of 4,906), 1,679 in 1921 (out of 4,355), 1,906 in 1931, and 2,300 in 1939. [Ed.]

Holocaust Period. Under Soviet rule (1939–41), the communal bodies were disbanded and all political activity outlawed. In 1940 the former political leaders and important businessmen were arrested. In spring 1941 young Jews were drafted into the Soviet army and placed in special work units. The city fell to the Germans in July 1941. On July 27 a pogrom broke out, led by the Ukrainian populace in which the Jews were murdered and robbed, and their sacred literature was burned. A provisional Jewish committee was set up in an attempt to prevent further persecution. The community had to pay a fine of 1,000,000 zlotys, but could not raise such a sum. Emissaries were sent to the German authorities in Peremyshlyany in an effort to lower the sum and delay payment, but met with partial success. The Jews of Glinyany were sent to a labor camp in Kurwice. The *Judenrat, headed by Aaron Hochberg, considerably assisted the community until the period between Nov. 20, 1942, and Dec. 1, 1942, when the remaining Jews were interned in Peremyshlyany ghetto. They perished there when it was liquidated in the summer of 1943. The city of Glinyany was taken by Soviet forces in August 1944, at which time only 20 Jewish survivors were found there. These left Glinyany in 1946. [Ar.W.]

Bibliography: M. Balaban, in: YE, 6 (c. 1910), 586; *Bleter far Geshikhte*, 4 pt. 3 (1953), 163; H. Halpern (ed.), *Megiles Gline* (1950); *Khurbn Gline* (1964); A. Korech (ed.), *Kehillat Glina 1473–1943, Toledoteha ve-Ḥurbanah* (1950).

GLIWICE (Ger. **Gleiwitz**), city in Silesia, Poland. It passed to Prussia in 1742, reverting to Poland in 1945. A "Jewish Street" is mentioned there in the Middle Ages. In 1587 the city council opposed further Jewish settlement and those already resident probably left soon afterward. In 1715 a Jew acquired the liquor privileges in Gliwice and built a home there; he converted to Christianity, and in 1753 opposed the acceptance of additional Jewish residents. However, the community grew from 62 in 1795, to 178 in 1812 (6.9% of the total population), and numbered 2,009 (16.5%) in 1867, 1,962 (3.17%) in 1905, and 2,200 (2%) in 1921, the industrialized city having grown much more rapidly than the Jewish community. The first synagogue, in use from 1812, was replaced in 1861. In 1932 the community maintained a *mikveh*, library, school (100 pupils), home for the aged (founded 1926), seven charitable and nine social organizations. [Ed.]

Holocaust and Contemporary Periods. There were 1,300 Jews living in Gliwice in 1932. When the Nazis came to power in 1933 the community was subjected to the anti-Semitic program adopted throughout Germany. On Nov. 10, 1938 (**Kristallnacht*), the Nazis burned down the large synagogue, and arrested all male Jews between the ages of 18 and 60. After two days of torture in prison, they were deported to *Buchenwald concentration camp where some died. The rest were sent home after three or six months' imprisonment. All the women were forced to do hard, humiliating work in the city. Jews were also compelled to leave their homes and settle in densely crowded living quarters with a minimum of one family per room. In May 1942, 586 Jews were deported to *Auschwitz, where all died. The several hundred who remained were liberated on Jan. 26, 1945, when the Soviet army captured the city. All these survivors left Gliwice after the war. Subsequently a small number of Jews from Poland settled there. There were 200 Jews living in the town in 1950. The new community had its own producers' cooperative (1962). A number emigrated after the Six-Day War. [S.Kr.]

Bibliography: B. Nietsche, *Geschichte der Stadt Gleiwitz* (1886), 599–606; FJW (1932–33), 104; M. Grinwald, in: *Zion*, 9 (1944), 143–5; S. Wenzel, *Juedische Buerger und kommunale Selbstverwaltung in preussischen Staedten, 1808–1845* (1967), 265; AJYB (1962).

°**GLOBOCNIK, ODILO** (1904–1945), Nazi executioner of Polish Jewry. Born in Trieste, Italy, Globocnik joined the Nazi Party in Austria in 1922 and was nominated *Gauleiter* of Vienna in reward for his part in the preparation of Austria's annexation in 1938, but was later dismissed for embezzlement. In September 1939, *Himmler appointed him S.S. and Police Leader of the Lublin district. He organized Jewish slave labor camps as industrial enterprises of the S.S., and in April 1942 he was put in charge of "Action Reinhard" (see *Holocaust, General Survey) to annihilate Polish Jewry and confiscate their property. He organized the death camps of *Belzec, *Sobibor, *Majdanek, and *Treblinka. Irregularities in his administration of confiscated Jewish property and conflicts of authority with Hans *Frank led to Globocnik's transfer to Trieste as Higher S.S. and Police Leader of the formerly Italian-occupied parts of Yugoslavia. He is believed to have poisoned himself in May 1945.

Bibliography: R. Hoess, *Commandant of Auschwitz* (1960); J. Tenenbaum, *Race and Reich* (1956), index; R. M. W. Kempner, *Ha-Mikẓo'a Hashmadah* (1963), index; J. Wulf, *Das Dritte Reich und seine Vollstrecker* (1961); Hilberg, *Destruction of the European Jews* (1961), index; Reitlinger, *Final Solution* (1953), index. [Y.Re.]

GLOGAU (Pol. **Głogó**), town in Silesia, W. Poland. Jews are first mentioned there in 1280. In 1299 the duke of Gross-Glogau granted them a charter of privileges. The community possessed a cemetery, a synagogue, inhabited a "Jew's lane," and engaged in moneylending, and the cloth and fur trade. The Jews of Glogau escaped persecution during the *Black Death, 1348–49, but in 1401 two Jews were burned to death for an alleged *Host desecration, and the synagogue and other buildings were destroyed in a riot by the populace in 1442. The community subsequently recovered and prospered until 1488, when Duke Hans, after first taxing them heavily, expelled them. Nevertheless, a few Jews continued to live outside the city bounds. After the expulsion of Silesian Jewry in 1582 the family of Israel Benedict was allowed to live in Glogau and received a letter of privilege in 1598. Protected by this, other members of his family and numerous fictitious relatives flocked to the city from Poland and Prague. A Jewish quarter was organized and a synagogue built in 1636. Despite the sufferings caused by the Thirty Years' War, the plague, a general conflagration in 1678, and local opposition, the community grew from 81 families in 1673 to 1,564 persons in 1725. After it returned to Prussia in 1745. *Frederick II confirmed the limited rights of the community in 1743. One of the most prosperous communities in Central Europe, Glogau Jewry overshadowed that of *Breslau. Since the beginning of the 18th century, the community possessed its own seal. The Jewish population gradually outgrew the confines of the Jewish quarter and totaled 2,000 in 1791 (one-fifth of Silesian Jewry). In the 19th century, the community decreased from 1,516 in 1812 (12% of the total population) to 1,010 in 1880 (5.4%), and 716 in 1900. Solomon and Eduard *Munk, Michael *Sachs, and David and Paulus *Cassel were born in Glogau. Solomon *Maimon was buried in the old cemetery. The community remained approximately the same size (around 600) until 1933. Many left during the Nazi persecutions and their numbers had declined to 120 by 1939. The community was not reestablished after World War II.

Bibliography: R. Berndt, *Geschichte der Juden in Gross-Glogau* (1873); M. Brann, *Geschichte der Juden in Schlesien* (6 vols. (1896–1917), passim; Brilling, in: *Juedische Zeitung fuer Ostdeutschland*, 8 (Nov. 6, 1931); FJW, 97; Germ Jud, 2 (1968), 279–80; Blaschke, in: *Ost und West*, 16 (1916), 185–92.
[Ed.]

GLOGAU, JEHIEL MICHAEL BEN ASHER LEMMEL HA-LEVI (c. 1740–1818), rabbi in Burgenland (Austria). Glogau took his name from his birthplace, where his father served as *dayyan*, before becoming rabbi in Eisenstadt. Around 1780 Glogau served as preacher of the *ḥevra kaddisha* of Vienna. On the death of his father in 1789 he succeeded him at Eisenstadt. He was in halakhic correspondence with Moses *Sofer, who held him in high esteem (*Ḥatam Sofer* OḤ, nos. 40, 80). His son Moses (d. 1837), who served as rabbi of Liben near Prague and then in Deutschkreutz (Burgenland), published the commentaries on *aggadah* of his father and grandfather together with his own work entitled *Ḥut ha-Meshullash bi-She'arim* (Vienna, 1821). The work contains sermons on the weekly readings of the Torah, each consisting of three parts: the sermon of his grandfather, entitled *Sha'ar Asher*, of his father, entitled *Sha'ar ha-Mayim*, and his own, *Sha'ar ha-Katan*.

Bibliography: M. Markbrieter, *Beitraege zur Geschichte der juedischen Gemeinde Eisenstadt* (1908), 53f.; J. J. Greenwald, *Ha-Yehudim be-Hungaryah* (1913), 73f.; P. Z. Schwartz, *Shem ha-Gedolim me-Ereẓ Hagar*, 1 (1913), 45a no. 127, 3 (1915), 17a no. 6; B. Wachstein, *Die Inschriften des alten Judenfriedhofes in Wien*, 2 (1917), 194 n. 1, 564 n. 17; idem, *Die Inschriften des alten Judenfriedhofs in Eisenstadt* (1922), 152 no. 426, 188 no. 594; idem, *Urkunden und Akten zur Geschichte der Juden in Eisenstadt* (1926), 469–71, 714; Patai, in: *Arim ve-Immahot be-Yisrael*, 1 (1946), 54.
[Y.Ho.]

GLOTZ, GUSTAVE (1862–1935), French historian. He was born at Haguenau and taught at the *lycée* in Nancy (1886–92), and Paris (1892–1907). In 1907 he became professor of Greek history at the Sorbonne. In 1920 he became a member of the Académie des Inscriptions et Belles Lettres, and in 1928 president of the *Institut de France*. Well known as a French patriot and as a fine scholar and a popular teacher, he was honored at his Sorbonne jubilee in 1932, when the *Mélanges Gustave Glotz* (2 vols., including bibliography) was presented to him. His work is notable for its special study of ancient Greek social and economic life. He directed the publication of the *Histoire générale*, in which the first three volumes of the *Histoire grecque* (1925–1936) are his work in collaboration with Robert Cohen. He contributed to the *Dictionnaire des antiquités grecques et romaines*. His other works include *Etudes sociales et juridiques sur l'antiquité grecque* (1906); *Le travail dans la Grèce ancienne* (1920; Eng. 1926); *La civilisation égéenne* (1923, Eng. 1925); and *La cité grecque* (1928; Eng., 1929). He was an editor of the *Revue des Etudes Grecques*.
[Ir.M.]

GLOUCESTER, county town in N. England. Its Jewish community is first mentioned in the financial records of 1158–59. It was again mentioned in connection with an alleged ritual murder in 1168. The Jewry was situated in the present East Gate Street, the synagogue being on the north side. Josce of Gloucester, a prominent financier under Henry II, apparently financed an illegal raid on Ireland. Under John, the community suffered greatly from royal exaction. Gloucester possessed an **archa*. It was one of the dower-towns of Queen Dowager Eleanor from which the Jews were expelled in 1275. The members of the community, first transferred to *Bristol, were afterward scattered. A small community was reestablished at the close of the 18th century but decayed in the middle of the 19th century. The last survivor died in 1886.

Bibliography: J. Jacobs, *Jews of Angevin England* (1893), 45–47, 376; Rigg-Jenkinson, Exchequer, passim; H. G. Richardson, *English Jewry under Angevin Kings* (1960), passim; C. Roth, *Rise of Provincial Jewry* (1950), 67–70; Roth, England, index.
[C.R.]

GLUBOKOYE (Pol. **Głębokie**), small town in Belorussian S.S.R., in Poland until 1793 and from 1921 to 1945. Jews are mentioned there in the middle of the 16th century. Within the framework of the Council of Lithuania (see *Councils of the Lands) Glubokoye came under the jurisdiction of the *Smorgon community. Samuel *Mohilever was rabbi there from 1848 to 1856. The community numbered 755 in 1766, 3,917 in 1897 (70% of the total population), and 2,844 in 1921 (63%).
[Ed.]

Holocaust Period. Between October 1939 and June 1941 Glubokoye belonged to the Soviet-occupied zone. In the early days of the Nazi occupation (July 1941), several Jews accused of being Communists were put to death. When many of the prisoners in the Soviet jail of nearby Berezwiecz were found dead the blame was placed on the Jews and a pogrom was prevented only after intercession by R. Josef Ha-Levi Katz. In early November 1941 a ghetto was set up in the town and the Jews there were grouped into two categories: those fit for work, and the sick and the aged. Jews from the nearby villages of Szarkowczyzna, Postawy, and Plissa were also brought to the ghetto and its population reached 6,000. On March 25, 1942, 105 Jews were arrested and shot. Following this *Aktion*, the youth tried to organize and make contact with the partisans. On June 19, 1942, about 2,500 Jews classified "unfit for work" were murdered in the Borek forest. In 1943 when Soviet partisans attacked targets in the vicinity of Glubokoye the Germans, fearing that contact might be established between the ghetto and the partisans, began to deport the Jews and liquidate the ghetto. On Aug. 20, 1943, members of the *Judenrat* were ordered to organize the Jews for deportation. Upon entering the ghetto, the Germans met with armed resistance by Jewish groups. Some Jews tried to break through the siege, but few succeeded. In order to break the resistance and to prevent a mass escape, the Germans set the ghetto on fire. Jews from Glubokoye who managed to escape joined partisan units, including the Kaganovich unit. About 60 survived the Holocaust. The community was not reconstituted after World War II. [AR.W.]

Bibliography: *Lite*, 1 (1951), 1551–53; *Yahadut Lita*, 1 (1959), index; Yad Vashem Archives.

GLUCK, ALMA (born **Reba Fiersohn;** 1884–1938), U.S. soprano. Born in Bucharest, Rumania, she was taken to New York as a child. When she left school she worked as a secretary, and it was not until her marriage

Alma Gluck, U.S. soprano. From M. Davenport, *Too Strong for Fantasy*, London, 1968.

to Bernard Gluck, in 1906, that she began taking singing lessons. In 1909 she obtained an engagement at the Metropolitan Opera, New York, where she remained for four years. Subsequently, after studying in Berlin with Marcella Sembrich, she concentrated on concert work. Her great success was enhanced by her recordings. In 1914, having divorced her first husband, she married the violinist Efrem Zimbalist. Her home in New York became the meeting place of distinguished musicians and she was a principal figure in the founding of the American Guild of Musical Artists. Her daughter by her first marriage became the novelist Marcia *Davenport.

Bibliography: M. Davenport, *Too Strong for Fantasy* (1967), index; G. Saleski, *Famous Musicians of Jewish Origin* (1949), 587–9; Baker, Biog Dict. [ED.]

GLUCKMAN, HENRY (1893–), South African physician and politician who was the only Jew to hold a cabinet post in the Union of South Africa. He represented a Johannesburg division in Parliament from 1938 until 1958, when he retired from politics to devote himself to industrial interests. Largely as a result of his work as chairman of the government's National Health Services Commission (1942–44), whose report influenced future health policy, the prime minister, General J.C. Smuts, in 1945 appointed him minister of health and housing. He held this portfolio until 1948 when the government went out of office. Gluckman was chairman of the Central Health Services and Hospitals Coordinating Council (1943–45) and of the National Nutrition Council (1945–48). He was a regional vice-president of the World Parliamentary Association. He served in the South African Medical Corps in both world wars and was president of the National War Memorial Health Foundation, and vice-president of the Jewish Ex-Service League.

Gluckman was an executive member of the Jewish Board of Deputies and vice-president of the Zionist Federation. Particularly interested in the Hebrew University, he was on its board of governors and was chairman and life-president of the South African Friends of the Hebrew University. [L.HO.]

GLUCKMAN, MAX (1911–), social anthropologist. Born and educated in Johannesburg, South Africa, and Rhodes scholar to Oxford, 1934, he was assistant anthropologist to the Rhodes Livingston Institute in North Rhodesia (now Zambia) from 1939 to 1941 and its director from 1941 to 1947. In 1947 he was appointed lecturer in social anthropology at Oxford and in 1949 professor of social anthropology at the University of Manchester. He did field research in Zululand from 1936 to 1938; in Barotseland, from 1939 to 1941; Tonga in North Rhodesia in 1944; and Lamba in 1946. Gluckman became an expert on African societies, the political systems of tribal society, and more generally political anthropology. His *Custom and Conflict in Africa* (1955) paid special attention to cultural change and the significance of conflict, which he regarded as a basic element in society. He was chairman of the Association of Social Anthropologists of the British Commonwealth from 1962 to 1966. He wrote *Administrative Organization of the Barotse Native Authorities* (1943); *Rituals of Rebellion in South-East Africa* (1954); *Custom and Conflict in Africa* (1955); *Order and Rebellion in Tribal Africa* (1963); *Politics, Law, and Ritual in Tribal Society* (1965); and *The Ideas in Barotse Jurisprudence* (1965). [E.FI.]

GLUCKSMAN, HARRY L. (1889–1938), U.S. communal worker. Glucksman was born in New York. A founder of the Jewish center movement in the U.S. and Canada, he joined the *National Jewish Welfare Board in 1917 when it was organized as a war service agency, and was executive director for 19 years until his death. Previously, Glucksman had served in executive capacities with the Jewish Big Brothers (N.Y.), the 92nd Street YMHA (N.Y.), and the New Orleans YMHA. An able administrator and organizer, Glucksman was widely consulted on various aspects of Jewish community life. He was a supporter of Zionism and was prominent in the American Jewish Committee, the New York YMHA, and the Jewish Board of Guardians. [ED.]

GLUCKSTEIN, English family of caterers. In 1872 ISIDORE GLUCKSTEIN (1851–1920) opened a small tobacconist's shop in London with his brother-in-law Barnett *Salmon. This concern developed into Salmon and Gluckstein, the largest firm of retail tobacconists in England, who sold out to the Imperial Tobacco Company in 1904. In 1887 Isidore Gluckstein was also one of the founders of the catering firm, J. Lyons and Company, together with his brother MONTAGUE GLUCKSTEIN (1853–1922), Alfred Salmon, son of Barnett Salmon, and Sir Joseph *Lyons. Montague Gluckstein conceived the idea of this popular catering establishment and played a leading part in its development, based on the principle of offering good food at moderate prices. He succeeded to the chairmanship of the company on the death of Lyons in 1917. ISIDORE MONTAGUE GLUCKSTEIN (1890–) was chairman of the company 1956–60, and president 1961–68.

Other members of the family were SIR SAMUEL GLUCKSTEIN (1880–1958), who was active in the London Country Council and occupied many posts in executive committees and was mayor of Westminster 1920–21; and SIR LOUIS HALLE GLUCKSTEIN (1897–), Conservative member of parliament from 1931 to 1945, chairman of the Greater London Council in 1968 and president of the Liberal Jewish Synagogue from 1944. [ED.]

GLUECK, ABRAHAM ISAAC (1826–1909), Hungarian rabbi. Glueck was born in Vertes and served as rabbi of Tolcsva for almost 50 years, until his death. His published works are *Be'er Yiẓhak* on tractate *Ḥullin* (1896), and on *Gittin* in two parts (1909–10), and responsa *Yad Yiẓhak*, in three parts (1902–08). R. Joseph ha-Kohen Schwartz published a complete volume entitled *Ẓafenat Pa'ne'aḥ* (1909), consisting of notes to the third part. Glueck also published the *Parashat Mordekhai* (1889) of Mordecai Benet, together with his own glosses. Many of his works were apparently lost in the Holocaust.

Bibliography: B. Z. Eisenstadt, *Dorot ha-Aḥaronim* (1913), 99f.; P. Z. Schwartz, *Shem ha-Gedolim me-Ereẓ Hagar,* 1 (1913), 8a–b, no. 71; *Magyar Zsidó Lexikon* (1929), s.v. [N.B.-M.]

GLUECK, NELSON (1900–1971), U.S. archaeologist and president of *Hebrew Union College. Glueck, who was born in Cincinnati, Ohio, received his rabbinic ordination from the Hebrew Union College there in 1923. Continuing

Nelson Glueck on an archaeological expedition. Courtesy Government Press Office, Tel Aviv.

his studies in Germany, Glueck received his Ph.D. at Jena in 1927. In 1928–29 he studied at the American School of Oriental Research in Jerusalem. Glueck began teaching Bible at Hebrew Union College in 1929, and while still a member of the faculty resumed his connection with the American School of Oriental Research. He was director of the Jerusalem School during 1932–33, 1936–40, and 1942–47, and field director of the Baghdad School in 1942–47. During World War II Glueck worked with the U.S. Office of Strategic Services, then was director of the Union of American Hebrew Congregations, to which he had been appointed in 1941.

A conspicuous figure among American archaeologists, Glueck undertook systematic excavations throughout Transjordan. In 1937 he uncovered the Nabatean Temple at Jebel el-Tannur, and in 1938 he began excavating the Iron Age site of Tell-el-Kheleifeh (Ezion-Geber), near Akaba. From 1952 onward he surveyed ancient sites in the Negev.

In 1947 Glueck was elected president of Hebrew Union College. The college, isolated geographically from the main centers of American Jewish life, also tended to be overshadowed by the burgeoning activities of its patron, the Union of American Hebrew Congregations. Avoiding philosophical controversy, Glueck successfully fought to maintain the independence of the college, and at the same time transformed its structure. In 1949 he succeeded Stephen Wise as president of the Jewish Institute of Religion in New York, and the amalgamation of the two schools followed. Branches of the combined institution were opened in Los Angeles and Jerusalem largely due to Glueck's enthusiasm. The buildings in Cincinnati were greatly enlarged and the granting of fellowships for postgraduate studies, particularly to Christian students of Judaica, was increased considerably.

In addition to contributions to learned journals, Glueck has published *Das Wort Ḥesed in alttestamentlichen Sprachgebrauche* (1927); *Explorations in Eastern Palestine* (4 vols., 1934–51); *The Other Side of the Jordan* (1940); *The River Jordan* (1946); *Rivers in the Desert* (1959); and *Deities and Dolphins: the Story of the Nabateans* (1966). On his 70th birthday, the festschrift *Near Eastern Archeology in the Twentieth Century* was published in his honor.

Bibliography: D. Lazar, *Rashim be-Yisrael,* 1 (1953), 322–6; *Current Biography,* 30 (July 1969), 28–30; *Time* (Dec. 13, 1963). [ED.]

GLUECK, SHELDON (1896–), U.S. criminologist. Born in Warsaw, Glueck was taken to the United States in 1903. In 1925 he became an instructor in criminology at Harvard and was professor of law from 1931. A member of the advisory committee on Rules of Criminal Procedure of the U.S. Supreme Court, he was also an adviser at the Nuremberg war crimes trials after World War II.

Glueck's work in criminology was largely accomplished with the help of his wife, ELEANOR GLUECK-TOUROFF (1898–), who held research posts in criminology at Harvard from 1928 to 1953. For over 30 years they carried out unique follow-up investigations of delinquent and criminal behavior to determine the effectiveness of various forms of correctional treatment. The research resulted in several important publications including *One Thousand Juvenile Delinquents* (1934). Later research into the early identification of delinquency and recidivism led to the development of prognostic tables to predict post-offense behavior of criminal offenders. The Glueck system of prediction enabled them to determine which children in the first grade would probably become persistent delinquents unless there was timely and effective intervention. The predictions were based on certain factors in the social background of the

Sheldon Glueck and his wife, Eleanor Glueck-Touroff, U.S. criminologists. Photo Lotte Meitner-Graf, London.

children such as parental discipline, relationship with parents, and the cohesiveness of the family. Validation studies of these prediction tables generally confirmed their accuracy, and were approved by a number of eminent criminologists and social scientists.

Among their many publications were *Unraveling Juvenile Delinquency* (1950), in which the Glueck Social Prediction Table is described, and *Predicting Delinquency and Crime* (1959), which incorporates various tables of prediction for different types of criminal and delinquent behavior. They also wrote *Ventures in Criminology* (1964). Among Sheldon Glueck's other writings were: *Mental Disorder and the Criminal Law* (1925); and *The Nuremberg Trial and Aggressive War* (1946). [Z.H.]

GLUECKEL OF HAMELN (1645–1724), Yiddish memoirist. Glueckel was born in Hamburg of a prominent patrician family. At 14 she was given in marriage to Ḥayyim

Glueckel of Hameln.

of Hameln, and when her husband moved to Hamburg, she was his adviser in all practical matters even while bearing and raising their 12 children. As a result, she was able to carry on his business and financial enterprises after his death in 1689. Eleven years later she married the banker Cerf Lévy of Metz where she lived until her death.

Glueckel's fame rests on her *Memoirs*, which she began to write at 46 in order to dispel the melancholy that overcame her after the death of her first husband and in order to acquaint her children and grandchildren with their family background. She completed writing the first five sections by 1699; then, after a pause of 16 years, she resumed her writing and completed the last two sections in 1719. Her original manuscript is lost but copies made by her descendants were preserved. In 1896, David *Kaufmann published the *Memoirs* for the first time in the original Yiddish, with a lengthy German introduction. Since then the *Memoirs* have been translated into German, Hebrew, and English (*Memoirs of Glueckl of Hameln*, tr. by M. Lowenthal, 1932), and have formed an important source for Central European Jewish history and culture and for linguistic and literary studies of older aspects of Yiddish. Though primarily a family chronicle and not intended for publication, the simple and intimate *Memoirs* unfolded a rich panorama of Jewish life in cities such as Hamburg, Altona, Hameln, Hanover, Metz, Berlin, and Amsterdam. Glueckel had an excellent memory, a kind temperament, a poetic gift of expression, a good traditional education, and a pious disposition. She was well versed in the legendary lore of the Talmud and had read the popular Yiddish ethical books. She often made use of parables, fables, folk tales, and stories that illustrated a moral. She was profoundly influenced by *tkhines* (devotional Yiddish prayers for women) and often echoed them in her meditations.

Bibliography: I. Zinberg, *Geshikhte fun der Literature bay Yidn*, 6 (1943), 275–9; N. B. Minkoff, *Glikl Hamel* (Yid., 1952); B. Z. Abrahams, *Life of Glueckel of Hameln* (1962); Shatzky, in: *Yivo Bleter*, 6 (1934), 138–44 (incl. bibl.). [S.L.]

°**GLUECKS, RICHARD** (1889–?), S.S.-*Brigadefuehrer* (major general), charged with participation in the mass murder of Jews in the "Final Solution" (see *Holocaust, General Survey). After serving as an artillery officer during World War I, Gluecks became a member of the Nazi Party and the S.S. In 1936 he was appointed chief of staff under Theodor Eike, inspector of concentration camps, and succeeded him in 1940. In 1941, when the Inspection Authority was absorbed into the "Economic and Administrative Main Office" (W.V.H.A.) of the S.S., Gluecks became head of Amtsgruppe D, which supervised the concentration camps (see Concentration *Camps). Under his jurisdiction, exploitation of prisoner's labor was introduced in the camps. He disappeared without trace at the end of World War II.

Bibliography: R. Hoess, *Commandant of Auschwitz* (1961), index; R. Hilberg, *Destruction of the European Jews* (1961), 605, 706, and index; IMT, *Trial of the Major War Criminals*, 24 (1949) index. [Y.Re.]

GLUECKSOHN (Glickson), MOSHE (1878–1939), Hebrew journalist and Zionist leader. Born in Cholynka, near Grodno, Gluecksohn began his Zionist activity in Western Europe among Jewish students. He was a delegate to the Sixth Zionist Congress (1903) and later congresses, joining the opposition to the Uganda Scheme. From 1908 to 1914 he was the secretary of the Ḥovevei Zion committee in Odessa. In 1910 Gluecksohn began to publish articles in Hebrew in *Haolam* and later also in *Ha-Shillo'aḥ*. After the February Revolution, 1917, he edited the Moscow Hebrew daily *Ha-Am*. After the Bolshevik Revolution he left for Palestine (autumn 1919). From 1923 to 1938 he edited the daily *Haaretz*, and during his period editorship the paper became an important Zionist organ, supporting the policy of Chaim Weizmann and the Zionist leadership and strongly opposing Revisionism. Gluecksohn was the ideological leader of Ha-No'ar ha-Ẓiyyoni and of progressive Zionism. He wrote monographs on Aḥad Ha-Am (1927) and Maimonides (1935). Active in public life as a leader of the General Zionist Party in Palestine, he was also a member of the Zionist General Council, Va'ad ha-Lashon ha-Ivrit (Hebrew Language Committee), and the Board of Governors of the Hebrew University. Kibbutz *Kefar Glickson is named after him. His *Ishim ba-Madda u-va-Sifrut* ("Personalities in Science and Literature") appeared after his death (1940–41; 2nd ed. 1963, with a preface by his wife).Two volumes of his collected works appeared posthumously: *Ishim ba-Ẓiyyonut* ("Zionist Personalities," 1940), and *Im Ḥillufei Mishmarot* ("Changing the Guard," 1965).

Bibliography: Bergman, in: *Haaretz* (July 2, 1943); G. Kressel, *Toledot ha-Ittonut ha-Ivrit be-Ereẓ Yisrael* (1964), index; A.

Carlebach, *Sefer ha-Demuyot* (1959), 306–11; Rabbi Binyamin (pseud.), *Keneset Ḥakhamim* (1960), 358–80.

[B.SCH./ED.]

GLUECKSTADT, town in Schleswig-Holstein, N.W. Germany; until 1864 under Danish rule. It was founded in 1616 by Christian IV of Denmark who in 1619 granted special privileges to induce a group of Hamburg Jews to settle there. By 1650, 130 Sephardi Jews had taken residence in the town. They opened a sugar refinery, a soap factory, and saltworks, and were active in foreign trade. The leader of the newly settled Sephardi community, Albertus *Denis, received permission to operate a mint. The Jews, known as members of the "Portuguese nation," had two representatives on the city council, and possessed a synagogue, school, cemetery, and printing press. The first rabbi was Abraham de Fonseca, who later moved to Hamburg. Due to the rising prosperity of *Altona, the city declined economically in the early 18th century and many Jews left; their privileges lapsed in 1732. Although the synagogue was completely rebuilt in 1767 only 20 families remained by then. The last rabbi died in 1813, and the synagogue was dismantled in 1895.

Bibliography: Cassuto, in: JJLG, 21 (1930), 287–317; idem, in: *Jahrbuch fuer die juedischen Gemeinden Schleswig-Holsteins*, 2 (1930–31), 110–8; H. Kellenbenz, *Sephardim an der unteren Elbe* (1958), index; M. Grunwald, *Portugiesengraeber auf deutscher Erde* (1902), index; Baron, Social[2], 14 (1969), 278ff. [ED.]

GLUECKSTADT, ISAAC HARTVIG (1839–1910), Danish financier. Glueckstadt, who was born in Fredericia, Denmark, started his business career as a private banker in Christiania (Oslo) in 1865; five years later he was made manager of the Norwegian Credit Bank. In 1872 he was recalled to Copenhagen as director of the new Landmandsbanken, which developed into the largest bank in Scandinavia under his farsighted management. From the outset, Glueckstadt recognized the importance of international connections, and did not confine himself to banking alone. Many important Danish commercial enterprises, among them the Copenhagen Free Port and the East Asiatic Company, owed a great deal to his initiative and support. For many years he was chairman of the board of delegates of the Jewish Community

Bibliography: *Dansk Biografisk Leksikon*, 8 (1936), 179–82; J. Schovelin, *Landmansbanken 1871–1921* (Copenhagen, 1921).

[JU.M.]

GLUSK (Glosk), ABRAHAM ABBA (second half of 18th century), Haskalah pioneer. According to one opinion he was born in Glussk (Lublin province) and to another, in the town bearing the same name in the province of Minsk. He is also identified with the "Glusker Maggid" whose works were burned for heresy in the courtyard of the Vilna synagogue. Glusk, who acquired a wide knowledge of philosophy and secular learning, left his native land in search of free ideas. After a long period spent wandering from city to city he reached Berlin where he met Moses *Mendelssohn. However he was persecuted by local Orthodox circles and the head of the Berlin community asked the authorities to expel him from the city on the pretext that he had no right of residence. Mendelssohn, however, who considered Glusk a profound thinker, enabled him to remain. Glusk later traveled in Germany, Holland, France, and England before returning home. His subsequent fate is unknown. The German poet A. von Chamisso wrote a poem dedicated to Glusk (1832).

Bibliography: Stanislavsky, in: *Voskhod*, 12 (1887), 122–8; *Ha-Karmel* (1871), 234–5; A. Kohut, *Mendelssohn und seine Familie* (1886), 51–53. [ED.]

GLUSKA, ZEKHARYAH (1895–1960), leader of the Yemenite community in Ereẓ Israel. Born in Nadir, Yemen, Gluska moved to Ereẓ Israel with his parents who settled in the Neveh Ẓedek quarter in Jaffa in 1909. In 1911 he joined the Ha-Po'el ha-Ẓa'ir Party and became one of the first members of the Histadrut. In 1921 he helped form the Ẓe'irei ha-Mizraḥ movement, which was formed to integrate Yemenite youth in Ereẓ Israel, and acted as its representative in the first Asefat ha-Nivḥarim. Gluska was a founder of Hitaḥdut ha-Teimanim ("Union of Yemenites") in Ereẓ Israel and its chairman from 1925. He became its representative in the central *yishuv* bodies and at Zionist Congresses. In 1949 he was elected on behalf of the Yemenite list to the First Knesset.

Bibliography: Tidhar, 3 (1958), 1515–16. [B.J.]

GLUSKIN, ZE'EV (1859–1949), Zionist. Born in Slutsk, Belorussia, Gluskin joined the Ḥovevei Zion in Warsaw in the 1880s, became a member of *Benei Moshe, and was among the founders of the Menuḥah ve-Naḥalah society, which established the settlement of Reḥovot. He was also one of the founders of the Aḥi'asaf publishing house, which introduced innovations in the publishing and distribution of Hebrew books. He participated in the establishment of the Carmel society (1896), which marketed and exported the wine produced in the settlements, and was its first director. In 1901 Gluskin took part in a Ḥovevei Zion deputation to Baron Edmond de Rothschild to persuade him to continue his settlement activities in Ereẓ Israel. In 1904 he was among the founders of the Geulah Company, which was established for the private purchase of land in Ereẓ Israel.

Gluskin went to Ereẓ Israel late in 1905 and took over the directorship of Aguddat ha-Koremim ("Vintners Association") and of its wine cellars in Rishon le-Zion and Zikhron Ya'akov. When World War I broke out, he went to Alexandria and helped organize aid both for the refugees from Ereẓ Israel and for Jews who had remained there. He supported the volunteer movement for the establishment of a Jewish regiment in the British Army from among the Ereẓ Israel refugees. He was director of the Geulah Company from 1925–46. He published his memoirs (1946), which contain valuable material on the history of the Jews and of Zionism in Russia and Ereẓ Israel.

Bibliography: D. Idelovitch, *Rishon le-Ẓiyyon* (1941), index; M. Smilansky, *Mishpaḥat ha-Adamah*, 3 (1954), 194–206; Y. Pogrebinsky, *Sefer "Ge'ullah"* (1956), 131ff., 233–5. [Y.S.]

GLUSSK (Yid. **Hlusk**), town in Belorussian S.S.R. Jews settled in Glussk in the third quarter of the 17th century. Jehiel b. Solomon *Heilprin was rabbi there and compiled the regulations of its *ḥevra kaddisha*. In 1717 the Jews paid a 600 zloty poll tax. In 1847 the town had a Jewish population of 3,148, in 1897, 3,801 (71% of the total population), and in 1926, 2,581 (58.3%). Glussk had no industry. Some of the Jews produced a special kind of tea (called Glussk tea) but most were gardeners, carpenters, horse merchants, and small traders. The community came to an end under the Nazi occupation. Most were sent to their death but entire families fled to the forest, where many of them fought in partisan units.

Bibliography: *Słownik geograficzny Królestwa Polskiego* 3 (1882), 78–79; *Yevrei v SSSR* (1929[4]), 51; *Sefer ha-Partizanim*, 1 (1958), 648–9; Y. Slutzky (ed.), *Sefer Bobruisk*, 2 (1967), 764–8.

[ED.]

GNAT, tiny insect. Included among the plagues of Egypt is *arov*, identified by one *tanna* as "a swarm of gnats" and "hornets" and by others as "a mixture of animals" (Ex. R. 11:3). In the Septuagint *arov* is rendered by the Greek word for "flies." In Egypt there are many species of gnats or mosquitoes, in particular *Culex* and the *Anopheles*, a conveyor of malaria. Their eggs are laid in bodies of water and the gnat develops by stages—larval, pupal, imaginal. Despite the inconvenience caused by the gnat, the rabbis stated that it, too, is important in the complex of ecological relations between creatures (Shab. 77b). They also declared that even "if all mortals were to gather together to create one gnat," they would fail to do so (Sif. Deut. 32).

Bibliography: Tristram, Nat Hist, 327; J. Feliks, *Animal World of the Bible* (1962), 125.

[J.F.]

GNESIN, MIKHAIL FABIANOVICH (1883–1957), Russian composer, teacher, and writer. Born in Rostov-on-Don, he studied with Lyadov and Rimsky-Korsakov at the St. Petersburg Conservatory. From 1910 to 1920 he taught at Rostov, Yekaterinodar, and Petrograd, and undertook study trips to Greece, Italy, France, Germany, and Palestine. He also made a survey of music education in the Jewish schools on behalf of the *Odessa Committee. During 1921 he stayed in Palestine, and then went to Germany where he was one of the founders of the Jibneh music publishing house and reorganized the activities of the *Society of Jewish Folk Music of which he had been one of the founders in 1908.

From 1923 to 1935 he was professor of composition at the Moscow Conservatory, where he also served as head of the pedagogical faculty and of the "studios for the development of the national music of the Soviet peoples." From 1935 to 1945 he taught composition at the Leningrad Conservatory, and from 1945 to 1951 headed the composition department at the music school which bore the names of himself and his sister who was also a musician. Gnesin's pedagogical activity included the creation of the basic plan for teaching music composition, which is still followed in the Soviet Union. In addition to his memoirs, he published a number of books on composition, aesthetics, Jewish music, and a study of Rimsky-Korsakov. As a composer he pioneered the new Russian symphonic style, and the use of material from the various peoples of the U.S.S.R. Of the 68 items in the list of his works, about a quarter bear "Jewish" titles. The sources for these were, as he himself declared, threefold: tunes of his maternal grandfather, the Vilna *badḥan* and singer Shayke Fayfer (Isaiah Fleytsinger); the synagogue tradition which he received from his first teacher, Eliezer *Gerovich, and the melodies he had collected in Palestine. The publication of his Jewish compositions was stopped in 1929 (see list, up to this date, in Sendrey, Music). Of his later works, the most noteworthy are *Song of the Old Homeland*, for orchestra, op. 30; *Wolochs* for string quartet and clarinet, op. 56, in two versions (1938, 1951); *Pastoral Elegy* for piano trio, op. 57

Mikhail Gnesin, Russian musician. Jerusalem, J.N.U.L., Schwadron Collection.

(1940); the opera *Abraham's Youth*, to his own libretto, op. 36 (1921–23); and the suite *A Jewish Orchestra at the Mayor's Ball*, from his music to Gogol's *Revizor* ("The Government Inspector"). His opera *Bar Kokhba*, to a libretto by Samuel Halkin, remained unfinished. Articles and memoirs by Gnesin were compiled and edited by R. V. Glezer and published as *M. F. Gnesin: statyi, vospominaniya, materialy* (1961).

Bibliography: A. N. Drozdov, *Michail Fabianowitsch Gnessin* (Rus. and Ger., 1927); *Istoriya russkoy muzyki*, 1 (1956); B. V. Asafev, *Russian Music from the Beginning of the Nineteenth Century* (1953), index; Baker, Biog Dict; Grove, Dict; Riemann-Gurlitt; M. Bronsaft [Gorali], *Ha-Askolah ha-Musikalit ha-Yehudit* (1940), 52–59.

[H.B-D.]

GNESSIN, MENAHEM (1882–1952), Israel actor and pioneer of the Hebrew theater. Menahem Gnessin, a brother of Uri Nissan *Gnessin, went to Palestine from the Ukraine in 1903 and for some years was a laborer and teacher in the

Menahem Gnessin (right) and Nahum Zemach, founders of Habimah, with Ḥannah Rovina in Moscow, 1918. Courtesy Keren Hayesod United Israel Appeal, Jerusalem.

villages. In 1907 he founded the Amateur Dramatic Arts Company for the presentation of plays in Hebrew. He staged Chirikov's *The Jews*, Gutzkow's *Uriel Acosta*, and other plays in Jaffa, Jerusalem, and the Judean settlements. Returning to Moscow in 1912, Gnessin and N. *Zemach established a Hebrew group which formed the nucleus of *Habimah. By 1923 Gnessin was in Berlin, organizing the Te'atron Ereẓ Yisraeli, which performed a one-act play, *Belshazzar* by H. Roche, with great success. In 1924 he took the group to Palestine and worked as an actor, teacher, and director. When Habimah reached Palestine in 1928, he joined the company. Gnessin wrote articles on the theater and published his memoirs *Darki im ha-Te'atron ha-Ivri, 1905–26* ("My Career in the Hebrew Theater," 1946).

Bibliography: M. Kohansky, *The Hebrew Theatre in its First Fifty Years* (1969), index.

[G.K.G.]

GNESSIN, URI NISSAN (1881–1913), Hebrew author who was the first to introduce the psychologically orientated prose style into Hebrew literature. Born in Starodub, Ukraine, Gnessin spent his childhood and youth in Pochep, a small town in the province of Orel. His father was head of a yeshivah and Gnessin studied in a *ḥeder*, later at his father's yeshivah where J. Ḥ. *Brenner was also a student. Besides his religious studies, Gnessin was interested in secular subjects, studying classical and modern languages and literatures. As a boy he already wrote poems and at 15 began publishing, together with Brenner, a literary monthly and a literary weekly for a small circle of friends and readers. These served as a forum for many of his early works. Nahum *Sokolow invited the young poet, then 18, to join the editorial staff of *Ha-Ẓefirah* in Warsaw; this marks the beginning of a productive period in his literary career. Gnessin published poems, literary criticism, stories, and translations in *Ha-Ẓefirah*. A small collection of short stories and sketches, *Ẓilelei ha-Ḥayyim* ("The Shadows of Life"), appeared in 1904.

At this time Gnessin began wandering from city to city, unable or unwilling to strike permanent roots. After a year's stay in Warsaw he moved to Yekaterinoslav, then to Vilna, where he worked for a time for the periodical *Ha-Zeman*, and then went to Kiev. Gnessin tried to study abroad but was not accepted since he did not have a formal education. Financial distress, hunger, and an inner restlessness beset Gnessin during his stay in Kiev, yet it was the time of his greatest prolificacy. However, plans to found a Hebrew literary organ and a publishing house did not materialize. In 1907 Gnessin left Kiev and at Brenner's invitation went to London (via Warsaw and Berlin, where he stayed for a short time) to co-edit **Ha-Me'orer* with Brenner. The periodical failed and there were violent disagreements between him and Brenner. London proved to be a severe disillusionment in other ways—the spiritual life of London Jewry was disappointing and his fatal heart disease, probably contracted in Kiev, began to affect him. In the autumn he immigrated to Ereẓ Israel but was unable to adjust. The country was a bitter experience for the young writer; his painful impressions found expression only in his letters however. He ascribes his disappointment at times to himself, at times to his environment which he saw as "Jews who trade in their Judaism." In the summer of 1908 Gnessin returned to Russia. He died in Warsaw four years later.

Gnessin's work, one of the major landmarks in Hebrew prose, is characterized by modern literary techniques and devices which he introduced into Hebrew literature. The interior monologue through which the reader receives an unmediated impression of the hero's continuous flow of ideas, sensations, feelings, and memories as they come into his consciousness was one of the main literary vehicles used by Gnessin to convey the psychological anxieties of his characters. He was among the first Hebrew writers to probe the problems of alienation and uprootedness, particularly as they affected the Jew in the modern age. Among his works four stories of his middle period are most outstanding and their impact on Hebrew prose is felt to this day: *"Haẓiddah"* ("Aside," 1905); *"Beinatayim"* ("Meanwhile," 1906); *"Be-Terem"* ("Before," 1909); and *"Eẓel"* ("By," 1913). His early work, *Ẓilelei ha-Ḥayyim*, fails to reveal an individualistic literary character, while later stories, like *"Ba-Gannim"* ("In the Gardens," 1909) and *"Ketatah"* ("A Quarrel," 1912), mark the transition to a new psychological style. Brenner, G. *Shofman, and Gnessin are among the first to cast the problems of the Jew of the age in a literary context. Gnessin poignantly describes the dilemma of the Jew whose world outlook is rooted in the values and spirit of the Jewish East European townlet, but who, at the same time, adopted the characteristics of a "citizen of the world" sharing the achievements and the deterioration of 20th-century culture. Gnessin's treatment of the theme is close to that of *Berdyczewski.

The four stories are autobiographical and Gnessin, under the guise of different names, is the protagonist. The plots, variations of the same theme, are about a man who leaves home, travels to distant lands, and becomes a "citizen of the world" only to find himself uprooted. A cosmopolitan, he is now completely alienated and lonely. After traveling far and wide, he returns home only to be faced by the awful realization that he has become an alien in his own homeland. At times he may only go as far as the next town, a center somewhat larger than his own hamlet, but the experience uproots and alienates him. The past becomes irretrievable, the gap unbridgeable, and he is cast in a strange, complex, and confusing world. The theme, apparently peculiar to contemporaneous Jewish intellectuals who had rejected religious tradition, merges in Gnessin with the more universal theme of perplexity, cultural strangeness, loss of God, and loss of roots. Out of his anguish, the lost son, wishing to comfort himself, cries: "Father, there is a God in heaven, isn't there, and He is so good!" *("Be-Terem")*. The very names of the stories imply the protagonist's detachment from time and place.

Scandinavian literature and the stories of Chekhov, his favorite author, had a marked influence on Gnessin. His sense of time as a factor in the life of man and of society resembles that of Marcel Proust. Through the associative technique, Gnessin focused the past and future in the present rendering the present less real than the past. He broke with the realistic trend then current in the Hebrew short story and became a "modern" author in the spirit of developments in world literature after World War I.

Gnessin's style is a flow of lyrical patterns which approaches poetic rhythm. His lyricism, however, is neither ambiguous nor vague and his description of details, objects, characters, and scenery is vivid and precise. One of Gnessin's stylistic devices is to reflect the inner world of his characters in all that surrounds them. This demands a descriptive realism and an avoidance of rhetoric. His language, despite certain Russianisms, captured the rhythms of the spoken tongue. His critical essays, which he signed U. Esthersohn, show a close affinity to the 19th-century school of symbolism. Among the works he translated are prose poems by Baudelaire and works by Chekhov, Heinrich Heine, S. Obstfelder, M. Spektor, and J. Wassermann.

For translations into English see Goell, Bibliography, 2102.

Bibliography: J. Ḥ. Brenner (ed.), *Haẓiddah* (memorial volume, 1917); B. Katz (Benshalom), *Uri Nissan Gnessin* (1935); S. Y. Penueli, *Brenner u-Gnessin ba-Sippur ha-Ivri shel Reshit ha-Me'ah ha-Esrim* (1965); Y. Zmora, *Ha-Mesapper Kav le-Kav* (1951); Z. Fishman, in: *Ha-Toren*, 10 (1923), 89–95; S. Nashkes, in: *Kitvei U. N. Gnessin*, 3 (1946), 221–35; Kressel, Leksikon (1965), 494–6.

[Le.G.]

GNIEZNO (Ger. **Gnesen**), city in Poland; first capital of Poland and center of the Catholic Church in that country until the beginning of the 14th century. Jews are mentioned there in 1267. Various charters of privilege granted to individual Jews or the community giving them rights of residence, and permission to organize defense and engage in commerce (1497, 1499, 1519, 1567, 1571, 1637, 1661) were destroyed in fires that periodically devastated the town. From the 13th to the middle of the 17th centuries, Gniezno Jewry remained one of the smaller communities in the kingdom, numbering 100 people in 30 houses at the end of the period. A representative from Gniezno participated in the provincial *(galil)* council of the communities of Great Poland in 1519. Several such councils were convened at Gniezno (in 1580, 1632, 1635, 1640, 1642). Local and visiting merchants and their agents dealt in wool and rags and collected tolls at the biannual fairs, and even attempted to carry on business outside the Jewish quarter (1643). The synagogue, built in 1582, was modeled after the one in Poznan. Eliezer *Ashkenazi was among the rabbis of Gniezno. The events surrounding the Swedish War (1655–59), as well as attacks led by the Jesuits and by the troops of Stephan *Czarniecki ended with the destruction of the community. In 1661 it reorganized outside the city walls. A new synagogue was built in 1680. In the first half of the 18th century the community suffered during the Northern War, and there was an outbreak of fire, as well as cases of *blood libel (1722, 1738). There were 60 Jews living in Gniezno in 1744. The community increased from the second half of the 18th century, particularly after Gniezno came under Prussian rule with the second partition of Poland in 1793, growing from 251 in the beginning of the period to 1,783 in the middle of the 19th century. It had cultural and welfare institutions, craftsmen's associations, a school, and a synagogue. The talmudic scholar Moses Samuel *Zuckermandel officiated as rabbi in Gniezno from 1864 to 1869. Subsequently many Jews emigrated to the German states and from the second half of the 19th century to America, especially after Gniezno was incorporated within independent Poland in 1919. The community numbered 750 in 1913 and approximately 150 in the 1930s. [D.Av.]

Holocaust Period. Before World War II nearly 150 Jews lived in Gniezno. During the Nazi occupation, the town belonged to Warthegau. During the first four months of the occupation, the town was emptied of all its Jewish inhabitants. A certain number escaped before and after the Germans entered, but the majority were deported on orders given on Nov. 12, 1939, by Wilhelm Koppe, the Higher S.S. and Police Leader of Warthegau. The orders called for the deportation of the entire Jewish population of Gniezno by the end of February 1940 to the territory of the General-gouvernement. On Dec. 13, 1939, 65 Jews from Gniezno, probably the last of the community, arrived in Piotrkow Trybunalski in the Radom district. After the removal of the Jews from Gniezno, the Germans razed the old Jewish cemetery and transformed it into a warehouse. No Jews resettled in the town after World War II. [De.D.]

Bibliography: Halpern, Pinkas, index; idem, *Yehudim ve-Yahadut be-Mizraḥ Eiropah* (1968), index: B. D. Weinryb, *Te'udot le-Toledot ha-Kehillot ha-Yehudiyyot be-Polin* (1950), index (=PAAJR, 19 (1950), Hebrew and English text); D. Avron, *Pinkas ha-Kesherim shel Kehillat Pozna* (1967), index; A. B. Posner, *Le-Korot Kehillat Gnesen* (1958); A. Heppner and J. Herzberg, *Aus der Vergangenheit und Gegenwart der Juden und der juedischen Gemeinden in den Posener Laendern* (1909), 405–13; D. Dąbrowska, in: BŻIH, 13–14 (1955), passim (on Holocaust).

GNOSTICISM, designates the beliefs held by a number of nonorthodox Christian sects flourishing in the 1st to 2nd centuries C.E., which developed mystical systems of philosophy based on the *gnosis* (Gr. "knowledge") of God. These systems were syncretic, i.e., mixtures of pagan magic and beliefs from the Babylonian and Greek world as well as from the Jewish. Judaism made an important contribution to the conceptions and the developments of gnosticism. One way in which Jewish motifs were infused into gnosticism was through the Bible, which was holy to Christianity and likewise through other Jewish literature—in Hebrew, Aramaic, and Greek—which was used by the Christians. The chapters on the Creation in Genesis were also of special influence. Special importance was also attributed to the account of the first man and his sin, which is interpreted by gnosticism as the downfall of the divine principle into the material world. From their negative attitude toward the world of natural existence and moral law which is meant to regulate man's behavior in this world, the gnostics came to a view of the God of Israel, the creator of the universe, as the god of evil, or an inferior god, and they strongly rejected his Law and its commandments. They interpreted the stories in the Bible in a way opposite to their meaning and intention: thus, for example, the original serpent is often seen by them as the bearer of the true "knowledge," of which God intends to deprive man; and Cain becomes a positive figure persecuted by God, etc.

Jewish influence on gnosticism is also evident in the use of names, concepts, and descriptions taken from the Hebrew or Aramaic, e.g., God, the creator of the universe, is called in some gnostic systems *Yaldabaot* (*Yalda Bahut*, according to some "the Child of Chaos"), other mythological or symbolic figures in gnosticism are: *Barbelo* (*Be-arba Eloha*, "in four gods," i.e., the father, the son, the female principle in the divine, and the first man), *Edem* (Eden), *Akhamot* (*ḥokhmot*, "wisdom," according to Prov. 9:1); the name of the gnostic Naassene sect is derived form *naḥash* ("serpent"); the mysterious words *"Ẓav la-ẓav ẓav la-ẓav kav la-kav kav la-kav ze'eir sham ze'eir sham"* (Isa. 28:10, 13) serve as the mystical designation of the three gnostic *Sefirot*.

In addition to these contributions unwittingly and unintentionally made by Judaism to gnosticism, there existed in Judaism itself, at the end of the Second Temple period, emotional and intellectual attitudes which were close to the spiritual world of gnosticism. It is possible that these had a more direct influence on the emergence of gnosticism or, at least, that they served as seeds for a few of its ideas. There are indications of this in the literature of the Dead Sea Sect. Common to both gnosticism and the Dead Sea Scrolls is the view of esoteric "knowledge" as a redemptive factor, which enables a group of select people to bridge the abyss separating the human from the divine, and to rise "from a spirit perverse to an understanding of you and to stand in one company before you with the everlasting host and the spirits of knowledge, to be renewed with all things that are and with those versed in song together" (Thanksgiving Psalms, 1QH 11:13–14), and to be those "who heard the glorious voice and saw the holy angels, men whose ears are opened and hear deep things" (War Scroll, 1QM 10:11).

The literature of the sect also reflects a dualistic outlook on the world conceiving a schism between the principle of good (the light) and the principle of evil (the darkness) each with its own hosts of angels and spirits. This view, however, in contrast to its expression in gnosticism, does not step beyond the framework of Jewish belief in divine unity. Even the feeling of disgust and revulsion with man and the impurity of his material basis ("the mystery of the flesh is iniquity"; Manual of Discipline, 1QS 11:9) does not culminate in the notion of distinction between matter *per se* and the divine spiritual world; "For the world, albeit now and until the time of the final judgment it go sullying itself in the ways of wickedness owing to the domination of perversity" (*ibid.*, 4:19), but God "created man to rule the world" (*ibid.*, 3:17–18). Thus, despite a certain spiritual kinship between the writings of the sect and the world of gnosticism, the former are not records of a "gnostic Judaism," but rather reflect certain general attitudes of mind shared at that time by others including Jews, which could be the point of departure for truly gnostic speculations.

There is no explicit mention in talmudic literature of gnosticism and its history. It is possible, however, that the appellation *Minim refers in some instances to gnostics.

See also *Dualism. For the influence of gnosticism on the history of Jewish mysticism, see *Kabbalah.

Bibliography: H. Graetz, *Gnostizismus und Judentum* (1846); C. W. King, *The Gnostics and Their Remains* (1872²); G. Scholem, *Jewish Gnosticism, Merkabah Mysticism, and Talmudic Tradition* (1960); Scholem, Mysticism, index; R. M. Grant, *Gnosticism and Early Christianity* (1959); K. Schubert, in: *Kairos*, 3 (1961), 2–15 (Ger.); M. Friedlaender, *Der vorchristliche juedische Gnostizismus* (1898).

[D.Fl.]

GOA, city and district on the W. coast of India, about 250 miles (400 km.) S. of Bombay, a Portuguese province from 1510 until 1961. The first Jew to be mentioned in Goa was

The standard of the Inquisition at Goa. From C. Roth, *History of the Marranos*, 1932.

Gaspar da *Gama who was kidnapped by Vasco da Gama in 1498 and baptized. From the early decades of the 16th century many New Christians from Portugal came to Goa. The influx soon aroused the opposition of the Portuguese and ecclesiastical authorities, who complained bitterly about the New Christians' influence in economic affairs, their monopolistic practices, and their secret adherence to Judaism. As a result of these complaints the Portuguese Inquisition was established in Goa in 1560, and lasted, apart from a temporary suspension from 1774 to 1778, for almost 250 years. Even before the Inquisition was formally established, a physician named Jeronimo Diaz had been burned in 1543 for maintaining heretical opinions. Many prominent New Christians became victims of the Inquisition in Goa. The great scientist Garcia de *Orta was not affected during his lifetime, but 12 years after his death, in 1580, his remains were exhumed, burned, and the ashes thrown into the ocean. In the latter part of the 16th century Coje *Abrahão served as interpreter to the Portuguese viceroys, despite ecclesiastical objections. Eighteenth-century travelers refer to the existence of a synagogue and organized Jewish communal life, but this is doubtful.

Bibliography: Roth, Mag Bibl, 105–6; Roth, Marranos, 394; E. N. Adler, *Auto De Fé and Jew* (1908), 139–51; J. M. T. de Carvalho, *Garcia d'Orta* (Sp., 1915); A. Baiao (ed.), *A inquisição de Goa*, 2 vols. (1945); Fischel, in: JQR, 47 (1956/57), 37–45.
[W.J.F.]

GOAT. The classification of the domesticated goat bred in Israel is disputed among scholars, some maintaining that it originates from the wild goat *Capra hircus*, hence the name of the domesticated goat as *Capra hircus mambrica*, others, that it originates from the wild *Capra prisca*, the name of the domesticated goat therefore being *Capra prisca mambrica*. The wild goat is apparently the *akko* mentioned as one of the permitted wild animals (Deut. 14:5). The goat of Ereẓ Israel has recurved horns, those of the he-goat being branched. Its bones have been found in excavations at *Megiddo and a drawing of it in excavations at *Gezer (dating from about 3,000 years ago). The goat has black hair (cf. Song 4:1), but a few have black hair with white or brown spots (cf. Gen. 30:32). This black hair may have symbolized sin, and for this reason it was chosen as a sin offering and for the scapegoat (see *Azazel; Lev. 16:8ff.). The expression *sa'ir* (lit. "hairy") for a he-goat (*ibid.*, 4:24) and *se'irah* for a she-goat (4:28) is connected with their long hair. The curtains of the Tabernacle were made of goat's hair, as were the black tents of the Bedouin—"the tents of Kedar" (Song 1:5). The she-goat is called *ez*, but *izzim* is also a general expression for the species, the kid being referred to as *gedi izzim* (Gen. 38:17) or *seh izzim* (Deut. 14:4); he-goats are called *attudim* (Num. 7:17) or *teyashim* (Gen. 30:35). The he-goat usually leads the flock and hence apparently the reference to it as "stately in going" (Prov. 30:29, 31). Another name for the he-goat is *ẓafir* (Dan. 8:5).

The importance of the goat lay in its flesh, that of the kid being particularly delicious (Gen. 27:9; 38:20; Judg. 13:15). Ancient peoples apparently boiled a kid in milk on idolatrous fertility festivals, the prohibition of seething "a kid in its mother's milk" (Ex. 23:19; 34:26; Deut. 14:21) being connected with this. From its threefold repetition, the sages deduced a general prohibition against eating meat with milk, as well as its concomitant laws (Kid. 57b). Goat's milk was widely used (cf. Prov. 27:27), being also regarded as a remedy for chest trouble. A *baraita*, however, tells of a pious man who reared a goat in his home for this purpose, but because he transgressed the prohibition of the sages against the breeding of goats, his colleagues rebuked him, calling the goat an "armed robber" (BK 80a), the goat being regarded as a robber since it jumps over fences and damages plants. A Greek inscription prohibiting the breeding of goats has been uncovered at Heracleas. According to the Mishnah (BK 7:7) "small cattle (goats and sheep) are not to be bred in Ereẓ Israel, but may be bred in Syria or in the deserts of Ereẓ Israel." After the destruction of the country's agriculture, especially following the Muslim conquest, goats were imported to Ereẓ Israel, and they increased in number. Some maintain that they were responsible for the erosion of the land by ruining the terraces, destroying the natural vegetation, and creating fissures on the slopes. The eroded soil was deposited in the valleys, blocking the flow of rivers to the sea and forming marshes such as those of the Valley of Jezreel, which were drained by Jews only in the present century. Even now goats, still kept in large numbers by the Bedouin, cause damage to Israel's natural woods by chewing the young shoots, thereby preventing them from growing to full height.

In the 1940s, the Jewish settlers introduced into the country the white European goat, distinguished for its yield of milk. In the Diaspora, particularly in Eastern Europe, the Jews in the towns and villages raised goats so as to have an independent supply of milk. In popular Jewish folklore

A wild goat and its kid on a scarab of the Late Bronze Age (1550–1200 B.C.E.). Found at Tell al-Fukhkār near Acre. Photo Ariel Berman, Haifa.

the goat is a well-known motif which finds expression in jokes ("the rabbi and the goat"), in folk songs ("the child and the goat," cf. *"Ḥad Gadya"*), as also in poems and paintings (e.g. those of *Chagall).

Bibliography: Dalman, Arbeit, 4 (1935), 171; 6 (1939), 186ff.; F. S. Bodenheimer, *Animal and Man in Bible Lands* (1960), 224, index, s.v. *Capra;* Feliks, in: *Teva va-Areẓ,* 7 (1964/65), 330–7.

[J.F.]

°GOBINEAU, JOSEPH ARTHUR, COMTE DE (1816–1882), French diplomat and essayist. Of his abundant literary efforts, only his *Essai sur l'inégalité des races humaines* (1853–55) is now remembered. In this essay Gobineau simplified to the extreme current opinions on the "racial factor" in history and the hierarchy of races, white, yellow, and black. According to him, only the white or "Aryan" race, the creator of civilization, possessed the supreme human virtues: honor, love of freedom, etc., qualities which could be perpetuated only if the race remained pure. Though he held the Jews in no particular aversion, Gobineau believed that the Latin and Semitic peoples had degenerated in the course of history through various racial intermixtures. Only the Germans had preserved their "Aryan purity," but the evolution of the modern world condemned them too to crossbreeding and degeneracy. Western civilization must be resigned to its fate. The success of the *Essai* was posthumous and, predictably, assured by Gobineau's German admirers. Chief of these was Richard *Wagner, who shared his cultural pessimism, and the literary society of Bayreuth, followed by a group of authors and anthropologists who founded the Gobineau-Vereinigung in 1894. Gobineau's influence on recent history, and especially on anti-Semitic ideology, was due less to his dilettante philosophy of history than to the construction given it by German and other fanatics.

Bibliography: L. I. Snyder, *The Idea of Racialism . . .* (1962); J. Buenzod, *La formation de la pensée de Gobineau et l'Essai sur l'inégalité des races humaines* (1967).

[L.Po.]

GOD. This entry is arranged according to the following outline:

IN THE BIBLE

The Bible is not a single book, but a collection of volumes composed by different authors living in various countries over a period of more than a millennium. In these circumstances, divergencies of emphasis (cf. Kings with Chronicles), outlook (cf. Jonah with Nahum), and even of fact (cf. Gen. 26:34 with 36:2–3) are to be expected. These factors have also affected the biblical presentation of the concept of God. There are passages in which Israel's monotheism is portrayed in unalloyed purity and incomparable beauty (I Kings 19:12; Isa. 40:18), and there are other verses in which folkloristic echoes and mythological reflexes, though transmuted and refined, appear to obscure the true character of the Hebrew concept of the divine (Gen. 2 and 3). Notwithstanding these discrepancies the Bible is essentially a unity; its theology is sui generis and must be studied as a whole to be seen in true perspective. This total view of biblical doctrine does not seek to blur differences and to harmonize the disparate; rather it resolves the heterogeneous elements into a unitary canonical ideology—the doctrine of the final editors of the Bible. It blends the thoughts, beliefs, and intuitions of many generations into a single spiritual structure—the faith of Israel—at the heart of which lies the biblical idea of God. It is this complete and ultimate scriptural conception of the Deity that will be described and analyzed in this section.

The One, Incomparable God. God is the hero of the Bible. Everything that is narrated, enjoined, or foretold in biblical literature is related to Him. Yet nowhere does the Bible offer any proof of the Deity's existence, or command belief in Him. The reason may be twofold: Hebrew thought is intuitive rather than speculative and systematic, and, furthermore, there were no atheists in antiquity. When the psalmist observed: "The fool hath said in his heart 'There is no God'" (Ps. 14:1), he was referring not to disbelief in God's existence, but to the denial of His moral governance. That a divine being or beings existed was universally accepted. There were those, it is true, who did not know YHWH (Ex. 5:2), but all acknowledged the reality of the Godhead. Completely new, however, was Israel's idea of God. Hence this idea is expounded in numerous, though not necessarily related, biblical passages, and, facet by facet, a cosmic, awe-inspiring spiritual portrait of infinite magnitude is built up. Paganism is challenged in all its aspects. God is One; there is no other (Deut. 6:4; Isa. 45:21; 46:9). Polytheism is rejected unequivocally and absolutely (Ex. 20:3–5). There is no pantheon; even the *dualism of Ormuzd and Ahriman (of the Zoroastrian religion) is excluded (Isa. 45:21); apotheosis is condemned (Ezek. 28:2ff.). Syncretism, as distinct from identification (Gen. 14:18–22), which plays a historical as well as a theological role in paganism, is necessarily ruled out (Num. 25:2–3; Judg. 18). Verses like Exodus 15:11—"Who is like Thee, O Lord, among the gods?"—do not lend support to polytheism, but expose the unreality and futility of the pagan deities. The thought is: Beside the true God, how can these idol-imposters claim divinity? The term "sons of gods" in Psalms 29:1 and 89:7 refers to angels, the servants, and worshipers of the Lord; there is no thought of polytheism (see E. G. Briggs, *The Book of Psalms* (ICC), 1 (1906), 252ff.; 2 (1907), 253ff.). The one God is also unique in all His attributes. The prophet asks: "To whom then will ye liken God? Or what likeness will ye compare unto Him?" (Isa. 40:18). Though the question is rhetorical, the Bible in a given sense provides a series of answers, scattered over the entire range of its teaching, which elaborate in depth the incomparability of God. He has no likeness; no image can be made of Him (Ex. 20:4; Deut. 4:35). He is not even to be conceived as spirit; the spirit of God referred to in the Bible alludes to His energy (Isa. 40:13; Zech. 4:6). In Isaiah 31:3, "spirits" parallels "a god" (*ʾel*, a created force) not the God, who is called in the verse YHWH. Idolatry, though it lingered on for centuries, was doomed to extinction by this new conception of the Godhead. It is true that the Torah itself ordained that images like the cherubim should be set up in the Holy of Holies. They did not, however, represent the Deity but His throne (cf. Ps. 68:5[4]); its occupant no human eye could see. Yet the invisible God is not a philosophical abstraction; He manifests His presence. His theophanies are accompanied by thunder, earthquake, and lightning (Ex. 19:18; 20:15[18]; Hab. 3:4ff.). These fearful natural phenomena tell of His strength; He is the omnipotent God (Job 42:2). None can resist Him (41:2); hence He is the supreme warrior (Ps. 24:8). God's greatness, however, lies not primarily in His power. He is omniscient; wisdom is His alone (Job 28:23ff.). He knows no darkness; light ever dwells with Him (Dan. 2:22); and it is He, and He only, who envisions and reveals the future (Isa. 43:9). He is the source of human understanding (Ps. 36:10[9]), and it is He who endows man with his skills (Ex. 28:3; I Kings 3:12). The classical Prometheus and the Canaanite Kôthar-and-Ḥasis are but figments of man's imagination. The pagan pride of wisdom is sternly rebuked; it is deceptive (Ezek. 28:3ff.); but God's wisdom is infinite and unsearchable (Isa. 40:28). He is also the omnipresent God (Ps. 139:7–12), but not as *numen, mana*, or *orenda*. Pantheism is likewise negated. He transcends the world of nature, for it is He who brought the world into being, established its laws, and gave it its order (Jer. 33:25). He is outside of time as well as space; He is eternal. Everything must perish; He alone preceded the universe and will outlive it (Isa. 40:6–8; 44:6; Ps. 90:2). The ever-present God is also immutable; in a world of flux He alone does not change (Isa. 41:4; Mal. 3:6). He is the rock of all existence (II Sam. 22:32).

The Divine Creator. God's power and wisdom find their ultimate expression in the work of creation. The miracles serve to highlight the divine omnipotence; but the supreme miracle is the universe itself (Ps. 8:2, 4[1, 3]). There is no theogony, but there is a cosmogony, designed and executed by the divine fiat (Gen. 1). The opening verses of the Bible do not conclusively point to *creatio ex nihilo*. The primordial condition of chaos (*tohu* and *bohu*) mentioned in Genesis 1:2 could conceivably represent the *materia prima* out of which the world was fashioned; but Job 26:7 appears to express poetically the belief in a world created out of the void (see Y. Kaufmann, Religion, 68), and both prophets and psalmists seem to substantiate this doctrine (Isa. 42:5; 45:7–9; Jer. 10:12; Ps. 33:6–9; 102:26; 212:2). *Maimonides, it is true, did not consider that the Bible provided incontrovertible proof of *creatio ex nihilo* (*Guide*, 2:25). The real criterion, however, is the overall climate of biblical thought, which would regard the existence of uncreated matter as a grave diminution of the divinity of the Godhead. God is the sole creator (Isa. 44:24). The celestial beings ("sons of God") referred to in Job 38:7, and the angels who, according to rabbinic *aggadah* and some modern exegetes, are addressed in Genesis 1:26 (cf. 3:22) were themselves created forms and not co-architects or co-builders of the cosmos. Angels are portrayed in the Bible as constituting the heavenly court, and as taking part in celestial consultations (I Kings 22:19ff.; Job 1:6ff.; 2:1ff.). These heavenly creatures act as God's messengers (the Hebrew *malʾakh* and the Greek ἄγγελος, from which the word "angel" is derived, both mean "messengers") or agents. They perform various tasks (cf. Satan, "the Accuser"), but except in the later books of the Bible they are not individualized and bear no names (see *Angels and Angelology). Nor are they God's only messengers; natural phenomena, like the wind (Ps. 104:4), or man himself, may act in that capacity (Num. 20:16). Some scholars think that since the Bible concentrated all divine powers in the one God, the old pagan deities, which represented various forces of nature, were demoted in Israel's religion to the position of angels. The term *shedim* (Deut. 32:17; Ps. 106:37), on the other hand, applied to the gods of the nations, does not, according to Y. Kaufmann, denote demons, but rather "no-gods," devoid of both divine and demonic powers. The fantastic proliferation of the angel population found in pseudepigraphical literature is still unknown in the Bible. It is fundamental, however, to biblical as well as post-biblical Jewish angelology that these celestial beings are God's creatures and servants. They fulfill the divine will and do not oppose it. The pagan notion of demonic forces that wage war against the deities is wholly alien and repugnant to biblical theology. Even Satan is no more than the heavenly prosecutor, serving the divine purpose. The cosmos is thus the work of God above, and all nature declares His glory (Ps. 19:2, 13ff.). All things belong to Him and He is the Lord of all (I Chron. 29:11–12). This creation theorem has a corollary of vast scientific and social significance: the universe, in all its measureless diversity, remains a homogeneous whole. Nature's processes are the same throughout the world, and underlying them is "One Power, which is of no beginning and no end; which has existed before all things were formed, and will remain in its integrity when all is gone—the Source and Origin of all, in Itself beyond any conception or image that man can form and set up before his eye or mind" (Haffkine). There is no cosmic strife between antagonistic forces, between darkness and light, between good and evil; and, by the same token, mankind constitutes a single brotherhood. The ideal is not that of the ant heap. Differentiation is an essential element of the Creator's design; hence the Tower of Babel is necessarily doomed to destruction. Although uniformity is rejected, the family unity of mankind, despite racial, cultural, and pigmentary differences, is clearly stressed in its origin (Adam is the human father of all men) and in its ultimate destiny at the end of days (Isa. 2:2–4). The course of creation is depicted in the opening chapter of the Bible as a graduated unfolding of the universe, and more particularly of the earth, from the lowest levels of life to man, the peak of the creative process. God, according to this account, completed the work in six days (that "days" here means an undefined period may be inferred from Gen. 1:14, where time divisions are mentioned for the first time; cf. also N. H. Tur-Sinai, in EM, 3(1958), 593). The biblical accounting of the days, however, is not intended to provide the reader with a science or history textbook but to describe the ways of God. Running like a golden thread through all the variegated contents of the Bible is the one unchanging theme—God and His moral law. Of far greater significance than the duration of creation is the fact that it was crowned by the Sabbath (Gen. 2:1–3), bringing rest and refreshment to the toiling world. The concept of the creative pause, sanctified by the divine example, is one of the greatest spiritual and social contributions to civilization made by the religion of Israel. The attempts to represent the Assyro-Babylonian *šabattu* or *šapattu* as the forerunner of the Hebrew Sabbath are without foundation. The former was a designation for the ill-omened 15th day of the month, and the notions associated with it are as polarically different from those of the Sabbath, with its elevating thoughts of holiness and physical and spiritual renewal, as a day of mourning is from a joyous festival.

God in History. The Sabbath did not mark the retirement of the Deity from the world that He had called into being. God continued to care for His creatures (Ps. 104), and man—all men—remained the focal point of His loving interest (Ps. 8:5[4]ff.). The divine providence encompasses both nations (Deut. 32:8) and individuals (e.g., the Patriarchs). Cosmogony is followed by history, and God becomes the great architect of the world of events, even as He was of the physical universe. He directs the historical movements *(ibid.)*, and the peoples are in His hands as clay in the hands of the potter (Jer. 18:6). He is the King of the nations (Jer. 10:7; Ps. 22:29). There is a vital difference, however, between the two spheres of divine activity. Creation encountered no antagonism. The very monsters that in pagan mythology were the mortal enemies of the gods became in the Bible creatures formed in accordance with the divine will (Gen. 1:21). Nevertheless, the stuff of history is woven of endless strands of rebellion against the Creator. Man is not an automaton; he is endowed with free will. The first human beings already disobeyed their maker; they acquired knowledge at the price of sin, which reflects the discord between the will of God and the action of man. The perfect harmony between the Creator and His human creation that finds expression in the idyll of the Garden of Eden was disrupted, and never restored.The revolt continued with Cain, the generation of the Flood, and the Tower of Babel. There is a rhythm of rebellion and retribution, of oppression and redemption, of repentance and grace, and of merit and reward (Jer. 18:7–10). Israel was the first people to write history as teleology and discovered that it had a moral base. The Bible declares that God judges the world in righteousness (Ps. 96:13); that military power does not presuppose victory (Ps. 33:16); that the Lord saves the humble (Ps. 76:10) and dwells with them (Isa. 57:15). The moral factor determines the time as well as the course of events. The Israelites will return to Canaan only when the iniquity of the Amorite is complete (Gen. 15:16); for 40 years the children of Israel wandered in the wilderness for accepting the defeatist report of the ten spies (Num. 14:34); Jehu is rewarded with a dynasty of five generations for his punitive action against the house of Ahab; and to Daniel is revealed the timetable of redemption and restoration (Dan. 9:24). It is this moral element in the direction of history that makes God both Judge and Savior. God's punishment of the wicked and salvation of the righteous are laws of the divine governance of the world, comparable to the laws of nature: "As smoke is driven away, so drive them away; as wax melts before fire, let the wicked perish before God . . ." (Ps. 68:2–3; cf. M. D. Cassuto, in *Tarbiz*, 12 (1941), 1–27). Nature and history are related (Jer. 33:20–21, 25–26); the one God rules them both. The ultimate divine design of history, marked by universal peace, human brotherhood, and knowledge of God, will be accomplished in "the end of days" (Isa. 2:2–4; 11:6ff.), even as the cosmos was completed in conformity with the divine plan. Man's rebellions complicate the course of history, but cannot change the design. God's purpose shall be accomplished; there will be a new heaven and a new earth (Isa. 66:22), for ultimately man will have a new heart (Ezek. 36:26–27).

God and Israel. Within the macrocosm of world history there is the microcosm of Israel's history. It is natural that in the context of national literature the people of Israel should receive special and elaborate attention, although the gentile world, particularly in prophetic teaching, is never lost sight of. The Bible designates Israel *ʿam segullah*, "a treasured people," which stands in a particular relationship to the one God. He recognized Israel as His own people and they acknowledge Him as their only God (Deut. 26:17–18). He redeems His people from Egyptian bondage, brings them to the promised land, and comes to their aid in periods of crisis. Israel's election is not, however, to be interpreted as a form of favoritism. For one thing, the Exodus from Egypt is paralleled by similar events in the histories of other peoples, including Israel's enemies (Amos 9:7). In truth, Israel's election implies greater responsiblity, with corresponding penalties as well as rewards: "You only have I singled out of all the families of the earth; therefore I will visit upon you all your iniquities" (Amos 3:2; see *Chosen People). The choice of the children of Israel as God's people was not due to their power or merit; it was rather a divine act of love, the fulfillment of a promise given to the Patriarchs (Deut. 7:7–8; 9:4–7). The Lord did, however, foresee that the spiritual and moral way of life pioneered by Abraham would be transmitted to his descendants as a heritage. Subsequently this concept found material expression in the covenant solemnly established between God and His people at Sinai (Ex. 24:7ff.). This covenant demanded wholehearted and constant devotion to the will of God (Deut. 18:13); it was an everlasting bond (Deut. 4:9). Thus to be a chosen people it was incumbent upon Israel to become a choosing people (as Zangwill phrased it). The rhythm of rebellion and repentance, retribution and redemption, is particularly evident in the story of Israel. Yet the fulfillment of the divine purpose is not in doubt. God's chosen people will not perish (Jer. 31:26–27). It will be restored to faithfulness, and in its redemption will bring salvation to the whole earth by leading all men to God (Jer. 3:17–18). Until that far-off day, however, Israel will remain God's witness (Isa. 44:8).

The Divine Lawgiver. The covenant that binds the children of Israel to their God is, in the ultimate analysis, the Torah in all its amplitude. God, not Moses, is the lawgiver; "Behold, I Moses say unto you" (cf. Gal. 5:2) is an inconceivable statement. It would not only be inconsistent with Moses' humility (Num. 12:3), but would completely contradict the God-given character of the Torah. However, notwithstanding its divine origin, the law is obligatory on Israel only. Even idolatry, the constant butt of prophetic irony, is not regarded as a gentile sin (Deut. 4:19). Yet the Bible assumes the existence of a universal moral code that all peoples must observe. The talmudic sages, with their genius for legal detail and codification, speak of the seven Noachian laws (Sanh. 56a). Although the Bible does not specify the ethical principles incumbent upon all mankind, it is clear from various passages that murder, robbery, cruelty, and adultery are major crimes recognized as such by all human beings (Gen. 6:12, 13; 9:5; 20:3; 39:9; Amos 1:3ff.). It would thus appear that the Bible postulates an autonomous, basic human sense of wrongdoing, unless it is supposed that a divine revelation of law was vouchsafed to the early saints, such as assumed by the apocryphal and rabbinic literatures (and perhaps by Isa.

24:5.) The Torah—which properly means "instruction," not "law"—does not, in the strict sense of the term, contain a properly formulated code; nevertheless, detailed regulations appertaining to religious ritual, as well as to civil and criminal jurisprudence, form an essential part of pentateuchal teaching. The halakhic approach is reinforced by a number of the prophets. For instance, Isaiah (58:13), Jeremiah (34:8ff.), Ezekiel (40ff.), and Malachi (1:8; 2:10) lent their authority to the maintenance of various religious observances. Ezra and Nehemiah rebuilt the restored Jewish community on Torah foundations. Yet paradoxically the Bible also evinces a decidedly "anti-halakhic" trend. In Isaiah the Lord cries: "What to Me is the multitude of your sacrifices . . . I have had enough of burnt offerings of rams and the fat of fed beasts . . . who requires of you this trampling of My courts? . . . Your new moons and your appointed feasts My soul hates . . . When you spread forth your hands, I will hide My eyes from you; even though you make many prayers, I will not listen" (1:11–15). Jeremiah not only belittles the value of the sacrifices (7:22); he derides the people's faith in the Temple itself: "The temple of the Lord, the temple of the Lord, the temple of the Lord are these" (7:4). Even the Book of Psalms, though essentially devotional in character, makes an anti-ritual protest: "I do not reprove you for your sacrifices . . . I will accept no bull from your house . . . For every beast of the forest is Mine, the cattle on a thousand hills . . . If I were hungry, I would not tell you; for the world and all that is in it is Mine. Do I eat the flesh of bulls, or drink the blood of goats?" (50:8–13). These and similar passages represent a negative attitude towards established cultic practices. No less inconsonant with Torah law seems the positive prophetic summary of human duty formulated by Micah (6:8): "He has told you, O man, what is good; and what does the Lord require of you but to do justice, and to love lovingkindness, and to walk humbly with your God?" A similar note is sounded by Hosea (2:21–22 [19–20]): "I will espouse you with righteousness and with justice, with steadfast love, and with mercy. I will espouse you with faithfulness; and you shall be mindful of the Lord"; by Amos (5:14): "Seek good, and not evil, that you may live"; and by Isaiah (1:17): "Learn to do good; seek justice, correct oppression; defend the fatherless, plead for the widow." The emphasis here is on moral and spiritual conduct; the ceremonial and ritualistic aspects of religion are conspicuously left unmentioned. The paradox, however, is only one of appearance and phrasing. Inherently there is no contradiction. The ostensibly antinomian statements do not oppose the offering of sacrifices, prayer, or the observance of the Sabbath and festivals. It is not ritual but hypocrisy that they condemn. Isaiah (1:13) expresses the thought in a single phrase: "I cannot endure iniquity and solemn assembly." Organized religion must necessarily have cultic forms; but without inwardness and unqualified sincerity they are an affront to the Deity and fail of their purpose. The underlying motive of the precepts is to purify and elevate man (Ps. 119:29, 40, 68). The Torah (Wisdom) is a tree of life and its ways are ways of peace (Prov. 3:17, 18). Sin does not injure God (Job 7:20), but is a disaster to man (Deut. 28:15ff.). It is heartfelt devotion that saves the *mitzvah* from becoming a meaningless convention and an act of hypocrisy (Isa. 29:13). The specific commandments are in a sense pointers and aids to that larger identification with God's will that is conterminous with life as a whole: "In all your ways acknowledge Him" (Prov. 3:6). Just as the divine wonders and portents lead to a deeper understanding of the daily miracles of providence, so the precepts are guides to the whole duty of man. Biblical religion is thus seen to be an indivisible synthesis of moral and spiritual principles, on the one hand, and practical observances on the other.

The Biblical Theodicy. The moral basis of providence, reinforced by the ethic of the Torah, also raises another kind of problem. Can the biblical theodicy always be justified? The issue is raised already in the Bible itself. Abraham challenges the divine justice: "Shall not the Judge of all the earth do right?" (Gen. 18:25). Moses echoes the cry in another context: "O Lord, why hast Thou done evil to this people?" (Ex. 5:22). The prophets are no less perplexed: "Why does the way of the wicked prosper? Why do all who are treacherous thrive?" (Jer. 12:1). The psalmist speaks for the individual and the nation in many generations, when he cries: "My God, my God, why hast Thou forsaken me?" (22:2 [1]), and the Book of Job is, in its magnificent entirety, one great heroic struggle to solve the problem of unwarranted human suffering. The biblical answer appears to point to the limitations of man's experience and understanding. History is long, but individual life is short. Hence the human view is fragmentary; events justify themselves in the end, but the person concerned does not always live to see the denouement. In the words of the psalmist: "Though the wicked sprout like grass and all evildoers flourish, they are doomed to destruction forever" (92:8–10; cf. 37:35–39). The brevity of man's years is further complicated by his lack of insight. God's purpose is beyond his comprehension: "For as the heavens are higher than the earth, so are My ways higher than your ways and My thoughts than your thoughts" (Isa. 55:9). In the final analysis, biblical theodicy calls for faith: "But the righteous shall live by his faith" (Hab. 2:4); "they who wait for the Lord shall renew their strength" (Isa. 40:31). It is not an irrational faith:—*Certum est quia impossibile est* (Tertullian, *De Carne Christi,* 5), but is necessitated by innate human intellectual limitations. In another direction the problem is even more formidable. God, the Bible states categorically, hardened Pharaoh's heart; nevertheless the Egyptian ruler was punished for this. Indeed his obduracy was induced in order to provide the occasion for his punishment (Ex. 7:3). Here the fundamental norms of justice by any standards are flagrantly violated. The explanation in this sphere of biblical theodicy is not theological but semantic. Scripture ascribes to God phenomena and events with which He is only indirectly concerned. However, since God is the author of all natural law and the designer of history, everything that occurs is, in a deep sense, His doing. Even in human affairs the king or the government is said to "do" everything that is performed under its aegis. Thus God declares in Amos 4:7: "And I caused it to rain upon one city, and I caused it not to rain upon another city," although the next clause uses passive and impersonal verbal forms to describe the same occurrences. The processes of nature need not be mentioned, since the laws of the universe are dictates of God. Similarly Exodus states indiscriminately that "Pharaoh hardened his heart" (8:28), that "the heart of Pharaoh was hardened" (9:7), and that "the Lord hardened the heart of Pharaoh" (9:12). In the end it is all one; what God permits He does. This interpretation does not, however, fit another area of divine conduct. Uzzah, the Bible states, was struck dead for an innocent act that was motivated by concern for the safety of "the ark of God" (II Sam. 6:6–7). Wherein lay the iniquity? Here the reason appears to be of a different character. Even innocent actions may in certain circumstances be disastrous. Uzzah's attempt to save the ark from falling was well meant, but it was conducive to irreverence. Man needs God's help; God does not require the help of man (Sot. 35a; for a similar thought cf. Ps. 50:12; another explanation is given by Kimḥi, II Sam. 6:6). In one thoughtless moment Uzzah could have reduced the sacred ark in the eyes of the people to the impotent level of the idols, which the prophets depicted with such scathing mockery. The same principle operated in the tragedy of Nadab and Abihu, and Moses explained the underlying principle in the words: "I will show Myself holy among those who are near Me" (Lev. 10:1–3).

The Limitation of the Infinite God. Is the Godhead subject to restriction? The irresistible conclusion to be drawn from biblical teaching is that such a limitation exists. Man's freedom to resist or obey the will of God is a restriction of the Deity's power that is totally unknown in the physical universe. It must be added, however, that this restriction is an act of divine self-limitation. In His love for man God has, so to speak, set aside an area of freedom in which man can elect to do right or wrong (Deut. 5:26; 30:17). In rabbinic language: "Everything is in the power of Heaven except the reverence of Heaven" (Ber. 33b). Man is thereby saved from being an automaton. It adds a new dimension to the relationship between God and man. Man may defect, but when, on the other hand, he chooses the path of loyalty, he does so from choice, from true love. Needless to say, without such freedom there could be neither sin nor punishment, neither merit nor reward. The divine humility, which permits human dissent, is also the grace to which the dissenter succumbs in the end. Man is a faithful rebel, who is reconciled with his Maker in the crowning period of history. God's self-limitation is thus seen as an extension of His creative power. Other biblical concepts that might be construed as restrictions of God's infinitude are, on closer scrutiny, seen not to be real limitations. The association of the Lord with holy places like the Tent of Meeting, the Temple, Zion, or Sinai does not imply that He is not omnipresent. In prophetic vision Isaiah saw the divine train fill the Temple, and at the same time he heard the seraphim declare: "the whole earth is full of His glory" (6:1–3). God's geographical association, or His theophany at a given place, signifies consecration of the site, which thus becomes a source of inspiration to man; but no part of the universe exists at any time outside God's presence. Sometimes God is depicted as asking man for information (Gen. 3:9; 4:9). On other occasions He is stated to repent His actions and to be grieved (Gen. 6:6). These are mere anthropomorphisms. The Lord knows all (Jer. 11:20; 16:17; Ps. 7:10), and unlike human beings He does not repent (Num. 23:19). Genesis 6:6 is not a contradiction of this thesis; its "human" terminology does not imply a diminution of God's omniscience, but emphasizes the moral freedom granted to man. In addition to spiritual option, the Creator, as has been stated, gave man knowledge. This finds expression, inter alia, in magical powers, which, in as much as they are "supernatural," constitute a challenge to God's will. In Moses' protracted struggle with Pharaoh, the Egyptians actually pit their magical powers against the Almighty's miracles. In the end they acknowledge their relative weakness and admit that they cannot rival "the finger of God" (Ex. 8:15). This is to be expected, for the divine wisdom is unbounded (Job 11:7), whereas human understanding is finite. Nevertheless the use of all forms of sorcery, even by non-Israelites, is strongly denounced (Isa. 44:25); to the Israelite, witchcraft is totally forbidden (Deut. 18:10–11). The differentiation between magic and miracles had deep roots in Hebrew monotheism. To the pagan mind magical powers were independent forces to which even the gods had to have recourse. The miracle, on the other hand, is regarded in the Bible as a manifestation of God's power and purpose. It is an attestation of the prophet's mission (Isa. 7:11); whereas divination and sorcery are either forms of deception (Isa. 44:25) or, where magic is effective, as in the episode of the witch of Endor (I Sam. 28:7ff.), it represents an abuse of man's God-given knowledge. There is no independent realm of witchcraft, however; all power, natural and supernatural, emanates from the one God. To the Israelite all that happens is wrought by God.

The Divine Personality. Though inconceivable, God is portrayed throughout the Bible as a person in contradistinction to the idols, who are dead, He is called the living God (II Kings 19:4, 16). He is neither inanimate nor a philosophical abstraction; He is the living source of all life. Anthropomorphisms abound in the Bible, but it is not by these that the divine personality, so to speak, is depicted. Anthropomorphic figures were intended to help early man to grasp ideas that in philosophical terms transcended the human intellect. God's essential personality is primarily reflected in His attributes, which motivate His acts. He is King, Judge, Father, Shepherd, Mentor, Healer, and Redeemer—to mention only a few of His aspects in His relationship to man. Different biblical teachers conceived God's character from different historical angles. Amos was conscious of God's justice. Hosea underscored the Lord's love, and made forgiveness and compassion the coefficient, as it were, of divinity: "I will not execute My fierce anger . . . for I am God and not man" (11:9). Ezekiel stresses that God does not desire the destruction of the wicked but that through repentance they may live (18:23). The heart of the matter is clearly stated in the Torah: "The Lord passed before him (Moses), and proclaimed, 'The Lord, the Lord, a God merciful and gracious, slow to anger, and abounding in steadfast love and faithfulness, keeping steadfast love for thousands, forgiving iniquity and transgression and sin, but who will by no means clear the guilty . . ." (Ex. 34:6–7). Maimonides was philosophically justified in insisting that God has no attributes and that the epithets applied to Him in the Bible really represent human emotions evoked by His actions (*Guide*, 2:54). The Bible, however, which is little interested in the speculative approach to the Deity, but teaches practical wisdom and religion as life, without the help of catechism or formulated dogmas, prefers to endow God with personality to which it gives the warmth and beauty of positive characterization. In sum, the divine nature is composed of both justice and love. The Bible recognizes that without justice love itself becomes a form of injustice; but in itself justice is not enough. It can only serve as a foundation; the superstructure—the bridge between God and man—is grace.

Between Man and God. Grace is the divine end of the bridge; the human side is existential devotion. Otherwise, what M. Buber felicitously called the "I—Thou" relationship cannot come into being. Hence, underlying all the commandments is the supreme precept: "And you shall love the Lord your God with all your heart, and with all your soul, and with all your might" (Deut. 6:5). This love is unqualified: "You shall be whole-hearted with the Lord your God" (Deut. 18:13). It calls for complete surrender; but this is not conceived as a narrow, if intense, religious attitude. It is broad-based enough to allow for deep-rooted spiritual communion. Man pours out his heart in prayer to God; it is to Him that he uplifts his soul in thanksgiving and praise; and it is also to Him that he addresses his most searching questions and most incisive criticism of life and providence. Sincere criticism of God is never rebuked. God reproaches Job's friends, who were on His side; but Job is rewarded despite his searing indictment of God's actions. The God-man relationship flowers in an evolutionary process of education: Man is gradually weaned from his own inhumanity, from atrocities, like human sacrifice (Gen. 22:2–14), from bestial conduct, and from wronging his fellowman. The goal again is love: "You shall love your neighbor as yourself" (Lev. 19:18). It is a corollary of the love of God: "I am the Lord." Reward and retribution play a role in the divine educational procedures; but their functions are limited—they are not ultimates. The eternal fires of hell are never used as a deterrent, though punishment of the wicked after death is obscurely mentioned (Isa. 66:24; Dan. 12:2), nor is paradise used as an inducement. The Torah-covenant is an unquenchable spiritual light (Prov. 6:23); but the "I—Thou" relationship does not end with the written word. God communes with man directly. The prophet hears the heavenly voice and echoes it; the psalmist knows, with unfaltering conviction, that his prayer has been answered and that salvation has been wrought before he actually experiences it. At one with God, man finds ultimate happiness: "In Thy presence is fullness of joy, in Thy right hand bliss for evermore" (Ps. 16:11).

The Hebrew term for the love that binds man to God (as well as to his fellowman) is *ʾahavah;* but sometimes the Bible uses another word, *yirʾah* (literally: "fear"), which seems to turn the "I—Thou" nexus into an "It" relationship. The psalmist declares: "The fear of the Lord is the beginning of wisdom" (111:10), and Ecclesiastes comes to the conclusion: "The end of the matter; all has been heard. Fear God, and keep His commandments, for this is the whole duty of man" (12:13). The picture is thus completely changed. The heavenly Father suddenly becomes a divine tyrant, before whom man cowers in terror, as does the unenlightened pagan before the demonic force that he seeks to appease. This might be consonant with the notion of "the jealous God" (Ex. 34:14), but it would appear to be irreconcilable with the concept of the God of *ḥesed* ("lovingkindness," "grace"). Here, too, this is not a theological but a semantic problem. *Yirʾah* does not signify "fear"; it is best rendered by "reverence." "Love" and "reverence" are not antithetic but complementary terms. They are two aspects of a single idea. *ʾAhavah* expresses God's nearness; *yirʾah* the measureless distance between the Deity and man (see *Love, Love and Fear of God). God spoke to Moses "mouth to mouth" (Num. 12:8), yet in his human frailty the Hebrew leader could not "see" his divine interlocutor (Ex. 33:20). The inner identity of "love" and "reverence" is reflected in the Torah's religious summary: "And now, Israel, what does the Lord your God require of you but to revere the Lord your God, to walk in all His ways and to love Him, and to serve the Lord your God with all your heart and with all your soul" (Deut. 10:12). Talmudic Judaism (Shab. 120a) drew a distinction between *ḥasidut* (steadfast love of God) and *yirʾat shamayim* ("reverence of Heaven"), but this represents a later development. In the Bible this bifurcation does not exist; "reverence of God" is by and large the biblical equivalent of "religion."

Likewise there is no spiritual contradiction between the "gracious" and the "jealous" God. "Jealousy" is an anthropomorphic term used to define God's absolute character, which excludes all other concepts of the Godhead. It does not detract from the divine love and compassion; it serves only to protect them. The sum of all the divine attributes finds expression in the epithet "holy." It is the highest praise that prophet and psalmist can give to the Lord (Isa. 6:3; Ps. 22:4 [3]), and since man is created in the image of God (Gen. 1:26), the attribute of holiness becomes the basis of the concept of "the imitation of God": "You shall be holy; for I the Lord your God am holy" (Lev. 19:2). The Bible makes it clear, however, that, in seeking to model himself on the divine example, it is primarily God's moral attributes that man must copy. Even as God befriends the sojourner and acts as the father of the fatherless and as the judge of the widow, so must man, on his human scale, endeavor to do (Deut. 10:18–19; cf. Sot. 14a). Indeed all that uplifts man, including the Sabbath and abstention from impurity, is comprised in the concept of the imitation of God. At the highest level Israel's ethic and theology are indissolubly linked.

To sum up: the biblical conception of God was revolutionary both in its theological and its moral implications. The pagan world may occasionally have glimpsed, in primitive form, some of the higher truths inherent in Israel's ethical monotheism. Egypt for a brief span attained to monolatry (Akhenaton's heresy); Babylon had a glimmering of a unified cosmic process; Marduk, Shamash, and Aton punished evildoers; and some Greek philosophers commended the imitation of the godhead. Yet no cult in antiquity even remotely approached the elevated conceptions associated with the one God of the Bible. This spiritual revolution not only eventually brought paganism to an end, but its inner dynamic gave birth, in time, to two daughter religions, Christianity and Islam, which, despite their essential differences from Judaism, are deeply rooted in biblical thought. [I.ABR.]

IN HELLENISTIC LITERATURE

Certain Jewish concepts of God were apparently known to the circle of Aristotle. His pupil Theophrastus (fourth century B.C.E.) said of the Jews that they were "the philosophers among the Syrians," because of their concept of the unity of God. The skeptic *Hecataeus of Abdera, the first of the Greek thinkers to attempt to define the substance of the Jewish concept of God, states that the Jews do not give form or image to God, because they regard the cosmos—which includes everything—as God. Their idea of the unity of God, according to Hecataeus, includes all existing things. Megasthenes, a Greek writer of the early third century, also notes that the important philosophers, outside of Greece, were the wise men of Israel. He arrived at this conclusion because of the fact that the unity of God was an accepted idea in Israel. Thus the Greek thinkers regarded the Jewish notion of divine unity as a view founded upon philosophic meditation in the spirit of the ideas common in their own circles, and in the spirit of the Ionian monists.

However, the primary quality of God according to Jewish teachings—ethical personalism—was not considered by the Greek writers. This idea of God's ethical will, which is beyond the universe and beyond nature and has absolute dominion over nature and over man, was far from the Greek mode of thought. Strangely no signs of influence of the Greek concept of God's unity is found in the early Jewish compositions in Greek. In the Septuagint, for instance, there is a recognizable tendency to avoid anthropomorphism (e.g., "And they saw the God of Israel" (Ex. 24:10) is translated as: "And they saw the place where the God of Israel stood"). This tendency, however, has deep roots in the Jewish concepts of God during the period of the Second Temple, which found expression in the abstention from uttering the Tetragrammaton or in applying to God terms taken from everyday usage. This should not be regarded as intentional avoidance of anthropomorphism, as there are no signs of such avoidance in the Bible. It rather expresses a reverence for the majesty of God, which compelled the choosing of special expressions relating to divine matters. In any event the Septuagint contains no trace of the terms or linguistic usages current in Greek philosophic literature. All those terms to which the philosophers gave a special abstract connotation, such as Nous ("Mind"), Cosmos ("Universe"), Psyche ("Divine Soul"), occur in the Septuagint not in their abstract philosophical sense but in their normal concrete daily usage. Even in the apocryphal Wisdom of Solomon—a book undoubtedly influenced by Greek philosophy—the concepts of God are no different from those found in the Bible. Although the author of the Wisdom of Solomon praises the value of Wisdom in his book and regards it as a sort of partner in the creation of the world, this idea does not in the slightest detract from the concept of the unity of God for God is the Creator of the world, and Wisdom is not regarded as an independent or separate entity from God. The moral value of Wisdom in the life of man is particularly stressed as a force which refines the spirit of man and elevates him to a higher intellectual moral level. In so doing the author reduces the importance of Wisdom as a cosmic force. Man, according to the Wisdom of Solomon, seeks a personal closeness with God; God reveals Himself by signs and wonders in the history of the Jewish nation and by utilizing reward and punishment. All this accords with what is found in the Bible. Yet in contrast to the later Jewish view, the author of the Wisdom of Solomon regards God as a creator from existent material (not *ex nihilo*) as in the doctrine of matter and form found in Plato. The philosopher *Aristobulus of Paneas (first half of 2nd century B.C.E.) already clearly expressed his opposition to anthropomorphism, and explains such expressions as "the hand of God," or "the voice of God" allegorically (see *Allegory) as the power of God, the expression of God's power of dominion in the world, etc. In the teaching of Aristobulus there is already a clear attempt to make the Jewish view of God correspond to the teaching of the Greek philosophers, even though it is difficult to determine to which school of philosophy Aristobulus himself belonged. The author of the Letter of *Aristeas too was influenced by Greek philosophy. God rules over all creatures and all are dependent upon Him, while He himself is not dependent upon any creature. The author of the Letter of Aristeas lays down that all men are aware of the unity of God as the Creator of everything, the director of everything, and the ruler over everything, but different peoples designate Him by different names (Letter of Aristeas 16). The name of the chief god current among the Greeks, Zeus, indicates his character as the source of life in nature and it too therefore is nothing else but a term for the one God.

Philo. The influence of Greek philosophy is especially strong on *Philo. Philo, under the influence of Plato, frequently uses for God the terms *τό ὄν, τό ὄν ὄντως* which in the teaching of Plato signify "existence" or "true existence" (see Timaeus, 27D–29D). Philo points to a basis for these in the expression "I am that I am" (cf. Som. 1:230–31, Ex. 3:14). There is no hint of such terminology in the Septuagint (the sentence: *Ἐγώ εἰμι ὁ ὤν*, used by the Septuagint for "I am that I am" has no connection with the above-mentioned terms used by Plato and Philo). Philo also uses such terms as *ἕν, μόνας*, "the one," "unity," etc., for the purpose of stressing God's transcendence over perfection, over all concepts of the good and the beautiful, and for His being above human comprehension. Such a degree of philosophic abstraction in the conception of God rules out any possibility of personal relations between man and God, examples of which are found in the Bible and the later literature. However as a Jew Philo was unable to content himself with mere abstraction, and he frequently raises the question of the relations of man to God, particularly on the methods by which man can come to apprehend God. Apprehension of God is possible, according to Philo, from two aspects: that of His existence, and that of His subsistence. A conception of God's existence can be achieved without great difficulty, since His works testify to this: the universe, man, and all other creatures. However many aberrations occur in such a conception, since many people do not distinguish the ruler of the world from the powers subject to him; these people are compared to one who ignores the chariot driver and thinks that the horses are directing the movement toward the goal with their own powers; in such a manner the distorted concepts of God current in the circles of idolaters are created. Philo battled with exceptional vehemence against the views of those who regard the various heavenly powers or other hidden forces as independent active causes. It is his opinion that sound human intelligence has the power to avoid such aberrations in the understanding of God and this was achieved, according to Philo, by the greatest of the Greek philosophers whose names he mentions with much respect. However, this recognition of God's existence founded upon contemplation of the material world is very far from perfect, since it judges the uncreated from the created, whereas it is impossible to judge the reality of God by the creatures He created. A more perfect apprehension of God's reality is attained by those who "apprehended him through Himself, the light through the light." This was achieved only by the few intimates of God who are in no need of external analogies as aids to the apprehension of God. This type of person is called by Philo, "Israel," i.e., according to his etymology, "seers of God" (Praem. 43ff.). This level of understanding of the Divine existence was attained by Moses. The conceptual level of apprehension of the Divine existence is the highest that a mortal can attain. For as a result of the frailty of human nature man does not possess the power to apprehend anything of the nature of the Divine. Even the sharpest vision is not capable of seeing Him who was not created, since man possesses no instrument which could prepare him to apprehend His image, and the most man can attain is the apprehension that the nature of God is not within the bounds of human apprehension. Nevertheless the attempt at such apprehension is not in vain. For even though the results of such effort will always be negligible, the effort itself elevates man and lifts him to a high degree of spiritual purity. Examples of such endeavor by man to apprehend the Divine nature are described in Philo's writings. After human intellect investigates everything to be found on earth, it turns to the contemplation of heavenly causes and partakes of their harmonious motion. From there it rises to the sphere of the intelligibles and at the time it contemplates the ideas of sensible things and absorbs their spiritual splendor, "a sober intoxication" (*νηφάλια μέθη*) assails it and elevates it to the level of prophecy. With a spirit full of supramundane yearnings it is elevated to the highest level of the intelligible world and already beholds itself approaching the King Himself in His glory. Now, however, when the craving for vision is greatest, dazzling beams of abounding light pour themselves over it and the brilliance of their glitter dims the eye of reason (Op. 69–72; Praem. 36f.). The impossibility of direct contact between God's nature and the sensible world created the concept of duality in Philo's understanding of the world, a concept much influenced by Plato. According to this view it does not become the majesty and elevation of God to be in direct contact with matter, and the forces within God or the activities overflowing from him fulfill the function of the intermediaries. The great gap between the sublime God and the perceptible world is bridged in Philo's teaching by the idea of level and intermediaries which serve as a connection between the absolute being of God and the changing level of the perceptible world. Angel, Idea, Logos—are the terms utilized by Philo to formulate the principles of the theory of levels whose influence upon subsequent religious thought was enormous.

[Y.G./ED.]

IN TALMUDIC LITERATURE

Abstract philosophical concepts, such as are found in Philo, are foreign to the thought system of the rabbis of the Talmud and Midrash. However, a marked tendency is discernible among them to present an exalted picture of God, as well as to avoid expressions that could throw the slightest shadow on the conception of His absolute Oneness. In the *Targums, the early Aramaic translations of Scripture, the name God is frequently rendered "*memra* ('word') of God." It is certain that no connection whatsoever is intended between this word and the "logos," or with the idea of an intermediary between God and the world. Were this the intention, the word "*memra*" would have been used in the Targum to such verses as: "The Lord sent a word unto Jacob" (Isa. 9:7); "so shall My word be that goeth forth out of My mouth" (*ibid.* 55:11); "He sent His word and healed them" (Ps. 107:20). It is precisely in these verses that the Targum employs the word *pitgam* ("word") or *nevu'ah* ("prophecy"). Even in the verse "By the word of the Lord were the heavens made" (Ps. 33:6) "word" is rendered by the Targums as *milta* ("word") of God. Nor is there any mention of the expression "*memra*" in the Targums of the account of creation. It is therefore certain that this word, which occurs only in the Targums, but not in the Talmud and the Midrash, was used only to guard against any idea which (in the minds of the common people for whom the Targum was intended) might militate against the exalted conception of the Divinity or tend to diminish the pure concept of God. For the same reason one finds many euphemisms employed as substitutes for the names of God, such as *Ha-Gevurah* ("Might"), *Raḥmana* ("the Merciful"), *Ha-Kadosh Barukh Hu* ("The Holy One, blessed be He"), or such terms as *Shamayim* ("Heaven"), *Ha-Makom* ("Omnipresent"), *Ribbono shel Olam* ("Lord of the Universe"), *Mi-she-Amar ve-Hayah ha-Olam* ("He who spoke, and the Universe came into being"), *Avinu she-ba-Shamayim* ("Our Father in heaven"), *Mi she-Shikken Shemo ba-Bayit ha-Zeh* ("He who caused His name to dwell in this house"). A special significance was given by the rabbis to the tetragrammaton, and to *Elohim*, the tetragrammaton denoting the attribute of mercy, and *Elohim*, that of judgment (Gen. R. 33:3). That this was a time-honored distinction is evident from its occurrence in Philo where, however, in conformity with the tradition of the Septuagint to translate the tetragrammaton by the Greek word *κύριος*, which corresponds more closely to the concepts of rule and judgment, the name is regarded as the symbol of the attribute of judgment, and the name *Elohim* (translated in the Septuagint by Θεός) as a symbol of the attribute of mercy. The idea of the unity of God, which was widely discussed in non-Jewish circles at the time, receives strong emphasis in the *aggadah*. The concept of the unity of God is based upon the premise that the cosmos, with all its activities, is inconceivable without the existence of a single power which determines and directs it in accordance with a preordained plan and in conformity with a definite purpose. In order to give concrete expression to this idea, the rabbis of the *aggadah* utilized various parables, whose prototypes are found in Philo. They were particularly fond of the parable of "the ship and the captain," or of "the building and its owner," or of "the building and its director" (Sif. Deut. 341; Gen. R. 12:12; Mid. Ps. 23 to 24:1ff.; Gen. R. 39:1). Just as it is impossible for the ship, for example, to reach its destination without a captain, so administration of the cosmos and of individuals is impossible without a directing and supervising force. Other parables frequently found in the *aggadah* were intended to bring about reverence for the might of God, whose awesomeness is rendered even greater for the very reason that it defies man's powers of comprehension. If the brilliance of the sun blinds the human eye, how much more so the light of God (Ḥul. 59b). Man is unable to observe more than a particle of His grandeur and sublimity. The rabbis of the *aggadah* also use the soul as an example in teaching this doctrine. If a man's own soul, the source of his life, is beyond his intellectual comprehension, how much less can he comprehend the Creator of the universe and the source of its life (Mid. Ps. to 103:1; Lev. R. 4:3).

The recognition of the oneness of God is regarded by the scholars of the Talmud as a cardinal principle of religion, concerning which mankind as a whole was commanded, the seven precepts binding upon Noachians including idolatry (see *Noachian Law).

If there is any difference between the biblical concept of God and that of the Talmud it lies in the fact that the God of the Talmud is more "homey," so to speak, than the God of the Bible. He is nearer to the masses, to the brokenhearted, to the ordinary person in need of His help. Only in this sense, does He at times appear to be an even greater epitomization of ethical virtues than the God of Scripture.

One finds no echo in the *aggadah* of the arguments for and against idolatry, such as occur in the Greek literature of that period. The *aggadah's* attacks on idolatry are much more extreme than those of the biblical period, the dominant note being one of contempt and disdain for those who presume to desecrate in a degrading and crude manner that which is most holy in human life—the service of God. In the course of their violent attacks on idolatry, the rabbis did not shrink from denouncing with equal vehemence the cult of emperor-worship, a type of idolatry for which Nimrod, Sisera, Sennacherib, Hiram, and Nebuchadnezzar served as the prototypes.

In apocalyptic circles, among those who expounded *Merkabah mysticism and those who entered *paradise, there is no discernible variation from the aggadic concept of God, the restrictions that the scholars of the Talmud placed upon the study of the esoteric doctrine of the *Ma'aseh Merkavah* and upon those of whom it was said that they "entered paradise" having a great deal to do with this. Despite this there were many in these circles "who looked and became demented," or "who cut down the saplings" (i.e., led astray the youth). The Talmud applied to them the term **minim* ("sectarians"), a term which also included Christians, Gnostics, and other sectarians, whom the rabbis regarded either as complete disbelievers (Sif. Deut. 32, 39) or as rejecting the oneness of God. Regardless of whether these sectarians were Jews or whether they wished to identify themselves with them, the rabbis made every effort to exclude them from the fold, at times taking drastic measures to do so. The reaction of the rabbis to the varying concepts of God that were widespread in their time was thus characterized by exceptional vigilance. Even more significant, however, was the complete absence, in their doctrine of the Deity, of any materialistic elements. Though, according to the rabbis, angels play an important role in the lives of human beings, this does not in the least affect the closeness of God to every person in his daily life: "When trouble comes upon a man, he does not burst upon his patron suddenly, but goes and stands at his door . . . and he calls his servant who announces: 'so and so is at the door'. . . . Not so, however with regard to the Holy One, blessed be He. If trouble comes upon a man, he should cry out neither to Michael nor to Gabriel, but let him cry out to me, and I shall answer him immediately" (TJ, Ber. 9:1, 13a).

The nearness of God is the predominating idea of the Talmud and Midrash. God mourns because of the evil decrees He has pronounced upon Israel; He goes into exile with His children; He studies Torah and gives His view on halakhic topics, and is overjoyed if the scholars triumph over him in *halakhah*. Every generation of Israel has been witness to the nearness of God. God revealed Himself at the Red Sea as a warrior; at Sinai as a sage filled with mercy; after the incident of the golden calf, as a congregational reader draped in a *tallit* ("prayer shawl"), instructing the people how to pray and repent. These metaphors are not intended anthropomorphically, but are rather devices for driving home the idea of God's nearness to his people, by the use of striking and daring images. The sages see no difference between God's closeness to Israel in the past and in the present. The idea of the selection of Israel and the greatness of its destiny stands, both in the past and in the present, at the very center of the relationship between God and His people, and complete confidence therefore exists that God will answer His people whenever they seek Him. The concept of God's nearness to man is also enshrined in the ethical teaching of the time, the rabbis enjoining man to imitate the attributes of God: "Just as He is merciful and compassionate, be thou too merciful and compassionate (Mekh., be-Shallaḥ 14:2; Sifra 19:1). [Y.M.G.]

IN MEDIEVAL JEWISH PHILOSOPHY

Medieval Jewish philosophy concentrated very heavily on problems concerning the existence and nature of God, His knowability, and His relationship to man and the world. Neither the Bible nor rabbinic literature contain systematic philosophic treatments of these topics, and it was only under the stimulus of Greek and Arabic philosophy that Jews engaged in such inquiries. In natural philosophy, metaphysics, and theology Jewish thought was influenced by *Kalām thinkers and by Arabic versions of neoplatonism and Aristotelianism. Fundamental to Jewish philosophic speculation about God was the conviction that human reason is reliable (within its proper limits), and that biblical theology is rational. Most medieval Jewish philosophers considered intellectual inquiry essential to a religious life, and were convinced that there could be no real opposition between reason and faith. Thus, *Saadiah Gaon held that, "The Bible is not the sole basis of our religion, for in addition to it we have two other bases. One of these is anterior to it; namely, the fountain of reason . . ." (*Book of Beliefs and Opinions*, 3:10). *Baḥya ibn Paquda believed that it is a religious duty to investigate by rational methods such questions as God's unity, because, of the three avenues which God has given us to know Him and His law, "the first is a sound intellect" (*Ḥovot ha-Levavot*, introduction; cf. 1:3). Even *Judah Halevi, who distrusted philosophy, said, "Heaven forbid that there should be anything in the Bible to contradict that which is manifest or proved" (*Kuzari*, 1:67). This attitude toward the relationship between reason and faith dominated medieval Jewish philosophy. It reached its highest, most elaborate, and most familiar expression in the thought of *Maimonides, and was reaffirmed by later philosophers, such as *Levi b. Gershom and Joseph *Albo.

The Existence of God. The first task of philosophical theology is to prove the existence of God, though medieval philosophers did not always begin their treatises with this topic. Of the familiar philosophic arguments for the existence of God, the ontological argument, i.e., that God's existence follows necessarily from a definition of what He is, seems to have been unknown to medieval Jewish thought. Emphasis was placed on the cosmological argument, according to which the existence of God was derived from some aspect of the world, such as the existence of motion or causality. Some attention was also given to the teleological argument, according to which the existence of God was derived from order existing in the world.

Teleological Argument. The simplest form of the teleological argument, the argument from design, was used by Saadiah and Baḥya. Both derided those who claim that the world arose by chance without an intelligent and purposive creator. They pointed out the high improbability (in their view, incredibility) that the extremely complex and delicately balanced order of the universe could have come about accidentally, since even ordinary artifacts are known to require an artisan. A more sophisticated version of this argument was offered by Levi b. Gershom. From the teleological nature of all existing things, i.e., the fact (as he supposed) that each thing is moved toward the realization of its own proper end, he concluded that all things together move toward their common ultimate end. This is the final cause of the world, namely God.

Cosmological Argument. In Saadiah's versions of the cosmological argument, following the Kalām closely, he deduced the existence of God from the creation of the world. He first demonstrated that the world must have been created in time out of nothing, and he then showed that such a world could only have been created by an omnipotent God whose essence is an absolute unity. Baḥya followed a similar method. His basic argument was that since the world is composite, it must have been put together at some point in time; it could not have made itself, because nothing can make itself; therefore, it must have been created, and the creator of the world we call God. The earliest Jewish philosopher to turn away from the Kalām in favor of a stricter Aristotelianism was Abraham *ibn Daud, and the most prominent by far was Maimonides (see *Aristotle and Aristotelianism). In contrast to the followers of the Kalām, Maimonides rejected the view that proofs for the existence of God are contingent on proofs of the creation of the world. He showed that in principle one cannot prove either that the world is eternal or that it was created, but went on to argue that even if we grant the eternity of the world, we can still demonstrate the existence of God. The arguments he used, two of which had already been set forth in Abraham ibn Daud's *Emunah Ramah*, are essentially cosmological. The most familiar of Maimonides' arguments is the argument from motion. Since things in the world are in motion and no finite thing can move itself, every motion must be caused by another; but since this leads to an infinite regress, which is unintelligible, there must be an unmoved mover at the beginning of the series. This unmoved mover is God. Another of Maimonides' arguments begins from the fact that the existence of all things in our experience is contingent, i.e., their existence begins and ends in time, so that each thing can be conceived as not existing. Contingent existence is unintelligible, unless there is at least one necessary existence, one being whose existence is eternal and independent of all cause, standing behind it. Maimonides laid great stress on the conception of God as necessary existence. This argument was the only one that Ḥasdai *Crescas found acceptable, though he was a severe critic of the Aristotelianism of his predecessors. In addition to other arguments, Saadiah and Judah Halevi offered a non-philosophical argument. Since the revelation at Sinai took place in the presence of 600,000 adults, there is public evidence that places the fact of God's existence beyond all reasonable doubt.

The Nature of God. For Judaism, the proof of God's existence is incomplete unless it also establishes His absolute unity. Though Jewish philosophers conceived this unity in different ways, none deviated from the fixed belief in God's unity. In reflecting on this question, practically all Jewish philosophers of the Middle Ages came to the conclusion that the unity of God necessarily implies that He must be incorporeal. This conclusion then required them to set forth figurative or metaphorical interpretations of the many biblical passages that ascribe bodily characteristics to God, because no proper philosophical understanding of God can accept a literal reading of these anthropomorphisms. As Abraham ibn Daud pointed out, Jewish thinkers were particularly sensitive to this problem because many non-Jews held the slanderous opinion that the Jews believe in a corporeal God. Thus, it is understandable that medieval Jewish philosophers devoted much attention to arguments for God's incorporeality and the detailed exegesis of anthropormorphic passages in Scripture. Some scholars even suggest that the primary purpose of Saadiah's philosophical work was to refute all claims that God is corporeal. Maimonides began his *Guide of the Perplexed* with an elaborate and comprehensive effort to refute all literal interpretations of passages in the Bible that speak of God as having corporeal features.

Divine Attributes. Having rejected the literal meaning of biblical statements about God, the medieval philosophers had to determine what may be considered a legitimate description of God. Can attributes of God, such as goodness, mercy, wisdom, and justice be predicated of Him positively? The bulk of medieval opinion held that one cannot properly say anything positive about God, for two reasons. First, ascribing multiple attributes to Him compromises His unity. Second, human language reflects the limitations of the human perspective, so that describing God by way of human predicates reduces Him to the finiteness of man. Therefore, a majority of the medieval philosophers held that nothing positive can be said about God. However, since there is no choice but to talk about God in some way, despite the limitations of human language, they had to find some interpretation of the divine attributes which would not be a positive one. The most widely accepted solution was to understand all the essential attributes, such as living, wise, powerful, which describe the divine nature, as negative, so that every seemingly positive assertion about God only says what He is not. For example, the statement, "God is wise," can only mean that He is not ignorant. In this way one may speak of God's nature in the language of men without compromising His unity and without reducing Him to human form. Because God transcends all knowledge and all experience, one can only affirm that He exists and even this must be interpreted as negating that He lacks existence and describes what He is solely in terms of negative attributes. This view was held with minor variations by Saadiah, Baḥya, Joseph ibn *Zaddik, Judah Halevi, Ibn Daud, and Maimonides. Besides these descriptions of God's nature which were interpreted as negative attributes, there are others, such as merciful and just, which appear to describe what God does rather than what He is. These could also not be interpreted positively since such positive predication of these descriptions, too, could compromise God's unity. These descriptions were therefore interpreted as attributes of action, i.e., as describing God's effects without, however attempting to account for a property in God which causes these effects. This non-positive predication of the attributes of action again safeguards divine unity. Maimonides gave the most subtle and comprehensive treatment to the problem of attributes. While holding rigorously to the negative interpretation of essential attributes, he also followed some of his predecessors in affirming the doctrine of attributes of action. Thus, a great calamity may be interpreted in human eyes as an expression of God's anger, and a seemingly miraculous rescue of men from danger will be understood as an instance of God's love and compassion. Two major figures of the late medieval period rejected the doctrine of negative attributes. Both Levi b. Gershom and Ḥasdai Crescas argued in favor of the view that if God is to be intelligible, His attributes must be understood as positive predications. They did not think that positive predication compromises the divine unity and perfection. Moreover, Levi b. Gershom believed that positive predicates could be applied to God literally because their primary meaning is derived from their application to God, while their human meaning is secondary. The position of Joseph Albo, the last of the medieval Jewish philosophers, is ambiguous. Although he affirmed the doctrine of negative attributes, he also tried to argue that the divine attributes have a descriptive-positive meaning.

Relation of God to Man and the World. In denying God's corporeality and in developing the doctrine of negative attributes, the philosophers went far toward protecting the unity of God. However in proclaiming this absolute metaphysical unity they also generated serious problems. If God is conceived as the metaphysical One, eternal, absolute, unique, and incomparable, how should His relationship to man and the world be understood? In every relation there is multiplicity, and in relations with the corporeal world there is also inescapable temporality. With respect to *creation the problem was often solved (or at least avoided) by invoking various forms of neoplatonic theories of emanation.

Divine Providence. The issue was particularly acute with respect to the question of divine providence and God's relationship to man. To remain consistent with the Bible and rabbinic teaching, the philosophers had to affirm the doctrine of *reward and punishment and, thus, support the view that God knows and is concerned about individual human life and action. Yet, such a God seems to be a temporal, changing being, not the absolute, eternal One. In a most radical statement Maimonides asserted that, "the relation between us and Him, may He be exalted, is considered as non-existent" (*Guide of the Perplexed,* 1:56). Maimonides tempered this view, however, and developed a theory according to which God shows providence to the human species. God is removed from any direct involvement with individual animals or with inanimate objects: "For I do not by any means believe that this particular leaf has fallen because of a providence watching over it; nor that this spider has devoured this fly because God has now decreed and willed something concerning individuals" (*ibid.,* 3:17). Moreover, according to Maimonides, the providential care of man is totally dependent on the level of the individual's intellectual development. As the human intellect develops in its highest form, it is brought into progressively closer contact with the divine nature which overflows toward it; for the individual human intellect is only a particularization of the divine overflow. "Now if this is so, it follows necessarily . . . that when any human individual has obtained . . . a greater proportion of this overflow than others, providence will of necessity watch more carefully over him than over others . . . Accordingly, divine providence does not watch in an equal manner over all the individuals of the human species, but providence is graded as their human perfection is graded . . . As for the ignorant and disobedient, their state is despicable proportionately to their lack of this overflow, and they have been relegated to the rank of the individuals of all the other species of animals" (*ibid.,* 3:18). Maimonides solved the problem by making providence an extension of the divine nature in the perfected human intellect, and thus succeeded in preserving God's unity and eternity. Similar views were held by Levi b. Gershom and Abraham *ibn Ezra. While the medieval Jewish philosophers succeeded in meeting the challenge of their intellectual environment, many Jews felt that in the process they had sacrificed the spiritual satisfactions of simple piety. As the French philosopher Pascal (17th century) once observed, the God of the philosophers is no substitute for the God of Abraham, Isaac, and Jacob. Many great Jewish teachers opposed such philosophical conceptions of God, because they felt that they robbed the Jew of his intimate relationship with a God who is loving and compassionate, as well as stern, judging, and commanding. In the centuries since the Middle Ages, Judaism has made room for both the God of the philosophers and the God who lives in the emotions and aspirations of simple, non-philosophical men. [MA.FO.]

IN KABBALAH

The kabbalistic view of God is in principle a derivation from the desire to abolish the contradiction between the two concepts: God's unity and God's existence. The emphasis of God's unity leads the philosopher to reject anything that could undermine that absolute unity—any attribute, determination, or quality that can be interpreted as an addition to His unity and as evidence for plurality. On the other hand, the emphasis on God's life which is characteristic of religious faith endangers His unity, since life is variegated by its very nature: it is a process and not a state. In the opinion of many kabbalists the divinity should be conceived of in the following two fundamental aspects: (1) God in Himself who is hidden in the depths of His being; (2) the revealed God who creates and preserves his creation. For kabbalists these two aspects are not contradictory but complement one another. Regarding God Himself the first aspect suffices, and in the opinion of some (Moses *Cordovero, and the Ḥabad Ḥasidism), one could doubt whether from this point of view anything at all exists apart from God. It is precisely the second view, however, that is required by religious faith: namely, a revealed God who can be recognized by His action and revelation.

In terms of God Himself, He has neither a name nor an attribute and nothing can be said of Him except that He is. This absolute divinity is usually called in Kabbalah **Ein-Sof* ("the Infinite"). *Ein-Sof* lacks any attributes, even more than, if one may say so, does the God of Maimonides. From the sayings of some early kabbalists, it is apparent that they are careful not even to ascribe personality to God. Since He is beyond everything—beyond even imagination, thought, or will—nothing can be said of Him that is within the grasp of our thought. He "conceals Himself in the recesses of mystery"; He is "the supreme cause" or "the great existent" (in *Berit Menuḥah*, Amsterdam, 1648), appellations which contain a negation of the personal nature of God. There were also kabbalists, however, who wished to give a personality to *Ein-Sof*, though in their opinion too this personality was indefinable: according to them the *Ein-Sof* is *ba'al ha-raẓon*, "the possessor of will" (Menahem Azariah da *Fano) hence it is possible to say of Him, as do faithful pious Jews, "Blessed be He"; "May He be blessed and exalted," etc. Both these conceptions are met with in the pages of the *Zohar. In favor of the personal character of *Ein-Sof* weighed the argument that even without the existence of emanations, the *Sefirot*, and the worlds, His perfection would not lack anything, hence one should not think that God acquired personality through the emanation of the "attributes" or the *Sefirot*, which determine for us the personal character of God. It should be said that, in the opinion of all kabbalists the *Ein-Sof* is divinity itself, but some kabbalists doubt whether it is also "God." For the life of the *Ein-Sof* is concealed within itself and is not revealed, while the religious man seeks the revelation of this concealed life. This revelation comes through the emanation of the *Sefirot*, which are the domain of the life of the revealed God. This emanation is not a necessity, according to the nature of the *Ein-Sof;* it is a voluntary activity of the emanator.

The special difficulty in connection with this view is that according to kabbalistic doctrine the ten *Sefirot* or worlds of heavenly *Parẓufim* ("configurations," in the Lurianic Kabbalah) are not created regions distinct from the *Ein-Sof*, like other creations, but are included within the divine unity (see *Emanation). The *Sefirot* are also attributes (and some kabbalists explicitly identify them with the "attributes of action" of the philosophers) but in actual fact they are more than attributes: they are the various stages at which God reveals Himself at the time of creation; they are His powers and His names. Each quality is one facet of his revelation. Hence every name applied to the divine is merely one of these qualities: *Eheyeh Yah, El, Elohim, Ẓeva'ot, Adonai*—each points to a special aspect in the revealed God, and only the totality of all these qualities exhausts the active life of God. It is this totality, its order, and its laws, in which the theology of the Kabbalah is fundamentally interested. Here the personality of God is manifested even if it is not developed: God revealed himself not only at Mt. Sinai; He revealed Himself in everything since the beginning of the creation, and will continue to reveal Himself until the end of time; His act in creation is His main revelation. From this position stems a certain dualism in the realm of the revelation of the divine: on the one hand there is *Ein-Sof* which is transcendental and its traces are not discernable in the creatures; yet on the other hand the traces of the living God, who is embodied in the world of the *Sefirot*, are found in everything and discernable in everything—at least to the mystic who knows how to interpret the symbolic language of outer reality. God is in His creation, just as He is outside of it. And if the *Sefirot*, active in the creation, are the "souls" and the inwardness of everything, then the *Ein-Sof* is the "soul of the souls." By the mere fact of being a creature, no creature is divine, though nevertheless something of the divine is revealed in it. The world of *Sefirot* then is the region of divine revelation per se, for the flow of divine life rises and descends in the stages of the *Sefirot*. The divine revelation emanates also upon the region of creation, through the "clothing" of the *Sefirot* in the mundane world.

In critical literature on Kabbalah opinions vary on the question to what extent the formulations of this fundamental standpoint are pantheistic. At various times a pantheistic view of God had been attributed in particular to the Zohar, to Moses Cordovero, and to Abraham *Herrera. Important in the theology of the Kabbalah is the new view of the divine presence, which is no longer a synonym for God Himself, but a name for the last *Sefirah* which is the passive and receptive element in God, although it is simultaneously active and emanating upon the creatures. The unity of God in the *Sefirot* is dynamic and not static and all explanations by kabbalists of the *Shema* ("Hear O Israel") testify to this: this is the unity of the stream of life flowing from the *Ein-Sof*, or, according to some opinions, from the will which is the first *Sefirah*. (See *Kabbalah.) [G.SCH.]

IN MODERN JEWISH PHILOSOPHY

Moses Mendelssohn. Moses *Mendelssohn, the first modern Jewish philosopher, believed that, "Judaism knows nothing of a revealed religion in the sense in which Christians define this term." The truths of religion, particularly those that have to do with the existence and nature of God, are principles of reason and, as such, are available to all men. Through rational reflection we know that God exists, that He is a necessary and perfect being, creator of the world, omnipotent, omniscient, and absolutely good. These truths, which constitute the essential grounds of salvation, are the elements of a natural religion shared by all men. What is peculiarly Jewish is not religion at all, but only divine legislation, God's revealed law, which binds and obligates the Jewish people alone and is the necessary condition of their salvation. True religion, on the other hand, is universal. God has made known to all men, through reason, the essential and eternal truths about His nature and the world He created.

Solomon Formstecher. Solomon *Formstecher was especially indebted to the idealist philosopher *Schelling for the metaphysical foundations of his theology. He conceived God as the "world-soul," which is the ultimate ground of the unity of all reality. While nature is the open manifestation of God in the world of our experience, it is only as spirit that God can truly be conceived. His essence is beyond all human knowledge, and to restrict God to the necessarily anthropomorphic conceptions of man borders on paganism. Formstecher believed that the world-soul is not in the world, but is prior to and independent of it. God is an absolutely free spirit, whose freedom is most clearly evident in His activity as creator of the world. Because of His absolute freedom, God is understood as the ultimate ethical being and as the ideal that man should strive to imitate and realize in his own ethical life.

Samuel Hirsch. Samuel *Hirsch taught a doctrine similar to that of Formstecher, although he was more dependent on the philosophy of *Hegel. He emphasized the centrality of the ethical even more than Formstecher did. Man discovers his freedom in his own self-consciousness. He knows himself, not as part of nature, but as an "I" who stands in freedom over against the world. God is conceived, on this human model, as a being who is absolutely free and supreme in power over all that exists. Through the miracles that He performs, God exhibits to man His absolute power and freedom. For Hirsch, Judaism is, above all, the religion of the spirit. Its highest purpose is the actualization of human freedom in the ethical life, because only in free and moral acts does man truly serve God.

Solomon Ludwig Steinheim. Unlike most of his contemporaries, Solomon Ludwig *Steinheim thought that philosophy and religion are radically opposed. He held that the true knowledge of God can be acquired only through revelation, and that scriptural revelation contradicts the canons of human reason. If God is conceived in purely rational terms, then His freedom must necessarily be denied, because rationality entails causal necessity. The God of reason is subject to causal rules, since, even as first cause, He is limited to that which reason finds possible. Such a God is not absolutely free. Neither is He a true creator, for according to the principle that nothing comes from nothing, He could not have created the world freely and *ex nihilo*. Steinheim rejected reason in favor of revelation, denied the principle of causality, and represented God as the true and free creator who stands above the limitations of rational necessity. Only through such a theology does man become free. Freedom is possible for man only if he subordinates his reason to the God of revelation, whose creative freedom provides the sole ground of genuinely human existence.

Nachman Krochmal. Nachman *Krochmal, although living in Eastern Europe, was more fully Hegelian than his Western Jewish contemporaries. They modified the prevailing philosophy to accommodate the personal God of traditional Judaism, but Krochmal developed a doctrine which borders on pantheism. He conceived God as Absolute Spirit, containing in itself all reality. Absolute Spirit has none of the characteristics of a personal God. Even as cause, He is impersonal: He causes the world only in the sense that He is its totality. The world is derived from God through emanation, which Krochmal understood as a form of divine self-limitation. In this Krochmal was affected by kabbalistic doctrines,which he combined with Hegelianism.

Hermann Cohen. Three figures of major importance appeared in the late 19th and early 20th centuries, Hermann *Cohen, Franz *Rosenzweig, and Martin *Buber. In his early years Cohen thought of God as a philosophical construct that served as the guarantor of morality and moral progress. The existence of God, according to this conception, cannot be proved. He is beyond all positive descriptions, and is thought of only as an "idea" in the technical Kantian sense. Though His nature is absolutely unknown to us, God as idea is the one absolutely necessary ground of morality. His reality is affirmed because the alternative of denying morality cannot be accepted. In his later years Cohen adopted more traditional language as he became more deeply concerned for Judaism. He then spoke of God as the Creator, the God of love, and the source of all being, who is absolutely one and unique.

Franz Rosenzweig. In Rosenzweig's view, God is not known through philosophic inquiry or rational demonstration. He is met in direct existential encounter, which is true revelation. In the anguished consciousness of his own creaturely contingency, man encounters God, who is the creator of the world, and above all he encounters dependence. This meeting reveals God as an all-powerful and loving father. His love for man results in commandments that bind every individual for whom the divine-human encounter is a reality.

Martin Buber. Like Rosenzweig, Buber stressed, above all, the personal quality of God. He is the Eternal Thou, whom one meets as the supreme partner in dialogue. This is not the depersonalized God of the philosopher-theologian, whose nature is expressed in a set of formal propositions. Man knows Him only as the Ever-Present, who meets him in true encounter. No effort to give a consistent definition of God succeeds. "Of course God is the 'wholly Other'; but He is also the wholly Same, the wholly Present. Of course He is the *Mysterium Tremendum* that appears and overthrows; but He is also the mystery of the self-evident, nearer to me than my I" (*I and Thou* (1937), 79).

Mordecai Kaplan. In the United States Mordecai *Kaplan developed a naturalistic view of God in conscious opposition to the traditional, supernatural views. Convinced that modern science makes it impossible to believe in a transcendent, personal God, Kaplan nevertheless saw value in retaining the idea and the name "God." He conceived God simply as that power in nature which makes possible the fulfillment of man's legitimate aspirations. Despite his commitment to scientific naturalism, Kaplan believed that the world is so constituted that valid human ideals are supported and helped toward realization by the cosmic process. It is this force making for human salvation that Kaplan called God. [Ma.Fo.]

ATTRIBUTES OF GOD

The discussion in Jewish philosophy of the attributes or predicates (Heb. *te'arim;* Arab. *ṣifāt*) of God is based on the problem of how God, whose essence is presumed to be unknowable, can be spoken of in meaningful terms.

Philo. Philo was the first to introduce the doctrine of the unknowability of God, which he derived from the Bible (see C. Siegfried, *Philo* (1875), 203–4; H. A. Wolfson, *Philo,* 2 (1947), 86–90, 119–26). He interprets Moses' prayer, "Reveal Thyself to me" (according to the Septuagint version of Ex. 33:18) as a plea for a knowledge of God's essence, and God's answer as pointing out that only His existence, and not His essence, can be known (Wolfson, op. cit., 86–87). From God's unlikeness to any other being follows His simplicity, i.e., essential unity, indivisibility, and His being "without quality," i.e., without "accidents" such as inhere in corporeal objects, and without "form," such as inheres in matter. God belongs to no class. He is without genus or species, and consequently no concept can be formed of Him (*ibid.*, 97–110). The scriptural passages describing God in anthropomorphic and anthropopathic terms must, therefore, be understood as serving a merely pedagogical purpose. Since God's essence is unknowable, all the predicates of God in Scripture describe Him only by what is known of Him through the proofs of His existence, and they refer only to the causal relation of God to the world. Philosophical discussion of the problem of God's attributes gained new impetus under the influence of Muslim philosophy, especially the Kalām.

Kalām. The most elaborate Jewish Kalām discussion of attributes is found in Saadiah's *Emunot ve-De'ot* (*Book of Beliefs and Opinions*, tr. by S. Rosenblatt, 1948). Saadiah finds in Scripture the following attributes assigned to God: He is one, living, omnipotent, omniscient, and unlike any other being. His unity and incomparability follow logically from the notion of "Creator" (1:1), as do the notions of existence, omnipotence, omniscience. The latter three attributes do not imply diversity in God. Just as the attribute of "Creator" does not add anything to the essence of God, but merely expresses His causal relation to the world, so do these three attributes, which explain the term Creator, add nothing to His essence, but merely denote the existence of a world created by Him (1:4). It would seem to follow that these three attributes are active, not essential attributes, but this is not Saadiah's ultimate meaning. Since these attributes, when applied to God (unlike the case when they are applied to man) are not distinct from God's essence, Saadiah upholds positive essential attributes (existence, omniscience, omnipotence), but reduces their meaning to that of God's causality as Creator. He does, however, distinguish between these essential attributes and attributes of action. Attributes such as merciful, gracious, jealous, and avenging are attributes of action in the sense that they express a certain affection for the creatures produced by the causality of God (1:12).

Neoplatonism. Jewish neoplatonic writings are marked by a new emphasis on the unity of God. At the same time the notion of the will of God was injected into the discussion. The extant writings of Isaac *Israeli, the earliest Jewish neoplatonist, contain few references to the attributes (see A. Altmann and S. M. Stern, *Isaac Israeli* (1958), 151–8). Solomon ibn *Gabirol's views are more explicit. In his *Mekor Ḥayyim* and his poem *Keter Malkhut*, Ibn Gabirol emphasizes God's unity (*Mekor Ḥayyim*, 3:4, 5:30). Negative terms are used particularly with reference to the "mystery" *(sod)* of the divine unity, concerning which we do not know "what it is," but which may be described as unaffected by plurality or change, or by attribute *(to'ar)* and designation *(kinnui)*. His negative interpretation of the divine attributes is, however, complicated by Ibn Gabirol's doctrine that matter and form, the two principles which constitute all created beings, derive from the essence and the will of God respectively. Matter (which is originally "spiritual" matter) proceeds from the very essence of God, and form is impressed upon, and diffused in matter by virtue of God's will. Ibn Gabirol's will tends to assume the character of an intermediate between God and the world and, in certain respects, shares in the divine absoluteness (*ibid.*, 5:37–9; 4:20). Baḥya ibn Paquda's elaborate treatment of the attributes in the *"Sha'ar ha-Yiḥud"* ("Chapter on Unity") of his *Ḥovot ha-Levavot* starts from the thesis that from the existence and order of the universe, the existence of one single creator can be inferred. Like Aristotle (*Metaphysics*, 5, 5, 1015b, 16–7), Baḥya distinguishes between the "accidental" and "absolute" senses of the term "one" and concludes that the truly One is God alone, who is incomparable and unique (1:8–9). Having established God's unity in the neoplatonic sense, Baḥya proceeds to discuss the meaning of the attributes, which may again be classified under two heads: essential attributes and attributes of action. The essential attributes are existence, unity, and eternity. They do not imply a plurality in God's essence, but must be interpreted negatively, i.e., God is not nonexistent; there is no plurality in Him; He is not a created thing. The attributes of action which describe God's actions either in anthropomorphic terms or in terms of corporeal motions and acts are used by Scripture in order to establish a belief in God in the souls of men (1:10), i.e., for pedagogical reasons.

Aristotelianism. In Jewish Aristotelianism the discussion of the divine attributes reached a new level, reflecting the influence of Avicenna and, subsequently, of *Averroes. The notion of God as the "necessary being" which was introduced by Avicenna, contested by al-*Ghazālī, and modified by Averroes, replaced, in some measure, the neoplatonic concept of the One. Moreover, the problem of the meaning of terms like "one" and "being" came to the fore, for even though these terms were predicated of God in a peculiar sense, they seemed also to bear a generic sense in which they were predicated of other beings as well. Al-*Fārābī held the notion that common terms of this kind are predicated of God "firstly" or "in a prior manner," and of other beings "secondly" or "in a posterior manner," i.e., that the perfections implied by the particular predicate derive from God as their cause or exemplar. According to Avicenna, the term "one" is predicated of God and other beings "in an ambiguous sense" (see H. A. Wolfson, in *Homenaje a Millás-Vallicrosa*, 2 (1956), 545–71), which implies the doctrine of the "analogy" of being (A. M. Goichon (tr.), *Ibn Sina, Livre des Directives et Remarques* (1951), 366–9, n. 2), a view which was not adopted by the first Jewish Aristotelians (Abraham ibn Daud and Maimonides), who substituted for it the notion of the purely homonymous character of these terms, that is that terms applied to God and other beings share only the name but not the meaning. Only under the influence of Averroes did the doctrine of the "analogy" of being eventually command the assent of Jewish Aristotelians (notably Levi b. Gershom, see below). Abraham ibn Daud, in his *Emunah Ramah* (ed. by S. Weil (1852), 48–57), follows Avicenna in establishing the existence of God as "the necessary being" in the sense that God's essence necessarily implies His existence, while in the case of all other beings their existence is only "possible" and extrinsic to their essence. True unity is therefore established in the case of God alone by virtue of His intrinsic necessary existence. Ibn Daud enumerated seven positive attributes: unity, truth, existence, omniscience, will, omnipotence, and being. These neither imply definitions of God nor constitute a plurality in Him. They have to be interpreted as either negations or as asserting God's causality. Unlike Avicenna, he asserts the homonymity of the term "being" in the case of God as compared with its application to all other beings. God's being is true and necessary because it alone has an underived and independent existence. The other eight attributes are explained by Ibn Daud as negative.

MAIMONIDES. The most incisive treatment of the attributes is found in Maimonides' *Guide of the Perplexed* (1:50–60). Maimonides argues that every attribute predicated of God is an attribute of action or, if the attribute is intended for the apprehension of His essence and not of His action, it signifies the negation or privation of the attribute in question (1:58). There cannot be affirmative essential attributes, i.e., affirmative predications relating to the essence of God which is unknowable (1:60). The anthropomorphic and anthropopathic descriptions of God in Scripture have to be understood as attributes of action, or as assertions of God's absolute perfection (1:53). Novel elements in Maimonides' discussion of attributes are his fivefold classification; his rejection of relational attributes; and his interpretation of negative attributes. Maimonides lists and discusses five kinds of attributes: (1) A thing may have its definition and through it its essence is predicated of it. In the case of God, who cannot be defined, this kind of attribute is impossible. (2) A part of a definition may be predicated. This, again, is inapplicable to God; for if He had a part of an essence, His essence would be composite. (3) A quality subsisting in an essence may be predicated. None of the genera of quality is applicable to God. (4) A relation to something other than itself (to time, place, or another individual) may be predicated of a thing. This is inadmissible in the case of God who is not related to time or place and not even to any of the substances created by Him. (5) The action performed by a certain agent may be predicated of him. This kind of attribute makes no affirmation of his essence or quality and is therefore admissible in the case of God (1:52). The "13 attributes of mercy" revealed by God to Moses (Ex. 34:6–7) are attributes of action. They do not denote affections (e.g., compassion) on the part of God, but merely express the actions proceeding from Him in terms drawn from analogous human experience. Maimonides makes the point that not only the many attributes of God used in Scripture, but also the four intellectually conceived attributes of existence, omnipotence, omniscience, and will are attributes of action and not essential attributes (1:53). Because of God's absolute uniqueness and unlikeness to anything else, God's essence is unknowable (1:55). The only correct way of speaking of God's essence is that of negation. Maimonides lists eight terms (existence and life, incorporeality, firstness, omnipotence, omniscience, will, and unity), all of which are interpreted as negative in meaning and as expressing the dissimilarity between God and all other beings, e.g., "God exists" means "God is not absent"; "He is powerful" means "He is not weak." The negation means that the term in question (e.g., "weak") is inapplicable to God. It also means that the affirmative term (e.g., "powerful") is equally inapplicable, and that it can only be used in an equivocal sense. Maimonides' doctrine of attributes reflects, fundamentally, Avicenna's position as represented by al-Ghazālī in his *Tahāfut al-Falāsifa'* (i.e., denial of essential attributes based on the concept of God's "necessary existence," which, in turn, is based on the Avicennian ontological distinction between essence and existence in the cases of all beings except God), but goes beyond Avicenna in rejecting relational attributes.

Post-Maimonidean Philosophy. In post-Maimonidean Jewish philosophy the influence of Averroes became increasingly pronounced. Averroes' attack on Avicenna's ontological distinction between essence and existence (*Tahāfut al-Tahāfut*, ed. by S. van den Bergh (1954), 179–81, and passim) achieved particular prominence and led to the adoption of the theory that the divine attributes did not imply homonymous terms, but rather that essence and existence are identical in all beings, including God.

LEVI BEN GERSHOM (GERSONIDES). The full implications of Averroes' critique of Avicenna appear in the doctrine of Levi b. Gershom (*Milḥamot Adonai*, 3:3). The attributes are not to be interpreted as equivocal in meaning. They are to be understood *secundum prius et posterius* (both by a priori and a posteriori reasoning). They do not thereby imply a kind of relation and similarity between God and other beings, nor do they involve plurality: "For not every proposition in which something is affirmed of something implies plurality of that thing" (see H. A. Wolfson, in JQR, 7 (1916/17), 1–44, 175–225). Gersonides quotes scriptural passages affirming God's oneness (Deut. 6:4) and existence (Ex. 3:14), and he concludes from them the attributes of intellect, life, goodness, omnipotence, and will must likewise be predicated of God in a positive sense.

ḤASDAI CRESCAS. The last significant development of the doctrine of divine attributes in medieval Jewish philosophy is found in Ḥasdai Crescas (*Or Adonai*, 1:3, 1–6). He distinguishes between the essence of God, which is unknowable, and essential predicates which are knowable. The latter are neither identical with God's essence nor merely accidental to it, but inseparable from it in the sense that the one cannot be thought of without the other. This distinction is not in conflict with the notion of God's absolute simplicity. Nor is God's unlikeness to any other being thereby denied. The attributes of omnipotence and omniscience may be predicated of God *secundum prius et posterius*. There are, however, some attributes which are, in the final analysis, negative in meaning, namely existence, unity, and eternity. These too apply to God and all other beings *secundum prius et posterius* and are thus not equivocal. Crescas thus firmly rejects denial of affirmative attributes, and suggests that such denial may be interpreted as really referring only to God's essence, where it is legitimate, but not to His essential attributes (1:3,3 end).

Modern Philosophy. In modern Jewish philosophy the divine attributes are no longer discussed with the stringency imposed by the medieval tradition as inherited from Philo and the neoplatonists and modified by the Aristotelians. Nevertheless, the concepts evolved by the medieval thinkers are not entirely lost. Both Moses Mendelssohn and Hermann Cohen reflect in different ways, according to their respective positions, essential elements of the earlier discussion. Mendelssohn deals with the attributes particularly in his small treatise *Die Sache Gottes oder die gerettete Vorsehung* (1784). He asserts in the name of "the true religion of reason" the conjunction in God of his "greatness" and His "goodness." The greatness of God contains two parts: His power or omnipotence and His wisdom or omniscience. Mendelssohn's discussion of the divine attributes (he does not use this term) is directed towards the problem of theodicy. The essential point is that the infinite wisdom of God is allied to His infinite goodness, which constitutes God's "justice." In its highest degree justice is "holiness" in which equity and mercy are included. The concept of the goodness of God implies that God's punishment of the sinner is meant for the sake of the sinner's improvement. Hermann Cohen presents his concept of the attributes of God in much closer dependence on the medieval Islamic and Jewish philosophers, particularly on Maimonides. The concept of the unity of God in Judaism, according to Cohen, must not be confounded with that of mere "oneness," which is merely negative in meaning. Cohen adopts the term "uniqueness" *(Einzigheit)*, which denotes God as the only Being in the true sense of the word, and signifies also His incomparability (Isa. 40:25), eternity, and causality (*Religion der Vernunft* (1929), 51–54, 70), as well as the concept of God as creator (*ibid.*, 73–77). He interprets Maimonides' theory of negative attributes as the absolute negation of negativity and the affirmation of positivity. Thus, propositions such as "God is not weak" are given in the logical form "God is not non-active" (*Juedische Schriften*, 3 (1924), 252, 257;

Religion der Vernunft, 72–73). Moreover, he links this interpretation with his own concept of *Ursprung* (*principium;* Gr. *arché*) as the thinking which alone can produce what may be considered as being, and which does not depend on the data of sense experience. Cohen interprets Maimonides' attributes of action as expressing the "correlation" between God and men (see A. Altmann, *In Zwei Welten* (1962), 377–99). They denote exemplars for man's action rather than qualities in God (*Religion der Vernunft,* 109ff., 252, 313). The attributes of action can be reduced to two: love and justice which, in Cohen's ethical monotheism, become "concepts of virtue for man" (*ibid.,* 475, 480). [A. ALT.]

JUSTICE AND MERCY OF GOD

Central among the biblical affirmations about God are those that emphasize His justice *(mishpat)* and righteousness *(ẓedakah)* on the one hand, and His mercy *(raḥamim)* and loving-kindness *(ḥesed)* on the other. God's justice and mercy are both affirmed in God's proclamation to Moses at Sinai before the giving of the Decalogue: "The Lord, the Lord, a God compassionate and gracious, slow to anger, abounding in kindness and faithfulness, extending kindness to the thousandth generation, forgiving iniquity, transgression, and sin; yet He does not remit all punishment, but visits the iniquity of the fathers upon children and children's children, upon the third and fourth generations" (Ex. 34:6–7). Justice and mercy are the bases of the covenant between God and the Israelites. God's mercy is revealed in the fact that he redeemed the people of Israel from slavery in Egypt to make them His people and contract a covenant with them: "When Israel was a child, I loved him, out of Egypt I called my son" (Hos. 11:1). His justice is revealed in the fact that He punishes the Israelites if they sin and do not uphold their side of the covenant: "You only have I known of all the families of the earth; therefore I will punish you all your iniquities"(Amos 3:2). Both the justice and mercy of God are evident in the biblical portrayal of God's relationship with Israel; "I will betroth you to me in righteousness and in justice, in steadfast love and in mercy" (Hos. 2:19). In exercising justice and punishing the people of Israel when they sin God reveals His power and lordship not only to Israel but to the world as a whole. God's justice is often tempered by His mercy: "My heart recoils within me, My compassion grows warm and tender. I will not execute My fierce anger, I will not again destroy Ephraim; for I am God and not man . . ." (Hos. 11:8–9). By exercising His mercy God hopes to encourage the people of Israel to uphold their side of the covenant and fulfill His demands as expressed in the Torah. The relationship between justice and mercy in God's attitude toward the people of Israel is intricate and varied, and while some biblical verses emphasize His justice and others, His mercy, it is impossible to say that one or the other is predominant.

In Post-biblical Judaism. This same intermingling of justice and mercy is to be discerned in the works of Philo and other post-biblical writings (see G. F. Moore, *Judaism in the First Centuries of the Christian Era,* 1(1927), 386–400). In rabbinic Judaism a vivid expression of this intermingling is found in a parable in Genesis Rabbah (12:15) comparing God to a king who in order to prevent a fragile goblet from shattering must mix hot and cold water when filling it. Thus the world exists because of the admixture of the attributes of mercy and justice (*middat ha-raḥamim* and *middat ha-din*). Behind this parable lies a complex development of biblical ideas in which the two divine appellations, the Tetragrammaton (YHWH) and *Elohim,* were understood to refer to the two main manifestations of God's providence: the first, to express the attribute of mercy; the second, that of justice (see A. Marmorstein, *The Old Rabbinic Doctrine of God,* pt. 1 (1927), 43–53, 181–208). The presence of both names in Genesis 2:4 signifies that mercy and justice were both necessary in order to make creation possible. Genesis Rabbah 39:6 expresses a similar notion: "If thou desirest the world to endure, there can be no absolute justice, while if thou desirest absolute justice the world cannot endure . . ." Insofar as God's justice and mercy are necessary for creation it is not only the community of Israel that is the major object of these divine activities but the world as a whole. Nonetheless, it must be recognized that rabbinic Judaism was more concerned with the divine activities of mercy and justice as they were directed toward the community of Israel. The fate of the Jewish people in the Roman period was a tragic impetus to this discussion. Faced, too, with the problem of the suffering of the righteous and the prosperity of the wicked, the rabbis examined the concept of divine justice and advanced a number of new interpretations of it in an effort to justify the apparent imbalance of suffering and prosperity in the world. It was suggested that ultimate reward and punishment would take place in the *afterlife, that suffering was a process of purification *(yissurin shel ahavah),* and that the individual often suffered for the sins of his ancestors or of the community at large.

While various trends in medieval Jewish philosophy and mysticism interpreted the divine attributes of justice and mercy differently, they all affirmed that these were qualities of God. In the face of the holocaust in the 20th century, some thinkers, for example, R. Rubenstein, have seriously questioned the concept of divine justice and mercy, while others, for example, Emil Fackenheim, maintain that it is a major obligation of Jewish religious thought to rediscover the meaning of the concept in the face of the contemporary situation.

See also *Suffering; *Good and Evil. [L.H.S.]

CONCEPTIONS OF GOD

Monotheism. The normative Jewish conception of God is theism, or more exactly, *monotheism. It conceives of God as the creator and sustainer of the universe, whose will and purposes are supreme. He is the only being whose existence is necessary, uncaused, and eternal, and all other beings are dependent on Him. God as conceived by Judaism transcends the world, yet He is also present in the world, and "the whole earth is full of His glory" (Isa. 6:3). He is a personal God, whom man can love with the highest and most complete love, while confronting Him as father, king, and master. He loves man and commands him, and his commandments are the criterion of the good. He is absolutely one, admitting no plurality in his nature, and absolutely unique, so that no other existing thing can in any way be compared to Him. This is essentially the picture of the biblical God as it was developed and understood in classical Jewish thought.

This conception of God contrasts sharply with the mythological gods, who have parents and children, eat and drink, have desires and passions. Judaism categorically rejected the mythological gods. However, a variety of more sophisticated conceptions of God confronted Judaism, presenting challenges and evoking responses.

Atheism. It might be supposed that the greatest threat to monotheism would be atheism, but throughout most of Jewish history this was not the case. In the Bible there is no awareness of genuine atheism. The biblical authors attacked idolatry and other mistaken conceptions of God. Frequently, they attacked those who deny that God is concerned with man and the world, but seemed unaware of men who did not believe in a superior power.

Atheism was known in the Middle Ages, and was countered by the various proofs for the existence of God that were common to all medieval philosophical theology. Yet, since the dominant medieval culture was overwhelmingly religious, atheism constituted only a minor threat. In modern times atheism became a significant and widely held doctrine, based on and reinforced by naturalistic scientific ideas and scientifically oriented philosophy. The classical proofs for God's existence have been largely discredited and no longer provide a satisfactory ground for theism. Modern theists usually offer arguments for the existence of God, but do not claim that they have proofs. These arguments, though not decisive, provide a justification for the theistic option, since it is claimed that these are matters about which no demonstrative certainty is possible. In the 20th century theistic belief usually rests on a combination of admittedly incomplete intellectual evidence and personal faith and commitment.

Polytheism and Dualism. Polytheism, the belief that there are many gods, was never a serious threat to normative Judaism, because it is a form of idolatry which could not be readily confused with biblical doctrine. Wherever polytheism appeared among Jews, recognized authorities rejected it vigorously.

Dualism was the only version of polytheism which made serious inroads into the cultural world of the Jews. Dualism teaches that there are two cosmic powers, each of which has dominion over one portion of the universe. The Zoroastrian version has a god of light and a god of darkness, while the Gnostics taught that there is a hidden god who is beyond all knowledge and the evident god who created and formed the world. Dualism is soundly rejected in a classical biblical passage which says, "I am the Lord, and there is none else, beside me there is no God . . . I form the light and create the darkness; I make peace and create evil; I am the Lord that doeth all these things" (Isa. 45:5,7). This forceful denial of dualism is repeated in a slightly modified form in the daily liturgy. The Talmud challenges the heresy of dualism explicitly with strong prohibitions against any deviations from standard liturgy that might have dualistic implications. Rabbinic rulings proscribe any form of prayer that suggests that there are *shetei reshuyot,* two independent powers controlling the world (Ber. 33b).

The medieval philosophers also argued against dualism. Saadiah Gaon dealt with the problem explicitly, offering three arguments against the dualistic position. He first showed that if the doctrine of one God is abandoned, there is no reason to restrict the cosmic powers to two. Arguments can then be made for almost any number one chooses. A second objection is that dualism makes unintelligible the fact that there is an ordered world, since, presumably, each power could frustrate the designs of the other. Finally, he argued that we cannot conceive of such powers as gods at all, since each would limit the other (*Beliefs and Opinions,* 2:2). Other medieval philosophers attacked dualism indirectly through their arguments for the necessary unity of God.

Though there are similarities between Kabbalah and *Gnosticism, the kabbalists did not succumb to the temptations of dualism. "On the contrary," says Gershom Scholem "all the energy of 'orthodox' Kabbalistic speculation is bent to the task of escaping from dualistic consequences; otherwise they would not have been able to maintain themselves within the Jewish community" (Scholem, Mysticism, 13).

Trinity. The Trinitarian conception of God is associated especially with *Christianity. Though Christian theologians normally intepret the Trinity as a doctrine of one God in three persons, Jewish thinkers rejected it categorically as a denial of the divine unity. Since only heretical Jewish sects could even entertain the possibility of a Trinitarian God, most Jewish anti-Trinitarian polemics were directed specifically against Christianity. Occasionally, kabbalistic doctrines seem to have a Trinitarian cast, as is the case in the thought of Abraham *Abulafia (*ibid.,* 123ff.). However, these Trinitarian formulations are always interpreted in such ways that they clearly do not refer to a triune God. Some Shabbateans (see *Shabbetai Ẓevi) developed a trinity consisting of the unknown God, the God of Israel, and the *Shekhinah* ("Divine Presence"; *ibid.,* 287ff.). Their heresy was vigorously attacked by official Jewish spokesmen.

Pantheism. A far more complex problem is posed by Jewish attitudes toward pantheism. This doctrine teaches that God is the whole of reality and that all reality is God. Because it does not involve any polytheistic notions and seems, therefore, compatible with standard Jewish doctrines about God's unity, pantheism found occasional followers among even highly respected Jewish thinkers. It also evoked great opposition, because it denies some of the fundamentals of Jewish monotheism. The pantheistic God is not a separate being who transcends the world, nor is he even a being who is immanent in the world. He is identical with the totality of the world. He is not a personal God; he neither commands men nor seeks their obedience. Consequently, there are almost no instances of pure pantheism within the normative Jewish tradition, though pantheistic tendencies have appeared at various times. They derive from an overemphasis on the immanence of God or an excessive stress on the nothingness of the world. They must be considered in any account of Jewish conceptions of God. Hermann Cohen expressed the extreme view of many thinkers when he stated categorically "Pantheism is not religion" (see *Ethik des reinen Willens* (1921[2]), 456–66.). Nevertheless, one can find various traces of pantheistic thought, if not actual pantheism, in many deeply pious Jewish thinkers. Some scholars attempted to put a pantheistic interpretation on the rabbinic use of *Makom* ("Place") as a name for God because "He is the place of the world, but the world is not His place" (Gen. R. 68). (The original significance of *Makom* as a divine name has no pantheistic connotations.) Philo also spoke of God as "Place" and for this reason is considered by some interpreters to have a pantheistic doctrine. H. A. Wolfson however, argues that for Philo the doctrine that God is the place of the world means that "God is everywhere in the corporeal world, thereby exercising His individual providence, but He is no part of the corporeal world and is unlike anything in it" (see his *Philo* (1947), 245ff.). The elements of pantheism which appeared periodically in the history of Jewish thought were almost always tempered by the use of theistic language and adjustments to theistic claims. Solomon ibn Gabirol conceived of reality as a graded continuum, moving from the Godhead through a series of levels of being down to the corporeal world (*Mekor Ḥayyim,* passim). His system seems pantheistic, because it treats all reality as one continuous emanation of the divine substance. Nevertheless, in his general religious orientation he returns to standard conceptions of a personal God who is the creator of the world. The thought of Abraham ibn Ezra exhibits a similar ambiguity. He used purely pantheistic language when he said that "God is the One. He is the creator of all, and He is all . . . God is all and all comes from Him" (Commentary to Genesis, 1:26; to Exodus, 23:21). Yet, there are countless places in his writings where he also uses strictly conventional theistic terminology. Wherever there is strong neoplatonic influence on Jewish thought a suggestion of pantheism is usually present. Pantheism also appears in mystical doctrines that stress the immanence of God. In the Kabbalah there is an ongoing struggle between pantheistic and theistic tendencies. The former often provide the doctrinal base of a kabbalistic system, while the latter determine the language in which the system is expressed. Scholem states, "In the history of Kabbalism, theistic and pantheistic trends have frequently contended for mastery. This fact is sometimes obscured because the representatives of pantheism have generally endeavored to speak the language of theism; cases of writers who openly put forward pantheistic view are rare . . . The author of the Zohar inclines toward pantheism . . . On the whole, his language is that of the theist, and some penetration is needed to lift its hidden and lambent pantheistic core to the light" (Mysticism, 222). The same tendency can observed in Ḥasidism. In a key passage R. *Shneur Zalman of Lyady asserted that "there is truly nothing besides Him" (*Tanya, Sha'ar ha-Yiḥud ve-ha-Emunah,* ch. 3); yet, he can hardly be called a pure pantheist when we consider the many conventional theistic formulations in his writings. Only in the case of Nachman Krochmal does there seem to be an instance of genuine Jewish pantheism. Krochmal ascribed true existence only to God, who is Absolute Spirit. In his thought only the Absolute Spirit truly exists, and he denies any other mode of existence. Krochmal was far less inclined than earlier Jewish thinkers to adopt language appropriate to a doctrine of a personal, theistic God.

Deism. Deism was still another conception of God that confronted Jewish theology. Deistic doctrine contains two main elements. First is the view that God, having created the world, withdrew himself from it completely. This eliminates all claims of divine providence, miracles, and any form of intervention by God in history. Second, deism holds that all the essential truths about God are knowable by unaided natural reason without any dependence on revelation. The vast bulk of Jewish tradition rejected both deistic claims. It is hardly possible to accept the biblical God and still affirm the deistic view that he is not related to the world. Numerous rabbinic texts are attacks on the Greek philosophers who taught such a doctrine. Similar attacks continued throughout the history of Jewish philosophy. Of the medieval philosophers, only Levi ben Gershom seems to have had deistic tendencies.

Among modern Jewish thinkers, Moses Mendelssohn is sometimes classified as a deist because he held that there is a universal natural religion, whose doctrines are known by reason alone. It does not seem correct, however, to identify Mendelssohn's God with the deistic God, because he ascribes to God qualities of personality and involvement with the world that are hardly in accord with standard deism (see Guttmann, Philosophies, 291ff.). However, Mendelssohn is open to varying interpretations, and Leo *Baeck was not alone when he propounded the view that for Mendelssohn "Judaism had become merely a combination of law and deistic natural religion." Over the centuries of its history Judaism has been exposed to a variety of conceptions of God, but none has ever been strong enough to overcome the basic Jewish commitment to monotheism. Other doctrines have influenced Jewish thought and have left their traces, yet, the monotheistic faith has consistently emerged as the normative expression of Jewish religion.

[MA.FO.]

Bibliography: IN THE BIBLE: Kaufmann Y., Toledot (incl. bibl.); Kaufmann Y., Religion; M. Buber, *I and Thou* (1937); EM, 1 (1950), 297–321; U. Cassuto, *The Documentary Hypothesis* (1961); A. J. Heschel, *The Prophets* (1962); R. Gordis, *The Book of God and Man* (1965). IN HELLENISTIC LITERATURE: J. Klausner, *Filosofim ve-Hogei De'ot,* 1 (1934); H. A. Wolfson, *Philo,* 2 vols. (1947). IN TALMUDIC LITERATURE: Ginzberg, Legends, index; M. Lazarus, *Ethics of Judaism,* 2 vols. (1900–01); G. F. Moore, *Judaism,* 2 vols. (1927), index; C. G. Montefiore and H. Loewe, *A Rabbinic Anthology* (1938), index; A. Marmorstein, *The Old Rabbinic Doctrine of God* (1927, repr. 1968); A. Cohen, *Everyman's Talmud* (1932), 1–71 and index; M. Guttmann, *Das Judentum und seine Umwelt* (1927); H. Cohen, *Religion der Vernunft aus den Quellen des Judentums* (1929²); P. Kuhn, *Gottes Selbsterniedrigung in der Theologie der Rabbinen* (1968). IN MEDIEVAL JEWISH PHILOSOPHY: Guttmann, Philosophies, index; Husik, Philosophy, index; D. Kaufmann, *Attributenlehre* (1875). IN THE KABBALAH: Scholem, Mysticism, index; idem, *Reshit ha-Kabbalah* (1948); I. Tishby, *Mishnat ha-Zohar,* 1 (1949), 95–282; M. Ben Gabbai, *Derekh Emunah* (1890, repr. 1967); M. Cordovero, *Elimah Rabbati* (1881, repr. 1961), Ma'ayan 1. IN MODERN JEWISH PHILOSOPHY: J. B. Agus, *Modern Philosophies of Judaism* (1941); Guttmann, Philosophies, index; S. H. Bergman, *Faith and Reason: An Introduction to Modern Jewish Thought* (1961). ATTRIBUTES OF GOD: D. Kaufmann, *Attributenlehre* (1875); idem, *Gesammelte Schriften,* 2 (1910), 1–98; H. A. Wolfson, in: *Essays and Studies in Memory of Linda R. Miller* (1938), 201–34; idem, in: *Louis Ginzberg Jubilee Volume* (1945), 411–46; idem, in: *Harvard Studies in Classical Philology,* 56–67 (1947), 233–49; idem, in: HTR, 45 (1952), 115–30; 49 (1956), 1–18; idem, in: *Mordecai M. Kaplan Jubilee Volume* (1953), 515–30; idem, in: JAOS, 79 (1959), 73–80; idem, in: *Studies and Essays in Honor of Abraham A. Neuman* (1962), 547–68; A. Altmann, in: BJRL, 35 (1953), 294–315; idem, in: *Tarbiz,* 27 (1958), 301–9; Guttmann, Philosophies, passim; S. Rawidowicz, in: *Saadya Studies* (1943), 139–65; A. Schmiedl, *Studien ueber juedische, insondere juedische-arabische Religionsphilosophie* (1869), 1–66; G. Vajda, *Isaac Albalag, Averroiste Juif, Traducteur et Annotateur d'Al-Ghazali* (1960), 34–129, and passim; idem, in: *Jewish Medieval and Renaissance Studies* (1966), 49–74.

GOD, NAMES OF. Various Hebrew terms are used for God in the Bible. Some of these are employed in both the generic and specific sense; others are used only as the personal name of the God of Israel. Most of these terms were employed also by the Canaanites, to designate their pagan gods. This is not surprising; since on settling in the Promised Land the Patriarchs and early Israelites made "the language of Canaan" their own (Isa. 19:18), the Hebrew language would naturally use the Canaanite vocabulary for terms designating their own Deity. It must be noted, however, that in the Bible these various terms, when used by the Israelites to designate their own Deity, refer to one and the same god, the sole God of Israel. At least from the time of Moses on this is certainly true, and it is probably true even from the time of Abraham. When Joshua told the tribes of Israel, assembled at Shechem, that their ancestors had "served other gods" (Josh. 24:2), he was referring to the ancestors of Abraham, as is clear from the context. The God who identified Himself to Moses as YHWH said He was "the God of Abraham, the God of Isaac, and the God of Jacob" (Ex. 3:6). Therefore, the terms "the Fear of Isaac" (perhaps rather, "the Kinsman of Isaac," Gen. 31:42, 53) and "the Mighty One of Jacob" (Gen. 49:24; Isa. 49:26), are synonymous with YHWH, even though these terms may have been specific titles by which the God of these partriarchs was known as their individual tutelary deity.

ʾEl. The oldest Semitic term for God is *ʾel* (corresponding to Akkadian *ilu(m),* Canaanite *ʾel* or *ʾil,* and Arabic *ʾel* as an element in personal names). The etymology of the word is obscure. It is commonly thought that the term derived from a root *ʾyl* or *ʾwl,* meaning "to be powerful" (cf. *yesh le-el yadi,* "It is in the power of my hand," Gen. 31:29; cf. Deut. 28:32; Micah 2:1). But the converse may be true; since power is an essential element in the concept of deity, the term for deity may have been used in the transferred sense of "power."

In Akkadian, *ilu(m),* and plural *ilū* and *ilānu,* is used in reference to any individual god as well as to divine beings in general; but it is not employed as the personal name of any god. In Ugaritic Canaanite, however, *il* occurs much more frequently as the personal name of the highest god *el* than as the common noun "god" (pl., *ilm;* fem., *ilt*). In the Ugaritic myths El is the head of the Canaanite pantheon, the ancestor of the other gods and goddesses, and the creator of the earth and its creatures; but he generally fades into the background and plays a minor role in the preserved myths.

In the Bible *ʾel* is seldom used as the personal name of God, e.g., *ʾEl-ʾElohei-Yisrael,* "El, the God of [the Patriarch] Israel" (Gen. 33:20; cf. Ps. 146:5). Almost always, *ʾel* is an appellative, with about the same semantic range as *ʾelohim* (see below). The word can thus be preceded by the article: *ha-ʾel,* "the [true] God" (e.g., Ps. 18:31, 33, 48; 57:3). Like *ʾelohim, el* can be employed in reference to an "alien god" (Deut. 32:12; Mal. 2:11) or a "strange god" (Ps. 44:21; 81:10). It can also have the plural form *ʾelim,* "heavenly beings" (Ex. 15:11). In contrast to the extremely common word *ʾelohim, el* occurs relatively seldom, except in archaic or archaizing poetry, as in Job and Psalms. But *ʾel* and, rarely, *ʾelohim* are used when the term is modified by one or more adjectives, e.g., "an impassioned God" (e.g., Ex. 20:5; 34:14), "a God compassionate and gracious" (e.g., Ex. 34:6; Ps. 86:15). Moreover, *ʾel,* not *ʾelohim,* is used when God is contrasted with man, i.e., the divine contrasted with the human (Num. 23:19; Isa. 31:3; Ezek. 28:9; Hos. 11:9; Job 25:4). As an element in theophoric names, *ʾel,* not *ʾelohim,* is used often as the first element, e.g., Elijah, Elisha, and Elihu, and even more often as the last element, e.g., Israel, Ishmael, and Samuel. Of special interest are the divine names of which El is the first element: *ʾEl ʿElyon, ʾEl ʿOlam, ʾEl Shaddai, ʾEl Roʾi,* and *ʾEl Berit.*

ʾEl ʿElyon. The Hebrew word *ʿelyon* is an adjective meaning "higher, upper," e.g., the "upper" pool (Isa. 7:3), the "upper" gate (II Kings 15:35), and "highest," e.g., the "highest" of all the kings of the earth (Ps. 89:28). When used in reference to God, the word can rightly be translated as "Most High." Since in reference to God *ʿelyon* is never preceded by the article *ha-* ("the"), is must have been regarded as a proper noun, a name of God. Thus, it can be used as a divine name meaning "the Most High" (e.g., Deut. 32:8; Isa. 14:14; Ps. 9:3) or in parallelism with YHWH (e.g., Ps. 18:14; 21:8; 83:19), El (Num. 24:16; Ps. 107:11), and Shaddai (Ps. 91:1).

Among the Canaanites, *ʾEl* and *ʿElyon* were originally distinct deities, the former attested by archaeological evidence from Ugarit in Western Syria, the latter by evidence from Phoenicia further south. Later, both terms were combined to designate a single god *ʾEl ʿElyon.* In the *Tell el-Amarna Letters of the 15th–14th centuries B.C.E., the Canaanites called El Elyon "the lord of the gods." According to Genesis 14:18–20, Melchizedek, king of Salem, was "a priest of God Most High *[ʾEl ʿElyon],*" and he blessed Abraham by "God Most High, Creator of heaven and earth." Abraham accepted the title "Most High" as merely descriptive of his own God; he swore by "YHWH, God Most High, Creator of heaven and earth." The combined form El Elyon occurs also in the Aramaic *Sefire inscriptions of the eighth century B.C.E. (see Pope, *El in the Ugaritic Texts* (1955), 54ff.) and in later Greek inscriptions as *Zeus Hypsistos.* Whereas for the pagans the term referred to the god who was supreme over the other gods, in Israel it referred to the transcendent nature of the one true God.

ʾEl ʿOlam. According to Genesis 21:33, "Abraham planted a tamarisk at Beer-Sheba, and invoked there the name of YHWH, the everlasting God." The Hebrew for "the Everlasting God" is *ʾel ʿolam,* literally, "the God of an indefinitely long time." Perhaps it was the title of El as worshiped at the local shrine of Beer-Sheba (cf. El Bethel, "the El of Bethel," in Gen. 35:7). Then Abraham would have accepted this Canaanite term as descriptive of his true God. In any case, the epithet is logical in the context, which concerns a pact meant for all times. The term by which Abraham invoked YHWH at Beer-Sheba is apparently echoed in Isaiah 40:28, where YHWH is called "the Everlasting God *[ʾelohei ʿolam],* the Creator of the ends of the earth" (cf. Jer. 10:10, *melekh ʿolam,* "the everlasting King"; Isa. 26:4, *ẓur ʿolamim,* "an everlasting Rock"). In Deuteronomy 33:27, where "the ancient God" *(ʾelohei qedem)* parallels "the everlasting arms" *(zeroʿot ʿolam),* the text is uncertain. Only in the late passage of Daniel 12:7 (probably translated from Aramaic) is the article used with *ʿolam:* "The man clothed in linen . . . swore by Him that liveth for ever *(be-ḥei ha-ʿolam).*"

ʾEl Shaddai. According to the literary source of the Pentateuch that the critics call the "Priestly Document,"

The 42-letter name of God inscribed on a silver arm amulet, worn as a protection against evil. Persia, 17th/18th century, 6¼×2½ in. (16×6.5 cm.). Tel Aviv, Einhorn collection. Photo David Harris, Jerusalem.

YHWH "appeared to Abraham, Isaac, and Jacob as El Shaddai" (Ex. 6:3). The traditional English rendering of the obscure Hebrew term *ʾEl Shaddai* as "God Almighty" goes back to ancient times. The Septuagint renders Shaddai as *Pantokrator,* "All-powerful"; this is followed by the Vulgate's *Omnipotens,* "Omnipotent." Apparently, this rendering is based on an ancient rabbinic interpretation, *sha,* "who," and *dai,* "enough," i.e., "He who is self-sufficient" (e.g., Ḥag. 12a); thus, the Jewish translators Aquila and Symmachus in the early centuries C.E. translated *shaddai* by Greek *hikanos,* "sufficient, able." But this definition can hardly be taken as the true etymology of the term. No fully satisfactory explanation of it has yet been accepted by all scholars. The term is usually explained as a cognate of the Akkadian word *šadū,* "mountain," but not in the sense that *ʾEl Shaddai* would mean "God the Rock" (cf. *ẓur,* "Rock," an epithet of God, e.g., Deut. 32:4, 30, 37).

Rather, *ʾEl Shaddai* would mean "ʾEl-of-the-Mountain," i.e., of the cosmic mountain, the abode of ʾEl; for the Patriarchs the term would mean "the God of Heaven." The ending *-ai* of *shaddai* would be adjectival, as in Ugaritic *ʾrṣy* (to be vocalized *ʾarṣai*), "She of the Earth," the name of one of the three daughters of the Ugaritic *ʾEl.* It may be objected that Akkadian *šadū* should be cognate with Hebrew *sadeh,* "open field"; and that therefore in Hebrew the divine name should have been *ʾEl Saddai.* It is possible, however, that the Patriarchs brought the term with them from Mesopotamia, and thus preserved the Akkadian shift of original *ś* to *š* in this word, contrary to the correct Hebrew distinction between original *ś* and *š*. Or, perhaps, Akkadian *šadū* is not cognate with Hebrew *sadeh,* but with Hebrew *shad,* "breast," which comes from proto-Semitic *tad;* the semantic development from rounded "breasts" to "hills" and "mountains" would not be impossible. Although no Ugaritic equivalent of *ʾEl Shaddai* has yet been found, in the Ugaritic poem about Baal and Anath (II AB, iv–v: 23–24, in Pritchard Texts, 131–3) it is said that Asherah "penetrates the *dd* [mountain?] of El and enters the pavilion of King Father Shunem [or the King, the Father of Years?]."

In the Bible the full name, *ʾEl Shaddai,* is used only in connection with Abraham (Gen. 17:1), Isaac (Gen. 28:3), and Jacob (Gen. 35:11; 43:14; 48:3). The word Shaddai alone occurs as God's name in the ancient oracles of Balaam (Num. 24:4, 16), in poetic passages (Isa. 13:6; Ezek. 1:24; Joel 1:15; Ps. 68:15; 91:1; and 31 times in Job), and even in archaizing prose (Ruth 1:20–21). Moreover, Shaddai is an element in very ancient Israelite names, such as Ammishaddai ("My Kinsman is Shaddai"; Num. 1:12) and Zurishaddai ("My Rock is Shaddai"; Num. 1:6).

ʾEl Roʾi. The divine name *ʾEl Roʾi* occurs in Genesis 16:13. After Hagar was driven away by Sarai (Sarah) and fled into the western Negev, at a certain spring or well she had a vision of God, "and she called YHWH who spoke to her, 'You are *ʾEl Roʾi.*'" The meaning of the word "Roʾi" in this context is obscure. By itself it can be either a noun, "appearance" (I Sam. 16:12), "spectacle, gazingstock" (Nah. 3:6), or a participle with a suffix of the first person singular, "seeing me," i.e., who sees me (Job 7:8). Therefore, *ʾEl Roʾi* could mean either "the God of Vision" (who showed Himself to me) or "the God who sees me." The explanation of the divine name that is given in the second half of the same verse (Gen. 16:13b) is equally obscure. As the Hebrew text now stands, it is usually rendered as "She meant, 'Have I not gone on seeing after He saw me *[aḥarei roʾi]*?'" (JPS, 1962), or, "She meant, 'Did I not go on seeing here *[halom]* after He had seen me?'" (E.A. Speiser, *Genesis* (1964), 117). In the following verse (16:14) it is stated: "Therefore the well was called *Beʾer-Laḥai-Roʾi.*" This name is explained in a footnote as "Apparently, 'The Well of the Living One Who sees me.'" (JPS). However, on the basis of the name of the well, E.A. Speiser (op. cit., p. 119) would emend the unvocalized Hebrew text of Genesis 16:13, *hgm hlm rʾyty ʾḥry rʾy,* to read *hgm ʾlhm rʾyty wʾḥy,* "Did I really see God, yet remain alive?" The name of the well he would then take to mean, "Well of living sight." Since the well was in the region occupied by the Ishmaelites (and Hagar was the mother of Ishmael), the divine name, *ʾEl Roʾi,* may have been proper to the Ishmaelites rather than to the Israelites.

ʾEl Berit. The divine name *ʾEl Berit* ("God of the Covenant") occurs only in Judges 9:46, where mention is made of "the house [i.e., temple] of *ʾEl Berit*" at Shechem. This is certainly the same sanctuary that is called "the house [i.e., temple] of *Baʿal Berit*" in 9:4. From the treasury of the temple of Baal-Berith the citizens of Shechem gave seventy silver shekels to Abimelech, the son of Jerubbaal (another name of Gideon) to aid him in his fight for the sole kingship of Shechem against the other sons of Jerubbaal *(ibid.).* A few years later, the rebellious citizens of Shechem were burned to death by Abimelech in the temple of El-Berith where they had taken refuge (9:46–49).

The Deuteronomist editor of the Book of Judges regarded Baal-Berith as a pagan god. But the case is not quite that simple. First of all, in early Israel the word *baʿal,* meaning "owner, master, lord," was often regarded more or less as a synonym of *ʾadon,* "lord" (see below under "*ʾAdonai*"), and so it could be used legitimately as a title of YHWH. Among the sons of King Saul, who was certainly not a worshiper of a pagan god, were those who bore the names of Merib-Baal, "the Lord contends" (?) and Eshbaal (originally, *ʾish-baʿal*), "man of the Lord," I Chron. 8:33, 34; 9:39, 40; and even one of King David's sons was called Beeliada (originally *baʿal-yadaʿ*), "the Lord knows" (I Chron. 14:7), who is called Eliada *(ʾel-yadaʿ),* "God knows" in II Samuel 5:16. Only after the time of Solomon was the word "Baal" recognized in Israel as the specific title of the Canaanite storm-god Hadad, and thereafter avoided by true Israelites as a title for YHWH. (Scribal tradition later changed the *baʿal* in older Israelite names to *boshet* ("shame") in the Books of Samuel and Kings; see *Euphemism and Dysphemism.) It is likewise uncertain what the *berit* ("covenant") refers to in the words Baal-Berith or El-Berith. Shechem was regarded as a sacred site by Abraham and Jacob, each of whom erected an altar there (Gen. 12:6–7; 33:19–20). In addition, Jacob's acquisition of land at Shechem (Gen. 33:19; cf. 48:22) and the connubium between the sons of Jacob and the sons of Hamor (as the Shechemites were then called) imply certain covenant agreements. Moreover, the strange name, "sons of Hamor" (*benei ḥamor,* "sons of the ass"), who is said to be the "father of Shechem" (Gen. 34:6), seems to have something to do with covenant making. From the *Tell-el-Amarna Letters (c. 1400 B.C.E.) it is known that there was a strong Hurrian element in Shechem. The Septuagint is therefore probably correct in reading *hḥry* ("the Horite," i.e., the Hurrian) instead of *hḥwy* ("the Hivite") of the Masoretic Text in describing the ethnic origin of "Shechem" (Gen. 34:2); moreover, the uncircumcised Shechemites (Gen. 34:14, 24) were most likely not Semitic Canaanites (see E. A. Speiser, op. cit., 267). It is also known that the slaughtering of an ass played a role among the Hurrians in the making of a covenant. Thus, Baal-Berith or El-Berith may have been regarded by the Shechemites as the divine protector of covenants.

Did the early Israelites perhaps regard El-Berith as the God of the covenant made between YHWH and Israel? It is a noteworthy fact that Joshua, who had apparently been able to occupy the region of Shechem without force because Israelites who—many scholars believe—had never been in Egypt were already living there, renewed the Covenant of Sinai with all Israel precisely at Shechem, the city sacred to El-Berith, "the God of the Covenant" (Josh. 8:30–35; 24:1–28). Therefore, even though the late Deuteronomist editor of the Book of Judges (it is conjectured by the adherents of the documentary hypothesis) considered Baal-Berith one of the pagan Canaanite *Baʿalim,* this term may well have been regarded in early Israel as one of the titles of YHWH.

ʾEloha, ʾElohim. The word *ʾeloha* "God" and its plural, *ʾelohim,* is apparently a lengthened form of *ʾEl* (cf. Aramaic *ʾelah,* Arabic *ʾilāh*). The singular *ʾeloha* is of relatively rare occurrence in the Bible outside of Job, where it is found about forty times. It is very seldom used in reference to a pagan god and then only in a late period (Dan. 11:37ff.; II Chron. 32:15). In all other cases it refers to the God of Israel (e.g., Deut. 32:15; Ps. 50:22; 139:19; Prov. 30:5; Job 3:4, 23). The plural form *ʾelohim* is used not only of pagan "gods" (e.g., Ex. 12:12; 18:11; 20:3), but also of an individual pagan "god" (Judg. 11:24; II Kings 1:2ff.) and even of a "goddess" (I Kings 11:5). In reference to Israel's "God" it is used extremely often—more than 2,000 times—and often with the article, *ha-ʾelohim,* "the [true] God." Occasionally, the plural form *ʾelohim,* even when used of the God of Israel, is construed with a plural verb or adjective (e.g., Gen. 20:13; 35:7; Ex. 32:4, 8; II Sam. 7:23; Ps. 58:12), especially in the expression *ʾelohim ḥayyim,* "the living God." In the vast majority of cases, however, the plural form is treated as if it were a noun in the singular. The odd fact that Hebrew uses a plural noun to designate the sole God of Israel has been explained in various ways. It is not to be understood as a remnant of the polytheism of Abraham's ancestors, or hardly as a "plural of majesty"—if there is such a thing in Hebrew. Some scholars take it as a plural that expresses an abstract idea (e.g., *zekunim,* "old age"; *neʿurim,* "time of youth"), so that *ʾElohim* would really mean "the Divinity." More likely, however, it came from Canaanite usage; the early Israelites would have taken over *ʾelohim* as a singular noun just as they made their own the rest of the Canaanite language. In the Tell-el-Amarna Letters Pharaoh is often addressed as "my gods *[īlāniʾya]* the sun-god." In the ancient Near East of the second half of the second millennium B.C.E. there was a certain trend toward quasi-monotheism, and any god could be given the attributes of any other god, so that an individual god could be addressed as *ʾelohai,* "my gods" or *ʾadonai,* "my lords." The early Israelites felt no inconsistency in referring to their sole God in these terms. The word *ʾelohim* is employed also to describe someone or something as godlike, preternatural, or extraordinarily great, e.g., the ghost of Samuel (I Sam. 28:13 cf. Isa. 8:19 "spirits"), the house of David (Zech. 12:8), the mountain of Bashan (Ps. 68:16), and Rachel's contest with her sister (Gen. 30:8).

ʾAdonai. The Hebrew word *ʾadon* is correctly rendered in English as "lord." In the Bible it is often used in reference to any human being who had authority, such as the ruler of a country (Gen. 42:30), the master of a slave (Gen. 24:96), and the husband of a wife (Gen. 18:12). In formal polite style a man, not necessarily a superior, was addressed as "my lord" (*ʾadoni;* e.g., Gen. 23:6, 15; 24:18); and several men could be addressed as "my lords" (*ʾadonai;* e.g., Gen. 19:2). Since God is "Lord *[ʾadon]* of all the earth" (Josh. 3:11), He is addressed and spoken of as "my Lord"—in Hebrew, *ʾAdonai* (literally, "my Lords," in the plural in keeping with the plural form, *ʾElohim,* and always with the "pausal" form of a long *ā* at the end). Originally, "*ʾadonai,*" especially in the combined form "*ʾadonai* YHWH" (e.g., Gen. 15:2, 8; Deut. 3:24; 9:26), was no doubt understood as "my Lord." But later, "*ʾAdonai*" was taken to be a name of God, the "Lord."

YHWH. The personal name of the God of Israel is written in the Hebrew Bible with the four consonants YHWH and is referred to as the "Tetragrammaton." At least until the destruction of the First Temple in 586 B.C.E. this name was regularly pronounced with its proper vowels, as is clear from the *Lachish Letters, written shortly before that date. But at least by the third century B.C.E. the pronunciation of the name YHWH was avoided, and Adonai, "the Lord," was substituted for it, as evidenced by the use of the Greek word *Kyrios,* "Lord," for YHWH in the Septuagint, the translation of the Hebrew Scriptures that was begun by Greek-speaking Jews in that century. Where the combined form ʾAdonai YHWH occurs in the Bible, this was read as ʾAdonai ʾElohim, "Lord God." In the early Middle Ages, when the consonantal text of the Bible was supplied with vowel points to facilitate its correct traditional reading, the vowel points for ʾAdonai with one variation—a *sheva* with the first *yod* of YHWH instead of the *ḥataf-pataḥ* under the *aleph* of *ʾAdonai*—were used for YHWH, thus producing the form YeHoWaH. When Christian scholars of Europe first began to study Hebrew, they did not understand what this really meant, and they introduced the hybrid name "Jehovah." In order to avoid pronouncing even the sacred name ʾAdonai for YHWH, the custom was later introduced of saying simply in Hebrew *ha-Shem* (or Aramaic *Shemāʾ,* "the Name") even in such an expression as "Blessed be he that cometh in the name of YHWH" (Ps. 118:26). The avoidance of pronouncing the name YHWH is generally ascribed to a sense of reverence. More precisely, it was caused by a misunderstanding of the Third Commandment (Ex. 20:7; Deut. 5:11) as meaning "Thou shalt not take the name of YHWH thy God in vain," whereas it really means "You shall not swear falsely by the name of YHWH your God" (JPS).

The true pronunciation of the name YHWH was never lost. Several early Greek writers of the Christian Church testify that the name was pronounced "Yahweh." This is confirmed, at least for the vowel of the first syllable of the name, by the shorter form Yah, which is sometimes used in poetry (e.g., Ex. 15:2) and the *-yahu* or *-yah* that serves as the final syllable in very many Hebrew names. In the opinion of many scholars, YHWH is a verbal form of the root *hwh,* which is an older variant of the root *hyh* "to be." The vowel of the first syllable shows that the verb is used in the form of a future-present causative *hiphʿil,* and must therefore mean "He causes to be, He brings into existence." The explanation of the name as given in Exodus 3:14, *Eheyeh-Asher-Eheyeh,* "I-Am-Who-I-Am," offers a folk etymology, common in biblical explanation of names, rather than a strictly scientific one. Like many other Hebrew names in the Bible, the name Yahweh is no doubt a shortened form of what was originally a longer name. It has been suggested that the original, full form of the name was something like *Yahweh-Asher-Yihweh,* "He brings into existence whatever exists"; or *Yahweh Ẓevaʾot* (I Sam. 1:3, 11), which really means "He brings the hosts [of heaven? or of Israel?] into existence." "The Lord of Hosts," the traditional translation of the latter name, is doubtful.

According to the documentary hypothesis, the literary sources in the Pentateuch known as the Elohist and the Priestly Document never use the name Yahweh for God until it is revealed to Moses (Ex. 3:13; 6:2–3); but the Yahwist source uses it from Genesis 2:4 on, thus implying that it was at least as old as Abraham. If the name is really so old, then Exodus 6:2–3 must be understood as meaning that from the time of Moses on, Yahweh was to be the personal name of the God who brought the people of Israel into existence by bringing them out of Egypt and established them as a nation by His covenant with them at Sinai.

Divine Epithets. Besides the above-mentioned divine names, rightly so called, the God of Israel is also given several epithets or appellatives that are descriptive of His nature. Only a few of these can be mentioned here.

Basic to Israel's concept of its God is the divine title given Him of "Creator of heaven and earth" (Gen. 14:19, 22). He is also called "the Creator of Israel (Isa. 43:15—unless this is to be emended to "the Mighty One of Israel; cf. Isa. 1:24); for His creative activity was regarded, not only as His initial bringing of the world into existence, but also as His continuous governing of the world (Isa. 29:16; 45:9; 64:7; Jer. 27:5; 31:35–36). To stress His transcendent sanctity, He is called "the Holy One" (Isa. 40:25; Hab. 3:3), and especially, "the Holy One of Israel" (e.g., Isa. 1:4; 5:19, 24). To point to His loving care for His flock, His Chosen People, He is called "the Shepherd of Israel" (Ps. 80:2; cf. 28:9; Hos. 4:16). Another common title of YHWH is "the Rock" (e.g., Deut. 32:4, 18, 31, 37; I Sam. 2:2; II Sam. 22:32; Isa. 44:8; Ps. 18:32), thus comparing Him to a high crag on which one finds refuge and safety.

The God of Israel is very often spoken of or addressed as "King" or "King of Israel," thus describing His sovereign rule over His Chosen People, to give them peace, happiness, and salvation (e.g., Isa. 41:2; 44:6; 52:7). The so-called "Enthronement Psalms of YHWH" (Ps. 47; 93; 96–99) emphasize the Lord's kingship over Israel. Prophetic oracles are proclaimed as pronouncements made by His Royal Majesty (Jer. 46:18; 48:15; 51:57;). Although before the time of Saul, Israel generally rejected the idea of human kingship as an encroachment on the Lord's sole rule over Israel (I Sam. 8:7; 12:12), at a later period the Chronicler did not hesitate to speak of the Davidic kings as the Lord's representatives seated on the royal "throne of YHWH" (e.g., I Chron. 17:14; 28:5; 29:23). Not only the nation, but also individual Israelites addressed the Lord as "King" (Ps. 5:3; 44:5; 84:4). It is disputed whether the term "King" was used of YHWH before the monarchical period in Israel. The rare use of this title for YHWH in the Pentateuch (Ex. 15:18, Num. 23:21; Deut. 33:5) may be due to later editing of additions made in these older books; however, even Gideon, in refusing to "rule over" Israel does not speak of YHWH as the king of Israel but says, "It is YHWH who is to rule over you" (Judg. 8:22–23). The term "King" is not mentioned in this passage. Certainly, at least in Israel's nomadic period, the idea of kingship, even as attributed to YHWH, was foreign to Israelite thought. The phrase "Ancient of days," which is employed as an epithet of God in modern times, is biblical in origin, but its use as a divine epithet is not.

For the use of the names of God as a basis for the documentary hypothesis see *Bible, cols. 906–7. See also *Mari.

Apocrypha. In the Apocrypha, as in the Hebrew Bible, the most common names for the deity are "God" (Gr. *Theos;* in Ben Sira usually *ʾElohim* but sometimes *ʾEl*), "Lord" (Gr. *Kyrios,* which no doubt generally stands for *ʾAdonai;* but Ben Sira commonly has *YHWH,* represented by three *yods* in the medieval mss.), "the Most High" (Gr. *ho Hypsistos,* probably for Heb. *ʿElyon,* but perhaps at times for *Ha-Gavoha* as in the Talmud), "the Lord Almighty" (Gr. *Kyrios Pantokrator* for Heb. *YHWH Ẓevaʾot*) or simply "the Almighty" (Gr. *ho Pantokratōr* for Heb. *Ẓevaʾot* alone), "the Eternal One" (Gr. *ho Aionios* (I Bar. 4:20, 22, 24, etc.) for Heb. *ʾEl ʿOlam*), etc.

Among the terms used for God that are more or less peculiar to the Apocrypha are: "the God of Truth" (I Esd. 4:40); "the Living God of Majesty" (Add. Esth. 16:16; cf. Talmudic Heb. *Ha-Gevurah*); "King of Gods and Ruler of every power" (Add. Esth. 14:12); "Sovereign Lord" (Lat. *Dominator Dominus;* IV Ezra 6:11); "Creator of all" (Heb. *Yoẓer ha-Kol;* Ecclus. 24:8; 51:12); and such terms as "the Praiseworthy God" *(El ha-Tishbaḥot);* "Guardian of Israel" *(Shomer Yisrael),* "Shield of Abraham" *(Magen Avraham),* "Rock of Isaac" *(Ẓur Yiẓḥaq)* and "King over the king of kings" *(Melekh Malkhei ha-Melakhim),* which are found in that passage of Ben Sira, inserted after 51:12 in the Greek, that has been preserved only in Hebrew.

An interesting passage occurs in IV Ezra 7:62 (132)–70 (140), where, based on Exodus 34:6–7, the author of this book lists seven names of the Most High: "I know that the Most High is called 'the Compassionate One,' because He has compassion on those who have not yet come into the world; and 'the Merciful One,' because He has mercy on those who repent and live by His law; and 'the Patient One,' because He is patient toward those who have sinned, since they are His creatures; and 'the Bountiful One,' because He would rather give than take away; and 'the One Rich in Forgiveness,' because again and again He forgives sinners, past, present, and to come, since without His continued forgiveness there would be no hope of life for the world and its inhabitants; and 'the Generous One,' because without His generosity in releasing sinners from their sins not one ten-thousandth part of mankind could have life; and 'the Judge,' because if He did not grant pardon to those who have been created by His word by blotting out their countless offenses there would probably be only a very few left of the entire human race."

The earliest occurrences (except for Dan. 4:23: "It is Heaven that rules") of the substitution of the word "Heaven" (God's abode) for "God" (Himself) are found in the Apocrypha: "In the sight of Heaven" (I Macc. 3:18), "Let us cry to Heaven" (I Macc. 4:10), "They were singing hymns and glorifying Heaven" (I Macc. 4:24), "All the people . . . adored and praised Heaven" (I Macc. 4:55), "With the help of Heaven" (I Macc. 12:15), and "From Heaven I received these [sons]" (II Macc. 7:11). In the Christian Gospels this usage is especially common in the Judeo-Christian Gospel of Matthew, where, e.g., "the kingdom of Heaven" corresponds to "the kingdom of God" in the parallel passages of Mark and Luke (Matt. 3:2=Mark 1:15; Matt. 5:3=Luke 6:20; et al.), but also in Luke 15:18, 21: "I have sinned against Heaven." This usage still persists in such modern English expressions as "Heaven help us!" [L.F.H.]

In the Talmud. The subject of the names of God in the Talmud must be considered under two heads, the prohibition of using the biblical divine names, and the additional names evolved by the rabbis.

THE PROHIBITION OF USE OF THE NAMES OF GOD. The prohibition applies both to the pronunciation of the name of God and its committal to writing, apart from its use in sacred writings. The prohibition against the pronunciation of the name of God applies only to the Tetragrammaton, which could be pronounced by the high priest only once a year on the Day of Atonement in the Holy of Holies (cf. Mishnah Yoma 6:2), and in the Temple by the priests when they recited the Priestly Blessing (Sot. 7:6; see also Ch. Albeck (ed.), *Seder Nashim* (1954), 387). As the Talmud expresses it: "Not as I am written am I pronounced. I am written *yod he vav he,* and I am pronounced *alef dalet*" (*nun yod,* i.e., *ʾAdonai;* Kid. 71a). The prohibition of committing the names of God to secular writing belongs to a different category. Basing themselves on Deuteronomy 12:4, the *Sifrei* (ad loc.) and the Talmud (Shev. 35a) lay it down that it is forbidden to erase the name of God from a written document, and since any paper upon which that name appears might be discarded and thus "erased," it is forbidden to write the name explicitly. The Talmud gives an interesting historical note with regard to one aspect of this. Among the decrees of the Syrians during the persecutions of *Antiochus Epiphanes was one forbidding the mention of the name of God. When the *Hasmoneans gained the victory they not only naturally repealed the decree, but demonstratively ordained that the divine name be entered even in monetary bonds, the opening formula being "In such and such a year of Johanan, high priest to the Most High God." The rabbis, however, forbade this practice since "tomorrow a man will pay his debt and the bond (with the name of God) will be discarded on a dunghill"; the day of the prohibition was actually made an annual festival (RH 18b).

It is, however, specifically stated that this prohibition refers only to seven biblical names of God. They are *ʾEl, ʾElohim* (also with suffixes), "I am that I am" (Ex. 3:14), *ʾAdonai,* the Tetragrammaton, *Shaddai* and *Ẓeva'ot* (R. Yose disagrees with this last, Shev. 35a–b). The passage states explicitly that all other names and descriptions of God by attributes may be written freely. Despite this, it became the accepted custom among Orthodox Jews to use variations of most of those names in speech, particularly *ʾElokim* for *ʾElohim,* and *Ha-Shem* ("the Name; and, for reasons of assonance, *ʾAdoshem*) for Adonai. The adoption of *Ha-Shem* is probably due to a misunderstanding of a passage in the liturgy of the Day of Atonement, the *Avodah.* It includes the formula of the confession of the high priest on that day. Since on that occasion he uttered the Ineffable Name, the text has "Oh, *Ha-Shem,* I have sinned," etc. The meaning is probably "O [here he mentioned the Ineffable Name] I have sinned," and from this developed the custom of using *Ha-Shem* for *ʾAdonai,* which is in itself a substitute for the Tetragrammaton (see also Allon, Meḥkarim, 1 (1957), 194ff.; S. Lieberman, *Tosefta ki-Feshutah (Moʿed),* 4 (1962), 755).

*Shabbetai b. Meir ha-Kohen (first half 17th century) states emphatically that the prohibition of erasure of the divine name applies only to the names in Hebrew but not the vernacular (*Siftei Kohen* to Sh. Ar. YD 179:8; cf. *Pitḥei Teshuvah* to YD 276:9), and this is repeated as late as the 19th century by R. Akiva Eger (novellae, ad loc.). Jehiel Michael Epstein, however, in his *Arukh ha-Shulḥan* (ḤM 27:3) inveighs vehemently against the practice of writing the Divine Name even in vernacular in correspondence, calling it an "exceedingly grave offense." As a result the custom has become widespread among extremely particular Jews not to write the word God or any other name of God, even in the vernacular, in full.

Rabbinical Names of God. The rabbis evolved a number of additional names of God. All of them, without exception, are references to His attributes, but curiously enough they are not included in the list of the permitted names enumerated in the passage in *Shevu'ot:* "the Great, the Mighty, the Revered, the Majestic," etc. (35a–b). The most common is *Ha-Kadosh barukh Hu* ("the Holy One, blessed be He"; in Aramaic, *Kudsha berikh Hu*). It is an abbreviation of "the Supreme King of kings, the Holy One blessed be He." The full formula is found in the Mishnah (e.g., Sanh. 4:5; Avot 3:1), but more often the abbreviation is found (e.g., Ned. 3:11; Sot. 5:5; Avot 3:2; 5:4; and Uk. 3:12); it is by far the most common appellation of God in the Midrash. Another name is *Ribbono shel Olam* ("Sovereign of the Universe"), normally used as an introduction to a supplication, as in the prayer of *Onias ha-Me'aggel for rain (Ta'an. 3:8). One of the most interesting names is *Ha-Makom* (lit. "the place," i.e., the Omnipresent; Av. Zar. 40b; Nid. 49b; Ber. 16b), and it is explained in the Midrash: "R. Huna in the name of R. Ammi said, 'Why do we use a circumlocution for the name of the Holy One, blessed be He, and call him *Makom?* Because He is the place of His world, but this world is not His [only] place' " (Gen. R. 68:49). The name *Ha-Raḥaman* ("the All-Merciful") is commonly used in the liturgy, particularly in the *Grace after Meals. In the Talmud, the Aramaic form, *Raḥmana,* is also found (Git. 17a; Ket. 45a), as it is in several prayers from the geonic period. So also *Shamayim* ("heaven") as in *Yirat Shamayim* ("Fear of God"; Ber. 16b.), however *Avinu she-ba-Shamayim* ("Our Father in Heaven"; Yoma 8:9) is also used. According to the Talmud (Shab. 10b) *Shalom* ("Peace") is also one of the names of God, as is the word *Ani* ("I") in Mishnah Sukkah 4:5, and in Hillel's statement (Suk. 53a) "If *Ani* is here, all is here," it is given the same connotation.

Reference is made to a "Name of 12 letters" and a "Name of 42 letters" (Ked. 71a). Of the former, it is stated that "it used to be entrusted to everyone, but when unruly men increased, it was confided only to the pious of the priesthood and they used to pronounce it indistinctly ("swallowed it") while their priestly brethren were chanting the benediction." R. Tarfon, who was a kohen, states that he once heard the high priest thus muttering it. Similarly the 42-lettered Name is entrusted only to those of exceptionally high moral character. Rashi (ad loc.) states that these names have been lost. According to the kabbalists the prayer *Anna be-Kho'aḥ,* found in the prayer book, and consisting of 42 words is connected with this latter name. Finally it should be mentioned that to the rabbis it is definite that the Tetragrammaton denotes God in His attribute of mercy and *ʾElohim* (which in fact means a "judge" (cf. Ex. 22:8, 27)) denotes Him in His attribute of justice.

See also *Shekhinah. [L.I.R.]

In Kabbalah. The Kabbalists emphasized the unfathomable nature of God by applying to Him the names such as *temira de-temirin* (the "hidden of hidden") and *attika de-attikin* (the "ancient of ancients") to indicate His eternity, and, borrowed from philosophy, *sibbat kol ha-sibbot, illat kol ha-illot* (the first cause), or *Ein Sof* ("without end," eternal). In addition to the above-mentioned forty-two letters, there is a mention in the Kabbalah of a forty-five lettered name derived from Proverbs 30:4 "what *(mah)* is His name," 45 being the numerical equivalent of the word *mah.* There is also mention of a seventy-two lettered name. This number was arrived at by a combination of the numbers of letters in the names of the twelve tribes, the Patriarchs, and the nine letters of the words *shivtei Yisrael* (the "Tribes of Israel"). For a full analysis see *Kabbalah. [Ed.]

In Medieval Jewish Philosophy. The multiple names of God in the Bible posed a special problem for medieval Jewish philosophers. Concerned to defend and explicate God's absolute unity, they found it necessary to treat the divine names in a way that eliminates any suggestion of plurality in God's being. They either reduced the multiple names to a single common meaning or showed that, among the numerous names, one alone was the proper and exclusive name of God. *Saadiah Gaon held that the two most widely used scriptural names, YHWH and *ʾElohim,* have a single meaning. This is in marked contrast to the above-mentioned teaching that one name stands for God's attribute of mercy and the other for His attribute of justice.

*Judah Halevi, Abraham *ibn Daud, *Maimonides, and

Joseph *Albo, all emphasized the Tetragrammaton as the only proper name of God. Judah Halevi held that all the other names "are predicates and attributive descriptions, derived from the way His creatures are affected by His decrees and measures" (*Kuzari*, 2:2; 4:1–3).

Maimonides declared that, except for YHWH, "All the names of God that are to be found in any of the books derive from actions" (*Guide of the Perplexed*, 1:61–64), but only the Tetragrammaton "gives a clear and unequivocal indication of His essence," a view which is shared by Albo (*Sefer ha-Ikkarim*, 2:28). For Halevi the meaning of YHWH is hidden, and for Ibn Daud it refers to God as master of the universe. The philosophers identified God as creator, first cause, first mover, first being, or necessary existence, but none of these technical philosophic terms can be considered names of God.

In Modern Jewish Philosophy. From Moses *Mendelssohn through Martin *Buber, modern Jewish philosophy exhibits two main tendencies with respect to the names of God. One line, moving from Mendelssohn through such thinkers as Solomon *Formstecher, Samuel *Hirsh, Nachman *Krochmal, and Hermann *Cohen, treats the names of God as primarily metaphysical. In his German translation of the Bible, Mendelssohn renders YHWH as "the Eternal"; Formstecher speaks of God as the "World-Soul"; and Krochmal conceives Him as "Absolute Spirit." In his extensive discussion of the traditional divine names, Cohen interprets all of them as pointing to God's unity and His uniqueness. YHWH refers to God as absolute Being; *Ehyeh-asher-ehyeh* (Ex. 3:14) relates to His eternal and unchanging nature; and **Shekhinah*, translated by Cohen as "Absolute Rest," refers to the unchanging divine nature.

In contrast, Franz *Rosenzweig and Martin Buber view the names as primarily religious and personalistic. In their translation of the Bible, they render YHWH by the personal pronouns YOU or HE. *Ehyeh* names the God who is always present to man and constantly participates in human concerns. Thus, Buber interprets Exodus 3:14 as saying, "I again and again stand by those whom I befriend; and I would have you know indeed that I befriend you." They consider the philosophic interpretation of the names as seriously inadequate in its failure to grasp the personal-religious reality which is fundamental to Judaism. Turning in a radically different direction, Mordecai *Kaplan developed a purely naturalistic conception of God. He refers to Him as "The Power that makes for salvation" and interprets this as "The Power that makes for the fulfillment of all valid ideals."

See also *God, Attributes. [MA.FO.]

Bibliography: IN THE BIBLE: A. E. Murtonen, *Philological and Literary Treatise on Old Testament Divine Names* (1952); M. Pope, *El in Ugaritic Texts* (1955); Albright, in: JBL, 54 (1935), 173–93; 67 (1948), 377–81; Freedman, *ibid.*, 79 (1960), 151–6; Abba, *ibid.*, 80 (1961), 320–8; Bailey, *ibid.*, 87 (1968), 434–8; Cohon, in: HUCA, 23 (1950–51), 579–604; Mowinckel, *ibid.*, 32 (1961), 121–33; Cross, in: HTR, 55 (1962), 225–9; Maclaurin, in: VT, 12 (1962), 439–63; Rendtorff, in: ZAW, 78 (1966), 277–92; Hyatt, in: JBL, 86 (1967), 369–77; A. Alt, *Der Gott der Vaeter* (1929); Finkelstein, in: *Conservative Judaism*, 23 (1969), 25–36. IN THE TALMUD: S. Esh, *Ha-Kadosh Barukh Hu: Der Heilige Er sei gepriesen* (1957); A. Marmorstein, *The Old Rabbinic Doctrines of God: The Names and Attributes of God* (1968²), 17–145.

GODAL, ERIC (1898–1969), German cartoonist. Born in Berlin, Godal began drawing topical illustrations and cartoons for *Acht Uhr Abendblatt* when in his twenties. He drew some of the first cartoons of Hitler and his stormtroopers, and when the Nazis seized power in 1933 escaped from Berlin when the men sent to arrest him surrounded the wrong house. Godal went to Prague, where he worked for the anti-Nazi daily *Prager Mittag* and for the satirical weekly *Der Simplicus* which had been founded as an answer to the famous weekly *Simplicissimus* of Munich, which had by then accepted the Nazi line. Godal reached the U.S. before World War II and contributed to various papers there. He returned to Germany in 1954 and worked for the *Hamburger Abendblatt* and the woman's magazine *Constanze*. He visited Israel in 1968 to write a series of illustrated articles. His memoirs, *Kein Talent zum Tellerwaescher*, were published in 1969. [ED.]

GODEFROI, MICHAEL HENRI (1813–1883), Dutch lawyer and statesman, who was the first Jew to hold a cabinet post in Holland and the first Jewish member of the Second Chamber of Parliament. Born into an emancipated

Michael Godefroi, 19th-century Dutch lawyer and statesman. Courtesy Amsterdam Municipal Archives.

Jewish family in Amsterdam, Godefroi became a judge of the Provincial Court of North Holland in 1846 and in 1849 entered the Second Chamber of the Netherlands Parliament where he remained until 1881. He became minister of justice from 1860 to 1862 and drafted a new legal code. Godefroi was active in Jewish affairs as chairman of the Hoofdcommissie tot de Zaken der Israëlieten. In 1857 he induced the Dutch government to defer its trade agreement with Switzerland until that country granted equal rights to her Jews. Likewise, in 1876 he successfully opposed the ratification of the Dutch-Rumanian commercial agreement because of Rumania's persecution of Jews. [H.BO.]

GODINER, SAMUEL NISSAN (1893–1942), Soviet Yiddish poet. From 1912 to 1918 he served in the Russian army. He was wounded during World War I, taken prisoner, escaped and joined the Red Army. From 1921 to 1923 he attended a Soviet literary institute in Moscow. His first short stories, published after 1921, dealt with the Russian civil war and employed the impressionistic symbolic style of the Kiev novelists David *Bergelson and *Der Nister. His later short stories followed the requirements of socialist realism. Godiner's most popular novel was *Der Mentsh mit der Biks* ("The Man with the Rifle," 2 vols., 1928). He translated Russian novels into Yiddish and wrote a drama *Dzhim Kuperkop* (1930). In June, 1941, when the Germans invaded Russia, Godiner left Moscow in order to fight with the partisans in the occupied region and died a hero's death, which was lamented by Ezra *Fininberg in the verses of *Fun Shlakhtfeld* ("From the Battlefield," 1943). His short novel, *Zaveler Trakt* (1938), was reprinted posthumously in New York in 1950.

Bibliography: LNYL, 2 (1958), 33ff.; Levin, in: S. N. Godiner, *Zaveler Trakt* (1950), 5–8 (introd.). [S.L.]

GODÍNEZ, FELIPE (c. 1585–c. 1639), Spanish playwright. Born in Moguer, Godínez became famous as a preacher in Seville. Jewish sympathies remained strong in his "New Christian" family: one of his grandparents was penanced by the Inquisition and an uncle fled to North Africa, where he reverted to Judaism. Old Testament themes inspired a number of Godínez' plays—*El divino Isaac, Las lágrimas de David, Amán y Mardoqueo o la reina Esther, Los trabajos de Job* and *Judit y Holofernes.* Of these, *Los trabajos de Job* is memorable for its pathetic evocation of the trials of its hero. Godínez also wrote works on the lives of Christian saints, as well as some comedies of intrigue typical of the period, notably *Aun de noche alumbra el sol.* The biblical works are considered his best. Godínez was arrested by the Inquisition and in November 1624 appeared at an auto-da-fé—one of the very few dramatists of the Spanish Golden Age to appear at an auto-da-fé in person. His property was confiscated, and he was deprived of his ecclesiastical offices and imprisoned for two years. After his release he moved to Madrid, where he was accepted in literary circles, although writers like Lope de Vega (1562–1635) satirized him because of his Jewish origin. Godínez nevertheless agreed to deliver Lope de Vega's funeral oration.

Bibliography: M. Méndez Bejarano, *Histoire de la Juiverie de Séville* (1922), 195–213; A. Valbuena Prat, *Historia de la literatura española,* 2 (1946), 148–9, 151; E. Diez Echarri and J. M. Roca Franquesa, *Historia de la literatura española e hispanoamericana* (1960), 513–4.

[K.R.S.]

GODOWSKY, LEOPOLD (1870–1938), pianist. Born in Soshly near Vilna, he was a child prodigy and early embarked on a widely acclaimed international concert career. His enquiries into the fundamentals of pianistic technique led him to the composition of etudes and pieces for both the elementary and virtuoso level, with special attention to left-hand technique. He also edited some of the standard etude works.

His son, also called LEOPOLD GODOWSKY (1900–), was a U.S. violinist and co-inventor, with Leopold *Mannes, of the Kodachrome color process. Though photography was only Godowsky's hobby, he was best known for his pioneering work in the development of color film. He was born in Chicago, but spent much of his youth in Berlin and in Vienna, where his father held prominent positions for several years. Godowsky met Leopold Mannes in a school in Connecticut when they were both 16 years old. While still at school they began experimenting to find a successful method of producing color film. They built a camera with three lenses and three filters, one for each primary color, and superimposed them on a single plate. Eventually, they produced a double-layered plate on which part of the spectrum could be photographed. Working at the Eastman Kodak laboratories in Rochester, N.Y., they succeeded by 1935 in developing three-color motion-picture film, and soon after followed with the process for stills. In 1938 they initiated research for Kodacolor, Ektacolor, and Ektachrome film and in 1939 they left Rochester. Godowsky built his own laboratory on his estate in Connecticut for further experiments. In addition, Godowsky was the first violinist of the San Francisco Symphony Orchestra and played in the Los Angeles Philharmonic. [ED.]

°**GOEBBELS, PAUL JOSEF** (1897–1945), Nazi leader and propaganda minister. Exempted from military service during World War I because of his clubfoot, Goebbels received a Ph.D. in literature and history in 1920. After some political searching, he made several unsuccessful attempts to write for liberal papers, most of which happened to be owned by Jews. He joined the Nazi Party in 1922. He never forgot his failure with liberal newspapers. After some soul-searching, Goebbels resolutely backed Hitler in the party's factional intrigues. In 1926 he was appointed *Gauleiter* ("district head") of Berlin, where he succeeded in building a strong party organization out of insignificant beginnings. The Nazi success at the polls in the early 1930s was due to a considerable extent to the propagandist genius of Goebbels, who had become chief of the party's propaganda department at the beginning of 1929. Appointed minister for people's information and propaganda after the Nazi accession to power, he became virtual dictator of Germany's communications media and artistic life. Goebbels' Manichean philosophy of a charismatic hero-leader opposed by powers of darkness (the latter personified by the Jew) was reflected in his propaganda. He was one of the instigators of the anti-Jewish boycott of April 1, 1933, and of **Kristallnacht* (1938), organizing the latter in Berlin and participating in the Nazi conference dealing with the aftermath of the pogrom, in which heavy sanctions were imposed on the Jews. Continually demanding new oppressive measures against the Jews, he was among the initiators of the *Final Solution (see *Holocaust, General Survey), doing his best to incite the killers by various propaganda methods. As *Gauleiter* of Berlin he strove to make it *judenrein,* i.e., "cleanse" it of its Jewish population. Goebbels stayed with Hitler to the end, killing himself and his family after Hitler's suicide.

Bibliography: L. P. Lochner, *Goebbels' Diaries 1942–1943* (1948); H. Heiber, *Josef Goebbels* (Ger., 1962); R. Manvell and H. Fraenkel, *Doctor Goebbels* (1960); E. K. Bramstead, *Goebbels and National Socialist Propaganda 1925–1945* (1965).

[Y.RE.]

°**GOERING, HERMANN WILHELM** (1893–1946), Nazi leader. A fighter pilot during World War I, Goering was awarded the highest military decoration ("Pour le Mérite"). In 1922 he joined the Nazi Party, becoming the first leader of its storm troops (S.A.). He was at Hitler's side during the Munich putsch of Nov. 9, 1923, and suffered a thigh wound, which caused his life-long drug addiction. He stood by Hitler through all the party's vicissitudes, boasting of being his leader's most faithful paladin. He participated in the intrigues that brought the Nazis to power and was appointed Hitler's minister of air transport and Prussian prime minister. In the latter capacity he formed the *Gestapo. Goering created the Nazi Air Force (Luftwaffe) and planned its strategies; he was as much responsible for its initial successes as for its later failures. In 1936 he was appointed "Plenipotentiary for the Four-Year Plan" to prepare Germany economically for war. Goering decided to use the property of German Jewry for financing Germany's rearmament, and he utilized his office to organize its expropriation. In the spring of 1938 he promulgated a set of orders obliging German Jewry, which by then included the Jews of Austria, to declare and register their property. The **Kristallnacht* in 1938 gave him the opportunity to realize his plans and set his "aryanization" into action to expropriate Jewish businesses and property. On Nov. 12, 1938, Goering convened a conference of Nazi officials and experts, including Josef *Goebbels and Reinhard *Heydrich. The conference decided to impose a fine of a billion marks on Germany's Jews to expiate the murder of vom Rath. Furthermore, all Jewish property was to be taken over by the Reich and the owners indemnified with government low-interest bonds at a price lower than the real value. Goering's expropriation methods later served as a pattern for looting Jewish property in the countries occupied during World War II. Continuing the policy set by the November Conference, on Jan. 24, 1939, Goering appointed Heydrich head of the newly formed central organization for Jewish emigration, the "Zentralstelle fuer juedische Auswanderung." At the start of World War II, Goering was appointed Hitler's successor. He organized the plunder of the occupied countries, especially the Soviet

Union. He collaborated with Alfred *Rosenberg in confiscating Jewish collections of art and used the loot to enlarge his own private collection. On July 31, 1941, Goering charged Heydrich with the implementation of Hitler's decision on the "Final Solution" (see *Holocaust, General Survey). He sent a representative to attend the *Wannsee Conference. He was involved in every phase of the destruction of European Jews and knew their fate. He was a fanatical anti-Semite (see his remarks at the Nov. 12, 1938 conference), but according to some authorities he saved individual Jews, at least before the start of the destruction process. With the decline of Germany's fortunes, Goering's influence waned. The failures of his Luftwaffe and his indolence and corruption made Hitler lose faith in him. Before committing suicide, Hitler stripped him of all his offices and had him arrested. Goering was condemned to death by the Nuremberg International Military Tribunal as a major war criminal, specific reference being made to his decisive role in the extermination of the Jews. He poisoned himself before the execution could take place.

Bibliography: *The Trial of the Major War Criminals* (1947), index; *Nazi Conspiracy and Aggression* (1949; includes indictment of Goering); W. Frischauer, *Rise and Fall of Hermann Goering* (1951); R. Manuell and H. Fraenkel, *Hermann Goering* (1962); E. Davidson, *Trial of the Germans* (1966), ch. 3; C. Bewley, *Hermann Goering and the Third Reich* (1962), 337–54; G. M. Gilbert, *Nuremberg Diary* (1947), 185–216.

[Y.RE.]

GOERLITZ, town in Silesia, E. Germany. The earliest extant sources attest to the presence of a Jewish community at the beginning of the 14th century but it was probably even older. It is known that there was a *Judengasse* on which both Jews and non-Jews were living in 1307. The cemetery dates from 1325, and the community owned a bathhouse and a synagogue as well. In this period the only occupation pursued by Jews which is attested in the sources was that of moneylending. The persecutions in the wake of the *Black Death brought the community to an end in 1349, but it was reestablished in 1364. After their expulsion in 1389, Jews were permitted to stay in Goerlitz only to participate in trade fairs.

Shortly before 1849 a new community was founded. A cemetery was acquired in 1850; the first synagogue was consecrated in 1870 and the second in 1911; the latter was destroyed in 1938. In 1880 there were 643 Jews in Goerlitz. In 1932, even before the Nazi regime, ritual slaughter was prohibited in Goerlitz. Separate areas for Jewish merchants were set up in the marketplace on Aug. 30, 1935. The number of Jews decreased rapidly, from 600 in 1931 to 376 in 1933 and 134 in 1939. The remnants of the community were wiped out during World War II.

Bibliography: FJW, 98–99; Germ Jud, 1 (1963), 504; 2 (1968), 282–3; Neubauer, Cat, no. 194.

[B.BR.]

°**GOETHE, JOHANN WOLFGANG VON** (1749–1832), German writer. As a boy, Goethe acquired a thorough knowledge of *Luther's translation of the Bible, which left its mark on his conversation, letters, and literary work. Among his youthful projects were a "biblical, prose-epic poem," *Joseph und seine Brueder* (the manuscript was discovered and published in facsimile by Paul Piper in 1920, but its authenticity has been questioned); *Belsatzar,* a tragedy in alexandrine verse; and a drama, *Isabel,* which was to end with Jezebel being hurled from a window. Goethe also mentions, among "youthful sins" which he condemned to the fire, a work inspired by the history of Samson. His notebooks show him wrestling with the Hebrew alphabet and with the Judeo-German dialect (*Judendeutsch*) which he heard on visits to the *Judengasse* of his native Frankfort. He records how, on one such occasion, when part of the ghetto burned down, he helped to quench the flames while other youngsters jeered at the hapless Jews. Goethe even planned a novel in which seven brothers and sisters were to correspond in seven languages, including *Judendeutsch;* the surviving *Judenpredigt* written in that dialect was intended for inclusion in this novel. In 1771 he reviewed Isachar Falkensohn *Behr's *Gedichte eines polnischen Juden.*

Goethe's *Faust* has almost 200 passages containing biblical parallels, beginning with the "Prologue in Heaven," for which the first chapters of Job served as a model, and ending with the final scene of Faust's death and ascension, whch was inspired by the biblical and talmudic accounts of the death of Moses. He never composed a major work on a biblical theme, however, because he realized the difficulties he would face in competing with the original text and in reconciling aesthetic and religious requirements.

After he moved to Weimar in 1775, Goethe's social life brought him into contact with many Jewish and converted Jewish intellectuals, including Heinrich *Heine, who did not impress him. Goethe allowed the artist Moritz *Oppenheim to paint his portrait and to illustrate his poetic idyll *Hermann und Dorothea* (1798). He opposed legislation aimed at liberalizing the position of Jews in German society. In general, however, Jews did not engage more than the periphery of his interest. Goethe's many Jewish biographers include Albert Bielschowsky, Ludwig Geiger, Richard Moritz Meyer, Eduard Engel, Georg Simmel, Emil *Ludwig, Friedrich *Gundolf, and Georg *Brandes.

Bibliography: L. Deutschlaender, *Goethe und das Alte Testament* (1923), incl. bibl.; H. Teweles, *Goethe und die Juden* (1925); G. Janzer, *Goethe und die Bibel* (1929), incl. bibl.; M. Waldman, *Goethe and the Jews* (1934); R. Eberhard, *Goethe und das Alte Testament* (1935), incl. bibl.; A. Spire, in: E.-J. Finbert (ed.), *Aspects du génie d'Israël* (1950), 183–99.

[S.L.]

GOETTINGEN, city in W. Germany. Jews are first mentioned there in the 13th century. The community, composed of a dozen families, had a synagogue and paid $4\frac{1}{2}$% of the city's taxes. It was destroyed in 1350 during the *Black Death persecutions, but in 1370 a charter giving

The synagogue of Goettingen, West Germany. Courtesy Yad Vashem, Jerusalem.

protection to the Jews of the city was re-endorsed. In 1591 the Jews were expelled from Goettingen. Several resettled in the city at the end of the 17th century, and in 1718 Jews were given permission to acquire real property. In the university quarter their numbers were limited to three families. Some Hebrew printing took place in Goettingen. Abraham Jagel's *Lekaḥ Tov* was published there in 1742, and Hebrew type was also used in A. G. Wachner's *Antiquitates Hebraeorum* (1742–43). The community numbered 43 in 1833, 265 in 1871, 661 (1.75% of the total population) in 1910, 411 in 1932, and 173 in 1939. In 1859 there was appointed at Goettingen University the first Jew to become a professor in a German university, the mathematician Moritz Abraham *Stern. The university was noted for its biblical scholars, most of whom were champions of the documentary hypothesis, from J. G. *Eichhorn and G. H. A. *Ewald to Paul de *Lagarde and Julius *Wellhausen. When James *Franck, the Nobel prizewinner, resigned his chair in 1933, a number of professors demanded that he be tried for sabotage; six other Jewish professors were put on compulsory leave, among them the mathematicians Otto *Neugebauer and *Richard Courant, as well as Nikolaus *Pevsner, and Eugen *Caspary. Most of the Jews remaining in Goettingen after the outbreak of World War II were deported to *Theresienstadt in 1942, and by October 20 of that year only nine remained. There were 26 Jews living in Goettingen in 1965.

Bibliography: Germ Jud, 2 (1968), 296–8; Yad Vashem Archives; PKG. [ED.]

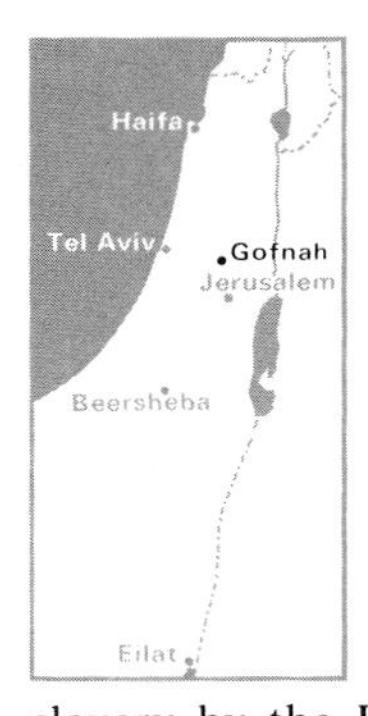

GOFNAH (Gufnah, or **Bet Gufnin;** Heb. גֻּפְנָה), town in N. Judea that is first mentioned in the Second Temple period. The Talmud refers to it as Bet Gufnin, a name derived from the Hebrew root *gefen* ("vine"). Gofnah replaced Timnah as the center of a toparchy in the time of Herod and continued to occupy this position in later times (Jos., Wars, 1:45; 3:55; Pliny, *Naturalis Historia,* 5:15, 30). In the middle of the first century B.C.E., the inhabitants of Gofnah were sold into slavery by the Roman general Cassius for failure to pay taxes, but they were freed shortly afterward by Antonius. The city was part of the area under the command of Hananiah b. Johanan in 66 C.E. during the Jewish War. Vespasian occupied it in 68 C.E., established a garrison there, and concentrated the priests and other important persons who had surrendered to him in the city (Jos., Wars, 6:115). Gofnah is also mentioned in the Talmud as a city of priests (Ber. 44a; TJ, Ta'an. 4:8, 69a). In the Middle Ages it continued to exist as Gafeniyyah. It is marked as a road station on the Peutinger Map; Eusebius places it 15 miles (24 km.) north of Jerusalem on the road to Neapolis (Onom. 168:16). Remains found there include a Jewish tomb with inscribed ossuaries, one of which mentions a Judah, son of Eleazar (in Aramaic); a Greek inscription, Salome daughter of Iakeimos, in a burial cave; a Roman villa; and a Byzantine church.

On the site of historical Gofnah there is now the Arab village of Jifnā (جفنا), which in 1967 had 655 inhabitants, of which 538 were Christians and the rest Muslims. Its Greek Orthodox church stands on Byzantine foundations. [M.A.-Y./E.O.]

GOG AND MAGOG (Heb. גּוֹג וּמָגוֹג). Gog and Magog are first mentioned together in Ezekiel 38–39 in the vision of the end of days, where the prophet describes the war of the Lord against "Gog, of the land of Magog, the chief prince of Meshech and Tubal." After the ingathering of Israel Gog will come up against Israel with many peoples from the furthest north to plunder it and carry away spoil. The Lord Himself will go to war against Gog and punish him "with pestilence, and with blood, and with overflowing rain," and His name will be magnified and sanctified in the eyes of many nations. Gog will die in the land of Israel and his place of burial will be called "the valley of *hamon Gog*" and for seven years the inhabitants of Israel will use the weapons of the enemy for fuel.

Since, in the list of the sons of Noah (Gen. 10:2), Magog is mentioned as the brother of Gomer and Madai, the most reasonable identification put forward is with Giges, also known as Gogo, king of Lydia, and Magog, with his country. That, however, does not affect in any way the symbolic nature of the name and the special character of Ezekiel's vision. Gog and his people are not historical enemies of Israel, like Babylonia and Assyria. They will attack simply out of a lust for violence and with the intention of destroying a peaceful kingdom. Indeed, other prophets prophesied about a people that would come up from the north to besiege Israel in the end of days, but Ezekiel, who prophesied after the destruction of the Temple, fixed the date of the last war after the ingathering of the exiles and the rebuilding of Jerusalem.

In the Septuagint the name Gog appears in two other places where it is not mentioned in the Hebrew text. In Numbers 24:7, Gog appears instead of Agag, and in Amos 7:1, the reading is "Gog," instead of *gizei* ("the mowings"). These variants indicate the antiquity of the connection between the war of Gog and the advent of the Messiah. Descriptions of the decisive, final war occupy an important place in the Apocrypha (En. 56:5; IV Ezra 13:5), but the names Gog and Magog appear only in the vision of the Hebrew Sibylline Oracles (3:319 and 512), and even there only as the name of a country between the rivers of Ethiopia, a country saturated with blood, for which a bitter fate is in store. In the *aggadah,* the names Gog and Magog were reserved for the enemy of Israel in the end of days, but the details are very different from those in Ezekiel. In Ezekiel, Gog is the king of Magog; in the *aggadah,* Gog and Magog are two parallel names for the same nation. Moses had already seen Gog and all his multitude coming up against Israel and falling in the valley of Jericho (Mekh. Be-Shalaḥ, 2), and Eldad and Medad prophesied concerning them (Sanh. 17a). The war of Gog and Magog is in essence a war against the Lord, and the whole of Psalm 2 is interpreted as referring to it (Av. Zar. 3b; Tanḥ. Noah 18; PdRK 79); God Himself will do battle with this enemy. The last of "the ten occasions of the Shekhinah's descent to the world" will be in the days of Gog and Magog (ARN[1], 34, 102). R. Akiva was of the opinion that the judgment of Gog would endure for 12 months (Eduy. 2:10). This judgment will bring great calamities upon Israel that will cause all previous calamities to fade into insignificance (Tosef., Ber. 1:13). Eliezer b. Hyrcanus connects it with the pangs of the Messiah and the great day of judgment (Mekh., Be-Shalaḥ 4: Shab. 118a). The war of Gog and Magog will be the final war, after which there will be no servitude, and it will presage the advent of the Messiah (Sif. Num. 76, Deut. 43; Sanh. 97b). In the Palestinian Targums the Messiah plays an active role in this war. Gog and Magog and their armies will go up to Jerusalem and fall into the hands of the Messianic king, but the ingathering of the exiles—contrary to what is said in Ezekiel—will come only after the victory (Targ. Yer., Num. 11:26; *ibid.,* Song 8:4). A kind of compromise is found in the Targum, namely, that the house of Israel will conquer Gog and his company through the assistance of Messiah the son of Ephraim (Targ. Yer., Ex.

40:11; cf. also Targ. Song 4:5). In the New Testament vision of John (John 20), the war of Gog and Magog takes place at the end of a millennium after the first resurrection, and in *Sefer Eliyahu* ("Book of Elijah"; Y. Kaufmann (Even Shemuel), ed.), *Midreshei Ge'ullah* (1954²), 46) Gog and Magog come after the days of the Messiah but before the final day of judgment.

From the biblical sources and the tradition of the rabbis, the stories about Gog and Magog passed to the Church Fathers. At the time of the Gothic migrations it was customary to identify the Goths with Gog and Magog. An ancient Christian tradition also identified Gog and Magog with the barbarian peoples whom Alexander the Great locked away behind iron gates next to the Caspian Sea but who are destined to break forth in the end of days. During the Islamic conquests, Christians identified the Muslim armies with Gog and Magog.

Bibliography: Kaufmann Y., Toledot, 3 (1954), 578–83; Ginzberg, Legends, index; P. Volz, *Die Eschatologie der juedischen Gemeinde im neutestamentlichen Zeitalter* (1934), 150ff.; J. Klausner, *The Messianic Idea in Israel* (1955); M. Waxman, *Galut u-Ge'ulah* (1952), 218–33.

[Ed.]

GOIIM (Heb. גּוֹיִם), name appearing in the Bible as "king of Goiim." Genesis 14:1, 9 mentions "Tidal king of Goiim," as one of the kings participating in a war during the time of Abraham. It is generally agreed that Tidal is Tudḫaliya, the name of five Hittite kings (Heb. תִּדְעָל; Ugaritic transliteration Tidʿl, Ttʿl). The only one who fits into this period from a chronological point of view is Tudḫaliya I (c. 1740–1710), though information is lacking about him in this respect. The word *goyim* is also used to indicate "nations" in general. There is an opinion that the connection between the two usages of the word *goyim* resembles that of *ummān-Manda* ("the horde, the armies of *'Manda'*"), the barbarian nation which helped the Babylonians destroy Harran, in 610 B.C.E. in Akkadian documents. Whereas the Hittite connection of Tidal and Goiim may be clear, if Goiim reflects the Akkadian *ummān*, the Hebrew name is simply a translation. Thus, there is reason to believe that the name Goiim in Hebrew simply means "nations" and is incomplete for "the nations of . . .," the actual name of Tidal's realm having been omitted in translation or lost in transmission. The usage in Joshua 12:23 is probably a corruption of Goiim to Gilgal (according to LXX), that is, the king Gilgal of Galilee instead of the king of Goiim of Gilgal (cf. Isa. 8:23).

Bibliography: M. Cassuto, in: EM, 2 (1954), 457–8; D. Wiseman, *Chronicles of Chaldaean Kings* (1956), 81, n. to l. 38; Jean Bottero, in: *Archives Royales de Mari*, 7 (1957), 224–5; E. A. Speiser, *Genesis* (Eng., 1964), 107–8; N. M. Sarna, *Understanding Genesis* (1966), 113.

[Ed.]

GOITEIN, BARUCH BENEDICT (c. 1770–1842), Hungarian rabbi and author. Goitein was born in the town of Kojetin, Moravia and studied in the yeshivah of Moses *Mintz in Budapest. He was appointed rabbi in Hőgyesz, in Hungary. Goitein's fame rests upon his *Kesef Nivḥar*, 3 parts, Prague, 1827–28; repr. of 2nd ed., 1966, an examination of, and commentary on, 160 talmudic themes. Although a product of the Hungarian method of study, the close approximation of his method with that customary in the Lithuanian yeshivot made his work very popular in talmudic circles. He resigned from his rabbinical office in 1841 and was succeeded the following year by his son Ẓevi Hirsch (Hermann; 1805–1860) author of *Yedei Moshe* (1905) on the 613 commandments.

Bibliography: P. Z. Schwartz, *Shem ha-Gedolim me-Ereẓ Hagar*, 1 (1914), 216 no. 20.

[E.H.]

GOITEIN, SHLOMO DOV (**Fritz,** 1900–), orientalist. Descended from a Hungarian family of rabbis, Goitein was born in Burgkunstadt. He emigrated to Palestine in 1923, and taught for four years at the Reali School in Haifa. In 1928 he joined the faculty of the Institute of Oriental Studies at the Hebrew University. He was appointed professor in 1947 and continued to teach at the Hebrew University until 1957, when he became professor of Arabic at the University of Pennsylvania, Philadelphia (until 1970). In 1938–48 he was also an inspector on behalf of the Department of Education of the government of Palestine.

During the first period of his scholarly activity, Goitein published a series of investigations of the religious institutions of Islam, such as prayer, and the Ramadan month of fasting, among others. The crowning achievement of his studies of ancient Islam was the publication of the fifth volume of al-Balādhurī's (9th century) historical work *Ansāb al-ashrāf* (1936).

During the second period of his research, Goitein dealt primarily with the cultural legacy of the Jews of Yemen. Among the results of this work were *Jemenica*, a collection of proverbs from central Yemen (1934; *From the Land of Sheba*, 1947) and the publication of the account by Ḥayyim Ḥabshush, who accompanied Joseph *Halevy, on his explorations in Yemen (Ar. text, 1941; Heb. tr., 1939).

In his third period, Goitein was mainly engaged in publishing documentary texts from the Cairo *Genizah, from which he derived conclusions about the history of the Jews in Mediterranean countries and about the general history of these texts (*A Mediterranean Society*, 1, 1967). He also wrote *Jews and Arabs—Their Contacts through the Ages* (1967³).

Shlomo Dov Goitein, orientalist. Courtesy Hebrew University, Jerusalem.

In addition to his works in Arab studies, Goitein also published works on biblical research, including *Iyyunim be-Mikra* (1958) and works on pedagogy, such as *Hora'at ha-Ivrit be-Ereẓ Yisrael* (1958³) and on the teaching of Bible in elementary and secondary schools (1960). [E.A.]

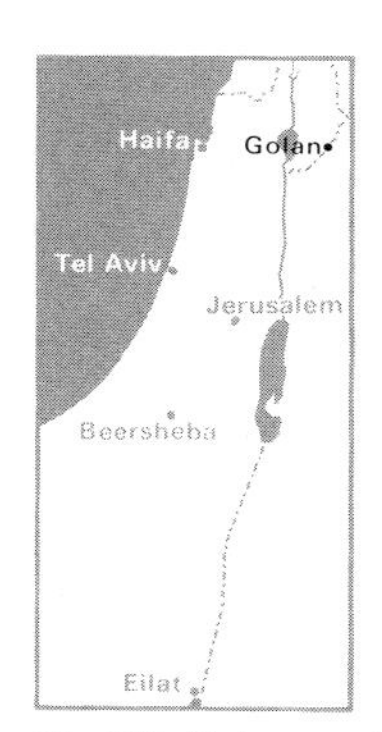

GOLAN (Heb. גּוֹלָן), a town of *Manasseh in *Bashan that was set aside as a city of refuge (Deut. 4:43; Josh. 20:8) and a levitical city of the family of Gershon (Josh. 21:27; I Chron. 5:56). It is mentioned as Giluni in the *Tell el-Amarna Letters. Although situated in Bashan, the city seems to have given its name to the entire district of Golan (or Gaulan) to the west of it. According to Eusebius it was a large village in Batanaea in the fourth century B.C.E. (Onom. 64:68). Schumacher has identified it with Sakhm al-Jawlān, a village 5 miles (8 km.) east of the Nahr al-ʿAllān (ʿAllān River), the eastern boundary of Gaulanitis. This identification is in conformity with the assumption that the city was located outside the district named for it, which ended at

Nahr al-ʿAllān. Others propose a more northerly location, in the region of *Maacah. There are several references to Golan in the Talmud; these, however, seem to refer to the district and not to the city (TJ, Meg. 3: 1, 73d).

For geography, archaeology, and settlement of the region see *Ramat ha-Golan.

Bibliography: R. Dussaud, *Topographie historique de la Syrie* ... (1927), 335, 343f.; Albright, in: *L. Ginsberg Jubilee Volume* (1945), 57 (Eng. section); EM, s.v. [M.A.-Y.]

GOLCUV JENIKOV (Czech. **Golčův Jeníkov;** Ger. **Goltsch-Jenikau**), town in E. Bohemia, Czechoslovakia. Jews appear to have settled in Golcuv Jenikov at the end of the 16th century. Documents indicate that there was a synagogue in 1659 which was rebuilt in 1806 and 1870; it continued in existence after World War II. Because of plague the Jews settled temporarily outside the town in 1681. In 1724 there were 28 families in Golcuv Jenikov; there were 613 Jews there in 1847 (27.8% of the total population), and 79 (3.9%) in 1931. The community had a Jewish German-language school from 1797 to 1907. R. Aaron *Kornfeld, whose yeshivah was the last in Bohemia, lived in Golcuv Jenikov. Those members of the community, who had not succeeded in leaving by 1942, were deported to Nazi extermination camps. The synagogue accessories were transferred to the Central Jewish Museum in Prague. After the Holocaust, some Jews returned to Golcuv Jenikov, where the Jewish quarter (rebuilt after a fire in 1808) and cemetery (the oldest monument dates from 1726) still existed in 1970. The synagogue was put at the disposal of the Prague State Jewish Museum in 1969. In nearby Habry (Habern), a Jewish community was founded in the 14th century. Its synagogue dates from 1650. Habry had 21 Jewish families in 1724; 120 families in 1848; 143 persons in 1893; and 28 in 1931. In 1898 it was incorporated in the Golcuv Jenikov community.

Bibliography: Maximovič, in: H. Gold (ed.), *Die Juden und Judengemeinden Boehmens in Vergangenheit und Gegenwart* (1934), 152–7; O. Kosta, in: *Židovská ročenka* (1970/71), 71–79. [J.HER.]

GOLD, BENJAMIN (1898–), U.S. labor leader. Gold, who was born in Bessarabia, Russia, was taken to the United States in 1910. In the following year, he started to work in the fur industry. Gold joined both the Socialist Party and the Fur Workers Union where he became identified with the union's left wing. During the 1920s a struggle took place between the union's left wing led by Gold (who had joined the Communist Party by 1925), and the more conservative wing. Gold, who became the general manager of the union's New York joint board in 1925, led a bitter strike in 1926 which lasted 17 weeks. The strike ended with the union winning only one of its major demands, a 40-hour work week. The American Federation of Labor then investigated the joint board and charged it with being Communist-controlled and corrupt. As a result of these charges, the union's executive council expelled Gold and his fellow officers. Gold and other left-wing needle trade unionists then formed the Needle Trades Industrial Union and the Fur Workers Industrial Union. During the Depression, Gold attended the Lenin School of Moscow. In 1935 the Fur Workers Industrial Union was disbanded and its members joined the new CIO International Fur Workers Union (which later became known as the International Fur and Leather Workers Union). In 1937 Gold became the union's president, while continuing to play an important role in the Communist Party. In 1948 the union was forced to leave the CIO as a result of that organization's investigation into Communist influence in a number of its member unions. Shortly afterward, Gold, in order to be eligible to sign the Taft-Hartley Act's loyalty pledge, which, in turn, would provide his union with the legal protection afforded by the act, resigned from the Communist Party. Gold continued as union president until he resigned in 1954. After resigning he worked as a fur cutter until his retirement. [AL.A.B.]

GOLD, HENRY RAPHAEL (1893–1965), U.S. rabbi and psychiatrist. Born in Grajewo, Poland, Gold was ordained rabbi by the Jewish Theological Seminary in 1916. He held rabbinical positions in Memphis (1916–18), Boston (1918–24), New Orleans (1924–28), and Dallas (1928–43). While in Dallas he took up the study of medicine, receiving an M.D. from Baylor University in 1934 and later teaching medical psychiatry there. He also served as a commissioner of the Dallas Housing Authority. On giving up his rabbinate in Dallas he moved to New York and entered private practice as a psychiatrist and psychologist. Gold was an active Zionist. At various times he served as president of Hapoel Hamizrachi and the National Council for Torah Education and as vice-president of the Union of Orthodox Jewish Congregations and of the Zionist Organization of America.

Bibliography: *New York Times* (Jan. 7, 1965). [S.D.T.]

GOLD, HERBERT (1924–), U.S. novelist. Gold, who was born in Cleveland, served in the U.S. Army during World War II. After the war he studied in Columbia and in Paris, finally settling in San Francisco, and eventually was appointed professor at the University of California at Berkeley. Gold's books deal with the search for love between men and women, parents and children. His style is witty yet compassionate. His most successful characters are young people who affect cynicism without being cynical, and who hide their real sensitivity behind a conventional mask. Gold's humor stems from the relentless truthfulness of his description of male and female relationships. His novels include *The Birth of A Hero* (1951), *The Prospect Before Us* (1954), *The Man Who Was Not With It* (1956), and *The Optimist* (1959). *Therefore Be Bold* (1960) is a humorous Jewish work set in the Middle West; *Love and Like* (1960) a collection of short stories; and *Salt* (1963) a satirical novel dealing with life in the impersonal metropolis. Gold also published essays on the contemporary American scene entitled *The Age of Happy Problems* (1962). In *Fathers* (1967), the novelist drew upon his own family experiences to tell of the Jewish immigrants who sought fulfillment in the United States. The book is notable for its description of the painful battles between the generations and the crippling effect of the break with the past. [SY.R.]

GOLD, HUGO (1895–), publisher and historian. Gold was born in Vienna. In 1924 he became the head of the publishing house Juedischer Buch- und Kunstverlag, formerly owned by his uncle Max *Hickl. From 1924 to 1939 he was the publisher and editor of the journal *Juedische Volksstimme*, and from 1931 to 1936 of the historical journal *Zeitschrift fuer die Geschichte der Juden in der Tschechoslowakei*. He edited the *Zeitschrift fuer die Geschichte der Juden* (Tel Aviv) from 1964. In 1940 Gold settled in Palestine. After World War II he established (in Tel Aviv) the Olamenu publishing house, which concentrates on books relating to Central European Jewry. Gold's main contributions as a historian are works on the history of the Jews in Czechoslovakia, Austria, and Bukovina, including *Die Juden und Judengemeinde Bratislava in Vergangenheit und Gegenwart* (1932); *Geschichte der Juden in Wien* (1966); *Max Brod, Ein Gedenkbuch 1884–1968* (1969); and *Gedenkbuch der untergegangenen Judengemeinden des*

Burgenlandes (1970). The works he wrote and edited are a major source of information about the destroyed Jewish communities in Central Europe. [Ed.]

GOLD, MICHAEL (**Irwin Granich**; 1893–1967), U.S. Communist author and journalist. Born in New York to poor immigrant parents from Rumania, Gold left school at the age of 13 and worked at various odd jobs to help support his family. He later attended City College night school and began to write his first sketches and poems, which from the start were politically radical in tone. After a brief and unhappy tenure as a special student at Harvard and an extended stay in Mexico in 1916–17, he returned to New York where he worked as a copy editor on the Socialist *Call* and contributed articles and poetry to *Masses*. He joined the Communist Party soon after its formation and became editor first of the *Liberator* (1920–22) and later of *New Masses* (1928–32), both of which were devoted to "proletarian" literature and culture. Gold also worked closely in these years with the left-wing New Playwrights' Theater and himself wrote several plays and a collection of short stories, *120 Million* (1929). In 1930 he published his autobiographical novel of the Lower East Side, *Jews Without Money*, whose stark imagistic prose has made it one of the best-known accounts of Jewish immigrant life in New York. Throughout the 1930s and '40s Gold wrote a regular column for the Communist *Daily Worker* but produced little of literary value. During the last years of his life he lived in San Francisco, where he contributed to the radical West Coast publication, *The People's World*. His books include *The Hollow Men* (1941) and *Change the World!* (1937), a collection of his newspaper columns.

Bibliography: M. Gold, *Mike Gold Reader*, ed. by S. Sillen (1954); Folsom, in: D. Madden (ed.), *Proletarian Writers of the Thirties* (1968), 221–51; C. Angoff, *Tone of the Twenties* (1966), 182–8; D. Aaron, *Writers on the Left* (1961), 84–90, 453. [Ed.]

GOLD, WOLF (**Ze'ev**; 1889–1956), rabbi, leader of religious Zionism. Born in Sczcyczyin, Poland, and descended from a long line of rabbis, Gold was ordained at the age of 17 and succeeded his father-in-law as rabbi in Juteka. In 1907 he emigrated to the U.S., where he served in several congregations: South Chicago, Scranton, Pennsylvania, Williamsburg, New York, San Francisco (where he strenuously fought Reform), and Brooklyn, New York. A man of handsome presence with a beautiful speaking voice, he was a powerful orator and capable organizer. Everywhere he engaged in educational and communal activities, founding a Hebrew school (Williamsburg Talmud Torah), a yeshivah ("Torah ve-Da'at"), a hospital ("Beth Mosheh," Brooklyn), a Hebrew teachers training college

Wolf Gold, leader of the American Mizrachi movement.

(San Francisco), and an orphanage (also in Brooklyn). Gold was from the beginning in the forefront of Zionist workers in the U.S.: in the *Order of the Sons of Zion, and the Zionist funds; he was a delegate to all Zionist Congresses and a member of the Zionist General Council from 1923. From 1913 he was active in the *Mizrachi movement, which, together with his lifelong friend M. *Bar-Ilan (Berlin), he organized in the U.S., and serving as president of the American Mizrachi 1932–35. From 1945 he represented the Mizrachi on the executive of the Jewish Agency and was a member of the Jewish delegation at the United Nations in 1946. Already in 1924 Gold went to Ereẓ Israel to assist in the religious propaganda work of the chief rabbinate and the Mizrachi in the new settlements. His experience led him to the idea of an agricultural yeshivah which was founded eventually (1938) in *Kefar ha-Ro'eh. He settled in Ereẓ Israel in 1935. With the establishment of the State of Israel he became a member of the Provisional Council of State and for some time headed the Jewish Agency's Department for the Development of Jerusalem and in 1951 the Department for Torah Education and Culture. In that capacity Gold did much for the establishment of schools and other educational institutions in various parts of the Diaspora—in North Africa in particular. He worked on the plans for a training institute for rabbis, teachers, youth leaders, etc. for the Diaspora, which after his death came into being as the Z. Gold Institute for Jewish Studies and Teachers' Seminary. A volume of his sermons, articles etc. was published in 1949 (*Nivei Zahav*), and a memorial volume of sermons in 1963 (*Ẓiyyon min ha-Torah*, ed. Z. Tabori).

Bibliography: EẒD, 1 (1958), 464–9, incl. bibl.; *Netivot*, no. 6 (1956), 7–16; S. Daniel, in: *Gevilim*, 1 (1957), 84–102; J. B. Soloveitchik, in: *Ẓiyyon min ha-Torah* (1963), 31–43; *Shanah be-Shanah 5731* (1970), 192–201; Z. Gold, *Lessons in Talmud* (1956), introd. [Ed.]

GOLDBERG, ALEXANDER (1906–), Israel chemical engineer. Goldberg, who was born in Vilna, went to England in 1914. He graduated in mining engineering and

Alexander Goldberg, Israel chemical engineer and president of the Haifa Technion. Courtesy Haifa Technion.

chemical engineering at the Royal School of Mines, London. He was a pioneer in the development of techniques of crop preservation, and subsequently worked with the raw-material group of the Hawker-Siddeley organization. During World War II he was responsible for producing metallic magnesium from seawater, and later for the production of the aluminum used in Britain's postwar prefabricated houses. In 1948 he went to Israel and headed Chemicals and Phosphates Ltd. thereby becoming a key figure in Israel's developing chemical industry. In 1965 he became president of the Haifa Technion. [S.A.M.]

GOLDBERG, ARTHUR JOSEPH (1908–), U.S. labor lawyer, secretary of labor, supreme court justice, and ambassador to the United Nations. Goldberg, who was born in Chicago, was the youngest of 11 children. After graduating from Northwestern University Law School

Arthur J. Goldberg speaking after receiving an honorary degree from the Hebrew University of Jerusalem, July 1968. Photo Werner Braun, Jerusalem.

(1929) at the head of his class, Goldberg began practicing law in Chicago. He soon developed a national reputation in labor law, a field then rapidly expanding in the wake of the intensive labor strife and legislation of the depression years and Roosevelt's New Deal. During World War II, he was appointed head of the labor division of the U.S. Office of Strategic Services (OSS), for which he helped to establish intricate clandestine operations with anti-Fascist trade union leaders behind Nazi lines. In 1948 Goldberg was appointed general counsel of the Congress of Industrial Organizations (CIO). In this capacity he played a crucial role in the prolonged negotiations between the CIO and its warring rival the AFL (American Federation of Labor) and was instrumental in drafting the merger agreement between them in 1955, after which he returned to private practice. His book *AFL-CIO: Labor United* was published the following year.

An early supporter of the presidential aspirations of John F. Kennedy, Goldberg was appointed to the cabinet as secretary of labor upon Kennedy's inauguration in 1961. Unlike his immediate predecessor, Goldberg took an activist view of the office. He vigorously strove to raise the national minimum wage and to increase federal unemployment benefits, while at the same time seeking to arbitrate a wide range of labor-management conflicts in order to implement Kennedy's anti-inflationary program by discouraging excessive wage hikes. His activities in this area alienated many of his old labor colleagues, causing the magazine *New Republic* to summarize his two years as labor secretary by remarking, "His contribution to the Kennedy administration has been notable for his forthright disregard of old ties with organized labor in shaping a new doctrine of the national interest in labor-management disputes."

In 1962 Goldberg was chosen by President Kennedy to replace the retiring Felix Frankfurter as a justice on the United States Supreme Court. During his term on the Court, Goldberg consistently voted with its liberal majority and wrote several key decisions protecting the rights of naturalized American citizens. The most significant decision written by him, however, was in the famous Escobedo Case of 1964, in which the Court ruled by a 5–4 majority that every accused prisoner had the constitutional right to be advised by a lawyer during police interrogation, thereby working a revolution in American criminal law.

In 1965 Goldberg resigned from the Court to become United States permanent representative to the United Nations. The high point of his U.N. career came during the Arab-Israel war of 1967, when throughout the six days of fighting he repeatedly and successfully argued the American position calling for a cease-fire without previous Israel withdrawal. He thereby earned the enmity of the Arab nations, who accused him of influencing American foreign policy on behalf of Jewish interests. Goldberg was also said to have had a major hand in the drafting of the November 1967 Security Council resolution which served as a basis for the Jarring Mission to the Middle East. In 1968 he resigned from his position, reportedly dissatisfied with President Johnson's "hawkish" policies in Vietnam and his own inability to moderate them. Leaving Washington, he settled in New York City, where he opened a law practice while taking an active behind-the-scenes role in local and statewide Democratic Party politics. In 1970 he ran unsuccessfully for the office of governor of New York State. Goldberg, who was active in Zionist and Jewish affairs, was president of the American Jewish Committee (1968–69) and chairman of the Jewish Theological Seminary's board of overseers (1963–69).

Bibliography: J. P. Frank, *The Warren Court* (1964), 165–85; D. P. Moynihan (ed.), *The Defences of Freedom: The Public Papers of Arthur J. Goldberg* (1966). [Ar.B.]

GOLDBERG, BAER (Dov) BEN ALEXANDER (known by his acronym **Bag**; 1800–1884), Polish scholar. Goldberg was born in Chlodna, near Lomza, Poland, and was orphaned at an early age. He studied Torah in dire poverty, but earned a reputation as a prodigy. Having tried his hand at business and teaching, in 1830 Goldberg became a private tutor for the family of the wealthy and learned Gershon Litinski in one of the villages of Suwalki district. When after some time the entire Litinski family converted to Christianity, he was slandered as having influenced them.

In 1843 he went to Berlin, where he was favorably received by the *maskilim*. However, lacking a formal education, he could not find employment there, and in 1847 went to England, where he managed with great difficulty to earn a living copying and publishing Hebrew manuscripts from the Oxford libraries. In 1853 he settled in Paris, earning his living there by copying and publishing Hebrew and Arabic manuscripts from the National Library. Altogether, Goldberg published 17 books and pamphlets and hundreds of articles in Hebrew periodicals, writing mainly under the name "Divrei Bag" ("Words of Bag") and "Gam Elleh Divrei Bag" ("These also are the words of Bag"). His writings exemplified all the virtues and weaknesses of one who is self-taught: diligence and an abundance of detail but written in ornate language and lacking organization.

Goldberg's main contribution to scholarship was the editing of such medieval works as *Ḥofes Matmonim* (1845), a collection of medieval texts; Isaac Israeli's *Yesod Olam* (1848); Ibn Janaḥ's *Sefer ha-Rikmah* in Judah ibn Tibbon's translation (1857); *Iggeret Sherira Ga'on* (1873); *Risalat R. Judah b. Koraish* (1867); and Abraham b. Moses b. Maimon's *Birkat Avraham* (1860, repr. 1960).

Bibliography: I. I. Goldbloom, in: *Oẓar ha-Sifrut*, 4 (1892), 542–51; B. Wachstein, *Hebraeische Publizistik in Wien* (1930), 71 (incl. bibl.); Kressel, Leksikon, 1 (1965), 412–3. [Ed.]

GOLDBERG, BEN ZION (1895–), Yiddish journalist. Descended from prominent rabbinical families in Lithuania, Goldberg went to the United States at the age of 12. In 1917 he married the youngest daughter of *Shalom Aleichem. After writing articles on psychology for the Yiddish daily *The Day* (1920), he expanded his horizon to politics, social problems, and literature. From 1924 to 1940 he was the paper's managing editor. As a daily columnist for more than 40 years, he exerted considerable influence on Jewish public opinion, often arousing heated controversies, particularly with his pronounced pro-Soviet orientation during his middle years. His books in English include *The*

Jewish Problem in the Soviet Union (1961) and *Travels in the Soviet Union* (1966).

Bibliography: LYNL, 3 (1960), 45–48. [S.L.]

GOLDBERG, BORIS (1865–1922), economist and Zionist. Born in Shaki (Sakiai), Lithuania, Goldberg studied at Hanover, where he graduated in 1891 as a chemical engineer. In 1898 he moved to Vilna. He joined the Ḥibbat Zion movement at an early age, and when the Zionist Organization was founded joined it at once. Goldberg was an ardent supporter of practical settlement work in Ereẓ Israel. He contributed articles to all existing Jewish periodicals in Russia, was a member of the editorial board of *Razsvet* and *Ha-Olam* and published studies on the demographic and social composition of Russian Jewry. Goldberg was a member of the Central Office of the Zionist Organization in Vilna, and, together with his brother I. L. *Goldberg, he headed the illegal Zionist activities in the Vilna region, for which he was imprisoned on several occasions. In 1906 he took part in the work of the League for Equal Rights for Russian Jews, and in 1917 he was a member of the National Council of Russian Jews. He left Russia in 1919 as a representative of Russian Jews to the Comité des Délégations Juives, which represented the Jewish people at the Versailles Peace Conference. He helped to transfer capital of Russian Jews to Palestine and was one of the founders of the Ha-Boneh Company and the Silikat building materials factory in Tel Aviv. He was wounded during the Arab riots of 1921 and died a year later in Tel Aviv.

Bibliography: N. Sokolow, *History of Zionism*, 2 (1919), index; I. Klausner, *Mi-Kattoviẓ ad Basel*, 2 vols. (1965), index; Tidhar, 1 (1947), 293, 483–4.

[Y.S.]

Boris Goldberg, Russian Zionist leader. Jerusalem, J.N.U.L., Schwadron Collection.

GOLDBERG, ISAAC (1887–1938), U. S. author. Born in Boston, Goldberg wrote *Sir William S. Gilbert* (1913); *The Story of Gilbert and Sullivan* (1928); *George Gershwin* (1931); *Major Noah: American-Jewish Pioneer* (1936); and *Queen of Hearts* (1936), a biography of Lola Montez. He did pioneering work in his surveys, *Studies in Spanish-American Literature* (1920) and *Brazilian Literature* (1922). Goldberg also translated into English some of the major Yiddish authors, such as David Pinski, Scholem Asch, and Yehoash. From 1923 to 1932 he was literary editor of *The American Freeman*.

Bibliography: Ewen, in: *American Hebrew* (Nov. 5, 1937).

[S.L.]

GOLDBERG, ISAAC LEIB (1860–1935), Zionist leader and philanthropist in Russia and Ereẓ Israel; brother of Boris *Goldberg. After studying at the Kovno yeshivah, he

Isaac Leib Goldberg, a leader of the Third Aliyah. Courtesy Central Zionist Archives, Jerusalem.

settled in Vilna, where he joined his uncle's business. One of the first members of the *Ḥibbat Zion movement (1882), he founded the Ohavei Zion society in Vilna. At the Ḥovevei Zion meeting in *Druzgenik in 1887, he sought to effect a compromise between the views of the Orthodox and the *maskilim*. He represented the Ḥovevei Zion committee in Vilna and was a member of *Benei Moshe. His home in Vilna became the center of Zionist and Jewish national activities. His wife, Rachel, was among the founders of Yehudiyyah Hebrew Girls School.

Goldberg was a delegate to the First Zionist Congress, representing the Ḥovevei Zion of Vilna; in 1900 he was appointed representative of the *Zionist Organization in the Vilna district. He took part in the establishment of the Geulah Company, whose aim it was to acquire land in Ereẓ Israel for private ownership, and of the Carmel Company for the marketing of wine produced in the Jewish settlements in Ereẓ Israel. In 1908 he established a farm at *Hartuv and purchased the first plot of land on Mount Scopus in Jerusalem for the future *Hebrew University. In 1906 he became a member of the Zionist Central Committee in Russia, and its office was located in his home. He lent his support to the Zionist periodicals in Vilna *Ha-Olam* and *Dos Yidishe Folk*. During World War I the Russian authorities forced him to live in Moscow, where he continued his Zionist activities. In 1919 he settled in Palestine, engaged in growing oranges, and made important contributions to improving the packing and marketing of citrus products. He was one of the founders of the *Haaretz* daily newspaper, which he supported financially. Goldberg was also a supporter of the Hebrew Language Committee. He left half his estate for the establishment of a fund for the Promotion of Hebrew Literature and Hebrew Culture in Ereẓ Israel, which was eventually handed over to the *Jewish National Fund, which devoted the income to Hebrew cultural projects.

Bibliography: N. Sokolow, *History of Zionism*, 2 (1919), index; S. Eisenstadt, *I. L. Goldberg*... (Heb., 1945); I. Klausner, *Mi-Kattoviz ad Basel*, 2 vols. (1956), index; Tidhar, 1 (1947), 293, 483–4. [Y.S.]

GOLDBERG, LEA (1911–1970), Hebrew poet and critic. Born in Koenigsberg, Eastern Prussia, she spent the early years of her childhood in Russia but after the Revolution her family returned to their home in Kovno, Lithuania. While still a schoolgirl, Lea Goldberg began to write Hebrew verse and

Lea Goldberg, Hebrew poet and critic. Government Press Office, Tel Aviv.

her first poem was published in *Hed Lita* in 1926. She attended the universities of Kovno, Berlin, and Bonn. Arriving in Tel Aviv in 1935, she joined the circle of modernist authors, whose mentor was Avraham *Shlonsky, and began publishing her poetry in *Turim*, the literary forum of the group. Shlonsky helped her compile her first volume of poetry *Tabbe'ot Ashan* ("Smoke Rings," 1935). After a career as a schoolteacher, she joined the editorial staffs of **Davar* and later *Mishmar* in the capacity of theater critic and eventually became editor of *Al ha-Mishmar*'s literary supplement. She also served on the staff of *Davar li-Yladim*, a popular children's magazine, was the children's book editor of Sifriyyat Po'alim, and the literary adviser to *Habimah, Israel's national theater. In 1952 she was invited to organize the Department of Comparative Literature at the Hebrew University of Jerusalem holding the chair until her death. A prolific and versatile writer, Lea Goldberg's literary talent found expression in many genres. Primarily a poet, she was also a literary critic, wrote a number of children's works, was a copious translator, and the author of a novel and a play.

Poetry. All of Lea Goldberg's poetry is written in the modern mode set by the school of younger poets that developed in Ereẓ Israel during the Mandate period. Influenced by the Russian Acmeist poets (a literary trend which rejected symbolism, aiming at concrete imagery and a clear unadorned style), she used traditional verse forms, expressing her modernism through a conversational style which eschewed the ornate rhetoric of many of her predecessors and the bombastic expressionism of her contemporaries. Her language though symbolic is simple and familiar in which ordinary words, images, rhythms, and rhymes have an astonishing freshness. The later verse is stripped of all "literary" pretensions; the poet thus strove to evolve a style of direct and unencumbered statement of the poetic experience. Lea Goldberg's tendency toward aesthetic intellectualism is modified by a lyrical delicacy. She refused to write ideological verse and unlike her contemporaries she rarely touched upon Jewish themes. Only in the aftermath of the Holocaust did she express her feelings in a Jewish framework (*Mi-Beiti ha-Yashan*, "From my Old Home," 1944). Universal in her approach, she wrote on childhood, nature, love (especially unfulfilled love), the quest for aesthetic expression, aging, and death. In her later years her central themes were resignation to the tragedy of existence and finding solace in the poetry unexpectedly discovered in ordinary phenomena. Among her outstanding poems are: "Mi-Shirei ha-Naḥal" ("The Songs of the Stream" in: *Al ha-Periḥah*, 1948) in which she employed natural symbols such as river, stone, tree, moon, and blade of grass to serve as a vehicle for the poetic presentation of aesthetic problems of the creative artists; "Be-Harei Yerushalayim" ("In the Hills of Jerusalem" in: *Barak ba-Boker*, 1956), one of her best landscape poems, set in Jerusalem, the city in which she resided for many years; and "Ahavatah shel Teresa di Mon" ("The Love of Therese du Meun," in *Barak ba-Boker*), a series of sonnets whose theme is a love affair between an aging medieval aristocrat and her young lover.

Criticism. An avid reader, Lea Goldberg was at home in the literature of all the major European languages. She was most familiar with Russian literature and wrote *Aḥdut ha-Adam ve-ha-Yekum bi-Yẓirat Tolstoy* ("The Unity of World and Man in Tolstoy's Works," 1959), as well as a collection of essays on Pushkin, Lermontov, Gogol, Turgenev, Herzen, and Chekhov entitled *Ha-Sifrut ha-Rusit ba-Me'ah ha-Tesha-Esreh* (1968). The latter was to have been part of a general history of the literature of the period, but she abandoned the project. Lea Goldberg was also well versed in Italian literature and wrote an introduction to Dante's *Divine Comedy* (*Mavo la-Komedyah ha-Elohit*, mimeograph, 1958) and a preface to her translation of selected poems by Petrarch (1957). In *Ḥamishah Perakim bi-Ysodot ha-Shirah* ("Five Chapters in the Elements of Poetry," 1957), a more systematic attempt at studying the problems of poetry, she discusses poetic theory, meter, rhyme, and symbol. Each chapter begins with a close reading of a Hebrew poem which is used to illustrate her specific hypothesis posited. In contrast to her generalizations about poetry, which reflect accepted literary criteria, the interpretations of specific works show an original and creative poetic mind. The same can be said about her study *Ommanut ha-Sippur* ("The Art of the Short Story," 1963).

Children's Literature. Lea Goldberg was one of Israel's most successful children's writers. She was able to enter the world of children, communicate with them, and establish a bond of friendship with all children not only through the written word but by live contact. She wrote about 20 works for children. A whole generation of Israelis grew up on her stories and poems (see *Children's Literature).

Prose Works. *Mikhtavim mi-Nesi'ah Medummah* ("Letters from an Imaginary Journey," 1937) and *Ve-Hu ha-Or* ("He Is The Light," 1946), the two major prose works of Lea Goldberg, are mainly autobiographical. The latter is set in Lithuania and describes the struggle of a young and sensitive girl student for identity, despite insecurities rooted in a background of mental illness in her immediate family. The earlier work, *Mikhtavim mi-Nesi'ah Medummah* hardly a novel because of its weak structure, refers to a later period in the author's life and gives an insight into her basically aristocratic view of the arts. The struggle between leftist politics and art is the theme of her single play *Ba'alat ha-Armon* ("Lady of the Manor," 1956) which is set in postwar Europe. The play (in English translation) was staged in New York but was not a critical success.

Translations. Among the many European classics that Lea Goldberg translated into Hebrew are: Tolstoy's *War and Peace* (1958), Chekhov's *Stories* (1945), Gorki's *Childhood* (1943), several plays and poems by Shakespeare (1957), selected poems by Petrarch (1957), Ibsen's *Peer Gynt* (1958), and *Aucassin et Nicolette* (1966). Together with Shlonsky she edited an anthology of Russian poetry (1942). Lea Goldberg started to paint in her later years and she illustrated several of her own books (*Aucassin et Nicolette*, for example). For English translations of her works see Goell, Bibliography, index.

Bibliography: E. Spicehandler, in: *Israel* (Spring 1961), 61–80; G. Yardeni, *Siḥot im Soferim* (1961), 119–32; G. Shaked, in: *Moznayim*, 3 (1956) no. 3, 86–190; idem, in: *Orot*, 38 (Jan. 1960), 45–49; D. Sadan, in: *Yerushalayim, Shenaton le-Divrei Sifrut ve-Ommanut* (1970), 17–22; R. Alter, in: *Commentary*, 49, 5 (1970), 83–86. [E.Sp.]

GOLDBERG, OSCAR (1885–1952), scholar and author, born in Berlin. Goldberg first studied medicine, but on the basis of personal parapsychological experiments he turned to esoteric mysticism. After Hitler's rise to power he emigrated to France and subsequently to the United States. He later returned to France and died in Nice. His first work, *Die fuenf Buecher Mosis, ein Zahlengebaeude* (1908) is an attempt to prove (in accordance with kabbalistic opinion) that the entire Torah is based on the letters of the Tetragrammaton. His basic theories are expressed in the works: *Die Wirklichkeit der Hebraeer* (vol. 1, 1925; no more were published); *Maimonides* (1935); and articles on Greek mythology in the monthly *Mass und Wert* (1937). Goldberg assumed that there were "metaphysical" peoples whose biological center was their "god" as opposed to peoples or groups who had lost their metaphysical power and were merely biological groups. *Die Wirklichkeit der Hebraeer* ("The Reality of the Hebrews") shows the Hebrews to be the outstanding example of a metaphysical people, which activates the vital link between it and its "center," i.e., its god, via the magical power of ritual and makes its god dwell within the world. The metaphysical reality of the genuine Hebrews consisted in the activation of the laws and statutes of the Torah (which must be understood in its most literal and exact interpretation). Later Judaism, beginning with "the religion of the prophets," was based on the deterioration of the magical powers of the Hebrews and the loss of the basic tools for the activation of their magical reality: the Tabernacle and the Ark of the Covenant. Every metaphysical people has a national god, and among these gods, which had perfect reality, the God of Israel is but the strongest. As the real magical power of metaphysics was weakened, there begins the process of the transformation of the ritual which possessed formal and material precision into an abstract universal "religion." The histories of religions constitute decline and not progress. The decline of true Hebraism, which worked miracles not according to circumstance but by order and fixed ritual, began during the reigns of David and Solomon. It reached its nadir in the "religiosity" of the Psalms. The transition from worship in the Temple to that in the synagogue typifies the decline of the metaphysical power to nothingness.

Goldberg accepted only the Pentateuch as a divine document in all its details and signs, and interpreted it magically, not "theologically." The Revelation of God is not an act of free grace to His creatures, but springs from the need of God Himself to find a dwelling place *(mishkan)* on earth. Goldberg views the system of Maimonides as the final expression of complete alienation from the true mission of the Hebraic existence, and as an intended blurring and abolition of the realistic principle which is the power to work miracles in favor of moralistic and abstract prattle. According to this system, Goldberg interpreted all details of other mythologies. He advocated the organization of the remnants of magical power which remained here and there, in order to find a way for the renewal of divine revelation. He stated his magical views in a clearly rationalistic way and linked them with modern biological philosophy. The kabbalistic origins of his thought are conspicuous and Goldberg himself recognized this despite his attempts to define specific differences between the spheres of the Torah and that of Kabbalah. Goldberg was hostile to Zionism, which he viewed as a secular renewal of a Jewish people without a metaphysical basis according to his definition.

For many years Goldberg led a small group which propagated his views in writing and orally. His most important disciple in philosophy was Erich Unger (d. 1951 in London). For some time his works and thoughts had considerable influence on circles of both Jewish and gentile intellectuals, scholars and writers such as the paleontologist E. Dacque, and the writer Thomas Mann. The latter depicted Goldberg in his novel *Doctor Faustus* (1947) as the character Dr. Chaim Breizacher.

Bibliography: J. Schechter, *Mi-Madda le-Emunah* (1953), 213–29; E. Unger, *Politik und Metaphysik* (1922); idem, *Das Problem der mythischen Realitaet* (1926); idem, *Wirklichkeit, Mythos, Erkenntnis* (1930); A. Caspary, *Die Maschinenutopie* (1927). [G.Sch.]

GOLDBERG, RUBE (Reuben Lucius; 1883–1970). U.S. cartoonist. Goldberg was best known for his sports cartoons, comic strips, humor panels, editorial cartoons, and sculpture. After studying engineering at the University of California, he drew sports cartoons for several years for the *Chronicle* and later for the *Bulletin* in his native San Francisco. In 1907 he went to New York, joined the staff of the *Evening Mail*, and for the next 30 years had an international following for his widely syndicated features. They included *Foolish Questions, Mike and Ike, Boob McNutt*, and the zany inventions of *Professor Lucifer Gorgonzola Butts*, who contrived complicated apparatus to perform simple tasks. Goldberg joined the *New York Sun* in 1938 as political cartoonist. His satirical drawing, *Peace Today*, won the Pulitzer Prize in 1947. The annual award of the National Cartoonists' Society, which he helped to found, was named "the Reuben" in his honor. [I.R.]

GOLDBERGER, IZIDOR (1876–1944), Hungarian rabbi and scholar. Goldberger, who was born in Bátorkeszi, Hungary, held appointments in Sátoraljaujhely (1903–1914) and Tata (1912–1944). He wrote on the history of Hungarian Jewry, especially on that of the Jews in Zemplén county (1910), and in the city of Tata (1914). He also wrote on the emancipation of Hungarian Jewry. Goldberger translated into Hungarian excerpts from the Mishnah (1905) and from the Midrash (1907).

Bibliography: *Dr. Goldberger Izidor tatai rabbi irodalmi működése, 1904–1914* (1915); *Magyar Zsidó Lexikon* (1929), 318; Wininger, Biog, 2 (1927), 441; 7 (1936), 14. [J.Z.]

GOLDBERGER, JOSEPH (1874–1929), U.S. physician and public health specialist. Goldberger, who was born in Giralt, Hungary, immigrated to the U.S. at an early age. From 1899 until his death he served in the U.S. Public Health Service in Washington, D.C. Goldberger's greatest contribution was his discovery of the etiology and therapy of pellagra and his introduction of nicotinic acid as a means of preventing the disease. He also made significant contributions in the study of infectious diseases and public health, particularly in the field of welfare of the poor.

Bibliography: S. R. Kagan, *Jewish Medicine* (1952), 549; *Biographisches Lexikon der hervorragenden Aerzte*, 1 (1932), s.v. [S.M.]

GOLDBLOOM, JACOB KOPPEL (1872–1961), Zionist leader. Born in Kletsk, then Poland, Goldbloom went to London in 1892, joined the Ḥovevei Zion and after meeting Herzl began to found Zionist societies in Whitechapel. He introduced the *"Ivrit be-Ivrit"* method of Hebrew teaching and taught many thousands of youngsters who enrolled in his "Redman's Road Talmud Torah" over the decades. From 1901 onward Goldbloom attended almost every Zionist Congress and was a member of the Zionist General Council. In 1935 he became chairman of the European executive of the Confederation of General Zionists. He served Herzl, Wolffsohn, Otto Warburg, Weizmann, Sokolow, and Nahum Goldmann with loyalty and devotion. Goldbloom was one of the architects of the British Zionist Federation and of its Synagogue Council. He wrote a utopian work in Hebrew entitled *Ḥag ha-Bikkurim be-Ereẓ Yisrael bi-Shenat 2016* ("Festival of the First Harvest in Ereẓ Israel in the Year 2016," 1920). In 1963 his remains were buried in Jerusalem. [Jo.Fr.]

GOLDBLUM, ISRAEL ISSER (Isidore; 1864–1925), Polish Hebrew writer and bibliographer. Goldblum was born in Vilna and studied in East European yeshivot . He devoted himself to the study and publication of Hebrew manuscripts in Berlin, Paris, London, Oxford, and Rome. The result of his researches he published under the pseudonym Yafag mainly in the periodical *Ha-Maggid.* He corresponded with the leading Jewish scholars of his time and published a collection of these letters (*Kevuẓat Mikhtavim,* 1895). He also published *Mi-Ginzei Yisrael be-Paris* (1894), on the Paris Hebrew manuscripts and *Ma'amar Bikkoret Sefarim* (1891). Some of his writings and letters are extant in manuscript at the Jewish Theological Seminary of America.

Bibliography: Kressel, Leksikon, 1 (1965), 409–10. [Ed.]

GOLDEN, DAVID AARON (1920–), Canadian lawyer and government official. Born in Sinclair, Manitoba, Golden practiced law in Winnipeg and lectured at the University of Manitoba Law School from 1945 to 1951. He was chief legal adviser of the department of defense production from 1951 to 1954 when he became deputy minister of defense production in the federal government. Golden left the government service to become president of the Air Industries Association of Canada in 1962. For a short period he served as deputy minister for industry but returned to the Air Industries Association in 1964 and in 1969 became founding president of Telesat Canada Corporation, the company responsible for the development of the Canadian communications satellite.

Bibliography: *Who's Who in Canadian Jewry 1965* (1965), 437. [B.G.K.]

GOLDEN, HARRY LEWIS (Herschel Goldhurst; 1902–), U.S. author, editor, and publisher. One of five children of immigrants from Austria-Hungary, Golden was

Harry Golden, U.S. author and editor. Courtesy *The Carolina Israelite,* Charlotte, N.C. Photo Declan Haun.

born on New York's Lower East Side. His father was an editor of the *Jewish Daily Forward.* Golden studied English literature, but left university without taking his degree. During the "Roaring Twenties" he was sentenced to five years imprisonment for running a Wall Street gambling den. On his release he moved south, changing his name to Golden and becoming a successful journalist. Golden is best known for his one-man newspaper, *The Carolina Israelite,* which he published from 1942 to 1969. He was much admired by American liberals for his witty and courageous stand in favor of Negro integration, attacking race hatred as absurd rather than criminal. His best-selling books *Only In America* (1958), *For 2¢ Plain* (1959), and *Enjoy* (1960) were drawn from some of his editorials. Much of their charm lies in their folkloristic description of Jewish immigrant life. His other works include *Mr. Kennedy and the Negroes* (1964); *So What Else Is New* (1964); and an autobiography, *The Right Time* (1969). In 1965 he published *A Little Girl is Dead* about the Leo *Frank case.

Bibliography: M. Levin (ed.), *Five Boyhoods* (1962), 37–78; T. Solotaroff, in: *Commentary,* 31 (1961), 1–13; *Current Biography Yearbook 1959* (1960), 150–2. [M.H.H.]

GOLDENBERG, BAERISH (1825–1898), Hebrew scholar, teacher, and poet. Born in Vishnevets (Volhynia), he studied in Tarnopol in the school established by Joseph *Perl, and in 1850 opened his own school there. The rest of his life was devoted to teaching, mainly in Tarnopol, but also for some time in other towns in Galicia and Rumania. He published many linguistic studies in the Hebrew journals of his time, articles and books (in German) on ancient Jewish history, and Hebrew poetry. His two major Hebrew books are *Ohel Yosef* (a biography of Joseph Perl and a history of his Tarnopol school, 1860) and *Or Ḥadash* (biblical commentaries and linguistic studies, 10 vols., 1889–97). He also edited the journal *Nogah ha-Yare'aḥ* (1872–80).

Bibliography: G. Bader, *Medinah va-Ḥakhameha* (1934), 59–60; N. M. Gelber, *Toledot ha-Tenu'ah ha-Ẓiyyonit be-Galiẓyah* (1958), 261; *Sefer Tarnopol* (1955), 94–95. [G.K.]

GOLDENBERG, H. CARL (1907–), Canadian lawyer, economist, and government adviser. Born in Montreal, Goldenberg became a queen's counsel in 1952. He lectured at McGill University in economics and political science from 1932 to 1936 and was an adviser to provincial governments on municipal finance before becoming a senior official in the Department of Munitions in 1940. Goldenberg was appointed special arbitrator or mediator in numerous strikes and industrial crises in all parts of Canada and as adviser, consultant, investigator, or commissioner on a wide variety of problems. He was chairman of the boards of inquiry into the sugar industries of Jamaica (1959–60) and Trinidad (1960–62), and was counsel for Newfoundland on the revision of the terms of union with Canada. He was special counsel for various Canadian provinces at Dominion-Provincial conferences and sat as a special commissioner to inquire into an alleged bread combine in Western Canada (1948). In 1968 Goldenberg was made an adviser to the prime minister, Pierre Trudeau, on constitutional affairs. [B.G.K.]

GOLDENBERG, LAZAR (1846–1916), Russian revolutionary and one of the first Jewish socialists in Russia. Goldenberg joined the revolutionary movement as a young man and was arrested. He escaped to Switzerland where he became secretary of the Slavic department of the International League of Socialist Revolutionaries. Goldenberg went to London in 1876 and established the Agudat ha-Soẓialistim ha-Ivrim (the Jewish Socialist Organization) with Aaron *Lieberman, which was probably the first of its kind in the world. On a visit to Rumania in 1881,

Goldenberg was seized and handed over to the Russian authorities but managed to escape a second time. He lived for ten years in New York where he organized the Russian revolutionary activities abroad and for many years afterward managed a publishing house in London which produced books on socialist subjects in Russian. From 1891 to 1900 Goldenberg published an English monthly *Free Russia.* His memoirs appeared posthumously (1924) in Russian in the Moscow periodical *Katorga i ssylka* (nos. 3, 4, 5, 6). [Ed.]

GOLDENBERG, SAMUEL LEIB (1807–1846), Hebrew journalist. Born in Bolechow (Bolekhov) into a wealthy family, he was one of the pioneers of the Haskalah in Galicia. In 1833 Goldenberg launched the periodical **Kerem Ḥemed* which was almost entirely devoted to scholarly articles (in the form of letters) and marked a development in Hebrew periodical literature. The leading modern Jewish scholars of the first half of the 19th century contributed to it.

Bibliography: Klausner, Sifrut, 2 (1952), 37–38. [G.K.]

GOLDEN CALF (Heb. עֵגֶל מַסֵּכָה, Ex. 32:4; עֶגְלֵי זָהָב I Kings 12:28), the golden image made by Aaron at the behest of the Israelites and venerated near Mount Sinai (Ex. 32). Exodus 32 relates that the Israelites, anxious about Moses' prolonged absence, demanded that *Aaron provide a god to lead them. Complying, Aaron collected the golden ornaments of the people and fashioned the gold into the shape of a calf or a small bull. Aaron probably intended the calf to represent the vacant throne of God, like the cherubim in the Tabernacle, but the image was immediately hailed by the people as a representation of the God who had brought Israel out of Egypt. Aaron then built an altar, and on the following day sacrifices were offered and the people feasted and danced and played. Thereupon the Lord told Moses of the apostasy of the "stiff-necked people," whom He proposed to destroy. Moses, however, interceded on behalf of the Israelites and persuaded the Lord to renounce His intended punishment. Carrying the Tablets of the Covenant down from Mt. Sinai, Moses saw the people dancing around the golden calf. In great anger Moses smashed the Tablets, melted down the image of the calf, pulverized the precious metal, and scattered the powdered gold over the available source of water, thus making the people drink it (verse 20); and there is doubtless a causal nexus between this and the plague that is reported in verse 35 (see Ordeal of *Jealousy).

Exodus 32 relates that Moses then upbraided Aaron for having "brought great guilt" upon the people. The parallel account in Deut. 9:20 relates that but for Moses' supplication on behalf of Aaron the Lord would have destroyed Aaron. Stern punishment was, however, meted out to the calf-worshipers, 3,000 of whom were slain by the *Levites who had responded to Moses' call for volunteers. Henceforth the Levites were consecrated to the service of the Lord. Despite Moses' prayer for divine forgiveness, the Lord threatened that on the day of His visitation punishment would overtake the people. Soon afterward a plague broke out among the Israelites (see above). In addition the Lord announced that He would no longer abide amid this "stiff-necked people." The Israelites mourned the departure of the Divine presence and stripped themselves of their ornaments (Ex. 33:1–6).

Critical View. The extant text of Exodus 32 is according to certain Bible critics an expansion of a basic narrative into several strata by secondary additions; for another interpretation see Cassuto (Exodus, ad loc.). The critical view does not see the chapter as a literary unity on the basis of inconsist-

"Adoration of the Golden Calf" by the French artist Nicolas Poussin, 1635. Oil on canvas, 5×7 ft. (1.52×2.13 m.). London, National Gallery.

encies. Others, however, believe that Aaronic authorship (and divine sanction) of the practice of calf symbolism was claimed from the very beginning by Jeroboam I and the priesthoods of Bethel and Dan, and that the version in Exodus 32, in boldly "representing Aaron, the ancestor of Israel's priestly caste, as a man of somewhat feeble character" (H. L. Ginsberg, in JBL, 80 (1961), 345) is motivated by a desire to discredit the practice which he instituted.

Calf and Bull Symbolism. The narrative of the golden calf cannot be understood without relating it to the erection of two golden calves in the temples of *Beth-El and *Dan by *Jeroboam I of Israel (I Kings 12:26ff.). Not only are the general features of the story similar in both accounts, but the explanatory formula in Exodus 32:4b, 8b—"These are your gods, O Israel, who brought you up out of the land of Egypt"—is virtually identical to the one in I Kings 12:28b. Scholars are divided on the question of the chronological relationship of the two accounts. The traditional view is that the Jeroboam incident is dependent on the Exodus story (see Cassuto, loc. cit.). Other scholars, however, hold the view that Exodus 32 presupposes I Kings 12.

The bull had an important role in the art and religious texts of the ancient Near East. The storm-god *Hadad is frequently represented standing on a bull. Taking these facts into account it is generally assumed (after H. Th. Obbrick) that Jeroboam's calves corresponded to the *cherubim of Solomon's Temple, i.e., they were regarded as seats or pedestals upon which the Lord was thought to stand invisible to human eyes. M. Haran remarks that if Jeroboam's calves were considered pedestals, then they were not meant to be an exact replica of cherubim connected with the *Ark of the Covenant because the Ark and its cherubim were kept in the publicly inaccessible Holy of Holies while the calves were placed in the courts of the Temple, where the people could see and kiss them (cf. Hos. 13:2). It is also possible that the calves were, from the beginning, meant to represent the Lord like the images in the sanctuaries of Micah and Dan (Judg. 17:4; 18:14, 15–31; cf. M. Haran, in B. Zvieli (ed.), *Siḥot ba-Mikra,* 1 (1968), 214; idem, in: *Biblica,* 50 (1969), 264).

In any case Jeroboam's initiative must have had some basis in an old tradition, otherwise he could not have succeeded in his enterprise. Jeroboam's bulls, contrary to the Ark symbolism, were meant to be accessible to worshipers in the temples (cf. I Kings 12:27); and thus they developed from symbols of the Lord to fetishes in their own right (cf. e.g., II Kings 17:16; Hos. 8:5–6; 10:5; 13:2). [Ed.]

In the Aggadah. The rabbinic attitude toward the episode of the golden calf is guided by the need to explain how the Children of Israel could demand an idol so soon after hearing the Ten Commandments and giving liberally to the erection of the Sanctuary and how Aaron could agree to the construction of the calf and still not forfeit his future role as high priest. The initiative in demanding the idol is attributed by some rabbis to the mixed multitude who joined the Israelites at the time of the Exodus (Ex. 12:38). Forty thousand of them, accompanied by two Egyptian magicians, *Jannes and Mambres, came to Aaron and claimed that it already was the sixth hour of the 40th day since Moses had left, the hour which he previously had designated for his return. They claimed that since he had not yet appeared he would never come. Satan added to the state of helplessness of the people by showing them a vision of Moses' bier which convinced them that he had died. Only then did they demand that Aaron produce a god for them (Shab. 89a; Tanḥ. B., Ex. 112–3). The error of the people consisted in including in their calculation the day of the ascent, whereas Moses had excluded it (Rashi, Shab. 89a). God was also blamed since He enslaved them in Egypt where they were exposed to the most idolatrous of ancient civilizations (Ex. R. 43:7) and for giving them an abundance of gold and silver when they left Egypt (Ber. 32a). *Hur, who is regarded as the son of Miriam and Caleb, attempted to dissuade the people from the sin and was put to death by them. Aaron feared that he would share the same fate (Lev. R. 10:3; Tanḥ. B., Ex. 112–3) and in accordance with his passion for the pursuit of peace (Avot 1:12; see *Aaron in the aggadah), felt it better to acquiesce than to permit the people to commit the unpardonable sin of slaying two leaders on the same day (Sanh. 7a). Hoping to gain time, he ordered them to bring the golden ornaments of their wives, relying on their known piety to refuse. The men thereupon donated their own jewelry (PdRE 45). Aaron then threw the gold into the fire, still hoping that Moses would return. Instantly, however, a calf appeared, alive and skipping, the result of a splinter which was thrown into the fire by the wicked Micah. This splinter, containing the words עלה שור (*aleh shor,* "Come up, Ox"; Joseph being compared to an ox; cf. Deut. 33:17), had previously been thrown into the Nile by Moses when he desired that Joseph's coffin rise to the surface so that he could transport his remains to Ereẓ Israel (Tanḥ. *Ki Tissa,* 19). According to another version, the Egyptian magicians made the calf move as if it were alive (Song R. 1:9, no. 3). Aaron then postponed the celebration to the next day again to gain time. Since God knew that Aaron was motivated by good intentions the high priesthood was not withheld from him (Lev. R. 10:3; Ex. R. 37:2). Nevertheless, he still was severely punished in that the subsequent death of two of his sons was attributed to his role in this incident (Lev. R. 10:5).

The tribe of Levi (Yoma 66b) and its 12 heads (PdRE 45) did not join the worship of the calf. The remaining Israelites were severely punished. Whoever sacrificed and burned incense died by the sword; whoever embraced and kissed the calf died by the plague; and whoever rejoiced in his heart died of dropsy (Yoma 66b). "There is not a misfortune that Israel has suffered which is not partly a retribution for the sin of the calf" (Sanh. 102a). [A.Ro.]

In Christianity. During the Roman period and long after, the golden calf episode was a source of embarrassment to the Jews in their relations with the increasingly aggressive Church, which fully exploited the story in its polemics with the Synagogue. Even Josephus, who was concerned only with pagan anti-Semitism, was evidently afraid that the biblical account might be employed by Alexandrian anti-Semites to lend credence to their allegation that the Jews worshiped an ass's head in the Temple (cf. Apion 2:80, 114, 120; Tacitus, Histories 5:4). Josephus accordingly omits the entire golden calf episode from his account of the Israelite migrations in the desert. Instead, he graphically depicts the deep anxiety of the Israelites concerning Moses and their joy when at last he came down from Mount Sinai (Ant. 3:95–99). Not only did Moses not break the tablets, but he actually displayed them to the rejoicing people (3:101–2). Josephus also omits any reference to Aaron, and the same is true of Philo who does not, however, completely suppress the golden calf narrative (Mos. 2:161–74, 271).

As early as the immediate post-crucifixion era, Stephen, the first Christian martyr, sharply denounced the Jews (but not Aaron who was held in veneration by the Church) for having made the golden calf, which became the fountainhead of Jewish crimes throughout their history, culminating in the crucifixion of Jesus (Acts 7:41–52). For the Church the golden calf episode served as proof that the divine covenant with Israel had never been consummated, so that the Jewish claim to a special relationship with the Almighty was unacceptable (see Smolar in bibl., p. 91). By worshiping the golden calf, the Jews had revealed their foolish, stubborn, unrepentant, and immoral character (*ibid.,* 100). Augustine also associated the calf cult with the worship of the devil, and the Jews who had drunk the water into which the powder of the golden calf had been cast with the body of the devil (*ibid.*, 100–1). The medieval identification of the Jew with the devil was no doubt influenced by this extreme patristic interpretation (*ibid.*, 101, n. 12).

While the rabbinic reaction to such violent attacks by the Church was bound to be militant, as has been seen, some of the criticism was frankly accepted, and the seriousness of the offense was by no means played down: Israel was compared to "a shameless bride who plays the harlot within her bridal canopy" (Shab. 88b). [M.A.]

See also *Aaron in the *aggadah;* *Hur in the *aggadah.*

For Golden Calf in the Arts see *Moses in the Arts.

Bibliography: IN THE BIBLE: O. Eissfeldt, in: ZAW, 17 (1940–41), 199ff.; Albright, Stone, 228ff.; U. Cassuto, *A Commentary on the Book of Exodus* (1965[4]), 284–97; T. J. Meek, *Hebrew Origins* (1960), 135ff.; M. Aberbach, in: JBL, 86 (1967), 129–40; L. Smolar and M. Aberbach, in: HUCA, 39 (1968), 91–116; S. E. Loewenstamm, in: *Biblica*, 48 (1967), 481–90. IN THE AGGADAH: Ginzberg, Legends, 3 (1954[4]), 119–34; 6 (1959[4]), 50–56. IN CHRISTIANITY: Smolar and M. Aberbach, loc. cit.

GOLDENE KEYT, DI (Yid. "The Golden Chain"), Israel Yiddish quarterly. It was founded under Histadrut (Labor Federation) auspices in 1949 and first edited by Abraham *Sutzkever and Abraham *Levinson, the latter being succeeded at his death in 1955 by Eliezer Pines. In the journal's first issue, Joseph *Sprinzak and others called for an end to the antagonism between Hebrew and Yiddish, since Hebrew was no longer the tongue solely of scholars, and Yiddish could no longer be derided as a jargon of the Diaspora. Its issues contained works by Yiddish masters and by young writers in Israel and the Diaspora; Yiddish translations of Hebrew literature; research into literary and linguistic problems; and surveys of Jewish cultural events. *Di Goldene Keyt* became recognized as the preeminent literary organ of Yiddish writers. [S.L.]

GOLDENSON, SAMUEL HARRY (1878–1962), U.S. Reform rabbi. Goldenson was born in Kalvarija, Poland, and was taken to the United States in 1890. He was ordained at the Hebrew Union College in 1904, then led congregations in Lexington, Ky. (1904–06), and Albany, N.Y. (1906–18). In 1918 Goldenson moved to Temple Rodef Shalom, Pittsburgh, where he established his reputation nationally. In 1934 he was appointed senior rabbi of Temple Emanu-El, New York, also serving as president of the Central Conference of American Rabbis (1933–35). Becoming rabbi emeritus in 1947, he devoted the last years of his career to preaching in small communities under the auspices of the Union of American Hebrew Congregations. Goldenson adhered to the older standpoint in American Reform Judaism, emphasizing the universal message of the prophets and showing little sympathy with Jewish nationalism and the revived interest in ceremonial. He was a lifelong advocate of social justice and was active in campaigns for civic betterment.

Bibliography: *New York Times* (Sept. 1, 1962). [AB.V.G.]

GOLDENTHAL, JACOB (1815–1868), Austrian orientalist. Goldenthal was born in Brody and became principal of the Jewish school in Kishinev, Russia, in 1843; in 1846 he settled in Vienna and taught oriental languages, rabbinics, and literature at the University of Vienna from 1849 until his death.

Goldenthal published several articles on medieval Jewish literature in *Kokhevei Yiẓhak* (5, 1846; 24, 1858). He edited the following medieval texts: Abraham ibn Ḥasdai's Hebrew translation of al-Ghazālī's Arabic *Mīzān al-'Amal, Sefer Moznei Ẓedek* (1939); Averroes' commentary on Aristotle's *Rhetoric*, translated to Hebrew as *Be'ur Ibn Roshd le-Sefer ha-Halaẓah le-Aristo* (1842); *Mesharet Moshe* (1845), an exposition of Maimonides' teaching on the concept of providence; Nissim b. Jacob's *Mafte'aḥ shel Manulei ha-Talmud* (1847), dealing with Talmud methodology; Moses Rieti's poem *Mikdash Me'at* (1851), on ancient philosophy and the history of Jewish literature; and Moses Narboni's commentary on Maimonides' *Guide, Be'ur le-Sefer Moreh Nevukhim* (1852). Goldenthal tried to revive Jost and Creizenach's periodical *Zion*, but only one issue, *Neue Zion* (1845), appeared. His correspondence with S. D. *Luzzatto was published in *Kokhevei Yiẓhak*. He also published the first Hebrew textbook for the study of Arabic, *Sefer Maspik li-Ydi'at Dikduk Lashon Arvi* (1857), and compiled a catalog of forty Hebrew manuscripts at the National Library of Vienna (1851).

Bibliography: J. Fuenn, *Knesset Yisrael*, 1 (1866), 541–2; Gelber, in: *Arim ve-Immahot be-Yisrael*, 66 (1955), 204–5. [S.M.S.]

GOLDENWEISER, ALEXANDER ALEXANDROVICH (1880–1936), U.S. anthropologist. Born in Kiev, Russia, the son of Alexander Solomonovich *Goldenweiser, Goldenweiser studied anthropology under Franz *Boas, and later taught anthropology and other social sciences at various institutions including Columbia University, the New School for Social Research, and the University of Oregon in Portland. He followed Boas in his attacks on certain intellectual positions then prevalent, such as unilinear evolutionism, geographical and biological determinism, and extreme diffusionism. Described by a contemporary as "the most philosophical of American anthropologists," Goldenweiser did little field work except for several brief trips to the Grand River Iroquois Reservation in Ontario. His main contributions were to anthropological and social theory, as in his article "The Principle of Limited Possibilities in the Development of Culture" in Journal of American Folklore, 26 (1913), in which he sought to explain convergences among traits of different cultures as due to a natural limitation on the number of possible forms. In addition, he contributed to the elucidation of such basic concepts as culture, culture patterns, and especially, totemism, the subject of his best-known monograph in which he rejected Durkheim's theory of the totemic origin of religion. He concerned himself too with various themes in the history of thought and helped organize the *Encyclopedia of Social Science*, for which he wrote a number of articles.

Bibliography: DAB, 22 (1958), 244–5; IESS, 6 (1968), 196–7. [E.FI.]

GOLDENWEISER, ALEXANDER SOLOMONOVICH (1855–1915), Russian jurist and criminologist. Born in Yekaterinoslav, Goldenweiser was a distinguished lawyer who became known for his advocacy of criminal law reform in Russia. He was considerably influenced by Tolstoy's novel *Resurrection* attacking the existing social order in Russia, which led him to argue in his well-known work, *Prestupleniye, kak nakazaniye, a nakazaniye—kak prestupleniye* (1908, *Crime as Punishment and Punishment as Crime*, 1909) that crime is a punishment for society and that society is criminal in imposing a punishment. He published several other works on criminal law reform, including *Sovremennaya sistema nakazaniy i yega budushchnost* (1896, "The Modern Penal System and its Future") and *Voprosy vmeneniya i ugolovnoy otvetstvennosti vi pozitivnom osveshchenii* ("Imputation and Criminal Responsibility . . .," 1902). [D.B.-R.-H.]

GOLDENWEISER, EMANUEL ALEXANDROVICH (1883–1953), U.S. economist. Goldenweiser was born in Kiev, went to the United States in 1902, studied at Columbia and Cornell universities, and, in 1907, joined the U.S. government service as an economist and statistician. He first served with the Immigration Commission and then with the Census Bureau and the Department of Agriculture. In 1919 he began working for the Federal Reserve Board, and from 1927 until his retirement was its director of research. He developed the Board's statistical services, frequently represented the Federal Reserve System nationally, and served on the government's principal technical committees on economics and finance. He was, moreover, one of the main U.S. designers of the International Monetary Fund and the World Bank. His many publications include: *Immigrants in Cities* (1909), *Farm Tenancy in the United States* (1924), *The Federal Reserve System in Operation* (1925), and *Monetary Management* (1949). [J.O.R.]

GOLDFADEN, ABRAHAM (1840–1908), Yiddish poet, dramatist, and composer, father of the Yiddish theater (see *Theater, Yiddish). Born in Staro Konstantinov, Ukraine, he received not only a thorough Hebrew education but also acquired a knowledge of Russian, German, and secular subjects. To avoid the draft, Goldfaden was sent to a government school at 15 and there came under the influence of his teacher Abraham Ber *Gottlober, a Hebrew writer who was also a lover of Yiddish. Graduation from this school in 1857 permitted Goldfaden to enter the rabbinical seminary at Zhitomir, which trained rabbis, teachers, and Jewish officials for government service. Under the guidance of sympathetic teachers, including such leaders of the Haskalah movement as E. Z. Zweifel, H. S. Slonimsky, and Gottlober, he was encouraged to compose Hebrew lyrics. The first of these were published in 1862 in *Ha-Meliẓ*. A year later Goldfaden's first Yiddish poems appeared in *Kol Mevasser*. In 1865 Goldfaden published a booklet of his Hebrew songs *Ẓiẓim u-Feraḥim*. In 1866, the year of his graduation as a teacher, his first collection of Yiddish songs *Dos Yudele* offered rich material for **badḥanim* and folksingers. It was followed by a supplementary booklet *Di Yudene* (1869). In 1875 he joined a former classmate Isaac Joel *Linetzki in founding and editing in Lemberg a short-lived humorous magazine *Der Alter Yisrolik*. Goldfaden then went to Rumania where he came in contact in Jassy with the *Broder Singers, who were singing and acting out Yiddish songs, including his own, in wine cellars and restaurant gardens. He then conceived the idea that the dramatic effect of the songs and impersonations could be heightened if they would be combined with prose dialogues and woven into an interesting plot. He gathered a few singers and rehearsed with them scenarios composed by himself. The first performances in October 1876 initiated the professional Yiddish theater. Encouraged by the enthusiastic reception accorded his performances in Jassy, Goldfaden engaged wandering minstrels and cantors' assistants as additional actors, toured other Rumanian cities, including Bucharest, and then went to Odessa. By 1880 his troupe was giving performances throughout Russia and his phenomenal success was encouraging theatrical ventures by other enterprising actors and librettists. The Yiddish theater expanded and flourished until 1883, when the Russian government, fearing this new mass medium, banned performances in Yiddish. This action compelled authors, actors, and producers to migrate to other lands. Yiddish theaters were established in Paris, London, and New York. In 1887 Goldfaden was invited by some of his actors who had moved to New York to join them, but when he arrived he encountered severe competition from producers who had preceded him and from scriptwriters who were even more prolific than he. He found Europe more congenial and returned to produce and direct performances of his plays in London, Paris, and Lemberg. He returned to the United States in 1903 and spent his last five years in New York.

Poster for Goldfaden's operetta, *Shulamis*, 1881.

Of Goldfaden's early plays, the most successful were *Shmendrik* (1877), a satirical comedy whose title-hero became a synonym for a gullible, good-natured person; *Der Fanatik oder di Tsvey Kuni Lemels* (1880), a Yiddish parallel to Molière's satiric comedy *Les précieuses ridicules*. The last two plays maintained their stage popularity uninterruptedly for many decades and were readapted for Israel audiences of the mid-1960s and the first of them was adapted into a film in Israel (English title: *The Flying Matchmaker*).

Goldfaden's more serious dramas began with the 1880s, a tragic decade for Russian Jewry. The romantic operetta *Shulamis* (1880) which represented the transition from his earlier period to his later one, alternated between gaiety and tragedy. In *Doctor Almosado* (1882), he reacted to the pogroms of 1881 and even though he transposed the scene of the dramatic action to 14th-century Palermo, his audience sensed its timeliness and its veiled references to their sad plight. In *Bar Kochba* (1887), an historical musical depicting the last desperate revolt of the Jews against their Roman oppressors, Goldfaden, an adherent of the Ḥovevei Zion movement, tried to stir his people with visions of ancient national grandeur and heroism. After Herzl's death, Goldfaden wrote his last play *Ben Ami* (1907), premiered a few days before his own death. It was to a large extent an adaption of George Eliot's Zionist novel *Daniel Deronda*, but the action was transposed to pogrom-ridden Odessa and the English aristocrat who admired the Jewish people was transformed into a Russian baron. The play ended with the pogrom victims and their noble savior experiencing regeneration as pioneers of Jewish national redemption on the soil of Zion.

Despite their slight literary value, many of Goldfaden's 60 plays—not all of them published—continued to be adapted by actors and producers and entered into the permanent repertoire of the Yiddish theater. His characters from Schmendrik and Kuni Lemel to Hotzmakh, the good-natured peddler, and Bobbe Yakhne, the malevolent witch, have been real figures to several generations of theatergoers. [S.L.]

Music. Goldfaden himself furnished the tunes to his plays, although he was unable to write music and played no instrument. He drew upon the most varied sources—synagogue chants and Jewish folksong, the non-Jewish folk and popular music of Eastern Europe, and Italian and French operatic arias. Many of the songs from his plays have remained popular: some were folksongs initially (such as the cradle song *Rozhinkes mit Mandlen* which he adapted and put into *Shulamis,* from where it achieved its fame), and others became folksongs. Goldfaden described his musical activity with engaging frankness in his short autobiography; A. Z. *Idelsohn's analysis of the melodies in *Shulamis* and *Bar Kokhba,* and his conclusions, are a fair appraisal both of Goldfaden's musical shortcomings and his merits. For the performance of *Di Kishefmakherin* ("The Witch") by the Jewish Chamber Theater of Petrograd in 1922, the music was rearranged by Josef *Achron. In 1947, "The Witch" was staged in Tel Aviv in Hebrew by the *Ohel Theater, on the 70th anniversary of its first performance. The text was adapted by Abraham Levinson as a play within a play—bringing Goldfaden himself and his contemporary audience on the stage—and the music was rearranged by Marc *Lavry. [B.B.]

Bibliography: LNYL, 2 (1958), 77–87; Z. Zylbercweig, *Leksikon fun Yidishen Teater,* 1 (1931), 275–367; *Goldfaden-Bukh* (1926); N. Meisel, *Abraham Goldfaden* (Yid., 1938); J. Shatzky (ed.), *Hundert Yor Goldfaden* (1940); N. B. Minkoff, *Literarishe Vegn* (1955), 29–40; S. Liptzin, *Flowering of Yiddish Literature* (1963), 33–51; Idelsohn, Music, 229, 447–53; Sendrey, Music, indexes.

GOLDHAMMER-SAHAWI, LEO (1884–1949), leader of the Zionist Organization in Austria, author, and journalist. Born in Mihaileni, Rumania, Goldhammer moved to Vienna in 1902 and became an adherent of Herzl. He devoted himself primarily to statistical-economic studies of the Jews, particularly those of Austria. He established and edited the early Zionist periodicals in Vienna, *Die Stimme* and *Die Hoffnung.* In 1907 he moved back to Rumania, returning to Vienna after World War I. Goldhammer was president of the Zionist Organization of Austria for many years. He took part, with B. *Borochov, in founding the World Union of *Po'alei Zion. He continued his Zionist activities until after the Nazi invasion of Austria (1938), finally settling in Haifa in 1939 and taking an active part in municipal affairs and the Aliyah Ḥadashah Party. Among his books are *Kleiner Fuehrer durch die Palaestina-Literatur* (1919), *Die Juden Wiens* (1927); a monograph on the Jews of Vienna in volume 1 of *Arim ve-Immahot be-Yisrael* (1946); and *Leopold Plaschkes* (1943).

Bibliography: MB (Aug. 5, 1949). [G.K.]

GOLDHAR, PINCHAS (1901–1947), Australian Yiddish writer. Born in Lodz, Goldhar began his literary career with poetry but soon turned to writing realistic short stories. In 1928 he left Poland and settled in Melbourne, where he operated a small dye-shop which supported his literary labors. He edited (and for a long period singlehandedly printed) the first Yiddish weekly in Australia. The pioneer of Yiddish literature in Australia, his stories focused upon the integration of the Polish-Jewish immigrant among the Australians. His *Dertseylungen fun Oystralie* ("Tales of Australia") appeared in 1939 and one volume of his collected works, *Gezamlte Shriftn* was published posthumously in 1949.

Bibliography: LNYL, 2 (1958), 56ff. [M.Rav.]

GOLDIN, EZRA (1868–1915), Hebrew and Yiddish author. Born in Luna, Grodno district, Goldin lived in Warsaw from 1886 to 1893 and then moved to Lodz. His first publication was a collection of poems *Shirei No'ar* ("Poems of Youth," 1887). Subsequently he turned to writing fiction, and his stories appeared in Hebrew and Yiddish literary journals, including *Ha-Ẓefirah* and *Ha-Meliẓ.* Several of his stories were published as separate books. In 1896 he published *Ha-Zeman,* a literary anthology to which many leading Hebrew writers of the day contributed. At the beginning of the century he abandoned his literary activity, took up commerce, and became a prosperous merchant. During World War I he fled from the approaching German army and spent his last days in Riga. Goldin's short stories idealized the traditional Jewish way of life, particularly its devotion to Torah. In his view the secularized Judaism of the new nationalism had yet to prove its legitimacy as a replacement for the old faith.

Bibliography: B. Z. Eisenstadt, *Dor, Rabbanav ve-Soferav,* 1 (1895), 12f.; H. I. Yanovsky, *Le-Dorotai,* 2 (1938), 180f.; Waxman, Literature, 4 (1960[2]), 151–4. [G.K.]

GOLDIN, JUDAH (1914–), U.S. scholar and teacher. Goldin was born in New York City and in 1939 was ordained by the Jewish Theological Seminary. He then taught religion, Jewish literature, and history at several institutions; in 1958 he began teaching classical Judaica at Yale University. Goldin was a fellow of the American Academy for Jewish Research and chairman of the Yale Judaica Research Committee. Goldin's particular scholarly concern was rabbinic Judaism, and he was a skillful and graceful translator. Among his works are *The Fathers According to Rabbi Nathan* (1955), an annotated translation; *Living Talmud* (1957), a compendium of medieval commentaries on *Avot;* and "The Period of the Talmud" (in L. Finkelstein (ed.), *The Jews . . . ,* 1 (1960[3]), 115–215). [J.Ri.]

GOLDING, LOUIS (1895–1958), English novelist. Born in Manchester, Golding joined an ambulance unit during World War I and served in Macedonia and France. *Sorrow of War* (1919), a book of poems, was followed by his first novel, *Forward from Babylon* (1920). During the 1920s Golding traveled widely and the many books reflecting his experiences include *Sicilian Noon* (1925); *Those Ancient Lands: Being a Journey to Palestine* (1928); *In the Steps of Moses the Lawgiver* (1937); *In the Steps of Moses the Conqueror* (1938); and a late work, *Good-bye to Ithaca* (1955). Louis Golding made his reputation, however, with *Magnolia Street* (1931), the first of a cycle of novels about Anglo-Jewish life. *Magnolia Street,* which was an international best-seller and was adapted for the stage, was based on his memories of Manchester, which in his books became "Doomington." The novel portrayed the tensions and sympathies governing the relations between Jewish and non-Jewish inhabitants of one particular street between 1910 and 1930. Golding projected himself into the book through his *alter ego,* the emancipated painter Max Emmanuel, whose brother (like the novelist's) died on active service in France in World War I. The second of the Doomington novels, *Five Silver Daughters* (1934), was set against the background of the Bolshevik Revolution and post-war Germany. Golding's ideal of racial harmony was personified by the eponymous hero of *Mr. Emmanuel* (1939), which was later made into a film of the same name (1945), while *The Glory of Elsie Silver* (1945) reflected his response to Nazism and his sympathy for Zionism. These he had already revealed in two studies: *The Jewish Problem* (1938) and *Hitler Through the Ages* (1939).

Not all Golding's novels were concerned with Jewish themes: *The Camberwell Beauty* (1935) dealt with black magic and the Mafia in Sicily; and *The Loving Brothers* (1952) told the story of two pairs of brothers, one of each pair being brilliant and the other criminal. Golding also wrote radio plays and books on sport. His other works include the novel *Day of Atonement* (1925); *James Joyce* (1933), a study; *The World I Knew* (1940); and *To the Quayside* (1954).

Bibliography: J. B. Simons, *Louis Golding, A Memoir* (1958).

[RE.W.]

GOLDMAN, family of U.S. investment bankers descended from Bavarian-born MARCUS GOLDMAN (1821–1904) and JOSEPH *SACHS, both of whom arrived in the United States in 1848. Goldman was a peddler in Pennsylvania and a clothing merchant in Philadelphia before he began his financial career in New York in 1869. Later he was joined by his son, HENRY GOLDMAN (1857–1937), and by Joseph Sachs's sons, SAMUEL SACHS, who married Marcus Goldman's daughter LOUISE, and HARRY SACHS. They formed the banking firm of Goldman, Sachs & Co., which cooperated with the London bankers Kleinwort and Japhet in channeling European capital into United States investments.

Friendship between Henry Goldman and the *Lehman Brothers partner, Philip Lehman, engendered joint underwritings for companies engaged in the manufacture and distribution of consumer goods. Henry Goldman, staunchly pro-German in World War I, retired in 1918. Under the guidance of Joseph *Duveen, he assembled an impressive art collection. Only two members of the Sachs family remained in the business as limited partners: Walter Edward Sachs (1884–) and Howard Joseph Sachs (1891–).

Bibliography: S. Birmingham, *Our Crowd* (1967), index; J. Wechsberg, *The Merchant Bankers* (1966), 285, 303–6; S. N. Behrman, *Duveen* (Eng., 1951), 286–90.

[H.G.R.]

GOLDMAN, BERNARD (1841–1901), Polish patriot and militant supporter of assimilation. Goldman was born in Warsaw, where his father was a Hebrew *maskil* and owned a printing press; his grandfather Jacob was a rabbi in Amsterdam. Goldman played an active role in the Polish revolutionary movements against czarist rule. After the demonstration held in Warsaw in 1861 he was exiled to Siberia, but escaped and returned to Warsaw to take part in the uprising of 1863. After its suppression he went abroad, traveled through Germany, and reached Paris, where he contributed to the organ of the Polish émigrés. He went to Vienna in 1867 and completed his law studies. In 1870 he settled in Lemberg where he initiated an extensive program for promoting education among the Jewish masses in Galicia. He organized cultural activities, including courses and libraries for spreading Polish culture and combating the pro-Austrian centralist movement. In opposition to the aspirations of the Shomer Yisrael society of German orientation, he founded the rival Doreshei Shalom and published a newspaper *Zgoda.* This resulted in the establishment of the *Agudat Aḥim, which later became the most prominent center of assimilationist activity in Poland.

In 1876 Goldman took his seat in the national Sejm (parliament) of Galicia as the delegate for Lemberg and in 1883 was elected to the Lemberg municipal council. Goldman was also active within the framework of the community administration, founding an organization of artisans, Yad Ḥaruẓim. In particular he promoted the development of a school network, which was named after him. This network provided a Polish-oriented education combined with the teaching of religious observance.

Bibliography: EG, 4 (1956), 314–5; N. M. Gelber, *Die Juden und der polnische Aufstand 1863* (1923), 221; M. Balaban, *Dzieje Żydów w Galicji* (1914); M. Bertold, *Żydzi w powstaniu 1863* (1913), 21–22, 30–31; Estreicher, *Almanach i leksykon żydostwa polskiego,* 1 (1937), 67–69; J. K. Urbach, *Udział żydów w walce o niepodległość Polski* (1938), 102–3; 150–1; *Polski słownik biograficzny,* 8 (1959–60), 210–1.

[M.LAN.]

GOLDMAN, EDWARD FRANKO (1878–1950), U.S. bandmaster, brother of Mayer Clarence *Goldman. Goldman was born in Louisville, Kentucky, and studied music at the National Conservatory, New York, where Anton Dvořak taught him composition. He began his career as solo cornetist in the Metropolitan Opera orchestra, and in 1911 formed his own band which from 1918 gave outdoor concerts on university campuses and in New York public parks. The band toured the U.S. and in 1945 performed for the U.S. armed forces in the Phillipines and Japan. It had a high standard of performance and an unusually extensive repertoire, and hence exerted a great influence on bands throughout the U.S. Goldman was a founder and first president of the American Bandmasters' Association. He was assisted by his son and associate conductor RICHARD FRANKO GOLDMAN (1910–).

[ED.]

GOLDMAN, EMMA (1869–1940), U.S. anarchist writer and lecturer, leading advocate of anarchism in the United States. Emma Goldman, born in Kovno, Lithuania, grew up there and in Koenigsberg and St. Petersburg, emigrating to the United States in 1885. Her independent spirit emerged early, and disputes with teachers and her father cut short her formal education. In the main she was self-educated, particularly in anarchist thought. Her long and close association with Alexander *Berkman was the most significant influence upon her in thought and deed. Unlike many anarchists, she moved beyond the small radical immigrant community, and her lectures and journal, *Mother Earth* (1906–18), aimed to illuminate the injustice and immorality of American society.

Emma Goldman became an open advocate of birth control in the years before World War I, which led to considerable notoriety. However, it was her vigorous opposition to conscription during the war that finally led the United States government to imprison her and ban *Mother Earth* from the mails. Emma Goldman had long been considered dangerous, and the combination of a technical weakness in her citizenship status and legislation which broadened the grounds for action against undesirable aliens, led to her deportation to the Soviet Union in 1919. By 1921 she fled that country, repelled by the suppression of the individual, which seemed as complete under Bolshevism as under capitalism.

While she continued to write and lecture, her active political career was ended except for vigorous efforts on behalf of the Catalonian anarchists in the Spanish Civil War. Her life was one of commitment to anarchism in theory, and to personal independence and radical political action in practice.

Emma Goldman continuously focused on the basic contention that the state was a coercive force that destroyed the differences among individuals and eliminated genuine freedom in defense of the conformity required by society. She stressed the freedom of the individual, responsive to self-developed standards of love and justice. Her demand for individual freedom never wavered, and she detested capitalism because of its inherent inequalities, which doomed the majority of persons to a toilsome and regimented life focused on material matters. She favored communism as the ultimate form of economic organization to break the link between work and income that enslaved men in Western capitalist states. To Emma Goldman, anarchism conformed to man's basic nature, and it would prove to be a workable and orderly system.

Emma Goldman's writings include *Anarchism and Other Essays* (1910); *My Disillusionment in Russia* (1923); *My Further Disillusionment in Russia* (1924); and *Living My Life* (2 vols., 1931).

Bibliography: R. Drinnon, *Rebel in Paradise* (1961). [I.Y.]

GOLDMAN, ERIC FREDERICK (1915–), U.S. historian. Goldman was born in Washington, D.C. He was professor of history at Princeton where he taught from 1940. Goldman served as president of the Society of American Historians from 1962 to 1969. He was a member of the academic council of the American Friends of the Hebrew University. Goldman's field of specialization was American history of the 20th century. His best-known books are: *Rendezvous With Destiny: A History of Modern American Reform* (1952) and *Crucial Decade, America 1945–1955* (1956), revised as *Crucial Decade—and After, America 1945–1960* (1961). In 1964 President Johnson named Goldman special consultant to the president. After his resignation (1966) Goldman published *The Tragedy of Lyndon Johnson* (1968). [O.I.J.]

GOLDMAN, HETTY (1881–), U.S. archaeologist. Her excavation of Halae, in the ancient Greek district of Boetia, was followed by excavations at the Ionian city of Colophon in Asia Minor and at Eutresis, a Bronze Age settlement in Boeotia. These were interrupted by the Greco-Turkish war in 1922. The peak of her career was her excavation at the south Anatolian city of *Tarsus, birthplace of the apostle Paul, which had been a flourishing site in the Bronze and Iron Ages as well as during Hellenistic and Roman times. Hetty Goldman's main interest was the relationship between the oriental cultures of the Eastern Mediterranean and the culture of the Greek world. She was one of the first members of the Institute for Advanced Study, Princeton, New Jersey. Her published woks include *Excavations at Eutresis in Boeotia* (1931) and *The Acropolis of Halae* (in *Hesperia*, 9 (1940), 381–514). She edited *Excavations at Gözlü Kule, Tarsus*, 3 vols. (1950–63).

Bibliography: S. S. Weinberg (ed.), *The Aegean and the Near East* (1956), studies presented to Hetty Goldman (includes bibliography). [P.P.K.]

GOLDMAN, MAYER CLARENCE (1874–1939), U.S. lawyer, born in New Orleans. Goldman became convinced that achievement of the American ideal of equality before the law required the state to provide qualified legal counsel for poor defendants. He vigorously advocated establishment of the office of Public Defender by state and local governments. He gave speeches and wrote for legal periodicals in support of this cause. He wrote a book, *The Public Defender* (1917), and was coauthor of a movie script on the subject. Goldman chaired the Public Defender committees of the American Lawyers Guild, the American Institute of Criminal Law and Criminology, and the New York State Bar Association. He initiated the Public Defender movement in New York and drafted Public Defender bills introduced in the State Legislature from 1915 to 1931. [B.G.L.]

GOLDMAN, MOSES HA-KOHEN (1863–1918), U.S. Hebrew teacher and journalist. A native of Pinsk, he studied at the Volozhin yeshivah and then under R. Isaac Hirsch *Weiss, in Vienna. Later he journeyed to London and, in 1890, settled in the United States where he became a teacher, a printer, and, finally, a journalist. He founded the short-lived Hebrew journal *Ha-Moreh* in 1894 and then edited (1901–02), first together with Nahum Meir *Schaikewitz, then by himself *Ha-Le'om*, which began as a Hebrew-Yiddish monthly and then appeared only in Hebrew. In 1909 he edited the first American Hebrew daily *Ha-Yom* which ceased publication after 90 days but reappeared briefly in 1913. The *Proverbs of the Sages* which he first published in *Ha-Le'om* with translations in English was republished in a separate book in New York (1916).

Bibliography: B. Z. Eisenstadt, *Ḥakhmei Yisrael ba-Amerika* (1903), 26f.; J. D. Eisenstein, *Oẓar Zikhronotai*, 1 (1929), 138; Kressel, Leksikon, 1 (1965), 421. [El.S.]

GOLDMAN, SOLOMON (1893–1953), U.S. Conservative rabbi. Goldman, who was born in Volhynia, Russia, was taken to the U.S. as a child. He studied at the Rabbi Isaac Elchanan Yeshivah and at the Jewish Theological Seminary

Solomon Goldman, U.S. Conservative rabbi. Zionist Archives and Library, New York.

where he was ordained (1918). After serving in Brooklyn and in Cleveland, where he established a Conservative congregation against stormy opposition, Goldman became rabbi of the Anshe Emet Synagogue of Chicago (1929) and held that position until his death. He became widely known as an orator, communal leader, and scholar, and popularized the cause of Zionism. Among the positions of leadership which he held were the presidency of the Zionist Organization of America and cochairmanship of the United Jewish Appeal. Rabbi Goldman edited a series of texts in modern Hebrew literature and wrote *Romance of a People*, a pageant performed at the Chicago World's Fair in 1933. Among his books are *A Rabbi Takes Stock* (1931), *The Jew and the Universe* (1936), *Crisis and Decision* (1938), and *Undefeated* (1940), all dealing with the Jewish people in modern times. In his last years he began the publication of a study of the Bible and its influence on world literature, of which three volumes were completed: *The Book of Books* (1948), *In the Beginning* (1949), and *From Slavery to Freedom* (1958). [J.Rl.]

GOLDMAN, YA'AKOV BEN ASHER (1856–1931), Hebrew journalist. Goldman was born in Jerusalem where he studied at the Eẓ Ḥayyim yeshivah. Influenced by the Haskalah at an early age, he contributed articles to the Hebrew press, including *Yehudah vi-Yrushalayim*, *Ha-Ẓefirah*,

Ha-Asif, Ha-Maggid, Ha-Meliẓ, and *Ḥavaẓẓelet.* In 1890 he moved to Jaffa, where he was among the leading figures in the Ashkenazi Jewish community and one of the founders of the Neveh Ẓedek quarter. For a time he served as chief Palestine correspondent for *Ha-Ẓefirah* and acting editor of *Ḥavaẓẓelet.* His articles include detailed historical accounts of modern Jewish settlement in Ereẓ Israel. At the turn of the century, Goldman became extremely religious. He abandoned his secular writing and devoted himself to biblical research. Late in life, he published two books on various topics (talmudic, religious, etc.).

Bibliography: Kressel, Leksikon, 1 (1965), 419. [G.K.]

GOLDMANN, EMIL (1872–1942), Austrian legal historian and Etruscan scholar. Goldmann studied law and taught German legal history at the University of Vienna from 1905 to 1938. In that year he publicly criticized the articles of the Nazi leader Alfred Rosenberg and was forced to flee to England. He became a lecturer at Cambridge University. In his study of German legal history in the early Middle Ages, Goldmann sought to trace the link with primitive ritual, thus evolving the ethnologic approach to legal history. He studied in depth the laws of primitive peoples. Goldmann's researches in legal history were published in the collection *Untersuchungen zur deutschen Staats- und Rechtsgeschichte* (1903), and his articles of Etruscan studies appeared in several volumes.

Bibliography: H. Lentze, *Oesterreichische Zeitschrift fuer Volkskunde,* 4 (1950), 76ff. [ED.]

GOLDMANN, NAHUM (1895–), statesman and Zionist leader, born in Visznevo, Lithuania. When Goldmann was two years old his family moved to Germany—first to Koenigsberg and from there to Frankfort. His father, Solomon Ẓevi Goldmann, was a writer and Hebrew

Nahum Goldmann, international Jewish leader. Government Press Office, Tel Aviv.

teacher, and young Goldmann grew up in an atmosphere suffused with the spirit of Judaism. At the age of 15 he published an anonymous article attacking Solomon *Reinach, the vice-president of *Alliance Israélite Universelle, that contributed to Reinach's resignation from his post. In 1913 Goldmann spent several months in Ereẓ Israel and reported his impressions in *Eretz Israel, Reisebriefe aus Palaestina,* published in 1914. During World War I he joined the staff of the Jewish section of the German Foreign Ministry. At that time Goldmann supported a pro-German orientation of the Zionist movement and sought means of gaining the Kaiser's support for the Zionist cause. After the war, Goldmann joined with Jacob *Klatzkin in publishing *Freie Zionistische Blaetter,* a Zionist periodical (1921–22). At this time the two men also conceived the idea of publishing a German-language Jewish encyclopedia, and in 1925 they founded a publishing house, "Eshkol," for this purpose. Three years later the first volume of the *Encyclopaedia Judaica* made its appearance. Hitler's rise to power prevented the completion of the venture, and when publication of the encyclopedia had to be interrupted, a total of ten volumes in German and two in Hebrew had been issued. (In the 1960s, Goldmann took the initiative in inaugurating the present English-language *Encyclopaedia Judaica.*)

In the early 1920s Goldmann joined Ha-Po'el ha-Ẓa'ir, but later left the party and became a member of the Zionist "radical" faction and in 1926 was elected its representative on the Zionist Actions Committee. He was critical of Weizmann's plan to coopt non-Zionists to the *Jewish Agency. He also denounced the Zionist leadership for its lack of interest in the political and cultural problems of Jewish masses in the Diaspora. According to his conception, Ereẓ Israel would not be capable of absorbing the entire Jewish people; it should serve as an inspiration and a source of life to the Jewish people and be a symbol and the principal instrument of its renascence.

Goldmann was the chairman of the Political Committee at the 17th Zionist Congress (1931) and played a decisive role in forging a majority to oppose the reelection of Weizmann as president of the Zionist Organization. Two years later, however, when the Radical faction was disbanded, Goldmann began to lean toward Weizmann and eventually to cooperate with him. In the same year, Goldmann was forced to leave Germany, and in 1935 he was deprived of German citizenship and became a citizen of Honduras. At the end of 1933, upon the death of Leo *Motzkin, he was elected chairman of the Comité des Délégations Juives, and in 1935 he became the representative of the Jewish Agency at the League of Nations (succeeding Victor Jacobson). Together with Stephen *Wise, he was the moving spirit in the organization of the *World Jewish Congress and at the first conference of the Congress, in 1936, was appointed chairman of its executive board. Shortly after the outbreak of World War II, he moved to New York.

During the Mandatory period Goldmann supported the idea of establishing a Jewish State. In 1931, during the debate on the "final goal" of Zionism and in 1935, as the head of the *General Zionist faction, he declared that the principal task of the Zionist Movement was to create among the Jewish people the momentum for the establishment of a Jewish State in Ereẓ Israel. In 1937, he was among the most ardent supporters of the Partition Plan, preferring sovereignty to territory. This attitude also prompted him to support *Ben-Gurion at the *Biltmore Conference. Henceforth, until May 1948, he took an active and sometimes decisive part in the diplomatic and public relations activities designed to bring about the immediate establishment of a Jewish state. When the State of Israel came into being, Goldmann was elected one of the two chairmen of the Executive of the Zionist Organization (Berl Locker was the other), and in 1956 he was elected president of the organization. Upon the death of Stephen Wise, he was also elected president of the World Jewish Congress.

Goldmann was largely responsible for initiating negotiations with the Federal Republic of Germany on the payment of *reparations to Israel and indemnification for Nazi victims. It was primarily Goldmann who arranged for the secret preliminary contact with German statesmen, mainly with Chancellor Konrad *Adenauer, before the official negotiations took place. It was also mostly at his initiative that the Claims Conference, which became the most comprehensive and representative world Jewish body, was established. He was elected president of the Conference and led its delegation in the negotiations with Germany.

Goldmann subsequently conducted similar negotiations with Austria. As a result of the work done by the Claims Conference, a Memorial Foundation for Jewish Culture was established in 1965, with Goldmann as its president. He initiated the creation of the Conference of Jewish Organizations (COJO) and became its president, founded the World Council of Jewish Education, took an active part in organizing the Conference of Presidents of Major American Jewish Organizations for Israel, was the chairman of the first international conference for Soviet Jewry (Paris, 1960), etc.

In the field of Zionist affairs, Goldmann participated in the formulation of the Jerusalem Program (1951; see *Basle Program) and conducted the negotiations with the Israel government that preceded the enactment of the law on the status of the World Zionist Organization and the signing of a covenant between the State of Israel and the Zionist Organization. He supported the concept of the centrality of the State of Israel in the life of the Jewish people, but opposed any attitude that negated the Diaspora (while at the same time refusing to accept the view held by many American Zionists that the American Diaspora was no longer to be regarded as an exile). Goldmann regarded the continued existence of the Jewish people in the Diaspora as threatened not by anti-Semitism, but by full emancipation and by the unparalleled prosperity of the Jews in most countries since World War II. He believed that the struggle of the Jewish people should now be directed to uphold the right of the Jews to be different from other peoples and preserve their uniqueness. This task, primarily an educational one, should be the main concern of the Jewish people and its leaders.

In 1962 Goldmann left the United States and became a citizen of Israel. He did not, however, take an active part in the internal political life of the country. He subsequently spent part of his time in Israel and part in Europe. In 1968 Goldmann took on Swiss citizenship "for personal and economic reasons."

Goldmann frequently voiced criticism of Israel's leadership, which he accused of narrow-mindedness, overestimating the power of the state and its military forces, lacking the proper attitude toward the Jewish people in the Diaspora, and of pursuing an inflexible policy. He advocated a more elastic and moderate policy toward the Arab states and also recommended that Israel moderate her criticism of Soviet policy vis-à-vis the Middle East and Jews living in the U.S.S.R. Declarations made by Goldmann in this vein periodically caused friction between him and leading Israel personalities; furthermore, the various offices held by Goldmann also raised the question of whether his criticism represented the view of the Zionist Organization, the World Jewish Congress, some other Jewish body, or only his personal opinion. Relations between Goldmann and Israel leaders took a further turn for the worse after the *Six-Day War, when the impression was created that Goldmann's identification with the State of Israel was rather less than that of many other Jewish leaders. It was against this background that several Zionist parties began to oppose his continuance in office as president of the organization, and at the 27th Zionist Congress (1968), Goldmann did not put forward his candidacy for the presidency. The *Autobiography of Nahum Goldmann* appeared in 1969. In 1970, a controversy was aroused by Goldmann's approach to the Israel prime minister in connection with a possible meeting between himself and *Nasser. When the Israel government expressed its disapproval, the matter was dropped.

Selections of Goldmann's articles and speeches have been published in two volumes: *Dor shel Ḥurban u-Ge'ullah* (1968) and *Be-Darkhei Ammi* (1968).

Bibliography: J. Draenger, *Nachum Goldmann*, 2 vols. (Ger., 1959, Fr., 1956); A. Carlebach, *Sefer ha-Demuyyot* (1959), 172–5; R. Vogel (ed.), *The German Path to Israel* (1969). [Ch.Y.]

GOLDMARK, Viennese and U.S. family. Joseph Goldmark (1819–1881), Austrian revolutionary leader and U.S. physician and chemist, was born in the province of Warsaw. He studied at Vienna University (1838), entered medical school in 1840, and took a research post in chemistry in 1845. When revolution broke out in Vienna in 1848 Goldmark was a hospital intern. He enlisted in the Academic Legion, became president of the Students Union, and was elected to the Reichstag. Accused of complicity in the murder of Minister of War Latour (for which he was later sentenced to death in absentia), Goldmark fled the country, and in 1850 left France for New York. In 1868 he was acquitted after voluntarily returning to Austria to stand trial on the murder charge. Goldmark first practiced as a physician in New York but achieved greater prominence through the practical application of his knowledge of chemistry. In 1857 he took out a patent for manufacturing mercury compound, and in 1859 he established a highly successful factory for making percussion caps and cartridges. Of his ten children, one married Louis D. *Brandeis and another Felix *Adler. A third daughter, Pauline Goldmark (1874–1962), was a well-known social worker and served as secretary of the national and New York consumer leagues. A son, Henry Goldmark (1857–1941), was a civil engineer engaged in railroad construction, and was the designer of the locks for the Panama Canal. The composer Karl *Goldmark was a half brother of Joseph Goldmark. Rubin Goldmark (1872–1936), U.S. musician, nephew of Karl Goldmark, was born in New York. Moving to Colorado for reasons of health, he directed the Conservatory of Music at Colorado College from 1895 to 1901. From 1902 he lived in New York, teaching piano and harmony and giving numerous lecture recitals throughout the United States and Canada. In 1911 he became director of the department of theory of the New York College of Music, and in 1924 head of the department of composition of the Julliard Graduate School. While Goldmark was known in his day as a composer (in 1910 his piano quartet won the Paderewski Chamber Music Prize), his influence as a teacher was more considerable. His pupils included Aaron *Copland, George *Gershwin, and Efrem *Zimbalist, and he was highly respected for his intellectual honesty, artistic integrity, and broad general culture. In 1956 City College, New York, named its music building in his honor.

Rubin Goldmark, U.S. musician. Courtesy Juillard School of Music, New York.

Bibliography: J. Goldmark, *Pilgrims of '48* (1930); *New York Times* (March 7, 1936); DAB, 22 (1958), 249–50; Grove, Dict, 3 (1954[5]), 699–701; MGG, 5 (1956), 481–5; O. Thompson (ed.), *Cyclopedia of Music and Musicians* (1956[7]), 682–3; Baker, Biog Dict (1958[5]), 583–4. [Ed.]

GOLDMARK, KARL (1830–1915), composer. Goldmark was the son of a cantor in the small town of Keszthely, and was sent to study in Vienna. He was financed by his half brother Joseph, who, however, was involved in the revolutionary activities of 1848 and had to leave the

Caricature of Karl Goldmark, Hungarian composer. Jerusalem, J.N.U.L., Schwadron Collection.

country. Karl himself was led out to be shot as a rebel, but was saved by the intervention of a friend. He settled in Vienna as a teacher, conductor, and composer, and displayed his great talent for orchestration in the overture *Sakuntala* (1865). His opera *Die Koenigin von Saba* (1875) and his *Laendliche Hochzeit* (1876) symphony, with a libretto by S.H.*Mosenthal, on which he worked for ten years, was an immediate success in Vienna and many other cities. Goldmark wrote other operas which had limited success, violin concertos, chamber music, choral music and songs. For a short time he was the teacher of Sibelius, and did much to encourage the performance of Wagner in Austria. His autobiography, *Erinnerungen aus meinem Leben* (1922), was translated into English in 1927 as *Notes from the Life of a Viennese Composer*.

Bibliography: O. Keller, *Karl Goldmark* (Ger., 1901); MGG; Riemann-Gurlitt; Grove, Dict; Baker, Biog Dict. [M.Ros.]

GOLDSCHEID, RUDOLF (1870–1932), Austrian sociologist and pacifist. Born in Vienna, where he lived throughout his life, Goldscheid was representative of a strongly ethically oriented group whose interest was in the problems of sociology and social philosophy. A cofounder of the German Sociological Society ("Deutsche Gesellschaft fuer Soziologie," 1909), he sided with the approach of the "Kathedersozialisten" (academic social reformers) against Max Weber's emphasis on a strictly objective, "value-free" orientation in the social sciences. As editor of the *Friedenswarte*, he was one of the most influential European pacifists. He was also editor of the *Annalen fuer Natur- und Kulturphilosophie*. His publications include: *Zur Ethik des Gesamtwillens* (1902); *Verelendungs- oder Meliorationstheorie* (1906); *Monismus und Politik* (1912); *Hoeherentwicklung und Menschenoekonomie* (1911); *Frauenfrage und Menschenoekonomie* (1913); and *Staatssozialismus und Staatskapitalismus* (1917). [W.J.C.]

GOLDSCHMIDT, ERNST DANIEL (1895–), librarian and scholar of Jewish liturgy. Goldschmidt was born in Koenigshuette (now Chorzow, Poland), where his father was rabbi. He served from 1926 to 1935 as librarian in the Prussian State Library, Berlin. Emigrating to Palestine in 1936, he joined the staff of the Jewish National and University Library (1936–62). Goldschmidt prepared critical editions of various liturgical texts. His various Passover *Haggadot* (with German translation, introduction, and notes, 1936, 1937; Hebrew, 1947, 1960^2) became very popular; the *Haggadah* by N. N. Glatzer (Eng., 1953, 1969^2) is based on Goldschmidt's work. In 1959 his edition of Maimonides' prayer text appeared; it was followed by *Siddur Tefillat Yisrael* (two rites) in 1964; *Seliḥot* according to both the Lithuanian and Polish rites in 1965; *Kinot* (liturgy for the Ninth of Av, Polish rite) in 1968; S. D. Luzzatto's introduction to his edition of the *Maḥzor Roma* was reissued by Goldschmidt (1966) with notes and an essay on the Roman rite. His edition of the High Holiday *maḥzor* (1970), which is a compendium of all the Ashkenazi rites, is of particular importance. [A.C.]

GOLDSCHMIDT, GUIDO (1850–1915), Austrian organic chemist. Goldschmidt was born in Trieste. From 1874 to 1891 he worked at the University of Vienna, becoming

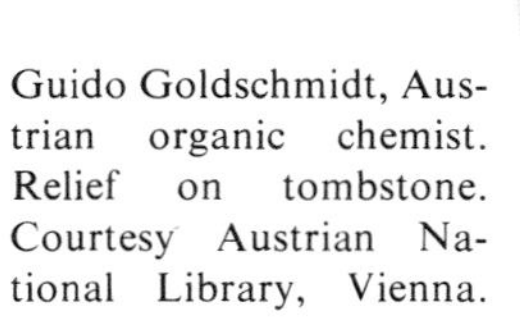

Guido Goldschmidt, Austrian organic chemist. Relief on tombstone. Courtesy Austrian National Library, Vienna.

professor there in 1890. In 1891 he became professor of chemistry at the German University of Prague. In 1907 he was elected rector of the university, but declined to accept the position, partly because he thought that it might precipitate anti-Semitic manifestations. He returned to the University of Vienna in 1911. He was one of the earliest organic chemists to elucidate the structure of an alkaloid, in his case papaverine; later he worked on other alkaloids, on polynuclear hydrocarbons (fluoranthene and others), on aldehyde condensations, etc.

Bibliography: *Berichte der Deutschen Chemischen Gesellschaft*, 49 (1916), 893–932; *Chemiker-Zeitung*, 39 (1915), 649; *Proceedings of the American Academy of Arts and Science*, 77 (1950). [S.A.M.]

GOLDSCHMIDT, HANS (1861–1923), German industrial chemist. He was born in Berlin, and was awarded his doctorate at Heidelberg in 1886. He became a partner with his brother in the firm of tin smelters and metallurgists founded by his father in Essen. In 1894 he invented the "Thermit" process, still used for welding heavy sections of iron and steel. Although industrial chemists were not really welcome in German learned societies, he became chairman of the Bunsengesellschaft fuer Angewandte Physikalische Chemie and of the Liebig Stipendien Verein. [S.A.M.]

GOLDSCHMIDT (née **Benas**), **HENRIETTE** (1825–1920), German suffragette and educator; wife of Rabbi Abraham Meir Goldschmidt of Leipzig. She was one of the founders of the German Women's League (Allgemeiner Deutscher Frauenverein) in 1865, organized petitions on behalf of women's rights to higher education and entry in professions (1867), and was a signatory to a petition to the Reichstag for protecting children born out of wedlock. In 1871 she founded the Society for Family Education and for Peoples' Welfare (Verein fuer Familienerziehung und Volkswohl) in Leipzig, and was instrumental in the establishment of a municipal educational institution which eventually comprised kindergartens, a seminary for kindergarten teachers, and a vocational school for girls with teachers' training courses. In 1911 she founded the first institution of higher education for girls in Germany. Henriette Goldschmidt wrote *Die Frauenfrage, eine Kulturfrage* (1870), as well as on education, publicizing the ideas of Froebel. Her works include *Was ich von Froebel lernte und lehrte* (1909).

Bibliography: H. Lange and G. Baeumer (eds.), *Handbuch der Frauenbewegung* (1901), index; J. Siebe and J. Pruefer, *Henriette Goldschmidt...* (Ger., 1922); M. Mueller, *Frauen im Dienste Froebels* (1928). [D.I.S.]

GOLDSCHMIDT, HERMANN (1802–1866), French astronomer and artist. Born in Frankfort, Goldschmidt studied painting in Munich and in 1836 settled in Paris where he became eminent as a vivid painter of historical events and portraits. In spite of his great artistic activity, astronomy became his hobby and love. An enthusiastic observer of the sky, Goldschmidt worked with simple devices and modest optical instruments. In the nine years between 1852 and 1861 he discovered 14 asteroids (or minor planets as these were then called). He also observed variable stars, double stars, comets, nebulae, and in 1860, in Spain, a total solar eclipse; his report was accompanied by three impressive oil paintings. In 1857 he received the Cross of the Legion of Honor and in 1861 the Royal Astronomical Society in London awarded him its Gold Medal. [A.BE.]

GOLDSCHMIDT, JAKOB (1882–1955), banker, born in Eldagsen, Hanover. Goldschmidt joined the Hanover banking house of H. Oppenheimer. In 1910 he formed his own firm Schwartz, Goldschmidt & Company and became one of Germany's leading bankers. In 1918 he became managing director of the Nationalbank fuer Deutschland which later merged with the Deutsche Nationalbank and the Darmstaedter Bank to form the Darmstaedter und Nationalbank. In 1931 the bank closed due to the failures of their main customers and the reluctance of the German authorities to assist the bank. Having become a major target of Nazi attacks, Goldschmidt left Germany in 1933 and settled in the United States in 1936. His wide-ranging business interests both in Europe and the United States included shipping, steel, power, mining, insurance, and aviation. He was an art collector, and supported many philanthropies and cultural institutions, including the New York Metropolitan Museum and the Museum of Modern Art. [J.O.R.]

GOLDSCHMIDT, LAZARUS (1871–1950), scholar, bibliophile, and translator of the Talmud into German. Goldschmidt, who was born in Plongian, Lithuania, studied first at the Slobodka yeshivah and later at the universities of Berlin and Strasbourg. His early studies were devoted to Ethiopian language and its literature. He published the Ethiopic version of the Book of Enoch (I Enoch) with Hebrew translation (1892) and *Biblioteca Ethiopica* (1895). Goldschmidt published an edition of the *Sefer Yeẓirah* (1894), a Hebrew translation of the Koran (1916), and prepared a new edition of Jacob Levy's *Woerterbuch zum Talmud und Midrasch* (1924). On the rise of Hitler to power in 1933 Goldschmidt left Germany for England and lived in London. His bibliographical works include *Hebrew Incunables* (1948), and the *Earliest Editions of the Hebrew Bible* (1950).

Goldschmidt's major contribution was his translation of the entire Babylonian Talmud into German. It appeared in two editions, a nine-volume work containing the original text and variant readings (1897–1935) and a 12-volume edition without the original text (1929–36). This translation, which was severely criticized by David Zvi *Hoffman (ZHB 1, 1896), was nevertheless considered to be an important and standard work in talmudic studies. Goldschmidt also prepared a subject concordance to the Babylonian Talmud which was published posthumously (1959). He also published a facsmile edition of the Hamburg manuscript of the order *Nezikin* of the Babylonian Talmud (1913). A controversial figure who engaged in sharp personal polemics against leading scholars of his time (Immanuel Loew, David Hoffman, and others), he published a number of pamphlets attacking his adversaries. In his youth, he published as a practical joke an Aramaic text entitled *Baraita de-Ma'aseh Bereshit* (1894), which he claimed to be an old Midrash. Later he admitted that this was a parody. Goldschmidt was a collector of rare books. His collection was acquired by the Royal Library in Copenhagen.

Bibliography: E. Neufeld, in: *Synagogue Review*, 16 (Dec. 16, 1941), no. 4. [ED.]

GOLDSCHMIDT, LEVIN (1829–1897), German jurist and politician, who made a significant contribution to the development of commercial law in Germany. Goldschmidt, who was born in Danzig, was professor of law at Heidelberg from 1860. An authority on mercantile law, he was a judge of the commercial court. He represented the National Liberal Party in the Reichstag from 1875 to 1877. Although actively interested in Jewish affairs as a member of the Deutsch-Israelitischer Gemeindebund and president of the Berliner Hilfsverein fuer juedische Studierende, he argued that the interests of the fatherland came before those of the Jews. His writings include *Handbuch des Handelsrechts* (1864–1868) and *Universalgeschichte des Handelsrechts* (1891).

Bibliography: J. Riesser, *Levin Goldschmidt* (Ger., 1897). [G.T.]

GOLDSCHMIDT, LUDWIG (1853–1931), German philosopher. Born in Sondershausen, he taught at Gotha from 1883 onward. He was a commentator on Kant, and forcefully opposed the Neo-Kantian interpretations. Goldschmidt's works were directed toward the devulgarization of Kant's philosophy. Like some of the other 20th-century Kantians, he opposed Einstein. Goldschmidt's writings include *Die Wahrscheinlichkeitsrechnung: Versuch einer Kritik* (1897); *Kant und Helmholtz* (1898); a new edition of Mellin's *Marginalien und Register zu Kants Kritik der Erkenntnisvermoegen* (2 vols., 1900–02); some attacks on other Kant interpreters, *Kantkritik oder Kantstudium?* (1901); *Baumanns Anti-Kant* (1906); *Kant und Haeckel* (1906); and *Gegen Einsteins Metaphysik* (1923). [R.H.P.]

GOLDSCHMIDT, MEIR ARON (1819–1887), Danish novelist, political writer, and journalist. Born in Vordingborg, Zealand, Goldschmidt was sent to Copenhagen for a year as a child and was impressed by the Jewish life of the capital. Although he matriculated in 1836, religious prejudice prevented him from studying medicine. He accordingly turned to journalism and in 1837 founded a liberal provincial weekly, *Nestved Ugeblad* (later renamed *Sjællandsposten*), whose policy brought him a heavy fine and a year's censorship. He later moved to Copenhagen and in 1840 founded *Corsaren*, a successful satirical weekly with a radical outlook. The paper attacked Denmark's conservative establishment, especially the absolute monarchy and the powerful civil service. Goldschmidt began his literary career with the novel *En Jøde* (1845; *The Jews of Denmark*, 1852). This told the story of a Danish Jew whose break with traditional Orthodoxy provokes his father's curse. His romance with a Christian girl ends unhappily and the hero ultimately becomes a moneylender. *En Jøde* contains some picturesque descriptions of Jewish customs and festivals, as does the story *Aron of Esther* in the collection *Fortællinger* ("Tales," 1846). During the years 1847–59 Goldschmidt published the periodical *Nord og Syd*, which largely consisted of his own articles on literature, theater, art, and politics. After the failure of the magazine *Hjemme og Ude,* which appeared briefly in 1861, he moved to England, but returned to Denmark in 1863, resolved to abandon his political involvements. The central figure of his long novel *Hjemløs* (1853–57), which he himself adapted into English as *Homeless, or a Poet's Inner Life* (1861), is a Danish gentile, but Goldschmidt introduces a cultured English Jew who teaches the hero that happiness and misery are balanced in each person's life and that men's sins must be atoned for on earth. The novelist called this ethical system "Nemesis," and it dominates his later works. These include two novels, *Arvingen* (Eng., *The Heir,* both 1865), and *Ravnen* ("The Raven," 1867); three Jewish short stories, *"Maser"* (1858, *"Avrohmche Nattergal"* (1871; English version in *Denmark's Best Stories,* 1928), and *"Levi og Ibald"* (1883); and *Livserindringer og Resultater* ("Memoirs and Results," 2 vols., 1877). Goldschmidt was an outstanding storyteller and the wordly yet pious and decent hero of his Jewish stories is one of the outstanding figures of Danish fiction.

Bibliography: G. Brandes, *Samlete Skrifter,* 2 (1900), 447–68; H. Kyrre, *M. A. Goldschmidt* (Danish, 1919); *Dansk Biografisk Leksikon,* 8 (1936). [F.J.B.-J.]

GOLDSCHMIDT, RICHARD BENEDICT (1878–1958), German geneticist. Goldschmidt, who was born in Frankfort, became a lecturer at Munich University in 1904. In 1913 he was selected to head a genetics department at the newly organized Kaiser Wilhelm Institute for Experimental Biology in Berlin. Before assuming his duties he went to Japan to obtain material for his studies on sex determination in the gypsy moth. World War I broke out while he was on his way home; as a result he spent three of the war years as a visiting professor at Yale University and the fourth interned as an enemy alien. Returning to Berlin after the war, he worked at the Kaiser Wilhelm Institute from 1919 to 1936, except for two years as a visiting professor at the University of Tokyo (1924–26). In 1936, as a result of the Nazi persecution, he emigrated to the United States. He was professor of zoology at the University of California in Berkeley until his retirement in 1948. In the course of his studies on the gypsy moth Goldschmidt discovered that sex is determined by a balance between genetic factors for maleness and femaleness present in all individuals. He found that the strength of these factors differed in different geographic races, and was able to produce predictable degrees of intersexuality by appropriate interracial hybridizations. These findings led him to conclude that the genes are responsible for determining the rate of physiological processes. He rejected the concept of linearly linked unitary

Richard Benedict Goldschmidt, German geneticist. Courtesy National Academy of Sciences, Washington, D.C.

genes; instead he regarded the chromosome as a single giant molecule. Mutations, in his view, were caused by breakages and rearrangements of the chromosomal material ("position effects"). Goldschmidt's views on evolution were also unorthodox; he maintained that new types evolved not through the selection and accumulation of small genetic differences but rather by major, single-step mutations ("hopeful monsters") that produced drastic changes in development. Although he stood almost alone as a dissenter, he was widely respected as a brilliant critic and eloquent polemicist. Goldschmidt's scientific works include: *Mechanismus und Physiologie der Geschlechtsbestimmung* (1920; *The Mechanism and Physiology of Sex Determination,* 1923); *Physiologiche Theorie der Vererbung* (1927; *Physiological Genetics,* 1938); *The Material Basis of Evolution* (1940); *Theoretical Genetics* (1955); and a number of textbooks, among them *Ascaris* (Ger., 1922; *Ascaris, The Biologist's Story of Life,* 1937). He also wrote *Portraits from Memory: Recollections of a Zoologist* (1956), and the autobiographical *In and Out of the Ivory Tower* (1960).

Bibliography: E. Caspari, in: *Genetics* (Jan. 1960), 1–5; A.V. Howard (ed.), *Chamber's Dictionary of Scientists* (1958), 191–2. [M.L.G.]

GOLDSCHMIDT, VICTOR (1853–1933), German crystallographer and inventor. Goldschmidt, who was born in Mainz, was appointed teacher at Heidelberg University in 1888, and professor in 1893. Among his publications were *Index der Krystallformen der Mineralien* (3 vols., 1887–91), a catalog of the forms on the crystals of minerals, and *Krystallographische Winkeltabellen* (1897), a collection of tables of angles in crystal formation. His chief work, however, was his *Atlas des Krystallformen* (1913–23), a compilation of all published figures of crystals of minerals, in nine volumes. His researches into number series appearing in crystal symbols resulted in his formulation of a theory of number and harmony involving a consideration of musical and color harmonies. Goldschmidt was the inventor of the bicircular goniometer, used in measuring angles. He was baptized.

Bibliography: L. Milch, in: *Festschrift Victor Goldschmidt* (1928), includes bibliography; C. Palache, in: *American Mineralogist,* 19 (1934), 106–11 (includes bibliography); L.J. Spencer, in: *Mineralogical Magazine,* 24 (1936), 287–9; *Neue Deutsche Biographie,* 6 (1964). [Ed.]

GOLDSCHMIDT, VICTOR MORITZ (1888–1947), Norwegian mineralogist, crystallographer, and geochemist. Goldschmidt was born in Zurich, son of Heinrich Jacob Goldschmidt (1857–1937) who became professor of chemistry at Oslo University in 1901. In 1914 Victor Goldschmidt was appointed professor of crystallography, mineralogy, and petrography at Oslo University. In 1929 he was appointed director of the mineralogical-petrographical institute at Goettingen, but in 1935 left Nazi Germany to return to Oslo. He was chairman of the Norwegian Friends of the Hebrew University in 1937. After the invasion of Norway in 1940, Goldschmidt was hunted by the Nazis and was arrested on several occasions. The underground succeeded in smuggling him to Sweden in December 1942 and from there he was flown to England, where he devoted himself to work connected with atomic energy. He returned to Oslo in 1946. Goldschmidt was one of the great mineralogists and crystallographers of his generation and is recognized as the founder of the new science of geochemistry. Already in his doctoral thesis in 1911 on the "Phenomena of Metamorphosis" he established a basis for classifying the metamorphic minerals according to general physico-chemical laws, proposed the concept of "stability limits" of minerals, and developed the idea of mineral facies that became the central idea in mineralogy-petrography. Later he developed the notion of type relationships of rocks and laid the foundations of genetic classification of magnetic rocks. Besides these main fields of work, he also explained the distribution of chemical elements in the earth's crust and defined the laws of distribution that result from the natural factors in elements themselves. Goldschmidt was also interested in problems of practical research including the formation of mineral pigments, the

Victor Moritz Goldschmidt, Norwegian mineralogist and geochemist. Courtesy Mineralogisk-Geologisk Museum, Oslo.

production of aluminum from silicates, the use of biotite as a fertilizer, and the use of olivine as a raw material for the production of materials resistant to chemical and heat reactions. Goldschmidt's main works were *Die Kontaktmetamorphose im Kristianiagebiet* (1911); *Geologisch-petrographische Studien* . . . (5 vols. 1912–21); *Geochemische Verteilungsgesetze der Elemente* (9 parts, 1923–38).

Bibliography: D. Oftedal, in: Geological Society of America, *Proceedings 1947* (1948), 149–54, includes bibliography; C. E. Tilley, in: Royal Society of London, *Obituary Notices* . . ., 17 (1948), 51–66; Norwegian Academy of Science, *Årbok 1947* (1948), 85–102.

[Y.K.B.]

GOLDSMID, English family, descended from AARON GOLDSMID (d. 1782), who settled in London in the second quarter of the 18th century and was active in the affairs of the Great Synagogue. BENJAMIN GOLDSMID (1755–1808) and ABRAHAM GOLDSMID (1756–1810), sons of Aaron, became prominent financiers in the City of London during the French revolutionary wars, when their competition with the old-established non-Jewish bankers resulted in the issue of Treasury loans on terms much more favorable to the government, and thereby initiated a new era in public finance. The brothers were active in the affairs of the Jewish community and in general philanthropy. They served in all the offices of the Great Synagogue and were associated with the establishment of both the Jews' Hospital and the Royal Naval Asylum. Their close familiarity with the sons of George III did much to break down social prejudice against Jews in England and to pave the way for emancipation. They were considered by Lord Nelson among his closest friends. Both of the brothers committed suicide. Their activity marked the displacement of the Sephardi element in London from their former hegemony. ALBERT GOLDSMID (1793–1861), Benjamin's son, entered the army in 1811, He fought in the Peninsular War at Waterloo, and reached the rank of major general. SIR ISAAC LYON GOLDSMID (1778–1859), son of Aaron Goldsmid's second son Asher, made a large fortune, partly by financing railway construction. He was made a baronet in 1841, being the first professing Jew to receive an English hereditary title. He was prominent in the struggle for Jewish emancipation in England and was one of the founders of the nonsectarian University College, London. He took a leading part in the establishment of the Reform synagogue. In 1846 he was created Baron de Palmeira by the king of Portugal. SIR FRANCIS HENRY GOLDSMID (1808–1878), the eldest son of Isaac Lyon, was the first Jewish barrister in England and for many years a member of Parliament, as was his brother FREDERICK DAVID GOLDSMID (1812–1866). SIR JULIAN GOLDSMID (1838–1896), the son of Frederick David, succeeded to the title and was for many years a member of Parliament and at one time deputy speaker. Like his father, he was also active in communal affairs as chairman

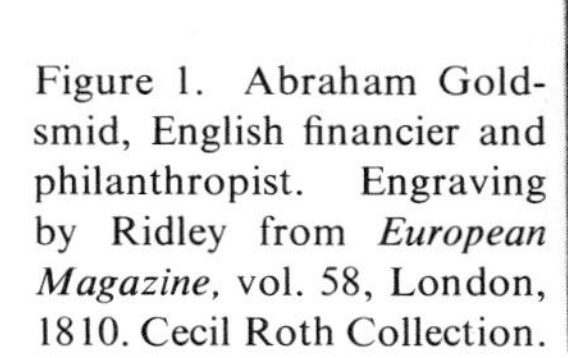

Figure 1. Abraham Goldsmid, English financier and philanthropist. Engraving by Ridley from *European Magazine*, vol. 58, London, 1810. Cecil Roth Collection.

of the Reform synagogue, of the *Anglo-Jewish Association, etc. On his death, the baronetcy was transferred to his cousin, Sir Osmond *D'Avigdor. ANNA MARIA GOLDSMID (1805–1889), daughter of Isaac Lyon, made a name as philanthropist and poet. SIR FREDERICK JOHN GOLDSMID (1818–1908), who belonged to the baptized branch of the family, was a distinguished orientalist, a major general in the army, constructed the first telegraph lines in Persia, and established the administrative system in the Congo (see also *D'Avigdor family).

Bibliography: A. J. Prijs, *Pedigree of the Family Goldsmit-Cassel of Amsterdam, 1650–1750* (1937); Hyamson, in: JHSET, 17 (1951–52), 1–10; Emden, *ibid.*, 14 (1935–39), 225–46; D. Marks and A. Loewy, *Memoir of Sir Francis Henry Goldsmid* (1882); Cope, in: *Economica*, 9 (1942), 180–206.

[C.R.]

Figure 2. Caricature of Sir Isaac Lyon Goldsmid by R. Dighton, 1824. Cecil Roth Collection.

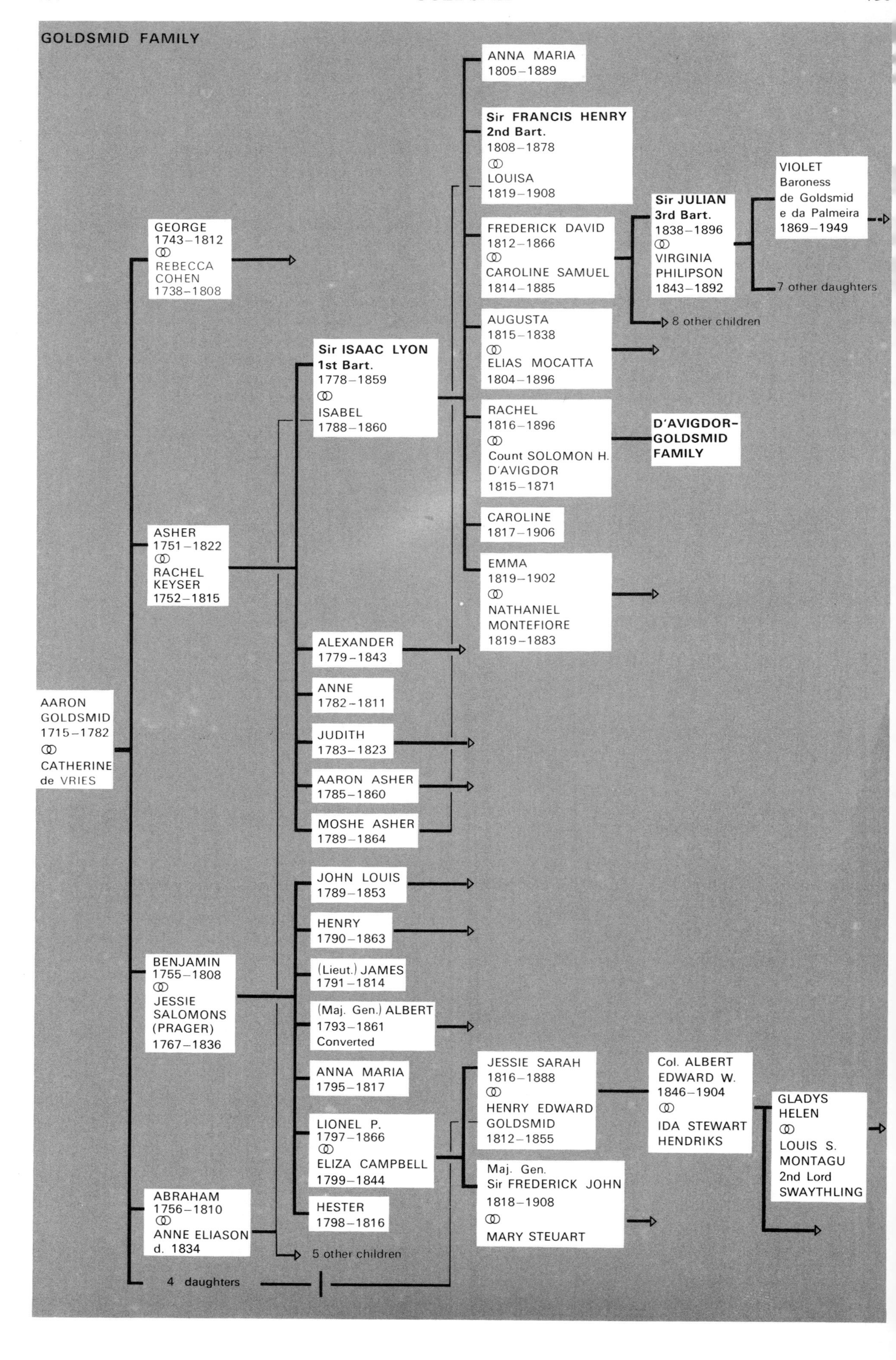
GOLDSMID FAMILY
AARON GOLDSMID 1715–1782 ⚭ CATHERINE de VRIES
GEORGE 1743–1812 ⚭ REBECCA COHEN 1738–1808
ASHER 1751–1822 ⚭ RACHEL KEYSER 1752–1815
BENJAMIN 1755–1808 ⚭ JESSIE SALOMONS (PRAGER) 1767–1836
ABRAHAM 1756–1810 ⚭ ANNE ELIASON d. 1834
4 daughters
Sir ISAAC LYON 1st Bart. 1778–1859 ⚭ ISABEL 1788–1860
ALEXANDER 1779–1843
ANNE 1782–1811
JUDITH 1783–1823
AARON ASHER 1785–1860
MOSHE ASHER 1789–1864
JOHN LOUIS 1789–1853
HENRY 1790–1863
(Lieut.) JAMES 1791–1814
(Maj. Gen.) ALBERT 1793–1861 Converted
ANNA MARIA 1795–1817
LIONEL P. 1797–1866 ⚭ ELIZA CAMPBELL 1799–1844
HESTER 1798–1816
5 other children
ANNA MARIA 1805–1889
Sir FRANCIS HENRY 2nd Bart. 1808–1878 ⚭ LOUISA 1819–1908
FREDERICK DAVID 1812–1866 ⚭ CAROLINE SAMUEL 1814–1885
AUGUSTA 1815–1838 ⚭ ELIAS MOCATTA 1804–1896
RACHEL 1816–1896 ⚭ Count SOLOMON H. D'AVIGDOR 1815–1871
D'AVIGDOR-GOLDSMID FAMILY
CAROLINE 1817–1906
EMMA 1819–1902 ⚭ NATHANIEL MONTEFIORE 1819–1883
Sir JULIAN 3rd Bart. 1838–1896 ⚭ VIRGINIA PHILIPSON 1843–1892
8 other children
VIOLET Baroness de Goldsmid e da Palmeira 1869–1949
7 other daughters
JESSIE SARAH 1816–1888 ⚭ HENRY EDWARD GOLDSMID 1812–1855
Maj. Gen. Sir FREDERICK JOHN 1818–1908 ⚭ MARY STEUART
Col. ALBERT EDWARD W. 1846–1904 ⚭ IDA STEWART HENDRIKS
GLADYS HELEN ⚭ LOUIS S. MONTAGU 2nd Lord SWAYTHLING

GOLDSMID, ALBERT EDWARD WILLIAMSON (1846–1904), English soldier. Born at Poona, India, Goldsmid entered the British Army in 1866, reached the rank of colonel in 1894, and served with distinction in the Boer War. Born of a long-assimilated family connected with the illustrious *Goldsmid family by marriage (though he was not descended from it), he became attracted to Judaism in maturity and was henceforth active in the life of Anglo-Jewry. In 1892 he went temporarily to the Argentine to supervise the *Jewish Colonization Association (ICA) colonies established there by Baron de *Hirsch. He was one of the founders of the *Maccabeans and of the *Jewish Lads' Brigade in London. A prominent member of the English Ḥovevei Zion (see *Ḥibbat Zion) movement, as early as 1891 he advocated the revival of Hebrew as a spoken language, welcomed Herzl's proposals with enthusiasm, became an ardent Zionist, and was a member of the *El-Arish Commission in 1903. Herzl was deeply impressed by him and thought of him as occupying high office in the Jewish State when it was established. Goldsmid is said to have been the model for George *Eliot's character Daniel Deronda.

Bibliography: Fraenkel, in: *Herzl Yearbook*, 1 (1958), 145–53; N. Sokolow, *History of Zionism* (1919); index; T. Herzl, *Diaries*, ed. by M. Lowenthal (1956), index. [C.R.]

GOLDSMITH, LEWIS (c. 1763–1846), English political journalist. Goldsmith, who was born in London, was never associated with Judaism and was probably baptized as a young man. His *The Crimes of Cabinets* (1805) censured the attempts to suppress the French Revolution. Later he took refuge in Paris where he established *The Argus*, an anti-English journal. The journal was suspended when he refused to attack the English royal family. Returning to England in 1809, he was tried for high treason but was acquitted. He then started the violently patriotic *Anti-Gallican* (subsequently *The British Monitor*), advocating the assassination of Napoleon. On the restoration of Louis XVIII, he returned to Paris where he became interpreter to the Tribunal of Commerce. Goldsmith published his *Statistics of France* in 1832. His daughter Georgiana (1807–1901) became the second wife of Baron Lyndhurst, Lord Chancellor of England, and a noted political hostess.

Bibliography: *Nouvelle Biographie Générale*, s.v.; DNB, s.v.; Rubens, in: JHSET, 19 (1955–59), 39–43. [C.R.]

GOLDSMITH, RAYMOND WILLIAM (1904–), U.S. economist. Born in Brussels, Belgium, Goldsmith lived in the U.S. from 1930 and during the years 1934–48 he served with the U.S. Securities and Exchange Commission, the War Production Board, and the National Bureau of Economic Research. He was U.S. adviser on the 1946 German currency reform and on the 1947–48 Austrian treaty negotiations. Goldsmith became professor of economics, first at New York University (1958–59) and later at Yale (from 1960). Money and banking were his major interests, and his works include: *The Changing Structure of American Banking* (1933); *A Study of Saving in the United States* (3 vols., 1955–56); *Financial Intermediaries in the American Economy* (1958); *The National Wealth of the United States in the Postwar Period* (1962); and *Financial Structure and Development* (1969). [J.O.R.]

GOLDSMITH, SAMUEL ABRAHAM (1892–), U.S. social worker. Goldsmith was born in New York. Following service as a field worker for the YMHA and the Jewish Welfare Board in New York City, Goldsmith served for ten years as executive director of the Bureau of Jewish Social Research. In this capacity he conducted detailed surveys of Jewish social services in many American cities. Their findings and recommendations profoundly affected the direction of American Jewish social and communal work. In 1930 Goldsmith was appointed executive director of the Jewish Federation and Jewish Welfare Fund of Chicago, a position he held until his retirement. He served as president of the National Conference on Jewish Social Welfare (1928–29) and of the Illinois Welfare Association (1948–49), and held numerous other positions of significant organizational responsibility. [K.D.R.]

GOLDSMITHS AND SILVERSMITHS. The two closely related professions of refining, casting, beating, and filigreeing silver and gold have occupied Jewish craftsmen uninterruptedly from biblical times to the present. The highly skilled nature of the work, the relatively constant value of the two precious metals and the universal demand for artifacts made of them, their ready transportability, and not least, their use throughout the ages in Jewish ritual and ceremonial objects, all help account for the fact that Jewish goldsmiths and silversmiths can be found in almost every period of Jewish history wherever Jewish communities existed. However, because their creations were so often melted down or plundered for their metallic worth, no identifiable work of any Jewish craftsman has survived from before late medieval times, except for the artifacts and cult objects that have been excavated.

Antiquity. Apart from archaeological finds—ear and finger rings, anklets, pendants, beads, eating and drinking utensils, and figures of gods and goddesses such as those uncovered at Beth-Shean, Tell al-ʿAjjūl and Tell al-Faraḥ—there is ample literary evidence from the Bible that both silver and gold were worked by Israelite craftsmen from the earliest times; indeed, according to the biblical narrative, the first two Jewish goldsmiths and silversmiths were the builders of the Tabernacle, *Bezalel and Oholiab. The many biblical injunctions against making silver and gold idols point in themselves to the widespread manufacture of such objects from the time of the Israelite conquest on, as borne out also by stories like that of Micah and his idol of silver (Judg. 17) or Jeroboam's golden calves (I Kings 12). Numerous passages in the Bible refer to silver and gold artifacts of all kinds and to the many silver and gold utensils in the Temple. Though neither of these metals was ever mined in Palestine, both were available throughout the ancient Near East; the Bible speaks of *Ophir and *Tarshish as sources, and this has been partly corroborated by a recently found eighth-century B.C.E. ostracon on which appear the words "gold from Ophir." Israelite craftsmen most probably learned to work both gold and silver directly

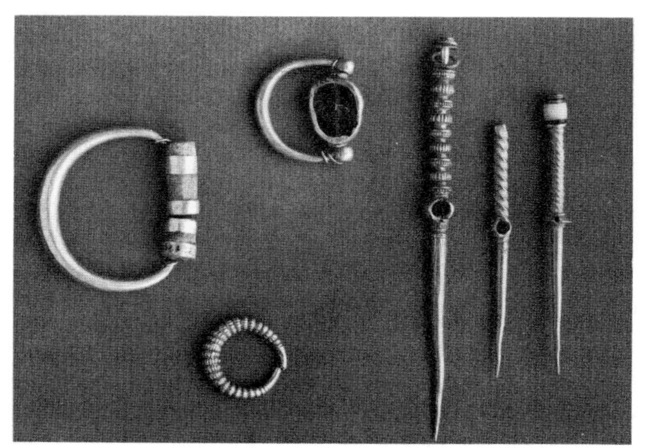

Figure 1. Gold jewelry of the Middle Canaanite period (23rd–16th centuries B.C.E.), found at Tell al-ʿAjjūl. Jerusalem, Israel Museum. Photo David Harris, Jerusalem.

Figure 2. Gold pendant with goddess holding scepter. Late Bronze Age (1550–1200 B.C.E.), found at Beth-Shean. Jerusalem, Rockefeller Museum, Israel Department of Antiquities.

from the Canaanites among whom they settled. In the time of Ezra and Nehemiah, to judge by two verses in the Book of Nehemiah (3:8, 31–32), they were organized into guilds. Such societies undoubtedly persisted later in the Second Temple period, and it is known that in the years preceding the destruction of the Temple goldsmiths occupied their own quarters in Jerusalem. The Mishnah (Mid. 3:8) and Josephus (15:390) write of a golden vine with grape clusters "a marvel of size and artistry" adorning the Herodian Temple. Several references to Jewish goldsmiths and silversmiths occur in the Mishnah and Talmud. Rabbi Eliezer, a *tanna* living in the first half of the second century, ruled that Jewish craftsmen could not make ornaments for idols but could supply gentile customers with "necklaces, earrings and finger rings"—a clear indication that such artisans competed for the non-Jewish trade as well. The Talmud (Sot. 49b; Shab. 59a) twice refers to a specific piece of gold jewelry, the "city of Jerusalem" *(yerushalayim shel zahav)* or "city of gold," apparently a pendant, engraved with an illustration of a wall encircling a city, that was customarily given to young brides. The first record of Jewish gold- and silversmiths active outside Palestine comes from the description in Suk. 51b of the great synagogue of Alexandria. It is stated that various groups of artisans, among them silversmiths and goldsmiths, sat each in their own pews, "so that when a poor man [i. e., artisan] entered there, he recognized the members of his own craft and turned to them to find means for the maintenance of himself and his family." This presumably refers to organized guilds. That Alexandria continued to harbor many Jewish gold- and silversmiths as late as the eve of the Muslim conquest, by which time the Jewish population of the city had greatly dwindled, is known from the writings of the sixth-century monk and geographer Cosmas Indicopleustes, who also mentions an even greater concentration of such Jewish craftsmen in Medina, where, he writes, 300 Jewish gold- and silversmiths lived in one quarter of the city. Presumably this records the beginnings of a tradition of Jewish gold and silver work in the southern Arabian peninsula.

Middle Ages and Modern Times. Like the practice of *crafts in general by Jews in the Middle Ages, the intricate craft of the goldsmith and silversmith continued to be a widespread Jewish occupation south of the Pyrenees and in the Mediterranean lands, while there was little activity among Jews in this profession north of this demarcation line. The specific combination of skills and financial acumen needed for the goldsmith's trade is evidenced in the information that has been preserved about the plying of this craft by Jews in Muslim countries. The records of the *Genizah* of Cairo show that goldsmithing was a common, lucrative, and highly specialized profession of Jews in Egypt and the surrounding area as far as Aden in the 11th and 12th centuries. In Iraq, Persia, Yemen, and the Maghreb many of the goldsmiths were Jews. That this was a

Figure 3. Silver filigree Torah finials *(rimmonim)* from Sicily, 15th century, preserved in the cathedral of Palma de Mallorca. Courtesy B. Torres, Cabildo Cathedral, Palma de Mallorca. Photo Yeronimo Juantous, Mallorca.

Figure 4. Silver tankard by Myer Myers, New York, 1745. Courtesy The New York Historical Society, New York.

widespread Jewish occupation in Muslim countries may be explained by the contempt in which artisans were held by the Arabs. In pre-Islamic Arabia there was a tribe of Jewish goldsmiths, the *Zuaynuga, who were defeated and forced to accept Islam by Muhammad. The preponderance of Jews in goldsmithing and silversmithing, particularly in the manufacture of jewelry, continued well into the modern period. In Baghdad, in 1844, 250 of 1,607 Jewish families employed in industry and trade were goldsmiths by profession. In Yemen in particular, the Jewish artisans attained a high standard of skill and artistry. Jews there even believed that the few Muslim goldsmiths were descendants of Jews who had been forcibly converted. The mass immigration to Israel after 1948 of the Jews of Yemen and other Arab countries helped to develop a local jewelry industry.

Jewish goldsmiths are among the first Jews mentioned in Muslim Spain, and are repeatedly referred to there in the following centuries. In Christian Spain Jewish goldsmiths were to be found in practically every sizable town; they were employed by the royal households and occupied their own row of shops in large cities like Tudela and Pamplona. The Augustinian eremites of Barcelona in 1399 commissioned a Jewish artisan to make them a silver reliquary. Jews manufactured Christian religious artifacts in violation of Jewish law and the antipope Benedict XIII in 1415 had to forbid Spanish Jews to produce such objects as goblets and crucifixes. Jewish silversmithing was expressly permitted in the 15th century: in Aragon in 1401 and in Castile in 1419. A magnificent pair of silver **rimmonim*, decorated with semiprecious stones and executed by a Spanish Jewish artist in Camarata (Sicily) in the 15th century, still survives in the Cathedral treasury in Palma de Majorca. Delicate filigree work surrounds the horseshoe arched repoussé areas and the Hebrew inscriptions. The expulsion from Spain in 1492 left many *Marranos in the Iberian peninsula and Balearic islands who now engaged freely in silversmithing and goldsmithing. Numbers of the exiles from Spain and Portugal entered these crafts in the Ottoman Empire. This was recognizable particularly in Walachia where Jews sometimes even headed the silversmith guilds. In Ereẓ Israel, in particular in Safed, goldsmithing was considered one of the profitable crafts for Jews in the 16th century. In Italy the refugees from Spain met local well-established Jews in the craft. An apostate of Ferrara, Ercole dei Fideli (before baptism, Solomon de Sessa), was celebrated in this renaissance environment for the ornamental daggers and other works he produced (1465–1519). The gold- and silversmith Abraham b. Moses Ẓoref ("goldsmith") is mentioned in Venice in the early 18th century. Jewish goldsmiths are found in Rome in 1726. In Bohemia-Moravia gold- and silversmithing developed as a flourishing craft among Jews from the 16th century. Emperor Rudolf II appointed Isaac Goldscheider ("gold refiner") elder of Bohemian Jewry in 1560. He was followed in the craft by his son Jacob. The profession became widespread there, as attested by the frequent appearance of the name Ẓoref on Prague tombstones until 1740. In the 18th century Jewish goldsmithing was combined with the Jewish trade in precious stones and metals centered in Amsterdam and Hamburg. The craft continued to develop. There were eight goldsmiths among the Jews who returned to Prague in 1749. Several families practiced the craft for successive generations. The program of "enlightenment" and "productivization" of the Jews, animating the legislation of Emperor *Joseph II, encouraged practice of the craft among Jews; a separate Jewish guild came into existence in 1805 and continued until the abolition of the guilds in 1859. There were 29 Jewish apprentices recorded in Prague in 1804 and in 1830 there were 55 goldsmiths. In Germany, Jews did not begin to enter the craft until the middle of the 19th century when, however, the general developments in Jewish society were tending to deflect them from occupation in crafts. Silesia was an exception, for Jewish goldsmiths and silversmiths were working there in the second half of the 18th century. In Poland-Lithuania Jews entered this craft as they entered others, as a result of the weakness of the guilds and the activities of Jews in the private towns of the nobility. In 1664 Hirsch Jelenowicz was officially called "goldsmith to His Majesty" in Poland. With the mass emigration of Jews from Eastern Europe to Western Europe and the Americas, Jewish goldsmiths—now combining the profession with watchmaking—joined the few Sephardi goldsmiths who had arrived there earlier. The most noted of early Jewish goldsmiths in the United States was Myer *Myers. Between 1725 and 1837, 50 Jewish goldsmiths are recorded in England. Thus in modern times Jewish goldsmiths in Northern and Central Europe severed

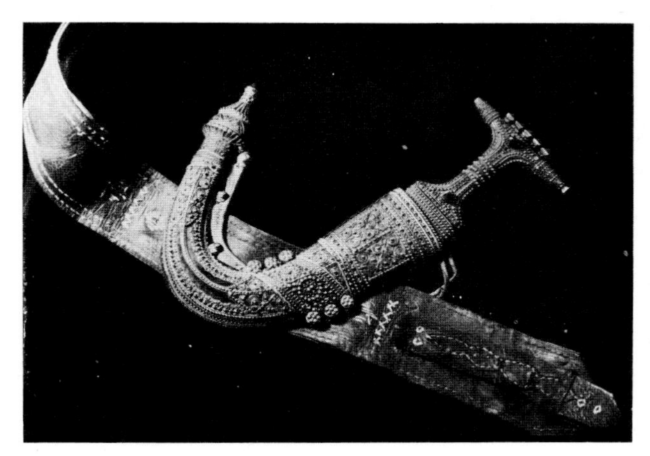

Figure 5. Silver filigree dagger worked by a Jewish silversmith in Yemen. Jerusalem, Israel Museum. Photo A. Bernheim, Jerusalem.

Figure 6. The "Sitaphornes Tiara" by Israel Roukhomovsky 1896. From I. Roukhomovsky, *Mayn Leybn un mayn Arbayt,* Paris, 1928.

the old connection with moneylending and pawnbroking and the trade became allied with formal banking, on the one hand, and with the making of delicate instruments and the watch trade, on the other. Jewish *art, in particular, the ornamentation of Torah scrolls, *mezuzot,* and similar cult objects, was influenced by the Christian artisans who did the work for Jews, especially in Northern, Central, and Eastern Europe in the early Middle Ages. Family names like Goldschmidt, Goldsmith, Goldsmid, Ẓoref or Soref, and Orefice (Italian) generally indicate that at some stage in its history the family derived its livelihood from goldsmithing. [H.W.]

Many Jewish goldsmiths and silversmiths became celebrated during the 19th century: best known was Israel Roukhomovsky, who worked in a small townlet near Odessa (Russia) at the turn of the century. In 1896 he was asked by a friend to make a golden tiara decorated with scenes from the *Iliad,* scenes in the daily life of the Scythians, and inscriptions referring to the gift of a tiara to King Sitaphornes by the people of Albia. In 1898 this work was sold to the Louvre as an archaeological find by a Viennese merchant. When in 1903 Roukhomovsky was invited to Paris, and there produced a similar work with his primitive tools, he managed to convince a team of archaeologists headed by Clermont-Ganneau that he was the craftsman who made the alleged Sitaphornes tiara.

In Palestine the *Bezalel School of Arts and Crafts, established by Boris *Schatz in 1906, created a style of its own by adapting the traditional artistry of the Yemenites to western forms and tastes. This "Bezalel style" continued to be produced in Israel, especially in the manufacture of ritual objects as well as jewelry. Among modern goldsmiths and silversmiths in Israel and the U.S.A. were many important artists; most renowned in the production of ritual objects, both in Jerusalem and New York, were Wolpert and Gumbel. [B.N.]

Bibliography: L. A. Mayer, *Bibliography of Jewish Art* (1967), index s.v. *Goldsmith* and *Ceremonial Art;* A. Wolf in: MGJW, 9 (1902), 12–74; 15 (1905), 1–58; 24 (1907), 103–17; M. Gruenwald,

Figure 7. Cover for the second Golden Book of the Jewish National Fund in gold and silver with ivory plaques and leather binding, by Ze'ev Raban, c. 1913. Jerusalem, J.N.F.

ibid., 74 (1925), 419f.; Y. Bronner, in: *Zeitschrift fuer die Geschichte der Juden in der Tschechoslowakei,* 1 (1931), 243–7; H. Flesch, in: *Die juedischen Denkmaeler in der Tschechoslowakei* (1933), 32–33; Baer, Urkunden, index; Baer, Spain, index; Y. W. Rosenbaum, *Myer Myers, Goldsmith* (1954); A. G. Grimwalde, in: JHSET, 18 (1953–55), 113–26; C. Roth, *The Jews in the Renaissance* (1959), 195–8; S. Simonsohn, *Toledot ha-Yehudim be-Dukkasut Mantova,* 2 vols. (1962–64) index s.v. *Ẓorefim;* M. Wischnitzer, *A History of Jewish Crafts and Guilds* (1965); A. Ben-Yakob, *Yehudei Bavel mi-Sof Tekufat ha-Ge'onim ad Yamenu* (1965), index s.v. *Ẓorefim;* O. Muneles (ed.), *Prague Ghetto in the Renaissance Period* (1965), 108–25; Ashtor, Korot, 1 (1966), 180; J. Hrasky, in: *Judaica Bohemiae,* 2 (1966), 19–40; 97–106; H. Bentov, in: *Sefunot,* 10 (1966), 413–83; J. M. Landau, *Ha-Yehudim be-Miẓrayim ba-Me'ah ha-Tesha-Esreh* (1967); S. D. Goitein, *A Mediterranean Society* (1967), index; W. Pillich, in: *Zeitschrift fuer die Geschichte der Juden,* 4 (1967), 79–82; B. Brilling, *ibid.,* 5 (1968), 21–26; 6 (1969), 137–46; idem, *Geschichte der juedischen Goldschmiedwerke in Schlesien* (1969); I. Roukhomovsky, *Zikhroynes fun mayn Leybn un fun mayn Shtetl* (1930); A. Kanoff, *Jewish Ceremonial Art* (1970).

GOLDSTEIN, ABRAHAM SAMUEL (1925–), U.S. lawyer and educator. Goldstein, who was born in New York City, was admitted to the Washington, D.C., bar in 1949. After two years as a law clerk to U.S. Circuit Court Judge David *Bazelon (1949–51), he practiced privately with a Washington law firm from 1951 to 1956. In the latter year, he was appointed a member of the Yale Law School faculty. Goldstein, an expert in U.S. criminal law and procedure, became a professor in 1961 and in 1970 was named the dean of Yale Law School. He also served as a consultant to the President's Commission on Law Enforcement and as a member of the Connecticut State Board of Parole. Active in Jewish affairs, he was a member of the board of directors of the New Haven Jewish Community Council. Goldstein wrote *The Insanity Defense* (1967). [ED.]

GOLDSTEIN, ALEXANDER (1884–1949), Russian Zionist leader. Born in Minsk, Goldstein studied law at the University of St. Petersburg and took an active part in Zionist student circles. In 1903 he published his first article (in Russian) and eventually became one of the outstanding writers on Zionist affairs, contributing to the Zionist monthly, *Yevreyskaya Zhizn,* and primarily to *Razsvet,* when this weekly was founded in 1907. He also traveled throughout Russia in order to promote the Zionist idea. He was one of the originators of the Helsingfors Program which sought to incorporate Diaspora activities into the Zionist program. At the Seventh Convention of Russian Zionists, held in Petrograd in 1917, Goldstein submitted a proposal to hold a national "referendum," which would demand equal rights for the Jews in the Diaspora as well as a national home for the Jews in Ereẓ Israel. In 1919 he left Russia, and, when Keren Hayesod was established, he entered its service and traveled extensively on its behalf. In 1933 he settled in Palestine, where he continued his work for Keren Hayesod.

Bibliography: Tidhar, 2 (1947), 793; *He-Avar*, 14 (1967), 3–87.

[G.K.]

GOLDSTEIN, ANGELO (1889–1947), politician and Zionist leader in Czechoslovakia. The son of a rabbi in Bohemia, he graduated in law. He was wounded during his service in the Austro-Hungarian army in World War I. After the war he practiced as an advocate in Prague. An active Zionist from his student days, he was among the founders of the Jewish party. At the death of Ludwig *Singer (1931) he took his place in parliament, and was reelected in 1935. An outstanding orator, he fought all attempts at discrimination against Jews. Goldstein was bitterly opposed by assimilationists and extreme Orthodox Jews. He acted as counsel in libel actions brought against the Jewish party (e.g., as counsel of Emil *Margulies in the Hirschler-*Weber case in 1928). Goldstein was one of the main propagandists of Zionism in the Czech language. He served on the Zionist General Council (1931–35) on behalf of the Progressive General Zionist faction. In 1939 he left for Palestine where he practiced as a lawyer.

Bibliography: *The Jews of Czechoslovakia* (1969), index.

[Y.Ge.]

GOLDSTEIN, EUGEN (1850–1931), German physicist. Goldstein was born at Gleiwitz in Upper Silesia and became a student of the German scientist Herman von Helmholtz (1821–1894). Most of Goldstein's research was devoted to radiant emissions, first at the University of Berlin and later at the Potsdam Observatory. He is best remembered for his studies of high-vacuum cathode ray tubes, leading to his discovery of "Kanalstrahlen," known in English as "canal rays." He found that these rays travel in the opposite direction from normal cathode rays. This was

Eugen Goldstein, German physicist. Jerusalem, J.N.U.L., Schwadron Collection.

highly significant for the understanding of radiation in general, as it was shown later that such rays consist of positively charged particles and this in turn led Rutherford to prove that these particles, called protons, must exist alongside uncharged neutrons to make up the nucleus of every atom.

Bibliography: I. Asimov, *Biographical Encyclopedia of Science and Technology* (1964), 403–4; Huntress, in: *Proceedings of the American Academy of Arts and Sciences*, 78 (1950), 29–30.

[J.E.H.]

GOLDSTEIN, FANNY (1888–1961), U.S. librarian. Born in Kamenets-Podolsk, Russia, Fanny Goldstein was taken to the United States at an early age. She entered the Boston public library system in 1913 and served as librarian of the West End branch from 1922 until her retirement in 1957, developing there a notable Judaica collection later housed in the main library. In 1954 she was appointed curator of Judaica, the first woman in America to receive this title.

Throughout her career she was active in promoting interest in Jewish books and writers among Jews and non-Jews alike. In 1925 she introduced the celebration of Jewish Book Week in Boston; it was subsequently made a national event. In 1940 she became the first chairman of the National Committee for Jewish Book Week and in 1941 was made honorary president of its successor organization, the Jewish Book Council of America. She was well known for her listings of Judaica published by the Boston Public Library, and those which appeared in the *American Jewish Year Book* (43 (1941/42), 499–517) and the *Jewish Book Annual* (5 (1946/47), 84–100; also vols. 11–16, 1952–59). In 1958 she presented her own large collection of Judaica to the Boston Public Library, where it is now maintained as the Fanny Goldstein Collection.

Bibliography: C. Angoff, in: JBA, 20 (1962/63), 70–72.

[H.J.A.]

GOLDSTEIN, HERBERT S. (1890–1970), U.S. rabbi. Goldstein was born and educated in New York City, receiving his B.A. (1911) and M.A. (1912) degrees from

Herbert S. Goldstein, U.S. rabbinic leader. Courtesy Yeshiva University, New York.

Columbia University. He graduated from the *Jewish Theological Seminary in 1914, and was also ordained by Rabbi Shalom Jaffe, vice-president of the *Union of Orthodox Rabbis. While still a seminary student, he assisted Rabbi Moses Z. Margolies at the prestigious Kehilath Jeshurun Congregation in New York. After graduation, he pioneered a new synagogue in Harlem, which was then populated by first-generation Jewish immigrants. To attract their American-born children, Goldstein organized a youth *minyan* and gradually evolved the congregation into a new form: an institutional synagogue which comprised social, educational, and sports activities in addition to religious services. After Harlem became a totally Negro neighborhood in the 1930s, he transferred his activities to the West Side (1937), where he had previously established a branch known as the West Side Institutional Synagogue. Goldstein also served as professor of homiletics at the Rabbi Isaac Elchanan Theological Seminary of *Yeshiva University, and was president of the *Synagogue Council of America, *Rabbinical Council of America, and the *Union of Orthodox Jewish Congregations. He was also active in the *Agudath Israel movement, and continually visited Ereẓ Israel to aid the activities of the Harry Fischel Institute for Research in Jewish Law and the Rabbi Herzog World Academy of Jewish Studies. Both these projects were supported by the philanthropic foundation established by his father-in-law, Harry *Fischel. He also wrote several books, including a commentary to the 613 commandments, and edited his father-in-law's autobiography. Despite the fact that he was a graduate of the Jewish Theological Seminary, Goldstein was a strictly Orthodox rabbi, belonging to the right wing of the English-speaking Orthodox rabbinate, and in this respect was unique.

[Ed.]

GOLDSTEIN, ISRAEL (1896–), U.S. Conservative rabbi and Zionist. He was born in Philadelphia and ordained by the Jewish Theological Seminary in 1918. In that year he

Israel Goldstein, Conservative rabbi and chairman of the Keren Hayesod.

was appointed rabbi of the prominent Congregation B'nai Jeshurun in New York, where he served until 1961. An ardent Zionist, Goldstein was president of the Jewish National Fund of America (1933–43), and vice-president (1934–43) and president (1943–45) of the Zionist Organization of America, and enjoyed the reputation of an outstanding orator and administrator. A member and officer of several Jewish, interfaith, and public organizations and commissions, he was a founder of the National Conference of Christians and Jews (1928) and of Brandeis College (1946). Elected first president of the World Confederation of General Zionists (1946), he served as chairman of both the United Jewish and Palestine Appeals (1947–48), treasurer of the Jewish Agency (1948–49), and first president of Amidar, the Israel national housing company (1948–49). During Goldstein's tenure as president of the American Jewish Congress (1951–58) that organization vigorously opposed McCarthyism and the restrictive McCarran-Walter Immigration Act, supported equal rights for American Negroes, and attempted to counter Arab anti-Israel propaganda. In 1961 Goldstein moved to Jerusalem and became world chairman of the Keren Hayesod-United Israel Appeal. His books include a history of his congregation *Century of Judaism in New York* (1930); sermons and essays, *Towards a Solution* (1940) and *American Jewry Comes of Age* (1955); and *Transition Years, New York-Jerusalem, 1960–1962* (1962). His wife BERTHA (1895–) was national president of the *Pioneer Women Organization (1947 to 1951) and was active in many women's organizations.

Bibliography: H. Schneiderman (ed.), *Two Generations in Perspective: Notable Events and Trends, 1896–1956* (1957). [ED.]

GOLDSTEIN, JOSEF (1837–1899), *ḥazzan* and composer. Goldstein was born and brought up in Hungary. His father, known as "Shmelke Ḥazzan," was *ḥazzan* of the town of Neutra, and Josef sang in his choir at the age of six. His father died when Josef was ten, and when he was 13, though still at school, he was made *ḥazzan* of the community. During the next five years, he conducted services in many Hungarian towns and at the Polish synagogue in Vienna, studied music in Prague, Florence, and Padua, and sang in concerts in Budapest and elsewhere. At the age of 18 he was appointed chief *ḥazzan* of the Leopoldstadt Synagogue in Vienna, and served there for over 40 years. He introduced the Polish-Jewish style of singing, which he also used for the songs in his book *Schire Jeschurun* (3 vols., 1862). The work contains melodies for all the services of the synagogue and settings of psalms for choir with organ accompaniment.

Bibliography: Idelsohn, Melodien, 6 (1932), 196–209, nos. 15–30; Friedmann, Lebensbilder, 2 (1921), 102–8; E. Zaludkowski, *Kultur-Treger fun der Yidisher Liturgie* (1930), 120–4; Sendrey, Music, index. [J.L.N.]

GOLDSTEIN, JUDAH JAMISON (1886–1967), U.S. judge and civic leader. Goldstein, who was born in Ontario, Canada, went with his family to New York's Lower East Side when a child. He began practicing law in 1907 and in 1911 became secretary to Alfred E. Smith, then majority leader of the New York State Assembly. In the wake of the Seabury probe of municipal corruption, Goldstein assisted in the investigation of New York City's magistrate courts and was then appointed to this court by Mayor Walker. In 1936 he received an interim appointment to the General Sessions Court and in 1939, despite the opposition of Tammany Hall, won a full term on that court. Defeated as the Republican-Liberal-Fusion candidate for mayor in 1945, he was reelected to the court in 1953. On the bench, Goldstein was a socially conscious and innovative justice who advocated more understanding and lenient treatment for youthful offenders. Prominent in Jewish community, welfare, and philanthropic activities, Goldstein was an active Zionist, a trustee of the Federation of Jewish Philanthropies, a member of the board of the Joint Distribution Committee, and a founder with Lillian *Wald of the East Side Neighborhood Association. He was president (for 32 years) of the well-known Grand Street Boys, the philanthropic organization composed of members who rose from slum childhoods to positions of power and prominence in New York City life. Goldstein wrote *The Family in Court* (1934), dealing with the requirements of the Family Court. [R.SK.]

GOLDSTEIN, JULIUS (1873–1929), German philosopher. Born in Hamburg, he taught at the Technische Hochschule in Darmstadt from 1901. He edited the literary journal *Der Morgen,* which dealt with Jewish topics, from 1925 until his death. Philosophically he was close to William James, whose *A Pluralistic Universe* he translated (1914). He wrote a great deal on contemporary civilization and culture. Goldstein's major works are *Untersuchungen zum Kulturproblem der Gegenwart* (1899); *Die empiristische Geschichtsauffassung David Humes . . .* (1902); *Wandlungen in der Philosophie der Gegenwart . . .* (1911) on James, Bergson and Eucken; *Die Technik* (1912); *Rasse und Politik* (1921), dealing with the Jewish question; *Aus dem Vermaechtnis des neunzehnten Jahrhunderts . . .* (1922); and *Deutsche Volks-Idee und deutsch-voelkische Idee* (1927).

Bibliography: *Der Morgen,* 5 (1929), no. 4. [R.H.P.]

GOLDSTEIN, KURT (1878–1965), neurologist and psychiatrist; coformulator of a test which measures the impairment of function in the case of brain injury in regard to abstract and concrete thinking, known as the Goldstein-Sheerer test. Goldstein, who was born in Katowice, Poland, was educated and worked in Germany. During World War I, he headed a special hospital for treating brain injuries. After the war, he was appointed professor at Frankfort University and in 1931 at Berlin University. With the coming of the Nazis, he was dismissed from his post, imprisoned, and then released. He then emigrated to the U.S. He headed a research laboratory at the Montefiore Hospital, New York from 1936 to 1940. Then he taught for five years at Tufts Medical College in Boston, and from 1946 was professor of psychology at the City College of New York. Through his medical work on patients with brain damage, Goldstein formed a holistic approach and questioned the idea that the brain was an assembly of mechanisms that performed particular functions. He conceived the brain as a single unit in whose every function, the whole personality is reflected. His many investigations covered problems of localization in the brain, the methods of adaption of an organism to injuries, and the behavior of

Opening page of Book Seven from *Mishneh Torah* by Maimonides. David and Goliath are illustrated in the bottom margin. The *Kaufmann Mishneh Torah* consists of four volumes and was written by Nathan bar Simeon ha-Levi in 1295 in Cologne, Germany. Budapest, Library of the Hungarian Academy of Sciences, Kaufmann Collection, ms. A77/I–IV, vol. II, fol.118 ($19\frac{3}{4} \times 13\frac{3}{4}$ ins/50 × 35 cm.).

patients with brain damage. His findings were collected in his books: *Psychologische Analysen hirnpathologischer Faelle* written in collaboration with A. Gelb (1920); *Der Aufbau des Organismus* (1934, *The Organism,* written in collaboration with A. Gelb, 1963[2]), which have become classic works in neurology. From his own wide and varied experience with speech disorders, resulting from central defects and lesions, he published *Ueber Aphasie* (1927);

Kurt Goldstein, neurologist and psychiatrist.

The Organism (1939); *Human Nature in the Light of Psychopathology* (1940); *After-effects of Brain Injuries in War* (1942); and *Language and Language Disturbances* (1948). [Li.H.]

GOLDSTEIN, SALWIAN (1855–1926), Russian historian. Goldstein was born in Warsaw to an assimilated family. In 1888 he began lecturing on Polish and Lithuanian antiquities at the Imperial Archaeological Institute at St. Petersburg. In 1908 he was among the founders of the Jewish Historical-Ethnographical Society and was in charge of its archives. Goldstein's main activity was the collection of documents and other material on the history of Russian Jewry. He organized the archives of S.*Bershadsky and cooperated in the preparation and editing of the collections of documents *Regesty i nadpisi* (3 vols., 1899–1913), and *Russko-yevreyskiy arkhiv* (vol. 3, 1903). He published studies in *Yevreyskaya starina* and similar publications and was a contributor to the *Yevreyskaya Entsiklopediya,* the Russian-Jewish encyclopedia. Goldstein belonged to the small group of scholars who endeavored to maintain some sort of independent Jewish scholarship under Soviet rule.

Bibliography: YE, 6 (1910), 660–1; *Yevreyskaya starina,* 12 (1928), 404–5. [Y.S.]

GOLDSTEIN, SIDNEY (1903–), mathematician and aerodynamicist. Goldstein, who was born in Hull, England, was lecturer in mathematics at Manchester University, and then a fellow of St. John's College, Cambridge (1931–45). Goldstein became a fellow of the Royal Society in 1937. He was chairman of the Aeronautical Research Council (1946–49), and professor of applied mathematics at Manchester University 1945–50. Goldstein went to Israel in 1950, as vice-president of the Technion in Haifa and dean of the department of aeronautical engineering. In 1955 he became professor of applied mathematics at Harvard University in the U.S. Goldstein wrote numerous papers on applied mathematics (most dealing with aeronautics), and he was editor and coauthor of *Modern Developments in Fluid Dynamics* (1938) and *Lectures in Fluid Mechanics* (1960). [S.A.M.]

GOLDSTEIN, SIDNEY EMANUEL (1879–1955), U.S. Reform rabbi. Goldstein, who was born in Marshall, Texas, was ordained at the Hebrew Union College in 1905. From 1905 to 1907 he held the position of assistant superintendent at New York's Mt. Sinai Hospital. When the Free Synagogue was founded by Stephen S. Wise in 1907, Goldstein became associate rabbi and established and directed its Social Service department. The services instituted by Goldstein included a child-placement service and a program for assisting former mental patients to readjust to life outside the institution. Goldstein was a vigorous supporter of the labor, woman's suffrage, and civil rights movements, regarding the rabbi as a pioneer in social and community reform and the synagogue as the instrument for

Sidney Goldstein, a founder of the Jewish Institute of Religion in New York. Courtesy Hebrew Union College, New York.

implementing them. A founder of the Jewish Institute of Religion, Goldstein was professor of social service at the Institute from 1922. Long interested in the field of marriage counseling, Goldstein served as chairman of both the New York State Conference on Marriage and the Family from 1936 to 1947 and the Jewish Institute on Marriage and the Family from 1937. His numerous public activities included: chairman of the Central Conference of American Rabbis' Commission on Social Justice (1934–36); chairman of the executive committee of the War Resisters League of America (1930–40); chairman of the Joint Committee on Unemployment (1930–34); and executive committee member of the State of New York Committee on Discrimination in Employment (1941–44). His book, *The Synagogue and Social Welfare* (1955), studied the meaning of the synagogue and its relation to American life. [Ed.]

GOLDSTUECKER, EDUARD (1913–), Czech literary historian, author, and diplomat. In his youth he was active in the Ha-Shomer ha-Ẓa'ir movement in Slovakia but later became a Communist. Following the Nazi occupation of Czechoslovakia in 1938, Goldstuecker fled to England, where he studied at Oxford. In 1945 he returned to Prague, joined his country's diplomatic service, and, after a tour of duty in London, was appointed Czechoslovakia's first minister to Israel (1949–51). Goldstuecker later figured in the *Slánský trial and in 1952 was sentenced to life imprisonment for "anti-State" activities. Released after eight years, he was appointed professor of German literature at Prague University. An outspoken critic of the Party's interference in cultural affairs, Goldstuecker published a collection of studies on Franz *Kafka, *Na téma Franz Kafka* (1964). As a result of his efforts Kafka, who until then was taboo in the Communist world, was "rehabilitated" in Czechoslovakia and some other states of the Communist bloc. After the liberalization of the Czechoslovak regime in January 1968, Goldstuecker was elected president of the Czechoslovak Writers' Union and a member of the Czech National Council. After the Soviet invasion of Czechoslovakia in August 1968, Goldstuecker was a major target of criticism by the anti-liberal elements. He left the country and accepted a visiting professorship at the University of Sussex, England. In 1970 Goldstuecker was one of several Czechoslovak public figures accused of being agents of "Zionism and Imperialism" and tried in absentia. Goldstuecker for his part maintained that his Jewish origin was a major reason for his persecution by "Stalinist ruling circles" in Czechoslovakia. [Av.D.]

GOLDWASSER, ISRAEL EDWIN (1878–), U.S. educator, financier, and philanthropist. Goldwasser was born in New York City, and began public school teaching in 1897. He eventually became a principal and the youngest district superintendent of schools in New York City (1914–17), publishing several educational works, including *Method and Methods in Teaching English* (1912) and *Yiddish English Lessons* (with Joseph Jablonower, 1914). In 1920 Goldwasser entered business as a factor, becoming president of an investment firm during the 1930's, and retired in 1954 after nearly 15 years with the Commercial Factors Corporation. Subsequently he served as an economic consultant and took a special interest in economic projects in Israel. Goldwasser was a leading figure in many Jewish communal organizations, such as the Federation of Jewish Philanthropies, of which he was the first executive director (1917–20). His son, EDWIN L. GOLDWASSER (1919–), was codirector of the National Accelerator Laboratory in Weston, Illinois, the world's largest atom smasher. [ED.]

GOLDWATER, family of early settlers in Arizona and the American West. Originally named "Goldwasser," the first of the family to reach America were the brothers MICHAEL and JOSEPH, who were born in Konin, Poland, in the 1820s. They emigrated first to Germany, then to England, where they worked as cap makers, and in 1852, along with Michael's young wife, to the United States. Attracted by the gold rush, they went West, selling whiskey and hardware to the miners and then settling in Los Angeles, where they operated a combined general store and saloon. In 1862 Michael Goldwater led a mule train to the gold-rush settlement of La Paz, Arizona, along the Colorado River. He remained in the area and later founded the town of Ehrenburg, which he named after a friend who had been killed by Indians. Subsequently he was joined by his brother Joseph and the two opened a large store in Phoenix and another in Prescott. Michael retired in 1883 and died in 1903, leaving the business, Goldwater Inc., to his sons MORRIS and BARON. Baron married an Episcopalian. Their son, BARRY M. GOLDWATER (1909–), served as U.S. senator from Arizona from 1952 to 1964 and again from 1968, and was the unsuccessful presidential candidate of the Republican Party in 1964.

Bibliography: O. Jensen, in: *American Heritage* (June 1964).

[ED.]

GOLDWATER, SIGMUND SCHULZ (1873–1942), U.S. consultant in hospital administration and design. Goldwater was born in New York City. Joining Mount Sinai Hospital in New York, he rose to the position of director, a post he held during 1917–29. At the same time, Goldwater became a registered architect, and gained an international reputation as an expert consultant in hospital design and administration. In 1914 New York Mayor John Mitchell appointed him health commissioner, later citing his accomplishments in reorganizing the department. Goldwater served as commissioner of hospitals under Mayor La Guardia for six years starting in 1934, and worked to rejuvenate the city's aging facilities. An advocate of extending private health insurance to lower income groups, Goldwater became president of the Associated Hospital Service in 1940. [R.SK.]

GOLDWYN (Goldfish), SAMUEL (1882–), U.S. *motion-picture producer. Born in Warsaw, he went to the U.S. at the age of 13. He worked in a glove factory and at the age of 30 owned a successful glove company. In 1913 Goldwyn entered the motion-picture industry as an associate of his brother-in-law, Jesse L. *Lasky, and Cecil B. de Mille. Their first production, *The Squaw Man,* perhaps the first feature-length film made in Hollywood, was an instant success. Two years later Goldwyn joined Edgar and Archibald Selwyn to form the Goldwyn Pictures Corporation (using the first syllable of Goldfish and the last of Selwyn), adopting the name as his own.

Samuel Goldwyn, U.S. film producer. Courtesy Jewish Theatrical Guild, New York.

The spectacular period of his career opened when in 1923 he began making films independently and a year later converted his interest in Goldwyn Pictures to form Metro-Goldwyn-Mayer. He endowed his films with talent and imagination, and left his own distinctive mark on them.

He introduced and produced many popular actors and hired distinguished writers including Maeterlinck, Robert Sherwood, and Lillian Hellman.

He became a legend in the film industry and many malapropisms were attributed to him. Goldwyn assigned his profits to the Samuel Goldwyn Foundation for assisting scholars and philanthropic causes. [JO.R.]

GOLDZIHER, IGNAZ (Isaac Judah; 1850–1921), Hungarian scholar, one of the founders of modern Islamic scholarship. Goldziher, born in Szekesfehervar (Stuhlweissenburg), attended the lectures of A. *Vambery at the University of Budapest while he was still a high-school pupil. He studied Arabic manuscripts at Leyden and Vienna and traveled in Egypt, Palestine, and Syria before becoming a lecturer at the University of Budapest in 1872. As his university teaching was unpaid until he became a professor in 1904, he earned his living as secretary of the Budapest Neolog Jewish community for 30 years. In 1900 he succeeded D. *Kaufmann as professor of religious philosophy at the Budapest Rabbinical Seminary. Goldziher was elected a member of the Hungarian Academy of Sciences long before his appointment to a professorship in the university. He was respected by Muslim scholars and received queries from them; he was invited to lecture at Fuad University in Cairo but did not accept the position. When the Jewish National Home was established in Palestine after World War I, it was hoped that Goldziher would use his influence in the Muslim world to help bring about a rapprochement between Jews and Arabs, but he was far from being a Zionist, and refused to act on this matter. Goldziher was the first to describe critically and comprehensibly the history of Islamic oral tradition (*hadith) and the various Islamic sects; he published many studies, still valuable, on pre-Islamic and Islamic culture, the religious and legal history of the Arabs, and their ancient and modern poetry. He was one of the initiators of the *Enzyklopaedie des Islam* (4 vols., 1913–36), and was among its contributors. Goldziher's principal works in this field are: *Beitraege zur Literaturgeschichte der Shīʿa und der sunnitischen Polemik* (1874); *Die Zâhiriten* . . . (1884); *Muhammedanische Studien* (2 vols., 1889–90; Eng. tr. *Muslim Studies,* ed. by S. M. Stern, 1967); *Abhandlungen* *zur arabischen Philologie* (2 vols., 1896–99); *Vorlesungen ueber den Islam* (1910, 1925²); and *Die Richtungen der islamischen Koranauslegung* (1920). Goldziher also made valuable contributions to Jewish scholarship. At the age of 12 he published *Si'aḥ Yiẓḥak*, an essay on the Jewish prayers. His doctoral dissertation was devoted to the 13th-century Arab-Jewish philologist and Bible commentator *Tanḥum Yerushalmi. He wrote for Hungarian and German Jewish periodicals and in various Festschriften on problems of Jewish scholarship, in particular about the relations between Islam and Judaism, and on Muslim criticism of the Pentateuch, the Talmud, and the "people of the book" in general. Goldziher's Islamic and Jewish studies complemented each other; he was able to draw many parallels between the two religions, pointing out their differences as well.

Among his major publications in Jewish studies are: *Der Mythos bei den Hebraeern* . . . (1876; *Mythology among the Hebrews* . . ., 1877); "Mélanges judéo-arabes" (in REJ, vols. 43–60, 1901–10); and "Islamische und juedische Philosophie des Mittelalters" and "Religion des Islams," in *Die Kultur der Gegenwart* (vol. 1 pt. 3, 1906). With W. Wundt and H. Oldenberg he edited *Allgemeine Geschichte der Philosophie* (1909). Goldziher reviewed critically various editions of the Arabic originals of important medieval philosophical and halakhic texts and himself edited pseudo-Baḥya's *Kitâb Ma'ânî al-Nafs* (1907). He also wrote on modern Hebrew poetry (in JQR, 14 [1902], 719–36). His general views on Judaism were presented in *A zsidóság lényege és fejlődése* ("Essence and Evolution of Judaism," 2 vols., 1923–24), and in a lecture delivered in Stockholm ("Tradition und Dogma" in AZDJ, 78 (1914), 6–8, 22–23, 33–35; Eng. tr. in *Reform Advocate*, 47 (1914), 39–42). Goldziher served on the editorial board of the *Jewish Encyclopedia* (1901–06), to which he contributed many articles. An *Ignace Goldziher Memorial Volume* was published in two parts (1948–58) by S. Loewinger, J. Somogyi, and A. Scheiber. A collection of his writings was edited in three volumes by J. Desomogyi as *Gesammelte Schriften* (1967–69), and a bibliography of his works was published by B. Heller, *Bibliographie des oeuvres* . . . (1927) and of his Hebrew writings was compiled by S. D. Goitein (in KS, 23 (1946/47), 251–7). After his death, Goldziher's valuable library and his extensive scholarly correspondence was acquired by the National and University Library in Jerusalem.

Bibliography: H. Loewe, *Ignaz Goldziher* (Ger., 1929); A. S. Yahuda, in: JC Literary Supplement (April 25, 1924); idem, in: *Der Jude*, 8 (1924), 575–92; L. Massignon, in: B. Heller, *Bibliographie des oeuvres de Ignace Goldziher* (1927), introduction; M. Plessner, in: I. Goldziher, *Harẓa'ot al ha-Islam* (1951), 289–309; J. Nemeth, in: *Acta Orientalia Academiae Hungariae*, 1 (1950–51), 7–24; S. Loewinger, in: S. Federbusch (ed.), *Ḥokhmat Yisrael be-Ma'arav Eiropah* (1958), 166–81.

[M.PL./ED.]

GOLEM (Heb. גֹּלֶם), a creature, particularly a human being, made in an artificial way by virtue of a magic act, through the use of holy names. The idea that it is possible to create living beings in this manner is widespread in the magic of many peoples. Especially well known are the idols and images to which the ancients claimed to have given the power of speech. Among the Greeks and the Arabs these activities are sometimes connected with astrological speculations related to the possibility of "drawing the spirituality of the stars" to lower beings (see *Astrology). The development of the idea of the *golem* in Judaism, however, is remote from astrology: it is connected, rather, with the magical exegesis of the *Sefer *Yeẓirah* ("Book of Creation") and with the ideas of the creative power of speech and of the letters.

The word *"golem"* appears only once in the Bible (Ps. 139:16), and from it originated the talmudic usage of the term—something unformed and imperfect. In philosophic usage it is matter without form. Adam is called *"golem,"* meaning body without soul, in a talmudic legend concerning the first 12 hours of his existence (Sanh. 38b). However, even in this state, he was accorded a vision of all the generations to come (Gen. R. 24:2), as if there were in the *golem* a hidden power to grasp or see, bound up with the element of earth from which he was taken. The motif of the *golem* as it appears in medieval legends originates in the talmudic legend (Sanh. 65b): "Rava created a man and sent him to R. Zera. The latter spoke to him but he did not answer. He asked, 'Are you one of the companions? Return to your dust.' " It is similarly told that two *amoraim* busied themselves on the eve of every Sabbath with the *Sefer Yeẓirah* (or in another version *Hilkhot Yeẓirah*) and made a calf for themselves and ate it. These legends are brought as evidence that "If the righteous wished, they could create a world." They are connected, apparently, with the belief in the creative power of the letters of the Name of God and the letters of the Torah in general (Ber. 55a; Mid. Ps. 3). There is disagreement as to whether the *Sefer Yeẓirah* or *Hilkhot Yeẓirah*, mentioned in the Talmud, is the same book called by these two titles which we now possess. Most of this book is of a speculative nature, but its affinity to the magical ideas concerning creation by means of letters is obvious. What is said in the main part of the book about God's act during creation is attributed at the end of the book to *Abraham the Patriarch. The various transformations and combinations of the letters constitute a mysterious knowledge of the inwardness of creation. During the Middle Ages, *Sefer Yeẓirah* was interpreted in some circles in France and Germany as a guide to magical usage. Later legends in this direction were first found at the end of the commentary on the *Sefer Yeẓirah* by *Judah b. Barzillai (beginning of the 12th century). There the legends of the Talmud were interpreted in a new way: at the conclusion of profound study of the mysteries of *Sefer Yeẓirah* on the construction of the cosmos, the sages (as did Abraham the Patriarch) acquired the power to create living beings, but the purpose of such creation was purely symbolic and contemplative, and when the sages wanted to eat the calf which was created by the power of their "contemplation" of the book, they forgot all they had learned. From these late legends there developed among the Ḥasidei Ashkenaz in the 12th and 13th centuries the idea of the creation of the *golem* as a mystical ritual, which was used, apparently, to symbolize the level of their achievement at the conclusion of their studies. In this circle, the term "*golem*" has, for the first time, the fixed meaning indicating such a creature.

In none of the early sources is there any mention of any practical benefit to be derived from a *golem* of this sort. In the opinion of the mystics, the creation of the *golem* had not a real, but only a symbolic meaning; that is to say, it was an ecstatic experience which followed a festive rite. Those who took part in the "act of creation" took earth from virgin soil and made a *golem* out of it (or, according to another source, they buried that *golem* in the soil), and walked around the *golem* "as in a dance," combining the alphabetical letters and the secret Name of God in accordance with detailed sets of instructions (several of which have been preserved). As a result of this act of combination, the *golem* arose and lived, and when they walked in the opposite direction and said the same combination of letters in reverse order, the vitality of the *golem* was nullified and he sank or fell. According to other legends, the word *emet* (אמת; "truth"; "the seal of the Holy One," Shab. 55a; Sanh. 64b) was written on his forehead, and when the letter *alef* was erased there remained the word *met* ("dead"). There are legends concerning the creation of such a *golem* by the prophet *Jeremiah and his so-called "son" *Ben Sira, and also by the disciples of R. *Ishmael, the central figure of the *Heikhalot* literature. The technical instructions about the manner of uttering the combinations, and everything involved in the rite, proves that the creation of the *golem* is connected here with ecstatic spiritual experiences (end of commentary on *Sefer Yeẓirah* by *Eleazar of Worms; the chapter *Sha'ashu'ei ha-Melekh* in N. Bachrach's *Emek ha-Melekh* (Amsterdam, 1648); and in the commentary on *Sefer Yeẓirah* (Zolkiew, 1744–45) attributed to *Saadiah b. Joseph Gaon). In the legends about the *golem* of Ben Sira there is also a parallel to the legends on images used in idol worship which are given life by means of a name; the *golem* expresses a warning about it (idol worship) and demands his own death. It is said in several sources that the *golem* has no intellectual soul, and therefore he lacks the power of speech, but opposite opinions are also found which attribute this power to him. The opinions of the kabbalists concerning the nature of the creation of the *golem* vary. Moses *Cordovero thought that man has the power to give "vitality" alone to the *golem* but not life *(nefesh)*, spirit *(ru'aḥ)*, or soul proper *(neshamah)*.

In the popular legend which adorned the figures of the leaders of the Ashkenazi ḥasidic movement with a crown of wonders, the *golem* became an actual creature who served his creators and fulfilled tasks laid upon him. Legends such as these began to make their appearance among German Jews in the 15th century and spread widely, so that by the 17th century they were "told by all" (according to Joseph Solomon *Delmedigo). In the development of the later legend of the *golem* there are three outstanding points: (1) The legend is connected with earlier tales of the resurrection of the dead by putting the name of God in their mouths or on their arm, and by removing the parchment containing the name in reverse and thus causing their death. Such legends were widespread in Italy from the tenth century (in *Megillat* *Aḥima'aẓ). (2) It is related to ideas current in non-Jewish circles concerning the creation of an alchemical man (the "homunculus" of Paracelsus). (3) The *golem*, who is the servant of his creator, develops dangerous natural powers; he grows from day to day, and in order to keep him from overpowering the members of the household he must be restored to his dust by removing or erasing the *alef* from his forehead. Here, the idea of the *golem* is joined by the new motive of the unrestrained power of the elements which can bring about destruction and havoc. Legends of this sort appeared first in connection with Elijah, rabbi of Chelm (d. 1583). Ẓevi Hirsch *Ashkenazi and his son Jacob Emden, who were among his descendants, discussed in their responsa whether or not it is permitted to include a *golem* of this sort in a *minyan* (they prohibited it). Elijah Gaon of Vilna told his disciple *Ḥayyim b. Isaac of Volozhin that as a boy he too had undertaken to make a *golem*, but he saw a vision which caused him to desist from his preparations.

The latest and best-known form of the popular legend is connected with *Judah Loew b. Bezalel of Prague. This legend has no historical basis in the life of Loew or in the era close to his lifetime. It was transferred from R. Elijah of Chelm to R. Loew only at a very late date, apparently during the second half of the 18th century. As a local legend of Prague, it is connected with the Altneuschul synagogue and with an explanation of special practices in the prayers of the congregation of Prague. According to these legends, R. Loew created the *golem* so that he would serve him, but was forced to restore him to his dust when the *golem* began to run amok and endanger people's lives. [G.SCH.]

In the Arts. The legends concerning the *golem*, especially in their later forms, served as a favorite literary subject, at first in German literature—of both Jews and non-Jews—in the 19th century, and afterward in modern Hebrew and Yiddish literature. To the domain of belles lettres also belongs the book *Nifla'ot Maharal im ha-Golem* ("The Miraculous Deeds of Rabbi Loew with the Golem"; 1909), which was published by Judah Rosenberg as an early manuscript but actually was not written until after the *blood libels of the 1890s. The connection between the *golem* and the struggle against ritual murder accusations is entirely a modern literary invention. In this literature questions are discussed which had no place in the popular legends (e.g., the *golem*'s love for a woman), or symbolic interpretations of the meaning of the *golem* were raised (the unredeemed, unformed man; the Jewish people; the working class aspiring for its liberation).

Interest in the *golem* legend among writers, artists, and musicians became evident in the early 20th century. The *golem* was almost invariably the benevolent robot of the later Prague tradition and captured the imagination of writers active in Austria, Czechoslovakia, and Germany. Two early works on the subject were the Austrian playwright Rudolf *Lothar's volume of stories entitled *Der Golem. Phantasien und Historien* (1900, 1904[2]) and the German novelist Arthur *Holitscher's three-act drama *Der Golem* (1908). The Prague German-language poet Hugo *Salus published verse on "Der hohe Rabbi Loew" and by World War I the theme had gained widespread popularity. The outstanding work about the *golem* was the novel entitled *Der Golem* (1915; Eng. 1928) by the Bavarian writer Gustav Meyrink (1868–1932), who spent many years in Prague. Meyrink's book, notable for its detailed description and nightmare atmosphere, was a terrifying allegory about man's reduction to an automaton by the pressures of modern society. Other works on the subject include Johannes Hess's *Der Rabbiner von Prag (Reb Loeb)*... (1914), a four-act "kabbalistic drama;" Chayim Bloch's *Der Prager Golem: von seiner "Geburt" bis zu seinem "Tod"* (1917; *The Golem. Legends of the Ghetto of Prague*, 1925); and *Ha-Golem* (1909), a story by the Hebrew writer David *Frischmann which later appeared in his collection *Ba-Midbar* (1923). The Yiddish dramatist H. *Leivick's *Der Golem* (1921; Eng., 1928) was first staged in Moscow in Hebrew by the Habimah Theater. Artistic and musical interpretations of the theme were dependent on the major literary works. Hugo Steiner-Prag produced lithographs to accompany Meyrink's novel (*Der Golem; Prager Phantasien*, 1915), the book itself inspiring a classic German silent film directed by Paul Wegener and Henrik Galeen (1920), and a later French remake by Julien Duvivier (1936). The screenplay for a post-World War II Czech film about the *golem* was written by Arnost *Lustig. Music for Leivick's drama was written by Moses *Milner; and Eugen d'Albert's opera *Der Golem*, with libretto by F. Lion, had its première at Frankfort in 1926, but has not survived in the operatic repertory. A more lasting work was Joseph *Achron's *Golem Suite* for orchestra (1932), composed under the influence of the Habimah production. The last piece of this suite was written as the first movement's exact musical image in reverse to symbolize the disintegration of the homunculus. *Der Golem*, a ballet by Francis Burt with choreography by Erika Hanka, was produced in Vienna in 1962. [ED.]

Bibliography: Ch. Bloch, *The Golem* (1925); H. L. Held, *Das Gespenst des Golems* (1927); B. Rosenfeld, *Die Golemsage und ihre Verwertung in der deutschen Literatur* (1934); G. Scholem, *On the Kabbalah and its Symbolism* (1965), 158–204; F. Thieberger, *The Great Rabbi Loew of Prague: his Life and Work and the Legend of the Golem* (1954).

GOLIATH (Heb. גָּלְיָת), Philistine warrior from the city of Gath (I Sam. 17:23) who advanced from the ranks of the Philistines when they faced the Israelites in battle in the Valley of Elah (I Sam. 17). Because of Goliath's great size, he is described as a *rafah* (Raphah; II Sam. 21:19–20; I Chron. 20:8), the *Rephaim being among the ancient people of Canaan who were regarded as giants (Deut. 2:11). Goliath was equipped with heavy armor and weapons— a bronze helmet, a coat of mail, bronze greaves, a bronze javelin slung between his shoulders, and a heavy

Miniature of Goliath about to be attacked by David, from the *British Museum Miscellany.* London, British Museum. Add. Ms. 11639, fol 523b.

spear with a head of iron. This fighting equipment was typical of that carried by warriors from the countries of the Aegean Sea, the region from which the *Philistines came. Goliath's defiant call for the battle to be decided by the outcome of a duel with a warrior from the enemy's camp (I Sam. 17:8–10) was also a customary practice among the peoples of that region, although there are parallels to such single combat in Egyptian sources also. His appearance and his boastful words struck terror into the poorly armed Israelite warriors. However, thanks to his courage, faith, and agility, the young *David managed to kill Goliath with a slingstone aimed at the Philistine's forehead (*ibid.* 17:50). David's victory caused the rout of the Philistine army (17:51–53). Goliath's head was brought to Jerusalem (17:54), while his sword was hung up and kept in the temple at Nob (21:10; 22:10). *Ahimelech the priest later returned the sword to David when he arrived at Nob in his flight from King Saul (21:10). In II Samuel 21:19 it is stated that Elhanan the Beth-Lehemite, one of David's captains, slew Goliath. This contradiction was noticed by the author of Chronicles, who attempted to resolve it by representing Elhanan as having killed "Lahmi, the brother of Goliath the Gittite" (I Chron. 20:5). Some scholars hold that Elhanan was David's original name, which was later changed to David. [B.O.]

In the Aggadah. Goliath was related to his vanquisher David, being descended from Orpah, Ruth's sister-in-law (Sot. 42b). Orpah was a woman of low character and morals, but as a reward for the 40 steps which she took in following Naomi before leaving for Moab, Goliath was permitted to flaunt his strength for 40 days before his downfall (Ruth R. 2:20). Goliath appeared "morning and evening," when the *Shema* was to be recited, to make Israel omit this affirmation of faith (Sot. 42b). The name Goliath is interpreted allegorically as a reflection of effrontery *(gillui panim)* in profaning the name of God. He is described as *"ish ha-beinayim"* ("champion") because he was built like a *binyan* ("building"; *ibid.*). "When David looked at Goliath and saw that he was a mighty man armed with all kinds of weapons, he said, 'Who can prevail against such as he?' But when David saw him reviling and blaspheming, he said: 'Now I shall prevail against him, for there is no fear of God in him'" (Mid. Ps., 36:2). David cast upon him the evil eye and he was struck with leprosy which rooted him to the ground (Lev. R. 21:2). When he fell, an angel pressed his face into the ground, choking the mouth which had blasphemed God (*ibid.* 10:7). [Ed.]

In Islam. In connection with the war of *Saul, who is known as Tālūt in the Koran, Muhammad relates that a number of the people of Israel doubted whether they could overcome Jālūt (Goliath) and his army. Allah however granted them courage and strength, and Dā'ūd (see *David) killed Goliath (Sura 2:250–2). The details of the duel between David and Goliath are retold in the post-Koranic literature as they are stated in the Bible. Muslim legend relates that Jālūt was one of the kings of Canaan; this is linked to the legend that he came from the Amalekites-Berbers. Goliath is briefly mentioned in the *Qaṣīda,* which is attributed to al-Samaw'al ibn ʿAdiyā: "and on the misfortune of ʿIfrīs when he rebelled against God and on Goliath when his fate caught up with him." According to J. W. (H. Z.) Hirschberg, the name ʿIfrīs is similar in form to Idrīs-Iblīs (Satan), which is a strange change of the Philistine name. However, it is possible that this is an allusion to the *aggadah* tracing Goliath's descent from Orpah (see above). According to Horowitz (see bibliography), the name Jālūt was influenced by the word *galut,* which Muhammad often heard in Medina. There is a spring in the valley of Jezreel (Israel) which is known to the Arabs as ʿAyn Jālūt (today En-Harod; cf. Judg. 7:1).

For Goliath in the Arts see *David, In the Arts. [H.Z.H.]

Bibliography: Y. Yadin, *The Art of Warfare in Biblical Lands,* 2 (1963), 265ff.; idem, in: *Eretz Israel,* 4 (1956), 68ff.; Sukenik (Yadin), in: JPOS, 21 (1948), 114–6; de Vaux, in: *Biblica,* 40 (1959), 495–508 (Fr.); de Boer, in: OTS, 1 (1942), 78–104. In the Aggadah: Ginzberg, Legends, index. In Islam: J. W. Hirschberg, *Der Dīwān des As-Samau'al ibn ʿAdijā'* . . . (1931), 2, 61; EIS³, 2 (1965), 406 s.v. *Djālūt,* incl. bibl.; J. Horovitz, *Koranische Untersuchungen* (1926), 106.

Mordecai Golinkin, Israel opera conductor. Photo Prior, Tel Aviv.

GOLINKIN, MORDECAI (1875–1963), conductor and pioneer of opera in Israel. Golinkin was born in Izluchistaya in the Ukrainian province of Kherson and as a boy sang in the choir of Phinehas *Minkowsky. In 1918 he became conductor at the Maryinsky Opera Theater in Petrograd. He conceived the idea of establishing an Opera in Palestine and gave a concert with the singer Chaliapin to raise funds for the project on which he published a pamphlet in 1920. In 1923 Golinkin immigrated to Palestine and in July of that year staged a performance in Hebrew of *La Traviata*, with local and guest singers, in Tel Aviv. His company, the Palestine Opera, gave intermittent opera performances until 1948, when he became conductor of the Israel Opera, a post he held until 1953. Golinkin's writings include *The Temple of Art* (1927, Hebrew and English), a volume of memoirs *Me-Heikhalei Yefet le-Oholei Shem* ("From the Palaces of Japheth to the Tents of Shem," 1947), and *Ha-Historyah ba-Opera* ("History in the Opera," 1961). [YE.G.]

°**GOLITSYN, COUNT NIKOLAI NIKOLAYEVICH** (1836–1893), Russian author and government official. While holding governmental positions in the *Pale of Settlement, and as editor of the semiofficial newspaper *Varshavskiy Dnevnik*, Golitsyn undertook an inquiry into the Jewish problem in Russia. He wrote studies and articles on the subject with an anti-Jewish approach during the 1870s, achieving the reputation among upper government circles of being an expert on the Jewish problem, and in 1883 was appointed by the ministry of the interior a member of the "High Commission for the Revision of the Current Laws Concerning the Jews" (the Von Pahlen Commission). In this connection, Golitsyn prepared a series of studies and memoranda, the most important of which was *Istoriya russkogo zakonodatelstva o yevreyakh 1649–1825 gg.* ("History of Russian Legislation Concerning the Jews 1649–1825"). The book, of 1,116 pages, provides an abundance of documents drawn from archives and is therefore of value. It was published in 1886 in 300 copies. Despite his anti-Jewish outlook, Golitsyn agreed with the conclusions of the Commission which recommended the gradual abolition of the restrictions against the Jews (1888).

Bibliography: YE, 6 (c. 1910), 623; Dubnow, Hist Russ, 1 (1916), 392ff.; 2 (1918), 74ff.; I. Levitats, *Jewish Community in Russia, 1772–1844* (1943), 91, 102–4. [Y.S.]

GOLL, YVAN (1891–1950), Franco-German poet and author. Born in Saint-Dié, Vosges, Goll studied at the universities of Strasbourg and Paris. He was at first active in German expressionist circles, publishing *Lothringische Volkslieder* (1912), *Der Panamakanal* (1912), *Der Torso* (1918), and *Die Unterwelt* (1919). During World War I he lived in Switzerland, where he married the writer Claire Studer. His sympathies transcended political boundaries, and he followed his *Requiem pour les morts de l'Europe* (1916) with a German version, *Requiem fuer die Gefallenen von Europa* (1917). After the war Goll settled in Paris. There, in 1924, he established the magazine *Surréalisme*. Goll was a friend of James Joyce and Stefan *Zweig and published the first German translation of Joyce's novel *Ulysses*. Until 1925 he continued to write in German, his books including *Das Herz des Feindes* (1920), *Der Eiffelturm* (1924), and the drama *Der Stall des Augias* (1924). Together with his wife, Goll published three anthologies of French verse: *Poèmes d'amour* (1925), *Poèmes de jalousie* (1926), and *Poèmes de la vie et de la mort* (1926). These were followed by four novels. Jewish themes constantly recur in the rich and complex work of this cosmopolitan poet. Prominent among them are loneliness, eternal wandering between two worlds and three languages, the haunting presence of poverty, war, and death, and the search for salvation in occult and kabbalistic speculation. The figures of Job and of the *Wandering Jew merge with the homeless poet himself in a major verse

Portrait of Yvan Goll on the cover of a collection of French poems published by Seghers, Paris. Courtesy Pierre L'Herminier, Paris.

collection *La Chanson de Jean sans Terre* (3 vols., 1936–39; *Jean sans Terre*, Eng., 1958), where the only certainty in a foundering universe is total annihilation. In 1939 Goll and his wife fled to the U.S. While they were living in New York he published the literary magazine, *Hémisphères*, and a volume of English poems, *Fruit from Saturn* (1946). In 1947 they returned to Paris, where he died. On his sickbed Goll reverted to writing in German. Two volumes of poetry appeared after his death: *Traumkraut* (1951) and *Neila* (1954), and two other posthumous works were *Abendgesang* (1954) and a play, *Melusine* (1956). Other late works of Yvan Goll are *Le Char Triomphal de l'Antimoine* (1949), *Les Géorgiques parisiennes* (1951), and *Les Cercles magiques* (1951). His scattered publications were collected by his widow in *Dichtungen: Lyrik, Prosa, Drama* (1960). His wife, CLAIRE GOLL (1901–), wrote *Éducation barbare* (1941), *Arsénic* (Fr., 1945), and a novella, *Der Selbstmord eines Hundes* (1964), which was illustrated by the Golls' close friend, Mark Chagall.

Bibliography: J.F. Carmody, *The Poetry of Yvan Goll* (1956); H. Friedmann and O. Mann, *Expressionismus* (1956), 192–203, 354; C. Heselhaus, *Deutsche Lyrik der Moderne von Nietzsche bis Yvan Goll* (1961), 420–30; J. Mueller, *Yvan Goll im deutschen Expressionismus* (1962). [C.A.V.]

GOLLANCZ, SIR HERMANN (1852–1930), rabbi and teacher. Gollancz was born in Bremen and was the brother of Sir Israel *Gollancz. He officiated at the Bayswater Synagogue (1892–1923) and taught Hebrew at University College, London (1902–24). In 1897, when he received the rabbinic diploma on the Continent from three Galician rabbis, he became the center of a controversy over whether the rabbinic title should be a recognized qualification for the Anglo-Jewish clergy with the ultimate result that the title was so recognized. Gollancz published a number of critical editions and translations from Hebrew, Aramaic, and Syriac, including a Hebrew and English edition of *Sefer Mafte'aḥ Shelomo* (1914) and also of Joseph Kimḥi's *Shekel ha-Kodesh* (1919). Hermann was the first English rabbi to receive a knighthood (1923).

Bibliography: Loewe, in: DNB (1922–1930), 350–1; H. Gollancz, *Personalia* (includes bibliography); P. H. Emden, *Jews of Britain* (1943), 123–5. [C.R.]

GOLLANCZ, SIR ISRAEL (1864–1930), English literary scholar. Gollancz, son of the Rev. Samuel Marcus Gollancz, minister of the Hambro Synagogue in London and a brother of Rabbi Sir Hermann *Gollancz, was lecturer in English at University College, London (1892–95), and then at Cambridge. In 1903 he was appointed professor of English at King's College, London. An outstanding Shakespearean scholar, Gollancz also made important contributions to the study of early English literature and philology. His works include an edition and translation of the 14th-century alliterative poem, *Pearl* (1891), an edition of Marlowe's *Dr. Faustus* (1897), *The Sources of Hamlet* (1926), and *The Caedmon MS of Anglo-Saxon Biblical Poetry* . . . (1927). He was also general editor of the Temple Classics and of the highly successful Temple Shakespeare. Gollancz did not confine his activities to the area of English literature. In 1902 he helped to found the British Academy, of which he remained secretary until his death. In this capacity he was instrumental in establishing the British School of Archaeology in Jerusalem in 1920. He was knighted in 1919. He took an interest in Jewish affairs, especially in the training of rabbis. He also served on the council of Jews' College, London, for some years.

Bibliography: DNB, supplement, 4 (1937), 351–2. [H.F.]

GOLLANCZ, SIR VICTOR (1893–1967), English publisher and author. The grandson of a *ḥazzan* and nephew of Rabbi Sir Hermann *Gollancz and Sir Israel *Gollancz, Victor Gollancz early rejected his family's religious Orthodoxy and all middle-class conservatism. Appalled by poverty and suffering, he sought to combat these ills through socialism and, later, pacifism. While an undergraduate at Oxford, he took a brief interest in Liberal Judaism, but was increasingly drawn toward Christianity, although he never formally converted. After a period as a classics teacher Gollancz entered publishing, and in 1928 founded his own publishing house. In 1936, together with John Strachey and Harold *Laski, he established the Left Book Club, whose aim was to expose Nazism and to "halt Hitler with war." Their success in providing informative books at low cost was a remarkable feat of political publishing. The club, which became a nationwide social and political movement, had some 60,000 members at its peak, but did not survive the Nazi-Soviet pact of 1939, which for Gollancz was an intolerable betrayal.

During World War II Gollancz campaigned for the National Committee for Rescue from Nazi Terror, an organization which tried to save some of Hitler's victims. Later he sponsored other humanitarian causes, such as the "Save Europe Now" campaign to alleviate starvation in Germany in the post-World War II period, the Association for World Peace (later known as "War on Want"), and the

Sir Victor Gollancz, English publisher.

British campaign against capital punishment. Although from 1945 onward he fought the Palestine policy of British foreign secretary Ernest Bevin and endeavored to secure the admission of Jewish refugees to Palestine, Gollancz behaved characteristically when he headed an organization for relief work for the Arabs during Israel's War of Independence and later for Arab refugees in the Gaza Strip. He advocated reconciliation between Jews and Germans and between Jews and Arabs. At the same time he was on the board of governors of the Hebrew University in Jerusalem from 1952 to 1964.

A *bon vivant* with mystic longings, a successful businessman who opposed capitalism, an idealist tortured by a guilt complex, Gollancz wrote on many subjects. His books include: *The Brown Book of the Hitler Terror* (1933); a translation (1943) of *Why I Am A Jew* by Edmond *Fleg; two autobiographical works addressed to his grandson, *My Dear Timothy* (1952) and *More for Timothy* (1953); *The Case of Adolf Eichmann* (1961), which expressed his total opposition to the trial of the Nazi criminal; and several religious anthologies and essays on music. He was knighted in 1965. [RE.W.]

GOLLER, IZAK (1891–1939), English author and rabbi. Born in Lithuania, Goller was taken to England as a child. He served congregations in Manchester, London, and finally the Hope Place Synagogue in Liverpool, where his advanced social views and outspoken addresses led to his dismissal in 1926. With characteristic defiance, Goller thereupon reestablished himself in the Young Israel (Zionist) Synagogue in Liverpool. His verse collection, *The Passionate Jew and Cobbles of the God-Road* (1923), violently denounced the atrocities committed against the Jews of Eastern Europe after World War I. It was followed by *A Jew Speaks!* (1926), a book of poetry and prose which, like many of Goller's subsequent publications, was illustrated with the author's original "cartoons." Goller's novel, *The Five Books of Mr. Moses* (1929), was dramatized as *Cohen and Son* (1937), a Jewish mystery play in "three acts, ten scenes, and a melody," and first performed in London in 1932. Other plays on Jewish themes were *Judah and Tamar, Modin Women,* and *A Purim Night's Dream* (all in 1931), and *The Scroll of Lot's Wife* (1937). A statement of his faith as a Jew was contained in *First Chapter—A Summary of the History of My People from Abraham of Ur to Herzl of Budapest* (1936).

Bibliography: Temkin, in: JC (June 30, 1939); G. E. Silverman, in: *Liverpool Jewish Gazette* (June 24, 1960); idem, in: *Niv ha-Midrashiyyah* (Spring 1970), 74–81, English section. [G.E.S.]

GOLLUF, ELEAZAR (d. 1389), courtier and agent of the royal family of Aragon; member of a prominent Saragossa family. In 1376 he was permitted to carry arms and exempted from wearing the Jewish *badge. From 1383 he served as agent of the infante John, son of Pedro IV of Aragon, and of his wife Violante. After John ascended the throne in 1387 Golluf served as "chief agent of the queen"—in fact her chief treasurer—a position that had not been held by a Jew in Aragon for a century. His ledgers are not preserved, and may have been intentionally destroyed even before the end of the Middle Ages. A devoted Jew, Golluf's activities in Jewish affairs extended beyond his own community. After Golluf's death, his son ISAAC converted to Christianity, first obtaining the king's promise that he should nevertheless inherit his father's property. His name as a Christian was Juan Sánchez de Calatayud. He was the grandfather of Gabriel *Sánchez, a leading official during the reign of Ferdinand and Isabella and a supporter of Christopher Columbus.

Bibliography: Baer, Spain, index s.v. *Alazar Golluf;* Baer, Urkunden, 1 (1929), 610–6; M. Serrano y Sanz, *Orígenes de la dominación española en América,* 1 (1918), 138, 502f.; Lóz de Meneses, in: *Sefarad,* 14 (1954), 110. [ED.]

GOLOMB, ABRAHAM (1888–), Yiddish writer and educator. Born in Lithuania, Golomb studied at yeshivot and at the University of Kiev. After teaching in Russia, he directed schools in Israel, Canada, and Mexico City. In his hundreds of articles and several volumes he expounded his ideology, "Integral Jewishness," which includes the language, festivals, religious observances, family relationships, and ideals of the Jews. This collective experience, he contends, is essential for the continued existence of the Jewish people. Like *Dubnow and *Aḥad Ha-Am, Golomb stresses the need for retaining Jewish distinctiveness in the Diaspora, holding that this will remain a continuing fact of Jewish historic life, no matter how much the Jewish center in Israel grows. Golomb called for maximum efforts to retain both Yiddish and Hebrew as national languages of the Jewish people. Diaspora communities which were giving up Yiddish and adopting alien tongues were becoming fossilized, incapable of future growth. Without Yiddish, the Jews outside Israel would be fragmentized into scattered dying remnants of a people. He asked for canonization of the finest products of the Yiddish language, as had been done with earlier holy works in Hebrew. Golomb enriched the Yiddish vocabulary of science and psychology. He supplemented his theoretical discourses with practical classroom texts. His selected works *Geklibene Shriftn* appeared in six volumes (1945–48).

Bibliography: Rejzen, Leksikon, 1 (1926), 464–6; S. Kahan, *Literarische un Zhurnalistische Fartseykhnungen* (1961), 259–62.

[S.L.]

GOLOMB, ELIYAHU (1893–1945), leader of Jewish defense in Palestine and main architect of the *Haganah. Born in Volkovysk, Belorussia, Golomb went to Ereẓ Israel in 1909 and was a pupil in the Herzlia High School's first graduating class of 1913. He organized his fellow graduates into the Histadrut Meẓumẓemet (approximately "The Inner Circle") for agricultural training, service in Jewish settlements, and the realization of Zionist ideals, and himself went to train at *Deganyah. At the outbreak of World War I he opposed the enlistment of young Jews as officers in the Turkish Army and insisted on the formation of an independent Jewish defense force. In 1918 Golomb was a founder and leading member of the movement to encourage volunteers for the *Jewish Legion, in which he served as a corporal. He hoped that the Legion would form the basis for a permanent official Jewish militia. While serving in the army, he became friendly with Berl *Katznelson and joined the *Aḥdut ha-Avodah Party upon its foundation in 1919. After his demobilization he became a member of the committee to organize the Haganah and was active in dispatching aid to the defenders of *Tel Ḥai (1920).

In contrast to the *Ha-Shomer policy, Golomb realized that Jewish defense was a matter for the Jewish population at large, and not the concern of an elite of fighters. He successfully propagated this idea among the leaders of the *yishuv*. From 1921 Golomb was a member of the Haganah Committee of the *Histadrut and, in 1922, was sent abroad to purchase arms; he was arrested by the Vienna police in July of that year. He purchased arms and organized pioneering youth in Europe until 1924. In 1931 he was one of the three representatives of the Histadrut in the Mifkadah ha-Arẓit, the parity National Command of the Haganah.

Golomb regarded the Haganah as the arm of the nation and of the Zionist Movement and thus brought it under the auspices of the national institutions, although these were unable to express their opinions on defense matters openly. In consequence, he was violently opposed to the dissident armed organizations, *Irgun Ẓeva'i Le'ummi and *Loḥamei Ḥerut Israel (Leḥi), but tried to avoid futile hatred and attempted to find ways of reuniting them with the main body. In 1939 and 1940 he and Berl Katznelson tried to reach an agreement with Vladimir *Jabotinsky and the Revisionists over the reunification of the Zionist movement and the formation of a single defense command.

Eliyahu Golomb, pioneer of Jewish defense in Palestine. Courtesy Keren Hayesod, United Israel Appeal, Jerusalem.

During the Arab riots of 1936–39 Golomb was one of the initiators of the "field units" *(pelugot sadeh)* that went out to confront Arab terrorists in combat. He thus supported active defense and the punishment of terrorists; but, for both moral and tactical reasons, he opposed indiscriminate reprisals against the Arab population. Golomb supported all forms of cooperation with the British authorities that permitted secret stockpiling of weapons and military training, but never forgot the fundamental conflict existing between the alien regime and the clandestine Haganah. He always opposed giving of information to the British concerning the strength and equipment of the Haganah. Golomb was among those who supported the enlistment of volunteers into the British Army during World War II and proposed the parachuting of Jews into occupied Europe. He was one of the founders and builders of the *Palmaḥ and prepared the Haganah for the future struggle of the Jewish people in Palestine. He inspired and educated many commanders of the Haganah and future officers of the Israel Defense Forces.

Golomb was active in Ereẓ Israel public life. He was a leader of Aḥdut ha-Avodah (later of *Mapai), and of the Histadrut; a member of the Va'ad Le'ummi, as well as a delegate to Zionist congresses. His articles appeared in the Hebrew labor press, and a number of them were collected into two volumes, *Ḥevyon Oz* (1950–54), which also included memoirs and reminiscences by his friends. His home in Tel Aviv was turned into a Haganah museum.

Bibliography: Dinur, Haganah, index; Z. Shazar, *Or Ishim* (1964²), 182–8; S. Avigur, *Im Dor ha-Haganah* (1962³), 143–73; M. Sharett, *Orot she-Kavu* (1969), 13–25; Y. Allon, *The Making of the Israeli Army* (1970).

[Y.E./H.H.B.-S.]

GOLOVANEVSK, small town S. of Uman in Ukrainian S.S.R. The Jewish population numbered 1,974 in 1847 and 4,320 (53% of the total population) in 1897. During the civil war of 1918–19 the community formed a strong *self-defense organization which deterred the peasants of the surrounding region from pogroms, and 2,000 refugees from neighboring localities found refuge in Golovanevsk. At the end of 1919, however, armed bands of peasants led by the hetman Sokolowski broke into the town, overcame the self-defense units, and carried out pogroms in which over 200 Jews lost their lives. There were 3,474 Jews (86% of the population) living in Golovanevsk in 1926. They were murdered after Golovanevsk was occupied by the Nazis in 1941.

Bibliography: I. Klinov, *In der Tekufah fun Revolutsye* (1923), 157–210; A. D. Rosental, *Megillat ha-Tevaḥ*, 2 (1931), 3–16. [Y.S.]

°**GOLUCHOWSKI, AGENOR, COUNT** (1812–1875), Austrian politician, minister of the interior, and three times governor of Galicia. A conservative and a fervent Polish patriot, he was an opponent of Jewish emancipation. Claiming to "discover" conflicts among the Jews, he aspired to lead the "enlightened" Jews against the Orthodox. However, in parliament, he was leader of those conservatives who, while masking their anti-Semitism, fought against any changes in the condition of the Jews. When the Lvov municipality had twice rejected the right of the Jews to quit the ghetto (1846, 1855), the problem came before Goluchowski as minister of interior; he gave the casting vote against the Jews. In 1857 he forbade Jews to employ Christian servants. While he introduced a project granting Jews the right to acquire real property in 1865, when his project was passed to a commission he made no attempt to defend it and it never became law.

Bibliography: W. Feldman, *Stronnictwa i programy*, 1 (1907), 47; M. Bałaban, *Dzieje Żydów w Galicji i w Rzeczypospolitej Krakowskiej* (1914), index; Ph. Friedmann, *Die galizischen Juden im Kaempfe um ihre Gleichberechtigung, 1848–1868* (1929), index; I. Schiper, *Żydzi w Polsce odrodzonej*, 1 (1932–33), 388–90; I. Shatzky, in: *Di Yidn in Poyln* (1946), 450; *Polski Słownik Biograficzny*, 8 (1959–60), 258–9; *Wielka Encyklopedia Powszechna*, 4 (1964), 311; J. Tenenbaum, *Galitsye, mayn alte Haym* (1952), 69–78; N. M. Gelber, *Toledot ha-Ẓiyyonut be-Galiẓyah*, 2 (1958), 632. [Ed.]

GOMBERG, MOSES (1866–1947), U.S. organic chemist, born in Yelizavetgrad (now Kirovograd), Russia. In 1884 his father was accused of anti-czarist activities and fled with his family to Chicago, U.S.A. In spite of financial hardship, Moses graduated at the University of Michigan. In 1896–97 he went to Germany to work with Baeyer at Munich and Victor Meyer at Heidelberg. He subsequently returned to the University of Michigan where he became professor of chemistry. During World War I, he undertook the (to him abhorrent) task of working out commercial production of mustard gas, and as a major in the ordinance department advised on the manufacture of smokeless powder and high explosives. Of his various activities in organic chemistry—including the diazo reaction that bears his name—he is best known for his work on free radicals and his demonstration that carbon can exhibit a valency of three instead of the normal four. He was president of the American Chemical Society in 1931.

Bibliography: Schoepele and Bachmann, in: *Journal of the American Chemical Society*, 69 (1948), 2921–25; E. Farber (ed.), *Great Chemists* (1962), 1211–17.

[S.A.M.]

GOMBINER, ABRAHAM ABELE BEN ḤAYYIM HA-LEVI (c. 1637–1683), Polish rabbi. After the death of his parents during the Chmielnicki massacres of 1648, Abraham left his birthplace, Gombin. In 1655 he went to Lithuania, and there studied with his relative, Jacob Isaac Gombiner. Later he went to Kalisz, where he was appointed head of the yeshivah and *dayyan* of the *bet din*. Abraham is best known for his *Magen Avraham* (Dyhernfurth, 1692), a commentary on the Shulḥan Arukh *Oraḥ Ḥayyim*, highly esteemed throughout Poland and Germany by scholars who followed it in their halakhic decisions, at times against the opinions of other codifiers. In his work Abraham reveals his acumen, depth of insight, and comprehensive knowledge of the entire halakhic literature. Abraham's main purpose was to reach a compromise between the decisions of Joseph *Caro and the glosses of Moses *Isserles, but he upholds the latter where no compromise can be arrived at. He regarded all Jewish customs as sacred and endeavored to justify them even where they were at variance with the views of the codifiers. He also thought highly of the Zohar and of the kabbalists Isaac Luria and R. Isaiah Horowitz, occasionally accepting their decision against that of the codifiers. *Magen Avraham* is written in a terse style, which scholars were at times hard put to understand until the appearance of R. Samuel ha-Levi *Kolin's extensive commentary, *Maḥaẓit ha-Shekel*.

ספר
זית רענן הילקוט
דעסויא

Title page of Abraham Gombiner's *Zayit Ra'anan*, a commentary on the *Yalkut Shimoni*, Dessau, Germany, 1704.

Abraham is also the author of *Zayit Ra'anan* (Dessau, 1704), a commentary on the *Yalkut Shimoni,* published together with some of his homilies on Genesis, *Shemen Sason. Zayit Ra'anan* was also published in abridged form in the margins of the *Yalkut,* in the 1876 edition and in all subsequent editions. His short commentary on the Tosefta of *Nezikin* was published by his grandson under the title *Magen Avraham* at the end of the *Leḥem ha-Panim* (Amsterdam, 1732) of his son-in-law, Moses Jekuthiel Kaufmann. A commentary to Job, Proverbs, and Ecclesiastes was attributed in error to him, having in fact been taken from the *Beit Avraham* of Abraham b. Samuel *Gedaliah.

Bibliography: Landshuth, Ammudei, 2; Fuenn, Keneset, 17, s.v. *Avraham b. Ḥayyim ha-Levi Gombiner;* M. Freudenthal, *Aus der Heimat Mendelssohns* (1900), 20f.; S. Knoebil, *Toledot Gedolei Hora'ah* (1927), 99–103; Ḥ. Tchernowitz, *Toledot ha-Posekim,* 3 (1947), 164–72; J. L. Maimon, in: Y. Raphael (ed.), *Rabbi Yosef Caro* (Heb., 1969), 62f.; M. Strashun, *Mivḥar Ketavim* (1969), 323–3.

[Sh.Ash.]

GOMEL (**Homel;** in Jewish sources, *Homiyyah*), city in Belorussian S.S.R. The beginning of Jewish settlement is apparently connected with the annexation of the town to Lithuania in 1537. The community of Belitsa (which became a suburb of Gomel in 1854) is mentioned in 1639 as one of the Lithuanian communities. During the *Chmielnicki massacres in 1648 many refugees from the Ukraine fled to Gomel, but the Cossack armies reached the city and massacred about 2,000 Jews there. When the Poles returned in 1665 the Jewish community was renewed. By 1765 there were 685 Jewish families living in the city. *Ḥabad Ḥasidism won many converts there, and in the mid-19th century one of its leaders, Isaac b. Mordecai *Epstein, served as rabbi.

The city was given the status of district capital in 1852, its geographical situation and position as a railroad junction making it an important commercial center. The annual fair attracted many Jewish merchants. The community increased from 2,373 in 1847, with an additional 1,552 in Belitsa, to 20,385 in 1897 (56. 4% of the total population). It had 30 synagogues, including the great synagogue built by Count Rumyantsev in the middle of the 19th century. While a few wealthy Jews in Gomel traded in forest products or were government contractors, many thousands of poor families lived in the "Rov," the valley described by J. Ḥ. *Brenner in his *Me-Emek Akhor* (1900). Toward the end of the 19th century a Jewish revolutionary movement, centered on the Bund, developed in Gomel. Zionism also gained many adherents there and several Hebrew schools were established. Zionists from Gomel settled in Ereẓ Israel and participated in the building of Ḥaderah; many were pioneers of the Second and Third Aliyah. In the summer of 1903 there was a pogrom in Gomel in which eight Jews were killed, many wounded, and much Jewish property looted. A *self-defense group was organized in which the Jewish political parties participated. Subsequently, 36 of its members were prosecuted by the authorities, in company with the perpetrators of the pogroms, and charged with committing pogroms against the Russian population. During World War I, thousands of refugees from the war zone took refuge in Gomel and several yeshivot moved there from Poland and Lithuania.

After the consolidation of the Soviet regime, Jewish religious and nationalist elements struggled against the Communist campaign to win over the masses. Nevertheless, the *ḥadarim* were closed down, beautiful synagogues were converted to secular purposes, and Jewish communal life came to an end. The rabbi of Gomel, R. Borishanski, was arrested for opposing the Communist suppression of the Jewish religion. The community decreased from 47,505 in 1910 (55%) to 37,745 in 1926 (43. 7%).

During the Nazi occupation the Jews who did not manage to escape from Gomel were murdered, but information on this period is sparse. The Jewish population of the whole district numbered 45,000 in 1959; the number of Jews in Gomel was estimated at about 20,000 in 1970. There is no synagogue in the city. (In 1963 a *minyan* was interrupted by the police, who dispersed those at prayer and took away two Torah scrolls and all religious articles.) There is a separate Jewish cemetery. A monument was erected in the vicinity of the city to the memory of local Jews massacred by the Nazis.

Bibliography: Nathan Hannover, *Yeven Meẓulah;* L. H. Kahanovich, in: *Arim ve-Immahot be-Yisrael,* 2 (1948), 187–269; idem, *Mi-Homel ad Tel Aviv* (1952); S. Levin, in: *Royte Bleter* (1929); I. Halpern, *Sefer ha-Gevurah,* 3 (1950), 46–62; B. G. Bogoraz-Tan (ed.), *Yevreyskoye mestechko v Revolyutsii* (1926), 157–219; M. Zinowitz, *Ha-Ẓofeh* (March 3, 1944; April 4, 1944).

[Y.S.]

GOMEL, BLESSING OF (Heb. בִּרְכַּת הַגּוֹמֵל, i.e., "He who bestows"), a thanksgiving benediction recited by those who have been saved from acute danger to life. Those who have crossed the sea or a wilderness, have recovered from illness, or been released from prison are especially obligated to pronounce this blessing (Ber. 54b). The Talmud *(ibid.)* derives the duty to recite the *Gomel* from the verses: "Let them give thanks unto the Lord for His mercy, And for His wonderful works to the children of men!" (Ps. 107:8, 15, 21, 31); and "Let them exalt Him also in the assembly of the people, And praise Him in the seat of the elders" (Ps. 107:32). The blessing should preferably be said in the presence of ten men ("assembly of the people"), two of whom should be rabbis (recited at the "seat of the elders"; Sh. Ar., OḤ 219:3), and should be pronounced within three days after the person has been delivered from danger. It has become customary to recite this blessing after being called to the Reading of the Law in the synagogue on Mondays, Thursdays, or Sabbaths. In many communities it is recited by women after childbirth in front of the Ark after the service. The wording suggested by the Talmud is: "Blessed is He who bestows lovingkindness" (Ber. 54b). The accepted text for the benediction is "Blessed art Thou . . . Who doest good unto the undeserving, and Who hast dealt kindly with me" (Yad, Berakhot 10:8). The congregation responds "He who hath shown thee kindness, may He deal kindly with thee for ever" (Hertz, Prayer, 487). A *Gomel* benediction can be recited by an entire community. In Israel, this benediction is also recited by military reservists after a stretch of active service.

Bibliography: Idelsohn, Liturgy, 114f.

[Ed.]

GOMER (Heb. גֹּמֶר), the firstborn son of *Japheth; the father of Ashkenaz, Riphath, and Togarmah (Gen. 10:2–3; I Chron. 1:5–6); and the name of a nation (Ezek. 38:6). Gomer is nowadays identified with the *Gi-mir-ra-a* of the Assyrian sources who are the Κιμμέριοι of the Greek sources. This migratory people, who made their first historical appearance in Eastern Asia at the end of the eighth century B.C.E., shook Asia Minor with campaigns of conquest in the seventh century.

On Gomer, daughter of Diblaim, see *Hosea.

Bibliography: M. J. Mellink, in: IDB, 2 (1962), 440 (incl. bibl.).

[Ed.]

GOMEZ, family of prominent early U.S. merchants. Lewis Moses (c. 1660–1740), who was the founder of this New York family, was probably born a Marrano in

Madrid, and lived in France and England before settling in New York about 1703. Three years later he was made a freeman of New York City, where he prospered in the import and export trade. Together with his sons he purchased considerable real estate in the city and in Ulster and Orange counties. Of Gomez' six sons, one died at sea in 1722; the other five, all merchants, figured prominently in community affairs. MORDECAI (1688–1750) was made a freeman in 1715 and was appointed interpreter to the Admiralty Court. DANIEL (1695–1780) became a freeman in New York in 1727; he died in Philadelphia. DAVID (1697?–1769) carried on a considerable fur trade with the Indians and was a naturalized British subject in 1740. ISAAC (1705–1770) bought a distillery in the Montgomerie Ward in the city in 1763, together with BENJAMIN (1711–1772), who lived in Charleston for a time. In 1729 Gomez and his sons, except Benjamin, purchased land which included the site of what was to be the Shearith Israel cemetery off Chatham Square. They posted a bond that the land would be a "burying place" for the use of the "Jewish nation." The family was among the original founders of Congregation Shearith Israel. The elder Gomez was one of the trustees who purchased land for the Mill Street Synagogue and was president of the congregation in 1730, when the synagogue was dedicated. Benjamin Gomez served as *parnas* four times, and during the period between 1730 and the Revolution, seven members of the Gomez family served as president.

Bibliography: H. Simonhoff, *Jewish Notables in America . . .* (1956), 112–6; D. de Sola Pool, *Portraits Etched in Stone* (1952), index; L. Hershkowitz (comp.), *Wills of Early New York Jews* (1967), index; Rosenbloom, Biogr Dict, s.v. *Gomez, Benjamin*[1], *Gomez, David*[1], *Gomez, Isaac*[1], *Gomez, Lewis (Louis) Moses*, incl. bibl. on all of them.

[L.HE.]

GÓMEZ, ANTONIO ENRÍQUEZ, or **HENRÍQUEZ** (pseudonym of **Enrique Enriquez de Paz;** 1600?–1662?), Spanish playwright and poet. Born in Segovia, the son of a Portuguese Marrano, Gómez had a distinguished military career, rising to the rank of captain and receiving the decoration of Knight of the Order of San Miguel. Together with his son, Diego Enríquez Basurto (who also became a well-known author), Gómez left Spain in about 1636 and lived for a time in France, where most of his books were published. He later moved to Holland, where he reverted to Judaism and was symbolically punished in absentia at an auto-da-fé in Seville on April 13, 1660.

Gómez was a lyric, dramatic, and epic poet, as well as a noted satirist. His major works include the *Academias morales de las musas,* dedicated to Anne of Austria (Bordeaux, 1642), and *El siglo pitagórico y vida de don Gregorio Guadaña* (Rouen, 1644). The latter, a novel in verse and prose, presents a series of 14 transformations of a soul in different bodies, satirizing various classes of society. Gómez also wrote *Luis dado de Dios a Luis y Ana* (Paris, 1645), dedicated to Louis XIII of France; *Torre de Babilonia* (Rouen, 1649); and a biblical epic about Samson, *El Sansón nazareno* (Rouen, 1656). In the prologue to this last work, Gómez refers to his authorship of 22 plays. These are mainly concerned with themes of honor, love, and friendship and half are based on biblical subjects. Gómez composed a ballad dedicated to the martyr Lope de *Vega (Juda el Creyente), who was burned at Valladolid on July 25, 1644.

It has been claimed that Gómez returned to Spain, assumed the name Fernando de Zárate, and wrote over 30 plays of purely Catholic inspiration. Recent investigations, however, have produced documents which suggest that he was eventually arrested as a judaizer and died in the cells of the Seville Inquisition.

Bibliography: Kayserling, Bibl, 49; J. Caro Baroja, *Judíos en la España moderna y contemporánea,* 3 (1961), index; H. V. Besso, *Dramatic Literature of the Sephardic Jews of Amsterdam in the XVIIth and XVIIIth Centuries* (1947), index; C. A. de la Barrera y Leirado, *Catálogo bibliográfico y biográfico del teatro antiguo español* (1860), 134–42; Roth, Marranos, 246, 333; Révah, in: REJ, 118 (1959–60), 50–51, 71–72.

[K.R.S.]

GÓMEZ DE SOSSA, ISAAC (late 17th century), *Marrano literary figure. Gómez de Sossa lived and worked in Amsterdam and, according to Miguel de *Barrios, was a Latin poet and an imitator of Virgil. He composed poems in praise of the works of other writers, and was responsible for a Spanish translation of Saul Levi *Morteira's Hebrew work on the divine origin of the Law. He was a member of the Academia de los Sitibundos, a literary society founded in 1676 by Manuel de Belmonte, and was one of the judges of its poetry contests. His younger brother, Benito Gómez de Sossa, was a minor writer in Amsterdam. Their father, Abraham Gómez de Sossa, had once served as physician-in-ordinary to the infante Fernando, the son of Philip III of Spain and governor of the Netherlands in 1632. Abraham Gómez de Sossa died in Amsterdam in 1667, and Isaac composed a Latin epitaph for his tombstone.

Bibliography: M. de Barrios, *Relación de los Poetas y Escritores Españoles de la Nación Judaica Amstelodama* (n. d.); Kayserling, Bibl, 74, 104; idem, *Sephardim* (Ger., 1859), 292.

[K.R.S.]

GOMPERS, SAMUEL (1850–1924), U.S. trade unionist. Gompers was born in London and after a few years of primary school was apprenticed in the cigar-making trade. When Gompers' family emigrated to America in 1863, settling on the Lower East Side of New York City, he joined a local of the Cigar Makers' National Union. From this point Gompers' life centered on trade union activities. He became a leader of the cigar makers' union in the 1870s, playing a major role in its reorganization (1879) through increased dues, sickness and death benefits, and substantial control of locals by the national officers. Gompers helped to establish the American Federation of Labor in 1886, and became its president. He also edited the official journal of the Federation from 1894 until his death. Most of Gompers' public activities were related to his position in the American Federation of Labor. From 1900 he served as a vice-president of the National Civic Federation, which sought to promote stable labor relations through collective bargaining and personal contact between labor leaders, industrialists, and bankers. Gompers received considerable criticism from labor sources because of these associations. He also played a prominent role in winning strong support from American trade unions for President Woodrow Wilson's war policies in 1917 and 1918; and he did much to protect organized labor's interests during World War I.

Gompers was a formative influence upon the American labor movement, as well as a spokesman for it. Although he would have preferred the former role, the decentralized American labor movement did not permit any one individual to exercise much influence over the constituent trade unions. Gompers often had to rely upon his reputation and influence in order to be effective, and he often had to accept the role of spokesman even when his own views differed. Thus, for instance, despite his personal belief in organizing black workers, Gompers acquiesced in the refusal of the AFL to attempt to enforce an anti-discrimination policy upon its affiliates. However, in most matters, his views became almost synonymous with those of the leading unions in the Federation.

Gompers argued that the improvement of workers' wages, hours, and employment conditions could only be accomplished through the formation of strong trade unions to exert direct economic pressure on the employer. The resulting collective bargaining agreements protected the basic interests of the worker. Such labor organizations must be independent of control by politicians, intellectuals, or

Samuel Gompers, U.S. trade unionist. From B. Mandel, *Samuel Gompers,* Yellow Springs, Ohio, 1963.

any non-labor source. This viewpoint in effect acknowledged that organized labor lacked the political power to achieve its objectives through legislation, and that the climate of opinion in the United States was usually hostile to trade unions so that apparent victories might be reversed quickly. Moreover, Gompers believed that men view economic and social questions in terms of their material interests, which meant that the worker could not expect continuing support from the middle class, since their objectives would inevitably conflict. Workers must therefore avoid dependence on legislation or political action.

Gompers maintained a vitriolic hostility to socialism almost throughout his presidency of the AFL. The socialists called for industrial unionism and political action, as opposed to Gompers' belief in craft unionism dedicated to the immediate interests of a relatively homogenous membership. The socialists viewed the labor organization as only the first step in the workers' struggle for social justice. Ultimately, Gompers accepted capitalism providing it could guarantee an adequate standard of living for the worker, and he had little patience with claims that the entire economic system had to be reordered to accomplish this.

Despite his immigrant background, Gompers demanded the restriction of immigration in order to protect the competitive position of workers in America. Although he called for the unionization of all workers, he basically accepted the decision of the AFL to concentrate on the skilled and retain the craft basis for organizing, which maintained the position of the existing trade unions. Clearly, Gompers was an effective leader for organized workers, but for the greatest part of the labor force his program had little validity since these workers were unorganized and likely to remain so. Gompers' career was thus marked by the paradox that he was an able trade unionist but a largely ineffective labor leader. His autobiography, *Seventy Years of Life and Labor* (2 vols.), was published posthumously in 1925.

Bibliography: B. Mandel, *Samuel Gompers* (1963); F. C. Thorne, *Samuel Gompers* (1957); R. H. Harvey, *Samuel Gompers* (1935); L. Reed, *Labor Philosophy of Samuel Gompers* (1930); DAB, 7 (1931), 369–73.

[I.Y.]

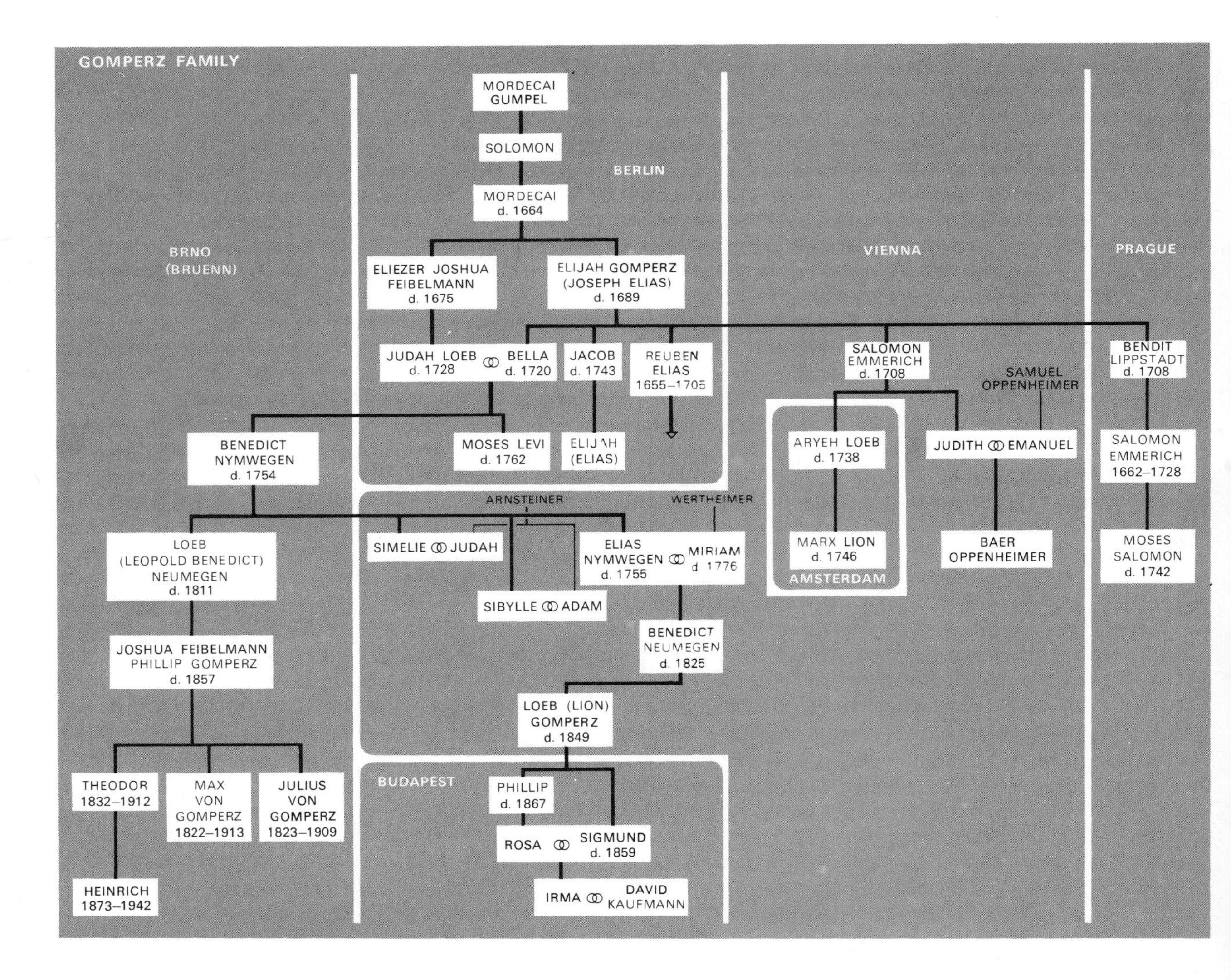

GOMPERTZ, English family, closely associated with the Hambro Congregation in London and known in the synagogue as Emmerich, after the family's place of origin. Joseph Gompertz (1731–1810) was an early member of the *Board of Deputies of British Jews. The sons of his brother Solomon Barent Gompertz (1729–1807) attained distinction in different spheres. Benjamin Gompertz (1779–1865) was a mathematician of genius, Fellow of the Royal Society, and writer on astronomy. When he was refused the post of actuary to the Guardian Insurance Office because of his faith, his brother-in-law N. M. *Rothschild established the Alliance Insurance Company (1824) in which he filled that position until 1848. He developed a mathematical law of human mortality which is still used in actuarial calculations. He proposed a plan for the amalgamation and reorganization of the Jewish charities in London. His brother Ephraim Gompertz (1776–1876) wrote *Theoretic Discourse on the Nature and Property of Money* (London, 1820), a pioneering work in the field of economics. Isaac Gompertz (1774–1856) was among the earliest Anglo-Jewish poets and was compared in his day to Dryden and Pope. His works include *Time or Light and Shade* (London, 1815); *The Modern Antique or, the Muse in the Costume of Queen Anne* (London, 1813); and *Devon, a Poem* (Teignmouth, 1825). He spent his last years in Devonshire and is buried in the Jewish cemetery of Exeter. Lewis Gompertz (1784–1861), the youngest of the Gompertz brothers, was an inventor who devoted himself to the cause of the humane treatment of animals. His *Moral Enquiries on the Situation of Men and Brutes* (London, 1824) led to the foundation of the Society (later Royal Society) for the Prevention of Cruelty to Animals, which he served devotedly as secretary. However, when it was reorganized on Christian sectarian lines in 1832 he was ejected. He then founded the Animals' Friend Society, with its influential periodical, *The Animals' Friend,* which he managed successfully until 1846, when his health failed and the society was disbanded. Gompertz was responsible for a number of patented inventions, many designed to lessen the sufferings of animals. His expanding chuck is still widely used in industry. In more recent times, the Gompertz family, no longer attached to Judaism, produced many army officers and the violinist Richard Gompertz (1859–1911).

Bibliography: D. Kaufmann and M. Freudenthal, *Familie Gompertz* (1907), 318–25; Roth, in: JHSET, 14 (1935–39), 8, 10, 14; P. Emden, *Jews of Britain* (1943), 167–74; Roth, Mag Bibl, index; DNB; *The Times* (July 12, 1965).

[C.R.]

GOMPERZ, name of a family widely dispersed throughout Central Europe. In records of the 14th century the old-German form of the name "Gundbert" began appearing as a surname for persons with the name Ephraim or Mordecai. Occurring in variant spellings as Gumpert, Gumpertz, Gomperts, Gumpel, etc., it became associated with a specific family prominent in the late 15th century, in the duchy of Juelich-Cleves, when Solomon ben Mordecai Gumpel received the right of residence in Emmerich. His immediate descendants settled in nearby Cleves, Wesel, and Nijmegen; branches of the family were eventually found in England, Amsterdam, Berlin, Frankfort on the Main, Prague, and America (Samuel *Gompers). David *Kaufmann, who married into the Budapest branch, traced, in cooperation with Max Freudenthal, the genealogy of the family (see bibliography).

Solomon's grandson Elijah (d. 1689) founded the family banking business in Wesel (Cleves) which soon became one of the largest in Prussia. His son Reuben Elias assisted in the rapid expansion of business. After moving to Berlin he became the first Jew to serve as a government official in Brandenburg; he subsequently became the chief inspector of taxes payable by the Jews in the duchies of Mark and Cleves (about 1700). He also acted as supplier to the army and to the court, and through these transactions came into contact with all the important Jewish court suppliers of his time, including Samuel *Oppenheimer, Leffmann *Behrends, and Behrend *Lehmann. Falsely accused of the attempted murder of Samson *Wertheimer, he was arrested by order of Frederick I and released a year later after payment of 20,000 talers.

Two members of the third generation of Court Jews in this family, Moses Levi and Elijah, established a banking and business house in Berlin at the beginning of the 18th century. In Prussia, members of the Gomperz family served as court purveyors to six rulers in the course of five generations. To Frederick I (1688–1713), the luxury-loving first king of Prussia, they supplied jewels, and to the soldier-king, Frederick William I (1713–1740), "tall fellows" for his guard. At the time of Frederick the Great (1740–1786) they changed their activities to minting. In conjunction with the Court Jew Daniel *Itzig they rented the minting monopoly. In Berlin, Aaron Elias Gomperz, physician, writer, and teacher of Moses Mendelssohn, became celebrated. Members of the Gomperz family also served as *Landesrabbiner* (Cleves and Silesia) and *Oberrabiner* (Ansbach). Many created influential positions for themselves, aided by their family relations with other Court Jews.

In Bohemia-Moravia a noteworthy member of the family was Salomon (Salman) Emmerich (1662–1728), who studied medicine at Leiden and practiced in Metz and Soest before establishing himself in Prague. He was the first Prague Jew to be freed by imperial order from wearing the obligatory neck-frill. His son Moses Salomon Gomperz (d. 1742) was permitted to practice medicine by Prague University after passing an examination, and was the first Jew to graduate from a German university, in Frankfurt on the Oder, in 1721.

The Bruenn (Brno) branch of the Gomperz family was founded by Loeb ben Bendit (Leopold Bendit or Benedict) Neumegen, from Nijmegen, Holland. His son Phillip Gomperz founded a successful bank. Three of his sons became celebrated: Theodor *Gomperz (1832–1912), classical philologist and historian of Greek philosophy; Max von Gomperz (1822–1913), industrialist, financier, and politician; Julius von Gomperz (1823–1909), president of the Jewish community from 1869, who initiated the Moravian communities organization and was active on behalf of the Jewish communities in Parliament. A hereditary title was conferred on him in 1879. Theodor's son Heinrich Gomperz (1873–1942) was also a classical philologist.

Bibliography: D. Kaufmann and M. Freudenthal, *Familie Gompertz* (1907); S. Stern, *The Court Jew* (1950), index; idem, *Der preussische Staat und die Juden* (1962), index s.v. *Gumperts;* H. Schnee, *Die Hoffinanz und der moderne Staat,* 3 (1955), index; G. Kisch, in: MGWJ, 78 (1934), 350–63; idem, in: HJ, 8 (1946), 169f., 175, 180; A. Shochat, *Im Ḥillufei Tekufot* (1960), index.

[M.Gra./H.W.]

GOMPERZ, THEODOR (1832–1912), Austrian classical philologist and historian of ancient philosophy. He was born in Bruenn, Moravia. From 1873 to 1901 Gomperz was professor of classical philology at the University of Vienna, and in 1882 was elected to the Academy of Sciences. His *Griechische Denker,* 3 vols. (1896–1909), is a monumental work which sets Greek philosophy, from its beginnings until after Aristotle, within the context of a history of science and of the general development of ancient civilization.

This work has been translated into many languages and is considered one of the basic works in its field. The author's empiricist-positivist bias is evident throughout. Gomperz, also active in public affairs and politics, served as a Liberal member of the Austrian upper house. In Jewish affairs, he took an extreme assimilationist stand and was violently opposed to Herzl and Zionism. His biography, letters, and notes were published by his son Heinrich as *Briefe und Aufzeichnungen* (1936). HEINRICH (1873–1942) was also a philosopher. He was baptized and was a professor in Vienna until 1934 when he was compelled to retire because of his refusal to join Dolfuss' Fatherland Front. In 1938 he emigrated to the U.S. In addition to the biography of his father, he published a new edition of his father's *Griechische Denker* (1922–31). He published a comprehensive study of Greek philosophy, *Die Lebensauffassung der griechischen Philosophen und das Ideal der inneren Freiheit* (1904), and *Philosophical Studies* (1953, edited by D. S. Robinson), which is a psychoanalytical study of Parmenides and Socrates.

Bibliography: THEODOR GOMPERZ: *Neue Deutsche Biographie*, 6 (1964); *Oesterreichisches Biographisches Lexikon*. HEINRICH GOMPERZ: Topitsch, in: *Wiener Zeitschrift fuer Philosophie, Psychologie und Paedagogik*, 5 (1954–55), 1–6; W. Ziegenfuss (ed.), *Philosophen-Lexikon*, 1 (1949). [O.I.S.]

GOOD AND EVIL.

In the Bible. A major corollary of the Jewish belief in the One God is that, seen in its totality, life is good. Viewing the cosmos as it emerged from chaos, God said, "It is good" (Gen. 1:10). In a monotheistic world view, a persistent problem is to account for the existence of evil in its many forms—natural catastrophes, pain and anguish in human life, moral evil, and sin. These facts must be fitted somehow within the design of the Creator as it is realized in the course of human history.

The problem of the existence of evil in the world was not given great prominence in the earlier books of the Bible, which are mainly concerned with positing general ethical-religious norms. In the later books, however, when the status of the individual vis-à-vis God gains in importance, it becomes necessary to account for the existence of evil in a world governed by a benevolent and omnipotent God. Jeremiah asks the perennial question concerning the prosperity of the wicked and the adversity of the righteous. This problem appears also in the Books of Isaiah, Job, and the Psalms. Various answers were given, which were later elaborated by the talmudists and the philosophers, but it should be noted that the idea of a heavenly reward is never mentioned in the biblical writings as a possible solution.

In Talmudic Literature. For the rabbis of the talmudic period the existence of evil in a world created by a merciful and loving God posed a number of theological problems, which they attempted to solve in a variety of ways. Although these solutions do not add up to a coherent theodicy, some of the more representative discussions indicate the general lines of rabbinic thought on the matter. First there is the issue of the existence of evil itself. The rabbis insisted that as good derives from God so, ultimately, does evil. This insistence was intended to discount any implications of duality, the idea of a separate deity from whom evil springs being complete anathema to the rabbis, who even say, "Man should bless God for the evil which occurs in the same way that he blesses Him for the good" (Ber. 33b). The same antidualistic motif is contained in the verse, "I am the Lord, there is none else; I form the light, and create darkness; I make peace, and create evil" (Isa. 45:6–7). (In the liturgy this is changed to "makes peace and creates all that exists," implying that evil itself is perhaps not a positive phenomenon at all, but mainly the absence of good.) Another vexing problem is why there is no just distribution of good and evil to the righteous and wicked respectively. This problem is dealt with in a number of different ways. On the one hand one finds the view that the issue is beyond the grasp of man's intellect, in support of which the verse, "I will be gracious to whom I will be gracious, and will show mercy on whom I will show mercy" (Ex. 33:19) is quoted (cf. Ber. 7a). On the other hand, a series of more partial solutions are proffered: the righteous man who suffers in this world is not wholly righteous, and the wicked man who prospers is not wholly wicked; or alternately the former is perhaps not a descendant of righteous ancestors, while the latter prospers because of the merit of his fathers (Ber. 7a); or evil is blamed on Satan and various malicious demons who are at the root of the trouble caused to the righteous (Ber. 6a; Gen. R. 84:3).

Perhaps the most widespread explanation of suffering in this world is that what the righteous undergo is punishment for every small sin they may have committed so that they will enjoy their full reward in paradise, while the wicked are rewarded in this world for any small amount of good they have to their credit so that in the world to come they will reap the full measure of the punishment they deserve (Ber. 4a; Eruv. 19a; Ta'an. 11a; Kid. 39b, Avot 2:16; Gen. R. 33:1; Yal., Eccles. 978). The sufferings of the righteous are also seen as a form of trial, "afflictions of love," enabling them to develop virtues such as patience and faith (Ber. 5a; BM 85a; Gen. R. 9:8; *Tanna de-Vei Eliyahu Zuta* 11). Support for this view is found in biblical verses such as "Happy is the man whom Thou disciplineth, O Lord, And teacheth out of Thy Law" (Ps. 94:12) and "It is good for me that I have been afflicted, In order that I might learn Thy statutes" (*ibid.* 119:71).

Another aspect concerning the evil caused by man himself is dealt with by viewing evil as the product of, if not identical with, the evil inclination (Ḥag. 16a). The evil inclination is a necessary factor in the continued existence of the world, for without it no man would build a house, marry, raise a family, or engage in trade (Gen. R. 9:9). Nevertheless, it is within man's grasp to control his evil inclination, against whose power the Torah was seen as an antidote (Kid. 30b). This control enables man to serve God with both his good and evil urges (Ber. 9:5); the one enabling him to continue in his this-worldly pursuits and the other helping him to grow in holiness. Despite an acute awareness of the extent of evil and suffering, both in the natural world and in the world of interhuman relations, and notwithstanding the limitations of the explanations they were able to offer by way of theodicy, the rabbis continually reaffirm the ultimate goodness of God and of His creation. This affirmation is even contained in the burial service, in a series of refrains emphasizing the perfection of God's world (Hertz, Prayer 1074). The rabbis advise man to accustom himself to say, "All that the Merciful One does is for the good" (Ber. 60b); and they assure him that the measure of God's reward exceeds that of His punishment (Yoma 76a). One *tanna*—*Nahum of Gimzo (Ish Gamzu)—was even renowned for his response to every occurrence: "This too is for the best" (Ta'an. 21a). [ED.]

In Medieval Jewish Philosophy. The answers given by *Philo to the problem of evil correspond, in certain respects, to those of the rabbis. If some righteous men suffer, he states, it is because they are not really perfect in their righteousness. Furthermore, the good which befalls the wicked is not a real good. Also, the suffering of the righteous may come from God as a trial or test, or because of the sins of their ancestors.

The need to account for the existence of evil in the world became even more acute with the manifestation of dualistic movements. Saadiah Gaon strongly rejects these dualist doctrines and affirms God's unity. Steeped as he was in the *Kalām tradition, he states that God conducts the world with infinite justice and wisdom. God, according to Saadiah, would not have created evil because evil does not have a separate existence *sui generis* but is nothing more than the absence of good. The sufferings of the righteous are either a requital for the few sins which they have committed, or they serve as an instrument of chastisement or trial, for which reward will be given in the afterlife. Saadiah thus upholds the doctrine of "afflictions of love."

The answer of Joseph al-*Basir, the 11th-century Karaite, is that the infliction of pain may, under certain circumstances, be a good instead of an evil, for it may ultimately result in a greater advantage. Thus, disease and suffering are either punishment for offenses committed, or are imposed with a view to later reward. Similarly, *Abraham b. Ḥiyya expresses the view that the righteous suffer in this world in order to try them and to increase their ultimate reward (*Meditation of the Sad Soul* (1969), 117ff.). Joseph ibn *Ẓaddik sees the evil which happens to the righteous as often being a natural occurrence without reference to reward and punishment. Sometimes, too, this evil is inflicted upon the good man for his sins, but ultimate reward and punishment are in the future life. Abraham *ibn Ezra sees the whole world as good. From God, he states, comes only good. Evil is due to the defect of the object receiving higher influence. To argue that because of a small part of evil the whole world, which is good, should not have been created, is foolish. Abraham *ibn Daud argues that it is impossible either according to reason or according to the Bible and tradition that evil or defect should come from God. If both good and evil come from God, He would have to be a composite. Besides, the majority of evils are negations, and cannot have been produced by any agent.

*Maimonides also views evil as a nonexistence, namely the absence of good, which could not have been produced by God. He distinguishes between three different kinds of evil. The first category is that of natural evils which befall man, such as landslides, earthquakes, and floods, or his having been born with certain deformities. The cause of this type of evil is the fact that man has a body which is subject to corruption and destruction. This is in accordance with natural law and is necessary for the continuance and permanence of the species. The second kind of evil is within the social realm, such as wars. This type of evil, Maimonides says, occurs infrequently and, of course, being wholly within the control of man, could not have been caused by God. Though difficult, its remedy is within the hands of man. The third class of evil, the largest and most frequent class, is the evil which the individual brings upon himself through his vices and excessive desires. Again the remedy is within man's power. Maimonides rejects the notion of "afflictions of love," holding instead that even the minutest pain is a punishment for some previous transgression. He explains that the tests mentioned in the Bible, such as God's request to Abraham to offer up his son, have a didactic purpose, to teach the truth of God's commandments and how far one must go in obeying them.

Joseph *Albo holds that perfect saints may have to endure agonies in order to atone for their people or for the entire world.

See also *Kabbalah, *Sin, *Adam, *Reward and Punishment, *Providence, *Free Will, *God, Justice and Mercy of God. [J.B.A./Ed.]

In Modern Jewish Philosophy. For Hermann *Cohen suffering stirs man's conscience and prods him to ethical action. Israel's election by God is tied up with the idea of Israel as the "suffering servant," i.e., the eternal prod of mankind's conscience. Evil in a metaphysical sense did not interest Cohen. He castigated metaphysical speculation about evil as an attempt to cover the existence of evil in society and as perverting the intent of suffering which should be to arouse sympathy in men.

The problem of evil played an important role in the philosophy of Martin *Buber. For Buber the source of evil was the failure to enter into relation, and conversely evil can be redeemed by the reestablishment of relations. "Good and evil, then, cannot be a pair of opposites like right and left or above and beneath, 'good' is the movement in the direction of home, 'evil' is the aimless whirl of human potentialities without which nothing can be achieved and by which, if they take no direction but remain trapped in themselves, everything goes awry" (*Between Man and Man* (1966[4]), 103). Man is not evil by nature, but his misuse of his nature generates evil. Some men can carry evil so far as to give it a kind of independent quality. However, evil is never an independent entity but such men crystallize it into a perverse resistance to the individual's self-fulfillment in relation. After World War II Buber did question the possibility of addressing God as "kind and merciful" in the light of what had happened to the Jews in Europe, but he nevertheless maintained the possibility of man redeeming evil. He denied the gnostic dualistic approach and maintained that man had it in his power to sanctify the world.

Abraham J. *Heschel, referring to a midrash about Abraham seeing a castle in flames (Gen. R. 39:1), asks: "The world is in flames, consumed by evil. Is it possible that there is no one who cares?" (*God in Search of Man* (1961[3]), 367). After considering the horrors of Auschwitz he questions: "What have we done to make such crimes possible? What are we doing to make such crimes impossible?" (*ibid.* 369). According to him nothing in the world is wholly good or wholly evil, everything is a mixture. Man's nature, his ego, and the relative rewards of evil in this world help evil to prevail. Fortunately, God is concerned about man's separating the good from the evil. God commands man and gives him the *mitzvot*, which are the tools by which man can overcome evil. "Evil is not man's ultimate problem. Man's ultimate problem is his relation to God . . . The biblical answer to evil is not the good but the holy. It is an attempt to raise man to a higher level of existence, where man is not alone when confronted with evil" (*ibid.* 376).

For Mordecai *Kaplan God is identical with certain principles in the universe whose analogues in human society lead to salvation, i.e., the achievement of the good for all mankind. The existence of evil in the world is due to the failure of man to act in accord with God, i.e., those principles. "When the conscience operates simultaneously through creativity, responsibility, honesty, and loyalty or love, it is the source of Divine Revelation . . . The function of conscience is not to philosophize or theologize concerning the problem of evil in the world. Conscience is the pain of the human spirit. The function of spiritual pain is not to have us speculate about it but to eliminate the cause . . . it is rather to impel us to make a religion of combating the man-made evils that mar human life . . ." (M. M. Kaplan, in *The Reconstructionist*, May, 1963).

See also *Eschatology, *World to Come, and *Reward and Punishment. [M.Gr.]

Bibliography: In Talmudic Literature: K. Kohler, *Jewish Theology* (1918); A. Marmorstein, *The Doctrine of Merits in Old Rabbinical Literature* (1920); A. Buechler, *Studies in Sin and Atonement* (1928); E. E. Urbach, *Ḥazal, Pirkei Emunot ve-De'ot* (1969). In Ancient and Medieval Jewish Philosophy: Guttmann, Philosophies, index, s.v. *evil;* Husik, Philosophy, index, s.v. *Evil, Problem of;* H. A. Wolfson, *Philo* . . . (1947), index, s.v. *Evil.* In Modern Jewish Philosophy: J. B. Agus, *Modern Philosophies of Judaism* (1941), 94–6, 108ff.; M. S. Friedman, *Martin Buber* (1960[2]), 11–15, 101–58; F. A. Rothschild, *Between God and Man* (1959), 191–7.

°**GOODENOUGH, ERWIN RAMSDELL** (1893–1965), U.S. scholar who specialized in the study of Judaism in the Hellenistic period. Goodenough was born in Brooklyn, New York. In 1923, he began teaching history at Yale University. While preparing his doctoral thesis, published as *The Theology of Justin Martyr* (1923), Goodenough came to the conclusion that many Hellenistic elements of early Christianity were derived not from the pagan world directly but from the already hellenized Judaism through which Christianity was first disseminated. Most of his later work was devoted to the study of this hellenized Judaism, especially *The Jurisprudence of the Jewish Courts in Egypt* (1929), *By Light, Light: The Mystic Gospel of Hellenistic Judaism* (1935), *The Politics of Philo Judaeus* (1938), *An Introduction to Philo Judaeus* (1940), and *Jewish Symbols in the Greco-Roman Period* (13 vols., 1953–68). Goodenough's reconstruction of Hellenistic Judaism from literary sources was often speculative. His account of the teachings of Philo, in particular, must be corrected in the light of H. A. *Wolfson's analysis of Philo's philosophy and demonstration of its many similarities to rabbinic teaching. But *Jewish Symbols in the Greco-Roman Period,* by its collection of Greco-Roman archaeological remains and its confrontation of these with pagan parallels, revealed an entire world of Judaism that previously had been known only in fragments and generally neglected. Consequently, this work began a new epoch in the study of ancient Judaism—this in spite of the fact that Goodenough's interpretation of the material is often unreliable. He probably underestimated the influence of rabbinic Judaism in the Greco-Roman diaspora; he far underestimated the penetration of rabbinic Judaism by Greco-Roman influences and ideas. Goodenough was active in many scholarly organizations, and edited *The Journal of Biblical Literature* from 1934 to 1942. [M.SM.]

GOODHART, ARTHUR LEHMAN (1891–), U. S. jurist. Born in New York, Goodhart studied in America and Britain and was an officer in the United States Army during World War I. In 1919 he became a lecturer in law at Cambridge University and was editor of the *Cambridge Law Journal* from 1921 to 1925. In 1931 Goodhart was appointed professor of jurisprudence at Oxford University. In this position he exercised considerable influence both as a lecturer and writer and his lucid exposition of legal problems, particularly in the field of contracts and torts, earned him a reputation as an outstanding jurist. He also served on several government legal committees, including the Royal Commission on the Police, the Monopolies Commission, and the Law Revision Committee.

In 1951 Goodhart was appointed master of University College, Oxford, the first Jew and the first American citizen to become master of an Oxford college. He was also the recipient of many other honors. He was made a king's counsel in 1943 and awarded a knighthood (honorary by virtue of his American citizenship). He was chairman of the International Law Association. His writings include *Essays in Jurisprudence and the Common Law* (1931); *Precedent in English and Continental Law* (1934); *The Government of Great Britain* (1946); and *Five Jewish Lawyers of the Common Law* (1950). He was also editor of the *Law Quarterly Review,* one of the most authoritative legal magazines in the world.

Goodhart took an interest in Jewish affairs and was a strong supporter of Israel. After the *Six-Day War he wrote several articles justifying the Israel position in international law. His son PHILIP J. GOODHART (1925–) was a Conservative Member of Parliament and a member of the British delegation to the Council of Europe and the United Nations.

Bibliography: *Current Biography Yearbook 1964* (1964), 159–61. [I.F.]

GOODMAN, BENNY (Benjamin David; 1909–), U.S. clarinetist and band leader. He learned to play the clarinet as a child in Chicago in a music instruction program fostered by a local synagogue. When he turned professional, he played in various well-known bands until he organized his own orchestra in 1933. Goodman became one of the founders of the "swing" style prevalent in the 1930s, and was called "The King of Swing." His was the first jazz ensemble in which both white and Negro musicians played

Benny Goodman, U.S. clarinetist and band leader. Courtesy Jewish Theatrical Guild, New York.

together. At the same time he developed a technical mastery which led to his appearances with symphony orchestras and chamber ensembles. Bartok dedicated his clarinet trio "Contrasts" to him in 1938, and Hindemith (1947) and *Copland (1948) each wrote a clarinet concerto for him. He wrote an autobiography, *The Kingdom of Swing* (1961), and authorized *Benny Goodman's Own Clarinet Method* (1941), edited by Charles Hathaway.

Bibliography: D. R. Connor, *BG—Off the Record* (1958); P. Maffei, *Benny Goodman* (1961); E. Condon and R. Gehman (eds.), *Eddie Condon's Treasury of Jazz* (1956), 258–74; N. Shapiro and N. Hentoff (eds.), *Jazz Makers* (1957), 175–86. [C.AB.]

GOODMAN, NELSON (1906–), U.S. philosopher. Goodman was born in Somerville, Massachusetts, and taught at Tufts College (1945–46), the University of Pennsylvania (1946–64), and at Brandeis University (from 1964). Goodman's most important works are *The Structure of Appearance* (1951), and *Fact, Fiction and Forecast* (1955). In the late 1950s he turned his attention to the theory of simplicity which was the main theme of his many contributions to philosophical journals. In attempting to eliminate superfluous entities in any complete description of the world, Goodman's work shows the influence of Bertrand Russell and W. Van Orman Quine.

Bibliography: A. Hausman and F. Wilson, *Carnap and Goodman, Two Formalists* (1967). [A.S.]

GOODMAN, PAUL (1875–1949), British Zionist and public figure. Born in Dorpat, Estonia, Goodman went to England in 1891. He was for many years secretary of the Spanish and Portuguese Congregation. Goodman became an active Zionist after hearing Theodor *Herzl address his first meeting in London (1896), and from that time until his death he served the Zionist Organization. He occupied various important positions in the Zionist Movement of

London and was honorary secretary of the Political Committee, appointed by Chaim *Weizmann and Naḥum *Sokolow, before the *Balfour Declaration was issued. Together with Arthur D. Lewis he edited the volume *Zionism: Problems and Views* (1916), was editor of the *Zionist Review* (1920–26 and 1934–38), and was a contributor to various Jewish encyclopedias and Zionist periodicals. Among his works are: *The Synagogue and the Church* (1908); *History of the Jews* (1911); *Moses Montefiore* (1925); *Zionism in England* (1930); *The Jewish National Home* (1943). He also edited *Chaim Weizmann: A Tribute on his Seventieth Birthday* (1945). A memorial tribute to him, entitled *The Rebirth of Israel* (1952), was published by the Zionist Federation of Great Britain.

Bibliography: *Paul Goodman on his Seventieth Birthday* (1945); *Current Biography Yearbook 1968* (1969), 153–7. [Jo.Fr.]

GOODMAN, PAUL (1911–), U.S. author, psychotherapist, and educator. The youngest of three children deserted by their father, Goodman was born and educated in New York City. At City College he was most influenced by the philosopher Morris Raphael *Cohen and by his reading of the Russian revolutionary author Kropotkin. A versatile writer, Goodman published verse collections such as *Stop-Light* (1942), *The Lordly Hudson* (1963), and *Hawkweed* (1967); novels including *The Empire City* (1959); plays (notably *Faustina,* 1949); short stories (*The Facts of Life,* 1946); and criticism. An account of life in New York over the previous three decades, *The Empire City,* was notable for its mingled comedy and sadness. From his earliest years Goodman's intelligence and experimental attitude toward literature gave him a place in the radical avant-garde, but it was only with the publication of *Growing Up Absurd* in 1960 that he became known to the wider public. The book is an indictment of the American "rat race" and a defense of those young people who do not choose to enter it. In the years that followed, Goodman came to be described as "the father-figure of the New Left" and as "a communitarian anarchist pacifist of protean intellect and prolific pen." Some other works were *Communitas* (1947), written in collaboration with his brother, the architect Percival *Goodman, which became a standard work on cities; *The Community of Scholars* (1962), a critique of the U.S. academic scene; *Utopian Essays and Practical Proposals* (1962); *The Society I Live in Is Mine* (1963); *Compulsory Mis-Education* (1964); and

Paul Goodman, U.S. author.

Like a Conquered Province: the Moral Ambiguity of America (1967); he also contributed to F. Perls, *Gestalt Therapy* (1951). Goodman taught at several universities and at the Institute for Gestalt Therapy (New York City and Cleveland). From 1964 to 1966 he was a full professor at the University of Wisconsin and then at San Francisco State College's experimental college. In the Massey Lectures, delivered over the Canadian broadcasting network, he described what he called an "empty society," which had "a tendency to expand meaninglessly for its own sake, and . . . to exclude human beings as useless." In 1967 Goodman published a journal, *Five Years: Thoughts in a Useless Time.*

Bibliography: *Current Biography Yearbook 1968* (1969), 153–7; R. Kostelanetz, in: *New York Times Magazine* (April 5, 1966), 70–71; S. J. Kunitz, *Twentieth Century Authors, First Supplement* (1955); G. Steiner, in: *Commentary,* 36 (1963), 158–63. [M.H.H.]

GOODMAN, PERCIVAL (1904–), U.S. architect. Goodman was born in New York, and studied there and in France. He was a versatile architect, an expert on city

Synagogue designed by Percival Goodman for Congregation Beth Emeth, Albany, N.Y., 1957. Courtesy Alvin Roth, Albany, N.Y.

planning, and a professor of architecture at Columbia University. Goodman designed furniture for mass production, wrote a book (*Communitas,* 1947), and illustrated the *Golden Ass* of Apuleius (1932). He had no previous religious background when he embarked on his fruitful career as a builder of synagogues. He said that the Nazi atrocities together with his readings of Martin Buber gave him the need for concrete expression of kinship.

Goodman's synagogues are brightly lit and tend to be small and intimate, as Goodman felt this encouraged a feeling of unity in the congregation and a sense of participation in the service. He humanized his design with the use of warm materials such as wood. He regarded the artist as an indispensable collaborator, and gave him an important place in his projects. In this respect he acted as a pioneer and helped to bring into being a flourishing modern synagogal art in the United States.

Goodman designed many synagogues, including the B'nai Israel synagogue in Millburn, New Jersey (1951), and Temple Beth-El, Springfield, Massachusetts (1952). His brother is the writer Paul *Goodman.

Bibliography: R. Wischnitzer, *Synagogue Architecture in the United States* (1955), 141ff.; A. Kampf, *Contemporary Synagogue Art* (1966), 37ff. [Ed.]

GOODMAN, TOBIAS (d. 1824), English scholar. Goodman, who was born in Bohemia, went to England at the close of the 18th century. In 1806 he was a schoolmaster in *Liverpool, where he is said to have preached the earliest synagogue sermons delivered in English. He was subsequently associated with the Westminster Synagogue in London, where he delivered various addresses, the earliest both delivered and published in English, on the death of the Princess Charlotte (1817) and of King George III (1820). Goodman published Jedaiah Penini's *Beḥinat Olam* with an English translation (1806). He was an active religious controversialist.

Bibliography: A. Barnett, *Western Synagogue through Two Centuries (1761–1961)* (1961), 48–51; Benas, in: *Transactions of the Historic Society of Lancashire and Cheshire*, 51 (1901), offprint, p. 17. [C.R.]

GOOR (Grasovski), YEHUDAH (1862–1950), educator and lexicographer. Born in Pohost, Belorussia, he studied at the yeshivah of Volozhin and in 1887 immigrated to Ereẓ Israel. At first he worked as an agricultural laborer and watchman in Rishon le-Zion and, after a year, as a clerk in Jaffa. He later became secretary of the *Benei Moshe society, participated in editing its publication *Ha-Mikhtavim me-Ereẓ Yisrael*, and became a teacher. With D. Yudelovitch he founded the first Histadrut ha-Morim ha-Ivrim (Hebrew Teachers' Association) in Ereẓ Israel. Goor was one of the pioneers of the *Ivrit be-Ivrit* method whereby Hebrew is taught without using any other language in explanation. He wrote several manuals on the study of Hebrew, Jewish history, natural sciences, the geography of Ereẓ Israel, and translated into Hebrew several of Hans Christian Andersen's tales, Daniel Defoe's *Robinson Crusoe*, and stories by Mark Twain, Dickens, and Jules Verne. In 1893, together with Eliezer Ben-Yehuda and D. Yudelovitch, he edited a newspaper for children, *Olam Katan* ("Small World"). From 1906 to 1929 he worked for the Anglo-Palestine Company, at first in Beirut (until 1911), and then in Jaffa-Tel Aviv. His activities with this institution included the purchase of lands for the *yishuv* in Tel Aviv and Haifa. While in Beirut, he helped to open a Hebrew kindergarten. During World War I, he and his family were exiled to Damascus, where he engaged in many beneficial activities for refugees in Palestine.

Yehudah Goor, Hebrew educator and lexicographer. Photo Prior, Tel Aviv.

Goor is best known for his work in Hebrew lexicography. Already in 1903, he prepared (together with Y. Klausner) a "pocket dictionary" and later several other small dictionaries (Hebrew-Hebrew, Hebrew-English, etc.). In 1920, he and D. *Yellin published an illustrated Hebrew dictionary, and from 1937 he was occupied with his major work, the *Millon ha-Safah ha-Ivrit* ("Dictionary of the Hebrew Language," published in an enlarged edition in 1947). In 1939, he prepared a *Leksikon le-Millim Zarot* ("Lexicon of Foreign Words"). Goor's was the first Hebrew dictionary in which Hebrew words were traced to the period in which they originated.

Bibliography: *Yehudah Grasovski Ish ha-Gevurot* (1942); Pograbinsky, in: KS, 28 (1952/53), 110–20 (bibliography). [Ir.G.]

GOOSE. The *barburim avusim* (AV, JPS "fatted fowl") included among the daily provision for Solomon's table (I Kings 5:3) have been identified with the goose, the word *barbur* being explained as derived from *bar* ("pure," "white"), and *avus* ("fattened"). Some, however, identify *barburim* ("swans" in modern Heb.) with hens (BM 86b) or with a variety of fowl that came from Barbaria, that is North Africa (Eccl. R. 2:7). The breeding of geese in Ereẓ Israel is extremely old, a picture of them being fattened having been preserved on a ninth-century B.C.E. ivory tablet found in excavations at Megiddo. In ancient Egypt geese were extensively bred and fattened. The Mishnah mentions goose breeding (Shab. 24:3; Ḥul. 12:1), and a distinction was made between the wild and the domesticated goose (TJ, BK 5:10, 5a; TB, BK 55a). According to folklore, "if a man sees a goose in a dream, he may hope for wisdom" (Ber. 57a).

Bibliography: F. S. Bodenheimer, *Animal and Man in Bible Lands* (1960), index, s.v. *Anser;* J. Feliks, *Kilei Zera'im ve-Harkavah* (1967), 133–4. [J.F.]

GORA KALWARIA (Yid. **Ger**; Heb. **Gur**), town 19 mi. (30 km.) S.E. of Warsaw, Poland. The town, known popularly as Nowy Jeruzalem, obtained a charter in 1670 which included a clause prohibiting the settlement of Jews there. Jews were first permitted to settle in the town after it passed to Prussian rule in 1795. Subsequently Gora Kalwaria became celebrated as the seat of the ḥasidic Gur dynasty, founded by Isaac Meir Alter and headed by his successors (see below). The community numbered 2,919 in 1897 (55.1% of the total population) and 2,691 in 1921 (48.9%). [Ed.]

Holocaust Period. On the eve of World War II there were approximately 3,500 Jews living in Gora Kalwaria. When the German Army entered on Sept. 8, 1939, a reign of terror began for the Jewish population. During April and May 1940 several hundred Jews from Lodz and nearby Pabianice and Aleksandrow were deported to Gora Kalwaria. In January 1941 all the Jewish inhabitants of the small localities around Gora Kalwaria, numbering approximately 300, were also concentrated there. On Feb. 25–26, 1941, all the Jews in the town were transferred to the Warsaw ghetto where they shared the fate of Warsaw Jewry. The Jewish community was not reconstituted after the war. [S.Kr.]

Gur dynasty. The Gur (Yid. *Ger*) ḥasidic dynasty, one of the most celebrated of the dynasties, existed in Poland from 1859 to 1939; subsequently the center moved to Ereẓ Israel, under the Gur rabbi residing in Jerusalem.

Gur Ḥasidism is based primarily on the trend in Ḥasidism developed by *Jacob Isaac of Przysucha (Peshiskha) and *Menahem Mendel of Kotsk (Kock) but has taken an individual direction. It also derives ideologically from the philosophy of *Judah Loew b. Bezalel of Prague (the Maharal).

Israel Alter, who became Gur rabbi in 1948. Photo Yacoby, Jerusalem.

The founder of the dynasty was Isaac Meir Rothenberg Alter (1789–1866), whose father R. Israel was a disciple of *Levi Isaac of Berdichev and rabbi of Gur. Isaac Meir grew up under the tutelage of Israel Hofstein, the *maggid* of *Kozienice, who influenced Isaac considerably. At an early age he distinguished himself in Torah study, showing originality and intellectual acumen. He subsequently studied under Aryeh Leib Zinz, rabbi of Polotsk, and won reputation as a brilliant young scholar.

After the death of the *maggid* of Kozienice, and a short period with the latter's son and successor Moses, Isaac Meir left him to become a disciple of *Simḥah Bunem of Przysucha, and after his death, of Menahem Mendel of Kotsk. He continued to give unreserved support to Menahem Mendel throughout the stormy controversy which divided Kotsk Ḥasidism and during the period when Menahem Mendel was in isolation, enabling Kotsk Ḥasidism to survive its acute internal crisis. After Mendel's death in 1859 Isaac Meir was acknowledged as their rabbi by the majority of the Kotsk Ḥasidim. His work entitled *Ḥiddushei ha-Rim* (Warsaw, 1875), novellae on Talmud tractates and the Shulḥan Arukh, became basic texts for study in the yeshivot and are still acknowledged as classic works on the *pilpul* (dialectical) method of exposition. Isaac Meir is frequently referred to by the name of his work as "Ḥiddushei ha-Rim." Isaac Meir displayed a ready awareness of public needs and was well acquainted with Jewish problems in Poland. He fought uncompromisingly to preserve the traditional Jewish way of life and headed opposition to the regulations imposing changes in dress issued by the government and upheld in Jewish circles by the *maskilim,* refusing to make concessions even when imprisoned by the authorities. During the Polish uprising of 1830 he was suspected of sympathizing with the Polish loyalists. He changed his name from Rothenberg to Alter. In his private life he experienced considerable suffering, losing his 13 children during his lifetime.

Although Isaac Meir derived the principal part of his teaching from the Przysucha-Kotsk school of Ḥasidism, in practice it revealed radical divergences. Instead of withdrawing from contact with the masses he tried to win them over, and interested himself in day-to-day problems. He made himself available to all who sought him out, receiving them kindly. However, like the Kotsk school he placed Torah study at the center of spiritual life. As one of the most eminent scholars in Poland of his day he developed among his followers enthusiasm for Torah learning. He also followed the Kotsk method in emphasizing profundity of thought in the search after truth and the inner promptings of the heart, and in continuous striving after self-perfection.

The period of his leadership, which lasted only seven years, had a formative influence on the development of Ḥasidism in Poland. Gur Ḥasidism became a powerful element in Orthodox Polish Jewry, and retained a leading position until the Holocaust.

Judah Aryeh Leib Alter (1847–1905), son of Abraham Mordecai (the eldest son of Isaac Meir), was orphaned as a child and brought up and educated largely by his grandfather. In 1870, after the death of *Ḥanokh of Aleksandrow, the successor of Isaac Meir as Gur rabbi, Judah Aryeh Leib became the head *(admor)* of Gur. In this position he wielded a wide influence and established the leadership of Gur Ḥasidism in Congress Poland. A distinguished scholar, modest in behavior, Judah Aryeh Leib won the confidence of rabbis and communal leaders throughout Jewry. Like his grandfather he also played a role in public affairs, concerning himself with contemporary Polish Jewish problems. Through his influence Ḥasidism in Poland dissociated itself from Zionism. Judah Aryeh Leib devoted much energy promoting Torah study and attracted many of the youth. His writings are collected under the title *Sefat Emet* (2 vols., 1905–08), after which he is also known. The five sections on the Pentateuch include addresses on Sabbaths and festivals, distinguished by the profundity of their ideas and clarity of exposition, and reflect the marked influence of Judah Loew b. Bezalel (the Maharal) of Prague. The sections on the Talmud, on tractates *Mo'ed* and *Kiddushin*, evidence his wide Jewish scholarship and ability to penetrate to the intended meaning and provide a lucid exposition of the problem, in contrast to the dialectical *pilpul* method followed by his grandfather.

Judah Leib was succeeded by his eldest son, Abraham Mordecai Alter (1866–1948), the last of the dynasty in Poland. Under his leadership Gur Ḥasidism reached the height of its influence. He restored the recitation of morning prayer to the regular time and enjoined a break during the Sabbath service for public study. A lover of order and precision, he gave Gur Ḥasidim an organized framework.

In the period preceding the Holocaust Abraham Mordecai was the most prominent figure in European Orthodox Jewry and one of the founders of *Agudat Israel. Particularly sympathetic toward young people and concerned with their needs, he was instrumental in establishing schools and youth organizations. As well as being a scholar, he was an ardent bibliophile. He visited Ereẓ Israel many times and acquired property there. On the outbreak of World War II he escaped from Gur to Warsaw, and finally to Ereẓ Israel in 1940. During and after the Holocaust he was active in rescue work and in the material and spiritual rehabilitation of refugees. He died on Shavuot at the height of the siege of Jerusalem in 1948 and was buried in the precincts of Yeshivah Sefat Emet which he had founded.

Abraham Mordecai's son, Israel Alter (1892–), succeeded him as Gur rabbi. A noted scholar of great personal charm, he had an influence far beyond the immediate circle of his followers. As head of the various Gur institutions and yeshivot he did much to enhance the reputation and influence of Gur Ḥasidism. Thousands of visitors traveled to his court in Jerusalem each year to see him and receive his blessing. [A.Y.G.]

Bibliography: *Bleter far Geshikhte,* 1 pt. 3–4 (1948), 146–8; *Megiles Poyln,* 5 pt. 1 (1961; Heb. and Yid.), 303, 305; T. Brustin-Bernstein, in: *Bleter far Geshikhte,* 4 no. 2 (1951), 103–19, passim; S. Weiss, in: *Sinai,* 8 (1941), 174–89; L. Grossman, *Shem u-She'erit* (1943), 20–21; O. Z. Rand (ed.), *Toledot Anshei Shem,* 1 (1950), 2–3; A. I. Bromberg, *Mi-Gedolei ha-Ḥasidut,* 2 (1951); 22 (1966); I. Alfasi, *Gur* (1954); A. I. Alter, *Me'ir Einei ha-Golah* (1954); M. Schwartzman, *Ha-Ma'or ha-Gadol* (1966); I. Frenkel, *Men of Distinction,* 1 (1967), 127–34; 2 (1967), 95–102; M. A. Lipschitz, *Hassidic School of Gur* (Diss., Univ. of Wisconsin, 1964).

GORDIMER, NADINE (1923–), South African novelist. She was born in the gold-mining town of Springs. Her first volume of short stories, *Face to Face* (1949), was followed by another collection entitled *The Soft Voice of the Serpent* (1953). Her first novel, *The Lying Days* (1953), essentially a work of autobiography, established what was to be the central theme of all her novels—the loss of innocence and the development of self-awareness and maturity. Her best-known work, *A World of Strangers* (1958), dealt with the friendship of a young British publisher and a black South African amid the stresses of apartheid. Her other novels include *Occasion for Loving* (1963), *The Late Bourgeois World* (1966), and *A Guest of Honor* (1970). She also published further collections of short stories, including *Friday's Footprint* (1960) and *Not For Publication* (1965) and, in collaboration with Lionel Abrahams, the anthology *South African Writing Today* (1967), which, like several more of her works, was banned in her own country. A courageous and respected writer, Nadine Gordimer displayed sensitivity and authority in her studies of the individual's fate within the peculiar circumstances of South African society. [M.Wa.]

GORDIN, ABBA (1887–1964), Yiddish and Hebrew writer. Born in the Vilna region, Gordin received a traditional Jewish education and was self-taught in general subjects. He wrote in Hebrew, Russian, and English as well as in Yiddish. As an ideologist of anarchism, he remained true to his convictions even in Communist Russia. He lived in Moscow and Leningrad until 1926, when he succeeded in escaping to New York, where he edited the periodical *Yidishe Shriftn* (1941–46). During the last seven years of his life he lived in Israel and edited the Hebrew-Yiddish periodical *Problemot*. In his early, pedagogical writings, Gordin sought a synthesis of biblical Judaism and classical anarchism. His memoirs of the post-1917 years, *Zikhroynes un Kheshboynes* ("Reminiscences and Reckonings," 1955–57), and *Draysik Yor in Lite un Poyln* ("Thirty Years in Lithuania and Poland," 1958), when he opposed communism and fought for anarchism, are a valuable, authentic, though one-sided, contribution to the history of the Bolshevik Revolution.

Bibliography: LYNL, 2 (1958), 139–40. [M.Rav.]

GORDIN, JACOB (1853–1909), playwright and journalist. In his stormy 18 years in America, Gordin wrote more than 100 plays for the Yiddish stage, most of which have been forgotten. Yet he must be reckoned the most important formative influence, after *Goldfaden, in the history of the modern Yiddish theater.

Born in Mirgorod, Ukraine, Gordin was writing for the Russian press at the age of 17. Though tutored in secular subjects at home, he was essentially self-educated. He tried his hand at business but failed and became in turn a farm laborer, a stevedore, and an actor in a Russian itinerant troupe, all the while writing for the Russian press. He finally settled in Yelizavetgrad (present-day Kirovograd) as a teacher in the local "russified" Jewish school.

Gordin's first political ideal was nurtured in a circle devoted to Ukrainian independence. Later, influenced by Tolstoy and by the dissident Stundists (a non-Orthodox Christian Evangelical sect in Russia), as well as by Russian populist and Jewish enlightenment currents, he founded his own sect, the Dukhovno-Bibliyskoye Bratstvo ("The Spiritual Biblical Brotherhood"), in 1880. He and his followers rejected post-biblical Judaism, claimed the Bible as the source for their rationalist ethics, repudiated commerce, and saw in agriculture the sole healthy and virtuous occupation. Gordin's obsession with occupational reform led him to write an article which grossly offended the Jewish community. Soon after the April 1881 pogroms, he published in the Russian press an open letter "To My Jewish Brethren" in which he argued that Jewish usury, love of money, and middleman occupations were to blame for Russian anti-Semitism. The "Brotherhood" was ineffectual; its efforts to build a communal colony failed. In 1891, the czarist police decided to disband the group, and Gordin, forewarned, fled to America.

Shortly after arriving in New York, which was to become his permanent home, Gordin applied to the Baron de *Hirsch Fund for aid in establishing a communal farm; he was refused. Family obligations, a pregnant wife and eight (eventually 14) children to support, made Gordin turn to journalism; he soon became a Yiddish journalist, and, by a further leap, a Yiddish playwright. Prior to his arrival in America, at the age of 38, Gordin had never written in Yiddish nor ever written a play.

Jacob Gordin, Yiddish playwright. Jerusalem, J.N.U.L., Schwadron Collection.

His first play *Sibirya* (1891), though an apprentice piece, reveals many of those qualities for which Gordin was to earn the title "Reformer of the Yiddish Stage." The Yiddish theater, as Gordin found it, was one of vulgar burlesque and of absurd and garish "historical operettas." In *Sibirya*, as in all of Gordin's plays, the characters speak good colloquial Yiddish rather than the affected germanized Yiddish favored by the bombastic style of the day. Gordin disciplined his ad-libbing comic actors and banned, or at least modified, the rhymed-couplet song-and-dance routine. He built suspense into his plays and made spectacle secondary to dramatic action. *Sibiryah*, however, also heralds Gordin's characteristic tendentiousness, stereotyping, moralizing, and excessive pathos. Yet the gentile judge in *Sibirya* is presented as a human being rather than as a caricature, something of an innovation, and indicative of the way in which Gordin's earnest view of the theater as school and temple yielded aesthetic fruit. But Gordin's melodramatic plays never ceased to be vehicles for his social gospel; he valued his art mainly for what it might teach.

Gordin's first great popular success *Der Yidisher Kenig Lir* (1892) made his reputation, as well as that of Jacob P. *Adler who was in the leading role. Henceforth, Gordin was to write many plays for virtuosi—the lead roles in *Mirele Efros* (1898) and *Di Shekhite* (1899) were created for Keni Liptsin, and those in *Sappho* (1899) and *Kreutzer Sonata* (1902) for Bertha *Kalish. Great actors respected Gordin and he in turn wrote great roles for them.

Gordin's use of borrowed plots was to become typical, and despite his open avowal of his sources, he was plagued with accusations of plagiarism. He adopted plots from Hugo, Hauptmann, Schiller, Gogol, Gorki, Sudermann, Grillparzer, Ibsen, Lessing, Gutzkow, Ostrovski, and others. From Shakespeare he took the skeletal plot of *King*

Lear for his *Yidisher Kenig Lir*—the title itself acknowledging the debt. The latter is essentially a Jewish play, a didactic melodrama which probes the problem of conflict between generations. The impulse behind its female analogue, *Mirele Efros*, possibly the most popular play in the Yiddish repertoire, came from Gordin's own Lear play rather than from Shakespeare. The world of *Mirele Efros* is a Jewish world, yet the play was performed successfully in nine languages. Gordin was frequently attacked for introducing alien matter into the Yiddish theater; some critics denied he was a Jewish writer at all.

Among the other popular Gordin plays may be mentioned *Got, Mensh un Tayvl* (1900), *Di Shvue* (1900), and *Khasye di Yesoyme* (1903). Only about a fourth of his plays have been printed, some in pirated editions; many exist in manuscript or have been lost. Gordin also wrote a score of one-act plays, largely to encourage amateur performers, and serious essays on the theater. He wrote widely for the press, but his stories and sketches are invariably marred by socialist moralizing.

Gordin came to love Yiddish but denied it the status of "national tongue." He viewed with pessimism the future of the American Yiddish theater whose temporary decline he lived to witness. His dying words were "finita la commedia." A quarter of a million Jews attended his funeral in New York City.

Gordin's works have not been well edited. The four basic collections are *Yankev Gordin's Ertseylungen* (1908); *Ale Shriftn* (4 vols., 1910); *Yankev Gordins Dramen* (2 vols., 1911); *Yankev Gordins Eynakters* (1917).

Bibliography: K. Marmor, *Yankev Gordin* (Yid., 1953), incl. bibl.; A. Cahan, *Bleter fun Mayn Lebn*, 3 (1926), 186–94; 4 (1928), 344–77; B. Gorin, *Di Geshikhte fun Yidishn Teater*, 2 (1923), 107–26; LNYL, 2 (1958), 142–53; S. Niger, *Dertseylers un Romanistn* (1946), 193–203; M. Winchevsky, *A Tog mit Yankev Gordin* (1909); Z. Zylbercwajg (ed.), *Leksikon fun Yidishn Teater* (1931), 391–461; idem, *Di Velt fun Yankev Gordin* (1964); Lifschutz, in: AJHSQ, 56 (1966/67), 152–62; Prager, in: *American Quarterly*, 18 (1966), 506–16.

[L.P.]

GORDIS, ROBERT (1908–), U.S. Bible scholar, author, and rabbi. Gordis was born in New York City, and ordained at the Jewish Theological Seminary in 1932. He served as rabbi of Temple Beth El of Rockaway Park, N.Y., from 1931 until his retirement in 1968, and while there established the first Conservative day school in the United States. A professor of Bible at the Seminary from 1940, Gordis also taught at Columbia University (1948–57), Union Theological Seminary (1960), and Temple University. He served as editor of the periodical *Judaism*, president of the Rabbinical Assembly and of the Synagogue Council of America, and consultant to the Center for the Study of Democratic Institutions.

Gordis' biblical scholarship has been in three major areas: Wisdom literature with special emphasis on the Books of Ecclesiastes and Job; the forms of rhetoric and biblical poetry; and aspects of the masorah and the preservation of the biblical text. Within the Conservative movement he was a spokesman for the centrist position, advocating change within the framework of the law. He has also written on the relationship of Judaism to contemporary problems, on the pertinent insights of the Jewish tradition to the issues facing Western civilization, and on the status of Judaism in the modern age. Among his books are: *Koheleth: the Man and His World* (1951); *Judaism for the Modern Age* (1955); *Faith for Moderns* (1960); *Root and the Branch* (1962); *Book of God and Man: A Study of Job* (1965); and *Judaism in a Christian World* (1966).

[J.R.]

GORDON, ABRAHAM (1874–1941?), socialist, active in Vilna. Of a poor family, Gordon became an engraver, from which profession he derived his Russian pseudonym "Rezchik." He took an active part in the Jewish workers' circles in Vilna and was influenced by populism. In the early 1890s Gordon led the opposition against the shift in aims of the workers' circles—from spreading general education and explaining socialist ideology in the Russian language to conducting propaganda in Yiddish on economic problems and the organization of strikes. Gordon fought the influence of the Social-Democrat intelligentsia (who later founded the *Bund) on the workers' movement. Even when remaining without supporters he continued to advocate his ideas for many years, and published a number of pamphlets. He was last reported in Vilna in 1940. The circumstances of his death are unknown.

Bibliography: E. Mendelssohn, in: *International Review of Social History*, 10 (1965), 271–3; LNYL, 2 (1958), 116–7; N. A. Buchbinder, *Di Geshikhte fun der Arbeter-Bavegung in Rusland* (1931), 69–70.

[M.M.]

GORDON, AHARON DAVID (1856–1922), Hebrew writer and spiritual mentor of that wing of the Zionist labor movement which emphasized self-realization through settlement on the land (the *ḥalutzim*); born in Troyanov, Russia. Gordon's grandfather was a noted scholar, and his father worked as a clerk for his famous relative, Baron Joseph *Guenzburg. Gordon studied Talmud, Bible, and Hebrew grammar with private tutors, as well as Russian and secular subjects on his own. As he was the only survivor of five children, his parents were anxious to have him exempted from military service, but he insisted on presenting himself for examination. When he was found medically unfit, he married and was given a responsible post in the financial management of Baron Guenzburg's estate, which he held, with interruptions, for 23 years. He was respected by the workers and junior officials, whose interests he tried to protect, often at the expense of his own. During this period he was active in educational and cultural work, especially among the youth. At first he was antagonistic to the modern Hebrew literature of his time, especially because of the hostility of many writers to Jewish religious tradition. In 1903, the village in which Gordon worked was sold to a new owner, and he had to find other employment. In this crisis, he decided, despite the opposition of his parents and his wife's family, to settle in Ereẓ Israel, and in 1904 he set out alone, bringing his wife and daughter over only five years later.

In Ereẓ Israel. Although he was now 48 and had never done physical work, he insisted on tilling the soil with his own hands. He worked as a manual laborer in the vineyards and orange groves of *Petaḥ Tikvah and *Rishon le-Zion and, after 1912, in various villages in Galilee, suffering all the tribulations of the pioneers: malaria, unemployment, hunger, and insecurity. From 1909 he wrote numerous articles, most of them published in **Ha-Po'el ha-Ẓa'ir*, embodying his original outlook on labor, Zionism, and the Jewish destiny, which became widely known as "the religion of labor," though he did not use the term. He spent his last years in *Deganyah, where he died in 1922.

Although Gordon was a delegate to the Eleventh Zionist Congress in 1913 and the Ha-Po'el ha-Ẓa'ir conference in Prague in 1920, he was never interested in political affairs as such. He believed that salvation for the Jewish people could come about only through the efforts of the individual to change himself. Thus, he was not enthusiastic about the *Balfour Declaration and the World War I *Jewish Legion. He opposed *Po'alei Zion and *Aḥdut ha-Avodah because of their ties with international socialism, believing that the

A. D. Gordon, Hebrew writer and Zionist philosopher. Courtesy Central Zionist Archives, Jerusalem.

Jewish workers in Ereẓ Israel must find their own way to a just, productive society through a life of labor. Although he held no official position, Gordon exercised a profound influence on the Jewish labor movement the world over through his writings and, even more, through his personal example. The *Gordonia youth movement, founded in 1925, was named after him and based largely on his ideas.

Gordon's Philosophy. Gordon's world view is rooted in the conviction that the cosmos has unity, that nature and man are one, and that all men are organic parts of the cosmos. Man is molded by the cosmos in two different ways: through his knowledge of the world and through his intuitive perception of the world, which can never be consciously known, yet can be lived. What we know is merely a fragment of what we are. A man becomes an individual by the way in which he opens himself to the immediacy of the experience of life. The human soul is related to a hidden part of the cosmos. It is in this "hidden" life that each man's individuality is rooted.

Gordon was conscious of the fact that his theory sets up a dichotomy between rational "knowledge" and "life." He compared their dualism with the relationship between the flame and the oil in a burning lamp. Consciousness and knowledge are the flame; life itself is the oil which nourishes it. The intellect achieves clarity by concentrating its light on a single sector of reality. However, the intellect pays a price for this clarity: it cuts off the living relationship between the sector which it investigates and the totality of the cosmos. The more a man penetrates nature with his knowledge, the less he can live it with his whole being. Yet the ultimate source of our deepest certainties is not the knowledge we may accumulate, but life itself. Living intuition speaks where our intellect fails us. The intellect is an important weapon in the struggle for survival. At the same time, however, it tends to isolate and alienate man from the cosmos as a whole.

In this tension Gordon discovers the source of religion. Through religion man begins to feel once again that he is an organic part of creation. God cannot be approached through the intellect, but man can reach God in an immediate living relationship. With the psalmist, Gordon says, "My soul thirsteth for God, the living God." A mystery to the intellect, God cannot be known, but He can be experienced and lived.

Gordon's friends found it difficult to accept his religious notions. For them religion had become ossified, irrelevant, a thing of the past. He attempts to meet their objections by making a distinction between form and content in religion. He concedes that as far as form is concerned, religion has lost much of its vitality. The content of religion originates in the religious individual; it is the expression of his sense of cosmic unity and purpose. But men tend to sanctify religious forms at the expense of religious content. Gordon claims that, though present-day religious thinking may be dead, God Himself can never die. He is a hidden mystery, yet we encounter Him in all we experience. Religion will not die so long as men live and think and feel. Its time has not passed—its time has not yet even come. True religion is of the future.

Man cut himself off from this source of rejuvenation when he left the soil and moved to the city. Nature is no longer the source of his inner renewal; he has reduced nature to a quantity of corn, or grain, or wood, which he buys or sells. Man's relationship with other men, things, and nature have become purely utilitarian. Authentic religion cannot live in such an atmosphere. If man is to rediscover religion, the proper balance between the two powers of the human soul—intellect and intuition—must be restored. The task of the intellect is to be the servant—the *shammash*—of intuition, not to overpower it. The proper balance between master and servant can be restored only by man's return to a direct relationship with nature.

"Our road leads to nature through the medium of physical labor." The return to nature through labor will enable man to rediscover religion and to regain a sense of cosmic unity and holiness. Gordon's religion has been defined as a "religion of labor." Gordon was strongly influenced by Tolstoy, who preached a similar return to nature; but unlike Tolstoy, Gordon attempted to practice what he preached.

Gordon opposed socialism in its Marxist form. He regarded Marxism as merely another creation of the intellect, a product of a technological and capitalistic civilization. The aim of Marxism is the reorganization of the social order, not the renewal of the human spirit. It seeks to change man by changing the regime, instead of seeking to change the regime by changing man. All attempts to transform human life through the introduction of a new social order are doomed to failure if they do not begin with what must come first: the living human being. A genuine inner renewal of society can be achieved not by an accidentally related mass, but only by an organically united community—the people. Nature has created the people as the connecting link between the cosmos and the individual. Mankind represents the unity not of states but of peoples. A people is a natural community embodying a living cosmic relationship.

For this reason cosmopolitanism must be replaced by what Gordon calls cosmo-nationalism. Cosmopolitanism is based on the assumption that the individual can be a citizen of mankind directly, without being a member of a specific historic people. This assumption is an illusion. Such an individual and such a mankind are mere abstractions. There are only men who are Russians, Germans, Frenchmen.

Gordon uses the phrase *am-adam* ("people-humanity,"

"people-incarnating humanity") to express his thinking on the role of the people in the fulfillment of man's destiny. Man was created in the image of God, and Gordon adds that the people has to be created in the image of God too. This "people-incarnating humanity" is the new ideal which Israel, returning to its land, is to exemplify in the eyes of all mankind. Gordon's cosmo-nationalism has genuine universalistic implications. No people must ever be permitted to place itself above morality. A people incarnates humanity only to the extent to which it obeys the moral law.

Here Gordon saw the challenge which the Jew faced in Ereẓ Israel. The recreation of such a nation—its realization—was to be the contribution of the reborn Jewish people to mankind. The creation of a nation which, at the same time, would be an integral part of humanity, is an extension of the original act of creation:

"We were the first to proclaim that man is created in the image of God. We must go farther and say: the nation must be created in the image of God. Not because we are better than others, but because we have borne upon our shoulders and suffered all which calls for this. It is by paying the price of torments the like of which the world has never known that we have won the right to be the first in this work of creation."

He saw the crucial test in the attitude of the Jews toward the Arabs:

"Our attitude toward them must be one of humanity, of moral courage which remains on the highest plane, even if the behavior of the other side is not all that is desired. Indeed their hostility is all the more a reason for our humanity."

Gordon's writings, entitled *Ketavim* (1951–54), appeared in three volumes, including a bibliography. There is also a selection of his writings in English entitled *Selected Essays* (1937).

Bibliography: S. H. Bergman, *Faith and Reason* (1961), 98–120; idem, *A. D. Gordon, l'homme et le philosophe* (1962); Ẓemaḥ Duran, in: A. D. Gordon, *Ha-Ummah ve-ha-Avodah* (1952), 11–52; M. M. Buber, *Israel and Palestine: The History of an Idea* (1952), last chapter; E. Schweid, *Ha-Yaḥid: Olamo shel A. D. Gordon* (1969); H. H. Rose, *The Life and Thought of A. D. Gordon* (1964); A. Hertzberg, *The Zionist Idea* (1960), 368–86; Rose in: *Judaism*, 10 (1961), 40–48.

[SH.H.B.]

GORDON, ALBERT I. (1903–1968), U.S. rabbi and sociologist. Gordon, who was born in Cleveland, Ohio, was ordained by the Jewish Theological Seminary. He served as rabbi of Adath Jeshurun Synagogue, Minneapolis, Minnesota (1930–46), as executive director of the United Synagogue of America (1946–50), and as rabbi of Temple Emanuel, Newton, Massachusetts (1950–68). While in Minnesota, Gordon served as a labor arbitrator for many industries for the National War Labor Board. He was a member of the faculty of Andover Newton Theological School, Boston University, and held many positions in the Jewish community. He wrote four sociological studies, which constitute a substantial contribution to the study of American Jewry: *Jews in Transition* (1949); *Jews in Suburbia* (1959); *Intermarriage: Interfaith, Interethnic and Interracial* (1964); and *The Nature of Conversion* (1967). He also wrote a series of booklets on marriage. [J.RI.]

GORDON, CYRUS HERZL (1908–), U.S. Semitic scholar. Born in Philadelphia, Gordon worked as a field-archaeologist in Jerusalem and Baghdad from 1931 to 1935, after which he taught Semitics at Johns Hopkins University (1935–38), Bible at Smith College (1938–41) and at Princeton (1939–42), Assyriology and Egyptology at Dropsie College (1946–56), and Near Eastern studies at Brandeis from 1956.

His *Ugaritic Grammar* (1940) and *Ugaritic Handbook* (1947) which revised the grammar and provided transliterated texts and glossaries were pioneer works in the field as were his *Ugaritic Literature* (1949) and later his *Ugaritic Manual* (1955; revised as *Ugaritic Textbook*, 1965).

Gordon's other major contribution has been in "Helleno-Semitics," the comparison of Eastern and Western civilizations, mainly through the study of early Greece and the Ancient Near East. His works on this subject include *Before the Bible* (1962; revised as *The Common Background of Greek and Hebrew Civilizations*, 1965), in which Gordon examines ancient Greek mythology in comparison to the biblical stories. In *Homer and the Bible* (1967) he tried to show the common background of all the East Mediterranean cultures.

These interests led him to regard the undeciphered Minoan tablets of Crete (Linear A) as possibly written in a language of Semitic origin. He suggested a translation of the Phaestos Disk of Crete and of Eteocretan inscriptions on the basis of Semitic linguistics. In 1966 he published these researches in *Ugarit and Minoan Crete* and *Evidence for the Minoan Language*. His other works on Semitics and archaeology are: *Nouns in the Nuzi Tablets* (1936); *Numerals in the Nuzi Tablets* (1938); *The Living Past* (1941), a summary of his studies on important excavations in the Middle East; and *Lands of the Cross and Crescent* (1948). He also wrote: *The Relationship between Modern and Biblical Hebrew* (1951); *Smith College Tablets* (1952), in which he published 110 cuneiform texts from the college collection; *Introduction to the Old Testament Times* (1953, revised as *The World of the Old Testament*, 1958); *Hammurabi's Code* (1957); *Adventures in the Nearest East* (1957), a popular description of important discoveries in the Middle East from the Dead Sea Scrolls to Ugaritic; *New Horizons in Old Testament Literature* (1960); *Ancient Near East* (1965); *Mediterranean Literature* (1967); and *Forgotten Scripts* (1968).

In 1968 Gordon declared that new knowledge about Phoenician word usage had made it likely that a previously rejected Phoenician tablet (found in 1872) was genuine and that the Phoenicians had gone to America from Ezion-Geber in the 19th year of Hiram, king of Tyre. [ED.]

GORDON, DAVID (1831–1886), Hebrew journalist and editor; one of the early supporters of Ḥibbat Zion. Born in Podmerecz near Vilna, he studied in a yeshivah and later turned to Haskalah and took up secular studies. In 1849 he settled in Sergei (Serbei), earning a meager livelihood as a teacher. In the mid-1850s he moved to England, where he remained until 1858, teaching Hebrew and German. In 1858 Gordon moved to Lyck when Eliezer Lipmann *Silbermann invited him to become assistant editor of the first Hebrew weekly, *Ha-Maggid*. In 1880 he officially became

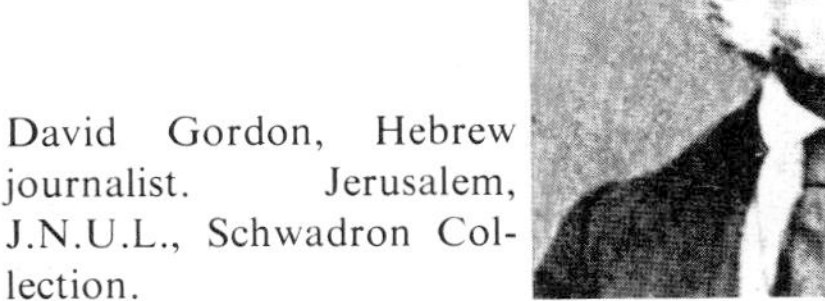

David Gordon, Hebrew journalist. Jerusalem, J.N.U.L., Schwadron Collection.

the editor of *Ha-Maggid*, a position he had long occupied unofficially. From 1879 to 1881 he published a weekly literary and scientific supplement to *Ha-Maggid*, called *Maggid Mishneh*. He also edited a German paper, *Lycker*

Anzeiger, and wrote for the *Times* and *Jewish Chronicle*. His articles in *Ha-Maggid* calling for Jewish national revival in Palestine were the first of their kind in Hebrew. When the Ḥibbat Zion movement was established in the early 1880s, he became one of its leading members and under his editorship *Ha-Maggid* became the Hebrew voice of the movement. Gordon also published several books and contributed to various Hebrew and Yiddish journals.

Bibliography: Waxman, Literature, 3 (1960), 335–7; G. Kressel (ed.), *Mivḥar Kitvei Gordon* (1942), with introd. and bibl. [G.K.]

GORDON, ELIEZER (1840–1910), rabbinical scholar. Gordon was born in the district of Minsk, and while still a young man was invited by R. Israel *Salanter to succeed him in Kovno as teacher of the younger pupils. Appointed in 1874 as rabbi of Kelme and head of its yeshivah, which now attracted many students, he became renowned as one of Lithuania's greatest and most pious rabbinical scholars. In 1884 he was appointed rabbi of Telz (*Telsiai) and head of its yeshivah, which, after the closing of the yeshivah of Volozhin, in 1858, became the spiritual center of Lithuanian Jewry. Gordon was one of the first to adopt what was known in Lithuanian yeshivah circles as "the method of logical comprehension," his lectures being distinguished for their penetrating analysis and their original and logical interpretations. He was also one of the first heads of Lithuanian yeshivah to introduce the study of *musar* ("ethics") into the curriculum, and he appointed adherents of the *Musar movement as *mashgiḥim* (student "supervisors"). Gordon took a special interest in the financial upkeep of the institution and was personally attentive to the needs of each of his students. So deep an attachment existed between them that even those of his students who later became estranged from his outlook and way of life continued to hold him in great personal esteem. As rabbi of Telz Gordon displayed great dedication and resoluteness. At times he would forego his salary; he interceded with the authorities to protect the rights of Russian Jewry; and he played an active part in internal Jewish matters. At every assembly of Russian rabbis Gordon was one of the principal speakers. In Vilna, in 1904, seeking to establish an organization that would embrace all of Orthodox Jewry, he helped found the Keneset Israel organization, regarded by some as the forerunner of *Agudat Israel. In 1910 the Telz yeshivah was destroyed by fire, and Gordon died in the same year, while on a visit to London, where he had gone to raise funds for its rebuilding, and was buried there. His only published work is *Teshuvot Rabbi Eli'ezer* (2 vols., 1912, 1940).

Bibliography: S. Assaf, in: *Ha-Ẓofeh* (Feb. 24, 1950); idem, in: *He-Avar*, 2 (1954), 34–45; D. Katz, *Tenu'at ha-Musar*, 2 (1950), 426–36; Z. A. Rabiner, *Ha-Ga'on Rabbi Eli'ezer Gordon* (1969).

[Z.K.]

GORDON, LORD GEORGE (1757–1793), English proselyte. A younger son of the third duke of Gordon, he entered Parliament in 1774 but attracted little notice until 1779 when he became president of the United Protestant League which opposed measures in relief of Catholic disabilities (1779). After the violent London "No-Popery" Riots (1780), Gordon was tried for high treason but was acquitted. He again appeared as Protestant champion in 1784 in the quarrel between the Dutch and Joseph II. He now began to be interested in Judaism. Although rebuffed by the London rabbinical authorities, he was circumcised in 1787, either in Holland or in Birmingham (where he lived for a time) assuming the name of Israel b. Abraham. He became scrupulous in religious observance, growing a long beard and rebuking those who were not as particular as himself. He was tried for libels on the British government and Marie Antoinette of France and sentenced in 1788 to imprisonment in Newgate, London. Here he surrounded himself with foreign Jews, ate only specially prepared food, refused to see any Jew who was not bearded, and held regular services with a *minyan* in his apartment. He died in prison, but was buried not in the Jewish cemetery but in the family burial plot.

Figure 1. Caricature of the English proselyte Lord George Gordon, published by W. Dickie in 1787. The weathercock indicates his change of faith, and his clothing mocks his decision to live as a Jew. Cecil Roth Collection. Photo David Harris, Jerusalem.

Figure 2. Lord George Gordon, wearing a broad-brimmed hat and smoking a pipe, receiving visitors in Newgate Gaol. A watercolor painted in 1793 by Richard Newton. Cecil Roth Collection.

Bibliography: P. de Castro, *Gordon Riots* (1926); Solomons, in: JHSET, 7 (1915), 222–71; P. Colson, *Strange History of Lord George Gordon* (1937); C. Roth, *Essays and Portraits in Anglo-Jewish History* (1962), 183–210; Roth, Mag Bibl, index.

[C.R.]

GORDON, HAROLD (1907–), U.S. rabbi and administrator. Gordon, who was born in Minneapolis, Minn., was ordained in Palestine. During World War II, he was chaplain in the North Atlantic Division of the Air Transport Command, flying over 250,000 miles to military bases in North America and Europe. Gordon was elected general secretary and chaplaincy coordinator of the New

York Board of Rabbis, the metropolitan organization of Orthodox, Conservative, and Reform rabbis, in 1946 and executive vice-president in 1956. As such, he directed a network of chaplains in hospitals, prisons, and other institutions, and coordinated the work of one of the largest rabbinic bodies in the world. He initiated the establishment of the International Synagogue at Kennedy Airport, the Brit Milah School, and the Brit Milah Board of New York.

[J.Ri.]

GORDON, JACOB (1877–1934), Canadian rabbi. Gordon was born in Danilowicz, and studied at Lithuanian yeshivot. He emigrated to Toronto in 1904 where he was recognized as the city's senior communal Orthodox rabbi. He helped found the Mizrachi movement in Toronto. In 1908 he helped establish the Simcoe Street *talmud torah,* the first in the city to use Hebrew as the language of instruction and precursor of the Associated Hebrew Schools. In 1919 Gordon addressed the founding conference of the Canadian Jewish Congress in Montreal on the subject of the five-day work week and its relationship to Sabbath observance. His writings include *Minḥat Ya'akov* (1914) and *"Dovev Siftei Yeshenim,"* on spiritualism, and *"Nezirut min ha-Basar,"* on vegetarianism, both in manuscript.

Bibliography: *Who's Who in Canadian Jewry* (1965), 114–5.

[B.G.K.]

GORDON, JEKUTHIEL BEN LEIB (18th century), kabbalist. Gordon went from Vilna to study medicine at the University of Padua. He became acquainted with Moses Ḥayyim *Luzzatto in Padua. At that time, Luzzatto was organizing his group for study and messianic activity. Gordon, who became his foremost disciple, was one of the first seven who signed the "regulations" of Luzzatto's circle around 1728. In 1729 Gordon wrote a letter in which he related in detail the activities of Luzzatto, especially the revelation of the *maggid,* the divine revelatory agent which disclosed to Luzzatto the *Zohar Tinyana* ("second Zohar"). Gordon described Luzzatto's many mystical powers and told of how various *ẓaddikim* were revealed to him. This letter fell into the hands of Moses *Ḥagiz, who saw that the activities recounted in the letter were close to Shabbatean practices, and asked the rabbis of Venice to intervene and stop them. Gordon supported Luzzatto in the ensuing controversy. He probably discontinued his medical studies to devote his energy to the activities of the group. A poem written by Luzzatto seems to indicate, with other sources, that Gordon was believed by Luzzatto and his circle to be a reincarnation (**gilgul*) of the soul of the hero Samson, who would be revealed in messianic times as Serayah from the tribe of Dan, and would be one of the leaders of the Israelite army in the apocalyptic wars. Gordon returned to Eastern Europe after Luzzatto had to cease his activities in Padua, but he probably continued to preach Luzzatto's teachings.

Bibliography: S. Ginzburg, *Ramḥal u-Venei Doro* (1937), 18–20 and passim; I. Tishby, *Netivei Emunah u-Minut* (1964), 169–72, 192–6; Y. David, in: *Tarbiz,* 31 (1961/62), 102–4; J. Dan, *ibid.,* 412–3.

[Y.D.]

GORDON, JUDAH LEIB (**Leon;** 1831–1892), Hebrew poet, writer , critic, and allegorist. One of the outstanding poets of the 19th century, Gordon was also a witty, incisive journalist who courageously militated against the ills in Jewish society. He advocated social and religious reform and fiercely denounced the rigidness of its leaders, especially the rabbis. His wrath was vented most directly in his poetry and in satirical feuilletons. Probably the severest critic of his time and a fiery exponent of the *Haskalah, Gordon is rightly considered one of its key spokesmen. He

Figure 1. Judah Leib Gordon, 19th-century Russian Hebrew poet and journalist. Courtesy Central Zionist Archives, Jerusalem.

embodied an age which ended with him, but at the same time he paved the way for such poets as Ḥayyim Naḥman *Bialik, Saul *Tchernichowsky, and others whom he had influenced. Bialik, his great admirer and successor as the "poet laureate" of Hebrew literature, called him "the mighty hammer of the Hebrew language."

Childhood and Education. Gordon was born in Vilna. His father was "a cultured and erudite man" who engaged as Judah Leib's first teacher Rabbi Lipa, the pupil of a disciple of the Gaon of Vilna. The boy was taught according to the Gaon's method which involved first the study of the Bible and Hebrew grammar, and then the study of Talmud (an unusual procedure in traditional Jewish education at that time). At 14 he already had the reputation of a prodigy. He was permitted to study without the guidance of a teacher and soon became thoroughly versed in rabbinic literature. His brother-in-law, the Yiddish poet Mikhel *Gordon, exercised a considerable influence on Judah Leib, who, at 17, began studying European culture and languages (Russian, German, Polish, French, and English). At 22 he graduated from the government teachers seminary in Vilna and in 1853 began his teaching career in various Jewish government schools in the Kovno province (Lithuania): in Ponevezh (1853–60); in Shavli (1860–65) where he taught French and other secular subjects in the higher grades of the government secondary school; and in Telz (1865–72).

First Steps in Literature (Ponevezh and Shavli Periods). Mikhel Gordon introduced Judah Leib to the Vilna circle of Hebrew *maskilim* whose leading members were Abraham Dov *Lebensohn, the outstanding Hebrew poet of the generation, and his son, the poet Micah Joseph *Lebensohn (Michal), Gordon's contemporary and friend. Both of them influenced his early literary efforts. At the behest of A. D. Lebensohn, Gordon transcribed Micah Joseph Lebensohn's manuscript poems, making minor editorial emendations, and when the latter died in 1852 at the age of 24, Gordon composed a eulogy to his memory, *"Hoi Aḥ"* ("O, Brother").

Gordon's first poems, *Shirei Higgayon* and *Shirei Alilah* (1851), were written under the influence of A. D. Lebensohn and his son. His first major work, *Ahavat David u-Mikhal* ("The Love of David and Michal," 1857), an epic, he dedicated to the "high priest," Lebensohn, who proofread and corrected it. Lebensohn also wrote a *haskamah* (a laudatory introduction) in verse to Gordon's book *Mishlei Yehudah* ("Judah's Parables," Vilna, 1859) which contains mostly translations and adaptations of works by Aesop, Phaedrus, La Fontaine, Lessing, and Krylov, as well as a few fables whose themes, while derived from the Bible, the *aggadah,* and the Midrash, are original in their rendering. The work became very popular and its reputation extended beyond the Hebrew reading public of Russia. Some of the fables were included in Karaite children's collections (in the Crimea and the Caucasus), and a chrestomathy compiled by M. *Steinschneider (Berlin, 1861) for D. Sassoon's Jewish school in Bombay includes many of Gordon's fables.

At this time, Gordon, besides composing poetry, already wrote polemic essays. In an article in the Hebrew periodical **Ha-Maggid* (signed "Dan Gabriel"), he advocated the translation of general literary works of universal human interest into Hebrew and denounced the opponents of such projects, accusing them of wishing "to drive out our Hebrew language from the lands of the living . . ." Gordon also reproached the German Jewish scholars, who published their Jewish studies in German, for their indifference to the Hebrew language. Thus already in the 1850s Gordon used the Hebrew language as a cudgel with which to rap Jewish society, especially the *maskilim* who failed to see in the revival of Hebrew a renaissance of the people itself.

Besides *Ha-Maggid,* Gordon published in *Ha-Karmel,* in L. Philippson's *Allgemeine Zeitung des Judenthums,* and in Russian-Jewish periodicals (e.g., *Raszvet, Den*). His articles in the non-Hebrew press were mostly on Hebrew literature. During the blood libel case in Shavli in which two Jews were accused of the murder of a little peasant girl (1861), he strongly denounced prejudice in the Jewish and in the general press, writing especially for *Golos,* a liberal Russian paper which came out for the rights of Jews, and on whose staff Gordon was employed.

Later Haskalah Activity. In 1865 Gordon became the principal of the Hebrew public school of Telz and later established a girls school in that city. He gave up teaching in 1872 and moved to St. Petersburg where he was secretary of the Jewish community and director of the *Society for the Promotion of Culture among the Jews. He held these offices simultaneously from 1872 to 1879 when he was incarcerated for purported anti-czarist activities. While imprisoned, and in banishment in Pudozh in the province of Olonets, he wrote *Ẓidkiyyahu be-Veit ha-Pekuddot* ("King Zedekiah in Prison," 1879), a historical biblical poem which reflects his prison experiences. Exonerated in 1880, he returned to St. Petersburg but was not reappointed to his former position. The passiveness with which the Jewish community leaders of St. Petersburg reacted to his imprisonment, with their failure to reinstate him after his release, was a blow to Gordon. Lacking any other income, he accepted A. *Zederbaum's invitation to become editor of the Hebrew daily **Ha-Meliẓ*.

Gordon was a prolific and versatile writer and editor. Besides editing, he wrote editorials and various columns (*"Halikhot Olam"* and *"Be-Mishkenot Ya'akov be-Ḥuẓ la-Areẓ"*) anonymously, and published stories, feuilletons, and book reviews under diverse pseudonyms. He turned the Hebrew feuilleton into an effective vehicle of expression. His poetry imitates the form of the biblical verse, but his prose style (stories and feuilletons) is a synthesis of biblical, talmudic, midrashic, and later Hebrew literature. Characterized by typical Hebrew scholarly humor, the style contains many puns and Gordon's literary and conceptual associations range over the whole body of Hebrew literature.

Gordon was also the science editor and literary critic of the Russian Jewish monthly *Voskhod* (1881–82), writing under the pseudonym *"Mevakker"* (Hebrew for "critic"). In "The History of Jewish Settlement in St. Petersburg," and "Attempts at Reforming the Jewish Religion," two articles published in *Voskhod,* he denounced basic reforms in the Jewish religion and the negative attitude to the Talmud taken by some. At the same time, however, he advocated moderate changes. Following a disagreement with his publisher, Gordon resigned from *Ha-Meliẓ* in May 1883 and began editing a collection of his poems which was published by the Jubilee Committee (4 vols., 1884), established in 1881 to honor the 25th anniversary of his writing career. He also worked on the staff of the 82-volume Russian encyclopedic dictionary, published by F. Brockhaus and I. *Efron, to which he contributed articles on Jewish history and Hebrew literature. Gordon's poetry of this period, which he published in the annual *Ha-Asif,* was mostly satirical and included some biting verse against Zederbaum, the publisher of *Ha-Meliẓ*. This, however, did not stop the latter from recalling Gordon to the editorship of his paper. Gordon returned in December 1885 and having meanwhile been completely cleared by the Russian secret police, his name now appeared on the masthead. He continued as editor for two years (December 1885–88), during which time *Ha-Meliẓ* became a daily.

Literary Periods in Gordon's Work. Gordon's work falls into three periods: (1) the romantic period; (2) the realistic period; (3) the period of national awakening.

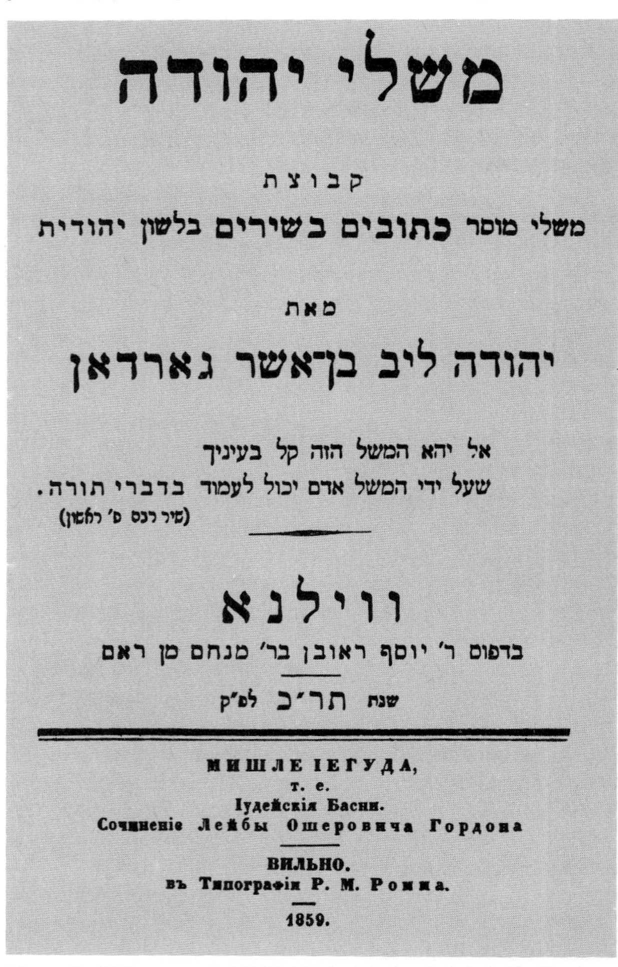

משלי יהודה

קבוצת

משלי מוסר כתובים בשירים בלשון יהודית

מאת

יהודה ליב בן־אשר גארדאן

אל יהא המשל הזה קל בעיניך
שעל ידי המשל אדם יכול לעמוד בדברי תורה.
(שיר רבה פ׳ ראשון)

ווילנא

בדפוס ר׳ יוסף ראובן בר׳ מנחם מן ראם

שנת תר״ב לפ״ק

МИШЛЕ IЕГУДА,
т. е.
Iудейскiя Басни.
Сочиненiе Лейбы Ошеровича Гордона

ВИЛЬНО.
въ Типографiи Р. М. Ромма.

1859.

Figure 2. Title page of *Mishlei Yehudah,* by Judah Leib Gordon, Vilna, 1859. Jerusalem, J.N.U.L.

THE ROMANTIC PERIOD. Influenced by the Haskalah and its exponents, he wrote long epics on biblical themes during this period, e.g., *Ahavat David u-Mikhal* (Vilna, 1857), "*David u-Varzillai*" (written between 1851 and 1856), and "*Asenat Bat Potifera*" (publ. in 1868). They are imbued with the Haskalah spirit and are of allegorical tenor, yet echo yearnings for a distant and enchanting biblical past.

THE REALISTIC PERIOD. In his poetry as well as in his polemical articles, Gordon was the foremost combatant against the ills of Jewish society and the intransigent religious conservatism of its leaders who, in his view, disregarded the reality of the modern age. He fearlessly chided the people and their leaders. In one of his letters he called himself "the national prosecutor." He became an advocate of the common people, the poor, and the oppressed. Among those whose cause he championed was the Jewish woman whom he saw deprived of rights and subordinate to the male. The heroine of the poem "*Kozo shel Yod*" ("The Point on Top of the *Yod*," completed in 1876) is the beautiful Bat-Shu'a (Gen. 38:12) who, after much suffering and hardships, succeeds in obtaining a divorce from her husband Hillel, a ne'er-do-well who had gone abroad to seek his fortune and had deserted her and their two children. An educated young man, a government employee, wants to marry Bat-Shu'a, but "Rav Vafsi ha-Kuzari" (the name being an anagram of the letters of the then well-known Rabbi Joseph Zechariah [Stern]) invalidates the divorce bill because the husband's name "Hillel" had not been signed in *plene,* lacking the letter *yod.* Bat-Shu'a therefore remains an **agunah* and poor. The poem is an outcry against the lot of the Jewish woman who, because of the "point of a *yod*," is denied happiness. In fighting for the rights of Jewish women, Gordon was influenced by the powerful Russian women's liberation movement of the 1860–70s. "*Kozo shel Yod*" became a catchword quoted by the fighters for women's rights: "Hebrew woman, who knows your life?/In darkness you came and in darkness shall go;/Your sorrow, your joy, your misfortune, your desires/In you are born, in you they die."

THE PERIOD OF NATIONAL AWAKENING. Gordon, like the *maskilim* of his generation, at first believed that isolation was at the root of all the troubles that plagued the Jews. "Be a Jew in your home and a man in the street," a line from his poem *Hakizah Ammi* ("My People Awake"), became the motto for a whole generation of *maskilim.* The source of the evil was the rabbis whom he considered intransigent and rigid adherents to the *halakhah* and to old customs and tradition. The only solution for Russian Jewry was to leave its narrow, confined existence and to adapt itself to the wider environment. He urged Jews to stop speaking Yiddish which he regarded as a jargon and to adopt Russian. He advocated universal general education, reform of religious customs, and prompted Jews to engage in more productive occupations, such as crafts, industry, and agriculture. Caught up in the liberal spirit that swept Russia at the time, Gordon firmly believed in Russian liberalism, especially after serfdom was abolished in 1861 and the Jews were granted some rights. He thought that adaptation to the non-Jewish environment would lead to a relationship of friendship and brotherhood between Jews and the people among whom they lived.

Gordon was to be disillusioned in Russian liberalism and in his whole conception of the viability of Jewish life in the Diaspora. This led him to reexamine his ideas and values in the light of everyday reality. With the growth of the anti-Semitic movement in Russia and in light of the ineptness of Russian liberalism, Gordon despaired of the Russian Jewish community ever integrating within the Russian environment and cultural milieu. He was also disappointed in the Jewish *maskilim,* particularly the young, who were carried away by the assimilationist trend, rejecting indiscriminately and forsaking Jewish values and the Hebrew language which Gordon loved and championed without reservation. In his poem "*Le-Mi Ani Amel*" ("For Whom Do I Labor?") he cries out in despair: "My enlightened brothers have learned science./They mock the old mother who holds the distaff/Forsake it [Hebrew] and let us each follow the language of his country." He concludes on an ominous note of dejection: "Oh, who can tell the future, who can tell me?/Perhaps I am the last of Zion's poets/And you, the last readers." Thus he protested against the assimilationist trend as well as against his adversaries who accused him of preaching russification.

The 1881 pogroms in southern Russia (instigated with the knowledge and perhaps the support of the government) completely crushed Gordon's spirit. He began to look upon emigration to Western countries as the only salvation for Russian Jewry. Gordon did not believe that the Ereẓ Israel of his time, under the yoke of a degenerate and cruel Turkish rule which closed the country to Jewish immigration, could absorb all the Jews who would want to settle there. He therefore advocated emigration to Western countries, particularly to the United States. In his powerful poem "*Aḥoti Ruḥamah*" ("Ruhamah, My Sister"), written in 1882 after the Russian pogroms, he pleaded for "the honor of Jacob's daughter whom the son of Hamor had violated." The use of biblical names—Dinah, daughter of Jacob, and Shechem, son of Hamor—enabled the poet to evade Russian censorship and to publish his poem of wrath against the Russian rioters in *Migdanot,* a literary supplement to *Ha-Meliẓ.* Gordon thunders in his wrath: "Abel's blood marks Cain's forehead!/And your blood too all shall behold/A mark of Cain, disgrace and eternal shame/On the forehead of the murderous villains."

He ends his poem: "Come, let's go, my sister Ruḥamah!" In "*Bi-Ne'areinu u-vi-Zekeneinu Nelekh*" ("We Shall Go, Young and Old"), a poem also written in the aftermath of the Russian atrocities, he calls out to the Jewish people: "Fear not, Jacob, be not dejected,/Thousands slaughtered will not deter!/Our God's voice calls from the storm/'Let's go, young and old'."

Gordon's changed attitude is manifest in his articles and feuilletons written when he returned as editor of *Ha-Meliẓ* which had become the organ of the *Ḥibbat Zion movement. He was sharply attacked by **Ha-Ẓefirah* and **Ha-Yom,* rival Hebrew papers. They accused him of disavowing the views he had preached all his life and of submitting, for material reasons, to the dictates of the owner of *Ha-Meliẓ.* Gordon, however, never actually joined the Ḥibbat Zion movement and did not explicitly endorse emigration to "Turkish" Ereẓ Israel as a solution for Russian Jewry. Settlement in Ereẓ Israel, without the renaissance of the nation, in his view, would be ineffectual, and such a revival depended on religious and cultural modifications: "Our redemption can come about only after our spiritual deliverance" (*Ha-Meliẓ,* 18 (1882), 209–16).

His writings, in which he fervently urged the revival of Hebrew and which express his great love for the Jews as a people, undoubtedly influenced the movement for national revival and later the Zionist movement. In his introduction to *Al Parashat Derakhim* ("At the Crossroads," 1895), *Aḥad Ha-Am, father of spiritual Zionism, notes his indebtedness to Gordon. Gordon's call, "O House of Jacob, come ye, and let us walk" (Isa. 2:5), in his article in *Ha-Karmel* (1866), in which he advocated enlightenment and rapprochement to Europe, eventually became the motto of the first *Bilu pioneers who turned their back on Europe and its enlightenment and emigrated to Erez Israel (1882) to rebuild its wilderness. Gordon, while not committing himself formally, actively upheld the Zionist cause. Thus his criticism (in Hebrew and Russian) of L. *Pinsker's *Autoemancipation* (1882) was favorable, as was his view on Britain's occupation of Egypt in 1882. Realizing that the occupation would increase Palestine's importance "as a corridor to Egypt and a center for Asian trade and that the British rule would attract many of our brethren throughout the Diaspora to Palestine to till the soil, build railways, and introduce new life in trade, property, and arts and crafts," he proposed the founding of "the society for those going to Palestine" in his article in *Ha-Meliz* (1882).

Gordon's place in Jewish literature as the poet of the Haskalah is undisputed. The aesthetic value of his writings, however, was questioned soon after his death and is still being contended. The dispute grew out of a literary atmosphere which had reexamined the values of the past. The last decade of the 19th century had witnessed cultural changes in society in general, and the Jewish community in particular, that affected literature and modified aesthetic taste. It was debated whether Gordon was a poet or merely a versifier. Strong views were voiced by both his admirers and his detractors but the former always prevailed.

There was no conflict between Gordon, the poet and visionary, and the Gordon who attempted to forge a new style, had mastered several languages, both classical and modern, and was a gifted translator. Among his translations are Byron's *Hebrew Melodies* (*Zemirot Yisrael*, 1884), the Pentateuch (from Hebrew into Russian, 1875), and classical fables which he translated from Russian into Hebrew *(Mishlei Mofet)*. Gordon also wrote in Russian and German on Judaism and Hebrew literature. His light, humoristic poems in Yiddish, a language he had always disparaged, were published in *Kol Mevasser*, a Yiddish weekly supplement (1862–72) to *Ha-Meliz*. At the request of friends, the poems were collected in a book and published under the title *Sihat Hullin* ("Small Talk," 1887, 1889[2]). At home in all of Jewish literature, Gordon was able to draw on its sources with remarkable versatility and ease. He invested obsolete expressions and idioms with fresh meaning and created new syntactical units. Bialik called him one of the greatest wizards in Hebrew of all times—a title his prodigious mastery and control of the language has deservedly earned.

Kitvei J. L. Gordon (2 vols., 1953–60), his collected works (prose and poetry), includes an autobiography and diary. His letters were published by I. J. Weissberg (*Iggerot Y. L. Gordon*, 2 vols., 1894).

Bibliography: A. B. Rhine, *Leon Gordon: An Appreciation* (1910), incl. bibl.; Waxman, Literature, 3 (1960[2]), 234–55; *Kitvei J. L. Gordon*, 1 (1953), introd. by J. Fichmann; *Mehkarim bi-Leshon Bialik vi-Yhudah Leib Gordon* (1953); Klausner, Sifrut, 4 pt. 2 (1942); *Leksikon fun der Yidisher Literatur un Prese* (1914); J. S. Raisin, *Haskalah Movement in Russia* (1913), index; *Sefer Zikkaron le-Soferei Yisrael ha-Hayyim Ittanu ka-Yom* (1889), 19–20; *Ha-Asif*, 6 (1893), 1855–56; Spiegel, *Hebrew Reborn* (1930), index; G. Karpeles, in: AZDJ, no. 43 (1892); YE, vol. 6, pp. 690–5.

[A.Z.B.-Y.]

GORDON, MIKHEL (1823–1890), Hebrew and Yiddish poet. Born in Vilna, he early came under the influence of the Haskalah circle of A. D. *Lebensohn. He began his literary career in 1847 with a Hebrew elegy on the death of Mordecai Aaron *Guenzburg, a member of this circle, and continued with Hebrew articles in various periodicals and the publication of two books in Hebrew. He rose to fame with his Yiddish songs which circulated in manuscript in the 1850s and 1860s and for which he also composed melodies. He published some of these Yiddish songs in *Di Bord . . . un andere . . . Yidishe Lider* ("The Beard and other Yiddish Songs," 1868), issued anonymously so as not to endanger his reputation as a Hebrew poet. His song *Shtey oyf Mayn Folk* ("Arise My People") was composed in 1869 and has generally been regarded as the classical poetic expression in Yiddish of the spirit of Jewish enlightenment in Russia. That year he also published a history of Russia in Yiddish. His late, pessimistic mood, intensified by his poverty and loneliness, is reflected in his final poems, published in 1889. In his early period, he influenced the Hebrew and Yiddish poetry of J. L. *Gordon, whose sister he married, and in his later period the ballads of S. S. *Frug and the folksongs of Mark *Varshavsky.

Bibliography: Rejzen, Leksikon, 1 (1926), 510–8; LNYL, 2 (1958), 129–34; I. Manger, *Noente Geshtalten* (1938), 150–63; Charlash, in: *S. Niger Bukh* (1958), 56–71; S. Liptzin, *Flowering of Yiddish Literature* (1963), 63–66. [S.L.]

GORDON (Goldberg), MILTON M. (1918–), U.S. sociologist. Born in Gardiner, Maine, Gordon taught at the University of Pennsylvania, Drew University, and Haverford and Wellesley colleges before being appointed professor of sociology at the University of Massachusetts in 1959. A specialist in the fields of social stratification and inter-group relations, he became widely known through his books, *Social Class in American Sociology* (1958) and *Assimilation in American Life* (1964). The latter, which analyzes the role of race, religion, and national origin in American social organization, is remarkable for its differentiation between cultural and structural pluralism and the formulation of the concept of the "ethclass," referring to social ranking within an ethnic group.

Gordon dealt with subjects of Jewish interest in several of his many papers and essays. They include "The Nature of Assimilation and the Theory of the Melting Pot" in *Current Perspectives in Social Psychology* by E. P. Hollander and R. G. Hunt (1967[2]) and "Marginality and the Jewish Intellectual" in *The Ghetto and Beyond: Essays on Jewish Life in America* (ed. Peter I. Rose, 1969). He was general editor of the *Ethnic Group in American Life* series.

[W.J.C.]

GORDON, SAMUEL LEIB (1865–1933), Hebrew writer and Bible scholar. Born in Lithuania, he emigrated to Palestine in 1898 and taught at the Jaffa Boys School. When the school was taken over by the *Alliance Israélite Universelle, he left for Warsaw (1901) where he established

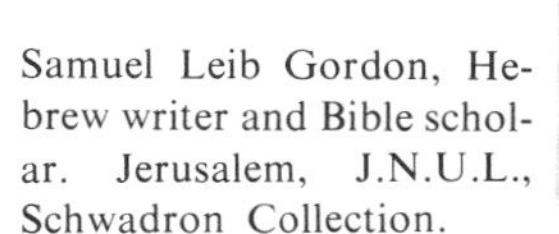

Samuel Leib Gordon, Hebrew writer and Bible scholar. Jerusalem, J.N.U.L., Schwadron Collection.

a Hebrew school for boys. In 1924, he returned to Palestine and devoted the latter years of his life to the composition of an extensive commentary on the Bible. Gordon contributed poems, articles, and translations to the Hebrew periodicals of the late 19th century, and also wrote extensively for children. His books include *Kinnor Yeshurun* (3 vols., 1891–93); *Torat ha-Sifrut* (2 vols., 1900), which was reprinted many times; and a revised edition of his poems, *Shirim u-Fo'emot* (with foreword by S. Halkin), which was published in 1955. He translated three books by I. *Zangwill, La Fontaine's *Fables*, and Shakespeare's *King Lear*. Gordon's textbooks played a vital role in Hebrew education in the Diaspora at the turn of the century; *Ha-Lashon* (3 vols., 1910–19) was one of his most popular works. He also edited several journals for the young: *Olam Katan* (1901–05), *Ha-Ne'urim* (1904–05), as well as *Ha-Pedagog* (1903–04), a journal of education to which the best writers of his generation contributed. [G.K.]

From 1907 he worked on a vocalized Bible commentary which was to provide a "new scientific pedagogical interpretation for advanced students and teachers, edited in the accepted traditional spirit." Known as *Shalag* after the initials of his name, it was largely based on German Bible criticism. Gordon explained words and subject matter simply and fully enough for school pupils and teachers without elaborating on the religious significance of the Bible. His introduction to the prophetic and hagiographic books deal with the literary aspect as well as with personalities and events. Gordon's commentary is still used extensively in the secondary schools in Israel, with the exception of those which are religiously oriented. [J.Lev.]

Bibliography: Ḥ. N. Bialik, *Devarim she-be-Al-Peh* (1935), 242–3; M. Gluecksohn, *Ishim ba-Madda u-va-Sifrut* (1941), 309–12; J. Fichmann, *Be-Terem Aviv* (1959); idem, *Ruḥot Menaggenot* (1953), 383–6; *Kitvei A. Levinson*, 1 (1957), 161–5; M. Y. Fried, *Yamim ve-Shanim*, 2 (1939), 147–50; H. A. Kaplan, *Pezurai* (1937), 198–201.

GORDONIA, pioneering Zionist youth movement that was founded at the end of 1923 in Galicia from small cells and grew into a world movement. The first groups of Gordonia were created under the influence of *Hitaḥadut, on the one hand, and by members who had left *Ha-Shomer ha-Ẓa'ir, on the other. The official name of the movement was chosen at the first world conference in Danzig (November 1928) as Histadrut ha-No'ar ha-Amamit ha-Ḥalutzit Gordonia (the People's Pioneering Association of Youth—Gordonia). The principles of the movement, which were set down at the same conference, were the "building up of the homeland, education of members in humanistic values, the creation of a working nation, the renaissance of Hebrew culture, and self-labor *(avodah aẓmit)*."

From its beginnings, the movement developed around two ideological bases. It aimed at reaching the lower classes of Jewish society (artisans, farmers and villagers, poor people, which constituted a large percentage of Galician Jewry), in contrast to Ha-Shomer ha-Ẓa'ir, which was composed principally of students; and it wished to mold these youth in the spirit of A. D. *Gordon's personality and teachings. Although Gordon, as a historical figure, was recognized by all the pioneering youth movements, Gordonia regarded his philosophy as its principal ideological source and adopted his world view. In contrast to the dogmatic attachment of Marxist movements to Marx, the relationship of Gordonia to Gordon was characterized by its lack of dogmatism, as reflected in Gordon's personality itself. Gordon's ideological image was not distinguished from his personality, and the combination of both was viewed as expressing free humanistic creativity (influenced by both the world at large and the Jewish world) that perpetuates independent, original thought which is always related to all facets of life. This philosophy was particularly attractive to those who had been disappointed by Marxism and did not believe that it was relevant to a youth movement wishing to build its future in Ereẓ Israel on the basis of labor. The Danzig Conference established 13 standards for the behavior of the individual in his personal life and in the movement, and in his relationship to the Jewish people, Ereẓ Israel, labor, socialism, etc. Although it had taken much from other youth movements, especially German ones, Gordonia meticulously maintained its unique character as a Jewish, Zionist, and Ereẓ Israel-oriented movement.

From Galicia Gordonia spread to the rest of Poland, Rumania, and the United States and, by World War II, had close to 40,000 members. At all its conferences, it stressed its identification with the Ereẓ Israel labor movement and its fundamental principle—personal fulfillment through *aliyah* and settlement within the framework of collective living and labor. The first Gordonia groups began to settle in Ereẓ Israel shortly after the riots of 1929, first in Ḥaderah and later in other places. These groups laid the foundation for kevuẓot of Gordonia in the rebuilt *Ḥuldah, which became the movement's center in Ereẓ Israel and contains the central archive of Gordonia, and in Kefar ha-Ḥoresh, Massadah, Ma'aleh ha-Ḥamishah, Nir Am, Ḥanitah, etc. These groups, which first merged into Iggud Gordonia, joined Ḥever ha-Kevuẓot in 1933 and also provided new members for established kevuẓot (Deganyah Alef and Bet, Geva, Ginnegar, etc.).

Later followed the merger of Gordonia with Maccabi ha-Ẓa'ir, which developed as a Jewish scouting movement in Germany and Czechoslovakia and whose members began to settle in Ereẓ Israel in 1932–33. Maccabi ha-Ẓa'ir set up its first settlements (Kefar ha-Maccabi, Ma'yan Ẓevi) in the framework of Ḥever ha-Kevuẓot in 1941, integrated with Gordonia, and thereafter the two movements served as a single framework for pioneering Jewish youth from Eastern and Western Europe. In 1937 a Gordonia movement came into being among Jewish youth in Palestine, and in 1945 it united with part of Maḥanot ha-Olim and founded Ha-Tenu'ah ha-Me'uḥedet (full name, Ha-Tenu'ah ha-Kelalit shel ha-No'ar ha-Lomed). After the Holocaust, attempts were also made abroad to unite pioneering youth movements with aims similar to those of Gordonia, and finally, when the *Iḥud ha-Kevuẓot ve-ha-Kibbutzim was created (in 1951), and after a series of mergers with Gordonia, *Ihud Habonim was founded.

Gordonia played a heroic role in Nazi-occupied Poland during World War II. In Warsaw, under the leadership of Israel Zeltzer and Eliezer Geller, a secret center of the movement was established on 23 Nalewki Street, which organized a considerable network of underground educational activities among its members of all age groups. The center, mainly through Geller's visits in the ghettos of Czestochowa, Opoczno, Bedin, Sosnowiec, Opatow, and other towns, contributed greatly to the resistance movement and also to the preparations for active revolts, particularly in Warsaw in 1943. Gordonia's Polish-language underground paper in Warsaw *Słowo Mlodych* was published in Hebrew translation in 1966 by the archives of Gordonia-Maccabi ha-Za'ir. From its foundation, the movement published newspapers and literature in a number of languages. Pinḥas *Lavon (Lubianiker) was the head of the movement from its foundation throughout its existence.

Bibliography: P. Lubianiker, *Yesodot* (1941); idem, in: *Derekh ha-No'ar* (1930), 47–73; idem, in: G. Chanoch (ed.), *Darkhei ha-No'ar* (1937), 17–26; Mandel, in: J. Cohen and D. Sadan (eds.), *Pirkei Galiẓyah* (1957), 270–81; A. Avnon (ed.), *Ittonut Gordonia be-Maḥteret Getto Varshah* (1966); I. and G. Kressel, *Mafte'aḥ le-ha-Po'el ha-Ẓa'ir (5668–5717)* (1968), s.v.; *Gordonia Report* (1938).

[M.Ma.]

GORELIK, SHEMARYA (1877–1942), Yiddish essayist and literary critic. Born in the Ukraine, he joined the Zionist movement in 1905, after having been an advocate of socialism. He wrote for various Zionist publications, and in 1908 joined S. *Niger and A. *Veiter in founding and editing *Literarishe Monatsshriften,* a Vilna literary monthly which attracted writers of diverse ideologies and furthered the Yiddish cultural resurgence that followed the 1908 *Czernowitz Yiddish Conference. The periodical gave expression to the new national and romantic-symbolist trends in Yiddish literature. During World War I, Gorelik lived in Switzerland, participated in pacifist agitations, and was sentenced to prison for six months. He later described his experiences during these years in a German volume, *Fuenf Jahre im Land Neutralia.* After the war, he lived in Germany and contributed to German Zionist periodicals, until forced to leave in 1933. He then settled in Palestine and wrote for the Hebrew press.

Gorelik's Yiddish essays were collected in five volumes (1908–24). A posthumous selection, with an introduction by his brother, M. Horelik, appeared in Los Angeles in 1947. A Hebrew translation of Gorelik's essays by Abraham Shlonsky, was published in Tel Aviv (*Massot,* 1937). As a literary critic whose studies were impressionistic, Gorelik was not primarily interested in stylistic innovations but rather sought to educate his readers by directing their attention to new insights and ideas.

Shemarya Gorelik, Yiddish essayist and literary critic. Lithograph by Hermann Struck. Courtesy Leo Baeck Institute, New York.

Bibliography: Rejzen, Leksikon, 1 (1926), 539–42; LNYL, 2 (1958), 163–5; J. Glatstein, *In Tokh Genumen* (1956), 98–102; S. Liptzin, in: *Maturing of Yiddish Literature* (1970), 75–77. [Ed.]

GOREN, CHARLES HENRY (1901–), U.S. bridge expert. Goren, who was born in Philadelphia into a Russian immigrant family, was admitted to the Pennsylvania bar in 1923 and practiced in Philadelphia. He had taken up bridge during his student days and eventually achieved master strength, abandoning the bar in order to play and write about bridge. Goren won the National Bridge Championship of America 31 times. As a writer, his many books and newspaper columns earned him widespread recognition. Goren's bridge methods are known for their simplicity and teachability. He cleverly synthesized the "honor trick" strategy of Culbertson with the "point-count" invented by Milton Work. His books include: *Contract Bridge in a Nutshell* (1946); *Point Count Bidding in Contract Bridge* (1949); *New Contract Bridge in a Nutshell* (1959); *An Evening of Bridge with Charles H. Goren* (1959); and *Goren's Hoyle Encyclopaedia of Games* (1961). [G.A.]

GOREN (Gruenblatt), NATAN (1887–1956), Hebrew author, journalist, and critic. Born in Vidzy, in the Kovno district of Lithuania, he moved to Vilna in 1903. He became active in Jewish revolutionary circles and was imprisoned several times during 1906–08. In 1910 he moved to Odessa, joining the prominent group of Hebrew and Yiddish writers who lived there. Subsequently he lived in Moscow, where he worked for the Stybel publishing house and for the journal *Ha-Am.* In 1921 he returned to Lithuania, taking up a leading position in Jewish education and in Hebrew and Yiddish letters. In 1935 he settled in Tel Aviv, where he taught in secondary schools, was active in the Writers' Association, and continued his literary work.

His articles, stories, and poems appeared, beginning in 1911, in numerous Hebrew and Yiddish journals in Europe, Palestine, and the United States. He published his first novel, *Feyvush,* in 1901, several other novels, and two collections of essays on modern Hebrew writers, *Mevakkerim be-Sifrutenu* ("Critics in Our Literature," 1944), and *Demuyyot be-Sifrutenu* ("Figures in Our Literature," 1953).

Bibliography: Z. Harkavi (ed.), *Sefer Natan Goren* (1958). [G.K.]

GOREN, SHLOMO (1917–), Israel rabbi. Born in Zambrow, Poland, he was taken in 1925 to Palestine where his father was one of the founders of Kefar Ḥasidim. At the age of 12, Goren entered the Hebron Yeshivah in Jerusalem where he soon became famous as a prodigy. He published his first work, entitled *Nezer ha-Kodesh* (1935) on Maimonides' *Mishneh Torah,* at the age of 17. In 1939, Goren published *Sha'arei Tohorah* on the laws of *mikveh.*

He joined the Haganah in 1936, and fought in the Jerusalem area during the War of Independence. During this war, he was appointed by the two chief rabbis, Herzog and Ouziel, as chief chaplain of the newly formed army. He subsequently distinguished himself for his bravery, qualified as a paratrooper, and rose to the rank of brigadier-general. He accompanied the troops during both the Sinai Campaign and the Six-Day War, and was the first to conduct a prayer service at the liberated Western Wall in 1967. Goren was responsible for the organization of the military chaplaincy and worked out the regulations for total religious observance in the army. He was responsible for numerous original responsa concerning specific problems of observance due to conditions of active warfare and technological progress. He also developed the principles for permitting the assumed widows *(agunot)* of missing soldiers to remarry. Particularly noteworthy were his decisions permitting the remarriage of the widows of those men who perished on the destroyer *Eilat* and the submarine *Dakar* in 1967/8.

In 1961 Goren received the Israel Prize for the first volume (on the order *Berakhot*) of his comprehensive commentary on the Jerusalem Talmud, entitled *Yerushalmi ha-Meforash* (1961). A collection of his halakhic and philo-

Shlomo Goren, chief chaplain of the Israel Defense Forces, blowing the *shofar* at the Western Wall, Jerusalem, during the Six-Day War, 1967. Courtesy Government Press Office, Tel Aviv.

sophical essays, mainly concerning the Festivals and Holy Days, was published in 1964 under the title of *Torat ha-Mo'adim*. In 1968, he was elected Ashkenazi chief rabbi of Tel Aviv-Jaffa.

Bibliography: Ehrlich, in: *Panim el Panim* (Oct. 4, 1967); D. Lazar, *Rashim be-Yisrael*, 2 (1955), 86–91. [Mo.P.]

°**GORGIAS,** Seleucid general in the war against the forces of *Judah Maccabee. Together with two other generals, *Ptolemy Macron and *Nicanor, Gorgias was sent against the Jews in 165 B.C.E. with a force of 40,000 foot soldiers and 7,000 cavalry. Gorgias set out from his camp near Emmaus with 6,000 soldiers, hoping to surprise Judah by night. Judah, however, succeeded in evading the Greek army and destroyed its main camp at Emmaus, after which Gorgias retreated in disorder. When, two years later, Judah and his brother *Simeon set out to Gilead and Galilee in order to protect the hard-pressed Jewish settlements there, they left the armies of Judea under the inexperienced command of *Joseph and Azariah, sons of Zechariah. Hoping to acquire a reputation for valor, the two commanders attacked the armies of Gorgias, who was at that time in command at Jamnia, but suffered a disastrous defeat.

Bibliography: Jos., Ant., 12:298, 305–12, 351; I Macc. 3:38; 4:1ff.; 5:55; II Macc. 10:14; 12:32–37; Schuerer, Hist, 31, 35; Klausner, Bayit Sheni, 1 (1951²), 57; 3 (1950²), 21, 23. [I.G.]

GORIN, BERNARD (pseudonym of **Isaac Goido;** 1868–1925), Yiddish writer, playwright, and drama critic; born in Lida, in Lithuania, Gorin began his literary career in 1889 with a story, *Zikhroynoys fun Kheder* ("Memoirs From the Ḥeder"), in Mordecai Spektor's *Hoysfraynd*. In 1890 he published a story, *Shakhne un Shrage*, in I. L. Peretz's *Yidishe Bibliotek*. In 1894 Gorin left Russia for New York, where he became active in the literary and theatrical world. In 1908 he joined the staff of the Yiddish daily *Jewish Morning Journal*, reviewing Yiddish plays. Gorin's most important work was the two-volume *Di Geshikhte fun Yidishn Teater* ("History of the Yiddish Theater," 1918) which lists 2,000 plays produced on the Yiddish stage. In 1927 Gorin's stories were collected and published in three volumes. He adapted Tolstoy's *War and Peace*, Lessing's *Nathan the Wise*, and Zola's novels for Yiddish readers.

Bibliography: Rejzen, Leksikon, 1 (1928), 531–7; Schulman, *Geshikhte fun der Yidisher Literatur in Amerike* (1943), 110–6; LNYL, s.v. [E. Sch.]

GORIZIA, city in N.E. Italy. Gorizia was part of the Austrian empire until 1918 though for centuries its culture had been Italian. Jews were first mentioned in 1348. In 1648 a ghetto was established. The community followed the Ashkenazi rite. The Jews of Gorizia were mostly money-lenders. After they had been expelled from the smaller Venetian towns in 1777, more Jews moved to Gorizia; in 1788 the town had a Jewish population of 270. After that date many prominent Jews were born in Gorizia, including Isaac Samuel *Reggio who was honorary rabbi there for some years. [A.Mil.]

Holocaust Period. In 1931 there were 288 Jews in the community of Gorizia. During the fascist persecutions 45 Jews were sent to extermination camps, in addition to four Jews from the neighboring town of Udine. After the war, and up to 1969, about 30 Jews remained in the community. In 1970 the community was annexed to that of *Trieste, ceasing to exist as an independent Jewish body. [S.D.P.]

Bibliography: G. Bolaffio, in: RMI, 23 (1957), 537–46; 24 (1958), 30–40, 62–74, 132–41.

GORKI (until 1932 **Nizhni Novgorod**), city on the Volga River, Russian S.F.S.R. It served as an entrepôt for the merchants of Russia and Russian Central Asia from the early 19th century. From 1835 Jewish merchants were permitted to attend its celebrated fairs where they were allowed to purchase goods and, with the exception of imported articles, sell them wholesale. A permanent Jewish community was founded by soldiers discharged from the army of Nicholas I (see *Cantonists), and in 1873 received permission to maintain a house of worship. On June 7, 1884, pogroms resulting in murder and looting broke out in Kanavino, a suburb of the city. The Jewish community of Gorki numbered 2,377 in 1897 (2.5% of the total population). It increased during World War I when refugees from the war zone arrived there, and in 1926 numbered 9,328 (5.2% of the total). According to the census of 1959 the Jewish population of Gorki oblast was 17,827; the majority apparently lived in the capital. In 1970 the Jewish population was estimated at about 30,000. There was a Jewish cemetery, but no synagogue. [Y.S.]

°**GORKI, MAXIM** (pseudonym of **Aleksey Maksimovich Peshkov;** 1868–1936), Russian author. Gorki was the outstanding pre-Revolutionary Russian writer who sided with Lenin and the Bolsheviks, but he also distinguished himself as a vigorous champion of the oppressed Jewish people in Russia. Raised in a primitive environment, where the Jews were seen through a strange accumulation of folklore, fantasy, and superstition, Gorki was intellectually at odds with such notions, although emotionally and artistically he sometimes could not help expressing them. His early revolutionary position—which despite periods of dissent and opposition to the Bolsheviks and even voluntary exile, eventually made him a supporter of the Soviet regime—was closely linked with his deep revulsion against Jew-baiting and pogroms, and his warm friendship for many Jewish writers and intellectuals. His story *Pogrom* (1918), inspired by the *Kishinev outrages of 1903, was no isolated example of Gorki's preoccupation with the Jewish fate in Russia; and in *Detstvo* (1914; *My Childhood,* 1915), the first part of his autobiography, Gorki movingly recalled a Jewish boy encountered in his youth. In 1916 Gorki coedited *Shchit* ("The Shield"), an anthology of statements in defense of the Jews drawn from Russian literature, and in his own contribution made it clear that he saw in the question of Jewish rights the whole issue of injustice under the Czarist system.

Gorki also showed sympathy for the Hebrew renascence and for Zionist aspirations in Ereẓ Israel. Most of Gorki's impassioned denunciations of anti-Semitism have been omitted from the 30-volume Soviet edition of his works (1949–55). Most of these omissions have been cataloged (B. Suvarin, in *Dissent,* winter 1965; B. D. Wolfe, *The Bridge and the Abyss* (1967), 162–3n.). Works not published in this edition include an article on the Hebrew poet *Bialik; another on the Kishinev pogrom; and an appeal to save the *Habimah theater, then still in the U.S.S.R.

His wife, Ekaterina Peshkova (née Volzhina, 1876–1965), was, after the October Revolution, for many years a kind of guardian angel of the political prisoners in the U.S.S.R. in her capacity as chairman of the "Political Red Cross." She was warmly remembered by many Jews, particularly Zionists, whom she helped in various ways during their imprisonment, sometimes obtaining for them the permission to emigrate to Palestine.

Bibliography: A. S. Kaun, *Maxim Gorky and His Russia* (1932); I. Weil, *Gorky: His Literary Development and Influence on Soviet Intellectual Life* (1966), contains bibl. of works in translation.

[I.W.]

GORLICE, town in S. E. Poland. In the early period of Polish rule Gorlice belonged to the district of Nowy Sacz where all the towns had been granted the privilege of excluding Jews *(de non tolerandis Judaeis),* excepting Nowy Sacz itself, where a Jewish community existed. A few Jewish families were living in Gorlice in 1765 and 1784. Jews settled there in the 19th century, living in an area near the marketplace. By 1880 the Jewish population formed half of the total of 5,000, and by 1900 their number had grown to 3,297 (51.2%). They dealt mainly in wine and corn. The town suffered severely during World War I. In 1921 there were 2,300 Jews (41%) living in Gorlice. [Ed.]

Holocaust Period. At the outbreak of World War II the Jewish population numbered between 4,500 and 5,000. Most of them fled to the Soviet-occupied part of Poland before the Germans entered on Sept. 6, 1939. The Germans immediately took hostages among Jews and Poles and detained them for a long time in prison. On the eve of Rosh Ha-Shanah, the Germans ordered that all Jews between 18 and 35 years old should appear daily at the magistrate's office for work. On the eve of the Day of Atonement, the Germans destroyed the interior of the main synagogue and later converted it into a stable. Religious Jews were singled out for particular persecution: Jews caught praying in small *minyanim* were killed; the *shoḥet,* who continued to slaughter poultry in secret, was shot with his family.

During the German occupation, a *Judenrat* consisting of seven members was set up in Gorlice. Its first president, Henryk Arnold, a man of integrity, was harassed by the Gestapo and finally killed in the *Judenrat* office for

Entrance to a cemetery near Gorlice, Poland, which contains mass graves from World War I. Jerusalem, C.A.H.J.P., Inv. 2519.

disobedience to German orders. The Jewish police in Gorlice were honest and helpful in protecting the population. A Jewish labor office was established to supply the Germans regularly with manpower. After the outbreak of the German-Soviet war (1941) a ghetto was established. An influx of refugees from larger towns, such as Cracow, caused an acute housing shortage. Disease spread, but there was no Jewish doctor available until a physician arrived from Cracow some time later. The *Judenrat* established a primitive hospital. A Jewish elementary school functioned, possibly also in the ghetto, where Hebrew was taught clandestinely.

In the spring of 1942 about 70 members of Zionist organizations were executed in Gorlice and the neighboring town of Biecz. In June 1942 a large fine was levied on the community, and houses were searched in order to confiscate valuables. In the summer increased numbers of young men were sent to distant labor camps in *Plaszow, Pustchow, and Frysztak. In early August, Jews from nearby Bobowa and Biecz were brought to Gorlice. On Aug. 12, 1942, another heavy fine, of 250,000 zlotys, was imposed for immediate payment. On the night of Aug. 13–14, 1942, the ghetto was surrounded by German and Ukrainian units. In the morning the Gestapo selected about 700 old and infirm people. They were taken to Garbic, where a mass grave was prepared. They were ordered to undress and were shot at the edge of the grave. The majority of the remaining Jews were sent to the death camp at Belzec. Many Jews managed to escape during the *Aktion* to fields, woods, or villages in the vicinity: encountering no help, most of them returned and were executed on the spot or included in the transport.

After this, about 700 able-bodied Jews remained in Gorlice. In the period to mid-September two further "selections" were made and most of the remaining Jews were sent to Belzec; after Sept. 14, 1942, there remained only the factory workers who lived in the factory buildings, and on Jan. 6, 1943, they were sent to the labor camps of Muszyna and Rzeszow.

After the war approximately 30 Jewish families returned to Gorlice. They found that their property had been looted, and that tombstones from the cemetery had been taken to construct pavements. An attempt was made at rehabilitation, and goods sent by the Landsmannschaft in the United States were distributed by a committee. However, anti-Semitism among the local population caused them to leave shortly afterward. [De.D.]

full-page border decoration and initial panel for "pour out thy wrath" from the *Darmstadt Haggadah*. The illustrations depict women upils with their teachers, and a Passover *seder* table. Written by Israel ben Meir of Heidelberg in the 15th century. Darmstadt, Hessiche andes- und Hochschulbibliothek, Cod. Or. 8, fol. 37v (14 × 9¾ ins/35.5 × 24.5 cm.).

Bibliography: An-Ski, *Der Yidishe Khurbn Fun Poyln, Galitsye un Bukovine* (1922); *Sefer Gorlizeh* (1962); Yad Vashem Archives, M/1209/1.

GORNI (pl. **Grana**), term used for the Jewish immigrants from Leghorn (Livorno), who began to settle in North Africa, especially in Tunisia, from the 17th century on. Livorno was called Leghorn(a) in Jewish sources (e.g., David Reuveni), as well as by English sailors, and Jews and Arabs in the Maghreb. The first syllable *Le* was used as an article, making al-Ghorn(a); from this came the appellative (al-)Gorni. Until the 1940s the Gorni constituted separate congregations in Tunis and in other towns of Tunisia, with their own administration, *bet din,* and communal institutions. At all times, these Jewish immigrants felt separate from the "Tuansa," i.e., the old residents of Tunisia.

Bibliography: Neubauer, Chronicles, 2 (1893), 167–9, 205, 208, 213–4; H. Z. Hirschberg, *Me-Erez Mevo ha-Shemesh* (1957), 22; Hirschberg, Afrikah, index; A. Milano, in: *Miscellanea di studi in memoria di Dario Disegni* (1969), 139–51. [H.Z.H.]

GORODENKA (Pol. **Horodenka**), city in Stanislav oblast, Ukrainian S.S.R. Jews first settled there under Polish rule during the middle of the 17th century. In 1743 the Polish landowner granted them by a privilege the right to live in the town and to engage in commerce (excluding trade in Christian religious appurtenances) and crafts. The community received land for building a synagogue and for a cemetery. Jews of Gorodenka were dealers in grain, timber, and salt, wine makers, distillers of brandy, beer brewers, tavern keepers, and leasers and managers of estates. According to the census of 1765, there were 863 Jewish families in Gorodenka and 133 Jews living in 14 villages in the vicinity, affiliated to the Gorodenka community. In the middle of the 18th century there was a group of Shabbateans and Frankists in the town. During the 1760s most of the Jews in Gorodenka joined the ḥasidic movement, among them Naḥman of Horodenko, one of the closest disciples of Israel b. Eliezer Ba'al Shem Tov.

The city passed to Austria in 1772. In 1794, 30 Jews in Gorodenka (12 families) joined to found an agricultural settlement. Despite their economic difficulties, the rate of taxation levied upon the Jewish population was five times higher than that for the Christian population. According to data of 1890, 4,340 of the 11,162 inhabitants of the town and of the 18 members of the municipal council were Jews. By the end of the 19th century a local *Benei Zion society had been founded, which by 1897 consisted of about 150 members. A Jewish boys' school financed by Baron *Hirsch functioned from 1898 until 1914. The first Hebrew school was opened in 1907. At the beginning of the 20th century, the community had a great synagogue and a number of *battei midrash* and ḥasidic prayer houses. In World War I the Jews in Gorodenka suffered severely under the Russian occupation. In 1916 Jewish houses were set on fire and nine local Jews were hanged on a charge of espionage.

Gorodenka was within Poland between the two world wars. The Jewish population numbered 3,048 (out of ,907) in 1921. Subsequently, about 2,000 emigrated to the United States, Canada, and South America, and hundreds of others to Ereẓ Israel. [A.Cy.]

Holocaust Period. Within a few days of the outbreak of war between Germany and the U.S.S.R., Gorodenka was occupied by Hungarian troops. The local Ukrainian populace immediately attacked the Jewish inhabitants, murdering and robbing them. Subsequently, Jews from Carpatho-Ruthenia (which had been annexed by Hungary) arrived in Gorodenka, having been driven from their homes. A local Jewish committee was set up to deal with the situation. Aid was extended to the local Jews and refugees. When the city came under German administration in September 1941 conditions deteriorated. Anti-Jewish measures were enacted, including restriction on free movement on the streets, compulsory wearing of the yellow *badge, and the institution of slave labor. In November the Jews were concentrated in a ghetto. On Dec. 4, 1941, they were assembled, allegedly to receive immunization against typhus, but were guarded by the Germans and their Ukrainian collaborators in the great synagogue. The following day they underwent a *"Selektion,"* and those classed as "nonproductive" were taken to mass graves dug between the villages of Michalcze and Simakowce, and murdered. On April 4, 1942, a second *Aktion* was carried out in which 1,500 were murdered. In May and June hundreds of Jews were taken from Gorodenka to Kolomyya, where they shared the fate of the Jews there. Some of the inmates fled to Tlusta, where they found temporary refuge. The ghetto was liquidated on Sept. 6, 1942. On March 24, 1944, Soviet forces returned to Gorodenka, but by then only a few Jews were left. They subsequently left for Poland in transit to Palestine. [Ar.W.]

Bibliography: M. Bałaban, *Spis Żydów i Karaitów ziemi Halickiej i powiatów Trembowelskiego i Kołomyjskiego w roku 1765* (1909), 18; M. Freudental, *Leipziger Messegaeste* (1928), 141; W. Tokarz, *Galicya w początkach ery józefińskiej ...* (1909), 356–7; B. Wasiutyński, *Ludność żydowska w Polsce w wiekach xix i xx* (1930), 100, 122; *Sefer Horodenka* (Heb. and Yid., with Eng. introduction, 1963).

GORODOK (Pol. **Gródek Jagielloński**), city in Lvov oblast, Ukrainian S.S.R., within Poland until 1772 and between the two world wars. The earliest information on the presence of Jews there dates from 1444. Jews were responsible for collection of customs and taxes in Gorodok for short periods. In 1550 King Sigismund II Augustus granted the town the privilege to exclude Jews *(de non tolerandis Judaeis),* but probably those already there remained. In 1662, after Gorodok had been devastated during the Crimean Tartars' invasions, the local governor *(starosta)* encouraged Jews to settle in the town and rehabilitate it; because of the objections of the townsmen, he assigned them a special quarter, "the Gnin." King John III Sobieski confirmed their right of residence in 1684. According to the census of 1765, there were 788 Jews living in the "Jewish town of Gnin" and 251 in neighboring villages. As a result of the difficult economic situation, the debts of the community increased, amounting to 3,212 zlotys in 1784.

The community numbered 2,952 in 1880 (29% of the total population), and 3,610 in 1900, with an additional 3,478 living in villages in the district. In World War I the Jews of Gorodok and its surroundings suffered severely during the fighting between the Russian and Austrian armies in 1915, and subsequently in 1918–19 during the struggle between the Poles and Ukrainians. There were 2,545 Jews living in the city itself (24% of the population) and 1,414 in the villages in 1921, and 3,281 in 1931. Between the two world wars most of them were occupied in crafts, hawking, and trade in agricultural products. [A.Cy.]

Holocaust Period. With the German invasion of Poland on Sept. 1, 1939, many Jewish refugees from western Poland arrived in the city, and by 1941 the Jewish population numbered over 5,000. From October 1939 until the outbreak of the German-Soviet war in June 1941 the city was occupied by the Soviets. In July 1941 the Germans captured Gorodok, and neighboring farmers, mainly Ukrainians, attacked the Jews there. Conscription into forced labor camps in Jaktorow and Winniki continued through the autumn of 1941 and 1942. On May 19, 1942, several hundred Jews were deported to Janowska camp in Lvov. On August 13, a large number were deported to the extermination camp in Belzec. On Jan. 21 and Feb. 3, 1943, additional deportations took place. The ghetto was liquidated in May 1943. The last Jews of Gorodok were shot and buried in mass graves near Artyszczow. [Ar.W.]

Bibliography: B. Wasiutyński, *Ludnośeć żydowska w Polsce . . .* (1930), 107, 115, 147, 151, 196, 212; I. Schiper, *Studya nad stosunkami gospodarczymi żydów w Polsce podczas sredniowiecza* (1911), 154, 239, 243.

GORODOK, town in Belorussian S.S.R., north of Vitebsk. The Jewish community was founded during the 18th century. In 1772, when Belorussia was annexed by Russia after the first partition of Poland, the town had 400 Jews, the majority of the population. In 1897 there were 3,413 Jews in Gorodok (68% of the total population), and in 1926, 2,660 (48.3%), most of whom were *Ḥabad Ḥasidim. The community was exterminated in 1941 during the German occupation.

There is also a townlet named Gorodok in *Molodechno oblast, Belorussian S.S.R. In 1897, it had 1,230 Jews, who constituted 75% of the population. Between the two world wars the townlet belonged to Poland. With the Nazi occupation in June 1941, the approximately 1,500 Jews were imprisoned in a ghetto, and about a year later the ghetto was liquidated. Those who survived, some 400, were transferred to the central ghetto of *Krasnoye, and fugitives from the ghetto played an active role in the local partisan movement.

Bibliography: Surkin, in: B. Karu (Krupnik) (ed.), *Sefer Vitebsk* (Heb., 1957), 233–4; *Sefer ha-Partizanim ha-Yehudim*, 1 (1958), 479. [Y.S.]

GORZOW WIELKOPOLSKI (Ger. **Landsburg an der Warthe**), town in Poland, before 1945 in Brandenburg. A Jewish quarter and synagogue are first mentioned in 1557, though the community probably originated in the 14th century. It ceased to exist in 1573 when Jews were expelled from the whole of Brandenburg. Toward the middle of the 17th century, Jews attended the Landsberg fairs and soon after renewed their permanent settlement in the city. In 1662 Solomon Kajjem Kaddish was rabbi of the city and in 1672 his authority was extended to include all Brandenburg. He was succeeded by Benjamin Wolff Liebmann. In 1690, 21 Jewish families lived in the city; their number had increased to 417 persons by 1717. In that year, however, all Jews without right of domicile were banished and only 96 remained. They were active in the wool trade and the leather industry. A synagogue was built in 1755, and was used until 1854. The community grew from 304 in 1817 to 730 in 1871, but declined to 435 in 1933. Six charitable organizations, a school, and a cemetery were maintained in 1932, as well as an old-age home which had been opened in 1928. The community diminished during the Nazi era to 180 in 1936 and 95 in 1939; eight of the community were deported to Czechoslovakia on Aug. 27, 1942.

Bibliography: B. Elsass, in: MGJV, 16 (1905), 95–103; MGADJ, 1 (1909), 9–29; FJW, 66; O. Lassaly, in: MGWJ, 80 (1936), 406–24; E. Keyser (ed.), *Deutsches Staedtebuch* (1939), 776; PK Germanyah; S. Stern, *Der Preussische Staat und die Juden*, 1 (1962), Akten, index; 2 (1962), Akten, nos. 45, 146, 170, 171, 172, 252, 269, 294. Part of the communal archives (1717–1912) are in the C.A.H.J.P., Jerusalem. [Ed.]

GOSHEN (Heb. גֹּשֶׁן), a grazing area in the N.E. of lowe Egypt, east of the delta. Goshen was the residence assigne to Jacob and his family, and it was there that the Israelite lived in Egypt (Gen. 45:10; Ex. 9:26). It is currentl assumed that the name is derived from the Semitic root גוש, i.e., compact, solid, and fertile land, suitable for grazin and certain types of cultivation. In the Bible Goshen i described as "the best part of the land" of Egypt (Gen 47:6). It is also called "the land of Rameses" (Gen. 47:11 and it was probably identical with or not far from the "fiel of *Zoan" (Tanis; Ps. 78:12, 43), the name of the Egyptia capital during the *Hyksos period. The Septuagint (Gen 46:28) renders Goshen as Heroonpolis (i.e., *Pithom, Ex 1:11), and once (Gen. 46:34) as "the Arab land of Gesem." Therefore it is generally assumed that Goshen is to be locate in Wādi Tumeilāt, which stretches from the eastern arm o the Nile to the Great Bitter Lake and is known to be excellen pasture land. Support for this identification is found in a papyrus (Pritchard, Texts, 259) from the end of the 13t century B.C.E. which describes how nomadic shepherd moved from the land of Edom, past the Merneptah fortres in Teku to the wells of Pithom in order to keep themselve and their cattle alive (cf. Gen. 45:10; 47:4). Teku is Wād Tumeilāt. The rulers of Egypt would therefore seem t have permitted nomadic Semitic tribes to come to Goshe and graze there.

Bibliography: P. Montet, in: RB, 39 (1930), 5 ff.; W. F. Albrigh in: BASOR, 109 (1948), 15; 140 (1955), 30–31; idem, *Yahweh an the Gods of Canaan* (1968), 79, 134; H. H. Rowley, *From Joseph t Joshua* (1950), index; H. Kees, *Ancient Egypt* (1961), index, s.v *Wadi Tumilat* [P.A.

GOSLAR, city in Lower Saxony, W. Germany. Jewis merchants from *Worms are mentioned there in 1074 an 1114. In 1252 the city demanded the rights to the taxes fro its Jewish settlement for itself, opposing the royal preroga tive on the Jews as *servi camerae;* royal taxes wer levied on them through the municipality from 1274. I 1312 the community paid a direct tax identical to that pai by Christians. The city council intervened on behalf of th community against the exactions of Emperor Louis I in 1336 and 1340. The community of Goslar did no suffer persecution even at the time of the *Black Death and the local form of the Jewish *oath was relatively free o degrading formulas. Problems of residence rights (*ḥeren ha-yishuv*) gave rise to bitter quarrels between old and ne settlers, which the municipal council was often called upo to arbitrate, and resulted in a split in the community in 133 which lasted for seven years. At that time there wer approximately 30 Jewish taxpayers.

The former synagogue of Goslar, Germany, now a bakery Courtesy Goslar Municipality.

From 1312 the city council issued an increasing number of *Judenbriefe* conferring rights and obligations on individual Jews, so that by 1340 at least half of the Jews in Goslar were not included in the community for taxation purposes. This process continued in the latter half of the 14th century, accompanied by increased taxation and decline of the community. By 1400 not even a *minyan* could be organized, and in 1414 several Jews secretly left for Brunswick to evade a heavy imperial tax. A *blood libel about 1440 contributed to the decline of the community. A community in Goslar is mentioned in 1615, when a *parnas* was installed and took the oath of office. The *pinkas* registering a community of nine members was begun in 1677. A synagogue was built in 1693.

The community numbered 43 persons in 1871 and 38 in 1933. On **Kristallnacht*, Nov. 10, 1938, the synagogue (consecrated in 1802), and Jewish shops and homes were attacked and looted. The well-preserved community archives were destroyed. Twenty-two members of the community perished during the Holocaust. A new community was organized, with 46 members in 1948, but declined soon afterward. It had eight members in 1970.

Bibliography: Germ Jud, 1 (1963), 117f.; 2 (1968), 283–95; M. Stern, in: *Israelitische Monatsschrift* (supplement to *Die Juedische Presse*), 40 (1909), 41–42, 45–47; 41 (1910), 6–7, 10–11; idem, in: *Israelitischer Lehrer und Cantor* (supplement to *Die Juedische Presse*), 31 (1900), 17–18; 32 (1901), 38–39; D. Loehr, in: *Friede ueber Israel*, 47 (1964), 147–9, 167–70; H. Fischer, in: *Zeitschrift der Savigny-Stiftung fuer Rechtsgeschichte, Germanistische Abteilung*, 56 (1936), 89–149; L. Rabinowitz, in: HJ, 2 (1940), 13–21.
[H.W.]

GOSLAR, HANS (1889–1945), a senior official of the Prussian government during the Weimar Republic and a leader of the *Mizrachi movement in Germany. Born in Hanover, Goslar wrote for periodicals, specializing in economic problems. He became an early adherent of Zionism and in 1911 published a book entitled *Die Krisis der juedischen Jugend Deutschlands* (1911). During World War I he served in Eastern Europe, where he came to know the Jewish masses and this profoundly revised his religious outlook. On his return to Germany in 1919, his activities in the German Social Democratic Party earned him the title of Ministerialrat and an appointment as director of the press section of the Prussian government, a post he retained until he resigned in 1932. In 1919 he published *Die Sexualethik der juedischen Wiedergeburt*, in which he urged a return to Jewish family ethics. He maintained his general Jewish, Zionist, and Mizrachi activities and published several books on Jewish as well as general themes. In 1933 Goslar moved to Amsterdam, where he continued his communal activities, especially on behalf of the rescue of Jews from Germany. He was a neighbor of Anne *Frank's family, and his daughter was Anne's friend, mentioned in Anne's diary on several occasions. In 1943 he was deported to the Westerbork concentration camp and in 1944 was transferred to *Bergen-Belsen, where he died shortly before the liberation. He also wrote *Juedische Weltherrschaft: Phantasiegebilde oder Wirklichkeit?* (1919).

Bibliography: Pick, in: MB (July 12, 1957); Y. Aviad, *Deyokenot* (1962), 235–7.
[G.K.]

GOSLAR, NAPHTALI HIRSCH BEN JACOB (c. 1700–?), rabbi and philosopher. Goslar acted as *dayyan* in his native *Halberstadt, but later moved to Amsterdam. Only in his 50th year did he begin to study Maimonides' *Guide* and religious philosophy in general. In his *Ma'amar Efsharut ha-Tivit* ("Treatise on Natural Potentiality," Amsterdam, 1762), composed in dialogue form and partly in rhymed prose, he criticizes the doctrine of an uncreated prime matter and polemicizes against deism. The appendix to the *Ma'amar* contains talmudic novellae under the title *Meromei Sadeh*. Goslar addressed two letters, dealing with theological problems, to his son Samuel who too was *dayyan* at Halberstadt (published in German translation by B. H. Auerbach, *Geschichte der israelitischen Gemeinde Halberstadt* (1866), 100ff., 199ff.).
[M.N.Z./Ed.]

GOSTYNIN, town in central Poland. The Jewish population numbered 157 in 1765, 634 in 1856, 1,849 in 1897, and 1,831 (27. 5% of the total) in 1921. Between 1823 and 1862 there were special residential quarters for the Jews. The old synagogue, destroyed by fire, was rebuilt in 1899. It was situated in the former Jewish lane, and a side alley there was popularly known as the "alley of the dead," recalling the location of the old Jewish cemetery. The ḥasidic leader and rabbi *Jehiel Meir Lipschuetz lived in Gostynin in the 19th century. There were 2,269 Jews living in Gostynin on the eve of World War II.

Holocaust Period. Immediately after the German army entered the town in Sept. 1939, mass arrests and attacks on Jews began along with requisition and looting of Jewish property. Jews were ordered to hew the old wooden synagogue into pieces and carry them to German inhabitants for fuel. They were ordered to pay two "contributions" (fines) in succession; when the president of the community was unable to collect the second sum in time, he sent a delegation to the Warsaw Jewish community (on a German suggestion) and received the required amount.

A ghetto was set up in Gostynin which was at first open, but subsequently surrounded by barbed wire. Order was kept by Jewish police. Most of the Jews left the ghetto every morning for hard labor assignments. In August 1941 transports of men and women began to be sent to labor camps in the Warthegau. The ghetto was liquidated on April 16–17, 1942, when nearly 2,000 Jews were sent to the death camp at Chelmno.

By the end of the war all traces of Jewish life in the town had been obliterated. The cemetery had been desecrated and destroyed, the tombstones hauled away, and the tomb *(ohel)* of the local *ẓaddik* destroyed. The few Jews from Gostynin who survived the Holocaust subsequently emigrated.

Bibliography: *Pinkes Gostynin: Yizkor Bukh* (1960); D. Dąbrowska, in: BŻIH, 13–14 (1955), 122–84 passim.
[De.D.]

GOTA, MOSES ZERAHIAH BEN SHNEUR (d. 1648), Turkish rabbi. Gota studied under Jehiel Basan and Joseph di Trani. After spending most of his life in Constantinople, he moved to Jerusalem and from there, to Hebron; financial difficulties compelled him to leave for Cairo, where he remained for the rest of his life. His contemporaries describe him as a great *posek* and as expert in Kabbalah. Apart from some responsa, all his works have remained in manuscript. They are: *Zeraḥ Ya'akov* on the *Beit Yosef* of Joseph *Caro; a commentary on Maimonides' *Mishneh Torah;* a supercommentary on Rashi's Pentateuch commentary; collected responsa and sermons. Some of his responsa are to be found in the Bodleian Library together with those of Eliezer Arḥa (rabbi in Hebron from 1634) and David *Habillo. Others appear in various works, among them in the collection of responsa *Zera Anashim* (1902). Gota's remains were interred on the Mount of Olives in 1650.

Bibliography: Conforte, Kore, 51; Frumkin-Rivlin, 2 (1928), 31; Fuenn, Keneset, 337.
[S.Mar.]

GOTEBORG (Gothenburg; Swed. **Göteborg)**, city in S.W. Sweden. In 1780 a number of Jewish families were granted permission to enter the area, and by 1792, 20 Jews lived in the city. Though the first synagogue was built in 1808, the

The liberal synagogue of Goteborg, Sweden, built 1855. Courtesy Mosaiska Fösamlinger, Goteborg.

congregation was unable to secure the services of a rabbi, Carl Heinmann, until 1837. After an attempt to introduce radical reform measures, opposed by the rabbi, two members of the congregation secured Heinmann's resignation in 1851, replacing him with the liberal German rabbi, Moritz Wolff, who led the community until 1899. Numbers of Polish and Russian Jews settled in Goteborg between 1903 and 1920. During World War II the Goteborg community absorbed many Jewish refugees from Denmark and also from Poland and Russia (1943–45). The Jewish population increased steadily and in 1968 reached 1,450, making Goteborg the third largest Jewish community in Sweden.

Bibliography: *Göteborgs mosaiska församling, 1780–1955* (1955); *Skrift till invigningen av mosaiska församlingens i Göteborg nuy församlingshus* . . . (1962); H. Valentin, *Judarna i Sverige* (1964).
[Ed.]

GOTHA, city in Thuringia, E. Germany. Jews from Gotha are mentioned in *Cologne in 1250 and later in *Erfurt. Eight members of the community were killed in connection with a *blood libel in Weissensee in 1303. The community suffered during the *Black Death persecutions (1349) and again in 1391. Though the community disappeared after the persecutions of 1459–60, a *mikveh (Judenbad)* is mentioned in 1564 and 1614. Until 1848 no Jews were allowed to live in the duchy of Gotha but restricted trading was permitted. The community formed after 1848 increased from 95 in 1872/3, to 236 in 1880, and 372 in 1910 (0.9% of the total population). A synagogue was built in 1903. In 1932 the prosperous community of 350 members maintained a synagogue, school, cemetery, library, and six social and charitable organizations. On Nov. 10, 1938, the synagogue was burned down and 28 men of the community were sent to *Buchenwald. The 80 remaining Jews had been deported by 1939. The community was not reestablished after World War II.

Bibliography: Germ Jud 1, 118–19; 2, 295–96; FJW, 372; PK.
[Ed.]

GOTLIEB, ALLAN (1928–), Canadian government official. Born in Winnipeg, Gotlieb lectured in law at Oxford from 1954 to 1956. He entered Canadian government service in 1957 and in 1962 was appointed a Canadian delegate to the 18-nation disarmament conference. Gotlieb was special lecturer on disarmament at Queen's University, Ontario, in 1965 and in the following two years was visiting professor of international institutions at Carlton University, Ottawa. In June 1967 he was appointed assistant under-secretary of state for external affairs and served as Canadian alternate delegate to the United Nations General Assembly. He was made deputy minister of communications in 1968. Gotlieb's writings include *Disarmament and International Law* (1965) and *Canadian Treaty-Making* (1968).
[B.G.K.]

GOTSFELD, BESSIE GOLDSTEIN (1888–1962), U.S. social worker and Zionist. Born in Poland, she migrated to the U.S. as a girl and in 1909 settled in Seattle. She was active in assisting Jewish immigrants from Russia to settle in that part of the U.S. In 1925 she was instrumental in founding the *Mizrachi Women's Organization, a religious Zionist group. She made her first visit to Palestine as a Mizrachi representative in 1930, for the purpose of establishing a girls' vocational training school. She stayed on to help resettle victims of Nazism, particularly children, in Palestine during the 1930s. Her interest in children is reflected in the numerous child care and vocational training centers, established at her initiative and built with U.S. funds raised by Mizrachi, in the course of her more than 25 years as Mizrachi representative in Israel. The childrens' village of Kefar Batyah is named after her. She served for many years as Mizrachi Women's honorary president.
[Ed.]

GOTTESFELD, CHONE (1890–1964), Yiddish humorist and writer of comedies. He emigrated to New York from Skala in eastern Galicia at the age of 18. From 1914 he wrote light sketches for the Yiddish *Jewish Daily Forward*. His most successful comedies were *Gevalt, Ven Shtarbt Er* ("Heavens, When Will He Die?") and *Parnosse* ("Livelihood"). Rudolph *Schildkraut and Maurice *Schwartz directed and acted in his plays. His humorous memoirs, *Vos Ikh Gedenk Fun Mayn Lebn* ("What I Remember of My Life"), appeared in 1960.

Bibliography: LNYL, 2 (1958) 24ff.; Z. Zylbercwajg, *Leksikon fun Yidishn Teater*, 1 (1931), 258ff.
[M.Rav.]

GOTTESMAN, U.S. family of philanthropists. Mendel Gottesman (1859–1942), industrialist, banker, and philanthropist, was born in Munkacs, Hungary, and emigrated to the United States in the 1880s. He pioneered in the paper and pulp industry, and later founded and became president of an investment banking company. Gottesman founded and supported several *talmud torahs* on the Lower East Side of New York, particularly between the 1890s and 1915, during which time he became associated with the forerunner of Yeshiv

University, the Isaac Elchanan Theological Seminary. In 1917 he organized the Gottesman Tree of Life Foundation, through which many of his charitable activities were carried out, including granting scholarships to Yeshiva University students. He served as treasurer of Yeshiva University for many years and as president of the Yeshiva Endowment Foundation, which he conceived and established from 1928 to 1942. DAVID SAMUEL GOTTESMAN (1884–1956), merchant and financier, was born in Munkacs, Hungary, the son of Mendel Gottesman. He became his father's partner in the wood pulp industry and later developed his own companies in that business and in investment banking. In 1941 he established the D. S. and R. H. Gottesman Foundation to donate funds for higher education, local welfare, Jewish studies, and other causes. Among the foundation's charitable contributions were four Dead Sea Scrolls, purchased for the State of Israel in 1955, and the donations of funds in 1961 for the construction of the Shrine of the Book in Jerusalem to house the Dead Sea Scrolls; the building is now part of the Israel Museum. BENJAMIN GOTTESMAN (1897–), born in New York City, the son of Mendel Gottesman, carried on his father's work in both business and philanthropic association with Yeshiva University. A trustee of the university, he was vice-president and treasurer of the Gottesman Tree of Life Foundation, one of the founders of the Albert Einstein College of Medicine of Yeshiva University, president of the Yeshiva Foundation Endowment Inc., and chairman of the Investment and Endowment Committee. Gottesman also served on the Investment Advisory Committee of *Hadassah, of which his wife ESTHER GOTTESMAN (1899–), born in New York City, was national treasurer. [ED.]

GOTTHEIL, GUSTAV (1827–1903), Reform rabbi, liturgist, and U.S. Zionist leader. Gottheil was born in Pinne, Posen. He was drawn to liberal Judaism at the University of Berlin, and studied with such scholars as Steinschneider and Zunz. During 1855-60 Gottheil was a teacher at the Reform Gemeinde in Berlin and preaching assistant to Samuel *Holdheim, who impressed him deeply. In Manchester, England, where he served the progressive Congregation of British Jews from 1869 to 1873, Gottheil mastered English, then joined Temple Emanu-El of New York City in 1873 as co-rabbi to the aging Samuel *Adler. Challenging the ethical culture theories of Felix Adler, son of Samuel Adler, Gottheil espoused a more traditional theistic Judaism, and was upheld by the congregation. He attempted to maintain a rabbinical school under Emanu-El's auspices during 1874-85, but it had very few students. Gottheil published a hymnal in 1886 and a devotional compilation *Sun and Shield* (1896). He voluntarily abandoned issuing his own prayer book in favor of the *Union Prayer Book*, which included a number of his translations and renderings. The most important American rabbi publicly to support Zionism during the First Zionist Congress in 1897, Gottheil, his son Richard *Gottheil, and Stephen S. *Wise were among the founders of the Federation of American Zionists. Gottheil was a teacher and friend to such young rabbis as Stephen S. Wise, Leon Harrison, and Samuel Schulman. In a sense he was a bridge from the German beginnings of Reform to its Eastern—as distinct from Midwestern—American flowering.

Bibliography: R. J. H. Gottheil, *Life of Gustav Gottheil, Memoir of a Priest in Israel* (1936). [B.W.K.]

GOTTHEIL, RICHARD JAMES HORATIO (1862–1936), U.S. orientalist. Gottheil was born in Manchester, England, the son of Gustav *Gottheil, and immigrated to New York with his parents in 1873. He taught Semitic languages at Columbia University from 1886 until his death, except for one year, 1920/21, at the University of Strasbourg; he was director of the Oriental Department of the New York Public Library from 1896 until his death and

Richard Gottheil, U.S. orientalist and educator. From *American Jewish Yearbook, 1937–38*, Jewish Publication Society, Philadelphia.

president of the American Oriental Society, 1933–34. Gottheil was an active Zionist and prominent in American Jewish life. Among other activities he served as president of the American Federation of Zionists, 1898–1904, president of the Society of Biblical Literature, 1902–03, and vice-president of the American Jewish Historical Society from 1904 on. He founded the Zeta Beta Tau Fraternity, originally a Zionist society, and was one of the founders of the *Jewish Institute of Religion in New York. Among the works Gottheil published, in addition to numerous articles in scholarly and general periodicals and books, are: *Zionism* (1914), *The Holy War* (1915), *The Belmont-Belmonte Family* (1917), and *The Life of Gustav Gottheil; Memoir of a Priest in Israel* (1936). Among the works he edited and translated are *A Treatise on Syriac Grammar by Mâr(i) Eliâ of Sôbhâ* (1887), and with W. H. Worrell, *Fragments from the Cairo Genizah in the Freer Collection* (1927). He was an editor of the *Jewish Encyclopedia* (1901–06) and the editor of the *Columbia University Oriental Series* (vols. 1–29, 1901–36).

Bibliography: G. A. Kohut, *Professor Gottheil—an Appraisal at Seventy* (1933); J. Bloch, in: JAOS, 56 (1936), 472–9; S. Rosenblatt, in: BASOR (Dec. 1936), 2–3. [ED.]

GOTTLIEB, ADOLPH (1903–), U.S. painter and exponent of abstract expressionism. In the 1930s Gottlieb exhibited regularly with a New York group of experimental expressionists known as "The Ten." From 1937 to 1939 he

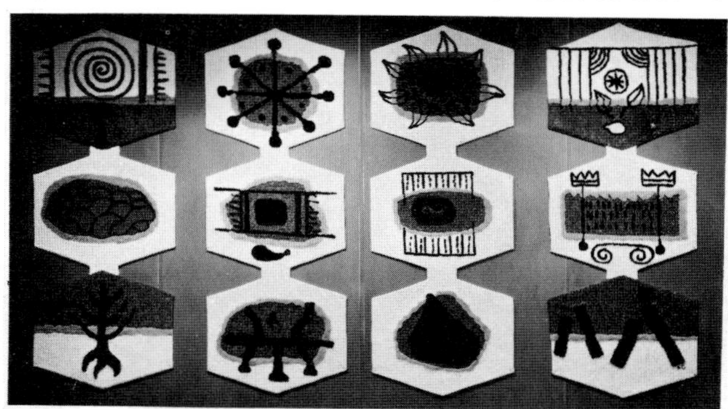

"The Jewish Holidays," tapestry designed by Adolph Gottlieb for Temple Beth-El, Springfield, Mass. Courtesy Union of American Hebrew Congregations, New York.

lived in Tucson, Arizona. The desert and the mood and expanse of western vistas can be found in successive phases of his surrealist iconography. In 1939 he returned to New York, where European surrealists influenced his creation of "Pictographs." The grid compartments in which he placed an eye, an arrow, a hand, all derived from primitive myth symbols which were retained as vaguer frameworks as his style grew freer during the 1950s. In addition to wide display and acquisition by museums in the U.S. and elsewhere, his work won first prize in the 1963 São Paulo Bienal. He designed ark curtains for Congregations B'nai Israel, Millburn, N.J., and Beth El, Springfield, Mass., and designed and supervised fabrication of a 1,300 square-foot stained glass facade for the Milton Steinberg Center, of the Park Avenue Synagogue, New York. In 1967 he was appointed to the Art Commission of the City of New York.

Bibliography: R. Doty and D. Waldman, *Adolph Gottlieb* (1968).

[R.Bro.]

GOTTLIEB, BERNHARD (1885–1950), dental scientist. Born in Kuty, Slovakia, Gottlieb trained in Vienna, where he did research in diseases of the teeth, specializing in the cause of caries. He was the first to describe the epithelial tissue which joins the tooth surface to the gum. During World War I he served as a dental surgeon on the Russian-Rumanian front. In 1921, he started to lecture at the University of Vienna, and was a pioneer in experimental animal studies which drew the attention of researchers in this field in Europe and the U.S. In 1938, under Nazi rule, Gottlieb was dismissed from his post at the university. With the help of some non-Jewish admirers he was able to leave Austria. Gottlieb was a keen talmudist, and identified with the cause and interests of a Jewish state in Ereẓ Israel. He went to Palestine where he spent two years teaching at the Hebrew University, and helped to set up dental clinics. In 1940, Gottlieb emigrated to the United States, where he was visiting professor at the Kellogg Foundation Institute at Ann Arbor, Michigan.

[J.Y.]

GOTTLIEB, FRANTIŠEK (1903–), Czech poet and author. Born in Klatovy, Gottlieb was an active Zionist in his youth, and made Jewish nationalism the ideological basis of his first book of poetry, *Cesta do Kanaan* ("The Way to Canaan," 1924), and of his earliest novel, *Zivoty Jiřího Kahna* ("The Lives of George Kahn," 1930, 1947²). In 1939, he emigrated to Palestine, but during World War II joined the Czechoslovak army in the Middle East. After the war, he returned to Prague, where he entered the Czechoslovak Foreign Ministry. His impressions of wartime Palestine are embodied in a volume of poems, *Dvojí nástup* ("Double Ascent, 1942, 1946²), and in two books of short sketches, *Čelem proti čelu* ("Head On," 1947) and *Jaro a poušť* ("Spring and Desert," 1956, 1962²). In 1966 he published a volume of poems, *Rozpjaty den.* Gottlieb was not deterred from dealing with Jewish themes after the Communist coup of 1948.

Bibliography: O. Donath, *Židé a židovství v české literatuře 19. a 20. století,* 2 (1930), index; J. Kunc, *Slovnik českých spisovatelů beletristů 1945–56* (1957); R. Iltis, in: *Jewish Quarterly,* 13 (Summer 1965), 11.

[Av.D.]

GOTTLIEB, HEINRICH (1839–1905), lawyer, communal leader, and writer, born in Lvov. He practiced law in Kalisz and Lvov. As deputy chairman of the Lvov community Gottlieb was responsible for its educational department, and did much to develop its activities. His book *Schulbetrachtungen* (1872) deals with educational questions. He also wrote studies on pedagogy, law, philosophy, natural sciences, and history, including a series of articles on the Jewish Khazar kingdom (in *Oesterreichische Wochenschrift,* nos. 13, 17, 21, and 48, 1894). He was editor of the Polish periodical *Ekonomista* and contributed to *Izraelita.* Gottlieb also wrote literary essays and poetry (*Weltuntergang,* 1888).

Bibliography: M. Bałaban, in: YE, 6 (c. 1910), 733–4.

[Ed.]

GOTTLIEB, HINKO (1886–1948), Yugoslav author, translator, and Zionist leader. Born in a Croatian village, Gottlieb made his name as a Zionist poet and writer on Jewish themes while he was still a student in Zagreb. After graduating he divided his activity between law practice and literary pursuits. His verse, which combined imagination and realism, reflected contemporary events and his whole output testified to his strong Jewish loyalties and his anti-Nazi sentiments. A prominent contributor to most Jewish publications in Yugoslavia between the world wars, Gottlieb founded the Jewish monthly *Ommanut,* which he edited from 1936 until 1941. He published Serbo-Croat translations of German, Yiddish, and Hebrew works, the latter for an anthology of modern Hebrew literature (1935), as well as translations from Heine (1936). A collection of his poems *Ijar, jevrejski maj* ("Iyyar, the Jewish May") appeared in 1935. As a lawyer, Gottlieb often defended Yugoslav communists and had contacts with Josip Broz, the World War II partisan leader who became President Tito. Following the Nazi invasion in 1941, Gottlieb was arrested and imprisoned in Vienna and then in Zagreb. He managed to escape and joined Tito's forces. In 1944 he was sent to Bari, Italy, where he organized the rescue of 1,500 Croatian Jews. In the following year he left Europe for Ereẓ Israel, where he completed and revised his stories of the Holocaust period. These later works include *Ključ od velikih vratiju* (*The Key to the Great Gate,* 1947), a novel which later appeared in Hebrew (1950); and the short story *Kadiš u šumi* ("Kaddish in the Forest," 1944), which has been acclaimed as one of the outstanding products of Jewish underground literature.

Hinko Gottlieb, Yugoslav writer and Zionist leader. Courtesy Federation of Yugoslav Jewish Communities, Belgrade.

Bibliography: S. Radej, in: *Jevrejski Almanah 1954;* V. Dedijer, *Josip Broz Tito* (1953); C. Rotem, in: *Jevrejski Almanah 1957/8,* idem, in: *Davar* (June 14, 1945 and Oct. 31, 1958).

[Zd.L./C.Ro.]

GOTTLIEB, HIRSCH LEIB (1829–1930), Hebrew journalist. Born in Szigetvar, Hungary, Gottlieb translated works of Goethe, Schiller, and others into Hebrew. In 1878, in his native town, he began to publish *Ha-Shemesh,* the first Hebrew paper in Hungary. Among those who contributed to the paper were the Hebrew writers R. A. *Broides, G. *Bader, and D. I. Silberbusch. As a result of the opposition of the rabbi of Szigetvar the paper was moved for a time to Kolomea, Galicia, where it appeared once under the name *Ha-Shemesh* and once as *Ha-Ḥarsah.* Gottlieb ceased publishing it at the turn of the century, returned to Szigetvar, and began to publish Yiddish newspapers. Because of open advocacy of Zionism in his Yiddish paper *Zion* he was persecuted by religious extremists, but he nevertheless persevered until the eve of World War I. Gottlieb was also a well-known humorist whose anecdotes and light verse were published in his newspaper and in his book of Yiddish verse, published posthumously.

Bibliography: *Tazlil*, 4 (1964), 44–65 (Hebrew translation of his autobiography); Yaari, in: KS, 35 (1959/60), 111–2. [G.K.]

GOTTLIEB, JACOB (1911–1945), Yiddish poet and essayist. Born in Kovno, Gottlieb was a descendant of the ḥasidic rabbis of Nowy Sacz. His first poetry collection, published at the age of 20, proved his mastery of various lyric styles as well as of blank verse. His poems were characterized by mystic imagery and treated universal themes such as love and nature as well as social and national subjects. He envisaged a coming world decline and another Jewish catastrophe. Three additional volumes of lyrics appeared in 1933, 1936, and 1938, and a study of H. *Leivick in 1939. He fled eastward from the Nazis, and he survived in Turkestan until almost the end of the war, but died of typhus in 1945. A posthumous selection of his poems, *Geklibene Lider,* was published in Montreal in 1959.

Bibliography: LNYL, 2 (1958), 18; J. Leftwich (ed.), *The Golden Peacock* (1961). [M.Rav.]

GOTTLIEB, JEDIDIAH BEN ISRAEL (d. 1645), talmudic scholar and itinerant preacher in Poland. He visited the major Jewish communities, especially Lvov (Lemberg), Cracow, and Lublin. His biblical and talmudic homilies (*Ahavat ha-Shem*) were published in Cracow in 1641, and again in Lublin in 1645. This work includes 50 different explanations of Deuteronomy 10:12. His biblical commentaries, printed in Cracow in 1644 in three volumes under the title *Shir Yedidut,* reflect Jewish social, religious, and economic life in Poland in the first half of the 17th century, prior to the catastrophe of the *Chmielnicki uprising. As a prominent preacher, Gottlieb had the courage to castigate the rich members of the Jewish communities for being overzealous in their pursuit of worldly riches. He enjoined them to bequeath part of their fortunes for community needs and scholars, rather than leave everything to their children. From Gottlieb's homilies it also transpires that Jews with drive and initiative easily found economic opportunities in trade and tax farming, and acquired considerable wealth. He expressed his preference for "self-made" men over those who acquired wealth by inheritance, and supported their claim to social status. Gottlieb is representative of the itinerant preachers of that period who sensed the spirit of the times and often aroused delight by clever, humorous, or anecdotal explanations of the texts.

Bibliography: H. D. Friedberg, *Ha-Defus ha-Ivri be-Krakov* (1900), 27; H. H. Ben-Sasson, *Hagut ve-Hanhagah* (1959), index. [Ed.]

GOTTLIEB, MAURYCY (1856–1879), Polish painter. Born in Drohobycz, in eastern Galicia, he was the son of a prosperous owner of an oil refinery. At the age of 13, he studied at the art school in Lemberg, and three years later at the Vienna Academy. Later, under the influence of his teacher at the Cracow Academy, professor Jan Matejko, an ardent champion of Polish nationalism, Gottlieb turned from German to Polish subject matter. Gottlieb was subjected to anti-Semitic taunts, and painted a self-portrait called "Ahasuerus," which referred to the legend of the Wandering Jew who was shunned by everyone. In 1876 he received a prize at Munich for his painting, "Shylock and Jessica." The noted publisher Bruckmann then commissioned him to make twelve illustrations for a deluxe edition of Lessing's drama *Nathan der Weise*. Yielding to anti-Semitic pressure, Bruckmann canceled the commission after seven of the illustrations had been finished. Gottlieb's next major work, "Jews praying on the Day of Atonement," was stimulated by his studying Heinrich *Graetz' *History of the Jews*. The picture caused a sensation in Jewish circles, and the Jewish press hailed it as a genuinely Jewish masterpiece. With the aid of a Viennese patron, Gottlieb went to Rome, where he

Figure 1. Maurycy Gottlieb, self-portrait, 1873. New York, Jewish Museum. Photo Frank Darmstaedter.

Figure 2. "The Artist's Mother" by Leopold Gottlieb, 1910, oil on canvas. Jerusalem, Israel Museum.

again met his teacher Matejko, who greeted him as "the most hopeful disciple of Polish art, whom I greet as my successor." After a few months in Rome, Gottlieb went back to Cracow, where he died at the age of 23. Considering the fact that Gottlieb's career covered only four or five years, his extant work is remarkable both in quality and quantity. "Shylock and Jessica" is so well and richly painted that the theatricality of the scene is overlooked, and "Jews Praying on the Day of Atonement" (which embodies a self-portrait) is an indisputable masterpiece. Gottlieb was also an excellent portraitist. His portraits are gems of psychological penetration in an era that often beautified and falsified its sitters. His portraits of girls and elderly women have delicacy, lightness of touch, and charm.

Maurycy's younger brother LEOPOLD GOTTLIEB (1883–1934), the 13th child of the Gottlieb family, studied in Cracow, Munich, and Paris, and for a while taught at the Bezalel School in Jerusalem. During World War I he was a lieutenant in the Polish Legion, and thereafter fought under Pilsudski in Poland's War of Independence. Among the numerous personalities who sat for him for portraits were Pilsudski and the writer Sholem Asch.

Bibliography: M. Narkiss (ed.), *Maurycy Gottlieb, Iggerot ve-Divrei Yoman* (1955); *Polski Słownik Biograficzny*, 8 (1959–60), 386–7; Roth, Art, 556–62, 808–10. [A.W.]

GOTTLIEB, YEHOSHUA (1882–c. 1940/41), Zionist journalist and leader in Poland during the interwar period. Born in Pinsk, Gottlieb began his Zionist activities in 1913, becoming a member of the central committee of the Zionist Organization in Poland in 1916. He served the movement mainly as a journalist, writing for the great Warsaw Yiddish dailies *Haynt* (1919–35) and *Moment* (1935–39), and was one of the outstanding newsmen and essayists of his time. In 1935 he was elected to the Sejm (Polish parliament). From 1927 to 1934 he was chairman of the Warsaw Journalists' Association and from 1924 to 1939 was a member of the Warsaw Jewish Community Council, serving as its deputy chairman from 1926 to 1930. He was one of the founders of the Et Livnot ("Time to Build") faction of the *General Zionists, which supported *Weizmann's idea of an "enlarged" *Jewish Agency. On behalf of his faction, Gottlieb worked diligently in support of the Fourth Aliyah (from 1924 on), which consisted mostly of middle-class Jews from Poland. When World War II broke out, he fled to Pinsk, where he was arrested by the Soviets soon after their entry into the city. He died in prison in Poland, according to one version, while another version has it that he had been taken to northern Kazakhstan.

Bibliography: LNYL, 2 (1958), 15–18; Kol, in: *Sefer Pinsk*, 2 (1966), 539–40; Remba, in: *Ḥerut* (Dec. 17, 1965). [G.K.]

GOTTLOBER, ABRAHAM BAER (pseudonyms **Abag** and **Mahalalel,** 1810–1899), Hebrew and Yiddish writer and poet. Born in Staro-Konstantinov (Volhynia), Gottlober was taken to Tarnopol (now Ternopol), Galicia, by his father at the age of 17. In Galicia he came in contact with the Haskalah, of which he was a staunch advocate most of his life, and met Joseph *Perl in 1828. Upon his return to Volhynia, his pious father-in-law, violently opposed to his secular studies, compelled him to divorce his wife. Gottlober, embittered by the affair, developed a hostility toward orthodoxy and Ḥasidism which found satiric expression in his writings. At 19 he remarried and moved to Podolia where, under the influence of Menahem Mendel *Levin's works, he began writing in Yiddish and in Hebrew. He wandered from place to place, living between 1830 and 1850 in Bessarabia, Berdichev, and Kremenets. In Kremenets he married for the third time and befriended I. B. *Levinsohn. Upon obtaining a government teaching license in 1850 he taught school until 1865 when he was appointed instructor of Talmud at the rabbinical seminary in Zhitomir. There he remained until the government closed down the seminary in 1873.

Hebrew Works. Gottlober's literary career extends over a 60-year period and though his writings are of a limited aesthetic value, they are a real, if modest, contribution to

Abraham Baer Gottlober, Hebrew and Yiddish writer. Jerusalem, J.N.U.L., Schwadron Collection.

the development of the modern Hebrew language and literature and to Yiddish literature. During the 1830–50 period, he published two collections of Hebrew poems: *Pirḥei ha-Aviv* (1837) and *Ha-Nizzanim* (1850). In 1874, on an extended sojourn in Vienna, he published his Hebrew translation of Lessing's *Nathan der Weise*, a number of nationalistic poems in Hebrew, and the short story *"Kol Rinnah vi-Yshu'ah be-Oholei Ẓaddikim"* (*Ha-Shaḥar* 1874/5). When the editor of *Ha-Shaḥar*, Perez *Smolenskin, attacked the Berlin Haskalah and wrote disparagingly of Moses *Mendelssohn, Gottlober broke with him and founded the Hebrew monthly *Ha-Boker Or* which appeared intermittently in Lemberg and later in Warsaw (1876–86). The periodical, mainly a vehicle for Gottlober's attack on Smolenskin's views, published also many of his short stories and studies in biblical exegesis, and in 1886 the second part of his memoirs, *Zikhronot mi-Ymei Ne'urai*. (The first part had appeared separately in Warsaw in 1881, while supplementary material was published in *Ha-Asif*, 1885.) With the demise of his journal, Gottlober left Warsaw and lived first in Dubno, then in Rovno, spending the last years of his life in Bialystok. While the poet's longing for Ereẓ Israel found some poetic expression in the 1870s, the 1881 pogrom shocked him into further national realization: he joined the Ḥibbat Zion movement and most of his poetry was now imbued with yearning for the Land of Israel. *Kol Shirei Mahalalel* (1890) is a collection of his poetry, original and translated, that had not appeared in the previous collections. A scholar, Gottlober also published a number of research and critical works. Among these are: *Bikkoret le-Toledot ha-Kara'im* (1865) a study of the history of the Karaites; *Iggeret Bikkoret* (1866), a critical work on modern Hebrew poetry; a translation of Moses Mendelssohn's *Jerusalem* (1867), and *Toledot ha-Kabbalah ve-ha-Ḥasidut* (1869), a history of the Kabbalah.

Yiddish works. Gottlober's most productive period in Yiddish writing was between the years 1840 and 1870. One of his earliest works, *Feldblumen*, a collection of lyrics, and *Di Farkerte Welt*, a didactic poem, were lost, but most of the poems were recovered in the 1920s and 1930s. Many of Gottlober's Yiddish works were published long after they had been written: his three-act comedy *"Der Dektukh oder Tsvey Khupes in Eyn Nakht"* was written in 1838 and published in 1876, and the poem, *"Der Bidne Yisrolik,"* written in 1843, appeared in 1876. Often depicted against a ḥasidic background, the works are written in an everyday dramatic speech into which the author introduced a satirical note. Gottlober's attitude toward Yiddish was ambivalent: while he saw it as a language "without literature, without grammar, and without logic," he also felt that he could address the Jewish public only in its own language. Among his best Yiddish works are: *Dos Lid finen Kugel* (1863), a parody on Schiller's poem *Lied von der Glocke; "Der Seim oder di Groyse Aseyfe in Vald, ven di Ḥayes Hoben Oysgekliben dem Layb far a Meylekh"* (1863, but written in 1842), a satiric fable in verse form, and *"Der Gilgul"* (1896), a sharp social satire which was first published in *Kol Mevasser* in 1871. *"Zikhroynes vegen Yudishe Shrayber"* (*Yudishe Folksbibliotek* 1, 1888) is his important nonfictional work in Yiddish. A collection of his Yiddish works appeared in 1927, *A. B. Gottlober's Yidishe Verk* (a. Fridkin and Z. Rejzen, eds.).

Initial Evaluation. Greatly overestimated in the prime of his career, Gottlober's writings have, nevertheless, left their mark on Hebrew and Yiddish letters. A facile writer, his style is fluent rather than compelling. Much of his writing is a direct attack on the obscurantism of the period and shows his firm support of the Haskalah. During the last 20 years of his life, however, he had become disappointed with the ideals of the Haskalah and had become one of the early champions of the nationalist movement and of the revival of Hebrew. While his poems are strongly marked by lyricism and often reflect his own experiences, his personal feelings were so closely interwoven with the public weal that much of his poetry bears a journalistic stamp. Its artistic value lies in the fact that it mirrors the aspirations and aesthetic criteria of his time. His incisive criticism influenced contemporary Hebrew poetry and led to greater metrical flexibility; his memoirs and short stories remain valuable for the interesting light they shed on many facets of Jewish life in Eastern Europe. Gottlober was also one of the first Hebrew writers to translate Russian poetry into Hebrew. His studies on the Karaites and on the Kabbalah, although highly imitative, served to draw attention to important but neglected areas of Jewish interest.

Bibliography: Klausner, Sifrut, 5 (1955[2]), 286–344 (includes bibliography); P. Shalev-Toren, *A. B. Gottlober vi-Yẓirato ha-Piyyutit* (1958); Rejzen, Leksikon, 1 (1926), 451–8; Waxman, Literature, 3 (1960[2]), 255–8; A. Fridkin, *A. B. Gottlober un Zeyn Epokhe* (1925).

[D.P.]

GOTTSCHALK, LOUIS REICHENTHAL (1899–), U.S. historian. Born in Brooklyn, N.Y., Gottschalk taught at the University of Chicago from 1927 where he was

Louis Gottschalk, U.S. educator and historian.

professor from 1935. Gottschalk was assistant editor (1929–43) and acting editor (1943–45) of the *Journal of Modern History* and president of the American Historical Association (1953). Gottschalk's main historical interests were the era of the French Revolution, modern European history in general, and historiography. His major works include: *Jean Paul Marat: a Study in Radicalism* (1927); *Era of the French Revolution* (1929); a multi-volumed study of Lafayette (in progress; 5 vols. 1935–1969); and *Understanding History: A Primer of Historical Method* (rev. ed., 1969). While maintaining exacting standards for the verification of past events, he recognized the influence of the historian's own environment on his interpretation. Gottschalk served on the International Commission for a Scientific and Cultural History of Mankind from 1956, becoming vice-president in 1962. Gottschalk was active in Jewish affairs, and was president of the Chicago Board of Jewish Education (1942–45); council member of the Conference on Jewish Social Studies; and chairman of the Union of Chicago B'nai B'rith Hillel Foundation from 1963.

Bibliography: R. Herr and H. T. Parker (eds.), *Ideas in History: Essays presented to Louis Gottschalk by his former students* (1965).

[J.I.S.]

GOTTSCHALK, MAX (1889–), Belgian social scientist and Jewish leader. Born in Liège, Gottschalk was a member of the bar at Liège and Brussels and joined the staff of the International Labor Office (1921–23). At the end of 1923, he was invited to join the Institute of Sociology of the Free

Max Gottschalk, Belgian sociologist.

University of Brussels as research professor, and was mostly occupied with problems of unemployment. The representative of the ILO for Belgium and Luxembourg (1923–40), Gottschalk became government commissioner for unemployment (1933–34) and president of the Social Security Board (1935–40). During World War II Gottschalk went to the United States, where he taught at the New School for Social Research in New York. After the war, he returned to the Institute of Sociology in Brussels, where he was president of the Center of Regional Economy and president of the International Council for Regional Economy (1958–68). On retiring from the Belgian and International Associations for Social Progress, he became honorary president of both these organizations.

His Jewish activities were religious, social, and intellectual. He presided over the Central Jewish Consistory of Belgium (1956–62). In the social field, he was vice-president of the *Jewish Colonization Association, board member of *Alliance Israélite Universelle and ORT-Union, and a founder of the Centrale d'Oeuvres Sociales Juives (United Jewish Appeal) in Brussels. He directed the Research Institute for Peace and Postwar Problems of the American Jewish Committee (1940–49) and from 1959, the Centre National des Hautes Etudes Juives, financed by the Belgian government. As president of the Belgian Committee for Refugees from Nazi Germany (1933–40), he was instrumental in the rescue of the passengers of the ship "St. Louis," that was sent back from Cuba and finally permitted to land in Antwerp (July 1939). Gottschalk wrote numerous publications in Jewish and non-Jewish fields.

[ED.]

GOTTSCHALL, MORTON (1894–1968), U. S. university teacher and administrator. Gottschall was born in New York City. He graduated from the City College of New York (1914), and became a tutor in history there. In 1919 he was named recorder of City College, a post he held for 15 years. During this period he also taught history and legal philosophy. In 1934 Gottschall was appointed professor and dean of the college, a capacity in which he served until his retirement in 1964. As dean he was known for his consideration for the individual student. He was head of a large college whose enrollment was mostly Jewish and with whose needs and aspirations he deeply sympathized. [L.F.S.]

GOUDCHAUX, MICHEL (1797–1862), French banker and politician. Born in Nancy, Goudchaux was a director of his father's bank there. In 1826 he became manager of the bank's Paris branch and helped found a working-class newspaper *Le National.* He participated in the revolution of July 1830 and was wounded when he placed himself at the head of an insurgent group. After the revolution, Goudchaux was made mayor of his district, member of the general council of the department of the Seine, and paymaster general in Strasbourg. In 1834, however, he returned to Paris and bitterly attacked the government's economic policies in a series of articles in *Le National.* Goudchaux became minister of finance in the Second Republic and in 1849, vice-president of the National Assembly. He was defeated in the elections of 1852 and devoted his life to philanthropic work, founding Jewish schools in Nancy. In 1857 he was elected to the Legislative Assembly but refused to swear the oath of allegiance to Napoleon III and did not take his seat.

Bibliography: R. Lazard, *Michel Goudchaux, son oeuvre et sa vie politique* (1907); Rabi (pseud.), *Anatomie du Judaïsme français* (1962), 65; JC (Jan. 9, 1863), 7. [S.C.]

GOUDSMIT, JOEL EMANUEL (1813–1882), Dutch lawyer. Goudsmit was the first Jew to become a university professor in Holland and member of the Royal Netherlands Academy of Sciences. Goudsmit, who was born in Leyden, graduated in law in 1842. After a period in practice he was appointed professor of Roman law at Leyden in 1859. As a writer he became famous through his *Pandecten-Systeem* (1866; *The Pandects,* 1873) which was translated into several languages. Also active in Jewish affairs, he was for many years chairman of the Society for the Promotion of the Welfare of the Jews in Holland. He publicly protested against anti-Semitic publications in Holland and advocated the rights of the Jews in Rumania. [H.Bo.]

°**GOUGENOT DES MOUSSEAUX, HENRI** (1805–1876), French anti-Semitic writer. A Catholic aristocrat who called himself "a soldier of Christ," Gougenot des Mousseaux was obsessed with demons and Jews. He is chiefly known for *Le Juif, le judaïsme et la judaïsation des peuples chrétiens* (1869). Published on the eve of the first Vatican council with the blessing of Pope *Pius IX, it was influential in Conservative circles in France before *Drumont's *France Juive.* The theme of the book is an alleged Jewish conspiracy to destroy Christianity and rule the world by means of 18th-century Liberalism and *Freemasonry. Translations appeared in 1876 in Austria and Rumania, and a second edition was published in France in 1886.

Bibliography: R. F. Byrnes, *Antisemitism in Modern France,* 1 (1950), passim; L. Poliakov, *Histoire de l'antisémitisme,* 3 (1968), 348. [Ed.]

GOULD, SAMUEL BROOKNER (1910–), U.S. educator and university administrator. Born in New York City, Gould studied at Bates College and New York, Oxford, Cambridge, and Harvard universities. He converted to Christianity during his undergraduate years. He taught English at William Hall High School, West Hartford, Conn. (1932–38) and served as head of the department of speech of the Brookline (Mass.) school system (1938–47). From 1947 to 1953 he was at Boston University, first as professor of radio and speech and director of the division of radio, speech, and theater, and then as assistant to the president. Gould's major contribution to education was in college and university administration as president of Antioch College (1954–58); chancellor of the University of California, Santa Barbara (1959–62); and president of the multi-campus State University of New York (1964–70). Appointed president of Educational Broadcasting Corporation in 1962, he took a leading role in raising the standards of American educational radio and television. [W.W.B.]

GOURD (Heb. דְּלַעַת; pl. דְּלוּעִים), a plant. It occurs in the Bible only in the form of a place-name Dilan, a town in the inheritance of Judah (Josh. 15:38), but it is frequently mentioned in talmudic literature. In modern Hebrew the word is applied to the gourd of the genus *Cucurbita,* now grown extensively in Israel, but since this genus originates in America the word undoubtedly designated some other plant in ancient times. From its many descriptions in talmudic literature, the reference is clearly to the calabash gourd *(Lagenaria vulgaris),* then a most important crop in Ereẓ Israel. Its large fruit, usually shaped like a broad-bellied bottle, was used as a vegetable when soft and when hard its shell was used as a container for liquid and food (Kil. 7:1). Vessels made from the fruit have been found in ancient Egyptian graves. Talmudic literature has many descriptions of the gourd. Its extremely smooth skin gave rise to the expression "he shaves himself as smooth as a gourd" (Sot. 16a). Various dishes were prepared from the soft fruit (Shev. 2:10), but its dried seeds are not fit for eating (TJ, Shev. 2:10, 34a). The plant has leaves which are very large and hard, and which could be written on in an emergency (Tosef., Git. 2:3); it has tendrils by which it climbs any support (TJ, Er. 1:1, 18b). Various strains of the gourd were grown, among which the Mishnah mentions the Syrian, Egyptian, Remuẓian, and Greek gourds (Kil. 1:5; Ned. 51a). Of these the last strain was the most important and so vigorous that one plant could cover an entire field (Kil. 3:7). Also used in the Talmud to designate the gourd, *kara,* apparently an Aramaic word, is included among the food eaten on the New Year (Ker. 6a). (For the correct meaning of *kikayon* in Jonah 4:6 et al. (AV, JPS "gourd") see *castor plant.)

Bibliography: Loew, Flora, 1 (1928), 542–8; J. Feliks, *Kile Zera'im ve-Harkavah* (1967), 66–71. [J.F.]

GOURI, HAIM (1923–), Hebrew poet and novelist. Born in Tel Aviv, Gouri served in the Palmaḥ from 1942 to 1947. He was sent on various missions by the Haganah to the displaced persons (DP) camps in Europe after World War II and was an officer in the Israel forces during the War of Independence. From 1954, he wrote a weekly column in the daily *La-Merḥav.*

His first poems were light verses which appeared in various publications of the Palmaḥ, and in 1943 he began to publish in literary magazines. *Pirḥei Esh* ("Flowers of Fire," 1949) was his first collection of poems. He published further volumes of poetry, as well as works of reportage, and a novel. He also translated French poetry and drama into Hebrew.

His early poetry, influenced by Natan Alterman, portrays a young boy's reactions to the newly discovered wonders of the world. Depicting mostly concrete situations where God, death, and time become tangible realities, most of these poems are void of abstractions. In *Pirḥei Esh* and *Ad Alot ha-Shaḥar* ("Till Dawn Breaks," 1950), the young maturing boy, in his first encounter with the adult world, assimilates the collective experiences of the Palmaḥ fighters, confronted by war and death, into an intimate personal experience. *Shirei Ḥotam* (1954) is marked by the poet's attempt to cling to the memory of distant experiences; he wishes to relive them, but, at the same time, emphasizes the gap existing between the original experience and life as now lived by his generation. His poetry became more cerebral; the early concrete grasp of reality was replaced by abstract expressions and conceptualizations.

Shoshannat ha-Ruḥot ("The Wind Rose," 1960) portrays Gouri's poignant awareness of the sharp contrast between his lost world, alive only in memories—recalled through symbols and emotions which are rooted in the poet's strong ties to his homeland, in a collective responsibility, and in the demands of the times made on the individual—and the present in which the poet sees his homeland as an alien land. He is torn between two extremes: the desire to escape his past, to live anonymously in an "alien" land and cast off his heavy burdens; and his regret at his own alienation and isolation. The past, from which the poet finds no escape, is also revealed in the clear relation between these later poems and Gouri's early work. The early language patterns, imparting a new meaning, recur; these combine with the poet's longing to convert every visual phenomenon and inner mood into a lofty aesthetic experience.

Gouri's novel *Iskat ha-Shokolad* (1965; *The Chocolate Deal,* 1968) presents the Holocaust through the experience of its two heroes, whose physical survival and well-being belie their psychological deformity. The author, using allusive dialogue, interior monologue, and symbolic references, creates a mood where the dividing line between the real and the imagined, the believable and the unbelievable, becomes blurred, the whole melting into a painful reality. Another work, *Mul Ta ha-Zekhukhit* (1962; French *La cage de verre,* 1964), is a chronicle of the Eichmann trial in Jerusalem.

Two major books published after the Six-Day War were: *Dappim Yerushalmiyyim* ("Jerusalem Pages," 1968), a miscellany, and *Tenu'ah le-Magga* ("Seek and Destroy," 1968), a collection of poems. The most important work in *Dappim Yerushalmiyyim* is a diary in which the author records his experiences as company commander of the Jerusalem brigade faced with the taking of Ammunition Hill, one of the strongest fortifications of Jerusalem. The work also includes feuilletons and sketches written before the war. The mood is strongly nationalistic. *Tenu'ah le-Magga* is a variation of the earlier theme, but the anguish of nostalgia for the past is relieved by a new element: personal youthful memories now search out the national collective reservoir on which the poet draws through his knowledge of the Bible. For the first time, biblical figures such as Joseph and his brothers, Samson, Absalom, and Amos appear in his poetry, drawn intimately, as if they had risen out of the poet's childhood world. The experience in *Tenu'ah le-Magga,* reminiscent of *Pirḥei Esh,* is the poet's rediscovery, at a higher level, of his identification with the collective experience of his nation, meeting it for the first time on the ancient battlefields in the Bible. A list of English translations of his work is in Goell, Bibliography, 826–48.

Bibliography: A. Huss, in: *Gazit,* 11 (1949), 63–5; S. Halkin, in: *Beḥinot be-Vikkoret ha-Sifrut . . .,* 1 (1952), 6–25; M. Brinker, in: *Massa,* 4 (1954); Ḥ. Bar-Yosef, in: *Eked,* 1 (1960/61), 136–8; G. Katznelson, in: *Moznayim,* 12 (1961), 277–81; G. Yardeni, *Tet Zayin Siḥot im Soferim* (1961), 167–81; A. Ukhmani, *Kolot Adam* (1967), 137–52.

[Ma.M.]

GOVERNMENT, PRAYER FOR THE, the prayer for the welfare of the government forms part of the synagogue ritual on Sabbath mornings and on the festivals. Its inclusion in the service is based on the Mishnah: "R.

Figure 1. Prayer for the well-being of Queen Anne, from an English *siddur,* London, 1714. London, British Museum, Ms. Harley 5703, fol. 9.

Ḥanina, Segan ha-Kohanim said: Pray for the welfare of the government; since but for fear thereof, men would swallow each other alive" (Avot 3:2). The idea is found as early as Jeremiah; the prophet counseled the Jews who were taken into the Babylonian captivity: "Seek the peace of the city whither I [i.e., the Lord] have caused you to be carried away captive, and pray unto the Lord for it; for in the peace thereof shall ye have peace" (Jer. 29:7).

The prayer for the welfare of the ruling powers of the State (king, government, etc.) and petitions for the welfare of the congregation, belong to the morning service and are recited before the Scrolls of the Law are returned to the Ark. The Sephardim recite it on the Day of Atonement after *Kol Nidrei.* The traditional version of the prayer starts: "May He Who dispenseth salvation unto kings and dominion unto princes, Whose kingdom is an everlasting kingdom, Who delivereth His servant David from the destructive sword . . . [etc.] . . . may He bless, preserve, guard, assist, exalt, and highly aggrandize our Sovereign . . .," the titles following.

In non-monarchic countries the prayer is recited for the welfare of the head of the state (the president) and the government. In modern times the prayer is recited in most synagogues in the vernacular. The wording has frequently been modified in accordance with the circumstances.

In Israel a new version of this prayer was formulated and approved by the Chief Rabbinate after the establishment of the State in 1948; it also includes a prayer for the welfare of all Jews in the Diaspora. The prayer is also recited in the U.S. at public services on special occasions such as Thanksgiving Day, July 4th, and Armistice Day

For samples of prayers for the government in the

Figure 2. Prayer for Count Sigmund Haimhausen, 19th-century benefactor of the community, in the Chodova Plana synagogue, western Bohemia. From *Die Juedischen Denkmaeler in der Tschechoslovakei*, Prague, 1933.

different rituals, see P. Birnbaum (ed.), *Daily Prayer Book* (1949), 379 (Orthodox); Hertz, Prayer, 506–7 (Orthodox); Rabbinical Assembly of America and United Synagogue of America, *Sabbath and Festival Prayerbook* (1946), 130 (Conservative); *Union Prayerbook*, 1 (1946), 148 (Reform).

Bibliography: Abrahams, Companion, clx–clix. [ED.]

GOZAN (Heb. גּוֹזָן ; Akk. **Guzana**), an Aramaean city on the western shores of the Habor River, a tributary of the Euphrates. The site of Gozan, now Tell Halaf, was first excavated and explored by M. von Oppenheim (1911–19; 1929). Although Tell Halaf—from which is derived the name of the "Halaf Period," a period in the development of northeastern Mesopotamian polychrome pottery—is in itself a key site in the history of civilization, its chief historical importance lies in the fact that it was the site of Gozan, the capital city of the Aramaean kingdom of Bīt Baḫiāni (see *Aram) which was established between the 11th and 10th centuries B.C.E. The remains of the administrative and cultic center of Gozan disclosed by the excavations at Tell Halaf are of great importance for the understanding of the development of the mixed Hittite-Hurrian-Mesopotamian peripheric architecture, art, religion, and changing way of life in the first millennium B.C.E. On one of the orthostats there is the first depiction of an Aramaean camel rider. Bīt Baḫiāni and Gozan are first mentioned in the annals of Adad Nirari II, king of Assyria. It is recorded that in his seventh campaign, around 894 B.C.E., he gained the submission of Abisalamu (Heb. Absalom) son of the House/Tribe Baḫiāni. Although there is further evidence of this submission in the Assyrian annals, further archaeological evidence seems to indicate that there was a short independent period in the history of Bīt Baḫiāni and its capital Gozan. The central figure during this period was (according to this Aramean inscription) Kappara, son of Ḥadijānu (from a new dynasty). It was he who erected the monumental architecture of Gozan during the latter part of the second half of the ninth century B.C.E. which was a period of severe crisis in Assyria, especially between the end of the reign of Shalmaneser III and that of Shamshi Adad V (between 827–810). This period of independence ended in 808 B.C.E. when according to the Eponym Canon (C^{b}I) Gozan was reconquered by Sammu-ramat (classical Semiramis), the queen mother, and her son Adad-Nirāri III. By 793 B.C.E. Gozan was already an organized Assyrian province. According to II Kings 17:6 inhabitants of Israel and Samaria were deported to the area along the "Habor River of Gozan." Assyrian documents discovered in Gozan and in other administrative centers contain information on the life of the inhabitants and deportees. Among these documents is a letter from Ḫabbishu of Samaria to the king (Waterman, no. 6331) which deals with various local affairs, mentioning several Hebrew-sounding names, such as *Ni-ri-ia-u* (Heb. Noriah), the *rab nikāsi*, overseer of income *(nekasīm)* and *Pa-al-ti-ia-u* (Heb. Paltijah), and also a woman, all "servants" to the local governor. Another document (Waterman no. 167) speaks of moving inhabitants from Gozan, perhaps to Dūr-Sharrukîn, the new capital of Sargon II, king of Assyria, according to his policy of population mixing. The sender reports that some people mentioned in his list are missing, for example, Ḫūli the gardener with his family of five. Finally, a deed of slave sale discovered in Gozan (in AFO, supplement 6, no. 111) contains many other Hebrew names, such as *Da-a-na-a* (Heb. Dinah); *Isīʿa* (Heb. Hosea), *Milkināme* (Heb. Malchiram), *Yasimē* (Heb. Ishmael?); but one of the witnesses is Rīmanni-Ishtār, an Assyrian. The documents date from the late eighth and seventh centuries.

Bibliography: E. Forrer, *Die Provinzeinteilung des assyrischen Reiches* (1920), index; L. Waterman, *The Royal Correspondence of the Assyrian Empire* (1930); Ebeling and Meisner, E. Unger, in: *Reallexikon der Assyriologie* (1938), 37; J. Friedrich et al., *Die*

Figure 3. Prayer of the Mantua community for Francis II, emperor of Austria 1792–1835. Cecil Roth Collection. Photo David Harris, Jerusalem.

Inschriften von Tell Halaf (1940); M. von Oppenheim, *Tell Halaf*, 2 vols. (1943–50); O. Callaghan, *Aram Naharaim* (1948); B. Maisler, in: BIES, 15 (1949/50), 83–85; A. Malamat, *ibid.*, 99–102; idem, *Ha-Aramim be-Aram Naharayim* (1952), 47ff.; H. Frankfort, *The Art and Architecture of the Ancient Orient* (1954), 172ff., passim; D. D. Luckenbill, *Ancient Records* (1968), index.

[P.AR.]

GOZHANSKY, SAMUEL (pseudonyms: **Ha-Moreh, "Lanu,"** 1867–1943) Bundist, born in Novovola, Belorussia. The son of a wagoner, Gozhansky graduated from the Teachers' Seminary in Vilna in 1888. He became a socialist and from 1891 to 1895 led the Jewish Social Democrats in Vilna, the pioneers of the *Bund. As almost their only writer in Yiddish, Gozhansky composed most of the explanatory pamphlets directed to the workers. The most important, the "Letter to Agitators" (1893–94; preserved in typescript in Russian, retranslated into Yiddish, 1939, and into Hebrew, 1967), primarily sets out the fundamentals of the ideology of the Jewish workers' movement. According to this, Jewish workers would obtain their social and political rights if they constituted "a recognizable force" of their own which would conduct "the national political struggle" for obtaining civil rights for all the Jews. The Jewish workers would join up with the general workers' movement as an independent body. Gozhansky was arrested for revolutionary activity in Bialystok in 1896 and exiled to Siberia. He returned in 1902. Subsequently he was active in the Bund in Warsaw, Vilna, and other places, standing as Bundist candidate in the elections for the second Duma, and contributing to the Bundist paper *Folkstseitung* During this period he was imprisoned several times. He was a member of the foreign committee of the Bund and as its delegate served as secretary of the Congress of the Russian Social Democratic Workers' Party in London in 1907. He wrote the pamphlets "Zionism" and "The Jewish Proletariat." During World War I Gozhansky lived in Tula. After the 1917 Revolution he edited the Bund organ *Dos Profesionele Lebn* in Petrograd (Leningrad). He joined the Communist Party in 1919 but was not active in the *Yevsektsiya (Jewish section).

Bibliography: *Revolyutsionnoye dvizheniye sredi yevreyev* (1930), index; LNYL, 3 (1958), 7–8; M. Mishkinsky, in: *Zion*, 31 (1966), 89–101.

[M.M.]

GOZLAN, ELIE (1876–1964), Algerian pedagogue and journalist. Gozlan took part in the First Zionist Congress in Basle in 1897, was the secretary-general of the Algiers Jewish Consistory, and was one of the founders of the Algiers branch of the World Jewish Congress. He established and edited the *Bulletin de la Fédération des Sociétés Juives d'Algérie* (1936–47), which he courageously published during the Vichy regime. With the collaboration of outstanding Catholic and Muslim personalities, he helped found the Union des Croyants Monothéistes in Algiers. The Union was temporarily effective in establishing harmonious relations among all elements of the Algerian population.

Bibliography: Elmaleh, in: *Maḥberet*, no. 15 (May 1961), 261–6 (French supplement).

[R.AT.]

°**GRABSKI, STANISLAW** (1871–1949), Polish statesman and economist; he was the most prominent ideologist of the *Endecja (N.D.) Party and its leader for many years. Grabski held office as minister of education in 1923. In 1925–26, before the May Revolution, he played a prominent role in the conclusion of an agreement *(ugoda)* between the Jewish Parliamentary Club and the Polish government headed by his brother Wladyslaw. In 1926, he became alienated from Endecja because of his opposition to Fascist circles. Grabski was inconsistent in his political opinions during World War II in the government-in-exile in London, and in 1946 he returned to Warsaw, having reconciled himself with the new regime.

WLADYSLAW GRABSKI (1874–1938) was Stanislaw's brother. Before World War I he was a National Democrat (Endecja) deputy in the Russian *Duma. In independent Poland after the war, where he was a deputy of the Sejm (parliament), he left the party and took an independent position, serving as minister of finance in several governments. When the Red Army invaded Poland in 1920, Grabski became prime minister for a short while, and again headed the government from 1923 to 1925. The financial policy and taxation system introduced by Grabski became a severe financial burden to Jewish merchants and shopkeepers. The resulting crisis in the economic life of Polish Jewry served as an impetus to emigration on the "Fourth Aliyah" to Palestine of 1924–26, which became known as the "Grabski *aliyah*."

Bibliography: *Polski Słownik Biograficzny*, 8 (1959–60), 519–28; J. Shatzky, in: *Algemeyne Entsiklopedye: Yidn*, 4 (1950), 226.

[M.LAN.]

GRACE AFTER MEALS (Heb. בִּרְכַּת הַמָּזוֹן, *Birkat ha-Mazon*), a central feature of the liturgical service in the Jewish home. It is considered to be a biblical ordinance, inferred from the verse "Thou shalt eat and be satisfied and bless the Lord thy God for the good land which He has given thee" (Deut. 8:10). If one is in doubt whether he has recited it it should be repeated rather than not said at all (Tur and Sh. Ar., OḤ 184; Maim., Yad, Berakhot 2:14; cf. Ber. 21a). Grace after Meals consists of four blessings and is recited only after a meal at which bread has been eaten. If bread is not eaten, a shorter form of grace is recited (for versions see below). The first blessing *(Birkat ha-Zan)* praises God for providing food for all His creatures. The second *(Birkat ha-Areẓ)* expresses Israel's particular gratitude for the "good land" God has given it, the redemption from Egypt, the covenant of circumcision, and the revelation of the Torah. The third benediction, called *Boneh Yerushalayim* and also *Neḥamah* ("consolation"), asks God to have mercy on Israel and to restore the Temple and the Kingdom of David. It includes a plea that He may always sustain and support Israel. To these three benedictions which form the core of the Grace a fourth *(Ha-tov ve-ha-metiv)* was added after the destruction of *Bethar. It combines thanks for God's goodness, with the prayer that He may fulfill specific desires (Ber. 48b–49b). It is followed by several petitions which begin with the word *Ha-Raḥaman* ("May the All-Merciful . . ."). Originally phrased to suit individual desires, the supplications have now become standardized. The number of these petitions varies greatly in different rites; the general Sephardi rite has some 15, while the Ashkenazi has nine.

According to the Talmud (Ber. 48b), the first benediction was instituted by Moses when the manna fell from heaven; the second by Joshua when he conquered Ereẓ Israel; the third by David and Solomon; and the fourth by the rabbis of *Jabneh in gratitude for the miracle that the corpses of the unburied dead of Bethar did not decay, and that permission was ultimately granted for their burial (see: *Bar Kokhba). Finkelstein however, points out that the fourth blessing was known to *Eliezer b. Hyrcanus (Ber. 48b) who died before the fall of Bethar, and to *Yose the Galilean (Tosef., Ber. 1:9) and *Ishmael (TJ, Ber 7:1, 11a), who do not mention the incident. He, therefore, suggests that this blessing may have originated in the early years of the reign of *Hadrian. The Book of Jubilees (22:6–9) quotes the original threefold blessing, and attributes it to Abraham. Josephus (Wars, 11:131) testifies to the custom of thanksgiving after meals, and traces it back to *Simeon

סדר ברכת המזון

ברוך

אתה ה' אלהינו מלך העולם הזן את
העולם כלו בטובו בחן בחסד וב
וברחמים הוא נותן לחם לכל בשר
כי לעולם חסדו:
ובטובו הגדול תמיד
לא חסר לנו
ואל יחסר לנו
מזון לעולם ועד בעבור שמו
הגדול כי הוא (אל) זן ומפרנס

The beginning of the Grace after Meals, *Birkat ha-Mazon*, from an 18th-century East European *siddur*. Cambridge University Library, Ms. Add. 1532, fol. 19.

b. Shetah (also mentioned in TJ, Ber. 7:2, 11b). The Book of Ben Sira (Ecclus. 36:12–14, 17–19) clearly follows parts of the third benediction, and the Christian thanksgiving prayer in the *Didache* (a Christian work of the last decade of the first century) chapter 10, also bears strong resemblances to the Jewish formula. Among Portuguese Jews the Grace is known as *benção*, and among Ashkenazim by the Yiddish term *benshn*, a corruption of the Latin "benedictio" (by way of Old French).

According to the Talmud (BB 60b) it is forbidden to forget the destruction of the Temple even during meals, and thus the recitation of Grace should be preceded on weekdays by Psalm 137. The custom, however, is not often observed. More common is the practice to recite Psalm 126 on Sabbaths and festivals, its optimistic vision better fitting the spirit of these days. The rabbis ordained that whenever three or more have eaten bread together, one of them must summon the others to say Grace with him (Ber. 7:1–5). In reply to the invitation "Gentlemen, let us say Grace," (in Sephardi usage "with your permission"), the others reply "Blessed be the name of the Lord henceforth and forever." The leader repeats the statement and then continues, "With your consent (in Sephardi usage "with the permission of Heaven") let us now bless Him of whose food we have eaten." The others then respond: "Blessed be He whose food we have eaten and through whose goodness we live." This formula is known as *zimmun*, and according to the Talmud (Ber. 45b; Ar. 3a) must even be recited by three women who eat together. According to one opinion in the Mishnah, the *zimmun* formula becomes increasingly elaborate as the number of participants grows to ten, a hundred, a thousand, and ten thousand; more numerous and more solemn epithets of God are added every time (Ber. 7:3; Meg. 4:3). In modern times, the word *Elohenu* ("our God") is inserted in the third line of the formula when the number of participants is ten or more. The custom of communal grace, originally used only when the participants numbered at least ten, can be traced back to the custom of **havurah* ("community") meals, held especially on the Sabbaths. The practice was widespread in the Second Temple period among the Pharisees, and certain sectarian groups such as the Essenes.

Grace may be recited in any language (Sot. 7:1), but must be said at the table from which one has eaten (Maim. Yad, Berakhot, 4:1) and on which some bread should be left until the conclusion of the benediction (Tos. to Ber. 42a and Sanh. 92a). It is followed by a blessing on a cup of wine. The codifiers differ as to whether the cup of wine is required only when Grace is recited with *zimmun* or even when it is recited individually (Sh. Ar., OH 182:1). It has become customary to have the cup of wine only at *zimmun* on Sabbaths, festivals, and other special occasions. Various changes are made in the grace to suit different circumstances. On Sabbaths and festivals a special section (*Rezeh* and *Ya'aleh ve-Yavo* respectively) is inserted in the third blessing and an additional petition added in the series of *Ha-Rahaman;* in the Ashkenazi rite the word *Magdil* (from Ps. 18:51) in the final *Ha-Rahaman* is changed to *Migdol* (from II Samuel 22:51). The change probably originated through the confusion, by some early editors of the *siddur*, between ב"בש"B.SH.B." (meaning "in II Samuel"), and 'בשב *be-Shabbat* ("on Sabbaths"). Special *Ha-Rahaman* petitions are also inserted on New Moons, Rosh Ha-Shanah, Sukkot, and Passover *seder*. On Hanukkah and Purim, **Al ha-Nissim* is said during the second blessing which is devoted to thanksgiving (Shab. 24a; cf. Rashi *ibid.*). At a wedding banquet, the third line of the *zimmun* is changed to read "Blessed be our God in whose abode is joy, of whose food we have eaten and through whose goodness we live" (Ket. 8a; cf. Rashi *ibid.*), and the seven wedding benedictions are recited at the conclusion of Grace (Maim. Yad, Berakhot, 2:9, 5:5). At the house of a mourner, a special prayer is substituted for the end of the third benediction, a change is made in the text of the fourth, and the *zimmun* is slightly changed (Ber. 46b; Sh. Ar., YD 379, OH 189:2). At the meal which follows a circumcision ceremony, the wording of the *zimmun* is changed to suit the occasion. Among the several lines which begin with *Ha-Rahaman* in the fourth blessing, a child, a guest (see Ber. 46a), and the master of the house may each insert passages to suit their particular circumstance (see Tur., OH 189). Since the establishment of the State of Israel, some families have also inserted a fourth *Ha-Rahaman* "May the All-Merciful bless the State of Israel, and all who work for her."

Shorter Forms. Ever since the formulation of a "complete" *Birkat ha-Mazon*, there have been shorter versions for extraordinary occasions. The guiding principle has been that the *mitzvah* of reciting *Birkat ha-Mazon* is commanded by the Torah, but the actual content has developed over the ages. Workmen who eat during working hours, therefore, may recite a shortened form, consisting of the first *berakhah*, the "blessing for the land," and mention of Jerusalem (Sh. Ar., OH 191:1). Children are required to recite only small sections. In cases of extreme emergency, he who says, "Blessed be the Merciful One, the King, the Master of this land" has fulfilled his obligation. The *siddur* of Saadiah Gaon contains a highly abbreviated version of *Birkat ha-Mazon*. Another shortened form is found in the *Magen Avraham* commentary to the Shulhan Arukh (OH 192:1). In general, shorter forms include the entire first *berakhah*, mention of the Covenant and the Torah as well as the blessing for the land in the second *berakhah*, and mention of Israel and the Davidic Kingdom in the third *berakhah*.

In the United States, the Conservative movement has evolved a shortened version based on this formula, used at public gatherings and summer camps (the traditional long form is usually recited on the Sabbath).

The Reform Prayer Book has a short version made up of two English paragraphs and concluding with the Hebrew ending of the traditional first *berakhah*.

When bread is not eaten there are two other forms of grace (known as *Berakhah Aḥaronah*—"final benediction") to be recited, depending on the nature of the food consumed. For food prepared from the five species of grain (wheat, barley, rye, oats, and spelt), wine, or the fruits of Ereẓ Israel (grapes, figs, olives, pomegranates, and dates) a short summary of the Grace after Meals is said. This is in the form of one benediction with insertions for the type of food eaten and for special occasions such as the Sabbath and festivals. This is called in the Talmud *Berakhah Me'ein Shalosh*—"the benediction summarizing the three" (benedictions of the regular grace). For any other food a short benediction (called in the Talmud *Ve-Lo-Khelum*, "Nothing" but popularly known by its first two words *(Bore Nefashot)* is recited (Ber. 37a–b; laws codified Sh. Ar., OḤ 207–8; texts Hertz, Prayer, 984, 988).

Bibliography: Finkelstein, in: JQR, 19 (1928/29), 211–62; Abrahams, Companion, 207ff.; ET, 4 (1952), 475–511; Heinemann, in: JJS, 13 (1962), 23–29.

[ED.]

GRACE BEFORE MEALS. The rabbis required a blessing before partaking of food since they considered it sacrilegious to "enjoy of this world without a prior benediction" (Ber. 35a). They instituted separate blessings for the various species of food, of which those over bread and wine are considered the most important. The blessing for bread, "Who bringest forth bread from the earth" (*Ha-moẓi leḥem min ha-areẓ;* Ber. 6:1), is based upon Psalms 104:14, and, when recited at the start of a meal, exempts one from the obligation to recite most additional blessings for the remaining courses (Sh. Ar., OḤ 177). Since this blessing is often the only one recited before a meal, the popular term for the grace before meals is *Moẓi*. The blessing for wine, "Who createst the fruit of the vine (*"Bore peri ha-gafen";* Ber. 6:1), is recited, even when the wine is drunk in the course of the repast and not at the beginning (Sh. Ar., OḤ 175, and see also 176).

Although the actual formulation of the blessings before meals was delineated during rabbinic times, the practice itself is of ancient origin. Thus in I Samuel 9:13 there is a reference to the people waiting for the prophet to bless the sacrifice before they would partake of its flesh. Josephus describes the grace before the meal recited by the *Essenes (Jos., Wars, 2:131). The rabbis attached great importance to the proper recitation of these blessings, and the father of R. Simeon b. Zevid was praised "as being a great man and well versed in the benedictions" (Ber. 38a).

Bibliography: Hertz, Prayer, 984–95; Idelsohn, Liturgy, 122; E. Levy, *Yesodot ha-Tefillah* (1952[2]), 279–81.

[ED.]

GRACIAN (Ḥen), SHEALTIEL BEN SOLOMON (14th century), Spanish rabbi, a contemporary of *Isaac b. Sheshet (Ribash) to whom he was related. Both apparently studied under R. Nissim Gerondi. After his marriage he lived in Fraga and was appointed rabbi of the community of Alcala in c. 1369, at which time he acceded to its request to affirm under oath that he would never leave this position. Later he regretted his hasty oath and requested Nissim Gerondi and Isaac b. Sheshet to absolve him of it, but they refused, and Isaac wrote him that "the truth is dearer to me—since both of us must respect it" (Ribash, no. 370). Around 1375 Shealtiel was appointed rabbi of Barcelona, in succession to Nissim who had died. R. Isaac b. Sheshet corresponded with him and mentions him in his responsa frequently and he states that, "he was a preeminent rabbinic authority . . . of outstanding scholarly attainments . . . and of foremost renown in Spain" (*ibid.*, no. 365). Isaac b. Sheshet asked him to mediate in a quarrel which arose between his daughter and her father-in-law. He urged him to lend his support, writing, "and should those in dispute with me, my enemies and their supporters, endeavor to incite you against me, do not listen to them" (*ibid.*, no. 415 end). However, Shealtiel disagreed with the stand which had been taken by Isaac b. Sheshet, and the outcome of the matter is unknown.

Bibliography: Baer, Urkunden, 1 (1929), 499f., 543, 705; A. M. Hershman, *Rabbi Isaac ben Sheshet Perfet and His Times* (1943), 24n.40, 66f., 87, 181f., 233, 242; Neubauer, Cat, no. 2218/4c.

[Y.HO.]

GRACIAN (Ḥen), ZERAHIAH BEN ISAAC BEN SHEALTIEL (13th century), physician, philosopher, and translator. Son of a prominent Barcelona family, Gracian emigrated to Italy. From 1277 to 1290 he lived in Rome, where he gave public lectures on exegetical and philosophical subjects. He was regarded as an expert on Maimonides' *Guide of the Perplexed*, and was frequently asked to solve problems posed by the book. One such reply, addressed to *Judah b. Solomon, a relative of Gracian's, was published in *Oẓar Neḥmad* (2 (1857), 121ff.). *Hillel b. Samuel of Verona, who probably met Gracian during the time he spent in Barcelona as a student of *Jonah Gerondi, also addressed himself to Gracian with philosophical questions. The exchange of views between the two scholars eventually took the form of a violent debate (two of Gracian's replies to Hillel have been published, *ibid.*, 124ff.).

Gracian was the author of the following works: (1) Commentary on Proverbs (1288–89), published by I. Schwartz in *Ha-Shaḥar*, under the title *Imrei Da'at* (also known as *Imrei Shefer*) and republished as a separate edition in 1871. (2) Commentary on Job (1290–91), published by Schwartz in *Tikvat Enosh* (1868). Both commentaries, written at the request of his disciples in Rome, combine philological and philosophical methods of exegesis and reveal Gracian's liberal views on matters of faith as well as his reluctance to make use of rabbinic sources and even of the prophets. In his commentary on Job Gracian criticizes the exegetes who preceded him, especially *Naḥmanides. (3) Commentary on the Pentateuch, or on certain portions of it, which, however, is no longer extant. (4) Commentary on parts of the *Guide* (1:1–71 and other passages, especially the 25 propositions appearing at the beginning of book 2). (5) Essays and comments on various problems. Gracian translated the following works from Arabic into Hebrew: (1) Maimonides' aphorisms; (2) *Galen's *De causis et symtomatibus;* (3) A part of Galen's *Katagenē;* (4) *Avicenna's *Canon*, not completed, perhaps because in the meantime Gracian had learned about the translation by Nathan ha-Me'ati; (5) Maimonides' shorter treatise on sexual intercourse; (6) Maimonides' treatise on drugs (of which only the introduction is still extant). All these translations seem to have been made at the same time (1277). At the request of Shabbetai b. Solomon, the rabbi of Rome, Gracian translated the following works (in 1284): Aristotle's *De anima;* *Averroes' middle commentaries on Aristotle's *Physics* and *Metaphysics;* paraphrase by *Themistius of Aristotle's *De caelo;* Al-*Fārābī's treatise on the nature of the soul (published by Z. H. Edelmann in

Ḥemdah Genuzah, 1856, and by Rosenthal, 1857); and the pseudo-Aristotelian *Liber de causis.*

Gracian and Hillel of Verona are to be credited with the propagation of philosophical studies among Jewish circles in Italy.

Bibliography: Steinschneider, in: *Oẓar Neḥmad,* 2 (1857), 229–45; Steinschneider, Uebersetzungen, 111–24*, 125, 146, 160, 262, 295, 652, 681, 764, 765; Steinschneider, Arab Lit, 213–19; Dukes, in: HB, 3 (1860), 99–100; Kirchheim, *ibid.,* 4 (1861), 125–6; Carmoly, in: *Oẓar Neḥmad,* 3 (1860), 109–10.

[U.C./Ed.]

GRADE, CHAIM (1910–), Yiddish poet and novelist. Born in Vilna, he became that city's most articulate literary interpreter. His father, a Hebrew teacher, died when Grade was a young boy, and his mother toiled at a fruit stand in Vilna's marketplace in order to give her son a good traditional education. By the age of 22, Grade had attended several yeshivot, studying seven years under the famed scholar-rabbi the *Ḥazon Ish and being attracted to the *Musar movement. Grade was one of the staunchest pillars of the literary movement *Young Vilna which, beginning in the early 1930s, sought both to synthesize secular Yiddish culture with new currents in world literature, and to bring the impoverished Jewish home into contact with the progressive forces of contemporary society.

In 1932 Grade published his first lyrics in the Vilna *Tog,* then edited by the literary historian Zalman *Rejzen, and soon afterward his poems appeared in leading Yiddish periodicals in Europe and America. His first book, *Yo* (1936), was acclaimed by critics for its stylistic elegance and its affirmation of faith in a possible synthesis of traditional and modern currents. His long poem "Musernikes" (1939), in which he depicted himself in the figure of Chaim Vilner, described the spiritual struggles of the yeshivah students torn between the Musar traditions and worldly temptations.

During World War II, Grade found refuge in Soviet Russia, and after the war dedicated a series of poems, *"Mit Dayn Guf oyn Mayne Hent"* ("With Your Body in My Hands") to his wife who perished in the Holocaust; in them love and personal tragedy take on national overtones; and in his volumes *Doyres* ("Generations," 1945), *Pleytim* ("Refugees," 1947), and *Shayn fun Farloshene Shtern* ("Light of Extinguished Stars," 1950), Grade mourns the victims of the Holocaust and describes the survivors. With this attempt at confronting the national Jewish tragedy, Grade becomes in a sense the national Jewish poet, as Bialik was in his day.

Returning from the Soviet Union to Poland in 1946, Grade went on to Paris, where he was active in revivifying Yiddish cultural life among the surviving Jews and where he headed the Yiddish literary club. In 1948 he was sent to the U.S. as a delegate to the Jewish Culture Congress. He settled in New York and began his association with the Yiddish daily *Jewish Morning Journal.* His novel, *Di Agune* ("The Abandoned Wife," 1961), depicts all segments of Jewish Vilna society between the wars; it appeared in a Hebrew translation in 1962. *Der Mentsh fun Fayer* ("The Man of Fire," 1962) included his poems on Israel and his elegies on the Ḥazon Ish, as well as on martyred Soviet Yiddish writers. In 1969 another volume of poetry appeared, *Oyf Mayn Veg tsu Dir ("On My Way to You").*

Grade is one of the rare interpreters of yeshivah life in modern Yiddish literature; with photographic accuracy, objectivity, and affection, he recreates the daily life of the yeshivah student and such scenes as rabbis discussing talmudic law. The poems to his mother in *Der Mames Tsavoe* ("My Mother's Will," 1949) are among the most outstanding lyrics in Yiddish; they are permeated with love and respect for his mother, who perished during the Holocaust. She is also the central figure of his first prose volume, *Der Mames Shabosim* ("My Mother's Sabbaths," 1955). This three-part work describes his orphaned childhood in Vilna, his life as a refugee in Soviet Russia, and his return to a destroyed postwar Vilna, decimated of its Jews and its Jewish institutions. Pre-World War II Jewish Vilna

Chaim Grade, Yiddish poet and novelist. Photo Hetz, Tel Aviv.

comes to life in the collection *Der Shulhoyf* ("The Courtyard of the Synagogue," 1958), written in some of the finest prose of the post-classical generation; it contains the novel *Der Brunem* (English translation *The Well,* 1967). His long novel of yeshivah life, *Tsemakh Atlas* (2 vols., 1967–68) was also translated into Hebrew (1968), and a volume of lyrics, together with a Hebrew translation, *Parmetene Erd* ("Parchment Earth") was published in Tel Aviv in 1968. One of Grade's best stories "My Quarrel with Hersh Rasseyner," a dramatic dialogue between a freethinking Yiddish writer and a pious yeshivah scholar, both survivors of the Holocaust, was included in I. Howe and E. Greenberg's *A Treasury of Yiddish Stories* (1954, 579–606). His poems in English translation appeared in J. Leftwich, *The Golden Peacock* (1961), and in R. Whitman's *Anthology of Modern Yiddish Poetry* (1966).

Bibliography: LNYL, 2 (1958), 335–8; E. Schulman, *Yung Vilne* (1946); J. Glatstein, *In Tokh Genumen* (1956), 348–54; S. Bickel, *Shrayber fun Mayn Dor* (1958) 366–73; I. Biletzky, *Essays on Yiddish Poetry and Prose Units* (1969), 233–42.

[I.H.B.]

GRADIS, family of ship owners and community leaders, of Marrano extraction, which flourished in Bordeaux from the 17th century. David Gradis (1665–1751) founded an import-export firm (David Gradis et fils, 1696) whose trade relations extended to England, Canada, and the French West Indies. His nephew Abraham (1699–1780) increased the firm's scope and prestige and was appointed royal purveyor in 1744. In 1748 he founded the Societé Gradis et fils under the auspices of the French government, and contracted to provide regular shipping services to Quebec for six years. For the entire period of the Seven Years' War (1756–63) his trade with Canada amounted to 9,000,000 livres. There were many losses, for more than half of the ships that he sent out were captured by the English, and he had trouble collecting from the state. Nevertheless, the Gradis House prospered greatly. In 1763, A. Gradis' friend Choiseul became the naval minister, and Gradis was given a contract to provision the French possessions in West Africa. In these transactions Gradis supplied spirits, gunpowder, knives, and cloth, taking his payment in slaves, whom he sold in San Domingo for sugar. In return for his services during the war, Gradis was praised by Louis XV through his minister Berryer, and later instanced by Abbé *Grégoire in support of arguments in favor of Jewish emancipation. Moses Gradis (1740–1788), a cousin of

PLATE 1. *Eruv Tavshilin* tablet, Germany, 1806. The blessing is recited to allow food to be cooked in preparation for the Sabbath when a festival falls on a Friday. 30×25¼ in. (76×64 cm.). Jerusalem, Israel Museum. Photo David Harris, Jerusalem.

PLATE 2. Short form of grace after meals, Italy, 18th century. 14×18 in. (35.5×45.7 cm.). Jerusalem, Michael Kaufman Collection. Photo David Harris, Jerusalem.

Abraham, inherited the firm after the latter's death. His brother, DAVID GRADIS (the Younger; 1742–1811), was a candidate for Bordeaux in the elections to the States General of 1789, and wrote several works on religion and philosophy. Similarly, his son BENJAMIN (1789–1858), and his grandson HENRI (1830–1905), divided their time between business, politics, and writing. Henri wrote *Histoire de la révolution de 1848* (2 vols. 1872), *Jérusalem* (1883), and *Le Peuple d'Israël* (1891). He was vice-mayor of Bordeaux and head of the Bordeaux *Consistory.

Bibliography: J. de Maupassant, *Abraham Gradis* (Fr., 1931); A. Hertzberg, *French Enlightenment and the Jews* (1968), index; H. Graetz, in: MGWJ, 24 (1875), 447–59; 25 (1876), 78–85; A. Cahen, in: REJ, 4 (1882), 132–44; 5 (1882), 258–67; B. G. Sack, *History of the Jews in Canada* (1964), 13–31, 261; S. Rosenberg, *The Jewish Community of Canada*, 1 (1970), index.

[ED.]

GRAEBER, SCHEALTIEL EISIK (1856–?), Hebrew writer and publisher. Born in Galicia, he became involved in the Haskalah movement at an early age. He wrote for various Hebrew journals, but his major contribution in Hebrew letters was as a publisher. He published the periodical *Ha-Ohev Ammo ve-Ereẓ Moladeto* (1881), the annual *Beit Oẓar ha-Sifrut* (from 1887), and the works of Italian Jewish scholars, such as S. D. Luzzatto (*Iggerot Shadal*, 1882–94) and M. I. Tedeschi. [G.K.]

°GRAES (Gratius), ORTWIN VAN DE (1480–1542), Dominican friar and fanatic anti-Jewish polemicist. He was coauthor (or translator) of Victor von *Carben's *De vita et moribus Judaeorum* (1509) and translated into Latin some of the polemics of Johann *Pfefferkorn, to whose *Judenfeind* (1509) he wrote an introductory poem *De pertinatia Judaeorum* ("On the Obstinacy of the Jews"). In 1513 Johannes *Reuchlin directed his defense in his controversy with Pfefferkorn mainly against Graes who was also the principal target of *Epistolae obscurorum virorum* (1515 and 1517). Graes's wordy reply (*Lamentationes obscurorum virorum*, Cologne, 1518) was no match for this savage satire. The *Praenotamenta* (1514) and *Defensio* (1516) against Reuchlin's *Augenspiegel* are also considered Graes's work.

Bibliography: Graetz, Hist, index; M. Brod, *Johannes Reuchlin und sein Kampf* (1965), 178ff.; J. Kracauer, *Geschichte der Juden in Frankfurt . . .*, 1 (1925), 247ff.; D. Reichling, *Ortwin Gratius . . .* (Germ., 1884).

[ED.]

GRAETZ, HEINRICH (1817–1891), Jewish historian and Bible scholar. Graetz was born in Xions (Ksiaz), Poznan, the son of a butcher. From 1831 to 1836 he pursued rabbinic studies in Wolstein (now Wolsztyn) near Poznan. There Graetz taught himself French and Latin and avidly read general literature. This brought him to a spiritual crisis, but reading S. R. *Hirsch's "Nineteen Letters on Judaism" in 1836 restored his faith. He accepted Hirsch's invitation to continue his studies in the latter's home and under his guidance. Eventually their relationship cooled; he left Oldenburg in 1840 and worked as a private tutor in Ostrow. In 1842 he obtained special permission to study at Breslau University. As no Jew could obtain a Ph.D. at Breslau, Graetz presented his thesis to the University of Jena. This work was later published under the title *Gnostizismus und Judentum* (1846). By then Graetz had come under the influence of Z. *Frankel, and it was he who initiated a letter of congratulations to Frankel for leaving the second *Rabbinical Conference (Frankfort, 1845) in protest, after the majority had decided against prayers in Hebrew. Graetz now became a contributor to Frankel's *Zeitschrift fuer die religioesen Interessen des Judentums*, in which, among others, he published his programmatic "Konstruktion der juedischen Geschichte" (1846).

Heinrich Graetz, Jewish historian. From *American Jewish Yearbook, 1941–42*, Jewish Publication Society, Philadelphia, Pa.

Graetz failed to obtain a position as rabbi and preacher because of his lack of talent as an orator. After obtaining a teaching diploma, he was appointed head teacher of the orthodox religious school of the Breslau community, and in 1850, at Hirsch's recommendation, of the Jewish school of Lundenburg, Moravia. As a result of intrigues within the local community, he left Lundenburg in 1852 for Berlin, where during the following winter he lectured on Jewish history to theological students. He then began to contribute to the **Monatsschrift fuer Geschichte und Wissenschaft des Judentums*, which Frankel had founded in 1851 and which he later edited himself (1869–88). He also completed the fourth volume (dealing with the talmudic period and the first to be published) of his *Geschichte der Juden von den aeltesten Zeiten bis zur Gegenwart* ("History of the Jews . . .," 1853). In 1853 Graetz was appointed lecturer in Jewish history and Bible at the newly founded *Jewish Theological Seminary of Breslau, and in 1869 was made honorary professor at the University of Breslau.

Visit to Ereẓ Israel. Between 1856 and 1870 eight further volumes of his *Geschichte der Juden* appeared, leaving only the first two volumes—dealing with the biblical period and the early Second Temple period—to be completed. These Graetz postponed until he could see Ereẓ Israel with his own eyes. This he did and on his return published a memorandum which was highly critical of the social and educational conditions and of the system of **Ḥalukkah* in particular. Graetz pleaded for a Jewish orphanage which was established at a later date, and continued to show an interest in the *yishuv* and its problems. After the *Kattowitz Conference he joined the *Ḥovevei Zion, but he resigned when it appeared to him that their activities had assumed a political character.

Biblical Studies. The first volume of the *History of the Jews* (to the death of Solomon) appeared in 1874 and the two parts of the second volume (to the revolt of the Hasmoneans) in 1875–76. As to biblical research, Graetz's approach to the Pentateuch was traditional, but in his studies on Prophets and Hagiographa he occasionally adopted radical views. He asserted the existence of two Hoseas and three Zechariahs. His commentaries on Song of Songs and Ecclesiastes (the latter written according to him in the time of Herod) were published in 1871 and his commentary to Psalms in 1882. These were generally not favorably received, though by making use of the old Bible versions and of talmudic Hebrew he was able to obtain some valuable results. Toward the end of his life it was Graetz's intention to publish a critical text of the Bible, but this project did not materialize.

Controversy with Treitschke. Graetz played a role in the struggle of German Jews against the new wave of anti-Semitic attacks. In 1879 the nationalistic Prussian historian *Treitschke violently attacked the 11th volume of the *History of the Jews* which dealt with recent times. He accused Graetz of hatred of Christianity, Jewish nationalism, and the lack of desire for the integration of Jews within the German nation (*Ein Wort ueber unser Judentum,* 1880). This led to a public debate in which both Jewish and non-Jewish writers participated. While most of them rejected Treitschke's virulent anti-Semitism, even Jewish writers dissociated themselves, with few exceptions, from Graetz's Jewish nationalism. Graetz in his reply in the press pointed out that in spite of their glorious past Jews had become interwoven in the life of Western Europe and that they were patriots in their respective countries. He rejected the accusation of hatred of Christianity. In a further attack Treitschke claimed that Graetz sought to establish a mixed Jewish-German culture in Germany, that he was a German-speaking "oriental" and a stranger to European-German culture, etc. Graetz retorted sharply, but assimilationist German Jewry showed its disapproval of Graetz by not inviting him to serve on the Jewish Historical Commission, set up in 1885 by the Union of Jewish Communities, with the purpose of publishing the sources for the history of the Jews in Germany. But a wider Jewish public, and the world of Jewish scholarship in particular, honored Graetz on the occasion of his 70th birthday; and a jubilee volume was published to celebrate the event. Graetz was invited to deliver the opening speech at the Anglo-Jewish Exhibition in London in 1887, which was published under the title of *Historic Parallels in Jewish History* (translated by J. Jacobs, 1887). In 1888 he was elected honorary member of the history department of the Academy of Madrid, a special distinction for a historian who had described the misdeeds of the Spanish Inquisition.

Popular History of the Jews. Between 1887 and 1889 an abridged edition of his great work was published in three volumes under the title *Volkstuemliche Geschichte der Juden* (1887–89; 10 editions to 1930; Eng. tr. 1930[4]), which became one of the most widely read Jewish books in Germany. Graetz's main work became the basis and the source for the study of Jewish history, and its influence is felt to this day. It was translated into many languages (see below). The Hebrew adaptation-translation of S. P. *Rabinowitz (with A. Harkavy, 1890–99) exerted much influence among the Hebrew-reading public of East European Jewry; so did the various English translations among English-speaking Jewry.

The Historian. The foundations of the outlook of Graetz on the Jewish people and its history appear to have been laid during his association with S. R. Hirsch and under the influence of his ideas concerning the great mission of the Jewish people. In general, Graetz remained faithful to these ideas to the end of his days. Graetz had set out his concept of Jewish history in his *Konstruktion der juedischen Geschichte* (1846, 1936; Heb. tr. *Darkhei ha-Historyah ha-Yehudit,* 1969). He started with a number of Hegelian definitions, but he considered the basic ideas of Judaism as eternal, changing only their external forms. The ideal form is harmony of the political and religious elements. Therefore Graetz regarded Judaism as a unique politico-religious organism, "whose soul is the Torah and whose body is the Holy Land." As for the latest exilic period in Jewish history, Graetz agrees that theoretical-philosophical ideas have taken over from the national-political principle: "Judaism became science." He feels, however, that the process is not yet concluded and that "it is the task of Judaism's conception of God to prepare a religious state constitution" in which it would achieve self-realization, i.e., in it the harmony of the religious and political elements will be restored. Graetz's ideas on the nature of Jewish history underwent further development. In an essay entitled *Die Verjuengung des juedischen Stammes* (in Wertheimer-Komperts' *Jahrbuch fuer Israeliten,* 1863; repr. with notes by Zlocisty in *Juedischer Volkskalender,* Brno, 1903; Eng. tr. in I. Lesser's *Occident* (1865), 193 ff.) he rejected the belief in a personal Messiah, and maintained that the prophetic promises referred to the Jewish nation as a whole. In this period (1860s) Graetz under the influence of M. Hess' *Rome and Jerusalem* did not believe in the political revival of the Jews and in the possibility of the creation of a Jewish center in Ereẓ Israel (see letters to Hess and the conclusion of his pamphlet *Briefwechsel einer englischen Dame ueber Judentum und Semitismus,* which he published anonymously in 1883; also under the title *Gedanken einer Juedin ueber das Judentum . . .,* 1885). The rediscovery of Graetz's diary and correspondence with Hess reveals the extent of his national and messianic fervor. He formulated the concept of the messianic people as the highest stage in the development of the messianic belief. From the Jewish people, endowed with special racial qualities of self-regeneration, will emerge the leadership for the final stage in universal history: eternal peace and redemption. But later he lost his original enthusiasm. Both in this pamphlet and in his essay "The Significance of Judaism for the Present and the Future" (in JQR, 1–2, 1889/90), he emphasized the historical and religious significance of continuous Jewish existence. He saw the main importance of Judaism in the ethical values which it was its task to impart to the world. Judaism is the sole bearer of monotheism; it is the only rational religion. Its preservation and the propagation of the sublime ethical truths to be found in Judaism, these are the tasks of the Jews in the world and this is the importance of Judaism for human culture.

The "History." Graetz's life work is his *History of the Jews,* and most of his other writings were merely preliminary studies or supplements to this gigantic structure. Even though attempts had been made before him by both Christians (Basnage) and Jews (Jost) to write a Jewish history, the work of Graetz was the first comprehensive attempt to write the history of the Jews as the history of a living people and from a Jewish point of view. With deep feeling, he describes the struggle of Jews and of Judaism for survival, their uniqueness, the sufferings of the Exile, and the courage of the martyrs, and in contrast, the cruelty of the enemies of Israel and its persecutors throughout the ages. Out of his appreciation of Judaism and his reaction against all that Christianity had perpetrated against Judaism, Graetz pointed out the failure of Christianity as religion and ethics to serve as a basis for a healthy society. He subjected its literary sources (the Gospels and the Epistles of Paul) to a radical, historical criticism. The writing of such a Jewish history in German for a public which in its vast majority identified itself with German nationalism and Christian culture was no easy task for a writer who did not have a very clear idea of the mission and the future of his nation. Graetz erred more than once on the side of inconsistency, excessive sentimentalism, and apologetics.

The Historiographer. From a historiographic point of view, the *History of the Jews* was a great and impressive achievement. Graetz made use of a vast number of hitherto neglected sources in several languages, though these were mainly literary sources; there was hardly any archival material on Jewish history available in his days. He adopted the philologic-critical method and succeeded in clarifying several obscure episodes in Jewish history. He described everything which appeared to him understandable and logical in the history of his people and emphasized the forces and the ideals which had assured its survival in periods of suffering and trial. Having studied the works of outstanding personalities, especially those with whom he felt a spiritual affinity (such as Maimonides), Graetz succeeded in painting a series of live historical portraits, stressing the role played by a particular figure in his epoch and in the history of the nation in general. His intuition as a historian was astonishing. Thus, for example, the documents discovered in the Cairo **Genizah* after the death of Graetz confirmed several of his surmises concerning the development of the *piyyut* and the period of the *geonim*. But Graetz the historiographer had his faults as well, among which was his excessive and rather naive rationalism. He showed no understanding for mystical forces and movements such as *Kabbalah and *Ḥasidism, which he despised and considered malignant growths in the body of Judaism. Graetz was not acquainted with and perhaps, subconsciously, not interested in the history of the Jews of Poland, Russia, and Turkey, and in his attachment to Haskalah expressed contempt bordering on hatred for "the fossilized Polish talmudists." He refers to Yiddish as a ridiculous gibberish. The social and economic aspect of history is neglected by Graetz, and even political and legal factors were used by him only as a foil for the description of sufferings or of the achievements of leading personalities ("Leidens- und Gelehrtengeschichte"). Graetz wrote in a lively and captivating though often over-rhetorical, and partisan, style.

Critics. In spite of his faults Graetz's work had a tremendous effect on Jews everywhere, but he was not short of critics either. S. R. Hirsch voiced strong criticism as early as the publication of the first volume in his *Jeschurun* (1885–86), calling it "the phantasies of superficial combinations." The breach between teacher and pupil was now complete, and Graetz took his revenge by some scathing criticism of Hirsch in the last volume of his history. From the opposite direction came Geiger's verdict that the work contained "stories but not history" (*Juedische Zeitschrift,* 4 (1866), 145ff.; cf. also Steinschneider's censure in HB, 3 (1860), 103f.; 4 (1861), 84; 6 (1863), 73ff.). Graetz replied to his contemporary critics in periodicals and in subsequent volumes of his history.

The "History": editions and translations. The great number of editions and translations (also of single volumes: cf. Brann, in MGWJ, 61 (1917), 481–91) of the *Geschichte* speak their own language of success. The various volumes were published in up to five editions until World War I. Several volumes of the last edition (11 vols., 1890–1909) were edited and annotated by M. Brann and others. The best known Hebrew translation is by S. P. Rabinowitz (1890–99). Yiddish translations appeared in 1897–98, 1913, and 1915–17. English translations: (1) without the notes and excurses, by Bella Loewy (5 vols., 1891–92), with an introduction and final retrospect by Graetz himself (1901); (2) the same with a sixth volume including P. Bloch's memoir, 1892–98; and (3) the "Popular History" (5 vols., 1919). French translations: volume 3 was translated by Moses *Hess under the title *Sinai et Golgotha* in 1867; and the whole work by M. Wogue and M. Bloch (1882–97). The work was also translated into Russian, Polish, and Hungarian.

Most of Graetz's other published work was preparatory to the main "History," and appeared in the *Monatsschrift* and in the *Jahresberichte* of the Breslau Seminary. On the occasion of Graetz's 100th birthday anniversary the *Monatsschrift* (vol. 61 (1917), 321 ff.) and the *Neue Juedische Monatshefte* (vol. 2 nos. 3–4, 1917/18) issued a series of studies on the life and works of the historian. A number of Graetz's essays, his early diaries (see Brann, in MGWJ, 62 (1918), 231–65), and some letters, etc. have been published in Hebrew (*Darkhei ha-Historyah ha-Yehudit* (1969), tr. by J. Tolkes, introd. by S. Ettinger and biography by R. Michael).

Bibliography: G. Deutsch, *Heinrich Graetz—a Centenary* (1917); J. Meisl, *Heinrich Graetz . . . zu seinem 100. Geburtstage* (1917); M. Brann (ed.), *Heinrich Graetz: Abhandhungen zu seinem 100. Geburtstage* (1917); idem, in: MGWJ, 62 (1918), 231–69; *ibid.*, 61 (1917), 212–5, 321–491 (various contributions, incl. bibls.); P. Bloch, *Heinrich Graetz: a Memoir* (1898; also in Graetz, Hist, 6 (1949), 1–86); E. Schmerler, *Ḥayyei Graetz* (1921), incl. bibl.; S. Dubnow, in: *Voskhod,* 12 nos. 1–9 (1892); Kaufmann, Schriften, 1 (1908), 212–82; I. Abrahams, in: JQR, 4 (1892), 165–203; M. Guedemann, in: *Neue Freie Presse* (Vienna, Oct. 20, 1891); idem, in: JJGL, 21 (1918), 45–55; H. Cohen, *Juedische Schriften,* 2 (1924), 446–53; S. Baron, *History and Jewish Historians* (1964), 269–75; I. Elbogen, in: *Festschrift S. Dubnow* (1930), 7–23; N. Rotenstreich, in: *Zion,* 8 (1943), 51–59; E. J. Cohn, in: G. Kisch (ed.), *Breslau Seminary* (1963), 187–203; I. Elbogen, *ibid.*, 205–21; S. Grayzel, *ibid.*, 223–37; G. Herlitz, in: YLBI, 9 (1964), 76–83; R. Michael, *ibid.*, 91–121; 13 (1968), 34–56. [S.Ett.]

°**GRAF, KARL HEINRICH** (1815–1869), German Protestant Bible scholar; born in Mulhouse, Alsace, and died in Meissen, Saxony. Graf began as a teacher of French and Hebrew in Paris and Meissen, where, in 1852, he became a professor. The hypothesis of his teacher, E. Reuss, that the prophetic books preceded the literary formulations of the Pentateuchal laws led Graf to the further hypothesis (*Die geschichtlichen Buecher des Alten Testaments,* 1866) that the Priestly Code, i.e., the source which includes Leviticus, which had until then been considered the earliest source of the Pentateuch, was actually the latest of the Pentateuchal sources. This contribution to the reconstruction of the history of ancient Israel was later developed by J. *Wellhausen. He also wrote commentaries on Moses' blessing (1857) and the Book of Jeremiah (*Der Prophet Jeremia,* 1862). [Ed.]

GRAJEWO, small town in Bialystok province, Poland. Jews settled there at the beginning of the 18th century. According to the 1765 census, there were 83 Jews aged over one year (17 families), of whom six families resided in their own houses and eleven in leased dwellings; 336 Jews were living in 38 villages in the vicinity. They leased taverns or were occupied as small traders or artisans (tailors, tinsmiths). Until 1862 Grajewo was included in the towns of the Russian-German border zone, where Jewish residence was subjected to various restrictions. In the 19th century many Jews in Grajewo exported agricultural produce to Eastern Prussia. The community numbered 197 (39% of the total population) in 1808, 727 (57%) in 1827, 1,457 (76%) in 1857, 4,336 in 1897 and 2,384 (39%) in 1921. There were anti-Jewish outbreaks in 1933. In November 1942 most of the Jews in Grajewo were sent to the death camp of *Treblinka.

Bibliography: R. Mahler, *Yidn in Amolikn Poyln in Likht fun Tsifern* (1958), index; B. Wasiutyński, *Ludność Żydowska w Polsce . . .* (1930), 37. [Ed.]

GRAJEWSKI, ARYEH LEIB (1896–1967), talmudic scholar, jurist, and journalist. Grajewski was born near Lomza in Poland and studied in the yeshivah of Israel Meir Ha-Kohen (the "Ḥafeẓ Ḥayyim"), in Radin and at Slobodka. At the age of 16 he was ordained rabbi by outstanding scholars. He left for Ereẓ Israel in 1913, but at the outbreak of World War I in 1914 he and his family were compelled to move to Egypt because of their Russian citizenship. On the initiative of Joseph Trumpeldor he participated in the founding of a school for the children of the refugees and exiles from Ereẓ Israel then in Alexandria. He assisted his father Simeon Ḥayyim, who was appointed Jewish chaplain to the British expeditionary force in the Near East. In 1919 he returned to Jerusalem where he taught Talmud in the Hebrew Gymnasium. In 1921 he went to Paris, completing his legal studies in the following year, taught Talmud at the Rabbinical Seminary of Paris, and was a member of the central council of the Federation of French Zionists, chairman of the Union of Jewish Students, director of a school preparing young refugees for teaching, president of the Paris union of Hebrew teachers, etc. He published poems, stories, and articles on Jewish and general topics in French newspapers (in *L'Intransigeant*, in which he ran a special section on Hebrew and Yiddish literature, in *Les Nouvelles Littéraires;* and in the *Revue du Levant*), in Jewish French-language newspapers, and in Hebrew papers in Ereẓ Israel and elsewhere; and he edited the French column of the Paris Yiddish paper, *Parizer Haynt*. He devoted himself mainly to research in Hebrew law and Talmud. His first articles in this field were published in Hebrew in *Ha-Toren* (no. 11, 1945), and in French in *Hamenora*. He was a regular contributor to the Jerusalem periodicals *Ha-Mishpat* and *Ha-Mishpat ha-Ivri*. In 1935 Grajewski returned to Ereẓ Israel and for two years was engaged in teaching, after which he devoted himself to law, practicing also as a rabbinic lawyer. He published a monograph on Joseph ibn Migash (1953, 1963[2]). He published *Dinei Perudin u-Ketatot ba-Mishpat ha-Ivri* (1948). He died in Jerusalem and bequeathed his library to the library of Hechal Shlomo in Jerusalem.

Bibliography: Tidhar, 3 (1949), 1465f. [Z.K.]

GRAJEWSKI, ELIEZER ZALMAN (1843–1899), rabbinic scholar, traveler, and journalist. Grajewski was born in Malyaty (Maletai), near Vilna. He served first as the rabbi of Kletsk and later of Orsha. In 1873, he visited Ereẓ Israel, where he became a strong supporter of the new settlers. Upon his return, he published reminiscences of his journey in *Ha-Ivri*. When the Mazkeret Moshe organization was founded to honor Sir Moses Montefiore, leading Russian rabbis advocated the appointment of Grajewski as its director in Ereẓ Israel, and for this purpose he went to England in 1876. He did not, however, obtain the appointment but instead was appointed rabbi in Liverpool in 1877. He also traveled extensively throughout the United States, where he lectured on the necessity of encouraging the upbuilding of Ereẓ Israel. In 1890 Grajewski settled in Jerusalem, where he lived for the remainder of his life, although he died in Rigrod, near the Prussian border, after having gone to Vienna for medical treatment. His published works include *Ginnat Egoz* (1887), consisting of sermons and talmudic novellae: *Ginzei Keneset Yisrael* (1877), and *Gevul Yam* (1889), two commentaries to the *Haggadah;* and *Si'aḥ Eli'ezer* (1896), explanations of *piyyutim* recited on special occasions.

Bibliography: Tidhar, 2 (1947), 618f. [A.Ro.]

GRANACH, ALEXANDER (Isaiah Gronach; 1890–1945), German and Yiddish actor of proletarian types, who distinguished himself in expressionist portrayals. Granach, who was born in Galicia, reached Berlin at the age of 15

Alexander Granach, German and Yiddish actor, in Ernest Toller's *Hoppla wir Leben*, c. 1924. Jerusalem, J.N.U.L., Schwadron Collection.

while traveling with a Yiddish troupe. He was accepted at Max *Reinhardt's school and joined the Reinhardt Theater in 1908. After World War I, he specialized in modern plays, but also won acclaim for his Shylock and his Mephistopheles. He also played in Yiddish, appearing in Sholem Asch's *God of Vengeance*, and presented Yiddish plays in New York in 1931. After a period in Poland and Russia, he settled in the U.S. in 1938. Here he staged *Shylock* and other plays in Yiddish, and acted minor parts in Hollywood.

Bibliography: A Zweig, *Juden auf der deutschen Buehne* (1928), index. [G.K.G.]

GRANADA, city and province in Andalusia, S. Spain. According to tradition in the legends of Spanish Jewry, some of the Jews exiled by Nebuchadnezzar settled in Granada (Solomon ibn Verga, *Shevet Yehudah*, ed. by A. Shochat (1947), 33–34), which they called "the pomegranate of Spain." Even the Moors thought that the Jews had founded the city, which they called *Gharnāṭat al-Yahūd* ("Granada of the Jews"). The earliest extant information on the Jewish community in Granada is that the garrison stationed in the city after its conquest by the Moors in 711 was composed of Jews and Moors. During the Umayyad period Granada was one of the most important communities in all Spain. In the 11th century as a result of the fragmentation of Andalusia—when Granada became an independent principality—Jews received a large share in its administration. *Samuel ha-Nagid was not only leader of his own people but also vizier and military commander in the state. Prominent Jews were also among his political opponents who fled from the principality after the victory of Samuel's faction (Ibn Daud, Tradition, 74). The Jewish position in the leadership of the state is explained by the conditions within the principality—controlled by a Berber military clique which did not strike roots within the state. In the many court intrigues the king could depend on a Jew who had no aspirations for the throne. At that time, most of Granada's population was Jewish, and Samuel led the Jews for the benefit of the state. Various libelous documents were issued against the position of the Jews, and were circulated through neighboring principalities. An anti-Jewish polemical tone was even voiced in their wars against Granada.

Samuel's son, Joseph ha-Nagid, fell victim to a mass revolt in 1066 in which the "[Jewish] community of Granada" perished along with him (*ibid.*, 76). According to a later testimony, "more than 1,500 householders" were killed (Ibn Verga, op. cit., 22). Soon afterward the Jews returned to a position of influence in Granada, however not for long. At the time of the conquest of the city by the Almoravid Ibn Tāshfīn in 1090, the community was destroyed and the *Ibn Ezra family was among the refugees. During the Almohad regime (1148–1212), only Jews who had converted to Islam were permitted to live in the city. The attempt of Jews and Christians to overthrow Almohad rule in 1162 met with failure. At first, Jews, together with Christians, were expelled from the town during the wars of the Reconquest (1232). They returned to Granada when the kingdom of Granada was ruled by the Muslim Naṣrid dynasty (1232–1492). There is no available information on the Jews of Granada during the 13th–15th centuries, yet it is known that several of the kings of Aragon sent Jews as legates to Granada.

After 1391 *Conversos found shelter in Granada, where they openly returned to Judaism. In the agreement of surrender signed between the king of Granada and Ferdinand and Isabella in 1491 it was stated that Jews who were natives of Granada and its environs, and designated to be transferred to Spain, would be granted protection; those who wished to leave the country for North Africa would be given the opportunity to do so. Conversos who returned to Judaism were given a deadline to leave the country. It was also agreed that no Jew would have the right of judgment over the Moors, and that Jews would not serve as tax collectors.

On March 31, 1492, the edict of expulsion of the Jews from Spain was signed in the recently captured Granada. The traveler Hieronymus Muenzer, who visited Granada in 1494–1495, states that Ferdinand ordered the razing of the Jewish quarter in 1492, where, according to Muenzer, 20,000 Jews resided. In addition to the families of Samuel ha-Nagid and Ibn Ezra, natives of Granada included Judah ibn *Tibbon, Saadiah b. Maimon *ibn Danān, Solomon b. Joseph ibn Ayyūb, and many other scholars and authors. The Jewish quarter in Granada was not located in a single place throughout the centuries of Muslim rule. It was moved, expanded, or contracted by the various dynasties which ruled the city. Ashtor estimates the total number of residents of 11th-century Granada at 26,000, of which 20% were Jews.

Bibliography: Harkavy, in: *Me'assef,* ed. by L. Rabbinowitz, 1 (1902), 1–56; Baer, Urkunden, 2 (1936), 394, 413; Baer, Spain, index; S. Katz, *The Jews in the Visigothic and Frankish Kingdoms of Spain and Gaul* (1932), 116; H. Muenzer, *Viaje por España y Portugal 1494–1495* (1951), 44; J. de Mata Carriazo, in: *Al-Andalus,* 11 (1946), 69–130; L. Torres-Balbas, *ibid.,* 19 (1954), 193f.; Schirmann, Sefarad, 1 (1954), 74–78; Ashtor, in: *Zion,* 28 (1963), 51f.; Ashtor, Korot, 1 (1966²), 204ff.; 2 (1966), 84–120; L. del Marmol Carvajal, *Historia del rebelion y castigo de los moriscos del reyno de Granada* (1600). [H.B.]

GRANADA, GABRIEL DE (b. 1629), Marrano, arrested for Judaizing by the Inquisition in Mexico in 1642. During his trial, although not under torture as is commonly supposed but under the frightening pressures of his surroundings, he implicated over 80 other people, including his mother, four aunts, grandmother, and brother. His father, Manuel de Granada, who had traveled to the Philippines, died before Gabriel's arrest; his mother, Maria de Rivera, starved herself to death in the Inquisition jail. The trial dragged on at least until September 1645 and Gabriel was not sentenced until April 16, 1646, when he was reconciled to the Church.

Bibliography: C. Adler (ed.), *Trial of Gabriel de Granada by the Inquisition in Mexico 1642–1645* tr. by D. Fergusson (1899, = AJHSP, 7 (1899), 1–134); AJHSP, index to vols. 1–20 (1914), and index to later volumes. [Ma.C.]

GRANIN, DANIEL ALEKSANDROVICH (pseudonym of **D. A. German;** 1918–), Soviet author. Granin, who was born and raised in Petrograd, became an engineer and worked for a number of years at various industrial enterprises. After serving in the Red Army in World War II, he turned to literature. His favorite theme was the clash between the professional and personal integrity of a scientist or a technocrat and the powerful political pressures exercised by the Communist bureaucracy. Granin's early works include *Variant vtoroy* ("Second Version," 1949) and the novel *Iskateli* (1954; *Those Who Seek,* 1956). The publication of his story *Sobstvennoye mnenie* ("One's Own Opinion") in 1956 was one of the most significant events of the post-Stalin "thaw." He justified his advocacy of independent thought as serving, in the final analysis, the best interests of the Soviet state. But it provoked the anger of Party bureaucrats because it was taken, not unreasonably, as implying that the party's policy of thought control was harmful to the country. Granin's best-known novel is *Idu na grozu* ("I Go Out Into the Storm," 1962), which has been credited with providing the best portrait of the world of Soviet scientists.

Bibliography: V. M. Akimov et al. (eds.), *Russkiye sovetskiye pisateli prozaiki* (1959), 571–9, includes bibliography. [M.F.]

GRANOTT (Granovsky), ABRAHAM (1890–1962), Israel economist, head of the *Jewish National Fund. Born in Folesti, Bessarabia, Granott was appointed secretary of the J.N.F. in 1919. After the transfer of the J.N.F. Head Office to Jerusalem in 1922, Granott settled in that city, becoming the Fund's managing director, chairman of its board of directors (1945), and president (1960). His plan for a joint land authority of the J.N.F. and the State of Israel served as

Abraham Granott, Israel economist. Portrait by P. Litvinovsky. Courtesy Jewish National Fund, Jerusalem.

the basis for the land legislation passed by the *Knesset in 1960. In 1948 Granott was cofounder and chairman of the Progressive Party (see *Independent Liberal Party) and was elected to the first Knesset in 1949, serving as chairman of its finance committee. His main contribution to Israel's economy consisted in establishing the principles for a progressive agrarian policy, which he formulated in a number of works such as *Land System in Palestine* (1952) and *Agrarian Reform and the Record of Israel* (1956). For a full bibliography of Granott's writings (in Hebrew, English, French, Spanish, German, etc.) up to 1951 see the appendix to his book *Be-Hitnaḥel Am* (1951).

Bibliography: Keren Kayemeth Leisrael, *Abraham Granott* (Heb., 1962); Y. Ronen (ed.), *Kalkalat Yisrael Halakhah le-Ma'aseh* (1963), 1–3. [Th.H.]

GRANOVSKY, ALEXANDER (pseudonym of **Abraham Azarch**; 1890–1937), Soviet theatrical director and founder of the post-Revolution Jewish State Theater. Born in Moscow and educated in St. Petersburg and Munich, Granovsky organized an amateur Yiddish drama group in 1918. In 1919 he was authorized to open a studio in Petrograd (Leningrad), and after six months he presented Maeterlinck's *The Blind* followed by Sholem *Asch's *The Sinner* and *Amnon and Tamar.* Granovsky aimed at the creation of a new Jewish style which would break with the Yiddish "primitive" tradition. His studio grew into a repertory theater, and and was finally called the "*Jewish State Theater." It moved to Moscow and presented works mainly by Jewish authors, *Shalom Aleichem, Sholem *Asch, A. *Goldfaden, I. L. *Peretz, *Mendele Mocher Seforim, and L. *Reznik, and plays by non-Jewish authors such as *Uriel Acosta* by K. F. Gutzkow and *Trouhadec* by Jules Romains. His method of production was exemplified in his presentation of Peretz's *Night in the Old Market* (1925), which relied largely on music, movement, lighting, and the "art of silence." In 1928–29 he toured Western Europe. He did not return to Russia, but staying in Berlin directed Arnold Zweig's *Sergeant Grischa* in German and *Uriel Acosta* for *Habimah (1930).

Bibliography: *Das Moskauer juedische akademische Theater* (1928); M. Kohansky, *The Hebrew Theater* (1969), 123f. [G.K.G.]

GRANT, BARON ALBERT (**Albert Gottheimer;** 1830–89), British financier. Born in Dublin, educated in London and Paris, Grant introduced in Britain the Crédit-Foncier type of mobilizing small investments for large projects. Many of his enterprises lacked solidity, and he was often attacked and lampooned. His companies, 37 in all, included public utilities and financial institutions in Europe and overseas. Their issued capital totaled 25 million sterling ($125 million), but eventually were worth only 5 million ($25 million). Grant also initiated slum clearance and collected paintings. He was member of parliament for Kidderminster, 1865–68 and 1874–80. He purchased Leicester Square (London), converted it into a public garden, and handed it over to the Metropolitan Board of Works in 1874. In 1868 he was ennobled by King Victor Emanuel of Italy. He died in comparatively poor circumstances at Bognor. [J.O.R.]

°**GRANT, ULYSSES SIMPSON** (1822–1885), victorious Union Army general of the Civil War and 18th president of the United States (1869–77). Grant's name has been linked irrevocably with anti-Jewish prejudice through his signature on General Order Number 11, issued at his headquarters of the Department of the Tennessee, located in Holly Springs, Miss., on December 17, 1862: "The Jews, as a class violating every regulation of trade established by the Treasury Department and also department orders, are hereby expelled from the department within twenty-four hours from the receipt of this order. Post commanders will see that all of this class of people be furnished passes and required to leave, and any one returning after such notification will be arrested and held in confinement until an opportunity occurs of sending them out as prisoners, unless furnished with permit from headquarters. No passes will be given these people to visit headquarters for the purpose of making personal application for trade permits." It cannot be proven indisputably whether this blanket condemnation and order of expulsion, executed in the area under Grant's military control in parts of the states of Kentucky, Tennessee, and Mississippi, was composed by Grant himself or by an underling, on the inspiration of an official of the War Department or in response to complaints by General W. T. Sherman, or in accordance with the wishes of gentile cotton-buyers in the area. Extensive research has uncovered much anti-Jewish prejudice on the part of military officers and civilian officials, but no conclusive key to the identity of the specific instigator of Grant's Order. The general himself had instructed one of his subordinates on Nov. 10, 1862, to insure that "no Jews are to be permitted to travel on the railroad south from any point . . . they are such an intolerable nuisance that the department must be purged of them." On the same day that he signed Order No. 11, he reported to an assistant secretary of war that "I instructed the commanding officer of Columbus [Mississippi] to refuse all permits to Jews to come South, and I have frequently had them expelled from the department . . . The Jews seem to be a privileged class that can travel everywhere . . ." An explanation which Grant offered on September 14, 1868, in the thick of the presidential campaign, implied that reports to him from the field and a reprimand from Washington had led him to issue and publish the order "without reflection and without thinking of the Jews as a sect or race to themselves but simply as persons who had successfully . . . violated an order . . ." It is also possible that the fact that Grant's own father was involved in business dealings with Jews at this time had something to do with his frame of mind.

Lincoln insisted that the order be revoked, despite Grant's unique facility for winning battles. Debates about the order took place on the floor of both the House and Senate, but opinion was divided fairly closely along party lines. During Grant's victorious presidential campaigns of 1868 and 1872, discussion of the anti-Jewish order appeared in the public and Jewish press, and some Jews and non-Jews were torn between their admiration for General Grant and their detestation of Order Number 11.

No single act or word, let alone edict, of another president or federal official, in all of American history, compares with the Grant order for rank generalization, harshness, or physical consequences. Yet Grant did not previously, nor subsequently, reveal animus toward Jews or Judaism. He appointed a number of Jews to important office during his presidency, offering the secretaryship of the Treasury to Joseph *Seligman, whose family included long-term friends of Grant dating back as far as 1849. In 1870 Grant appointed the former head of the American B'nai B'rith, Benjamin Franklin *Peixotto, to the unsalaried position of consul at Bucharest as part of an effort to persuade the Rumanian government to relent from its violent campaign of pogroms against its Jews. Simon *Wolf, a vigorous, albeit unofficial and unsupervised, representative of Jewish concerns in Washington, believed that Grant "did more on and in behalf of American citizens of Jewish faith, at home and abroad, than all the Presidents of the United States prior thereto or since." But Grant was a Republican, and so was Wolf, and Grant appointed Wolf recorder of deeds of the District of Columbia in 1869.

The Grant affair underlines the unconscious assimilation by many Americans of traditional anti-Jewish stereotypes, and the constant search for scapegoats which took place during the traumatic experience of the Civil War as it did in other periods of social and psychological crisis.

Bibliography: S. Wolf, *Presidents I Have Known* (1918), 63–98; J. Isaacs, in: AJA, 17 (1965), 3–16; B. Korn, *American Jewry and the Civil War* (1951), ch. 6; L. Gartner, in: AJHQ, 58 (1968), 24–117. [B.W.K.]

GRASSHOPPER. Among the insects mentioned in the Bible as permitted for food are those "that go upon all fours, which have jointed legs above their feet, wherewith to leap upon the earth" (see *Animals of the Bible). These are "the *arbeh* ("*locust") after its kinds, and the *solam* (AV, JPS, "bald locust") after its kinds, and the *ḥargol* (AV, "beetle"; JPS, "cricket") after its kinds, and the *ḥagav* (AV, JPS, "grasshopper") after its kinds" (Lev. 11:21–22; and see *Dietary Laws). The last three, each followed by the expression "after its kinds," refer to numerous species of grasshopper, there being, according to an *amora,* as many as 800 (Ḥul. 63b). Although in the Bible *ḥagav* applies to the grasshopper and not to the locust, it may have the latter meaning in the verse, "if I command the *ḥagav* to devour the land" (II Chron. 7:13), as it has in the Mishnah, which speaks of it as being at times a countrywide plague. In Israel there are many species of grasshopper, some small, others up to 2 in. (5 cms.) and more in size. The small grasshopper hiding in the high grass symbolizes the puniness of man when viewed from above (Num. 13:33; Isa. 40:22). All species of the grasshopper in Israel develop (like the locust) by metamorphosis, that is, the larva *(zaḥal)* has no wings but the adult has wings covering most of its body, an essential characteristic of the permitted grasshopper (Ḥul. 65b). In mishnaic and talmudic times the grasshopper was widely used as food, being also preserved in salt (Av. Zar. 2:7; et al.). There are Yemenite Jews who, on the basis of tradition as to their *kashrut,* still eat locusts and species of grasshopper.

It is difficult to identify "the *solam* after its kinds." The word means "destroying, eating," and refers to the grass-eating grasshopper, said to have the characteristic of being *gabbaḥat,* that is, apparently, having an arched back and slender feelers; many such species are found in Israel. Some identify it with the long-headed grasshopper of the genus *Acridium* (but see Av. Zar. 37a), i.e., with a species known as *ayyal kamẓa* which is *kasher* according to evidence from Second Temple times (Eduy. 8:4). With regard to the next permitted group "the *ḥargol* after its kinds," the sages stated that the outstanding characteristic of the *ḥargol* is "that it has a tail." This applies to the long-horned grasshopper of the family Tettigoniidae, whose female has a long protuberance which is a tube for the laying of eggs. Most of these species do no damage to agriculture, since they feed on insects and not on grass. Among them are also species whose imago is wingless, such as the *Saga* species, the largest grasshopper in Israel, and prohibited as food (see Ḥul. 65b).

Bibliography: Palmoni, in: EM, 1 (1950), 520–6, s.v. *Arbeh;* J. Feliks, *Animal World of the Bible* (1962), 116–8. [J.F.]

°**GRATIAN (Franciscus Gratianus;** d. before 1179), monk of Bologna. He is known for his canonical compilation *Decretum Gratiani,* assembled about 1140. The other title of the compilation, *Concordantia discordantium canonum,* clearly indicates its purpose, to bring together a large number of patristic texts and decrees of Church councils and popes, arranged in order of content. Though never officially adopted by papal authority, it was used in schools and synods, and from around 1159 was the manual of the Roman Curia. Among the thousands of texts assembled in the compilation only a few isolated ones concern the Jews. They include canon 61 of the Fourth Council of Toledo held in 633 (see *Church Councils), securing for children who are true Christians the belongings of their parents who have returned to Judaism (E. Friedberg (ed.) *Corpus Juris Canonici,* 1 (1871), 419: c. 7, C. 1, qu. 4). Others are canon 34 of the Council of Agde held in 506, imposing an eight-month instruction period for Jewish candidates for baptism, and canon 56 of the Fourth Council of Toledo, compelling Jews converted by force to remain Christians (*ibid.,* 1392: c. 93–94, D. 4, De cons.). One small group of texts concern mixed marriages, which must be dissolved and the children brought up by the Christian party; the converted Jews (of Spain) who have readopted Judaism, whose children must be given into the care of monasteries; converted Jews, who must avoid all contacts with their former coreligionists; and the prohibition on Christians eating the unleavened bread of Jews, living among them, consulting their physicians, bathing with them, or finally, sharing meals with them (various councils; *ibid.,* 1087: c. 10–14, C. 28, qu. 1).

Bibliography: A. Villien and J. de Ghellinck, in: *Dictionnaire de théologie catholique,* 6 (1920), 1727–51; J. Forchielli and A. M. Stickler (eds.), *Studia Gratiana,* 1 (1953–); *New Catholic Encyclopedia,* 6 (1966), s.v. [B.BL.]

°**GRATTENAUER, KARL WILHELM FRIEDRICH** (1770–1838), German anti-Semitic pamphleteer. In one of his widely circulated tracts attempting to rouse public opinion against Jewish emancipation *Wider die Juden* (1803, running into five editions), Grattenauer suggested that the Berliners remove Moses *Mendelssohn's bust and replace it with Voltaire's. Following in the wake of the latter's allegedly rationalist arguments against the Jews, Grattenauer was among the first to introduce the concept of race, thus heralding a new and ominous tendency in anti-Semitism, based no longer on religious but on pseudo-scientific grounds. "That the Jews are a very singular race, no historian or anthropologist can contest," wrote Grattenauer.

Bibliography: M. H. Brunschwig, *La lutte pour l'émancipation des Juifs en Prusse* (1946), index; L. Poliakov, *Histoire de l'antisémitisme,* 3 (1968), index; V. Eichstaedt, *Bibliographie zur Geschichte der Judenfrage, 1750–1848* (1938), index. [ED.]

GRATZ, U.S. family of merchants and community leaders in Philadelphia. The Gratz family was founded in the United States by BARNARD GRATZ (1738–1801), who was of Polish birth and who emigrated from London in 1754. After working in the mercantile house of David Franks, in 1757 he went into partnership with Michael Moses, and a few years later he and his younger brother MICHAEL (1740–1811) formed a long-lived partnership under the family

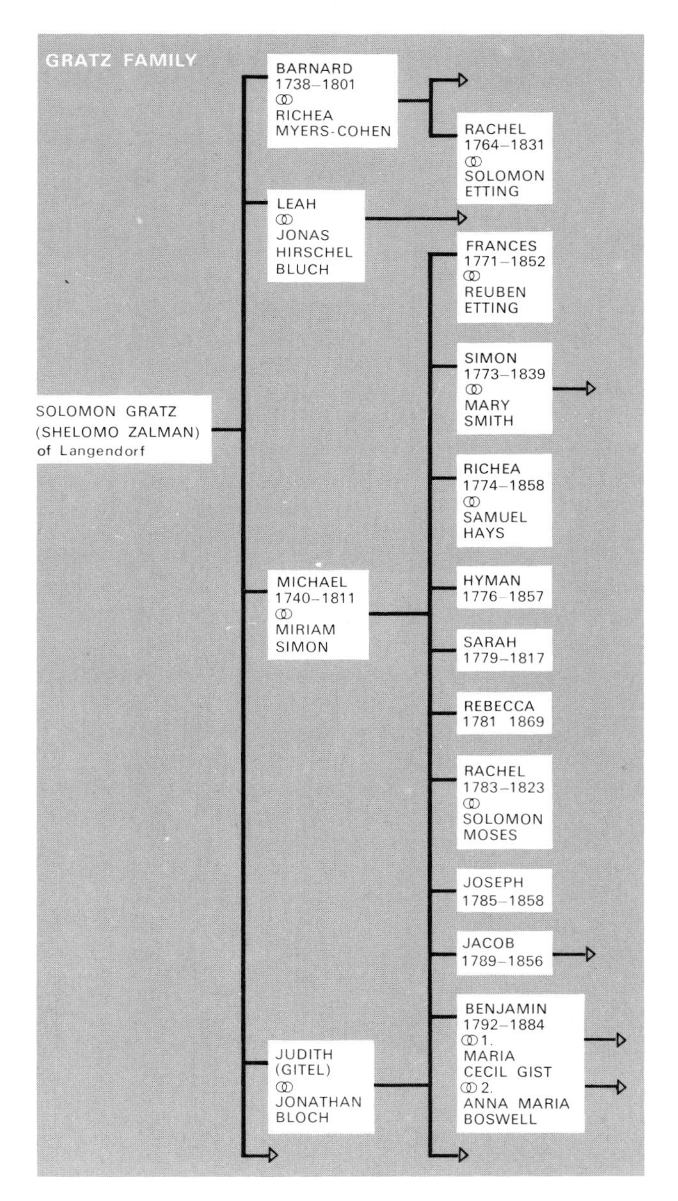

name as shippers and traders operating on the east coast and inland. As part of their trading operation, the partners sold *kasher* meat to the West Indies and conducted an

Figure 1. Right, Barnard Gratz, founder of the Philadelphia family noted for its services to both the Jewish community and the early American republic. Detail from a portrait by Charles Peale Polk. Cincinnati, Ohio, American Jewish Archives. Left, his brother and business partner, and co-worker, Michael Gratz. Detail from a portrait by Thomas Sully. Montreal, Henry Joseph Collection.

extensive and sometimes dangerous Indian trade. In the midst of a very busy social and business career Barnard, with other merchants, signed Non-Importation Agreements to boycott British goods during the Stamp Act and Townshend Act crises prior to the Revolution. Always deeply involved with Jewish communal activities, the brothers helped found the first Philadelphia synagogue, which in 1773 evolved into Congregation Mikveh Israel. Barnard Gratz was named its first *parnas,* and Michael was on the board of directors. The Gratz family supported the Revolution, as did many Philadelphia Jews, and supplied goods to the Continental Army. After the war, the Gratzes became involved in a successful struggle for equal rights in Pennsylvania. Always interested in western lands, the Gratzes supplied money to the Indian trader and agent George Croghan and to George Rogers Clark in his Revolutionary expedition to capture Detroit, and in 1794 invested in real estate around Louisville, Kentucky. Michael founded Gratzburg, in Otsego County, New York, in 1793.

Two of Michael's sons, SIMON (1773–1839) and HYMAN (1776–1857), carried on the family business. Hyman was elected director of the Pennsylvania Company for Insurance in 1818 and president in 1838. He founded *Gratz College. Both brothers participated in the affairs of the Pennsylvania Academy of Fine Arts and the Pennsylvania

Figure 2. Rebecca Gratz, communal worker. Portrait by Thomas Sully. From *American Jewish Yearbook 1923–24,* Jewish Publication Society, Philadelphia.

Botanical Gardens. Though Simon and his younger brothers JACOB (1789–1856) and BENJAMIN (1792–1884) married gentiles, through their sisters' marriages the family was related to other prominent Jewish families. Their sister FRANCES (1771–1852) married Reuben *Etting; RACHEL (1783–1823) married Solomon Moses; and RICHEA (1774–1858) married Samuel *Hays. Richea is reputed to have been the first Jewish girl to attend college in the United States. Others of the Gratz family achieved considerable careers in law and politics as well as in business. Another of Michael's sons, JOSEPH (1785–1858), was an ardent Federalist, as was his brother Hyman. Joseph was a director of the Philadelphia Institution for the Instruction of the Deaf and Dumb, and of the Atlantic Insurance Company.

Jacob joined the family firm in 1806, but soon left to form his own dry goods firm. He received an M.A. degree (1811) from the University of Pennsylvania. In 1824 and 1839 he was elected to the state legislature. His younger brother Benjamin also joined the family firm and studied at the University of Pennsylvania. He was admitted to the bar in 1816. One of the early Jewish residents of Kentucky, where the family held land, he helped organize the Lexington and Ohio Railroad in 1830 and in 1835 helped found the Lexington branch of the Bank of Kentucky. Perhaps the best known of the Gratz family was Michael's daughter REBECCA (1781–1869). She is reputed to have been the model for Rebecca in Walter Scott's novel Ivanhoe. She had a wide acquaintance, including many literary figures; her friend Washington Irving may have told Scott about her. Energetic in social welfare as in her friendships and her

Figure 3. Rachel Moses, daughter of Michael Gratz. Miniature on ivory by Edward Greene Malbone. From *Early American Jewish Portraiture,* New York, 1952.

inveterate letter writing, she aided in founding the Female Hebrew Benevolent Society (1819), the Hebrew Sunday School Society (1838), and the Philadelphia Jewish Foster Home and Orphan Asylum (1885) and worked with these organizations for many years.

Bibliography: E. Wolf and M. Whiteman, *History of the Jews of Philadelphia from Colonial Times to the Age of Jackson* (1957), index; W. V. Byars, *B. and M. Gratz Papers* (1916); D. Philipson (ed.), *Letters of Rebbecca Gratz* (1929); R. G. Osterweis, *Rebecca Gratz: A Study in Charm* (1935).

[L.HE.]

GRATZ COLLEGE, first Jewish teacher-training institution in the U.S. In 1856 Hyman *Gratz, Philadelphia merchant and philanthropist, bequeathed approximately $150,000 to Mikveh Israel Congregation to establish a college "for the education of Jews residing in the City and County of Philadelphia." The fund, which became operative in 1893, was used by the trustees to establish an institution for training Jewish teachers. The college was formally opened in November 1897, holding sessions in the Mikveh Israel Synagogue until 1909 when it moved into its own building. The Mikveh Israel Elementary School, meeting in the college building, served as a school for observation and practice under the supervision of the college. The original faculty of the college consisted of Henry Speaker, principal, Arthur Dembitz, and Isaac

Gratz College, Philadelphia, Pa.

*Husik. In 1905, Julius *Greenstone joined the faculty, and in 1933 he became principal.

Because of a growing need for Jewish teachers, the board entered into an arrangement in 1928 by which the college was to be managed jointly by the Gratz trustees and the Hebrew Education Society of Philadelphia, with the support of the Federation of Jewish Charities. Through this affiliation the college acquired the right to grant academic degrees, and the first such degree (B.H.L.) was awarded in 1952. In 1962 new quarters were completed, largely through a grant of the Federation of Jewish Agencies, which provides 75 per cent of the college operating budget. From 1962 Mitchell E. Panzer, a graduate of the college, was president of the board of overseers. Elazar Goelman was appointed dean of the college and director of its Division of Community Services in 1959. In 1960 the Philadelphia College of Jewish Studies became the Gratz College I.M. Wise Department (for the training of Reform religious teachers). The Samuel Netzky Adult Institute of Jewish Studies was organized in 1962. In 1967 Gratz College received accreditation by the Middle States Association of Colleges and Secondary Schools.

The college consists of six departments, including the Elementary School of Observation and Practice. It offers courses leading to teachers' diplomas and the academic degrees of Bachelor of Hebrew Literature, Bachelor of Religious Education, and Master of Hebrew Literature. Total enrollment in the entire institution during 1969–70 was 1,500, with 1,600 graduates at that date.

Bibliography: *Publications of the Gratz College* (1897); *Gratz College Bulletin* (1967/68); I. Margolis, *Jewish Teacher Training Schools in the United States* (1964), 6–66. [W.CH.]

GRAUBART, JUDAH LEIB (1861–1937), rabbi and halakhic scholar. Graubart was born in Szrensk, Russian Poland, and served as rabbi in Staszow. During World War I he was removed to the interior of Russia by the czarist regime to ensure the good behavior of the Jews of Staszow. Granted permission to travel, Graubart visited many communities in Russia, and in 1917, under the Kerensky government, he helped organize Hebrew scholars. Under the Bolsheviks he opposed Simon *Dimanstein's plan for Yiddish schools, advocating that Hebrew be taught as well. In 1920 Graubart emigrated to Toronto, where he became head of the Eitz Chaim *talmud torah* and the acknowledged spiritual leader of the city's Polish Jews. He organized a *kehillah* there on the East European prototype. Graubart's writings include *Ḥavalim be-Ne'imim* (5 vols., 1928–39), a work of responsa and *halakhot; Sefer Zikkaron* (1926), memoirs of his Russian period; *Yabbi'a Omer* (1936), a sermonic collection; *Devarim ki-Khetavam* (1931–32); and *Yamin u-Semol* (1929–30), rabbinic essays.

Bibliography: N. Shemen, in: Talmud Torah Eẓ Ḥayyim, *25 Yoriger Yovel Bukh* (1943), 13–45; idem, in: E. Ehrlich (ed.), *Sefer Staszow* (Eng., Heb., Yid., 1962); I. Rafael, in: EẒD, s.v. [B.G.K.]

GRAUMANN, SIR HARRY (1868–1938), South African mining magnate, industrialist, and financier. Born in England, Graumann went to South Africa at the age of 16 and engaged in mining in the Transvaal. He became a member of the Johannesburg Sanitary Board (forerunner of the town council) and was one of the city's four aldermen under the Kruger regime. During the Boer War (1899–1902), Graumann worked for Transvaal refugees in Capetown. After the war, he became the first Jewish mayor of Johannesburg. In 1912 he protested against the proposed restriction of Jewish immigration. He was elected to parliament in 1915. His memoirs, *Rand Riches and South Africa,* appeared in 1935. [ED.]

GRAUR, CONSTANTIN (1877–1940), Rumanian journalist. Born in Botosani, N. Moldavia, Graur started his career as a proofreader. He later edited newspapers in Galaţi and Ploesti, and went to Bucharest in 1919 to edit *Cuvîntul Liber* (The Free World). With other Rumanian journalists, he founded the magazine *Facla* ("The Torch"), but continued writing for other papers, including the Jewish periodicals *Infratirea* ("Union") and *Adam.* In 1921, he became the chief manager of two daily papers *Dimineata* ("Morning") and *Adevârul* ("Truth"), which came to be regarded as "Judaized," because of the number of their Jewish contributors. During Nazi demonstrations, copies of these papers were burned on the streets. Graur had a democratic outlook and campaigned for Jewish emancipation. His writings include: *Manasse, cercetare critică* ("Manasse, Critical Research," 1904), *Din istoria socialismului Român* ("From the History of Rumanian Socialism," 1912), *Socialiştii Români in slujba Germaniei* ("Rumanian Socialists in Germany's service" 1914), and *Cu privine la Franz-Ferdinand* ("Concerning Franz Ferdinand," 1935).

Bibliography: S. Podoleanu, *60 scriitori români de origine evreească,* 1 (1935), 137–42; T. Teodorescu-Branişte, Oameni şi *paiaţe* (1967), 355–9. [A.FE.]

GRAY, HERBERT (1931–), Canadian legislator and cabinet minister. Gray, who was born in Windsor, Ontario, was admitted to the Ontario bar in 1956 and practiced law in his native city. In 1962 he was elected M.P. for Windsor West and was returned in subsequent elections. Gray was named parliamentary seretary to the minister of finance in 1968 and was the first parliamentary secretary to pilot legislation through the House of Commons. In October 1969 he was made a member of the federal cabinet of Canada, the first Jew to be named to that body. He was named minister without portfolio with special responsibilities in the department of finance and in 1970 he was appointed minister of national revenue. M. A. *Gray was his cousin. [B.G.K.]

GRAY, MORRIS ABRAHAM (**Moishe Gourary**; 1889–1966), Canadian politician. Born in Russia, Gray emigrated to Canada in 1907 and settled in Winnipeg where he opened a travel agency. He served for four years on the Winnipeg public school board and was an alderman from 1931 to 1942. In 1941 he was elected to the Manitoba legislature as a member of the Cooperative Commonwealth Federation (CCF) and its successor, the New Democratic Party. In parliament he was a powerful advocate of social benefits, particularly for the sick and aged. Gray was a prominent Zionist and a member of the *Po'alei Zion for almost half a century. He was a founder of the Jewish Immigrant Aid Services of Canada (J.I.A.S.) and the *Canadian Jewish Congress and held senior executive posts in both organizations. He was also chairman of the Western Canada Association for Labor Israel. [B.G.K.]

GRAYZEL, SOLOMON (1896–), U.S. historian and communal leader. Grayzel was born in Minsk, Belorussia, but was educated in the United States. He was ordained by the Jewish Theological Seminary in 1921 and served as the first rabbi of Congregation Beth-El in Camden, N.J., continuing his studies at Dropsie College. In 1929, upon his

Solomon Grayzel, U.S. historian. Photo Maurice Robbins.

return from research studies abroad, he began teaching Jewish history at Gratz College in Philadelphia, continuing to teach there and serving as registrar until 1945. In 1939, he took an editorial position with the Jewish Publication Society of America, working under Isaac *Husik. At the latter's death in the same year he became the editor in chief, a position he held until 1966. He was elected to the presidency of the Jewish Book Council of America in 1945 and was connected with the *Jewish Book Annual* from its inception in 1942. From 1966 he taught Jewish history at Dropsie College.

Grayzel's major scholarly efforts centered on the relationship of Christians and Jews during the Middle Ages. His doctoral thesis, *The Church and the Jews in the XIIIth Century* (1933, 1966[2]), was followed by individual articles on related subjects which have appeared in the *Jewish Quarterly Review, Historia Judaica,* the *Hebrew Union College Annual,* and other publications. He also wrote a popular, one-volume *History of the Jews* (1947, 1968[2]), widely used as a textbook, and *A History of the Contemporary Jews* (1960).

Bibliography: A. A. Steinbach, in: *Jewish Book Annual,* 28 (1970), 110–115.

[Sl. B.]

GRAZ, capital of *Styria, considered one of the oldest Jewish settlements in Austria. Although a gravestone, excavated in 1577 and erroneously dated to 70 B.C.E., long led to the belief that the community was much older, adjacent Judendorf was recorded in documents dating from 1147. In Graz itself there is reliable evidence of the presence of Jews only in the last decades of the 13th century. At that time they made their living mostly through moneylending, particularly to the local nobility. By 1398 a community had come into existence, located in a Jewish quarter, headed by a *Judenmeister* and a **iudex Judaeorum,* and possessing a synagogue and a *mikveh.* Though expelled in 1439, the Jews returned by 1447. After the expulsion of the Jews from Styria in 1496, together with the rest of Austrian Jewry, almost four centuries passed before there was again a formal settlement of Jews in the town. Only in 1783 were they permitted to attend the yearly trade fairs then held in Graz. Individual families with special permits were allowed to settle in Graz after 1848. By 1863 a community had come into being and in 1868 the demand for special permits was rescinded; at that time an official organization of the community took place. From then on the community grew rapidly, partly because of economic factors. It numbered 566 in 1869 (0.7% of the total population), 1,238 in 1890, and 1,720 (1.1%) in 1934.

The community was able to finance its activities not only through the imposition of taxes on the Jews of Styria but on those of Carinthia and Carniola as well. Soon after its formal organization, a primary school was founded. By 1892 a large school was built; in 1895 an impressive synagogue was dedicated. The anti-Zionism of Graz's communal leaders was pronounced, but a large influx of refugees from Eastern Europe in the wake of World War I strengthened the Zionist movement considerably, and in 1919, the Zionists gained a majority in the community. The Jews in Graz were socially segregated, and in the later 1930s Graz was a center of Austrian National Socialism (known as the "capital of the insurrection" after 1938).

Immediately after the *Anschluss* (March 12, 1938), the Jewish cemetery was desecrated. The members of the community board were arrested and released only after prolonged negotiation. Local functionaries were anxious to make Graz the first town to be *Judenrein.* On the initiative of the head of the Jewish community, Elijah Gruenschlag, Adolf *Eichmann agreed to the transfer of 5,000,000 marks to facilitate the emigration of 600 Jews to Palestine, but the events of Nov. 10, 1938, put an end to the project. On the night of Nov. 9–10 (**Kristallnacht*), the synagogue was dynamited and burned to the ground. More than 300 Jews were taken to Dachau concentration camp, to be released three weeks later. All Jewish residents were driven from their homes, and some 80% of them found temporary asylum. Their subsequent fate is unknown, though most perished in the Holocaust. After World War II, 110 Jews settled in Graz. There were 420 in 1949 and 286 in 1950. A small synagogue in a communal center built on the site of the synagogue ruins was consecrated in 1968.

The historian David *Herzog was rabbi of Graz (1908–38), and the Nobel Prize laureate Otto *Loewi taught pharmacology at Graz University from 1909 to 1938. Wilhelm Fischer-Graz (1846–1932), a writer popular at the time for many novels, mainly set in the town itself or in Styria, worked in Graz as a librarian.

The synagogue and Jewish school in Graz, Austria, consecrated in 1895 and destroyed on *Kristallnacht,* November 10, 1938. Courtesy Meir Lamed.

Bibliography: J. E. Scherer, *Die Rechtsverhaeltnisse der Juden ...* (1901), 455–517; E. Baumgarten, *Die Juden in Steiermark* (1903), passim; A. Rosenberg, *Beitraege zur Geschichte der Juden in Steiermark* (1914), index; D. Herzog, *Die juedischen Friedhoefe in Graz* (1937); idem, in: MGWJ, 72 (1928), 159–67, 327; 75 (1931), 30–47; idem, in: ZGJT, 3 (1933), 172–90; F. Popelka, *Geschichte der Stadt Graz,* 2 (1935), 332–44; Rosenkranz, in: *Yad Vashem Bulletin,* 14 (1964), 40–41; Schwarz, in: J. Fraenkel (ed.), *The Jews of Austria* (1967), 391–4; Kosch, in: *Zeitschrift des Historischen Vereines fuer Steiermark,* 59 (1968), 33–43; Germ Jud, 1 (1963), 119; 2 (1968), 300–2; K. Hruby, in: *Judaica,* 25 (1969), 179–81; PK Germanyah; Yad Vashem Archives.

[M.La.]

GRAZIANO, ABRAHAM JOSEPH SOLOMON BEN MORDECAI (d. 1684), Italian rabbi. Graziano was born in Pesaro where he studied under Isaac Raphael Ventura. He lived for some time in Rome, proceeding from there to Modena where he studied under his grandfather, Nathaniel Trabot, who ordained him in 1647. He first served as a member of the *bet din* of Modena, where he was later appointed rabbi. His characteristic signature, *Ish Ger* ("a strange man") is a play on the first letters of his name and on his being a "stranger" in Modena. Abraham's leniency with regard to some local customs aroused the opposition of his contemporaries. He is known as the first collector of books and manuscripts among Italian Jews. He left no published works of his own; most of his rulings remain in manuscript and some are occasionally found in the work of his contemporaries. His commentary on the Shulḥan Arukh is mentioned in the *Zera Emet* (vols. 1,2) of Ishmael ha-Kohen. One of his responsa, from the year 1665, is written in Italian, interspersed with biblical verses and quotations in Hebrew. Of the 54 poems in his collected work, poems for festivals, births, weddings, and funerals, some have been published. His elegy on his brother, Aaron, who died in 1648, is of a high literary standard. Two elegies preserved at the beginning of *Ma'avar Yabbok* of Aaron of Modena are erroneously ascribed to him.

Bibliography: Baron, in: *Studies . . . A. S. Freidus* (1929), 122–37 (Heb. part); Jona, in: REJ, 4 (1882), 112–26; Mortara, Indice, 28 n. 1; Ghirondi-Neppi, 3; Kaufmann, in: MGWJ, 39 (1895), 350–7.

[S.MAR.]

GREAT POLAND (Heb. פּוֹלִין גָּדוֹל), historic administrative unit of Poland-Lithuania, and a Jewish historical geographical entity within the framework of the *Councils of the Lands. The region, which lay on both sides of the Warta River, consisted of the provinces of *Poznan, *Gniezno, *Kalisz, *Plock, Rawa, Sieradz, Leczyca, and Pomerania; in the Jewish organizational framework, it comprised 36 communities and mother communities, and over 60 small communities and subsidiary communities. Of the mother communities, the important communities of Poznan, Kalisz, *Leszno (Lissa), and *Krotoszyn attained a special status. The region was under Polish rule until the partitions of 1772 and 1793; largely under Prussian (later German) rule until 1918, with the interruption of the government of the grand duchy of Warsaw between 1807 and 1815; since World War I in independent Poland, with the interruption of Nazi German rule 1939–45.

The communities of Poznan, Gniezno, Kalisz, Plock, and others were founded in the 12th to 14th centuries, the legal basis for their development being laid down by the charter issued by Prince *Boleslav the Pious (1264). As throughout Poland-Lithuania, Jewish settlement in Great Poland developed considerably in the 16th to 17th centuries, while in the 18th century it underwent a decline. The Great Poland province (גָּלִיל, "circuit") in the Jewish autonomous framework was under the hegemony of the community of Poznan until the middle of the 17th century, passing to Kalisz until the beginning of the 18th century, and then to Leszno until the close of that century.

During the period under the hegemony of Poznan rights of residence were obtained and preserved by means of a prolonged and stubborn struggle. The Jewish organizational framework was developed in the form of a Council for the Province of Great Poland, or the Council of the Province of Poznan, which acted on behalf of the Jews as regional spokesman in contact with external powers, such as the ecclesiastical authorities and the municipality, and with internal bodies, such as the local community leadership and the Council of Four Lands. Among the Jewry of Great Poland there thus developed an independent regional consciousness, having a specific social significance, collective responsibility, and spiritual authority and tradition (of the "Great Poland rite"). The foundations were therefore laid for the conservative pattern which successfully withstood the storms accompanying the religious-social movements which swept this Jewry during the 17th and 18th centuries. During the period of leadership of the communities of Kalisz and Leszno, a period of chaos in Poland when there was a third wave of Jewish settlement, both the local and central organs of the Jewry of Great Poland were weakened and the communities plunged into an increasing state of insolvency and "debts to the state." After the area passed to Prussia (by stages, in the late 18th century) severe restrictions were imposed on the Jews of Great Poland. In consequence of the limitations placed on their numbers, thousands of Jews were expelled from the communities. The ideas of Haskalah began to spread there owing to the proximity to Berlin and the influence of Solomon *Maimon. Under the government of the grand duchy of Warsaw from 1807 to 1815 the chances of emancipation for the Jews in Great Poland vanished, and new taxes were imposed on them (the recruiting tax and the kosher *meat tax). As a result, an increasing number of Jews emigrated to the German states. Following the renewal of Prussian rule in 1815 the struggle for emancipation was again taken up (1848–50), because the general regulations and the "temporary measures" (1833) had not granted emancipation to all the Jews of the province (with a distinction between citizens and "tolerated" persons). In accordance with the "temporary measures," changes were made in the structure of the communities (1833–47); attempts were made to reorganize the Jewish educational institutions, and germanization and Haskalah became of increasingly important influence in the lives of the Jews of the region. The Prussian authorities supported the Jewish communities, which made up about 15% of the total population, since they were useful in suppressing the Polish element, which formed about one-half of the total population of the region; as a result of the Jews' pro-German orientation their relations with the Polish inhabitants became strained. On the other hand, tension arose between the German inhabitants and the Jews because of their economic success; these stresses resulted in increased waves of Jewish emigration to the West and overseas, so that a number of communities in Great Poland were depleted. When the region was incorporated into independent Poland after the end of World War I, the hostility of the Poles and Polish authorities toward the Jews was intensified in this area because of their pro-German tendencies. The social and economic ties of the communities there with Germany having been disrupted by the political changes, emigration appeared to many as the best solution. After the Nazi occupation the community of Great Poland came to an end.

See also *Poland.

The Council of the Land (Province) of Great Poland. Great Poland is important in the history of Jewish *autonomy through this institution. The beginnings of the Council are obscure; its formation, however, preceded that of the councils of the communities of the other parts of Poland (see *Councils of the Lands). At the earliest, its creation is connected with the charter issued to the Jews by Boleslav the Pious in 1264. The history of the Council falls into two periods: the period of consolidation, which continued up to 1519, and its subsequent history until 1764. Its achievements during the first period include the extension of rights of residence and their renewed ratification (1364, 1453); defense against the slander of having introduced the *Black Death (1348), as well as many other negotiations accomplished successfully by *shtadlanut* (see **shtadlan*); the appointment of a chief rabbi of the province or "provincial rabbi," the *Episcopus Judaeorum Poznaniae;* the extension of the area under his jurisdiction and the definition of the scope of his authority (1389–93, 1458, 1519). The Jewish leadership was also successful in its opposition to the officially appointed tax lessee, and was empowered to choose 11 assessors and five collectors (with the exception of Poznan and Kalisz) for estimating the amount of taxation (the *sekhum,* "sum"), its distribution and collection, and its transfer to the state treasury, the ministers, and the Council itself for its own internal requirements (1512–19). The history of the Council extends over a period of about 250 years (1519–1764). It met from once in three years to twice a year in various communities of the province of Rydzyna. During this period the Council extended its activities. A considerable part of these, of a general and standard nature, were drafted in the form of regulations, some of which have been preserved in the communal registers. The subjects it dealt with include livelihood, established claims, municipal affairs, disputes, loans, peddling, fairs, commerce in general and with non-Jews in particular, and Torah study. Responsibility for execution of the decisions was entrusted to the rabbi of the province and its communal leaders. The rabbi of the province was elected by 32 electors of the community of Poznan, in conjunction with (9–19) delegates from the province, by a majority vote for a period of three years. He acted as the rabbi of the community of Poznan and served as its *rosh yeshivah* (uninterruptedly from 1651). Until the middle of the 17th century he was assisted in his functions by one of the *dayyanim* of the province, chosen from the *dayyanim* of Poznan. Occasionally the influence of the rabbi of Great Poland extended beyond the borders of the province to the communities of Silesia (1540, 1583, 1626, 1637). The *parnasim* (leaders) of the communities usually acted as the *parnasim* of the province. The number of provincial *parnasim* varied between nine, six and eleven (1668, 1677, 1685, 1754). Of these, two to three were delegates from Poznan. The *parnas* of the Council was assisted by the *ne'eman* (treasurer) of the province, the *sofer* (secretary) of the province (generally the same person), the *shammai* (assessor) of the province, the *shammash* (clerk) of the province, and the *shali'aḥ* (emissary) of the province. They were chosen by the *parnasim* of the Council during its sessions. The *parnas* of the Council was empowered to impose a series of punishments, such as imprisonment, expulsion, fines, and the *ḥerem* (ban) to ensure that these functions were fulfilled (1669). He was occasionally assisted by the influence and connections of the *shtadlan* of the Poznan community.

Bibliography: A. Heppner-Herzberg, *Aus Vergangenheit und Gegenwart der Juden und der juedischen Gemeinden in den Posener Landen* (1902); B. Breslauer, *Die Auswanderung der Juden aus der Provinz Posen* (1909); R. Wassermann, in: *Zeitschrift fuer Demographie und Statistik der Juden,* 6 (1910), 65–76; L. Lewin, *Die Landessynode der grosspolnischen Judenschaft* (1926); U. U. Zarchin, *Jews in the Province of Posen* (1939).

[D.Av.]

GREECE (Heb. יָוָן, *Yavan*), country in S.E. Europe. This article is arranged according to the following outline:

SECOND TEMPLE PERIOD (to 330 C.E.)

Although the earliest known Jews on the Greek mainland are to be found only from the third century B.C.E., it is highly probable that Jews traveled or were forcibly transported to Greece by way of Cyprus, Ionia, and the Greek isles by various enemies of Judah during the biblical period (cf. Joel 4:6; Isa. 66:19; see *Javan). The first Greek Jew known by name is "Moschos, son of Moschion the Jew," a slave mentioned in an inscription, dated approximately 300–250 B.C.E., at Oropus, a small state between Athens and Boeotia. This date coincides with the reign of the Spartan king *Areios I (309–265), who, according to later sources, corresponded with the Judean high priest Onias (I Macc. 12:20–1, Jos., Ant., 12:225). If this fact is to be accepted (cf. S. Schueller, in: JSS, 1 (1956), 268), one can assume that such a correspondence entailed a certain amount of Jewish travel to Greece and is thereby possibly connected with the establishment of a local Jewish community. Further growth of the Jewish community probably took place as a result of the Hasmonean uprising, when numbers of Jews were sold into slavery. At least two inscriptions from Delphi (Frey, Corpus, 1 (1936), nos. 709, 710) from the middle of the second century B.C.E. refer to Jewish slaves. Among those Jewish fugitives to reach Sparta during the reign of Antiochus IV Epiphanes was the high priest Jason (II Macc. 5:9).

During the Hasmonean period the Jewish community in Greece spread to the important centers of the country, and from the list of cities in I Maccabees 15:23—probably dating to the year 142 B.C.E.—it appears that Jews already resided at *Sparta, Delos, Sicyon, Samos, *Rhodes, *Kos, Gortyna (on *Crete), Cnidus, and *Cyprus (cf. F. M. Abel, *Les Livres des Maccabées* (1949), 269). A similar list of Jewish communities in Greece is transmitted by Philo (*Legatio ad Gaium,* 281–2), and thus reflects the situation during the first century C.E.

Among those places containing Jews Philo lists "Thessaly, Boeotia, Macedonia, Aetolia, Attica, Argos, Corinth, and most of the best parts of the Peloponnesus. Not only are the mainlands full of Jewish colonies but also the most highly esteemed of the islands of Euboea, Cyprus, and Crete." That a sizable Jewish colony existed at Delos is further attested by the Jewish inscriptions in the area, including a number from the local synagogue (Frey, Corpus, 1 (1936), nos. 725–731; cf. Jos., Ant., 14:231–2, regarding Jews of Delos who are also Roman citizens). It may be assumed that the community at Rhodes was in close contact with the Judean king Herod, who is known to have generally supported the needs of the island (Jos., Wars 1:424; 7:21; Ant., 16:147). The Jews of Crete are also mentioned by Josephus in reference to the imposter claiming to be the prince Alexander, who had been put to death by Herod (Jos., Wars, 2:103). The second wife of Josephus was also a resident of Crete (Jos., Life, 427). The Jewish population of Greece probably grew considerably during and after the

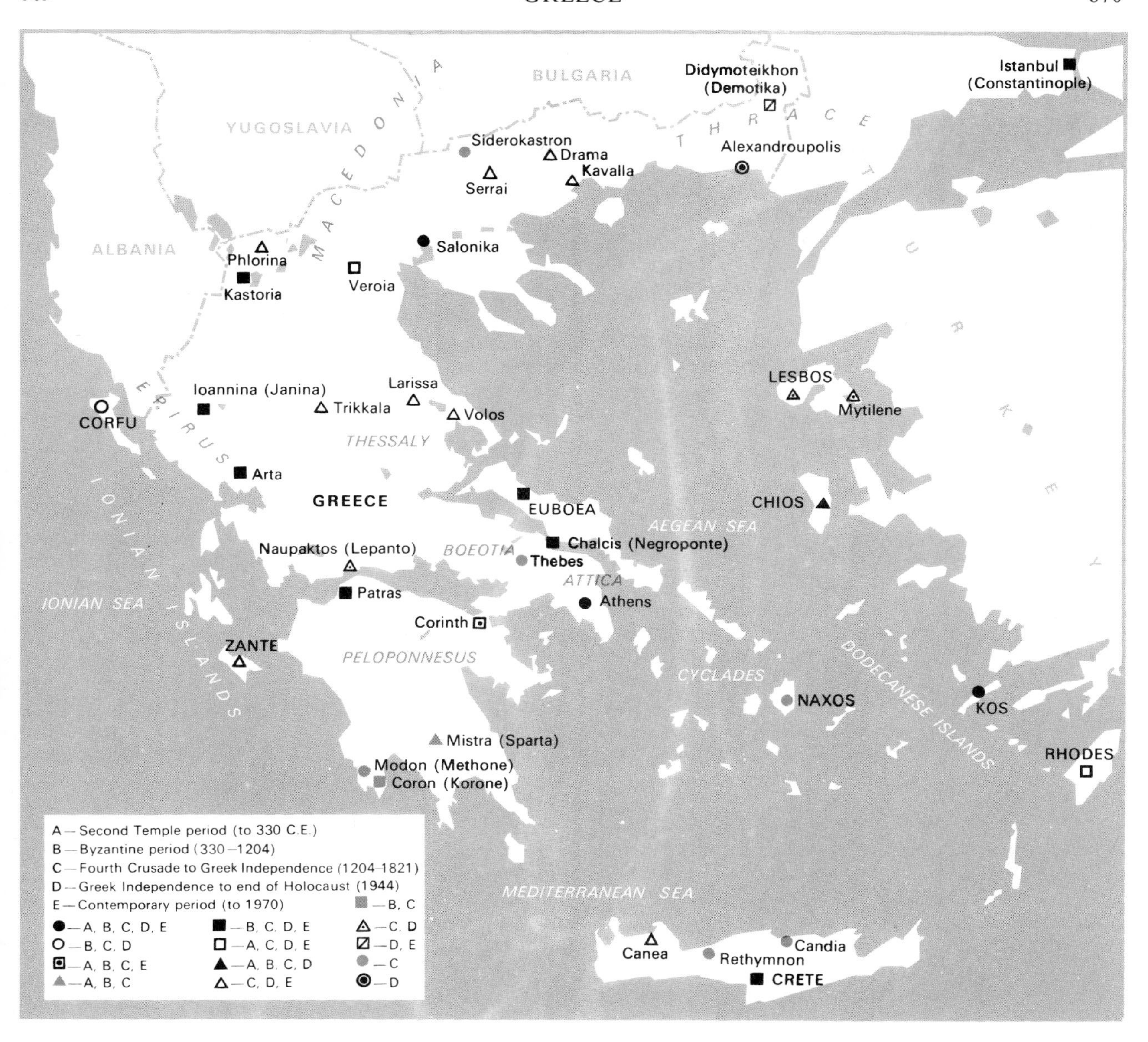

Major Jewish settlements in Greece. Jews are known to have settled in Greece in all the above periods, but in very few places was their settlement continuous, even within any specific period. Although there were Jews in many cities in the contemporary period, their numbers were insignificant except in Athens (1967, 2,800 approx.), Salonika (1968, 1,300 approx.), and Larissa (1967, 450 approx.).

Jewish War (66–70), and in one case Josephus relates that Vespasian sent 6,000 youths from Palestine to work for Nero at the Isthmus of Corinth (Wars, 3:540). An extremely large and powerful Jewish community also existed by the second century on Cyprus, for during the Jewish wars under *Trajan (115–7) the capital of Cyprus, Salamis, was laid waste by Jewish inhabitants and thousands of non-Jews were murdered. The consequence of this uprising, however, was a total ban on Jewish residence on the island, under pain of death (Dio Cassius 68:32; Eusebius, *Chronicon* 2:164). After Trajan, Hadrian (117–138) retorted with severe penal laws against the Jews, prohibiting circumcision, but these laws were allowed to lapse by Antoninus Pius (138–161), and henceforth the Jews were accorded a larger degree of tolerance. From the second century they were subject to the spiritual jurisdiction of a hereditary patriarch resident in Palestine. The Jews of the Diaspora early forgot Hebrew and adopted Greek (except for liturgical purposes), using a translation of the Bible—the Septuagint—which was begun at Alexandria under Ptolemy II. Apart from Cyprus, Greek Jews did not suffer any particular upheaval during the Roman period, and the ancient Jewish settlement served as a foundation for the Jewish settlement during the Byzantine period (from 330 C.E., see below)—when the capital of the Roman Empire was removed to Constantinople—and a basis for Jewish settlement in other Balkan countries (see individual countries).

[I.G.]

EARLY AND MIDDLE BYZANTINE PERIODS (330–1204)

Byzantium's secular institutions, with the emperor at their head, gave her long periods of stability, while in the West the Church added to the feudal disorder. These characteristics had their bases in the seventh-century Heraclian dynasty, which brought agrarian reform and a reorganization of the provinces, producing an army from small landowners and controlling the capital of the empire. The Heraclians were not only able to preserve their domains after Syria, Palestine, and Egypt had fallen and Constantinople had been besieged, but were also able to maintain their own authority against incursions from the outside. The struggle against Islam and the internal and external threats to imperial sovereignty were the dangers which faced Byzantium up to the First Crusade. Her successes in these realms shaped her external and internal policy. The emperor received and held the secular and ecclesiastical support of the people, enough so that this did not become a problem to the underlying unity of the empire. Religious conflicts which existed were largely resolved by the emperor, a believing Christian, who decided for the Church who was a heretic and who was not.

A far greater threat arose in the tenth century, when the Macedonian emperors had to fight against the attempts to destroy the foundations of Byzantine economic and military security through the acquisition of great estates, i.e., the liquidation of the smallholdings and the control of the soldiers settled upon them. Although the emperors were successful for a time, the end of the old order came in about the middle of the 11th century. Great landowners, partially independent from the emperor's influence, caused radical changes in the structure of Byzantine society. Additionally, the Normans in the western parts of the empire, the *Seljuks in Anatolia, and finally the Normans again—this time as Crusaders—succeeded in shattering the empire.

Byzantine Jewry in the seventh century is assumed to have continued in the status it held during the Roman period, as urban life was preserved and with it the main centers of Jewish population. Greece suffered greatly from Slavic incursions but the towns were hardly affected. *Salonika's Jewish history was unbroken and there were Jews in Rhodes and Cyprus.

The Middle Ages, for the Jew at least, begin with the advent to power of Constantine the Great (306–337). He was the first Roman emperor to issue laws which dramatically limited the rights of Jews as citizens of the Roman Empire, which were conferred upon them by Caracalla in 212. With the growth of Christianity the Roman emperors were influenced to further restrict the rights of the Jews. Constantine denied the Jews the right of proselytizing and prohibited intermarriage and Jewish possession of slaves. The legal status of the Jews was established by Christian Rome in the fifth century, when Theodosius II (408–450) introduced specific regulations into his codification of the laws, in his *Codex Theodosianus* (438). The Jewish community was recognized legally, even though not in a friendly manner, and religious worship was protected. In the sixth century, although more hostile and interfering, Justinian I (527–565) left the basic situation unaltered. It remained so in the seventh century also. Leo III (717–741), in the next imperial compilation of laws, the *Ecloga* ("Selections," 740), made no reference to the Jews. This preservation of legal status was very important to the Jewish community, as the Christian heretic had no legal status at all. Formal protection of the law minimally meant that the Jew had a place in the social structure.

Forced Conversion. In 632 Heraclius ordered the conversion of all Byzantine Jewry. This was a major point in his program of strengthening imperial unity, as he looked on the Jews as a political threat. Feeling that the Jews had shared in Persian military successes, he wanted to minimize their independence and influence within the empire. This policy of forced conversion was extended to Christian heretics but never took root for the Jews, who continued to be active in the civic life of the empire.

In 721 Leo III issued a decree, which later proved to be ineffectual, ordering all Jews to be baptized. In leading a new dynasty to power he, like Heraclius, wished to insure imperial unity and also may have suspected a lack of Jewish loyalty. The messianic movements to the East, having aroused fears in Leo's mind, had attracted Jewish support and may have caused the order to forcibly convert the Jews of the empire. In spite of these state actions Jewish prosperity still had room for existence in the empire and the results of the decree were as limited as they were in 632, even though some Jews left the empire and some converted outwardly. The termination of this decree seems to have been by 740.

The second Council of Nicaea in 787 reversed Leo's policy and criticized his handling of the Jews, proclaiming that Jews had to live openly according to their religion. According to Gregorios Asbestas, then metropolitan of Nicaea, the Jews who actually accepted Leo's inducements to convert were numerous enough to arouse this religious statement. Generally, these actions by Heraclius and Leo had little, if any, effect on the Jews of the empire.

Basil I (867–886), like his predecessors, also made an effort to convert the Jews forcibly, possibly to increase imperial unity but more probably to show his hand as a knowledgeable ruler in religious matters. Failing, where earlier Christians had, to persuade the Jews to convert, he issued a decree of forced conversion about 874. Like the Byzantine rulers before him, he failed in his efforts. The legal code of the period, the *Basilica,* made no basic changes in what Justinian had to say about the Jews, i.e., their legal status in religious and communal affairs continued to be recognized, and in some sense protected. Leo VI (886–912) apparently tried to follow in his father's policies but quickly gave it up.

Under Romanus I Lecapenus (920–944), who ruled in Constantine VII's (913–959) stead, further forced conversions, as well as persecutions, of the Jews were effected. This possibly happened by 932 and definitely by 943. His policy is known to have caused considerable migration to Khazaria. These acts may have been caused by Romanus' insecurity on the throne, as Constantine was the legitimate ruler and the former looked for ways to insure his position. In any event the persecutions were particularly severe, surpassing those of his predecessors. They were stopped quite suddenly when *Ḥisdai ibn Shaprut wrote to either Constantine or Helena, Romanus' daughter and the former's wife.

The last 250 years before the Fourth Crusade seem to have been a relatively quiet period for the Jews of the empire and it can be inferred that the situation actually improved and that no attempts were made by the authorities at coercing the Jews to convert. Further emphasis of this situation is provided by the fact that when the monk Nikon (tenth century) incited the inhabitants of Sparta to banish the Jews from their midst, his words were to no effect. In Chios an expulsion decree in 1062 was issued against those Jews who had recently settled there. There is no reason to believe that during the First Crusade in 1096, which took place during the reign of Emperor Alexius I Comnenus, the Jews were attacked when the Crusaders passed through the Balkans. The Jewish quarters, however, were looted. In the general panic which struck the Jewish world a messianic effervescence also came to the surface in Salonika, Adrianople, and other cities. It is related that certain communities left their homes for Salonika in order to sail to Palestine from there. A tremendous emotion seized the community of Salonika, where both the authorities and the archbishop showed a positive attitude to the messianic spirit.

Social and Economic Conditions. The legal disabilities of the Jews during the period, known from the *Basilica,* were minimal and included exclusion from service in the armed forces and the government, even though Jews had been employed as tax collectors on Cyprus during the first two

Figure 1. Athens synagogue, built 1903. Courtesy Athens Jewish Community.

decades of the 12th century. Jews were forbidden to buy Christian slaves, but this had little effect on them. No other restrictions existed concerning economic matters which did not also affect Christians. The charging of interest in trade and the purchase of land, except Church land, were permitted, although the emperors tried to control these matters for themselves. The question as to whether there was a specific Jewish tax seems to be open to a great deal of debate, but J. Starr (see bibl. *The Jews in the Byzantine Empire*) felt that such taxes did exist but were little enforced after the seventh century. In short, the taxes provided for by Theodosius II in 429, Justinian's *Corpus,* and again three centuries later in the Nomocanon had little more effect on the Jewish community in the later period than on the Christian one. Such legal restrictions which did exist included: the absence of the right of Jews to testify in cases involving Christians; the overriding imperial authority over religious matters between Jews; the right of Jewish testimony before Jewish judges only in civil litigation between Jews; the prohibition of Judaizing; and the necessity for Jews to take an oath in legal cases, which was contemptuous of the Jewish faith. Nevertheless, circumcision was officially permitted, the Sabbath and the Festivals were protected, synagogues were allowed, and even though the building of new ones was formally proscribed, the prohibition was not rigidly enforced. Although the Jew was restricted, he was in a much better position than Christian heretics. Jews were active as early as the seventh century as physicians and skilled artisans, particularly as finishers of woven cloth (e.g., in Sparta), dyers (in Corinth), and makers of silk garments (in Salonika and Thebes). Jews were also involved in commerce and farming and as owners of land.

In religious matters Hebrew remained the language of the Jews, although it was paralleled by the limited usage of Greek. Karaism began to appear in the empire in the tenth century (see Ankori, in bibl.) but only began to take root after the First Crusade. R. Tobiah b. Eliezer of Kastoria was an important Rabbanite spokesman. Aside from R. Tobiah little if any writing was apparently done in the areas of Midrash, Talmud, and *halakhah* during this entire period in Byzantium. There was literary activity in southern Italy, but then this area can only be included in the widest definition as to what was territorially part of Byzantine Greece. Additionally, about this time both Rabbanites and Karaites began to come to Byzantium from Muslim territory.

*Benjamin of Tudela, the 12th-century traveler, states that in his time there were Jews in Corfu, Arta, Aphilon (Achelous), Patras, Naupaktos, Corinth, Thebes, Chalcis, Salonika, Drama, and other localities. The Greek islands on which Jews lived were Lesbos, Chios, Samos, Rhodes, and Cyprus. He found the largest community in Thebes, where there were 2,000 Jews, while in Salonika there were 500, and in other towns from 20 to 400. The Jews of Greece engaged in dyeing, weaving, and the making of silk garments. After Roger II, the king of the Normans in Sicily, conquered some Greek towns in 1147, he transferred some Jewish weavers to his kingdom in order to develop the weaving of silk in his country. On Mount Parnassus Benjamin of Tudela found 200 farmers; there were also some serfs among the Jews. During the reign of the Byzantine emperor Constantine IX Monomachus (1042–1055), there were 15 Jewish families in Chios who were perpetual serfs to the Nea Moné monastery. The Jews of Chios paid a poll tax—in reality a family tax—which the emperor transferred to the monastery. The Jews of Salonika also paid this tax. The majority of the Jews conducted their trade on a small scale and with distant countries. The Greek merchants envied their Jewish rivals and sought to restrict their progress. *Pethahiah of Regensburg describes the bitter exile in which the Jews of Greece lived (see also *Byzantine Empire).

FOURTH CRUSADE AND LATE BYZANTINE PERIOD (1204–1453)

Greece from 1204 to 1821 was the subject of many conquests, divisions, reconquests, and redivisions at the hands of the Normans of Sicily, the Saracens, the Crusaders, the Venetians, the Genoese, the Seljuks, the Bulgars and the Slavs, the Byzantine emperors, the Cumans, the Ottoman Turks, and others.

Greek Rule. During this period Theodore Ducas Angelus, the Greek despot of *Epirus (?1215–30), who was defeated in 1230 by the czar of the Bulgars, John Asen II (1218–1241), was notorious for his cruelty. Theodore added the kingdom of Salonika to his domain in 1223 or 1224, holding it until 1230. He initiated an anti-Jewish policy which other Greek rulers followed after him. Theodore apparently enriched himself by confiscating the wealth of the Jews, and refused them redress against his abuses. He is also charged with proscribing Judaism. After Theodore was defeated by John Asen, he was condemned to death and two Jews were ordered to put out his eyes. When they took pity on him and did not fulfill the emperor's order, they were thrown from the summit of a rock.

The Greek rulers of the Empire of Nicaea were also harsh in their policy toward the Jews. John III Ducas Vatatzes (1222–54) apparently continued Theodore's decree against the Jews. The motive for persecuting the Jews is conjectural, but it seems to reflect the upsurge of nationalism in the provinces which remained under Greek rule. Jewish presence in the Latin states and in the areas ruled by the ambitious John Asen apparently strengthened the distrust which the Greek rulers had for their Jewish subjects in both Asia and Europe. Bulgaria's territorial expansion might have offered a degree of relief for the Jews, but the decline of the Latin Empire must have had a negative effect on them. By 1246 John III had entered Salonika and controlled the area from Adrianople to Stobi and Skoplje, including the town of Kastoria.

With the restoration of Byzantine rule (in the guise of the Nicaean Empire) over a large part of the Balkans, various Jewish communities felt the weight of the rulers' anti-Jewish policy. Little information is available on this but it can be assumed that the communities of Kastoria, Salonika, and several others suffered from the Greek advances. Once the Greek "rump state" of Nicaea had recovered Constantinople under the leadership of Michael VIII Palaeologus (1258–82), the anti-Jewish policy became outdated. He then began to resettle and reconstruct the ravaged capital, evidently realizing that his program required the cooperation of all elements, other than those who were then hostile (notably the Venetians and the subjects of the kingdom of Naples). It is not known whether there were Jews in Constantinople when Michael captured it, but after his conquest he renounced the policy of John III and made it possible for Jews to return and live there quietly.

From the end of the Latin Empire the Byzantine emperors began to recover part of the Peloponnesus, nevertheless being frustrated in part in their attempts by Murad I, who held Salonika from 1387 to 1405, and Murad II, who secured Salonika for the Ottoman Empire (1430–1913). The disintegration of the Byzantine Empire and in a large part its seizure by the Ottoman Turks led to generally favorable conditions for the Jews living within the Turkish sphere (see *Ottoman Empire; Covenant of *Omar).

Jewish Immigrations into Greece. The important Jewish communities which existed after the Fourth Crusade were Crete, Corinth, Coron (*Korone), *Modon, *Patras, and *Chios. The *Romaniots *(Gregos)*—the acculturized Jewish inhabitants of Greece—were Greek-speaking. Until recently Greek was still spoken by the Jews of Epirus, Thessaly, Ioannina, Crete, and Chalcis (see also *Judeo-Greek). From the end of the 14th century refugees immigrated from Spain to Greece, and from the end of the 15th century from Portugal and Sicily. In towns such as Trikkala, Larissa, Volos, and above all in Salonika the Sephardim introduced their own language and customs. With the flight of the Jews from Hungaria in 1376 (probably connected with the Black Death and the persecution of Jews in Eastern Europe at the time) many Jews settled in the towns of Kavalla and Siderokastron; they brought their special customs with them. As a result of Sultan Suleiman's journey to Hungaria in 1525, a number of Jews emigrated from there to Greece. The descendants of the Hungarian Jews were completely absorbed by the Sephardim after a few generations. A third group in Greek Jewry was that of the Italian-speaking Jews of Corfu, whose ancestors were expelled from Apulia in southern Italy.

During the 16th and 17th centuries the Jewish population increased with the addition of the Spanish Marranos, who fled to the countries dominated by the Turks, and after the persecutions of 1648, Polish refugees. The congregations *(kehalim)* were organized according to the regions of origin. Thus, during the 16th century in Patras there were the following *kehalim:* Kehillah Kedoshah Yevanim ("Greek Holy Community"), Kehillah Kedoshah Yashan ("Ancient Community," of Sicilian origin), Kehillah Kedoshah Ḥadash ("New Community," refugees from Naples and smaller Italian towns), and Kehillah Kedoshah Sephardim. In Arta there were *kehalim* whose founders had come from Corfu, Calabria, Apulia, and Sicily. [Ed.]

OTTOMAN (AND LATE VENETIAN) RULE (1453–1821)

The important communities during the Turkish (and late Venetian) periods were, in the first place, Salonika, which was probably the largest Jewish community during the 16–18th centuries and which until the beginning of the 20th century was populated by a majority of Jews; Naupaktos; Patras, whose merchants were known as courageous travelers who went as far as Persia; Arta; and Thebes, which was "renowned for its wisdom" (responsa of Elijah *Mizrahi (Constantinople, 1559–61), No. 71). On Crete the Jews played an important part in the transit trade; the island was also known for its rabbis and scholars, notably the *Capsali family, *Delmedigo, and others. There were also some Jews on Cyprus. After the conquest of Rhodes by the Turks in 1552, Jews from Salonika arrived on the island, where their commercial role became an important one. The island also became a stopping place for pilgrims on their way to Palestine. It was widely known for its rabbis, especially the rabbinical dynasty of the *Israel family.

When Sigismondo Malatesta conquered Mistra (Sparta) in 1465, he burned down the Jewish quarter. In 1532 when the forces of Andrea Doria attacked the Greek towns which were in the hands of the Turks, the Jews of Coron, Modon, and Patras suffered greatly. Their property was confiscated and they were taken captive. During the reign of Selim II (1566–1574) Don Joseph *Nasi was appointed duke of Naxos and the surrounding isles. In 1669 the Venetian armies attacked the island of Chios. To commemorate the miraculous stand against their siege, the local Jews annually celebrated "Purim of Chios" on Iyyar 8. With the Venetian invasion of the Peloponnesus in 1685, the Jews abandoned Patras in fear and fled to Larissa. They were also compelled to flee for their lives from the islands of the Aegean Sea. The Greeks of the Peloponnesus, who often rebelled against the Turks, massacred the Jews whom they considered allies of the Turks. During this period of confusion in the 18th century the communities of Patras, Thebes, Chalcis, and Naupaktos were destroyed.

Religious Culture Under Ottoman Rule. Besides Salonika, which during the 16th and 17th centuries was a major Jewish center, there were also important rabbis and scholars in the smaller communities of Greece. During the 16th and 17th centuries these included: Solomon Cohen (MaharSHaKH) of Zante and the Peloponnesus; Samuel b. Moses *Kalai, the author of *Mishpetei Shemu'el,* of Arta; Moses *Alashkar of Patras, the author of responsa; during the 18th century: Isaac Algazi, the author of *Doresh Tov;* Isaac Frances of Kastoria, the author of *Penei Yiẓḥak;* Ezra Malki of Rhodes, the author of *Malki ba-Kodesh* and other works; Jedidiah Tarikah of Rhodes, the author of *Ben Yadid* and other works; Isaac Obadiah of Patras, the author of *Iggeret Dofi ha-Zeman;* Eliezer b. Elijah ha-Rofeh ("the physician") Ashkenazi of Nicosia, Cyprus, the author of *Yosif Lekaḥ* on the Book of Esther.

Economic Situation of the Jews. During the Turkish period (1453–1821) the Jews of Greece were principally engaged in the crafts of spinning silk, weaving wool, and making cloth. They also controlled an important part of the commerce, moneylending, and the lease of the taxes. In the Greek islands under Venetian rule the Jews only engaged in retail commerce, as the larger type of commerce was the monopoly of the Venetian nobility. Under Turkish rule, however, the wholesale trade was concentrated in Jewish hands. The Jews succeeded in developing connections in Italy, France, Amsterdam, Hamburg, London, and in the Orient with Constantinople, Izmir, and Alexandria. The merchants of Kastoria traded in hides, furs, cattle, metals, and broken silver vessels. The Jews of Naupaktos were engaged in the trade of palm branches. At a later stage the tobacco, grain, sesame, hashish, and raw hides trades became those of the Jews. However in Thessaly, the Peloponnesus, and the Balkans the Jews engaged in peddling and tinsmithing, living in extreme poverty. In Salonika all the port activities were in Jewish hands and the port was closed on Sabbaths and Jewish festivals.

GREEK INDEPENDENCE (1821)–WORLD WAR II (1940)

With the outbreak of the Greek revolt in 1821 Greek Jewry suffered intensively because of its support of and loyalty to Ottoman rule. In those towns where the rebels gained the upper hand, the Jews were murdered after various accusations had been leveled against them. In the massacre of the Peloponnesus 5,000 Jews lost their lives; the remainder fled

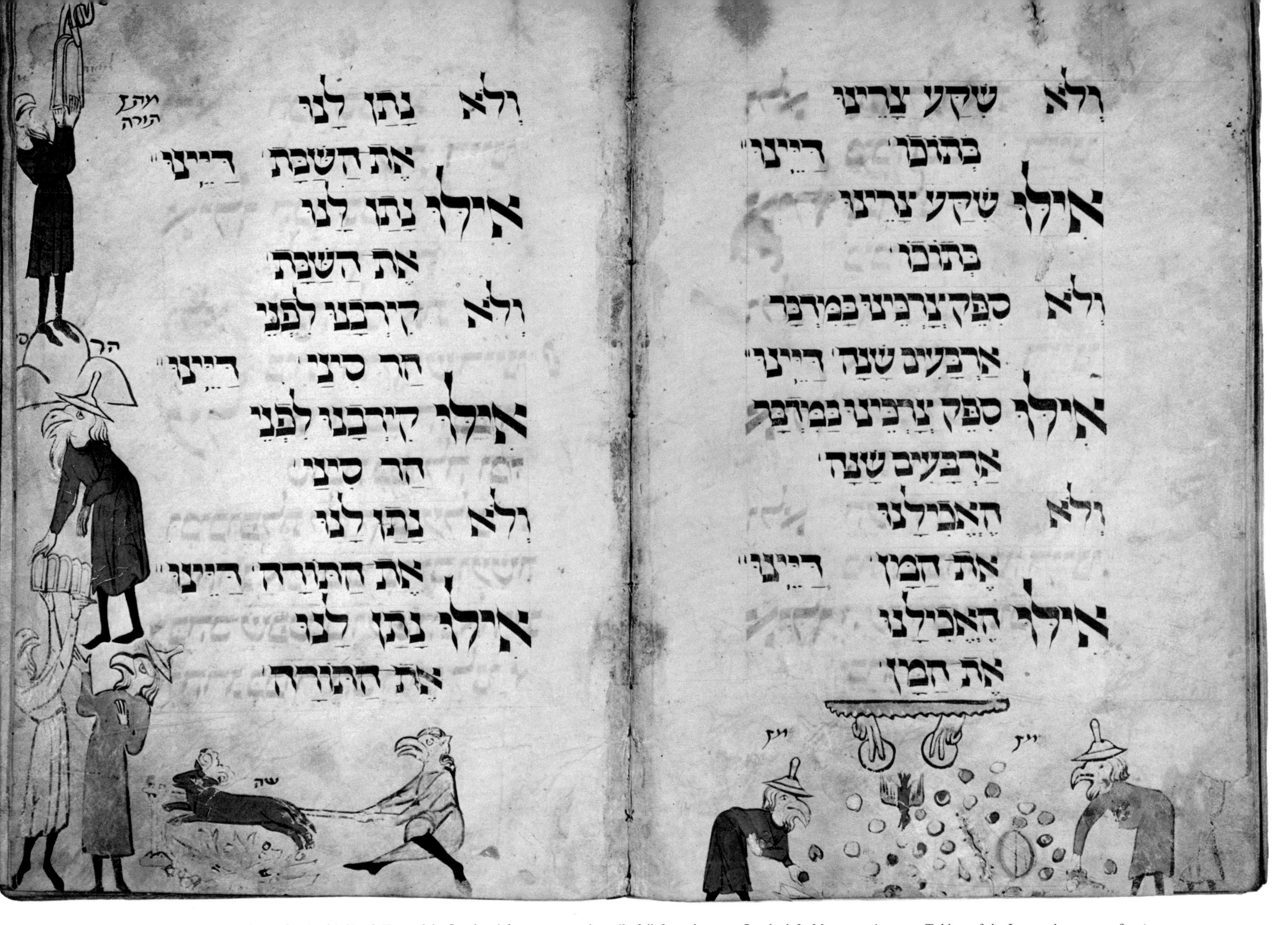
ולא שקע צרינו
בתוכו דיינו
אילו שקע צרינו
בתוכו
ולא ספק צרכינו במדבר
ארבעים שנה דיינו
אילו ספק צרכינו במדבר
ארבעים שנה
ולא האכילנו
את המן דיינו
אילו האכילנו
את המן

ולא נתן לנו
את השבת דיינו
אילו נתן לנו
את השבת
ולא קרבנו לפני
הר סיני דיינו
אילו קרבנו לפני
הר סיני
ולא נתן לנו
את התורה דיינו
אילו נתן לנו
את התורה

Dayyeinu, a double page from the *Birds' Head Haggadah.* On the right, manna and quails fall from heaven. On the left, Moses receives two Tablets of the Law and passes on five (an allusion to the Pentateuch) to the Israelites. Written by Menahem in South Germany, about 1300. Jerusalem, Israel Museum, ms. 180/57, folios 22v–23 ($10\frac{5}{8} \times 7\frac{1}{8}$ ins/27 × 18.5 cm.).

Figure 2. The Hayyim Pinhas dispensary of the Bikur Holim Hospital in Salonika. Courtesy David Benvenisti, Jerusalem.

to Corfu. From that time the condition of the Jews who lived among the Greeks, even within the boundaries of Turkish rule, began to deteriorate. From time to time there were blood libels, such as in Rhodes (Turkish until 1912; Italian until 1947) in 1840. In 1891 disorders broke out on the Greek islands; the Jews left in panic. During the same year there was also a blood libel in Corfu (Greek, from 1864). The Jews on the island, as well as on the neighboring island of Zante, were attacked. About 1,500 Jews left the Greek islands and settled in Italy, Turkey, and Egypt. Even the active participation of the Jewish citizens of Greece in the war against Turkey in 1897 was not mentioned in their favor; with the end of the hostilities in Thessaly, anti-Jewish riots broke out and an important part of the Jewish population was compelled to seek refuge in Salonika. At the beginning of the 20th century there were about 10,000 Jews in Greece. After the Balkan War (1912–13), with the annexation of further territories, which included Salonika, Chios, Crete (1908), Epirus, Kavalla, and Phlorina (1908), their numbers grew to 100,000.

After the population exchanges between Turkey and Greece as a result of the Treaty of Lausanne (1923) and the arrival in Salonika of 100,000 Greeks from Anatolia, the status of the Jews deteriorated because of the increased competition in commerce and the crafts. Many Jews were compelled to leave the city. On the other hand, the economic position of the Jews in the provincial towns of Epirus, Thessaly, Macedonia, and the islands did not arouse the jealousy of their neighbors. Until World War II the situation of the Jews in Greece was satisfactory. They controlled the markets of paper, textiles, medicines, glassware, ironware, wood, and hides, and were also represented in heavy industry, international commerce, and banking. Many Jews were also employed in manual labor as stevedores, coachmen, and fishermen, as well as in various handicrafts. The number of Jews in Greece on the eve of World War II was 77,000.

Civic and Cultural Conditions of the Jews. Greece recognized the civic and political equality of the Jews from the time of its establishment as a modern state in 1821. In 1882 legal status was granted to the Jewish communities. This status was confirmed on various occasions when laws defining the privileges and obligations of the communities were passed. The community councils, which were elected by general suffrage, were responsible for the religious, educational, and social affairs.

At the beginning of the 20th century the Alliance Israélite Universelle still maintained a number of Jewish schools in Greece. The Jewish schools were attached to the communities and did not have any attachment to religious or political trends. Jewish children attended the state schools and the religious studies were entrusted to *ḥazzanim*, who were content to teach the prayers in their traditional tunes. It was only in Corfu that the religious studies were of a higher standard. In those regions which were under Turkish rule until 1912, such as Thrace, Macedonia, and Epirus, there was a Jewish school in every community which was supported by the Alliance. The greatest concentration of Jewish schools was in Salonika. Between the two world wars there were 12 Jewish schools founded by the community, institutions of the Alliance, as well as private schools. In 1931 a law was passed which prohibited children of Greek nationality from attending foreign schools before they had completed their elementary education. This came as a fatal blow to the Alliance schools; the institutions of the Alliance amalgamated with the community schools in 1935. The Italians opened a seminary for the training of rabbis and teachers of Jewish subjects on the island of Rhodes, but it closed in 1938.

HOLOCAUST PERIOD

The Italian army attacked Greece on Oct. 28, 1940, and the Germans invaded on April 6, 1941. According to statistics of the *Salonika Jewish community, 12,898 Jews, among them 343 officers, served in the Greek army and several hundred Jews fell in battle. The entire country was occupied on June 2, 1941, and split up among the Axis (German, Italian, and Bulgarian) forces. Treatment of the Jews differed from one occupied zone to another.

German Zone. Salonika was taken by German troops on April 9, 1941. Anti-Jewish measures were at once instituted, beginning on April 12 when Jewish-owned apartments were confiscated and the Jewish inhabitants ordered to vacate them within a few hours. Three days later, the members of the Jewish community council and other prominent Jews were arrested. A "scientific" delegation arrived from Germany for the purpose of plundering the community of its valuable Hebrew books and manuscripts for transfer to the Nazi "Institute for Jewish Affairs" in Frankfort. Before long, the impoverishment of the community became overwhelming and the community council was unable to extend aid to all those who were in need. Contagious diseases spread and the death rate rose steeply, especially among the children. In July 1942 the men were sent on forced labor; a short while later, however, the community council made an agreement with the Germans, whereby it undertook to pay them the sum of 2,500,000,000 old drachmas, due Dec. 15, 1942, in consideration of which the Germans would refrain from drafting Jews for forced labor. At the end of 1942 Jewish-owned factories and groceries were confiscated and the well-known Jewish cemetery was destroyed. On Feb. 6, 1943, racial restrictions were introduced; Jews were ordered to wear a yellow badge and confined to a ghetto, while special signs had to be posted above windows and establishments belonging to Jews. Jews were also prohibited from using public transport and had to be indoors by sundown. The transfer to the ghetto, set up in a specially designated area, had to be completed by March 25, 1943. On February 25, the trade unions were ordered to expel their Jewish members; on March 1 the Jews had to declare all the capital in their possession, and 104 hostages were seized to ensure full compliance with this order. At this time, a rumor spread that the Jewish population was about to be deported to *Poland. The recently established Jewish underground warned the Jews of the danger confronting them, but little heed was taken and only about 3,000 escaped to Athens. The first transport of Jewish deportees left Salonika for the gas chambers on March 15, 1943, followed by further transports of 3,000 Jews each at intervals of two to three days. Thus, various sectors of the ghetto were systematically cleared of their inhabitants. Five transports left in the last two weeks of March, nine in April, and two in May; in June 820 Jews were dispatched to Auschwitz, the transport consisting of members and employees of the community council and teachers. On Aug. 2, 1943, skilled workers, "privileged" Jews, and a group of 367 Spanish citizens were sent to *Bergen-Belsen, where they remained until Feb. 7, 1944. On Aug. 7, 1,800 starving Jewish forced laborers were brought to Salonika and deported from there in the 19th and final transport from Salonika to the death camps. In all 46,091 Salonika Jews were deported—45,650 to Auschwitz and 441 to Bergen-Belsen—95% of whom were killed. The renowned Salonika community, the great center of Sephardi Jewry, came to an end.

Other Districts under German Occupation. On Feb. 3, 1943, the chief rabbi of Salonika, Rabbi Ẓevi Koretz, was ordered to ensure adherence to the racial restrictions in the provincial towns under the jurisdiction of German headquarters in Salonika. These were the towns in East Thracia, near the Turkish border, as well as Veroia, Edessa, and Phlorina in central and eastern Macedonia. On May 9, 2,194 Jews from these towns were sent to Auschwitz. A few Jews were saved by the local population and the chief of police, e.g., in the town of Katherine. Prominent Greeks, among them the archbishop of Athens and labor leaders, tried to assist the Jews, and there were Greeks who offered shelter and helped the Jews escape to the mountains.

ITALIAN ZONE. The Italian forces controlled Athens and the Peloponnesus. As long as the zone was held by the Italians, the Jews were not persecuted, the racial laws were disregarded, and efforts were made to sabotage the Italian racial policy. After the Italian surrender (Sept. 3, 1943), however, the Germans occupied the entire country, and on Sept. 20, 1943, Eichmann's deputy, Dieter *Wisliceny, arrived in Athens with detailed plans for the destruction of the Jews. Elijah Barzilai, the rabbi of Athens, was ordered by Wisliceny to provide a list of all the members of the Jewish community. Instead of doing so, the rabbi warned the Jews of Athens and himself fled to a provincial town. This enabled a considerable number of Athenian Jews to escape. On Oct. 7, 1943, Juergen *Stroop, the *hoehere SS und Polizeifuehrer* in Greece, published an order in the newspapers, dated October 3, for all Jews to register, on penalty of death. Archbishop Damaskinos gave instructions to all monasteries and convents in Athens and the provincial towns to shelter all Jews who knocked on their doors. On March 24, 1944, the Athens synagogue was surrounded by the Nazis and 300 Jews were arrested; another 500 Jews were routed out of hiding. They were first interned in a temporary camp at Haídar and later sent to their death in Auschwitz on April 2, along with other Jews caught in Athens. The rest of Athenian Jewry hid with their Greek-Christian neighbors. The Jewish partisans supplied food to those in hiding in cellars and attics.

BULGARIAN ZONE. A large part of Thrace and Eastern Macedonia remained under Bulgarian occupation, including the towns of Kavalla, Serrai, Drama, Besanti, Komotine, and Alexandroupolis (Dedeagach). Over 4,000 Jews from Thrace and over 7,000 from Macedonia were deported by the Bulgarians (see *Bulgaria, Holocaust) to the gas chambers in Poland; about 2,200 Jews survived.

The total number of Jews in Greece sent to death in the extermination camps is estimated at 65,000—about 85% of the entire Jewish population.

Jewish Resistance. The conquest of Athens by the Germans on April 27, 1941, marked the end of open warfare. Over 300 Jewish soldiers and 1,000 other Jews joined Greek partisan units. The Jewish partisans sabotaged German military centers and military factories, blew up German supply ships, and severed lines of communication. A group of 40 Jewish partisans took part in the blowing up of Gorgopotamo Bridge, causing a break in the rail link between northern and southern Greece. At the beginning of 1943 partisan units made up entirely or primarily of Jews were set up in Salonika, Athens, and Thessaly, under the command of Greek or British officers. The Salonika partisan units gathered information on troop movements in Macedonia and transmitted it to partisan headquarters in Athens. In Thessaly the national resistance organization, set up by the Jews in the towns of Volos, Larissa, and Trikkala, was under the command of an aged rabbi, Moses Pesaḥ, who roamed the mountains with a rifle in his hand. The courage and heroism displayed by the Jewish partisans earned them the praise of field marshal Wilson, the commanding officer of the Allied Forces in the Near East. Their main task was the establishment of contacts between the various parts of Greece and the Allied general headquarters in Cairo. The Jewish partisans also succeeded in hiding hundreds of Jews in the mountains and remote villages. Others worked for the Germans under assumed names in such places as the port of Piraeus and carried out acts of sabotage. The greatest single heroic act of the Greek-Jewish underground was the mutiny of 135 Greek Jews in Auschwitz; they were members of a *Sonderkommando,* charged with cremation of the corpses from the gas chambers. With the aid of a group of French and Hungarian Jews they blew up two crematoriums. Attacked by the SS guards and by five planes, the rebels held out for an hour until all 135 were killed.

CONTEMPORARY PERIOD

In the autumn of 1944, when Greece was liberated from Nazi occupation, over 10,000 Jews, almost all of whom were destitute, were in the country. A variety of factors (the general political instability, successive changes in the composition of the government, and the extended economic crisis) made the reconstruction of the Jewish community difficult. The Greek civil war also made emigration difficult for the Jews, as the majority of the men were obligated by the draft and could not receive emigration permits. After Greece's de facto recognition of the State of Israel a Greek cabinet committee decided (on Aug. 4, 1949) to permit Jews of draft age to go to Israel on condition that they renounce their Greek citizenship. Until the end of the 1950s about 3,500 Jews from Greece settled in Israel, 1,200 emigrated to the United States, and a few hundred others emigrated to Canada, Australia, South Africa, the Congo, and Latin American countries. In 1950 the number of Jews in Greece was about 8,000; in 1958 it was 5,209; and in 1967 about 6,500 Jews were scattered among 18 communities; 2,800 in Athens, 1,000 in Salonika (a number which rose to 1,300 by 1968), and 450 Jews in Larissa. As early as November 1944 a meeting of Athenian Jews elected a temporary council of 12 members that was recognized by the government as the representative of the Jewish community; in June 1945 the council was accorded legal status.

During the war, almost all of the synagogues had been destroyed or severely damaged; the synagogue in Athens was reconstructed, however, as were synagogues in other cities. A major obstacle to the reestablishment of Greek Jewry was the question of restitution of property that was confiscated during the occupation by the Nazis and compensation for the Nazi persecution. Although the anti-Jewish laws were repealed in most areas in 1944, they were canceled in Salonika only in June 1945. The question of compensation, however, involved a slower process. In 1949 the Organization for the Assistance and Rehabilitation of Greek Jews was established by official order to deal with this problem, but its work made no progress for a number of years. In spite of the lack of legal evidence as to who was deported to death camps, an agreement was signed in Bonn in March 1960 between the governments of West Germany and Greece on compensation to Nazi victims. About 62,000 claims for compensation were registered under this law; 7,200 of them were by Jews, of which about 6,000 were registered by Jews living outside Greece who had lost their Greek citizenship, and thus also their right to compensation.

During the first years after the liberation, Greek Jewry was materially supported by world Jewish organizations—the *American Jewish Joint Distribution Committee, the *Jewish Agency, etc. Only slowly did it rise above its state of poverty. As late as 1954 large numbers of survivors of the Holocaust continued to live in substandard conditions. Over the years the situation improved: unemployment decreased, and by the late 1960s the Jewish population included many artisans, merchants, retailers and wholesalers, industrialists (especially in clothing and textiles), free professionals, etc.

In spite of the stormy changes that passed over Greece after the war—and in spite of the influence of Nazi propaganda during the occupation—organized anti-Semitism was not evident in Greece, and the people generally refrained from activities motivated by hate against the Jews, except for some isolated incidents. Strong cultural contacts exist between the Jews and the Greeks, and the rate of intermarriage is on the rise.

A special problem arose from the fact that during the occupation a relatively large number of Jews participated in the struggle of the partisans and some of them afterward went over to the Communist camp. After the civil war the minister of defense issued a special order that clarified the position of the Jews who served in the E.LA.S. brigades. He emphasized that these Jews were not to be viewed as "Communists," since during the Nazi occupation they had no choice but to flee to the mountains. Nonetheless, a number of Jewish partisans were executed. Five Jews who were condemned to death and 21 others who were deported to the islands were freed on the condition that they emigrate to Israel and renounce their Greek citizenship. When the situation in Greece became more stable, the Jews slowly returned to civilian life. They participated in elections—and were even candidates on various party lists—and a few were absorbed into government positions.

In 1964 a Jewish school existed in Athens with 150 pupils. Other areas are deprived of Jewish educational activities because of the small number of children and a shortage of teachers. The religious and communal life of Greek Jewry is very weak. Synagogues are empty except during the High Holidays. In the 1950s, in addition to the rabbi in Athens, there were rabbis in Volos, Ioannina, and Larissa; later there was only the one rabbi in Athens who also served as the chief rabbi of Greek Jewry. The council of Jewish communities is affilated with the *World Jewish Congress and publishes a bimonthly; *WIZO carries on activities for women.

RELATIONS WITH ISRAEL

The relations between Greece and Israel have generally been cool. Greece was the only European country to vote against the U.N. partition plan for Palestine in 1947. After the establishment of the State of Israel, Greece recognized the new state de facto, but for a time did not establish diplomatic ties with it. Diplomatic representations were set up in Athens and Jerusalem only in 1952, but not on the level of an embassy or legation. Greece usually supports the Arab side in disputes brought before the U.N. However, shipping, air, and trade ties exist between the two countries. After the *Six-Day War of 1967, Arab terrorists made Athens the scene of attacks on Israel air communications. In 1970 seven Arab terrorists were convicted by Greek courts and sentenced to various prison terms, from two to 18 years, for attacks on an El Al plane, throwing a bomb at the El Al office, killing a Greek child, and trying to hijack a TWA plane. In August 1970 when Arab terrorists hijacked an Olympic Air Lines plane and demanded the release of the seven convicted terrorists, the Greek government submitted to their blackmail and released them. After that incident, Greek authorities seem to have taken special precautions against the renewal of Arab terrorist activities on Greek territory. [S.MAR.]

Figure 3. Memorial to the first six Jews of Salonika killed by the Nazis in 1943. Courtesy David Benvenisti, Jerusalem.

MUSICAL TRADITIONS OF GREECE AND THE BALKANS

The migration of Jews expelled from the Iberian Peninsula at the end of the 15th century toward the main centers of the Turkish Empire led to a synthesis of musical traditions in the Balkan Peninsula in which Spanish elements—of Mozarabic or medieval Christian origin—were deeply fused with Greco-Byzantine, Turkish, and Slavic ones. Three different types of such Jewish ethnomusical mosaics can still be discerned. The first is the Sephardi-style tradition. This one is evident in most of the Jewish communities of the Balkan Peninsula, whose main cultural centers, until World War II, were Salonika and Constantinople, and in the other important centers with strong local traditions of their own: Sarajevo, Sofia, Monastir, Edirne (Adrianople), Bucharest and Craiova in Rumania (Sephardi "branch settlements" in an Ashkenazi region), and Larissa and Volos in Greece. The common musical tradition of these centers, although called Sephardi, is different equally from that of the Arab-influenced communities of the Near East, the more Spanish style of Morocco, and the more Portuguese one of Western Europe (Leghorn, Amsterdam, Bayonne, etc.).

The second mosaic is the Byzantine-style tradition. This one is evident in some isolated centers of continental Greece, chiefly Ioannina and also Trikkala, Arta and Patras, Chalcis (Euboea, Negroponte), and in Crete. There a greater portion of the musical and liturgical traditions of the Byzantine period survived, in spite of the overwhelming influence of the Sephardi newcomers. A Greek dialect is preserved in both the language used by Jews and in the hymnographic tradition with melodic conventions of its own, which developed independently during the 16th–18th centuries. The Sephardi rite was adopted in the liturgy, but the *Romaniot traditions have not been forgotten. The music has followed the same lines of development as the Greek folk song, such as the rhythmic incorporation of ornamental flourishes.

The third mosaic is the Italianate-style tradition. This one is evident on the island of Corfu and its neighboring centers, such as Zante. This tradition especially reflects the liturgical and musical influence of southern Italy, from which area the Jews came to settle in Corfu as early as the 14th–15th centuries. A similar Italian influence, traceable to Venice, was apparent in the now-extinct Sephardi communities of Dalmatia, such as Split, Dubrovnik, and Vlona.

The chant of Balkan Sephardim, which is directly connected to that of the communities of Asia Minor (Izmir, Rhodes), presents a well-stabilized integration of Greek and Turkish elements. The scales of *Maqam Hijaz* and *Hijaz Car* are widely used; in secular and popular songs, the Phrygian ending (on *mi*) is frequent, while the *Maqam Sika (Siga)* is preferred for the reading of the Torah. The difference in style between the men's and women's repertoire is striking. The men's style is more orientalized, ornamented, influenced by the *papadiké* and *kalophonia* of Byzantine church song and by the style of Islamic culture. It is used mainly in the synagogue repertoire. The women, in their domestic repertoire in Hebrew or Ladino, have preserved a much more limpid and open way of singing, which in its phrasing, scales, and intervals is quite close to that of medieval Spain. The true *romances in archaic Spanish, which are often used as cradle songs, are less faithful to the Castilian source in the Balkans than in the Moroccan area. In addition to these, a particular type of popular or folk-style song developed during the past centuries. This tradition, which continued to develop until about two generations ago, hardly differed in its musical style from the contemporary Greek folk song and was not a "learned" one; but elements from the folklore and the life of the "Hebrew quarter" were often found in it. Some songs in Ladino were also for liturgical or domestic religious use, especially vernacular translations of Hebrew texts, such as the chants for removing the Torah scroll from the Ark, the homiletic translations of Jonah and of the *haftarah* of the Ninth of Av, songs of the *Haggadah*, and hymns for Simḥat Torah.

At Adrianople, a school of singers and poets—the *maftirim*—developed an extensive repertoire during the 16th and 17th centuries. This paralleled the traditions of mystic confraternities (such as *Shomerim la-Boker*) of Italy and of the *Bakkashot-singers of Aleppo. It depended largely on the *laḥan* technique (contrafacture), by which Greek, Turkish, Italian, and Arab songs served as melodic models and were indicated for this purpose at the head of each poem. A local stylistic overlay unified this heterogenic material—the nasalizing intonation, melodic ornamentation, and nostalgic-plaintive style of performance. Performance was mostly by a soloist, supported by refrains sung by the entire congregation or group and lacking any polyphonic features.

The earlier Byzantine ("Romaniot") style flourished much more overtly in the area where Greek is still the spoken language: at Ioannina (Janina), Chalcis, and partly also at Corfu. It is found both in the women's and in the men's songs. The women's songs show it in a peculiarly hard and sad form, with minimal ornamentation and flourishes. The men's synagogal chant is more influenced by the Greek *kalophonia* and the microtonic intonations of the surrounding Greek and Muslim cults (at Ioannina the synagogue itself is built on a plan similar to a mosque). Among the women there still exists a very ancient tradition of *μοιρολγία* funeral lamentations, mostly distichs or quatrains of short lines, with an archaic execution in responsive or antiphonic divisions between the singers. The women were also assigned the singing of paraliturgic hymns, often based on midrashic traditions, on Esther and the Feast of Purim (the hymn *κίνα γλῶσσα* is also widespread outside the Greek-speaking communities), the *Akedah, the Sabbath, and other religious themes. These songs flourished in the 17th–18th centuries, more or less during the same post-Shabbatean period that also gave rise to the mystic confraternities. This traditional literature of liturgical music constructed in rhymed distichs or quatrains, often with refrains or intercalations in Hebrew, reveals the existence of a more ancient homiletic tradition and is conserved both orally and in manuscripts. It reached its highest level in the 17th century with the poet-composer Samuel Hanen.

Three distinct traditions coexisted and still exist to some degree among the Corfiote communities in Tel Aviv and Trieste. One is that of the Italians or Pugghiesi (from Salento in Apulia-Puglia), which has remained the only important witness to the tradition of the medieval Jewish communities of southern Italy; the second is that of Greece, the "Romaniot" tradition similar to that of Ioannina; the third is the Sephardi one. Some paraliturgic hymns for Shavuot in four languages alternatively in each line of each quatrain (Greek, Italian, Ladino, and Hebrew) confirm this symbiosis. A well-known folk song in two languages, the lubricious quarrel between mother and daughter, provides a fair example of the differences of class and culture between the Greeks, more bourgeois and assimilated, and the more earthy Pugghiesi. However, the translations in the ancient Apulian dialect and the songs of this tradition, which are included in the Passover *Haggadah*, were the common property of all Corfiote Jews. A considerable number of manuscripts bear witness to the existence of a *Minhag Korfu*, rich in *piyyutim*. These also include an elegy on the destruction of the Temple, for the Ninth of Av, in the Apulian-Venetian dialect. The chant of the Pugghiesi shows a singular persistence of medieval styles, also preserved in Greco-Italic church chants (mainly in those of the 8th mode). The more recent religious chants both in the synagogue and the home, Sabbath hymns, and popular poems in Hebrew or in its Italian translation are performed in a spontaneous polyphony of three- and six-voice parts, which is similar to the folk usage of the gentile population in the Adriatic-Dalmatic area. [L.Le.]

Bibliography: General: B. D. Mazur, *Studies on Jewry in Greece* (1935); *Joshua Starr Memorial Volume* (1953). Second Temple and Roman Empire Period: Schuerer, Gesch, 3 (1909[4]), 55–57; Lewis, in: JSS, 2 (1957), 264–6. Byzantine Period: J. Starr, *The Jews in the Byzantine Empire, 641–1204* (1939); idem, *Romania—The Jewries of the Levant after the Fourth Crusade* (1949); idem, in: PAAJR, 11 (1942), 59–114; idem, in: JPOS, 15 (1935), 280–93; idem, in: *Byzantinisch-neugriechische Jahrbuecher*, 12 (1936), 42–49; idem, in: JQR, 38 (1947), 97–99; J. Parkes, *The Conflict of the Church and the Synagogue* (1934), index; J. R. Marcus, *The Jew in the Medieval World: A Source Book, 315–1791* (1938), 3–8; S. Krauss, *Studien zur byzantinisch-juedischen Geschichte* (1914); idem, in: *Recueil jubilaire en l'honneur de S. A. Rosanès* (1933), 53–67; M. Molho, *Histoire des Israélites de Castoria* (1938); E. S. Artom and M. D. Cassuto (eds.), *Takkanot Kandiyya ve-Zikhronoteha* (1943), passim; G. Ostrogorsky, *History of the Byzantine State* (1956, 1968[2]), index; Z. Ankori, *Karaites in Byzantium* (1959), 148–50; A. Sharf, in: *World History of the Jewish People*, second series, 2 (1966), 49–68; Perles, in: *Byzantinische Zeitschrift*, 2 (1893), 569–84; Kaufmann, *ibid.*, 7 (1898), 83–90; E. Csetényi, in: *Etudes orientales à la mémoire de Paul Hirschler* (1950), 16–20. Ottoman Rule and Independent Greece until 1940; M. Molho, in: *Homenaje a Millás Vallicrosa*, 2 (1956), 73–107 (Fr.); Rosanes Togarmah, passim; AZDJ, 54 (1890), 3–4. Holocaust Period M. Molho and J. Nehama, *In memoriam: Hommage aux victimes juives des Nazis en Grèce*, 3 vols. (1948–53); idem, *Sho'at Yehudei Yavan 1914–1944* (1965); I. Kabeli, *La Contribution des juifs à la libération de la Grèce* (1946); idem, *Trois étapes de la tragédie juive en Europe* (1946); idem, in: *YIVO Bleter*, 37 (1953), 205–12; idem, in YIVOA, 8 (1953), 281–8; Moissis, in: *Les Juifs en Europe (1939–1945)* (1949), 47–54; R. Hilberg, *Destruction of the European Jews* (1961) 442–53 and index; G. Reitlinger, *Final Solution* (1968[2]), 398–408 Melamed, in: *Cahiers de l'Alliance Israélite Universelle*, 95 (1956) 12–18; 96 (1956), 13–21; 97 (1956), 15–20; Roth, in: *Commentary* 10 (1950), 49–55; Elk, in: *Yad Vashem Bulletin*, 17 (1965), 9–15 Sabille, in: *Le Monde Juif*, 6 no. 49 (1951), 7–10; Neshamith, in *Mi-Bifnim*, 22 no. 4 (1960), 405–9; *Yedi'ot Beit Loḥamei ha-Getta'ot*, 22 (1960), 109–16; P. Friedman, in: *Joshua Starr Memorial Volume* (1953), 241–8 (bibliographical survey on Holocaust period in Greece). Contemporary Period: J. Neḥama, in: *Cahiers Sefardis*, 1 (1946/47), 12–15; AJYB, 49 (1947/48), 434–6; S. Modiano *ibid.*, 54 (1953), 294–300; M.G. Goldbloom, *ibid.*, 57 (1956), 359–65 V. Semah, *ibid.*, 61 (1960), 217–22; 66 (1965), 399–405; P. R. Argenti *The Religious Minorities of Chios* (1971).

GREEK AND LATIN LANGUAGES, RABBINICAL KNOWLEDGE OF. The nature and extent of the knowledge of Greek and Latin on the part of the rabbis are subjects of scholarly controversy, differing opinions even being based on the same data, since they lend themselves to several interpretations. Such data are the Greek quotation in Talmud and Midrash, rabbinical knowledge of Greco-Roman institutions, written historical sources, archaeology epigraphy, and certain changes in the Hebrew language The problem is compounded by fluid historical situation prevailing in late antiquity, such as the varying policy of Rome as the protagonist of Hellenism in the Near East and the degree of native assertion which, in Jewish Palestine, led to sporadic condemnations (Meg. 9a) and suppose prohibitions of Greek. Among these, those after 66 C.E. (T. Shab. 1:6, 3c) and during the "War of Quietus" (116 C.E. Sot. 9:14, etc.—a prohibition of the use of Greek, whic itself employed the Greek loanword *polemos* for "war"!) are probably real. However the ruling against the use of Greek in 65 B.C.E. because of an incident at the siege of Jerusalem, as cited in the Talmud (Sot. 49b; cf. Jos., Ant., 14:25–8) is probably legendary (although E. Wiesenberg argues that it was probably historical). The Tosefta (Av. Zar. 1:20) and *Menaḥot* 99b (c. 90 C.E. and before 135 C.E.) discourage the study of Greek wisdom. This very repetition of anti-Greek measures, however, and some endorsements (Yad. 4:6; TJ, Sanh. 10:1, 28a; Rabbi in: Sot. 49b; Meg. 1:8) and positive evaluations of Greek (Esth. R. 4:12; Gen. R. 16:4, 36:8) indicate the temporariness or ineffectiveness of prohibitions. The Talmud tries to harmonize these contradictions by declaring that Greek was permissible for foreign contacts only (Sot. 49b, et. al.) or as a social asset for girls (TJ, Sot. 9:16, 24c). Use of liturgical Greek is indicated in the Jerusalem Talmud (Sot. 7:1, 21b), possibly in *Sotah* 49b (Rabbi), et al.; and a sort of public or official instruction is reflected in the metaphorical "500" students of Greek of *Simeon b. Gamaliel II, c. 140 C.E. (Sot. 49b). Occasionally Greek wisdom is distinguished from Greek language but seems to be identical with it in the Hasmonean War report of Sot. 49b, etc. It may signify "sophistry" (Graetz) or the "rhetorical art" as preparation for administrators but hardly a full ephebic or philosophical-scientific education. Opinions as to rabbinic Greek thus differ widely: bilingualism or trilingualism (Hebrew, Aramaic, Greek), even a Palestinian version of the general Hellenistic vernacular *(koiné)* and a Judeo-Greek have been surmised, in opposition, for example, to the view that the midrashic use of Greek stances is merely a device to impress non-understanding audiences!

There is, however, complete unanimity that Latin was little known (cf. Git. 80a, et al.), Greek being for nearly a millennium the language of Macedonian, Roman, and Byzantine administrations and many semi-independent cities in Palestine (332 B.C.E.–636 C.E.) and of importance even in Parthia. Moreover, "Latin" loanwords in Hebrew (*dux, matrona*, Caesar, "legion," "family," a.o.) were often loanwords already in the Greek from which they had been borrowed. Estimates as to the ratio of Greek to Latin loanwords in rabbinic literature have been as high as one hundred to one.

In view of this deadlock of opinions, the problem under review must be examined through fresh approaches.

Languages in Contact. Insufficient use has been made so far of the discipline of modern linguistics in solving this task. Both Aramaic and Hebrew of this period underwent transformation not only in lexicography—c. 3,000 Greco-Roman loanwords—(which is generally acknowledged) but also in phonology (e.g., the gradual weakening of laryngeals in some localities, cf. Meg. 24b; Ber. 32a; Er. 53b; cf. E. Y. Kutscher, in: JSS, 10 (1965), 21–51); in syntax (especially the dissolution of the construct case into a prepositional phrase); the frequency of an absolute nominative before conditional clauses (cf. M. H. Segal, *Grammar of Mishnaic Hebrew* (1927, repr. 1958), 213–4) resembling the Greek genitive absolute. According to Bendavid (see below) certain usages of the Palestinian sages indicate quasi-mechanical transfer from the Greek and can be found in phraseology (e.g., Heb. *lashon ha-ra*, Gr. *kakoglossia*, "evil tongue"); in semantics (Heb. *batlan*, "scholar," and Gr. *scholastikos* both allude to "leisure"; Heb. *yishuv*, Gr. *oikoumene*, "habitation"); change of gender (biblical *makkel*, "staff," becomes feminine after Greek *bakteria* and *rhabdos*); the increase of reflexive verbs; and new properties of the prepositions. The verb, according to linguists the most conservative element in language, was affected by a new tense system, notably a precise present tense and compound tenses (with auxiliary verb), and the creation of Hebraized roots from the Greek, among them such important verbs as *ḳ-l-s*, "praise"; *k-r-z*, "proclaim"; *h-g-n*, "be proper"; *p-y-s*, "pacify" and "cast lots"; *ṭ-g-n*, "fry"; *ṭ-k(ḳ)-s*, "arrange"; *s-m-n*, "signify"; *ḳ-ṭ-r-g*, "accuse"; and *p-r-s-m*, "publicize." The loanwords cover all aspects of life but are especially prominent in certain areas of material civilization (architecture, agriculture, fashion, commerce, and technology) and public life (government, taxation, law, and warfare). Apart from the salient keywords of Greco-Roman civilization, such as "circus," "theater," "stadium," "hippodrome," "column," "icon," "colony," "metropolis," "triumph," "emperor," "senator," "tyranny," "pedagogue," and "philosopher," even indispensable terms of daily life are loanwords, such as "air," "sandal," "tome," "collar," "sum," "salary," "mint," "nausea," "diarrhea," "character," "person," "type," et al. (all preceding English examples being approximately identical with the Greco-Hebraic terms). Even proper names of rabbis are affected: Alexander, Antigonus, Boethus, Dosa, Pa(p)pus, Symmachus, Tarphon, etc., alongside basic religious terms: Sanhedrin, *bimah, afikoman*, "angel" (Targum), *kairos*, "mystery," "blasphemy," et al. (Of course thousands of other Greco-Roman terms in modern Hebrew have been added in the modern technological era.) The orthography of actual Greek words and of loanwords is fairly systematic (though difficult to date and subject to error in scribal tradition and reveals Greek language change, e.g., the Greek *upsilon* in certain diphthongs is already given as v (or f) as in Byzantine and modern Greek (Selevcus for Seleucus, avto- for auto-). All these observations, however, do not yet give any information regarding the rabbinic knowledge of written Greek sources, especially since Krauss's views of the derivation (see below) of certain loanwords from Homeric or rare Greek poetry have not been generally accepted.

Greek as an Intercultural Representative Prestige Language. This was especially true of public display, including inscriptions in the Temple (even its ritual objects, cf. Shek. 3:2), and on synagogues, epitaphs, etc. Some of the Greek in Palestinian cemeteries may belong here and may not be diaspora Greek. To claim that all rabbis were excluded from this vast sector of public life through ignorance or hostility is manifestly absurd. It has been assumed, however, that the opposition to Greek was strongest among some popular preachers who continued earlier Zealot attitudes (see below, Avi-Yonah, 71).

Greek as Professional Expertise. There is much justification for the claim that Jewish mercenaries, slaves, tax collectors, and certain artisans, e.g., sculptors for idolatrous customers, and the rulers, courtiers, and diplomats of the Hasmoneans and Herodians had to resort to Greek because of their social-economic functions. It seems that the *tannaim* and many leading Palestinian *amoraim*, as well as their Pharisaic predecessors, belong to a group of "technocrat" experts who could administer, legislate, interpret, edit law and literature, theologize, moralize, and console—precisely the abilities and functions of their Greco-Roman counterparts, the rhetorician-scholar-bureaucrats, from Cicero to Seneca (once practically vice-emperor), from Dio Chrysostom to Plutarch (a priest-magistrate). The rabbis' idealization of the Sage—the characteristic ideology of hellenized bureaucracies—their popular ethics and their uses of Hellenic myth, literary forms, and *Hermeneutics, their academic institutions and efforts at preserving tradition, suggest knowledge of their Greco-Roman colleagues. The presence of schools of law, philosophy, and exegesis in and near Palestine (Ashkelon, Beirut, Caesarea, Gederah, Gaza), the Roman administrative center in Caesarea, and wandering rhetors must have furthered the spread of "professional" Greek. True, most of the grecianized talmudic data could stem from audio-transmission of rhetorics, the expertise of Greco-Roman bureaucracy. Yet Greco-Hebrew legal terminology (*diatheke, hypotheke, epitropos, k(o)inonia*, cf. Prosbul, etc.), some talmudic science, and rabbinic use of isopsephy (*Gematria) are more technical than the usual orations. Actual Greek halakhic documents (e.g., a marriage contract) and numerous Greek translations of Hebrew literature indicate some measure of literary experience. (Not for all the latter could the aid of proselytes be claimed. In any case, the semilegendary portrayals of the translator *Aquilas, a proselyte, *Elisha b. Avuyah, the "heretic," and *Meir, a reputed descendant of proselytes, may belong to periods of native reassertion when it had become unthinkable that rabbis were fluent in Greek.) Moreover, the insistence on oral transmission may occasionally have been merely a literary pose in conformity with a general trend toward cynicism in rhetoric (cf. Diogenes Laertius, 6:2, 48). At this stage of history, Jewish tradition and its agents were probably highly literate and literacy-minded. The Greek knowledge of the

Hillelite dynasty to *Rabbi, 200 C.E., and beyond of *Joshua, Meir, and *Abbahu, must have been considerable, as their use of Hellenistic materials and disciplines, their friendliness toward Greek, and their contacts with the Roman government indicate. In later centuries, however, the increasing impoverishment of Palestine and the accompanying alienation from Christianized Rome may have modified this situation.

Comparative Studies of Other Hellenizing Cultures would further illustrate Judean situations: Cato the Elder, the Roman arch-conservative speaking excellent Greek; Roman senators outlawing Greek rhetoric; a similar mass of loanwords even within societies resisting Greek, such as the Western Roman Empire, the Syrian Church, and native Armenia and Egypt; and slaves, proselytes, and uprooted populations spreading the knowledge of Greek (in Judea: after the Maccabean wars, cf. E. E. Urbach's discussion of the "Canaanite slave," in: *Zion* 25 (1960), 141–89, Heb.).

All in all, the scarcity and ambiguity of talmudic sources and the problematics of the historical data do not lend themselves to generalizations. What type of "rabbi," for example, is mentioned in the Greek Leontius memorial of Bet She'arim (Frey, 1006). Did the rabbis debate with Christians in Aramaic or Greek? When they declared Greek as "suitable" for poetry and Latin for war (Est. R. 4:12), did they thereby evaluate languages or merely characterize these cultures in general? Do halakhic statements on Homeric books presuppose their intimate knowledge (TJ, Sanh. 10:1, 28a; Yad. 4:6)? Perhaps the true question is not whether the rabbis knew Greek slightly or in depth (even the rhetors used various aid books), but whether they knew it adequately for their purpose. Only additional finds, such as actual Greek literature or more Greek halakhic documents, will throw further light on these problems.

Bibliography: Frey, Corpus; S. Lieberman, *Greek in Jewish Palestine* (1942); idem, *Hellenism in Jewish Palestine* (1962[2]); M. Avi-Yonah, *Bi-Ymei Roma u-Bizantyon* (1962[3]), 67ff.; S. Krauss, *Griechische und lateinische Lehnwoerter im Talmud, Midrasch und Targum* (1898–99) (to be used with reservation: see G. Zuntz, in: JSS, 1 (1956), 129–40; cf. however, H. Rosén, in: JSS, 8 (1963), 56–72); E. Wiesenberg: in: HUCA, 27 (1956), 213–33; A. Sperber, *ibid.*, 12–13 (1937–38), 103–274; M. Schwabe, in: *Sefer Zikkaron le-Asher Gulak ve-li-Shemu'el Klein* (1942), 187–200; idem, in: *Eshkolot*, 1 (1954), 73–85; A. Halevi, in: *Tarbiz*, 29 (1960), 47–55, 31 (1962), 157–69, 264–80; A. Bendavid, *Leshon Mikra u-Leshon Ḥakhamim* (1967[2]), 111–8; 135–52, 183–90; H. A. Fischel, in: *Semicentennial Volume of the Middle West Branch of the American Oriental Society* (1969), 59–88; J. N. Sevenster, *Do You Know Greek?* (1968). [H.A.F.]

GREEK LITERATURE, ANCIENT. Greeks came into contact with the Land of Israel long before the Hellenistic period, but there is no information as to the impression made by Jews or Judaism upon them in the classical period. The only classical writings extant referring to the Jews are *Herodotus' *Histories*, but his acquaintance with them is at best highly superficial, and he considers them to be Syrians who practiced circumcision, which custom they had acquired from the Egyptians. Aristotle does mention a lake in Palestine, but without connecting it in any way with the Jewish people. Thus, although the ancient civilizations of Egypt, Babylon, and Persia were familiar to the Greek men of letters and philosophers—at least in their general outline even before the days of Alexander the Great—they were apparently completely ignorant of the specific religion and culture of Palestine.

This situation changed radically after Alexander the Great and the foundation of the various Macedonian kingdoms throughout the East. From earliest times descriptions of Jews and Judaism occur in the works of Greek authors, some of whom belonged to the school of Aristotle. Thus, Theophrastus, one of Aristotle's foremost pupils, in his work "On Piety" described the Jewish sacrificial rites as utterly different from those of the Greek, consisting entirely of holocausts, offered in the middle of the night. The Jews are described by him as philosophers whose custom it is to converse among themselves about theology at the time of the offering of the sacrifices and to gaze at the stars. His contemporary, Clearchus, who was also a member of the Peripatetic school, in his dialogue "On Sleep" gives the contents of a conversation supposedly held between Aristotle and a Jew in Asia Minor (see below). The Jews are also described as philosophers in the work of the traveler Megasthenes (see below).

More detailed, and in some respects more realistic, is the detailed description vouchsafed by *Hecataeus of Abdera, who spent a long time in Egypt at the beginning of the Hellenistic period. Hecataeus describes the origin of the Jewish people as resulting from an expulsion from Egypt of undesirable elements at the time of a plague. Their leader Moses, who excelled in ability and valor, conquered the land of Judea for the Jews, founded Jerusalem, erected the Temple there, and set down the constitution of the Jewish people. Hecataeus was familiar with the division into 12 tribes and was the first of the Greek writers whose works are still extant to note that the Jews make no images of their godhead, nor conceive Him to be of human form, since, according to him, the Jews equate their God with the heavens. Moses entrusted the keeping of the laws to the priests, whom he also appointed as judges. The Jewish constitution does not know the form of monarchy, and the high priest is described as the head of the Jewish nation. The position of high priest is filled by one of the priests, chosen from among the rest for his excellence of character and wisdom. Moses also commanded the Jews to raise all the children born to them, which is the reason for the rapid increase in their numbers.

At the beginning of the Hellenistic period, Judaism was known to Greek thinkers and men of letters only in the vaguest of outlines. Their impressions are not very different from those they had of other ancient civilized peoples of the East. Their tendency to consider the Jews to be the bearers of a philosophic religion is evident, and their descriptions are generally quite highly idealized. It should be noted that the descriptions of the Jews, not excluding that of Hecataeus, still lack any taint of that hostility which is characteristic of most of the later writers. This general attitude continues into the third century. Thus, Hermippus of Smyrna states that Pythagoras received some of his teachings from the Jews, and that his philosophy was influenced by Judaism.

From the third century B.C.E. on, however, with the crystallization of an anti-Jewish outlook, the Jews, their religion, customs, and origins, begin to be described in a definitely negative light. This new approach flourished in the anti-Jewish atmosphere of Egypt and was abetted not a little by the old tensions between Egyptians and Jews. As time passed, it continued to gather strength, fanned by the Greco-Jewish clash in Alexandria, particularly during the days of the early empire. Since the Greco-Alexandrian literature was one of the main cultural flowerings of the age, it was a very important instrument in the formation of informed public opinion throughout the Hellenistic world and the Roman Empire.

One of the most important authorities of this new, anti-Jewish spirit in Greek literature was the Egyptian priest, *Manetho. He seems already to have identified the Jews with the *Hyksos and Moses with the Egyptian priest Osarsiph, who was described by him as the leader of the lepers and the other unclean and defiling elements who had been harming the population of Egypt. It was probably at this time that the belief that the Jews worshiped an ass—the animal holy to the Egyptian god Seth-Typhon, Osiris' enemy—was evolved. Manetho was only one of the many mouthpieces for the anti-Jewish propaganda. Even more rabid than he was *Lysimachus of Alexandria. According to him also, the Jewish nation stems from the impure and undesirable elements who had been expelled from Egyptian society. Their leader, Moses, taught them to hate all mankind, and their opposition to the temples of other nations typifies their entire approach.

It was *Apion of Alexandria (first century C.E.) who collected this anti-Jewish material. Not only did he refine the literary form of the tradition concerning the Exodus, which was most derogatory to the Jews, but he also protested against the Alexandrian Jews' demands to be considered citizens of the city, spoke with contempt of the Jewish religious practices, repeated the statement that the Jews worshiped an ass, stressed their supposed hatred of foreigners, said that they had contributed nothing to human civilization, and saw in their lowly political status an expression of the worthlessness of their religion. Actually, Apion added little of his own, but in his works the anti-Jewish spirit was given free rein and his writings contain virtually the entire gamut of the anti-Jewish themes which formed the anti-Semitic stereotype in the ancient world, and they also left their mark on Latin literature.

In spite of the generally extreme anti-Jewish character of the Alexandrian Greek literature, which was not a little influenced by the national Egyptian tradition, one nevertheless finds at least one writer—Timagenes of Alexandria (second half of the first century C.E.)—who apparently preserved a more objective approach to the Jews and in his history even expressed admiration for the Hasmonean king Aristobulus I. Interest in Jews and Judaism was also shown by Greek writers outside Egypt, from Syria and other parts of the Greek world. Asia Minor was of first rank in the intellectual and cultural life of the Hellenistic-Roman period, and it was also liberally sprinkled with areas thickly populated by Jews. It is in the works of one of the writers from Asia Minor—the historian Agatharchides of Cnidus (second century B.C.E.)—that the first mention in Greek sources is found of the Sabbath rest. He notes with scorn that it was because of this superstition that Jerusalem, the capital of the Jews, was conquered by Ptolemy I.

In the wake of the conflict between the Jews and Rome and Pompey's conquest of Jerusalem, there was an increased interest in the history of the Jews and in their religious observances on the part of the Asia Minor writers. It found its expression, *inter alia,* in the writing of books devoted entirely to this subject. Among these, *Alexander Polyhistor's anthology is particularly interesting, consisting as it does largely of excerpts from other authors and particularly from Jewish-Hellenistic literature. Teucer of Cyzicus also wrote a special work on the Jews. *Apollonius Molon's book on the Jews enjoyed great influence. Apollonius was a rhetorician from Alabandus in Caria and some of the foremost men of Roman society were influenced by his works. He had some knowledge concerning Abraham, Isaac, Joseph, and Moses, and the biblical tradition is clearly reflected in his work. Nevertheless, his attitude toward the Jews was most negative, and he considered them to be the least capable of the barbarians (i.e., non-Greeks), a nation which had added nothing to the cultural store of mankind.

A different approach is to be found in the works of the historian and geographer *Strabo, from Amaseia in Pontus, who lived in the time of Augustus. In the 16th book of his geography he describes Moses as an Egyptian priest who rejected the Egyptian forms of divine worship which centered around the deification of animals, and likewise objected to the anthropomorphism of Greek theology. Moses' god was identified with the heavens and the natural world, and many people of discerning intellect were convinced by him and became his followers. Under Moses' leadership they gained control of what is now called Jerusalem and there he founded a polity in accord with his views. Strabo expresses his complete approval of this polity and adds that for some time Moses' successors continued to live according to his constitution and were truly just and God-fearing. However, in the course of time the priesthood—which among the Jews encompassed the political power as well—fell into the hands of superstitious men, and after them in the hands of those who had despotic leanings. The superstitions which were introduced gave rise to the Jewish laws concerning forbidden foods, circumcision, and the like. The tyranny engendered robbery and violence, and large portions of Syria and Phoenicia were subjugated by the Jews. In short, Strabo looked upon Judaism as a basically positive phenomenon, and lauds the pure belief in God which typified it in its early days, but according to him Judaism had in the course of time degenerated and become corrupt.

Among the representatives of Greek literature in Syria, the philosopher, historian, and polymath *Posidonius of Apamea is of importance. He also wrote concerning the Jews and undoubtedly influenced those who came after him, but his views concerning Jews and Judaism are still a mystery, since it is difficult to determine what is to be ascribed to him and what to his followers. An allusion to "the cold Sabbath" of the Jews is to be found in the works of the poet Meleager of Gadara (first century B.C.E.). More than any of the other Greco-Syrian writers, *Nicholas of Damascus was intimately connected with Jewish affairs. He wrote his "Universal History" under Herod's inspiration and spent many years in his court in Jerusalem. The history of Herod's reign and the events of contemporary Jewish history were assigned a very prominent place in his work. He also included biblical traditions in the earlier portions of the history. Unlike the other contemporary gentile authors, Nicholas dealt with the period of the Israelite monarchy, including such events as David's wars with the Arameans. Abraham is described by him as a king in Damascus.

Typical of the level of knowledge concerning Judaism current among the educated classes of the Hellenistic world in the first century B.C.E. is the material brought by the universal historian, Diodorus of Sicily. He mentions Moses among those lawgivers who ascribed their constitutions to divine inspiration, and he states that the God of the Jews was called Ἰάω. Elsewhere in his work—where he is apparently dependent upon Posidonius—he relates the origins of the Jewish people according to the version which grew up and became current in Greco-Egyptian circles; i.e., that the first Jews had been lepers who had been expelled for this reason from Egypt. The personality of Moses is also presented in a positive light by Pseudo-Longinus, a literary critic of first rank, in his excellent work "On the Sublime." The author, whose name has not come down, quotes the early part of the Book of Genesis (". . . and there was light . . ." etc.) as an excellent example of lofty and exalted style and in this connection also expresses praise for the Jewish lawgiver.

*Plutarch is the only Hellenistic writer of the period of the early Roman Empire from Greece proper who is known to have written about Judaism. Most of his comments respecting the Jewish religion are to be found in his "Table-Talk," where the essence of the Jewish ritual is discussed as well as the nature of the Jewish godhead, and one of the participants even explains the supposedly close connection between the Dionysian rites and the Jewish festival of Tabernacles. At any rate, the tone is serious and does not reflect any innate animosity toward Jews or Judaism, and this is equally true in respect of the parts dealing with Jewish history which appear in his biographies of famous people, although in his work "On Superstition" the conduct of the Jews on the Sabbath during wartime is brought in as an illustration of superstitious conduct—just as it was already stressed by Agatharchides of Cnidus at the very beginning of the Hellenistic period.

In short, it may confidently be stated that Judaism as a phenomenon was familiar to the writers of the later Hellenistic period and to those who wrote during the early days of the Roman Empire. Their information concerning the history of the Jewish people is scanty and the influence of Jewish literature, even in translation (the Septuagint), is extremely meager. The attitude toward Judaism in Greek literature is not monolithic. Whereas particular hatred for the Jewish people and its religion is the hallmark of the representatives of the Greco-Egyptian literary school, definite sympathy is reflected in the writings of Pseudo-Longinus, and writers like Strabo or Plutarch express a relatively balanced view. In the descriptions of Judaism, stress is usually laid upon the origin of the Jewish nation and its religion, upon the personality of Moses on the one hand and on contemporary events on the other.

The attitude toward Judaism continued to be a live issue during the second half of the second century C.E., even after the rebellions during the reigns of Trajan and Hadrian had greatly weakened the Jewish people, and its religious influence diminished because of the competition posed by the spread of Christianity. *Numenius of Apamea, the forerunner of the neoplatonic school, may have been influenced in his philosophic thought by Philo of Alexandria. Be that as it may, his attitude to Moses was one of open admiration, and he even compared Moses to Plato. *Galen treats the Jewish philosophical conceptions seriously and critically. He is familiar with the cosmogony of Moses and specifically states his preference for the Greek conceptions in the form in which they are expressed by Plato. Whereas, he states, according to the Jewish view God's will is sufficient cause for anything and everything, according to the Greek view certain things are physically impossible and God chooses the best out of the possibilities of becoming. Moses is censured for having omitted the *causa materialis* and having thus postulated the *creatio ex nihilo*.

The historian *Dio Cassius also makes some interesting remarks touching upon Jewish history, in connection with his general survey of the history of Rome. Pompey's conquest of Jerusalem gave him the opportunity to describe the nature of the Jewish religion. He states that the Jews differ from all the rest of mankind in respect of their way of life, but in contrast to some of his predecessors he does not explain Jewish separatism on the grounds of misanthropy. He stresses the monotheistic and abstract nature of the Jewish belief, noting particularly the observance of the Sabbath, the Jew's loyalty to his faith, and the phenomenon of proselytization. As a contemporary of the Severi, he appreciates the fact that the Jews, in spite of their repression in the period immediately preceding, had nevertheless preserved and eventually won the right to live freely according to their customs.

The struggle between paganism and Christianity brought in its wake a pagan reappraisal of its attitude toward Judaism. The polemical works against Christianity of Celsus of Porphyry and of Julian, who had been raised as a Christian, reflect some accurate knowledge of the Bible. But to the extent that they come to grips with the Jewish outlook their attacks are in fact aimed mainly against Christianity, the roots of which are in the sanctified Jewish tradition. Hence, in spite of Judaism's particularistic and intolerant attitude toward paganism, they evince a sincere readiness to try to understand it as a national religion, anchored in an ancient tradition, contrasting it in this way to revolutionary Christianity. As the domination of Christianity became a fact, pagan writers like the Antiochene rhetor Libanius began to see Judaism as being in the same defensive camp as the pagan Hellenistic tradition.

No less than in the regular literary sources, the influence of Judaism is also clearly reflected in the syncretistic magical texts of the ancient world and in *Hermetic writings. Both these genres are replete with Jewish elements. The name of the Jewish godhead and the names of the angels are extremely common in magical papyri, and the thread of the biblical cosmogony is inextricably woven into the fabric of Hermetic tradition. [M.ST.]

Alphabetical List of Ancient Greek Authors Mentioning Jews or Judaism. The writers whose names are marked with an asterisk in the list below form the subjects of articles in their appropriate alphabetical position in the Encyclopaedia.

AELIAN (Claudius Aelianus; c. 170–235 C.E.), Greek sophist. Aelian mentions the Jews in several places. In *Varia Historia,* 12, 35, he includes the Jewish Sibyllines (see *Apocalyptic Literature) in a list of *Sibylline oracles. In his *De Natura Animalium,* 6, 17, he tells of a snake enamored of a girl in Judea during the reign of Herod. He also mentions the deer on Mount Carmel.

AGATHARCHIDES OF CNIDUS (second century B.C.E.), Hellenistic historian and scholar. Agatharchides lived in Egypt during the reigns of Ptolemy VI Philomater (181–145) and Ptolemy VII Euergetes (145–116). His principal works are a history of Asia in ten books and a history of Europe in 49 books, neither of which is extant. Josephus, however (Apion, 1:205–12; Ant. 12:5–6), quotes a short passage from the latter work referring to the "superstition" of the Jewish defenders of Jerusalem which prevented them from fighting on the Sabbath.

***ALEXANDER POLYHISTOR** (c. 105–40 B.C.E.), of Miletus, author of "On the Jews."

ANTONIUS DIOGENES (c. 100 C.E.), author of a fictional romance on Thule, quoted in Porphyry's "Life of Pythagoras." He quotes the tradition to the effect that the philosopher was influenced by the peoples of the East. According to Antonius, Pythagoras visited the Egyptians, Arabs, Chaldeans, and Hebrews, and learned from them the accurate interpretation of dreams.

***APION** (c. 20 B.C.E.–45 C.E.), anti-Jewish writer from Egypt.

***APOLLONIUS MOLON** (first century C.E.), anti-Jewish writer from Cana.

APPIAN OF ALEXANDRIA (second century C.E.) author of a general history of Rome. Appian mentions the Jews and Jewish history in several places, especially in his books on Syria, Mithridates, and those dealing with the civil wars in Rome. Though he himself shared in the general apprehension during the Jewish uprisings in Egypt in 116 C.E., Appian shows no animosity toward the Jews.

***ARISTEAS** (second to first century B.C.E.), Greek historian, author of "On the Jews."

ARISTON OF PELLA (mid-second century C.E.), Palestinian author of a lost dialogue between a Jew and a Jewish convert to Christianity which apparently discussed the question of messianic prophecies in the Old Testament. Whether this work contained the passage on the *Bar Kokhba rebellion cited by *Eusebius or whether Ariston wrote a separate monograph on this war is not known.

ARRIAN (Flavius Arrianus; c. 96–c. 180 C.E.), Greek soldier, historian, and philosopher. Arrian is best known for his *Anabasis,* a history of Alexander the Great from his accession until his death, and *Parthica,* a history of the Parthians, of which only fragments have survived. In the former, Arrian recounts Alexander's capture of Gaza, though he is silent about Judea. On the other hand, in his *Parthica* (fragment 79), Arrian seems to have described in detail the suppression of the Jewish revolt in Mesopotamia in 116 C.E.

***ARTAPANUS** (second century B.C.E.), Alexandrian historian of the Jews.

***CELSUS THE PHILOSOPHER** (second century C.E.), Greek anti-Christian polemicist.

***CHAEREMON** (first century C.E.), stoic writer of Alexandria.

CHARAX OF PERGAMUM (probably second half of the second

century C.E.), writer of Asia Minor. In a passage extant in the geographical lexicon of the sixth-century Stephanus of Byzantium (s.v. Ἑβραῖοι), Charax states that the appellation "Hebrew" for the Jews stems from Abramon (Abraham). A similar explanation is given by *Artapanus.

CHOERILOS OF SAMOS (fifth century B.C.E.), Greek poet. Josephus quotes him (Apion 1, 172–5), stating that he refers to Jews who participated in Xerxes' expedition against Greece. However, the fact that they had round tonsures indicates that they probably were not Jews.

CLAUDIUS IOLAUS (or **Julius**), Phoenician historian of unknown date. The passage preserved from his writings in the sixth-century geographical lexicon of Stephanus of Byzantium gives the etymology of the name Judea as deriving from the legendary hero Oudaios (Οὔδαῖος), one of the men "sown" *(spartoi)* by Cadmus ("the man of the East," Heb. *Kedem*), who fought as the ally of Dionysius and is connected with the origins of Thebes. (This may explain the connection alleged by the Maccabees between the Jews and the Spartans.) Since the fragment mentions *Caesarea, the author cannot have antedated Herod the Great.

CLEARCHUS OF SOLI (in Cyprus; fourth and third centuries B.C.E.), Greek philosopher. Clearchus is generally regarded as a disciple of Aristotle, although his concepts of the soul have more in common with Platonism. In the fragment preserved in Josephus (Apion 1, 176–82) Clearchus describes a meeting between Aristotle and a Jew in Asia Minor. The Jew is defined in this context as hellenized, not only by virtue of the language he speaks but in his soul. The Jews in general are regarded as philosophers dwelling among the Syrians, akin to the Calani, the philosophers of the Indians. Lewy suggests that the Jew is a figment of Clearchus' imagination, similar to other Orientals who are represented as superior in wisdom to Greeks.

***CLEMENT OF ALEXANDRIA** (c. 150–c. 220 C.E.), Church Father.

CLEOMEDES (second century C.E.), author of an astronomical work permeated with Stoic concepts. Cleomedes mentions the Jews in passing when deprecating the vulgar idiom employed by Epicurus. He compares the Greek—vulgar but apparently good—spoken by the Jews with the language of the brothels and that common among women celebrating the Thesmophoria.

CONON I, one of the authors mentioned by Josephus (Apion 1:216) in the list of Greek writers who wrote in detail about the Jews. Some identify him with a writer of that name mentioned in Servius' commentary to Virgil (*Servius ad Aeneidem* 7:738), but this is doubtful. Still more doubtful is the identification of Conon with Conon II.

CONON II (late first century B.C.E. and early first century C.E.), a mythographer, contemporary of King Archelaus of Cappadocia. Fragments of Conon's work have been preserved in the library of Photius. Among his tales is one linking the myth of Perseus' rescue of Andromeda with the town of Jaffa. This connection is in fact very old and it can be traced to as early as the fourth century B.C.E. (in pseudo-Scylax).

DAMASCIUS (sixth century C.E.), the last head of the neoplatonist school. In his *Vita Isidori* he states that Theosebius, disciple of Hierocles, exorcised a demon from his master's wife by invoking the rays of the sun and the God of the Hebrews. He also tells in the same book that in the fifth century Marinus, successor of Proclus as chief of the neoplatonic school, was originally from Neapolis, modern Nablus (in the immediate vicinity of Shechem) a city built at the foot of Mount Gerizim, where there was a temple of Zeus Hypsistos which had been consecrated by Abraham, ancestor of the Hebrews. Marinus, he continues, was originally a Samaritan who later repudiated the doctrines of this sect (which he accused of having deviated from the faith of Abraham) and embraced Hellenism.

DAMOCRITUS (possibly first century B.C.E.), historian who wrote a work "On the Jews," in which he claimed that the Jews worshiped a golden ass head, and that every seven years they captured an alien whom they sacrificed to their god—the first occurrence in literature of the *Blood libel. *Apion has a similar account.

***DEMETRIUS THE HISTORIAN** (third century B.C.E.), chronicler from Alexandria.

DIO CASSIUS (c. 155–235), Greek author of a history of Rome.

DIO OF PRUSA (c. 40–120 C.E.), orator, called Chrysostom ("golden-mouthed") for his eloquence. According to the testimony of his biographer, Synesius (fourth century), Dio described the *Essenes as a utopian-like community living near the Dead Sea in the vicinity of Sodom.

DIODORUS OF SICILY (first century B.C.E.), author of a world history (called the "Library") in 40 books, from the creation of the world to Caesar's conquest of Britain in 54 B.C.E. Hecataeus of Abdera was the source for his account of the Jews (40. frag. 2). In 194 Diodorus notes that "Moyses" claimed to have received his laws from the god named Iao.

DIOGENES LAERTIUS (early third century C.E.), author of "Lives and Opinions of Eminent Philosophers," a eulogistic account of the ancient Greek philosophers. In the prologue (1, 9) he mentions the view of some writers which traces the origin of the Jews back to the Magi.

DIOS (**Dius;** of unknown date), author of a history of Phoenicia, in which (according to Jos., Apion, 1:112–5; Ant., 8:146–9) he relates that King Solomon sent riddles to King Hiram of Tyre, asking him to send him others in return, on the understanding that the one who failed to solve them would forfeit a sum of money. Hiram agreed and, unable to find the solutions, forfeited a large sum. Subsequently, however, with the aid of a Tyrian named Abdemun, Hiram not only solved Solomon's riddles but sent him others which Solomon could not solve, and had then to repay to Hiram more than he received.

DIOSCORIDES PEDANIUS of Anazarba (Anavarza, in Cilicia; mid-first century C.E.), pharmacologist. Dioscorides has a few references to medical materials found in Judea: the balsam, the Jews' stone, and scammony. Dioscorides exercised a great influence on medieval medicine. Ḥisdai ibn Shaprut took part in the revision of the Arabic translation of his work and Maimonides may have utilized it.

***EPICTETUS** (c. 100 C.E.), Greek Stoic philosopher.

ERATOSTHENES OF CYRENE (c. 275–194 B.C.E.), polymath, author of *Geographica,* a first-rate geography much used by *Strabo, who cites his description of Arabia (16:4,2), commenting upon the occupations of the inhabitants (including the Judeans) soil, flora, water supply, and distances. Strabo elsewhere (16:2, 44) cites Eratosthenes' theory that the region around Edom was once a lake and that the land came into existence as a result of volcanic eruptions.

EUHEMERUS (fourth century B.C.E.), writer. In his *Hiera Anagraphe* ("Sacred History"), he suggested that the gods had originally been benefactors of mankind who were subsequently worshiped because of their great deeds. Josephus cites him as establishing the antiquity of the Jews (Apion, 1:216).

***GALEN** (131–c. 201 C.E.) Greek physician and philosopher.

***HECATAEUS OF ABDERA** (fourth century B.C.E.), Greek historian and ethnographer.

HERACLITUS (c. 500 B.C.E.), Greek philosopher. Philo asserts that Heraclitus stole his theory of opposites from Moses, but condemns him for not believing in a divine agency beyond the world. "Heraclitean" views on the constant motion of all things and on the origin of the world in fire were known to and sometimes opposed by, medieval Jewish philosophers, e.g., *Saadiah Gaon.

***HERMES TRISMEGISTOS,** Greek mythological figure, alleged author of the *Hermetika.*

HERMIPPUS OF SMYRNA (third century B.C.E.), peripatetic biographer. He is quoted by Josephus (Apion, 1:163–5) as recording in his work on *Pythagoras that the soul of one of the latter's disciples imparted to him certain precepts, notably, to avoid passing a spot where an ass had collapsed, to abstain from thirst-producing water, and to avoid calumny, in the practice of which Pythagoras "was imitating and appropriating the doctrines of the Jews and Thracians." *Origen cites another work of Hermippus in which he states categorically that Pythagoras derived his philosophy from the Jews (so also Antonius Diogenes and Aristobulus). Attempts to connect Greek philosophers with the Orient are common, however (cf., e.g., Megasthenes), and based apparently on romantic speculation.

HERMOGENES (date unknown), author of a history of Phrygia in which he tells of the Phrygian Noah, Nannacos. Josephus mentions him (Apion, 1:216) among those historians who wrote of the Jews and testified to their antiquity.

HERODOTUS (fifth century B.C.E.), Greek historian. He notes that the Phoenicians and the "Syrians of Palestine," have, on their own testimony, learned the practice of *circumcision from the Egyptians (*Historiae,* 2:104; cf. Jos., Ant., 8:262; Apion, 1:169). Herodotus mentions that these Syrians and Phoenicians furnished and manned 300 warships for the Persian navy (7:89). As Herodotus does not use the name *Ioudaioi* ("Judeans"), it is uncertain if the "Syrians of Palestine" are Jews or possibly Philistines who, although originally uncircumcised (Judg. 14:3), later adopted that rite from the Egyptians.

***HOMER,** earliest Greek epic poet, author of the Odyssey and the Iliad.

HYPSICRATES OF AMISUS (in Pontos), first century B.C.E., historian. He is often cited by *Strabo and is probably his source for Bosphoran affairs. Hypsicrates' works seem to have dealt with the history and ethnography of the Near East and Africa and touched on Jewish affairs. He is quoted by Josephus (Ant. 14; 138–9) from Strabo as the source of information about the help given by *Antipater II and Hyrcanus III to *Julius Caesar.

LAETUS (La'itos), dating probably from the Hellenistic period. According to the second-century Christian apologist, Tatian, Laetus translated into Greek the historical works of three Phoenician historians: Theodotus, Hypsicrates, and Mochus, who included in their works an account of King Hiram, who gave his daughter in marriage to King Solomon (so also Menander of Pergamum; whereas I Kings 11:1 states merely that Solomon married Sidonian women) and donated all kinds of timber for the construction of the Temple.

***LYSIMACHUS OF ALEXANDRIA** (second–first century B.C.E.), author of mythographical work on Egypt.

***MANETHO** (third century B.C.E.), Egyptian priest and historian.

MEGASTHENES (c. 350–290 B.C.E.), ambassador of Seleucus Nicator at the court of the Indian king, Chandragupta. Megasthenes wrote a work on India idealizing the Indians. He apparently included in this work idealized descriptions of the Jews, whom he probably knew firsthand while at the court of Seleucus, to judge from his statement that both the Jews and Brahmans had already taught everything concerning nature that was taught by the ancient Greek philosophers.

MELEAGER OF GADARA (c. 140–70 B.C.E.) was of Syrian parentage and grew up in Tyre. The *Palatine Anthology,* which includes 130 of his love epigrams (vii. 419, 7–8), exhibits his knowledge of Eastern languages: "If you are a Syrian, Salam! If you are a Phoenician, Naidius! If you are a Greek, Chaire!" His Menippean satires, Cynic sermons in prose mingled with verse (a Semitic form called "maqāma" by the Arabs) are lost. In one of his epigrams (A. P. 5. 160), Meleager sighs for his sweetheart Demo who is naked in another's arms, and disparagingly concludes: "If thy lover is some Sabbath-keeper, no great wonder! Love burns hot even on cold Sabbaths," an allusion (cf. *Rutilius Namatianus*) probably to the fact that from a pagan point of view the Sabbath, with its numerous prohibitions, was "cold," i.e., "dull."

MENANDER OF EPHESUS (possibly second century B.C.E.) is probably identical with Menander of Pergamum quoted by Clement of Alexandria (*Stromateis* 1:114) as stating that "Hiram gave his daughter in marriage to Solomon at the time when Menelaus visited Phoenicia after the capture of Troy" (cf. *Laetus). He wrote a history of Phoenicia (in Ant. 8:144, Josephus says that Menander translated the Tyrian records from Phoenician into Greek) which included an account of *Hiram of Tyre, in whose reign "lived Abdemon, a young lad, who always succeeded in mastering the problems set by Solomon, king of Jerusalem" (Jos., Apion, 1:120; Ant. 8:146; cf. *Dios). Hiram also dedicated the golden pillar in the temple of Zeus, which, according to *Eupolemus (Eusebius, *Praeparatio Evangelica,* 9:34), was a present from Solomon. According to Josephus (Ant. 8:324), Menander also alluded to the drought which occurred during King Ahab's reign.

MENANDER OF LAODICEA (third century C.E.), author of rhetorical works. He mentions that Jews from all over the world flock to Palestine for their festal assembly *(panegyris).*

MNASEAS OF PATARA (in Lycia; probably second century B.C.E.), a disciple of *Eratosthenes. He wrote a Periegesis, a geographical work covering Europe, Asia, and Libya. According to Josephus (Apion, 2:112–4), Apion attributes to Mnaseas a story of how an Idumean named Zabidus duped the Jews into believing that he intended to deliver his god Apollo and thus gained entrance into the Temple, from which he stole the golden head of the ass allegedly worshiped by the Jews (cf. *Damocritus)—the first occurrence in literature of the canard that the Jews worshiped an ass. Since Mnaseas' words are known only at third hand, little weight attaches to the story, but it does illustrate the credulity (cf. *Herataeus, *Horace, etc.) widely ascribed to the Jews in antiquity.

NICARCHUS (date unknown), author of a book on the Jews in which he says that Moses was called Alpha because of the many leprous spots (*alphous;* cf. a similar canard in *Manetho) which he had on his body. (Alpha was an honorific title for senior members of the museum in Alexandria, and was regarded as synonymous with excellence.)

***NICHOLAS OF DAMASCUS** (first century B.C.E.), historian and philosopher.

NUMENIUS OF APAMEA (c. 150–200 C.E.), Greek philosopher, author of a lost work "On the Good" where he introduced the Jews to support his Platonic-Pythagorean view of God as incorporeal. A quotation in Eusebius, *Praeparatio Evangelica* 9:8, praises Moses; according to *Clement of Alexandria Numenius called Plato, whom he revered, "Moses speaking pure Greek."

PAUSANIUS (second century C.E.), author of the travel book "A Circuit of Greece" in Greek. He includes customs and historical data as well as an actual guide to sights. In his treatment of the area around Olympia he describes the Jordan's course, and in his book on Arcadia he speaks of the tomb of Queen *Helena of Adiabene in Jerusalem; elsewhere he mentions various peculiarities of Palestine.

PHILO OF BYBLOS (also called **Herennius Philo,** 64–161 C.E.), Greek author of a Phoenician history. Philo claimed that his history was a translation from the Phoenician of Sanchuniathon, whose sources go back to before the Trojan War. Many quotations from his history concerning religion are found in Eusebius' *Praeparatio Evangelica* (1:9, 22–10; 8). He is also said to have written, among other works, a history of the Jews in which he criticized Hecataeus of Abdera. Only fragments of his work survive.

PHILODEMUS (c. 110—c. 40/35 B.C.E.), Epicurean philosopher from Gadara in Palestine. He founded a school at Herculaneum, Italy, and may have been a teacher of *Horace. He wrote Cynic diatribes. According to Hadas (see bibl.) his erotic poetry shows some parallels with the Song of Songs.

PHILOSTRATUS (b.c. 172 C.E.), a native of the island of Lemnos, he studied rhetoric in Athens and later joined the literary and philosophic circle in Rome of Empress Julia Domna, wife of Septimius Severus. She commissioned him to write a literary life of Apollonius of Tyana, whom he presented as a divinely inspired sage, prophet, and reformer along Pythagorean lines. The work has several comments on the separateness of the Jews and on their bloody revolt against the Romans under Vespasian.

***PLUTARCH** (c. 46–c. 120), Greek biographer and moralist.

POLEMON OF ILIUM (c. 202–181 B.C.E.), Greek author of a lost history in which the Exodus was used to date the mythological Greek king Apis, according to Eusebius, *Praeparatio Evangelica,* 10:10, 15.

POLYBIUS OF MEGALOPOLIS (c. 210–128 B.C.E.), the most notable of the Hellenistic historians. Polybius did not devote much space to the Jews or Judaism in his universal history. His detailed description of the fourth Syrian war (book 5) makes no mention of Jerusalem or Judea, although it gives a comparatively lengthy account of the conquest of Palestine. He does, however, discuss the Jews in the context of the fifth Syrian war, as attested in the fragment from book 16 of his history, preserved in Josephus (Ant. 12:3, 135–6). Here Polybius records among other achievements of Antiochus III that those Jews who lived near the Temple of Jerusalem allied themselves with him. From another passage (Jos. Apion 2:53–54) it can be seen that a section of Polybius' work, now lost, also gave *Antiochus Epiphanes' impecunious state as his motive for plundering the Temple.

***PORPHYRY** (233–305), Greek philosopher and polemist.

***POSIDONIUS** (c. 135–c. 50 B.C.E.), Greek philosopher, biologist and scientist.

PSEUDO-HECATAEUS see *Hecataeus of Abdera.

PSEUDO-LONGINUS, name ascribed to the author of the Greek treatise "On the Sublime." The oldest manuscript of the treatise ascribes it to Dionysius Longinus. The only Longinus known however, was named Cassius not Dionysius, and the opening of this manuscript notes the author as "Dionysius or Longinus." The work must therefore be regarded as of uncertain date and authorship. The book tries to answer the question: "What are the characteristics of great writing?" In 9.9, the author cites Genesis as an example of greatness of thought: "Similarly, the lawgiver of the Jews, no ordinary man—for he understood and expressed God's power in accordance with its worth [cf. Jos., Ant. 1:15 for similarity of language]—writes at the beginning of his Laws: 'God said'—what?—'Let there be light,' and there was light; 'let there be land,' and there was land." The fact that Longinus gives only the substance of the biblical passage suggests an intermediate source, and since Longinus' treatise was written explicitly in answer to a work of *Caecilius of Calacte, who was apparently a Jew, the latter may well be the source. Another possible source is *Philo, whose language and sentiments resemble those of "Longinus" in chapter 44.

***PSEUDO-SCYLAX** (c. 350 B.C.E.), author of the *Periplous*.

PTOLEMY OF CHENNOS (early second century B.C.E.), of Alexandria, author of a lost "new" compilation of interesting facts, summarized in Photius. He derived Moses' supposed nickname, "Alpha," from the Greek word for leprosy, *alphoi* (cf. Nicarchus).

PTOLEMY OF MENDE (date unknown), an Egyptian priest who wrote in Greek a lost work on Egyptian chronology, quoted by Tatian in *Oratio ad Graecos,* 38, on the date of the Exodus. Apion made use of this work.

PTOLEMY THE BIOGRAPHER, brother of *Nicholas of Damascus. Like his brother, Ptolemy was a highly esteemed member of the literary circle which surrounded Herod I. After Herod's death, he sided with Antipas (Jos., Ant., 17:225; Wars, 2:21). A fragment of a work about Herod stating that the Idumaeans were Phoenician and Syrian in origin and were forcibly converted to Judaism (cf. Jos., Ant. 18:257–8) has been ascribed to him by Reinach (Textes, 88–89) but it may possibly belong to another Ptolemy.

PTOLEMY THE GEOGRAPHER (second century C.E.), Alexandrian astronomer and geograher. Among his many works was a "Geography" in eight books in which he fixed the longitude and latitude of thousands of places, including many in Palestine: Ptolemais (Acre), Sycaminon (Haifa), Mount Carmel, Caesarea Stratonis (Caesarea), Iope (Jaffa), Ascalon (Askelon), Tiberias, Neapolis (Nablus), Gaza, Lydda, Hierosolyma (Jerusalem). However, Ptolemy's locations are often in error.

***PYTHAGORAS** (c. sixth century B.C.E.), semi-legendary Greek philosopher and mystic.

SEXTUS EMPIRICUS (late second century C.E.), Greek physician and philosophical writer in whose works on Skepticism (extant) the Jewish abhorrence of pig's flesh is mentioned (*Pyrrhonic Sketches* 3:223).

***STRABO** (c. 63 B.C.E.–c. 24 C.E.), Greek geographer and historian.

TEUCER OF CYZICUS (c. 100–50 B.C.E.), Greek author. He wrote historical works on various subjects, including a Jewish history, as reported by Suidas. None of his works survive.

***THALLUS** (first century C.E.), Greek author of a universal history.

THEODOTUS (second century B.C.E.), Samaritan epic poet.

THEOPHILUS. Josephus (Apion, 1:216) includes one Theophilus in a list of Greek authors who mentioned the Jews at some length and whose writings testify to the antiquity of the Jewish people. His date and nationality are unknown but he may be identical with the Theophilus whom Alexander Polyhistor cites as a source for the story that King Solomon sent the gold left over from the building of the Temple to the king of Tyre. It is also possible that he is the Theophilus who is known to have been of the school of Zenodotus, the great Alexandrian scholar of the third century B.C.E.

***THEOPHRASTUS OF ERESOS** (c. 372–288 B.C.E.), Greek philosopher and pupil of Aristotle.

TIMAGENES OF ALEXANDRIA, historian of Alexandria who also lived in Rome during the Augustan Age. Timagenes was the author of a general history centering on Alexander and his successors. He refers to the Jews and possibly devoted a special section to Jewish history. The three relevant passages preserved from his writings deal with the policy of Antiochus Epiphanes of Judea, *Aristobulus I, and the wars of Alexander *Yannai. Timagenes is the only Alexandrian Greek historian who does not evince hostility toward the Jews.

TIMOCHARES (date unknown), author of a lost history in Greek of Antiochus IV Epiphanes (175–164 B.C.E.) or Antiochus VII Sidetes (138–128). His remarks on Jerusalem's topography are preserved in Eusebius, *Praeparatio Evangelica,* 9:35.

XENOPHON OF LAMPSACUS (second century B.C.E.), author of a fanciful travel book in Greek. He has been identified with Xenophon, author of a guide to Syria, quoted anonymously on the subject of Jerusalem's topography in Eusebius, *Praeparatio Evangelica,* 9:36.

ZOPYRION, an author, otherwise unknown, appearing in a list of Greeks who wrote specifically about the Jews and attested to their antiquity. Josephus (Apion, 1:216) criticizes him for inaccuracy.

See also *Hellenistic Jewish Literature.

Bibliography: Reinach, Textes (the basic source on the subject); Pauly-Wissoura; M. Radin, *The Jews Among the Greeks and Romans* (1915), 97ff.; D. Staehlin, in: W. v. Christ and W. Schmid, *Geschichte der griechischen Literatur,* 2, pt. 1 (1920[6]), 539ff.; I. Heinemann, in: Pauly-Wissowa, suppl. 5 (1931), 3–43; J. Lewy, *Olamot Nifgashim* (1960), 3–14; V. Tcherikover, *Hellenistic Civilization and the Jews* (1959), 287, 358ff.; M. Hadas, *Hellenistic Culture* (1959); F. Jacoby, *Die Fragmente der griechischen Historike* (1958); S. Lieberman, *Greek in Jewish Palestine* (1942); E. Schwartz, *Griechische Geschichtschreiber* 1957), 36ff.; E. Gabba, *Appiano e la storia delle guerre civili* (1956); Y. Gutman, *Ha-Sifrut ha-Yehudit ha-Helenistit* (1958); L. G. Westerink (ed. and tr.), *Damascius, Lectures on the Philebus* (1959).

GREEK LITERATURE, MODERN. The literary image of the Jew was molded in Greece by the Jews themselves, by Greek non-Jews and, indirectly, by the Turks. In ancient Greece, Jews were referred to as a "community of philosophers." In the Hellenistic period there was some anti-Jewish writing; but, in the main, Jews and Greeks enjoyed a friendly cultural relationship (see *Hellenistic Jewish Literature; *Greek Literature, Ancient).

Influence of the Bible. Probably no work contributed more to the harmonious relationship between *Hellenism and Judaism than the *Septuagint. But in the *Byzantine Empire, fanatical rulers enacted anti-Jewish decrees which altered the image of the Jew and even threatened his survival, e.g., the anti-Jewish decrees of *Constantine I, Novella 146 of *Justinian, as well as the anti-Jewish enactments of Basil I (867–886), as described in the *Chronicle* of *Ahimaaz b. Paltiel. The Greek Jews and the newly arrived Sephardi exiles from Spain, welcomed by Sultan Bajazet II, fared well under the *Ottoman Empire. Hebrew studies became popular and talmudic schools multiplied. Important achievements were an anonymous Polyglot Pentateuch (1547), the Book of Job (1576) and a medieval Greek translation of the Hebrew Bible in 1576 (see *Judeo-Greek). Jewish writing was revived again in the 18th and even more in the 19th centuries. Hebrew education was popularized in both synagogue and home by the Judeo-Greek translations. Among 20th-century Greek writers, G. Th. Vafopoulos wrote a tragedy based on the story of Esther (1934). Kosta Papapanayiotou published two dramas, one about Esther and the other about Rizpah, in 1963. Nikos Kazantzakis, in his *Sodhoma kye Ghomorra* (1956), relates the age of the Bible to the modern world which, in his view, has reverted to the corruption of the past. Despite his preference for the Old Testament over the New, Kazantzakis distorts rabbinic Judaism and the character of his own Jewish contemporaries. Ioanna Dhriva Maravelidhou, in her verse drama *Esther* (1967), pays homage to those Jews in the Persian Empire who were prepared for any sacrifice to preserve the idea of one God. In his book *Simon Bar Kochba,* published in 1966, Vassos Kaloyannis dealt with the epic Jewish struggle against Rome.

The Figure of the Jew in Modern Greek Literature. Contemporary prejudice marks the poetic "Story of the Little Jewess Marcada" (Venice, 1627), which tells of the heroine's abduction by her Christian lover and her subsequent apostasy. *I thisia tou Avraam* ("The Sacrifice of Abraham," 1696), a mystery play probably written in 1635 by the Cretan Kornaros (d. 1677), is the only masterpiece by a Greek of that time. The earliest surviving edition was printed in Venice in 1713. It may have been based on an earlier Italian drama and reveals both the influence of the Bible and a humanistic treatment of the Jew. In the *Thisia*, which continues to be revived in Greece almost annually and has been translated into all the major European languages, the author presents an anthropomorphic God and depicts Abraham not as a Hebrew patriarch but as a distraught father torn between love for his son and love of God.

For the next three centuries Greek writers devoted their efforts to liberating their country from the Turks. As a strategic measure against the revolutionary tide which finally led to the successful War of Greek Independence (1821–32), the Turks created a climate of covert hostility between Greek and Jew. It was not until almost all of Greece was liberated that a humanistic treatment of the Jew was again found in Greek literature. The novelist Gregorios Xenopoulos wrote a drama entitled *Rachel* (1909) on the expulsion of the Jews from Zante; Konstantinos Cavafy, the Alexandrian Greek poet, wrote a poem entitled "Of the Hebrews, A.D. 50," in which he philosophized ironically on the dangers of Jewish assimilation; and Nikolaos D. Vizinos published several refutations of the *blood libel.

The one Greek writer to portray the Jew in universal terms was Nikos Kazantzakis who devotes a chapter to the Russian Jew in his travel book *Ti idha sti Rousia* ("What I saw in Russia," 1928). Here he sees the Jew as a rebel and revolutionary by force of historical circumstance. In his autobiographical *Anafora ston Greko* (1961; *Report to Greco*, 1965) he shows profound sympathy for the suffering of the German Jewish students he met in Berlin. In Jerusalem, he longed not only for his own God but also for the Old Testament God, and he visited Mount Sinai to hear His voice as Moses heard it. Kazantzakis nevertheless remained bitterly opposed to Zionism, which he considered a reactionary delusion. Elsewhere, he showed admiration for Eliezer *Ben-Yehuda, the father of the Hebrew revival. In the novel with the Hebrew title *Todah Rabbah* (1934, English translation 1956), Kazantzakis portrays the Russian Jew as "one facet of a single consciousness that experienced and mirrored the complex, fluid, many-sided reality of the Soviet Union."

The playwright Spyros Melas turned to historical drama in *Judas*, first produced in Athens in 1934. In this play Judas is portrayed as a revolutionary leader who joins Jesus for the liberation of Judea. Manolis Georgiou Skoulidhis wrote *I ipothesis Dreyfus* ("The Dreyfus Case," 1960), in which he dramatized modern opinions about this famous trial. Pantelis Georgiou Prevelakyis, influenced by the ideology of his close friend Kazantzakis, wrote *O Lazaros* (1954), a drama in which he examined the attitude of an early Christian toward the new religion. A prose work by V. Ghazis on the Cain and Abel theme (1955) consists of seven allegorical accounts, the last of which predicts an eventual atomic war.

Several authors who were personally involved in World War II wrote works dealing with the Nazi occupation of Greece and their concentration camp experiences. One was Elias Venezis, whose play, *Block C*, was published in 1945. Venezis' novel *Okeanos* ("Ocean," 1956) gives a sympathetic portrait of a Jewish stowaway from Smyrna bound for the United States. Jacob Kampaneli, who spent the years 1943–45 in the Mauthausen concentration camp, wrote the first draft of a prose work on his experiences in 1947 and published a final version in 1965. His pro-Jewish sympathies are very evident, since after the liberation he remained in the camp until all the Jewish survivors who wished to had emigrated to Palestine. Other works on the concentration camp theme are the play *Epistrofi apo to Buchenwald* ("Return from Buchenwald," 1948) by Sotiris Patatzis and a long poem by Takis Olympios, *40382* (1965) inspired by the number branded on the arm of a girl who survived Auschwitz. A volume of poems by Sophia Mavroídhi Papadhaki (1905–), *To louloudhi tis tefras* ("The Flower of the Ashes," 1966), had its origin in a flower she saw growing among the ashes of Dachau. Papadhaki also wrote a life of David and short stories about Ruth and Jonah.

Vassos Kaloyannis was one of several non-Jewish authors to write about Jewish communities in Greece, which he did in his *Larissa, Madre d'Israel* ("Larissa, Mother of Israel," 1959). Demetrius Hatzis wrote about the Janina Jewish community in *I mikri mas polis* ("Our Small City") and the archimandrite Nikodemos Vafiadhis gave an account of the Jewish community of Didymotichon in his *I israilitikyi kyinotis Dhidhimotichou* (1954). The art critic Anghelos Georgios Procopiou, who spent a year in Israel, described his impressions of the country in his book *O Laos tis Vivlou*, "The People of the Bible." The image of the Jew in Greek literature is still clearly identified with the history of Judaism and the Bible. In modern times, however, Greek authors are trying to create an emphatic, three-dimensional image of the Jew as a Greek citizen whose sufferings must not be forgotten. George Zoghrafakyis (1908–), a non-Jewish writer from Salonika, who edited the works of Eliyia and published essays on modern Jewish figures such as *Herzl and *Agnon, should also be mentioned.

The Jewish Contribution to Greek Literature. Until World War II Salonika was the center of Greco-Jewish culture and Jewish authors wrote mainly in *Ladino, the language spoken by the majority of the Jewish community. Among the very few Jewish writers in Greek, who, between the two world wars, sought to interpret their background and traditions in terms of the contemporary world were the prominent journalist Moisis *Caïmis and the brilliant and prolific poet Joseph *Eliyia. After World War II Jewish writers in Greece showed a natural preoccupation with the tragic fate of their community during the Nazi occupation. J. Matarasso published the poignant *Kye omos oli tous dhen pethanan* ("Still They All have not Died," 1948); P. Chajidhimiou wrote a book of commemorative verse entitled *Bene Israel* (1957); and Joseph Matsas investigated the cultural achievements of the Jews in his native Ioannina. Although he wrote in French, Albert *Cohen, born in Corfu, used his native background as a setting for some of his novels.

Other Jewish writers returned to the path blazed earlier by Caïmis and Eliyia. They include the Zionist author Asher *Moissis; Raphael Konstantinis (1892–), who edited two Jewish periodicals; Julius Caïmis; Joseph (Pepo) Sciaki; Baruch Schiby; and the outstandingly successful Nestoras *Matsas, who converted during World War II but retained a burning interest in his Jewish heritage and the tragedy of his people.

Well-known Jewish Greek Writers. The writers whose names are marked with an asterisk in the list below form the subjects of articles in their appropriate alphabetical position in the Encyclopaedia.

CAÏMIS, JULIUS (1897–), author and translator, son of Moisis Caïmis. His works include *Exi kanones zoghrafikyes* ("Six Laws of Art," 1937); *Vivlikyes istories* ("Bible Stories"), based on rabbinic sources; and *La comédie grecque dans l'âme du théâtre d'ombres* (1935).

***CAÏMIS, MOISIS** (1864–1929), journalist.

***ELIYIA, JOSEPH** (1901–1931), poet.

MATSAS, JOSEPH (1920–), literary scholar and translator. A Greek resistance fighter, Matsas, who became president of the Jewish community in his native Janina, wrote studies of Greco-Jewish culture and Judeo-Greek poetry. His works include *Yianiotika evraïka traghoudhia* ("Ioannina Hebrew Songs," 1953) and *Ta onomata ton Evreon sti Yanina* ("The Names of the Ioannina Jews," 1955).
***MATSAS, NESTORAS** (1932–), author, artist, and film director.
***MOISSIS, ASHER** (1899–), author, translator, and Zionist leader.
SCHIBY, BARUCH (1906–), author and journalist of Salonika. Known mainly for his quarterly *Dhelfika tetradhia,* he was a prominent literary figure, a founder of the anti-Nazi resistance movement, and a leading Zionist. His *I fleghomeni vatos* ("The Burning Bush," 1968) discussed the origins of the Jews and various aspects of Judaism.
SCIAKI, JOSEPH (Pepo; 1917–), lawyer and author. He wrote *Pikres alithies* ("Bitter Truths," 1952), a book of short stories, one of which deals with Jewish life in Athens.

Bibliography: W. N. Stearns (ed.), *Fragments From Graeco-Jewish Writers* (1908); Fischer, in: *Jewish Affairs* (Aug. 1953), 23–29.

[R.D.]

GREEN, ABEL (1900–), U.S. theatrical journalist, editor of *Variety,* the chief theatrical paper in the U. S. While at New York University, Green wrote theatrical interviews for the New York *Sunday World. Variety* was founded by Sime Silverman in 1905 and Green succeeded him as editor in 1933. A chronicler of theatrical news, Green added to English theatrical slang with coinages which he called "un-King's English." A shrewd critic, Green once capsuled a film review with the succinct phrase, "It went in one eye and out the other." He was the author of *Mr. Broadway,* a film script of *Variety's* founder-editor; coauthor with Joe Laurie, Jr. of *Show Biz from Vaude to Video* (1952) and editor of *Variety Music Cavalcade* (1952) and *The Spice of Variety* (1953). [Jo.R.]

GREENACRE, PHYLLIS (1894–) U.S. psychiatrist. Phyllis Greenacre, who was born in Chicago, was appointed clinical professor of psychiatry at Cornell University Medical College in 1935. In 1942 she joined the faculty of the New York Psychoanalytic Institute and was its president from 1948 to 1950. One of her main interests was the subject of anxiety. In 1941 she published a paper in which she sought the roots of anxiety in the birth trauma of the fetus, as revealed in the newborn child and in the memory traces of the adult patient in psychoanalysis. Birth with its enormous sensory stimulation after the relaxed fetal state, in her view, produced a strong narcissistic drive and a defensive organization of anxiety in the infant. Her book *Trauma, Growth and Personality* appeared in 1952.

A further focus of Greenacre's interest was the sexual anomaly of fetishism. She stressed the magical value represented by the fetish in early life as a result of disturbed mother-child relationships. She wrote, too, on identity and its relation to body image stressing the role of visual perception and perceptual distortion in the fetish image of the genitals and face. In 1953 she edited *Affective Disorders.* Her analysis of the creative personality and imagination was set out in her study of two lives, *Swift and Carroll* (1955); her other publications include *The Quest for the Father: a Study of the Darwin-Butler Controversy* (1963).

Bibliography: A. Grinstein, *Index of Psychoanalytic Writings,* 2 (1957), 6 (1964).

[Lo.M.]

GREENBAUM, EDWARD SAMUEL (1890–1970), U. S. lawyer, soldier, and public servant. Greenbaum was born in New York, the son of Samuel, a Supreme Court Justice in New York, and Selina, president of the Jewish Working Girls Vacation Society. He entered law practice in 1915. A skillful attorney, Greenbaum dealt with diverse legal problems, and his clients included prominent public personalities. Greenbaum's public service career began in the 1920s when he participated in a study of U.S. legal practice. Reform of the courts became a lifelong interest: as a member of the Judicial Conference of the State of New York, he was a key campaigner for reorganization of the New York court system, finally achieved in 1960–61. Greenbaum enlisted in the army in World War I, retiring at its end as a major. Returning to active duty in 1940, he rose to brigadier general. During World War II he was a principal aide to the secretary of war and played a leading role in establishing War Department labor policy, for which he was awarded the Distinguished Service Medal in 1945. Public positions he held include Alcohol Control Commission chairman (1933); special assistant to the attorney general's office (1934–38); Long Island Railroad Commission counsel (1938); and alternate delegate to the United Nations (1957). He helped found the Jewish Big Brothers Organization; served on the executive committee of the Jewish Welfare Board, Armed Services Division; and was active on the American Jewish Committee and the Jewish Board of Guardians. He served as trustee of the Institute for Advanced Studies at Princeton. Greenbaum coauthored *King's Bench Masters,* a study of British pretrial practice (1932), and wrote an autobiography, *Lawyer's Job* (1967).

[B.G.L.]

GREENBERG, DAVID MORRIS (1895–), U.S. biochemist. Greenberg was born in Boston, obtained his doctorate at the University of California in 1924, and became professor of biochemistry at Berkeley in 1941. On his retirement in 1963, he worked as a research biochemist at the Oncologic Institute, University of California Medical School in San Francisco. Greenberg served on the U. S. Atomic Energy Commission and on the isotopes panel of the National Research Council. He was editor of the *Proceedings of the Society of Experimental Biology and Medicine,* and served as chairman of the California section of this society. Greenberg was a pioneer in the use of radioisotopes for biochemical investigations. He wrote *Aminoacids and Proteins* (1951), *Chemical Pathways of Metabolism* (1954), and *Metabolic Pathways* (1960). [S.A.M.]

GREENBERG, ELIEZER (1896–), Yiddish poet and literary critic. Born in Bessarabia, at an early age he was influenced by the poets Eliezer *Steinbarg, Jacob *Sternberg, and Moshe *Altman, who were pioneers of Hebrew and Yiddish literature in this Russian province on the Rumanian border. At 17, Greenberg emigrated to the United States, but impressions of his native town enriched his poetry throughout his life. His lyrics and essays began to appear in Yiddish periodicals and anthologies in 1919. Together with Elias *Schulman, he founded and edited *Getseltn* (1945–48), a periodical of verse and literary criticism, and with Irving *Howe, he edited an English anthology of short stories, *A Treasury of Yiddish Literature* (1954). His first booklet of poetry, *Gas un Avenues* ("Streets and Avenues," 1928), portrays New York as the symbol of the vaulting ambition of contemporary man. It was followed by the poems of *Fun Umetum* ("From Everywhere," 1934) and of *Fisherdorf* ("Fishing Village," 1938).

During the depression of the 1930s, a social proletarian tone appeared in his verses, but when tragedy struck the Jewish people a decade later he wrote the angry and despairing verses of *Di Lange Nakht* ("The Long Night," 1946), in which the whole earth was portrayed as a hospital of the sick and the delirious from which God had averted His face. In "Baynakhtiker Dialog" ("Night Dialogue") in *Eybiker Dorsht* ("Eternal Thirst," 1968) Greenberg reverted to calmer moods, again at peace with God and man. As a critic, Greenberg revealed sensitive insight in his studies on Moshe Leib *Halpern, H. *Leivick, and Jacob *Glatstein.

Bibliography: LNYL, 2 (1958), 391ff.; J. Glatstein, *In Tokh Genumen* (1956), 323–8; S. Bickel *Shrayber fun Mayn Dor* (1958), 144–7; S. D. Singer, *Dikhter un Prozaiker* (1959), 109–12. [S.L.]

GREENBERG, HAYIM (1889–1953), Zionist leader, essayist, and editor. Greenberg, born in the Bessarabian village of Todoristi in Russia, joined the Zionist movement while still a youngster and attracted immediate notice as a self-taught intellectual prodigy. In 1904 he attended the Zionist Congress in Helsinki as a correspondent, and while still in his teens moved to Odessa, where he emerged before long as a leading figure in Hebrew and Zionist letters, excelling as both an orator and an essayist on philosophical and political themes. With the outbreak of World War I, Greenberg moved to Moscow, where he edited the Russian-Jewish weekly *Razsvet* ("The Dawn"). After the Russian Revolution he served for a while as an instructor in medieval Jewish literature at the University of Kharkov and lectured at Kiev Academy. Arrested several times for Zionist activities by the Communist authorities, he left for Berlin in 1921, where he edited *Haolam* ("The World"), the official weekly of the World Zionist Organization.

Greenberg went to the U.S. in 1924 to become editor of the Yiddish Zionist publication *Farn Folk* ("For the People"), which later became *Der *Yidisher Kempfer* ("The Jewish Warrior"), and in 1934 became editor of the Labor Zionist monthly *The Jewish Frontier*. From 1934 he was a permanent member of the Central Committee of the Labor Zionist Organization of America. During World War II he served as head of the American Zionist Emergency Council, and in 1946 he was appointed director of the Department of Education and Culture of the Jewish Agency Executive in America. Greenberg's influence on Zionist activities during these years was great. Particularly noteworthy were his

Hayim Greenberg, Zionist leader and man of letters. Central Zionist Archives, Jerusalem.

accomplishments in winning the votes of several Latin-American delegations at the United Nations for the creation of a Jewish State, and later in helping to forge strong cultural ties between the new State of Israel and Jews the world over.

As an essayist in three languages, Yiddish, Hebrew, and English, Greenberg was distinguished by his breadth of knowledge, urbanity of approach, and deep moral earnestness. The core of his writings was devoted to expounding the philosophy of Zionism and attempting to demonstrate its consistency with the ideals of socialism, pacifism, and universalism to which he adhered. Collections of his essays have appeared in several volumes in Yiddish and in English, including: *The Inner Eye* (2 vols., 1953–64); *Yid un Velt* (1953); *Beytlakh fun a Tog-Bukh* (1954); *Mentshn un Vertn* (1954); and *Hayim Greenberg Anthology* (1968).

Bibliography: Gordis, in: *Judaism*, 2 (1953), 99–100; LNYL, 2 (1958), 398–404; Kressel, Leksikon, 1 (1965), 509–10; S. Bickel, *Shreiber fun Mayn Dor* (1958), 256–66. [H.H.]

GREENBERG, HENRY BENJAMIN (Hank; 1911–), U.S. baseball player. Greenberg, who was born in New York City, entered professional baseball in 1930. Three years later he joined the Detroit Tigers as a first baseman, and in 1934 helped them win their first American League pennant in 25 years. The Tigers were champions again in 1935, and Greenberg won the American League's Most

Hank Greenberg, U.S. baseball player. Courtesy Bloch Publishing Co., N.Y.

Valuable Player award. Injuries put him out of the game for a year (1936), but in 1938 he hit 58 home runs, two less than Babe Ruth's single-season home run record.

Converted into an outfielder in 1940, Greenberg led the Tigers to another pennant victory and won a second Most Valuable Player award. After service in the U.S. Army Air Corps in World War II, Greenberg rejoined the Tigers in the middle of the 1945 season and won the American League pennant on the last day of the season with a grand slam home run in the ninth inning. His hitting contributed to the Tigers' victory in the 1945 World Series. In 1946 he returned to first base, and won his third American League home run title. Greenberg was sold to the Pittsburgh Pirates in 1947 and ended his playing career after one season in the National League. He compiled a lifetime batting average of .313, hit 331 home runs and batted in 1,276 runs in 1,394 games. Greenberg was elected to the Baseball Hall of Fame in 1956.

Bibliography: B. Postal et al., *Encyclopaedia of Jews in Sports* (1965), 61–63. [J.H.S.]

GREENBERG, IRVING (1933–), U.S. Orthodox rabbi and educator. Greenberg was born in Brooklyn, N.Y. Rabbi of Young Israel of Brookline, Mass., from 1953–56, he served as Hillel director at Brandeis University and lecturer in Near Eastern Judaic studies (1957–58). In 1959 Greenberg joined the faculty of Yeshiva University, where he became professor of history. From 1965 he has been rabbi of the Riverdale Jewish Center. Greenberg is a leading exponent of the Musar movement. He is an active participant in dialogues with Conservative and Reform Jews, and has published many articles in scholarly and organizational publications. [L.Be.]

GREENBERG, LEOPOLD (1885–1964), South African judge, born in Calvinia, Cape Province. Raised to the bench at the age of 39, he became judge president of the Transvaal in 1938 and was elevated in 1943 to the Appellate Division of the Supreme Court, the highest judicial body in South Africa. He was acting chief justice in 1953 and served as officer administering the government in the absence of the governor-general. Known for his erudition, humanity, and caustic wit, he was acknowledged to be among South Africa's ablest judges. After his retirement in 1955, he sat on a judicial commission of inquiry into African disturbances in Johannesburg in 1957.

In Jewish life he was associated mainly with Zionist causes; for many years was honorary president of the Keren Hayesod, the Israel United Appeal, and the South African Friends of the Hebrew University. He was the first South African on the board of governors of the Hebrew University of Jerusalem, whose institute of forensic medicine, established from funds raised by South African Jewry, was named after him. [L.S.]

GREENBERG, LEOPOLD JACOB (1861–1931), editor of the *Jewish Chronicle* and one of the first Zionists in Britain. Born in Birmingham, Greenberg was at first active in the non-Jewish press as a publisher and owner of a news agency. He became involved in Jewish affairs and began to attract notice as one of *Herzl's first adherents in Britain. He promoted Herzl's ideas before the general and Jewish public, and it was he who arranged for Herzl to appear before the Royal Commission on Alien Immigration in London in 1902 (through his close ties with Joseph *Chamberlain, secretary for the colonies, who also came from Birmingham). Herzl entrusted him with various political missions in England, such as those connected with the *El-Arish project and the *Uganda Scheme, and eventually Greenberg served as Herzl's offical representative vis-à-vis the British government. Although he had supported the Uganda project, Greenberg did not join the *Territorialists. He became a leader of the British Zionist Federation and held various offices in the organization.

In 1907 he and his friends acquired the *Jewish Chronicle* in order to make it a Zionist organ and he was appointed editor in chief. He was a staunch fighter for Jewish rights and a particularly severe critic of the Czarist regime's attitude toward the Jews. Upon his appointment as editor, he gave up his official activities in the Zionist movement. Throughout the years, however, he persisted in his efforts to gain the support of various British circles for Zionism. After World War I, he opposed the official policy of the Zionist Organization, but his was a "loyal opposition." He was among the founders of *The Jewish Year Book* (1896–); *Young Israel,* a periodical for youth (1897); and other publications. Herzl described him as "the most able of all my helpers." In accordance with his last will, his ashes were taken to Deganyah and interred there (1932).

His son, Ivan Marion (1896–1966), joined the editorial board of the *Jewish Chronicle* in 1925 and served as its editor in chief from 1936 to 1946. During this period, he attacked the British government for its anti-Zionist policy in Palestine. He translated M.*Begin's book *Revolt* into English (1951). He was a leader of the *Revisionist Party in Britain.

Bibliography: C. Roth, in: *The Jewish Chronicle 1841–1941* (1949), 124–40 and index; Rabinowitz, in: I. Cohen (ed.), *Rebirth of Israel* (1952), 77–97; T. Herzl, *Complete Diaries,* 5 (1960), index; L. Stein, *Balfour Declaration* (1961), index. [G.K.]

GREENBERG, SAMUEL BERNARD (1893–1917), U.S. poet. Born in Vienna, Greenberg was taken to the U.S. in 1900; after a poverty-stricken life in New York City's ghetto he died from tuberculosis at the age of 24. Self-taught except for a few years in elementary school, he displayed remarkable precocity and power as a poet and was also a gifted artist. Influenced primarily by the American writers Emerson and Thoreau and by the English poets Keats, Shelley, and Browning, Greenberg wrote mystical poetry filled with vivid and strange imagery. His imperfect command of English grammar and vocabulary give his verse an unusual, surrealistic tone characteristic of some of the most sophisticated modernist poetry of the early 20th century. Greenberg might have remained unknown had not Hart Crane, the American poet, discovered his manuscripts in 1923. The poems had a profound effect on Crane and eventually, more than 20 years after Greenberg's death, a first selection (*Poems from the Greenberg Manuscripts,* 1939) was published which helped to establish his important place in American literary history. A second selection, *Poems by Samuel Greenberg,* was published in 1947. [B.W.]

GREENBERG, SIMON (1901–), U.S. rabbi and educator. Greenberg, who was born in Russia, was taken to the U. S. in 1905. He was ordained by the Jewish Theological Seminary in 1925. From 1925 to 1946 Greenberg was rabbi of Har Zion Temple, Philadelphia, Pa., one of the leading synagogues of the Conservative movement. He then returned to the Seminary to serve as provost (1946–51), executive director of the United Synagogue (1950–53), and as president of the University of Judaism in Los Angeles (1955–63). He was appointed professor of homiletics and education in 1948 and vice-chancellor in 1957. One of Conservative Judaism's most articulate spokesmen, Greenberg stressed the centrality of the Jewish people, the importance of Zionism and Hebrew, the religious character of American civilization, and the importance of Hebrew in Jewish education. Greenberg was a member of the Jewish

Simon Greenberg (right), vice-chancellor of the Jewish Theological Seminary, New York, with Saul Lieberman (left) and Mordecai Kaplan, 1959. Courtesy Jewish Theological Seminary, New York.

Agency Executive, president of the Rabbinical Assembly of America, and a leader of the World Council on Jewish Education. Greenberg's numerous writings include: *Living as a Jew Today* (1940); *Ideals and Values of the Prayer Book* (1940); *The First Year in the Hebrew School: A Teacher's Guide* (1946); *Foundations of a Faith* (1967); *Words of Poetry* (1970); and a series of brochures on the Conservative movement in Judaism. He also compiled the Harishon series of Hebrew textbooks. [J.R.]

GREENBERG, URI ZEVI (pseudonym **Tur Malka;** 1894–), Hebrew poet. He was born in Bialykamien, eastern Galicia and was descended from ḥasidic leaders (Meir Przemyslany on his father's side and the *Saraf,* Uri Strelisk, on his mother's). In his infancy his parents moved to Lvov where Greenberg received a traditional ḥasidic upbringing and education. His earliest poems, both in Hebrew and Yiddish, were published in 1912 in leading periodicals of the day. In 1915 he was drafted into the Austrian army and, after serving on the Serbian front, he deserted in 1917, returning to Lvov where he witnessed the Polish pogroms against the Jews in 1918—an event which made an indelible impression on him. After the war he published poems in both Yiddish and Hebrew and soon became a leader of a group of Yiddish expressionist poets (including Perez *Markish) and the editor of a short-lived avant-garde periodical, *Albatros* (1922–23). He spent a year in Berlin (1923) and then immigrated to Ereẓ Israel (1924).

Uri Zevi Greenberg, Hebrew poet. Government Press Office, Tel Aviv.

In Ereẓ Israel, Greenberg stopped writing in Yiddish and published in Hebrew exclusively. When *Davar*, the Labor daily, was founded in 1925, he participated as one of its regular columnists. His columns were headed *Mi-Megillat ha-Yamim ha-Hem* and *Shomer Mah mi-Leyl* and expressed strong views against Zionist sloganeering and calling for self-realization through pioneering. Between 1925 and 1927 he edited the booklets *Sadan* and *Sadna Dar'ah* in which he contended that Hebrew artists must abandon "the fixed confines of art, join the Jewish collective, and wrestle with and think out the complex of problems of Jewish national life." Although during this period he was committed to the Labor Zionist movement, he already began to express extreme ultranationalistic ideas which contradicted the official line. In the wake of the Arab riots of 1929, he broke with the Labor movement, joined the ranks of the nationalist Zionist Revisionist Party, and denounced both the British government and the Zionist leadership of the *yishuv* for betraying the Zionist dream. He became active in political life and was elected as a Revisionist delegate to the *Asefat ha-Nivḥarim* (the legislative body of the *yishuv*) and to several Zionist Congresses. Between 1931 and 1934 he lived in Warsaw where he was sent by the Revisionist movement to edit its Yiddish weekly *Di Velt*. Returning to Ereẓ Israel in 1936, in his poetry and articles he attacked the moderate socialist Zionist leadership and warned of the imminent danger to European Jewry. During the final struggle against Great Britain for national independence, he identified with the *Irgun Ẓeva'i Le'ummi and following the establishment of the State of Israel was elected to Israel's Knesset as a member for the Ḥerut Party, serving from 1949 to 1951. He was awarded the Israel Prize for Hebrew Literature in 1957.

In contrast to most Hebrew writers who were committed to a secularist-humanist Zionism, Greenberg asserts a religious mystical view of Zionism as the fulfillment of the Jewish historical destiny. The Jew is, in his view, wholly other than the non-Jew, having been elected by God at the beginning of time as a holy instrument of His will. The covenant made with the Jewish Patriarch, Abraham, and renewed at Sinai, is a meta-historical event which cannot be altered by time nor ignored by Jew or gentile. The Jew exists outside of history in an eternal dimension in which mere rationality has no validity. "What shall be in the future, has already occurred in the past and what was not, shall never be. Therefore I put my trust in the future, for I hold the shape of the past before me: this is the vision and the melody. Selah, Hallelujah, and Amen" (*Reḥovot ha-Nahar*, 1951, p. 37). In Greenberg's scheme the future shall bring about the fulfillment of God's promise to establish Jewish sovereignty and the Messianic redemption. Any attempt by the Jew to shirk his cosmic role, either by default or by an attempt to imitate the value system of the unelected (Europe, the gentiles), leads him to disaster. The secular nationalism or socialism of most contemporary Jews are superficial readings of the meaning of the Jewish destiny and can only lead to a holocaust. The call for the renewal of Jewish sovereignty is an imperative of the eternal mythos of Judaism. It is neither a sociological nor historical solution of practical human needs, but an absolute value which may exact any price which its realization requires. Halfhearted attempts at Zionist fulfillment are doomed to failure whether they are inhibited by moral niceties, which are derived from alien value systems, or are diffused by human selfishness.

In his Yiddish phase, *In Malkhus fun Tselem* ("In the Kingdom of the Cross," 1922) Greenberg already foresaw the European Holocaust. His poetry from then on is obsessed with this vision of horror (*Migdal ha-Geviyyot*, "The Tower of Corpses," in *Sefer ha-Kitrug ve-ha-Emunah*, 1936). Greenberg in *Reḥovot ha-Nahar* wrote one of the most moving dirges composed about the Nazi Holocaust. The tragedy, in his view, is the logical culmination of the 2,000-year confrontation between the cross and the star of David and the six million dead are an insuperable barrier which shall eternally separate Christian from Jew. For Greenberg the Holocaust puts into question not only God's theodicy but appears as a horrible practical joke which God and history have played on the Jew: "You promised to come one day to gather and lead them proudly to Zion and to renew their kingdom, raise their king. But, behold you did not come, O God; the enemy came and gathered them all, an ingathering of exiles for annihilation. Now there is no need for redemption. Sit, sit, God, in your heavens" (*Reḥovot ha-Nahar*, p. 249). God, the Redeemer of Israel has become "the keeper of the Jewish cemetery" (p. 250).

Greenberg's God however moves outside the rational dimension and in a sudden leap of faith the poet reasserts the vision of redemption: "Will the Messiah yet come? Amen, he shall surely come." Divine history, of which Jewish history is a part, is based on an irrational paradox. Thus, out of the ashes of the crematoria, redemption will come, and out of despair faith. The Holocaust and the vision of Jewish sovereignty are two sides of the same coin of history. Greenberg's personal poetry often sings of his agony as the suffering prophet-priest of the mythos of Jewish catastrophe and redemption. In the years preceding the Holocaust, he laments the tragic fact that the multitude did not heed his terrible message of the imminent massacres, reviling him as they had always spurned their prophets in the past. He is filled with revulsion at their obstinacy and their blind concern for material trivialities in the face of disaster: "God how did I ever get here, inside the swamps—a man of vision befouled by their mud?"

He associates his national poetry with his personal history which also turns into mythos. The Jewish home in Poland, its Eden-like security of faith, his mother and father, assume archetypal dimensions. His love poetry, too, is inhabited by these primordial symbols: mother and father, Adam and Eve, Eden, primeval forests, the sea, the moon, lakes, rivers; they form a mythical landscape not very different from that of much of his national verse.

In an age when poets were concerned with formal and aesthetic problems, Greenberg's poetry is one of engagement, his poetic energy is fired by his all-consuming ideological commitment. Often in his poetry the poetic line surrenders to the overwhelming force of his rhetoric with which he pounds his readers mercilessly. At other times his verse is terse and brilliantly lyrical. While philosophically he rejects European aesthetics and the European poetic tradition, in practice he sometimes uses its devices and forms. More frequently his formal resources are indigenously Jewish: the Bible, medieval dirges, and concepts and statements drawn from kabbalistic literature. His early commitment to expressionism is retained throughout and is evidenced by his rhetorical flourishes, changing rhythms within the poem and sometimes even in one single line, wild metaphors, free verse, and his frequently irregular rhyme patterns.

His anti-humanist approach and ultranationalism, although mitigated by a commitment to Jewish ethical values, is not representative of contemporary Jewish thought. But Hebrew literary criticism has recognized the poetic genius of Greenberg though it rarely shares his ideology. Not that Greenberg's views lack a genuine Jewish basis; they are often deeply rooted in the Jewish subconscious and when expressed expose the raw nerve of the Jewish historical experience. But Greenberg's ideology reflects only one aspect of the Jewish soul—the particularistic, aristocratic sense of election—and often ignores its universalistic humanist character.

U. Z. Greenberg's main works include:

In Yiddish: *Ergiz oyf Felder* (1915); *In Zaytens Roysh* (1919); *Krig oyf der Erd* (1921); *Farnakhtengold* (1921); *Mefiste* (1921, 1922[2]).

In Hebrew: *Eimah Gedolah ve-Yare'aḥ* (1925); *Ha-Gavrut ha-Olah* (1926); *Ḥazon Aḥad ha-Ligyonot* (1928); *Anacreon al Kotev ha-Izzavon* (1928); *Kelappei Tishim ve-Tishah* (1928); *Kelev Bayit* (1919); *Ezor Magen u-Ne'um Ben ha-Dam* (1930); *Sefer ha-Kitrug ve-ha-Emunah* (1937); *Min ha-Ḥakhlil ve-El ha-Kaḥol* (in *Lu'aḥ Haaretz*, 1949); *Al Da'at ha-Nes ha-Nikhsaf* (1951); *Mi-Tokh Sefer he-Agol* (in *Lu'aḥ Haaretz*, 1950); *Menofim Reḥokei Mahut* (*ibid.*, 1951, 1952); *Reḥovot ha-Nahar—Sefer ha-Ilyot ve-ha-Ko'aḥ* (1951); *Massa ve-Nevel* (in *Lu'aḥ Haaretz*, 1953); *Shirei Aspaklar be-Hai Alma* (*ibid.*, 1955); *Massekhet ha-Matkonet ve-ha-Demut* (in *Moznayim*, 1954); *Be-Fisat ha-Arig u-ve-Ḥelkat ha-Ḥevel* (*ibid.*, 1965).

For English translations see Goell, Bibliography, 776–825.

Bibliography: B. Kurzweil, *Bein he-Ḥazon le-vein ha-Absurdi* (1966) 3–99; J. H. Yeivin, *Uri Ẓevi Greenberg, Meshorer Meḥokek* (1938); idem (ed.), *Be-Ikkevei ha-Shir* (1949–50); J. Klausner, *Mi-Shenei Olamot* (1944), 209–15; idem, *Meshorerei Dorenu* (1956), 235–49; A. Liphshitz, *Uri Ẓevi Greenberg, Meshorer Adnut ha-Ummah* (1945); A. Ukhmani, *Le-Ever ha-Adam* (1953), 290–8; Y. T. Helman, *Hagut u-Demut* (1963), 124–41; S. Y. Penueli, *Demuyyot be-Sifrutenu ha-Ḥadashah* (1946), 124–30; idem, *Sifrut ki-Feshutah* (1963), 206–21; D. A. Friedman, *Iyyunei Shirah* (1964), 294–8; M. Ribalow, *Sefer ha-Massot* (1928), 146–59; Y. Rabinowitz, *Be-Ḥavlei Doram* (1959), 21–67; G. Katzenelson, *ibid.*, 21 (1966), 307–14; J. Friedlaender, *Iyyunim be-Shirat Uri Ẓevi Greenberg* (1966) (incl. bibl.); J. D. Abramsky, in: *Yad la-Kore*, 7 (1963–69), 79–86 (bibl.); Waxman, Literature, 4 (1960) 324–27.

[E.Sp.]

GREENEBAUM, Chicago family in second half of the 19th–20th centuries, originating in Eppelsheim, Germany; among the early Jewish settlers in Chicago. The brothers Michael and Jacob Greenebaum went to Chicago in 1846; the first of the family to arrive. Two other brothers, Elias and Henry, arrived in 1848. A few members of the family joined the California gold rush in 1849. However, the majority remained in Chicago and became involved in Jewish and civic affairs there.

Elias Greenebaum (1822–1919) worked for two years in a dry goods store after coming to Chicago and then became a clerk in the banking house of Richard K. Swift. In 1855 he and Henry founded the Greenebaum Brothers Banking House. In 1877 Elias organized the banking house under the firm name of Greenebaum Sons, which subsequently was incorporated as a state bank in 1911 under the name Greenebaum Sons Bank & Trust Company. The name was changed to Greenebaum Sons Investment Co. in 1921. Through consolidation with other companies it became successively the Bank of America, Central Trust Co. of Illinois, and Central-Republic Bank & Trust Co. Greenebaum and Associates and the Greenebaum Mortgage Co. still existed in 1970. Elias Greenebaum led the adherents of the Reform group when Chicago's only (at the time) congregation Kehilath Anshe Maarav split into Orthodox and Reform factions. He was a founder of the Juedischer Reformverein (1858), which founded Congregation Sinai, the first Reform congregation in Chicago (1861). He was director, treasurer, and vice-president of this congregation at various times.

Michael Greenebaum (1824–1894) became a tinner and plumber after his arrival in Chicago. Active in the Abolitionist movement, he led a crowd that freed a slave held prisoner by a U.S. marshall (1853). He founded and was the first president of the Hebrew Benevolent Society (1854), and a founder of the Chicago Public Library, the Chicago Historical Society, the Astronomical Society, the 82nd Illinois Volunteer Regiment of Veterans, and the Ramah Lodge of B'nai B'rith. Later, he was the first president of the District Grand Lodge 6 of B'nai B'rith. He also founded and was first president of the Zion Literary Society (1877).

Henry Greenebaum (1833–1914) was a hardware salesman, and then a clerk in Richard K. Swift's banking house before founding the Greenebaum Brothers Banking House with Elias. He later became president of the German Savings Bank. Henry served as secretary and honorary member of Orthodox Congregation B'nai Sholom, was a founder and first president of the United Hebrew Relief Association in 1859, a founder of Congregation Sinai, first president of Congregation Zion (Reform), and later first president of Isaiah Congregation. He was the first Jew to serve on the City Council, as alderman from the Sixth Ward (1856), was a presidential elector on the Douglas ticket (1860), represented Cook County on the first Equalization Board (1856), and was a member of the West Chicago Park Commission. He was also a patron of the arts, the first president of the Beethoven Society (1876), and the first president of the Orpheus Maennerchor.

Henry Everett Greenebaum (1858–1934), Elias' elder son, was born in Chicago. A partner in the family banking business, he became treasurer of the first Chicago Home for Aged Jews, in 1893. Moses Ernst Greenebaum (1858–1934), Elias' second son, was also a partner in the family banking business. He was chairman of the Chicago Community branch of the Jewish Welfare Board, vice-president of Michael Reese Hospital, treasurer of the Jewish Historical Society of Illinois, treasurer of the Citizens Association of Chicago, and president of Sinai Congregation (1906–29). James E. Greenebaum (b. 1866) was treasurer of the Chicago Home for Jewish Orphans in 1893. Edgar N. Greenebaum (b. 1890) served on the Chicago Board of Education. [M.A.G.]

GREENFIELD, ALBERT MONROE (1887–1967), U.S. financier and civic leader. Greenfield, who was born in Kiev, Ukraine, was taken to the U.S. at the age of five. He worked at several jobs before he entered the real estate field, founding Albert M. Greenfield and Company. By the time he was 30, Greenfield had amassed a multi-million dollar fortune. Upon his retirement in 1956, his company was one of the largest real estate firms in the U.S. Greenfield lost much of his first fortune when his Bankers Trust Company was compelled to close in the early days of the depression of the 1930s, and subsequently made another. In the 1950s and 1960s he took pride in his designation as "Mr. Philadelphia," because the Greenfield interests controlled so many department stores, hotels, and specialty shops, through his City Stores holding company, and because his participation was solicited for every conceivable philanthropic and civic cause. Greenfield was also extremely active politically and was considered a power in Philadelphia politics. He was a member of the Philadelphia Common Council (1917–20), and was extremely close to William S. Vare, the boss of the Philadelphia Republican machine. Although he seconded Herbert Hoover's nomination in 1928, from 1934 on he was identified with the Democratic Party (while continuing to give financial and other support to occasional Republican candidates). He served as a delegate to all the Democratic national conventions from 1948 through 1964. Greenfield was a member of the influential Jewish delegation which waited upon President Harry S. *Truman the night/morning he granted U. S. recognition to Israel. Greenfield was close to President Lyndon B. *Johnson, because he had been a member of the small group that supported Johnson for president in 1960. Greenfield was never wholly committed to a single Jewish cause or institution; he accepted the usual board memberships and honors, took pride in his early service as a trustee of the Jewish Institute of Religion, and in the decisive role which he played in the merger of three Jewish hospitals in Philadelphia in 1951. At one time, the National Conference of Christians and Jews briefly stimulated his interest, and through its agency he endowed a Center for Human Relations at the University of Pennsylvania. [B.W.K.]

GREENSTEIN, HARRY (1896–), U.S. social worker. Greenstein was born in Baltimore, Maryland. From 1928 until his retirement he served as executive director of the Associated Jewish Charities of Baltimore. Greenstein also served as State Relief administrator during 1933–36. He was director of welfare in the Middle East for the United Nations Relief and Rehabilitation Agency (UNRRA) from 1944–45 and in 1949 was the advisor to the American military governor on Jewish affairs in Germany. In the latter position, Greenstein was instrumental in the passage of the General Claims Law, which applied to reparations in the American zone and served as a basis for the 1952 Federal Supplementing and Coordinating Law in West Germany. He also helped to arrange for the care and resettlement of displaced persons. He was elected to the presidencies of the Baltimore Council of Social Agencies (1935–39), National Conference of Jewish Community Service (1937–38), and American Association of Social Workers (1939–40).

Bibliography: L. L. Kaplan and T. Schuchat, *Justice, Not Charity* (1967). [K.D.R.]

GREENSTONE, JULIUS HILLEL (1873–1955), U.S. educator and author. Greenstone was born in Mariampol, Lithuania, and emigrated to the United States in 1894. He studied at the City College of New York and the Jewish Theological Seminary of America, where he was ordained in 1900. In 1905 he joined the faculty of Gratz College, where he taught Jewish education and religion. He was principal of the college from 1933 to 1948. From 1902 on he maintained a modest Jewish bookshop in his home, toward which rabbis and everyone else interested in Jewish education gravitated to obtain books as well as advice and guidance. Greenstone was among the first American Jews to produce books of popular Jewish scholarship in English. His *The Religion of Israel* (1902) was later rewritten and expanded into *The Jewish Religion* (1920). *The Messiah Idea in Jewish History* (1906) was the first work in English to examine historically the messianic idea in Jewish literature. His commentaries on the biblical books Numbers and Proverbs appeared in the series *Holy Scriptures with Commentary*, published by the Jewish Publication Society (1939). He contributed articles to the *Jewish Encyclopedia* (1901). For some twenty years he contributed a popular though scholarly column to the Philadelphia weekly *Jewish Exponent*. Some of these essays were collected and republished in *Jewish Feasts and Fasts* (1945). [S.C.]

GREENWALD, JEKUTHIEL JUDAH (Leopold; 1889–1955), U.S. rabbi and scholar. Greenwald, born in Hungary, studied in yeshivot in that country and in Frankfort on the Main under Neḥemiah *Nobel. In 1924 he settled in the United States, where he was the rabbi of Orthodox congregations in New York and Columbus, Ohio. Greenwald, who wrote numerous monographs and articles in Hungarian, Yiddish, and Hebrew, was especially interested in rabbinic authorities and Jewish communities of Hungary, on which he wrote *Ha-Yehudim be-Ungarya* (1913) and *Toyznt Yor Idish Lebn in Ungarn* (1945). His work *Le-Toledot ha-Reformaẓyon ha-Datit be-Germanyah u-ve-Ungarya* (1948) is a history of the Reform movement in Germany and Hungary (this work contains a bibliography of Greenwald's work up to 1948 and an evaluation by C. Bloch, 1–28, second pagination). He also wrote works on the history of the Sanhedrin and biographies of leading rabbis, such as Joseph Caro and Moses Sofer. In the latter category are *Beit Yehonatan* (1908) about Jonathan *Eybeschuetz, and *Toledot Mishpaḥat Rosenthal* (1920) about the Rosenthal family, which included several rabbis. Greenwald compiled an important manual of traditional laws and rites of mourning, *Kol-Bo Avelut* (3 vols., 1947–52).

Bibliography: N. Katzburg, in: *Sinai*, 37 (1955), 277–81; 40 (1957), 313–4; Kressel, Leksikon, 1 (1965), 511–2; EẒD, 1 (1958), 589–96. [El.S.]

GREETINGS AND CONGRATULATIONS. Although Jews have adopted the languages of the countries in which they live, they have always tended to retain traditional forms of greetings and congratulations either in Hebrew or Yiddish and occasionally in Aramaic, and some of these forms of greetings are adaptations of biblical verses while others are taken from the liturgy. Many are merely the expression of an emotion in Hebrew or Yiddish without any literary source. In the list below the most common forms of greetings are given; the list does not include the many variations which sometimes exist nor does it include simple translations such as *boker tov* (=good morning).

The traditional salutation, "Blessed shalt thou be when thou comest in, and blessed shalt thou be when thou goest out" (Deut. 28:6), on a fragment from a Bible, Egypt (?), 13th century (?). Cambridge University Library, Or. Ms. 1080, J. 50.

		Hebrew	Literal meaning	Occasions when said	Origin and/or reference
GREETINGS AND CONGRATULATIONS–GENERAL FORMS OF					
1	Shalom or Shalom lekha	שָׁלוֹם / שָׁלוֹם לְךָ	Peace / Peace to you	As a common greeting equivalent to "hello," "goodbye," "good day."	Gen. 29:6, 43:27, Ex. 18:7; Judg. 6:24 I. Sam. 16:4
2	Shalom aleikhem	שָׁלוֹם עֲלֵיכֶם	Peace to you	As above.	
3	Aleikhem shalom	עֲלֵיכֶם שָׁלוֹם	To you, peace	Response to greeting No. 2.	
4	Barukh ha-ba	בָּרוּךְ הַבָּא	Blessed be the one who comes.	A common greeting, equivalent to "welcome." A child brought to the circumcision ceremony and a bride and groom approaching the wedding canopy are also greeted thus. The response to the greeting is No. 5 or 6.	Ps. 118:26
5	Barukh ha-nimẓa	בָּרוּךְ הַנִּמְצָא	Blessed be the one (already) present.	Response to greeting No. 4.	
6	Barukh ha-yoshev	בָּרוּךְ הַיּוֹשֵׁב	Blessed be the one who is sitting.	Response to greeting No. 4 Used by a guest to the host sitting at the head of the table.	
7	Shalom berakhah ve-tovah	שָׁלוֹם בְּרָכָה וְטוֹבָה	Peace, blessing and (all) good (to you).	General blessing used by Sephardi Jews.	
8	Ḥazak u-varukh	חֲזַק וּבָרוּךְ	Be strong and blessed.	As above. **Also used in Sephardi synagogues to a person who returns to his seat after having performed liturgical functions.**	
9	Yishar koḥakha or Yasher ko'akh	יִישַׁר כֹּחֲךָ (Yiddish)	May your strength (increase) go straight.	Congratulations for success and achievement. In traditional synagogues also extended to a person who has been called up to the Torah reading.	
10	Ḥazak ve-emaẓ	חֲזַק וֶאֱמָץ	Be strong and of good courage.	Congratulations for success and achievement. Also extended to a bar mitzvah boy after he has finished reading the *haftarah*.	e.g. Deut 31:23
11	Biz hundert un tsvantsik	(Yiddish)	(May you live) until the age of 120	A wish for long life.	
12	Tsu gezunt	(Yiddish)	Good health.	To a person who has sneezed; also to someone convalescing.	
13	*a.* Li-veri'ut	לִבְרִיאוּת	Good health.	As above.	
	b. Asuta	אָסוּתָא (Aramaic)	Good health.		
14	Refu'ah shelemah	רְפוּאָה שְׁלֵמָה	(May you have) a complete recovery.	Wish to a sick person.	
SABBATH AND HOLIDAY GREETINGS					
15	*a.* Shabbat shalom Gut shabes.	שַׁבַּת שָׁלוֹם (Yiddish)	Good Sabbath	The Sabbath greeting.	
	b. Shabbat hi mi-lizok u-refu'ah kerovah lavo	שַׁבַּת הִיא מִלִּזְעֹק וּרְפוּאָה קְרוֹבָה לָבוֹא	It is Sabbath and forbidden to make supplications but may you soon get well.	When visiting the sick on the Sabbath.	Shab. 12a.
16	*a.* Shavu'a tov *b.* A gute vokh	שָׁבוּעַ טוֹב (Yiddish)	A good week.	A greeting on Saturday night at the end of the Sabbath.	

No.		Hebrew	Literal meaning	Occasions when said	Origin and/or reference
17	Gut khoydesh	(Yiddish)	A good new month.	On new moons.	
18	Gut Yontev	(Yiddish) corrupted from the Hebrew Yom Tov	A good holiday (to you).	On holidays and festivals.	
19	*a.* Mo'adim le-simḥah *b.* Ḥag same'aḥ	מוֹעֲדִים לְשִׂמְחָה חַג שָׂמֵחַ	Joyous holidays. Joyous holiday.	On festivals. The response to which is No. 20.	
20	Ḥaggim u-zemannim lesason	חַגִּים וּזְמַנִּים לְשָׂשׂוֹן	Holidays and festivals for joy and gladness.	Response to No. 19a, 19b.	This wording is from the prayer for the three festivals.
21	Ve-hayita akh same'aḥ	וְהָיִיתָ אַךְ שָׂמֵחַ	You shall have nothing but joy.	On Sukkot, when visiting a person in his *sukkah*.	Deut. 16:15
	NEW YEAR AND DAY OF ATONEMENT				
22	*a.* Shanah tovah	שָׁנָה טוֹבָה	A good year (to you), or its more ample version:	During the Days of Penitence.	The wording is from the prayers *'Amidah and 'Avinu Malkenu*
	b. Le-shanah tovah tikkatevu (ve-teḥatemu)	לְשָׁנָה טוֹבָה תִּכָּתֵבוּ (וְתֵחָתֵמוּ)	May you be inscribed (and sealed) for a good year (i.e. in the Book of Life), or its shorter form:		
	c. Ketivah tovah	כְּתִיבָה טוֹבָה	A good inscription (in the Book of Life).		
23	Gam le-mar	גַּם לְמַר	To you too.	Response to one of the greetings in Nos. 22a, b, c. and 24 a, b.	
24	*a.* Ḥatimah tovah or	חֲתִימָה טוֹבָה	A sealing for good (to you), or its more ample version:	On the Day of Atonement, the day of "Sealing the book".	Wording from the prayerbook.
	b. Gemar ḥatimah tovah	גְּמַר חֲתִימָה טוֹבָה	A propitious final sealing (to you) (in the Book of Life).	As above. This form can be used until 'Hoshana Rabba.	
	ON JOYOUS OCCASIONS AND FAMILY EVENTS				
25	*a.* Mazzal tov	מַזָּל טוֹב	Good luck (i.e., may you enjoy a favorable zodiac constellation).	For joyous occasions, especially child-birth, betrothal, wedding, bar-mitzvah, etc. . .	Ashkenazi custom.
	b. Be-siman tov	בְּסִימָן טוֹב	As above	As above	Sephardi custom.
26	Barukh tihyeh	בָּרוּךְ תִּהְיֶה	Be you be blessed (too), (i.e., the same to you).	Response to Mazzal Tov wish.	
27	Le-ḥayyim or	לְחַיִּים	To life.	On taking a drink, usually alcoholic.	Shab. 67 b.
28	Le-ḥayyim tovim u-le-shalom	לְחַיִּים טוֹבִים וּלְשָׁלוֹם	Good life and peace (to you).	More ample form of No. 27.	
	DURING MOURNING				
29	Ha-Makom yenaḥem etkhem be-tokh avelei Ẓiyyon vi-Yrushalayim	הַמָּקוֹם יְנַחֵם אֶתְכֶם בְּתוֹךְ אֲבֵלֵי צִיּוֹן וִירוּשָׁלַיִם	May the Lord comfort you among all mourners for Zion and Jerusalem.	To a mourner during the week of mourning.	See: 'Mourning
	ON YAHRZEIT				
30	Ad bi'at ha-go'el	עַד בִּיאַת הַגּוֹאֵל	(May you live) until the coming of the Messiah.	On the yearly anniversary of the death of a relative.	Among German Jews.
	IN WRITTEN FORM ONLY (INITIALS)				
31	Ad me'ah shanah	עַד מֵאָה שָׁנָה (עמ"ש)	Until a hundred years.	In the heading of a private letter, after the addressee's name.	

		Hebrew	Literal meaning	Occasions when said	Origin and/or reference
32	Zekhuto yagen aleinu	זְכוּתוֹ יָגֵן עָלֵינוּ (זי״ע)	May his merit protect us.	After name of distinguished deceased; usually ḥasidic.	
33	Zikhrono li-verakhah or Zekher ẓaddik li-verakhah	זִכְרוֹנוֹ לִבְרָכָה (ז״ל) זֵכֶר צַדִּיק לִבְרָכָה (זצ״ל)	May his memory be for a blessing. May the memory of the pious be for a blessing.	After name of deceased; also in speech.	
34	Alav ha-shalom	עָלָיו הַשָּׁלוֹם (ע״ה)	Peace be on him.	As above.	
35	Natreih Raḥamana u-varkhei	נַטְרֵיה רַחֲמָנָא וּבַרְכֵיה (נר״ו) (Aramaic)	May God guard and bless him (you).	Written form of address.	
36	She-yiḥyeh le-orekh yamim tovim amen	שֶׁיִּחְיֶה לְאֹרֶךְ יָמִים טוֹבִים אָמֵן (שליט״א)	May he (you) live for many good days, Amen.	As above.	

°**GRÉGOIRE, HENRI BAPTISTE (Abbé Grégoire;** 1750–1831), Catholic clergyman, one of the activists of the *French Revolution. Grégoire led the campaign for the civic emancipation of the Jews before and during the Revolution. In the secular field, he held enlightened-revolutionary opinions, while in the religious field his outlook was neo-Jansenist. It was one of the principal expectations of the Jansenists that the Revolution would bring about the reform of the universe at the millennium and with it the return of Jews to the Christian religion and the Land of Israel. Grégoire adhered to these expectations, and the Jewish problem thus at first became the focal point upon which his secular activities and religious hopes converged. In 1785, Grégoire took part in a competition held by the Société Royale des Arts et Sciences of Metz on the question: "Are there possibilities of making the Jews more useful and happier in France?" His work, which shared the first prize, was published in 1789 under the title *Essai sur la régénération physique, morale, et politique des Juifs* (*Essay on the Physical, Moral and Political Reformation of the Jews,* London, c. 1791). In it Grégoire suggests that the Jews should be westernized and integrated within French society. He repeats the claim, which had already been voiced before him, that the main social and moral shortcomings of the Jews were due to the servitude to which they had been subjected. Amelioration of their status would also achieve reform of their character. Grégoire was, however, more extreme than C. W. *Dohm or *Mirabeau in pressing for the abolition of the fundamental causes of Jewish social and political separatism: communal autonomy, the Jewish quarters, Yiddish, and the "superstitious beliefs" to which the Jews adhered because they were misled by their rabbis. Grégoire however dismissed the traditional Christian claim that the Jews must suffer because of their sins as deicides. On this subject he said: "The oracles which announced the destruction of Jerusalem point out the distant moment at which the consequences of it are to end. The Deity directs every event in a manner agreeable to His supreme views; and perhaps He reserves for us the glory of realizing His designs in preparing by our humanity the revolution by which these people are to be reformed."

The opinions expressed in his work were the basis for his political and publicistic activities concerning the Jews from 1789 to 1806. Grégoire played an active and energetic role in raising the question of the Jews in the French National Assembly until emancipation was granted to them in September 1791. Among his other activities, he presented the delegation of Alsace-Lorraine Jews to the National Assembly on Oct. 14, 1789, in connection with which he published a *Motion en faveur des Juifs,* which was a summary of his *Essai* drafted in a more revolutionary spirit. In 1802, while on a tour of Europe, he preached, advocating the emancipation of the Jews. In 1806, he published a pamphlet in answer to *Bonald's objections to the civic emancipation of French Jews. After *Napoleon Bonaparte's rise to power, Grégoire gradually withdrew from political activity and became increasingly engrossed in his religious

Henri Grégoire, French clergyman who advocated the emancipation of the Jews. Courtesy Alliance Israélite Universelle, Paris.

and eschatological hopes, which centered on the expectation of the fall of Rome and the renewed establishment of a Jewish Jerusalem as the capital of a reconstituted Christian world. He organized a Franco-Italian circle which propagated these expectations. One of the members of this circle was A. Manzoni, a father of the Italian national movement. Later publications of his include *Observations nouvelles sur les Juifs, et spécialement sur ceux d'Allemagne* (2 vols., 1806), and *Histoire des sectes religieuses* (2 vols., 1810).

Bibliography: H. Carnot (ed.), *Mémoires de H. Grégoire* (1838); P. Grunebaum-Ballin, *L'Abbé Grégoire et les Juifs* (1931); idem, in: REJ, 121 (1962), 383–96; F. Ruffini, *La vita religiosa di Alessandro Manzoni*, 2 (1931); M. Ginsburger, in: *Festschrift zu S. Dubnows 70ten Geburtstag* (1930), 201–6; A. Hertzberg, *French Enlightenment and the Jews* (1968), index.

[B.M.]

°**GREGORY,** name of 16 popes.

Gregory I (the Great), pope 590–604; the most important of the earlier popes from the point of view of Jewish history. It was he who formulated the Jewish policy of the papacy, faithfully followed in subsequent generations in both its favorable and its unfavorable aspects. Complaining bitterly in his sermons of the obduracy of the Jews and their stony hearts, he took care that the canonical restrictions against them should be obeyed in all their rigor. Twenty-eight of his 800 extant letters deal with Jewish matters. He strongly objected to the observance of any ceremonies that savored of Judaism or tended to obscure the boundaries between Church and Synagogue. Although approving of the initial stages of the reactions against the Jews in Spain under the *Visigoths, nevertheless he insisted that the Jews should be treated with humanity, and endeavored to have their legal rights confirmed and respected. The Jews of Italy and other countries frequently appealed to Gregory for protection. He was indignant when synagogues were destroyed, and ordered them to be rebuilt. While condemning forced baptisms, he did not object to the offering of material benefits to prospective converts; although such actual converts might be insincere, their children would be brought up as faithful Christians. One of his epistles, beginning with the words *Sicut Judaeis*, emphasized that the Jews must be protected in the enjoyment of those rights guaranteed to them by law, and this phrase was prefixed (from the 12th century onward) to the traditional protective *bull generally issued by every pope on his accession. [C.R.]

Gregory IX, pope 1227–41. Shortly after his election, Gregory granted the crusaders against the *Albigenses a moratorium on their debts to Jews and canceled the interest due. In 1229, he laid down that a Jewish child who had been baptized by his converted father was to be entrusted to the father and not to the mother, if she remained Jewish. During the same year, he also ordered that strong measures be taken against Jews who refused to pay the church tithes (which were due on houses acquired from Christians). Although the collection of decretals drawn up by *Raymond of Peñafort (as a continuation of the decree of Gratian) in 1230 and promulgated by Gregory in 1234 includes Gregory the Great's letter on the protection of synagogues, it also contains two texts from the Third Lateran Council which are unfavorable to the Jews (see *Church Councils). Intervening against the Jews of Hungary, Castile, and Portugal in 1231, he insisted on the observation of the canons relating to the Jewish *badge and the prohibition on the appointment of Jews to public office. In 1233, in Germany, he also condemned the employment of Christian servants by the Jews. However, during the same year, he issued the protective bull *Etsi Judaeorum* and in 1235 reminded all Christians of the terms of the bull *Sicut Judaeis*. Similarly, on Sept. 5, 1236, he issued orders to several archbishops and bishops of southwestern and western France to compel the crusaders to make good the losses the Jews had suffered at their hands. On several occasions from 1237 on Gregory replied to the anxieties expressed by King Louis IX of France over the use which should be made of the money paid by the Jews, inevitably derived from usury; the pope advised the king to employ this money for the relief of Constantinople or the Holy Land. Nicholas *Donin turned to Gregory with his denunciation of the Talmud; however, although he issued the order impounding the Talmud for an examination of its contents, its actual condemnation was pronounced by Pope *Innocent IV.

Gregory X, pope 1271–76; one of the popes most kindly disposed toward the Jews. Renewing the bull of protection *Sicut Judaeis* in 1272, he added an important clause: an accusation against Jews based solely on the testimony of Christians was invalid; Jewish witnesses must also appear. Gregory vigorously combated the *blood libel, declaring that it was no more than an invention propagated in order to extort money from the Jews. He ordered that tribunals were not even to take such accusations into consideration: Jews who had been imprisoned on this charge were to be set free immediately, and in future a Jew was only to be arrested if actually caught in the act. At the Council of Lyons, in the summer of 1274, Gregory met *Nathan b. Joseph Official, with whom he had a lengthy discussion. In a memorandum drawn up for this council by Humbert of Romans in support of Gregory's policy, a long passage comes to the defense of the Jews against future attacks by crusaders. It should be noted, however, that Gregory also renewed the bull of Clement IV, *Turbato Corde,* which delivered the Jews (relapsed converts and their accomplices) into the hands of the Inquisition.

Gregory XIII, pope 1572–85. It may be common knowledge that this pope reformed the calendar, but it is less well-known that Jews most probably contributed to this. Gregory's policy toward the Jews cannot be distinctly characterized, since it swayed between relative favor and severity. Soon after his election, he protected the Jews in the ghetto of Rome who were in danger of being attacked by the soldiers. Further, an order issued by his notary threatened with hanging any non-Jew found in the ghetto or its vicinity without a valid reason. Gregory authorized once more moneylending with a maximum interest rate of 24%. A warrant of June 10, 1577 confirmed the statutes of the Jewish community and permitted the collection of taxes. In 1581, he guaranteed the safe-conduct of Jews coming into Italy or passing through the country. Although Marranos were also able to benefit from this concession, Gregory nevertheless allowed the Marrano Joseph Saralbo, who had returned to Judaism in Ferrara, to be condemned to the stake in 1583. Gregory was also responsible for organizing regular compulsory missionary sermons, often with the collaboration of apostate preachers (see *Sermons to Jews). The Jewish community was compelled to defray the costs of this institution, as well as the expenses of the House of *Catechumens. In order that converts should not be defrauded of their share in the family fortune, Gregory ordered that an inventory of a family's belongings be drawn up immediately after the baptism of one of its members. The bull *Antiqua Judaeorum improbitas,* of June 1, 1581, authorized the Inquistion directly to handle cases involving Jews, especially those concerning blasphemies against Jesus or Mary, incitement to heresy or assistance to heretics, possession of forbidden books, or the employment of Christian wet nurses. During the same year, however, following the intervention by Avtalion *Modena, Gregory suspended the order which he had just issued confiscating the books of several Jewish communities of Italy. In 1581, he also exempted the Jews from wearing the badge on certain occasions (journeys, visits to fairs). The new prohibitions against Jewish physicians treating Christian patients contributed to the decline of medical science among Italian Jews. However, shortly before his death, Gregory intervened with the Knights of Malta to obtain the release of Jewish prisoners in their hands, even though the ransom he offered was lower than the sum demanded. [B.BL.]

Bibliography: GREGORY I: S. Katz, in: JQR, 34 (1933/34), 113–36; B. Blumenkranz, *Juifs et chrétiens dans le monde occidental 430–1096* (1960), passim. GREGORY IX: S. Grayzel, *Church and the Jews in the XIIIth Century* (1966²), passim; Vogelstein-Rieger, 211, 232–37; L. Auvray (ed.), *Les registres de Gregory IX*, 4 vols. (1890–1955); E. Friedberg (ed.), *Décrétales* (1881); A. Clerval, in: *Dictionnaire de Théologie Catholique*, 6 (1924), 1805–6. GREGORY X: S. Grayzel, *Church and the Jews in the XIIIth Century* (1966²), index; Vogelstein-Rieger, 244f.; L. Gatto, *Il pontificato di Gregorio X* (1959), passim; P. A. Throop, *Criticism of the Crusade* (1940), 166ff. GREGORY XIII: Vogelstein-Rieger, 169–76; Roth, Italy, 315–7 and passim; Milano, Italia, 255–7 and passim; L. v. Pastor, *Storia dei Papi*, 9 (1955), passim.

GREGORY, SIR THEODORE (1890–1971), British economist. Gregory, who was born in London, taught at the London School of Economics from 1913 to 1919. He was professor of economics at the University of London from 1917 to 1937 and from 1929 to 1930 was dean of the faculty. In addition to his teaching activities, Gregory served from 1929 to 1931 on the Macmillan Committee on Industry and Finance which laid the basis for the renewal of Britain's financial system. At various times he also acted as an adviser to the governments of Australia, New Zealand, Greece, India, and the Irish Free State. His main fields were general and monetary economics, and his numerous publications include *Gold, Unemployment, and Capitalism* (1933), *The Gold Standard and its Future* (1932, 1935³), *India on the Eve of the Third Five-Year Plan* (1961), and *Ernest Oppenheimer and the Economic Development of Southern Africa* (1962). He was knighted in 1942. [J.O.R.]

°**GREGORY OF TOURS** (**Georgius Florentius**; 538–594), bishop of Tours from 573. Most of the information on the Jews in Merovingian France during the second half of the sixth century comes from Gregory. He was present at—and later participated in—the disputation held between King Chilperic and the Jew *Priscus in 581, which he describes in his *Historia Francorum*. This same work contains a report on the forced conversion of Jews in *Clermont-Ferrand in 576 and Chilperic's forcible attempt to impose conversion throughout his whole kingdom in 582. Gregory is also the source testifying to the ancient presence of Jews in Tours, Marseilles, Orléans, Bourges, and other places. His works contain invaluable information on the economic and social conditions of the Jews. The manner in which he often introduces Jews into his tales of miracles is curious: their function is in a sense a guarantee to the authenticity of his narrative. It was Gregory who introduced into the West two legends of oriental origin, concerning "the Jewish child of the blazing furnace" (who had taken communion and been punished by his father, but saved by the virgin Mary) and the desecrated icon (a painting representing Jesus, lacerated by the Jews, which had supposedly begun to bleed); these two legends are of grave significance because one was the distant source of the *blood libel and the other of the *Host desecration accusation.

Bibliography: B. Blumenkranz, *Auteurs chrétiens latins* (1963), 67–73; idem, *Juifs et chrétiens...* (1960), index; F. Cayre, *Patrologie* (1945), 264–67. [B.BL.]

GRENOBLE, capital of the Isère department, France, formerly capital of Dauphiné. A lamentation on the martyrdom of ten Jews from Grenoble was incorporated in the Bourguignon *maḥzor* in the second half of the 13th century. After the Jews were expelled from France in 1306, Dauphin Humbert I allowed a number of them to settle in Grenoble, offering them relatively favorable privileges. However, at the time of the *Black Death in 1348, 74 Jews were arrested and, after a trial lasting three months, were burned at the stake. Apart from isolated individuals, there were no Jews in Grenoble until 1717, when a group from Comtat Venaissin attempted to settle there; they were driven out by the city parliament. A new community was formed after the Revolution.

Holocaust and Postwar Periods. During World War II Grenoble, first occupied by the Italians, and later by the Germans, was an important center offering a base shelter for Jewish resistance of every kind: armed resistance, rescue of children, and hiding and "camouflage" of adults. The *Gestapo became especially active from 1943 on, made numerous arrests, and tortured and deported many people. Marc Haguenau (for whom a Jewish group of the French underground was named) was tortured and killed in Grenoble; the young Denis *Marx was killed there by Brunner, the former commandant of *Drancy. Léonce Bernheim, a noted Zionist leader, and his wife were arrested in the vicinity of Grenoble. The *Centre de Documentation Juive Contemporaine was clandestinely created in Grenoble by Isaac *Schneersohn. After the war, many refugees stayed in the city, and by 1960 the Jewish population numbered over 1,000. In the 1960s the Jewish population increased rapidly reaching about 5,000 in 1969, including immigrants from North Africa. The community engaged a rabbi and maintains a range of institutions, including a synagogue and community center.

Bibliography: Gross, Gal Jud (1897), 143; Ḥ. Schirmann, in: *Zion*, 19 (1954), 66; Z. Szajkowski, *Franco-Judaica* (1962), no. 310; idem, *Analytical Franco-Jewish Gazetteer* (1966), 205–9; A. Prudhomme, Histoire de Grenoble (1888), 138ff, 198. [G.LE.]

°**GRESSMAN, HUGO** (1877–1927), German Protestant theologian, student of the Bible and the ancient Orient. In 1902–07 he taught in Kiel; from 1907 until his death he was professor of Bible at the University of Berlin. His main scholarly work was on the history of Israel's religion. A disciple of Gunkel, his approach was based on the analysis of literary genres and motifs. He also sought to discover the influence of the Palestinian geographic milieu on the world view of Israel and on the way of life of the early inhabitants of Palestine. His priniciple works are: *Der Ursprung der israelitisch-juedischen Eschatologie* (1905); *Die aelteste Geschichtsschreibung und Prophetie Israels* (1910, 1921²); *Mose und seine Zeit* (1913); *Das Weihnachtsevangelium* (1914); and *Der Messias* (1929). He edited the *Altorientalische Texte zum Alten Testament* (1926²) and the *Altorientalische Bilder zum Alten Testament* (1927²); Gressman also edited the third edition of Bousset's *Die Religion des Judentums im spaethellenistischen Zeitalter* (1926³). [M.Z.S.]

GRILICHES, AVENIR (1822–1905), Russian engraver. Griliches was born in Vilna. He was self-taught, and attracted attention by engraving a striking resemblance of the czar. In 1871 he became one of the few Jews permitted to stay in St. Petersburg, where he was employed by the Imperial Mint. In 1889 and 1898 Griliches was listed officially as mint engraver at St. Petersburg. He is credited with engraving the state seals of Alexander III and Nicholas II, as well as the five ruble, one ruble, half ruble, and twenty kopeck coins. He produced some of the most distinguished Russian commemorative medals of the 1880s and 1890s. His son ABRAHAM (1852–c. 1916) also born in Vilna, graduated from the St. Petersburg Academy of Fine Arts in 1876. He was employed as an engraver at the Imperial Mint. Raised to the position of senior engraver, he is credited with striking some dies of the coinage of Nicholas II, as well as the 1912 Alexander III commemorative medal. Abraham Griliches was even more noted for his medals, for which he received awards at the Paris Exposition in 1889 and 1900. He was also an excellent gem engraver. [D.M.F.]

GRINBERG, ALEKSANDER ABRAMOVICH (1898–), Russian chemist. Grinberg studied at the University of Leningrad. In 1936 he was appointed professor of chemistry at the Lensovet Leningrad Technological Institute. In 1943 he became a corresponding member and in 1958 an academician of the U.S.S.R. Academy of Sciences, and in 1946 was awarded a Stalin Prize. He contributed many papers to Russian scientific journals, his major area being the chemistry of complex compounds. His book on this subject (1951) appeared in English as *Introduction to the Chemistry of Complex Compounds* (1962). [S.A.M.]

GRINKER, ROY RICHARD Sr. (1900–), U.S. neuropsychiatrist and psychoanalyst. Born in Chicago, Grinker taught at the University of Chicago from 1927. During World War II he rose to the rank of colonel in the U.S. Army Medical Corps. From 1946 Grinker was director of the institute for psychosomatic and psychiatric research and training at the Michael Reese Hospital in Chicago, and supervisory analyst at the Chicago Institute for Psychoanalysis. From 1951 he was clinical professor of psychiatry at the University of Illinois and in 1969 became professor of psychiatry at the University of Chicago's medical school.

Grinker was chief editor of the *Archives of General Psychiatry* from 1956. He also wrote many books and articles in his professional field. After publishing the textbook *Neurology* (1934, 1966[6]), Grinker collaborated with J. P. Spiegel in writing *Men Under Stress* (1945), an account of the treatment of war neuroses based on military personnel's experiences in North Africa. The two men developed the treatment of the emotionally traumatized soldier with a drug to promote a "catharsis" of his battle experiences. Grinker set out the results of his research in and therapy of psychosomatic disturbances in two books: *Psychosomatic*

Roy Grinker, U.S. neuropsychiatrist and psychoanalyst. Courtesy University of Chicago.

Research (1953) and (with F. P. Robbins) *Psychosomatic Case Book* (1954). He also devoted much attention to the theory of an integrated approach to normal and disturbed human behavior. He tried to elicit the relations between the intrapersonal physical and psychological systems and those with which the person interacts in his environment. Grinker's views were elaborated in two published symposia: *Toward a Unified Theory of Human Behavior* (1956), which he edited, and *Integrating the Approaches to Mental Disease* (ed. by H. D. Kruse, 1957). [Lo.M.]

GRISHABER, ISAAC (d. 1815), Hungarian rabbi. Born in Cracow, Grishaber went in 1782 to Hungary and was appointed rabbi of Paks. For an unknown reason he left this community and went to serve the community of Baja, but toward the end of his life he returned to Paks. He was in halakhic correspondence with Ezekiel *Landau, author of the *Noda bi-Yhudah,* and studied under him for a while in Prague, as well as with Moses *Sofer. Grishaber was resolute in his views and fought for them stubbornly and courageously. He was involved in a violent controversy in 1798/99 because of his dispute with Rabbi Aaron *Chorin over whether sturgeon is kasher. He published a pamphlet on the subject, *Makel No'am* (Vienna 1799), giving his reasons for forbidding this fish, with supporting letters from contemporary rabbis in Hungary and elsewhere.

Bibliography: P. Z. Schwartz, *Shem ha-Gedolim me-Ereẓ Hagar,* 1 (1913), 506 no. 227; A. Stern, *Meliẓei Esh al Ḥodshei Kislev-Adar* (1962[2]), 206 no. 67; D. Sofer, *Mazkeret Paks,* 1 (1962), 3–91.

[Sh.W.-H.]

GRODNO (Horodno), city in Belorussian S.S.R., formerly in *Poland-Lithuania. One of the oldest Jewish communities in the former grand duchy of *Lithuania (see *Poland-Lithuania), the Grodno community received a charter from Grand Duke Witold in 1389. This indicates the existence of a synagogue and cemetery and shows that Jews owned real property in the city and its environs and engaged in commerce, crafts, and agriculture. They were banished by the general decree of expulsion of the Jews from Lithuania in 1495 and their property was sequestered, but were permitted to return and to claim their possessions in 1503. During the 16th century the townsmen of Grodno were consistently hostile to the Jews, the artisans in particular. Grodno, however, became noted as a center of Jewish learning. By the end of the century a number of *battei midrash* and yeshivot had been established and Horodno was written by the Jews as though it were *Har-Adonai* ("the holy mount" in Hebrew). The community was spared during the *Chmielnicki massacres in 1648–49 and gave asylum to fugitives from the south, but later suffered from the Russian invasions of 1655–57 and subsequent invasions by the Swedes. The fanaticism of the Jesuits was from 1616 an additional spur to frequent calumnies against the Jews, and the kidnapping of Jewish children for forced conversion. The community became heavily involved in debt to pay for the defense and ransom of those victims. A *blood libel in 1790 resulted in the death of R. Eleazar b. Solomon of Virbalis (Verzhbolow). Another ritual murder accusation was made in 1816. One of the three principal communities in Lithuania, Grodno was represented on the Council of Lithuania (see *Councils of the Lands). It thus assumed responsibility for the care of Jewish affairs in general, while undertaking Jewish defense in libel cases in particular, since it was the seat of the Lithuanian court of appeal. The first Hebrew book to be published in Lithuania was printed in Grodno in 1788 in the Royal press. A second Hebrew press, established in Grodno in 1793, formed the kernel of the celebrated publishing and printing house owned by the *Romm family, whose early publications were in "Vilna and Grodno" (subsequently in Vilna).

Population Figures. In 1549 the Jewish population formed 17% of the total; in 1560 it numbered 1,000 according to one estimate, in 1764, 2,418 and in 1793, some 4,000. When Grodno passed to Russia with the third partition of Poland in 1795, the Jewish community was the largest in Lithuania after Vilna. The Jewish population numbered 8,422 in 1816 (85.3% of the total); approximately 10,300 in 1856–57 (63.3%); 27,343 in 1887 (68.7%); 27,874 in 1904 (64.1%); 34,461 in 1912 (c. 60%); 15,504 in 1916 (64.4%);

Figure 1. The wooden synagogue in Grodno, built in the latter half of the 18th century. Courtesy Yad Vashem, Jerusalem.

18,697 in 1921 (53.4%); and 21,159 in 1931 (42.6%). The decrease in the Jewish population during World War I was partly due to their expulsion to inner Russia by the Russian military authorities in 1915. The decrease relative to the general population after the war was due both to Jewish emigration from Grodno and to the official encouragement given to Poles to settle there after its conquest by the Poles in 1919.

Occupations. The principal traditional sources of income of Grodno Jews were commerce (principally in agricultural and timber products) and crafts, and more recently, industry. In 1887, 88% of commercial undertakings, 76% of factories and workshops, and 65.2% of real estate in Grodno were Jewish owned. The situation did not alter appreciably before World War I, but after Grodno's reversion to Poland the Jews were systematically ousted from their economic positions and from the middle of the 1930s a stringent anti-Jewish economic boycott was imposed. In 1921 there were 1,273 industrial enterprises and workshops in Jewish ownership, employing 3,719 persons (2,341 of them hired workers, of whom 83.2% were Jews), 34.6% for food processing (and tobacco), and 29% garment manufacturing. In 1937 there were 65 Jewish-owned large or medium-sized factories employing 2,181 workers, of whom 895 (41%) were Jews, as against 51 state-owned or non-Jewish enterprises employing 2,262 workers. Among the other main enterprises then owned by Jews were a large bicycle factory, a factory for artistic leather products, a glass factory, a lithographic plant, foundries, and breweries. Some of the plants proved good training grounds for potential immigrants to Palestine during the 1930s. The huge Y. Shereshevsky tobacco factory in Grodno employed, before World War I, some 1,800 workers and provided a livelihood for hundreds of families in subsidiary activities, nearly all Jewish. Work stopped on the Sabbath and Jewish festivals and it maintained a school for the children of the employees. The Polish government nationalized it in the 1920s, making it conform to the official pattern and the majority of the Jewish workers were forced out.

Rabbis and Authors. Among the notable rabbis serving in Grodno were Mordecai *Jaffe (16th century); Jonah b. Isaiah Te'omim, author of *Kikayon de-Yonah* (1630); Moses b. Abraham, author of *Tiferet le-Moshe* (1776); Joshua b. Joseph, author of *Meginnei Shelomo* (1715); Mordecai Suesskind of Rothenburg (17th century); and Simḥah b. Naḥman Rapoport of Dubno. The last to hold office was Benjamin Braudo (d. 1818). The dispute over the succession to the rabbinate after his death led to its abolition in Grodno and the appointment of *morei hora'ah* (decisors on law). The kabbalist and ethical pietist *Alexander Susskind, author of *Yesod ve-Shoresh ha-Avodah* and *Ẓavva'ah,* was a citizen of Grodno. Also renowned beyond Grodno in the 19th century was Nahum b. Uzziel—R. Noḥumke—a scholar who was famous for his devoted care of the poor.

Communal Institutions. In the 19th century, the Grodno community supported numerous *battei midrash* and societies formed by the **Mitnaggedim* for religious studies, which were attended regularly by people from all classes of the community. The famous scholar R. Shimon *Shkop headed the great "Sha'arei Hatorah" yeshivah in Grodno (1920–39). The Hebrew poet Abba Asher Constantin *Shapiro originated from Grodno. The Hebrew author Abraham Shalom *Friedberg and the Yiddish poet Leib *Naidus lived there. The Jewish community made outstanding provision for benevolent and welfare institutions. From the 18th century there existed the society for care of the sick (Bikkur Ḥolim). Some wealthy members of the community contributed lavishly toward establishing orphanages, hospitals, old-age homes, and an excellent trade school. One of the first loan and savings cooperative funds in Russia was opened in 1900.

Labor and Socialist Movements. A Jewish Socialist circle already existed in Grodno in 1875–76 where the first Jewish Socialists turned their attention to the working man. From the end of the 1890s the various trends of Jewish labor movements became increasingly active in Grodno, in particular in the tobacco factory. Central to the movement was the *Bund. The labor movements played an important part in organizing Jewish self-defense in Grodno in 1903 and 1907, and some Jewish youngsters there also avenged the bloodshed that resulted from the pogroms at *Bialystok. In the years between the two world wars the working movement fought for the rights of the Jewish worker to obtain employment and against anti-Jewish discrimination by the Polish government.

Zionism. A legal document of 1539 which deals with a Jewish couple who intended to leave Grodno for Jerusalem is almost a symbol of the strong roots later struck by the Ḥibbat Zion and Zionist movements in Grodno. Among Grodno Jews joining the early settlements in Ereẓ Israel in the 19th century was Fischel *Lapin, who settled in Jerusalem in 1863 and was a prominent communal worker. A society for settling in Ereẓ Israel was founded in Grodno in 1872, and a second acquired land in *Petaḥ Tikvah on its foundation in 1880, where a pioneer settler from Grodno was Mordecai *Diskin. The society of *Ḥovevei Zion in Grodno in 1890 gave generous support in building the Girls' Hebrew school in Jaffa. Grodno was one of the most active centers of Ḥovevei Zion, as also subsequently of the Zionist movement in Russia, in which the two brothers Bezalel and Leib *Jaffe were prominent. Zionist shekels were printed clandestinely in Grodno. Grodno remained one of the important centers of the Zionist movement and its constituent parties and youth movements between 1916 and 1939. During World War II, when Grodno was under Soviet rule (1939–41), a clandestine Zionist center there transferred intending immigrants to Ereẓ Israel via Vilna, then the capital of Soviet Lithuania. In the educational sphere, the reformed *ḥeder (ḥeder metukkan),* founded in Grodno in 1900 and providing instruction in Hebrew, was among the first and most successful of its type in Russia. Hebrew teachers' preparatory groups were introduced in 1901 and the famous "Pedagogic Courses" which trained numerous pioneer Hebrew teachers in 1907. After World War I the Grodno Zionists, headed by Noah Bas, instituted the Hebrew educational system *Tarbut. Jewish pioneers from Grodno emigrated in the successive *aliyot* from the beginning of the *Bilu movement, and Grodno youth were among the first to join the Second Aliyah. The Grodno *He-Ḥalutz association was among the first founded in Lithuania, and the Third Aliyah from Poland was initiated by Grodno pioneers.

Holocaust Period. Under Polish rule there were pogroms in Grodno as early as 1935. A large-scale pogrom took place between Sept. 18 and 20, 1939, during the Polish army's withdrawal from the town prior to the entry of the Soviet Army. The Nazis occupied Grodno on June 22, 1941, the day on which Germany attacked the Soviet Union. On July 7, 80 Jews in the professions were arrested and executed by the Nazi authorities. On Nov. 1, 1941, the Jews of Grodno were segregated into two ghettos, one for "skilled workers" in the small, overcrowded "synagogue quarter" *(Shulhof)* and the fish market; the other, which was smaller and reserved for the "unproductive," in the suburb of Slobodka. On Nov. 2, 1942, the ghettos were surrounded and sealed off, and their liquidation began. The liquidation took place in several stages. On Nov. 14–22, the Slobodka ghetto was destroyed and its inhabitants were taken "to work places" but in fact to their death in Auschwitz. That same month 4,000 people were expelled from the ghetto in the *Shulhof* to the transit camp of Kelvasin, 4 mi. (6 km.) from Grodno. Some of them died there as a result of the inhuman conditions, and the rest were expelled after a short period together with the Jewish population of the villages in the Grodno region, who were then sent to either Auschwitz or Treblinka. In a big Nazi *Aktion* on Jan. 17–22, 1943, 10,000 Jews were sent to the *Treblinka extermination camp. The rest were deported on March 12 to Bialystok. According to a Nazi source, 44,049 Grodno Jews were sent to the extermination camps, 20,577 Jews from Grodno itself, and 23,472 from neighboring townlets. Some 180 Jews remained in Grodno and the district, hidden among gentiles or otherwise concealed until the town was liberated by the Soviet Army in July 1944. Early in 1942, a Jewish underground resistance and defense movement was formed; members of Zionist youth movements, especially women, set up a communications center in Grodno for contact with the ghettos in *Vilna, *Bialystok, and *Warsaw; there was also a workshop for forging "Aryan" papers and travel permits for members of the movement engaged in rescuing Jews and in armed defense. Before the big *"Aktion,"* an unsuccessful attempt was made to assassinate Streblow, a chief executioner of Grodno Jewry. There was also an attempt to organize a mass escape from the Great Synagogue, which served as a collection center for deportation, and to assassinate Kurt Wiese, the other chief executioner of Grodno Jewry.

Figure 2. The *bimah* (reader's desk) in the Grodno wooden synagogue. Courtesy Yad Vashem, Jerusalem.

After World War II. Groups of Grodno Jewish partisans were active in forests. Some 2,000 Jews resettled in Grodno over a period of years following its liberation.

By the 1960s Grodno had no synagogue. The "old" synagogue was a storehouse; the "new" one was used as a sports hall. In the mid-1950s the Jewish cemetery was plowed up. Tombstones were taken away and used for building a monument to Lenin. There are four mass graves of Jews near the city, on which monuments were erected after World War II. One of them was repeatedly desecrated and damaged and there were several cases of graves being similarly treated.

Bibliography: Regesty, I–II; S.A. Friedenstein, *Ir Gibborim* (1880); Rabin, in: *He-Avar* (1957); *Grodno, dzieje w zarysie* (1936); Tenenbaum-Tamarof, *Dappim min ha-Deleikah* (1948); *Yedi'ot Beit Loḥamei ha-Getta'ot* (1957), no. 18–19, 53–62; H. Grosman, *Anshei ha-Maḥteret* (1965²), 172–84; *Grodner Opklangen,* no. 1–18 (Buenos Aires, 1949–1968).

[D.R.]

GRODZINSKI, ḤAYYIM OZER (1863–1940), talmudic scholar and one of the spiritual leaders of Lithuanian Orthodox Jewry, son of the talmudic scholar, Solomon David Grodzinski (1831–c. 1908). Grodzinski studied in the yeshivot of Eisheshok and Volozhin, where he was known as an *illui* ("prodigy"). In 1887 he was appointed one of the *dayyanim* of the *bet din* of Vilna, and he came to be regarded as its leading *dayyan.* Grodzinski was one of the initiators of the Vilna Conference of 1909, which resulted in the formation of the Orthodox Keneset Israel organization. He also participated in the founding conference of the Agudat Israel at Katowice in 1914, served as a leading member of that party's Council of Sages, and was the prime force for spreading its influence in and around Vilna. An initiator of the conference of rabbis at Grodno in 1924 which founded the Va'ad ha-Yeshivot ("Council of the Yeshivot") for the spiritual and material support of yeshivot and their students, he was the moving spirit behind the Council.

Grodzinski was a vehement opponent of Zionism and of secular education for Jews, his aim being to preserve the Torah milieu of the Lithuanian yeshivot and townlets intact. In 1934 he prevented the transfer of the Hildesheimer rabbinical seminary from Berlin to Tel Aviv. Asked by an Agudat Israel kibbutz whether it was permitted to settle on Jewish National Fund land, he advised its members "Let him who is firm in spirit stay steadfast in his place and not hurry to join the swelling stream . . . until God has mercy on His people and hastens his redemption." In 1929, when Isaac Rubinstein was chosen as chief rabbi of Vilna, Grodzinski's supporters sparked a violent controversy in the community.

Grodzinski's responsa were published in three volumes under the title of *Aḥi'ezer* (1922, 1925, 1939). In the introduction to the last volume, written on the eve of the Holocaust, he spoke of the fear and dismay that was rapidly descending upon the entire Jewish people, both in the Diaspora and (in a reference to the 1936–39 riots) in Ereẓ Israel. He wrote about the spiritual disintegration of the Jewish community, and its laxity in the observance of the

Sabbath, *kashrut*, and the laws of marital purity. All this he blamed on the Reform movement in the West and on secular education in the East. His sole consolation was in "the important work of preserving and strengthening Torah education" and in the fact that "the large and small yeshivot were the strongholds of Judaism . . . in Poland and Lithuania."

Bibliography: S. Rothstein, *Aḥi'ezer* (1946[2]); O. Z. Rand (ed.), *Toledot Anshei Shem* (1950), 21–22; O. Feuchtwanger, *Righteous Lives* (1965), 17–22; J. L. Kagan and H. B. Perlman, in: L. Jung (ed.), *Jewish Leaders* (1953), 433–56; A. Rothkoff, in: *Jewish Life* (May-June 1967). [H.H.B.-S.]

GRODZISK MAZOWIECKI, small town in Poland. It had 157 Jewish inhabitants in 1765, 790 in 1856, 2,154 in 1897, 2,756 in 1921 (out of 11,254), and 3,600 in September 1939. Grodzisk was the seat of a ḥasidic dynasty, founded by Elimelech of Grodzisk (d . 1892). His grandson R. Israel Shapiro, a scholar and writer of songs, who after World War I settled in Warsaw, perished in the Holocaust, as did Eliezer b. Abraham Ḥayyim of Falancz, rabbi in Grodzisk from 1913 to 1919. Members of the Grodzisk dynasty settled in Ereẓ Israel. During World War II, in November 1941, the Germans transferred the Jews of Grodzisk to the Warsaw Ghetto, and in 1942 to the death camp of Treblinka.

Bibliography: *Bleter far Geshikhte,* 1 pt. 3–4 (1948), 146–8. [Ed.]

GRODZISK WIELKOPOLSKI (Ger. **Graetz;** Yid. גריידיץ), town in W. Poland, formerly in the province of Posen (Prussia). Jews first settled there in 1634, but their number diminished during the Swedish wars (1655–60). Toward the end of the 17th century Jews from Grodzisk visited the Leipzig fairs. The Jewish population numbered 812 in 1765, 1,156 (half the total population) in 1793, and 1,634 in 1820. In 1820 the existing synagogue collapsed and a new one was opened in 1822. Rabbis of Grodzisk include Judah Loeb b. Solomon of Prague, who had to flee during the Northern War (1700–21); Gershon b. Jehiel Landsberg (c. 1726–40); Ẓevi Hirsch b. Benjamin (c. 1768–70), author of *Tiferet Ẓevi;* and Benjamin Schreiber (c. 1820–39). In the second half of the 19th century the noted talmudist and *ẓaddik* Elijah *Guttmacher, a forerunner of Zionism, lived in Grodzisk where many Jews, mainly from Congress Poland, used to visit him. In 1898 a society for the study of Jewish history and literature was founded there. Toward the end of the 19th century the Jewish population declined, numbering 240 in 1905, and 61 in 1921 (out of a total population of 5,604), and 71 in neighboring Buk (out of 3,408). In 1922 the community ceased to exist. The communal archives (including Guttmacher's correspondence) were transferred to Jerusalem. Rudolph *Mosse, the well-known publisher of the *Berliner Tageblatt,* who was born in Grodzisk, founded a hospital there in the name of his father who practiced as physician in the town.

Bibliography: A. Heppner and I. Herzberg, *Aus Vergangerheit und Gegenwart der Juden . . . in der Posener Landen* (1909), 420f.; Główny Urząd Staystyczny, *Skorowidz miejscowaśći Rseczypospolitej Polski,* 10 (1926), s.v.; I. T. Eisenstadt et al., *Da'at Kedoshim* (1897–98), 45. [Ed.]

GROJEC (Yid. **Gritse**), small town in Poland. The privilege granted to the town in 1744 prohibited Jewish settlement there; nevertheless Jews began to settle there in the 18th century; they are mentioned there in 1754. The community numbered 1,719 in 1856 (68.7% of the total population), 3,737 in 1897 (61.9%), and 4,922 in 1921 (56.3%). On the eve of World War II there were approximately 5,200 Jews living in Grojec. [Ed.]

Holocaust Period. With the entry of the German army on Sept. 8, 1939, terrorization of the Jewish population began. On Sept. 12, 1939, all men between the ages of 15 and 55 were forced to assemble at the market, and from there were marched on foot to Rawa Mazowiecka, about 37 mi. (60 km.) away. Many were shot on the way. During the spring of 1940 about 500 Jews from Lodz and the vicinity were forced to settle in Grojec. In July 1940 a ghetto was established and the plight of the Jewish inhabitants drastically deteriorated. They suffered from hunger, epidemics, and lack of fuel during the winter of 1940–41. In January 1941 about 1,000 Jews from nearby places were brought to the Grojec ghetto. On Feb. 23–24, 1941, about 2,700 of the Jews in Grojec were deported to the Warsaw Ghetto where they shared the fate of Warsaw Jewry. In September 1942 the ghetto in Grojec was liquidated. About 3,000 surviving Jewish inmates were deported to Bialobrzegi (a small town on the Warsaw-Radom highway), and from there were all sent to Treblinka death camp. In Grojec itself only 300 Jews remained, 83 of whom were deported after some time to a slave labor camp in Russia near Smolensk, where almost all were murdered. The last 200 Jews were executed in the summer of 1943 in a forest near Gora Kalwaria. After the war the Jewish community in Grojec was not reconstituted. Organizations of former Jewish residents of Grojec were established in Israel, France, the U.S., Canada, and Argentina. [S.Kr.]

Bibliography: *Megillat Gritse* (Yid. and some Heb., 1955); *Bleter far Geshikhte,* 1 pt. 3–4 (1948), 146–8; *Megillat Polin,* 5 (1961), 278; Halpern, Pinkas, 399.

GRONEMANN, SAMUEL (Sammy; 1875–1952), German author and Zionist leader. Gronemann, who was born in Strasbourg, West Prussia, was the son of Selig Gronemann (1845–1918), a rabbi and scholar who refused to endorse the anti-Zionist stand of the German "Protestrabbiner" in 1898. After studying at the Hildesheimer Rabbinical Seminary and at the University of Berlin, Gronemann qualified as a lawyer and then embarked on a career as a journalist, playwright, and novelist. While serving on the eastern front in World War I, Gronemann came in touch with Jewish communities in the occupied territories, and after the war ended he personally helped many Jewish refugees. Gronemann served as legal adviser to the Union of German Actors and Playwrights. His novels include *Tohuwabohu* (1920); *Hawdoloh und Zapfenstreich* (1924), in which the East European milieu is prominently featured; and *Schalet* (1927). He also wrote a Purim play entitled *Haman's Flucht* (1926). A noted wit, Gronemann's most successful works were his comedies which were adapted for the Hebrew stage after he settled in Tel Aviv in 1936. These include *Jakob und Christian* (1936), which mocked Nazi

Samuel Gronemann, German author and Zionist leader. Courtesy Central Zionist Archives, Jerusalem.

race theories; *Der Prozess um des Esels Schatten* (1945), a political satire; and *Die Koenigin von Saba* (1951). He is perhaps best remembered, however, for *Der Weise und der Narr: Koenig Salomo und der Schuster* ("The King and the Cobbler," 1942), a comedy in a legendary biblical setting. The Hebrew version by Nathan *Alterman, *Shelomo ha-Melekh ve-Shalmai ha-Sandelar* (1942), was performed by the *Ohel Theater in Tel Aviv. In 1965 it was set to music by Alexander Argov and performed by the *Cameri theater. It became the first successful Hebrew musical comedy and was performed in various countries. A pioneer German Zionist, Gronemann was a delegate to the Zionist congresses from 1901 onward and was for many years a member of the Zionist Actions Committee. His reputation for political impartiality brought him the presidency of the Zionist Congress court. Gronemann's memoirs, *Erinnerungen eines Jecken* (1947), are an important contribution to the history of the Zionist Movement in Germany. A traditionally observant Jew, he was an outspoken critic of Diaspora assimilationism, and also attacked certain aspects of ultra-Orthodoxy.

Bibliography: Tidhar, 3 (1958), 1383–4; D. Stern, *Werke juedischen Autoren deutscher Sprache* (1969), 153. [M.G.]

GRONINGEN, city and province in N. Netherlands. The first information about Jews there dates from 1573. Near the end of the 17th century a number of Jews came to the city of Groningen and its environs from adjacent Germany; religious services were held in a private home, but in 1691 these were prohibited by the municipal authorities and in 1710 the Jews were expelled from the city. However, some individual Jews are known to have come to the city in subsequent years and in 1744 the community leaders petitioned the authorities to approve the first statute of the Jewish community of Groningen. Ten years later they were given permission to erect a synagogue and a rabbi was chosen to serve the community which, by 1757, consisted of 30–40 families. Individual Jews were granted rights of citizenship and of membership in the guild of small retailers. In the second half of the 18th century Jewish communities developed in several towns in the district such as Winschoten, Veendam, Hoogezand, Sappemeer, and Stadskanaal. The Jews were chiefly engaged in the cattle trade, or dealt in haberdashery. In 1789 the community numbered 396. After 1848 the Orthodox members formed a separate congregation Teschuat Israel, erecting their own synagogue and acquiring a separate portion of the cemetery. The congregations reunited in 1881. In the second half of the 19th century Groningen became the seat of a chief rabbi. Despite the general increase in population, the number of Jews remained more or less stable, owing to emigration to the west of the country. In 1920 the Jewish population of the city was 2,369, and in 1931 about 2,500. In 1939, 2,411 Jews were living in Groningen, including 218 German Jews and 44 other foreign nationals. Jews from the towns and villages in the vicinity were forced to concentrate in the city Groningen after the German occupation. Altogether the Jews made up about 2.5% of the population. [M.Roz.]

Holocaust Period. One of the first victims of the Germans was the philosopher Leonard *Polak (1880–1941). In September 1941 all the Jewish children were evicted from the public schools and a separate Jewish elementary and high school was opened. From July 10, 1942, onward most of the Jewish inhabitants of Groningen were deported, with the exception of 150 Jewish partners of mixed marriages. Almost all the Jews perished, including the chief rabbi, S. Dasberg. Only ten survived the camps, while about 300 other Jews were left alive at the end of the war. In contrast to the neighboring province of Friesland, the non-Jewish population of Groningen did little to provide hiding places either for its own Jews or for those from elsewhere. [J.AN.]

Contemporary Period. The monumental synagogue in the Folkingestraat, which was inaugurated in 1906, was not reopened after the war and now serves as a small factory. Since 1945 services have been held in the former youth synagogue nearby. The only other Jewish congregation still existing in the province of Groningen is in Stadskanaal, which had 20 Jews in 1969, against a total of 16 Jewish congregations with some 4,250 Jews in 1940. In 1969 there were 150–180 Jews living in the city of Groningen. The process of emigration to the west of the country or to Israel continued. The synagogues of all the defunct congregations have been sold. Groningen now comes under the jurisdiction of the Chief Rabbinate of Utrecht. [H.Bo.]

Bibliography: I. Mendels, *De joodsche gemeente te Groningen* (1910); Boekman, in: *Mensch en maatschappij*, 10 (1935), 174–96; N. Rost, *De vrienden van mijn vader* (1956); H. Beem, *De verdwenen mediene* (1950).

GROPER, JACOB ASHEL (1890–1968), pioneer of Yiddish poetry in Rumania. Born in Mihaileni, Groper was active in furthering Yiddish culture while studying law at the University of Jassy. After spending most of his life in Rumania, he emigrated to Israel in 1964 and settled in Haifa. A participant in the 1908 *Czernowitz Yiddish Conference, he began to write in Rumanian, German, and Yiddish, but concentrated on Yiddish as of 1908. From 1914 his poems appeared in periodicals in Vilna, Lemberg (Lvov), Bucharest, and London, as well as in anthologies and in the volume *In Shotn fun a Shteyn* (1934). Some of his poems were translated into Rumanian and he edited a collection of Peretz's writings, *Y. L. Peretz* (1915). Groper was not a prolific writer, but he performed a valuable service in raising the prestige of Yiddish in Rumania. Widely known there by Jews and gentiles, Groper was considered by critics to be the outstanding Yiddish poet in Rumania. One of the many requests in his will was for his collected works to be published in Israel in Yiddish and in a Hebrew translation.

Bibliography: Rejzen, Leksikon, 1 (1926), 623–5; LNYL, 2 (1958), 364; S. Bickel, *Inzikh un Arumzikh* (1936), 100–3; idem, *Rumenia* (1961), 193–204. [S.L.]

GROPPER, WILLIAM (1897–), U. S. cartoonist and painter. New York-born Gropper supported himself by drawing cartoons for the New York *Tribune, Smart Set,*

"Old Tree and Old People" by William Gropper, 1939, oil on canvas, 20×22¼ in. (50.8×56.5 cm.). New York, Whitney Museum of American Art.

Bookman, Dial, Vanity Fair, New York *Post, New Republic,* and *The Nation* while he studied painting. He was also a contributor to such left-wing publications as *New Masses* and the Yiddish *Morning Freiheit.* During the Depression, he painted murals for public buildings for the Works Project Administration. Gropper, for years a leading painter in the American social realism movement—which was preoccupied with commenting upon political, social, and economic problems—used his art as a weapon in the fight for the betterment of the human condition. Groper's visit in 1948 to the ruins of the Warsaw Jewish Ghetto made a deep impression on him, and he began to paint Jewish subjects. In his work after 1948, the Jew of Eastern Europe is presented as the epitome of all suffering mankind. Gropper also designed stained-glass windows for a temple in River Forest, Illinois.

Bibliography: A. L. Freundlich, *William Gropper, Retrospective* (1968). [A.W.]

GROSS, ADOLF (1862–1937), lawyer, communal worker, and delegate in the Austrian parliament. Gross founded the Jewish Independent Party in Cracow, with the objectives of attaining equality of rights and a communal organization which would concern itself with the needs of the Jewish masses. In his profession Gross won a reputation as a jurist, and in public life as a political journalist and democratic mediator. He established a public company for the construction of cheap lodgings and founded consumer cooperatives. He achieved wide popularity as one of the most prominent members of the Cracow municipal council, on which he was active until 1897. In the electoral campaign for the Austrian parliament of 1907 his opponent was Ḥayyim *Hilfstein, a Zionist who exercised particular influence in assimilationist circles. However, Gross defeated him in the struggle for the Jewish vote. As a delegate, he joined the Polish Parliamentary Club in Vienna and collaborated with the Polish Socialist Party (P. P. S.). Gross was a member of the public committee for the relief of poor Jews in Galicia founded on the initiative of philanthropic societies in England, Germany, and Austria. In the various institutions he upheld his opposition to Zionism and also opposed an attempt to establish a Jewish secondary school in Cracow.

Bibliography: I. Tenenbaum, *Galitsye, mayn Alte Haym* (1952), 108, 127; I. Schwarzbart, *Tsvishn beyde Velt-Milkhomes* (1958), 170, 186; *Sefer Kraka* (1959), 123. [M.LAN.]

GROSS, CHAIM (1904–), U.S. sculptor. A native of Kolomea, Galicia, Gross went to the United States in 1921. Gross made sculptures for public institutions, including the Hadassah Medical Center in Jerusalem. He wrote the book: *The Technique of Wood Sculpture* (1957). He produced a large number of works in different media—wood, stone, bronze, pen and ink, and water color—but his contributions to wood sculpture are the most outstanding. The forests of the Carpathian mountains near his birthplace first taught him the qualities and potentialities of wood. He never camouflaged or overpolished its surfaces and never disguised its colors but respected its texture and grain. Among his favorite themes are female acrobats and mothers playing with small children.

Bibliography: J. V. Lombardo, *Chaim Gross, Sculptor* (1949); A. L. Chanin, in: C. Gross, *Fantasy Drawings* (1956), 716; L. Goodrich, in: *Four American Expressionists* (exhibition catalog; 1959). [A.W.]

GROSS, CHARLES (1857–1909), U.S. historian. Born and educated in Troy, N.Y., Gross continued his studies in Europe. His doctoral dissertation was expanded into a classic two-volume work, *The Gild Merchant* (1890). In 1888 he was appointed an instructor at Harvard, and he was made a full professor in 1901. Gross took an active part in Jewish life. At the Anglo-Jewish Exhibition in London in 1887, he lectured on "The Exchequer of the Jews in England in the Middle Ages." In 1893 he translated into English Kayserling's volume on Christopher Columbus and the Jews. He was also vice-president and a charter member of the American Jewish Historical Society. Among his most important works: *Select Cases from the Coroner's Rolls, 1265–1413* (1896), and *Select Cases Concerning the Law Merchant, A.D. 1270–1638* (1908–32), both of which he edited for the Selden Society; *Bibliography of British Municipal History* (1897) and *The Sources and Literature of English History from the Earliest Time to about 1485* (1900, 1915², 1951).

Bibliography: Jacobs, in: AJHSP, 19 (1910), 189–93. [H.L.A.]

GROSS, HEINRICH (Henri; 1835–1910), rabbi and scholar. Gross, who was born in Szenicz, Hungary, received his traditional rabbinical education as a student of Judah *Aszod, at the Breslau Jewish Theological Seminary, at Halle, Berlin, and also with L. *Zunz. For a time, he was private tutor in the home of Baron Guenzburg in Paris. Gross served as rabbi in Gross-Strelitz (Strzelce, Poland), and from 1870 in Augsburg, Bavaria. He specialized in the study of the lives of leading French rabbis and their communities in the Middle Ages and published his researches in learned journals. Gross's lasting contribution to Jewish scholarship is his *Gallia Judaica* (1897), "a geographic dictionary of France according to rabbinic sources," which was translated into French from the German manuscript by M. Bloch and published by the *Société des Etudes Juives.* This standard work was reproduced in 1969 with additional notes by S. Schwarzfuchs.

Bibliography: Wininger, Biog, 2 (1927), 525; 7 (1936), 34. [G.WE.]

Bronze *menorah* by Chaim Gross, 1968, height 24 in. (61 cm.). Pittsburgh, Pa., Harold J. Ruttenberg Collection. Photo Walter Russell, New York.

GROSS, NAPHTALI (1896–1956), Yiddish poet and folklorist. Born in Kolomea, Galicia, he emigrated to the U.S. in 1913 and worked as a typesetter and as a teacher in Yiddish schools. His first published poems appeared in the Montreal *Jewish Daily Eagle*. From 1943, Gross was on the staff of the New York *Jewish Daily Forward* where, from 1946, he wrote a weekly column *Mayselekh un Mesholim* ("Little Stories and Parables"), based on stories from readers. They appeared in collected form *(Mayselekh un Mesholim)* in 1955, illustrated by his brother, the artist Chaim *Gross. Naphtali Gross' major poetic works are *Psalmen* ("Psalms," 1919), *Der Vayser Rayter* ("The White Horseman," 1925), and *Idn* ("Jews," 2 vols., 1929 and 1938). In the 1920s, his neo-Romantic poems and ballads deviated from the dominant literary trend, and he was criticized by many for his preoccupation with religious motifs and with the idealization of the *shtetl* ("small town") at a time of revolution. Gross was also a successful translator. His translation of the Five Scrolls ranked him after only Yehoash as a Yiddish translator of the Bible. With Abraham *Rejzen, he translated the poems of Solomon ibn *Gabirol. His collected poems *Lider* (1958) contain a bibliography by E. H. Jeshurin. [SH. B.]

GROSS, NATHAN (1874–1922), a founder of *Po'alei Zion and general secretary of the *Jewish National Fund Head Office. Born in Tarnopol, Galicia, Gross moved to Vienna in his youth and worked as a clerk. At first he joined the Social Democrats, but when he became aware of the hostile attitude to Jews shown by the party's leaders (particularly those who were themselves Jews), he left the party. With the publication of Herzl's ideas of a Jewish state, Gross became a Zionist. He was among the organizers of the clerical union in Austria and in this manner contributed to the establishment of a Zionist labor movement. The first cells that he established in various places gradually coalesced into the Po'alei Zion movement, of which he and S. *Kaplansky became the chief spokesmen at Zionist Congresses and in the Zionist Movement. (As a consequence of new activities *Merḥavyah was founded, thereby realizing Franz *Oppenheimer's plan for the establishment of agricultural cooperatives in Ereẓ Israel.) In 1908 Gross was appointed general secretary of the head office of the Jewish National Fund situated first in Cologne and, in 1914, moving to The Hague. He retained this post until his death.

Bibliography: N. Agmon (Bistritsky, ed.), *Demuyyot*, 2 (1951), 277–9; M. Singer, *Be-Reshit ha-Ẓiyyonut ha-Soẓyalistit* (1958), 444.
[G.K.]

GROSSBERG, MENASSEH (c. 1860–?), rabbinical scholar. Born in Trestina, Russia, Grossberg led a wandering life, copying and publishing Hebrew manuscripts from libraries in Berlin, Paris, London, Amsterdam, Munich, and other cities. In the first decade of the 20th century he settled in London, copying manuscripts for European scholars at the British Museum and at Oxford. His many publications included: a Pentateuch commentary by Jacob of Vienna (*Peshatim u-Ferushim*, 1888, repr. 1967) from a Munich manuscript; Meshullam b. Moses' *Sefer ha-Hashlamah* on tractates *Berakhot, Ta'anit*, and *Megillah* (from a Hamburg manuscript, the first with an introduction by H. Brody (1893, repr. 1967), and the last as an appendix to *Peshatim u-Ferushim*); *Ḥiẓẓei Menasheh* (1901), a manuscript commentary on the Pentateuch by various medieval scholars also containing Jonathan of Lunel's novellae on *Horayot* (1901); *Sefer Yeẓirah* (1902); David b. Levi's *Sefer ha-Mikhtam* on *Megillah* (1904); *Megillat Ta'anit* (with an extensive introduction, 1906); and *Seder Olam Zuta* (also with introduction, 1910). Grossberg also published responsa and various halakhic treatises. [ED.]

GROSSER, BRONISLAW (pseudonyms: **Slawek; Zelcer;** 1883–1912), lawyer born in Miechow, Poland; one of the second generation of *Bund leaders. The son of a lawyer, he became a leader of the Warsaw socialist youth while still at secondary school. His experience of anti-Semitism made him conscious of his Jewish identity, and influenced by Bundists from Lithuania, he joined the Bund. Grosser was among those who in 1906 consistently supported the independence of the Bund, being against its return to the Russian Social Democratic party. He was a member of the advisory committee of the Social Democratic group in the Fourth Duma (1912) and was elected to the central committee of the Bund. An incisive writer and fluent speaker, Grosser was outstanding among the relatively few intellectuals who joined the Bund in Poland at that time. He defined his task as "defense of the interests of the Jewish workers in Poland, and within this framework defense of the interests of the country."

Bibliography: Rejzen, Leksikon, 1 (1926), 620–3; J. S. Hertz (ed.), *Doyres Bundistn*, 1 (1956), 319; *Polski Slownik Biograficzny*, 9 (1960–61), 6.
[M.M.]

GROSSINGER, JENNIE (1892–), U.S. resort owner and manager. Jennie Grossinger, born in a small town in Galicia, was taken to America by her parents at the turn of the century. The Grossingers lived in extreme poverty on New York's Lower East Side and Jennie went to work in a sweatshop after several years of public school. In 1912 she married her cousin, Harry Grossinger (1890–1964) and the following year the entire family moved to a farm in the Catskill Mountains near Liberty, N.Y. The farm was converted into a boardinghouse in 1914, and Grossinger's eventually grew under Jennie Grossinger's management into a giant resort of over 1,000 acres, whose 800 employees serve some 1,300 guests on an average day. She also wrote a cookbook *The Art of Jewish Cooking* (1958). Grossinger's is a center of Jewish activity, especially on behalf of Israel. [H.H.]

Jennie Grossinger, U.S. resort owner.

GROSSMAN, KURT RICHARD (1897–), German journalist. A pacifist after World War I, Grossman became general secretary of the *Deutsche Liga fuer Menschenrechte* (German League for Human Rights) in his home town, Berlin (1926), and organized its fight against injustice in German law courts. Grossman was active in cases such as that of the Russian war prisoner, Jacobowsky (executed and then adjudged innocent), and that of Walter Bullerjahn who had been imprisoned as the result of false witness. He wrote *Dreizehn Jahre "Republikanische" Justiz* (1932). Warned that the Nazis were about to arrest him, Grossman escaped to

Prague in 1933. There he established and directed the *Deutsche Fluechtlingsfuersorge* (Relief for Refugees from Germany) and wrote brochures against Nazism. In 1938 he went to Paris and in 1939 to New York. After World War II, Grossman became a recognized spokesman on problems concerning Jewish refugees and *restitution and compensation. Among the books written during his American years are: *Die Unbesungenen Helden: Menschen in Deutschlands dunklen Tagen* (1957); *Ossietzky: ein deutscher Patriot* (1963), which won the Albert Schweitzer Prize; and a history of restitution, *Die Ehrenschuld: Kurzgeschichte der Wiedergutmachung* (1967); *Emigration, Geschichte der Hitler-Fluechtlinge 1933–45* (1969). [F.R.L.]

GROSSMAN, MEIR (1888–1964), Zionist leader. Born in Temryuk in the Krasnodar Territory, Russia, Grossman at an early age became a contributor to the Russian press. For a while he lived in Warsaw, where he began contributing to the Yiddish press. In 1913 he went to Berlin to study, becoming a member of the central committee of *He-Ḥaver, the Zionist students' society, and editing its Russian and Hebrew organs.

On the day that World War I broke out, Grossman left for Copenhagen, and worked there as a correspondent for the Russian daily *Russkoye Slovo.* A few months after his arrival he began the publication of a Yiddish daily, *Kopenhagener Togblat* (later renamed *Yidishe Folkstsaytung*). At *Jabotinsky's suggestion he published a Yiddish fortnightly, *Di Tribune,* dedicated to publicizing the cause of a Jewish Legion, a World Jewish Congress, and equal rights for Jews. Jabotinsky also persuaded him to move to London, which he did in the fall of 1916, publishing *Di Tribune* there as a daily. The campaign for a Jewish Legion did not, however, yield immediate results, and when the paper closed, Grossman returned to Copenhagen.

After the February 1917 Revolution in Russia, Grossman returned to Petrograd, where he became a contributor to *Petrograder Togblat,* the daily founded by *Yiẓḥak Gruenbaum. After the October Revolution he was asked to move to Kiev and there edited several periodicals: *Der Telegraf,* a daily, together with Naḥman *Syrkin; *Oyf der Vakh,* Zionist weekly; and *Die Velt,* another daily. He was a member of the executive committee of Ukrainian Zionists, took part in the National Jewish Assembly and in the work of the Provisional National Council, and was a deputy of the Rada, the national council of the independent Ukraine. When hostilities broke out and the Bolsheviks invaded the Ukraine, Grossman, together with Abraham Coralnik, was sent abroad to inform the world of the situation and appeal for help. In London and in the United States, Grossman and Coralnik created aid organizations for Ukrainian Jews (1919).

At the end of 1919, Grossman joined Jacob *Landau, in establishing the Jewish Correspondence Bureau for the dissemination of news of Jewish interest. This bureau eventually became the *Jewish Telegraphic Agency (J.T.A.). Grossman left the J.T.A. in 1928 as a result of differences with Landau. In 1925 he had founded the *Palestine Bulletin,* an English-language daily in Jerusalem, that in 1932 became the *Palestine Post* (later the *Jerusalem Post*). After the 1920 riots in Palestine, Grossman criticized Weizmann's policies and called for his resignation. When Jabotinsky left the Zionist Executive and eventually founded the *Revisionist Party (in 1925), Grossman became one of his early supporters and was appointed deputy chairman of the new party's world center. In 1933 the party split on the issue of secession from the Zionist Organization; Grossman headed the minority, which opposed Jabotinsky and which was in favor of remaining in the *Zionist Organization. He then established the *Jewish State Party.

In 1934 he settled in Palestine, where he became the manager of Bank le-Hityashevut Amamit. In 1937 he caused a sensation at the Zionist Congress by reading from its rostrum confidential minutes of Weizmann's talks with

Meir Grossman, journalist and Zionist Revisionist leader. Central Zionist Archives, Jerusalem.

the British colonial secretary, Ormsby-Gore, in which Weizmann promised to influence the Zionist movement in favor of the partition plan of Palestine, though the Zionist General Council had adopted a resolution against the plan. Grossman's "suspension from membership in the Zionist General Council" by the Zionist court, for having disclosed confidential Zionist documents, caused a stir in the Jewish press the world over, particularly in the London *Jewish Chronicle.* He spent the World War II years in the United States. After the war the two factions of the Revisionist Party were reunited, and Grossman attended the Zionist Congress as a representative of the united party. He did not, however, join the *Ḥerut Party, and preferred to join the *General Zionists, becoming one of its representatives in the Executive of the Zionist Organization (1954–1960). When the General Zionist Party merged with the Progressive Party to form the Liberal Party, Grossman again did not follow his party's decision and resigned from the Zionist Executive. He continued his journalistic work and also participated in the activities of various public institutions. He took special interest in the situation of Soviet Jews and promoted the publication of Russian-language periodicals in Israel (*Vestnik Izraila,* and *Shalom*).

Bibliography: Tidhar, 4 (1950), 1927–28; LNYL, 2 (1958), 359–60. [I.K.]

GROSSMAN, MORTON IRVIN (1919–), U.S. gastroenterologist. Born and educated in Ohio, Grossman first served as assistant biochemist (1939–41) at Ohio State University Medical School and from 1950 to 1951 as professor of physiology in the Department of Clinical Sciences. From 1951 to 1955 he was chief of physiology in the Division of Medical Nutrition at Fitzsimons Army Hospital. In 1955 he joined the faculty of the University of California School of Medicine and was appointed chairman of the Department of Medicine in 1965. Grossman was consultant to the National Institutes of Health (1960–65) and a member of many professional societies. He served as editor of *Gastroenterology* (1960–65) and wrote many papers on the physiology of the alimentary tract, gastrointestinal hormones, and the physiology of nutrition. [F.R.]

GROSSMAN, VASILI SEMYONOVICH (1905–1964), Soviet Russian writer. Born to a traditional Yiddish-speaking family in the intensely Jewish town of Berdichev, he moved to Moscow as a young man and, after graduating from the university, worked for a time as a chemical engineer in the coal mines of Donbas. His short story *V gorode Berdicheve* ("In the Town of Berdichev," 1934), which described the Civil War in and around his home town, earned the praise of Maxim Gorki. Grossman's most important early work is *Stepan Kolchugin* (1937–40), a three-volume novel describing the Communist underground before the Reolution. He became famous as the author of *Narod bessmerten* ("The People is Immortal," 1942), the first important Soviet novel inspired by World War II. His second war novel, *Za pravoye delo* ("For the Just Cause"), the first part of which appeared in 1952, was never completed. It was found ideologically objectionable because of its underestimation of the Communist Party's role in the forging of victory over Nazism. Another cause of official displeasure probably was Grossman's emphasis on such "minor" traits of Nazism as the mass extermination of the Jews and its strong nationalism. Coming as they did at the height of Soviet anti-Semitic campaigns and the wave of glorification of everything Russian, Grossman's observations were against the official line. Somewhat earlier, Grossman and Ilya *Ehrenburg had tried to publish a "Black Book" of documentary evidence of Nazi crimes committed against the Jews on Soviet territory. The book was already set in type, but, as Ehrenburg points out in his memoirs, its publication was banned by the Soviet authorities. One volume was eventually published in Bucharest (1947) under the title *Cartea Neagră*, with a foreword by Grossman. A copy of the original manuscript is in the archive of Yad Vashem, Jerusalem.

Bibliography: V. M. Akimov et al. (eds.), *Russkiye Sovetskiye pisateli prozaiki*, 1 (1959), 609–25; D. Litani, in: *Yedi'ot Yad Vashem*, 23/24 (1960), 24–26 (on the Black Book). [M.F.]

GROSS-ZIMMERMANN, MOSHE (1891–), Yiddish essayist. Gross-Zimmermann, who was born in Galicia, lived in Vienna from 1908 and there wrote German impressionistic lyrics, one-act plays, and aphorisms. From 1918 to 1920, he edited a Yiddish newspaper *Juedische Morgenpost*. His essays on Yiddish, French, and German writers appeared in the Viennese monthly *Kritik*, as well as in leading Yiddish periodicals in Warsaw (notably *Heint*) and New York. In 1938 he settled in Palestine, joined the staff of the Hebrew daily *Davar*, and contributed to the Yiddish monthly *Di Goldene Keyt* and the Yiddish daily *Letste Nayes*. From 1950 he headed the Yiddish department of Kol Zion la-Golah (Israel's overseas broadcasts) and his weekly feuilletons were widely listened to in Eastern Europe. In his essays, collected in the volumes *Yidn tsvishn Yidn* (1956) and *Intimer Videranand* (1964), he displayed a rare mastery of style, marked by a subtle humor. [I.H.B.]

°**GROTIUS, HUGO** (**Huig de Groot;** 1583–1645), Dutch statesman, jurist, theologian, and historian. Grotius' contacts with Jews and Judaism were concerned with both political and spiritual matters. As a result of the flight of Marranos from Spain and Portugal to the Netherlands in the late 16th and early 17th century, and the consequent formation, without a firm legal basis, of sizable Jewish communities in *Amsterdam and other cities, the estates of Holland appointed Grotius to a commission "to amend the regulations for protecting Jews living in these lands from all scandals, anxieties, and sanctions." Grotius' report, known as *Remonstrantie*, appeared in 1615, but was not published in full until 1949. In the report Grotius posed three questions: whether it is desirable to allow Jews to settle in the country; whether it is advisable to permit them to follow their religious traditions; and in what ways it is possible to prevent difficulties affecting either Christianity or the state, through the presence in the land of Jews observing their religion. Grotius answered the first question in the affirmative. On the second point, he advised that the Jews be granted freedom of worship subject to limitations to prevent certain religious and political hazards.

Though some of his replies were noteworthy for their tolerance, others were hardly agreeable to Jews. Grotius ruled that all Jews who entered the state should be obliged to register with the city authorities, declaring that they believed in one God and that the words of Moses and the prophets were true. They were to be allowed to live in urban areas only, and their number was to be limited to 200 families in the provinces of Holland and Friesland and to 300 families in Amsterdam. They were to be granted the privilege of engaging in commerce and industry. Mixed marriages between Jews and Christians were to be prohibited. Yet the Jews were not to be compelled to conform to a particular style of dress nor to be separated from the rest of the residents in any other way. They must not be coerced to violate their Sabbath, nor should they desecrate Sundays and Christian holidays. Different penalties were fixed for those who might transgress these regulations. The *Remonstrantie* were accepted by the estates of Holland but were not adopted as a general law for the entire country.

Even more interesting are Grotius' intellectual contacts with Judaism. His conceptions of, and attacks on, Judaism were formed within the framework of Christian apologetics. He confesses his obligation to the Hebrew authors who, through their knowledge of the literature, language, and customs of their people, have revealed a special understanding of the Scriptures. Similar statements are found in the *Annotata ad Vetus Testamentum* (Paris, 1664). In his legal works Grotius quotes, in addition to the writings of Jewish authors who wrote in Greek (Philo and Josephus), the medieval Jewish commentators, as well as the Targum, Talmud, and Midrash. Occasionally his compositions contain Hebrew words and verses, and there can be no doubt that he had some knowledge of Hebrew and Aramaic; for example, he says in the *Annotata* that the beauty of the Song of Songs is marred in translations. His reported wide familiarity with Semitic languages nevertheless appears exaggerated. Many of his letters, especially to his friend Gerhard Johannes Vossius as well as to *Manasseh Ben Israel, indicate that he gained much of his information about Jews from the latter, whom he admired greatly. Because of the Jewish thread running through his works, which grew stronger in the course of time, Grotius was accused of leanings toward Judaism and of preferring Jewish to Christian biblical exegesis, accusations which, however, overlooked the spiritual ties between Protestantism and the Old Testament.

Bibliography: J. Meijer (ed.), *Hugo de Groot. Remonstrantie nopende de ordre dije in de landen van Hollandt ende Westvrieslandt dijent gestelt op de Joden* (1949), introduction; J. Meijer, in: HJ, 14 (1952), 133–44; idem, in: JSOS, 17 (1955), 91–104; I. Husik, in: HUCA, 2 (1925), 381–417; A. K. Kuhn, in: AJHSP, 31 (1928), 173–80; A Loewenstamm, in: *Festschrift . . . des Juedisch-Theologischen Seminars*, 2 (1929), 295–302; M. Balaban, in: *Festschrift . . . Simon Dubnow* (1930), 87–112; J. M. van Eysinga, in: *Mededeelingen der Koninklijke Nederlandse Akademie van Wetenschappen, Afdeling Letterkunde*, 13 (1950), 1–8; C. Roth, *Life of Menasseh Ben Israel* (1934), 146–8. [Sh.R.]

GROVES, SACRED. The concept of sacred groves arose out of the traditional mistranslation of the Asherah as a sacred grove near the altar. The Asherah is now known to have been a man-made cult object that was placed near the altar. (For a fuller discussion see *Asherah.) There were, however, sacred *trees. [T.S.F.]

GROZNY, capital of the Chechen-Ingush Autonomous Soviet Socialist Republic, S.W. European R.S.F.S.R. Situated on the Rostov-Baku railroad, it has been an oil-producing center since 1893. Until 1917 the city was outside the Pale of Settlement, but a community of *mountain (Tat) Jews existed there, which in 1866 numbered 928 persons living in 197 houses. In 1897 the Jewish population numbered 1,711 (11% of the total population) divided into two communities: mountain Jews and "Ashkenazim." In 1900 a synagogue built in oriental style was opened. The community suffered heavily during the civil war of 1918–21 and many Jews left the city. There remained 1,274 in 1926 (1.7% of the population). In World War II, during the summer of 1942, the German advance was halted just before reaching Grozny and the Jews of the city were saved from annihilation. The Jewish population according to the 1959 census numbered 4,981 in the towns of the Chechen-Ingush Autonomous Soviet Socialist Republic; it may be assumed that the majority lived in Grozny. By 1970 the number of Jews in Grozny was estimated at about 10,000. The only synagogue serving the "Tat" Jews, who reside in a Jewish quarter, was confiscated in 1962. [Y.S.]

GRUBY, DAVID (1810–1898), physician, born in Novi Sad, then Hungary; one of the poineers of modern microbiology and parasitology. Gruby left home while young and moved to Budapest, where he worked in a Jewish restaurant. As a Jew, he could not be accepted in a high school, so he stood outside the classroom door and listened to lessons. Eventually one of the teachers took pity on him, and arranged his admittance. Gruby studied medicine in Vienna and received his degree in 1834. Despite his being a Jew, he was appointed a surgeon at the university medical school. The university proposed that he be made a professor, on condition that he become converted to Christianity. Gruby rejected this proposal, left Vienna, and settled in Paris (1839). He was given a post at the Museum of Nature, and lectured there on normal and morbid pathology. From 1841 to 1852 he made a number of discoveries, from which evolved the new branch of mycology in both human and veterinary medicine, advancing the development of microbiology and parasitology. Gruby was the first to prove experimentally that a fungus was likely to be the cause of a specific disease in man. He was also one of the first to investigate parasitic worms and their life cycles. One of his most important discoveries, made in 1843, which represented a turning point in the history of microbiology, was the first description of the flagellate parasites of frogs' blood and tissues. Gruby called these parasites "trepanosomes." In the same year, working with the French veterinarian Delafond, he discovered microfilaria in the circulating blood of infested frogs, thus opening a new avenue for the investigation of filaria

David Gruby, pioneer of microbiology and parasitology. Courtesy Israel Medical Association, Jerusalem.

worms which constitute a widespread disease agent for man in tropical climates. He also did research on comparative anatomy, experimental physiology, experiments with chloroform and ether in anesthesia immediately after its introduction in Europe. He also investigated the composition of the lymph, the microscopic structure of the intestinal epithelium, and the treatment of war wounds. He was also one of the first to prepare microscopic photographs. From 1852 onward, he devoted his time to his large private practice. He was the private physician of Chopin, Liszt, Heine, and Dumas.

Bibliography: Kisch, in: *Transactions of the American Philosophical Society*, 44 (1954), 193–226. [S.A.]

°**GRUEBER, HEINRICH** (1891–), German pastor who saved Christians of Jewish extraction from Nazi persecution. Imprisoned in 1937 because of Christian religious opposition, he founded, after his release, the "Buero Grueber" for victims of the *Nuremberg Laws. The Buero aided non-Aryan Christians financially and helped them to emigrate. As a result of his protests in 1940 against the first deportations, Grueber was sent to the Sachsenhausen and later to the Dachau concentration camps. After his release in 1943, he secretly carried on with his work and at the end of the war set up an Evangelical Aid Society for Victims of Racial Persecution. He denounced all efforts to "whitewash" former Nazis and was a witness at the Eichmann trial held in Jerusalem in 1961. On his 70th birthday, the Grueber Grove was planted in Jerusalem. He wrote *Dona Nobis Pacem* (1957), *Leben an der Todeslinie: Dachauer Predigten* (1965[2]), and *Erinnerungen aus sieben Jahrzehnten* (1968).

Bibliography: *An der Stechbahn* (1957[2]); *H. Grueber, Zeuge pro Israel* (1963). [C.C.A.]

GRUENBAUM, ADOLF (1923–), U.S. philosopher of science and mathematics. Gruenbaum, who was born in Cologne, Germany, immigrated to the United States in 1938, and taught at Lehigh University (1950–60). He was appointed professor and director of the Center for the Philosophy of Science at the University of Pittsburgh in 1960. Gruenbaum's thorough knowledge of the physical and mathematical problems enabled him to analyze some of the basic philosophic questions that arose in connection with space and time. He tried to resolve some of the major difficulties involved in working out a consistent theory. He wrote several articles dealing with the philosophy of physics and mathematics, and the philosophy and methodology of the natural sciences. His major works are *Philosophical Problems of Space and Time* (1963) and *Modern Science and Zeno's Paradoxes* (1967). [R.H.P.]

GRUENBAUM, HENRY (1911–), Danish economist and politician. The son of a shoemaker, Gruenbaum was trained as an engraver but obtained a degree in economics. He joined the Labor Party, where he was active as an economist and statistician, and as editor of the party's paper *Socialdemokraten*. During World War II Gruenbaum was a leading member of the Danish Resistance. After the war he was principally concerned with price control and vocational training. In 1964 he became minister of economics and Nordic affairs and from 1965 to 1968 finance minister, in which capacity he deputized for the prime minister in the latter's absence. His publications include *Industrielt demokrati* (1947). [J.O.R.]

GRUENBAUM, MAX (1817–1898), German researcher in Jewish folklore and the popular languages of the Jews, one of the founders of Yiddish philology. He was born in Seligenstadt. In 1858 Gruenbaum was appointed director of the Hebrew Orphan Asylum in New York. In 1870 he returned to Europe, settled in Munich, and devoted himself to research. In the field of folklore, Gruenbaum investigated the history of aggadic themes and their influence on Islam. In the field of linguistics and literature Gruenbaum published his *Juedisch-deutsche Chrestomathie* (1882) and a selection from Yiddish literature. He was the first linguist to make a study of the structure and evolution of the Yiddish language. When he was 80 years old Gruenbaum published a chrestomathy of Judeo-Spanish which is important for the general research of Romance languages. Among his books were *Beitraege zur vergleichenden Mythologie aus der Haggadah* (1877); *Neue Beitraege zur semitischen Sagenkunde* (1893); *Die juedisch-deutsche Litteratur in Deutschland, Polen und Amerika* (1894) and *Juedisch-Spanische Chrestomathie* (1896).

Bibliography: F. Perles, in: AZDJ (Dec. 25, 1898); idem, in: M. Gruenbaum, *Gesammelte Aufsaetze* (1901), introduction (repr. in: *Juedische Skizzen* (1912), 61–64); ADB, 49 (1904), 589–94; Rejzen, Leksikon, 1 (1926), 635.

[M.PL.]

GRUENBAUM, YIZHAK (1879–1970), leader of the radical faction in General Zionism, one of the main spokesmen of Polish Jewry between the two world wars, and the first minister of the interior of the State of Israel. Born in Warsaw, Gruenbaum first studied medicine, but in 1904 took up law. He began Zionist activity and publicist writing during his student days. From the seventh Zionist Congress (1905) onward he served as a delegate to Zionist Congresses. He edited several newspapers in Polish, Yiddish (in Warsaw, St. Petersburg, and Paris) and Hebrew (he was a member of the editorial board of *Ha-Olam, Ha-Ẓefirah,* and other publications). As a speaker and author, he fought for his opinions with courage and perseverance. Gruenbaum was active in promoting Hebrew culture in Poland and in the *Tarbut organization. He tried to ensure that the struggle of the Jews in the Diaspora for their rights should be led by Zionists and was a central figure at the conference of Russian Zionists at Helsingfors, 1906 (see *Helsingfors program). In Poland, Gruenbaum created a pattern for Jewish policy which exploited all political methods in the struggle for the rights of the Jews of that country. During the elections to the Fourth Duma, in 1912, Gruenbaum had been active in rallying the Jewish parties in Warsaw to support the socialist candidate Jagiello, who had promised to press for equal Jewish rights against the anti-Semitic Polish nationalists. The right-wing camp, who viewed this as jeopardizing Polish national interests, called for an anti-Jewish boycott in response, which intensified anti-Semitism among the Polish public. During World War I, Gruenbaum stayed in Petrograd and it was only upon the conclusion of the war, in September 1918, that he returned to Warsaw, where he established the

Yiẓḥak Gruenbaum, Zionist, Polish Jewish leader, and Israel's first minister of the interior. Government Press Office, Tel Aviv.

Provisional National Council which played an important role in the campaign for civic and political rights of the Jews during the first years of independent Poland. In 1919 Gruenbaum was elected to the Sejm (parliament), and as a member of the constitution commission stood alone in the difficult struggle to guarantee the rights of the national minorities in the articles of the constitution of 1921. In reaction to the perverted election regulations which sought to prejudice fair representation of the national minorities, he participated, as initiator and organizer, in the formation of a "national minorities bloc." This achieved considerable success in the elections of 1922 in which the national minorities, and the Jews among them, obtained a considerable number of mandates. This policy of combining Jewish interests with those of the other national minorities in Poland resulted in sharp controversies within Polish Jewry and bitterness on the part of the Poles. Gruenbaum remained adamant in his policy, but the value and strength of the minorities bloc declined in the next elections as a result of the pressure of the Polish authorities and the divisions among the Jews. Thus, when anti-Semitic trends grew among the Germans and the Ukrainians in Poland during the 1930s, this policy was completely discarded. Gruenbaum continued to be a member of the Polish Sejm from 1918 until he left Poland in 1932. Over considerable periods of time, he also served as the chairman of the *koło* (club) of the Jewish members of the Sejm. His speeches in the Sejm, directed against the anti-Semitic policy of the Polish government, were outstanding for their pungency and militant spirit. In Zionist life Gruenbaum was vigorously and sharply opposed to the "enlargement" of the Jewish Agency by the co-optation of non-Zionists, and headed the radical Zionist faction known in Poland as Al ha-Mishmar. In 1932 he left for Paris. At the Zionist Congress of 1933 he was elected a member of the Jewish Agency Executive and then settled in Palestine. On the Executive he held the positions of head of the Aliyah Department (1933–35), and head of the Labor Department (1935–48), and he was also one of the leaders of the Organization Department (1935–46). He headed the publishing house Mosad Bialik from 1935 to 1948, was treasurer of the Jewish Agency from 1949 to 1950, and acted as its commissioner from 1950 to 1951; this last function was entrusted to him in order to supervise the propriety and honesty of the activities of the Agency administration. On the eve of the establishment of the State of Israel, Gruenbaum was a member of the People's Administration, in charge of internal affairs; in the Provisional Government (1948–49) he was minister of the interior, and the elections to the Knesset (1949) were organized under his guidance. In these elections, he appeared in a personal "Yiẓḥak Gruenbaum list," which was based on appreciation of Gruenbaum's personality and support of his struggle for the secularization in the state. The list received 2,514 votes, which was not enough to obtain a single seat. Subsequently, Gruenbaum remained active for many years in journalism and Zionist affairs, where his sympathies were now with its Leftist faction and he contributed frequently to the *Mapam* newspaper *Al ha-Mishmar.* He spent the last decade of his life in kibbutz Gan Shemuel. Gruenbaum's extremism in his orientations and the expression of his opinions focused upon his personality both hatred and a large measure of admiration. His principal writings are: *Ha-Tenu'ah ha-Ẓiyyonit be-Hitpatteḥutah* (4 vols., 1942–54); *Milḥamot Yehudei Polin* (1922, 1941[2]); *Bi-Ymei Ḥurban ve-Sho'ah* (1940–46), *Materjały w sprawie żydowskiej w Polsce* (2 vols., 1919–22); *Dor be-Mivḥan* (1951); *Penei ha-Dor* (2 vols., 1957–60); and *Ne'umim ba-Seim ha-Polani* (1963); and he edited the first and sixth volumes of *Enẓiklopedyah shel Galuyyot* (1953, 1959).

Bibliography: LNYL, 2 (1958), 380–6; A. Levinson, *Kitvei . . .* (1956), 215–20.

[H.H.B-S.]

GRUENBERG, KARL (1861–1940), economic and social historian. Gruenberg, who was born in Focsani, Rumania, studied and practiced law from 1885. In 1900 he became an associate professor of economics and in 1909 full professor at the University of Vienna. He was director of the Institute of Social Research at the University of Frankfort from 1924 until 1927 when he resigned because of ill health. Gruenberg wrote extensively on the agrarian history of the Austrian monarchy and the history of Socialism. Beginning in 1910 he published the *Archiv fuer die Geschichte des Sozialismus und der Arbeiterbewegung*. Gruenberg was murdered by a Nazi in Frankfort on the Main.

Bibliography: *Oesterreichisches biographisches Lexikon*, 2 (1959), 88. [Ed.]

GRUENBERG, LOUIS (1884–1964), U.S. composer. Born in Poland, near Brest Litovsk, Gruenberg was taken to the U.S. at the age of two. He studied in Berlin with Busoni, and made his debut as a pianist in 1912 at a concert of the Berlin Philharmonic, under Busoni's baton. In that year he composed a children's opera called "The Witch of the Brocken" which was followed by "The Bride of the Gods" (1913). After winning a prize for "The Hill of Dreams" (New York Symphony Society, 1919), Gruenberg devoted himself entirely to composition.

The League of Composers performed his "Daniel Jazz" in 1925. This was followed by "The Creation" (1923), into which he introduced Negro spirituals. In 1931 the Juillard School of Music commissioned and produced his opera "Jack and the Beanstalk."

Gruenberg's most important work was his opera "Emperor Jones," based on Eugene O'Neill's play of that name. Gruenberg was one of the first American composers to use elements of Negro spirituals and jazz in serious music. His opera "Green Mansions," based on W. H. Hudson's novel, was commissioned by the Columbia Broadcasting System and broadcast in 1937. Moving to California, Gruenberg wrote background music for films, and composed two other operas, "Queen Helena" (1936) and "Volpone" (1945), five symphonies, and various chamber works. He was one of the organizers of the League of Composers.

Bibliography: MGG, s.v.; Baker, Biog Dict, s.v. and suppl.; Grove, Dict, s.v. [J.Ga./Ed.]

GRUENBERG, SAMUEL (1879–1959), biblical scholar and communal worker. Gruenberg was born in Rumania and in 1920 was appointed lecturer in Bible exegesis, history and geography of Palestine, and modern Hebrew at the Berlin rabbinical seminary. He was active in the Mizrachi movement and founded the Welt-Verband Shomre Shabbos, presiding over its founding congress in 1930. Gruenberg emigrated to Palestine in 1936 and then served as the chairman of the Mo'aẓah Datit ("religious council") of Tel Aviv.

With A. M. Silbermann he edited the *"Menorah"-Woerterbuch*, a modern Hebrew-German, German-modern Hebrew dictionary (1920). Gruenberg's exegetical work appeared mainly as articles in German (collected under the title *Exegetische Beitraege*, 5 vols., 1924–33) and Hebrew (collected under the title *Li-Feshuto shel Mikra*, 1945). He also wrote *Zur Geschichte der Bibelexegese I, Nordfranzoesische Klassiker der Bibelexegese* (1928). Among his Hebrew works is *Niẓẓanim* (1906), a book of poetry. Gruenberg was the editor of the Hebrew section of Joseph *Wohlgemuth's *Jeschurun*, to which he contributed many studies.

Bibliography: I. Eisner, in: YLBI, 12 (1967), 46; Tidhar, 4 (1950), 1624–25. [Ed.]

GRUENBERG, SIDONIE MATSNER (1881–), U.S. educator, who exercised a dominant influence in advancing the study of guidance methods for parents and children. Sidonie Gruenberg was born in Austria and was educated in Germany and New York. In 1906 she joined the Child Study Association of America, became director (1923–1950), and served as consultant from 1950. Gruenberg wrote extensively for children and parents, and her books were translated into many languages. She was regarded as an authority on child-parent relationships and lectured in parent education, and was a member of the editorial boards of *Parents Magazine* and *Child Study*. She was chairman of the subcommittee of the White House Conference on Child Health and Protection (1930); a member of The White House Conference (1940) and The Mid-Century White House Conference (1950); director of the Public Affairs Commission (1947) and the Social Legislation Information Service (1947–61).

[R.E.O.]

GRUENEWALD, MAX (1899–), rabbi and communal leader. Gruenewald was born in Koenigshuette, Upper Silesia, Germany. Gruenewald served as rabbi in Mannheim and as president of the Jewish community of that city. He was a member of the Executive Committee of the *Reichsvertretung, which led the Jews of Germany during the Nazi period. In 1938 Rabbi Gruenewald arrived in Palestine, and in 1939 went to the U.S. at the invitation of the Jewish Theological Seminary of America. He served as rabbi of the Conservative Congregation B'nai Israel, Milburn, N.J., from 1944. Rabbi Gruenewald was the American chairman of the Leo Baeck Institute, honorary president of the American Federation of Jews from Central Europe and president of the Gustav Wurzweiler Foundation.

[J.Ri.]

GRUENFELD, JUDAH (1837–1907), Hungarian rabbi. Gruenfeld was born in Satoraljaujhely. He was one of the most important pupils of Abraham Judah Ha-Kohen Schwartz, rabbi of Beregszasz-Mad, and like his teacher frequented the court of the ḥasidic rabbi of Zanz. He lived for a time in Huszt, where Moses *Schick often consulted him on important problems. In 1883 he was appointed rabbi of Büdszentmihály, serving there until his death. His writings were not collected, but a substantial part of them were published by Joseph Schwartz in *Va-Yelakket Yosef* (1899–1917). Twenty-six important responsa were published in *Responsa Maharshag* (1961) by his son Simeon (1881–1930), who served first as *dayyan* of Munkacs and then succeeded his father at Büdszentmihály. Simeon was the author of *Responsa Maharshag*, Pt. 1 (1931) on both *Oraḥ Ḥayyim* and *Yoreh De'ah*, Pt. 2 (1939) on *Oraḥ Ḥayyim* alone. In 1961 the work was republished in Jerusalem with his additional responsa on *Ḥoshen Mishpat* and *Even ha-Ezer*. His responsa are distinguished by their clarity, their penetration, and their great erudition. He also wrote *Zehav Sheva* (1933) on the Pentateuch. He left more than 2,000 responsa in manuscript, novellae on several tractates, a large work on the *halakhot* of *mikva'ot*, and a work on *ta'arovot* (mixtures containing forbidden food). It is doubtful if these works have survived. [N.B.-M.]

GRUENHUT, DAVID BEN NATHAN (17th–18th centuries), German talmudist and kabbalist. In 1682 he printed Ḥayyim Vital's *Sefer ha-Gilgulim* ("On the Transmigration of Souls"), but was prevented from distributing it by the rabbinate of Frankfort, which opposed kabbalistic works because of the danger of Shabbateanism. Two years later, however, while at Heimerdingen, he published it again, this time through a Christian printer in Frankfort. After serving as rabbi for several years in neighboring towns (Idstein, Aue, and perhaps also Heimerdingen), he returned to Frankfort, becoming one of the scholars in the *bet ha-midrash* founded by David *Oppenheim. Gruenhut published *Tov Ro'i* (Frankfort, 1702), Jacob *Weil's work on the laws of ritual slaughter, to which he added his *Migdol David*, consisting of homilies and comments on Genesis. He published the *Sefer Ḥasidim* of *Judah he-Ḥasid with his own commentary (Frankfort, 1712) and in the following year Samuel *Uceda's *Midrash Shemu'el* (Frankfort, 1713). On friendly terms with *Eisenmenger and *Schudt before they published their anti-Semitic works, he wrote an adulatory preface to the former's edition of the Bible.

Bibliography: Fuenn, Keneset, s.v.; M. Horovitz, *Frankfurter Rabbinen*, 2 (1883), 54–55. [D.TA.]

GRUENHUT, ELEAZAR (Lazar; 1850–1913), rabbi and author. Gruenhut was born in Gerenda, Hungary, and in 1883 he was appointed rabbi of Temesvár. Impressed by the Haskalah and taking up the challenge he saw in it, he decided to augment his general education and acquire a scientific foundation for his Jewish studies. At the age of 40 he resigned his rabbinical post, left Temesvár, and moved to Berlin, where he studied at the Hildesheimer seminary and at the University of Berlin. He was especially influenced by Azriel *Hildesheimer and Abraham *Berliner. In 1892 he emigrated to Palestine and became head of the German-Jewish Orphanage. His introduction of secular studies there and his openly proclaimed Zionist views aroused the opposition of ultra-Orthodox circles in Jerusalem. Gruenhut was a prominent figure in the early Mizrachi. In addition to his communal and educational activities, Gruenhut continued his scholarly endeavors, mainly in Midrash and in Palestinian geography.

Bibliography: S. Ha-Cohen Weingarten, in: *Lu'aḥ Yerushalayim*, 7 (1946/47), 168–77; 8 (1947/48), 211–4. [J.H.]

GRUENHUT, MAX (1893–1964), criminologist and penal reformer. Gruenhut, who was born in Magdeburg, Germany, taught at Hamburg until 1922, when he went to Jena University. Later he went to Bonn as professor ordinarius. After the Nazi accession to power he emigrated to Britain where he was appointed reader in criminology at Oxford. In 1948 he published his widely acclaimed work, *Penal Reform*. Gruenhut, who became a practicing Lutheran, took a special interest in the development of the probation system. He devoted several publications to this subject, stressing the extramural method of peno-correctional treatment as a possible alternative to imprisonment in many cases. The United Nations asked Gruenhut to undertake an investigation of certain problems relating to the efficacy of probation. The results were issued by the UN Social Affairs Department in 1964.

Bibliography: Mannheim, in: *British Journal of Criminology*, 4 (1964), 313–5. [Z.H.]

GRUENING, ERNEST HENRY (1887–), U.S. journalist, administrator, and politician. Gruening was born in New York City to parents of German origin. He received a medical degree from Harvard in 1912, but decided on a career in journalism and joined the staff of the Boston *Evening Herald*. After serving as an artillery officer and on the War Trade Board's Bureau of Imports during World War I, Gruening edited *The Nation* from 1920 to 1923, winning fame for his crusades against U.S. economic exploitation of Latin America. In 1927 he moved to Maine and founded the muckraking Portland *Evening News*, which specialized in attacks on the power utilities. Gruening abandoned journalism as a profession in 1934 when he was appointed director of the Division of Territories and Island Possessions of the Department of the Interior, a post he held until 1939. From 1935 to 1937 he also served as relief and reconstruction administrator in Puerto Rico. Gruening became territorial governor of Alaska (1939–53), in which capacity he was a strong proponent of Alaskan statehood. When Alaska was admitted to the Union, Gruening was elected a U.S. senator (1958) and was reelected in 1962. He was defeated in his bid for a third term in the 1968 Democratic primary. Gruening's Senate career was marked by his vigorous opposition to American military intervention in Latin America and Vietnam and by his support for federal birth control programs and public power projects. His publications include: *Mexico and its Heritage* (1928); *Public Pays and Still Pays* (1931, 1964); *State of Alaska* (1954); and *Vietnam Folly* (1968). [H.S.]

GRUENWALD, MORITZ (1853–1895), Czech rabbi and scholar. Gruenwald was born in Ungarisch-Hradisch, Moravia. He studied at the Breslau rabbinical seminary and served as rabbi in various cities, among them Pisek, Bohemia, 1887–93, before becoming chief rabbi of Bulgaria, residing in Sofia, in 1893. He also directed and taught at the Sofia rabbinical seminary.

In 1881 Gruenwald founded and edited until 1885 *Das Juedische Zentralblatt Zugleich Archiv . . . Boehmen* (1882–85), a periodical intended for the congregations in which he served. He published a number of books, including *Einfluss der Bibel auf die Bildung von Redensarten in europaeischen Sprachen* (1883); *Zur romanischen Dialektologie*, on Ladino and Rashi's *Lo'azim* (1883) and works on Czech Jewish history. [ED.]

GRUMBACH, SALOMON (1884–1952), French socialist. Born in an Alsatian village, Grumbach went to Paris as a young man to become editor of *L'Humanité* under Jean Jaurès. During World War I he was Swiss correspondent of the paper and wrote French propaganda tracts on such subjects as *Le Destin de l'Alsace-Lorraine* (Lausanne, 1916) and *Germany's Annexionist Aims* (Engl., 1918) in both German and French. Elected a member of the central committee of the French Socialist Party (SFIO), he represented it at the Third Socialist International and was elected on the Socialist ticket to the French Chamber of Deputies in 1928. Grumbach was a member of the Chamber almost continually until 1948 and was successively vice-chairman and then chairman of its Foreign Affairs Committee. Following the fall of France in 1940, he was imprisoned and later assigned a place of forced residence but escaped in 1942 and joined the French resistance movement. After the war, Grumbach was reelected to the Chamber of Deputies and concerned himself with aid for refugees. He exercised influence on France's recognition of the State of Israel. He was also active in the World Jewish Congress, especially on behalf of the Jews of North Africa and was secretary-general of the world executive of *ORT.

Bibliography: JC (July 18, 1952), 19; *New York Times* (July 14, 1952), 17. [S.C.]

GRUNBERG, ABRAHAM (1841–1906), a leader of the *Ḥibbat Zion movement. Born in Kishinev, Grunberg became a merchant and estate owner and one of the first wealthy Jews to join the Ḥibbat Zion movement. He lent his support to L. *Pinsker in Odessa. In 1889, at the Ḥovevei Zion Conference at Vilna, he was elected to the committee of trustees (the other members of which were S. *Mohilever and S. J. *Fuenn), which replaced Pinsker at the head of the movement. In 1890 he helped obtain from the Czarist authorities the authorization for the Society for the Support of Jewish Agriculturists and Artisans in Syria and Palestine (the official name of the Odessa Committee of Ḥovevei Zion), and upon Pinsker's death (1892) he was elected president of the society, a post which he retained until a few months before his death. Grunberg also headed a delegation that discussed with Baron *Rothschild in Paris the methods of agricultural settlement in Ereẓ Israel (1901). He frequently served as a Jewish representative before the Russian authorities.

Bibliography: A. Druyanow (ed.), *Ketavim le-Toledot Ḥibbat-Ẓiyyon ve-Yishuv Ereẓ-Yisrael*, 2 (1925), index; 3 (1932), index.

[Y.S.]

GRUNFELD, ISIDOR (1900–), rabbi and author. Born in Tauberettersheim, Bavaria, Grunfeld studied law and philosophy at the universities of Frankfort and Hamburg, and rabbinics at yeshivot there. After practicing law at Wuerzburg, Bavaria, he settled in England in 1933, where he studied for the rabbinate and was ordained in 1938. He was minister of the Finsbury Park synagogue (1936–38), and served first as registrar and later (from 1939) as *dayyan* of the London Beth Din, from which office he retired owing to ill health in 1965. Among his numerous communal activities were those for the Jewish War Orphans in Europe, and the British Council for Jewish Relief and Rehabilitation. He was also active in Amnesty International and various peace movements. Grunfeld's literary work is chiefly concerned with S. R. *Hirsch's writings, editing English translations of his work with extensive introductions and notes (*Judaism Eternal*, 2 vols., 1956; *Horeb*, 2 vols., 1962; introduction to I. Levy's English translation of S. R. Hirsch's Pentateuch commentary, 1959). He also wrote *The Sabbath* (1954) and *Three Generations* (on the history of neo-Orthodoxy, 1958). His wife Judith (née Rosenbaum) was active in the Beth Jacob movement (religious girls' schools) and in the Jewish secondary schools movement in England.

Bibliography: JC (Oct. 28, 1960); *Jewish Review*, London (Nov. 4, 1961).

[ED.]

GRÜNVALD, PHILIP (**Fülöp**; 1887–1964), Hungarian historian. Grünvald was born in Sopron, the son of Mano Grünvald, rabbi of the Orthodox congregation there. In 1913 he started his teaching career at the Jewish secondary school in Budapest. From 1919 to 1948 he taught at the Jewish High School and from 1948 to 1958 he was its principal. From the early 1950s until his death he taught Jewish history at the Jewish Theological Seminary in Budapest. As a teacher he was held in great esteem, especially because of his absolute integrity and deep religious commitment. Grünvald also served the Jewish Museum of that city for 30 years, first as curator and later as director.

In 1927 he presented an outline for a history of the Jews in Hungary (in: *A Zsidó Gimnázium Értesitője*, 8 (1927), 12–29). Later, he dealt with the history of the Jews in Buda, *A zsidók története Budán* (1938). His other works dealt with aspects of the history of Jews in Hungary. His major work was the continuation of *Monumenta Hungariae Judaica*, with A. *Scheiber, he edited volumes 5–7 (1959–63) of this important historical work.

Bibliography: A. Scheiber, in: *Soproni Szemle*, 18 (1964), 187–8; idem, in: MHJ, 8 (1965), 11–17, incl. list of his works.

[AL.SCH.]

GRÜNWALD, AMRAM (d. 1870), Hungarian talmudist. Although he published no works he is extensively mentioned in the works of his contemporaries who referred difficult problems to him; e.g., Abraham S. B. Sofer in *Ketav Sofer* (OḤ, nos. 3, 94); Judah Aszod in *Teshuvot Maharia* Pt. 2 (no. 236); David Neumann, in *Nir le-David* (nos. 105,118). His ethical testament was published in the *Keren le-David* (1929) of his son Eliezer David Grünwald. Grünwald died in Csorna, Hungary.

[N.B.-M.]

His other son, MOSES (1853–1910), was a scholar and rabbi. He studied under Abraham Samuel *Sofer in Pressburg, but leaned to Ḥasidism and often visited R. Issachar Dov of *Belz. He served as rabbi in Homonna, Slovakia and Kisvarda, Hungary and from 1893 in Huszt, Carpatho-Russia, where he established one of the major Hungarian yeshivot. Grünwald wrote three works all with the title *Arugot ha-Bosem:* (1) responsa (1912); (2) a study of the talmudic principle of *Issur Ḥal al Issur* (more than one prohibition can apply to the same act; 1928); and (3) a commentary on the Pentateuch (1913). He also wrote *Mikveh Tohorah* on the laws of *mikveh* (1931). His will was published (1911) under the title *Hakhanah de-Rabbah*.

[Y.AL.]

Bibliography: P. Z. Schwartz, *Shem ha-Gedolim me-Ereẓ Hagar*, 2 (1914), 256 no. 13; A. Stern, *Meliẓei Esh al Ḥodshei Adar* (1938), 77b (on Amram Grünwald). S. N. Gottlieb, *Oholei Shem* (1912), 234; P. Z. Schwartz, *Shem ha-Gedolim me-Ereẓ Hagar*, 2 (1914), 9a, no. 142 (on Moses b. Amram Grünwald).

GRÜNWALD, JUDAH (1845–1920), Hungarian rabbi. Grünwald was born in Brezó (Brezova, now Czechoslovakia), and served as rabbi of Szobotisz for seven years, of Bonyhad a further seven years, of Surany for two and a half years, and of Szatmar (Satu-Mare) for 22 years. In Szatmar he founded a large yeshivah which achieved a wide reputation. After his death several of his works were published. The most important of them is the responsa *Zikhron Yehudah* (*Budapest-Satoraljaujhely*, 1923–28) in two parts. In part 1 (no. 187) he discusses whether one may associate with Zionists and expresses the fear that through Zionism "an opportunity will be given for us to be attacked and to make us disliked by the gentile countries." Another responsum (no. 200) to Joseph Ḥayyim Sonnenfeld in Jerusalem, dated 1913, on whether it is permitted to associate with the *Agudat Israel, was removed from the volume and replaced by a responsum on whether it is permitted to handle food and drink on the Day of Atonement in order to give it to children. Others of his published works are: (1) *Shevet mi-Yhudah* (2 pts., 1922), on the Pentateuch; (2) *Ḥasdei Avot* (1925), on the tractate *Avot;* (3) *Olelot Yehudah*, a commentary on Psalms (1927); and (4) *She'erit Yehudah* (1938), on the Pentateuch.

Bibliography: S. N. Gottlieb, *Oholei Shem* (1912), 425; P. Z. Schwartz, *Shem ha-Gedolim me-Ereẓ Hagar*, 1 (1914), 546 no. 292; A. Stern, *Meliẓei Esh al Ḥodshei Kislev–Adar* (1938), 526–36; *Sinai*, 5 (1939–40), 421–3; Weingarten, *ibid.*, 29 (1951), 98f.

[N.B.-M.]

GRUNWALD, MAX (1871–1953), rabbi, historian, and folklorist. Born at Hindenburg (now Zabrze, Silesia), Grunwald served as rabbi in Hamburg (1895–1903) and Vienna (1905–35). He settled in Jerusalem in 1938. Grunwald was a many-sided and productive scholar. He wrote on the history of the communities which he served (*Hamburgs deutsche Juden–1811*, 1904; *Portugiesengraeber auf deutscher Erde; Juden als Rheder und Seefahrer*, 1902; and on Vienna: *Geschichte der Juden in Wien* (for schools, 1926); *Wiener Ḥevra Kaddisha*, 1910; *Vienna*, 1936 (in the Jewish communities series of the Jewish Publication Society of America)). Grunwald also wrote on such famous Viennese Jews as S. Oppenheimer (*Samuel Oppenheimer und sein Kreis*, 1913) and S. Wertheimer and his descendants (in: *Juedische Familienforschung*, 1926). Of more general historical interest is his anthology of the accounts of Jewish participants in Napoleon's campaigns (*Die Feldzuege Napoleons . . .*, 1913).

Grunwald's main interest, however, was Jewish folklore, and his contribution in this field is of lasting importance. In 1897 he founded the *Gesellschaft fuer juedische Volkskunde* and edited and largely wrote its organ, the *Mitteillungen* (1897–1922), which was succeeded by the *Jahrbuecher fuer juedische Volkskunde* (1923–25). In this area he contributed also to other periodicals as well as to a number of Festschriften (J. Lewy, 1911; *Gaster Anniversary Volume, . . .*) and published important studies such as *Hebraeische Frauennamen* (1894–), *Eigennamen des alten Testaments* (1895), and in the related field of Jewish art *Holzsynagogen in Polen* (with others, 1934). Among Grunwald's other interests were Spinoza, on whom he had written his dissertation (1892) and a prize-winning *Spinoza in Deutschland* (1897). On the occasion of the international exhibition on hygiene in Dresden in 1911 he published a book on that subject, *Hygiene der Juden* (1912). He also edited a German prayer book for women (*Beruria*, 1913^2) and one for serving soldiers (*Gebetbuch fuer israelitische Soldaten im Kriege*, 1914). On the occasion of Grunwald's 70th birthday *Omanut*, the publication of the Bezalel Museum in Jerusalem, issued his bibliography (1941).

His son, KURT (1901–), was a banker, economist, and public figure in Jerusalem. He wrote on aspects of Jewish economic history including *Tuerkenhirsch* (1966), a study of Baron de *Hirsch. [E.F.]

GRUSENBERG, OSCAR OSIPOVICH (1866–1940), advocate in Russia also active in Jewish communal affairs, born in Yekaterinoslav. After completing his legal studies at the University of Kiev in 1889, he was invited to prepare for a professorship at the university on the condition, which he rejected, that he embrace Christianity. He settled in St. Petersburg and began to practice law, but as a Jew was only permitted to practice as an "assistant advocate." Although he soon won a reputation throughout Russia as a brilliant lawyer, it was only in 1905 that he was granted the title of a "certified lawyer." Grusenberg specialized in criminal cases and his appearance in political trials as the defender of liberals, revolutionaries, or representatives of minority groups always received wide publicity. He defended the writers Maxim Gorki, V. *Korolenko, and such political figures as P. Milyukov, and Leon *Trotsky, as well as the group of representatives of the First *Duma after the Vyborg proclamation of 1906 protesting against the dissolution of the Duma by the government.

Grusenberg gained greatest renown, however, in specifically Jewish trials. Inspired with a national Jewish consciousness, and pride in the history of his people, he displayed great ability in defending the persecuted and obtaining justice for fellow Jews. In defending unjustly accused Jews, he was not content merely to obtain redress of wrongs done to them as individuals, but also tried to vindicate Jewish honor; and was called by Jews "the national defender." He disagreed with Jewish leaders who preferred that Jewish causes of public interest should be defended in court by Russian lawyers. Grusenberg appeared in the trials following the pogroms of *Kishinev and *Minsk; P. *Dashevski, who had made an attempt on the life of P. *Krushevan, the instigator of the Kishinev pogrom, and D. *Blondes in Vilna (1900–02) were defended by Grusenberg. In the Blondes case some Jews were inclined to accept the relatively light penalty imposed on the defendant by the lower court, but Grusenberg insisted on bringing the case before a higher court in order to clear the name of the Jews absolutely. The high point in his life and in his career as a lawyer was his appearance in the *Beilis

Oscar Grusenberg, Russian advocate and champion of Jewish rights.

trial in 1913, which he considered was similar to the stand of the martyrs in the trials of the Inquisition. His success was the result not only of his brilliant forensic talents, his profound knowledge of criminal law, and mastery of court procedure but also of his knowledge of the psychology of the common Russian, an important factor since the fate of the defendant in criminal cases was decided by a jury consisting, as a rule, of people from all walks of life.

As a member of the Russian Constitutional Democratic Party, Grusenberg was also active in Russian political life. In the elections to the Second *Duma he was a candidate in Vilna province, but was defeated by the Poles. He was later a member of the advisory council to the Jewish representatives in the Third and Fourth Dumas. After the *Balfour Declaration Grusenberg drew closer to Zionism and in 1917 joined the "Jewish Bloc" organized by the Zionists. That year he was made a senator by Kerensky's Provisional Government. In 1918–19 during the Russian civil war Grusenberg headed the Jewish Council for Self-Defense and the Council for Aiding the Victims of Pogroms. In 1919 he was chosen as one of the representatives of Ukrainian Jewry to the *Comité des Délégations Juives in Paris. After the Soviets came to power, Grusenberg left Russia. He stayed from 1921 to 1923 in Berlin and from 1926 to 1932 in Riga. In 1929 he served as the representative of the Jews of Latvia at the founding of the enlarged *Jewish Agency and was chosen a member of its council. Grusenberg spent the last years of his life in France.

Besides legal articles published in Russian professional journals Grusenberg also wrote on Jewish subjects in *Voskhod* and in *Budushchnost*, edited by his brother Samuel.

He wrote a book on his experiences as an advocate, and in 1938 his memoirs appeared under the title *Vchera* ("Yesterday"). A collection of his essays and speeches in Russian, including some critical appreciations, was published posthumously in 1944.

In 1950 his remains were brought to Israel in accordance with his will.

Bibliography: S. Kucherov, in: *Russian Jewry 1860–1917* (1966), 219–52; A. A. Goldenweiser, *V zashchitu prava* (1952), 239–49; M. Samuel, *Blood Accusation* (1966), index. [S.K.]

GRYNBERG, BERL (1906–1961), Yiddish writer. Grynberg grew up in Warsaw and emigrated to Argentina in 1923. He worked in Cordoba and Buenos Aires as a printer and, for decades, as linotypist for the Yiddish daily *Di Prese*, where his earliest stories appeared. They aroused critical attention with their original combination of realistic and romantic characteristics. The stories often begin with actual happenings but soon become mystical and symbolic. The themes, landscapes, and characters of his six narrative volumes are both Argentinian and Jewish. He was profoundly influenced by Sholem Asch and David Bergelson. He was a victim of depressive moods and committed suicide.

Bibliography: LNYL 2 (1958), 392ff; S. Bickel, *Shrayber fun Mayn Dor* (1965), 377–80. [M.Rav.]

GRYNSZPAN (Gruenspan), HERSCHEL (1921–?), assassin of a German diplomat in Paris. Grynszpan, who was born in Hanover, Germany, into a family of Polish Jews, moved to Paris early in 1938. When he learned that Polish Jews, including his parents, were being deported from Germany (Oct. 28, 1938), he decided to assault the German ambassador in Paris in order to arouse public opinion in the West regarding the Nazi persecution of Jews.

Herschel Grynszpan, whose assassination of a German diplomat served as the pretext for the *Kristallnacht* of November 1938. Courtesy Yad Vashem Archives, Jerusalem.

Grynszpan shot at a German embassy official, Ernst vom Rath, who, mortally wounded, died two days later. His death served as a pretext for the November pogroms against Jews throughout Germany and Austria, termed **Kristallnacht*. Grynszpan was held for questioning by the French authorities, and the Germans accused him of being a tool of "world Jewry." When France capitulated, Grynszpan escaped to the Free Zone. However, he later returned to the Occupied Zone, where he was arrested and handed over to the Germans, who made elaborate preparations for a show trial. In the end, the whole affair was hushed up and Grynszpan disappeared without trace.

Bibliography: F. K. Kaul, *Der Fall des Herschel Grynspan* (1965); L. Steinberg, in: *Le Monde Juif*, 2 (1964), 17–25; WLB, 17 (1963), 56—bibliography. [Sh.E.]

GUADALAJARA, city in Castile, central Spain. A Jewish community already existed there at the time of the *Visigoths, for the Jews are said to have been entrusted, by Ṭāriq ibn-Ziyād, with the defense of the town after the Arab conquest in 714. Joseph *Ferrizuel (Cidellus), the physician of Alfonso VI, was active on behalf of the Jews there after the Christian reconquest in 1085. Most of the Guadalajara Jews earned their living from weaving, shoemaking, and tailoring. A tax of 11,000 maravedis, levied from the community as late as 1439, attests to its well-established financial situation. After the anti-Jewish persecutions of

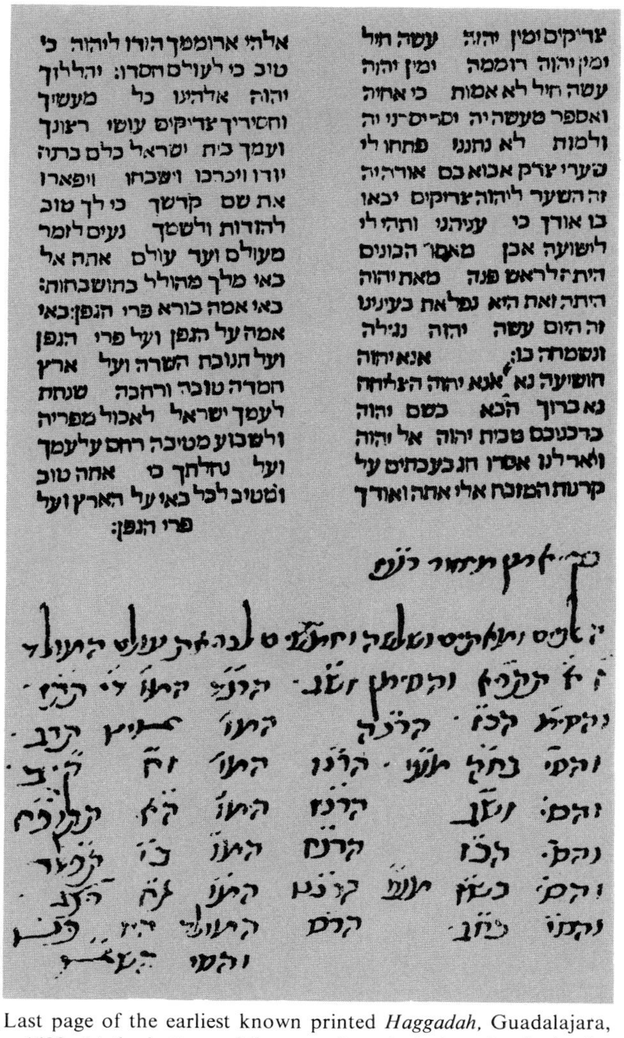

Last page of the earliest known printed *Haggadah*, Guadalajara, c. 1482. At the bottom of the page the calculations for the beginnings of the Hebrew months in the year 1493 have been added by hand. The copy of this *Haggadah* in the Jewish National and University Library, Jerusalem, is the only one known to exist.

1391, the order to confine the Jews and the Moors in separate sections of the city was rigorously enforced. Several Jews of Guadalajara acted as tax farmers even in the 15th century. The tax levied from the Jews of Guadalajara during the war against Granada was one of the highest paid by any Jewish community, amounting to 104,220 maravedis in 1488 and 90,620 maravedis in 1491.

Guadalajara was a foremost cultural center of Spanish Jewry and the birthplace of the *Kabbalah in Castile. *Moses de Leon and other important scholars of the 13th century were active in Guadalajara. *Isaac ibn Sahula, author of the *Meshal ha-Kadmoni,* was in practice there as a physician. The earliest-recorded Hebrew printing press in Spain was established in 1482 in Guadalajara by Solomon *Alkabeẓ who produced there in that year the commentary of David *Kimḥi on the later prophets and the *Tur Even ha-Ezer* of *Jacob b. Asher (1480–82). During the years before the expulsion of the Jews from Spain, residents included Isaac *Abrabanel and Isaac *Aboab II who directed one of the most important yeshivot in Castile. A document of 1499, concerning Jewish property in Guadalajara at the time of the expulsion, lists three synagogues and 36 Jewish houseowners. The exiles from Guadalajara established their own synagogue in Algiers in the early 16th century.

Bibliography: Baer, Spain, index; Baer, Urkunden, index; Suárez Fernández, Documentos, index. [H.B.]

GUADALUPE, town in Castile, W. Spain. Jewish landowners are recorded there in the second half of the 14th century. The community was annihilated in the wave of anti-Jewish riots which swept Spain in 1391, but was revived during the 15th century. In 1485, however, Jews were forbidden to live in Guadalupe by order of Nuño de Arévalo, the local inquisitor. In 1492, prior to the expulsion of the Jews from Spain, *veedores* (leaders) of the community sold the land of the old cemetery to the local bishop for 400 reals; a clause in the deed of sale states that the price was so low because of the kindnesses shown to the Jewish community by the bishop. The *Conversos in Guadalupe lived in a special street in the former Jewish quarter. Jews from Trujillo would stay at the homes of these Conversos, which became important centers for fulfilling the Jewish observances. Forty-six dossiers, almost all of 1485, are preserved concerning persons arraigned before a special tribunal sent by the Toledo Inquisition to uncover relapsed Conversos. Several Conversos who had entered the monastery of San Bartholomé de Lupiana near Guadalupe were tried there in 1489–90. The monks Diego de Marchena and García Çapata, whose conversion to Judaism caused a furor in the church in Spain, belonged to this monastery. They were burned at the stake as Jews.

Bibliography: A. Sicroff, in: *Studies . . . U. J. Benardete* (1965), 89–125; H. Beinart, in: *Tarbiz,* 26 (1956/57), 78; idem, in: *Scripta Hierosolymitana,* 7 (1961), 167–92; F. Fita, in: *Boletín de la Academia de Historia,* 23 (1893), 283; E. Escobar, in: *El Monasterio de Guadalupe,* 1 (1916), 62; Suárez Fernández, Documentos, index; Baer, Urkunden, index; Baer, Spain, index. [H.B.]

GUASTALLA, ENRICO (1828–1903), Italian soldier. Born in Guastalla, central Italy, Guastalla gave up his career as a businessman in 1848 to volunteer for the Piedmontese army in the struggle for the unification of Italy. He fought against Austria in 1848 and participated in the abortive capture of Rome from the pope in the following year. For several years he was editor of *Libertà e Associazione,* but his radical views came into conflict with the authorities and he fled to England, where he joined the radical patriot Giuseppe Mazzini. Guastalla returned to Italy in 1859 and joined Garibaldi in his campaigns of 1860 and 1866, being promoted major. He fought with Garibaldi in his attack on Rome and was taken prisoner with him at Aspromonte. The recipient of numerous awards, he was elected to the Italian parliament in 1865 and sat there for many years. [Mo.K.]

GUATEMALA, Central American republic, population 4,863,520 (1968), Jewish population c. 1,100. Documents in the archives of the Mexican Inquisition attest to the presence of Marranos in Guatemala during the colonial period. The origins of the present Jewish community, however, are to be found in the mid-19th-century immigration from Germany. The community formed by these immigrants was small and isolated from the Jewish world, and its descendants are no longer Jews. The most prominent members of this community were the Stahl family, which established cotton mills and for 30 years attended to the government's banking and financing needs. Jewish immigrants arrived at the beginning of the 20th century from Germany and Middle East countries, followed in the 1920s by East European Jews. Many of the latter came via Cuba and considered Guatemala only a transit stop until they could obtain visas to the United States.

Guatemala was not favorably disposed to Jewish immigration, which it attempted to limit. In 1932 the government ordered the expulsion within one month of all peddlers; although the actual expulsion was averted, peddling was prohibited, and many Jews faced ruin and were compelled to emigrate. The Jewish community was reduced to only 800 souls in 1939. In 1936 under the influence of the substantial German community in Guatemala, legislation was enacted to curb immigration of all people of Asian origin (among whom were included the Poles). Although never formally abolished, these laws have rarely been enforced since World War II, and after the war many Jewish refugees entered the country. The majority of the Jews live in Guatemala City, the remainder in Quetzaltenango and San Marcos. According to the 1965 census, out of 1,030 Jews, 276 were engaged in industry and commerce, 66 in the free professions, and 7 in agriculture. The same census indicated that the community had 74 mixed marriages, accounting for 27.2% of the Jewish population.

The community comprises three main groups: the German, the Sephardi, and the East European, each with its

Centers of Jewish settlement in Guatemala.

own institutions—the Sociedad Israelita de Guatemala and Bet-El (reform), Maguen David, and Centro Hebreo, respectively—and its own synagogue. Other organizations, unified under the Comité Central, include *B'nai B'rith, *Wizo, and two youth groups, the Maccabi and Guafty (the latter a Reform youth movement). The Organización Sionista de Guatemala comprises all Zionist groups. A Jewish school, called Instituto Albert Einstein, founded in 1957, is authorized by the Ministry of Education and has an enrollment of 100 children from kindergarten through preparatory levels. The Jewish press is all but nonexistent. The Spanish-language monthly, which appeared previously, ceased publication, and only a single communal information bulletin is published occasionally.

Guatemala has traditionally maintained excellent relations with Israel. Its representative to the United Nations in 1947, Jorge García Granados, was a member of the U.N. Special Commission for Palestine (UNSCOP) and worked tirelessly for the establishment of a Jewish state in part of Palestine. His book *The Birth of Israel* was published in 1949. The two governments have engaged in various projects cooperatively. Guatemala maintains an embassy in Jerusalem and in 1949 Israel established its embassy in Guatemala City.

Bibliography: J. Beller, *Jews in Latin America* (1969); F. Tenenbaum (ed.), *La comunidad Judía de Guatemala* (1963); A. Monk and J. Isaacson, *Comunidades Judías de Latinoamérica* (1968), 86–88; JJSO, 7 (1965), 302–3; J. Shatzky, *Yidishe Yishuvim in Lataynamerike* (1952).

[De.Al.]

GUEBWILLER, town in the Haut-Rhin department, E. France. In 1270 there was a community of at least 10 families in the town; from 1330 or earlier they owned a synagogue. However the community ceased to exist after the *Black Death persecutions (1348–49). Jews did not reappear in Guebwiller until the beginning of the 17th century. Their numbers did not grow to any extent until the 19th century (about 80 families in 1870), but subsequently declined once more. Several Jews from Guebwiller were deported by the Nazis. In 1969 a small community again existed. The present Rue des Tonneliers was formerly known as Rue des Juifs.

Bibliography: E. Scheid, *Histoire des Juifs d'Alsace* (1887), 107, 136, 249; C. Wetterwald, *Strassennamen von Gebweiler* (1928), 32; Z. Szajkowski, *Analytical Franco-Jewish Gazetteer* (1966), 251; Germ Jud, 2 (1968) 270–1.

[B.Bl.]

GUEDALLA, HAIM (1815–1904), philanthropist and supporter of Jewish settlement in Ereẓ Israel. Born in London, Guedalla was the scion of a Moroccan family. He married the niece of Moses *Montefiore. Through his association with the Montefiore family he became interested in Ereẓ Israel. In the period 1876–80, he was the chairman of the Turkish Bondholders of the General Debt of Turkey, and in view of the size of the debt—£250,000,000—he proposed that Ereẓ Israel be purchased from the Turks in exchange for the debt. George *Eliot, who was then taken up with the idea of the return of the Jews to their ancestral home, inspired this idea in him. There was considerable reaction to Guedalla's proposal in the Jewish world: some people treated it with amusement, while others (such as Y. M. *Pines) thought it worthy of consideration. Guedalla did in fact negotiate with Midhat Pasha, the grand vizier, but nothing came of the proposal. In 1863 Guedalla accompanied Moses Montefiore on a trip to Morocco to bring aid to its Jewish community, and on the way back he visited Spain. This trip was the beginning of his campaign designed to persuade the Spanish government to permit the return of the Jews, an aim which was in fact achieved in 1869. He also joined Montefiore on his fourth trip to Ereẓ Israel in 1855 and extended help to various institutions there. He published articles, pamphlets, and books dealing with Jewish affairs and supplied the funds for the English translation of *The Jewish Question of Russia* by Demidoff San Donato (1884).

Bibliography: JC (Oct. 7, 1904).

[G.K.]

GUEDALLA, PHILIP (1889–1944), English biographer, historian, and essayist. A member of an old Sephardi family, and the son of David Guedalla, a pioneer English Zionist, Philip Guedalla was educated at Oxford, where he excelled as a debater and actor, and later became a barrister. During World War I he was legal adviser to the ministry of munitions and the contracts department of the British War Office. After ten years at the bar, he retired in 1923 to devote himself to literature and politics. Guedalla's five attempts to secure election to Parliament as a Liberal M.P. failed; but his books on historical personalities and events, mostly of the 19th century, were an outstanding success. A witty speaker and writer, he developed a brilliant and highly individual style, often tinged with irony, in his works. These include *The Second Empire* (1922), on Napoleon III; *Palmerston* (1926); *Gladstone and Palmerston* (1928); a study of Wellington entitled *The Duke* (1931); *The Queen and Mr. Gladstone* (1933); *The Hundred Days* (1934), on Napoleon I's last campaign; *The Hundred Years* (1936), covering 1837–1936; *The Liberators* (1942); and *Middle East, 1940–42: A Study in Axis Power* (1944). He also wrote studies of famous personalities such as *Supers and Supermen* (1920) and *Masters and Men* (1923); two books of American interest, *Independence Day* (1926), which appeared in the U.S. as *Fathers of the Revolution* (1926), and *Conquistador* (1927); and published the works of Disraeli, to which he added his own introductory notes (1927). He was president of the British Zionist Federation, 1924–28, and in 1925 delivered his presidential address to the Jewish Historical Society of England on *Napoleon and Palestine*. Philip Guedalla was noted for his aphorisms, such as "Any stigma to beat a dogma," "History is the study of other people's mistakes," and "An Englishman is a man who lives on an island in the North Sea governed by Scotsmen." During World War II, at the age of 54, he became a squadron leader in the Royal Air Force. One of his last works was *Mr. Churchill: A Portrait* (1941).

Bibliography: DNB (1941–50); *The Times* (Dec. 18, 1944).

[G.E.S.]

GUEDEMANN, MORITZ (1835–1918), Austrian rabbi, historian, and apologete. Guedemann was born in Hildesheim, Prussia; he was ordained at the Breslau Jewish Theological Seminary, in 1862. Guedemann was appointed rabbi in Magdeburg in 1862. Four years later he went to Vienna as a *maggid* and in 1868 became a rabbi there. In matters of Jewish law and practice he took a conservative position, opposing, for example, the introduction of the organ and the omission of prayers relating to Zion, which contrasted with his liberal outlook in scholarly matters. In 1869 he was appointed head of the Vienna *bet din* and in 1891 became chief rabbi with Adolf *Jellinek and sole chief rabbi on the latter's death in 1894.

This period was one of rapid growth for the Vienna Jewish community and also of intensified political anti-Semitism. Guedemann played an active role in developing communal institutions. With Joseph Bloch he organized the Oesterreichisch-Israelitische Union (1886) and also helped found the *Israelitisch-Theologische Lehrenstalt in 1893. Though Guedemann had not been trained as a historian, most of his numerous contributions to scholarship were in that field. His major work was *Die Geschichte des Erziehungswesens und der Cultur der abendlaendischen Juden* (3 vols., 1880–88), the first systematic attempt to examine some of the underlying trends and institutions of medieval Jewish life in terms of their non-Jewish milieu. Other works include *Das juedische Unterrichtswesen waehrend der spanisch-arabischen Periode* (1873) and *Quellenschriften zur Geschichte des Unterrichts und der Erziehung bei den deutschen Juden* (1892). During the final decades of his life Guedemann devoted an increasing amount of his scholarly output to the refutation of academic anti-Semitism. His *Juedische Apologetik* appeared in 1906. [Is.Sch.]

Attitude to Zionism. When *Herzl was engaged in writing *Der Judenstaat,* he thought of three personages who would assist him in turning his idea into reality: Baron de *Hirsch, Baron *Rothschild, and Guedemann. It was to Guedemann that Herzl addressed one of his first letters (June 11, 1895) and his name appears frequently in Herzl's diary for the period in which Herzl began his preoccupation with political Zionism. In Herzl's eyes, Guedemann was not only Vienna's chief rabbi but one of the greatest authorities on Judaism, of which Herzl possessed only a very limited knowledge. But although opposed to the extreme Reform movement, Guedemann was in agreement with its attitude on the contemporary problem of the Jewish people. He could not understand why a Jew who had grown up among the German people and in the realm of its culture "should uproot himself by his own hands from the soil upon which he had grown," or, as he formulated it on one occasion, "Should I go from here, where the word Jew and all who bear that name are held up to shame, and leave the field to our enemies in order to form a majority in Palestine? No! A hundred thousand horses will not drag me from here, until I achieve revenge over the anti-Semites and joy over their downfall."

Over a period of many months, Herzl held meetings with Guedemann and exchanged letters with him. At the beginning, Guedemann was impressed by the idea of the *Judenstaat* and by its author; when the book came out, however, and caused a storm among the assimilationists, Guedemann's attitude underwent a decided change. For a while he wavered between support for Zionism and opposition to it; in the end, he published a book, *Nationaljudentum* (1897) in which he attacked Herzl's *Judenstaat.* In his book he sought to prove that not only was there no such thing as a Jewish people, but that it was the main task of the Jews to bring about the abolishment of nationalism. Both Herzl and *Nordau came out with sharp reactions to Guedemann's book. [G.K.]

Bibliography: B. Wachstein, *Bibliographie der Schriften Moritz Guedemanns* (1931); T. Herzl, *Complete Diaries,* 5 (1960), index; J. Fraenkel (ed.), *Jews of Austria* (1967), 111–29; Yerushalmi, in: S. Federbush (ed.), *Ḥokhmat Yisrael be-Ma'arav Eiropah* (1958), 187–98; I. Schorsch, in: YLBI, 11 (1966), 42–66; J. Fraenkel, *ibid.,* 67–82.

GUELMAN, JACOBO (1900–), Uruguayan politician. Born in Argentina, Guelman emigrated to Uruguay. He practiced medicine and joined the "Colorado" (Liberal) Party. A municipal councillor in Soriano, he was elected to the Chamber of Deputies in 1962. In 1966 he was elected senator and was a member of the Board of the Banco de Seguros del Estado. Guelman was active in Jewish communal affairs. [P.Li.]

GUENZBURG (also **Guensburg, Guenzberg, Ginzburg, Ginsburg, Ginzberg, Ginsberg, Ginzburger, Ginsburger**), family name common among East European Jews, especially in Russia. The first known Jews to call themselves by this name (after the beginning of the 16th century) came from the town of Guenzburg in Bavaria. Relatives of this family from neighboring Ulm who settled in Guenzburg used the name Ulma-Guenzburg, or simply Ulma. Abbreviated forms of Guenzberg, such as Guenz or Gaunz were also used. Some branches of the Guenzburg family later added Oettingen or Kliachko to form hyphenated names. When, early in the 19th century, the Russian authorities ordered the Jews to select family names, many in Poland, Lithuania, and Volhynia adopted the name Ginsburg, or a similar name, but these were not related to the emigrants from Guenzburg and their descendants in Bavaria.

The genealogy of the Guenzburg family has been traced back to Simeon Guenzburg (1506–1586), the grandson of Jeḥiel of Porto. The Guenzburg family produced numerous rabbis of note, including Aryeh *Gunzburg, author of *Sha'agat Aryeh,* in the 18th century, who, according to the family genealogy, was of the 11th generation to bear the name, and also the writer Mordecai Aaron *Guenzburg. The most celebrated branch of the family was that of the barons *Guenzburg.

Bibliography: B. Friedberg, *Zur Genealogie der Familie Guenzburg* (1885); D. Maggid, *Sefer Toledot Mishpeḥot Ginzburg* (1899). [S.K.]

GUENZBURG, distinguished Russian family of bankers, philanthropists, and communal workers, of whom three generations were active during the second half of the 19th and early 20th centuries in Russia and Paris. They gained a place in modern Jewish history for their efforts on behalf of Russian Jewry as semiofficial representatives before the czarist authorities as well as for their Jewish and general philanthropic activities. Horace Guenzburg was granted a baronetcy in 1871 by the archduke of Hesse-Darmstadt. In 1874 this title was also awarded to his father, Joseph Yozel Guenzburg. The title was made hereditary by Czar Alexander II. The most outstanding members of the family were: Baron Joseph Yozel (Yevsel) Guenzburg (1812–1878), son of Gabriel Jacob (1793–1853), who, according to the family genealogists, was of the 15th generation of the Guenzburg family. Born in Vitebsk he received a traditional education, and acquired wealth in the 1840s as a lessee of the liquor monopoly and later as an army contractor. In 1857 he settled with his family in Paris but retained his enterprises in Russia. In 1859 he founded the Joseph Yevsel Guenzburg Bank, in St. Petersburg, which rapidly became one of the chief financial institutions in Russia and contributed significantly to the development of credit financing in that country. He participated in financing railroad construction and the development of gold mines in the Urals, Altai, and Trans-Baikal Siberia.

Guenzburg tried to utilize his contacts with influential Russian circles to improve the situation of the Jews, and especially to win rights of permanent Jewish residence outside the *Pale of Settlement for specific categories of Jews, such as merchants, craftsmen, or demobilized soldiers. In this he was successful. The first synagogue in St. Petersburg was built as a result of his efforts. He was one of the founders of the *Society for the Promotion of Culture among the Jews of Russia in 1863 and supported its activities. Guenzburg provided scholarships for Jewish youth to encourage higher education, especially in medicine, and donated substantial sums to encourage Jews to engage in agriculture, which he regarded as an important step toward improving their situation. In addition to awarding prizes for agriculture, he devoted the income from his extensive estates in southern Russia to settling Jews on these lands. He died in Paris and was buried in the family sepulcher there. He had one daughter and four sons, some of whom engaged in his enterprises.

His second son, the best known, was Baron Horace (Naphtali Herz) Guenzburg (1833–1909), born in Zvenigorodka, in the province of Kiev. In addition to a general education, Horace received a Jewish education in his father's house. Among his teachers was the Hebrew writer Mordecai Sukhostaver, who for many years served as Joseph Yozel Guenzburg's secretary. Through him Horace became closely acquainted with the Hebrew poet Jacob *Eichenbaum who profoundly influenced him. While still a young man, Horace became his father's aide and principal partner in his financial enterprises as well as in his public activities. When his father established his bank in St. Petersburg, Horace became its acting director. His talents as well as his manners contributed to its success as one of the central financial institutions of Russia. His personal qualities gained him the respect and confidence of court circles. Among other activities he managed the financial affairs of the archduke of Hesse-Darmstadt, who appointed him consul-general in Russia (1868–72), the only instance when the Russian government consented to the appointment of a Jew as consul in its domains. The Russian government also showed its appreciation of Guenzburg's services by appointing him state councillor and awarding him orders of merit. Until 1892 he served as alderman in the St. Petersburg municipality. He was director of financial institutions, as well as a supporter and member of many non-Jewish social welfare institutions. In 1892 the Guenzburg bank suspended operations as a result of a crisis that was brought about by the suspension of credits by the Russian government.

Baron Horace (Naphtali Herz) Guenzberg, Russian Jewish financier. Jerusalem, Schwadron Collection, J.N.U.L.

Guenzburg's home in St. Petersburg was a meeting place for liberal scholars, authors, artists, and other intellectuals in the Russian capital. As well as a philanthropist Horace was a generous patron of scientific, cultural, and social institutions, and of promising writers, artists, and musicians. Among others the sculptor Mark *Antokolski benefited from Guenzburg's assistance early in his career.

In Russian society Horace's position and his contacts with the authorities helped him continue with greater effect the activities of his father on behalf of Russian Jewry and as patron of its communal affairs. During the period of reaction in Russia, he had to keep vigilant watch to prevent the promulgation of an ever increasing number of anti-Jewish decrees and to counteract the accusations against the Jews. When the new military service law was about to be passed in 1874 he succeeded in preventing the inclusion of special provisions directed against Jews. During the blood libel case in *Kutais in 1878 he encouraged the celebrated scholar, the convert Daniel *Chwolson, to write a book tracing the history of the blood libel, which he subsidized. In 1881–82 he attempted to establish a countrywide organization of Russian Jews, and he convened and headed conferences of representatives of Jewish communities in St. Petersburg to plan action against the pogroms then taking place in southern Russia. Guenzburg also urged the government to rescind the "Temporary Regulations" of 1882 (*May Laws), which had been promulgated by the minister of the interior, *Ignatyev, and he actively participated in the work of the Pahlen Commission (1883–88) which had been empowered to review the laws pertaining to Jews.

After his father's death, Horace headed the Jewish community in St. Petersburg, and also the Society for the Promotion of Culture among the Jews of Russia. After the 1905 pogroms he organized and headed a committee to aid the victims. He opposed the emigration of Jews from Russia, and as chairman of the ICA (*Jewish Colonization Association) committee in Russia, he urged that the funds donated by Baron Hirsch be spent in Russia to encourage agriculture and crafts among Jews. He supported publications of historical interest, including the collection of Russian laws pertaining to Jews edited by V. *Levanda, and other studies. Horace had 11 children.

His son, Baron David Guenzburg (1857–1910), was born in Kamenets-Podolski. He continued the family tradition of public and communal activity and philanthropy, but is mainly noted for his scholarly work in Judaic and oriental studies. He specialized in oriental subjects and linguistics, and medieval Arabic poetry, in the universities of St. Petersburg, Greifswald (Germany; 1879–80), and in Paris, and was a pupil of the Hebrew writer Ẓ. ha-Cohen *Rabinowitz, of A. *Neubauer, and of Senior *Sachs. The last, who was a tutor in the Guenzburg home in Paris, influenced David to study medieval Hebrew poetry. David gained a knowledge of most Semitic languages, and published a number of works. These include: the physician Isaac b. Todros of Avignon's *Be'er le-Ḥai* from the sole manuscript (1884); the first edition of *Sefer ha-Anak (Ha-Tarshish)* of Moses Ibn Ezra (1886); the diwan of the Spanish-Arab poet, Ibn Guzman (1896); studies of the foundations of Arabic poetry (in publications of the oriental department of the Royal Archeological Society, 1892–97); a comprehensive work on ancient Jewish ornamentation, *L'Ornement Hébreu,* in collaboration with the Russian art critic, V. V. Stasov (1903), which contained examples of Jewish illuminations from medieval Hebrew manuscripts, among them illuminated Bible manuscripts of oriental origin in a style which combined Byzantine and Arabic elements; a catalog and description of Arabic, Greek, and Coptic manuscripts in the Institute of Oriental Languages of the Russian Foreign Office; a book on the poetry of Lermontov (published posthumously in 1915; as a connoisseur of Russian poetry, Guenzburg was especially attracted by the Jewish and oriental elements in Lermontov's works); a number of studies published in Russian, French, German, and Hebrew periodicals and in jubilee

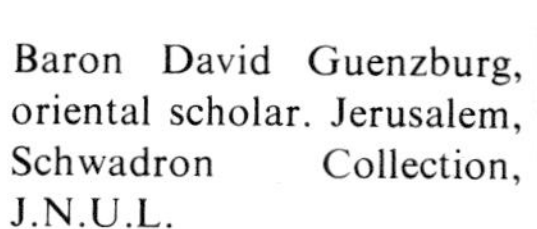

Baron David Guenzburg, oriental scholar. Jerusalem, Schwadron Collection, J.N.U.L.

volumes honoring scholars of his day. He also coedited the jubilee volume honoring A. *Harkavy. His library, which had one of the most important collections of Judaica, was one of the largest in private ownership in the world, and contained a valuable collection of manuscripts and books, including incunabula (presently in the Lenin State Library in Moscow).

Although more interested in scholarly than public activity, David was active in the St. Petersburg community, which he headed after his father's death, in the Society for the Promotion of Culture among the Jews in Russia, in ICA, and in the society to encourage crafts and agriculture among Russian Jews. In 1910 he headed a conference of Russian Jews to solve religious problems. He was also active in areas that related to his academic interests, and was chairman of the Ḥovevei Sefat Ever ("Society of Lovers of Hebrew"), a member of the committee of *Mekiẓei Nirdamim, a founder of the Society for Oriental Studies, a member of the scientific council of the Ministry of Education, as well as a founder member of other academic institutions in Russia and abroad, including the Société Asiatique of Paris. With Judah Leib Benjamin *Katzenelson (Buki ben Yogli) he was one of the editors in chief of the *Yevreyskaya Entsiklopediya* (Russian Jewish Encyclopedia), and responsible for the section dealing with geonic literature and the Arab period in Jewish history. The crowning achievement of his academic work was the creation of the Jewish Academy, officially named Higher Courses on Oriental Studies, which he established in St. Petersburg in 1908. This was a one-man project, for Guenzburg not only supported these courses with his funds, but was also its rector and lectured on Talmud, rabbinic literature, Semitic languages, Arabic literature, and medieval Jewish philosophy. Its lecturers included S. *Dubnow and J. L. B. Katzenelson, who headed it after Guenzburg's death. The academy, which continued until 1916, created a Russian school of Judaic scholarship, and was attended by Z. *Shazar, Joshua *Guttman, Y. *Kaufmann, and S. *Zeitlin, among other distinguished scholars and writers.

David's brother Pierre (d. 1948), an industrialist living in Paris, left for the United States in 1940. His wife Yvonne de la Meurthe (d. 1969) served for 20 years as honorary president of ORT. Their daughter married Sir Isaiah *Berlin.

Bibliography: D. Maggid, *Sefer Toledot Mishpeḥot Ginzburg* (1899); G. B. Slioberg, *Baron G. O. Guenzburg* (Rus., 1933); *He-Avar*, 6 (1958), 77–178. [S.K.]

GUENZBURG, ILYA YAKOVLEVICH (1860?–1939), Russian sculptor. Born into a traditional family in Vilna, Guenzburg attracted the attention of Mark *Antokolski at the age of eleven, and went with him to St. Petersburg where he studied under Antokolski himself. The art historian V. V. Stasov took an interest in his career. In 1878 he entered the St. Petersburg Academy of Arts where he received a gold medal for his "Lament of Jeremiah." After graduation in 1886, he traveled abroad for a year on a scholarship provided by Baron H. *Guenzburg, and returned to St. Petersburg, to continue his work. After the Russian Revolution he founded a Jewish Society at Petrograd for fostering art.

His work falls into three main groups: (1) scenes of children; (2) contemporary writers, artists, and scientists, e.g., Tolstoy, Tchaikovsky, Pasternak, and Mendeleyev; (3) abstract subjects, busts, and memorials (noted among them were those of Antokolski (in the Jewish cemetery of Leningrad) and that of V. V. Stasov). His sculptures were portrayed with realism, and included "A Child Before Bathing" and "The String" (depicting a child playing); both are in the Leningrad Museum. He published his memoirs, *Iz moyey zhizni* ("From My Life"; 1908), which is also of historical value on Jewish life in Russia.

Bibliography: *Ost und West* (March, 1904); YE 6 (c. 1910), 534–6. [Ed.]

GUENZBURG, MORDECAI AARON (1795–1846), Hebrew author and founder of the first modern Jewish school in Lithuania. Guenzburg was born in Salantai and earned a living as an itinerant tutor until 1835 when he settled permanently in Vilna. In 1841 he and the poet Solomon *Salkind founded a modern Jewish school, which he directed as headmaster until his death. Guenzburg became one of the leading spokesmen for the Vilna Haskalah, though he was a moderate who opposed radical change. He observed the practical *mitzvot* which, under Moses *Mendelssohn's influence, he viewed as social regulations for the benefit of the Jewish community. He opposed the extremism of both the Orthodox and the secularists. When Max *Lilienthal was invited to Russia by the authorities, Guenzburg joined the Vilna *maskilim* in attacking Lilienthal's attempts to win over the Orthodox and ridiculed his German ways and superficiality.

Guenzburg's books in the area of French and Russian history enjoyed wide circulation and helped improve his financial condition. In 1844 and 1862 (2 vols.) he published *Devir*, an anthology of letters, essays, and short stories, containing, among others, letters by Goethe, *Heine, and *Boerne, and a translation of the letters of Moses Montefiore's personal secretary, Eliezer *Halevi, who accompanied Montefiore on his first trip to Palestine. *Devir* also contained essays about the neglected Jewish communities in the Arab lands, China, and Ethiopia. *Devir* aroused in its readers a love for Palestine and influenced Abraham *Mapu and Kalman *Shullmann. His autobiography *Avi'ezer*, his most original work, appeared in 1864. Written in the style of Rousseau's confessions, it portrays the inner world of the Jewish child, and is a ringing attack on the *ḥeder* system of education. Stylistically, Guenzburg surpasses his contemporaries by far. For the sake of accuracy he resorted to mishnaic Hebrew, introducing talmudic phrases and neologisms, many of which became commonly accepted and are still in use, for example, *milḥemet magen* ("defensive war"), *milḥemet tigrah* ("offensive war"), *rahitim* ("furniture"), *beit-do'ar* ("post office"), etc. Guenzburg was the literary forerunner of P. *Smolenskin, J. L. *Gordon, M. L. *Lilienblum, and R. A. *Broides. His other works include: *Ittotei Rusyah Ha-Ẓarefatim be Rusyah* (1843), on the Franco-Russian War of 1812; *Pi ha-Ḥirot* (1843), a history of the wars of 1813–1815.

Bibliography: D. Maggid, *R. Mordecai Guenzburg 1795–1846* ... (Heb., 1897), includes bibliography; J. Fichmann, in: M. Guenzburg, *Ketavim Nivḥarim* (1911); Klausner, Sifrut, 3 (1960[3]), 120–70; J. S. Raisin, *The Haskalah Movement in Russia* (1913), 213–21; Waxman, Literature, index. [Ab.A./Ed.]

GUENZIG, EZRIEL (1868–1931), rabbi and scholar. Guenzig, who was born in Cracow, received the traditional talmudic education there. He later studied secular subjects in Berlin and philosophy and Semitics at Berne University. He served as rabbi in the Moravian communities of Dresnitz and Loschitz until 1918. After World War I, he settled in Antwerp, where he became head of the Taḥkemoni School and later was active as a bookseller. Guenzig's scholarly work was mainly concerned with the history of Haskalah in Galicia. However, he dealt with other subjects as well. He wrote on F. *Mieses (*Oẓar ha-Sifrut*, 3 pt. 5 (1890), 1–54), whose writing he prepared for publication. His other published works include: *Der Commentar des Karaeers Jephet ben Ali* (1898); *Der Pessimismus im*

Judenthume (1899); *Die Wundermaenner im juedischen Volke* (1921); and *Das juedische Schrifttum ueber den Wert des Lebens* (1924). Guenzig served as assistant editor of **Ha-Maggid*, and edited the seven volumes of the literary journal *Ha-Eshkol* (1898–1913). The first two volumes of the latter were edited with J. S. Fuchs.

Bibliography: G. Bader, *Medinah va-Ḥakhameha* (1934), 64–65; M. Mossler, in: *Haolam*, 19 (1931), 683–4; *Barkai* (Johannesburg; Feb.–March 1937), 7; (March–April 1937), 20; H. Gold (ed.), *Juden und Judengemeinden Maehrens* (1929), 319–20; Kressel, Leksikon, 1 (1965), 477–8.

[G.K.]

GUENZLER, ABRAHAM (1840–1910), Hungarian rabbinical publicist and polemicist. Born in Satoraljaujhely, Guenzler was gifted from youth with a talent for writing which he employed in defense of traditional Judaism. In 1868, he published a pamphlet, *Tokhaḥat Megullah*, in which he attacked Isaac Friedlieber's compilation *Divrei Shalom* and defended traditional Jewry against the Reform movement, then on the ascendant in Hungary.

Subsequently Guenzler moved to Sziget, a community of Ḥasidim and *maskilim*, where he began to publish a Hebrew weekly, *Ha-Tor*. It was the first Hebrew journal published in Hungary and exerted considerable influence. The revival of the Hebrew language was his main ambition, and in 1876 he published in Sziget a booklet, *Das Meter Moss*, most of which was in Hebrew because "there are people who understand Hebrew better than Yiddish." The journal was published in Sziget for three years (1874–76), but it seems that he could not maintain it there and moved with it to Kolomyya in Galicia and from there to Cracow. Meanwhile the pogroms against the Russian Jews broke out (1881). Guenzler accurately described them in *Ha-Tor*, with the result that the Russian government banned it from Russia. Since most of the journal's subscribers lived there (he had nearly 300 subscribers in Russia, and about 250 in Austria-Hungary), *Ha-Tor* ceased publication. Guenzler could not refrain, however, from commenting on contemporary and local issues. He published his articles in *Kol Maḥazike Hadas*, published fortnightly in Lemberg. Meanwhile R. Simeon Sofer of Cracow founded the weekly *Maḥazike Hadas* and Guenzler was appointed editor. The publishers of *Kol Maḥazike Hadas* sued Guenzler; eventually it was agreed that *Maḥazike Hadas* would stop publication and Guenzler would edit *Kol Maḥazike Hadas* but he was later forced to resign.

Bibliography: G. Bader, *Medinah va-Ḥakhameha* (1934), 65–66.

[N.B.-M.]

°**GUÉRIN, VICTOR** (1821–1891), French explorer of the Near East. Guérin was professor of rhetoric at various French universities and finally at Paris. In 1852 he traveled extensively in Greece, Egypt, Tunisia, and Ereẓ Israel. His works include a seven-volume *Description géographique, historique et archéologique de la Palestine* (1869–80), containing three volumes on Judea and two each on Samaria and Galilee. Guérin's work combines historical information (especially from the church fathers and crusader authors) with topographical descriptions; although he preceded the age of scientific archaeology, he noted many monuments which have since disappeared. He also wrote *La Terre sainte, son histoire, ses souvenirs* (2 vols., 1881–83) and *Jérusalem, son histoire, sa description, ses établissements religieux* (1889).

[M.A.-Y.]

GUGGENHEIM, U.S. family. Meyer Guggenheim (1828–1905), merchant and industrialist, was the progenitor of the American branch of the family. He was born in Langnau, Switzerland, and immigrated to the United States in 1848 with his father Simon, settling in Philadelphia. After a period of peddling, Meyer established successful stove polish, lye, and lace-embroidery businesses. In the late 1870s he purchased an interest in the Leadville mines in Colorado. Leaving the embroidery business, the firm of M. Guggenheim's Sons rapidly acquired and built silver, lead, and copper mines and smelters in the western United States, Mexico, and other countries. In 1901 the firm merged with the American Smelting and Refining Company, in which the Guggenheims played a dominant role. At the height of the family's fortune, the company was estimated to be worth over $500,000,000. Meyer's seven sons continued the family's business operations as Guggenheim Brothers, expanding their holdings from Alaska to the Congo.

Meyer Guggenheim, seated center, with his seven sons. Left to right: Benjamin, Murry, Isaac, Daniel, Solomon, Simon, William. From S. Birmingham, *Our Crowd*, New York, 1967. Photo Culver.

His eldest son, Isaac (1854–1922), was born in Philadelphia. He promoted the family's enterprises, including the Guggenheim Exploration Company. He was a contributor to the New York Federation of Jewish Charities, Jewish Theological Seminary, and Hebrew Union College. Meyer's second son, Daniel (1856–1930), became the leader of the Guggenheim Brothers' far-flung enterprises and was responsible for expansion and modernization. As president of American Smelting and Refining Company for nearly 20 years, he developed tin mines in Bolivia, diamonds in Africa, and nitrates in Chile. Progressive in labor relations, Daniel favored unionization and government economic legislation. With his brother Murry he endowed free band concerts in New York's Central Park; the Daniel and Florence Guggenheim Foundation; and the Daniel Guggenheim Fund for the Promotion of Aeronautics. He was a trustee of New York's Temple Emanu-El and one of the founders of the Jewish Theological Seminary. Meyer's third son, Murry (1858–1939), participated actively in managing Guggenheim Brothers and the American Smelting and Refining Company. His philanthropies included a free dental clinic in New York. The fourth son, Solomon Robert (1861–1949), developed the family's interests in Mexican and Chilean mining. A benefactor of New York's Mt. Sinai and Montefiore Hospitals and the New York Public School Athletic League, he formed the Solomon R. Guggenheim Foundation, which encouraged nonobjective art. The Guggenheim Museum in New York, designed by Frank Lloyd Wright, commemorates this interest. A fifth son, Benjamin (1865–1912), entered the family mining business and then withdrew from the partnership in 1900 to head International Steam Pump. He died in the sinking of the "Titanic."

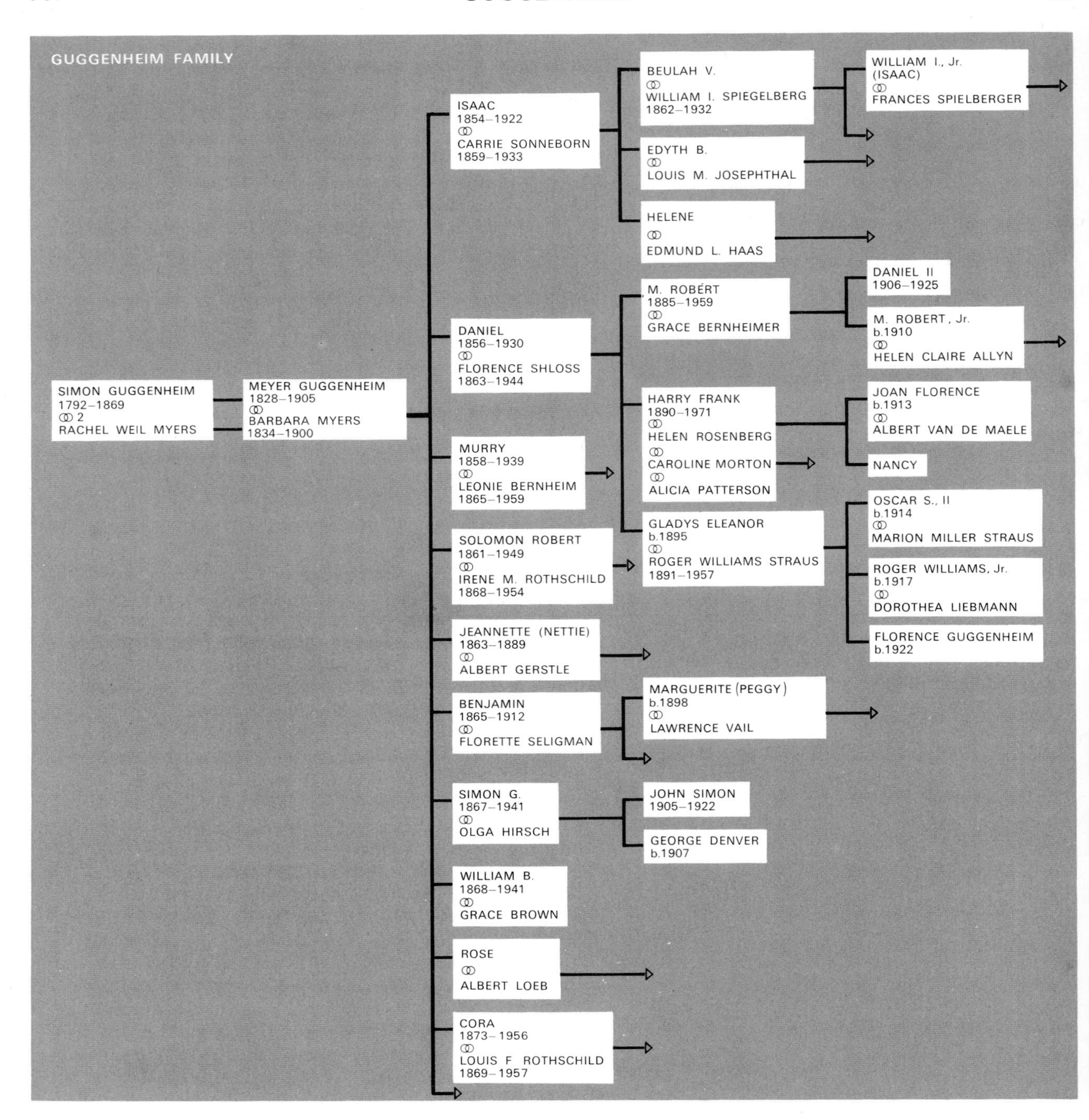

Meyer's sixth son, SIMON (1867–1941), was associated with the family's mining interests and, during 1907–13, served as United States senator from Colorado. In 1925 he established the John Simon Guggenheim Foundation which has provided fellowships to thousands of scholars, scientists, and artists. The seventh son, WILLIAM (1868–1941) managed company property until 1900, then withdrew from the family firm. His subsequent activities were public affairs, writing, and philanthropy.

Daniel's son HARRY FRANK (1890–1971) served the family's mining enterprises and was senior partner of Guggenheim Brothers. As president of the Daniel Guggenheim Fund for the Promotion of Aeronautics from its inception in 1926, he did much to advance aviation. He esestablished the Harry Frank Guggenheim Foundation. From 1929 to 1933 he served as United States ambassador to Cuba, and later founded and was president of the Long Island daily *Newsday*. Benjamin's daughter, MARGUERITE (Peggy; 1898–), spent most of her life in Europe, aiding the modern art movement, especially American abstract expressionism. Her home is a center for art display.

Bibliography: H. O'Connor, *Guggenheims: The Making of an American Dynasty* (1937); M. Lomask, *Seed Money* (1964); E. P. Hoyt, *Guggenheims and the American Dream* (1967).

[Mo.Ro.]

GUGGENHEIM, PAUL (1899–), Swiss jurist and authority on international law. Born in Zurich, Guggenheim became head of the Institute of International Law at the University of Kiel in 1927. Guggenheim became a member of the Permanent Court of Arbitration at The Hague in 1951 and judge ad hoc of the International Court of Justice in 1955. He represented a number of countries before The Hague court and also acted as arbitrator in many international disputes. He wrote extensively on subjects relating to international law. His books include *Lehrbuch des Voelkerrechts* (2 vols., 1948–51) and *Traité de Droit international public* (2 vols., 1953–54, second edition of the first volume, 1967). Guggenheim was president of the Central Committee of the Swiss community from 1944 to 1950. He wrote many scholarly articles on matters of Jewish interest such as Zionism, Palestine, Jewish postwar problems, minority rights, Swiss Jewish history, and the Jewish refugee problem. In 1960, he was elected president of the World Federation of the United Nations Association and in 1964 became its honorary president. [V.W.]

GUGGENHEIM-GRUENBERG, FLORENCE (1898–), pharmacist and historian, born in Berne, Switzerland. During the 1930s and 1940s she was active in Swiss Jewish national and international organizations, and from 1950 was president of the Juedische Vereinigung in Zurich. She was the editor of *Beitraege zur Geschichte und Volkskunde der Juden in der Schweiz,* a periodical devoted to the history and folklore of the Jews in Switzerland. Among her many works on Swiss Jewish history, dealing mainly with the communities of Lengnau and *Endingen, is Volume 1 of Augusta Weldler Steinberg's (ed.) *Geschichte der Juden in der Schweiz* (1966), a history of the Jews in Switzerland from the 16th century to the period after emancipation.

Bibliography: D. Stern (ed.), *Buecher von Autoren juedischer Herkunft in deutscher Sprache* (1967), 106–7. [Ed.]

GUGLIELMO DA PESARO (known as **Guglielmo Ebreo;** 15th century), Italian dancing master. He was a pupil of Domenichino da Piacenza, founder of the new school of dancing at the court of Ferrara, and taught in Florence, where he was apparently attached to the court of the Medici. Here he compiled (c. 1463) his "Treatise on the Art of Dancing," one of the most memorable works of the sort produced in Renaissance Italy. It includes two dances composed by the young Lorenzo de' Medici. In 1475 Guglielmo supervised the pageantry at a resplendent ducal wedding in Pesaro. After this he was apparently converted to Christianity under the name of Giovanni Ambrogio. He was then in the service of the Duchess of Milan who sent him to teach dancing at the Court of Naples. In 1481 he was dancing master to seven-year-old Isabella d'Este at Ferrara. Guglielmo introduced the fashion of the *moresche,* embodying both dance and mimicry, before the grand spectacle. He composed many *balletti* that were revolutionary for his time. His writing makes clear that he did not see as his final aim the mere compilation of dances. He attempted to explain the fundamentals of dancing, giving considerable thought to the relationship between dance and music. Guglielmo outlined six prerequisites for all dancers of which the first three were of enduring importance: *misura,* the dancer's ability to keep time to the musical rhythm; *memoria,* the ability to recollect steps in correct sequence; *partire del terreno,* the ability to do the right movement in space.

Miniature depicting Guglielmo da Pesaro with dance students, from his "Treatise on the Art of Dancing," Florence, c. 1463. Paris, Bibliothèque Nationale, Ms. Ital. 973 fol. 21v.

Though he intended only to compose dances for courtly balls, Guglielmo outlined the requirements for the artistic dancer for all time.

Bibliography: O. Kinkeldey, in: *Studies in Jewish Bibliography and Related Subjects—Freidus Memorial Volume* (1929), 329–72, includes bibliography; C. Roth, *The Jews in the Renaissance* (1959), 276–81, 363; F. Reyna, *Des origines du ballet* (1955), 42–49; A. Michel, in: *Medievalia et Humanistica,* 3 (1945), 121–4 (Eng.). [C.R./W.So.]

°**GUIDACERIO, AGACIO (Agathius Guidacerius;** 1477–1540), Italian Hebraist. A priest from Calabria, Guidacerio began studying Hebrew at Rome under Jacob Gabbai, who was apparently a Portuguese refugee. Under the patronage of Pope Leo X, Guidacerio served as first professor of Hebrew at the University of Rome from 1514 onward. He published a pioneering *Grammatica hebraicae linguae* (Rome, c. 1514) and an annotated edition of Song of Songs (Rome, 1524; Paris, 1531[2]). During the sack of Rome (1527), Guidacerio lost his library and subsequently fled to Avignon, from where he was called to Paris to become a royal reader at the College of the Three Languages. His other works include another Hebrew grammar, *Peculium Agathii-Mikneh Agathii* (Paris, 1537), and *Sefer ha-Diqduq—Grammaticae in sanctam Christi linguam institutiones* (Paris, 1539).

Bibliography: H. Galliner, in: HJ, 2 (1940), 85–101; C. Roth, *Jews in the Renaissance* (1959), 145. [G.E.S.]

GUILDS.

In Antiquity. There is evidence in the Bible of a certain unity among craftsmen. This appears to have played a role similar to that of the unions of artisans which assisted their members in the economic and social spheres in ancient Babylonia at the time of Hammurapi. In this period, association among the artisans was confined to the framework of the family, most of whose members were employed in the same profession over the generations, and took the form of concentration of a given group of craftsmen in a certain site in the town for residence and work. The Bible mentions a valley of craftsmen (I Chron. 4:14). In Jerusalem, there was "the bakers' street" (Jer. 37:21). During the period of the Return to Zion, after the Babylonian Exile, the social cells of the professions had consolidated and were acknowledged to the extent that some are mentioned as a group when the walls of Jerusalem were rebuilt: "between the upper chamber of the corner and the sheep gate repaired the goldsmiths and the merchants" (Neh. 3:32). Distinctive indications of the existence of craftsmen's unions according to families, and their concentration in particular streets, are found during both the Second Temple era and the talmudic period in Ereẓ Israel, Egypt, and Babylonia. However, the forms of professional organization prevailing in the Hellenistic world gradually gained in influence and appear to have obscured the unifying role of the family in many professions. This was replaced by a special association *(ḥavurah)* of the members of a given profession for defined purposes: the synagogue was a unifying factor for these associations. The place of the hereditary craft is still evident in the tradition recorded in the Mishnah concerning the families of craftsmen in the Temple (Shek. 5:1; Yoma 3:11; 38a).

From the period preceding the Bar Kokhba revolt there is evidence on the organization of the Tarsians (weavers of flax, so called after the industry of Tarsus, the capital of Cilicia) around special synagogues in Tiberias and Lydda (Meg. 26a; Naz. 52a; TJ, Shek. 2:6, 27a), while during the period which followed the revolt there appeared the "master" of the Tarsians (Av. Zar. 17b) and the chief of the

Figure 1. Scissors, guild sign of a tailor (Zalman Ḥayat=tailor), at the head of a tombstone in the old Prague cemetery, 1629. From *The Old Jewish Cemetery of Prague*, Prague, 1947.

slaughterers in Sepphoris during the days of Judah ha-Nasi (Tosef., Ḥul. 3:2). From the period of the *amoraim* there is mention of the studies of the "apprentice of the carpenter" (Mak. 8b) and the "apprentice of the smith" and his relations with "his master," the craftsman, who issues orders which he is expected to obey (BK 32b, see Shab. 96b). In a later Midrash there emerges the "company of donkey drivers" which, in partnership, engages in transportation; "they had a chief over the company" who directed its activities (Mid. Ps. 12:1). In Hierapolis, Phrygia, there were unions of dyers of purple stuff and carpet weavers, to whom someone bequeathed a sum of money in order to adorn his tomb on the festivals of Passover and Shavuot; presumably all, or the majority of, the members of these unions were Jews. In Alexandria there were found "the goldsmiths by themselves, the silversmiths by themselves, the weavers by themselves, and the Tarsians by themselves, so that a visitor could come and join his profession and thus earn his livelihood" (Tosef., Suk. 4:6).

Mutual assistance was then one of the declared objectives of the companies of craftsmen and there is a specification how "the woolworkers and dyers . . . the bakers . . . the donkey drivers . . . the sailors are authorized" to act and reach agreement among themselves for the benefit of their fellow craftsmen; they purchased their requirements in partnership; it was accepted to "observe a period of relaxation," i.e., an agreement to refrain from competition in the market and reduction of prices (see Tosef. BM, 11:24ff.; *Sefer ha-Shetarot* of Judah b. Barzillai al-Bargeloni, no. 57). Those whose work took them on the highways introduced a mutual insurance of their animals and implements employed in transportation (Tosef., *ibid.*). It is also known that Jews belonged to the general unions of craftsmen, though presumably they did not participate in their religious cults. [H.H.B.-S.]

Middle Ages and Early Modern Era. The guilds of the Middle Ages in Europe were thoroughly Christian in character and the Jew had no place in them. Since few Jews in Ashkenaz practiced crafts, they did not organize their own guilds, while the Jewish merchants were restricted in their professions and arranged their affairs through the general communal regulations. In the Byzantine Empire, in the 12th century, an authorization was granted to Jewish craftsmen by Manuel I (1143–1180) to establish guilds in their towns. In Sicily there were Jewish guilds of silk weavers, dyers, and carpenters during the 12th to 15th centuries. In 1541 the tailors' guild of Rome reached an agreement with the Christian guild of the city. In Christian Spain the occupations of the Jews were highly diversified and many engaged in crafts. They established associations *(ḥavurot)* active in the economic, social, and religious spheres. Solomon b. Abraham *Adret clearly formulated the legal character of the guilds: "every company which has a common interest is to be regarded as a town apart . . . this was customary in all the holy communities and no one ever raised any doubts as to this" (Rashba, Resp., vol. 4, no. 185). The responsa of R. *Asher b. Jehiel, Solomon *Adret, and *Isaac b. Sheshet Perfet provide information on the structure and activities of the "companies" in Spain. The regulations presented to the king by the company of Jewish shoemakers in Saragossa in 1336 for ratification include arrangements for financial assistance to colleagues in times of sickness, a compulsory arrangement for the visiting of the sick and participation in the rejoicing and mourning of members modeled on the arrangements of the Christian guilds. Also recorded are institutions for charitable purposes and special prayer designed for craftsmen (such as in Perpignan and Saragossa) and the *(bet)* "*midrash* of the weavers" (in Calatayud) "which were set aside . . . for the individuals of the company, and were not consecrated for everyone that comes" (Ribash, Resp., no. 331). A main development in Jewish guilds among Ashkenazi Jewry took place in Eastern Europe, in Bohemia-Moravia, and in Poland-Lithuania, with the increasing number of Jewish craftsmen in those countries. The earliest information on these goes back to the 16th century. Despite the violent opposition of the Christian guilds, the number of Jewish artisans increased considerably and they organized themselves in guilds during the 16th to 18th centuries after the pattern of the Christian guilds, and in order to protect themselves from them. In Prague, there were Jewish guilds of butchers, tailors, furriers, embroiderers, shoemakers, goldsmiths, hairdressers, and pharmacists. In several towns of Poland and Lithuania, such as Brody, Cracow, Lublin, Lvov, Lissa (Leszno), and Vilna, there were numerous Jewish guilds, with up to ten in one community.

The regulations of the Jewish guilds in Eastern Europe followed the spirit of the general guilds, but their social-religious content was influenced by Jewish customs and modes of life. Since they were essentially economic organizations, the Jewish guilds established rules on the relations between their members, the status of the craftsmen, the trainees and the apprentices, and the standards and quotas of production authorized to every craftsman. The guilds were concerned to prevent unfair competition between their members and to protect them from local craftsmen who were not organized in a guild or from craftsmen not living in the town. They cared for their members' welfare, assisted those in difficulties, and provided relief to the widows and orphans of guild members. They developed organized activity for the religious education of members and their children. All the craftsmen, trainees, and apprentices were compelled to take part in public prayers and to observe the Sabbath and festivals. The guilds also

Figure 2. Tombstone showing a stag, for the name Ẓevi, holding a mortar and pestle, guild sign for pharmacists. From *The Old Jewish Cemetery of Prague,* Prague, 1947.

formulated detailed rules for the election of committee members. Even though many guilds were first formed through the initiative of the communal administration, the relations between the two bodies gradually deteriorated until open clashes occurred during the 18th century between the guilds and the community leadership in Berdichev, Minsk, and Vitebsk. With the political and economic decline of Poland-Lithuania, the guilds lost their importance. In Russia, Austria, and Prussia, among which Poland was partitioned in the latter part of the 18th century, the guilds with their typical medieval structure were already on the verge of extinction. They ceded their place to modern forms of economic organization. Associations *(ḥavurot)* of craftsmen existing in many communities during the 19th century had slight economic influence and their function was confined to religious, cultural, and social activities. They continued until the 1930s. In Poland between the two world wars the *cechy* (guilds) legislation which limited the Jewish craftsmen was revived. As a result, the debate was renewed on the role and organization of the Jews in this modern reincarnation of the guilds. [M.W./Ed.]

Bibliography: M. Wischnitzer, *History of Jewish Crafts and Guilds* (1965); idem, in: HUCA, 23 pt. 2 (1950–51), 245–63; idem, in: JSOS, 16 (1954), 335–50; idem, in: *Zaytshrift far Yidisher Geshikhte, Demografie, un Ekonomik,* 2–3 (1928), 73–88; Juster, Juifs, 1 (1914), 486–7; T. Jacobovits, in: JJGJČ, 8 (1936), 57–145; M. Kremer, in: Zion, 295–325; idem, in: YIVOA, 11 (1956/57), 211–42; idem, in: *Bleter far Geshikhte,* 2 (1938), 3–32; I. Mendelsohn, in: BASOR (Dec. 1940), 17–21; Alon, Toledot, 1 (1953), 103–6; L. Frydman, in: *Yivo Bleter,* 12 (1937), 520–32; M. Hendel, in: *Oẓar Yehudei Sefarad,* 6 (1963), 77–84; I. Levitats, *The Jewish Community in Russia* (1943), index; I. Halpern, *Yehudim ve-Yahadut be-Mizraḥ Eiropah* (1969), 163–94.

GUINZBURG, HAROLD KLEINERT (1899–1961), U.S. publisher. Guinzburg, who was born in New York City, worked briefly as a journalist in Bridgeport and Boston. He later worked for the publishing house Simon & Schuster as a talent scout for new authors. In 1925 he and his friend George Oppenheim founded Viking Press, whose initial success resulted from the sale of quiz and "boner" books, though the firm later sponsored many prominent authors. A consistent innovator in the publishing field, Guinzburg founded the Literary Guild, one of America's first book clubs, in 1927; he sold his share in it in 1933, the same year that Viking again pioneered by establishing a special children's book department. During World War II he served both as chief of the Office of War Information's domestic bureau of publications (1943) and as head of it's London publications division (1944). His armed forces anthology *As You Were* (1943), which was edited by Alexander Woollcott, was the start of the immensely popular Viking Portable Library series. After the war, Guinzburg launched Viking's own paperback line, Compass Books. A staunch civil libertarian and member of the New York Chapter Board of the American Civil Liberties Union, he strongly opposed literary censorship and contended that any limitation of free expression was incompatible with democracy. He also served as a director of the American Book Publishers Council and as its president from 1956 to 1958, and as vice-president of the Jewish Telegraphic Agency. He contributed to *Books and the Mass Market* (1953). [Ed.]

GULAK, ASHER (1881–1940), historian of Jewish law. Gulak, who was born in Dackira, Latvia, obtained a diploma in law at Dorpat University in 1911, and pursued further legal study in Germany (1919–24). He returned briefly to Latvia, where he taught at government-sponsored courses for Jewish teachers, before settling in Palestine in 1925. Gulak was appointed lecturer (1926) and subsequently professor (1936) of Jewish law at the Hebrew University. He published books and numerous articles on talmudic and Jewish law, which were comparative studies on the Jewish, Greek, and Roman legal systems, as well as articles on current problems, particularly in the field of education. Gulak's pioneering four-volume work *Yesodei ha-Mishpat ha-Ivri* ("Foundations of Hebrew Law," 1922) was the first to present Jewish law systematically. This was followed in 1926 by an anthology of Jewish legal formularies and documents, *Oẓar ha-Shetarot ha-Nehugim be-Yisrael* (1926), later enlarged by his *Urkundenwesen im Talmud* (1935), *Le-Ḥeker Toledot ha-Mishpat ha-Ivri bi-Tekufat ha-Talmud* ("Researches in the History of the Talmudic Law of Property," 1929), and *Toledot ha-Mishpat be-Yisrael bi-Tekufat ha-Talmud* (1939), a similar study of the law of obligations.

Bibliography: Shochetman, in: KS, 17 (1940), 211–4; Alon, Meḥkarim, 2 (1958), 285–97; Kressel, Leksikon, 1 (1965), 436–7. [Ch.G]

GULL (Heb. שַׁחַף; AV "cuckow," JPS "sea-mew"), bird mentioned in the Bible as prohibited as food (Lev. 11:16; Deut. 14:15), the Hebrew name means "thin" or "swift of movement" and, on the basis of its rendering as λαρός in the Septuagint, refers to the gull. Eight species of the genus *Larus* are found in Israel. Feeding on sea fish and scraps of food, they follow ships for the offal thrown overboard. The gull also penetrates to inland regions of the country (even to the Negev) where it lives on worms and snails. To the family of the gull (Laridae) belong the *Sterna,* a genus of which two species are found in Israel, distinguished from the gull by being web-footed along the entire length of their toes.

Bibliography: J. Feliks, *Animal World of the Bible* (1962), 86; M. Dor, *Leksikon Zo'ologi* (1965), 330f. [J.F.]

GUMPERT, MARTIN (1897–1955), German author and physician. The son of a medical practitioner, Gumpert was born in Berlin and, after serving in the German Army Medical Corps during World War I, specialized in venereal

Martin Gumpert, German author and physician. Courtesy M. Steinhardt, Nahariyyah.

and skin diseases. In 1927, he became the head of a Berlin clinic for the treatment of these complaints and the director of a center for the study of deformities, on which he published a manual, *Die gesamte Kosmetik* (1931). Between 1933 and 1936, when the Nazis forced him out of medical practice, Gumpert began to write the first of a series of works that were to make him famous: a biography of Samuel Hahnemann, the originator of homeopathy (1934); and *Das Leben fuer die Idee* (1935; *Trail-Blazers of Science*, 1936), portraits of outstanding scientists. Gumpert emigrated to New York in 1936 and resumed his career as a dermatologist. He soon moved to a new specialization, geriatrics, strongly maintaining that society was frittering away millions of useful lives through compulsory retirement at the age of 65. Gumpert rapidly achieved medical distinction, heading the geriatric clinic in New York's Jewish Memorial Hospital from 1951 and gaining many professional honors. Two medical works in English advocating a new approach to the treatment of the aged were *You Are Younger Than You Think* (1944) and *The Anatomy of Happiness* (1951).

In his youth, Gumpert had written two collections of lyrics, *Verkettung* (1916) and *Heimkehr des Herzens* (1921). Other literary works in German written after his move to the U.S. include *Berichte aus der Fremde* (1937), poems; *Dunant: Der Roman des Roten Kreuzes* (1938; *Dunant: The Story of the Red Cross*, 1938); *Hoelle im Paradies* (1939), an autobiography; and a novel, *Der Geburtstag* (1948). He also contributed a short article on his friend and fellow exile, Thomas *Mann, *The Stature of Thomas Mann* (1946). From 1952 until his death, Gumpert edited a New York medical journal, *Lifetime Living*.

Bibliography: *Science Illustrated* (June 1946), 637–40; *New Yorker* (June 10 and 17, 1950); *Current Biography* (1951), 250–1; *New York Times* (April 19, 1955). [R.K.]

GUMPLOWICZ, LUDWIG (1838–1909), Austrian jurist and sociologist. He was born in Cracow, in Austrian Galicia (now Poland), and studied law at the University of Vienna. An ardent Polish patriot, he participated in the Polish insurrection against Russia in 1863, and as a consequence of the failure both of the rebellion and of subsequent nationalistic activities Gumplowicz had to leave Cracow and availed himself of an opportunity to become a *Privatdozent* in political science at the University of Graz. In 1862 he was appointed adjunct professor in political science, and 11 years later, in 1893, he received his full professorship. Gumplowicz was baptized, but retained a lively interest in Jewish affairs. Gumplowicz was a proponent of Jewish assimilation. He thought that the Jews, having no territorial basis and no common language, were lacking the prerequisite of a nationality. In a letter directed to Theodor Herzl and dated Dec. 12, 1899, he expressed this view in highly emotional language.

Academically, Gumplowicz remained isolated at a provincial university, but he had brilliant students, such as Franco Savorgnan and Franz Oppenheimer, and found himself recognized by early American sociologists. Gumplowicz was one of the first to achieve full emancipation for sociology from the nonsocial sciences by insisting that social phenomena and evolution are distinctive and can be understood only by reference to social causes. That which is unique about social phenomena arises from human groups in interaction rather than from the behavior of individuals abstracted from the influence of association and dissociation. According to Gumplowicz, social and cultural evolution is a product of the struggle between social groups. This struggle replaces individual struggle in his theory of evolution. Gumplowicz offers two basic hypotheses. One, the polygenetic hypothesis, asserting that the species man evolved from various older types at many different times and in many different places, so that between the races there is no blood bond; and two, the hypothesis that an unsurmountable antagonism exists between different groups and races. For Gumplowicz society was the sum total of conflicting ethnic groups, each group being centered around one or more common interests. Thus the struggle between these ethnic groups, which he called races, is relentless. Gumplowicz was pessimistic about progress. His polygenetic view precluded the possibility of unitary evolution. In every society and state partial evolution and progress have taken place; but in every society and state there have also been destruction and setbacks. Therefore, Gumplowicz holds that progress can be observed only in particular periods and particular countries.

Another important aspect of Gumplowicz's work includes the distinction he made between simple, limited groupings organized on the basis of consanguinity and community of culture, on the one hand, and compound groupings, such as the state, formed in the process of amalgamation of originally separate groups, such as masters and slaves or ethnic groups. In the state, ethnic groups merge into social classes, a common body of rights and obligations is developed, and internal conflict is toned down and possibly even composed. External conflict between states takes then the place of internal ethnic and class conflicts. Therefore, although Gumplowicz is classified often as a social Darwinist, he was actually one of the first social determinists. In his system, the individual and his motives were useless abstractions. The individual was the product of

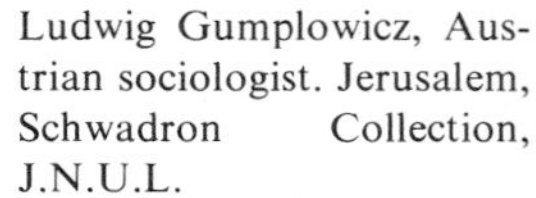

Ludwig Gumplowicz, Austrian sociologist. Jerusalem, Schwadron Collection, J.N.U.L.

group experiences; his morals derived from his relations in the particular groups to whom he belonged, whereas his notions of rights could be traced to the accommodative norms developed by the struggle of interest groups in his society.

Gumplowicz's most important works include: *Rasse und Staat* (1875), *Der Rassenkampf* (1893), and *Grundriss der Sociologie* (1885); the latter is his only work that has been translated into English by Frederick W. Moore, as *Outlines of Sociology* (1889) and reissued by Irving L. Horowitz (1962). An edition of all of Gumplowicz's writings, under the title *Ausgewaehlte Werke,* appeared in 1926. An evaluation of Gumplowicz as a Jew is contained in "Scholar and Visionary: the correspondence between Herzl and *Ludwig Gumplowicz*" (*Herzl Yearbook,* 1 (1958), 165–80).

Bibliography: B. Zebowski, *Ludwig Gumplowicz: eine Bio-Bibliographie* (1926); *The Times* (London, Aug. 20, 1909), 10a.

[W.J.C./AL.B.]

GUNDOLF, FRIEDRICH (pseudonym of **Friedrich Gundelfinger,** 1880–1931), German literary historian. One of the earliest disciples of Stefan George, Gundolf participated in George's cultural movement, *Blaetter fuer die Kunst,* and in 1920 published the first major study of the great writer. From 1911, Gundolf taught at Heidelberg University, and his lectures on literature were original in content and models of style. His studies covered a wide range: Caesar, Shakespeare, Paracelsus, Lessing, Klopstock, Goethe, Hoelderlin, Kleist, Nietzsche, Hofmannsthal, Rilke, and Stifter. He was partly responsible for the 10-volume German translation of Shakespeare's works

Friedrich Gundolf, German literary historian. Courtesy D.P.A., Frankfort.

which appeared under his editorship (1908–18). In his biographies of literary figures, Gundolf was not interested so much in the details of their daily lives as in the spirit revealed in their creative masterpieces, and he interpreted their unique *Gestalt* with a reverential awe. His publications, which incude *Goethe* (1916), *Caesar, Geschichte seines Ruhms* (1924), *Shakespeare und der deutsche Geist* (1911; 1959), and *Romantiker* (2 vols., 1930–31), combined intuition with a respect for facts. They served literary historians as examples of scholarship and style, and had profound impact.

Bibliography: V. A. Schmitz, *Gundolf, eine Einfuehrung in sein Werk* (1965); O. Heuschele, *Friedrich Gundolf, Werk und Wirken* (1947); E. Kahn, in: YLBI, 8 (1963), 171–83; W. Lewin, *ibid.,* 201–8 (Ger., with Eng. summary).

[S.L.]

°**GUNKEL, HERMANN** (1862–1932), German Bible scholar. Gunkel taught at the universities of Halle from 1888 to 1894 and 1920 to 1927, Berlin from 1894 to 1907, and Giessen from 1907 to 1920. The work of Gunkel has been a learned stimulant in biblical scholarship. His conviction that historical criticism, which seeks an ideal history of Israel based on the chronological and biographical terms and exemplified classically by the J. Wellhausen school, was inadequate in writing a history of Israel's literature led him to discover the importance of determining the oral prehistory of the written sources, and of classifying the source material into the appropriate categories of literary "forms." He thus pioneered the methods of form criticism to biblical studies, and introduced the traditional historical point of view in writing Israel's history. His first major work, *Schoepfung und Chaos in Urzeit und Endzeit* (1895, 1921), was a study into the popular mythology underlying the biblical ideas concerning the beginning and the end of the present world order. By piecing together the existing variants of the surviving texts, he made the first scholarly attempt to reconstruct the original myth of creation. His commentary on Genesis (1901, 1963[6]) argued for the great antiquity of the sagas, legends, and traditions of the first book of the Bible. The introduction, published separately and translated into English as *The Legends of Genesis* (1901, 1964[5]), was primarily interested in the characteristics of the legend as a genre and its historical development. His most successful attempt at a literary history of Israel, based primarily on an analysis of the types and forms of Israel's speech, appeared in the volume on *Die orientalischen Literaturen* (1906) in Hinneberg's series *Die Kultur der Gegenwart.* His approach has proved most fruitful in his studies on the Psalms: *Ausgewaehlte Psalmen* (1917[4]); *Die Psalmen uebersetzt und erklaert* (1926); and *Einleitung in die Psalmen* (published posthumously and under the joint authorship of J. Begrich, 1933), where the classification of Psalms is according to their principle types *(Gattungen)* and each type is related to a characteristic life setting *(Sitz im Leben).* Gunkel's book on Esther (1916, 1958[2]) is fundamental for understanding the literary character of the book. A number of crucial studies related to form criticism are found in two series of published essays: *Reden und Aufsaetze* (1913) and *Was bleibt vom Alten Testament* (1916; *What Remains of the Old Testament? and Other Essays,* 1928). His *Das Maerchen im Alten Testament* (1917) historically traces the genre of the folktale in the Bible in light of Near Eastern culture. In addition to his many writings he served as an editor of *Die Religion in Geschichte und Gegenwart* (1909–13 and 1927–32[2]), and, with W. Bousset, of the series *Forschungen zur Religion und Literatur des Alten und Neuen Testaments.*

Bibliography: *Festschrift . . . H. Gunkel* (1923), incl. bibl.; DB, s.v. (incl. bibl.); H. J. Kraus, *Geschichte der historisch-kritischen Erforschung des Alten Testaments* (1956), 309–34; H. F. Hahn, *The Old Testament in Modern Research* (1956), 119–28.

[Z.G.]

GUNZBERG, ARYEH LEIB (Loeb) BEN ASHER (1695–1785), talmudist. Born in Lithuania, Aryeh became assistant to his father on his appointment about 1720 as rabbi of the upper district in Minsk, comprising at the time 40 small communities. In 1733 he founded a yeshivah, which soon attracted students from Belorussia and Lithuania. Differences over methods of instruction between Aryeh Leib and Jehiel Heilprin, author of *Seder ha-Dorot* and head of another yeshivah in Minsk, led to much friction between both the teachers and students, Heilprin being opposed to the pilpulistic method used by Aryeh Leib to stimulate the minds of his students. In the introduction to his famous volume of responsa, *Sha'agat Aryeh,* however, Aryeh Leib himself is critical of the role of *pilpul* in establishing the "truth of the Torah." Finally compelled in 1742 to leave Minsk, he settled in one of the nearby towns where he continued to help his aged father. In 1750 he was appointed rabbi in *Volozhin, where among some of his notable disciples were Ḥayyim *Volozhiner and his brother

ספר

שאגת ארי'

והוא חלק א' מחלקי התשוב' מחברתי
פני הקטן ארי' המכונה ליב בהמ"ו
הגאון המפלא מהור"ר אשר זלה"ה
ממדינת ליטא ונקרא בפי כל רבי ליב

תחת ממשלת אדונינו המלך האדיר
והמיוחס מאוד פרידריך
השני מלך פרייסן הגם יר"ה ויתנשא
מלכותו מעלה למעלה אמן

נדפס פה ק"ק פ"פ דאדר
בדפוס של האדון דאקטאר ופראפעססאר
גרילא

בשנת מה אהבתי תור"תך כל
היום היא שיחתי

Sha'agat Aryeh, a collection of responsa by Aryeh Leib b. Asher Gunzberg, Frankfort on the Oder, 1755. Jerusalem, J.N.U.L.

Simḥah. Here he prepared his halakhic work, *Sha'agat Aryeh* (Frankfort on the Oder, 1755). He lived in poverty, became involved in disputes with the community leaders, and at the age of 69 wandered from city to city. He reached Germany and eventually accepted the position of *av bet din* in Metz (1765), becoming also head of a large yeshivah there. He remained in Metz until his death. Besides his *Sha'agat Aryeh*, Aryeh Leib published in his lifetime *Turei Even*, novellae on the tractates *Rosh Ha-Shanah*, *Ḥagigah*, and *Megillah* (Metz, 1781). His posthumously published works are: *She'elot u-Teshuvot Sha'agat Aryeh ha-Ḥadashot* (1874); *Gevurot Ari*, novellae on *Ta'anit* (1862); and *Gevurot Ari*, on *Yoma* and *Makkot* (1907).

Bibliography: *Ha-Me'assef*, 2 (1785), 161–8; Carmoly, in: *Israelische Annalen*, 2 (1840), 186, no. 15; Cahen, in: REJ, 12 (1886), 294ff.; B. Z. Eisenstadt, *Rabbanei Minsk ve-Ḥakhameha* (1898), 15ff.; D. Maggid, *Sefer Toledot Mishpeḥot Ginzburg* (1899), 35–52; S. J. Fuenn, *Kiryah Ne'emanah* (1915²), 163.

[M.N.Z./Ed.]

GUNZBURG, NIKO (1882–), Belgian jurist and criminologist. Born in Riga, Latvia, his family settled in Belgium when he was a boy. In 1923 he was appointed lecturer in law at the University of Ghent where he later became the first Jew to be made a professor. He founded its Institute of Criminology in 1937 and headed it until 1952 except during World War II when he was attached to the Belgian embassy in Washington. From 1953 to 1956, he was professor of law at the University of Djakarta, Indonesia. His works on penal law and criminology earned him an international reputation. They include: *Les transformations récentes du droit pénal* (1933) and *La trajectoire du crime; études sur le nouveau code Pénal du Brésil* (1941). A prominent figure in the Belgian Jewish community, Gunzburg was founder and president of the Central Committee for Jewish Welfare in Antwerp. He participated in the inaugural conference of the World Jewish Congress in 1936 and was chairman of the Council of Jewish Associations (1947–50). Gunzburg was also a passionate advocate of the use of the Flemish language and he was head of the society of Flemish Jurists.

[Z.H.]

GUNZENHAUSER (Ashkenazi), JOSEPH BEN JACOB (d. 1490) and Azriel, his son, pioneers in Hebrew printing. The Gunzenhausers went to Naples from Gunzenhausen in southern Germany and set up a Hebrew press, which from 1487 to 1492 produced an impressive range of books (see *Incunabula), in all about 12 volumes. Among them were the Hagiographa with various rabbinical commentaries (1487); Avicenna's medical *Canon*, the first and only edition of the work in Hebrew *(Ha-Kanon)*; and the first edition of Abraham ibn Ezra's Pentateuch commentary (1488). After Joseph Gunzenhauser's death his wife (or daughter) and son continued his work. The Gunzenhausers assembled a team of distinguished typesetters and correctors from Italy. Joshua Solomon Soncino, who began printing at Naples about this time, issued a prayer book of the Spanish rite for Gunzenhauser in May 1490.

Bibliography: D. W. Amram, *Makers of Hebrew Books in Italy* (1909), 63, 66; B. Friedberg, *Ha-Defus ha-Ivri be-Italyah* . . . (1956), 40ff.; A. Freimann (ed.), *Thesaurus Typographiae Hebraicae* . . . (1931), A57, 1ff.

[Ed.]

GURA-HUMORULUI, town in N. Rumania, in the historic region of Bukovina. Frescos with a tableau of the "Day of Judgment" painted between 1547 and 1550 depicting among others Turkish and Jewish figures are found in the Voronet monastery there. Jewish settlement began in Gura-Humorului under Austrian rule in 1835, with five Jewish families (in a total population of 700). They increased to 20 by 1848 and formed an organized community. Prayers were first held in a private house. The first synagogue was erected in 1869, and the Great Synagogue in 1871. As in the other communities of Bukovina, the influence of Ḥasidism was strong. At first occupied as craftsmen, merchants, and purveyors to the Austrian army, Jews later established workshops for wood processing and lumber mills. At the close of the 19th century, they played an important role in the industrialization of the town. The community numbered 130 persons in 1856, 190 in 1867, 800 in 1869, 1,206 in 1890, 2,050 in 1910, and 1,951 in 1927.

After the town passed to Rumania at the end of World War I, and throughout the period between the two world wars, the authorities endeavored to restrict the Jews in their economic activities while there were also occasional anti-Semitic outbreaks. The Zionist movement, formed locally at the beginning of the 20th century, had a large following. *Aliyah* to Ereẓ Israel began during the 1930s. At the time of the persecutions by the Rumanian Fascists, 2,954 local Jews and others who had gathered there from the surrounding area were deported in a single day (Oct. 10, 1941) to *Transnistria, where most of them died. After the end of World War II, the survivors returned to the town; they were joined by other Jewish inhabitants of the region who returned from their places of deportation, and numbered 1,158 in 1948. Nearly all the Jews there emigrated to Israel between 1948 and 1951.

Bibliography: H. Gold (ed.), *Geschichte der Juden in der Bukowina*, 2 (1962), 84–87.

[Y.M.]

GUREVICH, MOSHE (1874–1944), Bundist in Russia. Born in St. Petersburg, he came from a wealthy religious family. His grandfather Elhanan Cohen of Salant, a railroad contractor, carried on an independent struggle in St. Petersburg against the anti-Jewish czarist legislation. Many members of his family became revolutionaries. Gurevich studied at the universities of St. Petersburg and Berlin, joined the Social Democrats, and was active in St. Petersburg and Gomel. He later headed the *Bund in Vilna, and between 1901 and 1903 took a leading part in the Hirsh *Lekert affair and in opposing the *Independent Jewish Workers' Party. He was imprisoned for his socialist activities. After his release Gurevich went to the United States as an emissary of the Bund in 1905. He stayed there until his death, and was a member of the educational committee of the *Workmen's Circle from 1920 to 1922.

Bibliography: J. S. Hertz (ed.), *Doyres Bundistn*, 1 (1956), 269–73. [M.M.]

GURIAN (Gurfinckel), SORANA (1914–1956), Rumanian novelist and journalist who later wrote in French. Sorana Gurian was born in Komrat, Bessarabia. After her university studies she spent three years in France, then returned to Bucharest on the eve of World War II and joined the anti-Fascist underground. After the war she became a journalist, but in 1947 her article calling for freedom of expression led to the suppression of her work. Early in 1949 she escaped from Rumania and settled in Paris. Except for a two-year stay in Israel (1949–51), she spent the rest of her life in France, where she quickly established herself as a newspaper and radio political commentator, as well as an author. Sorana Gurian's first novel which made her famous, *Zilele nu se întorc niciodată* ("Never Do the Days Return," 1946), was the largely autobiographical story of an intellectual family in a Bessarabian town. *Intîmplări dintre amurg și noapte* ("Events Between Dawn and Night," 1946), a collection of stories, dealt with the sexual obsessions of lonely women. Her first book in French, *Les mailles du filet* (1950), a diary of the years 1947–49, had a factual authenticity which made it an important political document. She translated her first Rumanian novel as *Les jours ne reviennent jamais* (1952), and wrote a sequel to it: *Les amours impitoyables*, which appeared in 1953, and which dealt with the political scene in pre-World War II Rumania. Her last book, *Récit d'un combat* (1956), a record of her desperate search for

Sorana Gurian, Rumanian-French novelist and journalist.

treatment of the cancer from which she was dying, was enlivened by her thirst for life, her courage, and the support of her friends.

Bibliography: C. Malraux, in: *Évidences* (Oct. 8, 1956), 48–49; G. Marcel, in: *Arts et Spectacles* (Feb.–March, 1956); Manès Sperber, in: *Preuves* (Feb. 1956), 45–46; Y. Margolin, in: *Ha-Boker* (June 22, 1956), E. Sussmann, in: *Davar* (Aug. 17, 1956). [D.L.]

GURLAND, ḤAYYIM JONAH (1843–1890), Russian rabbi and scholar. Gurland was born in Kletsk, Belorussia, and was educated at the Vilna rabbinical seminary and at the University of St. Petersburg, where he studied Oriental languages with D. *Chwolson. He wrote his dissertation on the influence of Islamic philosophy, in particular the Mutakallimūn, Muʿatazilites, and Ashʿarians, on Maimonides. While employed at the Imperial Library of St. Petersburg, Gurland worked on the *Firkovich manuscripts, being one of the first to discover his forgeries; he published the results of this research as *Ginzei Yisrael be-St. Petersburg* (1865–67). In 1873 he was appointed inspector of the Jewish teachers' seminary in Zhitomir; there he published a Yiddish and Russian calendar, entitled in Hebrew *Lu'aḥ Yisrael* (1878–81), which also contained scholarly articles. After three years in Western Europe, he returned to Russia and founded a Jewish high school in Odessa. In 1888 the government appointed him rabbi of Odessa. In addition to contributing articles to the leading Hebrew periodicals, Gurland published a Hebrew version of D. Chwolson's work on the Tammuz cult in ancient Babylonia, *Ma'amar ha-Tammuz* (1864), and a seven-volume work on the persecutions of Jews in Russia during the 17th and 18th centuries, *Le-Korot ha-Gezerot al Yisrael* (1887–89), with a posthumous addendum (1893) to the last volume containing a biography of the author by D. Cahana.

Bibliography: Kressel, Leksikon, 1 (1965), 459–60; N. Sokolow, *Sefer Zikkaron le-Sofrei Yisrael* . . . (1899), 133–40. [ED.]

GURS (near Pau, Basses-Pyrénées), one of France's largest concentration camps during World War II. It was opened first for Republican Spanish refugees, later also for refugees from Austria and Germany, and, after the Franco-German armistice of June 1940, for Jews. Food supply and sanitary conditions in Gurs were worse than in the camps of the occupied territory of France. As a result 800 Jews died there in the winter of 1940. In 1941 there were 15,000 internees, including 7,200 German Jews who had been deported from the Palatinate and Baden, and about 3,000 Jewish refugees who had been arrested in Belgium on May 10, 1940, and sent first to the French concentration camp Saint-Cyprien and then to Gurs. In the second half of July 1942, Eichmann's delegate Dannecker inspected Gurs. Shortly afterward most of the internees were sent from Gurs to *Drancy, and from there to death camps. Deportations ended in the summer of 1943 when only 735 women, 250 men, and 215 children remained in the camp. The cemetery near the camp contains the graves of 1,200 Jews.

Bibliography: Z. Szajkowski, *Analytical Franco-Jewish Gazetteer* (1966), 214–2; J. Weill, *Contribution à l'histoire de camps d'internement dans l'Anti-France* (1946). [ED.]

GURSHTEIN, AARON (1895–1941), Soviet Yiddish literary historian. Gurshtein was born in the Ukraine. He studied Yiddish and Hebrew literature in Vilna and at the University of Petrograd. He taught literature at the University of Moscow and specialized in the Yiddish classical masters, *Mendele Mokher Seforim, I. L. *Peretz, and *Shalom Aleichem, whom he interpreted from a Marxist viewpoint. His essays also furthered the work of the best Soviet Yiddish writers, such as David *Bergelson, Der *Nister, and Shemuel *Halkin. During the thaw of the New Economic Policy (NEP), he welcomed the more liberal tendency to evaluate art aesthetically and not politically. His study *Vegn Undzer Kritik* ("About Our Criticism," 1925) was tolerant even of symbolist works. However, by 1933, when with M. *Viner he wrote *Problemes fun Kritik* ("Problems of Criticism"), he retreated from his earlier tolerance and accepted socialist realism as the only desirable artistic approach. In 1941 he died in action against the Germans. His death was lamented in elegiac verses by Ezra *Finenberg.

Bibliography: LNYL, 2 (1958), 204f. [S.L.]

GURVITCH, GEORGES (1894–1966), French sociologist. Born in Russia, Gurvitch was educated at the universities of Petrograd and Paris. Gurvitch taught at the universities of Petrograd and Strasbourg, and from 1948 until his death at the University of Paris. He also was editor of the *Cahiers Internationaux de Sociologie* and the *Journal of Legal and Political Sociology.* He was profoundly influenced by the philosophers Hegel and Bergson, the socialists Petrajizhky and P. A. Sorokin, and especially by the phenomenological school in philosophy. Gurvitch worked on a highly analytical level, dealing particularly with the sociology of law, the nature of groups and social classes, and later the character of social time. Among his major sociological writings are: *The Sociology of Law* (1942), *Essais de Sociologie* (1938), *Eléments de sociologie juridique* (1940), *La déclaration des droits sociaux* (1940), *La vocation actuelle de la sociologie* (1950), *Twentieth Century Sociology* (edited with W. E. More, 1945), *Traité de sociologie* (2 vols., 1958), *Industrialisation et technocratie* (edited with G. Friedmann, 1949), *Déterminismes sociaux et liberté humaine* (1955), *Dialectique et sociologie* (1962), and *The Spectrum of Social Time* (1964). He tried to increase awareness of (1) symbolic nuances in social life; (2) a series of conceptually distinct levels in human experience; (3) the importance of dialectical and oppositional mechanism in society; and (4) the relation between conceptions of time and human behavior. Gurvitch's distinction between microsociology and macrosociology has been widely accepted among sociologists, but his assertion that each uses distinct methods of investigation has been opposed by neopositivists and functionalists.

Bibliography: R. Toulemont, *Sociologie et pluralisme dialectique: introduction à l'oeuvre de Georges Gurvitch* (1955); P. Bosserman, *Dialectical Sociology* (1968).

[AL.B.]

GURWITSCH, AARON (1901–), U.S. philosopher and psychologist. Born in Vilna, he lectured at the Sorbonne from 1933. In 1940 he went to the U.S., where he taught at Brandeis University, Johns Hopkins University, and the New School for Social Research in New York. Gurwitsch was distinguished for his special philosophical approach to the problems of psychology. He sought to show the mutual relations which exist between the psychological image pattern, conceived in consciousness as an entity, and the conscious content which consciousness aims at when it knows or remembers it as conceived. He distinguished between the pattern and the content at which consciousness is aimed. This latter conception he called, after Husserl, *"noema."* The unity of the pattern and the *noema* are for Gurwitsch a "theme" *(thema).* The conscious horizon which surrounds the theme and which is liable to influence the shaping of its form in consciousness at every moment is called by him "the theoretical field." He tried to find phenomenological interpretations of other psychological theories such as those of W. James, J. Piaget, and Kurt *Goldstein. His writings include: "On the Intentionality of Consciousness" in: *Philosophical Essays in Memory of E. Husserl* (1940), 65–83; *Théorie du champ de la conscience* (1957; *Field of Consciousness,* 1964); "Phenomenological and Psychological Approach to Consciousness", in: *Philosophy and Phenomenological Research,* 15 (1955), 303–19; "Der Begriff des Bewusstseins bei Kant und Husserl," in: *Kantstudien,* 55 (1964), 410–27.

Bibliography: H. Spiegelberg: *The Phenomenological Movement,* 2 (1960), 630.

[A.GR.]

GURWITSCH (Gurvich), ALEXANDER GAVRILOVICH (1874–1954), Soviet Russian biologist. Gurwitsch was born in Poltava, Ukraine. After studying and teaching abroad he returned to Russia in 1906, and from 1907 until 1918 taught at the women's higher education courses in St. Petersburg. He was a professor at Simferopol University from 1918 to 1925 and at Moscow University from 1925 to 1930. For the next 18 years he worked at the All-Union Institute of Experimental Medicine in Leningrad. He was awarded a Stalin Prize in 1941.

Gurwitsch was one of the first scientists to study the effects of certain types of drugs on development. His concern with the problem of organization of embryonic growth led him to study the mechanics of cell division. In 1923 he began to publish a series of papers which aroused intense controversy. He claimed to have detected what he called "mitogenetic rays," a form of energy emitted by living cells, which he believed stimulated growth in other tissues. His original experiments were performed with onion roots. In a book published in 1937, *Mitogenetic Analysis of the Excitation of the Nervous System,* Gurwitsch attempted to extend his concept to explain the activity of the nervous system. The evidence on which these ideas were based was generally regarded as equivocal, and most biologists rejected his theories.

Bibliography: Blyakher and Zalkind, in: *Byulleten Moskovskogo obshchestva ispytaniya prirody,* 60 (1955), 103–8.

[N.LEV./ED.]

GUSIKOW, JOSEPH MICHAEL (1802–1837), musician. Descendant of a long line of *klezmerim,* Gusikow, who was born in Shklov, Belorussia, first took up the flute but had to abandon it because of incipient consumption. He then constructed an improved xylophone consisting of 15 (later 29) tuned wooden staves, with a chromatic range of two-and-a-half octaves laid upon supports of tied straw and beaten with two thin sticks, which he called "Holz und Stroh." With this instrument he began to tour Russia and in the mid-1830s Austria, when he appeared before the emperor. His repertoire by now included many virtuoso and salon pieces originally written for the piano (including concertos), operatic arias, and—his specialty—extempore variations on arias, Jewish and gentile folk tunes, and even national anthems, all without having had a single music lesson. Society lionized him, and his orthodox earlocks become a ladies' fashion—the coiffure à la Gusikow. Concerts in Germany, France, and Belgium followed. In Leipzig, Solomon *Plessner published a Hebrew ode in his praise (1836). In Brussels his instrument and manner of playing were analyzed by the musicologist Fétis. Gusikow's illness had in the meantime grown worse. He died at Aachen. Lamartine, Félix *Mendelssohn-Bartholdy and his sister Fanny, as well as numerous other musicians of discernment, all attested to his virtuosity and creative power. The English writer Sacheverell Sitwell was therefore not exaggerating when he described Gusikow as "the greatest untaught or impromptu musician there had ever been." One of his tunes was published by Abraham Moses *Bernstein in *Muzikalisher Pinkes* (1927), p. 114.

Bibliography: S. Sitwell, *Splendours and Miseries* (1943), 143–66; D. Sadan, *Ha-Menaggen ha-Mufla* (1947); Sendrey, Music, nos. 3529, 4098–98a, 5812–17.

[B.B.]

GUSS, BENJAMIN (1905–), Canadian lawyer. Born in Dorbian, Lithuania, Guss was taken to Saint John, New Brunswick, as a child. He was admitted to the Canadian bar and joined the Canadian Conservative Party, becoming national chairman of the Young Conservatives in 1944. He was master of the Supreme Court of New Brunswick and founder-chairman of the Legal Aid Committee of the Canadian Bar Association. Guss was a prominent figure in Jewish communal affairs as an area president of the Canadian Jewish Congress, and a founder of Canadian Young Judea.

[B.G.K.]

GUTENBERG, BENO (1889–1960), geophysicist. Born in Darmstadt, from 1912 to 1923 Gutenberg was assistant at the International Seismological Bureau at Strasbourg. He was then appointed teacher at Frankfort University, where he became professor in 1926. In 1930 he emigrated to the U.S. to take up the position of professor of geophysics and meteorology at the California Institute of Technology, Pasedena, where in 1946 he became director of the Seismological Laboratory. Gutenberg was the president of the International Association for Seismology (1951–54) and a member of the National Academy of Sciences in Washington. As one of the outstanding seismologists of the last decades, he confirmed the occurrence of earthquakes down to depths of 375 mi. (600 km.) and was the originator of the hypothesis of continental spreading (Fliess theory). He carefully analyzed the available information on the earth's interior and made the first exact determination of the earth's core at 1812 mi. (2,900 km.) below the surface and detected the "asthenosphere channel" at a depth of 62–124 mi. (100–200 km.). This discovery had a critical influence on identifying elastic waves produced by large artificial explosions. He also investigated the nature of the atmosphere. On the basis of the research of Lindemann and Dobson, Gutenberg revolutionized existing conceptions. He maintained that at the height of 31 mi. (50 km.) the temperature was probably as high as on the earth's surface, and that the composition of the atmosphere remained unchanged up to a height of 94 mi. (150 km.). He contributed much to modern geophysical ideas on the earth's crust and mantle. Among his works are *Seismische Bodenunruhe* (1924), *Der Aufbau der Erde* (1925), *Grundlagen der Erdbebenkunde* (1927), *Lehrbuch der Geophysik* (1929), the important *Handbuch der Geophysik* (1930), *Seismicity of the Earth* (with C. F. Richter, 1941), *Internal Constitution of the Earth* (1939), and *Physics of the Earth's Interior* (1959).

Bibliography: P. Byerly, in: *Science*, 131 (April 1960), 965–6; R. Stoneley, in: *Nature*, 186 (May 7, 1960), 433–4. [Ed.]

GUTFREUND, OTTO (1889–1927), Czech sculptor. Born in eastern Bohemia, Gutfreund was sent in his youth to study in Paris, and became a pioneer of cubism in sculpture. During World War I he joined the French Foreign Legion. His war experiences left a deep impression on his human and artistic development. Returning to Prague in 1920, he abandoned all earlier formalism and turned to simplified, stylized reality, choosing scenes from everyday life. Among his best work from the cubist period are "Anxiety" (1911), "Don Quixote" (1911), and "Hamlet" (1912). The period of his artistic maturity is best represented by the monumental group "Grandmother" (1922), the allegoric groups "Industry and Commerce" (1923), and the life-size statue of President Masaryk in Hradec Králové, which was removed when the Communists came to power in 1948. Gutfreund had probably a more profound influence on modern Czech sculpture than any other of his contemporaries.

Bibliography: Wander, in: *Das Zelt*, 1 (1924–25), 244–7; V. Kramář et al., *Gutfreund* (Cz., 1927); *Otto Gutfreund* (Cz., 1948), includes reproductions; *Příruční slovník naučný*, 1 (1962), plate opp. p. 305, no. 8; 2 (1963), 66, s.v. [Av.D.]

°**GUTHE, HERMANN** (1849–1936), German archaeologist. Guthe was born in Westerlinde, Germany, and appointed a professor at the University of Leipzig in 1884. He excavated at the *Ophel in Jerusalem on behalf of the Deutscher Palaestina-Verein in 1881 and discovered part of the eastern wall of the Temple Mount. He also copied the newly discovered *Siloam inscription. In 1904 he visited Megiddo and Madaba and copied the mosaic map found at the latter site. From 1911 to 1925 he was one of the directors of the Verein and editor of its Zeitschrift. His publications include *Palaestina in Bild und Wort* (1883–84), *Ausgrabungen bei Jerusalem* (1883), *Bibelwoerterbuch* (1903), and *Bibelatlas* (1926[2]). He collaborated in the *Kautzsch translation of the Bible, wrote *Geschichte des Volkes Israel* (1904), and published (with P. Palmer) *Die Mosaikkarte von Madeba* (1906).

[M.A.-Y.]

GUTHEIM, JAMES KOPPEL (1817–1886), U.S. Reform rabbi. Gutheim, trained in his native Westphalia as a teacher, went to the United States around 1843. In 1846 he went to Cincinnati to become rabbi of B'nai Yeshurun Congregation (today the Isaac M. Wise Temple), then in 1850 accepted an invitation to become the leader of Shaare Chesed Congregation of New Orleans. In 1853 he became

James K. Gutheim, U.S. Reform rabbi. Courtesy American Jewish Archives, Cincinnati, Ohio.

ḥazzan of the New Orleans Spanish-Portuguese Congregation, the Dispersed of Judah. After New Orleans was captured from the Confederacy, Gutheim refused to take the oath of allegiance to the Union and went into voluntary exile, serving the Jews of Montgomery, Alabama, and Columbus, Georgia, from 1863 to 1865. He returned to New Orleans after the war, and from 1868 preached in English at Temple Emanu-El of New York City. He was highly regarded as a pulpiteer in New York, and many of his sermons and addresses were printed in the *Jewish Times*, which published a volume of his efforts entitled *Temple Pulpit* (1872). Gutheim was the author of many hymns in English. He also prepared a translation of the fourth volume of Heinrich *Graetz's *History of the Jews*, of which the first five chapters were printed in the *Jewish Times* as early as 1869. The volume itself was published by the American Jewish Publication Society in 1874, marking the first appearance in America of Graetz's epoch-making book. Meanwhile, Gutheim had decided to return to New Orleans in 1872 to serve a new Reform congregation, Temple Sinai, which had been organized in 1870 and had already built a new synagogue, probably in order to attract Gutheim back to the city. Gutheim became the acknowledged leader of the Jews of New Orleans, and held important civic posts as well. He was a close friend and faithful supporter of Isaac Mayer *Wise in the development of the Union of American Hebrew Congregations and Hebrew Union College.

Bibliography: B. W. Korn, *American Jewry and the Civil War* (1951), 47–50; *Early Jews of New Orleans* (1969), 251–4; L. C. Littman, *Stages in the Development of a Jewish Publication Society* (unpubl. M.A.H.L. thesis, Hebrew Union College—Jewish Institute of Religion, N.Y.C.), 75, 78–93; J. G. Heller, *As Yesterday When It Is Past* (1942), 32–41; M. Heller, *Jubilee Souvenir of Temple Sinai* (1922), 48–52; L. Shpall, in: *Louisiana Historical Quarterly*, 12 (1929), 461–7.

[B.W.K.]

GUTMAN, ALEXANDER B. (1902–), U.S. physician. Born in New York City, he was educated in the U.S. and Austria. From 1951 he served as director of the department of medicine and physician in chief of New York's Mount Sinai Hospital. On his retirement in 1968 he was appointed professor of medicine at the Mount Sinai School of Medicine. Gutman was editor in chief of the American Journal of Medicine which he founded in 1946. He was also associate editor of the classic Cecil-Loeb *Textbook of Medicine* (1950–60). He served on many advisory boards and professional societies.

Gutman introduced the acid phosphatase test for prostatic cancer. He became one of the world's authorities on gout and his research into its cause and treatment resulted in new insights into this disease and brought him many honors, prizes, and awards. He made major contributions toward the understanding of the pathophysiology of purine metabolism.

Bibliography: *National Cyclopaedia of American Biography*, 1 (1960), 190. [F.R.]

GUTMAN, CHAIM (1887–1961), Yiddish humorist, satirist, and theater critic, better known under his pseudonym "Der Lebediker" ("the lively one"). He grew up in the province of Minsk, Russia, and in 1905 emigrated to the U.S., where he worked at various trades before opening a bookstore. He wrote some poetry but was more successful as a writer of epigrams and sketches for the humorous journal *Der Kibetzer.* He edited the comical weekly *Der Kundes,* and wrote witty columns for New York's Yiddish dailies. His language was rich, vivid, and colloquial, an American East-Side Yiddish employing some Anglicisms for local color. His sketches *Azoy hot geret Pompadur* ("Thus Spake Pompadour"; 1918), were followed by another seven humorous collections. A two-act comedy *Meshiekh oyf East Broadway* ("Messiah on East Broadway") was occasionally staged. His sketches enriched the repertoire of Yiddish comedians for several decades.

Bibliography: Rejzen, Leksikon, 1 (1926), 544–9; LNYL, 2 (1958), 177–80; A. Mukdoni (ed.), *Zamelbukh . . . Der Lebediker* (1938). [M.Rav.]

GUTMAN, NAHUM (1898–), Israel painter and illustrator. His work is a good example of the local expressionist painting typical of the 1920s and 1930s. Gutman, the son of the writer Simḥah *Ben-Zion, was taken to Ereẓ Israel from Rumania at the age of seven. He enrolled at the Bezalel School of Art in 1913 and studied under Boris *Schatz and Abel *Pann. After a brief period of service in the *Jewish Legion in World War I, Gutman continued his education in Vienna. He studied print making with Hermann *Struck in Berlin. Here he met *Bialik and illustrated his works. Gutman returned to Ereẓ Israel in 1926 and participated in the "Modern Artists" exhibition in Tel Aviv in 1927. He worked in oils and watercolors, made drawings, and also illustrated children's stories. Gutman designed scenery for the Ohel Theater in 1935 and a mosaic for the chief rabbinate building in Tel Aviv in 1961. His subjects were mainly landscapes, local scenes, and some portraits. He was influenced early in his career by landscape painters of the Paris School and his art developed a decorative feel, combining light and rapid line with pale, luminous colors. Gutman's literary talents expressed themselves mainly in the writing of prose, especially children's stories. Among the collections of short stories he published are: *Sippurim Meẓuyyarim* (1950), *Ir Ketannah va-Anashim bah Me'at* (1959), and many children's tales of which the best known is the series *Be-Ereẓ Lobengulu Melekh Zulu* (1940–). Books illustrated by Gutman include *Esther* (1932); *Passover Haggadah* (1952[2]); and Bialik's *Va-Yehi ha-Yom* (1965).

"A Synagogue in Safed," oil painting by Nahum Gutman, 1969/70.

Bibliography: Y. Haezrahi, *Naḥum Gutman* (Heb., 1965), with reprod.; U. Ofek, *Mi-Robinzon ad Lobengulu* (1963), 180–91; Z. Scharfstein, *Yoẓerei Sifrut ha-Yeladim* (1947), 117–22; Y. Fischer, in: B. Tammuz (ed.), *Art in Israel* (1966), 18–22. [Y.Fi.]

GUTMANN, DAVID MEIR (1827–1894), Ereẓ Israel pioneer. Born in Hungary in 1827, Gutmann fought in the Hungarian War of Independence in 1848, but was disillusioned by the Hungarian attitude toward Jews. In 1876 he sold his property and went with his wife to settle in Ereẓ Israel. In Jerusalem he was influenced by the visionary ideas of his friend Akiva Yosef *Schlesinger, gave large donations to charitable institutions, took part in land purchase and the establishment of new quarters outside the walls of the Old City, and also searched for land for agricultural settlement, despite the objection of several rabbis. He joined a group of Jerusalemites who, when they failed in attempts to purchase land near Jericho, acquired the Mullabis lands by the Yarkon River in 1878 and established Petaḥ Tikvah there. Gutmann was one of the founders of the settlement and suffered greatly on its behalf. He sold all his property in Jerusalem to pay the settlement's debts and conduct its law cases with the previous landowners. In his old age he was greatly impoverished. He died in Jaffa and was buried in Jerusalem.

Bibliography: Tidhar, 1 (1947), 304; EẒD, 1 (1958), 457–9; G. Kressel, *Em ha-Moshavot Petaḥ Tikvah* (1953), ch. 5. [G.Y.]

GUTMANN, EUGEN (1840–1925), German banker. Born in Dresden, the son of an old-established banking family, Gutmann, together with several partners, took over the banking house of Michael *Kaskel and formed the Dresdner Bank. After initial difficulties a branch which had been opened in Berlin came under Gutmann's guidance. He developed it into a leading national and international financial institution with worldwide interests that included railways in Turkey, mining in Bohemia, and banking in Latin America. Gutmann directed the bank for more than 40 years. Germany's defeat in 1918 and the subsequent economic collapse broke Gutmann's health, and in 1920 he retired.

Bibliography: S. Kaznelson, *Juden im deutschen Kulturbereich* (1959), 743–5; NDB, 7 (1966). [J.O.R.]

GUTMANN, JOSEPH (1923–), U.S. art historian. Gutmann, who was born in Wuerzburg, Germany, went to the United States in 1936. In 1959 he was ordained as rabbi. After teaching at Hebrew Union College and the University of Cincinnati, he was appointed professor of medieval art history at Wayne State University, Detroit, in 1969. His publications include: *Juedische Zeremonialkunst* (1963; *Jewish Ceremonial Art,* 1964); *Images of the Jewish Past: An Introduction to Medieval Hebrew Miniatures* (1965); and *Beauty in Holiness: Studies in Jewish Customs and Ceremonial Art* (1970). [Ed.]

GUTMANN, JOSHUA (1890–1963), scholar of Jewish Hellenism. Born in Belorussia, Gutmann studied with Chaim *Tchernowitz (Rav Ẓa'ir) in Odessa at the Slobodka Yeshivah, at Baron Guenzburg's Institute of Oriental (i.e., Jewish) Studies, and at the universities of St. Petersburg, Odessa, and Berlin. From 1916 to 1921 he taught in Odessa, and from 1921 to 1923 he was principal of the Hebrew Teachers' Seminary in Vilna. He settled in Berlin in 1923 and in 1925 joined the editorial board of the German *Encyclopaedia Judaica* and that of the Hebrew encyclopedia *Eshkol,* contributing hundreds of articles in a wide range of Jewish subjects; he also lectured at the Hochschule (Lehranstalt) fuer die Wissenschaft des Judentums. Gutmann emigrated to Palestine in 1933, at first teaching in the Reali school in Haifa and later becoming head of the Hebrew Teachers' Seminary in Jerusalem. From 1942 to 1953 Gutmann served on the editorial staff of the biblical encyclopedia *Enẓiklopedyah Mikra'it* and from 1946 to 1961 on that of the *Encyclopaedia Hebraica.* In 1949 he began teaching Jewish-Hellenistic studies at the Hebrew University. In 1954 with M. *Schwabe he founded *Eshkolot,* a periodical for classical studies, serving as its sole editor from 1956.

Gutmann's main work in Jewish Hellenism was the first two volumes of *Ha-Sifrut ha-Yehudit ha-Hellenistit* (1958, 1963), which deal with the beginnings of that literature. He also contributed to Hebrew, Russian, and English periodicals and to several Festschriften; he edited with M. Schwabe the Hans Lewy memorial volume, *Sefer Yoḥanan Levi* (1949). Gutmann's wide-ranging scholarship in both Judaism and the classics enabled him to make significant contributions to the understanding of the Hellenistic period in Jewish history and literature. He gave fresh insight into the Greek philosophers' interest in Judaism, which was an important element in the growth of Jewish Hellenism.

Bibliography: A. Fuks, S. Safrai, and M. Stern, *Al Profesor Yehoshu'a Gutmann* (1964), includes bibliography. [M.D.H.]

GUTMANN, WILHELM, RITTER VON (1825–1895), Austrian industrialist and philanthropist. Born in Lipnik (Leipnik, Moravia) and a pupil of the yeshivah there, he began his career as a commission agent in the coal business. Subsequently, in partnership with his brother David (1834–1912), he founded the firm of Gebrueder Gutmann (1853) which eventually controlled the bulk of the Austro-Hungarian coal trade, at first selling imported coal and later acquiring and developing coal seams in the Ostrava basin and in Galicia, thereby improving considerably the monarchy's trade balance. The Witkowitz Steel Works, which they established, developed into one of the outstanding firms on the continent, numbering the Viennese *Rothschilds and members of the nobility among its partners; after 1918 it became a joint-stock company. Following the Munich agreement (1938), lengthy negotiations took place between the Nazis and the Gutmann and Rothschild families; a price of £10,000,000 was offered but the deal was never concluded. The company became part of the Hermann Goering concern without being owned by it. After World War II, it became a Czechoslovakian state-owned enterprise.

Founder of the Oesterreichischer Industriellenklub and a member of the board of the Creditanstalt, Wilhelm was a member of the Lower Austrian Diet, where he supported German liberalism. Both brothers were knighted, Wilhelm in 1878 and David a year later. The Gutmanns were also active in Jewish affairs, Wilhelm as president of the Vienna Jewish community (1891–92) and David as head of the Israelitische Allianz in Vienna and the Baron de *Hirsch school fund for Galicia. They were cofounders of the *Israelitisch-Theologische Lehranstalt. Both gave generous support to Jewish and non-Jewish philanthropic institutions: among the Jewish foundations they established and supported were an orphanage for girls at Doebling, a childrens' hospital in Vienna, an institution for the crippled at Krems, and an old-age home in Lipnik. They defrayed Joseph *Bloch's expenses in the Bloch-*Rohling trial.

Max Gutmann (1857–1930), Wilhelm's son, studied mining engineering at Leoben Academy (Austria), gaining a worldwide reputation in the field and publishing several books on it. He was also an authority on labor relations and a pioneer in social insurance.

Bibliography: H. Gold, *Geschichte der Juden in Maehren* (1929), index; *Neue deutsche Biographie,* 7 (1966), 347–8; R. Hilberg, *The Destruction of the European Jews* (1967[2]), 66–72; K. Kratochuil, *Bankéři* (1962), index. [M.La./Ed.]

GUTT, CAMILLE (1884–), Belgian statesman. Born in Brussels, Gutt qualified as a lawyer and joined the Liberal Party. At the end of World War I he was appointed secretary-general to the Belgian delegation to the Reparations Commission and from 1920 to 1924 was chief secretary to the minister of finance. Gutt himself was minister of finance from 1934 to 1935 and from 1939 to 1940 when Belgium was overrun by the Germans. He escaped with the rest of the Belgian cabinet to Britain and held various ministerial posts in the Belgian government in exile until the Liberation. From 1946 to 1951 he was managing director of the International Monetary Fund. [Ed.]

GUTTMACHER, ALAN F. (1898–), U.S. professor of obstetrics and proponent of world population control. Born and educated in Baltimore, Maryland, he served as clinical

Alan F. Guttmacher, U.S. physician and educator. Courtesy Planned Parenthood Federation of America, New York.

professor of obstetrics and gynecology at Columbia University's College of Physicians and director of the department of obstetrics and gynecology at New York's

Mount Sinai Hospital until 1962 when he became president of the Planned Parenthood Federation of America, and in 1964 chairman of the medical committee of the International Planned Parenthood Federation (1964–68).

Guttmacher lectured and wrote extensively on the subject of world population control. His later books on the subject include *Babies by Choice or by Chance* (1959); *Pregnancy and Birth* (1962); *Planning your Family* (1965); and *Birth Control and Love* (1969). [F.R.]

GUTTMACHER, ELIJAH (1795–1874), rabbi and forerunner of the Ḥibbat Zion movement. Born in Borek, district of Posen, Guttmacher studied at various yeshivot, the most outstanding of which was that of R. Akiva *Eger in Posen. He also studied Kabbalah and acquired a good knowledge of German and general subjects. From 1822 he was the rabbi of Pleschen, and from 1841 until his death he served as rabbi in Grodzisk Wielkopolski (Graetz). His great erudition and his way of life, which was akin to that of the Ḥasidim in Eastern Europe, made his name famous in the Jewish world, and a stream of visitors made their pilgrimage to him, as to a ḥasidic *rebbe,* to obtain amulets for the cure of diseases and the solution of personal problems. In order to end this kind of veneration, he published a request asking people to refrain from approaching him on such matters; these appeals, however, were of no avail and he acquired the unsought position of the *rebbe* of West European Ḥasidim.

Guttmacher's inclination to mysticism and his preoccupation with problems affecting the Jews of his time led him to ponder the idea of redemption and its practical realization as a solution to the misery of the Jews. He was one of a small minority of rabbis who, despite their belief in the Messiah, did not think that the Jewish people should wait for the coming of redemption passively, but rather should do all in their power to hasten redemption by engaging in constructive work in Ereẓ Israel. Thus Guttmacher lent his support to Z. H. *Kalischer's efforts to organize potential settlers for Ereẓ Israel and propagated the idea in his letters and articles. He wrote,

Elijah Guttmacher, mystic and precursor of Ḥibbat Zion. Lithograph by Hermann Struck. Jerusalem, J.N.U.L., Schwadron Collection.

> "It is an error to believe that everyone will live his life in the usual manner and suddenly, one day, the gates of mercy will open, miracles will happen on heaven and earth, all the prophesies will be fulfilled, and all will be called from their dwelling places. This is not so, I say, and I add, that settling in the Holy Land—making a beginning, redeeming the sleeping land from the Arabs, observing there the commandments that can be observed in our day—making the land bear fruit, purchasing land in Ereẓ Israel to settle the poor of our people there—this is an indispensable foundation stone for complete redemption."

He reiterated this theme, or variations thereof, repeatedly and this provided invaluable support to the budding Ḥibbat Zion movement, which was opposed by both Orthodox and assimilationist rabbis. Guttmacher left behind many works on talmudic and kabbalistic subjects, only a small portion of which have appeared in print (many of the manuscripts are stored in Jerusalem archives). Among his works are: novellae on the *mishnayot* and the *Gemara* contained in the Talmud edition published by Romm; *Ẓafenat Pa'ne'aḥ* (1875), a book devoted to the tales of Rabbah b. Ḥana as told in *Bava Batra; Sukkat Shalom* (1883); and *Shenot Eliyahu* (1879); the latter two books are linked to the study groups established in Jerusalem at his inspiration.

Bibliography: N. Sokolow, *Hibbath Zion* (Eng., 1934), 17–28; A. I. Bromberg, *Ha-Rav Eliyahu Guttmacher* (1969); EẒD, 1 (1958), 448–56. [G.K.]

GUTTMACHER, MANFRED (1898–1966), U.S. criminologist and psychiatrist. His career was devoted to the study of the mentally disturbed, maladjusted offender. Born in Baltimore, he graduated from Johns Hopkins University in 1923. From 1930 to 1960 he was chief medical officer of the Supreme Court of Baltimore. He held the rank of colonel in the U.S. Army Medical Corps during World War II (1942–46), and served as chief psychiatric consultant to the Second Army. During 1948, he served as scientific adviser to the United Nations Social Commission, dealing with the causes and prevention of crime and the treatment of offenders. He taught at Johns Hopkins University, the University of Maryland, and at a number of other universities. His works include *Sex Offenses* (1961), *Psychiatry and the Law* (1952), and *Mind of the Murderer* (1960). [Z.H.]

GUTTMAN, JACOB (1845–1919), historian of Jewish philosophy, born in Beuther (Bytom), Silesia. Guttman studied at the University of Breslau, and at the Jewish Theological Seminary of that city. His doctoral thesis dealt with the relation between Spinoza and Descartes (*De Cartesii Spinozaeque philosophiis,* 1868). He served as rabbi in Hildesheim from 1874 to 1892, and in Breslau from 1892 until his death. From 1910 on he was president of the German Rabbinical Assembly *(Rabbinerverband).* Guttmann published a number of monographs, each of which gives a detailed exposition of the doctrine and sometimes of the sources of some medieval Jewish philosopher. These monographs are: *Die Religionsphilosophie des Abraham Ibn Daud aus Toledo* (1879); *Die Religionsphilosophie des Saadja* (1882); and *Die Philosophie des Salomo Ibn Gabirol* (1889). His study of Isaac Israeli appeared in Baeumker's *Beitraege zur Geschichte der Philosophie des Mittelalters* (vol. 10 no. 4, 1911). He also published important works dealing with the relation between Christian scholasticism and medieval Jewish philosophy. One of these, entitled *Das Verhaeltnis des Thomas von Aquino zum Judentum und zur juedischen*

Literatur (1891), studies the extent of the influence of Maimonides on Thomas Aquinas. In *Die Scholastik des 13. Jahrhunderts in ihren Beziehungen zum Judentum und zur juedischen Literatur* (1902), Guttmann discussed the influence of Maimonides, Gabirol, and Isaac Israeli upon

Jacob Guttman, German rabbi and historian. Jerusalem, J.N.U.L. Schwadron Collection.

William of Auvergne, Albertus Magnus, Duns Scotus, Roger Bacon, and others. Maimonides' influence on Christian thought is also discussed in "Der Einfluss der maimonidischen Philosophie auf das christliche Abendland," one of the two articles contributed by Guttmann to the volume *Moses ben Maimon* (1914), of which he was coeditor; the other one, entitled "Die Beziehungen des Religionsphilosophie des Maimonides zu den Lehren seiner juedischen Vorgaenger," dealt with the relation between Maimonides and earlier Jewish philosophers.

Bibliography: M. Brann, in: MGWJ, 64 (1920), 1–7; I. Heinemann, *ibid.*, 250–72; *Festschrift zum siebzigsten Geburtstag Jakob Guttmanns* (1915), incl. bibl. to date.
[Sh.P.]

GUTTMAN, JULIUS (Yiẓḥak; 1880–1950), philosopher and historian of Jewish philosophy; son of Jacob *Guttmann. He was ordained as rabbi by the Rabbinical Seminary of Breslau. From 1910 he lectured in general philosophy at the University of Breslau, and from 1919 in Jewish philosophy at the Hochschule fuer die Wissenschaft des Judentums in Berlin. In 1934 he migrated to Jerusalem, where he was professor of Jewish philosophy at the Hebrew University.

Guttmann's literary activity covered three areas: (1) sociological research, in which his criticism of L. Sombart's theory of the role of Jews in the evolution of economic systems is of special importance (see *Archiv fuer Socialwissenschaft und Sozialpolitik*, 36 (1913), 149–212); (2) philosophical investigations, in which Guttmann was especially influenced by the philosophy of *Kant (see his *Kants Begriff der objektiven Erkenntnis*, 1911), and by the new trend toward phenomenology; he believed in the existence of a priori principles for human consciousness; this attitude which he maintained until the end of his life (see especially his article in *"Eksistenzyah ve-Idei'ah"* ("Existence and Idea," in M. Buber and N. Rotenstreich (eds.), *Hagut* (1944), 153–73)) underlay much of his philosophical thinking. In his philosophy of religion he followed especially the later teachings of Schleiermacher and Rudolf Otto. All of Guttmann's research is marked by an attempt to offer a description of the phenomenology of thought, religion, and ethics, rather than by an attempt to define these areas by means of abstract definition; (3) Guttmann's major area of research was the history of Jewish philosophy, to which he devoted his magnum opus, *Die Philosophie des Judentums* (1933; Heb. trans., with corrections and additions by the author, *Ha-Filosofyah shel ha-Yahadut*, 1951; *Philosophies of Judaism* (from Heb. version), 1964). The subject of the book is "the Jewish religion and the attempts made through the ages to explain and justify it." Guttmann does not limit his discussion to the philosophy of the Middle Ages, but deals with Jewish philosophy from its biblical sources until modern times. His account of the history of Jewish philosophy reflects his conviction that the conception of God, described by the term "ethical Monotheism," forms the foundation of Judaism (*Ikkarei ha-Yahadut* (1951), 20–39), and he uses this conception for evaluating the Jewish "character" of each approach used by the various Jewish philosophical schools. While Guttmann holds that Jewish philosophy is primarily only a history of ideas taken from non-Jewish sources, he maintains, nevertheless, that the Jewish tradition influences each movement with its own particular nature.

Guttmann's book was criticized, from a fundamentally different approach, by Leo *Strauss in his *Philosophie und Gesetz* (1935). Strauss's articles have been collected under the title *Dat u-Madda* (1955), and his lectures edited by N. Rotenstreich as *Devarim al ha-Filosofyah shel ha-Dat* (1959).

Bibliography: F. Bamberger, in: YLBI, 5 (1960), 3–34; L. Roth, in: *Iyyun*, 2 (1951), 3–10 (see also bibliographies on pp. 11–19 and 182–4).
[J.Lev.]

GUTTMAN, LOUIS (Eliahu; 1916–), sociologist. Born in New York, he was educated at the University of Minnesota where he taught from 1936 to 1940. From 1941 to 1950 he taught at Cornell University; during the years 1941–45 he also served as an expert consultant to the U.S. War Department in the information and education division. A member of the Labor Zionist movement from his early youth, Guttman went to Israel in 1947, when he founded and became the director of the Israel Institute of Applied Social Research. He was appointed professor at the Hebrew University in 1954. Guttman's reputation rests on his work in methodology. The Guttman scale, which is described in "A Revision of Chapin's Social Status Scale," *American Sociological Review* (1942), ranks items in such a way that the statements appearing at the top of the scale must also check all the preceding ones. This is done by taking a number of random samples of population and then ranking the statements in the order in which they are consistently chosen by the respondents. Other contributions by Guttman appeared in P. Horst (ed.), *Prediction of Personal Adjustment* (1941); S. A. Stouffer (ed.), *Measurement and Prediction* (1949); and in P. L. Lazarsfeld (ed.), *Mathematical Thinking in the Social Sciences* (1954). The last contains Guttman's original approach to testing-factor analysis, the radex. The major difference between the radex and older forms of factor analysis is that it deals with the order of the factors, not just the common factors. The radex involves the notion that there is a difference in kind and a difference in degree between the tests used for analysis.
[W.J.C.]

GUTTMANN, MICHAEL (1872–1942), Hungarian talmudic scholar. Guttmann was born in Hungary and studied at the Budapest rabbinical seminary and at the University of Budapest. From 1903, the year of his ordination at the Budapest rabbinical seminary, to 1907 he was rabbi at Csongrád. He lectured on Jewish law from 1907 to 1921 at the Budapest seminary. From 1921 to 1933 he was rabbi and professor of Talmud and *halakhah* at the Breslau Jewish theological seminary and in 1925 he was visiting professor of Talmud at the Hebrew University of Jerusalem. In 1933 he was appointed head of the Budapest seminary. Guttmann combined a wide knowledge of the sources with an acute modern, critical approach. Among his publications in this field were *Einleitung in die Halacha*

(Budapest Seminary *Jahresberichte*, 1909, 1913); *Asmakhta* (Breslau Seminary *Jahresberichte*, 1924), on talmudic methodology; and *Beḥinat ha-Mitzvot* (*ibid.*, 1928) and *Beḥinat Kiyyum ha-Mitzvot* (*ibid.*, 1931), on the reasons for the observance of the commandments. He edited *Abraham b. Ḥiyya's textbook of geometry, *Ḥibbur ha-Meshiḥah ve-ha Tishboret* (introduction, 1903; the work itself 1912–13). Guttmann was one of the editors of *Ha-Ẓofeh le-Ḥokhmat Yisrael* (1911–14), editor of *Ha-Soker* (from

Michael Guttmann, Hungarian talmudist. Courtesy Alexander Guttmann, Cincinnati, Ohio.

1933), and of *Magyar Zsidó Szemle* and published articles in these and other periodicals in Hebrew, Hungarian, French, and German. He was also an editor of and contributor to the *Oẓar Yisrael* encyclopedia and the Eshkol Encyclopedia Judaica, in both the German and Hebrew editions. His *Das Judentum und seine Umwelt* (part 1, 1927) deals with the attitude of Judaism to the non-Jewish world. Written against the background of rising nationalism and anti-Semitism in Germany in the 1920s, when everything Jewish, and the Talmud in particular, was under virulent attack, it is completely apologetic. Guttmann planned as his major life work a vast talmudic encyclopedia, which would have been beyond the talents of most other scholars working alone. Only four volumes of Guttmann's *Mafte'aḥ ha-Talmud*, covering the letter *alef*, appeared (1910–30); the rest of the material was lost after his death when the Nazis occupied Hungary in 1944. Even this small installment is of major importance as a talmudic reference work.

Bibliography: D. S. Loewinger, in: S. Federbush (ed.), *Ḥokhmat Yisrael be-Ma'arav Eiropah*, 1 (1959), 130–47; idem (ed.), *Jewish Studies in Memory of M. Guttmann* (1946), incl. bibl.; A. Guttmann, in: *Bitzaron*, 8 (1943), 46–48. [M.D.H./Ed.]

GUTTMANN, ROBERT (1880–1942), Czech primitive painter. During his life, Guttmann was better known for his unusual personality than for his paintings. He was a familiar figure of the Jewish scene in Prague as he walked from one coffeehouse to another, his work rolled up under his arm, arranging impromptu exhibitions of his drawings and watercolor paintings. His subjects were mainly people, landscapes, and street scenes. However, his work was not taken seriously until after his death in the Lodz ghetto in 1942. It was only when his work was exhibited after World War II, that he was recognized as an original, genuine naive artist whose works—most of them now in the State Jewish Museum in Prague—were widely admired at a number of posthumous exhibitions. He was a lifelong Zionist. At the age of 17 he walked from Prague to Basle to attend the First Zionist Congress, and he made his way on foot to all subsequent Congresses held during his lifetime.

Bibliography: A. Heller, *Guttmann: eine psychologische Studie ueber den Maler Robert Guttmann* (1932). [Av.D.]

"Self Portrait in the Fruit Market" by Robert Guttmann, oil, 1941. Prague, State Jewish Museum.

°**GUTZKOW, KARL FERDINAND** (1811–1878), German nationalist author. Gutzkow was a prominent figure in the "Young Germany" literary movement where he led the reactionary wing, in contrast to the liberal trend influenced by Rahel *Varnhagen von Ense, *Heine, and *Boerne. Like *Goethe, Schlegel, and Brentano, Gutzkow expanded the theme of the *Wandering Jew in German literature, as for instance in his "Julius Moses Ahasver" (in: *Vermischte Schriften*, 2, 1842). Gutzkow also wrote a historical drama, *Uriel Acosta* (1846), in which the author's own emotional experiences and inner conflicts are echoed. Gutzkow had already treated this story in a tale, *Der Sadduzaeer von Amsterdam* (1833). Discrepancies between the drama and Acosta's actual life roused protests from H. *Jellinek and induced him to write a monograph on Spinoza's forerunner, *Uriel Acosta's Leben und Lehre* (1847).

See also Image of the Jew in *German Literature.

Bibliography: L. Poliakov, *Histoire de l'antisémitisme*, 3 (1968), index; G. Brandes, *Main Currents in Nineteenth Century Literature*, 6 (1923), index, J. G. Robertson, *A History of German Literature* (1959), index; V. Eichstaedt, *Bibliographie zur Geschichte der Judenfrage* (1938), index. [Ed.]

°**GUY, PHILIP LANGSTAFFE ORD** (1885–1952), archaeologist. Born in Scotland, he joined the excavations at Carchemish and Tell el-Amarna after World War I. From 1922 to 1925 he was chief inspector of antiquities in Palestine and excavated an Iron Age cemetery in Haifa. He directed the excavations at Megiddo (1925–35) where he introduced a method of balloon photography and cleared the mound to stratum V (Iron Age). As director of the British School of Archaeology in Jerusalem from 1938 to 1939 he began a survey of the Negev. He served in the British Army in World War II and rejoined the department of antiquities in 1947. He remained in Israel as chief of its division of excavations and survey until his death. He directed excavations at Bet Yeraḥ, Jaffa, and Ayyelet ha-Shaḥar. His publications include excavation reports of Tell el-Amarna and Megiddo, including the large volume *Meggido Tombs* (1938). He married a daughter of Eliezer *Ben-Yehuda.

[M.A.-Y.]

GUYANA (formerly **British Guiana**), state in N.E. South America, population: 647,000 (est. 1965); Jewish population: 40 persons (1960 estimate) living in the capital Georgetown. The earliest Jewish settlers in Guyana arrived during the Dutch rule which began in 1581. Jewish settlements, such as Nieuw-Middleburgh (built between 1648 and 1666 by Jews from Leghorn, Italy), were established in the region of Pomeroon. However, difficult climatic conditions, local wars, and slave uprisings caused the eventual emigration or assimilation of the Jewish community. Before the outbreak of World War II there was a handful of Jews in the capital, Georgetown, but there was neither an organized community nor a synagogue, Early in 1939, 165 Jewish refugees from Europe, who arrived on the S.S. *Koenigstein,* were not permitted to disembark, and shortly thereafter the government barred immigration. However, 130 Jews found refuge in the country during the war years but most of these eventually emigrated.

In 1939, in the wake of the failure of the *Evian Conference on the German refugee problem and in view of Britain's intention to severely restrict Jewish immigration to Palestine (see *White Paper), Britain proposed her crown colony Guiana as a site for Jewish immigration and settlement. Thus, in February 1939, an international investigating committee under the auspices of the Inter-Governmental Commission on Refugees, formed at Evian, arrived in the country to explore the proposed area. The land under consideration consisted of approximately 42,000 sq. mi. in the forest and swamp region of the interior. Neither the coastal region, which comprises 4% of the area of British Guiana but holds 90% of the country's population, nor the open region adjacent to it, were included in the proposed area.

The committee stated that although the region was not ideal for the settlement of European immigrants, the quality of the soil, the availability of important minerals, and the climatic and health conditions did not preclude their settlement. The committee

Report of the British Guiana Refugee Commission to the Advisory Committee on Political Refugees appointed by the President of the United States of America

Presented by the Secretary of State for the Colonies to Parliament
by Command of His Majesty
May, 1939

LONDON
PRINTED AND PUBLISHED BY HIS MAJESTY'S STATIONERY OFFICE
To be purchased directly from H.M. STATIONERY OFFICE at the following addresses:
York House, Kingsway, London, W.C.2; 120 George Street, Edinburgh 2;
26 York Street, Manchester 1; 1 St. Andrew's Crescent, Cardiff;
80 Chichester Street, Belfast;
or through any bookseller
1939
Price 4*d*. net

Cmd. 6014

Title page of the British Government's White Paper on Jewish refugee settlement in British Guiana, 1939. Jerusalem, J.N.U.L.

proposed a two-year trial period during which 3,000–5,000 sturdy young people with professional training would be sent to the region to test the practicality and the advisability of large-scale investment and development.

Many considered the British plan for Jewish settlement in British Guiana to be a political strategem. They pointed out that the same region was investigated in 1935 by an international commission and found unsuitable for the settlement of 20,000 Assyrians suffering persecution in Iraq. Not only had the commission stated unanimously that the region was unsuitable for settlement, but its conclusion had been accepted by the British government itself.

However, in May 1939, before British policy on Palestine was officially proclaimed in the White Paper, the British government published the report of its own investigating committee which found British Guiana to be a place for possible settlement. Prime Minister Neville Chamberlain announced that Jewish settlement in British Guiana would bring the establishment of a new community which would enjoy a large measure of autonomy and representation in the government of the colony. The program was described in government circles as a "New Balfour Declaration" and as a plausible alternative to the Jewish National Home in Palestine.

Once it had served its political end to make the "White Paper" more palatable, this settlement project was dropped. The British government explained that it was compelled to promise the region to the inhabitants of the West Indies, who had racial and religious ties with the people living there. In any case, the natives of British Guiana objected to foreign settlement, the British government said.

The only Jewish organization which was seriously involved in the British Guiana scheme was the *American Jewish Joint Distribution Committee on whose behalf Joseph A.*Rosen participated in the inquiry commission.

Relations with Israel. Since April 1967 Israel's ambassador to Colombia has also been non-resident ambassador to Guyana. Out of a desire to mobilize the Arab and Soviet blocs in the international arena, for support of its own conflicts, Guyana formerly adopted a hostile line toward Israel. However, from 1969 relations between the two countries improved substantially as a result of Guyana's supportive votes in the United Nations. Israel has extended a certain amount of technical assistance to Guyana.

Bibliography: *Report of the British Guiana Refugee Commission* . . . (1939); E. Liebenstein (Livneh), *Ha-Teritoryalizm he-Ḥadash* (1944), 11–16.

[AR.M.]

GYMNASIUM, ancient Greek institution devoted to physical education and development of the body (γυμνός, "naked"). Although originally established for functions of a purely athletic and competitive nature, the gymnasium eventually became dedicated to the furthering of intellectual, as well as physical aspects of Greek culture. During the Hellenistic period attendance at the gymnasium was recognized as the standard educational prerequisite for Greek youths wishing to attain citizenship in the *polis.* Thus, with the establishment of a Hellenistic administration in Jerusalem during the reign of *Antiochus IV Epiphanes, the high priest *Jason was given permission "to set up a gymnasium and ephebeum" (II Macc. 4:9). This act was abhorred by the vast majority of Palestinian Jews, who rightly considered the gymnasium a symbol of the Greek heathen culture chosen to supplant ancient Jewish law in Jerusalem (cf. I Macc. 1:13–15). The author of II Maccabees stresses that the gymnasium was erected adjacent to the Temple, and describes the priests abandoning their service at the altar "to participate in the unlawful exercises of the palaestra as soon as the summons came for the discus throwing" (I Macc. 4:14). Opposition to participation in the gymnasium was not as vehement among the Jews of Ptolemaic Egypt, and it may be assumed that the upper classes of Alexandrian Jewry were interested in obtaining this training for their youth. This interest was enhanced with the Roman conquest of Egypt, for Roman policy identified the graduates of the gymnasium as legitimate Greek "citizens," and only these might serve as the basis for local administration. It is therefore understandable that the Greek population of Alexandria was violently opposed to the enrollment of "non-Greeks" (i.e., Egyptians and Jews) among the *epheboi* (cf. the "Boule Papyrus," Tcherikover, Corpus 2 (1960), 25–29 no. 150). The Greek demands were eventually supported by the emperor Claudius (41 C.E.), who decreed, according to another papyrus (*ibid.*, no. 153), that the Jews "are not to intrude themselves into the games presided over by the gymnasiarchs.

Bibliography: E. Bickerman, *From Ezra to the Last of the Maccabees* (1962), 104ff.; A. H. M. Jones, *The Greek City* (1940), 220ff.; Tcherikover, Corpus, 1 (1957), 38ff., 73, 76; idem, *Hellenistic Civilization and the Jews* (1959). [I.G.]

GYONGYOS (Hung. **Gyöngyös**), city in N. Hungary. Jews are first recorded there in the 15th century, and in 1735 there was an organized community. The synagogue, built before the end of the 18th century, was destroyed in the great fire which devastated the city in 1917. The community always remained a *status quo ante community, though a separate Orthodox community was established in 1870. The first rabbi of the community was Feivel b. Asher Boskovitz; he was succeeded by Wolf Lippe (officiated 1840–50), a noted bibliophile. Eleazar Fuerst (1853–1893) founded a yeshivah in the town. The Jewish population numbered 2,250 in 1920, and 2,429 in 1941. Of these only 461 survived the Holocaust. There were 300 Jews in Gyongyos in 1946 and 414 in 1949.

Bibliography: R. L. Braham, *Hungarian-Jewish Studies*, 2 (1969), 143, 160, 180; *Magyar Zsidó Lexikon* (1929), 331–2; MHJ, index. [B.Y.]

GYÖR (Hung. **Györ;** Ger. **Raab**), city in N. W. Hungary, near the Austrian border. The earliest information on Jewish settlement there dates from the last third of the 14th century, though it is probable that an organized community had existed earlier. A Jews' Street is recorded in the municipal land register of 1567, and a synagogue is mentioned in the municipality's accounts. The Church, which would permit only Catholics to reside in the city, compelled the Jews to settle on the nearby Györ-Sziget island on the Danube River. A community was organized there in 1791 and a synagogue established in 1795. Jews did not settle in the city proper until 1840. In 1851 they formed a single community with the island Jews. A new synagogue was built in 1870. In 1871 a separate Orthodox community was organized. Noted rabbis of Györ were S. Ranschburg, J. Fischer, and E. Roth. The last stimulated the ideology of Jewish nationalism in the community; he was deported to Auschwitz in 1944.

The Jews of Györ, mainly manufacturers, artisans, and merchants, numbered 5,904 in 1920, and 7,220 in 1941.

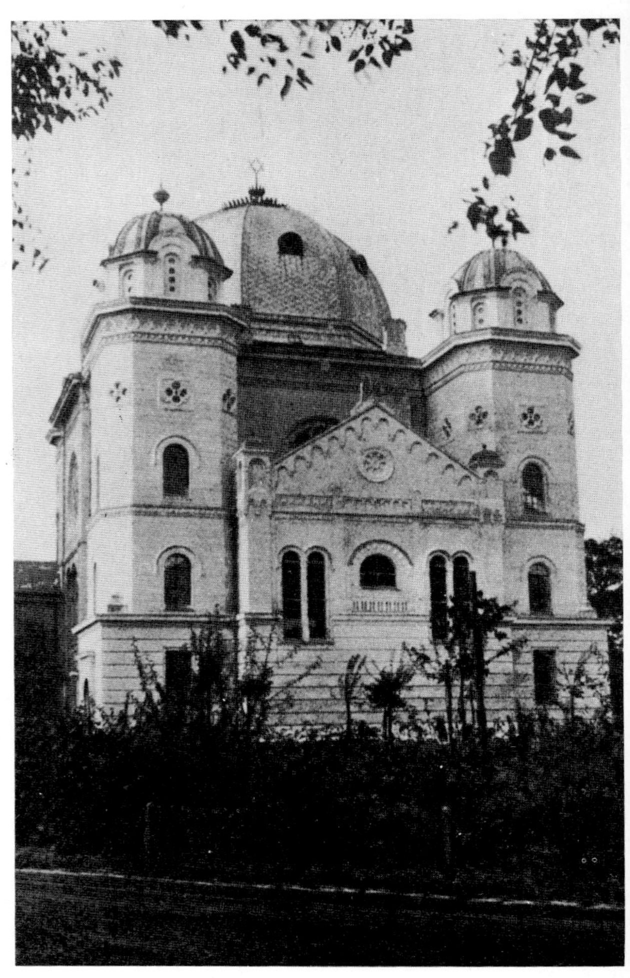

Synagogue in Györ, Hungary, built in 1870. Courtesy C.A.H.J.P., Jerusalem.

Between 1942 and 1944 the majority of male Jews were sent to labor camps. The Nazis occupied Hungary in March 1944, and on June 11, the remaining 5,200 Jews of Györ were deported to Auschwitz. After the war 700 survivors returned. In 1946 there were 950 Jews in Györ but in 1970 only 200 remained. The synagogue was sold in 1969.

Bibliography: J. Kemény, *Vázlatok a györi zsidóság történetéből* (1930); A. Scheiber, *Hebraeische Kódex-Ueberreste in ungarlaendischen Einbandstaefeln* (1969), 95–99; MHJ, 12 (1969), 10 (1967); 9 (1966); 8 (1965); 7 (1963); 6 (1961); 5 (2 pts., 1959–60), index locorum, s.v.; 4 (1938), index locorum s.v. *Rab;* 3 (1937), index s.v. *Györ megye, györi zsidók;* R. L. Braham, *The Hungarian Jewish Catastrophe; a selected and annotated bibliography* (1962), geographic index, s.v. [AL.SCH.]

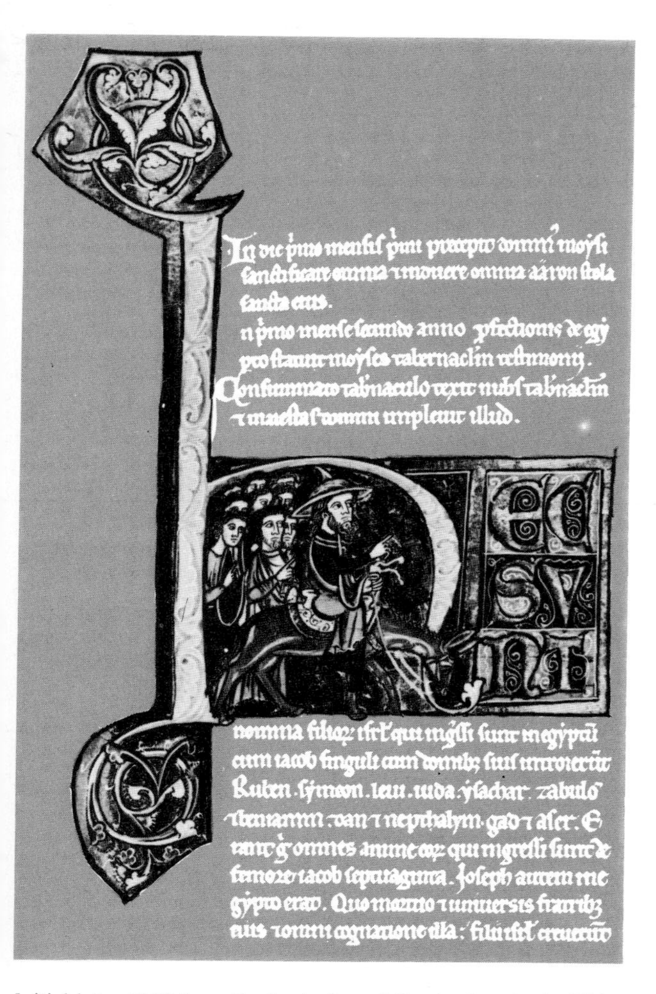

Initial letter "H" from the beginning of Exodus in a Latin Bible, France, 12th century. The illumination shows Jacob and his sons going down to Egypt. Amiens, Bibliothèque Municipale, Ms. 21, fol. 27.

HAAN, JACOB ISRAËL DE (1881–1924), Dutch poet and journalist. Born in Smilde, De Haan was the son of a cantor and the younger brother of the authoress Carry (de Haan) van *Bruggen. Abandoning his parents' Orthodoxy, De Haan set out on a career that was to lead him through many spiritual crises and much personal and political turmoil. He flirted with anarchism, socialism, and even Christianity, and in 1907 married a non-Jewish doctor. His first two works, the semi-autobiographical novels *Pijpelijntes* (1904) and *Pathologieën* (1906), revealed a tendency toward homosexuality, and their publication led to his dismissal from a teaching post and his expulsion from the Dutch Socialist Party. De Haan's wife then financed his study of law, in the course of which he visited Russia and published *In Russische gevangenissen* ("In Russian Prisons," 1913). After his graduation in 1916 he became a law tutor, but when he failed to secure a chair at Amsterdam University he decided to devote himself to writing, a course in which he was encouraged by two leading Dutch poets, F. W. van Eeden and A. Verwey. Shortly before World War I, De Haan had reverted to strict Orthodoxy, and had begun writing verse of an increasingly religious and mystical nature. He was already a Zionist, and now joined the *Mizrachi movement. In 1918, abandoning his wife and children, he settled in Palestine. Here he became the correspondent of the Amsterdam *Algemeen Handelsblad* and the London *Daily Express,* and at first adopted a Zionist position. He soon became disillusioned with both the religious and the secular leaders of the *yishuv,* and joined the ultra-orthodox *Agudat Israel, becoming the spokesman of the Jerusalem "Ashkenazi Council" headed by R. Ḥayyim *Sonnenfeld. He began sending regular anti-Zionist reports to the overseas press, and pro-Arab memoranda to the British Mandatory authorities and the League of Nations. His intrigues with the Arab nationalist leaders included the organization

Jacob Israël de Haan. Jerusalem, Schwadron Collection, J.N.U.L.

of an Agudist delegation to Amman in Transjordan, where he won the approval of King Hussein of the Hejaz. De Haan's political services to the enemies of the *yishuv* created a furore: his lectures at the government law school were boycotted by Jewish students, and he was repeatedly warned to cease his activities. De Haan ignored these warnings. On June 30, 1924, he was assassinated near the Sha'arei Ẓedek Hospital in Jerusalem, where he had attended evening prayers. His assailants were two members of the *Haganah, acting on instructions issued by their high command. Like his life, De Haan's death provoked great controversy. Outwardly the champion of unrelenting orthodoxy, De Haan was the victim of his own sexual proclivities. It is probable that his Arab friends, aware of his homosexuality, exploited the weakness to further their own political ends. De Haan's own verse collection, *Kwatrijnen* ("Quatrains," 1924), provides ample evidence of his inner conflicts and torments, which found expression in erotic reminiscences and blasphemous outbursts. His other works include the well-known collection of poems on Jewish themes, *Het Joodsche Lied* ("The Jewish Song," 2 vols., 1915–21), and two volumes of travel sketches, *Palestina* and *Jerusalem* (1921). His collected verse, *Verzamelde Gedichten*, appeared in 1952. De Haan's tragic end inspired Arnold *Zweig's novel *De Vriendt kehrt heim* (1932; *De Vriendt Goes Home*, 1934).

Bibliography: E. I. Israel, *Jacob Israël de Haan, de dichter van het Joodse lied* (1963); J. Meyer, *De zoon van een gazzan. Het leven van Jacob Israël de Haan* (1967), contains much hitherto unpublished information; A. Z. Ben-Yishai, *Ha-"Kadosh" De Haan. Ḥayyav u-Moto* (1925); Dinur, Haganah, 2 (1963), 251–3, 1142; H. Kana'an, in: *The Jewish Observer and Middle East Review* (July 31, 1964).

[H.Bo.]

HA'ANAKAH (Heb. הַעֲנָקָה), the gratuity which the master was enjoined to pay his Hebrew bound servant when the latter was set free. This institution is the source, in Jewish law, of the laws of severance pay, i.e., payment of compensation to employees on their dismissal. The term *ha'anakah* has been interpreted as deriving from the word *anak* (עֲנָק) in the sense of an ornament (around the neck, Prov. 1:9), i.e., that the bondsman must be "ornamented" with the gratuity, or in the sense of "loading on his neck" (Rashi and Ibn Ezra to Deut. 15:14).

Scriptural References. The duty of *ha'anakah* is enjoined in the Bible as both a negative and a positive precept—"when thou lettest him go free from thee, thou shalt not let him go empty," and "thou shalt furnish him liberally out of thy flock, and out of thy threshing floor, and out of thy winepress of that wherewith the Lord thy God hath blessed thee" (Deut. 15:13, 14)—and in this twofold manner has been included in the enumeration of the precepts (Maim., *Sefer ha-Mitzvot*, pos. comm. 196 and neg. comm. 233; *Semag, lavin* 178 and *asayin* 84; *Sefer ha-Ḥinnukh*, nos. 450, 484). The duty of *ha'anakah* arose upon completion of the six-year period of service (Deut. 15:12) and the grant was to be made out of the things with which the master's house had been blessed by virtue of the bondsman's service (Deut. 15:14; Kid. 17b; see statements of Eleazar b. Azariah). The duty of *ha'anakah* was enjoined as a reminder of the bondage in Egypt and exodus to freedom (Deut. 15:15), when the Israelites were "furnished" with property of their Egyptian masters (Sif. Deut. 120; Rashi and Rashbam, ad loc.). The institution of *ha'anakah*, unique to Jewish law as opposed to other ancient legal systems, was rooted in the special attitude toward a Hebrew bondsman, whose position was compared to that of a worker hired for a fixed term: ". . . for to the double of the hire of a hireling hath he served thee six years" (Deut. 15:18).

The Right to the Gratuity. It was laid down that the servant became entitled to the gratuity upon expiry of his term of service, or termination thereof on account of the Jubilee or his master's death, but not for reasons attributable to the servant himself, as, for example, when he gained his freedom by "deduction from the purchase price" (i.e., by refunding his master part of the price paid for himself, pro rata to the uncompleted term of his service): "you shall furnish to whomever you set free, but not to anyone who sets himself free" (Sif. Deut. 119; Kid. 16b). For this reason the gratuity right was forfeited by a runaway, notwithstanding intervention of the Jubilee. In the opinion of R. Meir, one who was freed by deduction from the purchase price remained entitled to the gratuity since it took place with the master's approval (Kid. 16b); on the other hand, some of the *tannaim* denied the gratuity right to one who was set free on account of his master's death (TJ, Kid. 1:2, 59c).

In the *Midrash Halakhah* the gratuity right was extended both to the one sold into bondage through the court on account of his theft (Ex. 22:2) and to one who sold himself into bondage on account of utter poverty (Lev. 25:39), nor were these cases distinguished in the Mishnah (see Ḥ. Albeck, *Shishah Sidrei Mishnah, Seder Nashim*, 409f.). In a *baraita* disputing opinions were expressed on this matter; some scholars holding that only one sold into bondage through the court and not one selling himself was entitled to gratuity, with R. Eliezer (Kid. 14b) holding that both were entitled thereto; this dispute was carried over into the codes (Yad, Avadim, 3:12; Tos. Kid. 15a, s.v. *idakh;* and commentaries). One of the grounds for the view that one who sold himself into bondage was not entitled to the gratuity was that in doing so voluntarily, he transgressed the prohibition, "For unto Me the children of Israel are servants; they are My servants" (Lev. 25:55) "and not the servants of servants" (Kid. 22b; *Yam shel Shelomo*, Kid. 1:22).

Substance of the Gratuity Right. In tannaitic times the gratuity was looked upon as a personal right of the freed servant which was not transferable on death (Sif. Deut. 119), but the *amoraim* held it to be part of his remuneration and therefore transmissible ". . . just as the wages of a hired servant belong to his heirs, so here too . . ." (Kid. 15a; cf. also the version of Elijah Gaon, loc. cit. and see *Minḥat Ḥinnukh* no. 482). Contrary to the principle of "R. Nathan's Lien" (see **Shi'abuda de-Rabbi Natan*) with regard to the general right to recover a claim from a third party indebted to the debtor, the gratuity right was not attachable by the servant's creditor (Kid. 15a–16b) and, according to the majority of the *posekim*, the creditor could not recover his debt from the amount of the gratuity—not even when the servant was already released and in possession of the gratuity payment (Maim. comm. to Kid. 1:2; cf. Nov. *Penei Yehoshu'a* Kid., final collection).

The duty of furnishing a gratuity was, according to the majority view of the scholars, independent of the measure of gain derived by the master from his servant's labor (Sif. *ibid.;* Kid. 17a/b and cf. contrary opinion of Eleazar b. Azariah), but all the scholars accepted that a minimum was payable (although disagreeing on the amount: Kid. 17a), together with an increment according to the measure with which the master has been "blessed," such increment being payable by the master with a "generous hand" (Sif. Deut., 119–20).

Two opposing views concerning the legal substance of the gratuity were expressed in the codes. According to some scholars it was not part of the servant's remuneration for his labor but derived from the institution of charity (*ẓedakah;* Shakh. to ḤM 86:3) or of waiver and gift (*Sema, ibid.*, 86:2 and see *Giddulei Terumah* to *Sefer ha-Terumot*,

An initial-word panel with marginal illustrations of a Passover table, for the opening text *ke-Ha Laḥma* from the *Joel ben Simeon Haggadah.* Written and partly illuminated in Germany and Italy by the scribe Joel ben Simeon of Bonn in the middle of the 15th century. London, British Museum, Add. ms. 14762, fol. 6 ($14\frac{7}{8} \times 11$ ins/37.5 × 28 cm.).

51:1:5); other *posekim*, following the *halakhah* of the *amoraim* concerning transmissibility at death, of the gratuity, took the view that the gratuity was mainly to reward the servant for services rendered "beyond his wages" (Beit ha-Beḥirah, Kid. 15a) and therefore it had to be considered as part of his remuneration (*Penei Yehoshu'a* Kid. 16b; *Mishneh la-Melekh*, to Yad. *ibid.*).

Severance Pay. Adaptation of the gratuity institution to one of general compensation for employees upon dismissal was first mentioned toward the end of the 13th century, when it was stated that notwithstanding the abolition of Hebrew bound service, which was linked with observance of the Jubilee year, the employer still had to pay a gratuity to his departing worker regardless of the period of service (*Sefer ha-Ḥinnukh*, 450). Although this was phrased at that time as a moral obligation only, later scholars found it possible to recognize this duty of the employer as legally binding. In recent times this development has been acknowledged in the decisions of various scholars, and particularly in the judgments of the rabbinical courts in Israel, in three different ways:

(a) In accordance with the principle of the bound servant's gratuity, in pursuance of the statements in the *Sefer ha-Ḥinnukh (ibid.)*, it was held that "... the intention of the Torah was to make it the employer's duty to be concerned about the worker's future so that the latter should not depart from his work empty-handed" (PDR, 3:286f.). Because Jewish law compared the position of a bound servant to that of a hired worker, it was concluded that the latter "certainly enjoys all the former's privileges ... the more so since he does not transgress a prohibition" (i.e., that of selling himself into bondage—see above; resp. Maharam of Rothenburg, ed. Prague, no. 85; see also *Yam ha-Gadol*, no. 22).

(b) A different approach was adopted by Benẓion *Ouziel (see his responsum quoted in *Teḥukat Avodah* (see bibl.) 132f.). Holding that the law of the gratuity could not properly be relied upon to support the existence of a full legal duty to compensate an employee upon his dismissal, he preferred to base this duty on the scriptural admonition, "That thou mayest walk in the way of good men, and keep the paths of the righteous" (Prov. 2:20) in the same way as it was relied upon in the Talmud with reference to exempting the hired worker in certain circumstances from liability for damage negligently caused to his employer (BM 83a). Although conceding that this talmudic principle was a matter of equity *(li-fenim mi-shurat ha-din)* rather than binding law, R. Ouziel followed the opinion of numerous *posekim* that it was nevertheless enforceable by the court (*Mordekhai* BM 257; Sh. Ar., ḤM 12:2, and *Rema ibid.*; also *Baḥ* HM 12), and therefore decided that the court, "having due regard to the respective positions of the parties and reasons for the worker's dismissal or for his own departure," was empowered to order an employer to compensate his worker.

(c) Since it was not generally accepted that an obligation solely *li-fenim mi-shurat ha-din* is enforceable by the court, some scholars preferred to base the principle of severance pay on the Jewish legal source of custom (see **Minhag*; PDR, 1:330f.). Thus the rabbinical courts, applying the rule that "custom overrides the law" has special reference to labor law (TJ, BM 7:1; 11b) and recognizing "the spread in our time of a usage to pay severance pay," have laid down that severance pay "is not a matter of grace but a claim under law" which is payable even if the employer be a charitable institution; in arriving at this decision the rabbinical courts incorporate also the principle of the gratuity, holding that particular significance attaches to custom in this instance, since "we find a basis for it in the Torah and *halakhah*," and this custom is founded on the Torah, the gratuity payable to the Hebrew bound servant "and therefore it is fit and proper" (PDR, 1:330f.; 3:286f.; 4:120).

It may be noted that R. Ouziel, in giving his above-mentioned decision (in 1945), specifically refrained from basing the severance pay obligation on custom—for the reason that such a usage was not yet sufficiently known and widespread. A mere ten years later the court, seeking a basis for full legal recognition of the severance pay duty, had reason to find as follows: "now that the custom has spread and become accepted in the whole country, and is common and practiced daily, it must be followed and the above-mentioned statements [of R. Ouziel] no longer apply." This is an illustration of great flexibility in recognizing the establishment of a custom.

In the years since the establishment of the State of Israel, the rabbinical courts have laid down a number of rules concerning the matter of severance pay, including the following provisions: compensation is to be paid at the customarily accepted rate, or if this be uncertain, as determined by the court (PDR, 1:332f.); it is payable also to a temporary employee—if he has worked for a period approximating two years *(ibid.)*, and also to a part-time employee (4: 129), but an independent contractor is not entitled to severance pay (3:272). An innovation was the rule that the employer is obliged to provide his worker with one month's prior notice of dismissal, or a month's remuneration in lieu thereof. This was deduced by the analogy of the landlord's duty, in Jewish law, to provide the tenant with a month's notice of eviction, in order that the latter be not deprived of a roof over his head; *a fortiori* in the case of a worker, so that he be given an opportunity to find an alternative source of livelihood. (Sh. Ar., ḤM 312:5; PDR, 4:130 and 3:281–3, where disputing opinions are quoted on the aptness of the analogy.)

In the State of Israel. In Mandatory times the obligation of severance pay was upheld in numerous judgments of the Mishpat ha-Shalom ha-Ivri. This fact contributed toward entrenchment of the usage, which came to be recognized as legally binding in a decision of the Mandatory High Court (Cohen v. Capun, in: *Palestine Law Reports* 7 (1940), 80, 88) and until 1963, custom alone formed the legal basis for the payment of severance pay under the general law. Thus the Supreme Court of Israel, in considering the antiquity of the above custom, stated: "It is common cause that the principle of severance pay is rooted in the scriptural duty of *ha'anakah*" (PD 5:275; 17, pt. 2:1255). The lack of statutory guidance led to many difficulties in the application of the custom. In 1963 the Severance Pay Law was enacted by the Knesset, with emphasis on the fact that the fundamental idea of this law derived from traditional Jewish law. The following are some of the law's main provisions:

A person dismissed by his employer after having been continuously employed for one year or—in the case of a seasonal employee—for two seasons in two consecutive years, is entitled to severance pay at the rate of a month's wages per year of employment for a "salaried employee" and two week's wages per year for employment for a "wage earner" (i.e., one whose remuneration is paid on the basis of a lesser period than one month; secs. 1, 12); in certain circumstances the employee is entitled to severance pay following his own resignation, i.e., reason of an appreciable deterioration of his conditions of employment, or on account of his or a member of his family's state of health, or the transfer of his residence (secs. 6–8, 11). The employee is also entitled to severance pay if his employment has ceased owing to the death of his employer, and for certain other reasons (sec. 4) and upon the employee's own death, severance pay is payable to his survivors (sec. 5). A person employed under a contract for a fixed period is entitled to severance pay at the end of the period, as if dismissed, unless the employer has offered to renew the contract (sec. 9). Severance pay is deemed to be wages payable in precedence to all other debts (sec. 27) and a composition and acknowledgment of discharge as to severance pay are invalid unless reduced to writing and expressly state that they relate to severance pay (sec. 29).

See also *Labor Law; *Slavery.

Bibliography: H. Baker, *Legal System of Israel* (1968), 189–94; M. Wager and P. Dickstein, *Pizzuyei Pitturin* (1940); S. B. Bar-Adon, *Dinei Avodah* (1942), 51–63; M. Finding, *Teḥukat ha-Avodah* (1945), 49f., 132f.; ET, 9 (1959), 673–87; Sh. Warhaftig, *Dinei Avodah ba-Mishpat ha-Ivri,* 2 (1969), 643–53, 1090–1100; M. Elon, in: ILR, 4 (1969), 87–89.

[M.E.]

HAARETZ, Israel daily newspaper published in Tel Aviv. After World War I a group of businessmen, headed by Y. L. *Goldberg and S. Salzmann, acquired a licence to publish a daily newspaper. On June 18, 1919, the first issue of *Hadashot Haaretz,* a name derived from an earlier weekly newspaper published by the Military government, was published in Jerusalem. Edited by N. *Touroff, the contributors were Hebrew writers and journalists, recent immigrants from Russia. E. *Ben-Yehuda and his son Ithamar *Ben-Avi also contributed, but after a short time they separated and founded *Do'ar ha-Yom.* At that time, too, the name of the newspaper was changed to *Haaretz.* At the end of 1922, M. *Glueckson was appointed editor and served until 1937 (the paper moved to Tel Aviv in 1923). Glueckson's influence on the paper was paramount during all his years as editor: he gave *Haaretz* its independent, liberal orientation, employing a large number of writers and journalists who were products of the journalistic tradition of the Russian Hebrew press. The only daily newspaper in Tel Aviv until 1925, *Haaretz,* in its literary supplement, brought together the best Hebrew writers and scholars in Israel and abroad. When S. Z. *Schocken acquired the paper in 1937, his son, G. Schocken became editor. *Haaretz* also publishes various supplements, among them the literary column *"Tarbut ve-Sifrut,"* as well as a weekly magazine for children *Ha-Areẓ Shellanu* (edited by Benjamin *Tammuz). In 1970 its daily circulation was 50,000 and its Friday edition reached 70,000.

גליון א
Price 1 P. T. מחיר הגליון גרוש מצרי
N 1

Hadashot Haaretz
(The Palestine News)
Daily newspaper

חדשות הארץ
עתון יומי לענייני החיים והספרות

Jerusalem, Wednesday, 18 June 1919 VOL. I. שנה א

א. מ. ברחוב
למצב היהודים והיהדות

חזום:
המחלקה האמריקאית של הועדה ביןהלאומית באי.
הד הפרעות ביהודי פולניה.
ממשלות ההסכמה מכירות את האדמירל קולטשק לבעל־בריתן.

Front page of the first issue of *Hadashot Haaretz,* the precursor of *Haaretz,* June 18, 1919. Jerusalem, J.N.U.L.

Bibliography: G. Kressel, *Toledot ha-Ittonut ha-Ivrit be-Ereẓ-Yisrael* (1964[2]), 118–52.

[G.K.]

HAARLEM, capital of North Holland province, Netherlands. In 1605 a few Portuguese Jews from Amsterdam obtained a charter from the municipality allowing them to settle freely and build a synagogue, on the condition that 50 families took residence in the town. Because of this condition no community was established at the time, but this liberal charter determined in practice the legal position of the Jews in the Netherlands. In the middle of the 18th century, a small Ashkenazi congregation was formed, led for 20 years by Simeon Boas of The Hague. The synagogue was consecrated in 1841 and enlarged in 1896. The Jewish population numbered 330 in 1819, 700 in 1913, and 1,200 in 1940. [F.J.H.]

Holocaust Period. Shortly after the capitulation of the Netherlands, Jews living in Haarlem and the vicinity who held foreign citizenship were expelled. About 1,500 Jews remained behind after the expulsion. One of the city's first elders (all of whom belonged to the Fascist Nationaal-Socialistische Beweging) initiated the decrees for restrictions against the Jews which were later to be extended over all of Holland. In March and April 1941 the Jews in Haarlem were forbidden to appear in public places or to leave their apartments. When Jewish children were evicted from public schools, a separate elementary school and high school were set up for them; the latter had 90 pupils. In February 1943, 100 Jewish hostages, including the chief rabbi, P. A. Frank, and two community leaders, were shot in retaliation for the murder of a German soldier. About two weeks later, the Jews of Haarlem were moved to Amsterdam, from where most of them were sent via *Westerbork to death camps. Only ten Jewish survivors returned after the war. [J.M.]

Contemporary Period. The synagogue was not reopened after the war and neither was the Joles Jewish hospital and home for the aged, part of the funds of which were transferred to Israel for the establishment of the Joles Old Age Home for Dutch and other aged immigrants in Haifa. The seaside resort of Zandvoort, which had a separate Jewish congregation before the war, was brought under the jurisdiction of Haarlem. A *kasher* restaurant-hotel with synagogue was opened there in 1965. In 1969 some 230 of the 170,000 inhabitants of Haarlem (including the adjoining municipalities of Bloemendaal, Heemstede, Zandvoort, and Beverwijk) were Jews. In 1970 the Rabbijn de Vries Jewish Old Age Home was officially opened in Haarlem. [H.Bo.]

Bibliography: M. Wolff, *Geschiedenis der Joden te Haarlem 1600–1890,* 2 vols. (1917–19); Brugmans-Frank, 384–5, 440; J. Presser, *Ashes in the Wind: The Destruction of Dutch Jewry* (1968), index.

HAAS, FRITZ (1886–), German zoologist. Born in Frankfort, Haas was the youngest of four children in a banker's family. His early interest in zoology was focused on mollusks, and his entire scientific career was devoted to a study of these animals. In 1911 he was appointed assistant keeper of invertebrate zoology at the Naturmuseum Senckenberg, Frankfort. In 1914 Haas was on a collecting visit to the Pyrenees and was stranded in Spain for the duration of World War I. He put these years to productive use, and did extensive investigations with Spanish mollusks, which resulted in more than a score of papers on the molluscan fauna of Spain. On returning to Germany after the war, he became editor of the *Archiv fuer Molluskenkunde* and in 1922 was promoted to keeper of invertebrate zoology. With the advent of the Nazi regime, Haas was removed from his posts in 1936, and fled to the U.S.A. In 1938 he was appointed curator of lower invertebrates at the Field Museum of Natural History, Chicago. Though officially retired, from 1959 Haas continued his scientific activity with vigor, publishing a number of important monographs during the following decade, including the definitive monograph on freshwater clams in *Das Tierreich*.

Bibliography: A. Solem, in: *Fieldiana: Zoology*, 53 no. 2 (1967), 71–144, includes bibliography of his writings. [M.L.G.]

HAAS, GEORG (1905–), Israel zoologist. Born in Vienna, Haas studied zoology and paleontology. From 1931 to 1932 he was a visiting investigator at the Kaiser Wilhelm Institute in Berlin, where he did research on protozoan cytology. In 1933 he emigrated to Israel and joined the staff of the Hebrew University of Jerusalem. He was appointed professor in 1954.

Although Haas' chief interest was the functional anatomy and evolution of reptiles, he also published extensively on the mollusks of Israel and on fossil reptiles and mammals of the region. A dedicated teacher, he had a seminal influence on the growth of zoological science in Israel, and many of Israel's outstanding zoologists were trained in his laboratory. [M.L.G.]

HAAS, LEO (1901–), Czech painter and cartoonist. His most important works were his drawings in the concentration camps of Nisko and Theresienstadt (Terezin) during World War II. In tortured lines and a grotesque expressionism, they captured the squalor and misery of human beings awaiting death. He hid the drawings in Terezin, but later recovered them, having survived Auschwitz, Sachsenhausen, and Mauthausen. Haas studied in Berlin and Vienna, and became director of a lithographic printing house in his birthplace, Opava. After the war, he returned to Czechoslovakia to become one of the leading political cartoonists of the Communist press. In 1955 he left for East Germany. He is represented in museums in Prague and East Berlin.

Bibliography: F. Hermann, et al. (eds.), *Terezin* (Eng., 1965), 156–61, 319. [Av.D.]

HAAS, LUDWIG (1875–1930), German politician. Born in Freiburg, Baden, Haas practiced law in Karlsruhe, where he was a city councillor from 1908 to 1919. In 1912 he entered the Reichstag as a member of the Progressive People's (later Democratic) Party. On the outbreak of World War I Haas volunteered for the army and was decorated for distinguished service on the Western front. At the end of 1915 he was seconded to the German military government of occupied Poland as head of the Jewish department, where he worked in close contact with Emanuel Carlebach and Pinḥas *Kohn in an attempt to reorganize Polish Jewry. The Jewish community statute, which was the fruit of this collaboration, regulated the life of Polish Jewry until the end of the Polish republic in 1939. After the 1918 revolution in Germany, Haas became minister of the interior in the first republican government of Baden. He continued to represent his party in the Reichstag, and became its chairman in 1929. Haas founded

Ludwig Haas, German politician.

the *K. C. Jewish student society at Freiburg and was active in the *Centralverein deutscher Staatsbuerger juedischen Glaubens* (Central Union of German Citizens of the Jewish Faith).

Bibliography: Schrag-Haas, in: BLBI, 4 (1961), 73ff.; Carlebach, in: YLBI, 6 (1961), 62ff. [Ed.]

HAAS, SOLOMON BEN JEKUTHIEL KAUFMANN (d. 1847), Moravian rabbi and author. Haas studied under Benjamin Wolf Loew, rabbi of Kolin, then became a member of the *bet din* of Holleschau and later rabbi of Strassnitz (Moravia). Haas is the author of glosses to all four parts of the Shulḥan Arukh. Those to *Yoreh De'ah, Oraḥ Ḥayyim,* and *Even ha-Ezer* were published under the title *Kerem Shelomo* (Pressburg, 1840, 1843, and 1846 respectively), which was highly praised by Moses *Sofer, Nehemiah *Trebitsch, and Haas's teacher Benjamin Wolf Loew. He later made extensive additions to it. Those to *Ḥoshen Mishpat* were published in the *Likkutei Ḥaver ben Ḥayyim* of F. Plaut (Munkács, 1855). Other works, still in manuscript, include a volume of sermons of considerable interest for the cultural history of the time, and a collection of poems, *Benot ha-Shir* (completed in 1820), consisting of secular songs and plays, some of them translated from German into Hebrew.

Bibliography: S. Wiener, *Kohelet Moshe* (1893–1918), 648, no. 5384; H. Gold, *Juden und Judengemeinden Maehrens* (1929), 520f. [Jo.H./Ed.]

HAAS, WILLY (1891–), German essayist, critic, and translator. Born in Prague, where he studied law, Haas belonged to the literary circle of Max *Brod, Franz *Werfel, and Franz *Kafka. Moving to Berlin, he founded and edited the influential weekly, *Die literarische Welt,* from 1925 to 1933. With the rise of Nazism Haas went to India and then worked for a film company in Britain. He returned to Germany in 1949 and joined the editorial staff of *Die Welt* in Hamburg. Haas dealt with the more profound problems of contemporary literary and cultural life and became one of postwar Germany's leading critics and essayists. In his autobiography, *Die literarische Welt* (1957), he gives a detailed account of his life in three countries. [R.K.]

HAASE, HUGO (1863–1919), German socialist leader. Born in Allenstein, East Prussia, and a lawyer by profession, Haase became a socialist with a deeply humanitarian approach. He was first elected to the Reichstag as a Social Democrat in 1897 and after August Bebel's death in 1912 led the socialist faction. At the second Socialist International, Haase worked for Franco-German friendship and the prevention of a European war. On the outbreak of World War I in August 1914 he was persuaded by the majority of the party that this was a war of self-defense and supported the German government, saying: "In the hour of danger we will not leave the Fatherland in the lurch." In 1915, however, he joined Karl *Kautski and Eduard *Bernstein in a plea to stop the war, and left the Social Democrats to form the Independent Social Democrat Party which fought against the government's annexationist policies. In 1918, on the defeat of Germany and the outbreak of revolution, Haase became one of six members of the provisional government and for a time shared the presidency of the Council of the People's Deputies. He soon resigned, on the ground that the majority Socialist Party had deviated from the strict socialist line toward the bourgeois democratic establishment, and he formed his own left-wing opposition group in the Weimar National Assembly. This urged the government to sign the Treaty of Versailles. Haase was assassinated by a German nationalist in October 1919.

Bibliography: E. Haase (ed.), *Hugo Haase, sein Leben und Wirken* (1929). [Ed.]

HA-ASIF (Heb. הָאָסִיף), six literary annuals, published in Warsaw, intermittently from 1884 to 1894 and edited by Nahum *Sokolow. *Ha-Asif* was the first attempt to bring Hebrew literature to the masses at a popular price: volume 1 reached a circulation of 12,000, an unusual achievement for the period. Editorial policy, which favored cultural Zionism, considered Ereẓ Israel as one of the solutions to the Jewish problem, "however, to put all our trust in one suggestion is a great danger." Consequently *Ha-Asif* favored constructive action on behalf of Diaspora Jewry mainly in the cultural and intellectual realms. *Ha-Asif's* ample volumes were filled with a variety of materials. The earlier volumes featured a practical, almanac-type section, which was dropped in the later issues, completely literary in content. Sokolow wrote the annual review in which literary matters were stressed. Among his colleagues were D. Frischmann, M. Weber, and I. Ḥ. Zagorodski. The contributors to the literary section included the leading authors of the period. Shalom Aleichem first published his original stories in Hebrew in *Ha-Asif*. In the Jewish studies section, which also occupied a prominent position, almost all Jewish scholars of note participated. Some published complete books (S. Bernfeld, translation of M. Kayserling's book on the Spanish and Portuguese Jews; *Ha-Asif* 4 (1887)). Others published ancient manuscripts. Sokolow's detailed reviews of new books and journals in Jewish studies dominated the criticism section. E. Atlas, another critic, published a series of sharp critical articles which are still of some relevance to contemporary criticism. Criticism of rabbinical literature—which, in general, was ignored by Hebrew periodicals—was published by Y. Suwalski (vol. 4). *Ha-Asif* also contained articles about the Jews of Ereẓ Israel in the 19th century (J. Goldman, vols. 1–4 and Z. Wissotsky, vols. 4 and 7). J. D. Eisenstein published a survey of Jewish life in the United States (vol. 2). It also contained a section devoted to general sciences, including medical, scientific, and technical materials. The first Hebrew article on the flora of Ereẓ Israel also appeared in *Ha-Asif*. The success of *Ha-Asif* brought about the appearance of similar annuals. According to Sokolow, the mass circulation of *Ha-Asif* was a main cause of the creation of the Hebrew press (1866).

Bibliography: G. Kressel (ed.), *Mivḥar Kitvei N. Sokolow,* 1–3 (1958–61), index; Waxman, Literature, 4 (1960) 452–4. [G.K.]

האסיף
לתקופת השנה
ספר־כולל מקדש לתורה ולחכמה, למחקר ולבקרת, לעניני הדת ולעניני העם, להליכות עולם ולמצב המדינה, ופרד בכלל לשני ראשים:
אוצר הידיעות | אוצר הספרות
ובתשלום הספר־הכולל, לוח שנתי עם כל הידיעות הדרושות לאלף הלוח, וחלק גדול להודעות מאת סוחרים ואנשי מעשה.
שנת תרמ"ה
נחום סאקאלאוו
ווארשא
בדפוס ר' יצחק גאלדמאן נ"י.
שנת תרמ"ד לפ"ק
„ГААСИФЪ"
Еврейскій историко-литературный и промышленный Сборникъ, съ приложеніемъ краткаго Календаря за 5645 годъ.
Изданіе Н. Соколова.
ВАРШАВА
1884

Front page of the first issue of the Hebrew literary annual *Ha-Asif*, Warsaw 1884. Jerusalem, J.N.U.L.

HAAVARA, a company for the transfer of Jewish property from Nazi Germany to Palestine. The Trust and Transfer Office Haavara Ltd., was established in Tel Aviv, following an agreement with the German government in August 1933, to facilitate the emigration of Jews to Palestine by allowing the transfer of their capital in the form of German export goods. The amounts to be transferred were paid by prospective emigrants into the account of a Jewish trust company (PALTREU—Palestina Treuhandstelle zur Beratung deutscher Juden) in Germany and used for the purchase of goods which the Haavara then sold in Palestine. The proceeds, in Palestine currency, were paid to the emigrants living in Palestine. The rate of exchange was adjusted from time to time by the Haavara according to the disagio, necessitated by the subsidy which the Haavara granted the Palestinian importers, to make up for the steadily deteriorating value of the Reich mark, so the German goods could compete with other imports. The ensuing disagio, borne by the emigrants, accordingly increased from 6% in 1934 to 50% in 1938. The major part of the transfer proceeds provided the 1,000 Palestine Pounds (then $4,990) necessary for a "capitalist" immigration certificate of the Mandatory administration, but also for other categories of immigration, such as youth aliyah, students, and artisans as well as for the transfer of public funds. The transfer, which weakened the boycott of German goods declared by many Jewish organizations around the world, met with considerable opposition. The controversy was settled at the Zionist

Congress in Lucerne (1935) which decided by a vast majority in favor of the transfer and placed the Haavara under the supervision of the *Jewish Agency. The Haavara continued to function until World War II, in spite of vigorous attempts by the Nazi Party to stop or curtail its activities. The total transfer amounted to LP 8,100,000 (Palestine Pounds; then $40,419,000) including LP 2,600,-000 (then $13,774,000) provided by the German Reichsbank in coordination with Haavara. The Haavara transfer was a major factor in making possible the immigration of approximately 60,000 German Jews to Palestine in the years 1933–1939, and together with the money invested by the immigrants themselves, in providing an incentive for the expansion of agricultural settlement and for general economic development.

Bibliography: E. Marcus, in: *Yad Vashem Studies*, 2 (1958), 179–204; S. Esh, in: *Am Yisrael be-Dorenu* (1964), 330–43; L. Pinner, in: *In zwei Welten* (1962), 133–66. [Lu.P.]

ḤABAD, trend in the ḥasidic movement founded by *Israel b. Eliezer Ba'al Shem Tov. Ḥabad was founded by *Shneur Zalman of Lyady, a disciple of *Dov Baer the *maggid* of Mezhirich and of *Menahem Mendel of Vitebsk. When Menahem Mendel emigrated to Ereẓ Israel (1777), Shneur Zalman replaced him as leader of the Ḥasidim of Belorussia; it was then that he began to formulate his specific doctrine, which he embodied in his work *Likkutei Amarim*, also known as *Tanya* (Slavita, 1796). His thesis develops a systematic theosophical doctrine on the conceptions of God and the world and of man and his religious obligations, based on the Kabbalah of Isaac *Luria in its original form combined with the Ḥasidism of the Ba'al Shem Tov and especially that of the *maggid* of Mezhirich. Ḥabad stresses intellectuality, hence its name *Ḥokhmah, Binah, Da'at* ("Wisdom, Understanding, Knowledge"), and thus emphasizes Torah study. In Ḥabad the leadership of the *ẓaddik* is mainly spiritual: encounters between him and the members of his congregation are devoted to the study of Torah and ethics and discussion of the problems of the community. Their concern for Jewish interests sometimes brought the

Figure 1. Shneur Zalman of Lyady, founder of Ḥabad. A micrographic portrait by Nethanel Ḥazan, using writing from the rabbi's *Likkutei Amarim (Tanya)*. From *Challenge*, London, 1970.

Figure 2. Ḥabad Ḥasidim celebrating the completion of the writing of a Torah Scroll, New York, 1970. The Scroll was begun by the previous Lubavicher Rebbe, Joseph Isaac Schneersohn, in 1942. From *Challenge*, London, 1970.

leaders of Ḥabad into conflict with the authorities, but sometimes they cooperated with them. In 1812 the founder of Ḥabad fled with the Russian armies before Napoleon's advance and instructed his followers to give active support to the Russian side. All Ḥabad *ẓaddikim*, with the exception of Menahem Mendel (1902–), who lived in the United States, were imprisoned by the Russian authorities and liberated only after special intervention. The Ḥabad Ḥasidim were the first ḥasidic teachers to establish yeshivot *(Tomekhei Temimim)* and they also developed a ramified speculative and propagandist literature. The first and principle center of Ḥabad until World War I was in Belorussia; from there it spread to isolated regions. The Ḥabad established a settlement in Ereẓ Israel and even reached central Russia. In Soviet Russia they conducted widespread clandestine activities and during the period between the two world wars transferred their center first to Latvia, then to Poland, and finally to the United States. After World War II they participated in rescue activities and also worked in European Displaced Persons' camps and among the Jews of North Africa.

Two large centers of Ḥabad Ḥasidism emerged in the U.S. and in Israel (*Kefar Ḥabad), but its emissaries were active in many countries.

For a full description, analysis and bibliography, see entries on *Shneur Zalman of Lyady, and *Shneersohn family. [A.Ru.]

HABAKKUK (Heb. חֲבַקּוּק; cf. Akk. *ḫambaququ* or *ḫabbaququ*, a fragrant herb), prophet at the time of the *Chaldeans' ascent to power (Hab. 1:6), a time apparently after the Egyptian defeat at Carchemish (Jer. 46:2) and Hamath, when the Babylonian forces under Nebuchadnezzar occupied the area. The Book of Habakkuk contains only three chapters (totaling 56 verses), and is traditionally divided into two parts according to content: narrative (chapters 1 and 2) and prayer (chapter 3). The narrative consists of a series of five short prophetic utterances. The first (1:2–4) is a complaint against God for allowing violence and injustice to prevail unchecked in the land, one of the greatest problems in biblical thought. Jeremiah, too, asks "Wherefore doth the way of the wicked prosper?" (12:1–2) as does Job. But Habakkuk differs from Jeremiah and Job in that he offers a prophetic answer. The second utterance (1:5–11) is a divine oracle prophesying that the instrument of judgment—the Chaldeans—is near at hand.

The description of the Chaldeans is ambivalent. On the one hand it implies that the Chaldeans are God's answer to the prophet's complaint, but on the other it is a typical biblical description of "the enemy" (e.g., Deut. 28:49–53; Isa. 5:26–30; Jer. 4:13; 5:15–17; 6:22–23). In 1:10 the prophet's ambivalence is even more profound when he speaks of the Chaldeans' power in language usually reserved for describing the power of God: "And they scoff at kings, and princes are a derision to them" (cf. "who brings princes to nought, and makes the rulers of the earth as nothing" Isa. 40:23) and in the last words of verse 11: "guilty men, whose own might is their god" (in 1QpHab it is written "he makes his own might to be his god"). Thus, the "deliverer" is none other than the wicked enemy who is unable to change injustice into justice, which compels the prophet to again ask the original question: why do the evil prosper? The ambivalent description of the Chaldeans and the reiteration of the original question have brought scholars to the idea that the Chaldeans are not the answer to the prophet's complaint but rather the reason for it. When he speaks of the injustice in the world, Habakkuk is referring to the Chaldeans and their deeds. Unlike others who asked in general terms why the unjust thrive, Habakkuk relates the question to a specific historical situation. The third utterance (1:12–17) asks why God allows the wicked to devour the righteous, to which the fourth utterance (2:1–5) responds: eventually the wicked shall fail, but the righteous shall live by their faith. The first biblical appearance of *qeẓ* ("end") in its apocalyptic sense is in Habakkuk, and subsequently in the Bible this usage is found exclusively in Daniel (8:19; 11:13, 27, 35; 12:4–13).

Ḥabakkuk the prophet, a sculpture better known as *Lo Zuccone* ("The Bald One") by Donatello, 1427–36. Florence, Museo dell' Opera del Duomo. Photo Alinari, Florence.

The fifth utterance (2:7ff.) takes the form of five parables that begin with "woe to him" and stress the punishment that the wicked will receive (some of the parables are found differently phrased in other books of the Bible, e.g., Isa. 14, 51; Jer. 22:13, which proves their popularity among the people of Judah). The fifth parable contrasts idols—brilliantly ornamented, but utterly lifeless and dumb—to the divine glory of God, which strikes the whole world dumb.

The prayer comprising chapter 3 is divided into four sections (3:1–2, 3–7, 8–15, 16–19), the second and third sections recalling God's deeds, and the first and fourth constituting the essence of the prayer. Most scholars hold that chapter 3 was not part of the original Book of Habakkuk and bears no connection to the first two chapters. Other scholars, however, believe the entire book to be a single, continuous literary piece, and view chapter 3, which describes the punishment of the wicked, as a response to the questions raised in chapter 1. The prayer opens with "Upon Shigionoth" (3:1) and closes in the manner of the Psalms with "For the Leader with string music" (*la-menaẓẓe'aḥ bi-neginotai;* 3:19). In a spirit similar to that found in the beginning of the Blessing of *Moses, the Song of *Deborah, and Psalm 77 (17ff.), the prophet entreats the return of God's compassion. The prayer refers to God's actions at the time of the Exodus from Egypt, the cosmic transformation during the Creation (mentioned in Isa. 51:9; Hab. 3:2), and God's deliverance of His people and His anointed one, smiting the wicked and "laying him bare from thigh to the neck" (3:13). After recounting the past, the prophet looks to the future and prays: "may I be relieved on the day of trouble, when the [Chaldean] people invade with their troops" (3:16). Habakkuk concludes by describing the effects of drought (3:17), a possible symbol of evil, but nevertheless expressing his hope and faith: "Yet I will rejoice in the Lord, I will exult in the God of my salvation" (verse 18).

The language of Habakkuk in general, and especially in the two middle sections of the prayer, is vigorous and rich, and abounds in the use of ancient poetic and rhetorical forms, of which analogous examples appear only in early biblical poetry (Blessing of Moses, Song of Deborah, etc.). It occasionally resembles Ugaritic poetry in construction, and at times also in the use of rhetoric (as in the use of climactic parallelism, 3:2, 8, 13), archaic diction, and mythical images of the wars of creation (the sun, the moon, the abyss, and rivers appear in the form of living creatures). Linguistic features which once argued for a late dating of the book (such as the absence of the definite article) have been proved to be signs of real antiquity.

According to *Seder Olam Rabbah* 20, Habakkuk lived at the time of Manasseh (698–642 B.C.E.). Critical scholars now contend that he lived in the time of Jehoiakim (608–598 B.C.E.), and some place him earlier, at the end of Josiah's reign (639–609 B.C.E.), when the Assyrian kingdom was destroyed. However, Y. Kaufmann dates the prayer to the brief reign of Jehoiachin (597 B.C.E.). The hypothesis of B. Duhm that the word *Kasdim* (Chaldeans, 1:6) is to be emended to Kittim (Heb. כִּתִּים), and that it refers to the campaigns of Alexander the Great, has not been found acceptable. The *Dead Sea Scrolls show that as early as the time of the Second Temple the word "Chaldeans" was interpreted as referring to the Roman campaigns in the Orient in the sixties of the first century B.C.E. (see *Pesher).

According to legend, Habakkuk was the son of the Shunammite woman (Zohar, 1:7; 2:44–45). This identification is apparently based on his name, for the verb *ḥbk* ("to embrace") is employed in connection with the annunciation of the birth of the woman's son in II Kings 4:16. In the apocryphal story of Bel and the Dragon, which tells of Daniel's exploits against Babylonian idolatry, Habakkuk is presented as a contemporary of Daniel, probably because both mention the arrival of the Chaldeans (Hab. 1:6; Dan. 1:1). In the same story he is considered to be the son of Jeshua the Levite (Bel, 1). This reference is apparently to a levite family called Jeshua, which is mentioned in Ezra 2:40, et al. According to Rabbi Simlai (2nd generation *amora*), Habakkuk based all the 613 commandments received by Moses on the single principle that "the righteous shall live by his faith" (Hab. 2:4; Mak. 23b–24a). [Y.M.G./D.Br.]

In the Arts. The prophet Habakkuk has inspired no literary works of major importance, but is of some significance in art and music. He is identified with the prophet brought by an angel to nourish Daniel in the lions' den, and thus his attributes are an angel and a basket of bread. In Christian typography he is one of the prophets who foresaw the Nativity. He appears alone on the wooden doors of Santa Sabina, Rome (fifth century); in the ninth-century *Christian Typography* of Cosmas Indicopleustis (Vatican); and on the door of the Vierge Dorée (Amiens Cathedral, 13th century). The famous 15th-century statue by Donatello known as *Lo Zuccone* ("The Bald One") represents Habakkuk. Formerly in the Florence Campanile, it is now in the Museo dell' Opera del Duomo, Florence. A 17th-century statue by Bernini in the Chigi Chapel at Santa María del Popolo, Rome, shows the angel lifting Habakkuk by his hair. He is frequently seen in company with Daniel. There are examples on fourth-century sarcophagi; on a sixth-century Coptic textile; again in the Cosmas Indicopleustis manuscripts; on a 13th-century bas-relief from the portal of the Virgin, Laon Cathedral; and on stained-glass windows in Auch (16th century) and Cambridge (17th century).

The psalm-like third chapter of Habakkuk is included among the *cantica* in the liturgy of all Christian denominations, and is generally sung to a simple psalmodic formula. There are a few art-music settings of this section, such as F. Giroust's *Domine quidvi auditionem* for chorus (1779) and, in the 20th century, cantatas entitled *Habakkuk* by György Kósa (1954) and Jacques Berlinski (b. 1913). [Ed.]

Bibliography: B. Duhm, *Das Buch Habakuk* (1906); E. Sellin, *Das Zwoelfprophetenbuch* (1930); M. D. Cassuto, in: *Keneset*, 8 (1943), 121–42; W. H. Ward, *Habakkuk* (ICC, 1911, 1948[3]); W. F. Albright, in: H. H. Rowley (ed.), *Studies in Old Testament Prophecy Presented to T. H. Robinson* (1950), 1–18; Kaufmann Y., Toledot, 3 (1960), 360–8; O. Eissfeldt, *The Old Testament, an Introduction* (1965), 416–23 (incl. bibl.); Ginzberg, Legends, index; M. H. Segal, *Mevo ha-Mikra*, 2 (1967[4]), 488–90.

HABAKKUK, PROPHECY OF, book attributed to Habakkuk, in an appendix to the sixth-century lists of Apocrypha, the Stichometry of Nicephorus and that of Pseudo-Athanasius. It is mentioned together with works of Baruch, Ezekiel, and Daniel. Further, the title of **Bel and the Dragon* in the Septuagint (but not Theodotion) reads: "From the prophecy of Habakkuk son of Jesus of the tribe of Levi." This story tells how Daniel was cast into a lion's den. On the sixth day of his imprisonment Habakkuk was taking food to the reapers in the field in Judea, when he was seized by the hair and miraculously transported to Babylon, where he gave the food to Daniel. This story appears in the *Life of Habakkuk* in the Pseudo-Epiphanian *Lives of the Prophets* (ed. Torrey, 28ff.) in a somewhat different version. The *Life* also ascribes to Habakkuk *inter alia* visions of the destruction, restoration, and subsequent destruction of the Temple. These might perhaps also reflect the Habakkuk apocryphon. The story is also known (apparently from Christian sources) in later Jewish works such as Josippon, *Chronicle of Jerahmeel* (ed. Gaster, 220ff.), and *Sefer Yuḥasin* (1925), 238.

Bibliography: M. R. James *Lost Apocrypha* (1920); Charles, Apocrypha, 1 (1913), 652; A. Kahana, *Ha-Sefarim ha-Ḥiẓoniyyim*, 1 (1936), 554–5. [M.E.S.]

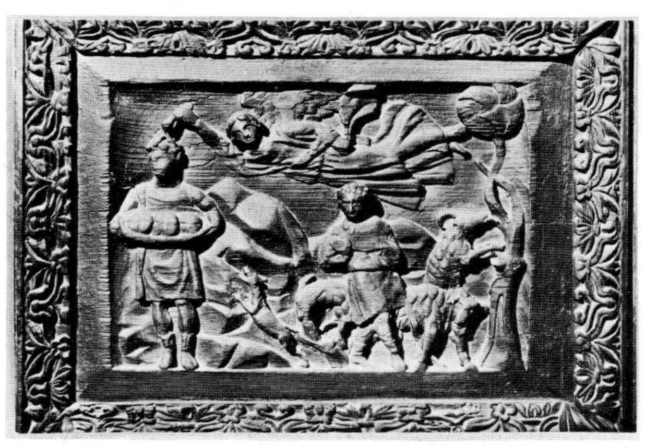

Angel lifting Habakkuk by his hair to transport him to Daniel in Babylon. Detail illustrating the apocryphal story, from the carved wooden doors of the church of Santa Sabina, Rome, fifth century.

HABAS, BRACHA (1900–1968), Hebrew writer and editor; wife of David *Hacohen. Born in Alytus, Lithuania, she was taken to Palestine in 1907. After a period of teaching she turned to journalism, serving on the editorial board of the newspaper *Davar* (1935–53) and of the Am Oved publishing house. Among other publications she edited *Davar li-Yladim* and *Devar ha-Shavu'a*. Her books include: *Ḥomah u-Migdal* ("Stockade and Tower," 1939); *Korot Ma'pil Ẓa'ir* ("Story of a Young Immigrant," 1942); *Derakhim Avelot* ("Paths of Mourning," on the D.P. camps and the Jewish Brigade, 1946); *David Ben-Gurion ve-Doro* (1952); *Pagodot ha-Zahav* ("Golden Pagodas," Burmese legends, 1959); *Benot Ḥayil* (on Palestinian ATS volunteers, 1964); *Ḥayyav u-Moto shel Joop Westerweel* ("The Life of Joop Westerweel," 1964); *Tenu'ah le-Lo Shem* ("Movement without a Name," on volunteer work by veteran settlers among new immigrants, 1965); *He-Ḥaẓer ve-ha-Givah* ("The Yard and the Hill," the story of kevuẓat *Kinneret, 1968). A list of her works translated into English appears in Goell, Bibliography, 28, 88, 96.

Bibliography: J. Harari, *Ishah va-Em be-Yisrael* (1958), 470f.; R. Katznelson, *Massot u-Reshimot* (1947), 207; *Kol Kitvei... G. Schoffmann*, 5 (1960), 130f.; Tidhar, 3 (1949), 1128f.; 16 (1967), 5001f. [G.K.]

ḤABBĀN, town in central Hadhramaut (S. Arabian Peninsula). Zekharya al-Ḍāhiri (mid-16th century), who traveled in the Hadhramaut region, expressly states that there were no Jews there. Ḥabbān and some surrounding villages seem to have been the only places in that part of South Arabia where Jews lived during the 19th and 20th centuries. The numbers of Jews in Ḥabbān given by travelers in the 19th century (2,000, 1,000, and 200 Jews) seem very vague. A. *Tabib mentions 200 men (above 13 years old) and S. Yavnieli (Jawnieli) only 30 families.

The Jews of Ḥabbān were a distinctive group among South Arabian Jews. Desert dwellers of unusual appearance, tall with delicate features, they had long hair reaching down over their shoulders but no sidelocks and moustache, which they plucked; additionally, they tied ribbons around their heads. The women tied nets decorated with silver jewelry around their heads and also wore wide silver belts. Their political status was similar to that of other Jews of the Arabian Peninsula; they paid a poll tax as "protected Jews," but nevertheless they occasionally suffered from persecutions and riots. The Jews of Ḥabbān are descendants of one family and are divided into four households—Maʿṭūf, Hillel, Shamūkh, and Mayfaʿ—which lived separately in various parts of the city and numbered around 30 families in 1911–12. This division into households is

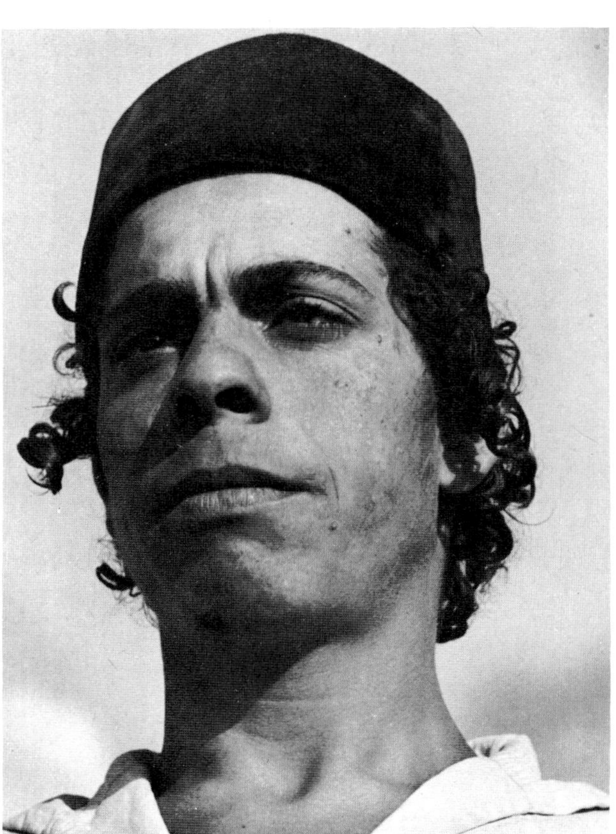

Figure 1. An immigrant from Ḥabbān, photographed shortly after his arrival in Israel, 1951. Courtesy Keren Hayesod, United Israel Appeal, Jerusalem.

reminiscent of the tribal formation of desert dwellers. Besides these family divisions, there were also some slight differences in their prayer customs. Additionally, there are no *kohanim* or levites among the Ḥabbān Jews. The difficult economic conditions under which they lived compelled the men to abandon their families for several months at a time in order to travel to distant Arab localities, where it was possible for them to make a living. This life of wandering had a negative effect on their spiritual life, as they normally returned to their village only for the High Holidays and Passover. The Jewish community paid a very small tax—20 reals per year. Because they were a very small minority, they lived in relative security. They recall no persecution, and their youths even wore knives openly in their belts like the Arabs. Though they were isolated and far removed, they jealously guarded their religion and traditions. They possessed the halakhic works which were accepted among the Jews of Yemen and preserved a special way of life through dance and song, especially at wedding celebrations and on Purim.

The Ḥabbān Jews were mainly silversmiths and goldsmiths who made jewelry and ornaments. A minority raised sheep and camels. Most of the Jews of neighboring al-Bayḍā were hawkers and a small number were goldsmiths; they numbered some 50 families in 1911–12. In addition, some 40 families lived in nearby Bayḥān. During the 1940s the Jewish population of Ḥabbān grew to 60 families. In 1949 when the Jews learned that it was possible to emigrate to Israel, they made all the necessary preparations. Some were even afraid to travel from village to village to earn their livelihood, for fear that the Israel emissaries would not find them. In 1950 an emissary from Israel arrived to organize the exodus, which was finally carried out in two stages—from Ḥabbān to Aden and from Aden on the "magic carpet" operation to Israel. The operation, however, failed to proceed smoothly, as the Arabs of Ḥabbān attempted to prevent Jewish emigration to Israel. A number of Muslims demanded that the governor forbid the Jews to leave before paying their debts (originally small, but inflated by a high rate of interest). The emissary in the end succeeded in reducing the amount of payment and when it was paid, the Jews were allowed to leave. Almost all of them went to Israel in the same year, together with other Yemenite Jews.

After their *aliyah* they settled at Moshav Bareket, where they numbered about 100 families (800 individuals); some others settled at Kefar Shalem (near Tel Aviv). Due to a high natural rate of increase and lower death rate in relation to their former one in Yemen, they have increased in number. In 1970 they numbered around 180 families. Because of the limited space in their moshav they have been forced to spread out to neighboring settlements. The Jews of Ḥabbān, including the young people, continue to maintain their religious heritage and their close family ties. They marry almost exclusively among themselves, but their unique folklore is gradually disappearing.

See also *Ḥimyar and *South Arabia for further information on Ḥabbān and Hadhramaut.

Bibliography: E. Brauer, *Ethnologie der jemenitischen Juden . . .* (1934), index; A. Tabib, *Golat Teiman* (1931); S. Jawnieli, *Massa le-Teiman* (1952), 36–37, 222–8; M. Zadoc, *Yehudei Teiman* (1967), 259–62; J. Shaari, in: *Harrel, Kovez Zikkaron . . . Rephael Alshekh* (1962), 231–5; T. Ashkenazi, in: *Sinai,* 22 (1947/48), 248–57; idem, in, JQR, 38 (1947/48), 93–96.

[ME.W./Y.R./H.J.C.]

ḤABBAR, pl. **ḤABBAREI,** persecutors of the Jews in Babylon, mentioned in the Babylonian Talmud. They created hardships for Jews, forbidding them to light lamps on their (the Ḥabbarei's) festive days (Shab. 45a; Git. 17a), to perform burials and slaughter of animals (Yev. 63b) in accordance with Jewish law, and interfering with the proper observance of the festivals by the Jews (Bezah 6a; see Rashi *ibid.*). The rise of the Ḥabbarei in Babylon may be established as

Figure 2. A woman from Ḥabbān in traditional dress and jewelry, 1951. Courtesy Keren Hayesod, United Israel Appeal, Jerusalem.

occurring between the death of R. Ḥiyya the Great and that of Rabbah Bar Bar Ḥana, i.e., at the end of the first quarter of the third century C.E. (Yev. 63b). It is possible that the Ḥabbarei were Zoroastrian priests, fire worshipers, whose influence increased in Babylon in the course of that century, after the rise to power of the Sassanid dynasty.

Bibliography: Kohut, Arukh, 3 (1926), 339f.; S. Krauss, *Tosefot Arukh ha-Shalem* (1937), 178f.; J. Obermeyer, *Landschaft Babylonien* (1929), 262f. [M.BE.]

HABE, HANS (pseudonym of **János Békessy;** 1911–), Budapest-born German novelist whose works reflect fierce opposition to the Nazis. Habe became the League of Nations correspondent of the *Prager Tagblatt* in 1935. On the outbreak of World War II he enlisted in the French army. He escaped from a German POW camp in 1940, and served in the U. S. forces for the rest of the war. In 1945 he founded the American-backed Munich *Neue Zeitung.* Habe's novels include *Drei ueber die Grenze* (1937; *Three over the Frontier,* 1939), *Weg ins Dunkel* (1951; first published as *Walk in Darkness,* 1949), and *Im Namen des Teufels* (1956; *Agent of the Devil,* 1959). The autobiographical *Ob Tausend Fallen* (1943; first published as *A Thousand Shall Fall,* 1941) describes the ordeal of foreign volunteers and loyal French troops deprived of arms and encouragement by the incompetent and defeatist French high command. His book on the assassination of President John F. Kennedy, *Der Tod in Texas* (1964), appeared in the U.S.A. as *The Wounded Land.* Habe also wrote an autobiography, *All My Sins* (1957); *Die Mission* (1965; *The Mission,* 1966), based on the *Evian conference of 1938; and *Christopher and His Father* (1967), which deals with the question of Federal Germany's remorse. [ED.]

HABER, family of German bankers. SALOMON (SAMUEL) HABER (1764–1839), born in Breslau, moved to Karlsruhe toward the end of the 18th century, and set up a banking and finance house. He and his sons were prominent in the early industrial development of Baden and Wuerttemberg, and from about 1820 S. Haber and Sons became one of Europe's leading bankers. In 1829 hereditary nobility was bestowed on Salomon's son LOUIS (LUDWIG; 1804–1892). Frequent marriages with other Jewish moneyed families fortified the Habers' financial and social status, but when in 1847 the bank experienced difficulties it was the government of Baden which came to the rescue, and not the family connections. Louis' brother MORITZ (1798–1874) took part in the formation of the Bank fuer Handel und Industrie in Darmstadt, the forerunner of the Darmstaedter Bank. Together with his brother Louis he was also among the founders of the Vienna Kreditanstalt (1855), and in 1863 of the Bodenkreditanstalt. The youngest of the brothers, SAMUEL (1812–1892), settled in Paris where Moritz had to take refuge after he had killed his opponent in a duel in Karlsruhe.

Bibliography: H. Schnee, *Die Hoffinanz und der moderne Staat,* 4 (1963), 68–86. [J.O.R.]

HABER, FRITZ (1868–1934), German physical chemist and Nobel laureate. Haber was born in Breslau, the son of a prosperous chemical and dye merchant and an alderman of the city. After a period in industry and business, he went in 1893 to the Technische Hochschule at Karlsruhe, and in 1906 became professor of physical and electrochemistry. His work on carbon bonds led to a rule bearing his name. Turning to electrochemistry, he wrote *Grundriss der technischen Electrochemie auf theoretische Grundlage* (1898) and was a co-developer of the glass electrode. In 1905 he wrote *Thermodynamics of Technical Gas Reactions.* His

Fritz Haber, German physical chemist and Nobel Prize winner. Sketch by Arnold Bursch, 1917. Courtesy Margaret W. Bruch.

most important work, started in 1904, was the synthesis of ammonia from hydrogen and nitrogen. His laboratory demonstration interested Bosch, Bergius, and the Badische Anilin- und Sodafabrik companies, and they eventually developed the process into a commercial operation. Haber and Bosch were awarded the Nobel Prize in chemistry in 1918 "for the synthesis of ammonia from its elements"; this work of Haber was to be invaluable to the German military effort in World War I. In 1911 he was made director of the new Kaiser Wilhelm Research Institute in Berlin-Dahlem, and in 1914 this was turned over to war work, particularly gas warfare, starting with chlorine and ending with mustard gas. After Germany's defeat, he reconstituted his Institute, and in the 1920s it became probably the leading center of physical chemistry in the world. Haber was president of the German Chemical Society, and of the Verband deutscher chemische Vereine (which he created), and after some months spent in Japan he created the Japan Institute in Berlin and Tokyo.

Haber left the Jewish faith, and with the Nazi accession to power in 1933 was not immediately threatened but he was ordered to dismiss all the Jews on the staff of his institute. He refused and resigned. His health, already poor, deteriorated. He went to a sanatorium in Switzerland, where he died. In 1952 a tablet was unveiled in Haber's memory at the Kaiser Wilhelm Institute.

Bibliography: M. H. Goran, *The Story of Fritz Haber* (1967), incl. bibl.; R. Stern, in: YLBI, 8 (1963), 70–102. [S.A.M.]

HABER, SAMUEL L. (1903–), U.S. economist and organization executive. Haber, who was born in Harlau, Rumania, was taken to the U.S. in 1911. He worked as a researcher on labor and economic problems (1925–43), then served in the U.S. Army, 1943–46. In 1947 Haber became director for Germany of the American Jewish Joint Distribution Committee, where he headed an extensive program for approximately 200,000 D.P.s. In 1954 Haber was sent to Morocco to organize a comprehensive Jewish welfare program and in 1957 he established a welfare program for

Jews in Poland, becoming the first JDC representative permitted to function in that country since 1950. After serving as assistant director general of JDC's European headquarters in Geneva (1958–64) and assistant executive vice-chairman in New York (1964–67), Haber was appointed to succeed the murdered Charles *Jordan as Joint executive vice-chairman in 1967. [Ed.]

HABER, SHAMAI (1922–), Israel sculptor. He was born in Lodz, Poland, and in 1935 emigrated to Palestine where he studied in Tel Aviv and fought in the War of Independence. From 1949 he lived in Paris. He worked close to nature, and created portraits under the influence of such French masters as Charles Despiau. In 1954 he turned to abstraction. In 1962 he produced his first monumental

Monumental sculpture by Shamai Haber at Naḥal Sorek, 1962. Courtesy Israel Atomic Energy Commission, Yavneh.

work for the atomic reactor building at Naḥal Sorek (Nebi Rubin) in Israel. In 1965, together with Yitshak *Danziger, he created a monumental composition for the Israel Museum, Jerusalem. When he turned to abstraction Haber worked in stone. He used large blocks and assembled them in such a manner as to create a static relationship between the volumes and the spaces between them. The solitary presence of his sculpture in its surroundings has an archaic quality which is increased by his method of working the stone. [Y.Fi.]

HABERLANDT, GOTTLIEB (1854–1945), German plant physiologist. Born in Ungarisch-Altenberg, Hungary, Haberlandt rose to a professorship first at the University of Graz (Austria) and later at the University of Berlin. His contributions in the field of plant responses to environmental stimuli helped to establish plant physiology as a significant separate discipline within the biological sciences. In 1884 Haberlandt described the important relationship between the anatomy of plants and their physiological capacities in a classic volume, *Physiologische Pflanzenanatomie* (1884; *Physiological Plant Anatomy*, 1914). In utilizing function as a basis for establishing structural categories he anticipated 20th-century interest in physiological plant ecology. Later works include *Das Reizleitende Gewebesystem der Sinnpflanze* ("Stimuli Transmitting Tissue System of the Mimosa," 1890) and *Sinnesorgane im Pflanzenreich* ("Sense Organs of the Plant Kingdom," 1901) as well as numerous research reports dealing with the mechanism of plant tropisms, the significance of transpiration in the migration of nutrients, and the general functions of the vascular system.

Bibliography: *Neue Deutsche Biographie*, 7 (1966), includes bibliography. [G.H.F.]

HABERMANN, ABRAHAM MEIR (1901–), bibliographer and scholar of medieval Hebrew literature. Born at Zurawno (Galicia), Habermann from 1928 was librarian at the Schocken Library in Berlin. He immigrated to Palestine in 1934 and served as director of the Schocken Library in Jerusalem until 1967. From 1957 he taught medieval literature at Tel Aviv University (professor, 1969) and taught at the Graduate Library School of the Hebrew University. He was editor of the department of bibliography (Jewish printers) for the *Encyclopaedia Hebraica*, and the department of medieval Hebrew poetry for the *Encyclopaedia Judaica*. Habermann began his study of medieval literature in 1925, specializing in the Ashkenazi *piyyut* from the time of R. Ephraim ben Jacob of Bonn. A prolific writer, his books include: *Ha-Madpisim Benei Soncino* (1933); *Gevilim; Me'ah Sippurei Aggadah* (1942); *Ha-Genizah* (1944); *Toledot ha-Sefer ha-Ivri* (1945); *Ha-Piyyut* (1946), *Ateret Renanim*, *piyyutim* and songs for Sabbath and festivals (1967); *Ha-Sefer ha-Ivri be-Hitpatteḥuto* (1968); *Sha'arei Sefarim Ivriyyim* (1969); and *Toledot ha-Piyyut ve-ha-Shirah* (1970), which is the first attempt at a survey of the history of Hebrew *piyyut* and poetry and its development in various cultural centers from post-biblical times to the Haskalah period. Habermann edited and compiled such diverse medieval works as: *Piyyutei Rashi* (1941); *Seliḥot u-Fizmonim* of R. Gershom Me'or ha-Golah (1944); *Gezerot Ashkenaz ve-Ẓarefat* (1946); *Niẓoẓot Ge'ullah*, an anthology of redemption and messianism (1949); *Maḥberot Immanu'el ha-Romi* (1950); *Even Boḥan* of Kalonymus ben Kalonymus (1956); and studies of the Dead Sea Scrolls, *Edah ve-Edut* (1952), and *Megillot Midbar Yehudah* (1959).

Bibliography: Kressel, Leksikon, 1 (1965), 568f. [Y.Ho.]

ḤABIB, ḤAYYIM BEN MOSES BEN SHEM TOV (16th century), rabbinical author. One of the Jews exiled from Portugal in 1497 who escaped to Fez. In 1505 he compiled over 3,000 responsa of Solomon b. Abraham *Adret, in *Sefer ha-Battim*. Ḥ. J. D. *Azulai heard of the existence of the manuscript in Fez. Joseph Samon, the author of *Edut Bi-Yhosaf*, eventually took it to Jerusalem, where it came into the possession of Sussman Jawitz (1813–1881), father of the historian Ze'ev *Jawitz who had emigrated to Jerusalem from Warsaw (see introduction to *Berakhah Meshulleshet*, Warsaw, 1863). *Sefer ha-Battim* was published by Sussman's son Abraham, together with the glosses of Isaac Goldman who had also published Adret's novellae on tractate *Menaḥot*. Ḥabib's characteristic signature: "Ḥayyim b. Moses ibn Ḥabib whose knees did not kneel to Baal, nor to fire and wood," is probably an allusion to his flight from Portugal.

Bibliography: Fuenn, Keneset, 355; J. M. Toledano, *Ner ha-Ma'arav* (1911), 86; Azulai, 2 (1852), 21 no. 131. [S.MAR.]

ḤABIB, MOSES BEN SOLOMON IBN (c. 1654–1696), Turkish rabbi and author. Born in Salonika, he was a descendant of *Levi ben Ḥabib. He went to Jerusalem in his youth. He studied in the yeshivah of Jacob *Ḥagiz and from c. 1677 to 1679 he traveled as an emissary of Jerusalem, reaching as far as Budapest. In 1688 Ḥabib was appointed head of the yeshivah in Jerusalem maintained by the philanthropist Moses ibn Ya'ish, of Constantinople. In the following year, on the death of Moses Galante, Ḥabib was appointed to succeed him as chief rabbi of Jerusalem (1689). His grandson, Jacob *Culi, who published most of his grandfather's works, also had in his possession a number of other manuscripts which he used in his own work *Me-Am Lo'ez* (Constantinople, 1733). A manuscript of his sermons is in the National Library in Jerusalem. The ascription to him of the *Eẓ ha-Da'at* (printed in *Or Ẓaddikim*, Salonika, 1799) has been questioned by S. Hazan.

He wrote the following works: *Get Pashut* (Ortakoi, 1719), on the laws of divorce and *ḥaliẓah; Shammot ba-Areẓ* (Constantinople, 1727), consisting of *"Yom Teru'ah,"* on the tractate *Rosh Ha-Shanah*, *"Tosafot Yom ha-Kippurim,"* on the tractate *Yoma*, and *"Kappot Temarim,"* on the tractate *Sukkah* (Constantinople, 1731); and *Ezrat Nashim* (*ibid.*, 1731), on the laws of *agunah*. Ḥ. J. D. *Azulai states that most of Ḥabib's responsa were lost at sea; however some have survived, and have been published, part in *Kol Gadol* (Jerusalem, 1907), and part in the works of contemporary scholars (*Devar Sha'ul*, 1927). Moses also wrote a commentary on the Jerusalem Talmud entitled *Penei Moshe* of which tractates *Berakhot*, *Pe'ah*, and *Demai* are extant in manuscript (Sassoon Ms. 592).

Bibliography: S. Hazzan, *Ha-Ma'alot li-Shelomo* (1859); Rosanes, Togarmah, 4 (1935), 326–8; 5 (1938), 14; Frumkin-Rivlin, 2 (1928), 89–91; M. D. Gaon, *Yehudei ha-Mizraḥ be-Ereẓ Yisrael*, 2 (1938), 241; Yaari, Sheluḥei, 298f.; J. Molcho, in: *Oẓar Yehudei Sefarad*, 5 (1962), 81ff.; Scholem, Shabbetai Ẓevi, 1 (1959), 200f.; D. S. Sassoon, *Ohel Dawid*, 1 (1932), 104–6; Lieberman, in: *Sefer ha-Yovel . . . A. Marx* (1950), 313–5; Benayahu, in: *Tarbiz*, 21 (1950), 58–60. [S.MAR.]

Title page of *Get Pashut*, Moses ibn Ḥabib's work on the laws of divorce and *ḥaliẓah*, Ortakoi, Turkey, 1719.

ḤABIBA, JOSEPH (beginning of the 15th century), Spanish talmudic scholar. Virtually no biographical details are known of Ḥabiba. His teachers were *Nissim b. Reuben (the Ran) and Ḥasdai *Crescas. Author of novellae to the Talmud and a commentary on Isaac *Alfasi known as the *Nimmukei Yosef*, he is regarded as the last of the **rishonim* to comment on the Talmud and the *Hilkhot ha-Rif*. It was previously thought that Ḥabiba wrote commentaries only to those tractates of Alfasi on which Nissim b. Reuben did not comment, but it is now believed that his commentary covered the whole work. Only his commentaries to tractates *Mo'ed Katan, Yevamot, Bava Kamma, Bava Meẓia, Bava Batra, Sanhedrin*, and *Makkot* have been published in editions of the Talmud, but his commentaries to the tractates *Megillah* and *Pesaḥim* (1960) and to *Gittin* (1963) and *Avodah Zarah* in M. J. Blau (ed.), *Shitat ha-Kadmonim al Massekhet Avodah Zarah* (1969) have been published. His commentaries on *Berakhot, Shabbat, Ta'anit*, and *Ḥullin*, are still in manuscript. Of his novellae to the Talmud there have been published: *Shevuot* (in *Beit ha-Beḥirah* of Menahem ha-Meiri; Leghorn, 1795), and *Ketubbot* and *Nedarim* (in the *Ishei ha-Shem*, *ibid.*, 1795, new ed. 1960).

In his commentary Ḥabiba usually quotes the *geonim*, the Spanish **posekim* until *Jacob b. Asher, and Yom Tov *Vidal of Tolosa. According to Malachi ha-Kohen (in his *Yad Malakhi*), Ḥabiba differs from Nissim in that he quotes the aforementioned authors and *Yom Tov b. Abraham Ishbili, and in that he commences each of the novellae with "the author says" and concludes with "thus for the words of the author," something not found in the works of other *rishonim*. It is this characteristic, as well as the numerous quotations from the works of Yom Tov Ishbili and Asher b. Jehiel, which serve as indubitable indications of the author of the *Nimmukei Yosef*. Ḥabiba's style is direct and succinct. Some see his commentaries as aimed at encouraging the study of Talmud rather than the *Hilkhot ha-Rif*, which, through its wide circulation, tended to displace the study of the Talmud. Consequently *Nimmukei Yosef* is regarded as a supplement rather than a commentary, the addition of passages of the Talmud omitted by Alfasi making the talmudic text readily available to the student. The *Nimmukei Yosef* is a valuable source for clarifying the opinions and approach of various *rishonim*, since in addition to quoting from their actual works he also gives oral traditions handed down by their pupils. He was highly regarded in later generations as an authoritative *posek*.

Bibliography: Malachi b. Jacob ha-Kohen, *Yad Malakhi* (Przemysl, 1888 ed.), 154d; Weiss, Dor, 5 (1904[4]), 760f.; H. Tchernowitz, *Toledot ha-Posekim*, 1 (1946), 163f.; M. J. Blau (ed.), in: J. Ḥabiba, *Nimmukei Yosef al Massekhtot Megillah u-Fesaḥim* (1960), introd.; M. Margalioth (ed.), *Hilkhot ha-Nagid* (1962), 79; Waxman, Literature, 2 (1960), 112. [Y.HO.]

ḤABIL, the name of four places inhabited by Jews at the time of their emigration from Yemen (1948–49). All four are located in the southernmost regions of present-day

Yemen, or close to its border. Among the *genizah* fragments there is a letter of appointment from a *gaon* to a person, whose name has not been preserved, requesting that the latter undertake the collection of funds for the Babylonian Academy. A letter was sent to the inhabitants of al-Ṣawīl and al-Ḥabil, which was to be read to them so that they would make their contributions; these were to be sent to the head of the academy in San'a or the emissaries of the academies in Yaman and Yamāma.

Bibliography: S. D. Goitein, in: *Tarbiz*, 31 (1961/62), 360–1.

[H.Z.H.]

HABILLO, DAVID (d. 1661), kabbalist of Safed and Jerusalem and emissary from Jerusalem. Habillo was the outstanding pupil of the kabbalist Benjamin b. Meir ha-Levi of Safed, whom he accompanied when he moved to Jerusalem. Ḥ. J. D. Azulai relates that the veteran rabbis of Jerusalem told him that Habillo lived there in 1652 and had a heavenly mentor *(maggid)*. Habillo wrote a commentary on *Sefer Yeẓirah* which has remained in manuscript. During the 1650s he went to Turkey as an emissary from Jerusalem. He met Abraham Yakhini in Constantinople before 1660 and also the youthful *Shabbetai Ẓevi, who almost certainly learned Kabbalah from Habillo. When Shabbetai Ẓevi was subsequently compelled to leave Constantinople, he proceeded to Smyrna with Habillo, who died there on the ninth of Av. After his death a dispute arose between his son, JUDAH HABILLO, who claimed the inheritance left in Smyrna by his father, and the heads of the Jerusalem community, who claimed the money as the proceeds of the mission on their behalf. Ḥayyim *Benveniste, the *av bet din* of Smyrna, decided in favor of the son.

Bibliography: Azulai, 1 (1852), 23a no. 17; A. Freimann, *Inyanei Shabbetai Ẓevi* (1912), 141 no. 9; Frumkin-Rivlin, 2 (1928), 29, 34, 69f.; Yaari, Sheluḥei, 154, 283, 287; G. Scholem, in: *Zion*, 13–14 (1948–49), 61f.; Scholem, Shabbetai Ẓevi, 1 (1957), 138–40, 154.

[A.YA.]

HABILLO (Xabillo), ELIJAH BEN JOSEPH (Maestro Manoel, second half 15th cent.), Spanish philosopher and translator of philosophical writings. Habillo was an admirer of Christian scholasticism, and translated some of the works of the Christian scholastics from Latin into Hebrew, including: Thomas *Aquinas' *Quaestiones disputatae, Quaestio de anima ("She'elot ba-Nefesh"), De animae facultatibus* (*"Ma'amar be-Koḥot ha-Nefesh,"* published by A. Jellinek in *Philosophie und Kabbala*, 1854), *De universalibus ("Be-Inyan ha-Kolel"),* and questions on Aquinas' treatise *De ente de essentia ("She'elot Ma'amar be-Nimẓa u-ve-Mahut");* William of Occam's three treatises entitled *Summa totius logicae ("Perakim be-Kolel"),* to which he added an appendix, and *Quaestiones Philosophicae;* and the pseudo-Aristotelian *Liber de causis ("Sefer ha-Sibbot").* It is also supposed that Habillo translated anonymously Vincenz of Beauvais' *De universalibus* under the title *Ma'amar Nikhbad be-'Kelal'* (see M. Steinschneider, Parma Ms. no. 457[7]).

Bibliography: S. Munk, in: OLZ, 7 (1904), 725; Munk, Mélanges, 303; Steinschneider, Uebersetzungen, 265, 470, 477, 483.

[ED.]

HABILLO, ELISHA (called **Mercado;** 1719–1792), rabbi of Sarajevo. Habillo studied under David *Pardo, author of *Shoshannim le-David.* He wrote *Avodat ha-Tamid* (Sarajevo, 1788), a commentary on the Sephardi liturgy for the whole year, together with the order of service for weekdays, with brief laws and explanations. In this work the author at times cites the explanations of Nehemiah *Ḥayon, only to dissociate himself from them at the end. He published his teacher's book of prayers for festivals, *Shifat Revivim* (Leghorn, 1787), including in the original his elegy on the ill-treatment by the Turks of the Sarajevo Jews who fled from the Austrians, and added a number of his poems. Habillo also wrote a commentary on the Passover *Haggadah* and on the Grace after Meals.

Bibliography: M. D. Gaon, *Yehudei ha-Mizraḥ be-Ereẓ Yisrael*, 2 (1938), 242; Frumkin-Rivlin, 3 (1929), 97; Rosanes, Togarmah, 5 (1938), 177.

[S.MAR.]

HABIMAH (Heb. "the Stage"), repertory theater company; founded in Moscow in 1917 as the first professional Hebrew theater in the world, and now the National Theater of Israel. Its initiator was Nahum David *Zemach, who was joined by Menahem Gnessin and the actress Ḥannah *Rovina in Warsaw, but World War I halted their efforts. They met again in Moscow in 1917 and were soon joined by a number of young Jewish actors. Their idea was not simply to found a theater but to give expression to the revolutionary change in the situation of the Jewish people and especially to the revival of Hebrew. Zemach turned to the

שנת חמשת אלפים שש מאות
תשעים וחמש לבריאת העולם אנו
החתומים מטה הנחנו ביום ב' לשבוע
ט' סיון במעמד קהל רב. את אבן
היסוד לבנין „בית הבימה" בתל-אביב
שהוא המשכן הראשון לתיאטרון בישראל.

In the year five thousand six hundred and ninety five after the creation of the world, on Monday, the ninth day of Sivan, (10.6.35) and in the presence of a vast multitude, we the undersigned, laid the corner stone of the Habima House in Tel-Aviv, which is to be the first dwelling-place of a theatre in Israel.

Arthur Wauchope.

Figure 1. Document recording the laying of the cornerstone of the Habimah Theater in Tel Aviv, 1935. The photograph above shows Sir Arthur Wauchope, the high commissioner for Palestine, signing the document, while Meir Dizengoff and Ḥannah Rovina look on. From "National Theatre Habimah," Tel Aviv, 1970.

Figure 2. Members of the original Habimah company in Moscow, c. 1920. Seated, right to left: Moshe Halevy, Shoshana Avivit, David Vardi, Naḥum Zemach, Menahem Gnessin, Haye'le Gruber. Standing: A. Viniar, Ḥannah Rovina, Reuven Persitz, Rachel Staroviotz, Miriam Elias, Shlomo Katz. Courtesy Israel Gur, Jerusalem.

great Russian theater director Konstantin Stanislavski and adopted his famous "method." It was, in fact, their idealism which enabled the Habimah actors to overcome the great initial difficulties, first of all the economic problem of the revolutionary period. David Vardi, one of its founding members, wrote in his diary in September, 1918: "Today we held a meeting . . . On the agenda was the food problem. It was decided to send two members out to the country, to look for potatoes and flour . . . We were each allotted a [role]. Mine was to bring potatoes from the he-Ḥalutz farm to the Habimah cooperative kitchen . . ."

There were also political problems. The Yevsektsiya, the Jewish section of the Communist Party, lodged a protest with Stalin, the People's Commissar of Nationalities, against Habimah's very existence. Stalin, however, overruled their intervention (1920). In this struggle Zemach succeeded in enlisting the support of leading artists, writers, and political personalities, as, e.g., Lunacharski, the commissar for education and culture, who proved a true friend of Habimah. Maxim *Gorki was also an enthusiastic supporter. Habimah introduced plays of a type that had never been staged by Jewish troupes, and they were directed by great teachers, all of them non-Jewish disciples of Stanislavski.

Habimah first performed in 1918, presenting four one-act plays by Jewish writers. It became one of the four studios of the Moscow Art Theater. Habimah scored its greatest triumph with S. *An-Ski's *The Dybbuk*, which was the third play it staged. Bialik translated it into Hebrew and Joel Engel composed its musical score. Its first performance took place on Jan. 31, 1922, and it established Habimah's reputation, as well as that of Yevgeni Vakhtangov, a young director of Armenian origin who had been delegated to Habimah by Stanislavski.

The Dybbuk owed its triumph to its outstanding orchestration, its forceful symbolism, and its glaring contrasts, but mainly to the boundless enthusiasm of the company in its acting and singing. Even in the mass scenes, every person on the stage gave his individual, distinct contribution; every Ḥasid and every beggar stood for something different, and yet together they formed a team. Vakhtangov's method, which was an endless process of refining, came to its perfect expression in the beggars' dance in Act II. In 1926 Habimah left Soviet Russia and went on a tour abroad. *The Dybbuk* was hailed as an unusual phenomenon. In 1927, when Habimah arrived in the United States, the company split. Zemach and several actors decided to stay in the country. According to David Vardi, "differences arose between Zemach and some of the younger actors, who had taken a giant step forward, of which Zemach hardly took note."

Habimah visited Palestine in 1928–29 and presented two productions, *Ha-Oẓar* ("The Treasure") by Shalom Aleichem and *Keter David* ("David's Crown") by Calderon, both under the direction of the Russian Alexander Diki. In 1930 the company went to Berlin, where it performed *Twelfth Night*, directed by Michael Chekhov, and *Uriel da Costa*, under the direction of Alexander Granovski. It finally settled in Palestine in 1931. In the course of time it added to its repertoire a great variety of plays derived both

Figure 3. Shimon Finkel in the title role of the Habimah production of Ibsen's *Peer Gynt,* 1952. Courtesy Israel Gur, Jerusalem.

from Jewish literature (of messianic and biblical content) and from world literature. It sought to foster dramas depicting Jewish life in the Diaspora, which it succeeded in presenting with extraordinary authenticity. Its aim was to present all phases of Jewish historical experience.

For the next 17 years Habimah was under the direction of its own members, mainly Barukh Chemerinsky and Ẓevi Friedland, the former concentrating on Diaspora dramas and original Hebrew plays, and the latter on world drama. Eventually Habimah also invited foreign directors, such as Leopold Lindberg, Leopold Jessner, and Tyrone Guthrie. It was Guthrie's 1948 production of *Oedipus Rex* which inaugurated a new era in the life of the company.

In the period in which Habimah relied mainly on its own directors, progress was slow. Each new performance became a festive occasion and Habimah had its admirers, a Habimah "circle," and a youth studio, as well as its own

Figure 4. The renovated Habimah Theater, 1970. Courtesy Government Press Office, Tel Aviv.

periodical *(Bamah);* but the company failed to keep pace with the cultural and social transformation of the *yishuv.* It did not rid itself of expressionistic oddities, and young people, as well as immigrants from the West, kept away. It also did not absorb the young talent which was crying out for a chance to prove its mettle. The graduates of the company's school for the most part joined the *Cameri, whose founding caused a crisis for Habimah.

In April 1948, Habimah went on a tour of the United States, presenting four productions (*The Dybbuk, The Golem, Keter David,* and *Oedipus Rex*). Although acclaimed by the critics, Habimah failed to attract audiences. When the company returned to Israel in July, it had nothing in its repertoire to express the heroic period of the national struggle. There was also conflict over the company's organization. For years there had been opposition to the continued existence of Habimah as a "collective," for it was argued that such a structure had become an obstacle to the company's progress because of the undue protection that it provided to members who had failed to attain the required artistic standard. This conflict was to remain unresolved for another two decades. Relief came from an unexpected quarter, the "generation of 1948." Yigal Mossinson's play *Be-Arvot ha-Negev* ("In the Negev Desert") had its premiere in February 1949 and met with an enthusiastic response. It expressed the spirit of the times, the highlights being Aharon Meskin's masterful

Figure 5. Scene from the Habimah production of *Inherit the Wind* by Jerome Lawrence and Robert E. Lee. Left to right: Shraga Friedman, Shimon Finkel, Ari Warshawer. Courtesy Israel Gur, Jerusalem.

acting and the play's portrayal of the new Israel-born generation.

In the following years Habimah enlisted directors of world renown: André Barsac from France, Alexander Bardini from Poland, Sven Malmquist from Sweden, John Hirsch from Canada, and Lee Strasberg and Harold Clurman from the United States. Under their direction, Habimah successfully mounted high-quality productions. At the same time, it continued to employ its own directors—Ẓevi

Friedland, Israel Becker, Shimon Finkel, Shraga Friedman, and Avraham Ninio.

In 1958, on the 40th anniversary of its first performance in Moscow, Habimah was awarded the title of "National Theater of Israel." The honorific award could not, however, conceal the company's shortcomings. There was neither an artistic authority nor a true collective, and conflicts between various factions, as well as financial difficulties, threatened the theater's very existence. Finally, in 1969, the members decided to dissolve the "collective." The Ministry of Education and Culture appointed its representatives to the management of Habimah, and a new administering director, Gavriel Zifroni, took over. In 1970 Habimah dedicated its renewed beautiful hall in the center of Tel Aviv. In the same year the veteran actor Shimon Finkel was appointed artistic director.

Bibliography: M. Kohansky, *The Hebrew Theatre* (1969), 76–85, 113–26 and index; N. Zemaḥ, *Be-Reshit ha-Bimah* (1966); Y. Bertonov, *Orot mi-be'ad la-Masakh* (1969); M. Gnessin, *Darki im ha-Te'atron ha-Ivri* (1946).

[Ed.]

ḪABIRU (Ḫapiru), an element of society in the Fertile Crescent during the greater part of the second millennium B.C.E. From their earliest appearance in documents of the 18th century B.C.E., the Ḫabiru constitute a class of dependents. In the early Assyrian and Babylonian period (18th–17th centuries) they appear in Cappadocia and in the kingdoms of Larsa, Babylon, Mari and the surrounding areas as bands of warriors attached to, and maintained by, the local rulers. Fifteenth-century documents of Alalakh (northern Syria) list the members of the Ḫabiru military units belonging to the adjacent towns. Nuzi documents of the same periods mention Ḫabiru units and individuals as receiving protection from the state. However, what is unique in these Nuzi documents is the number of contracts entered into between individual Ḫabiru men and women and wealthy citizens in which the relationship partakes of the character of both slavery and adoption. Hittite documents of the 14th and 13th centuries B.C.E. list the gods of the Ḫabiru among others who are signatories to international alliances. Hittite cult documents place the Ḫabiru (Ḫapiri) at the head of a list of subject and enslaved peoples or classes. Akkadian documents from Ugarit mention "the Ḫabiru [=SA. GAZ] of the Sun [=king of Heth]" and in Ugaritic alphabetic script *Ḫlb ʿprm* i.e., the Ḫabiru quarter of the city of Halbu (not identical with the great city of Ḥalab). From the 15th to the 12th centuries the *ʿpr.w* appear in Egyptian documents as captives from Palestine-Syria, and as slaves of the state.

Along with their appearance as dependents and protégés in lands of stable government, independent groups of Ḫabiru appear in times of disintegrating rule and lack of central control. In the Mari period of clashes between nations and cities, the Ḫabiru appear as robber bands which attacked and plundered settlements, either on their own or together with residents of nearby settlements. Similarly in Palestine-Syria during the *Tell el-Amarna period (15th–14th centuries B.C.E.) when Egyptian rule was weak, the confusion that resulted from the clashes between the local princes and the Egyptian governors provided an opportune time for the bands of Ḫabiru to run wild. On their own, together with local people, or as mercenaries helping either the city princes or the Egyptians they contributed greatly to the general confusion that was characteristic of the period.

The Ḫabiru were of varied origin. In Mari, a band of auxiliary soldiers was called Iamutbalian Ḫabiru ("Iamutbalāju Ḫa-bi-ru"), the former being the name of a western Semitic tribe and of the territory west of Baghdad. Documents from Mari and Alalakh cite cities as the origin of most of the Ḫabiru listed. Some of the Ḫabiru in Nuzi came from Akkad, Assyria, etc. A significant element among the Ḫabiru of the El-Amarna period were mutineers against the local kings. Their names also testify to a varied ethnic makeup: an early Babylonian list includes Akkadian and Western Semitic names; in Alalakh the names are principally non-Semitic (which corresponds with the surroundings); and in Nuzi there is a mixture of Akkadian and non-Semitic names. The ease with which they absorbed everyone who wished "to be a Ḫabiru" (in the language of the documents) indicates that they were not distinguished by ethnic unity.

All those called Ḫabiru shared a common inferior status. Almost all were fugitives from their original societies, and, as strangers without rights, they made themselves dependent on lords. For a few it is specifically noted that they were fugitives from authority or from personal calamities, or ordinary scoundrels (cf. similar bands in Israel during the biblical period: Judg. 9:4, 26ff.; 11:3; and especially David's band, I Sam. 22:2). The circumstances in which the Ḫabiru emerged are unclear. There are vague indications of a western-Semitic origin: their name; a settlement of Amorite (=MAR.TU; see *Amorites) soldiers of the early Babylonian period, named *Ḫa-bi-ri* (KI); the fact that the documents about them begin to appear at the height of Amorite migration to Mesopotamia. It is possible that Amorite unfortunates, stripped of land and possessions, formed the original core to which a rabble of paupers, refugees, and criminals was attracted in the course of time, without consideration of ethnic origin.

Ugaritic and Egyptian writings indicate that the root of the word Ḫabiru is *ʿapiru* (noun form). The existence of the *ʿayin* in the cuneiform, in the sign *ḪA*, points to a western-Semitic origin, since ordinarily the initial *ʿayin* becomes an *ʾalef* in Akkadian which is not the present case. These writings also establish the pronunciation of the second syllable (*BI* in cuneiform, hence either *bi* or *pi*) as *pi*, which makes less likely, but does not altogether rule out the word's derivation from the root *ʿ-B-R*.

In many sources the ideogram SA.GAZ is interchangeable with the term "Ḫabiru." This ideogram is translated in late lexicographical lists by the word *ḫa-ba-tu*, meaning "robber," but also migratory workers, who in El-Amarna letter no. 318:11–12 are kept apart from the Ḫabiru. (The later lexical identifications are not conclusive evidence.) It is probable that in many places the ideogram was pronounced Ḫabiru, but there is no definite proof for this. Some read the ideogram as *ša-ga-šu* based on the variants SA.GA.AZ, SAG.GAZ, meaning "murderer" (as in Akkadian) or "restless, foul" (as in Aramaic and Arabic). In any event, it is clear that both SA.GAZ and Ḫabiru had a negative connotation, to the extent that at times (and many such instances appear in the El-Amarna letters) the terms were used as synonyms for mutineers and paupers. [Mo.G.]

Ḫabiru and the Hebrews. Although the problem of the connection between the Ḫabiru and the Hebrews should be discussed from the point of view of the latter (see *Hebrews), certain points should be made here. The earlier stages of the problem are summarized by M. Greenberg (in bibl., 4–12, esp., 91–96; see R. de Vaux, W. F. Albright, M. P. Gray, J. Weingreen, and E. F. Campbell in bibl.; see also *Tell el-Amarna).

There is no basis for identifying the Ḫabiru with the "Hebrews" as basic identities, because it is clear that the Ḫabiru are a social element, while "Hebrews" are the people of Israel. On the other hand (not returning again to the philological problem, because the differences in punctuation cannot help, while the presence of an *ʿayin* is definite), it is certain that Abraham was called *ʿivri* because he fulfilled certain "pre-biblical" social structure identifications; other parts of the Israelites also could fulfill, for a short time, this traditional identification based on this structure (cf. Campbell, in bibl., 14). It is possible that the negative impact of this structure is felt in the definition of *'eved 'ivri* (Ex. 21:2) or in the *'ivrim* mentioned in connection with Saul in I Samuel 13–14 (although they may not be Israelites at all). It is impossible to identify the Israelite conquest with that of the Ḫabiru in the Tell el-Amarna letters for various fundamental reasons (including chronological ones); but although the latter is not mentioned in the biblical sources at all, the two conquests are typologically identical in certain respects. It is to be pointed out, however, that the Israelite conquest is a moving dynamic activity while that of the Ḫabiru is a stationary local-social one and its dynamics are social (chain reactions). The term Ḫabiru and also perhaps the traditional pre-biblical term "Hebrew" in this point of comparison is a framework of social transformation or a temporary aberration from order which has nothing to do with the conquest of the Israelites as a people. For other points, e.g., the question of 'Eb(e)r[i] as the eponym of the Hebrews in genealogy (e.g., Gen. 11:14ff.), see *Hebrews. [ED.]

Bibliography: J. Bottéro, *Le problème des Ḫabiru* . . . (1954); M. Greenberg, *The Ḫab/piru* (1955); idem, in: *Tarbiz*, 24 (1955), 369–79; M. P. Gray, in: HUCA, 29 (1958), 180–2; W. F. Albright, in: BASOR, 163 (1961), 53–54; E. F. Campbell, *Bi. Ar*, 23 (1960), 10, 13–16; J. Weingreen, in: *Fourth World Congress of Jewish Studies, Papers*, 1 (1967), 63–66 (Eng. section); P. Artzi, in: JNES, 27 (1968), 166–7; R. de Vaux, *ibid.*, 221–8 (incl. bibl.).

HA-BOKER (Heb. הַבֹּקֶר "The Morning"); (1) Daily Hebrew newspaper, published in Warsaw under the editorship of David *Frischmann from Jan. 14, 1909, until Aug. 20, 1909 (180 editions). Published with the Yiddish daily *Haynt*, to which Frischmann was a regular contributor, *Ha-Boker* was politically non-aligned. The editor was very exacting in the stylistic standard of the paper, and intent upon attracting as contributors the best Hebrew writers and intellects of the day. Translations from world literature were also published in *Ha-Boker*. The paper had

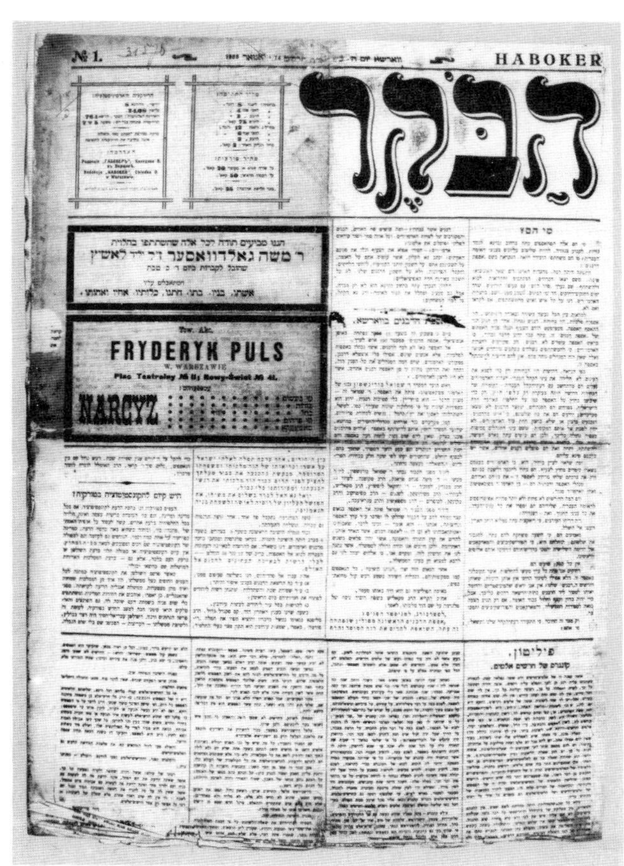
№ 1.

HABOKER

הבקר

FRYDERYK PULS

NARCYZ

First issue of the Warsaw Hebrew daily *Ha-Boker*, January 14, 1909. Jerusalem, J.N.U.L.

regular writers in London (Asher *Beilin), and in the United States (A. Fleishman), and occasional contributors elsewhere. Two current events filled up entire editions: the discovery of the *agent provocateur*, *Azeff, and the rebellion of the Young Turks in Turkey. Especially through the treatment of the latter, *Ha-Boker* took the stand, opposed to the official Zionist opinion, namely that the Young Turks would aggravate the already negative Turkish position on the Zionist undertaking (which indeed proved the case). Extensive debates were conducted, too, on the topic of Yiddish-Hebrew, and the "Hebrew in Hebrew" teaching method.

(2) Daily Hebrew newspaper published in Tel Aviv, 1935–65. Right-wing circles of the *yishuv* founded *Ha-Boker* as their organ for General Zionism. The orientation of the paper was formulated in the first edition by M. *Dizengoff. A brief period of groping was followed by consolidation in the editorial staff, especially after J. H. Heftman became editor in chief (he served intermittently as sole editor or as coeditor with Perez *Bernstein). *Ha-Boker* is credited with several journalistic innovations in the country, especially with vivid reporting, then in its pioneering stages. The literary supplement was edited for years by Baruch *Karu (Krupnik). After Heftman's death, Y. Gruman served as the paper's editor, followed by P. Bernstein and G. Ẓifroni. With the formation of the Liberal Party (1961), which consolidated the two branches of General Zionism, this paper served as its organ, and as a forum for publicists and writers in sympathy with the party. Finally, with the formation of the Ḥerut Liberal Party bloc (*Gaḥal) in 1965, the two party newspapers, *Ḥerut* and *Ha-Boker*, were replaced by a new paper, *Ha-Yom*.

Bibliography: G. Kressel, *Toledot ha-Ittonut ha-Ivrit be-Ereẓ-Yisrael* (1964[2]), 162–6. [G.K.]

HA-BONIM (Heb. הַבּוֹנִים), moshav shittufi in central Israel, by the seacoast, 6 mi. (10 km.) northwest of *Zikhron Ya'akov, affiliated with Tenu'at ha-Moshavim, founded in 1949 by graduates of the Iḥud Habonim youth movement from South Africa and other English-speaking countries. They were later joined by Israel-born youth and new immigrants from other countries. The economy is based on citriculture, livestock, etc. In 1968 there were 150 inhabitants. [E.O.]

HABOR (Heb. חָבוֹר), a river flowing through Mesopotamia for 218 mi. (350 km.) from north to south in the region of el-Jazira, the area between the Euphrates and Tigris rivers. It rises from Mt. Kharagah, and is joined by five tributary streams, emptying into the Euphrates north of Mari. The surrounding region was productive in antiquity; grain was raised mainly in the north while in the southern Habor Valley sheep and cattle, and later also horses, were raised. Beyond the northern Habor lay an important trade route, which started at Nineveh, the Assyrian metropolis, and ran by way of Nisibis, Gozan, and Haran to Carchemish on the Euphrates. This route was apparently used in the days of Abraham and even before. On the evidence of the remains excavated at Chagar Bazar, the Habor Valley was first settled in the Neolithic period. In the 18th century B.C.E., many attempts were made to channel the river's waters by means of dams and canals, as is known from the Mari letters of that period. In the 16th–14th centuries B.C.E. the region of the Habor was in the center of the mighty kingdom of Mitanni, and the area was reduced to ruins until it was revived in the tenth century B.C.E. The city of

Gozan (Tell Halaf) became especially important, and according to the Bible the river was apparently named after it. The Assyrian conquest of the Habor district began in the ninth and eighth centuries. When insurrections in the conquered cities increased, one city after another was destroyed and the inhabitants deported. In their place Tiglath-Pileser III settled the Israelite exiles from Transjordan (I Chron. 5:26), and later Sargon II settled the exiles from Samaria there (II Kings 17:6; 18:11; cf. Pritchard, Texts, 284–5). Documents found in the excavations of Gozan prove the presence of Israelite exiles in this city (see *Gozan and Assyrian *Exile).

Bibliography: F. Sarre and E. Hertzfeld, *Archaeologische Reise in Euphrat und Tigris-Gebiet*, 1 (1911); J. Seidmann, *Die Inschriften Adadniraris II* (1935); C. J. Gadd, in: *Iraq*, 7 (1940), 22ff.; J. Kupper, in: *Archives Royales de Mari*, 3 (1950), 2, 5, 80; J. Lewy, in: *Orientalia*, 21 (1952), 265–92, 393–425. [M.A.-Y.]

ḤABSHUSH, ḤAYYIM (**Ḥayyim b. Yaḥya b. Salim Alfityḥi;** d. 1899), Yemenite writer. Ḥabshush was a descendant of a distinguished rabbinical family in *San'a, Yemen. His craft of copper engraving stimulated his interest in antiquities and in *Sabean inscriptions. Ḥabshush served as a guide to the scholar Joseph *Halévy who went to Yemen in 1869, disguised as a Jerusalem rabbi, in order to search out Sabean inscriptions. Ḥabshush led him and later Eduard *Glaser through areas previously not visited by Europeans. Ḥabshush is known for his book *Masot Ḥabshush* ("The Travels of Ḥabshush"), a description of his travels with Halévy, written at Glaser's request about 20 years after the journey. The importance of the book lies not only in its content, but also in its language—a combination of the popular Arabic dialect of Sana and literary Hebrew—and its literary charm.

Ḥabshush is also the author of *"Halikhot Teiman,"* episodes in the history of Yemenite Jewry berween 1668 and 1817 and published in *Sefunot*, 2 (1958), under the title *"Korot Yisrael be-Teiman."*

Bibliography: S. D. Goitein (ed.), *Masot Ḥabshush* (1939); idem, *Travels in Yemen* (1941); idem, in: KS, 14 (1947/48), 256–70; E. Brauer, *Ethnologie der jemenitischen Juden* (1934), 11–13. [.Я.Y]

ḤABSHUSH, SHALOM BEN YAḤYA (c. 1825–1905), head of a yeshivah in San'a, Yemen, *dayyan*, and author. A goldsmith by profession, he kept aloof from public office and communal affairs, and devoted himself to the study of the Torah. He was the last head of the San'a yeshivah, which closed down in 1905, during a siege and famine. He wrote two works, which were published together (Aden, 1893): *Korban Todah*, explanations and novellae on the *Mekor Ḥayyim* of R. Yaḥyā Ṣāliḥ b. Jacob, dealing with the laws of ritual slaughter and *terefot;* and *Shoshannat ha-Melekh*, an abridged version of the responsa *Pe'ulat Ẓaddik* of R. Yaḥyā Ṣāliḥ. It was written and possibly copied by the author himself in 1862. The abridged responsa are presented in the form of *halakhot* and verdicts. In the margins he added the *Gan Shoshannim*, which indicates the source of the *halakhah*. The part on *Oraḥ Ḥayyim* and *Yoreh De'ah* was published together with R. David Mizraḥi's commentary on the Shulhan Arukh, *Shetilei Zeitim* (2 vols. 1886–96).

Bibliography: S. Gridi (ed.), *Shoshannat ha-Melekh* (1967), introduction. [Y.R.]

HACKENBURG, WILLIAM BOWER (1837–1918), U.S. silk manufacturer and philanthropist. After becoming secretary of the Hebrew Relief Society in 1858, Hackenburg devoted a great deal of his time to doing philanthropic work in his native Philadelphia. He was a founder of the Jewish Hospital, being largely responsible for its development into a major public institution, a trustee of both the Baron de Hirsch Fund and Dropsie College, and a vice-president of the Board of Delegates of American Israelites. In 1878 he

William Hackenburg, U.S. philanthropist. From *American Jewish Historical Society Journal*, vol. 48, 1958/59.

supervised the latter organization's compilation of a statistical survey of American Jewry. He was also active in Russo-Jewish refugee relief work. [S.D.T.]

HACOHEN, DAVID (1898–), Israel politician and diplomat. Born in Gomel, Russia, the son of Mordecai ben Hillel *Hacohen, he was taken to Ereẓ Israel in 1907. During World War I, Hacohen served in the Turkish Army in Anatolia. From 1923 he served in various economic enterprises of the *Histadrut and was one of the founders and directors of Solel Boneh. During World War II he was *Haganah liaison officer to the British Army and was closely connected with the Free French forces (his house in Haifa served as the site of their radio transmission to the Vichy-occupied Levant). For many years, Hacohen served as a member of the Arab-Jewish Haifa Municipality under the British Mandate. Together with other *yishuv* leaders, he was arrested by the British on "Black Saturday" (June 29, 1946) and interned at Latrun. A *Mapai member of the Knesset from 1949, Hacohen was chairman of its Foreign Affairs and Security Committee. He was many times leader of the Knesset delegations to the Interparliamentary Union and was twice a member of its executive. In 1953–55 Hacohen was Israel's first ambassador to Burma. His book, *Yoman Burma* (1963), is a record of his mission there. His second wife was Bracha *Habas.

Bibliography: Tidhar, 3 (1958), 1121–22; D. Lazar, *Rashim be-Yisrael*, 1 (1953), 135–41. [B.J.]

HACOHEN, MORDECAI BEN HILLEL (1856–1936), Hebrew writer and Zionist. At the age of 18 he began publishing in Hebrew periodicals, such as *Ha-Levanon*, *Ha-Ẓefirah*, and *Ha-Kol*, and, from 1876, was on the editorial staff of *Ha-Shaḥar*. In 1878/9 Hacohen, who was influenced by *Smolenskin's nationalism, published a long article sharply criticizing the Haskalah movement for having caused a spiritual crisis among the Jewish youth of East Europe. No less effective was his article in *Ha-Meliẓ* (1879), depicting the dire economic plight of Russian Jewry. In 1878 he moved to St. Petersburg. In 1880 he wrote a comprehensive survey of Jewish agriculturalists in modern Russia for the Russo-Jewish periodicals. Hacohen joined the *Ḥibbat Zion movement in 1881 and, in the same year, published in *Ha-Maggid* his article *"Kumu ve-Na'aleh Ziyyon"* ("Arise and Let Us Go to Zion"), the first of a series on the new movement. In 1886 he wrote from a Jewish nationalist standpoint the first comprehensive survey of Smolenskin's career. He visited Palestine at the end of 1889 and published his impressions in *Ha-Meliẓ*. In 1891, in his native town of Mogilev, Hacohen founded two societies for promoting settlement in Palestine, visiting the country again on their behalf in that year. He reported on his journey in *Lu'aḥ Aḥi'asaf* 9 (1901) and 11 (1903) criticizing the colonizing activities of the Ḥovevei Zion and of their agent, Ze'ev Tiomkin. A delegate to the first Zionist Congress (1897), he was the first to deliver a speech in Hebrew. In 1907 he settled in Palestine. Hacohen, who was one of the founders of Tel Aviv, played an active part in the economic and cultural life of the *yishuv*. He helped to start the monthly youth magazine *Moledet*, of which he later became an editor. He was also one of the organizers of the Association of Hebrew Writers. Hacohen's articles are characterized by their practical approach to contemporary problems, as exemplified by his demand that Jewish nationalism be given a sound economic basis. Especially noteworthy is his essay on *"The Literary Vision of Israel and Its Land,"* as expressed in the works of Smolenskin, George Eliot, Disraeli, and Baharav (*Ha-Shilo'aḥ*, vols. 2, 6, 11). His memoirs and diaries are also of historical and cultural importance.

Mordecai ben Hillel Hacohen, Hebrew writer. Jerusalem, J.N.U.L., Schwadron Collection.

His Hebrew works include: collection of articles and stories (2 vols., 1904); *Kevar*, memoirs (1923); *Olami*, memoirs (5 vols., 1927–29); *Milḥemet ha-Ammim*, a diary of World War I (5 vols., 1929–30); *Athalta* (2 vols., 1931–42), a collection of articles on Ereẓ Israel in the years 1917–20; *Ḥayyim Naḥman Bialik* (1933); *Be-Sivkhei ha-Ya'ar ve-od Sippurim* (1934); and *Sefer Shemot*, biographical sketches of Hebrew writers and of Zionist workers (1938). A selection of Hacohen's Yiddish writings was published in the miscellany *In Mame Loshen* (1935). Some of Hacohen's articles in Russian, "Jerusalem and its Region" (1909) and "On the Balance of Trade of Jaffa Harbor" (1913), were reprinted in pamphlet form. On the 50th and 60th anniversaries of the beginning of his literary work, miscellanies were published in his honor, *Mi-Boker ad Erev* (1925) and *Or le-Et Erev* (1934), which also contain biographical and bibliographical material about him.

[G.El.]

HACOHEN, RAPHAEL ḤAYYIM (1883–1954), rabbi and communal leader. Born in Shiraz, Persia, he was taken by his parents to Jerusalem in 1890. After a thorough rabbinical education, he began to take an active part in all communal affairs of the *yishuv* and the then small settlement of Persian Jews. He founded an organization, Agudat Ohavei Zion, which aimed to improve the economic and cultural situation of the Persian Jews in Jerusalem. A devoted Zionist, he was a delegate to the Convention ("Kenesiyyah") in Zikhron Ya'akov, organized by M. *Ussishkin in 1903. In 1922 he signed a memorandum to the Zionist Congress, outlining the conditions and requirements of the Persian Jewish colony in Jerusalem. In 1912 he established a Hebrew printing press in Jerusalem, which published many works of *Judeo-Persian literature. He himself was the author of *Shir u-Shevaḥah* (1905; 1921[2]), a collection of songs and *pizmonim* of his family and of the Jews of Shiraz, and of an "Autobiography."

Bibliography: M. D. Gaon, *Yehudei ha-Mizraḥ be-Ereẓ Yisrael*, 2 (1938), 303–4.

[W.J.F.]

HADAD, an early Semitic god, one of the chief gods of the *Amorites and, later, the *Canaanites. In Akkadian documents Hadad appears as Adad Addu and in Ugaritic as "Hd." Hadad was god of the mountains, thunder, rain, and storm, and by parallelism, fertility. He has been identified with "Baal-shamin, the lord of the heavens." The cult of Hadad existed in Syria from the earliest period up to Roman times. The bullock was sacred to him, and the sheaf of wheat, symbol of fertility, was one of his symbols. His consort was Atarʿata (called Atargatis, "the Syrian goddess," in Greek sources).

The centers of the Hadad cult were Damascus and Baalbek, where he was identified with the sun god. He was depicted on Syrian reliefs as a bearded man standing astride a bullock, holding shafts of lightning in his hands. In a later period he was depicted as a tall man wrapped in a tight garment decorated with emblems of the heavenly bodies, holding a threshing board in one hand and ears of grain in the other; next to him stand two bullocks. The Hadad cult spread throughout Canaan, where he was evidently identified with Baal of the Carmel, whom Elijah the prophet denounced (I Kings 18). In Palestine Hadad was also identified with the god Rimmon, who was worshiped in the Valley of Megiddo (cf. ". . . as the mourning of Hadadrimmon in the plain of Megiddon," Zech. 12:11).

In the Hellenistic period an altar was erected to Hadad near Acre. He and Atarʿata were also the chief gods of Hieropolis in Syria, but during the Hellenistic-Roman period the cult of the goddess gained in importance. When the Syrian cult spread west to the Greek and Roman cities, Hadad played only a secondary role.

Hadad appears in the Bible as the name of Edomite kings (Gen. 36:35; I Kings 11:14–25; I Chron. 1:46, 50) and is also a component of the names of Aramean kings (II Sam. 8:3; I Kings 20:1).

Bibliography: A. Deimel, *Pantheon Babylonicum* (1914), 43ff.; G. Dossin, in: *Syria*, 20 (1939), 171–2; Albright, Stone, 160, 176, 187–8, 332; S. Moscati (ed.), *Le Antiche Divinitá Semitiche* (1958).

[M.A.-Y.]

HADAMARD, JACQUES SALOMON (1865–1963), French mathematician. Born in Versailles, Hadamard held chairs of mathematics at the Collège de France from 1897 and the Ecole Polytechnique from 1912 until his retirement in 1935. He was elected a member of the Academy of Sciences in 1912 and was the first to be awarded the Feltrinelli Prize founded by the Italians in 1955 to compensate for the absence of a Nobel Prize for mathematicians. A brother-in-law of Alfred *Dreyfus, Hadamard took an active interest in the Dreyfus case, and for 60 years was a member of the central committee of the Ligue des Droits de l'Homme founded at the time of the Zola trial in 1898. The dangers of Hitlerism were recognized by Hadamard at an early stage. He was a free-thinker, but worked to alleviate the plight of German Jewry. He was a member of the French Palestine Committee and of the administrative board of the Hebrew University of Jerusalem. He escaped from France in 1941 to the United States, and moved to England to engage in operational research with the Royal Air Force. Hadamard produced important work in analysis, number theory, differential geometry, calculus of variations, functional analysis, partial differential equations, and hydrodynamics, and inspired research among successive generations of mathematicians. He published numerous papers and books. His *An Essay on the Psychology of Invention in the Mathematical Field* (1945; *Essai sur la psychologie de l'invention dans le domaine mathématique*, 1959) was published many years after his retirement.

Bibliography: Mandelbrojt and Schwartz, in: *Bulletin of the American Mathematical Society*, 71 (1965), 107–29; Cartwright, in: *Journal of the London Mathematical Society*, 40 (1965), 722–48.

[B.S.]

HADAS, MOSES (1900–1966), U.S. classical scholar and humanist. After graduating from Emory University, Hadas proceeded to Columbia University, at the same time pursuing studies at the Jewish Theological Seminary of America, from which he received his rabbinical diploma. Appointed instructor in Greek at the former institution in 1925, he became associate professor in 1946 and full professor in 1953. Three years later he was elected to the prestigious John Jay Chair in Greek, which he occupied until his death. During World War II he served with the Office of Strategic Services in North Africa and Greece.

Hadas' cardinal contribution to classical studies in the United States was to bring them out of the narrower confines of textual criticism into the broad area of general humanistic interest. This he did through a series of spirited and elegant renderings of the Greek dramatists and romances (e.g. Heliodorus) and of Caesar, Tacitus, Seneca, and other writers. He also wrote popular histories of Greek and Latin literature (1950, 1952); a broad, if sometimes controversial, survey of the Greco-Roman age, entitled *Hellenistic Culture: Fusion and Diffusion* (1959); a study (with Morton Smith) of classical aretalogy; and, in a lighter vein, an entertaining ancilla to classical reading. Many of these works appeared in inexpensive paperback editions, and thus introduced the ancient masterpieces to the general reader.

Hadas was a major figure at Columbia University. Alike through the humanity of his writings and the urbane temper of his character and outlook, he left an indelible impress on several generations of students and readers, and he was among the foremost to remove the traditional fustian from classical studies.

Outside of the classical field, Hadas produced, among other works, a delightful rendering of Joseph ben Meir *Zabara's *Book of Delight* (1932) and *Fables of a Jewish Aesop* (1966), a translation of the fox-fables of the 12th century *Berechiah ha-Nakdan. In his earlier years he was prominently identified with the Menorah movement in American universities. [TH.H.G.]

HADASSAH, THE WOMEN'S ZIONIST ORGANIZATION OF AMERICA, largest Zionist organization in the world and one of the largest women's organizations in the U.S. In 1969 Hadassah had 1,350 chapters and groups and over 318,000 members. It is, according to its constitution, "a voluntary, non-profit organization dedicated to the ideals of Judaism, Zionism, American democracy, healing, teaching and medical research." Its program is carried out on two fronts: in Israel where it sponsors medical training, research, and care, along with special education, and in the United States where members participate in fund raising and Jewish educational activities which serve many members as a vehicle for Jewish identification.

Early History. Hadassah began as one of several Zionist women's study circles organized in scattered regions of the United States at the turn of the 20th century. Like many others, the New York groups were called "Daughters of Zion." Henrietta *Szold became an active member and leader of the Harlem group, which she joined in 1907. Touring Ereẓ Israel in 1909, she was impressed by the beauty of the country but appalled by the misery and disease and the limited medical facilities, and decided to bring the situation before her study circle upon her return in 1910. Invitations were issued to a meeting "for the purpose

Figure 1. The first Hadassah nurses' unit with Henrietta Szold, front row, far right. Courtesy Hadassah, New York.

of discussing the feasibility of forming an organization for the promotion of Jewish institutions and enterprises in Palestine and the fostering of Jewish ideals." In 1912 the Hadassah chapter of the national Daughters of Zion was formed, gradually followed by chapters in other cities. The organization sponsored two visiting nurses in Palestine (1913) whose expenses were partly underwritten by philanthropist Nathan *Straus. By 1914, when the Daughters of Zion held their first convention, the seven attending chapters voted to change their name to Hadassah. In 1916 the World Zionist Organization called upon Hadassah to organize a medical relief group to deal with the wartime health emergency. The American Zionist Medical Unit which eventually sailed for Palestine in the summer of 1918 consisted of 44 physicians, nurses, sanitary engineers, dentists, and administrative staff. It was to be supported jointly by Hadassah and the Joint Distribution Committee, with two lay administrators, Alice *Seligsberg and Adolph Hubbard. Within a few years the organization became known as the Hadassah Medical Organization, an all-pervading medical presence in Palestine offering medical aid to Arabs as well as Jews.

Hadassah Medical Organization In Israel. The organization set up an infant welfare station, malaria control unit, playgrounds, school luncheons, home visiting, and distribution of pasteurized milk. It founded the Hadassah Training School for Nurses, now known as the Henrietta Szold-Hadassah School of Nursing, the first in Palestine, which graduated its first class in November 1921. Henrietta Szold herself had arrived in Palestine in 1920 to serve on the executive committee of the Hadassah Medical Organization. She laid the foundations for Hadassah's continuing approach, based on education and professional standards, with the ultimate aim of turning its programs over to the people of the country. By the late 1960s, many Hadassah hospitals, dispensaries, and special programs, including school lunches, child health and welfare centers, and playgrounds, had been presented by Hadassah to and were run by Israel's municipalities or by the government.

The concept of a *Hebrew university, an early Zionist dream realized in 1925 with the opening of buildings on Mount Scopus in Jerusalem, also advanced Hadassah service. Simultaneous with the steady expansion of Hadassah's clinical and medical services, negotiations continued between Hadassah, the University, and a body of American Jewish physicians interested in founding a modern hospital and medical school in Palestine. One of the original University institutes—Microbiology—developed into the faculty of science, with growing medical research departments. An agreement between the University and Hadassah in 1936 created the Hebrew University-Hadassah Medical

Figure 2. The Hebrew University-Hadassah Medical Center on Mount Scopus. Courtesy Hadassah Medical Organization, Jerusalem. Photo Alfred Bernheim, Jerusalem.

Center, a graduate school instituted in 1938. A year later the Rothschild-Hadassah-University Hospital, designed by Eric *Mendelssohn, opened on Mount Scopus. By 1944 the medical needs of immigrants streaming into Palestine resulted in a joint effort to establish the Hebrew University-Hadassah Medical School for undergraduates. Ground was broken on Mount Scopus in 1947, but hostilities postponed implementation, and in May 1948 the Medical Center was evacuated as a result of an Arab ambush which killed 75 professors, doctors, and nurses.

THE HEBREW UNIVERSITY-HADASSAH MEDICAL SCHOOL. After the 1948 war Hadassah doctors and nurses continued to function in makeshift buildings in Jerusalem. The Hebrew University-Hadassah Medical School was launched in 1949 in temporary quarters, and in 1952 ground was broken for the new Hadassah-Hebrew University Medical Center. In that year the medical school graduated its first class, and by 1970 it had graduated 1,218 doctors of medicine. The Medical Center in Ein Karem, dedicated in 1960, became the new complex for the Hadassah Medical Organization a year later. The facilities included the Rothschild-Hadassah University Hospital, a 700-bed teaching hospital with diagnostic and research laboratories, maternity and infant care pavilion, and outpatient department handling 250,000 visits annually; the Henrietta Szold-Hadassah School of Nursing and Nurses' Residence; the Hebrew University-Hadassah Medical School; and the Hebrew University-Hadassah School of Dentistry founded by the Alpha Omega Dental Fraternity. The synagogue on the grounds contains 12 stained-glass windows created

Figure 3. Aerial view of the Hadassah medical center complex at Ein Karem, 1970. Courtesy Hadassah Medical Organization, Jerusalem. Photo Emka, Jerusalem.

for Hadassah by Marc *Chagall. Additional space was allotted for a variety of medical specialties. The division of social medicine offers health education, research, and treatment. Hadassah-trained physicians serve as emissaries to teach and train personnel and set up health services in underdeveloped Asian and African countries. After the return to Mount Scopus following the Six-Day War in 1967, Hadassah commenced the reconstruction of its buildings and the School of Occupational Therapy moved into its permanent home there.

Youth Aliyah, Vocational Training, and J.N.F. Hadassah's concern with Israel's health needs expanded during the 1930s to include the problems of young Jewish refugees. From 1935 it actively supported *Youth Aliyah, an immigration program organized in Germany in 1933 by Recha *Freier for the transfer of adolescents and their resettlement in agricultural settlements in Palestine. Henrietta Szold was Palestine director of Youth Aliyah until her death. Since 1935 Hadassah has been the principal agency in the U.S. supporting Youth Aliyah, annually providing about 40% of its total world budget. From 1935 to 1970 over $60,000,000 was contributed by Hadassah. These funds were used to train and rehabilitate over 135,000 children from 80 lands in 267 Youth Aliyah installations, kibbutzim, youth villages, and day centers.

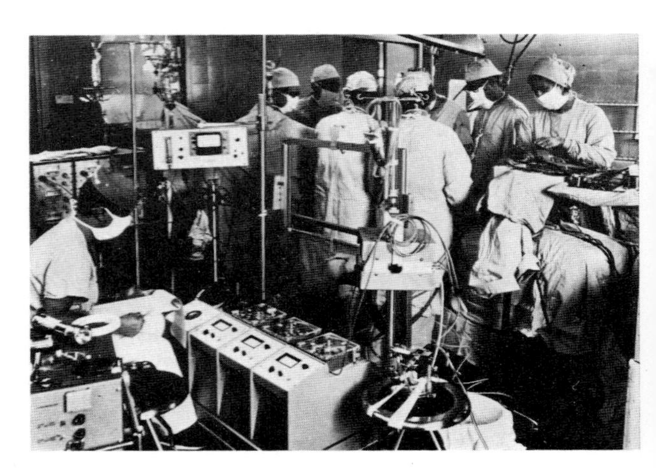

Figure 4. Open-heart surgery at Hadassah Hospital, Jerusalem, 1970. Courtesy Hadassah Medical Organization, Jerusalem. Photo Werner Braun.

Hadassah's vocational training plan, initiated in 1942, was an outcome of Henrietta Szold's earlier recognition of the need for technically trained personnel in a rapidly developing country. The Alice L. Seligsberg Vocational High School for Girls, first of its kind in Palestine, opened in Jerusalem in 1942, later to become the Hadassah Alice Seligsberg Comprehensive High School with a full academic curriculum for boys and girls. The Louis D. Brandeis Vocational Centers, begun with a bequest from the Brandeis estate, opened in 1944. They include the schools of Fine Mechanics and Precision Instruments with departments for tool and die-making and industrial electronics and printing and typography. In 1970, the two institutions were merged to form the coeducational Hadassah Comprehensive High School (Seligsberg-Brandeis). Hadassah-Neurim, a vocational training center at Kfar Vitkin, is run together with Youth Aliyah and with support from the Israel government. In 1944 the Vocational Guidance Bureau, later renamed the Vocational Guidance Institute, was created for testing and research, and has been assigned projects for the U.S. government. In 1968 all the non-medical educational and training programs were included in the Hadassah-Israel Education Services.

Figure 5. Annual convention on the fiftieth anniversary of Hadassah, New York, 1962. Photo G. D. Hachett, New York.

An active participant in programs designed to build and strengthen Israel, Hadassah became involved in the Jewish National Fund in 1925 and assumed responsibility for reclaiming tens of thousands of acres. By 1966 it had participated in planting 83,000,000 trees and reclaiming over 150,000 acres (625,000 dunams) of land, and in special reclamation projects in the Aravah and central Galilee.

U.S. Activities. Hadassah's Israel projects depend for their growth and development upon its U.S. membership. The program is a combination of fund raising and communal and educational activities, implemented through two New York membership corporations: Hadassah, the Women's Zionist Organization of America which charters and services the regions, chapters, and groups throughout the United States, and Hadassah Medical Relief Association, Inc., through which Hadassah carries out its Israel program. The program in Israel is under the direct supervision of the volunteer Hadassah Council in Israel. The overall administration of Hadassah is vested in the National Board. Policy decisions are made by the board and by the national convention, which is held annually, composed of delegates from regions, chapters, and groups.

Hadassah's programs in the United States and in Israel are largely supported by membership dues and contributions. Methods for raising funds vary, and include a wide range of cultural and social activities. In 1968 the total raised was $12,122,083, with $6 million earmarked for the Hadassah Medical Organization, over $2 million for Youth Aliyah, $650,000 for Hadassah Israel Education Services, $700,000 for Jewish National Fund, and over $150,000 for U.S. youth activities.

EDUCATION. Begun as a study group, Hadassah's program in the United States is basically one of education. National professional and lay leadership provides the membership with special materials and publications on U.S. and Zionist affairs and Jewish education. The program providing information on current developments in the Middle East and United States policy particularly as it relates to the Middle East also serves as a public relations medium for Zionism and the vehicle for working with various inclusive organizations. Internationally, Hadassah is a nongovernmental organization of the United Nations and an accredited observer to the United States Mission.

Hadassah's Jewish education program encourages the study of Jewish history and heritage, and the study of Hebrew through special courses and the support of Hebrew culture organizations. In addition, Hadassah publishes a monthly, the *Hadassah Magazine,* which reaches over a million readers. The Hadassah Program Department provides a variety of materials for meetings.

U.S. YOUTH ACTIVITIES. Hadassah has been actively involved in the education of U.S. Jewish youth. The Zionist youth movement, *Young Judea, organized in 1909, was later adopted as a project by Hadassah. In 1940 its activities came under the jurisdiction of the American Zionist Youth Commission, a joint effort of Hadassah and the Zionist Organization of America, and in 1967 it became part of Hadassah's youth program. Junior Hadassah was organized in 1920 and, like its parent organization, emphasized service to Israel through a series of special projects and a program of participation in American, Jewish communal, and Zionist life. In 1967 the entire Hadassah youth movement was reorganized as Hashachar ("The Dawn") under the sole sponsorship of Hadassah. The program offers activities in the U.S. and Israel for boys and girls in four age divisions from nine to 25: nine to 14, Junior and Intermediate Judea; 14 to 18, Senior Young Judea; 18 to 25, Hamagshimim. The Hadassah youth commission sponsors eight summer camps throughout the United States.

[GL.R.]

HADASSI, JUDAH (ha-Avel) BEN ELIJAH (12th century), *Karaite scholar of Constantinople. His greatest work is the *Eshkol ha-Kofer* (or *Sefer ha-Peles*), which according to his own testimony he began in 1148. The work is arranged according to the Ten Commandments and alphabetically. Written partly in verse, it explains the *mitzvot* and the *halakhot* and the reasons for their observance in accordance with the specific commandment on which they depend. It represents an encyclopedic corpus of Karaite belief and knowledge as it existed in the author's time. According to Hadassi, Karaite doctrine derives and may be learned from the Torah and the Prophets by way of a complete system of homiletical exposition, which he specifies in detail. The discussion on the *mitzvot* is preceded by a comprehensive treatment of the rules of vocalization and grammar in the Bible. Hadassi believed in man's free will in matters of faith and methods of Torah study. The rationalist trend in Karaism is recognizable in his attacks on the legends in the Talmud and the customs and interpretations of the *Rabbanites. There is also a certain measure of social criticism in his argument that the Rabbanites circumvent the prohibition against lending money on interest. Hadassi sharply attacked Christianity and Islam, but, like his Karaite predecessors, he attributed the corruption of Christianity to the Apostles, especially St. Paul; he stated that "Jesus was an exemplary, wise, and righteous man from the first . . . the scholars encompassed him . . . and killed him as they killed other pious men who criticized them."

The description given of the world and nature by Hadassi evidently reflected the current beliefs of the Jews living in the Byzantine Empire. He had an unqualified belief in astronomy and accepted demons and sorcerers. He knew of strange creatures in distant lands—a mixture of images from rabbinic legends, ancient mythology, and Eastern tales—and also of "the tribes of Jeshurun hidden beyond the Sambatyon River." Hadassi was thus a compiler rather than an original thinker, and in spite of his anti-Rabbanite bias he drew much of his material from Rabbanite sources. His Hebrew style, however, unlike that of his Rabbanite contemporaries, is awkward and not easily understandable and the rhymed arrangement often makes it obscure. *Eshkol ha-Kofer* was published by the Karaite press in Eupatoria, Crimea (1836). A few hymns by Hadassi are included in the official Karaite prayer book.

Bibliography: S. Pinsker, *Likkutei Kadmoniyyot* (1860), 223–5 (first pagination); B. Frankl, in: MGWJ, 31 (1882), 1–13, 72–85, 268ff.; W. Bacher, *ibid.*, 40 (1896), 14ff.; idem, in: JQR, 8 (1895/96), 431–44; L. Nemoy, *Karaite Anthology* (1952), 235–377; Z. Ankori, *Karaites in Byzantium* (1959), index s.v. *Yehudah Hadassi.*

[H.H.B.-S.]

ḤADDAD, EZRA (1903–), educator, author, and journalist. Ḥaddad mastered several languages, including Hebrew. He published Hebrew poems in the Jewish weekly *Yeshurun* (Baghdad, 1921) and from 1926 to 1951 he directed the Jewish schools al-Waṭaniyya and Shammāsh in Baghdad. After his immigration to Israel in 1951, he held leading executive positions in the Histadrut. In addition to his Hebrew poems, Ḥaddad published an Arabic translation of the Travels of Benjamin of Tudela (1945) together with notes and an introduction. He also wrote a textbook for the study of Arabic.

Bibliography: A. Ben-Jacob, *Yehudei Bavel* (1965), 307f.

[H.J.C.]

ḤADERAH (Heb. חֲדֵרָה), town in central Israel, in the northern Sharon, founded in 1890 by members of Ḥovevei Zion from Vilna, Kovno, and Riga who had bought the land a few months earlier. The area was swampy and infested with malaria, and the settlers underwent great suffering, with more than half dying of malaria in the first 20 years of Ḥaderah's existence. In 1895 Baron Edmond de *Rothschild began aiding the village, sending Egyptian workers to lay out the first drainage network and planting large eucalyptus groves; the eucalyptus tree soon became Ḥaderah's symbol. Dr. Hillel *Joffe worked indefatigably in combating the malaria at Ḥaderah. Although the disease ceased to constitute a problem from the late 1920s, the last vestiges of the swamps disappeared only in 1945, when a larger canal leading to the sea was dug. Whereas field and vegetable garden crops initially constituted main farm branches, citrus groves began to be planted before World War I and were greatly enlarged in the 1920s and 1930s. With the construction of the Lydda-Haifa railway in 1918/19, Ḥaderah became a railway station, and with the completion of the Ḥaderah-Petaḥ Tikvah highway in 1937, it also became an important crossroads, connected with Haifa in the north and the Jezreel Valley in the east. The number of inhabitants increased from 152 in 1898 to 320 in 1914, 450 in 1922, 3,372 in 1931, and 11,819 in 1948. Ḥaderah became a regional center, and in 1936 it received municipal council status. During the first years of Israel's independence, after 1948, Ḥaderah doubled its population. In 1961 it had 26,000 and in 1968, 31,100 inhabitants; of the latter, 40% were Israel-born, 33% hailed from Europe and America, and 27% from Asia and Africa. Although agriculture (carp ponds, bananas, cattle, poultry, beehives, flowers, etc., in addition to citrus and various field and garden crops) continues to develop, industry has become the main element in the town's economy. Concentrated on a dune area in the northwest, it includes the American Israel Paper Mills and Alliance Tire and Rubber Company (each with over 1,000 employed in 1970), food-preserve plants, and other enterprises. As the center of a sub-district, Ḥaderah fulfills administrative functions and has the Hillel Joffe hospital and educational institutions. The large municipal area of 12,695 acres, extending over the sand dunes west to the seashore, provides ample space for expansion of residential and industrial quarters.

A pottery ossuary of the Chalcolithic period found in the Ḥaderah area. Jerusalem, Rockefeller Museum, Israel Department of Antiquities.

The name Ḥaderah is derived from the Arabic *al-Khaḍrā'* ("the Green"), referring to the color of the former swamp vegetation and to the algae-covered water of Naḥal Ḥaderah. The area around Ḥaderah was first settled in the Chalcolithic period; house-shaped pottery ossuaries with painted decorations from this time were found in excavations there in 1936. Bronze Age remains, as well as ruins of buildings, mosaics, and a Roman bridge, were also discovered. In the crusader period the city was called Lictera after the Arabic name al-Khuḍayra. Because of the many swamps in its vicinity, the site was abandoned after the Crusades.

Bibliography: L. I. Shneorson, *Mi-Pi Rishonim* (1963); E. Hadani, *Ḥaderah, 1891–1951* (Heb., 1951); *Yedi'ot Ḥaderah*, nos. 1–3 (1965–68); M. Smilansky, *Ḥaderah* (Heb. 1930, 1936²); *Histadrut ha-Ovedim ha-Ivrim ha-Kelalit be-Ereẓ-Yisrael, Ḥaderah ha-Ovedet-le-Yovlah 1891–1941* (1941).

[S.H.]

ḤAD GADYA (Aram. חַד גַּדְיָא; "An Only Kid"), initial phrase and name of a popular Aramaic song chanted at the conclusion of the Passover **seder.* Composed of ten stanzas, the verse runs as follows: A father bought a kid for two *zuzim;* a cat came and ate the kid; a dog then bit the cat; the dog was beaten by a stick; the stick was burned by fire; water quenched the fire; an ox drank the water; a *shoḥet* slaughtered the ox; the *shoḥet* was killed by the Angel of Death who in punishment was destroyed by God. Each stanza repeats the previous verses closing with the refrain: *"ḥad gadya," "ḥad gadya."* Jewish commentators have invested *Ḥad Gadya* with a hidden allegorical meaning in which the kid symbolizes the oppressed Jewish people. It was bought by the father (God) for two coins (Moses and Aaron). The devouring cat stands for Assyria; the dog is Babylon; the stick represents Persia; the fire Macedonia; the water is Rome; the ox, the Saracens; the *shoḥet,* the Crusaders; and the Angel of Death, the Turks who in those days ruled Palestine. The end of the song expresses the hope for messianic redemption: God destroys the foreign rulers of the Holy Land and vindicates Israel "the only kid." Other commentators have tried to interpret *Ḥad Gadya* as an allegorization of the *Joseph legend or of the relationship between body and soul as reflected in Jewish mysticism. The best-known Jewish interpretations of *Ḥad Gadya* are: (1) *Kerem Ein Gedi,* by Judah b. Mordecai Horowitz (Koenigsberg, 1764); (2) a commentary by Jonathan *Eybeschuetz (Neubauer Cat Bodl. 1 (1886), no. 2246); (3) two commentaries by the Gaon of Vilna (e.g., in the *Haggadah Migdal Eder,* Vilna, 1923); (4) and a commentary by R. Moses *Sofer *(ibid.).* Most scholars agree, however, that the song was borrowed from a German folk song of the Hobelbanklied type *("Der Herr der schickt den Jokel aus")* which, in turn, is based on an old French

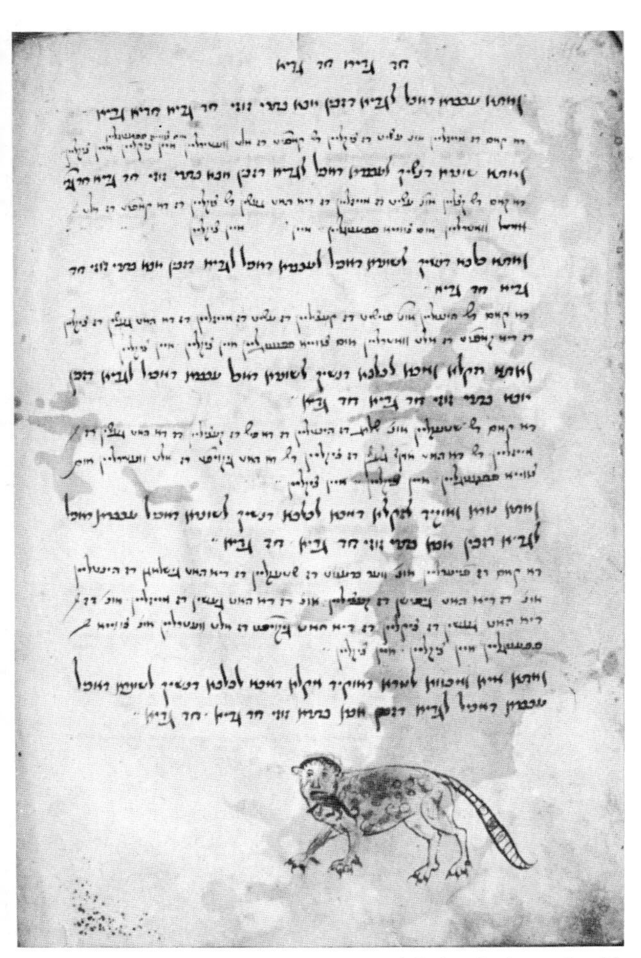

Figure 1. Part of the text of the song *Ḥad Gadya*, in Aramaic with a Yiddish translation, from the *Sereni Haggadah*, Italy, 15th century. Jerusalem, The Italian Synagogue. Photo Rolf M. Kneller, Jerusalem.

nursery song. Joseph *Jacobs (in notes to his "English Fairy Tales," London, 1893) points to the analogy of *Ḥad Gadya* with Don Quixote and with certain Persian and Indian poems. The riddle of the motif and meaning of *Ḥad Gadya* was also dealt with by Christian writers, notably by Hermann von der Hardt, in his *Ḥad Gadia Historia Universalis Judaeorum in aenigmate* (Helmstadt n.d.) and also by J. C. *Wagenseil, and by J. C. G. *Bodenschatz. The song seems to have originated in the 16th century and appears for the first time in a *Haggadah* printed in Prague (1590). It was never part of the Sephardi and the Yemenite rituals. It was incorporated into the **Haggadah* (like the other concluding songs, see: "**Eḥad Mi Yode'a*") for the amusement of the children so that they might not fall asleep before the end of the *seder*.

Figure 2. Pewter plate for Passover, with figures illustrating *Ḥad Gadya*, Germany, 18th century. Ardmore, Pa., Sigmund Harrison Collection.

Bibliography: Kohler, in: ZGDJ, 3 (1889), 234–6; D. Goldschmidt, *Haggadah shel Pesaḥ, Mekoroteha ve-Toledoteha* (1960), 96–98; M. Kasher, *Haggadah Shelemah* (1961), 190f.; A. M. Habermann, in: *Maḥanayim*, 55 (1961), 140–3; D. Sadan, *ibid.*, 144–50; For detailed bibl. see Kohut, in: JE, 6 (1904), 128, and Davidson, Oẓar, 2 (1929), 224 no. 39.

[ED.]

Figure 3. Woodcut illustrations for *Ḥad Gadya* for the *Haggadah* by Jacob Steinhardt, 1923. Jerusalem, B. M. Ansbacher Collection.

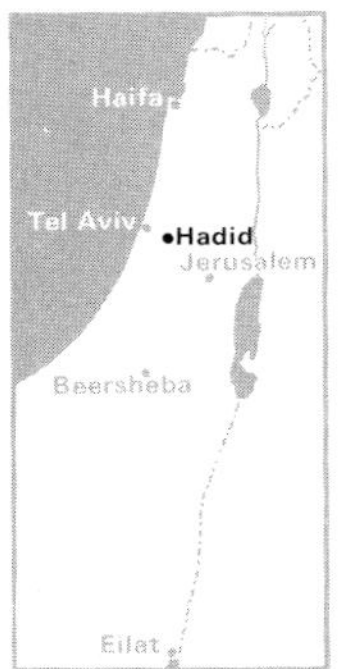

HADID (Heb. חָדִיד), city in the northern Shephelah, in the western part of the territory of *Benjamin. It is mentioned together with *Lydda and *Ono among the cities to which the Babylonian exiles returned (Ezra 2:33; Neh. 7:37; 11:34). The city had strategic importance; it was fortified by the Hasmonean *Simeon who camped nearby during Tryphon's invasion (I Macc. 12:38; 13:13—Adida). The battle between the Nabatean King Aretas and Alexander *Yannai took place near Hadid, and Vespasian later conquered it (Jos., Ant. 13:392; Wars 4:486). According to the Mishnah, it was already fortified in Joshua's time (Ar. 9:6). Eusebius describes it as being east of Lydda (Onom. 24:24—Aditha) and it also appears on the *Madaba Map (no. 59). A mosaic pavement with figurative nilotic scenes was found there in 1940. The ancient town was situated on a hill northwest of the abandoned Arab village of al-Ḥadītha, $3\frac{1}{2}$ mi. (6 km.) east of Lydda. In 1951, 60 Yemenite immigrant families founded a settlement called Ḥadid near the village.

Bibliography: Yeivin, in: *Eretz Israel*, 3 (1954), 35; Avi-Yonah, *ibid.*, 2 (1953), 49; Alt, in: PJB, 24 (1928), 71–72; M. Noth, *Das Buch Joshua* (1938), 93ff.; Abel, in: RB, 35 (1926), 218; Beyer, in: ZDPV, 56 (1933), 233.

[M.A.-Y.]

HADITH, the Islamic tradition, i.e., the *sunna* (actions, sayings, virtues, opinions, and ways of life of *Muhammad). The hadith is one of the four fundamentals which form the background of *fiqh* (Islamic jurisprudence). It encompasses all the relationships between man and God and between man and man including methods of prayer, fasting, pilgrimage, marital laws, and commercial affairs. The believer must be acquainted with the *sunna* of the Prophet and model his life in accordance with it; any deviation from the traditional path is a *bid'a* ("a harmful innovation").

The first to hand down the hadith were the companions *(ṣaḥāba)* of Muhammad, who followed the course of Muhammad's life and heeded his words. After his death, masses of believers went to the companions in order to hear the *sunna* of the Prophet. The men of the second generation continued to propagate the tradition which they had received from the *ṣaḥāba*, handing it down to their followers. Thus, a chain of traditionalists was formed, of the *isnād* ("support"), which preceded the texts *(matn)* themselves or the main part (of the teaching). At first, the hadith was handed down orally. A few of the traditionalists, however, wrote down the traditions for their personal use; these lists (*ṣaḥīfa*, "sheet") aided subsequent traditionalists, as well as the editors of the hadith. The editing of collections of the hadith began at the end of the Umayyad period; the editors adopted two different methods: *musnad*, the classification of traditions according to the names of the traditionists and *muṣannaf*, their classification according to subject, and edited according to the content. The oldest extant documents are a fragment on papyrus of the *ṣaḥīfa* by Ibn Lahī'a (d. 790), found in Egypt and containing traditions which are mainly of an eschatological nature; the collection by Mālik ibn Anas (d. 795), *al-Muwaṭṭa*, a section of the collection of Abdallah ibn Wahb (d. 812), also written on papyrus, which contains the sayings of the Prophet, the first caliphs, and the men of the second generation, mainly on ways of behavior and virtues; and the *musnad* of Aḥmad ibn *Ḥanbal, which contains about 30,000 hadiths.

From the beginning of Islam the believers attributed great importance to the hadiths as complementary and explanatory material to the Koran. The principle that certain traditions of the Prophet were nullified by later sayings of the Prophet was accepted; many works were written on the subject. The most eminent Muslim scholars dedicated their efforts to the clarification of the unusual words which are found in the hadith.

The struggle between social movements, political parties, and various religious trends within Islam gave rise to an abundance of hadiths which were attributed to the Prophet. Some contradicted others, thus confusing the Muslim scholars of tradition. A special science was established which is concerned with meticulous investigation into the reliability of the men of the *isnād*, as to character, talent, propriety, and ideological attachment to the various social and political groups. The hadiths were classified as "genuine" (*ṣaḥīḥ*, the best category), "fair" (*ḥasan*, the middle category), and "weak" *(ḍa'īf)* and were divided accurately and systematically according to their frequency, the number of authorities in the *isnād*, the relationship which existed between them (oral or written tradition), etc. During the ninth century six collections of hadiths (*muṣannaf*, see above) were written and accepted as reliable by Muslims: al-Bukhāri (d. 870), Muslim (d. 875), Abu Dā'ūd (d. 888), al-Tirmidhī (d. 892), al-Nasā'ī (d. 915), and Ibn Māja (d. 886). The works of al-Bukhāri and Muslim were particularly esteemed; the former contains 7,275 hadiths selected by the author from about 200,000 hadiths after a most meticulous examination. In the course of time many collections of hadiths were compiled; some are more comprehensive but as esteemed as the six aforesaid works, which have been edited and commented upon in detail by Muslim scholars. The great interest in the hadith gave rise to a special movement of "searchers of knowledge" *(ṭullūb al-'ilm)*, who wandered around the world in search of the scholars of the hadith in order to listen to their teachings. The influence of Judaism on the development of the *ḥadith* is evident not only in their content (see **Qiṣaṣal-Aubiya* ("The Legends of the Prophets") and *Bible in Islam) but also in the form in which they have been handed down. There is a striking similarity between the *isnād* and the chain of masoretes in tannaitic and amoraic literature in the *halakhah* and the *aggadah* (cf. also the concept of "a ruling received by Moses at Sinai" and the opening of the tractate *Avot:* "Moses received the Torah at Sinai and handed it down to Joshua, Joshua to the Elders, the Elders to the prophets, . . ."). Judaism has also influenced the hadiths which deal with the daily conduct of man, man's relationship to God, ethics, piety, various customs, as well as legal affairs, marital laws, and rites. The influence of Christianity on the hadith is not as apparent.

Bibliography: I. Goldziher, *Muhammedanische Studien*, 2 (1890), 1–274; idem. *Vorlesungen ueber den Islam* (1925[2]); A. J. Wensinck, *Handbook of Early Mohammedan Tradition* (1927); S. Bialoblocki, *Materialien zum islamischen und juedischen Eherecht* (1928), 3–19; H. Lammens, *L'Islam* (1941[2]), 87–107; E. I. J. Rosenthal, *Judaism and Islam* (1961), index.

[M.I.K./H.Z.H.]

HADRACH (חַדְרָךְ), city in Syria. Its identification is established by the biblical reference to the "land of Hadrach" in context with Damascus, Hamath, Tyre, and Sidon (Zech. 9:1). Some scholars also emend Ezekiel's description of the country's northern border from "the way of [Heb. *ha-derekh*] Hethlon" to "Hadrach-Hethlon," and accordingly locate it between the Mediterranean and Zedad (Ezek. 47:15). The city Hazrak is mentioned in an inscription of Zakir, king of Hamath and Luʿat (Lʿs; c. 780 B.C.E.), who captured the city and resisted its invasion by a coalition of kings from northern Syria and southern Anatolia. In the eighth century, the Assyrians stormed the city three times before Tiglath-Pileser III succeeded in conquering it in c. 738 B.C.E. He reduced it to an Assyrian province, bearing its name; an Assyrian governor is still found there in 689 B.C.E.

Since Hadrach appears in Assyrian documents together with Mt. Saua (apparently Mt. al-Zāwiya), scholars locate the land of Hadrach between the valley of Unqi (Antiochia) in the north, Hamath in the south, and the Orontes in the west. The location of the city Hadrach, however, is disputed; it is most likely Kharake, near Mu'arat e-Nu'aman.

A note from R. Joseph b. Dormaskit to R. Judah indicates that in talmudic times Hadrach was thought to be located in the vicinity of Damascus (Sif. Deut. 1). In the Middle Ages, the seat of Gaon Solomon b. Elijah and his yeshivah was called Hadrach; this is possibly the city Javbar, two miles (3 km.) northeast of Damascus, where remains of an ancient synagogue have been found. Hadrach was still mentioned by the travelers of the sixteenth and seventeenth centuries, as the place where the "Synagogue of the Prophet Elijah" whose ruins subsist to this day, was situated.

Bibliography: M. Noth, in: ZDPV, 52 (1929), 124–41; A. Dupont-Sommer, *Les Araméens* (1949), 51, 55, 62 f.; Mann, Texts, 2 (1935), 230 n. 215; A. Malamat, in: *Eretz Israel*, 1 (1951), 81ff.; B. Z. Luria, *Ha-Yehudim be-Suryah* (1957), 214, 243; I. Ben-Zvi, *She'ar Yashuv* (1965), 484ff.; Luckenbill, Records, index.

[M.A.-Y.]

HADRAMAUT (Hadhramaut, Hadramawt), region on S. coast of the Arabian Peninsula; politically refers to the Hadramaut states. For the history of its Jewish population see *Ḥabbān; *South Arabia. [Ed.]

HADRAN (Heb. הַדְרָן; Aram. "we returned"), a term indicating both the celebration held on the completion of the study of a tractate of the Talmud *(siyyum)* and the type of discourse delivered on that occasion. The origin of the term is the formula found at the end of the chapters of the tractates of the Talmud—"*hadran alakh* chapter so-and-so" (at a later date the words "*ve-hadrakh alan*" were added). Two explanations of the term have been given: "We shall return to thee"; and indicating "beauty" or "splendor," a form of farewell salutation to the tractate comparable to "Homage to thee, O Altar!" (Suk. 4:5, see Lieberman, in: *Alei Ayin, Minḥat Devarim . . . S. Schocken* (1948–52), 81 n.33). The celebration and feasting held on such an occasion are mentioned in the Talmud (Shab. 118b–119a) and it is laid down that the meal ranks as a religious one (Sh. Ar., YD 246:26). As a result it can exempt a person from the obligation of fasting, as for instance on the Fast of the *Firstborn on the eve of Passover (*Mishnah Berurah*, OḤ 470:10), or exempt those who have adopted the custom of fasting on the anniversary of their parents' death. On it one may partake of meat and wine during the days of mourning between the First of *Av until the Ninth of Av (Isserles to Sh. Ar., OḤ 551:10). The essential elements of prayer recited at the conclusion of the study of a tractate (printed at the end of each tractate in most editions of the Talmud), which includes the enumeration of the ten sons of Rav Pappa as a kind of incantation, is already mentioned by *Abraham b. Isaac of Narbonne in the *Sefer ha-Eshkol* (Z. B. Auerbach's edition, 2 (1968), 49, Sefer Torah no. 14; = S. Albeck's edition, 1 (1935), 159) in the name of *Hai Gaon, who observes that they refer to scholars from different eras and that they were not all the sons of the same Rav Pappa. It also includes the expanded version of the *Kaddish de-Rabbanan*. The discourse delivered at this celebration took on a special character. By recourse to ingenious *pilpul* it aimed at connecting the end of the tractate with its beginning or with the beginning of the next tractate to be studied. A special literature of this type thus developed, which began to appear mainly at the beginning of the 18th century (the first discourse of this class is perhaps the one at the end of the novellae on *Bava Kamma* (1631) of Meir *Schiff (published Hamburg, 1747)). Because of their pilpulistic character they gave rise to opposition and criticism.

Concluding page of a tractate of the Talmud with the words "*hadran alakh . . .*" Babylonian Talmud, *Bava Meẓia*, Schulsinger edition, New York.

Bibliography: J. Widler, *Hadar Yiẓḥak* (1940); S. K. Mirsky, *Siyyumei ha-Massekhtot ba-Mishnah u-va-Talmud ha-Bavli* (1961); Preshel, *ibid.*, 265–94 (listing 282 *hadranim*); Leiter, in: *Sinai*, 33 (1953), 56–61; Margaliot, in: *Ba-Mishor*, 7 (1945), 8 no. 277; Y. Z. Stern, in: TB, Ber. 236 (Third pagination).

[S.Z.H.]

°**HADRIAN, PUBLIUS AELIUS,** Roman emperor, 117–138 C.E. According to all the indications, Hadrian did not entertain any hostility toward the Jews at the beginning of his reign. On the contrary, it would appear that the Jews hoped for an improvement in their situation. Hadrian's first act, the execution of Lusius *Quietus, the governor of Judea, certainly appealed to the Jews. There is apparently an echo of the hopes raised by Hadrian's accession in the *Sibylline Oracles, which state that the man whose name is like that of the sea (H–adrian–Adriatic) will act favorably toward the Jews (5:46–50). There may also have been contacts between the Jews and the Roman government. Although there is no explicit information to that effect, it would appear that rumors began to spread that the Temple was to be rebuilt (cf. Gen. R. 64:10), but nothing practical resulted. It is not certain whether Hadrian issued decrees against Jewish observance before the *Bar-Kokhba War (132–135). One opinion holds that the Jews were affected, even if unintentionally, by a decree issued by Hadrian forbidding castration, which was interpreted as including a prohibition of circumcision. Others reject any connection between this decree and circumcision, and are of the opinion that the decrees against circumcision and other observances were enacted after the war.

The emperor also decided to erect a gentile city on the site of destroyed Jerusalem to be named *Aelia Capitolina after himself. According to Dio Cassius this decision was made about two years before the Bar-Kokhba War and it is regarded by many as one of the chief causes of the Jewish revolt, even though the project was implemented only after the revolt had been crushed. Hadrian frequently visited parts of the empire. He visited Judea in 130 C.E., but there is no knowledge of any contact between him and the Jews during this visit, although in talmudic literature many conversations of Hadrian with R. *Joshua b. Ḥananiah are reported. According to those who date Hadrian's anti-Jewish decrees, especially with regard to Aelia Capitolina, before the revolt, the visit resulted in fanning the flames of discontent. A reference to the visit has been preserved in a coin which shows the province of Judea, in the guise of a woman, greeting the emperor on his arrival. It should be borne in mind, however, that the official view represented on the coin in no way reflects the attitude of the Jews. From Judea Hadrian proceeded to Egypt, returning in 131. During his sojourn in Judea and the neighboring countries

Reverse of a coin of the Emperor Hadrian, with a woman representing the province of Judea, at the right of the altar, greeting the emperor. First century C.E. London, British Museum.

the Jews outwardly kept the peace, but in 132 the revolt broke out in full force. Despite some initial successes of the rebels, Hadrian's commander, Julius Severus, succeeded eventually in crushing the revolt (see *Bar Kokhba). It was then, most probably, that Hadrian issued the harsh restrictive edicts against the study of the Torah and the practice of Judaism, including circumcision, making their observance capital offenses. Presumably it was in the subsequent persecutions that R. *Akiva and other rabbis were martyred (see the Ten *Martyrs). It was then also that Aelia Capitolina was constructed on the ruins of Jerusalem. A temple to Jupiter Capitolinus and an equestrian statue of the emperor were erected on the site of the Temple. These edicts of Hadrian remained in force until the time of his heir, Antoninus Pius, and in cruelty and scope they recall the decrees of Antiochus 300 years earlier. Hadrian's decrees give eloquent expression to the detestation felt by the emperor, "the friend of culture and enlightenment," for Judaism and his complete inability to understand it, as well as to the gulf between Judaism and the world of the Roman Empire. [U.R.]

In the Aggadah. To the rabbis, Hadrian was a symbol of wickedness and cruelty. His name is usually accompanied by the epithet "the wicked" or by the imprecation "may his bones rot" in Hebrew or Aramaic. In addition the appellation "the wicked kingdom" refers very frequently to Rome in the days of Hadrian. All manner of stories are related about the murder of Jews at the command of Hadrian after the fall of *Bethar. On the verse, "the voice is the voice of Jacob" (Gen. 27:22) R. Johanan states that it refers to the voice of Emperor Hadrian, who "killed 80,000 myriads of people in Bethar" (Gen. R. 65:21; Lam. R. 1:16; 45). Nevertheless Hadrian appears in the *aggadah* in a more genial role which tends to emphasize his contacts with Jews, both scholars and the common people. He is said to have had discussions with Joshua ben Ḥananiah on the creation of the world (Gen. R. 10:3), and on resurrection, in which there appears the legend of the **luz*, the indestructible nut (coccyx) of the spinal column (*ibid.*, 28:3). Similarly, stories are told of him walking through Ereẓ Israel before the Bar Kokhba War and conversing with farmers. One of them describes him asking a centenarian who was planting fig trees whether he expected to eat of its fruits. The old man answered that as he had found fruit trees when he was born, so he was planting them for his children. Three years later, after the war, the man presented him with a basket of figs from that planting and Hadrian filled the basket with gold pieces (Lev. R. 25:5). These stories seem to be connected with the devastation caused by the war and the subsequent restoration of the previous fertility of the land, a fact specifically mentioned in connection with the aftermath of the war (TJ, Pe'ah 7:1, 20a). [L.I.R.]

Bibliography: Weber, in: CAH, 11 (1936), 294–324. For Hadrian and the Jews, see bibliography on Bar Kokhba. IN THE AGGADAH: Ginzberg, Legends, index; M. Radin, *Jews among the Greeks and Romans* (1915), 343–4.

°**HADRIAN (Adrian) I,** pope (772–795). Under Hadrian's papacy the Second Council of Nicaea, which condemned iconoclasm, was held in 787. On several occasions when Hadrian intervened personally in the controversy over graven images, and again in letters to Empress Irene and to Charlemagne, he fulminated against the Jewish respect for the biblical command against images; finally he compared the iconoclasts—whom the Council of Nicaea eventually declared heretics—with the Jews. In several edicts attempting to regulate relations between Christians and Jews he forbade Christians to celebrate Passover with the Jews, to accept unleavened bread from the Jews, and to rest on the Sabbath "after the Jewish fashion." In a letter addressed in 794 to the bishops of Spain, Hadrian complained in passing that he had learned that "many people who claim to be Catholics live freely with Jews and unbaptized pagans, sharing both food and drink with them." He urged the bishops to see that nothing of the sort occurred again and that the regulations laid down by Church Fathers were followed.

Bibliography: B. Blumenkranz, *Les auteurs chretiens latins...* (1966), 142ff. [B.BL.]

HADUTA (also known as **Ḥedvata) BEN ABRAHAM** (c. 6th century), one of the early *paytanim* in Ereẓ Israel. His **piyyutim* form a distinct group in *piyyut* literature because of their special subject material: a series of hymns commemorating the 24 watches (**mishmarot*) of priests (cf. I Chron. 24:7–18), practiced in the time of the Second Temple. One *kerovah* is dedicated to each watch. A prayer commemorating the watches dated 1034, found in the Cairo *Genizah*, gives evidence of the custom of the Palestinian Jews, whereby on each Sabbath the name of the division belonging to that Sabbath was proclaimed. It thus emerged that Haduta's *kerovot* were not *kinot* ("dirges") for the Ninth of *Av, as had been supposed, but were recited in the Palestinian synagogues each Sabbath.

The hymns mention many details concerning the names and the dwelling places of the watches. They are thus an important source of information for research of Palestinian topography. Possibly the priests were still concentrated in certain defined localities in Haduta's time.

Haduta (הֶדְוָתָא, הֲדוּתָא) sometimes signed his name (חֲדוּתָה, חֶדְוָתָה; with ח and ה instead of ה and א), and it is unlikely that there were two or three hymnologists of the same name.

Bibliography: Epstein, in: *Tarbiz*, 12 (1940/41), 78; Habermann, in: YMḤSI, 5 (1939), 80 n.; J. H. Schirmann, *Shirim Ḥadashim min ha-Genizah* (1965), 13–22; Zulay, in: *Ginzei Kaufmann*, 1 (1949), 36–38; idem, in: *Tarbiz* 22 (1950/51), 28–42; P. Kahle, *Masoreten des Westens*, 1 (1927), texts; YMḤSI, 5 (1939), 111–20, texts. [M.Z.]

HA-EFRATI (Tropplowitz), JOSEPH (c. 1770–1804), Hebrew poet and dramatist. Born in Tropplowitz, Silesia, he was a tutor for several years, during which he wrote the first acts of *Melukhat Sha'ul* ("Saul's Kingdom"), a drama that was completed in Prague in 1793. Although many of his poems were published in the first issues of *Ha-Me'assef*, his principal work remains *Melukhat Sha'ul*. The Yiddish translation became part of the traditional **Purimshpil* ("Purim play") in many Lithuanian and Polish towns. *Melukhat Sha'ul*, the first modern Hebrew drama of the

Haskalah period, is noteworthy for its new egalitarian and humanistic ideas. Evidently influenced by Shakespeare, Goethe, Schiller, and von Haller, as well as M. Ḥ. *Luzzatto, Ha-Efrati was particularly successful in his depiction of a man in the grip of irrational forces. Yet critics have argued that the play's weakness lies in its flat characterizations of all personages except Saul. David, Jonathan, and Michal represent abstract ideas rather than lifelike characters. Ha-Efrati, however, improved upon all the numerous attempts throughout the Middle Ages to dramatize the tragedy of Saul. He portrayed the pathos of a suffering hero, ridden with envy and guilt, torn by fears and loneliness, and not merely a proud and jealous king. The drama very likely influenced J. L. *Gordon's *David u-Varzillai* and *Ahavat David u-Mikhal* (1857). Parts of a newly discovered book of Ha-Efrati's Hebrew poems were published by A. Z. Ben-Yishai (*Beḥinot,* 11 (Fall 1957), 59–71).

Bibliography: Klausner, Sifrut, 1 (1952), 193–9; J. L. Landau, *Short Lectures on Modern Hebrew Literature* (1938²), 86–95; *Melukhat Sha'ul* (1968), introd. by G. Shaked; A. Yaari, in: KS, 12 (1935/36), 384–8; Kressel, Leksikon, 2 (1967), 32–33.

[Ed.]

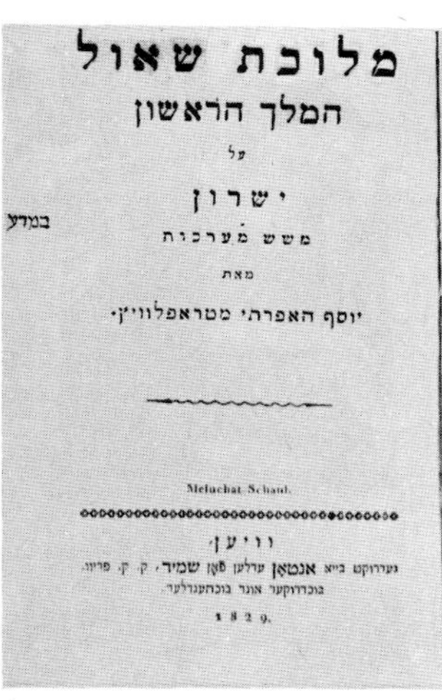

מלוכת שאול
המלך הראשון
על
ישרון
משש מערכות
מאת
יוסף האפרתי מטראפלוויין.
במדע

Meluchat Schaul.

וויען.
געדרוקט בייא אנטאן עדלען פאן שמיד, ק. ק. פריוו. בוכדרוקער אונד בוכהענדלער.
1829.

Title page and frontispiece of *Melukhat Sha'ul*, the Hebrew drama completed by Joseph Ha-Efrati in 1793. Vienna, 1829. Jerusalem, J.N.U.L.

HA-EMET (Heb. הָאֱמֶת, "The Truth"), the first Hebrew socialist periodical, published in Vienna during the summer of 1877. The idea of issuing a socialist organ for Jews originated in the revolutionary circles of Vilna. The editor and publisher (under the pseudonym Arthur Freeman) was Aaron Samuel *Liebermann. After he fled from Russia in 1875, Liebermann had at first attempted, unsuccessfully, to establish a bilingual periodical, *Ha-Pattish* ("The Hammer"), in Yiddish and in Hebrew, for both the Jewish masses and the *maskilim.* He received the support of the Jewish students' circle in Berlin, as well as Jewish revolutionaries such as Lazar *Goldenberg, Aaron *Zundelevich, and non-Jewish revolutionary leaders like P. Lavrov and V. Smirnov, editors of the periodical *Vperyod.* In its prospectus Liebermann announced that *Ha-Emet* would not concern itself with "religious and national issues" but with "the necessities of life"—"bread and work" and "the spoon and the fork question," which "took precedence over all other contemporary problems." The publication of the newspaper was motivated by "our love for our people solely in their capacity of human beings" and by a particular responsibility felt toward them "being conscious of their lives and their afflictions." As a newspaper issued legally, *Ha-Emet* maintained a cautious tone. Liebermann himself wrote almost all the aricles (which were unsigned). It included poems by J. L. *Levin (*Yahalal),* who with M. Kamyonski actively promoted the newspaper in Russia. Its agent in Galicia and Ukraine was Rabbi A. Eisner. The publication of *Ha-Emet* provoked wide controversy in the Jewish press. The newspaper closed down after three issues through lack of funds and the prohibition on its entry into Russia. Its direct successor was **Asefat Ḥakhamim,* whose editor M. *Winchevsky was influenced by Liebermann. Photographic editions of *Ha-Emet* were published by Ẓ. Krol with appendixes (1938), and in Jerusalem (1967).

[M.M.]

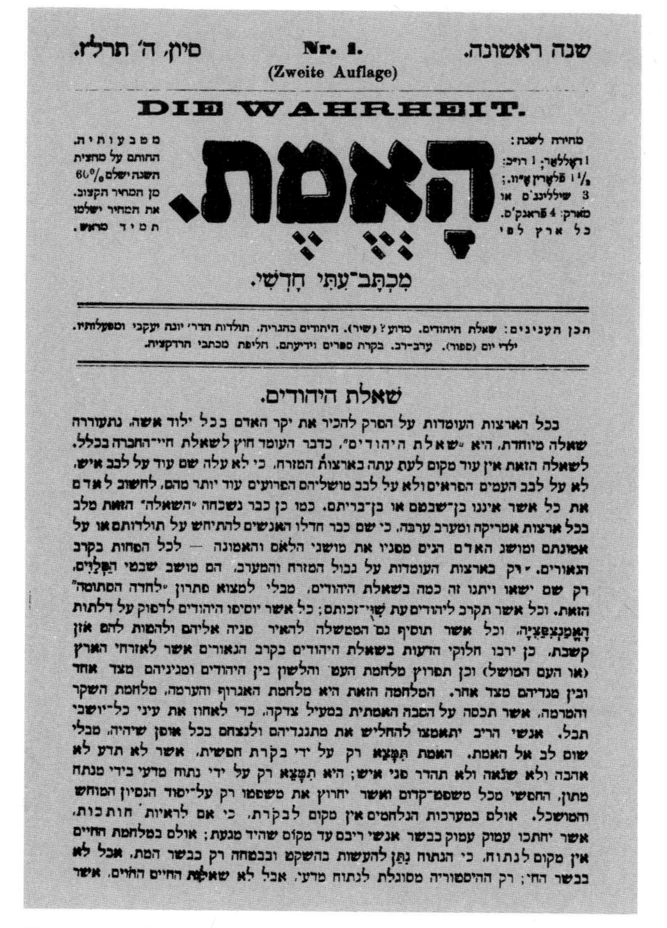

שנה ראשונה. Nr. 1. סיון, ה׳ תרלז.
(Zweite Auflage)

DIE WAHRHEIT.

מחירה לשנה:
1 ראללער; 1 רויכ:
1½ פלארין ע״וו.;
3 שיללינג׳ס או
מארק: 4 פראנק׳ס.
כל ארץ לפי

הָאֱמֶת.

מסבעותית.
התותם על מחצית
השנה ישלם 60%
מן המחיר הקצוב.
את המחיר ישלמו
תמיד מראש.

מִכְתָּב־עִתִּי חָדְשִׁי.

תכן הענינים: שאלת היהודים. מדוע? (שיר). היהודים בהגריה. תולדות הדר׳ יונה יעקבי ומפעלותיו. ילדי יום (ספור). ערב־רב. בקרת ספרים וידיעתם. חליפת מכתבי הרדקציה.

שאלת היהודים.

בכל הארצות העומדות על הפרק להכיר את יקר האדם בכל ילוד אשה, נתעוררה שאלה מיוחדת, היא „שאלת היהודים", כדבר העומד חוץ לשאלת חיי־החברה בכלל. לשאלה הזאת אין עוד מקום לעת עתה בארצות המזרח, כי לא עלה שם עוד על לבב איש, לא על לבב העמים הפראים ולא על לבב מושליהם הפרועים עוד יותר מהם, לחשוב לאדם את כל אשר איננו בן־שבטם או בן־בריתם. כמו כן כבר נשכחה „השאלה" הזאת מלב בכל ארצות אמריקה ומערב ערבה, כי שם כבר חדלו האנשים להתיחש על תולדותם או על אמונתם ומושג האדם הנים מפניו את מושגי הלאם והאמונה — לכל הפחות בקרב הנאורים. „רק בארצות העומדות על גבול המזרח והמערב, הם מושב שבטי הַפְּלָיִים, רק שם ישאו ויתנו זה כמה בשאלת היהודים, מבלי למצוא פתרון „לחדה הסתומה" הזאת. וכל אשר תקרב ליהודים עת שָׁוֶי־זכותם; כל אשר יוסיפו היהודים לדפוק על דלתות הָאֱמַנְצִפַּצְיָה, וכל אשר תוסיף גם הממשלה להאיר פניה אליהם ולהטות להם אזן קשבת, כן ירבו חלוקי הדעות בשאלת היהודים בקרב הנאורים אשר לאזרחי הארץ (או העם המושל) וכן תפרוץ מלחמת העט והלשון בין היהודים ומגיניהם מצד אחד ובין מנגדיהם מצד אחר. המלחמה הזאת היא מלחמת האגרוף והערמה, מלחמת השקר והמרמה, אשר תכסה על הסבה האמתית במעיל צדקה, כדי לאחוז את עיני כל־יושבי תבל. אנשי הריב יתאמצו להחליש את מתנגדיהם ולנצחם בכל אופן שיהיה, מבלי שום לב אל האמת. האמת תִּמָּצֵא רק על ידי בקרת חפשית, אשר לא תדע לא אהבה ולא שנאה ולא תהדר פני איש; היא תִּמָּצֵא רק על ידי נתוח מדעי בידי מנתח מתון, החפשי מכל משפט־קדום ואשר יחרוץ את משפטו רק על־יסוד הנסיון המוחש והמושכל. אולם במערכות הנלחמים אין מקום לבקרת, כי אם לראיות חותכות, אשר יחתכו עמוק עמוק בבשר אנשי ריבם עד מקום שהיד מגעת; אולם במלחמת החיים אין מקום לנתוח, כי הנתוח נִתָּן להעשות בהשקט ובבטחה רק בבשר המת, אבל לא בבשר החי; רק ההיסטוריה מסוגלת לנתוח מדעי, אבל לא שאלת החיים החיים, אשר

Front page of the first issue of *Ha-Emet,* the first Hebrew socialist periodical, Vienna, Sivan, 5637 (1877). Jerusalem, J.N.U.L.

HAETZYONI, YEHUDAH (1868–1938), Zionist in Germany and an aide of *Herzl. Haetzyoni was born in Jerusalem, but upon his father's death, his mother remarried and took him along with her to Vienna, where he studied medicine. In 1896, when the first exhibition of Ereẓ Israel products was opened in Berlin, he became its chief propagandist, accompanying the exhibition on a tour of Germany and urging the Jews to settle in Ereẓ Israel. After the pre-publication of a synopsis of Herzl's *Der Judenstaat* Haetzyoni wrote an article in *Zion* (vol. 2, 1896), a periodical published by W. *Bambus, in which he emphasized the importance of Ereẓ Israel as the territory for the future Jewish state and of the revival of the Hebrew language. Herzl reacted to Haetzyoni's article in a letter (dated Feb. 7, 1896), in which he addressed Haetzyoni as "old friend," and enclosed galley proofs of *Der Judenstaat.* At this stage Haetzyoni's Zionist activities ceased. He moved to Marrakesh, Morocco, and became physician to the sultan and the German legation. Haetzyoni published descriptions of Moroccan Jewry in *Ha-Meliẓ.* After World

War I he settled in Lithuania, where he taught at Jewish high schools in Vilkaviskis and Ukmerge (Vilkomir). He died in a home for the aged in Kaunas. His reminiscences of the birth of Zionism and his meetings with Herzl were published in *Ha-Olam* (Feb. 25, 1932) and *Hed Lita* (15 (1924), 15–16).

Bibliography: *Be-Misholei ha-Ḥinnukh* (Kaunas, Dec. 1938), 24–27. [G.K.]

HAEZRAHI (originally **Brisker**), **YEHUDA** (1920–), Hebrew novelist and playwright. Born in Jerusalem, he served in the British Army during World War II. He wrote several novels and plays, as well as numerous articles and sketches. Haezraḥi's works include: *Ke-Ẓel Over* (1946), a novel; *Ananim ba-Sa'ar* (1947), a collection of stories; *Im Shaḥar* (1959), two novellas; a collection of three plays (1960)—*Ha-Te'omim, Ha-Mishtammet,* and *Ha-Seruv;* a novel, *Panim u-Massekhah* (1963); *Beit ha-Sefarim ha-Le'ummi ve-ha-Universita'i* (1967), a history of the national library at the Hebrew University; and *Ir Even ve-Shamayim* (1968), a belletristic description of Jerusalem. He edited albums of the paintings of *Alva (1954), Nahum *Gutman (1965), and Yossi *Stern (1965). (A list of his works translated into English appears in Goell, Bibliography, 67.)

His wife, Pepita Haezrahi (1921–1963), taught philosophy at the Hebrew University of Jerusalem. She published works in English and in Hebrew in the fields of philosophy, aesthetics, and ethics.

Bibliography: M. Avishai, *Bein ha-Olamot* (1962), 157–73; A. Cohen, *Soferim Ivriyyim Benei Zemannenu* (1964), 109–18; Kressel, Leksikon, 1 (1965), 58. [G.K.]

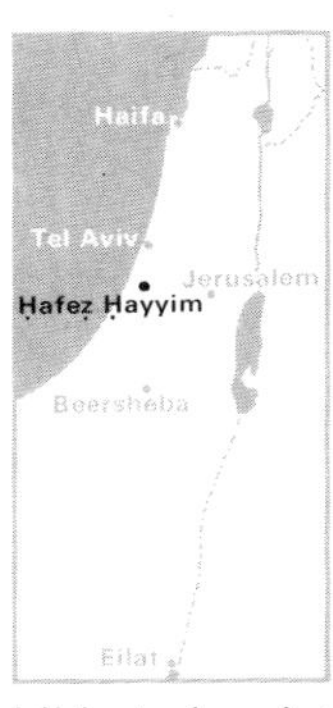

ḤAFEẒ ḤAYYIM (Heb. חָפֵץ חַיִּים), kibbutz in the southern Coastal Plain of Israel, 3 mi. (5 km.) S.E. of Gederah, affiliated with *Po'alei Agudat Israel. In 1937 Ha-Kibbutz ha-Me'uḥad members founded a village there, Sha'ar ha-Negev, but later moved north to establish their permanent settlement, *Kefar Szold. Afterward an Orthodox group, graduates of the Ezra youth movement in Germany, who previously worked on land near *Afulah, took over the site (1944). The kibbutz has intensive farming and also developed hydroponics to permit the literal observance of the **shemittah* precepts. Ḥafeẓ Ḥayyim runs a guest house and recreation home. The kibbutz is named after Rabbi *Israel Meir ha-Kohen (Ḥafeẓ Ḥayyim). In 1968 its population was 360. [E.O.]

Working in hydroponics at kibbutz Ḥafeẓ Ḥayyim during the sabbatical year, *shemittah,* 1959. Courtesy Keren Hayesod, United Israel Appeal, Jerusalem.

HAFFKINE, WALDEMAR MORDECAI (1860–1930), bacteriologist. Born and educated in Odessa Haffkine studied under the Nobel prizewinner Elie *Metchnikoff. He was offered a teaching post provided he converted to the Russian Orthodox Church, which he refused to do. Invited in 1889 by Metchnikoff, then at the Pasteur Institute, Paris, to become its librarian, he was later made assistant to the director. In 1892 Haffkine developed the first effective vaccine against cholera. Lord Dufferin, British ambassador to France, formerly viceroy in India, persuaded him to substitute India for Siam as the field-test area to combat cholera. In 1893, with a group of doctors and laboratory workers, Haffkine went through India inoculating, with excellent results, villagers who had volunteered for treatment. In 1896, when plague struck Bombay, the government sent him there to develop a vaccine against the plague. He succeeded within three months. Germany, Russia, China, and France sent scientists to study his methods and demands for his vaccine flooded his laboratory. In 1897, Queen Victoria named him Companion of the Order of the Indian Empire and in 1899 he was granted British citizenship.

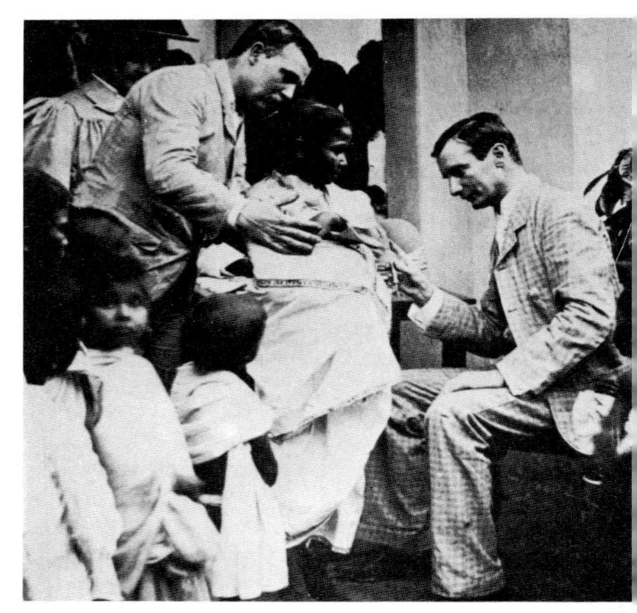

Figure 1. Waldemar Haffkine, seated, inoculating school children during a cholera epidemic in Bengal, 1896. Courtesy Edythe Lutzker, New York.

In 1902 plague struck the Punjab, which received large quantities of vaccine. Nineteen of the tens of thousands inoculated contracted tetanus and died. Haffkine was charged with sending contaminated vaccine. An inquiry was launched as a result of which Haffkine was suspended and his pay forfeited. In 1904 he presented evidence in his defense at the Lister Institute, London, and the Pasteur Institute. Although Haffkine defended himself in the official inquiry and, subsequently, in scientific circles, it was only after the *London Times,* on July 29, 1907, published a long scientific defense of Haffkine that the Government exonerated him. Haffkine returned to Calcutta with neither the promotion nor the salary increase he had been promised, to continue laboratory research until compulsory retirement at the age of 55.

Later Haffkine settled in Paris, where he participated actively in various Jewish organizations' efforts to create an independent Jewish state in Palestine. In 1919, with others, he presented a petition to the Peace Conference in Versailles, stressing minority rights for Jews in Eastern Europe.

Figure 2. First day cover and stamp in memory of Waldemar Haffkine, issued by the Indian Post Office in 1964. Courtesy Edythe Lutzker, New York.

In 1925 the Plague Research Laboratory he had founded in Bombay was renamed the Haffkine Institute in his honor. An observant Jew most of his life, in 1929 he created the Haffkine Foundation in Lausanne, bequeathing to it his fortune of $500,000, and stipulating that the interest be used to foster religious, scientific, and vocational education in yeshivot in Eastern Europe.

Bibliography: S. A. Waksman, *Brilliant and Tragic Life of W. M. W. Haffkine, Bacteriologist* (1964), incl. bibl.; M. A. Popovsky, *Fate of Dr. Haffkine* (1963); E. Lutzker, in: *Actes du XIe Congrès International d'Histoire des Sciences* (1965), 214–9, (Eng.) incl. bib.; idem, in: *Acts of the XXIst International Congress of the History of Medicine* (1968); M. Einhorn, in: *Harofé Haivri*, 38 (1965), 362–334 (Eng.).

[ED.L.]

HAFKA'AT SHE'ARIM (Heb. הַפְקָעַת שְׁעָרִים), raising the price of a commodity beyond the accepted level, or that fixed by a competent authority.

Profiteering and Overreaching. The law of *Hafka'at She'arim* ("profiteering") is analogous to that of overreaching (**ona'ah*, "misrepresentation"), it being the object of the law in both cases to preserve a fair and just price. However, the law of overreaching—fraudulent or innocent (i.e., mistaken)—stems from a biblical prohibition (Lev. 25:14): the law was fixed that if the price exceeded the value by one-sixth, the seller must return this part to the purchaser; if the price was higher yet, the purchaser might demand cancellation of the transaction; conversely, if the price was too low, the law applies *mutatis mutandis* in favor of the seller. The law of profiteering on the other hand has its source in rabbinic enactment designed to prohibit the setting of prices in excess of the customarily accepted ones, even if the purchaser is aware of and agrees to the inflated price; ". . . even when he [the seller] says 'it cost me one *sela* and I want to earn two on it,' he has not transgressed the law of *ona'ah* but he is prohibited by rabbinic enactment from making a profit of more than one-sixth in essential commodities" (*Beit ha-Beḥirah*, BM 51b).

Price-fixing and Control; Prohibition against Profiteering. It would seem that in the mishnaic period there were fixed prices, apparently determined by a competent authority (BM 4:12, 5:7). There is evidence that in Jerusalem—prior to the destruction of the Temple—the market commissioners "did not supervise prices but measures only" (Tosef., BM 6:14); in Babylonia (at the commencement of the third century C.E.) there was supervision of prices at the instance of the *exilarch (TJ, BB 5:11, 15a; TB, BB 89a). The sages of that period were divided, however, on this matter. Some expressed the opinion that "price inspectors do not need to be appointed" and that competition between merchants would suffice to stabilize the price while others were of the opinion that it was incumbent on the court to supervise the prices because of the "swindlers" who hoarded commodities toward a time when they might be in short supply in order to sell them at a high price (TJ and TB, BB 89a). In the course of time the view favoring price supervision apparently became generally accepted (BB 89a; Yoma 9a) and thus it was decided in the codes: "but the court is obliged to determine prices and to appoint commissioners for this purpose, to prevent everyone from charging what he likes . . ." (Yad, Mekhirah 14:1; Tur and Sh. Ar., ḤM 231:20).

The scholars compared profiteering to the transgressions of "giving short measure of the ephah" (deceit with regard to *weights and measures) and to that of charging interest on loans (BB 90b; and see *Usury). In their opinion, the profiteer transgresses the biblical injunction "that thy brother may live with thee" (Lev. 25:36; *Sma* ḤM 231:43) and they regarded profiteers as "bandits who prey on the poor . . . on whom they concentrate their attention" (Meg. 17b and Rashi, *ibid.*). The prescribed punishment for them: "flagellation and they are compelled to sell at the market price" (Yad, Genevah, 8:20; Tur and Sh. Ar., ḤM 231:21). Authority to determine prices was given not only to the court, but also to local communal representatives: "and the townspeople are authorized to fix prices" (of wheat and wine, so as to maintain the price in a particular year—Rashi) "and measures and workers' wages, which they may enforce by means of punishment" (i.e., fines; cf. BB 89a and Rashi; Tosef. BM 11:23; BB 8b; see also **takkanot ha-Kahal*). It appears that already in the talmudic period, the law of profiteering was only applied to essential commodities such as wheat, oil, and wine, and this was confirmed in the codes: "prices [of nonessentials] are not determined but everyone may charge what he likes" (Yad, Mekhirah 14:2 and standard commentaries ad loc.; Tur and Sh. Ar., ḤM 231:20).

The maximum profit generally permitted to the seller was one-sixth (BB 90a). Some of the authorities took the view that this rate applied to one selling his merchandise in bulk, without toil (a wholesaler); a shopkeeper, however, "selling his merchandise little by little, might have his toil and overheads accounted for in addition to a profit of one-sixth" (Tur and Sh. Ar., ḤM 231:20). They also decided that the rules concerning profiteering were only to take effect if imposed as measures of general application to all vendors, otherwise the individual could not be obliged to adhere to the permitted maximum rate of profit *(ibid)*.

Stringent Supervision in Ereẓ Israel. Particular care was taken to maintain a cheap supply of essential products in Ereẓ Israel, where no middleman between producer and consumer was tolerated: "it is forbidden to speculate in essential commodities in Ereẓ Israel but everyone shall bring from his barn and sell so that these [commodities] may be sold cheaply" (Tosef. Av. Zar. 4:1; BB 91a, Yad, Mekhirah 14:4; Sh. Ar. ḤM 231:23); however, it was decided that in the case of a commodity in free supply or where a middleman worked to prepare and process the product, such as baking bread from wheat, profit-making was permitted, even in Ereẓ Israel (Tosef. Av. Zar. 4:1; BB 91a and *Rashbam*, *Yad Ramah* and *Beit ha-Beḥirah ibid;* Yad, Mekhirah 14:4; Sh. Ar., ḤM 231:23).

Measures to Prevent Profiteering. The sages sought in various ways to eliminate the factors which made for a climate for profiteering. Thus it was forbidden to hoard produce bought on the market, lest this cause prices to rise and bring losses to the poor, and in a year of famine no hoarding at all was permitted (not as much as a "cab of carobs"), not even of the produce harvested from one's own field (BB 90b; Yad, Mekhirah 14:5–7). In later *halakhah* storing of produce from the producer's own field was permitted, even in a famine year, for the sustenance of his family (Tur., ḤM 231:29) for a period of one year (Sh. Ar., ḤM 231:24). Produce hoarders, like profiteers, were compared to those who charged interest on loans (BB, 90b). In order to prevent profiteeing, it was not permitted to export essential products from Ereẓ Israel, since this might cause a shortage and a consequent rise in prices (BB 90b–91a, Yad, Mekhirah 14:8; Sh. Ar., ḤM 231:26). With the same object in mind the rabbis laid down that the proclamation of a public fast (on account of drought) should not be announced for the first time on a Thursday as this would cause panic (out of fear of famine) at a time when everyone was preparing for the Sabbath, and this might lead to profiteering (Ta'an. 2:9).

In their war against profiteers the scholars made use of a deliberate *interpretation of the law. At a time when the numerous sacrifices required to be brought by a woman who had given birth caused the price of a pair of sacrificial birds (two doves) to be raised to a golden dinar (25 silver dinars), Simeon b. Gamaliel the Elder vowed: "I shall not sleep this night until a pair sells for a dinar" (i.e., silver; Ker. 1:7). He entered the court and taught that a woman who had had five definite births (and thus should bring five sacrifices) need bring one sacrifice only and might eat of the *zevaḥim* ("sacrificial animals"), i.e. is ritually pure, and that "the remainder is not obligatory upon her; that same day the price of sacrificial birds stood at a quarter [of a silver dinar per pair]." (*ibid.*); Rashi (Ker. 8a) comments: "though he interpreted the word of the law leniently, it was a time to campaign for the Lord (*et la'asot la-shem*) for if no remedy had been found, not even one [sacrifice]would have been brought." Some 1,600 years later, when the fishmongers of Nikolsburg, Moravia, greatly raised the price of fish, "having seen that the Jews were not deterred by expensive prices from buying fish for the Sabbath," the Nikolsburg community enacted a *takkanah* which prohibited everyone from buying fish for a period of two months. Asked whether this *takkanah* did not in some measure slight the honor of the Sabbath, M. M. *Krochmal, chief rabbi of Moravia, replied that in order to enable also the poor "to honor the Sabbath by [eating] fish" it were better not to buy fish for a few Sabbaths so as to bring down the prices, and he quoted the statements of Simeon b. Gamaliel (above), as a clear practical illustration of the saying: "it is well to desecrate one Sabbath, so that many Sabbaths be observed" (*Ẓemaḥ Ẓedek*, no. 28).

In the State of Israel. In the State of Israel there are a number of laws designed to combat profiteering in essential commodities. The Commodities and Services (Control) Law, 5718–1957, provides for various means of supervision over commodities declared to be subject to control by the minister charged with implementation of the law, enforcible on pain of imprisonment, fine, and closing down of a business, etc. The Tenants' Protection Laws, 5714–1954 and 5715–1955, control maximum rentals for residential and business premises and also limit the right of ejectment to grounds specified in these laws only. These laws are supplemented by the provisions of the Key Money Law, 5718–1958. The Restrictive Trade Practices Law, 5719–1959, restricts, amongst others, the artificial manipulation of price levels at the hands of a monopoly or cartel. In the Knesset debates preceding the passing of these laws, some members relied on Jewish law in support of their arguments (*Divrei ha-Keneset* vol. 7, p. 564; vol. 14, p. 1822; vol. 18, p. 2176; vol. 21, p. 169; vols. 23, pp. 372, 374, 383; vol. 24, pp. 2478, 2514).

Bibliography: Gulak, Yesodei, 1 (1922), 64–66; P. Dickstein, in: *Ha-Mishpat ha-Ivri*, 1 (1925/26), 15–55; ET, 10 (1961), 41–49.

[M.E.]

HAFSIDS, Berber dynasty which ruled Ifrīqiyā (Tunisia) and eastern Algeria from 1228 to 1574; descendants and onetime disciples of the Almohads. The Hafsids' center was Tunis but their rule extended at times throughout Algeria, reaching the borders of Morocco. Under Hafsid rule Tunis underwent a cultural and commercial efflorescence, during which time many Jews prospered due to the increasingly close relations with Christian countries in the 13th and 14th centuries. The Jewish merchants of Tunis traded with their brethren in these countries, especially Italy. The presence in Tunis of Christian merchants, another minority group, lightened the burden of the Jews. The mid-16th century saw the advent of the Spanish and Portuguese in the Hafsid ports in retaliation against the acts of the corsairs. The Jews, some of whom were recent exiles from Spain, feared Spanish rule. Many fled from the large cities into the desert and others had to be ransomed from the Spanish at great cost. The Ottoman Turks put an end to the Hafsid kingdom.

Bibliography: Hirschberg, Afrikah, 1 (1965), 274–6, 326–8; EIS, 2 (1927), 216–8.

[ED.]

HAGANAH, the underground military organization of the *yishuv* in Ereẓ Israel from 1920 to 1948. The idea of establishing a defense organization that would protect the *yishuv* throughout Ereẓ Israel was born during the Ottoman period. The head of *Ha-Shomer, Israel *Shoḥat, sent a memorandum to the Executive of the Zionist Organization at the end of 1912, suggesting the establishment of a country-wide organization for self-defense around Ha-Shomer.

Initial Organization. With the British conquest of Ereẓ Israel, it seemed that there would be no need for a Jewish defense organization, for a European power had assumed responsibility for the preservation of civil order with the aid of legally constituted forces from the *yishuv*. Especially in favor of this position was Vladimir *Jabotinsky. He viewed the perpetuation of the *Jewish Legion, which was established in the framework of the British army during World War I as a garrison in Palestine, as the best assurance of the peace and security of the *yishuv*. The Arab assault on the Jewish settlements in Upper Galilee in March 1920 (see *Tel Ḥai), the imminent danger to the settlements in Lower Galilee in the summer of 1920, and, above all, the failure of the self-defense activities openly organized by Jabotinsky during the Passover riots in Jerusalem in 1920 destroyed these illusions. Those who regarded themselves responsible for the defense of the *yishuv*, members of Ha-Shomer and soldiers of the Jewish Legion, came to realize that it was impossible to depend upon the British authorities and that the *yishuv* must create an independent defense force, completely free of foreign authority—in a word, an underground—for both security and political considerations. In contrast to Ha-Shomer, this organization should encompass masses of people and be subordinate to a public Jewish authority. The *Aḥdut ha-Avodah (A) conference at Kinneret in June 1920 accepted Ha-Shomer's resolution to disband and declared its own responsibility "to concern itself with the arrangement of defense matters." A committee was chosen "to organize a defense organization," and among its members were Shoḥat and Eliahu *Golomb. In September 1920 the *Gedud ha-Avodah (the "Joseph Trumpeldor Labor and Defense Legion") was established with the participation of ex-members of Ha-Shomer. In addition to their tasks as workers and guards, the members of the Gedud were to serve as a reserve force for the Haganah. In December 1920, the *Histadrut accepted responsibility for guard and defense matters at its founding convention, and at the first Histadrut council in

March 1921, a defense committee was set up, consisting of Israel Shoḥat, Eliahu Golomb, Joseph *Baratz, Ḥayyim *Sturmann, and Levi Shkolnik (*Eshkol), and the first steps were taken toward training members and purchasing arms.

The riots of May 1921 caught the new defense organization unprepared, but they proved the necessity for its existence. Members were sent to Vienna to begin organizing the consignment of arms (revolvers and ammunition) to Palestine by various means (in beehives, refrigerators, steamrollers, etc.). In addition, the first course for Haganah instructors was run under the command of an ex-Legionnaire, Elimelekh Zelikovich ("Avner"). On Nov. 2, 1921 ("Balfour Day"), an organized group of defenders repelled an attack of an Arab mob on the Jewish quarter of the Old City of Jerusalem and prevented the slaughter of its inhabitants.

During the 1920s. At the outset of Haganah activities, there was friction in the organization's leadership, originating in disagreement over defense systems between ex-Ha-Shomer people and Golomb's group. The Histadrut leadership supported Golomb's group, and the friction finally led to the disassociation of the Ha-Shomer people from the activities of the Haganah and their concentration in the Gedud ha-Avodah, in which they created an underground within an underground by developing an independent network to acquire arms, providing training courses, and pursuing an unsuccessful attempt to develop ties with the Soviet Union (1926). Their major achievement was the arms' cache at Kefar Giladi.

When the ex-Ha-Shomer members left the Haganah framework, the leadership of defense affairs remained, in effect, in the hands of an ex-Legionnaire, Yosef Hecht, who received his salary from the Histadrut Executive and maintained loose contact with the secretary of the Histadrut, David *Ben-Gurion. He was aided in his work, especially in the northern areas, by Shaul Meirov (*Avigur) of kevuẓat Kinneret. In the 1920s the Haganah was composed of separate branches in the major cities, a few moshavot, and a few kevuẓot and kibbutzim. In the cities there were also local committees composed of people who collected money for defense purposes. Each city had a Haganah commander who received a salary from the local Haganah committee. All the rest of the members, whose number did not exceed a few hundred, served as volunteers, training on Saturdays and in the evenings—mostly with revolvers and hand grenades—and being mobilized for guard duty on the border line between the *yishuv* and the Arab population during critical days (the anniversary of the *Balfour Declaration—November 2, the Ninth of Av, the festival of al-Nabī Mūsā in Jerusalem, etc.). A national officers' course, which was held on Mount Carmel near Haifa (1925), strengthened the contact between the handful of commanders. From time to time, meetings were held between the chief commanders, who formulated the "Constitution of the Haganah" in 1924. Primitive arms caches were set up in Shekhunat Borochov near Tel Aviv, in Geva, Kinneret, and Ayyelet ha-Shaḥar. In reality, the Haganah in the 1920s was an underground of such limited scope that it was not necessary to subject its activities to civilian control. Characteristic of the spirit of this period were activities such as the assassination of Jacob Israel de *Haan in June 1924 or the blowing up of a house near the Western Wall in September 1927 in response to Arab provocation of Jewish worshipers.

The riots of August 1929 brought about a complete change in the Haganah position. During the first days of the riots, when there were almost no British security forces in the country and the Arab police force did not carry out its tasks, the meager number of Haganah volunteers with their limited supply of arms filled the gap and saved the Jewish communities of Jerusalem, Tel Aviv, and Haifa from mass slaughter. In contrast, massacre and destruction of property were rampant in those places in which the Haganah was absent or in which its organization was deficient (Hebron, Safed, Moẓa). A deep impression was made by the defense of Ḥuldah, in which a handful of Haganah members fought against thousands of Arab attackers until British forces evacuated them. Old rivalries were forgotten during the riots, and ex-members of Ha-Shomer joined the Haganah fighters and took part in organizing the defense of the cities and the settlements. They also turned their central arms cache in Kefar Giladi over to the Haganah.

1931–1935. After 1929, the need to maintain, expand, and strengthen the Haganah was recognized by all parts of the *yishuv*. Its central command, i.e., Hecht, was ordered to broaden the framework of the Haganah and facilitate greater public control over the organization and its activities, and the civil institutions of the *yishuv* were also called upon to provide full cooperation with the Haganah command. Hecht, who objected to these changes because they went against his concept of the clandestine nature of the Haganah, was relieved of his command. The crisis of command led to the secession of a group of commanders in Jerusalem, led by Avraham Tehomi, that joined together with Revisionist groups to form the *Irgun Ẓeva'i Le'ummi (I.Ẓ.L.) in 1931. In the same year civil institutions of the *yishuv* arrived at an agreement, by which the national command of the Haganah was established on the basis of equal representation—three representatives of the Histadrut (Golomb, Dov *Hos, and Meir Rutberg) and three non-labor representatives (Dov Gefen, Issachar Sitkov, and Sa'adyah Shoshani). The moving spirit in the command was Golomb, whose personal influence was greater than his position as one of the six members of the command and whose modest apartment on Rothschild Boulevard in Tel Aviv was open night and day to people of the Haganah and served as a kind of headquarters of the organization.

The years 1931–35 were a period of quiet development for the Haganah. The structure of the organization hardly changed, and the major administrative work was centered in the three urban branches, whose commanders were Ya'akov Pat (Jerusalem), Elimelekh Zelikovich (alias

Figure 1. Cache of hand grenades in a Tel Aviv tannery. Courtesy Haganah Historical Archives, Tel Aviv.

Avner, Tel Aviv), and Ya'akov Dostrovsky (*Dori, Haifa). These branches constituted the mainstay of the organization, and the membership in each branch numbered in the hundreds. Training methods, however, did not change and were concentrated, as before, in the study of the revolver and hand grenade in the cities and the use of the rifle in the villages. The influence of the national command strengthened with the institution of systematic annual officers' courses (in Ḥuldah and Gevat) and the development of the communications branch (consisting basically of visual communication—flags, lanterns, heliographs) and intelligence. The national command also handled the acquisition of arms, especially from abroad. In 1935 rifles and rifle ammunition began to be sent in barrels of white cement from Belgium. On Nov. 18, 1935, the British authorities confiscated 537 barrels containing arms in Jaffa port, and the incident aroused substantial excitement among the Arabs of Palestine. The Haganah also began to develop workshops to produce hand grenades. The rural settlements began to organize into "blocs," and by 1936 about 20 of these blocs were in existence. At the head of each was a bloc commander who was responsible for the training of its members, acquiring arms and protecting them, and gathering intelligence on the security situation in the area. The position of the Haganah in each bloc was largely dependent upon the initiative of its commander.

During this period, the basic principles of the Haganah consolidated as follows: to maintain complete independence of any non-Jewish factor; to accept the authority of the Jewish national institutions—especially the Political Department of the *Jewish Agency; to maintain a national framework independent of political parties; and to shun militarism for its own sake. The organization was built upon the devotion and voluntary service of thousands of members. The British authorities were aware of the existence of the Haganah, but initially took no serious steps to follow its activities, arrest its commanders or members, or find its arms caches.

The Policy of Restraint. 1936–39, the years of Arab rebellion, in which the *yishuv* in both the cities and the countryside was under a perpetual siege and was attacked by Arab guerilla bands, were the years in which the Haganah matured and developed from a militia into a military body. It confronted riots by using methods learned from the previous disturbances. The Jewish quarters and settlements in the cities and countryside were surrounded by defense devices: wire fences, concrete positions, trenches, communication trenches, and floodlights. The Arabs made practically no attempts to attack these fortified areas, but they destroyed the harvests in the fields, chopped down orchards and forests, tried to disrupt Jewish transportation on the

ALL YOUR SHOPPING NEEDS AT Spinney's Limited

THE PALESTINE POST

Back to Normality LEADER, PAGE FOUR

Palestine Maritime Lloyd LIMITED

JERUSALEM TUESDAY, APRIL 21, 1936

VOL. XII. 3023. PRICE: TEN MILS

Italian Troops Near Addis Ababa

Inhabitants Reported Evacuating Capital

7 MORE DEAD IN FRESH OUTBREAKS IN JAFFA

OFFICIAL COMMUNIQUES

58 Injured Include 26 Jews - Rest of Palestine Reported Quiet

THE DEAD

Figure 2. Front page of *The Palestine Post,* April 21, 1936, two weeks after the outbreak of the Arab rebellion. Jerusalem, J.N.U.L.

Figure 3. A guard at one of the Stockade and Watchtower settlements, 1936. Courtesy Haganah Historical Archives, Tel Aviv.

roads, and set out on a terrorist campaign that affected casual passersby, women, and children.

With the outbreak of the riots, the Jewish Agency declared that the *yishuv's* response to Arab acts of terror would be "restraint"*(havlagah).* In addition to the moral side of the question, the Jewish Agency believed that a policy of restraint would lead to a positive response from the British authorities who would provide the beleaguered Jews with arms. In fact, the authorities cooperated with the Jewish Agency by establishing a broad formation of Jewish auxiliary police *(ghafirs)* dressed in special police uniforms and provided with arms (rifles, and, after a time, light machine guns). During the period of the riots, this formation developed, and its members were formed into the Jewish Settlement Police (J.S.P.), whose stations were placed in all agricultural settlements and in many urban quarters in the country. This force served as a cover for the activities and training of members of the Haganah. Later the members of the Haganah began to "go beyond the fence" and to develop forms of active fighting; escorts and reconnaissance units went into the fields and roads and other groups set ambushes for Arab terrorists. In 1937 field squads (Peluggot Sadeh) were established under the command of Yiẓḥak *Sadeh and Elijah Ben-Ḥur, trained specifically for war against terrorist gangs. These units gained battle experience with the establishment of the Special Night Squads (S.N.S.) under the command of Orde *Wingate, a British captain who was a proven friend of the Jewish cause. During the years of the riots, the Haganah protected the establishment of over 50 new settlements in new areas of the country (the *Stockade and Watchtower settlements). All attacks of Arab gangs that came to uproot these settlements (the largest of these were the attacks on Tirat Ẓevi, Ḥanitah, and Ma'oz) were repulsed.

In 1937 I.Ẓ.L. split and part of its members, together

he Passover *seder* meal, within an architectural framework. A full-page miniature from the *Erna Michael Haggadah*. Germany, Middle Rhine, c. 1400.
erusalem, Israel Museum, ms. 180/58, fol. 40 ($13\frac{3}{4} \times 10\frac{1}{8}$ ins/35×25.5 cm.).

with its commander, Tehomi, returned to the Haganah. Only the Revisionist members continued the independent existence of the organization. It did not engage particularly in defending the *yishuv,* but in 1937–38 it carried out counter-terrorist acts against Arab civilians on the roads and in markets, from which the Haganah disassociated itself for moral and political reasons. Unofficial cooperation with the British authorities did not deflect the Haganah from its independent course. The demand of the authorities that the Haganah be disbanded and its arms be turned in was rejected, and the Haganah even increased its efforts to enlarge its supply of arms. The underground industry for the production of arms was enlarged. In 1937 an agreement was reached between the emissary of the Haganah, Yehudah *Arazi, and the Polish government whereby the Poles would supply the Haganah with arms (rifles, ammunition, and machine guns) that would be transported to Palestine in steamrollers and various types of machinery. Haganah instructors in Poland were also allowed to utilize Polish arms in training young Jews who were going to settle in Palestine. The Haganah was active in organizing the clandestine emigration of Zionist youth from Europe that began in 1934, and until the outbreak of World War II, it assisted the landing of close to 6,000 "illegal" immigrants on the shores of Palestine.

At the end of the riots in Palestine, the number of men and women in the 20 branches of the Haganah reached 25,000. Its arms stores contained about 6,000 rifles and more than 220 machine guns (in addition to the arms of the J.S.P.). Changes were made in its high command. In 1937, Yoḥanan *Ratner was appointed head of the national command by the Executive of the Jewish Agency, and at the end of 1939 a general staff was established, headed by Ya'akov Dostrovsky (Dori). In order to finance the activities of the Haganah, a special system of donations and taxes, called Kofer ha-Yishuv, was organized, which continued to exist until the establishment of the State of Israel.

During World War II. With the anti-Zionist turn in British policy (White Paper of May 1939), a clash of opinion broke out in the *yishuv* in relation to the Haganah's main task. Non-labor circles wished to limit its activities to guarding settlements and urban quarters against Arab attackers. The Jewish Agency, however, wanted to turn the Haganah into the military arm of the *yishuv*'s struggle against the British White Paper policy, which was also the desire of most members of the Haganah. In 1941 the crisis was settled with the establishment of a security committee composed of representatives of all circles in the *yishuv* and given control over the Haganah.

With the outbreak of World War II, the Haganah

Figure 4. A Special Night Squad on its way to guard the Iraq Petroleum Company pipeline to Haifa, 1937. Courtesy Haganah Historical Archives, Tel Aviv.

Figure 5. Yiẓḥak Sadeh, commander of the Special Night Squads, at Ḥanitah in 1938 with two Haganah members: Moshe Dayan (left) and Yigal Allon (right). Courtesy Haganah Historical Archives, Tel Aviv.

was faced with new problems. On the one hand, it actively supported the volunteering to the Jewish units that were established in the framework of the British army. Many of the founders and members of the Haganah joined these units and did much to foster Jewish leadership in them and preserve their Zionist character. The members of the Haganah also developed networks for the clandestine acquisition of arms within the British army, and they cared for Jewish survivors and refugees in the countries of Europe in which they were stationed at the close of the war.

Figure 6. Members of the Haganah High Command at Kibbutz Mishmar ha-Emek, 1942. 1.Yiẓḥak Sadeh, 2.Israel Galili, 3.Yehudah Arazi, 4.Yigael Yadin, 5.Yiẓḥak Dubno, 6.Ya'akov Dori, 7.Alex Zur, 8. Moshe Sneh, 9. Eliahu Golomb. Courtesy Haganah Historical Archives, Tel Aviv.

At the same time, the general staff continued its activities in Palestine and developed the defense forces of the Haganah itself. Its members were divided into a "Guard Force," based on older members, for the static defense of the settlements, and a "Field Force," based on younger members (up to the age of 35), who were trained for active defense activities. A special paramilitary youth movement (*Gadna) was established to train youth between the ages of 14 and 18. In addition, courses were held for commanders of all ranks, among which the most important was the annual course for platoon leaders at Juʿāra near Ein ha-Shofet). The secret arms industry also expanded and produced mortars, shells, and submachine guns. National general defense programs were formulated in the *yishuv* (Program A in 1941, Program B in 1945). Finally the intelligence service of the Haganah (Shay—short for *sherut* *yedi'ot*) was developed and reached a very high level of effectiveness.

In 1941, a mobilized formation of the Haganah—the *Palmaḥ (short for *Peluggot Maḥaẓ*—"crack units")—was established. It was a regular underground army whose units were located in kibbutzim in all parts of the country. The members of the Palmaḥ earned a substantial amount of their living expenses by agricultural labor (14 days a month), and they received excellent training. When the German army stood at the gates of Egypt, contact was reestablished between the Haganah and the British military authorities and joint efforts were carried out in which hundreds of Palmaḥ members received commando training by British officers. At a later time, a paratroop unit was established in this cooperative framework, and 32 of its members parachuted in Europe into enemy territory to organize Jewish youth in Nazi-occupied territory for resistance against the Nazis. From the end of 1939, the Haganah legally published a monthly entitled *Ma'arakhot* that was devoted to military thought and studies of military planning.

In general, however, the British authorities were hostile to the Haganah and saw it as an obstacle to their anti-Jewish policy. In 1939–40 many members of the Haganah were imprisoned and searches were carried out to locate the arms caches. The British military forces met with opposition that gradually reached the stage of bloodshed (Ramat ha-Kovesh, 1943), and show trials were held against Haganah members accused of stealing arms from British military depots. In 1944 the dissident underground organizations (I.Ẓ.L. and *Loḥamei Ḥerut Israel—Leḥi) began attacking the British, against the established policy of the Jewish Agency. The Haganah was charged with stopping the activities of I.Ẓ.L. after the latter refused to heed the warnings of the Jewish Agency. This task (called the "saison") was carried out mainly by volunteers from the Palmaḥ. This mission aroused bitter feelings, even in the ranks of those who carried it out, mainly because some of the imprisoned members of I.Ẓ.L. were turned over to the British authorities.

The Policy of Resistance. A short time after the end of World War II, when it became clear that the British government would not abandon its anti-Zionist policy of the 1939 White Paper, the Jewish Agency charged the Haganah with leading the "Jewish resistance movement" against this policy. A special committee (Committee X) was established to control the activities of this movement. The implementation of the resistance plan was entrusted to Moshe *Sneh, then head of the national command, and Yiẓḥak Sadeh, acting chief of staff. In order to coordinate all underground activities, an agreement was arrived at with I.Ẓ.L. and Leḥi. The insurgent activities in this common framework began on Nov. 1–2, 1945, with the coordinated attack on rail lines and equipment. At the center of the resistance activities was the "illegal" mass immigration from Europe and North Africa, whose organization on land and sea devolved on the Haganah and its various arms: the *Beriḥah and the Organization ("Mosad") for "*Illegal" Immigration. In Palestine, units of the Palmaḥ destroyed army and police equipment, and the Haganah organized mass demonstrations that clashed with the British police and army. In addition to these, I.Ẓ.L. and Leḥi carried out their activities with the approval of the Haganah. The activities were accompanied by illegal written and oral propaganda (the *Ḥomah* wall newspaper and the clandestine broadcasts of the *"Kol ha-Haganah"*). On June 17, 1946, these activities reached their height with the blowing up of all the bridges on the borders of Palestine by the Haganah

Figure 7. *Theodor Herzl*, a Haganah "illegal" immigrant ship captured by the British, being brought into Haifa port, April 1947. Courtesy Keren Hayesod, United Israel Appeal, Jerusalem.

forces. About two weeks later, on June 29 ("Black Saturday"), the British authorities responded by imprisoning the members of the Jewish Agency Executive and the Va'ad Le'ummi and by vigorous searches in the kibbutzim in order to catch members of the Palmaḥ and uncover the arms caches of the Haganah (a large store was uncovered at Yagur).

After "Black Saturday," the Executive of the Jewish Agency called for a pause in the resistance, but I.Ẓ.L. and Leḥi refused to obey this order and continued their armed attacks. The Haganah limited its armed struggle to attempts to score direct hits against the operational devices installed to interfere with "illegal" immigration (radar devices, boats that deported immigrants to Cyprus, etc.). The "illegal" immigration also increased and reached new heights with the refugee ship *Exodus 1947* (summer 1947) and the two giant ships, *Pan Crescent* and *Pan York*, which set sail at the end of 1947 with 15,000 immigrants on their decks. These actions were greatly aided by the Haganah delegation to Europe, headed by Naḥum Kramer (Shadmi), that organized Haganah units in the Jewish D.P. camps in Central Europe and Italy and in other Jewish population centers (France, Rumania, Hungary, etc.). In Palestine the Haganah concerned itself with the security of settlements in new areas of the country, such as the northern Negev (11 settlements were established simultaneously at the close of the Day of Atonement, 1946), the Judean Mountains, and Upper Galilee. A substantial number of these settlers received military training in the Palmaḥ.

The commissions of inquiry that visited Palestine at the time (the Anglo-American Commission and the Special Commission on Palestine) met with representatives of the Haganah and drew conclusions that substantially affected the formulation of policy in 1947, namely, that in the event that a political solution desired by the Jews was arrived at, the Haganah would be able to withstand any attack, whether by the Arabs of Palestine or those of the neighboring states, without outside aid. In the spring of 1947, when a political solution began to be worked out (namely the U.N. plan for the partition of Palestine), David Ben-Gurion took it upon himself to direct the general policy of the Haganah, especially its preparation for the impending Arab attack, and appointed Israel *Galili head of the national command. The Haganah budget was substantially increased, and the purchase of arms was expanded by the emissary of the Haganah, Ḥayyim Slavin, who concentrated upon the acquisition of machinery to manufacture arms and ammunition from the United States. Preparations were made for the formation of new services and first and foremost an air force, which was initiated in the framework of the Haganah before the outbreak of World War II. By the eve of the War of Independence there were 45,000 members in the Haganah, about 10,000 of whom were in the Field Force and more than 3,000 in the Palmaḥ.

The War of Independence. At the outbreak of the War of Independence, the Haganah was prepared for its defense tasks. The Jewish settlements were fortified, and in accordance with a Haganah tradition from the days of Tel Ḥai, even settlements completely cut off from the main areas of Jewish settlement were not abandoned (such as the Eẓyon Bloc, the settlements of the Negev, and Yeḥi'am), although holding them cost the Haganah great efforts. The Haganah also increased its retaliatory actions against the attacks of Arab gangs on Jewish traffic, and the movement of vehicles was guarded by armed escorts. A general mobilization was declared in the *yishuv,* but the first major blows of the war fell on the mobilized formations of the Haganah, the J.S.P., and units of the Palmaḥ, which in a short period of time comprised three brigades (Yiftaḥ, Harel, and Negev). At the same time the quick mobilization and training of the Field Force began, and it was divided into seven brigades (Golani, Karmeli, Alexandroni, Kiryati, Givati, Eẓyoni, and the Seventh Brigade). Superhuman efforts were made to purchase arms of every type, including heavy arms and planes in America and Europe.

In the first four months of the war the Haganah engaged mainly in defending the positions of the *yishuv.* One of the reasons for its defensive stance was the presence of the British army, which, during its evacuation from the country, interfered in battles, usually to the advantage of the Arabs. Great achievements were made in these defensive actions, such as repulsing an attack on Tirat Ẓevi, the Eẓyon Bloc, and convoys to Jerusalem and other places, but losses were very heavy (about 1,200 civilians and soldiers, including the thirty-five fighters, called the "Lamed He," on a mission to the Eẓyon Bloc and 42 people in a convoy to Yeḥi'am). The feeling in the *yishuv* and in the world at large was that the Haganah had overrated its ability to withstand the attacking forces, and this feeling made itself felt in the international attitude to the Jewish prospects in the Palestine conflict.

In the beginning of April 1948, however, a great change took place in the activity of the Haganah, that was connected with the completion of the organization of the new brigades and the first large shipments of arms that had arrived from Europe. The beginning of this turn came with Operation Naḥshon, in which the road to besieged Jerusalem was broken through and the major fortifications on the hills on both sides of the road were captured. During the same period, the attacks of semi-regular Arab forces on Mishmar ha-Emek and Ramat Yoḥanan, whose purpose was to break through to Haifa, were repulsed. A series of conquests began, starting with the capture of Tiberias (April 18) and followed by the battle for Haifa, which ended with Haganah forces holding the entire city. Safed was captured on May 12, and the next day Arab Jaffa surrendered to the Haganah command. With the evacuation of British forces from Jerusalem, Haganah forces controlled the new city, but the Jewish quarter of the Old City was forced to surrender to the Arab Legion of Transjordan on May 28. The Eẓyon Bloc also fell to the Arab Legion.

On May 15, 1948, Haganah forces faced the armies of the surrounding Arab states that had invaded Palestine. These were large armies whose equipment, including cannons and tanks, outweighed that of the Haganah. The assault of the Syrian army on the northern Jordan Valley was halted in a series of desperate battles, in which the Haganah used its first cannons. Forces of the Iraqi army were stopped at the borders of the hills of Samaria. The assault of the Arab Legion and the Egyptian army on Jerusalem, accompanied by indiscriminate cannon bombardment on the city, was repulsed. Heavy battles were waged in the Latrun area on the highway to Jerusalem. When the Haganah proved unable to occupy the Latrun area it paved a temporary road to the city, south of Latrun (the "Burma Road"), and thus insured communication with Jerusalem. In the south, the advance of the Egyptian army was halted by the Palmaḥ, the Givati Brigade, and members of the settlements in the area, including Yad Mordekhai and Negbah.

In the midst of these battles, the provisional government of Israel decided to turn the Haganah into the army of the state. The transition was basically a formality, but it symbolized the end of an era. In the Order of the Day of May 31, 1948, the minister of defense, David Ben-Gurion, announced that with the establishment of the State of Israel, the Haganah abandoned its underground character and became the regular army of the state. The name of the Haganah was incorporated into the official name of the army of the new state: Ẓeva Haganah le-Israel (*Israel Defense Forces).

See also *Israel, State of, Historical Survey (1880–1948), *Israel Defense Forces (1880–1948), *Ha-Shomer, *Palmaḥ, *War of Independence.

Bibliography: Dinur, Haganah; Z. Gilad and M. Meged (eds.), *Sefer ha-Palmaḥ,* 2 vols. (1955); *Ha-Haganah be-Tel-Aviv* (1956); Y. Avidar, *Ba-Derekh le-Ẓahal* (1970); Y. Bauer, *From Diplomacy to Resistance* (1970); N. Lorch, *The Edge of the Sword* (1968[2]); M. Mardor, *Strictly Illegal* (1964); Y. Allon, *Shield of David* (1970); idem, *The Making of Israel's Army* (1970). [Y.S.]

HAGAR (Heb. הָגָר), Egyptian maidservant of *Sarah (Sarai). The tradition involving Hagar is preserved in two narrative cycles. The passage in Genesis 16:1–16 records how Hagar was given to Sarai's husband Abram as a concubine (1–13). When Hagar conceived, she became contemptuous of Sarai, who, in turn, abused her until she fled into the desert (4–6). There, by a spring, Hagar encountered an angel, who exhorted her to return (7–9) and gave her a favorable oracle concerning her future son to be named *Ishmael (10–12). Hagar named the place in honor of the event (13–14). Finally, she bore Ishmael (15). The second tradition (Gen. 21:8–21) records that after Sarai—now Sarah—had borne Isaac, she demanded the expulsion of Hagar and her son. According to the Septuagint, she was distressed to see Ishmael playing "with her son Isaac." Upon receiving divine reassurance (12–13), Abraham reluctantly banished Hagar (14ff.) to the desert, where she and Ishmael were saved from death by divine intervention (17ff.).

The legal systems of Mesopotamia, Abraham's birthplace, provide analogues to the situations encountered in these passages (see *Patriarchs, *Nuzi). The Code of Hammurapi (par. 146) stipulates that in certain circumstances, a concubine who bore children to her master and claimed equality of status with her mistress could be punished but not sold. Likewise, a Nuzi marriage contract stresses the obligation of a wife to provide her husband with a concubine who may never be sold (Pritchard, Texts, 220, 3).

Contemporary critical scholarship regards the first tradition as predominantly J (Jahwist), with P (Priestly) inserts comprising verses 1a, 3, 15–16; the second is agreed to be entirely E (Elohist). As a whole, however, the literary transmission of these narratives has long presented difficulties. The problems are both literary and chronological. The

Figure 1. Hagar depicted in a miniature from *Weltchronik*, a 14th-century German illuminated manuscript by Rudolph von Ems. Left, Hagar, carrying her son Ishmael, is sent away by Abraham; right, Ishmael stands behind Hagar as an angel speaks to her. Stuttgart, Wuerttembergische Landsbibliothek HB XIII 6 fol. 51v. Courtesy Bildarchiv Foto Marburg.

literary problems arise from the fact that both accounts involve the banishment of Hagar (16:6; 21:14), the encountering of an angel who provided an oracle (16:7–12; 21:17–18), and the presence of a well (16:14; 21:19). It has been suggested that two independent versions of Hagar's banishment originally existed, the first referring to her pregnancy and the second to the time after Isaac's birth. Consequently, some scholars resolve the assumed conflation by judging 16:9 to be a late redaction whose purpose was to give sequence to the narratives; others assume that the naming of Ishmael was deleted in the second tradition. These difficulties are lessened if the narratives are considered separate crystallizations of the Hagar-Ishmael saga, each one limited and both integrated by the root *šmᶜ* (**שמע**; 16:2, 11; 21:12, 17). Each would serve both as an independent version of the etiology of the Ishmaelite-Hagarite tribes and a literary foil for the Isaac theme interwoven through it. However, the combination has introduced a chronological problem which did not exist when these traditions stood alone. According to Genesis 16:16, Abraham was 86 years old when Ishmael was born and 100 when Isaac was born (21:5), which would make Ishmael more than 14 years old at the time of his banishment (21:10ff.). This difficulty has resulted in various attempts to account for the conflation, as, e.g., the view that an account of the banishment of Hagar and her young son was combined with an account of the birth of Isaac in Abraham's old age.

Hagar's name appears to have been derived from the gentilic *Hagrim* or *Hagri'im,* which appears in Minean, Nabatean, Sabean, Palmyrene, and Hellenistic inscriptions. It also appears in the masoretic text as a gentilic (Ps. 8:7; I Chron. 5:10, 19–20; cf. II Sam. 23:36 with I Chron. 11:38). The historical relationship of the Ishmaelite and Hagarite tribes would then be expressed genetically by the etiological saga of Genesis 16 and 21. The etymology of Hagar is obscure, but some scholars have connected it with an Old South Arabic word meaning "city, area." [M.F.]

In the Aggadah. Hagar was the daughter of Pharaoh. When "Pharaoh saw the deeds performed on Sarah's behalf in his house, he gave Hagar to Sarah, saying; 'Better let my daughter be a handmaid in this house than a mistress in another's'" (Gen. R. 45:1). According to Philo (Abr., 251), Sarah testified about Hagar her handmaid, not only that she was a free woman of noble disposition, but also that she was a Hebrew in her way of life. Hagar was given to Abraham after he had dwelt ten years in the land of Canaan (Gen. 16:3) since a man having no children from his wife for ten years may not abstain any longer from the duty of propagation (Yev. 6:6). As soon as Hagar was with child she began to slander Sarah, saying to the ladies who came to visit her mistress, "My mistress Sarah is not inwardly as she appears outwardly. She pretends to be a woman of piety, but she is not, as she has prevented conception in order to preserve her beauty" (Gen. R. 45:4). When this came to the notice of Sarah she took Abraham to task for remaining silent at these taunts and she also made Hagar do servile work despite the fact that Abraham objected to any burden being added to that of childbearing (Gen. R. 45:6). Five times after she had fled from Sarah an angel visited Hagar, who, quite accustomed to the appearance of these celestial beings in Abraham's household, was not at all startled (Gen. R. 45:7). When Hagar came to the wilderness, she took up the idol-worship of the house of her father Pharaoh (*ibid.;* PdRE. 30). However, she gave it up when it proved worthless (Targ. Yer. Gen. 21:16). Hagar is identical with Keturah, whom Abraham married after the death of Sarah (Gen. 25:1). She was so called, because after having gone astray after idols, she again attached herself to a life of virtue (*keturah,* lit. "attached"; Zohar, Gen. 133b; Gen. R. 61:4).

For the figure of Hagar in Islam see *Abraham; *Ishmael, sections on Islam. [E.E.H.]

Figure 2. Hagar expelled by Abraham, a drawing by Rembrandt van Rijn. Amsterdam, Rijksmuseum.

Bibliography: D. H. Mueller, *Die Gesetze Hammurabis* (1903), 139–41; J. Skinner, *Genesis* (ICC, 1910); F. Dornseiff, in: ZAW, 52 (1934), 67; R. de Vaux, in: RB, 56 (1949), 26ff.; E. A. Speiser, *Genesis* (1964); N. M. Sarna, *Understanding Genesis* (1966), 127–9; Ginzberg, Legends, 1 (1909), 223, 231–2, 237–9.

HAGBAHAH, GELILAH (Heb. הַגְבָּהָה וּגְלִילָה; "lifting and rolling" of the Torah scroll), the elevation and subsequent rolling together of the Scroll of the Law in the synagogue. *Hagbahah* is the raising of the open Torah scroll, so that the congregation may see the writing and testify: "And this is the Law which Moses set before the children of Israel" (Deut. 4:44). "According to the word of the Lord by Moses" (Num. 9:23). In the Sephardi ritual, Deuteronomy 4:24, 33:4, is immediately followed by Psalms 18:31. In the Reform ritual, "This Torah is a tree of life to those who hold fast to it; and of them that uphold it everyone is rendered happy" (Prov. 3:18) is recited instead. In the Ashkenazi ritual, this rite is performed after the reading from the Pentateuch and before the reading from the

Figure 1. *Hagbahah*, the raising of the Torah scroll in a synagogue. Drawing by Bernard Picart, 1724. Amsterdam, Stedelijk Museum.

Prophets (*haftarah*). One person lifts up the Torah scroll in such a way that the congregation can see three columns of the writing. He then sits down and another person rolls the scroll, binds it, dresses it with a mantle, and replaces its various ornaments. This part of the rite is called *gelilah* ("rolling together"). In many ḥasidic synagogues *hagbahah* is made with an open scroll before the reading from the Torah and again after the reading, with a closed scroll which is then bound. In the Sephardi ritual, *hagbahah* is performed before the reading from the Pentateuch. The person who takes the Torah scroll from the ark opens it and carries it open to the reading platform. According to the Talmud, the person who performs the *gelilah* ceremony is honored even more than those who are called to the actual

Figure 2. *Hagbahah* in a Ḥabad school in North Africa. From *Challenge*, London, 1970.

reading of the Pentateuch (Meg. 32a, see also: Sh. Ar., OḤ 134). In some places, it has become the custom to let the *gelilah* be performed even by minors (under the age of bar mitzvah) who are not qualified to be called to the Pentateuch reading. In the Western Sephardi rite, however, *hagbahah* is performed only by an honorary official or members of an honorary brotherhood (levantadores).

Bibliography: ET, s.v., *Gelilah* and *Hagbahah;* Eisenstein, Dinim, s.v.; E. Munk, *The World of Prayer*, 1 (1961), 175. [Ed.]

HAGEN, town in North Rhine-Westphalia, W. Germany. A small Jewish community came into existence in Hagen during the early years of the 18th century. Among the town's 675 inhabitants in 1722 were four Jewish families, two of them glassmakers and two slaughterers. Little is known of the community in the following decades, but in 1799 there is evidence of a significant settlement of 23 Jews, mostly engaged in peddling. During the 19th century their numbers increased, and they were particularly prominent in the development of the textile industry. In this period they established a school and finally built a synagogue in 1859. By 1897 there were 470 Jews among the population. On the eve of the Nazi regime in 1930, there were 679 Jews in Hagen. The synagogue was destroyed in 1938 and the Jews were deported between 1942 and 1943. By 1956 there were again 20 Jews living in Hagen; the synagogue was rebuilt in 1960.

Bibliography: Hagen Municipality, *Gedenkbuch zum tragischen Schicksal unserer juedischen Mitbuerger* (1961). [Z.F.]

HAGENBACH, village in Bavaria, W. Germany. The existence of a Jewish community in Hagenbach was first noted through its suffering during the *Rindfleisch massacres (1298). Nothing more is known of it until 1478, when the expulsion of Jews from nearby *Bamberg increased the numbers and importance of the Jewish communities in Hagenbach and the neighboring villages. The various communities lived under the protection of the country gentry and formed an association to provide common rabbinic leadership and to represent their shared interests before the governmental authorities. The local **Memorbuch,* an important historical document, records that a synagogue and cemetery were consecrated in 1737. In 1813 an independent rabbinate was established, with its seat in Hagenbach, embracing 14 other small communities. In 1867 the community (totaling 126 persons) was united with that of *Baiersdorf, while in 1894 both were included in the rabbinate of Bamberg. The Jewish population numbered 88 in 1900 and only 24 in 1933. The community was not reestablished after World War II.

Bibliography: PK Bavaria; M. Weinberg, in: JJLG, 18 (1927), 203–16; A. Eckstein, *Geschichte der Juden im ehemaligen Fuerstbistum Bamberg* (1898), 48, 51. [Ed.]

HAGGADAH, PASSOVER (Heb. הַגָּדָה; "telling"), a set form of benedictions, prayers, midrashic comments and psalms recited at the **seder* ritual on the eve of *Passover. This entry is arranged according to the following outline:

INTRODUCTION

The *Haggadah* is based on the *seder* service prescribed by the Mishnah (Pes. 10), which had apparently been conducted in the form of a banquet. The observance of the precepts at the *seder*—the eating of the *pesaḥ* (the *paschal sacrifice), **mazzah* ("unleavened bread"), and **maror* ("bitter herbs"); the drinking of **arba kosot* ("four cups of wine"); and the recital of the story of the exodus from Egypt (the narrative of the *Haggadah*) were integrated into this banquet celebration. Essentially, the *Haggadah* is an account of the Egyptian bondage, a thanksgiving to God for the redemption, and, in Temple times, a thanksgiving for the acquisition of the Land of Israel. After the destruction of the Second Temple, the latter was replaced by a prayer for the ultimate redemption. The purpose of the *Haggadah* (*"Ve-higgadta le-vinkha"*—"And thou shalt tell thy son," Ex. 13:8), one of the central commandments of the day, is represented by the narrative itself. Not written by any particular author, or group of authors, the *Haggadah* is not a "literary composition" in the accepted sense of the term. Its narrative is a collection of excerpts from the Bible, Mishnah, and Midrash, interpolated with the ritual performances: the **Kiddush,* the benedictions recited on the performance of precepts, and for food, *Grace after Meals, and the **Hallel.* Gradually, stories, psalms, and songs were added. Many recensions of the *Haggadah,* differing from one another to a greater or lesser degree, have been preserved in various manuscripts, mostly dating from the 13th to the 15th century, and also in fragments from the Cairo **Genizah.* Some halakhic works also contain the text of, and commentaries on, the *Haggadah* (see below: Manuscripts and Editions). In keeping with its compilatory character and the varied nature of its sources, the literary or logical nexus between the different sections of the *Haggadah* is not always discernible. The quotations, derived from a multiplicity of sources, have mostly been adapted to the needs of the *seder* service.

COMPONENT PARTS

(1) The **Kiddush.* It is not specific to the *seder* service but is prescribed for all the festivals. (2) **Ha Laḥma Anya* ("This is the bread of affliction") are the opening words of a declaration in Aramaic, designating the *mazzah* as the bread of affliction and inviting the needy to join the meal. It ends with "This year we are here, next year may we be in the Land of Israel. This year we are slaves, next year may we be free men" (figure 1). There seems to be no clear connection between the three statements of the declaration. It appears to be a folk composition which was added to the *seder* liturgy after the destruction of the Temple. (3) **Mah Nishtannah* ("How is this night different"), popularly known as "the four questions," is according to the Mishnah (Pes. 10:4) apparently a formula with which the father can instruct his son. This formula passed through a number of stages till it assumed the forms which are to be found in the different recensions that are in use today. (4) *Avadim Hayinu* ("We were bondmen") is an introduction to the formal narration of the exodus from Egypt, based on the views of Samuel (Pes. 116a). Passages of unknown origin supplement the narration stressing its importance. (5) *Ma'aseh be-Rabbi Eli'ezer . . . Amar Rabbi Elazar* ("It is told of R. Eliezer . . . R. Eleazar b. Azariah said") is a story concerning the leading *tannaim,* followed by a discussion between them, whose purpose it is to emphasize the importance of the narration. While the story is preserved only in the *Haggadah,* the debate is cited in the Mishnah (Ber. 1:5) and in halakhic Midrashim (Sif. Deut. 130; Mekh., Pisḥa 16). (6) The *baraita* of the Four Sons, also preserved in a halakhic Midrash (Mekh., Pisḥa 18) and in the Talmud (TJ, Pes. 10:4, 37d), but in a recension differing considerably from *Haggadot* in use today, incorporates all the biblical verses enjoining the narration of the exodus (Deut. 6:20; Ex. 12:26; 13:8; 13:14). It adapts them to four different types of "sons": the wise, the wicked, the simple, and the disinterested, who should be instructed according to the *halakhah* "that according to the understanding of the son the father instructs him" (Pes. 10:4). (7) *Yakhol me-Rosh Ḥodesh* ("It might be thought that [this exposition should begin] from the New Moon [of Nisan]") is a tannaitic commentary on Exodus 13:8 (Mekh., Pisḥa 17), adducing exegetical proof that the narration of the exodus story is obligatory on the eve of Passover. (8) *Mi-Teḥillah Ovedei Avodah Zarah Hayu Avoteinu* ("In the beginning, our fathers worshiped idols") is an introduction to the narration of the exodus story based on Rav as opposed to Samuel's view (see above *Avadim Hayinu*). (9) A tannaitic Midrash on *Arami oved avi* (Deut. 26:5–8)—"An Aramean would have destroyed my father" (usually rendered: "A wandering Aramean was my father") which, according to the Mishnah (Pes. 10:4), everyone is obliged "to expound." This commentary, also preserved in the Midrashim based on the

Figure 1. Two pages from the *Birds' Head Haggadah*, an illuminated manuscript in which the faces are distorted to conform with the biblical prohibition of graven images. S. Germany, c. 1300. Jerusalem, Israel Museum.

Figure 2. Page of the *Barcelona Haggadah* with the first part of the section giving the initial letters of the rituals of the seder. Below the letters are figures performing the rituals. Barcelona, 14th century. London, British Museum, Add. Ms. 14761, fol. 27v.

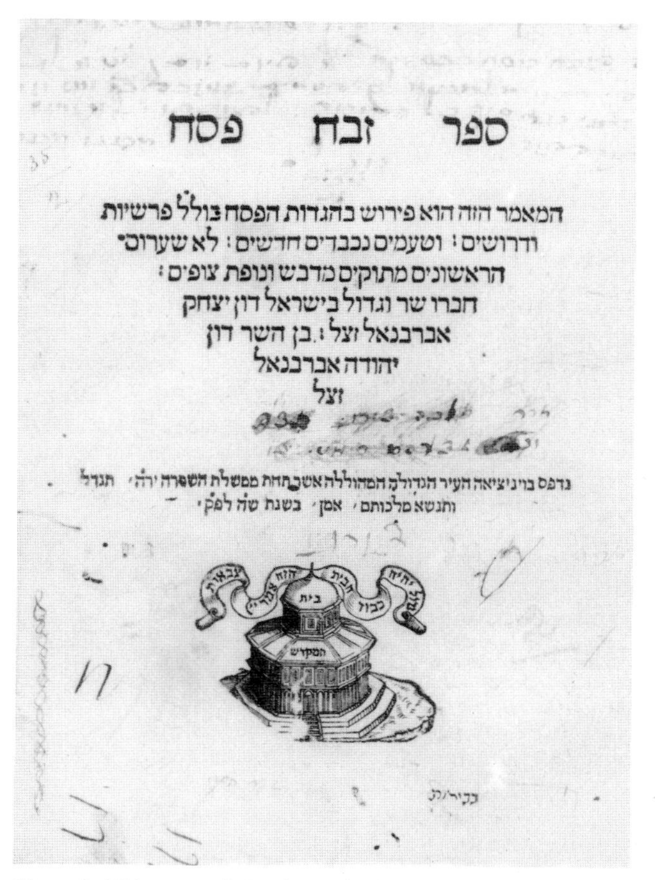

ספר זבח פסח

המאמר הזה הוא פירוש בהגדות הפסח כולל פרשיות
ודרושים: וטעמים נכבדים חדשים: לא שערום
הראשונים מתוקים מדבש ונופת צופים:
חברו שר וגדול בישראל דון יצחק
אברבנאל זצל: בן השר דון
יהודה אברבנאל
זצל

נדפס בויניציאה העיר הגדולה המהוללה אשר תחת ממשלת השררה יר״ה תגדל
ותנשא מלכותם אמן בשנת שה לפק

Figure 3. Title page of *Zevaḥ Pesaḥ*, the *Haggadah* commentary by Isaac Abrabanel. Venice, 1545. Jerusalem, J.N.U.L.

Figure 4. Part of the *Dayyeinu* poem with illumination of the opening and closing words of each verse. The hare hunt at the bottom of the page represents a mnenomic device (see *Abbreviations, Figure 2.). From the *"Brother" to the Rylands Spanish Haggadah,* Spain, 14th century. London British Museum, Or. Ms. 1404, fol. 15v.

Figure 5. Page of the 14th-century *Sassoon Spanish Haggadah,* with the passage "And the Lord brought us out of Egypt with a mighty hand and an outstretched arm," illustrated by the children of Israel, in medieval dress, leaving a walled town. Letchworth, England, Sassoon Collection, Ms. 514.

Figure 6. "The wise son" in a page from the 15th-century *Cincinnati Haggadah* from southern Germany, copied and possibly illustrated by Meir b. Israel Jaffe of Heidelberg. Cincinnati, Hebrew Union College.

Figure 7. Full-page miniature from the *Golden Haggadah,* an early 14th-century illuminated manuscript, probably from Barcelona. Upper right, Jacob blessing Pharaoh; upper left, Jacob blessing Ephraim and Manasseh; lower right, the death of Jacob; lower left, throwing the male Israelite children into the Nile. British Museum, Add. Ms. 27210, fol. 8v.

Figure 8. Page from the *Darmstadt Haggadah*, an illuminated manuscript from central Rhineland, Germany, second quarter of the 15th-century. Darmstadt, Hessische Landes- und Hochschulbibliothek, Cod. Or. 8, fol. 10v.

Figure 9. Page from the *Kaufmann Haggadah*, a late 14th century illuminated manuscript from Spain. Moses is shown leading the Israelites while the Egyptians watch from the tower, Pharaoh rides in pursuit, and a dog barks. Budapest, Library of the Hungarian Academy of Sciences, Kaufmann Collection. Ms. A. 422 fol. 43.

Figure 10. Page from the *Sarajevo Haggadah*, a 14th-century illuminated manuscript, probably executed in Barcelona; showing Rabban Gamaliel teaching his students. Sarajevo, National Museum, fol. 25*.

Figure 11. Page from the *Washington Haggadah*, a 15th-century illuminated manuscript from Italy. Elijah is shown riding into Jerusalem on a donkey with a family from the *seder*. Washington, D. C., Library of Congress.

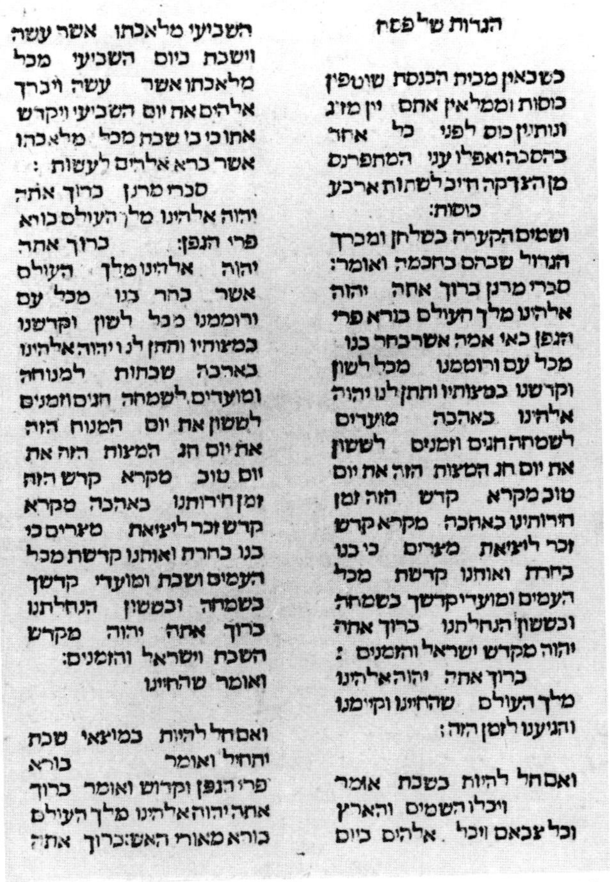

הגדות של פסח

כשבאין מבית הכנסת שוטפין
כוסות וממלאין אתם יין מזוג
ונותנין כוס לפני כל אחד
בהסבה ואפילו עני המתפרנס
מן הצדקה חייב לשתות ארבע
כוסות:
ושמים הקערה בשלחן ומברך
הגדול שבהם בחכמה ואומר:
סברי מרנן ברוך אתה יהוה
אלהינו מלך העולם בורא פרי
הגפן ברוך אתה אשר בחר בנו
מכל עם ורוממנו מכל לשון
וקדשנו במצותיו ותתן לנו יהוה
אלהינו באהבה מועדים
לשמחה חגים וזמנים לששון
את יום חג המצות הזה את יום
טוב מקרא קדש הזה זמן
חירותינו באהבה מקרא קדש
זכר ליציאת מצרים כי בנו
בחרת ואותנו קדשת מכל
העמים ומועדי קדשך בשמחה
ובששון הנחלתנו ברוך אתה
יהוה מקדש ישראל והזמנים:
ברוך אתה יהוה אלהינו
מלך העולם שהחיינו וקיימנו
והגיענו לזמן הזה:

ואם חל להיות בשבת אומר
ויכלו השמים והארץ
וכל צבאם ויכל. אלהים ביום
השביעי מלאכתו אשר עשה
וישבת ביום השביעי מכל
מלאכתו אשר עשה ויברך
אלהים את יום השביעי ויקדש
אתו כי בו שבת מכל מלאכתו
אשר ברא אלהים לעשות:
סברי מרנן ברוך אתה
יהוה אלהינו מלך העולם בורא
פרי הגפן: ברוך אתה
יהוה אלהינו מלך העולם
אשר בחר בנו מכל עם
ורוממנו מכל לשון וקדשנו
במצותיו ותתן לנו יהוה אלהינו
באהבה שבתות למנוחה
ומועדים לשמחה חגים וזמנים
לששון את יום המנוח הזה
את יום חג המצות הזה את
יום טוב מקרא קדש הזה
זמן חירותנו באהבה מקרא
קדש זכר ליציאת מצרים כי
בנו בחרת ואותנו קדשת מכל
העמים ושבת ומועדי קדשך
בשמחה ובששון הנחלתנו
ברוך אתה יהוה מקדש
השבת וישראל והזמנים:
ואומר שהחיינו

ואם חל להיות במוצאי שבת
יתחיל ואומר בורא
פרי הגפן וקדוש ואומר ברוך
אתה יהוה אלהינו מלך העולם
בורא מאורי האש: ברוך אתה

Figure 12. First page of the earliest known printed *Haggadah*, produced in Guadalajara, Spain, in 1482 by Solomon b. Moses Alkabeẓ. The only known copy of this incunabulum is at the Jewish National and University Library, Jerusalem.

Figure 13. Page from the *Prague Haggadah*, 1526, with Gothic ornamental border including figures of Adam and Eve (upper right and left), Samson with the gates of Gaza (middle right) and Judith with the head of Holofernes (middle left). Jerusalem, J.N.U.L.

Figure 14. Colophon page from the *Mantua Haggadah*, 1560, which reproduced the text of the *Prague Haggadah*, using new decorations. Jerusalem, J.N.U.L.

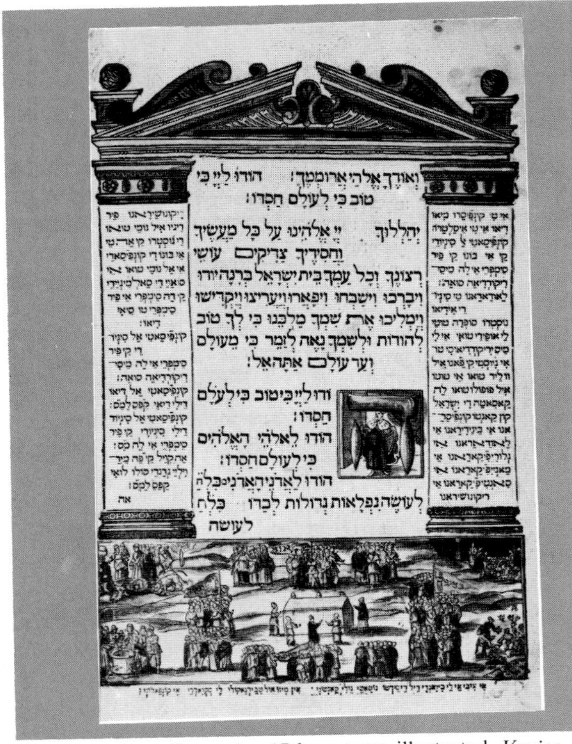

Figure 15. Page from the 17th-century illustrated *Venice Haggadah*, 1609, with the text in the center and Ladino translation on the columns at the sides. Jerusalem, Israel Museum. Photo David Harris, Jerusalem.

Figure 16. Title page of the 1712 edition of the *Amsterdam Haggadah*, the first *Haggadah* to use copper engraved illustrations. Jerusalem, Michael Kaufman Collection. Photo David Harris, Jerusalem.

Figure 17. Cover and title page of a German army *Haggadah* used during World War I. Pictured on the cover are Franz-Joseph of Austria (right) and Wilhelm II of Germany. Bruenn, 1915. Jerusalem, B. M. Ansbacher *Haggadah* Collection.

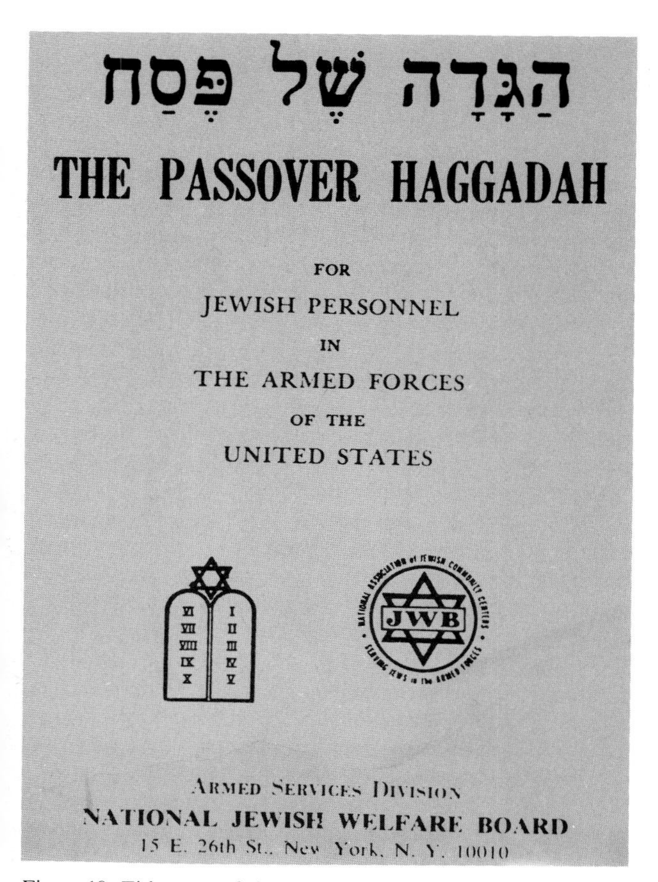
הַגָּדָה שֶׁל פֶּסַח

THE PASSOVER HAGGADAH

FOR

JEWISH PERSONNEL

IN

THE ARMED FORCES

OF THE

UNITED STATES

JWB

ARMED SERVICES DIVISION

NATIONAL JEWISH WELFARE BOARD

15 E. 26th St., New York, N. Y. 10010

Figure 18. Title page of the *Haggadah* issued for U.S. soldiers by the National Jewish Welfare Board during World War II. Jerusalem, B. M. Ansbacher *Haggadah* Collection.

Figure 19. Page from a *Haggadah* issued for soldiers of the Haganah in 1948, with illustrations by A. Alweil. Jerusalem, B. M. Ansbacher *Haggadah* Collection.

Sifrei (Sif. Deut. 26:5 (301), especially Mid. Lek. Tov, and Mid. Hag., ad loc.), is a haphazard selection of aggadic interpretations. In the *seder* ritual, it is prefaced with "Blessed be He who observes His promise . . . Go and learn what Laban the Aramean sought . . .," a passage not found in the Midrashim and apparently composed in the post-talmudic period. (10) Commentaries of the *tannaim* on the miracle of the plagues and the division of the Red Sea during the exodus from Egypt are recited. In most Jewish communities these have been seen as a continuation of the preceding Midrash; their source is the *Mekhilta* (*Va-Yehi be-Shallah* 6). (11) *Kammah Ma'alot Tovot la-Makom Aleinu* ("How many goodly favors has the Almighty bestowed upon us") is a poem in two versions which is preserved only in the Passover *Haggadah.* The poem was composed during the Second Temple period and seems to have no direct connection with the *seder* service. (12) The Mishnah of Rabban Gamaliel. It explains the significance of the Passover sacrifice, the unleavened bread, and the bitter herbs. Taken from the Mishnah (Pes. 10:5), it was reworded (in a question-and-answer form) during the post-talmudic period. (13) *Be-Khol Dor va-Dor* ("In every single generation") is a passage from the Mishnah (Pes. 10:5), or from an expanded Mishnah *(baraita),* which had been supplemented by a statement of Rava (Pes. 116b). (14) The first two chapters of *Hallel* are recited, as prescribed in the Mishnah following Bet Hillel (Pes. 10:6). (15) The benediction for redemption "Who redeemed us" is based on the ruling of R. Tarfon and R. Akiva in the Mishnah. After observing the commandments to eat unleavened bread and bitter herbs, the meal is eaten, followed by Grace after Meals. (According to the opinion of scholars such as Elbogen, Ginzberg, and Finkelstein, etc. it is obvious from the text of the *Mah Nishtannah* that at some stage in the development of the *seder* service this part of the ritual followed rather than preceded the meal.) The company then continues with the second part of the *Haggadah.* (16) *Shefokh Ḥamatkha* ("Pour out Thy wrath") is a collection of verses whose theme is a supplication for vengeance on the nations that have oppressed Israel. The custom to recite these verses is attested since medieval times; their number and order differ according to the various rites. (17) The last part of the *Hallel* is recited, as specified in the Mishnah (Pes. 10:7). (18) *Yehallelukha Adonai Eloheinu al Kol Ma'asekha* ("All Thy works shall praise Thee") is a benediction of praise ("Birkat ha-Shir") in accordance with R. Judah's view (Pes. 118a). (19) The Great *Hallel* (Ps. 136). Its recital became obligatory at a later date. (It is based on the *baraita* of R. Tarfon *(ibid.).*) (20) *Nishmat Kol Ḥai* ("The breath of all that lives"), another version of the *Birkat ha-Shir* ("Benediction over the Song") is recited, in accordance with the view of R. Johanan *(ibid.).*

RITUAL ACTS

The text of the *Haggadah* is also divided according to the prescribed ritualistic acts of the *seder* service. Each textual section is headed by a descriptive phrase which, in some rites, is chanted as a separate litany. The sections are: *kaddesh* (the *Kiddush;* figure 2), *u-reḥaẓ* ("washing" of the hands), *karpas* (eating the "herbs" dipped in salt-water), *yaḥaẓ* ("dividing" the middle *maẓẓah*), *maggid* (the "narration"), *raḥaẓ* ("washing" the hands for the meal), *moẓi-maẓẓah* (the "benediction" over the *maẓẓah*), *maror* (eating the "bitter herbs"), *korekh* (eating "bitter herbs with *maẓẓah*"), *shulḥan arukh* (the "meal"), *ẓafun* (eating of the **Afikoman*—the "last *maẓẓah*"), *barekh* ("Grace after Meals"), *hallel* (recitation of the second part of *Hallel*), and *nirẓah* (the closing formula). This Passover *Haggadah* and *seder* ritual follows the practice of the Pumbedita and Sura academies of Babylonia and was adopted by all the Jewish communities in the Diaspora. It completely superseded the ancient Palestinian recension which differed from it in certain respects (such as the omission of sections 4–7 listed above.

TEXTUAL ELABORATIONS

A tendency, however, existed to elaborate on the text of the *Haggadah* with midrashic and poetic sections. These additions are neither obligatory nor universally accepted: e.g., the tannaitic exposition *Ani Adonai ve-lo Aḥer* ("I the Lord and no other"; *Maḥzor Vitry,* 293) and an interpretation of *ve-natan lanu et mamonam* ("and gave us their substance"; the *siddur* of Saadiah Gaon, 143), the latter is derived from the *Mekhilta de-R. Simeon b. Yoḥai,* and was adapted to the *seder* ritual. Similarly, certain benedictions were expanded through the interpolation of *piyyutim* (e.g., in the *siddur* of Saadiah Gaon, 144). Among oriental communities it is customary to recite in the first part of the *seder* service the hymn "And ye shall say: This is the offering of the Passover." In later times, hymns and roundelays were gradually incorporated into the *Haggadah,* and sung at the end of the *seder:* **Az Rov Nissim* ("Of old, Thou didst Perform most Miracles at Night"; from a *kerovah* by *Yannai); *Omeẓ Gevuratekha* ("The Strength of Thy Might"; from a *kerovah* by R. Eleazer *Kallir); **Ki Lo Na'eh* ("For to Him Is it Becoming"; by an anonymous *paytan*); and *Ḥasal Seder Pesaḥ* ("Accomplished is the Order of the Passover"; from a *kerovah* by R. Joseph Tov Elem *Bonfils). Other hymns introduced are just folk songs composed for the entertainment of children, e.g., **Addir Hu* ("Strong is He"); **Eḥad Mi Yode'a* ("Who Knows One?"); **Ḥad Gadya* ("One Only Kid"). In other communities different *piyyutim* have been adopted: e.g., "On Passover in Egypt my Captives went forth Free"; "From the House of Iniquity, Seat of my Strifes" or "Home of my Medanite [captors]" (both are in the *Maḥzor Carpentras*); or "Who Wrought Wonders in Egypt" (*Maḥzor Romania,* Constantinople, 1510). In northern France it was customary to sing at the end of the *seder* "The Lovers Sing with Ringing Voice" (*Maḥzor Vitry,* 298).

COMMENTARIES

Textual difficulties in the *Haggadah* called for the annotation of the text. The earliest commentaries were written in a talmudic style and can be found in the halakhic works of the school of Rashi and his disciples (e.g., in *Maḥzor Vitry; Ha-Orah,* ed. by S. Buber, 1905; *Siddur Rashi,* ed. by S. Buber and J. Freimann, 1911; *Ha-Pardes,* ed. by D. Ehrenreich, 1824). The commentary attributed to R. *Samuel b. Meir is written in the same style. A more comprehensive and profound exposition is found in *Shibbolei ha-Leket* by R. Zedekiah b. Abraham *Anav (13th century; ed. by S. Buber, 1886), in which are incorporated some annotations by Isaiah di *Trani, as well as interesting novellae, by the author's brother. The two important commentaries composed in the 14th century were by R. *Aaron b. Jacob ha-Kohen of Lunel (in *Orḥot Ḥayyim;* it also appeared in **Kol bo*) and by R. David b. Joseph *Abudarham (in his commentary on the prayer book; Venice, 1566). These early commentators merely annotated the text. They were not concerned with the investigation of the historical aspect of the *Haggadah* and did not refer to the sources of its different texts. This simple explanatory type of commentary came to a close in the 15th century with *Afikoman* by R. Simeon b. Ẓemaḥ *Duran, which until that time was the only commentary published as a separate book. After the 15th century, the commentators

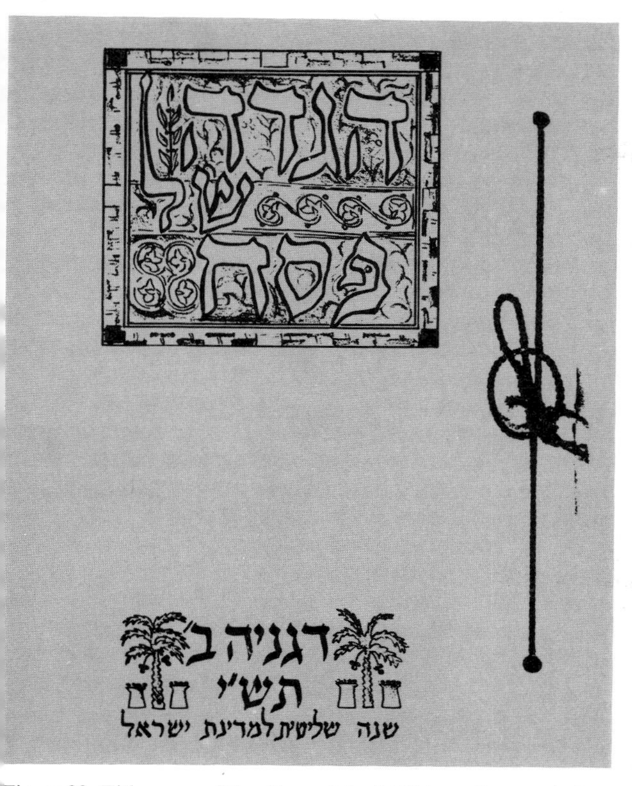

Figure 20. Title page of the *Haggadah* of Kibbutz Deganyah Bet, 1950. Jerusalem, B.M. Ansbacher *Haggadah* Collection.

Figure 21. Emergency *Haggadah* of the Israel Defense Forces with abridged ritual and large print, for soldiers on front-line duty, 1967. Jerusalem, B. M. Ansbacher *Haggadah* Collection.

ncluded material of their own in their expositions, both as an elaboration on the narrative and as a discussion of philosophical and theological concepts. R. Isaac *Abrabanel in *Zevaḥ Pesaḥ* (Venice, 1545; figure 3) poses 100 questions which he answers at length. With reference to the verse "Know thou of a surety . . ." (Gen. 15:13), he asks: "What benefit have we derived from the exodus from Egypt, in view of the fact that we are once again in exile?" In his reply he discusses the significance of the exile and the ways of Providence at great length, without establishing any direct connection with the text. The commentary thus becomes a separate discourse. Subsequent commentators, who followed his style, mostly annotated in an aggadic vein, while a few gave mystical interpretations, e.g., R. Eliezer *Ashkenazi in *Ma'asei Adonai* (Venice, 1583); R. *Judah Loew b. Bezalel (the Maharal) of Prague in *Gevurot Adonai* (Cracow, 1582), in which he also expounds halakhic matters; and the kabbalists R. Moses *Alshekh and R. Isaiah *Horowitz. The best known later commentators are: R. Jacob *Emden, R. *Elijah b. Solomon Zalman of Vilna, Jacob of Dubno, Jacob b. Jacob Moses *Lorberbaum (of Lissa), and Moses *Sofer (Schreiber) who wove their homiletic compositions round and into the Passover *Haggadah.* R. Ḥayyim Joseph David *Azulai (18th century), known for his critical approach, also follows the above method in his commentaries on the *Haggadah,* though occasionally the critical view is discernible. Only in the 19th century did scholars begin to analyze the text, to clarify its sources, and to determine the original wording. This method was adopted by H. *Edelman, E. *Landshuth, D. *Cassel, M. Friedmann, and D. *Goldschmidt, whose commentaries were published in articles or in book form.

MANUSCRIPTS AND EDITIONS

Through the generations the Passover *Haggadah* has been one of the most popular works—perhaps the most popular—in Jewish religious literature. Many recensions, differing from one another to a greater or lesser degree, have been preserved in various manuscripts mostly dating from the 13th to the 15th century, and also in fragments from the Cairo *Genizah.* These manuscripts originate from all countries in which Jews have lived. Some halakhic works also contain the text of and commentaries on the *Haggadah.* Others are found in daily or festival prayer books; the majority, however, are separate works for use on the eve of Passover only. These manuscripts have not yet been adequately investigated; only a selected few, particularly the illuminated copies, have engaged the attention of scholars. In the seventh or eighth century the *Haggadah* was apparently compiled as a separate work by the *geonim.* The oldest extant version however is in the prayer book *(siddur)* of Saadiah Gaon (10th century; ed. by I. Davidson, S. Assaf and B. I. Joel, 1941); other early versions are found in Maimonides' *Mishneh Torah* (12th century) and in *Maḥzor Vitry* (11th century). Since the 15th century, the *Haggadah* has had more than 2,700 editions, either with or without commentaries. Later editions have included as many as 200 commentaries. The Haggadah has been translated into vernaculars used by Jews, e.g., Yiddish, Ladino, Judeo-Greek, Judeo-Arabic (in its various dialects), and Judeo-Persian, which are often printed together with the *Haggadah.* Oral vernacular renderings are traditional in those communities which have no printed literature in their spoken idiom (e.g., in modern Aramaic). The *Haggadah* has been rendered into a number of languages, and the translation, whether with or without commentary, is often included in the editions. "Emended" editions, which do not give the traditional but a substitute version, are customary in certain communities, e.g., the *Haggadah* of S. *Maybaum (1891), Caesar *Seligmann (Frankfort, 1913), Guggenheim (Offenbach, 1927), the *Central Conference of American Rabbis (from 1905 onward), the Union of Liberal and Progressive

Synagogues in London (1953), and the *Reconstructionist movement in the U. S. The tendency to "reform" the *Haggadah* exists also in Israel, especially in nonreligious kibbutzim which tend to emend the text of the *Haggadah* from year to year; as a rule, these editions do not appear in print, but in cyclostyled form only. The Karaites have composed a Passover *Haggadah* of their own, which is completely different from that of the Rabbanites, and consists of biblical verses and a few benedictions. It has been printed several times (Pressburg, 1879; Odessa, 1883; Vilna, 1900; Ramleh, 1953). *Haggadah* editions based on scientific analysis and research are by: H. Edelman (1845); E. L. Landshuth (*Maggid me-Reshit,* with an introduction, 1855); J. D. *Eisenstein (*Oẓar Perushim ve-Ẓiyyurim al Haggadah shel Pesaḥ,* 1920); C. *Roth (in English, 1939); D. Goldschmidt (with a commentary in Hebrew; 1947) and with an introduction on the history of the *Haggadah* and the texts of all the midrashic and paytanic additions in 1960; and M. M. *Kasher (containing Mss. recensions, *genizah* fragments, and a collection of commentaries, as well as a lengthy introduction, 1955). [D.G.]

ILLUMINATED MANUSCRIPTS

Introduction. During the 13th to 15th centuries the Passover *Haggadah* was one of the most popular Hebrew illuminated manuscripts in Sephardi as well as Ashkenazi or Italian communities.

The popularity of the *Haggadah* for embellishment at that time was the result of the fusion of several factors. To begin with, the crystallization of its text into a single received and authoritative version made it easier to extract the Passover *Haggadah* from the complete annual cycle of prayers contained in the *siddur* and to copy it as a separate book. Such a book, the record of the most important private, domestic ritual, performed with the entire family gathered around the Passover table, was a much more personal object, less subject to communal prescription and prohibition, and so lent itself to the expression of personal taste in enrichment more than any other sacred codex. Being instructive in nature, the illustrations may have served as a means of holding the interest of the children through the long Passover eve ceremony. Because of its comparatively small size, it was not too expensive for the head of a family to commission or purchase, nor too laborious for scribe to write and artist to illuminate. Nor is it a coincidence that, just at the time when illuminated *Haggadah* manuscripts began to appear as separate books, that is to say during the 13th century, new developments were coming to the fore in European manuscript production. The social and economic growth of town life at this period fostered an increase in the number of secular workshops concerned with the manufacture of books. Interest in learning and need for the written means of its transmission coincided with a feeling of freedom and security in the more established towns. At the same time, new techniques in the preparation of parchment, inks, colors, gold leaf, and other materials brought the acquisition of illuminated manuscripts within the reach of many citizens.

Even so, not every household in the Jewish community could afford to possess an illuminated *Haggadah.* Only the richer Jews, who, especially in Spain, were employed by princes or their courtiers and were therefore better acquainted with beautifully illuminated codices, would have the means to attempt the imitation of the fashion for such objects by commissioning the illumination of Hebrew books. Such commissions would present the artist with the problem of a subject matter which was new to him, and the problem was met by the fusion of traditional Jewish themes, motifs, and, iconography with the more fashionable styles and layout of contemporary Christian illumination, according to the style of the artist and the taste of his patron. In the 14th and 15th centuries, especially in Germany, a more popular type of illuminated *Haggadah* was developed which could reach many more patrons and more easily satisfy the growing demand. The pattern, system, and choice of subject in the illuminated *Haggadot* were influenced by Greek and Latin illuminated manuscripts, chiefly psalters, of a type common in the princely courts of Europe.

Types of Illustration. The range of *Haggadah* illumination was obviously dependent in the first place on the contents of the book, which can be roughly divided into four categories: textual, ritual, biblical, and eschatological. These four categories may be applied to all illuminated *Haggadot* of the 13th to the 15th centuries, whether Ashkenazi, Sephardi, or Italian. The most common textual illustrations are of the main elements of the Passover ritual according to Rabban *Gamaliel: *pesaḥ* (paschal lamb), *maẓẓah* (unleavened bread), and *maror* (bitter herb). In fact, the *maẓẓah* and *maror* may have been the earliest textual illustrations in the *Haggadot* of the ninth and tenth centuries and, judging from the fact that an example was found in the Cairo **Genizah,* may have derived from Egypt, Palestine, or Mesopotamia. Decorated initial words were common to most Hebrew illuminated manuscripts, though some were peculiar to the *Haggadot.* One example is the decorative construction of bold initial words, written one under the other on either side of the page, for the poem *Dayyeinu* ("It would have sufficed us"; figure 4 and color plate between columns 1452 and 1453). This construction exists in eastern *Haggadot,* as well as in those included in the prayer book. In some *Haggadot* Rabban Gamaliel himself and his pupils are illustrated, as well as other rabbis mentioned in the text. Other textual illustrations include the "four sons," described in the narrative; the wise son was depicted as a rabbi, the wicked son as a soldier, the simple one as a boy, and the one who "does not know how to ask" as a jester. Some of the decorations are pictorial witticisms, such as the one of the man pointing at his wife while reciting *maror zeh*—"this bitter herb"—or literal representations of the text, like the man leaving prison as an illustration to Psalm 118:3–7 in the *Sassoon Spanish Haggadah* (figure 5 and color plate between columns 1388 and 1389). In Italian and Ashkenazi *Haggadot* there are even more literal illustrations of the Hebrew text, such as that of a man dressed for travel coming out of a town gate placed beside the text which begins, "Come out and learn what Laban the Aramite sought to do to Jacob"; or the picture of a naked woman to illustrate Ezekiel 16:7 as in the *Joel b. Simeon *Haggadah* in the British Museum.

The ritual illustrations are for the most part didactic, beginning with the preparations for Passover—the baking of the *maẓẓot,* the killing of the paschal lamb, and the cleansing of the house and the dishes. Other illustrations show people reciting the *Haggaddh* in the synagogue (color plate between columns 1324 and 1325)—a custom which was known in Spain—or leaving the synagogue; the family sitting round the *seder* table; the washing of the hands; the pouring, lifting, or drinking of the four cups of wine; the hiding and finding of the *afikoman;* and the eating of the various herbs. These genre scenes of medieval Jewish life depict the customs of various European communities by portraying their daily and festive dress, household utensils, furniture, and buildings and may have been invented at the time by the Jewish artists themselves for use in the *Haggadah.* Most interesting of all the categories are the biblical pictures. They begin as illustrations of the biblical and midrashic texts contained in the *Haggadah*, with the chief emphasis on the story of the Exodus, preceded by the history of the Patriarchs. The cycle was sometimes broadened to include other episodes ranging from the Creation, as in the Spanish *Sarajevo Haggadah* (see below), to Jonah under his gourd in the *Yahuda Haggadah* (Israel Museum, Jerusalem) and the *Second Nuremberg Haggadah* (Schocken Library, Jerusalem; color plate between columns 1260 and 1261). Sometimes these biblical illustrations and the ritual pictures are intermingled. For example, the smearing of the lintel with blood is incorporated into a cycle of the preparations for Passover in the *Rylands Spanish Haggadah* (John Rylands Library, Manchester, England); and the baking of *mazzot* is introduced into the Exodus story in the *Birds' Head Haggadah* (see below).

Many legendary episodes from early Midrashim are depicted along with the biblical illustrations, some being found in Sephardi as well as Ashkenazi *Haggadot*. Only a few can be mentioned here: Abraham cast into the fire by Nimrod; Joseph's meeting with the angel on his way to his brothers in Dothan, as in the *Golden Haggadah* (see below); Joseph's coffin thrown into the Nile by the Egyptians in the *Sarajevo Haggadah;* the testing of Moses by means of gold and a live coal in the *Kaufmann Haggadah* (see below); Zipporah feeding Moses in prison for seven years in the *Yahudah Haggadah;* and Moses receiving two tablets of the Law and passing on five—the Pentateuch—in the *Birds' Head Haggadah*. Some biblical illustrations are quite literal, such as a tongueless dog barking at the Israelites coming out of Egypt to illustrate Exodus 11:7 in the *Kaufmann Haggadah*.

The eschatological illustrations refer to the ultimate destiny of the Jewish nation and the fate of the individual Jew. One such representation is the entry of the righteous into paradise (Psalm 118:19), which is depicted in the *Birds' Head Haggadah*, for example, as the three Patriarchs led by an angel. In many *Haggadot* the passage "Pour out Thy wrath upon the nations that know Thee not" (Psalm 79:6) is an invitation to eschatological illustration. In the *Kaufmann Haggadah* an angel is seen pouring the contents of a cup over a group of people.

More common in Ashkenazi *Haggadot* is an illustration associated with the prophet Elijah, the traditional harbinger of the Messiah, who is to come riding on as ass, bringing vengeance on the unbelievers who have destroyed Israel and redeeming the Jewish nation. The custom of opening the door to Elijah during the recital of "Pour out Thy wrath" is illustrated in the *Washington Haggadah*. The final verse of the *Haggadah*, "Next year in Jerusalem," is illustrated in the *Birds' Head Haggadah* by a rendering of the newly built Jerusalem and its Temple, with Jews adoring it, while in the *Sarajevo Haggadah* the facade of the Temple is depicted (color plate between columns 1132 and 1133). In the *Second Nuremberg Haggadah* the prophet Elijah is seen riding a donkey with the Israelites following him to Jerusalem.

Regional Schools. Three types of *Haggadot* are distinguishable on the basis of their illustrations and the way these are placed: Ashkenazi, Sephardi, and Italian. While some features are common to all schools, each regional school has some local trait peculiar to its *Haggadah*.

The rich Spanish *Haggadah* is usually composed of three parts: the text; full-page biblical miniatures; and a collection of the *piyyutim* recited in the synagogue during Passover week and on the Sabbath before Passover. The text of the Spanish *Haggadah* is very sparsely illustrated, mainly with textual and ritual representations, and the *piyyutim* section is barely decorated. The most significant artistic section is that of the full-page miniatures. The best known of about a dozen surviving specimens of this rich type of Spanish *Haggadah* are the *Sarajevo*, the *Kaufmann*, and the *Golden Haggadah*.

The full-page biblical miniatures that preceded the Spanish *Haggadot* may have been derived from the manner of illuminating the Latin psalter in England and France during the later Middle Ages, which in its turn was based on the "aristocratic" type of Greek psalter illumination of earlier Byzantine schools.

The Ashkenazi *Haggadot*, from France and Germany, are all decorated with illustrations in the margins surrounding the text. There are two main groups; the earlier one places ritual and biblical illustrations, literal representations of the text, adjoining the passages they interpret. Good examples are the 13th-century *Dragon Haggadah* from France, now in Hamburg, Germany, and the *Birds' Head Haggadah* of about 1300. The later group contains a consecutive cycle of pictures from any of the books of the Bible, placed with no direct relation to the *Haggadah* text. Examples of this decoration can be found in Jerusalem in the Schocken Library and in the *Yahuda Haggadah*. The famous *Darmstadt Haggadah*, of the first half of the 15th century, has very few textual and ritual illustrations, and none is biblical. Equally few appear in the *Erna Michael Haggadah* in the Israel Museum (color plate between columns 1068 and 1069). Joel b. Simeon of Bonn was responsible for many illuminated *Haggadot*, both in Germany and in Italy; his best in the German style is the one in the British Museum (color plate between columns 1004 and 1005). A crude but expressive example of his transition period is the *First Nuremberg Haggadah* in the Schocken Library. The *Washington Haggadah* illuminated in the Florentine style is one of his best.

The third type of *Haggadah*, the Italian, may have been the earliest of the three and the model for the others. Since no early Italian *Haggadah* has survived, however, the type must be reconstructed from later examples which have already been subject to other influences. In the 15th century, the Italian *Haggadot* must have been influenced mainly by the Ashkenazi type, since they contain marginal illustrations only. In the first half of the century the Ashkenazi influence is apparent chiefly in the general overall design. Following an influx of Jews expelled from Germany, a new group of Italo-Ashkenazi *Haggadot* emerged in which, though the style is Italian, the script and layout are Ashkenazi. In this group are the numerous manuscripts executed in the workshops of Joel b. Simeon, and those influenced by him. The *Haggadah* in the sumptuous *Rothschild Miscellany* in the Israel Museum is illustrated on traditional Ashkenazi lines in the Ferrarese style of about 1470.

The most outstanding examples of the illuminated *Haggadot* are discussed in greater detail below.

[B.N.]

Examples of Illuminated Haggadot. BIRDS' HEAD HAGGADAH (Israel Museum, Jerusalem, Ms. 180/57). So named because many of the human figures are depicted with birds' heads, this is probably the oldest surviving Ashkenazi illuminated *Haggadah* manuscript. It was discovered in 1946 by Mordekhai *Narkiss. It was copied in the south of Germany late in the 13th century by a scribe named Isaac who also copied the first volume of the *Leipzig Maḥzor*. Its illumination consists mainly of marginal text illustrations, depicting historical scenes from Exodus, and ritual as well as eschatological scenes. The style of the illumination, the bright colors, and the decorative motifs, though somewhat primitive, indicate its Upper Rhenish origin. Its name is imprecise because the artist uses other methods of human distortion, such as a boy with a bulbous nose, angels with blank faces, and Egyptians in helmets with lowered visors. The manuscript was reproduced in facsimile in

1967 accompanied by an introductory volume of essays (color plate between columns 876 and 877). [B.N.]

CINCINNATI HAGGADAH is a 15th-century illuminated script in the library of the Hebrew Union College, Cincinnati. It was copied in square Ashkenazi script on 69 vellum leaves by the scribe Meir b. Israel *Jaffe of Heidelberg. It is decorated with painted initial-word panels, a decorative border, and miniatures in the margin illustrating the Passover ceremony and the text. The style of the miniatures and decorations indicate that the manuscript was executed in the late 15th century in southern Germany. Landsberger suggested that the scribe was also the artist of the *Haggadah*. This theory however has been challenged on the grounds that more than one artist seems to have worked on this manuscript. Moreover, it is unlikely that a scribe-artist would paint miniatures which obliterate his own script, as happens on several folios (figure 6). [J.GUT.]

DARMSTADT HAGGADAH is an early 15th-century manuscript preserved in the Darmstadt Landesbibliothek (Cod. Or. 8). Its richly decorated folios are unusual for *Haggadot*. It was copied about 1430 by Israel b. Meir of Heidelberg in square Ashkenazi script. Its decoration contained initial-word panels, a few fully framed borders, and two full-page miniatures. The illustrations consist mainly of teachers, with male and female students, some in small frames and others in many-storied gothic frames, an unusual iconographic feature. The origin of these types must have been on contemporary "Heroes and Heroines tapestries" or frescoes showing Hebrew, pagan, and Christian worthies. The miniatures depict a hunting scene and a spring of youth. Little room is left in the manuscript for the text. Though the artist of the miniatures is unknown, the fact that the 15th-century art was not wholly dependent on church and court workshops made the emergence of an outstanding Jewish illustrator among the expert Jewish calligraphers possible. A facsimile reproduction was produced in 1927 in Leipzig (figure 8 and color plate between columns 812 and 813). [R.W.]

GOLDEN HAGGADAH (British Museum Add. Ms. 27210) is the earliest and most sumptuous of the illuminated Sephardi *Haggadot*. It contains the text of the *Haggadah*, a collection of 100 *piyyutim*, and 15 full-page miniatures illustrating the biblical story from Adam naming the animals up to the exodus from Egypt. The style of the miniatures and the text illustrations suggest that it was executed in Barcelona in the first quarter of the 14th century. It is based on the northern French gothic style of the late 13th century. The full-page miniatures, divided into four compartments each painted on a burnished gold background, were executed by two artists. The *iconography of the scenes derives from the illustrations of contemporary Latin manuscripts and from Jewish aggadic iconography which may go back to early Jewish Bible illumination. There is a companion manuscript of the second half of the 14th century in the British Museum (Or. Ms. 2884). A facsimile reproduction was produced in 1970 in London and New York (figure 7).

KAUFMANN HAGGADAH (Budapest, Library of the Hungarian Academy of Sciences, Kaufmann Collection, Ms. A422) is a 14th-century Spanish manuscript composed of two parts: 14 full page miniatures (fols. 1v–10, 57v–60) and an illustrated *Haggadah* (fols. 11v–56). The *Kaufmann Haggadah* has an incomplete miniature cycle of Exodus. The manuscript is incorrectly bound, as the entire group of full-page miniatures is dispersed, with some attached to the beginning of the manuscript (fols. 1v–10) and others to the end (fols. 57v–60). The facsimile edition of the manuscript, by the Hungarian Academy of Sciences in 1954, did even more to hinder an understanding of the cycle by printing the miniatures on both sides of the pages and omitting alternate blank pages, thus preventing a correct reconstruction of the sequence. The episodes represented in the extant miniatures begin with the discovery of the infant Moses and end with Miriam's song after crossing the Red Sea, with one miniature of the preparations for Passover eve (fol. 2). Among the biblical illustrations are many midrashic ones such as Moses removing Pharaoh's crown from his head. In most cases these illustrations are within the large, painted, initial-word panels, but sometimes they appear in the margins between the extended foliage scrolls. The *Haggadah* also contains some red, green, and purple filigree-work panels. The text illustrations are elaborate and contain, besides the usual rabbis, four sons, *mazzah*, and *maror*, some repetitions of the biblical episodes depicted in the full-page miniatures, such as the labor of the Israelites (fol. 15v), the throwing of the male children into the river (fol. 27v), and the Israelites coming out of Egypt (fol. 43).

The Italianate style of the illumination is pronounced. In describing this *Haggadah* in the introductory volume of *Die Haggadah von Sarajevo*, J. von Schlosser attributed the style to northern Italy. In fact, it is Castilian of the late 14th century, characterized by many Italian stylistic elements. The Byzantine-Bolognese figure style and the very colorful, fleshy leaves support this assumption, as does the triple-towered castle—the emblem of the Kingdom of Castile—which is depicted in the center of the round, decorated *mazzah* surrounded by four naked personifications of the winds blowing trumpets (figure 9).

SARAJEVO HAGGADAH (Sarajevo National Museum) is a 14th-century Spanish illuminated manuscript composed of the traditional three parts: 34 full-page miniatures (fols. 1v–34); illuminated *Haggadah* text (fols. 1*–50*); and *piyyutim* and Torah readings for Passover week (fols. 53*–131*). It is by far the best-known Hebrew illuminated manuscript, and has been reproduced in part twice during the last 70 years with scholarly introductions by H. Mueller and J. von Schlosser, and by C. Roth. The full-page miniatures in the *Sarajevo Haggadah* display the widest range of subjects even among the rich Spanish *Haggadot*, from the Creation of the World to Moses blessing the Israelites and Joshua before his death, followed by illustrations of the Temple, preparations for Passover, and the interior of a Spanish synagogue. There are few full-page miniatures; most are divided horizontally into two framed sections, with some in four sections. Although the greater part of the iconography of the miniatures is derived from Latin Bible illumination of the Franco-Spanish school, some Jewish elements can be detected, as in the abstention from representation of God or any heavenly beings. Other Jewish aspects can be found in the text illustrations of the *Haggadah*, such as a miniature of Rabban Gamaliel and his students, and the *mazzah* and *maror*. Stylistically, the illuminations are related to the Italian-gothic school prevailing in Catalonia in the 14th century. That the *Sarajevo Haggadah* originates from the Kingdom of Aragon can be inferred from three coats of arms displayed in the manuscript. The *Haggadah* reached the Sarajevo Museum when in 1894 a child of the city's Sephardi Jewish community brought it to school to be sold, after his father had died leaving the family destitute (figure 10 and color plate between columns 1132 and 1133). [B.N.]

WASHINGTON HAGGADAH (Library of Congress in Washington, D.C.) consists of 39 vellum leaves, 6 by 9 in. (15×22.5 cm.), written in square Ashkenazi script, completed by Joel b. Simeon in 1478. It has painted initial-word panels, and many marginal illustrations of the Passover ceremonies and the Exodus story. Although the illustrations depict German customs, their stylistic features and decorative elements indicate a late 15th-century northern Italian origin. The illustrations are closely related to those in other manuscripts believed to have been executed in the northern Italian workshop of the same scribe-illustrator. A facsimile was produced in 1965 with a preface by Lawrence Marwick (figure 11). [J.GUT.]

PRINTED EDITIONS OF ILLUSTRATED HAGGADOT

Introduction. The earliest known edition of the *Haggadah* to be printed separately was produced in Spain at Guadalajara about 1482, on 12 pages in double column. Only a single copy is known to exist, and it may well be that other, perhaps earlier, editions have disappeared (figure 12). The bibliography of the Passover *Haggadot* published by A. Yaari in 1960 includes 2,717 entries, but taking into account omissions and later editions, there can be no doubt that the total to the present date is at least 3,000. In the text of the *Haggadah* included in the prayer book according to the Italian rite (Casalmaggiore, 1486), there is a conventional representation of the *mazzah*, as in some of the earliest *Haggadah* manuscripts, and these may be considered the earliest known illustrations to the printed *Hagga-*

dah. The crudely executed but by no means ignorant illustrations in the Latin *Ritus et celebratio Phase* (Frankfort, 1512) by the Christian Hebraist Thomas Murner, drawn by his brother Beatus, may have been inspired by a Jewish model. In the extremely rare *Seder Zemirot u-Virkat ha-Mazon* (Prague, 1514) there are figure woodcuts on the same subjects which appear later in illustrated *Haggadot,* and may derive from some lost edition. Of the earliest known illustrated edition, hypothetically attributed to Constantinople about 1515, only fragments remain. From the worn state of some of the blocks it may have been a reprint. From these fragments it is obvious that the whole work must have been lavishly illustrated.

Prague Edition (1526). The continuous record of the illustrated printed *Haggadah* begins with the *Prague edition of 1526 (figure 13). This magnificent work, with its profuse marginal cuts and decorations and its superb borders, is among the finest productions of the 16th-century press. The beauty of the work lies above all in the disposition of the type and the exquisite balance of the pages. Its most remarkable feature is three pages with engraved borders in monumental gothic style. The printers and publishers were Gershom Solomon Kohen Katz and his brother Gronem (Geronim). The artistic work was apparently executed partly by Ḥayyim Shaḥor (Schwartz), Gershom Kohen's collaborator, who sometimes signed his initials, and partly by a gentile assistant. Some of the decorative features were derived from non-Jewish works, including the Nuremberg chronicle of 1484. In recent years the Prague *Haggadah* has been reproduced repeatedly in facsimile. The cuts and illustrations in the publication were long imitated, deteriorating progressively as the years went by. The Prague edition of 1556 retained some of the original elements but this was not the case with the one published in 1590 or with other commonplace editions that continued to appear in Prague and elsewhere down to the mid-18th century. An interesting new edition, apparently by Ḥayyim Shaḥor, appeared in Augsburg in 1534. This, however, had little influence and only one complete copy is preserved.

Mantua Edition (1560, 1568). The next important step in the record of the illustrated *Haggadah* was the Mantua edition of 1560, published by the *shammash,* Isaac b. Samuel. This reproduced the text of the Prague edition page for page and letter for letter in facsimile, but introduced new illustrations and marginal decorations which had already been used in non-Jewish publications and were in conformity with Italian taste. The format was repeated with remarkable success in another edition published in Mantua in 1568 by a non-Jewish firm which concealed its identity under the name Filipponi. The marginal decorations were specially recut for this production, which rivals the Prague edition of 1526 (figure 14).

Venice Editions. The Mantua editions served as precise models for a group of illustrated *Haggadot* in smaller format produced in rapid succession at the turn of the century (1599, 1601, 1603, and 1604) in Venice, which had become the great center of Jewish publishing. These converted the hybrid but impressive Mantua editions into a cohesive but unimpressive unity, reproducing every accidental decoration and copying every accidental marginal detail. The major illustrations at the foot of the pages were expanded into an entirely fresh series of 17 engravings, some of them appearing more than once. These illustrated the *seder* service, the subject matter, and the story of the Exodus. Thus, this is the first *Haggadah* which is consistently and systematically illustrated.

In 1609 the veteran printer Israel ha-Zifroni of Guastalla planned an edition with completely new illustrations. Printed for him by Giovanni da Gara, it was set in bold type, each page within an engraved architectural border. The illustrations were placed at the top or foot of almost every page in the early part of the volume, and more sparsely toward the end. There was one important innovation in this edition: in a series of small panels on an introductory page, the various stages in the Passover celebration are illustrated with men and women dressed in contemporary fashion; a later page similarly illustrates the ten plagues. These features were henceforth to become usual in illustrated *Haggadot.*

The illustrations of the first part of the service (before the meal) are almost wholly devoted to the exodus, while those in the second part (after the meal) deal with the biblical story in general and with the messianic deliverance. In 1629 a further edition based on ha-Zifroni's with a similar format was published in Venice by the Bragadini press. This continued to be reproduced, without any basic change but with increasingly worn types and indistinct blocks, until late in the 18th century. The illustrations continued to be copied in *Haggadot* printed in the Mediterranean area, especially in Leghorn, almost to the present day. Thus the pattern of the traditional illustrated *Haggadah* was established (figure 15).

Amsterdam Editions. In 1695 there appeared in Amsterdam a new edition of the illustrated *Haggadah* which followed closely, in its general layout as well as in detail, the example of the now accepted Venetian prototype. The illustrations were, however, much improved by being engraved on copper. The artist was *Abraham b. Jacob, a former Protestant preacher. He chose many of the same incidental scenes as had appeared in the Venice *Haggadot,* but he drew them afresh, basing his work on the biblical pictures in the *Icones Biblicae* by Matthew Merian the Elder; he probably used the second edition of the work which had appeared in Amsterdam in c. 1655–62. Abraham b. Jacob also used miscellaneous scenes taken from other works by Merian. Thus the four sons of the *Haggadah* text (depicted together for the first time in one illustration) are miscellaneous figures brought together from various publications of Merian, without any attempt at grouping. The "wise son" and the "son who could not ask," for example, come from an engraving of Hannibal sacrificing before the altar, while the scene of the sages celebrating at Bene-Berak is reproduced—with some alterations—from Merian's picture of the feast given by Joseph to his brethren. The first map of Ereẓ Israel known in a Jewish publication was added on a folding page at the end of the book. A further edition of the work was produced in Amsterdam in 1712, with minor differences, and the name of the artist was omitted from the title page (figure 16).

As the Venice *Haggadah* of 1609/29 was widely imitated in southern Europe, so the Amsterdam editions had an enduring influence on the *Haggadot* produced in the Ashkenazi world. The pictures were imitated, if not copied, time after time with increasing indistinctness in innumerable editions illustrated with woodcuts or steel engravings. Such editions appeared in Frankfort in 1710 and 1775, in Offenbach in 1721, and in Amsterdam in 1765 and 1781. Throughout the 19th century and down to the present day the illustrations, including the four sons and the Passover at Bene-Berak, continued to be reproduced in ever-decreasing quality in hundreds of cheap *Haggadot* published on both sides of the Atlantic. The Amsterdam editions also inspired a number of illustrated *Haggadot* by 18th-century German Jewish manuscript artists, some of whom even improved on the original.

Some Later Editions. A few independently conceived *Haggadot* of the later period may be mentioned: the Trieste edition of 1864 with 58 original copper engravings of considerable artistic merit by K. Kirchmayer; the Prague edition of 1889 with illustrations by the Slovak artist Cyril Kulik; and the curious lithograph edition published in Poona in 1874 for the benefit of the *Bene Israel community. In the 20th century, editions have appeared illustrated (or in some cases entirely executed) by artists of the caliber of Joseph *Budko, Jakob Steinhardt, Arthur *Szyk, Albert *Rothenstein, and Ben *Shahn, and in Israel by J. Zimberknopf and David Gilboa, the last being written in scroll form. The modified *Haggadot* produced for the kibbutzim are also almost always illustrated, sometimes by local artists (see figures 17, 18, 19, 20, and 21). [C.R.]

MUSICAL RENDITION

Chanting and singing the texts of the *Haggadah* is generally observed in all Jewish communities, each one according to its peculiar style and custom. Although the celebration of the *seder* night is a family affair in which nobody is obliged to sing, it is customary to do so according to the example set by one's parents. From a musical point of view, the *Haggadah* text offers opportunities for solo chant as well as for responsorial and community singing. The scope of singing styles encompasses the simple chant (of the narrative and didactic sections), a more developed and melodious recitation that blends well with the responses of the company (for psalms and the old-style hymns), and melodies sung by all those present (for the more recent songs). The melodic recitations often come close to the simpler forms of synagogue chant; the Ashkenazi reader, for instance, largely uses the *Adonai Malakh Shteyger,* while the Jews of Iraq employ their *Tefillah* mode for some chapters. The psalms of the **Hallel* are usually intoned to the ancient patterns of psalmody (see Jewish *Music), and sung with great enthusiasm; already in the *Gemara* a proverb is quoted which says that singing the *Hallel* "cracks the ceiling" (TJ and TB, Pes. 7:12). The stanzas of the medieval poems that conclude the *Haggadah,* however, are given veritable song tunes in contemporary and past popular styles. These tunes vary from family to family and constitute a still unexplored treasure of folklore. Melodies in the folk style are normally attached to the poems *Addir Hu, Ki Lo Na'eh (Addir bi-Melukhah), Eḥad Mi Yode'a,* belonging to the widely disseminated category of "counting songs," and *Ḥad Gadya*. Less frequent are *Ḥasal Seder Pesaḥ* and the two acrostical hymns following it, as well as certain psalm verses and responsorial refrains in the earlier sections. The homelike atmosphere of *Haggadah* reading also permitted singing these poems in the vernacular. In the Ashkenazi community, this custom is not attested later than the 18th century, when it appears to have been abandoned. The Sephardim, however, not only continue singing the poems in the Ladino vernacular, but extend this even to more formal chapters such as *Ha Laḥma Anya.* There is an example from Bulgaria in which every Ladino verse is repeated immediately in Bulgarian and Turkish; the Bulgarian version was to serve the young generation, the Turkish text was meant for the older one, while Ladino was for all.

At some places it is regarded as a merit and even a duty to extend the celebration of the *seder* night by joyful singing, eventually accompanied by dance steps, for as long as possible. This custom, of course, has its roots in mystical concepts, but it did not remain confined to such circles and is honored by eastern and western communities as well. Ḥasidic *niggunim* ("melodies") are most often inserted by Ashkenazi celebrants. The *Haggadah* was also adapted by the Reform tendencies; there were several additions of music in rather dull style, but the substance was not touched. Kibbutzim in Israel have either designed their own tunes out of old and new elements or embellished tradition by additional songs and melodies. Israel songs (in the "classical" style of the 1940s and 1950s) are largely employed for stressing the national and seasonal aspects of Passover, and these tunes display their full charm in the traditional setting. A widely used "Kibbutz *Haggadah*" setting is that by Yehudah *Sharett. Another side-development was the use of the *Haggadah* for an oratorio, jointly undertaken by Max *Brod and the composer Paul *Dessau in 1933–35. There the traditional text has been expanded by selected scenes from the Bible and Midrash, and the music combines a declamatory style with the harsh harmonies of that period and full orchestral accompaniment. [H.Av.]

Bibliography: Haggadah: E. Baneth, *Der Sederabend* (1904); A. Berlinere, *Randbemerkungen zum taeglichen Gebetbuche,* 2 (1912), 47ff.; Finkelstein, in: HUCA, 23 (1950–51), pt. 2, pp. 319–37; idem, in: HTR, 31 (1938), 291–317; 35 (1942), 291–332; 36 (1943), 1–18; M. Friedmann (Ish-Shalom), *Me'ir Ayin al Seder ve-Haggadah shel Leylei Pesaḥ* (1895); D. Goldschmidt, *Haggadah shel Pesaḥ ve-Toledoteha* (1960), introduction (cf. reviews by E. E. Urbach in KS, 36 (1961), 143ff., and J. Heinemann in *Tarbiz,* 30 (1960/61), 405ff.); Z. Carl, *Mishnayot im Be'ur Ḥadash: Pesaḥim* (1927), introduction; J. Lewy, *Ein Vortrag ueber das Ritual des Pessachabends* (1904); Marx, in: JQR, 19 (1927/28), 1ff.; Stein, in: *Jewish Studies,* 8 (1957), 13–44; Zunz, Vortraege, 133–5; ET, 8 (1957), 177–93. **Illuminated Manuscripts:** Mayer, Art, index; B. Narkiss, *Hebrew Illuminated Manuscripts* (1969), index. BIRDS' HEAD HAGGADAH: M. Spitzer (ed.), *The Birds' Head Haggadah of the Bezalel National Art Museum in Jerusalem* (1967), bibliography in introductory volume, pp. 123–4. CINCINNATI HAGGADAH: Landsberger, in: HUCA, 15 (1940), 529–58. DARMSTADT HAGGADAH: B. Italianer, *Die Darmstaedter Pessach-Haggadah* (1927–28); R. Wischnitzer, in: P. Goodman (ed.), *Passover Anthology* (1961), 295–324. GOLDEN HAGGADAH: Margoliouth, Cat, no. 607; Gutmann, in: SBB, 7 (1965); Mayer, Art, no. 1792 (102–4, 106–7); B. Narkiss, *The Golden Haggadah* (1970). KAUFMANN HAGGADAH: Mayer, Art, no. 1792 (187–99, pls. xxxi–xxxv); no. 2061; no. 2302; B. Narkiss, in: KS, 34 (1958/59), 71–79; 4 (1966/67), 104–7. SARAJEVO HAGGADAH: Mayer, Art, index and nos. 1792, 2235–7; no. 2969 (nos. 30, 41). WASHINGTON HAGGADAH: Landsberger, in: HUCA, 21 (1948), 73–103; Gutmann, in: SBB, 7 (1965), 3–25. **Printed Editions:** Mayer, Art, index; S. Wiener, *Bibliographie der Oster-Haggadah* (1949²), contains a list of 884 editions between 1500 and 1900; idem, in: SBB, 7 (1965), 90–125 (addenda of 330 editions); A. Yaari, *Bibliografyah shel Haggadot Pesaḥ* (1960). **Music:** E. Werner, in: SBB, 7 (1965), 57–83; M. Brod, in: *Musica Hebraica,* 1–2 (1938), 21–23; B. Bayer, in: *Dukhan,* 8 (1966), 89–98; Idelsohn, Melodien, 2 (1922), nos. 16–26; 3 (1922), nos. 14–16; 4 (1923), nos. 76, 78, 79; L. Algazi, *Chants Sephardis* (1958), nos. 23–28; Levy, Antología, 3 (1968), nos. 189–316; A. Schoenfeld, *Recitative und Gesaenge . . . am ersten und zweiten Abende des Ueberschreitungs-festes* (1884); E. Piattelli, *Canti liturgici ebraici di rito italiano* (1967), 168–9.

HAGGAHOT (Heb. הַגָּהוֹת "glosses"; "corrections"), a term used both to mean the examination of manuscript and printed works in order to correct errors and in the sense of "glosses," i.e., notes and brief comments on the text.

This entry is arranged according to the following outline:

In the Bible, the verb, *haggiyyah* means to enlighten (cf. Ps. 18:29), and Kutscher conjectures that originally it had the same meaning when applied to books, since the main task of the *maggiha* (person making the *haggahah*) in the early period was to go over faded writing in order to "brighten" it.

Correction of Errors. *Haggahah* has been an integral element of writing and printing from the beginning since it is humanly impossible to avoid error. The types of error (both the authors' and the copyists') and correspondingly the categories of *haggahot* can be classified in two main groups.

Correction in the Content. This type of correction was mostly done by the author himself. In early literature with a large circulation the *haggahah* was done by scholars and experts. It was reported of Isaac Ruba, a *tanna* in the school of Judah ha-Nasi, that he had a corrected text of the Mishnah (TJ, Ma'as. Sh. 5:1, 55d). At a later period the *amora* Zeira complained that contemporary scholars did not correct the Mishnah in their possession in accordance with the version of R. Isaac *(ibid.)*. *Haggahot* of this type were done both on the basis of original and established texts, but at times they were also made at the discretion of the *maggiha*. Various scholars have pointed out *haggahot* of this later type which have found their way into the text of the Mishnah. Fragments of the *Mishneh Torah* of Maimonides in the author's own handwriting were discovered in the Cairo *Genizah* by M. Lutzki, who published them at the end of the Schulsinger edition (1947), and from them it is possible to trace the process of corrections and emendations whereby the final work was created. Manuscripts of Maimonides' commentary to the Mishnah, likewise thought to be in his own hand, have also been discovered and contain many of the author's *haggahot;* in some of them he changes his mind and gives a different opinion. The text of the *Ba'alei ha-Nefesh* of Abraham b. David of Posquières in the edition of Y. Kafaḥ (1965), a text emended by the author following the *hassagot* ("criticisms") of Zerahiah b. Isaac ha-Levi Gerondi, is a similar example. From this type of correction the "*Haggahot* literature" (see below) later developed.

Correction of Stylistic or Graphic Errors. This category consists essentially of technical mistakes resulting from such common copyists' errors as repeating the same word twice (dittography), omitting one of two similar adjacent letters or words (haplography), and missing words or lines because the same word occurs further on in a passage (homoioteleuton). In early times (and in Yemen until quite recently) there was also a class of errors which resulted from the practice of the "publishers" of those days of appointing a group of people (mainly slaves), skilled writers who wrote from dictation exactly what they heard (to this type belong such errors as *eilav,* "unto him," for *el av,* "unto father"). This type of error was obviated in copying the text of the Bible because of the prohibition against copying from dictation. The correction of such errors, made by others than the author himself, was done by comparing the text with an early or authoritative copy which adhered closely to the original text.

In early days a checked, original copy was deposited in the Temple, library, or archives, and whenever necessary the correct text was determined by it. The Midrash (Deut. R. 9:9) reports a tradition of a special **Sefer Torah* written by Moses and placed in the ark so that the correct text could be established (see S. Lieberman, *Hellenism in Jewish Palestine* (1950), 85f.). There are also reports of *Sifrei Torah* that were preserved in the Temple for the same purpose, and from them the *Sefer Torah* of the king was checked by the supreme *bet din.* The scroll was called "the Temple scroll," and texts were examined by a group of "book correctors" in the Temple, whose wages were paid from the public funds of the Temple treasury (Ket. 106a, Lieberman op. cit., 22); according to some commentators these correctors also examined the scrolls belonging to individuals and were also paid from the communal treasury. Similar scrolls were known which were regarded as especially accurate because they had been written by an expert scribe and had been meticulously checked; such a scroll was called "a checked *(muggah)* scroll." Examples were those written by Assi (Lieberman op. cit., 25). A medieval manuscript of the *Mishneh Torah* exists (Neubauer, Bod. Cat, no. 577) which was corrected on the basis of the author's text, and Maimonides confirms this by his signature at the end of the manuscript. Later this manuscript was kept at the *bet din,* and it was forbidden to use it for any purpose other than correcting later copies (according to the instructions in the colophon).

Uncorrected Torah scrolls were regarded as unauthoritative, and it was forbidden not only to use them but even to keep them (Ket. 19b); at a later period this prohibition was extended to include halakhic works (Sh. Ar., YD, 279). A complete set of halakhic rules was laid down for the correction of *Sifrei Torah*—their fitness for public reading being conditional on many details, including accurate *haggahah.* A scroll containing a certain number of errors was disqualified, and it was forbiden to correct it since the *haggahah* would spoil its appearance. If the errors were less numerous, an added letter could be erased or a missing one inserted. In the event of an error in the Divine Name, which it is forbidden to erase, it was sometimes the practice to peel off a layer from the parchment (Pitḥei Teshuvah to Sh. Ar., YD 276:2). The *haggahah* of *Sifrei Torah* is a purely technical task, as the text itself is naturally never emended and no discussion on the text of the Bible is found in talmudic literature (Lieberman, op. cit. 47). In some places, the scribe was made responsible for the *haggahah* (Resp. Rashba, pt. 1. no. 1056). There is evidence of the existence of corrected manuscripts of the Mishnah, such as "in an accurate Mishnah corrected from that of R. Ephraim" (*Maḥzor Vitry,* ed. by S. Hurwitz (1923[2]), 536). The following correctors of the Mishnah are known from the era of printing: Joseph Ashkenazi; the "*tanna* of Safed," Samuel Lerma; Soliman Oḥana; Menahem de Lonzano; Bezalel Ashkenazi; and his pupil Solomon Adani.

Influence of Haggahot on Text. The failure to distinguish between the two types of *haggahah,* as well as between corrections based on accurate texts and sources and those based on the judgment of the scribe, together with an exceptional caution against changing the actual text, caused the *haggahot* to be relegated to the margin instead of the text itself being corrected. As various copyists failed to appreciate this, the *haggahot* were subsequently incorporated into the body of the text. A critical examination in later ages revealed and indicated places where external *haggahot* had been arbitrarily and artificially included in the text (the question of the different sources of the material of the Babylonian Talmud and its transmission, which are known to have influenced the text, belongs to a different category). The *geonim* already pointed out this phenomenon (see M. M. Kasher, in *Gemara Shelemah,* Pesaḥim pt. 1 (1960), introd.). Despite this, it should be noted that in the main the text of the authoritative halakhic literature was meticulously preserved because of its importance in legal decisions and in leading a life in accordance with *halakhah.* The Jerusalem Talmud and the various halakhic and aggadic Midrashim were not preserved in a sufficiently corrected form, however, because the attitude to them was less punctilious.

The *haggahot* of various scholars affected the text of the Talmud, and this custom apparently became so widespread that *Gershom b. Judah of Mainz (who is stated to have copied books, among them the Bible) found it necessary to impose a ban on those who emended books, although it seems that this step was unsuccessful in completely eradicating the practice. A few generations later Jacob *Tam came out sharply against the emendation of books (introduction to *Sefer ha-Yashar*). He described the method of his grandfather, Rashi, stating that he did not emend the text itself but noted his emendations in the margin. It was Rashi's pupils who corrected the text in conformity with these notes, and Tam criticizes them for it. He also differentiates between *haggahah* which consisted of erasing words and that which was merely addition. Among other things he reveals that his brother Samuel b. Meir (Rashbam) also frequently made *haggahot* in the body of the text. It is important to note that the present text of the Babylonian Talmud is considerably influenced by Rashi's emendations, in contrast to the *haggahot* of the tosafists and other scholars. Perhaps this fact is to be attributed to the atttitude of Tam. In the age of printing this same process is encountered. Many of the *haggahot* of Solomon Luria have been introduced into the printed text of the Talmud, though he noted them in a special book and they were originally published in this form. In later editions of the Talmud, however, the text was already emended according to his notes (see below). The *haggahot* of Samuel Edels (the Maharsha), who was opposed to *haggahot* of the text (see his introduction), were nevertheless incorporated in the text.

PROOFREADERS. During the age of printing the influence of proofreaders and printers on the texts of books became increasingly important, and today it is occasionally possible to trace the methods of different proofreaders. After it had been established beyond doubt that the Leiden manuscript of the Jerusalem Talmud is the one from which the first edition was published in Venice (1523, by Bomberg), Lieberman showed in his essay on the tractate *Horayot* in the Jerusalem Talmud how great a share the proofreader—Cornelius Adelkind—had in establishing the present text (*Sefer ha-Yovel*... C. Albeck, 1963, 283–305). The research of R. N. N. Rabbinovicz on the text of the Babylonian Talmud provides a great deal of information on the activities of its first proofreaders. The most prominent of them was Ḥiyya Meir b. David, one of the rabbis of Venice, who was given the responsibility of correcting the whole Talmud edition by Bomberg in the course of three years (1520–23), as well as the commentary of Asher b. Jehiel. The proofreader of the first tractates of the Soncino Talmud (1484) was Gabriel b. Aaron Strasburg, and Rabbinovicz shows that his work is very faulty.

Gradually notes and corrections in the margins of books increased until they at times assumed the character of a textual apparatus. Still later these notes were even collected and issued in the form of independent works in which the word *haggahot* generally appeared in the title. The word is applied to many books, though their contents and character differ from one another.

Haggahot Literature. In the *haggahot* literature which developed, two main groups can be distinguished, the first constituting additions and supplements to the contents of the work—glosses—and the other consisting of emendations and notes to the text. The most prominent and best known of the first group were compiled on works of codification. An additional characteristic common to books of this category is that they lack formal structure and, since they were not authoritative, they were subjected to later adaptation and editing.

GLOSSES ON THE CODES. Such glosses were added to the great halakhic code, *Hilkhot ha-Rif*, of Isaac *Alfasi. Only fragments remain of the earliest gloss, the *haggahot* of his pupil, Ephraim (Abraham b. David, *Temim De'im* no. 68 and citations in the *Ha-Ma'or* of Zerahyah ha-Levi). One of the important motives for such works is the tendency to make the code reflect the views of the scholars of a particular country, and also apply to other spheres of the *halakhah*. It was with this aim that the great halakhic compilation, the *Mordekhai* of Mordecai b. Hillel, consisting of the rulings and responsa of German and French scholars, was compiled on the *Hilkhot ha-Rif*. In the manuscripts, however, the *Mordekhai* appears as a gloss to the work itself. The *Mordekhai* was not edited by its compiler and there are different versions and editions. In the 13th century Meir ha-Kohen, Mordecai's colleague and according to some his brother-in-law (both were pupils of Meir b. Baruch of Rothenburg), wrote his *haggahot*, called **Haggahot Maimuniyyot*, on the *Mishneh Torah*. It attempted to add to Maimonides' rulings the opinions and decisions of the scholars of Germany and France, and the views and responsa of Meir of Rothenburg occupy a prominent part of the work. As a result of this amalgamation of halakhic rulings there emerged a work which could serve as an authoritative halakhic code in different centers.

The *haggahot* of the tosafist *Perez b. Elijah of Corbeil to the *Tashbeẓ* of Samson b. Zadok was written for a similar purpose. Perez noted the customs and halakhic decisions of his teacher, Meir of Rothenburg, and added the customs and rulings of the French scholars. He also wrote *haggahot* to the *Sefer Mitzvot Katan (Semak)* of *Isaac b. Joseph of Corbeil, which are mainly a summation of the views of the early scholars. Because of the succinctness and brevity of the *Semak*, *haggahot* were added to it by many scholars from different localities. The best known are the as yet unpublished *haggahot* of Moses of Zurich (see Urbach, Tosafot, 450). To the comprehensive *Piskei ha-Rosh* of Asher b. Jehiel, who moved from Germany to Spain at the beginning of the 14th century, was added the *Haggahot Asheri* of Israel of Krems (14th century). In the main this consists of summarized quotations from the *Or Zaru'a* of Isaac b. Moses of Vienna and of the rulings of Hezekiah b. Jacob of Magdeburg (13th century) from whom he collected the rulings of Isaac b. Samuel.

The best-known *haggahot*, which had a decisive influence on the establishment of the *halakhah*, are those of Moses *Isserles of Cracow to the Shulḥan Arukh. Their purpose was both to supplement the rulings of Joseph Caro, who based himself upon the three *posekim*, Isaac Alfasi, Maimonides, and Asher b. Jehiel, with the rulings of the scholars of Germany, France, and Poland, and also to note the customs and decisions which were accepted by Ashkenazi Jewry where they differed from those accepted by the Sephardim. The *haggahot* of Isserles were noted on the margins of the Shulḥan Arukh and are based upon his *Darkhei Moshe* (Resp. Rema 131:3), and were copied and circularized by his pupils (on Sh. Ar. OḤ, Hilkhot Niddah, Cracow, 1570, on the whole Sh. Ar., *ibid.*, 1578). The notes and source references to the *Haggahot ha-Rema* were added later by others (first in the Cracow, 1607 edition). Isserles also compiled *haggahot* to other works such as *The Guide of the Perplexed* of Maimonides and the *Mordekhai*. With a similar purpose, Jacob Castro, chief rabbi of Egypt, also wrote *haggahot* to the Shulḥan Arukh—*Erekh Leḥem* (Constantinople, 1718)—which reveal many similarities with those of Isserles, but were not widely used.

This category of *haggahot* had several consequences, both positive and negative. On the one hand, they preserved fragments of large works which have been lost, apparently because of their size and the difficulties of transporting and copying them, or because they were superseded by the codes. On the other hand, it is possible that the abridgments and summaries actually contributed to the original works being forgotten (some were later rediscovered, e.g., the *Or Zaru'a, Ravyah,* and others).

TEXTUAL NOTES AND EMENDATIONS. In the *haggahot* literature of the second category, those of Solomon b. Jehiel *Luria of Lublin to the Babylonian Talmud are outstanding in their scope and importance. According to his sons, who published them separately under the title *Ḥokhmat Shelomo* (Cracow, 1581–82), he had no intention of committing his *haggahot* and comments to book form, but they served him as "notes and a prolegomenon to his major work, the *Yam shel Shelomo.*" These *haggahot* were written in the margin to the Bomberg edition of the Talmud in which he studied. Although the proofreaders of this publishing house were noted scholars (see above), this edition contains many mistakes and errors. The *haggahot* were made by comparing the text with sources and parallels, and according to his sons, Luria made use of manuscripts of the Talmud, of Rashi, and of the *tosafot* in his possession. In the Talmud published at that time in Constantinople by the brothers Yavetz, these *haggahot* were appended to the various tractates, and sometimes corrections were made according to the *haggahot* in the body of the work and indicated in the margin. In the later editions they were incorporated into the text and cannot be detected without special investigation (numerous examples are to be found in the *Dikdukei Soferim* of R. N. N. Rabbinovicz). Luria also wrote *haggahot* to many other halakhic works. A. Berliner saw his *haggahot* to Maimonides in the town of Sokol (see Assaf in bibl.).

Also known are the *Haggahot ha-Baḥ* of Joel *Sirkes of Cracow, which he also inscribed on the margins of the first editions of the Talmud in which he studied. They were first published in Warsaw in 1824 as a separate work and thenceforth in the later editions of the Talmud. Like those of Luria, these *haggahot* greatly affect the understanding of the text of the Talmud and its commentaries, but in contrast to those *haggahot* which in many cases were based upon manuscripts, Sirkes' corrections were mainly according to linguistic considerations and internal comparisons within the Talmud itself. Among the outstanding scholars who devoted themselves to *haggahot* and emendations in this sense was *Elijah the Gaon of Vilna. According to tradition, his corrections and amendments covered the whole range of talmudic, midrashic, and kabbalistic literature. Although he himself published none of his *haggahot,* some were printed later, but not all have survived in an accurate and original form. Among his published *haggahot* are some of those on the Babylonian Talmud (in late editions starting Vienna, 1816–26), on the *Mekhilta* (Vilna, 1844), the order *Zera'im* of the Jerusalem Talmud (Koenigsberg, 1858), *Sifrei* (1866), Tosefta (firstly independently and later in the Vilna edition of the Talmud), and the *Sifra* (1959). Scholars have concerned themselves with the question whether Elijah of Vilna's *haggahot* are also based upon manuscripts and early versions or are the outcome of his own discretion. With regard to the Tosefta, S. Lieberman (*Tosefet Rishonim,* 3 (1939), introd.) has established that in essence they are derived from quotations of the text in the works of the *rishonim,* and apparently those on the Jerusalem Talmud also belong to this category.

In this category of *haggahot* are works which are less well known but of considerable importance, since through them the original readings of manuscripts and early printed works, from which the *haggahot* were taken, have been preserved. This phenomenon is especially notable in the works of Sephardi rabbis of recent centuries, who had access to manuscripts which they used frequently. Among them are *Haggahot Tummat Yesharim* (Venice, 1622) on *Avot de-Rabbi Nathan,* the *Sifra,* Alfasi, etc. Many such *haggahot* are also enshrined in the works of Ḥ. J. D. Azulai, who saw and used more manuscripts and early printed editions than any other author. In his first work, compiled in his youth, the *Sha'ar Yosef* (Leghorn, 1757) on *Horayot,* he made extensive use for the first time of the well-known manuscript of the Babylonian Talmud (now Ms. Munich no 95, issued in photographed facsimile by H. L. Strack in Leiden in 1912), from which he corrected texts of the Talmud. His other works (see Benayahu's lists, p. 185–252) constitute a rich source of knowledge on the nature and existence of manuscripts in talmudic literature and of *haggahot* from them. This category of *haggahot* contained in the works of the Oriental scholars, which has scarcely been investigated, contains a considerable amount of material both on texts and contents of the works and is a fruitful field for historical and literary research into the history of talmudic literature.

Bibliography: Y. Kutscher, *Ha-Lashon ve-ha-Reka ha-Leshoni shel Megillat Yeshayahu ha-Shelemah mi-Megillot Yam ha-Melaḥ* (1959), 462f.; S. Lieberman, *Hellenism in Jewish Palestine* (1950), 20–27, 83–99; idem (ed.), Maimonides, *Hilkhot ha-Yerushalmi* (1947), introd.; Y. Kafaḥ (ed.), Abraham b. David, *Ba'alei ha-Nefesh* (1965), introd.; Epstein, Mishnah (1948), 168ff., 201, 352, 424–595, 1269–75, 1284–90; E. S. Rosenthal; in: PAAJR, 31 (1963), 1–71 (Heb. pt.); idem, in: *Sefer Ḥ. Yalon* (1963) 281–337; R. N. Rabinovitz, *Ma'amar al Hadpasat ha-Talmud,* ed. by A. M. Habermann (1952); M. Kasher, in: *Gemara Shelemah,* Pesaḥim pt. 1 (1960), introd.; E. M. Lipschuetz, in: *Sefer Rashi* (1956), 190–3, 236; B. Benedikt, in: KS, 26 (1949/50), 322–38 (on *Haggahot* of R. Ephraim); S. Kohen, in: *Sinai,* 9–16 (1941–45), esp. 9 (1941), 265f., 12 (1943), 99–106 (on the *Mordekhai;* idem, *ibid.,* 11 (1942), 60f. (on *Haggahot Maimuniyyot*); Urbach, Tosafot, 436f. (on the *Mordekhai*), 437f. (on *Haggahot Maimuniyyot*), 439, 453ff. (on *Haggahot* of Perez of Corbeil), and index 590 s.v. *nusḥa'ot:* I. Nissim, in: *Sefunot,* 2 (1958), 89–102 (on *Haggahot* of J. Castro and J. Ẓemaḥ); idem, in: *Sinai-Sefer Yovel* (1958), 29–39 (on *Haggahot* of Isserles); A. Sier, *Ha-Rema* (1957), 59ff. (ditto); S. Assaf, in: *L. Ginzberg Jubilee Volume,* Heb. pt. (1946), 455–61 (on S. Luria's *Ḥokhmat Shelomo*); S. K. Mirsky, in: *Horeb,* 6 (1942), 51–55 (on Joel Sirkes' *Bayit Ḥadash*); J. H. Levin, *Aliyyot Eliyahu* (1963), 79ff. (on *Haggahot* of Elijah of Vilna); K. Kahana, in: *Ha-Ma'ayan,* 2 no. 1 (1955), 24–41 (ditto); S. Goren, in: J. L. Maimon (ed.), *Sefer ha-Gra,* 4 (1954), 45–107 (ditto); M. Vogelmann, *ibid.,* 108–10 (ditto); M. Benayahu, *Rabbi Ḥ. Y. D. Azulai* (Heb., 1959), 81ff.

[S.Z.H.]

HAGGAHOT MAIMUNIYYOT, a comprehensive halakhic work which is one of the most important sources for the halakhic rulings of the scholars of Germany and France. Its author was the distinguished pupil of *Meir b. Baruch of Rothenburg, Meir ha-Kohen of Rothenburg (end of the 13th century). He compiled it as a supplement and notes (see **Haggahot*) to the *Mishneh Torah* of Maimonides, and its first part was published in the Constantinople edition of the *Mishneh Torah* (1509), and has appeared in all subsequent editions. Of it, Levi ibn Ḥabib writes (Responsa, ed. Lemberg No. 130): "If the author of the *Haggahot* is a small man in your eyes, he is great in the eyes of all Israel." It may originally have been written on the margins of the *Mishneh Torah,* as it appears in early manuscripts, and as seems to be the case from the passages to which the words "written in the margin" are appended. Of the 14 books of the *Mishneh Torah,* the only books to which there are no *Haggahot* are *Hafla'ah, Zera'im* (save for a fragment at its end), *Avodah, Korbanot,* and *Tohorah.* The chief aim of the author was to attach the rulings of the scholars of Germany and France to the work of Maimonides, whose decisions and conclusions are in the main based upon the traditions and rulings of the scholars of Spain. This aim was the result of the great preoccupation with Maimonides' work in the school of Meir of Rothenburg (who also compiled works connected with Maimonides—see Urbach, 434ff.), as well as the need felt to adapt the work of Maimonides, which was spreading more and more as a comprehensive halakhic work, for use also in Germany and France.

The work is divided into two sections, one of glosses and notes attached to the *Mishneh Torah*, and the other—also called *Teshuvot Maimuniyyot* (first published in the Venice ed. of 1524)—appended at the end of each book of the *Mishneh Torah* and containing responsa by German and French scholars relevant to the topics dealt with in the body of the work. It is difficult to determine whether this division is the work of the author himself or was effected by a later editor, although it is early and already appears in early manuscripts of the work. This division is not absolute, however, and in the section of glosses one can still find responsa which, apparently in view of their brevity and direct connection with the *halakhah* under discussion, were not given separately (for examples see Urbach, 436 n. 20). On the other hand, the section of responsa contains non-responsa material (*ibid.*, n. 21).

There are differences between the editions of 1509 and 1524, some of which are material. The wording of the glosses in the Venice edition (from which the later editions were printed) is more original and the author generally speaks in the first person, while the wording of the 1509 edition shows signs of being a later version, and has obviously passed through adaptation and abbreviation at the hands of a later editor. In many places in the 1509 edition the passages end with the words: "thus far the language of R. M. K." (=R. Meir ha-Kohen); the editor even comments on the words of Meir ha-Kohen (see to Hilkhot Zekhiyyah u-Mattanah 11:19; "however may the All-Merciful pardon Meir ha-Kohen..."). Certain passages appear in the Constantinople version which are absent from the Venice version, and vice versa. The Constantinople edition contains additions that may have been added by the editor, most of them taken from the *Sefer Mitzvot Gadol (Semag)* of Moses of Coucy, the *Sefer Mitzvot Katan (Semak)* of Isaac of Corbeil, the *Sefer ha-Terumah* of Baruch b. Samuel of Mainz, the *Ha-Roke'aḥ* of Eleazar of Worms, the *Seder Olam* of Simḥah of Speyer, etc.

From Urbach's comparison of the two editions there can be no doubt about the identification of Meir ha-Kohen as the author of the glosses, nor is there any reason to assume that other authors participated in it, as was assumed by S. Cohen and J. Wellesz. The close connection between the sections of the book is also beyond doubt, and there is no need to assume that Meir ha-Kohen made use of a preexisting collection of responsa. The section of glosses (Venice edition) contains references in many places to the section of responsa (see the list in Wellesz, p. 52, to which many additions can be made). It is difficult to determine whether these references are the author's own or the editor's. They do not, however, seem to replace responsa included in the glosses of the original work, which when taken out were left as mere references (see, e.g., the *Haggahot* Sheluḥin ve-Shutafin, 5 no. 6). The section of responsa is on the books *Nashim* (37 items), *Kedushah* (27), *Hafla'ah* (7), *Nezikin* (22), *Kinyan* (40), *Mishpatim* (71), and *Shofetim* (20), and contains a valuable collection of the responsa of the author's teacher Meir of Rothenburg, which in some cases gives a reading of greater value than other sources, while others are unknown from any other source. Also cited in it are responsa by Jacob Tam, Isaac b. Samuel ha-Zaken, Samson of Sens (copied from the *Nimmukim* of his pupil Jacob of Courson, who collected them into a book—see Resp. to Ma'akhalot Asurot, no. 13), and his brother Isaac b. Abraham, Simḥah b. Samuel of Speyer, Baruch b. Samuel of Mainz, etc.

No biographical details of Meir ha-Kohen are known other than that he was, according to some, the pupil of Meir of Rothenburg; Mordecai b. Hillel ha-Kohen, the author of the *Mordekhai*, was his brother-in-law and colleague (Ishut 9, no. 1); and he lived in Rothenburg (Responsa to Shofetim, no. 16, where the reading should be "here Rothenburg" and not "in it, in Rothenburg"; see *Sefer ha-Parnas* (1891), no. 269). He attended upon his teacher when the latter was imprisoned in Wasserburg (Shab. n. 6) and later in the fortress of Ensisheim (to Tefillah 14:5, according to the Constantinople ed.), and there discussed halakhic matters with him. His teacher sent halakhic responsa to him (Sefer Torah 7 n. 7; Tefillah 15 n. 1; Ishut 3 n. 15). In one responsum (Resp. Maharam of Rothenburg, ed. Prague, no. 78) he addressed him thus "the lips of the priest preserve decisive Torah opinion [cf. Mal. 2:7], my intimate associate R. Meir ha-Kohen."

The supplements and variants of the Constantinople edition, which is now rare, were published in the El ha-Mekorot edition of the *Mishneh Torah* (1954–56), and in the Po'alei Agudat Israel edition (1944) to the books *Madda* through *Nashim*. A substantial number of manuscripts are known (in Jerusalem, Oxford, British Museum, Cambridge, Sassoon, and other libraries), but they have not yet been investigated and examined. The attempt of Allony to fix the date of the writing of the Cambridge manuscript (13.1) of the *Mishneh Torah* as 1230 instead of 1170 is a mistake, for he did not notice that it contains the *Haggahot Maimuniyyot*. I. Z. Kahana, who began to issue a critical edition of the rulings and responsa of Meir of Rothenburg (vols. 1–3, 1957–63), drew a great deal from the *Haggahot Maimuniyyot*, utilizing four manuscripts of the work.

Bibliography: Azulai, 2 (1852), 33 no. 23; Weiss, Dor, 5 (1904[4]), 77f.; S. Kohen, in: *Sinai*, 10 (1942), 10; Wellesz, in: *Ha-Goren*, (1908), 35–59; N. Allony, in: *Aresheth*, 3 (1961), 410; Urbach, Tosafot, 434–6.

[S.Z.H.]

HAGGAI (Heb. חַגַּי; "born on a festival"), prophet from the post-Exilic period whose book is the tenth in the Minor Prophets. His extant prophecies, which consist altogether of 38 verses, date from the second year of the reign of Darius I king of Persia, i.e., 520 B.C.E., between the first of Elul and the 24th of Kislev. It appears, however, that the prophet was previously well-known to the people, and that his words carried weight (1:12). The author of Ezra-Nehemiah notes the important role he played in the rebuilding of the Temple (Ezra 5:1; 6:14).

His prophecies deal mainly with the construction of the Temple, and with the great events which the nation will experience in the future as a result of it. Haggai turns first to *Zerubbabel, son of Shealtiel, governor of Judah, and to Joshua, son of Jehozadak, the high priest (1:1–3), and then to the people (1:3–11), encouraging them not to postpone the construction of the Temple, but to begin immediately. He claimed that all the mishaps of poverty, famine, and drought which befell the nation were caused by the delay in the work. The people listened to Haggai's words despite their fears (1:13; 2:5) and, led by Zerubbabel and Joshua, they began work on the 24th of Elul. Although the new Temple seemed small and poor "and as nothing in your eyes" (2:3), Haggai encouraged them by saying that the size of the building would not determine its value for future generations. He proclaimed that with the renewal of the Temple construction, God's covenant with His people would be renewed, as in the days of the exodus from Egypt. However, the first condition for the return of the Divine Spirit is the beginning of the work (2:4–5). The prophet also had a messianic vision of the time to come: God will shake all the universe and the wealth of all the nations will

Haggai prophesying in an illustration from the *Conradin Bible*, Italy, 13th century. Baltimore, Md., Walters Art Gallery, Ms. W. 152, fol. 24.

come to the Temple; its glory will be greater than the glory of the First Temple (2: 6–9).

Three months later, on the 24th of Kislev (2:10–19), when the Temple's foundations were laid, Haggai proclaimed two new prophecies. He turned to the priests to seek guidance from them (cf. Jer. 18:18 "instruction from the priest"). He asked what the law is concerning a man who carries hallowed meat in the skirt of his garment which touches any food. They replied that the food does not become holy, but if a man made unclean by a dead body touches the food, the food does become unclean. From this, Haggai drew a parallel for the people: as long as the Temple was not built, despite the fact that sacrifices were being offered on the altar, the people were unclean. Only when the Temple is rebuilt will the Lord's lovingkindness return. In support of this, he declared that from that day on they shall be blessed. That very day (2:20ff.) the prophet uttered a messianic oracle about Zerubbabel. He announced that God was about to shake the heavens and earth and overthrow the kingdom of Persia ("the strength of the kingdoms of the nations"). He will destroy "everyone by the sword of his brother" (2:22), and then Zerubbabel's turn will come. While Jeremiah prophesied about Jehoiakim (22:24), "though Coniah the son of Jehoiakim king of Judah were the signet ring on My right hand, yet I would pluck thee thence," Haggai turned the curse into a blessing for his grandson Zerubbabel: "I will take you . . . and make you like a signet ring" (2:23). Like other prophets before him, Haggai envisioned the end of idolatry and the renewal of the kingdom of Israel. He was first, however, to prophesy about the exalted role destined for the Second Temple in the life of Israel and the entire world. The language of the book is that of simple prose which however occasionally becomes florid (1:5–11; 2:6–9, 21–23). The prophet uses phrases from the Torah (cf. Haggai 2:5 with Ex. 24:8; Haggai 2:12 with Lev. 6:20; etc.). He alludes to Isaiah's prophecy about the honor which the nations will bring to the Temple in the future (Isa. 60), to Jeremiah's words (Jer. 22:24) which he reinterprets; and to the prophecies of Ezekiel (Ezek. 37:27) about the holy spirit resting upon the new Temple. He is similar to Zechariah, his contemporary, in his views concerning the honor to be paid the Temple in the future (Zech. 6:15, 8:20–23) and the greatness of Zerubbabel (*ibid.*, 3:8). It is assumed that the book was edited by the prophet's disciples. The sages (BB 15a) attributed its editing to the elders of the Great Assembly.

Bibliography: General: Ackroyd, in: JJS, 2 (1951), 163–76; 3 (1952), 1–13, 151–6; idem, in: JNES, 17 (1958), 13–27; Bentzen, in: RHPR, 10 (1930), 493–503; H. W. Wolff, *Haggai* (1951); K. Galling, *Studien zur Geschichte Israels im persischen Zeitalter* (1964); Hess, in: *Rudolph Festschrift* (1961), 109–34; Kaufmann, Y., Toledot, 4 (1956), 215, 225. Special Studies: Bloomhardt, in: HUCA, 5 (1928), 153–95; Budde, in: ZAW, 26 (1906), 1–28; James, in: JBL, 53 (1934), 229–35; Kittel, Gesch, 3 pt. 2 (1929), 441–57; Noth, in: ZAW, 68 (1956), 25–46; Siebeneck, in: CBQ, 19 (1957), 312–28; Waterman, in: JNES, 13 (1954), 73–78; J. W. Rothstein, *Juden und Samaritaner* (1908). [Y.M.G.]

HAGGAI (or **Ḥagga;** fl. c. 300 C.E.), Palestinian *amora*. Probably born in Babylon (TJ, Or 3:1, 63a; TJ, Av. Zar. 3:14, 43c), he went to Palestine, where after initial difficulties (Av. Zar. 68a) he became a prominent member of the academy of Tiberias and one of the principal pupils of *Zeira whom he often accompanied (TJ, Dem. 3:2, 23b) and in whose name he transmitted sayings (TJ, Kid. 3:2, 63d). In a dispute with *Ḥanina in a case of marital law, Haggai was praised by R. Hilla as a scholar of sound judgment *(ibid.)*. Because of his important position in the academy he opened each study session while *Yose and Jonah closed them (TJ, RH 2:6, 58b). Haggai was also the pupil (according to Frankel, *Mevo ha-Yerushalmi*, 79b–80b, the associate) of Yose (BB 19b; TJ, Pes. 4:3, 31a; TJ, Kid. 3:3, 64a; see TJ, Shab. 1:5, 4a, where Yose calls him "rabbi"; cf. TJ, RH 2:6, 58b). In a case brought before *Aḥa he supported the view of his teacher Yose by an oath "By Moses," a formula often employed by him (TJ, Naz. 5:1, 54a; TJ, 4:3, 24a, etc.). Like Yose he held the view that the reason for the interdiction against looking at the kohanim while they are reciting the Priestly Benedictions is because it may distract them from proper concentration (TJ, Ta'an. 4:1, 67b).

His close pupil and associate was *Mana, the head of the academy in Sepphoris, who participated in Haggai's scholarly discussions *(ibid.)*. Once Mana visited his sick teacher on the Day of Atonement and gave him permission to drink, but Haggai declined to avail himself of it (TJ, Yoma 6:4, 43d). His daughter was involved in lawsuits because she squandered her property (TJ, BB 10:15, 17d). His son Eleazar was a pupil of Mana's academy in Sepphoris (TJ, Shek. 7:3, 50c). Haggai appears to have lived for a while in Tyre (TJ, Ket. 2:6, 4a) and some sources hint at the fact that he migrated to Babylonia in the days of *Abbaye and *Rabbah since he is quoted in the Babylonian Talmud as having had discussions with them (e.g., BM 113b but see Dik. Sof. BM 169b, n. 100). The Haggai who ordered *Jacob of Kefar Nibburaya to be punished by flagellation for falsely interpreting Scripture to the effect that fish must be slaughtered in the same way as animals and that the son of a gentile mother may be circumcised on the Sabbath is probably this Haggai and not *Haggai of Sepphoris.

Bibliography: Bacher, Pal Amor, 3; Hyman, Toledot, s.v.; J. L. Maimon, *Yiḥusei Tanna'im ve-Amora'im* (1963), 229–30; Ḥ. Albeck, *Mavo la-Talmudim* (1969), 323–5. [Ed.]

HAGGAI OF SEPPHORIS (third century C.E.), Palestinian *amora.* Born in Babylonia, one of the principle pupils of *Huna (the exilarch), he emigrated to Palestine where he joined the pupils of R. *Johanan. There is considerable confusion between him and another *amora* of the same name (see preceding entry). In fact, most authorities, including the classical ones (*Yiḥusei Tanna'im ve-Amora'im,* s.v. *Haggai*), do not distinguish between the two. Even accepting that there were two distinct men called Haggai (and there were more, see Albeck, *Mavo la-Talmudim,* 391), it remains difficult to determine which events recorded apply to the one and which to the other. Haggai transmitted halakhic rules in the names of Abba b. Avda, Abbahu, Isaac, Johanan b. Lakhish, Joshua b. Levi, Samuel b. Naḥamani, etc. When the coffin of his teacher Huna (probably the exilarch mentioned above, see Tos. to MK 25a; and TJ, Kil. 9:4, 32b–c) was brought (in 297 C.E.) to Palestine to be placed in a cave (sepulcher) at the side of *Ḥiyya's remains, Haggai was chosen to place his teacher's coffin there, a special honor and privilege (MK 25a). According to another version (TJ, Ket. 12:3, 35a) he was at that time an old man of over 80 and people suspected that he wished to enter the cave only to die at that chosen spot. Thus he asked that a rope be attached to his feet so that he might be pulled out from the cave after the burial of Huna.

In *Genesis Rabbah* (9:3) he quotes, in R. Isaac's name, an interpretation of I Chronicles 28:9 to teach that "even before thought is born in a man's heart, it is already revealed to God." Further (Gen. R. 60:2), based upon Genesis 24:12, he states that everybody needs God's grace, since even Abraham, in whose merit favor is granted to the whole world, was in need of divine grace for the success of the choice of a bride for Isaac. It is stated that when he appointed officials *(parnasim)* he handed them a Torah scroll to symbolize that authority comes only from the Law, as it is written, "By me kings reign . . . by me princes rule" (Prov. 8:15–16).

Bibliography: Bacher, Pal Amor; Hyman, Toledot, s. v.; J. L. Maimon, *Yiḥusei Tanna'im ve-Amora'im* (1963), 229–30; Ḥ. Albeck, *Mavo la-Talmudim* (1969), 287.

[ED.]

ḤAGIGAH (Heb. חֲגִיגָה); the last tractate—according to the customary arrangement—of the order **Mo'ed* in the Mishnah, Tosefta, and the Babylonian and Jerusalem Talmuds. It is also called *Re'iyyah* (so in the Zuckermandel edition of the Tosefta). The Mishnah contains three chapters. Chapters 1:1–2:4 deal with the laws of peace-offerings which were offered during the festivals (hence the name of the tractate) and with kindred subjects such as the duty of *pilgrimage (*re'iyyah,* "appearance," hence the alternative name of the tractate), and the laws of sacrifices during the festival in general. From 2:5 until the end of the tractate it deals with the laws of ritual purity and impurity connected with sacred objects and the Temple. The *mishnayot* 1:8–2:1 are entirely different from the rest of the tractate and have a character of their own. The conjecture of Nachman *Krochmal seems probable, that the original tractate *Ḥagigah* commenced with these two *mishnayot,* which are a kind of introduction to the different categories of *halakhah* (which include laws of *Ḥagigah*) whose purpose is to emphasize the relationship of the Midrash to the *halakhah* and the tendency to depart from the previous method of deriving *halakhot* from direct exposition of Scripture (see **Midrash Halakhah*). Chapter 1:7 is an addition from the Tosefta. Most of the Mishnah of *Ḥagigah* was already arranged apparently during the Temple period and most of the scholars mentioned in it belong to that period. According to Epstein the *halakhot* of *Ḥagigah* were already arranged at the latest in the time of Herod. The Tosefta similarly contains three chapters and deals with similar themes, and the same applies to the two Talmuds except that the Talmud of the tractate contains an abundance of *aggadah,* particularly on the cosmogony and *Merkabah mysticism, and the four "who entered paradise" (TJ, Ḥag. 2:1; Ḥag. 13b–15a). *Ḥagigah* was translated into English by I. Abrahams in the Soncino edition of the Talmud (1938).

Bibliography: Ḥ. Albeck, *Shishah Sidrei Mishnah* 2 (1958), 387–90; Epstein, Tanna'im, 46–52; (1952), 75; E. E. Urbach, in: *Beḥinot,* 3 (1952), 75.

[ED.]

HAGIOGRAPHY. Although hagiographies, embellished accounts of biblical worthies, are not unknown in previous ages, particularly in the apocrypha (e.g., Lives of the *Prophets and Martyrdom of *Isaiah), in the Middle Ages they developed as a specific genre of literature, of which they constitute a major type (see *Fiction, Hebrew). These may be divided into two main categories according to the protagonist portrayed: (a) hagiographies whose heroes are ancient Jewish sages and martyrs (biblical and talmudic characters); (b) hagiographies whose heroes are medieval scholars, rabbis, and martyrs. Different fields of medieval literature have adapted the hagiography to their specific needs. Ethical literature used it to exhort in the footsteps of the hero (see *Exemplum); Hebrew historical writings usually substituted the hagiography for the biography of medieval

Engraving illustrating the tractate *Ḥagigah,* showing pilgrims going up to Jerusalem for a festival; from a Hebrew-Latin Mishnah, illustrated by Mich. Richey, Amsterdam, 1700–1704, J.N.U.L.

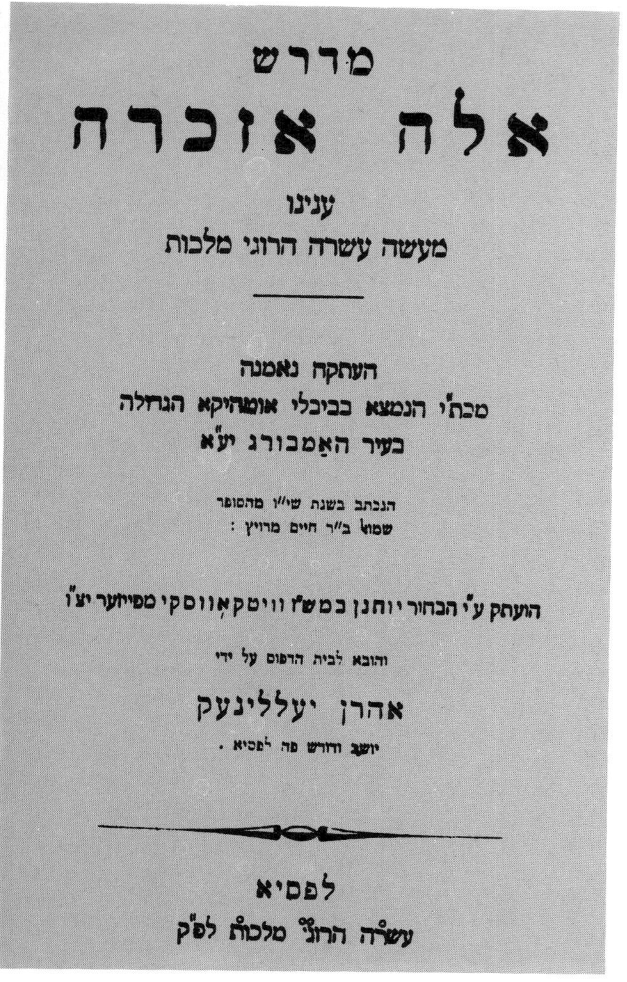

מדרש
אלה אזכרה
ענינו
מעשה עשרה הרוגי מלכות

העתקה נאמנה
מכת"י הנמצא בביבלי אטהיקא הגדולה
בעיר האמבורג יע"א

הנכתב בשנת שי"ו מהסופר
שמואל ב"ר חיים מרויץ :

הועתק ע"י הבחור יוחנן כמש"ז וויטקאווסקי מפיזער יצ"ו

והובא לבית הדפוס על ידי
אהרן יעללינעק
יושב ודורש פה לפסיא .

לפסיא
עשר"ה הרוג"י מלכו"ת לפ"ק

Hebrew title page of a Hebrew-German edition of *Midrash Elleh Ezkerah,* a medieval version of the story of the Ten Martyrs, edited by A. Jellinek. Leipzig, 1853. Jerusalem, J.N.U.L.

and ancient Jewish scholars. Medieval collections of Hebrew stories abound with hagiographic material; while in kabbalistic and ḥasidic literature, the hagiography was a formal literary device to convince the reader of the veracity of the Jewish mystics' visions.

Use of Biblical and Talmudic Material. Biblical and talmudic stories were freely adapted. In *Midrash Va-Yisa'u* (in A. Jellinek, *Beit ha-Midrash,* 3 (1938[2]), 1–5), a narrative about Jacob and his sons, the characters are portrayed as medieval knights who fight over Shechem and other cities, in the same way as the Crusaders had fought in the capture of a city. Abraham and Moses were also subjects of individual works, embellished by hagiographic additions. So were the lives of talmudic sages; the medieval Midrash *Pirkei Rabbi Eliezer,* for instance, opens with a hagiographic account of *Eliezer b. Hyrkanus. One of the most typical examples of medieval hagiography is the story of the *Ten Martyrs, known also as *Midrash Elleh Ezkerah* (ed. by A. Jellinek, 1853). Some of the material is drawn from talmudic sources, but most of its treatment is within the framework of medieval themes and literary conventions. It is an account of the tortures inflicted by the Romans on ten martyrs, most of them *tannaim* (the ten martyrs had not been contemporaries and could not have been executed together); the story also inspired the composition of prayers and *piyyutim,* and became the cornerstone of Hebrew medieval martyrologic hagiography.

Use of Contemporary Stories and Personages. Hagiography of the Middle Ages which centered around medieval characters contains historical and biographical details, as well as fiction. Some of the legends included are entirely original, while others thematically belong to international hagiographic motifs. The miracle associated with Rashi when still in his mother's womb (that a wall opened to let his pregnant mother hide from a group of soldiers) is told about many other sages, and has nothing whatsoever to do with Rashi's personality or biography. Sometimes the heroes of such legends are purely fictional, and the hagiography thus is not even related to a historical personality.

The development of the hagiography in the Middle Ages is perhaps best exemplified by the evolvement of cycles of hagiographies centered around the leaders of the Ḥasidei Askhenaz: *Samuel he-Ḥasid, R. *Judah he-Ḥasid, his son, and *Eleazar ben Judah of Worms. The earliest known versions were found (in manuscript) and published by N. *Bruell (*Jahrbuecher fuer Juedische Geschichte und Literatur,* 9 (1889), 1–71). Different versions are extant in many later Hebrew and Yiddish collections. There are no hagiographies about these rabbis from their own time (12th and 13th centuries); the stories begin to appear in the 14th and 15th centuries. However, many of the hagiographies from these cycles point to the fact that the elaborate narrative about one of these rabbis sprang from a much simpler story that was told and written by that writer himself. In the simple narrative, the hero's name is not mentioned nor did he see himself as the hero. In one of his theological works, R. Judah he-Ḥasid has a five-line story about a rabbi who miraculously discovered some clothes that had been stolen from one of his pupils. A hagiography written in the 15th century, about R. Judah, contains a long and well-developed legend about the rabbi's discovery of a treasure which had been entrusted to a Jew and stolen from him, thus endangering the lives of a whole Jewish community. The core of the narrative is the same, but the plot was elaborated upon, many details were added, and the anonymous hero became R. Judah he-Ḥasid himself. Short descriptions, such as the one by R. Judah he-Ḥasid in Ḥasidei Ashkenaz literature of sorcerers and demons, were later expanded into hagiographies describing contests between the pietist sages and gentile sorcerers in the working of miracles and sorcery. While these early theological works receded into oblivion, the stories to which they gave birth survived and evolved into the fully developed genre of hagiography.

Ibn Ezra and Other Spanish Jewish Scholars. One of the most prominent heroes of medieval Hebrew hagiography was R. Abraham *ibn Ezra. Nothing in his actual biography justifies the stories told about him, except that he was a traveler, and visited many countries in the East and in the West. Abraham ibn Ezra became the "traveling hero" of a cycle of hagiographic legends. Disguised so that nobody would recognize him, in a dramatic moment he would reveal his true identity. In these tales, Ibn Ezra pokes fun at proud rich men, helps Jews in danger, is the hero of both popular jokes and tragic legends. Ibn Ezra was a hero of fiction up to modern times, and in the 19th century, stories describing his miraculous adventures were still being printed.

Other Spanish Jewish scholars also became central figures of hagiographies. The beginnings of the Jewish center of learning in Spain were described by Abraham *Ibn Daud in his *Seder ha-Kabbalah* by means of the hagiographical story "The Four Captives." *Judah Halevi's pilgrimage to Jerusalem was the focus of a cycle of hagiographical stories; and this most rationalistic of Spanish Jewish scholars did not escape legends which told about his later adherence to the Kabbalah.

Martyrologic Hagiography. The martyrologic hagiography developed especially in Germany during the Crusades of the 11th–13th centuries. Thousands of Jewish martyrs became subjects of legends. The best known revolves about R. *Amnon, the alleged author of the prayer *_U-Netanneh Tokef._ Many other martyrs were described in a similar hagiographic manner in collections of historical writings and stories.

Hagiography and Kabbalah. The most powerful creative force of Jewish hagiography in the Middle Ages was the Kabbalah. Kabbalists of the 12th and 13th centuries told legends about their teachers and mystical mentors. The first kabbalistic scholar in Provence, head of a school of kabbalists, Rabbi *Isaac Sagi Nahor ("the blind"), was described by his disciples as capable of distinguishing between a "new" and an "old" soul, i.e., between persons whose souls had entered the human form for the first time and souls that had transmigrated from previous existences (see *Gilgul). In Spain, there were kabbalists who wove wonderful tales about the mystics of Germany. R. *Isaac ha-Kohen of Segovia (the second half of the 13th century) told about the powers of Eleazar of Worms who, according to him, traveled on a cloud whenever he had an urgent trip to make.

The Zohar and Later Kabbalistic Writings. The Zohar is full of hagiographic references to R. *Simeon b. Yoḥai, his son *Eleazar, and his disciples. Their wondrous deeds are incorporated into the homiletics that make up the whole work. When R. Simeon b. Yoḥai studied, for example, birds stopped flying all around, fire encircled him, and wonderful events happened to people in his vicinity. Among the many miracles attributed to him and his disciples by the author of the Zohar, some are founded solely in myth, e.g., the legends about his contradicting God's will and his prevalence, or his fight with the powers of darkness, the _Sitra Aḥra_ ("The Other Side," i.e., Satan). The Zohar influenced later kabbalistic writings in which the same approach toward the mystics is adopted. Two anonymous 14th-century Spanish works, _Sefer ha-Kaneh_ (Prague, 1610) and _Sefer ha-Peli'ah_ (Korets, 1784), have for their central characters members of the family of the _tanna_ R. *Neḥuna b. ha-Kaneh. A whole set of hagiographical stories is woven around each member of the family. Many of these stories describe a meeting of the heroes with heavenly powers.

The deterioration of the situation of the Jews in Spain (at the end of the 14th and during the 15th century) gave birth to a new kind of hagiography, also associated with the Kabbalah: stories about sages who had attempted to hasten the redemption in one way or the other. Some of these include much historical data, like the stories about the martyr Solomon *Molcho; others are purely fictional, like the story about *Joseph Della Reina, who almost succeeded in overcoming and enslaving Satan and *Lilith, but at the last moment, failed and became enslaved by them instead. From this period onward, Jewish hagiography is mostly concerned with messianic expectations and activity.

Isaac Luria and Other Sages of Safed. The hagiographic cycle of stories about Isaac *Luria (who lived in Safed in the years 1570–72, were the first to be compiled into a book. His disciples preserved and wrote legends describing his superhuman powers. There are two main versions of the cycle of stories about him: _Shivḥei ha-Ari,_ a collection of letters written by R. *Solomon Shlumil of Dreznitz, who described not only Luria, but other sages in Safed, and a later work, *_Toledot ha-Ari_ which was dedicated to Luria almost exclusively. It includes more than 50 stories. Some of them describe mostly his supernatural knowledge, his ability to know the past and the future, what was happening at great distances and in heaven, and his power to read the thoughts and the hearts of other people. The other stories, which seem to be later additions to the original cycle, describe miracles which he was said to have performed. Even when taking into consideration these later additions, the dominant hagiographic motif in these cycles is the supernatural knowledge of Luria, and not the miracles he performed.

Luria's greatest pupil, R. Ḥayyim *Vital, unlike his teacher, did not leave it to later generations to write and to compile the hagiographic stories about him. He did it himself. He kept a diary which was published under the title _Sefer ha-Ḥezyonot_ (1866) and previously, in a shorter version, as _Shivḥei Rav Ḥayyim Vital_ (1826). Like his teacher Luria, Vital also had messianic aspirations. Basing himself on the conjurations of witches, sorcerers, his own visionary dreams and his teacher's sayings he saw himself destined for great deeds. Luria and Vital are also connected with the first famous version of "The Dibbuk" story (told in different versions in _Sefer ha-Ḥezyonot_ and in _Shivḥei Rav Ḥayyim Vital_). The theme of the *_dibbuk_ later became one of the standard motifs in Jewish hagiography: the ability to drive out evil powers or strange souls which had taken hold of a human body.

The stories about the great sages of Safed spread throughout the Jewish world. Their development varied in form and according to geographic locales. In the east hagiographic cycles had for their central figures especially R. Ḥayyim Joseph David *Azulai and R. Ḥayyim b. Moses *Attar; in the west and in Eastern Europe R. *Judah b. Bezalel Loew and R. Joel Ba'al Shem became the heroes of such legends. In the 18th and 19th centuries up to the beginning of the 20th century hagiographic stories about sages of later ages (after Luria) were still being collected and published.

Modern Jewish Hagiography. Modern Jewish hagiography is connected with the ḥasidic movement which began in Eastern Europe in the second half of the 18th century. With the publication of *_Shivḥei ha-Besht_ (Berdichev, 1815) the genre was brought to its highest artistic expression. The book is a compilation of hagiographic stories about the founder of the ḥasidic movement and his disciples, collected from manuscripts. The stories, written both in Hebrew and in Yiddish (since the 16th century, Yiddish being the main medium of expression for hagiographic stories in Eastern Europe), had circulated among the Ḥasidim since the *Baal Shem Tov's death in 1760.

Later ḥasidic leaders and their followers used the *_Shivḥei ha-Besht_ as a model for the writing of hagiographic stories about later ḥasidic sages. Consequently, there are hagiographic collections about almost every major ḥasidic rabbi, even those who lived in the early 20th century. The stories in these compilations are often about several sages and may be arranged according to a main theme, e.g., _The Revelation of the Ẓaddikim,_ a collection of stories about the ways in which the greatness of the ḥasidic sages was revealed (see, e.g., S. Gavriel, _Hitgallut ha-Ẓaddikim_ (1905)).

Side by side with the development of ḥasidic hagiography, another kind of hagiography came into being. These were hagiographies about the *_Lamed-Vav Ẓaddikim,_ the thirty-six anonymous and mysterious holy men, because of whose humble manner, just deeds, and virtue the world continues to exist. Many of the motifs of this cycle of legends are taken from older tales and hagiographies. Together with the ḥasidic stories, they take Hebrew hagiography into the 20th century.

Bibliography: J. Meitlis, _Das Ma'assebuch_ (1933); idem, in: _Di Goldene Keyt,_ 23 (1955), 218–234; G. Scholem, in: _Tarbiz,_ 6 (1935), no. 2, 90–98; idem, _Judaica_ (Ger., 1963), 216–25; _Mishnat ha-Zohar,_ ed. by F. Lachover and J. Tishby, 1 (1957[2]), introd. [Y.D.

ḤAGIZ, family of Spanish origin which emigrated to Morocco after the expulsion decrees of 1492, and settled in Fez, where some of its representatives were at the head of the Castilian community of *Megorashim* ("the exiled"). ABRAHAM ḤAGIZ (I) (died before 1563) arrived in Fez with the Spanish exiles when still very young. He was brought up and educated there and is the signatory of a *takkanah* of 1545. SAMUEL ḤAGIZ (II) (died c. 1570) was probably the younger brother of Abraham; his grandson, Samuel Ḥagiz (II), in his *Mevakkesh ha-Shem* mentions some of his grandfather's biblical commentaries and credits him with directing an important yeshivah, as is also confirmed by his disciple, Samuel b. Saadiah ibn Danan. In the *takkanot* of Fez, Samuel's signature is almost always found together with those of the other Castilian rabbis and it also appears on ordinances and decisions of the years 1545, 1559, and 1568. JACOB ḤAGIZ (d. 1634), a signatory of the Castilian *takkanot* of Fez between 1588 and 1608 (cf. *Kerem Ḥemed;* s.v. *Malkei Rabbanan*), is probably the son of Samuel Ḥagiz (I) and not the grandfather of Jacob *Ḥagiz, the author of *Halakhot Ketannot*. There is a controversy about this relationship which has not been resolved (J. Ben-Naim in his *Malkhei Rabbanan* completely confuses the two). SAMUEL ḤAGIZ (II) left Fez, his birthplace, about 1590, remained for some time in Tripoli, North Africa, then traveled to Venice where, in 1597, he published *Mevakkesh ha-Shem,* sermons on the Pentateuch, and *Devar Shemu'el,* a homiletic commentary on Deuteronomy. He then emigrated to Ereẓ Israel and settled in Jerusalem. ABRAHAM ḤAGIZ (II), signatory of decisions in Fez dated 1638, 1640, and 1647, remained in Morocco after the departure of Samuel (II), probably his older brother. Members of the family also settled in Ereẓ Israel. See also *Ḥagiz, Jacob and *Ḥagiz, Moses.

Bibliography: J. Ben-Naim, *Malkhei Rabbanan* (1931), 10b, 16b, 55b, 72a, 123a; J. M. Toledano, *Ner ha-Ma'arav* (1911), 80, 83, 102–4, 110, 134. [H.Z.]

ḤAGIZ, JACOB (Israel; 1620–1674), Jerusalem scholar. He was the son of Samuel Ḥagiz, who was rabbi of Fez, and son-in-law of Moses *Galante. During his youth he resided in various communities in Italy. In 1658 he emigrated to Jerusalem, where he headed a yeshivah founded and maintained by the Vega brothers of Leghorn, in which secular subjects and Spanish were also studied. Jacob himself, in addition to his Torah study, occupied himself with philosophy, astronomy, medicine, and grammar. He instituted several **takkanot* in Jerusalem, mainly in the field of divorce procedure. In contrast to his father-in-law, Jacob was a vehement opponent of *Shabbetai Ẓevi from the beginning, being one of the first to regard him as a false messiah, and he was one of those who excommunicated him in 1665. In 1673, he went to Constantinople, in order to publish his *Leḥem ha-Panim* but died before achieving this.

He was also the author of: *Eẓ ha-Ḥayyim,* a commentary to the Mishnah (*Mishnayot,* Leghorn, 1652–56); *Halakhot Ketannot* (Venice, 1704), responsa; *Tehillat Ḥokhmah,* a talmudic methodology, published with the *Sefer Keritot* of *Samson of Chinon (Verona, 1647); *Ein Yisrael,* an adapted edition of the *Ein Ya'akov* of Jacob ibn Habib with the additions of Leone Modena (Verona, 1645); *Petil Tekhelet* (Venice, 1652) a commentary on the *azharot* of Solomon ibn Gabirol; *Dinei Birkat ha-Shaḥar, Keri'at Shema u-Tefillah,* laws of the morning blessings, of the reading of the *Shema* and of the *amidah* (Verona, 1648); *Almenara de la Luz* (Leghorn, 1656), a Spanish translation of the *Menorat ha-Ma'or* of Isaac *Aboab.

Bibliography: Scholem, Shabbetai Ẓevi, index; M. Benayahu, in: HUCA, 21 (1948), 1–28 (Heb. sect.); idem, in: *Sinai,* 34 (1954), 172ff.; Frumkin-Rivlin, 2 (1928), 61–64. [D.TA.]

ḤAGIZ, MOSES (1672–?1751), scholar, kabbalist and opponent of Shabbateanism; son of Jacob *Ḥagiz. He was born in Jerusalem and studied with his grandfather, Moses *Galante. He appears to have quarreled in his youth with the rabbis and lay leaders of Jerusalem, for when in 1694 he left Ereẓ Israel to collect money to found a yeshivah in Jerusalem, damaging letters were sent after him to the communities to which he turned. Moses visited Egypt and then Italy, where in 1704 he published his father's *Halakhot Ketannot.* He traveled by way of Prague to Amsterdam where he made contact with Ẓevi Hirsch *Ashkenazi, then rabbi of the Ashkenazi community, and collaborated with him in an energetic struggle against Shabbateanism and its secret adherents. When in 1713 Ashkenazi and Moses refused to retract the excommunication of the Shabbatean Nehemiah *Ḥayon, a fierce quarrel broke out between them and the elders of the Portuguese community. In 1714 when Ashkenazi resigned his rabbinical office and left Amsterdam, Moses was compelled to leave with him. He went first to London with Ashkenazi, there continuing the fight against Ḥayon and his allies, and then to Altona, home of Jacob *Emden, Ashkenazi's son, where he resumed the struggle against Shabbateanism. Among those he attacked were Michael Abraham *Cardoso and even Jonathan *Eybeschuetz, and he took the offensive against Moses Ḥayyim *Luzzatto, inducing the rabbis of Venice to excommunicate him. In 1738 Moses returned to Ereẓ Israel and settled in Safed. He died in Beirut and was taken to Sidon for burial.

A talmudic scholar of the first rank and a prolific writer, Moses was assisted by a good grounding in secular knowledge and by a command of several foreign languages. In Altona he was friendly with Johann Christopher *Wolf, who mentions him in his *Bibliotheca Hebraica.*

His works include: *Leket ha-Kemaḥ,* novellae on the Shulḥan Arukh, *Oraḥ Ḥayyim* and *Yoreh De'ah* (Amsterdam, 1697), and *Even ha-Ezer* (Hamburg, 1711); responsa *Shetei ha-Leḥem* (Wandsbeck, 1733); the ethical treaties *Ẓerror ha-Ḥayyim* and *Mishnat Ḥakhamim* (*ibid.,* 1728–31 and 1733 respectively); *Elleh ha-Mitzvot* (Amsterdam, 1713), on the numeration of precepts in Maimonides' *Sefer ha-Mitzvot,* on the Oral Law, and on Kabbalah; *Sefat Emet* (Amsterdam, 1697); and *Parashat Elleh Masei* (Altona, 1738), on the sanctity of the land of Israel. His literary activity also included the editing of many early books.

Bibliography: Scholem, Shabbetai Ẓevi, index; M.Benayahu, in: HUCA, 21 (1948), 1–28 (Heb. sect.); Frumkin-Rivlin, 2 (1928), 124–34; A. M. Luncz, in: *Yerushalayim,* 1 (1882), 119f.; M. D. Gaon, *Yehudei ha-Mizraḥ be-Ereẓ Yisrael,* 2 (1938), 243–5; Yaari, Sheluḥei, 363–71; Y. Nadav, in: *Sefunot,* 3–4 (1960), 303, 307–10, 326; M. Friedmann, *ibid.,* 10 (1966), 483–619, passim. [D.TA.]

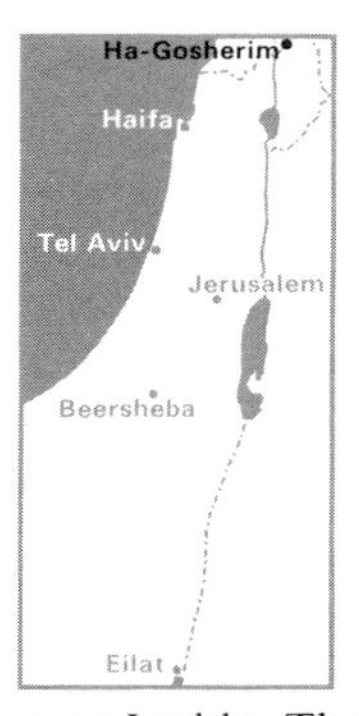

HA-GOSHERIM (Heb. הַגּוֹשְׁרִים), kibbutz in the Ḥuleh Valley, Israel, affiliated with Ha-Kibbutz ha-Me'uḥad, first founded in 1943 as a Ha-Po'el ha-Mizrachi moshav called Neḥalim, the fourth of the "Ussishkin Fortresses" (see *Tower and Stockade). It was taken over in the summer of 1948 by the present group, whose nucleus is composed of settlers from Turkey. The settlers of Neḥalim meanwhile established themselves at the former *Templar colony of Wilhelma near Lydda. The 1951–52 split in Ha-Kibbutz ha-Me'uḥad brought new settlers—veteran members of *Kefar Giladi and other kibbutzim—to Ha-Gosherim in order to remain within their movement's framework. The kibbutz developed intensive and irrigated farming and opened a large guest resort which benefits from the proximity of the Ḥurshat Tal Nature Reserve with its giant Tabor oaks, lawns, and pools fed by the Dan River. Ha-Gosherim, meaning "Bridge Builders," refers to the local topography—the Jordan headstreams, Iyyon (*Ijon), Senir, and Dan, spanned by a number of bridges. In 1968 the kibbutz had a population of 412. [E.O.]

HAGOZER, JACOB AND GERSHOM (first half of the 13th century), father and son, *mohalim* (practitioners of circumcision, hence the name *Gozer,* a synonym for *mohel*) in Germany. Little is known of Jacob except that he composed a book on the laws of circumcision which served as the basis for a more comprehensive work on the same subject by Gershom, who also made use of the work of his uncle *Jacob b. Yakar of Worms. Gershom's works covered every aspect of the subject. Large sections from it were copied word for word and incorporated into two works by two anonymous *mohalim.* All that is known of the author of the first is that he was a nephew of *Ephraim of Bonn and that he knew Jacob personally, received oral traditions from him, and quoted his customs and conduct. This author added many aggadic passages in praise of the precept of circumcision and its virtues, many local customs and medical details concerning circumcision, and various sermons delivered at such ceremonies. The book is of considerable value for its picture of the life of the Jews of Germany at that time and also contains important quotations from earlier literature for which there is no other source.

This *mohel,* like Gershom, introduced hygienic improvements into the circumcision ceremony and brought about the abolition of many unsound practices of ultra-conservative *mohalim.* The author of the second work was a pupil of *Eliezer b. Joel ha-Levi, himself a *mohel,* and quotes him and Gershom freely. At the end of the book is appended a collection of relevant passages from other works. The two books were published by Jacob Glassberg in his *Zikhron Berit la-Rishonim* (1892). They were the first books in the rabbinic literature of Germany wholly devoted to the laws of circumcision, and probably the first works in the whole of German rabbinic literature dealing with one specific subject.

Bibliography: Mueller, in: J. Glassberg, *Zikhron Berit la-Rishonim* (1892), introd. [I.T.-S.]

HAGRONIA (Lat. **Agranium**), town on the Euphrates. It served as a kind of citadel for the town of *Nehardea, as its name Akra ("fort") di Hagronia (BB 73b) testifies. After Nahardea declined as a religious center following its partial destruction by Pappa bar Nazar in 259 C.E. (see *Odenathus), most of its Jews settled in Hagronia. Its Jewish community, though not large (BB 73b), was of considerable importance. Rava, head of the Pumbedita academy from 338 to 52, went from Maḥoza to Hagronia to proclaim a public fast (Ta'an. 24b) and it is reported that the exilarch lectured there during the second half of the fourth century (Yoma 78a). Its scholars were termed "the elders of Hagronia" (Shab. 11a). Many talmudic scholars are known to have been born there—Avimi (BM 77b), Judah (Av. Zar. 39a), Samuel b. Abba (BK 88a), Hilkiah (Yev. 9a), Eleazar (Ta'an. 24b), and Mordecai (Sot. 46b).

Bibliography: Neubauer, Géog., 347f.; A. Berliner, *Beitraege zur Geographie und Ethnographie Babyloniens im Talmud und Midrasch* (1883), 31f.; J. Obermeyer, *Die Landschaft Babylonien im Zeitalter des Talmuds und des Gaonats* (1929), 265–70; Neusner, Babylonia, 2 (1966), 248. [M.Be.]

HAGUE, THE (Dutch **'s Gravenhage** or **Den Haag;** Fr. **La Haye**), the seat of the government of the Netherlands and capital of South Holland province. Jewish settlement in The Hague began in the last quarter of the 17th century, whe Sephardi notables from Amsterdam moved there to be clos to the seat of the government. The first synagogue wa consecrated in 1698, and in 1703 the wealthy De *Pint family established its own synagogue. In 1709, an officia congregation named Ḥonen Dal was founded, and late Jacob *Pereira established a separate congregation calle Beth Jacob. The magnificent synagogue of the Sephardim built on the model of the Great Synagogue in Amsterdam was consecrated in 1726. A poorer Ashkenazi grou followed the Sephardim to The Hague; they acquired cemetery in 1698. Their synagogue, built in 1722, was late destroyed by fire and reconstructed in 1844.

Figure 1. Engraving of the Sephardi synagogue in The Hague constructed in 1726 and sold by the Jewish community afte World War II. Cecil Roth Collection. Photo David Harris Jerusalem.

The Hague community flourished particularly in the 18t century. The central figure in the Ashkenazi communit was the wealthy banker Tobias Boas (1696–1782), the so of a Polish immigrant, who was instrumental in preventin the expulsion of the Jews from Bohemia by having Dutc pressure applied on *Maria Theresa (1744–45). Active a the same time was the chief rabbi of the Hague communit Saul Halevi (1748–85). The favorable attitude of the cit authorities toward the Jews found expression in th decision to exchange the stone bridges for wooden bridges in order to make the city suitable for an **eruv,* which woul allow moving around it on the Sabbath (1692). Thoug some Hebrew works were printed in The Hague in 1739, more important press was opened about 1775 by Loe Soesmans, who had been active as a printer in Amsterdan and Leiden. He and his sons printed a number of liturgica and poetical items with J. H. Muninkhuizen until 1781. A the end of the 18th century, grave economic crises befell th Jews of The Hague as a result of the general economi situation and later the annexation to France, and from the on the community lost its importance from a Jewish and general point of view.

The Jewish community in The Hague, which numbere about 2,400 in 1809, grew to 17,400 in 1939 (among then only about 300 Sephardim and about 2,000 refugees fron Germany). The rabbi of the Ashkenazi community was als chief rabbi for the whole area. In cooperation with th municipality the community developed a special education al system for Jewish children: those children whose parent so desired were concentrated in certain public schools an given lessons in Jewish subjects, which were incorporate into the general curriculum. On the eve of World War II most of the Jews were well off.

Holocaust Period At the time of the German occupatio

(May 1940), 13,862 Jews lived in The Hague: 1,609 of them were of foreign nationality and 4,320 were half-Jewish. The Hague was the center of German occupation rule, and special measures against the Jews were taken during the very first months, e.g., they were forbidden access to many streets. At the beginning of the occupation period, The Hague was the seat of the Jewish Coordination Committee (J.C.C.), a representative body set up by the Jewish communities and major national organizations. After the Joodse Raad *(Judenrat)* for Amsterdam had been formed, the J.C.C. was dissolved and a representative of the Joodse Raad, Henri Edersheim, was appointed for The Hague; in many ways he was able to act independently from Amsterdam. In charge of the execution of anti-Jewish measures was Franz Fischer, commander of the *Sicherheits polizei,* who became notorious for his cruelty. During the first years, Jewish life was maintained as far as circumstances allowed; for example, four Jewish schools existed with a total of 226 pupils. During the summer of 1942, however, deportations began, and after only one year The Hague was practically *Judenrein.* A strange part was played at the time by the economist F. Weinreb, a member of Agudat Israel, who managed to dupe the *Sicherheits polizei* with imaginary plans for the mass emigration of rich Jews, thus obtaining deferment of deportation for many of them. He was finally arrested, but, liberated again by the Germans, he went into hiding until the end of the war. He was sentenced by a Dutch court for collaboration, but even years later public opinion was divided over the question of whether an injustice had been committed in Weinreb's case. In 1945, there were only 1,283 Jews in The Hague.

See also *Netherlands: Holocaust. [J.M.]

Contemporary Period. The number of Jews in The Hague and its satellite towns (Scheveningen, Wassenaar, Rijswijk, Voorburg, etc.)—with a total population of 750,000—was 1,700 in 1969, of whom 1,475 were affiliated with the Ashkenazi congregation and 225 with the Liberal one. Two of the Ashkenazi synagogues that existed in 1940 were still in use: the monumental synagogue in the Wagenstraat, constructed in 1844 in what was then the center of the Jewish quarter, and one in the seaside resort of Scheveningen (the latter following East European rite). The monumental Sephardi synagogue at the Prinsessegracht, constructed in 1726, was not reopened after the war—as hardly any Sephardim were left in The Hague—and was sold by its trustees to a real-estate owner. The Liberal congregation, which was founded in 1931, met on hired premises. The Hague and its surrounding district had an Ashkenazi Chief Rabbi of their own. A modern communal center was opened in the annex of the Wagenstraat synagogue in 1962. Many of the Jewish institutions that existed in The Hague in 1940, such as the orphanage, continued to exist only in a legal sense and annually transferred much of their revenue to Israel. The Jewish old-age home was modernized and expanded and in 1969 had 83 beds. The presence of the Israel Embassy in The Hague gave an added dimension to local Jewish life. [H.Bo.]

Figure 2. Main Ashkenazi synagogue in The Hague, built in 1844. Photo M. Ninio, Jerusalem.

Bibliography: M. Henriques Pimentel, *Geschiedkundige aanteekeningen betreffende de Portugeesche Israelieten in den Haag* (1876); D. S. van Zuiden, *De Hoogduitsche Joden in's Gravenhage . . .* (1913); S. Seeligmann, *Het geestelijk leven in de Hoogduitsche Joodsche Gemeente te's Gravenhage* (1914).

HAGUENAU, Alsatian town in the Bas-Rhin department, E. France. The earliest information on the presence of Jews in Haguenau dates from 1235; in that year a blood libel was perpetrated against the Jews of the town, but thanks to the protection of the emperor, whose **servi camerae* they were, they escaped harm. The Jews had to pay taxes to both the emperor and the municipality. The latter also protected them effectively, especially in 1338 against the *Armleder bands, but unsuccessfully at the time of the *Black Death: by February 16, 1349, the Jewish community had been destroyed. The first synagogue (the courtyard of which was used in 1352 for the wheat market) stood on the former Rathausplaetzel, later the Place de la République; the *mikveh* was situated on the bank of the Moder, on the site of the present municipal hospital. In 1354, the Jews returned to Haguenau and formed a new community. A house (number 8 of the present Rue du Sel) was then used as a synagogue. A good deal of Hebrew type was used in books printed in Haguenau between 1517 and 1520, among them works by *Reuchlin and *Melanchthon. In 1528, *Joseph (Josel) b. Gershom of Rosheim obtained from the emperor the abrogation of an expulsion order issued by the town. Haguenau subsequently became a refuge for the Jews of the surrounding district on various occasions. During the second half of the 17th century, several Jews who had fled from Poland settled there. From 1660, there has been a rabbi in Haguenau. Notable rabbis included Meyer Jaïs, later chief rabbi of Paris, who held office in Haguenau between 1933 and 1938.

The community of Haguenau consisted of 34 families in 1735, 64 in 1784, and 600 souls on the eve of World War II. Of these, 148 persons died in deportation or on the battlefield. In 1968, the community numbered about 300. The present synagogue on the Rue des Juifs (plundered by the Nazis and later renovated) was erected in 1821. The cemetery is known to have existed from the 16th century, but it was probably established during the Middle Ages. For a long time, it also served all the Jews of the region. The oldest epitaph preserved there dates from 1654.

Bibliography: M. Ginsburger, in: Germ Jud, 1 pt. 2 (1963), 121ff., 2 pt. 1 (1968), 318ff.; E. Scheid, in: REJ, 2 (1881), 73–92, 3 (1881), 58–74, 4 (1882), 98–112, 5 (1882), 230–9, 8 (1884), 243–54, 10 (1885), 204–31; A. Marx, *Studies in Jewish History and Booklore* (1944), 326f.; J. Bloch, *Historique de la Communauté Juive de Haguenau . . .* (1968); Z. Szajkowski, *Analytical Franco-Jewish Gazetteer 1939–1945* (1966), index.

[B.Bl.]

HA-ḤINNUKH (Heb. הַחִנּוּךְ ; "the Education"), an anonymous work on the 613 precepts (see *Commandments, 613) in the order of their appearance in Scripture, giving their reasons and their laws in detail. The various attempts to identify the author have proved unsuccessful; the most widely held view is that he was *Aaron b. Joseph ha-Levi of Barcelona, the identification being based on an obscure allusion in the introduction: "A Jew of the house of Levi of Barcelona." From certain references in the book (precept 400) it has been concluded that the author was a pupil of Solomon b. Abraham *Adret. The first edition (Venice, 1523) gives "Rabbi Aaron" as the author. In the opinion of S. H. Kook the basis for this identification lies in the introduction to precept 95: "out of fear of drawing near to the tabernacle of the Lord, the levites my brethren *[aḥai]* were purified and Aaron offered them." The proofreader of the second edition (*ibid.,* 1600–01) in fact based himself on this passage but he is mistaken because it is the biblical Aaron who is referred to and the text should read: "and the levites after *[aḥar]* being purified" (cf. Num. 8:21). This identification was already questioned by Ḥ.J.D. Azulai and other scholars, who have shown it to be completely without foundation. Elsewhere the name of the author is given as Baruch (David ibn Zimra, *Meẓudat David,* precept 206). The book was compiled at the end of the 13th century. Some deduced the date of its composition from the date 1257 mentioned in precept 326 with reference to the sabbatical years, but the passage in question is taken from the novellae of Solomon b. Abraham Adret to *Avodah Zarah* 9a. The Vatican library contains a manuscript written in 1313.

The name of the book is taken by some as referring to its educational aim, to which in fact the author alludes at the end of the introduction: "To touch the heart of my young son and his companions in that each week they will learn the precepts that are included in the weekly portion of the Law" (see also *Meẓudat David,* precept 397). This is the reason both for the order in which the commandments are given, and its contents, which are mainly for the purpose of study and not to give the *halakhah.* The work follows a definite pattern: (1) a definition of the essence of the precept; (2) its source in the Written Law and the connection with its development in the Oral Law; (3) the principles of the precept and its reasons; (4) its main details. The book is mainly based on the *Sefer ha-Mitzvot* and the *Mishneh Torah* of Maimonides, at times whole sections being copied verbatim (precepts 173, 485). The author used Ibn Ḥasdai's Hebrew translation of the *Sefer ha-Mitzvot.* He also used the works of other authors, including those of Alfasi and chiefly of Adret and Naḥmanides. The uniqueness of the work lies in the section dealing with the explanation of the principles of the precepts, especially "the simple description" (precept 98). His explanations are based on common sense. His style and presentation are clear and understandable befitting its educational aim for youth and ordinary people. Many editions of the work have appeared. The best known is that containing the commentary *Minḥat Ḥinnukh* of Joseph *Babad. Other well-known authors to devote compositions to it include Judah *Rosanes and Isaiah *Pick. It has been issued according to the first edition with notes, variant readings, and an introduction by C. B. Chavel (1962[5]).

Bibliography: C. B. Chavel (ed.), *Sefer ha-Ḥinnukh* (1962[5]), introd., and 797–806; H. Heller (ed.), *Sefer ha-Mitzvot le-Rabbenu Moshe ben-Rabbi Maimon* (1914), 8f. (introd.); S. H. Kook, *Iyyunim u-Meḥkarim,* 2 (1963), 316–20; Munk, in: ZHB, 11 (1907), 186–8; D. Rosin, *Ein Compendium der Juedischen Gesetzeskunde aus dem vierzehnten Jahrhundert* (1871); J. Rubinstein, in: J. Babad, *Sefer Minḥat Ḥinnukh ha-Shalem,* pt. 3 (1952), 151ff. (bibliographical list of editions of *Sefer ha-Ḥinnukh*). [S.Z.H.]

HAHN, ALBERT L. (1889–1968), German banker and economist. Hahn was born in Frankfort and during the 1920s joined the Deutsche Effekten- und Wechselbank, in which his family had a sizable interest. In 1929 he became professor of economics at the University of Frankfort. In 1939 he went to the U.S., and taught at the New School for Social Research in New York. He left the U.S. in 1950 and eventually returned to his teaching career at Frankfort University. Hahn's main concern was the theory of money and credit. He consistently advocated a stable currency as a prime social safeguard. His many publications include: *Volkswirtschaftliche Theorie des Bankkredits* (1920); *Common Sense Economics* (1956); *Fuenfzig Jahre zwischen Inflation und Deflation* (1963); and *Ein Traktat ueber Waehrungsreform* (1964). [J.O.R.]

HAHN, JOSEPH BEN MOSES (c. 1730–1803), German talmudic scholar. Hahn was *dayyan* of the *bet din* of the combined communities of Hamburg, Altona, and Wandsbeck and was beloved as the preacher in the old as well as in the new *klaus* in Hamburg which was renamed after him. In the *Emden-*Eybeschuetz controversy he sided with the

Portrait of Joseph Hahn, German talmudic scholar, by J. Nathan. Jerusalem, Sir Isaac and Lady Wolfson Museum in Hechal Shlomo. Photo David Harris, Jerusalem.

latter. In 1789, Saul *Berlin, the ill-famed son of R. Ẓevi Hirsch Berlin, published under the nom de plume Obadiah b. Baruch, *Miẓpeh Yokte'el,* a criticism of the *Torat Yekuti'el* (Berlin, 1772) of Raphael *Kohen, the famous rabbi of the three communities. Hahn presided over the *bet din* which excommunicated the author on the grounds of his having libeled ha-Kohen. In another case he ruled that the body of a Jewish woman, executed by the civil authorities for poisoning her mother-in-law and sister-in-law, should be reburied in a Jewish cemetery without religious qualification or restriction, as she had been mentally disturbed at the time. He was said to have had an encyclopedic mind and memory.

Bibliography: E. Duckesz, *Chachme AHW* (1908), Germ. pt. 34, Heb. pt. 97f.; idem, *IVOH Lemoschaw* (1903), 66f.; E. L. Landshuth, *Toledot Anshei ha-Shem u-Fe'ulatam ba-Adat Berlin* (1884), 90. [M.T.]

HAHN (Nordlingen), JOSEPH YUSPA BEN PHINEHAS SELIGMANN (1570–1637), German rabbi and author. Hahn spent all his life in Frankfort. He was present during the *Fettmilch riots, the subsequent expulsion of the Jews from the city in 1614, and their triumphant return two years later after Fettmilch was hanged. Hahn was head of the Frankfort *bet din* and of the local yeshivah. When there was no other incumbent, he also filled the office of communal rabbi. Hahn was a contemporary and colleague of Isaiah *Horowitz (Shelah). Hahn is best known for his book *Yosif Omeẓ* (Frankfort, 1723). In 1718, Joseph Kosman, one of Hahn's descendants, published his own *Noheg Ka-Ẓon Yosef* in Hanau, in which he quoted freely from his kinsman's work, sometimes without indicating his source. Hahn's *Yosif Omeẓ* deals mainly with the laws and customs of the Jewish calendar and liturgy, particularly those prevalent in contemporary Frankfort. He quotes the custom of reciting the hymn "**Lekhah Dodi*" on Friday evenings as a "new" one, recently introduced. Hahn deliberately substitutes his own phrases for those which, in the original, refer to "going out" to meet the Sabbath, since this custom obtained only in Ereẓ Israel, where the hymn was composed; the words he substituted retain the acrostic of the author's name. Hahn also voiced his displeasure at the new custom of delaying the commencement of the evening service on the first night of *Shavuot until a late hour.

The *Yosif Omeẓ* is a valuable source book for the history of the contemporary Frankfort Jewish community. Hahn mentions, for instance, the local Purim (Adar 20), instituted to commemorate the hanging of Fettmilch (no. 1107–09). He also records the comparatively slight damage suffered by the community as a result of the passage of soldiers through the area during the Thirty Years' War. The *Yosif Omeẓ* is written in a pious vein, and the concluding chapters are devoted to ethics. In the sections on pedagogy, Hahn deplored the ignorance of the Bible prevalent among rabbis of his day. He suggested that a boy who showed no sign of progress in the study of the Talmud by the age of 13 be withdrawn from its study and taught Bible instead.

Bibliography: M. Horovitz, *Frankfurter Rabbinen*, 2 (1883), 6–18; J. Horovitz, in: *Festschrift . . . A. Freimann* (1935), 35–50; idem, in: *Festschrift . . . J. Freimann* (1937), 78–93; S. Esh (ed.), *Koveẓ le-Zikhro shel Eli'ezer Shamir* (1957), 155–62.

[A.T.]

HAI BAR RAV DAVID GAON, head of the *Pumbedita academy from 890 to 898. Hai was *dayyan* in Baghdad for for many years before he became *gaon;* he transferred the academy of Pumbedita to Baghdad (*Sha'arei Simḥah* of R. *Isaac ibn Ghayyat, 1 (1861), 63–64). None of his responsa has been preserved, but some of those attributed to R. "Hai" without further definition, may be his. Harkavy attributes the *Sefer ha-Shetarot* ("Book of Documents") to him, but Wertheimer, L. Ginzberg, and Assaf hold more plausibly that the author of the *Sefer ha-Shetarot* was the famous *Hai b. Sherira. Several early Karaite scholars attributed to Hai a book of polemics against the Karaites on the subject of the intercalation of the month and the arrangement of the calendar; many scholars believe that this was Hai b. David.

Bibliography: Mann, in: JQR, 11 (1920/21), 434–5; S. Assaf, *Sefer ha-Shetarot de-Rav Hai Ga'on* (1930), 7–8; Ibn Daud, Tradition, 52, 37, 129; Abramson, Merkazim, 911.

[M.Mar.]

HAI BEN NAHSHON, *gaon* of *Sura from 885–896. Both Hai's father and paternal grandfather, Zadok, had preceded him as *geonim* of Sura. In one of the few of his responsa which have been preserved he opposes the recitation of **Kol Nidrei* on the eve of the Day of Atonement, since in his opinion authority for the granting of absolution from vows is no longer to be obtained. It seems that the Karaite al-*Kirkisani was referring to Hai b. Nahshon when he wrote that the *gaon* Hai and his father translated the *Sefer ha-Mitzvot* of Anan from Aramaic to Hebrew. If any credence can be given to this statement it can only mean that they subjected the work to a critical examination, or that they translated it in order to dispute with him and challenge his views.

Bibliography: S. J. L. Rapoport, *Teshuvot Ge'onim Kadmonim* (1848), 9a–b; J. Mueller, *Mafte'aḥ Teshuvot ha-Ge'onim* (1891), 151–7; Lewin, in: *Ginzei Kedem*, 2 (1923), 1–3; S. Assaf, in: *Tarbiz*, 4 (1933), 36, 199f.

[M.Mar.]

HAI BEN SHERIRA (939–1038), *gaon* of Pumbedita and molder of the *halakhah* and the most prominent figure of his time. Of his youth nothing is known. From 986 he was the *av bet din* in the academy of *Pumbedita, acting as the deputy to his father Sherira *gaon;* in this role he left his mark upon the mode of studies and general orientation of the academy. According to some, he had a share in composing the *Iggeret Rav Sherira* (see *Sherira). Some time after he and his father had been released from prison, where they had been kept on a false charge, he became the *gaon* of Pumbedita, while his father was still alive, a position which he held for 40 years (998–1038). Although his position had been vied for by Samuel b. Hofni the latter withdrew his claim to the gaonate when Hai married his daughter. Students came to Hai's academy from Byzantium and from western Christian countries, from where queries were also sent to Hai. His ties with Spain and his influence upon *Samuel ha-Nagid in particular are well known.

Aside from his preeminence in rabbinic knowledge, he was well acquainted with the Persian and Arabic languages and with Arabic literature. While he permitted children to be taught Arabic writing and arithmetic, he warned against the study of philosophy (this was said in a letter ascribed to him and addressed to Samuel ha-Nagid). He criticized his father-in-law, Samuel b. Hofni, "and others like him, who frequently read the works of non-Jews."

Hai occupies a central position in the history of the **halakhah*. Later generations regarded him as the supreme authority, declaring that "he, more than all the *geonim*, propagated the Torah in Israel . . . both in the east and in the west . . . No one among his predecessors can be compared to him, who was the last of the *geonim*" (*Abraham ibn Daud, *Sefer ha-Kabbalah*). The measure of his influence and the volume of his responsa, decisions, and comments can be gauged from the fact that approximately a third of all extant geonic responsa are his (some of them in conjunction with his father).

In his writings Hai set out in detail his approach to the principles of faith and to the requirements of community leadership. In his *piyyutim* he expressed with much bitterness his sense of living in exile from Ereẓ Israel. He was a mystic, who ascribed sanctity to the **heikhalot* literature, believing that whoever studied it in holiness and purity could ascend to the world of the angels and of the divine chariot (*merkavah*). Contrary to the view of his father-in-law, he believed "that God performs signs and awe-inspiring acts through the righteous, even as He did through the prophets." But he vigorously opposed those who believed that the divine names and charms were efficacious in changing the course of nature, declaring emphatically that its laws cannot be modified by such means. Vehemently antagonistic to any tendency toward anthropomorphism, he maintained that anthropomorphic passages in the *aggadah* were to be interpreted metaphorically. In his formulation of the ideals and values of the complete Jew, he described the rewards for observing divine precepts. These rewards greet the righteous and form "groups that go to meet the Divine Presence" and say to the righteous: "Ascend to your grade, stand in your division (in heaven), you who have conquered your evil inclination . . . who have borne the yoke of the commandments, and in your fear of Him have endured suffering."

Hai drew special attention to the duty of the *dayyanim* to guide and admonish the people, as well as their responsibility for its conduct and their accountability for its sins. He demanded that strong measures be taken against dissenters and thieves, and under certain circumstances even permitted recourse to Jewish courts of law. He was opposed to the absolute annulment of vows on the eve of the Day of Atonement, his formulation of the **Kol Nidrei* prayer being: "Of all vows . . . which we have vowed . . . and have omitted to fulfill either through neglect or under constraint we pray that the Lord of heaven may absolve and pardon us." He adopted a tolerant attitude towards traditional local liturgical practices, but was opposed to delving into the reasons for them, insisting on "the observance of institutions introduced by those superior to our generations in learning and in caliber" (lit. "number"). He retained his physical and mental energies to the end. At the age of 99, a few months before his death, he replied with remarkable vigor to questions submitted to him. After his death, Samuel ha-Nagid eulogized him, saying: "During his lifetime he acquired all the choicest wisdom," and though "he left no child, he has, in every land, both east and west, children whom he reared in the Torah" (*Ben Tehillim,* 11). [H.H.B.-S.]

Of Hai's works the following are extant: (1) fragments of the Arabic original of *Sefer Shevu'ot* (*Kitāb al-Aymān;* "A Treatise on Oaths"), and a Hebrew rendering by an unknown translator of the entire work entitled *Mishpetei Shevu'ot* (Venice, 1602; Hamburg, 1782); (2) fragments of the Arabic original of *Sefer ha-Mikkaḥ ve-ha-Mimkar* (*Kitāb al-Shirā wa-al-Baye;* "Treatise on Commercial Transactions"). This, his chief literary production, was translated into Hebrew by Isaac *al-Bargeloni (Venice, 1602; Vienna, 1800), and another version is extant in manuscript; (3) *Sefer ha-Shetarot* ("Treatise on Documents"), containing the texts of various documents, such as a *ketubbah,* a *get,* etc. (published by Assaf in *Tarbiz,* 1 (1930), supplement). Fragments of Hai's commentary on several tractates of the Babylonian Talmud have also been preserved. The ascription of certain other works to Hai has, in recent years, been rejected.

To Hai are ascribed some 25 poems, most of which are prayers, *seliḥot,* and *piyyutim,* a few of them didactic poems on laws and etiquette and eulogies of contemporary personalities. Most of these are in meter and rhyme, but in form and content reveal very little similarity to Arabic poetry. For poetic power, pride of place should be given to a group of five *seliḥot* (not *kinot*) for the Ninth of *Av; these are without meter and rhyme and voice a bitter and vehement complaint in the manner of Job against the suffering endured by the Jewish people in exile in the face of its great faith in God. Hai's authorship of several poems, and even the fact of his having written poetry at all, which was questioned in modern times (from the beginning of research into the poetry of the Middle Ages) has now been confirmed. [J.Lev.]

Bibliography: S. Naschér, *Der Gaon Haia und seine geistige Thaetigkeit* (1867?); Weiss, Dor, 4 (1904[4]), 155–71; J. N. Epstein, *Der gaonaeische Kommentar zur Ordnung Tohorot* (1915), 1–36· Assaf, in: *Ha-Ẓofeh le-Ḥokhmat Yisrael,* 7 (1923), 277–87; idem, in: *Tarbiz,* 17 (1945/46), 28–31; Assaf, Ge'onim, 198–202; Kroll, in: *Mizraḥ u-Ma'arav,* 4 (1929/30), 347–51; E. E. Hildesheimer, *Mystik und Agada im Urteile der Gaonen R. Scherira und R. Hai* (1931); H. Brody, *Piyyutim ve-Shirei Tehillah me-Rav Hai* (1937); J. L. Fishman (Maimon; ed.), *Rav Hai Ga'on* (1938); H. Tchernowitz, *Toledot ha-Posekim,* 1 (1946), 95–105; Abramson, in: *Sefer Yovel J. N. Epstein* (1950), 296–315; idem, in: *Talpioth,* 5 (1952), 773–80; Weill, in: *Sefer Assaf* (1953), 261–79; Baron, Social[2], index.

HAIDAMACKS, paramilitary bands that disrupted the social order in Polish Ukraine during the 18th century. The name originated from the Turkish word *haida* meaning "move on!" The Haidamack movement was mainly the outcome of the social ferment which had already developed in the Ukraine toward the end of the 16th century and reached a peak in the Cossack uprising led by *Chmielnicki in 1648. The Haidamacks were mainly peasant serfs who had fled from the Polish landowners to the steppes beyond the River Dnieper. They were joined by poorer elements among the townsmen, sons of the impoverished nobility and clergy, members of heretical sects who had fled from Russia, and even Jewish renegades. The Haidamacks ambushed travelers or attacked small settlements, not for political reasons but principally for robbery accompanied by murder. However, they unwittingly served the political ends of the Russian administrators and the Russian Orthodox clergy since their persistent attacks helped to erode the position of the Polish kingdom in this period.

The Haidamack bands are first mentioned in documents dating from the beginning of the 18th century, but received a strong impetus in 1734, when dissensions broke out among the Polish nobility over the election of a new king. In 1768 the most violent Haidamack outbreak took place, known as Koliivshchina or (in Polish) Kolizczyzna, headed by Maxim Zhelesnyak (see below), in which religious, national, and social elements combined. The expulsion of the Jews or their destruction had long been the avowed purpose of insurgents in the Ukraine in the period of Chmielnicki and even earlier. The monks, who were the chroniclers of the period and the recorders of popular tales, glorified murder of the Jews and confiscation of their property as if they were deeds of piety. In addition, the Jews were a convenient target to attack because the competition in trade and commerce with the townsmen was so keen that the latter showed no disposition to defend Jews and would even divulge the movements of Jewish merchants to the Haidamacks. Most of the Jews were helpless against the brigands, and the Polish state authorities were not always able to defend them. The propaganda of the Russian Orthodox priests only intensified the hatred against the Jews. In this area the rivalry between the clergy of the Orthodox and Catholic churches accounts for the sharp rise in the number of *blood libels against the Jews from the fourth to sixth decades of the 18th century precisely in the region where the Haidamacks were active.

Most of the attacks made by the Haidamacks against the Jews took the form of robbery and murder of merchants traveling on the highway and assaults on Jewish tenant farmers living in isolated places and on inhabitants of small defenseless towns. During the years when the revolts increased (1734, 1750, 1768) even heavily fortified places were attacked, claiming large numbers of Jewish victims: 27 Jews were slaughtered in Korsun in 1734; 35 were murdered in Pavoloch in 1736. In the same year the Haidamacks captured the town of Pogrebishche and murdered 14 Jews; many others were wounded and their property robbed. Massacres of Jews took place in various towns in 1738 and 1742. A wave of attacks was perpetrated in 1750: Jews were killed in Vinnitsa, Volodarka, and in other cities. But these calamities were overshadowed by the wholesale massacres that took place in 1768 (known as the persecutions of Ukraine or of *Uman). Initially, about 700 people were killed in the city of Fastov including many scores of Jews.

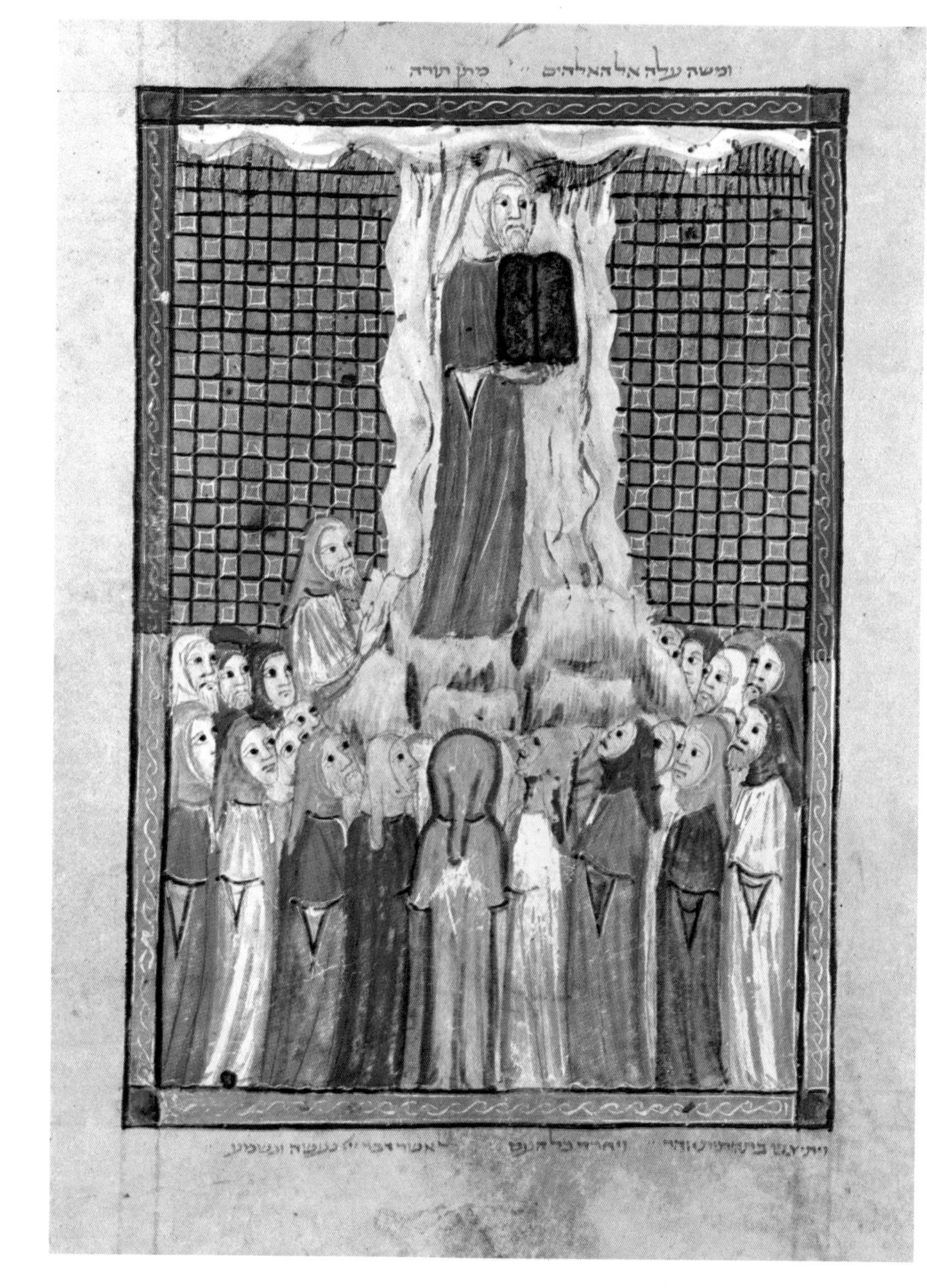

Two of a series of full-page miniatures from the *Sarajevo Haggadah*. The page on the right depicts Moses standing on top of the flaming Mount Sinai holding the Tablets of the Law. To the left of him stands Joshua, and the Israelites who encircle the mountain. The page on the left depicts a stylized façade of the Temple with three gates. The middle gate has a conched arch which contains the Ark of the Covenant covered by the wings of the cherubim, and the Tablets of the Law. Spain, 14th century. Yugoslavia, Sarajevo National Museum, folios 30 and 32 ($8\frac{1}{8} \times 6\frac{1}{4}$ ins/22×16 cm.).

In the townlet of Lysyanka a Jew, a Polish priest, and a dog were hanged side by side to indicate the equality of their respective religions.

Zheleznyak, an active leader of the gangs, massacred the Jews who had been unable to escape from Zhabotin, Kanyev, and Korsun before going on to the fortified city of Uman, to which many thousands of Poles and Jews had streamed from other places out of terror of the Haidamacks. The treachery of the Cossack commander Gonta led to the surrender of the city on June 19, 1768, and there ensued a frightful massacre of its inhabitants. The Jews attempted to hide but were unsuccessful. Some fought heroically until slain by the enemy. The majority of Jews were murdered in the synagogue. A number of prominent Jews, required to pay a ransom, were brutally murdered after they had complied. The number of Jewish victims ran into thousands, the slayers sparing neither women nor children. The synagogues were razed and the Torah scrolls desecrated and burned. According to some records the number of victims reached 20,000, both Poles and Jews. Some of the Jews in the surrounding districts who attempted to flee to the border city of Balta, half of which was situated in Turkish territory, were caught by brigands, who laid waste to the city. The Jews in the entire southeastern portion of Poland were seized with terror. They placed their hopes on the commander of the Polish army, Branicki, and a special prayer was composed in his honor. Although Branicki himself did not take part in the war against the Haidamacks, he had severely punished their leaders and was for this reason regarded by the Jews as the savior of Polish Jewry. The revolt was suppressed by the Russian and Polish troops. The rebels were tried by Polish punitive units and the Haidamack movement came to an end. The memory of the Haidamacks lingered in Ukrainian lore and entered the national literature (*Haydamaky* (1841), by Taras Shevchenko). It became a legacy of the Ukrainian national movement, and the Ukrainian partisan bands who perpetrated pogroms on the Jewish population in 1919–20 and 1941–44 were referred to as Haidamacks.

Bibliography: F. Rawita-Gawroński, *Historya ruchów hajdamackich*, 2 vols. (1913[2]); idem, *Żydzi w historji i literatur ze ludowej na Rusi* (1923); A. A. Skalkovski, *Nayezdy gaydamak na zapadnuyu Ukraynu v xviii stoletii, 1733–1768* (1845); *Arkhiv yugo-zapadnoy Rossii*, pt. 3, vol. 3 (1876); H.J. Gurland, *Le-Korot ha-Gezeirot al Yisrael*, 3 (1888), 7 (1892); Dubnow, Hist Russ, index.

[S.Ett.]

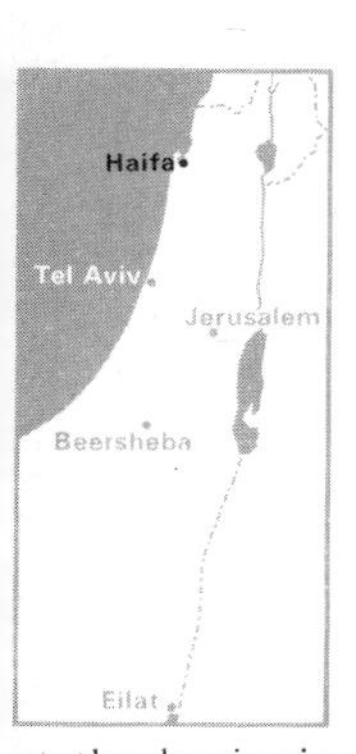

HAIFA (Heb. חֵיפָה), port in Israel and commercial and administrative center of the north of the country, with about 200,000 inhabitants in 1970. The city extends over the northwest side of Mt. Carmel and the coastal strip at its northern slope, and over the southern end of the Zebulun Valley and the northern edge of the Carmel Coast.

Early History. The earliest settlement in Haifa's vicinity was located at Tell Abu Hawam, a small port town founded at the beginning of the 14th century B.C.E. (Late Bronze Age) and was in existence until the Hellenistic period. The city was not a part of the area regarded as sanctified by the exiles returning from Babylon (see *Israel, Historical Boundaries). Haifa is possibly mentioned in the Persian period in the list of cities attributed to the geographer Scylax, between the bay and the "Promontory of Zeus" i.e., the Carmel. In the Hellenistic period the city moved to a new site, south of Bat Galim (the old port had apparently become blocked by sand). Tombs from the Roman period, including Jewish burial caves, have been found in the vicinity. The major city in the region was Shikmonah, which Eusebius even identifies with Haifa (*Onomastikon*, ed. by E. Klostermann (1904), 108:31). Haifa is mentioned in Jewish sources as the home of R. Avdimos (Avdimi, Dimi) and other scholars (Tosef., Yev. 6:8). It was a fishing village whose inhabitants, like the people of Beth-Shean and Tivon, could not distinguish between the pronunciation of the gutturals *ḥet* and *ayin* (TJ, Ber. 2:4). According to the Talmud, the murex (shellfish yielding purple dye used for the *tallit*) was caught along the coast from Haifa to the Ladder of Tyre (Shab. 26a). Politically Haifa throughout this period belonged to the district of *Acre. Its Jewish inhabitants were on hostile terms with the Samaritans in neighboring Castra, a fortress built by the Romans. A *kinah* speaks of the destruction of the Jewish community, along with other communities, when the Byzantines reconquered the country from the Persians in 628. Haifa is not mentioned in the sources dealing with the first 400 years of Muslim rule in Ereẓ Israel. It appears again only in the mid-11th century: in 1046 the Persian traveler Nasir-i Khusrau relates that large sailing ships were built there. He also mentions date palms that he found there and the sand used by goldsmiths. In 1084, the *gaon* *Elijah ha-Kohen went from Tyre to Haifa to proclaim the New Year on the soil of Ereẓ Israel and to renew the ordination of rabbis and the gaonate there.

On the eve of the First Crusade Haifa is described as an important and well-fortified city. The Crusaders pushing southward initially spared the city but later laid siege and conquered it with the help of the Venetian navy (summer 1100). All Haifa's Jewish defenders (who comprised the majority of the city's population) and its Egyptian garrison were slaughtered, bringing to an end another brief but flourishing chapter in Haifa's history. During the Crusader era Jews apparently did not resettle in Haifa. The city remained a small fortress and an insignificant port under the shadow of its mighty neighbors, Acre and Caesarea; during this period it was the capital of a seigniory held by a Crusader family, Garcia Alvarez. The fortress of Haifa was destroyed in 1187 when Saladin dealt a crushing blow to Crusader rule. It was returned under the peace treaty of 1192 to the Franks during the Third Crusade (1192–1265). In the mid-13th century the city's fortifications were rebuilt by Louis IX, king of France, but in 1265 Haifa again fell, this time to the Mamluk sultan Baybars who drove the remaining Crusaders from the country. During Baybars' systematic destruction of the coastal cities of Ereẓ Israel and Syria (to prevent their reoccupation by the Franks), Haifa was also razed (1291) and did not revive throughout the period of Mamluk rule. The Carmelite Order was founded on Mt. Carmel in 1156, but the monastery was destroyed by the Muslims in 1291. From the time of its conquest by the Muslims until the 15th century, Haifa was either uninhabited or an unfortified small village. At various times there were a few Jews living there, and both Jews and Christians made pilgrimages to Elijah's cave on Mt. Carmel.

Ottoman Rule. Haifa was apparently deserted at the time of the Ottoman conquest (1516). The first indication of its resettlement is contained in a description by the German traveler Raowulf who visited Ereẓ Israel in 1575. Haifa is subsequently mentioned in accounts of travelers as a half-ruined, impoverished village with few inhabitants. The expansion of commercial trade between Europe and Ereẓ Israel from the beginning of the 17th century improved Haifa's position. More and more boats began anchoring at the safer Haifa port in preference to the plugged-up bay at Acre. Haifa's revival as a flourishing port city is also to be credited to the emirs of the Turabay family, who ruled part

Figure 1. Panorama of Haifa from Mount Carmel. Courtesy Ministry of Tourism. Photo David Harris, Jerusalem.

of Ereẓ Israel at that time, and also Haifa. These local rulers also gave permission to the Carmelite monks to reestablish themselves in 1631, but only four years later the Muslims turned their church into a mosque. Later the monastery was rebuilt; in 1775 it was ransacked, and in 1821 it was destroyed by Abdullah, pasha of Acre. It was reestablished in 1828 and exists to this day.

At the beginning of the 18th century a new local ruler Zahir al-ʿUmar gained control of northern Ereẓ Israel and set up his capital in Acre. In 1742 Haifa again came into existence as a village or a small town located at the foot of Mt. Carmel near the present-day Bat Galim quarter. It had a small Jewish community and a synagogue. In the middle of the century Zahir annexed Haifa as well. Unfortified and spread over a wide and vulnerable plain, Haifa was almost captured in 1761 by the Turks. To prevent its falling into his enemies' hands, Zahir ordered his soldiers to raze the city to the ground and scatter boulders in the anchorage; thus the ancient city of Haifa was demolished. Zahir provided his growing capital with a safe alternative port of call 1⅓ mi. (2 km.) southeast of ancient Haifa, on a strip of coast at the foot of the Carmel at an easily defensible point. Unlike the ancient city of Haifa, the new port was situated on the crossroad from Acre to Jaffa. Zahir walled in the area and built another fortress on the slope above (known as the Burj, located on the site of Castrum Samaritanorum). The new city of Haifa grew up within these walls—retaining its old name.

18th–19th Centuries. Haifa gradually recovered and increased from an estimated 250 settlers in old Haifa at the beginning of the 18th century to 4,000 a century later. R. Naḥman of Bratslav spent Rosh Ha-Shanah of 5559 (1798) with the small Jewish community of Haifa. The composition of the population changed, mainly due to the growing influence of the Carmelite monks, so that in 1840 about 40% of the city's inhabitants were Christian Arabs living alongside the Muslim majority. Despite severe difficulties and opposition from the local inhabitants and the authorities, the Carmelite monks, with the aid of France, managed to hold on to the dark crypts above "Elijah's Cave" and also erected nearby the Stella Maris monastery. Its cornerstone was laid in 1827 and construction was carried out without incident under the Egyptian rule in force in Ereẓ Israel at that time (1831–40) which was well-disposed to Christians in general and especially to those under French protection.

The Egyptian conquest of Ereẓ Israel lent much impetus to Haifa's development, which was especially to the disadvantage of its rival Acre. The steamboats, which made their appearance at this time in eastern Mediterranean ports and contributed to the economic rebirth of Ereẓ Israel, used Haifa rather than Acre as their port of call. The consular representatives therefore began leaving Acre (which was also dominated by Muslim extremism) to settle in Haifa, with its large Christian population and better climate; the latter took over more and more of Acre's export trade, which had consisted largely of grain, cotton, and sesame seeds. In 1858 the walled city of Haifa was already overcrowded and the first houses began to be built outside the ancient city on the mountain slope. Ten years later the first German Templars arrived in the country from Wuerttemberg and built a colony, which became a model residential suburb, just west of Haifa. The members of this sect made important contributions to Haifa's development—they introduced the stagecoach, paved roads, and set up a regular coach service to Acre and Nazareth. The

Templars also established Haifa's first industrial enterprises and applied modern methods in agriculture, crafts, and commerce. Toward the end of the century the Germans enlarged their settlement and built the first residential quarter on the top of the Carmel (near the present-day Merkaz ha-Carmel). In 1905 Haifa's position and importance was further strengthened when it was connected up with the Hejaz railroad which was then being laid between Damascus and the Arabian Peninsula; most of the exports from the fertile lands of the Hauran now passed through Haifa.

Revival of Jewish Settlement. Haifa's Jewish community expanded gradually. Very few Jews had apparently settled there when the ancient city was rebuilt at the beginning of Turkish rule. In 1742 it contained a small Jewish community, composed mainly of immigrants from Morocco and Algeria. In 1839 there were 124 Jews in Haifa; in 1864, 384; in 1871, 760; and in 1901, 1,041. Up to this time North African Jews still comprised the majority of the community, which also contained some Sephardi Jews from Turkey and a few Ashkenazim. (In 1917 the number of Jews rose to 1,400 of whom a third were of North African origin, a third Sephardi, and a third Ashkenazi.) In the last quarter of the century, the Jews comprised about one-eighth of the total population. They lived in the *Ḥarat al-Yahūd* ("Jewish quarter") inside the poor Muslim district in the eastern part of the lower city. Most of them barely subsisted by petty trade and peddling in Haifa or nearby villages. The importance of the Jewish community in the city increased with the arrival of members of the First and Second Aliyah from East Europe, mostly from Russia. From the 1880s onward, and especially in the early 20th century, extensive Jewish commercial and industrial activity sprang up. During his visit to Ereẓ Israel in 1898–99, Theodor Herzl recognized Haifa's numerous potentialities as the future chief port and an important inland road junction. In his *Altneuland* (1902), the description of Haifa occupies a central place in his vision of rebuilt Israel. The laying of the cornerstone of the *Technion in 1912 marked the high point of the intensified Jewish activities and was a signal for further development projects.

On the eve of World War I, Haifa with more than 20,000 inhabitants and a constantly expanding export-import trade, was the key city of northern Ereẓ Israel. A progressive European minority added to its cosmopolitan character and an extensive network of schools, most of them Catholic, provided a high standard of education. New residential quarters were added in the east and west and on the southern slopes of the Carmel and eventually embraced the ancient site of the city.

Figure 2. The Dagon granary at Haifa port. Courtesy Dagon, Battei Mamgurot le-Yisrael, Haifa. Photo Erev.

British Mandate Period. On September 23, 1918, after four centuries of Turkish rule, Haifa was captured in fierce battles by the British forces. During the British Mandate, Haifa rapidly grew into a large modern city in which the Jewish population played an increasingly predominant role. In 1919 the Haifa-Lydda railroad was added to the narrow gauge Haifa-Ẓemaḥ-Dara line. In the 1920s and 1930s the road network which linked up the various parts of Haifa was greatly improved and extended.

The 1922 census recorded a population of 25,000 in Haifa, of whom more than 9,000 were Muslims, slightly fewer Christian Arabs, and more than 6,000 Jews. According to the 1931 census, it contained 50,403 residents, including about 20,000 Muslims, 15,923 Jews, and about 14,000 Christians. By 1944 the number of inhabitants had grown to 128,000 of whom 66,000 were Jewish, 35,940 Muslim, 26,570 Christian, and 3,000 Bahais. At the end of the Mandate (1948) the Jews comprised nearly two-thirds of the population (about 100,000 out of 150,000). The completion of the large harbor in 1934 produced a great burst of prosperity and Haifa became the main and practically only port of international repute in Ereẓ Israel, taking precedence over Jaffa. Haifa's economy was further strengthened by the completion in 1939 of the oil pipeline from Iraq to its Mediterranean terminus at Haifa and the large oil refineries near the city. At this time the port facilities encouraged many new industries, some of them the largest in the country (textiles, glass, bricks, petroleum products, cement, metal, ceramics, etc.), in Haifa and the vicinity, especially in the Zebulun Valley. Tension between the city's Arab and Jewish residents, in the Mandate period, however, impeded Haifa's development. The riots of 1936–39 in particular adversely affected the city's economy and business dwindled between the conflicting sides as well as trade with Syria and Lebanon. The Arab population, mainly concentrated in the lower city, obstructed the Jews on their way to the adjoining industrial areas and to the port and services adjacent to it (marine shipping companies, banks, transport, insurance, etc.), as more and more Jews from the 1920s onward settled in the Hadar ha-Carmel section (the continuation of the Herzliyyah district founded before World War I). Hadar ha-Carmel developed rapidly around the Technion, which was inaugurated in 1925. The Mandate authorities granted some municipal autonomy to the new Jewish quarter. The Jewish settlement in this period also climbed higher up on the slope around Merkaz ha-Carmel, in the Aḥuzzat Herbert Samuel quarter, and in Neveh Sha'anan. When the land in the Zebulun Valley on the coast of the bay was purchased in 1928, the Zionist movement made its first venture into comprehensive urban planning for which it engaged the British city planner Patrick Abercrombie. The area stretching from the southeast corner of the bay up to Acre was divided into functional regions—an industrial zone in the south near the port; a residential area in the center in which from 1930 onward the Kerayot were built (Kiryat Ḥayyim, Kiryat Bialik, Kiryat Motzkin, Kiryat Yam); and an agricultural belt in the north.

Toward the end of the British Mandate, both the Jews and the Arabs attempted to gain control over the city. The hostilities which broke out at the end of 1947 reached a peak on April 21–22, 1948, when the British suddenly decided to evacuate the city. In a lightning military action, the Haganah captured the Arab quarters and took over the city. Only about 3,000 of Haifa's 50,000 Arab residents chose to remain in the city; the rest, in response to the Arab High Command's orders, refused to accept Jewish rule and abandoned their homes.

1948–1970. Late in 1948 Haifa's population numbered

97,544, of whom 96% were Jews. At the end of 1950 there were 140,000 inhabitants; at the end of 1952, 150,600; at the end of 1955, 158,700; in 1961, 183,021; and at the end of 1967, 209,900 inhabitants. The city was the second largest in the country (until the unification of Jerusalem in 1967). The built-up area of Haifa continued to expand along the shore area and on the slopes and ridges of the Carmel. The lower city (whose former nucleus had been largely left in ruins in 1948) was rebuilt as the "City"—Haifa's main business section. The population density on Hadar ha-Carmel (also a center for retail trade, services, and entertainment) increased until residents started moving to the upper Carmel. Housing projects on a large scale were erected, including extensive suburbs such as Kiryat Eliezer on the coast and southern Romemah on a ridge of the Carmel.

In the 1950s and 1960s a number of changes were made in the functional arrangement of the city with Haifa and Acre being conceived as the axes of a comprehensive regional scheme. In the Haifa Bay area the industrial zone extends north along the coastal dune strip up to Acre and constitutes the "Steel City." Residential quarters have been built east of this zone. On Mt. Carmel the crest and narrow spurs branching off to the west and east are reserved for building and parks and orchards fill the gorges. Downtown Haifa has extended westward, spilling over southward into the Carmel Coast area.

After the establishment of the State of Israel, the port was greatly expanded and modernized and became the home port of Israel's fast-growing navy. The piers were tripled in number, the water level deepened, and many port facilities added, such as the Dagon storage silos with a 75,000 ton capacity. In 1954 an auxiliary port was built at the Kishon River outlet, its pier was lengthened in 1964 to 2,099 ft. (640 m.). A shipyard for building and repairing ships, a floating dock, and a jetty for Israel's fishing fleet were also built in the Kishon area (1959). In 1951, 1,370 ships called at Israel ports (excluding oil tankers), of which 1,168 entered Haifa port. In 1967, 2,372 ships called, including 1,545 at Haifa and 765 at Ashdod port (which began operations in 1966). Haifa continued to be almost the exclusive embarkation and debarkation sea point in Israel (about a quarter of a million passengers passed through Haifa in the peak year of 1965).

Haifa's industry continued expanding in this period, especially in the bay area. Two factories in Israel for the production and assembly of cars were set up there, as well as large chemical and petrochemical industries, an industrial and craft center, a plant for producing organic fertilizers from waste, a plant for purifying sewage water, and numerous other industrial enterprises. Also located in Haifa are the national offices of the Israel Railways (including their large workshops), the Israel Electric Company, Solel Boneh (Israel's largest contracting company), Zim (the largest shipping company), and others. Employment in the port area, which provides work for a tenth of the city's population, and in Haifa's varied industry, even in the Mandate period drew a very large working force to the city, which is the best organized in the country.

From 1951 until his death in 1969, the mayor of Haifa was Abba *Khoushi, formerly the secretary of the Haifa labor council. He did much to develop and beautify the city. The annual city budget rose from IL 86,000 ($346,775) in 1948–49 to IL 86,000,000 ($24,571,428) in 1968–69.

The *Bahai sect, with its world center in Haifa, built a gold-domed sanctuary and cultivated one of the finest and largest gardens in the country. Another unique feature of the city is the "Carmelit," Israel's only subway, which was set up in 1959.

Figure 3. Haifa port. Courtesy Keren Hayesod, United Israel Appeal, Jerusalem.

The educational system has received particular attention. Haifa University College was founded in 1963 by the municipality under the academic supervision of the *Hebrew University. It was granted independent status and in 1970 it offered courses in the humanities and social sciences and had a department for training high school teachers. Enrollment in 1969/70 totalled 3,600 and the academic staff numbered 340. In the previous year 189 degrees were conferred. In 1967 the college was transferred to the university campus (designed by the architect Oscar Niemeyer) on the summit of the Carmel. Various cultural and social centers, public buildings, and museums have been built to house among others, the naval museum, the Museum of Modern Art, the Japanese Art Pavilion, the *Haifa Municipal Theater, and the Haifa Symphony Orchestra. One of the best-known community centers is the James de Rothschild Center. In 1963 a Jewish-Arab youth center, Bet Gefen, was opened through the efforts of Abba Khoushi, to help integrate the minority youth.

Bibliography: R. Hecht, *Sippurah shel Ḥeifah* (1968); Z. Vilnay, in: *Sefer ha-Shanah shel Ereẓ Yisrael*, 1 (1923), 125–9; idem, *Ḥeifah be-Avar u-va-Hoveh* (1936); J. Schattner, in: IEJ, 4 (1954), 26ff.; Hamilton, in: QDAP, 4 (1935), 1 ff.; J. Braslavski (Braslavi), in: BJPES, 12 (1945/6), 166–7; idem, *Le-Ḥeker Arẓenu* (1954), index; E. G. Rey, *Les colonies fraques de Syrie*. . .(1883), 431; Prawer, Ẓalbanim, index; V. Guérin, *Description géographique . . . Samarie*, 2 (1875), 252 ff.; Mann, Egypt, index; EIS, s.v.; L. Oliphant, *Haifa, or Life in Modern Palestine* (1887); A. Carmel, *Toledot Ḥeifah bi-Ymei ha-Turkim* (1969); S. Klein, *Toledot ha-Yishuv ha-Yehudi be-Ereẓ Yisrael* (1935), index; *Ḥeifah ba-Asor le-Yisrael* (1959).

[A.CA.]

HAIFA MUNICIPAL THEATER, Haifa repertory company, founded in 1961 by the Haifa Municipality. It was the first theater in Israel to be initiated by a public body, as well as the first with a paying membership (subscribers were guaranteed five new productions each season). The theater was warmly welcomed by residents of Haifa, and from its inception had 12,000 subscribers. Unlike other theaters in Israel, the Haifa Municipal Theater began in a magnificent building with up-to-date stage equipment and a municipal subsidy which guaranteed its solvency. Its budget in 1967 was IL2 million, of which IL420,000 was subsidy. However, since there never was a theater in Haifa before, it had difficulty in recruiting actors. Despite this handicap, it succeeded in presenting several excellent productions, among them Berthold Brecht's *The Caucasian Chalk Circle*, which was performed with great success in Israel in 1962 and at the Venice Festival in 1963, and Shakespeare's *Richard III* (1966), both staged by the Haifa Municipal Theater's first artistic director, Yosef *Millo. The repertoire

Haifa Municipal Theater, opened in 1961. Courtesy Government Press Office, Tel Aviv.

of the Haifa Municipal Theater consists of classical, contemporary, and original Hebrew plays. In 1970 it recruited the avant-garde group of young actors and directors, led by Oded Kotler, who constituted *Bimat ha-Saḥkanim.* [M.K.]

HAIMOWITZ, MORRIS JONAH (1881–1958), Yiddish writer. Born in Mir, Russia, where he studied at the yeshivah, he emigrated to the United States in 1902, spending the rest of his life in New York. Haimowitz published his first story, *"Blondzhendik"* ("Erring"), in the *Fraye Arbayter Shtimme* in 1905. He then joined Di Yunge (a movement of young writers) and coedited their anthology *Yugend* (1907–08), where he published his stories and essays. Later, he was one of the editors of the miscellany *Literatur* (1910), and of the almanac *Die Naye Heym* (1914). Haimowitz' novels about Jewish life in America, and historical novels about Jesus and Shabbetai Ẓevi, displayed an understanding of human nature and of historical events. In the novel about Jesus *Arum dem Man fun Natseres* ("About the Man of Nazareth," 1924), he presented an interesting interpretation and characterization of the early Christian movement and of its leading personalities. He portrayed himself in the character of Levin in the novel *Oyfn Veg* ("En route," 1914).

Bibliography: Rejzen, Leksikon, 1 (1926), 1137–39, LNYL, 3 (1960), 717–9. [E.SCH.]

HAINDORF, ALEXANDER (1782–1862), German educator and physician. In 1825 he founded at Muenster, Westphalia, an institution for the advancement of crafts among Jews and the training of teachers for Jewish elementary schools. An endowment by Haindorf's father-in-law enabled the school to train about 350 artisans in 50 years. The school had such an excellent reputation that the Prussian government permitted Christian pupils to attend it; in 1830 they outnumbered the Jews. One of Haindorf's aims was to promote the amalgamation of Judaism and Christianity, and in "slow and cautious imparting of Christian education" he saw a step in this direction.

Bibliography: Steinberg, in: JZWL, 2 (1863), 1–11; M. Eliav, *Ha-Ḥinnukh ha-Yehudi be-Germanyah* (1960), 285, 295–6, 310. [M.LA.]

HAITI, republic on the Caribbean island of Hispaniola, with a Jewish population of less than 50 persons (1970). Columbus landed there during his first voyage in 1492. The first Jewish settlers arrived in Haiti from Brazil shortly after the island was conquered by the French in the 17th century. Many were employees of French sugar plantations and some acquired their own land, but French policy tended to divest Jews of their colonial possessions and thus obstructed the development of the community. Individual Jews arrived with French commercial enterprises, and there seems to have been a group of *Crypto-Jews in the city of Jeremie as well. In 1683 Jews were expelled from all French colonies in the West Indies, including Haiti. Those few who remained served as officials in French trading companies, especially in Jeremie. No vestiges of the first Jewish settlement were left after the revolutionary wars which were accompanied in 1804 by the massacre of nearly all the French population. Around 1830, in the wake of the Polish rebellion, several Jewish families arrived in Haiti. These new immigrants were quickly absorbed in the upper echelons of Haitian society. Jewish life in Haiti began in 1890 with the arrival of about 30 families, mainly from Lebanon, Syria, and Eygpt. They engaged primarily in the cloth trade. The Jewish population in Haiti in 1915, at the time of the American occupation, is considered to have been less than 200 persons. During the 20 years of the occupation, many of these Jews immigrated to the United States and to South American countries. In the 1930s new Jewish immigrants arrived from Germany, Austria, Poland, Rumania, and Hungary. Although the Haitian government has traditionally frowned on white immigration, asylum was granted to refugees. At the beginning of World War II the newcomers numbered about 100; after the war the Jewish population numbered about 35 to 40 families. Until 1938 immigration laws were benign, the only prerequisite being the possession of $100; as of that year the sum was raised to $1,000 and a government permit was required in addition.

By 1957 there were about 200 Jews in Haiti, but steady emigration during the next decade diminished the community to about ten families, most of whom lived in the capital, Port-au-Prince. The Jews of Haiti were never able to organize any communal institutions. Neither a school nor a synagogue has been established, and rabbis and cantors have been brought from abroad for the High Holidays and special occasions. The ambassador of Israel in Panama is accredited as nonresident ambassador of Israel to Haiti. An Israel Technical Cooperation Mission is located in Port-Au-Prince and is engaged in a project of agricultural and cooperative development.

Bibliography: J. Beller, *Jews in Latin America* (1969); A. Tartakower, *Shivtei Yisrael,* 3 (1969), 130–1. [J.BAR.]

HAJDU, MIKLÓS (1879–1956), Hungarian journalist and author. Born in Gölle, Hajdu studied in Budapest. From 1897, he was on the editorial boards of *Budapesti Napló* ("Budapest Daily") and *A Nap* ("The Day"), later becoming editor of the latter. Bright in style, *A Nap* was the first "boulevard" type paper in Hungary. Hajdu had a keen interest in Jewish communal life and was one of the leaders of the liberal Isaiah Religious Society. He supported the Zionist cause before World War I, and after the revolution of 1918 continued the struggle against assimilation within the framework of the Pest Neolog community. His literary works describe Jewish village life in western Hungary, and include: *Gilead* (1914) and *Szeniczei Savuot* ("The Shavuot of Szenice," 1939). In 1939 he emigrated to Ereẓ Israel and settled in Tel Aviv.

Bibliography: *Magyar Zsidó Lexikon* (1929), 337–8; *Magyar Életrajzi Lexikon* (1964), 657. [B.Y.]

HAJEK, MARKUS (1861–1941), laryngologist. Hajek, who was born in Yugoslavia, served in Vienna as assistant in the Rudolf Hospital and the University Polyclinic, and then became professor of laryngology at the University of

Vienna. Hajek made fundamental contributions to anatomic, pathological, and clinical subjects in rhinolaryngology. He developed a systematic and scientific approach in the

Markus Hajek, laryngologist. Jerusalem, J.N.U.L., Schwadron Collection.

diagnosis and therapy of sinus ailments based on anatomical and pathological studies. He conducted studies on tuberculosis of the upper respiratory tract. He devised many practical instruments, suggested a new method of operation on frontal sinusitis, and improved the technique of extralaryngeal operations for cancer of the larynx. Hajek had to emigrate when the Nazis annexed Austria and died a destitute refugee in London. Among his publications are: *Pathologie und Therapie der entzuendlichen Erkrankungen der Nebenhoehlen der Nase* (1899) which was translated into English in 1926; *Syphilis of the Oral Cavity, Pharynx and Nasopharyngeal Cavity* (1928).

Bibliography: S. R. Kagan, *Jewish Medicine* (1952). [S.M.]

HAJJĀJ (Hagège), DANIEL (1892–), Tunis-born publicist and Judeo-Arabic writer who emigrated to Paris in 1959. Hajjāj published, translated, adapted, and edited over 30 novels and worked on several local papers, while at the same time being employed in a series of professions—including pharmacist and typographer. Among his writings in Judeo-Arabic are "The Barber's Assistant" (1930), a short story followed by a collection of 1,000 Tunisian, Judeo-Arabic proverbs *(Mille proverbes tunisiens),* arranged in alphabetical order and "Tunisian Judeo-Arabic Literature" (1939), a survey of Judeo-Arabic literature and writers. He also founded and edited the scientific and artistic periodical *La Gaieté Tunisienne* (1913–15, 1933).

Bibliography: Attal, in: *Studies and Reports of the Ben Zvi Institute,* 3 (1960), 56–59, 46–48 (Heb. part). [R. AT.]

HA-KARMEL (Heb. הַכַּרְמֶל), Hebrew periodical published in Vilna under the editorship of S. J. *Fuenn. It first appeared as a weekly (1860–70) and later as a monthly (1871–80). *Ha-Karmel* was required by terms of its license to publish a Russian supplement. This supplement was a more extreme advocate of the enlightenment than its Hebrew equivalent. Fuenn was a moderate *maskil* who tried to bridge the gap between the traditionalist and liberal elements. He supported the policy of the Russian government toward the Jews, closer association of the Jews with the Russian nation and its culture, and advocated the transition to labor, especially agriculture. Among the contributors to *Ha-Karmel* were A. B. Lebensohn, Ẓ. H. Katzenellenbogen, M. Plungian, E. Zweifel, J. Eichenbaum, A. B. Gottlober, J. L. Gordon, Kalman Schulmann, J. Reifmann, A. Harkavy, Solomon Buber, S. Rubin, R. A. Braudes, and J. M. Pines. For a short time (1866–68),

שנה ראשונה

הכרמל

מכתב עתי לבני ישראל

בשפת קדש, עם נוספות בלשון רוססיא ואשכנז.

יוצא לאור מדי שבוע בשבוע

על ידי

שמואל יוסף בן יצחק פין.

ו' תמוז תרכ. ווילנא № 1

הדר הכרמל

קומי שפת יפת בת השמים!
ולשון אל ראשון! ראשך הרימי
תן כל סופריך שמו לך ידים
לשום על ארץ האסרים הנעימי
עתה לבוא נקראת גם הכרמלה
עדי בת אבינו אל יעקב סלה!

Front page of the first issue of the Hebrew periodical *Ha-Karmel,* published in Vilna, 6 Tammuz, 5620 (1860). Jerusalem, J.N.U.L.

Ha-Karmel's editorial policy became more liberal and a number of articles by more radical authors appeared (A. U. Kovner, A. J. Paperna, and L. Kantor). Editorials came out in support of M. L. Lilienblum who also began to contribute to it. However, it soon resumed its more moderate course. The number of subscribers fluctuated between 300 and 500. *Ḥevrat Mefizei ha-Haskalah,* to which the periodical devoted much space from the time of the founding of that society (1863), supported *Ha-Karmel,* although not pleased with its moderate position. The literary level of the periodical was generally low, its language flowery, the poems (with the exception of those of J. L. Gordon) and stories few and poor, and the articles written in a cumbersome style. Permeated with a spirit of Russian patriotism, *Ha-Karmel* supported the Russification policy in the regions of Lithuania and Poland. The paper devoted much space to news of Jewish life in Vilna and its surroundings.

Bibliography: S. J. Fuenn, in: *Ha-Karmel,* 1 (1860), 372–3; Klausner, Sifrut, 4 (1954), 11–20; G. Elkoshi, in: *He-Avar,* 13 (1966), 66–97; 14 (1967), 105–42; Y. Slutsky, *ibid.,* 14 (1967), 153–8. [Y.S.]

HAKDAMAH (Heb. הַקְדָּמָה), introduction to a book. The first known *hakdamah* is the introduction to the *Halakhot Gedolot. In effect it is a sermon in praise of the Torah which its author saw fit to place at the beginning of his book as a preface. In medieval literature the *hakdamah* served as a literary genre and halakhic authors regarded themselves duty bound to attach a *hakdamah* to their works. Generally speaking the author in his *hakdamah* gives his motives for writing the book, and says something about its contents, but very often the *hakdamah* has important literary value of its own. Spanish and Italian authors also gave their *hakdamot* an aesthetic form by means of rhyme, meter, and even verses and complete poems, and some of them are literary gems. Especially noteworthy are those of Naḥmanides who wrote many fine *hakdamot*, of especial merit being those to his *Milḥamot ha-Shem* and his *Torat ha-Adam*. Some *hakdamot* are complete works, both in scope and in quality, and of these the introduction of Menahem b. Solomon *Meiri to his commentary *Beit ha-Beḥirah* on *Avot* is especially noteworthy. Occasionally the contents, purpose, and scope of the book cannot be fathomed without the *hakdamah*. Because the ordinary reader usually omits the reading of the *hakdamah*, some authors literally adjured copyists not to copy their works without the introduction, as did, for example, the author of **Ha-Ḥinukh*. So important was the *hakdamah* regarded that a popular proverb has it that "a book without a *hakdamah* is like a body without a *neshamah*" ("soul"). [I.T.-S.]

The *hakdamah* attained full development with Saadiah Gaon, in the tenth century. A systematic thinker, he found it necessary to explain what had motivated him to treat the particular subject he had chosen, thus laying the foundation of his thesis as well as apprising the reader of the content of the book he was presenting. He followed this pattern in his *siddur* and particularly in his philosophical work, the *Sefer ha-Emunot ve-ha-De'ot*. In his rather lengthy introduction he states that he wrote this book in order to resolve the doubts and confusions of his contemporaries concerning their traditional faith. The method followed by Saadiah Gaon was further developed and perfected by Moses Maimonides. He used his prefaces to certain orders, tractates, and chapters of the Mishnah, to sections of his great code, the *Mishneh Torah*, to expound his own philosophical ideas, in addition to elucidating such recondite subjects as the various degrees of ritual impurity dealt with in the order of *Tohorot* or the plants mentioned in the order of *Zera'im*. Thus, in the "Eight Chapters" prefacing his commentary on the tractate *Avot*, he unfolds a complete system of ethics while in his introduction to the tenth chapter of the tractate *Sanhedrin*, where the afterlife is mentioned, he discusses resurrection, listing what he regards as the fundamentals of Jewish belief, the 13 "principles" of Judaism. Maimonides' philosophical magnum opus, the *Guide of the Perplexed*, has both a short dedicatory preface addressed to his favorite pupil for whom it was written, as well as a fairly extensive general introduction, outlining his understanding of the text of Scripture, which, according to him, cannot always be taken literally. He also cautions the reader not to judge the merit of his book by a few isolated statements but to consider it in its totality and with the same seriousness with which it was written. Among the medieval Jewish scholars whose prefaces to their works are worthy of note, Abraham ibn Ezra stands high on the list. In a rhymed introduction to his commentary on the Pentateuch, after dismissing as worthless four other methods of interpretation, he summarizes his own approach, namely that of a critical understanding of the biblical text, making use of all the aids of philology available, regardless of the conclusions to which such an approach may lead.

The prefaces of books by medieval Jewish authors started out, like those of the Muslim writers of the time, with praise of God. With the introduction of printing it became customary for publishers, editors, and even proofreaders to write prefaces asking the indulgence of the readers for typographical errors and mistakes due to other causes. [S.R.]

ḤAKHAM (Heb. חָכָם; lit. "wise" or "sage"), title given to rabbinic scholars. Originally, it was inferior to the title "rabbi" since a scholar who possessed *semikhah* was called "rabbi" while the lesser savant was called *ḥakham*, or "sage" (BM 67b f.). Afterward it was also utilized for ordained scholars (Tosef., Yev. 4:6). Another talmudic distinction was between *ḥakham* and *talmid* ("disciple"). The disciple was only expected to answer inquiries that pertained directly to his studies, while the sage was required to respond to questions in all areas of rabbinic scholarship (Kid. 49b). The title *ḥakham* was also used as a formal designation of the third in rank after the *nasi* and *av bet din* of the Sanhedrin (Hor. 13b).

Sephardi Jews later used the title *ḥakham* for their local rabbis (in London and Amsterdam, applied to the rabbi of the Spanish and Portuguese congregations, it is written Haham), and reserved the more honorable designation of rabbi for preeminent scholars (David Messer Leon, *Kevod Ḥakhamim*, ed. by S. Bernfeld (1899), 63f.). Turkish Jewry designated its chief rabbi as **ḥakham bashi*. [Ed.]

ḤAKHAM, SIMON (1843–1910), author and Bible translator. Ḥakham was born in Bukhara, the son of a scholarly Baghdad emissary. He emigrated to Jerusalem in 1890. During his years in Jerusalem, he was active as editor, publisher, translator, and author. Among his major publications are *Shir ha-Shirim* (1904[2]), *Midrash Petirat Moshe* (1897), prayers and *piyyutim* for holidays (1902), *Pitron Ḥalomot* (1901), the Passover *Haggadah* (1904), and *Targum Sheni* to *Megillat Esther* (1905). He edited and published *Sefer Shahzadeh we-Sufi ve-hu Sharḥ al ha-Sefer *Ben ha-Melekh ve-ha-Nazir* (1907) by Abraham ben Samuel ha-Levi (ibn) *Ḥasdai, which Elijah b. Samuel had translated into Judeo-Persian in 1684. He also published a Judeo-Persian translation of parts of the Shulḥan Arukh under the title *Likkutei Dinim* (1901–03), prepared by Abraham Aminoff, the leading rabbi of the Jerusalem Bukharan colony. He translated Abraham Mapu's biblical novel *Ahavat Ẓiyyon* (1912[2]), and brought out part of the famous *Sefer Sharḥ Shahin al ha-Torah* (1902–04) by the 14th-century Judeo-Persian epic poet Maulana *Shahin of Shiraz, along with some of his own poetry.

His translation of the Bible into the Judeo-Persian of the Bukharan Jews was a monumental achievement which ranks him with the great Bible translators. He began his **tafsir* in 1906, and it appeared in successive volumes along with the Hebrew text, *Targum Onkelos*, and Rashi. By the time of his death he had completed the Pentateuch and the Prophets up to Isaiah 41:9; his collaborators completed the translation of the whole Bible.

Bibliography: Yaari, in: *Moznayim*, 3 pt. 48 (1932), 10–12; idem, in: KS, 18 (1941/42), 382–93; 19 (1942/43), 33–55, 116–39; Fischel, in: L. Finkelstein (ed.), *The Jews* (1960[3]), 1180–82; Fischel, in: L. Jung (ed.), *Jewish Leaders* (1964[2]), 535–47. [W.J.F.]

ḤAKHAM BASHI, the title of chief rabbi in the Ottoman Empire, composed of the Hebrew work *ḥakham* ("sage," "wise man") and the Turkish word *bashi* ("head," or "chief"). At the end of 1836 or the beginning of 1837 the Ottoman authorities confirmed the first *ḥakham bashi* in Constantinople (see *Istanbul). According to a report in the official gazette of the empire this gesture was made at the request of those members of the community in the capital who were subjects of the sultan. They had no Christian-European powers behind them and were jealous of the honor of official confirmation that the government accorded to the Greek and Armenian patriarchs. This was in fact a turning point in the policy of the Ottoman authorities, who hitherto had not interfered in the internal affairs of the Jewish community and for centuries past had given no official status to its representatives. The original copies or authentic texts of the *berat hümayun* (imperial confirmation of appointments) occurring from 1836 onward, which were also granted to chief rabbis in Adrianople, Salonika, Izmir (Smyrna), Broussa (now Bursa), and Jerusalem, show that there was indeed a policy, the significance and consequences of which went beyond mere confirmation or appointments. Implicitly contained was an official recognition of the Jewish *millet.

A *berat* was concerned with three interrelated matters: the religious powers of the *ḥakham bashi,* his powers as representative of the government, and the permission to read the Torah. Within his area of jurisdiction the *ḥakham bashi* was the supreme authority in all religious matters and in charge of all *ḥakhamim* and heads of the community. He alone was authorized to ban and excommunicate offenders and prohibit their religious burial. The person and official residence of the *ḥakham bashi* enjoyed immunity which extended also to the *ḥakhamim* and officials subordinate to him. Disagreements on religious questions between *ḥakhamim* and the local Muslim authorities were to be settled before the supreme authorities of the empire in Constantinople. As representative of the government the *ḥakham bashi* was responsible for the collection of government taxes. Government officials had to lend his officials every assistance in performing this task and place guards at their disposal. To protect his officials from molestation and restrictions when traveling, they were excused from wearing distinctive Jewish clothing and permitted to carry arms. They were thus exempt from two important provisions of the Covenant of *Omar. By an order of 1850 the religious heads of the four millets were required to collect the poll tax. Regarding the permission to read the Torah, the intention to grant rights to the community as a whole is conspicuous in a clause figuring in all *berat* texts; it declared that the reading of the Torah in the *ḥakham's* house and in other houses is permitted in the Jewish religion, as is hanging veils and candelabra where such reading takes place. This declaration was tantamount to the permission to establish permanent synagogues, and it constituted an ingenious circumvention of a prohibition contained in the Covenant of Omar, which was a source of many difficulties and an occasion for incessant extortion. The *berats* issued in provincial towns to the *ḥakham bashi* state expressly that they were granted upon the recommendation of the *ḥakham bashi* of Constantinople, who was thus the head of all the rabbis in the empire. This was why, in the event of a disagreement among the members of a community concerning the appointment of the local *ḥakham bashi,* the disputants would try to influence the *ḥakham bashi* of Constantinople. His decision not infrequently was based on other than objective considerations. From certain (especially Tripolitanian and Iraq) sources it appears that a *ḥakham bashi* was sometimes sent from the capital without the local community having been consulted.

It is clear that while the *ḥakham bashi's* official functions enhanced his importance and prestige, they were not in themselves sufficient to grant him supremacy in the field of *halakhah* and religious jurisdiction. In fact, this post was sometimes assigned to a simple schoolteacher. Besides the *ḥakham bashi* who was described in French as temporal head (a translation of the Arabic-Turkish term *shaykh zamani*), there were *ḥakhamim* bearing the designation *rav ha-kolel* (chief rabbi) or spiritual head *(shaykh rūḥi).* It happened sometimes that a *ḥakham bashi* who had resigned or been deposed subsequently served as *rav ha-kolel,* just as *rav ha-kolel* (see *Kolel) was occasionally appointed *ḥakham bashi.* The powers vested in the *ḥakham bashi* show that he was regarded by the Ottoman authorities as their representative vis-à-vis the Jewish population, performing official functions on behalf of the Jews, and he was so regarded by the Jews themselves. His situation was further

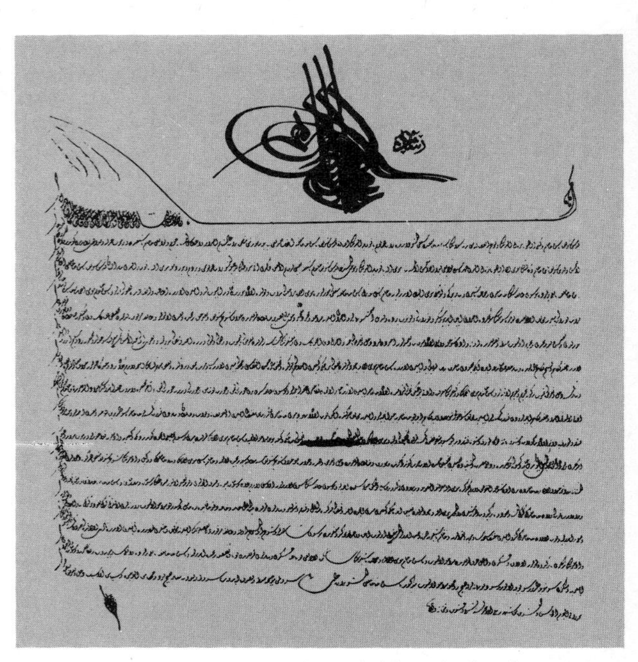

Firman appointing Jacob Meir as *ḥakham bashi* of Jerusalem, 1911. From E. Gaon and M. Laniado (eds.), *Zikhron Me'ir, A Jubilee Book,* Jerusalem, 1936.

complicated by dissension betweeen strictly traditionalist, anti-modernist members of the community and those favoring a general education and reforms in communal affairs. This situation accounts for the fact that of the five such chief rabbis officiating in the years 1836–63, three were deposed by the community and one was dismissed by the government because of his non-Turkish nationality. Three continued in office in the post of *rav ha-kolel,* which seems to indicate that they had been deposed as a result of clashes between the different factions within the community.

The first *ḥakham bashi* in Jerusalem was appointed by imperial firman in 1841. His Hebrew title **rishon le-Zion* was used by the Sephardi chief rabbis of Jerusalem. The "Organizational Regulations of the Rabbinate," confirmed by imperial firman in 1865 (see *Millet and *Community), describe in the first 15 clauses the status and powers of the *ḥakham bashi* as the head of the Jewish millet in the empire. The powers of the provincial chief rabbis have always been defined in the firmans issued on their appointment. In 1835 Tripolitania again came under the direct rule of the Sublime Porte who introduced there the same order that existed throughout the empire. The first *ḥakham bashi* was appointed by imperial firman in 1874 and therefore Tripoli is not mentioned in the "Organizational Regulations of the Rabbinate" of 1865. The title became so common that it referred to the head of every small community. The title *ḥakham bashi* is still in use in the Turkish republic, which has in Constantinople the largest Jewish community of the territories which once belonged to the empire, except Israel. After Iraq's separation from the Ottoman Empire and the establishment of the British Mandate, Baghdad Jewry was presided over by the deputy *ḥakham bashi* and spiritual head of Baghdad. This title was abolished in Iraq in 1932 and the title *raʾīsal ḥakhāmim* came into use.

Bibliography: M. Franco, *Essai sur l'histoire des Israélites de l'Empire Ottoman...* (1897), 151–2; A. Galanté (ed.), *Documents officiels turcs concernant les Juifs...* (1931), 32–50; *Appendice...* (1941), 4–8; H. Z. Hirschberg, in: A. J. Arberry (ed.), *Religion in the Middle East,* 1 (1969), 187, 196–201. [H.Z.H.]

HAKHEL (Heb. הַקְהֵל; "assemble"). The Bible enjoins that "At the end of every seven years, at the time of the year of release, at the Feast of Tabernacles" there is to take place an assembly of the whole people, "men, women, children, and the stranger that is within your gates." The purpose of this assembly is "that they may hear and so learn to revere the Lord your God and to observe faithfully every word of this Teaching" (Deut. 31:10–13). This ceremony, called *Hakhel* ("assemble") after the opening word of verse 12, is mentioned only once in the Talmud (Sot. 7:8), but in great detail and includes an interesting historical incident. The Mishnah lays it down *(ibid.)* that the date referred to is on the first day of the festival of Sukkot after the close of the seven year period of **shemittah*, i.e., on the 15th day of the first month of the eighth year.

The Mishnah connects this ceremony with another passage which deals with an entirely different subject, namely the duties of the king as laid down in Deuteronomy 17:14–20 and which it calls "the Chapter of the King." According to the Mishnah it was at the *Hakhel* ceremony that the king read that and other passages. It is possible that the coalescing of these passages is due to the similarity of wording between the two, the passage quoted above, and the passage with regard to the king "that he may learn to fear the Lord his God to keep all the words of this law and these statutes to do them" (*ibid.*, 17:19).

The Mishnah states that a wooden platform was set up in the Temple court upon which the king sat. "The minister *(ḥazzan)* of the synagogue used to take a scroll of the Torah and hand it to the chief of the synagogue, and the chief of the synagogue gave it to the deputy high priest who handed it to the high priest who handed it to the king. The king received it standing and read it while seated." The passages read were not "all the words of the Torah" but selected passages from Deuteronomy; from the beginning to 6:19, the last verses of which are the first paragraph of the **Shema*, the second paragraph of the *Shema* (11:13–21), 14; 22–27; 26:12–15; 17:14–20 ("the Chapter of the King"), and 27:15–26. He concluded the reading with eight benedictions, of which seven were identical with those pronounced by the high priest on the Day of Atonement (see Sot. 7:6) and the eighth (the fourth in number) for the festival instead of the one for pardon of sin pronounced by the high priest.

The continuity of the description of the ceremony in the Mishnah is interrupted by the information that despite the rule that the king read the passages while seated, "King Agrippa read it standing, for which he was praised by the rabbis," and continues with the moving story of the king, conscious of his mixed descent, bursting into tears when he read "thou mayest not put a foreigner over thee who is not thy brother" (Deut. 17:15) and the assembled people called out "thou art our brother." Most scholars identify this Agrippa who was so beloved of the people with *Agrippa I, who reigned from 41–44 C.E., the first of which years coincides with the year of *shemittah*. Others, however, ascribe it to *Agrippa II. In recent years in Israel an attempt has been made to revive a symbolical form of the *Hakhel* ceremony.

Bibliography: ET, 10 (1961), 443–52; A. Beuchler, in: *II. Jahresbericht der Israelitisch-Theologischen Lehranstalt in Wien* (1895), 11–14; S. Goren, *Torat ha-Mo'adim* (1964), 127–38; S. J. Zevin, *Le-Or ha-Halakhah* (1957[2]), 135–45.

[L.I.R.]

HAKHNASAT KALLAH (Heb. הַכְנָסַת כַּלָּה; "bringing in the bride" i.e., under the wedding canopy), a rabbinic commandment to provide a dowry for brides and to rejoice at their weddings (Maim. Yad., Avelim 14:1). The term is popularly applied to the provision of dowry for the poor brides. The precept is of such importance that it is permissible to interrupt even the (public) study of Torah in order to fulfill it (Meg. 3b and Tos. ad loc.). It is reckoned in the prayer book as among those deeds "for which a man enjoys the fruits in this world, while the stock remains for him for the world to come." (Hertz, Prayer, 17, version of Pe'ah 1:1 and Shab. 127a). A man who raises an orphan and enables her to marry is considered as continually doing acts of righteousness and justice (Ps. 106:3; Ket. 50a).

Communal charity collectors are permitted to use the funds they collected for other purposes for the dowry of poor brides (Sh. Ar., YD 249:15, and Siftei Kohen ad loc.). The Mishnah specified the minimum sum of 50 *zuz* to be given to a bride, but "if there was more in the poor funds they should provide for her according to the honor due to her" (Ket. 6:5). This minimal sum of "50 *zuz*" must be reassessed in every generation in accordance with its own economic conditions (Turei Zahav to Sh. Ar. YD 250:2). As in other aspects of communal Jewish charity, specific organizations were formed to supervise the collection and distribution of funds for the dowries and trousseaux of poor girls and orphans. These groups were often called Hakhnasat Kallah societies. In the ghetto of Rome, during the 17th century, for example such a society functioned actively (Roth, Italy, 364). Samuel Portaleone, an Italian preacher, in his description of seven charity boxes which existed in Mantua, Italy, in 1630, lists among them *hakhnasat kallah* (JQR, 5 (1893), 510). Hakhnasat Kallah societies have continued to function throughout the Jewish world.

In addition to aiding poor brides, the precept also demands that a person attend and rejoice at the marriage of any bride. It was considered meritorious to accompany the bride from her father's home to where the wedding ceremony was to take place (Rashi to Meg. 29a). This aspect of *hakhnasat kallah* may also be fulfilled by accompanying the bridegroom to the *bedekin* ("covering" the face) of the bride (Beit Shemu'el to Sh. Ar. EH 65:1). While it is also customary to dance before the bride and to praise her, Bet Shammai held that the virtues of the bride are not to be exaggerated, and that she is only to be praised "as she truly is." Bet Hillel, on the other hand, ruled that every bride should be regarded and praised as "beautiful and graceful" (Ket. 16b–17a).

The fulfillment of the precept of *hakhnasat kallah* should be performed humbly, modestly and in privacy, thus complying with the dictum "to walk humbly with thy God" (Micah 6:8; Suk. 49b).

See also *Charity, *Dowry, and *Marriage Ceremonies.

Bibliography: ET, 9 (1959), 136–43; Baron, Community, 1 (1942), 362ff., 2 (1942), 332f., 3 (1942), 212f.; I. Abrahams, *Jewish Life in the Middle Ages* (1920), 326; I. Levitats, *Jewish Community in Russia* (1943), 252; H. H. Ben-Sasson, *Hagut ve-Hanhagah* (1959), index.

[ED.]

HA-KIBBUTZ HA-ARẒI HA-SHOMER HA-ẒA'IR, a union of kibbutzim in Israel, founded in 1927 by the first collective settlements of *Ha-Shomer ha-Ẓa'ir pioneers. It regards itself as an avant-garde nucleus of the future socialist society in Israel and adheres strictly to the principles of collective life of its members and the collective education of their children. In 1970, Ha-Kibbutz ha-Arẓi comprised 75 kibbutzim with a population of about 30,000.

For further details see *Kibbutz Movement, Ha-Kibbutz ha-Arẓi ha-Shomer ha-Ẓa'ir. [ED.]

HA-KIBBUTZ HA-DATI, a union of religious kibbutzim in Israel, established in 1935 by members of *Ha-Po'el ha-Mizrachi. It combines religious practice with collective life and labor and exerts a political influence in the *National Religious Party by strengthening its left-wing faction, "*La-Mifneh." Many of the religious kibbutzim are located in dangerous border areas. Some of them, e.g., those of the Eẓyon Bloc, were overrun and destroyed by Arab forces during the *War of Independence. In 1970 Ha-Kibbutz ha-Dati comprised 13 settlements with a population of about 4,000.

For further details see *Kibbutz Movement, Ha-Kibbutz ha-Dati. [Ed.]

HA-KIBBUTZ HA-ME'UḤAD, a union of kibbutzim in Israel founded at a conference in Petaḥ Tikvah in 1927 by the first "large" kevuẓot, established primarily by pioneers of the Third Aliyah, including previous groups of *Gedud ha-Avodah ("Labor Legion"). In 1951 a split occured in its ranks due to political and ideological tensions between *Mapai and the left-wing *Aḥdut ha-Avodah. The Mapai-oriented members seceded, eventually founding the *Iḥud ha-Kevuẓot ve-ha-Kibbutzim. In 1970, Ha-Kibbutz ha-Me'uḥad numbered about 60 kibbutzim with a population of about 25,000–30,000.

For further details see *Kibbutz Movement, Me'uḥad. [Ed.]

ḤAKIM, SAMUEL BEN MOSES HA-LEVI IBN (?1480–after 1547), rabbi in Egypt and Turkey. Samuel came from a distinguished family of Spanish origin who had settled in Egypt. His father, Moses, was a personal friend of the governor of Egypt and, when difficulties arose, intervened on behalf of the Jews. Samuel studied in Egypt under the *nagid,* Jonathan ha-Kohen *Sholal, and at the beginning of the 16th century he was already regarded as one of the eminent Egyptian rabbis. He later left Egypt for Constantinople, where he also occupied an important position in the Jewish community, but it is difficult to ascertain in which year he made this move. According to a responsum it was c. 1517, but this seems to be a mistake for c. 1527, since there is extant a *haskamah* signed by Samuel and R. *David b. Solomon ibn Abi Zimra in Egypt in the year 1527 (Neubauer, Chronicles, 1 (1887), 158), a date confirmed by two manuscripts. His departure for Constantinople could not therefore have taken place before 1527, unless it be supposed that two scholars of the same name lived in Cairo at the same time, which is very difficult to accept. The problem of two Samuel b. Moses ha-Levi ibn Ḥakim (Hakam) is further complicated by the existence of Samuel Hakan who is definitely not identical with Samuel Ḥakim. Samuel was a friend of Moses *Hamon, physician to Sultan Suleiman. He frequently engaged in sharp polemics with the important rabbis of his time and even strongly criticized a halakhic ruling made by *Shalom Shakhna b. Joseph of Lublin on the laws of *sivlonot* (the gifts given by the bridegroom to his bride on the occasion of their engagement) which appeared at the end of the novellae of *Aaron ha-Levi of Barcelona (?) to *Kiddushin* (1904), which perhaps points to contacts between the rabbis of Constantinople and Poland. In 1547 he published a collection of responsa of *Isaac b. Sheshet Perfet (Ribash) in Constantinople. The book was published in sections and Samuel followed the accepted Constantinople custom of distributing the sections to purchasers on the Sabbath, in the synagogue. *Isaac ibn Lev complained that this custom was tantamount to engaging in business on the Sabbath. Samuel pointed to the precedent of the similar sale of such books as *Toledot Adam ve-Ḥavvah* (1516) of *Jeroham b. Meshullam and *Toledot Yiẓhak* (1518) of Isaac *Caro. Furthermore, he said, the greatest rabbis had not protested against it.

Only a small number of Samuel's many responsa have survived; some are preserved in the works of his contemporaries such as the responsa of Joseph *Caro and *Levi ibn Ḥabib, and a few responsa are still extant in manuscript. He is frequently mentioned in contemporary and later responsa. Ḥakim was on friendly terms with the *Karaites of Constantinople and was well acquainted with their customs. In one of his responsa written before 1533 (still in manuscript) he expresses the opinion that they sin inadvertently, not deliberately, and should not be treated as apostates or the illegitimate offspring of forbidden marriages. It is therefore permitted to intermarry with them, to drink their wine, to eat of their *sheḥitah,* and to accept them as witnesses in matters of personal status. This original opinion, for which no parallel or supporting view could be found either in his own or in succeeding generations, aroused the most vehement opposition of the other authorities. Among them were David b. Solomon ibn Abi Zimra (Responsa, pt. 2 no. 796), Moses *di Trani (Responsa, pt. 1, no. 37), and Bezalel Ashkenazi (Responsa, no. 3). There are extant glosses by Ḥakim to the novellae of Solomon b. Abraham *Adret on the tractate *Shabbat,* as well as a short introduction to the *Masoret Seyag la-Torah* of Meir ha-Levi *Abulafia. The place and date of Ḥakim's death are unknown.

Bibliography: C. Bernheimer, in: REJ, 66 (1913), 102; S. Assaf, in: *Alim,* 1 (1934–35), 73–75; idem, in: *Minḥah le-David* (1935), 223, 236–7; idem, in: *Zion,* 1 (1936), 213–4; idem, *Be-Ohalei Ya'akov* (1943), 185–6; Assaf, Mekorot, 220, 221, 255–6; idem, in: *Sinai,* 4 (1939), 532–50; Ashtor, Toledot, 2 (1951), 481–4; A. Yaari, *Ha-Defus ha-Ivri be-Kushta* (1967), 14, 103. [A.D.]

°ḤĀKIM BI-AMR ALLAH (AL-), the sixth caliph (996–1021) of the Ismā'īlī *Fatimid dynasty, which ruled in North Africa, Egypt, Palestine, Syria, and wide areas of the Arabian Peninsula. In the year 400 A.H. (1009–10 C.E.) a major change took place in al-Ḥākim's attitude toward the Muslim and Ismā'īlī traditions and he issued proclamations which were decisive for the development of the *Druze faith and community, of which he was the founder. The harassment of Christians, which had begun several years previously, was intensified, and the Church of the Holy Sepulcher in Jerusalem was burned down. According to Christian and Muslim sources these persecutions also included the Jews, but these reports should be treated with caution. A *Megillat Miẓrayim* ("Egyptian Scroll") from 1012, which is extant in two versions, mentions al-Ḥākim as the protector of the Jews, who allegedly assembled in the Great Synagogue of Fostat to thank God that the caliph had saved them from a rioting mob. This favorable appraisal is confirmed in letters written by the heads of the Palestinian and the Fostat yeshivot which mention that al-Ḥākim subsidized their institutions. After 1012 the persecution also included the Jews; synagogues were burned, and there were instances of forced conversion to Islam. The difficulties ceased only in the last years of al-Ḥākim (1017–20). Christians and Jews were permitted to rebuild their places of worship and forced converts were allowed to return to their former religion. At that time al-Ḥākim openly presented himself as the incarnation of the deity. The two above-mentioned events undoubtedly were related. Early in 1021 al-Ḥākim disappeared, and it is believed that he was murdered. A rumor spread among his followers that he was hiding on Mount al-Muqaṭṭam (near Cairo) and would appear again in the fullness of time (after a thousand years). The first article of the Druze faith is that al-Ḥākim was the last incarnation of the deity; he cannot have died, and his followers, therefore, are awaiting his return *(raj'a).* Al-Ḥākim's personality and Druze doctrines influenced later Jewish mystic movements. Joseph *Sambari (17th cent.) recounts in his chronicle *Divrei Yosef* (Paris, Alliance Israélite Universelle, Hebrew manuscript no. 22–23) the story of al-Ḥākim's persecutions. According to this version, the persecution of the Jews was caused by the Arabic translation of the Passover *Haggadah*, which tells of the drowning of the Egyptian king. Al-Ḥākim thought that this referred to him and forbade further translations of the *Haggadah*. Sambari further states that al-Ḥākim was murdered by his sister in the year 411 A.H., i.e., 1033.

Bibliography: S. de Sacy, *Exposé de la religion des Druzes*, 2 vols. (1838); Mann, Egypt, 1 (1920), 30–7; 2 (1922), 35–6, 70; H. Z. Hirschberg, in: A. J. Arberry (ed.), *Religion in the Middle East*, 2 (1969), 332–5; EIS[3], 2 (1965), s.v. Durūz.

[H.Z.H.]

HAKKAFOT (Heb. הַקָּפוֹת), term used to designate ceremonial processional circuits both in the synagogue and outside it, on various occasions.

Such circuits are mentioned in the Bible. There were, for instance, seven circuits around Jericho (once a day for six days, and seven times on the seventh day; Josh. 6:14–15). The Mishnah records that the *lulav* was carried around the Temple altar during the seven days of *Sukkot (Suk. 3:12). Although the *Gemara* makes no mention of similar circuits during Sukkot in the post-Temple period, both Hai Gaon (B. M. Lewin, *Oẓar ha-Ge'onim* (1934), Sukkah, 60, no. 151), and Saadiah Gaon (in his *Siddur*) mention the custom of making a circuit around the synagogue with the *lulav* and *etrog* on Sukkot. Nowadays a single circuit is made around the *bimah* on each of the first six days of Sukkot (except for the Sabbath) during the chanting of **hoshanot* at the close of the *Musaf* service. On *Hoshana Rabba, the seventh day of Sukkot, the procession around the *bimah* is repeated seven times. It is related that on this day, Hai Gaon used to make a pilgrimage to Jerusalem, and there make seven processional circuits around the Mount of Olives (*Sefer Ḥasidim*, ed. by J. Wistinetzki (1924[2]), no. 630). The Torah scrolls are carried around the synagogue in processional circuits during both the *Ma'ariv* and *Shaharit* services on *Simḥat Torah (a custom first mentioned by Rabbi Isaac Tyrnau, 14th–15th century; *Minhagim* (Lunéville (1806), 51a)). The Ḥasidim perform these *hakkafot* also at the conclusion of the *Ma'ariv* service on *Shemini Aẓeret. In Reform congregations, these *hakkafot* are performed on Shemini Aẓeret. In Israel where Simḥat Torah coincides with Shemini Aẓeret, many congregations perform *hakkafot* again after *Ma'ariv* at the completion of the festival.

Hakkafot are also performed on a number of other occasions. For instance, Torah scrolls are carried around in a processional circuit during the dedication of both synagogues and cemeteries. In a number of communities, it is customary for the bride to make either three or seven

Les ACAFOTH ou les sept tours, autour du CERCUEIL.

Figure 1. Engraving of *hakkafot* around a coffin by members of the burial society of the Amsterdam Portuguese Synagogue. From B. Picart, *Cérémonies et coutumes religieuses*, Amsterdam, 1723–43.

Figure 2. *Hakkafot* on Simḥat Torah in Tel Aviv, 1965. Courtesy Government Press Office, Tel Aviv.

hakkafot around the bridegroom during the wedding ceremony. The Sephardim and Ḥasidim walk around a coffin seven times prior to burial. It is also customary to walk around the cemetery when praying for the sick.

On all of these occasions one may note the juxtaposition of the "magic circle" with the mystical figure of seven, and the implied attempt to dissuade *shedim* ("evil spirits") from intruding upon the object of attention. With regard to the funerary *hakkafot* it has been suggested that the purpose is to ward off the spirits of the dead man's unborn children and to appease them with symbolic gifts of money. It is also significant that *Ḥoni ha-Me'aggel's miracles were performed after he had made a circuit (in the form of a drawn circle), around the place on which he stood (Ta'an. 19a, 23a).

Bibliography: ET, 10 (1961), 539; Eisenstein, Dinim, 105.

[H.RA.]

ḤALAFTA (early second century C.E.), *tanna*, father of the well-known *tanna* *Yose. Ḥalafta lived in *Sepphoris where he was a leader of the community (Tosef., Ta'an. 1:14; RH 27a). His colleague was *Johanan b. Nuri who discussed *halakhah* with him; seemingly among his associates were also *Akiva (BB 56b, where Ḥalafta is called Abba Ḥalafta as also in Shab. 115a; Tosef., BB 2:10; Tosef., Kelim, BM 1:5), *Ḥanina b. Teradyon (Ta'an. 2:5), and *Eleazar b. Azariah (Tosef., Kelim, BB 2:2). It is possible that in the last years of the Temple he was living in Jerusalem since he transmits an incident about Gamaliel the Elder (Tosef., Shab. 13:2). Several statements by him in *halakhah* and *aggadah* have been preserved, some by his son Yose (Kelim 26:6; Tosef., Bek. 2:19, et al.).

Bibliography: Hyman, Toledot, s.v.; J. Kanowitz, *Ma'arekhot Tanna'im*, 2 (1967), 107–9.

[Z.K.]

ḤALAFTA BEN SAUL (early third century C.E.), Palestinian *amora*. Ḥalafta taught *beraitot* which are cited both in the Jerusalem Talmud (Ber. 1:8, 3c; Pe'ah 2:6, 17a; Shev. 2:7, 34a; Hag. 3:7, 79d, et al.) and in the Babylonian (Zev. 93b; MK 10a; see Dik. Sof. *ibid.*). It is possible that he is to be identified with the Taḥlifa b. Saul who taught a *baraita* quoted in the Babylonian Talmud (Men. 7b, et al.). An *aggadah* is also cited in his name Ber. 29a). It has been suggested by some that he was the brother of Johanan b. Saul, and Yose b. Saul, a pupil of *Judah ha-Nasi.

Bibliography: Judah b. Kalonymos, *Yiḥusei Tanna'im ve-Amora'im*, ed. by J. L. Maimon (1963), 311f.; Hyman, Toledot, 454, s.v.; Margalioth, Ḥakhmei, 313f., s.v.

[Z.K.]

HA LAḤMA ANYA (Aram. הָא לַחְמָא עַנְיָא; lit. "Behold the poor bread"), opening words of an introductory paragraph of the Passover **Haggadah.* The announcement is in Aramaic, and is proclaimed at the **seder* service immediately after the conclusion of the *karpas* ceremony (in which greens are dipped in salt water; see, *Passover *seder*).

The announcement is composed of three unrelated sentences. The first reads, "Behold this poor bread (or, 'bread of poverty'), which our fathers ate in the land of Egypt." This points to the centrality of the *mazzah* ("the unleavened bread") in the Festival of Passover. The second sentence invites the poor to the Passover meal: "Let anyone who is hungry come in and eat; let anyone who is needy come in and make Passover." The third sentence reads, "This year we are here; next year we shall be in the land of Israel; this year we are slaves, next year we shall be free men."

The origins and exact purport of the *Ha Laḥma Anya* are obscure. Most early portions of the *Haggadah* were written in Hebrew and are mentioned in the Mishnah. The language and content of this announcement, however, suggest that it was composed in Babylon after the destruction of the Temple. The second sentence does find an almost exact analogy in the Talmud (Ta'an, 20b), where R. Huna is said to have exclaimed before his meals "Let every needy person come and eat." Mattathias Gaon, in the 9th century, claimed that this sentence of *Ha Laḥma Anya* had always been a *minhag avoteinu* ("custom of our fathers"; B. M. Lewin, *Ozar ha-Ge'onim,* 3 (1930), *Pesaḥim* 112). Had this sentence been the central feature of the announcement, however, the *Ha Laḥma Anya* would be expected to open the *Haggadah,* and to precede the **kiddush* and *karpas.*

The present version of the announcement is probably a combination of several texts which date from the talmudic and post-talmudic period. It has undergone several modifications. *Maimonides (Yad, appendix to *Ḥamez u-Mazzah*) cites the present version with minor changes and a small addition. *Saadiah Gaon's text opens with the third sentence, and is followed by the second. He omits the first sentence altogether. In certain late medieval manuscripts, the first sentence reads, "Behold like this poor bread . . ." Most texts, including those of Maimonides and *Judah Loew b. Bezalel, have the simple version in use today, "Behold the poor bread."

Bibliography: Davidson, Ozar, 2 (1929), 116, no. 2; Liber, in: REJ, 82 (1926), 217–9; E. D. Goldschmidt, *Haggadah shel Pesaḥ ve-Toledoteha* (1960), 7–9; M. M. Kasher, *Haggadah Shelemah* (1955), 5–8 (Hebrew pagination). [HA.BL.]

Illuminated opening from *Ha Laḥma Anya* from the *Sarajevo Haggadah,* Spain, 14th century. Sarajevo, National Museum, fol. 3*.

HALAKHAH. This article is arranged according to the following outline:

Definition
Dogmatics of the Halakhah
  Sources of Authority
    The Written Law
    Statements Handed Down by Tradition
    The Oral Law
      Interpretation of the Written Law
      Halakhah Given to Moses at Sinai
      Logical Deduction
    Sayings of the Scribes
      The Authority of the Sages
    Custom
Development of Halakhah
  The Early Period
  The Tannaitic Period
  The Amoraic Period
  Codification of the Halakhah
The Authority of the Halakhah

DEFINITION

The word "*halakhah*" (from the root *halakh,* "to go"), the legal side of Judaism (as distinct from *aggadah,* the name given to the non-legal material, particularly of the rabbinic literature) embraces personal, social, national, and international relationships, and all the other practices and observances of Judaism. In the Bible the good life is frequently spoken of as a way in which men are "to go," e.g., "and shalt show them the way wherein they are to go and the work that they must do" (Ex. 18:20). Originally the term *halakhah* (pl. *halakhot*) had the meaning of the particular law or decision in a given instance, as in the frequent expression "this is a law given to Moses on Sinai" *(*Halakhah le-Moshe mi-Sinai).* This usage persisted, but side by side with it there developed the use of *halakhah* as a generic term for the whole legal system of Judaism, embracing all the detailed laws and observances. For instance, the Talmud (Shab. 138b) comments on "the word of the Lord" (Amos 8:12) that this means the *halakhah.*

The study of the *halakhah* in the rabbinic period and beyond it became the supreme religious duty. Because of its difficult subject matter and its importance for practical Judaism this study took precedence over that of any other aspect of Jewish teaching. Typical is the rabbinic saying that after the destruction of the Temple, God has nothing else in His world than the four cubits of the *halakhah* (Ber. 8a). The superiority of halakhic study over aggadic was expressed in the parable of the two merchants, one selling precious stones, the other small ware. Only the connoisseur comes to buy from the former (Sot. 40a).

The general assumption in the classical Jewish sources is that the *halakhah* in its entirety goes back to Moses, except for various later elaborations, extensions, applications, and innovations in accordance with new circumstances. Thus

Maimonides (Yad, intro.) counts 40 generations backward from R. Ashi, the traditional editor of the Babylonian Talmud, to Moses and he concludes: "In the two Talmuds and the Tosefta, the *Sifra* and the *Sifrei,* in all these are explained the permitted and the forbidden, the clean and the unclean, the liabilities and lack of liability, the unfit and the fit, as handed down from person to person from the mouth of Moses our teacher at Sinai." But the verdict of modern scholarship is that the *halakhah* has had a history and that it is possible to trace the stages in its development with a considerable degree of success (see below). [L.J.]

DOGMATICS OF THE HALAKHAH

Sources of Authority. Like other legal systems, the *halakhah* is composed of different elements, not all of equal value, since some are regarded as of Sinaitic origin and others of rabbinical. Five sources can be differentiated:

THE WRITTEN LAW. According to the traditional concept of halakhic Judaism, the Written Law is not a collection of legal, religious, ethical statutes and the like deriving from separate sources, but a law uniform in nature and content and a revelation of the will of God—a revelation that was a single nonrecurring historical event (at Sinai). This law is considered to be a book of commandments, positive and negative, numbering 613 (see *Commandments, the 613).

STATEMENTS HANDED DOWN BY TRADITION (Kabbalah). On the verse "These are the commandments" (Lev. 27:34), the *Sifra* (*Be-Ḥukkotai,* 13:7) comments, "Henceforth no prophet may make innovations." Thus such commandments or injunctions the source of which is in the words of the prophets or the Hagiographa (referred to as Kabbalah) are generally regarded as of Sinaitic force, on the assumption that the prophets received them as an interpretation or as a *halakhah* given to Moses at Sinai. Thus, e.g., it is inferred from Jeremiah 32:44: "and subscribe the deeds, and seal them, and call witnesses," that the signature by witnesses to a document is a Sinaitic law (Git. 36a). At times, however, the *amoraim* conclude that the verse is to be regarded as a mere support (**asmakhta),* and the matter does not come within the definition of Torah law. An ambivalent attitude on their part toward traditional statements can be discerned; there is even in the Babylonian Talmud a rule: inferences concerning statements of the Torah may not be drawn from statements contained in Kabbalah (Ḥag. 10b; BK 2b; Nid. 23a).

From the dogmatic point of view, however, the statement of Naḥmanides (on principle 2 of Maimonides' *Sefer ha-Mitzvot*) and his differentiation seem correct; namely that wherever in the prophets and Hagiographa statements are made as commands and injunctions, they are merely an explanation of the Torah and have the same authority as the Oral Law, as tradition, while where statements are made by way of narrative, as "relating some event" (e.g., the case of sale in the Book of Nehemiah) they are of rabbinic status. The same applies to those laws designated in the Talmud as **takkanot* ("regulations") of the prophets, even if attributed to Moses himself. For the concept *de-rabbanan* ("of rabbinical authority") is not chronological but qualitative, so that such statements can be *de-orayta* (of Sinaitic authority) even if first revealed in the words of a late prophet, and *de-rabbanan* even if attributed to Moses, if they were transmitted as a *takkanah* or the confirmation of an ancient custom (e.g., the seven days of bridal festivity, the seven days of mourning).

THE *ORAL LAW. This includes: the interpretation of the Written Law transmitted, according to the sages, in its entirety with its details and minutiae at Sinai; *halakhah,* e.g., given to Moses at Sinai in the restricted sense; and logical deduction.

Interpretation of the Written Law. This interpretation consists of two elements: that regarded as certainly handed down at Sinai; that intrinsically inherent in the written word, but made manifest through the interpretation of Scripture by means of the accepted hermeneutical rules (see *hermeneutics). According to talmudic tradition anything transmitted directly by tradition counts as *de-orayta* and is in every way equivalent to the Written Law, while difference of opinion is found with regard to *halakhah* inferred only by means of interpretation since the Talmud itself has no systematic dogma on the subject.

Maimonides and Naḥmanides differ on this. According to the former (*Sefer ha-Mitzvot,* principle 2), anything inferred by interpretation is *de-orayta* only if supported by a tradition. If the Talmud does not clearly testify to its having been transmitted, then it is "the words of the *soferim*" or *de-rabbanan.*

On the other hand Naḥmanides holds (gloss, ad loc.) that anything derived by interpretation is also *de-orayta* whether or not supported by a talmudic tradition, unless the Talmud states explicitly that this is *de-rabbanan* (in the language of the Babylonian Talmud: "It is *de-rabbanan,* the verse being a mere support"). Both from the statements of Maimonides, as well as from those of Naḥmanides, it follows that *halakhot* inferred by interpretation of Scripture may be divided into three categories: *halakhah* received from Sinai where the purpose of the interpretation is to explain it and to connect it with the scriptural verse; in these cases there is no dispute as to the content of the *halakhah* since the interpretation at times merely serves a mnemotechnical purpose; *halakhah* not received from Sinai, but deduced by the sages from the scriptural verse, where the interpretation is in most cases to the point and included in the meaning of the verse; *halakhah* which all agree to be an innovation and *de-rabbanan,* the purpose of the interpretation being to find a support for it in Scripture (e.g., the rabbinic injunction against marrying relatives of the second degree, derived from Lev. 18:30: "Therefore shall ye keep My charge" (Yev. 21a)).

Halakhah Given to Moses at Sinai. This designation is given to ancient *halakhot* for which there is no scriptural support (or at the most very faint support). Examples are quantities (in connection with **issur ve-hetter* and things ritually unclean and clean, such as an olive's bulk, a quarter of a log, etc., Er. 4a), or that **tefillin* must be square (Meg. 24b) and written on parchment (Shab. 79b). It is difficult to decide whether in the early tannaitic period they actually regarded such *halakhot* as having been given at Sinai or whether the term "at Sinai" is employed merely to indicate their antiquity in order to increase their holiness and thus to immunize them against challenge (see the commentaries of Samson of Sens and Asher b. Jehiel to Yad. 4:3; Jair Ḥayyim Bacharach, in his *Ḥavvot Ya'ir* (no. 192) enumerates about 70 such *halakhot*). See also **Halakhah le-Moshe mi-Sinai.*

Logical Deduction. Sometimes the authors of the Talmud say of a certain *halakhah,* "it is self-evident," and as such it does not require scriptural proof since it is regarded as axiomatic; such as "whoever wishes to claim anything in the possession of his fellow must bring proof." To this category belong, strictly speaking, also fundamental concepts such as **ḥazakah,* the *majority rule, etc., since the scriptural verse addressed is only intended to provide a support for the *halakhah.* It is not the verse which is the source but logical reasoning and analogy.

SAYINGS OF THE SCRIBES (elders). In talmudic literature, the expression *mi-divrei soferim* (of scribal origin) has two meanings: a statement in principle from the Torah but its explanation is of scribal origin (see above, and e.g., Sanh.

88b); a statement decreed or enacted originally by the *soferim,* like "the second degrees of forbidden marriages are of scribal origin" (Yev. 2:4). What follows applies to the second meaning. Everything whose source is in statements of the scholars throughout the generations, from Moses to the present time, is called *de-rabbanan.* These teachings include: positive enactments *(takkanot)* made to protect the principles of religion and Torah, and negative enactments *(gezerot)* decreed to prevent breaches. From the verse: "According to the law which they shall teach thee ... thou shalt not turn aside from the sentence which they shall declare unto thee, to the right hand, nor to the left" (Deut. 17:11) it was inferred that it is a positive precept to obey the great *bet din* not only in everything applying to the text of the Torah, but also in everything that they found necessary to enact, and a warning is issued to anyone disregarding it.

The Authority of the Sages. In the Talmud the authority of the sages was defined as follows:

The sages have the power to abolish a biblical injunction (Yev. 89b–90b) in certain circumstances, such as: in monetary matters, on the basis of the rule that "deprivation of ownership by the *bet din* is valid": where it is a case of the passive act of "refraining from an action" *(shev ve-al ta'aseh),* as where they forbade the **lulav* and **shofar* to be handled and used on the Sabbath, lest they be carried in a public domain (thus the rabbinic prohibition is the cause of the biblical precept being ignored!).

The *bet din* has the power to temporarily disregard a biblical precept in order to reinforce observance. Similarly the court "may inflict flagellation and other punishment not in accordance with Torah law, in order to erect a protective fence round the Torah," but such acts may not be defined as *halakhah*—which would imply that the ruling is of a permanent character. So too, if they saw a temporary need to suspend a positive precept, or to transgress an injunction, in order to bring many back to religion, or to save the community from being ensnared in a transgression, all in accordance with the need of the time but not for future generations (Maim. Yad, Sanhedrin 24:4; Mamrim 2:4). The classical example is Elijah offering sacrifice on Mt. Carmel at the time the Temple existed (when sacrifice outside it was prohibited, Zev. 4b).

No restriction may be imposed upon the congregation if the majority cannot abide by it (BB 60b). So too no restriction may be imposed that would cause substantial loss (see, e.g., MK 2a) or excessive trouble. "It is preferable for them to transgress inadvertently rather than deliberately" (Beẓah 30a).

No court can abolish the decision of another contemporary court unless it be greater in wisdom and in number. The possibility of abolishing a restriction thus depends upon an important limitation: "It must be greater in wisdom and number" (Eduy. 1:5; for the meaning of this rule, which apparently prevents all possiblity of abolishing a *bet din* ruling, see Weiss, Dor, pt. 2, sec. 7 and Albeck in the supplements to Mishnah *Nezikin*).

At times the sages gave their pronouncements the same, and at times, even greater validity than those of the Torah. As an example "These days, enumerated in Megillat Ta'anit, are forbidden [for fasting], along with both the preceding and the following day. As to Sabbaths and New Moons, fasting on them is forbidden, but it is permitted on the preceding and following days. What is the difference between them? The latter are of biblical origin and words of the Torah require no reinforcement, whereas the former are of scribal authority and the words of the scribes require reinforcement" (RH 19a). Thus they were more stringent about the fulfillment of their *takkanot* than about the enactment of the Torah itself, because for the latter no danger of negligence was anticipated, as it was with their regulations. Many of the edicts and *takkanot* are anonymous, just as the early *halakhah* in general is anonymous: according to dogmatic conception they were all enacted and accepted by a vote of the great *bet din* in which, too, all disputed matters were decided. The modern historical approach, too, is close to this view, even though the concept "the great *bet din*" was not identical in all periods (see Ḥ. Albeck, in: *Zion,* 8 (1942/43), 85–93, 165–78; L. Finkelstein, *The Pharisees,* 1962[3]). Notwithstanding, many *takkanot* and edicts are mentioned that are connected with the names of definite persons or places, such as Joshua b. Gamla, Simeon b. Shetaḥ, Bet Shammai and Bet Hillel, Gamaliel the Elder, Johanan b. Zakkai, Gamaliel of Jabneh, the scholars of Usha, Judah ha-Nasi, etc. There are also many *halakhot* that are attributed to biblical personalities such as Moses, Joshua, Samuel, David, Solomon, Hezekiah, Daniel, the prophets (and the men of the Great *Synagogue). The individuals enumerated appear as heads of *batei din.*

The distinction between the concepts *de-orayta* and *de-rabbanan* in the whole field of *halakhah* actually derives from the *amoraim,* but it already existed in the time of the *tannaim* and is recognizable by the penalties fixed for transgressions of the different categories, and there is also found the explicit expression "statements of the scribes" in contrast to "statements of the Torah" (e.g., Yev. 2:4; Par. 11:5–6; Yad. 3:2; Zev. 99b). But the views of the *tannaim* and *amoraim* on this matter do not completely coincide, and at times a matter which according to tannaitic sources appears to be *de-orayta* becomes in the era of the *amoraim de-rabbanan.* The difference between the two concepts *de-orayta* and *de-rabbanan* not only expresses itself in penalties (thus, e.g., the sacrifices which one who transgresses the words of the Torah must bring as an atonement for his iniquity are not imposed as an obligation on one transgressing a prohibition of the sages, but on the other hand the sages have the right to flog one transgressing their words with "stripes of correction" in order to punish and reform him); there is also a difference in the halakhic consideration: "In the case of doubt with regard to a biblical injunction the stringent view is accepted, in the case of rabbinical, the lenient" (Beẓah 3b; TJ, Er. 3:4).

CUSTOM. The word custom (Heb. *minhag*) has various meanings in talmudic literature, and not all have the same force, even though all serve as sources of *halakhah.*

Religious custom which can be relied upon where the *halakhah* is unclear: "Every *halakhah* that is unclear in the *bet din* and you do not know its nature, go and see how the community conducts itself and conduct yourself accordingly" (TJ, Pe'ah 7:5). Here the concept of custom is close to the concept of "consensus" in Muslim law in its original stage: the people as a whole do not err, and therefore custom decides the matter; its nature is as the nature of the *halakhah.* In the Babylonian Talmud this idea is expressed in the words, "Go and see how the public are accustomed to act" (Ber. 45a) and this too is what Hillel certainly meant when he said: "Leave it to Israel; if they are not prophets, they are the children of prophets" (Pes. 66a).

Religious custom that is not publicly proclaimed as the official *halakhah* (see Ta'an 26b); here too, as in the previous section, the reference is not to a new custom but to fixing the norm in a *halakhah* concerning which there is a dispute, in accordance with the existing custom.

A custom that is in contradiction to the theoretical *halakhah* but by virtue of being a public custom, and that of conscientious people, has the power to cancel the *halakhah* (TJ, Yev, 12:1; Sof. 14, ed. Higger, 270f.). In these cases, the custom replaces the *halakhah.*

A custom introduced by a definite group—such as the citizens of a town, a group of pious men, women, professional groups, etc.—in some area of religious, social, or legal life, additional to the existing *halakhah*, serves as a source of *halakhah* which may not be altered and has the same authority as the words of the sages (see, e.g., Pes. 4:1; BM 7:1; et al.). [B.D.-V.]

See also *Minhag.

DEVELOPMENT OF HALAKHAH

The Early Period. Codes of law are found in the Pentateuch (Ex. 21–23:19; Lev. 19; Deut. 21–25) together with smaller collections and numerous individual laws. Biblical criticism explains the differences in style and the contradictions between one collection and another on the grounds that these groups of laws were produced in different circles at diverse times, e.g., in one collection the tithe is given to the levite (Num. 18:20–32) whereas in Deuteronomy it is retained by the farmer himself to be eaten in the place of the central sanctuary (Deut. 14:22–26). This kind of solution was not open to the Pharisaic teachers so that the early *halakhah* reconciles the two passages by postulating two tithes, the first *(ma'aser rishon)* to be given to the Levite and the second *(ma'aser sheni)* to be eaten in the place of the central sanctuary. Moreover, according to the traditional view, God conveyed to Moses together with the Written Law *(torah she-bi-khetav)* an Oral Law *(torah she be-al peh)*. This latter embraced both the specific "laws given to Moses at Sinai" and the many interpretations of the written text now found in the rabbinic literature.

One of the main points at issue between the Sadducees and the Pharisees was the validity of this doctrine of the Oral Law, the Pharisees affirming and the Sadducees denying it. But this is to oversimplify the problem. It is obvious that some process of interpretation of the written texts must have begun at the earliest period since many of the texts are unintelligible as they stand (though this is very different from the affirmation that the interpretation was uniform and handed down unimpaired from generation to generation). Buying and selling, for example, are mentioned in the Pentateuch without any indication of how the transfer of property was to be effected. The law of divorce (Deut. 24:1–4) speaks of a "bill of divorcement," but gives no information on how this is to be written. Ezekiel 44:31 would seem to be an interpretation of the laws found in Exodus 22:30 and Deuteronomy 14:21 (Weiss, Dor, 1 (1904[4]), 44–45). Jeremiah 17:21 is an interpretation of what is involved in Sabbath "work." It would appear certain that by about 400 B.C.E., after the return from Babylon and the establishment of the Second Temple, the Pentateuch had become the Torah (the Written Law) and there had begun to develop an oral interpretation of the Pentateuchal texts.

The identity of the men of the Great Synagogue, who are said to have flourished immediately after the return, is still a major problem, as is the relationship of this body to the "Scribes" (*soferim*; according to Frankel, *Darkhei ha-Mishnah* (1923), 3–7 et al.), the men of the Great Synagogue were the executive of a movement of Pentateuchal interpretation of which the "Scribes" formed the general body. However, more recent studies have demonstrated that the *soferim* were simply a class of biblical exegetes inferior in status to the "sages" so that it is illegitimate to speak of the period of the "Scribes" (Kaufmann, Y., Toledot, 4 (1960), 481–5; E. Urbach, in: *Tarbiz*, 27 (1957/58), 166–82). The Midrash process, in which the texts were carefully examined for their wider meaning and application, no doubt had its origin in this period. Another vexed question is whether the Midrash of a particular text is the real source of the law said to be derived from it or whether the law came first with the Midrash no more than a peg on which to hang it. The most convincing way of coping with the evidence on this matter is to suggest that the earliest Midrashim were in the nature of a real derivative process by means of which the deeper meaning and wider application of the texts were uncovered (although this must not be taken to exclude the existence of actual traditions for which texts were subsequently found). In the later Midrash the process is reversed.

The whole period down to the age of the Maccabees—on any showing the formative period in the history of the *halakhah*—is shrouded in obscurity. Y. Baer (in *Zion*, 17 (1951/52), 1–55) has argued that there was little pure academic legal activity at this period and that many of the laws originating at this time were produced by a kind of rule of thumb in which pious farmers in a comparatively simple form of society worked out basic rules of neighborly conduct, much in the same way as this was done among the Greeks in the age of Solon. Some of these rules can possibly still be detected among the earliest strata of the Mishnah, e.g., in the first chapter of *Bava Kamma*, which includes a formulation of the law of torts worded in the first person.

There are references in the sources to five pairs of teachers—the *zugot* ("pairs," *duumviri*)—beginning with Yose b. Joezer and Yose b. Johanan in the time of the Maccabees and ending with Hillel and Shammai in the time of Herod. The ethical maxims of these teachers are recorded in the Mishnah (Avot 1:4–5) but little legal material has been transmitted in their name. At this time, it was said, there was no legal debate in Israel (Tosef., Ḥag. 2:9), i.e., the law was known or where in doubt was decided by the "great court" in Jerusalem.

Historically considered there is no question, however, of a uniform *halakhah*, even at this early period, handed down from generation to generation in the form the *halakhah* assumes in the tannaitic period. Apart from the great debates on legal matters between the Sadducees and the Pharisees, the *halakhah* in the books of the Apocrypha (and the writings of the Qumran sect) is not infrequently at variance with the *halakhah* as recorded in the Mishnah and the other tannaitic sources (e.g., the law of false witnesses in Susannah conflicts with the Pharisaic law as recorded in the Mishnah, Mak. 1:4). Even in the Pharisaic party itself the schools of Hillel and Shammai at the beginning of the present era differed on hundreds of laws, so that it was said that there was a danger of the Torah becoming two *torot* (Sanh. 88b).

A major problem here is the motivation behind the approaches of the two rival schools. The theory associated with L. Ginzberg (*On Jewish Law and Lore* (1955), 102–18) and L. Finkelstein (op. cit.) finds the differences in the different social strata to which the schools belonged. The school of Shammai, it is argued, was legislating for the upper classes, the wealthy landowners and aristocrats, while the school of Hillel was legislating for the poorer urban workers and artisans. Thus according to the school of Hillel the legal definition of a "meal" is one dish, whereas according to the school of Shammai it is at least two dishes (Beẓah 2:1). In most societies the woman has a much more significant role among the upper classes than among the lower. Hence the school of Hillel rules that a valid marriage can be effected by the delivery to the woman of the smallest coin—a *perutah*—whereas the school of Shammai demands the much larger minimum amount of a *dinar* (Kid. 1:1). The school of Shammai only permits the divorce of a wife if she is unfaithful whereas the school of Hillel permits it on other grounds (Git. 9:10). While there is undoubtedly some truth in the theory of social motivation it is too sweeping to be entirely adequate. Other motives, such as different exegetical methods were also at work (see Alon, *Meḥkarim*, 2 (1958), 181–222).

The Tannaitic Period (c. 1–220 C.E.). The debates between the schools of Hillel and Shammai set in motion new debating processes among the rabbinic teachers of first- and second-century Palestine, the *tannaim*. Prominent in the second century were the rival schools of R. Akiva and R. Ishmael, who differed in their concept of the Torah revelation and, as a result, in their attitude toward the scope of the *halakhah* (see A. J. Heschel, *Torah min ha-Shamayim* (first 2 vols., 1962, 1965). According to R. Ishmael's school "the Torah speaks in the language of men" (Sif. Num. 15:31) and it is therefore not permissible to derive new laws from such linguistic usages as the infinitive absolute before the verb. According to the school of R. Akiva it is legitimate to do this and to derive laws from the use of the particles *gam* ("also") and *et* (the sign of the accusative), for example in Pesaḥim 22b, since in the view of this school no word or letter of the Torah can be considered superfluous or merely for the purpose of literary effect. A later teacher characterized the methods of the Akiva school by telling of Moses on high asking God why He had affixed the decorative "crowns" to some of the letters of the Torah. God replies that after many generations there will arise a man, Akiva b. Joseph by name, "who will expound upon each tittle heaps and heaps of laws." Moses then asks permission to see Akiva and is transported across time to enter Akiva's academy where he is unable to follow the arguments! Moses is distressed but is later comforted when Akiva replies to the question of his disciples: "Whence do you know this?" by stating: "It is a law given to Moses at Sinai" (Men. 29b).

At the end of the second century R. Judah ha-Nasi edited the Mishnah, in which were summarized all the legal debates and decisions of the *tannaim*. Judah ha-Nasi is better spoken of as the editor of the Mishnah, not its author, since it is clear that his compilation is based on earlier formulations, particularly those of R. Akiva and his disciple R. Meir. Indeed it is possible to detect various early strata embedded in the final form the Mishnah has assumed. For instance, the Mishnah (Pes. 1:1) records a rule that a wine cellar requires to be searched for leaven on the eve of Passover and then records a debate between the schools of Hillel and Shammai on how this rule is to be defined.

The Amoraic Period (c. 220–470 C.E.). Once the Mishnah had been compiled it became a sacred text second only to the Bible. The word of the post-mishnaic teachers in both Palestine and Babylon (the *amoraim*) was confined chiefly to discussion and comment on the Mishnah and to the application of its laws (and those found in the other tannaitic sources). It became axiomatic that no *amora* had the right to disagree with a *tanna* in matters of law unless he was able to adduce tannaitic support for his view. It must not be thought, however, that the *amoraim* were only concerned with practical application of the *halakhah*. A good deal of their work was in the field of abstract legal theory in which purely academic questions were examined and debated (see M. Guttmann, in *Devir*, 1 (1923), 38–87; 2 (1923), 101–64).

The *halakhah* of the Palestinian *amoraim* was eventually collected in the Jerusalem Talmud, that of the Babylonian *amoraim* in the Babylonian Talmud. With the "closing" of the Talmud this work virtually became the infallible source of the *halakhah*. Occasionally in the Middle Ages, as Weiss (Dor, 3 (1904[4]) 216–30) has demonstrated, authorities would disagree with talmudic rulings. Maimonides, for example, disregards in his code any laws based on a belief in the efficacy of magic even though the laws are found in the Talmud and are not disputed there. Some of the *geonim* tended to adopt a more lenient attitude toward the talmudic laws governing the relations between Jews and gentiles on the grounds that the gentiles in their milieu (the Muslims) were not idolaters. But such exceptions were few. The history of post-talmudic *halakhah* is founded on the appeal to the Talmud as the final and overriding authority. "To it [the Talmud] one must not add and from it one must not subtract" (Maim., Comm. to Mishnah, intro.). Of the two Talmuds the Babylonian became the more authoritative for a number of reasons. The *halakhah* of the Babylonian Talmud is more highly developed and more comprehensive; the Babylonian Talmud is later than the Jerusalem and hence able to override the decisions of the latter; the textual condition of the Babylonian Talmud is in a more satisfactory state; the Babylonian *geonim* at Sura and Pumbedita were in direct succession to the Babylonian *amoraim* (so that the Babylonian Talmud became "our Talmud") and the hegemony of the teachings of Babylonia was considerably strengthened as a result of political developments, including the emergence of Baghdad as the seat of the caliphate. Maimonides (Yad, intro.) states the accepted view: "All Israel is obliged to follow the matters stated in the Babylonian Talmud. Every city and every province are to be coerced to follow all the customs which the sages of the Talmud followed and to obey their decisions and follow their enactments since all the matters in the Talmud have been accepted by all Israel. And those sages who made the enactments or introduced the decrees or ordained the customs or decided the laws, teaching that the decision was so, were all the sages of Israel or the majority of them. And they heard by tradition the main principles of the whole Torah generation after generation reaching back to the generation of Moses our teacher on whom be peace."

Rules for determining the actual decision in law from the labyrinth of legal debate and discussion that is the Talmud are provided by the Talmud itself and by the savoraic additions to the Talmud, and other rules were widely accepted by the post-talmudic authorities. The following, in addition to those mentioned above, are some of the more important of these rules which enabled the Talmud to serve as the final authority in *halakhah* even though it is not itself a code of law.

Where there is a debate between an individual sage and his colleagues the view of the majority is adopted (Ber. 9a). The school of Hillel is always followed against the school of Shammai (Er. 6b). In the many matters debated by Rav and Samuel the view of Rav is followed in religious matters and that of Samuel in civil law (Bek. 49b). Except in three specified cases the opinion of R. Johanan is followed against that of R. Simeon b. Lakish (Yev. 36a). Similarly, except in three specified cases the opinion of Rabbah is followed against that of R. Joseph (BB 114b). The decision of Rava is followed against that of Abbaye except in six specified cases (Kid. 52a). Wherever a talmudic debate concludes with the statement "the law is . . ." *(ve-hilkheta)* this ruling is adopted. The lenient opinion is adopted when there is a debate regarding the laws of mourning for near relatives (MK 26b). The rulings of later authorities are generally preferred to those of earlier ones (from Rava onward) on the grounds that the later scholars, though aware of the opinions of the others, still saw fit to disagree with them (*Sefer Keritut*, 4:3, 6). It is generally accepted that where a ruling is conveyed in a talmudic passage anonymously *(setama)* this implies unanimity among the final editors and is to be followed even if elsewhere in the Talmud the matter is a subject of debate (see Tos. to Ber. 20b and Yev. 116a). Halakhic decisions are not generally to be derived from aggadic statements (based on TJ, Pe'ah 2:4; see ET, 1 (1951[3]), 62). This rule was not applied consistently and was occasionally departed from, particularly in the French and German schools in the Middle Ages for whom the entire talmudic material, including the *aggadah*, tended to be invested with infallible authority.

In spite of the "closing" of the Talmud (occasioned chiefly by the disturbed conditions at the end of the fifth century when the great Babylonian schools were closed for a fairly long period) and its acceptance as the final authority, new legislation could still be introduced under the heading of *takkanah* ("enactment"), of which there are many examples in the Talmud itself. By means of the *takkanah* it was possible to cope with new circumstances not covered by the talmudic law. From time to time the principle, found in the Talmud, was resorted to that "a court can inflict penalties even when these run counter to the Torah" if the times require it (Yev. 90b; see above). In Spain, for example, in the Middle Ages, the courts assumed the power to inflict capital and corporal punishment even though this right had long been taken from them according to the strict letter of the law (see Baron, Community, 1 (1942), 168–9 and notes).

Codification of the Halakhah. Teachers of the *halakhah* in the Middle Ages and afterwards were of two main types. Firstly there were the legal theoreticians such as Rashi and the tosefists, whose main activity consisted of exposition of the classical legal texts of the Talmud and other early rabbinic works. These were known as the *mefareshim* ("commentators") and their writings were naturally utilized to determine the practical law even though this was not their own province. Secondly there were the *posekim* ("decision-makers") whose opinions in practical legal matters were accepted because of their acknowledged expertise in this field. The activity of the *posekim* was of two kinds: responsa and codification. Questions of law on which direct guidance from the Talmud was not forthcoming were addressed to the great legal luminaries and from time to time these responsa were collected, helping to form the basis for new codifications of the *halakhah*. Both the new and older laws were frequently classified and codified. The process of responsa and subsequent *codification has continued down to the present.

One of the earliest codes was the **Halakhot Gedolot* of Simeon Kayyara (ninth century). Isaac *Alfasi compiled an abbreviated, and with regard to some texts an expanded, version of the Babylonian Talmud in which only the conclusions of the talmudic discussions were recorded so as to provide a digest of talmudic *halakhah* in its practical application. Where the Babylonian Talmud has no rulings Alfasi followed decisions found in the Jerusalem Talmud. *Maimonides compiled his gigantic code, the *Mishneh Torah* (called, after his death, the *Yad ha-Ḥazakah*), in which he presented the final decisions in all matters of *halakhah*, including those laws which no longer obtained in his day, such as the laws of the sacrificial cult. *Asher b. Jehiel, known as the Rosh (Rabbenu Asher), compiled a code in which due weight was given to the opinions of the French and German authorities which frequently differed from those of the Spanish authorities as recorded by Maimonides. Asher's son, *Jacob b. Asher, followed in his father's footsteps in his code known as the *Tur* ("row," pl. *Turim*, properly the "Four Rows," so called because the work is divided into four parts).

By the time of Joseph *Caro there was much confusion in the whole realm of practical *halakhah*. In addition to the many differences between the codes, Jewish communities tended to differ in their application of the laws so that, as Caro remarks (*Beit Yosef*, intro.), the Torah had become not two *torot* but many *torot*. In his great commentary to the *Tur*, called *Beit Yosef*, Caro sought to remedy the situation by working out a practical guide for a uniform application of the *halakhah*. His method was to follow a majority opinion whenever the three earlier codes of Alfasi, Maimonides, and the *Tur* disagreed and to rely on other authorities whenever this method of deciding was not possible. Caro's *Shulḥan Arukh contains the gist of his decisions as worked out in the *Beit Yosef*. Unfortunately, however, Caro's method weighted the scales in favor of the Spanish schools, since these were generally in accord with the views of Alfasi and Maimonides, against the German views as represented by Asher b. Jehiel and the *Tur*. The Shulḥan Arukh was thus incapable of serving as a practical guide to the German Jews and their followers in Poland, which from the 16th century became a foremost center of Jewish life. The remedy was provided by Moses *Isserles of Cracow who added notes to the Shulḥan Arukh, known as the *Mappah*, in which the German-Polish practices were recorded where these differed from the opinions of the Shulḥan Arukh. The Shulḥan Arukh, together with the *Mappah*, became the most authoritative code in the history of the *halakhah*, partly, at least, because it was the first code to be compiled after the invention of printing and so sure of the widest dissemination.

The Shulḥan Arukh marked a turning point in the history of the *halakhah*. Even when later authorities departed from its rulings they did so reluctantly. Adherence to the Shulḥan Arukh became the test of Jewish fidelity. The "Shulḥan Arukh Jew" became the supreme type of Jewish piety. Earlier rabbinical authorities were known as **rishonim* while later ones were known as **aḥaronim*. Rabbinic authority even in modern times is much more reluctant to disagree with the *rishonim* than the *aḥaronim*.

THE AUTHORITY OF THE HALAKHAH

Halakhah is the distinctive feature of Judaism as a religion of obedience to the word of God. It united Jews of many different temperaments, origins, and theological opinions, though the view ("pan-halakhism" as A. J. Heschel called it) that submission to the *halakhah* is all that is demanded of the Jew is a travesty of traditional Judaism. The major practical differences between Orthodox and Reform Judaism depend on the different attitudes of these groups to the *halakhah*. Orthodoxy considers the *halakhah*, in its traditional form, to be absolutely binding, whereas Reform, while prepared to be guided by the legal decisions of the past in some areas, rejects the absolute binding force of the traditional *halakhah*. Conservative Judaism adopts a midway position, treating the traditional *halakhah* as binding but feeling freer to interpret it and attempting to preserve the dynamic principle of legal development which, it claims, is typical of the talmudic period. The Orthodox rabbi, when faced with new halakhic problems raised, for instance, by the invention of printing and the use of electricity, will try to arrive at a decision by applying directly the ancient halakhic principles in the new circumstances. The Reform rabbi will be more inclined to consider the religious demands of the new age and will tend to operate within non-halakhic categories. The Conservative rabbi will try to utilize these latter in working out a fresh interpretation of the traditional *halakhah*. [L.J.]

Bibliography: Weiss, Dor; Frankel, Mishnah; Halevy, Dorot; G. F. Moore, *Judaism in the First Centuries of the Christian Era*, 3 vols. (1927–30); J. Kaplan, *The Redaction of the Talmud* (1933); Ḥ. Tchernowitz, *Toledot ha-Halakhah*, 4 vols. (1934–50); idem, *Toledot ha-Posekim*, 3 vols. (1946–47); J. Z. Lauterbach, *Midrash and Mishnah*, in his *Rabbinic Essays* (1951), 163–256; B. Cohen, *Law and Ethics in the Light of Jewish Tradition* (1957); idem, *Law and Tradition in Judaism* (1959); ET, 9 (1959), 241–339; M. Kadushin, *The Rabbinic Mind* (1965²), includes bibliography; Z. H. Chajes, *The Student's Guide Through the Talmud* (1960²).

HALAKHAH LE-MOSHE MI-SINAI (Heb. הֲלָכָה לְמֹשֶׁה מִסִּינַי; "a law given to Moses at Sinai"). As part of the *Oral Law, a number of laws, possessing biblical authority but neither stated in Scripture nor derived by hermeneutical principles, are stated in rabbinic literature to be "laws given to Moses at Sinai." The term occurs only three times in the Mishnah (Pe'ah 2:6; Eduy. 8:7; Yad. 4:3) but is found frequently together with terms of similar import, in the other sources of rabbinic Judaism, particularly in the Talmud (such as—"there is a received *halakhah*"; "there is a received tradition"; or simply "received"). Similarly, according to the Jerusalem Talmud (Shab. 1:4, 3b) the expression "in truth they said" also belongs to this category (however, see BM 60a and Rashi s.v. *be-emet*).

Among the laws said to have been given to Moses at Sinai are: the 18 defects which render an animal **terefah* (Ḥul. 42a); the duty of walking round the altar with willows and the feast of water drawing, both on the festival of Tabernacles (Suk. 34a); the underside and duct of the *tefillin*, the parchment of the *tefillin*, that the straps of the *tefillin* be black and the *tefillin* themselves square (Men. 35a), and that they should have a knot (Er. 97a); the minimum quantities of forbidden foods to constitute an offense and the rules regarding interpositions on the body which invalidate a ritual immersion (Er. 4a); that only half the damage is to be paid when damage is done by pebbles flying from under an animal's feet (BK 3b); and that doubtful cases of levitical defilement, if occurring in the public domain, are to be treated as pure (Ḥul. 9b). It will be seen that all these refer to long-established rules which could not have been known without a tradition to that effect. The medieval commentators point out that on occasion the term, *halakhah le-Moshe mi-Sinai,* is used of much later enactments and is not always to be taken literally, but refers to a *halakhah* which is so certain and beyond doubt that it is as though it were a *halakhah* given to Moses at Sinai (Asher ben Jehiel *Hilkhot Mikva'ot,* 1 (at the end of his *Piskei ha-Rosh* to *Niddah*) and his *Commentary to Mishnah,* Yad. 4:3). In most cases, however, they explain it literally, i.e., that these *halakhot* were transmitted by God to Moses at Sinai. Modern scholarship is skeptical on the whole question, but it is clear that the rabbis themselves did believe in the existence of laws transmitted verbally to Moses.

See also *Halakhah.

Bibliography: Weiss, Dor, 1 (1904[4]), index; W. Bacher, in: *Studies in Jewish Literature ... K. Kohler* (1913), 56–70 (Ger.); Ḥ. Tchernowitz, *Toledot ha-Halakhah,* 1 (1934), 29–36; L. Strack, *Introduction to the Talmud* (1945), 9; J. Levinger, *Darkhei ha-Maḥashavah ha-Hilkhatit shel ha-Rambam* (1965), 50–65.

[L.J.]

HALAKHOT GEDOLOT (Heb. הֲלָכוֹת גְּדוֹלוֹת), halakhic code belonging to the geonic period.

Nature of the Code. The *Halakhot Gedolot* gives a systematic and comprehensive summary of all the talmudic laws. Although in general it follows the order of the tractates of the Talmud, it groups together the various *halakhot* scattered in the Talmud according to their logical order, and, contrary to the procedure adopted in the Mishnah and *Gemara,* first states the general principle before giving the details. It also assigns new names to certain groups of *halakhot,* and embodies laws (such as those dealing with sacrifices and some of those applicable to the priests) which were no longer observed after the destruction of the Temple. The decisions are founded on those of the Talmud and on the halakhic principles laid down by its sages. The work is based on the Babylonian Talmud but the author also makes use to some extent of the Jerusalem Talmud, which he refers to as "the Talmud of the West." Other sources are the responsa of Babylonian *geonim* and the halakhic work of the same period *Sefer ha-Ma'asim shel Benei Ereẓ Yisrael. Halakhot Gedolot* spread throughout Jewry, and in the course of time decisions of *Yehudai Gaon and those of a later date were incorporated into it. The earlier authorities often quote excerpts from it which are different, or entirely absent, from the extant work.

The *Halakhot Gedolot* has an introduction—it is the first rabbinic work to have one—and it is generally held that it was directed against the *Karaites and others who rejected the Oral Law. It is in two parts, the one comprising aggadic statements in praise of the Torah and its students; the other enumerating, for the first time, the 613 *commandments mentioned in the Talmud (Mak. 23b). They are classified according to the degree of punishment incurred in transgressing them and according to their common character. This list of 365 negative and 248 positive commandments, which provided the basis for similar elaborations in various **azharot,* was severely criticized by Maimonides in his *Sefer ha-Mitzvot,* and defended by Naḥmanides.

Recensions of the Work. The work is extant in two recensions. The one *(Halakhot Gedolot 1),* published in Venice in 1548, is the Babylonian recension, which is the earlier and which preserves the original version. It was this recension that was used by the French and German scholars. The other *(Halakhot Gedolot 2)* was published by A. Hildesheimer on the basis of the Vatican manuscript

Title page of the Babylonian recension of *Halakhot Gedolot,* a code of all the talmudic laws, published in Venice, 1548. Jerusalem, J.N.U.L.

(1892) and is, in the opinion of scholars, identical with *Halakhot Gedolot shel Ispamya* ("Spain"; Tos. to Yev. 48a, see below), the version used by the scholars of Spain, southern France, and Italy. Various excerpts from this Spanish recension are not found in *Halakhot Gedolot 1*, having been omitted by copyists. Moreover, the former contains later additions, commentaries, and supercommentaries, and also the names of *geonim* who lived after Simeon Kayyara (see below), the last *gaon* to be mentioned in it being Ẓemaḥ b. Paltoi (890 C.E.). This recension, which may have been compiled in North Africa (Kairouan), was called by the northern French scholars *Halakhot Gedolot shel Ispamya,* having reached them from Spain by way of southern France. There may also have been other recensions of the work, for a southern French author mentions "our *halakhot* of Simeon Kayyara that came from Ereẓ Israel" (*Ha-Ittur,* pt. 2 (1874), 22c), while various excerpts from *Halakhot Gedolot,* not contained in the other recensions, have been found in the Cairo *Genizah.*

Date and Authorship. The authorship and date of the *Halakhot Gedolot* have been the subject of many studies and given rise to conflicting views. The work has been variously ascribed to Sherira Gaon (A. E. Harkavy (ed.), *Teshuvot ha-Ge'onim,* no. 376; *Zikkaron la-Rishonim ve-gam la-Aḥaronim,* 1/4 (1887)), Hai Gaon (D. Cassel (ed.) *Teshuvot Ge'onim Kadmonim* (1848) no. 87, et al.), by the scholars of Spain and Provence to Simeon Kayyara and to Yehudai Gaon by those of northern France and Germany. In his *Sefer ha-Kabbalah,* Abraham ibn Daud states that Simeon Kayyara lived before Yehudai Gaon and that the latter was the author of **Halakhot Pesukot,* written in 741 C.E., which "he compiled from *Halakhot Gedolot*" (Ibn Daud, Tradition, 47f., see also 127, n.18–19). S. J. Rapoport, following Abraham ibn Daud, held that *Halakhot Gedolot* is composed of two parts: the original *Halakhot Gedolot* of Simeon Kayyara and *Halakhot Pesukot* of Yehudai Gaon, which the latter's pupils incorporated into the former work. According to Rapoport, Yehudai Gaon's statements in *Halakhot Gedolot* can be recognized in two ways: by the Aramaic in which various passages are written, and by the word *pesak* ("legal decision"), which is associated with several statements and which, according to him, derive from *Halakhot Pesukot.* This, however, has been controverted by S. D. Luzzatto (*Beit ha-Oẓar,* 1 (1847), 53a f.). Graetz maintained that the work was written by Simeon Kayyara who lived at the end of the ninth or the beginning of the tenth century, some 150 years after Yehudai Gaon had composed *Halakhot Pesukot.* I. Halevy held that the author of *Halakhot Gedolot* was a younger contemporary of the writer of *Halakhot Pesukot,* the latter work being a compilation of Yehudai Gaon's practical decisions, while the former, more theoretical work has its source in the Talmud. A. Epstein contended that *Halakhot Gedolot* was written in Sura by Simeon Kayyara about 825 and that its main sources were Aḥa of Shabḥa's *She'eltot* and Yehudai Gaon's *Halakhot Pesukot.* Seventy years later there was compiled the second recension of the work, the *Halakhot Gedolot shel Ispamya,* the first recension being ascribed by them to Yehudai Gaon.

Simeon Kayyara came from Bozrah in Babylonia, as is attested by Hai Gaon. The city of Bozrah is mentioned twice in *Halakhot Gedolot* (in *Hilkhot Ḥallah* and in *Hilkhot Eruvin*) and was under the spiritual authority of Sura. Indeed, many of the laws and customs mentioned in the work conform to those of Sura, and several of its legal decisions are cited in the name of *geonim* of Sura.

The work has been reprinted several times: Venice (1548), Lemberg (1804), Vienna (1811), Berlin (1888–92, ed. by A. Hildesheimer). The various editions include comments by Solomon Salem (Amsterdam, 1764), notes by S. A. Traub (1875), and the commentary *Sefat Emet* by A. Margalioth (1894).

Bibliography: Rapoport, in: *Kerem Ḥemed,* 6 (1841), 236ff.; Graetz, in: MGWJ, 7 (1858), 217, 228; Halberstamm, *ibid.,* 8 (1859), 379–86; 31 (1882), 472–5; Graetz-Rabbinowitz, 3 (1893), 261; Reifmann, in: *Ha-Maggid,* 5 (1862), 293f.; Gottheil, in: MGWJ, 36 (1887), 457–61; Weiss, Dor, 4 (1904[4]), 29–37; Schorr, in: *Jubelschrift . . . L. Zunz* (1884), 127–41 (Heb. pt.); A. Hildesheimer, in: *Jahresbericht des Rabbiner-Seminars zu Berlin 5646* (1885/86); idem (ed.), *Halakhot Gedolot al pi Ketav Yad Romi* (1892), introd.; Halevy, Dorot, 3 (1923), 200f.; A. Epstein, in: *Ha-Goren,* 3 (1902), 46–81f. (*Kitvei A. Epstein,* 2 (1957), 378–409); L. Ginzberg, *Ginzei Schechter,* 2 (1929), 48–101, 110f., 201f.; L. Ginzberg, *Geonica,* 1 (1909), 95–111; Epstein, in: MGWJ, 61 (1917), 127–32; idem, in: *Tarbiz,* 10 (1939), 119–34; 283–308; 13 (1942), 25–36; 16 (1945), 79–82; Marx, in: ZHB, 13 (1909), 70–73; H. Tchernowitz, in: *Ha-Tekufah,* 5 (1923), 240–79; idem, *Toledot ha-Posekim,* 1 (1946), 70–78; Frankl, in: JJLG, 14 (1921), 208–16; V. Aptowitzer, *Mavo le-Sefer Ravyah* (1938), 230–3; idem, *Meḥkarim be-Sifrut ha-Ge'onim* (1941), 28, 30f., 78, 82; Waxman, Literature, 1 (1938[2]), 284–6; S. Assaf, *Teshuvot ha-Ge'onim* (1942), 39, 44; idem, *Tekufat ha-Ge'onim ve-Sifrutah* (1955), 168–70; H. L. Strack, *Introduction to the Talmud and Midrash* (1945), 163f.; S. K. Mirsky (ed.), *She'iltot de-Rav Aḥai Ga'on,* 1 (1960), 12–16 (introd.).

[Y.Ho.]

HALAKHOT KEẒUVOT (Heb. הֲלָכוֹת קְצוּבוֹת), a collection of *halakhot* belonging to the geonic era, attributed to *Yehudai Gaon. *Halakhot Keẓuvot* contains *halakhot* pertaining to the mishnaic order *Mo'ed* and also laws of divorce, wine of gentiles, mourning, *tefillin, ẓiẓit, mezuzah, terefot,* and a special chapter entitled *Shimmush Bet Din* dealing with legislation coming within the jurisdiction of the *bet din,* such as matrimonial and civil laws. The work, written for the most part in fluent simple Hebrew, does not give the sources of the *halakhah* and confines itself to laws of practical application. It is clear now that the *Halakhot Keẓuvot* is not by Yehudai. Some suppose the book to have been written in Ereẓ Israel, but in the opinion of M. Margalioth, it was composed in southern Italy during the second half of the ninth century, shortly before 863. The author draws on the one hand on *Halakhot Pesukot* (as he did not have in his possession the **Halakhot Gedolot*), and on the other on a Palestinian halakhic work similar to *Sefer ha-Ma'asim.* Many of the customs cited in the work are contrary to those of the *geonim* but conform with those prevailing in Italy, and the redemption money of a firstborn (see **Pidyon ha-Ben*) is given in Italian currency. Likewise, many of its linguistic forms are found only in the works of Italian scholars and the book was known and accepted in Italy for centuries, Italian scholars making extensive use of it. Differences in traditional *halakhot* are attributable to special traditions existing in the place of composition.

Although the book was hardly recognized in Babylonia, the *geonim* paying no attention to it and ignoring it as a source in their decisions, in the European countries it came to be regarded as authoritative. Among those making use of it are *Gershom b. Judah, *Hananel, Judah al-Bargeloni, and Melchizedek of Siponto, and whole sections from it are quoted in works emanating from the school of Rashi, e.g., *Sefer ha-Pardes, Sefer ha-Orah, Siddur Rashi, Maḥzor Vitry, Ma'aseh ha-Ge'onim,* and others. The chief importance of the book is historical, since it is the first halakhic work composed in Europe, and reflects the customs, methods of study, and style of the Jews of southern Italy, the first Torah center in the West. *Halakhot Keẓuvot* was first published by C. M. Horowitz in the collection *Beit Nekhot ha-Halakhot* (*Toratan shel Rishonim,* 1881).

Bibliography: V. Aptowitzer, *Meḥkarim be-Sifrut ha-Ge'onim* (1941), 27, 84, 91–95; M. Margalioth (ed.), *Halakhot Keẓuvot* (1942), 1–60; Hartom, in: KS, 19 (1942/43), 84–86; Hildesheimer, in: *Sinai*, 13 (1944), 271–87; 14 (1944), 21–32, 82–94; H. Tchernowitz, *Toledot ha-Posekim*, 1 (1946), 112–6; idem, in: *Melilah*, 2 (1946), 238–42; Assaf, Ge'onim, 170. [M.MAR./ED.]

HALAKHOT PESUKOT (Heb. הֲלָכוֹת פְּסוּקוֹת; "Decided Laws"), the first known halakhic work of the *geonim*, written in the eighth century and attributed to *Yehudai Gaon or to his pupils. It confines itself to those *halakhot* which are of practical application, arranging them according to subject matter: laws of *eruvin*, Sabbath, Passover, etc. Its language is the Aramaic of the Talmud (for the most part giving the actual wording of the Talmud) and it generally follows the order of the Talmud, only occasionally combining isolated or scattered *halakhot*. The author makes use of the halakhic Midrashim and the Tosefta and there are a few quotations from the Jerusalem Talmud and the *Sefer ha-Ma'asim*. In addition there are cited many explanations and traditions of the *savoraim* handed down by the *geonim*, and mention is made of some of the scholars belonging to the period of the *savoraim*.

Although much of the material in the *Pesukot Halakhot* corresponds to that of the *She'iltot* of R. *Aḥa and it is therefore probable that the author utilized it, it is also possible that both drew upon a common source, a collection of early interpretations available in the academy. Although the *geonim* ascribe the work to Yehudai Gaon, it should not be assumed that he compiled it himself. In order to explain away the fact that many of the *halakhot* in the *Halakhot Pesukot* differed from the accepted *halakhah*, the *geonim* and *rishonim* propagated the tradition that Yehudai was blind and that his disciples wrote the work ascribed to him. Yehudai is in fact frequently mentioned in the work, generally as *rosh metivta*, and his son, Joseph, is also mentioned once in the *Hilkhot Re'u*, the Hebrew translation of the work. Further evidence of the work not being wholly that of Yehudai may be seen in its inclusion of *Terefot de-Ereẓ Yisrael*, to which Yehudai was vehemently opposed (see Margalioth, in *Talpioth*, 8, 1963), although it may be that an early copyist added to the Babylonian work a section dealing with the *halakhot* in Ereẓ Israel to provide a parallel between the Babylonian and the Ereẓ Israel laws.

In consequence of this work, Yehudai achieved a reputation enjoyed by few in his time. *Pirkoi b. Baboi, his pupil, says of his master, "for many years there has been none like him . . . and he never said anything that he had not heard from his teacher . . . and Mar Yehudai of blessed memory added, 'I have never given any answer to a question for which there was no proof from the Talmud and I learned the law from my teacher, who had it from his own teacher.'" The intent of the above is apparently to emphasize the fact that the work is based on the two pillars of Talmud and tradition and, indeed, it contains no independent views, giving only the words of the talmudic sages or the traditions of the *savoraim* and early *geonim*.

Halakhot Pesukot filled a great need. Yehudai was in constant contact with the communities outside Babylon which turned to him with halakhic problems, and his realization that not every one could find his way in the Talmud, and that it was impossible to turn to the *geonim* with every problem, led him to take on himself the task of giving the essence of the Talmud, the halakhic conclusion without the involved discussion. The work became indispensable almost as soon as it appeared, "most people turning to the digested *halakhot* saying, 'what concern have we with the Talmud?'" Paltoi, the *gaon* of Pumbedita, opposed this practice, fearing it would cause people to abandon the study of Torah (*Ḥemdah Genuzah*, no. 110).

Many adaptations and abridgments of the book were made, of which fragments have been found in the *genizah*. The scholars who published them gave them the names which were common among the *rishonim*, e.g., *Halakhot Ketu'ot, Halakhot Ketannot*, etc. One of these adaptations is the **Halakhot Keẓuvot*, compiled in southern Italy during the first half of the ninth century.

The most important adaptation, which became even more widespread than the original, eventually displacing it, is the **Halakhot Gedolot* (Venice, 1548) which absorbed most of the *Halakhot Pesukot*, and added to it a great deal of material from the sources. The *Halakhot Pesukot* was translated into Hebrew and Arabic shortly after it was written. The Hebrew translation (published from an Oxford Ms. by A. L. Schlossberg with an introduction by S. Z. H. Halberstamm in Versailles in 1886) was given the name *Hilkhot Re'u*, since it begins with Exodus 16:29, of which "*Re'u*" is the first word. The translation, executed in Ereẓ Israel, is the first of halakhic material from Aramaic into Hebrew to survive. Its literary standard is not high and many passages which it was difficult to translate were left in the original Aramaic. The translation contains many of the peculiarities of the style and script characteristic of the Jerusalem Talmud and the *Sefer ha-Ma'asim*. The beginning and end of the manuscript are defective, although the Cairo *Genizah* contains many excerpts from which the missing portions could be restored. In general, there is a need for a new scientific edition, since that of Schlossberg is defective and full of errors.

Many fragments of the Arabic translation have also come down, most containing a section of the Aramaic original, followed by the translation, although there are also fragments of a consecutive translation. In all probability there were a number of Arabic translations, testimony to the great popularity of this first halakhic code after the compilation of the Talmud.

Until 1911 *Halakhot Pesukot* was known only through quotations in the books of the early scholars. In that year, however, a manuscript of the work was found by David Sassoon in San'a, the capital of Yemen, and was published by his son Solomon (1951). This unique manuscript is in a fragmentary state; both the beginning and the end are lacking, as well as portions in the body of the text. (Many individual pages of the missing section, however, have been found in the Cairo *Genizah*.) *Hilkhot Terefot* from the *Halakhot Pesukot* have been published recently from several remnants.

Bibliography: Azulai, 1 (1852), 63 no. 8, s.v. *Yehudai Ga'on;* Epstein, in: *Tarbiz*, 8 (1937), 16–31; 10 (1939), 283–308; idem, in: JQR, 4 (1913/14), 423–33; 5 (1914/15), 97–8; V. Aptowitzer, *Meḥkarim be-Sifrut ha-Ge'onim* (1941), 27–28; Ḥ. Tchernowitz, *Toledot ha-Posekim*, 1 (1946), 78–84; Assaf, Ge'onim, 167–8; Hildesheimer, in: *Sefer ha-Yovel shel "Sinai"* (1958), 566–72; Abramson, in: *Sinai*, 23 (1948), 75 n. 19; idem, in: *Tarbiz*, 18 (1946/47), 42 n.12; Margalioth, in: *Talpioth*, 8 (1963), 307–30 (text of *Hilkhot Terefot*); Bruell, Jahrbuecher, 9 (1889), 128–33; 232–44; Poznański, in: REJ, 63 (1912), 232–44; Waxman, Literature, (1960²), 281ff. [M.MAR.]

HALBERSTADT, city in E. Germany. The earliest document testifying to the presence of Jews in Halberstadt dates from 1261; in it the city promises its protection to the Jews "as in the past." It is probable that Jews were already settled in the city in 1189. A Jewish community *(Judendorf)* possessing a synagogue was first mentioned in 1364; it comprised 11 families in 1456, mainly occupied in moneylending. The Jews were expelled from Halberstadt in 1493; although some returned in the 16th century, they were expelled once more in 1595. Shortly afterward, several Jews again settled in the city and built a synagogue, which was destroyed during the Thirty Years War. In 1650 ten Jewish families were granted privileges allowing them to engage in business and moneylending, but forbidding them to build a synagogue. They were permitted to elect a rabbi in 1661. The authorities protected the Jews from the jealousy of Christian merchants and as a result the community had grown to 118 families (639 persons) by 1699. In 1689 Behrend *Lehmann, the powerful *Court Jew of Saxony and protector of the community, established a *bet midrash,* the renowned *klaus* (1707), and in 1712 permission was granted to build a new synagogue. Halberstadt then served as a center for the smaller communities in its environs (e.g., *Halle and *Magdeburg) and was the largest Jewish community in Prussia. Occupations of Jews in this period ranged from simple handicraft to finance and industry. The community was world renowned as a center for Torah study and philanthropy in the 17th and 18th centuries. In 1795 a school for children of poor families, called Hazkarat Ẓevi, was opened. It existed until shortly before the destruction of German Jewry. In the 1850s and 60s some Hebrew works were printed in Halberstadt. A beautiful *maḥzor* was issued by H. Meyer; J. Z. *Jolles' *Melon ha-Ro'im* was edited by Y. F. Hirsch and printed at the press of J. Hoerling's widow (1859); B. H. *Auerbach's controversial *Sefer ha-Eshkol* appeared in 1867–79; and Elijah of Vilna's *Adderet Eliyahu* was published there. In the 19th and early 20th century the Hirsch family was outstanding in the industrial sphere and for its philanthropic activities.

Halberstadt was the center of Orthodox Jewry in Germany and until 1930 the central organizations of German Orthodox congregations and other Orthodox bodies were situated there. Several famous rabbis served in Halberstadt, including Ẓevi Hirsch *Bialeh, Hirschel *Levin, and members of the *Auerbach family. In 1933 there were 706 Jews in Halberstadt (1.4% of the total population). With the rise of Nazism, and its consequent

Figure 1. Watercolor of the Halberstadt synagogue, 19th century. Jerusalem, Sir Isaac and Lady Wolfson Museum in Hechal Shlomo. Photo David Harris, Jerusalem.

Figure 2. Title page of the *memorbuch* of the Halberstadt community, 1695. Jerusalem, C.A.H.J.P.

economic and social pressure, many Jews began to leave. The community reacted to persecution by developing a complex of cultural and educational institutions, and formal relationships were retained with the governmental authorities. On Nov. 10, 1938 the synagogue was demolished and 90 Torah scrolls were desecrated in the streets; all males under 40 were arrested. Between 1939 and 1942, 186 persons were deported; none returned.

Bibliography: Germ Jud, 1 (1963), 123–4; 2 (1968), 317–9; B. H. Auerbach, *Geschichte der israelitischen Gemeinde Halberstadt* (1866); E. Lehmann, *Der polnische Resident Behrend Lehmann* (1885); S. Stern, *Der preussische staat und die Juden,* 1 (1962), Akten, no. 104–35, 54a–370, p. 531ff.; 2 (1962), Akten, no. 454–95; idem, *The Court Jew* (1950), index; M. Koehler, *Beitraege zur neueren juedischen Wirtschaftsgeschichte. Die Juden in Halberstadt und Umgebung bis zur Emanzipation* (1927); Y. Levinsky, in: *Reshumot,* new series, 1 (1945), 142–50; J. Meisl, *ibid.,* 3 (1947), 181–205; H. B. Auerbach, in: BLBI, 10 (1967), 124–58, 309–35; idem, in: *Zeitschrift fuer Geschichte der Juden,* 6 (1969), 11f., 19f., 151f., 155f.; PKG. [Z.Av.]

HALBERSTADT, ABRAHAM BEN MENAHEM MENKE (d. 1782), German rabbi. Halberstadt studied under his father who was *dayyan* of Halberstadt, as well as under Jonathan *Eybeschuetz. In 1733 he published the Shulḥan Arukh, *Yoreh De'ah* in Amsterdam. In addition to his talmudic learning he acquired a profound knowledge of grammar, mathematics, and astronomy. In his interesting correspondence with his Berlin friend Jeremiah (who has been identified either with Jeremiah b. Naphtali Hirsch of Halberstadt or with Jeremiah b. Ephraim Segal who died in 1788), he expresses his views on the problems of contemporary German Jewry. In a letter written in 1774 he stresses the importance of the study of grammar and the Bible, and in another letter the next year he expresses his admiration for Moses *Mendelssohn and N. H. *Wessely, and suggests that the latter's *Yein Levanon* be used by rabbis as a basis for their sermons. He affirmed that the ignorance of grammar and secular subjects by many rabbis was the cause for their inability to understand correctly certain passages of the Talmud. In a letter in 1770, while emphasizing that all the accusations against Eybeschuetz were baseless, he nevertheless severely censured Eybeschuetz' careless conduct, and condemned the negative character of many of his pupils. His glosses to the Talmud, *Penei Avraham,* have remained in manuscript. He published the *Ba'alei Nefesh* (Berlin 1762) of *Abraham b. David (Rabad), adding to it glosses published in Venice (1741). He died in Berlin.

Bibliography: B. H. Auerbach, *Geschichte der israelitischen Gemeinde Halberstadt* (1866), 78, 98ff., 187–97; L. Landshuth, *Toledot Anshei ha-Shem,* 1 (1883), 120.

[Y.Ho.]

HALBERSTADT, MORDECAI (also known as **Mordecai of Duesseldorf;** d. 1770), rabbi and grammarian. Born in the town of Halberstadt at the beginning of the 18th century, Mordecai studied under Abraham b. Judah Berlin, the local rabbi, and Ẓevi Hirsch Ashkenazi, the head of its yeshivah. He proceeded to Frankfort in 1730 where he studied under Jacob ha-Kohen, author of *Shav Ya'akov,* whose rulings and responsa he quotes in his *Ma'amar Mordekhai* (nos. 10, 69, 70, et al.). He taught at the Halberstadt yeshivah and, on the recommendation of Jacob ha-Kohen, was appointed *av bet din* of Griesheim near Frankfort (*Ma'amar Mordekhai,* nos. 2, 8, 14). He later served as rabbi of Darmstadt, and then at Duesseldorf (no. 23), where he remained until the end of his life. Requested by Samuel Heilmann of Metz and Joshua *Falk of Frankfort to join in the ban against Jonathan *Eybeschuetz and to give his opinion about the amulets, Halberstadt was reluctant to attack Eybeschuetz personally and instead recommended that they content themselves with adverse criticism of the activities of the circles close to Shabbateanism. He was the author of the responsa, *Ma'amar Mordekhai* (Bruenn, 1790). Responsum no. 30 deals with the case of an animal in whose stomach was found a needle adhering to the midriff. The scholars of the Rhineland regarded such an animal *kasher* on the basis of responsa by Solomon Ephraim *Luntschitz and Isaiah *Horowitz (*ibid.,* 41b). Halberstadt proved with profound acumen that these alleged responsa were forgeries by the Bonn informer, Krauss, "who forged and testified falsely in the names of those great scholars." *Leḥem Eden,* a pamphlet containing the glosses of Halberstadt's son, Menahem Mendel Halberstadt, is appended to the book. Mordecai Halberstadt also compiled a work on grammar that has remained in manuscript. His grandson, who published the *Ma'amar Mordekhai,* refers to him as "Mordecai *Balshan* [the 'linguist'], because of his profound knowledge of the holy tongue and Hebrew grammar."

Bibliography: B. H. Auerbach, *Geschichte der israelitischen Gemeinde Halberstadt* (1866), 74–76, no. 11; idem (Ẓevi Binyamin), *Berit Avraham* (1860), 24f.; P. Frankl, in: *Nachlath Zvi,* 8 (1937), 79.

[Y.Ho.]

HALBERSTAEDTER, LUDWIG (1876–1949), Israel radiologist. Born at Beuthen (Bytom), Silesia, he was appointed head of the department of radiotherapy at the Cancer Institute at the University of Berlin in 1919, becoming professor there in 1929. When the Nazis came to power in 1933, he settled in Ereẓ Israel, where two years later he was made professor of radiology and radiotherapy at the Hebrew University, Jerusalem. He was also head of the radiobiology department of the university and director of the cancer department at the Hadassah University Hospital.

Halberstaedter was a radiobiologist and radiotherapist of international reputation. A pioneer in several fields, he investigated the nature of monkey malaria and together with von Prowazek discovered the Halberstaedter-Prowazek bodies widely believed to present a stage in the life history of the causal virus of trachoma.

Bibliography: S. R. Kagan, *Jewish Medicine* (1952), 537–8.

[Ed.]

HALBERSTAM, ḥasidic dynasty, originating in western Galicia in the mid-19th century. The most important personality in the dynasty was its founder, Ḥayyim ben Leibush (1793–1876). Born in Tarnogrod, on his mother's side Ḥayyim was a descendant of Ḥakham Ẓevi (Ẓevi Hirsch *Ashkenazi). Ḥayyim's father directed a *ḥeder.* In 1830 he was appointed rabbi of Nowy Sacz (Zanz). As a youth Ḥayyim was brought to *Jacob Isaac the *ḥozeh* ("seer") of Lublin who strongly influenced him and he became a Ḥasid; he studied under Naphtali of *Ropczyce and Ẓevi Hirsch of *Zhidachov. Ḥayyim also studied with Ẓevi Hirsch of *Rymanow, Shalom Rokeaḥ of *Belz, and Israel of *Ruzhin. Ḥayyim administered his yeshivah in the best scholarly tradition of the old-style yeshivot in Poland. He would not permit his pupils to cultivate Ḥasidism until a late stage. Thus both Ḥasidim and *mitnaggedim* were attracted to his yeshivah. Known as strict in matters of learning and observance, he conducted his "court" modestly and discreetly and avoided the splendor and luxury customary at the "courts" of other *ẓaddikim* in that period. The main event in his public life was the dispute between the Ḥasidim of Zanz and Sadagora, which aroused a controversy that spread beyond Galicia and also involved the leading non-ḥasidic rabbis. The principal cause of the dispute lay in the basic difference between the Zanz pattern of Ḥasidism with its stress on traditional learning and ecstatic expression in religious life and the manner of life adopted by Israel of Ruzhin and followed by his descendants. They lived in almost literally royal style, in the utmost luxury and splendor, which aroused resentment and opposition particularly of the Ḥasidim of Zanz, and also of the conservative Ḥasidim of Galicia generally. The publication of Dov Baer of Lyova, the youngest son of Israel of Ruzhin, in which he renounced Ḥasidism and expressed his support of the Haskalah, gave the Ḥasidim of Zanz a weapon against the dynasty of Ruzhin. Ḥayyim issued a letter in which he openly expressed his strong reservations about the way of life of the Sadagora Ḥasidim. It was circulated throughout Galicia, and a stormy debate between the two ḥasidic groups ensued. A rabbinical convention in the Ukraine called for the excommunication of Ḥayyim and even demanded that he should be handed over to the authorities. The dispute reached Ereẓ Israel, where it took on an added dimension in affecting the financial arrangements of the *ḥalukkah,* and apportionment of the money from Poland, to support the community in Ereẓ Israel. A number of rabbis, including Joseph Saul *Nathanson of Lvov and Dov Berush *Meisels, rabbi of Warsaw, Ḥayyim's brother-in-law, attempted to conciliate the opposing parties. The Hungarian rabbis intervened without success. After several months the dispute died down, but Ḥayyim remained consistent in his opinions on the matter. Ḥayyim wrote: *Divrei Ḥayyim* (Zolkiew, 1864), on ritual purity and divorce laws; responsa *Divrei Ḥayyim* (Lemberg, 1875), and *Divrei Ḥayyim* (Munkacz, 1877), ḥasidic sermons on Torah and the festivals. His works reveal a profound knowledge of the Talmud and commentaries, the *midrashim,* and medieval philosophical literature. He quotes widely from Judah Halevi's *Kuzari,* Maimonides, Naḥmanides, and Abraham ibn Daud. From later literature, he cites Isaiah Horowitz, Judah Loew of Prague, the prayer book of Jacob Emden, and his teachers in Kabbalah and Ḥasidism. An opponent of asceticism, Ḥayyim was an exponent of the ecstatic mode of prayer and developed the ḥasidic melody. In his writings he emphasized the duty of charity and criticized *ẓaddikim* who lived luxuriously.

Ḥayyim had eight sons. The most important was EZEKIEL SHRAGA OF SIENIAWA (1811–1899), considered a scholar and strict in matters of *halakhah.* He was responsible for the transcription and publication of Abraham b. Mordecai *Azulai's commentaries on the *Zohar, *Or ha-Ḥammah* (1896–98) and *Zohorei Ḥammah* (1881–82), and Ḥayyim *Vital's *Sefer ha-Gilgulim* (1875). In 1878 Akiva ha-Kohen Lieber of Yasienica studied with him and edited his posthumous work *Divrei Yeḥezkel* (Sieniawa, 1906), novellae, sermons on the Torah and for the holidays, and a few responsa. Of other sons also influential were BARUCH of Gorlice (1826–1906); DAVID of Kshanow (1821–1894); AARON of Zanz (d. 1906), *ẓaddik* and rabbi of Zanz and later of the region. SOLOMON BEN MEYER NATHAN OF BOBOVA (1847–1906), grandson of Ḥayyim, founded a large yeshivah; he attracted youth and many Ḥasidim. His son BEN ZION (1873–1941) became celebrated for the beautiful melodies he composed and also attracted many Ḥasidim. He perished in the Holocaust. Ben Zion's son, SOLOMON, found refuge in the United States where he established a ḥasidic center in the Boro Park section of Brooklyn. In December 1959 he also founded the small settlement of Bobova, near Bat Yam, which has subsequently become a center for Bobova Ḥasidim in Israel. Several descendants of Ḥayyim Halberstam moved to Slovakia where they served as rabbis. One of them, JACOB SAMSON OF CZCHOW, settled in Klausenburg (Cluj), Transylvania, in 1917. Another descendant is

Jekuthiel Judah Halberstam, the Klausenburg Rebbe. From G. Krantzler, *Williamsburg, A Community in Transition,* New York, 1960.

JEKUTHIEL JUDAH (1904–), who later became the Klausenburg Rebbe. Although his wife and 11 children perished in the Holocaust, Jekuthiel survived and reestablished his court in the Williamsburg section of Brooklyn. In 1956 he founded Kiryat Zanz near *Netanyah in Israel. He later permanently settled in Kiryat Zanz, along with many of his Ḥasidim.

Bibliography: R. Mahler, in: *Proceedings of the Fourth World Congress of Jewish Studies,* 2 (1968), 223–5; A. Marcus, *Ha-Ḥasidut* (1953), 266–74, 277; Horodezky, Ḥasidut, index; I. Even, in: *Ha-Ivri,* 6 (1916), no. 1–no. 28; E. Roth, in: *Talpioth,* ed. by S. K. Mirsky, 6 (1953), 346–58; M. Zailikovitz (ed.), *Yalkut ha-Ro'im* (1896); *Keneset ha-Gedolah* (1869); W. Ehrenkranz, *Makkel Ḥovelim* (1869); M. Buber, *Tales of the Hasidim,* 2 (1966³), 208–15; H. Rabinowicz, *The World of Hasidim* (1970), 227; G. Kranzler, *Williamsburg* (1964), 150, 178, 209.

[P.ME.]

HALBERSTAM, ISAAC BEN ḤAYYIM (1810–1880), talmudist and author. Halberstam was born in Brody, and belonged to a distinguished rabbinical family. He was a brother-in-law of Dov Berush *Meisels, rabbi in Cracow and Warsaw, in partnership with whom he directed a banking establishment in Cracow. After losing his fortune, Halberstam devoted himself exclusively to study. His novellae to the Pentateuch, arranged in the order of the weekly portions, were published by his son, Solomon Zalman Ḥayyim, under the title *Si'aḥ Yiẓḥak* (1882).

Bibliography: I. Halberstam, *Si'aḥ Yiẓḥak* (1882), preface; Z. Horowitz, *Kitvei ha-Ge'onim* (1928), 90.

[ED.]

HALBERSTAM, SOLOMON (Zalman) ḤAYYIM (known from his acronym as **ShaZḤaH**; 1832–1900), Polish scholar and bibliophile. Halberstam was born in Cracow and studied with his father, Isaac Halberstam, an eminent talmudist. During his years as a successful merchant in Bielsko (Bielitz), Poland, he collected rare books and manuscripts. He studied some and lent others to Jewish scholars. Halberstam was one of the founders of the *Mekiẓe Nirdamim society. In addition to scholarly articles and notes to the works of other scholars, he published with introductions and notes some of the manuscripts from his library, among them being *Yom Tov b. Abraham's novellae on tractate *Niddah, Ḥiddushei ha-Ritba* (1868); Abraham *ibn Ezra's *Sefer ha-Ibbur* (1874); and *Judah b. Barzillai's *Sefer ha-Shetarot* (1898) and *Perush Sefer Yeẓirah* (1885). In 1890 he published *Kohelet Shelomo,* a catalog of his manuscripts which listed 411 items. After Halberstam's death most of his manuscripts were sold to the Judith Montefiore College in Ramsgate, England, and are now at Jews' College, London. The majority of the printed books in his library and a small part of his manuscript collection were acquired by the Jewish Theological Seminary in New York and the library of the Vienna community. Most of his correspondence is preserved in the library of the Jewish Theological Seminary. Halberstam also wrote notes to Ḥ. Michael's bibliographical work *Or ha-Ḥayyim* (in the Mosad ha-Rav Kook edition, 1965).

Bibliography: N. Sokolow (ed.), *Sefer Zikkaron le-Soferei Yisrael ha-Ḥayyim Ittanu ha-Yom,* (1889), 28; G. Bader, *Medinah ve-Ḥakhameha* (1934), 76–77; Davidson, in: *Yad va-Shem . . . A. S. Freidus* (1929), 1–14 (Heb. sect.); Zeitlin, Bibliotheca, index; B. Wachstein et al. (eds.) *Hebraeische Publizistik in Wien,* 2 (1930), 17; Shunami, Bibl., 890.

[A.M.H.]

HALBWACHS, MAURICE (1877–1945), French sociologist. In social psychology he investigated the problems of memory considered as a social fact and the influence of collective memory and tradition on beliefs, and traced the delicate interconnections between psychology and sociology. He combined an avid concern with sociographic investigation in various fields with his strong bent for theorizing in works on demographical statistics, on which subject he contributed to the *Encyclopédie Française.* He taught at the universities of Caen, Strasbourg, and Paris (after 1935), and a few months before his deportation and murder by the Nazis he was nominated to occupy the chair of social psychology at the College de France. He perished in the Buchenwald concentration camp. Among his works were: *La théorie de l'homme moyen: Essai sur Quetelet et la statistique morale* (1913); *Les cadres sociaux de la mémoire* (1925, 1952²); *L'évolution des besoins dans les classes ouvrières* (1933); *Morphologie sociale* (1934); *Esquisse d'une psychologie des classes sociales* (in *Enquêtes Sociologiques* . . ., 1938; repub. posthum., 1955; *The Psychology of Social Class,* 1958); *La topographie légendaire des Evangiles en Terre Sainte* (1941); *Psychologie collective* (1942), *Mémoire et Société* (1949), posthumous.

Bibliography: Alexandre, in: *Année Sociologique,* 1 (1949), 3–10; Cuvielier, in: J. S. Roucek, *Contemporary Sociology* (1958), 716ff.; G. Gurvitch and E. Moore (eds.), *Twentieth Century Sociology* (1945).

[E.FI.]

HA-LEVANON (Heb. הַלְּבָנוֹן, "Lebanon"), the first Hebrew newspaper in Ereẓ Israel. *Ha-Levanon,* edited by Jehiel *Brill, Joel Moses *Salomon, and Michael Cohen, first appeared in Jerusalem in March 1863. The paper was established as the organ of the **ḥalukkah* trustees at a time of strife within the Jerusalem Ashkenazi community.

כבוד

מחברת ראשונה

הלבנון

שנה עשירית

לָדַעַת חָכְמָה וּמוּסָר לְהָבִין אִמְרֵי בִינָה (משלי א).

באר היטב

(הסוף מנו' 10 שנה תשיעית)

Title page of an 1873 issue of *Ha-Levanon*'s literary supplement *Kevod ha-Levanon*. Jerusalem, J.N.U.L.

Throughout the paper's career, Brill, the editor in chief and the paper's moving spirit, consistently held that Jews living in the old city of Jerusalem should found suburbs outside the city's walls in which to live. Further, the *yishuv* living on the *ḥalukkah* should turn to productive occupations, particularly farming. At the same time, however, Brill objected to Ḥovevei Zion's fervent advocacy of the settlement of Ereẓ Israel, claiming that the movement's plans were impracticable, fired as they were by imagination rather than by a thorough knowledge of conditions in the country. He did approve of feasible programs of settlement and throughout the years urged Ḥovevei Zion to adopt a realistic attitude. Among the settlement programs supported by *Ha-Levanon* were *Moẓa and Petaḥ Tikvah.

Contributors to the paper included journalists and scholars from abroad as well as from Jerusalem. *Ha-Levanon* engaged in a bitter controversy with the rival paper, *Ḥavaẓẓelet*, established in Jerusalem during the summer of 1863. As a result both papers closed down in 1864. After a year's interval, Brill revived *Ha-Levanon* in Paris, where it appeared as a biweekly until 1868 when it became a weekly. Although published in Europe, the paper appeared in Jerusalem on a monthly basis and continued to print much news of Ereẓ Israel, most of its articles, in fact, being devoted to *yishuv* affairs. The paper, especially in its literary supplement *(Kevod ha-Levanon)*, printed diverse studies on Judaism and belles lettres (mostly translations), with leading local and foreign writers as contributors. Trapped in the siege of Paris during the Franco-Prussian War (1870–71) and the Commune, Brill depicted the latter for *Ha-Levanon*, and eventually he left for Germany where he revived *Ha-Levanon* in Mainz (1872) as a supplement of the German Orthodox paper *Israelit*. Becoming the Hebrew organ of Orthodoxy, it provided the forum for a bitter controversy with the religious Reform movement of M. L. *Lilienblum, J. L. *Gordon, and others. Concurrently, Brill continued to support every constructive plan relating to the *yishuv*. The Russian pogroms of the early 1880s brought about an ideological reorientation in *Ha-Levanon*. Brill severed his connection with the Orthodox circles and became a zealous advocate of the settlement of Ereẓ Israel. He conducted propaganda campaigns in Russia, and was responsible for the immigration to Ereẓ Israel of Jewish farmers who later founded the village of Ekron. At the end of 1882 *Ha-Levanon* ceased publication. In 1884 Brill settled in London, where he revived *Ha-Levanon* in 1886, but the paper closed on Brill's death that same year. A pioneer of the modern press in Ereẓ Israel, *Ha-Levanon* provided during its 20 years of existence the first opportunity for Hebrew journalists in Ereẓ Israel.

Bibliography: G. Kressel, *Ha-Levanon ve-ha-Ḥavaẓẓelet* (1943); idem, *Toledot ha-Ittonut ha-Ivrit be-Ereẓ Yisrael* (1964), 27–41; S. L. Zition, in: *Ha-Olam*, 6 (1912), nos. 28, 30, 31, 33, 35, 36, 38; R. Malachi, in: *Meyer Waxman Jubilee Volume* (1967), 70–142; G. Yardeni, *Ha-Ittonut ha-Ivrit be-Ereẓ Yisrael ba-Shanim 1863–1904* (1969), 17–29; Z. Ravid, in: *Hadoar*, 42 (1963), 18–22.

[G.K.]

HALEVI, EZEKIEL EZRA BEN JOSHUA (1852–1942), one of the most prominent scholars and poets of Iraqi Jewry in recent generations; born in Baghdad and died in Jerusalem. In 1897 Halevi emigrated to Ereẓ Israel and settled in Jerusalem. He earned his livelihood as a preacher; he was also a communal worker, president of the committee of the Iraqi community, and one of the founders of the yeshivah Shoshannim le-David. Of more than ten books which he wrote, five were published, including: *Arugat ha-Bosem* (1905), on the *aggadah; Tehillah ve-Tiferet* (1914), a commentary on the Book of Psalms; and also his *Simḥat Yom Tov* (c. 1934), which was a commentary on the Passover *Haggadah*.

Bibliography: A. Ben-Jacob, *Yehudei Bavel* (1965), 133, 194, 205; Tidhar, 11 (1961), 3843.

[A.B.-Y.]

HALEVI, JOSEPH ẒEVI BEN ABRAHAM (1874–1960), Israel rabbi and halakhic authority. Halevi was born in Slobodka and studied in its famous yeshivah. In 1891 he settled in Ereẓ Israel, where in 1897 he was appointed *dayyan* and assistant to his father-in-law, Naphtali Herz ha-Levi, the first Ashkenazi rabbi of Jaffa. In 1902 on the death of his father-in-law, he served for a time as rabbi of Jaffa, but when A. I. *Kook was appointed rabbi of Jaffa, Halevi was appointed head of the first permanent *bet din* established there. During Kook's absence from Ereẓ Israel in World War I he took over his functions as rabbi of the Ashkenazi community and together with Ben Zion *Ouziel represented the Jewish community of Jaffa-Tel Aviv before the Turkish government. Following the expulsion of Jews from Jaffa-Tel Aviv by the Turks, Halevi went to Petaḥ Tikvah and to Rishon le-Zion, returning to Jaffa after the entry of the British into Ereẓ Israel. He continued to fill the office of *av bet din* also during the rabbinates of Aaronson (1923–1935), Amiel (1936–1945), and Unterman (from 1947).

Halevi was a prolific author. Most of the 17 books he wrote deal with the *halakhot* and precepts applying to the land of Israel, maintaining that with the beginning of the "ingathering of the exiles" attention should again be paid to these laws. The following are some of his works: *Hora'at Sha'ah* (1909), an exposition of the principles permitting the working of the land in the Sabbatical year by selling it to a gentile; *Hashkafah li-Verakhah* (1930), on the laws of the separation of the tithes; *Aser Te'asser* (1935), on *terumot* and *ma'aserot* ("tithes"); *Neta ha-Areẓ* (1939), *Zera ha-Areẓ* (1941), *Kerem ha-Areẓ* (1943), *Leḥem ha-Areẓ* (1950); *Ḥovat Giddulei ha-Areẓ* (1953), dealing with the laws of *orlah, kilayim (*mixed species) of seeds and trees, kilayim of the vineyard, the law of *ḥallah and the laws of *leket, shikhḥah, and pe'ah; Amirah Ne'imah (1948; second series 1955 in two parts), halakhic expositions and novellae; Va-Tomer Ẓiyyon, 2 pts. (1950–58), homilies on the Pentateuch; Torat ha-Korbanot (1959), an exposition of 288 halakhot in Maimonides' laws of the sacrifices. Most of his works follow a standard pattern. The basis is the text from Maimonides' Mishneh Torah, to which he adds the decisions of rishonim and the decisions based upon new developments. Although there is an element of casuistry in his works, in the main he aims at giving the practical halakhah. In 1958 he was awarded the Israel Prize.

Bibliography: Ha-Ẓofeh (March 3–4, 1960, Apr. 1960); Tidhar, 1 (1947), 354f.; S. J. Zevin, Soferim u-Sefarim, 1 (1959), 59–70; I. Goldschlag, in: Shanah be-Shanah (1961), 361–63; Yahadut Lita, 3 (1967), 84.

[Y.Ho.]

HA-LEVI, SASSON BEN ELIJAH BEN MOSES (also known as **R. Sasson Smuḥa**; 1820–1910), Baghdad rabbi and disciple of R. Abdullah *Somekh. Ha-Levi held the position of dayyan from 1841 to 1876. In 1860 he intervened to prevent the expropriation from Jewish hands of the traditional tomb of the prophet Ezekiel in the village of Kifl. From 1876 to 1879 he was ḥakham bashi of Baghdad. A controversy then broke out between him and several members of the community, who deposed him and appointed R. Elisha Dangoor in his place. A dispute ensued between the two during the years 1880 to 1885. The majority of the rabbis supported Dangoor, while some of the wealthy sided with Ha-Levi. The matter reached the chief rabbi of Constantinople, who decided in favor of the former. Ha-Levi composed two piyyutim, which have been included in books of liturgical hymns.

Bibliography: A. Ben-Jacob, Yehudei Bavel (1965), 162f.

[A.B.-Y.]

HALÉVY (19th–20th centuries), French family of authors. Léon Halévy (1802–1883) was born in Paris. He was the younger son of Elie Halfon *Halévy and younger brother of the composer Jacques François Fromental *Halévy. A scholar of distinction, Léon Halévy became assistant professor of French literature at the Ecole Polytechnique in 1831 and head of the antiquities department in the Ministry of Education six years later. Although his connection with the community was intermittent and he married a non-Jewess, he never abandoned Judaism. He evidently found official prejudice strong enough to prevent his advancement, and in 1853 retired from public life and became a writer. Doctrinally a Saint-Simonian, he was critical of the development of post-biblical Judaism, favoring a reformist return to the "primitive faith" on semi-Christian lines. Halévy's works include Résumé de l'histoire des juifs anciens (1825) and its sequel, Résumé de l'histoire des juifs modernes (1828). He also wrote two volumes of verse, rhymed translations and plays, which included tragedies and dramas such as Luther (1834) and Electre (1864) and some popular vaudeville comedies.

Léon's son, Ludovic Halévy (1834–1908), was a writer whose comedies, librettos, novels, and stories dealt with the gay life of the French during the Second Empire. In collaboration with Henri Meilhac he wrote the text for Bizet's opera Carmen (1875), and librettos for several operettas by Jacques *Offenbach, including La belle Hélène (1865); La Vie parisienne (1866); La Grande-Duchesse de Gérolstein (1867); and La Périchole (1868). Their play Le Réveillon (1872), based on a German drama, was later adapted for Johann Strauss' Die Fledermaus. Their greatest success was the comedy Frou-Frou (1870). With H. Crémieux, Halévy wrote the libretto for Offenbach's Orphée aux enfers (1858). His other works include the novels Un Mariage d'amour (1881) and L'Abbé Constantin (1882), and several volumes of memoirs, notably L'Invasion (1872). He was elected to the Académie Française in 1884. In his later years he revealed a consciousness of his Jewish heritage. Ludovic Halévy's two sons were the philosopher and historian Elie *Halévy (1870–1937), and the historian and essayist Daniel Halévy (1872–1962). Although the latter graduated in Semitics and at first supported *Dreyfus, he became a reactionary and a convert to Catholicism. In later years Daniel Halévy even betrayed anti-Semitic tendencies, defending Marshal *Pétain and the arch-anti-Semite Charles *Maurras. His ideological break with his old Dreyfusard friend Charles *Péguy provoked the latter's indignant criticism in Notre jeunesse (1910). Daniel Halévy's works include: Apologie pour notre passé (1910), polemics with Péguy; Charles Péguy et les cahiers de la quinzaine (1918, 1941); Cahiers verts (1921–27); La Fin des notables, a history of the Third Republic (2 vols. 1930–37); and Nietzsche (1944).

Bibliography: Catane, in: Evidences, 46 (1955), 7–13; Szajkowski, in: JSOS, 9 (1947), 35, 43–44; A. Silvera, Daniel Halévy and his Times (1966); G. Weill, in: REJ, 31 (1895), 261–73.

[M.C.]

HALÉVY, ÉLIE (1870–1937), French philosopher and historian. He was the son of Ludovic *Halévy and brother of Daniel *Halévy. He was raised as a Protestant (his mother's religion). He became professor at the Ecole libre des Sciences politiques where he taught English history and European socialism. A Dreyfusard and a secular rationalist, he was a founder of the Revue de Métaphysique et de Morale and the Société française de Philosophie. His first work, La Théorie platonicienne des sciences (1896), dealt with Plato's negative dialectic as a way to positive construction. He applied this theory in a basic study of the Benthamite movement, La formation du radicalisme philosophique, 3 vols. (1901–04; The Growth of Philosophic Radicalism, 1928). His important Histoire du peuple anglais au XIXe siècle, 5 vols. (1912–32; A History of the English People in the 19th Century, 1924–34) covering the periods 1815–41, and 1895–1914 (he died before completing the rest), was an anti-Marxist interpretation of English history, stressing the role of religious factors in English political stability. He also wrote The World Crisis of 1914–18 (1930), L'ère des tyrannies (1938) against fascism and communism, and Histoire du socialisme européen (1948; from his notes). Halévy favored transforming collective belief through compromise rather than fanaticism as the means to international peace. At the end of his life he was pessimistic, convinced that war was inevitable and that the fascist and communist tyrannies would be perpetuated. He played an important role in English as well as in French intellectual life.

Bibliography: Brunschvicg, in: Revue de Métaphysique et de Morale, 44 (1937), 679–91; C.C. Gillispie, Journal of Modern History, 22 (1950), 232–49; M. Richter, International Encyclopedia of the Social Sciences, 6 (1968), 307–10.

[R.H.P.]

HALÉVY, ELIE HALFON (1760–1826), writer and poet in Hebrew and French. Born into an illustrious Jewish family in Fuerth, Bavaria, he received an Orthodox upbringing. As a young man he moved to Paris where he served as cantor, secretary of the community, and teacher. In Paris he acquired a broad general education and was greatly influenced by classical French literature. From 1817 to 1819 he edited and published a weekly journal in French, L'Israélite Français, which called for "Jewish enlightenment," and was animated by strong French patriotism. His only published book, Limmudei Dat u-Musar ("Teachings

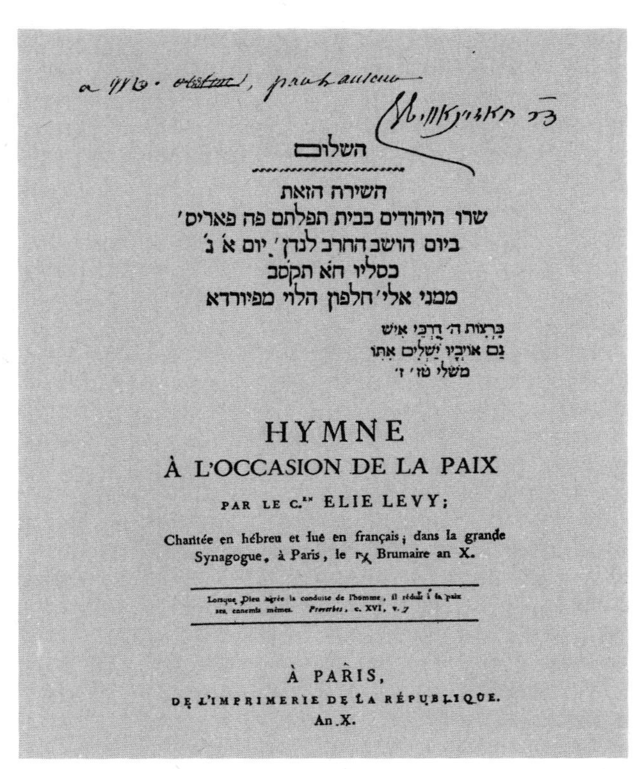

השלום

השירה הזאת
שרו היהודים בבית תפלתם פה פאריס'
ביום הושב החרב לנדן'. יום א' ג'
כסליו הא תקסב
ממני אלי' חלפן הלוי מפיורדא

בִּרְצוֹת ה' דַּרְכֵי אִישׁ
גַּם אוֹיְבָיו יַשְׁלִים אִתּוֹ
משלי טז' ז'

HYMNE
À L'OCCASION DE LA PAIX
PAR LE C.EN ELIE LEVY;

Chantée en hébreu et lue en français; dans la grande Synagogue, à Paris, le 18 Brumaire an X.

Lorsque Dieu agrée la conduite de l'homme, il réduit à la paix ses ennemis mêmes. *Proverbes*, c. XVI, v. 7

À PARIS,
DE L'IMPRIMERIE DE LA RÉPUBLIQUE.
An X.

Hymn written by Elie Halfon Halévy for the synagogue service celebrating the Treaty of Amiens. Paris, 1802. Jerusalem, J.N.U.L.

of Religion and Ethics," 1829), was a catechism for Jewish religious instruction. The tract is written in the spirit of the Haskalah and includes the decisions of the *Sanhedrin convened by Napoleon in 1807. His most important literary work, the poem *Ha-Shalom* ("Peace"), commemorated the cease-fire between France and England in 1802, when it was sung as a hymn, in both Hebrew and French, in the Great Synagogue of Paris. The poem was printed with a French and German translation by the imperial printing press in Paris, and reprinted in R. Fuerstenthal's *Ha-Me'assef* (1829, pp. 216–26). Written in the form of a classic Greco-Roman ode, it reflects the stormy period of the French Revolution and the subsequent wars and mirrors both the patriotic mood and the atmosphere of fear prevalent at the time. It remains a classic of the early period of modern Hebrew literature. Halévy was the father of the composer Jacques Francois Fromental *Halévy and the author and playwright Léon Halévy (see *Halévy family).

Bibliography: Klausner, Sifrut, 1 (1950²), 322–5; I. Zinberg, Sifrut, 5 (1959), 260–2.

[G.El.]

HALEVY (Rabinowitz), ISAAC (1847–1914), Polish rabbinical scholar and historian. Halevy was born in Ivenets, now Belorussia. After studying at the Volozhin yeshivah, he

Isaac Halevy, rabbinical scholar and historian. Jerusalem, J.N.U.L., Schwadron Collection.

settled in Vilna as a businessman, later turning to scholarship. Interested in Jewish education, he tried to find a way to reconcile the character of religious schools with the demands of the Russian government for reform. He lived in various cities, including Pressburg (Bratislava), Homburg, and Hamburg, in the last serving as *Klausrabbiner*. It was Halevy's idea of a world organization for Orthodox Jewry that led to the founding of *Agudat Israel in 1912. He took the initiative in founding the Juedisch-Literarisch Gesellschaft in Frankfort, whose yearbook (JJLG) appeared from 1903 to 1933. Halevy's major work, *Dorot ha-Rishonim* (6 vols., 1897–1939; repr. 1967) is a grandly conceived history of the Oral Law, the talmudic-rabbinic tradition from biblical times to the *geonim*. Halevy brought a vast talmudic erudition, ingenuity, and originality to his work, but in extra-rabbinic studies he was self-taught; he knew neither Latin nor Greek and quoted classical sources from their translations into German. Halevy worked "backward." Commencing with the savoraic and geonic period, he proceeded to that of the *amoraim* and the *tannaim*, and then to that of the *soferim* and the "men of the Great *Synagogue." The last volume deals with the biblical period and is a sustained attack on the critical school and attempts, following D. Z. *Hoffman, to prove the validity of the traditional view. The main purpose of the work was to demolish the historical theories advanced by such scholars as N. *Krochmal, S. J. *Rapaport, Z. *Frankel, H. *Graetz, and I. H. Weiss on the development of *halakhah* from earliest times. For Halevy, trained as he was in the old school, the Oral Law was revealed on Mount Sinai and was handed down unchanged; rabbinic controversies and the Palestinian-Babylonian differences in law and custom concern only the details of rabbinic enactments and extensions of the laws of the Torah. In his criticism of the historical school, which he accuses of tendentious misinterpretation, he writes with animosity and invective, and critics were not slow to point to the obvious shortcomings, both scholarly and literary, of *Dorot ha-Rishonim*. Nevertheless, it remains a major contribution to Jewish historical research.

Bibliography: O. Asher Reichel, *Isaac Halevy: Spokesman and Historian of Jewish Tradition* (1969); M. Auerbach (ed.), *Sefer ha-Zikkaron le-Y. I. Halevy* (1964); H. Schwab, *Chachme Ashkenaz* (Eng., 1964), 62f.

[Y.Ho.]

HALÉVY, JACQUES (François) FROMENTAL ÉLIE (1799–1862), French operatic composer. He was born in Paris, the son of Elie Halfon Halévy. He entered the Paris Conservatory at the age of ten, studied composition with Cherubini, and won the Rome Prize in 1819 for his cantata "Herminie." He taught at the conservatory from 1816, becoming professor of counterpoint and fugue in 1833, and of composition in 1840. His students included Bizet (who later became his son-in-law) and Gounod. Halévy's fame rests primarily on his grand opera "La Juive" (1835), and his comic opera "L'Eclair" of the same year, achievements which he never equaled. He composed about 20 operas (among them "Le Juif errant"; 1852), five cantatas, and ballets. His writings include memoirs of his activity in the Académie des Beaux Arts, of which he became permanent secretary in 1854.

Halévy's operatic style was greatly influenced by Meyerbeer, especially in the dazzling orchestration that was much in favor at the time. In "La Juive," a renaissance story of a prince in love with a Jewess (libretto by Scribe), he portrayed effective characters in situations of dramatic tension: Eleazar's aria "Rachel, quand du Seigneur" has remained one of the star items in the repertoire of dramatic tenors.

Halévy's attitude to Judaism seems to have been consciously neutral. In 1820 he composed a "Marche Funèbre et De Profundis" for three voices (text: Ps. 130 in

Hebrew), for the memorial service to the Duc de Berry in the synagogue in the Rue Saint-Avoye, now Rue du Temple. His cantata "Noé" (Noah) was completed post-

Jacques Halévy, French opera composer. From *Juedisches Athenaeum*, Leipzig, 1851.

humously by Bizet. Richard Wagner wrote in praise of Halévy's works, and also arranged a potpourri for two violins from his *La Reine de Chypre* (1841).

Halévy's brother Léon (see *Halévy family) wrote one of the first biographies of Halévy, *F. Halévy, ses oeuvres* (1863).

Bibliography: MGG, s.v.; Grove, Dict., s.v.; M. Curtis, in: *Musical Quarterly*, 39 (1953); Sendrey, Music, index. [J.T.]

HALÉVY, JOSEPH (1827–1917), French orientalist and Hebrew writer. Halévy began his career as a Hebrew teacher in his native Adrianople, Turkey, and later taught in Bucharest, Rumania. In 1868 he visited Ethiopia under the auspices of the Alliance Israélite Universelle to study the *Falashas. His report (not published), affirming the Jewishness of that forgotten tribe, led to a widespread philanthropic campaign on their behalf. The scientific results of his journey on the Falashas' language, literature, and customs, important in themselves, interested the French Académie des Inscriptions et Belles Lettres, which subsequently commissioned Halevy to explore Southern Arabia for Sabean inscriptions. For self-protection he traveled in the guise of a Jerusalem rabbi collecting alms for the poor. Ḥayyim *Ḥabshush, a Yemenite Jew who acted as Halevy's guide, described this expedition in *Travels in Yemen* (Arabic text, ed. and summarized in Eng. by S. D. Goitein, 1941; Heb. tr., *Masot Ḥabshush*, 1939).

The rich scientific harvest was 686 inscriptions, which were partly in Minean, a sister language of Sabean. Halévy published them under the title *Études Sabéennes* (1875; = *Journal Asiatique*, 1 (1873), 305–365; 2 (1874), 497–585). He also wrote reports of his journeys, *Rapport sur une Mission*

Joseph Halévy, orientalist and Hebrew writer. Jerusalem, J.N.U.L., Schwadron Collection.

Archéologique dans le Yémen (1872), and *Voyage au Nadjran* (1873). The researches were of importance not only for the knowledge of Sabean language and culture but for biblical studies as well. In 1879 Halévy began teaching Ethiopic at the Ecole Pratique des Hautes Etudes in Paris and became the librarian of the Société Asiatique. In 1893 he founded the *Revue Sémitique d'Epigraphique et d'Histoire Ancienne*, to which he contributed a great many articles on Semitic epigraphy and Bible studies. In the latter, published separately as *Recherches Bibliques* (5 vols. 1895–1914), he interpreted the first 25 chapters of Genesis on the basis of Babylonian-Assyrian discoveries, rejecting the Graf-Wellhausen *documentary hypothesis. He also discussed problems in the Bible in the *Revue des Etudes Juives*, *Revue Critique*, and *Revue de l'Histoire des Religions*. Halévy dealt with recently discovered parts of the Hebrew texts of Ben Sira in *Le nouveau fragment hébreu de l'Ecclésiastique* (1902); with the origins of Christianity in *Etudes évangéliques* (1903); and with Ethiopian, particularly Falasha, literature in *Seder Tefillot ha-Falashim* (1876), *Te'ezaza Sanbat* ("Sabbath laws"; 1902), *La guerre de Sarsa-Dengel contre les Falachas* (1907), and others.

Prompted by his "Semitic" pride, Halévy argued obstinately against the view that Sumerian was a non-Semitic language, which with Sumerian culture and cuneiform scripts preceded its Semitic successors. Halévy rejected this now generally accepted theory, believing Sumerian to be not a language but a hieratic, artificial script invented by the Assyrian-Babylonian priesthood for its own purposes. One of his works on this subject is his *Le Sumérisme et l'histoire babylonienne* (1900). In contrast to the assimilationist trend among French Jewry, Halévy was an ardent Hebraist and *Ḥovev Zion*. In his youth he was a regular contributor to Hebrew periodicals, such as *Ha-Maggid*, *Ha-Levanon*, and *Yerushalayim*, both in prose and in poetry, which were later collected and published under the title *Maḥberet Melizah va-Shir* (1894). The titles of his poems, such as *"Admat Avotai"* ("Land of My Fathers"), *"Al ha-Yarden"* ("By the Jordan,") and *"Tikvati"* ("My Hope") revealed his strong attachment to Ereẓ Israel. Halévy translated into Hebrew poems by Schiller, Byron, Victor Hugo, and others. In an article in *Ha-Maggid* of 1861 he proposed the establishment of a society, Marpei Lashon, for the development of the Hebrew language, an idea later realized in the Va'ad ha-Lashon ha-Ivrit and its successor, the Academy of Hebrew Language.

Bibliography: N. Sokolow, *Ishim*, 4 (1935), 144–92; F. Perles, in: *Ost und West*, 17 (1917), 105–10; M. Schorr, in: *Deutsche Literaturzeitung*, nos. 19–20 (May 12, and 19, 1918), 595–601, 627–33; D. Sidersky, *Quelques portraits de nos maîtres des études sémitiques* (1937), 59–63; M. Eliav, in: *Tarbiz*, 35 (1966), 61–67; T. B. Jones, *Sumerian Problem* (1969), 22–47. [H.J.P.]

HALEVY, MOSHE (1895–), Israel theatrical director and founder of the *Ohel Theater. He studied engineering in Moscow before joining the newly formed Habimah Studio as assistant director (1917). He left the company early, however, to found his own theater in Palestine and in 1925 established Ohel, a workers' theater under the auspices of the Histadrut. His first production, based on stories by I. L. *Peretz, was a great success, especially in the kibbutzim which, for many years, were to provide Ohel's main audiences. In his production of *Fishermen (Op Hoop van Zegen)* by Heijermans, he demonstrated his belief in the theater as an instrument for social betterment. For 25 years he directed almost all Ohel's productions, but left the company after disagreements in 1951. He engaged in other ventures, among them a small traveling Moshe Halevy Theater (1960), which continued until 1967. His autobiography *Darki Alei Bamot* ("My Stage Career") appeared in 1954.

Bibliography: Tidhar, 2 (1947), 953–4. [M.K.]

Drawing of Moshe Halevy, Israel theater director, by Reuven Rubin, 1948.

ḤALFAN, ELIJAH MENAHEM (16th century), Italian physician, rabbi, and kabbalist. Elijah was the son of the astronomer Abba Mari Ḥalfan and grandson of Joseph *Colon. He was one of the Italian rabbis approached to express his view of Henry VIII's divorce from Catherine of Aragon, on which he gave an affirmative opinion. He was also a supporter of Solomon *Molcho. Both these facts aroused the opposition of the physician Jacob *Mantino who feared that the close relationship with the English king as well as with the messianic agitation of Molcho would render the pope unfavorably disposed toward the Jews. Ḥalfan wrote responsa (including one in which he favored instructing non-Jews in the Torah; Ms. Kaufmann, no. 156:1 from 1545) and Hebrew poems (several verses are extant in Ms.; Neubauer, Cat, no. 948:1, 6). In a halakhic decision dated 1550, Elijah's name appears together with that of Meir Katzenellenbogen of Padua among others (Resp. Rema 56). He owned a valuable library in Venice, a catalog of which was published by A.Z.Schwarz (*Die Hebraeischen Handschriften der Nationalbibliothek in Wien* (1925), 145ff.).

Bibliography: Carmoly, in: *Revue Orientale,* 2 (1842), 133f.; K.Lieben, *Gal Ed* (1856), German section, 171 no. 168, Hebrew section, xlv no. 17; Michael, Or, no. 394; Kaufmann, in: JQR, 9 (1896/97), 500–8; idem, in: REJ, 27 (1893), 51–58; Vogelstein-Rieger, 2 (1895), 51–53; U. Cassuto, *Gli Ebrei a Firenze* (1918), 272; A. Z. Aescoly, *Ha-Tenu'ot ha-Meshiḥiyyot be-Yisrael* (1956), 271–3; Tishby, in: *Perakim,* 1 (1967–68), 135–7. [U.C./Ed.]

HALFNAUS (Ḥalfan, Chalfan), family which migrated from Provence to Italy after 1394 and later moved to Prague and Vienna. The family was linked with the famous *Kalonymus family which was prominent in the Middle Ages. Most of its members were physicians and were well known for their scholarship in science and literature. Abba Mari, a son-in-law of Joseph *Colon, lived in Italy and published in 1490 an elegy and a work on astronomy. His son was *Elijah Menahem. Another Abba Mari (d. 1586) was a physician in Prague. His son Elias (1561–1624) lived first in Prague and was granted his licence as a physician by Rudolf II (1598). With Aaron *Maor Katan (Lucerna) he later achieved prominence as a physician and *dayyan* in Vienna, and was also known as a book collector. He was even proposed as an army surgeon.

A second Ḥalfan family living in Vienna later changed its name to Wechsler. Its members included Eliezer ben Uri Shraga Phoebus (d. 1670), who was head of the community and was apparently the last person to be buried before the 1670 expulsion. His son Uri Shraga Phoebus (c. 1640–1707) headed a yeshivah in Prague. His *Dat Esh*, responsa and novellae on Maimonides' *Yad Hilkhot Kilayim,* was published in Berlin in 1743.

Bibliography: B. Wachstein, *Die Inschriften des alten Judenfriedhofes in Wien,* 1 (1912), index s.v. *Chalfan;* Kisch, in: JGGJC, 6 (1934), 15; Engelmann, in: *Juedische Familienforschung,* no. 4 (1937), 803–5; Bruck, in: HJ, 9 (1947), 161–70. [M.La.]

ḤALFON (Khalfon), ABRAHAM (late 18th century), rabbi in Tripoli. Information about Ḥalfon is limited to the fact that his book, *Ḥayyei Avraham* (Leghorn, 1826), was published posthumously by his son Raḥamim. The *haskamot* (recommendations) for the book were written by two emissaries from Tiberias, Joseph ibn Samon and Samuel Shoshanah, indicating Ḥalfon's ties to that town. The book contains traditional explanations of the commandments in the Shulḥan Arukh (*Oraḥ Ḥayyim* and *Yoreh De'ah*). The explanations, based on the Talmud, the *Zohar, Ketem Paz* (a commentary on the Zohar), *Sefer Ḥasidim,* and *Penei David* by Ḥayyim Joseph David *Azulai, are lucidly and attractively presented and avoid wearying casuistry. The book was published in several succeeding editions: 1844, 1857, 1861. Several other works by him, halakhic and homiletical, are still in manuscript. [Ed.]

ḤALFON BEN NETHANEL HA-LEVI ABU SAʿĪD (12th century), wealthy businessman in Egypt. Ḥalfon's affairs extended from India and Yemen to Spain. Numerous letters, addressed to him from furthest parts of the Jewish Diaspora, which bear evidence of his generosity and wealth, have been found in the Cairo *Genizah.* He was a close friend of *Judah Halevi, who also appears to have been his relative. Some of the letters which were sent by the latter to Ḥalfon have been preserved. It seems that the contacts between them dated from the time of Ḥalfon's visit to Spain in order to arrange personal affairs. Halevi then wrote poems and letters in the former's honor which were published by H.*Brody. When on his way to Ereẓ Israel, Halevi stayed at Ḥalfon's home in Cairo from 1140 to 1141. One of Ḥalfon's brothers was R. Moses b. Nethanel, the *av bet din* of the tribunal of the *gaon* *Maẓli'aḥ b. Solomon Ha-Kohen.

Bibliography: S.D.Goitein, *A Mediterranean Society* (1967), 213, 256, 297, 380; idem, in: *Sinai,* 33 (1953), 228–30; idem, in: *Tarbiz,* 24 (1955), 21–47, 134–49; 25 (1956), 393–412; 28 (1959), 346–61; 31 (1962), 366–8; 35 (1966), 274–7; Schirmann, *ibid.,* 9 (1938), 295; Strauss, in: *Zion,* 7 (1941/42), 145–51; Abramson, in: KS, 29 (1953/54), 136–7, 142. [A.D.]

HALHUL (Heb. חַלְחוּל), town in the territory of Judah mentioned once in the Bible together with Beth-Zur and Gedor (Josh. 15:58). An Idumean village called Aluros (identical with Halhul) is referred to by Josephus (Wars 4:522) as a fortified city which was destroyed by Simeon b.Giora along with Hebron during the Jewish War (66–70/73). Jerome mentions the city Alula belonging to

Jerusalem near Hebron (Eusebius, Onom., 87:11–12). The "tomb of Jonah" was shown there. In the 14th century Jews were living in Halhul and according to tombstone lists compiled by medieval Jewish travelers, the grave of the prophet Gad was located there. Today, the Muslim Arab village Ḥalḥūl is located at the highest spot of the Judean Hills about 3,347 ft. (1020 m.) above sea level, 2.5 mi. (4 km.) north of Hebron. As a result of the proximity of Hebron, Ḥalḥūl expanded in the 1950s and 1960s; in 1968 the village had over 6,000 inhabitants. Fruit orchards and particularly vineyards constituted its principal farming branch.

Bibliography: Nestle, in: ZDPV, 34 (1911), 79; E. Mader, *Altchristliche Basiliken und Lokaltraditionen in Suedjudaea* (1918), 35ff. [M.A.-Y.]

HALICZ (Russ. **Galich**), small town formerly in Poland, now in Stanislaw oblast, Ukrainian S.S.R. The earliest information relating to Jews in Halicz dates from 1488. In 1506, the Jews there were granted a remission of their taxes because of hardship caused by war. Halicz had one of the few organized *Karaite communities to exist continuously in Eastern Europe. It was founded by Karaites from Lvov. They were accorded the same rights "as other Jews" by the Polish monarch in 1578. Until the close of the 18th century the Karaites formed the majority of the Halicz community. Records of 1627 show that 24 houses there were owned by Karaites and only a few by Rabbanites. Subsequently the Rabbanite community increased. In 1765 it numbered 258, while there were 99 Karaites, and in 1900 there were 1,450 Rabbanites and 160 Karaites. In 1921 there were approximately 1,000 Rabbanites and 160 Karaites, who lived in a separate street and worshiped in their own synagogue, built at the end of the 16th century. The number of Rabbanites remained approximately the same in 1939, while the number of Karaites diminished to 100.

The Karaite community looked for cultural guidance to their spiritual center in the East, since the forefathers of the founders came from Crimea and their native language was Tatar. When the links with the parent center became attenuated, the cultural level of the Karaites in Halicz became so poor that by the first half of the 17th century there was no one in the community qualified to serve as *ḥakham* (or *ḥazzan*). The situation improved with the arrival of an emissary from Jerusalem, David Ḥazzan, around 1640. He was followed (c. 1670) by two brothers, Joseph and Joshua. Joseph, who earned the encomium "Ha-Mashbir" ("the provider"), discharged the duties of *ḥakham* and composed *piyyutim* which were included in the Karaite prayer book. His descendants served as *ḥakham-im-ḥazzanim* of the Halicz Karaite congregation until the beginning of the 19th century, when the office was held by members of the Leonovich family. Karaite autonomy was recognized by the Austrian government during the period when Halicz was administered by Austria. Abraham, the first of the Leonovich *ḥakhamim*, was one of the Karaites to be influenced by the ideas of *Haskalah. He corresponded with some of the luminaries of the movement, including Naḥman *Krochmal and Abraham *Geiger, who on their part took an interest in Karaism. Later, around the beginning of the 20th century, with the strengthening of the Polish cultural influence, most of the Karaites tended toward assimilation while a few drew closer to the Rabbanites. No further information is available.

Bibliography: M. Balaban, in: *Studya historyczne* (1927), 1–93; R. Fahn, *Le-Korot ha-Kara'im be-Galizyah* (1870), 2–16. [S.K.]

HALICZ (Heb. **הֶעלִיץ, Helicz, Halic, Helic**), family of printers in Cracow in the 16th century. Three brothers, Samuel, Asher, and Elyakim, sons of Ḥayyim Halicz, established Poland's first Jewish press there in about 1530. Their name indicates that the family originally came from the small town of Halicz on the Dniester in eastern Galicia. Their type and page arrangements show they learned their craft (and probably obtained type and equipment) in Prague. It is likely that they left Prague because a royal order of 1527 designated Gershom *Kohen as Bohemia's sole Hebrew printer; all other Hebrew print shops closed, and the brothers probably could find no further work there. The decorative borders for their opening pages were certainly brought by them from Prague. Three works listed by *Zunz as being from Cracow in 1530 were probably the earliest products of their press. These were: a Pentateuch; Tur, *Yoreh De'ah;* and a Passover *Haggadah* (all otherwise unknown). Their earliest surviving works, both dating from 1534, were *Issur ve-Hetter* by R. Isaac Dueren and *Mirkevet ha-Mishneh,* a Hebrew-Yiddish Bible dictionary by a R. Anshel. Yet evidently they did not prosper, and Asher dropped out.

In 1535 Samuel and Elyakim produced R. David Cohen's *Azharot Nashim* in Yiddish, a work dealing with religious laws for women. Then Elyakim alone issued a Yiddish version of Asher b. Jehiel's *Oraḥ Ḥayyim.* Samuel spent 1536 in Oels, Silesia, where he and his brother-in-law printed a book of *Tefillot mi-Kol ha-Shanah* ("Prayers for All Year") in large type. However, his books and equipment were destroyed in a fire and he returned to Cracow.

It was probably economic misery or possibly excessive pressure from the Polish church that made the three undergo baptism in 1537; they became Andreas (Samuel), Johannes (Elyakim), and Paul (Asher; or perhaps Asher became Andreas, and Samuel was Paul). Repelled by their act, the Jews boycotted them and would not even pay their debts. At the brothers' plea, King Sigismund I issued a decree dated March 28, 1537, commanding that Poland's Jews might buy only their books; no others were to print or sell Jewish works, and none might be brought in from other countries, on pain of a stiff fine. Yet, under tacit excommunication by the Jews, their plight only worsened. Believing, though, that the royal decree must improve matters, Johannes resumed printing in 1538–39, issuing mainly books for popular use.

Through their bishop, the desperate Halicz brothers sought and obtained a new royal decree on December 31, 1539, ordering the Jews of Cracow and Posen to buy their entire stock of some 3,350 volumes, valued at 1,600 florins. Pleading poverty, the two Jewish communities had their coreligionists in Lemberg (Lvov) included in the order. The complete stock of books was paid for in three years and destroyed. The Halicz firm went out of existence. In 1540 Johannes began printing Latin and Polish theological works. Paul, who became a Catholic missionary among the Polish Jews, printed a New Testament (Cracow, 1540–41), in a Judeo-German transcription of Luther's translation. He also produced *Elemental oder Lesebuechlein* (Hundsfeld, 1543), an instruction book in Hebrew for gentiles. Lukasz Halicz, a printer in Posen (1578–93), was apparently his son. Samuel returned to Judaism. After working as a bookbinder in Breslau, he went to Constantinople (c. 1550) and resumed Hebrew printing. He subsequently printed: the Scriptures (1551/52; repenting of his conversion in the colophon); the "Story of Judith" (1552/53); and R. Isaac Dueren's *Issur ve-Hetter,* retitled *Sha'arei Dura* (1553). In 1561–62, when Samuel was no longer living, the name of Ḥayyim b. Samuel Ashkenazi, apparently his son, appears as the printer of the responsa of R. Joseph ibn Lev in part 2.

Bibliography: M. Balaban, in: *Soncino-Blaetter,* 3 (1929/30), 1–9, 36–44; idem, *Yidn in Polyn* (1930), 183–95; Ḥ. D. Friedberg,

Toledot ha-Defus ha-Ivri be-Polanyah (1950), 1–4; A. M. Habermann, in: KS, 33 (1957/58), 509–20; B. Schlossberg, in: *Yivo Bletter*, 13 (1938), 313–24.

[C.W.]

HALIFAX, Atlantic Ocean port and capital of Nova Scotia province, Canada. The Jewish population in 1970 was 1,200. Until recently it was believed that Jews first came to Canada after the British conquest of Quebec in 1759–60. It is now known that shortly after the British founded Halifax as a military base in 1749, a Jewish settlement existed there. Recorded as merchants in 1752 were Israel Abrahams, Isaac Levy, Isaac Solomon, and Nathan Nathans (d. 1778), who by later records lived in Halifax for 27 or 28 years. These settlers, some of whom had families, seem to have come up from the neighboring and older British colonies of New England. Shortly after 1749 a burial ground was set aside for Halifax Jews. By 1758, however, a committee of the assembly and council recommended that the space be used as a site for a workhouse. Samuel *Hart was in Halifax in the 1790s and sat in the House of Assembly for the town of Liverpool from 1793 to 1799. He, not (as hitherto supposed) Selim *Franklin, was thus the first Jew to sit in a Canadian legislature. The Halifax Jewish community later dwindled and virtually vanished; in 1861, the first year for which a census of Jewish population exists, three Jews were living in the city. In 1881 there were at least 16 and ten years later, only two more. By 1901, however, the figure rose to 102. It more than doubled by 1911 and grew slowly but steadily thereafter. The 1961 census showed 1,188 Halifax Jews. By 1902 an Orthodox synagogue, the Baron de Hirsch Hebrew Benevolent Society, also known as Beth Israel Synagogue, had been founded. The building was demolished in 1917 in a disastrous explosion caused by the collision of a steamship carrying TNT with another ship, but was soon reestablished. A Conservative congregation, Shaar Shalom, also serves the community. The Canadian Jewish Congress and the Federated Zionist Organization of Canada maintain a joint regional office for the Atlantic provinces of Canada in Halifax. The city had a Jewish mayor, Leonard A. Kitz, from 1955 to 1957.

[B.G.K.]

HALKIN, ABRAHAM SOLOMON (1903–), orientalist and educator; brother of Simon *Halkin. Halkin, who was born in Novo-Bykhov, Russia, was taken to the U.S. in 1914. Halkin was lecturer in Semitic languages from 1928 to 1950 and from 1950 to 1970 professor of Hebrew at the City College of New York. He also taught at the Jewish Theological Seminary from 1929 to 1970. In 1970 he settled in Jerusalem. Halkin edited: part two of al-Baghdādī's *Muslim Schisms and Sects ("al-Farq bayna al-Fira'q")* (1935); the Arabic original and three Hebrew versions of Maimonides' *Iggeret Teiman* (1952); Ibn Aknin's Arabic commentary on the Song of Songs with a Hebrew translation, *Hitgallut ha-Sodot*... (1964); and *Zion in Jewish Literature* (1964). He also worked on a new critical edition and Hebrew translation of Moses Ibn Ezra's *Kitāb al-Muḥāḍara wa-al-Mudhākara,* a classic work on Hebrew poetics, and wrote the introduction to a new edition of J.A. Montgomery's *The Samaritans: The Earliest Jewish Sect* (1968). He was editor of the Encyclopaedia Judaica's department of Judeo-Arabic literature and medieval translations.

[Ja.L.]

HALKIN, SHMUEL (1897–1960), Soviet Yiddish poet. Born in Rogachev, Belorussia, Halkin grew up in a ḥasidic home and early came under the influence of Hebrew poetry and wrote Hebrew lyrics. When publication in Hebrew was banned in Soviet Russia, he turned to Yiddish and was encouraged by Peretz *Markish in Kiev and by David *Hofstein in Moscow. His first book of lyrics, *Lider,* appeared in 1922. Other volumes of poems and plays followed between 1929 and 1948. Until 1924, Halkin belonged to a Zionist circle and contemplated settling in Palestine, as is evident from a Hebrew song, *Shir ha-Ḥaluẓah,* written at this time and published in Israel after his death. In his autobiography, he acknowledged the influence of Judah Halevi and Solomon ibn Gabirol in the shaping of his lyric personality. Attacked for his Jewish nationalism, his nostalgic despair, and his deviation from the Communist party line on literature, he was compelled to recant his literary heresies. Thereafter, he avoided controversial themes and published Yiddish translations of English, American, and Russian classics, but his sublimated love for the Jewish people continued to find veiled expression. *Shulamis* (1940), a dramatic poem, based on *Goldfaden, and a verse drama, *Bar Kokhva* (1939), were staged by Yiddish theaters. In the latter he describes in a communist-ideological spirit the social and class differences between Bar Kokhba and R. Akiva on the one hand and the rich classes of Judea on the other. However, the poem also expresses a desire for the national freedom of the Jews, a fact which, considering the times, was daring and uncommon in Russia.

Shmuel Halkin, Soviet Yiddish poet. Courtesy Genazim, Tel Aviv.

His dramatic poem on the Warsaw Ghetto uprising was scheduled for the Moscow Yiddish Theater in 1948, but the theater was closed when the Jewish Anti-Fascist Committee was liquidated that year and Halkin was arrested as one of its prominent members and exiled to Siberia. He was released in 1955 when his health broke down in prison. He was rehabilitated in 1958 and a Russian translation of his poems then appeared. After his death in 1960, his native city named a street after him, and in 1966 a selection of his Yiddish lyrics was issued in Moscow. He was a cousin of Simon and Abraham S. *Halkin.

His play *Ghettogrod* is about the destruction of European Jewry. After his return from exile he published a poem, *The Confessions of Socrates* (*Parizer Tsaytung,* 1956/57), in which Halkin gives expression through the mouth of the doomed philosopher, to his own thoughts during the period of his imprisonment. He translated into Yiddish some of Shakespeare's plays and also some of the works of Pushkin, Gorki, and other Russian authors.

Bibliography: LNYL, 3 (1960), 41ff.; J. Glatstein, *In Tokh Genumen* (1947), 350–8, C. Madison, *Yiddish Literature* (1968), 409–11.

[S.L.]

HALKIN, SIMON (1898–), Hebrew poet, novelist, and educator. Born in Dobsk near Mohilev, Russia, he emigrated to the United States in 1914. He taught at the Hebrew Union College School for Teachers in New York City (1925–32), and after settling in Ereẓ Israel in 1932, he taught English at a Tel Aviv high school. In 1939, he returned to America and became professor of Hebrew literature at the Jewish Institute of Religion in New York. He was appointed professor of Modern Hebrew Literature at the Hebrew University in 1949.

Simon Halkin, Hebrew writer and educator. Courtesy Hebrew University, Jerusalem. Photo Werner Braun, Jerusalem.

In Halkin's works, metaphysical flights coalesce with earthly desires. This dichotomy already appears in his first novel *Yeḥi'el ha-Hagri* (1928) whose main character is torn between love of God and love of woman. It receives a more mature expression in *Be-Yamim Shishah ve-Leilot Shivah* (1929), a cycle of 36 sonnets; in *"Al Ḥof Santa Barbara"* (1928); and in *"Tarshishah."* These and other poems were collected in *Al ha-I* ("On the Island," 1945). Other motifs in Halkin's poetry are the tension between the death wish and the will to live, the loss of religious faith and the consolation which comes with the acceptance of the agony of living. In *Ma'avar Yabbok* ("The Ford of the Jabbok," 1965), Halkin deals in depth with the death motif. The speaker, obsessed with the love of his dead lover, discovers that the memory of love alone is able to sustain him through the agony of living. *"Ya'akov Rabinowitz be-Yarmouth"* is Halkin's maturest treatment of this theme. The poem depicts an encounter with a dead friend and writer and the ensuing dialogue across the chasm of death is punctuated by the knowledgeable irony of two men who have lived long and have learned the secret of resignation.

Halkin's works in literary criticism include *Arai va-Keva* ("Transient and Permanent," 1952), his unedited lectures on the history of modern Hebrew literature (mimeographed), and his English *Trends in Modern Hebrew Literature* (1950). The latter is a socio-historical appraisal of Hebrew writing during the last 200 years. Though a long-time resident of the United States, he expresses a negative attitude toward American Judaism and insists that its spiritual resources are limited, a view which permeates his unfinished novel *Ad Mashber* (1945) and his monograph *Yehudim ve-Yahadut ba-Amerikah* (1946).

Of his numerous translations, that of Walt Whitman's *Leaves of Grass* (1952) is outstanding. He also translated Shakespeare's *Merchant of Venice* (1929) and *King John* (1947); Jack London's *Before Adam* (1921) and *The Sea Wolf* (1924); and Shelley's *A Defense of Poetry* (1928).

A list of English translations of his work appears in Goell, Bibliography, index.

Bibliography: Malachi, in: *Yad la-Kore*, 3 (1951–53), 32–38; A. Epstein, *Soferim Ivrim ba-Amerikah*, 1 (1952), 172–208; *Gilyonot*, 23 (1949), 133–44; Kressel, Leksikon, 1 (1965), 617f.; Waxman, Literature, 4 (1960^{2}), 1073f.; R. Wallenrod, *Literature of Modern Israel* (1956), index.

[El.S.]

ḤALLAH (Heb. חַלָּה), a form of bread (II Sam. 6:19). The term also applies to the portion of dough set aside and given to the priest (Num. 15:19–20). The etymology of the word is traced either to the Hebrew root for "hollow" and "pierce" (Heb. חלל, *ḥll*), suggesting a perforated and/or rounded loaf, or to the Akkadian *ellu* ("pure"), referring to the bread's sacral use. Until new evidence allows more precision, however, *ḥallah* must be rendered "loaf" (parallel to the Hebrew word *kikkar*, cf. Ex. 29:23; Lev. 8:26). In the Bible, *ḥallah* is a bread offering subsumed under *minḥah*, the grain sacrifice. Commonly used in an unleavened form, and only rarely in a leavened form (Lev. 7:13; probably Num. 15:20), the bread is made with or without oil (Ex. 29:2, 23; Lev. 2:4; 7:12; 8:26; 24:5; Num. 6:15, 19).

[J.Mi.]

Post-Biblical. According to the rabbis, the precept of setting aside *ḥallah* applies to dough kneaded from one of the *five species of grain (Ḥal. 1:1), since only from them can the bread (referred to in Num. 15:19: "when you eat of the bread of the land" etc.) be made, although Philo (Spec. 132) limits it to wheat and barley alone. The time of setting aside the *ḥallah* was derived by the sages from the words, "Of the first of your dough"—which they interpreted as meaning "as soon as it becomes dough"—hence one may eat casually of dough before it forms a ball in the case of wheat, and a lump in the case of barley (Sif. Num. 110), i.e., when the kneading is finished. If, however, it had not been set aside from the dough it must be set aside from the baked bread *(ibid.)*. The Septuagint translates the word *ḥallah* as baked bread (ἄρτος), and both Philo and Josephus (Ant. 4:71) also imply that the precept of setting aside the *ḥallah* applies to baked bread. The quantity of dough from which *ḥallah* must be taken is not explicitly stated in the Bible, and Shammai and Hillel already differed on the quantity (Eduy. 1:2). In later generations, however, the quantity was fixed, based on the words "Of the first of your dough," which was taken to mean "as much as your dough was," viz, "the dough of the wilderness." How much was this? It is written (Ex. 16:36): "Now an *omer* is the tenth part of an *ephah*" (Er. 83a–b). It was accordingly laid down that dough is liable for *ḥallah* if it is kneaded from a bulk of at least 43 1/5 medium-size eggs (approximately $1\frac{3}{4}$ kg.; Maim. Yad, Bikkurim 6:15; Sh. Ar., YD 324:1), and as a mnemonic the sages pointed out that the numerical value of the word *ḥallah* is 43. Since the Bible does not specify the amount of *ḥallah* to be given, according to the letter of the law even a single barley corn exempts the whole dough, but the sages fixed a quantity in accordance with the size of the whole dough: "a householder whose dough is usually small sets aside 1/24; a baker sets aside 1/48." According to biblical law the obligation to separate *ḥallah* applies only to Ereẓ Israel, and "even in Israel there is no Torah obligation except when all Israel [i.e., the majority] are there" (cf. Ket. 25a). So that the obligation of *ḥallah* should not be forgotten, however, the rabbis made it obligatory to separate it nowadays too, and even outside Ereẓ Israel.

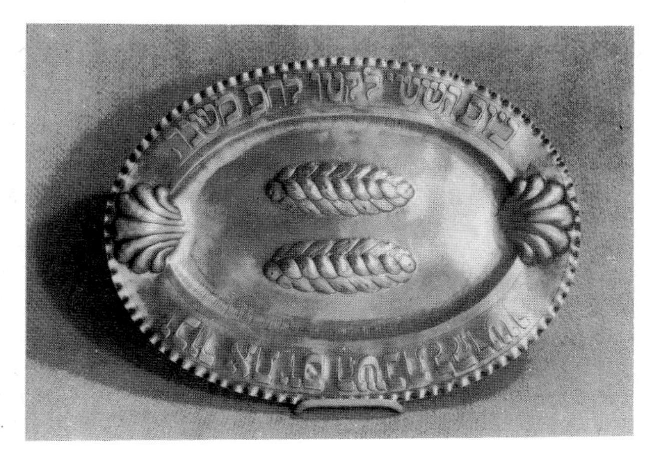

Figure 1. Silver *ḥallah* platter. Formerly Detroit, Charles Feinberg Collection. Photo Manning Bros., Detroit.

Figure 2. Girls learning to make *ḥallah*. From *Challenge*, Lubavich Foundation, London, 1970.

Ḥallah is one of the 24 perquisites of the priest (cf. Ezek. 44:30): "in order that the priests, who are always occupied with Divine service, should live without any exertion" (*Sefer ha-Ḥinnukh*, no. 385). *Ḥallah* must be eaten by priests in a state of ritual purity; the commoner who eats it deliberately is liable to the penalty of **karet*, and if eaten inadvertently must pay its value plus an added fifth to the priest, in the same way as a commoner who eats **terumah*. Nowadays since the obligation to give *ḥallah* is rabbinic and the priests are unable to eat it because of ritual uncleanness, it is customary to set aside an olive's bulk from any dough liable for *ḥallah* and to burn it. The precept of *ḥallah* is the subject of a special tractate of the Mishnah in the order *Zera'im* that bears its name and the Jerusalem Talmud also has a *Gemara* to it. The word *ḥallah* is popularly employed for the special Sabbath loaves.

For illustations see *Food, vol. 6, cols. 1419–20.

[I.BU.]

Bibliography: IN THE BIBLE: D. Z. Hoffman, *Sefer Va-Yikra*, 1 (1953), 107; Ben-Yehuda, Millon, 2 (1960), 1559; K. Elliger, *Leviticus* (Ger., 1966), 46. POST-BIBLICAL: Mishnah, *Ḥallah;* Maim., Yad, Bikkurim, 5–8; Sh. Ar., YD 322–30; Epstein, Tanna'im, 269–75; Ḥ. Albeck (ed.), *Shishah Sidrei Mishnah*, 1 (1958), 271–3.

ḤALLAH (Heb. חַלָּה), tractate in the order *Zera'im* dealing with the laws of **ḥallah* and its separation. The first chapter discusses the species liable to *ḥallah* and to the tithes, chapter 2 fruits from outside Ereẓ Israel entering and vice versa, and the laws of ritual purity and impurity in the kneading of the dough as well as the minimum quantities which established liability. Chapter 3 deals with the details of the laws of dough, and chapter 4 with the combination of different species and the laws of *ḥallah* in Syria and various parts of Israel. In chapter 4:10 and 11 have been preserved traditions from the time of the Temple about the bringing of *ḥallah*, first fruits, and firstborn animals from outside Ereẓ Israel to Jerusalem. It has *gemara* in the Jerusalem but not in the Babylonian Talmud. The Tosefta has only two chapters and the order of its *halakhot* differs from that of the Mishnah. Chapter 2:7–9 gives "the 24 priestly perquisites" and these have been added to the Mishnah in several manuscripts. It was translated into English by H. Danby in *Mishnah* (1933).

Bibliography: Ḥ. Albeck (ed.), *Shishah Sidrei Mishnah*, 1 (1958), 271–3; Epstein, Tanna'im, 269–75.

[ED.]

HALLE, city in E. Germany. Although Jews may well have been present in Halle at the end of the 11th century, the first definite information on their settlement in the city comes from the second half of the 12th century. Then under the protection of the archbishop of Magdeburg, they were hated by the burghers: in 1206 their houses were burned or looted—some were killed and the rest expelled from the city. However, in the mid-13th century there were again Jews in Halle, living in a special quarter, and mainly engaged in moneylending. In 1261, most of their property was confiscated by the archbishop, serving as a cause for a two-year war between the archbishop and the burghers. During persecutions accompanying the *Black Death (1350) the community was destroyed, but in the 14th and 15th centuries Jews returned once more to Halle. The renewed community existed until 1493, when the expulsion of the Jews was decreed. It possessed both a synagogue and a *mikveh*, and a cemetery existed long before 1350. Toward the end of the 17th century the elector of Brandenburg allowed several Jews to settle in Halle, to the dismay of the burghers. In 1693 a Jewish cemetery was officially designated and a synagogue dedicated in 1700. The government recognized the community in 1704. About 1708 a Hebrew printing press was set up in Halle by J. H. Michaelis, for whom the wandering proselyte printer Moses b. Abraham and his son Israel (of Amsterdam) printed a Hebrew Bible (1720). With the help of generous patrons, in 1709 Moses himself began to print some Talmud tractates.

The number of Jews in Halle increased from 12 families in 1700 to 50 in the middle of the 18th century. They were emancipated in 1808 and the community, numbering 150 persons, was given a constitution. In 1840 there were 167 members of the community, 443 in 1864, 660 in 1900, 1,902 in 1920, and 1,100 in 1933 (0.5% of the total population). On Nov. 10, 1938 the synagogue and communal center were

Copperplate engraving from a title page of a Hebrew-Latin Mishnah, illustrating the tractate *Ḥallah*, showing women kneading dough and giving the dough-offering *(ḥallah)* to the kohanim. Amsterdam, 1700–1704. Jerusalem, J.N.U.L.

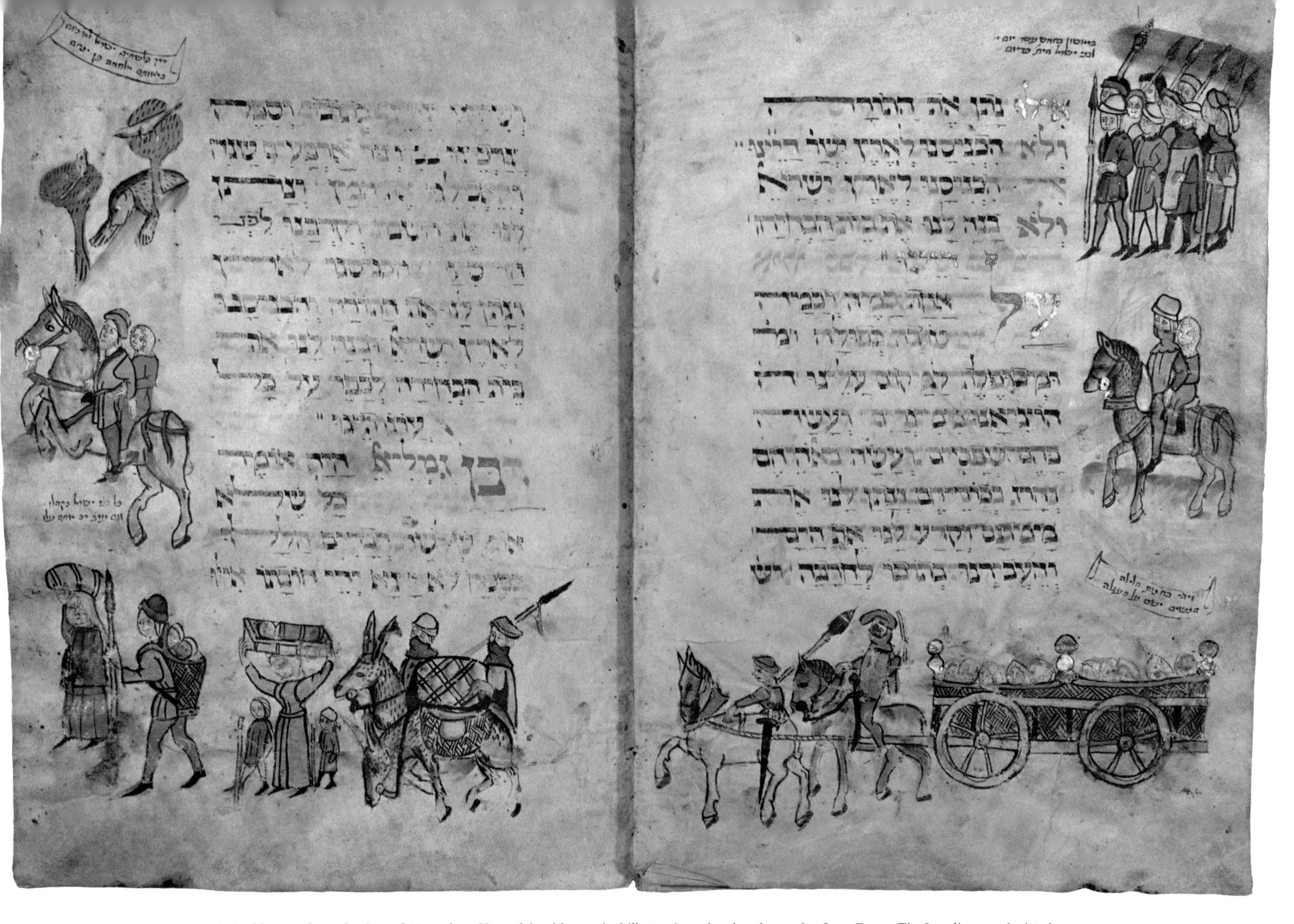

A double page from the *Second Nuremberg Haggadah,* with marginal illustrations showing the exodus from Egypt. The Israelites are depicted as armed soldiers, on horseback, in a carriage, and on foot. The illustrations are accompanied by rhymed explanations. Germany, mid-15th century. Jerusalem, Schocken Library, ms. 24 087, folios 19v–20 ($10\frac{1}{8} \times 7\frac{1}{8}$ ins/25.5 × 18 cm.).

emolished. Two hundred men were arrested and sent to Buchenwald; three of them lost their lives. In 1939 only 37 Jews remained in Halle and on July 1, 1944, 92 were still ving there. The community was renewed after World War and numbered 50 in 1966 (.02% of the population).

Bibliography: Germ Jud, 1 (1963), 124–30, 508–12; 2 (1968), 19–22; S. Neufeld, *Die Halleschen Juden im Mittelalter* (1915); S. chultze-Gallera, *Die Juden zu Halle im Mittelalter* . . . (1922); G. isch, in: *Sachsen und Anhalt; Jahrbuch der historischen ommission fuer die Provinz Sachsen und fuer Anhalt*, 4 (1928), 32–66; 5 (1929), 332–46; 6 (1930), 306–36; idem, in: ZGJD, 2 930), 166–8; H. D. Friedberg, *Toledot ha-Defus ha-Ivri* . . . (1937), 4–75; T. Tykocinski, in: MGWJ, 57 (1908), 32–43; S. Stern, *er preussische Staat und die Juden*, 1 (1962), index; 2 (1962), o. 513–67.

[Z.Av.]

ALLE, MORRIS (1923–), U.S. linguist. Born in iepaja, Latvia, Halle was educated in American universi- es, and began his teaching career as an instructor of ussian at North Park College, Chicago. Thereafter he ctured at Chicago and at Harvard, and in 1951 he joined e faculty of the Massachusetts Institute of Technology, here he became professor of modern languages in 1961.

Halle was renowned for his research in linguistic science. ussian, Slavic, and English were the languages most often volved in Halle's linguistic studies. He also focused on the nguistic aspects of Swedish, Arabic, German, Polish, ld and American English, the dialects of Southern ussia, and—in one case—Hebrew ("The Term *Canaan* in ledieval Hebrew," by R. Jakobson and M. Halle, in *For 1ax Weinreich on his 70th Birthday* (1964), pages 147– 72). Halle noted the implications of the computer for nguistics, and co-authored "On the Recognition of Speech y Machine" (in *Proceedings of the International Conference 1 Information Processing 1959* (1960), 252–6). He received cognition for his book, *The Sound Pattern of Russian* 959), and for two books he co-authored, *The Sound attern of English* (1968), and *Preliminaries to Speech nalysis* (1952, 5th repr. 1963). [Ed.]

ALLEGUA, family of White Jews in *Cochin. Originally om Aleppo, Syria, the family provided communal leaders om the 17th century until the present day. One of the first corded members was Moses Hallegua (Aleguo), whose ombstone is dated 1666. The title and office of the *mudaliar* ead of the autonomous Jewish community in Cochin) fell the Hallegua family when this hereditary position ecame vacant. When *Anquetil-Duperron visited Cochin 1757, Joseph Hallegua held the office. Hayyim Joseph ALLEGUA, who moved to Bombay, was instrumental in ublishing in 1846 the Marathi translation of the Passover *laggadah* of the *Bene Israel.

Bibliography: J. H. Lord, *Jews in India* (1907), 97; Fischel, in: *erzl Yearbook*, 4 (1961–62), 316–8; J. J. Cotton, *List of 1scriptions . . . in Madras* (1905), 274, no. 1550.

[W.J.F.]

ALLEL (Heb. הַלֵּל), the general term designating Psalms 13–118 when these form a unit in the liturgy. These psalms re essentially expressions of thanksgiving and joy for ivine redemption. *Hallel* is recited in two forms: (a) The full" *Hallel*, consisting of Psalms 113–118. It is chanted in e synagogue on *Sukkot, *Hanukkah, the first day of Passover (the first two days in the Diaspora), *Shavuot Tosef., Suk. 3:2, Ta'an. 28b), and (in many synagogues) srael *Independence Day. *Hallel* is also recited during the assover **seder* service (Tosef., Suk. 3:2), when it is known s *Hallel Mizri* ("Egyptian *Hallel*") because of the exodus rom Egypt which the *seder* commemorates (Ber 56a; cf. Rashi ad loc.). On this occasion it is recited in two parts Pes. 10:5–7; Maim. Yad, Hamez u-Mazzah 8:5). (b) The "half" *Hallel*, consisting of the "full" *Hallel*, excepting Psalms 115:1–11, and 116:1–11. According to the Yemenite rite, the order is slightly different, based on Maimonides (Yad, Hanukkah 3:8). It is recited in the synagogue on the *New Moon (Ta'an. 28b; but see also Ar. 10a–b) and on the last six days of Passover (Ar. 10b).

The term *Hallel ha-Gadol* ("Great *Hallel*") refers only to Psalm 136 (Tosef. Ta'an. 3:5) which is recited during **Pesukei de-Zimra* at the morning service on Sabbaths and on festivals (Tos. to Ta'an 26a). It is the daily psalm on the last day of Passover (Sof. 18:2), and is added to the *seder Hallel* (Pes. 118a; TJ, Pes. 5:7, 32c). According to the Mishnah (Ta'an 3:9), this psalm was sung on joyous communal occasions, e.g., the long-awaited rain after a period of severe drought.

In the Talmud, various origins are attributed to the custom of chanting *Hallel*. R. Eleazar claims that it was Moses and the people of Israel who first recited *Hallel;* R. Judah states that it was the Prophets who instituted its recitation for every occasion that the people of Israel should be redeemed from potential misfortune (Pes. 117a). The Talmud relates that *Hallel* was recited by the levites in the Temple (Tos. to Pes. 95b), and it was also chanted on Passover eve while the paschal lambs were being slaughtered (Pes. 5:7). *Hallel* became part of the synagogue service at an early stage, and in talmudic times, communities in Erez Israel added it to the end of the evening service for Passover (TJ, Pes. 10:1, 37c). This practice later spread to the Diaspora (Sof. 20:9), and is still the custom among Oriental Jews and Hasidim (Sh. Ar., OH 487:4; but see Isserles ad loc.) and in most synagogues in Israel.

Hallel is recited on all major biblical festivals, with the exception of *Rosh Ha-Shanah and the Day of Atonement; the solemnity of those occasions, when each mortal's destiny and fate is being decided, is deemed unsuitable for psalms of joy (Ar. 10b). Similar considerations caused these psalms to be omitted in a house of mourning on the New Moon and Hanukkah (Magen Avraham to Sh. Ar., OH 131:4). *Hallel* is not recited on *Purim, since the scroll of Esther is considered the festival's *Hallel* (Ar. 10b; Meg. 14a). One rabbinic tradition is that only the "half" *Hallel* is recited on the last six days of Passover because joy is mitigated by the calamity that then befell the Egyptian host when pursuing the Israelites (see Meg. 10b); another reason given is because no different sacrifice was offered each day (Ar. 10b). On Sukkot the *lulav* is waved during the refrains of Psalm 118:1–4, 25, and 29 (Suk. 3:9). *Hallel* may be recited at any time during the day (Meg. 2:5), although in the synagogue it is recited immediately after the morning service (RH 4:7). Special benedictions are recited before and after *Hallel* except at the *seder* service when no benediction is recited before it.

There is a difference of opinion among the early authorities as to whether the obligation to recite the *Hallel* is to be considered biblical or rabbinical (see *Sefer Mitzvot Katan* 146, *Yere'im ha-Shalem* 262; Maim. Yad, Hanukkah 3:6; *Sefer ha-Mitzvot*, ch. 1). The recitation on the New Moon is considered to be a custom (Ta'an. 28b), and there are some opinions that it is only recited in congregational prayers on that day. Similarly there are authorities who ruled that for the full *Hallel* the benediction should read "Blessed art Thou . . . who hast commanded us to finish *(ligmor)* the Hallel" instead of the customary "to read *(likro)* the Hallel." According to the *tosafot* (Sot. 32a, s.v. *Keri'at Shema*), *Hallel* may be recited in any language (see also Tosef., Sot. 7:7). It should be read standing (*Shibbolei ha-Leket* 173; Sh. Ar., OH 322:7), except at the *seder* service. Various traditions are related to the manner in which the *Hallel* is chanted. In some communities, it was

The beginning of the *Hallel* from the *Barcelona Haggadah*, Spain, 14th century. The first word *Hallelujah* is incorporated in a picture of worshipers in a synagogue. London, British Museum, Add. Ms. 14761, fol. 65v.

sung antiphonally (Tosef., Sot. 6:2); in others (as is still the practice among Yemenite Jews) the congregation responded with *hallelujah* after each half of a verse (Suk. 3:10; TJ, Shab. 16:1, 16c). Among Ashkenazi Jews, it is customary to repeat Psalm 118:1, 21–29 (see Suk. 3:10 and 39a). Opinions and customs differ regarding the recital of Hallel on Israel Independence Day.

For musical rendition see *Psalms.

Bibliography: Abrahams, Companion, 184ff.; Zeitlin, in: JQR, 53 (1962/63), 22–29; Finkelstein, in: HUCA, 23 (1950–51), part 2, 319–37; E. Levy, *Yesodot ha-Tefillah* (1952²), 209–13; ET, 9 (1959), 390–432; Idelsohn, Liturgy, 134, 158–9. [Ed.]

HALLELUJAH (Heb. הַלְלוּיָהּ), liturgical expression occurring 23 times, exclusively in the Book of Psalms. Apart from 135:3, it invariably appears as either the opening (106, 111–3, 135, 146–50) or closing word of a psalm (104–6, 113, 115–7, 135, 146–50) or in both positions (106, 113, 135, 146–50). In all cases, with the exception of 135:3 and 147:1, the term is not part of the body of the psalm. This fact, together with its total nonappearance in those psalms cited in other biblical books (cf. Ps. 106:48 with I Chron. 16:36) and its restriction to the last divisions of the Psalter (cf. Ber. 9b), suggest a late coinage.

It is generally agreed that Hallelujah means, "praise [ye] the Lord." The plural imperative form of the verb would indicate that the term was a directive to the worshiping congregation in the Temple by the presiding functionary which was meant to evoke a public response. In the course of time it became an independent cultic exclamation so that the Greek-speaking Jews simply transliterated it (LXX, Ἀλληλούϊα). On the other hand, a consciousness of its composite nature is preserved in amoraic discussions as to whether the Hebrew should be rendered by the scribes as one word or two (Pes. 117a; Sof. 5:10, TJ, Suk. 3:12, 53d TJ, Meg. 1:11, 72a). A novel explanation is given by R Joshua b. Levi who regards the final syllable as a superlative suffix and who translates the term, "praise Him with many praises" (Pes. 117a). [N.M.S.]

In Music. The tradition of rendering the word Hallelujah at the beginning and/or end of a psalm, by a special melodic phrase is certainly very old, judging by its survival in the usages of many Jewish communities. In some of them, the word is even added at the end of each verse on some occasions. The Yemenites prefix "Hallelujah" or "Ve-Hallelujah" to certain festive *piyyutim*, which are therefore called *Halleluyot*. Christian tradition attests the practice of "Hallelujah-singing" from the earliest periods especially in a form which may or may not have been taken over from Jewish practice: songs on the single word, in which the "lu" and "jah" syllables were drawn out as long flourishes, until they became the so-called *Jubilus*—a wordless ecstatic outpouring. In the Middle Ages these long Hallelujahs began to serve as the basis, in the lower or middle voice, of elaborate compositions in which the upper voices uttered a poetic expression of praise. Sometimes the word itself was split—as in the 13th-century three-voiced "*Alle*-psallite-cum-*luja*" (see A. T. Davison and W. Apel (eds.), *Historical Anthology of Music*, 1 (1964²), 35). During the Renaissance and Baroque periods the *Jubilus*-like setting of the word *Alleluia* is found again, of course in the form of elaborate polyphonic compositions; the word also became a favorite vehicle for canons. The tradition continues until today, for example: the "Hallelujah chorus" in Handel's *Messiah*, Mozart's *Alleluja* for soprano and orchestra (actually the second part of his motet *Exsultate, jubilate*, K. 165), and the great *Alleluja* pieces in William Walton's *Belshazzar's Feast* (1929–31) and Arthur Honegger's *Le Roi David* (1921). [B.B.]

Bibliography: In Music: G. Reese, *Music in the Middle Ages* (1940), index, s.v. *Alleluia;* B. Staeblein, in: MGG, 1 (1949), 331–50; E. Gerson-Kiwi, in: *Festschrift Heinrich Besseler* (1961), 43–49 (Eng.).

HALLER'S ARMY (**"Blue Army"**), force of Polish volunteers organized in France during the last year of World War I, responsible for the murder of Jews and anti-Jewish pogroms in Galicia and the Ukraine. The group was organized on the initiative of the Polish National Council (K.N.P.), achieved French recognition in June 1917, and with the appearance in Paris in July 1918 of General Józef Haller, known for his struggles for Polish freedom within the framework of the Polish legions, command was transferred to him. The political direction lent by the National Council in Paris, headed by Roman *Dmowski, gave the group an extreme nationalistic character. The army had about 50,000 men who moved to the southeast front in Poland during the months of April, May, and June, 1919. The addition of Haller's substantial forces to the regular Polish army enabled the Poles to conquer eastern Galicia. Foreign officers and the ties with France kept Haller's forces independent of the official Polish command, a fact exploited by Haller's soldiers (called the "Hallerczycy") for undisciplined and unbridled excesses against Jewish communities in Galicia. Attacks on individual Jews on the streets and highways, murderous pogroms on Jewish settlements, and deliberate provocative acts became commonplace. While these may have been o the initiative of individual soldiers, they were known to their officers, if not openly supported by them. In 1920, during the Polish offensive toward Kiev resulting from the Pilsudski-Petlyura alliance, anti-Jewish pogroms occurred in the region.

Józef Haller (1873–1960), who was a member of the Sejm (parliament) from 1922 to 1927, became a member of the Polish government-in-exile during World War II.

Bibliography: A. Micewski, *Z geografii . . . politycznej II Rzeczypospolitej* (1964). [M.LAN.]

HALLGARTEN, family of U.S. bankers. LAZARUS HALLGARTEN (d. 1875), a native of Frankfort, Germany, arrived in New York in 1848 and in 1850 opened an office for exchanging immigrants' currency. By establishing connections with Frankfort and other European banking centers, he and his partners developed a successful foreign exchange business. During the 1860s the firm became prominent as one of the largest gold bullion dealers in the United States. For its role on "Black Friday" (September 24, 1869) in stabilizing the price of gold which had been skyrocketed by the speculations of Jay Gould, the firm received official recognition by the United States Treasury. During the latter part of the 19th century the firm was engaged in the reorganization of the country's major railroads, and expanded its trading in bonds and stocks. In 1881 it became a member of the New York Stock Exchange. Meanwhile, Lazarus' sons CHARLES (1838–1908) and JULIUS (d. 1884) had joined the firm, and the financing of industrial combines became a major field for Hallgarten & Co. World War I saw an intensification of the firm's domestic business, and between the two world wars the firm acted as fiscal agents for many foreign governments, and established offices and representations in almost all the European financial centers. With the passing of the 1934 Securities and Exchange Act it limited itself to underwriting and general brokerage business. As late as 1950 the majority of the firm's active members were direct descendants of a partner of Lazarus Hallgarten. Most of the Hallgartens were interested in community activities as well as in the arts. Lazarus' son, Charles, who moved to Frankfort and conducted the firm's banking affairs there, was especially active in philanthropic work. He held a leading position in the *Alliance Israélite Universelle, the Hilfsverein der Deutschen Juden, and the Jewish Colonization Association, and helped to organize efforts for the relief and emigration of the Jewish victims of the Russian pogroms. He was the founder of the Gesellschaft zur Erforschung Juedischer Kunstdenkmaeler (Society for Research of Monuments of Jewish Art). He also helped to found an association for public education and a legal aid office for women.

Bibliography: R. Hallgarten, *Charles L. Hallgarten* (Ger., 1915); *Reden gehalten bei der Beerdigung des Herrn Charles L. Hallgarten* (1908); W. Emrich, *Bildnisse Frankfurter Demokraten* (1956), 2–25; NDB, 7 (1966). [J.O.R.]

HALLO, RUDOLF (1896–1933), German art historian, friend and successor of Franz *Rosenzweig as head of the Freies Juedisches Lehrhaus in Frankfort. Hallo was born in Kassel to a prominent family of court Jews and artisans, which included Israel Aron *Hammerschlag of Prague and his grandson and namesake, who was made a Court Jew in 1657 by Frederick William of Brandenburg. The family tradition of painting, gilding, and synagogue decoration began in 1816, when Simon Hallo became an apprentice housepainter, the medieval painters' guild having opened to Jews in the wake of the Emancipation. The firm Gebrueder Hallo was founded in 1891 and moved to Tel Aviv in 1935. Trained in classical art at the University of Goettingen, Rudolf Hallo contributed significantly to the founding of Jewish art history as a discipline and also wrote on biblical and archaeological subjects. His interest in art history, especially Jewish and Hessian provincial art and handiwork, carried on the family tradition on an academic level.

Franz Rosenzweig was the son of his mother's closest friend. Hallo married Gertrude Rubensohn, also a friend of Rosenzweig and one of his circle (see Rosenzweig's *Briefe*, 285, 288). Upon his incapacitation Rosenzweig designated Hallo to succeed him as head of the Lehrhaus (*Briefe*, 354). Because of differences between the two men concerning educational policy, which stemmed from deeper disagreements in philosophical outlook (cf. *Briefe*, 364, 365), Hallo resigned at the end of the summer trimester of 1923 (*Briefe*, 373). He returned to his native Kassel, and there became curator at a state museum, where he created a department of Jewish art. He continued writing and lecturing. Among Hallo's works are *Juedische Kunst aus Hessen und Nassau* (1933), *Juedische Volkskunst in Hessen* (1928), *Rudolph Erich Raspe* (1934, posthumously), *Geschichte der juedischen Gemeinde Kassel* (1931), and *Judaica* (1932, separate printing from *Religioese Kunst aus Hessen und Nassau*).

His son, WILLIAM W. HALLO (1928–), Assyriologist, was born in Kassel. He immigrated to the United States in 1940. Hallo taught Bible and Semitic languages at Hebrew Union College in Cincinnati (1956–62), and from 1962 taught Assyriology at Yale University, serving as curator of the Babylonian collection there. He published extensively on ancient Near Eastern and biblical subjects.

Bibliography: R. Hallo, *Geschichte der Familie Hallo* (1930); F. Rosenzweig, *Briefe* (1935); N. N. Glatzer, *Franz Rosenzweig: His Life and Thought* (1953), index; Wininger, Biog., vol. 7, 52. [J.KR.]

HALPER, ALBERT (1904–), U.S. novelist. His first novel, *Union Square* (1933), on a radical theme, was an immediate success. His experiences in a mail order house in his native Chicago and in the Chicago central post office found expression in his novels *The Chute* (1937), *The Little People* (1942), and *The Golden Watch* (1953), a story of a West Side Chicago Jewish family. *The Chute* showed Halper in retreat from the Jewishness of his immigrant parents, presenting a wholly negative picture of American Jewish life. In *Sons of the Fathers* (1940), however, he portrayed Jewish customs and ceremonies with objectivity and even sympathy. *Atlantic Avenue* (1956) is a story of violence in New York City.

Bibliography: F. Champney, in: *Antioch Review*, 2 (1942), 628–34; S. Liptzin, *Jew in American Literature* (1966), 183–6. [S.L.]

HALPER, BENZION (1884–1924), Hebraist, Arabist, and editor. Halper was born in Zhosli (Zasliai), Lithuania. He emigrated to Germany and from there to England. In 1907 he began studying Semitics at the University of London. While at the university he also studied at Jews' College. In 1910 he spent a year in Egypt under university auspices. During this period he contributed regularly to the Hebrew periodical *Ha-Yehudi*. In 1911 Halper went to New York and worked as classifier and copyist of *genizah* fragments in the library of the Jewish Theological Seminary of America. In 1912 he became a Fellow at Dropsie College in Philadelphia, and from 1913 taught there in the departments of rabbinics and cognate (Semitic) languages. In 1923 he was advanced to the rank of associate professor of cognate languages. He also served the college as custodian of manuscripts. From 1916 to 1924 Halper was editor of the Jewish Publication Society of America.

Among the *genizah* fragments brought to Dropsie College by Cyrus Adler, Halper discovered a portion of *Sefer* *ha-Mizvot* ("Book of Precepts") by the tenth-century halakhist and philosopher *Ḥefeẓ b. Yaẓli'aḥ. He translated it into Hebrew and published both the original Arabic text and the translation with an introduction and critical

Benzion Halper, Hebrew and Arabic scholar. *American Jewish Yearbook 1924–25*, Jewish Publication Society, Philadelphia, Pa.

notes as *The Book of Precepts* (1915). His scholarly and at the same time popular anthology, *Post-Biblical Hebrew Literature* (Hebrew and English, 2 vols., 1921), presented some previously unpublished texts as well as critical notes and a glossary. Under the title *Shirat Yisrael* (1924), he published an edition and Hebrew translation of *Kitab al-Muḥadara wal-Mudhakara* ("Book of Discussions and Remembrances") by the 12th-century Hebrew poet, Moses *ibn Ezra, dealing with Hebrew prosody and, more generally, with Jewish life and literature. Halper's last important work was the *Descriptive Catalogue of Geniza Fragments in Philadelphia* (1924), which identifies and describes in detail nearly 500 fragments. Halper's first major essay, entitled "The Participal Formations of Geminate Verbs" (in ZAW, 30 (1910), 42–57, 99–126, 201–28), discussed Hebrew roots from אבב to תפף. His major studies included "The Scansion of Medieval Hebrew Poetry" (in JQR, 4 (1914), 153–224), "An Autograph Responsum of Maimonides" (*ibid.*, 6 (1916), 225–9), "A Dirge on the Death of Daniel Gaon" (*ibid.*, 10 (1920), 411–20), and analyses of *genizah* discoveries and Jewish literature in Arabic (in *Ha-Tekufah*, 1923, 1924, 1928).

Bibliography: C. Adler, in: AJYB, 26 (1924), 459–71; J. N. Simchoni, in: *Ha-Tekufah*, 23 (1927), 490–500; I. M. Elbogen, *ibid.*, 24 (1928), 541–2. [M.B.-H.]

HALPERIN, YEḤIEL (1880–1942), Hebrew educator. Born in Priluki, Ukraine, Halperin taught in Y. Adler's "progressive *ḥeder*" in Gomel and later in S. L. *Gordon's in Warsaw. In 1909 he established the first Hebrew kindergarten in Warsaw, and, in 1910, a Hebrew seminary for kindergarten teachers. At the outbreak of World War I (1914) Halperin moved to Odessa where he established a similar seminary. Emigrating to Palestine in 1920, he served as a supervisor of Hebrew kindergartens from 1922 to 1925, and was appointed head of the Kindergarten Department of the Teachers' Seminary and of the Levinsky Kindergartens in Tel Aviv (1926). In 1936 he founded a special college for kindergarten teaching in Tel Aviv, which continued to function until 1941. Halperin published a journal devoted to the interests of the Hebrew kindergarten, *Ha-Ginnah* (in Odessa, from 1918; then in Jerusalem, from 1922). His collected works were published posthumously in three volumes: *Shi'urim be-Torat Ḥinnukh ha-Tinokot* (1944); *Be-Keren Zavit* (1945), kindergarten play songs; and *Mah Sipper Yare'aḥ Li* (1952), eight legends.

Bibliography: Epstein, in: *Hed ha-Ḥinnukh*, 17 (1943), 59–62; I. Gruenbaum, *Penei ha-Dor*, 1 (1957), 316–9; Spivak, in: D. Levin (ed.), *Al ha-Rishonim* (1959), 63–68. [G.El]

HALPERN, BENJAMIN (Ben, 1912–), U. S. sociologist, educator, and Zionist. Halpern, who was born in Boston, Massachusetts, was active in the Zionist movement and Jewish affairs from his youth. He served as national secretary of the He-Ḥalutz Organization of America (1936–37), managing editor of the *Jewish Frontier* magazine (1943–49), and associate director of the departments of culture, education, and publications of the Jewish Agency (1949–56). In 1956 Halpern became research associate in Middle Eastern studies at Harvard University. He began his association with Brandeis University in 1962 and was subsequently appointed professor of Near Eastern studies there. He was a member of the Jewish Agency Executive from 1968. Halpern's scholarly work was closely associated with his Jewish and Labor Zionist commitments and interests. His numerous publications, many of which were published in *Jewish Frontier* and *Midstream* magazines, deal chiefly with problems of Zionism, Israel society, and the role of the Jews in U. S. society. In his *The American Jew: A Zionist Analysis* (1956), which deals with both the implications and realities of assimilation and differences and similarities between U.S. Jews and other Jewish communities, Halpern contends that Jews will never be completely accepted into U.S. life as long as they remain Jews. Halpern's most important book is *The Idea of the Jewish State* (1969[2]), which traces the development of Zionism both as an ideology and a movement. [W.J.C.

HALPERN, GEORG GAD (1878–1962), economist and leading figure in the economic activities of the Zionist Organization. Born in Pinsk, Halpern studied economics in Germany (his doctoral dissertation was entitled *Die juedischen Arbeiter in London*, 1903). He became active in Zionist affairs in his youth and, beginning in 1903, he attended all Zionist Congresses. During the period of the *Democratic Fraction, he became a close associate of Chaim Weizmann and throughout the years served as an adviser for and administrator of the financial affairs and economic institutions of the Zionist Organization. He also wrote on economic affairs for the German press and was the director of an oil company. From 1921 to 1928 he was a director of the *Jewish Colonial Trust in London. Halpern was the moving force behind various economic institutions sponsored by the Zionist Organization: the Anglo-Palestine Bank, the Palestine Electric Corporation, *Keren Hayesod, the Land Development Co., etc. He settled in Palestine in 1933, founded the Migdal Insurance Co. (1934), and was a member of the board of Bank Leumi.

Bibliography: Tidhar, 10 (1959), 3613; *Sefer Pinsk* (1966), 508–9 [G.K

HALPERN (Halperin), ISRAEL (1910–), Israel historian. Halpern was born in Bialystok, Poland, emigrated to Ereẓ Israel in 1934, began his teaching career at the Hebrew University in 1949, and became professor in 1963. His main interest was the history of East European Jewry, particularly *pinkasim* ("registers"). His publications include *Pinkas Va'ad Arba Araẓot* ("Minutes of the Council of the Four Lands," 1945); *Ha-Aliyyot ha-Rishonot shel ha-Ḥasidim le-Ereẓ Israel* ("Early Ḥasidic Immigration to Palestine," 1956); and *Takkanot Medinat Mehrin* ("Moravian Community Enactments," 1952). He also edited *Sefer ha-Gevurah* (3 vols., 1941, 1951[2]), a historical-literary anthology of Jewish self-defense and martyrdom, and *Beit Yisrael be-Polin* (2 vols., 1948–54), a collection of essays on Polish-Jewish history. Halpern took a leading part in the work of the Israel Historical Society, and was coeditor of the journals *Zion* and *Shivat Ẓiyyon*, publications devoted to the history of Zionism. He was the brother of Lipman *Halpern, the neurologist. [Er

HALPERN, LIPMAN (1902–1968), Israel neurologist, brother of the historian Israel *Halpern. Born in Bialystok, Poland, Halpern settled in Ereẓ Israel in 1934. In 1938 h was invited to start a neuropsychic outpatient clinic at the Hadassah University Hospital, Jerusalem and became head of the newly formed department of neurology in 1941. He was appointed to the faculty of medicine being formed at the Hebrew University-Hadassah Medical School in 1946, becoming dean of the faculty in 1965 and playing an active part in the development of medical education in Israel. In 1953 he was awarded the Israel Prize for Medicine. Halpern won an international reputation for his research on extrapyramidal diseases, the sensory functions, functions of the frontal brain, and the dynamics of aphasia of polyglots. His major work was a study of posture and its relations to the functions of the organism and the influence of sensory stimuli on posture. He also drew attention to the influence of color on the organism. Among his publications is *Le Syndrome d'induction sensorimotrice* (1951). [ED.]

HALPERN, MOSHE LEIB (1886–1932), Yiddish poet. Born in Galicia, he emigrated to the United States in 1908, after participating in the Czernowitz Yiddish Language Conference. In the same year his first poems were published. In New York and Montreal he lived in poverty and loneliness, finding relief from his misery in composing sardonic verses. From 1910 until the end of World War I he participated in the anthologies of the insurgent literary group *Di Yunge*, and was hailed as the group's most robust and independent poet. His first collection of poems, *In New York* (1919), went through three editions and assured him recognition as a major Yiddish poet. It was followed by *Di Goldene Pave* ("The Golden Peacock," 1924). Halpern represented the immigrant Jewish youth of the early 20th century who saw freedom tainted by social injustice. He hated social falsehood and cultural sickness and his undisciplined verses alternated between a strident assertion of individualism and a profound sympathy for the underprivileged.

Bibliography: Rejzen, Leksikon, 1 (1926), 769–72; LNYL, 3 (1960), 31–38; Z. Weinper, *M. L. Halpern* (Yid., 1940); E. Greenberg, *M. L. Halpern* (Yid., 1942); J. Leftwich, *Golden Peacock* (1939). [S.L./SH.B.]

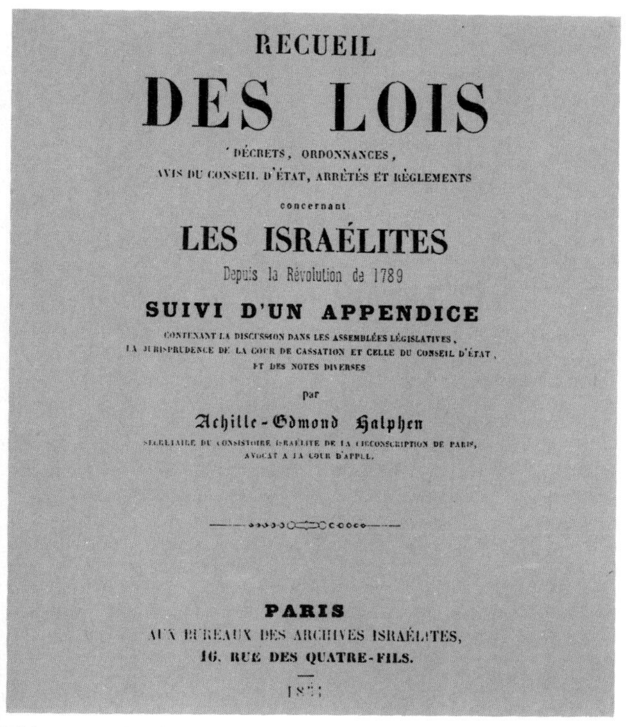
RECUEIL
DES LOIS
DÉCRETS, ORDONNANCES,
AVIS DU CONSEIL D'ÉTAT, ARRÊTÉS ET RÈGLEMENTS
concernant
LES ISRAÉLITES
Depuis la Révolution de 1789
SUIVI D'UN APPENDICE
CONTENANT LA DISCUSSION DANS LES ASSEMBLÉES LÉGISLATIVES,
LA JURISPRUDENCE DE LA COUR DE CASSATION ET CELLE DU CONSEIL D'ÉTAT,
ET DES NOTES DIVERSES
par
Achille-Edmond Halphen
SECRÉTAIRE DU CONSISTOIRE ISRAÉLITE DE LA CIRCONSCRIPTION DE PARIS,
AVOCAT A LA COUR D'APPEL.

PARIS
AUX BUREAUX DES ARCHIVES ISRAÉLITES,
16, RUE DES QUATRE-FILS.
18[illegible]

Title page of Achille-Edmond Halphen's collection of laws concerning the Jews in France from 1789 to 1850. Paris, 1851. Jerusalem, J.N.U.L.

HALPHEN, family of Alsatian origin. They included ACHILLE-EDMOND HALPHEN, who compiled the standard collection of documents on French Jewish history *Recueil des lois, décrets, ordonnances . . . concernant les Israélites depuis la Révolution de 1789* (1851); FERNAND HALPHEN (1872–1918), Parisian composer, who was a pupil of Massenet and Fauré, and composed several orchestral pieces and songs, a one-act opera, and a sonata for violin and piano; GEORGES-HENRI HALPHEN (1844–1889), mathematician, born in Rouen, who taught at the Ecole Polytechnique in Paris and became a member of the Académie des Sciences: in 1881 his work on the classification of curves was granted an award by the Berlin Academy; ALICE FERNAND-HALPHEN (d. 1963) author of a monograph on Gracia Mendes *Nasi (1929); and LOUIS *HALPHEN, historian.

Bibliography: Sendrey, Music, nos. 7889–90 (on F. Halphen); H. Poincaré, *Savants et écrivains* (1910), 125–40; E. Picard, *Mélanges de mathématiques et de physiques* (1924), 1–11. [ED.]

HALPHEN, LOUIS (1880–1950), French historian. Born in Paris, he taught medieval history at the University of Bordeaux from 1910 until 1928 when he became a lecturer in the Paris Ecole des Hautes Etudes and later professor of medieval history at the University of Paris. In 1940 he fled to unoccupied France and taught at the University of Grenoble from 1941 until 1943, after which the Nazis took the city and he went into hiding. In 1944 he returned to Paris and resumed his teaching career at the Sorbonne. Halphen first gained importance as a medieval historian through two publications *Le Comté d'Anjou au XIe siècle* (1906) and *Etudes sur l'administration de Rome au Moyen Age 751–1252* (1907). He adhered strictly to the sources of which he had full command. In his *Initiation aux études d'histoire du Moyen Age* (1940, 1952[3]), he provided an exposition of his methodology as a guide for young scholars. Among his works of broader scope are *L'essor de l'Europe, XIe–XIIIe siècles* (1932, 1948[3]), and *Les Barbares* (1926; 1948[5]) which he wrote for the series *Peuples et Civilisations*. In these books he emphasized the importance of relating European history to Asian and Islamic history. He also wrote *Charlemagne et l'empire Carolingien* (1947).

Bibliography: *Mélanges d'histoire du Moyen Age dédiés à la mémoire de Louis Halphen* (1951), xv–xxiii (list of his publications). [J.B.S.]

HALPRIN, ROSE LURIA (c. 1896–), U.S. Zionist leader, born in New York City of a traditional Jewish family. She studied Hebrew and attended the Teachers' Institute of the Jewish Theological Seminary of America, Hunter College,

Rose Halprin, U.S. Zionist leader. Courtesy Central Zionist Archives, Jerusalem.

and Columbia University. Rose Halprin served as president of Hadassah during 1932–34 and 1947–51. During 1934–39 she lived in Palestine, where she was Hadassah's Palestine correspondent. She was Hadassah's first representative to the Zionist General Council from 1939 to 1946. In 1946 she was elected to the Executive of the Jewish Agency for Palestine and continued in that office for more than 20 years. In 1955 she became acting chairman and from 1960 to 1968 she was chairman of the American Section of the Jewish Agency. During her Hadassah career, Rose Halprin served in many capacities. She was a member of the Board of Governors of the United Jewish Appeal and of the Hebrew University in Jerusalem. [GL.R.]

HALSMAN, PHILIPPE (1906–), U.S. photographer. Halsman, who was born in Latvia, opened a photo studio in Paris and soon gained a reputation as a portrait and fashion photographer. The coming of the Nazis to France forced him to flee to the U.S. By 1956 his work was appearing on the cover of *Life* magazine, which sent him on several assignments round the world. He received international acclaim for his portraits and in 1966 the United States engraved as postage stamps two of Halsman's portraits, one of Adlai Stevenson and the other of Albert Einstein. He was elected the first president of the American Society of Magazine Photographers (ASMP). He published

Philippe Halsman, U.S. photographer. Photo Yvonne Halsman.

the following books: *The Frenchman: Photographic Interview with Fernandel* (1949); *Piccoli: A Fairy Tale* (1953); *Dali's Mustache . . .* (1954); *Jump Book* (1959); and *Halsman on the Creation of Photographic Ideas* (1961). [P.P.]

ḤALUKKAH (Heb. חֲלֻקָּה), financial allowance for the support of the inhabitants of Ereẓ Israel from the contributions of their coreligionists in the Diaspora. In a wider sense, *ḥalukkah* denotes the organized method of this support and the institutions responsible for it, especially after the end of the 18th century. The support given by the Jews of the Diaspora to their brothers in Ereẓ Israel was customary even in ancient times and there are references to it in the periods of the Mishnah and the Talmud. Rabbis left Ereẓ Israel to seek contributions abroad for the support of Torah scholars. During the Middle Ages and especially during the following centuries, this method of support for the inhabitants of Palestine became widespread and encompassed the whole of the Jewish world. The fundamental idea on which the *ḥalukkah* is based is the conviction that Ereẓ Israel held the central position in the religious and national consciousness of the people, hence the special importance accorded to the population residing there. This population is not to be considered as any other entity of Jews, but rather as the representative of the whole Jewish people, the guardian of all that is sacred in the Holy Land; in this role it merits the support of the whole people. The Jews, in the lands of their dispersion, both communities and individuals, were conscious of their duty toward the *yishuv* and considered their support of it as an act of identification with it.

In the 16th century organized methods for the collection of contributions were established in large Jewish centers; the charity-boxes named for R. Meir Ba'al ha-Nes ("The Miracle-Worker") were a popular instrument for the collection of contributions. Communities and national communal organizations urged the public to fulfill its duty and contribute toward the *yishuv*. The communal organizations of Poland, Lithuania, Moravia, and elsewhere included special clauses in their regulations concerning the Palestinian funds and their collection, and even appointed officials for this purpose. The contributions were usually transferred to Palestine through commercial centers and harbor towns which maintained relations with the Orient. From the beginning of the 17th century, Venice was such a center and funds from Poland and Germany passed through there. In the 17th–18th centuries Leghorn also served this purpose. Amsterdam became a center for the contributions of Western Europe from the 17th century onwards. The most important center for the Palestinian funds was Constantinople; it was near Palestine and the capital of the Turkish government. There was also a spiritual affinity between its rabbis and those of Palestine. Contributions from Eastern Europe also passed through there. The Constantinople center not only handled contributions but also intensively encouraged their collection. During the first quarter of the 18th century, the community in Constantinople undertook the improvement of the financial position of the Jerusalem community and tried to extricate it from its heavy debts. A special tax was levied for this purpose and the expenses of Jerusalem were subject to the control of Constantinople.

From the beginning of the 19th century, Vilna attained a special importance as the center for the collection of contributions from Russia, and the Ashkenazi *Perushim* (followers of the Gaon R. Elijah of Vilna) community in Jerusalem depended on this center. In accordance with the (internal) Jewish regulations of 1823, this center had exclusive authority for the collection of all contributions in Russia; its decisions on the distribution of funds to beneficiaries and general expenses were binding. The Amsterdam center, which was reorganized at the beginning of the 19th century under the leadership of Ẓevi Hirsch *Lehren (1784–1853), was also of great importance. It appointed collectors in the important communities of Western Europe and received annual pledges from them. These funds were then distributed between the various communities of Palestine, according to a fixed scale and with the consent of the leaders of the *yishuv*. Besides these centers, which in their time served several countries, there were similar national centers at Frankfort, Vienna, Prague, Pressburg, etc. The collection of contributions was made more efficient by special emissaries who left Palestine for the Diaspora and who described the difficulties in Ereẓ Israel in order to encourage the public in their duty toward the *yishuv*. These missions from Palestine, together with the support of the *yishuv*, were an ancient institution and played an important part in the mutual relationship and binding ties between the Diaspora and the Holy Land. The emissaries of Palestine reached the most far-flung areas of the Jewish world. Apart from this main object, they also gave religious and spiritual guidance, some of these emissaries being prominent scholars.

After the beginning of the 17th century, objections were raised against these missions in order to reduce the expenses involved in them. It was suggested that the collection of funds and their transfer be carried out by the communities themselves. The leaders of the *yishuv* opposed this plan for fear that the living relationship between Palestine and the Diaspora would be ruined; and with the absence of personal contacts, the needs of Palestine Jewry would not be satisfied. In spite of the objections, emissaries continued to visit the Oriental countries. On the other hand, the objections of the Amsterdam center were more determined and these missions were stopped in 1824. The leaders of the *yishuv* agreed to this arrangement but tried to circumvent it periodically by sending emissaries to Western Europe for special needs. Lehren was, however, adamant in his decision. At first, the contributions collected were destined for the scholars and the needy, without any distinction as to their land of origin. With time, however, especially during the last third of the 18th century, a tendency to allocate contributions to a defined section of the *yishuv* came into existence. This development was connected with the new Ashkenazi settlement in the country, and from then onward became a characteristic of the *ḥalukkah*. The first *Ḥasidim to emigrate to Palestine during the last quarter of the 18th century regularly received support from their colleagues in their country of origin. Similar arrangements existed for the *Perushim* who emigrated to Palestine and formed their own community at the beginning of the 19th century. As the Ashkenazim were a small minority and the funds contributed, according to prolonged tradition, were remitted to the Sephardi community, the former felt the necessity to assign the incomes from Eastern Europe for themselves alone. Once their numbers increased, the Ashkenazim requested that a portion of the contributions from the rest of Europe also be given to them. After the 1820s these demands were accepted and from that time regular arrangements were made between the two communities concerning ratios for dividing the income from Western Europe and other countries where Ashkenazi and Sephardi communities existed.

Until the end of the first third of the 19th century, there were two principal sections within the Ashkenazi community, the Ḥasidim and the *Perushim*. In the late 1830s, the Ashkenazi community began to break up into organizations based on the countries and regions of origin in Europe. One such organization, known as **kolel*, was characteristic and exclusively confined to the Ashkenazi *yishuv* in Palestine of the 19th and early 20th centuries. This sub-division into *kolelim* was due to economic factors, especially the desire of the emigrants of a given country to ensure themselves the incomes from their country of origin. The sub-division into *kolelim* was almost nonexistent among the Sephardim because they were not dependent on the *ḥalukkah* to the same extent as the Ashkenazim. However, even among them there were some who considered themselves to be discriminated against. Thus, the Georgians and the North Africans broke away from the general Sephardi community. The breaking-up process began in the 1830s when the immigrants from Germany and Holland formed their own *kolel*, the *kolel Hod* (abbreviation for Holland ve-Deutschland). In 1845 the *kolel Varsha* (Warsaw) was established and consisted of members of Polish origin who were dissatisfied with the leadership of the *Perushim* and who felt themselves discriminated against.

The fragmentation process was especially intensified in the 1850s when six *kolelim* were founded by emigrants of Eastern and Central European countries and regions. In 1858 the *kolel Hungaryah* (Hungary; *Kolel Shomerei ha-Ḥomot*, "*Kolel* of the Guardians of the Walls"), the most important one of the period, was established. The pupils of R. Moses Sofer, who had emigrated to Palestine, and those immigrants who had come from the countries of the Austro-Hungarian Empire during the 19th century belonged to this *kolel*. It was one of the largest *kolelim*, both numerically (about 2,500 souls in 1913), and in its real estate holdings; as such it was an influential factor in Jerusalem's communal life. Many of the members of this *kolel* stood out because of their religious zealotry and their opposition to any innovation. The *Neturei Karta* ("Guardians of the City"), the zealous faction of Jerusalem's religious Jews, emerged from this group. On the other hand, the first agricultural pioneers also came from this *kolel*. A further wave of subdivisions occurred in the 1870s, when another five *kolelim* were established. All of these, except one, separated themselves from the ḥasidic *kolel*, whereas those of the 1840s and 1850s had broken away from the old Ashkenazi community. In 1913 there were 26 Ashkenazi *kolelim* in Jerusalem.

The leadership of the *kolelim* was composed of rabbinical personalities. Abroad, a president, who was generally the most prominent rabbi of that country, was the head of the *kolel*. With the ḥasidic *kolelim*, it was the *rebbe* of that trend. Wealthy volunteers worked under the guidance of the president; the *kolel* leaders in Palestine, also prominent rabbis, were appointed by the leaders abroad, as were the communal workers and officials. The *kolel*, which functioned according to set regulations, was in close relationship with the country of origin of its members. The Sephardi *kolel* was led by the Sephardi chief rabbi, assisted by a council of rabbis.

The *ḥalukkah* arrangements were different with the Sephardim and the Ashkenazim. With the former *ḥalukkah* was only distributed to such scholars whose study was their profession, in accordance with the principle that the purpose of *ḥalukkah* was to support those who studied the Torah. The poor of the community only benefited from the *ḥalukkah* indirectly. The justification for this system was that the Sephardim were integrated in the country. They could earn their livelihood and were not dependent solely on *ḥalukkah*. In practice, with the absence of regular support, there were many poor in the community. In addition to the *ḥalukkah* for individuals, the Sephardi *kolel* also set aside a part of its income for general community expenditure. The *ḥalukkah* of the Ashkenazim was divided on the basis of a fixed sum per head. In addition to this, scholars received an additional allocation in accordance with their status. Occasionally, there were supplementary allocations derived from special contributions which the *kolel* received apart from its regular income. The *ḥalukkah* allocations differed from *kolel* to *kolel*, according to the income and the number of members. In 1913 the *ḥalukkah* of the Hungarian *kolel* was 100 francs for every person each year, while that of the Holland-German *kolel* was 360 francs for a couple with a further 80 francs for a child. These were the two most firmly established *kolelim*. Generally, the *ḥalukkah* allocation was far from sufficient to provide for the requirements of those who received it, and as the possibilities of gaining a livelihood were extremely limited in Jerusalem, most of the *ḥalukkah* beneficiaries lived in poverty. They and their *kolelim* were generally in debt. In light of this, there was a great deal of friction between the individual members of *kolelim* and between the *kolelim* themselves. Furthermore, the *kolel* leaders were targets for attack. The echoes of these *kolel* and *ḥalukkah* controversies were also heard abroad; there were many discussions in halakhic literature over these questions.

The division within the Ashkenazi community required the establishment of a body which would concern itself with the general interests of the community and deal with such matters as the *kolelim* were not involved in. Consequently, the Va'ad ha-Kelali ("General Committee") of the Ashkenazi *kolelim*, on which each *kolel* had a representative, was established in 1866. The committee preoccupied itself with

זכרו מרחוק את ה' וירושלם
תעלה על לבבכם

קול קורא לעזרה

קורלאנד וליפלאנד

בארץ אפריקא ומדינת טראנסוואל

שלום לכם מירושלם עיר קדשינו

אחינו היקרים

אם אשכחך ירושלם. אם לא אזכרכי. אם לא אעלה את ירושלם

קופות רבי
מאיר בעל הנס

יעקב שפירא נ"י שוב בעה"ק ירושלם תובב"א

שבתי זצ"ל

שמעו נא אחינו הרחמנים

בן עירך העני עמך

כי על כן אחינו היקרים

ביתו קופה של צדקה לעלוי נשמת רמבעה"נ בעד כולליט
ווילנא וזאמוט קורלאנד וליפלאנד

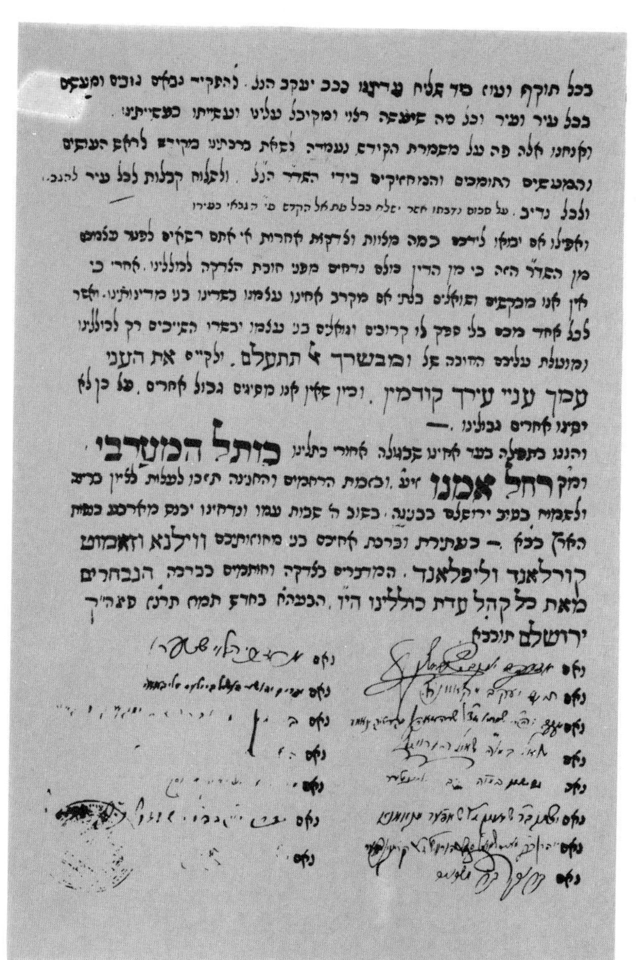

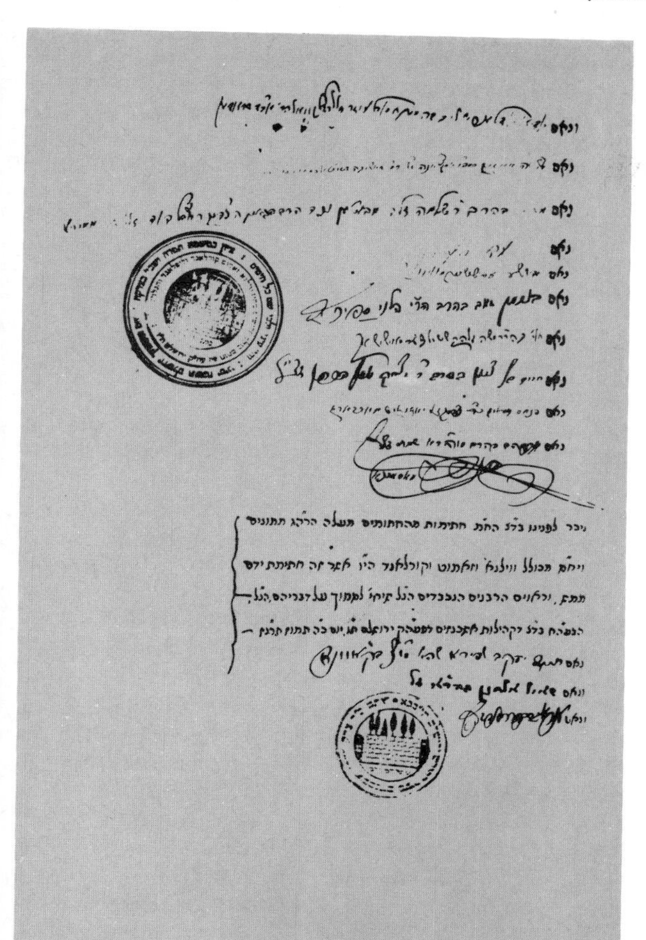

Document from the Jerusalem *kolel* of Kovno, Vilna, Courland, and Livonia, appointing Jacob Shapiro as emissary to the Jewish communities of the Transvaal in South Africa, 1897.

The letter, written in highly flowery language, opens with a reference to the love of Zion which inspired Elijah b. Solomon Zalman (Gaon of Vilna), "a messenger of the Lord of Hosts," to establish the Ashkenazi community of Jerusalem (Perushim). The Meir Ba'al ha-Nes Fund was established for their support by coreligionists abroad, who placed charity boxes in every home.

According to the letter, the settlement in Jerusalem originally known as the *kolel* of Vilna was at one time the distributing center for all funds sent from Russia for Ashkenazim in Jerusalem. As the years passed, however, different regional groups had established their own *kolelim*, and the Vilna *kolel's* receipts had accordingly decreased to a critical level. An emissary sent to Lithuania the previous year had returned empty-handed, but with the advice that someone be sent to South Africa to raise funds from the many Lithuanian Jews now prospering there. For this mission the *kolel* had appointed Jacob Shapiro, a *shoḥet* of Jerusalem, whom the letter authorizes to establish committees in every community and to issue receipts.

Every Jew in South Africa is urged to place a R. Meir Ba'al ha-Nes collection box in his home for the oldest and largest *kolel* in Jerusalem, which comprises over 2,000 souls, including hundreds of widows and orphans, old people, and great and pious rabbis.

The document ends with a promise of prayers at the Western Wall and Rachel's Tomb for the Jews of the Diaspora. It is signed by the 25 members of the council of the *kolel*, and attested by members of the Ashkenazi *bet din* of Jerusalem. This document was presented to the South African Jewish Board of Deputies by L. I. Rabinowitz, Jerusalem.

the general requirements of the community, such as the rabbinate, religious education, welfare, taxes, payments to the government, and the support of scholars. The committee also distributed *ḥalukkah* to persons who were not members of any *kolel.* Later its income came principally from America but also from other regions in accordance with arrangements made with various *kolelim,* though these were not always honored by the *kolelim,* who generally gave preference to their own particular interests.

The *ḥalukkah* was a decisive factor in the existence and the development of the Jewish population in Palestine. Its importance grew during the 19th century, when immigration reached serious proportions. At that time Palestine was economically poor and was ruled by a retarded and corrupt government. Under these circumstances the *yishuv* could not have existed, much less have grown, had it not been organized within the framework of the *kolelim,* who provided for their people and gathered money from abroad. (The other non-Muslim communities in Palestine were also supported to a large extent from abroad.) The *kolelim,* who were responsible for the *ḥalukkah* distributions, played an important role in the development of urban settlement, especially outside the walls of the Old City in Jerusalem. The Jewish quarters, which were built after 1869 on the initiative of the *kolel* leaders, were an important factor in the territorial expansion of the Jewish population of Jerusalem. The Jewish population in the other three "holy cities"—Hebron, Safed, and Tiberias—also was essentially reliant on the *ḥalukkah.*

From the middle of the 18th century, criticism of the ways and manners of life of the *yishuv* increased in the Jewish world of Western Europe. The *ḥalukkah* and its arrangements were the center of criticism in the writings of L. A. *Frankl, who visited Palestine in 1856, the historian *Graetz (1872), and Samuel *Montagu, in his report in 1875. The principal objection was that the *ḥalukkah* was also distributed to those who were neither scholars nor needy.

The criticism of the *ḥalukkah* intensified when the Ḥibbat Zion movement, which sought to build a society based on its own labor, was established. It challenged the very system of *ḥalukkah* and belittled its importance. The heads of the *kolelim* rejected this criticism and explained the necessity of the *ḥalukkah* in the prevailing social and economical situation. They also stressed its merits for the maintenance of the *yishuv,* the integration of immigrants, and the construction of new quarters. Even so, the deficiencies of the *ḥalukkah* were not unknown to members of the old *yishuv,* and calls for reform were voiced. The public discussion of this matter became one of the principal topics of the Hebrew writers in Palestine and abroad. The negative attitude toward *ḥalukkah* held by the Ḥovevei Zion was passed on to Zionist ideology, which regarded the old *yishuv* unfavorably. Current historical literature has been more favorable toward the old *yishuv* in light of its place as an important link in the renewal and revival of Ereẓ Israel. Consequently, the *ḥalukkah* is also looked upon with less criticism. With the beginning of the new *yishuv,* the importance of the *ḥalukkah* decreased continually, and after World War I it was limited to the circles of the old *yishuv.* In these circles, some *kolelim* still exist, but they have lost their former public importance. In practice, they have become charitable societies and their principal income is derived from their property and contributions given out of traditional sympathy.

Bibliography: Luncz, in: *Yerushalayim,* 7 (1906), 25–40, 181–201; 8 (1907), 306–21; 9 (1911), 1–62, 187–213; Malachi, in: *Lu'aḥ Ereẓ Yisrael,* 18 (1912/13), 81–102; Yaari, Sheluḥei, passim; L. A. Frankl, *Nach Jerusalem,* 2 (1858), 43–51, 58–60; S. Montagu, *Report . . . to the Sir Moses Montefiore Testimonial Fund* (1875); Eberhard, in: *Mitteilungen und Nachrichten des Deutschen Palaestina Vereins,* 14 (1908), 17–29; A. M. Hirsch, in: *Historia Judaica,* 14 (1952), 119–32; Rivlin, in: *Zion,* 2 (1927), 149–72; Frumkin-Rivlin, 138–57; Baron, in: *Sefer ha-Shanah li-Yhudei Amerikah,* 6 (1942), 167–79; idem, in: JSOS, 5 (1943), 115–62, 225–92; E. Hurwitz (ed.), *Mosad ha-Yesod* (1958[2]); Y. Z. Kahana, in: *Sinai,* 43 (1958), 125–44; B. Gat, *Ha-Yishuv ha-Yehudi be-Ereẓ Yisrael, 1840–1881* (1953), passim; Rivlin, in: *Yad Yosef Yiẓḥak Rivlin* (1964), 108–50; J. J. Rivlin and B. Rivlin (eds.), *Iggerot ha-Pekidim ve-ha-Amarkalim me-Amsterdam* (1965); J. Rivlin, *Megillat Yosef* (1966), 149–216; Weinstein, in: *Bar Ilan Yearbook,* 6 (1968), 339–56 (Heb.); M. M. Rothschild, *Ḥalukkah* (1969); J. Meisel, *Heinrich Graetz* (1917), 142–51. [N.K.]

HAM (Heb. חָם), one of the three sons of Noah. Although he is always placed between Shem and Japheth (Gen. 5:32; 6:10, et al.), he appears to have been the youngest of the three (9:24). The Bible relates how Ham observed Noah drunk and naked in his tent. He was apparently insensitive to his father's honor. In contrast, when he told his brothers of the incident, they at once covered Noah, doing so with the utmost delicacy (9:22–23). When Noah became aware of what had transpired, he cursed Canaan for his immodesty: "Cursed be Canaan; the lowest of slaves to his brothers" (9:24–25). The reason for Noah cursing Canaan, and not Ham, is not clear. Actually "Ham the father of" in verses 18b and 22 seems to be a somewhat crude link between verses 18–19 and 20ff., in which Noah's sons are Shem, Japheth, and Canaan (see *Canaan, Curse of). The Bible does not specify the nature of Ham's sin. Rabbinic exegesis attributes great sinfulness to him in order to explain the severity of the punishment (Sanh. 70a; TJ, Ta'an. 1:6,64a). However, Ugaritic epic poetry makes it clear that the disgrace of a drunken father was considered by the Canaanites to be a crime of the utmost gravity. Ham had four sons, Cush, Mizraim, Put, and Canaan, who became the progenitors of numerous nations (Gen. 10:6–20). The presence of Canaan and of South Arabian tribes (Sheba, Dedan) in this genealogy is surprising, since by linguistic criteria these peoples were Semitic. To overcome this discrepancy between linguistic and racial characteristics it has been suggested that Cush is to be identified with the Kassites, who ruled Babylonia in the second millennium B.C.E., rather than with Nubia; that Mizraim might be Muzri, in southeast Cappadocia, instead of Egypt; and that in general the nations mentioned in the genealogy are to be sought in Asia Minor rather than Eastern Africa or Southern Arabia. None of these theories has found much acceptance. As the home of the most important nations descended from Ham, Egypt is poetically called "Ham" in one psalm whose date is controversial (Ps. 78:51), and "the land of Ham" in two late psalms (Ps. 105:23, 27; 106:22; cf. Genesis Apocryphon, 19:13). Egypt is apparently the nucleus of the Hamite genealogy, the others having been added because of geographical proximity or political ties. [M.Wu.]

In the Aggadah. Ham's descendant (Cush) is black skinned as a punishment for Ham's having had sexual intercourse in the ark (Sanh. 108b). When Ham saw his drunken father exposed, he emasculated him, saying, "Adam had but two sons, and one slew the other; this man Noah has three sons, yet he desires to beget a fourth" (Gen. R. 36:5). Noah therefore cursed Canaan (Gen. 9:25), Ham's fourth son, since through this act he was deprived of a fourth son (Gen. R. 36:7). According to another opinion, Ham committed sodomy with his father (Sanh. 70a) and Noah cursed Canaan because Ham, together with his father and two brothers, had previously been blessed by God (Gen. R. loc. cit.). Another tradition attributes the curse to the fact that it was Ca

The sin of Ham (Gen. 9:20–24) depicted in a Hebrew illuminated manuscript, the *Harrison Miscellany*, Italy, 18th century. Ardmore, Pa., Sigmund Harrison Collection.

naan who castrated Noah. Ham was nevertheless to blame because he informed his brothers of their father's nakedness (PdRE 23). Canaan was so wicked that his last will and testament to his children was: "Love one another, love robbery, love lewdness, hate your masters, and do not speak the truth" (Pes. 113b). Ham was also punished in that his descendants, the Egyptians and Ethiopians, were taken captive and led into exile with their buttocks uncovered (Isa. 20:4; Gen. R. 36:6). Ham was responsible for the ultimate transfer to Nimrod of the garments which God had made for Adam and Eve before their expulsion from the Garden of Eden. From Adam and Eve these garments went to Enoch, and from him to Methuselah, and finally to Noah, who took them into the ark with him. When the inmates of the ark were about to leave their refuge, Ham stole the garments and kept them concealed for many years. Finally, he passed them on to his firstborn son, Cush, who eventually gave them to his son, Nimrod, when he reached his 20th year (PdRE 24; *Sefer ha-Yashar*, Noaḥ, 22). [A.Ro.]

Bibliography: A. Reubeni, *Shem, Ḥam ve-Yafet* ... (1932), 71–182; J. Skinner, *A Critical and Exegetical Commentary on Genesis* (1912), 181–7, 200–4; Jeremias, Alte Test; *Eretz Israel*, 3 (1954), 18–32; U. Cassuto, *A Commentary on the Book of Genesis* (1964); Ginzberg, Legends, 1 (1942), 166–73, 177; 5 (1947), 188–95.

HAM (Heb. הָם), biblical city in Transjordan where Chedorlaomer, king of Elam, and his allies defeated the Zuzim in their campaign against the rebellious Canaanite kings (Gen. 14:5). In this biblical reference, Ham appears between Ashteroth-Karnaim and Kiriathaim, both of which are located in Transjordan, and it has therefore been identified with Tel Ham, 4½ mi. (7 km.) south of Arbel (Irbid) in

Gilead. The identification of Ham with a place of the same name in the list of Thutmose III (no. 118) is doubtful. At Tel Ham three megalithic walls and pottery from the Early Canaanite period have been found but no remains from the Patriarchal (Middle Bronze) Age have been uncovered there so far.

Bibliography: Maisler (Mazar), in: *Kovez ha-Ḥevrah la-Ḥakirat Erez Yisrael va-Attikoteha*, 4 (1945), 68; Bergman, in: JPOS, 16 (1936), 237ff.; Glueck, Explorations, 1 (1951), 165f.; Aharoni, Land, index.

[M.A.-Y.]

ḤAMA (of Nehardea; fourth century), Babylonian *amora* and head of the *Pumbedita academy from 356–377 C.E., in succession to *Naḥman b. Isaac. Ḥama was a native of *Nehardea (BB 7b and Rashi *ibid.*) and the term "*amoraim* of Nehardea" is stated to apply specifically to him (Sanh. 17b). He was evidently a disciple of Rabbah, whose teachings he transmitted (Ket. 86a). Ḥama's teachings and practices are referred to in several places in the Talmud (Ber. 22b; MK 12a, et al.). His legal decisions were approved by later generations as the authoritative law (BB 7b; Shevu. 48b). Ḥama made a living by selling goods where they were cheap at the higher cost prevailing in other markets, the purchaser transporting the goods there at Ḥama's risk (BM 65a; cf. 69b). It is stated that King Shapur of Persia asked Ḥama about the biblical source of Jewish burial rites (Sanh. 46b), which being quite different from those of the Persians seemed strange to him. Ḥama did not know. When Aḥa b. Jacob heard of this, he said "The world is run by fools! Why did he not cite the verse [Deut. 21:23] 'Thou shalt surely bury him the same day'?" However, since Shapur I—it is unlikely that Shapur II (310–379) is being referred to, since he was not on close terms with the Jews—reigned from 241 to 272, the reference is probably to another, earlier, Ḥama.

Bibliography: Hyman, Toledot, 456–8, s.v.; Margalioth, Ḥakhmei, 316, s.v.; Ḥ. Albeck, *Mavo la-Talmudim* (1969), 408f.

[Z.K.]

ḤAMA BAR BISA (end of second century C.E. to third century), Palestinian scholar, contemporary of *Judah ha-Nasi. He was the father of Oshaiah, and at times is referred to simply as "Father of Oshaiah" (MK 24a). He lived in the southern part of the country (TJ, Nid. 3:2). Judah ha-Nasi praised him before Ishmael b. Yose b. Ḥalafta (Nid. 14b; TJ, Nid. 2:1). Ḥama b. Bisa was a judge, and his halakhic teachings are mentioned in the Jerusalem Talmud in his name, as they were transmitted by Yose b. Ḥanina (TJ, Shev. 2:2, 33d.) and Judah b. Pazzi (TJ, Suk. 1:1, 52b), and there is also a reference to a question Ḥama posed before Ḥiyya pertaining to a halakhic matter (TJ, Nid. 3:2). In the Babylonian Talmud too, there is a quotation in his name on a question of *halakhah* (MK 24a). It is related that he had left his home and city for twelve years in order to devote his time to the study of Torah. Upon his return he did not wish to startle his family by his sudden reappearance. He stopped at the *bet ha-midrash* and sent word to his family, informing them of his arrival. His son Oshaiah came to welcome him but was unrecognized by the father. They engaged in scholarly discourse, and R. Ḥama was deeply impressed with the young man's erudition, regretting his failure to give his son an adequate education because of his long absence from home. To his great surprise he finally learned the identity of his son (Ket. 62b). Bisa, Ḥama's father, was also a prominent scholar. To these three generations of scholars, Bisa, Ḥama, and

Oshaiah, Rami b. Ḥama applied the verse (Eccles. 4:12): "A threefold cord is not quickly burst asunder" (Ket. 62b; BB 59a). Opinion is divided as to whether this Oshaiah is identical with *Oshaiah Rabbah, the compiler of the *beraitot* (cf. Tos. to BB. 59a).

Bibliography: Bacher, Pal Amor; Frankel, Mevo, 85b; Hyman, Toledot, 458; Ḥ. Albeck, *Mavo la-Talmudim* (1969), 160. [Z.K.]

ḤAMA BAR ḤANINA (third century), Palestinian *amora*. He lived in the period of Judah Nesi'ah (Shab. 38a), the grandson of Judah Ha-Nasi (but cf. TJ, Shab. 3:1, 5d for a different reading), and may have headed an academy at *Sepphoris as his father *Ḥanina b. Ḥama had done (TJ, Shab. 6:2, 8a). Like his ancestors Ḥama was wealthy and built a synagogue in Sepphoris (TJ, Pe'ah 8:9, 21b). One of his close friends was *Oshaiah, and once, while visiting the synagogues of Lydda with him, Ḥama exclaimed: "What vast treasures have my ancestors sunk here [in erecting the synagogue]." Oshaiah responded: "How many lives have your ancestors sunk here! For were there not many needy people here who studied Torah in great poverty?" (TJ, Pe'ah 8:9, 21b; Shek. 21a). Although often mentioned as participating in halakhic discussions (Shab. 147b; TJ, Shab. 5:3,7c et al.), he distinguished himself particularly in the field of *aggadah*. Many of his homilies are quoted in his name by the aggadist R. *Levi II, especially in Midrash *Tanḥuma. He explained the curtailed form of the Divine name and the word for "throne" in Exodus 17:16 to teach that as long as Amalek's offspring exists, God's name and throne are not complete (Tanḥ. B., Deut. 45), and Psalms 29:4, to the effect that at the Revelation at Mount Sinai, God spoke to the young and strong with power, whereas to the old and weak with majesty (Song R. 5:16).

Commenting on Deuteronomy 13:5, "Ye shall walk after the Lord your God," he asked: "How can man walk after God, of whom it is written 'The Lord thy God is a consuming fire'?" (Deut. 4:24) and explained that it comes to teach that "as God clothed the naked [i.e., Adam], visited the sick [i.e., Abraham after his circumcision], comforted the mourning [i.e., Isaac after the death of his father], and buried the dead [i.e., Moses], so should man pursue similar deeds of lovingkindness in imitation of God's ways" (Sot. 14a). Among his many other beautiful statements in the *aggadah* may be mentioned, "If a man sees that he prays and is not answered, he should pray again" (Ber. 32b) and "Great is penitence for it brings healing to the world" (Yoma 86a). He expounded Proverbs 18:21, "death and life are in the power of the tongue," to teach that by the power of speech a man can kill another man even at a distance (Ar. 15b). Hyman distinguishes between two scholars by the same name, the second one being the pupil of R. *Hiyya b. Abba (an *amora* of the third generation, c. 290–320).

Bibliography: Bacher, Pal Amor; Hyman, Toledot, 460–1; Ḥ. Albeck, *Mavo la-Talmudim* (1969), 237f. [ED.]

HAMADAN, city in W. Iran. Hamadan, biblical Ecbatana, the summer residence of *Darius, has had a record of Jewish association from biblical times. According to Ezra 6:2 the decree issued by *Cyrus the Great permitting the Jews to rebuild their Temple in Jerusalem was found in the royal archives there. The Talmud regards Hamadan, with Halah and Nehavend (Kid. 72a), as "the cities of Media and Persia." An ancient Pahlevi source ascribes the founding of this city to Queen *Shushandokht, Jewish wife of Yazdegerd I (fifth century). In the eighth century, *Yudghan of Hamadan headed the messianic sectarian movement initiated by *Abu ʿIsā of Isfahan. That Hamadan had a large Jewish community in the 11th and 12th centuries is attested by *Benjamin of Tudela (c. 1162), who estimates its numbers at 30,000 (or 50,000 according to another reading) and by the *Iggerot* of the *gaon* *Samuel b. Ali which states that a yeshivah existed there under the auspices of the Jewish authorities in Baghdad. *Rashīd al-Dawla, the Persian Jewish vizier, historian, and scholar, was born in Hamadan. Like the rest of Persian Jewry, the Hamadan community suffered during the persecutions under the Safavid shahs. Under the Qājār dynasty (1794–1925), the Jews of Hamadan were subjected to missionary activities of Christians and the *Bahai movement, and to legal discriminations of all kinds. However, an *Alliance Israélite Universelle school was established in 1901, and in 1912 the first Zionist group was set up in Hamadan. Among the early pioneers of the subsequent *aliyah* was Menahem Levi, the local rabbi and director of the Alliance school; after settling in Jerusalem he became a central figure in all affairs concerning the Persian community.

According to Jewish tradition (expressed in gaonic literature, by Benjamin of Tudela, *Shahin, *Babai ibn Lutf and others), the mausoleum in the center of Hamadan houses the tombs of Mordecai and Esther. The Hebrew inscriptions on these tombs have been repeatedly investigated by European scholars, especially by Ernst *Herzfeld, and show that these cenotaphs, which should be dated to the end of the 13th century, were erected by the mother of two brothers, physicians in the service of the Īl-khān rulers, both bearing the title "Jamāl al-Dawla." In any case, Persian Jews regarded these tombs as holy sites, and made them the object of annual pilgrimages in which Muslims also participated. [W.J.F.]

In 1948 the number of Jews was estimated at 3,000–6,000, but when the economic situation of the community deteriorated, many left for Israel and elsewhere. According to the 1956 census, 1,714 Jews lived in the town, most of them in the crowded Jewish quarter. According to the 1966 census only 402 Jews were left in Hamadan. In 1949 the Alliance Israélite Universelle school was attended by 1,605 pupils, the number falling to 428 Jewish pupils in 1961. In 1948 an Alliance Israélite Universelle teachers seminary also functioned and had 23 students. The Oẓar ha-Torah school, which had 356 pupils in 1949, closed a few years later. In 1968 the town had a branch of the Iranian Jewish Women's Organization and the Youth Organization *(Kanun Javanan)*.

See also *Iran. [H.J.C.]

Bibliography: J. Obermeyer, *Die Landschaft Babylonien* (1929), 110–8; E. E. Herzfeld, *Archaeological History of Iran* (1935), 104ff.; R. Abrahamian, *Dialectes des Israélites de Hamadan et d'Ispahan* (1936); L. Lockhart, *Famous Cities of Iran* (1939), 46–52.

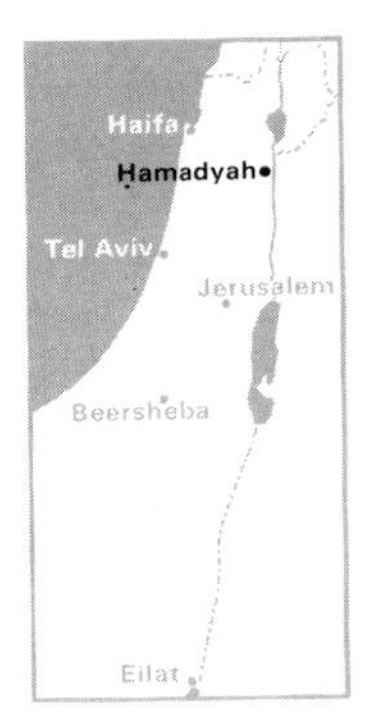

ḤAMADYAH (Heb. חֲמַדְיָה), kibbutz in the Beth-Shean Valley, affiliated with Iḥud ha-Kibbutzim. It was first founded as a *Tower and Stockade settlement by a moshav group in 1939, but was taken over by kibbutz Ḥermonim in 1942. Their initial difficulties were considerable due to the hot and dry climate and their proximity to the then Arab town Beth-Shean. A security problem again arose after the *Six-Day War (1967) when Ḥamadyah underwent frequent artillery barrages from Transjordan. The kibbutz has developed various agricultural branches, and opened two industrial enterprises for furniture (mainly doors) and plastics. Ḥamadyah's name, meaning "God-cherished," was adapted from an adjacent Arab village named after the Turkish sultan ʾAbd al-Ḥamīd. In 1968 its population was 260. [E.O.]

HA-MAGGID (Heb. הַמַּגִּיד, "The Declarer"), the first Hebrew newspaper. *Ha-Maggid* began publication in 1856 in Lyck, eastern Prussia, under the editorship of Eliezer Lipmann *Silbermann. Silbermann, whose writing talents were limited, was nevertheless a genuine pioneer in Hebrew journalism. Although periodicals had existed for a hundred years prior to the founding of *Ha-Maggid,* the problems of running a newspaper were different from those of running a literary, scientific, and social journal. The paper lacked journalists, publishers, and a news agency. Because the rhetorical biblical Hebrew of the time was not adapted to reporting news and making comments on current affairs, a new journalistic idiom had to be developed.

Ha-Maggid appeared as a weekly (except during its first few months) until it ceased publication in 1903. Until 1890 it was published in Lyck, then in Berlin, and from 1892 in Cracow. The paper grew in importance under David *Gordon, editor from 1858 to 1886, who made the paper of interest to all Jews by reporting both Jewish and general news. *Ha-Maggid* became a fount of information on Jewish life throughout the world during the second half of the 19th century. In a series of articles in 1863 and 1869, a time when the Hebrew press was either opposed or indifferent to nationalist ideas, Gordon took a strong stand in favor of Jewish settlement in Palestine. After the 1881 pogroms in Russia, *Ha-Maggid* fervently advocated Jewish nationalism and settlement in Ereẓ Israel. In this respect it served as a precedent for many of the Hebrew papers that followed.

שנה ראשונה

ליק יום ד׳ ר״ח סיון התרט״ז ליצירה

נומער 1

המגיד

מכתב קורות הימים

יגיד ליעקב מהנעשה בכל חלקי תבל בין כל יושבי חלד אשר ינעם ואשר ראוי לדעת לכל איש ישראלי — לתעלתו ולתועלת השפה העבריה הנחמדה.

אליעזר ליפמאן זילבערמאן.

וְהָאֱמֶת וְהַשָּׁלוֹם אֱהָבוּ. זכרי׳ ח׳.

Front page of the first issue of *Ha-Maggid,* the first Hebrew newspaper. Published in Lyck, Prussia, 1 Sivan 5616 (1856). Jerusalem, J.N.U.L.

Throughout the years the paper devoted a special section to Judaic studies, in which the greatest scholars of the day participated. Like most other papers of that period, *Ha-Maggid* espoused moderate Haskalah, i.e., accommodating the religious and traditional heritage to the needs of the time, insofar as the accommodation was not in violation of Jewish law. *Ha-Maggid's* contributors included representatives of all trends of thought. The paper also developed popular sections for science and technology (e.g., a medical section) thereby making Hebrew richer and more adaptable. After Gordon's death (1886) the paper began to decline, a process accelerated by the establishment that year of the Hebrew daily, **Ha-Yom*. In its later years *Ha-Maggid* was moved to Galicia and became the organ of the local Ḥovevei Zion movement. The paper's last editor, S. M. Laser, founded the weekly **Ha-Mizpeh* (1904) after *Ha-Maggid* ceased publication in 1903.

Bibliography: C. L. Zitron, in: *Ha-Olam,* 6, no. 1–2 (1912), 4, 6, 8, 10–12; D. Gordon, *Mivḥar Ma'amarim,* ed. by G. Kressel (1942); Posner, in: *Yad la-Kore,* 4–5 (1958–59), 89–94; J. Barzilai, in: *Bitzaron,* 37 (1957/58), 78–88, 178–90; H. Toren, in: *Anakh,* 1 (1954), 232–41.

[G.K.]

HAMAN (Heb. הָמָן), son of Hammedatha, the Agagite, according to the *Scroll of Esther, an official in the court of Ahasuerus who was superior to all the king's other officials. Resentful of *Mordecai the Jew, who was the only one among the servants of the king in the royal court who would not bow down to him, Haman decided to exterminate all the Jews, "the people of Mordecai" (3:6). To determine the day of the destruction he cast a lot *(pur),* and then received the consent of the king to publish a royal decree throughout the entire Persian kingdom proclaiming the extermination. Through Mordecai, however, the news reached Esther, who immediately set about saving her people. She invited Haman and the king to a feast lasting two days, and on the second day revealed to the king, in Haman's presence, the evil designs that the latter harbored against her people. In his anger, the king ordered that Haman be hanged on "the tree which Haman has prepared for Mordecai" (Esth. 7:10), and that his hanging be followed by that of his sons. The king then issued a decree permitting the Jews "to gather and defend themselves" on the day that had been set aside for their extermination (Esth. 8:11). This decree and the victory of the Jews over their enemies were the reasons for the establishment of the holiday of *Purim.

Various explanations have been offered to explain the name and designation of the would-be exterminator of the Jews. The names of both Haman and his father have been associated with haoma, a sacred drink used in Mithraic worship, and with the Elamite god Humman. The name Haman has also been related to the Persian *hamayun,* "illustrious," and to the Persian name Owanes. A name that is similar, if not identical, to that of the father is Haumadatha (הומדת; Cowley, Aramaic, 8:2, 9:2), the name of a Persian military commander in the Jewish colony at Elephantine. An attempt has been made to relate Agag to the tribe of Agazi, that dwelt close to the Medes and is mentioned in the Annals of Sargon II (Luckenbill, *Ancient Records,* 2 (1927), 23, 58). In view, however, of the fact that the author of Esther traces Mordecai's line back to the Benjamite Kish, father of Saul (2:5), and that he implies in 3:4 that anyone who was told that Mordecai was a Jew would immediately understand that it would be degrading for him to do obeisance to Haman, he must have intended the designation of Haman as "the Agagite" to indicate descent from Saul's opponent *Agag, king of Amalek (Deut. 25:17–19; I Sam. 15; cf. Jos., Ant., 11:209). Although

Haman leading Mordecai through the streets of Shushan. Haman's wife, Zeresh, mistaking him for Mordecai, dumps slops on him. Poland, late 19th century; from *Święta żydowskie w przeszłości i teraźniejszości,* Cracow, 1908.

Saul displayed leniency toward Agag (I Sam. 15:9), the latter's distant descendant was not only a personal rival of Mordecai but an inveterate "enemy of the Jews" (Esth. 3:10, 8:1, 9:10; cf. 7:6) who had to be destroyed along with his ten sons (7:10, 9:6–10; cf. Ex. 17:8–16 and Deut. 25:17–19).

In the Septuagint and the apocryphal *Additions to Esther,* the designation Agagite is replaced by the inexplicable terms Bugaean (LXX 3:1; 9:10; Add. Esth. 12:6) or Macedonian (LXX 9:24; Add. Esth. 16:10). The *Additions to Esther* describes Haman as bent upon delivering the Persian kingdom to the Macedonians (16:14). [B.Po.]

In the Aggadah. In the Midrashim (Esth. R. 7–8; *Targum Sheni; Midrash Abba Guryon* and others) Haman is depicted as a foe of Israel typical of the times in which these writers of the Midrashim lived. The enemies of Israel maintained that the Jews were ungrateful to their benefactors and mocked the faithful of the nations in whose midst they dwelt. The feast that Ahasuerus prepared at the beginning of his reign is attributed by these same Midrashim to the evil designs of Haman, whose purpose was to undermine Israel with exotic foods and incestuous orgies, so that the Jews who attended this feast, against Mordecai's advice, would bring down upon themselves the destruction ordained by Heaven (Esth. R. 7:13). However, the decree was annulled as a result of the cries of the schoolchildren who were studying with Mordecai because they also were involved in the decree of extermination. A humorous piece of folklore relates that Haman was a barber for 22 years in the town of Kefar Karzum (Kefar Karnayim in Transjordan, or Kerazim), and his father was a bath attendant in the town of Koranis and these professions stood them in good stead later when Mordecai had to be dressed and bathed after he had been weakened by fasting. There is an interesting *aggadah* to the effect that all the various trees put forward a claim, on the basis of their virtues, that Haman should be hanged on them. The thornbush was chosen, however, since because it had no virtues, the wicked Haman should be hanged on it (Esth. R. 9:2).

Haman continued to be regarded as the prototype of the enemy of the Jews throughout the ages. It became customary to make a loud noise in the synagogues to drown out his name whenever mentioned in the Purim reading of the Book of Esther. [Y.M.G.]

In Islam. Hāmān, according to the Koran, was one of the foremost advisers of Pharaoh-Firʿawn. He built a tower for his master, who planned to climb up to the God of Moses (Sura 28:5, 7, 38; 40; 38; 51:38–39). In Suras 29:38 and 40:25–26 Hāmān appears together with Firʿawn and Qārūn (Korah), who was also Moses' enemy. [H.Z.H.]

Bibliography: I. Scheftelowitz, *Arisches im Alten Testament* (1901–03); L. B. Paton, *The Book of Esther* (ICC, 1908); P. Renard, in: DBI, 1 (1912), 433ff.; H. H. Schaeder, *Iranische Beitraege,* 1 (1930); J. Lewy, in: HUCA, 14 (1939), 127ff. In the Aggadah: Ginzberg, Legends. In Islam: Vajda, in: EL²; Kisāʾī, *Qiṣaṣ* ed. by I. Eisenberg (1922), 202; H. Speyer, *Biblische Erzaehlungen . . .* (1961), 412.

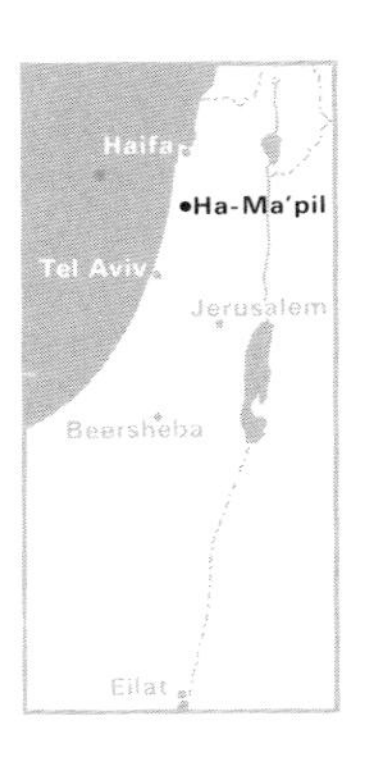

HA-MA'PIL (Heb. הַמַּעְפִּיל), kibbutz in central Israel in the Ḥefer Plain, affiliated with Ha-Kibbutz Ha-Arẓi Ha-Shomer ha-Ẓa'ir, founded in 1945 by pioneers from Eastern and Central Europe, some of whom were veterans of World War II. It engages in intensive farming, and runs a stocking factory. The name, meaning "ascender," alludes to the *ha'apalah* (*Illegal Immigration). [E.O.]

HAMASHBIR HAMERKAZI, the main wholesale supplier for consumers' cooperatives and labor settlements in Israel; the first economic agency to be established by the labor movement in Ereẓ Israel. It was founded (as Hamashbir) in 1916, during the economic crisis of World War I, to supply the working population with reasonably priced goods, and was reorganized as Hamashbir Hamerkazi in 1930. In addition to its wholesaling activities, it has developed the consumers' cooperative movement all over the country, opened large stores in the main towns, and established factories, mainly in the textiles and food-processing industries, which have been transferred to a separate company, Hamashbir Hamerkazi Le-Taasia. Hamashbir is affiliated to the *Histadrut, whose economic arm, Ḥevrat ha-Ovedim, is entitled to appoint a representative on its general management and intervene in matters of principle. Its general conference, consisting of delegates from collective and cooperative villages and of cooperative societies, elects a 71-member council, which appoints a general management of 21, which, in turn, chooses the ten-man active management. Its turnover in 1968 was IL376 million ($107 million) and it supplied 800 cooperative stores in town and country.

Bibliography: Histadrut, Makhon le-Meḥkar Kalkali ve-Ḥevrati, *Meshek ha-Ovedim 1960–1965* (1967); I. Avineri (ed.), *Ha-Lu'ah ha-Ko'operativi shel Medinat Yisrael* (1968). [L.A.S.]

HA-MAVDIL (Heb. הַמַּבְדִּיל; "who distinguishes"), name of a hymn sung in the *Havdalah ceremony at the close of the Sabbath. The acrostic yields the name of the author Isaac the Younger (probably Isaac b. Judah *ibn Ghayyat of

Spain (1030–1089)). There are two versions of the hymn; in both the refrain starts: "May He who maketh a distinction between holy and profane pardon our sins (in most versions: "and our wealth"); may he multiply our offspring as the sand and as the stars in the night." The hymn was probably composed for the concluding service *(Ne'ilah)* of the Day of Atonement. One version is still recited as a *selihah piyyut* in the *Ne'ilah* service of some of the Sephardi rites (e.g. Algeria); the other, and better known version, has become the standard hymn for the *Havdalah* service in all Jewish rites, including the Karaite one.

See **Havdalah.*

Bibliography: Zunz, Poesie, 14ff.; Hertz, Prayer, 750ff.; Davidson, Oẓar, 2 (1929), 147ff., nos. 741ff.

[Ed.]

HAMBRO, JOSEPH (1780–1848), merchant and financier. Born in Copenhagen, the son of Joachim Hambro (1747–1806), a silk and cloth merchant, Joseph started his career as a peddler in the streets of his native city. At the age of 13 he went to Hamburg to be trained in a commercial firm and after his return prospered as a wholesale dealer. Hambro was the first in Denmark to run a steam mill, and traded with the Danish West Indies. The government commissioned him to arrange a Danish-English public loan and to regulate economic relations between Denmark and Norway after the peace treaty of 1814. In 1820 Hambro was appointed court banker by the king of Denmark. At the age of 60 he settled in London, where later he was buried as a Jew in the presence of the chief rabbi although he had married a gentile. In his bequest Hambro left considerable sums to the community in Copenhagen. His son, Carl Joachim Hambro (1808–1877), was baptized with his father's consent at the age of 15. He established the great banking firm of Hambros (1839), which also negotiated public loans and was active in the financing of Danish railways and in the founding of the Great Northern Telegraphic Company. Neither father nor son forgot the community of Copenhagen although they remained aloof from the London Jewish community.

Bibliography: J. Wechsberg, *Merchant Bankers* (1966), 21–98; H. Faber, *Danske og Norske i London* (1915); *Dansk Biografisk Leksikon,* 9 (1936), 13–15.

[Ju.M.]

HAMBURG, city and state in W. Germany, including the cities of *Altona and *Wandsbeck from 1937.

The Sephardi Community. The first Jews to settle in Hamburg were wealthy Marranos from Spain and Portugal who went to the city at the end of the 16th century. At first they sought to conceal their religion in their new place of residence. When it was discovered that they had been observing Jewish customs, some of the inhabitants demanded their expulsion, but the city council, pointing to the economic benefits accruing from their presence, opposed the measure. Among the Jews were financiers (some of whom took part in the founding of the Bank of Hamburg in 1619), shipbuilders, importers (especially of *sugar, coffee, and *tobacco from the Spanish and Portuguese colonies), weavers, and goldsmiths. In 1612 the Jews of Hamburg paid an annual tax of 1,000 marks and by 1617 this sum was doubled. The kingdoms of Sweden, Poland, and Portugal appointed Jews as their ambassadors in Hamburg. Those who had come to Hamburg from Spain and Portugal continued to speak the languages of their native lands for two centuries and about 15 books in Portuguese and Spanish were printed in Hamburg from 1618 to 1756. (From 1586 Hebrew books, especially the books of the Bible, had been published in Hamburg by Christian printers, mostly with the help of Jewish personnel.)

As early as 1611 Hamburg had three synagogues, whose congregations jointly owned burial grounds in nearby Altona. In 1652 the three congregations combined under the name of Beth Israel. Uriel da *Costa lived in Hamburg in 1616–17; the local physician Samuel da *Silva wrote a pamphlet attacking him; the excommunication of da Costa by R. *Leone Modena was read publicly in the Hamburg synagogue. Shabbateanism swept the community in 1666; so certain were they of the imminence of the Messiah that the governing board of the community announced that the communal buildings were for sale. The rabbi, Jacob b. Aaron *Sasportas, was one of the few not carried away by the prevailing enthusiasm. When in 1697 the city unexpectedly raised the annual tax levied against the Jews to 6,000 marks, the majority of the rich Jews of Hamburg (most of whom belonged to the Spanish-Portuguese congregation) moved to Altona and Amsterdam.

Figure 1. The Bornplatz Synagogue in Hamburg, built in 1906, and destroyed in 1938 during *Kristallnacht.* Courtesy Hamburg Municipality.

Among the prominent Jews of Spanish and Portuguese origin who lived in Hamburg were the physician and author Rodrigo de Castro (1550–1627), R. Joseph Solomon *Delmedigo (1622–25 in Hamburg), the physician and lexicographer Benjamin *Mussafia (1609–1672), the grammarian and writer Moses Gideon *Abudiente (1602–1688), the rabbi and writer Abraham de Fonseca (d. 1651), and the poet Joseph *Ẓarefati (d. 1680).

The Ashkenazi Community. From about 1600, German Jews were admitted to Wandsbeck and in 1611 some of them settled in Altona, both cities under Danish rule. By 1627 German Jews began to settle in Hamburg itself, although on festivals they continued to worship at Altona, where the Danish king had permitted the official establishment of a congregation and the building of a synagogue in 1641. They submitted their disputes to the jurisdiction of the rabbi of the Altona congregation. Shortly thereafter the three communities banded together to form one congregation, a union that was to be broken temporarily in the 1660s. Many Jews, fleeing from persecutions in Ukraine and Poland in 1648, arrived in Hamburg where they were helped by the resident Jews. However, the refugees soon left for Amsterdam since at that time the Christian clergy in Hamburg was inciting the inhabitants to expel the Ashkenazi Jews from the city, an expulsion which took place in 1649. Most went to Altona and a number to Wandsbeck; only a few remained in Hamburg, residing in the homes of the Spanish-Portuguese Jews. Within a few years many of those who had been driven out returned to Hamburg, and in 1656 a number of refugees from *Vilna also found asylum there.

The three Ashkenazi congregations—Altona, Hamburg, and Wandsbeck— reunited in 1671 to form the AHW congregation, with the seat of their rabbinate in Altona. One of the most famous rabbis of the merged congregation was Jonathan *Eybeschuetz who was appointed to the post

Figure 2. The new Hamburg synagogue and community center built in 1960. Courtesy Hamburg Municipality. Photo Conti Press.

in 1750. His equally famous adversary, Jacob *Emden, lived in Altona. R. Raphael b. Jekuthiel *Kohen, who served the community for 23 years, was one of the fiercest opponents of *Mendelssohn's translation of the Pentateuch (1783). The AHW congregation ceased to exist in 1811 when the French authorities imposed a single consistorial organization; the Ashkenazim and Sephardim united to form one congregation, the Altona community retaining its own rabbinate which was also recognized by the Jews of Wandsbeck until 1864.

Hamburg Jews were molested during the *Hep! Hep! riots of 1819. However, by 1850 they were granted citizenship, due in large measure to the efforts of Gabriel *Riesser, a native of Hamburg.

The Reform movement, which began in Berlin, eventually reached Hamburg. A Reform temple was dedicated in 1818, and in 1819 a new prayerbook was published to accord with the liturgical ritual of the new congregation. The rabbinate in Hamburg published the opinions of noted Jewish scholars to discredit the temple (entitled *Elleh Divrei ha-Berit*, Altona, 1819) and prohibited the use of its prayer book. Isaac *Bernays, leader of the community from 1821 to 1849, espoused the cause of "modern Orthodoxy" and sought to endow the traditional divine service with greater beauty. In his day controversy flared up again when the Reform congregation occupied a new building and the more radically abridged and revised version of its prayerbook *Siddur ha-Tefillah* was issued (1844). At the time the Orthodox rabbi was Jacob *Ettlinger, founder of an anti-Reform journal.

Other German Jews who lived in Hamburg included *Glueckel of Hameln, the merchant and philanthropist Salomon *Heine (the uncle of Heinrich Heine), Moses Mendelssohn, the poets Naphtali Herz *Wessely and Shalom b. Jacob *ha-Kohen, Isaac *Halevy, the author of *Dorot ha-Rishonim*, the art historian A. *Warburg, the philosopher Ernst *Cassirer, the psychologist William *Stern, Albert *Ballin, and the financiers Max *Warburg and Karl *Melchior. Among Orthodox rabbis of recent times worthy of note is Nehemiah *Nobel and among the Reform, C. *Seligmann and P. *Rieger. In 1884 the fortnightly *Laubhuette* and in 1900 the weekly **Israelitisches Familienblatt* began to be issued in Hamburg. The municipal library and the library of the University of Hamburg contain a large number of Hebrew manuscripts, listed by M. *Steinschneider. Nearly 400 Hebrew books were printed in Hamburg in the 17th–19th centuries. In the 19th century, the Jewish printers issued mainly prayer books, the Pentateuch, mystic lore, and popular literature.

The Jewish congregation of greater Hamburg was the fourth largest community in Germany. In 1866 there were 12,550 Jews at Hamburg and in 1933 about 19,900 (1.7% of the general population), including more than 2,000 at Altona. The last rabbi was Joseph *Carlebach, who was deported in 1942 and killed by the Nazis.

Holocaust Period. In the years 1933–37 more than 5,000 Jews emigrated; on Oct. 28, 1938 about 1,000 Polish citizens were expelled. The pogrom of *Kristallnacht* (Nov. 9–10, 1938), in which most synagogues were looted and closed down, caused an upsurge of emigration. In 1941, 3,148 Jews were deported to Riga, Lodz, and Minsk. In 1942, 1,848 Jews were deported to *Auschwitz and *Theresienstadt. In ten subsequent transports to Theresienstadt 370 were deported. Approximately 7,800 Hamburg Jews lost their lives in the Nazi era (153 mentally ill were executed and 308 committed suicide). In this period the community was led by Max Plaut and Leo Lippmann (who committed suicide in 1943). A few hundred Jews, privileged or of mixed marriage, outlived the war. A concentration camp, Neuengamme, was situated near the city. A total of 106,000 inmates passed through its gates and more than half of them perished.

Since World War II. On May 3, 1945 Hamburg was liberated by British troops who offered aid to the few hundred Jewish survivors. On September 18 a Jewish community was organized, which reopened the cemetery, old age home, *mikveh*, and hospital soon after. By March 18, 1947 the community totaled 1,268, its numbers changing due to emigration, immigration, and a high mortality rate. In January 1970 there were 1,532 Jews in Hamburg, two-thirds of whom were above 40 years old. In 1960 a 190-bed

Figure 3. The Portuguese synagogue in Hamburg, the last Sephardi synagogue in Germany, taken over by the Ashkenazi community in 1930.

Hamburger Tageblatt

Die Reichsparteileitung an alle Nationalsozialisten:

Marschbefehl gegen die Juden!

Endlich auch der Hamburger Anzeiger verboten! / Stahlhelmkommissare in Braunschweig

Am Sonnabend schlagen wir los!

Der Kampf gegen die jüdischen Geschäfte

Figure 4. Front page of the *Hamburger Tageblatt* of March 29, 1933, containing the Nazi order for a general anti-Jewish boycott to begin on Saturday, April 2. From O. Wolfsberg-Aviad et al., *Die Drei-Gemeinde,* Hamburg, 1960.

hospital was opened and a large modern synagogue consecrated. Herbert Weichmann (b. 1896) was elected Buergermeister in 1965. An institute for Jewish history was founded in 1966, its driving spirit being the gentile Erich Lueth, whose main activity was the promoting of Jewish-Christian understanding.

Bibliography: H. Kellenbenz, *Sephardim an der unteren Elbe . . .* (1958); H. Krohn, *Die Juden in Hamburg,* 1 (1969); 2 (1970); A. Cassuto, *Gedenkschrift anlaesslich des 275-jaehrigen Bestehens der portugiesisch-juedischen Gemeinde in Hamburg . . .* (1927); M. Grunwald, *Portugiesengraeber auf deutscher Erde . . .* (1902); M. Grunwald, *Hamburgs deutsche Juden bis zur Aufloesung der Dreigemeinden . . .* (1904); O. Wolfsberg et al., *Die Drei-Gemeinde . . . Altona-Hamburg-Wandsbeck* (1960); H. Gonsierowski, *Die Berufe der Juden Hamburgs von der Einwanderung bis zur Emanzipation* (1927); L. Dukes, *Uebersicht alter . . . Anstalten . . . Vereine . . . Stiftungen der Deutsch- und der Portugiesisch-israelitischen Gemeinde in Hamburg* (1841); J. S. Schwabacher, *Geschichte und rechtliche Gestaltung der portugiesisch-juedischen und der Deutsch-israelitischen Gemeinde zu Hamburg* (1914); Glueckel von Hameln, *Life of Glueckel of Hameln . . .* (1962); E. Lueth, *Hamburgs Juden in der Heine-Zeit* (1961); H. Krohn, *Die Juden in Hamburg, 1800–1850 . . .* (1967); E. Duckesz, *Iwoh lemoschaw . . .* (1903); H. Goldstein (ed.), *Die juedischen Opfer des Nationalsozialismus in Hamburg* (1965); B. Brilling in: *Zeitschrift des Vereins fuer Hamburgische Geschichte 55* (1969), 219–44.

[Z.Av.]

HAMBURG, ABRAHAM BENJAMIN (Wolf; 1770–1850), German talmudic scholar. Hamburg was born in Fuerth and studied at the yeshivah of R. Meshullam-Solomon Kohn, the chief rabbi of Fuerth. He succeeded his teacher as head of the yeshivah, and in 1820 was appointed *moreh-ẓedek* ("spiritual leader") of the congregation, serving also as cantor and *mohel.* The appointment of a new chief rabbi, however, was indefinitely postponed and Hamburg was hard put to combat the inroads of the Reform movement into the community. In his correspondence with Moses *Sofer, who describes Hamburg as a "great man of high stature," he talks of his difficulties in building a communal *mikveh* (see M. Sofer, *Ḥatam Sofer, Yoreh De'ah* (1958²), no. 214; *Even ha-Ezer,* 1 (1958²), no. 82). By 1830, the adherents of the Reform movement had obtained a majority in the communal administration and had him removed from all his positions, except from that in the Klaus synagogue in which he had vested rights (it had been founded by one of his ancestors, Baermann Fraenkel). His yeshivah was closed and his opponents enlisted the help of the police in expelling his students, who numbered more than 100, from Fuerth. Ultimately, Hamburg himself was driven from the city and died heartbroken.

Hamburg's published works include sermons, responsa, talmudic novellae, and memorial addresses. *Sha'ar Zekenim* (Sulẓbach, 1830) consists of sermons, eulogies, and ethical tracts. The latter half of the work also contains responsa addressed to former pupils and rabbinical contemporaries. *Simlat Binyamin* (Fuerth, 1840–41), Hamburg's other major work, is in three parts. The first contains responsa on *Oraḥ Ḥayyim* and *Yoreh De'ah,* and the second under the title *Naḥlat Binyamin* on *Even ha-Ezer* and *Ḥoshen Mishpat,* as well as *aggadot;* this section deals at length with the laws of circumcision. In the third section under the title *Sha'ar Binyamin* (unpublished) the author includes his own interpretations, additions, and novellae. One of his eulogies is in honor of his teacher, Solomon Kohn (*Kol Bokhim . . .,* Fuerth, 1820). He also paid homage to Sir Moses *Montefiore in a poem on his visit to Fuerth in 1841 together with Adolphe *Crémieux, on their return from the Orient. Hamburg taught and inspired a number of eminent disciples, among them Seligmann-Baer *Bamberger, and Moses Sofer.

Abraham Hamburg, German talmudic scholar. Jerusalem, J.N.U.L., Schwadron Collection.

Bibliography: Fuenn, Keneset, 304–5; Loewenstein, in: ZGJD, 2 (1888), 90; idem, in: JJLG, 6 (1909), 209–14, 225. [Ed.]

HAMBURGER, JACOB (1826–1911), German rabbi and scholar. Hamburger, who was born in Loslaw (Wodzislaw, Poland), served as rabbi in Neustadt (near Pinne, Poland) and Mecklenburg-Strelitz (Prussia). His most important work was his two-volume *Real-Encyklopaedie fuer Bibel und Talmud,* the first such work ever published in the German language (1874–83) dealing with the Bible and Talmud respectively. This he later extended into a three-volume *Real-Encyklopaedie des Judentums* (1874–1900, 1904–05³), the third volume dealing with post-talmudic Judaism. Hamburger also began to write *Geist der Hagada,* an alphabetical anthology of talmudic and midrashic sayings, but only completed the letter A (1857). He also contributed the section on the Karaites and other matters to Winter and Wuensche's standard work on post-biblical literature, *Juedische Litteratur seit Abschluss des Kanons* (1894–96).

Bibliography: N. Sokolow (ed.), *Zikkaron le-Soferei Yisrael . . .* (1889), 29. [A.C.]

ḤAMDĪ, LEVI BEN YESHU'AH (1861–1930), hymnologist, *ḥazzan,* and preacher. Ḥamdī was born in San'a, Yemen, and emigrated to Palestine in 1891; he died in Jerusalem. In Yemen he was a Hebrew teacher, and his *ḥeder* was renowned for its progressive educational methods. In Jerusalem he became a Torah scribe, and also wrote amulets, charms, and lots. Many came to him believing that he was a man of great powers and a miracle worker. His strange behavior, possibly connected to his chronic illness and the death of his children in infancy, included self-mortification and fasts. He even exiled himself to Egypt in order to achieve the remission of his sins. Ḥamdī is generally known as a poet and *ḥazzan.* As a kabbalist, he thought that the poetry of Yemen was mystical and holy. He assisted A. Z. *Idelsohn in his research into Jewish melodies, and sang many Yemenite melodies for the latter to record. Ḥamdī composed hymns and prayers of supplication on such themes as the exile, the redemption, and Ereẓ Israel. In Yemen, he wrote prayers expressing his yearning for Ereẓ Israel. *Koveẓ Shirim,* a collection of his hymns and prayers, was published in Jerusalem in 1966.

Bibliography: Idelsohn, in: *Reshumot,* 1 (1925), 3–68; M. D. Gaon, *Yehudei ha-Mizraḥ be-Ereẓ Yisrael,* 2 (1938), 257–8; Geshuri, in: *Ha-Ẓofeh* (1939), no. 270.

[Y.R.]

HAMEIRI (Feuerstein), AVIGDOR (1890–1970), Hebrew poet, novelist, and translator. Hameiri was born in Dávidháza, Carpatho-Ukraine (then Hungary). His first Hebrew poem *"Ben he-Atid,"* which appeared in the weekly

Avigdor Hameiri, Israel writer. Courtesy *Jerusalem Post.*

Ha-Miẓpeh (1907), was followed by others in various Hebrew journals. His first volume of verse, entitled *Mi-Shirei Avigdor Feuerstein,* was published in 1912. In 1916 he was captured by the Russians while serving as an Austrian officer on the Russian front, imprisoned in Siberia, and released in 1917 after the October Revolution. In 1921 he emigrated to Palestine, joined the staff of the daily *Haaretz,* and edited several critical journals. In Tel Aviv, he founded the first Hebrew social satirical theater Ha-Kumkum (1932). Hameiri published various novels, short stories, and poetry collections that gave literary expression to his war experiences, the Third Aliyah, and later, the Holocaust. He also translated into Hebrew works of Heine, Schiller, Arnold Zweig, Stefan Zweig, etc.

Hameiri belongs to the earliest exponents of expressionism in Hebrew poetry. Sustained pathos, and strained and occasional exaggerated figures of speech characterize his work. He attacked the stagnation of Jewish life, described the gruesomeness and the frenzy of hatred that engulfed all of humanity during World War I and particularly the vulnerability of Jews to its consequences. After he settled in Palestine, he castigated the new Jewish society for not realizing its declared ideals. The key figures in his poetry are his mother, whom he lost in his childhood, and his grandfather, who raised him; the former becomes the symbol of Jewish motherhood and the latter—age-old Israel. Hameiri's power as a storyteller is revealed mainly in his realistic war stories. Their central theme is the peculiarly tragic fate of the Jewish soldier fighting wars which are not his. He loathes the bloodshed and the bestiality of combat, and yet, since he is an outsider, is unable to find comfort in the companionship of his fellow soldiers. In 1968 he was awarded the Israel Prize.

Sefer ha-Shirim ("The Book of Poems," 1933) contains his complete poetry up to its publication. His subsequent works of poetry included *Ha-Moked ha-Ran* ("The Singing Pyre," 1944), collected poems from 1933 to 1944; *Ḥalomot shel Beit-Rabban* ("Schoolboy Dreams," 1945), and *Be-Livnat ha-Sappir* ("In a Pavement of Sapphire," 1962). His works of fiction include the novel *Ha-Shigga'on ha-Gadol* (1950; *The Great Madness,* 1952); *Be-Geihinnom shel Mattah* ("Lower Hell," novel, 1932); *Tenuvah* ("Produce," 1947²); *Ha-Mashi'aḥ ha-Lavan* ("The White Messiah," novel, 1948); *Bein Laylah le-Laylah* ("Between the Nights," short stories, 1944); and *Sodo shel Socrates* ("Socrates' Secret," historical novel, 1955). A list of his works translated into English appears in Goell, Bibliography, 861–81, 2123–34.

Bibliography: S. Streit, *Penei ha-Sifrut,* 2 (1939), 280–91; Waxman, Literature, 4 (1960), 174–8, 320–4; R. Wallenrod, *The Literature of Modern Israel* (1956), index; S. Halkin, *Modern Hebrew Literature* (1950), 121, 154; S. Sanet, *Eifoh Hem ha-Yom?* (1970), 21–27.

[G.El.]

HAMEIRI (Ostrovsky), MOSHE (1886–1947), rabbi and Mizrachi leader in Ereẓ Israel. Born in Karlin, Belorussia, Hameiri settled in Ereẓ Israel in 1897. He studied at yeshivot in Jerusalem and was ordained by Ḥayyim Berlin and A. I. Kook, becoming rabbi of the *Ekron settlement in 1912. Active from his youth in the Mizrachi movement, in 1919 he became one of the chief planners and organizers of the religious school system in Palestine. Hameiri taught Talmud at the Mizrachi Teachers' Seminary in Jerusalem. He was a member of the Va'ad Le'ummi executive, heading its department of local religious communities. Hameiri helped to organize the Chief Rabbinate in Palestine and was one of the founders of the Kiryat Moshe quarter in west Jerusalem. His books include *Ha-Middot she-ha-Torah Nidreshet Bahen* ("The Principles by Which the Torah is Expounded," 1924), *Mevo ha-Talmud* ("Introduction to the Talmud," 1935), a textbook for schools and teachers' seminaries, *Toledot ha-Mizrachi be-Ereẓ Yisrael* ("The History of Mizrachi in Ereẓ Israel," 1944), and *Irgun ha-Yishuv ha-Yehudi be-Ereẓ Yisrael* ("The Organization of the Jewish Yishuv in Ereẓ Israel," 1942).

Bibliography: EẒD, 2 (1960), 122–5; *Sefer Ish ha-Torah ve-ha-Ma'aseh* (1946), for his 60th birthday, includes bibliography.

[Ed.]

HA-MELIẒ Heb. הַמֵּלִיץ, "The Advocate"), the first Hebrew paper in Russia. *Ha-Meliẓ* was founded in Odessa in 1860 by Alexander *Zederbaum with the assistance of his son-in-law, A. J. Goldenblum. Zederbaum obtained the license to publish the paper through his connections with the czarist authorities. *Ha-Meliẓ* was long the organ of the moderate Haskalah movement in Russia, although at times it served the extreme wing of the Haskalah, publishing the writings of M. L. *Lilienblum and J. L. *Gordon, advocates of religious reform. In the literary sphere, *Ha-Meliẓ* was involved in a bitter controversy concerning A. U. *Kovner and his destructive criticism of Hebrew literature (Kovner also sharply criticized *Ha-Meliẓ* in his *Ẓeror Peraḥim,* 1868). Appearing in Russia, where censorship was severe, *Ha-Meliẓ* defended the czarist

שנה שניה

המליץ

בין עם ישרון ובין הממשלה, בין האמונה ובין ההשכלה.

№ 2.

פקודות הממשלה.

זאת תורה

Front page of *Ha-Meliz*, October 12, 1861, the first Hebrew newspaper in Russia, founded in Odessa in 1860. Jerusalem, J.N.U.L.

regime, but also criticized it surreptitiously. Zederbaum introduced into *Ha-Meliz* the Hebrew journalistic article with all its virtues and defects and attracted contributors from among the best authors in Russia, such as *Mendele Mokher Seforim. After ten years in Odessa, *Ha-Meliz* was transferred to St. Petersburg (1871) where it appeared until it ceased publication in 1904. As *Ha-Meliz* was pro-Russian, it advocated Haskalah, Jewish agricultural settlement in Russia, occupation in trades, and improving education while fostering traditional and religious values. Accordingly, it held a reserved attitude toward nationalist and Zionist ideals which were gaining impetus in the early 1880s. Only as Zionism grew stronger, and under the influence of A. S. *Friedberg, one of the paper's editorial assistants, did *Ha-Meliz* become the organ of the Ḥibbat Zion movement in Russia. In response to the growing interest in Zionism in the 1880s, *Ha-Meliz*, which had been a weekly, became a semiweekly in 1883 and a daily from 1886, until it ceased publication. For different reasons the paper did not appear for periods of various lengths, from a few months in 1871–72 and in 1879, to a few years, from 1874 to 1877. *Ha-Meliz* flourished in the 1880s and 1890s, particularly under the editorship of the poet Judah Leib *Gordon (1880–83, 1885–88). Promoting Hebrew literature in Russia during the second half of the 19th century, *Ha-Meliz* published the earliest writings of Aḥad Ha-Am, Bialik, and scores of other Hebrew authors and scholars in Russia and abroad. *Ha-Meliz* also published controversy which, descending to the personal level, bore negative consequences. When *Ha-Meliz* became the organ of the Ḥibbat Zion movement in Russia it published the best nationalist-Zionist journalism. For many years *Ha-Meliz* published various literary collections, introducing writers of all political and religious factions. On Zederbaum's death in 1893, the paper ceased to appear for a few months until it was taken over by Leon *Rabinovich who served as its last editor.

Bibliography: S. L. Zitron, in: *Ha-Olam*, 7 (1913), passim; 8 (1914), passim; S. Bernstein, *Be-Ḥazon ha-Dorot* (1928), 74–102; R. Malachi, in: *Hadoar*, 40 (1961), no. 13–27, passim; Kressel, Leksikon, 2 (1967), 703f. [G.K.]

HAMELN (Hamelin), city near Hanover, W. Germany. Jews are first mentioned in the privileges granted to the town in 1277. The formula of the Jewish oath of Hameln, almost identical with the earlier formula of Dortmund, was recorded in the municipal ledger. In the early years of Jewish settlement there were no more than about ten Jewish families, engaged mostly in moneylending under the protection of the municipal authorities. By the middle of the 14th century the number of Jews had grown significantly, and in 1344 they opened a synagogue. Shortly thereafter however, during the *Black Death persecutions (1349–50), the community ceased to exist. For the next two centuries only individual Jews settled in Hameln. By the middle of the 16th century their members had increased and a "Jewish Street" is mentioned in 1552. In 1590 Duke Henry Julius banished all the Jews from his provinces, but the Hameln town council, claiming its traditional right to control the fate of the Jews in the town, determined to ignore the order. Nevertheless, most of the Jews left. In her memoirs, *Glueckel of Hameln indicates that only two Jewish families lived there in 1660.

By the end of the 17th century the Hameln community had increased and a number of its members were among those attending the Leipzig fairs (1691–1763). A new cemetery was consecrated in 1743. There were appointed rabbis resident in the city until 1782. The 12 Jewish families in Hameln in 1777 had declined to five families in 1814 and risen again to ten only in 1830. In 1832 the community was put under the jurisdiction of the rabbinate of Hanover and a school was established. A new synagogue was dedicated in 1879. The Jewish population numbered 86 in 1845; 149 in 1875; and 170 (0.6% of the total) in 1931. The synagogue was destroyed in 1938 and the remainder of the community (44 in 1939) deported. In 1963 a memorial to the Jews of Hameln was erected in the city.

The synagogue of Hameln, Germany. Designed by Edwin Oppler, it was built in 1879 and destroyed by the Nazis. Courtesy Hameln Municipality.

Bibliography: Germ Jud, 2 (1968), 323–34; A. Neukirch, *Hamelner Renaissance* . . . (1950); A. Reimer, *Juden in niedersaechsischen Staedten des Mittelalters* (1907), passim; H. Spanuth and R. Feige (eds.), *Geschichte der Stadt Hameln* (1963). Part of the communal archives (1709–1844) are in the Central Archives for the History of the Jewish People in Jerusalem. [Z.Av./Z.F.]

HAMENAḤEM, EZRA (1907–), Hebrew writer. Born in Skoplje, Serbia, he settled with his family in Ereẓ Israel in 1914. After receiving a religious education in the Old City of Jerusalem, he worked in a Jerusalem bank and then at *Mosad Bialik, the Am Oved publishing house, and as editor of literary programs on the Israel radio. In the late 1930s, he began writing about the old and new cities of Jerusalem, particularly about their oriental Jewish community. His collections of short stories include *Bein ha-Ḥomot* (1941), *Afar ha-Areẓ* (1948), *Be-Ẓel ha-Yamim* (1956), and *Sippurei ha-Ir ha-Attikah* (1968).

Bibliography: A. Cohen, *Soferim Ivriyyim Benei Zemannenu* (1964), 144–6; Y. Keshet, *Maskiyyot* (1953), 261–72; R. Wallenrod, *Literature of Modern Israel* (1956), 188. [G.K.]

HA-ME'ORER (Heb. הַמְעוֹרֵר; "the Awakener"), a Hebrew monthly published in London in 1906–07 and edited by J. Ḥ. *Brenner. *Ha-Me'orer* began publication after the failure of the Russian revolution of 1905. While living in London, Brenner was involved in the Jewish and general labor movements there. Through this monthly, dominated by his sharp and nonconformist thinking, Brenner hoped to establish a Hebrew center in England at a time when there were few Hebrew papers in Russia. He was severely critical of complacency in Hebrew literature, which resisted original thought, and of the Jewish labor movement in Russia, which promoted Yiddish instead of Hebrew. In particular, Brenner denounced what he considered hollow verbiage current in the Jewish workers' movement on the one hand, and in the Zionist movement and its literature on the other.

Ha-Me'orer was the periodical in which Brenner first crystallized the approach characterizing the periodicals he later edited. His reactions to current affairs and to literature were a model of original, non-conventional thinking. In addition to printing stories and plays of his own and others, he also published poems, essays, and translations of Ibsen, Wilde, and Maeterlinck. Contributors to *Ha-Me'orer* were authors, old and young, who appreciated the editor's attempts to maintain a Hebrew paper single-handedly. After appearing for less than two years, however, the paper could no longer maintain itself and ceased publication. *Ha-Me'orer* greatly influenced young Jews and particularly the generation of the Second *Aliyah*.

Bibliography: Kressel, Leksikon, 1 (1965), 369–72; idem, in: *La-Merḥav* (Sept. 26, 1969). [G.K.]

ḤAMEẒ (Heb. חָמֵץ; "fermented dough"; cf. Ex. 12:39). *Ḥameẓ* is prohibited in Jewish religious usage in two instances, one of which has a purely theoretical application at the present day, while the other is of topical application. The first was the prohibition against offering up *ḥameẓ* of any kind (or honey) on the altar as a concomitant of sacrifices (Lev. 2:11, where it is referred to as *se'or*). *Se'or* and *hameẓ* are by no means synonymous. *Se'or* refers to the leavening agent, while *ḥameẓ* is the new dough to which the *se'or* is added, and it is expressly called *leḥem ḥameẓ* ("leavened bread"; Lev. 7:13). This distinction is clearly shown by Exodus 12:15: "Seven days you shall eat unleavened bread *(maẓẓot)*; on the first day you shall remove leaven *(se'or)* from your houses, for whoever eats leavened bread *(ḥameẓ)* from the first day to the seventh day that person shall be cut off from Israel." Further corroboration of this distinction is furnished by a linguistic criterion: *se'or* is never used with the verb *akhal* ("eat"), since it is too sour to be edible. The leavened bread mentioned with regard to the sacrifices is given directly to the priest or is consumed by the worshiper (cf. Lev. 2:12, 7:13; 23:17, 20). The instructions for the making of shewbread contain no prohibition of the use of leaven (Lev. 24:5–9) since it was not consumed but merely displayed. However post-biblical tradition prohibits it (Jos., Ant. 3:142, 255ff.; cf. Men. 5:1). It was permitted, however, as part of the sacrificial meal (Lev. 7:13). The other is the complete prohibition of *ḥameẓ* (or anything containing it) during *Passover, which includes its consumption, deriving any benefit from it, and retaining it in one's possession (Ex. 12:19). To this the rabbis added the prohibition after Passover of leaven which had been in one's possession during the festival (Pes. 2:2; 28b; Sh. Ar., OḤ 448). However, the author of the "Passover Papyrus" of Elephantine (Cowley, Aramaic, 21, p. 60ff.) felt that it sufficed to keep the leaven out of sight, i.e., stored away. Nonetheless he did follow the *halakhah*, in opposition to the stricter Samaritan view (a restored text), in maintaining that only fermented grain but not fermented fruit (wine) was included under the definition of leaven (H. L. Ginsberg, in: Pritchard, Texts, 491, esp. n. 6).

The criterion for rendering grain *ḥameẓ* is that on decomposition it ferments. This characteristic was stated to apply only to the five species of grain, usually translated as "wheat, barley, spelt, rye, and oats" (but see *Five Species). Other grains which, instead of fermenting, "rotted," were not regarded as coming within the prohibition of *ḥameẓ*; in this class, as is specifically stated, belong rice and millet (Pes. 35a). Despite this fact, Ashkenazi authorities, in contrast to Sephardi, not only forbid the use of rice (and millet) on Passover, but extend the prohibition to include a whole additional range of products which they regard as belonging to the category of *kitniyyot* ("pulse") or even "doubtful *kitniyyot*," including such foods as beans, peas, maize, and peanuts, since flour is made from them and thus people might come to use ordinary flour in such a way as to make it *ḥameẓ*. In practice, among Ashkenazi Jews the only flour used on Passover is "*maẓẓah* meal" (i.e., ground *maẓẓah*) and potato flour, while the Sephardim use rice.

Prohibited *ḥameẓ* is divided into three categories of descending stringency: *ḥameẓ gamur*, that which is "completely" *ḥameẓ*, i.e., one of the above fermented doughs and such derivatives as whisky; *ta'arovet ḥameẓ*, that which has in it an admixture of even the smallest amount of *ḥameẓ*; and *ḥameẓ nuksheh*, roughly, *ḥameẓ* which is unsuitable for food, such as writer's paste (Pes. 3:1). It is only for the first that the penalty of *karet* is involved, although Maimonides (Yad, introd., negative commandment no. 198) regards the word *maḥmeẓet* (Ex. 12:19) as referring to *ta'arovet* which is therefore, according to him, forbidden by the Bible. The penalty of *karet* is involved, and the minimum amount for which liability is incurred is an olive's bulk.

Whereas the prohibition of most forbidden food is nullified if it is accidentally mixed in more than 60 times its volume of permitted food and this applies even to leaven mixed in permitted food being prepared for Passover prior to the festival—during Passover *ḥameẓ* can never be nullified in this way; the most minute admixture renders everything with which it has been mixed forbidden as *ta'arovet*. As a result, practically every food product which has not been specially prepared under supervision in order to ensure the complete absence of *ḥameẓ* is regarded as belonging to this category. For the same reason all vessels which have been used during the year are forbidden for use during the festival, unless they have been cleansed in accordance with halakhic requirements (see *Passover).

The period which it takes for flour mixed with water to begin fermenting is stated as the time it takes to walk a (Roman) mile (Pes. 46a); the authorities have established this as 18 minutes. This, however, applies to normal conditions and varies according to the circumstances. Thus, on the one hand, if the temperature of the water is above normal the process is accelerated; on the other hand, the ontinuous manipulation of the dough delays, and even revents, fermentation (OḤ 459; for details see *Mazzah).

Ḥasidim, believing that there is a possibility that some of ie flour in the mazzah may have remained unbaked, take p the extreme attitude of not eating mazzah or mazzah ieal which has been soaked in water during the whole of ie seven days of Passover; they permit it only on the eighth ay (which obtains in the Diaspora).

The prohibition of ḥamez commences from the time that ie paschal sacrifice used to be offered, at midday on the 4th of Nisan, but the period has been extended to two ours earlier (Pes. 28b).

Leaven in Jewish Thought. Leaven is regarded as the ymbol of corruption and impurity. The "yeast in the ough" is one of the things which "prevents us from erforming the will of God" (Ber. 17a). The idea was reatly developed in the Kabbalah. The New Testament lso refers to "the leaven of malice and wickedness" which s contrasted with "the unleavened bread of sincerity and ruth" (I Cor. 5:8). Similarly the word is applied to what vas regarded as the corrupt doctrine of the Pharisees and adducees (Matt. 16:12; Mark 8:15).

It was applied particularly to the admixture of elements f impure descent in a family. (Fermented) "dough" was ontrasted in this context with "pure sifted flour." Thus, vith regard to purity of family descent, "All the countries re regarded as dough compared to Erez Israel, while Erez srael is regarded as dough compared to Babylonia" (Kid. 1a). Ezra did not leave Babylonia until he had made its 'Jewish population pure sifted flour" (by bringing up those f doubtful descent to Erez Israel, *ibid.* 69b). The widow of a man of doubtful descent is referred to as a "dough widow" (Ket. 14b).

Bibliography: S. Zevin, *Ha-Mo'adim ba-Halakhah* (1959[7]), 231ff. [L.I.R.]

ḤAMEZ, SALE OF (Heb. מְכִירַת חָמֵץ). No *ḥamez (leaven) may be present, or seen, in the house of a Jew during Passover. In addition to the prohibition against eating ḥamez or deriving any benefit from it, the Pentateuch explicitly states: "Seven days shall there be no eaven found in your houses" (Ex. 12:19), "neither shall here be leaven seen with thee, in all thy borders" (Ex. 13:7). Any ḥamez which a Jew has kept over Passover becomes forbidden forever (Pes. 2:2 and 29a; Sh. Ar. OḤ, 448:3).

Disposal of Ḥamez. The disposal of all ḥamez which is in the possession of a Jew is carried out after the **bedikat ḥamez* ("search for leaven") has taken place on the eve of the 14th of Nisan. According to the *halakhah,* the ḥamez may be disposed of in three ways. It may be burnt (which must be done before 10 o'clock on the morning of the 14th of Nisan). It may be annulled by declaring, "May all leaven in my possession, whether I have seen it or not, whether I have removed it or not, be annulled and considered as the dust of the earth." It may also be sold. Since the first method might involve hardship, especially where large quantities of foodstuffs are involved, or where the ḥamez is used for business purposes, the ḥamez is sold to a non-Jew. This applies only to foodstuffs; utensils which have been used for ḥamez need only be washed and stored separately.

The Legal Character of the Sale. The transaction by which the ḥamez is sold must be of a legal character, carried out by means of a bill of sale. The purchaser must both lease the place in which the ḥamez is stored, and buy the ḥamez itself. The gentile thus becomes the legal owner of the ḥamez which the Jew, if he so desires, may buy back after Passover. The completion of the sale is effected by the signing of the contract and by the transfer of money, usually in the form of a down payment (see Modes of *Acquisition). The rabbinic insistence that such a bill of sale be in accordance with the requirements of the *halakhah,* and the inconvenience which would result were every Jew to attempt to sell his own ḥamez gave rise to the formal sale of the ḥamez. The Jewish vendor merely appends his signature to a composite document which grants power of attorney to sell his ḥamez to an agent (usually the local rabbi) who, in turn, arranges the contract with the non-Jewish buyer. The agent buys the ḥamez back after Passover, and restores it to its original owners. All the contracts are written in Hebrew although it has been suggested that the vernacular be used for the bill of sale so as to ensure the Gentile's understanding of the contract.

Stages of Development of the Transaction. Four distinct stages in the evolution of the transaction whereby ḥamez is sold can be traced in rabbinic literature. The first sales, referred to in the Talmud (Pes. 2:1; Tosef., Pes. 1:7; Shab. 18b; Pes. 13a, 21a), were clearly of a simple nature. Although the *Gemara* does not discuss any details, such a sale presumably involved the physical transfer of ḥamez from Jew to non-Jew "in the market place" (Pes. 13a). The beginning of the second stage, by which it became common practice to sell ḥamez to a non-Jew with the mutual understanding that the Jew would buy it back after Passover, is hinted at in the Tosefta (Pes. 1:24, also in TJ, Pes. 2:2, 28d). Although the author of *Halakhot Gedolot* (ed. by I. Hildesheimer (1892), 136) stipulated that there must be no suggestion of such an intention, the practice had clearly earned rabbinic consent by the time of the compilation of the Shulḥan Arukh (OḤ 448:3). The condition that the ḥamez must be physically transferred from the property of the Jew to that of the non-Jew still remained (*Magen Avraham,* Sh. Ar., OḤ 448:3). It was the observation of Joel *Sirkes (*Bayit Ḥadash,* OḤ 448)—that this caused considerable inconvenience to merchants—which initiated a new chapter in the history of the sale of ḥamez. He suggested that such inconvenience might be avoided by selling (or later leasing) the room in which the ḥamez was stored to the non-Jew, a transaction which involved a small down payment and the physical transfer only of the key to the room. In later times the official nature of the transaction was stressed by the writing of a bill of sale. A copy of such a document (in Judeo-German) written by R. Ezekiel *Landau of Prague is preserved in his son Samuel Landau's responsa (*Shivat Ziyyon* 11); others were sometimes printed in *Haggadot.* The final stage in the evolution of the sale of ḥamez was introduced by R. *Schneur Zalman of Lyady. Objecting to the blatant legal fiction involved in Sirkes' method, he proposed the idea of a "general" sale, with an agent acting on behalf of the Jewish vendor. Despite the opposition of numerous rabbis, including Solomon b. Judah Aaron *Kluger of Brody and R. Joseph Saul *Nathanson, this proposal has generally been accepted as the form of the sale of ḥamez.

See **Bedikat Ḥamez.*

Bibliography: S. J. Zevin, *Ha-Mo'adim ba-Halakhah* (1963[10]), 245–55. [H.Ra.]

HAMILTON, city in Ontario, Canada; Jewish population (1970), estimated 4,200; total population, 298,000; Greater Hamilton, 460,000. In 1851 there were only three Jews in Hamilton but six years later the numbers had increased sufficiently to permit the formation of the Hebrew Benevolent Society Anshe Sholom of Hamilton, which purchased a burial site. In 1863 the Anshe Sholom Congregation was incorporated as a synagogue, the fourth in Canada. In contrast to other Jewish communities in Canada, although, parallel to conditions in the United States, Anshe Sholom was composed in its earlier years predominantly of German Jews. In other contemporary synagogues in Ontario the membership was an admixture of English, German, and East European Jews. Its women's welfare group, the Deborah Society, founded in 1873, kept its minute books in German as late as the 1890s, the only synagogue group in Canada known to do this. Perhaps because of this factor it was ahead of other Canadian synagogues in adopting Reform practices. Edmund Scheur, who settled in Hamilton in 1871 (when it had 177 Jews), initiated mixed seating. Though Anshe Sholom was Canada's first Liberal synagogue, it was slow to adopt classical Reform and was more conservative in its rituals than others. Bernard Baskin served the congregation from 1949.

Hamilton's second synagogue, Beth Jacob, now its largest, like many others in Canada dates from the influx of East European Jews from czarist Russia after 1882. A local factor was the secession of some dissidents from the liberalizing Anshe Sholom congregation. A charter for the Beth Jacob Synagogue was obtained in 1887 (there had been a *minyan* from 1883) and in 1889 a church building was purchased and renovated, which served for 67 years. In 1956 the congregation was affiliated to the Conservative movement. The Adas Israel congregation started in 1914 as a *shtibl* and was known as the Polish synagogue. In 1959 a new impressive building was erected and the synagogue became Hamilton's largest Orthodox institution, also sponsoring a Jewish day school, Hamilton Hebrew Academy. Two other Orthodox congregations exist, the Agudath Achim, founded by Rumanian Jews, and the Ohav Tzedeck.

The United Hebrew Association was founded in 1916 and in 1932 was absorbed into the Jewish Social Services, which embraced case work, free loan, immigrant aid, and other welfare services. In 1933 all local Jewish organizations (then 24, in 1970 more than 30) united to form the Council of Jewish Organizations.

Outstanding citizens of Hamilton have been Jacob N. Goldblatt (19th century); Kenneth D. Soble (1911–1966), broadcasting executive and public housing head; Rabbi Samuel Levine (1878–1953), *rosh bet din;* Joseph A. Sweet (1897–), county court judge from 1958; and David Steinberg, judge of the juvenile and family court from 1969.

Synagogue of Congregation Anshe Sholom, Hamilton, Ontario, founded in 1863. Photo Hardwick Studio, Hamilton.

Bibliography: A. D. Hart (ed.), *Jew in Canada* (1926), index; B. G. Sack, *History of the Jews in Canada* (1945), index; L. Kurman, in: *Canadian Jewish Reference Book and Directory* (1963), 342–7; S. Rosenberg, *Jewish Commity in Canada* (1970), index. [B. G. K.]

ḤAMIẒ, JOSEPH BEN JUDAH (d. c. 1676), physician, philosopher, kabbalist, and communal leader. Born in Venice, from his youth Ḥamiẓ devoted himself to Torah and scholarship and was one of the outstanding pupils of Leone *Modena. In 1624 he received the degree of doctor of medicine and philosophy at the University of Padua. At the same time the rabbis of Venice decided to ordain him as rabbi. In honor of his graduation, his teacher and colleagues published a "collection of eulogies and poems" under the title *Belil Ḥamiẓ* (Venice, 1624; also in: *Seridim,* 1938). To Modena's distress, Ḥamiẓ came under the influence of esoteric teachings and joined the kabbalistic circles of Moses *Zacuto and *Aaron Berechiah b. Moses of Modena. In 1658 he and Zacuto published an expanded edition of the *Zohar Ḥadash* with glosses on the *Zohar, entitled *Derekh Emet.* During the same period Ḥamiẓ began to write a commentary on the Zohar but ceased this work because he decided to move to Jerusalem. Thereafter all traces of him are lost.

During recent years two collections of his works have been found. I. Tishby discovered that a manuscript in Oxford University Library (Ms. Bod. 2239) is a collection of Ḥamiẓ's works written during the years 1667–75. From its contents it is clear that he was associated with Shabbatean circles and was active in the movement. E. Kupfer discovered that Ms. Parma 1283 was written by Ḥamiẓ in the town of Zante, where he stayed around 1666 on his way from Venice to Ereẓ Israel with his family. Apparently he delayed there because of the troubles that befell him: his wife and many members of his family who had accompanied him from Venice died in Zante. While staying there, he practiced as a physician, devoted much of his time to Torah, and was active in the life of the Jewish community. In 1674 he promoted the conference for the union of the communities in Zante, and was chosen to introduce **takkanot* for the united community.

From his writings in the Parma manuscript, it is clear that despite his devotion to Kabbalah and his association with Shabbatean activists he continued to be in doubt and disturbed. Even in his later years, side by side with kabbalist writings there are philosophical ideas and studies based on the school of Maimonides. Among the works in this collection is the *Pirkei ha-Musar u-Middot,* which he wrote as a kind of testament for his children.

Bibliography: M. Benayahu, *Iggerot R. Shemu'el Abohav ve-R. Moshe Zakut u-Venei Ḥugam,* 2, 8 (1955); I. Tishby, in: *Sefunot,* 1 (1956), 80–117; Scholem, Shabbetai Ẓevi, 2 (1957), index; E. Kupfer, in: KS, 40 (1965), 118–23; idem, in: *Sefunot* (in print). [E.K.]

HA-MIẒPEH (Heb. הַמִּצְפֶּה; "the Watchtower"), a Hebrew weekly newspaper. Appearing in Cracow from 1904 to 1921 (with intervals during World War I), *Ha-Miẓpeh* was edited by Simon Menahem Laser. Laser, the last editor of **Ha-Maggid* which ceased publication in 1903, wanted to maintain the Hebrew press in Galicia. His new paper had a religious Zionist orientation and was the faithful organ, without official status, of the *Mizrachi movement. At the same time it fought the opponents of Zionism, including both Ḥasidim and assimilationists. *Ha-Miẓpeh* reached its highest popularity at the time of the elections for the Austrian parliament, when it fought with extraordinary vigor the government-approved anti-Zionist pact between assimilationists and the ḥasidic rabbis. The paper also combated negative manifestations in the Zionist movement. Laser encouraged literary talents in Galicia. He discovered S. Y. *Agnon (then still known as Czaczkes), Avigdor *Hameiri, U. Z. *Greenberg, and many others who later became famous in Hebrew literature. Apart from Laser's journalistic pieces, the paper published studies, poems, stories, essays, feuilletons, and a humorous section for Purim. It was maintained throughout the years by Laser's efforts and without any subvention, even during World War I when he revived the paper after it had been forced to close.

Nr. 1.

המצפה

HAMICPE

עתון שבועי

מחיר גליון בודד 30 הלר.

Kraków, 14. września 1917.

גליון א.

התקוה הראשנה.

Front page of the Hebrew weekly newspaper *Ha-Mizpeh*, edited by Simon Laser, Cracow, September 14, 1917. Jerusalem, J.N.U.L.

Laser was among the few who understood the nature of the Bolshevik regime's attitude toward the Jews, the problematic nature of the Balfour Declaration, and other political issues.

Bibliography: G. Kressel (ed.), *Al ha-Mizpeh, Mivḥar Kitvei Shimon Menaḥem Laser* (1969). [G.K.]

ḤAMMAT GADER (Heb. חַמַּת גָּדֵר; **Emmatha, El Ḥamme),** ancient site in the Yarmuk Valley S.E. of Lake Kinneret. Ḥammat contained hot springs and attracted settlers from earliest times. In talmudic times it was included in the territory of *Gadara, and the Talmud thus refers to it as "Ḥammat of Gadara." It was heavily populated in this period, and many visitors from the south, the Golan, and Galilee, including Judah ha-Nasi and his pupils, came to bathe in the springs. The Romans also used the springs during the bathing season. The ruins of large bathhouses still stand in the valley. [E.Cı.]

In the Modern Period. The five thermal springs of Ḥammat Gader (the waters of the hottest and richest in minerals have a temperature of 124°F (51°C)) intermittently served local inhabitants for healing purposes. The place became a station on the narrow-gauge railway branch that connected Haifa through Ẓemaḥ with the Hejaz railway (traffic on the line was finally halted in 1946 when the Palmaḥ blew up a bridge crossing the Yarmuk near Ḥammat Gader). The border of the British Mandate of Palestine protruded eastward into the narrow Yarmuk gorge for 3 mi. (5 km.), thus creating a wedge, including Ḥammat Gader, of a few hundred meters width only, between Transjordanian and Syrian territory. In Israel's War of Independence (1948), the Syrians occupied the place when advancing toward Lake Kinneret; in the 1949 Armistice Agreement, the Ḥammat Gader tongue returned to Israel sovereignty, although it was declared a demilitarized zone where only the previous (i.e., Arab) inhabitants were permitted to return. Nevertheless in 1951, Syrian forces occupied Ḥammat Gader and held it until 1967. The Syrians turned the spot into a rest center for their officers and officials, building a mosque, hotel, bathhouses, and other installations. In the Six-Day War (1967), Ḥammat Gader returned to Israel control. In the ensuing years, it was repeatedly shelled from Jordanian positions on the steep slope directly above it, and mines planted by terrorists caused a number of losses to Israel civilians. Because of the security situation, plans for developing Ḥammat Gader as a farming, tourist, and recreation center had to be postponed, and the group preparing to settle there had to erect its collective village, Mevo Ḥammat, 3 mi. (5 km.) to the northwest on the Golan plateau. [E.O.]

Bibliography: Albright, in: BASOR, 35 (1932), 12; Glueck, *ibid.*, 49 (1933), 22; E. L. Sukenik, *The Ancient Synagogue of el-Ḥammeh "Hammath-by-Gadara"* (1935); idem, in: JPOS, 15 (1935), 101–80; EḤA, s.v.

Aerial view of El Ḥamme, built on the ancient site of Ḥammat Gader, showing the bridge over the River Yarmuk and, in the background, the minaret of the mosque in the military rest center established by the Syrians. Photo Ze'ev Radovan, Jerusalem.

HAMMATH (חַמַּת), city in the territory of Naphtali mentioned in the Bible together with Rakkath and Chinnereth (Josh. 19:35). Its name indicates the presence of hot springs. Most scholars identify Hammath with Hammath-Dor, a city of refuge and a levitical city (Josh. 21:32), which is generally located at Hammath Tiberias, south of Tiberias. No remains from the biblical period, however, have thus far been uncovered there, and the site of the ancient town should probably be identified with the early remains within the confines of Roman Tiberias. Hammath was famous for its hot baths in the Second Temple period (Jos., Wars 4:11; Jos., Ant. 18:36); when Tiberias rose to prominence in talmudic times, Hammath, one mile away and joined to Tiberias for halakhic purposes, also became well known (Meg. 2b; Tosef., Er. 7:2; TJ, Er. 6 (5); 13). After the destruction of the Second Temple, priests of the Maziah course settled there (*Baraita of the Twenty-Four Mishmarot*, 24); the Emmaus mentioned in the Mishnah *Arakhin* 2:4 may refer to the place. R. Meir was one of the many talmudic scholars who lived there. A Jewish community is attested there up to the time of the Cairo *Genizah*.

During the excavation of the foundations of bathhouses, two synagogues were discovered; the first was excavated by N. Slouschz in 1920 and the other by M. Dothan in 1961–63. The first, belonging to the transitional type of synagogue, consisted of a basilica-shaped hall without an apse. The facade oriented to Jerusalem contained four small marble columns which apparently supported a marble lintel above the Ark of the Law. The synagogue was paved with mosaics; fragments of the "*seat of Moses" (cathedra) were found there, as well as a stone seven-branched *menorah*, carved in relief and decorated with a "button and leaf" pattern in the form of pomegranates. In the second synagogue four building phases were distinguished. (1) The earliest structure consisted of a public building (probably not a synagogue) with rooms surrounding a central courtyard. (2) A synagogue from the third century C.E. (3) Directly above this synagogue and using its columns was another synagogue built in the form of a basilica with an outstanding mosaic pavement which contained (from north to south): a dedicatory inscription flanked by two lions; a zodiac of a high artistic standard with the sun god Helios on his chariot in the center and representations of the four seasons in the corners; the Ark of the Law with *menorot* and other ritual articles. Inscriptions in Greek and one in Aramaic commemorate several builders, especially a certain "Severus, the pupil of the most illustrious patriarchs." The building, 47 ½ ft. (14 ½ m.) wide, contains a nave with two aisles east of it and to the west of it, an aisle, and a hall (women's gallery?). The synagogue is attributed to the beginning of the fourth century C.E.; in a later period a stationary *bamah* ("platform") was installed and the entrance was moved from the southern to the northern side. (4) Above the site of this synagogue another one was built in the sixth century with a slightly different orientation. It was basilica in shape, 62 x 49 ft. (19 x 15 m.) with an apse and a mosaic pavement with geometric designs.

Bathhouses have again been built at Hammath Tiberias in modern times. They are fed by five springs whose waters reach a temperature of 140°–144° F (60°–62° C) and contain graphite, iron, and magnesium chloride. Of curative value, they are widely used, especially in the winter

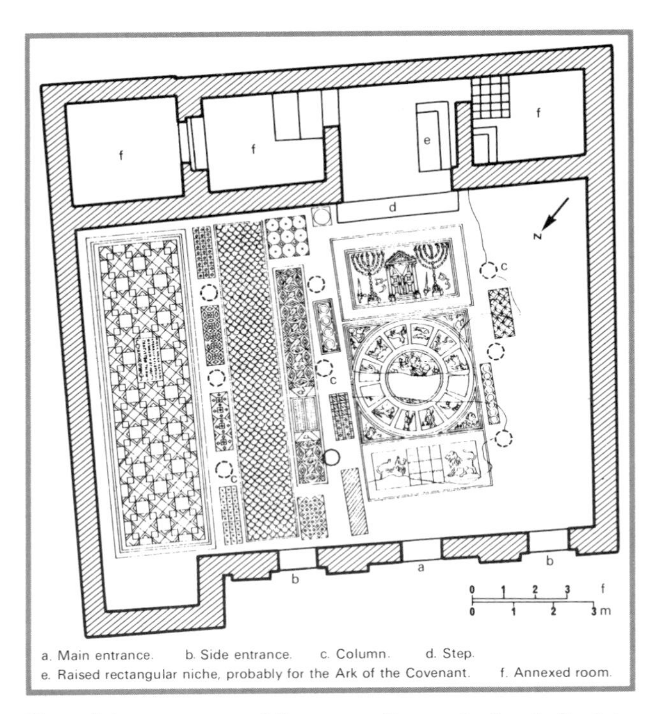

Plan of the synagogue of Severus at Hammath, first half of the fourth century, C.E. Courtesy M. Dothan, Israel Department of Antiquities, Jerusalem.

Greek inscription on the floor mosaic in the synagogue of Severus at Hammath, listing the names of Severus and other builders, first half of fourth century C.E. Courtesy M. Dothan, Israel Department of Antiquities, Jerusalem.

seasons. The grave of R. *Meir Ba'al ha-Nes is reputed to be near Hammath Tiberias, and a large synagogue is situated on the site. The grave site became famous in the Jewish world beginning in the 18th century because of the collection boxes, named after R. Meir, widely distributed by emissaries of charitable institutions. It is an ancient custom to hold festivities and build bonfires near the grave on the 14th of Iyyar.

Bibliography: Slouschz, in: JPESJ, 1(1921), 5–39, 49–52; W. F. Albright, in: BASOR, 19 (1925), 10; M. Dothan, in: IEJ, 12 (1962), 153–4; idem, in: *Qadmoniot*, 1 (1968), 116–23; A. Saarisalo, *Boundary between Issachar and Naphtali* (1927), 128 n. 1; M. Noth, *Das Buch Josua* (1938), 90–91; D. W. Thomas, in: PEFQS, 65 (1933), 205; 66 (1934), 147–8.

[M.A.-Y.]

HAMMERSTEIN, U.S. family closely associated with the development of opera and the popular musical theater in U.S. Its two most famous members were Oscar Hammerstein I (1847–1919) and his grandson, Oscar II (1895–1960). Born in Berlin, OSCAR HAMMSERSTEIN I ran away from home, reached New York in 1863, and worked in a cigar factory. He soon became an important and wealthy figure in the industry. His passion, however, was for building opera houses. The Harlem Opera House, built in the 1880s, was his first. The Victoria (1899) was a successful vaudeville theater managed by his son WILLIAM. Altogether he built ten opera houses and theaters in New York, in addition to an opera house in Philadelphia (1908) and one in London (1911). His Manhattan Opera House (1906), a venture in which his son ARTHUR (1873–1955) was closely involved, competed with the dominant Metropolitan Opera House until 1910, when the Metropolitan bought it out for $1,200,000. In its time the Manhattan helped to make grand

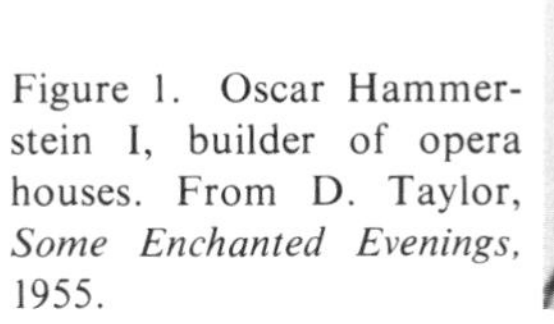

Figure 1. Oscar Hammerstein I, builder of opera houses. From D. Taylor, *Some Enchanted Evenings*, 1955.

opera exciting by bringing new talent and works to American audiences. His later ventures were less successful. OSCAR HAMMERSTEIN II, librettist, was born in New York, the son of William Hammerstein. He played an important role in developing the "musical play" into an integrated dramatic form. He worked for his uncle Arthur as a stage manager. By 1920 he had produced the books for three musicals. *Wildflower* (1923) was his first real success. Subsequently he collaborated on such Broadway musicals as *Rose Marie* (1924), *Desert Song* (1926), and *Show Boat* (1927). After some years in Hollywood, he formed his partnership with the composer Richard *Rodgers in 1943. Together they produced a series of successful musicals with a style and form of their own. These included *Oklahoma* (1943), *Carousel* (1945), *South Pacific* (1949), which won a Pulitzer Prize, *The King and I* (1951), and *The Sound of Music* (1959). The Rodgers and Hammerstein Foundation, New York, established a fund for cancer research in 1963, at the Hebrew University Hadassah Medical School, Jerusalem.

Figure 2. Oscar Hammerstein II, librettist and pioneer of musical comedy. From D. Taylor, *Some Enchanted Evenings*, 1955.

Bibliography: J. F. Cone, *Oscar Hammerstein's Manhattan Opera Company* (1966); *Fact Book Concerning the Plays of Richard Rodgers and Oscar Hammerstein* (1954).

[H.C.]

Upper part of the stele of Hammurapi, showing him receiving his laws from the sun god, c. 1792–1750 B.C.E. From L. H. Grollenberg, *Atlas of the Bible*, London, 1967.

HAMMURAPI ([the spelling of the name with a "p" rather than a "b" seems assured by the writing *'mrp'* in Ugaritic] apparently "the [divine] kinsman is a healer," but interpreted by post-Kassite Babylonian tradition as *kimta rapaštu*, "widespread kinfolk"), the sixth king (1792–50 B.C.E.) of the first dynasty of Babylon, one of several Amorite kingdoms which rose in southern Babylonia in the aftermath of the fall of the third dynasty of Ur.

Sources for the reign of Hammurapi are his own inscriptions, including the lengthy prologue to the code which bears his name; year names in date formulas which, in keeping with established tradition, list an outstanding military, political, or domestic event by which the year is known; letters, both from Hammurapi's own chancellery, and from other centers, especially the large political archive from *Mari in the upper Euphrates valley; business documents; and legal texts. Since Hammurapi's Babylon has not been excavated, his own diplomatic archive has not been uncovered.

When Hammurapi assumed the throne, Babylon was a small city-state, his predecessors having limited themselves to maintaining their local rule against the ambitions of similar states in the vicinity and against the incursions of nomads. As seen from a document written in the generation before Hammurapi, and from the contemporaneous Mari letters, the situation in southern Babylonia during the early Old Babylonian period was such that each ruler managed to govern within the limited confines of his city-state, while the open interurban spaces were given over to the control of nomadic and seminomadic tribes who roamed the area. It was Hammurapi's accomplishment to weld these several city-states into a cohesive base from which to embark on the wider conquest of the rest of Mesopotamia.

To his contemporaries, Hammurapi was a somewhat lesser figure than he is thought to be today—a minor king in comparison to others, according to a Mari letter. Indeed, for the first ten years or so of his reign, Babylon seems to have been at least partially subservient to Assyria, then ruled by Shamshi-Adad I. After the death of the latter during, or just after, Hammurapi's tenth year, Assyria began to decline, and a complicated political and military maze took form in Babylonia, expressing itself in a system of ephemeral alliances and counter alliances and reciprocal demands for military aid, each king continually jockeying for a more advantageous position. The serious rivals of Hammurapi were then Zimri-Lim of Mari, Rim-Sin of Larsa, and Ibal-pi-El of Eshnunna, together with his Elamite allies.

For the middle 20 years or so of Hammurapi's reign, nothing militarily or politically decisive occurred and the year names of this period reflect in the main a time of intensive civic building and canal making. By the 29th year of his reign Babylon must have been strong enough to take on its rivals. This year initiates ten years of intensive campaigning, which gave Hammurapi control of all of Mesopotamia. After a long period of seemingly friendly relations, Rim-Sin of Larsa was defeated in the 30th year of Hammurapi's reign; a coalition of forces from Assyria, Eshnunna, and Elam was defeated in the 31st year; Mari, in the 32nd; and Assyria was finally subdued in the 36th and 38th years. This seems to be the limit of Hammurapi's conquests, and there is no reason to identify him with *Amraphel of Genesis 14.

Hammurapi is best known for the so-called Code of Hammurapi (see *Mesopotamia). This is a misnomer, at least to the extent that it is not comprehensive. Modern scholarship tends to view the code as an abstract formulation of actual precedents in the form of ad hoc decisions of the king gathered from the state archives, plus an undetermined smaller element of deliberate, reforming legislation, all this cast in the traditional form of law codes consisting of a prologue, body of law, and epilogue. The actual function, if any, of this code is unknown, and it is never referred to in contemporary legal texts. The code reflects a tripartite division of society: an upper level of free men *(awīlum),* a class of state dependents (*muškēnum,* cf. Heb. *misken,* "poor"), and a slave caste *(wardum),* with no social mobility between classes. In other basic aspects, the code shows fundamental points of contact with the slightly older Eshnunna code, as well as with the Book of the *Covenant in Exodus 20ff.

The small amount of Old Babylonian literature preserved shows that this was a period of great and original creativity in Akkadian literature. It produced, furthermore, the last reliable formulation of the Sumerian traditions, and present knowledge of Sumerian language and literature is based, to a large extent, on the products of the contemporary scribal school. In religion, the rise of Marduk, the local god of Babylon, to the status of a great god, concomitant with the political rise of Babylon, should be noted.

Bibliography: C. J. Gadd, in: CAH², vol. 2, ch. 5 (1965; incl. bibl., 55–62); J. J. Finkelstein, in: JCS, 20 (1966), 95–118.

[AA.SH.]

HAMNUNA, the name of several Babylonian *amoraim.* (1) HAMNUNA SABA ("the elder"), a pupil of Rav (BK 106a), mid-third century C.E. He transmitted his teacher's sayings (Er. 16b; et al.). Rav was fond of Hamnuna and taught him a number of apothegms (Er. 54a). He succeeded Rav as the head of the academy of Sura. According to the Talmud, statements of "the school of Rav" emanated from Hamnuna (Sanh. 17b). There are both halakhic and aggadic statements in his name, and many of the latter emphasize the duty of study of the Torah and the gravity of its neglect, e.g., "Jerusalem was destroyed only because they neglected the teaching of schoolchildren" (Shab. 119b); "Man is judged first in respect of study of Torah alone" (Kid. 40b). The Talmud also cites formulae of prayers uttered by him, some apparently composed by him (Ber. 11b; 17a; 58a; et al.). Hamnuna was an associate of Ḥisda (Shab. 97a; et al.) and Ḥisda once became so enthusiastic at his exposition that he said: "Would that we had feet of iron so that we could always run and listen to you" (see Ber. 41b and Rashi *ibid.*). It is stated that his body was transported for burial to Ereẓ Israel where miraculous events occurred on that occasion (MK 25a–b).

(2) HAMNUNA, an *amora* of the beginning of the fourth century C.E. A native of Harpania in Babylonia (Yev. 17a), he resided in Harta of Argiz in the vicinity of Baghdad where he taught (Er. 63a; Shab. 19b). He was a pupil and colleague of Ḥisda (Er. 63a) who praised him highly to *Huna (Kid. 29b). He also studied under R. Judah (Shevu. 34a) and Ulla (Yev. 17a).

(3) HAMNUNA ZUTA ("the younger"), fourth century C.E. The formula of the Confession of Sin, which he was accustomed to recite on the Day of Atonement, the opening words of which are: "O my God! Before I was formed, I was not worthy," is included in the liturgy of that day. When requested to sing a song at the wedding of Mar, the son of Ravina, he sang: "Woe to us, that we must die!" asking his colleagues to join in with the refrain: "Where is the Torah and where is the Commandment that they may shield us?" (Ber. 31a).

Other *amoraim* of the same name, some with and some without appellations, who lived in the third and fourth centuries and whom it is difficult to identify, are referred to in the talmudic sources.

Bibliography: Hyman, Toledot, 376–9; Ḥ. Albeck, *Mavo la-Talmudim* (1969), 281–3, 197f.

[Z.K.]

HAMON, family of Spanish and Portuguese origin which lived in Turkey. ISAAC HAMON (second half of 15th century) was a physician in the court of King Abdallah of Granada. With the Spanish expulsion the family settled in the Ottoman Empire, where its members rapidly achieved fame as physicians of considerable influence in the courts of the sultans. JOSEPH HAMON "THE ELDER" (d.c. 1518), a native of Granada, was court physician to the sultans Bayazid II (1481–1512) and Selim I (1512–20). Hamon accompanied the latter in his military expedition to Egypt from 1516 to 1517 and died in Damascus during the return journey. His influence at the court of the sultan enabled him to assist his coreligionists when they were in danger. The best known and most important member of the Hamon family was his son MOSES (c. 1490–c. 1554), who succeeded his father as the physician of the sultan Selim I and was also physician to Suleiman the Magnificent (1520–1566). Moses soon became the leading court physician. He also wielded extensive influence as a result of his connections with the powerful court party, led by Roxolana-Khūrram, the favorite wife of Suleiman, and her son-in-law, the chief vizier Rustum Pasha. Shortly before his death, he was dismissed as a result of court intrigues. In times of need Moses employed his influence to help his brother Jews. For example, he obtained a firman from Suleiman the Magnificent protecting the Jews from *blood libels. According to this decree, all such libels were to be brought by the accusers before the Royal Dīwān instead of before an ordinary judge. Hamon also intervened with Sultan Suleiman in the affair of the properties of Gracia Mendes *Nasi, which had been confiscated in Venice. When the community of Salonika appealed to him (between 1539 and 1545) for assistance in dealing with powerful members who had disturbed the communal discipline by flouting new regulations, he had them brought to Constantinople where they were penalized by the government, which upon his request also sent a judge and an official to supervise the execution of the regulations.

Moses and his descendants (who are referred to as Evlad-i Musa, "children of Moses," in official documents) were exempted from the payment of certain taxes in recognition of their services to the country. Moses, who accompanied Suleiman in his campaign against Persia in 1534, returned from Baghdad with R. Jacob b. Joseph *Tavus, who, with the financial support of Moses, published the Torah, together with his own Persian translation and the Arabic translation of *Saadiah Gaon in 1546. In the synagogue, which was named after him, Moses maintained a yeshivah which was headed by R. Joseph *Taitaẓak of Salonika. He owned a valuable and rare collection of manuscripts, which included the *Codex Dioscorides* (a famous pharmaceutical work) of the sixth century which is now in Vienna. He also wrote several works on medicine, including an important one on dental cure, which is to be found in the Istanbul University Library.

JOSEPH (d. 1577), son of Moses, was the physician of Suleiman the Magnificent and Selim II (1566–74). From the latter, he obtained the renewal of the rights of the Jews of Salonika in 1568. It appears that between 1559 and 1560, he maintained relations with the renowned Jewish physician in Salonika, *Amatus Lusitanus. Joseph belonged to the literary circle of Constantinople, which was led by Gedaliah *ibn Yaḥia and which included the poets Saadiah Longo and Judah Zarko. ISAAC (16th–17th century), the son of

Joseph, was also a physician. He declined a proposal of the Spanish government, which offered him a sum of money if he would influence the Ottoman government in negotiating a peace treaty with Spain. He was the father of the poet Aaron ben Isaac *Hamon.

Bibliography: Solomon Ibn Verga, *Shevet Yehudah*, ed. by A. Shochat (1947), 56, 92, 144; H. Gross, in: REJ, 56 (1908), 1–26; 57 (1909), 56–78; Rosanes, Togarmah, 1 (1930²), 93, 126; 2 (1938), 4, 56–57, 286–98; 3 (1938), 354–6; A. H. Freimann, in: *Zion*, 1 (1936), 192, 205; S. Krauss, *Geschichte der juedischen Aerzte* (1930), 4, 55; A. Galante, *Histoire des Juifs d'Istanbul* (1941), 10; U. Heyd, in: *Oriens*, 16 (1963), 152–70; B. Lewis, in: *Bulletin of the School of Oriental and African Studies, University of London*, 14 (1952), 550–63.

[S.MAR.]

HAMON, AARON BEN ISAAC (early 18th century), Hebrew poet. Hamon, who lived in Constantinople and Adrianople, wrote a preface to Reuben Mizraḥi's *Ma'yan Gannim* (Constantinople, 1721); a poem published in Isaac *Cheleby's *Semol Yisrael* (Constantinople, 1723), in which all the words begin with the letter ש *(sin)*; and a considerable number of devotional poems. The latter are included in the poetry collections of Turkish Jews, and some of them even in the Karaite liturgy. He was influenced by the poetry of Israel *Najara and the latter's contemporaries. Hamon's poetry was popular and widely read.

Bibliography: Zunz, Poesie, 358; Michael, Or, 135 no. 283; S. Landauer, *Katalog . . . Strassburg* (1881), 63 no. 41; Gross, in: REJ, 56 (1908), 26; 57 (1909), 78; Benjamin Raphael b. Joseph (ed.), *Shirei Yisrael be-Ereẓ ha-Kedem* (1926), 81, 86, 177, 191, 204, 208; Davidson, Oẓar, 4 (1933), 359.

[J.H.SCH.]

HAMON, LEO (1908–), French lawyer and politician. Born in Paris to a family of Polish immigrants, Hamon practiced as a lawyer and following the fall of France in 1940 joined the Resistance. He was a member of the French Provisional Assembly (1944–45) and sat as a senator for the Seine department from 1945 to 1958. Hamon was a founding member of the Movement Republicain Populaire (M.R.P.) but in 1954 joined the pro-Gaullist Jeune République. He continued to support de Gaulle after the latter became president of France in 1958 and in June 1969 was appointed spokesman of the French cabinet. Hamon was a professor of law at the University of Dijon from 1959 to 1960 and for the next four years at the Institut des Hautes Etudes d'Outre-mer. He served as vice-chairman of the national television planning committee from 1965 to 1969. His writings include: *Le Conseil d'Etat juge du fait* (thesis, 1932); *De Gaulle dans la République* (1958); and *La France et la guerre de demain . . .* (1967). [ED.]

HAMOR (Heb. חֲמוֹר; "ass"), the leading citizen of the town of Shechem in the time of the patriarch Jacob; his son was called Shechem (see *Dinah). Jacob bought a parcel of land from the sons of Hamor and built an altar upon it (Gen. 33:19–20). Joseph's bones were buried on this ground by the children of Israel when they returned from Egypt (Josh. 24:32). There are mutually contradictory data on the ethnic character of Hamor. In Genesis 34:2 he is called a Hivite, prince of the land. In the Septuagint he is called Εμμωρ ὁ Χορραῖος i.e., Hamor the Horite; while Genesis 48:22 indicates that the Amorites ruled in Shechem.

Hamor and his son were killed by Simeon and Levi in revenge for Shechem's dishonoring of their sister Dinah, after which the city was plundered and destroyed (Gen. 34). This deed aroused the anger of their father, Jacob (Gen. 34:30), and echoes of this linger in his deathbed blessings (Gen. 49:5–6). In S. Yeivin's view, this story would appear

Simeon and Levi avenge the honor of their sister Dinah by slaying Hamor and his son Shechem (Gen. 34). French miniature, 13th century. London, British Museum, Ms. Harley 4381, fol. 30.

to be an early description of the domination by two of the Israelite tribes over a region of the land; therefore there is no mention of wars of conquest in the region of the hills of Ephraim in connection with the settlement of the land by the tribes.

The name Hamor had already been associated with the dwellers of Shechem in the days of *Abimelech: "Who is Abimelech and who is Shechem that we should serve him? Did not the son of Jerubbaal and his officer, Zebul, once serve the men of Hamor, the father of Shechem?" (Judg. 9:28). W. F. Albright believes, on the basis of Mari documents in which the phrase "to kill an ass" means "to conclude an alliance," that the phrase "the men of Hamor" as applied to the Shechemites during this period designates them as "allies." F. Willesen found further evidence for this hypothesis in a South Arabian inscription in which the word *ḥmrn* seems to mean entering into an alliance. The temple of the Shechemites is called Beth-El-Berith ("house of the god of the covenant or alliance"; Judg. 9:46). On the basis of the Arslan Tash (between Carchemish and Harran) tablets, Albright tried to identify the god bearing this epithet as the Canaanite Horon (see *Beth-Horon), god of treaties. The name Hamor (Himār) also occurs as a proper name among the early Arabs.

Bibliography: S. Yeivin, *Meḥkarim be-Toledot Yisrael ve-Arzo* (1960), 143–4; E. Meyer, *Die Israeliten und ihre Nachbarstaemme* (1906), 416; G. Ryckmans, *Les noms propres sud-sémitiques*, 1 (1934), 105; Albright, Arch Rel, 113; Von Soden, in: *Die Welt des Orients*, 3 (1948), 187, 213; Willesen, in: VT, 4 (1954), 216–7; W. Robertson-Smith, *The Religion of the Semites* (1956), 468; E. Nielsen, *Schechem* (Eng., 1959²), passim.

[E.STE.]

ḤANA BAR ḤANILAI (end of the third century C.E.), Babylonian *amora*. Ḥana belonged to the circle of R. *Huna (Meg. 27a), for whom he showed great respect, regarding himself as his pupil. When he saw R. Huna carrying his tools on his shoulder, he took them from him to relieve him of his burden (Meg. 28a). Ḥana was, apparently, a leader of the community in his city (Meg. 27a). He was well known for his wealth and famed for his charity. R. *Ḥisda states that there were 60 bakers working in his house during the day and a similar number during the night to provide bread for the poor; that his hand was always in his purse, ready to extend help to any deserving poor, sparing them the embarrassment of waiting; that the house had entrances on all four sides to facilitate their entry and anyone who entered the house hungry left it sated; also, that when there was famine in the land, he left food outside, in order that the poor who were ashamed to take it during daylight could help themselves in the darkness (Ber. 58b). Very little is known of his halakhic views; only once is he mentioned in a discussion with Ḥisda.

Bibliography: Judah b. Kalonymus, *Yiḥusei Tanna'im ve-Amora'im*, ed. by J. L. Maimon (1963), 330f.; Margalioth, Ḥakhmei, 323f., Hyman, Toledot, 464f. [Z.K.]

ḤANA BEN BIZNA (third–fourth century C.E.), Babylonian *amora*. Ḥana was primarily an aggadist, most of his statements being quoted in the name of Simeon Ḥasida (Ber. 7a; 43b; Yoma 77a, et al.), whose name is otherwise unknown. One of them is, "Better that a man throw himself into a fiery furnace than put his neighbor to shame in public" (BM 59a, et al.). His contemporary, *Sheshet, admitted that Ḥana was his superior in the field of *aggadah* (Suk. 52b). Ḥana was judge in Pumbedita in *Naḥman b. Isaac's time (Ket. 50b; BK 12a) but he is also mentioned as being in Nehardea where, in spite of criticism he allowed himself to frequent pagan barber shops (Av. Zar. 29a). The *amora* *Joseph relied on his judgment in matters of *halakhah* (Suk. 47a).

Bibliography: Judah b. Kalonymus, *Yiḥusei Tanna'im ve-Amora'im*, ed. by J. L. Maimon (1963), 327–30; Hyman, Toledot, 463f., s.v.
[Z.K.]

HANAMEL (or **Hananel**; Heb. חֲנַנְאֵל, חֲנַמְאֵל), high priest in 37/36 B.C.E., reappointed in 34. According to the Mishnah (Par. 3:5) Hanamel was an Egyptian. However, Josephus states that he was a Babylonian. He was appointed high priest by Herod, who deliberately disregarded the obvious choice, Aristobulus, the younger brother of Mariamne. Herod's choice was dictated by his desire to withhold this office from any member of the Hasmonean family. In face of the protests of Alexandra and Mariamne, Herod was obliged to depose Hanamel and appoint Aristobulus in his stead, but Hanamel was restored to office after the murder of Aristobulus on Herod's instructions. The Mishnah mentions Hanamel as one of the high priests during whose term of office the *red heifer was burned.

Bibliography: Schuerer, Gesch, 2 (1907[4]), 269; Halevy, Dorot, 1 pt. 3 (1923), 114ff.; Klausner, Bayit Sheni, 4 (1950[2]), 12–14, 42; A. Schalit, *Hordos ha-Melekh* (1964[3]), 62–64, 363, 376, 379, 512.
[A.SCH.]

HANAN THE EGYPTIAN (second century C.E.), *tanna*, one of "those who argued before the sages" in *Jabneh (Sanh. 17b). Apparently a native of Alexandria, Egypt, he is mentioned once in a *baraita* in the Babylonian Talmud (Yoma 63b). In another *baraita* there is reference to another "Hanan the Egyptian," named as "one of the judges who heard civil cases in Jerusalem" (Ket. 105a): this Hanan must, therefore, have lived three to four generations before his namesake. Nothing is known of him, and it seems that he is considered in the Talmud as unimportant (see Tos. to Ket. 105a, s.v. *de-ḥashuv*).

Bibliography: Hyman, Toledot, 471.

[Z.K.]

HANANEL BEN ḤUSHI'EL (d. 1055/56), scholar, *posek*, and commentator. Hananel was born in Kairouan, the son of *Ḥushi'el b. Elhanan. The early authorities refer to him as "of Rome," lending credence to the suggestion of Italian origin. Like his father, he was accorded the title *resh bei rabbanan* ("chief among the rabbis") by the Babylonian academies. After his death in Kairouan the title passed to *Nissim Gaon, his pupil. Hananel's most important work, which has not been completely preserved, was his commentary on the Talmud. Unlike Rashi, he limited himself to the subject matter only and did not give a running commentary, his main intention being to sum up the discussion and decide the *halakhah*. He relied greatly on the *geonim*, and in particular upon *Hai Gaon to whom he refers as "the *gaon*" without further qualification. In many places the commentary of Hananel is simply a word for word copy of Hai's commentary, sometime without acknowledgment. When he writes "we have received" a certain explanation—which contradicts the opinion of the *geonim*—the reference is to traditions received from his father or earlier Italian scholars, upon whose teaching he drew. The commentary contains explanations of many difficult words, chiefly in Arabic or Greek, most of which found their way into the *Arukh* of *Nathan b. Jehiel of Rome. Hananel was the first to make frequent use of the *Jerusalem Talmud, and he regularly compares it with discussions in the Babylonian Talmud. In consequence some scholars have exaggerated the importance of his influence upon the spreading of the study of the Jerusalem Talmud in particular. In addition to the Jerusalem Talmud, he also includes much from the Tosefta and the halakhic Midrashim in his commentary. It is not certain whether the commentary covered all the six orders of the Talmud, and in particular whether he wrote commentaries to those tractates whose subjects have no practical application. The following of his commentaries are extant: *Berakhot* (collected from published books and manuscripts in B. Lewin, *Oẓar ha-Ge'onim*, 1 (1928), appendix; the whole of the order *Mo'ed* (published in the standard editions of the Talmud); most of the order *Nashim* (also in *Oẓar ha-Ge'onim*, 7–11 (1936–42)); most of the order *Nezikin* (in the standard Talmud); and a fragment to tractate *Ḥullin* (ed. by B. Lewin, in: *Sefer ha-Yovel—J. L. Fishman* (1926), 72–79). The commentaries to *Horayot* (in standard Talmud edition) and *Zevaḥim* (the last three chapters, ed. by I. M. Ben-Menahem (1942)) attributed to him are not by him. This list shows that he also wrote commentaries to sections not of practical application (e.g., the second half of tractate *Pesaḥim* and the fragment of *Ḥullin* which includes chapter II).

Hananel's commentary gained wide circulation soon after its appearance, and served as the main bridge between the teaching of the Babylonian *geonim* and the scholars of North Africa and that of the scholars of Europe and Ereẓ Israel. *Eliezer b. Nathan was the first of the scholars of France and Germany to make use of and disseminate it, and Nathan b. Jehiel of Rome was the first of the Italian scholars. In Ereẓ Israel it was used first by *Nathan *(Av ha-yeshivah)* and in Spain by the author of *Sha'arei Shavu'ot* (see *Isaac b. Reuben). Among the scholars of North Africa, extensive use was made of it by Isaac *Alfasi who copied very many of his rulings, both in his name and anonymously; in fact, the whole of Alfasi's work is based upon it. From Alfasi it passed to the scholars of Spain after him, such as *Joseph ibn Migash, *Maimonides, Meir ha-Levi *Abulafia, and others. In Germany and France the tosafists based themselves to a considerable extent on Hananel, and he is frequently quoted by them. All the *rishonim* laid great store on the readings of the Talmud embedded in his commentary, and he himself several times emphasized his readings. In addition to his commentary he wrote a *Sefer Dinim* whose nature is not known (see S. Assaf, *Teshuvot ha-Ge'onim* (1942), 51), and there are a number of citations from a book in *Hilkhot Terefot*. The *rishonim* quote his commentary to the Pentateuch and fragments of it have been collected by A. Berliner (in *Migdal Ḥananel*, 1876) and by J. Gad (*Sheloshah Me'orot ha-Gedolim*, 1950). Some of the *rishonim* erroneously attributed to Hananel the anonymous **Sefer Mikẓo'ot*.

Bibliography: S. J. L. Rapoport, in: *Bikkurei ha-Ittim*, 12 (1831), 11–33; *Migdal Ḥananel* (1876), includes biography; S. Poznański, in: *Festschrift . . . A. Harkavy* (1908), 194–8 (Heb. pt.); Kohut, Arukh, 1 (1926²), 12–13 (introd.); V. Aptowitzer, in: *Jahresbericht der Israelitisch-Theologischen Lehrenstalt in Wien*, 37–39 (1933), 3–50; (=*Sinai*, 12 (1943), 106–19); S. Abramson, in: *Sinai*, 23 (1948), 57–86; idem, *Rav Nissim Ga'on* (1965), index; Urbach, Tosafot, index.

[I.T.-S.]

HANANEL BEN SAMUEL (first half of 13th century), Egyptian (?) talmudist. There are no biographical details of Hananel, but he is known to have composed commentaries, which Ḥ. J. D. Azulai saw in manuscript, to the *Halakhot* of Isaac *Alfasi on several tractates of the Talmud. The commentaries to *Eruvin* (Margoliouth, Cat, no. 479) and *Kiddushin* (Neubauer, Cat, no. 438/7) are extant, but they have not yet been published. S. Abramson in his *Rav Nissim Ga'on* (1965) excerpted from the commentary to *Eruvin* many of the quotations there from Nissim Gaon's commentary on that tractate. According to one view Hananel was head of the academy of Fostat in Egypt and Peraḥyah b. Nissim was his pupil. According to Steinschneider, his father was the *nagid* Abu Manzur, Samuel b. Hananiah, but in the opinion of Mann this is impossible.

Bibliography: Steinschneider, Arab Lit, 227 nos. 166–7; S. D. Luzzatto, in: *Ha-Levanon*, 3 (1866), 285f.; idem, in: *Literaturblatt des Orients*, 11 (1850), 242–5; Carmoly, in: *Ha-Karmel*, 6 (1867), 94; J. Horovitz, in: ZHB, 4 (1900), 155–8; S. Poznański, *ibid.*, 186; Mann, Egypt, 1 (1920), 195 n. 2; S. Assaf, in: KS, 23 (1946/47), 237f.

[S.Z.H.]

HANANIAH (Ḥanina), nephew of Joshua b. Hananiah (second century C.E.), *tanna*. Some are of the opinion that Hananiah was the son of Judah b. Hananiah who is mentioned in a single source as the author of an aggadic statement (Sif. Deut. 306), but there is no doubt that his teacher was his uncle *Joshua b. Hananiah (Nid. 24b), and probably for this reason he is usually referred to as "Hananiah, nephew of Joshua b. Hananiah," though sometimes he is referred to simply as Hananiah (Shab. 12a, 20a, et al.). He was one of the leading figures of his generation and when he fell ill "*Nathan and all the notables" came to visit him (Ḥul. 47b). He was known chiefly as a halakhist, although there are *aggadot* in his name. He is not mentioned in the Mishnah. In his youth Hananiah lived in Ereẓ Israel. When in Simonia, he gave a ruling without having authority to do so. R. Gamaliel expressed his displeasure until Joshua sent him a message, "It was on my instructions that Hananiah gave the ruling" (Nid. 24b). On one occasion Hananiah went to Babylon during the lifetime of his uncle and then returned to Ereẓ Israel (Suk. 20b). It may be this visit which is referred to in the incident that while on their journey: "they remembered Israel . . . and they burst into tears and rent their garments . . . and returned to their place, saying: 'Dwelling in Israel is equivalent to all the precepts of the Torah' " (Sif. Deut. 80).

Subsequently, for a reason that is not clear (Eccles. R. 1:8, 4), he returned to Babylonia where he remained until his death. In the well-known *baraita* that enumerates those scholars to whose locality it is worth going to study, he is mentioned: "After Hananiah, the nephew of Joshua, to the exile" (Sanh. 32b). Hananiah was the greatest of the scholars in Ereẓ Israel at the time of the Hadrianic persecutions which followed the failure of the Bar Kokhba revolt in 135, and with his departure the power of the Sanhedrin was diminished. As a result Hananiah permitted himself "to intercalate the years and to fix the new moons" in exile, in conformity with the *halakhah* that the greatest among the ordained scholars of the generation may do so outside Ereẓ Israel if he has not left his equal in the land. He continued to do so after the persecutions abated and Ereẓ Israel again became the center of Torah, because he regarded himself as the outstanding scholar of the generation and the scholars of Ereẓ Israel as inferior to him. The Jews of Babylonia followed his calendar, and in consequence the scholars of Ereẓ Israel took vigorous steps against him. Representatives were sent from Ereẓ Israel to Babylonia, but even after *Judah b. Bathyra of Nisibis demanded that the authority of the center in Ereẓ Israel be accepted, Hananiah refused to obey (TJ, Ned. 6:8; TB, Ber. 63a–b).

Bibliography: Halevy, Dorot, pt. 2 (1923), 190–205; Hyman, Toledot, s.v.; Allon, Toledot, 1 (1958), 151–2; 2 (1961), 75–6; A. Burstein, in: *Sinai*, 38 (1956), 32–7; 40 (1957), 387–8.

[Z.K.]

HANANIAH (Ḥanina) BEN ḤAKHINAI (sometimes referred to simply as **Ben Ḥakhinai;** middle of the second century C.E.), *tanna* in Ereẓ Israel. Ḥananiah was "one of those who debated before the sages" in *Jabneh (Sanh. 17b). He was one of the distinguished pupils of *Akiva (Tosef. Ber. 4:18), who also taught him mystic lore (Tosef., Ḥag. 2:2; Ḥag. 14b). He studied with Akiva in Bene-Berak for 12 years without once returning home (Ket. 62b), and his wife was held up as an example of a "helpmeet for him" because of her forbearance (Gen. R. 17:3). He then dwelt apparently in Sidon from where he sent a query to Akiva (Nid. 52b). He is quoted three times in the Mishnah, *Kilayim* 4:8, *Makkot* 3:9, and in *Avot* 3:4, where he states: "He who wakes up at night, or he who goes on his way alone, and turns his heart to idle thoughts, sins against himself." He is also mentioned several times in the Tosefta, one of his dicta there being: "He who deals falsely with his fellow denies God" (Shevu. 3:6). He also knew many languages (TJ, Shek. 5:1, 48d). According to one version in a late Midrash he was one of the *Ten Martyrs.

Bibliography: Hyman, Toledot, s.v.

[Z.K.]

HANANIAH (Ḥanina) BEN TERADYON (second century C.E.), *tanna* during the *Jabneh era, and martyr. Hananiah was head of the yeshivah of *Sikhnin in Galilee (Sanh. 32b). Only a few of his sayings in *halakhah* (Tosef. Mik. 6:3, Men. 54a) and *aggadah* (Avot 3:2) have been preserved. When the news of the martyrdom of Akiva at Caesarea reached *Judah b. Bava and Hananiah, they said that his death was an omen that the land of Israel would soon be filled with corpses and the city councils (*Boule) of Judea abrogated. Their forecast was fulfilled (Sem. 8:9, Higger's edition p. 154–5). They were apparently referring to the destruction of Judea which followed the crushing of the *Bar Kokhba revolt and to the ensuing religious persecution by Hadrian. Hananiah himself was a victim of those persecutions. He was sentenced to death for teaching the Torah and holding public gatherings in defiance of the prohibition against it, in order to foster Judaism. Unlike *Eleazar b. Parta who was arrested with him, Hananiah, when interrogated, admitted that he had been teaching Torah, since it was a divine command. He was sentenced to

Hananiah b. Teradyon, the martyr, being burned at the stake. Detail from Benno Elkan's *menorah* at the Knesset, Jerusalem 1956. Photo Yiẓḥak Amit, kibbutz Zorah.

be burnt at the stake, his wife to be executed, and his daughter sold to a brothel. All three accepted their fate with equanimity, justifying the way of God, except that Hananiah was distressed that he had devoted himself only to study and not to philanthropic activity (although he was a charity overseer).

He was burnt at the stake wrapped in the *Sefer Torah* (which he had been holding when arrested). In order to prolong his agony tufts of wool soaked in water were placed over his heart so that he should not die quickly. In answer to the wonder of his daughter at the fortitude with which he bore his sufferings, he answered, "He who will have regard for the plight of the *Sefer Torah*, will also have regard for my plight." It is stated that the executioner *(quaestionarius)*, moved by his sufferings, removed the tufts and increased the heat of the fire, and when Hananiah expired he too jumped into the flames, whereupon a heavenly voice proclaimed that the two "are assigned to the world to come" (Av. Zar. 17b–18a; Sif. Deut. 307; Sem. 8:12, Higger's edition p. 157–9). His daughter, who had been consigned to a brothel, preserved her virtue, and was eventually ransomed by *Meir who had married her sister, the learned *Beruryah (on the halakhic dispute between the son and daughter of Hananiah, cf. Tosef. Kel. BK 4:17). It is related that one of Hananiah's sons associated with robbers (possibly the reference is to a group of political rebels) and when he was put to death, Hananiah would not permit him to be eulogized but applied to him censorious verses from the Bible (Lam. R. 3:16, No. 6; Sem. 12:13, D. T. Higger's edition p. 199–200). In the stories of the *Ten Martyrs in the **heikhalot* literature, the account of Hananiah's martyrdom is embellished with mystical additions.

Bibliography: Bacher, Tann; E. E. Urbach, in: *Sefer Yovel le-Yiẓhak Baer* (1960), 61–64. [M.D.H.]

HANANIAH (Ḥanina) OF SEPPHORIS, Palestinian *amora* (late fourth century., C.E.). Probably a disciple of R. Phinehas, many of whose teachings he transmitted (TJ, Ma'as. 3:3, 50c; TJ, Or. 1:8, 61c, et al.), he is mentioned frequently in halakhic and aggadic conflict with his friend and contemporary Mana b. Jonah (TJ, Ḥal. 2:2, 58c; TJ, Pes. 3:1, 30a, et al.; also, TJ, Ber. 3:1, 6a; TJ, Ket. 1:2, 25b) who may have been his brother (TJ, MK 3:5, 82d). After the death of R. Jonah, Hananiah was head of the academy of Sepphoris, but later resigned from his post in favor of Mana, and assumed the position of student under him (TJ, Ma'as. Sh. 3:9, 54c; TJ, Yev. 3:4, 4d, et al.). Because of this R. Hananiah was listed among those "who have relinquished their crown in this world, to inherit the glory of the world to come" (TJ, Pes. 6:33a). There is a geonic tradition to the effect that Hananiah emigrated to Babylonia (*Teshuvot ha-Ge'onim* Harkavy, §248), where he joined the circle of Rav Ashi (BB 25b; Ḥul. 139b); however it is obvious that, for chronological reasons, it is necessary to differentiate between the two Hananiahs.

Bibliography: Hyman, Toledot, s.v.; Z. W. Rabinowitz, *Sha'arei Torat Bavel* (1961), 406–7; Ḥ. Albeck, *Mavo la-Talmudim* (1969), 393–4. [Z.K.]

HANANIAH SON OF AZZUR (Heb. חֲנַנְיָה בֶּן עַזּוּר), of Gibeon, "false prophet," contemporary of the prophet *Jeremiah (Jer. 28:1). Hananiah prophesied that Judah would be freed of the yoke of Babylon, that the Temple vessels would be returned, and that Jeconiah (i.e., Jehoiachin), the son of *Jehoiakim, king of Judah, would be restored as king in Jerusalem. The setting of his prophecy, as proclaimed in the fourth year of Zedekiah's reign of Judah (593 B.C.E.; Jer. 28:2–4), was the gathering of the representatives of Edom, Moab, Ammon, Tyre, and Sidon in Jerusalem to plan a coordinated activity against *Nebuchadnezzar. Jeremiah argued against this treaty in the name of God, for it would not succeed. He put a yoke on his neck to symbolize the yoke of Nebuchadnezzar and the kingdom of Babylon imposed by God for three generations (*ibid.* 27:1ff.). Thus, the "prophets" in Judah who predicted that all the Temple vessels and Jeconiah would be returned from Babylon were speaking false prophecies. It is not known whether Hananiah prophesied together with those "prophets," or separately, though his prophecy coincided with theirs. To Hananiah Jeremiah responded "Amen" in bitter irony, but he added that a true prophet can only be one whose prophecies for good are fulfilled (cf. Deut. 18:18–22). Thus, in two years they would know if Hananiah spoke the truth. Hananiah, to give credence to his words, broke the yoke off Jeremiah's neck in public, as a sign of the breaking of the yoke of Nebuchadnezzar (Jer. 28:10–11). Jeremiah proclaimed that the act was, on the contrary, not a symbol of the breaking of the yoke, but of the replacement of the wooden yoke by an iron one. He also predicted that Hananiah would die in that same year, and three months later Hananiah died (28:16–17). [Y.M.G.]

In the Aggadah. Hananiah was one of the prophets who misused the gifts with which he had been divinely endowed (Sif. Deut. 84). He is particularly criticized for using Jeremiah's prophecy of the defeat of Elam (Jer. 49:35), as the basis of his own forecast that a similar fate would befall the Babylonians (Jer. 28:2). He reached this conclusion, not as a result of prophecy, but by reasoning, arguing: "If Elam, which only came to assist Babylon, will be broken; how much more certain is it that Babylon itself will be destroyed" (Sanh. 89a). Jeremiah then challenged Hananiah to give some sign to indicate the validity of his prophecy that God would perform this miracle "within two full years" (Jer. 28:3). Hananiah retorted that Jeremiah first had to give some sign that his prophecies of gloom would be fulfilled. Initially reluctant to do so (because God's evil decrees can always be averted by repentence), Jeremiah eventually prophesied that Hananiah would die that same year. This prophecy was fulfilled; the reference to his death in the "seventh month" (which commences a new year), indicates that he died on the eve of Rosh Ha-Shanah, but commanded his family to keep the death secret for a few days in an attempt to discredit Jeremiah (TJ, Sanh. 11:5). [Ed.]

Bibliography: W. Rudolph, *Jeremia* (Ger., 1947), index. In the Aggadah: Ginzberg, Legends, 4 (1947), 297–8; 6 (1946), 389; I. Ḥasida, *Ishei ha-Tanakh* (1964), 158.

HANAU, city near Frankfort, W. Germany. The earliest documentary evidence for the presence of Jews in Hanau dates from 1313. During the *Black Death persecutions in 1349 the Jewish community of Hanau was destroyed and its synagogue confiscated. There were no more Jews in the city until 1429 when there were again two Jewish families living there. In 1603 Count Philip Ludwig II granted ten Jewish families a privilege *(Judenstaettigkeit)* allowing them to settle in Hanau, build a special quarter *(Judengasse),* and erect a synagogue, which was dedicated in 1608. Previously, Jewish families had brought their dead to Frankfort and then Windecken for burial, but a cemetery was consecrated in Hanau itself in 1603. By 1607 the community had grown to 159; 100 years later there were 111 families, or 600 to 700 individuals, resident in the city. In 1659 a conference of notables representing five Jewish communities took place in Hanau. Among the many talmudic scholars active in Hanau in the 17th and 18th centuries, best known was R. Tuviah Sontheim (1755–1830), *Landrabbiner* from 1798, and chief rabbi for the whole province of Hanau from 1824 to 1830. He was followed in office by Samson Felsenstein (1835–82).

In the 17th and 18th centuries Hanau developed into an important center of Hebrew printing. From Hans Jacob Hena's press, which was established in 1610, issued such important works as responsa by Jacob *Weil, Solomon b. Abraham *Adret, and Judah *Minz as well as Jacob b. Asher's *Arba'ah Turim.* Employing both Jews and gentiles, this press produced a great number of rabbinic, kabbalistic, and liturgical items within about 20 years. A hundred years later Hebrew printing was resumed in the city by H. J. Bashuysen, who published Isaac Abrabanel's Pentateuch commentary (1709). In 1714 Bashuysen's press was taken over by J. J. Beausang and was active until 1797.

During the last quarter of the 18th century several Court

The burning of the 17th-century Hanau synagogue by the Nazis, November 1938. Courtesy Hanau Municipality.

Jews lived in Hanau, mainly occupied as suppliers of the army. From 1806 the Jews were allowed to live in any part of the town, but full emancipation was not granted until 1866. The community numbered 540 persons in 1805, 80 families in 1830, 447 persons in 1871, and 657 at the turn of the century. In 1925 there were 568 Jews in Hanau and 447 in 1933. At that time there existed a synagogue, a cemetery, three charitable societies, and a religious school attended by 75 children.

Jews were active in many aspects of the commercial and industrial life of the town. However, Nazi economic boycotts had a telling effect so that the number of Jews had dwindled by May 1939 to 107. On Nov. 9/10, 1938, the synagogue was burned to the ground; the site was later cleared and title to it transferred to the city. The teachers' quarters owned by the community were demolished and many gravestones at the Jewish cemetery were overturned. The last 26 Jews of Hanau were deported in 1942 to Auschwitz and Theresienstadt. Another five Jews, partners of mixed marriages, remained in the town.

In 1968, a few Jews resided in Hanau.

Bibliography: L. Loewenstein, *Das Rabbinat in Hanau nebst Beitraegen zur Geschichte der dortigen Juden* (1921:=JJLG, 14 (1921), 1–84); Germ Jud, 2 (1968), 336–7; H. Schnee, *Die Hoffinanz und der moderne Staat,* 2 (1954), 352–60; E. J. Zimmermann, *Hanau Stadt und Land*... (1903), 476–521; L. Rosenthal, *Zur Geschichte der Juden im Gebiet der ehemaligen Grafschaft Hanau*... (1963); FJW, 187–8; L. Una, in: *Juedisches Litteratur-Blatt,* 20 (1891), 10–11, 14–15, 19, 23, 80–81; E. J. Zimmermann, in: *Hanauisches Magazin* (*Hanauer Anzeiger,* June 1, 1924).

[C.T.]

HANAU, SOLOMON ZALMAN BEN JUDAH LOEB HA-KOHEN (1687–1746), Hebrew grammarian. Born in *Hanau where his father served as cantor, Solomon Hanau taught at Frankfort. There, in 1708, he published *Binyan Shelomo,* a Hebrew grammar written in the form of casuistic criticism of earlier grammarians. The criticism led to resentment, and the leaders of the Frankfort community demanded that he add to his work an apology to those whom he had "offended." Hanau moved to Hamburg. There he taught for a number of years and continued his linguistic research. He published *Sha'arei Torah* (Hamburg, 1718). The book was based on "natural inquiry" (i.e., on independent investigation of the language, deviating from traditional grammar wherever the author deemed it necessary). A brief essay on the scriptural accents, *"Sha'arei Zimrah,"* was added to the book. *Yesod ha-Nikkud* (Amsterdam, 1730) is another minor work on the subject. His most famous work, *Ẓohar ha-Tevah* (Berlin, 1733), published in at least 12 editions, includes all his grammatical innovations. It influenced numerous grammarians of the Haskalah and the Revival period of the Hebrew language and was the book which set *Ben Yehuda (according to the latter's own statement) on the course which made him revive spoken Hebrew. Hanau answered the attacks of his adversaries in *Kurei Akkavish* (Fuerth, 1744).

In *Binyan Shelomo,* Hanau had already mentioned the linguistic "errors" (i.e., non-biblical forms) contained in contemporaneous prayer books, and in *Sha'arei Tefillah* (Jessnitz, 1725, and three other editions) he recorded a number of these errors with his corrections. Apparently the book aroused the anger of the conservatives, and Hanau was compelled to leave Hamburg. He went to Amsterdam; a few years later he returned to Germany where he wandered from city to city (among others, Fuerth and Berlin), and died in Hanover. In 1735, while in Copenhagen, Hanau was engaged as a private tutor to Naphtali Hirz *Wessely, then aged ten; Hanau, it seems, instilled in his pupil an affection for the Bible and the study of the Hebrew

ספר

בנין שלמה

נדפס בעיר המהוללה

פראנקפורט דמיין

שנת תי"ו חיים לפ"ק

בדפוס מטיאס אנדרע:

Title page of *Binyan Shelomo*, a Hebrew grammar by Solomon Zalman b. Judah Loeb ha-Kohen Hanau. Frankfort, 1708 (sic).

language. Several essays by Hanau have survived in manuscript form, including: *Ma'aseh Oreg*, an explanation of the grammatical passages in Rashi's commentary on the Torah; *Mishpat Leshon ha-Kodesh*, philosophical writings and commentaries on the Bible; *Shivah Kokhevei Lekhet*, a work in Yiddish on the calendar. [Ch.M.R.]

HANDALI, JOSHUA BEN JOSEPH (17th century), Turkish rabbi. Handali was born in Skopje in Yugoslavia. In his youth he moved to Salonika, where he studied under Ḥayyim Shabbetai. His first work, written in 1613, was a pamphlet on the laws pertaining to gifts from a groom to his bride *(sivlonot)*. He was recognized as a halakhic authority and various Balkan communities turned to him with their problems. In 1621 he moved to Safed, where he was one of the pioneers of the Jewish resettlement. He later settled in Jerusalem where he is mentioned as being involved in the Shabbetai Ẓevi controversy. Toward the end of his life he interested himself in Kabbalah. Some of his responsa are included in his *Penei Yehoshu'a* (included in the collection *Me'orot ha-Gedolim*, Constantinople, 1739), and others in the *Benei Aharon* by Aaron Lapapa (Smyrna, 1674).

Bibliography: Frumkin-Rivlin, 2 (1928), 32. [S.Mar.]

HANDELSMAN, MARCELI (1882–1945), Polish historiographer. Born in Warsaw, Handelsman served as professor of general history at Warsaw University from 1915. He was head of the Warsaw Institute for History, and a member of the Académie des Sciences Morales et Politiques in Paris. Handelsman's historical research covered several fields. His first study dealt with punishment in early Polish law (*Kara w najdawniejszym prawie polskim*, 1907). His main areas of interest were the history of Poland from the time of its first partition in 1772, the Napoleonic era, and Franco-Polish relations. In these fields he published the following books: *Napoléon et la Pologne, 1806–07* (1909); *Francja-Polska 1795–1845* (1926); *Les Idées françaises et la mentalité politique en Pologne au XIXE* siècle (1927). Handelsman also wrote essays of general historical importance, on the development of the present-day nationalism, and on methodology and the interpretation of history. He had a progressive-realistic attitude to historical research and opposed the romantic-conservative school. Although he had converted to Christianity Handelsman was sent by the Germans to the Nordhausen concentration camp where he died.

Bibliography: W. Moszczenska, in: *Kwartalnik Historyczny*, 63, no. 3 (1956), 111–50; Polska Akademia Nauk, *Polski Słownik Biograficzny* (1960–61); A. B. Boswell, in: *Slavonic and East European Review*, 25 (1946), 247–9. [Ed.]

HANDLER, MILTON (1903–), U.S. attorney. Handler was born in New York City. He graduated from Columbia Law School (1926) and served on its faculty from 1927. A specialist in trademarks and antitrust law in both private and public practice, Handler held posts on the National Labor Board (1933–34), U.S. Treasury Department (1938–40), Lend Lease Administration (1942–43), Foreign Economic Administration, of which he was special counsel, and the U.S. attorney general's national committee to study antitrust laws (1953–55). During the movement for Israel independence, Handler was chairman of the American Jewish Conference's Palestine Committee, member of the American Zionist Emergency Council (1944–48), and coauthor of a report on Palestine submitted to the United Nations in 1947. In 1969 he was appointed chairman of the American Friends of the Hebrew University. Handler's books and articles include *Antitrust in Perspective* (1957), and *Cases and Materials on Trade Regulation* (ed., 1967[4]). His wife, Miriam Handler, was active in American Jewish support for Israel. She served on the U.S. Manpower Commission Training Within Industry (1943–45), was a member of the Hadassah National Board from 1947, and held other leadership positions with the American Friends of the Hebrew University and the American-Israel Cultural Foundation. [Ed.]

HANDLER, PHILIP (1917–), U.S. biochemist. Born on a New Jersey farm, Handler taught at Duke University, North Carolina, from 1939. He was a professor of biochemistry there from 1950 and in 1960 assumed the chair of biochemistry at the university. Handler's early research dealt with pellagra, a dietary deficiency disease. He and his collaborators showed that the vitamin nicotinic acid was a component of NAD and NADP, two coenzymes important in electron transfer in cells. Handler's later research was concerned with niacin and choline deficiency, purine metabolism, hypertension, and parathyroid tumors. Handler served at various times as president of the American Society of Biochemists and of the Federation of American Societies for Experimental Biology. He held leading positions in the National Science Foundation, including the chairmanship of the National Science Board, its policy-making body. In 1964 Handler was appointed to the President's Science Advisory Committee. In the same year he was elected to membership of the National Academy of Sciences and in 1969 became president of the Academy. He was coauthor of *Principles of Biochemistry* (1954) and from 1957 was the editor of *Geriatrics*.

Bibliography: *Current Biography Yearbook* (1964), 174–6. [S.A.M.]

HANDLIN, OSCAR (1915–), U.S. historian. Handlin, who was born in Brooklyn, New York, became professor of history at Harvard. He also directed the Center for the

PLATE 1. Spice box in silver filigree, with semiprecious stones and enameled panels. France or Germany, late 17th century. Height 12 in. (30 cm.). Jerusalem, Sir Isaac and Lady Wolfson Museum in Hechal Shlomo. Photo David Harris, Jerusalem.

PLATE 2. Velvet *ḥallah* cover embroidered in gold. Central Europe, 18th century(?). 25×22 in. (63.5×55.8 cm.). Jerusalem, Michael Kaufman Collection. Photo David Harris, Jerusalem.

PLATE 3. Articles used in the *havdalah* ceremony. Left to right: Silver candle holder, Germany, early 18th century, 12½ in. (33 cm.); gold *kiddush* goblet, Germany, early 17th century, 5½ in. (15 cm.); silver and gilt spice box, Austria, 1817, 11 in. (29 cm.); Jerusalem, Israel Museum. Photo David Harris, Jerusalem.

Study of Liberty at Cambridge, Massachusetts (1958–66), and in 1966 assumed the directorship of the Charles Warren Center for the Study of American History. His works include: the Pulitzer Prize-winning study of American immigrants, *The Uprooted* (1951); *Boston's Immigrants* (1941); *Chance or Destiny* (1955); *Al Smith and His America* (1958); *The Newcomers: Negroes and Puerto Ricans in a Changing Metropolis* (1959); and *The Americans* (1963). By applying sociological insights to historical research, Handlin brought new evidence to bear on many controversial issues in American history such as the nature of the Populists, the origins of anti-Semitism, the economic foundations of colonial slavery, and the conservatism of American immigrants. A vice-president of the American Jewish Historical Society, his contributions to American Jewish history include: *Adventure in Freedom: Three*

Oscar Handlin, U.S. historian. Courtesy Harvard University News Office, Cambridge, Mass.

Hundred Years of Jewish Life in America (1954); and (with his wife, Mary Flug) "A Century of Jewish Immigration to the United States," in AJYB, 50 (1948), 1–84. [H.L.T.]

HANFMANN, GEORGE MAXIM ANOSSOV (1911–), U.S. archaeologist. Hanfmann was born in St. Petersburg (Russia) and was educated at the University of Berlin. With the advent of the Nazis he was forced to leave Germany and went to Harvard. He became curator of classical art at the Fogg Art Museum in 1946 and professor in 1956. From 1958 he excavated at *Sardis in Asia Minor. He was largely responsible for the discoveries of the ruins and partial reconstruction of the Sardis synagogue. His earlier work specialized in Etruscan sculpture but he extended his work by dealing with the interrelation between Greek and

George Hanfmann, U.S. archaeologist. Courtesy Fogg Art Museum, Cambridge, Massachusetts.

neighboring Near Eastern cultures in the Homeric and post-Homeric archaic age. Hanfmann's works include: *Season Sarcophagus in Dumbarton Oaks,* 2 vols. (1951); *Etruskische Plastik* (1956), and *Roman Art* (1964). [P.P.K.]

HANGCHOW, coastal capital of Chekiang province, E. China. It was the largest city in the world during the 14th century. At that time, a Jewish community with a synagogue existed there. The Arab traveler Ibn Baṭṭūṭa in the first half of the 14th century described Hangchow as consisting of six cities, each with its own wall, and an outer wall surrounding the whole. Ibn Baṭṭūṭa "entered the second city through a gate called the Jews' Gate. In this city live the Jews, Christians, and sun-worshiping Turks, a large number in all." The Chinese Jew, *Ai T'ien, during a visit to Peking in 1605, told Matteo Ricci, the Jesuit missionary, about the presence of numerous Jews and the existence of a synagogue in Hangchow. Nothing is known of the further history of the community.

Bibliography: H. A. R. Gibb, *Ibn Baṭṭūṭa, Travels in Asia and Africa 1325–1354* (1929), 293; A. C. Moule, *Christians in China before the Year 1550* (1930), 3. [R.L.]

ḤANĪF (pl. **Ḥunafā**), Arabic term which occurs many times in the Koran in connection with true monotheism. The primary meaning and the origin of the word is still to be determined. In pre-Islamic times it seems to have been used for adherents of Hellenistic culture. Muhammad uses it as a term for the God-fearing, righteous men in the pre-Islamic period, who followed the original and true religion. Abraham was one of them, Muhammad is his true follower, and Islam is the reappearance of the true faith distorted by Judaism and Christianity (e.g., Sura 10:105; 16:121, 124; 30:29). According to Muhammad's biographers, many such God-seekers who lived in Arabia during his lifetime, such as *Umayya ibn Abī al-Ṣalt, did not accept his prophetic mission to the Arabs. In later usage *ḥanīf* means Muslim.

Bibliography: V. V. Bartold, *Muzulmanskiy mir* (1917), 48 (*Mussulman Culture,* 1934); Wensinck, in: *Acta Orientalia,* 2 (1924), 191; K. Ahrens, *Muḥammad als Religionsstifter* (1935), 17, N. 3; J. W. Hirschberg, *Juedische und christliche Lehren* (1939), index; N. A. Faris and H. W. Glidden, in: JPOS, 19 (1941), 1–13; W. Montgomery Watt, in: *Encyclopaedia of Islam,* 3 (1966²), s.v. [H.Z.H.]

ḤANINA (Hananiah; Comrade of the Rabbis; end of the third–beginning of the fourth century), Palestinian *amora.* Ḥanina was born in Babylonia; in his youth he migrated to Ereẓ Israel and studied under Johanan among others (Men. 79b; Ber. 5b; et al.). Johanan was greatly distressed because he was unable to ordain him, but Ḥanina comforted him, saying: "It is because we are descendants of Eli the Priest; we have a tradition that none of this family is destined to be ordained" (Sanh. 14a). For this reason he was called *ḥaver* ("comrade") of the rabbis. He is frequently mentioned together with Oshaya, who was also a priest of the family of Eli that emigrated to Ereẓ Israel; they may have been brothers (*Yiḥusei Tanna'im ve-Amora'im* (1963, 388)). Both earned their living by sandal-making. In illustration of their great piety, the Talmud relates that their workshop was in the market of the harlots for whom they made shoes, yet they never raised their eyes to look at them. The harlots, recognizing their piety, used to swear "by the lives of the holy rabbis of Israel" (Pes. 113b). Ḥanina's halakhic sayings are cited in the Talmud. Problems were directed to him (TJ, Ber., 1:1, 2b; MK 3:5, 82b), and in reply to a query about abolishing an accepted custom, he replied: "Since your ancestors were accustomed to forbid this, do not change the custom of your ancestors, that they may rest in peace" (TJ, Pes. 4:1, 30d). He sent *halakhot* in the name of Johanan from Ereẓ Israel to Babylonia (Yev. 58b). He disputed with Ilai in *halakhah* (Shab. 84b), and had discussions with Zeira (RH 13a). He also had connections with Rabbah and repeated *beraitot* before him (BM 6b; et al.). Some are of the opinion that Rabbah (b. Nahamani was his brother (see *Yuḥasin,* s.v. Rabbah bar Nahamani).

Bibliography: Bacher, Pal Amor; Hyman, Toledot, s.v.; Ḥ. Albeck, *Mavo la-Talmudim* (1969), 241–3. [Y.D.G.]

ḤANINA BAR ḤAMA (early third century C.E.), Palestinian scholar of the transitional generation from *tannaim* to *amoraim*. Ḥanina was born in Babylon (TJ, Pe'ah 7:4, 20a), and studied there under a scholar called Hamnuna (TJ, Ta'an. 4:2, 68a). He went to Ereẓ Israel and lived in Sepphoris where he was a distinguished pupil of Judah ha-Nasi (TJ, Nid. 2:7, 50b). He transmitted information about the rulings and customs of his teacher (TJ, Ber. 3:5, 6d) who greatly admired him (Av. Zar. 10b). He was friendly with Ishmael b. Yose, with Bar Kappara, and with Ḥiyya, in whose presence Ḥanina boasted of the sharpness of his intellect, saying, "Were the Torah, God forbid, to be forgotten in Israel, I would restore it by means of my dialectics" (Ket. 103b; BM 85b). Ḥanina's colleagues were Rav, Jonathan, and Joshua b. Levi, and he went with the last to visit the Roman proconsul in Sepphoris (TJ, Ber. 5:1, 9a). According to the Jerusalem Talmud Ḥanina was not ordained by Judah ha-Nasi during the latter's lifetime, because he was vexed with him over a certain matter, but he ordered his son Gamaliel who succeeded him to ordain him (TJ, Ta'an. 4:2). According to a *baraita* quoted in the Babylonian Talmud, however (Ket. 103b), Judah ha-Nasi ordered before his death: "Ḥanina b. Ḥama shall preside," which Rashi explains as meaning to preside over the college. This indeed seems to be the meaning of the phrase in its context which deals with the appointments to be made in the college after Judah's death. Further it is stated that Ḥanina refused to accept this appointment "because R. Afes was two and a half years older than he." Afes was appointed, and only after his death did Ḥanina accept the office. Among his most prominent pupils were Johanan and Simeon b. Lakish and also Eleazar, who frequently transmits in his name. Eleazar's statement in the name of Ḥanina: "The disciples of the wise increase peace in the world, as it says [Isa. 54:13]: and all thy children shall be taught of the Lord, and great shall be the peace of thy children. Read not *banayikh* ["thy children"] but *bonayikh* ["thy builders"]" (Ber. 64a; et al.) has become famous and is incorporated in the daily prayer book.

Ḥanina lived to a very advanced age (Ḥul. 24b). He earned a living by trading in honey (TJ, Pe'ah 7:4, 20b) and also practiced medicine, in which he was regarded as an expert (Yoma 49a). He harshly rebuked his fellow citizens of Sepphoris and bemoaned their hardheartedness (TJ, Ta'an, 3:4, 66c). He emphasized the value of rebuke in his statement: "Jerusalem was destroyed only because they did not rebuke each other" (Shab. 119b). He frequently spoke in praise of Ereẓ Israel (TJ, Pe'ah 7:4, 20b) and explained the description of Ereẓ Israel as *ereẓ ẓevi* (lit. "land of the hind," JPS "beauteous," AV "glorious"; Dan. 11:41) as follows: "Just as the skin of the hind cannot hold its flesh; so the land of Israel when it is inhabited can provide space for everyone, but when it is not inhabited it contracts" (Git. 57a). Ḥanina was strongly opposed to anyone leaving the land of Israel, and said of him, "He has abandoned the bosom of his mother, and embraced the bosom of a stranger" (TJ, MK 3:1, 81c). He was especially opposed to a priest leaving the country, even for religious reasons (*ibid.*).

Ḥanina's aggadic statements are numerous. He was of the opinion that the planets influence Israel too, and that "the constellation of the hour is the determining influence" (Shab. 156a). This influence, however, does not limit the activity of divine providence, since both witchcraft and constellations are subject to the providence of the creator "for if there be no decree from Him, they can do him no harm" (Rashi to Ḥul. 7b; cf. Sanh. 67b). The overall power of providence is stressed in his saying: "No man bruises his finger here on earth, unless it was so decreed against him in heaven" (Ḥul. 7b). But this emphasis does not nullify the value of man's freedom of will: "Everything is from heaven, excepting cold draughts, as it is written [Prov. 22:5]. Cold draughts [thus he understands the words usually rendered "thorns and snares"] are in the way of the froward; he that keepeth his soul holdeth himself far from them" (BM 107b). Moreover it is certain that no one should rely upon his constellation or upon providence in all that pertains to his character, since "Everything is in the hand of heaven except the fear of heaven" (Ber. 33b), but the attainment of the fear of heaven is not given to all men equally and for the same effort (*ibid.*). Ḥanina stressed the heinousness of profaning the Divine Name: "The Holy One was indulgent of idolatry—but He was not indulgent of the profanation of the Name" (Lev. R. 22:6); "It is better for a man to commit a transgression in secret—and not profane the Name of Heaven in public" (Kid. 40a). Among his other noteworthy sayings are, "He who lifts a hand against his fellow, even without smiting him, is called a sinner" (Sanh. 58b); "Let not the blessing of a common person be light in your eyes" (Meg. 15a); "The son of David will not come until the haughty in Israel are extinct" (Sanh. 98a).

Bibliography: Bacher, Pal Amor; Hyman, Toledot, s.v.; E. E. Urbach, in: *Sefer ha-Yovel le-Yeḥezkel Kaufmann* (1960), 141–6.
[Z.K.]

ḤANINA (Ḥinena) BAR PAPA (Pappi; end of third and beginning of fourth century C.E.), Palestinian *amora*. Ḥanina belonged to the circle of R. Johanan's pupils, Abbahu, Isaac Nappaḥa, Ammi, etc., though he only once actually quotes R. Johanan himself (TJ, BK 10:2, 71b.). He was renowned in the field of *aggadah*, and was considered an excellent preacher (Sot. 9a, et al.). He may have learned his *aggadah* from Samuel b. Naḥman whom he calls "rabbi" (TJ, Shev. 4:3, 35b). He was considered a paradigm of holiness (Kid. 81a) and even the night spirits feared him. It is related of him that he distributed alms at night (TJ, Pe'ah 8:9, 21b). When the Angel of Death came to take him, he requested another 30 days in which to revise his learning. The Angel of Death, who respected him deeply, granted this request, and when he died a pillar of fire separated him from the people (Ket. 77b).

Bibliography: Judah b. Kalonymus, *Yiḥusei Tanna'im ve-Amora'im*, ed. by J. L. Maimon (1963), 376–8; Margalioth, Ḥakhmei, 346–8, s.v.; Hyman, Toledot, 494–7, s.v.; Ḥ. Albeck, *Mavo la-Talmudim* (1969), 239f.
[Z.K.]

ḤANINA BEN ABBAHU (c. 300), Palestinian *amora*. Ḥanina was the son of the famous *Abbahu who lived in Caesarea. He studied under his father and transmitted teachings in his name, as well as about him (Kid. 33b; TJ, Bik. 3:7, 65d; et al.) but later his father sent him to study at the yeshivah of Tiberias. When his father heard that instead of devoting himself to study there he was engaging in works of benevolence, he sent him a message: "Is it because there are no graves in Caesarea [cf. Ex. 14:11; the reverential interment of the dead being one of the highest of benevolent activities] that I sent you to Tiberias? For it has already been decided that study takes precedence over good deeds" (TJ, Pes. 3:7, 30b). Ḥanina apparently returned to Caesarea (TJ, Ket. 4:15, 29b) where he was a *dayyan* (TJ, Yev. 2:4, 3d) and is referred to also as "Ḥanina of Caesarea" (Song R. 1:20, no. 3). In addition to *halakhah*, aggadic sayings were transmitted in his name (TJ, Shab. 6:9, 8d; Lam. R. Proem 34; *ibid.* 2:1, no. 2; et al.).

Bibliography: Frankel, Mevo, 87b–88a; Hyman, Toledot, s.v.; Ḥ. Albeck, *Mavo la-Talmudim* (1969), 327–8.
[Z.K.]

IANINA BEN ANTIGONUS (first half of second entury C.E.), *tanna.* Ḥanina was a kohen (Bek. 30b), and it s highly probable that in his youth he lived in Jerusalem efore the destruction of the Temple and remembered ertain details of that period (Tosef., Ar. 1:15; see also Kid. :5). Similarly, many of the teachings quoted in his name re on the subject of the Temple and its vessels (Bek. 6:3, 4,); Tosef., Shek. 3:15; Tosef., Suk. 4:15; et al.), which is he main subject matter of his quoted statements. He also ransmitted a halakhic tradition in the name of R. Eleazar Iisma (Tosef., Tem. 4:10). His son, too, was well known, nd R. Judah and R. Yose sought his judgment on uestions of ritual purity (Bek. 30b).

Bibliography: Hyman, Toledot, 479–80. [Z.K.]

IANINA BEN DOSA (first century C.E.), *tanna.* Ḥanina ved in Arav in lower Galilee (north of the valley of Bet Ietofah) and was a disciple-colleague of *Johanan b. akkai. Ḥanina was distinguished for his extreme piety. It said of him "that he was praying when a scorpion bit him, ut he did not interrupt his prayer. His pupils went and ound it dead at the entrance to its hole. They said: Woe to e man bitten by a scorpion, but woe to the scorpion that ites Ben Dosa" (Tosef., Ber. 3:20; and cf. TJ, Ber. 5:1 and er. 33a). The sages applied to him the phrase (Ex. 18:21) men of truth" (Mekh., Malek 2). They held him up as an xample of a completely righteous man (Ber. 61b), and escribed him as "one for whose sake God shows favor to is entire generation" (Ḥag. 14a). He refused to benefit om the property of others though he was destitute, and ich remarkable things are related about this conduct that was stated, "Every day a divine voice proclaims from Mt. Ioreb: The whole world is sustained by the merit of my son Ianina, and Ḥanina my son subsists on a *kav* of carobs om one week to the next" (Ber. 17b).

He was zealous in observing precepts: e.g., in the bservance of the Sabbath, which he kept from midday on riday (Gen. R. 10:8); in separating tithes (TJ, Dem. 1:3); nd in returning lost property to its owner (Ta'an. 25a). His rayers were regarded as being specially accepted, and as a esult he was frequently requested to pray for the sick and ose in trouble (Ber. 34b; Yev. 121b). When the son of ohanan b. Zakkai fell ill, Ḥanina prayed for him and he ecovered. Johanan b. Zakkai claimed that he himself ould not have succeeded in achieving this and when his ife asked, "Is Ḥanina greater than you?" he replied, "No! ut he is like a servant before the king, and I am like a ourtier before the king" (Ber. 34b). The *aggadah* speaks xtensively of the miracles that happened for him (Ta'an. 4b–25a; ARN[1] 8, 38). On one Sabbath eve at twilight he aw his daughter sad. He said to her: "Why are you sad?" he replied: "I exchanged my vinegar can for my oil can, nd I kindled the Sabbath light with vinegar." He said to er: "My daughter, why should this trouble you? He who ommanded the oil to burn will also command the vinegar o burn" (Ta'an. 25a).

More has been transmitted about his pious deeds and his onders than about his dicta, and the little preserved is in e field of *aggadah,* confining itself to emphasis on the nportance of good deeds: "He whose deeds exceed his isdom, his wisdom shall endure; but he whose wisdom xceeds his deed, his wisdom will not endure. He in whom e spirit of his fellow creatures takes delight, in him the pirit of the All-present takes delight; and he in whom the pirit of his fellow creatures takes not delight, in him the pirit of the All-present takes not delight" (Avot 3:9–10). It as said that: "When Ḥanina b. Dosa died, men of deeds eased and piety came to an end" (Sot. 9:15). Of his wife o it was said that she resembled her husband in piety (BB 74b) and like him was "accustomed to miracles" (Ta'an. 25a).

Bibliography: Bacher, Tann; Hyman, Toledot, s.v.; G. B. Zarfati, in: *Tarbiz,* 26 (1956/57), 130ff.; E. E. Urbach, *Ḥazal* (1969) index. [Z.K.]

ḤANINA BEN GAMALIEL (mid-second century C.E.), *tanna.* He was a son of Rabban *Gamaliel of Jabneh, and an older brother of the patriarch *(nasi)* *Simeon b. Gamaliel, who quotes his teachings (Tosef., Nid. 7:5). Ḥanina was apparently a disciple of *Tarfon (see Ned. 62a; Kid. 81b). He differed on *halakhah* with *Akiva (Nid. 8a) and with Yose ha-Gelili (Men. 5:8), and engaged in halakhic discussions with the disciples of Akiva (Tosef., Av. Zar. 4 (5): 12; Tosef., Nid. 4:5; et al.). He was also well-versed in the *aggadah* (MK 23a) and many *aggadot* are quoted in his name. He apparently died young, and because of this his younger brother was appointed to the position of *nasi.*

Bibliography: Hyman, Toledot, s.v. [Z.K.]

ḤANINA (Aḥonai) KAHANA BEN HUNA (the second half eighth century), *gaon* of Sura (769–774). A priest belonging to a significant priestly family, he let his nails grow, saying "the Temple will soon be rebuilt and they will require a priest qualified for *melikah*" (slaughtering the sacrificial bird by pinching the back of its neck; Yev. 1:15). Ḥanina was a student of *Yehudai b. Naḥman Gaon. His interpretations and rulings, found in the *Halakhot Gedolot,* were highly regarded by succeeding *geonim.* The value of the *sela* coin as determined by him has been incorporated in the text of the Talmud (Bek. 50a). Ḥanina was the teacher of Jacob b. Mordecai ha-Kohen, who was known among the *geonim* for his independent views, and also of a Samuel, the first portion of whose *Midrash Asefah* has been included in the *Halakhot Gedolot,* in collections of geonic responsa, and also in the Midrashim of Yemen. Some passages of Ḥanina's works have been included in the Yalkut Shimoni.

Bibliography: B. M. Lewin (ed.), *Iggeret R. Sherira Ga'on* (1921), 108; idem, *Oẓar ha-Ge'onim (Ta'anit),* pt. 2 (1932), 30; L. Ginzberg, *Geonica,* 2 (Eng., 1909), 31, 94, 113; Baron, Social^2, 7 (1958), 259f.; J. Mueller, *Mafte'aḥ li-Teshuvot ha-Ge'onim* (1891), 72. [M.H.]

ḤANINA SEGAN HA-KOHANIM (first century C.E.), *tanna* living in the last years of the Second Temple, the designation *Segan ha-Kohanim* referring to the fact that he was deputy high priest (cf. Yoma 39a). He transmitted details about the Temple service both from his knowledge of his father's customs (Zev. 9:3) and from those of the other priests (Pes. 1:6; Eduy. 2:1–2), and about other customs prevalent in Temple times (Eduy. 2:3; Men 10:1; et al.). On the basis of his testimony cited in *Pesaḥim* 1:6, an extensive and ramified discussion is developed in the Babylonian Talmud (Pes. 14a–21a). The Mishnah also gives information about the customs of his family in the Temple (Shek. 6:1). His intense love of the Temple is expressed by a remark in connection with the prohibition against bathing on the Ninth of Av: "The house of our God merits that for its sake a man should forego an immersion once a year" (Ta'an. 13a). Two *halakhot* in his name are found in the Tosefta (Ter. 9:10; Neg. 8:6), both dealing with the laws of ritual purity. His aggadic sayings extol the virtue of peace: "Great is peace which is equal to the whole act of creation." He says that the word "peace" in the priestly blessing refers to domestic peace (Sif. Num. 42), and he enjoins, "Pray for the peace of the ruling power, since but for fear of it men would have swallowed up each other alive" (Avot 3:2), and in praise of Torah: "Everyone who takes the words of the Torah to heart . . . will have removed from him fear of the sword, fear of famine, foolish thoughts . . . fear of the yoke of human beings" (ARN[1] 20, 70). According to Maimonides (Commentary to Mishnah, introd.), Simeon b. ha-Segan (cf. Shek. 8:5; Ket. 2:8) was the son of Ḥanina.

Bibliography: Hyman, Toledot, s.v. [Z.K.]

ḤANITAH (Heb. חֲנִיתָה), kibbutz situated on the Israel-Lebanese frontier in western Upper Galilee, 4½ mi. (7 km.) E. of Rosh ha-Nikrah. Ḥanitah, affiliated with Iḥud ha-Kevuẓot ve-ha-Kibbutzim, was founded in 1938, at the height of the Arab riots, as a *tower and stockade outpost, with the aim of gaining a foothold in a region until then devoid of Jewish settlement, and of closing the border gap through which armed gangs used to infiltrate from Lebanon. Ḥanitah became the epitome of the defense settlement and its foundation was the subject of the first Hebrew opera *Dan ha-Shomer* by *Shin Shalom and Marc *Lavry. First established by a *Haganah unit at a site known as "lower Ḥanitah" the settlement had to repel incessant attacks, two defenders falling the very night it was founded. A month later, "upper Ḥanitah" was set up on the permanent site at the top of the ridge. In 1939, a group of settlers from Eastern Europe took over. Arduous reclamation work was required to carve cultivable land (mainly for deciduous fruit orchards and vineyards) out of the rocky terrain overgrown

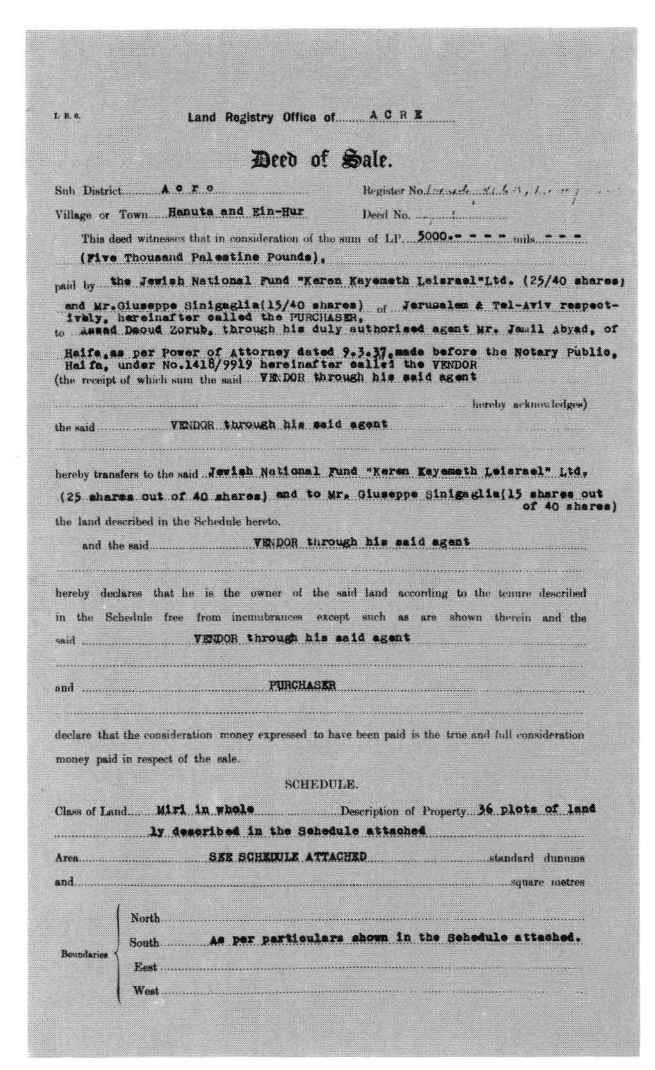

L.R.8. Land Registry Office of ACRE

Deed of Sale.

Sub District Acre Register No.

Village or Town Hanuta and Ein-Hur Deed No.

This deed witnesses that in consideration of the sum of LP. 5000.- - - - mils - - -

(Five Thousand Palestine Pounds),

paid by the Jewish National Fund "Keren Kayemeth Leisrael"Ltd. (25/40 shares) and Mr.Giuseppe Sinigaglia(15/40 shares) of Jerusalem & Tel-Aviv respectively, hereinafter called the PURCHASER,

to Assad Daoud Zorub, through his duly authorised agent Mr. Jamil Abyad, of Haifa, as per Power of Attorney dated 9.3.37, made before the Notary Public, Haifa, under No.1418/9919 hereinafter called the VENDOR

(the receipt of which sum the said VENDOR through his said agent hereby acknowledges)

the said VENDOR through his said agent

hereby transfers to the said Jewish National Fund "Keren Kayemeth Leisrael" Ltd, (25 shares out of 40 shares) and to Mr. Giuseppe Sinigaglia(15 shares out of 40 shares)

the land described in the Schedule hereto,

and the said VENDOR through his said agent

hereby declares that he is the owner of the said land according to the tenure described in the Schedule free from incumbrances except such as are shown therein and the said VENDOR through his said agent

and PURCHASER

declare that the consideration money expressed to have been paid is the true and full consideration money paid in respect of the sale.

SCHEDULE.

Class of Land Miri in whole Description of Property 36 plots of land ly described in the Schedule attached

Area SEE SCHEDULE ATTACHED standard dunums

and square metres

Boundaries
North
South As per particulars shown in the Schedule attached.
East
West

Figure 1. Transfer of Ḥanitah to the Jewish National Fund by its Arab owner, 1937. Jerusalem, J.N.F.

Figure 2. Kibbutz Ḥanitah in 1946. Courtesy J.N.F., Jerusalem.

with wild brush. Forests were planted and ancient woodlands in the vicinity restored. Ḥanitah established a large rest resort and a metal factory for steel-cutting tools. Its population in 1968 was 390. Its name dates back to the second and third centuries C.E. and is preserved in the form Ḥanita (חניתא; Tosef., Shev. 4:9 and TJ, Dem. 2:1, 22b), today Khirbat Ḥānūtā at the site of the kibbutz. [E.O.]

HANKIN, YEHOSHUA (1864–1945), Ereẓ Israel pioneer, instrumental in acquiring large tracts of land for Jewish settlement. Born in Kremenchug, Ukraine, Hankin went to Ereẓ Israel in 1882 with his father, who was one of the founders of Rishon le-Zion. In 1887 the family moved to Gederah where he established friendly relations with the Arab *felaḥeen* and landowners, which helped him in negotiating for the purchase of land for the expansion of Jewish settlement. His first purchase, in 1890, was of the lands on which Reḥovot was established, and a year later he bought the land on which Ḥaderah was founded; he also purchased the lands on which the *Jewish Colonization Association (ICA) settlements in the Galilee and elsewhere were set up. In 1908, when the Zionist Organization began to engage in practical work in Ereẓ Israel and established the Palestine Land Development Corporation (for the purchase and cultivation of land for the *Jewish National Fund and private purchasers), Hankin joined this company. As early as 1897 he had negotiated for the purchase of the Jezreel Valley lands, but the first sale there was delayed until 1909 when Hankin at last succeeded in buying the lands of Kafr

Yehoshua Hankin, early Zionist pioneer. Courtesy Central Zionist Archives, Jerusalem.

Fūla (10,000 dunams), on which Merḥavyah, the first Jewish settlement in the valley, was established. In 1915 he was exiled to Anatolia, Turkey, by the Turkish authorities, returning to Palestine three years later. In 1920 he purchased a large tract of land (51,000 dunams) in the Jezreel Valley, on which many agricultural settlements were later established (En-Harod, Tel Yosef, Nahalal, and others), and as a result he became known as "The Redeemer of the Valley." Seven years later he submitted to the Zionist leadership a daring 20-year plan for the acquisition of Palestinian lands; from 1932 he served as director of the Palestine Land Development Corporation. Hankin wrote *Jewish Colonization in Palestine* (1940, ed. and tr. by E. Koenig). He died in Tel Aviv and was buried on Mt. Gilboa opposite the land he redeemed in the Jezreel Valley, near the Harod spring. During his lifetime, he purchased more than 600,000 dunams of land, most of which passed into the possession of the Jewish National Fund. The moshav Kefar Yehoshu'a in the Jezreel Valley is named after him.

Bibliography: U. Yaari-Poleskin, *Yehoshu'a Hankin ha-Ish u-Mifalo* (1933); M. Smilansky, *Mishpaḥat ha-Adamah,* 3 (1951), 207–81; Tidhar, 2 (1947), 752–5; M. Sharett, *Orot she-Kavu* (1969), 102–8; E. Ashbel (ed.), *Shishim Shenot Hakhsharat ha-Yishuv* (1970).

[G.El.]

HANNAH (Heb. חַנָּה; "graciousness, favor"), wife of Elkanah, of the family of Zuph from Ramathaim-Zophim in the hill country of Ephraim; mother of the prophet *Samuel. Hannah appears in the Bible in connection with the birth of Samuel. Together with Elkanah and her co-wife Peninnah, she used to make the pilgrimage annually to the Temple in Shiloh to offer sacrifices (I Sam. 1:2–7; 2:19; the Septuagint and a fragment from Cave 4 at Qumran in 1:24). Though the favored wife of her husband, she was unhappy because she was childless for many years and taunted about it by her co-wife. As she once stood in the Temple, pouring out her bitter anguish inaudibly, with only her lips moving, and vowing to dedicate any son born to her to the Temple and the service of God, *Eli the high priest at Shiloh observed her and chided her for her apparently drunken behavior. On ascertaining its true cause, however, he added his blessing to her pleas. Hannah gave birth to a son, Samuel, and after weaning him brought him to the Temple, offered a sacrifice and a song of thanksgiving, and left him with Eli to serve in the Temple for life. Each year she would return to bring him a small cloak, when she went up with her husband to offer the yearly sacrifice. Eli blessed her and Hannah bore three more sons and two daughters (I Sam. 2:21).

The story of Hannah and the birth of Samuel is one of the most charming in the Bible. It is similar to other stories of barren mothers who late in life bore sons destined to be leaders of the nation, and to the story of *Rachel who was also the favored wife of her husband. Hannah's pledging her son before his birth is similar to the action of Samson's mother (Judg. 13), who pledged him as a *nazirite. This was a common practice of the period (although it was later forbidden—"a woman shall not pledge her son as a nazirite," Naz. 4:6). Amos 2:11–12 refers to prophets and nazirites jointly. It is worth noting that according to the Septuagint and the fragment from Qumran, Hannah dedicates her son specifically "as a nazirite for all time" who is forbidden to partake of wine and spirits (similarly in Ecclus. 46:13; Jos., Ant., 5:347). According to R. Nehorai (Naz. 9:5; Maim. Yad, Nezirut, 3:16) Samuel was a nazirite like Samson.

[J.M.G.]

In the Aggadah. Hannah was one of the seven prophetesses (Meg. 14a). It was on her instigation that

Hannah (right) with her husband Elkanah and co-wife Peninnah, from the *Conradin Bible,* S. Italy, 13th century. Baltimore, Md., Walters Art Gallery, Ms. W. 152.

Elkanah took a second wife after ten years of marriage without children (PR 43, 181b). Once Peninnah had given birth, however, she ceaselessly taunted Hannah (cf. I Sam. 1:6), constantly reminding her of her childlessness (PR 43, 182a–b). The expression "O Lord of hosts" (I Sam. 1:11), which she was the first to use, implies: "Of all the hosts You have created, is it so hard to give me one son" (Ber. 31b), and to have contained the suggested criticism of God: "To which host do I belong? If the heavenly, then I will never die; if the mortal, then I should be able to give birth" (PR 43, 179b). The triple repetition of the phrase "thy handmaid" refers to her contention that she had not transgressed any of the three transgressions for which women die in childbirth (Ber. *ibid.,* cf. Shab. 2:6). Hannah was so assured of the righteousness of her case that not only did she "hurl words at God" *(ibid.)* but she even volunteered to feign adultery, so that she would have to undergo the ordeal of water, after which, according to the Bible, "she will be cleansed and shall conceive seed" (Num. 5:28; Ber. *ibid.*).

[Ed.]

Bibliography: H. P. Smith, *Critical and Exegetical Commentary of the Books of Samuel* (ICC, 1899), 3–19; M. Z. Segal, *Sifrei Shemu'el* (1964[2]), 1–20; Cross, in: BASOR, 132 (1953), 15–26.

HANNAH AND HER SEVEN SONS, a story told in II *Maccabees, Chapter 7, of seven brothers who were seized along with their mother by *Antiochus IV Epiphanes, presumably shortly after the beginning of the religious persecutions in 167/166 B.C.E., and commanded to prove their obedience to the king by partaking of swine's flesh. The brothers defiantly refused to do so. Encouraged in their resolve by their mother, they were executed after being put to frightful tortures. When the mother was appealed to by the king to spare the youngest child's life by prevailing upon him to comply, she urged the child instead to follow in the path of his brothers, and she herself died shortly thereafter.

The accounts of the manner in which she met her death differ. According to IV Maccabees, she threw herself into the fire. The Midrash states that she lost her reason and threw herself to her death from a roof, while according to *Josippon* she fell dead on the corpses of her children. The story, along with that of the martyrdom of the aged priest Eleazar (II Macc. 6:18–31), became the subject of the book known as the Fourth Book of Maccabees. In rabbinic literature the story is recounted as an instance of martyrdom

Hannah lamenting her martyred sons. Detail from a page of the *Hamburg Miscellany,* Mainz(?), Germany, c. 1427, illustrating a *piyyut* for Ḥanukkah. Hamburg, State and University Library, Cod. Heb. 37, fol. 79v.

during the Hadrianic persecution (Lam. R. 1:16, no. 50; Git. 57b; PR 43:180; SER 30:151). The martyrs were venerated in the Roman Catholic calendar of saints (Aug. 1) as the "Seven Maccabee Brothers," although the mother is also mentioned with them, their martyrdom being considered a prefiguration of later Christian martyrdoms. According to Antiochene Christian tradition, the relics of the mother and sons were interred on the site of a synagogue (later converted into a church) in the Kerateion quarter of Antioch. On this and other grounds, it has been suggested that the scene of the martyrdom was Antioch rather than Jerusalem.

Whatever its historical substratum, the story in II Maccabees and in all subsequent sources is doubtless an adaptation of a stock form of a terrible tragedy (cf. I Sam. 2:5 and Isaiah di Trani's commentary; Job 1:2, 19; Ass. Mos. 9; Jos., Ant. 14:429; BB 11a; Sem. 8:13). Drawing directly on II Maccabees, *Sefer Josippon* (c. 953) restored the story to its original Epiphanian setting. Although in II Maccabees and *Gittin* the name of the mother is not given, in other rabbinic accounts she is called Miriam bat Tanḥum, while in Syriac Christian accounts she is called Shamone and/or Maryam. However, the obvious association with I Samuel 2:5 impelled a Spanish reviser of the *Josippon* (ed. Constantinople, 1510, 4:19) to name the anonymous mother of II Maccabees "Hannah," by which name she has become famous, thanks to the dissemination of the longer (Spanish) version of *Josippon* and the medieval *piyyutim* in Hebrew, Arabic, and Judeo-Persian which are based on it. The shorter recension of the work (ed. Mantua, c. 1480, 126f.) and the literature based on it continued to refer to her anonymously. The story has inspired many legends on the place of the martyrs' burial, as well as works of art, poetry, and drama on their martyrdom, down to modern times.

Bibliography: G. D. Cohen, in: *Sefer ha-Yovel . . . Kaplan* (1953), 109–22; H. M. Michlin, in: *Mizraḥ u-Ma'arav,* 3 (1928/29), 194–9; J. Gutman, in: *Sefer Yoḥanan Levi* (1949), 25–37; F. M. Abel, *Les Livres des Maccabées* (1949), 370–84; E. J. Bickerman, in: *Byzantion,* 21 (1951), 63–83 (Fr.); M. Hadas (ed.), *The Third and Fourth Books of Maccabees* (1953), 91ff.; Nissim b. Jacob, *Ḥibbur Yafeh me-ha-Yeshu'ah,* ed. and tr. by H. Z. Hirschberg (1954), 58ff., introduction; T. W. Manson, in: BJRL, 39 (1956/57), 479–84.

[G.D.C.]

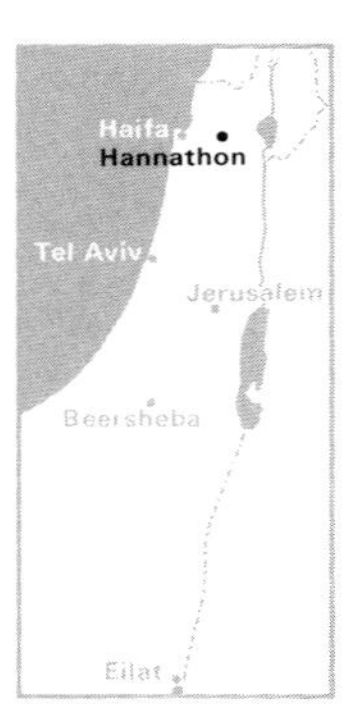

HANNATHON (Heb. חַנָּתֹן), city in the territory of Zebulun between Rimmon and Iphtahel (Wadi al-Malik) in Lower Galilee (Josh. 19:13–14). It is mentioned in two el-Amarna letters as Ḥinnatuni or Ḥinnatuna (ed. Knudtzon, 8, 245); in one it is referred to as the place where the kings of Shimron and Acre attacked a Babylonian caravan which was on its way to Egypt, and in the other, as the place where the king of Acre freed Labayu, king of Shechem, after he had been captured at Megiddo. Tiglath-Pileser III mentions Hannathon (Ḥinatuna) among the cities captured during his Galilean campaign in 733 B.C.E., together with Kanah and Jotbah. The site is generally identified with Tell al-Badaywiyya at the western end of the Bet Netofah Valley, on an important road near Rammun, Kanah, and Jotapata. Pottery dating from the Middle Bronze, Late Bronze, and Iron Ages has been found there. An alternative identification locates Hannathon at Khirbat al-Ḥarbaj in the southern end of the plain of Acre (but see *Achshaph).

Bibliography: Alt, in: PJB, 21 (1925), 62ff.; Y. Aharoni, *Hitnaḥalut Shivtei Yisrael ba-Galil ha-Elyon* (1957), index; Aharoni, Land, index; Albright, in: BASOR, no. 11 (1923), 11; idem, in: AASOR, 2–3 (1923), 23f.

[M.A.-Y.]

ḤANNELES, JUDAH LEIB BEN MEIR (d. 1596), rabbi and author, probably from Posen; known by the initials of his name, as "Maharlaḥ" (**M**orenu **ha**-**R**av **L**eib **H**anneles). Judah, the son of Meir of Tannhauser, was one of nine brothers, among them *Eliakim Goetz b. Meir, a leading scholar of Posen, Jacob *Temerls, and Akiva of Hotzenplatz. He is the author of *Va-Yiggash Yehudah,* a commentary on the *Arba'ah Turim* of *Jacob b. Asher, which he explains word by word, noting each halakhic ruling, giving its source and citing the various opinions. In his commentary Judah sought to complete the *Beit Yosef* of Joseph *Caro; he disagrees with Caro in several instances and also gives more accurate versions of the *Arba'ah Turim,* of which Caro was not aware. At times he even disagrees with Jacob b. Asher. He began the publication of his work toward the end of his life, and died before it was completed. His brother, Jacob Temerls, continued with the publication of *Oraḥ Ḥayyim* (Lublin, 1596–99). In the later editions of the *Arba'ah Turim,* beginning with that of Dyhernfurth (1791–96), a second corrected edition of *Va-Yiggash Yehudah* on *Oraḥ Ḥayyim* was published, in which the sources were omitted. Although the *Ḥiddushei ha-Ga'on Leib Ḥanneles* on *Oraḥ Ḥayyim* printed in the standard text of the *Arba'ah Turim* have been wrongly ascribed to him (being a selection of glosses from commentators compiled by the brothers Michael Simon and Joseph Maya the sons of the printer, Jehiel Maya), they nevertheless include many selections from Ḥanneles' work.

Bibliography: Eliakim Goetz ben Meir, *Even ha-Shoham u-Me'irat Einayim* (Dyhernfurth, 1733), 5 (introd.); Hoffman, in: *Magazin fuer juedische Geschichte und Literatur,* 1 (1874), 8; H. D. Friedberg, *Toledot Mishpaḥat Shor* (1901), 14–15; S. Wiener, *Kohelet Moshe,* 5 (1904), 549, no. 4512; H. Tchernowitz, *Toledot ha-Posekim,* 2 (1947), 299–300.

[ED.]

HANNOVER, ADOLPH (1814–1894), Danish scientist and physician, known for his experimental studies in histology and microscopic technique. Hannover's detection of a plant parasite on the salamander was of vital importance to medicine for it proved for the first time the

Adolph Hannover, Danish medical scientist. Courtesy Israel Medical Association, Jerusalem.

significance of vegetative contagious matter in the transmission of infectious diseases. Hannover's use of chromium acid as a hardening agent contributed to microscopic technique. His treatises on the microscopy of the nervous system, on the construction of microscopes, on the retina, and on the nature of cancer were translated into many languages.

Bibliography: M.A. Hannover: *Adolph Hannovers fædrene og mødrene Slægt* (1914).

[Ju.M.]

HANNOVER, NATHAN NATA (d. 1683), preacher, kabbalist, lexicographer, and chronicler. During the *Chmielnicki massacres which started at the end of 1648, he had to leave his birthplace in Volhynia and he wandered through Poland, Germany, and Holland for several years. His sermons, delivered during those years of wandering, were compiled into a book covering the entire Pentateuch. In 1653 he went to Italy. In the same year in Venice, he published *Yeven Meẓulah* ("Miry Pit"), dealing with the Chmielnicki persecutions. He associated with the great kabbalists of the period: Samuel Aboab and Moses Zacuto of Italy; and those who had come from Ereẓ Israel—Ḥayyim Cohen, Nathan Shapira, and Benjamin ha-Levi of Safed. He studied the Kabbalah doctrines of the school of Isaac Luria for a number of years and enjoyed the munificence of patrons in Leghorn in 1654 and in Venice in 1655–56.

In 1660 in Prague, Hannover published *Safah Berurah* ("Clear Language"), a Hebrew-German-Latin-Italian conversation lexicon, text, and guidebook for travelers, and in 1662, *Sha'arei Ẓiyyon* ("The Gates of Zion"), a collection of prayers for *tikkun ḥaẓot* ("midnight prayers"), and for other kabbalistic rituals of the Lurianic school. These two books were the result of his studies in Italy. In 1662, he was appointed president of the *bet din* and head of the yeshivah in Jassy, Walachia, which was then a Turkish province. He was still in Jassy in 1666, the "year of redemption," when the Messiah was due according to the beliefs of the Shabbatean movement. He is mentioned among those who wrote to Lithuania to announce the event. He spent about ten years in Jassy and, according to tradition, in Pascani too. He then moved to Ungarisch Brod, Moravia, on the Hungarian border, where he was preacher and religious judge. He was killed, while praying with the community, by Turkish soldiers who raided the town.

Hannover was a prolific writer, but most of his works, sermons and writings on the Kabbalah, were lost. Apart from the sermon *Ta'amei Sukkah,* printed in Amsterdam, 1652, and a kabbalistic writing on Purim, preserved in manuscript, only the three books published in his lifetime are extant. The subject matter and the style of these works are diverse, yet each had considerable influence for a long time. The prayer book, *Sha'arei Ẓiyyon,* was reprinted over 50 times, chiefly in Italy, Holland, and Central and Eastern Europe. The book served as a channel for introducing into the ordinary prayer book certain elements of the Lurianic Kabbalah, such as the *Berikh Shemei* prayer. *Safah Berurah* also had several editions, being published both under its own title and other titles in its original form and in a modified version. Up to the 19th century, it was used for the study of foreign languages in Central and Eastern Europe. It is still an important source for research into the Yiddish and the Hebrew used in the author's time.

The small book *Yeven Meẓulah,* on the Chmielnicki pogroms of 1648–52, has relatively few personal experiences of the author. It is mainly based on eyewitness accounts of others and hearsay evidence (including information Hannover found in print). This was the manner of writing of chroniclers of the period. Hannover's broader vision, lucid language, and simple and graceful manner of relating events gave the book an appeal it still retains. Among the Ashkenazi Jews, it was reprinted in the original version and in Yiddish translation, in almost every generation (including Hebrew edition, 1945; Yiddish edition, 1938), It was translated into French (1855), German (1863), Russian (1878), Polish (1912), and English (*Abyss of Despair,* 1950). The book has also been a source of information on the massacres of the Chmielnicki period to modern writers and poets like S. Asch and Minsky. Some historians have followed the narrative uncritically, without submitting it to historical analysis.

Bibliography: I. Israelson, in: YIVO, *Historishe Shriftn,* 1 (1929), 1–26 (cf. 2 (1937), 684–5, notes by Halevy); M. Weinreich, in: *Tsaytshrift far Yidishe Geshikhte, Demografye . . . ,* 2–3 (1928), 706–16; I. Nacht, in: *Reshumot,* 1 (1946), 164–7; N. Prylucki, in: *YIVO Bleter,* 1 (1931), 414ff.; I. Shatzky, in: *Gezerot Taḥ* (1938), 9–159; Elbogen, Gottesdienst, 200, 390.

[I.H.]

ספר שערי ציון

אלה דברי קבלה

נדפס באמשטרדם

Title page of Nathan Nata Hannover's *Sha'arei Ẓiyyon,* a collection of kabbalistic prayers. Amsterdam, 1671. Jerusalem, J.N.U.L.

HANNOVER, RAPHAEL LEVI (1685–1779), mathematician and astronomer. Born in Weikersheim, he worked as a bookkeeper in the house of Oppenheimer in Hanover, where he met the philosopher Leibniz and became his devoted pupil, studying mathematics, astronomy, and natural philosophy. He wrote two books in Hebrew on astronomy: *Luḥot ha-Ibbur,* astronomical tables for the Jewish calendar (Leiden-Hanover, 1756–7; Dessau, 1831), and *Tekhunat ha-Shamayim ve-Khol Ẓeva'am u-Mahalakham* (Amsterdam, 1756). He left several unpublished manuscripts.

Bibliography: Zinberg, Sifrut 3 (1957), 306. [G.K.]

HA-NO'AR HA-IVRI–AKIBA, pioneering and scouting Zionist youth movement with special attachment to the traditional values of Judaism. The movement was founded in Cracow as an organization of Jewish students in non-Jewish high schools. In 1924 Akiba united with similar youth organizations in western Galicia and assumed the character of a pioneering Zionist youth movement. A group that left the movement constituted the nucleus of the youth movement of the *General Zionists, Ha-No'ar ha-Ẓiyyoni. Akiba was active in Poland and to a lesser degree in Austria, Czechoslovakia, Greece, Yugoslavia, Bulgaria, and Palestine between the two World Wars, during the Holocaust, and almost until the establishment of the State of Israel. Its pioneering members began to settle collectively in Palestine in 1930. They were among those who fought for Jewish labor in Petaḥ Tikvah, Be'er Ya'akov, Ekron, and Ḥaderah and were among the founders of Neveh Eitan, Usha, Bet Yehoshu'a, Bustan ha-Galil, Benei Zion, etc.

Before the Holocaust, the membership of the movement reached 30,000. At the 21st Zionist Congress (1939), the last before the war, the movement was represented by six delegates. The ideological foundation of Akiba was based on the following principles: both assimilation—as a pragmatic means to solve the Jewish problem—and the leftist movements—especially Communism—lead to the destruction of Judaism. The efforts of assimilationists for generations have ended in failure, and the same is true of leftist movements, which denied Jewish national identity. Akiba advanced the desire to create an original Jewish experience through a pioneering way of life in Ereẓ Israel and viewed Zionism as the perpetuation of Jewish history.

Akiba educated its members toward a positive attitude to the traditional Jewish way of life. This emphasis was important among semi-assimilated youth who had been drawn away from Judaism. Its guiding principle was that even those who doubted the values of faith must agree that the traditionally religious way of life embodies the original creation of the Jewish people and its unifying quality was still valid in the present. Therefore the behavior in public and in Jewish institutions should not contradict the traditional way of life. During the Holocaust, the leaders of Akiba were among the heads of the Jewish fighting organizations and participated in the armed revolts in the Cracow ghetto (1942) and the Warsaw ghetto (1943). The ideological leader of the movement was Yoel Dreiblatt.

Bibliography: *Ha-Tenu'ah ha-Ḥalutzit be-Aguddat ha-No'ar ha-Ivri Akiva* (1940); Y. Dreiblatt, *Ziv Mo'adei Yisrael* (1946); G. Davidson, *Yomanah shel Yustinah* (1953); *Sefer Cracow* (1953), 263–70, 286–9; *Cracow Memorial Journal* (1968), 939–45. [Mo.Si.]

HA-NO'AR HA-OVED VE-HA-LOMED (Heb. "Working and Student Youth"), Israel youth movement for boys and girls aged 9–18. It is an integral part of the *Histadrut. It was founded as Ha-No'ar ha-Oved in 1926 to conduct educational activities among working youth aged 13–18 and improve their wages and working conditions. Its founder and mentor was David *Cohen. The movement ran evening classes, which were taken over by the state in 1955; labor exchanges, taken over by the State Employment Service in 1959; and youth groups for ages 10–12, 13–15, and 16–18. Most of the instructors came from the kibbutzim of *Iḥud ha-Kevuẓot ve-ha-Kibbutzim and *Ha-Kibbutz ha-Me-'uḥad. In 1933 a group of members founded its first kibbutz, *Na'an, and it has provided founding members for about 40 kibbutzim in all. In 1959 Ha-No'ar ha-Oved merged with Habonim–Ha-Tenu'ah ha-Me'uḥedet to form the present organization. In 1970 it had about 100,000 members; somewhat more than one-third were working boys and girls and belonged to the trade sections, and the rest, most of them still at school, belonged to the educational groups. While it has no formal party affiliation, most of its youth leaders belong to the *Israel Labor Party.

Bibliography: *Ba-Ma'aleh, Itton ha-No'ar ha-Oved* (1926–); *Ittim, Ḥoveret Ezer la-Madrikh* (1966–); *Aleh, Itton Ḥativat No'ar ha-Iḥud* (1966–). [Ed.]

ḤANOKH BEN MOSES (d. 1014), Spanish talmudist. The biography of Ḥanokh the son of *Moses b. Ḥanokh, is told in Abraham *ibn Daud's *Sefer ha-Kabbalah* (*The Book of Traditions,* ed. by G. D. Cohen (1967), 65–71). On the death of his father in about 965, Ḥanokh was appointed rabbi of Córdoba and as a result was virtually chief rabbi of the whole of Muslim Spain. Joseph *ibn Abitur, who was his equal in knowledge of Torah and excelled him in secular knowledge, competed with him for the post, but *Ḥisdai ibn Shaprut decided in Ḥanokh's favor. When Ḥisdai died, the struggle was renewed, and on this occasion the caliph, al-Ḥakam II al-Mustanṣir (961–76), confirmed the appointment of Ḥanokh; whereupon Ibn Abitur was put under the ban and left Spain. However, when the caliph died and the vizier al-*Manṣūr took control of the kingdom in Spain, a Jewish merchant, Jacob *ibn Janu rose in power. The latter supported Ibn Abitur, Ḥanokh was dismissed from office, and Ibn Abitur was invited to return to Spain. Ibn Abitur did not accept the invitation. Subsequently, Ibn Janu was imprisoned by al-Manṣūr and Ḥanokh was restored to office, serving until his death. From all the information that is available, it appears that Ḥanokh followed his father in all matters. He was an outstanding talmudic scholar, some of whose responsa were included in the contemporary gaonic responsa. Like his father, he worked to establish an independent Torah center in Spain. R. *Hai Gaon complains bitterly that Ḥanokh did not answer his letters. He had important disciples, the greatest of whom was *Samuel ha-Nagid.

Bibliography: Abramson, Merkazim, 84–90; idem, in: *Tarbiz,* 31 (1961/62), 196ff.; Ashtor, Korot, 1 (1966[2]), 233–48; M. Margalioth, *Hilkhot ha-Nagid* (1962), index. [E.A.]

ḤANOKH OF ALEKSANDROW (1798–1870), ḥasidic *ẓaddik* and leader; son of Phinehas ha-Kohen of Lutomirsk. He became a disciple of *Simḥah Bunim of Przysucha (Pshiskhah) and *Menahem Mendel of Kotsk, and served as rabbi in *Aleksandrow near Lodz, and later in Nowy Dwor, and in Pressnitz. Ḥanokh spent most of his life in the circles of the Ḥasidim of Przysucha and their successors in Kotsk and Gur, and in 1866 Ḥanokh succeeded Isaac Meir *Alter as leader of Gur Ḥasidism (see *Gora Kalwaria). He settled in Aleksandrow which had become a center for Kotsk-Gur Ḥasidism. Ḥanokh continued the Kotsk trend in a mystical religious interpretation. He emphasized the value of Torah study which he termed "internal worship." Ḥanokh taught that every *mitzvah* must be performed from within and not merely externally. Man should dedicate his entire being to the performance of a *mitzvah* and in turn receives the strength of his being from the *mitzvah* which he performs. His devotion effects a transformation in the world order and causes a divine emanation. Ḥanokh taught that while a man should occupy himself with the entire Torah and all the *mitzvot*, he should select one *mitzvah* for his particular attention. Of himself Ḥanokh states: "I have chosen the quality of humility."

Ḥanokh believed that everyone could follow the path of Ḥasidism by his own efforts, and that the *ẓaddik* was merely a guide. However, a compelling attachment exists between the *ẓaddik* and his community: "The true leader successfully serves God with the aid of the Ḥasidim who gather round him." Ḥanokh emphasized joy and happiness in life, but his joviality concealed a serious thinker. His teachings are distinguished by brevity and acuity. Only a few of his writings—responsa on halakhic questions, letters and sermons, poems and riddles—have survived in manuscript. Most of his teachings were recorded by his disciples and are published in *Ḥashavah le-Tovah* (1929); his stories and sayings are collected in *Si'aḥ Sarfei Kodesh* (1923).

Bibliography: P. Z. Gliksman, *Tiferet Adam* (1923), 56–58; L. Grossman, *Shem u-She'erit* (1943), 12; A. Y. Bromberg, *Mi-Gedolei ha-Torah ve-ha-Ḥasidut*, 14 (1958); L. I. Newman, *Hasidic Anthology* (1963), index; M. Buber, *Tales of the Hasidim*, 2 (1966[3]), 312–8.

[E.Z.]

ḤANOKH ZUNDEL BEN JOSEPH (d. 1867), commentator on the Midrash. Ḥanokh lived in Bialystok (Poland), and devoted himself to writing commentaries on the Midrash. They are largely based upon the earlier commentators such as the *Mattenat Kehunnah* of Berman Ashkenazi, the *Yefeh To'ar* of Samuel Jaffe Ashkenazi, and the *Yedei Moshe* of Abraham Heller Ashkenazi, but he adds original comments. In the *Eẓ Yosef* he strives to give the plain meaning of the text and establish the correct readings, while the *Anaf Yosef* is largely homiletical (published together as *Yalkut al Petirat Aharon u-Moshe*, Warsaw, 1874). In addition to his commentaries on the classical Midrashim, the *Rabbah* (1829–34), and the *Tanḥuma* (1833), he also wrote commentaries on other midrashic works, such as the **Seder Olam Rabbah* (1845), *Midrash Shemu'el* (1860), *Aggadat Bereshit* (1876), and the *aggadot* in the *Ein Ya'akov* of Jacob ibn Ḥabib (1883). He also wrote a commentary on *Pirkei Avot* (1892), and *Olat ha-Ḥodesh* (1859), consisting of the prayers for the new moon, with a commentary. His commentaries on *Yalkut Shimoni* and the *Mekhilta* are still in manuscript.

Bibliography: Fuenn, Keneset, 312; Joel, in: KS, 13 (1936/37), 513 no. 1, 519 no. 19.

[Y.Ho.]

HANOVER (Ger. **Hannover**), city in W. Germany. Sources dating from 1292 note the presence of Jews in Hanover's "old city" (Altstadt). The period was one of significant expansion for the city and, therefore, Jewish moneylenders were welcomed and promised protection by the city council. A municipal law of 1303 prohibited anyone from molesting the Jews "by word or deed." The Jewish community grew significantly, and by 1340 ritual slaughter was permitted in the city. During the *Black Death persecutions the Jews were driven from the city. In 1369–71 only one Jew lived in Hanover until he, too, was expelled by the council, with the permission of the duke. In 1375 the dukes yielded to the city the privilege of admitting Jews and retaining their taxes. Shortly thereafter historical records again attest to the presence of Jews in the city. By 1500 several Jews also lived in the "new city" (in 1540, there were three families in the old city, and five in the new). During this period the Jews

Figure 1. The Hanover synagogue, opened in 1870, enlarged in 1900, and destroyed by the Nazis in 1938. Courtesy Hanover Municipality. Photo Hermann Friedrich.

maintained a synagogue and a rabbi. In 1451 the bishop of Muenden forced the Jews of Hanover to wear the distinguishing *badge, and in 1553 the Jews were compelled to listen to the court preacher Urbanus Rhegius in the synagogue. Between 1553 and 1601 the dukes issued six orders of expulsion against the Jews, but they were either canceled or not carried out. Apparently the Jews who were under the protection of the city were not affected by these orders. In 1588 the council forbade all business connections with Jews, and for a long time Jews did not live in the "old city."

In 1608 the residence of six Jewish families in the "new city" is mentioned, but when they opened a synagogue it was destroyed by the burghers (1613). In the 17th century the dukes permitted the settlement of several wealthy Jews in the "new city." At the request of the Court Jew Leffmann *Behrens, a resident of Hanover, a rabbinate was founded for the Duchy of Hanover. In 1704 a synagogue was established in Behrens' home. In 1710 only seven Jewish families lived in the city, but subsequently their numbers increased considerably, reaching 537 in 1833. Hanover became an important center of Jewish learning and increasingly the residence for important Jewish figures in the financial world. A larger synagogue was built in 1870 and expanded in 1900. From 1848 to 1880 Solomon *Frensdorff, the masoretic scholar, headed a teachers seminary. Hebrew printing took place in Hanover during the 18th and 19th centuries. Among the more significant works produced was Jacob b. Asher's commentary on the Pentateuch (1838). Prominent rabbis of Hanover include Nathan *Adler (1831–45) and Selig Gronemann (1844–1918). The Jewish population numbered 1,120 in 1861 (1.9% of the total population), 3,450 in 1880 (2.8%), 5,130 in 1910 (1.7%), 4,839 in 1933 (1.1%), and 2,271 in 1939 (0.5%). On the eve of World War II Hanover had one of the ten largest Jewish communities in Germany, with over 20 cultural and welfare institutions. Despite the many overt anti-Semitic acts directed against Hanover Jewry from the beginning of the Nazi regime the community was not critically affected until the latter part of 1938. It reacted to Nazi rule by

Figure 2. The new synagogue of Hanover, opened in 1963. Courtesy Hanover Municipality. Photo Hermann Friedrich.

intensifying its Jewish educational system, particularly its youth organizations, and preparing its residents for emigration. The destruction of the community began in earnest in 1938 when the synagogues were destroyed and Jews terrorized. Some 2,900 Jews from Hanover were deported to the concentration camps between 1941 and 1945. After the war 66 survivors of the prewar community returned. In 1963 a new synagogue was opened; in 1966 there were 450 Jews in Hanover (0.03% of the total population).

Former German State. The Duchy of Hanover was formed out of the former territories of *Brunswick and Lueneburg in the 17th century. Duke Ernst August (1679–98) obtained the title of elector through the services of Leffmann Behrens, whose descendants continued in the service of the crown till the middle of the 19th century. Other prominent families of Court Jews were David, Cohen, and Gans. The dukes established their rights of taxation and guardianship over the Jews, expressed in the **Judenordnung* of 1723, in force until 1842, which severely restricted the number of Jews there. In 1808 the Jews of Hanover received civil rights either through annexation of the territory to France or its incorporation in the newly created Kingdom of Westphalia. These rights were abolished in 1815, and the basic 1842 legislation concerning the Jews confirmed discrimination against them by expressly excluding Jews from state posts. The Jewish oath was rescinded only in 1850. The Jews finally achieved emancipation three years after Hanover passed to Prussia (1866).

Bibliography: H. Bodemeyer, *Die Juden: ein Beitrag zur Hannoverschen Rechtsgeschichte* (1855); Wiener, in: *Jahrbuch fuer die Geschichte der Juden und des Judenthums*, 1 (1860), 167–216; idem in: MGWJ, 10 (1861), 121–36, 161–75, 241–58, 281–97; 13 (1864), 161–84; M. Zuckerman, *Dokumente zur Geschichte der Juden in Hannover* (1908); S. Gronemann, *Genealogische Studien ueber die alten juedischen Familien Hannovers* (1913); Blau, in: *Zeitschrift fuer Demographie und Statistik der Juden*, 8 (1912), 70–75; 10 (1914), 110–6; S. Stern, *The Court Jew* (1950), index; *Leben und Schicksal: zur Einweihung der Synagoge in Hannover* (1963); Germ Jud, 2 (1968), 337–40; A. Loeb, *Die Rechtsverhaeltnisse der Juden im . . . Hannover* (1908); *Pinkas ha-Kehillot* (1963); S. Freund, *Ein Vierteljahrtausend Hannoversches Landrabbinat 1687–1937* (1937); H. Schnee, *Die Hoffinanz und der moderne Staat*, 2 (1954), 11–85; BJCE.

[Z.Av.]

HANSON, NORMAN LEONARD (1909–), South African architect. Hanson made a major contribution to the town planning of Ashkelon in Israel, designed the national headquarters of the South African Zionist Federation in Johannesburg (his birthplace) and the mining and geology block at the Witwatersrand University. He served on its faculty of architecture for many years. Hanson was president of the Institute of South African Architects in 1947. In 1963, he left South Africa to take up the chair of architecture at Manchester University. [L.Ho.]

HANTKE, ARTHUR (Menahem; 1874–1955), Zionist leader. Born in Berlin, the son of a religious family from the district of Posen, Hantke was in 1893 a founding member of the Juedische Humanitaetsgesellschaft, a society of Jewish students in Berlin, which in the course of time adopted a Jewish national outlook. He joined the Zionist Organization soon after it was founded in 1897. In 1905 he became a member of the Zionist General Council of the World Zionist Organization and was appointed director of the office of the Zionist Federation in Germany. From 1910 to 1920 he served as president of this organization. At the Tenth Zionist Congress held in Basle (1911) he was elected to the Zionist Executive, a post in which he was responsible for financial and organizational affairs. During World War I he was charged with important political tasks, one of which was to establish contact with the German Foreign Ministry on behalf of the Zionist Organization. After the publication of the *Balfour Declaration in London he attempted to obtain similar declarations from the Central Powers and succeeded in obtaining a pro-Zionist statement from the Austro-Hungarian foreign minister, Count Czernin (Nov. 17, 1917). After the war he lived for a time in London, where he continued to deal with organizational affairs of the Zionist Organization. In 1920 he was put in charge of the Central European department of the *Keren Hayesod and of the Berlin office of the Zionist Organization. In 1926 Hantke settled in Palestine, and from then he

Arthur Hantke, Zionist leader. Courtesy Central Zionist Archives, Jerusalem.

served (with L. *Jaffe until 1948) as the managing director of the head office of the Keren Hayesod in Jerusalem. The moshav Even Menaḥem on the Israel-Lebanese border is named after him.

Bibliography: K. Blumenfeld, *Erlebte Judenfrage* (1962), index; R. Lichtheim, *Toledot ha-Ẓiyyonut be-Germanyah* (n.d.), index; I. Gruenbaum, *Penei ha-Dor*, 2 (1960), index; Z. Shazar, *Or Ishim*, 1 (1963[2]), 108–18.

[Mi.H.]

ḤANUKKAH (Heb. חֲנֻכָּה; "dedication"), an annual eight-day festival commencing on the 25th of Kislev. According to a well-founded tradition it was instituted by Judah *Maccabee and his followers. The term *ḥanukkah* is found in Hebrew and in Aramaic (ḥanukta) in rabbinic literature, while in Greek it is ὁ ἐγκαινισμὸς τοῦ Ηυσιαστηρίου, "dedication of the altar," (I Maccabees 4:59) and τὰ ἐγκαίνια, "feast of the dedication" (John 10:22, where it is an abbreviation of *ḥanukkat ha-mizbe'aḥ*, "dedication of the altar," of I Maccabees, and of *ḥanukkat beit Ḥashmonai*, "dedication of the Hasmonean Temple" in rabbinic literature). The sources which refer to Ḥanukkah yield little information on

1

סדר ברכת המזון

ומטיב לכל ומכין מזון לכל
בריותיו אשר ברא · ברוך אתה ה'
הזן את הכל

נודה לך ה' אלהינו על
שהנחלת לאבותינו
ארץ חמדה טובה
ועל שהוצאתנו ה' אלהינו מארץ
מצרים ופדיתנו מבית עבדים ועל
בריתך שחתמת בבשרנו ועל
תורתך שלמדתנו ועל חקיך ש
שהודעתנו ועל חיים חן וחסד
שחוננתנו ועל אכילת מזון שאתה
זן ומפרנס אותנו תמיד בכל יום
(ובכל עת ובכל שעה)
בחנוכה ובפורים אומרים
(כאן על הניסים :)

סדר ברכת המזון

20

על הניסים
ועל הפורקן ועל הגבורות ועל
התשועות ועל המלחמות ש
שעשית לאבותינו בימים ההם
בזמן הזה :

בימי

מתתיהו בן יוחנן כהן גדול
וחשמונאי ובניו כשעמדה
מלכות יון הרשעה על
עמך ישראל להשכיחם
תורתך ולהעבירם מחקי
רצונך · ואתה ברחמיך

מרדכי ואסתר בשושן
הבירה כשעמד עליהם
המן הרשע בקש להשמיד
להרוג ולאבד את כל
היהודים מנער ועד זקן
טף ונשים ביום אחד ב

2

Figure 1. "Lighting of the Ḥanukkah Candles" by Moritz Oppenheim, Germany, 1880. Jerusalem, Israel Museum. Photo David Harris, Jerusalem.

Figure 2. The *Al ha-Nissim* prayer included in the Grace after Meals on Ḥanukkah and Purim, from an 18th-century Eastern European *siddur*. Cambridge University Library, Ms. Add. 1532.

Figure 3. Woodcut from *Sefer Minhagim* showing the Ḥanukkah lamp being lit in a synagogue. Printed by Proops, Amsterdam, 1707. Jerusalem, J.N.U.L.

Figure 4. Israel child lighting Ḥanukkah candles. Courtesy Government Press Office, Tel Aviv.

3

4

the institution of the festival. They were composed long (perhaps even generations) after its establishment; legends seem to be inextricably interwoven with the historical traditions. I Maccabees (4:36–59) states that Judah Maccabee, after defeating Lysias, entered Jerusalem and purified the Temple. The altar that had been defiled was demolished and a new one was built. Judah then made new holy vessels (among them a candelabrum, an altar for incense, a table, and curtains) and set the 25th of Kislev as the date for the rededication of the Temple. The day coincided with the third anniversary of the proclamation of the restrictive edicts of Antiochus Epiphanes in which he had decreed that idolatrous sacrifices should be offered on a platform erected upon the altar. The altar was to be consecrated with the renewal of the daily sacrificial service, accompanied by song, the playing of musical instruments, the chanting of **Hallel,* and the offering of sacrifices (no mention of any special festival customs is made). The celebrations lasted for eight days and Judah decreed that they be designated as days of rejoicing for future generations. Ḥanukkah, as the festival that commemorates the dedication of the altar, is also mentioned in the scholium of **Megillat Ta'anit,* as well as in the traditional **Al ha-Nissim* ("We thank Thee for the miracles") prayer for Ḥanukkah.

In II Maccabees (1:8; 10:1–5), the main aspects of Ḥanukkah are related as in I Maccabees. The book adds, however, that the eight-day dedication ceremony was performed on an analogy with *Solomon's consecration of the Temple (2:12). The eight days were celebrated "with gladness like the Feast of Tabernacles remembering how, not long before, during the Feast of Tabernacles, they had been wandering like wild beasts in the mountains and the caves. So, bearing wands wreathed with leaves and fair boughs and palms, they offered hymns of praise" (10:6–8). Ḥanukkah is, therefore, called *Tabernacles (1:9), or Tabernacles and Fire (1:18). Fire had descended from heaven at the dedication of the altar in the days of Moses and at the sanctification of the Temple of Solomon; at the consecration of the altar in the time of *Nehemiah there was also a miracle of fire, and so in the days of Judah Maccabee (1:18–36, 2:8–12, 14; 10:3).

Josephus, whose history of Ḥanukkah is based on I Maccabees, does not mention the term Ḥanukkah and concludes: "From that time onward unto this day we celebrate the festival, calling it 'Lights'" (φῶτα, Ant. 12:325). He explains that the festival acquired this name because the right to serve God came to the people unexpectedly, like a sudden light *(ibid.)*.

None of these writings mentions the kindling of lights on Ḥanukkah. Reference is first made in a *baraita:* "The precept of light on Ḥanukkah requires that one light be kindled in each house; the zealous require one light for each person; the extremely zealous add a light for each person each night. According to Bet *Shammai: 'On the first day, eight lights should be kindled, thereafter they should be progressively reduced' while Bet *Hillel held that: 'On the first night one light should be kindled, thereafter they should be progressively increased'" (Scholium to *Megillat Ta'anit;* Shab. 21b). Another *baraita* states that the Hasmoneans could not use the candelabrum in the Temple since the Greeks had defiled it. They, therefore, took seven iron spits, covered them with zinc, and used them as a candelabrum (Scholium to *Megillat Ta'anit*). Indeed the sages of the second century C.E. observe that the candelabrum of the early Hasmoneans was not made of gold (Men. 28b; et al.). This tradition forms the core of the story, a later version of which relates that the Hasmoneans found in the Temple "eight iron bars, erected them, and kindled lights in them" (PR 2:5). Another *baraita* ascribes the eight-day celebration of Ḥanukkah to the kindling of the Temple candelabrum. It states that on entering the Temple, the Hasmoneans discovered that the Greeks had defiled all the oil, except for one cruse, which contained enough oil to keep the candelabrum burning for only one day. A miracle, however, happened and they kindled from it for eight days; in its commemoration a festival lasting eight days was instituted for future generations (Scholium to *Megillat Ta'anit;* Shab. 21b; cf. also **Megillat Antiochus*). All these stories seem to be nothing but legends, and the authenticity of the "oil cruse" story has already been questioned in the Middle Ages.

Certain critics conjectured that the origin of Ḥanukkah was either a festival of the hellenized Jews or even an idolatrous festival that had occurred on the 25th of Kislev. Antiochus had, therefore, chosen the day to commence the idolatrous worship in the Temple. No allusion can be found in the sources to bear out this surmise. Ḥanukkah is also not connected in any way, except in calendrical coincidence, with the celebrations of the shortest day of the year (the birthday of the sun), or with the feasts of the Greek god Dionysius.

Most of the Ḥanukkah traditions complement one another, and what is lacking in one may be found in the other. Probably, during the eight-day dedication of the altar by Judah Maccabee, a second Tabernacles (analogous to the Second *Passover) was held because the festival had not been celebrated at its proper time. They observed the precept of taking the **lulav* in the Temple though not the precept of sitting in tents, for this was done at its proper time even by the partisans in the mountains. The custom of Simḥat Bet ha-Sho'evah ("the water-drawing festival"), with its kindling of torches and lamps in the courts of the Temple and the city of Jerusalem, seems likely to have been transferred as well from *Sukkot to Ḥanukkah. This was the general pattern of the festival as Judah instituted it. Before long, however, the custom of taking the *lulav* during Ḥanukkah was abolished and forgotten in time. The author of I Maccabees, who lived in Alexander Yannai's time, was unaware of the custom although it was still remembered in the Diaspora and is recorded by Jason of Cyrene and by the author of II Maccabees. Hints of a connection between Ḥanukkah and Sukkot are also preserved in rabbinic literature. The rejoicing with lights and illuminations in the Temple (after which Ḥanukkah came to be called Urim, "Lights") also became less common after a time so that Josephus no longer knew why the name "Lights" was given to the festival. By then, however, the custom of kindling lights on Ḥanukkah had spread to places outside Jerusalem, lights being kindled in the streets or in the homes. This variety of customs associated with Ḥanukkah is reflected in the *baraita* which discusses the controversy between the schools of Shammai and Hillel (see above) seemingly about the second half of the first century C.E. The custom of kindling the Ḥanukkah lights was then fixed by the sages as a rule for each man; thus it spread throughout Israel, and when other festive days mentioned in *Megillat Ta'anit* were revoked, Ḥanukkah remained as a holiday (RH 18b–19b). Consequently, Ḥanukkah evolved from a distinct Temple festival into a popular family one.

The *halakhah* prescribes that lighting the Ḥanukkah lamp should take place between "sunset and until there is no wayfarer left in the street. The lamp should be placed outside the entrance of the house. If a person lives on an upper story, it should be set on the window, nearest to the street. If he is in fear of the gentiles, the lamp may be placed inside the inner entrance of the house, and in times of danger, the precept is fulfilled by setting it on the table" (Scholium to *Megillat Ta'anit;* Shab. 21b). "Danger" not

5

6

Figure 5. Children portraying Judah Maccabee and his soldiers in an American Hebrew school Ḥanukkah production, 1948. From *Congregation Shearith Israel Diamond Anniversary;* 1884–1959; Dallas, Texas.

Figure 6. Silver *dreidel* (top) for Ḥanukkah, Poland, 19th century. Jerusalem, Israel Museum. Photo R. Milon, Jerusalem.

Figure 7. Isser Unterman, Ashkenazi chief rabbi of Israel, kindling the first light at the Western Wall in Jerusalem, 1968. Courtesy Government Press Office, Tel Aviv.

Figure 8. A participant in the annual Ḥanukkah torch relay from Modi'in to Jerusalem. Courtesy Government Press Office, Tel Aviv.

7

8

Figure 9. Lead Ḥanukkah *dreidel* with wooden casting mold, Poland, 20th century. Jerusalem, Israel Museum. Photo R. Milon.

only existed in Ereẓ Israel during the Hadrianic persecution, but also in Babylonia, where Jews feared the *Hobarei who were fire worshipers (Shab. 45a). Perhaps because of the danger involved, Jews in Babylonia were most particular in the observance of the Ḥanukkah precepts; they decided that "because its purpose is to publicize the miracle," it takes precedence over the purchase of wine for *Kiddush* on the Sabbath (Shab. 23b). "Women are also obliged to kindle the Ḥanukkah lamp since they were also included in the miracle" (Shab. 23a). The precept is best fulfilled by kindling with olive oil; however, any oil may be used *(ibid.).* The Ḥanukkah lamp and the Ḥanukkah light may not serve any practical purpose (Shab. 21b). On kindling the lights, two benedictions are recited, one is a blessing on the lights and the other for the miracle; on the first night, *"She-Heḥeyanu"* (the blessing for the season) is added. The kindling of the light is followed by a short prayer which begins with the words *"Ha-Nerot Hallalu"* ("these lamps"; Sof. 20:4). A summary of the event, i.e., *Al ha-Nissim . . . Bi-Ymei Mattityahu* ("In the days of Mattathias") is recited in the **Amidah* prayer and in the Grace after Meals. The entire *Hallel* is said on each of the eight days. The reading of the law is from the portion of the Torah which describes the sacrifices brought by the princes at the dedication of the sanctuary, and the kindling of the candelabrum (Num. 7:1–8:4); special **haftarot* are prescribed for the Sabbaths of Ḥanukkah. **Taḥanun* is not said and it is forbidden to eulogize the dead or to fast.

In medieval times, Ḥanukkah became such a popular festival it was said "Even he who draws his sustenance from charity, should borrow, or sell his cloak to purchase oil and lamps, and kindle" the Ḥanukkah light (Maim. Yad, Megillah va-Ḥanukkah, 4:12). In some communities, women did not work while the lights were burning, and often even during the whole of Ḥanukkah. It became the custom to feast on Ḥanukkah and, relying upon late Midrashim which associate the story of *Judith with Ḥanukkah, cheese was customarily eaten. Pancakes *(latkes)* are eaten in many Ashkenazi communities, and in Israel doughnuts *(sufganiyyot)* have become customary food for the festival. *"*Ma'oz Ẓur Yeshu'ati"* ("Mighty Rock of my Salvation"), a hymn composed in Germany by a 13th-century poet about whom nothing is known except his name Mordecai, is usually sung in the Ashkenazi ritual after the kindling of the lights. The Sephardim recite Psalm 30. The origin of the custom to have an additional light, the *shammash* ("servant") with which the Ḥanukkah lights are kindled, is based on two injunctions: not to kindle one Ḥanukkah light with another; and not to use the Ḥanukkah lights for illumination.

Ḥanukkah celebrations were also expressed in ways of which the halakhists disapproved, e.g., in card playing which became traditional from the end of the Middle Ages. On Ḥanukkah, children play with a *dreidel* or *sevivon* ("spinning top"), and also receive gifts of "Ḥanukkah money." Among Sephardim, special feasts for the children and competitions for youths are arranged. In countries where Christmas became a popular family festival, Ḥanukkah, particularly among Reform Jews, assumed a similar form. In modern Israel, Ḥanukkah symbolizes mainly the victory of the few over the many, and the courage of the Jews to assert themselves as a people which was the impetus of the national renaissance. This view found literary and artistic expression and is also reflected in such customs as the torch relay race which sets out from *Modi'in where the revolt broke out and the Hasmoneans are buried.

In Israel giant Ḥanukkah lamps, visible for great distances, are kindled during the feast atop public buildings, such as the Knesset building in Jerusalem.

Bibliography: O.S. Rankin, *The Origins of the Festival of Hanukkah . . .* (1930); idem, in: *The Labyrinth,* ed. by S.H. Hooke (1935), 161–209; E. Bickerman, *The Maccabees* (1947), 42–44; S.J. Zevin, *Ha-Mo'adim ba-Halakhah* (1963[10]), 156–81; T.H. Gaster, *Purim and Hanukkah in Custom and Tradition* (1950); idem, *Festivals of the Jewish Year* (1955); V. Tcherikover, *Hellenistic Civilization and the Jews* (1959), index; E. Solis-Cohen Jr., *Hanukkah* (1960); Krauss, in: REJ, 30 (1895), 24–43, 204–19; 31 (1896), 39–50; Lévi, in: REJ, 30 (1895), 220–31; 31 (1895), 119–20; Hochfeld, in: ZAW, 22 (1902), 264–84; Leszynsky, in: MGWJ, 5 (1911), 400–18; Liber, in: REJ, 63 (1912), 20–29; Hoepfel, in *Biblica,* 3 (1922), 165ff.; R. Marcus, *Law in the Apocrypha* (1927), 90–93; Finkelstein, in: JQR, 22 (1931/32), 169–73; Lichtenstein, in: HUCA, 8–9 (1931/32), 275f.; Zeitlin, in: JQR, 29 (1938/39), 1–36; Alon, Meḥkarim, 1 (1957), 15–25; Petuchowski, in *Commentary,* 29 (1960), 38–43.

[M.D.H.]

ḤANUKKAH LAMP (also known as **ḥanukkiyyah** and Ḥanukkah **menorah**). It is probable that the richly decorated Ḥanukkah lamp of medieval and modern times had its origin in the simple, pear-shaped Greco-Roman λύχνος (clay lamp), with aperture for the wick and one for the oil reservoir, that was in universal use throughout the Mediterranean world in the centuries before and after the beginnings of the Common Era (figure 2). During Ḥanukkah in talmudic times these lamps were mounted on elongated vertical bases, many of which were found in excavations and which were in use until recently by Jews of Yemen and Persia. There was in use in talmudic times the Greco-Roman *polymixos,* a many mouthed lamp which was made of clay, stone, or bronze with eight apertures for wicks fed by a central reservoir on whose surface geometrical or symbolic designs often appear. An early example carved from stone is published here for the first time. The lamp was unearthed in a cave in Jerusalem (figure 4). This particular lamp is the source of all later stone Ḥanukkah lamps of similar design found in Yemen, North Africa, France, and other places (figure 5). A marble Ḥanukkah lamp of similar type from medieval times, inscribed with the Hebrew verse, "For the commandment is a lamp and the teaching is light" (Prov. 6:23), was found in Avignon, southern France (Paris, Klagsbald Collection (figure 3)).

Another important type of the Ḥanukkah lamp was a circular lamp in the shape of a pointed star. An archaeological stone lamp from Persia or Babylonia is illustrated here (figure 9). This example portrays the tradition in Babylonia and Persia, which was allowed according to the Babylonian Talmud, if the lights did not resemble one flame (מדורה) (Shab. 23b). This tiny lamp may have been made for a traveler's use. Ceramic lamps with eight apertures found in excavations in Ereẓ Israel—some adorned with Jewish symbols—were certainly used as Hanukkah lamps (see figure 4, cf. 7 fig. 2). Metal lamps were also used in the talmudic period and are mentioned in the Talmud (Shab. 44a; Ḥul. 9a, Pes. 14a). Bronze Ḥanukkah lamps of eight apertures surely existed even though no examples of this type have as yet been unearthed in excavations. An example of such a bronze lamp, unearthed in northern Babylonia, decorated with seven branched candelabra and with seven spouts, is illustrated here (figure 6).

In mishnaic times, according to the *halakhah* of the *tannaim*, the Ḥanukkah lamp had to be positioned outside the entrance of the house to affirm publicly the Ḥanukkah miracle. To prevent the lights from being extinguished by the winter winds of the Ḥanukkah season of ancient Israel and Babylonia, the Jews must have inserted the lamps into "a glass lantern." Lanterns were in use in talmudic times and they are mentioned in the Mishnah and Tosefta (Kel. 2:4; Tosef., Kelim, BB 7:11). Lanterns, which were in turn placed on pedestals, as mentioned in both the Talmud (Shab. 44a) and New Testament (Luke 11:33), and which have been uncovered at archaeological excavations, were customary in antiquity. The Talmud (Shab. 22a) states that the *menorah* must be on the right. On passing through the entrance to a positioned to the left of the door, while the *mezuzah* is home with these objects so placed, the Jew fulfilled the biblical phrase: "How beautiful and how pleasant are you" (Song 7:7), according to the tractate *Soferim* (20:3) which explains further: "How beautiful are you with the *mezuzah* and how pleasant are you with the Ḥanukkah lamp."

Later the lamps for Ḥanukkah were mainly made of metal. It is known, for example, that R. Meir b. Baruch of Rothenburg refused to use clay lamps as one may not use old clay lamps for Ḥanukkah according to tractate *Soferim* 20:3. He also mentions his teacher Shmuel hanging a metal lamp on his door (Tur, OḤ 673). The metal Ḥanukkah lamp that developed during the Middle Ages generally had a back-wall, from which it was hung against the wall, and eight oil spouts. The master light or *shammash* generally stood to one side or at the top, whether in the middle or on the left, and quite often there was no *shammash* at all. The back-wall of the Ḥanukkah lamp stems from the medieval situation, in accordance with the rules of *halakhah*, according to which the Ḥanukkah lamp was to be placed outside, near the door. In times of danger, however, the rabbis permitted the lighting of the Ḥanukkah lamp inside the home. In order still to comply with the injunction "*mezuzah* on the right and Ḥanukkah lamp on the left," the lamp was hung inside at the entrance opposite the *mezuzah*. The great rabbinic authority Isaac b. Abba Mari of Marseilles (12th century) states in his work *Sefer ha-Ittur:* "he who can place the Ḥanukkah lamp outside puts it outside. And if not, on the entrance." Meir of Rothenburg also relates that he saw his teacher fixing the Ḥanukkah lamp on the doorposts. Originally the back-wall was a hanging device, and the trefoil on top of most back-walls is a remnant of its use. German Jewry was accustomed to kindle the Ḥanukkah lights near the door until as late as the 17th century. Spanish communities throughout the world maintained this custom until recently. Thus lamps from Spanish Morocco are often inscribed with the verse from Deuteronomy 28:6: "Blessed are you at your coming and blessed are you at your leaving" (figure 8).

The Ḥanukkah lamp with a back-wall originated in Spain. The oldest back-walled Ḥanukkah lamp (Narkiss no. 21) dating from the 13th century was discovered in Lyons, in the south of France; and is now in Paris in Musée Cluny. The *shammash* is on the same line but at a right angle to the other spouts. Similar lamps are in other collections, including the Israel Museum (figure 7). The early Jewish communities of southern France were fundamentally Sephardi and wholly under Spanish influence. This type of lamp is decorated with Gothic rose windows, quatrefoils, and arched colonnades. The Ḥanukkah lamp with its arabesque curls and the palm leaf in its top comes from Muslim Spain (figure 10). So also the tiny Ḥanukkah lamp (height: 83 mm.) with its arabesques shows its origin from Muslim Spain (figure 11). The *shammash* in this lamp is still in the same line with the spouts, without any distinction, as in the early Bezalel lamp (Narkiss no. 16). This type of lamp was spread throughout the world by the Spanish Jews and similar lamps with the same arabesques were found in Morocco, Italy, and Poland. A lamp constructed in the form of two twisting serpents whose heads meet to complete a Gothic triangle (figure 14) is a common motif of Islamic art, and is found in the remnants of the Jewish art of Spain as well. The serpent is itself an old Jewish symbol. A copy of this lamp, with certain additions, appeared later in Eastern Europe (figure 12). The motif is common in the side panels of Polish lamps and also reached as far as Cochin, India.

The predominant Spanish origin can also be traced in later examples. The beaten brass lamps of Morocco (figure 15) and Holland (figure 13) sometimes resemble one another to the extent that it is difficult to differentiate between them. This striking similarity emphatically demonstrates the common Sephardi origin. In the medieval Moslem and Oriental world, the decoration on the back-wall of Ḥanukkah lamps tended to be more simple. It was characteristic in some areas to have glass burners inserted in holders below the brass back-wall, which was sometimes decorated with "a hand of Fatimah" to ward off evil spirits. The star-shaped lamp hanging from the ceiling was also employed by the Jews in Spain and commonly used in Italy, Holland, and Germany. The great rabbinic authority of 14th-century Provence, Menahem b. Solomon *Meiri, allows the kindling of Ḥanukkah lights in this lamp "without any doubt," although Ḥanukkah lamps with lights "in the round," which look like one flame, were forbidden (Shab. 23b). In one of the miniatures of the Spanish *Sarajevo Haggadah* (text, folio 31 v, figure 19) this type of lamp is depicted hanging over the *seder* table. This can also be seen in the south German *Erna Michael Haggadah* (figure 16).

During the Renaissance in Italy, the lamp evolved further decorative enrichment in the style of that period. One Italian Renaissance lamp (figure 21) depicts an urn from which the holy fire rises. The urn is flanked by guardian lions. This motif springs from Jewish tradition and is connected with the story of the Maccabees, who hid the defiled altar and then built it anew. This story is developed in talmudic sources and in the Books of the Maccabees, both of which were known to Italian Jewry. This motif has its source in an old tradition in Jewish painting from Spain. The annals of the Inquisition in Spain tell of an illustrated Scroll of Lamentations found in the home of a Marrano, Juan Dias. One of the pictures showed flames coming up as if from a burning stove. Juan Dias explains, "this is the holy fire from the holiest of holies. Jeremiah the prophet took this fire and hid it in order that enemies, who were about to destroy Jerusalem, should not take it with them. God said to the prophet that this fire will appear when God returns" (H. Beinart, *Anusim be-Din ha-Inkviziẓyah* (1965), 26). In 16th-century Italy the back-wall grew in ornateness: it was generally cast in copper, bronze, or brass and was decorated with tritons, cherubs, urns, masks, and cornucopiae in the Renaissance style (figure 25). Frequently, back-walls were engraved with depictions of biblical or apocryphal scenes, such as Judith carrying the head of Holophernes, an episode traditionally associated with the Ḥanukkah festival (figure 20). Some backs bore architectural designs (figure 24), others the coats of arms of noble patrons; thus, an entire series of bronze 16th-century Ḥanukkah lamps are adorned with the armorial bearings of cardinals of the Catholic Church, whose sacerdotal hats are held aloft by baby cherubs (figure 22).

The baroque style of the Italian Ḥanukkah lamp merged into the rococo, which continued to prevail, on the whole, until the period of the Enlightenment. In the 18th century back-walls occasionally bore designs emblematic of the person to whom they belonged, as was the case with a silver Ḥanukkah lamp made in 1709 by the London silversmith J. Ruslen for Eliah Lindo, which showed the prophet Elijah being fed by the ravens (figure 17). In Prague a common type of lamp had side-panels representing Moses and Aaron, with the Swedish hat, the badge of the community, surmounting the centerpiece (figure 28).

The Jews of Germany had a peculiar culture of their own and were not highly susceptible to the influence of Spanish Jewry—not at the time of their greatness and certainly not during the period of their decline. German custom differed from that of Spain. A tale of Meir of Rothenberg relates that "he would kindle in small metal vessels," most likely adding another vessel every day (figures 23 and 29). The early Ashkenazi back-walled lamps (the Figdor lamp in New York's Temple Emmanuel (Narkiss, no. 17 figure 31) and the Klagsbald lamp (Synagoga 208)) are probably of the 14th century, which can be deduced from their script and decoration. They may have been made in Italy by Ashkenazi Jews. From the Middle Ages up to the 18th century, all different sources, ranging from rabbinic writings through books on customs by non-Jews such as *Kirchner, *Buxdorf, and *Bodenschatz, point to the use by German Jews of a lamp in the form of a star (*Judenstern*). This lamp was hung from the ceiling and regularly used as a Sabbath lamp. During Ḥanukkah, however, even as late as the 17th century (Buxdorf), the lamp was hung near the door in the old tradition (figure 27). German Jews also employed the eight-branched standing *menorah*, especially in synagogues (figure 33). Unfortunately, early examples are nonexistent, as these metal lamps were confiscated during wars to be used for casting weaponry.

Only during the 17th and 18th centuries did the back-walled Ḥanukkah lamp become common in Germany, becoming more popular apparently under the influence of Eastern Europe. These back-walled lamps of German origin are usually finely crafted from pewter (figure 32) and silver (figure 30), executed in the main by non-Jewish artisans at the direction of Jewish clients. At this period the Jews in Germany were at times under the spiritual influence of the centers of Torah in Eastern Europe. Nearly all their rabbis came from there.

The back-walled Ḥanukkah lamp came to Eastern Europe during the 16th century, introduced through Spanish Jewish refugees who fled to this area. The small lamp (figure 26), with its arabesque curls, proves the Spanish origin and is, indeed, a copy of old Sephardi lamps of this type. The Polish Jews only added legs, as their custom was to place the lamp on the windowsill or on a table during the lighting ceremony. Only a few examples of this type of 16th-century Polish lamp still exist. It may be that Mordecai Yoffe refers to just such a lamp when he writes about "a special vessel for Ḥanukkah lights which has eight spouts" לבוש החור כל חנוכה תרע״ו ס״ק ה׳. After some time, the Jews of Eastern Europe freed themselves from the attachment to the Spanish-style lamp (figure 35). Jewish craftsmen abounded in Eastern Europe. Artisans who cast in brass and silversmiths who worked in filigree (figure 40) and repousse were rooted in Jewish tradition. With great artistic sensitivity they enriched the appearance of the Ḥanukkah lamp with a breathtaking variety of Jewish symbols: deer and lions, eagles and other birds, *menorah* and Temple facade, Torah crowns, gates, columns, etc. (see figure 38). Eight-branched standing lamps were also cast, particularly for synagogue use (figure 36).

The Spanish-Portuguese Jews in Holland maintained their old traditions, brought from Spain. From these Jews have come down very beautiful sheet brass lamps, hammered, cut out, and engraved (figure 13). They also cast lamps of brass, these lamps reflecting both the old tradition and signs of their new surroundings. Dutch Jews produced back-walled lamps of silver (Narkiss 130) and pewter as well, and utilized the eight-branch standing form, often standing on a base with three legs in the form of serpents. Also utilized were brass and silver star-shaped hanging lamps with eight openings. Such lamps were hung from a hook near the door, serving as a Sabbath lamp in the Jewish home during the entire year.

The Jews of North Africa in general and the Jews of Morocco in particular distinguished themselves in fine craftsmanship. In the Middle Ages North African Jewry used Ḥanukkah lamps of stone and glazed pottery. According to tractate *Soferim* old used pottery was not considered proper for use in Ḥanukkah lights. In order to bring them into conformity with halakhic requirements pottery lamps were glazed (as was also done later in Germany). When Spanish Jewry sought refuge in North Africa they brought with them their tradition of fine work and artistic sense. They knew well how to fuse their own traditions with the Islamic culture of North Africa, since, after all, they were hardly strangers to the Islamic culture in Spain. The lamps of North African Jewry thus show a great variety of forms and motifs. These Ḥanukkah lamps display skilled artisanship in casting and in engraved, pierced, and hammered-brass sheet (figures 15 and 37; Narkiss 70–72). This is particularly apparent in the communities of Spanish Morocco.

In Iraq and Persia the Jews maintained an ancient tradition of round Ḥanukkah lamps of stone or metal, this tradition stemming from the period of the Babylonian Talmud. During the last centuries, they employed round silver standing lamps which were occasionally 18th century lamps, intended for wall-hanging, utilizing rings for glass oil containers (figure 18). There are also Iraqi late back-walled lamps decorated with the "hand of Fatimah." During the last 400 years, Persian Jews were persecuted and poor. For Ḥanukkah lamps they used simple brass cups, adding one on each day. Some examples of these cups, wrought in silver, have appeared from Meshed. They used also round Ḥanukkah lamps from stone, clay, bronze, and brass.

1

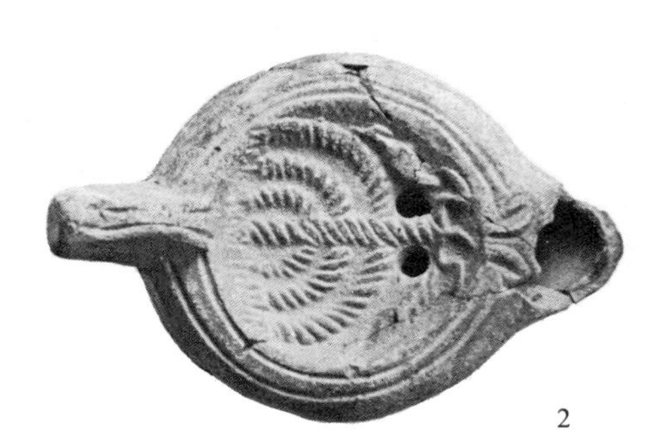

2

3

4

5

Figure 1. Stone eight-spout lamp. Jerusalem, Talmud period. The back grooves probably served as receptacles for used wicks and oil containers. Width 7½ in. (19½ cm.). Tel Aviv, Einhorn Collection. Photo David Harris, Jerusalem.

Figure 2. Ceramic *lycanos* oil lamp with seven-branched *menorah* in relief. Alexandria, fourth century C.E. Jerusalem, Israel Museum, Reifenberg Collection. Photo R. M. Kneller, Jerusalem.

Figure 3. Stone lamp from Avignon, 12th century. The inscription reads "For the commandment is a lamp and the teaching is light" (Prov. 6:23). Paris, V. Klagsbald Collection. Photo Communauté, Paris.

Figure 4. Clay eight-spout *polymixos* decorated with birds. Ereẓ Israel, Talmud period. Width 4 in. (10 cm.). Tel Aviv, Einhorn Collection. Photo David Harris, Jerusalem.

Figure 5. Stone lamps. The triangular one, from Yemen, 18/19th century, has the *shamash* in front. The other two, from Morocco, 19th century, have nine spouts in a row. Jerusalem, Israel Museum. Photo David Harris, Jerusalem.

6

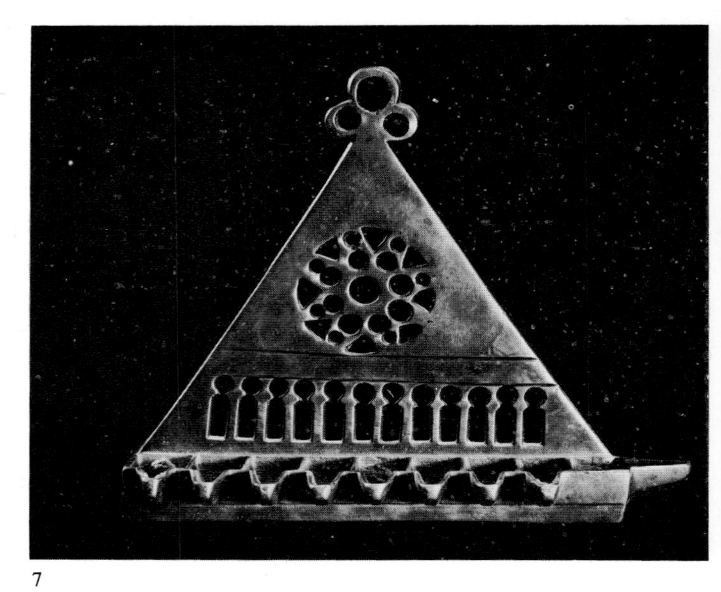

7

9

8

10

Figure 6. Bronze seven-spouted *polymixos* lamp from North Babylonia, third/fourth century. Width 5½ in. (8 cm.). Tel Aviv, Einhorn Collection. Photo David Harris, Jerusalem.

Figure 7. Bronze lamp from Lyons, France, 14th century. The back wall is decorated with a rose window and arcades. Jerusalem, Israel Museum. Photo David Harris, Jerusalem.

Figure 8. Brass lamp with cut-out greeting from Spanish Morocco, 17th century. Width 10 in. (15.5 cm.). Tel Aviv, Einhorn Collection. Photo David Harris, Jerusalem.

Figure 9. Star-shaped stone lamp, believed to be from Babylonia or Persia, sixth/seventh century C.E., diam. 2½ in. (6.4 cm.). The size indicates that it may have been for use by a traveler. Tel Aviv, Einhorn Collection. Photo David Harris, Jerusalem.

Figure 10. Brass back-walled lamp with arabesque motifs, thought to be from Spain, 14/15th century. Width 7½ in. (19 cm.). Tel Aviv, Einhorn Collection. Photo David Harris, Jerusalem.

11

12

13

14

15

Figure 11. Brass traveler's lamp, thought to be from Spain, 14th century. Width 3 in. (7.5 cm.). Tel Aviv, Einhorn Collection. Photo David Harris, Jerusalem.

Figure 12. Brass lamp from Poland, 18th century, with snake motif. Width 8½ in. (22 cm.). Tel Aviv, Einhorn Collection. Photo David Harris, Jerusalem.

Figure 13. Beaten-brass lamp from Holland, 18th century. Decorated with twin hearts and discs, with a *menorah* in the center. Width 8¾ in. (22.5 cm.). Tel Aviv, Einhorn Collection. Photo David Harris, Jerusalem.

Figure 14. Brass lamp from Spain, 14th century, with twisting serpents. Width 6 in. (15 cm.). Tel Aviv, Einhorn Collection. Photo David Harris, Jerusalem.

Figure 15. Beaten brass lamp from Morocco, 19th century. Figures include twin gates with rosettes, palms, and birds, and a *magen David* in the center. Width 9¾ in. (25 cm.). Tel Aviv, Einhorn Collection. Photo David Harris, Jerusalem.

16

17

18

19

Figure 16. Illuminated page from the *Erna Michael Haggadah* showing a hanging star-shaped lamp used by German Jews. Middle Rhine, c. 1400. Jerusalem, Israel Museum, Ms. 180/58, fol. 40.

Figure 17. Silver lamp with back wall showing Elijah fed by ravens, made for Eliah Lindo by John Ruslen, London, 1709. London, Jewish Museum, Felix Nabarro Collection. Photo Warburg Institute, London.

Figure 18. Brass lamp from Baghdad, 18th century. Glass burners are inserted in holders. The "hands of Fatimah" are intended to ward off evil spirits. Jerusalem, Israel Museum. Photo David Harris, Jerusalem.

Figure 19. Illuminated page from the *Sarajevo Haggadah* showing the hanging lamp used by Spanish Jews. Barcelona(?), 14th century. Sarajevo, National Museum, fol. 31*v.

20

21

22

Figure 20. Brass lamp from Italy, 16th century, with two winged cherubs blowing horns, surmounted by Judith holding Holophernes' head. Beneath her name in Hebrew is a leg, possibly a guild or crest symbol. Width 8 in. (20 cm.). Tel Aviv, Einhorn Collection. Photo David Harris, Jerusalem.

Figure 21. Bronze lamp from Italy, 17th century, with relief on back panel of lions guarding the holy fire. Width 6½ in. (16.5 cm.). Cecil Roth Collection. Photo Werner Braun, Jerusalem.

Figure 22. Back panel of a lamp from Italy, 16th century, with the coat of arms of Cardinal Acquaviva in the center, supported by two cherubs and with a tasseled cardinal's hat above. Paris, M. Kugel Collection.

Figure 23. Tin lamp from Germany, 19th century, in the form of little chairs. A chair was probably added each day of the festival. Jerusalem, Sir Isaac and Lady Wolfson Museum in Hechal Shlomo. Photo David Harris, Jerusalem.

23

Additional Italian Lamps

Figure a. Bronze, 16th-century lamp with a fleur-de-lis, symbol of the city of Florence. Cecil Roth Collection.

Figure b. Bronze, 16th-century lamp, with crenellated back wall. Haifa, Ethnological Museum and Folklore Archives. Photo Oskar Tauber, Haifa.

Figure c. Bronze, 17th-century ornate lamp. Haifa, Ethnological Museum and Folklore Archives. Photo Oskar Tauber, Haifa.

Figure d. Cast brass lamp, an early 19th-century copy of a 17th-century type. Formerly Detroit, Michigan, Feinberg Collection Photo Manning Brothers, Ann Arbor, Michigan.

a

b

c

d

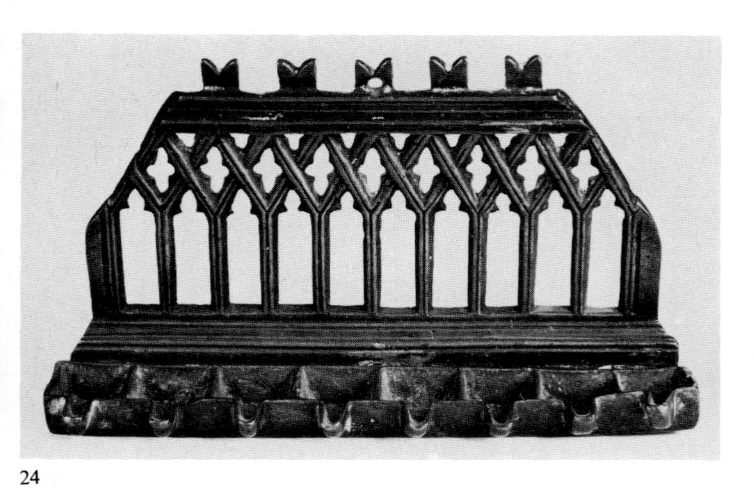

24

25

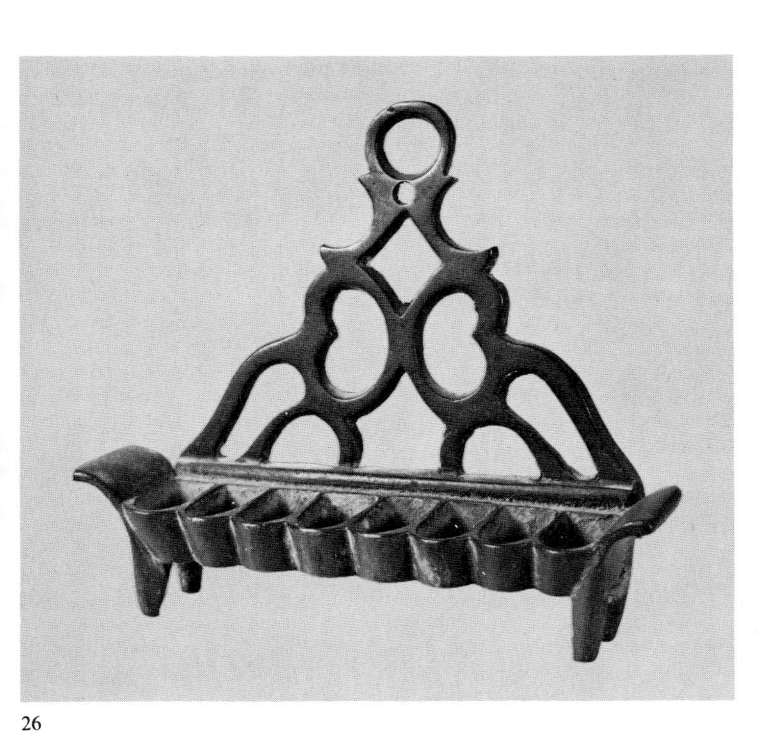

26

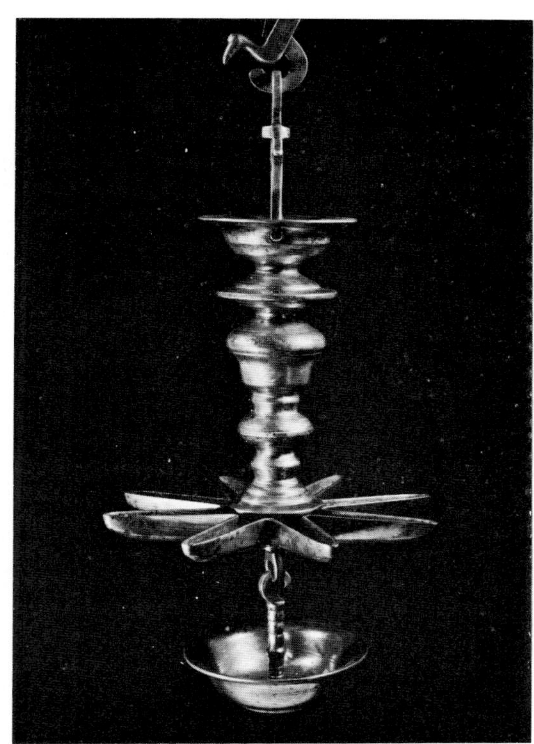

27

28

Figure 24. Bronze lamp in Gothic style from Spain or southern France, 16th century trefoil arches, quatrefoil windows, and split battlements. Width 5½ in. (14 cm.). Tel Aviv, Einhorn Collection, Photo David Harris, Jerusalem.

Figure 25. Brass lamp in Renaissance style from Italy, 16th century. Width 9 in. (23 cm.). Cecil Roth Collection. Photo Werner Braun, Jerusalem.

Figure 26. Brass lamp from Poland, 17th century, with arabesque back wall indicating Spanish origin. The legs were added in order to place the lamp on a window-sill. Width 6 in. (15 cm.). Tel Aviv, Einhorn Collection. Photo David Harris, Jerusalem.

Figure 27. Hanging brass lamp from Germany, 18th century. Jerusalem, Israel Museum. Photo David Harris, Jerusalem.

Figure 28. Brass lamp of Czech origin, late 18th century, with side panels representing Moses and Aaron. Prague, Jewish Museum.

29

Figure 29. Lead lamp from Eastern Europe, 19th century, in the form of little chairs, each inscribed with the initial letters for the Hebrew phrase, "a great miracle happened there." Jerusalem, Israel Museum. Photo David Harris, Jerusalem.

30

Figure 30. Silver lamp from Augsburg, Germany, 18th century. In relief are the blessings in Hebrew and a lit *menorah* flanked by Moses and Aaron, while the standing figures include Judah Maccabee, Judith, and the *shammash* holder; the legs are in the form of bears. Width 11½ in. (29 cm.). Jerusalem, Israel Museum. Photo David Harris, Jerusalem.

Figure 31. The Figdor lamp from Germany, 14th century, with the inscription from Proverbs 6:23, and three medallions with a dragon and two lions. New York, Temple Emanuel, Lehman Collection. Formerly Vienna, A. Figdor Collection.

Figure 32. Pewter lamp from Horb, Germany, 18th century, 8 in. (20 cm.). Cecil Roth Collection. Photo Werner Braun, Jerusalem.

31

32

33

34

35

Figure 33. Silver standing lamp from Germany, 19th century. Width 28 in.(71 cm.). Detroit, Charles Feinberg Collection. Photo Manning Bros., Highland Park, Michigan.

Figure 34. Cast brass hanging-type lamp from Cochin, India, 19th century, with floral decorations and animals. Width 11 in. (28 cm.). Cecil Roth Collection. Photo Werner Braun, Jerusalem.

Figure 35. Brass lamp from Eastern Europe, 18th century, with birds and lions flanking a stylized *menorah* on the back wall. Width 9½ in. (24 cm.). Tel Aviv, Einhorn Collection. Photo David Harris, Jerusalem.

36

37

Figure 36. Brass lamp for synagogue use from Poland, 17th century. Width 42 in. (106 cm.). Formerly Detroit, Charles Feinberg Collection. Photo Manning Bros., Highland Park, Michigan.

Figure 37. Cast and engraved brass lamp from Morocco, inscribed with the name of the artist, Moshe Kohen, and the date corresponding to 1744. Jerusalem, Israel Museum. Photo David Harris, Jerusalem.

38

39

40

'igure 38. Brass lamp from Poland, 18th century, with gate in center of back wall. Width 11 in. (28 cm.). Tel Aviv, Einhorn Collection. 'hoto David Harris, Jerusalem.

'igure 39. Brass lamp from Cochin, 18th century. Width $8\frac{3}{4}$ in. (22 cm.). Tel Aviv, Einhorn Collection. Photo David Harris, Jerusalem.

'igure 40. Silver filigree lamp from Galicia, 18th century. The crown was added at a later date. Formerly Detroit, Charles Feinberg 'ollection. Photo Manning Bros., Highland Park, Michigan.

Little study has been made of Ḥanukkah lamps of Cochin, India. This small and distant Jewry is astonishing in the richness of forms evident in their lamps. They were influenced by Spanish Jewry. The Portuguese conquest in India really began in only about 1500, but two bronze lamps (in the Cecil Roth Coll., figure 34, and in the Einhorn Coll.) are old castings from the Middle Ages, displaying a Romanesque style. Their origin probably lies in the early contact between Spanish Jewry and the Far East resulting from Spanish and Portuguese voyages of exploration and commerce. These sailors and merchants were happy to find their Jewish brethren in India. Other Ḥanukkah lamps from India show a fusion of their Sephardi origin with the influence of the surrounding Indian milieu (figure 39).

In the modern period, the festival of Ḥanukkah took on a renewed meaning, the Ḥanukkah lights symbolizing the national Renaissance of the Jewish people. An abundance of new *menorot* were made in Israel and the Diaspora. A few of these were both original and artistic. Worth mentioning are the Ḥanukkah lamps of "*Bezalel" at the beginning of this century. Boris *Schatz, the founder of "Bezalel," sought an original Jewish style by combining traditional Jewish motives with the style and workmanship of the Middle East. Worth mentioning as well are the lamps of artistic value wrought by the sculptor Mark Schwarz (Menorah 1927, p. 61) and the lamp of Benno Elkan with the five Maccabean brothers (Menorah, 1929, page 617).

Bibliography: K. Freyer, in: *Moaus Zur: ein Chanukkahbuch* (1918); R. Wischnitzer, in: REJ, 89 (1930), 135–46; P. Romanoff, in: E. Solis-Cohen (ed.), *Hanukkah; The Feast of Lights* (1937), 83–92; M. Narkiss, *Menorat ha-Ḥanukkah* (1939), with Eng. summary.

[Y.El.]

HA-OGEN (Heb. הָעֹגֶן; "the anchor"), kibbutz in central Israel in the Ḥefer Plain, affiliated with Kibbutz Arẓi Ha-Shomer ha-Ẓa'ir, founded in 1947. The founding settlers from Czechoslovakia and Austria were later joined by new members from other countries. In 1969 Ha-Ogen had 500 inhabitants and engaged in intensive farming, ran a plastic-tube factory, and was partner in a rubber factory.

[E.O.]

Plastics factory at kibbutz Ha-Ogen. Courtesy Government Press Office, Tel Aviv.

HAOLAM, the central organ of the World Zionist Organization, published as a weekly from 1907 to 1950 (except for short intervals). Established on the initiative of N. *Sokolow during his service as general secretary of the World Zionist Organization, *Haolam* was a Hebrew counterpart of *Die *Welt,* the German-language official organ of the Zionist Organization. Like *Die Welt,* for most of the years of its existence *Haolam* also had a yellow cover which, according to *Herzl, symbolized the transformation of the shameful "yellow badge" to a color of pride and respect. At first *Haolam* was edited in Cologne—the residence of David *Wolffsohn, then president of the Zionist Organization—and printed in Berlin. Sokolow, who was preoccupied with other affairs, left most of the editing to his assistant, A. Ḥermoni. It soon became clear that Western Europe was not the appropriate place to publish a Hebrew paper; moreover, most of the members of the Zionist Executive regarded the paper as a burden upon the budget. As a result, at the end of its second year of publication (December 1908), the paper was moved to Vilna, where it became the organ of the Zionist Organization in Russia, under the editorship of A. *Druyanow. In the spring of 1912, upon the initiative of M. M. *Ussishkin *Haolam* was moved to Odessa and continued its publication there until the outbreak of World War I.

Publication was resumed in 1919, in London, which had by then become the seat of the Zionist leadership, with Abraham *Idelson as editor (until 1921). Idelson planned to transfer the paper to Berlin, which had become a center of Hebrew literary activity in the early postwar period, but he died before achieving his aim. It was not until 1923 that Idelson's plan was realized, and H. *Greenberg, S. *Perlman, and M. *Kleinmann became the new editors. The former two soon left the editorial board, leaving Kleinmann as the sole editor until his death in 1948. In 1924, when conditions in Germany took a turn for the worse, *Haolam's* editorial offices were again moved to London. For several years the printing was done in Paris. Its final move took place in 1936, when the paper was transferred to Jerusalem which by then had also become the headquarters of the World Zionist Organization. Upon Kleinmann's death, his two assistants, M. Chartiner and M. Cohen, became its editors until February 1950, when the paper ceased to exist.

For two generations, *Haolam* served as a faithful reporter of events and developments in Zionist and Jewish affairs. It also had a literary section, which published articles and the complete works in installments of outstanding Hebrew authors and scholars (such as Sokolow's book on *Spinoza, A. A. *Kabak's work on Solomon *Molcho, S. L. *Zitron's history of Hebrew journalism, stories by *Mendele Mokher Seforim, etc.). The paper carried excellent informational columns, and A. Litai's column on events taking place in the *yishuv* has retained its value as an important historical source.

Bibliography: A. Ḥermoni, *Be-Ikkevot ha-Bilu'im* (1952), 128–66; *Haolam* (Feb. 21, 1950), last issue, includes its history.

[G.K.]

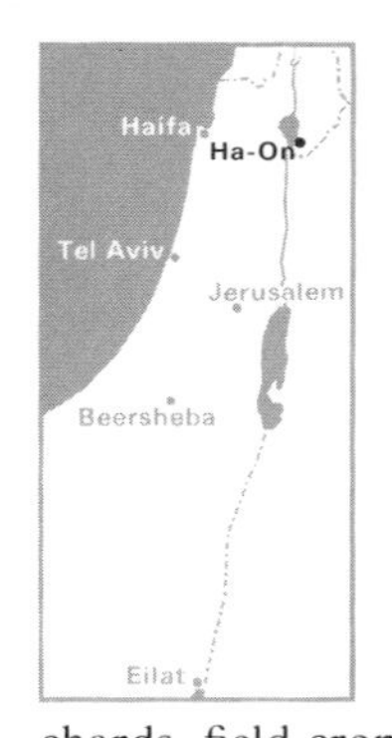

HA-ON (Heb. הָאוֹן; "strength"), kibbutz on the eastern shore of Lake Kinneret, Israel, south of *Ein Gev, affiliated with Iḥud ha-Kevuẓot ve-ha-Kibbutzim, founded in 1949. Some of its members are Israel-born, and others came from Eastern Europe and other countries. Until the *Six-Day War (June 1967) the kibbutz was constantly exposed to the Syrian gun emplacements directly above it on the Golan Plateau. Its economy includes bananas, date palms, fruit orchards, field crops, carp ponds, and dairy farming. Ha-On is also a partner in the Lake Kinneret fishing cooperative and runs a metal factory.

[E.O.]

HA-OVED HA-ẒIYYONI (Heb. "The Zionist Worker"), Israel labor movement founded as a *Histadrut faction at Ra'ananah on Nov. 22–23, 1935, by pioneer immigrants of General Zionist Youth from Eastern Europe, many of them members of kibbutzim. In Ereẓ Israel, these pioneers belonged to the General Zionist Organization but opposed its policy of boycotting the Histadrut. They worked inside the General Zionist movement to ensure its classless character and inside the Histadrut, which they regarded as the home of all trends in Jewish labor, to oppose class tendencies and the adoption of socialist symbols. There was much controversy on this subject inside the General Zionist movement, especially during the five years between a first gathering at Petaḥ Tikvah in 1930 and the foundation conference in 1935. Ha-Oved ha-Ẓiyyoni worked for the implementation of the principle of Jewish labor as an essential element in the upbuilding of the nation but not as a matter for class conflict. It established and built kibbutzim and moshavim for the implementation of the pioneering Zionist idea but not as instruments for socialism and demanded the establishment of nonparty labor exchanges allocating work on the basis of individual rights and qualifications.

After 1948, Ha-Oved ha-Ẓiyyoni helped to establish the *Progressive Party and became part of its successor, the *Independent Liberal Party. It established six kibbutzim (in the framework of the movement of Ha-No'ar ha-Ẓiyyoni), 13 moshavim, five moshavim shittufiyyim, and five youth villages. In the Histadrut, it favors workers' participation in management and profits. It supports the maintenance of a pluralistic economy, with encouragement for all sectors. In the 1969 Histadrut elections it received 5.69% of the vote.

[M.Kol]

HA-PARNAS, SEFER (Heb. סֵפֶר הַפַּרְנָס), work by Moses Parnas, one of the pupils of *Meir b. Baruch of Rothenburg, who lived in the first half of the 14th century. Almost nothing is known of its author. His work was well known to the scholars of Germany in the 15th century, such as Jacob *Moellin, Joseph *Colon, Israel *Isserlein, and Israel *Bruna. It was afterward lost, but was published in 1891 with notes by David *Luria as far as section 17, as well as those of its publisher, Moses Samuel Horowitz. This book is very typical of the works belonging to "the school of Meir of Rothenburg," and its author cites traditions, customs, rulings, and teachings of his master based both upon what he himself had seen, as well as culled and abridged from other collections, such as *Tashbeẓ* by Samson b. Zadok.

Bibliography: Urbach, Tosafot, 439.

[I.T.-S.]

ספר

הפרנס

מהרב רבינו משה פרנס מרוטנבורג אשר כתבו עפ״י
מהר״ם רוטנבורג ז״ל כמבואר במבוא.

הספר היקר הזה היה טמון בכת״י ערך שש מאות שנה ועתה יוצא לאור
הדפוס בפעם הראשונה עם הגהות וביאורים עד סי׳ י״ז מהגאון ר׳
דוד לוריא ז״ל. והגהות על כל הספר מהמו״ל הרב הגדול
מה׳ משה שמואל הורוויץ נ״י מווילנא.

גם נלוה לו כת״י מהגאון החסיד רבינו אליהו (הגר״א
מווילנא) ז״ל לקוטים על הרמב״ם והסמ״ג.

ובסופו שלש שו״ת מכונה בשם קונטרס

ידי מש״ה

כהרב המו״ל אשר נשא ונתן עם הרב הגאון מהור״ר
שלמה הכהן נ״י מו״ץ דפה.

ווילנא

בהוצאות ובדפוס ר׳ אברהם צבי נ״י לבית קאצינעלינבוגין.
שנת תרנ״א לפ״ק

Title page of *Sefer ha-Parnas* by Moses Parnas of Rothenburg, which cites traditions, rulings, and teachings of his master, Meir b. Baruch of Rothenburg. Vilna, 1891. Jerusalem, J.N.U.L.

HAPAX LEGOMENA (Gr. "once said"), words which are only once recorded in a certain kind of literature. Since the interest in Middle Hebrew lexicography arose comparatively late, Middle Hebrew texts are frequently not well-established philologically and new texts are often discovered, the interest in hapax legomena in Hebrew is, for all practical purposes, limited to the Bible or, more precisely, to biblical Hebrew. There are in biblical Hebrew about 1,300 hapax legomena (yet their precise number cannot be stated, since the exact definition is not clear as to whether or not they include homonymic hapax legomena). Most of them (about 900) are not too difficult to interpret, being derived from well-known biblical roots (as *ʿemdah*, Micah 1:11, *moʿomad*, Ps. 69:3, both denoting "standing ground," being derived from the well-known root **עמד**, "to stand"). About 400, however, cannot be derived from known biblical roots and are therefore more difficult to interpret. Occurring only once, their exact meaning is more difficult to establish from context than that of words attested more often. Except for this fact and the possibility that hapax legomena may have arisen through error in transmission, the philological treatment of hapax legomena does not differ from that of words occurring more often. The meaning of both is elucidated by comparison with other Semitic languages, which often makes it possible to establish the etymology of the word treated. Middle Hebrew has, of course, a special standing in this matter. Since the Bible, because of its small size and limited topics, has preserved only a small part of Hebrew vocabulary, it is often due to mere chance that a word occurs only once in the Bible, though there may be ample examples of it in Middle Hebrew (as in the case with *sullam* "ladder," Gen. 28:12). Even the sages of the Mishnah did not understand the hapax legomenon *ve-teʾteʾtiha*, "and I will sweep it" (Isa. 14:23), except with the help of vernacular speech, as used by Rabbi's handmaid (RH 26b). Hapax legomena sometimes belong to removed subject matters (as Isa. 3:18ff., describing the ornaments of Zion's daughters), and there are relatively many hapax legomena denoting animals, plants, and diseases (as *letaʾah* "lizard," Lev. 11:30; *luz*, "almond tree," Gen. 30:37; *ḥarḥur*, "fever," Deut. 28:22) and loan words (as *ʾappiryon*, "litter," Song 3:9). The Book of Job, with its special style and many Aramaisms, contains a relatively large proportion of hapax legomena, 145 in number, among them 60 without derivation from known biblical roots. The (much larger) Book of Isaiah has 201 hapax legomena, among them, again, 60 without derivation.

In Hebrew literature hapax legomena are called *ʾen lo ʾaḥ*, *ʾen lo ḥaver*, *ʾen lo reʿa ba-Miqraʾ*, "it has nothing alike, no brother, no fellow, no comrade in the Bible," or *millim bodedot*, "isolated words." *Saadiah Gaon wrote in Arabic *Kitāb al-Sabʿīn Lafẓa min Mufradāt al-Qurʾan* ("The Book of Seventy Hapax Legomena in the Bible"), dealing with over 90(!) hapax legomena, which he explains by means of mishnaic words. It stands to reason that this book originally contained 70 words, and was expanded later, either by Saadiah himself or by others, yet preserving its original name. Although it is one of the oldest and most important philological works in the history of Hebrew linguistics, it is in its intention a polemic work against Karaites, endeavoring to prove the value of tradition from the linguistic point of view: without mishnaic Hebrew even the linguistic interpretation of the Bible is impossible.

Bibliography: I. M. Casanowicz, in: JE, 6 (1904), s.v.; B. Klar, in: *Meḥkarim ve-Iyyunim* (1954), 159–75; N. Allony, in: *Goldziher Memorial Volume*, 2 (1958), 1–48 (Heb. section); idem, in: HUCA, 30 (1959), 1–14 (Heb. section); Ch. Rabin, in: EM, 4 (1962), 1066–70.

[J.Bl.]

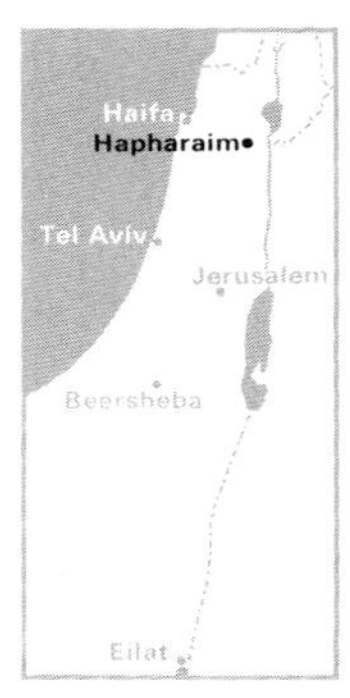

HAPHARAIM (Heb. חֲפָרַיִם), town in the territory of Issachar (Josh. 19:19), located between Chesulloth and Shunem on one side and Shion and Anaharath on the other. A place with the same name is mentioned in the Mishnah (Men. 8:1) as the source of fine wheat supplied to the Second Temple. Eusebius (Onom. 28:26) identified it with Aphraia, 6 mi. (10 km) north of Legio (al-Lajjūn near Megiddo), which may point to the vicinity of Afulah. Recent scholars, relying on the spelling Afarayim in talmudic literature (Tosef. Men. 9:2; TB, Men. 83b), have proposed its identification with *Ophrah of Gideon (Judg. 6:11), and perhaps the *ʿfr* in the list of Thutmose III. The site of Hapharaim is possibly at al-Tayyiba in the hills north of the Jezreel Valley (see map). Another suggested identification, with Khirbat al-Farriyya near Megiddo, is less probable.

Bibliography: G. Dalman, *Sacred Sites and Ways* (1935), 219; Abel, Geog, 2 (1938), 343, 402; Albright, in: JBL, 58 (1939), 183; M. Noth, *Das Buch Josua* (1953³), 117; EM, s.v.

[M.A.-Y.]

HAPOEL (Heb. "The Worker"), Israel workers' sports organization, affiliated with the *Histadrut. It had its beginnings in a Haifa soccer team in 1924. The countrywide association was organized in 1926 with a twofold aim: to provide opportunities for physical education and sport for the masses of Palestinian youth and to involve them in the labor movement. Hapoel members pioneered in naval and other activities in order to assist "illegal" immigration into Palestine. They also helped to establish settlements and were active in the *Haganah, the pre-state Jewish defense organization. Through Hapoel's efforts the number of swimming pools in the country increased and floodlit playing fields were opened making possible nighttime basketball and volleyball. Hapoel organized the Lake Kinneret swims in which some 10,000 swimmers participate annually, road marches, and long-distance foot races as well as sports conventions *(Poeliad)* with international participation. Hapoel's teams and individual contestants won championships in most of the fields of Israel sport. The organization also encourages sports activities in various places of work, such as factories, shops, etc. Since 1927 Hapoel has been affiliated with the International Labor Sports Organization. After the establishment of the state it played an important role in encouraging and organizing sports activities in the underdeveloped African countries. In 1968 there were more than 85,000 members of Hapoel in 600 branches throughout the State of Israel.

Mass calisthenics at the opening of the Hapoel International Games at Ramat Gan, Israel, 1966. Government Press Office, Tel Aviv.

Bibliography: I. Paz and A. Lahav, *Alafim ve-Allufim* (1961), with notes in Eng.

[Ye.A.]

HA-PO'EL HA-MIZRACHI, religious pioneering and labor movement in Ereẓ Israel. Religious pioneers who settled in Ereẓ Israel in 1920–21 banded together and in April 1922 founded Ha-Po'el ha-Mizrachi, whose program stated that it "aspires to build the land according to the Torah and tradition and on the basis of labor, to create a material and spiritual basis for its members, strengthen religious feeling among the workers, and enable them to live as religious workers." The new framework was a product of the Third *Aliyah, which included many young people marked by their religious consciousness. They were pioneers and workers who viewed settling in Ereẓ Israel as a *mitzvah,* a religious commandment and task, but did not find a place in the existing labor community, despite the fact that socially they belonged to it. They opposed the prevalent view among workers in the 1920s that regarded religion as obsolete and adherence to the *mitzvot* as an obstacle to the building of the land according to socialist principles. The ideology of the new religious labor group was developed for the most part by Shemuel Ḥayyim *Landau, Isaiah *Shapira, Nehemiah Aminoaḥ, Isaiah Bernstein, Shelomo Zalman *Shragai, and Shimon Geshuri. It was called Torah va-Avodah (Torah and Labor), after the saying: "The world stands on three things: Torah, divine service (*avodah*—literally, work), and deeds of loving-kindness" (Avot 1:2). The sources of this ideology also included ideas from Polish Ḥasidism and from the system of "Torah with *Derekh Ereẓ*" of Samson Raphael *Hirsch.

The concept of Torah va-Avodah emphasized the demand for social justice and a productive life as an essential condition of the return to the homeland and as an integral part of a full religious life in Judaism. In view of the desiccation of Jewish life in the Diaspora, even greater emphasis should be placed on those elements which were practically excluded from Jewish existence outside Ereẓ Israel. The ideology proclaimed that complete Judaism is a synthesis of religious, social, moral, national, and political elements, realized mainly through personal commitment and creativity. All these aspects of national life must be inspired by the Written and Oral Law. Special emphasis was placed on the demand for social justice. "Only he who earns his living by his own labor is certain that his livelihood is free from the labor of others, from exploitation and fraud." "Morality and justice are links in a long chain of sanctification and purification of life, which originates in the acceptance of the rule of God." This outlook led its followers along the path of productivization and especially toward cooperative and collective agricultural settlement.

From its earliest appearance there were conflicts between Ha-Po'el ha-Mizrachi and *Mizrachi because of the former's socialist trends, though technically it was an organizational part of Mizrachi. On the other hand, it had differences with the *Histadrut, because of Ha-Po'el ha-Mizrachi's religious concept of the Jewish people, its opposition to the class struggle, and its demand for obligatory arbitration in labor disputes. In practice, it appeared as an independent element in the labor market. After an unsuccessful attempt to join the Histadrut in the 1920s, Ha-Po'el ha-Mizrachi acted as a part of the world Mizrachi movement. In 1925, however, it created a special body of its own in the Diaspora called Ha-Berit ha-Olamit shel Tenu'at Torah va-Avodah, which included Mizrachi youth groups and the pioneering Mizrachi movements in different countries. Thus Ha-Po'el ha-Mizrachi united an ideological movement, a labor federation, and a political party in one body.

As an ideological movement, Ha-Po'el ha-Mizrachi propagated its ideas and opinions in its organ *Netivah* (edited by Geshuri), in pamphlets and books in the Torah va-Avodah Library, and later on in *Moreshet*. It attracted to its ranks the religious kevuẓot united in *Ha-Kibbutz ha-Dati and established the pioneering youth movement *Benei Akiva, which later on founded the yeshivah high school under the initiative of Moshe Ẓevi *Neriah. As a labor federation, Ha-Po'el ha-Mizrachi was active in the same areas as the Histadrut. It established employment bureaus and welfare institutions and was active developing Jewish labor, the *Haganah, and the organization of pioneering and "illegal" immigration. It founded economic enterprises such as Bank Ha-Po'el ha-Mizrachi; a mortgage bank, Adanim; the financial tool of the settlements, Yaniv; the construction company for housing, Mash'hav; and several cooperatives, united under one roof, Merkaz ha-Mosedot ve-ha-Mifalim ha-Kalkaliyyim shel ha-Po'el ha-Mizrachi. It also organized young religious workers in Ha-No'ar ha-Dati ha-Oved and established the sports organization, Eliẓur. In 1935 its women members organized the Women's League of Ha-Po'el ha-Mizrachi and later united with the Women's Mizrachi Organization of the *National Religious Party.

As early as the 1920s the movement started its settlement activity. At first, the common form was the *moshav ovedim, which seemed more suitable for the members of Ha-Po'el ha-Mizrachi than the kevuẓah or kibbutz. Sedeh Ya'akov, established in 1927 in the western Jezreel Valley, was the movement's first moshav. Ha-Po'el ha-Mizrachi had to overcome the opposition of the Histadrut and of the official Zionist institutions before it was recognized as an independent factor in settlement. Before 1948 eight moshevei ovedim were established, all in areas of regional settlement projects of the Zionist Organization. During the great immigration of the 1950s, Ha-Po'el ha-Mizrachi was allocated 20% of the settlement. In the course of five years, 40 moshavim of new immigrants, and later on, another ten, were added. In addition, four moshavim shittufiyyim were founded. All these were organized in the Iggud ha-Moshavim shel Ha-Po'el ha-Mizrachi, whose organ is *Ma'anit* (established in 1951).

From the early 1930s groups for collective settlement sprang up within Ha-Po'el ha-Mizrachi. These first religious kevuẓot or kibbutzim were formed by members of *Berit Ḥalutzim Datiyyim* (Baḥad) in Germany, the trainees of the Mizrachi youth *hakhsharah* ("training") in Poland, and later on, by the Ha-Shomer ha-Dati in Poland and in Galicia. They established Ha-Kibbutz ha-Dati in 1935. It established settlements from 1937, the first being *Tirat Ẓevi (after Ẓevi Hirsch *Kalischer) in the Beth-Shean Valley. Ha-Kibbutz ha-Dati followed a policy of *hityashevut gushit* ("bloc settlement"), concentrating a number of settlements in one area in order to develop fully its social-religious ideas and its strength as a religious factor in society. This policy forced it to go to the farthest frontiers of the existing settlement areas. A bloc of religious kibbutzim was created in the Beth-Shean Valley, the Eẓyon bloc in the Hebron mountains, and another bloc in the vicinity of Gaza. Before the establishment of the state (1948) Ha-Kibbutz ha-Dati movement numbered 16 settlements, ten already set up and the rest about to be settled. Because of their location on the borders of the *yishuv*, the *War of Independence dealt them a severe blow. The Eẓyon bloc (including the three religious kibbutzim Kefar Eẓyon, Massu'ot Yiẓḥak, and Ein Ẓurim) was completely wiped out, most of the settlements at the approach to Gaza were destroyed (Be'erot Yiẓḥak and Kefar Darom), and the movement lost seven percent of its adult population. After the war, 12 of these settlements remained, and three became moshavim shittufiyyim.

The relations of Ha-Po'el ha-Mizrachi with the Histadrut developed after some violent conflicts in the late 1920s and the early 1930s concerning labor, settlement, and cooperation. In 1928 an agreement was reached on the distribution of labor and participation in Kuppat Ḥolim. The agreement did not fulfill the anticipated hopes, and Ha-Po'el ha-Mizrachi abrogated it in 1941. Despite the friction, more cooperation was achieved between the two federations after the establishment of general labor bureaus in the early 1940s. In the course of time, Ha-Po'el ha-Mizrachi joined the agricultural center of the Histadrut, its trade union department, and the teachers organization. However, the trend for a complete merger was never realized though its demand became even greater in light of the great religious *aliyah* after the establishment of the state. The majority in Ha-Po'el ha-Mizrachi preferred an independent framework. Ha-Kibbutz ha-Dati organized in the 1930s the religious sector of *Youth Aliyah. It directs the activities of *Benei Akiva, absorbs *Naḥal groups, and maintains *ulpanim* for new immigrants.

Ha-Po'el ha-Mizrachi entered politics almost from its inception, at first mostly as a function of its labor activity and of its affiliation with Mizrachi. In the Zionist Organization it acted as a part of Mizrachi. However, gradually Ha-Po'el ha-Mizrachi developed independent activity in the *yishuv* institutions and also in the Zionist Organization. From the 19th Congress in 1935, it was represented on the Zionist Executive by Moshe Ḥayyim *Shapira, who from that time served as head of Ha-Po'el ha-Mizrachi. It was represented on the Va'ad Le'ummi Executive by Shragai and later on by Zerah *Wahrhaftig. In the last elections of the Asefat ha-Nivḥarim in 1944, Ha-Po'el ha-Mizrachi received 9.5% of the total vote. It became a major factor in the religious community of the *yishuv*. The relations between Ha-Po'el ha-Mizrachi and Mizrachi were tense throughout their existence as separate organizations, while they were united only in the world center of the body called Mizrachi-Ha-Po'el ha-Mizrachi. The antagonism between the two was particularly bitter in Ereẓ Israel, where Mizrachi belonged to the non-labor camp and Ha-Po'el ha-Mizrachi had an agreement with the Histadrut. But the increasing strength of Ha-Po'el ha-Mizrachi in Ereẓ Israel led it more and more to a take-over of Mizrachi instead of separating from it. This trend eventually led to their merger and the establishment of the *National Religious Party.

From the 1930s, when political activity began to occupy a prominent place in Ha-Po'el ha-Mizrachi, three main factions emerged in it. The El ha-Makor group leaned to the right, supporting the strengthening of ties with Mizrachi (as opposed to attachment to the labor movement) and advocating political activism against the Mandatory regime. La-Mifneh constituted the left wing, demanding the strengthening of links with the labor camp, joining the Histadrut, and seceding from the Mizrachi organization. It demanded political moderation, in the spirit of Chaim *Weizmann's policy, and more concern for settlement and movement activity. In the middle was the "centrist" faction, which took a compromising stand on political questions in the *yishuv* and Zionist policy. The main struggle for leadership in Ha-Po'el ha-Mizrachi took place between the "centrist" faction and the faction of the left-wing La-Mifneh.

In 1937 Ha-Po'el ha-Mizrachi was among the opponents of the partition plan, though, on the whole, it was closer than Mizrachi to Weizmann's leadership, stressing its loyalty to the Zionist and *yishuv* institutions and supporting the unification of all the forces of the country, including the dissident underground organizations (*Irgun Ẓeva'i Le-'ummi and *Loḥamei Ḥerut Yisrael). Though its demands concerning religious matters, such as observance of the Sabbath and *kashrut* in public institutions, etc., were its political raison d'être, it took also an active stand on general questions, such as labor problems, immigration, defense, settlement, and social matters. With the establishment of the state, political matters came to the fore. Despite the foundation of the United Religious Front in the First Knesset, in which all religious parties took part (with the exception of Ha-Oved ha-Dati, which was represented by *Mapai), Ha-Po'el ha-Mizrachi maintained a certain independence, as, e.g., on the question of the conscription of women who were released from military service for religious reasons. In 1949 it defined its position by demanding to change the law of compulsory conscription of religious women to that of compulsory national service for them, and, as long as the law was not changed, it called on every observant young woman to be drafted into the religious units of the Naḥal.

Ha-Po'el ha-Mizrachi emphasized the need for religious Jews to participate actively in public life and deal with the general objectives of the people and the state, thus preserving a live connection between the religious tradition and public life, especially in legislation. Hence its approach to topical political questions (as, e.g., the integrity of the area of Ereẓ Israel after the *Six-Day War), appropriate legal arrangements affecting the entire nation (marriage and divorce), the public way of life (Sabbath law, observances of Sabbath and *kashrut* in the Israel Defense Forces), official religious institutions (the rabbinate, religious councils), and especially the securing of religious education for all who wish it. In the Knesset and the government, Ha-Po'el ha-Mizrachi acted as a compromising and unifying element both on foreign and domestic policy. It participated in practically all governments, twice causing a government crisis, first regarding religious education in immigrant camps, and again on the question of the items "religion" and "nationality" in the registration of population (known colloquially as the "Who is a Jew?" problem).

In 1956 Ha-Po'el ha-Mizrachi decided to merge with Mizrachi, both in Israel and in the Zionist Organization, and in July 1956 the National Religious Party was established. The unified party acts in accordance with Ha-Po'el ha-Mizrachi principles. Thus, it was an initiator of the Government of National Unity prior to the Six-Day War in 1967. It demanded action on the Arab refugee problem by settling them in Judea and Samaria and flexibility in negotiations with Arab states. Ha-Po'el ha-Mizrachi is organized in 104 branches in 74 settlements. According to a census of 1969, it numbered nearly 100,000 members.

See also *Mizrachi, *Mizrachi-Ha-Po'el ha-Mizrachi, *National Religious Party.

Bibliography: J. Salmon, *Ha-Po'el ha-Mizrachi be-Ereẓ Yisrael, Kronologyah u-Bibliografyah 1920–28* (1968); Y. Raphael, *Madrikh Bibliografi le-Sifrut Ẓiyyonit Datit* (1960); N. Ammino'aḥ, *Al ha-Mabbu'a* (1968); S. Don-Jechia, *Admor-Ḥalutz* (1961); idem, *Ha-Mered ha-Kadosh* (1960); S. Z. Shragai, *Ḥazon ve-Hagshamah* (1956); Y. Bernstein, *Ye'ud va-Derekh* (1956).

[M.U.]

HA-PO'EL HA-ẒA'IR (Heb. "The Young Worker"), Ereẓ Israel labor party founded by the first pioneers of the Second Aliyah. Its full name was Histadrut ha-Po'alim ha-Ẓe'irim be-Ereẓ Israel—and it was called Ha-Po'el ha-Ẓa'ir for short. Ha-Po'el ha-Ẓa'ir was founded in Petaḥ Tikvah in the autumn of 1905 on the initiative of Shelomo *Ẓemaḥ and Eliezer *Shoḥat, who were among the first arrivals of the Second Aliyah in 1904. Its name symbolized the new character of the Jewish worker of the Second Aliyah, to be distinguished from that of the earlier workers (who had been organized since the beginning of the 1890s) and from *Po'alei Zion (the first of whose members began to arrive in the country at the same time). The new idea was expressed in the words carried as a motto on its newspaper for years: "An indispensable condition for the realization of Zionism is the conquest of all branches of labor in Ereẓ Israel by the Jews." Certain modifications were made in this definition after the revolution of the Young Turks (1908) because of the misunderstanding that might be aroused by the word "conquest." The wording was then changed to "the increase of Jewish workers in Ereẓ Israel and their consolidation in all branches of labor."

The uniqueness of this party was in its being the first indigenous workers' party in Ereẓ Israel. It groped to formulate an exact program for its activities, but its direction was clear to its founders and its members, and it was formulated a few years after the party's foundation by one of its first ideologists and the editor of its paper, Yosef *Aharonovitch. These were: to introduce the principle of labor into the official work program of Zionism; to spread the idea of the "conquest of labor" among the farmers and employers in Ereẓ Israel; to win over Jewish youth and inspire them to join the ranks of the "conquerors of labor"; and to pave the way for and assist the workers in Ereẓ Israel, who would set out to establish their place in labor.

From its foundation, Ha-Po'el ha-Ẓa'ir opposed Po'alei Zion because of the latter's acceptance of international socialism and the theory of the class struggle, which Ha-Po'el ha-Ẓa'ir felt were incongruous with the situation in Ereẓ Israel. There were also disagreements between the two movements over the relationship to Yiddish; Po'alei Zion began to publish its paper, *Onfang*, in Yiddish in 1907 (but later changed over to Hebrew) and fought for the use of Yiddish abroad. Nonetheless, there was complete cooperation between the two parties in almost every sphere of practical activity, in spite of the perpetual polemics in their newspapers. The idea of labor, which was the fundamental principle of Ha-Po'el ha-Ẓa'ir and its great innovation in Ereẓ Israel, was exalted a few years later by A. D. *Gordon (who never formally joined the party, but maintained strong ties with it and its press through his life) as an absolute and cosmic value in the life of man and in his inner and spiritual worlds. Labor was transformed from a means of livelihood into a supreme value, as an answer to the moral demand of the Jews.

At the time, the "conquest of labor" meant basically the competition of Jewish workers in the Jewish villages with Arab labor who demanded lower wages. There were members of the party who wished to propose other means of rooting the Jewish worker in the soil of Ereẓ Israel, e.g., by settlement on the land, and also requested the inclusion of

בעל הבית ובני ביתו שאומרים ההגדה

A full-page miniature from a "Sister" to the *Golden Haggadah*. The illustration depicts a *ḥazzan* ("cantor") in a Spanish synagogue reading the *Haggadah* to those members of the community who are unable to do so in their homes. Spain, Barcelona (?), 14th century. London, British Museum, Or. ms. 2884 fol. 17v ($9\frac{1}{8} \times 7\frac{1}{2}$ ins/23.3 × 19 cm.).

ity workers in the party's program. Eventually, a compro-
nise was reached between the "conquest of labor" in the
illages and the establishment of independent agricultural-
vorkers' settlements. The members of Ha-Po'el ha-Ẓa'ir
vere among the founders of the "mother of kevuẓot,"
Deganyah; among the initiators of the idea of the moshav
vedim (e.g., E. L. Joffe); and the founders of the first
noshav, *Nahalal, after World War I. Politically the party
vas able to express its ideas only after the revolution of the
'oung Turks. It formulated them as "a Jewish majority,
ealthy in the economic and cultural sense." This political
rticle was also connected with the "conquest of labor" and
vith rooting the Jewish laborer in Ereẓ Israel by perpetual
ncouragement of immigration (the party even published a
nanifesto which called for *aliyah*). The constitutional
reedom afforded by the Turkish revolution was not
egarded as valuable in itself, except as a means of reaching
Jewish majority in Ereẓ Israel.

The members of Ha-Po'el ha-Ẓa'ir participated in
uarding the settlements and self-defense activities, but
heir relationship to *Ha-Shomer, which was established by
nembers of Po'alei Zion, was one of reserve. The same is
rue of participation in volunteering for the *Jewish Legion
t the end of World War I. However, there were those who
upported enlistment in the Legion, and when the support-
rs eventually constituted a majority, the minority (which
ncluded A. D. *Gordon and other leaders) continued to
ppose it. The party participated in Zionist congresses,
eginning with the Eighth Congress in 1907, and main-
ained ties with the *Ẓe'irei Zion movement abroad. Before
World War I, the party took steps to establish a world
rganization, an aspiration that was realized after the war
t the Prague Conference (1920), which created the
Hitaḥadut from Ha-Po'el ha-Ẓa'ir in Palestine and Ẓe'irei
Zion abroad.

Ha-Po'el ha-Ẓa'ir did not join *Aḥdut ha-Avodah (A)
vhen it was formed in 1919 to unite all the workers of Ereẓ
srael because it regarded Aḥdut ha-Avodah as a branch of
he world movement of Po'alei Zion. On the other hand, it
articipated in the establishment of the *Histadrut in 1920.
n it Ha-Po'el ha-Ẓa'ir was a minority party, facing an
Aḥdut ha-Avodah majority (26 delegates to 37 from Aḥdut
a-Avodah at the first conference, 36 to 69 at the second
onference, 54 to 108 at the third conference) and struggling
gainst it. A representative of Ha-Po'el ha-Ẓa'ir, Joseph
*Sprinzak, was the first workers' representative from Ereẓ
srael to become a member of the Zionist Executive (1921).
Members of Ha-Po'el ha-Ẓa'ir were also among the leaders
of the Agricultural Workers' Organization in Galilee and
Judea (Ha-Histadrut ha-Ḥakla'it ba-Galil u-vi-Yhudah)
before World War I, which was the first nucleus of a roof
organization for Second Aliyah workers, and were also the
ounders of the agricultural press in Hebrew, which
eflected the agricultural experience of Jewish laborers (the
editor was E. L. Joffe and among the first contributors was
Berl *Katznelson).

The ideological evolution of Ha-Po'el ha-Ẓa'ir did not
cease after World War I, especially with the rise of Chaim
*Arlosoroff, who coined the term "popular Socialism," as
distinct from the class struggle. Arlosoroff was influenced by
the ideas of Gustav *Landauer and Martin *Buber (also a
member of the party and among the participants in the
Prague Conference) and the practical experience of his
party in Ereẓ Israel. With the first consolidation of the
kibbutz federations in the 1920s (*Ha-Kibbutz ha-Me'u-
ḥad), the bloc of small kevuẓot was consolidated into Ḥever
ha-Kevuẓot with ties to Ha-Po'el ha-Ẓa'ir (see Iḥud
ha-Kevuẓot ve-ha-Kibbutzim). In the controversy over
forms of collective settlement (between the kibbutz and
moshav), the party's stand was equally in favor of both
forms. Ha-Po'el ha-Ẓa'ir adopted *Gordonia abroad, the
first of whose members settled in Palestine in 1929 during
the discussions over the merger with Aḥdut ha-Avodah.
The pioneers of *Ha-Shomer ha-Ẓa'ir who arrived in
Palestine with the Third Aliyah were also close to Ha-Po'el
ha-Ẓa'ir, and only later did they part ways.

Ha-Po'el ha-Ẓa'ir had extensions in a number of
countries, the most outstanding of which was in Germany.
This branch was created after World War I, and its
outstanding figures were Martin Buber, Georg *Landauer,
Arlosoroff, and others. Ha-Po'el ha-Ẓa'ir's *aliyah* bureau in
Vienna was a very impressive instrument after World War
I; it was created by members of the party in Palestine and
assisted and directed the first immigrants of the Third
Aliyah. Ha-Po'el ha-Ẓa'ir created the first labor newspaper
in Ereẓ Israel, called *Ha-Po'el ha-Ẓa'ir* (1907 in stencil and
printed from 1908). With the cessation of publication
during World War I, it was replaced by several journals
until it could resume publication in 1919 (until 1970). The
party also had a publishing house during the Second Aliyah
called La-Am, which published tens of popular scientific
pamphlets (in Hebrew translation), and after the war it
published a social-literary monthly, *Ma'abarot*, edited by
Jacob *Fichmann (1919–21). Ha-Po'el ha-Ẓa'ir laid the
groundwork for the new Hebrew literature in Ereẓ Israel,
and the best of its authors contributed to the party's
periodicals and publications.

During its existence, the party held 21 conferences. At
the last one (1929), it was decided by a large majority to
merge with Aḥdut ha-Avodah. The union was carried out in
the following year through the creation of a common party:
Mifleget Po'alei Ereẓ Israel (Ereẓ Israel Workers' Party)—
*Mapai. The most outstanding personalities in Ha-Po'el
ha-Ẓa'ir, throughout its existence, were A. D. Gordon,
Joseph *Vitkin, Joseph Aharonovitz, Yiẓḥak *Elazari-Volcani, E. L. Joffe, Joseph Sprinzak, Shelomo *Shiller, Eliezer
*Kaplan, Shemuel *Dayan, Ẓevi Yehudah, Joseph *Baratz,
and others.

Bibliography: J. Shapira, *Ha-Po'el ha-Ẓa'ir* (1967), detailed bibl. 492–6; I. and G. Kressel, *Mafte'aḥ le-ha-Po'el ha-Ẓa'ir (5668–5717)* (1968). [G.K.]

HA-PO'EL HA-ẒA'IR (Heb. הַפּוֹעֵל הַצָּעִיר; "The Young
Worker"), first newspaper of the labor movement in Ereẓ
Israel; founded in 1907. After five years as a biweekly,
Ha-Po'el ha-Ẓa'ir became a weekly, which it remained until
it ceased publication in 1970. During its lifespan, the paper
attained a continuity of publication enjoyed by no other
Hebrew periodical. There were, however, periods during
which the paper did not appear: it was discontinued in
1915 and renewed in the fall of 1918. *Ha-Po'el ha-Ẓa'ir* was
edited by Yosef *Aharonovitch until 1923, and then by
Yiẓḥak *Laufbahn until his death in 1948, and finally by
Israel *Cohen. It was the organ of the Ha-Po'el ha-Ẓa'ir
Party. When that party merged with *Aḥdut ha-Avodah to
become Mifleget Po'alei Ereẓ Israel (*Mapai), the paper
became the organ of Mapai (1930), and from 1968 of
Mifleget ha-Avodah ha-Yisre'elit (*Israel Labor Party).
Ha-Po'el ha-Ẓa'ir reflected the development of the Israel
labor movement. The pioneers of this movement could not
identify with the existing Hebrew papers, and established
Ha-Po'el ha-Ẓa'ir with the meager resources at their
disposal. The paper's ideology, expressed in its motto: "An
indispensable condition for the realization of Zionism is the
conquest of all branches of labor in Ereẓ Israel by the Jews,"
attracted all Second Aliyah workers until the founding of the
*Po'alei Zion paper *Ha-Aḥdut* in 1910. *Ha-Po'el ha-Ẓa'ir* expressed the party's persistent demand that the Zionist Orga-

nization implement practical Zionism, and also encouraged the use of Hebrew as the common language of the *yishuv*. *Ha-Po'el ha-Ẓa'ir* became the most distinguished paper in Ereẓ Israel during the Second Aliyah. Its contributors were among the best Hebrew authors and journalists, some of whom first appeared in print in this paper. Among the early regular contributors were: A. D. Gordon, J. Ḥ. Brenner, Ya'akov Rabinowitz, Rabbi Binyamin, S. Y. Agnon, Yiẓḥak Elazari-Volcani (then Wilkanski), and Moshe Smilanski. Its excellent literary supplement was edited during its first years by Devorah *Baron. A complete index of authors and subjects in *Ha-Po'el ha-Ẓa'ir* during the 50 years 1907–57 was compiled by Isa and G. Kressel in 1968.

Bibliography: Y. Laufbahn (ed.), *Arba'im Shanah* (1947); *Ha-Po'el ha-Ẓa'ir* (June 12, 1957; Sept. 26, 1967); G. Kressel, in: *Asufot*, 4 (1954), 44–65; 5 (1957), 108–20. [G.K.]

HAPSBURG (Habsburg) MONARCHY, multi-national empire in Central Europe under the rule of the Hapsburg dynasty from 1273 until 1918; from 1867 known as Austro-Hungary. Its nucleus was *Austria and it included at different times countries with considerable Jewish populations (*Bohemia and *Moravia, and *Hungary from 1526), parts of Italy between 1713 and 1866. With the annexation of *Galicia (1772) and *Bukovina (1775) it became the state with the largest Jewish population in Europe. As the Hapsburgs were also Holy Roman Emperors, they were the supreme lords of the empire's **servi camerae regis* (servants of the treasury), the Jews. The legal position of the Jewish communities varied, according to the differing legal status of the Hapsburgs in their hereditary lands (Austria, *Carinthia, *Syria, etc.), the countries of the Bohemian crown, the countries of the crown of St. Stephen (Hungary, *Transylvania, Croatia-Slavonia, and the Banat), Galicia, Bukovina, and from 1908 Bosnia and Herzegovina. However it was based in principle on juridical and religious autonomy. After the marriage of *Maria Theresa to Francis Stephen, duke of Lorraine (1736), the Hapsburgs also bore the title of "King of Jerusalem."

During the period of the Counter-Reformation the Hapsburgs, protagonists of militant Catholicism, were influenced by the spirit of religious intolerance. Still, they tended to protect the Jews in their domains, in part because of Jewish fiscal contributions at a time of domestic and foreign war. They frequently sided with the Jews against the Estates, who were, as a rule, unfriendly to the Jews. However it was the declared policy of the Hapsburgs to limit the number of Jews in their domains (see *Familiants Laws). Nevertheless Jewish communities often turned to the monarch with considerable success to annul decrees of banishment legislated by local authorities. The Hapsburg Empire was the first to conscript Jews for *military service, and *Joseph II's Toleranzpatents were the first laws to lift humiliating restrictions. From 1848 enjoyment of civil rights was made independent of religious affiliation, and from 1867 Jews enjoyed full civic equality in the empire. Jewish participation in the economic life of the empire was significant, particularly in its industrialization.

At the beginning of the 19th century developing nationalist ideologies of peoples within the empire were seeking expression with centrifugal effect. Jews were one of the elements besides the army, bureaucracy, nobility, and the Catholic Church, to support the dynasty in preserving the empire's unity. Jews throughout the empire developed their own particular brand of patriotism and on the emperor's birthday synagogues were crowded. Both the emperor and the Jews recognized their mutual interest, with the Jews considering the sovereign to be their sole recourse against the anti-Semitic tendencies of nascent nationalisms. *Francis Joseph I in particular won the gratitude of the Jews for his frequent statements against anti-Semitism (see *Christian Social Party, Austria; Karl *Lueger; Georg von *Schoenerer; Karl Hermann *Wolf; Ernst *Schneider). Jewish politicians such as Adolf *Fischhof and Otto *Bauer were particularly aware of the danger to the monarchy in the conflicts between the nationalities, and they suggested remedies. Joseph Samuel *Bloch created an ideological foundation for Jewish patriotism. Theodor *Herzl's ideas were influenced by the monarchy's problem of contending with its competing nationalities. The dismemberment of the Hapsburg Empire brought into being successor states with nationalistic policies that indeed often proved to be disadvantageous for their Jewish minorities.

Alleged Jewish Descent. Anti-Semitic propaganda claimed that the Hapsburgs were contaminated with Jewish blood, the protruding lower lip characteristic of many of them being considered a racial mark! The allegation was based on the assertion that Roger II of Sicily (1095–1154), whose offspring intermarried with the Hapsburgs, had married a *Pierleoni, a sister of the Jewish antipope *Anacletus II. The claim became notorious when the Austrian noble Adalbert von Sternberg declared around 1900 that he could have Jewish blood only through his kinship to the Hapsburgs. Modern research dismisses the allegation.

Bibliography: R. A. Kann, *The Habsburg Empire* (1957); idem, *The Multinational Empire . . ., 1848–1918* (1950); J. E. Scherer, *Die Rechtsverhaeltnisse der Juden in den deutsch-oesterreichishen Laendern* (1901), 339–452; A. Sternberg, *Paepste, Kaiser, Koenige und Juden* (1926); A. Czelitzer, in: *Juedische Familien-Forschung*, 23 (1930), 282–3; J. Prinz, *Popes from the Ghetto* (1966), 248 n. 83; G. Schimmer, *Statistik des Judentums in den im Reichsrathe vertretenen Koenigreichen und Laendern* (1873); idem, *Die Juden in Oesterreich nach der Zaehlung vom 31. December 1880* (1881); Baron, Social[2], 9 (1965), 194ff.; 332–4; 14 (1969), 147–223; Z. von Weisel, in: J. Slutsky and M. Kaplan, *Ḥayyalim Yehudim be-Ẓivot Eiropah* (1967), 17–29. See also bibl. for *Austria. [M.LA.]

HARAN (Harran; Heb. חָרָן; Akk. *Harrāni(m)*, "Caravan-station").

Name and Location. Haran is located some ten miles north of the Syrian border, at the confluence of the wadis which in winter join the Balikh River just below its source. It is strategically located about halfway between Guzana (Gozan) and Carchemish on the east-west road which links the Tigris and the Mediterranean, at the very point where the north-south route along the Balikh links the Euphrates to Anatolia. It is thus the traditional crossroads of the major routes from Mesopotamia to the west and the northwest (cf. Ezek. 27:23), and its very name in Akkadian (and Sumerian) implies as much. The biblical name Paddan-aram (Gen. 25:20 et al.), "the Aramean highway," seems to identify the same site by a synonym reflecting its later role as a center of Aramean settlement.

In the "Patriarchal Age." In 1959, a single sounding near the center of the great mound of Haran yielded some pottery of Middle Bronze I type, but for the rest of its history the archaeological record is unavailable and written sources provide the sole evidence. They first mention Haran in an Old Babylonian itinerary as an important crossroads and in a letter addressed to Yasmaḫ-Addu (=Adad), the Assyrian viceroy at Mari (c. 1790 B.C.E.). Another letter shows that Haran was an important center of the semi-nomadic "Benjamites." It alerts the king of Mari to the conclusion of a formal alliance between Asdi-takim, who was then king of Haran, and the (other) kings of Zalmaqum on the one hand, and the sheiks and elders of the "Benjamites" on the other hand. This alliance was concluded in the temple of the moon-god Sin at Haran. The land of Zalmaqum was the object of an extended campaign by Šamši-Addu (=Shamshi-Adad) I of Assyria (c. 1815–

1782 B.C.E.) and probably became subject to him together with Haran. With his death, however, the Old Assyrian Empire broke up and Haran was thus, apparently, an independent principality at the very time when, presumably, the biblical traditions reflect the sojourn of the Terahides in the area (Gen. 11:25). The migration of the Terahides parallels what appears to have been the movement of the moon cult from Ur to Haran, and the personal names of the Terahides reflect the geographical names of the Haran area. Specifically Serug, the grandfather of Terah, may be compared with the town of Sarugi (modern Seruj), some 35 miles west of Haran, and Nahor, his father (and second son) with the town of Nahur, probably located on the Upper Habor River due east of Haran. Terah's own name has been identified with Til (-sha)-Turahi on the Balikh south of Haran and his third son, Haran, recalls the name of the town, although the two names are spelled differently in Hebrew. At all events, the Mari letters document a political, social, and economic state of affairs in the latitude of Haran which makes entirely plausible the settlement there of at least five generations of pastoral Terahides. Albright has further suggested that they took advantage of the strategic position of Haran to engage in a far-flung trade, based on donkey caravans, in conjunction with Abraham and Lot, the son of his brother Nahor, who, he suggests, journeyed onward to Damascus, Canaan, and Sinai.

In the Late Second Millennium. Haran is not mentioned in the cuneiform sources of the Mitannian period. However, it probably belonged to that Hurrian state and was captured by the Hittites along with other Mitannian centers when it is first heard of again in the 15th century. Matiwaza, son-in-law of Shuppiluliuma, conquered the legitimate Mitannian ruler, Shuttarna III, with the help of Shuppiluliuma's son Piyashilli of Carchemish and presently had to cede Haran and his other conquests west of the Habor River to the latter. The first mention of Haran in Middle Assyrian documents occurs under Adad-Nirari I (c. 1304–1273 B.C.E.), who briefly conquered the Hittite vassal states as far as the Euphrates. His son Shalmaneser I (c. 1272–1243 B.C.E.) repeated these feats, as did his grandson Tukulti-Ninurta I (c. 1242–1206 B.C.E.), but in the 12th century newly entrenched waves of Aramean settlers began to make the region their own and the invasions of the Sea Peoples (c. 1200 B.C.E.) upset all of the traditional balance of power in the Near East. By the end of the 12th century, Haran was a center of Aramean settlement ruled by pretended or actual successors of the early Hittite royal houses. Hence the biblical names of this region, Aram Naharaim and Paddan-aram.

As Assyrian Crownland. While it is uncertain precisely when Haran passed under direct Assyrian rule, it is clear that it was one of the first of the more distant provinces to do so, for it always enjoyed a special status within the empire; was loyal to the king when other provinces revolted; never the object of a recorded Assyrian campaign in the first millennium; and even harbored the last Assyrian defenders when the cities of Assyria proper had already collapsed. In the years 615–12 B.C.E., the last king of Assyria, Ashur-uballit II, made a final desperate attempt at Haran to save the empire, and it was not until he fled Haran in 609 B.C.E. that the fate of Assyria was finally sealed. In the Neo-Babylonian period Haran was one of the centers of Nabonidus' religious-political activity.

Bibliography: C. H. W. Johns, *An Assyrian Doomsday Book* (1901); W. F. Albright, in: JBL, 43 (1924), 385–93; idem, in: BASOR, 163 (1961), 36–55; G. Dossin, in: *Mélanges Syriens . . . R. Dussaud* (1939); J. Levy, in: HUCA, 19 (1945–46), 405–89; B. Maisler (Mazar), in: *Zion*, 11 (1946), 1–16; R. T. O'Callaghan, *Aram Naharaim* (1948); Seton Lloyd and W. Brice, in: *Anatolian Studies*, 1 (1951), 77–112; D. S. Rice, *ibid.*, 2 (1952), 36–84; C. J. Gadd, *ibid.*, 8 (1958), 35–92; D. J. Wiseman, *Chronicles of Chaldaean Kings* (1961); H. Tadmor, in: *Assyriological Studies*, 16 (1965), 351–63.

[W.W.H.]

HARARI, family of rabbis from Aleppo. The founder of the family was MOSES (d. 1649). ISAAC BEN MOSES (d. 1810), rabbi of Aleppo and author of *Zekhor le-Yiẓḥak* (Leghorn, 1818), died in Safed. NISSIM BEN ISAIAH (d. 1830), referred to as Rafoul, was the author of *Alei Nahar* (Jerusalem, 1903). He died in Aleppo. MOSES BEN ISAAC (d. 1816) was *dayyan* in Aleppo, emigrated to Ereẓ Israel, and died in Jerusalem. R. ḤAYYIM SOLOMON (d. 1888) held the position of *Ḥakham Bashi* in Damascus at the end of the 19th century. During the 20th century SHALOM (SELIM; d. 1938), who was born in Jaffa, achieved distinction. He studied law in Constantinople and after the revolution of the Young Turks, he was appointed judge in Beirut and later was member of the Court of Appeals in Jerusalem. After the occupation of Lebanon by the French, he lived there and practiced law. In the 1930s he became president of the Jewish community of Beirut, where he died.

[H.J.C.]

HARARI (Blumberg), ḤAYYIM (1883–1940), educator and author in Ereẓ Israel. Born in Dvinsk (then Russia), he began teaching at the Herzlia High School in Tel Aviv in 1906. One of the pioneers of the Hebrew theater, he established an amateur group called Ḥovevei ha-Bamah ha-Ivrit, in which he participated as a director, actor, and translator of plays. He contributed to the Hebrew press in Russia and Ereẓ Israel and edited two volumes on the festivals entitled *Sefer ha-Ḥanukkah* (1937) and *Sefer Tevet, Shevat, Adar* (1941). His articles and stories were collected in an anthology entitled *Kitvei Ḥayyim Harari* (2 vols., 1941–42).

His wife, YEHUDIT (1885–), educator and public figure in Ereẓ Israel, was the daughter of Aaron *Eisenberg, a founder of Reḥovot. In 1903 she founded the second Hebrew kindergarten in Ereẓ Israel in Reḥovot. She also taught at the Herzlia High School and the Levinsky Teachers Training College in Tel Aviv and was headmistress of the model school attached to the college. She published articles in the Hebrew press, and her books include *Bein ha-Keramim* (1947) and *Ishah va-Em be-Yisrael* (1959).

Their son, IZHAR (1908–), parliamentarian and lawyer, was born in Jaffa. He was active in the *Haganah and *Ẓahal and was a member of the Knesset for the *Progressive (later *Liberal and *Independent Liberal) Party from 1949. He joined the *Israel Labor Party in 1968. He was the founder and chairman of the Israel Foreign Policy Association.

Bibliography: Tidhar, 1 (1947), 497f.; 2 (1947), 831f.; 4 (1950), 1717f.

[A.A./B.J.]

HARARI, SIR VICTOR RAPHAEL (1857–1945), Egyptian Jewish financier from Cairo. He began his career at the Egyptian ministry of finance, where he rose to the position of director general of the accounts department. In 1929 he was elected to the board of directors of the Egyptian National Bank and headed the boards of directors of many economic enterprises. He was knighted by King George V in 1928.

Bibliography: J. Landau, *Ha-Yehudim be-Miẓrayim* (1967), 17, 174–5.

[H.J.C.]

HARBIN (Chinese: **Ha örl pin**), the capital of Heilung Kiang Province, in N. Manchuria, China. The modern development of Harbin began at the close of the 19th century, with the beginning of the Russian penetration of Manchuria. When Russia was granted the concession to build the Chinese Eastern Railway under the Russo-Manchurian treaty of 1898, Harbin became its administrative center with a 30-mi. (50 km.)-wide zone along the railway. In the same year, a number of Russian Jewish families went to Harbin with the official consent of the czarist government, which was interested in speedily populating the area, and which, consequently, granted them better status than that of the Jews in Russia. Among the first Jews were F. I. Rif, the brothers Samsonovich, and E. I. Dobisov. Along with other minority groups (such as Karaites), the Jews were granted plots of land on the outskirts of the town. Not being allowed to work directly on the railway, they were active as shopkeepers and contractors.

By 1903 a self-administered Jewish community existed in Harbin, numbering 500 Jews. After the Russo-Japanese War of 1905, many demobilized Jewish soldiers settled in Harbin, followed by refugees from the 1905–07 pogroms. By 1908 there were 8,000 Jews in the city, and a central synagogue was built in 1909. Several institutions came into being within the community, including clubs, a home for the aged, and a hospital providing care for all other nationalities as well. A *ḥeder* was established in Harbin in 1907 and a Jewish secondary school (Yevreyskaya Gimnaziya) in 1909, which had 100 pupils in 1910. However, 70% of the Jewish pupils attended non-Jewish schools, because a numerus clausus did not exist for Jews in Harbin. The influx of Jewish refugees during World War I, the Russian Revolution (1917), and the Russian civil war sharply increased the Jewish community, which reached its peak—10,000–15,000—in the early 1930s. It numbered about 5,000 in 1939. A Jewish National Bank was established in Harbin in 1923 as well as a Jewish library. Between 1918 and 1930 about 20 Jewish newspapers and periodicals were also established. All were in Russian except the Yiddish *Der Vayter Mizrekh,* appearing three times a week with a circulation of 300 in 1921–22. The Russian-language weekly *Yevreyskaya Zhizn* ("Jewish Life," which until 1926 was called *Sibir-Palestina*) appeared from 1920 to 1940 with a circulation throughout Manchuria and North China. The Zionist movement, led by Abraham Kaufman, and several youth clubs played a major part in the life of the community. Until 1921 Harbin Zionists were affiliated to the Russian and Siberian Zionist Organization and participated in their conferences. When Zionism was outlawed in the Soviet Union, Harbin became an island of Russian-language Zionism. In the years from 1924 to 1931 the Soviet regime, largely preoccupied with internal problems, exercised only limited influence on Manchurian territory. During this time the Jews of Harbin enjoyed the same rights as all other foreigners, and were left alone to prosper. However, in 1928, when the Chinese Eastern Railway was handed over to the Chinese, an economic crisis broke out and many Jews left Harbin, some to the Soviet Union, others to Shanghai, Tien-Tsin, etc. This situation changed drastically for the worse with the Japanese occupation of Manchuria (1931–45) and the establishment of a puppet regime, under which Jews were subjected to terror and extortion. The treatment became even more oppressive in World War II when the Japanese, as Axis partners, and under the influence of Russian right-wing emigrés, adopted an anti-Semitic policy. During Japanese rule, Jewish national life was kept alive by Zionist youth movements, particularly *Betar and *Maccabi, which organized Jewish cultural activities. Betar, which was the strongest Zionist youth organization, published a Russian-language magazine *Ha-Degel* ("The Flag"). Until 1950 four synagogues existed in Harbin. Many Jews left Manchuria before the outbreak of World War II, for the U.S., Australia, Brazil, and other countries. During 1945–47, Harbin was under Soviet occupation, and Jewish community leaders were then arrested and sent to the Soviet interior. About 3,500 of the former "Chinese" Jews, most of them from Harbin, live in Israel, where they play an active role in all walks of life.

ОДНОДНЕВНАЯ
ГАЗЕТА ЖУРНАЛ
КО ДНЮ ОТКРЫТИЯ
ЕВРЕЙСКОЙ БОЛЬНИЦЫ
В ХАРБИНЕ
ИМЕНИ М.А. и Е.С. НАФТАЛИНЫХ
О-ВА "МИШМЕРЕС-ХОЙЛИМ"
Почетный экземпляр

Front page of a special issue of the Harbin daily journal in honor of the opening of the Jewish hospital, October 21, 1931. Jerusalem, J.N.U.L.

Bibliography: I. Cohen, *Journal of a Jewish Traveller* (1928), 160–81; H. Dicker, *Wanderers and Settlers in the Far East* (1962), index; *Yevreyskaya zhizn,* nos. 3–4 (1939); N. Robinson, *Oyfleyzing fun di Yidishe Kehiles in Khine* (1954); S. Rabinowitz, in: *Gesher,* 2 (1957), 121–68. [R.L./N.DR./ED.]

HARBURG, E.Y. (Edgar "Yip"; 1898–), U.S. songwriter. After traveling through Latin America working for newspapers, he turned to writing lyrics for Broadway musicals. His particular vein was the so-called "socially conscious," and his "Brother Can You Spare a Dime?" which he wrote during the depression of the 1930s became a classic. He wrote the lyrics and coauthored the book for the witty musical *Finian's Rainbow* (1947) and wrote lyrics for *The Wizard of Oz, Cabin in the Sky,* and other popular films. His songs "Over the Rainbow" and "Happiness is a Thing Called Jo" won Academy Awards. [Jo.R.]

HARBY, ISAAC (1788–1828), U.S. author, journalist, teacher, and pioneer of Reform Judaism. Harby was born in Charleston, South Carolina. He became both teacher and journalist at the age of 16. He then began to study law, but the death of his father in 1805 left him the main support of a large family. He returned to teaching, opening a school at

Edisto Island and then at Charleston. Finding journalism more profitable, Harby worked on various Charleston newspapers, editing several of his own not too successfully. A play, *Alberti,* was successful in Charleston in 1819, but Harby soon returned to teaching. After his wife's death in 1827, he left Charleston to establish a school in the more prospering metropolis of New York, but died soon after. Many tributes were paid him, including the publication of a memorial volume by his friend Abraham *Moise. A man of rare literary taste, and author of excellent dramatic criticisms, Harby played an important role in the establishment of the Reformed Society of the Israelites, the pioneer effort of Jewish religious reform in the United States. In 1824 a group of 47 members of Charleston's Congregation Beth Elohim unsuccessfully petitioned the congregation's board to modify the ritual, remove the Spanish and Portuguese archaisms and permit explanatory discourses in English. Later that year the Reformed Society of Israelites was organized. On its first anniversary, Harby delivered a discourse outlining the Society's aims; in 1827 he was elected president. His departure for New York and subsequent death left a void. Other leaders left Charleston,

Figure 1. Silhouette of Isaac Harby, teacher and pioneer of U.S. Reform Judaism. Waltham, Mass., American Jewish Historical Society.

also for economic reasons, and by 1833 the Society dissolved. A number of Harby's literary, political, and religious essays appear in J. Blau and S. Baron (ed.), *Jews of the United States,* 3 (1963).

Bibliography: L. C. Moise, *Biography of Isaac Harby* (1931); Kohler, in: AJHSP, 32 (1931), 35–53; Fagin, in: AJA, 8 (1956), 3–13.

[M.H.St.]

HARDEN, MAXIMILIAN (1861–1927), German journalist and polemist. He edited his periodical *Die Zukunft,* founded in 1892, with vigor, erudition, and an eye for

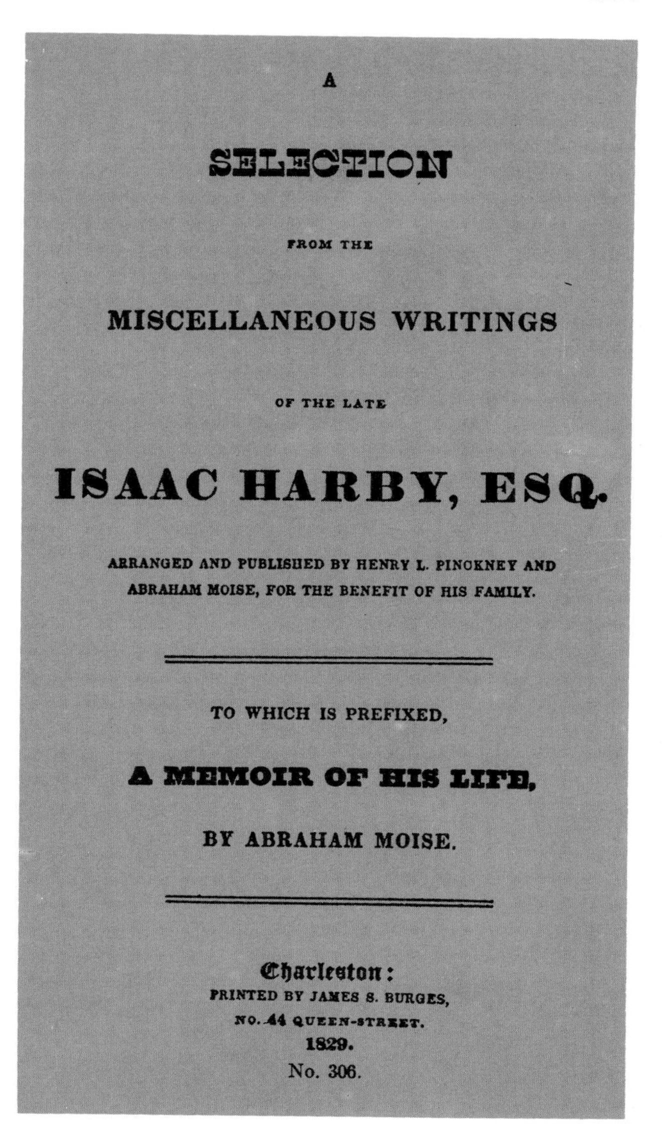

A

SELECTION

FROM THE

MISCELLANEOUS WRITINGS

OF THE LATE

ISAAC HARBY, ESQ.

ARRANGED AND PUBLISHED BY HENRY L. PINCKNEY AND ABRAHAM MOISE, FOR THE BENEFIT OF HIS FAMILY.

TO WHICH IS PREFIXED,

A MEMOIR OF HIS LIFE,

BY ABRAHAM MOISE.

Charleston:
PRINTED BY JAMES S. BURGES,
NO. 44 QUEEN-STREET.
1829.

No. 306.

Figure 2. Title page of selected writings of Isaac Harby. Charleston, S. C., 1829. Waltham, Mass., American Jewish Historical Society.

intrigue that often exposed society and government circles. Born Witkowski in Berlin, he reacted violently against his Jewish origin, was baptized at 16, and changed his name. But he could not escape his ancestry, and among his German contemporaries he was the symbol of Jewish arrogance which they said was undermining Prussian militarism. His political articles written under the pen name "Keut" revealed a talent for satire. Two collections were published, *Apostata* (1892) and *Literatur und Theater* (1896). With irony and courage, Harden attacked William II and the neo-Byzantinism which surrounded him, championing the cause of the aging ex-chancellor Bismarck. *Die Zukunft* became the most influential German weekly of its time and the mouthpiece of liberal opposition to the Kaiser. For subjecting the monarch to ridicule, Harden was twice imprisoned. In 1906–07 he brought about the downfall of Prince zu Eulenburg, the Kaiser's most influential adviser, with revelations about his private life that scandalized the monarchy. During World War I he criticized the German high command and, after the abdication of the Kaiser, the revolutionary regime. In his later years he showed an interest in Jewish affairs. In 1900 he published Walter Rathenau's article *"Hoere Israel"* in *Die Zukunft,* and later expressed appreciation of the Zionist movement. *Die Zukunft* ceased publication in 1922; and an attempt was made on Harden's life that same year. Harden collected his articles in four volumes, *Koepfe* (1910–24). He also published *Krieg und Friede* (1918).

Maximilian Harden, German journalist. From H. F. Young, *Maximilian Harden, Censor Germaniae,* The Hague, 1959.

Georg Witkowski (1863–1939), his younger brother, was a leading German literary historian. He also embraced Lutheranism, but his abandonment of Judaism did not protect him from Nazi persecution. Witkowski lectured at the University of Leipzig, specializing in literature of the era of Goethe. His works include the *Geschichte des literarischen Lebens in Leipzig* (1909), and *Das deutsche Drama des neunzehnten Jahrhunderts* (1923). Between 1909 and 1933 Witkowski edited the *Zeitschrift fuer Buecherfreunde.*

Bibliography: H. F. Young, *Maximilian Harden, Censor Germaniae* (1959); Gottgetreu, in: YLBI, 7 (1962), 215–46. [S.L.]

°**HARDENBERG, KARL AUGUST VON** (1750–1822), Prussian chancellor from 1810, instrumental in enacting the edict concerning the civil status of the Jews (March 3, 1812). While minister of the principality of *Bayreuth-Ansbach (1792) he had already dealt with the problem of Jewish rights and was in social contact with David *Friedlander and other members of the Berlin community. Considering that Jewish emancipation was a vital part of the general Prussian reforms, he stated that he was not prepared to approve any law which was based on more than four words: equal rights, equal duties. He did not, therefore, approve of the restrictions still contained in the edict. At the Congress of Vienna (1815) he once more advocated Jewish rights. While there, he was a frequent guest in Fanny von *Arnstein's house. He tried unsuccessfully to have Eduard *Gans appointed to Berlin University while Gans was still Jewish. D. F. *Koreff was his personal physician, adviser, and protégé. After 1815 Hardenberg continuously opposed the Prussian king and his reactionary ministers, who repudiated their promises of justice and equality for the Jews made during the Napoleonic wars, but since he remained in a minority in the cabinet his support was ineffectual.

Bibliography: S. W. Baron, *Die Juden-Frage auf dem Wiener Kongress* (1920), index; M. J. Kohler, *Jewish Rights at the Congress of Vienna (1814–15)* (1918), 63–83; Freund, *Die Emanzipation der Juden in Preussen,* 1 (1912), 165ff.; H. Spiel, *Fanny von Arnstein* (1962), index; H. G. Reissner, *Eduard Gans* (1965), index; H. Fischer, *Judentum, Staat und Heer in Preussen* (1968), index; R. Dukas, *Die Motive der preussischen Judenemanzipation von 1812* (1916), 53ff.; A. Eckstein, in: *Festschrift Martin Philippson* (1916), 267–74; F. Morgenstern, in: JSOS, 15 (1953), 253–75. [M.La.]

HARDMAN (Salutski), JACOB BENJAMIN (1882–1968), U.S. labor leader and writer. Hardman, born Jacob Benjamin Salutsky in Vilna, joined the Marxist Social Democratic Party as a young man, working as an organizer in Vilna in 1906 and in Kiev in 1907. After several arrests, he was exiled in 1908 by the czarist government for illegal political activities. Arriving in the United States in 1909, Hardman was elected secretary of the Jewish Language Federation of the Socialist Party at its founding in 1912. From 1914 to 1920 he edited *Naye Welt,* the federation's Yiddish weekly. Hardman joined the national executive of the Communist Worker's Party in 1921, but was expelled in 1923 for his criticism of the Jewish left's pro-Bolshevik line and its nihilistic approach to Jewish problems. From 1925 to 1944 he edited *The Advance,* organ of the Amalgamated Clothing Workers Union, and was a member of the executive of the Conference for Progressive Labor Action (1927–34). During World War II Hardman helped organize the American Labor Press Association, of which he became president, and from 1945 to 1953 he was editor of the periodical *Labor and Nation.* He was also editor of *American Labor Dynamics in the Light of Post-War Developments* (1928), *Clothing Workers in Philadelphia* (1940), and *House of Labor* (1951), and during the 1950s was director of research of the Columbia University project "Trends in Union Leadership."

Bibliography: M. Epstein, *Jews and Communism* (1959), passim; *New York Times* (Jan. 31, 1968), 38. [Ed.]

HARE (Heb. אַרְנֶבֶת, *arnevet*), according to the Pentateuch one of the prohibited animals (Lev. 11:6; Deut. 14:7). The Hebrew word is connected with the Akkadian *annabu* ("the jumper"). The Vulgate translates it from the Greek λαγώς ("a hare") as *lepus.* In spite of this the Septuagint gives the translation δασύπους, that is, "the hairy-legged." The Talmud explains that the wife of *Ptolemy Philadelphus, who according to tradition appointed 72 elders to translate the Pentateuch, was named Λαγώς and the translators made the change, apprehensive that the king might say: "The Jews have mocked at me and put my wife's name [as an unclean animal] in the Pentateuch" (Meg. 9b; TJ, Meg. 1:11, 71d).

The description in the Pentateuch of the *arnevet* as a ruminant raises a difficulty since the hare is not one, and hence some cast doubt on this identification. The reference, however, is apparently to the movement of its jaws when it eats and perhaps also to its habit of regurgitating the food it eats in the early morning hours and of later chewing it again, as in rumination.

In Israel there are three species of hare: in the coastal lowland, in the mountains, and in the Negev. It is extensively hunted, but its rapid propagation prevents its extermination. The *halakhah* mentions "the wool of hares" among those to which the law of *sha'atnez* ("the prohibition of wearing material containing wool and linen") does not apply (Shab. 27a), the reference here being apparently to the rabbit—*Dryctolagus cuniculus*—which the Romans bred extensively and which may have been introduced into Ereẓ Israel in mishnaic times. Some mistakenly identify the *shafan* (AV "coney"; JPS "rock-badger"), *coney, mentioned in the Pentateuch

Hare *(arnav),* left with three types of rabbit *(arnevet).* Courtesy J. Feliks, Jerusalem.

alongside the hare, with the rabbit, and this is its common usage in modern Hebrew.

Bibliography: J. Feliks, *Animal World of the Bible* (1962), 41; M. Dor, *Leksikon Zo'ologi* (1965), 46f. [J.F.]

HAREL (Heb. הַרְאֵל), kibbutz in the Jerusalem corridor, east of Ḥuldah, affiliated with Kibbutz Arẓi ha-Shomer ha-Ẓa'ir, founded in October 1948. Harel was established on a site where hard battles had been fought four months earlier (see *Israel War of Independence). The first settlers were *Palmaḥ veterans of the Harel Brigade who had fought in the area and in Jerusalem; they were later joined by immigrants from various countries. Farming is based on deciduous fruit orchards, crops, etc. Carob plantations and large forests have been planted in the vicinity, in the middle of which stands the Harel panorama tower. [E.O.]

HA-REUBENI (Rubinowitz), EPHRAIM (1881–1953), botanist and pioneer in Ereẓ Israel. Born in Novo-Moskovsk, Ukraine, Ha-Reubeni settled in Ereẓ Israel in 1906 and worked as teacher of natural science in various high schools. In 1907 he founded the first museum of botany in Ereẓ Israel. Together with his wife Hannah (d. 1956) he founded in 1912 the Museum of Flora of the Bible and Talmud, in Rishon le-Zion. In 1936 they were transferred to the Hebrew University. He joined the academic staff of the Hebrew University in 1926 and in 1935 was appointed lecturer in botany of the Bible and Talmud. Ha-Reubeni contributed much to the investigation of plants in Ereẓ Israel, their uses and associated folklore. On the basis of their research, together with linguistic studies of plant names in Hebrew, Aramaic, Arabic, and other languages, the Ha-Reubenis did much to explain the ancient Hebrew botanical terms and to identify the plants mentioned in the Bible and Talmud. They wrote *Meḥkarim bi-Shemot Ẓimḥei Ereẓ Yisrael* (1930) and *Oẓar Ẓimḥei Ereẓ Yisrael* (1941).

Bibliography: C. Tartakower, in: *Menorah,* 2 no. 3 (Ger., 1924), 1–2; Tidhar, 12 (1962), 3946–47; *Ha-Teva ve-ha-Areẓ,* 7 (1947), 303 (bibliography). [S.Bo./Ed.]

HAR HA-MELEKH (Heb. הַר הַמֶּלֶךְ; "king's mountain"; Aramaic *Tur Malka*), a hilly district in Judah. It should probably be identified with the toparchy of Orine ("the mountain," Pliny, *Natural History,* 5:7), i.e., the district of Jerusalem in Hasmonean times, since according to the Talmud "any mountain that is in Judah is Har ha-Melekh" (TJ, Shev 9:2, 38d). Its original borders thus extended from Gibeah of Saul in the north to Solomon's Pools in the south and from Kiriath-Jearim in the west to the ascent of Adummim in the east. The word *melekh* ("king") apparently indicates the Hasmonean kings beginning with Alexander Yannai. Har ha-Melekh contained fields and vegetables gardens and its fowls were sent to the Temple. After the destruction of the settlements in the district during the Bar Kokhba War (132–135), Har ha-Melekh was attached to the territory of *Aelia Capitolina. Its Jewish inhabitants were expelled and its produce, which continued to be supplied to Caesarea, was considered gentile produce and thus exempt from tithes. In later talmudic literature the true extent of its area was forgotten and villages in the Bet Guvrin district (e.g., Kefar Bish, Kefar Shiḥlayim) were erroneously attributed to Har ha-Melekh. The alleged number of its villages reached fantastic proportions ("60,000 myriads") and their populations are also highly exaggerated (TB, Git. 57a; Lam. R. 2:2, no. 4). B.Z. Luria proposed to locate Har ha-Melekh in the Mt. Ephraim range, in the direction of the Carmel, between Kefar Otenai and Narbata.

Bibliography: S. Klein, *Ereẓ Yehudah* (1939), 239ff.; B. Z. Luria, *Yannai ha-Melekh* (1961), 38ff.; Press, Ereẓ, s.v. [M.A.-Y.]

ḤARIF, family, many of whose members were rabbis in Poland from the 16th to the 19th centuries. Some regard the family as descended from *Shalom Shakhna b. Joseph of Lublin. They included Moses ha-Zaken ("the elder") ben Israel (16th–17th centuries)—the first to be given the epithet *ḥarif* ("sharp-witted")—who served as rabbi of Kremienec, Lvov, and Uleynov. He was the author of *Seder Gittin* (still in mss.) which was in the possession of Ephraim Zalman Margolioth. Israel, his son, headed a yeshivah in Lvov and was *av bet din* of Uleynov. Moses Phinehas (1625–1702), son of Israel, was chief rabbi of Lvov, and presided over the Council of Four Lands in 1685. He was an opponent of the Shabbateans, and added supplements to his grandfather's *Seder Gittin.* Israel, second son of Israel b. Moses, was born on the day his father died, and was given his name. He was *av bet din* of Alik. Of the sons of Moses Phinehas, Ẓevi Hirsch (d. 1737) was the *av bet din* of Jaworow, and Jacob was *av bet din* of Leszniow and the province of Podolia. One son of Jacob, Judah Leib, was *av bet din* of Korow, and another, Saul (first half of 18th century), *av bet din* of Olesko, and later of Brody where he founded a *bet midrash* called after him. Moses Ḥayyim ben Eleazar (1690–1760), grandson of Moses Phinehas, was rabbi of Komarno, Zloczow (1719), and Lvov (1724). After a violent controversy between him and Jacob Joshua *Falk concerning the rabbinate of Lvov, which arose out of an allegation by a proselyte that Moses Ḥayyim had influenced him to become a Jew, he was compelled to flee to Khotin, which was under Turkish rule, and he died there. Jacob Isaac (?1710–1771), son of Moses Ḥayyim, changed his name to Hochgelerter, and in 1740 was appointed rabbi of Zamosc. His son Joseph (1740–1807) was rabbi of Jampol and Zamosc. His halakhic glosses, *Ḥiddushei Mahari,* were published in the *Zera Aharon* (Zolkiew, 1757). *Mishnat Ḥakhamim* (Lvov, 1792), the first part of his commentary to Maimonides' *Mishneh Torah,* was also published. His sons were Ḥayyim ben Joseph (1770–1809), rabbi of Ostrowiec, Hrubieszow, and Grabowiec, author of halakhic novellae entitled *Ḥut ha-Meshullash,* appended to his father's *Mishnat Ḥakhamim,* and Isaac ben Joseph (1771–1825), rabbi of Tarnograd, Chelm, and Zamosc, author of *Zikhron Yiẓḥak* (c. 1822), consisting of responsa and homilies.

Bibliography: G. Sochestow, *Maẓẓevat Kodesh,* 4 (1869), 73b–74b; H. N. Dembitzer, *Kelilat Yofi,* 1 (1888), 86a–88a; S. Buber, *Anshei Shem* (1895), 130, 158–62, 195f.; J. Cohen-Ẓedek, *Shem u-She'erit* (1895), 58f.; idem, in: *Ha-Goren,* 1 (1898), 28–31; Ẓ. (H.) Horowitz, in: *Ha-Ivri,* 11 no. 13 (1921), 8–10; 11 no.14 (1921), 8f.; idem, *Kitvei ha-Ge'onim* (1928), 28–30, 59–61; idem, *Toledot Mishpaḥat Horowitz* (n.d.), 21 n.41; idem, in: MGWJ, 72 (1928), 494ff.; M. Bersohn, *Słownik biograficzny uczonych żydów polskich XVI, XVII, i XVIII wieku* (1905), 68f. [Y.Ho.]

ḤARIF HA-LEVI, family of rabbis and scholars in Poland in the 17th and 18th centuries. The founder of the family was Solomon ben Isaac Abraham of Przemysl (d. 1638), a pupil of Joshua *Falk, and son-in-law of Joseph ha-Kohen. He was rabbi of Lemberg when he died. His elder son, Isaac Segal, was the son-in-law of Samuel *Edels, and rabbi of Rymanow. He was the ancestor of many generations of rabbis and scholars including Ephraim Zalman *Margalioth of Brody and Samuel Kamnitzer, great-grandfather of Eisik Segal of Lemberg. Solomon's second son, Moses Segal, was rabbi of Polna and later head of a yeshivah in

Lemberg. Moses' son, JOSEPH SEGAL (d. 1702), was rabbi of Przemysl and the Ḥakham Ẓevi (Ẓevi Hirsch *Ashkenazi) said of him that his only transgression was his disobedience of the *takkanah* of Usha which laid it down that one should not give more than one fifth of one's income to charity. JEKUTHIEL ZALMAN SEGAL, son of Joseph, was the first rabbi of Drohobycz, appointed in 1670. Of his six sons, all of whom were rabbis, the most distinguished was ISAAC HA-LEVI. NATHAN NETA, another son of Jekuthiel, was rabbi and *av bet din* of Lemberg. He died apparently in 1776.

Bibliography: Ḥ. N. Dembitzer, *Kelilat Yofi*, 1 (1888), 41–42b; S. Buber, *Anshei Shem* (1895), 203f.; J. Cohen-Ẓedek, in: *Ha-Goren*, 1 (1898), 24, 26, 28 (second pagination); E. Z. Margaliot, *Ma'alot ha-Yuḥasin* (1900), 34–36; Margaliot, in: *Sinai*, 31 (1952), 92; Z. Horowitz, *Kitvei ha-Ge'onim* (1928), 47, 69f. [Y.Ho.]

HARIRI, family of kabbalists of the village of Ḥarir, in the district of Irbil, Kurdistan. ISAAC BEN MOSES (17th century), the founder of the family, lived in this village during the first half of the 17th century. He wrote the kabbalistic work *Naḥalat ha-Shem* and a number of religious *piyyutim*. His son PHINEHAS, who was attracted to Shabbateanism, was also a *paytan* and author. The sons of Phinehas, ḤAYYIM and ISAAC, were rabbis in the townlet of Rawanduz, in the district of Irbil. ABRAHAM BEN PHINEHAS (19th century) left six works in manuscript. His son MOSES was a teacher for beginners in Köi in the district of Irbil, and owned a large library of religious books. He wrote at least three works, of which *Va-Yivḥar Moshe* was published in Baghdad in 1930. Moses' son Isaac was rabbi in Rawanduz.

Bibliography: A. Ben-Jacob, *Kehillot Yehudei Kurdistan* (1961); index. [H.J.C.]

ḤARIZI, ABU ISAAC ABRAHAM (fl. c. 1100), Hebrew poet of Toledo, Spain. Moses ibn Ezra mentions him in his poetics (tr. by B. Halper, *Shirat Yisrael* (1924), 74) as being a contemporary of Joseph ibn Sahl (1124). Judah *al-Ḥarizi praises Abraham's verses in two passages in the *Taḥkemoni* (ed. by Kaminka (1899), 39, 41). It is uncertain whether he belonged to the same family as Judah al-Ḥarizi. A number of poems, known to have been composed by a "Ḥarizi" (*Maḥzor Aleppo, Siftei Renanot*, Karaite Rite and Ms.), may be Abraham's. There were, however, also other Ḥarizis (Ms. Adler 135 contains poems by a Simḥah Ḥarizi).

Bibliography: Sachs, in: *Oẓar Ḥokhmah*, 2 (1861), 37; Brody, in: A. Berliner, *Aus meiner Bibliothek* (1898), 6 (Heb. sect.); Habermann, in: *Mizraḥ u-Ma'arav*, 4 (1930), 18–21; J. H. Schirmann, *Shirim Ḥadashim min ha-Genizah* (1965), 284. [J.H.SCH.]

HARKAVY, ALBERT (Abraham Elijah; 1835–1919), Russian orientalist, scholar of Jewish history and literature. Harkavy was born in Novogrudok, Belorussia. He studied at Lithuanian yeshivot and at the universities of St. Petersburg, Berlin, and Paris. On his return to Russia in 1870 he began teaching ancient oriental history. The opposition in certain circles to the appointment of a Jew to a university lectureship prompted the Russian government to cancel his post, and he was transferred to the department of Jewish literature and oriental manuscripts at the Imperial Library in St. Petersburg. In 1877 he was made head of that department, remaining in that position for the rest of his life.

Harkavy started his literary and scientific work in 1861, publishing articles mainly in *Ha-Karmel* and *Ha-Meliẓ* on the natural and physical sciences and on current problems in education and literature. At about that time Harkavy started his research on the origin of the Jewish community in Russia. His efforts were part of the general efforts of the Wissenschaft des Judentums school to secure equality for Russian Jews. They based their claims on the ancient Jewish heritage in Russian language. Harkavy argued his theories in several essays and articles, and especially in his first

Albert Harkavy, orientalist and historian of Russian Jewry. Jerusalem, Schwadron Collection, J.N.U.L.

Russian book, *O yazyke yevreyev, . . . i o slavyanskikh slovakh, vstrechayemykh u yevreyskikh pisateley* (1865), which also appeared in Hebrew as *Ha-Yehudim u-Sefat ha-Slavim* ("The Jews and the Slavic Language," 1867).

Harkavy claimed that the Jewish community in Russia was formed by Jews who migrated from the region of the Black Sea and Caucasia, where their ancestors had settled after the Assyrian and Babylonian exiles. These people, who preserved an ancient Jewish heritage, which they spread among the *Khazars, expanded through the Khazar kingdom westward to Czechoslovakia. Their spoken language was Slavic, at least from the ninth century on; not until the 17th century did it change to Yiddish, and that was because many Ukrainian Jews fled the 1648–49 pogroms to Poland, where Yiddish was spoken. This theory concerning the origins of Russian Jewry led to Harkavy's research into the history of the Khazars, the most important of which is his essay *Skazaniya yevreyskikh pisateley o khazarakh i khazarskom tsarstve* ("Jewish Authors' Reports on the Khazars and the Khazar Kingdom," 1874). The reports were few and sketchy but Harkavy showed uncanny knowledge and acumen in their interpretation.

An important part of his work was publishing Jewish manuscripts by Jewish authors which were in the possession of the St. Petersburg library, with his comments and critical notes. Among them were works by the later *geonim*, including Saadiah Gaon, Samuel b. Hophni, and Hai Gaon; and the Spanish sages, including Samuel ha-Nagid, Joseph ha-Nagid, Judah Halevi, and Abraham ibn Ezra. He also published manuscripts in the journals *Me'assef Niddaḥim* (16 issues, 1878–80) and *Ḥadashim Gam Yeshanim* (20 issues, 1886–1907); in the series of monographs he edited, *Zikkaron le-Rishonim ve-gam le-Aḥaronim* (7 issues, 1879–82), and in other publications.

Significant information in Jewish history is included in his comments on volumes three to eight of H. Graetz's *Geschichte der Juden*. Among the manuscripts he published were geonic responsa and the long version of "The Letter of King Joseph of the Khazars to R. Ḥisdai ibn Shaprut" and other manuscripts that the library acquired from the Karaite scholar Abraham Firkovich.

While working on Karaite documents it occurred to Harkavy that Firkovich had forged many of the manuscripts and tombstone epitaphs. He proved this claim in a series of articles and essays, of which the most significant were *Altjuedische Denkmaeler aus der Krim mitgetheilt von Abraham Firkowitsch 1839–1872* ("Ancient Jewish Monuments from Crimea . . .," 1876) and *Po voprosu o iudeyskikh drevnostyakh naydennykh Firkovichem v*

Krymu ("On Jewish Antiquities Found by Firkovich in Crimea," in *Zhurnal Ministerstva narodnago prosveshcheniya,* 1877). Harkavy's keen, systematic analysis in this controversy placed him in the first rank of Jewish scholars of his time. Since Firkovich used his forgeries to obtain equality for the Karaites (but not for all the Jews) in Russia, Harkavy felt he was fighting for the whole of Jewry. The controversy escalated when the learned apostate Daniel *Chwolson of the University of St. Petersburg took Firkovich's side and defended his theories. Of his many articles about the Karaites the most significant are the one on Anan (in *Voskhod,* 1900) and his extensive research *Ocherki istorii karaimstva* ("Notes on the History of the Karaites," 1896–1900).

Harkavy published in Russian a description of Samaritan scrolls of the Torah found in the St. Petersburg public library (1874), and with H. L. Strack a description in German of the Bibles found in Firkovich's collection (1875). He devoted a special essay in German, *Neuaufgefundene hebraeische Bibelhandschriften* (1884), to biblical manuscripts he acquired later. These descriptions are important from both paleographic and historical points of view, as the manuscripts contain various notes and comments added by the authors and copyists. Harkavy was esteemed by the czarist regime, and in the 1890s he was awarded a hereditary noble title and made an honorary member of several scientific societies in various countries. He was active in the Jewish community of St. Petersburg as the *gabbai* of the central synagogue and as a member of Mefiẓei Haskalah be-Yisrael and Mekiẓei Nirdamim societies. A listing of his entire work through 1907, including 392 titles, was published by D. Magid with corrections and supplements by S. A. Poznański in a Festschrift published on the occasion of Harkavy's 70th birthday, *Zikkaron le-Avraham Eliyahu* (1908).

Bibliography: Y. Guttman, in: *Ha-Shilo'aḥ,* 24 (1871), 161–70; S. Assaf, in: *Kobez al Jad,* 11 (1936), 191–243; Z. Harkavy, in: S. K. Mirsky (ed.), *Ishim u-Demuyyot be-Ḥokhmat Yisrael...* (1959), 116–36.

[A.N.P.]

HARKAVY, ALEXANDER (1863–1939), lexicographer of Yiddish and author. Harkavy, a grandson of the rabbi of Novogrudok and a relative of the orientalist and historian Albert *Harkavy, was born in Novogrudok, Belorussia. He had a traditional Jewish education and showed an early interest in languages, acquiring some knowledge not only of Hebrew but also of Russian, Syriac, German, and—particularly—Yiddish in his teens. In 1878 Harkavy went to Vilna, where he was befriended by the Yiddish author Isaac Meir *Dick. He wrote his first work in this period, in Yiddish. He earned a living as a bookkeeper for *Romm, the Hebrew-Yiddish publishing house. After the pogroms of 1881

Figure 1. Alexander Harkavy, Yiddish lexicographer. From *American Jewish Yearbook 1940–41,* Jewish Publication Society, Philadelphia, Pa.

Harkavy joined the *Am Olam movement and emigrated to the United States, intending to settle in a Jewish collective agricultural colony. When the project did not materialize he

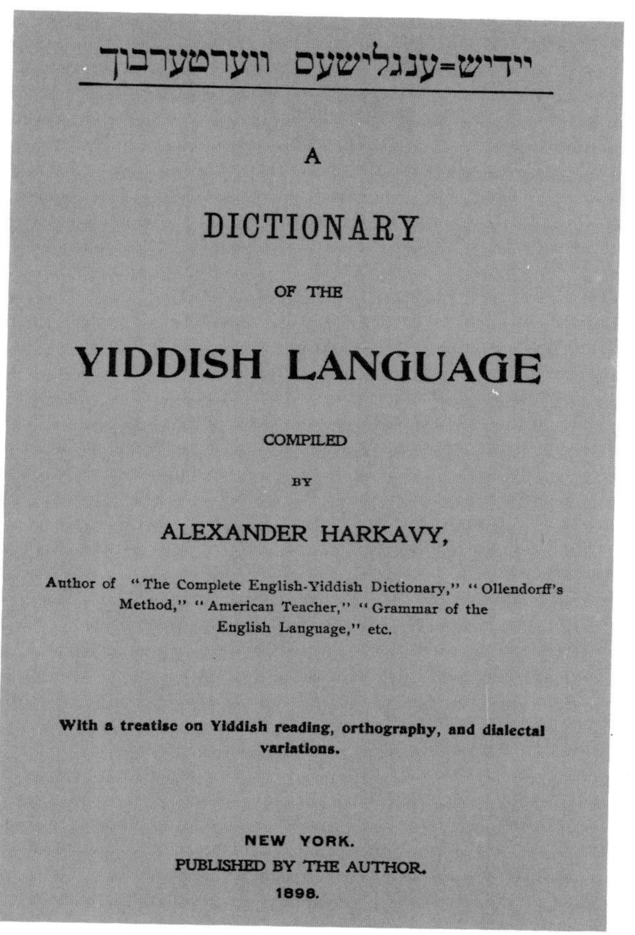

יידיש-ענגלישעס ווערטערבוך

A

DICTIONARY

OF THE

YIDDISH LANGUAGE

COMPILED

BY

ALEXANDER HARKAVY,

Author of "The Complete English-Yiddish Dictionary," "Ollendorff's Method," "American Teacher," "Grammar of the English Language," etc.

With a treatise on Yiddish reading, orthography, and dialectal variations.

NEW YORK.

PUBLISHED BY THE AUTHOR.

1898.

Figure 2. Title page of Harkavy's Yiddish-English dictionary, New York, 1898. New York Public Library.

found what work he could, as a stevedore, a farm laborer, a dishwasher, learning English intensively and then tutoring English and Hebrew privately.

Harkavy's love of Yiddish soon crystallized into a vocation, but for about 10 years his search for a steady income sent him wandering. He was in Paris in 1885, returned to New York in 1886, taught Hebrew at a *talmud torah* in Montreal in 1887, went to Baltimore in 1889 and there founded the short-lived periodical *Der Yidisher Progres,* and returned once more to New York in 1890. A year later his first popular textbook, *Englishe Lerer,* was published. Almost 100,000 copies were sold. Through this and other books in the "English self-taught" genre, such as his guide to writing letters, *Englishe Brifnshteler* (1892); through his Yiddish translations of classics; through his classroom lectures and popular expositions of American history and culture; and above all through his Yiddish dictionaries, he became the teacher par excellence of two generations of immigrants. He translated *Don Quixote* into Yiddish as *Geshikhte fun Don Kikhot* (1910) and revised the King James English Bible and translated it into Yiddish for an edition in which the English and the Yiddish appeared side-by-side (1926). His popular expositions included *Columbus, Entdeker fun Amerike* (1892). He taught U.S. history and politics for the New York Board of Education and Yiddish literature and grammar at the Jewish Teachers' Seminary in New York, and he lectured as well for the Workmen's Circle. Harkavy wrote a column called "Kol-Boi" ("Everything in It") for the *Abend-Post* and occasional articles for many Yiddish, Hebrew, and English papers and journals. He also wrote *Perakim me-Ḥayyai* ("Autobiographic Chapters," 1935). Harkavy's most lasting achievements were in lexicography. His English-Yiddish and Yiddish-English dictionaries, encompassing about 40,000 Yiddish words, went through at least 22 editions and reprints. His crowning work was the *Yiddish-English-Hebrew Dictionary* (1925; fourth reprint, 1957).

See *Yiddish Language.

Bibliography: B. G. Richards, in: AJYB, 42 (1941), 153–64; Y. Mark, in: JBA, 26 (1968/69); I. Shatzky, *Harkavis bio-bibliografye* (1933); B. Tshubinski, in: *Leksikon fun der Nayer Yidisher Literatur*, 3 (1960).

[Mor.Sch.]

ḤARLAP, JACOB MOSES BEN ZEBULUN (1883–1951), Ereẓ Israel rabbi. Ḥarlap was born in Jerusalem, where his father, who had immigrated from Poland, was a *dayyan* in the *bet din* of Moses Joshua Judah Leib Diskin. His main teacher was the Jerusalem scholar, Ẓevi Michael Shapira and under his influence Ḥarlap engaged in *Kabbalah and practiced asceticism. After Shapira's death, Ḥarlap published *Ẓevi la-Ẓaddik* (1907), in his memory, and arranged his writings for publication, publishing his halakhic work *Ẓiẓ ha-Kodesh* (two parts, 1920–1951) with his own additions. When Rabbi A. I. *Kook arrived in Ereẓ Israel in 1904, Ḥarlap immediately came under his influence, and a bond of unusual intimacy developed between them which was strengthened by their common interest in Kabbalah and their leaning toward mysticism and poetic meditation. Ḥarlap was particularly attracted by Kook's thought which stressed the special role of the Jewish people as a whole, the sanctity of the land of Israel, and the Zionist movement and its upbuilding of Ereẓ Israel—a first stage in the future messianic redemption.

When in 1908 the Sha'arei Ḥesed district of Jerusalem was established outside the Old City, Ḥarlap was appointed its rabbi. In 1912 he was appointed to the Eẓ Hayyim yeshivah. In 1918 he was one of the chief speakers at the meeting of the rabbis of Jerusalem with Chaim *Weizmann demanding that the Zionist movement confine itself to the political field, but he refused Weizmann's offer that he undertake the conduct of religious affairs in the *yishuv*. When the Merkaz ha-Rav yeshivah was founded in Jerusalem by Kook, Ḥarlap was invited to serve as head of the yeshivah and he continued in this post until his death. After the death of Rabbi Kook in 1935, many expected Ḥarlap to be chosen as chief rabbi, and in any case he was later regarded by many as his natural successor. On the establishment of the State of Israel Ḥarlap expressed orally and in writing his belief in "the beginning of the redemption"; at the same time he demanded an amelioration of religious standards. Ḥarlap never left Ereẓ Israel during his life and regarded it as a merit "that I never departed from holy confines and never [breathed] the air [or trod the] ground of the land of the gentiles."

Jacob Ḥarlap, Jerusalem rabbi and scholar. Courtesy Yeshivat Beth Zevul, Jerusalem.

Ḥarlap's main halakhic work is *Bet Zevul*, comprising his halakhic discourses, novellae on the Talmud and on Maimonides' *Mishneh Torah*, and halakhic responsa, in six parts, of which two were published in his lifetime (1942 and 1948) and the others between 1957 and 1966. His books on Jewish thought and religious meditation bear the general title *Mei Merom*. Seven volumes were published (1945ff.), among them a discussion of Maimonides' *Shemonah Perakim*, tractate *Avot*, the High Holidays, and repentance. The central idea of these works is the need to purify one's heart, and sanctify one's life. The aim of the Torah is the perfection of man in thought and in action, the penetration of "the light and spark of holiness that dwells within the people of Israel" into "the depth of the nation's soul which will bring about the redemption." Among his other works are: *Hed ha-Ḥayyim ha-Yisre'eliyyim* (1912); *Tovim me-Orot* (1920), a defense of A. I. Kook's *Orot; El Am ha-Shem* (1943), some of his sermons and articles; *Imrei No'am* (1947), "words of comfort, and encouragement to the people of Israel"; and *Hed Harim* (1953), a collection of his letters to A. I. Kook.

Bibliography: J. S. Rabinson, *Ha-Rav Rabbi Ya'akov Moshe Ḥarlap* (1936); S. Daniel, in: *Mizpeh, Shenaton "Ha-Ẓofeh"* (1953), 645–70; J. Rubinstein, in: *Hadoar*, 32 (1953), 93; J. Gershony, *ibid.*, 40 (1961), 53–55; H. Lifschitz, in: *Sinai*, 32 (1953), 246–52; idem, in: S. Federbush (ed.), *Ḥazon Torah ve-Ẓiyyon* (1960), 287–303; S. Bornstein, in: *Sinai*, 43 (1958), 418–28; EZD, 2 (1960), 371–90; *Or ha-Mizraḥ*, 10 no. 3–4 (1962), 1–22; K. P. Tchursh, *ibid.*, 17 (1968), 77–80.

[Z.K.]

HARLAU (Rum. **Hârlău**), town in Moldavia, N. E. Rumania. A Jewish physician served the prince of Moldavia, Stephen the Great, in Harlau at the end of the 15th century. In the early 18th century some Jewish craftsmen, immigrants from Poland, were exempted from taxes. In 1768 a Jew was authorized to establish a factory for window glass and a paper mill in Harlau. From 1751 the documents mention the "Jews' Guild," which in 1834 became the local community organization. The oldest of the five synagogues in Harlau was built at the end of the 17th century. The community had a primary school (founded c. 1900), which was erected with the assistance of the *Jewish Colonization Association. There were also a *talmud torah*, a *mikveh*, and two Jewish cemeteries.

Anti-Semitic persecutions led half of the Jewish population of Harlau to emigrate to the United States during 1899–1900. However, at the same time Jews expelled from the villages settled in Harlau, and so the Jewish population did not decrease. The community numbered 784 in 1803, 2,254 (56.6% of the total) in 1886, 2,718 (59%) in 1899, and 2,032 (22.3%) in 1930. The majority of both craftsmen and merchants enumerated in Harlau in 1913 were Jews. Following emancipation in 1919 the Jews took an active part in the municipal council. A small cooperative credit bank was founded in Harlau with the aid of the American Jewish Joint Distribution Committee. Rabbis of Harlau included Israel Isaacson (b. 1895), a deputy in the Rumanian parliament, who settled in Israel. During World War II some of the Jews in Harlau were deported to Botosani, and others to Jassy. There were 1,936 Jews living in Harlau in 1947. In 1969 approximately 60 Jewish families were living there and they maintained a synagogue.

Bibliography: M. Schwarzfeld, *Ochire asupra evreilor din România*... (1887), 38; E. Schwarzfeld, *Impopularea, reîmpopularea şi întemeierea tîrgurilor şi tîrguşoarelor in Moldova* (1914), 21, 22; S. Savin, in: *Revista cultului mozaic*, 19 (1965), no. 119; M. Carp, *Cartea Neagră*, 1 (1946), 66, 158, 200, 202; PK Romanyah, 1 (1970), 112–4.

[Th.L.]

HARMAN (Herman), AVRAHAM (1914–), Israel diplomat and president of the Hebrew University. Born in London, Harman, who studied law at Oxford, settled in Palestine in 1938. From 1939 to 1940 he was in Johannesburg as a staff member of the South African Zionist Federation and then returned to Jerusalem to head the English Section of the Youth Department of the Jewish

Abraham Harman, Israel diplomat and president of the Hebrew University. Courtesy Hebrew University, Jerusalem.

Agency. From 1942 to 1948 he was the head of the Information Department of the Agency, and after the establishment of the State of Israel Harman became deputy director of the Press and Information Division of the Israel Foreign Ministry. In 1949 he was appointed Israel consul-general in Montreal, Canada, and then became the director of the Israel Office of Information and counselor to the Israel delegation to the United Nations (1950–53). After a two-year period as the Israel consul-general in New York, Harman returned to Jerusalem in 1955 and was appointed a member of the Jewish Agency Executive, heading its Information Department. In 1959 he was appointed Israel ambassador to the United States, a post he held until 1968. His warm identification with the Jewish community and its problems brought him personal popularity wherever he served. Upon his return to Israel, Harman was appointed president of the Hebrew University, Jerusalem.

His wife, ZENA (1914–), was born in London and educated at the London School of Economics and Political Science. She served on several Israel delegations to the U.N. In 1964 she was elected chairman of UNICEF (the United Nations Children's Emergency Fund). In 1969 she was elected to the Seventh Knesset on behalf of the Israel Labor Party.

[ED.]

HARO (Faro), city in Castile, northern Spain. A charter *(fuero)* given to the city by Alfonso VIII (1158–1214) granted the Jews in Haro, who had aided him during the war against Navarre, a series of privileges which included arrangements concerning their security, the indemnity to be paid for the murder of a Jew, and release from various taxes. Jews were permitted to fish in the river, to establish mills, and to engage in dyeing. The *fuero* was later endorsed by Sancho IV (1284–95) and Ferdinand IV (1295–1312). Alfonso settled some Jews in the fortress but they also lived in the unwalled sections of the city. In 1305 they were authorized to choose their own judges in suits involving members of different faiths. An organized community continued to exist throughout the 15th century. Jews owned lands and vineyards which they leased to Christians and Muslims. Some were potters. Prominent in the 15th century were the tax farmer Don Solomon Zadik and Samuel Cubo who represented the community in 1476 in a dispute with the town council regarding pasture land and the slaughterhouse. A census in 1492 at the time of the expulsion of the Jews from Spain showed that the community numbered 48 taxpayers.

Bibliography: Baer, Spain, index; Baer, Urkunden, index; D. Hergueta, *Noticias históricas de la Ciudad de Haro* (1906), 61, 208, 242, 267; Cantera, in: *Sefarad,* 2 (1942), 327; 22 (1962), 87ff.; León Tello, *ibid.,* 15 (1955), 157–69; Suárez Fernańdez, Documentos, 68, 76.

[H.B.]

Figure 1. Illustration from the *Sarajevo Haggadah,* showing the head of the family distributing *ḥaroset* (above) and *mazzot* (below). Spain, 14th century. Sarajevo, National Museum, fol. 33v.

ḤAROSET (Heb. חֲרוֹסֶת), paste made of fruit, spices, wine, and *mazzah* meal which forms part of the *seder rite on *Passover eve. It is symbolic of the mortar that the Jews made when they were slaves in Egypt. The word is of unknown origin. It has been suggested that it may stem from *ḥeres* (חֶרֶס, "clay"), because of the color resemblance. The ingredients vary in different communities; in most western countries, it is made of apples, chopped almonds, cinnamon, red wine, and *mazzah* meal. In many Sephardi communities, however, the fruits, etc. that grew in Ereẓ Israel in Bible times—grapes, wheat (*mazzah* meal), dates, figs, olives, apricots, pomegranates, and almonds—are used. North Africans also include pine-nuts and hard-boiled eggs, flavoring the paste with piquant and often pungent spices, such as ginger. Yemenites add other

Figure 2. A silver *ḥaroset* container, Ereẓ Israel, 20th century, inscribed with verses explaining why *ḥaroset* is eaten during the Passover *seder.* Jerusalem, Sir Isaac and Lady Wolfson Museum in Hechal Shlomo. Photo David Harris, Jerusalem.

seasoning: e.g., chili pepper. In Israel, the bland occidental mixture is turned into a dessert by adding bananas, dates, candied peel, orange juice, and sugar. It is often served as a course of the meal.

Bibliography: M. Kasher, *Haggadah Shelemah* (1955), 62–64.

[M.L.B.-D.]

HAROSHETH-GOIIM (Heb. חֲרֹשֶׁת הַגּוֹיִם), biblical locality, the seat of *Sisera, commander of the army of Jabin king of Canaan (Judg. 4:2). When Sisera heard that *Barak was assembling his army at Mount Tabor, he advanced from Harosheth-Goiim to the brook of Kishon, where Barak defeated him and drove his army back to Harosheth-Goiim (*ibid.* 4:12–16). Various scholars have proposed to identify the site with either Khirbat al-Harbaj or Tell al-ʾAmar near al-Ḥārithiyya. These identifications, however, are disputed by B. Mazar, who argues that Harosheth-Goiim is not the name of a city but a general term designating the forested regions of central Galilee (cf. *Gelil ha-goyim,* "Galilee of the nations," Isa. 8:23), over which Sisera attempted to impose his rule. The root חרש in Hebrew and related languages means "forest"; the Septuagint also translates Harosheth as *drymos,* "forest" (Judg. 4:16).

Bibliography: Abel Geog, 2 (1938), 343f.; Maisler (Mazar), in: HUCA, 24 (1953), 81–84; Y. Aharoni, *Hitnaḥalut Shivtei Yisrael ba-Galil ha-Elyon* (1957), 101f.; Aharoni, Land, index.

[M.A.-Y.]

HARRIS, SIR DAVID (1852–1942), South African mining magnate, soldier, and politician. A cousin of Barney *Barnato, Harris went to South Africa from London in 1871, and made on foot the 600-mile journey from Durban to the diamond mines at Kimberley, where he worked for a time as a digger. He became associated with Cecil Rhodes, and from 1897 to 1931 was a director of De Beers Consolidated Mines, founded by Rhodes and Barnato. On Barnato's death in 1897, Harris was elected to his seat in Parliament, where for 32 years he was esteemed as an authority on the diamond industry. Harris fought in several frontier wars in the Cape Colony, rising to the rank of lieutenant colonel. In the Boer War (1899–1902) he commanded the town guard of Kimberley during the historic 125-day siege. He was mentioned in dispatches and decorated for his services. Later he was knighted. Harris

Sir David Harris, South African mining magnate and member of parliament. From D. Harris, *Pioneer, Soldier and Politician,* London, 1931.

was one of the founders of the Griqualand West Hebrew Congregation and was its president for many years. His benefactions to the community included the site on which the Kimberley synagogue was built in 1875. In Parliament he frequently spoke on immigration and other matters of Jewish concern. Known as the "grand old man" of Kimberley, Harris told the story of his life in *Pioneer, Soldier and Politician* (1931).

[L.Ho.]

HARRIS, ZELLIG SABBETAI (1909–), U.S. linguist. Harris was born in Russia and was taken to the United States as a child of four. He graduated from the University of Pennsylvania and joined the faculty there in 1931. He was appointed professor of linguistics in 1947. In the late 1930s his interests shifted from Semitics to general linguistics. His early work was primarily devoted to the development of procedures of linguistic analysis. His purpose was to devise a set of precisely formulated methods which, applied to data of a particular language, would yield a grammatical description of this language. This was completed in the late 1940s, and Harris then turned his attention to the study of connected discourse. He observed that formal operations of a general nature could be applied to the utterances of a discourse, reducing it to a "normalized" form. Procedures analogous to those of structural linguistics could then be applied, finally yielding a structural analysis of the discourse. This work led to an intensive investigation of the properties of the formal operations ("transformations"). Other investigations resulted in the development of computer programs for the analysis of language structure, many studies of the detailed properties of English syntax, and more abstract investigation of the formal properties of linguistic structures. Harris' major publications on his work are *Methods in Structural Linguistics* (1951); *String Analysis of Sentence Structure* (1962); *Discourse Analysis Reprints* (1963); *Mathematical Structures of Language* (1968). Harris helped to develop the adult education program for Israel kibbutzim centered in Givat Ḥavivah.

[N.C.]

HARRISBURG, capital city of Pennsylvania. Of a total population of 209,501 in the metropolitan area there are 5,500 Jews (1969). The first Jewish settlers in Harrisburg were immigrants from Germany and England; they arrived in the 1840s and assembled regularly for Sabbath and holiday services under the leadership of Lazarus Bernhard. In 1852 this group drew up the constitution for the first synagogue, Ohev Shalom, which was Orthodox until 1867, when it adopted Reform. Philip D. Bookstaber served as its rabbi from 1924.

Other congregations that formed since then are Chizuk Emunah (1884), now Conservative; Kesher Israel Congregation (1902), the leading Orthodox institution in central Pennsylvania, Temple Beth El (1926), Conservative, and Machzike Hadas (1904), Lubavich ḥasidic. Eliezer *Silver, who served as rabbi of Kesher Israel from 1907 to 1925, founded many of the community's services, including the Harrisburg Hebrew School, a *talmud torah;* the Hebrew Free Loan society; and Transient Home. Yeshiva Academy founded in 1944 by David L. Silver, rabbi of Kesher Israel, and Aaron S. Feinerman, is a day school providing religious and secular instruction for elementary and junior high pupils. The Jewish Community Center was founded in 1915 as a Y.M.H.A. by Leon Lowengard; its name was changed in 1941. United Jewish Community, founded in 1933, serves as a central fund-raising agency and speaks officially for the community on both Jewish matters and Jewish-gentile community relations. The Harrisburg Jewish community had the highest per capita donation in the country to the U.J.A. emergency fund during Israel's Six-Day War. For decades its leading philanthropist was businesswoman Mary Sachs.

Until the 1940s most Jews were engaged in the merchandising of food, clothing, and furniture; the scrap business; and peddling. In the 1960s many were engaged in manufacturing clothing, food distribution, retail merchandising, the professions, and state government positions. In 1968 attorney Gilbert Nurick was the first Jew to head the

Ohev Shalom, the synagogue established by the first Jewish settlers in Harrisburg, Pennsylvania, in the middle of the 19th century. Courtesy Jewish Community Center, Harrisburg, Pa.

State Bar Association. The first community college in the state, Harrisburg Area Community College, was established mainly because of the efforts of Bruce E. Cooper, chairman of its board. In 1969 for the first time, a Jew, William Lipsitt, was judge of the county court. Despite Jewish participation in a wide range of communal affairs, discrimination persists in exclusion from country clubs and Masonic lodges. [D.L.Sɪ.]

HARRISSE, HENRY (1829–1910), U.S. historiographer. Born in Paris, Harrisse emigrated to the United States in 1849. After teaching in South Carolina, he became professor of French at the University of North Carolina and simultaneously prepared for the bar at its Law School. In 1857, he settled in Chicago and four years later in New York, dividing his time between the practice of law and writing on philosophy, French literature, and historiography. In New York, he met Samuel Barlow, the eminent attorney and Americana bibliophile, who stimulated his interest in the period of discovery. Together they published *Notes on Columbus* (1866). Harrisse's *Bibliotheca Americana Vetustissima,* which evaluated every book referring to America from 1493 to 1551 (1866; repr. 1922, 1958), established his reputation and, when he returned to Paris (1866) to practice law, he was acknowledged as an authority in American studies.

Among his other books on the period of discovery are: *Notes pour servir à l'histoire, à la bibliographie et à la cartographie de la Nouvelle-France et des pays adjacents, 1545–1700* (1872); *Ferdnand Colomb, sa vie, ses œuvres . . .* (1872); *Christophe Colomb, son origine, sa vie, ses voyages, sa famille et ses descendants* (2 vols., 1884–85); *The Discovery of North America* (1892); *Americus* (Eng., 1895); *John Cabot, the Discoverer of North America . . .* (1896); and *The Diplomatic History of America. Its First Chapter . . .* (1897).

Bibliography: H. Cordier, *Henry Harrisse* (Fr., 1912); R. G. Adams, *Three Americanists* (1939). [M.A.Bʀ.]

HARRY, MYRIAM, pen name of Mme. **Emile Perrault,** née Shapira (1875–1958), French author. She was born in Jerusalem, the daughter of Moses William *Shapira; her mother was a former Protestant deaconess. Myriam was educated in Berlin and Paris, where she became secretary to the French critic, Jules Lemaître. She led an active life and many of her experiences found their way into her stories. Her sensitivity to human suffering lent depth and color to such works as *La Conquête de Jérusalem* (1903), *La Divine chanson* (1911), *La petite fille de Jérusalem* (1914), *Siona chez les Barbares* (1918), *Siona à Paris* (1919), and *Le Tendre cantique de Siona* (1922). Myriam Harry also wrote accounts of her travels in Tunisia, Egypt, the Levant, Madagascar, Persia, Indo-China, and Palestine. Three of these, *Les Amants de Sion* (1923), *La Nuit de Jérusalem* (1928), and *La Jérusalem retrouvée* (1930), show clearly her sympathy for the Zionist movement.

Bibliography: A. Mailloux, *Myriam Harry* (Fr., 1920); *Le Monde* (March 12, 1958). [M.C.]

HART, English family, sons of Hartwig (Naphtali Hertz) Moses, formerly of Breslau, later of Hamburg. The elder son Aaron Hart (Uri Phoebus; 1670–1756) first studied and taught in Poland. After 1705 he was appointed rabbi of the Ashkenazi community in London in succession to Judah Loeb b. Ephraim Anschel. The appointment was largely due to the influence of his wealthy brother Moses. Aaron was implicated in a dispute concerning the divorce of a member of the community, in defense of which he published his *Urim ve-Tummin* (1707), the first book printed entirely in Hebrew in London and his only literary production. He continued as rabbi of the Great Synagogue until his death. His authority was recognized in the Jewish communities that were springing up in the provincial towns, and he may be regarded as being informally the first chief rabbi of Great Britain. Edward Goldney, an English conversionist, engaged in a disputation with him in the last years of his life. His brother Moses (1675–1756) emigrated to England about 1697. Partly through the assistance and support of his cousin, the magnate Benjamin *Levi, he amassed a fortune as a broker. In 1722 he rebuilt the Ashkenazi synagogue (later the Great Synagogue) at his own expense and continued to control it until his death. He was highly regarded in government circles and was partly responsible for British diplomatic efforts at intervention at the time of the expulsion of the Jews from *Prague in 1745.

Figure 1. Moses Hart, English financier and synagogue benefactor. From a portrait formerly in the board room of the Great Synagogue, London.

Figure 2. Aaron Hart, regarded as the first English chief rabbi. Jerusalem, J.N.U.L., Schwadron Collection.

Bibliography: C. Roth, *History of the Great Synagogue* (1950), index; Busse, in: JHSET, 21 (1968), 138–47; Kaufmann, *ibid.*, 3 (1899), 105ff.; Adler, in: *Papers... Anglo-Jewish Historical Exhibition* (1888), 230–78; E. Goldney, *Friendly Epistle to Deists and Jews* (1759); DNB, s.v.

[C.R.]

HART, AARON (1724–1800), early settler in Canada. Hart was a native of London of Bavarian-born parents. He immigrated to New York via Jamaica about 1752. At the time of General Jeffrey Amherst's capture of Montreal in 1760, Hart was a commissary officer with the British troops. He stayed in Canada, settling in Trois Rivières, where he acquired considerable property and engaged in fur trade and other commercial pursuits. As seigneur of Becancour, Hart recruited a militia battalion which bore his name. The second post office established in British Canada was located in his home, with Hart as postmaster. He played a leading role in the public life of Trois Rivières, and was considered responsible for developing the town into an important trading center. The Hart family was identified with this city for more than a century. To avoid marrying outside his faith, Hart sailed to England and married his cousin Dorothea Catherine Judah, whose brothers had also settled in Trois Rivières. His prayer book reveals that he was an Ashkenazi Jew and kept his family records in Yiddish. By the time he died, Hart was reputed to be the wealthiest man in the British colonies.

Bibliography: Rosenbloom, Biogr Dict; R. Douville, *Aaron Hart* (Fr., 1938); A. Tessier, in: *Cahiers des Dix*, 3 (1938), 217–42; S. Rosenberg, *Jewish Community in Canada* (1970), index.

[B.G.K.]

HART, ABRAHAM (1810–1885), first important U.S. Jewish publishing executive and leading Philadelphia Jew of his generation. Hart was born in Philadelphia of German-Dutch parents. On the death of his father in 1823, he secured a job with Carey and Lea, the prominent publishing house founded by Matthew Carey. In 1829 he and Edward L. Carey established their own firm, E. L. Carey & A. Hart, which was soon in the first rank of American publishers. Among the authors they published were Macaulay, Thackeray, Longfellow, and James Fenimore Cooper. Although Carey died in 1845, Hart continued to use the name Carey and Hart until 1850, when his publications began to appear under the imprint A. Hart which he used until he retired in 1854. With his fortune made, Hart gave his time to civic activities and to investments in such fields as mining and sewing machines. He served as president of Mikveh Israel Congregation of Philadelphia for more than 30 years (1841–64 and 1867–76). Hart presided at the 1845 meeting that inaugurated the *Jewish Publication Society and was its president until a fire in his own building in 1851 wiped out almost the entire stock of the society's books. He was active in the agitation for a presidential pronouncement on the *Mortara Case in 1858. For three years beginning in 1866 he was president of the *Board of Delegates of American Israelites. Hart was treasurer of the *Hebrew Education Society in the years 1848–75 and was the first president of *Maimonides College. During his time no Jewish development of note in Philadelphia, and virtually none nationally, took place without his support.

Abraham Hart, U.S. publisher and philanthropist. From *American Jewish Historical Society Journal,* Vol. 48, 1958–59.

Bibliography: H. S. Morais, *Jews of Philadelphia* (1894), 53–58 and index; E. Wolf and M. Whiteman, *History of the Jews of Philadelphia* (1957), 352–3.

[B.W.K.]

HART, BENJAMIN (1779–1855), early Canadian army officer and magistrate. Hart was born in Trois Rivières, the third son of Aaron *Hart. In February 1811 he applied for a commission in the Lower Canada militia. Thomas Coffin,

Bank note issued by Hart's Bank, Trois Rivières, Canada, c. 1835. From A. D. Hart (ed.), *The Jew in Canada,* Toronto, 1926.

commander of the district, responded a year later advising against it on the grounds that Christian soldiers would not tolerate Jews in their midst. In August 1812 he wrote the governor refuting the objection with letters from a Catholic officer and a Protestant chaplain and pointing out Coffin's "private resentment" at being defeated by Benjamin's brother Ezekiel in the 1807 election. Nothing came of this exchange but despite this snub Benjamin Hart provided the sum of £1,000 to assist the paymaster in his needs. Shortly afterward Hart enlisted and saw active service in the War of 1812. Hart was justice of the peace in Montreal in 1837, and in the rebellion of that year and the following, he read the Riot Act and took an active role in quelling the disturbances, both as an army officer and magistrate. In 1826 he was president of the Shearith Israel Synagogue in Montreal.

Bibliography: Rosenbloom, Biogr Dict; J. J. Price, in AJHSP, 23 (1915), 137–40; S. Rosenberg, *Jewish Community in Canada* (1970), index.

[B.G.K.]

HART, BERNARD (1763–1855), American merchant, father of Congressman Emanuel B. *Hart. Hart was born in London to a family which probably originated in Fuerth.

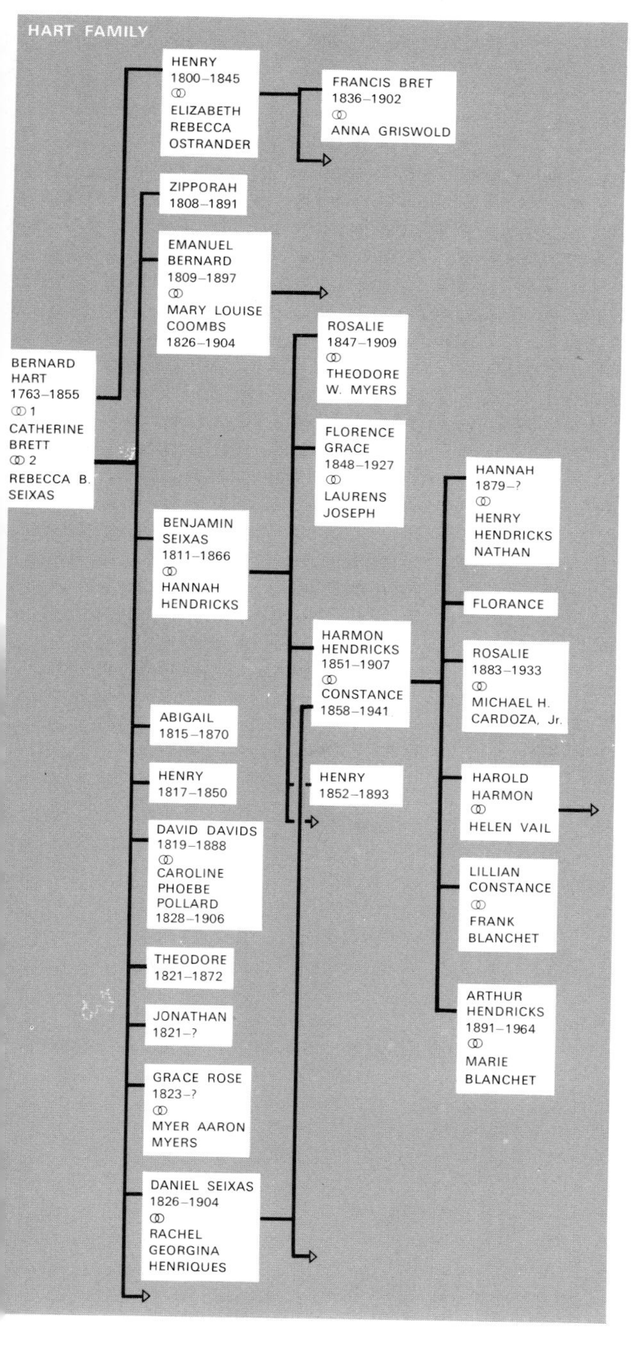

He had emigrated to Canada by 1776–77, and appears to have lived and traded in both Montreal and New York City until about 1800. In 1799 he was married to a non-Jewess, Catherine Brett, either in Canada or New York, but the

Bernard Hart, American merchant. From H. Simonhoff, *Jewish Notables in America*, New York, 1956.

marriage was a brief one. Catherine bore him one son, Henry, in whom Bernard took no interest aside from financial support. Henry's son was the literary figure Bret Harte. By the time of Bernard Hart's second marriage, in 1806, to Rebecca Seixas, niece of *ḥazzan* Gershom Mendes *Seixas, Hart had become *parnas* of Shearith Israel Congregation in New York, a post which he held for three years. He was active in the affairs of the congregation for many years, especially in its burial society. Hart is reported to have served as a quartermaster in the New York State Militia in 1787, and as a major during the War of 1812. He was a member of the committees which established the first New York Exchange office in 1792, and the New York Stock and Exchange Board in 1817, serving as secretary of the latter 1831–53.

Bibliography: Rosenbloom, Biogr Dict, s.v.; D. Pool, *Portraits Etched in Stone* (1952), index; H. Simonhoff, *Jewish Notables in America* (1956), 239–42.

[B.W.K.]

HART, CECIL M. (1883–1940), Canadian ice hockey pioneer. Born in Bedford, Quebec, a direct descendant of Aaron *Hart, Canada's first Jewish settler, Cecil Hart organized, managed, and played for the Star Hockey Club from 1900 to 1922. In 1910 he formed the Montreal City Hockey League, and his Stars became champions in 1914–15 and 1916–17. Hart organized the first international amateur hockey series between Canada and the United States. Entering professional hockey in 1921, Hart secured the Montreal Canadians of the National Hockey League for a group of businessmen and became manager. For six straight seasons they reached the championship playoffs. The Canadians won the Stanley Cup (emblematic of the world professional championship) in 1929–30 and 1930–31.

Bibliography: B. Postal et al. (eds.), *Encyclopedia of Jews in Sports* (1965), 333–4.

[J.H.S.]

HART, DANIEL (1800–1852), Jamaican lawyer and politician. A merchant in Kingston for over 30 years, Hart was the first Jew to be granted civil and political privileges in Jamaica. He was the senior representative for the Parish of St. Mary in the Jamaican House of Assembly and in 1851 was appointed *custos rotulrum* ("parish registrar"). For many years, he was an alderman and a member of the assembly for the city and parish of Kingston, as well as a justice of the peace and assistant judge of the Court of Common Pleas.

[B.H.]

HART, EMANUEL BERNARD (1809–1897), New York City Democratic politician and leader of Jewish institutions. Hart was born in New York City, son of Bernard Hart, a New York Stock Exchange member, and Rebecca Seixas Hart. He began his political activity in 1832 as a

Jacksonian Democrat, and became a member of the Tammany Society. He served for two terms as an alderman in New York City (1845–46). Defeated in his first campaign for the federal Congress, Hart won on the second try and served from 1851 to 1853. Among many other positions which he held throughout a long, but not particularly distinguished career of office-holding were: surveyor of the Port of New York (1857–62); a commissioner of Immigration (1870–73); a New York Excise commissioner (1880–83); disbursing agent at the New York custom house (1885–89); cashier in the New York County sheriff's office (1889–93). He was also an officer in the New York State Militia. In earlier years when he was not on the public payroll, Hart was a stock and bond broker, and in later years he was a merchant. Hart was a member of Shearith Israel Congregation, as was his father, and served as president of the Mount Sinai Hospital (1870–76), when the hospital's new structure on Lexington Avenue was dedicated. He was also president of the Hebrew Home for the Aged and Infirm.

Bibliography: Davis, in: AJHSP, 32 (1931), 99–111; M. U. Schappes (ed.), *Documentary History of the Jews in the United States* (1950), 285–6, 641. [B.W.K.]

HART, EPHRAIM (1747–1825), U.S. communal leader and stockbroker. Hart, who was born in Fuerth, Bavaria, went to New York before the outbreak of the American Revolution. After the British captured New York (1776), Hart moved to Philadelphia. He was one of the first members of the Spanish and Portuguese Synagogue in Philadelphia, dedicated in 1782. He returned to New York in 1787, became a stockbroker, and also speculated successfully in real estate. Hart was a charter member of the Board of Stock Brokers (1792). He served as an elector of Congregation Shearith Israel (1787) and was a founder of its burial society Hebra Hesed ve Emet (1802). Hart sat in the New York State Senate (1810) and was a business associate of John Jacob Astor. [Ed.]

HART, ERNEST ABRAHAM (1836–1898), British physician, medical editor, and humanitarian. Born and educated in London, during the Crimean War (1854) Hart led his fellow students in a successful appeal to the Admiralty to improve the status of the naval doctors aboard ship. At 20 he qualified as a specialist in opththalmology and in 1864 became an ophthalmologic surgeon and lecturer at St. Mary's Hospital in London. He introduced new methods in dealing with eye diseases, particularly in the treatment of aneurysm. Later he was appointed aural surgeon and dean of the medical school.

In 1858 he had begun writing for the medical journal, *Lancet*, and shortly thereafter was named coeditor. In 1866 he accepted the editorship of the *British Medical Journal*, the official publication of the British Medical Association. He expanded and improved the journal and through his efforts the membership of the Association increased rapidly. As chairman of its Parliamentary Bills Committee, he undertook a number of projects to eliminate the ills which militated against public health and sound social conditions in Britain. His exposure of the deplorable state of the London workhouse infirmaries led to the establishment of the Metropolitan Asylums Board and to better treatment of the sick among the poor. He campaigned against the evil of baby farming and it was largely through his efforts that the Infant Protection Act was passed in 1872. Hart had a large part in securing legislation ensuring the quality of the milk supply in cities, in abating the smoke nuisance, bettering working conditions in factories and safeguarding the health of workers. He worked for the amelioration of the plight of Irish peasants and for reclaiming of wasteland in Ireland. He attacked the Indian Government for its neglect in eliminating the conditions which produced cholera. He denounced the fraud of hypnotism and mesmerism in a series of articles, which appeared under the title of "The Eternal Gullible."

As a young man he had advocated the granting of equal rights to Jews in the columns of *Frazier's* magazine and in 1877 he published *The Mosaic Code*, which dealt with the hygienic laws of the Bible. [Ed.]

HART, EZEKIEL (1767-1843), early Canadian political figure. Hart was born in Trois Rivières, the second son of Aaron *Hart. He succeeded his father as seigneur of Becancour. In 1807 he was elected to the legislature of Lower Canada for Trois Rivières. Because of the sharp rivalry between the French and English camps he was prevented from taking his seat at the following session of the legislature in 1808. Regarding him as a member of the English faction the French-speaking deputies pointed out that as a Jew he could not take the oath "on the true faith of a Christian." He was reelected in May 1808, and in April 1809, he was again prevented from being seated.

Bibliography: Rosenbloom, Biogr Dict, 52; J. J. Price, in: AJHSP, 23 (1915), 43–53; S. Rosenberg, *Jewish Community of Canada* (1970), index. [B.G.K.]

HART, HERBERT LIONEL ADOLPHUS (1907–), British philosopher of law. From 1932 to 1940 he practiced at the Chancery Bar, and from 1939 to 1945 served in the British War Office. He returned to Oxford in 1945, becoming a fellow of University College, and professor of jurisprudence in 1952. His major writings include *Causation in the Law* (with A. M. Honoré, 1959); *The Concept of Law* (1961); *Punishment and the Elimination of Responsibility* (1962); *Law, Liberty and Morality* (1963); *The Morality of the Criminal Law* (1964). Each of these works is characterized by the application of the techniques of contemporary philosophy to areas of serious legal and moral contention. In general, Hart's work stands in opposition to philosophical determinism, the notion that nobody can act differently from the way he does, and therefore cannot be held responsible for what he does. To accept this point of view would risk blurring the general recognition that a man's fate should depend upon his choice, and with it the whole way of conceiving human relationships. Not only in the law or in morally crucial situations, but also in our everyday transactions we view one another as responsible and not "merely as alterable, predictable, curable, or manipulable things." [A.S.]

HART, ISAAC (d. 1780), U.S. merchant. Hart, a Loyalist, left England about 1750, and established himself in Rhode Island. He soon became one of the wealthiest merchants in the colony, and his prominent position made Hart a leader of *Newport's Jewish community. He served on the committee which raised funds for the building of Newport's Touro synagogue, was one of the purchasers of the land it stands on, and his firm, Naphthali Hart and Company, erected the building. In 1780 the revolutionary government of Rhode Island exiled him with other Loyalists, and in December he was killed, supposedly during an American raid on Fort George in New York.

Bibliography: Rosenbloom, Biogr Dict, s.v. [N.O.]

HART, JACOB (1745–1814), kabbalist and grammarian He was the first native-born English scholar of this type in the modern period. A jeweler by profession, Hart took an active part in communal affairs in London and received rabbinical ordination in Europe some time between 1800 and 1804. Under his Hebrew name of Eliakim b. Abraham he published various works in Hebrew on religion, Kabbalah, and grammar. They include *Asarah Ma'amarot,* of which five treatises only were published, three of them in England (1794–99); *Milḥamot Adonai,* a polemic in defense of religion against science and philosophy, sharply criticizing Voltaire and other rationalist writers; *Binah la-Ittim,* a computation of the date of the end of the world *(keẓ)* according to the Book of *Daniel, predicting it for 1843; *Ẓuf Novelot* on kabbalistic subjects; an abridgment of *Novelot Ḥokhmah* by Joseph Solomon *Delmedigo with notes and a commentary in which Hart attempted to prove *creatio ex nihilo.* Two of his works were published in Berlin in 1803, *Ma'yan Gannim,* an abridgment of *Ginnat Egoz* by Joseph b. Abraham *Gikatilla, and *Ein ha-Kore* on the Hebrew vowels, which contends that the Ashkenazi pronunciation is correct. In the same year Hart published in Roedelheim the grammatical treatise *Ein ha-Mishpat.* His works indicate that Hart was a man of broad general education.

Bibliography: A. Barnett and S. Brodetsky, in: JHSET, 14 (1940), 207–23; A. Barnett, *The Western Synagogue through Two Centuries* (1961), index. [C.R.]

HART, JOEL (1784–1842), U.S. doctor. Hart was born in Philadelphia and educated at the Royal College of Surgeons in London. Establishing himself in New York, Hart became a leader of the city's medical community. He was one of the charter members of the Medical Society of the County of New York (1806), and was among the group that founded the College of Physicians and Surgeons in 1807. Hart gave up his practice in 1817 to become United States consul at Leith, Scotland, a position he held until 1832. He then returned to New York where he practiced medicine until his death.

Bibliography: Rosenbloom, Biogr Dict, s.v. [N.O.]

HART, MOSS (1904–1961), U.S. playwright. Born and raised on New York's East Side, Hart wrote his first play when he was 12 and gained early experience as a producer in Jewish clubs. His first success was *Once in a Lifetime* (1930), a satire on Hollywood written in collaboration with George S. *Kaufman. With Kaufman he went on to write *Face the Music* (1932), a satire on New York municipal government which became an Irving *Berlin revue; *As Thousands Cheer* (1933), a revue with music by Irving Berlin; *Merrily We Roll Along* (1934), a satire on Broadway; and two famous comedies, *You Can't Take It With You* (1936), which won a Pulitzer Prize, and *The Man Who Came To Dinner* (1939). On his own, Hart wrote the satirical *George Washington Slept Here* (1940); the musical libretto for the *Lady In The Dark* (1941); and *The Climate of Eden* (1952). Hart's direction of *My Fair Lady,* the 1957 musical based on Shaw's *Pygmalion,* was widely acclaimed. Hart's autobiography, *Act One* (1959), a modest but moving story, was filmed shortly after his death.

Moss Hart, directing actress Audrey Hepburn. Courtesy Jewish Theatrical Guild, New York.

Bibliography: J. Gould, *Modern American Playwrights* (1966), 154–67. [B.G.]

HART, MYER (d. 1797), early American merchant, and a founder of the town of Easton, Pennsylvania, in 1752. Hart, an immigrant to the colonies, prospered with the town, and by 1763 was Easton's largest taxpayer and civic leader. Although he became a British subject in 1764, he actively supported the American Revolution. Hart was appointed to the Pennsylvania State Commission charged with the care of British prisoners of war, and in 1778 he testified that, despite contradictory reports, the Englishmen were well treated. In 1782 he moved to Philadelphia; his business there failed some years later.

Bibliography: E. Wolf and M. Whiteman, *History of the Jews of Philadelphia* (1957), index; Rosenbloom, Biogr Dict, s.v. incl. bibl. [N.O.]

HART, SAMUEL (c. 1747–1810), Nova Scotia merchant and politician. Hart is known to have settled in the British colony of Nova Scotia, to have been a dry goods merchant in Halifax in the 1780s, and to have lived at Maroon Hall, in Preston. He was a member of the small Jewish community which existed in Nova Scotia in the second half of the 18th century and which dwindled and expired by the mid-19th century. From 1793 to 1799 Hart was a member of the Nova Scotia House of Assembly for Liverpool Township, thus becoming the first Jew to sit in a legislative body in territory that was later to become Canada. [B.G.K.]

HART, SOLOMON ALEXANDER (1806–1881), English painter. Solomon was the son of a Plymouth silversmith, who moved with his family to London in 1820. First apprenticed to an engraver, Hart entered the Royal Academy as a student in 1823; three years later he exhibited a miniature portrait of his father. He continued for a time to paint miniatures for a livelihood. In 1828 he showed his first oil at the British Institute, and, two years later, "Elevation of the Law" (now in the Tate Gallery, London), also called "Interior of a Jewish Synagogue at the Time of the Reading of the Law" (depicting the interior of the former Polish synagogue in London). An associate of the Royal Academy in 1835 and a full member five years later, he was professor of painting at the Royal Academy from 1854 to 1863. In his last eighteen years he served there as librarian. Hart's crowded canvases usually illustrate famous episodes of English history, and are done in the formal, dignified academic style that matured in the Regency period. Paintings on Jewish themes are also frequent. His "Rejoicing of the Law in the Ancient Synagogue at Leghorn" represents the procession of the Scrolls on Simḥat Torah. His painting "Manasseh ben Israel" was destroyed in the London blitz during World War II. [A.W.]

HARTFORD, capital of Connecticut. Population (1969 est.) of greater Hartford, 300,000; Jewish population, 30,000.

Early History. Hartford's town records reveal an early Jewish presence in colonial times. General court proceedings in 1659 mention a certain "David the Jew," an itinerant peddler; in 1661 a party of Jews in the city was given permission "to sojourn in Hartford seven months";

in 1667 "Jacob the Jew" transported horses to New York; in 1669 "David Jew" and "Jacob Jew" were among the 721 inhabitants listed in the town records. Advertisements in *The Hartford Courant* in 1788 and 1801 contain references to a thoroughfare known as "Jew Street," but whether it was actually inhabited at the time by Jews or Jewish merchants is unknown.

Jewish settlement in Hartford did not begin in earnest, however, until the 1840s with the first wave of immigrants from Germany. In 1847 Congregation Beth Israel was formed with an initial membership of six; four years later it had 150 members "of thriving business and good standing in society." A B'nai B'rith lodge was established in 1851, and in 1854 a *Frauen Verein* was organized to provide mutual aid and serve as a center of social activities. In 1856 Beth Israel acquired its first permanent structure, a refurbished Baptist church, and engaged Rabbi Isaac Mayer (1809–1898), who served for 12 years. With growing affluence and acculturation, the congregation erected a new synagogue in 1876, and in 1878 dropped its traditional orientation to join the Reform Union of American Hebrew Congregations.

East European Immigration. As a result of the great East European immigration to America, Hartford's Jewish population increased from 1,500 in 1880 to over 7,000 in 1910 and to almost 20,000 by 1920. The new immigrants founded the Adas Israel Synagogue in 1884, the Agudas Achim Synagogue in 1887, and six other Orthodox synagogues in the ensuing years. Two East European rabbis, Isaac S. Hurewitz, who served in Hartford from 1893 to 1935, and Zemach Hoffenberg, who served from 1899 to 1938, ministered to these congregations. Other Jewish institutions and organizations sprang up: the Hartford Sick Benefit Association and the Hebrew Ladies Benevolent Society in 1898; the B'nai Zion Society, which sponsored a group of 12 Zionist clubs, also in 1898; the Hebrew Institute Talmud Torah in 1901; the Hebrew Home for the Aged in 1907, the Hebrew Home for Children in 1907; the Council of Jewish Women in 1910; and a chapter of the Labor Zionist Farband in 1914. In 1912 some 30 of these organizations merged to form the United Jewish Charities. A Hadassah chapter was set up by Henrietta Szold in 1914, and in 1918, through the joint efforts of five local branches of the Workmen's Circle, the Labor Lyceum opened its doors. Among the immigrants were some who added new dimensions to Hartford's economic life: expert furriers from Russia helped make Hartford a center of the fur trade, and skilled Jewish carpenters and cabinetmakers introduced the reproduction of antique furniture.

Post-World War I. Between the two world wars, with the cutoff of mass immigration, Hartford's Jewish community grew at a slower pace; this period was primarily one of further consolidation and integration into the general life of the city. Hartford's first Conservative congregation, the Emanuel Synagogue, was organized in 1919. Its first Jewish country club, the Tumble Brook Country and Golf Club, was opened in 1922. Mount Sinai Hospital, the first and only Jewish hospital in the state, was established in 1923. The weekly *Jewish Ledger*, founded by Samuel Neusner in 1929, with Rabbi Abraham J. Feldman as editor, has chronicled Jewish activity in the city. In 1935 a Jewish Community Council was formed, and in 1937, the Jewish Welfare Fund; the merger of these two organizations into a single Federation in 1945 united all Jewish communal and philanthropic endeavors under one roof. A Yeshiva Day School, established in 1940, had 12 grades, with several hundred students, in 1970.

During the post-World War II period, Jewish community life in Greater Hartford centered around the city's

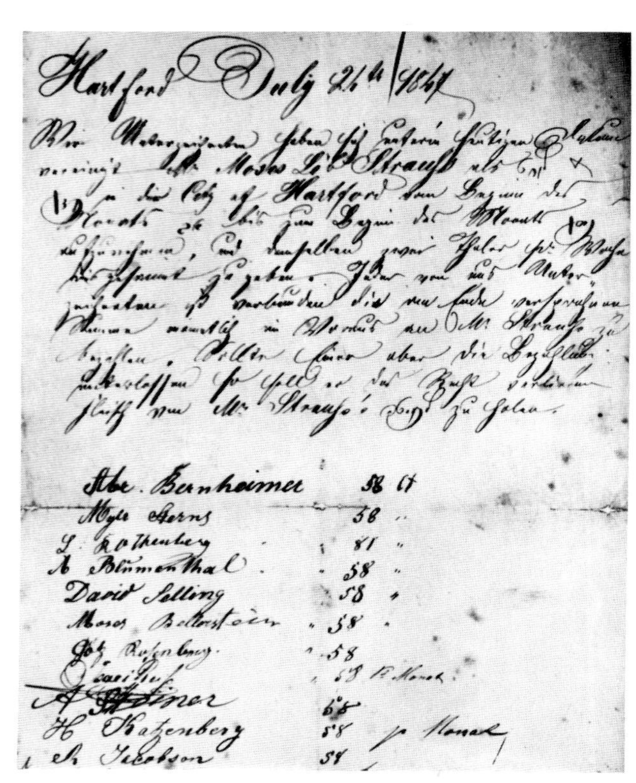

Agreement appointing Moses Leib Straus *shoḥet* and *ḥazzan* of Hartford, Connecticut, and specifying the monthly contributions of members of the congregation towards his remuneration of two dollars a week, 1847. Courtesy Morris Silverman, Hartford, Conn.

synagogues—11 Conservative, 8 Orthodox, and 3 Reform and around its Jewish Community Center, built in 1955, with over 7,000 members. Prominent rabbis in the community have included Morris *Silverman (1923–), Abraham J. Feldman (1925–), Abraham Avrutick (1946–), and William Cohen (1946–). In all, Greater Hartford had 132 Jewish philanthropic, religious, cultural, and social organizations (1970).

The economic life of the Jewish population is concentrated in the professions and in business. Over one-fifth of Hartford's doctors, approximately one-third of its dentists and attorneys, and one-half of its certified public accountants are Jews. Jews own over half of Hartford's retail businesses, although less than two percent of the city's commercial bank executives and barely one percent of the executives in the ten largest insurance companies are Jewish. At the University of Hartford Jews comprise roughly 20% of the faculty and 33% of the student body. As is the tendency elsewhere, Hartford's Jews moved in increasing numbers to the suburbs, so that in 1970 the majority lived outside the city proper.

Jews in Public Life. Between 1860 and 1969, 102 Jews were elected to city and town councils; 34 served in the state legislature since 1919. In 1933 Herman P. *Kopplemann became the first Jew from Hartford to be elected to Congress, where he served four terms. Some Hartfordites holding public office are Morris Silverman, chairman and member of the Connecticut State Commission on Human Rights and Opportunities from 1943; Bernard Shapiro, state welfare commissioner during 1959–70; Elisha Freedman, city manager, from 1963; M. Joseph Blumenfield, U.S. District Court judge from 1964; and Louis Shapiro and Abraham S. Bordon on the state judiciary. Annie Fisher was the first Jewish district superintendent of schools. Hartford's best-known Jewish citizen is Abraham A. *Ribicoff, who was governor of Connecticut and then elected to the Senate.

Jews have played an active role in Hartford's educational and cultural life. They are prominent in the University of Hartford, and the Hartford Symphony Orchestra.

Bibliography: M. Silverman, *Hartford Jews: 1659–1969* (1970).

[Mo.S.]

HARTGLAS, MAXIMILIAN MEIR APOLINARY (1883–1953), Zionist leader in Poland during the interwar period. Born in Biala Podlaska, Hartglas studied law at Warsaw University and from 1907 to 1919 practiced his profession in Siedlce. After serving in the czarist army in World War I and in the Polish army in the Polish-Soviet war in 1920, he was elected a member of the Sejm (Polish parliament). Joining Y. *Gruenbaum in a faction that opposed the Polish government's discriminatory policy toward the Jews, he was instrumental in obtaining the repeal of anti-Semitic czarist laws in Poland's former Russian provinces. Hartglas served as the defense attorney in several famous Polish trials, in which the true reason for the indictment was the fact that the accused were Jews. At an early age he took part in the struggle for Polish independence, Jewish defense, and Zionist activities. He was among those who formulated the theory of the Diaspora work program for Zionism at the *Helsingfors Conference (1906). Hartglas served as chairman of the Polish Zionist Organization and of the "club" of Jewish deputies in the Sejm. He settled in Palestine in 1940 and joined the staff of the *Jewish Agency. Upon the establishment of the state (1948), he became director general and later legal adviser of the Ministry of the Interior. Throughout his life he published articles on the problems of Polish Jewry and Zionism in various languages, to which he added Hebrew after his settlement in Israel.

Bibliography: LNYL, 3 (1960), 73–74; Tidhar, 3 (1958), 1129–30; *Polski Słownik Biograficzny*, 9 (1960–61), 295; A. Haftka, in: I. Schiper (ed.), *Żydzi w Polsce odrodzonej*, 10 (1933), 313–59.

[G.K.]

HARTMANN, HEINZ (1894–1970), psychoanalyst. Hartmann, who was born in Vienna, was leading theoretician in psychoanalysis and a pioneer in the field of psychoanalytic ego psychology. In 1939 he published his paper *Ich-Psychologie und Anpassungsproblem*, translated into English in 1958 as *Ego Psychology and the Problem of Adaptation*. Like Anna *Freud, he emphasized the activities of that psychic construct, the ego, as no less important than that of the drives, the id. He pointed out the importance of man's adapting to an "average expectable environment" as a function of the ego. In the same paper, he defined the "conflict-free sphere of the ego"—where patterns of behavior develop independently of unconscious intrapsychic conflict; they do so either, primarily, through inborn autonomous ego functions or, secondarily, by gaining autonomy from the conflicts which helped bring them about. A student of Freud, Hartmann amplified and elaborated numerous aspects of psychoanalytic theory, including the relation of intrapsychic events and of psychoanalysis to the environment, to society, and to the social sciences. He emigrated to Switzerland in 1938 and in 1941 settled in the United States. He served as president of the International and New York Psychoanalytic Associations (1951–57 and 1952–54 respectively). In 1959 he was made honorary president of the International Association.

Bibliography: L. Eidelberg (ed.), *Encyclopedia of Psychoanalysis* (1968), index; A. Grinstein, *Index of Psychoanalytic Writings*, 2 (1957) 7 (1964); R. M. Loewenstein, in: F. Alexander et al., *Psychoanalytic Pioneers* (1966), 469–83, includes bibliography.

[R.Mo.]

HARTMANN, MORITZ (1821–1872), German author and revolutionary. Hartmann was born in Dušniky, near Přibram, Bohemia. One of the first Jewish youngsters in Bohemia to receive a general high school education, Hartmann demonstratively abandoned Judaism as a youth, although he never formally converted to Christianity. Extolling the Hussites and the revived Czech national feeling of his time in *Kelch und Schwert* (1845) and *Boehmische Elegien*, he transferred the Jewish yearning for Zion to the Czech longing for independence and spoke of Prague as the "Slavic Jerusalem." Austrian objections to Hartmann's pro-German sympathies resulted in his flight to Leipzig and eventually to Paris, where he met *Heine and George Sand. Returning to Prague in 1847, he was briefly imprisoned and then became the central figure in "Young Bohemia," a group of German writers which included Siegfried *Kapper (later Hartmann's brother-in-law) and Friedrich Hirsch-Szarvady, later a Hungarian nationalist. Faced with the anti-Jewish excesses of the 1840s, Hartmann blamed the Czech people for the Prague disturbances and for the anti-Semitic tendencies of Czech nationalist leaders such as Karel *Havliček-Borovský. He turned to German liberalism, and in 1848 he was elected delegate to the revolutionary German national assembly in Frankfort, where he was a popular idol of the extreme left and was made a member of the assembly's delegation to Vienna.

Following Windischgraetz's suppression of the revolution, Hartmann became a fugitive and expressed his disappointment and anger with the liberals in his satirical *Reimchronik des Pfaffen Mauritius* (1849). His experiences during the 1848 Revolution and abortive Baden uprising were summarized in *Bruchstuecke revolutionaerer Erinnerungen* (1861). Hartmann earned his living as a foreign correspondent, particularly during the Crimean War (1854), after which he moved first to Paris and then to Geneva, where he taught German literature from 1860 onward and married a Protestant. Following the general amnesty of 1868 he returned to Vienna and joined the editorial staff of the *Neue Freie Presse*. The many novellas which Hartmann published during the 1850s–1860s include a few stories on Jewish themes. His collected works in ten volumes appeared posthumously in 1873–74 and a selection of his letters (ed. R. Wolkan) in 1921.

His son, Ludo Moritz Hartmann (1865–1924), was a prominent Austrian Social Democrat and, as a result of his

Moritz Hartmann, German writer and revolutionary. Engraving by A. Weger. New York, Leo Baeck Institute.

atheism and political activities, was denied a chair in history at the University of Vienna until after the fall of the Hapsburgs in 1918. Ludo Hartmann founded the *Vierteljahresschrift fuer Sozial- und Wirtschaftsgeschichte,* his major work being a comprehensive *Geschichte Italiens im Mittelalter* (4 vols., 1897–1915). He was the Austrian republic's ambassador in Berlin from 1918 until 1921.

Bibliography: O. Wittner, *Moritz Hartmanns Jugend* (1903); idem, in: Moritz Hartmann, *Gesammelte Werke* (1906–07), vols. 1–2, *Moritz Hartmanns Leben und Werke;* O. Donath, in: JGGJČ, 6 (1934), 323–442 passim; M. Grunwald, *Vienna* (1936), index; J. Goldmark, *Pilgrims of '48* (1930), index; H. Bergmann, in: G. Kisch (ed.), *Czechoslovak Jewry, Past and Future* (1943), 22–24; G. Kisch, *In Search of Freedom* (1949), index; A. Hofman, *Die Prager Zeitschrift "Ost und West"* (1957), index; *The Jews of Czechoslovakia* (1968), index.

[Ed.]

HARTOG, LEVIE DE (1835–1918), jurist and orientalist. Born at Gorinchem, Holland, he was professor of public law at the University of Amsterdam from 1877 to 1906, and served from 1887 on the board of trustees of the Nederlands Israëlietisch Seminarium, the Jewish theological seminary of Amsterdam. Hartog published a textbook on Dutch public law, collated the Leiden manuscripts for M. Steinschneider's *Alfabeta de-Ben-Sira* (Berlin, 1858), and wrote a biography in Dutch of his teacher of oriental languages, R. P. Dozy. [F.J.H.]

HARTOG, SIR PHILIP JOSEPH (1864–1947), British educator. His mother was Marion Moss who with her sister Celia had published pioneer sketches of Jewish history in English. Hartog, who was born in London, began his career as lecturer in chemistry at Owens College, Manchester (1891). He became academic registrar of the University of London in 1903. Hartog did extensive chemical research and published the results of his investigations on the thermochemistry of the sulphites, the flame spectrum of nickel compounds, and the latent heat of steam. He was associated with the founding of the School of Oriental and African Studies in London. He was a member of the Viceroy's Commission on the University of Calcutta, India, in 1917. From 1920 to 1925 Hartog served as the first vice-chancellor of the University of Dacca, Bengal. He was instrumental in the creation of the National Foundation for Educational Research, London, to study the nature and purpose of school examinations. He played a leading role in the improvement of school and college examinations. In 1930 Hartog was knighted for distinguished public service. In 1933 he went to Palestine as chairman of the committee of inquiry on the organization of the Hebrew University in Jerusalem. In the same year he became chairman of the

Sir Philip Joseph Hartog, British author and educator. From M. Hartog, *P. J. Hartog; a Memoir . . .,* London, 1949.

Jewish Professional Committee to assist refugees from Germany. He was chairman of the Liberal Jewish Synagogue and active in the Anglo-Jewish Association and Board of Deputies of British Jews. Hartog's works include: *The Writing of English* (1907), *Blaise Pascal* (1927), *Joseph Priestly and his Place in the History of Science* (1931), *Some Aspects of Indian Education, Past and Present* (1939), and *Words in Action* (1947).

Hartog's brother, Numa Edward (1865–1871), was a mathematician who had attracted attention when in 1869 he had graduated as Senior Wrangler at Cambridge University but as a Jew had not been admitted to a fellowship. Their cousin was the philosopher H. *Bergson.

Bibliography: M. H. Hartog. P. J. Hartog: *a Memoir by his Wife Mabel Hartog* (1949). [Er.S.]

HARTOGENSIS, BENJAMIN HENRY (1865–1939), U.S. jurist, historian, and civic leader. Hartogensis, born in Baltimore, was a lifelong resident there, practicing law from 1893. He wrote for the Baltimore *Sun* and *Baltimore American,* and for Jewish publications, including the (Philadelphia) *Jewish Exponent,* of which he was an associate editor, and the *Publications of the American Jewish Historical Society.* Hartogensis' major interests were legal and historical, particularly the history of religious liberty in America, including Jewish law (especially marital) and biblical influences on American law. A leader in civic and Jewish organizations, Hartogensis was a founder of Baltimore's night schools, and the Baltimore branch of the Alliance Israélite Universelle. He established the Jewish legal section of the Baltimore Law Library. [R.S.G.]

HARZFELD (Postrelko), AVRAHAM (1888–), labor leader in Ereẓ Israel. Born in Stavishche, Ukraine, he studied at the yeshivot of Berdichev and Telz, receiving a rabbinical diploma. In 1906 he joined the Russian Socialist Zionist Party (S.S.), for which he was twice arrested and imprisoned for two years in Vilna. In 1910 he was sentenced to life imprisonment with hard labor in Siberia, but in 1914 escaped from Siberia and reached Ereẓ Israel, where he worked as an agricultural laborer in Petaḥ Tikvah and was active in the labor movement. During World War I he played an important role in helping Jews who had been arrested by the Turks, including members of the secret *Nili group. Harzfeld was a member of *Po'alei Zion (1914–19), *Aḥdut ha-Avodah (1919–30), and *Mapai (from 1930) and was one of the founders of the *Histadrut in 1920. From 1919 he was a prominent member of the Histadrut's earlier Central Agricultural Council (Ha-Merkaz ha-Ḥakla'i) and in over 40 years of office played an important role in planning agricultural settlement in Palestine. He initiated many settlement projects and followed with dedication and diligence the development of new settlements throughout the country. For more than 40 years, including the difficult *Tower and Stockade period, there was hardly an

Avraham Harzfeld (front row, hand raised) with the first settlers at Ḥanita, March 1938. Courtesy J.N.F., Jerusalem.

establishment of a new settlement at which Harzfeld was not personally present. He was a member of the Zionist General Council from 1921, a member of the directorate of the Jewish National Fund from 1949, and a Mapai Knesset member in the first, second, and third Knesset. He became known for the "ḥasidic" atmosphere of enthusiastic group singing, which he introduced in intervals at the meetings of Zionist and *yishuv* bodies.

Bibliography: S. Kushnir, *The Village Builder: biography of A. Harzfield* (1967).

[G.El.]

ḤASAN, ABU ALI JEPHETH IBN BUNDĀR (second half of 11th century), thought to be one of the first of the Yemenite *negidim* who lived in Aden between the 11th and early 14th centuries. His name indicates he was of Persian origin. According to genizah fragments and tombstone inscriptions, Jewish leadership was transferred from San'a to Aden, because of the rising importance of the latter's port as a center of trade between Egypt and India. According to documents connected with Ḥasan's name, he was active during the second half of the 11th century until approximately its close. One of the documents contains the date 1409 of the Seleucid era (1097/98 C.E.).

As a wealthy man who engaged in trade with India and served as a "traders' official" in Aden, i.e., a colleague and representative of the traders, Ḥasan was also a public leader. He was called "the head of the communities," meaning that he had authority over the Jewish communities of southern Yemen. His title *nagid* is found in the eulogy of the Tunisian trader Abraham b. Peraḥyah b. Yajo for his son Maḍmūm: "and all the community called him *nagid* the son *[nin]* of a *nagid* " (*nin* being son according to Targ. Onk., Gen. 21:23). Ḥasan's descendants were also wealthy traders who signed agreements with tribal chiefs and pirates in control of the sea routes from Egypt, by way of the Red Sea, to India, thus assuring freedom of navigation and trade. They were also called *negidim* and were active in public life in Yemen. They had connections mainly with the Palestinian academy in Egypt.

Bibliography: E. Strauss, in: *Zion*, 4 (1939), 217–31; S. D. Goitein, in: *Sinai*, 33 (1953), 225–37; idem, in: Jewish Theological Seminary, N.Y., *Sefer ha-Yovel... M. M. Kaplan* (1953), 45, 51–53; idem, in: *Tarbiz*, 31 (1961/62), 357–70; idem, in: Y. Ratzaby (ed.), *Bo'i Teiman* (1967), 15–25; idem, in: JQR, 53 (1962/63), 97; E. Subar, *ibid.*, 49 (1958/59), 301–9; J. Mann, in: HUCA, 3 (1926), 301–3.

[El.B.]

ḤASAN (Hussein) BEN MASHI'AḤ (tenth century), Karaite scholar. According to *Ibn al-Hītī he lived in Baghdad, where he held religious *disputations with the Christian scholar Abu Ali ʿIsā ibn Zarʿa. *Sahl b. Maẓli'aḥ states that Ḥasan had disputations with Saadiah Gaon (d. 942), which seems chronologically unlikely. Ḥasan also wrote a polemical treatise against Saadiah, passages of which are incorporated in the *Eshkol ha-Kofer* of Judah *Hadassi and in a manuscript in Leningrad. A remark of *Ibn Ezra in the introduction to his commentary on the Pentateuch suggests that Ḥasan wrote biblical commentaries.

Bibliography: S. Poznański, *Karaite Literary Opponents of Saadiah Gaon* (1908), 15f.; Mann, Texts, 2 (1935), index.

[L.N.]

ḤASDAI (Ḥisdai), name of four Babylonian exilarchs. Ḥasdai ben Bustanai lived in the 7th century. Both he and his brother Baradoi served as exilarchs following the death of their father, *Bustanai, in about 670. The two brothers attempted to undermine the position of the sons of their father's Persian wife, alleging that she had the status of a female prisoner of war who had not been manumitted. Ḥasdai ben Baradoi (d. 733?) was exilarch at the beginning of the 8th century. He was the father-in-law of R. Natronai b. Nehemiah, the head of the Pumbedita academy. Various legends are told about him in Arab chronicles. His son *Solomon was exilarch from 733 to 759, if not later. His second son, David, was the father of *Anan, founder of the Karaite sect. Ḥasdai ben Natronai was exilarch during the first half of the 9th century.

Ḥasdai ben David ben Hezekiah (The Second) was exilarch in the 12th century (d. before 1135). During this period the office of exilarch gained in prestige and its bearers had great influence at the court of the caliph Muhammad al-Muktafi, who appointed him as exilarch. Benjamin of Tudela, the 12th-century traveler, reports that Ḥasdai was one of the teachers of David *Alroy, the false Messiah. His son Daniel took his place as exilarch. Abraham *ibn Ezra may have met him during his visit to Baghdad in 1139. He died a year before *Pethahiah of Regensburg's visit to Baghdad in about 1175.

Bibliography: M. N. Adler (ed.), *Masot Binyamin mi-Tudela*, (1907), 54 (Eng. pt.); Pethahiah of Regensburg, *Sibbuv*, ed. by L. Gruenhut (1905), 9; S. Poznański, *Babylonische Geonim im nachgaonaeischen Zeitalter* (1914), 115–8; Ch. Tykocinski, in: *Devir*, 1 (1923), 145–79; J. Mann, in: *Sefer... S. A. Poznański* (1927), 23; Mann, Texts, 1 (1931), 208–9, 211, 228; S. Abramson, in: KS, 26 (1950), 93–94.

[A.D.]

HASENCLEVER, WALTER (1890–1940), German poet and playwright. Born in Aachen of a Jewish mother and a non-Jewish father, Hasenclever served in the German army during World War I but his experiences made him a pacifist. After 1918 he worked for a time as a foreign correspondent in Paris and the U.S. Leaving Germany in 1933, he eventually settled in France. After the French collapse in 1940, Hasenclever was twice interned and, fearing the arrival of the Nazis, committed suicide in a detention camp near Aix-en-Provence. A friend of the critic Kurt Pinthus and of Franz *Werfel, Hasenclever was an early expressionist who became famous with his revolutionary drama, *Der Sohn* (1914). This dealt with the conflict between the generations and preached resistance to blind authority. Three verse collections were *Der Juengling* (1913), *Tod und Auferstehung* (1917), and *Gedichte an Frauen* (1922). His pacifist ideas were expressed in the tragedy *Antigone* (1917), while satire and pathos distinguished such later dramas as *Die Menschen* (1918), *Der Retter* (1919), *Gobseck* (1922), and *Mord* (1926). In *Jenseits* (1920) Hasenclever briefly turned to the occult. From the late 1920s he wrote plays in a more comic or ironic spirit, such as *Ehen werden im Himmel geschlossen* (1929) and *Napoleon greift ein* (1930). He also wrote German versions of foreign plays and films, one of his collaborators being Ernst *Toller. His drama *Muenchhausen* appeared posthumously in 1947.

Bibliography: K. Pinthus, in: W. Hasenclever, *Gedichte, Dramen, Prosa* (1963), 6–62; H. Kesten, *Meine Freunde, die Poeten* (1959), 229–36; A. Soergel and C. Hohoff, *Dichtung und Dichter der Zeit*, 2 (1963), 274–81.

[Ed.]

HA-SHAḤAR (Heb. הַשַּׁחַר), Hebrew journal which was published and edited in Vienna by Peretz *Smolenskin from 1868 to 1884. During these 16 years, 12 volumes of *Ha-Shaḥar* were published. In theory *Ha-Shaḥar* was a monthly; in practice, however, the financial and organizational difficulties caused prolonged interruptions in its regular appearances. In his first article *"Petaḥ Davar"* ("Preface") Smolenskin describes its aims: the diffusion of *Haskalah; war against its Orthodox opponents, especially the Ḥasidim; war against assimilationists and religious reformers; and defense of the national values of the nation and the Hebrew language. Smolenskin molded the image of *Ha-Shaḥar* as an independent and militant journal. *Ha-Shaḥar* was initially designed mainly for Russian Jews. Because of Russian restrictions against the Hebrew press, however, it was published in Vienna, from where copies were sent to the offices of the censor in Russia before distribution through agents in Russia. Sometimes, an article which the censor was liable to reject was published in a special supplement, and sent to the subscribers in Russia in sealed envelopes separately from the regular copy. Outside Russia as well, *Ha-Shaḥar* acquired a large audience of readers, especially in Austria, Galicia, and Rumania. The number of subscribers to the annual fluctuated between 800 to 1,300.

Subscriptions covered only a part of the expenses even though the publisher did not pay fees to his writers and carried out himself a large part of the proofreading and the distribution of the copies to the subscribers. Smolenskin invested his own money in *Ha-Shaḥar* and was supported by contributors from among the well-to-do *maskilim*, and subsidies from the *Alliance Israélite Universelle in Paris and the Ḥevrat Mefiẓei ha-Haskalah ("Society for the Dissemination of the Haskalah") in St. Petersburg.

Ha-Shaḥar published belles lettres and articles dealing with Jewish scholarly matters and current affairs. Among the Hebrew writers of the generation who contributed were M. D. *Brandstadter, R. A. Broides, the poets J. L. *Gordon, A. B. *Gottlober, J. L. *Levin (Yehalel), I. *Kaminer, S. *Mandelkern, and M. M. *Dolitzki. There, too, Smolenskin published his novels *(Ha-To'eh be-Darkhei ha-Ḥayyim, Simḥat Ḥanef, Kevurat Ḥamor, Ha-Yerushah, Nakam Berit)*. The works are written mainly

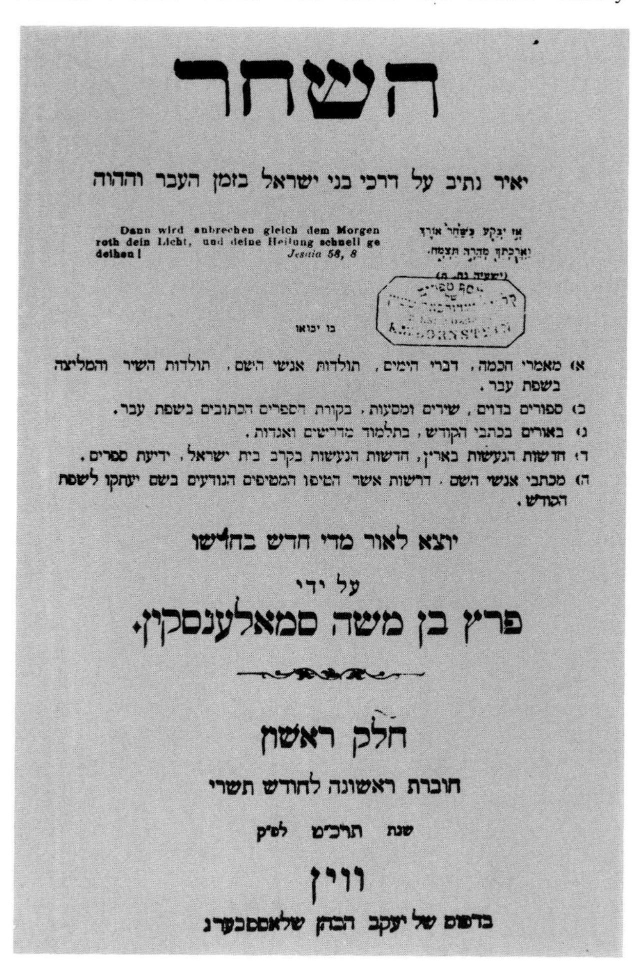

השחר

יאיר נתיב על דרכי בני ישראל בזמן העבר וההוה

אז יבקע כשחר אורך וארכתך מהרה תצמח.
(ישעיה נח, ח)

Dann wird anbrechen gleich dem Morgenroth dein Licht, und deine Heilung schnell gedeihen! *Jesaia 58, 8*

בו יבואו

א) מאמרי חכמה, דברי הימים, תולדות אנשי השם, תולדות השיר והמליצה בשפת עבר.
ב) ספורים בדוים, שירים ומסעות, בקורת הספרים הכתובים בשפת עבר.
ג) באורים בכתבי הקודש, בתלמוד מדרשים ואגדות.
ד) חדשות הנעשות בארץ, חדשות הנעשות בקרב בית ישראל, ידיעת ספרים.
ה) מכתבי אנשי השם, דרשות אשר הטיפו המטיפים הנודעים בשם יעתקו לשפת הקודש.

יוצא לאור מדי חדש בחדשו

על ידי

פרץ בן משה סמאלענסקין.

חלק ראשון

חוברת ראשונה לחודש תשרי

שנת תרכ״ט לפ״ק

ווין

בדפוס של יעקב הכהן שלאססבערג

Front page of the first issue of the Hebrew journal *Ha-Shaḥar*, Vienna, Tishri, 1868. Jerusalem, J.N.U.L.

in the flowery *maskil* style. Most condemn the rabbinical orthodoxy of the time and especially the Ḥasidim, but at the same time assail the assimilationist *maskilim*. Socialistic undertones are heard especially in Yehalel's poetry (*"Kishron ha-Ma'aseh,"* and others).

In the area of Judaic studies *Ha-Shaḥar* published works of scholars from Western and Eastern Europe, including Solomon *Rubin, David *Kahana, Y. *Reifman, S. *Buber I. H. *Weiss, S. *Sachs, Meir *Ish-Shalom (Friedmann), A. *Jellinek, J. H. *Gurland, A. E. *Harkavy, Ḥ. Z. *Lerner, A. *Krochmal, E. Shulman, and D. Holub. *Ha-Shaḥar* also published letters of Jewish scholars and authors of the early Haskalah: S. J. *Rapoport, S. *Luzzatto, and J. *Perl. Most of the book reviews were written by Smolenskin.

Of prime historical importance were the articles which dealt with current problems. Smolenskin himself published his major articles on Jewish problems in which he introduced his nationalist ideology. These views, and especially his attack on *Mendelssohn, the cultural hero of the Haskalah, alienated many of his supporters, and by the end of 1880 Smolenskin was forced to discontinue publication. With the rise of the Ḥibbat Zion movement in the wake of the pogroms of 1881, Smolenskin renewed the publication of *Ha-Shaḥar* which now openly advocated the Ḥibbat Zion program for Jewish settlement in Ereẓ Israel. Smolenskin filled *Ha-Shaḥar* with dozens of articles on the new movement. He attacked the Alliance Israélite Universelle, which had once supported him, for their opposition to Jewish settlement in Ereẓ Israel. E. *Ben-Yehuda, M. L. *Lilenblum, A. S. *Freidberg, A. A. *Sirotkin, and others now wrote in *Ha-Shaḥar*. In spite of his weakening state of health, Smolenskin continued to publish *Ha-Shaḥar* until his death, after which his brother, Y. L. Smolenskin, published the last four copies, completing the 12th volume.

Bibliography: Klausner, Sifrut, 5 (1955[2]), index; A. Sha'anan, *Ha-Sifrut ha-Ivrit ha-Ḥadashah li-Zerameha*, 2 (1962), 44–47; A. Kristianpoller, *Die hebraeische Publizistik in Wien*, abt. 3 (1930).

[Y.S.]

HA-SHILO'AḤ (Ha-Shillo'aḥ; Heb. הַשִּׁלוֹחַ), Hebrew literary, social, and scientific monthly in Russia until World War I. Founded in 1896, *Ha-Shilo'aḥ* was first edited by *Aḥad Ha-Am in Odessa and Warsaw and printed in Berlin and Cracow until after the Russian revolution of 1905. From 1907 to 1919 it was edited and printed in Odessa, while from 1920 until it ceased publication in 1926, it was edited and printed in Jerusalem. Altogether 46 volumes appeared in 23 years of publication (there were intervals during which the monthly did not publish, e.g., the Russian revolution of 1905, in 1915 under the czarist regime, in 1919 under the Soviet regime).

Aḥad Ha-Am intended *Ha-Shilo'aḥ* to be a journal devoted to Zionism, Jewish scholarship, and belles lettres in a style accessible to the general reader. Not believing in art for art's sake, he was interested in making literature serve the monthly's general objectives of Zionism and "usefulness" to the people. This approach was attacked by young authors (*Berdyczewski, in particular) and the controversy helped determine the course of Hebrew literature in the early 20th century. *Ha-Shilo'aḥ* expressed Aḥad Ha-Am's bitter antagonism to Herzl and political Zionism, which elicited a strong reaction from the Zionist movement. The writing in *Ha-Shilo'aḥ* was free of rhetoric, the result of the great effort Aḥad Ha-Am spent, as his letters testify, in guiding the writers and editing their work. Thus the monthly, which only printed material of high quality, was from its inception a novelty in Hebrew periodicals. Aḥad Ha-Am's successor, Joseph *Klausner, who edited the monthly from 1903 until it ceased publication, followed a

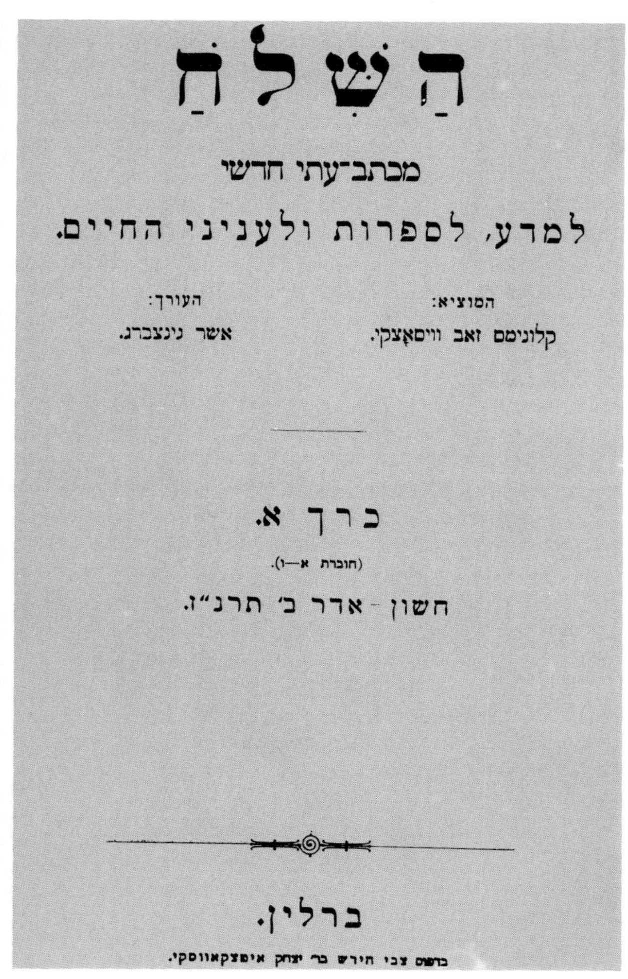
הַשִּׁלֹחַ

מכתב־עתי חדשי

למדע, לספרות ולעניני החיים.

המוציא: קלונימס זאב וויסאצקי.

העורך: אשר גינצברג.

כרך א.

(חוברת א—ו).

חשון - אדר ב׳ תרנ״ז.

ברלין.

בדפוס צבי הירש בר יצחק איטצקאווסקי.

Title page of the first volume of *Ha-Shilo'aḥ*, the Hebrew literary journal founded by Asher Ginsberg (Aḥad Ha-Am) in 1896. Jerusalem, J.N.U.L.

similar policy, but devoted more space to belles lettres and the works of such authors as J. Ḥ. *Brenner, I. L. *Peretz, S. *Asch, Z. *Shneour, and S. *Tchernichowsky. Ḥ. N. *Bialik, many of whose works were printed in *Ha-Shilo'aḥ*, coedited volumes 13–21. Most of Aḥad Ha-Am's essays also appeared in *Ha-Shilo'aḥ*, both while he was editor and after.

Ha-Shilo'aḥ revolutionized all genres of Hebrew literature and journalism. It became a model of Hebrew writing, both in form and content, and authors regarded it as an honor to publish in the journal. Indeed, the writings in *Ha-Shilo'aḥ* remain of interest and value today both for the subject matter and the style they introduced into Hebrew literature. Unlike Aḥad Ha-Am, Klausner was an adherent of political Zionism, yet *Ha-Shilo'aḥ* reflected all the trends within Zionism. When Klausner immigrated to Ereẓ Israel in 1920, *Ha-Shilo'aḥ* resumed publication in Jerusalem, and from 1925, Jacob *Fichmann, editor of the literary section, coedited the monthly. In Jerusalem the journal did not enjoy the same importance as it had in Russia. There were already a number of newspapers and periodicals in Ereẓ Israel where, in addition, the atmosphere in which *Ha-Shilo'aḥ* had thrived in Russia was lacking. A bibliography of the writings and authors printed in *Ha-Shilo'aḥ* was compiled by Joshua Barzilai-Folman (1964).

Bibliography: Aḥad Ha-Am, *Iggerot*, 1–6 (1956–60²); Ḥ. N. Bialik, *Iggerot*, 1–5 (1937–39); J. Klausner, *Darki li-kerat ha-Teḥiyyah ve-ha-Ge'ullah*, 1–2 (1955²); B. Shoḥetman, in: *Sefer Klausner* (1937), 525f.; idem, in: *Gilyonot*, 21 (1947), 101–7; Waxman, Literature, 4 (1960), 404ff.

[G.K.]

HASHKIVENU (Heb. הַשְׁכִּיבֵנוּ; "cause us to lie down"), initial word of the second benediction after the *Shema* of the daily evening prayer. This prayer for protection during the night is mentioned in the Talmud (Ber. 4b) and is considered as an extension of the *Ge'ullah* benediction which precedes it. There are two versions of this prayer, the Sephardi liturgy employing a shorter version for Friday evenings in view of the discouragement of supplication on the Sabbath (TJ, Ber. 4:5, 8c; also I. Davidson et al. (eds.), *Siddur Rav Sa'adyah Ga'on* (1941), 27 and iii). The prayer closes on weekdays with the benediction: "Blessed art thou, O Lord, who guardest thy people Israel for ever" (which uses the Babylonian text), whereas on Friday evening it ends: "Blessed art thou, O Lord, who spreadest the tabernacle of peace over us, over Israel and over Jerusalem" (which was the Palestinian text). The Midrash to Ps. 6) attributes the inclusion of the prayer in the evening service to the fact that the *ẓiẓit*, which perform a protective function, are not worn during the night.

Bibliography: Elbogen, Gottesdienst, 99–109.

[ED.]

HA-SHOMER (Heb. הַשּׁוֹמֵר, "The Watchman"), association of Jewish watchmen in Ereẓ Israel, which was active between 1909 and 1920. It was founded by pioneers of the Second *Aliyah, many of whom had been active in revolutionary movements and Jewish self-defense in Russia, and were critical of the methods used to protect life and property in the Jewish settlements based upon non-Jewish guards (Bedouin, Circassian, Mughrebim, etc.). Most of them were members or sympathizers of the *Po'alei Zion Party. On the initiative of Israel *Shoḥat, about ten of them, including Izhak *Ben-Zvi and Alexander *Zeid, met in Jaffa in 1907 and founded a secret society called Bar-Giora, which aimed at winning the right to work and keep guard in the settlements and develop Jewish settlement in new areas. It adopted as its watchword a line from Ya'akov *Cahan's poem *"Biryonim"* ("Zealots"): *"Be-dam va-esh Yehudah naflah, be-dam va-esh Yehudah takum"* ("By blood and fire Judea fell; by blood and fire Judea shall rise"). The members of Bar-Giora were given responsibility for the protection of Sejera (now Ilaniyyah) in lower Galilee, and, in 1908, of Mesḥa (Kefar Tavor). On the initiative of Bar-Giora a wider organization, called Ha-Shomer, was established in April 1909 at a meeting in Mesḥa. It was headed by a committee of three: Shoḥat, Israel *Giladi, and Mendel Portugali. Bar-Giora, in effect, merged with the new body. Within three years, Ha-Shomer assumed responsibility for the protection of seven villages, among them Ḥaderah, Reḥovot, and Rishon le-Zion. Other settlements passed also to an all-Jewish guard system. Within a short time the Jews in Ereẓ Israel no longer relied on the protection of foreign consuls and powerful neighbors, but were capable of defending their lives and property. Ha-Shomer based its methods on a close study of the conditions in the country, the ways of the Ottoman authorities, and the character of the Arab bedouin and peasants. The *shomerim* spoke Arabic, wore a mixture of Arab and Circassian dress, and carried modern weapons; some of them became expert horsemen. In 1914 they numbered about 40, with another 50–60 candidates for membership and temporary auxiliaries; at harvest time, they could deploy some 300 men. Candidates had to undergo a year's trial and take a ceremonial oath after being approved by a two-thirds majority at the annual general meeting. The *shomerim*, with their picturesque dress and armament, were prominent in the life of the new *yishuv* and played an important part in settling new and disputed land. They were widely known in the Zionist movement, which supported them. *Yizkor*, a memorial volume in

Figure 1. A Ha-Shomer group, 1910. Courtesy Central Zionist Archives, Jerusalem.

honor of their casualties, in Hebrew, Yiddish and German, had a great influence after World War I on Diaspora Jewish youth. Ha-Shomer was criticized by some circles, especially the supporters of the *Ha-Po'el ha-Ẓa'ir party, because of its independence and the fear that it might anger the Arabs. On the outbreak of World War I, Ha-Shomer had to go underground, and two of its leaders, Manya and Israel Shoḥat, were exiled in 1915 to Anatolia. Its difficulties were intensified by internecine dissensions, as a result of which a group of members, headed by Israel Giladi, left and founded southwest of Metulah the settlement of Kefar Giladi. In 1916 it started to recover: its members collected and stored arms, and organized the protection of Jewish property. Ha-Shomer opposed the espionage activities of *Nili because it endangered the Jewish community, and decided to execute Yosef *Lishanski, one of the Nili group who had escaped, in case he fell into the hands of the Turkish authorities and betrayed the secrets of the defenders. Lishanski was caught by the Turks, however, and told them all he knew. As a result, twelve *shomerim* were interrogated in Damascus and four of them imprisoned. During the British campaign in Palestine, members of Ha-Shomer joined the *Jewish Legion, while others joined the mounted police, which kept order in Galilee, and played a prominent part in the defense of *Tel Ḥai and Jerusalem. However, new elements in the *yishuv*'s leadership demanded the reorganization of defense on a broader basis under the discipline of the recognized Jewish authorities, public and political bodies. On the proposal of some of its new members, led by Eliyahu *Golomb and Yiẓḥak *Tabenkin, it was decided that the organization should disband and its members serve as the basis for a new defense system. On June 15, 1920, *Aḥdut ha-Avodah accepted the responsibility for the reorganization of defense, and Ha-Shomer ceased to exist as a separate body. Its members continued, however, to maintain contact and made an important contribution to the *yishuv*'s defense and its constructive efforts. Ha-Shomer was the first body in the Zionist movement and the Jewish *yishuv* which believed that the existence of an organized Jewish armed force would be a decisive factor in the realization of Zionism, and its example was an inspiration to the *Haganah and the pioneering youth movements.

Figure 2. Ha-Shomer members with their flag, bearing the motto, "By blood and fire Judea fell; by blood and fire Judea shall rise." The Union Jack had been sewn to the flag before the presentation to the Jewish Legion serving with the British army in World War I. Standing, second from left, is Ya'akov Pat; next to him, Raḥel Yanait. Courtesy Haganah Historical Archives, Tel Aviv.

Bibliography: *Kovez̧ Ha-Shomer* (1937), Sefer Ha-Shomer (1957); Dinur, Haganah, 1 pt. 2 (1956), index; Y. Ya'ari-Poleskin, *Ḥolemim ve-Loḥamim* (1964[3]); S. Sheva, *Shevet ha-No'azim* (1969), passim; Z. Nadav, *Mi-Ymei Shemirah ve-Haganah* (1955); Y. Allon, *The Making of Israel's Army* (1970).

[Y.S.]

HA-SHOMER HA-ẒA'IR, Zionist-socialist pioneering youth movement whose aim is to educate Jewish youth for kibbutz life in Israel. Ha-Shomer ha-Ẓa'ir had its roots in two youth movements that came into being in Galicia (then a province of the Austro-Hungarian Empire) before World War I: Ẓe'irei Zion, which emphasized cultural activities; and Ha-Shomer, primarily a scouting movement (based on the British model). During the war, when many thousands of Jews from the eastern part of the empire took refuge in Vienna, the two movements merged and took on the name Ha-Shomer ha-Ẓa'ir (1916). At the same time a similar development took place among the Jewish youth movements in the Russian part of Poland.

The early years of the movement coincided with the immediate postwar period, which was marked by a national and social awakening among the peoples of Europe, the October Revolution in Russia, and the great hope of standing on the threshold of an era of peace and progress. The ideology of the new movement was also profoundly affected by the persecutions to which East European Jewry was exposed at the time (the Petlura pogroms in the Ukraine, the pogrom in Lvov, etc.). On a spiritual level, Ha-Shomer ha-Ẓa'ir drew its inspiration from the *Ha-Shomer in Ereẓ Israel; the writings of A. D. *Gordon, J. Ḥ. *Brenner, J. *Trumpeldor; as well as from the romantic aura surrounding the revolutionary anti-czarist underground and its heroes. Other influences on the movement are to be found in the Free Youth Movement (the Wandervogel) as it was first developed in Germany before World War I and in the new philosophy, literature, psychology, and pedagogy of the time, which called for a reevaluation of existing modes of life and thought. Thus, Ha-Shomer ha-Ẓa'ir sought to create a synthesis between Jewish culture and the rebuilding and defending of Ereẓ Israel, on the one hand, and universal cultural and philosophical values, on the other, and this was to become a characteristic aspect of the movement's ideology.

Educational Method. Another characteristic of Ha-Shomer ha-Ẓa'ir is its educational method, which provides for an organic combination of "training and study groups" with the independent culture and life of youth as practiced by the Free Youth Movement, and also utilizing the symbols and the discipline of scouting. The movement puts special emphasis on the training of the individual and the development of the personality (in its early years Nietzsche's *Thus Spake Zarathustra* was very popular in the ranks of the movement). The basic pedagogic unit of Ha-Shomer ha-Ẓa'ir is the *kevuẓah* (in which the sexes are not mixed), several of which, of the same age groups, combine for certain activities to form larger, coeducational units, such as the *peluggah* ("company") and *gedud* ("batallion"). There are three age groups—the young level (age 11–14), known as *kefirim* ("cubs"), *benei midbar* ("sons of the desert"), or *benei Massada* (sons of Massadah); the intermediate level (15–16), known as *ẓofim* ("scouts"); and the adult level (from 17 upward) known as *bogerim* ("adults"), as well as *keshishim* ("oldsters") and *magshimim* ("implementers, those who fulfill"). Each level has its own program, which is adapted to its emotional needs and intellectual capacity. A local branch is a *ken* ("nest"), and it is headed by *hanhagat ha-ken* ("*ken* leadership"); a district branch is *ha-galil* and is headed by *hanhagat ha-galil;* while a national federation is headed by *ha-hanhagah ha-rashit* ("chief leadership") and the entire world movement is headed by *ha-hanhagah ha-elyonah* ("supreme leadership").

Before World War II, the Warsaw headquarters of the movement published two periodicals, both in Hebrew: *Ha-Shomer ha-Ẓa'ir,* which served as the organ of the movement as a whole and its adult level, and *Ha-Miẓpeh,* which was the organ of the intermediate level. There was also a Ha-Shomer ha-Ẓa'ir publishing house in Warsaw, which put out books of educational content. The various national branches also had their own organs, either in Hebrew or the local languages.

Personal Fulfillment. Ha-Shomer ha-Ẓa'ir is also noted for its application of the principle of personally fulfilling the ideals of the movement. It fosters among its adherents radicalism in the original sense of the term—the search for the root of things and the demand for consistency of thought, analysis, and action; this leads to the principal obligation of the individual—that of personal fulfillment of ideals and conclusions. As a result, the movement took up the struggle against assimilation (including "Red" assimilation, i.e., the widespread phenomenon of Jewish youth and intellectuals being drawn entirely into communist or socialist movements, denying their Jewish identity, and abandoning Jewish values and their responsibility for the fate of the Jewish people). It fostered the use of Hebrew—as opposed to the local language—and created pioneering Jewish atmosphere in its groups, a pedagogic measure culminating in the paramount obligation of its members—*aliyah* and life in a kibbutz. The strict application of the principle of personal fulfillment resulted in tens of thousands of young people passing through the ranks of Ha-Shomer ha-Ẓa'ir and being forced to leave the movement for failing to settle in Israel, failing to join a kibbutz, or failing to fulfill other demands put upon them by the movement. There were, of course, thousands who stood the test and settled in Ereẓ Israel in kibbutzim of Ha-Shomer ha-Ẓa'ir.

Ha-Shomer ha-Ẓa'ir insists on the organic continuity of its program, from the youngest level up to the personal fulfillment by its adult members in the form of membership in a kibbutz in Israel. The principle of personal fulfillment also accounts for the profound educational influence exerted by the *kevuẓah* leader. This derives not only from his way of life and the quality of his performance as their instructor, but also from the conviction on the part of the young members that whatever their leader demands of them, he is about to fulfill himself—settling in Israel and joining a kibbutz.

Beginnings in Ereẓ Israel. During the Third Aliyah, (1919–23) some 600 members of Ha-Shomer ha-Ẓa'ir settled in Ereẓ Israel. There was no institutional link between the various groups of these settlers or between them and the movement abroad. As a result, the strength of this first wave of Ha-Shomer ha-Ẓa'ir settlers was dissipated: they were dispersed all over the country and, to some degree, were not absorbed in kibbutz life. Furthermore, the removal of the most mature and most active members from the tasks they had fulfilled as instructors and guides caused a general slackening in the activities of the movement abroad. A severe crisis of "individualism" set in, known in the annals of the movement as "the great drift." It was not until 1927, when the *Kibbutz Arẓi Ha-Shomer ha-Ẓa'ir was founded, that a permanent framework was established for the organized absorption of Ha-Shomer ha-Ẓa'ir settlers in Ereẓ Israel and for the guidance of the movement abroad. In the period of the Third and Fourth Aliyah (up to 1926), Ha-Shomer ha-Ẓa'ir evolved its ideology. Slanted toward Marxism, it represented a synthesis between Zionism and socialism, between pioneering construction and class war. When the *Histadrut was founded (1920), the Ha-Shomer ha-Ẓa'ir kibbutzim failed to find a common language with any of the existing parties, and, instead of joining any of them, they declared themselves an independent group. Apart from its tasks in the kibbutzim, in the settlement of newcomers, and in education, the Kibbutz Arẓi also became a framework for the joint development of political ideology ("ideological collectivism") and for joint political action in the Histadrut and the Zionist Movement.

The World Movement. The World Federation of Ha-Shomer ha-Ẓa'ir was founded in Danzig in 1924. It had been preceded by the establishment of Ha-Shomer ha-Ẓa'ir movements in Rumania, Lithuania, Latvia, the U.S.S.R. (in addition to the existing movements in Galicia, Poland, and Austria), and by the initiation of efforts on the part of the kibbutzim in Ereẓ Israel to cooperate in the organized and concentrated guidance of the movement abroad. More branches were founded in the period between the First and Second World Convention (the latter also held at Danzig in 1927) in Czechoslovakia, the U.S., Canada, Belgium, and Bulgaria. The founding of the Kibbutz Arẓi greatly enhanced the influence of Ha-Shomer ha-Ẓa'ir in Ereẓ Israel upon the movement abroad. Ha-Shomer ha-Ẓa'ir in the U.S.S.R., Latvia, and, to some degree, in Lithuania, however, did not accept the independent political orientation of the majority of the movement, and members of the movement in these countries who settled in Israel found their way to the *Aḥdut ha-Avodah Party (which in 1930 merged with *Ha-Po'el ha-Ẓa'ir to become *Mapai), and did not join the Kibbutz Arẓi upon its establishment. When the Kibbutz Arẓi was in its early stage, there was still hope that the split in the ranks of the movement would eventually heal, and thus the Second Convention decided to regard the Kibbutz Arẓi only as the "principal path for the movement." The Russian-Latvian minority in Israel, however, not only failed to join Kibbutz Arẓi, but became one of the founders of *Ha-Kibbutz ha-Me'uḥad (linked to Aḥdut ha-Avodah and later to Mapai); disappointed in its expectations, the Third Convention (held in Vrutky, Czechoslovakia in 1930) decided that the Kibbutz Arẓi was now the only correct path for the Ha-Shomer ha-Ẓa'ir. The Russian-Latvian minority responded by seceding from the movement and forming "Neẓaḥ" (No'ar Ẓofi-Ḥalutzi—Ha-Shomer ha-Ẓa'ir—Scouting Pioneering Youth, see below).

On the Eve of World War II and the Holocaust. At the time of the Fourth World Convention (Poprad, Czechoslovakia, 1935), Ha-Shomer ha-Ẓa'ir had reached the height of its strength and achievements: groups in Hungary, Germany, Yugoslavia, France, Britain, Switzerland, Tunisia, Egypt, and South Africa had joined the movement, and there were encouraging beginnings in Latin America; membership totaled 70,000, with the majority about to go to Palestine or undergoing agricultural training, and with the adult members active in *He-Ḥalutz, the League for Labor Ereẓ Israel, the elections to the Zionist Congress, etc.

The rising tide of fascism in Eastern and Central Europe forced the movement to organize itself for self-defense and for the continuation of its activities under conditions of semilegality or, if this should become necessary, as an underground movement.

When World War II broke out, large numbers of members seeking to escape from the invading German forces converged upon Vilna. A part of this Vilna group eventually joined other refugees in fleeing to the Soviet Union, where they fought in the ranks of the Red Army. Some succeeded in reaching Ereẓ Israel before the German-Russian war broke out (June 1941). Others, however, were ordered by the movement to return to Nazi-occupied territory, where they became outstanding activists of the Jewish resistance, the Jewish partisans, and the ghetto fighters. Mordecai *Anielewicz, the commander of the revolt in the *Warsaw ghetto, was a member of Ha-Shomer ha-Ẓa'ir movement, and elsewhere in the Polish ghettos and in other countries under Nazi occupation the movement's members were among the leaders of the uprisings.

The Postwar Period. After the war, the surviving members of the movement prepared for *aliyah* and took an active part in the organization of the "illegal" immigration to Ereẓ Israel and the rehabilitation and reeducation of the surviving refugee children in the displaced persons camps in Germany and Italy. In the wake of the political developments in Eastern and Central Europe, the little that had remained of the movement soon dissolved. Henceforth, Ha-shomer ha-Ẓa'ir centered its activities particularly upon Latin America, and members from this area are to be found in most of the movement's kibbutzim in Israel. Branches of the movement continue to exist also in North America, Western Europe, South Africa, and Australia. The Fifth World Convention, held in 1958, was the first to meet in Israel, which had by then become the seat of the headquarters of the movement. Branch offices also existed in Paris, New York, and Buenos Aires. Their task was to direct the work of the emissaries of Kibbutz Arẓi dispatched to the various countries.

Ha-Shomer ha-Ẓa'ir in Israel. The Israel Federation of Ha-Shomer ha-Ẓa'ir naturally occupies a special place among the various branches. When the federation was first established (in 1930), the principles and methods applied by the movement in its work in the Diaspora had to be adapted to the conditions prevailing in Ereẓ Israel, where the problems of Jewish youth are radically different and where the kibbutz is not far away. The relative importance of the Israel movement in the World Federation and as a reservoir of manpower for the Kibbutz Arẓi has grown from year to year, and it has also been playing an ever-increasing role in the establishment of new Ha-Shomer ha-Ẓa'ir kibbutzim and the consolidation of existing kibbutzim. The first kibbutz founded by graduates of the movement in Ereẓ Israel was Nir David in the Beth-Shean Valley, established in 1936. (See also *Mapam).

U.S.-Canada. The movement was founded in North America in 1923. Ha-Shomer ha-Ẓa'ir has found it difficult to make headway in the American Jewish community, with its economic prosperity, its lack of a youth-movement tradition, and the philanthropic character of its Zionist movement. Nevertheless, there are a number of kibbutzim in Israel in which U.S. Ha-Shomer ha-Ẓa'ir graduates predominate (such as Ein ha-Shofet, Kefar Menahem, Hazor, Galon, Sasa, and Barkai). In the course of time, the American movement was also instrumental in the establishment of adult groups (Americans for Progressive Israel, linked to Mapam in Israel), made up of people who were attracted by the Zionist-socialist orientation of Ha-Shomer ha-Ẓa'ir. In the U.S., the movement has its own organ, *Young Guard* and maintains branches in Detroit, Boston, New York, Los Angeles, and, in Canada, in Montreal and Toronto, as well as training farms for the specific purpose of preparing for *aliyah* and kibbutz life.

Great Britain. The movement was founded in Great Britain in the late 1930s, by Ha-Shomer ha-Ẓa'ir members among the refugees from the continent, and by members of He-Ḥalutz and Habonim, who were attracted by Ha-Shomer ha-Ẓa'ir ideology. While it made progress during the war and the immediate postwar period, the movement has not succeeded in recovering the losses in its ranks caused by the *aliyah* of its founders and leading members (in the period 1946–1950), nor has it yet been able to reach the second generation, British-born Jewish youth. Branches exist in Manchester and in London. In Israel, Ha-Shomer ha-Ẓa'ir settlers from Britain are found primarily in the kibbutzim Ha-Ma'pil, Ha-Zore'a, Yasur and Zikim.

South Africa. Founded in 1935, the movement has branches in Johannesburg and Capetown. In Israel, South African *ḥalutzim* of the movement have settled in Shuval, Barkai, Naḥshon, and Zikim.

Australia. Australian Ha-Shomer ha-Ẓa'ir was founded in 1953, with branches in Melbourne and Sydney. Its settlers in Israel are concentrated mainly in Nirim. [P.M.]

Neẓaḥ. Neẓaḥ was established in 1930 as the result of a split in Ha-shomer ha-Ẓa'ir, and was disbanded during World War II. The origins of Neẓaḥ are in the Ha-Shomer ha-Ẓa'ir in Russia at the beginning of the Soviet regime. During this period many groups of Jewish scouts existed in Russia; some were affiliated with *Maccabi, while others had no affiliations.

Ha-Shomer Ha-Ẓa'ir in Russia held its clandestine founding convention in Moscow in 1922 and established itself as a country-wide movement. During David *Ben-Gurion's visit to Russia in 1923 the movement's basic ideology became personal fulfillment through *aliyah* and pioneering in Ereẓ Israel. Although illegal and persecuted by the authorities, Ha-Shomer ha-Ẓa'ir grew in size and had as many as 20,000 adherents throughout Soviet Russia. Its last "Information Page" was circulated as late as 1932, and there is evidence that some of its groups continued to exist even after that date.

The first *ḥalutzim* of this movement went to Palestine in 1924 and founded a Ha-Shomer ha-Ẓa'ir kibbutz from the U.S.S.R. on the shores of Lake Kinneret (now kibbutz Afikim). Their underground existence in Russia had prevented their attending the founding convention of the world movement of Ha-Shomer ha-Ẓa'ir and upon their arrival in Ereẓ Israel they discovered that there were substantial differences between them and the movement that developed outside Russia. They advocated membership in one of the existing labor parties (from 1930 this party was Mapai). They also opposed the creation of Ha-Kibbutz ha-Arẓi as a separate federation of kibbutzim of Ha-Shomer ha-Ẓa'ir and proposed joining kibbutzim from other movements in a single federation (which later became ha-Kibbutz ha-Me'uḥad); they disagreed with the ideological transformation which took place in Ha-Shomer ha-Ẓa'ir, and turned it from a pioneering youth movement into a political body advocating, in one of its planks, the "socialist revolution" in the leftist meaning of the term.

The struggle inside Ha-Shomer ha-Ẓa'ir went on for six years, ending in the secession of the Russian Ha-Shomer ha-Ẓa'ir from the movement and the creation of Neẓaḥ, which adhered to the original ideology of the Russian Ha-Shomer ha-Ẓa'ir. The new movement was composed of the Ha-Shomer ha-Ẓa'ir from Russia, Latvia, Estonia, and

Lithuania, and was later joined by the *Blau-Weiss (or Tekhelet Lavan) movement, in Austria, Czechoslovakia, and Yugoslavia. It also maintained close ties with the Borissia movement of Transylvania, and, in its last years, with the *Iḥud Habonim in England and America. Members of Neẓaḥ may be found in Afikim, Kefar Giladi, Ein Gev, Kinneret, Ne'ot Mordekhai, and other kibbutzim. Most of them became members of Mapai (from 1968, the Israel Labor Party). [J.I.]

Bibliography: D. Leon, *The Kibbutz* (1964); A. Ben-Shalom, *Deep Furrows* (1939); I. L. Lindheim, *Parallel Quest* (1962); *Israel Horizons* (1953–); *Young Guard* (1934– ; title varies); *Hashomer Hatzair* (Johannesburg, 1936–56); *Labour Israel* (1948–59); *Sefer Ha-Shomer ha-Ẓa'ir*, 3 vols. (1956–64); *Sefer Ha-Shomer ha-Ẓa'ir*, 3 vols. (1956–1964); *Sefer Ha-Shomerim 1913–1933* (1934); P. Merḥav, *Toledot Tenu'at ha-Po'alim be-Ereẓ-Yisrael* (1967); A. Ophir, *Afikim be-Maḥazit Yovelah* (1951); D. Horowitz, *Ha-Etmol Shelli* (1970), 73–152.

ḤASIDEI ASHKENAZ, a social and ideological circle, with a particular religious outlook, in medieval German Jewry. The first centers of the movement were Regensburg in southern Germany and the communities of Speyer, Worms, and Mainz on the Rhine; from there, its influence spread over most of Germany and, to a certain extent, to France also. Its main literature was composed during the first half of the 13th century. This movement developed in the spiritual and social atmosphere of the Jewish communities in German towns of the 12th and 13th centuries. **Kiddush ha-Shem* (martyrdom) was an extremely important factor in its formation. Another significant factor was the challenge of the Christian pietist movements. It reacted against the pressure from these trends in Christianity and was also influenced by them. Added to these was the movement's feeling of spiritual supremacy derived from its own strength and duties to God and the nation. [Ed.]

The Literature of the Circle. The literature of the Ḥasidei Ashkenaz developed in two different directions. The movement produced some ethical works, intended to influence the mass of the Jews and direct them toward rigorous observance of the commandments and the moral values of Judaism (see *Ethical Literature). Most important of these works was the *Sefer *Ḥasidim*, which continued to influence Jewish ethical thought throughout the centuries, and remained an active force in shaping Jewish ethics until modern times.

The second direction in which the Ḥasidei Ashkenaz developed was the writing of a vast body of esoteric works, some containing mystical elements. According to the traditions of the Ḥasidim themselves, this esoteric lore reached them through a long chain of verbal tradition, beginning in Italy in the eighth century. This tradition was carried mainly by the *Kalonymus family, which was transferred in the ninth century from Italy to Germany by one of the Carolingian emperors. Most of the prominent leaders of the Ḥasidei Ashkenaz were members of this family, notably *Samuel b. Kalonymus he-Ḥasid ("the Pious") in the second half of the 12th century, his son *Judah b. Samuel he-Ḥasid (d. 1217), and his pupil, *Eleazar b. Judah b. Kalonymus of Worms (d. c. 1230). The tradition continued to flourish in this family, and prominent among its bearers are some of the descendants of Judah he-Ḥasid: Moses, his son; *Eleazar b. Moses ha-Darshan; and *Moses b. Eleazar, Judah's great-grandson. Other writers belonging to this circle were disciples of Eleazar of Worms, among them *Abraham b. Azriel, author of **Arugat ha-Bosem* and *Isaac b. Moses of Vienna, author of *Or Zaru'a*. The Kalonymus family represents the central group of the Ḥasidei Ashkenaz, authors of esoteric literature. There were, however, other groups or individuals who wrote such works without being in close touch with the core. Most of these works remained anonymous and very little is known about the place and time in which they were written. One of the most important is the **Sefer ha-Ḥayyim*, written about the turn of the 13th century by a ḥasidic scholar who was deeply influenced by Abraham *ibn Ezra in formulating his theology, which also includes elements similar to some kabbalistic ideas. Another anonymous writer was the author of *Sefer ha-Navon*, a commentary on the verse *"Shema Israel"*; the author had no direct connection with the main group of the Kalonymus family, though apparently he had access to at least one work written by Judah he-Ḥasid.

Besides these scattered, anonymous writers it seems that there existed a group of mystical writers in the 12th and 13th centuries who are distinguished by their use of a pseudepigraphic *baraita* attributed to *Joseph b. Uzziel, known in Hebrew literature as the grandson of Ben Sira, the legendary son of the prophet Jeremiah (see *Ben Sira, Alphabet of). The *baraita* is mainly cosmological, closely related to *Sefer *Yeẓirah*. One of the earliest commentaries on this *baraita* is attributed to a scholar called Avigdor ha-Ẓarefati. Among the works which originated in this group was the commentary on *Sefer Yeẓirah* attributed to *Saadiah Gaon (not to be confused with Saadiah's true commentary on that work). The best-known writer of this group is *Elhanan b. Yakar, who lived in the first half of the 13th century in England and France and wrote two commentaries on *Sefer Yeẓirah* and a theological work, *Sod ha-Sodot*.

The theology of the Ḥasidei Ashkenaz aroused some controversy in Ashkenazi Jewry; in *Ketav Tamim* Moses *Taku attacked their ideas as expressed in Judah he-Ḥasid's *Sefer ha-Kavod*, in the *Sefer ha-Ḥayyim*, which Taku erroneously attributed to Abraham ibn Ezra, and in the sources of these ideas, especially the works of Saadiah Gaon, *Emunot ve-D'eot* and the commentary on the *Sefer Yeẓirah*.

Various sources were used in the formulation of Ashkenazi ḥasidic esoteric thought. There were, undoubtedly, some external, Christian influences, especially some of the neoplatonic medieval writings. In most cases these sources are unknown; only in one case, that of Elhanan b. Yakar, has it been established that he made use of material included in medieval Christian theological works. It is possible that some ideas came to the Ḥasidei Ashkenaz through verbal, not written, sources. As for the Jewish sources, the Ḥasidim made extensive use of *heikhalot* and *Merkabah literature, which they copied and quoted extensively, thus preserving some texts which might otherwise have been lost. They also made use of the works of some of the first medieval theological writers in Hebrew: Shabbetai *Donnolo, *Abraham b. Ḥiyya, and *Judah ha-Nasi of Barcelona; of special significance was the influence of Abraham ibn Ezra and there is hardly a ḥasidic work which does not, directly or indirectly, reflect his influence. However, the basic ideas of the Ashkenazi ḥasidic thinkers came from Saadiah Gaon, whose writings were known to them not in the 12th-century translation by Judah ibn *Tibbon, but from an earlier, poetic paraphrase in which the discursive, philosophical character of the works had been obliterated. No wonder, therefore, that the Ḥasidei Ashkenaz saw Saadiah as a mystic, similar to the ninth-century *Aaron of Baghdad (Abu Aharon) who came from Babylonia to Italy, and on whom they relied for some mystical knowledge, especially in the interpretation of prayer.

Theology. The basic idea which the Ḥasidei Ashkenaz tried to teach was the unity and incorporeality of God, opposing all anthropomorphic descriptions of God. In this, their teachings were similar to those of the Jewish philosophers in Spain. The difference, however, lies in their concept of the intermediary powers between God and man. The Ḥasidei Ashkenaz accepted from Saadiah Gaon the idea that a supreme power, the *Kavod* ("Divine Glory"), also called the **Shekhinah*, is the subject of all the anthropomorphic descriptions of God in the Bible, but they differ from him in their concept of the essence of the *Kavod.* According to Saadiah the *Kavod* was created and was one of the angels, though supreme above all. Most of the Ḥasidei Ashkenaz described the *Kavod* as a divine being, emanating from God himself (though they did not have a special word for the concept of emanation, as did the kabbalists). Some writers even described a whole world of many *Kevodot*, thus using the neoplatonic concept of a ladder of emanated beings descending from the Godhead toward the created world. *Kavod* plays a prominent part in the doctrines of the Ḥasidei Ashkenaz; the soul is connected with the *Kavod*, or even emanates from it, and receives its spiritual sustenance from it. Some of the many writings on prayer, prayer exegesis, and instructions on the right way to pray, emphasize that prayer should be directed toward the Godhead itself and not the *Kavod*, thereby suggesting that there were tendencies in the circles of the Ḥasidei Ashkenaz to consider the *Kavod* as a divine entity toward whom prayers should be directed. However, all of them regarded the *Kavod* as the major divine entity exerting influence on events in the lower world.

The theology of the Ḥasidei Ashkenaz is deeply grounded in the idea of divine immanence, and they emphatically state that the Godhead is itself present within all created things, and not the *Kavod.* In this, Saadiah's influence is again paramount. The immanence of God is clearly expressed in the oldest remaining work of the Ḥasidei Ashkenaz, the **Shir ha-Yiḥud*, which was probably composed at the end of the 12th century. The idea of immanence was so central to their theology, that it was questioned why a man should turn toward heaven while praying when God was present everywhere. The answer was that in heaven dwelt the *Kavod*, and this was the revealed part of God, a sign toward which man should turn, though not one toward which he should direct his prayers.

The Ḥasidei Ashkenaz did not regard the regular laws of nature, man, and society as revealing God's true nature. These laws were arbitrary, and sometimes their purpose was adverse to God's intentions; that is, they were created in order to serve as a trial *(nissayon)* for the just and pious who must overcome them. Wonders and unusual happenings, however, and certainly the miracles which occur in the world, do reveal God's true nature, and the pious and learned scholar can interpret them in order to understand better the ways and nature of God. In this connection the Ḥasidim made extensive use of demonological phenomena, regarding them as a kind of miracle and trying to divine some theological moral from the analysis of such phenomena. Thus their literature contains probably the largest extant body of demonological and magical information in medieval Hebrew literature.

Secretly the Ḥasidei Ashkenaz also dealt in messianic speculation, though they tried to conceal this (thus it is almost unmentioned in *Sefer Ḥasidim*). Believing that the messianic age was about to dawn, probably around 1240, they expected retribution to be meted out to the gentiles for all the sufferings undergone by German Jewry in the dreadful age of the Crusades. [Y.D.]

The followers of Ḥasidut Ashkenaz regarded themselves as bearers of a religious consciousness deeper than that generally prevailing and subject to religious duties severer than the accepted ones. The maximum was asked of the person able and willing to take upon himself the "restrictions of Ḥasidut," while a lesser standard sufficed for those who had not entered its circle. From the *tovim* (the "good"), the Ḥasidim (the "pious"), and the *ẓaddikim* (the "righteous"), a maximum of emotional fervor and utmost purification of soul and thought were demanded, together with exact attention to the details of both major and minor precepts. The other members of the community at large were divided into the *ra'im* ("evil ones") and the despotic ones—whom the Ḥasidim fought against—and the *peshutim* ("simple ones")—whom the Ḥasidim guided inasmuch as they were capable of observing and feeling. In its relations with the community and its institutions, the Ḥasidei Ashkenaz therefore fluctuated between two contrasting attitudes: between the desire for leadership and service, and the tendency among its members to seclude themselves in order to live their exalted individual lives.

Their Symbolism. The array of symbols of Ḥasidei Ashkenaz is based to a considerable extent on faith in the strength of the Holy Names and the mystic power of the letters of the Holy Language (Hebrew) and their combinations; these are the channels of man's communication with the celestial worlds, through study and prayer: "every blessing and prayer . . . everything . . . according to its measure and its weight, its letters and its words; if it were not so, then our prayers would, God forbid, be comparable to the song of the uncircumcised nations." Love of the Creator played a dominant role in the doctrine of the Ḥasidei Ashkenaz and among the duties of the Ḥasid; this love must saturate all his senses and resources; its strength must lead him toward joy so that no void remained in his instincts through which sin or the thought of it might penetrate. In the writings of the Ḥasidim the fervor of their emotional love and joy is expressed in symbols and parables drawn from the experiences and emotions of sexual relationships.

"Prayer is called a service like the service on the altar; when the Temple existed, the angels rose heavenward in the flame of the sacrifices . . . and today . . . they rise in the prayer which issues from the heart; for prayer is like a ladder. If there is no devotion behind the words of any blessing, the ladder stops there." The perfection of the "ladder" is so conceived that "the pronunciation of every word must be prolonged, so that there is devotion in a man's heart for every word that issues from his mouth" (*Sefer Ḥasidim* no. 11). Inner devotion is achieved through external methods: the letters should be counted. Melodies should be appropriate: "For supplications and demands, a melody which causes the heart to weep; for words of praise, a melody which causes the heart to rejoice." However, he who is not a Ḥasid may be content with general devotion; simple men and women may be exempted from reciting the prayers in Hebrew, and in certain cases even exempted from saying them in their established form; as long as they devote their hearts to their Father in Heaven.

The supreme manifestation of love for God is *Kiddush ha-Shem* ("the sanctification of the Holy Name," i.e., martyrdom), a glory for which the Ḥasid yearns. In this act, he wages the war of the people of God against Christian heresy and serves the Creator by sacrificing his body. The Ḥasidim were among "the first of the martyrs" during periods of persecution. Their courage, their service of the *Kavod* and the Lord, and their self-sacrifice became an example for others.

In ḥasidic doctrine concerning the world and man, there

are numerous occult elements. The Jew lives in a world and in a community in which, to a certain extent, the dead continue their association with the living; demons and spirits also encompass man from all sides and Judah he-Ḥasid even believed that they obeyed the *halakhah*. Sorcery is a concrete factor and a common occurrence in people's lives, and the teachings of the Ḥasidim contain many instructions and rules of conduct which serve as a protection against these powers. In these conceptions can be discerned the imprint of Christian superstitions current in their surroundings.

Ethical Views. The Ḥasidim make no reference to two inclinations in man—toward the "good" and the "evil"—and it appears that man is regarded as having only "one inclination"; the way in which this is used determines whether a deed is good or evil. The Ḥasidim therefore taught that the instincts, desires, and longings of the heart were to be turned toward the good side. According to them, mortification of the body was a method of repentance. They taught "commensurate repentance," that is, the acceptance, measure for measure, of affliction and degradation in return for the pleasure and the reward gained from sin; in some details these ideas show the influence of the notions and practices of repentance current among Christian monks. Mortification, however, had a merit of its own: the sufferings of the righteous vindicate the masses: "the Messiah bears the sins" of the nation and it is incumbent upon the Ḥasidim to adhere to this principle. In this approach there is undoubted evidence of Christian influence.

In relations between man and man, they demanded of themselves a mode of behavior according to "the law of Heaven," the application of absolute justice in the fullest sense of its spiritual significance and content; the "law of the Torah" was sufficient only for the man who was not a Ḥasid. There were some Ḥasidim who decided: "When two people come before the rabbi for him to dispense justice, if these two are of a quarrelsome disposition, the rabbi will apply the law of the Torah, even though a contrary decision would be reached according to the law of Heaven; if, however, these two are good and God-fearing men and heedful of the words of the rabbi, he must apply the law of Heaven, even if the law of the Torah requires the opposite." A practical example of this was their willingness to admit the testimony of "honest women." In their statements on the "two laws" lie occasional criticisms of the *halakhah* because of their demand for perfection of the soul. Some said that the punishments detailed in the Torah "corresponded to man's conception of what is unlawful"—that is, in respect of social codes of behavior, but "do not correspond to instinctive awareness"—that is, they do not accord with the standard by which the Ḥasid assesses sin, which gives due consideration to temptations and the difficulty of overcoming them.

From the words of the Ḥasidim there emerges a kind of Cynical indifference toward those who mock them; to bear insult in this fashion they regarded as a pious virtue. In this they reveal the reaction of a minority which is resolute in its opinion and convinced of its uniqueness in the face of possible attacks from the majority and a clash with accepted habits. Their place in society can thus be deduced from this aspect of their doctrine. In the eyes of the Ḥasidim "humility for the sake of Heaven" is a virtue which elevates the soul of the individual, and through this the public attains stability and unity. Their extreme candor and their belief in the single uniform instinct in man brought them to realize the dialectic tension which is entailed when the way of life of the minority becomes known and honored by the many. They describe how "others honor themselves with their humility . . . they are greater than us and yet do not want to take precedence over anyone, as if to say, we are humble."

Social Doctrine. The social doctrine of the Ḥasidim assumes that the original and desirable situation is complete equality in respect of property and social status; inequality is the result of sin. However, they attributed moral significance to the unequal distribution of riches: wealth is given to the rich so that they may sustain the poor. In accordance with this, they were accustomed to give a tenth of their money to charity. Because of this outlook, the Ḥasidim were troubled by the problem of the criterion of uniformity—which does not draw any distinction between rich and poor—in the imposition of taxes and public obligations on individuals. They justified the prevalence of this system in public life through the fear that if individual considerations were taken into account, the "evil ones" would attempt to evade their responsibilities. However, they required that "good ones" judge for themselves, after the general imposition, their ability and duty to see whether they were capable of making restitution to the poor for that which had unjustly been taken from them. R. Judah b. Samuel he-Ḥasid and his colleagues even advised a man to forgo the public honor of a *mitzvah* purchased in the synagogue if someone was prepared to acquire it for a higher price; the reward for this *mitzvah* would belong to him who had relinquished it if he secretly gave to the poor the sum he had previously paid in public for the *mitzvah*.

This outlook resulted in some tension between the circle of the Ḥasidim and the community leaders on several occasions. The writings of the Ḥasidim contain a critical account of these leaders and their deeds; clashes between the leaders of the Ḥasidim and the community are also mentioned. It is evident that the Ḥasidim disapproved of several principles of the leadership, while many others in the community objected to the attempt at practical application of the doctrines of the Ḥasidim within the communities.

To the Ḥasidim family life is the basis and framework of piety. Love between man and woman is legitimate as long as it does not lead to sin; they also considered that this love had a definite spiritual content. A man fasts and prays in order to win the woman he loves. In their writings, they gave considerable thought to matchmaking, believing that love and family descent were commendable and desirable factors and considerations. Family descent was also regarded as a basic element in the preservation of the proper way of life of the community. However, they considered money as a negative factor and consideration in matchmaking, although they did not ignore its importance in practice.

Along with their emotional depth and mysticism, the Ḥasidim also preserved the tradition of meditation and study. Their respect for books is profound: in the *Sefer Ḥasidim*, the "righteous" bewail the fact that their libraries are scattered after their deaths. They believed that it was commendable not to haggle over the price of a book.

The attitude of the Ḥasidim to the non-Jewish world is imbued with the bitterness of those who battle against a successful foe and suffer cruel oppression. But even here, in several instances, it is possible to recognize the influence of the spiritual environment of Christianity and current ideas.

The Ḥasidei Ashkenaz became influential in the Jewish world, while at the same time they adapted many and profound elements foreign to that world. They were marked by a refinement of feeling and simplicity of thought, and were woven together by bonds of personal honesty and responsibility before the Creator. Even at its height, the movement comprised only a small group within German Jewry, but as a result of the example of its leading personalities and its growth from the spiritual climate of the time, it succeeded in leaving its imprint. The testaments and customs of the leading Ḥasidim greatly influenced the general way of life, as well as specific details, conceptions of *halakhah*, and the versions of prayers. From the second half of the 13th century onward they even exerted some influence over Spanish Jewry. The Jews of Poland-Lithuania of the late Middle Ages also pointed out with pride that "we are of the lineage of the Ḥasidei Ashkenaz," although the atmosphere of their social and religious life had undergone many changes since the time of the Ḥasidim.

[Ed.]

Bibliography: J. Dan, *Torat ha-Sod shel Ḥasidei Ashkenaz* (1967); idem, in: JJS, 17 (1966), 73–82; M. Guedemann, *Ha-Torah ve-ha-Ḥayyim*, 1 (1897); Scholem, Mysticism, 80–118; idem, *Ursprung und Anfaenge der Kabbala* (1962), s.v. *Chasidim, deutsche;* A. Cronbach, in: HUCA, 22 (1949), 1–147; J. Trachtenberg, *Jewish Magic and Superstition* (1939), index; M. Harris, in: JQR, 50 (1959), 13–44; Y. Baer, in: *Zion*, 3 (1938), 1–50; 18 (1953), 91–108; 32 (1967), 129–36; idem, in: *Meḥkarim . . . le-Gershom Scholem* (1968), 47–62; J. N. Simhoni, in: *Ha-Ẓefirah* 42 (1917); E. E. Urbach, in: *Zion*, 12 (1947), 149–59; Urbach, Tosafot, 141–94, 285–370; idem, *Sefer Arugat ha-Bosem* . . . (1963), 177–85; H. H. Ben-Sasson (ed.), *Toledot Am Yisrael*, 2 (1969), index.

ḤASIDEI UMMOT HA-OLAM (Heb. חֲסִידֵי אֻמּוֹת הָעוֹלָם, lit., "The pious ones of the nations of the world"), a rabbinic term denoting righteous gentiles. The concept is first found (albeit in a limited form) in the Midrash. The *Yalkut Shimoni*, for instance, explains that the verse "Let thy priests be clothed with righteousness . . ." (Ps. 132:9) refers to "the righteous of other nations who are priests to the Holy One in this world, like Antoninus and his type" (Yal. Isa. 429). The notion that the *ḥasidei ummot ha-olam* also merit a place in the world to come (a true sign of their worthiness) is found in the Tosefta, which teaches that they are as eligible as any member of the House of Israel to a share in the hereafter (Tosef., Sanh. 13:2). This dictum is twice codified by Maimonides (Yad, Teshuvah 3:5), who also defines the concept (Yad, Melakhim 8:11): "All who observe the Seven Commandments"—obligatory to the descendants of Noah—are *ḥasidei ummot ha-olam*, provided that they are motivated by belief in the divine origin and the authenticity of Moses' prophecy, and not by mere intellectual cogency. In the latter case they are to be considered only as "wise ones of the other nations" (*ḥakhmeihem*, according to some versions). Without specifically naming the righteous gentiles, Maimonides also equates "all human beings who ardently seek God . . . desire to worship Him, to know Him, and to walk uprightly in His ways . . .," with priests and levites (Yad, Shemittah 13:13).

The concept of *ḥasidei ummot ha-olam* was elaborated and embellished in medieval Jewish literature. It is mentioned by such philosophers as Hasdai *Crescas (*Or Adonai* no. 364:4) and *Abrabanel (introduction to commentary to Isaiah), R. Isaac *Arama states, "Every true pious gentile is equal to a 'son of Israel' " (*Akedat Yiẓḥak*, ed. Venice, ch. 60). The concept is mentioned in a legal context in the Shulḥan Arukh (YD 367:1, Be'er ha-Golah). The Zohar states that all gentiles who do not hate Israel, and who deal justly with the Jews, qualify as *ḥasidei ummot ha-olam* (Exodus, 268a).

Since World War II the term has been used for those non-Jews who helped Jews to escape the Nazi persecutions. See *Righteous of the Nations.

Bibliography: Zunz, Gesch, 388; M. Guttmann, *Das Judentum und seine Umwelt*, 1 (1927), 171.

[Ha.Bl.]

ḤASIDIM (Heb. חֲסִידִים, "pietists"), term used in rabbinic literature to designate those who maintained a higher standard in observing the religious and moral commandments. The various definitions in rabbinic literature of the *ḥasid*, and the more numerous accounts given there of them and their actions, clearly indicate that the image of the *ḥasid* was not identical at all times and in all circles. The sources reflect a broad spectrum of religious types, each distinguished in its own way, but common to all is a divergence from what was regarded as conventional behavior and the normal standard.

The precise period of the *ḥasidim ha-rishonim* ("first ḥasidim") mentioned in rabbinic literature cannot be determined. Statements about them recount their virtues, which were utter devotion to fulfilling the *mitzvot* with a total disregard of any danger, extreme solicitude for human relations to the extent of transcending the strict requirements of the law, a fear of sin expressed by avoiding anything that might possibly lead astray or to the commission of sin, and by a constant readiness to undergo purification and to seek atonement for any doubtful sin by offering sacrifices. Before praying the early *ḥasidim* would wait an hour in order to direct their hearts to God (Ber. 5:1), nor did they interrupt their prayers even in the face of possible danger (Tosef., Ber. 3:20; TB, Ber. 32b). They refrained on a weekday from doing anything that involved the slightest apprehension of ultimately desecrating the Sabbath (Nid. 38a). They would bury thorns and glass deep in their fields, "placing them three handbreaths deep in the ground so that the plow might not displace them" and people stumble over them (Tosef., BK 2:6). The *tanna* R. Judah stated that "the early *ḥasidim* were eager to bring a sin offering," but since they did not inadvertently commit sins "they made a free-will vow of naziriteship that they might bring a sin offering" (Tosef., Ned. 1:1; TB, Ned. 10a). They were accustomed to make a free-will offering of a suspensive guilt offering *(asham talui)*, and this type of sacrifice "became known as the guilt-offering of the *ḥasidim*" (Ker. 6:3; Tosef., Ker. 4:4).

Akin to the *ḥasidim ha-rishonim* are the "*ḥasidim* and men of action" *(ḥasidim ve-anshei ma'aseh)*. This phrase does not indicate two distinct groups of people—the *ḥasidim* were so called on account of the special good deeds which they performed and the miracles vouchsafed them by virtue of these good deeds. The only extant tradition states that during the Rejoicing of the Water-drawing *(simḥat bet ha-sho'evah)* "they used to dance with lighted torches and sing songs and praises." Some of them used to say "Happy my youth, that has not put to shame my old age"; others, "Happy my old age, that has atoned for my youth" (Suk. 5:4; Tosef., Suk. 4:2). Outstanding representatives of the "*ḥasidim* and men of action" were *Ḥoni ha-Me'aggel, his grandsons *Abba Hilkiah and Hanan ha-Neḥba (Ta'an. 23a), and *Ḥanina b. Dosa who lived at the end of the Second Temple period and whom the Mishnah regards as the last of the "men of action" (Sot. 9:15; the reading in TJ is "*ḥasidim*"). These men did not belong to the class of the halakhists, and there was even certain opposition between them (cf. Ta'an. 23a; Ber. 34b). The statement of Ḥanina b. Dosa that "he whose actions exceed his wisdom, his wisdom shall endure, but he whose wisdom exceeds his actions, his wisdom will not endure" (Avot 3:9) clearly reveals the difference between the "men of action" and the sages. Expressive of their deep faith and implicit belief in God's omnipotence are the deeds of the "*ḥasidim* and men of action" and the remarks that accompanied them on various occasions. Thus Ḥanina b. Dosa entertained no doubts when he said, "He who commanded oil to burn will also command vinegar to burn" (Ta'an 25a), for to them the miraculous was regarded as quite natural. When a poisonous lizard bit Ḥanina b. Dosa and died, he brought it on his shoulder to the *bet ha-midrash*, commenting simply:

Embroidered hanging for a *sukkah*, silk, gold, and silver thread on taffeta, Italy(?), 18th century. It depicts the celebration of the Feast of the Drawing of Water and shows three pious men of action performing dances and acrobatics as described by R. Simeon b. Gamaliel, head of the Sanhedrin. The central figure is making the ritual bow, the *kiddah*. Washington, Smithsonian Institution, Cooper Hewitt Museum of Design.

"See, my sons, it is not the lizard that kills, it is sin that kills" (Ber. 33a). The contents, motifs, and form of several stories related in the sources about "a certain *ḥasid*" (e.g., Tosef., Pe'ah 3:8; TJ, Shab. 15:3, 15a; BK 50b, 80a) indicate that the stories refer to these early ones (BK 103b). A difficulty is posed by the statement that "wherever the Talmud speaks of a certain *ḥasid* it refers either to Judah b. Bava or Judah b. Ilai" (Tem. 15b). However, this may mean no more that that these *tannaim* were the ones who reported such stories.

Despite the differences in time and conditions, the conduct and deeds of the *ḥasidim* and men of action bear a certain resemblance to the stories in the Bible about the earlier prophets, in that their influence derived not from the power of their exhortations but from the force of their deeds, courage, and sense of dedication. The rabbis gave expression to this in their homiletical interpretation of Genesis 2:5, "And there was not man to till the ground," on which they commented: "There was no man to cultivate people's allegiance to God, such as Elijah and Ḥoni ha-Me'aggel" (Gen. R. 7; and see Theodor-Albeck, 117, n. 5).

The early *ḥasidim* created no organization or sect but were active as individuals, each in his own vicinity and time. Nor can they be identified with the *Essenes, as various scholars from the 19th century onward (Frankel, Geiger, Derenboug, Kohler) have sought to do, for what is known about them does not accord with the descriptions of the Essenes in Philo, Josephus, Pliny, and others. Y. Baer has assigned to the "early *ḥasidim*" a central place in the history of Second Temple times, identifying them with the sages who flourished in the pre-Hasmonean period. Thus he contends that the Great Synagogue was a development of *ḥasidim* and sages, that its continuity was preserved by the **zugot*, and that these *ḥasidim* are to identified with the Essenes and with Philo's *Therapeutae. He believes that they were the first exponents of the *halakhah* as embedded in the earliest layers of the Mishnah, and that they laid the foundations of the entire structure of faith as reflected in the ascetic-spiritual-martyrological aspects of statements in the *aggadah*, Midrash, and Philo's writings. This account of them does not, however, accord with what is reported in rabbinic sources about the early *ḥasidim* and their activities. They were not the creators of the ancient *halakhah*, nor the initiators of a philosophic and mystical teaching. The fact that they lived a simple and modest life with a minimum of material needs—"Ḥanina my son is satisfied with a *kav* of carobs from one Sabbath eve to another" (Ta'an. 24b)—does not constitute asceticism. Manifestations of abstinence among talmudic scholars are not remnants of outworn ancient ascetic teaching of the early *ḥasidim*, but are connected with the circumstances of a much later period. Moreover, the tannaitic period preserved a memory of them as being specifically distinguished and separated from the sages as a whole. Furthermore, the type of *ḥasid* of that period differed in outlook from the early *ḥasidim*. Thus *Hillel, who in his teachings incorporated ideas inherited from the early *ḥasidim*, is the author of the aphorism that "an ignorant person cannot be a *ḥasid*" (Avot 2:5). Nor could there be any piety without the study and knowledge of the Torah (see ARN[1] 12, 56; ARN[2] 27, 56). When Hillel died, they said of him: "Alas, the humble man, alas the *ḥasid* [is no more]" (Tosef., Sot. 13:4), his eminence in the Torah having been combined with humility (Lev. R. 1:5), and with implicit trust in the Almighty (Ber. 60a), and "all his actions were for the sake of Heaven." But Hillel, whose personality comprised many other aspects too, was not regarded as one of the early *ḥasidim*, and yet precisely he and those who followed in his footsteps represent the *ḥasid*-sage.

Generally the term *ḥasid* came later to refer to ideal and exemplary behavior in some sphere of life. A *ḥasid* is one who declares "what is mine is yours, and what is yours is yours" (Avot 5:10) and "He whom it is hard to provoke and easy to pacify" (*ibid.* 5:11). This and other definitions are far removed from the ways of the early *ḥasidim*. There was moreover a definite line of abstinence and of extreme asceticism which reached full maturity and became a characteristic feature of the *ḥasid* only in the amoraic period. This trend started after the destruction of the Second Temple "when the abstinent ones increased in Israel" (Tosef., Sot. 14:11), seeking in fasts a substitute for atonement, now denied to them with the cessation of sacrifices. At the beginning of the second century these expressions of abstinence vanished but reappeared to spread with greater force during the persecutions following the Bar Kokhba revolt. Ben Azzai, of whom it was said that "whoever sees Ben Azzai in a dream can hope to attain piety" (Ber. 57b), proclaimed extreme abstinence from all earthly pursuits, declaring, "Let the world be sustained by others" (Tosef., Yev. 8:4; Yev. 63b). A similar circumstance is reflected in R. Meir's homiletical interpretation that "Adam was a great *ḥasid*" (see Er. 18b; Gen. R. 20, ed. Theodor-Albeck, 195). At the end of the tannaitic period there once again appear sages who, in their extreme demands, spontaneous reactions, and miraculous deeds, are reminiscent of the early *ḥasidim* and the men of action. Of such a type was *Phinehas b. Jair who defined and enumerated the steps leading to *ḥasidim* regarded by him as a stage in the attainment of the holy spirit (Sot. 9:15).

In the amoraic period extreme conclusions were drawn from Akiva's principle that suffering is to be lovingly accepted as the ultimate goal of anyone who serves God, the same interpretation being applied to man's normal suffering—and not only to times of persecution—as a punishment for sins. But while a *ḥasid* therefore prays that he may suffer, not everyone is privileged to have such prayers answered, and accordingly some pious *amoraim*, instead of awaiting suffering, deliberately afflicted and mortified themselves. This was done by Ḥiyya b. Ashi (Kid. 81b), Zera (BM 85a), Mar b. Ravina (Pes. 68b). Not that all the *amoraim* agreed that self-denial entitled one to be called a *ḥasid* (Ta'an. 11b), Simeon b. Lakish declaring that "a scholar may not afflict himself by fasting because thereby he lessens his heavenly work" *(ibid).* There were also *amoraim* called *"ḥasid,"* such as Amram the Ḥasid (Kid. 81a; Git. 67b), Simeon the Ḥasid (Ber. 43b) and Mar Zutra (Ned. 7b), who acquired this title not on account of acts of mortification but of other virtues and deeds. The Ḥasid Huna declared anyone who has a fixed place for prayer to be a *ḥasid* (Ber. 6b), R. Alexandri that "whoever hears someone curse him and keeps silent is called a *ḥasid*" (Mid. Ps. to 16:11). A certain criticism was leveled against "the *ḥasidim* of Babylonia"—the *amoraim* Huna, Ḥisda, and Naḥman—in the Babylonian Talmud itself which disparagingly contrasted their humility and courtesy with those of the Ereẓ Israel sages, although the latter were known for their hardness (Meg. 28b; and see Ḥul. 122a). In principle, the *ḥasid* is one who does more than is required of him by the letter of the law, and *halakhot* which go beyond the strict legal requirements are termed by the *amoraim* "the Mishnah of the *ḥasidim*" (TJ, Ter. 8:10, 46b; or "the measure of the *ḥasidim*" (BM 52b). The popular test of a *ḥasid* was if his prayer for rain was answered (Ta'an. 23b). In the days of both the *tannaim* and the *amoraim* the sages were displeased with ignorant people who adopted the standards of the *ḥasid* (Shab. 121b; and see TJ, Av. Zar 2:3, 41a). Simeon b. Lakish even maintaining that "if an ignorant man is a *ḥasid*, do not dwell in his vicinity" (Shab. 63a). On R. Joshua's statement in the Mishnah that a foolish *ḥasid* is to be included among those who bring destruction upon the world, the two Talmuds quote instances of the *ḥasid* who, on account of his rigid observance of the *mitzvot* and of his abstinence, refrains from saving his fellow from death (TJ, Sot. 3:4, 19a; TB Sot., 21b).

Colloquially, the term "*ḥasid*" was used to designate a just, upright, and good person, this inexact usage being sometimes found also in literary sources: "it fits him to become just, *ḥasid*, upright, and faithful" (Avot 6:1); "even as the earlier righteous men were *ḥasidim*" (ARN[1] 8, 38; and see TJ, Sanh. 6:9, 23c, where *Simeon b. Shetaḥ and someone who flourished in the days of King David are referred to as *ḥasidim*). Inscriptions on Jewish epitaphs at Bet She'arim and in Italy contain, alongside *δίκαιος* ("righteous"), the term *ὅσιος* which is found in the Septuagint both for *ḥasid* and for *yashar*, an upright man.

Bibliography: Frankel, Mishnah (1923[2]), 14, 42; idem, in: *Zeitschrift fuer die religioesen Interessen des Judenthums*, 3 (1846), 441–61; idem, in: MGWJ, 2 (1853), 30–40, 61–73; A. Buechler, *Types of Jewish-Palestinian Piety* (1922); L. Gulkowitsch, *Die Bildung des Begriffes Ḥasid* (1935); S. Lieberman, *Greek in Jewish Palestine* (1942), 69–78; Y. F. Baer, in: *Zion*, 18 (1953), 91–108; idem, *Yisrael ba-Ammim* (1955); Sarfatti, in: *Tarbiẓ*, 26 (1957), 126–48; Avigad, in: *Eretz Israel*, 5 (1959), 182; E. Urbach, in: *Sefer Yovel le-Y. Baer*, 48–68; idem, *Ḥazal, Pirkei Emunot ve-De'ot* (1969), index; Jacobs, in: JJS, 8 (1957), 143–54; Safrai, *ibid.*, 16 (1965), 15–33; Falk, in: *Sefer Zikkaron . . . B. De Vries* (1969), 62–69. [EH]

ḤASIDIM, SEFER (Heb. סֵפֶר חֲסִידִים, "Book of the Pious"), major work in the field of ethics, produced by the Jews of medieval Germany. It comprises the ethical teachings of the *Ḥasidei Ashkenaz movement in the 12th and early 13th centuries. Two versions of the book have survived, one printed in Bologna and the other found in manuscript in Parma.

Tradition attributes the entire *Sefer Ḥasidim* to R. *Judah he-Ḥasid (the Pious) of Regensburg (d. 1217), the great teacher of Ashkenazi Ḥasidism. There is some proof, however, that the first two *"maḥbarot"* (groups into which the book is divided) of the Parma version were written by Judah's father, R. Samuel b. Kalonymus he-Ḥasid. This is substantiated by a study of their style. These two *"maḥbarot"* discuss the fear of God and repentance. Some of the passages in *Sefer Ḥasidim* bear close similarity, in language and ideas, to the ethical introductions to the *Roke'aḥ*, the halakhic work by R. *Eleazar of Worms. A number of scholars, therefore, conclude that R. Eleazar, R. Judah's most prominent disciple, was the author of some of the passages in *Sefer Ḥasidim*, and probably its editor. It is equally possible, however, that R. Eleazar used portions of the *Sefer Ḥasidim* in his writings, as he did with other mystical works of his teacher. No conclusive proof is to be found as to what extent R. Eleazar participated in the authorship of the work; whereas there is a clear statement by R. Judah's son, Moses, describing how R. Judah wrote two pages of *Sefer Ḥasidim* (Ms. Guenzburg 82, 64b) in the last week of his life. It can be concluded that *Sefer Ḥasidim* was written by R. Judah he-Ḥasid, and that some material was added to it from the writings of his father R. Samuel. A problem nevertheless exists regarding the origin and development of the work. Some of the earliest quotations from the *Sefer Ḥasidim* found in the Ashkenazi ḥasidic writings of the first half of the 13th century are in neither of the two known

A man leaving prison, holding his chains, illustrates the text of Psalms 118 :5 ("I called upon the Lord in distress, the Lord answered me"). Initial-word panels in two pages from the *Sassoon Spanish Haggadah* of the 14th century. Letchworth, Sassoon Collection, ms. 519, pages 138–139 ($9\frac{7}{8} \times 6\frac{1}{2}$ ins/25 × 16.5 cm.).

II.

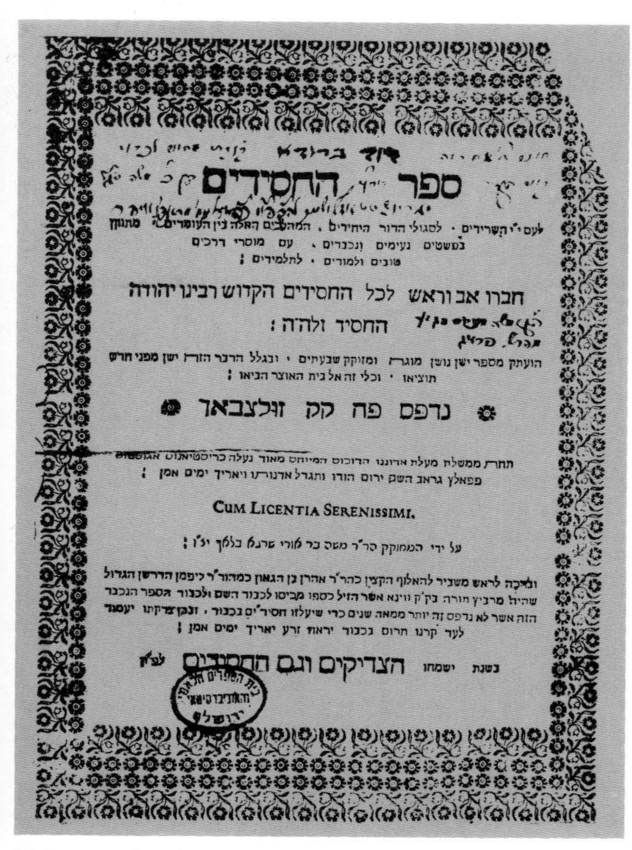
ספר החסידים
עם י״ו השרידים · לסגולי הדור היחידים . המהלכים האלה בין העומדים · מתנוקן
במשפטים נעימים ונכבדים . עם מוסרי דרכים
טובים ולמורים · לתלמידים ׃

חברו אב וראש לכל החסידים הקדוש רבינו יהודה
החסיד זלה״ה ׃

הועתק מספר ישן נושן מוגר״ה ומזוקק שבעתים · ובגלל הדבר הזו״ת ישן מפני חדש
תוציאו · וכלי זה אל בית האוצר הביאו ׃

נדפס פה קק זולצבאך

תחת ממשלת מעלת אדוננו הדוכוס המיוחס מאוד נעלה כריסטיאנוס אגוסטוס
פפאלץ גראב השם ירום הודו ותגדל אדנותו ויאריך ימים אמן ׃

Cum Licentia Serenissimi.

על ידי המחוקק הר״ר משה בר מורי שרגא בלאך יצ״ו ׃

ובהיכה לראש משביר להאלוף הקצין כהר״ר אהרן בן הגאון כמהור״ר ליפמן הדרשן הגדול
שהיה מרביץ תורה בק״ק ווינא אשר הזיל כספו מכיסו לכבוד השם ולכבוד הספר הנכבד
הזה אשר לא נדפס זה יותר ממאה שנים כדי שיעלזו חסידים בכבוד · וזכן צדקתו יעמוד
לעד קרנו תרום בכבוד יראה זרע יאריך ימים אמן ׃

בשנת ישמחו הצדיקים וגם החסידים לפ״ק

Title page of *Sefer Ḥasidim*, the 13th-century Ashkenazi ethical work. Sulzbach, Austria, 1685. Jerusalem, J.N.U.L.

versions. It is possible that parts of the original *Sefer Ḥasidim* were lost early in the development of the two versions that survived.

Many of the passages in *Sefer Ḥasidim* are homiletic and exegetic in nature, explaining the ethical, and sometimes the philosophical or mystical, meanings of biblical verses or talmudic sayings. Most of the passages, however, discuss only ethics, and do so in direct connection with everyday life. *Sefer Ḥasidim* is the prime example of pragmatic and realistic ethical teachings in Jewish ethical literature; it takes into account the special characteristic of every case, the psychology of the person discussed, the historical and economic situation, and the person's special relationship to other people. This approach renders *Sefer Ḥasidim* the most important historical source for the study of everyday Jewish life in medieval Germany; it throws light especially on economic and religious relations of Jews with gentiles. The book has some descriptions of actual incidents, clarifying the situation in Germany during and after the disasters brought by the crusaders on Jews in Germany and France. Later Jewish ethical works influenced by *Sefer Ḥasidim* retained its strict and uncompromising adherence not only to the commandments, but to the entire body of religious ethics. The book instructs the pious man how to resist temptation and avoid any situation which may lead to sin. It teaches how to dress, to speak, to pray, to work, and to sleep; how to choose a wife and to select friends; how to harmonize between the necessities of existence and the requirements of religious life; which city is suitable for a pious person to live in and which is not; the right relationship between teacher and pupil; how to choose a righteous teacher; in what fields one may have commercial contact with gentiles and how to treat them, and many other subjects. No other Hebrew work in ethics covers so much ground and devotes such close attention to realistic detail. All later writers in the field of ethics in Ashkenazi literature used *Sefer Ḥasidim* as a basis; many of them added very little to what they had taken from it. After the 15th century, writers of *halakhah* used the work as an authority, sometimes the final authority, on the Jewish way of life.

The Bologna version was printed in 1538 and later in numerous other places (including Jerusalem 1957, edited by R. Margaliot). The Parma manuscript was published by J. Wistinetzky (Berlin, 1891–94) and in 1924 at Frankfort, with an introduction by J. Freimann. The manuscripts found in a number of libraries are incomplete, each containing only a tenth of the whole work. Scholars who have compared the two versions reached the conclusion that the Parma one was the earlier and more reliable. It comprises more than 1,900 passages, whereas the Bologna version has less than 1,200. The Parma version has many duplications and inconsistencies, which were either omitted or harmonized in the Bologna edition. There the passages are better arranged and a system is apparent, whereas the Parma manuscript seems, in places, unedited and chaotic. The Bologna edition was probably edited and changed later by an editor who may have lived in France, probably before 1300. In the Parma version the transliterated vernacular words are in "German," whereas in the Bologna edition they are in "French."

The book is compiled from independent passages *(simanim)*, arranged in groups *(maḥbarot)*, sometimes under titles describing the subject of the single group *(maḥberet)*, e.g., "witchcraft," "books," "prayer," etc. Titles such as "This is the Book of the Just" *(Sefer Ḥasidim)*, "*Sefer Ḥasidim* on the Book of Proverbs," or "This also is *Sefer Ḥasidim*" are to be found in the Parma version as well. It is evident that the book was compiled from smaller collections which themselves were compiled from independent passages.

Bibliography: J. Wistinetzki and J. Freimann (eds.), *Sefer Ḥasidim* (1924[2]), 1–73; Simḥoni, in: *Ha-Ẓefirah* (1917), passim; Scholem, Mysticism, 80–99; Harris, in: JQR, 50 (1959), 13–44; idem, in: PAAJR, 31 (1963), 51–80; Cronbach, in: HUCA, 22 (1949), 1–147; Baer, in: *Zion*, 3 (1938), 1–50; S. G. Kramer, *God and Man in the Sefer Ḥasidim* (1966).

[Y.D.]

ḤASIDISM, a popular religious movement giving rise to a pattern of communal life and leadership as well as a particular social outlook which emerged in Judaism and Jewry in the second half of the 18th century. Ecstasy, mass enthusiasm, close-knit group cohesion, and charismatic leadership of one kind or another are the distinguishing socioreligious marks of Ḥasidism.

This article is arranged according to the following outline:

HISTORY

Beginnings and Development. The movement began in the extreme southeast of *Poland-Lithuania, and was shaped and conditioned by the tension prevailing in Jewish society in the difficult circumstances created by the breakup of Poland-Lithuania in the late 18th century and the three partitions of the country. This combined with the problems inherited as a result of both the *Chmielnicki massacres and the *Haidamack massacres. The framework of Jewish leadership was shaken, and the authority and methods of Jewish leaders were further undermined and questioned in the wake of the upheaval brought about by the false messianic and kabbalistic movements of *Shabbetai Ẓevi and Jacob *Frank, the shadow of the latter lying on Ḥasidism from its inception. As well as furnishing an ideological background, *Kabbalah, combined with popular traditions of ecstasy and mass enthusiasm, provided constructive elements for a new outlook in religious and social behavior. The earlier messianic movements and authoritarianism of the community leaders prevailing at that time, combined with the necessarily individualistic leadership of the opposition to such authoritarianism, coalesced to accustom the Jewish masses to charismatic as well as authoritative leadership. Mystic circles in Poland-Lithuania in the 18th century combined to create ḥasidic groups *(ḥavurot)* with a distinct pattern of life, mostly ascetic, sometimes with their own synagogue (for example, the so-called *kloyz* of the ascetic Ḥasidim of *Brody). These circles were noted for their special behavior during prayer, for their meticulous observance of the commandments, and also by their daily life. Their prayers were arranged for the most part according to the Sephardi version of Isaac *Luria. They were not looked upon favorably by the official institutions of the community because of the danger of separatism and because of their deviation from the accepted religious customs. Some among them secluded themselves, and spent their days fasting and undergoing self-mortification. Others were ecstatic—"serving the Lord with joy." These groups were quite small and closed; their influence upon the general public was very small.

At first, *Israel b. Eliezer Ba'al Shem Tov (the Besht) appears to have been one of a number of leaders characterized by ecstatic behavior and an anti-ascetic outlook. A popular healer who worked with magic formulas, amulets, and spells, he attracted to his court, first at Tolstoye and then at Mezibezh, people who came to be cured, to join him in ecstatic prayer, and to receive guidance from him. Israel also undertook journeys, spreading his influence as far as Lithuania. After his "revelation" in the 1730s, which marked the beginning of his public mission, he gradually became the leader of ḥasidic circles; drawn by his personality and visions, more and more people were attracted to the ḥasidic groups, first in Podolia, then in adjacent districts in southeast Poland-Lithuania. Unfortunately it is not possible to fix their number but more than 30 are known by name. Both Israel himself and his whole circle were deeply convinced of his supernatural powers and believed in his visions. Some who came within his orbit continued to oppose him to some degree (see *Abraham Gershon of Kutow, *Naḥman of Horodenko, and *Naḥman of Kosov); under his influence others turned away from ascetic talmudic scholarship to become the theoreticians and leaders of Ḥasidism and Israel's disciples (see *Dov Baer of Mezhirech and *Jacob Joseph of Polonnoye). At his death (1760) Israel left, if not a closely knit group, then at least a highly admiring and deeply convinced inner circle of disciples, surrounded by an outer fringe of former leaders of other ḥasidic groups who adhered to him while dissenting from his views to some extent, and a broad base of devout admirers in the townships and villages of southeast Poland-Lithuania. His outlook and vision attracted simple people as well as great talmudic scholars, established rabbis, and influential **maggidim*.

After a brief period of uncertainty (c. 1760–66), the leadership of the second generation of the movement passed to Dov Baer of Mezhirech (known as the great *maggid* of Mezhirech), although he was opposed by many of Israel's most prominent disciples (e.g., Phinehas Shapiro of Korets and Jacob Joseph of Polonnoye), and many of this inner circle of his opponents withdrew from active leadership, a fact of great significance for the history of Ḥasidism. Nevertheless, Ḥasidism continued to propagate and spread. *Toledot Ya'akov Yosef* (1780), by Jacob Joseph of Polonnoye, embodied the first written theoretical formulation of Ḥasidism, transmitting many of the sayings, interpretations, and traditions of Israel Ba'al Shem Tov, and Jacob Joseph continued with these expositions in subsequent works. From Dov Baer's court missionaries went forth who were successful in attracting many scholars to Ḥasidism and sending them to the master at Mezhirech to absorb his teaching. Due to illness he did not often meet with his disciples. Unlike the Ba'al Shem Tov he was not a man of the people, and favored young scholars whose intellectual foundation did not dampen their ecstatic tendencies. From the new center at Volhynia, Ḥasidism thus spread northward into Belorussia and Lithuania and westward into Galicia and central Poland (see *Shneur Zalman of Lyady, *Levi Isaac of Berdichev, Aaron (the Great) of *Karlin, and Samuel Shmelke *Horowitz). At this time Ḥasidism even penetrated into the center of opposition to it, in Vilna. Many local ḥasidic leaders became influential as communal leaders and local rabbis.

Ḥasidic groups went to Ereẓ Israel creating a far-flung and influential center of ḥasidic activity, notably in Tiberias. Israel Ba'al Shem Tov intended to go to Ereẓ Israel, but for some unknown reason turned back when in the middle of the journey. His brother-in-law Abraham Gershon of Kutow went there in 1747, settled in Hebron, and six years later moved to Jerusalem where he established contact with the mystical group "Beth El," which had been founded by the Yemenite kabbalist Sar Shalom *Sharabi. Other Ḥasidim went to Ereẓ Israel, some settling in Tiberias. The newcomers made no notable impression on the Jews settled there. In 1777 a group of Ḥasidim of Ryzhin emigrated to the Holy Land under the leadership of *Menahem Mendel of Vitebsk. There were many who joined the caravan who were not members of the ḥasidic camp, and it numbered at the time of its arrival in Ereẓ Israel about 300 people. The newcomers settled in Safed but after a short while Menahem Mendel and some of his followers moved to Tiberias. Some remained in Safed, others moved to Peki'in, and so it was that the Ḥasidim spread over Jewish Galilee. Even in the very year of their immigration persecution against the Ḥasidim began in Galilee, for **Mitnaggedim* in Lithuania sent collections of

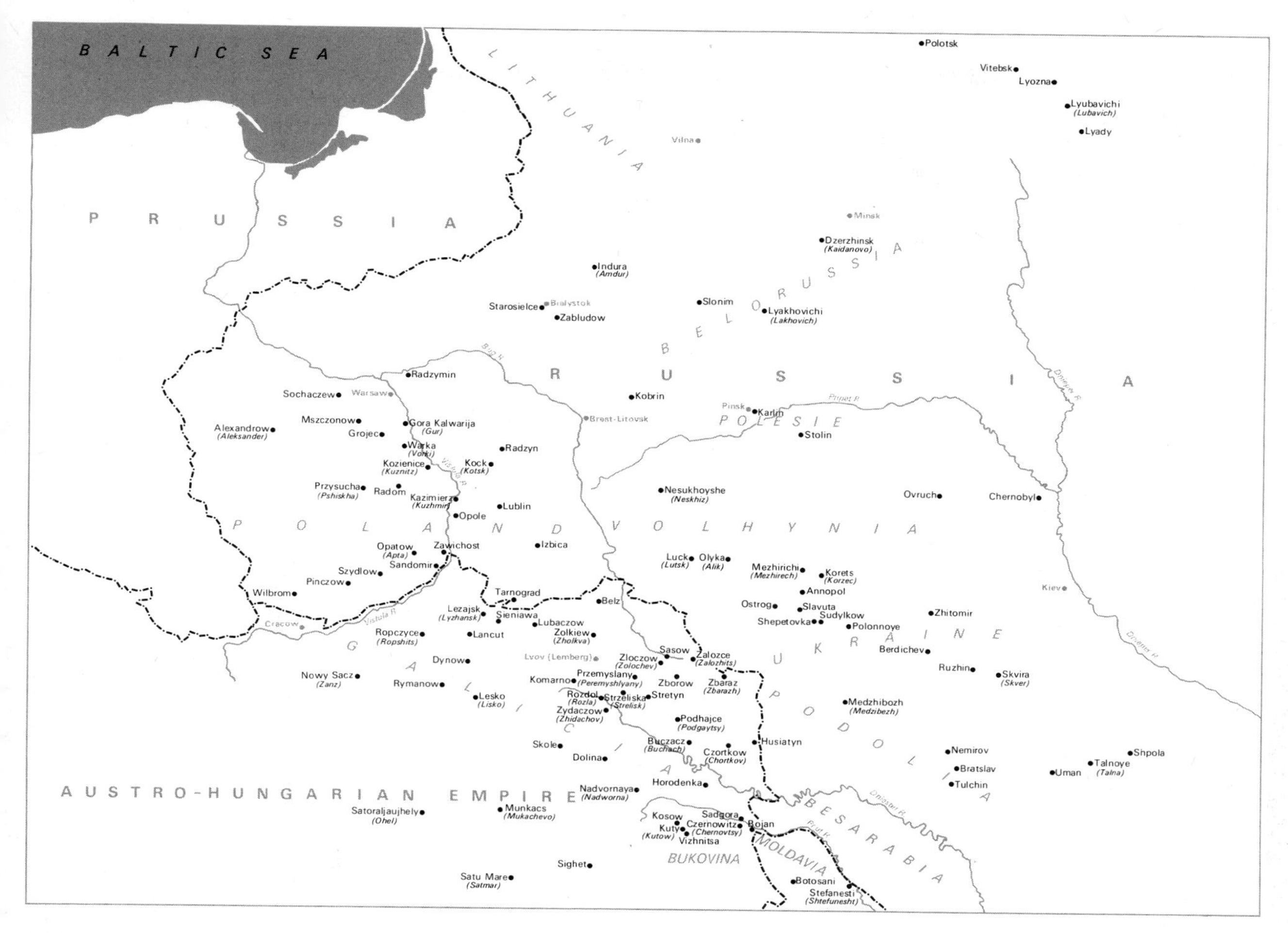

Main centers of Ḥasidism in Europe. Alternate names in Yiddish, Polish, Russian, and German are given in parentheses.

"evidence" against the Ḥasidim after they had left. The Sephardim in Safed participated in the controversy and sided with the *Mitnaggedim.* In 1784 Menahem Mendel built a house for himself and in it there was a synagogue. The Ḥasidim sent emissaries to collect money on their behalf and laid the foundation in Ryzhin, Lithuania, and in other places for the permanent support of the Ḥasidim of the Galilee.

The basic pattern of ḥasidic leadership and succession emerged in the third generation of the movement (c. 1773–1815). The spread and growth of Ḥasidism, both geographically and in numbers, the diversified and illustrious leadership of charismatic individuals who became heads of local centers, each developing his own style of teaching and interpretation of the ḥasidic way of life, the breakup of former lines of communication and of cultural ties caused by the partitions of Poland-Lithuania (1772, 1793, and 1795), and last but not least the pressures brought to bear on ḥasidic communities by the struggle against Ḥasidism—all these factors contributed to the decentralization of leadership of the ḥasidic world and consequently to an ever-growing diversification of ḥasidic thought and variation in the ḥasidic way of life. From this generation onward, there were always a number of contemporaneous leaders, each claiming the allegiance of his followers. In the main, both leadership and allegiance were handed down from generation to generation and thus arose both the dynasties of ḥasidic *ẓaddikim* and the hereditary camps of their followers. At times the living charismatic force reasserted itself anew, as in the case of *Jacob Isaac ha-Ḥozeh ("the seer") of Lublin, who began to lead a community in the lifetime of his master, *Elimelech of Lyzhansk, without his blessing, or Jacob Isaac *Przysucha who led a community in the lifetime of his master, though without leaving him. Descent from the first leaders of Ḥasidism did not inevitably guarantee preeminence (see *Abraham b. Dov of Mezhirech) nor was it a defense against bitter attacks on unconventional leadership (see *Naḥman of Bratslav, the great-grandson of the Ba'al Shem Tov).

In this third generation, the new pattern of leadership assured the victory of Ḥasidism over its opponents and its increasing spread throughout Eastern Europe. With the inclusion of Galicia in the Austrian Empire, Ḥasidism also gained adherents among Hungarian Jewry (see *Teitelbaum family, *Mukachevo). At this time Ḥasidism also developed systematic schools of theology, such as the more intellectual and study-centered *Ḥabad Ḥasidism. Some ḥasidic personalities, like Levi Isaac of Berdichev, were venerated by all Jewry as models of piety and love of humanity. The spiritual outlook and pattern of leadership of the practical *ẓaddik* (see below) also crystallized in this generation. Clearly, with such diversification in leadership and attitudes, from this generation on there was considerable and open tension between the various dynasties and courts of Ḥasidism, which sometimes flared up into bitter and prolonged conflicts (see, for example, *Naḥman of Bratslav, *Belz, *Gora Kalwaria (Gur), *Mukachevo, *Kotsk).

By the 1830s the main surge of the spread of Ḥasidism was over. From a persecuted sect it had become the way of life and leadership structure of the majority of Jews in the Ukraine, Galicia, and central Poland, and had sizable groups of followers in Belorussia-Lithuania and Hungary. With the great waves of emigration to the West from 1881,

Figure 1. "Ḥasidim in a *bet midrash*" by Isidor Kaufmann. New York, Oscar Gruss Collection. Photo Frank Darmstaedter, New York.

Ḥasidism was carried into Western Europe and especially to the United States. In the West its character was gradually, but ever more rapidly, diluted and its influence became more external and formal. With the abatement of the struggle against Ḥasidism by the end of its third generation and its acceptance as part of the Orthodox camp, Ḥasidism attained the distinction of being the first religious trend in Judaism since the days of the Second Temple which had a self-defined way of life and recognizable rite of worship, but yet was acknowledged (albeit somewhat grudgingly) by those who differed from it as a legitimate Jewish phenomenon.

Opposition to Ḥasidism. This recognition came only after a bitter struggle. However, only in Lithuania and possibly Ryzhin in the last 30 years of the 18th century did this struggle show clear signs of an organized movement. Except for this period, the opposition to Ḥasidism was confined to local controversies. The anti-ḥasidic camp was inspired by the ideas, fears, and personality of *Elijah b. Solomon Zalman, the Gaon of Vilna, who influenced the communal leadership to follow him in his opposition to Ḥasidism. To the Gaon, Ḥasidism's ecstasy, the visions seen and miracles wrought by its leaders, and its enthusiastic way of life were so many delusions, dangerous lies, and idolatrous worship of human beings. Ḥasidic stress on prayer seemed to him to overturn the Jewish scale of values in which study of the Torah and intellectual endeavor in this field were the main path to God. Aspersions were also cast on Ḥasidism because of the supposed hidden influence of the secret teachings of Shabbateanism and in particular of the almost contemporaneous Jacob Frank. Various ḥasidic changes in the knives for **sheḥitah*, and even more so in their change from the Ashkenazi to the Sephardi prayer rite, were seen as a challenge to Orthodoxy and a revolutionary rejection of traditional authority.

Writings of rabbis contemporaneous with the Besht reveal some suspicion and derision (Moses b. Jacob of Satanov in his *Mishmeret ha-Kodesh,* Solomon b. Moses *Chelm in his *Mirkevet ha-Mishneh,* and Ḥayyim ha-Kohen *Rapoport). In 1772 the first and second **ḥerem* were proclaimed against the Ḥasidim; ḥasidic works were burned; and the first pamphlet against Ḥasidism, *Zemir Ariẓim ve-Ḥorvot Ẓurim,* was published. The Ḥasidim countered with a *ḥerem* of their own and with burning the *Zemir Ariẓim;* at the same time Menahem Mendel of Vitebsk and Shneur Zalman of Lyady tried to approach Elijah of Vilna, but to no avail. In 1781 another harsh *ḥerem* was proclaimed against the Ḥasidim: "They must leave our communities with their wives and children . . . and they should not be given a night's lodging; their *sheḥitah* is forbidden; it is forbidden to do business with them and to intermarry with them, or to assist at their burial."

The struggle sharpened during the 1780s and in particular in the 1790s. Not infrequently both Ḥasidim and their opponents denounced each other to the secular authorities (see *Avigdor b. Joseph Ḥayyim, *Shneur Zalman of Lyady), leading to arrests of various ḥasidic leaders and mutual calumnies of a grave nature. With the crystallization of the movement of the *Mitnaggedim* in Jewish Lithuania on the one hand and the appearance of the *Haskalah as an enemy common to all Orthodoxy on the other, the bitterness and ferocity of the struggle between Ḥasidism and its opponents abated, though basic differences remained on estimation of the Jewish scale of values, the place of the leadership of *zaddikim*, and the permissibility of certain ecstatic traits of the ḥasidic way of life; sometimes latent and sometimes active, these differences never wholly subsided. The code for the Jews which came out in Russia in 1804 permitted each Jewish sect to build special synagogues for itself and to choose special rabbis for itself, and thus legalization was given to the Ḥasidim in Russia. In the conflict between the *Mitnaggedim* and the Ḥasidim, it was the Ḥasidim who were eventually victorious.

The wars of Napoleon and especially his Russian campaign (1812) aroused a strong reaction among the Jewish community. The Jews of Poland and Russia were located on opposite sides of the front. These wars gave birth to many ḥasidic traditions, whose degree of trustworthiness is unknown. According to them *zaddikim* "participated" in the battles, giving their magical thrust for one side or the other. In addition to the legendary material, there are two tested facts. Levi Isaac of Berdichev was at the top of the list of Jewish contributors to the war effort of the Russians against Napoleon (1807). Shneur Zalman of Lyady ordered his Ḥasidim to spy on behalf of Russia, by explaining that "if Bonaparte wins the wealthy among Israel would increase and the greatness of Israel would be raised, but they would leave and take the heart of Israel far from Father in Heaven" *(Beit Rabbi)*.

Modern Period. In the late 19th century and up to World War II various ḥasidic dynasties and camps entered the political life of modern parties and states. Ḥasidim were the mainstay of *Agudat Israel (and see also *Maḥzike Hadas).

This change constituted a new stage in the development of the ḥasidic movement. Alongside the spiritual leaders a growing class of secular activists developed. The expansion of the ḥasidic camp and its penetration to positions of authority and public responsibility in the communities gained influence for the activists who recognized the authority of the *zaddik* and submitted to his leadership. Yet, sometimes the *zaddik* was only a tool in their skillful hands. Through all of this Ḥasidism finally lost more and more of its spiritual character; it was eventually cut off from its kabbalistic sources and turned instead to organization.

To be sure, this process did not take place without sharp battles, and even in later generations there were *zaddikim* who tried to raise anew the foundations of the Ḥasidism of the Ba'al Shem Tov. Generally, the institutionalization of Ḥasidism continued to a greater degree and notable changes took place in its content. Spontaneity gave way to routine forms.

In the second half of the 19th century the expansion of Ḥasidism stopped. With the greater—albeit moderate—tendencies toward the secularization of Jewish life, Ḥasidism shut itself in and passed from a position of attack to one of defense. The ideas of the Enlightenment, national and socialist ideals, and the Zionist movements shook the traditional Jewish way of life. Ḥasidism strongly opposed any change in the way of life and in spiritual values and alienated itself from the new forces which rose up among the Jews. The movement of Ḥibbat Zion was not welcomed in the courts of the *zaddikim*. At the end of the 19th and the beginning of the 20th centuries, the Jewish workers' movements were outside the ḥasidic camp. The numbers of Ḥasidim did not decline, but its power of attraction was failing. Only in one area did Ḥasidism produce something new: namely, a strong emphasis on Torah study. The first ḥasidic yeshivah was founded, apparently, by Abraham Bornstein of Sochaczew in the 1860s. At the end of the century the *zaddikim* of Lubavich founded yeshivot of "Tomekhei Temimim." An attempt was also made to establish a yeshivah at Gur in Poland. It seems that by the study of Torah the ḥasidic leaders sought to immunize the ḥasidic youth from the "harmful influences" from outside With this they repeated, in essence, the attempt of the *Mitnaggedim* of Lithuania, who were defending themselves from Ḥasidism.

In World War I (1914–18) and the first few years following it, the distribution of Ḥasidism changed. Many of the *zaddikim* who lived in the area of the battles were driven out of their towns or were forced to leave because of economic difficulties and threats to security. The vast majority of them escaped to the big cities and some of them remained there after the war. The collapse of the Austro-Hungarian Empire and the formation of new countries sometimes cut off masses of Ḥasidim from their leaders and they found themselves politically in Rumania or Czechoslovakia. However, the most important and most tragic event in the lives of the Ḥasidim was the cutting off of the Russian branch, as the result of the Bolshevik regime.

The changes which took place in Jewish society in Eastern Europe in the period between the two World Wars (1918–39), and the problems which then faced the Jews, left their imprint upon the Ḥasidim of those countries. Ḥasidism continued in its conservatism. It was the main sector, and at times the only part of the Jewish population, which carefully maintained the tradition of dress, language, and education. The majority of Ḥasidim strongly opposed the Zionist movement and especially religious Zionism; they did not even encourage emigration to Ereẓ Israel which was growing during those years, although they did not interfere with it. However, many Ḥasidim did join the waves of emigration to Ereẓ Israel. Some of them founded Bene-Berak, Kefar Ḥasidim, etc., and others settled in cities and concentrated themselves in special ḥasidic *minyanim*. They remained loyal to the *zaddikim* abroad, naming themselves after them, and maintained their connections.

Figure 2. Ḥasidim in the Meah She'arim quarter of Jerusalem. Photo Zwy Bassey, Jerusalem.

Figure 3. Gur Ḥasidim wearing their Sabbath and festival *kapotes* (black silk coats) and *spodiks* (fur hats) on their way to the Western Wall in Jerusalem. Photo David Eisenberg, Jerusalem.

During the Holocaust the ḥasidic centers of Eastern Europe were destroyed. The masses of Ḥasidim perished and, together with them, most of the ḥasidic leaders. *Ẓaddikim* who survived moved to Israel or went to America and established new ḥasidic centers there. Although many Ḥasidim were active in Ereẓ Israel and were enthusiastic supporters of the foundation of the State of Israel (see e.g., *Kozienice, *Gur, Lubavich-*Schneersohn), for some of them this was a very late development, while others retained a bitter and active hostility to everything modern in Jewish life and culture and in particular to the State of Israel (see Joel *Teitelbaum of Satmar).

In the 20th century the philosophy of Martin *Buber and A. J. *Heschel and the works of such writers as Isaac Leib *Peretz helped to mold neo-Ḥasidism, which consequently had a considerable influence on modern Jewish culture and youth.

[A.Ru.]

United States. Ḥasidim emigrated to the U.S. within the great Jewish migration of 1880–1925, where they generally formed part of the larger body of pious immigrant Jews while frequently establishing *shtiblekh* of their own. They seem to have been less successful than non-ḥasidic immigrant Jews in transmitting their style of religious life to the next generation, because, apart from their *ẓaddikim,* who had remained in Europe, they apparently felt a fatalistic impotence to perpetuate the Judaism they knew. After World War I several *ẓaddikim* went to the U.S., including the Twersky dynasties from the Ukraine and the Monastritsh *ẓaddik*. They gathered followers but lacked the means and the sectarian fervor to establish a ḥasidic movement. This enervation ended with the arrival in 1940 of R. Joseph Isaac *Schneersohn, the *Lubavicher rebbe,* and the general revival of Orthodox Judaism in the U.S. from that date. A network of yeshivot and religious institutions was founded under the control of R. Joseph Isaac Schneersohn and his successor R. Menahem Mendel Schneersohn, and the unprecedented practice was initiated by Lubavich Ḥasidim of vigorously evangelizing Jews to return to Orthodoxy. The Lubavich Ḥasidic movement achieved wide attention and exercised some influence on the U.S. Jewish community.

Following World War II, surviving Polish and especially Hungarian Ḥasidim came to the U.S., including the *ẓaddikim* of Satmar (R. Joel Teitelbaum), Klausenburg-Sandz (Halberstam), and Telem (R. Levi Isaac Greenwald). The Hungarian Ḥasidim exhibited no interest in winning over other Jews and remained self-segregated. A small community of Ḥasidim, followers of the *ẓaddik* of Skver, established the suburban township of New Square, Rockland County, near New York City. Most Hungarian Ḥasidim concentrated in a few neighborhoods of New York City, shunned the daily press and the mass media, and rejected secular education with grudging acceptance of the state's minimum standards. Most controversial was the relentless hostility toward the State of Israel, especially of Satmar Ḥasidim, who published tracts and conducted public demonstrations against it. [L.P.G.]

Ḥasidic Way of Life. Leadership Patterns. The personality and activities of Israel Ba'al Shem Tov, and the theories and traditions transmitted in his name and developed and augmented by his followers and disciples, shaped the pattern of leadership in Ḥasidism: the leader was the *ẓaddik,* whose charismatic personality made him the paramount authority in the community of his followers. Tensions already evident at the time Dov Baer of Mezhirech assumed the leadership of the Ḥasidim, and the splintering of the leadership after his death, caused variations and sometimes deviations in this pattern, but in its essentials it remained unchanged.

All ḥasidic leadership is characterized by an extraordinary magnetism, given expression through various activities and symbols. The *ẓaddik* is believed in, devoutly admired, and obediently followed. From the end of the third generation of Ḥasidism, a dynastic style of leadership often developed, with generation after generation of a certain dynasty of *ẓaddikim* following in the main its own specific interpretation of the ḥasidic way of life and communal cohesion (e.g., the more intellectual and theoretical pattern with the Lubavich-Schneersohn dynasty at the head of the Ḥabad wing; the enthusiastic and revolutionary teachings, style of leadership, and communal pattern of the Kotsk dynasty).

Laying differing stress on the various elements of ḥasidic belief and life-style, the *ẓaddik* provides the spiritual illumination for the individual Ḥasid and the ḥasidic community from his own all-pervasive radiance, attained through his mystic union with God. This union and the ensuing enrichment of his soul are used for the sake of the people, to lead them lovingly to their creator. The *ẓaddik* is a mystic who employs his power within the social community and for its sake. A wonder-healer and miracle-worker, in the eyes of his followers he is a combination of confessor, moral instructor, and practical adviser. Also a theoretical teacher and exegetical preacher, with a style of preaching peculiar to *ẓaddikim,* he expounds his ḥasidic *torah* (Hebrew for the teaching of the *ẓaddikim*) at his table (in ḥasidic parlance *der tish*) surrounded by his followers, generally during the third meal on the Sabbath *(se'udah shelishit).* For the individual Ḥasid, joining the court of his *ẓaddik* is both a pilgrimage and a revitalizing unification with the brotherhood gathered at the court, united around and through the *ẓaddik.* The Ḥasid journeyed to his *ẓaddik's* court at least for the High Holidays (although this practice later weakened) to seek his blessing, which was also entreated from afar. He submitted a written account of his problems (known as a *kvitl*), usually accompanying this with a monetary contribution (*pidyon,* short for *pidyon nefesh,* "redemption of the soul"). The money went toward the upkeep of the *ẓaddik* and his court (who were not dependent on or supported by any single community) and was also used to provide for the needs of the poor in the ḥasidic community. Serving as intermediaries between the *ẓaddik* and the Ḥasidim were the *gabbai* (the administrative head of the court) or the *meshammesh* (the *ẓaddik's* chamberlain), who from the first generation onward mediated between the *zaddik* and the Ḥasid in matters of *kvitl* or *pidyon*. In Ḥasidism the *zaddik* is conceived of as the ladder between heaven and earth, his mystic contemplation linking him with the Divinity, and his concern for the people and loving leadership tying him to earth. Hence his absolute authority, as well as the belief of most ḥasidic dynasties that the *zaddik* must dwell in visible affluence.

The Prayer Rite and Other Customs. From its beginnings Ḥasidism developed its own prayer rite. In fact, the ḥasidic version of the prayers, though called *Sephard*, is not identical with the Sephardi rite, nor with the Ashkenazi, but is a combination of: (1) the Polish Ashkenazi rite; (2) changes made by Isaac Luria; and (3) the Sephardi rite of Palestine upon which Luria based his changes. The result is a patchwork and was a source of great confusion. The ḥasidic version itself is not uniform and there are many differences between the various ḥasidic prayer books. The first ḥasidic prayer book was that of Shneur Zalman of Lyady (Shklov, 1803). The main differences in ḥasidic prayer are: the recitation of the collection of verses beginning with I Chronicles 16:8 (*"hodu"*) before **Pesukei de-Zimra;* in the *Kedushah*, they recite *Nakdishkha* in *Shaharit* and in *Minḥah*, *Keter* in *Musaf* (see **Kedushah*). Prayer for the Ḥasid is ecstatic and loud, involving song, body movements, shaking, and clapping.

In the first generations of Ḥasidism, while it was still a minority belief in most communities and under bitter attack, the Ḥasidim opened their own small prayer houses, called *shtiblekh*, a name which continued to be used. The separateness of the ḥasidic community was aggravated by their insistence on a specific type of highly sharpened (*geshlifene*) *sheḥitah* knife, a demand which both necessitated and permitted a separate ḥasidic *sheḥitah* with its own income and organization. The reason for this custom has not been sufficiently explained.

As by the mid-19th century Ḥasidism prevailed in most communities of the Ukraine, Volhynia, central Poland, Galicia, and in many in Hungary and Belorussia, the pattern of leadership based on the *zaddik* changed the character of local community leadership to a considerable extent. Local leaders and rabbis became subject to the authority of the *zaddik* whose followers were the most influential ḥasidic group in a given community.

The image and memory of past and present *zaddikim* are shaped and kept alive through the ḥasidic tale (*ma'aseh*), which is recounted as an act of homage to the living link between the Ḥasid and his God. As well as embodying the sayings of such teachers as Israel Ba'al Shem Tov, Levi Isaac of Berdichev, Naḥman of Bratslav, and Menahem Mendel of Kotsk, these tales reflect popular philosophy to a great extent.

The insistence of Ḥasidism from its inception on joy (*simḥah*) as the prime factor in the good Jewish life and the essential element of divine worship led to the importance of the ḥasidic dance and song as expressions of piety and group cohesion, whether in the *shtiblekh* in the individual community or when united together at the *zaddik's* court and table. Ḥasidic influence was spread, but was also further splintered, by the widespread custom of giving support and something approaching the status of *zaddik* to descendants of a dynasty who did not become *zaddikim* (the so-called *einiklakh*, "the grandsons"). Various other specific ḥasidic customs (e.g., the rushing to the *zaddik's* table to obtain a portion of the remnants (*shirayim*) of the food he had touched) were contributing factors to the closeness of the ḥasidic group. The ecstatic prayer of the *zaddik*—mostly when reciting the Song of Songs or the *Lekhu Nerannenah* prayer on the entry of the Sabbath—which figures frequently in ḥasidic tales, was a powerful element in holding the group together.

The elements of ḥasidic song, dance, and tale later became influential in modern Jewish youth movements and helped to shape neo-Ḥasidism. From the end of World War I, the Ḥabad-Lubavich movement led the underground struggle to maintain Jewish religious life and culture under

Figure 4. A *Farbrengen* (ḥasidic gathering) with Rabbi Menahem Mendel Schneersohn, the Lubavicher Rebbe, in Brooklyn, New York, in the 1960s.

Figure 5. "A Ḥasid studying" by Lazar Krestin, 1902. Cincinnati, Ohio, Hebrew Union College Museum.

communist regimes (see *Russia). Some ḥasidic dynasties took part in the creation of agricultural settlements in Israel (*Kefar Ḥasidim, *Kefar Ḥabad). In recent times, groups of young Jews in the United States have demonstrated their allegiance to protest movements through turning to ḥasidic modes of expression to embody their enthusiasm, specific cohesion, and adherence to Jewish identity. [A.RU.]

BASIC IDEAS OF ḤASIDISM

Creator and Universe. While it is true that many of the basic ideas of Ḥasidism are grounded in earlier Jewish sources, the Ḥasidim did produce much that was new if only by emphasis. With few exceptions, ḥasidic ideas are not presented systematically in the ḥasidic writings, but an examination of these writings reveals certain patterns common to all the ḥasidic masters. Central to ḥasidic thought is an elaboration of the idea, found in the Lurianic Kabbalah, that God "withdrew from Himself into Himself" in order to leave the primordial "empty space" into which the finite world could eventually emerge after a long process of emanations. This "withdrawal" *(ẓimẓum)*, according to Ḥabad thought especially and to a considerable degree also to ḥasidic thought in general, does not really take place but only appears to do so. The infinite divine light is progressively screened so as not to engulf all in its tremendous glory so that creatures can appear to enjoy an independent existence. The whole universe is, then, a "garment" of God, emerging from Him "like the snail whose shell is formed of itself."

In a parable attributed to the Ba'al Shem Tov a mighty king sits on his throne, situated in the center of a huge palace with many halls, all of them filled with gold, silver, and precious stones. Those servants of the king who are far more interested in acquiring wealth than in gazing at the king's splendor spend all their time, when they are admitted to the palace, in the outer halls, gathering the treasures they find there. So engrossed are they in this that they never see the countenance of the king. But the wise servants, refusing to be distracted by the treasures in the halls, press on until they come to the king on his throne in the center of the palace. To their astonishment, once they reach the king's presence, they discover that the palace, its halls, and their treasures are really only an illusion, created by the king's magical powers. In the same way God hides Himself in the "garments" and "barriers" of the cosmos and the "upper worlds." When man recognizes that this is so, when he acknowledges that all is created out of God's essence and that, in reality, there are no barriers between man and his God, "all the workers of iniquity" are dispersed (*Keter Shem Tov*, I, 5a–b). In its context this parable refers to prayer. Man should persist in his devotions and refuse to be distracted by extraneous thoughts. But the idea that all is in God is clearly implied. The verse: "Know this day, and lay it to thy heart, that the Lord He is God in heaven above and in the earth beneath; there is none else" (Deut. 4:39) is read as: "there is nothing else." In reality there is nothing but God, for otherwise the world would be "separate" from God and this would imply limitation in Him (*Keter Shem Tov*, I, 8b).

The ḥasidic leader R. Menahem Mendel of Lubavich observes (*Derekh Mitzvotekha* (1911), 123) that the disciples of the Ba'al Shem Tov gave the "very profound" turn to the doctrine of the oneness of God so that it means not alone that He is unique, as the medieval thinkers said, but that He is all that is: "That there is no reality in created things. This is to say that in truth all creatures are not in the category of 'something' *[yesh]* or a 'thing' *[davar]* as we see them with our eyes. For this is only from our point of view since we cannot perceive the divine vitality. But from the point of view of the divine vitality which sustains us we have no existence and we are in the category of complete nothingness *[efes]* like the rays of the sun in the sun itself . . . From which it follows that there is no other existence whatsoever apart from His existence, blessed be He. This is true unification. As the saying has it: 'Thou art before the world was created and now that it is created'—in exactly the same manner. Namely, just as there was no existence apart from Him before the world was created so it is even now."

As a corollary of ḥasidic pantheism (more correctly, panentheism) is the understanding in its most extreme form of the doctrine of divine providence. The medieval thinkers limited special providence to the human species and allowed only general providence so far as the rest of creation is concerned. It is purely by chance that this spider catches that fly, that this ox survives, the other dies. For the Ḥasidim there is nothing random in a universe that is God's "garment." No stone lies where it does, no leaf falls from the tree, unless it has been so arranged by divine wisdom.

Particularly during prayer but also at other times man has to try to overcome the limitations of his finite being to see only the divine light into which, from the standpoint of ultimate reality, he and the cosmos are absorbed. This transcendence of the ego is known in ḥasidic thought as *bittul ha-yesh*, "the annihilation of selfhood." Humility *(shiflut)* does not mean for Ḥasidism that man thinks little of himself but that he does not think of himself at all. Only through humility can man be the recipient of God's grace. He must empty himself so that he might be filled with God's gifts.

Optimism, Joy, and Hitlahavut. Ḥasidic optimism and joy *(simḥah)* are also based on the notion that all is in God. If the world and its sorrows do not enjoy true existence and the divine light and vitality pervade all, what cause is there for despair or despondency? When man rejoices that he has been called to serve God, he bestirs the divine joy above and blessing flows through all creation. A melancholy attitude of mind is anathema to Ḥasidism, serving only to create a barrier between man and his Maker. Even over his sins a man should not grieve overmuch: "At times the evil inclination misleads man into supposing that he has committed a serious sin when it was actually no more than a mere peccadillo or no sin at all, the intention being to bring man into a state of melancholy *[aẓvut]*. But melancholy is a great hindrance to God's service. Even if a man has stumbled and sinned he should not become too sad because this will prevent him from worshiping God" (*Ẓavva'at Ribash* (1913), 9). Some ḥasidic teachers, however, draw a distinction between man's "bitterness" *(merirut)* at his remoteness from God and "sadness." The former is commendable in that it is lively and piercing whereas the latter denotes deadness of soul. A further result of the basic ḥasidic philosophy is *hitlahavut*, "burning enthusiasm," in which the soul is aflame with ardor for God whose presence is everywhere. Man's thought can cleave to God, to see only the divine light, and this state of attachment *(devekut)*, of always being with God, is the true aim of all worship.

Love and Fear. The study of the Torah, prayer, and other religious duties must be carried out in love and fear. The bare deed without the love and fear of God is like a bird without wings. A ḥasidic tale relates that the Ba'al Shem Tov was unable to enter a certain synagogue because it was full of lifeless prayers, which, lacking the wings of love and fear, were unable to ascend to God. As observant Jews the Ḥasidim did not seek to deny the value of the deed but they taught repeatedly that the deed could only be elevated when carried out in a spirit of devotion. R. Ḥayyim of Czernowitz writes (*Sha'ar ha-Tefillah* (1813), 7b): "There is a man whose love for his God is so strong and faithful that he carries out each *mitzvah* with superlative excellence, strength and marvelous power, waiting in longing to perform the *mitzvah*, his soul expiring in yearning. For, in accordance with his spiritual rank, his heart and soul know the gracious value of the *mitzvot* and the splendor of their tremendous glory and beauty, infinitely higher than all values. And how much more so the dread and fear, the terror and trembling, which fall on such a man when he performs a *mitzvah*, knowing as he does with certainty that he stands before the name of the Holy One, blessed be He, the great and terrible King, before Whom 'all the inhabitants of the earth are reputed as nothing; and He doeth according to His will in the host of heaven' [Dan. 4:32], who stands over him always, seeing his deeds, for His glory fills the earth. Such a man is always in a state of shame and lowliness so intense that the world cannot contain it, especially when he carries out the *mitzvot*. Such a man's *mitzvot* are those which fly ever upward in joy and satisfaction to draw down from there every kind of blessing and flow of grace to all worlds."

This idea was applied to all man's deeds, not only to his religious obligations. In all things there are "holy sparks" *(niẓoẓot)* waiting to be redeemed and rescued for sanctity through man using his appetites to serve God. The very taste of food is a pale reflection of the spiritual force which brings the food into being. Man should be led on by it to contemplate the divine vitality in the food and so to God Himself. In the words of the highly charged mythology of the Lurianic Kabbalah, the "holy sparks" released by man provide the *Shekhinah* with her "Female Waters" which, in turn, cause the flow of the "Male Waters" and so assist "the unification of the Holy One, blessed be He, and His *Shekhinah*" to produce cosmic harmony. Because of the importance of man's role for the sacred marriage and its importance in the ḥasidic scheme, the Ḥasidim adopted from the kabbalists the formula: "For the sake of the unification of the Holy One, blessed be He, and His *Shekhinah*" *(le-shem yiḥud)* before the performance of every good deed, for which they were vehemently attacked by R. Ezekiel Landau of Prague (*Noda bi-Yhudah*, YD no. 93). (The redemption of the "holy sparks" was one of the reasons given for ḥasidic fondness for tobacco. Smoking a pipe served to release subtle "sparks" not otherwise accessible.)

Kavannah and Ẓaddikism. Is this program of sustained contemplation, attachment, and utter devotion to God really possible for all men? The ḥasidic answer is generally in the negative. This is why the doctrine of ẓaddikism is so important for Ḥasidism. The holy man, his thoughts constantly on God, raises the prayers of his followers and all their other thoughts and actions. In the comprehensive work on ẓaddikism, R. Elimelech of Lyzhansk's *No'am Elimelekh*, the *ẓaddik* appears as a spiritual superman, with the power to work miracles. He is the channel through which the divine grace flows, the man to whom God has given control of the universe by his prayers. The *ẓaddik* performs a double task: he brings man nearer to God and he brings down God's bounty to man. The *ẓaddik* must be supported by his followers. This financial assistance is not for the sake of the *ẓaddik* but for the sake of those privileged to help him. By supporting the *ẓaddik* with their worldly goods his followers become attached to him through his dependence on them, which he readily accepts in his love for them. Their welfare thus becomes his and his prayers on their behalf can the more readily be answered. The *ẓaddik* even has powers over life and death. God may have decreed that a person should die but the prayers of the *ẓaddik* can nullify this decree. This is because the *ẓaddik's* soul is so pure and elevated that it can reach to those worlds in which no decree has been promulgated since there only mercy reigns.

But if such powers were evidently denied to the great ones of the past how does the *ẓaddik* come to have them? The rationale is contained in a parable attributed to the Maggid of Mezhirech (*No'am Elimelekh* to Gen. 37:1). When a king is on his travels he will be prepared to enter the most humble dwelling if he can find rest there but when the king is at home he will refuse to leave his palace unless he is invited by a great lord who knows how to pay him full regal honors. In earlier generations only the greatest of Jews could attain to the holy spirit. Now that the *Shekhinah* is in exile, God is ready to dwell in every soul free from sin.

Social Involvement. The social implications of ḥasidic thought should not be underestimated. The sorry conditions of the Jews in the lands in which Ḥasidism was born were keenly felt by the ḥasidic masters who considered it a duty of the highest order to alleviate their sufferings. In the ḥasidic court the wealthy were instructed to help their poorer brethren, the learned not to look down on their untutored fellows. The unity of the Jewish people and the need for Jews to participate in one another's joys and sorrows was repeatedly stressed. The preachers who seemed to take a perverse delight in ruthlessly exposing Jewish shortcomings were taken to task by the Ba'al Shem Tov and his followers. The *ẓaddik* was always on the lookout for excuses for Jewish faults. R. Levi Isaac of Berdichev is the supreme example of the *ẓaddik* who challenges God Himself to show mercy to His people.

From the numerous anti-ḥasidic polemics (collected e.g., by M. Wilensky, *Ḥasidim u-Mitnaggedim*, 1970) we learn

Figure 6. Rabbi Fridman, the Boyaner Rebbe, blessing wine and food before allotting the *shirayim* (the remaining portion) to his Ḥasidim. Photo Yacoby, Jerusalem.

which of the ḥasidic ideas were especially offensive to their opponents. The doctrine that all is in God was treated as sheer blasphemy. The doctrine, it was said, would lead to "thinking on the Torah in unclean places" i.e. it would obliterate the distinction between the clean and the unclean, the licit and the illicit. The alleged arrogance of the claims made for the *zaddik* were similarly a cause of offense. The ḥasidic elevation of contemplative prayer over all other obligations, especially over the study of the Torah, seemed to be a complete reversal of the traditional scale of values. The doctrine of *bittul ha-yesh* was criticized as leading to moral irresponsibility. The bizarre practice of turning somersaults in prayer, followed by a number of the early Ḥasidim as an expression of self-abnegation, was held up to ridicule, as was ḥasidic indulgence in alcoholic stimulants and tobacco. The resort of the Ḥasidim to prayer in special conventicles (the *shtiblekh*), their adoption of the Lurianic prayer book, their encouragement of young men to leave their families for long periods to stay at the court of the *zaddik*, were all anathema to the *Mitnaggedim* who saw in the whole process a determined revolt against the established order. [L.J.]

TEACHINGS OF ḤASIDISM

Origins of Ḥasidic Teachings. The teachings of Ḥasidism are as notable for their striking content as they are for the colorful literary form in which they are cast. Their sources, however, are readily traceable to kabbalistic literature and to the *musar* literature of Safed deriving from it. The first generation of ḥasidic teachers usually embodied their teachings in terse aphorisms. These, too, reflect the influence of the aforementioned literature. The first evidence of the spread of ḥasidic teaching dates from the 1750s and comes from the anti-ḥasidic polemical writings of the *Mitnaggedim*, their implacable opponents. Authentic ḥasidic teachings appeared in print only at the beginning of the 1780s. These published teachings of the Ḥasidim make no reference to the doctrines ascribed to them by their mitnaggedic opponents. For this curious fact, two possible explanations suggest themselves. Either the *Mitnaggedim* were guilty of exaggeration and distortion in their hostile description of ḥasidic doctrine or, in the interim, a process of internal criticism had moderated original ḥasidic teachings in the decades preceding their publication. The likelihood is that both factors were at work. This does not mean to imply, however, that the teachings of Israel b. Eliezer (the Ba'al Shem Tov) recorded by his disciples are to be regarded as having been censored, thus casting doubt on their authenticity. What is to be inferred is that the antinomian and anarchistic doctrines taught by certain circles were not incorporated into classical Ḥasidism. While no evidence of the specific character of such teachings is available, there can be no doubt of the existence of such groups.

The teachings of the earliest circles of Ḥasidim were transmitted in the name of Israel Ba'al Shem Tov, Judah Leib Piestanyer, Naḥman of Kosov, Naḥman of Horodenko (Gorodenka), and others. This was a group of decided spiritual (pneumatic) cast which also fashioned for itself a particular communal life-style, a community built not on family units but rather on meetings organized around prayer circles. As a matter of principle, this pattern served as the basis for the development of the classic ḥasidic community.

It may be said that for the first time in the history of Jewish mysticism, ḥasidic thought reflects certain social concerns. There is present a confrontation with distinctly societal phenomena and their transformation into legitimate problems in mysticism as such. This concern is expressed not in the establishment of specific liturgical norms or formulas devised for the convenience of the congregation but in such doctrines as the worship of God through every material act, and the "uplifting of the sparks" *(nizozot)*. In the teachings of the Ba'al Shem Tov and his circles these doctrines involved a sense of social mission.

Worship Through Corporeality (Avodah be-Gashmiyyut). One of the most widespread teachings of Ḥasidism from the very beginnings of the movement is the doctrine calling for man's worship of God by means of his physical acts. In other words, the human physical dimension is regarded as an area capable of religious behavior and value. From this assumption, a variety of religious tendencies followed. To be especially noted is the extraordinary emphasis placed on the value of such worship and the subsequent attempt to limit it to a devotional practice suitable only for spiritually superior individuals. In the teachings of the Ba'al Shem Tov, this doctrine developed in uncontrolled fashion, culminating in the tenet that man must worship God with both the good and the evil in his nature.

The ideological background of worshiping God through such physical acts as eating, drinking, and sexual relations was suggested by the verse "in all thy ways shalt thou know Him" (Prov. 3:6). For if it is incumbent upon man to worship God with all his natural impulses by transforming them into good, then obviously the realization of such an idea demands involvement in that very area in which these impulses are made manifest—the concrete, material world. In addition, the revolutionary views concealed within the interstices of the teachings of the Ba'al Shem Tov make it clear that corporeal worship *(avodah be-gashmiyyut)* saves man from the dangers of an overwrought spiritualism and retreat from the real world. This is expressed by Jacob Joseph of Polonnoye, a disciple of the Ba'al Shem Tov, in the name of his teacher: "I have heard from my teacher that the soul, having been hewn from its holy quarry, ever ought to long for its place of origin, and, lest its reality be extinguished as a result of its yearning, it has been surrounded with matter, so that it may also perform material acts such as eating, drinking, conduct of business and the like, in order that it [the soul] may not be perpetually inflamed by the worship of the Holy One blessed be He, through the principle of the perfection *[tikkun]* and maintenance of body and soul" (*Toledot Ya'akov Yosef*, ch. *Tazri'a*). The point made here in advocacy of corporeal worship is largely psychological and not theological.

The theological concept designed to reinforce the affirmation of corporeal worship is grounded in the dialectical relationship that operates between matter and spirit. In order to reach the spiritual goal, man must pass through the material stage, for the spiritual is only a higher level of the material. The parables of the Ba'al Shem Tov of the "lost son" point to the theological function served by the concept of "corporeal worship." The son, in foreign captivity, enters the local tavern with his captors, all the time guarding within him a hidden secret which is none other than the key to his redemption. While his captors drink only for the sake of drinking, he drinks in order to disguise his true happiness which consists not in drinking but rather in his "father's letter"—his secret—informing him of his impending release from captivity. In other words, there is no way to be liberated from the captivity of matter except by ostensibly cooperating with it. This ambivalent relation to reality forms a supreme religious imperative.

Social Consequences of the Doctrine of "Corporeal Worship." The dialectic tension between matter and spirit or between form and matter—the conventional formulation in Ḥasidism—assumes social significance and the polar terms come to denote the relationship between the *zaddik* and his congregation. In this context, the opposition between spirit and matter is conceived so as to create a seeming tension between the inner content of the mystical act and the forms of social activity. It is within the community, however, that mystical activity should be achieved though, of course, in hidden fashion. Those who surround the *zaddik* are incapable of individually discerning the moment in which the transformation of the secular into the holy occurs. This indispensable transformation can be experienced only communally. Therefore, the community of Ḥasidim becomes a necessary condition for the individual's realization of the mystical experience. It became the imperative of Ḥasidism to live both in society and beyond its bounds at one and the same time. The social and psychological conditions necessary for fulfillment of "corporeal worship" are rooted not alone in the disparity between form and matter, i.e., between the masses and the *zaddik*, but rather in the inner spiritual connection between the two. Only the presence of a basic common denominator makes possible the appearance of a mystical personality which grows dialectically out of otherwise disparate elements. The *zaddik* represents the "particular amid the general." The absence of such integration precludes the consequent growth of the spiritual element.

In the teachings of the Ba'al Shem Tov, little stress is placed on the theories of the Lurianic Kabbalah centering in the "uplifting of the sparks." Nevertheless, these theories later served as the theoretical justification for the necessity of *avodah be-gashmiyyut*. The Lurianic theory, as interpreted by the Ḥasidim, maintains that through contact with the concrete material world by means of *devekut* ("communion" with God), and *kavvanah* ("devotional intent"), man uplifts the sparks imprisoned in matter. In this context, the concept of *avodah be-gashmiyyut* carries with it a distinct polemical note, since it is asserted that its validity has particular application to the sphere of social life. Thus, a major religious transvaluation finds expression in the creation of a new system of social relations. This is exemplified in the instructions given by the Ba'al Shem Tov granting permission to desist from *devekut* during prayer in order to respond to some social need. He indicates that should a man be approached during a period of *devekut* by a person wishing to talk to him or seeking his assistance he is permitted to stop praying since in this latter action (i.e., in directing his attention from prayer to his fellow) "God is present." Here, the temporary abandonment of the study of Torah *(bittul Torah)* and of *devekut* is justified by the fact that this encounter too constitutes part of the spiritual experience of the "spiritually perfect man." As a result, the meaning of religious "perfection" is determined by a new system of values.

In the teachings of the Ba'al Shem Tov's disciple, Dov Baer, the Maggid of Mezhirech, these motives disappear. The direction of thinking assumes a completely typical spiritualistic character. *Avodah be-gashmiyyut* is conceived of as an indispensable necessity although it is covertly questioned whether every man is permitted to engage in it. A pupil of one of the Maggid's disciples, *Meshullam Feivush of Zbarazh, specifically states that it was not the Maggid's intention to proclaim *avodah be-gashmiyyut* as a general practice but rather as a practice intended for an elite immune to the danger of the concept's vulgarization. One of the Maggid's most important disciples, Shneur Zalman of Lyady, mentions the practice with a touch of derision. Nevertheless, it came to occupy a central place in the literature of Ḥasidism. The meaning and limits of the concept served as a focal point of an ongoing controversy among the movement's proponents.

Figure 7. Ḥasidim in their weekday beaver hats. Photo Zwy Bassey, Jerusalem.

The Ethos of Ḥasidism. From the moment that the formula *yeridah le-zorekh aliyyah* ("the descent in behalf of the ascent") became established in the context of the emphasis placed upon it by the Ba'al Shem Tov, a certain perturbation of the traditional system of ethical values in Judaism was imminent. Although the precise limits of the descent into the region of evil were still open to debate, the acceptance in principle of man's mandate to "transform" evil into good, through an actual confrontation of evil in its own domain, was an idea definitely unwelcome in any institutionalized religion. The classical example of dealing with this problem propounded in the teachings of the Ba'al Shem Tov was that of the encounter with evil in the sphere of human impulses: "A man should desire a woman to so great an extent that he refines away his material existence, in virtue of the strength of his desire." The significance of this statement lies in its granting a warrant to exhaust the primordial desires without actually realizing them; it is not a dispensation for the release of bodily desires through physical actualization but through their transformation. This concept is of great importance to an understanding of the significance of confronting evil, as it points to the peculiar inner logic implicit in the idea of *avodah be-gashmiyyut* as found expression in the ethical sphere.

Within the framework of the concept of "descent" *(yeridah)*—a concept over which Ḥasidism wavered a great deal—can be included the idea of the "descent" of the *zaddik* toward the sinner in order to uplift him. This "descent" carries with it bold ethical implications in that it justifies the "descent" into the sphere of evil and demands the consequent "ascent" from the domain of sin. A moral danger is of course implicit in the real possibility that a man may "descend" and thereafter find himself unable to achieve the consequent ascent. Here again, the very act of confronting evil requires an independent valuation, admitting of no previous criticism or censorship, although such confrontation was regarded as the special prerogative of men of "spirit," i.e., the *zaddikim*. Thus, out of the teachings of the Ba'al Shem Tov arose a primary imperative to turn toward material reality and the worldly inferior sphere. If only in moral terms, this demand grew from a basic ethic-religious claim that man is not at liberty to abstain from the task of transfiguring the material world through good.

The teachings of the Maggid of Mezhirech reveal a more restrained doctrine on the one hand, and an interiorization of spiritual problems on the other, evidenced by the greater degree of introspection and inwardness characteristic of the mystic. In the Maggid can be discerned a tendency toward an increasing spiritualization, accompanied by greater moral restraint. Among the followers of the Maggid, however, developments took place in very different directions. In the courts of some *zaddikim* the influence of the thinking of the Ba'al Shem Tov was apparent in the doctrines they broadcast, propagating social responsibility and a communal mysticism. These centers of teaching developed primarily in Galicia, the Ukraine, and also in Poland at the court of the rabbi of Lublin. This last school reached a crisis point during the period of its heirs in *Przysucha, *Kotsk, and *Izbica, when it began to cast doubt on the large majority of accepted ḥasidic doctrines, especially on their moral significance. At the same time Ḥabad Ḥasidism in Belorussia developed in the direction of a rationalized religious life by preserving pre-ḥasidic moral biases, and by shunning the mystical adventurism of the Ba'al Shem Tov and even the Maggid of Mezhirech, which in its attempt to spiritualize reality, had propounded as necessary the confrontation with evil and laid down the conditions for this conflict, while seeing in the "uplift of the sparks" its great mission. Nevertheless in the person of Dov Baer, son of Shneur Zalman of Lyady, the founder of Ḥabad Ḥasidism, can be discerned a thinker with a tendency toward a pure and aristocratic mysticism, a fact which establishes his affinity to the views of the Maggid of Mezhirech, although this holds true only in terms of this aristocratic bent. In terms of an "ethical mentality," as it were, Dov Baer is a representative of his father's line of thought.

Prayer. In the second and third generation of Ḥasidism, some Ḥasidim testified to the fact that, in their view, the major innovation of the Ba'al Shem Tov lay in his introducing in prayer a fundamentally new significance as well as new modes of praying. The author of *Ma'or va-Shemesh,* a disciple of Elimelech of Lyzhansk, writes, "Ever since the time of the holy Ba'al Shem Tov, of blessed and sanctified memory, the light of the exertion of the holiness of prayer has looked out and shone down upon the world, and into everybody who desires to approach the Lord, blessed be He . . ." This can be understood to mean that the Ḥasidim saw in the doctrine of the Ba'al Shem Tov two things as essentially one: the radiance (of the light of holiness) and new hope, and the revived exertion (involved in the holiness of prayer). These dual motifs began to function as guidelines for ḥasidic prayer, in the following senses:

(1) The origins of prayer lie in the conflict with the external world, known as "evil thoughts." Prayer requires a great effort of concentration if man is to overcome the tendency of the plenitude of exterior reality to permeate his consciousness. This quite natural permeation to which man responds instinctively is considered in Ḥasidism as the "wayfaring" of thought and as such is the very opposite of its concentration, which requires a negation of the world, a turning away from it, and is based on man's ability to achieve pure introspection devoid of all content. The function of this introspection is to achieve the utter voiding ("annihilation") of human thought and to uplift the element of divinity latent in man's soul. The transformation of this element from a latent to an active condition is understood as true union with God, the state marking the climax of *devekut* ("clinging to God," "communion with God"). Prayer, then, is regarded as the most accessible foundation for the technique of *devekut* with God. The spiritual effort involved in prayer was considered so strenuous as to give rise to the ḥasidic dictum "I give thanks to God that I remain alive after praying."

(2) The two stages described as constituting the process of prayer are: *dibbur* ("speech") and *maḥashavah* ("thought"). In passing through the first of these stages man contemplates the words of the prayer through visualizing their letters. Concentrated attention on these objects before his eyes gradually depletes the letters of their contours and voids thought of content, and speech, the reciting of the prayers, becomes automatic. Man continues to recite the prayers until an awesome stillness descends upon him, and his thought ceases to function in particulars; he establishes a connection with the divine "World of Thought" which functions on transcendent and immanent perceptible levels at one and the same time. This immanent activity is identical with the revelation of the "apex," the inner "I." In the wordplay of the Ḥasidim: "the I (אני) becomes Nought" (אין); in the "flash of an eye" a condition of utter annulment is established, and this is the state of nothingness the mystic seeks to achieve.

(3) For Ḥasidism the significance of prayer lies neither in beseeching the Creator and supplicating Him, nor in focusing attention on the contents of prayer. Rather, prayer is primarily a ladder by means of which a man can ascend to *devekut* and union with the Divinity. Ḥasidism did not embrace the Lurianic doctrine of *kavvanot* since it failed to accord with the primary intent of *devekut*. However, in spite of all the individualistic tendencies inherent in prayer through *devekut,* the Ḥasidim did not belittle the importance of communal worship, nor did they demand of the Ḥasid that he achieve *devekut* outside the bounds of the community and the halakhic framework of prayer. When there arose problems of prayer through *devekut* within the framework of the time sequence conventionally set for prayer, there were those Ḥasidim who chose to dispense with the framework, and even allowed a man to worship outside of the time limits set for prayer, provided that he infused his prayer with *devekut*. However, as a result, the Ḥasidim quite rapidly felt themselves in danger of jeopardizing the framework of the *halakhah,* and, for the most part, they recanted and accepted the authority of the existing frameworks.

(4) *Devekut,* which became the banner under which Ḥasidism went forth to revitalize religious life and modify the traditional hierarchy of values in Judaism, quickly led to a confrontation between it and the daily pattern of existence of the Ḥasid. Not only was traditional worship and its significance brought face to face with new problems, the same held true for *talmud torah*. The reason for this lay not in a fundamental revolt against the study of the Torah as such, but rather in the fact that *devekut* laid claim to the greater part of man's day and left little time for learning. In this confrontation *devekut* gained the ascendency, though there can be discerned in ḥasidic sources a tendency to strike a balance with the problematic nature of prayer, in order to prevent the study of Torah being swallowed up in mysticism. In the 19th century a distinct reaction in the direction of scholarship at the expense of *devekut* took place in certain ḥasidic "courts."

The performance of the *mitzvot,* too, and all man's actions attendant upon them, was overshadowed by *devekut,* as the fulfilling of the *mitzvot* was assessed in terms of the *devekut* achieved by man. In the new hierarchy of values the *mitzvah* itself became a means—and only one of several—to *devekut.* The widespread ḥasidic slogan "Performance of the *mitzvah* without *devekut* is meaningless" bears supreme testimony to the fact that the new mystical morality came to terms with traditional Jewish patterns on a new plane.

The existential status of man was conceived anew in Ḥasidism, and an attitude of resignation toward the world was emphasized. The Ḥasid was asked to rejoice in order to obviate any possibility of self-oriented introspection which might lead him to substitute, as his initial goal, personal satisfaction for the worship of God. The Ḥasidim went to great lengths to crystallize the primary awareness that they were first and foremost "sons of the higher world."

ḤASIDIC LITERATURE

Ḥasidic literature comprises approximately 3,000 works. No comprehensive bibliography is as yet available, although partial bibliographies exist, mostly as part of the general catalog of Hebrew literature. These include such works as *Seder ha-Dorot, Shem ha-Gedolim he-Ḥadash, Oẓar ha-Sefarim,* and *Beit Eked Sefarim,* in which ḥasidic works are listed. In more detailed fashion, the literature of Ḥasidism has been catalogued by G. *Scholem in his *Bibliographia Kabbalistica* (1933). A detailed bibliography of Bratslav Ḥasidism can be found in the pamphlet known as *Kunteres Elleh Shemot* (1928), also edited by G. Scholem. In addition, there is a detailed bibliography of Ḥabad Ḥasidism, compiled by A. M. Habermann, called *Sha'arei Ḥabad,* which can be found in the Salman Schocken jubilee volume *Alei Ayin* (1952).

Ḥasidic literature began to appear in print in 1780; the first published work was *Toledot Ya'akov Yosef* (Korets, 1780) by Jacob Joseph of Polonnoye. The following year saw the publication of *Maggid Devarav le-Ya'akov* (Korets, 1781), a work of the teachings of Dov Baer of Mezhirech. The earliest works of Ḥasidism were printed at Korets (Korzec), Slavuta, Zhitomir, Kopust, Zolkiew, Przemysl, Leszno, Josefov, and at several other places. Speculative works were the first type of ḥasidic literature published; it was only in the 19th century that anthologies of ḥasidic tales came into their own, and successive anthologies began to appear in print. Several manuscripts of major importance in the canon of speculative writings, which were composed in the 18th century, were first published in the 19th century. As they gradually acquired authoritative standing among the Ḥasidim, these works were frequently reprinted.

Speculative Literature. The great bulk of Ḥasidism's speculative literature was compiled in the manner of homiletic discourses *(derashot)* on selected passages from the weekly Torah readings as well as from other portions of Scripture. For the most part, it consists of recorded literature and not original writings. The homiletic framework, traditionally used for expository purposes throughout the literature of Judaism, served as background for ḥasidic ideas as well. The reader can immediately feel the ḥasidic "pulse" in each and every homiletic sermon, which reveals the presence of a distinct type of propaganda, designed to spread the aims and ideas of its authors. The associative context underlying these homiletic sermons is highly complex, for it relies not only upon exegesis of scriptural passages but also on the vast range of rabbinic literature throughout the ages, on the literature of the *halakhah* from the *rishonim* to the *aḥaronim,* on the early and Lurianic Kabbalah, and on the *musar* literature of Spain and Safed. The language of these writings is influenced by the oral nature of the *derash,* in which scant attention is paid to either syntax or to artifices of style, and the idiomatic characteristics of Yiddish have left their mark on the sentence structure of the Hebrew.

Expository Pamphlets and Letters. Conscious of the need to clarify the complexities of their teachings, in order to define them with as great a degree of precision as possible, the Ḥasidim adopted a special form of writing, the expository pamphlet. This was not done with the intention of creating a new literary genre, but as a way of replying to contemporary problems over which opinion was divided. Among the important literature of this class are the *Tanya* (Slavuta, 1796) by Shneur Zalman of Lyady and *Kunteres*

Figure 8. A young Ḥasid wearing a gold-striped *kaftan* and a fur *streimel.* Photo Zwy Bassey, Jerusalem.

ha-Hitpa'alut by his son, Dov Baer. In this class, too, fall Dov Baer's prefaces to several other works. In addition, the prefaces to the writings of *Aaron of Starosielce, Shneur Zalman's foremost disciple, should be classified as belonging to this genre, although they can stand as a class of their own. Similarly, the *Derekh Emet* (1855) by Meshullam Feivush of Zbarazh, is close to an expository pamphlet in its content, while in form it is epistolary. Treatises of the explanatory type, shorter and more compressed, appear in several well-known letters, such as those of *Ḥayyim Ḥaikel of Amdur, Menahem Mendel of Vitebsk, and *Abraham b. Alexander Katz of Kalisk, and a type of epistolary literature, known as the *"Iggerot ha-Kodesh"* of Shneur Zalman of Lyady and Elimelech of Lyzhansk, was widely dispersed; among the richest of these collections of letters is the *Alim li-Terufah* (1896) by Nathan Sternherz of Nemirov, a disciple of Naḥman of Bratslav. Apart from this category of writing there exists a wealth of epistolary literature dealing with both current affairs and with the social problems of the Jewish communities of the time; these letters are primarily of historical importance.

Kabbalistic Writings. Notwithstanding the differences of opinion within the ḥasidic community over the relative importance of close study of the Lurianic Kabbalah—differences resulting from a variety of factors—Ḥasidism counted among its adherents several of the leading kabbalists of the age. While Elijah b. Solomon, the Gaon of Vilna, expressed particular interest in the Kabbalah of the Zohar, ḥasidic kabbalists were largely influenced by Cordoverianic and Lurianic Kabbalah. Outstanding among ḥasidic writers of kabbalistic texts were the *maggid* *Israel of Kozienice, Ẓevi Hirsch of Zhidachov, and Jacob Ẓevi Jolles, author of a lexicon of Lurianic Kabbalah entitled *Kehillat Ya'akov* (1870). It is noticeable that the kabbalistic commentaries of these Ḥasidim are not always integrated within the framework of their ḥasidic teachings, but here and there it is possible to discern traces of ḥasidic thought in their commentaries on the Zohar and on the *Eẓ Ḥayyim*

Figure 9. Ḥasidic Dance, woodcut by Jakob Steinhardt, 1961. Jerusalem, B. M. Ansbacher Collection.

of Ḥayyim *Vital. A more pronounced attempt at integrating the two trends of thought, though in the direction of Kabbalah, becomes evident when the works in question are ḥasidic writings which attempt to locate their origins and sources of continuity in the Kabbalah.

Halakhic Writings. Eighteenth-century Ḥasidism did not give rise to many halakhic treatises; the best-known works of this type are the *Shulḥan Arukh* (Kopust, 1814) by Shneur Zalman of Lyady, and the writings of his grandson, the Ẓemaḥ Ẓedek. Polish Ḥasidism revitalized the scholastic tradition; prominent scholars among them were Isaac Meir of *Gur, author of *Ḥiddushei ha-Rim,* and Gershon Ḥanokh of Radzyn (see *Izbica-Radzyn), who reinstituted the custom of wearing a blue-fringed garment, or *ẓiẓit tekhelet*. Galician Ḥasidism, too, had outstanding men of learning like Ḥayyim *Halberstam of Zanz, author of *Divrei Ḥayyim* (1864), and Isaac Judah Jehiel of Komarno.

Liturgy. Although it was not ḥasidic practice to create a new liturgy, nevertheless exceptional cases are known in which Ḥasidim composed and instituted novel prayers. There were those Ḥasidim who were accustomed to add Yiddish words to their prayers, and there were also prayers which were composed and recited as additions to the conventional liturgy. Typical examples of these additional and spontaneous prayers are found in Bratslav Ḥasidism. Phinehas of Korets paid particular attention to modifications in the liturgy and even added changes of his own, which have come down in manuscript only. The *Siddur ha-Rav* of Shneur Zalman of Lyady did much to establish specific liturgical norms for the adherents of Ḥabad Ḥasidism.

Vision Literature. Visions were favorably regarded by the Ḥasidim, but they were allowed scant publicity and their publication was limited. In spite of this there remain a few writings which hint at the existence of visionaries. Writings by one of them, Isaac Eizik of Komarno, were widely circulated; a selection appeared in print: *Megillat Setarim* (1944).

Narrative Literature. The literature of the ḥasidic movement is generally known largely through its treasury of tales and legends. The first collections appeared in the early 19th century; the earliest of these was the *Shivḥei ha-Besht* ("Praises of the Ba'al Shem Tov"), edited by the *shoḥet* of Luniets, and published in 1805 in Kopust. This purported to be a documentary monograph, but there is no doubt that it is simply a collection of stories which, however, contain a measure of historical fact. To some extent the *Shivḥei ha-Besht* is an imitation of the *Shivḥei ha-Ari* (Constantinople, 1766); however, there are few examples of this *shevaḥim* genre in ḥasidic literature. Few biographies or autobiographies appear in ḥasidic writings; exceptions are Nathan Sternherz of Nemirov on Naḥman of Bratslav and the works of some 20th-century biographers.

From the mid-19th century, hundreds of story anthologies began to appear. These early anthologies should not be seen as truly documentary; rather they are stories reflecting the ethos of Ḥasidism. Each story consists of a specific lesson embedded in a social or historical situation, narrating a single event and expressed in the conventional manner of "once upon a time . . ." From this point, the narrative situation evolves into a moral homily. The stories have a simple narrative basis; the time element is insignificant and there are no epic descriptions. The events of the story serve only as a framework for the lesson it contains, and the situation is of a spiritual and not a historical nature. In this manner, the epigrammatic element is also highlighted. It is characteristic of this type of story to recount events in the first person, thus lending the narrative a touch of authenticity, that is, the air of having been passed down by word of mouth from generation to generation. At times the stories are told in the name of some famous person, mentioned by name; at others, they are presented in the name of "a certain Ḥasid." Every ḥasidic dynasty saw to it that collections of its own stories were compiled. Fairly frequently, collections were published containing stories belonging to several dynasties, originating in the same geographical region, such as Poland, Galicia, and Ukraine.

The tradition of collecting and publishing ḥasidic tales continued down to the present century, still deriving its authority from the oral tradition. Some better-known collections are: *Sefer Ba'al Shem Tov* (1938), *Mifalot Ẓaddikim* (1856), *Teshu'ot Ḥen* (Berdichev, 1816), *Nifla'ot ha-Sabba Kaddisha* (2 vols., 1936–37), *Irin Kaddishin* (1885), *Nifla'ot ha-Rabbi* (1911), *Si'aḥ-Sarfei Kodesh* (1923), *Ramatayim Ẓofim* (1881), *Abbir ha-Ro'im* (1935), *Heikhal ha-Berakhah Iggera de-Pirka* (1858), *Kehal Ḥasidim* and *Siftei Ẓaddikim* (1924). Several 20th-century men of letters have compiled collections of ḥasidic tales, notably *Berdyczewski, Martin Buber, Eliezer *Steinman, and Judah Kaufman (Even Shemuel). Buber's anthology was published in English as *Tales of the Ḥasidim.*

INTERPRETATIONS OF ḤASIDISM

From its beginnings the ḥasidic movement has attracted the attention of both supporters and opponents in each succeeding generation. Anti-ḥasidic polemics were in print even before the movement's own writings were first published. Although in the main, complaints were voiced against the eccentric practices of the sect, among the accusations can be discerned matters of principle which were destined to figure prominently on both sides in the modern debate over Ḥasidism.

Early Opposition. The earliest opponents of Ḥasidism, such as Moses b. Jacob of Satanov, author of *Mishmeret ha-Kodesh* (Zolkiew, 1746), charged the Ḥasidim with avarice, boorishness, and contempt of the *halakhah.* In the 1770s, more adverse testimony began to accumulate; among the more important of these are the works of Israel Loebel, *Ozer Yisrael* (Shklov, 1786) and *Sefer ha-Vikku'aḥ* (Warsaw, 1798). Loebel accused the Ḥasidim of changing the liturgical conventions from the Ashkenazi to the Sephardi; of praying according to Isaac *Luria's doctrine of *kavvanot;* of praying with exaggerated joy when proper devotion demands tears and repentance; and of praying with wild abandon and with accompanying bodily movements. Solomon of Dubna, a follower of Moses *Mendelssohn, reproached the Ḥasidim for pride and high-handedness, and for a propensity to drunkenness. A more inclusive attack, embracing a wide range of accusations dealing mainly with the Ḥasidim's changes in traditional Jewish ways and practices, was made by Mendelssohn's teacher, Israel of Zamosc, author of *Nezed ha-Dema* (Dyhernfurth, 1773). Inveighing against both the spiritualism of their religious demands and the "moral corruption" of *ẓaddik* and Ḥasid alike, Israel of Zamosc pointed to evidence of the movement's bias toward separatism revealed in their changes in customs, such as the wearing of white and the adoption of the blue-fringed garment *(ẓiẓit tekhelet)* with the fringes worn on the outside. Among the ritual and spiritual claims of the Ḥasidim he denounced: the pretension to a profound religiosity; the practice of ritual bathing prior to morning and evening prayers in order to become worthy of the Divine Spirit; abstinence and fasting; spiritual arrogance; the claim to be "visionary" seers; breaking down the "walls of the Torah"; advocating the doctrine of "uplifting the sparks" *(niẓoẓot)* in the act of eating according to the doctrine of *tikkun;* and introducing a "new liturgy of raucousness." Among their immoral practices he counted cupidity, hypocrisy and abomination, gluttony, and inebriation.

Israel of Zamosc did not assemble his charges into an ordered exposition of the nature of Ḥasidism; nevertheless, they served as the basis for an interpretation of Ḥasidism which found expression in the writings of the most profound, systematic, and recondite of Ḥasidism's opponents—Ḥayyim of Volozhin (*Volozhiner), a disciple of Elijah b. Solomon Zalman, the Gaon of Vilna. In his book *Nefesh ha-Ḥayyim* (Vilna, 1824), in which the term Ḥasid is discreetly omitted, the principles of an interpretation of Ḥasidism as a novel religious phenomenon are first adumbrated. Ḥayyim of Volozhin presented Ḥasidism as a spiritual movement which ignores a cardinal principle in Judaism, namely that where the very nature of a *mitzvah,* as well as its fulfillment, is jeopardized by an idea, the latter should be set aside. Equally, where new values—lofty though they may be—threaten to come into conflict with tradition, the latter should be upheld. He rarely voiced an objection to specific ḥasidic practices but objected on a theoretical basis to matters of fundamental belief in Ḥasidism which appeared to him as dangerous. In so doing, he managed to detach his polemic from its historical context. Ḥayyim of Volozhin saw the spiritual uniqueness of Ḥasidism as follows:

(1) Ḥasidic teachings imparted a new significance to the concept of "Torah for its own sake," an idea which Ḥasidism understood as "Torah for the sake of *devekut*" ("communion") with God. According to Ḥayyim the study of the Torah for itself alone (and not for the sake of *devekut*) had a value transcending the fulfillment of the *mitzvot* themselves. (2) Ḥayyim objected to the centrality in ḥasidic thought of the necessity for "purity of thought," since in his opinion the essence of the Torah and *mitzvot* did not necessarily lie in their being performed with "great *kavvanah* and true *devekut*." Here, Ḥayyim of Volozhin pointed out the opposition between mysticism and the *halakhah.* He emphasizes the dialectic process by which the performance of a *mitzvah* with excessive *kavvanah* leads to the destruction of the *mitzvah.* The very act of fulfilling the *mitzvah* is the fundamental principle and not the *kavvanah* accompanying its performance. He therefore challenged Ḥasidism on a matter of basic principle: performing *mitzvot* for the sake of heaven, he stated, is not a value in itself. (3) He regarded the ḥasidic attempt to throw off the yoke of communal authority as social amoralism. (4) He objected to the practice of praying outside the specified times set for prayer and to the consequent creation of a new pattern of life.

Ḥasidism and Haskalah. By the 1770s Ḥasidism had already come under the fire of the Haskalah. In Warsaw Jacques Kalmansohn published a scathing criticism of the social nature of Ḥasidism, as did Judah Leib Mises in his *Kinat ha-Emet* (Vienna, 1828). However, the writer who displayed the most striking talent for caricature and pointed satire sarcasm was Joseph *Perl of Tarnopol in his booklet *Ueber das Wesen der Sekte Chassidim aus ihren eigenen Schriften gezogen im Jahre 1816* ("On the Essence of the Ḥasidic Sect, Drawn from their own Writings in the Year 1816"; Jerusalem, National Library, Ms. Var. 293). The intent of his essay was to portray the material and spiritual conditions of the Ḥasidim in the lowest terms and to exert pressure on the Austrian authorities to force all the Ḥasidim to receive a compulsory education within the state-run school system. Perl's major contention was that as a socio-religious phenomenon Ḥasidism was an anti-progressive factor owing to its spiritual insularity and its social separatism: in spirit it was idle and passive and as a social group it was unproductive.

A more ambivalent view of Ḥasidism appears in the memoirs of Abraham Baer *Gottlober (*Abraham Baer Gottlober un Zayn Epokhe,* Vilna, 1828), who, when he later adopted the principles of the Haskalah, became convinced that it was Ḥasidism which had facilitated the spread of the Haskalah movement, in that it constituted a critical stage in the life of Judaism. Ḥasidism, according to Gottlober, threw off the yoke of rabbinical authority and in so doing opened the first sluicegate for the advance of the Haskalah.

ספר

לקוטי אמרים

חלק ראשון הנקרא בשם ספר

של בינונים

מלוקט מפי ספרים ומפי סופרים קדושי

עליון נ"ע מיוסד על פסוק כי

קרוב אליך הדבר מאוד בפיך ובלבבך

לעשותו · לבאר היטב איך הוא קרוב

מאד בדרך ארוכה וקצרה בעזה"י

נדפס

בסלאוויטא

תחת

יר"ה :

בשנת כי קרוב אליך הדבר מאוד בפיך ובלבבך

לעשותו לפ"ק

Figure 10. Title page of *Sefer Likkutei Amarim* known as the *Tanya,* by Shneur Zalman of Lyady, founder of the Ḥabad movement of Ḥasidism, Slavuta, 1796. Jerusalem, J.N.U.L.

Figure 11. Ḥasidim dancing in the courtyard of the tomb of Simeon bar Yoḥai in Meron, during the celebration of Lag ba-Omer, May 1970. Courtesy Government Press Office, Tel Aviv.

He also believed that Ḥasidism lay at the root of the crisis involving the Shulḥan Arukh. It displaced Shabbateanism and the Frankist movement, and tarnished the glory of "rabbinism." Gottlober evinced a particular admiration for the Ḥabad Ḥasidism because of their affinity to the Haskalah. However, Ḥasidism itself he regarded as a social movement which was disintegrating in its very essence because its criticism was internally directed.

Toward the end of the 1860s and the beginning of the 1870s there began to appear in print selections of the writings of E. Z. *Zweifel, under the title *Shalom al Yisrael,* a work which came to the defense of Ḥasidism, attempting to interpret its teachings on the basis of Ḥasidism's own authentic sources. In his balanced and informed argument, the author undertook an analysis of fundamental ḥasidic sayings and teachings, pointing out their significance and underlining, too, their uniqueness in comparison with Kabbalah. As a *maskil,* he had, of course, reservations about the "popular" elements of Ḥasidism, and about a number of its social aspects. Among the *maskilim* most influenced by *Shalom al Yisrael* was Micha Josef Berdyczewski, whose interpretation of Ḥasidism in his book *Nishmat Ḥasidim* (1899) was couched in romantic terms. Viewing the movement as a Jewish renaissance, an attempt to break down the barriers between man and the world, he saw in Ḥasidism "joy and inner happiness" and the opportunity to worship the Lord in many different ways.

Martin Buber and his Successors. Martin Buber was influenced by Berdyczewski, and in principle adopted his opinions, but his thesis was far more profound. Buber's first works on Ḥasidism are written in the spirit of mysticism, such as *Die Geschichten des Rabbi Nachman* (1906; *Tales of Rabbi Nachman,* 1962[2]) and *Die Legende des Baalschem* (1908; *Legend of the Baal-Shem,* 1969[2]). From his existentialist teachings, which he developed and consolidated during the 1930s and 1940s, Buber utilized the principle of dialogue as a criterion for understanding the essence of Ḥasidism, which he saw as giving support to the direct encounter, active and creative, between man and the world surrounding him. According to Buber, especially in his mature work *Be-Fardes ha-Ḥasidut* (1945), the dialogue of encounter reveals the reality of God; the cosmos is potentially holy, the encounter with man makes it actually holy. Buber sought to locate the origin of this fundamental concept, which he called pan-sacramentalism, in the ḥasidic doctrine of the worship of God through the corporeal and worldly dimensions of man's being, and attempted to view through this aspect the revival of Judaism that found expression in Ḥasidism as opposed to the *halakhah.* The ḥasidic renaissance was seen by Buber as a fresh and living religious phenomenon, and also as a process of social and communal consolidation of novel educational importance. He believed that the *ẓaddikim* gave expression to this new educational and religious meaning, for every *ẓaddik* represented a special experience acquired as a result of the encounter through dialogue. Particularly emphasizing the concrete and historical import of Ḥasidism, Buber placed little value on the abstract ideas of Ḥasidism, the intellectual games of the Kabbalah, and its millenarian hopes and expectations, being convinced that Ḥasidism had liberated itself from these elements and constructed a realistic experience of life. Buber understood the ḥasidic imperative "Know Him in all thy ways" as transcending the bounds of the *mitzvot* as religious experience over and above the *halakhah.* The element of mystery in Ḥasidism has been studied by Hillel Zeitlin.

A scathing attack on Berdyczewski and Buber was made by the Zionist *maskil* Samuel Joseph Ish-Horowitz, who, early in the 20th century, brought out a series of articles which later appeared in booklet form under the title of *Ha-Ḥasidut ve-ha-Haskalah* (Berlin, 1909). "Modern" Ḥasidism, known as neo-Ḥasidism, was taken to be that of Berdyczewski and Buber. In his work, the Ḥasidism of the Ba'al Shem Tov is depicted as a wild, undisciplined movement, while the Ba'al Shem Tov himself is shown as a charlatan influenced by his rustic surroundings and by the Haidamak movement. According to Horowitz, Ḥasidism contributed no new truths or ways of looking at the world: it simply appropriated to itself the vocabulary of the Kabbalah without fully understanding its implications, and colored it with quasi-philosophical notions "belonging to the household mentality and chronic psychology of the ghetto." Modern or neo-Ḥasidim (specifically Berdyczewski and Buber) attempted to discover in Ḥasidism ethical values and a positive popular force, in particular in the ḥasidic "joy," which they interpreted as a protest against the dejection produced by the conditions of the Diaspora, but for Horowitz the Shabbatean movement was to be preferred to Ḥasidism, as it took an upright stand, advocating a breaking free of the bonds of the Diaspora and the ghetto. Horowitz dismissed the claims that Ḥasidism was a movement of revival and revolt as little more than arrant nonsense; Ḥasidim, far from rebelling against the rabbinate, kept the *mitzvot,* minor as well as major. He contended that the neo-Ḥasidim were deceiving themselves by interpreting the values of Ḥasidism in secular terms, which he regarded a perversion of history in the spirit of a new humanism. He believed that Ḥasidism was continuity and not revolt, and that the neo-Ḥasidim did violence to its true nature by viewing it as a revolutionary movement in Jewish history.

In recent years a criticism of Buber's views of Ḥasidism has been put forward by Gershom Scholem and Rivka Schatz. Opinion is also divided on the messianic significance of Ḥasidism, between Benzion Dinur and Isaiah Tishby, on the one hand, and Scholem on the other. J. G. Weiss (1918–1969) did remarkable work on Ḥasidism in many of his essays, most of which appeared in the *Journal of Jewish Studies.* He contributed much to the understanding of Bratslav Ḥasidism. Rivka Schatz's *Ha-Ḥasidut ke-Mistikah* ("Ḥasidism as Mysticism," 1968), a phenomenological analysis of Ḥasidism on the basis of available texts, attempts to answer certain fundamental questions concerning the spiritual aims of Ḥasidism and assesses the value attaching to ḥasidic innovations. [R.S.U.]

THE MUSICAL TRADITION OF ḤASIDISM

Problems of Definition and Research. By one definition, the field of ḥasidic music would include all music practiced in ḥasidic society. By another, and related, definition, any music performed in "ḥasidic style" is ḥasidic. A further possibilty could be to define ḥasidic music by its content, i.e., by those musical elements and forms which distinguish this from any other music. So far, such distinctions have not been formulated according to the norms of musical scholarship. The Ḥasidim themselves also possess criteria—formulated in their own traditional terms—according to which they judge whether a melody is "ḥasidic" or not, and to which dynasty-style and genre it belongs. These, too, have not yet been translated into ethnomusicological terms. Moreover, none of the extant studies of ḥasidic music has as yet managed to furnish a systematic description of the ḥasidic repertoire or even part of it.

A pioneer effort was made by Abraham Ẓevi *Idelsohn, the tenth volume of whose *Thesaurus* is devoted to ḥasidic songs. Idelsohn based his analyses on very loosely defined form and scale types—criteria which are not sufficient for an exclusive and thorough definition. The fundamental difficulty lies in the anthologistic character of the body of material which he assembled as a base for his analysis. Idelsohn's 250 items include vocal music, instrumental music, liturgical pieces, dance tunes, folk songs in Yiddish, etc., and are taken from various and often distant dynastic repertoires. Such a generalization could only be achieved if the material had first been analyzed by ethnographic subunits, such as one dynastic repertoire, or one genre (dance tunes, prayer melodies, or instrumental music, etc.). A comparative summary of these would then reveal the basic aspects of ḥasidic music as such. Nowadays the location of these units has itself become difficult, because of the far-reaching changes which have occurred during the last 50 years in the ḥasidic communities—especially as a result of the Holocaust. The original communal frameworks were for the most part destroyed, although attempts were made to reconstruct them in other places (chiefly in Israel and the U.S.). For some dynasties this proved impossible, since all that remained of them were a number of survivors living in various countries who could, at best, try to preserve the remnants of the tradition in their personal memory. Other dynasties did achieve a renascence around new geographical centers; but the interference of new external and internal factors could not but cause radical changes in the traditional patterns—including all aspects of the musical repertoire. Ḥabad Ḥasidism, for instance, professes a declared intention of reviving the traditional tunes, but the modern media of communication (recordings, concert performances, and the use of musical notation) have influenced both the material and its carriers, causing a noticeable standardization and impoverishment of the repertoire among the younger generation.

Two opposing tendencies can be discerned in the present-day repertoire. On the one hand, there is the attempt to preserve the traditional functions with their traditional melodies as strictly as possible (the *tish,* rabbi's table assemblies, and Sabbath and festival prayer customs). On the other hand, original elements appear in, and are stimulated by, those functions in which both the adherents of diverse dynasties and non-ḥasidic Jews come together and influence each other, such as weddings, *Simḥat Torah celebrations, and the *hillulot* of *Lag ba-Omer and the Seventh of Adar. These have created a distinctive repertoire, which arose mainly in Israel and the U.S. after World War II; it is made up chiefly of dance tunes and "rejoicing tunes," which were originally linked with specific functions and dynasties and have now been detached from their earlier setting and adopted by this "pan-ḥasidic" public. Here, many melodies have been furnished with new words; individual dynastic traits have been eroded; and the repertoire has absorbed a number of recently composed melodies. On the other hand, this repertoire has not accepted those melodies which were too exclusively associated with a specific dynasty, or the slow *tish* tunes. This "pan-ḥasidic" phenomenon is mainly found among those Ḥasidim whose communities did not achieve a renascence after the Holocaust, such as Zanz, Sadigora, Boyana, Dzykow, etc.

The historical dimension of ḥasidic music poses problems of its own. Above all it must be asked whether ḥasidic music developed out of an existing tradition and repertoire or was created as a new style in response to the new social and spiritual conditions established by the rise and development of ḥasidic society. If there was a continuity, the divergent dynastic styles grew out of codified local traditions, and the common elements are the result of the interactions and interrelations between the dynasties. If a new "ḥasidic" style was already created at the beginning of the movement, the dynastic proliferations could have caused a parallel proliferation of musical styles. In any case one must take into account the dynastic filiations and interrelations, geographical proximity or isolation, and the importance of the "court musicians" and **klezmerim* as transmitters of musical elements from one dynastic center to another.

Local gentile music (folk and popular)—Russian, Ukrainian, Polish, Rumanian, Hungarian, and Turkish—left a strong stamp on ḥasidic music, which sometimes gave rise to opinions that ḥasidic music could not be considered as an individual ethnomusical unit. Such an attitude disregards the obvious processes of transformation and re-creation which occurred in these tunes during their adoption by ḥasidic society and its musically creative personalities (see example 1). In itself, this widespread and constant adoption of gentile tunes was often based on a conscious ideology, namely the kabbalistic theory of the *niẓoẓot* ("divine sparks") inherent in every melody or folktale motive, which therefore could and should be "lifted up" from the "sphere of impurity" to which they had sunk from the "sphere of holiness." Thus the Ḥasidim went out to learn the local shepherds' and the peasants' songs (see example 2), took over military marches, and did not disdain even the ditties of the pothouses (see example 1). The original text could be justified as being allegorical, or have allegorical explanations added. Sometimes a new text was fitted to the melody, but in most cases the words were discarded, leaving a wordless *niggun.* Sometimes the memory of the original song was preserved, not infrequently together with a story (apocryphal or real) of how it came to be "lifted up" and by whom—such as the song represented in example 2, and the famous "cock's song" of Rabbi Isaac Eizik *Taub of Kalov. In most cases, however, the gentile ancestry of a ḥasidic tune can only be verified through a comparison with the relevant ethnic material. Such comparisons have frequently been made with insufficient and imprecise data, and not rarely by impression and memory only.

The Place of Music in Ḥasidic Thought. From the earliest ḥasidic writings onward the importance of prayer with *kavvanah* is emphasized to establish the link between man and his Creator. In the opinion of some *ẓaddikim* and their adherents, music and singing were ranked even higher for this purpose than explicit prayer. Since most ḥasidic song is textless, such a predominance of the melodic over the textual aspect may well be directly linked with this doctrine. The melodic primacy characterizes even the sung parts of ḥasidic prayer; instead of rendering the text, the ḥasidim actually render the melody associated with the text, into which the words are freely interpolated. Some of these renditions often sound as if the text did not exist at all. An extreme example is the singing of the Sabbath **zemirot* by the Slonim Ḥasidim, which is entirely textless, although the words accompany the melody and are dwelt upon "in thought."

Great significance is also attached to the movements of the body during prayer: moving the torso and the hands and clapping. It is therefore understandable that ḥasidic thinkers always attributed great virtues to the dance, which combines music and motion.

A thorough survey of the musical evidence in the literary sources, and their interaction with oral traditions, is not yet available, but a beginning has been made at the Jewish Music Research Center at the Hebrew University of Jerusalem. One of the major difficulties of establishing a documentable historical survey is that much of the literature of the founding and early periods of Ḥasidism was only printed much later. The literary evidence can be divided provisionally into the following categories.

(1) Traditional kabbalistic doctrines: their applications to music—especially as regard the aspects of prayer-contemplation, probably also the use of bodily movement to incite, express, and sustain ecstasy, and especially the concept of "joy in worship"—are only implicit in earlier writings, but become explicit in later ones. The kabbalistic interpretations of the **shofar,* its tones and its liturgical functions, were taken over into much of ḥasidic literature (see, e.g., the writings of Jacob Joseph of Polonnoye).

(2) The musical activities of the *ẓaddikim:* stories such as these began with the *Baal Shem Tov himself (who sang with the children when he brought them to the **ḥeder* when he was a teacher's assistant, who also functioned occasionally as a precentor, and to whom several melodies are attributed). These also include stories about the creation of particular melodies by *ẓaddikim* or their "court musicians," and the miraculous properties which were often attributed to such melodies.

(3) Sayings of *ẓaddikim* about the virtues of music: these appear either as part of a story, as above, or as independent maxims and discourses in the writings of the *ẓaddikim* or their disciples ("I once heard from my rabbi . . .").

(4) Musical elements in the world of the ḥasidic tales: the most fascinating—and as yet most puzzling—of these are to be found in the tales of R. Naḥman of Bratslav (see especially the "Tale of the Seven Beggars").

(5) Miscellaneous stories and sayings about music in the life of ḥasidic communities: a most valuable external contribution is furnished by the polemic writings of the opponents of Ḥasidism who, from the beginning, constantly poured their scorn on the ḥasidic predilection for singing and dancing. By their very vehemence and undoubted exaggerations they demonstrate the difference between the two cultures, and the force of the musical element in Ḥasidism from its inception. Because the earliest ḥasidic literature only rarely contains explicit descriptions of the musical activities of the *ẓaddikim* and their followers (for reasons which are as yet unclear), these anti-ḥasidic writings are all the more important as historical sources. As for notated historical sources, it must be remembered that, until modern times, ḥasidic music was neither created nor preserved by musical notation. For the possibility of survivals in 18th-century cantorial manuals, see *Music.

The Place of Music in Ḥasidic Life. The function of music in ḥasidic life is intrinsically different from that of other communities. These distinguish between music of the synagogue—which is the center of religious life—and music belonging to everyday life. In ḥasidic society the house of the *ẓaddik* is the spiritual and religious center, while the *shtibl* is only a place for prayer. The aura of sanctity which enveloped everything that took place in the *ẓaddik's* house therefore extended itself also to those musical activities of the ḥasidic community which were not a part of liturgical activity. In consequence, the boundary between sacred and secular music became blurred: secular forms such as marches and waltzes could be taken over for prayer tunes, and tunes used for ḥasidic dances could be furnished with texts from the liturgy. Since the dance was considered a sanctified action, dancing was and still is found even in the synagogue, before, between, and after certain prayer services. Since dance tunes appear even in the liturgical framework itself, this may explain why such tunes are found even where actual dancing is not customary. On the periphery of the ḥasidic repertoire there is also music such as folk-songs in Yiddish and other languages, children's songs, and the songs of the **badḥanim* (jesters at weddings). While the Ḥasidim do not see these as ḥasidic music proper, they have adopted the social phenomenon of the *klezmerim* in its entirety. Nowadays *klezmerim* take part in all *semaḥot* ("rejoicings"), such as weddings and the *hillulot* ("folk-festivals") of *Lag ba-Omer, the Seventh of Adar, and *Simḥat Bet ha-Sho'evah (Feast of Water Drawing). The repertoire of the *klezmerim* includes various kinds of instrumental music: marches, waltzes, the tunes called "Meron tunes" in Israel and "Bulgar" and "Terkishe" (Turkish) elsewhere, as well as melodies related to the vocal domain. In Jerusalem, where instrumental performance is traditionally forbidden in ḥasidic circles as a sign of mourning for the destruction of the Temple, the tonal color of the *klezmer* ensemble is often skillfully imitated at such "rejoicings" by a kind of "mouth music."

The Ḥasidic "Niggun." *Niggun* (Yid. *nign,* from *nagen,* which probably meant "singing" in biblical Hebrew) is the ḥasidic term for a musical unit, i.e., a "tune," be it sung or played. The *niggun* is the central musical manifestation of ḥasidic life. The form is not applied to the **nusaḥ,* the cantillation of the *masoretic accents, or the various folk and popular songs which Ḥasidism shares with the general Jewish culture. The latter are all conditioned by the textual factor, while the *niggun,* even when sung with words, is conceived as a completely autonomous musical entity. Most *niggunim* are sung without any words, with the frequent use of carrier syllables such as *Ah, Ay, Oy, Hey, Bam, Ya-ba-bam,* etc. Others have a partial text underlay. One *niggun* may also be sung to various texts. Where a *niggun* has a fixed text, the setting shows that the melody came first and the words were fitted to it afterward; even where it is known that a *niggun* was composed specifically for a certain text, the result sounds as if the text had been adapted to the melody. *Niggunim* are classified by the Ḥasidim themselves according to the following criteria:

(1) *Tish* ("Table") *niggunim.* These constitute the major part of the repertoire sung at the assembly of the rebbe's table. Other terms for them are "meditation *[maskhshove] niggunim,*" "mystical adhesion *[devekut] niggunim,*" "moral *[moralishe] niggunim,*" "assembly *[hitva'adut] niggunim,*" etc. They are lengthy and drawn out, sometimes metrical, sometimes in free rhythm, and sometimes in combinations of metrical and free sections. One of the most widespread types resembles a slowed-down mazurka, with the first beat changed from ♪.♬ to ♬♪., perhaps under the influence of Hungarian rhythm (see mus. ex. 4). The *niggunim* in free rhythm are related to the cantorial recitative. In some dynasties, such as Ḥabad and Vizhnitsa, these *niggunim* show the influence of East European folk forms, such as the

Rumanian *doina;* in others, such as Modzitz and *Bobov, they are influenced by West European art music (operatic melodies, polyphonic voice-divisions). The length of such a *niggun* may vary. It is divided into sections, called "fall" or by the Aramaic term *bava* ("gate"), which may number from two to seven and in exceptional cases reach 32, as in the *Ezkerah* of R. Israel *Taub of Modzitz (M. S. Geshuri, *Neginah ve-Ḥasidut be-Veit Kuzmir u-Venoteha,* pt. 2 (1952), 9–18). Most *tish niggunim* are textless. The texts of the others are generally taken from the Sabbath and Sabbath eve **zemirot* and a few also from the liturgy (see mus. ex. 5).

(2) Dance *Niggunim.* Most ḥasidic dance tunes belong to one type which can be defined by the following characteristics. The structure is periodic and symmetric, in multiples of four bars. The number of sections is from two to four. Common forms are A-A[1], A-B, A-B-C, A-B-C-B, the bipartite forms being the most frequent. The range is generally not more than one octave; sometimes only a fifth or a sixth. The number of motifs is small, mostly two or three and not more than six. Sometimes an entire *niggun* is made up of a single motif and its development (see mus. ex. 6). The most common tonal framework is that of the minor hexachord (*a* mode), extended sometimes by a lower or higher second. Others of these *niggunim* show a melodic relationship to the *Shtayger *Ahavah Rabbah* (see mus. ex. 7). About half of the dance *niggunim* repertoire has texts taken from biblical verses or from the liturgy, which are frequently short and fitted to the melody by constant full or partial repetition—a practice typical of the dance *niggun.* A related category is the "rejoicing" *(simḥah) niggunim,* which possess all the above characteristics but are sung more slowly and without dancing (see mus. ex. 8).

(3) Instrumental music. The concept of the *niggun* also embraces melodies of a strongly instrumental character, such as waltzes, marches, and the "Meron" or "Bulgar" tunes. The gentile waltzes and marches, having been transferred to new functions—*"tish"* and liturgy—in which they are unconnected with movement, have consequently undergone melodic and rhythmic changes, especially a marked slowing. On the other hand, the "Meron" tunes, which belong in part to the repertoire of the non-ḥasidic community, have remained the property of the *klezmerim.* Their character is a mixture of East Balkanic, Turkish, and Near Eastern traits (A. Hajdu, "The Meron Tunes," in *Yuval,* vol. 2, 1970).

Musical Styles. As already stated, the Ḥasidim themselves differentiate between the melodies pertaining to the various dynasties, but these distinctions have not yet been translated in terms of musicological analysis. Nevertheless, the stylistic particularities of certain dynasties can already be recognized, while others do not seem to have a style of their own. Information on the music of the "Ḥasidic heartlands"—Podolia, Volhynia, and Western Ukraine—is as yet insufficient; the few collected tunes do not show any stylistic singularities. In the more westerly dynasties—Bobov, Gur, and Modzitz—there is a strong Western influence, which expresses itself in a harmonic-tonal conception traceable to operatic melodies, modern cantorial creations, and (in Modzitz) polyphonic elaboration. Rumanian and Hungarian influences appear in dynasties in Transylvania and the Carpathian mountains such as Vizhnitsa, Maramaros, Satmar, Munkacs, and Kalov. The melodic framework, which lacks tonal-harmonic fundament, shows the traits found in the surrounding ethnic cultures: modes related to minor, pentatonics, and some scales with the augmented second. The *tish niggunim* of the Vizhnitsa Ḥasidim are distinguished by their length. Bratslav Ḥasidism shows the influence of its Ukrainian surroundings. The melodies are mostly short, simple in form, and in general do not exceed the range of one octave. Their melodic elements do not differ significantly from those of the Carpathian and Transylvanian dynasties described above. The northern area—Belorussia and Lithuania—comprises the centers of Ḥabad, Karlin, and Slonim Ḥasidism. Russian motifs and traits of performance are found in the Ḥabad repertoire, although part of it is also influenced by the Rumanian *doina* style. The singing of the Karlin Ḥasidim is distinguished by a strong rhythmic emphasis on every beat, while the melodic range is limited and often does not exceed the fifth, and the melodies are built on progression by seconds and on the variational repetition of brief motifs (see mus. ex. 9). Since the Karlin Ḥasidim are now concentrated in Israel, and this style is closely related to several styles found in the Near East, the question arises whether these traits were already present in the original Karlin repertoire, or whether they entered and dominated it only after the reconstitution of the community in Palestine and Israel; but in the absence of older recordings and notations it must remain unanswered. The Slonim Ḥasidim have a peculiar style, without parallel in other dynasties, characterized by the constant but irregular shifting of the melodic phrases upwards, by chromatic and even microtonal displacement, with the consequent shifting of the tonal center. None of the many possible reasons for this practice can be proved. The impression created by the constant displacement is one of wide-ranging melodies, although the motifs and phrases themselves are actually of a very small range. The upward shift is also found in other dynasties, such as Ḥabad, but there only as an imperceptible "creeping."

Sources. While the study of the oral traditions belongs to "ḥasidic ethnomusicology" which is only in its beginnings, the literature on the written traditions is already relatively extensive. Most of it, however, is in the form of anthologistic-anecdotal collections. The available notations from the oral traditions are, in most cases, valid only as preliminary or confirmatory evidence; they generally lack the needed documentation, are done by manual notation (i.e., following a singer, or the writer's memory, and not transcribed from recordings), and the notation itself is schematic and not infrequently distorting, due to lack of ethnomusicological notational techniques.

The first recordings of Jewish music produced in the U.S. included Ḥasidic melodies, performed by *klezmer* ensembles. After World War II some dynasties in the U.S. began to propagate their melodies on records. However, all these are arrangements: for cantor with instrumental ensemble, cantor and choir, or choir with or without instrumental accompaniment, and in each case with professional harmonizations in varying degrees of sophistication. In some of the records, chiefly those of the Ḥabad *niḥo'aḥ* productions, the choir at least is made up of Ḥasidim, which makes these records somewhat more authentic.

[AN.H./YA.MA.]

Bibliography: Horodetzky, Ḥasidut; idem, *Leaders of Hassidism* (1928); Dubnow, Ḥasidut; idem, in: *Ha-Shillo'aḥ,* 7 (1901), 314–20; A. Walden, *Shem ha-Gedolim he-Ḥadash* (1864); M. Bodek, *Seder ha-Dorot he-Ḥadash* (1865); A. Z. Zweifel, *Shalom al Yisrael,* 4 vols. (1868–73); S. Shechter, *Studies in Judaism,* 1 (1896), 1–45; A. Markus ("Verus"), *Der Chassidismus* (1901); I. Berger, *Zekhut Yisrael,* 4 vols. (1902–10); M. Ben-Yehezkel (Halpern), in: *Ha-Shillo'aḥ,* 17–22 (1907–10); idem, *Sefer ha-Ma'asiyyot,* 6 vols. (1968[3]); S. J. Horowitz, *Ha-Ḥasidut ve-ha-Haskalah* (1909); C. Bloch, *Die Gemeinde der Chassidim: ihr Werden und ihre Lehre* (1920); A. Kahana, *Sefer ha-Ḥasidut* (1922); A. Z. Aescoly, *Le Hassidisme* (1928); idem, in: *Beit Yisrael be-Polin,* 2 (1954), 86–141; Y. A. Kamelhaar, *Dor De'ah* (1933); T. Ysander, *Studien zum best'schen Hasidismus in seiner religionsgeschichtlichen Sonderart* (1933); Z. Fefer, in: *Sefer ha-Shanah li-Yhudei Polanyah,* 1

(1938), 233–47; Y. Raphael, *Ha-Ḥasidut ve-Ereẓ Yisrael* (1940); idem, *Sefer ha-Ḥasidut* (1955²); Scholem, Mysticism; idem, in: *Zion*, 6 (1941), 89–93; 20 (1955), 73–81; idem, in: *Hagut . . . S. H. Bergman* (1944), 145–51; idem, in: *Review of Religion*, 14 (1949/50), 115–39; idem, in: *Molad*, 18 (1960), 335–56; idem, in: *Commentary*, 32 (1961), 305–16; I. Tishby, in: *Keneset*, 9 (1945), 238–68; Y. Y. Grunwald, *Toyzent Yor Yidish Leybn in Ungarn* (1945); I. Halpern, *Ha-Aliyyot ha-Rishonot shel ha-Ḥasidim le-Ereẓ Yisrael* (1946); idem, in: *Zion*, 22 (1957), 194–213; M. Buber, *Hasidism* (1948); idem, *Origin and Meaning of Hasidism* (1960); A. I. Bromberg, *Mi-Gedolei ha-Ḥasidut*, 24 vols. (1949–69); J. G. Weiss, in: *Zion*, 16 (1951), 46–105 (second pagination); idem, in: *Alei Ayin* (1952), 245–91; idem, in: *Erkhei ha-Yahadut* (1953), 81–90; idem, in: JJS, 4 (1953), 19–29; 8 (1957), 199–213; 9 (1958), 163–92; 11 (1960), 137–55; idem, in: *Tarbiz*, 27 (1957/58), 358–71; idem, in: HUCA, 31 (1960), 137–47; idem, in: *Meḥkarim . . . Gershom Scholem* (1968), 101–13; E. Steinman, *Be'er ha-Ḥasidut*, 10 vols. (1951–62); idem, *Garden of Hasidism* (1961); A. Shochat, in: *Zion*, 16 (1951), 30–43; M. Gutman, *Mi-Gibborei ha-Ḥasidut* (1953²); J. S. Minkin, *Romance of Hasidism* (1955²); B. Dinur, *Be-Mifneh ha-Dorot* (1955), 83–227; idem, in: *Zion*, 8–10 (1942–45); H. M. Rabinowicz, *Guide to Hassidism* (1960); idem, *World of Hasidism* (1970); S. H. Dresner, *The Zaddik* (1960); S. Werses, in: *Molad*, 18 (1960), 379–91; A. Wertheim, *Halakhot ve-Halikhot be-Ḥasidut* (1960); H. Zeitlin, *Be-Fardes ha-Ḥasidut ve-ha-Kabbalah* (1960); Y. L. Maimon (ed.), *Sefer ha-Besht* (1960); R. Mahler, *Ha-Ḥasidut ve-ha-Haskalah* (1961); A. Rubinstein, in: *Areshet*, 3 (1961), 193–230; idem, in: KS, 38 (1962/63), 263–72, 415–24; 39 (1963/64), 117–36; idem, in: *Tarbiz*, 35 (1965/66), 174–91; idem, in: *Sefer ha-Shana shel Bar-Ilan*, 4–5 (1967), 324–39; S. Poll, *Hasidic Community of Williamsburg* (1962); L. I. Newman, *Hasidic Anthology* (1963); S. Federbush (ed.), *Ha-Ḥasidut ve-Ẓiyyon* (1963); A. Yaari, in: KS, 39 (1963/64), 249–72, 394–407, 552–62; M. A. Lipschitz, *Faith of a Hassid* (1967); R. S. Uffenheimer, *Ha-Ḥasidut ke-Mistikah* (1968), with Eng. summary; S. Ettinger, *Toledot Yisrael ba-Et ha-Ḥadashah*, ed. by H. H. Ben-Sasson (1969), index s.v. *Ḥasidim* and *Ḥasidut;* M. Wilensky, *Ḥasidim u-Mitnaggedim* (1970); W. Z. Rabinowitsch, *Lithuanian Hasidism* (1970). Musical Tradition: Sendrey, Music, nos. 2700–30, 6913, 7414, 7824, 7995, 8024, 9121, 9129, 9138–39, 9176, 9189, 9404–79, 9536; A. Z. Idelsohn, *Thesaurus of Hebrew Oriental Melodies*, 10 (1932); M. S. Geshuri (ed.), *La-Ḥasidim Mizmor* (1936), incl. bibl.; idem, *Neginah ve-Ḥasidut be-Veit Kuzmir u-Venoteha* (1952); idem, *Ha-Niggun ve-ha-Rikkud be-Ḥasidut*, 3 vols. (1956–59); H. Mayerowitsch, *Oneg Shabbos, Anthology of Ancient Hebrew Table Songs (Zemiroth)* (1937); V. Pasternak, *Songs of the Chassidim* (1968); J. Stutschewsky (ed.), *Rikkudei Ḥasidim* (1947); idem, *Niggunei Ḥasidim*, nos. 1–7 (1944–46); idem, *Me'ah ve-Esrim Niggunei Ḥasidim* (1950); idem, *Niggunim Ḥasidiyyim, Shabbat* (1970); S. Y. E. Taub, *Kunteres Ma'amarim (Kunteres Tiferet Yisrael)*, nos. 1–8 (1941–48), includes music supplement in each issue; J. Talmud, *Rikkudei Ḥasidim Yisre'eliyyim* (1956); M. Unger, *Khasides un Yontev* (1958); idem, *Di Khasidishe Velt* (1955); C. Vinaver, *Anthology of Jewish Music* (1953); S. Zalmanov (ed.), *Sefer ha-Niggunim* (1949).

Example 1. Ḥabad. *Nie Zhuritsi Khloptsi.* "Rejoicing" and dance *niggun* for a devotional gathering *(hitva'adut)* and festive occasions, derived from a Ukrainian song. Said to have been sung by the followers of the "Middle Admor," R. Dov Ber b. Shneur Zalman of Lyady, on their pilgrimages to his court. The second and third sections are probably an original ḥasidic development of the basic tune. This is also sung to a Yiddish text, *Gits nit kayn Nekhten.* Recorded by Y. Mazor at Kefar Ḥabad, 1969 (Jerusalem, J.N.U.L., National Sound Archives, Yc 121/16–17). Transcription Y. Mazor.

Example 2. Kalov. *Vald, Vald,* attributed to R. Isaac of Kalov. Present distribution not ascertained. Recorded by Y. Mazor in Jerusalem, 1967, from a descendant of a family of Zhikiv ḥasidim (Jerusalem, Israel Institute for Sacred Music, M 72/943). Transcription Y. Mazor. R. Isaac is said to have taken the tune from a shepherd's love song, changing the words in the second part to demonstrate the allegorical meaning: "Forest (Diaspora), how enormous thou art/Rose *(Shekhinah),* how far thou art./Were the forest (Diaspora) not so great/then were the rose *(Shekhinah)* not so far.

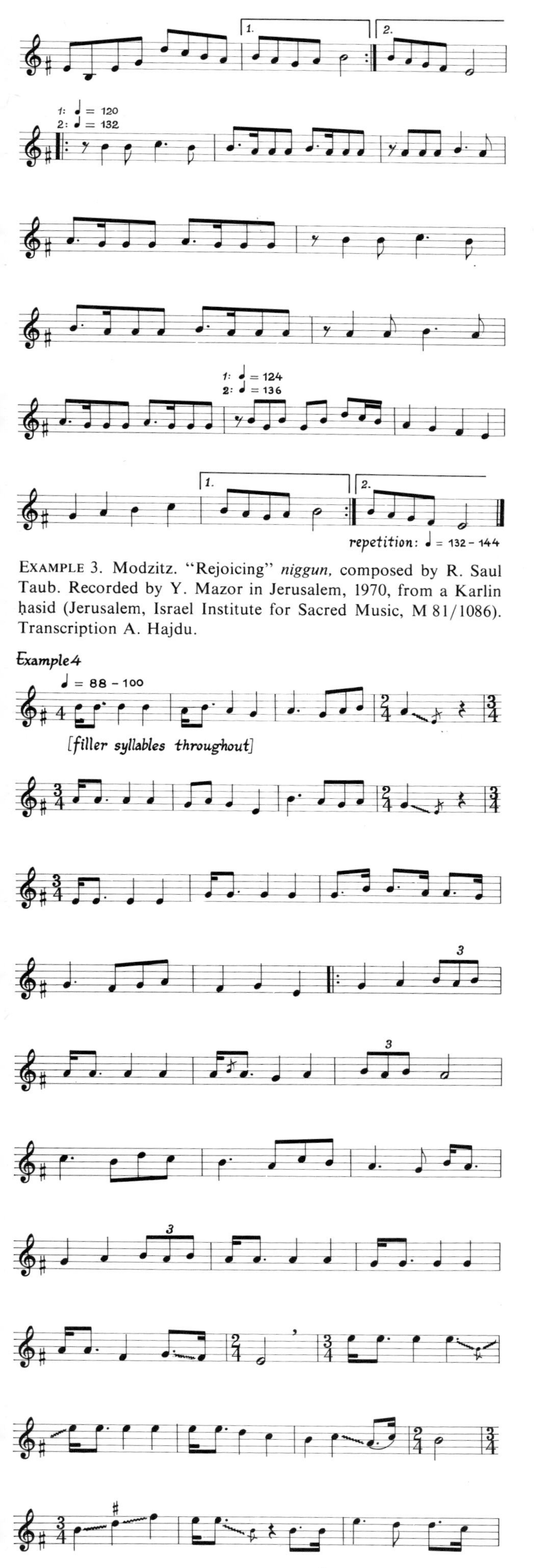

EXAMPLE 3. Modzitz. "Rejoicing" *niggun,* composed by R. Saul Taub. Recorded by Y. Mazor in Jerusalem, 1970, from a Karlin ḥasid (Jerusalem, Israel Institute for Sacred Music, M 81/1086). Transcription A. Hajdu.

EXAMPLE 4. Karlin. Textless *niggun,* sometimes also sung to the words of *Yah Ekhesof.* Believed to be old. Recorded by Y. Mazor in Jerusalem, 1970, when sung at a Karlin wedding before the entry of the bridegroom (Jerusalem, Israel Institute for Sacred Music, M 74/962). Transcription A. Hajdu.

EXAMPLE 5. Ḥabad. *Avinu Malkenu* ("Our Father, our King"), *niggun* for a devotional gathering, sometimes also sung during the *Avinu Malkenu* prayer. Attributed to R. Shneur Zalman of Lyady. From S. Zalmanoff (ed.), *Sefer ha-Niggunim,* 1949.

EXAMPLE 6. Pan-ḥasidic. Dance *niggun*, of unknown provenance, nonspecific in function. Recorded by Y. Mazor in Bene-Berak, 1967, as played by a Jerusalem *klezmer* group (Jerusalem, Israel Institute for Sacred Music, M 39/490). Transcription A. Hajdu.

EXAMPLE 7. Ḥabad. "Rejoicing" and dance *niggun* for devotional gatherings and festive occasions. Recorded by Y. Mazor at Kefar Ḥabad, 1967, on the "Feast of Redemption" (19th Kislev), at the devotional meeting in the yeshivah (Jerusalem, Israel Institute for Sacred Music, M 33/514). Transcription A. Hajdu.

EXAMPLE 8. Ḥabad. "Rejoicing" *niggun*, for various occasions. Sometimes sung to the text *Ashrenu mah tov ḥelkenu* ("Blessed are we, how goodly is our portion"). From S. Zalmanoff (ed.), *Sefer ha-Niggunim*, 1949.

EXAMPLE 9. Karlin. Opening *niggun* for the *hakkafot*. At present sung also in many other ḥasidic communities. Recorded by Y. Mazor, in the *Yeshivat ha-Matmidim*, Jerusalem, on Simḥat Torah night 1966 (Jerusalem, Israel Institute for Sacred Music, M 33/514). Transcription A. Hajdu. In Israel the tune was used by the pioneers of the Fourth Aliyah (1924–1931) as a wordless dance-song, and adapted by M. Ravina to the text of *Kol Dikhfin* in the Passover *seder*.

HASKALAH (הַשְׂכָּלָה), Hebrew term for the Enlightenment movement and ideology which began within Jewish society in the 1770s. An adherent of Haskalah became known as a *maskil* (pl. *maskilim*). The movement continued to be influential and spread, with fluctuations, until the early 1880s. Haskalah had its roots in the general Enlightenment movement in Europe of the 18th century but the specific conditions and problems of Jewish society in the period, and hence the objectives to which Haskalah aspired in particular, all largely differed from those of the general Enlightenment movement. Haskalah continued along new and more radical lines the old contention upheld by the Maimonidean party in the *Maimonidean Controversy that secular studies should be recognized as a legitimate part of the curriculum in the education of a Jew. For Jewish society in Central Europe, and even more so in Eastern Europe, this demand conflicted with the deeply ingrained ideal of Torah study that left no place for other subjects. As in medieval times, secular studies were also rejected as tending to alienate youth from the observance of the precepts and even from loyalty to Judaism.

The Haskalah movement contributed toward *assimilation in language, dress, and manners by condemning Jewish feelings of alienation in the *galut* and fostering loyalty toward the modern centralized state. It regarded this assimilation as a precondition to and integral element in *emancipation, which Haskalah upheld as an objective. The *maskilim* also advocated the productivization of Jewish occupation through entering *crafts and *agriculture. The emphasis placed on these common objectives naturally varied within Jewish society in different countries and with changing conditions. Greater emphasis was placed on assimilation and it became more widespread in Western and Central Europe than in Eastern Europe. Here the struggle for secular education and productivization was continuous and strong (see also Haskalah in Russia, below).

Beginning and Background of Haskalah. Moses *Mendelssohn is generally considered to be the originator of the Haskalah movement (the "father of the Haskalah"). However, this opinion has to be corrected in that a desire for secular education had already been evinced among the preceding generation of German Jews, and some individual Jews in Poland and Lithuania, during the 1740s. Knowledge of European languages could be found among members of the upper strata of Jewish society there many years before. Mendelssohn considered that a Jewish translation of the Bible into German was "a first step toward culture" for Jews. It seems, however, that he was

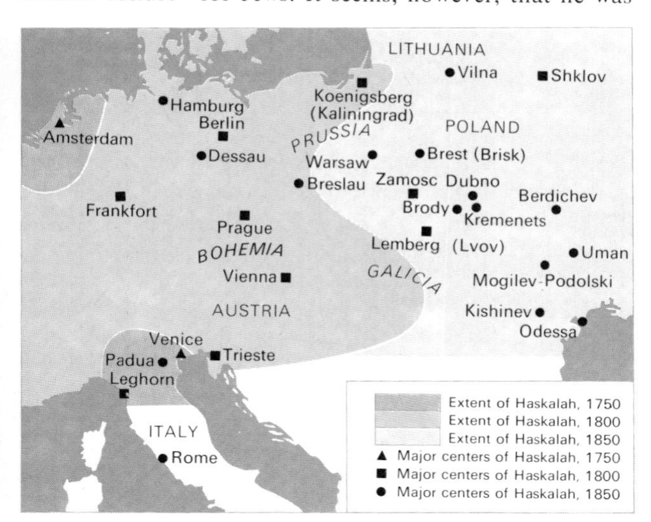

The spread and main centers of the Haskalah in Europe. From H. H. Ben Sasson (ed.), *History of the Jewish People*, Tel Aviv, 1969.

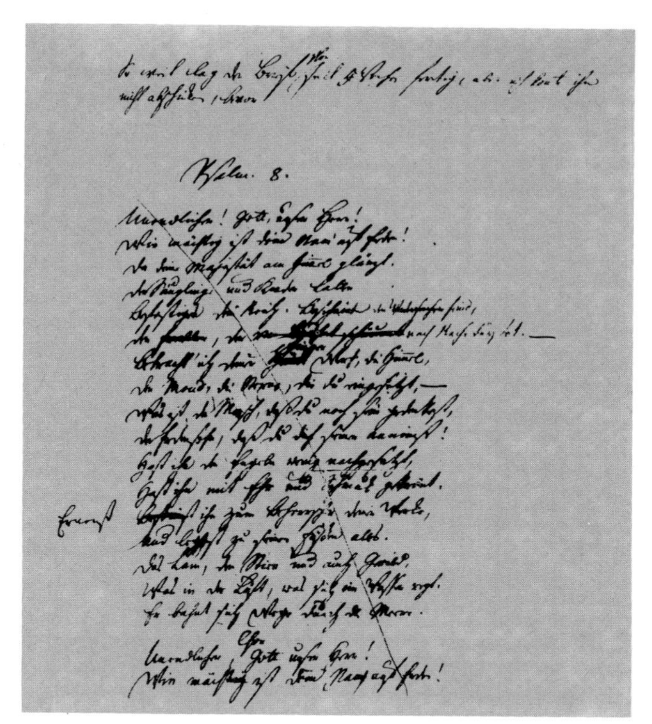

Figure 1. Page of the Psalms from the manuscript of Moses Mendelssohn's German translation of the Bible, published in Berlin in 1783. Jerusalem, J.N.U.L., Schwadron Collection.

doubtful about encouraging the spread of Haskalah among Jewry. When in the early 1780s it was proposed to translate certain works into Hebrew so as to lead the Jewish people to abandon "its ignorance and the opposition to every sensible reform," Mendelssohn "thought that any enterprise of this sort would indeed not be harmful, but neither would it be very beneficial" (see Solomon Maimon, *An Autobiography* (1947; repr. 1967), 97). Mendelssohn was opposed to *education of Jewish and non-Jewish children together; he was also against the **Toleranzpatent* issued by Emperor Joseph II, fearing that the method of education proposed there would lead Jews to *apostasy.

The birth and growth of the Haskalah movement were considerably facilitated by the policies of the absolutist regimes of Germany, Austria, and Russia during the 18th century, which deprived the Jewish community leadership of its coercive authority, such as exercise of the right of **ḥerem* ("ban"). Large-scale commercial transactions undertaken by the *Court Jews at this time brought the upper classes of Jewish society in contact with non-Jewish circles, and as a result there formed a section of the Jewish community which diverged from the traditional way of life. Others open to influence by Haskalah were individual Jews, frequently Jewish peddlers who often migrated to new localities without a communal organization or rabbis, where the individual was consequently left to himself. The literature and ideas of the Enlightenment penetrated in particular through the influence of the women who acquired a knowledge of French language and culture. Such Jews began to experience a feeling of inferiority in relation to non-Jewish culture; they began to frequent non-Jewish society, especially the intellectual *salons, and to campaign for emancipation, firm in the faith of its positive consequences for Jews.

Haskalah operated as an active trend within German Jewry in the space of one generation. Its influence first spread in *Galicia (which passed to Austria with the partition of Poland) and later in Lithuania and other provinces of the Russian *Pale of Settlement.

There were also countries where attitudes similar to those adopted by the Haskalah circles in Germany had been manifest among Jews earlier, where they were unaccompanied by disintegration of Jewish tradition. In Italy, men who had studied medicine and were well acquainted with philosophy and the classics, as well as Christian theological literature, held rabbinical positions. The prestige won by Jewish physicians of note was generally considered an asset and encouragement to the Jewish community (see Isaac Cantarini, *Et Kez* (Amsterdam, 1710), 1b). In Italy also, study of Kabbalah was compatible with secular studies (see Jacob Frances, in: I. Frances, *Metek Sefatayim*, ed. by H. Brody (1892), 74; Moses Ḥayyim *Luzzatto).

Early stirrings of a positive appreciation of secular culture among Jews had even appeared in Germany by the first half of the 18th century and were manifest earlier among some traditional scholars and leaders like Tobias b. Moses *Cohn the physician, author of *Ma'aseh Tuviyyah*, Jonathan *Eybeschuetz, or Jacob *Emden. More positive and active participation in general culture still combined with a traditional outlook is reflected in Israel *Zamosc and Aaron Elias Gomperz, who wrote his *Ma'amar ha-Madda* (1765) to point out the importance of the sciences (see also below).

The specific approach characterizing Haskalah was expressed by those to whom secular culture and philosophy became a central value which raises man to the highest spiritual level, possibly not below that of religious meditation, and for whom it symbolized the sublime aspect of man, who by his initiative can achieve progress in and dominate nature. They considered that such culture would elevate both the human and social stature of the Jew. The new spirit prompted a number of Haskalah writers to compose works popularizing science in Hebrew, like Mordecai Gumpel b. Judah Leib Schnaber (d. 1797; published under the name Marcus George Levisohn). Articles on natural sciences were published in the first Hebrew secular monthly *Ha-Me'assef* (see below) by Baruch Lindau (1759–1849) and Aaron Wolfsohn Halle.

המאסף
לשתי התקופות הראשונות
משנת
התקמח
Nebst einer deutschen Zugabe.
Königsberg und Berlin, 1788.
In der orientalischen Buchdruckerey.

Figure 1. Title page of an issue of *Ha-Me'assef*, the first Hebrew monthly. Koenigsberg and Berlin, 1788. Jerusalem, J.N.U.L.

Haskalah, like its parent the European Enlightenment movement, was rationalistic. It accepted only one truth: the rational-philosophical truth in which reason is the measure of all things. During the 1740s some of the youth had already begun to study Maimonides' *Guide of the Perplexed*. Haskalah accepted Enlightenment *Deism, giving it a specifically Jewish turn. Gotthold Ephraim *Lessing, in the parable of the Three Rings in *Nathan der Weise*, rejected the claim of any religion to represent the absolute truth. Mendelssohn held that there was nothing in the Jewish faith opposed to reason and that the revelation on Mount Sinai did not take place to impart faith but to give laws to a nation, because faith cannot be achieved by decree, while the laws which were given on that occasion were designed to serve as the laws of a unique Jewish theocratic state. Mendelssohn thus attempted to remove Judaism from the struggle between Enlightenment and revealed religion. The attitude of such Jews toward tradition underwent a radical change. The conception of Divine Providence in favor of Israel, the belief in the election of Israel, and the religious reasons advanced for the exile of Israel were weakened and the anticipation of Israel's future redemption began to wane.

While Mendelssohn and Naphtali Herz *Wessely, the pioneer of Haskalah education, did not doubt the sanctity and the authority of the Oral Law, they tried to demote the study of Talmud from its supreme position in Jewish education. Mendelssohn, in his letter to Naphtali Herz *Homberg, stressed the importance of actions and the study of the Bible in order to preserve the society of "true theists" (i.e., Judaism), while the Talmud is not mentioned there at all. This anti-talmudic mood was widespread. Study of the Talmud was not included in the curriculum of the "Free School" founded in Berlin in 1778 (see below). Wessely expressed this approach in the words: "We were not all created to become talmudists." Representing the most radical wing of Haskalah, David *Friedlaender was openly glad that the yeshivot were declining. The Talmud was also criticized in Russia. Abraham *Buchner, a teacher in the rabbinical seminary of Warsaw, even wrote a book entitled *Der Talmud in seiner Nichtigkeit* ("The Talmud in its Emptiness," 2 vols., 1848). In Galicia, Joshua Heschel *Schorr claimed that although the Talmud was historically important, its legal decisions were outdated socially and spiritually and hence no longer binding. Later Moses Leib *Lilienblum, too, considered the Talmud important but demanded from the rabbis, in the name of the "spirit of life," reform in *halakhah*.

In Western Europe and the German states, especially the northern German states, observance of *halakhah* was already being neglected before the advent of the Haskalah movement. Mendelssohn reacted sharply against the tendency to ignore the burden of the precepts found among persons close to him, some of whom even denied Divine Revelation to Moses. Among the *maskilim* who frequented Mendelssohn's home there were, according to Solomon *Dubno, "a group of men who were to be suspected of having discarded the yoke of the Torah." This negation of halakhic precepts, which was often coupled with contempt

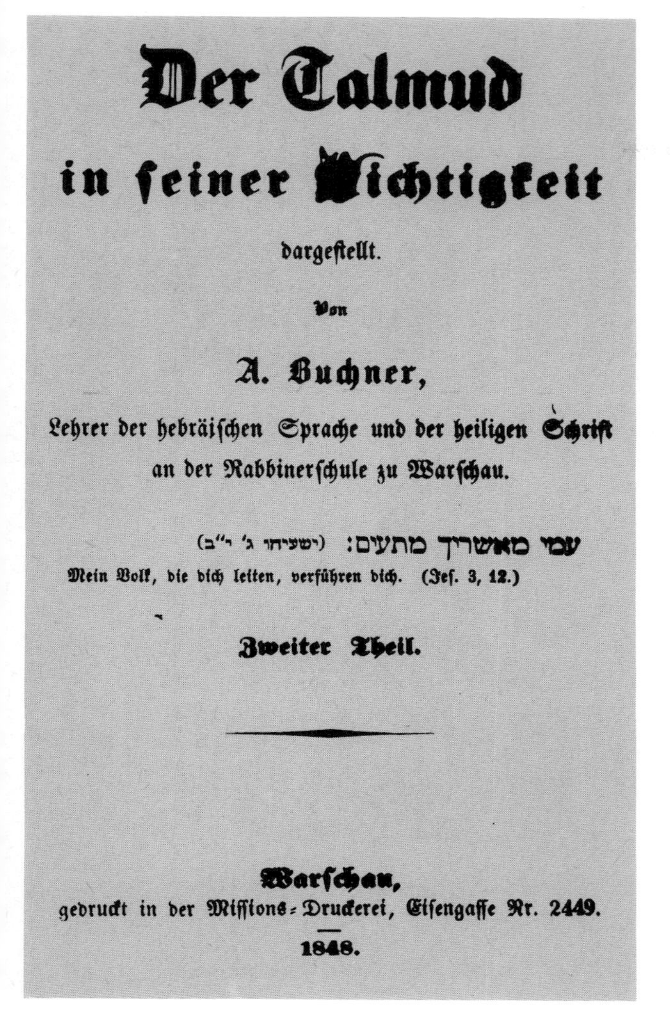

Der Talmud

in seiner Nichtigkeit

dargestellt.

Von

A. Buchner,

Lehrer der hebräischen Sprache und der heiligen Schrift

an der Rabbinerschule zu Warschau.

עמי מאשריך מתעים: (ישעיהו ג׳ י״ב)

Mein Volk, die dich leiten, verführen dich. (Jes. 3, 12.)

Zweiter Theil.

Warschau,

gedruckt in der Missions-Druckerei, Eisengasse Nr. 2449.

1848.

Figure 2. Title page of *Der Talmud in seiner Nichtigkeit* ("The Talmud in its Emptiness") by Abraham Buchner, Warsaw, 1848. Jerusalem, J.N.U.L.

toward the whole of Judaism, also served as a factor leading to mass apostasy among the Jewish bourgeoisie of *Berlin and its surroundings.

Linguistic Assimilation. Linguistic assimilation increasingly became a hallmark of Haskalah. In Germany, as well as in Alsace-Lorraine, wealthy Jews had begun to have their children taught German and French at the close of the 17th century to facilitate both their business and social contacts with non-Jews. French became the language of the "elite" in Jewish circles, where the reading of general literature became widespread. In the 1780s there were "the daughters of Israel, who are all able to speak the language of the gentiles with eloquence, but cannot converse in Yiddish" (*Ha-Me'assef* (1786), 139). By the 1790s the younger generation of the Jewish bourgeoisie of Berlin had begun to adopt German as their spoken language. A negative attitude toward Yiddish developed. German writers had claimed in the past that the Jews had been able to deceive non-Jews by the use of Yiddish in business transactions, and as a result decrees had been issued compelling Jews to write their commercial documents and keep their books in German.

Apparently Mendelssohn was influenced by these claims and even thought that Yiddish was ridiculous, ungrammatical, and a cause of moral corruption. He initiated translation of the Pentateuch into German, in order to induce Jews to use this language (see *Bible: Translations, German). Wessely approved wholeheartedly of the measures which Joseph II introduced against the use of Yiddish (*Ha-Me'assef* (1784), 178). David Friedlaender called for the removal of Yiddish as the language of instruction in the *ḥeder* and Jewish schools; in his opinion the use of Yiddish was responsible for unethical conduct and corruption of religion. He translated the prayers into German, "the language spoken by the inhabitants of these regions," because the Yiddish translations "were repulsive to the reader in their style and contents" (*Ha-Me'assef* (1786), 139). The *maskil* Zalkind *Hourwitz also suggested that the Jews be prohibited from employing either Yiddish or Hebrew for bookkeeping and business contracts, not only for transactions between Jews and Christians but also between Jews themselves, in order to prevent fraud.

A move against Yiddish in favor of the "mother tongue" (in this case, Dutch) was initiated by the *maskilim* in the *Netherlands during the period of French rule there. A Jewish weekly began to appear in Dutch in 1806. In 1808 a society was formed in Amsterdam for translation of the Bible and the prayer book into Dutch, as well as for the publication of textbooks in Hebrew and Dutch, the establishment of new schools, and the training of suitable teachers for them. King Louis Bonaparte issued a decree in February 1809, in force from Jan. 1, 1811, prohibiting the use of Yiddish in documents. Sermons in the synagogues were to be delivered in Dutch, while Dutch was to be the language of instruction for Jewish youth. The *consistory of the Netherlands ordered that notices in the synagogues be published in Dutch only, and all correspondence between the communities and the consistory was to be conducted in Dutch only. In France, the *maskilim* encountered no difficulties in their struggle against Yiddish in favor of French. French had been widely spoken among Jews before the Haskalah period. *Berr Isaac Berr preferred Mendelssohn's German translation of the Pentateuch to the one existing in Yiddish until a proper Jewish-French translation had been made. In Hungary, the *maskilim* were active in substituting Hungarian for the Yiddish vernacular during the 1840s. Hungarian became the language of instruction in the Jewish schools of several communities and preachers even began to employ this language in synagogues.

Development of Hebrew. Hebrew was not only of central importance to people like Jacob Emden and Jonathan Eybeschuetz, who apparently wished that Jews should be able to speak fluent Hebrew; Mendelssohn also considered the Hebrew language a national treasure. In his *Kohelet Musar,* 3 issues (1750), he called for an extension of its frontiers, on the example of other living languages. Cultivation of Hebrew was also one of the aims of the *Biur,* the commentary on the Pentateuch initiated by Mendelssohn. For these scholars Hebrew meant biblical Hebrew. Study of the Bible held a central position in the educational program of the Haskalah movement, whereas both the content of the Talmud and even more so the style of Hebrew used in the 18th century, and by earlier Ashkenazi rabbis, drove Haskalah scholars to reject the post-biblical layers in the Hebrew language. The interest shown by German gentile scholars in the Bible and its language also contributed to a certain extent to the preference of Haskalah circles for biblical Hebrew, though from the beginning some voices expressed reservations toward this extremist approach (see also *Ha-Me'assef* (1784), 185).

Ha-Me'assef served as the organ of the Haskalah in its Hebrew aspect. It was published regularly between 1783 and 1790, with difficulties until 1797, and revived from 1809 to 1811. It was published by the Doreshei Leshon Ever ("Friends of the Hebrew Language") in Koenigsberg founded in 1783, and renamed in 1786 Shoḥarei ha-Tov ve-ha-Tushiyyah ve-Doreshei Leshon Ever ("Seekers of Good and Wisdom and Friends of the Hebrew Language"). Even *Ha-Me'assef* published articles in German; its publication ceased through extreme assimilation of the adherents of Haskalah, in particular in Germany and Austria. German attracted younger and progressive circles. The literary contribution by the so-called **Me'assefim* generation was an important stage in the development of Hebrew language and literature. Hebrew became a vehicle for secular and professional scientific expression. They also contributed much to research in grammar and purity of expression. In Eastern Europe Hebrew remained the language of Haskalah literature for a longer period, appealing to a much wider public with deeper roots in Jewish culture than in Central and Western Europe. The *maskilim* there further developed and enlivened Hebrew (see Haskalah in Russia, below).

Education. The adherents of Haskalah shared the rationalist belief in the boundless efficacy of a rational education. They therefore turned to a change in the curriculum and methods of teaching as the main means of shaping a new mode of Jewish life. The first school to be guided by this ideal was founded in Berlin in 1778 and named both Freischule ("Free School") and Ḥinnukh Ne'arim ("Youth Education"). It was primarily designed for children of the poor and was without fee. The curriculum included study of German and French, arithmetic, geography, history, natural sciences, art, some Bible studies, and Hebrew. The school had a revolutionary effect on Jewish education, for it heralded the transfer of the center of gravity from Jewish studies to general subjects. The school was successful from the beginning; only half of its 70 first pupils came from poor homes. Wessely's welcome of Joseph II's educational proposals for Jews (*Divrei Shalom ve-Emet,* 4 pts. (1782–85)) and his call to the Jews of Austria to establish schools on this pattern were an outcome both of the success of the Freischule as well as the fear that if Jews themselves did not take the initiative, Jewish children would be compelled to attend the state schools. In this work Wessely set out both a detailed program and a basic philosophy for Haskalah education. German Jews of the upper social strata were ready for this program, though it aroused much rabbinical opposition, influenced from outside Germany.

In the same year (1785), the bishop of Mainz admitted 19 Jewish boys to the general school without difficulties. Many programs for Haskalah education were proposed, some drawing on the experience of Italian Jewish and Sephardi schools, whose curricula were considered near to Haskalah aims. The question of education was widely discussed in *Ha-Me'assef.* Some radical *maskilim* demanded that German and arithmetic should be taught to begin with and Hebrew reading and writing be added at a later stage. David Friedlaender sought to introduce German as the language of instruction in all subjects and the teaching of selected chapters of the Bible of ethical value to both boys and girls. In regard to religious instruction, he also suggested that only the ethical precepts be taught.

The *maskilim,* who despised the old-style Polish teachers, the *melammedim,* whom they considered uncouth and uncultured, were not satisfied with criticism alone. On their initiative new schools sprang up in Berlin, Dessau, and Frankfort on the Main, among other places, in which Hebrew and general studies were taught. A limited number of hours were usually devoted to Hebrew studies, while study of the Talmud was almost completely abandoned. Several educators wrote textbooks where the educational aims of the Haskalah movement found expression. The first to be written were the *Toledot Yisrael* (Prague, 1796), on Jewish history by Peter *Beer; *Imrei Shefer* (Vienna, 1816)

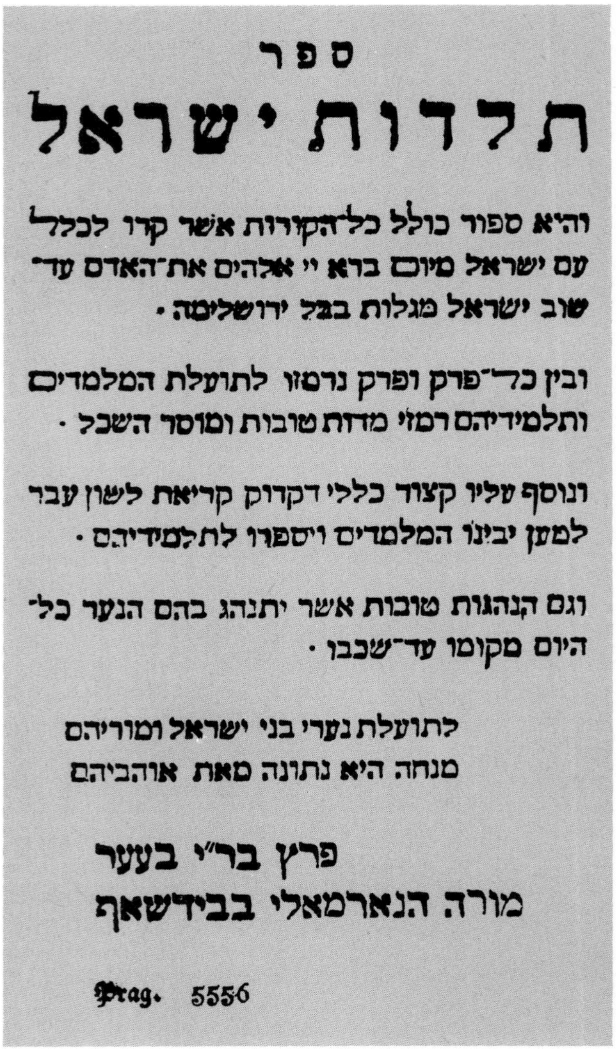

ספר
תלדות ישראל

והיא ספור כולל כל־הקורות אשר קרו לכלל
עם ישראל מיום ברא יי אלהים את־האדם עד־
שוב ישראל מגלות בבל ירושלימה ·

ובין כל־פרק ופרק נרמזו לתועלת המלמדים
ותלמידיהם רמזי מדות טובות ומוסר השכל ·

ונוסף עליו קצור כללי דקדוק קריאת לשון עבר
למען יבינו המלמדים ויספרו לתלמידיהם ·

וגם הנהגות טובות אשר יתנהג בהם הנער כל־
היום מקומו עד־שכבו ·

לתועלת נערי בני ישראל ומוריהם
מנחה היא נתונה מאת אוהביהם

פרץ בר״י בעער
מורה הנארמאלי בבידשאף

Prag. 5556

Figure 3. Title page of the first Haskalah textbook, *Toledot Yisrael,* a history of the Jews by Peter Beer, Prague, 1796. Jerusalem, J.N.U.L.

and *Bne-Zion* (Ger., *ibid.,* 1812), religious and moral readers for young people by Naphtali Herz Homberg. In 1807 a confirmation ceremony for boys in German, in imitation of the Christian custom, was introduced in the school at Wolfenbuettel, whence it spread to the other Jewish schools in Germany.

The influence of Haskalah also penetrated to Orthodox circles who were compelled to respond to the demands of the times. Even R. Ezekiel *Landau agreed that it was necessary "to know language and writing"; although "Torah is the main thing," "one should grasp both." R. *David Tevele of Lissa conceded to the emperor's request "to teach the children to speak and write the German language for an hour or two." The first "integral" schools (in which Jewish and general subjects were taught) were opened by the Orthodox in Halberstadt and Hamburg (see also Samson Raphael *Hirsch; *Neo-Orthodoxy). Haskalah brought a considerable change in the education of girls. The daughters of the wealthy generally studied under private teachers. The *maskilim* also began to show concern for the education of the daughters of the poor. Schools for girls were established in the 1790s in Breslau, Dessau, Koenigsberg, and Hamburg. The curriculum generally included some Hebrew, German, the fundamentals of religion and ethics, prayers, and arithmetic; there were also schools where the writing of Yiddish, handiwork, art, and singing were taught.

Schools with curricula based on the educational ideals of Haskalah were also established in France and other Western European countries. On the example of the "integral" schools in Germany, similar schools were also founded in East European countries. In 1813 a school was founded by Josef *Perl in Tarnopol (Galicia), where in addition to Bible, Mishnah, *Gemara,* and Hebrew grammar, the subjects of Polish, French, arithmetic, history, and geography were also taught; the language of instruction was German and there were also classes for girls. A similar school was established in Lvov in 1845. In Warsaw, three schools in which the language of instruction was Polish were established by Jacob *Tugendhold in 1819; two schools for girls were also established here.

With the foundation of the new schools, the problem of training teachers arose. Isaac *Euchel, David Friedlaender, and Judah Loeb *Jeiteles were among the first *maskilim* to raise this problem. Special institutions were established, but on many occasions the rabbinical seminaries also served this purpose. The first teachers' training seminary was opened in Kassel in 1810 by the consistory of the kingdom of Westphalia, followed by others through the first half of the 19th century. A seminary for teachers and rabbis was opened in Amsterdam in 1836 and a seminary for teachers in Budapest in 1857. Secondary schools did not develop anywhere. Only the Philanthropin school at Frankfort extended its curriculum in 1813 to include a secondary science-orientated section providing six years' studies after the four years of elementary classes. Some private institutions of a commercial-science orientation were established in Berlin. Those who went on to secondary studies generally attended non-Jewish institutions.

Government Intervention in Jewish Education. The educational ideals of Haskalah largely coincided with the aims set out for "improvement of the Jews" (see emancipation) and their education as conceived by "enlightened" absolutist rulers. Typical were the edicts issued by Joseph II for the Jews of Bohemia (1781), Moravia (1782), Hungary (1783), and Galicia (1789). The Jews were ordered to establish "normal" schools or to send their children to the state schools; Jews were also permitted to enter secondary schools and universities. Anyone who studied Talmud before completing the school curriculum was liable to be sentenced to a term of imprisonment; marriage was prohibited without a certificate of school attendance.

As a result of these edicts, 42 schools were opened in Moravian communities by 1784, 25 in Bohemia by 1787, and about 30 in Hungary by the end of the 1780s. In Galicia 104 schools were established but were closed down in 1806 during the period of reaction for fear of the "harmful" influence of the "anti-religious" Jewish teachers. Naphtali Herz Homberg was appointed to supervise the program in Galicia. In most German states the process of government intervention in the education of the Jews occurred at the beginning of the 19th century. Usually the Jews were ordered to establish secular schools for the education of their children or to send them to the general schools. There were also some states in Germany which at first did not authorize the Jews to establish separate schools and preferred that education be given to the Jewish children in the *ḥeder* or the public schools. In Prussia the general schools were opened to Jewish children in 1803; until 1847 the separate Jewish schools were recognized only as private schools. The trend toward Germanization was especially marked among the large Jewish population in the Polish region of former *Great Poland.

Some states also intervened in regard to yeshivot. They began to demand that the rabbis should have a general education and especially instruction in philosophy. In 1820 Francis I of Austria issued a decree obliging rabbis to study sciences and employ the language of the country in prayers and sermons. A rabbinical seminary, the first of its kind, was opened in Padua in 1829. This was followed up in many states and in different forms through the first half of the 19th century.

The advocates of "improvement of the Jews" (see *emancipation; C. W. von *Dohm) considered the restructuring of their occupations from moneylending and trade to productivization through taking up crafts and agriculture to be an essential element in and precondition for accomplishing both betterment of their character and their position. In the main the *maskilim* accepted this social and economic program as well as the criticism of Jewish life it implied. They hoped that productivization would bring a moral regeneration as well as change the *image of the Jew for enlightened Christians. In the new schools established by the *maskilim* in Germany (see above), instruction in crafts was also introduced and some also took care that their graduates should be apprenticed to Christian craftsmen. In various German states, societies to care for the interests of Jewish apprentices were organized. In Berlin a society for the Promotion of Industry was established in 1812 following the emancipation law issued in Prussia that year. Its objective was "to awaken and promote as much as possible the creative spirit among members of the Jewish religion by means of support and encouragement" and to "courageously refute the old-established opinion that we supposedly have an exclusive tendency to commerce" (see also *Joseph II; *Crafts). Naphtali Herz Homberg advocat-

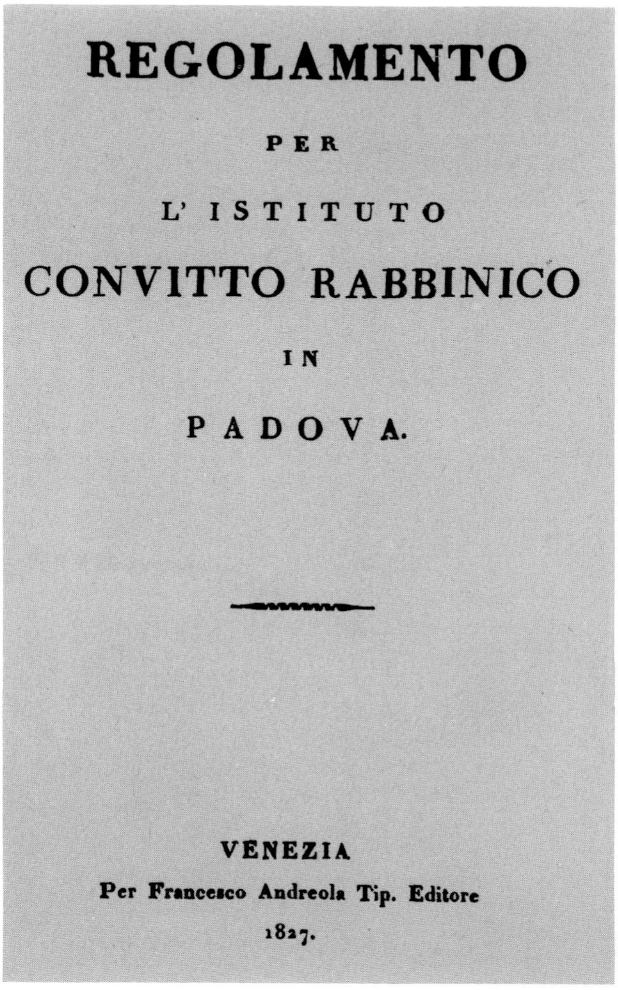
REGOLAMENTO

PER

L' ISTITUTO

CONVITTO RABBINICO

IN

PADOVA.

VENEZIA

Per Francesco Andreola Tip. Editore

1827.

Figure 4. Title page of the regulations of the Padua rabbinical seminary, opened in 1829, the first to oblige aspiring rabbis to study secular subjects. Jerusalem, J.N.U.L.

ed manual work which he considered was necessary from the moral as well as economic aspect. Homberg based his opinion on sayings of the rabbis in the Talmud in praise of labor and condemned the prevailing attitude of contempt toward the "worker" within Jewish society. Like Mendelssohn, he did not completely reject commerce from the aspect of its utility for society, but considered that the creativity of manual labor surpassed commerce from the aspect of social morality. Phinehas Elijah *Hurwitz complained that "the majority of our people do not want their sons to be taught crafts because they say with pride and arrogance that the occupation of crafts is shameful for us." He considered that commerce contributed to hatred of the Jews and to the allegation widespread among non-Jews that the Talmud teaches the Jews how to deceive them.

Cooperating with the authorities of the enlightened absolutist states and other regimes to promote general education and productivization among Jews, with the majority agreeing on the need for improvement of the Jews and the desirability of their assimilation, Haskalah circles found it natural to emphasize the complete loyalty which Jews acknowledged to the secular rulers as their protectors, and to the country and state as the framework for their security of life and autonomy. The *maskilim* did not content themselves with the traditional prayers for the king. Laudatory poems were written in honor of Frederick the Great of Prussia, noted for his "love" of the Jews. The Austrian emperor, Joseph II, was also honored with enthusiastic poems of praise and thanksgiving. Their enthusiasm for reform led a number of *maskilim* to advise the authorities how to "improve" the Jews without paying attention to whether these improvements were desired by them or not. Some collaborated with the authorities and bypassed the regular heads of the Orthodox communities without scrupling to slander them, a method used by Naphtali Herz Homberg and his staff of teachers in Galicia.

Trends in Ideology. An ahistoric stand, inclination to assimilation, and desire for emancipation helped to erode messianic hopes in Jewish society, at the close of the 17th and the first half of the 18th century, a trend apparent in Amsterdam, Italy, and Germany. The general anti-messianic position taken by *maskilim* was aided by the failure of the *Shabbetai Ẓevi movement. Jacob Emden quoted Jonathan Eybeschuetz as having preached that the main achievement of the Messiah for the Jews would be that "they would find clemency among the nations"—a traditional expression for attainment of a better legal and social status. The messianism of Jacob *Frank was oriented to nihilistic religious experience and to the conditions of contemporary Jewish existence in Poland. Some have regarded these attitudes as the catalysts of the anti-halakhic movement and the weakening of messianic hopes in Haskalah. Mendelssohn adhered in principle to the messianic hope, though he considered that it did not have "any influence on our civic behavior"—at least not in places where "they have treated the Jews with tolerance"; in his view the redemption would come through the Divine Will alone, though he once gave his opinion that the return of the Jewish people to Ereẓ Israel could be a political-secular event, during a world war. A few *maskilim*, according to Mordecai Schnaber, equated the Messiah with the reign of universal peace and toleration. Zalkind Hourwitz in his *Apologie des Juifs* (Paris, 1789) thought like Mendelssohn that the effect of messianic faith on the actual behavior of Jews was similar to the influence of the certainty of death on human activity; "this does not prevent them . . . from building, sowing, and planting in every place where they are permitted to do so."

After emancipation was attained a further weakening of messianic faith set in. When latter-day *maskilim* began to combine Haskalah ideology with a nationalist Jewish attitude their anti-messianic stand became a starting point for aspirations for redemption by natural agency (see *Ḥibbat Zion; *Zionism). Mendelssohn, however, regarded the Torah as a kind of divine legislation intended for the Jewish society and state only; but he saw this type of Jewish unity as a society of theists; nationalism per se was absent in his theory regarding the Jews.

Many *maskilim* identified themselves emotionally and expressly as "Germans." In his German writings, Mendelssohn repeatedly uses the phrase "we Germans," and he criticized use of the expression "Germans and Jews" instead of "Christians and Jews" by Johann David *Michaelis. After Jewish emancipation had been attained in France in 1791, Berr Isaac Berr proclaimed: "By Divine Mercy and the government of the people, we have now become not only men, not only citizens, but also Frenchmen." The *Assembly of Jewish Notables convened by Napoleon in 1806 coined the term "Frenchmen of the Mosaic religion." It also declared that "the Jews are no longer a nation" and that "France is our fatherland." From 1807 the appellation *"israélite"* in France (in German *"Israelit"*) also spread to the German states. The change expressed trends to assimilation as well as a tendency to efface former appellations for Jews that had become connected with an odious image. Both fitted in with Haskalah ideology.

Haskalah ideology was one of the foundations of the *Reform movement in the Jewish religion. The idea of reform had already been conceived by David Friedlaender in 1799. Through his influence the first steps in reform were taken by Israel *Jacobson, in the state of Westphalia. Friedlaender himself began to introduce reform in religion in Berlin after the Jews of Prussia had obtained their emancipation in 1812. He called for exclusion from the prayer book of all prayers for the return to Zion and the dirges on the destruction of the Temple, and demanded that prayers be recited in German; with this he also desired that the "society of true theists," after the expression of Mendelssohn, continue to exist. Haskalah ideology was also the basis for the efforts and achievements of the founders of the *Wissenschaft des Judentums in 1819 (see also Zacharias *Frankel; Abraham *Geiger; Marcus *Jost; Moritz *Steinschneider; Solomon Judah *Rapoport; Nachman *Krochmal; Samuel David *Luzzatto; Leopold *Zunz).

The beginnings of a renewed modern interest in Jewish history are already found in the generation of Mendelssohn and Wessely. In *Ha-Me'assef*, a special section was set aside for "biographies of eminent Jewish personalities" in which popular articles were written on Maimonides, Don Isaac Abrabanel, Moses Raphael de Aguilar, Isaac Orobio de Castro, and others. In these articles the first efforts were also made to bring to light ancient sources. The program of *Ha-Me'assef* also included the publication of works on the biographies of "living Jewish scholars." Accordingly Isaac *Euchel wrote a biography of Mendelssohn, and David *Friedrichsfeld a biography of Wessely (the two works were however published after the deaths of Mendelssohn and Wessely). In addition, a section of *Ha-Me'assef* was to deal with "the innovations taking place among our people which concern all the Jews, on their freedom in some countries, and the education of their youth . . . for the utility of youth with a quest for knowledge." Biographies of eminent Jewish personalities were also published in *Shulamit*. However, serious research into Jewish history on a wide scale was taken up by Haskalah circles when the poet and scholar Solomon *Loewisohn published his work *Vorlesungen ueber die neuere Geschichte der Juden* in Vienna in 1820, the first Haskalah attempt to present a general view of Jewish history from the earlier Diaspora period down to the time of the author.

Haskalah thus became one of the mainsprings of a renewed study of the nature of Judaism and the fate of the Jewish people. Mendelssohn attempted to demonstrate the superiority of Judaism over Christianity in his description of Judaism as a rational religion and of the practical precepts as the laws of the former Jewish state (and possibly also a future state) and as symbols of the ideals of the rational faith. Mendelssohn apparently thought that even at the millennium, when the whole world would submit to the "yoke of the Kingdom of Heaven," the Jews would still be obliged to observe the precepts because their function as "symbols," as educational factors, would never be abrogated. This was because Mendelssohn did not believe in the entire perfectibility of mankind in any period, seeing that "the whole of humanity is in constant motion, either in ascent or decline." Even though Mendelssohn did not say so explicitly, it may be assumed that his references to the election of Israel and its mission were not only intended to explain the past but also to indicate the situation in the future.

During the 19th century further attempts were made in the Haskalah camp to define the nature of Judaism. Some regarded Judaism as a "spiritual religion" in contrast to the idolatrous religions which were "religions of nature" and in contrast to Christianity, which served as the battleground between the elements in the Jewish "spiritual religion" and the idolatrous elements (Solomon *Formstecher). Others regarded Judaism as a moral religion, a religion of the heart and the emotions, in contrast to Hellenism, the religion of cold reason (S. D. Luzzatto, and others). N. Krochmal defined the faith of Israel as belief in the Infinite "Absolute Spiritual One" and considered this to be the secret of the eternity of the Jewish people. The growing development of historical consciousness supplanted traditional views on the fate of Israel in Haskalah thought. Exile was no longer conceived as a chastisement meted out by Providence, but the result of natural historical factors. In the West, emancipation was generally regarded as the end of the Exile (see *Galut). However, the difficult struggle for emancipation, which in Germany extended over several decades, awakened some doubts on the future of the Jews in Europe and here and there some far-reaching conclusions, such as emigration to America or a return to Palestine (Mordecai Manuel *Noah; *Salvador; Moses *Hess). [Az. S.]

Haskalah in Russia. Haskalah was introduced into Russia from Western Europe, particularly Germany. It was brought to the communities of Lithuania and Ukraine by merchants, physicians, and itinerant Jewish scholars from the close of the 18th century. As early as the 1780s some Jews in towns of Lithuania and Poland were subscribers to the *Biur* of Moses Mendelssohn and *Ha-Me'assef* of the German *maskilim*. The earliest *maskilim* in Eastern Europe were Israel Zamosc, Solomon Dubno, Judah *Hurwitz, Judah Loeb *Margolioth, Baruch *Schick, and Mendel *Lefin. They maintained direct relations with the *maskilim* of Berlin, but when spreading Haskalah in their own environment based themselves formally on the views of *Elijah b. Solomon Zalman, the Gaon of Vilna, and regarded themselves as his disciples. Baruch Schick, who published several works on mathematics and astronomy, wrote in his introduction to his translation of Euclid (Amsterdam, 1780) that he had heard the Gaon state that "in proportion to a man's ignorance of the other sciences, he will be ignorant of one hundred measures of the science of the Torah." Solomon Dubno contributed to the *Biur,* Mendelssohn's commentary on the Bible. Phinehas Hurwitz published the *Sefer ha-Berit* (Bruenn, 1797), a type of encyclopedia of various sciences, combining ethical observations and research in the spirit of moderate Haskalah. *Manasseh b. Joseph of Ilya, who was persecuted by the zealots for his free ideas, also belonged to this circle. As customary at this time, all these authors sought and obtained the written approval of outstanding rabbis for their works.

At the close of the 18th century the wealthy *maskil* Joshua *Zeitlin established a center for *maskilim* and traditional Torah scholars on his estate near Shklov. In his large library they were able to dedicate themselves to their studies and religious perfection. Included in this group were Baruch Schick and Mendel Lefin of Satanov. These *maskilim* made use of their relations with the Russian authorities as merchants, purveyors, and physicians, and submitted proposals to the administration for the improvement of the situation of the Jews by admitting them to various crafts, by the encouragement of agricultural settlement, and by the opening of modern schools for the Jews (memoranda of Jacob Hirsch of Mogilev, 1783; of

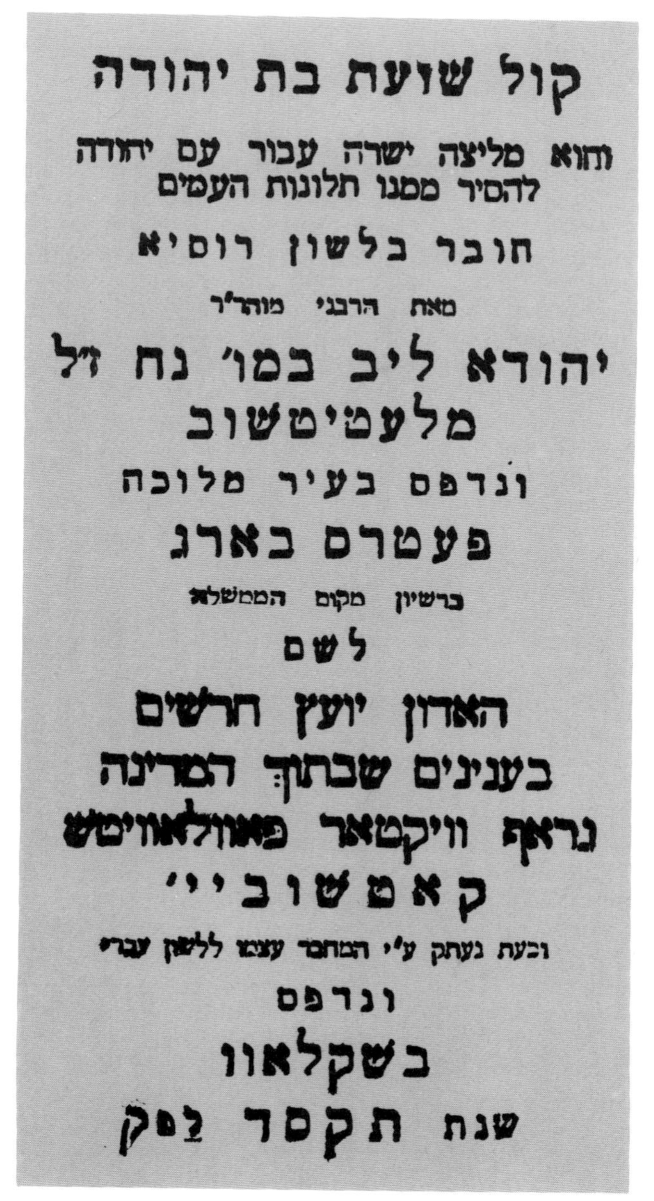
קול שועת בת יהודה
והוא מליצה ישרה עבור עם יהודה
להסיר ממנו תלונות העמים
חובר בלשון רוסיא
מאת הרבני מוהר"ר
יהודא ליב במו' נח ז"ל
מלעטיטשוב
ונדפס בעיר מלוכה
פעטרס בארג
ברשיון מקום הממשלה
לשם
האדון יועץ חרשים
בענינים שבתוך המדינה
גראף וויקטאר פאוולאוויטש
קאטשובייי
ובעת נעתק ע"י המחבר עצמו ללשון עברי
ונדפס
בשקלאוו
שנת תקסד לפק

Figure 5. Title page of *Kol Shavat Bat Yehudah,* Judah Leib Nevakhovich's Hebrew translation of his Russian pamphlet on the ideology of the St. Petersburg *maskilim.* The original was published in 1802, the Hebrew version in Shklov in 1803. Jerusalem, J.N.U.L.

Nathan Note *Notkin of Shklov, 1797; of the physician Jacob Elijah Frank of Kreslavka (Kraslava), 1800). The *maskilim* already concerned themselves with spreading education among the masses during this period. While having reservations against the use of Yiddish, they wrote works in that language for the education of the people. The physician Moses Markuse published *Sefer Refu'ot* in Poritsk, Volhynia, in 1790 in which he offered, as well as medical advice, guidance on the education of children. In 1817 the merchant Chaim Ḥaykl *Hurwitz of Uman published his *Tsofnas Paneakh,* an adaption of the work of J. Campe, *Die Entdeckung von Amerika.*

A small group of *maskilim* organized themselves in the new community which was established in St. Petersburg at the close of the 18th century. Their outlook was expressed in the Russian pamphlet *Vopl docheri iudeyskoy* (1802), published in a Hebrew version, *Kol Shavat Bat Yehudah,* in Shklov a year later. Written on the occasion of the debate on the Jewish problem which then took place within the Russian government, it took up the defense of the Jewish people, and included a plea that kindness and mercy be shown to it. A few years later its author, Judah Leib *Nevakhovich, became an apostate, as did his patron, the merchant Abraham *Peretz, the son-in-law of Nathan Note Notkin. These conversions, as well as the information concerning the epidemic of conversions among the *maskilim* of Germany, stiffened the hostility and suspicions felt by the mass of Jews in Russia toward the *maskilim.* They became a considerable obstacle in the spread of Haskalah there.

During the 1820s the Haskalah movement was revived in Lithuania and Southern Russia. Its promoters were emigrants from Galicia, such as the "Brodysts" in *Odessa, as well as Jews from Courland, influenced by German culture, and the inhabitants of the townlets bordering upon Prussia and Courland (Raseiniai; Zagare). During this period the *maskilim* gained a hold in Vilna, one of the centers of commerce with Western Europe. The *maskilim,* who dressed in German style and insisted on speaking pure German among themselves instead of Yiddish, which they regarded as a corrupted German dialect, were referred to by the masses as "Deytshen" or "Berliners." One of their main aims was to establish modern Jewish schools in which the pupils would be taught general subjects and Jewish studies in the German language. In 1822, Hirsch Hurwitz (son of the above-mentioned Chaim Ḥaykl Hurwitz) founded a school in Uman based on the "Mendelssohnian system." Of even greater importance was the foundation of a Jewish school in Odessa under the direction of Bezalel *Stern (1826). Similar schools were subsequently founded in Riga, Kishinev, and Vilna. During those years, the program of the *maskilim* was elaborated by Isaac Dov (Baer) *Levinsohn (Ribal) of Kremenets in his *Te'udah be-Yisrael* (Vilna, 1828) and *Beit Yehudah* (*ibid.,* 1839). The essence of this program was the establishment of a network of elementary schools for boys and girls in which the pupils would study Jewish and general subjects, as well as some kind of a profession; it also included the foundation of high schools for the more talented children, the promotion of productivization, particularly agriculture, among the Jewish masses, and departure from Yiddish in favor of "the pure German or Russian language."

The *maskilim* endeavored to organize themselves under the difficult conditions for free organization in general and for the Jews in particular during the reign of Czar *Nicholas I. In many towns small groups of *maskilim* were established, among them the Shoḥarei Or ve-Haskalah ("Seekers of Light and Education") society founded by Israel Rothenberg in Berdichev, the Maskilim Society in Raseiniai, and the Maskilim Group led by the author Mordecai Aaron Guenzburg in Vilna, which established its own synagogue, Taharat ha-Kodesh, in 1846. Harassed by censorship, they struggled to publish their works, which included the first Hebrew literary periodical there, *Pirḥei Ẓafon* (Vilna, 1841). Among them a modern Hebrew literature began to emerge. Mordecai Aaron Guenzburg wrote stories based on Jewish, general, and Russian history, adapted from non-Jewish sources or collected from other authors in this period. During the following years, Kalman *Schulmann proceeded with this enterprise. A number of poets wrote on secular subjects in lyrical Hebrew, many expressing the ideas of Haskalah. The most prominent in this group were Abraham Dov *Lebensohn (Adam ha-Kohen), whose first collection of poems, *Shirei Sefat Kodesh,* was published in Leipzig in 1842, his son Micah Joseph *Lebensohn (Mikhal), and the leading Haskalah poet, Judah Leib *Gordon. Abraham *Mapu created the Hebrew novel, and his *Ahavat Ẓiyyon* (Vilna, 1853) has become a landmark in the history of Hebrew literature. Despite their opposition to Yiddish, the Haskalah authors wrote works in this language in order to propagate their ideas among the masses by means of stories and works of popular science. The most outstanding of these authors, Isaac Meir *Dick, wrote hundreds of stories which were published in Vilna and Warsaw. Israel *Axenfeld and Solomon *Ettinger wrote stories and plays in the Haskalah spirit. Many of their works could not be published because of the censorship and were circulated in manuscript.

Even in the period of oppression and anti-Jewish legislation during the reign of Nicholas I, the *maskilim*

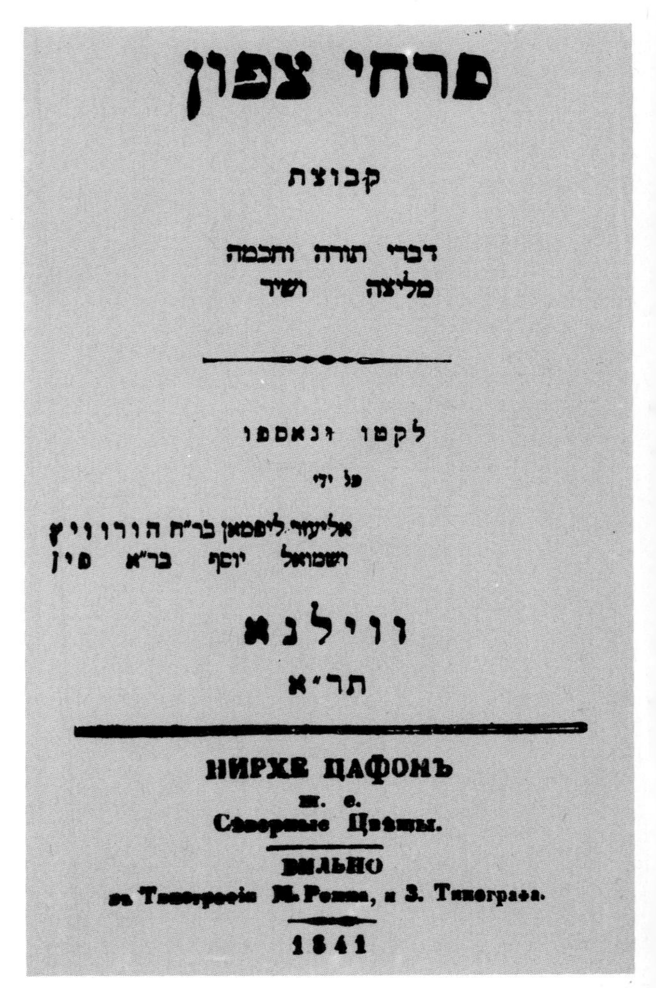
פרחי צפון

קבוצת

דברי תורה וחכמה
מליצה ושיר

לקטו ונאספו
על ידי
אליעזר ליפמאן בר"ח הורוויץ
ושמואל יוסף בר"א פין

ווילנא
תר"א

ПИРХЕ ЦАФОНЪ
т. е.
Сѣверные Цвѣты.

ВИЛЬНО
въ Типографіи М. Ромма, и З. Типографа.

1841

Figure 6. Title page of an early issue of *Pirḥei Ẓafon,* the first Hebrew literary periodical to be published in Vilna. Jerusalem, J.N.U.L.

looked upon the Russian government as a supporting force in their struggle for the realization of their ideas. In memoranda submitted to the authorities, they called for the imposition of reforms on the masses, such as change of their traditional dress for the European clothes of the period, and the strict supervision of Hebrew printing presses which were to be reduced to two or three in the whole country in order to make this possible. The government accepted these proposals and had them enforced. The *maskilim* found particular satisfaction in the government's program to establish a network of governmental Jewish schools in which the language of instruction would be German (later Russian). During the early 1840s the government entrusted Max *Lilienthal, the principal of the Jewish school of Riga, with the execution of this program. He was assisted by the local *maskilim* in every town. During the 1840s and 1850s many such schools were founded in the towns of the Pale of Settlement. Their Jewish teachers were drawn from *maskilim* circles who were granted the status of government functionaries. In Vilna and Zhitomir, government rabbinical seminaries were established. Their students were exempted from military service and were trained in view of becoming the future teachers and rabbis of the Jewish communities. In these schools and seminaries, which were financed by special taxes imposed on the masses (*candle tax), a new class of *maskilim* was educated. They received their education in Russian, and their ties with the Hebrew language and Jewish tradition were flimsy.

Haskalah received considerable stimulus through economic changes, particularly when a wide class of Jews engaged in liquor contracting emerged. As a result of their contracts with government officials, they and their employees required a knowledge of the Russian language, arithmetic, and other sciences. There thus arose a whole class of thousands of families who were no longer dependent on Jewish society from the economic and social point of view. These Jews wore the non-Jewish dress, neglected the observance of the religious precepts, shaved their beards, and were drawn closer to the Russian language and culture. The *maskil* of the former generation had been self-taught, familiar with Jewish literature, whose principal education was drawn from German literature, as well as from the *Ḥokhmat Yisrael* ("Jewish Science") literature. In contrast, the new *maskil* received his education in a Russian-Jewish school or in a general Russian school and was conspicuous for his considerable alienation from Jewish tradition.

The period of the important reforms at the beginning of the reign of *Alexander II and the suppression of the Polish uprising in 1863 gave a strong impetus to the spread of Haskalah among the masses of Jewish youth. The Jewish press, whose founders, journalists, and publishers were essentially *maskilim*, played a decisive role in this development. Among newspapers outstanding for their struggle in favor of Haskalah were the Hebrew **Ha-Meliẓ* (founded in 1860) and the Yiddish **Kol Mevasser* (1862), issued by A. *Zederbaum and first published in Odessa. The first newspapers issued by the Russian-orientated *maskilim* also appeared in Odessa, **Razsvet* and *Sion* (in 1860/61) and *Den* (1869–71), to which the leading Russian *maskilim* contributed. The older authors were joined by new ones, among them S. J. Abramovitz (later *Mendele Mokher Seforim), who wrote in Hebrew and Yiddish, I. J. *Linetzky (Yiddish), L. *Levanda, and G. Bogrov (Russian). Their writings produced a more advanced stage in Haskalah ideology, which found its expression in the saying of the poet J. L. Gordon: "Be a man when you go out and a Jew in your home." This press called for an alliance between the Jewish *maskilim* and the Russian government in order to fight "those in darkness" from within, especially the Ḥasidim and their *ẓaddikim*, and to support the governmental Russification policy throughout the Pale of Settlement. During the 1860s the institution of *kazyonny ravvin* ("government-appointed rabbi") was introduced. Its candidates were drawn from the ranks of the *maskilim* who had been educated in the Russian-Jewish schools.

In 1863, on the initiative of the richest Jews of the capital (the *Guenzburg, *Polyakov, and *Rosenthal families), the Ḥevrat Mefiẓei ha-Haskalah ("*Society for the Promotion of Culture among the Jews of Russia") was founded in St. Petersburg. This society came to the assistance of *maskilim* in the provincial towns, particularly high-school students, and encouraged the publication of Haskalah literature in Hebrew, Yiddish, and Russian.

Most of the *maskilim* believed the general assumption that Russia, in the wake of the other European states, was about to declare the emancipation of the Jews. The rights which had been granted to certain Jewish circles, such as the large-scale merchants (1859), intellectuals (1861), craftsmen (1865), and members of the medical profession (physicians, pharmacists, male nurses, midwives, etc.), seemed to point in that direction. The introduction of the general obligation of military service (1874), which included important concessions in the conditions and period of service for those with a Russian education, prompted many parents to send their children to the Russian schools. While in 1870 only 2,045 Jewish children studied in Russian secondary schools, by 1880 their numbers had increased to 8,000.

During this period there were two marked trends among the *maskilim*. One called for a rapid association with the Russian nation, even to the point of assimilation. The Hebrew language (and all the more so Yiddish) was merely regarded as a temporary instrument for spreading Haskalah among the retarded masses. At most, adherents to this trend recognized the need for the promotion of *Wissenschaft des Judentums* in the Russian language. This was the path which had been adopted by West European Jewry and along which Russian Judaism was also to be led. On the other hand, the standard-bearers of a nationalist ideology which called for the fostering of the Hebrew language and loyalty to Jewish nationalism also raised their voices. The voice of this trend was the newspaper **Ha-Shaḥar* (1868–84), published by Peretz *Smolenskin in Vienna but particularly addressed to Russian Jewry. Smolenskin sharply criticized the Mendelssohnian Haskalah and called for the promotion of Jewish nationalist values. During this period, however, he was a lone voice. To the majority of the *maskilim* it appeared that the historical evolution which had taken place in Western Europe would also overtake Russian Jewry. Some opinions considered this evolution to be natural and desirable, even drawing some far-reaching conclusions from it (A. U. *Kovner), while others expressed their regrets with regard to it (J. L. Gordon, in *Le-Mi Ani Amel*, 1871).

A significant change, however, occurred in the lives of the Russian Jews during the 1870s. The breakthrough into the general economy and Russian culture by the Jews resulted in the emergence of a powerful anti-Jewish movement, whose spokesmen included leading Russian intellectuals (Aksakov; Dostoyevski). A press inciting the Russian masses against the Jews and warning them of "domination" by the Jews, especially intellectuals, over the country was created. The reaction that set in in Russia in the wake of Alexander II's assassination at first resulted in anti-Jewish pogroms (1881–83) and later in severe restrictions of Jewish rights. One of these, the *numerus clausus, was especially destined to bar the way of the Jewish youth to the Russian schools.

The *maskilim* reacted to this situation in various ways. Those of the older generation attempted to adhere to their policies and placed their faith in "progress" which would eventually be victorious and bring the anticipated emancipation. This circle of Jewish-Russian intelligentsia centered around the newspaper **Voskhod* (St. Petersburg, 1881–1906). A considerable section of Jewish youth joined the Russian revolutionary movement with the hope that the fall of the czarist regime would eliminate all restrictions, and that the Jews would be assimilated and rapidly absorbed within the Russian people so that the Jewish problem would automatically disappear. Another section of the older generation and the intellectual Jewish youth resorted to Jewish nationalism. They established the *Ḥibbat Zion movement which considered that the solution of the Jewish problem in Russia lay in the emigration of the Jews to Ereẓ Israel where they would engage in productive occupations. They called for an alliance with the Jewish masses who were attached to their traditions and language in order to realize this project. The organ of this sector was the Jewish-Russian newspaper *Razsvet* (1879–83) and later *Ha-Meliẓ*. Haskalah, as an ideological trend on the Jewish scene, now ceded its place to the new trends, all of which—even if they violently criticized Haskalah from various directions—had received many of their ideas from it.

Even if from the historical point of view Russian Haskalah was a continuation of the Central European it nevertheless possessed an originality stemming from the particular character of Russian Jewry. The large number of Jews in that country and their great concentrations in the towns and townlets of the Pale of Settlement prevented the Haskalah movement from degenerating into a rapid course of assimilation and disintegration, as had occurred in Western Europe. In Russia the new Hebrew literature became a permanent fact and not an ephemeral phenomenon as in the West. Haskalah produced, even if in opposition to its own ideology, a secular literature in Yiddish, especially of Yiddish fiction. It gave rise to an alert Jewish press in three languages, Hebrew, Yiddish, and Russian. It also bequeathed to the nationalist movement, and particularly to the Zionist movement, the idea of productivization of the Jewish masses and their transition to labor in general and agricultural work in particular.

See also *Hebrew literature; *History. [Y.S.]

Bibliography: Z. Yavetz, in: *Keneset Yisrael*, 1 (1896), 89–152; S. Bernfeld, *Dor Ḥakham* (1896); idem, *Dor Tahpuḥot*, 2 vols. (1897); Graetz, Hist, 5 (1895); Dubnow, Weltgesch, 8 (1928); 9 (1929); Y. Kaufmann, *Golah ve-Nekhar*, 2 (1930); B. Offenburg, *Das Erwachen des deutschen Nationalbewusstseins in der preussischen Judenheit* (1933); M. Wiener, *Juedische Religion im Zeitalter der Emanzipation* (1933); J. Katz, *Die Entstehung der Judenassimilation in Deutschland und deren Ideologie* (1935); idem, *Tradition and Crisis* (1961), 260–74; A. Orinovsky, in: *Rishonim: Koveẓ Mukdash la-"Kursim ha-Pedagogiyyim ha-Grodna'iyyim"* (1936), 174–89; Baron, Social, 3 (1937); P. Sandlar, *Ha-Be'ur la-Torah shel Moshe Mendelssohn* (1941); G. Scholem, *Mi-Tokh Hirhurim al Ḥokhmat Yisrael* (1945; repr. from: *Lu'aḥ ha-Areẓ* (1945), 94ff.); Y. Fleishman, in: *Erkhei ha-Yahadut* (1953); E. Simon, in: *Sefer ha-Yovel . . . Mordekhai Menaḥem Kaplan* (1953), 149–87; R. Mahler, *Divrei Yemei Yisrael, Dorot Aḥaronim*, 2 (1954), 57–88, 223–43; 3 (1955), 34–94, 169–72; 4 (1956), 9–90; idem, *Ha-Ḥasidut ve-ha-Haskalah* (1961); B. Dinur, *Be-Mifneh ha-Dorot* (1955), 231–54; idem, in: *Tarbiz*, 20 (1959), 241–64; B. Katz, *Rabbanut, Ḥasidut, Haskalah*, 1 (1956), 140–266; 2 (1958), 122–251; Zinberg, Sifrut, 3 (1958), 260–335; 5 (1959), 13–143, 258–99; 6 (1960); J. Klausner, in: *Yahadut Lita*, 1 (1960), 405–12; M. Eliav, *Ha-Ḥinnukh ha-Yehudi be-Germanyah bi-Ymei ha-Haskalah ve-ha-Emanẓipaẓyah* (1960); Y. Slutski, in: *Zion*, 25 (1960), 212–37; A. Schochat, *Im Ḥillufei Tekufot* (1960); idem, in: *Ha-Molad*, 23 (1965/66), 328–34; I. E. Barzilay, *Shelomo Yehudah Rapoport (Shir) 1790–1867* (Eng. 1969); idem, in: PAAJR, 24 (1955), 39–68; 25 (1956), 1–38; idem, in: JSOS, 21 (1959), 165–92; S. Ettinger, in: H. H. Ben-Sasson (ed.), *Toledot Am Yisrael*, 3 (1969); Z. Rejzen, *Fun Mendelssohn bis Mendele* (1923); M. Erik, *Etyudn tsu der Geshikhte fun der Haskole* (1934); H. S. Kazdan, *Fun Ḥeder un Shkoles bis CYShO* (1956), 19–64. HASKALAH IN RUSSIA: J. S. Raisin, *The Haskalah Movement in Russia* (1913); S. Spiegel, *Hebrew Reborn* (1930); D. Patterson, *The Hebrew Novel in Czarist Russia* (1964); J. Meisel, *Haskala, Geschichte der Aufklaerungsbewegung unter den Juden in Russland* (1919); S. Tsinberg (Zinberg), *Istoriya yevreyskoy pechati v Rossii* (1915); E. Tcherikower, *Istoriya Obshchestva dlya rasprostraneniya prasveshcheniya mezhdu yevreyami v Rossii* (1913); P. Marek, *Ocherki po istorii Prosveshcheniya* (1909); 9 (1958[2]), 130–4, 225–38; Klausner, Sifrut, 3–4 (1953–54); R. Mahler, *Divrei Yemei Yisrael, Dorot Aḥaronim*, 4 (1956), 53–68; Y. Slutski, *Ha-Ittonut ha Yehudit-Rusit ba-Me'ah ha-19* (1970); J. Shatzky, *Kultur Geshikhte fun der Haskole in Lite* (1950); I. Sosis, *Di Geshikhte fun di Yidishe Gezelshaftlekhe Shtremungen in Rusland in 19th Yorhundert* (1929); M. Erik, *Etyudn tsu der Geshikhte fun der Haskole* (1934).

HASKAMAH (**Askamah;** Heb. הַסְכָּמָה, אַסְכָּמָה; "agreement," "approbation"), in Jewish literature, a term with several meanings: (1) Rabbinic approval and approbation of the legal decisions of colleagues, usually attached to the original legal decision and circulated with it. These *haskamot* sometimes amplify the original, by including additional sources and pointing out implications. (2) In the Spanish and later also in the Italian and Oriental communities, the term was used for the statutes and ordinances enacted by the communities (see *Ascama). (3) In the philosophical literature of the Middle Ages, "consensus," "harmony between entities," "pre-established harmony" (see Klatzkin, Thesaurus Philosophicus 1, 185–6). (4) More commonly, the recommendation of a scholar or rabbi to a book or treatise. This entry deals with the last meaning.

Origins and History. Various opinions have been offered on the origin or development of the *haskamah* for books. Some see the influence of the *approbatio* of the Church, others see it as resulting from the papal action of 1553 in the dispute between the publishing houses of *Bragudini and Giustiniani which resulted in the burning of the Talmud (see *Censorship). The first *haskamah* appeared in the 15th century, in the *Agur* by Jacob Landau (Naples, c. 1490), the first Hebrew book printed during its author's lifetime; it was signed by seven rabbis. The *haskamah* for Elijah Levita's *Sefer ha-Baḥur* (Rome, 1519) signed by the rabbi of Rome, threatens excommunication for republication within ten years. Thus the *haskamah* fulfilled the function of a copyright, the period of protection extending from five to 25 years. The *haskamah* in Joseph Caro's *Bedek ha-Bayit* (Venice, 1606) is signed by three rabbis (the number of *haskamot* varied from book to book); and it concluded with a declaration by the sexton that he has read it in all the synagogues of Venice. With the introduction of title pages in the 16th century, *haskamot* came to be printed at the beginning rather than at the end of a book.

Thus, the *haskamah* developed from a recommendation to an expression of approval to a method of protecting the author's rights and finally to a form of self-censorship to protect the Jewish community against the church censorship and later to counteract kabbalistic, pseudo-messianic, and Haskalah tendencies. Thus, at the Rabbinical Synod of Ferrara of 1554, it was enacted that no book should receive its first printing without prior approbation of three rabbis of the particular region. Similar *takkanot* were issued in Poland in 1594 and 1682. Such restrictions were used to prevent the spread of the heretical Shabbatean doctrines, or to protect the printers of the expensive Talmud editions. This led to many disputes and litigations. The majority of *haskamot* issued in the 17th and 18th centuries originated in the centers of Hebrew printing, such as Venice, Amsterdam,

The poem *Dayyeinu* ("it would have sufficed") from the *Mocatta Haggadah*. The words *illu* ("if") in the panel on the right are written in decorated zoo- and anthropomorphic letters while the words *dayyeinu* on the left are embellished with grotesque animals. Within the elongated panels the words are architecturally structured. The margin contains a micrographic motif. Spain, 13th century. London, University College, the Mocatta Library, ms. 1, fol. 38v ($9\frac{1}{2} \times 6\frac{7}{8}$ ins/24 × 17.5 cm.).

הסכמה

מהרב הגאון הגדול , החכם הכולל כק״ש מוהר״ר
אברהם אבלי מווילנא נ״י , בהרב הגדול מוהר״ר
אברהם שלמה ז״ל ,

קול התורה נשמע בארצנו , וזמיר החכמה הגיע עדינו , כי
נראה קסת הסופר בימינו , ספירת דברים דברי חכמה ובינה , כמסמרות
נטועים וכדרבונה , פעמי שולמית בתורה ובחכמה להכינה , ומה הדרבן
מכוון להביא חיי העו״הז אף דברי חכמים הגם שעיקרן לחיי עד עם כל
זה בחכמתם מכוונים גם חיי עו״הז לכוננה , ולכן נקראו אבות שגם הם
מביאים לחיי עו״הז כמו האב · אפס כי לא רבים יחכמו ללקט מפניני
פנימה אמרות טהורות ללבות דבריהם כגחלי אש , אשר אם לבה מלבה
והיה לאש בוערת , ואשר הם כחדום בלשתם לשון זהב ואדרת, לזאת
יקרו בעיני מאד מליצינו ורעינו , אשר לטובת בני עמינו , בחבורתם
נרפא לנו , לרפאות משבח ה׳ ההרוס כי יוסיפו לספר בשבח הא״ש
ארשנ״ו הרעננה ארשת שפתינו , שפת לשון עבר ואשורית , זכה וצחה
מלובנת בקמוניא אשלג ובורית , וילמדנו דעת סדר הלמוד ללמד לבני
יהודא , לתורה ולתעודה , בישראל שמו , כי העד העיד בעמו , ויתן
אומר אמרי שפר , ככל הכתוב פה בספר , לשובב נתיבות ולגדור פרץ ,
בלמוד התורה והחכמה וגם בדרך ארץ , ויישר לישורון הדרך הנכוחה ,
לדעת לשון וספר ולאחוז במלאכה , או במסחר הראוי לעשוה ככה ,
ולדרוש שלום העיר המחוז והפלך , ולעשות הטוב והישר בעיני אלקים
ומלך , ויחזק חרש זה כל דבריו את צורף באמרות ה׳ הצרופות , או
בדברי חז״ל בעלי אספות , הן כל אלה פעל ועשה גבר חכם בעוז , יקר
מפז , החכם המפואר והורני מופלג הרב מוה׳ יצחק בער מקרעמניץ יצ״ו ,
חזיתי איש מאור מעיר במלאכתו לפני מלכים יתיצב , גזרהו ספיר אבן
מחצב , וספרו זה ראו חכמים ויאשרוהו , שרים ורוזנים ויהללוהו ,
סופרים הביטו ונהרו , ומשוררים יצאו לקראתו ושרו , עד שעלה והגיע
למרום מצבו , כי עד מקום שאדונינו הקיר״ה במסבו , הובא להתבונן
בו מה טיבו , ויחוננהו הקיר״ה כרוב נדבת לבו , למען יצא לאור
לראות באבו , הן מאן חשוב ומאן ספון ומאן מעייל אזובי הקיר , לא
ראי

Haskamah given by Abraham Abele b. Abraham Solomon, rabbi of Vilna, to *Te'udah be-Yisrael* by Isaac Dov (Baer) Levinsohn, one of the leaders of the Haskalah. Vilna, 1828. Jerusalem, J.N.U.L.

and Constantinople. *Haskamot* were usually written in a combination of Hebrew and Aramaic, frequently using the florid style of rabbinic writings. They sometimes contain bibliographic, biographic, and geographic data, which, though not always exact, are an important source for historians and scholars, and bibliographers like Roëst, Wachstein and Wiener utilized this source.

Abuses. *Haskamot* have been much abused. Often their place and date were intentionally altered. Some writers, eager to have *haskamot* appended to their works, forged signatures and *haskamot*, as was the case in Nehemiah Ḥayon's *Ha-Kolot Yeḥdalun* (Amsterdam, 1725). Earlier *maskilim* used forged approbations to their works in order to deceive the pious reader. Others printed only part of the book which had received the *haskamah*, and some authors published their books on inferior paper with unclear type. As a result some *haskamot* included such specifications as "the condition of this *haskamah* that the printing of this book should be completed within two years" or "on condition that the printer should print the book on white paper with black ink." These factors, and others as well, made many rabbis reluctant to write *haskamot*. Samson *Wertheimer was ready to approve only the works of relatives or scholars who were poor. Some writers of approbations made no secret of the fact that they had been given to help the author financially (see Abraham ha-Kohen's *Beit Ya'akov*, Leghorn, 1792). Some rabbis denied *haskamot* to any book which dealt with Jewish law; others were ready to add their names only if a well-known rabbi had already given his *haskamah*. Still others protested that they had no time to read the entire book, or that they were not sufficiently acquainted with the subject; which did not prevent some from granting their approbation merely on the reputation of the author. Some authors were not eager to obtain the *haskamah* of rabbis who could not read the work; thus Moses Mendelssohn did not request *haskamot* for his books, nor did Raphael ha-Kohen for his *Torat Yekuti'el* (Berlin, 1772); other authorities disapproved of them altogether (Responsa *Ḥatam Sofer* ḤM 41), Ezekiel Landau used his *haskamah* to the Prague Pentateuch of 1785, to express his disapproval of Mendelssohn's Pentateuch edition. Between 1499 and 1850, 3,662 haskamot were issued, the majority in Eastern Europe. Authors of religious books are still anxious to print a *haskamah* by a prominent rabbi or authority. In secular works the worldwide custom of using a preface or an introduction by a well-known authority fulfills the same role.

Bibliography: L. Loewenstein, *Index Approbationum* (1923); I. S. Reggio, *Iggerot Yashar* (1834–36); B. Wachstein, in: MGWJ, 71 (1927), 123–33; I. Halperin (ed.), *Pinkas Va'ad Arba Araẓot* (1945), index; M. Carmilly-Weinberger, *Sefer ve-Sayif* (1966), xii–xiv, 177–85; Shunami, Bibl., 501

[M.C.-W.]

HASKELL, ARNOLD LIONEL (1903–), British ballet critic and author. In 1927 Haskell started his career with a firm of London publishers, devoted himself to ballet and in 1930 was joint founder of the Camargo Society, which was influential in the revival of ballet in England. For three years Haskell was critic of the *Daily Telegraph* (1935–38). He was director of the Royal Ballet School from 1946 and a governor of the Royal Ballet from 1957. In 1954 he advised the Dutch government on the formation of a National Ballet. His books on ballet were important in the cultivation of popular taste. Among them were *Balletomania* (1934), a word he introduced into the English language; *Diaghileff* (1935); *The Making of a Dancer* (1946); *In His True Centre* (1951), his autobiography; *The Russian Genius in Ballet* (1963); *What is Ballet?* (1965); and *Heroes and Roses* (1966).

[Ed.]

HASMONEAN BET DIN (Heb. בֵּית דִּין שֶׁל חַשְׁמוֹנָאִים); according to a talmudic source (Sanh. 82a; Av. Zar. 36b) "the court of the Hasmoneans decreed that an Israelite who had intercourse with a heathen woman is liable to punishment on account of "נִשְׁגָּא" (NaSHGA), a mnemonic designating four counts of liability: נִדָּה (*niddah;* "a menstruating woman"), שִׁפְחָה (*shifḥah;* "a maidservant"), גּוֹיָה (*goyah;* "a gentile"), and אֵשֶׁת אִישׁ (*eshet ish;* "a married woman"). A second tradition in the Talmud has Z instead of A, designating *zonah*, "harlot." There is no further mention of this Hasmonean court, and it has therefore been suggested, that the reference is to a temporary court set up early in the Hasmonean revolt, to fill the void created by the death of the religious leaders of the period. If this is so, it would appear that this court was responsible for the ruling that defensive battle is permissible on the Sabbath (I Macc. 2:39–41). However, it is more likely that the court was created after the establishment of Hasmonean rule in Palestine following the early successes of Judah and his brothers. Derenbourg claims that the court existed toward the end of the second century B.C.E., during the reign of Simeon and the first years of John *Hyrcanus. He further suggests that Hyrcanus changed the name of the court from Bet Din shel Ḥashmona'im to *Sanhedrin during the last years of his rule, following the schism with the Pharisees. Other scholars tend to identify the Hasmonean court with the "sons of the Hasmoneans" mentioned in the Mishnah (Mid. 1:6; in Yoma 16a, Av. Zar. 52b the reading is "house of Hasmoneans") as having "hidden away the stones of the altar which the Greek kings had defiled," but there is insufficient proof of this. Likewise, there is no reason to identify, as does I. H. Weiss, the Hasmonean *bet din* with the "Great Synagogue" of priests and elders that officially appointed Simeon high priest and leader of the nation (I Macc. 14:28; see *Asaramel). The most likely solution of the problem is that the Hasmonean court "was the private council of the Hasmoneans at the peak of their power." If this is so, the Hasmonean court was established by John Hyrcanus toward the end of his reign, or by his son Alexander Yannai during his struggle against his Pharisaic enemies. This court may have been responsible for the harsh treatment of the Pharisaic rebels. It was composed of Sadducean followers of the Hasmonean king (cf. Jos., Ant., 13:408ff., which relates how the Pharisees avenged their martyrs in the days of Queen Alexandra).

Bibliography: Derenbourg, Hist, 84ff.; Weiss, Dor, 1 (1904[4]), 102f.; Frankel, Mishnah, 43. [I.G.]

HASMONEANS (Gr. Ἀσαμωναίος; Heb. חַשְׁמוֹנָאִים), title for Maccabees in Josephus (Ant., 12:263), Mishnah (Mid. 1:6), and Talmud (Shab. 21b), but nowhere occurring in the Book of Maccabees. Josephus derives the name from the great-grandfather of Mattathias, Asamonaios. Probably the name is to be connected with the village of Heshmon (Josh. 15:27). It has also been suggested to connect the name with Hushim (I Chron. 8:11) or the place Hashmonah (Num. 33:29, 30). The Hasmoneans headed the rebellion against the Seleucid kingdom, established an autonomous Jewish state, annexed the most important regions of Ereẓ Israel, and absorbed a number of neighboring Semitic peoples into the Jewish people. These achievements were not only of major importance to Jewish history, but also left their impact on humanity as a whole. The successful rebellion of the Hasmoneans assured the continued existence of the Jewish religion and contributed to the decisive influence

Expansion of the Hasmonean kingdom, 167–142 B.C.E. After Zev Vilnay (ed.), *New Israel Atlas*, Jerusalem.

of monotheism in Western culture and history. Through the policy of the Hasmoneans, initiated after the rebellion, the Jewish people ceased to play a marginal role in history and exercised influence for generations to come.

The Hasmoneans were a priestly family, probably one of those which had moved from the territory of Benjamin to the lowlands of Lydda in the last days of the First Temple. They belonged to the Jehoiarib division of priests, who lived in *Modi'in on the border of Samaria and Judea. When the restrictive edicts of Antiochus were extended to the country towns and villages of Jewish Palestine, *Mattathias b. Johanan, then the head of the family, raised the banner of revolt in Modi'in, uniting under his leadership all those who were opposed to Antiochus' policy. After Mattathias' death in 167/166 B.C.E., his son *Judah Maccabee, a military genius, succeeded him as leader of the revolt. He scored a number of victories against the Seleucid army, and achieved the conquest of Jerusalem and the purification and rededication of the Temple in 164 B.C.E. (see: *Ḥanukkah). Judah continued to strive for the autonomy of Judea. He won additional victories against the Seleucid forces and in 161 B.C.E. established an alliance with Rome. Though Judah's death in battle slowed down somewhat Judea's progress toward independence, his brothers Jonathan and *Simeon continued his policy, taking advantage of the waning political star of the Seleucid dynasty to strengthen their own influence and to extend the borders of Judea. They annexed the districts of Lydda, Ramathaim, Ephraim, and the Ekron region, conquered Jaffa port, and seized control of the fortresses of the Acra in Jerusalem and Beth-Zur. The appointment of *Jonathan Apphus, the youngest son of Mattathias, to the high priesthood in 152 B.C.E., made this office one of the Hasmoneans' main sources of power. In 143–142 B.C.E., Demetrius II recognized the independence of Judea, and in 140 B.C.E. a decree was passed by the Great Assembly in Jerusalem confirming Simeon as high priest, ruler, and commander of the Jewish people and making these offices hereditary. Simeon's son, *John Hyrcanus (134–104 B.C.E.), continued the territorial expansion. He conquered Idumea, Samaria, and portions of Transjordan, and forcibly converted the Idumeans to Judaism. The internal crisis produced by a rift between the Hasmoneans and the Pharisees began during his reign. John's heir, *Aristobulus I (104–103 B.C.E.), was the first Hasmonean to arrogate to himself the title of king. Aristobulus continued the policy of conquest, compelling the Itureans in the north to become proselytes. During the reign of his brother, Alexander Yannai (103–76 B.C.E.) who succeeded him, the Hasmonean state reached the zenith of its power. The whole of the sea coast, from the Egyptian border to the Carmel, with the exception of Ashkelon, was annexed to Judea. Yannai also extended his rule over some of the Greek cities of Transjordan and strove to establish absolute authority as king and as high priest. It was his latter capacity which brought him into open conflict with the Pharisees. Yannai's wife, Salome Alexandra (76–67 B.C.E.), continued her husband's foreign policy, but reached an understanding with the Pharisees on internal affairs. Pompey's annexation brought the independence of the Hasmonean state to an end. Though the Romans allowed *Hyrcanus II, the oldest son of Alexander Yannai, to remain high priest and ethnarch, they abolished the monarchy and also detached large areas from Judea. Much had been gained, however— Judea proper, as well as Galilee, Idumea, many parts of Transjordan, the coastal plain and the coastal belt remained Jewish in character and culture for a long time as a result of the Hasmoneans' policy. The last to attempt to restore the former glory of the Hasmonean dynasty was *Antigonus

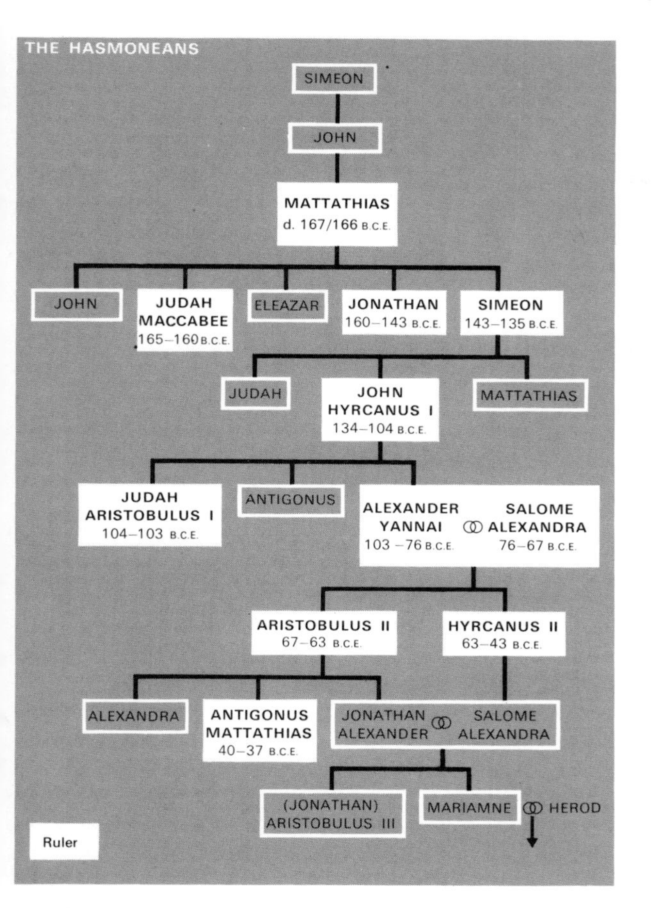

Mattathias, with the help of the Parthians. His defeat and death in 37 B.C.E. at the hands of the Romans brought the Hasmonean rule to a close, and prepared the way for Herod. Herod, however, at the height of military success had strengthened his position by betrothal to Mariamne, the granddaughter of Hyrcanus II whom he consequently married. The popularity of his sons by her, Alexander and Aristobulus, and of their grandson (Herod Agrippa I) was due to their Hasmonean descent. [M.ST.]

In the Arts. A vast number of literary works have been inspired by the heroism of Mattathias and the embattled Maccabees and by the martyrdom of Hannah and her Seven Sons, as recounted in the Apocrypha. In 1722 Antoine Houdar de La Motte published his French lyrical tragedy *Les Machabées,* but it was not until the 19th century that the subject achieved wider popularity among writers. I. B. Schlesinger's Hebrew epic *Ha-Ḥashmona'im* (1816) was followed by *Die Mutter der Makkabaeer* (Vienna, 1820), a late historical drama by the German visionary Zacharias Werner, and by a more conventional tragedy, Alexandre Guiraud's *Les Machabées, ou le Martyre* . . . (Paris, 1822). Interest in the theme

Figure 1. The Hasmoneans confronted by the Seleucid armies which, according to I Macc. 6:30 had 32 elephants. From a Low German Bible, Quentel, Cologne, 1478–80. Leipzig University, *Gesautkatalog der Wiegendrucke*, 1925–38, 4307–8.

first reached a peak in the mid-19th century wih dramas including *Die Makkabaeer* (1854) by Otto Ludwig, J. Michael's *Die Hasmonaeer* (1856; with music by V. Lachner), and a traditional Jewish interpretation of the story by Leopold Stein (1810–1882), also entitled *Die Hasmonaeer* (1859). Three later treatments of the subject were poems by Seligmann *Heller entitled *Die letzten Hasmonaeer* (1965); *The First of the Maccabees* (1860), a historical novel by the U. S. Reform pioneer Isaac Mayer *Wise; and Minnie Dessau Louis' *Hannah and her Seven Sons* (1902). In the Far East, Joseph *David (Penker) produced *The Maccabeans* (1921), a drama in Marathi. Between the world wars, the Brazilian novelist Antonio Castro published *A Judéa e os Macabeus* (1930) and Izak *Goller wrote *Modin Women* (1931), one of his plays on biblical themes. Under the impact of Nazism, the Holocaust, and the birth of the State of Israel, several Jewish writers returned to the heroic theme of the Hasmonean revolt. Abraham Lavsky published a Yiddish historical novel, *Di Khashmonayim Helden oder di Makkabeyer* (1941) the U.S. author Howard *Fast wrote the novel *My Glorious Brothers* (1948). Of these, Fast's was easily the outstanding and best known work. A work on a related theme was the Israel author Moshe *Shamir's historical novel *Melekh Basar va-Dam* (1954; *The King of Flesh and Blood,* 1958), which dealt with the career of the later Hasmonean ruler Alexander Yannai. Innumerable plays and stories devoted to the Ḥanukkah festival have been written for children, including many by Jewish authors and religious leaders in the United States.

The Maccabean wars have proved somewhat less attractive to artists. *Maccabeans,* a painting by the Austrian artist Jehuda Epstein, shows the beginning of the Jewish revolt. Boris *Schatz sculptured a heroic figure of Mattathias, formerly in the Royal collection, Sofia, Bulgaria. Gustave Doré produced dramatic engravings of Mattathias' call to arms and of the heroic death of Eleazar, brother of Judah, who was crushed by an elephant which he slew in battle (I Macc. 6). Another episode (I Macc. 9)—the battle of Jonathan and Simeon against Bacchides, a friend of the Syrian king, as transmitted by Josephus—was treated by the 15th-century French artist Jean Fouquet in his illuminations to the *Jewish War* and *Antiquities of the Jews.* Jonathan Maccabee appears on tapestries woven in Brussels in the 15th century, of which three portions have been preserved, showing Jonathan's coronation and receipt of gifts from other kings. A subject more commonly treated was the story of the seven martyred brothers, "Maccabees" only by association with the Apocryphal books (II Macc. 7), who preferred torture and death to being compelled to eat the flesh of swine. This became very popular in medieval Europe: the seven "Maccabean Martyrs" were canonized, Christians holding them to represent the Church Militant, while Antiochus symbolized the Antichrist. A church of the Seven Holy Maccabees stood in Lyons, France, and there was a chapel of the Maccabees in the cathedral of Saint Pierre, Geneva. Artists represented the Martyrs with amputated hands, together with Hannah, their mother. The Virgin with seven swords sometimes appears beside the figure of the latter. The theme also occurs in an eighth-century fresco at Santa Maria Antiqua, Rome; in medieval illuminated manuscripts; on the 13th-century southern portal of Chartres Cathedral; and in a 15th-century painting attributed to the Maître de Saint-Gilles (Amiens Museum). In the late Renaissance Jacopo Bassano painted the same subject. [ED.]

In music there were a few compositions about the Hasmoneans dating from the late 18th and early 19th centuries, of which only Ignaz Seyfried's melodrama *Die Makkabaeer* (c. 1835) was of significance. Anton *Rubinstein's opera *Die Makkabaeer* (première in Berlin, 1875), for which Solomon *Mosenthal wrote the libretto after Otto Ludwig's drama, had only a brief stage career, yet it became a source of pride for East-European Jewry. The aria *Leas Gesang* became a favorite at musical recitals and it was also arranged for instrumental combinations. Together with *Der heilige Sabbath* it can be found in the *Lider-Zamelbukh* edited by S. Kisselgoff (1911), with the text translated into Yiddish by A. Rivesman and into Hebrew by Saul *Tchernichowsky (no. 83–4). A comparison with the ḥasidic dance *Ladier Chabadnitze* (no. 62) in the same collection shows where the roots of the melody lie. Michael *Gnessin's *Makkavei,* a Russian "symphonic movement" for soloists, choir, and orchestra, was written after the composer's visit to Ereẓ Israel in 1922 and was first performed in 1925. Handel's oratorio *Alexander Balus* (1777; première in 1748), with libretto by Thomas Morrell, touches on the Maccabean theme.

Figure 2. Detail showing the five Hasmoneans from the *menorah* by Benno Elkan at the Knesset, Jerusalem. Photo Yiẓhak Amit, Kibbutz Zorah.

The theme of the Seven "Maccabean" Martyrs also achieved a degree of popularity from the end of the 17th century and throughout the 18th, inspiring an opera by Johann Wolfgang Franck (1679) and oratorios by various composers, including Attilio Ariosti (1704), Francesco Conti (1732), and Antonio Sacchini (1770). In Johann Heinrich Rollle's *Thirza und ihre Soehne* (1781), the story is ostensibly about Christian martyrs, but the characters and content are identical with the history of the Maccabees. A later example is Vittorio Trento's opera *I sette Maccabei* (1818).

The "Story of Hannah" has a permanent and honored place in the religious folksong traditions of Mediterranean and Near Eastern Jewry and it is generally sung by women on the Ninth of Av. The songs are in the vernacular and their poetical and musical form resembles the historical ballads of the various surrounding gentile cultures: only the tradition as such is the common "Jewish" element. The poems are not infrequently found in manuscripts or printed booklets of *kinot*, but the tradition is basically oral and it probably occurs throughout the vast area from North Africa to Persia and from the Ladino-speaking communities of Greece and Turkey to the Yemen.

See also *Judah Maccabee in the Arts. [B.B.]

Bibliography: E. J. Bickerman, *The Maccabees* (1947); R. H. Pfeiffer, *History of New Testament Times* (1949), 5–45; W. R. Farmer, *Maccabees, Zealots, and Josephus* (1956); V. Tcherikover, *Hellenistic Civilization and the Jews* (1959); M. Stern, *Ha-Te'udot le-Mered ha-Ḥashmona'im* (1965); Schuerer, Hist, index, s.v. *Asmoneans;* Meyer, Ursp, 2 (1921), 205–78; B. Maisler (Mazar), in: *Yedi'ot ha-Ḥevrah ha-Ivrit la-Ḥakirat Ereẓ Yisrael ve-Attikoteha*, 8 (1941), 105–7.

HA-SOLELIM (Heb. הַסּוֹלְלִים; "the Trail Blazers"), kibbutz in Lower Galilee, Israel, 5 mi. (8 km.) northwest of *Nazareth, affiliated with Iḥud ha-Kevuẓot ve-ha-Kibbutzim and aligned politically to Ha-No'ar ha-Ẓiyyoni (Independent Liberals) movement. It was founded in 1949 as the first Jewish settlement in the region. The original settlers were Israel-born and other veterans of World War II, who were later joined by new immigrants from North America. In 1969 various fruit orchards, beef cattle, and field crops constituted its principal farm branches. The *Bet Netofah Storage Lake for the National Water Carrier is located near the kibbutz. In 1968 there were 216 inhabitants. [E.O.]

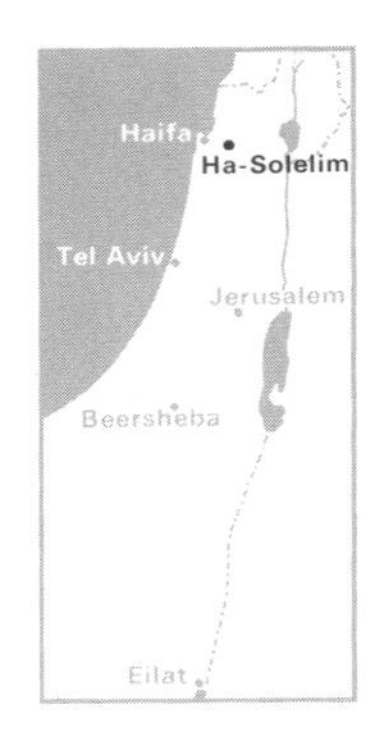

HASSAGAT GEVUL (Heb. הַסָּגַת גְּבוּל), a concept which originally had specific reference to the unlawful taking of another's land; later it was extended to embrace encroachment on various economic, commercial, and incorporeal rights of others.

Encroachment on Land. In Scripture. The original meaning of the term *hassagat gevul* was the moving (cf. *nasogu aḥor*, Isa. 42:17) of boundary stones or other landmarks from their resting places into the bounds of another's adjoining area of land, for the purpose of annexing a portion of the latter to one's own land. Naḥmanides' comment on the passage, "Thou shalt not remove thy neighbor's landmark, which they of old time have set, in thine inheritance which thou shalt inherit in the land that the Lord thy God giveth thee to possess it" (Deut. 19:14), is that Scripture speaks here "in terms of the present," i.e., of the usual situation, since it is common for landmark removal to take place in respect of ancient landmarks set up "of old time" which are not generally known and familiar. The prohibition against removal of the landmark is repeated in the enumeration of curses for recital on Mount Ebal (Deut. 27:17). The exact marking of land boundaries was already emphasized in patriarchal times, as may be gathered from the description of the field in *Machpelah bought by Abraham from Ephron the Hittite (Gen. 23:17), and this was also the case in other countries of the ancient East. Many boundary stones, engraved with invocations and curses against their removal, have been found in ancient Babylonia.

Removal of the landmark is exhorted against and castigated in the books of the prophets and the hagiographa (Hos. 5:10; Prov. 22:28, 23:10). In Proverbs too the reference is to the "present" and usual situation, namely removal of ancient landmarks set by earlier generations. In the Book of Hosea the castigation is directed against the princes, the strong, and in Proverbs it is hinted that the weak, the fatherless, were the main sufferers. In Job too removal of the landmark is mentioned among other injustices perpetrated on orphans, widows, and the poor (24:2–4).

In the Talmud. In the talmudic period the abovementioned passage from Deuteronomy 19:14 was given a literal interpretation and the special prohibition against landmark removal was held to be applicable to land in Ereẓ Israel only. The fact that the enjoinder, "Thou shalt not remove the landmark," appears after it is already stated that "Thou shalt not rob," was held to teach that anyone who uproots his neighbor's boundaries breaks two prohibitions, robbery and removal of the landmark, but that this was the case in Ereẓ Israel only, since it is written ". . . in thine inheritance which thou shalt inherit in the land . . ." *(ibid.)*, and outside Ereẓ Israel only one prohibition (robbery) is transgressed (Sif. Deut. 188). The *halakhah* was likewise determined in later times (Maim. Yad, Genevah 7:11; Sh. Ar., ḤM 376:1).

Land robbery, even outside Ereẓ Israel, has been regarded with great severity in Jewish law. The Talmud speaks of persons specially engaged in land measuring and the fixing of precise boundaries; surveyors are specifically instructed to make accurate calculations—down to the last fingerbreadth—and not to measure for one in summer and for the other in winter, since the measuring cord shrinks in summer (and expands in winter; BM 107b and Rashi *ibid.*; 61b; BB 89a; Maim. Yad, Genevah 8:1–3; Sh. Ar., ḤM 231:16–18).

In the Codes. It is explained that the general distinction made in Jewish law between *genevah* and *gezelah* (see *Theft and Robbery)—the former taking unlawfully by stealth and the latter openly with violence—applies also to the matter of trespass on land: "a person who removes his neighbor's landmark and encloses within his own domain even as much as a fingerbreadth from his neighbor's domain is a robber if he does so with violence and a thief if he does so stealthily" (Yad, Genevah 7:11; Sh. Ar., ḤM 376; from the *Semag, Lavin,* 153 it also appears that this was understood to be the version of Sif. Deut. 188). The opinion was expressed by some of the *poseḳim* that the prohibition against robbery or theft—in relation to trespass on land—forms part of the *de-rabbanan* (Oral Law) and not the *de-oraita* (Written Law) law, since land is never stolen but always remains in its owner's possession; this opinion is however contrary to the plain meaning of the above-mentioned statements in *Sifrei* (Tur, ḤM 371:10, 376; *Perishah, ibid., Sma.* to YD 371:2).

The great severity with which trespass on land has been regarded in Jewish law is illustrated in a responsum of Solomon b. Abraham *Adret (Rashba) concerning the following matter: "A person trespassed and built a wall within his neighbor's yard, thereby appropriating therefrom a cubit of land to his own, and then built a big house supported on this wall; now the owner of the yard comes to demolish the other's whole building." Asked whether in terms of the *takkanat ha-shavim* ("*takkanah* of restitution," see *Theft and Robbery) the trespasser might pay for the value of the land taken without having to demolish the building in order to restore the land to its owner, Rashba replied in the negative: "the *takkanat ha-shavim* was instituted in respect of movable property only, and in respect of land it was not stated that he [the injured party] should sell his property and break up his inheritance" (Resp. vol. 3, no. 188).

Widening of the Concept. The first manifestations of a widening in the doctrine of *hassagat gevul* are traceable back to talmudic times, when various *halakhot* were derived from the doctrine by way of **asmakhta*. Thus the doctrine was cited in support of the prohibition against withholding from the poor (all or anyone of them) their gleanings from the produce of the field (Pe'ah 5:6; on the meaning of the term *olim* and *al tasseg gevul olim,* see Albeck, *Mishnah, ibid.*). The prohibition against *hassagat gevul* was similarly invoked to lend a quasi-legal recognition to an individual's right (copyright) in respect of his own spiritual or intellectual creations: "Whence can it be said of one who interchanges the statements of Eliezer with those of Joshua and vice versa, so as to say of pure that it is unclean and of unclean that it is pure, that he transgresses a prohibition? It is taught: 'you shall not remove your neighbor's landmark'" (Sif. Deut. 188). Even the prohibition against marrying a pregnant woman or one weaning a child (i.e., by another man, for reasons of the possible threat to the welfare of the embryo or child), is supported by the doctrine of *hassagat gevul* (Tosef. Nid. 2:7; see also Mid. Tan., Deut. 19:14; Comm. R. Hillel, Sif. Deut. 188).

Trespass on Economic, Commercial, and Incorporeal Rights. Post-talmudic economic and social developments fostered the need to give legal recognition and protection to rights which had not become crystallized within any accepted legal framework during the talmudic period. Some of these rights found legal expression and protection through an extension of the prohibition against landmark removal, so as to embrace also encroachment on another's economic, commercial, and spiritual confines.

Tenancy Rights. Jewish places of settlement in the Middle Ages were restricted—at times voluntarily, at other times perforce—to particular streets or quarters. Hence the demand by Jews for dwellings in these particular places frequently exceeded the available supply, and sometimes a prospective Jewish tenant would offer a landlord a higher than customary rental in order to have the existing tenant evicted, the more so since the *halakhah* excluded neither an offer to pay a high rental nor eviction of a tenant upon termination of his lease. In order to fill the breach against this undesirable social phenomenon, various *takkanot* were enacted in the different centers of Jewish life. These *takkanot,* aimed at protecting tenants from eviction, were reconciled with the principles of Jewish law through a widening of the doctrine of *hassagat gevul* to take in also the tenant's right to remain in occupation of the premises hired by him. The earliest of these *takkanot,* akin in content to the tenants' protection laws found in many modern legal systems, are attributed to the time of *Gershom b. Judah (tenth century; for the text, see Finkelstein, Middle Ages, 31).

In a 13th-century *takkanah* of the community of Crete (Candia) it was laid down that: "a person shall not encroach on his neighbor's boundaries by evicting him from his home . . . from today onward no Jew shall be permitted . . . to offer an excessive payment or rental to any landlord in order to gain occupation of his house . . . and thereby cause him to evict the existing Jewish tenant, for this is a transgression against 'cursed be he that removes his neighbor's landmark,'" not only was the offender to be fined, but the *takkanah* also prohibited anyone to hire the house in question for a full year from the date of its being vacated (*Takkanot Kandyah,* ed. Mekiẓe Nirdamim, p. 16). Similar *takkanot* were customary in different Jewish centers during the Middle Ages (see, e.g., Ferrara *takkanot* of 1554, in: Finkelstein, Middle Ages 93f., 302, 305).

Trespass in Matters of Commerce and the Crafts. In tannaitic times the opinions of most sages inclined in favor of free commercial and occupational competition (BM 4:12, 60a-b; BB 21b). In the third century C.E., moral censure of someone setting up in competition with a fellow-artisan was expressed by some of the Palestinian *amoraim,* although without any legal sanction (Kid. 59a; Mak. 24a; Sanh. 81a). In the same century, in Babylonia, *Huna laid down the legal principle that a resident of a particular alley operating a handmill could stop a fellow-resident from setting up in competition next to him, because this involved an interference with his source of livelihood (BB 21b). This view was not, however, accepted as *halakhah,* and at the end of the fourth century it was decided by Huna b. Joshua that one craftsman could not restrain a fellow craftsman and resident of the same alley from setting up business (in the same alley), nor even the resident of another town from setting up in the same town, as long as the latter paid taxes to the town in which he sought to ply his craft (BB 21b). Even so, however, there was no definition of the legal nature and substance of even this limited right of restraint, nor was it enforced by any sanctions upon infringement, such as the payment of compensation.

With the restriction of Jewish sources of livelihood in the Middle Ages, and the resulting intensified competition, the whole question once more came to the fore. A Jew who with much effort and money had succeeded in acquiring a monopoly in a particular commercial field stood to lose his investment and livelihood through the competition of a fellow-Jew. From the tenth century onward, the question of a right of monopoly, its scope and sanctions, came to be widely discussed in the literature of the responsa and the codes. This discussion took in the *ma'arufyah* (a form of private monopoly) *takkanah*, which prohibited encroachment on the *ma'arufyah* of a fellow-Jew (*Or Zaru'a*, BM 10a, no. 28). Legally, the *ma'arufyah* right was a full-fledged right, capable of being sold (Resp. *Ge'onim Kadmoniyyim* 151) and was even discussed in relation to whether it passed on inheritance (Resp. *Ḥakhmei Ẓarefat va-Loter* 87). The law of the *ma'arufyah* was not free of dispute, and as late as the 16th century Solomon *Luria differed thereon in a number of material respects (Resp. Maharshal, 35, 36; *Yam shel Shelomo*, Kid. 3:2); yet he too recognized extension of the doctrine of *hassagat gevul* to include a prohibition against infringement of another's livelihood, and the majority of the *posekim* accepted the overall law of the *ma'arufyah* (Sh. Ar., ḤM 156:5 and standard commentaries; *Ir Shushan*, ḤM 156:5; *She'erit Yosef* 17).

Various *takkanot* have come down concerning the restriction of competition, particularly with reference to the acquisition of a right of lease or concession. In medieval times, particularly in Poland, a substantial proportion of the tax-collection concessions granted in respect of the wine trade, mints, border-customs, salt-mines, distilleries and saloons, etc., were concentrated in the hands of Jews, and various *takkanot* were enacted to restrict the competition in this field that had led to higher rentals and reduced profits (Halpern, Pinkas, 11f.; *Pinkas Medinat Lita*, nos. 46, 73, 87, 104; Resp. Baḥ., Yeshanot 60; *Masot Binyamin* 27; Resp. Maharam of Lublin 62; *Takkanot Medinat Mehrin*, p. 86, no. 259; *Ḥavvat Ya'ir*, 42).

Setting up in competition with a fellow-artisan or professional was similarly restricted in various fields. Thus a *melammed* ("teacher") was prohibited from encroaching on a colleague's confines by taking one of the latter's pupils into his own *ḥeder* (Takk. Cracow of 1551 and 1638, quoted by P.H. Wettstein, in: *Oẓar ha-Sifrut*, 4 (1892), 580 (2nd pagination) and it was likewise decided with reference to ritual slaughterers (*Ba'ei Ḥayyei*, ḤM pt. 2, 80; *Naḥalah li-Yhoshu'a*, 29; *Mishpat Ẓedek*, vol. 3, no. 14), the offender in this case being regarded as a robber who could be deprived of the remuneration received for such *sheḥitah* (Resp. *Divrei Ḥayyim*, pt. 2, YD 20) which might possibly even be declared ritually unfit (Resp. Shneur Zalman of Lyady, 9; see also Meshullam Roth, *Kol Mavasser*, pt. 1, no. 17).

An interesting development in this field is related to the office of rabbi. As late as the 15th century, it was decided by Israel *Isserlein and Jacob *Weil that a scholar holding the office of rabbi in a particular town could not restrain another from holding a similar office there, even though the latter would interfere with the former's prospects of earning remuneration in return for services such as arranging weddings, divorces, and the like. This decision was based on the reasoning that accepting a remuneration for such services was essentially contrary to the *halakhah* and its permissibility was not easily justifiable, and therefore it could hardly be recognized as an occupation or source of livelihood to be protected from the encroachment of competitors (*Terumat ha-Deshen, Pesakim u-Khetavim* 128; Resp. Maharyu, 151; *Rema*, YD 245:22). This *halakhah*, however, underwent a change in the light of new economic and social realities. Already in the mid-17th century it was stated that even if competition of this kind was not prohibited in law, "perhaps there is reason for protesting against it on the grounds of custom" (*Siftei Kohen* to Sh. Ar., YD 245:22, n.15); and at the commencement of the 19th century the change was also given legal recognition when Moses *Sofer (Resp. *Ḥatam Sofer*, ḤM 21) explained that the rule which held the law of *hassagat gevul* to be inappropriate to the rabbinate was only applicable "to that particular period when a rabbi was not engaged in the same way as a worker . . . but every scholar led the community in whose midst he lived and as such remuneration for *gittin* and *kiddushin* came to him naturally . . . but nowadays a rabbi is engaged—sometimes from another town—for remuneration, in the same way as any other worker and the community is obliged to provide him with his livelihood; we are not deterred from the acceptance of such reward, and therefore any one encroaching on the rabbi's confines is in the position of a craftsman setting up in competition with his neighbor, and a rabbi who does so is disqualified from his position" (Resp. *Shem Aryeh*, OḤ 7).

The legal basis for the restriction of competition, with imposition of sanctions, was found in an extension of the legal doctrine of *hassagat gevul* to include encroachment on the confines of another's trade and source of livelihood. An interesting insight into the manner in which the said extension was arrived at is offered in the method of interpretation adopted by Solomon *Luria (despite his advocacy of greater freedom of competition). In the case of a person ousted by his neighbor from a concession to a customs post, Luria reasoned that the defendant might be held liable for the pecuniary loss suffered by the other party even though it was decided law that there is no liability for **gerama* (a form of indirect damage) in tort. Luria relied on Roke'aḥ's statement that anyone interfering with another's source of livelihood falls within the enjoinder, "cursed is he who removes his neighbor's landmark," a statement Luria explained on the basis that this passage seemed to be redundant in the light of the prior scriptural injunction, "you shall not remove your neighbor's landmark," unless it was accepted that this passage related to trespass in the field of bargaining. Luria's decision accordingly was that the customs post be restored to the first concessionary without cost, or the defendant compensate him for the damage caused (Resp. Maharshal 89). Other scholars regarded trespass on a neighbor's trading interests as an integral part of the prohibition against trespass on another's right of tenancy (see Resp. Maharam of Padua 41).

Copyright. The first hints at recognition in Jewish law of the ownership of incorporeal property were given as early as tannaitic times. Thus it was stated, "a person who eavesdrops on his neighbor to reproduce his teachings, even though he is called a thief, acquires for himself" (Tosef., BK 7:13), and support for the prohibition against interchanging one scholar's statements with another's was found (Sif. Deut. 188) in the passage, "Thou shalt not remove thy neighbor's landmark." At the end of the 12th century the same passage was quoted by Judah he-Ḥasid in warning an heir against complying with a direction in the will of his deceased father to inscribe the latter's name as the author of a book, even though it was known to have been written by someone else (*Sefer ha-Ḥasidim*, ed. Mekize Nirdamim, nos. 17–32). It was nevertheless only from the 16th century onward that copyright became a defined legal right, protected by sanctions and partially based on the extended doctrine of *hassagat gevul*.

As in other legal systems, this development arose from the spread of printing and a need for the protection of printers' rights. As early as 1518 as approbation (*haskamah*) to the *Sefer ha-Baḥur* of *Elijah Levita contained a warning, on pain of ban, against anyone reprinting the book within the following ten years. In the mid-15th century, when Meir *Katzenellenbogen complained to Moses Isserles about the appearance of a rival edition of Maimonides' *Mishneh Torah* (shortly after his work had been printed by Katzenellenbogen), Isserles responded by imposing a ban on anyone purchasing the *Mishneh Torah* from Katzenellenbogen's competitor (Resp. Rema 10). Thereafter it became customary to preface books with approbations containing a warning against trespass in the form of any unauthorized reprint of the particular book within a specified period. Halakhic literature contains detailed discussions on various aspects of encroachment on printers' rights. Thus Isserles imposed his abovementioned ban on anyone purchasing the *Mishneh Torah*, because in that instance it would not have availed against the printer, a non-Jew. Other scholars held the opinion that the ban should be imposed, not on the purchasers of the book—as this would cause study of the Torah to be neglected—but on the printer instead, except if he be a non-Jew (*Zikhron Yosef*, ḤM 2; Resp. *Ḥatam Sofer*, ḤM 89). Unlike Isserles, who confined the operation of his ban (to purchasers) within the country concerned only, other scholars extended operation of the ban to printers everywhere (Resp. *Ḥatam Sofer*, ḤM 41 and 79). In most cases the period of the prohibition varied from three to 15 years, but was sometimes imposed for as long as 25 years. Some of the scholars held that a prohibition imposed against trespass on a printing right takes effect from the date of the approbation in which it has been formulated, but other scholars held the prohibition to come into effect upon commencement of the printing (Halpern, Pinkas 486; Resp. *Shem Aryeh*, ḤM, 20; *Mayim Ḥayyim*, YD 44; Resp. *Sho'el u-Meshiv*, pt. 1, no. 44).

The above prohibition was mainly justified on grounds of the printer's need for an opportunity to recover his heavy outlay through the subsequent sale of the printed product, since reluctance to undertake any printing in the absence of such protection was likely to send up the price of books and cause study of the Torah to be neglected by the public. In this regard there was a fundamental difference of opinion among scholars concerning the fate of the prohibition once the printer had sold the whole of his edition, i.e., prior to expiry of the period of his protection. According to some scholars the prohibition remained fully effective against all other printers, but others held that continuation of the printer's protection, after he had already obtained his remuneration, was itself likely to cause the price of books to rise and to contribute to the neglect of study (*Ḥatam Sofer*, ḤM 79; *ibid.* Addenda no. 57; *Parashat Mordekhai*, ḤM 7; *Tiferet Ẓevi*, YD 62; *Mayim Ḥayyim*, YD 44; *Pitḥei Teshuvah*, YD 236:1; *Ateret Ḥakhamim*, YD 25). This was the central halakhic issue in the dispute, at the beginning of the 19th century, between the respective printers of the Slavuta edition of the Talmud (the brothers Shapiro) and the Vilna-Grodno edition (the widow and brothers Romm).

Out of this discussion grew the recognition given, in later generations, of the existence in Jewish law of a full legal right in respect of one's own spiritual creation. Thus Joseph Saul *Nathanson, rabbi of Lvov, distinguished between printing the work of others, e.g., the Talmud, and printing one's own work, stating that in the latter event "it is clear that he has the right thereto for all time . . . for with regard to his own [work] a person is entitled to decree that it shall never be printed without his permission or authority . . . and this right avails him against the world at large" (*Sho'el u-Meshiv*, pt. 1, no. 44). In support of this opinion, Nathanson had reference to the copyright offered the patent-holder of an invention under general Polish law, adding that the effect of an author's restriction against any reprint of his work within a specified period was not to prohibit what would otherwise be permissible, but, on the contrary, to authorize others to reprint his work upon expiry of the period specified because "even if no express restriction is imposed . . . this remains prohibited as *hassagat gevul* by the law of the Torah" *(ibid.)*. A similar view was expressed by Naphtali Ẓevi Judah *Berlin concerning the individual's right in respect of his own teachings; he held that the individual might treat these as he would his own property—save for its total destruction, because it was a *mitzvah* to study and to teach others (*Meshiv Davar*, pt. 1, no. 24).

This view was not, however, generally accepted by the halakhic scholars. Thus Isaac *Schmelkes saw no reason why others might not reprint a book—even if first printed by the author himself—once the original edition had been completely sold; "everyone retains the right to study and to teach . . . why should another not be able to benefit his fellow men and print and sell cheaply?" (*Beit Yiẓḥak*, YD, pt. 2 no. 75). In his opinion Nathanson's analogy of a patent-right offered no real support for the correctness of his view, since in that case the perpetuity of the right derived from royal charter, without which others might freely copy the inventor's model, and furthermore, a work relating to the Torah was to be distinguished from any other work of the spirit inasmuch as "the Torah was given to all free of charge . . . not to be used with a view to gaining remuneration" *(ibid.)*. At the same time Schmelkes conceded the validity of a restriction imposed against reprint of a book within a specified period, not as a matter of *halakhah*, but in pursuance of the general law of the land, by virtue of the rule of **dina de-malkhuta dina* ("the law of the land is law").

The doctrine of *hassagat gevul* strikingly illustrates one of the paths for the development of Jewish law, namely extension of the content of a legal principle beyond its original confines, in a search for solutions to problems arising through changes in social and economic conditions.

Bibliography: Gulak, Yesodei, 1 (1922), 172–5; Gulak, Oẓar, 355, 359f.; S. Funk, in: JJLG, 18 (1927), 289–304; Z. Markon, in: *Ha-Mishpat*, 2 (1927), 192–201; Herzog, Instit, 1 (1936), 127–36; L. Rabinowitz, *Ḥerem Hayyishub* (Eng., 1945), 122–6; Z. Falk, *Ha-Kinyan ha-Ruḥani be-Dinei Yisrael* (1947); E. Rivlin, in: *Emet le-Ya'akov . . . Freimann* (1937), 149–62; F. Baer, in: *Zion*, 15 (1949/50), 35f.; ET, 9 (1959), 542–6; J. Katz, *Tradition and Crisis* (1961), 59f.

[M.E.]

HASSAGOT (Heb. הַשָּׂגוֹת), name given to rabbinic works wholly devoted to the criticism, usually negative, of earlier books. *Hassagot* literature is a part of a much wider literary genre, including **tosafot* on the one hand, and on the other, supplements in the style of the *Sefer ha-Hashlamah* of *Meshullam b. Moses. They appeared initially in the time of *Saadiah Gaon, when rabbinical "books" in the modern sense were first written, the first book of *hassagot* apparently being one by *Mevasser against Saadiah. *Hassagot* literature reached its peak in the 12th century, especially in Provence, the best known author of such works undoubtedly being *Abraham b. David of Posquières *(ba'al ha-hassagot)*. From the 14th century onward this class of literature began to decline, taking more and more the form of **haggahot*, limited in content and generally relegated to the margins of the books.

Only a small number of *hassagot* works were thus termed by their authors. The first such is Jonah *ibn Janaḥ's work against the grammatical works of Judah *Ḥayyuj. It was translated from the original Arabic into Hebrew by Judah ibn *Tibbon, and given the title *Sefer ha-Hassagah*, thus giving the word *hassagah* its present meaning. *Zerahiah ha-Levi, a friend of Ibn Tibbon, also uses this term with the same meaning in the introduction to his *Sefer ha-Ma'or*. Some *hassagot* works (such as the above-mentioned book of Mevasser) confine themselves to exposing the errors of the text under review, but most offer alternative views and opinions, and sometimes as in the case of Abraham b. David, even defend, explain, and supplement the text in question. *Hassagot* literature embraces a wide range of subjects, including *halakhah*, theology, and grammar. Likewise, writers of *hassagot* differ in their aims, from Mevasser who attacked, apparently on a personal background, the whole of Saadiah's literary work, classifying his *hassagot* according to chapter headings, through *Dunash b. Labrat who wrote *hassagot* on the works of his teacher Saadiah with pure academic interest on linguistic and biblical subjects alone, to Naḥmanides, who was prolific as a writer of *hassagot* (on the *Sefer ha-Mitzvot* of Maimonides, the *Sefer ha-Ma'or* of Zerahiah ha-Levi, and on the *hassagot* of Abraham b. David on *Alfasi). The *hassagot* of Naḥmanides were all written with the sole purpose of defending his predecessors, Alfasi and the author of the **Halakhot Gedolot*, against the criticisms which had been leveled against them.

Some *hassagot* were written in order to justify local customs, such as those of Zerahiah on Alfasi, and some in order to undermine a scholar's authority, such as those of Meir *Abulafia on Maimonides. Most writers of *hassagot* confine themselves to important and prominent personalities, such as those mentioned above. Of the critics of Alfasi, mention should be made of his pupils, Ephraim and Joseph *ibn Migash, whose books are not extant. Particularly noteworthy are the scholars of *Lunel, whose *hassagot* of Maimonides were written for their own instruction and were sent by them to Maimonides in order to elicit replies from him.

The *hassagot* have a style of their own. They are brief, pungent, and provocative. Their sometimes astonishing brusqueness is merely external and, in practice, was not taken amiss. The brevity of style was designed to strike a chord of decisiveness.

Bibliography: Jonah ibn Janaḥ, *Sefer ha-Rikmah*, ed. by M. Wilensky, 1 (1964²), 19 n. 7; M. Zucker (ed. and tr.), *Hassagot al Rav Sa'adyah Ga'on* (introd.); I. Twersky, *Rabad of Posquières* (1962), 128–98; B. Z. Benedikt, in: *Sefer Zikkaron ... B. de Vries* (1969), 160–7.

[I.T.-S.]

HASSAN, Spanish-Moroccan family whose most famous member in Spain was JAHUDA ABEN HAÇEN, the ambassador of Aragon to Granada in 1287. A refugee in Morocco, SHEMAYYAH HASSAN countersigned *takkanot* ("regulations") in Fez (c. 1575). During the 17th century, his family settled in Salé and Tetuan. Shem Tov and DAVID HASSAN extended their affairs to Gibraltar, where SIR JOSHUA *HASSAN was the first head of government (1964–69). In 1790, the Spanish consul in Tetuan, SOLOMON HASSAN, was hanged upon the order of the sultan Moulay Yazd. A branch of the family then settled in Mogador, whence RAPHAEL HASSAN (d. after 1825), author of *Leḥem Oni* (1834), left for London. In Tetuan, the financier SALVADOR HASSAN (d. after 1879) represented Spain and Italy, and his sons represented Portugal in Tangier, where they founded an important banking company.

Bibliography: S. Romanelli, *Ketavim Nivḥarim (Massa ba-Arav)*, ed. by H. Schirmann (1968), 135 f.; A. Leared, *A Visit to the Court of Morocco* (1879), 84–86; I. Laredo, *Memórias de un viejo Tangerino* (1935), 425f.

[D.Co.]

HASSAN, SIR JOSHUA (Abraham; 1915–), Gibraltar lawyer and politician. Born in the British colony of Gibraltar to a Sephardi family of North African origin, Hassan was admitted to the bar in 1939. Mayor of Gibraltar from 1945 to 1950 and again from 1953, he was chief member of the Legislative Council from 1950 to 1964. In that year he became chief minister, a post equivalent to that of premier, and championed the right of the colony to remain under British rule and not to be transferred to Spain. He lost the position as a result of the elections in 1969. Hassan was a devoted and observant Jew and president of the management board of the Jewish community. He was also active in Zionist affairs and was president of the Jewish National Fund Commission for many years. Even while holding the highest offices, Hassan continued to go from house to house collecting the contents of the J.N.F. boxes. He became a queen's counsel in 1954 and in 1963 received a knighthood.

[ED.]

ḤASSĀN IBN ḤĀSSAN (second half of tenth century), Spanish astronomer, who was called by some **Ḥassān ibn Mar Ḥassān** and by others **Ali ibn Mar Ḥassān.** It seems that Ḥassān was not his father's personal name but his family name. Ḥassān was a *dayyan* in Cordoba. That he lived in the tenth century can be inferred from the date 972 C.E., which he used in his calculations. He was an astronomer who followed the system of al-Battānī, writing three works which were in the possession of Jewish astronomers in Spain and in Eastern countries during the Middle Ages but were later lost.

Bibliography: Ashtor, Korot, 1 (1966²), 197, 297.

[E.A.]

HASSIDEANS (Assideans; Greek form of Hebrew *Ḥasidim;* "pious ones"), religious group or sect which originated in about the third or fourth century B.C.E. It centered around the revival and promotion of Jewish rites, study of the Law, and the uprooting of paganism from the land. The date of origin cannot be known with certainty. The Hassideans are first mentioned by name during the persecutions of Antiochus IV (Ephiphanes), king of Syria (175–164 B.C.E.), when its members joined the Maccabean opposition led by Mattathias in his revolt against the Syrians. They formed the nucleus of the Maccabean revolt and refused to compromise in any way with the Hellenizing policy of the Syrians. The Hassideans were exposed to torture and death for their refusal to desecrate the Sabbath and other Jewish observances. In I Maccabees 2:41 it is recorded that they were "mighty men in Israel ... such as were devoted to the Law." In I Maccabees 4 they are described as welcoming peace with the Syrians when the latter offered them assurances of religious liberty. The Hassideans ceased to cooperate with the Hasmoneans (the successors of Judah the Maccabee) in their fight for political independence.

Certain references to the **Ḥasidim* are found in the Psalms (12:2, 30:5, 31:24, 38:28, et al.), but it is doubtful that these accounts refer to the Hassideans. The passages speak of the efforts of the Hassideans to observe the Law, their persecutions by their adversaries, and their struggles against their enemies. References to *Ḥasidim* in the Mishnah and the Talmud (Ber. 5:1, Hag. 2:7, Sot. 3:4, Avot 5:10 and Nid. 17a) may refer to the Hassideans or merely to pious individuals of a later period. The Talmud refers to the strict observance of the commandments by *Ḥasidim*, to their ardent prayers, which they would not renounce even at the risk of their lives, and to their rigid observance of the Sabbath. Because of their meticulous observances the Hassideans have been linked with the *Essenes, but scholarly consensus places them as the spiritual forerunners of the *Pharisees.

Bibliography: J. W. Lightly, *Jewish Sects and Parties in the Time of Jesus* (1925); R. T. Herford, *Judaism in the New Testament*

Period (1928); S. Zeitlin, *History of the Second Jewish Commonwealth: Prolegomena* (1933); idem, *Rise and Fall of the Judean State*, 2 vols. (1962–67); Baron, Social [2], 1–2 (1952); N. H. Snaith, *Jews from Cyrus to Herod* (1956); Schuerer, Hist, index, s.v. *Pious;* R. Kaufman, *Great Sects and Schisms in Judaism* (1967). [M.Man.]

HATCHWELL, SOL (or **Suleika;** 1820–1834), Jewish martyr of Morocco, where she is known as "Sol ha-Ẓaddikah," After Sol Hatchwell had visited Muslim friends in her native Tangier, two Moors testified that she had recited the *Shahāda* (Muslim declaration of faith). In spite of her vigorous protests, she was henceforth, according to Muslim law, considered a Muslim. Her case was brought before the sultan, who ordered that she be brought from Tangier to Fez. Despite alternating offers of honor and threats, she refused to renounce Judaism. Condemned to death, she was publicly beheaded in Fez. For a long time, her martyrdom remained a historical topic, inspiring numerous Jewish and non-Jewish authors. The authors of legends, novels, plays, and *kinot* adopted the story of the "Jewish heroine" as their theme; the painter Dehodencq depicted her in his painting known as "The Torment of the Jewess." Her tomb in the cemetery of Fez became the site of pilgrimages of both Jews and Muslims.

Bibliography: H. de la Martinière, *Souvenirs du Maroc* (1919), 8; L. Godard, *Description et histoire du Maroc* (1860), 83–84; L. Voinot, *Pèlerinages judéo-musulmans au Maroc* (1948), 50–51; L. Brunot and E. Malka, *Textes judéo-arabes de Fès* (1939), 213–7; Attal, in: *Sefunot*, 5 (1961), 507; D. Corcos, in: JQR, 55 (1964/65), 56; Hirschberg, Afrikah, 2 (1965), 304f. [D.Co.]

HA-TEKUFAH (Heb. הַתְּקוּפָה; "The Season"), Hebrew periodical devoted to literary, scientific, and social subjects which appeared (first as a quarterly, then as an annual) intermittently between 1918 and 1950. *Ha-Tekufah* received the financial backing of Abraham Joseph *Stybel, a philanthropist who had placed David *Frischmann in charge of launching Hebrew literary projects on an unprecedented large scale. Accordingly, Frischmann established both the Stybel publishing house, and launched *Ha-Tekufah*, serving as the editor of both projects. The first volume of *Ha-Tekufah* appeared in Moscow early in 1918, before the Bolshevik regime had decided to suppress Hebrew literature. Frischmann published the works of the world's best authors and scholars. The literary standards of the periodical were high. Frischmann encouraged young authors, for example, Eliezer *Steinman. In all respects and not least for its beautiful graphic work, *Ha-Tekufah* was a rare phenomenon in Hebrew literature. Following the suppression of Hebrew in Russia, Frischmann moved to Warsaw where he published issues 5–15 After his death in 1922, he was succeeded by Ya'akov *Cahan and F. *Lachower. When Stybel's publishing house underwent a crisis, *Ha-Tekufah* was moved to Germany and volumes 24–27 (1928–30) were edited in Berlin by Benzion *Katz, S. *Tchernichowsky, and S. *Rawidowicz. The twin volume 26/27 (1930) lists Berlin–Tel-Aviv as its places of publication. Volumes 28–29 (1936) were edited by Ya'akov Cahan and published in Tel Aviv. Finally, *Ha-Tekufah* moved to the United States, volumes 30–35 (1946–1950) appearing in New York, edited by E. *Silberschlag and Aaron *Zeitlin (the last volume by Zeitlin alone).

Ha-Tekufah is a treasure trove of Hebrew literature of all genres, including belle lettres by many of the leading writers of the time. Its scholarly articles and translations were also by the leading figures in their field. The contributors to *Ha-Tekufah* are listed in an index appended to volume 25 (author's name only), and in an index (authors and subjects) to all the volumes prepared by J. Barzilai-Folman (1961).

התקופה

העורך: דוד פרישמאן המוציא: אברהם יוסף שטיבל

יוצאת ארבע פעמים בשנה

תמוז—אלול, תרע״ח

ספר שלישי

Title page of the third issue of *Ha-Tekufah*, Moscow, summer 1918. Jerusalem, J.N.U.L.

Bibliography: B. Z. Katz, in: *Ha-Ẓefirah*, no. 24 (1927), 36, 42, 54, 60; idem and A. Zeitlin, in: *Hadoar* (1956), no. 37; P. Birnbaum, *ibid.* (1968), no. 36. [G.K.]

HA-TIKVAH (Heb. הַתִּקְוָה; "The Hope"), anthem of the Zionist movement, and national anthem of the State of Israel. The poem was written by Naphtali Herz *Imber, probably in Jassy in 1878, and first published as *Tikvatenu* ("Our Hope") in his *Barkai*, 1886 (with the misleading note "Jerusalem 1884"). Its inspiration seems to have been the news of the founding of *Petaḥ Tikvah; the themes of the poem, together with those of Imber's *Mishmar ha-Yarden* ("Guarding the Jordan"), show the influence of the German *Die Wacht am Rhein* and *Der Deutsche Rhein* (the "River" and "As long as" motives) and the Polish patriots' song which became the national anthem of the Polish republic ("Poland is not lost yet, while we still live"). In

Figure 1. The Rumanian folk song, *Carul cu boi* ("Cart and Oxen"), the main source for the melody of *Ha-Tikvah*, from D. Idelovitch, ed., *Rishon le-Ẓiyyon*, 1941.

1882 Imber read the poem to the farmers of *Rishon le-Zion, who received it with enthusiasm. Soon afterward—probably in the same year—Samuel Cohen, who had come to Palestine from Moldavia in 1878 and settled in Rishon le-Zion, set the poem to a melody which he consciously based on a Moldavian-Rumanian folk song, *Carul cu Boi* ("Cart and Oxen"; see figure 1). In an

HATIKVAH

Kol od ba-levav penimah	As long as deep in the heart
Nefesh Yehudi homiyyah,	The soul of a Jew yearns,
U-le-fa'atei mizraḥ kadimah	And towards the East
Ayin le-Ẓiyyon ẓofiyyah.	An eye looks to Zion
Od lo avedah tikvatenu	Our hope is not yet lost
Ha-tikvah bat shenot alpayim,	The hope of two thousand years,
Lihyot am ḥofshi be-arẓenu	To be a free people in our land
Ereẓ Ẓiyyon vi-Yrushalayim.	The land of Zion and Jerusalem.

Former Version

Od lo avedah tikvatenu	Our hope is not yet lost
Ha-tikvah ha-noshanah,	The age-old hope,
Lashuv le-ereẓ avoteinu	To return to the land of our fathers
La-ir bah David ḥanah.	To the city where David dwelt.

atmosphere in which new songs and adaptations became folk songs almost overnight because folk songs were needed, and at a time when no one thought of copyright, the melody became anonymous in an astonishingly swift process of collective amnesia. Thus even Abraham Zvi *Idelsohn, who settled in Jerusalem in 1906, approached it as a purely folkloric phenomenon; in his *Thesaurus* (vol. 4, 1923) he published the first of his comparative analyses of the melody, which have been widely accepted and copied since, not always with the proper credit. The true history of *Ha-Tikvah* was rediscovered independently by Menashe *Ravina and by an Israel amateur musicologist, Eliahu Hacohen. The Moldavian *Carul cu Boi* is itself only one of the innumerable incarnations of a certain well-known melodic type (or pattern) found throughout Europe in both major and minor scale versions. Probably the earliest

Figure 2. The melody and text of *Ha-Tikvah* as sung in Israel. From *La-Menaẓẓeḥ Shir Mizmor,* a songbook for soldiers published by the Histadrut in 1968.

printed version of *Ha-Tikvah* with its melody is found in S. T. Friedland, *Vier Lieder mit Benutzung syrischer Melodien . . .* (Breslau, 1895).

Many, but not all, of the changes which intervened between the original text and early forms of the melody of *Ha-Tikvah* and the current version (Fig. 2) can still be retraced through songbooks, memoirs, etc. Some of these arose spontaneously; others were made on purpose, either to modify the text according to contemporary opinion or literary criteria, or to achieve the Sephardi syllable-stress instead of the old-fashioned Ashkenazi stress of the original. The standard harmonization is the one established in 1948 by the Italian conductor Bernardino Molinari, who orchestrated *Ha-Tikvah* for the *Israel Philharmonic Orchestra; another orchestration by Paul *Ben Haim is also current. The first English translation of the poem was made by Israel *Zangwill, the first German one by Heinrich *Loewe. In religious Zionist families there is a tradition of singing Psalm 126 *(Be-Shuv Adonai et Shivat-Ẓiyyon)* with the **zemirot* to the melody of *Ha-Tikvah.* The words can be found in several of the traditional collections of religious poetry published in Near Eastern communities during the past 50 years, and was therefore entered by Israel *Davidson in his *Oẓar.*

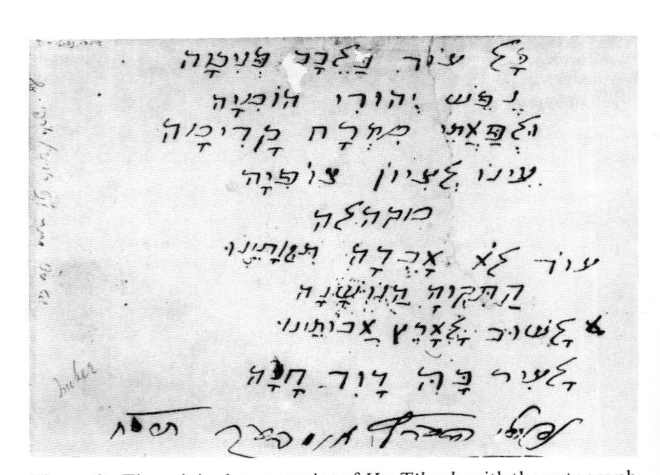

Figure 3. The original manuscript of *Ha-Tikvah,* with the autograph of its author, Naftali Herz Imber. Jerusalem, J.N.U.L., Schwadron Collection.

Two competitions for a Zionist anthem, the first proclaimed in *Die Welt* in 1898 and the second by the Fourth Zionist Congress in 1900, came to nothing because of the unsatisfactory quality of the songs composed or suggested. At the Fifth Zionist Congress in Basle in 1901 one of the sessions concluded with the singing of what was still called *Tikvatenu.* During the Sixth Zionist Congress (Basle, 1903), it was sung by dissenting factions. The Seventh Zionist Congress (Basle, 1905) ended with an "enormously moving singing of *Ha-Tikvah* by all present"—a moment which can be said to have confirmed its status. Although already proposed by David *Wolffsohn, the formal declaration of *Ha-Tikvah* as the Zionist anthem was only made at the 18th Zionist Congress in Prague in 1933. Under the Mandate, *Ha-Tikvah* was the unofficial anthem of Jewish Palestine. At the Declaration of the State on May 14th, 1948, it was sung by the assembly at the opening of the ceremony and played by members of the Palestine symphony orchestra at its conclusion. However, *Ha-Tikvah* was not given official status as a national anthem by a proclamation of the Knesset.

Bibliography: JC (Jan. 3, 1902), 32; (Aug. 28, 1903), viii and passim; (Aug. 4, 1905), 24; (Aug. 11, 1905), 19; Idelsohn, Melodien, 4 (1923), 116; 9 (1932), xix; Idelsohn, Music, 222–3; E. Hacohen, in: *Gittit,* no. 37 (June 1968), 4–5; M. Ravina, *Ha-Tikvah* (Heb., 1969), incl. bibl.; Goell, Bibliography, 895–900. [B.B.]

HATRED (Heb. שִׂנְאָה), overt or covert ill will. The Torah explicitly prohibits hatred of one's fellow in the verse "Thou shall not hate thy brother in thine heart" (Lev. 19:17). Hatred is understood by the rabbis as essentially a matter of mental disposition, as implied in the phrase "in thine heart." One who expresses hostility to his fellow through word or deed, although he violates the commandment "love thy neighbor" and injunctions against injury, insult, vengeance, etc., is not, according to most rabbinic authorities, guilty of the specific sin of hatred referred to in Lev. 19:17 (Sifra, Kedoshim; Ar. 16b; Maim. Yad, De'ot 4:5, *Sefer ha-Mitzvot,* prohib. 302; *Ḥinnukh* 238). The reasons are, apparently, that covert hatred is the more vicious form *(ibid.)* and that a person can defend himself against open hostility (I. M. Kagan, *Ḥafeẓ Ḥayyim* (Vilna, 1873), 13, n. 7). The Talmud is emphatic in its denunciation of hatred. Hillel taught that the essence of the entire Torah is, "What is hateful to you, do not do to others," all else being "commentary" (Shab. 31a). Hatred of one's fellow creatures "drives a man out of this world" (Avot 2:16). One who hates his fellow is considered a murderer (DER, 11).

Gratuitous Hatred (Heb. שִׂנְאַת חִנָּם). According to the Talmud gratuitous hatred is the most vicious form of hatred, and the rabbis denounce it in the most extreme terms. In their view the Second Temple was destroyed as punishment for this sin (Yoma 9b; cf. Story of Kamẓa and Bar Kamẓa, Git. 95b). It is equal to the three paramount sins of idolatry, fornication, and murder (Yoma 9b).

Halakhic Implications of Hatred. According to all rabbinic authorities one who hates (that is, one who, out of enmity, has not spoken to his fellow for three days) is ineligible to serve as a judge in cases involving his enemy; according to some he may not even be a witness (Sanh. 27b). Certain relatives of a woman (e.g., mother-in-law, step-daughter) may not testify concerning the death of her husband, for fear they may harbor hidden enmity (Yev. 117a).

Permissible Hatred. It is proper to hate the wicked. "Do not I hate them, O Lord that hate Thee?" (Ps. 139:21); "The fear of the Lord is to hate evil" (Prov. 8:13). The same thought is expressed in the Talmud (Pes. 113b). Exhortations to hate all manner of evil abound in the Bible (e.g, Ex. 18:21; Ps. 26:4). God Himself hates every form of immorality (e.g., Deut. 12:31; Isa. 1:14; Ps. 5:6) because of its harm to mankind, since God Himself cannot be affected (Saadiah Gaon, *Beliefs and Opinions,* 4:4). The enjoinder to hate evildoers applies, however, only to impenitent and inveterate sinners, those who pay no heed to correction (Maim. Yad, Roẓe'aḥ 13:14; *Ḥinnukh,* 238).

The Bible, nevertheless, distinguishes between the person as such and the sinner in him, "As God, I have no pleasure in the death of the wicked, but that the wicked turn from his way and live" (Ezek. 33:11). One must assist even the wicked in transporting his burden (Ex. 13:5) for otherwise "he may tarry [by the wayside]" and endanger his life (BM 32b; Pes. 113b). Furthermore, in order to learn to subdue one's baser inclinations, one must give priority to aiding the wicked over the good (BM 32b; Maim. Yad, Roẓe'aḥ 13:13). Thus, the true object of proper hatred is the sin, not the sinner, whose life must be respected and whose repentance effected. Beruryah, wife of Rabbi Meir, offered her interpretation of Psalm 104:35, "Let sins [*in loco*—sinners] cease out of the earth," and thereby admonished her husband to pray not for the destruction of sinners but for their regeneration (Ber. 10a). It is forbidden to rejoice at the downfall of even those sinners whom it is proper to hate: "Rejoice not when thine enemy falleth" (Prov. 24:17). Thus, since one can never be certain of one's motives, of the absolute wickedness of the sinner, and of whether one has discharged or is indeed even capable of completely discharging his obligation to reform the sinner, the rabbis stress the obligation of loving all men: "Be of the disciples of Aaron, loving peace and pursuing peace, loving your fellow creatures and drawing them near to the Torah" (Avot 1:12).

Bibliography: J. D. Kranz, *Sefer ha-Middot* (1967), 202–27; G. F. Moore, *Judaism in the First Centuries of the Christian Era,* 2 (1946), 89ff.; M. Lazarus, *Ethics of Judaism,* 2 vols. (1900), passim; A. Cohen, *Everyman's Talmud* (1949), 210ff.; E. Bar-Shaul, *Mitzvah ve-Lev* (1966), 167–77.

[J.H.SH.]

HATVANY-DEUTSCH, a 19th-century family of Hungarian industrialists and landowners, originally from the province of Arad. In the 20th century members of the family achieved distinction as painters, writers, and patrons of the arts. Its founder was IGNAC DEUTSCH (1803–1873), who established Hungary's first sugar refinery in the 1820s. Under his sons, BERNÁT and JOZSEF (I) DEUTSCH, the business expanded and made an immense contribution to the Hungarian national economy. As a reward the brothers were raised to the nobility in 1879 and authorized to add "de Hatvan" ("Hatvany") to their surname, the town of Hatvan, east to Budapest, having become the center of their industrial operations.

József I's son, SÁNDOR HATVANY-DEUTSCH (1852–1913), was, like his father and grandfather, born in Arad. He continued the development of the family business and founded the Hungarian manufacturers' association, but he was also a noted patron of the arts. He helped to establish various charitable institutions and received a barony in 1908. Sándor's sons gained distinction in Hungarian cultural life. The elder, LAJOS HATVANY (1880–1961), author, literary critic, and journalist, wrote in Hungarian and German. Born in Budapest, he entered the literary life of the Hungarian capital and, as a young man, was a founder of the literary periodical *Nyugat.* A generous supporter of aspiring writers, he was a prominent champion of Endre Ady (1877–1919), the great Hungarian poet. Among the journals which Lajos Hatvany edited before and during World War I was *Pesti Napló* ("Pest Journal"). His political outlook was radical and he took an active part in the democratic October Revolution of 1918. At the outbreak of the Communist Revolution of 1919 he went to Vienna, but returned to Budapest in 1927 and gave himself up for trial. He was found guilty of treason and libeling the Hungarian people, and sentenced to a short term in prison. On his release he resumed his writing career, but with the advent of the Hitler regime, he was again forced to leave the country in 1938. He spent World War II in England and returned to Hungary in 1947. During the 1950s he was condemned to silence, and was only granted recognition after 1959.

Lajos Hatvany's studies and criticisms were thorough. A convinced assimilationist and himself converted, he never ceased to deal with the problem of the Hungarian attitude toward Jews, and of Jewish assimilation and nationalism. His great trilogy, *Urak és emberek* ("Gentlemen and People," vol. 1, 1927; complete, 1963[2]), depicts the history of a Jewish family at the turn of the century and is a clear reflection of his own internal struggle. An English version of the first part appeared in New York as *Bondy jr.* (1931). His other works include *Die Wissenschaft des Nichtwissenswerten* (1908), a satire on philological exaggerations; *Die Beruehmten* (1913), a drama; *Das verwundete Land* (1921); *Gyulai Pál estéje* ("The Sunset of Paul Gyulai," 1911, 1960[2]); and *Ady—cikkek, emlékezések, levelek* (1959[2]).

The second son of Sándor was the painter FERENC HATVANY (1881–1958). Like his brother Lajos, he was born in Budapest and converted to Christianity. As a student he came under the influence of Adolf *Fényes. He acquired a fine collection of 19th-century French paintings and some of his own nudes and still lifes are displayed in the Budapest Museum of Fine Arts. He settled in Paris about 1947 and died in Lausanne.

The descendants of Ignac Deutsch's other son, Bernát, also attained importance in Hungarian public life and a few of them remained within the Jewish fold. Bernát's son, JOZSEF (II) HATVANY-DEUTSCH (1858–1913), collaborated with his cousin Sándor in the development of the sugar industry, and his banking and other financial interests made him one of the wealthiest Jews in Hungary. Active in Jewish communal affairs, he was a trustee and benefactor of the Budapest rabbinical seminary and a generous supporter of the Hungarian Jewish Literary Society (IMIT). He also established pioneering welfare and sickness benefit schemes for workers in his factories. In 1908 József II, like Sándor, was created a baron and became a member of the Hungarian parliament's upper house. He died in Germany. József II's children were the author LILI HATVANY (1890–), the political writer ANTONIA HATVANY-DEUTSCH (1894–), and the industrialist and writer BERTALAN HATVANY (1900–). Born in Budapest, Bertalan was a successful businessman, and a patron of literature, one of the writers whom he supported being the great Hungarian poet, Joseph Attila (1905–1937). An active Zionist and a generous contributor to the movement, he held views similar to those of the **Berit Shalom* on the problem of peace between Jews and Arabs. Bertalan Hatvany left Hungary in 1939, spent some time in Australia, and then settled in Paris. His early travels are reflected in books such as *Ázsia és a nacionalizmus* ("Asia and Nationalism," 1931); *Ázsia lelke* ("The Soul of Asia," 1935, which includes much of Jewish interest, including impressions of Ereẓ Israel); *Konfuciustól Nehemiásig* ("From Confucius to Nehemiah," 1936); *A kínai kérdés története* ("History of the Chinese Question," 1938); and *Az út és az ige könyve* ("The Book of the Way and the World," a translation of Tao-te King, 1957).

Bibliography: B. Kempelen, *Magyarországi zsidó e zsidó eredetű családok,* 2 (1938), 61–64; A. Szerb, *Magyar irodalomtörténet* (1943); *Magyar Zsidó Lexikon* (1929), s.v.; *Magyar Irodalmi Lexikon,* 1 (1963), s.v.; UJE, 5 (1941), 249–50.

[B.Y.]

°**HAUPT, PAUL** (1858–1926), U.S. orientalist and Bible scholar. He taught from 1880 at the University of Goettingen. In 1885 he was appointed to head the incipient Oriental Seminary in Johns Hopkins University in Baltimore, U.S., but he continued to lecture at Goettingen each summer until the outbreak of World War I. His more than 500 publications in German and English (as well as one Hebrew article on the Pentateuchal sources, 1895) and his training of several generations of Semitic philologists significantly influenced American biblical and oriental studies.

The scholarly writings of Haupt are governed by the empirical historical method with full employment of linguistic and philological data. His first essay, "The Oldest Semitic Verb Form" (in JRAS, 1878), showed that the Akkadian present is probably the most archaic verb form preserved in the extant Semitic languages. His biblical commentaries on the Song of Songs (1902), Ecclesiastes (1905), Nahum (1907), Esther (1908), and Micah (1910) emphasize Hebrew metrics. In *Purim* (1906) he discussed the origin of the Purim festival, tracing it to the Persian Nauroz feast, and in *Midian and Sinai* (1909; = ZDMG, 63 (1909), 506–30) he argued for the historical and cultural maturity of the Mosaic era. In his semipopular writings, Haupt was very productive, but whimsical and pontifical. Influenced by the writings of E. Burnouf, he wrote two learned articles on the Aryan ancestry of Jesus, which were later used by the Nazis as propaganda against the Jews. His original writings were supplemented by his editorial work on important series of Orientalia and Biblica. He edited with W. R. Harper the early volumes of *Hebraica* and with Friedrich Delitzsch the *Assyriologische Bibliothek* and *Beitraege zur Assyriologie und semitischen Sprachwissenschaft.* Three series of oriental studies published by Johns Hopkins University were under his supervision. He also edited the *Polychrome Bible* (1893, 1896–1904) and with H. H. Furness edited the English translation of selected portions.

Bibliography: *Oriental Studies Dedicated to P. Haupt* (1926), includes bibliography; Albright, in: *Beitraege zur Assyriologie und semitischen Sprachwissenschaft,* 10 no. 2 (1928), xiii–xxii.

[Z.G.]

HAURAN (Heb.חַוְרָן), region in northeastern Transjordan, today part of Syria. The name occurs for the first time—as *Hauranu*—in the account of Shalmaneser III's expedition against Hazael of Aram-Damascus in 841 B.C.E. Tiglath-Pileser III in 733/2 B.C.E. turned it into an Assyrian province called Haurina. This is apparently the Hauran mentioned by Ezekiel in the only biblical reference to the place (47:15–18). In describing the ideal boundaries of Ereẓ Israel, Ezekiel cities on the north "Hazer-Haticcon [probably Hazer-Inum] which is by the border of Hauran" and on the east "between Hauran and Damascus." The Septuagint reads here "Auranitis"; the suffix *-itis* indicates that it was a Ptolemaic administrative district. In 198 B.C.E the district of Hauran was taken from the Ptolemies by the Seleucids and with the decline of that kingdom it became the possession of the Itureans who held it also at the beginning of Roman rule. In order to restrain the inhabitants of adjacent *Trachonitis who were in the habit of raiding the convoys of Damascus, Augustus in 23 B.C.E. assigned the Hauran (together with Trachonitis and Batanaea) to Herod who settled Jews there in military colonies (Jos., Ant., 15:343; Wars, 1:398). It remained in the domain of the Herodian dynasty, passing from Herod's son Philip to Agrippa I and Agrippa II and with the death of the latter it was attached to Syria. At the end of the third century the Hauran was transferred to Provincia Arabia of which it remained a part until the end of Byzantine rule. The Hauran flourished during the Roman period when many cities were founded there including Canatha and Dionysias-Soada. As it was located in Jewish territory, the Hauran was one of the places in the Second Temple period where beacons were lit to announce the approach of Rosh Ha-Shanah and the festivals. After the signals were received at the Hauran from Agrippina (Grapina)-Kawkab al-Hawā they were transmitted to Bet Bitlin (RH, 2:4). The Hauran's border with the Nabatean kingdom in the Roman period can be very precisely established by inscriptions and eras used for dating purposes. The border included al-Mushannaf, Bosana (Būsān), Ḥabrān, Dionysias-al-Suwayda, and Karak in the Hauran. In Roman times it is therefore apparent that the concept of the Hauran had expanded and also included the fertile valley known today as al-Nuqra. The borders of Hauran thus reached Arabia along Wadi al-Dhahab in the south, the slopes of the Jebel el-Druze (Druze Mountain) in the east, Trachonitis in the north, and the Bashan (in the limited sense) and the city of Dion in the west.

Jewish settlement in the Hauran continued in talmudic times; several rabbis bore its name (e.g., Ḥunya de-Berat Huran; TJ, Shek. 1:1, 46a). In the fourth and fifth centuries

Christianity became deeply rooted in the Hauran as is indicated by the participation of bishops from the Hauran in church councils and the many ruins of churches found there. These churches inherited the independent style of the Eastern tradition which had evolved in the architecture and ornament of the buildings of the Hauran as early as Roman times and which also influenced synagogues in the Galilee. As in other border districts, Arabic influence increased in the Hauran in the Byzantine period. It was incorporated in the kingdom of Benu Ghassān under Byzantine protection but in 634 the Arabs conquered it without undue effort. The Hauran thereafter declined until *Druze from Lebanon began settling there in the 18th century. Following the riots in Lebanon between Druze and Christians in 1860, Druze settlement in the Hauran increased considerably and the region today is called Jebel el-Druze (Mount of the Druzes). Geographically the term Hauran comprises three separate concepts: (1) Mt. Druze itself, 5,900 ft. (1,800 m.) high; (2) the mountain, its slopes, and the el-Nuqra valley; and (3) all of the eastern part of northern Transjordan from Damascus to the Yarmuk. About 80,000 Druze live in the region.

Bibliography: S. Klein, *Ever ha-Yarden* (1925), 19–21; Tcherikover, in: *Tarbiz*, 4 (1933), 233, 361; Avi-Yonah, Geog, index; E. Fouer, *Die Provinzeinteilung des assyrischen Reiches* (1920), 52, 63; Elliger, in: PJB, 32 (1936), 68–69; Noth, *ibid.*, 33 (1937), 37–40; Epstein (Elath), in: PEFQS (1940), 13ff.; D. Sourdel, *Les cultes de Hauran a l'époque romaine* (1952); M. Dunand, *Le Musée de Soueida* (1934).

[M.A.-Y.]

HAURWITZ, BERNHARD (1905–), U.S. meteorologist. Born in Glogau, Germany, Haurwitz was educated at the University of Leipzig, where he became a member of the staff. With the coming of Hitler he emigrated to the U.S. and worked at the universities of Harvard and Toronto, Canada, until 1937. From 1937 to 1941 he was meteorologist of the Dominion of Canada and held the post of assistant professor at the Massachusetts Institute of Technology. From 1947 to 1959 he directed the department of oceanography and meteorology of New York University. In 1959, he became professor of astrophysics and physics at the University of Colorado, where he remained until 1964. In 1966, he was also appointed a professor at the University of Texas.

Haurwitz wrote many articles and several books, some of which were standard textbooks. These include *Dynamic Meteorology* (1941) and (with J. M. Austin) *Climatology* (1944). He served on the Board of Governors of the Hebrew University of Jerusalem. [D.Ash.]

HAUSDORF, AZRIEL ZELIG (1823–1905), a precursor of the *Ḥibbat Zion movement and pioneer of Jewish settlement in Ereẓ Israel. Born in Myslowice, Silesia, Hausdorf attended a yeshivah until the age of 20, when he went to London. He left in 1847, to settle in Jerusalem. He was a translator and expert on Jewish subjects for the Austrian consul and also represented the Jews at the Prussian consulate. He thus helped to protect the rights of refugees from Russia and Poland who did not enjoy the protection of a foreign power. When Baron Gustave de *Rothschild visited Ereẓ Israel, Hausdorf assisted him in founding the Misgav la-Dakh Hospital in the Old City of Jerusalem. He was a founder of the Ḥevrat Ahavat Zion, formed by members of Kolel Hod (Holland-Deutschland community), which bought a plot of land in the vicinity of the Temple Mount (1858), in order to found the Battei Maḥaseh quarter for the poor. The *kolel* sent him to Holland and Germany, where he acquired the support of Ẓevi Hirsch *Kalischer. He helped to acquire various plots of lands (near Jaffa and at Moẓa).

Bibliography: E. Hausdorf, *Zelig Hausdorf u-Fe'ulotav le-Hatavat ve-Haramat Maẓẓav Eḥav* (1905); P. Grajewsky, *Zikkaron la-Ḥovevim ha-Rishonim*, 1 (1927), 24–26; 2 (1929), 45–47; Yaari, Sheluḥei, 805–7; Eliav, in: *Sinai*, 61 (1967), 298–315.

[G.B.-Y.]

HAUSDORFF, FELIX (1868–1942), German mathematician. Hausdorff was born in Breslau, and was professor of mathematics at Greifswald from 1913 to 1921 and at Bonn from 1921 until his retirement in 1935. Together with his wife he committed suicide in 1942 in order to avoid the deportation order of the Gestapo. Hausdorff was an authority on set theory and its applications to sets of points and real analysis. His textbook *Mengenlehre* (Leipzig, 1935) is recognized as one of the great classics of set theory. The depth and simplicity of his research into fundamental problems was a source of inspiration in the rapid development of modern mathematics. Hausdorff was devoted to music and literature and published belles lettres under the pen name of Paul Mongré.

Bibliography: *Poggendorff's biographisch-literarisches Handwoerterbuch der exakten Naturwissenschaften*, 7a (1958), 402.

[B.S.]

HAUSER, HENRI (1866–1946), French historian. Hauser was born and educated in Oran, Algeria, but made his career in France. He was professor of ancient and medieval history at the University of Clermont-Ferrand (1893), taught modern history at the University of Dijon (1903), and after 1921 economic history at the University of Paris. Hauser's works include: *L'enseignement des sciences sociales* (1903); *Travailleurs et marchands dans l'ancienne France* (1920); and *Les débuts du capitalisme* (1927). In *L'impérialisme américain* (1905), he prophesied the decline of Europe and dominance of the United States, and his *Méthodes allemandes d'expansion économique* (1915) pertained largely to the role German industry had upon the outbreak of World War I. When the Nazis occupied France in 1940, he fled to the south where, in hiding and despite failing eyesight, he completed a study on the economic thought of Richelieu.

Bibliography: *American Historical Review*, 52 (1946), 221f., obituary.

[G.S.]

HAUSER, PHILIP MORRIS (1909–), U.S. sociologist. He was born in Chicago where he also studied. From 1938 until 1947 he was deputy director at the U.S. Bureau of the Census; in 1947 he was appointed professor of sociology at the University of Chicago. He was president of the American Sociological Association 1967–68. Hauser worked on various studies of population, urban problems, and city planning. Hauser continued the ecological emphasis of the Chicago School of Sociology, and channeled it demographically. An internationally known demographer, Hauser was an active proponent of population control in the United States and elsewhere. He also took an active interest in the civil rights movement. His works include *Government Statistics for Business Use* (1946), *Population and World Politics* (1958), *The Study of Population* (1959), *Housing a Metropolis* (1960), *Population Perspectives* (1961), *Urbanization in Latin America* (1961), *The Population Dilemma* (1963), *The Study of Urbanization* (1965) and *Handbook for Social Research in Urban Areas* (1967). [W.J.C.]

HAUSNER, BERNARD (1874–1938), rabbi, Polish Zionist leader, and representative of Poland in Palestine. Born in Czortkow, Galicia, he studied at the University of Vienna and at the rabbinical seminary there, graduating in 1901. He taught religion at the secondary schools of Lemberg (1899–1914) and was rabbi and spiritual leader of the Lemberg Jewish community for the two years that the city was occupied by the Russians (1914–16). He also served as military chaplain in the Austrian army on various fronts (1916–18). After the war he became a leader of the Zionist movement, particularly of Mizrachi, in Poland. He served as a member of the Sejm (Polish parliament) from 1922 to 1927, when he settled in Palestine. In 1926 Hausner published a treatise in Polish on the financial rehabilitation of Poland, which earned him the reputation of an economic expert. In Palestine, he served first as economic adviser to the Polish government and later (1932–34) as Polish consul in Tel Aviv. Both in Poland and Palestine, Hausner took an active part in public affairs and published essays on Jewish subjects (in Polish), as well as a Polish translation of the *maḥzor*. [G.K.]

His son GIDEON HAUSNER (1915–), Israel lawyer, was born in Lemberg, Poland, and was taken to Palestine in 1927. He went into private legal practice in Jerusalem but was Israel's attorney general from 1960 to 1963. Hausner was chief prosecutor in the *Eichmann trial, on which he wrote *Justice in Jerusalem* (1966). From 1965 Hausner was a member of the *Knesset for the Independent Liberal Party. [B.J.]

Bibliography: Tidhar, 9 (1958), 3316–17; EẒD, 2 (1960), 19–23.

ḤAVAẒẒELET (Heb. חֲבַצֶּלֶת), Hebrew newspaper, first published in Jerusalem in 1863, discontinued after approximately one year, revived at the end of 1870, and continued until close to the outbreak of World War I. Founded by Israel Bak, a pioneer of the Hebrew press, *Ḥavaẓẓelet* began publication after *Ha-Levanon* on July 13, 1863 in the wake of a controversy which broke out in Jerusalem concerning the affairs of the Eẓ Ḥayyim school. It opposed the position taken by *Ha-Levanon*, its journalistic rival. So fierce was the dispute that both papers were forced to discontinue publication in 1864. When *Ḥavaẓẓelet* resumed publication in 1870, Bak's son-in-law, I. D. Frumkin, gradually moved into the editorial staff, and soon became its editor. In the last years of the paper his son Gad Frumkin also served as editor.

The paper was the organ of the Ḥasidim, who were a minority among the general Ashkenazi *yishuv* in Jerusalem, mainly composed of *Mitnaggedim*. *Ḥavaẓẓelet* opposed the leadership of the Ashkenazi *yishuv* and supported the programs for the settlement of Israel (see S. *Berman, Rabbi J. *Alkalai) which were opposed by Ashkenazi rabbis of Jerusalem. In 1873 it launched an attack against the controllers of the *ḥalukkah* funds and those countered with a boycott against *Ḥavaẓẓelet* and its editor. Frumkin advocated the "productivization" of the Jewish community in Israel, especially by means of agriculture, and opposed Sir Moses Montefiore's programs because of his excessive sympathy for those in charge of the *ḥalukkah*. He encouraged young forces from among the members of the *yishuv* to participate in the newspaper.

Ḥavaẓẓelet appeared originally as a monthly, and from the second copy of the second year as a weekly, continuing as such for several decades. Only in its last years was the format enlarged, and the paper was published three times a week (1908–10); in the end it was printed again as a weekly. In 1870–71 a Yiddish supplement *(Die Roze)* came out. The literary supplement was called *Pirḥei Ḥavaẓẓelet*. In 1882, under the editorship of A. M. Luncz, there was published a foreign language supplement called *Gazette de Jerusalem*, and in 1884, the supplement *Mevasseret Ẓiyyon* appeared under the editorship of Eliezer Ben-Yehuda.

After the pogroms in Russia in the beginning of the 1880s the paper advocated *aliyah* and encouraged the first immigrants to settle on the land of Petaḥ Tikvah. With the arrival of the first wave of *aliyah* from Russia and from Yemen, the paper endeavored to ease their absorption both in agricultural work and in Jerusalem. Frumkin invited Ben-Yehuda to Jerusalem from Paris to work on the *Ḥavaẓẓelet*. Ben-Yehuda's publication of his own independent newspaper, *Ha-Ẓevi* in the autumn of 1884, gave rise to an antagonism between *Ha-Ẓevi* and *Ḥavaẓẓelet: Ḥavaẓẓelet* soon became the mouthpiece of the older generation of the *yishuv* in Jerusalem, while *Ha-Ẓevi* supported the new *yishuv*, especially the agricultural villages. The former, which in the beginning had been in opposition to the *ḥalukkah*, now became its loyal supporter. It now rejected the program of enlightenment that it had advocated in the 1870s, turned against the modernists of the *yishuv*, and later opposed political Zionism.

No 4 Jerusalem 17 — 8 ... 1631 ירושלים י׳ חשון תרל״א שנה ראשונה

חבצלת

מבשרת ציון

HABAZELETH

מבשר שלום ירושלם . משמיע חדשות מארץ סוריא , מודיע נעלמות מארץ מצרים . וארץ הודו , הקרובים אלינו . וכל דבר הדרוש לחפץ לבב אחינו דורשי ציון .

יוצא לאור מאת ישראל ב״ק וחביריו

למען ציון לא אחשה, ולמען ירושלם לא אשקט עד יצא כנוגה צדקה , וישועתה כלפיד יבער (ישעי׳ ס״ב)

Pour l'amour de sion Je ne me tairai Point, et Pour l'amour de Jerusalem Je ne serai point en repos. Jusqu'a ce que sa Justice sorte comme une splendeur, et que sa delivrance allume comme une lampe: [Esaie 62]

תוכן הענינים

שלום ירושלם

Front page of the fourth issue of the Jerusalem newspaper, *Ḥavaẓẓelet*, 17 Ḥeshvan, 5631 (1870). Jerusalem, J.N.U.L.

Gad Frumkin tried to revive the flagging spirit of the *Ḥavaẓẓelet* at the beginning of the present century, but his energy was curbed by his father. While this newspaper died out, a new press with an entirely different direction rose in its place. *Ḥavaẓẓelet* nevertheless raised a generation of writers and scholars, mainly from the old *yishuv*, who later filled distinguished positions in literature, science, and public life in Jerusalem and Ereẓ Israel. In 1954 a selection of the writings of I. D. Frumkin from the volumes of the *Ḥavaẓẓelet*, together with a comprehensive introduction and comments, was published in Jerusalem.

Bibliography: G. Kressel, *"Ha-Levanon" ve "Ha-Ḥavaẓẓelet"* (1943); idem, *Toledot ha-Ittonut ha-Ivrit be-Ereẓ Yisrael* (1964; see cap. 1); G. Yardeni, *Ha-Ittonut ha-Ivrit be-Erez Yisrael bi-Shenot 1863–1904* (1969), 17–81, 107–162; A. Frumkin, *In Friling fun Idishn Sotsialism* (1940); G. Frumkin, *Derekh Shofet bi-Yrushalayim* (1955); D. Idelovitch (ed.), *Kovez Ma'amarim le-Divrei Yemei ha-Ittonut be-Erez Yisrael*, 2 (1936), 28–38; S. Ha-Levi, *Ha-Sefarim ha-Ivriyyim she-Nidpesu bi-Yrushalayim* (1963).

[G.K.]

HAVDALAH (Heb. הַבְדָּלָה; "distinction"), blessing recited at the termination of Sabbaths and festivals, in order to emphasize the distinction between the sacred and the ordinary, with regard to the Sabbath (or festival) that is departing and the ordinary weekday. *Havdalah* is one of the most ancient blessings: according to the Talmud "the men of the Great *Synagogue instituted blessings and prayers, sanctifications and *Havdalot* for Israel" (Ber. 33a). Some authorities hold that the obligation to recite the *Havdalah* derives from the Pentateuch. According to the Babylonian Talmud, it was originally inserted in the *Amidah*, but subsequently "when they became richer—they instituted that it should be said over the cup of wine; when they became poor again—they inserted it again into the prayer" *(ibid.)*. Three views are mentioned in the Jerusalem Talmud (Ber. 5:2, 9b): (1) *Havdalah* was originally inserted in the *Amidah* and then also transferred to the cup of wine "for the benefit of the children"; (2) it was originally instituted over the cup of wine; (3) it was instituted in both places at the same time. Because of these variations, there were four opinions, already in the time of the *tannaim*, on the place of *Havdalah* in the *Amidah*. Moreover, in accordance with most of the *tannaim*, the present practice is to recite the proper *Havdalah* blessing over the cup of wine, while in the *Amidah* only mention of it should be made. At a much later date, in the middle of the medieval period, the custom began to develop of reciting *Havdalah* over a cup of wine in the synagogue as well, in order to exempt those who had no wine (cf. Ta'an. 24a).

The text of the *Havdalah* ceremony over a cup of wine developed over a long period of time and, in the Ashkenazi version, a number of verses were added at the beginning as "a good omen" (Tur, OḤ 296:1). These usually commence with, "Behold, God is my salvation," etc. (Isa. 12:2–3). This introduction is followed by three blessings—over wine, spices, and light—inserted in the *Havdalah* arrangement much before the time of *Bet Hillel and Bet Shammai, who already differed about their text and order (Ber. 8:5), even though R. Judah ha-Nasi instituted the last two over the cup of wine merely for the benefit of his household (Pes. 54a). The purpose of the blessing over light—"Who createst the light of the fire"—is to show that work is now permitted and to stress the departure of the Sabbath. The blessing over the wine itself stems from the duty to recite *Havdalah* over a cup of wine, as in the case of **Kiddush*. The reason for the blessing over spices has not been clarified. The *rishonim* explained it as compensation to the Jew for the loss of the "additional soul" which traditionally accompanied the Jew throughout the Sabbath (see Ta'an. 27b; Sof. 17:5; and see Tos. to Pes. 102b); other reasons have also been suggested (Tur, OḤ 296).

The *Havdalah* blessing itself, the fourth and final, according to the order of the prayer, was known from early times in various versions, differing primarily in the number of distinctions (e.g. "between the Sabbath and the other days of the week") they contained. In the Talmud (Pes. 103b; TJ, Ber. 5:2, 9b) it is laid down that "He who would recite but few distinctions, must recite not less than three, but he who would proliferate must not recite more than seven." R. Judah ha-Nasi, however, recited only one, the distinction "between the holy and the profane" (Pes. loc. cit.). Poetic versions containing seven distinctions have been preserved in the *Genizah* fragments (see Zulay in bibl.). Similarly with its wording in the *Amidah* of which various versions are known in the liturgies, of the different communities and in the *Genizah* fragments (see Zulay, bibl.).

Havdalah over a cup of wine is customary also when the Sabbath is immediately followed by a festival, since the festival's stringency is less than that of the Sabbath (Ḥul. 26b). Combined in this case with the *Kiddush*, its wording is: "Who makest a distinction between holy and holy." The order of this *Kiddush-Havdalah* is indicated by the well-known acrostic **yaknehaz* (*yayin* ("wine"), *Kiddush*, *ner* ("candle"), *Havdalah*, *zeman* ("season" = *she-heḥeyanu*)). This *Havdalah* is mentioned in the evening blessing for the sanctification of the day and the combined formula, fixed by *Rav and *Samuel in Babylonia, is known as "the pearl of Rav and Samuel" (Ber. 33b). When the termination of the festival is followed by a working day, *Havdalah* is recited without candle or spices.

There are many customs connected with *Havdalah:* the pouring of some of the wine on the ground as an omen of blessing (cf. Er. 65a), and hence the custom of overfilling the cup (Turei Zahav to OḤ 296:1); passing the last drop of wine in the cup over the eyes (cf. PdRE 20), and extinguishing the lamp with the remaining drops; when saying the blessing over the light, some look at their fingernails and some at the lines on their palms (S. Assaf, *Sifran shel Rishonim* (1935), 177). After *Havdalah* it is customary to chant special hymns, the best known being: "May He who sets the holy and the ordinary apart," originally instituted for the termination of the Day of Atonement, and "Elijah the prophet." Other songs and hymns said before or after *Havdalah* are mostly based upon the Jerusalem Talmud (loc. cit.). [I.T.-S.]

The Spice Box (Hadas). In the ceremony of *Havdalah*, it is customary for a box of aromatic *spices to be handed round accompanied with an appropriate blessing. In medieval Europe, sweet-smelling herbs such as myrtle (Heb. *hadas*) were generally used for this purpose. For this reason, the spice box came to be known as a *"hadas"* when spices were substituted for herbs. The moment of transition is marked by Rabbi Ephraim of Regensburg in the 12th century, who recorded that he said the blessing not over a branch of myrtle, but over spices contained in a special glass receptacle. This is probably the earliest mention of a special spice box. The earliest extant example, however, dates from about 1550. It originated from the synagogue at Friedberg, Germany and is now in the Jewish Museum, New York. Another example, dated 1543, was formerly in the Landesmuseum at Kassel but was lost when the museum was destroyed by the Nazis. The spice box has taken a large variety of forms, and has inspired craftsmen to fantasy and often to whimsy. Among the Ashkenazi Jews it often took the form of a fortified tower. It has been suggested that this form was adopted because spices, which came from the Orient, were so valuable that they had to be stored in the castle or city hall. It is also thought to have been derived from the ritual implements of the Church, such as the monstrance and thurible, which also took this form, as the implements of the Church were executed by the same gentile craftsmen as those of the synagogue. A "Jewish monstrance" commissioned from a Frankfort silversmith in 1550 is thus probably a spice box. The tower form could be imitated from a local tower or church steeple, surrounded by a balustrade, surmounted with a pennant and carrying a clock face indicating the conclusion of the Sabbath. It was executed in silver, sometimes engraved to resemble masonry, and later in filigree. Human and animal figures were placed around the tower: biblical worthies, soldiers, musicians, various synagogal officials such as the *shoḥet* (ritual slaughterer) with his knife, the scribe with his pen and inkwell, the *Schulklopfer* with his hammer (who woke worshipers for morning prayers), or sometimes a Jew holding a beaker of wine and performing *Havdalah*. A variant of the tower form was executed in northern Italy in the 18th century, where it was covered with delicate filigree work, studded with semiprecious stones and adorned with enamel plaques depicting scenes from the Bible. Spice boxes were also made in many other forms, such as

Figure 1. "Conclusion of the Sabbath," a painting by Moritz Oppenheim showing the preparations for the *Havdalah* ceremony in a mid-19th-century German household. The father pours the wine, and the youngest member of the family holds the lighted candle. New York, Oscar Gruss Collection. Photo Frank Darmstaedter, New York.

Figure 2. *Havdalah* service at a Lubavicher student weekend retreat, Minneapolis, Minnesota. From *Challenge,* London, 1970.

Figure 3. *Havdalah* set representing the Garden of Eden. The tree trunk, supporting the wine cup, has five branches of pierced fruit which serve as spice containers. A serpent is twined around the stand supporting the tray used for extinguishing the *Havdalah* candle. Silver and gilt repoussé; Germany, 18th century, height 9½ in. (23 cm.). Formerly Feinberg Collection, Detroit. Photo Manning Bros., Highland Park, Mich.

Figure 4. *Havdalah* spice box in the form of a windmill. Palestine, early 20th century. Silver, height 6 in. (15 cm.). Jerusalem, Michael Kaufman Collection. Photo David Harris, Jerusalem.

Figure 5. Silver spice box for the *Havdalah* ceremony, a decorated tower, height 9½ in. (23 cm.). Made in Frankfort, c. 1550, it was originally in the synagogue of Friedberg. New York, Jewish Museum.

6

7

Figure 6. Silver spice box, Persia, 19th century, height 11 in. (28 cm.). Jerusalem, Michael Kaufman Collection. Photo David Harris, Jerusalem.

Figure 7. Woodcut showing the examining of fingernails during the *Havdalah* ceremony, from a *minhagim* book, Venice, 1601. Oxford, Bodleian Library.

Figure 8. Silver filigree spice boxes. Left, in the form of a house, Russia, 19th century, length 2½ in. (6 cm.). Center, capped by a flag, Poland, 18th century, height 6 in. (15 cm.). Right, with small flag decorated with a *magen David*, Palestine, early 20th century, height 4½ in. (11 cm.). Jerusalem, Michael Kaufman Collection. Photo David Harris, Jerusalem.

8

animals, fish, birds, flowers and fruit, and even windmills. There was also the simpler form of round, square, or rectangular boxes. On occasion the spice box was combined with the taperholder used in the *Havdalah* ceremony. The spices were contained in a drawer beneath the taper, which was sometimes supported by a figure. In the East small jars and boxes were used to keep the herbs. In Persia these were jars with elongated necks, sometimes filled with rose water. As a result of the revival of Jewish ritual and synagogal art in Israel and the United States after World War II, spice boxes have been designed and executed by eminent artists in a contemporary manner. [ED.]

Bibliography: M. Brueck, *Pharisaeische Volkssitten und Ritualien* (1840), 108–25; A. Jawitz, *Mekor ha-Berakhot* (1910), 44–47; Abrahams, Companion 172f., 145, 190f.; I. Elbogen, in: *Festschrift . . . I. Lewy* (1911), 173–87; Mann, in: HUCA, 2 (1925), 318f.; Finesingen, *ibid.*, 12–13 (1937–38), 347–65; Zulay, in: *Sefer Assaf* (1953), 303–6; ET, 8 (1957), 67–102; Narkiss, in: *Eretz Israel*, 6 (1960), 189–98.

ḤAVER, 16th-century family of rabbis, originally from Damascus. The best-known members of the family are Isaac and his son Ḥayyim. ISAAC (d. 1541) was a rabbi and *posek* (also a physician according to Moses *Basola), and head of the Sicilian community of Damascus before 1522. He discussed halakhic problems with Jacob *Berab I. He died in Damascus and in 1564 his remains were taken by his son ḤAYYIM, to Safed for burial. Ḥayyim was already an important rabbi of Safed before his father's death, since his signature appears on a ruling of 1536 together with those of other great Safed halakhists (see Responsa *Avkat Rokhel*, of Joseph Caro, no. 124). He was apparently called to Damascus to succeed his father. In 1546, in accordance with his father's custom, Ḥayyim sent to Safed from Damascus the yearly calendar of the Sicilian community. He appears to have returned to Safed after a number of years and to have become one of the members of the *bet din* of Moses di *Trani, his signature appearing on a halakhic ruling of 1557 together with that of Di Trani and Shem Tov Bibas (Moses di Trani, Responsa *Mabit*, 1:287). A ruling by Ḥayyim from his Damascus period appears in *Avkat Rokhel* (no. 114). He died in Safed. ISAAC, one of his sons, is mentioned in a responsum of 1567 (*Mabbit*, 2:88). Apparently JOSHUA ḤAVER, the friend of Israel *Najara and a merchant in Syria, was also a member of this family.

Bibliography: Ashtor, Toledot, 2 (1951), 494; Assaf, in: KS, 22 (1945/46), 244; Frumkin-Rivlin, 1 (1929), 82; Rosanes, Togarmah, 2 (1938), 144; 3 (1938), 240; R. J. Z. Werblowsky, *Joseph Karo, Lawyer and Mystic* (1962), 92 n. 6. [A.D.]

ḤAVER, ḤAVERIM (Heb. חָבֵר, pl. חֲבֵרִים; "member"), the name for those belonging to a group that undertook to observe meticulously both the laws of *terumah* ("heave-offering") and *ma'aser* ("tithing") as well as the regulations of impurity and purity. The regulations binding the obligations of the *ḥaver* were already laid down in the time of Hillel and Shammai, since Bet Hillel and Bet Shammai differ about the details. A candidate for membership of the group was not immediately accepted as a full *ḥaver*, but was subjected to a period of education and probation. The candidate declared his readiness "to accept the obligations of a *ḥaver* in the presence of three *ḥaverim*" (Bek. 30b). In the first stage, when he was called *ne'eman* ("trustworthy") he undertook "to tithe what he eats, what he sells, and what he buys" (Dem. 2:2; Tosef., *ibid.* In the view of R. Meir, at this stage too "he may not be the guest of an *am ha-areẓ*"). He was then accepted "for wings," i.e., one who washed his hands before eating and before touching ritually clean food (Tosef., Dem. 2:11; S. Lieberman, *Tosefta ki-Feshutah* (see bibliography), pt. 1, 214). In the final stage he undertook more stringent obligations of ritual purity, undertaking

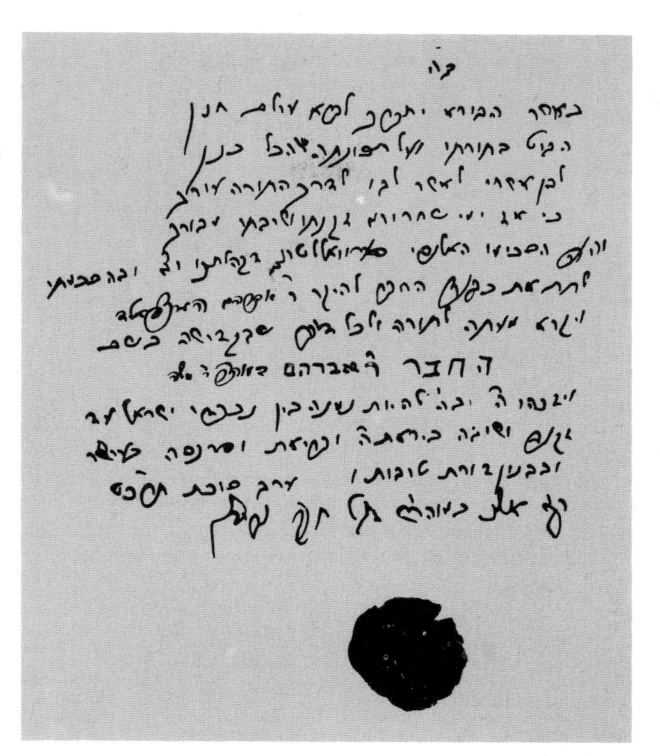

Document conferring the title of *ḥaver* on Abraham Herzfeld, Poland, 1868. Jerusalem, C.A.H.J.P., P22/14.

"that he would not give *terumah* or *ma'aser* to an *am ha-areẓ*, nor prepare ritually clean food for him, and that he would eat ordinary food in a state of ritual purity" (Tosef., *ibid.*, 2:2; Lieberman, *ibid.*, 210; see Dem. 2:3). After undertaking to observe all the obligations of a *ḥaver* he underwent a period of probation—30 days according to Bet Hillel and 12 months according to Bet Shammai—before being accepted as a full *ḥaver*. Anyone could join the group, including women and slaves (Tosef., Dem. 2:16–17), on condition that they undertook to fulfill the aforementioned obligations. No candidate was exempted from the conditions of acceptance ("even a scholar had to undertake them," *ibid.*, 2:13). Joining the group of *ḥaverim* meant separation from those who were not *ḥaverim*—from the *am ha-areẓ*—raising many problems in daily life, even in the life of the family, when some members were *ḥaverim* while others were not. In pursuit of their aims the *ḥaverim* did not isolate themselves from society or create special centers for themselves, nor did they form an organized group with officeholders having particular functions. Detailed *halakhot* were evolved to regulate relations between them and their environment in all spheres of life.

It is not possible to determine the exact period of the group's first emergence. The fact that the *halakhot* dealing with the *ḥaver* were mainly transmitted in the names of the *tannaim who lived after the Bar Kokhba revolt does not suffice to support the opinion of A. Buechler (see bibliography) who ascribed them to the era of Usha and even assigned them to the priests of Galilee. Not only is this contradicted by some sources, as stated, that Bet Shammai and Bet Hillel differed on details of these *halakhot* (see Tosef., Av. Zar. 3:9–10 for the period of Rabban Gamaliel), but other evidence also conflicts with the opinion of Buechler. It has long been recognized that the arrangement for accepting *ḥaverim* is reminiscent of the description given by Josephus (Wars, 2:137) of the acceptance into the fold of the Essenes, and parallels have been pointed out with the school of the Pythagoreans. The discovery of the Scroll of the *Manual of Discipline in the Judean desert throws new and important light on the subject. It is a document of a society in Ereẓ Israel, describing its life and regulations. There are indeed differences between the two; the Dead Sea group was a fraternity whose members lived communally and shared their possessions. Nevertheless the regulations with regard to ritual purity and many of the arrangements for initiation were common to both, and the same phrases and expressions occur in both. It seems reasonable to suppose that the various groups of *ḥaverim* among the Pharisees too were not all of one character and certainly did not always conduct themselves in all matters with the same degree of stringency. The differences are still reflected in those tannaitic statements which incorporate earlier *halakhot*.

It seems that originally when the *ḥaverim* were few in number their regulations were more stringent, but as they came to be accepted by wider circles a more lenient tendency developed. There are explicit references to this effect. "At first they said that a *ḥaver* who becomes a tax collector is to be expelled. Later they said that as long as he is a tax collector, he is not trusted, but if he withdraws from it, he is to be trusted" (Tosef., Dem. 3:4). It would also appear that *halakhot* which are quoted as disputes between *tannaim* are in actual fact merely transmissions of *halakhot* from different times, as for instance: if they regret becoming *ḥaverim*, they can never again be accepted, so claims R. Meir; R. Judah says: If they regret it publicly they can be accepted, but if clandestinely (i.e., they disregarded the regulations in private, but behaved in public as *ḥaverim*) they are not to be accepted (because of their hypocrisy); R. Simeon and R. Joshua b. Korḥa say: They may be accepted in both cases (*ibid.* 2:9). Meir's view represents the remnant of the strict rules of a group of *ḥaverim*, which, by the way, have a parallel in the scroll of the Manual of Discipline 7:1: "And if he cursed . . . then he shall be set apart and never again return."

The fact that most of the *halakhot* of the *ḥaverim* were taught during the era of Usha does not point to the time they came into existence but to the fact that at that time the regulations were renewed with the purpose of making *halakhot*, which at one time were of concern to small groups of *ḥaverim*, into the *halakhot* of the community as a whole. Meir took a stringent view while his colleagues favored a more lenient one. The renewal of these *halakhot* after the Bar Kokhba revolt can be ascribed to the general tendency towards asceticism then prevailing. However, it seems that, in practice, these stringencies were confined to scholars and their disciples, so that in the time of the *amoraim* "*ḥaver*" became a synonym for a scholar, so that it was said "The *ḥaverim* are none other than the scholars" (BB 75a; cf. the expression "*ḥaverim* of Torah" TJ, Ber. 1:1, 2d; Tanḥ., Niẓẓavim, 4; Lieberman in: *Tarbiz*, 2 (1930/31), 106), and it seems that in Babylon the Palestinian *amoraim* were called "*ḥavurah*" ("group of *ḥaverim*"; Shab. 111b; "the lion of the *ḥavurah*"; Pes. 64a).

The Post-Talmudic Period. In the academies of Babylon during the geonic period the three scholars sitting in the first row after the seven heads of the *kallah called *allufim ("chiefs") were known as *ḥaverim*. At the close of the geonic period this title was also bestowed upon important scholars outside the academy, such as Jacob b. Nissim and Saadiah b. Ephraim of Kairouan. In the academies of Ereẓ Israel, an ordained scholar was called "*ḥaver* of the Great Sanhedrin," and the 70 members of the academy were called collectively "*ḥavurta kadishta*" ("holy association"). The five *ḥaverim* after the *gaon* and the head of the academy were referred to by number, "third of the *ḥavurah*," "fourth of the *ḥavurah*," etc. A candidate for the *ḥavurah* was called *me'uttad la-ḥavurah* ("destined for the *ḥavurah*"). The designation was also widened figuratively into "the most eminent *ḥaver* of the *ḥavurah*," "the splendor of the *ḥaverim*," "the glory of the *ḥaverim*," etc. In the 11th century the title *ḥaver* was added to the names of the *dayyanim* heading the communities of Ereẓ Israel, Syria, and Egypt, who were apparently ordained by the yeshivah of Ereẓ Israel. The title was also current in the academy of Fostat (a letter of 1441 mentions "our teacher and master R. Pethahiah Kohen, the *ḥaver* of the Great Sanhedrin"). In Arabic-speaking countries the term "*ḥaver*" became a synonym for an educated man and a scholar and found its way into the Arabic language. The Jewish scholar in Judah Halevi's *Kuzari* is called in the Arabic original "Al-Ḥibr." In France, Italy, and Germany, it was used as a designation for young scholars, *benei ḥavurah* (*Or Zaru'a*, pt. 2, nos. 91 and 329; see Urbach, in: *Tarbiz* 10 (1938/39) 32 n.17). Only in the 14th century when the appointment of a rabbi in Germany depended upon ordination and the granting of the title *morenu*, did the title *ḥaver* become an indication of official recognition of exceptional merit in Torah learning. Its attainment was bound up with the fulfillment of certain conditions which varied from country to country and from one period to another. In the *takkanot* of the communities and regional councils of Poland, Lithuania, and Moravia, the conditions of the right to bear this title, together with a preferred status in the community, concessions in taxation, and other privileges, were laid down. The additional privileges granted to the bearers of the title brought the communal leaders to lay down the conditions for attaining the titles, even though they were granted by rabbis. The decline of the institutions for Torah study at the end of the 17th century in Poland and Lithuania brought with it also a modification of the requirements for the title of *ḥaver*, and it tended to become a mere title of respect.

Bibliography: A. Buechler, *Der galilaeische ʿAm-ha ʾAreṣ des zweiten Jahrhunderts* (1906); J. Lévy, *La légende de Pythagore de Grèce en Palestine* (1927), 236–63; Allon, in: *Tarbiz*, 9 (1937/38), 1–10, 179–95 (=Alon, Meḥkarim, 1 (1957), 148–76); Geiger, Mikra, 80–87; Lieberman, in: JBL, 71 (1952), 199–206; idem, *Tosefta ki-Feshutah*, 1 (1955), 209–33; Ch. Rabin, *Qumran Studies* (1957); Urbach, in: *Sefer Yovel le-Y. Baer* (1960), 68; Neusner, in: HTR, 53 (1960), 125–42; Zunz, Lit Poesie, 284f.; S. Poznański, *Inyanim Shonim ha-Noge'im li-Tekufat ha-Ge'onim* (1909), 46, 59, 62; idem, *Babylonische Geonim im nachgaonaeischen Zeitalter* (1914), 103 n. 1; Mann, Egypt, 1 (1920), 54, 182, 264, 272, 277f.; 2 (1922), 348; Assaf, Geonim, 99; J. Katz, *Masoret u-Mashber* (1958), 227f., 267. [EH]

ḤAVER IR or **Ḥever Ir** (Heb. חֲבֵר עִיר; חֶבֶר עִיר), a phrase whose exact vocalization and therefore meaning is uncertain. If the reading is *ḥaver ir* (lit. "an associate of the city"), it refers to an individual; if it is *ḥever ir* (lit. "a town association") the reference is to a specific association or organization. The latter reading could also imply a congregation or the religious quorum (*minyan*) required for public worship. The Mishnah (Ber. 4:7) records a difference of opinion as to whether the individual may himself recite the *Musaf* prayers or whether they may only be said publicly by the *ḥever ir*. In this context the phrase seems to mean a *minyan*. A similar conclusion is reached from the discussion concerning the differences between the order of the sounding of the *shofar* during private worship and public *ḥever ir* (RH 34b).

The rules regarding deportment at a funeral and in a house of mourning seem to indicate that the phrase refers to a specific communal fraternal society. The *ḥever ir* must participate in a man's funeral but not a woman's (Sem. 11:2). Neither was the *ḥever ir* obligated to extend condolences on the day that people gather the bones of relatives for reburial in ossuaries (Sem. 12:4). When the *ḥever ir* was present at the house of mourning, visitors were permitted to bring less costly food, since there were then many people to be fed (Ḥul. 94a; Sem. 14:13). In Jerusalem, there originally were *ḥavurot* ("associations") for participating in joyful events such as marriage and circumcision and in gathering the remains of the dead and comforting mourners (Tosef. Meg. 4 (3):15; Sem. 12:5). It may be that these *ḥavurot* were the precursors of the *ḥever ir*, or that they functioned together with it. They differed in that the *ḥavurot* were voluntary organizations whereas the *ḥever ir* was officially appointed by the townspeople as their representatives in performing these meritorious deeds.

Nevertheless, there are also instances where *ḥaver ir* seems to be the correct reading. After transient visitors to a town are assessed for charity, they may demand reimbursement for distribution to the poor in their own communities before their departure. However, when a *ḥaver ir* is in charge of the communal charity, no refund is granted and the *ḥever ir* uses it at his discretion (Meg. 25a–b, Rashi ad loc.). Likewise, the poor man's tithe could be given to the *ḥaver ir* who used it at his discretion (Tosef., Pe'ah 4:16). A kohen who had a disqualifying blemish was not permitted to utter the Priestly Benediction publicly, since the people would be distracted by it. If he is also a *ḥaver ir*, however, he may recite the benediction, since he is so well known that they will pay no attention to his disability (Tosef., Meg. 4 (3):29).

Bibliography: Geiger, Mikra; T. Horowitz, in: *Festschrift zum Geburstage Jacob Guttmanns* (1915), 125–42; idem, in: JJLG, 17 (1926), 241–314; S. Krauss, *ibid.*, 125–42; S. Ginsburg, *Perushim ve-Ḥiddushim ba-Yerushalmi*, 3 (1941), 410–32; S. Lieberman, *Tosefta ki-Feshuta*, 1 (1955), 190. [H.Fr.]

HAVILAH (Heb. חֲוִילָה), name mentioned five times in the Bible, both as a personal and place name. The name Havilah was applied to the territory watered by the Pishon River (Gen. 2:11), which was noted for choice gold, bdellium, and lapis lazuli (Gen. 2:12). Josephus and most Church Fathers identified the land of Havilah with the Ganges Valley. While the proper identification is still unknown, there are various theories concerning its location. The association of the land of Havilah with the products mentioned above supports Y. M. Grintz's identification of Havilah with Aualis, an Abyssinian district mentioned in Greek and Latin sources. This Havilah, or Aualis, is perhaps the Meluḫḫa referred to in cuneiform records and identified as the Egypt of the period of the Cushite dynasty; however, this latter point is especially questionable in relation to Havilah. Friedrich Delitzsch located the land of Havilah in the Syrian Desert, west and south of the Euphrates. P. Haupt, who regarded the Pishon as the belt of water formed by the Kerkha, Persian Gulf, and Red Sea, identified Havilah with Arabia. In E. A. Speiser's view, the identification of the whole geographic background revolves around the proper location of the biblical Cush, which is identified either as an African kingdom (Ethiopia) or as the Mesopotamian kingdom of the Kassites (Akk. Kaššû). Speiser prefers the latter identification. Thus the background of Havilah remains that of the Garden of *Eden in Babylonia (Persian Gulf). According to Cassuto, the common element in all five references to Havilah is the ethnic ties between the various peoples located on either bank of the Red Sea. The Bible, however, distinguishes the Havilah that serves as one of the boundaries of Ishmaelite territory from all other places named Havilah, with the qualifying phrase "by Shur, which is close to Egypt" (Gen. 25:18). It was in the area between this Havilah and Shur that Saul defeated the Amalekites and captured Agag, their king (I Sam. 15:7). The personal name Havilah appears in the Table of Nations (Gen. 10:7=I Chron. 1:9) and in Abrahamic genealogies (Gen. 10:29=I Chron. 1:23). In the former, Havilah is one of the five sons of *Cush the son of Ham. In the latter, Havilah is the sixth generation in lineal descent from Shem. The latter Havilah, the son of Joktan, apparently stands for a locality in South Arabia, as do Hadoram (Gen. 10:27), Sheba (Gen. 10:28), and Ophir (Gen. 10:29).

See also *Dedan.

Bibliography: F. Delitzsch, *Wo lag das Paradies?* (1881), 301; W. F. Albright, in: JAOS, 42 (1922), 317ff.; idem, in: AJSLL, 39 (1922), 15ff.; J. A. Knudtzon, *Die El-Amarna Tafeln* (1915); F. Hommel, *Grundriss der Geographie und Geschichte des alten Orients* (1926), 272 n. 1, 556 n. 4, 570; D. D. Luckenbill, *Ancient Records of Assyria and Babylonia*, 1 (1925), 170; J. Skinner, *Genesis* (ICC, 1930), 62–66; S. A. Montgomery, *Arabia and the Bible* (1939), 39; E. A. Speiser, *Oriental and Biblical Studies* (1967), 23–34; Y. M. Grintz, *Moẓa'ei Dorot* (1969), 35–50. [M.I.G.]

ḤAVIV-LUBMAN, AVRAHAM DOV (1864–1951), pioneer of Jewish settlement in Ereẓ Israel. Born on a Jewish agricultural settlement, Graitzevo, near Mogilev, Ḥaviv-Lubman joined the Ḥovevei Zion movement and, in 1885, moved to Ereẓ Israel. He went to live in Petaḥ Tikvah with his uncle, Mordekhai Lubman, who worked as a land surveyor for Baron Edmond de *Rothschild. He disliked the settlement's traditional way of life and moved to Rishon le-Zion, where he struggled together with others against the baron's paternalistic management of the new agricultural settlement. He was a founder of the Aguddat ha-Koremim ("The Vintners' Association"), which took over the supervision of the baron's wine cellars. For 16 years he was at intervals head of the local council of Rishon le-Zion. He wrote memoirs of his childhood and the early days of settlement in Ereẓ Israel entitled *Mi-Sippurei ha-Rishonim le-Ẓiyyon* (1934) and *Benei Dori* (1946), as well as a monograph on Rishon le-Zion (1929).

Bibliography: J. Ḥurgin, *Dov Ḥaviv-Lubman* (Heb., 1942); D. A. Yanovsky, in: *Mi-Sippurei ha-Rishonim le-Ẓiyyon* (1934), 3–8; D. Idelovitch, *Rishon le-Ẓiyyon* (1941), 419–21. [Y.S.]

HAVRE, LE, major port, N. France. From about the beginning of the 18th century, Jews, especially from *Bordeaux and its environs, wished to settle in Le Havre. In 1714, *Louis XIV ordered the town to expel all foreign Jews except "those who call themselves 'Portuguese.'" Around 1725, however, two Jewish families of German origin, the Hombergs (who were converted after a while) and the Lallemends, settled in Le Havre and obtained letters of naturalization. In 1776 the town once more refused several Jews permission to reside there in spite of their "royal passports" (actually valid for Paris). An organized community was founded in the mid-19th century. A new community, reconstituted after World War II, had a population of about 1,000 in 1969 and possessed a synagogue and community center.

Bibliography: A.-E. Borely, *Histoire de la ville du Havre . . .*, 3 (1881), 441ff. [B.Bl.]

HAVVOTH-JAIR (Heb. חַוֹּת יָאִיר), an area in northern *Gilead (Num. 32:41; I Kings 4:13; I Chron. 2:22), also ascribed to the *Bashan and to the *Argob district, that was part of the kingdom of *Og of Bashan (Deut. 3:14; Josh. 13:30). According to A. Bergman (Biran), the city of *Ham was originally the center of the region. After Og's defeat at *Edrei, the region was occupied by *Jair, son of Manasseh, and named after him (Num. 32:41). A nomadic population called Ya'uri, Yari, or Yaḥiri, is known from Assyrian documents to have been in the area of the Euphrates beginning with the 13th century B.C.E., and some scholars assume that groups of these nomads reached Gilead and were gradually incorporated into the Israelite tribes. The meaning of *havvoth* is apparently "villages," i.e., groups of tent camps of nomads or seminomads surrounded by loose stone walls (in the *Nuzi documents, the word *khawu* designates a stone wall around a field). The half-tribe of Manasseh, cattle breeders who had settled in Transjordan, probably had many such camps and moved with their herds from one to another in search of pasture (Num. 32). According to Judges 10:3–5, Havvoth-Jair was named for *Jair, the Gileadite, who judged Israel for 22 years and was buried at Kamon (modern Qamm) in Gilead. According to I Chronicles 2:22, however, it may have received its name from Jair, son of Segub, of the tribe of Judah. The villages of Jair are again mentioned in Solomon's sixth administrative district under the son of Geber from Ramoth-Gilead; the villages were joined to Argob in Bashan (I Kings 4:13). The area was later lost to Aram and annexed by Geshur (I Chron. 2:23). *Jeroboam II seems to have retaken it for a short time (I Chron. 5:11–17), but it was finally conquered and depopulated by *Tiglath-Pileser III (I Chron. 5:26).

Bibliography: G. A. Smith, *Historical Geography of the Holy Land* (1896[4]), 551–2; Abel, Geog, 2 (1938), 71–80; Bergman, in: JPOS, 16 (1936), 235–7; EM, s.v. [M.A.-Y.]

HAWAII, the 50th state of the United States; admitted in August 1959. Jewish beginnings in Hawaii are shrouded in myth. Ebenezer Townsend, Jr., a sailor on the whaling ship *Neptune,* wrote in the ship's log on Aug. 19, 1798, that the king came aboard ship and brought "a Jew cook with him." This may or may not be true, but it is the first mention of Jews in connection with Hawaii.

A Torah scroll and *yad* ("pointer") owned by the royal family of Hawaii show a connection between it and the early Jewish community. How the scroll and *yad* came into the possession of King David Kalakaua is not clear. The *Daily Pacific Commercial Advertiser* of Dec. 24, 1888, states that Queen Liliuokalani, Kalakaua's successor, had the scroll draped around the inside of the tent at Her Majesty's bazaar. The scroll, which has disappeared, was borrowed from the descendants of the royal family for use by the Jewish community on holidays as late as 1930. The *yad* is now in the possession of the only synagogue in the state, Temple Emanuel, a Reform congregation.

It is believed that Jewish traders from England and Germany first went to Hawaii in the 1840s. A few American Jews went from California at the end of the 19th century, but there was no organized Jewish community until the founding of the Hebrew Benevolent Society in 1901. The same year marked the consecration of a Jewish cemetery at Pearl City Junction. In 1922 the National Jewish Welfare Board (JWB) established the Aloha Center for Jewish military personnel. In 1938 the Honolulu Jewish community was established. Temple Emanuel was organized in 1951. The temple has a membership of 175 families.

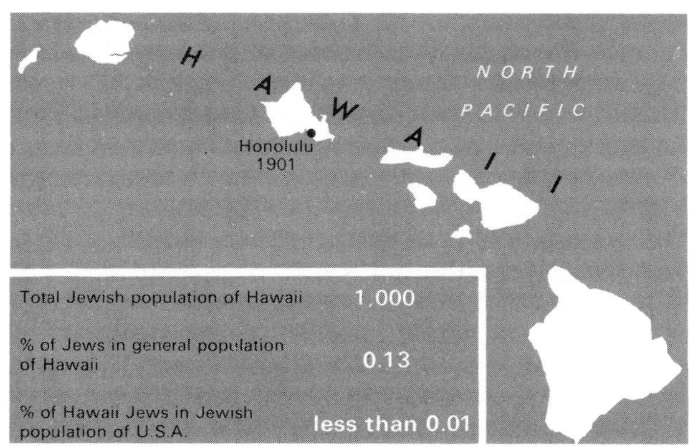

Jewish population of Hawaii.

The total Jewish population is given as 1,000, but an article in the Honolulu *Star Bulletin* of Jan. 25, 1967, estimates that the state may have as many as 4,000 Jews on both Oahu and the other islands, and that most of these Jews are unaffiliated with any aspect of Jewish life. The population is both youthful and largely transient. Most of the Jews have arrived since World War II; some were stationed there during the war, and after the war returned with their families. A few have been there for 40 years or more. Very few Jews are in business; the majority are in the professions—medicine, law, university teaching, government services, both federal and state, etc. A men's club and sisterhood are affiliated with the temple. A B'nai B'rith Lodge and a Hadassah Chapter have been organized. Temple services are held regularly. There is no real feeling of community as it is known in cities on the mainland of the United States; Jews live everywhere, are active in all aspects of Hawaiian life, and feel very much at ease in Hawaii's multiracial society. [G.C.S.]

HAWK, bird of prey. Two genera of hawk are found in Israel, the *Accipiter* and the *Falco,* these being referred to respectively in the Bible as *neẓ* (AV, JPS = hawk) and *taḥmas* (AV, JPS = "nighthawk"), mentioned among the unclean birds that are prohibited as food (Lev. 11:16; Deut. 14:15). The *neẓ* is generally identified with the sparrow hawk *(Accipiter nisus),* which nests on trees in various places in Israel, pounces in flight on its victims, particularly small birds, and is recognizable by its bright abdomen streaked with dark lateral stripes. It winters in Israel and some migrate to southern lands, as mentioned in Job (39:26). The Pentateuch refers to "the *neẓ* after its kinds." In Israel there are two other transmigratory species that belong to this genus. But the expression *neẓ* may also include other genera of birds of prey. Thus, for example, the *aggadah* says that Israel is like a dove which the *neẓ* seeks to devour (Song R. 2:14, no. 2), the reference here being to a bird of prey larger than the hawk, such as the *buzzard which preys upon doves (the *Accipiter* hunts only small birds: see Ḥul. 3:1) or the saker falcon *(Falco cherrug)* which in certain countries is trained to pursue birds and animals. Of the genus *Falco* there are several species in Israel, the most common being the non-migratory kestrel *(Falco tinnunculus)* which preys upon birds and field mice and is apparently the biblical *taḥmas,* a word meaning "robber, bandit."

Bibliography: E. Smolly, *Ẓipporim be-Yisrael* (1959[2]), 85; R. Meinertzhagen, *Birds of Arabia* (1954), 366ff.; J. Feliks, *Animal World of the Bible* (1962), 64f. [J.F.]

°**HAY, JOHN MILTON** (1838–1905), U.S. statesman who supported Rumanian and Russian Jewish rights. Hay was a secretary of state under presidents William McKinley and Theodore Roosevelt from 1898 to 1905. He was involved in U.S. diplomatic representations during this period on behalf of Rumanian and Russian Jews. In 1902, at the urging of American Jewish leaders including Oscar S. Straus and Jacob H. Schiff, Hay addressed a note to the signatories of the Berlin Treaty of 1878 protesting Rumania's violation of that treaty by its restrictions on Jews. Following the *Kishinev pogrom of 1903, again after Jewish pressure and with an eye to domestic political considerations, Hay publicized a protest petition drawn up by B'nai B'rith.

Bibliography: T. Denett, *John Hay: From Poetry to Politics* (1933), 395–400; N. W. Cohen, *Dual Heritage* (1969), 83–131.
[Mo.Ro.]

ḤAYDĀN, town in N. Yemen. The Jews who were concentrated in the towns of Ḥaydān, Sada, and the surrounding villages were known as Ḥayā'idna. A document from 1670, dealing with the division of a house in Sanʿa among three brothers of the Ḥaydānī family, indicates that they were from Ḥaydān. The Ḥayāʾidna are distinguishable from Yemenite Jews by their tall stature and developed physique. They were not subject to persecutions and harsh decrees as were the other Yemenite Jews. The restriction on the height of Jewish houses, which had to be lower than Muslim buildings, was not strictly enforced in the Ḥaydān area. Because they were few in number and far removed from the ruling center and their Jewish brethren, they enjoyed a certain measure of freedom and even wore swords and guns like the Muslims. Many of them were expert in the art of repairing the weapons of the Arabs, which was practically unknown to the Jews of other areas. They were also silversmiths. The Jewish population of Ḥaydān is mentioned in the account of the traveler R. Baruch b. Samuel of Pinsk, who visited Ḥaydān in 1833. The writer and businessman A. *Tabib, who was born in Ḥaydān, wrote two pamphlets which include a great deal of important information on the ethnology of the Jews of northern Yemen, including the towns of Ḥaydān and Sada. He also recounts a number of legends and folk tales from these places. One person from the community of Ḥaydān states that the Jews are descended from the first Exile (of the seven Exiles) from Ereẓ Israel; arriving there, they remained for 25 generations until moving on to Sanʿa. His historical lists include the important information that in 1906, a short time after the rise of the imām Yaḥya (1904), 250 people died in Ḥaydān, most of them from hunger.

Tabib also records interesting recollections about the *aliyah* of the Jews of Ḥaydān to Palestine. These Jews began to immigrate to Palestine in 1907. They settled in Reḥovot and Rishon le-Zion and engaged in agriculture, playing a leading role in the promotion of Jewish labor. Their countrymen, who arrived on the "magic carpet" in 1949, settled in nearby Kiryat Ekron and Kefar Gevirol ha-Nagid (near Reḥovot).

Bibliography: A. Tabib, *Golat Teiman* (1931); idem, *Shavei Teiman* (1932); E. Brauer, *Ethnologie der jemenitischen Juden* (1934), index; S. Jawnieli, *Massa le-Teiman* (1952); A. Koreaḥ, *Sa'arat Teiman* (1954), 146–8.
[Y.R./H.Z.H.]

HAYDEN, MELISSA (1928–), U.S. ballerina. Her dramatic power and virtuoso technique marked her as one of the outstanding dancers in America. Born Mildred Herman in Toronto, Canada, she trained early to be a dancer and at 17 went to New York, where she attended the School of American Ballet. After dancing in the ballet corps of Radio City Music Hall, she joined Ballet Theater in 1945, became a soloist, and joined the New York City Ballet in 1950. During her first season there she danced leading roles in *Illuminations, The Duel,* and *Age of Anxiety.* She also created roles in George Balanchine's *Agon, Firebird, Midsummer Night's Dream,* and other works of the repertoire. In 1963, she danced *Swan Lake* and *Coppélia* with the National Ballet of Canada. In her book *Melissa Hayden—Offstage and On* (1963) she explained her approach to dancing for the benefit of young people.
[M.B.S.]

HAYES, ISAAC ISRAEL (1832–1881), U.S. explorer. Born in Chester, Philadelphia, Hayes volunteered in 1853 as ship's surgeon on Kane's expedition to the North Pole in search of Sir John Franklin. His ship was icebound in Kane's Basin for two years, during which time Hayes took part in many sledge expeditions, on one of which he discovered and explored Grinnell Land. With nine of the ship's crew he also attempted to reach Opernavik (Greenland), and get help for the stranded ship (1854). Although he was forced to return to the ship, the following summer the whole crew made use of the route he had taken to make their escape. In 1860 Hayes sailed from Boston in command of the schooner *United States* in an attempt to discover the open water which he maintained surrounded the North Pole. After wintering in Kane's Basin, he continued north by sledge. He finally observed what he thought was the open polar sea but which in fact was the Kennedy Channel, which opens into the Arctic via the Mall Basin. He returned to Boston in 1861. He made his last trip to the Arctic in 1869, when he was accompanied by the American artist, William Bradford. Later in life he became a member of the New York Assembly.

The careful notes made by Hayes on his expeditions were a valuable contribution to natural history, meteorology, glaciology, and hydrology, and were included in the annals of the exploration society. He also took the first photographs of the Arctic. His writings include: *An Arctic Boat Journey* (1860); *Physical Observations in the Arctic Seas 1860 and 1861* (1867); *The Open Polar Sea* (1867), *Cast Away in the Cold* (1868); *The Land of Desolation* (1871).

Bibliography: E. K. Kane, *Arctic Explorations: The Second Grinell Expedition* (1856); G. W. Cullum, in: *Journal of the American Geographic Society,* 12 (1881), 110–24.
[ED.]

HAYES, SAUL (1906–), Canadian lawyer and community executive. Hayes, who was born in Montreal, became executive director of the United Jewish Relief Agencies of Canada in 1940, and of the Canadian Jewish Congress in 1942. He was appointed executive vice-president of the latter in 1959. Hayes participated in the San Francisco Conference on International Security in 1945. As executive head of the Canadian Jewish Congress, Hayes drafted numerous briefs, presented memoranda on behalf of Canada's Jewry, and was deeply involved in numerous missions affecting the status of Jews as Canadian and world citizens.
[B.G.K.]

HAYNT (הײַנט), leading Yiddish daily in Warsaw before World War II. It was founded in 1908 by the Hebrew-Yiddish journalist Samuel Jacob Jackan and two Zionists, the brothers Noah and Nehemiah *Finkelstein, as a continuation of the daily *Yidishes Tagblat,* which they had published from 1906. Its first issue appeared on Jan. 22, 1908, with Jackan as editor and a staff that included David *Frischman, Hillel *Zeitlin, Hirsch David *Nomberg, and Moshe Bunem *Justman ("B. Yeushzon"). *Haynt* supported Zionist ideology and in 1909 reached the unprecedented circulation of 70,000. In 1910 another Yiddish daily *Der Moment* was founded in Warsaw, edited by Ẓevi *Prylucki, which attracted some members of *Haynt*'s staff. In the ensuing continuous competition *Haynt* maintained its lead. It attracted readers by publishing stimulating articles, and thrilling novels in serial form, and also offering prizes (among them a trip to Ereẓ Israel). By 1914 its circulation had risen to more than 100,000. Its staff at that time included Sholem *Asch, Menahem *Boraisha, Abraham *Goldberg, Shemarya *Gorelik, Z. Wendroff, A. L. Jacobowitz, J. A. Leizerowicz, H. D. Nomberg, David Frischmann, Isaac Leib *Peretz, and *Shalom Aleichem. *Haynt* took a firm Jewish national stand in the elections to the fourth *Duma in 1912. It also fought the assimilationists in Warsaw in the Jewish communal elections of that year. In 1915, *Haynt* was closed down by the Russian authorities but reopened a few months later, when Warsaw was captured by the Germans. In independent Poland *Haynt* was deprived of many readers in the Ukraine and other regions not included in Poland's boundaries. It reached an agreement with the daily *Dos Yidishe Folk,* published from 1919 by the Zionist Organization of

Poland, becoming an organ of the Zionist Organization and replacing Jackan by Yehoshua *Gottlieb as editor. From 1921 Abraham Goldberg was the editor, but the paper's basic policy was determined by Yiẓḥak *Gruenbaum. In 1932 *Haynt* passed to the ownership of a cooperative composed of members of the editorial board and employees. After Goldberg's death in 1933, Aaron Einhorn and Moshe Indelmann edited the paper until its last issue on Sept. 22, 1939, on the eve of the German

№ 151

Major HAJNT

הײַנט

POLSKI BANK HANDLOWO-PRZEMYSŁOWY

Spółka Akcyjna w Krakowie

ODDZIAŁ WARSZAWSKI

Wierzbowa 9 (Plac Teatralny)

300,000,000

100,000,000

MODES

BALTIC AMERICA LINE

106

PRZENDZA

Stow. Wzajem. Pomocy Ekspedytorów

Front page of the Warsaw Yiddish daily, *Haynt*, July 2, 1922. Jerusalem, J.N.U.L.
J.N.U.L.

occupation of Warsaw. Leading contributors of *Haynt* included Vladimir *Jabotinsky (until 1933), B. Singer, I. J. Singer, Osias *Thon, Gershon Levin, Jacob *Lestschinsky, Z. *Segalowitch, Nahum *Sokolow, Ephraim *Kaganowsky, Ezriel *Carlebach, Z. *Shneour, and M. *Kipnis. It also issued periodicals in Yiddish and Polish, as well as two newspapers in Hebrew: the daily *Ha-Boker* (1909), edited by David Frischmann, and the weekly *Ba-Derekh* (1932–37).

Bibliography: *Haynt, 1908–1928, Yubiley Bukh* (1928); *Haynt, Yubiley Bukh 1908–1938* (1938); *Fun Noentn Over*, 2 (1956), 1–237.

[G.El.]

HA-YOM (Heb. הַיּוֹם, "the Day"), the first Hebrew daily newspaper. Published in St. Petersburg for 25 months, Feb. 12, 1886, to March 12, 1888, *Ha-Yom* was edited by Judah Leib *Kantor, who enjoyed the regular help of David *Frischmann and Judah Leib *Katzenelson. The Hebrew press had existed for 30 years when *Ha-Yom* appeared, and the Hebrew newspapermen of that time regarded the venture with skepticism and even derision. But Kantor's persistence overcame all obstacles and the paper appeared daily, in large format, with news gathered by telegrams received directly from the Russian telegraphic agency.

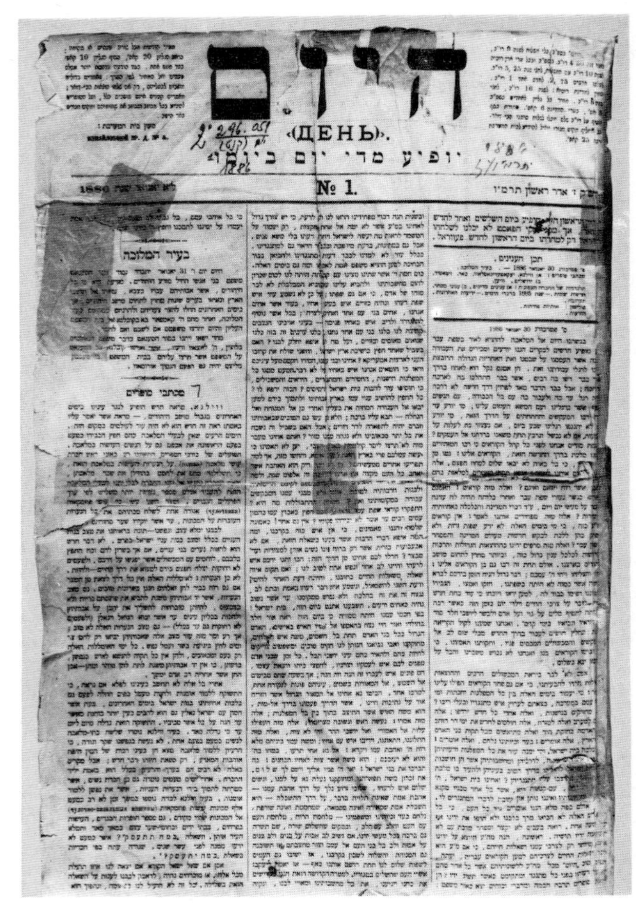

היום

«ДЕНЬ».

№ 1.

First issue of *Ha-Yom*, the first Hebrew daily newspaper. St. Petersburg, February 12 (Julian calendar: Jan. 31), 1886. Jerusalem,

Another innovation was *Ha-Yom's* simple and clear style, by means of which Kantor hoped to dislodge the stilted Hebrew still dominant in the press. The editor proved that a Hebrew paper could report on political and social events as efficiently as a paper in any other language and *Ha-Yom* actually became a European-style daily. The editorials and political articles were usually written by Kantor, while Frischmann regularly published feuilletons as well as the first of his famous literary letters, and Katzenelson contributed articles on science. Reporters from London, the U.S., and other Jewish centers contributed to the paper, which also printed substantial reports from Ereẓ Israel. However, the paper could not hold its ground owing to the rivalry with *Ha-Meliẓ* and *Ha-Ẓefirah*, which by the admission of its editors, Judah Leib *Gordon and Nahum *Sokolow respectively, reluctantly became dailies in order to compete with *Ha-Yom*. Another cause for its failure was its reserved and even cool attitude toward the Ḥibbat Zion movement. The paper proved, as Kantor said in his introduction to the first issue, that "the Hebrew language had the resources to discuss everyday life as it did in the old days."

Bibliography: N. Sokolow, *Ishim* (1958), 153–91; R. Malachi, in: *Ḥerut* (Dec. 31, 1965); Kressel, Leksikon, 2 (1967), 781; J. S. Geffen, in: AJHSQ, 51 (1961/62), 149–67.

[G.K.]

ḤAYON, NEHEMIAH ḤIYYA BEN MOSES (c. 1655–c. 1730), kabbalist with Shabbatean tendencies. Because of the bitter dispute which centered around Ḥayon, the information about his life is full of contradictions and must be sifted critically. His ancestors came from Sarajevo, Bosnia. From there, his father moved to Ereẓ Israel after spending several years in Egypt where, according to his own testimony,

Ḥayon was born. As a child, he was taken to Jerusalem, grew up in Shechem (Nablus) and in Jerusalem, and studied under Ḥayyim Abulafia. At the age of 18 he returned to Sarajevo with his father and married there. His enemies claimed that from that time on he was known for his adventures. He traveled widely throughout the Balkans and spent several years in Belgrade until its occupation by Austria in 1688. He may have joined his father as an emissary to Italy for the ransoming of captives from Belgrade. According to the testimony of Judah Brieli, Ḥayon was in Leghorn in 1691. Later he served for a short time in the rabbinate of Skoplje (Üsküb), Macedonia, at the recommendation of one of the great rabbis of Salonika.

He returned to Ereẓ Israel c. 1695 and lived for several years in Shechem (Nablus). After his first wife's death, Ḥayon married the daughter of one of the scholars of Safed. Ḥayon was well versed in exoteric and esoteric lore. From his youth, he was attracted to Kabbalah and he knew the Shabbatean groups intimately. His kabbalistic doctrine evades the issue of Shabbetai Ẓevi's messianic claims, but is based on principles common to Shabbeteanism. When Ḥayon received the pamphlet *Raza de-Meheimanuta* ("The Mystery of the True Faith"), attributed to Shabbetai Ẓevi by his sectarians, he claimed that he himself wrote it and that it was revealed to him by Elijah or by the angel *Metatron. Changing its name to *Meheimanuta de-Khula* he began to write a detailed commentary. In the meanwhile, he lived briefly in Rosetta, Egypt, and from that time he became known as one who engaged in practical Kabbalah. When he returned to Jerusalem (c. 1702–05), hostility developed between him and R. Abraham Yiẓḥaki who for several years leveled many accusations against Ḥayon (but never directly accused him of Shabbeteanism). Later, he returned to Safed and from there he went to Smyrna, apparently intending to publish his long commentary to *Meheimanuta de-Khula* and to find supporters for a yeshivah, which he wished to establish in Jerusalem. On his return to Jerusalem, the rabbis began to harass him and he was forced to leave Ereẓ Israel. He went to Italy via Egypt (1710–11). According to the testimony of Joseph *Ergas, in Leghorn, Ḥayon disclosed to him his belief in Shabbetai Ẓevi. In 1711, in Venice, he published his small book *Raza de-Yiḥuda* on the meaning of the verse on the unity of God, *Shema Yisrael,* as an abridgment of his larger work to which he added, in the meantime, a second commentary. The rabbis of Venice gave approbations to this booklet without understanding its intent. The book did not arouse controversy. Later, Ḥayon moved to Prague where he was received with great honor in scholarly circles and gained approval for *Oz le-Elohim,* his main work, and *Divrei Neḥemyah,* a book of sermons. David Oppenheim approbated *Divrei Neḥemyah* and Ḥayon altered the approbation to include the kabbalistic *Oz le-Elohim* as well. R. Naphtali Cohen, who at first befriended Ḥayon, kept him at a distance after a rumor got about that connected him with the *Doenmeh in Salonika. Ḥayon traveled via Moravia and Silesia to Berlin where, in 1713, supported by the wealthy members of the community, he succeeded in publishing *Oz le-Elohim.* It was daring of Ḥayon to publish a text which in many manuscripts was circulated then as a work of Shabbetai Ẓevi. With great acumen, he tried to prove in his two commentaries that this doctrine was firmly based in the classical texts of the Kabbalah. In some passages, he criticized the works of *Nathan of Gaza and Abraham Miguel *Cardozo, in spite of his doctrine being basically close to Cardozo's. Ḥayon's innovations were a new formulation of the principles of the beginning of Emanation and the difference between the First Cause which he calls "*Nishmata de-Kol Ḥayyei*" ("Soul of All Living Beings") and the *Ein-Sof* ("The Infinite Being"). What the kabbalists call *Ein-Sof* is in his opinion only the extension of the Essence (of God) or the *Shoresh ha-Ne'lam* ("the Hidden Root," i.e., God), but paradoxically enough this Essence is finite and it possesses a definite structure, **Shi'ur Komah* ("Measure of the Body of God"). Ḥayon thought that Isaac Luria's doctrine of **Ẓimẓum* ("withdrawal") must be understood literally and not allegorically. His doctrine of the three superior *parẓufim* ("aspects of God"), *attika kaddisha, malka kaddisha,* and *Shekhinah,* differs from the theories of other Shabbateans only in details and in terminology. His book may by defined as a strange mixture of basically Shabbatean theology and exegetical acumen by which he read the new theses into the *Zohar and the Lurianic writings. He prefaced his book with a long essay in which he argued, apparently hinting at the unorthodox sources of his thought, that it is lawful to learn Kabbalah from everyone, not only from those who conform to traditional Orthodox criteria. *Divrei Neḥemyah* contained a long sermon in which it was possible to see an indirect defense of the apostasy of the Doenmeh sect in Salonika, but which could also be interpreted as criticism of them. In June 1713 Ḥayon left Berlin for Amsterdam. Apparently he knew of the hidden Shabbatean tendency of Solomon *Ayllon, rabbi of the Sephardi congregation. Indeed, Ḥayon received the patronage of Ayllon, his *bet din,* and the *parnasim* of the community. However, a bitter and complex struggle developed between the supporters of Ḥayon and those of Ẓevi *Ashkenazi, the rabbi of the Ashkenazi community, and of Moses *Ḥagiz who knew of Ḥayon's early quarrels in Ereẓ Israel and recognized the Shabbatean "heresy" in his opinions, when they investigated his book. In this controversy, relevant factors (the true views of Ḥayon and his Shabbateanism) and personal factors (the arrogant behavior of Ẓevi Ashkenazi, personal antagonisms) are mingled. Essentially, the accusers of Ḥayon were right but from a formal and procedural point of view the Sephardi *bet din* was right. The quarrel aroused strong emotions, at first in Amsterdam, in the summer and the winter of 1713, and it swiftly spread to other countries. Naphtali Cohen apologized for his previous approval of Ḥayon and excommunicated him. So did Italian rabbis to whom both sides turned to for support. The leaders were Judah Brieli of Mantua and Samson Morpurgo of Ancona. Most of the participants in the controversy had not actually seen the books of Ḥayon and depended only on the letters from both sides. The major pamphlets against Ḥayon are: *Le-Einei Kol Yisrael* (the judicial decision of Ẓevi Ashkenazi and letters from him and from Naphtali Cohen; Amsterdam, 1713); *Edut le-Yisrael* (*ibid.,* 1714); works by Moses Ḥagiz including *Milḥamah la-Adonai ve-Ḥerev la-Adonai,* also including the letters of many Italian rabbis (Amsterdam, 1714); *Shever Poshe'im* (London, 1714); *Iggeret ha-Kena'ot* (Berlin, 1714); *Tokhaḥat Megullah ve-ha-Ẓad Naḥash* by Joseph Ergas (London, 1715); and *Esh Dat* by David Nieto (London, 1715). This book and several leaflets also appeared in Spanish. The *bet din* of the Sephardim published in Hebrew and in Spanish *Kosht Imrei Emet* (Amsterdam, 1713; in Spanish, *Manifesto*). Ḥayon answered his critics in several books and pamphlets in which he defended his views but denied that they contain any Shabbatean doctrine. They include *Ha-Ẓad Ẓevi Ashkenazi;* (Amsterdam, 1714); *Moda'a Rabba* (1714, including his biography); *Shalhevet Yah* (against Ergas), also including the pamphlets *Pitkah min Shemaya, Ketovet Ka'aka,* and *Iggeret Shevukin* (1714). His polemics against Ergas' *Ha-Ẓad Naḥash,* called *Naḥash Neḥoshet,* is found in Ḥayon's handwriting (Oxford, Ms. 1900). Because of the controversy he had aroused, Ḥayon did not succeed in publishing his second comprehensive work on Kabbalah, *Sefer Ta'azumot*. A complete manuscript of the work is preserved in the library of the *bet din*, formerly that of the *bet ha-midrash*, in London (62).

Ẓevi Ashkenazi and Moses Ḥagiz were forced to leave Amsterdam. However, the intervention of the rabbis of Smyrna and Constantinople, who excommunicated Ḥayon and condemned his works in 1714, decided the struggle against Ḥayon, whose supporters advised him to return to Turkey in order to obtain the annulment of the excommunication. Ḥayon returned and attempted to achieve this but he succeeded only partially. In his old age, he went back to Europe where in the pamphlet *Ha-Kolot Yeḥdalun* (1725) he published some documents in his favor. His journey was unsuccessful because Moses Ḥagiz again came out against him in the booklet *Leḥishat Saraf* (Hanau, 1726) where he threw suspicion on several of the documents, or on the circumstances under which they were signed. Most of the communities did not allow him access and even Ayllon refused to receive him in Amsterdam. Ḥayon wandered to North Africa and apparently died there before 1730. According to Ḥagiz, his son converted to Catholicism in order to take revenge on his father's persecutors and was active in Italy.

Bibliography: Graetz, Hist, 5 (1949), 215–31; D. Kahana (Kogan), *Toledot ha-Mekubbalim, Shabbeta'im, ve-ha-Ḥasidim* (1913), 123–7; Kauffmann, in: *Ha-Ḥoker*, 2 (1894), 11–15; Scholem, in: *Zion*, 3 (1929), 172–9; Sonne, in: *Kobez al jad*, 2 (1937), 157–96; Herling, in: *Amanah*, 1 (1939), 259–74; idem, in: KS, 15 (1939), 130–5; Kahana, in: *Sinai*, 21 (1947), 328–34; A. Freimann (ed.), *Inyanei Shabbetai Ẓevi* (1912), 117–38; Friedmann, in: *Sefunot*, 10 (1966) 489–618; Levi, in: RI, 8 (1911), 169–85; 9 (1912), 5–29. [G.Sch.]

HAYS, family established in the New World in the first quarter of the 18th century, when Michael Hays (d. 1740) emigrated from Holland to New York. Michael's sons Jacob (d. 1760), Solomon, Isaac (d. 1765), and Judah (1703–1764) and their descendants flourished in the American colonies. Jacob was active in building Congregation Shearith Israel in New York City in 1730. Jacob's sons Benjamin (d. 1816), Michael (1753–1799), and David (1732–1812) became farmers in Westchester County, and all actively supported the American cause during the Revolution, Benjamin by fighting in the army, Michael by permitting colonial troops to use his farm to store supplies. To keep the rebel army from utilizing the stores, the British army seized Michael's farm in 1776 and did not restore it until 1782. After the war Michael served in the New York State Constitutional Convention. The youngest brother, David, operated a store in Bedford in addition to his farm. He married into the *Etting family. While he was serving with the American army, Loyalists, who were attempting to keep supplies from reaching the colonial forces, burned his home, his store, and the rest of Bedford on the night of July 9, 1779. David's eldest son, Jacob (1772–1850), converted to Christianity and in 1802 was appointed high constable (chief of police) of the City of New York, a position he held until a year before his death.

See also Isaac *Hays.

Bibliography: Rosenbloom, Biogr Dict. [N.O.]

HAYS, ARTHUR GARFIELD (1881–1954), U.S. lawyer and civil liberties advocate. Hays, who was born in Rochester, New York, practiced law in New York for 20 years. In 1925 he abandoned his private practice to become general counsel of the American Civil Liberties Union. He represented clients without remuneration in numerous cases involving the violation of freedoms guaranteed by the Bill of Rights. Hays served as co-counsel with Clarence Darrow in 1925 in the celebrated Scopes anti-evolution case which became known as the "monkey trial." Although Scopes was convicted for violating a state law which prohibited the

Arthur G. Hays, U.S. civil liberties lawyer. Courtesy American Civil Liberties Union. Photo Blackstone Studios, New York.

teaching of any theory that denied divine creation, the trial compelled the State of Tennessee to abandon the enforcement of this law. Hays was involved in the defense of Sacco and Vanzetti, and the Scottsboro Negroes whose death sentence for alleged rape was reversed by the U.S. Supreme Court. He also defended Dmitrov and other Communists tried in Germany for the Reichstag fire, pleading through a German as the Nazis would not permit Hays, a Jew, to plead himself. After World War II, he helped the occupation forces to re-create democratic institutions in Germany. Hays was never prepared to confine his defense of liberty only to the causes for which he had sympathy. Thus, although he detested Nazism, he joined the attorney of Friends of New Germany in seeking an injuction against a police commissioner in New Jersey who had closed all halls to Nazi meetings (1937). He wrote several books, among them *Trial by Prejudice* (1933), *Democracy Works* (1939), and his autobiography, *City Lawyer* (1942). [A.Re.]

HAYS, DANIEL PEIXOTTO (1854–1923), U.S. lawyer. Hay who was born in Westchester County, New York, received his LL.B. from Columbia University Law School in 1875. A member of an old and prominent New York Jewish family, he was the grandson of Benjamin Etting Hays (1779–1858) and a descendant of Jacob Hays (see *Hays family), who went to New York Colony in the 1720s. Active in New York City and Westchester County politics for many years, Hays served as president of the Harlem Democratic Club, as delegate to several New York State Democratic conventions, and was appointed head of New York City's Municipal Civil Service Commission by Mayor Gilroy. Hays vigorously supported the presidential candidacy of Grover Cleveland in *City and Country*, a Nyack, New York, newspaper owned by him. Hays was also extremely active in Jewish communal affairs, serving on the executive committee of the Union of American Hebrew Congregations, as trustee and secretary of the Jewish Publication Society, and president of the Young Men's Hebrew Association. He was also a founder of the *American Hebrew*. His *Collected Poems* appeared in 1905. [Ab.K.]

HAYS, ISAAC (1796–1879), U.S. physician. Hays, a descendant of Michael Hays's son Isaac (see *Hays family), was born in Philadelphia. He graduated from the University of Pennsylvania (1816) and received an M.D. there (1820). An oculist, he was one of the pioneers in the study of astigmatism and color blindness, and he invented a scalpel for use in cataract surgery. Hays's contribution extended beyond his specialty. He was the editor of several important journals, one of the founding members of the American

Medical Association (1847), and wrote the code of medical ethics which has been adopted throughout the United States.

Bibliography: Rosenbloom, Biogr Dict, s.v. *Hays, Isaac*[3]. [N.O.]

ḤAYYAT, JUDAH BEN JACOB (c. 1450–c. 1510), kabbalist. Ḥayyat was born in Spain and studied Kabbalah under Samuel ibn Shraga. Around 1482 he addressed basic questions on Kabbalah to Joseph *Alcastil, who answered him at length. After the expulsion of the Jews from Spain in 1492 he suffered many hardships on sea voyages and in North Africa. In 1494 he reached Italy and for several years lived in Mantua where at the request of Joseph *Jabez he wrote in the early 16th century a detailed commentary on *Ma'arekhet ha-Elohut*, an early kabbalistic work that was widely circulated among contemporary kabbalists in Italy. The commentary, entitled *Minḥat Yehudah*, was published together with the *Ma'arekhet* in Ferrara in 1558 and in several later editions. It is considered one of the outstanding works of Kabbalah in the generation of the Spanish Expulsion. More than a commentary on the *Ma'arekhet* it is an independent, systematic work whose intention and major views differ greatly from those in the book which it supposedly intends to expound.

Ḥayyat was a radical representative of the Kabbalah of the *Zohar, in contrast to the Kabbalah of Abraham *Abulafia, which was accepted in Italy, and to the semi-philosophical Kabbalah of Isaac b. Abraham ibn *Latif, which Ḥayyat harshly criticized. He was one of the first to quote at length passages of the Zohar and the *Tikkunim* and based his kabbalistic theory on their sayings. He had reservations about philosophical commentaries on the Kabbalah which circulated in Italy. He also disputed against the *Iggeret Ḥamudot* of Elijah of *Genazzano which identified the **Ein Sof* ("the Infinite") with the first *Sefirah* ("emanation"). Concerning the essence of the *Sefirot*, Ḥayyat mainly concurred with the view of Menahem *Recanati. The process of creation is explained, according to him, by the double movement of expansion and contraction of the divine will. Creation is nothing but a realization into actuality through the divine will of the potential hidden unity of the *Ein-Sof*. Ḥayyat had a recognizable influence on all 16th–17th century Kabbalah. Even those who falsely wrote under names of earlier authors used his works at length. His supercommentary on Recanati's commentary to the Pentateuch has not been preserved.

Bibliography: G. Scholem, in: *Tarbiz*, 24 (1954/55), 174–206; E. Gottlieb, in: *Studies in Mysticism and Religion Presented to G. Scholem* (1968), 63–86 (Heb. section). [G.Sch.]

ḤAYYIM ABRAHAM RAPHAEL BEN ASHER (d. 1772), Jerusalem rabbi and kabbalist. Ḥayyim was a member of the *bet din* of Raphael *Meyuḥas, and later *av bet din* in Jerusalem. Toward the end of his life, in 1771, he was appointed *rishon le-Zion* (Sephardi chief rabbi). In 1731 (or 1734) he published in Constantinople the *Sha'arei Kedushah* of Ḥayyim *Vital. Between the years 1734 and 1765 he traveled as an emissary of Jerusalem, seeking contributions in Constantinople, Italy, France, and Egypt. Raphael was a signatory of the *Shetar Hitkasherut* ("articles of association") of the society of kabbalists. Head of the yeshivah Yefa'er Anavim in Jerusalem, established by him when he was on a mission in Jerusalem in 1791, he cosigned the *takkanah* forbidding bachelors between the ages of 20 and 60 from residing in Jerusalem. He gave approbations to many works, among them the *Ḥut ha-Meshullash* of Judah Diwan, and the *Shulḥan Gavoha* of Joseph Molkho. He died during a famine and plague that raged in Jerusalem.

Bibliography: Frumkin-Rivlin, 3 (1929), 98f.; Yaari, Sheluḥei, 289–91; Rosanes, Togarmah, 5 (1938), 240, 243; Katsh, in: *Sefunot*, 9 (1964), 323–35. [S.Mar.]

ḤAYYIM BEN ABRAHAM HA-KOHEN (c. 1585–1655), kabbalist, born in Aleppo. His ancestors went to Ereẓ Israel after the expulsion from Spain (1492) and later settled in Aleppo. Ḥayyim was the disciple of Ḥayyim *Vital during his last years in Damascus and he left an interesting story about his growing attachment to the study of Kabbalah under his teacher. Later, he was one of the rabbis of Aleppo. Ḥayyim wrote numerous works in the course of a 20-year period, which are listed in the introduction to his book *Torat Ḥakham*. During a long sea voyage which he undertook in order to bring these manuscripts to print, the ship was attacked by pirates off Malta. He saved himself by jumping into the sea near the coast, but all his manuscripts were lost. He states that he decided to write them again. Around 1650 he set out again for Constantinople where he stayed two to three years. The first part of his book *Mekor Ḥayyim*, a detailed kabbalistic commentary on the rules of the Shulḥan Arukh was published here. At the end of 1652 he was in Smyrna; later he went to Venice and returned through Zante to Aleppo. Through the mediation of Samuel *Aboab of Verona he had published in Venice the large volume of sermons, *Torat Ḥakham* (1654), with the kabbalist Moses *Zacuto acting as proofreader. Another part of *Mekor Ḥayyim*, called *Tur Bareket*, was published by the brothers Raphael and Abraham b. Danan in Amsterdam in 1654. In the same year Ḥayyim set out again

טור ברקת
ממקור חיים יונקת ·
חיים הכהן
חיים קלבריז
יצחק לוריא
בבית
עמנואל בנבנשתי
נדפס
באמשטרדם
שנת

Title page of *Tur Bareket*, a kabbalistic commentary on the laws of festivals and fasts by Ḥayyim b. Abraham ha-Kohen, Amsterdam, 1654. Jerusalem, J.N.U.L.

for Italy where he published two additional parts, *Tur Piteda* and *Tur Yahalom* (Leghorn, 1655). He died in Leghorn during the publication of his last book which thus remained incomplete, and only single sections have survived as pamphlets. All his commentaries on the Shulḥan Arukh have been published in two volumes (1878). In Leghorn, he introduced Nathan *Hannover to Isaac *Luria's Kabbalah. Hannover included in his *Sha'arei Ẓiyyon* a lament by Ḥayyim for the *Tikkun Ḥaẓot* (midnight prayer), *Kol be-Ramah Nishma*, which has since become part of every edition of this midnight liturgy. Among his commentaries on the Five Scrolls, only *Ateret Zahav* on Esther, explained both according to the literal meaning (*peshat*) and the Kabbalah, in the author's handwriting (Jerusalem, J.N.U.L., Ms. 8° 1581), and *Torat Ḥesed* on Ruth, have been preserved. The last, however, was published by the kabbalist David Lida as his own, under the title *Migdal David* (Amsterdam, 1680). This plagiarism was known in kabbalist circles even before it was made public by Ḥ. J. D. *Azulai in *Shem ha-Gedolim*. In his books Ḥayyim quotes only portions from throughout the *Zohar, and sometimes also the sayings of his teacher Vital, but most of his presentation is not based on other sources "and all his words are as if written from Sinai" (Nathan Hannover, introduction to *Sha'arei Ẓiyyon*). A prayer book with *kabbalistic meditations by Ḥayyim is extant in several manuscripts (two at the Ben-Zvi Institute in Jerusalem). Ḥayyim "was very careful not to write amulets," and was also opposed to those who spent too much time in prayer, wasting thus the whole day upon mystical meditations. Among kabbalists he was considered as more of a theoretical scholar than a practical mystic.

Bibliography: Michael, Or, no. 844; M. Benayahu in: *Sinai*, 34 (1953), 162–64, 194–7; idem, *Sefer Toledot ha-Ari* (1967), index.

[G.Sch.]

ḤAYYIM BEN BEZALEL (c. 1520–1588), talmudic scholar. Ḥayyim was born in Posen, and was the elder brother of the famous *Judah Loew b. Bezalel of Prague (the Maharal) who mentions him in his responsa (no. 12). He studied in the yeshivah of Shalom *Shakhna at Lublin where he was a contemporary of Moses *Isserles. Ḥayyim settled in Worms in 1549 where he lived in the home of his uncle, Jacob b. Ḥayyim, the local rabbi, succeeding him in 1563. He subsequently left to become rabbi of Friedberg, remaining there until his death.

When Isserles published his *Torat Ḥattat* on *issur ve-hetter* (on the dietary laws), Ḥayyim published a vigorous polemic against it in his *Vikku'aḥ Mayim Ḥayyim*. The introduction to the work was couched in such strong language both against Isserles and Joseph *Caro that it was omitted from editions after the first (Amsterdam, 1712), but has been reproduced in full by Tchernowitz (see bibl.). Ḥayyim's criticism was a general one against all those who presumed to publish halakhic codes which purported to give the final definitive *halakhah*, since they lead to neglect of the early authorities and can be used with disastrous results by the unlearned. Of Joseph Caro he comments that after saying "who am I to decide between the opposing views of the great authorities?" he then proceeds to do so. "It is like a man who says 'I have the greatest respect for what you say, but you are lying'!" The main target of his criticism, however, is Isserles' work. The *Torat Ḥattat* ("Law of the Sin-Offering") was rightly named, he said, since it, albeit unwillingly, causes people to sin, and it "even borders on *ḥillul ha-Shem* (Profanation of the Name of God)." In the same way as Moses set up the Copper Serpent with the best of intentions, yet when it became an object of idolatry Hezekiah did not hesitate to destroy it, so would he act with regard to this work of the "later Moses." He felt that Isserles should at least have stated that his work was only to be used by qualified scholars. (He himself had spent 16 years in composing a similar work, but only for his private use, and when one of his students purloined it and copied it, he sternly reproved him and destroyed the copy.) In addition to his general criticism he specified three reasons for his opposition. (1) Isserles had amended the code of Caro which reflected the Sephardi *minhag* to make it accord with the Polish, but he had completely ignored the differences between the Polish and the German *minhag*, which was more authoritative and ancient. (2) He had introduced a new element of leniency when "considerable loss" or "exceptional circumstances" (*she'at ha-deḥak*) were involved. (3) He abolished the *halakhah* in favor of unsubstantiated custom.

Ḥayyim wrote a number of other works. His *Sefer ha-Ḥayyim*, which he wrote in two months while he was confined to his house on account of a plague in 1578, is a moral and ethical dissertation. In style and language it is reminiscent of the pietistic works, and in fact his brother refers to him as "he-Ḥasid." His *Eẓ Ḥayyim* on Hebrew grammar (written in 1579) is still in manuscript. He was inspired to write it because of the criticism of Christian Hebrew scholars who accused the Jews not only of neglecting the study of Hebrew in favor of the Talmud, but even of forbidding it. He admits that he used the grammatical works of these detractors as one of his sources. He attributes the neglect of the study of Hebrew grammar to the fact that in the "bitter and long exile . . . it was impossible to encompass all subjects in the curriculum, for which reason alone the early authorities, especially the Ḥasidei Ashkenaz, confined their instruction to the Talmud" (Introduction). He also wrote *Be'er Mayim Ḥayyim*, a supercommentary on Rashi's Pentateuch commentary, and *Iggeret ha-Tiyyul* (Prague, 1605) consisting of explanations of talmudic passages using the methods of **Pardes*, in alphabetical order.

Bibliography: A. Gottesdiener, in: *Azkarah . . . A. I. Kook*, 4 (1937), 265f.; Ḥ. Tchernowitz, *Toledot ha-Posekim*, 3 (1947), 91–100; A. Siev, *Ha-Rema* (1957), 47–49; H. H. Ben Sasson, *Hagut ve-Hanhagah* (1959), 15, 35 n. 3.

[A.T.]

ḤAYYIM BEN HANANEL HA-KOHEN (second half of the 12th century), French tosafist. Ḥayyim lived in Paris and was a distinguished disciple and admirer of Jacob *Tam about whom he said that he would have defiled himself (referring to the prohibition against defilement of a kohen through contact with the dead) had he been present at his death (cf. Tos. to Ket. 103b). Ḥayyim wrote *tosafot* to several talmudic tractates and is quoted in the printed *tosafot* and in many other *rishonim*. "On him" said Isaac the Elder, "rested the honor of the entire generation." Ḥayyim opposed immigration to Palestine, stating that "in our generation the commandment to live in Palestine does not apply," as it was impossible to observe many commandments connected with the land (*ibid.*, 110b). However, he considered Jewish existence in the Diaspora as temporary. Ḥayyim was the grandfather of *Moses b. Jacob of Coucy, author of the *Semag*, and among his most prominent disciples was *Samson b. Abraham of Sens.

Bibliography: Urbach, Tosafot, 107–10; V. Aptowitzer, *Mavo le-Sefer Ravyah* (1938), 250.

[Z. M. R.]

ḤAYYIM (Eliezer) BEN ISAAC "OR ZARU'A" (late 13th century), German rabbi and halakhic authority, called "Or Zaru'a" after the famous work composed by his father, *Isaac b. Moses of Vienna. Ḥayyim was orphaned in his early youth. His principal teacher was Meir b. Baruch of Rothenburg, whose opinions he frequently cited. He also studied under such eminent scholars as Asher b. Jehiel and Ḥayyim b. Moses of Wiener-Neustadt. His permanent places of residence were Regensburg, Neustadt, or Cologne and he is said to have spent some years in France.

Ḥayyim's responsa (Leipzig, 1865; repr. Jerusalem, 1960) are especially valuable for the light they shed on the people, places, and events of his time. Thus he mentions (no. 110) a rabbinical synod which he attended at Mainz in about 1288, in which one of the matters discussed was the taxes imposed on the Jews by Rudolf of Hapsburg. In the same responsum he refers in passing to R. Meir of Rothenburg's imprisonment (see also no. 164). Some of the responsa provide important source material on Jewish-Christian relations in the 13th century. Most of Ḥayyim's decisions are based on those of the French and German halakhic authorities, particularly on his father's *Or Zaru'a*. His abridged version of that codification, which he entitled *Kiẓẓur Or Zaru'a* (or *Simanei Or Zaru'a*), summarized each section of the original work, omitted the legal discussions, and included his own views together with those of other scholars. From the many references to the *Kiẓẓur Or Zaru'a* in German rabbinic literature of the 14th and 15th centuries it is clear that his abridgment enjoyed long popularity. Ḥayyim also wrote *derashot* (homilies) dealing with regulations for the festivals, which are extant in manuscript. An important aspect of Ḥayyim's work is the lively correspondence he conducted with many of his contemporaries. It is believed that he addressed inquiries even to the Spanish scholar Solomon b. Abraham *Adret (Resp. Rashba, pt. 1, no. 572).

Bibliography: Wellesz, in: MGWJ, 48 (1904), 211–3; idem, in: REJ, 53 (1907), 67–84; 54 (1907), 102–6; Freimann, in: JJLG, 12 (1918), 314 (index), s.v. *Chajim Elieser b. Isak Or Sarua*; M. Pollak, *Juden in Wiener-Neustadt* (1927), 8, 35, 39; Urbach, Tosafot, index, s.v. *Ḥayyim b. Yiẓḥak*. [S.E.]

ḤAYYIM BEN JEHIEL ḤEFEẒ ZAHAV (13th century), German talmudist. Ḥayyim studied under his father and under *Samuel of Evreux. Many of his responsa are included in the responsa of *Meir b. Baruch of Rothenburg (ed. by M. Bloch, 1895, nos. 188–9, 209, 241, 249, 296–8, 339–41, 355–6, 382–3, 461–3). In a responsum (no. 241) he affirms that he filled the post of "emissary of Kolonia," probably Cologne. It has been therefore assumed by some that he was a member of the Cologne *bet din* and represented the community before the government. He was probably given the appellation "*Ḥefeẓ Zahav*" because of his book bearing this title, but from the endings of many of the responsa (nos. 189, 241, 339) it can also be deduced that his father was the author of the book. It appears that Ḥayyim was a colleague of Samuel b. Menahem, the teacher of Meir of Rothenburg, since in one responsum (no. 188) he refers to him as "my associate." This Ḥayyim is not to be identified with Ḥayyim b. Jehiel, the brother of *Asher b. Jehiel.

Bibliography: Michael, Or, no. 876; H. Gross, in: MGWJ, 34 (1885), 313f.; Germ Jud, 1 (1934), 151, 484; 2 (1968), index; I. Agus, *Rabbi Meir of Rothenburg*, 1 (1947), xxvi, 106, 129, 131, 146–8, 160f. [Y.H.]

ḤAYYIM BEN SAMUEL BEN DAVID OF TUDELA (14th century), talmudic scholar of Tudela, Spain. Ḥayyim was a pupil of Solomon b. Abraham *Adret, and the latter's responsa contain a number addressed to Ḥayyim. For some time Ḥayyim was in France, where he studied under *Perez b. Elijah. His main work is the *Ẓeror ha-Ḥayyim* (published in 1966), consisting of the laws appertaining to blessings, prayer, Sabbaths, and festivals, arranged according to the order of the calendar; it is based on views of various French, Provençal, and Spanish scholars but chiefly upon his teachers, Adret and Perez, though he does not mention them by name. His other work, *Ẓeror ha-Kesef*, on topics in *Ḥoshen Mishpat*, is still in manuscript. These books (referred to by the *rishonim* as the *ẓerorot*, "bundles") were in the possession of later scholars (but cf. Resp. Ribash, no. 396), who made use of and quoted them. This was particularly so in the case of the 16th-century Safed scholars, including Joseph *Caro. In this work, Ḥayyim alludes to a book of sermons he wrote, and Masud Ḥai Roke'aḥ, at the beginning of his *Ma'aseh Roke'aḥ* (Venice, 1742), quotes Ḥayyim's commentary to the tractate *Mo'ed Katan*, which is also cited by Bezalel *Ashkenazi in *Kelalei ha-Shas* (in Ms.). Among Ḥayyim's relations was Joseph ha-Dayyan, referred to respectfully several times in the responsa of Isaac b. Sheshet (Ribash).

Bibliography: Michael, Or, no. 904; S. H. Yerushalmi, *Mavo le-Sefer Ẓeror ha-Ḥayyim* (1966). [I.T.-S.]

ḤAYYIM BEN SOLOMON TYRER OF CZERNOWITZ (c. 1760–1816), rabbi and ḥasidic leader; born near *Buchach, Galicia. A disciple of *Jehiel Michael of Zloczów, he later served as rabbi in Mogilev, Kishinev, Czernowitz and district, and Botosani. He had a profound knowledge of rabbinical literature and mysticism, was an eloquent preacher and a talented writer. He did much to spread Ḥasidism and opposed the spread of *Haskalah in Rumania. His resistance to certain government decrees forced him to relinquish his office in Czernowitz in 1807. In 1813 he emigrated to Ereẓ Israel and settled in Safed. He wrote the following works, which were published in many editions: *Siddur shel Shabbat* (Mogilev, 1813); *Be'er Mayim Ḥayyim* (Sudilkov, 1820, with Pentateuch; Czernowitz, 1849); *Sha'ar ha-Tefillah* (Sudilkov, 1825); and *Ereẓ ha-Ḥayyim* (Czernowitz, 1861).

Bibliography: Frumkin-Rivlin, 3 (1929), 78; S. J. Schulsohn, in: *Jeschurun*, 15 (1928), 419–26. [A.Ru.]

ḤAYYIM ḤAYKL BEN SAMUEL OF AMDUR (d. 1787), ḥasidic leader in Lithuania. At first *ḥazzan* in Karlin, and a teacher in the little town of Amdur (Indura), near Grodno, he was attracted to *Ḥasidism through Aaron the Great of *Karlin. Ḥasidic sources relate that he subjected himself to excessive fasting and self-mortifications before he made the acquaintance of Dov Baer, the Maggid of Mezhirech. Becoming one of Dov Baer's most prominent disciples he founded a ḥasidic center in Amdur after the death of his teacher in 1773. A profound thinker and an enthusiastic and fearless propagandist of Ḥasidism, Ḥayyim was the ḥasidic personality most hated by the *Mitnaggedim* in Lithuania in the 1780s, and was a considerable factor in the outbreak of a second round of polemics between the two factions in 1781. He is described in somber tones in the literature of the *Mitnaggedim*, especially in the writings of *David of Makow. In *Shever Poshe'im* (in M. Wilensky, *Ḥasidim u-Mitnaggedim*, vol. 2, 1970) he and his associates are discussed with scorn. The *Mitnaggedim* persecuted him to such an extent that Ḥayyim was compelled to leave Amdur for a while and to stay in a village. He was undeterred by these persecutions, however, and continued to lead his congregation as *ẓaddik* until his death, bequeathing his position to his son Samuel.

Ḥayyim taught that God is infinite and men cannot comprehend Him. However, there is much latent power in man's intellect and by losing his own sense of being, he can be drawn nearer to and be united with his source. Ḥayyim therefore preached a complete negation of the human will before the divine will. The observance of a *mitzvah* was interpreted as an act desired by God and it is only this desire of God's which imparts validity to the *mitzvah.* It is also forbidden to serve God for the purpose of attaining the World to Come or other rewards. Ḥayyim is revealed as an extreme spiritualist: "We should forget ourselves as a result of our adhesion to Him." One should despise this world: "He who prays for his sustenance should be ashamed for doing so." If "I have set the Lord always before me, then I have no time to consider the events which befall me, for God surely knows of my needs better than I do myself." When a man stands before the Creator, all his limbs should tremble for fear of the Lord so that he does not know where he is standing, so much has he meditated on His essence. If, at that time, evil thoughts enter his mind, he should not repel them. On the contrary, this gives him the opportunity to elevate these thoughts to their source. If a man has sinned, he should rather endeavor to unite himself to the soul of the *ẓaddik*, as a result of which he will adhere to God.

His sermons were collected in *Ḥayyim va-Ḥesed* (1891, 1953²), including "rules of behavior," and letters to his followers, some of which had been previously published in *Iggeret ha-Kodesh* (Warsaw, 1850).

Bibliography: M. Wilensky, *Ḥasidim u-Mitnaggedim* (1970), index; M. H. Kleinemann, *Mazkeret Shem ha-Gedolim* (1967²), 49–55; W. Rabinowitsch, *Lithuanian Ḥasidism* (1970), index; R. Schatz, *Ha-Ḥasidut ke-Mistikah* (1968), index; A. Rubinstein, in: *Aresheth*, 3 (1961), 193–230

[MO.HAL.]

ḤAYYIM JUDAH BEN ḤAYYIM (17th–18th century), talmudist, rabbi of Janina (Ioannina), Greece. Ḥayyim Judah was born in Salonika, where he studied under Solomon *Amarillo, whose daughter he married. Toward the end of his life he emigrated to Jerusalem, where he had many disciples, among them Solomon Havdalah, a member of the *bet din* of Abraham Yiẓḥaki and in his old age rabbi of Jerusalem. Ḥ. J. D. *Azulai speaks of having seen a volume of Ḥayyim's responsa in manuscript. He carried on a halakhic correspondence with Samuel Florentin, author of the responsa *Me'il Shemu'el*, and others. His responsa are found in the works of others, e.g., *Kerem Shelomo* (Salonika, 1719) and *Zera Avraham* (Constantinople, 1732).

Bibliography: Fuenn, Keneset, 356; Azulai, 1 (1852), 58, no. 28; Rosanes, Togarmah, 4 (1935), 329; 5 (1938), 287.

[S.MAR.]

ḤAYYIM PALTIEL BEN JACOB (late 13th–early 14th century), German talmudic scholar. Ḥayyim Paltiel was a pupil of *Eliezer of Touques, and also, apparently, of *Meir b. Baruch of Rothenburg. He traveled through the cities of Bohemia and served as rabbi of Magdeburg. His questions to Meir of Rothenburg are included in the Cremona (1557, nos. 32–34), Prague (1608, no. 226), and Lemberg (1860, no. 507, et al.) editions of the latter's responsa and a number of his responsa to other scholars are also included in these collections. Of great historical importance is the responsum (Lemberg ed. no. 476) he wrote in 1291 from Magdeburg on the subject of the **Ḥerem ha-Yishuv*. He was one of the first—if not the first—to add the self-effacing epithet *tola'at* ("worm") to his formal signature, Ḥayyim Paltiel Tola'at (abbreviated to *Ḥapat*). One of his responsa to two of his pupils was forwarded by them to *Asher b. Jehiel for his opinion (Resp. Rosh, Kelal 30, no. 4). Ḥayyim Paltiel's chief importance lies in his *Sefer ha-Minhagim*, which contains the customs for the whole year, referring to benedictions, prayers, and festivals, according to the Ashkenazi rite. The work was later used by Abraham *Klausner, who adapted and amended it, and added other customs and explanations. The connection between the work of Klausner and that of Ḥayyim Paltiel was first suggested by H. J. Ehrenreich in the introduction to his edition of Klausner's *Minhagim* (1929), and was proved beyond doubt when Paltiel's work was discovered and published in *Kirjath Sepher* by D. Goldschmidt (see bibliography). Ḥayyim Paltiel thus emerges as one of the first authors of the **Minhagim* books, which gained wide popularity in 14th-century Germany and which laid the foundation for the spread of the version known in essence as *nosaḥ Ashkenaz* ("the Ashkenazi rite"). It is probable that he is identical with the Ḥayyim Paltiel whose biblical explanations are extensively quoted in a still unpublished manuscript of a Bible commentary by a 14th-century French scholar.

Bibliography: Ziemlich, in: MGWJ, 30 (1881), 305–16; Abraham Klausner, *Sefer ha-Minhagim*, ed. by H. J. Ehrenreich (1929), introd.; D. Goldschmidt, in: KS, 23 (1946/47), 324–30; 24 (1947/48), 73–83; Urbach, Tosafot, 456.

[I.T.-S.]

ḤAYYIM (Ben) SHABBETAI (known as **Maharḥash—Morenu Ha-Rav Ḥayyim Shabbetai;** before 1555–1647), rabbi in Salonika. He studied under Aaron *Sason, and subsequently became head of the yeshivah of the "Shalom" community. Many of his pupils became leading authorities such as *Solomon ha-Levi, Isaac Barki, Ḥasdai ha-Kohen *Peraḥyah, and David *Conforte. It is not clear whether Jacob Ruvio or Ḥayyim Shabbetai was appointed to the post of chief rabbi by the leaders of the Salonikan communities in 1638, but certainly after Ruvio's death in 1640, Ḥayyim Shabbetai served as chief rabbi. In point of fact, he had been referred to as "the great rabbi" as early as 1622. He devoted himself assiduously to congregational matters, introducing many important regulations, and was regarded as the outstanding halakhic authority of his time, questions being addressed to him from communities near and far. Only part of his works have been published. These include: novellae on the tractate *Ta'anit* and on the last chapter of tractate *Yoma*, published in the *Torat Moshe* of his son Moses (Salonika, 1797); responsa on *Even ha-Ezer* (Salonika, 1651); and *Torat Ḥayyim* (3 parts, Salonika, 1713, 1715, 1722), responsa. The second part of this last work is preceded by a *Kunteres ha-Moda'ah ve-ha-Ones*, on contracts entered into under duress, which was published separately (Lemberg, 1798) with a commentary by Jeremiah of Mattersdorf and his son Joab. Ḥayyim also wrote *Torat ha-Zevaḥ*, on the laws of slaughtering and inspection and *Seder Gittin* (unpublished). Many additional responsa are to be found in the works of his contemporaries and disciples. He was succeeded as rabbi of Salonika by his son Moses.

Bibliography: Conforte, Kore, index; Michael, Or, 412; Toiber, in: KS, 8 (1932), 275f.; Rosanes, Togarmah, 3 (1938), 175–8; I. S. Emmanuel, *Gedolei Saloniki le-Dorotam*, 1 (1936), 294–6, no. 448; idem, *Maẓẓevot Saloniki*, 1 (1963), 298–301, no. 685; Benayahu, in: *Sinai*, 34 (1954), 164f.

[A.D.]

ḤAYYOT, MENAHEM MANISH BEN ISAAC (d. 1636), Polish and Lithuanian rabbi. Ḥayyot's father served as rabbi of Prague. He himself was rabbi of Turobin, Moravia, apparently while very young, and later became a rabbi in Vilna. No biographical details of him are known but he is quoted in the works of many of his great contemporaries, such as Ephraim of Vilna in his *Sha'ar Efrayim* (Sulzbach, 1688) and Samuel Bacharach of Worms in his *Ḥut ha-Shani* (Frankfort, 1679). His son-in-law was Joseph Josefa *Horowitz. His tombstone was the oldest in Vilna. Of his works the following have been published: *Kabbalat Shabbat*, also entitled *Zemirot le-Shabbat* (Prague, 1621), Sabbath songs; an elegy, *Kinah le-Ḥurban*, on the fire in Posen in 1590 (Prague, 1590?), and a fragment of his supercommentary to Abraham ibn Ezra to Exodus 3:15 (see Herschkowitz, bibliography). In the catalogue of David *Oppenheimer there is mention also of a manuscript of *Derekh Temimim* (no. 375) by Ḥayyot, a commentary to the weekly portion of the Law, *Balak*, giving the plain meaning as well as homiletical and kabbalistic interpretations.

Bibliography: S. J. Fuenn, *Kiryah Ne'emanah* (1915²), 67–70; H. N. Maggid-Steinschneider, *Ir Vilna* (1900), 1f.; M. Herschkowitz, in: *Sinai*, 59 (1966), 97–127. [Y.AL.]

ḤAYYUJ, JUDAH BEN DAVID (c. 945–c. 1000), Hebrew grammarian. About his life little is known. He was born in Fez and arrived at Cordova in 960 when the dispute between *Menahem b. Jacob ibn Saruq and *Dunash b. Labrat was at its height, and sided with Menahem.

His works include: (1) *Teshuvot al Dunash ben Labrat* written with Menahem's students Isaac ibn Kapron and Isaac ibn *Gikatilla), which is his only work written in Hebrew. (2) *Kitāb al-Tanqīṭ* or *Kitāb al-Nuqat* ("Book of Vocalization") was translated into Hebrew by Abraham ibn Ezra, and is a continuation of (1). It includes a mixture of grammatical and masoretic matters, dealing mainly with nouns. (3) *Kitāb al Dhawāt Ḥurūf al-Līn* ("Book of Hollow Verbs"), translated into Hebrew by Moses ha-Kohen ibn Gikatilla, by Ibn Ezra, and by Isaac b. Eliezer ha-Levi (1458); parts of an anonymous translation have been found. (4) *Kitāb al-Dhawāt al-Mathalayn* ("Book of Reduplicated Verbs"), translated into Hebrew by Moses ha-Kohen ibn Gikatilla and Ibn Ezra (entitled *Pe'alei ha-Kefel*). (5) *Kitāb al-Natf* ("Book of Plucked Feathers"); Ibn Ezra called the book *Sefer ha-Karḥah* ("Book of Baldness"), and this later became corrupted to *Sefer ha-Rokḥah*. In this book he intended to explain all the difficult verses in the Bible by linguistic method. There are extant parts on Joshua, Judges, Kings, Isaiah, Jeremiah, and Ezekiel, which include discussions of individual words, as well as a discussion on the importance of the *meteg* and other accents for understanding the Hebrew language. (1) was published by Z. Stern in 1870. The originals and the Hebrew translations of (2) (3) and (4) were published by J. L. Dukes (1844), G. W. Nutt (1870), and M. Jastrow (1897). The Arabic original of (5) was partially published by P. Kokovtsov (see bibl.).

In his two works on the verb, Ḥayyuj developed the view that all Hebrew roots are made up of three letters, one of which, however, may be interchanged when conjugated with a weak letter, and may be elided or assimilated to a letter with a *dagesh*. This is a departure from the earlier view which recognized two-letter roots (תם, קם, רע, בל) and even some one-letter roots (ויט ויז).

His works spread rapidly throughout the Eastern countries and even became popular in Germany. Jonah ibn Janaḥ completed the material which he discusses in his book *Kitāb al-Mustalḥaq*. Moses ha-Kohen ibn Gikatilla prepared a synopsis in *Mukhtaṣar Ḥayyuj* (synopsis of Ḥayyuj's works); copies of these books were found in the *Genizah* in Cairo. Several works imitating Ḥayyuj were written, including *Sefer ha-Shoham*, by Moses Nesi'a, and *Sefat Yeter* by Isaac b. Eliezer ha-Levi. All the work on Hebrew language and biblical exegesis since Ḥayyuj has been based on his ideas, and much of what he said, as well as his terminology in translation, is used to this day.

Bibliography: W. Bacher, *Die grammatische Terminologie des Jehuda b. Dawid Hajjug* (1882); idem, in: J. Winter and A. Wuensche, *Die juedische Litteratur*, 2 (1894), 159–61; B. Drachman, *Die Stellung und Bedeutung des Jehuda Hajjug* (1885); M. Jastrow (ed.), *The Weak and Geminative Verbs in Hebrew by Abu Zakariyya Yahya ibn Dawud of Fez* (1897); Steinschneider, Arab Lit, 119; S. Poznański, in: JQR, 16 (1925/26), 237–66; H. Hirschfeld, *Literary History of Hebrew Grammarians and Lexicographers* (1926), 35–40; P. Kokovtsov, *Novye materialy . . .*, 2 (1916), 1–74 (Russ. pt.), 1–58; S. Pinsker, *Likkutei Kadmoniyyot* (1860), index; D. Yellin, *Toledot Hitpatteḥut ha-Dikduk ha-Ivri* (1945), 113f.; Abraham b. Azriel, *Arugat ha-Bosem*, ed. by E. E. Urbach, 2 (1947), 140; N. Allony, in: *Minḥah li-Yhudah [Zlotnick]* (1950), 67–83; idem, in: BM, 16 (1963), 90–105; P. Kokovtsov, *Mi-Sifrei ha-Balshanut ha-Ivrit* ed. by N. Allony (1970). [N.AL.]

ḤAYYUN, ABRAHAM BEN NISSIM (d. 1500), Portuguese scholar; a pupil of Joseph b. Abraham *Ḥayyun, rabbi of Lisbon. He was among the Jews who left Portugal after the decree of expulsion was issued in 1496, settling in Constantinople. He wrote *Imrot Tehorot*, an ethical work (Constantinople, 1515–20; Salonika, 1595; and Jerusalem, 1876), and *Ma'amar be-Mofetim*, on miracles described in the Bible (mentioned by Abraham b. Solomon Ḥayyun at the end of Joseph Ḥayyun's *Millei de-Avot*).

Bibliography: M. Kayserling, *Geschichte der Juden in Portugal* (1867), 74; Benjacob, Oẓar, 41 no. 786; A. Yaari, *Ha-Defus ha-Ivri be-Kushta* (1967), 79, 128. [ED.]

ḤAYYUN, JOSEPH BEN ABRAHAM (d. 1497), last rabbi of the Jewish community of Lisbon before the expulsion. Among his distinguished disciples were Abraham b. Nissim *Ḥayyun and Joseph *Jabez. While Ḥayyun was still in Lisbon, Isaac *Abrabanel consulted him on various halakhic questions, concerning one of which he composed a tract, *Maggid Mishneh*. After the decree of expulsion from Portugal was issued in 1496, Ḥayyun went to Constantinople, where he died shortly afterward. His

Millei de-Avot by Joseph b. Abraham Ḥayyun, rabbi of Lisbon Venice, 1606. Jerusalem, J.N.U.L.

published works are a commentary on the Book of Psalms (Salonika, 1523), and *Millei de-Avot*, a commentary on *Avot* (Constantinople, 1578; republ. Venice, 1606); a number of his notes on the order of the *haftarot* are included in *Likkutei Man* (Amsterdam, 1764). Other works remain in manuscript.

Bibliography: Benjacob, Oẓar, 324 no. 1106, 641 no. 380; Ben-Sasson, in: *Sefer Yovel le-Y. Baer* (1960), 217ff., 220; idem, in: *Zion*, 28 (1961), 56ff., 60; A. Yaari, *Ha-Defus ha-Ivri be-Kushta* (1967), 128. [ED.]

HAZAEL (Heb. חֲזָאֵל; "God has taken note"), king of Aram-Damascus (c. 842–798 B.C.E.). Hazael was a usurper—called by the Assyrians "son of a nobody"—who murdered Ben-Hadad (perhaps in reality Hadadezer, see *Ben-Hadad) and founded a dynasty in Damascus during the unsettled period that also witnessed the accession of *Jehu in Israel and *Athaliah in Judah.

According to I Kings 19:15–16, Hazael was to be anointed king of Damascus by *Elijah, as Jehu was to be anointed king of Israel. When, thereafter, Ben-Hadad lay ill, *Elisha informed Hazael, a royal servant, that Ben-Hadad's illness was not fatal, but that Hazael would nevertheless be king. Hazael thereupon smothered Ben-Hadad and usurped the throne (II Kings 8:7–15). Hazael immediately began the attacks on Israel predicted by Elisha, attacking *Ramoth-Gilead and seriously injuring Joram of Israel (II Kings 8:28–29).

During the campaigns of Shalmaneser III in the West, Aram, under Ben-Hadad (or Hadadezer), had stood at the head of a southern Syrian coalition which effectively repulsed the Assyrian armies under Shalmaneser at the battle of *Karkar in 853, and thereafter in 848 and 845. In 841, when Shalmaneser again campaigned in the West, Hazael alone resisted, withstanding a siege of Damascus, while Tyre, Sidon, and Israel became vassals of Assyria. A punitive campaign by Shalmaneser in 838 again failed to subdue Damascus, and the Assyrians withdrew, leaving Hazael the undisputed power in southern Syria. Hazael then began a series of attacks on Israel which resulted in the period of Aram's greatest territorial control and Israel's greatest weakness. At the end of the reign of Jehu, Hazael conquered all the Israelite lands east of the Jordan, and took possession of the highlands of Galilee (II Kings 10:32–33; Amos 1:3). After Jehu's death he overran the entire territory of Israel, proceeding south along the coast to Gath on the border of Judah (II Kings 12:18–19). Hazael completely humbled the kingdom of Israel throughout the reign of Jehoahaz (II Kings 13:1–3, 7, 22), dominated the trade routes to Arabia, probably conquered all of Philistia, and even threatened Jerusalem, retreating from the city only upon the payment of a heavy tribute by Joash, king of Judah (II Kings 12:19; cf. II Chron. 24:23–24). So great was Hazael's power and domination over Israel and Judah that the resumed expeditions of Assyria under Adad-Nirari III in 805 were viewed as a liberation, and Adad-Nirari was acclaimed a deliverer (II Kings 13:5).

Of the few artifacts remaining from Hazael's reign, of note is the ivory bed plaque inscribed as "belonging to our Lord Hazael" *(lmr'n ḥz'l)* that was discovered at Arslan Tash (the Assyrian provincial capital Hadattu).

Bibliography: E. Kraeling, *Aram and Israel* (1918); R. de Vaux, in: RB, 43 (1934), 512–8; B. Maisler [Mazar], in: JPOS, 18 (1938), 282–3; idem, in: D. N. Freedman and E. F. Campbell (ed.), *The Biblical Archaeologist Reader*, 2 (1964), 144–5; W. W. Hallo, *ibid.*, 160–4; M. F. Unger, *Israel and the Arameans of Damascus* (1957), 75–82, 160–3. ASSYRIAN SOURCES: Luckenbill, Records, 1 (1926), nos. 575, 578, 699, 672, 681; E. Michel, in: *Die Welt des Orients*, 2 (1947), 57–58; 3 (1948), 265–6, 268–9. [T.S.F.]

HAZAI, SAMU (1851–1942), Hungarian army officer and minister. Born in Rimszombat, Hazai graduated from the military academy in Vienna. He taught at the Ludovika Military Academy of Budapest and at the officer's school, of which he later became director. He was made Hungarian minister of defense in 1910 and was later given a barony and raised to the rank of fieldmarshal-lieutenant. During World War I, Hazai instituted several emergency laws, and later was in charge of recruitment for the entire Austro-Hungarian army. After the collapse of the empire in 1918 he was arrested for a short time by the Hungarian revolutionary government, and later played no further part in public affairs. Hazai converted to Christianity in his youth and had no interest in Jewish matters. [ED.]

ḤAZAK (Heb. חֲזַק; "be strong"), a salutation of well-wishing based on Moses' address to Joshua "Be strong and of good courage" (Deut. 31:7; 31:23; cf. II Sam. 10:12; Haggai 2:4). A fuller version, *Ḥazak, ḥazak ve-nitḥazzak* ("Be strong, be strong, and let us be strengthened"), is recited at the Torah reading in the synagogue when one of the five books of the Pentateuch is terminated (Isserles to Sh. Ar., OḤ 139:11). In the Sephardi ritual, the person who returns to his seat after having been called up to the *Reading of the Law is greeted by his neighbors with *Ḥazak u-varukh* ("Be strong and blessed"); he replies *Barukh tihyeh* ("Be blessed"), or *Kulkhem berukhim* ("Be you all blessed").

See also *Greetings and Congratulations.

Bibliography: Eisenstein, Dinim, 129. [ED.]

ḤAZAKAH (Heb. חֲזָקָה; lit. "possession," "taking possession"), a term expressing three main concepts in Jewish law: (1) a mode of acquiring ownership; (2) a means of proving ownership or rights in property; (3) a factual-legal presumption *(praesumptio juris)* as to the existence of a particular fact or state of affairs. In its first connotation *ḥazakah* creates a new legal reality, unlike the latter two cases where it is merely instrumental in proving or presuming an existing one. For *ḥazakah* in its connotation of possession see also *Evidence, *Ownership, *Property. For (1) see *Acquisition, Modes of.

ḤAZAKAH AS PROOF OF OWNERSHIP

Immovable Property. Possession per se of immovable property (*karka* or *mekarke'in*, lit. "land," as opposed to *metaltelin*, "movable property") known to have belonged to another does not displace the title of the legal owner (*mara kamma*, "first owner") thereto, for "land is never stolen" (*karka einah nigzelet;* BK 95a; TJ, BK 10:6, 7c) and "is always in the possession of its owner" (BM 102b). The possessor is accordingly required to prove that he acquired the property in a legally recognized way. If, however, he has held undisturbed possession in the manner of an owner for a period of three consecutive years, without protest from the previous owner, the possessor's plea that he purchased the property or received it as a gift (from the first owner or his father) and that the deed thereto has been lost, is believed. Where his possession is not accompanied by such a claim of right *(she-ein immah ta'anah)* but merely with the contention that "no one ever said anything to me," the *ḥazakah* is not established (BB 3:3). Where the property is purchased or inherited from another, the holder's mere plea (some scholars require proof on his part) that the deceased or seller held possession of the property in the manner of an owner, for even one day, will validate the occupier's *ḥazakah*, for "he cannot be expected to know how his father came by the property" (Rashbam, BB 41a). For this reason the court would "plead the cause" of the heir or purchaser (BB 23a), to the effect that he came by the property in lawful manner.

In Jewish law *ḥazakah* is part of procedural law only (as "mere evidence," *Yad Ramah*, BB 170a; for this reason the laws of *ḥazakah* are treated by Maimonides in *hilkhot To'en ve-Nitan* and not in the book on *Kinyan*), in contrast with the Roman law *usucapio* of the Twelve Tables, which is a matter of the substantive law whereby ownership is created by virtue of possession for a period of two years. The *ḥazakah* of Jewish law is somewhat akin to the possession in the Roman *praescriptio longi temporis* of the end of the second century C.E., according to which possession of property for ten or 20 years effectively established title, if accompanied by *iusta causa*. There, however, possession is equally effective even if it transpires that ownership was acquired in a defective manner *ab initio*, in contrast with the Jewish law, where "he who possesses a field by virtue of a deed which is found to be defective, his *ḥazakah* is not established" (Tosef., BB 2:2; BB 32b; cf. TJ, Shevu. 6:2, 37a, where a contrary opinion is expressed).

PERIOD OF POSSESSION. According to some *tannaim* (BB 36b and BB 3:1; *Tanna Kamma*) *ḥazakah* always requires possession for a period of three full years (this period is mentioned already in the Hammurapi code, sec. 30–31). Rava, a Babylonian *amora* of the first half of the fourth century, explains the length of this period on the ground that it is not customary for a purchaser to preserve his title deed for longer than three years, and that thereafter the first owner is not entitled to demand production of the purchaser's deed (BB 29a). In the case of a field producing one annual crop only, the period is 18 months according to Ishmael and 14 months according to Akiva, i.e., a period sufficient for the cultivation and enjoyment of three crops; a period covering the production of three crops—even if enjoyed in one year—is sufficient, according to Ishmael, in the case of a field of diverse trees whose fruits are harvested in different seasons (BB 3:1). According to Judah, a *tanna* of the second century, the period of three years applies in the case of an absent (abroad, "in Spain") owner (BB 3:2), but one year suffices where both the first owner and the occupier are present in the same country (Tosef., BB 2:1; according to BB 41a *ḥazakah* is immediately effective in the latter case). An analogous distinction is made in the Roman *praescriptio longi temporis*, between possession *inter absentes* (20 years) and *inter praesentes* (10 years). Some scholars (Gulak, Karl) are of the opinion (based on BB 3:2) that in ancient *halakhah* the law of *ḥazakah* was applicable only when both parties were in the same country; at the commencement of the amoraic period, this *halakhah* was interpreted as having been instituted because of "conditions of emergency" (BB 38a–b), whereby there was no means of travel between various districts within Ereẓ Israel; in times of peace, however, *ḥazakah* is effective even in the absence of the first owner. However, the question of the operation of *ḥazakah* between parties in different countries remained a disputed one even during the early amoraic period (TJ, BB 3:3, 14a).

MANNER OF EXERCISING POSSESSION. Possession must be held "in the manner in which people normally use the particular property" (Yad, To'en ve-Nitan 11:2); it must therefore be held for an uninterrupted period, unless it is local custom to cultivate the field one year and leave it fallow the next (BB 29a). It is a requirement that the possessor not only cultivate the field, but that he also enjoy its fruits, "for the essence of *ḥazakah* is the gathering of fruit ...," without which evidence of all his other activities on the land will not avail (TJ, BB 3:3, 14a; BB 36b).

PROTEST. Protest on the part of the first owner within the period of three years interrupts the occupier's *ḥazakah*, because it has the effect of warning the occupier to preserve his title deed as proof of ownership. In ancient *halakhah* this protest (variously called עֲרָר or עַרְעָר (*arar*; Tosef., BB 2:4; TJ, BB 3:3; BB 39b) and מְחָאָה (*meḥa'ah*; BB 29a, 39a et al.) by the *amoraim* of Ereẓ Israel and Babylonia respectively), served the procedural function of commencing litigation (analogous to the Roman *litis contestatio*) and was accordingly required to be made before the court. Doubt was already cast on this requirement by the *amoraim* of Ereẓ Israel (TJ, BB 3:3), and according to the Babylonian *amoraim* protest requires no more than that it should be made known to the public (*gillui milta le-rabbim*) by the first owner, or that he make a statement before witnesses that he maintains his interest in the property (BB 39b). In the fourth century the Babylonian *amoraim* prescribed a formula for the protest: "*Peloni* is a robber who occupies my land by robbery and on the morrow I shall bring suit against him," but an unqualified statement: "*Peloni* is a robber" is not an effective protest (BB 38b–39a), lest the occupier plead that "he merely insulted me and therefore I did not look to my deed" (Yad, To'en 11:7). Protest before two witnesses—not necessarily in the presence of the occupier—suffices, for the fact thereof is bound to come to the occupier's notice one way or another (BB 38b, 39b; Yad, To'en 11:5).

Any reasonable explanation for the lack of protest is a bar to effective *ḥazakah*. For this reason *ḥazakah* does not operate between husband and wife or parent and child, each in respect of the other's property, for in these cases the one party is not fastidious about the other's use of the property (BB 3:3; *Teshuvot ha-Rashba ha-Meyuḥasot le-ha-Ramban*, no. 93). In suits between other related parties, the issue of *ḥazakah* is decided by the court on the merits of the evidence in each case, depending on "whether one brother relied on the other in the running of his affairs," etc. (Resp. Rashba, pt. 1, no. 950; Tur and Sh. Ar., ḤM 149:6–8). Nor is *ḥazakah* gained by artisans (building contractors), *partners, metayers (אריסין—tenants receiving a share of the crop; see *Hiring and Letting), and guardians (see *Apotropos; BB 3:3), for they occupy by license (*reshut*; BB 42b; TJ, BB 3:5) and there is therefore no purpose in making protest against them. Possesion will also not lead to *ḥazakah* when the first owner is unable to make protest, whether for lack of communication with the occupier because of emergency conditions (BB 38a–b; see above) or because the occupier came on the property by the use of force, "like those of a certain family who are prepared to commit murder for monetary gain" (BB 47a). The exilarchs ("of that time") were also barred from gaining *ḥazakah* because the property owners "stood in awe of them" (i.e., of making protest; Yad, To'en 13:2; BB 36a; Rashbam ad loc.; Joseph b. Samuel *Tov Elem, *Teshuvot Ge'onim Kadmonim* no. 48, ascribes the lack of protest to the pleasure derived by the owners from the exilarch's use of their property). Nor could others gain *ḥazakah* over the property of the exilarchs, for the latter did not "hasten" to protest, because they were able to take forcible possession of their property or because they were not particular, on account of their wealth, about others using their property (BB 36a and Rashbam *ibid.*; *Ge'onim Kadmonim*, no. 48; *Bet ha-Beḥirah*, BB 36a). A non-Jew who acquires forcible possession and a Jew who derives his title through him do not gain *ḥazakah* over the property of a Jew (BB 35b), though in the time of R. Joseph, in Babylonia, it was decided otherwise, for there was a "judicial system which permitted no person to exercise duress against any other person" (*Beit ha-Beḥirah*, BB 36a and Git. 58b).

PLURALITY OF OCCUPIERS AND SUCCESSIVE OWNERS. *Ḥazakah* may be gained through someone occupying on behalf of the person claiming *ḥazakah*, as in the case of the tenant to whom the claimant lets the dwelling (BB 29a); and possession by one partner on behalf of another is similarly effective if each of them has occupied the property for part of the three-year period, provided that this partnership arrangement between them was publicly known (BB 29b; *Beit ha-Beḥirah*, BB 29b; Yad, To'en 12:5—"since they are partners, they are as one"). The required period for *ḥazakah* is cumulative both as against successive "first owners" and in favor of successive possessors, who respectively derive title from their predecessors (Tosef., BB 2:7–8). At the commencement of the amoraic period, Rav determined that the combined period for which possession was held by both the seller and the purchaser would only be cumulative in the case of a sale by deed, as in this manner the matter would become public and the "first owner" aware that a cumulative *ḥazakah* was challenging his ownership.

Aspects of Ḥazakah in Post-Talmudic Times. Aspects of *ḥazakah* were discussed by the *posekim* against the prevailing social and communal background. One matter discussed was the application of *ḥazakah* to a permanent seating place in the synagogue, which became an asset capable of being alienated and inherited (Sh. Ar., ḤM 162:7; Rema and *Pitḥei Teshuvah* ad loc.). Some of the scholars recognized the application of *ḥazakah* thereto (Meir ha-Levi Abulafia and others), but stress was laid on the difficulty of establishing uninterrupted synagogue attendance at all appointed services for three years—a requirement for effective *ḥazakah* (*Shitah Mekubbeẓet* and Nov. Ritba to BB 29b). Some scholars excused absence on account of illness or mourning (*Beit ha-Beḥirah* BB 29a) and even occasional absence for pressing business reasons (Responsa Rashba pt. 1, no. 943; Tur, ḤM 140:16; *Beit ha-Beḥirah* BB 29a differs), and the latter view prevailed (*Beit Yosef* ḤM 141:2; Rema ḤM 140:8). On the other hand, *ḥazakah* was generally not recognized as extending to public and communal property such as consecrated property, *talmud torahs,* charitable institutions, and the like, for "who shall make protest?" (Rashba, pt. 1 no. 642), and when recognized, *ḥazakah* was held to be effective only under special circumstances and in respect of property in the care of appointed officials or seven representative citizens (Tur and Sh. Ar., ḤM 149 end).

Deed of sale for a synagogue pew, Amsterdam, 1792. Jerusalem, C.A.H.J.P., 851 (2).

Many of the discussions of this period centered around relationships between Jews of different social status and between Jews and their gentile neighbors. The talmudic *halakhah* precluding others from gaining *ḥazakah* of the property of exilarchs and vice versa was discussed by Solomon b. Abraham *Adret and *Asher b. Jehiel in relation to the property of Jews who held official positions and exercised authority. Both decided that the cases were not analogous, for the exilarchs functioned as "quasi-royalty" and ". . . in these generations a Jew who should find favor with the king does not impose such awe . . ." as would deter the owner of property from protesting (Resp. Rosh 18:17; Resp. Rashba, pt. 1, no. 941; Tur, ḤM 149:13; *Sma* ḤM 149, no. 18; *Siftei Kohen* ḤM 149, n. 12). The question of *ḥazakah* in relation to a non-Jew or a Jew deriving title through him was frequently treated and the decision made dependent on the prevailing attitude of the central government toward the particular Jewish community: "in a case where the Jew can bring the non-Jew before the court of the land, a Jew deriving title through a non-Jew has *ḥazakah*" (Ravyah, quoted in *Mordekhai* BB 3:553; Rah quoted in the Nov. Ritba, BB 35 and see Ha-Ittur's dissenting opinion; cf. also Tur and Sh. Ar., ḤM 149:14 and 236:9; BB 55a and commentators ad loc.). Some of the *halakhot* of *ḥazakah* relating to immovable property were applied also in the matter of *Ḥezkat ha-Yishuv* ("the right of domicile").

Movable Property. Contrary to the rule in the case of immovable property, "movables" are in the *ḥazakah* of the person having the physical possession thereof even if the plaintiff brings witnesses that the movables are known to belong to him, and the former's plea that he acquired them according to law is accepted (Yad, To'en 8:1; Tur, ḤM 133:1; source of the rule: BB 3:3; Tosef., BB 2:6; only "the launderer has no *ḥazakah*"), except when the chattels are known to be stolen property (BK 68b, 94b; Sh. Ar., ḤM 354:2). The authorities were in dispute on the requirement of a plea of right on the part of the possessor in the case of movables (*Shitah Mekubbeẓet* BB 28b). *Ḥazakah* of movables is gained forthwith, possession for a period of two or three days and sometimes even one hour—depending upon the subject matter—being sufficient (BB 36a and Rabbenu Gershom ad loc.; also Rashbam BB 42a). However, not every *tefisah* ("taking of possession," "seizure") establishes valid *ḥazakah,* thus ". . . if they saw him hiding articles under his garments and he came out and said 'these are mine' he is not believed," unless there is a reasonable explanation for this type of behavior, as in the case of articles which are habitually concealed and the like (Shevu. 46a–b).

The rule excluding the operation of *ḥazakah* as between "first owners" and possessors standing in a special relationship toward each other (see above) applies also to movables, e.g., in the case of the artisan, the bailee, etc. (BB 3:3; Tosef., BB 2:5–6). Similarly it does not operate in respect of "articles which are made to be given on loan or hire" (Shevu. 46a–b), where the first owner may account for the fact that movables of this type are found in the hands of the possessor on these grounds. On the other hand, the first owner's claim that these movables were stolen from him is not believed, for this is an admission that they were not lent and "we do not presume a man to be a thief" (Shevu. 46b; Rosh and Ran ad loc.). Most commentators include in the category of "articles which are made to be given on loan or hire," all chattels "which are likely to be lent by their owners" (Rif and Ran to Shevu. 46b). According to this view, only chattels which their owners fear may be damaged, such as certain types of books (Rashi to Shevu. 46b), or those which are particularly valuable, such as articles of silver and gold (*Terumat ha-Deshen,* no. 335), are not to be considered as made to be given on loan or hire. This view is opposed by Maimonides, who holds that such a view in effect invalidates in respect of most movables—the principle that a thing must be considered to be the property of the person in whose possession it is found. Maimonides distinguishes between articles which are "likely to be given on loan or hire"—in which category he places all movables—and things which are "made to be given on loan or hire," defined by him as articles which in a particular locality are specifically made with a view to their being borrowed or hired for a fee and not for sale or home use, such as "large copper kettles for cooking at celebrations," etc., *ḥazakah* being included in the latter case only (Yad, To'en 8:9); other articles may also come within the latter category but only where their owner has witnesses to prove that he has constantly lent or hired them out and that he holds them for such purpose (To'en 8:9 and 10 and Rabad's stricture thereon).

Special Categories of Movables. In the case of slaves, a period of three years is required for effective *ḥazakah* (BB 3:1). Animals (livestock) were apparently deemed to be like other movables in the tannaitic period, i.e., *ḥazakah* was effective immediately; this may be deduced from the existence of a special ruling precluding shepherds from acquiring *ḥazakah*, as in the case of the artisan and bailee (Tosef., BB 2:5). At the commencement of the amoraic period, Simeon b. Lakish determined that the normal rule of *ḥazakah* did not apply in respect of livestock (BB 36a), for they "stray from place to place" (TJ, BB 3:1, 13d) and therefore "the fact of detaining it under his hand does not constitute proof, for it went of its own accord into his *reshut*" (i.e., domain; Yad, To'en 10:1). Differing opinions were expressed with regard to establishing *ḥazakah* in respect of chattels not falling within the normal rule, e.g., articles made to be given on loan or hire and livestock; some of the *posekim* expressed the opinion that in these cases *ḥazakah* is never established; others held that it is established after a period of three years; and some held that there is no fixed period for effective *ḥazakah*, the court having the discretion to decide the matter in each case (*Yad Ramah* BB 36a; Rashbam BB 36a; Nov. Ritba BB 36a; Nov. Rashba BB 46a; Tur, ḤM 133:10 and 138:1–2; Resp. Maharam of Rothenburg, ed. Prague, no. 180).

See also *Limitation of Actions. For *ḥazakah* in relation to servitudes (*ḥezkat tashmishim*) and torts see *Servitudes.

ḤAZAKAH AS A LEGAL-FACTUAL PRESUMPTION

This occurs in a number of forms:

(1) A legal presumption of the continued existence of a once-ascertained state of affairs, until the contrary be proved—"an object is presumed to possess its usual status" (Nid. 2a), e.g., that the flesh of an animal is presumed to be forbidden as having been cut from a living animal until it is ascertained that it was ritually slaughtered; once slaughtered, the animal's flesh is presumed to be permitted unless the manner in which it became *terefah* becomes known (Ḥul. 9a); that the husband is alive at the time that the bill of divorce is handed to the wife, even though he was old or ill when the agent or *shali'aḥ* left him (Git. 3:3); similarly the presumptions of normal health and fitness, referred to variously as *ḥezkat ha-guf* (Ket. 75b), *ḥezkat bari* (Kid. 79b; BB 153b), and *ḥezkat kashrut* (BB 31b).

(2) A legal presumption of the existence of a fixed and accepted custom or of the psychological nature of man, such as the following: that an agent fulfills his mandate (Er. 31b); that a woman does not have the impudence to declare (falsely) in her husband's presence that he has divorced her (Yev. 116a) and she is therefore believed; that a debtor does not settle his debt before due date, therefore his plea (without proof) that he repaid the debt before due date is not believed (BB 5a–b); that a **ḥaver* does not allow anything which is untithed to leave his hands and therefore if he dies leaving a silo full of produce, this is presumed to have been tithed (Pes. 9a); that no man affixes his signature to a document unless he knows the contents thereof, and he cannot therefore plead that he did not read or understand its contents (PDR 1:293–5).

(3) Legal presumptions permitting a conclusion of fact to be inferred from particular surrounding circumstances. Presumptions of this kind were relied upon even in cases of capital punishment, as if the conclusion had been proved by the evidence of witnesses: "we flog . . . stone and burn on the strength of presumption" (Kid. 80, and examples there quoted), "even where there is no testimony on the matter" (Rashi ad loc.). Similarly, in certain circumstances a woman reputed to be married to a particular man was held to be his wife (Yad, Issurei Bi'ah, 1:21, as per TJ, Kid. 4:10).

Support for the validity of the latter presumptions was found in the law of the Torah that the penalty for "one who curses or smites his father" is death: "how do we know for sure that he is his father? Only by way of presumption" (Yad and TJ, loc. cit.; in Ḥul. 11b, the aforesaid *halakhah* concerning "one who smites his father" serves as a basis for deduction of the *majority rule). [M.E.]

IN THE MIDDLE AGES AND EARLY MODERN TIMES

Ḥazakah was one of the main normative concepts of Jewish economic and social life. In the course of time it was applied to the most varied rights and objects: e.g., right of settlement in a given community, rights over a certain clientele, as well as rights to seats in a synagogue, and the right to exercise certain honorific functions at religious services.

Since it fitted into the structure and spirit of the guilds and civic economy and social morality, *ḥazakah* developed and proliferated. Based in principle on talmudic law (see above), its widening application came through communal authorities enacting new **takkanot* to meet new circumstances (see *Arenda, *Councils of the Lands, **Ḥerem ha-Yishuv*, **Ma'arufyah*, and *Poland-Lithuania). For that reason it was mainly the lay leaders of the communal administration (*kahal*), not the rabbi, who passed final judgment on the protection of tenancy and other acquired rights. The dispensation of *ḥazakah* ultimately rested upon the goodwill of the community and its leaders. As a result, practices varied in different communities, from town to town, and certainly from country to country. The prohibition on settling in a community without permission (*ḥerem ha-yishuv*) was the source of one of the main forms of *ḥazakah*. *Ḥazakah* proper generally applied to tenant protection, whereby no Jew was permitted to rent from a gentile owner a house occupied by another Jewish tenant without the latter's consent, a right the latter usually acquired after three years of occupancy. The purpose of the prohibition was to prevent raising the rents of old or new tenants. An ordinance attributed to *Gershom b. Judah stated that the house of a gentile from which a Jew had been evicted might not be leased by another Jew for an entire year. Even houses owned by Jews were included in similar decisions by the conference of Candia in 1238 and by some halakhists. At a meeting of elders in Ferrara in 1554 it was resolved:

"whereas there are some who infringe the *takkanah* of R. Gershom, which forbids any Jew from ousting another Jew from a house rented from a Christian landlord, and whereas such offenders claim that when the landlord sells his house the Jewish tenant thereby also loses his *ḥazakah*, we therefore decree that though the Christian owner sell his house, the right of the Jewish tenant to retain possession is unchanged; any Jew who ousts him is disobeying the *takkanah* of R. Gershom and also this *takkanah*, now newly enacted."

In Italy this law, which was recognized by the authorities, was called *jus gazaga* or *casaca*. The Lithuanian Council of the communities adopted a rule in 1623 that a house owned by a gentile and rented to a Jew who had a *ḥazakah* on it might be sold to another Jew by permission of the head of the *bet din*. The buyer thereby also acquired the *ḥazakah*. However, if he did not move into the house himself, he had to grant the tenant priority in occupying the house. The same ordinance was made to apply to a store in the market-place which was also governed by the three-year *ḥazakah* rule; in this case the buyer had to recompense the tenant for his *ḥazakah* costs. Although few *ḥazakah* records remain for Polish Jewry in the days when its council functioned, the communal law was enforced in Poland also. The practice was particularly prevalent in countries where Jews could not own lands, or were restricted to crowded ghettos or voluntarily inhabited Jewish quarters. The rule was a necessity to prevent exorbitant rent. In Spain, where Jews could own land, the *ḥazakah*, or *praescription*, applied to ownership of land as well as to rentals. Since *ḥazakah* was an important property right, it was negotiable, testable, and used as a dowry. The *kahal* made it an important source of income.

In Russia *ḥazakah* persisted long after the abolition of the *kahal* in 1844. The leaders of the Minsk community sold possession of a gentile's store to a Jew and bound every future *kahal* to protect this man's right to the acquired option on the property. The same enforcement of acquired rights was practiced with equal stringency within the Jewish community: merchants were shielded against outside competition; there were rules against the importation of meat and wine and many other protectionist regulations; artisans could acquire a form of *ḥazakah* on a customer, *ma'arufyah*, whereby no other craftsman was permitted to do work for him; a person could acquire rights to a seat in the synagogue, to a Torah Scroll, or to ornaments loaned to the congregation for its use. The term *ḥazakah* also applied to tenure of communal workers. In Moravia a law was passed that a rabbi who refused to appear in court to be tried, or engaged in trade, could lose his tenure and be dismissed.

See also Jewish *Autonomy. [I.L.]

Bibliography: Z. Frankel, *Der gerichtliche Beweis nach mosaisch-talmudischem Rechte* (1846), 437–74; M. Bloch, *Das mosaisch-talmudische Besitzrecht* (1897), 13–48; J. Lewin, in: *Zeitschrift fuer vergleichende Rechtswissenschaft*, 29 (1913), 151–298; J. Kohler, *ibid.*, 31 (1914), 312–5; J. S. Zuri, *Mishpat ha-Talmud*, 4 (1921), 19–28; Gulak, Yesodei, 1 (1922), 16f., 168–75; 4 (1922), 99f., 105, 114–28; A. Gulak, *Le-Ḥeker Toledot ha-Mishpat ha-Ivri bi-Tekufat ha-Talmud*, 1 (1929) (*Dinei Karka'ot*), 95–108; J. L. Kroch, *Ḥazakah Rabbah* (1927–63); Z. Karl, in: *Ha-Mishpat ha-Ivri*, 4 (1932/33), 93–112; Herzog, Instit, 1 (1936), 225–73; A. Karlin, in: *Sinai*, 22 (1947/48), 223–34; J. N. Epstein, *Mevo'ot le-Sifrut ha-Amora'im* (1962), 246–8; ET, 1 (1951[3]), passim (articles beginning with "*Ein Adam . . .*"); J. Unterman, in: *Sinai*, 54 (1964), 4–10; Z. Warhaftig, *Ha-Ḥazakah ba-Mishpat ha-Ivri* (1964); Elon, Mafte'aḥ, 72–79; J. Algazi, *Kehillat Ya'akov*, 2 (1898), 64a–87b ("*Kunteres Middot Ḥakhamim*"). IN THE MIDDLE AGES AND EARLY MODERN TIMES: I. Abrahams, *Jewish Life in the Middle Ages* (1920); Baron, Community, 3 (1942); Newman, Spain; I. Levitats, *Jewish Community in Russia* (1943); S. Dubnow, *Pinkas Medinat Lita* (1925); I. Halpern, *Pinkas Va'ad Arba Arazot* (1945); idem, *Takkanot Medinat Mehrin* (1952); H. H. Ben-Sasson, *Hagut ve-Hanhagah* (1959), index.

ḤAZAN, YA'AKOV (1899–), Israel political leader, a leading ideologist of *Mapam. Born in Brest Litovsk Ḥazan was a founder of the Hebrew Scout movement in Poland, which developed into *Ha-Shomer ha-Ẓa'ir. He was also a founder of He-Ḥalutz in Poland. In 1923 he moved to Palestine where he worked in the citrus groves and at swamp drainage before settling at kibbutz *Mishmar ha-Emek. A founder of *Ha-Kibbutz ha-Arẓi, the central kibbutz organization of Ha-Shomer ha-Ẓa'ir, he represented the movement in Zionist, *yishuv*, and Histadrut institutions. He was a member of the Mapam Central Committee, a member of the Knesset from its foundation, and a regular contributor to the movement's press. In 1969 he was one of the architects of Mapam's alignment with the *Israel Labor Party. [A.A.]

Ya'akov Ḥazan, a leading ideologist of Israel's Mapam party. Courtesy Government Press Office, Tel Aviv.

HAZAZ, ḤAYYIM (1898–), Hebrew writer. Born in Sidorovichi (Kiev province), Hazaz received a traditional and secular education, studying Hebrew and Russian literature. From the age of 16 (1914), when he left home, to 1921 he moved from one large Russian city to another. During and after the Russian Revolution he worked in Moscow on the Hebrew daily *Ha-Am* and at the time of the *Denikin and Wrangel pogroms he was in the Ukraine from where he escaped to the Crimean Mountains (1920). Hazaz went to Constantinople in 1921 where he lived about a year and a half and then moved to Western Europe, spending nine years in Paris and Berlin. The German capital had for a short time in the early 1920s become the Hebrew literary center after the Russian one had been destroyed by the revolution. Early in 1931 he left for Ereẓ Israel and settled in Jerusalem. Hazaz was politically active much of his life. He was the president of the Israel-Africa Friendship Association from 1965 (when it was founded) until 1969. After the Six-Day War (1967) Hazaz was prominent in the Land of Israel movement calling for settlement in the territories occupied during the war and for their permanent inclusion in the State of Israel.

Early Period—Russia. Hazaz began his literary career in Russia, publishing in *Ha-Shilo'aḥ* (1918, 274–84) under the pseudonym Ḥ. Ẓevi "*Ke-Vo ha-Shemesh*," a sketch, followed half a year later by his only short poem, "*Al ha-Mishmar*," dedicated to Saul Tchernichowsky. "*Meri*" and "*Ma'amar Moshe Rabbenu*" also appeared in *Ha-Shilo'aḥ* (1925, 1926), but under his own name. Hazaz published much during this period; his stories were well received and he gained wide acclaim. Many of his stories are set against the background of the Russian Revolution, among these are: "*Mi-Zeh u-mi-Zeh*" ("From This and That," in *Ha-Tekufah*, 21 (1924), 1–32); "*Pirkei Mahpekhah*" ("Chapters of the Revolution," *ibid.*, 22 (1924), 69–97); and "*Shemu'el Frankfurter*" (*ibid.*, 23 (1925), 81–184). The overall theme is the fate of the Jewish *shtetl* and the chaos and destruction wrought in its traditional way of life by the revolution whose impact is however only implicitly expressed. It is reflected in the interaction of forces from within and from without rather than directly represented by any single character. In all three stories only one non-Jewish revolutionary appears. Hazaz' fundamental interest in the revolution is thus on the level of human relations and understanding where it sowed bewilderment and confusion. The brief and concise description of events, trends, emotions, and characters and the fragmentary dialogue lend reality and immediacy to the narrative. However, the division of characters into the young revolutionary generation on the one hand and the anti-revolutionary older generation on the other is somewhat schematic. The general pervading mood is one of destruction in which the old world is wrenched from its axis while the new world is as yet not clearly focused. Thus the older generation, in the throes of tragedy, gains the sympathy of the reader. The young, however, are neither accused nor derided and even the irony directed against them is mild. Hazaz rewrote two of the stories: *"Mi-Zeh u-mi-Zeh"* became *"Nahar Shotef"* ("Flowing River," 1955, 1958, 1968), and *"Pirkei Mahpekhah"* became *Daltot Neḥoshet* ("Copper Doors," 1 vol., 1956; 2 vols., 1968). Best among the revolutionary stories, *"Shemu'el Frankfurter,"* has as a protagonist a revolutionary idealist, a Jesus-like figure, whose noble character leads him to a martyr's death. The story was excluded from his collected works and the author has stated that it needs rewriting (*Ma'ariv*, Sept. 26, 1969). At this time Hazaz also wrote a number of works not on the *shtetl* theme. *"Ḥatan Damim"* ("Bridegroom of Blood," in *Ha-Tekufah*, 23 (1925), 149–72), a prose poem, unfolds against the stark Midian desert. Zipporah, the wife of Moses, is portrayed as a tragic figure abandoned by her husband who had become a man of God. Modern in tone, the work is a lyrical masterpiece. It appeared in all of Hazaz' editions (in four slightly different versions) including a bibliophilic edition. *Be-Yishuv shel Ya'ar* ("In a Forest Settlement," 1930), Hazaz' first novel, is set in the early 1900s during the Russo-Japanese war. The plot centers around a Jewish family living among gentiles "in a forest settlement" and evolves against a background of revolutionary ideas and the disintegration of tradition. The gentile characters are tall strong woodcutters closely tied to their native soil. On the surface the members of the Jewish family seem to be living peacefully but beneath the apparent calm lurks the reality of the Jew's rootlessness. This alienation casts him simultaneously in a derisive and in a tragic light. The Jewish characters seem to be haunted by a fatalistic pessimism which affects everything they do. Thus they view their moving to the countryside and their abandoning of traditional values as determined by fate. The parodic and satiric figure of the young *melammed*, a revolutionary who expounds Marxian theories, also believes that his failure to be active in political affairs is predetermined by fate. The

Ḥayyim Hazaz, Hebrew writer. Courtesy Government Press Office, Tel Aviv.

underlying symbol of cutting down the trees is imbued with Jewish characteristics. *Be-Yishuv shel Ya'ar* has not been included in any edition of Hazaz' works. He called it "a book full of printing errors and sown with some wild oats. This book does not exist for me" (*Ma'ariv*, Dec. 29, 1967), and yet he thought of rewriting it (*Ma'ariv*, Sept. 26, 1969).

Ereẓ Israel. *Reḥayim Shevurim* ("Broken Millstones," 1942) marks the beginning of Hazaz' Ereẓ Israel period. Six stories are still set in the Jewish *shtetl* while the remaining three depict life in Ereẓ Israel. The themes of the Diaspora stories—poverty, the *bet ha-midrash* and Torah study, interest on loans, loafers' banter, *maskilim* and gentiles, and riots—were also treated by his predecessors, but his individualistic outlook and style invested them with new meaning, originality, and verve. In *"Shelulit Genuzah"* ("The Hidden Puddle"), the protagonist, Eliah Kotlik, a pauper, runs away from his ever-nagging wife. The story is built upon a series of "flights" which reach their climax in his escape from Reb Kamatzel, who owes him money. Kotlik's last flight is of a moral nature motivated by the precept of the Torah not to harass an impoverished debtor. The contrast between the first and last flights points up the spiritual growth of the hero: the fleeing victim of the first flight turns into the fleeing persecutor of the last. On another level, the last flight reveals the shortcomings of the value system of modern society in contrast to that of traditional Judaism. Despite its debased material conditions, the Judaism of the *shtetl* was imbued with a great humanitarian spirit. Kotlik's jump into the muddy puddle is thus a symbolic act: he disturbed "... the stagnant puddle which had been contemplating the heavens." *"Adam mi-Yisrael"* ("A Jew") is a story episodic in structure whose narrator, the protagonist's son, relates the wanderings of his father from *bet midrash* to *bet midrash* and his death at the hand of rioters. A *shtetl's* mute cry on the day of a riot permeates *"Ashamnu"* ("We Have Sinned"), an ideational story. The quelled attempt at rebelling against the conventional behavior of the *galut* Jew in the face of danger serves but to heighten the anguish of the writhing *shtetl*. The tone, bitter and hostile, carries a note of choked helplessness. The structural framework of *"Dorot Rishonim"* ("First Generations") is a retrospective view of the destroyed *shtetl* on which Hazaz lavishes praise. The aura of stability and spiritual harmony of the *shtetl* is however disturbed by a sense of imminent danger. Ereẓ Israel is the locale of *"Ha-Tayyar ha-Gadol"* ("The Big Tourist"). The protagonist, a grotesque character, is drawn against the background of a satiric-humoristic description of the numerous holy historical sites that seem to spring up all over Ereẓ Israel. Hazaz' second major work, *Ha-Yoshevet ba-Gannim* ("Thou That Dwellest in the Gardens," 1944), is a novel which narrates the experiences of three generations of Yemenites living in Ereẓ Israel. The generation of elders is represented by an old man who dreams of the Messiah and tries to calculate his advent. Moving in a visionary world of his own, his sanity at times is doubted. His son represents the second generation that has thrown off the burden of the traditions of Yemenite-Jewish culture, but at the same time has not adapted to the cultural milieu of Israel. The third generation, the young daughter, though alive to the new environment, is unable to strike deep roots in the new culture and her integration remains superficial. *Avanim Roteḥot* ("Boiling Stones," 1946), his third book, is comprised of ten stories, the first of which is the second edition of *"Ḥatan Damim." "Galgal ha-Ḥozer," "Ba'alei Terisin,"* and *"Yeraḥem ha-Shem"* are sketches of Yemenite life. *"Harat Olam"* and *"Ḥavit Akhurah"* depict the life of German-Jewish immigrants in Ereẓ Israel. Humor and tragedy become inextricably intertwined especially when a ludicrous, grotesque, and mixed-up Israeli intrudes upon their life and creates even greater confusion. *"Esh Bo'eret"* and *"Drabkin"* are insights into the lives of immigrants from Eastern Europe. The former describes the naive devotion of *ḥalutzim* who, despite overwhelming hardships, escaped from Russia. In the latter the protagonist, Drabkin, is an embittered Zionist who in the Diaspora had dedicated his life to the rebuilding of the homeland but in Ereẓ Israel was unable to find a significant role to play in its life. Drabkin's rejection is psychological. Having been badly received on arrival he projects his frustrations onto his ideals. The gap between ideals and their practical realization is questioned by a number of Hazaz' heroes. In *"Ha-Derashah"* ("The Sermon"), perhaps the most famous of his works, the hero, Yudke, strongly criticizes the accepted notions of Zionism. He objects to Jewish history which he describes as a boring chronicle of massacre and futility; a history created by the gentiles rather than willed by the Jewish people. He exhorts the Haganah leaders to wipe this humiliating and soiled record of a sorely tried people from the consciousness of the "new Jew." Jews of the past, he argues, wallowed in the tragedy of exile, they really did not wish to be redeemed. Traditional Judaism while praying for redemption was actually bent on preventing it. The story has many artistic flaws; on the first level it is clearly didactic and verbose. Another level, however, which gives the story dramatic impact, is created by the hero, a psychologically motivated round character, whose inner conflicts become apparent during his sermon; by the catcalls which his speech evokes; and by the network of imagery interwoven through the fabric of the story.

Hazaz' most comprehensive work, *Ya'ish* (4 vols., 1947–52), is set within an ethnological framework and traces the life of Ya'ish, a young Yemenite Jew. An ascetic and a dreamer, he abandons his mysticism upon his arrival in Ereẓ Israel. The work is a deep psychological probing into the inner recesses of Ya'ish's mind. Hazaz demonstrates an amazing familiarity with Yemenite culture and its rich religious heritage. These form a closely woven pattern within which the trials and conflicts of the protagonist are enacted. The emotional range and tenion of the hero's struggles are filtered through the agonizing experience of a man whose fertile imagination and hallucinations are those of a kabbalist, whose perception is deep and penetrating, and whose inner struggles reveal a suffering divided soul. A network of symbols is woven through the fabric of the story highlighted by such fantasy scenes as Ya'ish's ascent to heaven where he converses with the angels. The Yemenite world with its local color and folklore is vividly and realistically conveyed and Ya'ish's life, steeped in mysticism, stands out in sharp relief against the backdrop of the humdrum life of the community. During the time that Hazaz wrote *Ya'ish*, he also published *Be-Keẓ ha-Yamim* ("At the End of Days," 1950) a play set in Germany (Ashkenaz) during the time of *Shabbetai Ẓevi; the theme of redemption not only creates the mood but is the motivating force of the dramatis personae. Despite the historical setting, the confrontation of ideas and concepts transcends time and place. The hero, a zealous advocate of messianism, faces a hostile public led by the rabbi who is the very embodiment of rationalist orthodoxy. The central theme of the drama is similar to that of *"Ha-Derashah"*: Jews suffer exile because they lack the courage to be redeemed. *Daltot Neḥoshet* (1956), an adapted and extended version of *"Pirkei Mahpekhah,"* was considerably revised stylistically. The author expanded the descriptive passages and restrained the expressionistic outbursts of the narrator whose personal feelings and attitude toward the revolution are now that of an outsider, the "objective observer." Instead of the earlier stormy fearful mood, the style is freighted with minute ironic descriptions. A retrospective tone weaves its way through the fabric of the story deflecting, and at times distorting, the narrator's angle of vision. *Ḥagorat Mazzalot* ("The Zodiac," 1958) is a collection of three stories: *"Ofek Natui," "Ḥuppah ve-Tabba'at,"* and *"Nahar Shotef."* The plot of *"Ofek Natui"* ("Horizon") unfolds against the background of the Lachish region, an area developed for agricultural settlement in the 1950s; the theme is again the basic Jewish problem of Diaspora versus "redemption." The protagonist of *"Ḥuppah ve-Tabba'at"* ("Canopy and Wedding Ring") is an old Tel Avivian woman who lost all her sons in the Holocaust. She supports herself through peddling notions in cafes and donates her last penny toward the writing and consecration of a *Sefer Torah*. This symbolic act underlines her death which comes to her while she has a vision on the seashore. She leaves life, in which she was an alien, to go to a world where she belongs. *Nahar Shotef*, an adaptation of *"Mi-Zeh u-mi-Zeh,"* shows similar stylistic changes as those effected in *Daltot ha-Neḥoshet*. *Be-Kolar Eḥad* ("In the One Collar," 1963; translated into French and Swedish) harks back to the struggle waged by the Jewish underground against the British in Palestine. The protagonists, young Jewish fighters condemned to death, cheat the hangman by committing suicide (the story is based on an actual occurrence). The question of Diaspora, redemption, and **kiddush ha-Shem* is also a major theme here. The concept of self-sacrifice for an ideal holy to man is present in all of Hazaz' works.

A revised edition of all his writings appeared in 1968. Hazaz more than once rewrote many of his works and while claiming that he remained faithful to the essence of his writings (*Moznayim*, 26 (1968), 261), he also insisted that whoever only read his early writings, without rereading them in the later editions, would not know him (*Ma'ariv*, Dec. 29, 1967). Hazaz' writings are extensive geographically, historically, and ethnographically. Geographically, he ranges over an area that extends from the far north of Russia to the south of Yemen, from Germany in the west to Ereẓ Israel in the east. Historically his creative imagination encompasses biblical times, prior to the revelation at Mount Sinai, extending to the Second Temple period before the destruction of the Temple, the messianic dreamers in Germany, the prerevolutionary period and the revolution years in Russia, the riots in the Diaspora and in Ereẓ Israel, the Holocaust generation and the one that has been resuscitated out of its own ashes, the fighters for Israel's freedom, and the new settlement in Israel. Ethnographically he roams over much of the Diaspora (from Russia to Yemen), probing into the life of different segments of the Jewish people and portraying them in their original dwellings and in their new homes. His themes form a network of fundamental ideas and phenomena of contemporary Jewish life, which he relates to the history of the nation. The modern Jewish period he sees as a link in the great chain of Jewish national history and of the different Jewish historical epochs: "These are multivariant parts of culture of one national personality which have been welded together" (*Hed ha-Ḥinnukh*, no. 37 (1968), 7). This concept of unity is also reflected in Hazaz' style and language whose imagery and multiplicity of meaning are rooted in the ancient sources, thus encompassing and integrating simultaneously sources and originality. The wealth of his linguistic associations and his original imagery, at once real and fictitious, are the hallmarks of his style. Hazaz in his writings drew on his very wide knowledge of Talmud and Midrash to weave an intricate literary pattern. Thus many of his references and allusions are somewhat obscure to the average modern reader. In his revisions he has tended to minimize Arabic idioms which he had used extensively to create an effect of colloquial speech. He also deleted kabbalistic and *gematria* allusions and plays on cryptic words to arrive at a more limpid style. All his revisions thus have a sense of novelty and freshness. A movement from the tragic to the grotesque and satiric can be discerned in most of Hazaz' writings, especially in his later works. He uses different stylistic devices to achieve the tragic-comic. In his Russian tales the *shtetl* often rises to tragic stature, only to sink into caricature. A juxtaposition of sublime beliefs and the pettiness of those who profess them strikes the tragic-comic note in the Yemenite tales: thus the exalted redemptive theme of *Ha-Yoshevet ba-Gannim* is offset by parody; and the tragic moments in *Ya'ish* are undermined by the absurd. The play *Be-Keẓ ha-Yamim* borders on the tragic-grotesque. Hazaz was awarded the Israel Prize for Literature in 1953.

For English translations see: Goell, Bibliography, 2140–69, 2648, 2817; see also Spicehandler, in *Ariel* 1967.

Bibliography: M. Avishai, *Shorashim ba-Ẓammeret* (1969), 107–20; A. Ukhmani, *Le-Ever Adam* (1953), 248–82; J. Bahat, *S. Y. Agnon ve-Ḥ. Hazaz—Iyyunei Mikra* (1962), 175–257; idem, in: *Ha-Ḥinnukh*, 3–4 (1967), 121–7; idem, in: *Tarbiz*, 39 (1969/70), 390–414; idem, in: *Hasifrut*, 2 (1970), 538–64; A. Ben-Or, *Toledot ha-Sifrut ha-Ivrit be-Dorenu*, 2 (1955), 97–131, includes bibliography; I. Halpern, *Ha-Mahpekhah ha-Yehudit* (1967), 518–45; I. Zmora, *Shenei Mesapperim—Ḥ. Hazaz ve-Ya'akov Horovitz* (1940), 9–32; I. Cohen, *Demut el Demut* (1949), 56–115; D. Kena'ani, *Beinam le-Vein Zemannam* (1955), 37–93; F. Lachower, *Rishonim va-Aḥaronim*, 2 (1935), 182–94; B. Y. Michali, *Ḥayyim Hazaz; Iyyunim bi-Yẓirato* (1968); D. Miron, *Ḥayyim Hazaz* (1959); D. Sadan, *Avnei Boḥan* (1951), 237–51; S. Y. Penueli, *Demuyyot be-Sifrutenu ha-Ḥadashah* (1946), 131–43; idem, *Ḥulyot be-Sifrutenu ha-Ḥadashah* (1953), 171–85; idem, *Sifrut ki-Feshutah* (1963), 297–324; S. Kremer, *Re'alizm u-Shevirato* (1968), 149–73; J. Keshet, *Havdalot* (1962), 170–232; E. Schweid, *Shalosh Ashmorot* (1964), 71–89. [J.BAH.]

HA-ẒEFIRAH (Heb. הַצְּפִירָה, "The Dawn"), a Hebrew paper appearing in Warsaw intermittently between 1862 and 1931. Founded as a weekly in 1862 by Ḥayyim Selig *Slonimski, *Ha-Ẓefirah* was devoted to science and technology, the only Hebrew paper of its kind during the 1860s and 1870s. The space devoted to news and Jewish scholarship was negligible. Slonimsky, who had written scientific books in Hebrew from the 1830s, sought a regular forum for tracing the development of the sciences, which were expanding rapidly in those years. *Mendele Mokher Seforim, writing on science and technology, contributed regularly, but Slonimsky was the principal contributor to most issues. The paper ceased publication after six months when the editor was appointed principal of the rabbinical school in Zhitomir. When that institution closed down in 1874, Slonimsky revived *Ha-Ẓefirah*. Unable to obtain a permit in Russia, he published the paper in Berlin in the summer of 1874, with the aid of J. L. *Kantor. Although still mainly devoted to the sciences, Kantor introduced into the paper topical articles, political commentaries, and reports from Russia and other countries. Finally, Slonimsky obtained his licence and the paper again appeared in Warsaw from September 1875 until it ceased publication.

In Warsaw, too, Slonimsky devoted the bulk of the paper to science and the rest to sections then common in the Hebrew press. In 1876, however, when Nahum *Sokolow began writing for the paper, its character changed as he increasingly supplemented scientific writing with topical articles and surveys of current affairs. Originally only a regular contributor, Sokolow became acting editor, then chief editor, and finally the author of almost all articles appearing in the paper. In the early 1880s he gradually reduced the size of the science section and made the paper more like its contemporaries, only more vibrant. Thanks to his introduction of variety into the paper's content, *Ha-Ẓefirah* enjoyed a wide circulation. Sokolow's name became synonymous with *Ha-Ẓefirah* and his articles on

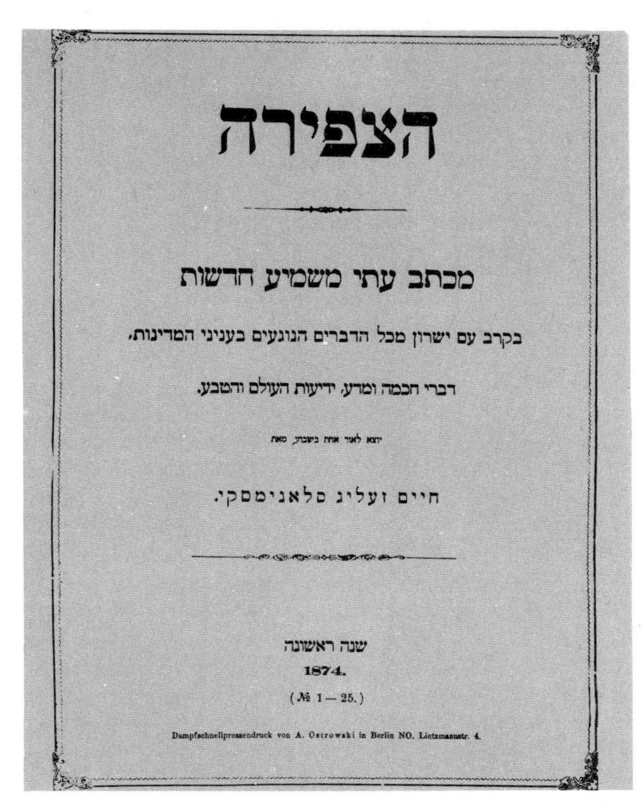
הצפירה

מכתב עתי משמיע חדשות

בקרב עם ישרון מכל הדברים הנוגעים בעניני המדינות,

דברי חכמה ומדע, ידיעות העולם והטבע.

יוצא לאור אחת בשבוע, מאת

חיים זעליג סלאנימסקי.

שנה ראשונה

1874.

(№ 1 — 25.)

Dampfschnellpressendruck von A. Ostrowski in Berlin NO. Lietzmannstr. 4.

Title page of the first volume of the revived publication of *Ha-Ẓefirah*, a Hebrew paper devoted largely to science and technology, Berlin, 1874. Jerusalem, J.N.U.L.

various subjects attracted many readers both among the *maskilim* and the Ḥasidim. Following *Ha-Yom's* lead, *Ha-Ẓefirah* became a daily in 1886, and began to provide an opportunity for new writers. Because Sokolow was deeply rooted in Polish Jewry, the paper served as the principal organ of Polish Jewry for almost two generations. *Ha-Ẓefirah* also printed reports from most of the Jewish centers throughout the world, particularly Ereẓ Israel and the United States. Sokolow realized the importance of innovation and novelty in journalism. Accordingly, he periodically changed the paper's format and writing style, to meet changing tastes. The attitude of Sokolow and the paper toward the Ḥibbat Zion movement and political Zionism was at first reserved, but after the First Zionist Congress *Ha-Ẓefirah* was faithful to Herzl.

Ha-Ẓefirah ceased publication early in 1906 when Sokolow became secretary of the World Zionist Organization. In 1910 the paper was revived with Sokolow as regular contributor, but edited by several of his disciples. During World War I the paper again ceased publication, but was reissued as a weekly in 1917 and as a daily in 1920. It did not appear from 1921 to 1926, when it was revived only to be discontinued again in 1928. *Ha-Ẓefirah* appeared for the last time in 1931, the year it permanently ceased publication. Among the paper's later editors were Isaac *Nissenbaum, Yiẓḥak *Gruenbaum, Joseph Heftman, and A. A. *Akaviah.

Bibliography: Kressel, Leksikon, 2 (1967), 481–7, 504–7. [G.K.]

ḤAẒER, ḤAẒERIM (Heb. חָצֵר,חֲצֵרִים), (1) a biblical term for seminomadic settlements on the edge of the Negev that were fenced in but not walled. The *ḥaẓerim* occupy an intermediate position between nomadic encampments and settled towns (Josh. 21:12, where it is translated as "villages"), but in the course of time some of them developed into towns (cf. Hazar-Gaddah, Hazar-Shual, Josh. 15:27–28, etc.). A similar meaning is apparently expressed by the term *ḥagar* (from the root meaning "to fence in"). Place

names combined with *ḥagar* are frequently mentioned in the Negev in the lists of *Shishak's conquests; in later sources the term refers to the Roman *limes*. The Avvim, who were absorbed by the invading Caphtorim (Philistines), also lived in *ḥaẓerim* in the south as far as Gaza (Deut. 2:23). In the Targum Yerushalmi, *Ḥaẓerim* is considered a locality and is identified with Rafah. [M.A.-Y.]

(2) ḤAẒERIM (Heb. חֲצֵרִים), kibbutz in the northern Negev, Israel, 4½ mi. (7 km.) W. of Beersheba, affiliated with Iḥud ha-Kevuẓot va-ha-Kibbutzim, founded by graduates of Youth Aliyah, among them "Teheran Children" and Israel-born youth on the night of Oct. 6, 1946, on which ten other new settlements were simultaneously set up in the South and Negev. In the first ten years of its existence, Ḥaẓerim sought ways to treat its desert loess soils and overcame isolation and siege in the *War of Independence (1948). In 1969 the kibbutz economy was based on field crops (mostly irrigated), fruit orchards, cattle, and an industrial enterprise, "Netafim," for drip irrigation equipment. [E.O.]

Bibliography: (1) Maisler, in: *Sefer . . ., J. N. Epstein* (1950), 317ff.; J. Braslavsky, *Le-Ḥeker Arẓenu* (1954), 255ff.

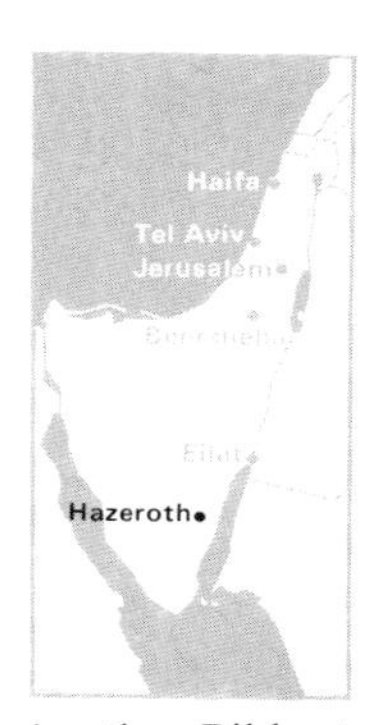

HAZEROTH (Heb. חֲצֵרוֹת, *ḥaẓerot*). (1) The second station of the Israelites on their journey eastward from Mount Sinai to Ezion-Geber between Kibroth-Hattaavah and Rithmah in the wilderness of Paran (Num. 11:35; 33:17–18). At Hazeroth, Miriam and Aaron "spoke against" Moses because he had married "a Cushite woman," and in punishment Miriam was "shut up" for seven days, during which the people waited there (*ibid.* 12:16). Hazeroth is also mentioned in the Bible together with Di-Zahab (Deut. 1:1). Its identification is dependent on the location of Mount Sinai. Those scholars who accept the traditional view of Mount Sinai at Jebel Musa identify Hazeroth with the oasis of ʿAyn al-Ḥaḍra, northwest of Dhahad (Di-Zahab?). Others who identify Mount Sinai with Jebel Ḥilāl locate Hazeroth at another ʿAyn al-Ḥaḍra in its vicinity. (2) A Hazeroth is mentioned on the Samaria ostraca among the places paying tribute of wine and oil to Samaria in the time of the Israelite kingdom. It is possibly identical with ʿAṣīra al-Shamāliyya, 3 mi. (5 km.) north of Shechem.

Bibliography: (1) Ms. W. M. F. Petrie, *Researches in Sinai* (1906), 262; Abel, Geog, 2 (1938), 214, 344; C. S. Jarvis, *Yesterday and Today in Sinai* (1931), 161, 171f.; (2) Ms. G. A. Reisner, et al., *Harvard Excavations at Samaria*, 1 (1924), 228ff. [M.A.-Y.]

ḤAẒEVAH (Heb. חֲצֵבָה), moshav in the central Aravah Valley, southern Israel, about 2½ mi. (4 km.) S. of Sodom, affiliated with Tenu'at ha-Moshavim. It was founded in 1965 as a *Naḥal border outpost settlement. The moshav lies about 3 mi. (5 km.) southeast of the spring, oasis, and ancient site by that name (*Notitia Dignitatum*, ed. by O. Seeck (1876) gives *Eisiba*, ʿAyn Ḥuṣub in Arabic), where Iron Age sherds were found. Under Roman rule, Ḥaẓevah was a border castle at an important road junction, and a military unit, the second cohort of the Gratiana Legion, was stationed there. Under the British Mandate, a police station was set up near the spring which is the most abundant in the Israel part of the Aravah Valley. In November 1948, the occupation of Ḥaẓevah by Israel forces lifted the siege of Sodom and led to the conquest of the whole Negev. In the early 1950s an experimental station, mainly for the propagation of forest trees, was established at the oasis. In the 1960s, the existence of rich groundwater reserves in the area was confirmed. Two small settlements exist nearer the spring, a village of private farmers and a group of immigrants, mainly from North America. [E.O.]

HAZKARAT NESHAMOT (Heb. הַזְכָּרַת נְשָׁמוֹת; "mentioning of the souls"), memorial prayer. In the Ashkenazi ritual, it is said after the reading of the Torah, during the morning service of the last day of Passover, Shavuot, and Sukkot (the three pilgrimage festivals), and on the Day of Atonement. In the Sephardi rite it is recited also on the Day of Atonement eve before *Ma'ariv*.

The prayer is divided into three sections; the principal part opens the prayer with the words, *"Yizkor Elohim"* ("May God remember . . . the soul . . ."). In common language the prayer has therefore become known as *Yizkor* or *Mazkir*. *Hazkarat Neshamot* expresses the fervent hope that the departed souls will enjoy eternal life in God's presence. There is evidence that this custom dates back to the period of the Hasmonean wars (c. 165 B.C.E.) when *Judah Maccabee and his men prayed for the souls of their fallen comrades and brought offerings to the Temple in Jerusalem as atonement for the sins of the dead (II Macc. 22:39–45). The belief that the meritorious deeds of descendants can atone for the departed appears frequently in aggadic literature (Hor. 6a; TJ, Sanh. 10:4, 29c; Sif. Deut. 210; Tanḥ. Berakhah 1; et al.). However, *Hai Gaon and his pupil *Nissim b. Jacob (c. 1000 C.E.) opposed the custom of praying for the departed on festivals and on the Day of Atonement, and of donating to charity on their behalf. They believed that only the actual deeds performed by a person during his lifetime count before God. Nevertheless,

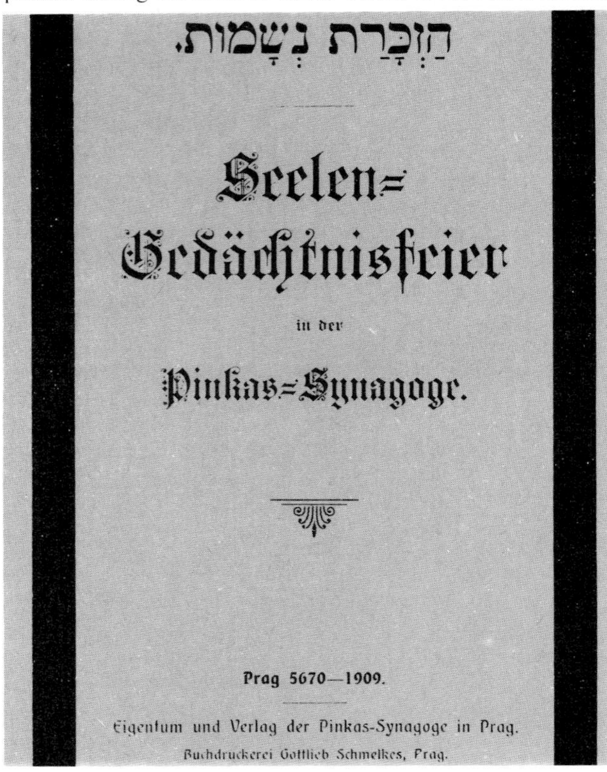
הַזְכָּרַת נְשָׁמוֹת.

Seelen=
Gedächtnisfeier
in der
Pinkas=Synagoge.

Prag 5670—1909.

Eigentum und Verlag der Pinkas-Synagoge in Prag.
Buchdruckerei Gottlieb Schmelkes, Prag.

Title page of the *Hazkarat Neshamot* recited at the Pinkas Synagogue, Prague, 1909. Jerusalem, E. Grodesky Collection.

the memorial prayer became one of the most popular and cherished customs, especially in the *Ashkenazi ritual. Historically, it gained its significance through the *Crusades and through the severe persecutions that took place in Eastern Europe during the 17th century when thousands of Jews died as martyrs. They were all inscribed in the death rolls (called *kunteres* or *memorbuch*, or *yizker-bukh*) of their communities and commemorated in the memorial prayers held on the three festivals, on the Day of Atonement and, in some congregations, on the Sabbaths during the **Omer* period (between Passover and Shavuot). In time, the death rolls came to include names not only of martyrs, but also of other members of the community, and the custom of memorial prayers for individuals evolved. After the memorial prayer for relatives, in the Ashkenazic rite the prayer **El Male Raḥamim* is recited for those who have died. Nowadays, a special prayer is frequently added for the victims of the Nazi Holocaust and for the Jewish soldiers who died in wars, particularly in Israel. The traditional memorial service concludes with the recital of **Av ha-Raḥamim*. The Torah Scroll(s) which had been taken out for the Reading of the Law is (are) returned to the Ark and the *musaf* service follows. In the Sephardi ritual, instead of reciting the *Hazkarat Neshamot* after the Torah service, everyone who is called to the Torah, after blessing it, recites a memorial prayer for his relatives. *Hazkarat Neshamot* mentions charitable offerings "for the repose of the departed souls" (Sh. Ar., OḤ 621:6) and in Orthodox synagogues, it is customary to promise donations during the service. It is also customary that those whose parents are still alive leave the synagogue during the entire *Hazkarot Neshamot* prayer. In the Conservative ritual, several introductory readings and appropriate Psalm verses in Hebrew and in the vernacular, as well as sections for meditation and special responsive readings in that language, were added to the traditional text of *Hazkarat Neshamot*. In the Reform ritual, the memorial service is held only on the last day of Passover and on the Day of Atonement as part of the late afternoon service before **Ne'ilah*. This service consists of a shortened version of the traditional text, the recital of Psalm 23 and of selected poems by Ibn *Gabirol, *Judah Halevi, and *Baḥya b. Joseph, and of readings and meditations expressing the transience and evanescence of life and the merits of those who have lived an exemplary life. Solemn music accompanies this *Hazkarat Neshamot* service which concludes with the entire congregation reciting the **Kaddish*. Synagogues are usually well attended by both men and women on the days that *Hazkarat Neshamot* is said; in some congregations these days have become occasions for major sermons by the rabbi.

See also **Ashkavah*.

Bibliography: ET, 8 (1957), 603–9; S. Hurwitz (ed.), *Maḥzor Vitry* (1923²), 392; Eisenstein, Yisrael, 96f.; M. Silverman, *High Holiday Prayer Book (Conservative)* (1939), 321–31; idem, *Sabbath and Festival Prayer Book (Conservative)* (1946), 221–7; *Union Prayer Book (Reform)*, 1 (1959), 268–73; 2 (1945³), 306–24; Hertz, Prayer, 1106–08; P. Birnbaum, *High Holiday Prayer Book* (1951), 727–34; Petuchowski, *Prayerbook Reform in Europe* (1968), index.

[M.Y.]

ḤAZKUNI, ABRAHAM (b. 1627), rabbi and kabbalist. Ḥazkuni, who was born in Cracow, was a disciple of Yom Tov Lipmann *Heller. He published a summary of Isaac *Luria's *Sefer ha-Kavvanot* under the title *Zot Ḥukkat ha-Torah* (Venice, 1659). His commentary on the *Zohar, *Shetei Yadot* consisting of two parts, *Yad Ramah* and *Yad Adonai*, was lost through the negligence of the printer, with the exception of eight pages which are preserved in Oxford and New York (JTS). Ḥazkuni's son Jacob later published his father's commentary on the Pentateuch under this same title (Amsterdam, 1726). Ḥazkuni also wrote *Zera Avraham*, a two-part work containing casuistic *derashot* on the Torah; *Yode'a Binah*, of unknown content; and novellae to the tractates *Beẓah* and *Mo'ed Katan*. He died in Tripoli.

Bibliography: Fuenn, Keneset, 24; Michael, Or, no. 92; P. H. Wetstein, in: *Ha-Eshkol* 7 (1913), 173–4; Neubauer, Cat, no. 1729, 6.

[Sh.A.H./Ed.]

HA-ẒOFEH (Heb. הַצּוֹפֶה), (1) daily Hebrew newspaper, published in Warsaw from 1903 to 1905. Following the journalistic tradition of **Ha-Yom*, *Ha-Ẓofeh* was well-balanced in its presentation of items of both Jewish and general interest, and upheld a Zionist point of view. Published daily, without interruption, the paper was managed by Y. A. Eliashov who also provided substantial financial support. Its first editor, A. *Ludvipol, was succeeded by H. D. *Nomberg. Ludvipol's regular staff included Simon *Bernfeld, Reuben *Brainin, A. L. Levinsky, I. L. *Peretz, and J. *Klausner, each of whom contributed material in his own field, e.g., stories, critical essays on Hebrew, Jewish and general literature, articles of political content, and feuilletons. Among the many other contributors to *Ha-Ẓofeh* were: Hillel *Zeitlin, *Mendele Mokher Seforim, S. *Asch, Ḥ. N. *Bialik, S. *Ben-Zion, Y. D. *Berkowitz, I. *Bershadski, Y. *Gruenbaum, S. *Tchernichowsky, Ya'akov *Cahan, S. A. *Horodezky, V. Z. *Jabotinsky (he began his Hebrew writing here), M.L. *Lilienblum, J. *Fichmann, Itzhak *Katzenelson, Yaakov *Rabinowitz, Judah *Steinberg, Jacob *Steinberg, and Moshe *Smilansky.

Ha-Ẓofeh was bitterly opposed to the *Uganda Scheme. During the Sixth *Zionist Congress (1903), it reached the peak of its circulation (almost 15,000 subscribers), because of its reporting of Herzl's opening remarks on Uganda in a telegram (something hitherto unheard of in the Hebrew press), and also because of its representation at the Congress by Brainin, Bernfeld, Ludvipol, and Ḥermoni. A free copy of all of Bialik's poems was presented to its subscribers while subscribers to **Ha-Shilo'aḥ* were granted a substantial discount. The newspaper was discontinued in 1905, during the first Russian revolution, mainly because members of the *Bund struck against the publishing house in which the paper was published.

Ha-Ẓofeh conducted the first short-story contest in Hebrew literature. Y.D. Berkowitz won first prize, and his story was published, together with other worthy entries and the opinions of the judges, in *Koveẓ Sippurim* (1904).

(2) Hebrew organ of the *National Religious Party published in Israel from 1937. Religious periodicals with a nationalistic orientation began to appear with the founding of the *Mizrachi movement, and were published in many European countries, in the United States, and in Israel. *Ha-Ẓofeh* first appeared in Jerusalem on August 4, 1937, edited by *Rabbi Binyamin, who also wrote the greater part of each copy. The paper, which appeared three times a week, was discontinued after 16 copies, but was renewed, as a daily, in Tel Aviv (Dec. 17, 1937). Rabbi Meir *Bar-Ilan (Berlin), who had been editor in chief of the paper in Jerusalem, remained in that capacity. Mordekhai *Lipson became editor of the daily *Ha-Ẓofeh*, assisted by Y. Bernstein and S.B. Feldman. Following internal contention over the nature of the newspaper, *Ha-Ẓofeh* became the organ of the worldwide Mizrachi movement. Its editors were Y. Bernstein and from 1951, S. *Don-Yaḥia (S. Daniel). The newspaper embraces all fields of the modern daily and includes all the usual sections. The weekly literary supplement of *Ha-Ẓofeh* focuses special attention on Jewish studies, both in Israel and abroad.

Bibliography: (1) E. E. Friedman, *Sefer ha-Zikhronot* (1926), 275–314; J. Klausner, in: *Ha-Boker* (Jan. 2, 1953); Y. Rabinowitz, in: *Davar* (Jun. 1, 1945). (2) *Ha-Ẓofeh* (Jan. 20, 1939); (Jan. 6, 1948); (June 6, 1954); (Sept. 18, 1963); S. Daniel, in: *Sefer ha-Shanah shel ha-Ittona'im* (1963), 36–39; G. Kressel, *Toledot ha-Ittonut ha-Ivrit be-Ereẓ Yisrael* (1964), 166–72.

[G.K.]

HAZOR (Heb. חָצוֹר), a large Canaanite and Israelite city in Upper Galilee. It is identified with Tell al-Qidāḥ (also called Tell Waqqāṣ), 8¾ mi. (14 km.) north of the Sea of Galilee and 5 mi. (8 km.) southwest of Lake *Ḥuleh. The city was strategically located in ancient times and dominates the main branches of the Via Maris ("Way of the Sea") leading from Egypt to Mesopotamia, Syria, and Anatolia.

Canaanite Hazor is mentioned in the Egyptian Execration Texts (19th or 18th century B.C.E.) and is the only Palestinian town mentioned (together with Laish) in the Mari documents (18th century B.C.E.) where it appears as a major commercial center of the Fertile Crescent with caravans traveling between it and Babylon. It is also frequently mentioned in Egyptian documents of the New Kingdom: in the city lists of Thutmoses III (where it appears together with Laish (*Dan), *Pella, and *Kinnereth), and of Amenhotep II and Seti I. In the *Tell-Amarna letters, the kings of Ashtaroth and Tyre accuse Abdi-Tirshi, king of Hazor, of taking several of their cities. The king of Tyre furthermore states that the king of Hazor left his city to join the *Habiru. In other letters, however, Abdi-Tirshi—one of the few Canaanite rulers to call himself king—proclaims his loyalty to Egypt. Hazor is also referred to in the Papyrus Anastasi I (probably from the time of Ramses II).

The Bible contains a direct reference to the role of Hazor at the time of Joshua's conquests. *Jabin, king of Hazor, headed a league of several Canaanite cities against Joshua in the battle at the waters of *Merom: "And Joshua turned back at that time, and took Hazor, and smote the king thereof with the sword: for Hazor beforetime was the head of all those kingdoms . . . and he burnt Hazor with fire . . . But as for the cities that stood on their mounds, Israel burned none of them, save Hazor only—that did Joshua burn" (Josh. 11:10–13). Hazor is also indirectly mentioned in the prose account of *Deborah's wars (Judg. 4) in contrast to the "Song of Deborah" (Judg. 5) which deals with a battle in the Jezreel Valley and does not mention Hazor. According to I Kings 9:15, the city was rebuilt by Solomon together with *Megiddo and *Gezer. The last biblical reference to Hazor records its conquest, with other Galilean cities, by *Tiglath-Pileser III in 732 B.C.E. (II Kings 15:29). In Hasmonean times, Jonathan and his army, marching northward from the Ginnosar (Gennesar) Valley during his wars against Demetrius, camped on the plain of Hazor near *Kedesh (I Macc. 11:76). Josephus locates the city above Lake Semachonitis (Ant. 5:199).

Hazor was first identified with Tell al-Qidāḥ by J. L. Porter in 1875 and again by J. Garstang in 1926. The latter conducted soundings at the site in 1928. Four large campaigns of excavations—the James A. de Rothschild Expedition—took place between 1955 and 1958, under the direction of Y. Yadin on behalf of the Hebrew University, with the aid of P.I.C.A., the Anglo-Israel Exploration Society, and the Israel government. A fifth campaign took place in 1968.

The site of Hazor is composed of two separate areas—the tell proper covering some 30 acres (120 dunams) and rising some 130 ft. (40 m.) above the surrounding plain, and a large rectangular plateau, about 175 acres (700 dunams) in area, north of the tell. The latter is protected on its western side by a huge rampart of beaten earth and a deep fosse, on the north by a rampart and on the other sides by its natural steep slopes reinforced by glacis and walls.

Figure 1. Aerial photograph of Hazor showing the tell proper (1), the plateau north of the tell (2), and the rampart of beaten earth west of the plateau (3). Courtesy Yigael Yadin, Jerusalem.

Lower City. Garstang had concluded from his soundings that the large plateau (enclosure) was a camp site for infantry and chariots and since he found no Mycenean pottery (which first appears in the area after 1400 B.C.E.), he dated Hazor's final destruction to about 1400, the date he ascribed to Joshua's conquest. The excavations, however, revealed that the enclosure was not a camp site but that the entire area was occupied by a city with five levels of occupation. It was first settled in the mid-18th century B.C.E. (Middle Bronze Age II), to which the fortifications date, and was finally destroyed sometime before the end of the 13th century B.C.E. The discovery of Mycenean and local ware from the 13th century helped to disprove Garstang's date of its fall. Seven areas in different parts of the lower city were excavated and the same chronology was found in all. The first city (stratum 4) was followed by a settlement (stratum 3) from the end of the Middle Bronze Age II (17th–16th centuries) which was razed by fire. The city was rebuilt in the Late Bronze Age I (stratum 2, 15th century). This stratum represents the peak of Hazor's prosperity together with the 14th-century city (stratum Ib) in which times Hazor was the largest city in the area in the land of Canaan; City Ib suffered destruction in undetermined circumstances. The last settlement in the lower city (stratum Ia) was a reconstruction of the previous one and with its fall, before the end of the 13th century, occupation ceased in the lower city. Its destruction, both here and in the contemporary city on the tell, is to be ascribed to the conquering Israelite tribes, as is related in detail in the Book of Joshua.

In the southwestern corner of the lower city (area C) a small sanctuary was found on the foot of the inner slope of the rampart. It dates from stratum Ib and was rebuilt in Ia. A number of basalt steles and statuettes were found in a niche in one of the walls, one with two hands raised toward a divine lunar symbol—a crescent and a circle, and a statuette of a seated male figure with its head intentionally broken off. Benches for offerings line the walls of the temple. A pottery cult mask was found in a potter's workshop nearby as well as a bronze standard plated with silver and bearing a relief of a snake goddess.

Rock-cut tombs with an elaborate network of tunnels connecting them were found in the eastern sector of the lower city (area F), dating from the earliest stratum. A large building (probably a temple) with thick walls was constructed there in the next city which used the older tunnels for a drainage system. In the next stratum (stratum II) a temple was built. In stratum 1b the area assumed a definite cultic character and a large monolithic altar with depressions for draining the sacrificial blood stood there.

In several areas, a large number of infant burials in jars were found beneath the floors of houses from stratum III.

Four superimposed temples were found in area H, at the northern edge of the lower city. The earliest (stratum III) consisted of a broad hall with a small niche—a sort of holy of holies. South of the hall was a raised platform reached by several finely dressed basalt steps. The next temple was substantially the same in plan but a closed court was added and an open courtyard south of it. The court was entered through a broad propyleum. The courtyard contained a large rectangular *bamah* ("high place") and several altars. A clay model of a liver, inscribed in Akkadian, found in a pile of debris nearby, was intended for use by the priest-diviners and mentioned various evil omens. A bronze plaque of a Canaanite dignitary wrapped in a long robe was also found. In stratum 1b, the temple was composed of three chambers built on a single axis from south to north: a porch, a main hall, and a broad holy of holies with a rectangular niche in its northern wall. In its general plan it resembles several temples found at Alalakh in northern Syria as well as the temple of Solomon. A row of basalt orthostats (which may have belonged originally to the previous temple) forming a dado around the interior of the porch and the holy of holies which is very similar to some found at Alalakh and other sites, shows distinct evidence of northern influence. On either side of the entrance to the porch stood a basalt orthostat with a lion in relief (only one was found, buried in a pit). The following temple (stratum 1a) shows only minor alterations. Two round bases found in front of the entrance to the hall are apparently similar to the *Jachin and Boaz of Solomon's temple. The many ritual vessels (probably reused from the previous temple) include a basalt incense altar, with the emblem of the storm god in relief—a circle with a cross in the center, ritual tables and bowls, a statuette of a seated figure, cylinder seals and a scarab bearing the name of Amenhotep III. Outside the sanctuary were found fragments of a statue of a deity with the symbol of the storm god on its chest. The god had stood on a bull-shaped base.

A succession of city gates and walls ranging in date from the founding of the city to its final end was found in area K on the northeastern edge of the lower city. The gate from stratum III was strongly fortified, with towers on either side and three pairs of pilasters in the passage. A casemate wall adjoining it is the earliest example of this type found thus far in Ereẓ Israel. A similar series of gates was found in the 1968 season on the eastern edge of the lower city.

Upper City. Five areas were excavated on the tell proper where 21 levels (with additional sub-phases) of occupation were uncovered. Settlement began here in the 27th century B.C.E. (end of the Early Bronze Age II), and, after a gap between the 24th and 22nd centuries, it was resettled in the Middle Bronze Age I (stratum XVIII). From the period of Hazor's zenith (15th century) parts of a large palace (the residence of the king?) and temple were uncovered which contained part of an orthostat with a lioness in relief similar to the lion orthostat from the contemporary temple in the lower city. Stratum XIII, the last Late Bronze Age city on the tell, shows the same signs of destruction in the 13th century as were found in the lower city. The upper city, however, in contrast, was resettled after a short interruption, but not in the form of a true city. Most of its constructions are still of a seminomadic character—silos, hearths, and foundations for tents and huts. These remains are essentially identical with those of the Israelite settlements in Galilee in the 12th century and indicate that the majority of this settlement occurred only after the fall of the cities and provinces of Canaan.

Stratum XI is an 11th-century, unfortified Israelite settlement, with a small high place. Only from the time of Solomon onward did Hazor return to its former splendor, though on a smaller scale than in Canaanite times. Solomon rebuilt and fortified the upper city (stratum X) with a casemate wall and a large gate with three chambers on either side and two towers flanking the passage. These are identical with the fortifications he constructed at Gezer and Megiddo (cf. I Kings 9:15). The following city was destroyed by fire and rebuilt by the House of *Omri in the ninth century (stratum VIII) which erected a strong citadel covering most of the western part of the tell (area B). The

Figure 2. Reconstruction of a sanctuary found in the lower city of Hazor, 14th–13th century B.C.E. Jerusalem, Israel Museum. Courtesy Yigael Yadin, Jerusalem.

Figure 3. A part of the upper city of Hazor, showing Solomon's gate (1), a casemate wall of the tenth century B.C.E. (2), and a large storehouse, thought to have been built in the ninth century B.C.E. by the House of Omri (3). Courtesy Yigael Yadin, Jerusalem.

citadel is symmetrical in plan with two long halls running from east to west and surrounded on three sides by chambers. The entrance was ornamented with proto-Aeolic capitals and a monolithic lintel. Near the citadel were a number of public buildings. The citadel was strengthened in the eighth century and continued in use until Hazor's conquest by Tiglath-Pileser III in 732 B.C.E.

A large storehouse with two rows of pillars in the center (mistakenly interpreted as Solomon's stables by Garstang) also dates to stratum VIII (House of Omri). Stratum VI (eighth century) was destroyed by an earthquake, possibly the one which occurred in the days of *Jeroboam II, mentioned in the Book of Amos. The last fortified city at Hazor is represented by stratum V, and after its destruction by the Assyrians the city remained uninhabited except for a temporary unfortified settlement (stratum IV). A large citadel in stratum III was evidently constructed by the Assyrians and continued in use in the Persian period. Another citadel, from stratum I, is attributed to the second century, i.e., the Hellenistic period.

In the 1968 season a large underground water system was discovered at the center of the southern edge of the mound facing the natural spring below. It has the same plan (although on a much larger scale) as the famous one at Megiddo, and was hewn out of the rock at the same period, i.e., the ninth century B.C.E. (Hazor stratum VIII).

Bibliography: Y. Yadin et al., *Hazor,* 4 vols. (Eng., 1959–64); Y. Yadin, in: D. W. Thomas (ed.), *Archaeology and Old Testament Study* (1967), 245ff. (includes bibl.); Y. Yadin, *The Biblical Archaeologist*, vol. 32 no. 3, 50ff.

[Y.YA.]

ḤAẒOR (ha-Gelilit; Heb. (חָצוֹר (הַגְּלִילִית), development town with municipal council status in eastern Upper Galilee, N.E. of Rosh Pinnah and 2½ mi. (4 km.) S. of the mound of ancient Hazor. The site was chosen in 1950 and its first housing schemes were ready in 1953, taking in immigrants from the Rosh Pinnah *ma'barah* and newcomers and having a population of 895 by the end of that year. Large numbers of immigrants, principally from Middle East and North African countries, were housed at Ḥaẓor, but many of them left after a short interval, due to poor local conditions. Later, when economic opportunities improved, the population grew again and reached 5,250 at the end of 1969. Ḥaẓor's assets are a good position for communications, a rich farming hinterland in the Ḥuleh Valley, an ample water supply, and the availability of level ground for industrial enterprises. A drawback is the proximity of two other towns—Safed and Kiryat Shemonah. The economy is founded on industrial enterprises (fruit and vegetable dehydration and preserves, knitting, toys, ceramics, carpets) and on hired labor provided for farming villages of the vicinity.

[S.H.]

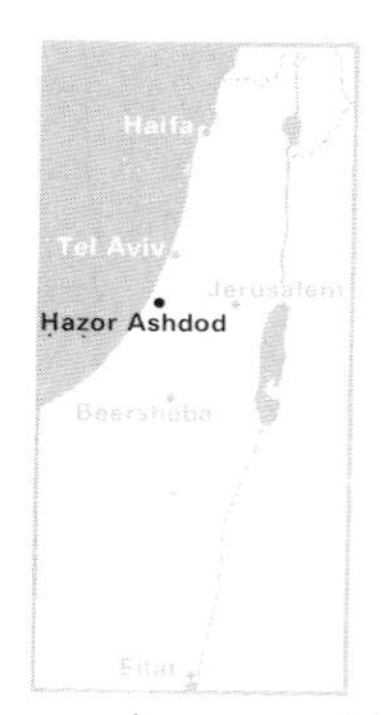

ḤAẒOR ASHDOD (Heb. חָצוֹר אַשְׁדּוֹד), kibbutz in the southern Coastal Plain of Israel, affiliated with Kibbutz Arẓi Ha-Shomer ha-Ẓa'ir. It was founded together with ten other settlements in the south and the Negev on Oct. 6, 1946, by a group which had previously founded *Gevulot as a Negev outpost. The members were joined by pioneer youth from the U.S., Bulgaria, and other countries. In 1968, Ḥaẓor Ashdod had 535 inhabitants, engaged in intensive farming, cattle, and running a metal foundry. The name Ḥaẓor is assumed to be historical as it is mentioned by Eusebius (Onom. 20:1; 30:22, et al.). The name of the nearest city, *Ashdod, was later added to distinguish between the kibbutz and the development town *Haẓor, situated in Galilee.

[E.O.]

HA-ZORE'A (Heb. הַזּוֹרֵעַ; "the Sower"), kibbutz on the western outskirts of the Jezreel Valley, Israel, affiliated with Kibbutz Arẓi Ha-Shomer ha-Ẓa'ir. It was founded in 1936, during the Arab riots, by a group of the Zionist pioneer Werkleute movement from Germany. Later, immigrants from Bulgaria, Syria, and other countries joined the settlement, which in 1968 had 610 inhabitants. Its economy is based on highly intensive farming and enterprises for furniture and for polyethylene covers for agricultural use. The Manasseh Forest, one of Israel's largest forests, is located nearby. Ha-Zore'a has an art and antiquities museum, Bet Wilfred Israel, housing inter alia Wilfred *Israel's Far Eastern art treasure collection.

[E.O.]

Timber at kibbutz Ha-Zore'a's furniture factory. Courtesy Jewish National Fund, Jerusalem.

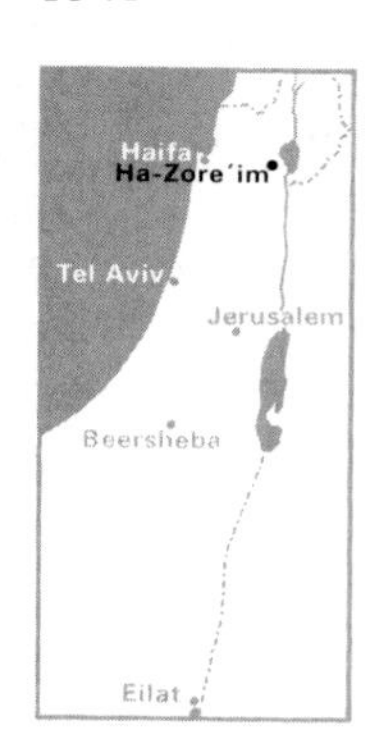

HA-ZORE'IM (Heb. הַזּוֹרְעִים), moshav in eastern Lower Galilee, Israel, affiliated with the Ha-Po'el ha-Mizrachi moshav association. It was founded in 1939 on land provided by the Palestine *Jewish Colonization Association. The settlers, who came from several countries, engage mainly in raising field crops, livestock, and orchards. Remnants of an ancient village assumed to be Serungiya (or Sirgunya) in the talmudic period (Gen. R. 1:6) were found here. The present settlement initially bore this name but the name of the founding group ("the Sowers") was later officially recognized. In 1968 its population was 300. [E.O.]

ḤAZZAN (Ḥazan), Turkish family, apparently of Spanish origin. Many of its members were scholars. In addition to Israel Moses b. Eliezer *Ḥazzan, the following members of the family may be mentioned. Joseph ben Elijah Ḥazzan (d. after 1694) was a pupil of Joseph *Trani, colleague of Ḥayyim *Benveniste in Constantinople, and the teacher of Abraham Israel Ze'evi. From Constantinople he proceeded to Smyrna, and from there to Jerusalem, where he died. He was the author of *Ein Yehosef* (Smyrna 1735), on *Bava Meẓia,* and some responsa—most of his responsa were destroyed in a fire together with other manuscripts; *Ein Yosef* (Smyrna, 1675), homilies on the weekly readings of the Bible; and a commentary on the *Ein Ya'akov,* to which he refers in the preface to the *Ein Yosef.* A commentary on the Pentateuch has also remained in manuscript. Ḥayyim (d. 1712), his son, was one of the rabbis of Smyrna. He later served as a rabbi in Egypt and then proceeded to Jerusalem. Queries were addressed to him from different countries. During 1704–07, together with Abraham Rovigo, he traveled in Western Europe as an emissary of the Jerusalem community. He continued alone to Eastern Europe and died in Mir, Lithuania. He was the author of *Shenot Ḥayyim* (Venice, 1693), sermons on the Pentateuch, as well as novellae and responsa left in manuscript. His son David (18th century) was one of the scholars of Jerusalem, where he had been born. In the 1720s he traveled in Western Europe as an emissary of the Jerusalem community, then proceeded to Smyrna, where he established a printing press. David was the author of *Ḥozeh David* (Amsterdam, 1724), a commentary on the Psalms; *Kohelet Ben David* (Salonika, 1748), on Ecclesiastes; *Agan ha-Sahar* (Salonika, 1750), on Proverbs; and other works.

Jacob Ḥazzan (d. 1802), a Jerusalem scholar, was also an emissary of the Jerusalem community from 1770 to 1775 in Turkey, Western Europe, and Poland. Joseph Raphael ben Ḥayyim Joseph (1741–1820), known as *ha-Yare'aḥ* from the first letters of his name (Y-osef R-aphael b. Ḥ-ayyim), was a rabbi in Smyrna. In 1811 he proceeded to Hebron and after two years went to Jerusalem where he was appointed *rishon le-Zion.* He was the author of *Ḥikrei Lev* (7 vols., Salonika-Leghorn, 1787–1832), novellae on the four parts of the Shulḥan Arukh, and *Ma'arekhei Lev* (Salonika, 1821–22) in two parts, homilies. His sons were Eliezer, Elijah Raḥamim, Isaac, and Ḥayyim David; Ḥayyim *Palaggi was his grandson. Eliezer (d. 1823) was a rabbi in Jerusalem, where he died. His works, *Ḥakor Davar, Ammudei ha-Arazim,* on the *Sefer Yere'im* of Eliezer of Metz, and kabbalistic novellae have remained in manuscript. He was the father of Israel Moses *Ḥazzan. Elijah Raḥamim (d. 1840) was a rabbi of Smyrna and the author of *Oraḥ Mishpat* (Salonika, 1858), on the Shulḥan Arukh *Ḥoshen Mishpat.* He left in manuscript responsa, sermons for Sabbaths and festivals, and *Even ha-Mikkaḥ,* on the *Mikkaḥ u-Mimkar* of *Hai Gaon. A number of his responsa are contained in the *Ḥikrei Lev* of his father. Ḥayyim David (1790–1869) was born in Smyrna. At the age of 20 he went to Constantinople and in 1840 he was appointed rabbi in Smyrna. He settled in Jerusalem in 1855 and in 1861, succeeding Ḥayyim Nissim Abulafia, was appointed *rishon le-Zion.* He was the author of *Torat Zevaḥ* (Salonika, 1852), on the law of *sheḥitah; Nediv Lev* (2 pts. Salonika-Jerusalem, 1862–66), responsa; *Yitav Lev* (Smyrna, 1868), homilies; *Yishrei Lev* (*ibid.,* 1870), various novellae; and other works in manuscript. Solomon Ḥazzan (d. 1856) was rabbi of Alexandria and died in Malta. He was the author of *Sefer ha-Ma'alot li-Shelomo* (1894), a compilation of biographies of scholars not included in the *Shem ha-Gedolim* of Ḥ. J. D. Azulai. Elijah Bekhor ben Abraham (d. 1908), grandson of Ḥayyim David, was born in Smyrna. In 1872–74 he went to North Africa as an emissary of the Jerusalem community. In 1874 he was appointed rabbi of Tripoli and from there went to Alexandria, where he died. He was the author of *Ta'alumot Lev* (Leghorn-Alexandria, 1879–1902), responsa in four parts; *Neveh Shalom* (Alexandria, 1894), on the customs of Alexandria; *Zikhron Yerushalayim* (Leghorn, 1874), on love of the Holy Land; and other works.

Bibliography: Frumkin-Rivlin, index; M. D. Gaon, *Yehudei ha-Mizraḥ be-Ereẓ Yisrael,* 2 (1937), 245–53; Rosanes, Togarmah, vols. 4 and 5, passim; A. Galante, *Les Juifs d'Izmir* (1937), passim; Yaari, Sheluḥei, index; idem, in: *Aresheth,* 1 (1958), 218 (index); M. Benayahu, *Rabbi Ḥayyim Yosef David Azulai* (1959), index; B. Tarajan, *Les communautés israelites d'Alexandrie* (1932), 51–2, 54–8.

[S.Mar.]

ḤAZZAN (pl. **Ḥazzanim,** Heb. חַזָּן, חַזָּנִים), cantor officiating in a synagogue; used in this specific sense since the Middle Ages. The word frequently occurs in talmudic sources, where it denotes various types of communal officials, most prominently the *ḥazzan ha-keneset.* This official performed certain duties in the synagogue, such as bringing out the Torah scrolls for readings (Sotah 7:7–8) and blowing a trumpet to announce the commencement of the Sabbath and festivals (Tosef., Suk. 4:12). He was not, however, regularly required to chant the synagogue service but could do so by request (TJ, Ber. 9:1, 12d); in talmudic times there was no permanent cantor and any member of the congregation might be asked to act as *sheli'aḥ ẓibbur* (TJ, Ber. 5:3, 9c). It was during the period of the *geonim* that the *ḥazzan* became the permanent *sheli'aḥ ẓibbur.* Among the factors which contributed to this change were the increasing complexity of the liturgy and the decline in the knowledge of Hebrew, together with a desire to enhance the beauty of the service through its musical content. The *ḥazzan ha-keneset,* who traditionally guarded the correct texts and selected new prayers, was a natural choice. When **piyyutim* began to take an important place in the liturgy of the synagogue, it was the *ḥazzan* who would recite them and provide suitable melodies. Some of the *paytanim* were themselves *ḥazzanim.* The recitation of the *piyyutim* was called *ḥizana* (*ḥizanatun*) by the Arabic-speaking *paytanim* and the Hebrew equivalent *ḥazzanut* (*ḥazzaniyyah* among Sephardi communities) came to refer to the traditional form of chanting the whole service, and later to the profession of cantor also.

During the Middle Ages the status of the *ḥazzanim* rose, and they were given better salaries, longer tenure of office, and more communal tax exemptions. The post of *ḥazzan* was "the most permanent and continuous synagogue office, one which underwent relatively few changes after the early Middle Ages" (Baron, Community, 2 (1942), 100). In Northern Europe eminent rabbis served as *ḥazzanim,*

Figure 1. A *ḥazzan*, from the *Birds' Head Haggadah*, S. Germany, c. 1300. The human face is not used to avoid disobeying the Second Commandment. Jerusalem, Israel Museum. Photo David Harris, Jerusalem.

among them Jacob *Moellin ha-Levi (Maharil) of Mainz (c. 1360–1427), who established strict norms for Ashkenazi *ḥazzanim* and some of whose chants are still in use. Gradually, the qualifications demanded of a *ḥazzan* became fixed. He was required to have a pleasant voice and appearance, to be married, to have a beard, to be fully familiar with the liturgy, to be of blameless character, and to be acceptable in all other respects to the members of the community (Sh. Ar., OḤ 53:4ff.). These strict requirements were modified occasionally, but were rigorously enforced on the High Holy Days. Ironically, the growing popularity of the *ḥazzan* made him the most controversial communal official. His dual role of religious representative and artistic performer inevitably gave rise to tensions (which persist in modern times). In many communities priority was given to a beautiful voice and musical skill over the traditional requirements of learning and piety. Leading rabbis castigated the *ḥazzanim* for needless repetition of words and for extending their chanting of the prayers with the sole purpose of displaying the beauty of their voices.

The emancipation of European Jewry led to important changes in the style and content of synagogue music. Traditional melodies were now set down in musical notation with harmonies to be sung by *ḥazzan* and choir. New melodies were composed under the influence of modern European musical trends and techniques. The pioneer in this field was Solomon *Sulzer, chief *ḥazzan* in Vienna from 1825 to 1890; he was closely followed by Samuel *Naumbourg of Paris, Louis *Lewandowski of Berlin, Hirsch *Weintraub of Koenigsberg, Moritz *Deutsch of Breslau, Abraham *Baer of Goteborg, Sweden, and many others. The ḥasidic movement, where the rabbi recited the prayers, and parts of the Reform movement which substituted the plain reading of the liturgy for the office of *ḥazzan*, remained outside this development. Indeed the joyful tunes of the Ḥasidim gradually became popular with many orthodox communities. The use of the organ and mixed choirs introduced by the *Reform movement radically changed cantorial music. Hebrew and German prayer texts were chanted to German chorale tunes; these replaced the traditional prayer music. Rabbi Isaac M. Wise, architect of American Jewish Reform, substituted the plain reading of liturgy for the office of *ḥazzan*. Only a few houses of worship retained *ḥazzanim* (e.g., Alois Kaiser) who tried to develop a tradition of American synagogue music. Classical reform in the U.S.A. was modified under the impact of the Zionist movement and East European immigration, and pressure grew to restore traditional forms of worship. Two *ḥazzanim* who became professors, A. W. Binder at the *Jewish Institute of Religion and A. Z. Idelsohn at the *Hebrew Union College, reintroduced traditional liturgy and music into Reform rabbinical studies.

The period from the end of the 19th century until World War II is described as the "Era of Golden *Ḥazzanut*." Cantorial music had a singular appeal to the Jewish masses, who would fill their synagogues to overflowing in order to hear an outstanding *ḥazzan*. Improved communications enabled leading *ḥazzanim* to tour Jewish communities on a far greater scale than previously, thus increasing their reputations, sometimes to legendary proportions. They were equated with the great operatic tenors of the time, whose style they grew to imitate. Even non-Jews were attracted to the synagogues to hear famous *ḥazzanim* and Gershon *Sirota was invited annually to sing for the czar. Following the mass emigration of Jews from Eastern Europe to the U.S., great *ḥazzanim* like Sirota, Josef *Rosenblatt, Mordechai *Herschman and Zavel *Kwartin gave concert tours in America, where all of them, except Sirota, remained. They were able to command enormous salaries and fees for concerts and High Holy Day services.

A major factor in building up the reputations and perpetuating the fame of the great *ḥazzanim* was the development of sound recordings, beginning with the first cantorial disk made by Sirota in 1903. Furthermore, lesser *ḥazzanim* adopted the style and melodies of the great cantors which they learnt from the records, and the singing of famous musical compositions became a chief attraction of synagogue services. In the post war period prominent *ḥazzanim* included Moshe *Koussevitzky and his brothers Jacob, Simchah, and David, Leib *Glanz, Israel Alter, Moshe Ganchoff, Pierre Pinchik, Leibele Waldman, Sholom Katz, and, in the younger generation, Moshe Stern. Some, such as Richard *Tucker and Jan *Peerce, achieved international fame as operatic tenors, but retained their contact with the synagogue through recordings and High Holiday and Passover services. In Israel the development of *ḥazzanut* lagged behind the U.S. However, the regular radio programs devoted to both Ashkenazi and Sephardi *ḥazzanut* have a large following. Many of the world's leading *ḥazzanim* have sung in Israel and a cantorial conference was held there in 1968. *Ḥazzanim* serve in the chaplaincy corps of the Israel army, but only the large towns employ *ḥazzanim* on a regular basis. A number of successful *ḥazzanim* have been attracted to the U.S., Great Britain, and South Africa, where the financial rewards are much greater. Most major Jewish communities in the world now have professional associations of *ḥazzanim* and several bulletins and journals are regularly published. An important factor in assuring the future development of *ḥazzanut* is the growth of cantorial training schools, in the U.S. (at Yeshiva University, the Jewish Theological Seminary, and the Hebrew Union College) in Great Britain (at Jews' College), and in Israel (at the Selah Seminary in Tel Aviv, and elsewhere).

Figure 2. *Ḥazzan* at the reader's desk, from an illuminated Scroll of Esther, Alsace, 19th century. Paris, Victor Klagsbad Collection.

See also Jewish *Music.

Bibliography: Baron, Community, index; Baron, Social², index; Idelsohn, Music; Sendrey, Music, 65–66, 75–80, 91–97, 201–7, 211ff., 336–7; Jewish Ministers Cantors' Association of America, *Di Geshikhte fun Khazzones* (Yid. and Eng., 1924); idem, *Khazzones* (Yid. and Eng., 1937); idem, *50 Yoriger Yovl Zhurnal* (Yid. and Eng., 1947); P. Gradenwitz, *Music of Israel* (1949); H. H. Harris, *Toledot ha-Neginah ve-ha-Ḥazzanut be-Yisrael* (1950); I. Rabinovitch, *Of Jewish Music* (1952); N. Stolnitz, *Negine in Yidishn Lebn* (Yid. and Eng., 1957); I. Shalita, *Ha-Musikah ha-Yehudit ve-Yozereha* (1960); I. Heskes (ed.), *The Cantorial Art* (1966); A. M. Rothmueller, *Music of the Jews* (1967²). [H.K./Ed.]

Alphabetical List. The following is a list of well-known persons in the various fields of modern synagogal music. The names marked with an asterisk are the subject of individual entries in the appropriate alphabetical position in this encyclopedia. In the use of the descriptive terms, the following distinctions have been made: editor—of a publication of or on synagogal music; collector—of important manuscripts and similar materials, unpublished, published partially, or published by others; composer—of prominent creative activity in either the traditional practice of "ḥazzanic composition" or in religious music.

***ABRASS, OSIAS** (Joshua; 1829–1883), *ḥazzan* and composer.

***ADLER, HUGO CHAIM** (1894–1955), *ḥazzan* and composer.

***ALGAZI, ISAAC** (1882–1964), *ḥazzan.*

***ALGAZI, LEON** (Yehudah; 1890–1971), choral director, composer, and editor.

***ALMAN, SAMUEL** (1877–1947), choral director and composer.

ALTER, ISRAEL (1901–), *ḥazzan* and composer. Born in Lvov, Alter studied music in Vienna. A powerful tenor with a wide range, he began his career as *ḥazzan* at Vienna's Brigittenauer Temple-Verein when he was 20. In 1925 he moved to Hanover, where he remained for ten years before becoming chief *ḥazzan* of the United Hebrew Congregation in Johannesburg, South Africa. He went to the U.S. in 1961, and became a faculty member of the School of Sacred Music of the Hebrew Union College. Alter published his cantorial compositions in *Shirei Yisrael* (2 vols., 1952–57), and in *Cantorial Recitatives for Hallel, Tal, Geshem* (1962), and his musical settings of Yiddish poems in *Mayne Lider* (1957). He also edited some of David Eisenstadt's liturgical works in *Le-David Mizmor* (n.d.).

***ALTSCHUL, JOSEPH** (Yoske Slonimer; 1840–1908), *ḥazzan.*

***BACHMANN, JACOB** (1846–1905), *ḥazzan* and composer.

***BAER, ABRAHAM** (1834–1894), *ḥazzan* and editor.

***BAUER, JACOB** (1852–1926), *ḥazzan.*

***BEER, AARON** (1738–1821), *ḥazzan* and collector.

BEIMEL, JACOB (c. 1875–1944), *ḥazzan.* Born in Parichi, Belorussia, where his father was also a cantor, as a child he sang in Bobruisk and Berdichev. He studied music in Odessa and Berlin, became cantor in Berlin, where he conducted the Mendelssohn Choir, and later served in Copenhagen. In 1915, he went to the U.S. and conducted choral concerts. He held posts in New York and later in Philadelphia. His works and adaptations of synagogue music, his folk songs and ḥasidic melodies, were published in the quarterly *Jewish Music Journal* (Eng. and Yid., 1934–35), which he edited in the U.S.

BELZER, NISSI see *Spivak, Nissan.

BERGGRÜN, HEINRICH (1838–1889), *ḥazzan* and composer. Born in Warsaw, Berggrün was a music teacher in Vilna, and later a violinist at the Grand Theater, Warsaw. He studied singing in Milan, became choirmaster in Odessa, was appointed *ḥazzan* in Posen, and chief cantor in Hanover in 1870. His compositions include: "Festival *Kaddish*" for *ḥazzan* and choir on the occasion of the jubilee of the Hanover synagogue, 1892; "Complete *Kaddish*" for *ḥazzan* and choir, 1889.

***BERLIJN, ANTON** (1817–1870), composer, conductor, and *ḥazzan.*

***BERLINSKY, HERMANN** (1910–), composer.

BERNSTEIN, ABRAHAM MOSHE (1866–1932), *ḥazzan* and composer. Born in Shatsk, in the Russian province of Minsk, Bernstein was a cantor in Bialystok and choir director for cantor Baruch Leib Rosowsky in Riga before being appointed cantor of the Taharas Kodesh synagogue in Vilna (1893–1923). A prolific composer, he set to music more than 150 Hebrew and Yiddish poems, the best known being *Zamd und Stern* and *Hemeril* ("The little hammer"). He compiled a collection of folksongs, *Muzikalisher Pinkos* (1927) and a cantorial collection, *Avodas Haborei* (3 vols., 1931). His son was the Israel composer Aviassof Bernstein (Barnea; 1903–1957).

***BINDER, ABRAHAM WOLFE** (1895–1966), choral director and composer.

***BIRNBAUM, ABRAHAM BEER** (1864–1922), *ḥazzan* and editor.

***BIRNBAUM, EDUARD** (1855–1920), *ḥazzan,* writer, and collector.

***BLANES, JACOB** (1877–1943), *ḥazzan.*

BLAUSTEIN, ABRAHAM (1836–1914), *ḥazzan.* Born in Riga, Blaustein became a cantor in Lomza, later in Vilna, and then settled in Germany. In 1877 he was appointed chief cantor of Bromberg (now Poland), a position he held until his death. He edited a weekly paper for cantors and founded an association for raising professional standards.

***BLINDMAN, YERUHAM** (Yerukhom ha-Koton; c. 1798–1891), *ḥazzan* and composer.

***BLUMENTHAL, NISSAN** (1805–1903), *ḥazzan* and composer.

BRANDON, OHEB (Oeb) ISAAC (c. 1830–1902), Dutch *ḥazzan.* Brandon was one of the best-known Sephardi *ḥazzanim* of Amsterdam, serving the congregation from 1861 to 1902. He wrote a guide for *ḥazzanim* which was probably partly a translation of the Hebrew guide, *Seder Ḥazzanut,* preserved in the community's archives. Brandon's work gave minutely detailed information about the melodies used on various occasions. It also dealt with local traditions such as the allocation of functions during services and included a chapter on the Portuguese phrases used for annuncements in the synagogue. Brandon had considerable influence on his successors, especially Jacob *Blanes.

BROD, DOVIDL (Strelisker, David; 1783–1848), Hungarian *ḥazzan.* Born in Brody, Brod officiated in synagogues as a child prodigy but received no musical training. Although destined originally for the rabbinate, he entered business. His business failed and he became a professional *ḥazzan* in Althofen, Austria, in 1822. In 1830 he moved to Budapest where he served as *ḥazzan* until his death. Unable to read a musical score he improvised his own melodies and though he left no written record of his compositions, most of the *ḥazzanim* of Hungary and Galicia and their pupils owed their style and their melodies to his inspiration.

CHAGY, BERELE (1892–1954), *ḥazzan* and composer. Born in Dagdo, Russia, Chagy took his first position as *ḥazzan* in Smolensk at the age of 18, but left after three years for the U.S. He held positions in Detroit, Boston, and Newark and in 1932 went to Johannesburg, South Africa, where he remained for five years. On his return to the U.S. he became *ḥazzan* at Temple Beth-El in Brooklyn, New York, a post which he held until his retirement. Chagy attained great popularity through his concerts and recordings and was praised for his clear, ringing, tenor voice, with a naturally graceful and flexible coloratura. In 1937 he published *Tefillot Chagy*, containing 87 recitatives for Sabbath services.

CHERSONER, WOLF see *Shestapol, Wolf.

DAVID, SAMUEL see *Musicians, Jewish.

***DEUTSCH, MORITZ** (1818–1892), *ḥazzan*, composer, and editor.

DUQUE, SIMON DAVID (1897–), one of the last two *ḥazzanim* of the Portuguese Synagogue of Amsterdam, Holland. Born in Amsterdam, he was appointed *ḥazzan* in 1923. Duque was chosen from among three candidates because of his adherence to the Amsterdam tradition. He also aimed at an operatic style. His *ḥazzanut* had many moving features particularly his *Kedushah* for Sabbath *Musaf* and *Ve-Hu Raḥum* for the evening service. His falsetto was famous.

EHRLICH, HERMANN (Zvi; 1815–1879), German *ḥazzan* and composer. Born in Meiningen, Ehrlich was *ḥazzan* of the little town of Berka, and edited a periodical, *Liturgische Zeitschrift*, which aimed at improving synagogue music. Contributors included Jewish scholars, teachers, and *ḥazzanim*. He also published collections of synagogue music, choral songs and recitatives for festivals, and a book on singing for schoolteachers. He composed *Juedisches Musik-Album* (1910) for voice and piano.

EPHROS, GERSHON (1890–), *ḥazzan*. Born in Poland, he went to Palestine at 20, and studied under the musicologist A. Z. *Idelsohn, for whom he also conducted a choir. Later he emigrated to the U.S. where he received appointments as *ḥazzan* and taught singing in schools. Ephros composed liturgical music for soloists, choir, and organ, and arranged ḥasidic dances and Israel songs. His main work is his *Cantorial Anthology* in five volumes (1929–57), a practical collection of older and recent works for all the synagogue services of the year, which also contains some of Ephros' own compositions.

FEINSINGER, JOSHUA (Shaye; 1839–1872), Russian *ḥazzan*. Born in Lithuania, Feinsinger was taught singing by his father, himself a *ḥazzan*. After completing his musical training, he became chief *ḥazzan* in the Polish town of Leczyca. In 1868 he was appointed chief *ḥazzan* in Vilna. Possessing a phenomenal voice and originality of expression, Feinsinger became famous as one of the greatest *ḥazzanim* of the mid-19th century. His most notable compositions were for the **Yoẓer* prayers for the *Sefirah* Sabbaths.

***FREED, ISADORE** (1900–), composer and choral director.

FRIEDE, SHALOM (1783–1854), Dutch *ḥazzan*. Born in Amsterdam, he served as *ḥazzan* from 1809 until his death. His collection of about 200 melodies for various prayers, preserved in manuscript in the Hebrew Union College, Cincinnati, added considerably to the knowledge of Polish cantoral and ḥasidic music. Of this collection, 15 melodies were published by A. Z. Idelsohn in *Oẓar Neginot Yisrael*. His preference for Polish and ḥasidic chants is reflected in his own compositions.

FRIEDMANN, ARON (1855–1936), German *ḥazzan*. Born in Szaki, Lithuania, Friedmann studied in Berlin and in 1882 was appointed chief *ḥazzan* of the Old Synagogue of the Berlin community, a post he held until 1923. He received the title of Koeniglicher Musikdirektor, Royal Academy of Art, Berlin, 1907. In 1901, he published *Shir li-Shelomoh*, a collection of cantorial music in traditional style for the prayers of the year. He also wrote *Der synagogale Gesang* (1904) and *Lebensbilder beruehmter Kantoren* (3 vols., 1918–27), containing biographies of 19th-century *ḥazzanim*.

***FRIEDMANN, MORITZ** (1823–1891), *ḥazzan* and editor.

***GEROWITCH, ELIEZER** (1844–1913), *ḥazzan* and composer.

***GLANZ, LEIB** (1898–1964), *ḥazzan* and composer.

***GOLDSTEIN, JOSEF** (1837–1899), *ḥazzan*.

HAST, MARCUS (Mordechai; 1840–1911), *ḥazzan* and composer. Born in Praga, near Warsaw, Hast served as *ḥazzan* in Warsaw, Torun, and Breslau, and from 1871 in the Great Synagogue, in Duke's Place in London. He published the traditional repertoire of the London synagogue, together with some of his own compositions, in *Oẓar ha-Rinnah ve-ha-Tefillah* (1874, with Michael *Bergson); *Seder ha-Avodah* (1879); and *Avodat ha-Kodesh* (1910). He also composed some cantatas and oratorios on Jewish subjects (*Bostanai, Azariah, The Death of Moses, The Destruction of Jerusalem*), conducted the Amateur Choral Society, and founded the Association of Cantors of Great Britain. Some of his synagogal compositions were included in the collections edited by his son-in-law Francis Lyon *Cohen.

***HENLE, MORITZ** (1850–1925), *ḥazzan*.

***HERSCHMAN, MORDECHAI** (1888–1940), *ḥazzan*.

***IDELSOHN, ABRAHAM ZVI** (1882–1938), musicologist and *ḥazzan*.

***JACOBI, FREDERICK** (1891–1952), composer.

***JADLOWKER, HERMANN** see *Musicians, Jewish.

***JAPHET, ISRAEL MEYER** (1818–1892), choral director and composer.

***JASSINOWSKY, PINCHAS** (1886–1954), *ḥazzan* and composer.

KAISER, ALOIS (1840–1908), *ḥazzan* and composer. Born in Hungary, Kaiser sang as a boy with Salomon *Sulzer. From 1859 to 1863 he was *ḥazzan* in Vienna, then went to Prague and three years later to the U.S. where he officiated until his death at the Oheb Shalom Congregation in Baltimore. Kaiser's intention in his compositions and arrangements was to provide music for the American synagogue, based on the traditional melodies but stripped of all "unnecessary ornamentation." With William Sparger he was responsible for the first edition of the *Union Hymnal* (1897) for the Conference of American Rabbis and edited *A Collection of the Principal Melodies of the Synagogue from the Earliest to the Present* (1893).

KARLINER, BARUCH (c. 1810–1871 or 1879), *ḥazzan*. Taking his name from the Russian town of Karlin where he first became a *ḥazzan*, Karliner also served other communities including Pinsk and Brisk. He had neither a particularly tuneful voice nor any musical knowledge, but would compose "when the spirit came upon him," even if this occurred during a part of the service which was not usually sung. His choir was accustomed to his sudden digressions from the rehearsed repertoire and when these occurred would continue to accompany him in his own style. His compositions, notable for their power and bold modulations, were written down by members of his choir and had a great influence on the following generations of *ḥazzanim*.

***KARNIOL, ALTER YEHIEL** (1855–1929), *ḥazzan*.

KASHTAN, SHLOMO see *Weintraub, Solomon.

KATZ, SHOLOM (1919–), *ḥazzan*. Born in Oradea, Rumania, Katz studied voice in Budapest and Vienna and was *ḥazzan* in Kishinev, Bessarabia, until he was deported in 1941. At the Bralow, Ukraine, concentration camp, he was taken out to be shot but requested permission to sing the prayer for the dead. The officer in charge was so impressed by his voice that he spared him and allowed him to escape. In 1947 he emigrated to the U.S. and became *ḥazzan* of the Beth Sholom Congregation in Washington, D.C. A powerful tenor with an extensive range and exceptional voice control, Katz developed an individualistic, unhurried and dramatic style.

KHERSONER, WOLF see *Shestapol, Wolf.

***KIRSCHNER, EMANUEL** (1857–1938), *ḥazzan* and composer.

***KOHN, MAIER** (1802–1875), *ḥazzan*.

***KORNITZER, LEON** (1875–1947), *ḥazzan*, choral director, and editor.

***KOUSSEVITZKY, MOSHE** (1899–1966), *ḥazzan*.

***KWARTIN, ZAVEL** (Zevulun; 1874–1953), *ḥazzan*.

LACHMANN, ISAAK (1838–1900), *ḥazzan*. Born in Dubno, Lachmann was a pupil of Joshua (Pitshe) *Abrass and Bezalel Odesser, and served in Berent, Stolp, Lauenburg, and, after 1873, in Huerben. He published studies on synagogal music in *Der juedische Kantor*. In 1899 he published the collection *Abodat Jisrael*, which followed the south-German tradition.

***LEONI, MYER** (1740–1796), *ḥazzan* and singer.

***LEWANDOWSKI, LOUIS** (1821–1894), choral director and composer.

***LEWENSOHN, JOEL DAVID** see *Loewenstein-Straschunsky, Joel David.

LION, MEIR see *Leoni, Myer.

LIPSCHITZ (Lipschuetz), **SOLOMON BEN MOSES** (1675–1758), German *ḥazzan* and writer. Born in Fuerth, the son of a *ḥazzan*, Lipschitz practiced his profession as a *ḥazzan* in several communities, including Prague and Frankfurt, before settling in Metz in 1715. His book *Te'udat Shelomo* (Offenbach, 1718) combines instructions and moral precepts for the *ḥazzan* with the writer's personal reminiscences—both of them valuable historical evidence.

***LOEWENSTEIN-STRASCHUNSKY, JOEL DAVID** (Vilner Balebessl; 1816–1850), *ḥazzan*.

LOMZER, ḤAYYIM see *Wasserzug, Ḥayyim.

***LOVY, ISRAEL** (1773–1832), *ḥazzan* and composer.

LYON, MEYER see *Leoni, Myer.

MALAVSKY, SAMUEL (1894–), *ḥazzan*. Born in Smela, near Kiev, Ukraine, Malavsky sang as a *meshorer* with various *ḥazzanim*. He went to the U.S. in 1914 and auditioned for Josef *Rosenblatt, thus beginning a lifelong association. Malavsky sang duets with Rosenblatt in concerts and on recordings, as well as officiating as *ḥazzan* in many leading congregations. In 1947 he formed the Malavsky family choir, "Singers of Israel," with his two sons and four daughters. They achieved great international popularity through their appearances in synagogues, concerts, and on recordings. Malavsky created a unique style for his family choir by introducing a strongly marked beat and syncopation into the traditional Eastern European *ḥazzanut*.

MARAGOWSKY, JACOB SAMUEL see *Morogowsky, Jacob S.

***MINKOWSKY, PINCHAS** (1859–1924), *ḥazzan*, writer, and composer.

MINSKER, SENDER see below Polachek, Sender.

***MOROGOWSKY, JACOB SAMUEL** (Zeidel Rovner; 1856–1942), *ḥazzan* and composer.

***NADEL, ARNO** (1878–1943), writer, choral director, composer, and collector.

***NAUMBOURG, SAMUEL** (1815–1880), *ḥazzan*, composer, and editor.

***NOWAKOWSKY, DAVID** (1848–1921), choral director and composer.

ODESSER, BEZALEL see *Shulsinger, Bezalel.

NE'EMAN, YEHOSHUA LEIB (1899–), Israel *ḥazzan*, writer, and teacher. Born in Jerusalem, Ne'eman sang as a *meshorer* with A. Z. Idelsohn and other *ḥazzanim* and studied liturgical music and singing with Solomon Rosowsky. His lyric tenor voice and emphasis on correct pronunciation and accentuation of the prayers made him a popular *ḥazzan* in many of Jerusalem's synagogues. He was often accompanied by his choir, Shir Ẓiyyon. From 1948 Ne'eman was lecturer in biblical cantillation at the Academy of Music in Jerusalem, and from 1958 to 1965 was director of the school for *ḥazzanim* for the Israel Institute for Sacred Music. He wrote extensively on biblical cantillation including *Ẓelilei ha-Mikra* (1955), and also published *Nusaḥ la-Ḥazzan* (1963, with demonstration records). Rosowsky based his *The Cantillation of Bible* (1957) on Ne'eman's renderings which he accepted as the pure representation of the Ashkenazi tradition.

OYSHER, MOISHE (1907–1958), *ḥazzan*. Born in Lipkon, Bessarabia, and taken to Canada in 1921, Oysher joined a Yiddish theatrical company, appeared on the Yiddish stage in New York, and led his own company in Buenos Aires, 1932. Returning to New York 1934, he decided to become a *ḥazzan* like his father and grandfather. He conducted services in New York, and was noted for ḥasidic interpretations of the traditional prayers. He starred in Yiddish films, *The Cantor's Son*, *Yankel the Blacksmith*, and *Der Vilna Balebesel*, and made numerous recordings.

***PARDO, DAVID** (d. 1701), *ḥazzan*.

***PEERCE, JAN** (1904–), singer and *ḥazzan*.

PILDERWASSER, JOSHUA SAMUEL see *Weisser, Joshua S.

PINCHIK, PIERRE (**Pinchas Segal**; c. 1900–), *ḥazzan*. Born in Zhivitov, Ukraine, the young Pinchik was sent to live with his grandfather in Podolia. His singing in the local yeshivah attracted the attention of one of his teachers who arranged for Pinchik to be taught music and piano and to study voice at Rostov. He became *ḥazzan* in Leningrad and subsequently made his way to the U.S., where his ḥazzanic talent was quickly recognized. His style was best expressed in his widely acclaimed performances and recordings of *Raza de-Shabbat*, which represent his successful attempt to evoke the mystical dimension of prayer.

POLACHEK, SENDER (also known as Sender Minsker; 1786–1869), Polish cantor. Born in Gombin, Polachek received instruction from Cantor Nahum Leib Weintraub, brother of Solomon *Weintraub. For over 30 years Polachek was cantor in Minsk (hence his additional name) and became famous for his melodic gifts. Having no knowledge of musical notation, he committed none of his works to writing, but he achieved an original style which deeply affected his hearers and which became known as the "Sender Steiger."

***PUTTERMAN, DAVID** (1901–), *ḥazzan* and editor.

***RAVITZ, SHELOMOH** (188?–), *ḥazzan*.

***RAZUMNI, EPHRAIM ZALMAN** (Solomon; 1866–1904), *ḥazzan*.

***RIVLIN, SHELOMOH ZALMAN** (1844–1962), *ḥazzan* and teacher.

ROITMAN, DAVID (1884–1943), *ḥazzan* and composer. Roitman was born in Dorozhinki, Russia, and studied with several *ḥazzanim*, notably Jacob Samuel *Morogowsky (Zeidel Rovner). He was *ḥazzan* in Vilna (1909–12), St. Petersburg (1912–17), and Odessa, before emigrating to the U.S. in 1921. From 1924 until his death he officiated at Congregation Shaare Zedek in New York. Roitman had a light, flexible, lyric tenor voice with an exceptional falsetto. He was noted for his clarity of rendition and his power of improvisation, while still maintaining an overall simplicity of expression. His compositions *Ashamnu mi-Kol Am* (in: G. Ephros (ed.), *Cantorial Anthology*, 2 (1940), 145–6) and *Raḥel Mevakah al Baneha*, both deeply moving liturgical laments achieved widespread popularity. In 1961, L. Avery published *Selected Recitatives of Cantor David Roitman*.

***ROSENBLATT, JOSEF** (Yossele; 1880–1933), *ḥazzan* and composer.

***ROSOWSKY, BARUCH LEIB** (1841–1919), *ḥazzan*.

***ROSOWSKY, SOLOMON** (1878–1962), composer and writer.

ROTHMUELLER, ARON MARKO (1918–), composer, singer, writer.

ROVNER, ZEIDEL see *Morogowsky, Jacob Samuel.

***SAMINSKY, LAZARE** (1882–1959), composer, choral director and writer.

***SCHALIT, HEINRICH** (1886–), composer.

SCHERMAN, PINCHAS see below Szerman, Pinchas

***SCHMIDT, JOSEF** (1904–1941), singer and *ḥazzan*.

***SCHORR, BARUCH** (1823–1904), *ḥazzan* and composer.

SHERMAN, PINCHAS see below Szerman, Pinchas.

***SHESTAPOL, WOLF** (**Wolf Khersoner**; c. 1832–1872), *ḥazzan* and composer.

***SHULSINGER, BEZALEL** (**Bezalel Odesser**; c. 1790–c. 1860), *ḥazzan*.

***SINGER, JOSEPH** (1841–1911), *ḥazzan* and writer.

***SIROTA, GERSHON** (1874–1943), *ḥazzan*.

SLONIMER, YOSKE see *Altshul, Joseph

***SPIVAK, NISSAN** (Nissi Belzer; 1824–1906), *ḥazzan*.

STARK, EDWARD (1863–1918), U.S. *ḥazzan* and composer. The son of a *ḥazzan*, Stark became *ḥazzan* of Temple Emanu-El in San Francisco in 1893 and remained there for 20 years. He was one of the most influential musicians in the service of the American Reform Synagogue. His compositions evince the influence of Sulzer and *Lewandowski and the style of the classical oratorio, but are based for the most part on traditional Jewish thematic material. He insisted on the use of the *ḥazzan* as soloist, thus reversing previous trends in the Reform synagogue. Under the title *Anim Zemiroth*, he published compositions for the Sabbath and the High Holidays (1909–13). In *Day of God* (1898) he arranged the *Kol Nidrei melody for soprano solo, choir, and small orchestra.

STRASCHUNSKI, JOEL DAVID (1816–1850), *ḥazzan*. See *Loewenstein-Straschunski, Joel David

STRELISKER, DAVID see above Brod, Dovidl.

***SULZER, SALOMON** (1804–1890), *ḥazzan* and composer.

SZERMAN, PINCHAS (1887–1942), *ḥazzan*. Born in Staszow, Poland, he sang as a boy with his elder brother, Abraham Isaac, then *ḥazzan* in Krashnik. Szerman studied in A. B. *Birnbaum's school for *ḥazzanim* in Czestochowa, and in 1909 was appointed *ḥazzan sheni* (assistant *ḥazzan*) at the Tlomacka Street Synagogue in Warsaw. Holding this post until the outbreak of World War II, he served together with the chief *ḥazzanim*, Gershon Sirota and Moshe Koussevitzky, and the choral directors Leo Loew and David Eisenstadt. Szerman was held in high esteem not only for his flexible baritone voice and his unaffected style, but also for his learning and character. He was one of the founders of the *Aggudat ha-Ḥazzanim* (Cantors' Association), in Poland, and served as its president and the editor of its journal *Di Khazonim Velt.*

***TUCKER, RICHARD** (1916–), singer and *ḥazzan.*

UNGAR, BENJAMIN (1907–), *ḥazzan.* Born in Jaslo, Galicia, Poland, Ungar studied with several notable cantors and composers before taking his first position as *ḥazzan* in Magdeburg, Germany. From there he moved to Stendal and in 1938 went to Israel. He officiated in several Tel Aviv synagogues and in 1959 became chief *ḥazzan* of the Tel Aviv Great Synagogue. The possessor of a powerful and rich tenor voice, Ungar gained a reputation through his many concert, radio, and television appearances, and became known internationally through his records and concert tours. In 1966 he became chairman of the Association of Cantors of Israel.

VILNER BALEBESSI see *Loewenstein-Straschunski, Joel David.

***VINAVER, CHEMJO** (1900–), choral director and writer.

WALDMAN, LEIBELE (c. 1907–1969), *ḥazzan.* Born in New York city, Waldman was recognized as a child prodigy and officiated as a *ḥazzan* and appeared in concerts while still a youth. He held positions in Boston, Passaic, and New York and sang regularly on the radio, rapidly becoming most popular. He possessed a warm, well-rounded, lyric baritone voice which, together with his clear diction and easy-flowing style, was particularly suited to the liturgical pieces and Yiddish religious folksongs which he performed in concerts and on his numerous records.

***WASSERZUG, HAYYIM (Hayyim Lomzer;** 1822–1882), *ḥazzan* and composer.

***WEINTRAUB** (Kashtan), **SOLOMON** (1781–1829, *ḥazzan* and Weintraub, Ẓevi Hirsch Alter (1811–1882), *ḥazzan.*

***WEISSER** (Pilderwasser), **JOSHUA SAMUEL** (1882–1952), *ḥazzan* and composer.

***YASSER, JOSEPH** (1893–), musicologist and choral director.

YASSINOWSKI, PINHAS see *Jassinowski, Pinhas.

YERUHAM HA-KOTON see *Blindman, Yeruham.

***ZARFATI, JOSEF** (18th century), *ḥazzan.*

ZALUDKOWSKI, ELIJAH (1888–1943), *ḥazzan* and writer. He was a son of the well-known *ḥazzan* of Kalisz, Noah Zaludkowski (1859–1931), known as "Reb Noaḥ Lieder." Elijah studied with his father and other *ḥazzanim,* and also at conservatories in Milan and Berlin. He held posts as *ḥazzan* in Warsaw, Vilna, and Liverpool, England, and in 1926 went to the U.S. where he officiated in New York and Detroit. Zaludkowski wrote *Di Kultur-Treger fun der Yidisher Liturgie* (1930), containing useful biographies of famous *ḥazzanim,* and published his father's and his own liturgical compositions in *Tefillat No'aḥ va-Avodat Eliyahu.*

***ZILBERTS, ZAVEL** (1881–1949), choral director, composer, and *ḥazzan.*

ḤAZZAN, ISRAEL MOSES BEN ELIEZER (1808–1863), rabbi and author. Ḥazzan was born in Smyrna, and in 1811 went with his father to Jerusalem, where he studied in the yeshivah of his grandfather Joseph Raphael Ḥazzan (see *Ḥazzan family). In 1842 Israel was appointed a member of the *bet din* in Jerusalem and in 1844 journeyed to London as an emissary of the Jerusalem community. During his stay in London he wrote a pamphlet, *Divrei Shalom ve-Emet,* against a pamphlet issued by the recently established Reform movement in England; and another pamphlet against the decisions of the Rabbinical Synod at Brunswick under the title *Kinat Ẓiyyon* (Amsterdam, 1846). The same year he joined a group established for the purpose of fighting the Reform movement. He later went to Rome, where he was appointed rabbi (1847–54), and interceded on behalf of the Jews of Italy in the court of Pope Pius IX. From Rome he proceeded to Corfu, where he was rabbi for five years. He was then invited to Alexandria, serving as rabbi and *av bet din* there until the end of 1862. He then settled in Haifa but died in Beirut, where he had gone on account of ill-health. His remains were taken for burial to Sidon since it was regarded as being within the borders of Ereẓ Israel. Ḥazzan also wrote *Naḥalah le-Yisrael* (Vienna, 1851), on the obligation of deciding laws of inheritance according to Torah; *Kedushat Yom Tov* (*ibid.,* 1855), against the attempt in Italy to abolish the second day of the festivals; and *She'erit ha-Naḥalah* (Alexandria, 1862), a dispute between a merchant and two emissaries of Ereẓ Israel. It was later combined with the *Naḥalah le-Yisrael* (1862) but is part of a work *Neẓaḥ Yisrael,* which has remained in manuscript and is an attack on the *Vikku'aḥ al Ḥokhmat ha-Kabbalah* of S. D. *Luzzatto. Other works are *Iyyei ha-Yam,* in two parts (pt. 1 Leghorn, 1869; pt. 2 is still in manuscript), a commentary on the responsa of the *geonim,* and *Kerakh shel Romi* (Leghorn, 1876), responsa. Still in manuscript are *Ḥoker Lev,* responsa, and *Yismaḥ Lev,* sermons preached in Jerusalem and during his activity as an emissary.

Bibliography: Frumkin-Rivlin, 3 (1929), 303; A. Galanté, *Les Juifs d'Izmir* (1937), 74f.; M. D. Gaon, *Yehudei ha-Mizraḥ be-Ereẓ Yisrael,* 2 (1938), 251f.; Yaari, Sheluhei, 176f., 729–32.

[S.Mar.]